PRAISE FOR *The Bedford Anthology of American Literature*

"In a number of respects, this anthology is exceptional. *The Bedford Anthology* has two major advantages: a realistic balance of texts that acknowledges the frequent practice of assigning novels and autobiographies in full, and an incredibly fruitful, focused approach guided by questions of print culture and its attendant questions of authorship, circulation, and reception of literary texts."

— Matt Cohen
Duke University

"Unlike many other anthologies, I can see myself teaching almost everything included here. Not only is the anthology representative, but it also serves to focus on some of the chief issues in American studies today."

— Rosemary Fithian Guruswamy
Radford University

"Susan Belasco and Linck Johnson have done a fine job conceptualizing a kind of American literature anthology not currently available. Their focused attention to reading, writing, and print culture will remind students (and all of us) of the significance of literature as a way of knowing. As I read I also considered whether the introductory American survey I teach would need significant revision if I were to use an anthology like this one. I found I could teach *my* course with *their* book."

— Pattie Cowell
Colorado State University

"I admire this anthology a great deal. But what recommends it, finally, is not simply its economies but the acuity of its choices, the unobtrusive depth of its learning, and its pedagogical and historical imaginativeness."

— Richard Millington
Smith College

"My overall reaction to this anthology is that it is one of the most thoughtfully organized and written anthologies of American literature that I have seen in recent years. Rich in visual materials, which are especially effective for an undergraduate audience, it is equally fulfilling in the content and choice of selections."

— Sharon M. Harris
University of Connecticut

"In sum, this text offers the best view of the cultural mosaic that is 'American Literature' that I have ever seen. I love the clear organization, and the various helpful apparati, especially the historical contextualizations of a work's particular 'place and time.'"

— Thomas Gannon
University of Nebraska

"Its selections are judiciously made, its introductions sound and focused on the real-world concerns of authorship in American history, its contextual material diverse, enriching, and to-the-point. I think that instructors who want for their undergraduate students a manageable anthology with an essential and diverse selection of texts, engaging biographical introductions, and contexts that ground the literature practically in the world of reading, publishing, and authorship will find *The Bedford Anthology of American Literature* a very attractive choice."

— Robert D. Habich
Ball State University

"I know many American literature professors who have forsworn using anthologies in the survey courses because of their unwieldiness, cost, and symbolic 'comprehensiveness.' This volume rethinks the concept of anthology. It takes a sophisticated, forward-looking curricular position and invites us all to rethink how we introduce students to American literature."

— Susan Tomlinson
University of Massachusetts, Boston

"The introductions are acute and generous without being overwhelming; they suggest depth without going into detail that might be stultifying to the new student of American literature."

— Daneen Wardrop
Western Michigan State University

The Bedford Anthology of American Literature

VOLUME TWO
1865 to the Present

Susan Belasco
University of Nebraska, Lincoln

Linck Johnson
Colgate University

Bedford / St. Martin's
BOSTON · NEW YORK

For Bedford / St. Martin's

EXECUTIVE EDITOR: Stephen A. Scipione
SENIOR DEVELOPMENTAL EDITOR: Maura Shea
SENIOR PRODUCTION EDITOR: Lori Chong Roncka
PRODUCTION SUPERVISOR: Jennifer Peterson
EXECUTIVE MARKETING MANAGER: Jenna Bookin Barry
MARKETING MANAGER: Adrienne Petsick
ASSOCIATE DEVELOPMENTAL EDITOR: Abby Bielagus
EDITORIAL ASSISTANT: Erin McGhee
PRODUCTION ASSISTANT: Lidia MacDonald-Carr
COPYEDITOR: Mary Lou Wilshaw-Watts
TEXT DESIGN: Judith Arisman, Arisman Design Studio
COVER DESIGN: Donna Lee Dennison
COVER ART: *Angel's Flight*, 1931, by Millard Sheets (32.17). Museum Associates /
    LACMA, Gift of Mrs. L. M. Maitland. Photo © Museum Associates / LACMA.
COMPOSITION: Stratford/TexTech
PRINTING AND BINDING: Quebecor World Taunton

PRESIDENT: Joan E. Feinberg
EDITORIAL DIRECTOR: Denise B. Wydra
EDITOR IN CHIEF: Karen S. Henry
DIRECTOR OF MARKETING: Karen Melton Soeltz
DIRECTOR OF EDITING, DESIGN, AND PRODUCTION: Marcia Cohen
MANAGING EDITOR: Elizabeth M. Schaaf

Library of Congress Control Number: 2006921308

Copyright © 2008 by Bedford / St. Martin's

Manufactured in the United States of America.

2   1   0   9   8
f   e   d   c   b   a

For information, write: Bedford / St. Martin's, 75 Arlington Street, Boston, MA
02116 (617-399-4000)

ISBN-10: 0-312-41208-8 (Volume Two)
ISBN-13: 978-0-312-41208-1

ISBN-10: 0-312-48299-X (Volume One)
ISBN-13: 978-0-312-48299-2

For Max Johnson and Stephen Jenkins

Preface

The Bedford Anthology of American Literature is designed to meet the challenge of teaching courses that cover American literature from its beginnings to the present day. That challenge has grown even more daunting during the last three decades, as the canon has expanded dramatically. We have been studying, teaching, and writing about American literature for over thirty years, yet like all teachers we grapple with questions about the selection, organization, and presentation of material, especially in relation to a changing student population. Indeed, even as instructors have recognized the claims of a growing number of writers and kinds of writings for a place on our syllabi, college students have become increasingly diverse in their backgrounds, experiences, and preparation for literary study. At the same time, rapid changes in technology have profoundly shaped students' understanding of language and communication, as well as their responses to both texts and textbooks.

The Bedford Anthology of American Literature takes a new approach to anthologizing American literature. The editors of any anthology inevitably build upon the work of earlier editors, and we have learned much from our predecessors and colleagues. Seeing anthologies of American literature become thicker and heavier, or expand into multiple volumes, however, we are concerned by the impact of that development on instructors and students alike. How, in the limited span of a semester or a quarter, can an instructor hope to cover the ever-growing list of writers and works or assign more than a relatively small number of the selections in most anthologies? And how do students respond when they find themselves skipping over large portions of an expensive anthology? Moreover, although we are deeply committed to anthologies as the most effective medium for representing the full range of American literature, we know from direct experience and the comments of other instructors that students find it awkward and unappealing to read certain kinds of works, especially novels and other extended prose narratives, in the somewhat cumbersome format of an anthology.

The Bedford Anthology of American Literature represents an effort to preserve the strengths of traditional anthologies while responding to changes in both the canon and in teaching methods that have emerged during the last thirty years. At every stage of our work on this anthology, we have been guided by the needs of instructors and their students. We have drawn on our extensive experiences at a wide range of institutions, and we have communicated with hundreds of instructors in colleges and universities across the country about how a new anthology might best meet their needs and the needs of contemporary college students. While the texts, notes, and introductions are based on current scholarship in the field, to which we are deeply indebted, *The Bedford Anthology of American Literature* is a tool for teaching and learning, and it aims at broad representation rather than comprehensive coverage. It consequently provides a rich but not unlimited range of choices to instructors facing the daunting task of creating syllabi and reading assignments of representative works from every period of American literature.

Two of the major pedagogical challenges facing teachers of the American literature survey course are engaging students in the readings and helping them understand history and context. We have, therefore, sought to bring together in an attractive format texts chosen on the basis of their literary or historical importance, their inherent interest, and their proven effectiveness in the classroom, either when studied on their own or in relation to other texts in the anthology. In addition to a core of commonly taught texts that instructors rely on, we have included rarely anthologized texts that have proven to be very successful in the classroom. We have also given some prominence to various kinds of life writings, which we view as a vital element in American literature and which we have found to be particularly attractive to students. In a further effort to stimulate student interest in and understanding of literary texts, as well as of their vital social, political, and cultural contexts, we have also incorporated features, including illustrations, that show the changing material conditions in which literary works were produced. We have thus sought to offer in reasonably compact volumes a foundation of essential texts that instructors need with a substantial amount of additional material to help them construct their own surveys of American literature. For students, our anthology offers a variety of ways to read and think about American literature and, we hope, fosters a greater understanding and appreciation of it.

Features of *The Bedford Anthology of American Literature,*
Volumes One and Two

A Teachable Collection of Literary Works. The selection of writers and works has been shaped by the new understandings of and approaches to American literature that have emerged during the last three decades. The selections consequently reflect the rich diversity of American literature, especially in terms of gender, race, and ethnicity. At the same time, the selection of writers and texts has been guided by what is actually taught in survey courses of American literature, based on extensive analysis of syllabi and reviews by over five hundred instructors nationwide.

An Apparatus Designed and Written for Students.   We have sought to make the introductory materials in the anthology lively and readable, while providing other features designed to engage the interest of students and enhance their appreciation and understanding of the texts. Biographical introductions highlight important aspects of the authors' backgrounds and experiences, while charting the course of their careers as writers. Marginal quotations, most often an appreciative observation by another writer, call attention to the characteristics or value of the author's work, and Web site references point to further information. Individual prose works and groups of poems are separately introduced in a selection headnote that provides information about the writing and publication of the works, as well as brief comments on their distinctive features or literary and historical significance. Explanatory notes are provided for each text and are designed to foster reading comprehension and assist students in understanding a work, not to provide critical commentary on the text. Indeed, we have consistently sought to provide contexts for reading texts and to raise questions designed to stimulate discussion rather than to offer interpretations of the texts.

Abraham Cahan
[1860-1951]

Abraham Cahan

This photograph was taken when Cahan was twenty-three, about two years after his arrival in New York City.

Abraham Cahan was born on July 7, 1860, in Podberezy, a shtetl or Jewish community in Russia. His parents were Sarah and Shakne Cahan, a teacher at a Hebrew school. When Cahan was about five years old, the family moved a short distance away to the larger city of Vilna. Both Podberezy and Vilna were situated in the Pale of Jewish Settlement, the area in eastern Russia where all Jews were required by law to live. The language spoken in the shtetl was Yiddish, a dialect combining words from Hebrew and several European languages, especially German. From an early age, Cahan developed a deep understanding of the value and importance of language through his intensive study of Hebrew, the Jewish Bible, and the Talmud, the body of Jewish civil and ceremonial law and legend. But he later decided to pursue secular studies at the Vilna Teacher Training Institute for Jewish students, which he attended from 1876 to 1881. While there, he was drawn to the revolutionary politics and socialism of students who opposed the political autocracy of Russia. The assassination of Czar Alexander II in 1881 prompted a wave of repression and violence directed against Russian Jews. Cahan, who had secured a job teaching in a school at Velizh, came under suspicion for possessing radical publications. Certain that he would be arrested and probably executed, Cahan fled Russia, joining more than 13,000 other Jews who left the country in 1882.

After a long and dangerous journey across Europe to England, Cahan booked a passage in steerage from Liverpool to New York City. During the voyage, he began to study English with the help of a Russian-English dictionary and a sailor who knew a few Russian words. Admitted through Ellis Island into the United States on June 7, 1882, Cahan joined thousands of other Jewish immigrants who had settled in the Lower East Side of Manhattan, then known as the "Ghetto." Even as he undertook the difficult task of earning a living in the overcrowded, impoverished section of the city, Cahan set about learning English. By the next year, his language skills were sufficient for him to begin teaching English to immigrants at the Young Men's Hebrew Association. In 1885, he met and married Aniuta (Anna) Bronstein, an immigrant from Kiev, Russia. Increasingly active in city politics and organized labor, Cahan formally joined the Socialist Labor Party in 1887. He soon began lecturing and writing articles in English on Jewish life in the city for several newspapers in New York. Revising a lecture he had delivered at the New York Labor Lyceum, Cahan also published "Realism," which appeared in the *Workman's Advocate* in 1889. As he later described it in his autobiography, the essay was "a philosophic consideration of the nature of art," based on his study of contemporary art and his reading of William Dean Howells, Henry James, and the Russian novelist Leo Tolstoy. Naturalized as an American citizen on June 8, 1891, Cahan continued to write articles in both English and Yiddish and edited a socialist newspaper published in Yiddish, the *Arbeter Tsaytung,* or "Worker's Journal."

He also began to write fiction. Cahan's first short story in English, "A Providential Match," appeared in *Short Stories* in 1895, the same year he published a serialized novel in Yiddish in the *Arbeter Tsaytung.* His efforts were strongly encouraged by William Dean Howells, who in 1895 told Cahan, "It is your duty to write." Buoyed by the support of an American writer he greatly admired, Cahan translated and published his serialized novel as *Yekl: A Tale of the New York Ghetto* (1896), which Howells enthusiastically reviewed in the *New York World.* "Suddenly I was known in American literature," Cahan later recalled. But he could not support himself and his family through fiction alone. In 1897, he helped establish what would become the leading Yiddish newspaper in the world, the *Jewish Daily Forward.* Cahan subsequently edited the newspaper for a total of fifty years. But he also continued to write in English for other New York newspapers and to publish articles and stories in magazines, including the prestigious *Atlantic Monthly.* A collection of five of his stories, *The Imported Bridegroom and Other Stories of the New York Ghetto,* was published in 1898. In a review of the volume, Howells once again praised Cahan's realism, observing that "the author handles [his materials] so skillfully that he holds the reader between a laugh and a heartache, and fashions into figures so lifelike that you would expect to meet them in any stroll through Hester-street," the busy artery at the heart of the Jewish community in New York City.

From that point on, Cahan was a prominent writer in both English and Yiddish. As the editor of the *Forward,* he was known for his articles on social reform and labor policy. Although he published a second novel in English, *The White Terror and the Red: A Novel of Revolutionary Russia* (1905), Cahan increasingly wanted to concentrate on journalism. At the invitation of the editors of *McClure's Magazine,* however, he wrote an extended fictional piece loosely based on some of the events of his life, *The Autobiography of an American Jew: The Rise of David Levinsky,* which was serialized in the magazine from April through July 1913. In revised form, Cahan later published it as *The Rise of David Levinsky: A Novel* (1917), now widely regarded as one of the most important works of early Jewish American fiction. During the same period, he began to write his actual autobiography, *The Education of Abraham Cahan,* which was published in five volumes between 1916 and 1936. Cahan continued to devote his energies to the *Forward,* serving as a spokesperson for American Jews and, after two visits to Palestine, becoming active in the Zionist movement. He also had the satisfaction of seeing many of his early fictional works reprinted in new editions. "Socialist leader, novelist, critic, and newspaper man," as he was described in the obituary in the *New York Times,* Cahan died on August 31, 1951.

Cahan's "A Ghetto Wedding."   This story was first published in the *Atlantic Monthly* only two months before it appeared in Cahan's collection *The Imported Bridegroom and Other Stories of the New York Ghetto* (1898).

[Cahan] sees his people humorously, and he is as unsparing of their sordidness as he is compassionate of their hard circumstance and the somewhat frowsy pathos of their lives.
—William Dean Howells

bedfordstmartins.com/ americanlit *for research links on Cahan*

An Emphasis on Complete Works.   In choosing selections for the anthology, we have sought to include complete texts – rather than excerpts – whenever possible. In Volume Two, we have included portions of extended works of nonfiction that can be effectively excerpted, including Sarah Winnemucca Hopkins's *Life among the Piutes*, Booker T. Washington's *Up from Slavery*, and W. E. B. Du Bois's *The Souls of Black Folk*. But all poems are printed in their entirety, and we have selected sketches, stories, or novellas rather than excerpts from novels. Lengthy works of fiction, which we believe students find far more comfortable to read as separate texts, are not included in the anthology. While we hope that many instructors will find the selections from key writers fully adequate for their purposes, we understand that other instructors may well wish to supplement the anthology with longer works of fiction. In order to make such works available for packaging with the anthology or for independent purchase, Bedford / St. Martin's has published the Bedford College Editions, attractive (and very competitively priced) reprints of five of the most frequently taught American novels: Nathaniel Hawthorne's *The Scarlet Letter*, Harriet Beecher Stowe's *Uncle Tom's Cabin*, Herman Melville's *Benito Cereno*, Mark Twain's *Adventures of Huckleberry Finn*, and Kate Chopin's *The Awakening*.

An Organization Designed for Greater Coherence and Comprehension.   The overall organization of the anthology is chronological. Volume One begins with Native American origin tales and concludes with the Civil War. Volume Two covers writers from 1865 to the present. Each volume, in turn, is divided into three **literary periods**. Within each of those periods, we have divided selections into related groups of authors or kinds of texts. Such **chapter groupings** are designed to serve several purposes. First, they bring into close proximity within the anthology works that might naturally be taught together, thus creating fruitful juxtapositions and helping instructors create coherent syllabi. We have also sought to address a problem we have often encountered when teaching with anthologies. Students sometimes find it difficult to relate the general information provided in a period introduction to the specific selections that follow or tend to forget much of that information by the time they read selections toward the end of the period. In addition to an introduction to each period, we also offer an introduction to each group of selections within the period, focusing on the specific cultural, historical, and especially literary backgrounds students may need in order to read those selections with understanding and appreciation.

A Unifying Theme on the History of Reading and Writing in America Provides Contexts for the Literature.   A thematic thread – the history of reading and writing in America – is woven throughout both volumes to assist students in understanding the context of the works and to emphasize the role literature has played in the unfolding story of culture and history in what became the United States. In the period introductions, as well as in the introductions to groups of authors and texts within each period, we emphasize developments such as the growth of literacy, the expansion of the educational system, changes in the production and distribution of books, and the emergence and increasing importance of periodicals in the literary culture of the United States. We further develop that theme in our introductions to authors, in which we indicate the ways such developments shaped their writings and literary careers, as well as in our

American Literature
1914–1945

The Emergence
of Modern American Drama

DURING THE EARLY DECADES of the twentieth century, "Broadway," the area around Times Square in New York City, at once symbolized and dominated theater in the United States. Many of the plays performed by hundreds of touring companies originated on Broadway, where the number of theatrical productions rose from seventy during the 1900–01 season to a peak of almost three hundred during 1926–27, after which the audience for theater was eroded by the growing popularity of "talkies" in the movies and the onset of the Great Depression. Operettas were especially popular on Broadway, as were musical extravaganzas such as Florenz Ziegfeld's *Follies,* which he produced virtually every year from 1907 through 1927.

◄ The Wharf Theatre
In the summer of 1916, the Provincetown Players gave their first public performances in a converted, 25 × 35 foot fishing shack at the end of Lewis Wharf in Provincetown, Massachusetts. Members of the group rigged up rudimentary lighting, created benches by resting planks on sawhorses, and built a 10 × 12 foot stage in the ramshackle building, which many theater historians view as the birthplace of modern American drama.

773

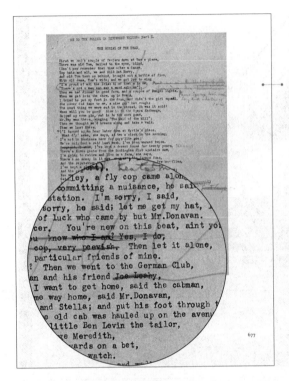

headnotes to selections, in which we discuss the writing and initial publication of the works. The history of reading and writing is further delineated in illustrations ranging from **manuscript pages**, including the opening page to T. S. Eliot's original typescript version of *The Waste Land* through a wide array of printed materials, such as the frontispiece to the original 1912 edition of Mary Antin's *The Promised Land*.

"American Contexts" Highlight a Wide Range of Writings under Compelling Topics. In addition to the works of the individual authors included in the anthology, briefer selections from many other writers are gathered together in clusters of related works called "**American Contexts**." Those sections focus on topics ranging from "Colonial Diaries and Journals" to "'Mine Eyes Have Seen the Glory': The Meanings of the Civil War" in Volume One and, in Volume Two, from "'The America of the Mind': Critics, Writers, and the Representation of Reality" to "'Inventing the Truth': The Contemporary Memoir." Such clusters are designed to extend the range and resonance of the anthology by introducing additional voices and other kinds of writing, from diaries, journals, and memoirs to editorials, critical essays, political speeches, and social criticism. Although individual selections within those clusters could of course be assigned separately, the "American Contexts" are designed as coherent units, most often intended to be taught as either an introduction or a coda to a larger period or grouping in the anthology. Some clusters invite discussion of distinctive genres, while others allow an opportunity to explore contested ideological issues, critical controversies, cultural developments, and responses to events such as the Civil War.

"Through a Modern Lens" Helps Students Make Connections between Writers from the Past and the Present. In order to bring later perspectives to bear on some of the writers and texts in Volume One, we have included brief sections throughout the volume under the general rubric "**Through a Modern Lens**." These include but are not limited to N. Scott Momaday's recent celebration of Native American origin and creation stories, Robert Lowell's exploration of one of the most prominent eighteenth-century writers in "Mr. Edwards and the Spider," and a tribute by the contemporary African American poet Kevin Young to Phillis Wheatley. In addition to revealing connections across time and space, the "Through a Modern Lens" feature offers rich opportunities for discussion of a number of connected issues: the imaginative effort required to understand the attitudes, conditions, and modes of expression of earlier periods; the sometimes tense rela-

American Contexts

"MAKE IT NEW":
POETS ON POETRY

IN HIS TRANSLATION OF THE *TA HIO* ("The Great Learning") of the ancient Chinese philosopher Confucius, the influential modern poet and critic Ezra Pound reaffirmed, "Renew thyself daily, utterly, make it new, and again new, make it new." The exhortation "make it new," a phrase that Pound later used as the title of a collection of his essays, consequently became a kind of shorthand for the complex and often conflicting agendas of American poets during the early decades of the twentieth century.

As the following commentaries by poets suggest, there was considerable disagreement among them about the ways in which poetry could be made new and what constituted the new poetry. In her introductory essay in the first issue of *Poetry: A Magazine of Verse* in 1912, its founder and editor Harriet Monroe affirmed that "all forms, whether narrative, dramatic, or lyric, will be acceptable." Monroe subsequently published a wide range of poetry in her magazine, which strongly encouraged both established and emerging poets in the United States. During the decades following the founding of *Poetry*, however, all of the elements of poetry – form, language, rhythm, rhyme, and subject matter – were topics of serious discussion and debate. Divisions emerged even within the first organized group of modern poets writing in English, the imagistes or imagists. Pound, the first leader of the group, described their fundamental aesthetic values and

538

---

poetic techniques in an essay published in *Poetry* in 1913. But he soon came into conflict with Amy Lowell, who was determined to democratize what Pound, using the French term, called imagisme and she called imagism, primarily in an effort to make such modern poetry seem less foreign or alien to audiences in the United States. As Lowell embarked on a crusade for imagism in essays such as "The New Manner in Modern Poetry," Pound moved in other directions, working with other new poets such as T. S. Eliot. In his 1919 essay "Tradition and the Individual Talent," Eliot challenged poets and critics who rejected "tradition" by emphasizing the vital connections between modern poets and poets of the past, a European tradition extending back to the ancient Greek poet Homer.

During the period from the 1920s through World War II, many poets grappled with questions about the function and status of poetry in the modern age. For poets of the Harlem Renaissance, questions about the language, sources, and subject matter of poetry were central to the contested issue of whether there was or could be what Langston Hughes described as "any true Negro Art in America." James Weldon Johnson rejected the tradition of dialect poetry, which he argued was not "capable of giving expression to the varied conditions of Negro life in America." Hughes, who frequently wrote in dialect, encouraged African American poets to produce work that was racial in both subject and treatment, drawing inspiration from indigenous traditions of music such as spirituals and jazz. In her essay "Modern Poetry," the poet and painter Mina Loy also emphasized the close relations between poetry and music, as well as the vital connections between "the renaissance in poetry" and the "composite language" forged by members of various races and immigrant groups in the United States. Hart Crane suggested that urban life and technological advances opened up new subjects for poets, exploring what in his 1930 essay "Modern Poetry" he described as the "function of poetry in a Machine Age." The poet most closely associated with rural New England, Robert Frost, reaffirmed some of the traditional forms and functions of poetry in "The Figure a Poem Makes" (1939), published near the end of the Great Depression. During that period of economic crisis, many viewed modern poetry as immaterial, and it was

MAKE IT NEW

ESSAYS BY

EZRA POUND

新
日 日 新

LONDON
FABER AND FABER LIMITED
24 RUSSELL SQUARE

Ezra Pound,
Make It New
The title of this 1934 collection of essays is Pound's translation of the four Chinese characters on the title page, which may more literally be translated "make new, day by day, make new."

bedfordstmartins.com/
americanlit for research links on the authors in this section

---

Occom through a Modern Lens

IN THE LATE EIGHTEENTH CENTURY, works by Native Americans who wrote in English were published by several printers, including Thomas and Samuel Green, descendants of a prominent family of colonial printers. The Greens printed dozens of sermons and religious books on their press in New London, Connecticut. They published Samson Occom's collection of hymns and spiritual songs, as well as his sermon on the execution of Moses Paul. Occom's works went through several editions during the eighteenth century and enjoyed considerable popularity. But Occom's autobiographical sketch existed only in manuscript until it was finally published in 1982. Since then, he has been the object of considerable attention by scholars, including James Ottery, a professor of English, a member of the Brothertown Indian Nation, and a descendant of Occom, whose name he spells *Occum*. Ottery wrote the following poem as he was contemplating the "silences" in Occom's "Diary," which he kept over many years and in which he wrote *A Short Narrative of My Life.* Some commentators have stressed Occom's failure to mention some of the devastating events of his life in his narrative, while scholars have emphasized its limitations as a source of ethnographic information about Native Americans. In contrast, playing off observations by nonnative critics and quotations from Occom's narrative, Ottery meditates on the obstacles that confronted a Native American attempting to put his "life into words in the language / that wasn't his mother tongue." The text, which incorporates Occom's words, is taken from the online publication of the poem (http://work.colum.edu/~jottery/IntroCW/NAC/SamsonOccum.htm).

The Reverend Mr. Samson Occom
This portrait of Occom, described in an accompanying caption as the "first Indian Minister that ever was in Europe," was published in London during or shortly after his triumphant fund-raising tour of England. Occom wrote his brief narrative of his life soon after his return to America.

410

James Ottery
[b. 1953]

THE DIARY OF SAMSON OCCUM

He put his life into words: his life
as a Presbyterian preacher,[1] his life
as a preacher and teacher before that
in the Society for Propagating the Gospel in New England,
two years of his life spent raising   5
money in old England for the Indian Charity School
in Connecticut, "funds misdirected"
for the founding of a white Dartmouth College instead.
He put his life into words, in the language
that was not his mother tongue, the language   10
not learned until he was 16;
in the language that was not his
until he reached the age of 16,
he wrote of his life until then in very few words
of the language that wasn't his mother tongue –   15

    I was born a Heathen
    and Brought up in Heathenism
    until I was between 16 & 17 Years of age,
    at a place call'd Mohegan . . .[2]

He put his life into words in the language   20
that wasn't his mother tongue, the English learned
first when he was 16,
(he would begin reading Hebrew at 21,
until "after a year of study" he would stop,
because "his *eyes* would fail him"),   25
in the language that was not his mother tongue
he would write:

    Having Seen and heard Several Representations,
    In England and Scotland [two words crossed out]

---

1. *Presbyterian preacher:* Occom was ordained a Presbyterian minister in 1759.
2. *I . . . Mohegan:* The opening lines of Occom's narrative.

411

tions between later readers and writers and earlier texts; and the ongoing influence of earlier authors on writers in the twentieth and twenty-first centuries, even as the works of those later writers reveal markedly different aesthetic values, literary practices, and philosophical or religious convictions.

Appealing Two-Color Design and Extensive Illustration Program Make Literature Inviting and Accessible for Today's Readers.   Each volume in *The Bedford Anthology of American Literature* includes more than two hundred carefully selected illustrations, ranging from engravings published in early travel narratives and examples of Native American arts to portraits of writers, paintings or photographs of contemporary scenes, and a wide range of images illustrating the history of literary and print culture, including manuscript pages, broadsides, periodicals, and the covers, frontispieces, and title pages of books. Although their inclusion is in part designed to enhance the attractiveness of and the experience of reading selections in the volumes, the primary purpose of the illustrations is pedagogical. Through our own teaching and in discussions with many other instructors, we have discovered that students increasingly respond to such visual materials, especially those that help them connect with authors and grasp the cultural, material, and social conditions in which literary works were produced. In fact, many of the selections in both volumes of this anthology were first published in illustrated books or periodicals, and such illustrations can generate fruitful discussions about both the literary work and its initial audience. In various ways, those and other illustrations raise questions about identity – the role of class, gender, race, and religion – and about self-representation and the representation of reality, questions that we believe may offer useful points of departure for a discussion of the central concerns and broader contexts of the literary texts. Thumbnails of some of the illustrations are used as visual markers in the timelines, which along with several maps are designed to help students negotiate the long history and the complex geography covered in *The Bedford Anthology of American Literature*.

A Note on Editorial Procedures

In general, we have taken the texts in the anthology from the first printings or from authoritative modern editions of early books and manuscripts. As far as is practicable, we have sought to reproduce the texts as they were originally written or published, retaining their historical features in order to preserve the flavor of the authors' styles and familiarize students with changes in English usage and the conventions of capitalization, punctuation, and spelling. Since spelling was not standardized until the late eighteenth century, we do not alter British spellings, such as *humour*; early variant spellings that can be clearly understood, such as *chearful* for *cheerful*; early past tense forms, such as *learnt* for *learned*; or contractions that were commonly used in early texts, such as *us'd* for *used* and *tho'* for *though*. To aid students in their reading of early texts, we have provided footnotes for many terms that are now archaic or obsolete. We have altered early printer's conventions that would cause confusion, such as the long *s* in *Bleffings*, which is printed as *Blessings*. We have silently expanded some abbreviations,

1896, effectively marking the end of Indian resistance to the army and policies of the United States. After that, the struggle for Indian rights increasingly shifted to politics and print culture. Charles A. Eastman (Ohiyesa) began his literary career with a popular account of his traditional Lakota upbringing, *Indian Boyhood* (1902). Another indigenous writer, Zitkala-Ša, exploited the literacy she had gained in English at an "assimilation school" for Indians to challenge the policies of assimilation and to preserve the traditions of Native Americans.

Immigration also raised questions about how the so-called alien populations might be assimilated into American society and culture. In the period from 1865 to 1914, during which the population of the country grew from 40 million to over 100 million people, more than 25 million immigrants arrived in the United States. The most profound symbol of America's welcome to immigrants ultimately became the Statue of Liberty

Immigrants in the United States, 1900
As this map illustrates, most of the millions of immigrants who arrived in the United States in the decades following the Civil War settled in the East, Midwest and West, where foreign-born inhabitants exceeded 30 percent of the population of some states in 1900.

elegiac volumes of poetry about the war, and Elizabeth Stuart Phelps offered consolation to the grief-stricken country in her novel *The Gates Ajar,* in which a young woman mourning the death of her brother, killed in the war, finds comfort in the Spiritualist belief that those who have gone to heaven retain a vital link to their loved ones left behind on earth. Phelps's best-selling novel was published in 1868, the year that General John Logan, commander of the Grand Army of the Republic, issued a proclamation designating May 30 as a memorial day "for the purpose of strewing with flowers or otherwise decorating the graves of comrades who died in defense of their country during the late rebellion, and whose bodies now lie in almost every city, village, and hamlet churchyard in the land." Even before his official proclamation, the decoration of the graves of soldiers who had died in the war had become a common ritual of mourn-

COMPARATIVE TIMELINE, 1865-1914

Dates	American Literature	History and Politics	Developments in Culture, Science, and Technology
1865–1869	1865 Walt Whitman, *Drum-Taps* 1865 Henry James, "The Story of a Year," his first signed story, in the *Atlantic Monthly* 1865 Mark Twain, "Jim Smiley and His Jumping Frog" in the *New York Saturday Press*	1865 Thirteenth Amendment abolishes slavery in the United States 1865 Confederate general Robert E. Lee surrenders at Appomattox Courthouse 1865 Abraham Lincoln is assassinated and Andrew Johnson becomes president	1865 *The Nation* begins publication in New York City 1865 William Booth founds religious group later named Salvation Army
	1866 Herman Melville, *Battle-Pieces and Aspects of the War* 1866 John Greenleaf Whittier, *Snow-Bound* 1867 John W. De Forest, *Miss Ravenel's Conversion from Secession to Loyalty* 1868 Elizabeth Stuart Phelps, *The Gates Ajar*	1866 Ku Klux Klan is formed 1867 Congress passes first of the Reconstruction Acts 1868 Fourteenth Amendment grants citizenship to all persons born in the United States, including former slaves 1868 Ulysses S. Grant elected president 1869 Elizabeth Cady Stanton and Susan B. Anthony establish the National Woman Suffrage Association	1866 Metropolitan Museum of Art founded in New York City 1867 Karl Marx, *Das Kapital* 1868 *Overland Monthly* begins publication in San Francisco 1869 Union Pacific and Central Pacific Railroads form transcontinental rail system 1869 Opening of Suez Canal

the continent, large portions of which had become U.S. territory as part of the treaty ending the Mexican War in 1848. American artists celebrated manifest destiny in paintings and stories of heroic pioneers bringing "civilization" to the West. But that process was viewed in a far different light by one of the first Mexican American writers to publish in English, María Amparo Ruiz de Burton. Describing her response to the term *manifest destiny* in a letter written in 1871, Ruiz de Burton angrily exclaimed: "Of all the evil phrases ever invented in order to create buffoons, there is not one phrase more detestable for me than that one, the most offensive, the most insulting; my blood rises to the top of my head when I hear it, and I see as if in a photographic instance, all that the Yankees have done to make Mexicans suffer – the robbery of Texas; war; [and] the robbery of California."

Advertisement for Western Lands
Railroad companies lured passengers and settlers by selling land in the West. By the time this poster was printed in 1872, the Burlington & Missouri Railroad Company ran from Chicago across Illinois and Iowa and deep into Nebraska.

further marginalizing the Mexican American population, especially in southern California. In her novel *The Squatter and the Don* (1885), Ruiz de Burton dramatizes the cultural clashes, racial tensions, and struggles over land between Anglo-American squatters and a Mexican American landowner in California.

The settlement of the West proved to be even more disastrous for Native Americans. In a last-ditch effort to preserve their way of life and to protect their lands from the relentless encroachment of white settlers, the Lakota (Sioux) and Cheyenne fought and won the battle of Little Bighorn in 1876. But the federal government swiftly overcame their resistance and redrew the boundary lines of Indian reservations, opening up vast portions of them to American settlers. The white reformer Helen Hunt Jackson documented the brutal history of the mistreatment of Native Americans in *A Century of Dishonor* (1881), a copy of which she sent to every member of Congress. Sarah Winnemucca Hopkins, the first Native American woman to publish a book in the United States, also pleads the cause of the Indians in *Life among the Piutes: Their Wrongs and Claims* (1883). Such efforts did little to alter the harsh policies of the federal government toward the Indians. Federal troops massacred more than one hundred unarmed Lakota at Wounded Knee, South Dakota, on January 16,

San Carlos Apache Indian Reservation
Many bands of Apache were forcibly relocated from their traditional homelands, which once extended across Arizona and New Mexico, to this reservation in southeastern Arizona, established in 1872. Katherine Taylor Dodge took this photograph of men, women, and children waiting in line for supplies outside an agency building on "issue day" in 1899.

including early abbreviated forms like y^e (the) and y^t (that) and abbreviations of the books of the Bible. We have also corrected obvious typographical errors, but we have altered punctuation, spelling, or other features of a text only in instances where the reading comprehension of students might be compromised. When we have made such alterations, we indicate them in notes or the headnote to the text, where we cite the published source of the text. Each text is followed by the year of its first printing or original composition and, when it is different, the year of publication of the edition from which the text is taken.

Print and Multimedia Ancillaries to Support
The Bedford Anthology of American Literature,
Volumes One and Two

Bedford College Editions reprint enduring literary works in a handsome and readable format that can be affordably packaged with either volume of the anthology. The literary works include: Nathaniel Hawthorne's *The Scarlet Letter*, edited by Susan S. Williams (Ohio State University); Harriet Beecher Stowe's *Uncle Tom's Cabin*, edited by Stephen Railton (University of Virginia); Herman Melville's *Benito Cereno*, edited by Wyn Kelley (Massachusetts Institute of Technology); Mark Twain's *Adventures of Huckleberry Finn*, edited by Gregg Camfield (University of the Pacific); and Kate Chopin's *The Awakening*, edited by Sharon M. Harris (University of Connecticut). The text of each work is lightly but helpfully annotated to aid readers without dictating how they should read. Prepared by eminent scholars and teachers, the editorial matter in each volume includes a chronology of the life of the author; an illustrated introduction to the contexts and major issues of the text in its time and ours; an annotated bibliography for further reading in backgrounds, criticism, and online; and a concise glossary of literary terms. The text of the work is also accessible online at an accompanying Web site (visit **bedfordstmartins.com/americanlit**), where it can be searched electronically.

Award-Winning Trade Titles Available for Packaging at Significant Savings.   Add more value and choice to your students' learning experiences by packaging *The Bedford Anthology of American Literature* with any of a thousand titles from Farrar, Straus & Giroux, Picador, St. Martin's Press, and other Macmillan trade publishers – at discounts of up to 50 percent off the regular price. To learn more, or to package a Macmillan trade book with *The Bedford Anthology of American Literature*, contact your local Bedford / St. Martin's sales representative. To see a complete list of titles available for packaging, go to **bedfordstmartins.com/tradeup**.

Resources for Teaching THE BEDFORD ANTHOLOGY OF AMERICAN LITERATURE, Volume One by Lisa Logan, University of Central Florida; Volume Two by Michael Soto, Trinity University. This extensive instructor's manual includes entries for every author and every thematic cluster and offers approaches to teaching; sample syllabi with tips on planning the course; connections to other authors and texts; classroom-tested suggestions for discussion, writing, and oral presentations; and print and multimedia resources for fur-

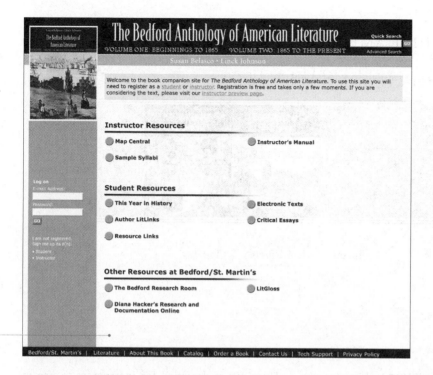

ther research. The instructor's manual is available in a combined print volume – or as downloadable files from the companion Web site.

Background Readings for Teachers of American Literature, compiled by Venetria K. Patton, Purdue University. This collection of critical essays for instructors provides an overview of recent changes in the field of American literary studies. The twenty-three readings include important scholarship, newer critical approaches, and practical ideas from experienced teachers. Organized by various approaches ranging from historical context to race and ethnicity and gender and sexuality, this professional resource is relevant to a wide range of courses in American literature, from surveys to graduate seminars.

Companion Web Site at **bedfordstmartins.com/americanlit.** This site is equipped with student and instructor resources that include annotated research links (LitLinks) for almost every author in the anthology, as well as for broader topics in American literature; maps, including all of the maps in the book plus access to many more at Map Central; This Year in History, which offers snapshots of important literary, historical, and cultural moments; additional critical essays directly related to several selections in the anthology; the instructor's manual (downloadable); and sample syllabi.

Instructor DVD, *Archive America*.   This DVD is designed for instructors to use in classroom presentations to help contextualize literary works in a manner that captures students' attention. The focus is on major themes in American literary history, which are brought to life through a rich collection of material that includes art, contextual documents, maps, audio recordings, and video clips.

Acknowledgments

The Bedford Anthology of American Literature is the product of the most challenging, enjoyable, and rewarding work the editors have ever undertaken. We have taken equal pleasure and satisfaction in working with and learning from others who share our deep commitment to teaching American literature. This anthology is the result of a truly collaborative effort, not only between the editors, but also among the hundreds of dedicated people who have helped shape the contents, design, and features of the anthology, including our colleagues, the staff at Bedford / St. Martin's, the authors and editors of the companion and ancillary texts, the members of our Editorial Advisory Board, and the hundreds of reviewers and survey respondents whose thoughtful comments have so enriched our understanding of the needs of instructors and their students at a wide range of institutions all across the United States.

We are delighted to thank all of those who have contributed to our work on this anthology, both directly and indirectly. From graduate school onward, we have learned from our teachers, students in our classes, and our colleagues. We would especially like to remember the late E. Hudson Long of Baylor University and the late Joseph L. Slater of Colgate University, two remarkable individuals with distinguished careers in the study and teaching of American literature. For their support and stimulating conversation, we want to thank our valued colleagues at Colgate University and the University of Nebraska, Lincoln: Peter Balakian, Sarah Bay-Cheng, Michael Coyle, George Hudson, Neill Joy, Jane Pinchin, Phillip Richards, and Sarah Wider; and Grace Bauer, Stephen Behrendt, Robert Bergstrom, Franz Blaha, Kwakiutl Dreher, Kalenda Eaton, Thomas C. Gannon, Melissa Homestead, Maureen Honey, Tom Lynch, Amelia Montes, Marshall Olds, Linda Pratt, Kenneth Price, Guy Reynolds, Joy Ritchie, Gregory Rutledge, Gerry Shapiro, Judy Slater, and Nick Spencer. We are also deeply and directly indebted to the authors of the *Resources for Teaching* THE BEDFORD ANTHOLOGY OF AMERICAN LITERATURE for their many excellent suggestions: Lisa Logan, University of Central Florida, and Michael Soto, Trinity University. Venetria K. Patton, Purdue University, editor of *Background Readings for Teachers of American Literature*, offered us several excellent ideas as she compiled the essays for that volume. For their excellent contributions to *Archive America*, the Instructor DVD, we would like to thank Amanda Gailey, University of Georgia; Vicky Gailey; Andrew Jewell, University of Nebraska, Lincoln; John David Miles, Duke University; Darcie Rives, Augustana College; Jefferson Slagle, Ohio State University; Laura Tohe, Arizona State University; Stefanie Wortman, University of Missouri, Columbia. The editors of the novels in the Bedford College Editions series also made numerous suggestions: Gregg Camfield, University of the Pacific; Sharon M. Harris, University of Connecticut; Wyn Kelley, Massachusetts Institute of Technology; Stephen Railton, University of Virginia; and Susan S. Williams, Ohio State University. Members of our Editorial Advisory Board have provided detailed reviews, sound advice, and helpful support on Volumes One and Two. Volume One board members include David J. Carlson, California State University, San Bernardino; Matt Cohen, Duke University; Pattie Cowell, Colorado State University; Paul Crumbley, Utah State University; William Merrill Decker, Oklahoma State University; Thomas C. Gannon, University of Nebraska, Lincoln; Sharon M. Harris, University of Connecticut; Lisa Logan, University of Central Florida; Richard Millington, Smith College; Barbara Packer, University of California, Los Angeles; Venetria Patton, Purdue University; Sarah Robbins, Kennesaw State University; Michael Soto, Trinity University; Zabelle Stodola, University of Arkansas at Little Rock; and Susan S. Williams, Ohio State University. Volume Two board members include Elizabeth Ammons, Tufts University; Stephanie Browner, Berea College; Donna Campbell, Washington State University; David Chinitz, Loyola University Chicago; Michael Coyle, Colgate University; Robert Donahoo, Sam Houston State University; AnaLouise Keating, Texas Woman's University; Linda Morris, University of California, Davis; Paul Sorrentino, Virginia Polytechnic Institute and State University; Michael Soto, Trinity University; Nicholas Spencer, University of Nebraska, Lincoln; and Susan Tomlinson, University of Massachusetts, Boston.

Throughout the years that we have been working on *The Bedford Anthology of American Literature*, we have been helped and guided by a large number of instructors at a variety of institutions. For their suggestions on Volume One, we are thankful to Stacy Alaimo, University of Texas at Arlington; James Albrecht, Pacific Lutheran University; Joseph Alkana, University of Miami; Scott Ash, Nassau Community College; Dorothy Baker, University of Houston at University Park; Matthew Bell, Emerson College; Peter

Bellis, University of Miami; Alfred Bendixen, California State University, Los Angeles; Tyler Blake, Mid-America Nazarene University; Cheryl Bohde, McLennan Community College; Ashlee Brand, South Texas Community College; Virginia Brooks, Palm Beach Community College, North; Matthew Brown, California State University, Chico; Donna Burney, Howard Payne University; Tracy Butts, California State University at Chico; Donna Campbell, Washington State University; Kevin Coots, Ashland Community College; Deborah Core, Eastern Kentucky University; Robert Cummings, University of Georgia; Jennifer Daniels, Northern Virginia Community College at Annandale; Jean Darcy, Queensborough Community College; Christine Doyle, Central Connecticut State University; James Egan, Brown University; Gregory Eiselein, Kansas State University; Karen English, San Jose State University; John Ernest, University of New Hampshire; Patricia Flanary, Lexington Community College; Annamaria Formichella-Elsden, Buena Vista University; Theresa Gaul, Texas Christian University; Rosemary Guruswamy, Radford University; Paul Gutjahr, Indiana University; Robert D. Habich, Ball State University; Carol Henderson, University of Delaware; Desiree Henderson, University of Texas at El Paso; Laura Henigman, James Madison University; William Hug, Jacksonville State University; Jocelyn Adkins Irby, Tennessee State University; Miranda Johnson-Parries, Old Dominion University; Patricia Kalayjian, California State University, Dominguez Hills; Valerie Karno, University of Rhode Island; Jimmie Killingsworth, Texas A&M University; Mark Knockemus, Northeastern Technical College; Cecilia Koncharr-Farr, College of Saint Catherine; Erika Kreger, San Jose State University; Peggy Kulesz, University of Texas at Arlington; Linda Leavell, Oklahoma State University; Jian-Zhong Lin, Eastern Connecticut State University; Lisa MacFarlane, University of New Hampshire; Stephen J. Martelli, Massasoit Community College; Stephen Mathis, Northern Essex Community College; David Mazel, Adams State College; Anthony Michel, California State University, Fresno; Bruce Michelson, University of Illinois; Quentin Miller, Suffolk University; Sally Mitchell, Temple University; Randall Moon, Hazard Community College; Wesley Mott, Worcester Polytechnic Institute; James Nagel, University of Georgia; Randy Nelson, Davidson College; Lisa Norwood, Drake University; Sandra Oh, University of Miami; Patricia Okker, University of Missouri-Columbia; B. Parris, University of Washington; David Payne, University of Georgia; Nancy Penney, Lord Fairfax Community College; Jeff Perkins, Somerset Community College; Leland Person, University of Cincinnati; John Pleimann, Jefferson College; Sharon Reedy, Pellissippi State Technological Community College; Donna Reiss, Tidewater Community College at Virginia Beach; Connie Richards, Salisbury State University; David M. Robinson, Oregon State University; Lois Rudnick, University of Massachusetts, Boston; Dorothy Seyler, Northern Virginia Community College at Annandale; Alan Silva, Hamline University; Jack Summers, Central Piedmont Community College; Timothy Sweet, West Virginia University; James Tanner, University of North Texas; Robert Tilton, University of Connecticut; Herbert Tucker, University of Virginia; Joseph Urgo, University of Mississippi; Edward Vega, Palm Beach Community College; Beverly Voloshin, San Francisco State University; Daneen Wardrop, Western Michigan University; Steven Ware, Puget Sound Christian College; Eric Weil, Shaw University; Ellen Weinauer, University of South Mississippi; Cindy Weinstein, California Institute of Technology; Carol Westcamp, University of Arkansas at Fort Smith; Warren

Westcott, Tennessee State University; Gary Williams, University of Idaho; and Michael Ziser, University of California, Davis.

For their helpful comments on Volume Two, we are thankful to Larry Adams, University of North Alabama; Robin Andreasen, South Texas Community College; George Bailey, Northern Essex Community College; Ashley Bourne, J. Sargent Reynolds Community College; Stephen Brennan, Louisiana State University; Judith Budz, Fitchburg State College; Christopher Bundrick, University of Texas-Pan American; Mark Cantrell, University of Miami; Shelby Cochran, Gadsden State Community College; Jean Lee Cole, Loyola College in Maryland; Bonny Copenhaver, Volunteer State Community College; Fenobia Dallas, Saginaw State University; Ann Fisher-Wirth, University of Mississippi; Glenda Frank, Fashion Institute of Technology; Geoff Grimes, Mountain View College; Darrin Grinder, Northwest Nazarene University; Joseph Haske, South Texas College; Kathleen Hicks, Arizona State University; John Hildebrand, University of Wisconsin-Eau Claire; Donna Hollenberg, University of Connecticut; Charles Johanningsmeier, University of Nebraska, Omaha; David Jones, University of Wisconsin-Eau Claire; Roberta Keller, Blue Ridge Community College; Liz Marconi, Massassoit Community College; Pamela Matthews, Texas A&M University; Linda McCloud, Broward Community College; Jason McEntee, South Dakota State University; Amelia Montes, University of Nebraska, Lincoln; Ben Olguin, University of Texas at San Antonio; Venetria Patton, Purdue University; Jonathan Price, California State University, Sacramento; Roberta Proctor, Palm Beach Community College; Jonathan Sponsler, Lehigh Carbon Community College; Cecilia Tichi, Vanderbilt University; Kendra Vaglienti, Brookhaven College; Ryan Van Cleave, Clemson University; and Amir Zubari, University of Miami.

Staff members of the University of Nebraska, Lincoln, and Colgate University libraries have helped us locate texts and solve bibliographic problems; we are especially appreciative of Kathy Johnson and Carl Peterson. We have also benefited from the several students who served so ably as research assistants for this project: Soojin Ahn, Jaclyn Cruikshank, Amanda Gailey, Ramon Guerra, Elizabeth Lorang, Janel Simons, and Stephanie Veverka. We are also grateful to the many students in our classes in American literature who have provided ideas and inspiration throughout our teaching careers at several colleges and universities.

Working with the extraordinarily talented staff members of Bedford / St. Martin's has been an enriching educational experience as well as a constant pleasure. The first member of the editorial staff we met at Bedford / St. Martin's was executive editor Steve Scipione, and we have come to depend on his expert professional opinions and high good humor. Our untiring editor, Maura Shea, provided strong support and wise counsel on an almost daily basis for four years. In her absence during a brief leave, we greatly valued the help and good cheer of Laura Arcari. Joan Feinberg, president of Bedford / St. Martin's, imaginatively guided a long series of stimulating discussions about American literature in general and our anthology in particular. Karen Henry, executive editor, has been a constant source of sound advice and soothing reassurance. Other members of the editorial staff — Denise Wydra, Kaitlin Hannon, Abby Bielagus, Erin McGhee — have also helped in many ways, large and small. We also want to thank the members of the new media staff who have taught us much about the technical possibilities of Web sites and DVDs: Harriet Wald, Dan Cole, Kim Hampton, and Coleen O'Hanley. Lori Chong

Roncka and the other members of the production staff, Marcia Cohen, Elizabeth Schaaf, and Lidia MacDonald-Carr patiently made hundreds – perhaps thousands – of invaluable suggestions. We greatly respect and admire the members of the art and design staff: Donna Dennison, Anna Palchik, Judith Arisman, Shelby Disario, Rose Corbett Gordon, Martha Friedman, and Linda Finigan. We also thank Virginia Creeden for her work on permissions and Jenna Bookin Barry and Adrienne Petsick for teaching us about marketing plans.

Finally, our wonderful family members and good friends have offered enthusiastic encouragement and happy diversions: Peggy Belasco; Bill Belasco and Teresa Morales; Janet and Steve Jenkins; Lance Johnson; Roslyn and Vincent Reilly; Michael Meyer and Gina Barreca; Dewey and Rebekah Mosby; Reagan Sides and Kirby Gosnell; and Pamela Stockton.

We lovingly dedicate *The Bedford Anthology of American Literature* to Max Johnson and Stephen Jenkins, our familial connections to the next generation of college students.

Susan Belasco
Linck Johnson

About the Editors

Susan Belasco (B.A., Baylor University; Ph.D., Texas A&M University), professor of English and women's studies at the University of Nebraska, Lincoln, has taught courses in writing and American literature at several institutions since 1974, including McLennan Community College; Allegheny College; California State University, Los Angeles; and the University of Tulsa. The editor of Margaret Fuller's *Summer on the Lakes* and Fanny Fern's *Ruth Hall*, she is also the coeditor of three collections of essays: *Approaches to Teaching Stowe's "Uncle Tom's Cabin," Periodical Literature in Nineteenth-Century America*, and *Leaves of Grass: The Sesquicentennial Essays*. The editor of "Walt Whitman's Periodical Poetry" for the *Walt Whitman Archive* (**whitmanarchive.org**), she is a past president of the Research Society for American Periodicals.

Linck Johnson (B.A., Cornell University; Ph.D., Princeton University), the Charles A. Dana Professor of English at Colgate University, has taught courses in writing and American literature and culture since 1974. He is the author of *Thoreau's Complex Weave: The Writing of "A Week on the Concord and Merrimack Rivers," with the Text of the First Draft*; the Historical Introduction to *A Week* in the Princeton University Press edition of the *Writings of Henry D. Thoreau*; and numerous articles and contributions to books. The recipient of a National Endowment for the Humanities Fellowship at the American Antiquarian Society, he is a member of the Editorial Board of the *Collected Works of Ralph Waldo Emerson*.

Contents

≡ AMERICAN LITERATURE, 1865–1914 ≡

Writing "American" Lives

≡ AMERICAN LITERATURE, 1914–1945 ≡

Modernisms in American Poetry

AMERICAN CONTEXTS
"MAKE IT NEW": POETS ON POETRY

The Emergence of Modern American Drama

At Home and Abroad: American Fiction between the Wars

AMERICAN CONTEXTS
FROM THE GREAT WAR TO THE GREAT DEPRESSION: AMERICAN WRITERS AND THE CHALLENGES OF MODERNITY

≡ AMERICAN LITERATURE SINCE 1945 ≡

From Modernism to Postmodernism

AMERICAN CONTEXTS
"INVENTING THE TRUTH": THE CONTEMPORARY MEMOIR

The Bedford Anthology
of American Literature

VOLUME TWO

1865 to the Present

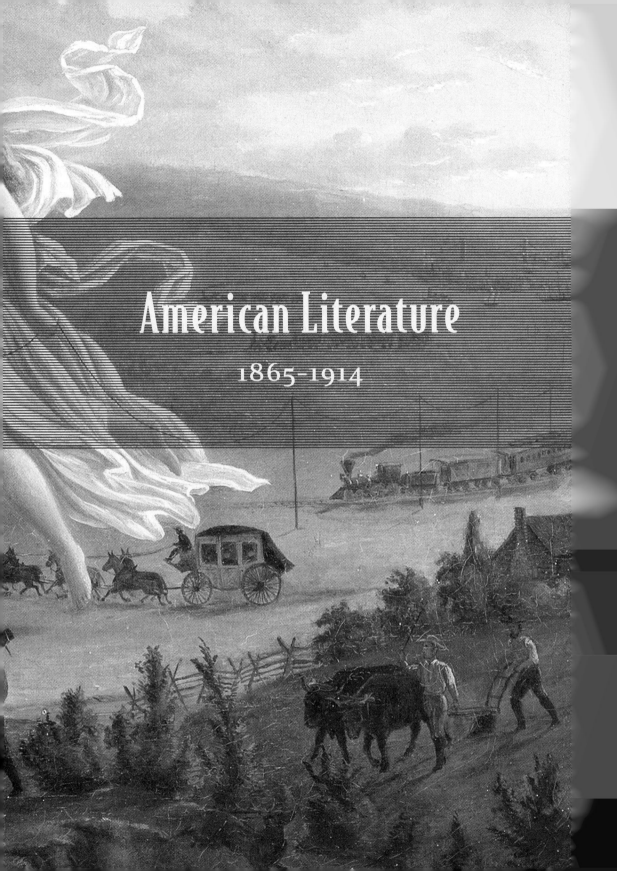

American Literature

1865–1914

$\mathcal{F}$OLLOWING THE CIVIL WAR, Northerners and Southerners could agree on little except the extent to which the country had been transformed by the traumatic experience of the four years between the attack on Fort Sumter in April 1861 and the surrender of the last Confederate forces in May 1865. "Society has been completely changed by the war," a Louisiana planter mournfully observed in 1865. But the conflict did not simply end slavery, sweep away the aristocratic plantation system, and devastate the landscape of the South. It also hastened changes that radically transformed life in the North. George Ticknor, a retired professor at Harvard College, wrote in 1868 that the war had created a "great gulf between what happened before in our century and what has happened since, or what is likely to happen hereafter. It does not seem to me as if I were living in the country in which I was born." The gulf between life before and after the war continued to expand during the following decades, as millions of settlers moved into the West and as unprecedented levels of immigration stimulated rapid industrialization in the North. Paradoxically, even as the reunited country developed into a world power, it was increasingly divided along lines of class, ethnicity, and race in a period that ushered in a modern and ever more multicultural America.

The Aftermath of the Civil War

In the years immediately following the end of hostilities, the nation struggled to come to terms with the terrible toll of the Civil War. Experts estimate that as many as 620,000 Americans died in the war, roughly 360,000 Union and 260,000 Confederate troops, and that more than 400,000 were wounded. Walt Whitman and Herman Melville published

◀ (OVERLEAF)

American Progress

This chromolithograph, based on an 1872 painting of the same title by John Gast, reveals the conceptions many Americans then shared about "manifest destiny." In an elaborate explanation of the patriotic symbolism of the picture, the publisher described it as an illustration of "the grand drama of Progress in the civilization, settlement and history of our civilization," personified by a female figure "floating westward through the air bearing on her forehead 'The Star of Empire.'" In one hand she carries a book, "the emblem of Education and the testimonial of our national enlightenment," while with the other hand she stretches out the wires of the telegraph. She hovers over forms of technology and transportation, including the newly completed transcontinental railroad, and hunters, miners, and homesteaders crossing the Great Plains. Before them, "fleeing from 'Progress,'" are wild game and the Indians, "moving Westward, ever Westward." In fact, many Indian tribes fought to retain their traditional homelands until the federal army finally forced them onto reservations to make room for the millions of settlers who poured into the West during the decades following the Civil War.

elegiac volumes of poetry about the war, and Elizabeth Stuart Phelps offered consolation to the grief-stricken country in her novel *The Gates Ajar*, in which a young woman mourning the death of her brother, killed in the war, finds comfort in the Spiritualist belief that those who have gone to heaven retain a vital link to their loved ones left behind on earth. Phelps's best-selling novel was published in 1868, the year that General John Logan, commander of the Grand Army of the Republic, issued a proclamation designating May 30 as a memorial day "for the purpose of strewing with flowers or otherwise decorating the graves of comrades who died in defense of their country during the late rebellion, and whose bodies now lie in almost every city, village, and hamlet churchyard in the land." Even before his official proclamation, the decoration of the graves of soldiers who had died in the war had become a common ritual of mourn-

COMPARATIVE TIMELINE, 1865–1914

Dates	American Literature	History and Politics	Developments in Culture, Science, and Technology
1865–1869	1865 Walt Whitman, *Drum-Taps* 1865 Henry James, "The Story of a Year," his first signed story, in the *Atlantic Monthly* 1865 Mark Twain, "Jim Smiley and His Jumping Frog" in the *New York Saturday Press*	1865 Thirteenth Amendment abolishes slavery in the United States 1865 Confederate general Robert E. Lee surrenders at Appomattox Courthouse 1865 Abraham Lincoln is assassinated and Andrew Johnson becomes president	1865 The *Nation* begins publication in New York City 1865 William Booth founds religious group later named Salvation Army
	1866 Herman Melville, *Battle-Pieces and Aspects of the War* 1866 John Greenleaf Whittier, *Snow-Bound* 1867 John W. De Forest, *Miss Ravenel's Conversion from Secession to Loyalty* 1868 Elizabeth Stuart Phelps, *The Gates Ajar*	1866 Ku Klux Klan is formed 1867 Congress passes first of the Reconstruction Acts 1868 Fourteenth Amendment grants citizenship to all persons born in the United States, including former slaves 1868 Ulysses S. Grant elected president 1869 Elizabeth Cady Stanton and Susan B. Anthony establish the National Woman Suffrage Association	1866 Metropolitan Museum of Art founded in New York City 1867 Karl Marx, *Das Kapital* 1868 *Overland Monthly* begins publication in San Francisco 1869 Union Pacific and Central Pacific Railroads form transcontinental rail system 1869 Opening of Suez Canal

ing in the North and the South. L. Nella Sweet's hymn "Kneel Where Our Loved Ones Are Sleeping," which was published in 1867, was thus dedicated "To the Ladies of the South who are Decorating the Graves of the 'Confederate Dead.'"

Even as the nation mourned, it struggled with questions about how and under what terms to unite the North and the South. In his final speech, delivered a few days before his assassination in April 1865, Abraham Lincoln described the daunting task of bringing together the bitterly divided country and of reconstructing the South. "No one man has authority to give up the rebellion for any other man," Lincoln somberly observed. "We simply must begin with, and mould from, disorganized and discordant elements. Nor is it a small additional embarrassment that we, the loyal people, differ among ourselves as to the mode, manner, and means of reconstruction." The differences in the North over the "means of reconstruction"

Dates	American Literature	History and Politics	Developments in Culture, Science, and Technology
1870–1879	1870 Bret Harte, *The Luck of the Roaring Camp and Other Sketches*	1870 U.S. population: 39,818,449	1870 First meteorological report issued by Weather Bureau, later National Weather Service
		1870 Fifteenth Amendment grants voting right to all qualified males, regardless of race or previous condition of servitude	
		1871 "Great Fire" of Chicago	1871 P. T. Barnum opens "Greatest Show on Earth" in Brooklyn
		1871 Revolution in France following defeat in Franco-Prussian War	
		1872 Congress designates Yellowstone as the first national park	1872 Claude Monet's painting *Impression, Sunrise* prompts first reference to Impressionists
	1873 Mark Twain and Charles Dudley Warner, *The Gilded Age*	1873 Financial panic leads to economic depression in United States	1873 Christopher Latham Sholes patents first typewriter
			1874 Joseph F. Glidden patents barbed wire
		1875 Civil Rights Act guarantees all Americans, regardless of race, equal access to public accommodations	
	1876 Mark Twain, *The Adventures of Tom Sawyer*	1876 Lakota (Sioux) and Cheyenne defeat Colonel Custer and his troops at battle of Little Bighorn	1876 American technological advances, including telephone, displayed at Centennial Exhibition in Philadelphia
		1876 Rutherford B. Hayes elected president	1876 Founding of National League of Professional Baseball Clubs

became even more apparent after Lincoln's death, as Congress wrangled with the new president, Andrew Johnson of Tennessee, who reportedly declared, "This is a country for white men, and as long as I am president, it shall be a government for white men." In 1866, Johnson vetoed the Fourteenth Amendment, which would have granted citizenship to all persons born in the United States, including former slaves. The veto outraged moderates and generated growing support in Congress for the "Radical Republicans," who favored greater support for former slaves and a more "radical" reconstruction of the South. Overriding the veto of the amendment, which was formally adopted by the states two years later, Congress passed the first of the Reconstruction Acts in 1867.

African Americans made strong gains during the following decade of Reconstruction. President Johnson's repeated vetoes

"We simply must begin with, and mould from, disorganized and discordant elements. Nor is it a small additional embarrassment that we, the loyal people, differ among ourselves as to the mode, manner, and means of reconstruction."

Dates	American Literature	History and Politics	Developments in Culture, Science, and Technology
1870–1879 (cont.)	1877 Sarah Orne Jewett, *Deephaven* 1878 Henry James, *Daisy Miller*	1877 Withdrawal of federal troops from the South signals end of Reconstruction 1878 "Susan B. Anthony Amendment" granting women right to vote is introduced in Congress 1879 Congress enacts law permitting women lawyers to argue cases before Supreme Court	1877 All-England Lawn Championship is first played at Wimbledon, England 1878 A. A. Pope manufactures first bicycles, called *wheels* 1879 Thomas Edison invents lightbulb
1880–1889	1880 José Martí, *Impressions of America* 1881 Joel Chandler Harris, *Uncle Remus* 1881 Henry James, *The Portrait of a Lady*	1880 U.S. population: 50,155,783 1880 James A. Garfield elected president 1881 Garfield is assassinated and Chester Arthur becomes president 1881 Founding of Federation of Organized Trades and Labor Union, later known as American Federation of Labor 1882 Chinese Exclusion Act	1881 Booker T. Washington organizes Normal and Industrial Institute for Negroes, later Tuskegee Institute 1882 Ottmar Mergenthaler invents linotype machine

of civil-rights legislation led to his impeachment by an angry Congress. He survived by a single vote, but in 1868 the Republican Party replaced Johnson as their presidential nominee with General Ulysses S. Grant, the Civil War hero who subsequently served two terms as president. Grant presided over the passage of the Fifteenth Amendment (1870), which provided voting rights to all qualified adult males, regardless of race or previous condition of servitude. The amendment enabled African American men to participate fully in the political process, both as voters and as representatives on the state and national level, and several African Americans were consequently elected to Congress. Reconstruction reached its high-water mark when Congress passed the sweeping Civil Rights Act of 1875. The law guaranteed all Americans, regardless of their race, access to public accommodations and facilities — such as restaurants, theaters, trains, and other public transportation — and protected their right to serve on juries.

Dates	American Literature	History and Politics	Developments in Culture, Science, and Technology
1880–1889 (cont.)	1883 Sarah Winnemucca Hopkins, *Life among the Piutes*	1883 Supreme Court declares Civil Rights Act of 1875 unconstitutional	1883 First performance of Buffalo Bill's Wild West Show
		1884 Grover Cleveland elected president	1884 Completion of Washington Monument
		1884 Financial panic leads to economic depression in United States	
	1885 María Amparo Ruiz de Burton, *The Squatter and the Don*		1885 *Good Housekeeping* magazine begins publication in Holyoke, Massachusetts
	1885 Mark Twain, *Adventures of Huckleberry Finn*		
	1886 Sarah Orne Jewett, *A White Heron and Other Stories*	1886 "Haymarket Affair," culmination of violent labor strife in Chicago	1886 Dedication of Statue of Liberty in New York harbor
		1887 "Golden Jubilee" marking fiftieth year of Queen Victoria's reign in England	
		1888 Benjamin Harrison elected president	1888 George Eastman patents Kodak camera
	1889 Mark Twain, *A Connecticut Yankee in King Arthur's Court*	1889 Oklahoma land rush as "Indian Territory" is opened to white settlers	1889 Jane Addams founds Hull House, settlement house in Chicago
1890–1899	1890 Emily Dickinson, *Poems*	1890 U.S. population: 62,947,714	1890 Jacob Riis, *How the Other Half Lives: Studies among the Tenements of New York*
		1890 Massacre of Lakota (Sioux) by federal troops at Wounded Knee, South Dakota	
		1890 Wyoming is first state to give women right to vote	

The following year, however, Reconstruction came to an abrupt end as a result of the disputed presidential election of 1876. Samuel J. Tilden, a Democrat from New York, won the popular vote but fell one vote short of the necessary majority of the electoral vote because of disputed returns in four states, three of them in the South. An electoral commission set up by Congress awarded the four states and the election to the Republican candidate, Rutherford B. Hayes. In what became known as the Compromise of 1877, the Republicans gained support for the commission's decision by offering southern Democrats in Congress a number of concessions, including the withdrawal of federal troops from the South.

The withdrawal of the troops, which had been deployed to ensure free elections and to protect black populations from attacks by whites who were determined to retain political power in the South, delivered a fatal blow to the civil rights and political aspirations of African Americans. The

Dates	American Literature	History and Politics	Developments in Culture, Science, and Technology
1890–1899 (cont.)	1891 William Dean Howells, *Criticism and Fiction* 1891 Mary E. Wilkins Freeman, *A New England Nun and Other Stories*		1891 The Music Hall, new Carnegie Hall, opens in New York City
	1892 Ambrose Bierce, *Tales of Soldiers and Civilians*	1892 Grover Cleveland elected president	1892 Pledge of Allegiance is first recited in public schools on Columbus Day
	1892 Charlotte Perkins Gilman, "The Yellow Wall-Paper"	1892 Federal immigration center opens at Ellis Island in New York harbor	1892 *Vogue* magazine begins publication in New York City
	1893 Stephen Crane, *Maggie: A Girl of the Streets (A Story of New York)*	1893 American plantation owners depose Queen Liliʻuokalani of Hawaiʻi; land later annexed by United States (1898)	1893 *McClure's Magazine*, famous for "muckraking" journalism, begins publication in New York City 1893 World's Columbian Exposition in Chicago
	1894 Kate Chopin, *Bayou Folk*	1894 Eugene Debs, president of the American Railway Union, is jailed during Pullman strike in Chicago	
	1895 Stephen Crane, *The Red Badge of Courage*	1895 Cuban war of independence from Spain begins	1985 *Bookman Magazine* coins term *bestseller*

federal government effectively ceased to enforce the Fourteenth and Fifteenth Amendments, and the Supreme Court declared the Civil Rights Act of 1875 unconstitutional in 1883. Southern states soon began to enact legal codes – the so-called Jim Crow laws, named after a grotesque character who performed in "blackface" in popular minstrel shows – that legalized segregation. The states also adopted poll taxes and discriminatory literacy tests that disenfranchised many black voters. The African American activist Ida B. Wells led a crusade against lynching, but Congress refused to pass an antilynching law, and African Americans suffered growing violence at the hands of organized white terror groups such as the Ku Klux Klan. In 1896 the Supreme Court affirmed the legality of segregation laws in the case of *Plessy v. Ferguson*, which challenged a Louisiana law that required blacks to ride in separate railroad cars, ruling that the law was constitutional and that such "separate but equal"

Dates	American Literature	History and Politics	Developments in Culture, Science, and Technology
1890-1899 (cont.)	1896 Paul Laurence Dunbar, *Lyrics of Lowly Life*	1896 Supreme Court affirms constitutionality of "separate but equal" accommodations for whites and African Americans in *Plessy v. Ferguson*	1896 *Everybody's Magazine* begins publication in New York City
		1896 William McKinley is elected president	
	1897 E. A. Robinson, *Children of the Night*		1897 Sigmund Freud defines Oedipus complex
	1898 Abraham Cahan, *The Imported Bridegroom and Other Stories of the New York Ghetto*	1898 Spain cedes Cuba, Puerto Rico, Guam, and the Philippines to United States in treaty ending Spanish-American War	1898 Marie Curie discovers elements polonium and radium, coining term *radio-activity*
	1899 Charles W. Chesnutt, *The Wife of His Youth and Other Stories of the Color Line*	1899-1902 Boer War between British and descendants of Dutch settlers in South Africa	
	1899 Kate Chopin, *The Awakening*	1899-1913 Philippine Insurrection	
	1899 Frank Norris, *McTeague: A Story of San Francisco*		
1900-1909	1900 Theodore Dreiser, *Sister Carrie*	1900 U.S. population: 75,994,575	1900 Number of daily newspapers in United States is 1,400; there are 3,500 magazines, with estimated readership of 65 million

accommodations did not stamp the "colored race with the badge of inferiority."

African Americans suffered cultural as well as legislative and judicial setbacks. The growing indifference of many white Americans to the struggle for freedom and racial equality was revealed in changing interpretations of the meaning of the Civil War. John W. De Forest announced his pro-Union plot and theme in the title of his early novel about the war, *Miss Ravenel's Conversion from Secession to Loyalty* (1867), in which one of the central characters defined the conflict as the culminating act in "the drama of human liberty," a "struggle for the freedom of all men, without distinction of race and color." In Albion Tourgée's popular novel *A Fool's Errand* (1879), he attributes the ultimate defeat of that larger struggle to Southern racial bias and recalcitrance, indicting the federal government for its failure to check the crimes of the Ku Klux Klan and to

Dates	American Literature	History and Politics	Developments in Culture, Science, and Technology
1900–1909 (cont.)	1900 Pauline Hopkins, *Contending Forces; or, A Romance Illustrative of Negro Life North and South*	1900 U.S. troops help suppress Boxer Rebellion against foreign presence in China	1900 *Colored American Magazine* begins publication in Boston
	1901 Booker T. Washington, *Up from Slavery*	1901 McKinley is assassinated and Theodore Roosevelt becomes president	
	1902 Zitkala-Ša, *Old Indian Legends*	1902 Cuba gains independence	1902 First movie theater opens in Los Angeles
	1903 Mary Austin, *The Land of Little Rain*		1903 Wright brothers' first flight at Kitty Hawk, North Carolina
	1903 Jack London, *The Call of the Wild*		1903 *Ladies' Home Journal* becomes first magazine to circulate one million copies of a single issue
	1903 W. E. B. Du Bois, *The Souls of Black Folks*		
		1904 Theodore Roosevelt elected president	
	1905 Edith Wharton, *The House of Mirth*	1905 First Russian Revolution	
	1905 Willa Cather, *The Troll Garden*		
	1906 Upton Sinclair, *The Jungle*	1906 San Francisco earthquake and fire	
	1907 *The Education of Henry Adams*		1907 First radio broadcast
		1908 William Howard Taft elected president	1908 Henry Ford introduces Model T

transform the culture of the South during Reconstruction. But writers and publishers soon shifted their attention from the bitter aftermath of the conflict to the battles of the Civil War. In innumerable works – such as the *The Personal Memoirs of U. S. Grant* (1885), which sold more than 300,000 copies within a year – former Union and Confederate soldiers recalled the fortitude and heroism displayed by combatants (almost invariably white soldiers and leaders) on both sides of the conflict. Concepts such as "honor" and "glory," which the authors of those accounts frequently evoked, had no place in Ambrose Bierce's unflinching short stories about the horrors of battle or in the most famous and best-selling novel about the war, Stephen Crane's *The Red Badge of Courage* (1895). Like most of the authors of histories, memoirs, and other popular writings about the Civil War at that time, however, Bierce and Crane largely ignored the causes and consequences of the war, which many white Americans

Dates	American Literature	History and Politics	Developments in Culture, Science, and Technology
1900-1909 (cont.)		1909 Formation of National Association for the Advancement of Colored People	1909 Charlotte Perkins Gilman begins publication of *Forerunner*
1910-1914	1912 Mary Antin, *The Promised Land* 1912 Sui Sin Far, *Mrs. Spring Fragrance* 1913 Willa Cather, *O Pioneers!*	1910 U.S. population: 91,972,266 1910 Beginning of Mexican Revolution 1911 Death of 146 women in Triangle Factory fire in New York City generates support of workers' unions and reform of labor laws 1912 Woodrow Wilson elected president 1914 World War I begins in Europe	1912 *Titanic* sinks with loss of more than 1,500 lives 1912 *Poetry: A Magazine of Verse* begins publication in Chicago 1913 Armory Show of modern art in New York City 1914 Opening of Panama Canal

Edmonia Lewis,
Forever Free

The figures of two slaves, with their chains broken, rejoice in and offer prayerful thanks for the Emancipation Proclamation of 1863. Lewis, of mixed African American and Native American ancestry, sculpted the figures in 1867, at a time when many Americans hoped that Reconstruction would usher in a new era of freedom and equality in the United States.

came to view as a tragic and unnecessary conflict that had destroyed an idyllic plantation system in the South.

That "plantation myth" and its attendant racial stereotypes took deep root in American culture. A host of white writers contributed to the development of the myth, including Joel Chandler Harris, who published several collections of his popular *Uncle Remus* stories between 1881 and 1906, and especially Thomas Nelson Page, a white supremacist who in essays, poetry, novels, and stories such as those collected in *Ole Virginia* (1887) evoked a world of contented slaves and their benign masters in the antebellum South. In response to Page and his many imitators, the African American writer Charles W. Chesnutt sought to subvert the plantation myth by writing a series of stories about slavery, some of which were collected in *The Conjure Woman* (1899). Another African American writer, Pauline Hopkins, traces the bitter fortunes of a black family before and after the Civil War in her most famous novel, *Contending Forces; or, A*

Romance Illustrative of Negro Life North and South (1900). But their realistic portrayals of slavery and the experiences of African Americans were overshadowed by romantic depictions of the "old South," as well as by works such as Thomas Dixon's hugely popular and viciously racist "Clan Trilogy" (1902-07), novels about Reconstruction in which the villains are emancipated slaves and the heroic defender of Aryan civilization is the Ku Klux Klan. The emerging technology of film also perpetuated the plantation myth. Based on popular "Tom Shows," one of the first feature films

Thomas Nast, *Is This a Republican Form of Government?*

Published in *Harper's Weekly* in 1876, this engraving of a man kneeling by the bodies of murdered African Americans protests the federal government's failure to protect black populations from growing violence in the South. In the background – behind debris labeled "Work Shop," "School," and "Home" – a sign reads, "The White Liners Were Here," a reference to one of a number of white terrorist groups, which also included the White League and the Ku Klux Klan. The caption below the drawing reads, "Is this a republican form of government? Is this protecting life, liberty, or property? Is this equal protection under the laws?"

was *Uncle Tom's Cabin*, subtitled *Slavery Days*, a distorted version of Harriet Beecher Stowe's antislavery novel in which even at a slave auction the slaves were shown "singing, dancing, shooting craps, and otherwise enjoying themselves," as the scene in the movie was described in the catalog for the film published by the Thomas A. Edison Company in 1903.

In the face of widespread racism and discrimination, African Americans divided over the ways in which they might seek to gain equality and civil rights in the United States. In numerous speeches and writings, including his warmly received autobiography, *Up from Slavery* (1901), Booker T. Washington affirmed that African Americans should devote their energies to economic and educational advancement, rather than pressing for social equality and political rights. W. E. B. Du Bois, who rejected Washington's accommodation to the attitudes and values of white America, offered a far more sweeping view of the aspirations, claims, and rights of African Americans in *The Souls of Black Folk* (1903). Urging African Americans to settle for nothing less than full social and political equality, Du Bois subsequently helped establish the National Association for the Advancement of Colored People, founded in 1909.

Expansion, Industrialization, and the Emergence of Modern America

The struggle to reunite the North and the South coincided with the settlement of the West. During the Civil War, Congress passed the Homestead Act (1862), which offered settlers title to 160 acres of public land after they worked it for five years, and the Pacific Railroad Act, which provided subsidies to the Union Pacific and Central Pacific companies to build a railroad line across the West to California. Railroads, which spread across the West after the completion of the transcontinental system in 1869, also sold at low rates the vast tracts of land they had received as government subsidies. Lured by cheap land and the promise of freedom and opportunity, millions of settlers went west. Some were former Union soldiers, claiming the land grants they had earned for their service during the Civil War. Others were jobless or poor farmers from the East who sought better lands in the West. Still others were immigrants from across Europe, many of whom settled in areas that were viewed as harsh and inhospitable, especially the arid Great Plains. After the end of Reconstruction in 1877, thousands of African Americans sought freedom from racial oppression in the South by moving west, especially to Kansas. Led by a former slave, Benjamin "Pap" Singleton, the African American homesteaders called themselves *Exodusters*, sharing the hope of many other settlers that they would find a promised land in the West.

With its settlement, the country fulfilled what many Americans conceived to be their "manifest destiny" to expand across the western part of the continent, large portions of which had become U.S. territory as part of the treaty ending the Mexican War in 1848. American artists celebrated manifest destiny in paintings and stories of heroic pioneers bringing "civilization" to the West. But that process was viewed in a far different light by one of the first Mexican American writers to publish in English, María Amparo Ruiz de Burton. Describing her response to the term *manifest destiny* in a letter written in 1871, Ruiz de Burton angrily exclaimed: "Of all the evil phrases ever invented in order to create buffoons, there is not one phrase more detestable for me than that one, the most offensive, the most insulting; my blood rises to the top of my head when I hear it, and I see as if in a photographic instance, all that the Yankees have done to make Mexicans suffer – the robbery of Texas; war; [and] the robbery of California."

Advertisement for Western Lands

Railroad companies lured passengers and settlers by selling land in the West. By the time this poster was printed in 1872, the Burlington & Missouri Railroad Company ran from Chicago across Illinois and Iowa and deep into Nebraska.

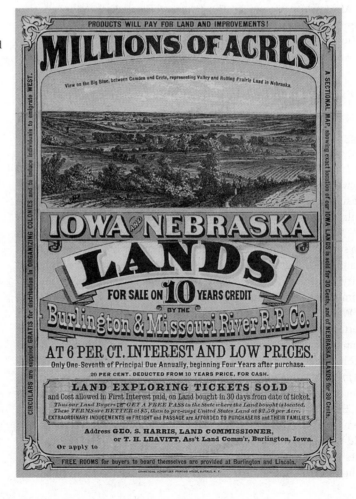

As railroads reached into more and more areas that had once been part of Mexico, Anglo-Americans arrived in large numbers, overwhelming and further marginalizing the Mexican American population, especially in southern California. In her novel *The Squatter and the Don* (1885), Ruiz de Burton dramatizes the cultural clashes, racial tensions, and struggles over land between Anglo-American squatters and a Mexican American landowner in California.

The settlement of the West proved to be even more disastrous for Native Americans. In a last-ditch effort to preserve their way of life and to protect their lands from the relentless encroachment of white settlers, the Lakota (Sioux) and Cheyenne fought and won the battle of Little Bighorn in 1876. But the federal government swiftly overcame their resistance and redrew the boundary lines of Indian reservations, opening up vast portions of them to American settlers. The white reformer Helen Hunt Jackson documented the brutal history of the mistreatment of Native Americans in *A Century of Dishonor* (1883), a copy of which she sent to every member of Congress. Sarah Winnemucca Hopkins, the first Native American woman to publish a book in the United States, also pleads the cause of the Indians in *Life among the Piutes: Their Wrongs and Claims* (1883). Such efforts did little to alter the harsh policies of the federal government toward the Indians. Federal troops massacred more than one hundred unarmed Lakota at Wounded Knee, South Dakota, on January 16,

San Carlos Apache Indian Reservation

Many bands of Apache were forcibly relocated from their traditional homelands, which once extended across Arizona and New Mexico, to this reservation in southeastern Arizona, established in 1872. Katherine Taylor Dodge took this photograph of men, women, and children waiting in line for supplies outside an agency building on "issue day" in 1899.

1896, effectively marking the end of Indian resistance to the army and policies of the United States. After that, the struggle for Indian rights increasingly shifted to politics and print culture. Charles A. Eastman (Ohiyesa) began his literary career with a popular account of his traditional Lakota upbringing, *Indian Boyhood* (1902). Another indigenous writer, Zitkala-Ša, exploited the literacy she had gained in English at an "assimilation school" for Indians to challenge the policies of assimilation and to preserve the traditions of Native Americans.

Immigration also raised questions about how the so-called alien populations might be assimilated into American society and culture. In the period from 1865 to 1914, during which the population of the country grew from 40 million to over 100 million people, more than 25 million immigrants arrived in the United States. The most profound symbol of America's welcome to immigrants ultimately became the Statue of Liberty,

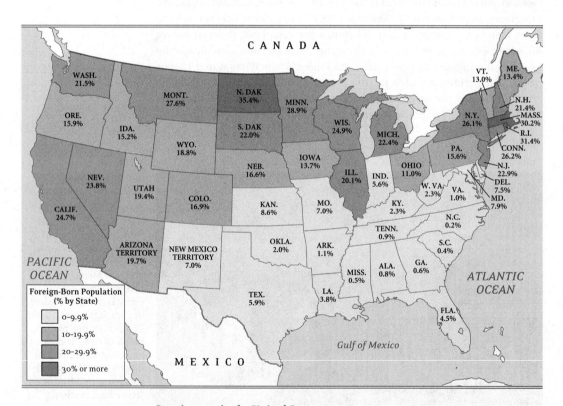

Immigrants in the United States, 1900

As this map illustrates, most of the millions of immigrants who arrived in the United States in the decades following the Civil War settled in the East, Midwest, and West, where foreign-born inhabitants exceeded 30 percent of the population of some states in 1900.

given by the people of France in honor of the celebration of the U.S. centennial in 1876. But many Americans contested the meaning of the monument, which was not erected in New York harbor until 1886. The dignitaries who spoke at the opening ceremonies emphasized the political symbolism of the statue, which was then called *Liberty Enlightening the World*. As early as 1883, however, the Jewish American poet Emma Lazarus affirmed a different meaning of the monument in her poem "The New Colossus," which she wrote to help raise funds for the construction of the base for the Statue of Liberty. For Lazarus, the uplifted torch that *Liberty* holds was not a symbol of political enlightenment but a guiding light and welcoming gesture to immigrants from Europe. That meaning became more firmly associated with the statue after 1903, sixteen years after Lazarus's death, when her friend Georgina Schuyler had the words of "The New Colossus" inscribed on a bronze plaque that was attached to a wall in the base of the Statue of Liberty. Many subsequently understood the statue to be speaking the famous concluding lines of the poem:

> Give me your tired, your poor,
> Your huddled masses yearning to breathe free,
> The wretched refuse of your teeming shore.
> Send these, the homeless, tempest-tost, to me,
> I lift my lamp beside the golden door!

The nation was often far less welcoming than those lines suggest. Thousands of men had been brought from China to California to work in gold fields and later on the western portion of the transcontinental railroad, and their labor was crucial to the completion of the vast project. After that, however, they were unwelcome in the West and throughout the United States. In response to growing anti-Chinese sentiments, Congress in 1882 passed the Chinese Exclusion Act, which prevented people from China from entering the country unless they were joining relatives and prohibited Chinese immigrants from becoming citizens of the United States. Three years later, when money was being raised for the erection of the Statue of Liberty, a Chinese immigrant named Saum Song Bo wrote a letter of protest to the *New York Sun*. "The statue represents Liberty holding a torch which lights the passage of those of all nations who come into this country," he bitterly observed. "But are the Chinese allowed to come? As for the Chinese who are here, are they allowed to enjoy liberty as men of all other nationalities enjoy it? Are they allowed to go about everywhere free from the insults, abuse, assaults, wrongs and injuries from which men of other nationalities are free?" Immigrants from southern and eastern Europe, as well as from Ireland, also generated anxiety and hostility among many native-born Americans, who viewed the newcomers, most of whom were Catholics or Jews, as threats to

"The statue represents Liberty holding a torch which lights the passage of those of all nations who come into this country. . . . But are the Chinese allowed to come?"

Chinese Exclusion Act

This handbill announcing a rally to celebrate the enactment of the 1882 law reveals the depth of hostility toward Chinese immigrants, especially in the West. The handbill also reveals the racial prejudice that generated widespread support for the law, which was hailed with the words "Hip! Hurrah! The White Man is on Top."

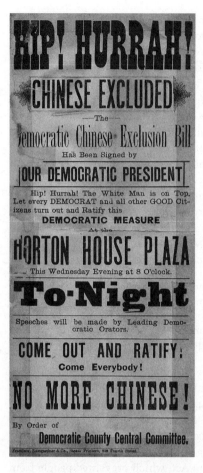

Protestant America. In "Unguarded Gates," a well-received poem first published in the influential *Atlantic Monthly* in 1892, Thomas Bailey Aldrich describes with dismay the "wild motley throng" passing through New York harbor, bringing with them "unknown gods and rites," "tiger passions, here to stretch their claws," and "strange tongues . . . alien to our air." Aldrich's concern about the impact of the new arrivals on American culture and society was echoed in numerous magazine and newspaper articles on "the immigration question" and what it meant to be an "American."

Immigration and rapid industrialization also generated growing conflicts between labor and corporations, or trusts, controlled by a few wealthy men. During what historians call "the Gilded Age," industrialists such as Andrew Carnegie, J. P. Morgan, and John D. Rockefeller amassed huge fortunes through cutthroat business practices and exploitation of labor. The flood of immigrants created a massive surplus of labor in the United States, where wages further declined during the depressions following the financial panics of 1873, 1884, and 1893. In 1890, eleven million of the country's twelve million families earned less than $1,200 a year, and the average income for that group was only $380. The low wages and long hours, as well as the appalling living and working conditions of most laborers, led to calls for political reform and the emergence of trade unions, including the Federation of Organized Trades and Labor Unions (later renamed the American Federation of Labor) in 1881. Five years later, the federation initiated a call for a national strike for an eight-hour workday. After strikers clashed with replacement workers at the McCormick Machine Harvesting Plant in Chicago, police retaliated by killing two of the striking workers. At a protest meeting called the following day at Haymarket Square, a bomb exploded, killing eight policemen. The arrest, trial, and conviction of eight men accused of the bombing, all of whom the judge sentenced to death, radicalized trade unionists like

Emma Goldman, a Jewish immigrant from Russia who became a leader of the anarchist movement in the United States. In 1894, the president of the American Railway Union, Eugene Debs, was imprisoned during the Pullman strike in Chicago. Debs, who came to believe that Americans should replace capitalism with a new cooperative system, subsequently helped form the Socialist Party, running for president five times on that ticket.

Chicago, the site of some of the most bitter and violent labor disputes of the period, came to symbolize both the dark realities and what many viewed as the bright promise of urban and industrial America. Harsh conditions in rural America prompted many on farms and in small towns to

VOL.17 NO.440   MARCH 22.1890.   PRICE 10 CENTS.

Judge

ENTERED AT THE POST OFFICE AT NEW YORK AS SECOND-CLASS MATTER.   COPYRIGHT 1890 BY THE JUDGE PUBLISHING CO.

THE PROPOSED EMIGRANT DUMPING SITE.

STATUE OF LIBERTY—"Mr. Windom, if you are going to make this island a garbage heap, I am going back to France."

"The Proposed Emigrant Dumping Site"

In this anti-immigration cartoon, used on the cover of the conservative magazine *Judge* in 1890, a frowning Statue of Liberty lifts her skirts as new immigrants are "dumped" onto her already overcrowded island, a symbol of the United States.

seek better lives in Chicago. Immigrants from abroad also swelled the population of the booming metropolis, which rose from roughly 100,000 in 1860 to nearly two million by 1900. Swiftly rebuilding after the "Great Fire" of 1871, the city won a competition to host the World's Columbian Exposition of 1893, a celebration of the four hundredth anniversary of Columbus's landing in America. But the exposition actually celebrated Chicago's economic power and the industrial advances of the United States. Twenty-seven million people visited the exposition, drawn there by the debut of the Ferris wheel, one of the most popular attractions; the nightly electric light shows powered by the huge dynamos displayed in the Palace of Mechanic Arts; and five thousand exhibits in the nearly two hundred buildings erected on landfill along the shore of Lake Michigan. The centerpiece of the exposition was the Court of Honor, a massive complex of plaster-clad, neoclassical buildings arranged around a vast reflecting pool, which came to be known as the "Great White City." That gleaming city bore little resemblance to the sprawling metropolis beyond the gates of the exposition or to other cities in the United States. Indeed, while mil-

World's Columbian Exposition, Chicago
Frances B. Johnson took this photograph of crowds of people touring the exposition grounds, including portions of the "Great White City," in 1893.

Downtown Chicago
This photograph of the congested intersection of Dearborn and Randolph streets was taken in 1910, by which time Chicago's population had grown from just over 100,000 in 1860 to more than two million people.

lions were flocking to the Columbian Exposition, the social reformer Jane Addams and her associates published *Hull House Maps and Papers*, a study of the grim living and working conditions in the industrial area around Hull House, a settlement house that provided educational programs and other services to immigrants in Chicago.

Writers of fiction also began to explore the realities of the new urban and industrial order in the United States. The tumultuous life of American cities was the subject of a growing number of stories and novels, including Stephen Crane's *Maggie: A Girl of the Streets (A Story of New York)* (1893), Frank Norris's *McTeague: A Story of San Francisco* (1899), and Theodore Dreiser's *Sister Carrie* (1900). Novelists also focused on corrupt practices of corporations, which were the primary focus of journalists and writers known as "muckrakers," a reference to their digging in the dirt, or "muck," to uncover corruption in politics and big business. One of the most influential of their works was Upton Sinclair's *The Jungle* (1906), a best-selling novel he wrote when the socialist newspaper *Appeal to Reason* commissioned him to investigate the exploitation of immigrant workers in the meat-packing industry in Chicago. Writers such as Abraham Cahan, a Jewish immigrant from Russia, drew upon their own direct experiences to illuminate the lives of new arrivals. In *Yekl: A Tale of the New York Ghetto* (1896) and *The Imported Bridegroom and Other Stories of the New York Ghetto* (1898), Cahan revealed just how difficult conditions were for many of those who passed through the "golden door" into the United States.

Even as millions of immigrants came to America from countries around the world, the United States aggressively sought to expand its influence and territory abroad. In 1893, American sugar-plantation owners deposed Queen Lili'uokalani of Hawai'i, which the United States annexed in 1898. That year, the country demonstrated its growing industrial and military might in the Spanish-American War. In the treaty that ended the brief war, Spain ceded control of Cuba, Puerto Rico, Guam, and the Philippines to the United States. Although it reluctantly granted independence to Cuba, the United States annexed Puerto Rico, Guam, and the Philippines. Anti-imperialists protested the betrayal of American political traditions, and many of those who had supported the war as an effort to liberate Spanish colonies opposed their annexation and were appalled by the brutal suppression by U.S. troops of the long Philippine Insurrection of 1899–1913. Revealing the attitudes of many Protestant Anglo-Americans toward "alien" groups at home and abroad, however, President McKinley argued that the Philippines "were unfit for self-government," so "there was nothing left for us to do but to take them all, and to educate the Filipinos, and uplift and civilize and Christianize them."

Innovation, Technology, and the Literary Marketplace

The industrialization that led to the country's emergence as a world power was accelerated by developments in technology that also transformed virtually every aspect of life in the United States. A host of new inventions were introduced between 1865 and 1914, including the lightbulb, the telephone, the typewriter, the radio, the motion picture, the automobile, and the airplane. There were equally significant changes in the technology of publishing, ranging from new methods of making paper to innovations in printing illustrations, the use of automated presses, and especially Ottmar Mergenthaler's invention in 1882 of the linotype machine, a revolutionary typesetting machine that Thomas Edison hailed as the "Eighth Wonder of the World."

W. R. Leigh, *A Modern Composing Room*

This illustration of linotype machines appeared in a series of articles, "The Business of a Newspaper," in *Scribner's Magazine* in 1897. In the accompanying text, the author explains, "Instead of type set from a case by hand there is now used the linotype machine, so-called because it casts a line of type at a time. . . . One operator on such a machine can do the work of five or six hand compositors."

Along with improved methods of distribution, those technologies helped a growing number of publishers meet the ever-increasing demand for printed materials of all kinds. One of the most striking developments in the period following the Civil War was the surge in reading, which was encouraged by the growing number of libraries in the United States. In 1876, when statistics on libraries were first compiled, there were 2,500 libraries with twelve million volumes. By 1900, the number of libraries had doubled, and their holdings had increased to forty million volumes. Those who could afford to purchase books had increasing access to them, especially in cities. Although as many as 90 percent of books published before World War I were sold by other means, including by subscription, bookstores grew in number and size by 1900. Since literacy rates were high, the population was expanding rapidly, and nearly 80 percent of all children attended school by the end of the century, publishers were assured of a steady supply of readers for both books and periodicals in the United States. As publishing became a big business, the term *bestseller* entered the American language, apparently coined for the lists that *Bookman Magazine* began to publish in 1895.

Not all kinds of writing benefited equally from the expansion of the literary marketplace, in which poetry assumed a diminishing role. Many of the poets who had been popular before the Civil War continued to publish, including Rose Terry Cooke and Sarah Morgan Bryan Piatt, and especially Henry Wadsworth Longfellow and John Greenleaf Whittier, who gained his greatest fame with the publication of *Snow-Bound* (1866), a nostalgic evocation of a simpler, rural world that had been destroyed by the Civil War. The child-oriented work of "schoolroom poets" such as Longfellow and Whittier, as well of popular poets such as Eugene Field and James Whitcomb Riley, strongly shaped public taste in poetry, making it difficult for more challenging and unconventional poets to gain an audience. Few read Walt Whitman, who published the first edition of his *Leaves of Grass* in 1855 and who revised and expanded the volume of poems through six more editions, including the final "deathbed" edition of 1891-92. After Emily Dickinson's death, Mabel Loomis Todd and Thomas Wentworth Higginson published the first of three volumes of her poems in 1890. The volumes sold well, as did the work of the pioneering African American poet Paul Laurence Dunbar, though he reached an even larger audience through his stories and novels. So did many white authors who wrote both poetry and fiction, including Stephen Crane, who published two collections of his poems, and Willa Cather, whose first book was a volume of poems, *April Twilights* (1903). One of the few American writers who devoted himself exclusively to poetry, Edwin Arlington Robinson struggled to earn a living. Certainly, the limited market for poetry was discouraging to established and would-be poets. "Poetry may get printed in newspapers, but no man makes money by it for the simple reason that nobody cares a fig for it," the revered poet William Cullen Bryant sourly observed shortly before his death in 1878. "The taste for it is something old-fashioned; the march of the age is in another direction; mankind are occupied with politics, railroads, and steamboats."

"Poetry may get printed in newspapers, but no man makes money by it for the simple reason that nobody cares a fig for it."

In contrast to poetry, fiction thrived in the new mechanical age. By the turn of the century, the novel had become the most popular of all literary genres, accounting for more than 25 percent of book production in the United States. In 1860, Ann Sophia Stephens published the first of the so-called dime novels, *Malaeska: The Indian Wife of the White Hunter*. Such mass-produced tales of adventure – which authors churned out in as little as a week and which frequently cost only a nickel – sold millions of copies during the following decades. Horatio Alger's *Ragged Dick* series, urban versions of the rags-to-riches story, were also enormously popular, as were family novels such as Louisa May Alcott's *Little Women* (1868-69) and its many sequels. One of the most famous writers of the period and the first celebrity author in the United States was Mark Twain, who made a fortune from his series of bestsellers, including the *Adventures of Huckleberry Finn* (1885). Other bestsellers ranged from historical romances such as Lew Wallace's biblical epic *Ben-Hur* (1880) to *The Call of the Wild* (1903), Jack London's internationally acclaimed novel

Mrs. Ann S. Stephens, *Malaeska: The Indian Wife of the White Hunter*

The woodcut cover illustration was added in this early reissue of the first, and one of the most popular, of "Beadle's Dime Novels."

about a sled dog in the wilds of the Klondike. European and especially English writers such as Arthur Conan Doyle and Rudyard Kipling continued to provide stiff competition, but American novelists benefited by the passage in 1891 of the Chase Act, which brought the United States into accord with an agreement for copyright protection signed in 1886 by a number of nations in Europe. The adoption of international copyright laws finally put European and American writers on a more equal footing, since American publishers thereafter had to pay royalties to authors whose works were first published outside the United States.

American fiction was also nourished by the growth of periodicals in the decades following the Civil War. During the war years, there were roughly 400 daily newspapers in the United States. By 1880, there were 850, and that number reached 1,400 by the turn of the century. Newspapers devoted a good deal of space to poetry and especially to prose fiction, which was a staple of a multiplying number of magazines in the United States. After struggling during the war years, when periodicals published in the North lost most of their Southern readers, magazines rebounded swiftly. Almost

"Mark Twain Incorporated" (detail)

The name *Mark Twain* gained such cultural currency that Samuel Clemens registered it as a trademark and incorporated himself as a commercial enterprise in 1908. He thus sought to secure perpetual copyright for his work by assigning all his copyrights, along with his pseudonym, to the Mark Twain Company. The *New York World* satirized the event in a cartoon in which Twain – dressed in his signature white suit and holding his customary cigar – is shown joining a small and seedy-looking group of capitalists, labeled "The Malefactors of Great Wealth Club."

immediately, the dominance of the *Atlantic Monthly* and *Harper's Monthly*, both of which had been established during the 1850s, was challenged by a series of prominent new literary magazines, including the *Galaxy* (1866), *Lippincott's* (1868), and *Scribner's Monthly* (1870), all published in the East; and the *Overland Monthly* (1868), which was published in San Francisco and featured writing about the West. During the following decades, the number of magazines exploded, from 700 during the Civil War to 2,400 in 1880 to roughly 3,500 at the turn of the century, by which time magazines had an estimated readership of sixty-five million people in the United States. Readers were attracted by the colorful covers, lavish illustrations, and modest cost of magazines such as *McClure's*, *Munsey's*, and the *Saturday Evening Post*, which achieved huge circulations by lowering their cover prices and funding themselves primarily through advertisements. Magazines became such a prominent feature of American life during the period that it has been described as the era of the magazine, the primary vehicle for public expression of culture in the United States.

The growth of periodicals gave added impetus to the development of one of the most vital forms of American literature, the short story. The story that launched Twain's lucrative career, "Jim Smiley and His Jumping Frog," was published in the *New York Saturday Press* in 1865, the year Henry James published his first signed work, "The Story of a Year," in the *Atlantic Monthly*. The first editor of the *Overland Monthly* was Bret Harte, whose enormously popular short stories helped create the vogue for regional or "local color" fiction in the United States. The short story soon became recognized as one of the major contributions of prose writers in the United States. "Almost as soon as America began to have any literature at all it had good short stories," Brander Matthew observed in 1885; "for fifty years the American short story has had a supremacy which any competent critic could not but acknowledge." Although newspapers and magazines continued to serialize novels, the short story became the most popular literary feature of periodicals. Suggesting that American writers had "brought the short story nearer perfection in an all around sense than almost any other people," the influential writer and critic William Dean Howells attributed that development to commercial success and "excellence" of American magazines, adding, "[I]t is probable that, aside from the pictures, it is the short stories that please the readers of our best magazines."

Magazines also revealed the important role of women as both consumers and producers of culture in the United States. The women's rights movement received a major setback in 1870, when the Fifteenth Amendment extended suffrage to African American men but not to black or white women. Thereafter, the movement increasingly focused its attention on the right of women to vote, which was not gained until the "Susan B. Anthony Amendment," first introduced in Congress in 1878, was finally adopted as the Nineteenth Amendment in 1920. Even as the American suffragists agitated through marches and public protests, activists such as Charlotte Perkins Gilman pursued a wide range of feminist issues in print. Gilman, for example, wrote for national periodicals such as the *New-England Magazine* and for her own journal, the *Forerunner.* Women faced strong opposition in their struggle for political rights and social equality, and they remained economically subordinate to men. By the end of the century, however, female education was expanding rapidly, at both the high-school and college levels, and a growing number of women were joining the labor force and entering professions that had previously been barred to them. The expanding economic and cultural roles of women was illustrated by the emergence of a series of magazines specifically designed to appeal to their interests and tastes. The most important women's magazine of the antebellum period, *Godey's Lady's Book*, ultimately succumbed to competition from a host of prominent magazines, including

> *"Almost as soon as America began to have any literature at all it had good short stories."*

"Mr. Gibson's American Girl"

Charles Dana Gibson's portrait of "the Gibson girl," the earliest visual stereotype of the ideal American woman, was used on the cover of the February 1903 issue of the *Ladies' Home Journal*, the first time a magazine of any kind circulated a million copies of a single issue.

THE MAGAZINE WITH A MILLION

THE LADIES' HOME JOURNAL

MR. GIBSON'S AMERICAN GIRL

FEBRUARY 1903   TEN CENTS

Harper's Bazar (1866), later renamed *Harper's Bazaar, Good Housekeeping* (1885), and the *Ladies Home Journal* (1883), the first magazine of any kind to circulate a million copies of a single issue, in February 1903. In addition to advertisements for women's clothing and accessories, as well as a wide range of articles on fashion, housekeeping, medicine, politics, and the arts, women's magazines published a good deal of short fiction, vigorously competing for readers with other mass-market magazines.

The growth of periodicals and the popularity of short stories offered opportunities for a wide range of American authors who emerged between the 1880s and the beginning of World War I. White women writers claimed a growing share of the market for fiction, including Edith Wharton, Sarah Orne Jewett, Mary E. Wilkins Freeman, Kate Chopin, Willa Cather, and Mary Austin. All of those writers produced novels as well as short fiction. But all of them began their careers by writing for newspapers or magazines and continued to do so, as did white male writers such as Ambrose Bierce and the novelists Stephen Crane, Theodore Dreiser, Jack London, and Frank Norris. At the same time, periodicals began to reflect the growing diversity of the country. The work of a few African American writers appeared in prominent national magazines. In 1887, Charles W. Chesnutt became the first African American writer to be published in the prestigious *Atlantic Monthly*, and Paul Laurence Dunbar later published stories in *Harper's Weekly* and the *Saturday Evening Post*. In 1900, Pauline Hopkins helped establish the *Colored American Magazine*, designed to feature the work and celebrate the achievements of African Americans. The following year, the *Outlook* serialized Booker T. Washington's *Up from Slavery*, even as W. E. B. Du Bois published a critique of Washington's leadership in the *Dial*, later revising the essay for *The Souls of Black Folk* (1903). The Native American writer Zitkala-Ša published essays and stories in several national magazines, as did Sui Sin Far, an immigrant of mixed Chinese and English ancestry who later collected some of her stories in *Mrs. Spring Fragrance* (1912). Following in the footsteps of immigrant writers such as Abraham Cahan, Mary Antin wrote an autobiographical account of what she described as her "assimilation into American ways," *The Promised Land*, which was serialized in the *Atlantic Monthly* in 1912.

By then, the United States bore little resemblance to the exhausted and grieving country that had emerged from the Civil War. In the summer of 1913, 50,000 white veterans of the war, former soldiers of both the Union and the Confederacy, gathered for a grand reunion commemorating the fiftieth anniversary of the Battle of Gettysburg. "Nothing could possibly be more impressive or more inspiring to the younger generation than this gathering," a journalist observed in the *Washington Post*. "But even more touching must be the emotions of these time-worn veterans, as they assemble on an occasion that in itself constitutes a greater victory than that of half a century ago, and one too, in which every section of a reunited country has common part." Indeed, as the reunion symbolized, many of the sectional divisions between the North and the South had been overcome, though largely at the expense of African Americans. The frontier had closed with the settlement of the West, largely at the expense of Mexican Americans and Native Americans. At the same time, immigration, industrialization, and urbanization had generated growing divisions in the country between wealth and poverty, as well as along lines of religion and ethnicity. The primarily agricultural country of the antebellum years gave way to an industrial colossus, whose military might and imperialistic ambitions had been demonstrated in the Spanish-American War of 1898. Many American writers had earlier used the Civil War as a symbol of what came to be called the "loss of American innocence." Certainly, if that "innocence" was not lost, it was at least deeply shaken by the traumatic conflict that ended in 1865. As many of the writings published during the following decades illustrate, it was further undermined by the tumultuous cultural, economic, political, and social developments during the half century between the end of the Civil War and the beginning of World War I, in August 1914.

Realism, Regionalism, and Naturalism

IN ADDITION TO TRIGGERING MASSIVE economic, political, and social dislocations, the Civil War generated a seismic cultural shift. The aftershocks were clearly registered in American literature, as writers responded to the altered circumstances, landscapes, and mood of the country during the decades following the war. The disillusionment and skepticism generated by the bloody conflict and its aftermath helped spur the development of a literary movement known as "realism." With its emphasis on representing things as they actually are, realism may be understood as a reaction against idealism, the representation of things as they should be, and

◄ George Bellows, *Cliff Dwellers* (1913)

Bellows captures the effects of immigration and urbanization in his realistic depiction of the tenement district of New York City. Although many of his contemporaries may well have viewed the work as an illustration of the "alien" nature of the people crowding the streets and apartment buildings, the title of the painting may well associate the new arrivals with some of the earliest inhabitants of the continent, the Native Americans of the Anasazi culture, who built the ancient cliff dwellings in the Southwest.

romanticism, both in the common sense of that term and in the narrower literary sense of writings that emphasize emotion, imagination, intuition, and the primacy of the individual. Just as there were realistic elements in many of the writings of the "Romantic Period" of American literature, from roughly 1830 to 1865, so were there romantic elements in many of the writings of the "Realistic Period," from roughly 1865 to the beginning of World War I. Nonetheless, most realists challenged or at least questioned some of the fundamental tenets of romanticism — the belief in the nobility and inherent goodness of the individual, an expansive faith in human progress, and the idealization of nature. Certainly, the romantic idealism of earlier writers such as Ralph Waldo Emerson, Margaret Fuller, Henry

Thomas Anshutz, *The Ironworkers' Noontime* (1880)

Realism became a significant force in American painting as well as literature in the decades following the Civil War. In what is widely regarded as the first realistic (especially by the standards of the time) and fully realized treatment of industrial subject matter by an American painter, Thomas Anshutz here depicts the noontime break of workers at a nail factory in Wheeling, West Virginia.

David Thoreau, and other transcendentalists proved to be difficult to sustain in the face of the carnage of the Civil War and the actualities of the new urban and industrial order in the United States.

Broader cultural movements spurred the development of American literary realism. What historians sometimes call the "second scientific revolution" strengthened the belief that new knowledge could be gained only through close observation of the natural world and that truth must be based on empirical evidence. The scientific method influenced the literary methods of the realists, who emphasized the importance of objectivity, observation, and the unbiased or unsentimental reporting of the observed phenomena of American life. The writings of the realists were related to and stimulated by the work of late-nineteenth-century American philosophers such as Charles Sanders Peirce, William James, and other participants in the philosophical movement called "pragmatism," the doctrine that the value of any belief, idea, or theory is dependent on its outcome or utility. Pragmatists reject moral absolutes, measuring the value of any truth, or conception, by its practical consequences and outcomes, as manifested in the conduct, ethical choices, and experiences of those who accept that conception as the "truth." American literary realism was also influenced by the work of British novelists such as Charles Dickens, George Eliot, and Anthony Trollope, as well as by the writings of a wide range of European writers, including Honoré de Balzac, Gustave Flaubert, Guy de Maupassant, and Ivan Turgenev. With their emphasis on the development of characters, their use of common language, their close attention to the details of specific locales, and their choice of plots mirroring the realities of ordinary lives, such fiction writers were popular among both authors and audiences in the United States.

The emergence of realism inspired a lively debate in postwar periodicals about the purposes and goals of American literature. The pages of literary magazines and even many newspapers were full of articles and commentaries on what constituted realism in fiction. George Parsons Lathrop, a critic and writer, offered the following definition in the *Atlantic Monthly* in 1874:

> Realism sets itself at work to consider characters and events which are apparently the most ordinary and uninteresting, in order to extract from these their full value and true meaning. It would apprehend in all particulars the connection between the familiar and the extraordinary, and the seen and the unseen of human nature. Beneath the deceptive cloak of outwardly uneventful days, it detects and endeavors to trace the outlines of the spirits that are hidden there; to measure the changes in their growth, to watch the symptoms of moral decay or regeneration, to fathom their histories of passionate or intellectual problems. In short, realism reveals. Where we thought nothing worthy of notice, it shows everything to be rife with significance.

Lathrop defined realism in a way that made it particularly useful and appealing to writers in the United States. During the decades before the Civil War, American writers had frequently commented on the difficulty of writing a romance in their native country, where "there is no shadow, no antiquity, no mystery, no picturesque and gloomy wrong, nor anything but a commonplace prosperity, in broad and simple daylight," as Nathaniel Hawthorne put it in his preface to *The Marble Faun* (1861). By suggesting that the materials of realism were "characters and events which are apparently the most ordinary and uninteresting," Lathrop affirmed the literary value of what Hawthorne and others had described as the commonplace actualities of life in the United States. Indeed, experiences and situations that others might dismiss as merely trivial or uneventful were for Lathrop potentially "rife with significance," a rich resource for writers committed to the faithful representation of everyday aspects of American life.

One of the earliest and most influential proponents of literary realism in the United States was the critic and novelist William Dean Howells. Born and raised in Ohio, where he worked as a journalist and printer, Howells became a major figure in the eastern literary establishment, first as an assistant editor (1866-70) and then as editor of the prestigious *Atlantic Monthly* (1871-81). During his years at the *Atlantic,* he advanced the cause of realism through his own fiction and by publishing the work of numerous writers from across the nation. Howells later promoted realism in his regular columns for another influential periodical, *Harper's Monthly Magazine.* "Realism is nothing more and nothing less than the truthful treatment of material," he succinctly stated in 1889. Throughout his long career, Howells tirelessly sought to guide the literary tastes of the American public away from the Romantic and sentimental toward what he viewed as the ordinary and true. "Let fiction cease to lie about life; let it portray men and women as they are, actuated by the motives and the passions in the measure we all know," he urged; "let it not put on fine literary airs; let it speak the dialect, the language, that most Americans know – the language of unaffected people everywhere – and there can be no doubt of an unlimited future, not only of delightfulness but of usefulness, for it."

"Let fiction cease to lie about life; let it portray men and women as they are, actuated by the motives and the passions in the measure we all know; . . . let it not put on fine literary airs; let it speak the dialect, the language, that most Americans know – the language of unaffected people everywhere – and there can be no doubt of an unlimited future, not only of delightfulness but of usefulness, for it."

Two of the many writers Howells championed illustrate the breadth of his literary sympathies as well as the range of literary realism in the United States. When he was an assistant editor of the *Atlantic Monthly,* Howells was asked by the senior editor whether the magazine should publish an early story by Henry James. "Yes, and all the stories you can get from the writer," Howells replied, explaining in one of his later essays: "I admired, as we must in all that Mr. James has written, the finished workmanship in which there is no loss of vigor; the luminous and uncommon use of words, the originality of phrase, the whole clear and beautiful style." Howells was an equally strong supporter of the work of the other most famous American realist, Mark Twain, who in background and literary practice could not have been more different from James. The cosmopolitan James, who was born in New York City and spent much of his life in Europe, is best known for his novels and stories of Americans traveling abroad, including *Daisy Miller* (1878). Twain, who grew up on the frontier in Missouri and served his literary apprenticeship in the far West, emerged out of the tradition of "Southwestern humor," humorous sketches and tall tales told in thick regional dialects. Although many critics tended to dismiss his popular writings as mere entertainment, Howells invited Twain to contribute to the *Atlantic Monthly*, where his series of autobiographical sketches *Old Times on the Mississippi* appeared in 1876. Along with many other writers of the period, Twain looked back to the time before the Civil War, which he nostalgically re-created in his first novel, *The Adventures of Tom Sawyer* (1876). Twain, however, offered a far more complex and darker version of that past in his *Adventures of Huckleberry Finn* (1885).

Twain's writings illustrate a number of features of "regionalism," a broad movement that encompassed a wide range of writers in various parts of the United States. As the nation's expanding population became more diverse and spread out across the continent, American writers began to redraw the literary map of the country. Twain's earliest work was influenced by Bret Harte, whose stories of miners, gamblers, and other low-life characters in California helped usher in the vogue of what was known as "local-color" writing, which became a staple of national, mass-circulation magazines after 1880. As some scholars have emphasized, local-color writing was in part a response to the growing pressures and threats of rapid social change during the late decades of the nineteenth century. By representing the characters and customs, as well as the peculiarities of dialect, dress, and manners of a specific region, local-color writers sought to preserve traditions threatened by the new urban and industrial order that emerged after the Civil War. Sarah Orne Jewett's sketches appealed to yearnings for the simpler life of provincial New England, while Mary Austin vividly described the remote and unspoiled landscapes of the far West. At the same time, Jewett and Austin emphasized the ways in which the natural environment shapes the lives of individuals, while other regional writers exposed the difficult conditions of life in various parts of the United States. The popular local-color writer Mary E. Wilkins Freeman and the poet Edwin Arlington Robinson, for example, dramatized the economic, emotional, and psychological struggles of people living in rural areas and decaying towns in the interior of New England. Willa Cather, who was celebrated for her pioneering stories of life in her native Nebraska, often evoked the claustrophobic world of the small town, the sameness of

Eastman Johnson, *Cranberry Harvest, Nantucket Island* (1880)

Many writers and painters responded to rapid social change in the United States by depicting ways of life that were threatened by industrialization and urbanization, including this communal scene in which families of men, women, and children work together harvesting cranberries on the isolated and as yet undeveloped island of Nantucket.

rural routines, and the grinding poverty experienced by many settlers on the Great Plains.

Both realism and regionalism were frequently vehicles for social criticism and satire. Ambrose Bierce debunked romantic myths about the nobility and grandeur of the Civil War by exposing the horrors of battle in his *Tales of Soldiers and Civilians* (1892). Early in her career, the feminist and activist Charlotte Perkins Gilman adopted the strategies of psychological realism in "The Yellow Wall-Paper" (1892), a harrowing story that illustrates the confinement and oppression of women in American society at that time. Her concern with the restricted role of women in a patriarchal society was shared by Kate Chopin, who developed that theme in local-color stories about Creole life in Louisiana and in her controversial novel *The Awakening* (1899), and by Edith Wharton, who wrote a series of stories and novels in which she satirized the debased values and hollow lives of the wealthy elite of New York City. In a different part of the city and at the other end of the social scale, the Jewish American writer and journalist Abraham Cahan depicted life in the "Ghetto," the area on the Lower East Side of New York City where more than a million Jews fleeing persecution in Russia and eastern Europe settled between the 1880s and 1914. Another immigrant writer, Sui Sin Far, focused on the trials of Chinese Americans, who were widely viewed as "heathens" and often subjected to hostility and violence in cities like San Francisco. At the same time, African American writers like Charles W. Chesnutt and the poet Paul Laurence Dunbar sought to subvert romanticized visions of slavery and denigrating stereotypes of black people, while Pauline Hopkins reveals the grim consequences of racial discrimination and hatred in the numerous stories and novels she published in the *Colored American Magazine*.

Even as writers enriched the diversity and extended the range of American realism, some of its basic assumptions were challenged by writers who participated in a new literary movement called "naturalism." A major force behind the emergence of naturalism was the work of Charles Darwin, especially the "social Darwinism" popularized by the English philosopher

Winslow Homer, *The Gulf Stream* (1899)

Homer's famous painting, which a critic in 1906 described as a powerful depiction of human isolation and vulnerability amidst "the cruelty of the elements and the elemental creatures of the sea," has much in common with the contemporary writings of the naturalists, who frequently depicted the struggle of characters for survival against the hostile forces of nature and the environment.

Herbert Spencer. Spencer held that Darwin's theories of evolution through natural selection also apply to individuals or groups within society, which consequently operate under the natural law of "survival of the fittest." In effect, as the naturalists understood Darwin and Spencer, man is simply an animal struggling for survival in a competitive jungle and driven by the same internal and external forces that operate on other animals. As the French novelist Émile Zola famously puts it in *The Experimental Novel* (1880), the fullest theoretical statement of the principles of naturalism, human beings are "human beasts." Zola also affirms that the novel is a scientific experiment that arrives at the truth about humanity and society by demonstrating the determining effects of a changing environment on a particular hereditary makeup. Although the line between realism and naturalism is often blurred, realists tend to emphasize the role of individual choice or volition, while naturalists emphasize the ways in which human behavior is determined by biological, economic, and environmental forces, both social and natural. Rather than a source of solace or a spiritual resource, naturalists view "nature" as an indifferent backdrop for the struggles and strivings of human beings. Indeed, in many naturalistic works characters struggle for survival against the seemingly hostile forces of nature, symbolized by the threatening ocean waves in Stephen Crane's "The Open Boat" (1897) and the harsh climate of the Klondike in Jack London's "The Law of Life" (1901).

The naturalists were also determined to depict experiences and explore places that had for the most part remained outside the boundaries of realism. An important site of naturalistic writing was the city, or urban "jungle," which was both the setting and a central metaphor in works by Crane, Theodore Dreiser, and Frank Norris. In a review of Norris's *McTeague* (1899), which is based on a sensational murder case in San Francisco, William Dean Howells suggests that the brutal work raises fundamental questions about the future of fiction in the United States. "Whether we shall abandon the old-fashioned American ideal of the novel as something which may be read by all ages and sexes, for the European notion of it as something fit only for age and experience, and for men rather than women; whether we shall keep to the bounds of the provincial proprieties, or shall include within the imperial territory of fiction the passions and motives of the savage world which underlies as well as environs civilization, are points which this book sums up and puts concretely," Howells observes. Disturbed and deeply ambivalent about such an "expansion" of the subject matter of the American novel, Howells argued that Norris's "true picture of life is not true, because it leaves beauty out." But the naturalists insisted that realists such as Howells left out far more, from sexual drives to

". . . whether we shall keep to the bounds of the provincial proprieties, or shall include within the imperial territory of fiction the passions and motives of the savage world which underlies as well as environs civilization, are points which this book sums up and puts concretely."

the socioeconomic forces that so powerfully shaped the lives of the great mass of people struggling for survival in the United States.

The naturalists, or what some critics then called "new realists," offered a dark and disturbing vision of American life at the turn of the twentieth century. Even as they aspired to scientific objectivity and disclaimed any moral or ethical purpose, however, many naturalists also sought to arouse concern and indignation about the conditions they described. Their depictions of urban life had much in common with shocking exposés such as *How the Other Half Lives: Studies among the Tenements of New York* (1890), in which the Danish immigrant and reformer Jacob Riis documents through descriptions and photographs the squalid living conditions in the slums of New York City. Some naturalistic writings also overlapped the investigative journalism of the muckrakers, who exposed the abuses of corporations and corruption in government in an effort to bring about reform. In his final novels and stories, Frank Norris thus focused on the ruthless practices of the railroad monopolies and speculators who controlled the price of wheat, hoping that his writings would encourage the public to turn against big business and consequently "get fair treatment and not be abused." Indeed, in their efforts to truthfully engage the actualities of American life, including the experiences of women, minorities, and immigrants crowded into urban slums, both realists and naturalists often gave added force to efforts on behalf of social reform in the United States.

American Contexts

"THE AMERICA OF THE MIND": CRITICS, WRITERS, AND THE REPRESENTATION OF REALITY

DURING THE DECADES FOLLOWING the Revolution, writers in the United States persistently called for the creation of a distinctly American literature, one that would establish the new nation's cultural independence from England and Europe. After the Civil War, in what Henry James termed the "era of discussion," the debate over what would constitute such a literature escalated. In an article published in the *Nation* in January 1868, John William De Forest wondered whether the "Great American Novel," which he defined as "the picture of the ordinary emotions and manners of American existence," might not now be at hand. De Forest was skeptical, and some other critics doubted that the novelist could find sufficiently rich materials amid the mundane realities of life in the United States. In response to such doubts, James Herbert Morse in an 1883 essay emphasized the vitality of "American life," which had "mastered a continent and developed its enormous resources," "freed a nation of slaves," and "survived a war of almost incredible disintegrating properties." Affirming that "such a life is rich enough to meet the largest demands of the novelist," Morse concluded: "America has much to learn from Europe. We cannot greatly boast abroad of ease and elegance in social life, of art and learning, of fine culture and manners; but of variety of movement, of free action and growth, of that satisfaction that comes from being alive all over, we have enough and to spare. Life here is not thin, except to the thin."

Morse's sense of the opportunities available to American authors was shared by many critics and writers during the decades following the Civil War. "Peace too has its infinite resources," Thomas Wentworth Higginson proclaimed in 1867. As the other selections included in the following section indicate, however, there was wide disagreement about the nature, purpose, and scope of American fiction. In response to those who insisted that writers should focus solely on American scenes and themes, Julian Hawthorne objected: "It is silly and childish to make the boundaries of the America of the mind coincide with those of the United States." Hawthorne was defending writers of the so-called international school, especially Henry James, who emphasized the fiction writer's imaginative freedom to explore a wide range of experiences and situations. At the same time, Lafcadio Hearn and Hamlin Garland protested what they viewed as the ongoing domination of New England in American fiction, which they argued must include the experiences and perspectives of writers from the South and the West. Although the critical debate was dominated by white males, a "Lady from Philadelphia" suggested that "The Coming American Novelist" might well be a woman and an African American. There was a growing consensus that American fiction would be characterized by realism, or truth to the experience of life in the United States, a position championed by the influential critic and novelist William Dean Howells. In a famous statement, Howells suggested that realists should focus on "the more smiling aspects of life, which are the more American." But the limits of realism were challenged by naturalists such as Frank Norris, who was determined to treat the widest range of experience, from life in the slums to "the mystery of sex," areas into which American literature had rarely ventured. Indeed, as American society was transformed by growing immigration, industrialization, and urbanization, critics and writers increasingly questioned what constituted the true reality of life in the United States.

bedfordstmartins.com/ americanlit for research links on the authors in this section

Thomas Wentworth Higginson

[1823-1911]

Born in Cambridge, Massachusetts, and educated at Harvard University, Thomas Wentworth Higginson was among the most remarkable individuals of nineteenth-century America. Trained as a Unitarian minister, he became a militant abolitionist and later served as colonel of the first

Thomas Wentworth Higginson

This engraving is based on an undated photograph, probably taken soon after the Civil War.

regiment of African American soldiers in the Civil War. After the war, he devoted himself to literature and social reform, especially women's suffrage and equal rights for African Americans. A prolific writer, Higginson contributed to major literary magazines, served as the assistant editor of the *Atlantic Monthly*, and published a number of books, including *Army Life in a Black Regiment* (1870) and biographies of Margaret Fuller, Henry Wadsworth Longfellow, and John Greenleaf Whittier. He was a friend and correspondent of Emily Dickinson and after her death Higginson coedited two volumes of her poetry. He also encouraged a wide range of American writers in a country that was still viewed by many as indifferent to the arts. "Our brains as yet lie chiefly in our machine shops," Higginson observes in "A Plea for Culture" (1867), in which he affirms the importance of a liberal arts education as the foundation for a truly significant national culture. Arguing that the value of a nation depends on its intellectual achievements rather than its material wealth, Higginson at the end of the essay considers the prospects for the emergence of an American literature that might finally be ranked with the national literatures of Europe. The text is taken from the first printing in the *Atlantic Monthly*, January 1867.

From A PLEA FOR CULTURE

It is observable that in English books and magazines everything seems written for some limited circle — tales for those who can speak French, essays for those who can understand a Latin quotation. But every American writer must address himself to a vast audience, possessing the greatest quickness and common-sense, with but little culture; and he must command their attention as he may. This has some admirable results: one must put some life into what he writes, or his thirty million auditors will go to sleep; he must write clearly, or they will cease to follow him; must keep clear of pedantry and unknown tongues, or they will turn to some one who can address them in English. On the other hand, these same conditions tempt one to accept a low standard of execution, to substitute artifice for art, and to disregard the more permanent verdict of more select tribunals. The richest thought and the finest literary handling which America has yet produced — as of Emerson, Hawthorne, and Thoreau[1] — reached at first but a small audience, and are but very gradually attaining a wider hold. Rénan[2] has said that every man's work is superficial, until he has learned to content himself with the approbation of a few. This is only one half the truth; but it is the half which Americans find hardest to remember.

---

1. **Emerson, Hawthorne, and Thoreau:** Ralph Waldo Emerson (1803-1882), Nathaniel Hawthorne (1804-1864), and Henry David Thoreau (1812-1862), who came to be viewed as among the most important American writers of the period before the Civil War.
2. **Rénan:** Joseph Ernest Renan (1823-1892), French philosopher and writer famous for his *Life of Jesus* (1863).

But American literature, though its full harvest be postponed for another hundred years, is sure to come to ripeness at last. Our national development in this direction, though slow, is perfectly healthy. There are many influences to retard, but none to distort. Even if the more ideal aims of the artist are treated with indifference, it is a frank indifference; there is no contempt, no jealousy, no call for petty manoeuvres. No man is asked to flatter this vast audience; no man can succeed by flattering; it simply reserves its attention, and lets one obtain its ear if he can. When won, it is worth the winning — generous in its confidence, noble in its rewards. There is abundant cause for strenuous effort among those who give their lives to the intellectual service of America, but there is no cause for fear. If we can only avoid incorporating superficiality into our institutions, literature will come when all is ready, and when it comes will be of the best.

· · ·

Above all other races and all other times, we should be full of hearty faith. It is but a few years since we heard it said that the age was dull and mean, and inspiration gone. A single gunshot turned meanness to self-sacrifice, mercenary toil to the vigils of the camp and the transports of battle.[3] It linked boyish and girlish life to new opportunities, sweeter self-devotions, more heroic endings; tied and loosed the threads of existence in profounder complications. That is all past now; but its results can never pass. The nation has found its true grandeur by war, but must retain it in peace.

Peace too has its infinite resources, after a nation has once become conscious of itself. It is impossible that human life should ever be utterly impoverished, and all the currents of American civilization now tend to its enrichment. This vast development of rudimentary intellect, this mingling of nationalities, these opportunities of books and travel, educate in this new race a thousand new susceptibilities. Then comes Passion, a hand straying freely through all the chords, and thrilling all with magic. We cannot exclude it, a forbidden guest. It re-creates itself in each generation, and bids art live. *Rouge gagne.*[4] If the romance of life does not assert itself in safe and innocent ways, it finds its outlet with fatal certainty in guilt; as we see colorless Puritanism touched with scarlet glory through the glass of Hawthorne.[5] Every form of human life is romantic; every age may become classic. Lamentations, doubts, discouragements, all are wasted things. Everything is here, between these Atlantic and Pacific shores, save only the perfected utterance that comes with years. Between Shakespeare in his cradle and Shakespeare in *Hamlet,* there was needed but an interval of time, and the same sublime condition is all that lies between the America of toil and the America of art.

[1867]

---

3. **A single gunshot . . . battle:** The Civil War officially began when South Carolina forces fired on Fort Sumter on April 12, 1861.
4. *Rouge gagne:* Literally, "red wins" (French).
5. **Puritanism . . . glass of Hawthorne:** A reference to Hawthorne's *The Scarlet Letter* (1850), a historical romance set in Puritan New England.

Lafcadio Hearn

[1850-1904]

Lafcadio Hearn

This photograph shows Hearn in 1889, shortly before he left for Japan.

The son of a Greek mother and an Irish father, Lafcadio Hearn was born in Greece and educated in England and France. His adult life divided into two distinct parts in two different worlds. In 1869, he immigrated to the United States, where he lived until 1890, when he left for Japan. There, he taught English literature at the Imperial University of Tokyo, became a Japanese citizen, taking the name of Koizumi Yakumo, and wrote more than a dozen books on Japanese life and culture. During the twenty-one years he lived in the United States, he published articles and stories in various national magazines. He also worked as a journalist, first in Cincinnati and then in New Orleans, where he wrote regularly on literature for the *Item*. In the following editorial, published in that newspaper on June 18, 1881, Hearn laments the fact that American literature was still dominated by representations of fashionable society as viewed from the perspective of New England. Urging the claims of other classes and regions, he emphasizes the need for truly American works of fiction that would explore the full range of life in the United States. The text is taken from *Editorials by Lafcadio Hearn*, edited by Charles Woodward Hutson (1926).

RECENT AMERICAN NOVELS

There has been what we might call a literary spurt lately among the younger school of American writers to catch up with the trans-Atlantic English literature of fiction. We refer especially to society fiction – to novels illustrating American society as British novels portray various phases of English society. We are represented, not largely, but well, in historical romance not American, but written by Americans, and European romances written by natives of the United States. But as regards novels illustrating American life proper we have had few productions of late years. At the same time there is a quantity of light American literature produced with this very aim, never attained though incessantly pursued. Some publishers have taken a good step in this direction by issuing series of anonymous novels intended to be peculiarly American. The intention was excellent, but its fulfillment has been found very difficult indeed. No fine American romance has been called into life by this new phase of enterprise. The creations it has begotten are imitations mostly of English or French novels, with nothing American about them except here and there a bit of scene painting from New England or Virginia. There is a curious similarity about all these romances; they are all the production of one particular school. Those who write have all breathed the same educational atmosphere, been guided by similar social influences, read the same literature, studied the same philosophy, traveled in the same countries, and studied art-ideas from the same standpoint. And all this study and thought and feeling and experience, is not only confined within the narrow circle of a certain preconceived Boston sentiment; but under the influence of that sentiment to such an extent everything is pedantically colored. There is much fine writing, much elegance of expression, much evidence of scholarship; but no idea whatever of studying American life from a standpoint not New English. The idea of seeking for the beautiful and the picturesque in the lower strata of society as well as in the upper, of studying agricultural home life as well as Fifth Avenue[1] drawing-room personages, of portraying distinctly national and local characteristics, of picturing phases of existence to be found in the United States only, does not seem to enter into the mind of these novelists. And this is the reason that in spite of style and scholarship and fine taste, the finest of those productions will find no readers within a few years. They teach nothing new, reproduce nothing of striking interest, contain nothing which may not be found in European contemporary novels in a far more acceptable shape.

The characteristics of the upper class of society are similar in all highly civilized countries; and even the tone of cultured thought has a universal resemblance. Differences of nationality create only the faintest tints of variation, For strong and characteristic color and sentiment, we must study not this hothouse growth of fashionable intellectuality, which resembles a flower that may be found in the private conservatories of all climates and countries; but rather the wild plants, the natural blossoms of human life. Bret Harte did this. Elizabeth Stuart Phelps did it. Oliver Wendell Holmes did it; and Hawthorne and Irving before him.[2] What is wanted now is something distinct and unique and truthful, which cannot be found in the factitious life of drawing-rooms, but in the workshops and factories, among the toilers on river and rail, in villages fringing the sea line or hidden among the wrinkles of the hills, in mining districts and frontier towns, in the suburbs of vast industrial centers, in old-fashioned communities about which quaint traditions cling, among men who, without culture, have made themselves representatives of an enormous financial force, and among those who, in spite of culture, have remained unable to rise above the condition of want, in the office of the merchant, and the residence of the clerk, and the home of the servant, and the rented rooms of the laborer.

[1881, 1926]

---

1. **Fifth Avenue:** The most fashionable residential street in New York City.
2. **Bret Harte . . . Irving before him:** Hearn cites the diverse examples of Bret Harte (1836-1902), who was known for his stories about the often harsh realities of the West, especially California; Elizabeth Stuart Phelps (1844-1911), the author of *The Silent Partner* (1871), a story about New England mill girls; Oliver Wendell Holmes (1809-1904), poet and essayist who also wrote stories exploring abnormal psychology; Nathaniel Hawthorne (1804-1864), best known for *The Scarlet Letter* (1850), a historical romance set in Puritan New England; and Washington Irving (1783-1859), whose most famous stories were set in Dutch communities in the Catskill Mountains of New York State.

Julian Hawthorne

[1846-1934]

Julian Hawthorne

This engraving is based on an undated photograph, probably taken during the 1870s.

The son of the novelist Nathaniel Hawthorne, Julian Hawthorne was educated in the United States but spent much of his early life in England. Hawthorne was the author of popular novels such as *Bresant* (1873) and *Garth* (1877), as well as books about his famous father, *Nathaniel Hawthorne and His Wife* (1884) and *Hawthorne and His Circle* (1903). Hawthorne was also a frequent contributor to a variety of literary magazines, including the *Atlantic Monthly, Harper's New Monthly Magazine,* the *Century Magazine,* and the *North American Review,* where he published "The American Element in Fiction." In the essay, Hawthorne vigorously defends writers of what was then called the "international school," especially Henry James, whose stories and novels frequently concerned the experiences of Americans traveling in Europe. In opposition to those who insisted that works of American literature must be set in the United States, Hawthorne argues that authors who brought an American perspective to bear on their characters and material were also creating a distinctly national literature. The text is taken from the first printing of the essay in the *North American Review,* August 1884.

From THE AMERICAN ELEMENT IN FICTION

That must be a very shallow literature which depends for its national flavor and character upon its topography and its dialect; and the criticism which can conceive of no deeper Americanism than this is shallower still. What is an American book? It is a book written by an American, and by one who writes as an American, that is, unaffectedly. So an English book is a book written by an unaffected Englishman. What difference can it make what the subject of the writing is? Mr. Henry James lately brought out a volume of essays on "French Poets and Novelists."[1] Mr. E. C. Stedman recently published a series of monographs on "The Victorian Poets."[2] Are these books French and English, or are they nondescript, or are they American? Not only are they American, but they are more essentially American than if they had been disquisitions upon American literature. And the reason is, of course, that they subject the things of the old world to the tests of the new, and thereby vindicate and illustrate the characteristic mission of America to mankind. We are here to hold up European conventionalisms and prejudices in the light of the new day, and thus afford everybody the opportunity, never heretofore enjoyed, of judging them by other standards, and in other surroundings than those amidst which

---

1. **"French Poets and Novelists":** A collection of literary essays published in 1878 by the American novelist Henry James (1843-1916).
2. **"The Victorian Poets":** A volume of literary criticism on British writers published in 1875 by the American critic Edmund C. Stedman (1833-1908).

they came into existence. In the same way, Emerson's "English Traits"[3] is an American thing, and it gives categorical reasons why American things should be. And what is an American novel except a novel treating of persons, places, and ideas from an American point of view? The point of view is *the* point, not the thing seen from it.

But it is said that "the great American novel," in order fully to deserve its name, ought to have American scenery. . . . It is silly and childish to make the boundaries of the America of the mind coincide with those of the United States. We need not dispute about free trade and protection here; literature is not commerce, nor is it politics. America is not a petty nationality, like France, England, and Germany; but whatever in such nationalities tends toward enlightenment and freedom is American. Let us not, therefore, confirm ourselves in a false and ignoble conception of our meaning and mission in the world. Let us not carry into the temple of the Muse[4] the jealousies, the prejudice, the ignorance, the selfishness of our "Senate" and "Representatives," strangely so called! Let us not refuse to breathe the air of Heaven, lest there be something European or Asian in it. If we cannot have a national literature in the narrow, geographical sense of the phrase, it is because our inheritance transcends all geographical definitions. The great American novel may not be written this year, or even in this century. Meanwhile, let us not fear to ride, and ride to death, whatever species of Pegasus[5] we can catch. It can do us no harm, and it may help us to acquire a firmer seat against the time when our own, our very own winged steed makes his appearance.

[1884]

---

3. Emerson's "English Traits": A travel book and work of cultural criticism published in 1856 by Ralph Waldo Emerson (1803-1882), who by the time of his death was widely considered to be one of the major American writers.
4. the temple of the Muse: In Greek and Roman mythology, the Muses were the nine goddesses who presided over the arts and sciences.
5. Pegasus: The winged horse of Greek mythology, a favorite of the nine Muses and a symbol of poetic inspiration.

Henry James

[1843-1916]

Henry James is best known for his short stories and novels, including *Daisy Miller* (1878) and *The Portrait of a Lady* (1880-81), both of which are set in Europe (see James, p. 130). He was also a prolific writer of literary criticism who sought to establish fiction, often dismissed as trivial entertainment, as a significant art form. His most famous critical essay is "The Art of Fiction," first published in the English journal *Longman's Magazine* and reprinted in James's collection *Partial Portraits* (1888). Responding to the "laws of fiction" that had been laid down in an essay by the English novelist Walter Besant, James delivers his most significant statement of the general principles governing the writing of fiction. In the following excerpt, probably the most famous passage in the essay, he addresses two of Besant's central points: that, as James summarizes them, "the novelist must write from his experience, [and] that his 'characters must be real and such as might be met with in actual life.'" The text is taken from the first printing in *Longman's Magazine*, September 1884.

From THE ART OF FICTION

It goes without saying that you will not write a good novel unless you possess the sense of reality; but it will be difficult to give you a recipe for calling that sense into being. Humanity is immense and reality has a myriad forms; the most one can affirm is that some of the flowers of fiction have the odour of it, and others have not; as for telling you in advance how your nosegay should be composed, that is another affair. It is equally excellent and inclusive to say that one must write from experience; to our supposititious aspirant such a declaration might savour of mockery. What kind of experience is intended, and where does it begin and end? Experience is never limited and it is never complete; it is an immense sensibility, a kind of huge spider-web, of the finest silken threads, suspended in the chamber of consciousness and catching every air-borne particle in its tissue. It is the very atmosphere of the mind; and when the mind is imaginative – much more when it happens to be that of a man of genius – it takes to itself the faintest hints of life, it converts the very pulses of the air into revelations. The young lady living in a village has only to be a damsel upon whom nothing is lost to make it quite unfair (as it seems to me) to declare to her that she shall have nothing to say about the military. Greater miracles have been seen than that, imagination assisting, she should speak the truth about some of these gentlemen. I remember an English novelist, a woman of genius, telling me that she was much commended for the impression she had managed to give in one of her tales of the nature and way of life of the French Protestant youth. She had been asked where she learned so much about this recondite being, she had been congratulated on her peculiar opportunities. These opportunities consisted in her having once, in Paris, as she ascended a staircase, passed an open door where, in the household of a *pasteur*,[1] some of the young Protestants were seated at table round a finished meal. The glimpse made a picture; it lasted only a moment, but that moment was experience. She had got her impression, and she evolved her type. She knew what youth was, and what Protestantism; she also had the advantage of having seen what it was to be French; so that she converted these ideas into a concrete image and produced a reality. Above all, however, she was blessed with the faculty which when you give it an inch takes an ell,[2] and which for the artist is a much greater source of

---

1. *pasteur:* Minister or pastor (French).
2. an ell: A former measure of length, approximately 45 inches.

strength than any accident of residence or of place in the social scale. The power to guess the unseen from the seen, to trace the implication of things, to judge the whole piece by the pattern, the condition of feeling life, in general, so completely that you are well on your way to knowing any particular corner of it – this cluster of gifts may almost be said to constitute experience, and they occur in country and in town, and in the most differing stages of education. If experience consists of impressions, it may be said that impressions *are* experience, just as (have we not seen it?) they are the very air we breathe. Therefore, if I should certainly say to a novice, "Write from experience, and experience only," I should feel that this was a rather tantalising monition if I were not careful immediately to add, "Try to be one of the people on whom nothing is lost!"

[1884]

Anonymous
(A "Lady from Philadelphia")

This article was published in "Our Monthly Gossip," a regular feature offering literary news and commentary in *Lippincott's Magazine.* During the 1880s, *Lippincott's* was a successful national literary magazine published in Philadelphia. The magazine regularly printed serializations of novels, including popular English works such as Oscar Wilde's *The Picture of Dorian Gray* and Arthur Conan Doyle's late Sherlock Holmes tale *The Sign of the Four. Lippincott's* also published the work of American fiction writers, including Henry James, Julian Hawthorne, and Rebecca Harding Davis, as well as the African American poet Paul Laurence Dunbar. The following excerpt from the article in "Our Monthly Gossip," identified in the table of contents as the work of a "Lady from Philadelphia," was among the first suggestions that the "Coming American Novelist" might well be not only an African American but also a woman. The text is taken from the first printing in *Lippincott's Magazine,* April 1886.

From THE COMING AMERICAN NOVELIST

When we come to formulate our demands of the Coming American Novelist, we will agree that he must be native-born. His ancestors may come from where they will, but we must give him a birthplace and have the raising of him. Still, the longer his family has been here the better he will represent us. Suppose he should have no country but ours, no traditions but those he has learned here, no longings apart from us, no future except in our future – the orphan of the world, he finds with us his home. And with all this, suppose he refuses to be fused into that grand conglomerate we call the

Lippincott's Monthly Magazine

In this poster advertising the January 1895 issue of *Lippincott's*, a woman is shown meditating on something she has just read in the popular magazine, which she still holds open in her hand.

"American type." With us, he is not of us. He is original, he has humor, he is tender, he is passive and fiery, he has been taught what we call justice, and he has his own opinion about it. He has suffered everything a poet, a dramatist, a novelist need suffer before he comes to have his lips anointed. And with it all he is in one sense a spectator, a little out of the race. How would these conditions go towards forming an original development? In a word, suppose the coming novelist is of African origin? When one comes to consider the subject, there is no improbability in it. One thing is certain — our great novel will not be written by the typical American. After a time the Yankee type will be replaced by some new combination from the effect of our life on the nations swarming to our shores; and, as far as nationality goes, The Novel might as well then be written by the African as by this new combination. Thus far he has given us the only national music we have ever had. Indeed, we may go further and assert that the plantation-songs are the only melodies in our day that are not growths from Handel or Beethoven. They are far more original than Wagner, because he is a legitimate result of a progress in logical lines. Given Gluck and Beethoven, and Wagner is certain after a time.[1] Of course by "plantation-songs" such music as Foster's "Old Folks at Home" is not meant,[2] but the song of the African himself, not the one written for him and then sung by the white people. Whether the peculiar swing and rhythm of his melodies is a vague recollection of Africa or the offspring of his civilization, it is distinctive in musical history. . . .

Yet farther: I have used the generic masculine pronoun because it is convenient; but Fate keeps revenges in store. It was a woman who, taking the wrongs of the African as her theme, wrote the novel that awakened the world to their reality,[3] and why should not the coming novelist be a woman as well as an African? She — the woman of that race — has some claims on Fate which are not yet paid up.

[1886]

---

1. **and Wagner is certain after a time:** The author traces a direct line of descent through a series of influential German composers, from Christoph Willibald von Gluck (1714-1787), George Frederick Handel (1685-1759), and Ludwig von Beethoven (1770-1827) to Richard Wagner (1813-1883), then viewed by many as the most advanced and innovative composer of the period.
2. **Foster's "Old Folks at Home" is not meant:** "Old Folks at Home" was an enormously popular ballad published in 1851 by Stephen Collins Foster (1826-1864), a white Northerner who wrote many songs about plantation life, as distinct from what came to be called "Negro spirituals," songs composed and originally sung by slaves in the South. Such "slave songs" were gaining growing popularity through performances throughout the North by the Jubilee Singers, a vocal group organized at Fisk University in 1871.
3. **It was a woman . . . reality:** The author refers to Harriet Beecher Stowe, author of the enormously popular and influential antislavery novel *Uncle Tom's Cabin* (1851-52).

William Dean Howells

[1837-1920]

William Dean Howells was at once a major novelist and the most influential American literary critic of the late nineteenth century (see Howells, p. 109). His fullest statement about the art of fiction was *Criticism and Fiction*, based in large part on the "Editor's Study" columns he wrote for *Harper's New Monthly Magazine* from 1886 until 1892. As he said in the first of those monthly columns, Howells proposed to "talk over with the reader — who will always be welcome here — such matters of literary interest as may come up from time to time, whether suggested by the new books of the day or other accidents of the literary life." Howells was a strong and consistent champion of realism, which he defined as the "truthful treatment of material." In the following commentary on the nature of American fiction, revised in part from his "Editor's Study" of September 1886, Howells suggests that such a truthful representation of American life would inevitably focus on its "more smiling aspects," since the actualities of life in the United States were sharply different from those in England and Europe. The text is taken from the first edition of *Criticism and Fiction* (1891).

From CRITICISM AND FICTION

It is the difference of the American novelist's ideals from those of the English novelist that gives him his advantage, and seems to promise him the future. The love of the passionate and the heroic, as the Englishman has it, is such a crude and unwholesome thing, so deaf and blind to all the most delicate and important facts of art and life, so insensible to the subtle values in either that its presence or absence makes the whole difference, and enables one who is not obsessed by it to thank Heaven that he is not as that other man is.

There can be little question that many refinements of thought and spirit which every American is sensible of in the fiction of this continent, are necessarily lost upon our good kin beyond seas, whose thumb-fingered apprehension requires something gross and palpable for its assurance of reality. This is not their fault, and I am not sure that it is wholly their misfortune: they are made so as not to miss what they do not find, and they are simply content without those subtleties of life and character which it gives us so keen a pleasure to have noted in literature. If they perceive them at all it is as something vague and diaphanous, something that filmily wavers before their sense and teases them, much as the beings of an invisible world might mock one of our material frame by intimations of their presence. It is with reason, therefore, on the part of an Englishman, that Mr. Henley[1] complains of our fiction as a shadow-land, though we find more and more in it the faithful report of our life, its motives and emotions, and all the comparatively etherealized passions and ideals that influence it.

In fact, the American who chooses to enjoy his birthright to the full, lives in a world wholly different from the Englishman's, and speaks (too often through his nose) another language: he breathes a rarefied and nimble air full of shining possibilities and radiant promises which the fog-and-soot-clogged lungs of those less-favored islanders struggle in vain to fill themselves with. But he ought to be modest in his advantage, and patient with the coughing and sputtering of his cousin who complains of finding himself in an exhausted receiver[2] on plunging into one of our novels. To be quite just to the poor fellow, I have had some such experience as that myself in the atmosphere of some of our more attenuated romances.

Yet every now and then I read a book with perfect comfort and much exhilaration, whose scenes the average Englishman would gasp in. Nothing happens; that is, nobody murders or debauches anybody else; there is no arson or pillage of any sort; there is not a ghost, or a ravening beast, or a hair-breadth escape, or a shipwreck, or a monster of self-sacrifice, or a lady five thousand years old in the whole course of the story; "no

---

1. **Mr. Henley:**   The English poet and critic William Ernest Henley (1849–1903).
2. **an exhausted receiver:**   That is, a container from which all of the air has been withdrawn, or a vacuum.

promenade, no band of music, nossing!" as Mr. Du Maurier's Frenchman said of the meet for a fox-hunt.[3] Yet it is all alive with the keenest interest for those who enjoy the study of individual traits and general conditions as they make themselves known to American experience.

These conditions have been so favorable hitherto (though they are becoming always less so) that they easily account for the optimistic faith of our novel which Mr. Hughes notices.[4] It used to be one of the disadvantages of the practice of romance in America, which Hawthorne more or less whimsically lamented,[5] that there were so few shadows and inequalities in our broad level of prosperity; and it is one of the reflections suggested by Dostoïevsky's novel, The Crime and the Punishment,[6] that whoever struck a note so profoundly tragic in American fiction would do a false and mistaken thing — as false and as mistaken in its way as dealing in American fiction with certain nudities which the Latin peoples seem to find edifying. Whatever their deserts, very few American novelists have been led out to be shot, or finally exiled to the rigors of a winter at Duluth; and in a land where journeymen carpenters and plumbers strike for four dollars a day the sum of hunger and cold is comparatively small, and the wrong from class to class has been almost inappreciable, though all this is changing for the worse. Our novelists, therefore, concern themselves with the more smiling aspects of life, which are the more American, and seek the universal in the individual rather than the social interests. It is worth while, even at the risk of being called commonplace, to be true to our well-to-do actualities; the very passions themselves seem to be softened and modified by conditions which formerly at least could not be said to wrong any one, to cramp endeavor, or to cross lawful desire. Sin and suffering and shame there must always be in the world, I suppose, but I believe that in this new world of ours it is still mainly from one to another one, and oftener still from one to one's self. We have death too in America, and a great deal of disagreeable and painful disease, which the multiplicity of our patent medicines does not seem to cure; but this is tragedy that comes in the very nature of things, and is not peculiarly American, as the large, cheerful average of health and success and happy life is. It will not do to boast, but it is well to be true to the facts, and to see that, apart from these purely mortal troubles, the race here has enjoyed conditions in which most of the ills that have darkened its annals might be averted by honest work and unselfish behavior.

Fine artists we have among us, and right-minded as far as they go; and we must not forget this at evil moments when it seems as if all the women had taken to writing hysterical

---

3. **Mr. Du Maurier's Frenchman . . . fox-hunt:** A scene in *Pictures of English Society* (1884), by the popular English writer George du Maurier (1834-1896).

4. **Mr. Hughes notices:** The English critic Eilian Hughes, in his essay "Present Day Novels: English versus American" (1899).

5. **Hawthorne . . . lamented:** Nathaniel Hawthorne (1804-1864), in the preface to his final novel *The Marble Faun* (1864), which is set in Italy.

6. **The Crime and the Punishment:** *Crime and Punishment* (1866), a tragic tale of poverty, suffering, murder, and redemption by the Russian novelist Fyodor Dostoevsky (1821-1881). In the following passage, Howells alludes to a central event in the life of Dostoevsky, who in 1849 was arrested for his involvement in revolutionary politics, sentenced to death, and placed before a firing squad. His sentence was commuted at the last moment, and he was instead exiled to Siberia.

improprieties, and some of the men were trying to be at least as hysterical in despair of being as improper. If we kept to the complexion of a certain school – which sadly needs a school-master – we might very well be despondent; but, after all, that school is not representative of our conditions or our intentions. Other traits are much more characteristic of our life and our fiction. In most American novels, vivid and graphic as the best of them are, the people are segregated if not sequestered, and the scene is sparsely populated. The effect may be in instinctive response to the vacancy of our social life, and I shall not make haste to blame it. There are few places, few occasions among us, in which a novelist can get a large number of polite people together, or at least keep them together. Unless he carries a snap-camera his picture of them has no probability; they affect one like the figures perfunctorily associated in such deadly old engravings as that of "Washington Irving and his Friends."[7] Perhaps it is for this reason that we excel in small pieces with three or four figures, or in studies of rustic communities, where there is propinquity if not society. Our grasp of more urbane life is feeble; most attempts to assemble it in our pictures are failures, possibly because it is too transitory, too intangible in its nature with us, to be truthfully represented as really existent.

[1891]

---

7. **"Washington Irving and his Friends"**: A popular engraving based on the painting *Washington Irving and His Literary Friends at Sunnyside* by Christian Schussele, who depicted an imaginary gathering of fifteen American writers at Irving's home, though Irving and three of the other writers were dead by the time the picture was painted in 1863.

Hamlin Garland

[1860–1940]

Hamlin Garland

This undated photograph was apparently taken during the 1890s.

Born in Wisconsin, Hamlin Garland later lived for extended periods in both Boston and southern California. His early experiences of the rigors of midwestern farm life shaped his prolific literary career, during which he published nearly fifty books and five hundred articles in a wide range of newspapers and literary magazines. His best-known works are *Main-Travelled Roads* (1891), a collection of short stories; *Crumbling Idols* (1894), a collection of essays on American literature; and his autobiographies, *A Son of the Middle Border* (1917) and *A Daughter of the Middle Border* (1921), for which he won the Pulitzer Prize. Garland firmly supported realism and local color in fiction, believing that the writer "spontaneously reflects the life which goes on around him." In "Literary Emancipation of the West," Garland advocates a "literature of national scope." Challenging the supremacy that Boston had claimed and held "in American literature for more than a half a century," Garland sought to promote writers of the South and the West: "The horizon widens each year, including more cities, more writers, more lovers of light and song, more makers of literature."

The text of the following excerpt from the end of the essay is taken from
the first printing in the *Forum*, October 1893.

From LITERARY EMANCIPATION OF THE WEST

Original creation moves in cycles. Each age of strong creative capability reveals life in
its own fashion. That is, each creative age in the past uttered its own truth as over
against the conventionalized dogmas of its teachers. I believe such a period of literary
breaking-away has come in America. Whitman announced it, but could not exemplify it
in popular form.[1] He voiced its force, its love of liberty and love of comrades, but he was
the prophet, not the exemplar. He said well that the real literature of America could not
be a polite literature. The nation is too great, too sincere. There is coming in this land
the mightiest assertion in art of the rights of man and the glory of the physical universe
ever made in the world. It will be done not by one man, but by many men and women. It
will be born not of drawing-room culture, nor of imitation, nor of fear of masters, nor
will it come from homes of great wealth. It will come from the average American home
in the city, as well as in the country. It will deal with all kinds and conditions. It will be
born of the mingling seas of men in the vast interior of America, because there the problem of the perpetuity of our democracy, the question of the liberty as well as the nationality of our art, will be fought out. This literature will be too great to submit to the
domination of any literary centre or literary master. With cities of half-a-million inhabitants scattered from Pittsburg to Seattle, New York and Chicago will alike be made
humble. Stand up, O young man and woman of the West! Stand erect! Face the future
with a song on your lips and the light of a broader day in your eyes. Turn your back on
the past, not in scorn, but in justice to the future. Reject the scholasticism of the East.
Cease trying to be correct, and become creative. This is our day. The past is not vital. It is
a highway of dust, and Homer, Aeschylus, Sophocles, Dante, Shakespeare are milestones.[2] Libraries do not create great poets and artists; they seldom aid, and they often
warp and destroy them. To know Shakespeare is good. To know your fellow-men is better. All that Shakespeare knew of his fellows you may know of your fellows, but not at
second-hand, not through Shakespeare, not through the eyes of the dead, but at first
hand.

---

1. **Whitman announced . . . popular form:** In the preface to *Leaves of Grass* (1855), Walt Whitman
(1819-1892) proclaims, "The American bard shall delineate no class of persons nor one or two out of the
strata of interests nor love most nor truth most nor the soul most nor the body most . . . and not be for the
eastern states more than the western or the northern states more than the southern." Although he was
revered by many writers, during his lifetime Whitman never gained a wide audience in the United States.
2. **It is a highway of dust . . . milestones:** Garland associates what he earlier calls "the scholasticism of the
East" with what he views as a sterile tradition of European literature from ancient epic poet Homer, who
lived about 850 BCE, and the Greek dramatists Aeschylus (526-456 BCE) and Sophocles (c. 496-406 BCE)
through the Italian poet Dante Alighieri (1265-1321) to William Shakespeare (1564-1616), who was by then
considered to be the greatest writer in English.

In closing let me say: I hope I have made it clear that our position is not one of attacking the East, or Eastern literary men. We are simply attacking the false and fatal idea of culture, based upon past models rather than upon truth. We are speaking for a broader outlook for American literature. We are standing for a literature which shall rise above culture, above library centres and literary masters, to sincerity of accent and to native democracy of sentiment, and, above all, to creative candor.

[1893]

Frank Norris

[1870–1902]

Frank Norris was deeply influenced by the naturalism of the French novelist Émile Zola, who argued that novelists should use methods of scientific objectivity to study human beings in relation to their surroundings (see Norris, p. 323). Zola's work influenced Norris's major novels, especially *McTeague* (1899), as well as his numerous literary essays, some of which were collected in *The Responsibilities of the Novelist*, published posthumously in 1903. Among the most famous of those essays is "A Plea for Romantic Fiction," which first appeared in the Boston *Evening Transcript*, the newspaper in which Norris published many of his critical statements. In the essay, Norris rejects the realism of writers such as William Dean Howells, who argued that American novelists should represent "the more smiling aspects of life" in the United States. In contrast, Norris urges the advantages of "Romance," not in the common sense of amorous tales of adventure, but as a form of the novel that "takes cognizance of the variations from the type of normal life," including the "sordid" and the "unlovely." This text is taken from the first printing in the Boston *Evening Transcript*, December 18, 1901.

A PLEA FOR ROMANTIC FICTION

Let us at the start make a distinction. Observe that one speaks of Romanticism and not of sentimentalism. One claims that the latter is as distinct from the former as is that other form of art which is called Realism. Romance has been often put-upon and overburdened by being forced to bear the onus of abuse that by right should fall to sentiment; but the two should be kept very distinct, for a very high and illustrious place will be claimed for Romance, while sentiment will be handed down the scullery stairs.

Many people today are composing mere sentimentalism, and calling it and causing it to be called Romance, so that with those who are too busy to think much upon these subjects, but who none the less love honest literature, Romance too has fallen into disrepute. Consider now the cut-and-thrust stories. They are all labelled Romances, and it is very easy to get the impression that Romance must be an affair of cloaks and daggers, or moonlight and golden hair. But this is not so at all. The true Romance is a more serious business than this. It is not merely a conjurer's trick box, full of flimsy quackeries, tinsel and clap traps, meant only to amuse, and relying upon deception to do even that. Is it not something better than this? Can we not see in it an instrument, keen, finely tempered, flawless – an instrument with which we may go straight through clothes and tissues and wrappings of flesh down deep into the red living heart of things?

Is all this too subtle, too merely speculative and intrinsic, too "precieuse"[1] and nice and "literary"? Devoutly one hopes the contrary. So much is made of so-called Romanticism in present day fiction, that the subject seems worthy of discussion, and a protest against the misuse of a really noble and honest formula of literature appears to be timely – misuse, that is, in the sense of limited use. Let us suppose for the moment that a Romance can be made out of the cut-and-thrust business. Good heavens, are there no other things that are romantic, even in this – falsely, falsely called – humdrum world of today? Why should it be that so soon as the novelist addresses himself – seriously – to the consideration of contemporary life he must abandon Romance and take up that harsh, loveless, colorless, blunt tool called Realism?

Now, let us understand at once what is meant by Romance and what by Realism. Romance – I take it – is the kind of fiction that takes cognizance of variations from the type of normal life. Realism is the kind of fiction that confines itself to the types of normal life. According to this definition, then, Romance may even treat of the sordid, the unlovely – as for instance, the novels of M. Zola.[2] (Zola has been dubbed a Realist, but he is, on the contrary, the very head of the Romanticists.) Also, Realism, used as it sometimes is as a term of reproach, need not be in the remotest sense or degree offensive, but on the other hand respectable as a church, and proper as a deacon – as, for instance, the novels of Mr. Howells.[3]

The reason why one claims so much for Romance, and quarrels so pointedly with Realism, is that Realism stultifies itself. It notes only the surface of things. For it Beauty is not even skin-deep, but only a geometrical plane, without dimensions of depth, a mere outside. Realism is very excellent so far as it goes, but it goes no farther than the Realist himself can actually see, or actually hear. Realism is minute, it is the drama of a broken tea-cup, the tragedy of a walk down the block, the excitement of an afternoon call, the adventure of an invitation to dinner. It is the visit to my neighbor's house, a formal visit, from which I may draw no conclusions. I see my neighbor and his friends – very, oh, such very! probable people – and that is all. Realism bows upon the doormat and goes away and says to me, as we link arms on the sidewalk: "That is life." And I say it is not. It is not, as you would very well see if you took Romance with you to call upon my neighbor.

1. **"precieuse"**: Precious, in the sense of fastidious or overrefined (French).
2. **M. Zola**: Émile Zola (1840-1902), French writer whose naturalistic novels strongly influenced Norris.
3. **Mr. Howells**: William Dean Howells (1837-1920), American novelist, editor, critic, and champion of realism.

Lately you have been taking Romance a weary journey across the water – ages and the flood of years – and haling her into the fubsy, musty, worm-eaten, moth-riddled, rust-corroded "Grandes Salles"[4] of the Middle Ages and the Renaissance, and she has found the drama of a bygone age for you there. But would you take her across the street to your neighbor's front parlor (with the bisque[5] fisher boy on the mantel and the photograph of Niagara Falls on glass hanging in the front window) would you introduce her there? Not you. Would you take a walk with her in Fifth avenue, or Beacon street, or Michigan avenue?[6] No indeed. Would you choose her for a companion of a morning spent in Wall Street, or an afternoon in the Waldorf-Astoria?[7] You just guess you would not.

She would be out of place, you say, inappropriate. She might be awkward in my neighbor's front parlor, and knock over the little bisque fisher boy. Well, she might. If she did, you might find underneath the base of the statuette hidden away, tucked away – what? God knows. But something which would be a complete revelation of my neighbor's secretest life.

So you think Romance would stop in the front parlor and discuss medicated flannels and mineral waters with the ladies? Not for more than five minutes. She would be off upstairs with you, prying, peeping, peering into the closets of the bedroom, into the nursery, into the sitting-room; yes, and into that little iron box screwed to the lower shelf of the closet in the library; and into those compartments and pigeon-holes of the "secretaire"[8] in the study. She would find a heartache (may-be) between the pillows of the mistress's bed, and a memory carefully secreted in the master's deedbox. She would come upon a great hope amid the books and papers of the study table of the young man's room, and – perhaps – who knows – an affair, or, great heavens, an intrigue, in the scented ribbons and gloves and hairpins of the young lady's bureau. And she would pick here a little and there a little, making up a bag of hopes and fears, and a package of joys and sorrows – great ones, mind you – and then come down to the front door, and stepping out into the street, hand you the bags and package, and say to you – "That is Life!"

However it may be abroad, in America so many women are taking advantage of the educational opportunities offered them that a number of colleges and universities are growing apprehensive lest the preponderance of their students be of the feminine gender, and in at least two universities there is talk of limiting the attendance of women.[9] For even here the prejudice exists to such an extent that it is felt to be a shame to a university to have more women than men in it.

---

4. "Grandes Salles": Large halls or rooms (French).
5. bisque: Delicate porcelain.
6. Fifth avenue, or Beacon street, or Michigan avenue: Fashionable residential streets in New York City, Boston, and Chicago.
7. Waldorf-Astoria: Elegant hotel in New York City.
8. "secretaire": Desk (French). A secretary is a type of desk with cubbies and shelves often hidden by a hinged door that opens to form a work surface.
9. However it may be abroad . . . women: The following three paragraphs on the education and capacities of women were omitted from the version of Norris's essay published posthumously in *The Responsibilities of the Novelist and Other Literary Essays* (1903).

But it is not "manlike education" which they are trying to secure. It is merely education. It is knowledge – facts – theories – truth – speculation – all of which belongs to anyone with eyes to see and ears to hear, and muliebrity[10] is no bar to the acquirement of these things.

As to the foundress of the Babylonian wall and the builder of the Pyramid, Mr. Lang[11] has us on the hip. We cherished the belief that certain excellent ancient ladies did these things, but we can relinquish that fond faith. He might, however, have dealt one blow at a time. It would have been more endurable. In regard to Jean d'Arc,[12] however – can even Mr. Lang be sure that another such as she will not appear?

Romance does very well in the castles of the Middle Ages and the Renaissance chateaux, and she has the entrée[13] there and is very well received. That is all well and good. But let us protest against limiting her to such places and such times. You will find her, I grant you, in the chatelaine's chamber and the dungeon of the man-at-arms;[14] but, if you choose to look for her, you will find her equally at home in the brownstone house on the corner and in the office building downtown. And this very day, in this very hour, she is sitting among the rags and wretchedness, the dirt and despair of the tenements of the East Side of New York.

"What?" I hear you say, "look for Romance – the lady of the silken robes and golden crown, our beautiful, chaste maiden of soft voice and gentle eyes – look for her among the vicious ruffians, male and female, of Allen street and Mulberry Bend[15]?" I tell you she is there, and to your shame be it said that you will not know her in those surroundings. You, the aristocrats, who demand the fine linen and the purple in your fiction; you, the sensitive, the delicate, who will associate with your Romance only so long as she wears a silken gown. You will not follow her to the slums, for you believe that Romance should only amuse and entertain you, singing you sweet songs and touching the harp of silver strings with rosy-tipped fingers. If haply she should call to you from the squalor of a dive, or the awful degradation of a disorderly house, crying: "Look, listen! This, too, is life. These, too, are my children, look at them, know them and, knowing, help!" Should she call thus, you would stop your ears; you would avert your eyes, and you would answer, "Come from there, Romance. Your place is not there!" And you would make of her a harlequin, a tumbler, a sword dancer, when, as a matter of fact, she should be by right divine a teacher sent from god.

---

10. **muliebrity:** The quality or characteristics of being a woman. The English word was coined to supply the missing opposite of *virility*.

11. **Mr. Lang:** Andrew Lang (1844-1912), prolific British writer and scholar whose most famous work on folklore and primitive religions was *Myth, Ritual and Religion* (1887). The magnificent city of Babylon, which was surrounded by a massive wall, and the pyramids of Egypt were among the architectural wonders of the ancient world.

12. **Jean d'Arc:** St. Joan of Arc (1412-1431), the religious and military leader who led French troops to a series of stunning military victories over the English. Later burned at the stake as a heretic, she was canonized in 1920.

13. **entrée:** The right to enter or be included (French).

14. **chatelaine's chamber and the dungeon of the man-at-arms:** The private room of the mistress of a castle and the prison cell of a medieval cavalryman.

15. **Allen street and Mulberry Bend:** Streets in the slums of New York City.

She will not always wear the robe of silk, the gold crown, the jewelled shoon,[16] will not always sweep the silver harp. An iron note is hers if so she choose, and coarse garments, and stained hands, and, meeting her thus, it is for you to know her as she passes — know her for the same young queen of the blue mantle and lilies.[17] She can teach you, if you will be humble to learn. Teach you by showing, God help you, if at last you take from Romance her mission of teaching, if you do not believe that she has a purpose, a nobler purpose and a mightier than mere amusement, mere entertainment. Let Realism do the entertaining with its meticulous presentation of tea-cups, rag carpets, wall paper and hair-cloth sofas, stopping with these, going no deeper than it sees, choosing the ordinary, the untroubled, the commonplace.

But to Romance belongs the wide world for range, and the unplumbed depths of the human heart, and the mystery of sex, and the problems of life, and the black, unsearched penetralia of the soul of man. You, the indolent, must not always be amused. What matter the silken clothes, what matter the prince's houses? Romance, too, is a teacher, and if — throwing aside the purple — she wears the camel's hair and feeds upon the locusts, it is to cry aloud unto the people, "Prepare ye the way of the Lord, make straight his path."[18]

[1901]

---

16. **shoon:** An early plural form of *shoe.*

17. **queen of the blue mantle and lilies:** The Virgin Mary, who is traditionally depicted wearing a blue mantle and who is associated with the purity of the lily.

18. **"Prepare . . . path":** See Matthew 3:3, where the words are spoken by the prophet John the Baptist, who is clothed in camel's hair and who survives on locusts and wild honey.

Mark Twain
(Samuel L. Clemens)

[1835-1910]

"Mark Twain," probably the most familiar figure in American literary history, first came before the public in 1863, when an itinerant journalist named Samuel L. Clemens adopted that pen name to sign his letters in the *Territorial Enterprise*, an obscure newspaper published in what was then the Nevada Territory. Clemens had been born nearly twenty-eight years earlier, on November 30, 1835, in Florida, Missouri. His family later moved to Hannibal, a town on the Mississippi River. There, in what he later described as "a heavenly place for a boy," Clemens unconsciously began to gather material for some of his most memorable works. He also began to gain the journalistic experience that would ultimately lead him to a career in writing. Shortly after his father's death in 1847, Clemens was apprenticed to a local printer. In 1851 he went to work for his brother, who had bought a newspaper in Hannibal. When Clemens was eighteen, he left home and drifted around the country for several years, still supporting himself as a printer and journalist. In 1857, however, Clemens pursued his childhood dream of becoming a steamboat pilot, a lucrative trade he plied until the outbreak of the Civil War in 1861 effectively ended commercial traffic on the Mississippi River. Following a brief stint in a pro-Southern militia unit in Missouri, Clemens turned his back on the war and headed west, his mind full of get-rich schemes. When those failed, he once again took up the pen, first in a series of unsigned letters and then as "Mark Twain." "It is an old river term, a leads-man's call, signifying two fathoms — twelve feet," Clemens explained to the editor of the *Territorial Enterprise*. "It has a richness about it; it was always a pleasant sound for a pilot to hear on a dark night; it meant safe water."

It was as "Mark Twain" — initially his literary persona and increasingly his public role — that Clemens would thereafter be known. He followed the spreading fame of that name from Nevada across the Sierra Nevada to California and finally back across the country to New York City. But he was then either celebrated or dismissed as a popular entertainer, the prolific generator of humorous newspaper sketches rather than serious literary work. His first book was a collection of such sketches, while his second book was a direct outgrowth of his newspaper work: *The Innocents Abroad* (1869), a comic and satirical account of a tour of Europe and the Holy Land based on letters originally published in the *Alta California* and the *New-York Tribune*. Flush with confidence and the substantial proceeds from that book, Twain in 1870 married Olivia Langdon, daughter of a wealthy family from Elmira, New York. The couple soon began a family and moved into a mansion in Hartford, Connecticut, where one of their neighbors was Harriet Beecher Stowe, the revered author best known for her influential antislavery novel *Uncle Tom's Cabin* (1851). Only then, having worked his way up to affluence and social respectability in the East, did Twain begin

Mark Twain

This photograph of Samuel L. Clemens was taken in 1867, shortly after he gained fame as "Mark Twain."

All modern American literature comes from one book by Mark Twain called Huckleberry Finn.
—Ernest Hemingway

to explore and exploit his wide experience and vivid memories of life along the Mississippi River in the years before the Civil War. Twain first wrote *Old Times on the Mississippi* (1875), a series of magazine sketches about his years as a steamboat pilot that he later incorporated into a book, *Life on the Mississippi* (1883). He followed those sketches with his first novel, *The Adventures of Tom Sawyer* (1876). In that popular "boy's book," as the genre was known, Twain told the story from the point of view of a genteel adult narrator. Twain took a different approach in the sequel he began to write in 1876. Using Tom Sawyer's disreputable and semiliterate friend Huck Finn as the narrator of the novel, Twain offered a triumphant demonstration of the power of colloquial speech in the *Adventures of Huckleberry Finn*, which he finally published in 1885.

That acclaimed book ultimately overshadowed Twain's other writings, but during the following decades he produced a wide range of work, including novels, stories, and travel books. Although many of those works were set in the past or in distant places, or both, Twain remained deeply engaged in contemporary life in the United States. In a novel set in medieval England, *A Connecticut Yankee in King Arthur's Court* (1889), he mounted a thinly veiled attack on the social injustices and political inequalities generated by the growing disparity between the rich and the poor in the industrial North. Twain explored the implications of miscegenation and the corrosive effects of slavery and racism in *The Tragedy of Pudd'nhead Wilson* (1895), a novel set in the antebellum South. He protested the ongoing oppression of African Americans even more directly in an extended essay, "The United States of Lyncherdom" (1901), a bitter response to the wave of violence that had been unleashed against blacks in the South after the end of Reconstruction. Indeed, the writer from a slaveholding state who had earlier worked so hard to become a respected figure in northern society and its literary culture — and whom many would come to view as the most quintessentially "American" of all the country's authors — became one of the sharpest critics of society and politics in the United States, both in the North and in the South. During the final decade of his life, Twain composed his lengthy *Autobiography*, some chapters of which he published in the *North American Review* in 1906-07. Organizing the work in the sequence in which his memories surfaced, rather than as a chronological narrative, Twain recalled scenes and events ranging from his joyous boyhood in Missouri to the devastating loss of his wife in 1904 and the deaths of two of his three daughters, one from meningitis in 1896 and the other from heart failure brought on by an epileptic seizure in December 1909. Shortly after describing those agonizing experiences in his *Autobiography*, Twain died at his home in Redding, Connecticut, on April 21, 1910.

bedfordstmartins.com/ americanlit *for research links on Twain*

Twain's "Jim Smiley and His Jumping Frog."   This sketch spread the fame of "Mark Twain" beyond the West. He had heard a version of this often-told story at a gold camp in California and wrote it down at the request of his friend "Artemus Ward," the pen name of C. F. Browne, a popular comic writer who was putting together a collection of sketches in 1865. When the story arrived too late to be included in the volume, it was published in the *New York Saturday Press,* from which it was widely reprinted in newspapers all around the United States. Twain subsequently revised it several times, notably as the title story of his first book, *The Celebrated Jumping Frog of Calaveras County and Other Sketches* (1867), and even more substantially for his *Sketches, New and Old* (1875). In all of the versions, however, a key element is the ironic interplay between the two narrators: the condescending stand-in for the educated audience – "Mark Twain" in the earliest version – and the garrulous old Simon Wheeler, the colloquial teller of the tale, who may well have the last laugh. The text is taken from the first printing in the *New York Saturday Press,* November 18, 1865.

JIM SMILEY AND HIS JUMPING FROG[1]

Mr. A. Ward,

Dear Sir: – Well, I called on good-natured garrulous old Simon Wheeler, and I inquired after your friend Leonidas W. Smiley, as you requested me to do, and I hereunto append the result. If you can get any information out of it you are cordially welcome to it. I have a lurking suspicion that your Leonidas W. Smiley is a myth – that you never knew such a personage, and that you only conjectured that if I asked old Wheeler about him it would remind him of his infamous *Jim* Smiley, and he would go to work and bore me nearly to death with some infernal reminiscence of him as long and tedious as it should be useless to me. If that was your design, Mr. Ward, it will gratify you to know that it succeeded.

I found Simon Wheeler dozing comfortably by the bar-room stove of the little old dilapidated tavern in the ancient mining camp of Boomerang, and I noticed that he was fat and bald-headed, and had an expression of winning gentleness and simplicity upon his tranquil countenance. He roused up and gave me good-day. I told him a friend of mine had commissioned me to make some inquiries about a cherished companion of his boyhood named Leonidas W. Smiley – Rev. Leonidas W. Smiley – a young minister of the gospel, who he had heard was at one time a resident of this village of Boomerang. I added that if Mr. Wheeler could tell me anything about this Rev. Leonidas W. Smiley, I would feel under many obligations to him.

Simon Wheeler backed me into a corner and blockaded me there with his chair – and then sat down and reeled off the monotonous narrative which follows this paragraph.

---

1. "Jim Smiley and His Jumping Frog": When Twain later revised the story, he altered the title to "The Notorious Jumping Frog of Calaveras County." The county, which is in the foothills of the Sierra Nevada, directly east of San Francisco, was the center of mining activity during the California gold rush of 1849.

He never smiled, he never frowned, he never changed his voice from the quiet, gently-flowing key to which he turned the initial sentence, he never betrayed the slightest sus-picion of enthusiasm – but all through the interminable narrative there ran a vein of impressive earnestness and sincerity, which showed me plainly that so far from his imagining that there was anything ridiculous or funny about his story, he regarded it as a really important matter, and admired its two heroes as men of transcendent genius in finesse . . . To me, the spectacle of a man drifting serenely along through such a queer yarn without ever smiling was exquisitely absurd. As I said before, I asked him to tell me what he knew of Rev. Leonidas W. Smiley, and he replied as follows. I let him go on in his own way, and never interrupted him once:

There was a feller here once by the name of *Jim* Smiley, in the winter of '49 – or maybe it was the spring of '50 – I don't recollect exactly, somehow, though what makes me think it was one or the other is because I remember the big flume wasn't finished when he first come to the camp; but anyway, he was the curiousest man about always betting on anything that turned up you ever see, if he could get anybody to bet on the other side, and if he couldn't he'd change sides – any way that suited the other man would suit *him* – any way just so's he got a bet, *he* was satisfied. But still, he was lucky – uncommon lucky; he most always come out winner. He was always ready and laying for a chance; there couldn't be no solitry thing mentioned but what that feller'd offer to bet on it – and take any side you please, as I was just telling you: if there was a horse race, you'd find him flush or you find him busted at the end of it; if there was a dog-fight, he'd bet on it; if there was a cat-fight, he'd bet on it; if there was a chicken-fight, he'd bet on it; why if there was two birds setting on a fence, he would bet you which one would fly first – or if there was a camp-meeting he would be there reglar to bet on parson Walker, which he judged to be the best exhorter about here, and so he was, too, and a good man; if he even see a straddle-bug start to go anywheres, he would bet you how long it would take him to get wherever he was going to, and if you took him up he would foller that straddle-bug to Mexico but what he would find out where he was bound for and how long he was on the road. Lots of the boys here has seen that Smiley and can tell you about him. Why, it never made no difference to *him* – he would bet on *anything* – the dangdest feller. Parson Walker's wife laid very sick, once, for a good while, and it seemed as if they warn't going to save her; but one morning he come in and Smiley asked him how she was, and he said she was considerable better – thank the Lord for his inf'nit mercy – and coming on so smart that with the blessing of Providence she'd get well yet – and Smiley, before he thought, says, "Well, I'll resk two-and-a-half that she don't, anyway."

Thish-yer Smiley had a mare – the boys called her the fifteen-minute nag, but that was only in fun, you know, because, of course, she was faster than that – and he used to win money on that horse, for all she was so slow and always had the asthma, or the dis-temper, or the consumption, or something of that kind. They used to give her two or three hundred yards' start, and then pass her under way; but always at the fag-end[2] of the race she'd get excited and desperate-like, and come cavorting and spraddling up,

---

2. **fag-end:** Tiring or exhausting conclusion of an event or occasion.

and scattering her legs around limber, sometimes in the air, and sometimes out to one side amongst the fences, and kicking up m-o-r-e dust, and raising m-o-r-e racket with her coughing and sneezing and blowing her nose — and always fetch up at the stand just about a neck ahead, as near as you could cipher it down.

And he had a little small bull-pup, that to look at him you'd think he warn't worth a cent, but to set around and look ornery, and lay for a chance to steal something. But as soon as money was up on him he was a different dog — his under-jaw'd begin to stick out like the for'castle of a steamboat, and his teeth would uncover, and shine savage like the furnaces. And a dog might tackle him, and bully-rag him, and bite him, and throw him over his shoulder two or three times, and Andrew Jackson — which was the name of the pup — Andrew Jackson would never let on but what he was satisfied, and hadn't expected nothing else — and the bets being doubled and doubled on the other side all the time, till the money was all up — and then all of a sudden he would grab that other dog just by the joint of his hind legs and freeze to it — not chaw, you understand, but only just grip and hang on till they threwed up on the sponge, if it was a year. Smiley always came out winner on that pup till he harnessed a dog once that didn't have no hind legs, because they'd been sawed off in a circular saw, and when the thing had gone along far enough, and the money was all up, and he came to make a snatch for his pet holt, he saw in a minute how he'd been imposed on, and how the other dog had him in the door, so to speak, and he 'peared surprised, and then he looked sorter discouraged like, and didn't try no more to win the fight, and so he got shucked out bad. He gave Smiley a look as much as to say his heart was broke, and it was *his* fault, for putting up a dog that hadn't no hind legs for him to take holt of, which was his main dependence in a fight, and then he limped off a piece, and laid down and died. It was a good pup, was that Andrew Jackson, and would have made a name for hisself if he'd lived, for the stuff was in him, and he had genius — I know it, because he hadn't had no opportunities to speak of, and it don't stand to reason that a dog could make such a fight as he could under them circumstances, if he hadn't no talent. It always makes me feel sorry when I think of that last fight of his'on, and the way it turned out.

Well, thish-yer Smiley had rat-terriers and chicken cocks, and tom-cats, and all them kind of things, till you couldn't rest, and you couldn't fetch nothing for him to bet on but he'd match you. He ketched a frog one day and took him home and said he cal'lated to educate him; and so he never done nothing for three months but set in his back yard and learn that frog to jump. And you bet you he *did* learn him, too. He'd give him a little hunch behind, and the next minute you'd see that frog whirling in the air like a dough-nut — see him turn one summerset, or maybe a couple, if he got a good start, and come down flat-footed and all right, like a cat. He got him up so in the matter of ketching flies, and kept him in practice so constant, that he'd nail a fly every time as far as he could see him. Smiley said all a frog wanted was education, and he could do most anything — and I believe him. Why, I've seen him set Dan'l Webster down here on this floor — Dan'l Web-ster was the name of the frog — and sing out, "Flies! Dan'l, flies," and quicker'n you could wink, he'd spring straight up, and snake a fly off'n the counter there, and flop down on the floor again as solid as a gob of mud, and fall to scratching the side of his head with his hind foot as indifferent as if he hadn't no idea he'd done any more'n any frog might do. You never see a frog so modest and straightfor'ard as he was, for all he was so gifted. And when it come to fair-and-square jumping on a dead level, he could get over more ground at one straddle than any animal of his breed you ever see. Jumping on a dead level was his strong suit, you understand, and when it come to that, Smiley would ante up money on him as long as he had a red.[3] Smiley was monstrous proud of his frog, and well he might be, for fellers that had travelled and ben everywheres all said he laid over any frog that ever *they* see.

Well, Smiley kept the beast in a little lattice box, and he used to fetch him downtown sometimes and lay for a bet. One day a feller — a stranger in the camp, he was — come across him with his box, and says:

"What might it be that you've got in the box?"

And Smiley says, sorter indifferent like, "It might be a parrot, or it might be a canary, maybe, but it ain't — it's only just a frog."

And the feller took it, and looked at it careful, and turned it round this way and that, and says, "H'm — so 'tis. Well, what's *he* good for?"

"Well," Smiley says, easy and careless, "he's good enough for *one* thing I should judge — he can out-jump any frog in Calaveras county."

The feller took the box again, and took another long, particular look, and give it back to Smiley and says, very deliberate, "Well — I don't see no points about that frog that's any better'n any other frog."

"Maybe you don't," Smiley says. "Maybe you understand frogs, and maybe you don't understand 'em; maybe you've had experience, and maybe you ain't only a amature, as it were. Anyways, I've got *my* opinion, and I'll resk forty dollars that he can out-jump any frog in Calaveras county."

And the feller studied a minute, and then says, kinder sad, like, "Well — I'm only a stranger here, and I ain't got no frog — but if I had a frog I'd bet you."

And then Smiley says, "That's all right — that's all right — if you'll hold my box a minute I'll go and get you a frog"; and so the feller took the box, and put up his forty dollars along with Smiley's, and set down to wait.

So he set there a good while thinking and thinking to hisself, and then he got the frog out and prized his mouth open and took a teaspoon and filled him full of quail-shot — filled him pretty near up to his chin — and set him on the floor. Smiley he went out to the swamp and slopped around in the mud for a long time, and finally he ketched a frog and fetched him in and give him to this feller and says:

"Now if you're ready, set him alongside of Dan'l, with his fore-paws just even with Dan'l's, and I'll give the word." Then he says, "One — two — three — jump!" and him and the feller touched up the frogs from behind, and the new frog hopped off lively, but Dan'l give a heave, and hysted up his shoulders — so — like a Frenchman, but it wasn't no use — he couldn't budge; he was planted as solid as a anvil, and he couldn't no more stir than if he was anchored out. Smiley was a good deal surprised, and he was disgusted too, but he didn't have no idea what the matter was, of course.

The feller took the money and started away, and when he was going out at the door he sorter jerked his thumb over his shoulder — this way — at Dan'l, and says again, very

---

3. **red:** That is, a "red cent," so called because of the high copper content in the penny before the Civil War.

deliberate, "Well – *I* don't see no points about that frog that's any better'n any other frog."

Smiley he stood scratching his head and looking down at Dan'l a long time, and at last he says, "I do wonder what in the nation that frog throwed off for – I wonder if there ain't something the matter with him – he 'pears to look mighty baggy, somehow" – and he ketched Dan'l by the nap of the neck, and lifted him up and says, "Why blame my cats if he don't weigh five pounds" – and turned him upside down, and he belched out about a double-handful of shot. And then he see how it was, and he was the maddest man – he set the frog down and took out after that feller, but he never ketched him. And —

[Here Simon Wheeler heard his name called from the front-yard, and got up to go and see what was wanted.] And turning to me as he moved away, he said: "Just sit where you are, stranger, and rest easy – I ain't going to be gone a second."

But by your leave, I did not think that a continuation of the history of the enterprising vagabond Jim Smiley would be likely to afford me much information concerning the Rev. Leonidas W. Smiley, and so I started away.

At the door I met the sociable Wheeler returning, and he buttonholed me and recommenced:

"Well, thish-yer Smiley had a yaller one-eyed cow that didn't have no tail only just a short stump like a bannanner, and —"

"O, curse Smiley and his afflicted cow!" I muttered, good-naturedly, and bidding the old gentleman good-day, I departed.

Yours, truly,

Mark Twain
[1865]

Twain's "A True Story, Repeated Word for Word as I Heard It." This story was told to Twain by a cook at Quarry Farm in Elmira, New York, where the Clemenses spent their summers. The printed version was particularly significant because it was the first piece Twain published in the most distinguished periodical in the United States, the *Atlantic Monthly*, where it appeared in 1874. Its editor, William Dean Howells, was then virtually the only member of the literary establishment who took Twain seriously as a writer, and the periodical consequently opened up to him a new and radically different audience. In response, the humorist offered a piece that was anything but funny, the poignant account of a former slave. Such stories, often transcribed by Northern abolitionists, had been a staple of the antislavery crusade before the Civil War. Here, in the waning period of Reconstruction, the story was transcribed by a writer who had grown up in a slave state, whose family had owned a slave, and who had briefly served in a pro-Southern militia unit in Missouri before moving west and finally settling in the East. At the same time, Twain's ear for southern vernacular speech gave the story a particular force and authenticity, anticipating his masterly deployment of such speech in the *Adventures of Huckleberry Finn*. The text is taken from the first printing in the *Atlantic Monthly*, November 1874.

A TRUE STORY, REPEATED
WORD FOR WORD AS I HEARD IT

It was summer time, and twilight. We were sitting on the porch of the farm-house, on the summit of the hill, and "Aunt Rachel" was sitting respectfully below our level, on the steps, – for she was our servant, and colored. She was of mighty frame and stature; she was sixty years old, but her eye was undimmed and her strength unabated. She was a cheerful, hearty soul, and it was no more trouble for her to laugh than it is for a bird to sing. She was under fire, now, as usual when the day was done. That is to say, she was being chaffed without mercy, and was enjoying it. She would let off peal after peal of laughter, and then sit with her face in her hands and shake with throes of enjoyment which she could no longer get breath enough to express. At such a moment as this a thought occurred to me, and I said: –

"Aunt Rachel, how is that you've lived sixty years and never had any trouble?"

She stopped quaking. She paused, and there was a moment of silence. She turned her face over her shoulder toward me, and said, without even a smile in her voice: –

"Misto C —, is you in 'arnest?"

It surprised me a good deal; and it sobered my manner and my speech, too. I said: –

"Why, I thought – that is, I meant – why, you *can't* have had any trouble. I've never heard you sigh, and never seen your eye when there wasn't a laugh in it."

She faced fairly around, now, and was full of earnestness.

"Has I had any trouble? Misto C —, I's gwyne to tell you, den I leave it to you. I was bawn down 'mongst de slaves; I knows all 'bout slavery, 'case I ben one of 'em my own se'f. Well, sah, my ole man – dat's my husban' – he was lovin' an' kind to me, jist as kind as you is to yo' own wife. An' we had chil'en – seven chil'en – an' we loved dem chil'en jist de same as you loves yo' chil'en. Dey was black, but de Lord can't make no chil'en so black but what dey mother loves 'em an' wouldn't give 'em up, no, not for anything dat's in dis whole world.

"Well, sah, I was raised in ole Fo'ginny, but my mother she was raised in Maryland; an' my *souls!* she was turrible when she'd git started! My *lan'!* but she'd make de fur fly! When she'd git into dem tantrums, she always had one word dat she said. She'd straighten herse'f up an' put her fists in her hips an' say, 'I want you to understan' dat I wa' n't bawn in de mash to be fool' by trash! I 's one o' de ole Blue Hen's Chickens, *I* is!' 'Ca'se, you see, dat's what folks dat's bawn in Maryland calls deyselves, an' dey's proud of it. Well, dat was her word. I don't ever forgit it, beca'se she said it so much, an' beca'se she said it one day when my little Henry tore his wris' awful, an' most busted his head, right up at de top of his forehead, an' de niggers didn't fly aroun' fas' enough to 'tend to him. An' when dey talk' back at her, she up an' she says, 'Look-a-heah!' she says, 'I want you niggers to understan' dat I wa' n't bawn in de mash to be fool' by trash! I 's one o' de ole Blue Hen's Chickens, *I* is!' an' den she clar' dat kitchen an' bandage' up de chile herse'f. So I says dat word, too, when I's riled.

"Well, bymeby my ole mistis say she's broke, an' she got to sell all de niggers on de place. An' when I heah dat dey gwyne to sell us all off at oction in Richmon', oh de good gracious! I know what dat mean!"

Aunt Rachel had gradually risen, while she warmed to her subject, and now she towered above us, black against the stars.

"Dey put chains on us an' put us on a stan' as high as dis po'ch, – twenty foot high, – an' all de people stood aroun', crowds an' crowds. An' dey 'd come up dah an' look at us all roun', an' squeeze our arm, an' make us git up an' walk, an' den say, 'Dis one too ole,' or 'Dis one lame,' or 'Dis one don't 'mount to much.' An' dey sole my ole man, an' took him away, an' dey begin to sell my chil'en an' take *dem* away, an' I begin to cry; an' de man say, 'Shet up yo' dam blubberin',' an' hit me on de mouf wid his han'. An' when de las' one was gone but my little Henry, I grab' *him* clost up to my breas' so, an' I ris up an' says, 'You shan't take him away,' I says; 'I'll kill de man dat totches him!' I says. But my little Henry whisper an' say, 'I gwyne to run away, an' den I work an' buy yo' freedom.' Oh, bless de chile, he always so good! But dey got him – dey got him, de men did; but I took and tear de clo'es mos' off of 'em, an' beat 'em over de head wid my chain; an' *dey* give it to *me*, too, but I didn't mine dat.

"Well, dah was my ole man gone, an' all my chil'en, all my seven chil'en – an' six of 'em I haint set eyes on ag'in to dis day, an' dat 's twenty-two year ago las' Easter. De man dat bought me b'long' in Newbern, an' he took me dah. Well, bymeby de years roll on an' de waw come. My marster he was a Confedrit colonel, an' I was his family's cook. So when de Unions took dat town, dey all run away an' lef' me all by myse'f wid de other niggers in dat mons'us big house. So de big Union officers move in dah, an' dey ask me would I cook for *dem*. 'Lord bless you,' says I, 'dat 's what I 's *for*.'

"Dey wa' n't no small-fry officers, mine you, dey was de biggest dey *is;* an' de way dey made dem sojers mosey roun'! De Gen'l he tole me to boss dat kitchen; an' he say, 'If anybody come meddlin' wid you, you jist make 'em walk chalk; don't you be afeard,' he say; 'you's 'mong frens, now.'

"Well, I thinks to myse'f, if my little Henry ever got a chance to run away, he'd make to de Norf, o' course. So one day I comes in dah whah de big officers was, in de parlor, an' I drops a kurtchy, so, an' I up an' tole 'em 'bout my Henry, dey a-listenin' to my troubles jist de same as if I was white folks; an' I says, 'What I come for is beca'se if he got away and got up Norf whah you gemmen comes from, you might 'a' seen him, maybe, an' could tell me so as I could fine him ag'in; he was very little, an' he had a sk-yar on his lef' wris', an' at de top of his forehad.' Den dey look mournful, an' de Gen'l say, 'How long sence you los' him?' an' I say, 'Thirteen year.' Den de Gen'l say, 'He wouldn't be little no mo', now – he's a man!'

"I never thought o' dat befo'! He was only dat little feller to *me*, yit. I never thought 'bout him growin' up an' bein' big. But I see it den. None o' de gemmen had run acrost him, so dey couldn't do nothin' for me. But all dat time, do' *I* didn't know it, my Henry *was* run off to de Norf, years an' years, an' he was a barber, too, an' worked for hisse'f. An' bymeby, when de waw come, he ups an' he says, 'I 's done barberin',' he says; 'I 's gwyne to fine my ole mammy, less'n she's dead.' So he sole out an' went to whah dey was recruitin', an' hired hisse'f out to de colonel for his servant; an' den he went all froo de battles everywhah, huntin' for his ole mammy; yes indeedy, he'd hire to fust one officer an' den another, tell he'd ransacked de whole Souf; but you see *I* didn't know nuffin 'bout *dis*. How was *I* gwyne to know it?

"Well, one night we had a big sojer ball; de sojers dah at Newbern was always havin' balls an' carryin' on. Dey had 'em in my kitchen, heaps o' times, 'ca'se it was so big. Mine you, I was *down* on sich doin's; beca'se my place was wid de officers, an' it rasp' me to have dem common sojers cavortin' roun' my kitchen like dat. But I alway' stood aroun' an' kep' things straight, I did; an' sometimes dey'd git my dander up, an' den I'd make 'em clar dat kitchen, mine I *tell* you!

"Well, one night – it was a Friday night – dey comes a whole plattoon f'm a *nigger* ridgment dat was on guard at de house, – de house was headquarters, you know, – an' den I was jist a-*bilin'!* Mad? I was jist a-*boomin'!* I swelled aroun', an' swelled aroun'; I jist was a-itchin' for 'em to do somefin for to start me. An' dey was a-walzin' an a-dancin'! *my!* but dey was havin' a time! an' I jist a-swellin' an' a-swellin' up! Pooty soon, 'long comes *sich* a spruce young nigger a-sailin' down de room wid a yaller wench roun' de wais'; an' roun' an' roun' an' roun' dey went, enough to make a body drunk to look at 'em; an' when dey got abreas' o' me, dey went to kin' o' balancin' aroun', fust on one leg an' den on t'other, an' smilin' at my big red turban, an' makin' fun, an' I ups an' says, '*Git* along wid you! – rubbage!' De young man's face kin' o' changed, all of a sudden, for 'bout a second, but den he went to smilin' ag'in, same as he was befo'. Well, 'bout dis time, in comes some niggers dat played music an' b'long' to de ban', an' dey *never* could git along widout puttin' on airs. An' de very fust air dey put on dat night, I lit into 'em! Dey laughed, an' dat made me wuss. De res' o' de niggers got to laughin', an' den my soul *alive* but I was hot! My eye was jist a-blazin'! I jist straightened myself up, so, – jist as I is now, plum to de ceilin', mos', – an' I digs my fists into my hips, an' I says, 'Look-a-heah!' I says, 'I want you niggers to understan' dat I wa' n't bawn in de mash to be fool' by trash! I 's one o' de ole Blue Hen's Chickens, *I* is!' an' den I see dat young man stan' a-starin' an' stiff, lookin' kin' o' up at de ceilin' like he fo'got somefin, an' couldn't 'member it no mo'. Well, I jist march' on dem niggers, – so, lookin' like a gen'l, – an' dey jist cave' away befo' me an' out at de do'. An' as dis young man was a-goin' out, I heah him say to another nigger, 'Jim,' he says, 'you go 'long an' tell de cap'n I be on han' 'bout eight o'clock in de mawnin'; dey's somefin on my mine,' he says; 'I don't sleep no mo' dis night. You go 'long,' he says, 'an' leave me by my own se'f.'

"Dis was 'bout one o'clock in de mawnin'. Well, 'bout seven, I was up an' on han', gittin' de officers' breakfast. I was a-stoopin' down by de stove, – jist so, same as if yo' foot was de stove, – an' I'd opened de stove do wid my right han', – so, pushin' it back, jist as I pushes yo' foot, – an' I'd jist got de pan o' hot biscuits in my han' an' was 'bout to raise up, when I see a black face come aroun' under mine, an' de eyes a-lookin' up into mine, jist as I 's a-lookin' up clost under yo' face now; an' I jist stopped *right dah,* an' never budged! jist gazed, an' gazed, so; an' de pan begin to tremble, an' all of a sudden I *knowed!* De pan drop' on de flo' an' I grab his lef' han' an' shove back his sleeve, – jist so, as I 's doin' to you, – an' den I goes for his forehead an' push de hair back, so, an' 'Boy!' I says, 'if you an't my Henry, what is you doin' wid dis welt on yo' wris' an' dat sk-yar on yo' forehead? De Lord God ob heaven be praise', I got my own ag'in!'

"Oh, no, Misto C —, *I* hain't had no trouble. An' no *joy!*"

[1874]

Twain's *Old Times on the Mississippi.*   In the following sketches — the first three of seven he published in the *Atlantic Monthly* in 1875 — Twain offered his earliest account of his experiences before the Civil War, which he would soon draw upon even more fully in his first two novels, *The Adventures of Tom Sawyer* and the *Adventures of Huckleberry Finn.* When the first of the sketches was about to appear, Twain suggested that the overall title of the series be changed to something like "Piloting on the Mississippi in the Old Times" or "Steamboating on the Mississippi in the Old Times," since he found himself writing about only one aspect of that period: his experience first as a cub pilot and then as a pilot during the years 1857-61. "I am about the only man alive who can write about the piloting of that day — and no man has ever tried to scribble about it yet," he told his friend William Dean Howells, the editor of the *Atlantic.* "Its newness pleases me all the time — and it is about the only new subject I know of." Certainly the sketches display not only his humor but also the pleasure Twain took in engaging that fresh material and reliving in memory one of the most satisfying periods of his life, over which he cast such a nostalgic glow in *Old Times on the Mississippi.* The text is taken from the first printing in the *Atlantic Monthly,* January–March 1875.

Hannibal, Missouri

This perspective map of the town where Mark Twain grew up, published in 1869, shows steamboats plying the Mississippi River. But the great age of steamboats had ended with the Civil War, and their demise was further hastened by the construction of railroads along the banks of the river, as illustrated in the foreground of the map.

OLD TIMES ON THE MISSISSIPPI

I

When I was a boy, there was but one permanent ambition among my comrades in our village on the west bank of the Mississippi River. That was, to be a steamboatman. We had transient ambitions of other sorts, but they were only transient. When a circus came and went, it left us all burning to become clowns; the first negro minstrel show that came to our section left us all suffering to try that kind of life; now and then we had a hope that if we lived and were good, God would permit us to be pirates. These ambitions faded out, each in its turn; but the ambition to be a steamboatman always remained.

Once a day a cheap, gaudy packet[1] arrived upward from St. Louis, and another downward from Keokuk. Before these events had transpired, the day was glorious with expectancy; after they had transpired, the day was a dead and empty thing. Not only the boys, but the whole village, felt this. After all these years I can picture that old time to myself now, just as it was then: the white town drowning in the sunshine of a summer's morning; the streets empty, or pretty nearly so; one or two clerks sitting in front of the Water Street stores, with their splint-bottomed chairs tilted back against the wall, chins on breasts, hats slouched over their faces, asleep — with shingle-shavings enough around to show what broke them down; a sow and a litter of pigs loafing along the sidewalk, doing a good business in water-melon rinds and seeds; two or three lonely little freight piles scattered about the "levee;" a pile of "skids" on the slope of the stone-paved wharf, and the fragrant town drunkard asleep in the shadow of them; two or three wood flats at the head of the wharf, but nobody to listen to the peaceful lapping of the wavelets against them; the great Mississippi, the majestic, the magnificent Mississippi, rolling its mile-wide tide along, shining in the sun; the dense forest away on the other side; the "point" above the town, and the "point" below, bounding the river-glimpse and turning it into a sort of sea, and withal a very still and brilliant and lonely one. Presently a film of dark smoke appears above one of those remote "points;" instantly a negro drayman, famous for his quick eye and prodigious voice, lifts up the cry, "S-t-e-a-m-boat a-comin'!" and the scene changes! The town drunkard stirs, the clerks wake up, a furious clatter of drays follows, every house and store pours out a human contribution, and all in a twinkling the dead town is alive and moving. Drays, carts, men, boys, all go hurrying from many quarters to a common centre, the wharf. Assembled there, the people fasten their eyes upon the coming boat as upon a wonder they are seeing for the first time. And the boat *is* rather a handsome sight, too. She is long and sharp and trim and pretty; she has two tall, fancy-topped chimneys, with a gilded device of some kind swung between them; a fanciful pilot-house, all glass and "gingerbread," perched on top of the "texas" deck[2] behind them; the paddle-boxes are gorgeous with a picture or with gilded rays above the boat's name; the boiler deck, the hurricane deck, and the texas deck are

---

1. **packet:** A nineteenth-century term for a small ship or boat that traveled regularly between two ports, originally carrying mail.
2. **"texas" deck:** The level on a steamboat that includes the pilothouse and officers' quarters.

fenced and ornamented with clean white railings; there is a flag gallantly flying from the jack-staff; the furnace doors are open and the fires glaring bravely; the upper decks are black with passengers; the captain stands by the big bell, calm, imposing, the envy of all; great volumes of the blackest smoke are rolling and tumbling out of the chimneys – a husbanded grandeur created with a bit of pitch pine just before arriving at a town; the crew are grouped on the forecastle; the broad stage is run far out over the port bow, and an envied deck-hand stands picturesquely on the end of it with a coil of rope in his hand; the pent steam is screaming through the gauge-cocks; the captain lifts his hand, a bell rings, the wheels stop; then they turn back, churning the water to foam, and the steamer is at rest. Then such a scramble as there is to get aboard, and to get ashore, and to take in freight and to discharge freight, all at one and the same time; and such a yelling and cursing as the mates facilitate it all with! Ten minutes later the steamer is under way again, with no flag on the jack-staff and no black smoke issuing from the chimneys. After ten more minutes the town is dead again, and the town drunkard asleep by the skids once more.

My father was a justice of the peace, and I supposed he possessed the power of life and death over all men and could hang anybody that offended him. This was distinction enough for me as a general thing; but the desire to be a steamboatman kept intruding, nevertheless. I first wanted to be a cabin-boy, so that I could come out with a white apron on and shake a table-cloth over the side, where all my old comrades could see me; later I thought I would rather be the deck-hand who stood on the end of the stage-plank with the coil of rope in his hand, because he was particularly conspicuous. But these were only day-dreams – they were too heavenly to be contemplated as real possibilities. By and by one of our boys went away. He was not heard of for a long time. At last he turned up as apprentice engineer or "striker" on a steamboat. This thing shook the bottom out of all my Sunday-school teachings. That boy had been notoriously worldly, and I just the reverse; yet he was exalted to this eminence, and I left in obscurity and misery. There was nothing generous about this fellow in his greatness. He would always manage to have a rusty bolt to scrub while his boat tarried at our town, and he would sit on the inside guard and scrub it, where we could all see him and envy him and loathe him. And whenever his boat was laid up he would come home and swell around the town in his blackest and greasiest clothes, so that nobody could help remembering that he was a steamboatman; and he used all sorts of steamboat technicalities in his talk, as if he were so used to them that he forgot common people could not understand them. He would speak of the "labboard"[3] side of a horse in an easy, natural way that would make one wish he was dead. And he was always talking about "St. Looy" like an old citizen; he would refer casually to occasions when he "was coming down Fourth Street," or when he was "passing by the Planter's House," or when there was a fire and he took a turn on the brakes of "the old Big Missouri;" and then he would go on and lie about how many towns the size of ours were burned down there that day. Two or three of the boys had

---

3. **"labboard"**: The apprentice engineer's pronunciation of "larboard," the side of a ship on the left of a person facing forward.

long been persons of consideration among us because they had been to St. Louis once and had a vague general knowledge of its wonders, but the day of their glory was over now. They lapsed into a humble silence, and learned to disappear when the ruthless "cub"-engineer approached. This fellow had money, too, and hair oil. Also an ignorant silver watch and a showy brass watch chain. He wore a leather belt and used no suspenders. If ever a youth was cordially admired and hated by his comrades, this one was. No girl could withstand his charms. He "cut out" every boy in the village. When his boat blew up at last, it diffused a tranquil contentment among us such as we had not known for months. But when he came home the next week, alive, renowned, and appeared in church all battered up and bandaged, a shining hero, stared at and wondered over by everybody, it seemed to us that the partiality of Providence for an undeserving reptile had reached a point where it was open to criticism.

This creature's career could produce but one result, and it speedily followed. Boy after boy managed to get on the river. The minister's son became an engineer. The doctor's and the postmaster's sons became "mud clerks;" the wholesale liquor dealer's son became a bar-keeper on a boat; four sons of the chief merchant, and two sons of the county judge, became pilots. Pilot was the grandest position of all. The pilot, even in those days of trivial wages, had a princely salary — from a hundred and fifty to two hundred and fifty dollars a month, and no board to pay. Two months of his wages would pay a preacher's salary for a year. Now some of us were left disconsolate. We could not get on the river — at least our parents would not let us.

So by and by I ran away. I said I never would come home again till I was a pilot and could come in glory. But somehow I could not manage it. I went meekly aboard a few of the boats that lay packed together like sardines at the long St. Louis wharf, and very humbly inquired for the pilots, but got only a cold shoulder and short words from mates and clerks. I had to make the best of this sort of treatment for the time being, but I had comforting day-dreams of a future when I should be a great and honored pilot, with plenty of money, and could kill some of these mates and clerks and pay for them.

Months afterward the hope within me struggled to a reluctant death, and I found myself without an ambition. But I was ashamed to go home. I was in Cincinnati, and I set to work to map out a new career. I had been reading about the recent exploration of the river Amazon by an expedition sent out by our government. It was said that the expedition, owing to difficulties, had not thoroughly explored a part of the country lying about the head-waters, some four thousand miles from the mouth of the river. It was only about fifteen hundred miles from Cincinnati to New Orleans, where I could doubtless get a ship. I had thirty dollars left; I would go and complete the exploration of the Amazon. This was all the thought I gave to the subject. I never was great in matters of detail. I packed my valise, and took passage on an ancient tub called the Paul Jones, for New Orleans. For the sum of sixteen dollars I had the scarred and tarnished splendors of "her" main saloon principally to myself, for she was not a creature to attract the eye of wiser travelers.

When we presently got under way and went poking down the broad Ohio, I became a new being, and the subject of my own admiration. I was a traveler! A word never had tasted so good in my mouth before. I had an exultant sense of being bound for mysterious lands and distant climes which I never have felt in so uplifting a degree since. I was in such a glorified condition that all ignoble feelings departed out of me, and I was able to look down and pity the untraveled with a compassion that had hardly a trace of contempt in it. Still, when we stopped at villages and wood-yards, I could not help lolling carelessly upon the railings of the boiler deck to enjoy the envy of the country boys on the bank. If they did not seem to discover me, I presently sneezed to attract their attention, or moved to a position where they could not help seeing me. And as soon as I knew they saw me I gaped and stretched, and gave other signs of being mightily bored with traveling.

I kept my hat off all the time, and stayed where the wind and the sun could strike me, because I wanted to get the bronzed and weather-beaten look of an old traveler. Before the second day was half gone, I experienced a joy which filled me with the purest gratitude; for I saw that the skin had begun to blister and peel off my face and neck. I wished that the boys and girls at home could see me now.

We reached Louisville in time — at least the neighborhood of it. We stuck hard and fast on the rocks in the middle of the river and lay there four days. I was now beginning to feel a strong sense of being a part of the boat's family, a sort of infant son to the captain and younger brother to the officers. There is no estimating the pride I took in this grandeur, or the affection that began to swell and grow in me for those people. I could not know how the lordly steamboatman scorns that sort of presumption in a mere landsman. I particularly longed to acquire the least trifle of notice from the big stormy mate, and I was on the alert for an opportunity to do him a service to that end. It came at last. The riotous powwow of setting a spar was going on down on the forecastle, and I went down there and stood around in the way — or mostly skipping out of it — till the mate suddenly roared a general order for somebody to bring him a capstan bar. I sprang to his side and said: "Tell me where it is — I'll fetch it!"

If a rag-picker had offered to do a diplomatic service for the Emperor of Russia, the monarch could not have been more astounded than the mate was. He even stopped swearing. He stood and stared down at me. It took him ten seconds to scrape his disjointed remains together again. Then he said impressively: "Well, if this don't beat hell!" and turned to his work with the air of a man who had been confronted with a problem too abstruse for solution.

I crept away, and courted solitude for the rest of the day. I did not go to dinner; I stayed away from supper until everybody else had finished. I did not feel so much like a member of the boat's family now as before. However, my spirits returned, in installments, as we pursued our way down the river. I was sorry I hated the mate so, because it was not in (young) human nature not to admire him. He was huge and muscular, his face was bearded and whiskered all over; he had a red woman and a blue woman tattooed on his right arm, one on each side of a blue anchor with a red rope to it; and in the matter of profanity he was perfect. When he was getting out cargo at a landing, I was always where I could see and hear. He felt all the sublimity of his great position, and made the world feel it, too. When he gave even the simplest order, he discharged it like a blast of lightning, and sent a long, reverberating peal of profanity thundering after it. I could not help contrasting the way in which the average landsman would give an order, with

the mate's way of doing it. If the landsman should wish the gangplank moved a foot farther forward, he would probably say: "James, or William, one of you push that plank forward, please"; but put the mate in his place, and he would roar out: "Here, now, start that
gangplank for'ard! Lively, now! *What*'re you about! Snatch it! *snatch* it! There! there! Aft
again! aft again! Don't you hear me? Dash it to dash! are you going to *sleep* over it! *'Vast*
heaving. 'Vast heaving, I tell you! Going to heave it clear astern? WHERE're you going
with that barrel! *for'ard* with it 'fore I make you swallow it, you dash-dash-dash-*dashed*
split between a tired mud-turtle and a crippled hearse-horse!"

I wished I could talk like that.

When the soreness of my adventure with the mate had somewhat worn off, I began
timidly to make up to the humblest official connected with the boat — the night watchman. He snubbed my advances at first, but I presently ventured to offer him a new chalk
pipe, and that softened him. So he allowed me to sit with him by the big bell on the hurricane deck, and in time he melted into conversation. He could not well have helped it, I
hung with such homage on his words and so plainly showed that I felt honored by his
notice. He told me the names of dim capes and shadowy islands as we glided by them in
the solemnity of the night, under the winking stars, and by and by got to talking about
himself. He seemed oversentimental for a man whose salary was six dollars a week — or
rather he might have seemed so to an older person than I. But I drank in his words hungrily, and with a faith that might have moved mountains if it had been applied judiciously. What was it to me that he was soiled and needy and fragrant with gin? What was
it to me that his grammar was bad, his construction worse, and his profanity so void of
art that it was an element of weakness rather than strength in his conversation? He was
a wronged man, a man who had seen trouble, and that was enough for me. As he mel-
lowed into his plaintive history his tears dripped upon the lantern in his lap, and I cried,
too, from sympathy. He said he was the son of an English nobleman — either an earl or
an alderman, he could not remember which, but believed he was both; his father, the
nobleman, loved him, but his mother hated him from the cradle; and so while he was
still a little boy he was sent to "one of them old, ancient colleges" — he couldn't remember which; and by and by his father died and his mother seized the property and "shook"
him, as he phrased it. After his mother shook him, members of the nobility with whom
he was acquainted used their influence to get him the position of "loblolly-boy[4] in a
ship;" and from that point my watchman threw off all trammels of date and locality and
branched out into a narrative that bristled all along with incredible adventures; a narrative that was so reeking with bloodshed and so crammed with hair-breadth escapes and
the most engaging and unconscious personal villainies, that I sat speechless, enjoying,
shuddering, wondering, worshiping.

It was a sore blight to find out afterwards that he was a low, vulgar, ignorant, sentimental, half-witted humbug, an untraveled native of the wilds of Illinois, who had
absorbed wildcat literature and appropriated its marvels, until in time he had woven

---

4. **loblolly-boy:** An assistant to a ship's surgeon, responsible for feeding ill patients, but figuratively the
phrase meant a country bumpkin whose position is at the very bottom of a ship's hierarchy.

odds and ends of the mess into this yarn, and then gone on telling it to fledgelings like me, until he had come to believe it himself.

II. A "Cub" Pilot's Experience; or, Learning the River

What with lying on the rocks four days at Louisville, and some other delays, the poor old Paul Jones fooled away about two weeks in making the voyage from Cincinnati to New Orleans. This gave me a chance to get acquainted with one of the pilots, and he taught me how to steer the boat, and thus made the fascination of river life more potent than ever for me.

It also gave me a chance to get acquainted with a youth who had taken deck passage — more's the pity; for he easily borrowed six dollars of me on a promise to return to the boat and pay it back to me the day after we should arrive. But he probably died or forgot, for he never came. It was doubtless the former, since he had said his parents were wealthy, and he only traveled deck passage because it was cooler.[5]

I soon discovered two things. One was that a vessel would not be likely to sail for the mouth of the Amazon under ten or twelve years; and the other was that the nine or ten dollars still left in my pocket would not suffice for so imposing an exploration as I had planned, even if I could afford to wait for a ship. Therefore it followed that I must contrive a new career. The Paul Jones was now bound for St. Louis. I planned a siege against my pilot, and at the end of three hard days he surrendered. He agreed to teach me the Mississippi River from New Orleans to St. Louis for five hundred dollars, payable out of the first wages I should receive after graduating. I entered upon the small enterprise of "learning" twelve or thirteen hundred miles of the great Mississippi River with the easy confidence of my time of life. If I had really known what I was about to require of my faculties, I should not have had the courage to begin. I supposed that all a pilot had to do was to keep his boat in the river, and I did not consider that that could be much of a trick, since it was so wide.

The boat backed out from New Orleans at four in the afternoon, and it was "our watch" until eight. Mr. B——, my chief, "straightened her up," plowed her along past the sterns of the other boats that lay at the Levee, and then said, "Here, take her; shave those steamships as close as you'd peel an apple." I took the wheel, and my heart went down into my boots; for it seemed to me that we were about to scrape the side off every ship in the line, we were so close. I held my breath and began to claw the boat away from the danger; and I had my own opinion of the pilot who had known no better than to get us into such peril, but I was too wise to express it. In half a minute I had a wide margin of safety intervening between the Paul Jones and the ships; and within ten seconds more I was set aside in disgrace, and Mr. B—— was going into danger again and flaying me alive with abuse of my cowardice. I was stung, but I was obliged to admire the easy confidence with which my chief loafed from side to side of his wheel, and trimmed the ships so closely that disaster seemed ceaselessly imminent. When he had cooled a little he told

---

5. deck passage . . . cooler: "'Deck' passage — i.e., steerage passage." [Twain's note]

me that the easy water was close ashore and the current outside, and therefore we must hug the bank, up-stream, to get the benefit of the former, and stay well out, down-stream, to take advantage of the latter. In my own mind I resolved to be a down-stream pilot and leave the up-streaming to people dead to prudence.

Now and then Mr. B— called my attention to certain things. Said he, "This is Six-Mile Point." I assented. It was pleasant enough information, but I could not see the bearing of it. I was not conscious that it was a matter of any interest to me. Another time he said, "This is Nine-Mile Point." Later he said, "This is Twelve-Mile Point." They were all about level with the water's edge; they all looked about alike to me; they were monotonously unpicturesque. I hoped Mr. B— would change the subject. But no; he would crowd up around a point, hugging the shore with affection, and then say: "The slack water ends here, abreast this bunch of China-trees; now we cross over." So he crossed over. He gave me the wheel once or twice, but I had no luck. I either came near chipping off the edge of a sugar plantation, or else I yawed too far from shore, and so I dropped back into disgrace again and got abused.

The watch was ended at last, and we took supper and went to bed. At midnight the glare of a lantern shone in my eyes, and the night watchman said: –

"Come! turn out!"

And then he left. I could not understand this extraordinary procedure; so I presently gave up trying to and dozed off to sleep. Pretty soon the watchman was back again, and this time he was gruff. I was annoyed. I said: –

"What do you want to come bothering around here in the middle of the night for? Now as like as not I'll not get to sleep again to-night."

The watchman said: –

"Well, if this an't good, I'm blest."

The "off-watch" was just turning in, and I heard some brutal laughter from them, and such remarks as "Hello, watchman! an't the new cub turned out yet? He's delicate, likely. Give him some sugar in a rag and send for the chambermaid to sing rock-a-by-baby to him."

About this time Mr. B— appeared on the scene. Something like a minute later I was climbing the pilot-house steps with some of my clothes on and the rest in my arms. Mr. B— was close behind, commenting. Here was something fresh – this thing of getting up in the middle of the night to go to work. It was a detail in piloting that had never occurred to me at all. I knew that boats ran all night, but somehow I had never happened to reflect that somebody had to get up out of a warm bed to run them. I began to fear that piloting was not quite so romantic as I had imagined it was; there was something very real and work-like about this new phase of it.

It was a rather dingy night, although a fair number of stars were out. The big mate was at the wheel, and he had the old tub pointed at a star and was holding her straight up the middle of the river. The shores on either hand were not much more than a mile apart, but they seemed wonderfully far away and ever so vague and indistinct. The mate said: –

"We've got to land at Jones's plantation, sir."

The vengeful spirit in me exulted. I said to myself, I wish you joy of your job, Mr. B—; you'll have a good time finding Mr. Jones's plantation such a night as this; and I hope you never *will* find it as long as you live.

Mr. B— said to the mate: —

"Upper end of the plantation, or the lower?"

"Upper."

"I can't do it. The stumps there are out of water at this stage. It's no great distance to the lower, and you'll have to get along with that."

"All right, sir. If Jones don't like it he'll have to lump it, I reckon."

And then the mate left. My exultation began to cool and my wonder to come up. Here was a man who not only proposed to find this plantation on such a night, but to find either end of it you preferred. I dreadfully wanted to ask a question, but I was carrying about as many short answers as my cargo-room would admit of, so I held my peace. All I desired to ask Mr. B— was the simple question whether he was ass enough to really imagine he was going to find that plantation on a night when all plantations were exactly alike and all the same color. But I held in. I used to have fine inspirations of prudence in those days.

Mr. B— made for the shore and soon was scraping it, just the same as if it had been daylight. And not only that, but singing —

> "Father in heaven the day is declining," etc.

It seemed to me that I had put my life in the keeping of a peculiarly reckless outcast. Presently he turned on me and said: —

"What's the name of the first point above New Orleans?"

I was gratified to be able to answer promptly, and I did. I said I didn't know.

"Don't *know*?"

This manner jolted me. I was down at the foot again, in a moment. But I had to say just what I had said before.

"Well, you're a smart one," said Mr. B—. "What's the name of the *next* point?"

Once more I didn't know.

"Well this beats anything. Tell me the name of *any* point or place I told you."

I studied a while and decided that I couldn't.

"Look-a-here! What do you start out from, above Twelve-Mile Point, to cross over?"

"I – I – don't know."

"You – you – don't know?" mimicking my drawling manner of speech. "What *do* you know?"

"I – I – nothing, for certain."

"By the great Caesar's ghost I believe you! You're the stupidest dunderhead I ever saw or ever heard of, so help me Moses! The idea of *you* being a pilot – *you!* Why, you don't know enough to pilot a cow down a lane."

Oh, but his wrath was up! He was a nervous man, and he shuffled from one side of his wheel to the other as if the floor was hot. He would boil a while to himself, and then over-flow and scald me again.

"Look-a-here! What do you suppose I told you the names of those points for?"

I tremblingly considered a moment, and then the devil of temptation provoked me to say: –

"Well – to – to – be entertaining, I thought."

This was a red rag to the bull. He raged and stormed so (he was crossing the river at the time) that I judge it made him blind, because he ran over the steering-oar of a trading-scow. Of course the traders sent up a volley of red-hot profanity. Never was a man so grateful as Mr. B— was: because he was brim full, and here were subjects who would *talk back.* He threw open a window, thrust his head out, and such an irruption followed as I never had heard before. The fainter and farther away the scowmen's curses drifted, the higher Mr. B— lifted his voice and the weightier his adjectives grew. When he closed the window he was empty. You could have drawn a seine through his system and not caught curses enough to disturb your mother with. Presently he said to me in the gentlest way: –

"My boy, you must get a little memorandum-book, and every time I tell you a thing, put it down right away. There's only one way to be a pilot, and that is to get this entire river by heart. You have to know it just like A B C."

That was a dismal revelation to me; for my memory was never loaded with anything but blank cartridges. However, I did not feel discouraged long. I judged that it was best to make some allowances, for doubtless Mr. B— was "stretching." Presently he pulled a rope and struck a few strokes on the big bell. The stars were all gone, now, and the night was as black as ink. I could hear the wheels churn along the bank, but I was not entirely certain that I could see the shore. The voice of the invisible watchman called up from the hurricane deck: –

"What's this, sir?"

"Jones's plantation."

I said to myself, I wish I might venture to offer a small bet that it isn't. But I did not chirp. I only waited to see. Mr. B— handled the engine bells, and in due time the boat's nose came to the land, a torch glowed from the forecastle, a man skipped ashore, a darky's voice on the bank said, "Gimme de carpet-bag, Mars' Jones," and the next moment we were standing up the river again, all serene. I reflected deeply a while, and then said, – but not aloud, – Well, the finding of that plantation was the luckiest accident that ever happened; but it couldn't happen again in a hundred years. And I fully believed it *was* an accident, too.

By the time we had gone seven or eight hundred miles up the river, I had learned to be a tolerably plucky upstream steersman, in daylight, and before we reached St. Louis I had made a trifle of progress in night-work, but only a trifle. I had a note-book that fairly bristled with the names of towns, "points," bars, islands, bends, reaches, etc.; but the information was to be found only in the note-book – none of it was in my head. It made my heart ache to think I had only got half of the river set down; for as our watch was four hours off and four hours on, day and night, there was a long four-hour gap in my book for every time I had slept since the voyage began.

My chief was presently hired to go on a big New Orleans boat, and I packed my satchel and went with him. She was a grand affair. When I stood in her pilot-house I was so far above the water that I seemed perched on a mountain; and her decks stretched so far away, fore and aft, below me, that I wondered how I could ever have considered the little Paul Jones a large craft. There were other differences, too. The Paul Jones's pilot-house was a cheap, dingy, battered rattle-trap, cramped for room: but here was a sumptuous glass temple; room enough to have a dance in; showy red and gold window-curtains; an imposing sofa; leather cushions and a back to the high bench where visiting pilots sit, to spin yarns and "look at the river;" bright, fanciful "cuspadores" instead of a broad wooden box filled with sawdust; nice new oil-cloth on the floor; a hospitable big stove for winter; a wheel as high as my head, costly with inlaid work; a wire tiller-rope; bright brass knobs for the bells; and a tidy, white-aproned, black "texas-tender," to bring up tarts and ices and coffee during mid-watch, day and night. Now this was "something like;" and so I began to take heart once more to believe that piloting was a romantic sort of occupation after all. The moment we were under way I began to prowl about the great steamer and fill myself with joy. She was as clean and as dainty as a drawing-room; when I looked down her long, gilded saloon, it was like gazing through a splendid tunnel; she had an oil-picture, by some gifted sign-painter, on every state-room door; she glittered with no end of prism-fringed chandeliers; the clerk's office was elegant, the bar was marvelous, and the bar-keeper had been barbered and upholstered at incredible cost. The boiler deck (*i.e.*, the second story of the boat, so to speak) was as spacious as a church, it seemed to me; so with the forecastle; and there was no pitiful handful of deckhands, firemen, and roust-abouts down there, but a whole battalion of men. The fires were fiercely glaring from a long row of furnaces, and over them were eight huge boilers! This was unutterable pomp. The mighty engines – but enough of this. I had never felt so fine before. And when I found that the regiment of natty servants respectfully "sir'd" me, my satisfaction was complete.

When I returned to the pilot-house St. Louis was gone and I was lost. Here was a piece of river which was all down in my book, but I could make neither head nor tail of it: you understand, it was turned around. I had seen it, when coming up-stream, but I had never faced about to see how it looked when it was behind me. My heart broke again, for it was plain that I had got to learn this troublesome river *both ways.*

The pilot-house was full of pilots, going down to "look at the river." What is called the "upper river" (the two hundred miles between St. Louis and Cairo, where the Ohio comes in) was low; and the Mississippi changes its channel so constantly that the pilots used to always find it necessary to run down to Cairo to take a fresh look, when their boats were to lie in port a week, that is, when the water was at a low stage. A deal of this "looking at the river" was done by poor fellows who seldom had a berth, and whose only hope of getting one lay in their being always freshly posted and therefore ready to drop into the shoes of some reputable pilot, for a single trip, on account of such pilot's sudden illness, or some other necessity. And a good many of them constantly ran up and down inspecting the river, not because they ever really hoped to get a berth, but because (they being guests of the boat) it was cheaper to "look at the river" than stay ashore and pay board. In time these fellows grew dainty in their tastes, and only infested boats that had an established reputation for setting good tables. All visiting pilots were useful, for they were always ready and willing, winter or summer, night or day, to go out in the yawl and help buoy the channel or assist the boat's pilots in any way they could. They were like-wise welcome because all pilots are tireless talkers, when gathered together, and as they talk only about the river they are always understood and are always interesting. Your true pilot cares nothing about anything on earth but the river, and his pride in his occu-pation surpasses the pride of kings.

We had a fine company of these river-inspectors along, this trip. There were eight or ten; and there was abundance of room for them in our great pilot-house. Two or three of them wore polished silk hats, elaborate shirt-fronts, diamond breastpins, kid gloves, and patent-leather boots. They were choice in their English, and bore themselves with a dignity proper to men of solid means and prodigious reputation as pilots. The others were more or less loosely clad, and wore upon their heads tall felt cones that were sug-gestive of the days of the Commonwealth.

I was a cipher in this august company, and felt subdued, not to say torpid. I was not even of sufficient consequence to assist at the wheel when it was necessary to put the tiller hard down in a hurry; the guest that stood nearest did that when occasion required — and this was pretty much all the time, because of the crookedness of the channel and the scant water. I stood in a corner; and the talk I listened to took the hope all out of me. One visitor said to another: —

"Jim, how did you run Plum Point, coming up?"

"It was in the night, there, and I ran it the way one of the boys on the Diana told me; started out about fifty yards above the wood pile on the false point, and held on the cabin under Plum Point till I raised the reef — quarter less twain — then straightened up for the middle bar till I got well abreast the old one-limbed cotton-wood in the bend, then got my stern on the cottonwood and head on the low place above the point, and came through a-booming — nine and a half."

"Pretty square crossing, an't it?"

"Yes, but the upper bar's working down fast."

Another pilot spoke up and said: —

"I had better water than that, and ran it lower down; started out from the false point — mark twain — raised the second reef abreast the big snag in the bend, and had quarter less twain."

One of the gorgeous ones remarked: "I don't want to find fault with your leadsmen, but that's a good deal of water for Plum Point, it seems to me."

There was an approving nod all around as this quiet snub dropped on the boaster and "settled" him. And so they went on talk-talk-talking. Meantime, the thing that was run-ning in my mind was, "Now if my ears hear aright, I have not only to get the names of all the towns and islands and bends, and so on, by heart, but I must even get up a warm per-sonal acquaintanceship with every old snag and one-limbed cotton-wood and obscure wood pile that ornaments the banks of this river for twelve hundred miles; and more than that, I must actually know where these things are in the dark, unless these guests are gifted with eyes that can pierce through two miles of solid blackness; I wish the piloting business was in Jericho and I had never thought of it."

At dusk Mr. B— tapped the big bell three times (the signal to land), and the captain emerged from his drawing-room in the forward end of the texas, and looked up inquir-ingly. Mr. B— said: —

"We will lay up here all night, captain."

"Very well, sir."

That was all. The boat came to shore and was tied up for the night. It seemed to me a fine thing that the pilot could do as he pleased without asking so grand a captain's permission. I took my supper and went immediately to bed, discouraged by my day's observations and experiences. My late voyage's note-booking was but a confusion of meaningless names. It had tangled me all up in a knot every time I had looked at it in the daytime. I now hoped for respite in sleep; but no, it reveled all through my head till sunrise again, a frantic and tireless nightmare.

Next morning I felt pretty rusty and low-spirited. We went booming along, taking a good many chances, for we were anxious to "get out of the river" (as getting out to Cairo was called) before night should overtake us. But Mr. B——'s partner, the other pilot, presently grounded the boat, and we lost so much time getting her off that it was plain the darkness would overtake us a good long way above the mouth. This was a great misfortune, especially to certain of our visiting pilots, whose boats would have to wait for their return, no matter how long that might be. It sobered the pilot-house talk a good deal. Coming up-stream, pilots did not mind low water or any kind of darkness; nothing stopped them but fog. But down-stream work was different; a boat was too nearly helpless, with a stiff current pushing behind her; so it was not customary to run down-stream at night in low water.

There seemed to be one small hope, however: if we could get through the intricate and dangerous Hat Island crossing before night, we could venture the rest, for we would have plainer sailing and better water. But it would be insanity to attempt Hat Island at night. So there was a deal of looking at watches all the rest of the day, and a constant ciphering upon the speed we were making; Hat Island was the eternal subject; sometimes hope was high and sometimes we were delayed in a bad crossing, and down it went again. For hours all hands lay under the burden of this suppressed excitement; it was even communicated to me, and I got to feeling so solicitous about Hat Island, and under such an awful pressure of responsibility, that I wished I might have five minutes on shore to draw a good, full, relieving breath, and start over again. We were standing no regular watches. Each of our pilots ran such portions of the river as he had run when coming up-stream, because of his greater familiarity with it; but both remained in the pilot-houses constantly.

An hour before sunset, Mr. B—— took the wheel and Mr. W—— stepped aside. For the next thirty minutes every man held his watch in his hand and was restless, silent, and uneasy. At last somebody said, with a doomful sigh.

"Well, yonder's Hat Island — and we can't make it."

All the watches closed with a snap, everybody sighed and muttered something about its being "too bad, too bad — ah, if we could *only* have got here half an hour sooner!" and the place was thick with the atmosphere of disappointment. Some started to go out, but loitered, hearing no bell-tap to land. The sun dipped behind the horizon, the boat went on. Inquiring looks passed from one guest to another; and one who had his hand on the doorknob, and had turned it, waited, then presently took away his hand and let the knob turn back again. We bore steadily down the bend. More looks were exchanged, and nods of surprised admiration — but not words. Insensibly the men drew together behind Mr. B— as the sky darkened and one or two dim stars came out. The dead silence and sense of waiting became oppressive. Mr. B— pulled the cord, and two deep, mellow notes from the big bell floated off on the night. Then a pause, and one more note was struck. The watchman's voice followed, from the hurricane deck: –

"Labboard lead, there! Stabboard lead!"

The cries of the leadsmen began to rise out of the distance, and were gruffly repeated by the word-passers on the hurricane deck.

"M-a-r-k three! M-a-r-k three! Quarter-less-three! Half twain! Quarter twain! M-a-r-k twain! Quarter-less" –

Mr. B— pulled two bell-ropes, and was answered by faint jinglings far below in the engine-room, and our speed slackened. The steam began to whistle through the gauge-cocks. The cries of the leadsmen went on – and it is a weird sound, always, in the night. Every pilot in the lot was watching, now, with fixed eyes, and talking under his breath. Nobody was calm and easy but Mr. B—. He would put his wheel down and stand on a spoke, and as the steamer swung into her (to me) utterly invisible marks – for we seemed to be in the midst of a wide and gloomy sea – he would meet and fasten her there. Talk was going on, now, in low voices: –

"There; she's over the first reef all right!"

After a pause, another subdued voice: –

"Her stern's coming down just *exactly* right, by *George!* Now she's in the marks; over she goes!"

Somebody else muttered: –

"Oh, it was done beautiful – *beautiful!*"

Now the engines were stopped altogether, and we drifted with the current. Not that I could see the boat drift, for I could not, the stars being all gone by this time. This drifting was the dismalest work; it held one's heart still. Presently I discovered a blacker gloom than that which surrounded us. It was the head of the island. We were closing right down upon it. We entered its deeper shadow, and so imminent seemed the peril that I was likely to suffocate; and I had the strongest impulse to do *something,* anything, to save the vessel. But still Mr. B— stood by his wheel, silent, intent as a cat, and all the pilots stood shoulder to shoulder at his back.

"She'll not make it!" somebody whispered.

The water grew shoaler and shoaler by the leadsmen's cries, till it was down to –

"Eight-and-a-half! E-i-g-h-t feet! E-i-g-h-t feet! Seven-and" –

Mr. B— said warningly through his speaking tube to the engineer: –

"Stand by, now!"

"Aye-aye, sir."

"Seven-and-a-half! Seven feet! *Six*-and" –

We touched bottom! Instantly Mr. B— set a lot of bells ringing, shouted through the tube, "*Now* let her have it – every ounce you've got!" then to his partner, "Put her hard down! snatch her! snatch her!" The boat rasped and ground her way through the sand, hung upon the apex of disaster a single tremendous instant, and then over she went! And such a shout as went up at Mr. B—'s back never loosened the roof of a pilot-house before!

There was no more trouble after that. Mr. B— was a hero that night; and it was some little time, too, before his exploit ceased to be talked about by river men.

Fully to realize the marvelous precision required in laying the great steamer in her marks in that murky waste of water, one should know that not only must she pick her intricate way through snags and blind reefs, and then shave the head of the island so closely as to brush the overhanging foliage with her stern, but at one place she must pass almost within arm's reach of a sunken and invisible wreck that would snatch the hull timbers from under her if she should strike it, and destroy a quarter of a million dollars' worth of steamboat and cargo in five minutes, and maybe a hundred and fifty human lives into the bargain.

The last remark I heard that night was a compliment to Mr. B—, uttered in soliloquy and with unction by one of our guests. He said: –

"By the Shadow of Death, but he's a lightning pilot!"

III. The Continued Perplexities of "Cub" Piloting

At the end of what seemed a tedious while, I had managed to pack my head full of islands, towns, bars, "points," and bends; and a curiously inanimate mass of lumber it was, too. However, inasmuch as I could shut my eyes and reel off a good long string of these names without leaving out more than ten miles of river in every fifty, I began to feel that I could take a boat down to New Orleans if I could make her skip those little gaps. But of course my complacency could hardly get start enough to lift my nose a trifle into the air, before Mr. B— would think of something to fetch it down again. One day he turned on me suddenly with his settler: –

"What is the shape of Walnut Bend?"

He might as well have asked me my grandmother's opinion of protoplasm. I reflected respectfully, and then said I didn't know it had any particular shape. My gunpowdery chief went off with a bang, of course, and then went on loading and firing until he was out of adjectives.

I had learned long ago that he only carried just so many rounds of ammunition, and was sure to subside into a very placable and even remorseful old smooth-bore as soon as they were all gone. That word "old" is merely affectionate; he was not more than thirty-four. I waited. By and by he said, –

"My boy, you've got to know the *shape* of the river perfectly. It is all there is left to steer by on a very dark night. Everything else is blotted out and gone. But mind you, it hasn't the same shape in the night that it has in the day-time."

"How on earth am I ever going to learn it, then?"

"How do you follow a hall at home in the dark? Because you know the shape of it. You can't see it."

"Do you mean to say that I've got to know all the million trifling variations of shape in the banks of this interminable river as well as I know the shape of the front hall at home?"

"On my honor you've got to know them *better* than any man ever did know the shapes of the halls in his own house."

"I wish I was dead!"

"Now I don't want to discourage you, but" –

"Well, pile it on me; I might as well have it now as another time."

"You see, this has got to be learned; there isn't any getting around it. A clear starlight night throws such heavy shadows that if you didn't know the shape of a shore perfectly you would claw away from every bunch of timber, because you would take the black shadow of it for a solid cape; and you see you would be getting scared to death every fifteen minutes by the watch. You would be fifty yards from shore all the time when you ought to be within twenty feet of it. You can't see a snag in one of those shadows, but you know exactly where it is, and the shape of the river tells you when you are coming to it. Then there's your pitch dark night; the river is a very different shape on a pitch dark night from what it is on a starlight night. All shores seem to be straight lines, then, and mighty dim ones, too; and you'd *run* them for straight lines, only you know better. You boldly drive your boat right into what seems to be a solid, straight wall (you knowing very well that in reality there is a curve there), and that wall falls back and makes way for you. Then there's your gray mist. You take a night when there's one of these grisly, drizzly, gray mists, and then there isn't *any* particular shape to a shore. A gray mist would tangle the head of the oldest man that ever lived. Well, then, different kinds of *moonlight* change the shape of the river in different ways. You see" –

"Oh, don't say any more, please! Have I got to learn the shape of the river according to all these five hundred thousand different ways? If I tried to carry all that cargo in my head it would make me stoop-shouldered."

"*No!* you only learn *the* shape of the river; and you learn it with such absolute certainty that you can always steer by the shape that's *in your head,* and never mind the one that's before your eyes."

"Very well, I'll try it; but after I have learned it can I depend on it? Will it keep the same form and not go fooling around?"

Before Mr. B— could answer, Mr. W— came in to take the watch, and he said, –

"B—, you'll have to look out for President's Island and all that country clear away up above the Old Hen and Chickens. The banks are caving and the shape of the shores changing like everything. Why, you wouldn't know the point above 40. You can go up inside the old sycamore snag, now."[6]

So that question was answered. Here were leagues of shore changing shape. My spirits were down in the mud again. Two things seemed pretty apparent to me. One was, that in order to be a pilot a man had got to learn more than any one man ought to be allowed to know; and the other was, that he must learn it all over again in a different way every twenty-four hours.

That night we had the watch until twelve. Now it was an ancient river custom for the two pilots to chat a bit when the watch changed. While the relieving pilot put on his gloves and lit his cigar, his partner, the retiring pilot, would say something like this: –

---

6. **inside the old sycamore snag, now:** "It may not be necessary, but still it can do no harm to explain that 'inside' means between the snag and the shore" – M. T. [Twain's note]

"I judge the upper bar is making down a little at Hale's Point; had quarter twain with the lower lead and mark twain[7] with the other."

"Yes, I thought it was making down a little, last trip. Meet any boats?"

"Met one abreast the head of 21, but she was away over hugging the bar, and I couldn't make her out entirely. I took her for the Sunny South – hadn't any skylights forward of the chimneys."

And so on. And as the relieving pilot took the wheel his partner[8] would mention that we were in such-and-such a bend, and say we were abreast of such-and-such a man's wood-yard or plantation. This was courtesy; I supposed it was *necessity*. But Mr. W— came on watch full twelve minutes late, on this particular night – a tremendous breach of eti-quette; in fact, it is the unpardonable sin among pilots. So Mr. B— gave him no greeting whatever, but simply surrendered the wheel and marched out of the pilot-house without a word. I was appalled; it was a villainous night for blackness, we were in a particularly wide and blind part of the river, where there was no shape or substance to anything, and it seemed incredible that Mr. B— should have left that poor fellow to kill the boat trying to find out where he was. But I resolved that I would stand by him any way. He should find that he was not wholly friendless. So I stood around, and waited to be asked where we were. But Mr. W— plunged on serenely through the solid firmament of black cats that stood for an atmosphere, and never opened his mouth. Here is a proud devil, thought I; here is a limb of Satan that would rather send us all to destruction than put himself under obli-gations to me, because I am not yet one of the salt of the earth and privileged to snub captains and lord it over everything dead and alive in a steamboat. I presently climbed up on the bench; I did not think it was safe to go to sleep while this lunatic was on watch.

However, I must have gone to sleep in the course of time, because the next thing I was aware of was the fact that day was breaking, Mr. W— gone, and Mr. B— at the wheel again. So it was four o'clock and all well – but me; I felt like a skinful of dry bones and all of them trying to ache at once.

Mr. B— asked me what I had stayed up there for. I confessed that it was to do Mr. W— a benevolence: tell him where he was. It took five minutes for the entire preposterous-ness of the thing to filter into Mr. B—'s system, and then I judge it filled him nearly up to the chin; because he paid me a compliment – and not much of a one either. He said, –

"Well, taking you by-and-large, you do seem to be more different kinds of an ass than any creature I ever saw before. What did you suppose he wanted to know for?"

I said I thought it might be a convenience to him.

"Convenience! Dash! Didn't I tell you that a man's got to know the river in the night the same as he'd know his own front hall?"

"Well, I can follow the front hall in the dark if I know it *is* the front hall; but suppose you set me down in the middle of it in the dark and not tell me which hall it is; how am *I* to know?"

---

7. **mark twain:** "Two fathoms. Quarter twain is 2 1/4 fathoms, 13 1/2 feet. Mark three is three fathoms." [Twain's note]

8. **partner:** "'Partner' is technical for 'the other pilot.'" [Twain's note]

"Well, you've *got* to, on the river!"

"All right. Then I'm glad I never said anything to Mr. W—."

"I should say so. Why, he'd have slammed you through the window and utterly ruined a hundred dollars' worth of window-sash and stuff."

I was glad this damage had been saved, for it would have made me unpopular with the owners. They always hated anybody who had the name of being careless, and injuring things.

I went to work now, to learn the shape of the river; and of all the eluding and ungrasp-able objects that ever I tried to get mind or hands on, that was the chief. I would fasten my eyes upon a sharp, wooded point that projected far into the river some miles ahead of me, and go to laboriously photographing its shape upon my brain; and just as I was beginning to succeed to my satisfaction, we would draw up toward it and the exasperat-ing thing would begin to melt away and fold back into the bank! If there had been a con-spicuous dead tree standing upon the very point of the cape, I would find that tree inconspicuously merged into the general forest, and occupying the middle of a straight shore, when I got abreast of it! No prominent lull would stick to its shape long enough for me to make up my mind what its form really was, but it was as dissolving and changeful as if it had been a mountain of butter in the hottest corner of the tropics. Nothing ever had the same shape when I was coming down-stream that it had borne when I went up. I mentioned these little difficulties to Mr. B—. He said, —

"That's the very main virtue of the thing. If the shapes didn't change every three sec-onds they wouldn't be of any use. Take this place where we are now, for instance. As long as that bill over yonder is only one hill, I can boom right along the way I'm going; but the moment it splits at the top and forms a V, I know I've got to scratch to starboard in a hurry, or I'll bang this boat's brains out against a rock; and then the moment one of the prongs of the V swings behind the other, I've got to waltz to larboard again, or I'll have a misunderstanding with a snag that would snatch the keelson out of this steamboat as neatly as if it were a silver in your hand. If that hill didn't change its shape on bad nights there would be an awful steamboat grave-yard around here inside of a year."

It was plain that I had got to learn the shape of the river in all the different ways that could be thought of, — upside down, wrong end first, inside out, fore-and-aft, and "thort-ships," — and then know what to do on gray nights when it hadn't any shape at all. So I set about it. In the course of time I began to get the best of this knotty lesson, and my self-complacency moved to the front once more. Mr. B— was all fixed, and ready to start it to the rear again. He opened on me after this fashion: —

"How much water did we have in the middle crossing at Hole-in-the-Wall, trip before last?"

I considered this an outrage. I said:

"Every trip, down and up, the leadsmen are singing through that tangled place for three quarters of an hour on a stretch. How do you reckon I can remember such a mess as that?"

"My boy, you've got to remember it. You've got to remember the exact spot and the exact marks the boat lay in when we had the shoalest water, in every one of the two thousand shoal places between St. Louis and New Orleans; and you mustn't get the shoal soundings and marks of one trip mixed up with the shoal soundings and marks of another, either, for they're not often twice alike. You must keep them separate."

When I came to myself again, I said, –

"When I get so that I can do that, I'll be able to raise the dead, and then I won't have to pilot a steamboat in order to make a living. I want to retire from this business. I want a slush-bucket and a brush; I'm only fit for a roustabout. I haven't got brains enough to be a pilot; and if I had I wouldn't have strength enough to carry them around, unless I went on crutches."

"Now drop that! When I say I'll learn[9] a man the river, I mean it. And you can depend on it I'll learn him or kill him."

There was no use in arguing with a person like this. I promptly put such a strain on my memory that by and by even the shoal water and the countless crossing-marks began to stay with me. But the result was just the same. I never could more than get one knotty thing learned before another presented itself. Now I had often seen pilots gazing at the water and pretending to read it as if it were a book; but it was a book that told me nothing. A time came at last, however, when Mr. B— seemed to think me far enough advanced to bear a lesson on water-reading. So he began: –

"Do you see that long slanting line on the face of the water? Now that's a reef. Moreover, it's a bluff reef. There is a solid sand-bar under it that is nearly as straight up and down as the side of a house. There is plenty of water close up to it, but mighty little on top of it. If you were to hit it you would knock the boat's brains out. Do you see where the line fringes out at the upper end and begins to fade away?"

"Yes, sir."

"Well, that is a low place; that is the head of the reef. You can climb over there, and not hurt anything. Cross over, now, and follow along close under the reef – easy water there – not much current."

I followed the reef along till I approached the fringed end. Then Mr. B— said, –

"Now get ready. Wait till I give the word. She won't want to mount the reef; a boat hates shoal water. Stand by – wait – wait – keep her well in hand. *Now* cramp her down! Snatch her! snatch her!"

He seized the other side of the wheel and helped to spin it around until it was hard down, and then we held it so. The boat resisted and refused to answer for a while, and next she came surging to starboard, mounted the reef, and sent a long, angry ridge of water foaming away from her bows.

"Now watch her; watch her like a cat, or she'll get away from you. When she fights strong and the tiller slips a little, in a jerky, greasy sort of way, let up on her a trifle; it is the way she tells you at night that the water is too shoal; but keep edging her up, little by little, toward the point. You are well up on the bar, now; there is a bar under every point, because the water that comes down around it forms an eddy and allows the sediment to

---

9. **learn:** "'Teach' is not in the river vocabulary." [Twain's note]

sink. Do you see those fine lines on the face of the water that branch out like the ribs of a fan? Well, those are little reefs; you want to just miss the ends of them, but run them pretty close. Now look out – look out! Don't you crowd that slick, greasy-looking place; there ain't nine feet there; she won't stand it. She begins to smell it; look sharp, I tell you! Oh blazes, there you go! Stop the starboard wheel! Quick! Ship up to back! Set her back!"

The engine bells jingled and the engines answered promptly, shooting white columns of steam far aloft out of the scape pipes, but it was too late. The boat had "smelt" the bar in good earnest; the foamy ridges that radiated from her bows suddenly disappeared, a great dead swell came rolling forward and swept ahead of her, she careened far over to larboard, and went tearing away toward the other shore as if she were about scared to death. We were a good mile from where we ought to have been, when we finally got the upper hand of her again.

During the afternoon watch the next day, Mr. B— asked me if I knew how to run the next few miles. I said: –

"Go inside the first snag above the point, outside the next one, start out from the lower end of Higgins's woodyard, make a square crossing and" –

"That's all right. I'll be back before you close up on the next point."

But he wasn't. He was still below when I rounded it and entered upon a piece of river which I had some misgivings about. I did not know that he was hiding behind a chimney to see how I would perform. I went gayly along, getting prouder and prouder, for he had never left the boat in my sole charge such a length of time before. I even got to "setting" her and letting the wheel go, entirely, while I vaingloriously turned my back and inspected the stern marks and hummed a tune, a sort of easy indifference which I had prodigiously admired in B— and other great pilots. Once I inspected rather long, and when I faced to the front again my heart flew into my mouth so suddenly that if I hadn't clapped my teeth together I would have lost it. One of those frightful bluff reefs was stretching its deadly length right across our bows! My head was gone in a moment; I did not know which end I stood on; I gasped and could not get my breath; I spun the wheel down with such rapidity that it wove itself together like a spider's web; the boat answered and turned square away from the reef, but the reef followed her! I fled, and still it followed – still it kept right across my bows! I never looked to see where I was going, I only fled. The awful crash was imminent – why didn't that villain come! If I committed the crime of ringing a bell, I might get thrown overboard. But better that than kill the boat. So in blind desperation I started such a rattling "shivaree"[10] down below as never had astounded an engineer in this world before, I fancy. Amidst the frenzy of the bells the engines began to back and fill in a furious way, and my reason forsook its throne – we were about to crash into the woods on the other side of the river. Just then Mr. B— stepped calmly into view on the hurricane deck. My soul went out to him in gratitude. My distress vanished; I would have felt safe on the brink of Niagara,

10. "shivaree": An early term for a noisy and discordant mock serenade; also spelled *charivari.*

with Mr. B— on the hurricane deck. He blandly and sweetly took his tooth-pick out of his mouth between his fingers, as if it were a cigar, – we were just in the act of climbing an overhanging big tree, and the passengers were scudding astern like rats, – and lifted up these commands to me ever so gently: –

"Stop the starboard. Stop the larboard. Set her back on both."

The boat hesitated, halted, pressed her nose among the boughs a critical instant, then reluctantly began to back away.

"Stop the larboard. Come ahead on it. Stop the starboard. Come ahead on it. Point her for the bar."

I sailed away as serenely as a summer's morning. Mr. B— came in and said, with mock simplicity, –

"When you have a hail, my boy, you ought to tap the big bell three times before you land, so that the engineers can get ready."

I blushed under the sarcasm, and said I hadn't had any hail.

"Ah! Then it was for wood, I suppose. The officer of the watch will tell you when he wants to wood up."

I went on consuming, and said I wasn't after wood.

"Indeed? Why, what could you want over here in the bend, then? Did you ever know of a boat following a bend up-stream at this stage of the river?"

"No, sir, – and I wasn't trying to follow it. I was getting away from a bluff reef."

"No, it wasn't a bluff reef; there isn't one within three miles of where you were."

"But I saw it. It was as bluff as that one yonder."

"Just about. Run over it!"

"Do you give it as an order?"

"Yes. Run over it."

"If I don't, I wish I may die."

"All right; I am taking the responsibility."

I was just as anxious to kill the boat, now, as I had been to save her before. I impressed my orders upon my memory, to be used at the inquest, and made a straight break for the reef. As it disappeared under our bows I held my breath; but we slid over it like oil.

"Now don't you see the difference? It wasn't anything but a wind reef. The wind does that."

"So I see. But it is exactly like a bluff reef. How am I ever going to tell them apart?"

"I can't tell you. It is an instinct. By and by you will just naturally *know* one from the other, but you never will be able to explain why or how you know them apart."

It turned out to be true. The face of the water, in time, became a wonderful book – a book that was a dead language to the uneducated passenger, but which told its mind to me without reserve, delivering its most cherished secrets as clearly as if it uttered them with a voice. And it was not a book to be read once and thrown aside, for it had a new story to tell every day. Throughout the long twelve hundred miles there was never a page that was void of interest, never one that you could leave unread without loss, never one that you would want to skip, thinking you could find higher enjoyment in some other thing. There never was so wonderful a book written by man; never one whose interest was so absorbing, so unflagging, so sparklingly renewed with every re-perusal. The passenger who could not read it was charmed with a peculiar sort of faint dimple on its surface (on the rare occasions when he did not overlook it altogether); but to the pilot that was an *italicized* passage; indeed, it was more than that, it was a legend of the largest capitals with a string of shouting exclamation points at the end of it; for it meant that a wreck or a rock was buried there that could tear the life out of the strongest vessel that ever floated. It is the faintest and simplest expression the water ever makes, and the most hideous to a pilot's eye. In truth, the passenger who could not read this book saw nothing but all manner of pretty pictures in it, painted by the sun and shaded by the clouds, whereas to the trained eye these were not pictures at all, but the grimmest and most dead-earnest of reading-matter.

Now when I had mastered the language of this water and had come to know every trifling feature that bordered the great river as familiarly as I knew the letters of the alphabet, I had made a valuable acquisition. But I had lost something, too. I had lost something which could never be restored to me while I lived. All the grace, the beauty, the poetry had gone out of the majestic river! I still keep in mind a certain wonderful sunset which I witnessed when steamboating was new to me. A broad expanse of the river was turned to blood; in the middle distance the red hue brightened into gold, through which a solitary log came floating, black and conspicuous; in one place a long, slanting mark lay sparkling upon the water; in another the surface was broken by boiling, tumbling rings, that were as many-tinted as an opal; where the ruddy flush was faintest, was a smooth spot that was covered with graceful circles and radiating lines, ever so delicately traced; the shore on our left was densely wooded, and the sombre shadow that fell from this forest was broken in one place by a long, ruffled trail that shone like silver; and high above the forest wall a clean-stemmed dead tree waved a single leafy bough that glowed like a flame in the unobstructed splendor that was flowing from the sun. There were graceful curves, reflected images, woody heights, soft distances; and over the whole scene, far and near, the dissolving lights drifted steadily, enriching it, every passing moment, with new marvels of coloring.

I stood like one bewitched. I drank it in, in a speechless rapture. The world was new to me, and I had never seen anything like this at home. But as I have said, a day came when I began to cease noting the glories and the charms which the moon and the sun and the twilight wrought upon the river's face; another day came when I ceased altogether to note them. Then, if that sunset scene had been repeated, I would have looked upon it without rapture, and would have commented upon it, inwardly, after this fashion: This sun means that we are going to have wind to-morrow; that floating log means that the river is rising, small thanks to it; that slanting mark on the water refers to a bluff reef which is going to kill somebody's steamboat one of these nights, if it keeps on stretching out like that; those tumbling "boils" show a dissolving bar and a changing channel there; the lines and circles in the slick water over yonder are a warning that that execrable place is shoaling up dangerously; that silver streak in the shadow of the forest is the "break" from a new snag, and he has located himself in the very best place he could have found to fish for steamboats; that tall, dead tree, with a single living branch, is not going to last long, and then how is a body ever going to get through this blind place at night without the friendly old landmark?

No, the romance and the beauty were all gone from the river. All the value any feature of it had for me now was the amount of usefulness it could furnish toward compassing the safe piloting of a steamboat. Since those days, I have pitied doctors from my heart. What does the lovely flush in a beauty's cheek mean to a doctor but a "break" that ripples above some deadly disease? Are not all her visible charms sown thick with what are to him the signs and symbols of hidden decay? Does he ever see her beauty at all, or doesn't he simply view her professionally, and comment upon her unwholesome condition all to himself? And doesn't he sometimes wonder whether he has gained most or lost most by learning his trade?

[1875]

Twain's "The Private History of a Campaign That Failed."   This account of Twain's brief experience in the pro-Southern militia in his home state of Missouri was published in 1885 in the *Century Illustrated Monthly Magazine,* which had begun publication four years earlier as a successor to *Scribner's Monthly Magazine.* From the beginning, the *Century* featured numerous articles about the Civil War, and in November 1884 the magazine launched an ambitious series of lavishly illustrated reminiscences written by soldiers who had fought on both sides of the conflict. Dozens of their accounts appeared in the magazine before the Century Company published a four-volume set based on the series, *Battles and Leaders of the Civil War* (1887-88), which became the best-selling and most frequently cited of all works on the Civil War. Twain's contribution to the series, which was not included in the published set, was distinctive in several ways. "Decisive battles, the leading characteristics of army life on each side of the lines, and the lives of the most prominent commanders, North and South, will be the subjects of the papers," the editors observed when announcing the commencement of the series in the *Century.* Twain's subject was far different, and the antiheroic tone of "The Private History of a Campaign That Failed" was in sharp opposition to the overall tone of the series, which the editors hoped would teach the generation that had grown up since the war "how the men who were divided on a question of principle and State fealty, and who fought the war which must remain the pivotal period of our history, won by equal devotion and valor that respect for each other which is the strongest bond of a reunited people." The text and one of its accompanying illustrations are taken from the first printing in the *Century,* December 1885.

THE PRIVATE HISTORY
OF A CAMPAIGN THAT FAILED

You have heard from a great many people who did something in the war; is it not fair and right that you listen a little moment to one who started out to do something in it, but didn't? Thousands entered the war, got just a taste of it, and then stepped out again, permanently. These, by their very numbers, are respectable, and are therefore entitled to a sort of voice, not a loud one, but a modest one; not a boastful one, but an apologetic one. They ought not to be allowed much space among better people – people who did something – I grant that; but they ought at least to be allowed to state why they didn't do anything, and also to explain the process by which they didn't do anything. Surely this kind of light must have a sort of value.

Out West there was a good deal of confusion in men's minds during the first months of the great trouble – a good deal of unsettledness, of leaning first this way, then that, then the other way. It was hard for us to get our bearings. I call to mind an instance of this. I was piloting on the Mississippi when the news came that South Carolina had gone out of the Union on the 20th of December, 1860. My pilot-mate was a New Yorker. He was strong for the Union; so was I. But he would not listen to me with any patience; my loyalty was smirched, to his eye, because my father had owned slaves. I said, in palliation of this dark fact, that I had heard my father say, some years before he died, that slavery was a great wrong, and that he would free the solitary negro he then owned if he could think it right to give away the property of the family when he was so straitened in means. My mate retorted that a mere impulse was nothing – anybody could pretend to a good impulse; and went on decrying my Unionism and libeling my ancestry. A month later the secession atmosphere had considerably thickened on the Lower Mississippi, and I became a rebel; so did he. We were together in New Orleans, the 26th of January, when Louisiana went out of the Union. He did his full share of the rebel shouting, but was bitterly opposed to letting me do mine. He said that I came of bad stock – of a father who had been willing to set slaves free. In the following summer he was piloting a Federal gun-boat and shouting for the Union again, and I was in the Confederate army. I held his note for some borrowed money. He was one of the most upright men I ever knew; but he repudiated that note without hesitation, because I was a rebel, and the son of a man who owned slaves.

In that summer – of 1861 – the first wash of the wave of war broke upon the shores of Missouri. Our State was invaded by the Union forces. They took possession of St.

Louis, Jefferson Barracks, and some other points. The Governor, Claib Jackson, issued his proclamation calling out fifty thousand militia to repel the invader.[1]

I was visiting in the small town where my boyhood had been spent – Hannibal, Marion County. Several of us got together in a secret place by night and formed ourselves into a military company. One Tom Lyman, a young fellow of a good deal of spirit but of no military experience, was made captain; I was made second lieutenant. We had no first lieutenant; I do not know why; it was long ago. There were fifteen of us. By the advice of an innocent connected with the organization, we called ourselves the Marion Rangers. I do not remember that any one found fault with the name. I did not; I thought it sounded quite well. The young fellow who proposed this title was perhaps a fair sample of the kind of stuff we were made of. He was young, ignorant, good-natured, well-meaning, trivial, full of romance, and given to reading chivalric novels and singing forlorn love-ditties. He had some pathetic little nickel-plated aristocratic instincts, and detested his name, which was Dunlap; detested it, partly because it was nearly as common in that region as Smith, but mainly because it had a plebeian sound to his ear. So he tried to ennoble it by writing it in this way: *d'Unlap*. That contented his eye, but left his ear unsatisfied, for people gave the new name the same old pronunciation – emphasis on the front end of it. He then did the bravest thing that can be imagined, a thing to make one shiver when one remembers how the world is given to resenting shams and affectations; he began to write his name so: *d'Un Lap*. And he waited patiently through the long storm of mud that was flung at this work of art, and he had his reward at last; for he lived to see that name accepted, and the emphasis put where he wanted it, by people who had known him all his life, and to whom the tribe of Dunlaps had been as familiar as the rain and the sunshine for forty years. So sure of victory at last is the courage that can wait. He said he had found, by consulting some ancient French chronicles, that the name was rightly and originally written d'Un Lap; and said that if it were translated into English it would mean Peterson: *Lap*, Latin or Greek, he said, for stone or rock, same as the French *pierre*, that is to say, Peter; *d'*, of or from; *un*, a or one; hence, d'Un Lap, of or from a stone or a Peter; that is to say, one who is the son of a stone, the son of a Peter – Peterson. Our militia company were not learned, and the explanation confused them; so they called him Peterson Dunlap. He proved useful to us in his way;

---

1. **The Governor . . . to repel the invader:** Claiborne F. Jackson (1806–1862), the governor of Missouri from 1861 to 1862, was a staunch secessionist who tried to lead the state out of the Union. The delegates to a convention held in St. Louis in March 1861 voted overwhelmingly against both secession and coercive efforts to force the Southern states back into the Union. Even as federal troops occupied the state, Jackson reorganized its militia into the Missouri State Guard, which was supplied with arms by the Confederacy. In June, after federal troops attacked the state guard's gathering at "Camp Jackson," the governor called out 5,000 militiamen "to defend the state from invasion." In response, Twain joined a pro-Southern militia unit, though he and others technically pledged their support to the state and federal constitutions, not to the Confederacy. In fact, there was considerable confusion and uncertainty among some men in the state guard, since Missouri remained part of the Union despite the ongoing efforts of the governor. During his brief time in the militia, which he abandoned at the end of July, Twain did not participate in any of the battles between federal troops and the state guard.

he named our camps for us, and he generally struck a name that was "no slouch," as the boys said.

That is one sample of us. Another was Ed Stevens, son of the town jeweler, – trim-built, handsome, graceful, neat as a cat; bright, educated, but given over entirely to fun. There was nothing serious in life to him. As far as he was concerned, this military expedition of ours was simply a holiday. I should say that about half of us looked upon it in the same way; not consciously, perhaps, but unconsciously. We did not think; we were not capable of it. As for myself, I was full of unreasoning joy to be done with turning out of bed at midnight and four in the morning, for a while; grateful to have a change, new scenes, new occupations, a new interest. In my thoughts that was as far as I went; I did not go into the details; as a rule one doesn't at twenty-four.

Another sample was Smith, the blacksmith's apprentice. This vast donkey had some pluck, of a slow and sluggish nature, but a soft heart; at one time he would knock a horse down for some impropriety, and at another he would get homesick and cry. However, he had one ultimate credit to his account which some of us hadn't: he stuck to the war, and was killed in battle at last.

Jo Bowers, another sample, was a huge, good-natured, flax-headed lubber; lazy, sentimental, full of harmless brag, a grumbler by nature; an experienced, industrious, ambitious, and often quite picturesque liar, and yet not a successful one, for he had had no intelligent training, but was allowed to come up just any way. This life was serious enough to him, and seldom satisfactory. But he was a good fellow anyway, and the boys all liked him. He was made orderly sergeant; Stevens was made corporal.

These samples will answer – and they are quite fair ones. Well, this herd of cattle started for the war. What could you expect of them? They did as well as they knew how, but really what was justly to be expected of them? Nothing, I should say. That is what they did.

We waited for a dark night, for caution and secrecy were necessary; then, toward midnight, we stole in couples and from various directions to the Griffith place, beyond the town; from that point we set out together on foot. Hannibal lies at the extreme south-eastern corner of Marion County, on the Mississippi River; our objective point was the hamlet of New London, ten miles away, in Ralls County.

The first hour was all fun, all idle nonsense and laughter. But that could not be kept up. The steady trudging came to be like work; the play had somehow oozed out of it; the stillness of the woods and the somberness of the night began to throw a depressing influence over the spirits of the boys, and presently the talking died out and each person shut himself up in his own thoughts. During the last half of the second hour nobody said a word.

Now we approached a log farm-house where, according to report, there was a guard of five Union soldiers. Lyman called a halt; and there, in the deep gloom of the overhanging branches, he began to whisper a plan of assault upon that house, which made the gloom more depressing than it was before. It was a crucial moment; we realized, with a cold suddenness, that here was no jest — we were standing face to face with actual war. We were equal to the occasion. In our response there was no hesitation, no indecision: we said that if Lyman wanted to meddle with those soldiers, he could go ahead and do it; but if he waited for us to follow him, he would wait a long time.

Lyman urged, pleaded, tried to shame us, but it had no effect. Our course was plain, our minds were made up: we would flank the farm-house – go out around. And that is what we did.

We struck into the woods and entered upon a rough time, stumbling over roots, getting tangled in vines, and torn by briers. At last we reached an open place in a safe region, and sat down, blown and hot, to cool off and nurse our scratches and bruises. Lyman was annoyed, but the rest of us were cheerful; we had flanked the farm-house, we had made our first military movement, and it was a success; we had nothing to fret about, we were feeling just the other way. Horse-play and laughing began again; the expedition was become a holiday frolic once more.

Then we had two more hours of dull trudging and ultimate silence and depression; then, about dawn, we struggled into New London, soiled, heel-blistered, fagged with our little march, and all of us except Stevens in a sour and raspy humor and privately down on the war. We stacked our shabby old shot-guns in Colonel Ralls's barn, and then went in a body and breakfasted with that veteran of the Mexican war.[2] Afterwards he took us to a distant meadow, and there in the shade of a tree we listened to an old-fashioned speech from him, full of gunpowder and glory, full of that adjective-piling, mixed metaphor, and windy declamation which was regarded as eloquence in that ancient time and that remote region; and then he swore us on the Bible to be faithful to the State of Missouri and drive all invaders from her soil, no matter whence they might come or under what flag they might march. This mixed us considerably, and we could not make out just what service we were embarked in; but Colonel Ralls, the practiced politician and phrase-juggler, was not similarly in doubt; he knew quite clearly that he had invested us in the cause of the Southern Confederacy. He closed the solemnities by belting around me the sword which his neighbor, Colonel Brown, had worn at Buena Vista and Molino del Rey;[3] and he accompanied this act with another impressive blast.

Then we formed in line of battle and marched four miles to a shady and pleasant piece of woods on the border of the far-reaching expanses of a flowery prairie. It was an enchanting region for war – our kind of war.

We pierced the forest about half a mile, and took up a strong position, with some low, rocky, and wooded hills behind us, and a purling, limpid creek in front. Straightway half the command were in swimming, and the other half fishing. The ass with the French name gave this position a romantic title, but it was too long, so the boys shortened and simplified it to Camp Ralls.

We occupied an old maple-sugar camp, whose half-rotted troughs were still propped against the trees. A long corn-crib served for sleeping quarters for the battalion. On our left, half a mile away, was Mason's farm and house; and he was a friend to the cause. Shortly after noon the farmers began to arrive from several directions, with mules and horses for our use, and these they lent us for as long as the war might last, which they judged would be about three months. The animals were of all sizes, all colors, and all

---

2. **Mexican war:** The Mexican War (1846–48), at the conclusion of which the United States gained California and a vast territory in the Southwest, was a training ground for many soldiers and officers who later fought in the Civil War, including Ulysses S. Grant and Robert E. Lee.

3. **Buena Vista and Molino del Rey:** Decisive American victories in the Mexican War.

breeds. They were mainly young and frisky, and nobody in the command could stay on them long at a time; for we were town boys, and ignorant of horsemanship. The creature that fell to my share was a very small mule, and yet so quick and active that it could throw me without difficulty; and it did this whenever I got on it. Then it would bray — stretching its neck out, laying its ears back, and spreading its jaws till you could see down to its works. It was a disagreeable animal, in every way. If I took it by the bridle and tried to lead it off the grounds, it would sit down and brace back, and no one could budge it. However, I was not entirely destitute of military resources, and I did presently manage to spoil this game; for I had seen many a steamboat aground in my time, and knew a trick or two which even a grounded mule would be obliged to respect. There was a well by the corn-crib; so I substituted thirty fathom of rope for the bridle, and fetched him home with the windlass.

I will anticipate here sufficiently to say that we did learn to ride, after some days' practice, but never well. We could not learn to like our animals; they were not choice ones, and most of them had annoying peculiarities of one kind or another. Stevens's horse would carry him, when he was not noticing, under the huge excrescences which form on the trunks of oak-trees, and wipe him out of the saddle; in this way Stevens got several bad hurts. Sergeant Bowers's horse was very large and tall, with slim, long legs, and looked like a railroad bridge. His size enabled him to reach all about, and as far as he wanted to, with his head; so he was always biting Bowers's legs. On the march, in the sun, Bowers slept a good deal; and as soon as the horse recognized that he was asleep he would reach around and bite him on the leg. His legs were black and blue with bites. This was the only thing that could ever make him swear, but this always did; whenever the horse bit him he always swore, and of course Stevens, who laughed at everything, laughed at this, and would even get into such convulsions over it as to lose his balance and fall off his horse; and then Bowers, already irritated by the pain of the horse-bite, would resent the laughter with hard language, and there would be a quarrel; so that horse made no end of trouble and bad blood in the command.

However, I will get back to where I was — our first afternoon in the sugar-camp. The sugar-troughs came very handy as horse-troughs, and we had plenty of corn to fill them with. I ordered Sergeant Bowers to feed my mule; but he said that if I reckoned he went to war to be dry-nurse to a mule, it wouldn't take me very long to find out my mistake. I believed that this was insubordination, but I was full of uncertainties about everything military, and so I let the thing pass, and went and ordered Smith, the blacksmith's apprentice, to feed the mule; but he merely gave me a large, cold, sarcastic grin, such as an ostensibly seven-year-old horse gives you when you lift his lip and find he is four-teen, and turned his back on me. I then went to the captain, and asked if it was not right and proper and military for me to have an orderly. He said it was, but as there was only one orderly in the corps, it was but right that he himself should have Bowers on his staff. Bowers said he wouldn't serve on anybody's staff; and if anybody thought he could make him, let him try it. So, of course, the thing had to be dropped; there was no other way.

Next, nobody would cook; it was considered a degradation; so we had no dinner. We lazied the rest of the pleasant afternoon away, some dozing under the trees, some smoking cob-pipes and talking sweethearts and war, some playing games. By late supper-time all hands were famished; and to meet the difficulty all hands turned to, on an equal footing, and gathered wood, built fires, and cooked the meal. Afterward everything was smooth for a while; then trouble broke out between the corporal and the sergeant, each claiming to rank the other. Nobody knew which was the higher office; so Lyman had to settle the matter by making the rank of both officers equal. The commander of an ignorant crew like that has many troubles and vexations which probably do not occur in the regular army at all. However, with the song-singing and yarn-spinning around the camp-fire, everything presently became serene again; and by and by we raked the corn down level in one end of the crib, and all went to bed on it, tying a horse to the door, so that he would neigh if any one tried to get in.[4]

We had some horsemanship drill every forenoon; then, afternoons, we rode off here and there in squads a few miles, and visited the farmers' girls, and had a youthful good time, and got an honest good dinner or supper, and then home again to camp, happy and content.

For a time, life was idly delicious, it was perfect; there was nothing to mar it. Then came some farmers with an alarm one day. They said it was rumored that the enemy were advancing in our direction, from over Hyde's prairie. The result was a sharp stir among us, and general consternation. It was a rude awakening from our pleasant trance. The rumor was but a rumor — nothing definite about it; so, in the confusion, we did not know which way to retreat. Lyman was for not retreating at all, in these uncertain circumstances; but he found that if he tried to maintain that attitude he would fare badly, for the command were in no humor to put up with insubordination. So he yielded the point and called a council of war — to consist of himself and the three other officers; but the privates made such a fuss about being left out, that we had to allow them to be present. I mean we had to allow them to remain, for they were already present, and doing the most of the talking too. The question was, which way to retreat; but all were so flurried that nobody seemed to have even a guess to offer. Except Lyman. He explained in a few calm words, that inasmuch as the enemy were approaching from over Hyde's prairie, our course was simple: all we had to do was not to retreat *toward* him; any other direction would answer our needs perfectly. Everybody saw in a moment how true this was, and how wise; so Lyman got a great many compliments. It was now decided that we should fall back on Mason's farm.

It was after dark by this time, and as we could not know how soon the enemy might arrive, it did not seem best to try to take the horses and things with us; so we only took the guns and ammunition, and started at once. The route was very rough and hilly and rocky, and presently the night grew very black and rain began to fall; so we had a troublesome time of it, struggling and stumbling along in the dark; and soon some person slipped and fell, and then the next person behind stumbled over him and fell, and so did the rest, one after the other; and then Bowers came with the keg of powder in his

---

4. **tying a horse . . . get in:** "It was always my impression that that was what the horse was there for, and I know that it was also the impression of at least one other of the command, for we talked about it at the time, and admired the military ingenuity of the device; but when I was out West three years ago I was told by Mr. A. G. Fuqua, a member of our company, that the horse was his, that the leaving him tied at the door was a matter of mere forgetfulness, and that to attribute it to intelligent invention was to give him quite too much credit. In support of his position, he called my attention to the suggestive fact that the artifice was not employed again. I had not thought of that before." [Twain's note]

arms, whilst the command were all mixed together, arms and legs, on the muddy slope; and so he fell, of course, with the keg, and this started the whole detachment down the hill in a body, and they landed in the brook at the bottom in a pile, and each that was undermost pulling the hair and scratching and biting those that were on top of him; and those that were being scratched and bitten scratching and biting the rest in their turn, and all saying they would die before they would ever go to war again if they ever got out of this brook this time, and the invader might rot for all they cared, and the country along with him — and all such talk as that, which was dismal to hear and take part in, in such smothered, low voices, and such a grisly dark place and so wet, and the enemy may be coming any moment.

The keg of powder was lost, and the guns too; so the growling and complaining continued straight along whilst the brigade pawed around the pasty hillside and slopped around in the brook hunting for these things; consequently we lost considerable time at this; and then we heard a sound, and held our breath and listened, and it seemed to be the enemy coming, though it could have been a cow, for it had a cough like a cow; but we did not wait, but left a couple of guns behind and struck out for Mason's again as briskly as we could scramble along in the dark. But we got lost presently among the rugged little ravines, and wasted a deal of time finding the way again, so it was after nine when we reached Mason's stile at last; and then before we could open our mouths to give the countersign, several dogs came bounding over the fence, with great riot and noise, and each of them took a soldier by the slack of his trousers and began to back away with him. We could not shoot the dogs without endangering the persons they were attached to; so we had to look on, helpless, at what was perhaps the most mortifying spectacle of the civil war. There was light enough, and to spare, for the Masons had now run out on the porch with candles in their hands. The old man and his son came and undid the dogs without difficulty, all but Bowers's; but they couldn't undo his dog, they didn't know his combination; he was of the bull kind, and seemed to be set with a Yale time-lock; but they got him loose at last with some scalding water, of which Bowers got his share and returned thanks. Peterson Dunlap afterwards made up a fine name for this engagement, and also for the night march which preceded it, but both have long ago faded out of my memory.

We now went into the house, and they began to ask us a world of questions, whereby it presently came out that we did not know anything concerning who or what we were running from; so the old gentleman made himself very frank, and said we were a curious breed of soldiers, and guessed we could be depended on to end up the war in time, because no government could stand the expense of the shoe-leather we should cost it trying to follow us around. "Marion *Rangers!* good name, b'gosh!" said he. And wanted to know why we hadn't had a picket-guard at the place where the road entered the prairie, and why we hadn't sent out a scouting party to spy out the enemy and bring us an account of his strength, and so on, before jumping up and stampeding out of a strong position upon a mere vague rumor — and so on and so forth, till he made us all feel shabbier than the dogs had done, not half so enthusiastically welcome. So we went to bed shamed and low-spirited; except Stevens. Soon Stevens began to devise a garment for Bowers which could be made to automatically display his battle-scars to the grateful, or conceal them from the envious, according to his occasions; but Bowers was in no humor for this, so there was a fight, and when it was over Stevens had some battle-scars of his own to think about.

Then we got a little sleep. But after all we had gone through, our activities were not over for the night; for about two o'clock in the morning we heard a shout of warning from down the lane, accompanied by a chorus from all the dogs, and in a moment every-body was up and flying around to find out what the alarm was about. The alarmist was a horseman who gave notice that a detachment of Union soldiers was on its way from Hannibal with orders to capture and hang any bands like ours which it could find, and said we had no time to lose. Farmer Mason was in a flurry this time, himself. He hurried us out of the house with all haste, and sent one of his negroes with us to show us where to hide ourselves and our tell-tale guns among the ravines half a mile away. It was rain-ing heavily.

We struck down the lane, then across some rocky pasture-land which offered good advantages for stumbling; consequently we were down in the mud most of the time, and every time a man went down he blackguarded the war, and the people that started it, and everybody connected with it, and gave himself the master dose of all for being so foolish as to go into it. At last we reached the wooded mouth of a ravine, and there we huddled ourselves under the streaming trees, and sent the negro back home. It was a dismal and heart-breaking time. We were like to be drowned with the rain, deafened with the howl-ing wind and the booming thunder, and blinded by the lightning. It was indeed a wild night. The drenching we were getting was misery enough, but a deeper misery still was the reflection that the halter might end us before we were a day older. A death of this shameful sort had not occurred to us as being among the possibilities of war. It took the romance all out of the campaign, and turned our dreams of glory into a repulsive night-mare. As for doubting that so barbarous an order had been given, not one of us did that.

The long night wore itself out at last, and then the negro came to us with the news that the alarm had manifestly been a false one, and that breakfast would soon be ready. Straightway we were lighted-hearted again, and the world was bright, and life as full of hope and promise as ever — for we were young then. How long ago that was! Twenty-four years.

The mongrel child of philology named the night's refuge Camp Devastation, and no soul objected. The Masons gave us a Missouri country breakfast, in Missourian abun-dance, and we needed it: hot biscuits; hot "wheat bread" prettily criss-crossed in a lat-tice pattern on top; hot corn pone; fried chicken; bacon, coffee, eggs, milk, buttermilk, etc.; and the world may be confidently challenged to furnish the equal to such a break-fast, as it is cooked in the South.

We staid several days at Mason's; and after all these years the memory of the dull-ness, the stillness and lifelessness of that slumberous farm-house still oppresses my spirit as with a sense of the presence of death and mourning. There was nothing to do, nothing to think about; there was no interest in life. The male part of the household were away in the fields all day, the women were busy and out of our sight; there was no sound but the plaintive wailing of a spinning-wheel, forever moaning out from some distant room, the most lonesome sound in nature, a sound steeped and sodden with homesickness and the emptiness of life. The family went to bed about dark every night, and as we were not invited to intrude any new customs, we naturally followed theirs.

Those nights were a hundred years long to youths accustomed to being up till twelve. We lay awake and miserable till that hour every time, and grew old and decrepit waiting through the still eternities for the clock-strikes. This was no place for town boys. So at last it was with something very like joy that we received news that the enemy were on our track again. With a new birth of the old warrior spirit, we sprang to our places in line of battle and fell back on Camp Ralls.

Captain Lyman had taken a hint from Mason's talk, and he now gave orders that our camp should be guarded against surprise by the posting of pickets. I was ordered to place a picket at the forks of the road in Hyde's prairie. Night shut down black and threatening. I told Sergeant Bowers to go out to that place and stay till midnight; and, just as I was expecting, he said he wouldn't do it. I tried to get others to go, but all refused. Some excused themselves on account of the weather; but the rest were frank enough to say they wouldn't go in any kind of weather. This kind of thing sounds odd now, and impossible, but there was no surprise in it at the time. On the contrary, it seemed a perfectly natural thing to do. There were scores of little camps scattered over Missouri where the same thing was happening. These camps were composed of young men who had been born and reared to a sturdy independence, and who did not know what it meant to be ordered around by Tom, Dick, and Harry, whom they had known familiarly all their lives, in the village or on the farm. It is quite within the probabilities that this same thing was happening all over the South. James Redpath recognized the justice of this assumption, and furnished the following instance in support of it. During a short stay in East Tennessee he was in a citizen colonel's tent one day, talking, when a big private appeared at the door, and without salute or other circumlocution said to the colonel:

"Say, Jim, I'm a-goin' home for a few days."

"What for?"

"Well, I hain't b'en there for a right smart while, and I'd like to see how things is comin' on."

"How long are you going to be gone?"

" 'Bout two weeks."

"Well, don't be gone longer than that; and get back sooner if you can."

That was all, and the citizen officer resumed his conversation where the private had broken it off. This was in the first months of the war, of course. The camps in our part of Missouri were under Brigadier-General Thomas H. Harris. He was a townsman of ours, a first-rate fellow, and well liked; but we had all familiarly known him as the sole and modest-salaried operator in our telegraph office, where he had to send about one dispatch a week in ordinary times, and two when there was a rush of business; consequently, when he appeared in our midst one day, on the wing, and delivered a military command of some sort, in a large military fashion, nobody was surprised at the response which he got from the assembled soldiery:

"Oh, now, what'll you take to *don't*, Tom Harris!"

It was quite the natural thing. One might justly imagine that we were hopeless material for war. And so we seemed, in our ignorant state; but there were those among us who afterward learned the grim trade; learned to obey like machines; became valuable soldiers; fought all through the war, and came out at the end with excellent records. One of the very boys who refused to go out on picket duty that night, and called me an ass for thinking he would expose himself to danger in such a foolhardy way, had become distinguished for intrepidity before he was a year older.

I did secure my picket that night — not by authority, but by diplomacy. I got Bowers to go, by agreeing to exchange ranks with him for the time being, and go along and stand the watch with him as his subordinate. We staid out there a couple of dreary hours in the pitchy darkness and the rain, with nothing to modify the dreariness but Bowers's monotonous growlings at the war and the weather; then we began to nod, and presently found it next to impossible to stay in the saddle; so we gave up the tedious job, and went back to the camp without waiting for the relief guard. We rode into camp without interruption or objection from anybody, and the enemy could have done the same, for there were no sentries. Everybody was asleep; at midnight there was nobody to send out another picket, so none was sent. We never tried to establish a watch at night again, as far as I remember, but we generally kept a picket out in the daytime.

In that camp the whole command slept on the corn in the big corn-crib; and there was usually a general row before morning, for the place was full of rats, and they would scramble over the boys' bodies and faces, annoying and irritating everybody; and now and then they would bite some one's toe, and the person who owned the toe would start up and magnify his English and begin to throw corn in the dark. The ears were half as heavy as bricks, and when they struck they hurt. The persons struck would respond, and inside of five minutes every man would be locked in a death-grip with his neighbor. There was a grievous deal of blood shed in the corn-crib, but this was all that was spilt while I was in the war. No, that is not quite true. But for one circumstance it would have been all. I will come to that now.

Our scares were frequent. Every few days rumors would come that the enemy were approaching. In these cases we always fell back on some other camp of ours; we never staid where we were. But the rumors always turned out to be false; so at last even we began to grow indifferent to them. One night a negro was sent to our corn-crib with the same old warning: the enemy was hovering in our neighborhood. We all said let him hover. We resolved to stay still and be comfortable. It was a fine warlike resolution, and no doubt we all felt the stir of it in our veins — for a moment. We had been having a very jolly time, that was full of horse-play and school-boy hilarity; but that cooled down now, and presently the fast-waning fire of forced jokes and forced laughs died out altogether, and the company became silent. Silent and nervous. And soon uneasy — worried — apprehensive. We had said we would stay, and we were committed. We could have been persuaded to go, but there was nobody brave enough to suggest it. An almost noiseless movement presently began in the dark, by a general but unvoiced impulse. When the movement was completed, each man knew that he was not the only person who had crept to the front wall and had his eye at a crack between the logs. No, we were all there; all there with our hearts in our throats, and staring out toward the sugar-troughs where the forest foot-path came through. It was late, and there was a deep woodsy stillness everywhere. There was a veiled moonlight, which was only just strong enough to enable us to mark the general shape of objects. Presently a muffled sound caught our ears, and we recognized it as the hoof-beats of a horse or horses. And right away a figure appeared in the forest path; it could have been made of smoke, its mass had so little sharpness of outline. It was a man on horseback; and it seemed to me that there were others behind him. I got hold of a gun in the dark, and pushed it through a crack between the logs, hardly knowing what I was doing, I was so dazed with fright. Somebody said "Fire!" I pulled the trigger. I seemed to see a hundred flashes and hear a hundred reports, then I saw the man fall down out of the saddle. My first feeling was of surprised gratification; my first impulse was an apprentice-sportsman's impulse to run and pick up his game. Somebody said, hardly audibly, "Good — we've got him — wait for the rest." But the rest did not come. We waited — listened — still no more came. There was not a sound, not the whisper of a leaf; just perfect stillness; an uncanny kind of stillness, which was all the more uncanny on account of the damp, earthy, late-night smells now rising and pervading it. Then, wondering, we crept stealthily out, and approached the man. When we got to him the moon revealed him distinctly. He was lying on his back, with his arms abroad; his mouth was open and his chest heaving with long gasps, and his white shirt-front was all splashed with blood. The thought shot through me that I was a murderer; that I had killed a man — a man who had never done me any harm. That was the coldest sensation that ever went through my marrow. I was down by him in a moment, helplessly stroking his forehead; and I would have given anything then — my own life freely — to make him again what he had been five minutes before. And all the boys seemed to be feeling in the same way; they hung over him, full of pitying interest, and tried all they could to help him, and said all sorts of regretful things. They had forgotten all about the enemy; they thought only of this one forlorn unit of the foe. Once my imagination persuaded me that the dying man gave me a reproachful look out of his shadowy eyes, and it seemed to me that I could rather he had stabbed me than done that. He muttered and mumbled like a dreamer in his sleep, about his wife and his child; and I thought with a new despair, "This thing that I have done does not end with him; it falls upon *them* too, and they never did me any harm, any more than he."

In a little while the man was dead. He was killed in war; killed in fair and legitimate war; killed in battle, as you may say; and yet he was as sincerely mourned by the opposing force as if he had been their brother. The boys stood there a half hour sorrowing over him, and recalling the details of the tragedy, and wondering who he might be, and if he were a spy, and saying that if it were to do over again they would not hurt him unless he attacked them first. It soon came out that mine was not the only shot fired; there were five others, — a division of the guilt which was a grateful relief to me, since it in some degree lightened and diminished the burden I was carrying. There were six shots fired at once; but I was not in my right mind at the time, and my heated imagination had magnified my one shot into a volley.

The man was not in uniform, and was not armed. He was a stranger in the country; that was all we ever found out about him. The thought of him got to preying upon me every night; I could not get rid of it. I could not drive it away, the taking of that unoffending life seemed such a wanton thing. And it seemed an epitome of war; that all war must be just that — the killing of strangers against whom you feel no personal animosity; strangers whom, in other circumstances, you would help if you found them in trouble, and who would help you if you needed it. My campaign was spoiled. It seemed to me that I was not rightly equipped for this awful business; that war was intended for men, and I for a child's nurse. I resolved to retire from this avocation of sham soldier-ship while I could save some remnant of my self-respect. These morbid thoughts clung to me against reason; for at bottom I did not believe I had touched that man. The law of probabilities decreed me guiltless of his blood; for in all my small experience with guns I had never hit anything I had tried to hit, and I knew I had done my best to hit him. Yet there was no solace in the thought. Against a diseased imagination, demonstration goes for nothing.

The rest of my war experience was of a piece with what I have already told of it. We kept monotonously falling back upon one camp or another, and eating up the country. I marvel now at the patience of the farmers and their families. They ought to have shot us; on the contrary, they were as hospitably kind and courteous to us as if we had deserved it. In one of these camps we found Ab Grimes, an Upper Mississippi pilot, who afterwards became famous as a dare-devil rebel spy, whose career bristled with desper-ate adventures. The look and style of his comrades suggested that they had not come into the war to play, and their deeds made good the conjecture later. They were fine horsemen and good revolver-shots; but their favorite arm was the lasso. Each had one at his pommel, and could snatch a man out of the saddle with it every time, on a full gallop, at any reasonable distance.

In another camp the chief was a fierce and profane old blacksmith of sixty, and he had furnished his twenty recruits with gigantic home-made bowie-knives, to be swung with the two hands, like the *machetes* of the Isthmus. It was a grisly spectacle to see that earnest band practicing their murderous cuts and slashes under the eye of that re-morseless old fanatic.

The last camp which we fell back upon was in a hollow near the village of Florida, where I was born — in Monroe County. Here we were warned, one day, that a Union colonel was sweeping down on us with a whole regiment at his heels. This looked decid-edly serious. Our boys went apart and consulted; then we went back and told the other companies present that the war was a disappointment to us and we were going to dis-band. They were getting ready, themselves, to fall back on some place or other, and were only waiting for General Tom Harris, who was expected to arrive at any moment; so they tried to persuade us to wait a little while, but the majority of us said no, we were accus-tomed to falling back, and didn't need any of Tom Harris's help; we could get along per-fectly well without him — and save time too. So about half of our fifteen, including myself, mounted and left on the instant; the others yielded to persuasion and staid — staid through the war.

An hour later we met General Harris on the road, with two or three people in his com-pany — his staff, probably, but we could not tell; none of them were in uniform; uniforms had not come into vogue among us yet. Harris ordered us back; but we told him there was a Union colonel coming with a whole regiment in his wake, and it looked as if there was going to be a disturbance; so we had concluded to go home. He raged a little, but it was of no use; our minds were made up. We had done our share; had killed one man, exterminated one army, such as it was; let him go and kill the rest, and that would end the war. I did not see that brisk young general again until last year; then he was wearing white hair and whiskers.

In time I came to know that Union colonel whose coming frightened me out of the war and crippled the Southern cause to that extent — General Grant. I came within a few hours of seeing him when he was as unknown as I was myself; at a time when anybody could have said, "Grant? — Ulysses S. Grant? I do not remember hearing the name before." It seems difficult to realize that there was once a time when such a remark could be rationally made; but there *was*, and I was within a few miles of the place and the occasion too, though proceeding in the other direction.

The thoughtful will not throw this war-paper of mine lightly aside as being valueless. It has this value: it is a not unfair picture of what went on in many and many a militia camp in the first months of the rebellion, when the green recruits were without discipline, without the steadying and heartening influence of trained leaders; when all their circumstances were new and strange, and charged with exaggerated terrors, and before the invaluable experience of actual collision in the field had turned them from rabbits into soldiers. If this side of the picture of that early day has not before been put into history, then history has been to that degree incomplete, for it had and has its rightful place there. There was more Bull Run material scattered through the early camps of this country than exhibited itself at Bull Run. And yet it learned its trade presently, and helped to fight the great battles later. I could have become a soldier myself, if I had waited. I had got part of it learned; I knew more about retreating than the man that invented retreating.

[1885]

Twain's "The War Prayer."   Twain was generally supportive of the Spanish-American War of 1898, which he viewed as an effort to liberate subject peoples from the despotism of Spanish rule, especially in Cuba. Under the terms of the treaty that ended the brief, eight-month war, Cuba gained independence, but Spain ceded Puerto Rico and Guam to the United States, which was also allowed to purchase the Philippine Islands. The war was consequently followed by the Philippine-American War (formerly known as the "Philippine Insurrection"), a bloody and protracted conflict between American troops and Filipinos seeking independence from the United States. Twain was appalled by his country's brutal military occupation of the islands, where between 250,000 and a million Filipinos, the vast majority of them civilians, died before the rebellion finally subsided at the end of 1913. "There must be two Americas," Twain bitterly observed early in the conflict, "one that sets the captive free, and one that takes a once-captive's new freedom away from him, and picks a quarrel with him with nothing to found it on; then kills him to get his land." His response to the Philippine-American War is also revealed by "The War Prayer," which Twain dictated in 1904-05 and then submitted to *Harper's Bazar* (later named *Harper's Bazaar*). After the editor rejected it as "not quite suited to a woman's magazine," Twain told a friend that he did not think the story would be published in his lifetime, adding, "None but the dead are permitted to tell the truth." Indeed, since he was under contract to write exclusively for the publishing firm of Harper & Brothers, Twain could not publish "The War Prayer" elsewhere, and the story did not appear until several years after Twain's death. The text is taken from its first printing in the collection *Europe and Elsewhere* (1923), edited by Twain's literary executor Albert Bigelow Paine.

THE WAR PRAYER

It was a time of great and exalting excitement. The country was up in arms, the war was on, in every breast burned the holy fire of patriotism; the drums were beating, the bands playing, the toy pistols popping, the bunched firecrackers hissing and spluttering; on every hand and far down the receding and fading spread of roofs and balconies a fluttering wilderness of flags flashed in the sun; daily the young volunteers marched down the wide avenue gay and fine in their new uniforms, the proud fathers and mothers and sisters and sweethearts cheering them with voices choked with happy emotion as they swung by; nightly the packed mass meetings listened, panting, to patriot oratory which stirred the deepest deeps of their hearts, and which they interrupted at briefest intervals with cyclones of applause, the tears running down their cheeks the while; in the churches the pastors preached devotion to flag and country, and invoked the God of Battles, beseeching His aid in our good cause in outpouring of fervid eloquence which moved every listener. It was indeed a glad and gracious time, and the half dozen rash spirits that ventured to disapprove of the war and cast a doubt upon its righteousness straightway got such a stern and angry warning that for their personal safety's sake they quickly shrank out of sight and offended no more in that way.

Sunday morning came — next day the battalions would leave for the front; the church was filled; the volunteers were there, their young faces alight with martial dreams — visions of the stern advance, the gathering momentum, the rushing charge, the flashing sabers, the flight of the foe, the tumult, the enveloping smoke, the fierce pursuit, the surrender! — them home from the war, bronzed heroes, welcomed, adored, submerged in golden seas of glory! With the volunteers sat their dear ones, proud, happy, and envied by the neighbors and friends who had no sons and brothers to send forth to the field of honor, there to win for the flag, or, failing, die the noblest of noble deaths. The service proceeded; a war chapter from the Old Testament was read; the first prayer was said; it was followed by an organ burst that shook the building, and with one impulse the house rose, with glowing eyes and beating hearts, and poured out that tremendous invocation —

> "God the all-terrible! Thou who ordainest,
> Thunder thy clarion and lightning thy sword![1]

---

1. "God . . . sword!": A variant of the opening lines of a familiar Protestant hymn: "God the All-terrible! King, who ordainest / Thunder thy clarion, the lightning thy sword, / Show forth thy pity on high where thou reignest; / Give to us peace in our time, O Lord."

Then came the "long" prayer. None could remember the like of it for passionate pleading and moving and beautiful language. The burden of its supplication was, that an ever-merciful and benignant Father of us all would watch over our noble young soldiers, and aid, comfort, and encourage them in their patriotic work; bless them, shield them in the day of battle and the hour of peril, bear them in His mighty hand, make them strong and confident, invincible in the bloody onset; help them to crush the foe, grant to them and to their flag and country imperishable honor and glory —

An aged stranger entered and moved with slow and noiseless step up the main aisle, his eyes fixed upon the minister, his long body clothed in a robe that reached to his feet, his head bare, his white hair descending in a frothy cataract to his shoulders, his seamy face unnaturally pale, pale even to ghastliness. With all eyes following him and wonder-ing, he made his silent way; without pausing, he ascended to the preacher's side and stood there, waiting. With shut lids the preacher, unconscious of his presence, contin-ued his moving prayer, and at last finished it with the words, uttered in fervent appeal, "Bless our arms, grant us the victory, O Lord our God, Father and Protector of our land and flag!"

The stranger touched his arm, motioned him to step aside — which the startled min-ister did — and took his place. During some moments he surveyed the spellbound audi-ence with solemn eyes, in which burned an uncanny light; then in a deep voice he said:

"I come from the Throne — bearing a message from Almighty God!" The words smote the house with a shock; if the stranger perceived it he gave no attention. "He has heard the prayer of His servant your shepherd, and will grant it if such shall be your desire after I, His messenger, shall have explained to you its import — that is to say, its full import. For it is like unto many of the prayers of men, in that it asks for more than he who utters it is aware of — except he pause and think.

"God's servant and yours has prayed his prayer. Has he paused and taken thought? Is it one prayer? No, it is two — one uttered, the other not. Both have reached the ear of Him Who hearest all supplications, the spoken and the unspoken. Ponder this — keep it in mind. If you would beseech a blessing upon yourself, beware! lest without intent you invoke a curse upon a neighbor at the same time. If you pray for the blessing of rain upon your crop which needs it, by that act you are possibly praying for a curse upon some neighbor's crop which may not need rain and can be injured by it.

"You have heard your servant's prayer — the uttered part of it. I am commissioned of God to put into words the other part of it — that part which the pastor — and also you in your hearts — fervently prayed silently. And ignorantly and unthinkingly? God grant that it was so! You heard these words: 'Grant us the victory, O Lord our God!' That is suf-ficient. The *whole* of the uttered prayer is compact into those pregnant words. Elabora-tions were not necessary. When you have prayed for victory you have prayed for many unmentioned results which follow victory — *must* follow it, cannot help but follow it. Upon the listening spirit of God the Father fell also the unspoken part of the prayer. He commandeth me to put it into words. Listen!

"O Lord our Father, our young patriots, idols of our hearts, go forth to battle — be Thou near them! With them — in spirit — we also go forth from the sweet peace of our beloved firesides to smite the foe. O Lord our God, help us to tear their soldiers to bloody shreds with our shells; help us to cover their smiling fields with the pale forms of their patriot dead; help us to drown the thunder of the guns with the shrieks of their wounded, writhing in pain; help us to lay waste their humble homes with a hurricane of fire; help us to wring the hearts of their unoffending widows with unavailing grief; help us to turn them out roofless with their little children to wander unfriended the wastes of their desolated land in rags and hunger and thirst, sports of the sun flames of summer and the icy winds of winter, broken in spirit, worn with travail, imploring Thee for the refuge of the grave and denied it — for our sakes who adore Thee, Lord, blast their hopes, blight their lives, protract their bitter pilgrimage, make heavy their steps, water their way with their tears, stain the white snow with the blood of their wounded feet! We ask it, in the spirit of love, of Him Who is the Source of Love, and Who is the ever-faithful refuge and friend of all that are sore beset and seek His aid with humble and contrite hearts. Amen."

(*After a pause.*) "Ye have prayed it; if ye still desire it, speak! The messenger of the Most High waits."

It was believed afterward that the man was a lunatic, because there was no sense in what he said.

[1904–05, 1923]

William Dean Howells
[1837–1920]

William Dean Howells was born in Martinsville (now Martin's Ferry), Ohio, on March 1, 1837, the son of a printer and publisher, William Cooper Howells, and his wife, Mary Dean Howells. Their increasingly large family moved from town to town in Ohio, as the utopian Socialist and abolitionist William Cooper Howells struggled to earn a living in the precarious newspaper business. Howells later recalled that from the age of twelve to nineteen he had "worked pretty steadily 'at case,'" that is, setting type. "I have to lament an almost entire want of schooling," he added. "However, my father had ardent literary tastes, and an excellent library and I studied and read as I could. . . . I learned with little or no help Spanish and German, a trifle of Latin and a soupçon of Greek." Inspired by his voracious and wide-ranging reading in drama, especially Shakespeare, fiction, and poetry, Howells began to write at an early age. By the time he was fifteen, he was working as a reporter for a newspaper edited by his father in Columbus, the *Ohio State Journal,* in which Howells's first poem was published in 1852. Although he was initially distressed that his proud father had printed the poem without his knowledge, Howells promptly began submitting his poems for publication. He published his first story in yet

William Dean Howells

This photograph of Howells was taken sometime during his years as editor of the influential *Atlantic Monthly,* 1871–81.

[Howells] seems to be almost always able to find that elusive and shifty grain of gold, the RIGHT WORD.

—Mark Twain

another newspaper edited by his father, the *Ashtabula Sentinel,* where Howells's "A Tale of Love and Politics," subtitled "Adventures of a Printer Boy," appeared in 1857.

Howells's youthful apprenticeship in the newspaper business soon began to pay dividends. He wrote a regular column from the state capitol in Columbus for the *Daily Cincinnati Gazette* and then joined the editorial staff of the *Ohio State Journal,* for which he wrote reviews, poems, and stories. Howells also published poems in more prominent eastern periodicals, including the *New York Saturday Press.* But his greatest early triumph came in August 1859, when James Russell Lowell accepted one of Howells's poems for publication in the prestigious *Atlantic Monthly.* In 1860, Howells published his first book, *Poems of Two Friends,* with his fellow journalist James John Piatt. A strong supporter of the Republican Party, Howells was hired to write a campaign biography of its presidential candidate, Abraham Lincoln. Having earned enough money for a trip east, Howells visited Boston, where he met Lowell and other members of the literary establishment in New England, including Henry Wadsworth Longfellow, Ralph Waldo Emerson, Nathaniel Hawthorne, and Henry David Thoreau. Howells then went to New York City, where he sought out Walt Whitman. Soon after Howells went back home, he met his future wife, Elinor Mead, a transplanted easterner who was impressed that someone from Ohio had published a poem in the *Atlantic Monthly.* When Lincoln became president in 1861, he rewarded Howells by appointing him American consul to Venice, Italy, where he remained throughout the Civil War.

Following his return to the United States in 1865, Howells emerged as one of the country's most influential critics, editors, and writers. Now married and a new father, Howells first moved to New York and then settled his family in Boston. Revising articles he had written for the *Boston Daily Advertiser* during his years in Venice, a city he loved, Howells wrote *Venetian Life,* a major commercial success published in 1866. That year, he was hired to work at the *Atlantic Monthly,* first as an assistant editor (1866–71) and then as its editor (1871–81). During his years at the magazine, Howells published the work of a wide range of American writers in the *Atlantic Monthly,* including his friends Henry James and Mark Twain. Beginning with his first novel, *Their Wedding Journey* (1871), Howells also serialized some of his own work in the magazine. After he left the editorship of the *Atlantic Monthly* to devote himself to writing fiction, Howells published two of his most celebrated novels, *A Modern Instance* (1882) and *The Rise of Silas Lapham* (1885). He also continued to write for periodicals, including *Cosmopolitan*, the *Nation*, and especially *Harper's New Monthly Magazine*. His move from Boston to New York City, where he became the associate editor of *Harper's* in 1886, represented a seismic shift in American publishing away from its traditional center in New England. In his monthly columns for the magazine, the "Editor's Study" (1886-92) and the "Editor's Easy Chair" (1899-1909), Howells promoted the work of a host of emerging writers from around the country, including Abraham Cahan, Charles W. Chesnutt, Stephen Crane, Paul Laurence Dunbar, Mary E. Wilkins Freeman, Sarah Orne Jewett, Frank Norris, and Edith Wharton.

During the final decades of his life, Howells became deeply involved in political and social issues. Those concerns are reflected in *Annie Kilburn* (1888), which exposes the human costs of industrialization, *A Hazard of New Fortunes* (1890), with its emphasis on the stark contrasts between wealth and poverty in New York City, and *A Traveler from Altruria* (1894), in which Howells satirizes life in the United States from the point of view of a visitor from a utopian republic. An outspoken critic of the Spanish-American War of 1898, Howells also strongly supported radical causes, including trade unionism, women's rights, and racial equality, becoming one of the founding members of the National Association for the Advancement of Colored People in 1909. When he turned seventy five in 1912, he was asked to prepare a statement to be read to the schoolchildren in New York City. "While I would wish you to love America most because it's your home, I would have you love the whole world and think of all the people in it as your countrymen," Howells responded with his characteristic candor and clarity. "You will hear people more foolish than wicked say 'Our country, right or wrong,' but that is a false patriotism and bad Americanism. When our country is wrong she is worse than other countries when they are wrong, for she has more light than other countries, and we somehow ought to make her feel that we are sorry and ashamed for her." Just as his social and political views mirrored the earlier radicalism of his father, Howells at the end of his long life explored his Ohio boyhood in a volume of reminiscences, *Years of My Youth* (1915), and two semiautobiographical novels, *New Leaf Mills* (1913) and *The Leatherwood God* (1916). The author of over one hundred books of drama, fiction, poetry, travel, and literary criticism, Howells died at the age of eighty-three on May 11, 1920.

bedfordstmartins.com/ americanlit for research links on Howells

Howells's "Editha."   Writing about the short story, Howells observed that American writers had perfected the genre, in part because of the popularity of magazines and the public demand for brief, readable works. Although he preferred to write novels, Howells also wrote dozens of short stories. Few of them were as pointed or as political as "Editha," which Howells wrote in response to the Spanish-American War of 1898, an example of what he and other critics decried as the growing imperialism of the United States. The war was in part generated by American support for the

Cuban struggle for independence from Spain during the 1890s. The brutal suppression of the Cuban revolt aroused strong anti-Spanish sentiment in the United States, where public opinion was further inflamed by sensational coverage in the press. In February 1898, the U.S. battleship *Maine* blew up in Havana harbor, killing 266 American sailors. Blaming Spain, the press clamored for intervention, and two months later Congress declared what came to be called the "Newspaper War." Howells, who condemned the war as "a wicked, wanton thing," protested by signing petitions and later by writing "Editha." The story was published in *Harper's New Monthly Magazine,* for which Howells also wrote a monthly editorial column, and which devoted more space to political and social commentary after it came under new leadership in 1900. The text, including one of the three original illustrations, is taken from the first printing of the story in the January 1905 issue of *Harper's.*

Editha

This illustration is one of three that appeared in the first printing of Howells's story in *Harper's*. It's caption read, "Keep it – keep it – and read it sometime."

EDITHA

The air was thick with the war feeling, like the electricity of a storm which has not yet burst. Editha sat looking out into the hot spring afternoon, with her lips parted, and panting with the intensity of the question whether she could let him go. She had decided that she could not let him stay, when she saw him at the end of the still leafless avenue, making slowly up toward the house, with his head down, and his figure relaxed. She ran impatiently out on the veranda, to the edge of the steps, and imperatively demanded greater haste of him with her will before she called aloud to him, "George!"

He had quickened his pace in mystical response to her mystical urgence, before he could have heard her; now he looked up and answered, "Well?"

"Oh, how united we are!" she exulted, and then she swooped down the steps to him. "What is it?" she cried.

"It's war," he said, and he pulled her up to him, and kissed her.

She kissed him back intensely, but irrelevantly, as to their passion, and uttered from deep in her throat, "How glorious!"

"It's war," he repeated, without consenting to her sense of it; and she did not know just what to think at first. She never knew what to think of him; that made his mystery, his charm. All through their courtship, which was contemporaneous with the growth of the war feeling, she had been puzzled by his want of seriousness about it. He seemed to despise it even more than he abhorred it. She could have understood his abhorring any sort of bloodshed; that would have been a survival of his old life when he thought he would be a minister, and before he changed and took up the law. But making light of a cause so high and noble seemed to show a want of earnestness at the core of his being. Not but that she felt herself able to cope with a congenital defect of that sort, and make his love for her save him from himself. Now perhaps the miracle was already wrought in him. In the presence of the tremendous fact that he announced, all triviality seemed to have gone out of him; she began to feel that. He sank down on the top step, and wiped his forehead with his handkerchief, while she poured out upon him her question of the origin and authenticity of his news.

All the while, in her duplex emotioning, she was aware that now at the very beginning she must put a guard upon herself against urging him, by any word or act, to take the part that her whole soul willed him to take, for the completion of her ideal of him. He was very nearly perfect as he was, and he must be allowed to perfect himself. But he was peculiar, and he might very well be reasoned out of his peculiarity. Before her reasoning went her emotioning: her nature pulling upon his nature, her womanhood upon his manhood, without her knowing the means she was using to the end she was willing. She had always supposed that the man who won her would have done something to win her; she did not know what, but something. George Gearson had simply asked her for her love, on the way home from a concert, and she gave her love to him, without, as it were, thinking. But now, it flashed upon her, if he could do something worthy to *have* won her — be a hero, *her* hero — it would be even better than if he had done it before asking her; it would be grander. Besides, she had believed in the war from the beginning.

"But don't you see, dearest," she said, "that it wouldn't have come to this, if it hadn't been in the order of Providence? And I call any war glorious that is for the liberation of people who have been struggling for years against the cruelest oppression. Don't you think so too?"

"I suppose so," he returned, languidly. "But war! Is it glorious to break the peace of the world?"

"That ignoble peace! It was no peace at all, with that crime and shame at our very gates." She was conscious of parroting the current phrases of the newspapers, but it was no time to pick and choose her words. She must sacrifice anything to the high ideal she had for him, and after a good deal of rapid argument she ended with the climax: "But now it doesn't matter about the how or why. Since the war has come, all that is gone. There are no two sides, any more. There is nothing now but our country."

He sat with his eyes closed and his head leant back against the veranda, and he said with a vague smile, as if musing aloud, "Our country – right or wrong."

"Yes, right or wrong!" she returned fervidly. "I'll go and get you some lemonade." She rose rustling, and whisked away; when she came back with two tall glasses of clouded liquid, on a tray, and the ice clucking in them, he still sat as she had left him, and she said as if there had been no interruption: "But there is no question of wrong in this case. I call it a sacred war. A war for liberty, and humanity, if ever there was one. And I know you will see it just a I do, yet."

He took half the lemonade at a gulp, and he answered as he set the glass down: "I know you always have the highest ideal. When I differ from you, I ought to doubt myself."

A generous sob rose in Editha's throat for the humility of a man, so very nearly perfect, who was willing to put himself below her.

Besides she felt, more subliminally, that he was never so near slipping through her fingers as when he took that meek way.

"You shall not say that! Only, for once I happen to be right." She seized his hand in her two hands, and poured her soul from her eyes into his. "Don't you think so?" she entreated him.

He released his hand and drank the rest of his lemonade, and she added, "Have mine, too," but he shook his head in answering, "I've no business to think so, unless I act so, too."

Her heart stopped a beat, before it pulsed on with leaps that she felt in her neck. She had noticed that strange thing in men; they seemed to feel bound to do what they believed, and not think a thing was finished when they said it, as girls did. She knew what was in his mind, but she pretended not, and she said, "Oh, I am not sure," and then faltered.

He went on as if to himself without apparently heeding her, "There's only one way of proving one's faith in a thing like this."

She could not say that she understood, but she did understand.

He went on again. "If I believed – if I felt as you do about this war – Do you wish me to feel as you do?"

Now he was really not sure; so she said, "George, I don't know what you mean."

He seemed to muse away from her as before. "There is a sort of fascination in it. I suppose that at the bottom of his heart every man would like at times to have his courage tested; to see how he would act."

"How can you talk in that ghastly way!"

"It *is* rather morbid. Still, that's what it comes to, unless you're swept away by ambition, or driven by conviction. I haven't the conviction or the ambition, and the other thing is what it comes to with me. I ought to have been a preacher, after all; then I couldn't have asked it of myself, as I must, now I'm a lawyer. And you believe it's a holy war, Editha?" he suddenly addressed her. "Or, I know you do! But you wish me to believe so, too?"

She hardly knew whether he was mocking or not, in the ironical way he always had with her plainer mind. But the only thing was to be outspoken with him.

"George, I wish you to believe whatever you think is true, at any and every cost. If I've tried to talk you into anything, I take it all back."

"Oh, I know that, Editha. I know how sincere you are, and how — I wish I had your undoubting spirit! I'll think it over; I'd like to believe as you do. But I don't, now; I don't, indeed. It isn't this war alone; though this seems peculiarly wanton and needless; but it's every war — so stupid; it makes me sick. Why shouldn't this thing have been settled reasonably?"

"Because," she said, very throatily again, "God meant it to be war."

"You think it was God? Yes, I suppose that is what people will say."

"Do you suppose it would have been war if God hadn't meant it?"

"I don't know. Sometimes it seems as if God had put this world into men's keeping to work it as they pleased."

"Now, George, that is blasphemy."

"Well, I won't blaspheme. I'll try to believe in your pocket Providence," he said, and then he rose to go.

"Why don't you stay to dinner?" Dinner at Balcom's Works was at one o'clock.

"I'll come back to supper, if you'll let me. Perhaps I shall bring you a convert."

"Well, you may come back, on that condition."

"All right. If I don't come, you'll understand."

He went away without kissing her, and she felt it a suspension of their engagement. It all interested her intensely; she was undergoing a tremendous experience, and she was being equal to it. While she stood looking after him, her mother came out through one of the long windows, on to the veranda, with a catlike softness and vagueness.

"Why didn't he stay to dinner?"

"Because — because — war has been declared," Editha pronounced, without turning.

Her mother said, "Oh, my!" and then said nothing more until she had sat down in one of the large Shaker chairs, and rocked herself for some time. Then she closed whatever tacit passage of thought there had been in her mind with the spoken words, "Well, I hope *he* won't go."

"And *I* hope he *will*," the girl said, and confronted her mother with a stormy exaltation that would have frightened any creature less unimpressionable than a cat.

Her mother rocked herself again for an interval of cogitation. What she arrived at in speech was, "Well, I guess you've done a wicked thing, Editha Balcom."

The girl said, as she passed indoors through the same window her mother had come out by, "I haven't done anything — yet."

In her room, she put together all her letters and gifts from Gearson, down to the with-ered petals of the first flower he had offered, with that timidity of his veiled in that irony of his. In the heart of the packet she enshrined her engagement ring which she had restored to the pretty box he had brought it her in. Then she sat down, if not calmly yet strongly, and wrote:

"GEORGE: I understood — when you left me. But I think we had better emphasize your meaning that if we cannot be one in everything we had better be one in nothing. So I am sending these things for your keeping till you have made up your mind.

"I shall always love you, and therefore I shall never marry any one else. But the man I marry must love his country first of all, and be able to say to me,

> 'I could not love thee, dear, so much,
> Loved I not honor more.'[1]

"There is no honor above America with me. In this great hour there is no other honor.

"Your heart will make my words clear to you. I had never expected to say so much, but it has come upon me that must say the utmost.   EDITHA"

She thought she had worded her letter well, worded it in a way that could not be bet-tered; all had been implied and nothing expressed.

She had it ready to send with the packet she had tied with red, white, and blue ribbon, when it occurred to her that she was not just to him, that she was not giving him a fair chance. He had said he would go and think it over, and she was not waiting. She was pushing, threatening, compelling. That was not a woman's part. She must leave him free, free, free. She could not accept for her country or herself a forced sacrifice.

In writing her letter she had satisfied the impulse from which it sprang; she could well afford to wait till he had thought it over. She put the packet and the letter by, and rested serene in the consciousness of having done what was laid upon her by her love itself to do, and yet used patience, mercy, justice.

She had her reward. Gearson did not come to tea, but she had given him till morning, when, late at night there came up from the village the sound of a fife and drum with a tumult of voices, in shouting, singing, and laughing. The noise drew nearer and nearer; it reached the street end of the avenue; there it silenced itself, and one voice, the voice she knew best, rose over the silence. It fell; the air was filled with cheers; the fife and drum struck up, with the shouting singing, and laughing again, but now retreating; and a single figure came hurrying up the avenue.

She ran down to meet her lover and clung to him. He was very gay, and he put his arm round her with a boisterous laugh. "Well, you must call me Captain, now; or Cap, if you prefer; that's what the boys call me. Yes, we've had a meeting at the town hall, and every-body has volunteered; and they selected me for captain, and I'm going to the war, the big

---

1. I . . . more: The famous lines are from "To Lucasta, Going to the Wars," by the English poet Richard Lovelace (1618-1658).

war, the glorious war, the holy war ordained by the pocket Providence that blesses butchery. Come along; let's tell the whole family about it. Call them from their downy beds, father, mother, Aunt Hitty, and all the folks!"

But when they mounted the veranda steps he did not wait for a larger audience; he poured the story out upon Editha alone.

"There was a lot of speaking, and then some of the fools set up a shout for me. It was all going one way, and I thought it would be a good joke to sprinkle a little cold water on them. But you can't do that with a crowd that adores you. The first thing I knew I was sprinkling hell-fire on them. 'Cry havoc, and let slip the dogs of war.'[2] That was the style. Now that it had come to the fight, there were no two parties; there was one country, and the thing was to fight the fight to a finish as quick as possible. I suggested volunteering then and there, and I wrote my name first of all on the roster. Then they elected me — that's all. I wish I had some ice-water!"

She left him walking up and down the veranda, while she ran for the ice-pitcher a goblet, and when she came back he was still walking up and down, shouting the story he had told her to her father and mother, who had come out more sketchily dressed than they commonly were by day. He drank goblet after goblet of the ice-water without noticing who was giving it, and kept on talking, and laughing through his talk wildly. "It's astonishing," he said, "how well the worse reason looks when you try to make it appear the better. Why, I believe I was the first convert to the war in that crowd to-night! I never thought I should like to kill a man; but now, I shouldn't care; and the smokeless powder lets you see the man drop that you kill. It's all for the country! What a thing it is to have a country that *can't* be wrong, but if it is, is right anyway!"

Editha had a great, vital thought, an inspiration. She set down the ice-pitcher on the veranda floor, and ran up-stairs and got the letter she had written him. When at last he noisily bade her father and mother, "Well, good night. I forgot I woke you up; I sha'n't want any sleep myself," she followed him down the avenue to the gate. There, after the whirling words that seemed to fly away from her thoughts and refuse to serve them, she made a last effort to solemnize the moment that seemed so crazy, and pressed the letter she had written upon him.

"What's this?" he said. "Want me to mail it?"

"No, no. It's for you. I wrote it after you went this morning. Keep it — keep it — and read it sometime —" She thought, and then her inspiration came: "Read it if ever you doubt what you've done, or fear that I regret your having done it. Read it after you've started."

They strained each other in embraces that seemed as ineffective as their words, and he kissed her face with quick, hot breaths that were so unlike him, that made her feel as if she had lost her old lover and found a stranger in his place. The stranger said, "What a gorgeous flower you are, with your red hair, and your blue eyes that look black now, and your face with the color painted out by the white moonshine! Let me hold you under my chin, to see whether I love blood, you tiger-lily!" Then he laughed Gearson's laugh, and

---

2. **Cry . . . war:** The line is from Mark Antony's soliloquy following the assassination of Caesar in Shakespeare's *Julius Caesar,* 3.1.273.

released her, scared and giddy. Within her wilfulness she had been frightened by a sense of subtler force in him, and mystically mastered as she had never been before.

She ran all the way back to the house, and mounted the steps panting. Her mother and father were talking of the great affair. Her mother said: "Wa'n't Mr. Gearson in rather of an excited state of mind? Didn't you think he acted curious?"

"Well, not for a man who'd just been elected captain and had to set 'em up for the whole of Company A," her father chuckled back.

"What in the world do you mean, Mr. Balcom? Oh! There's Editha!" She offered to follow the girl indoors.

"Don't come, mother!" Editha called, vanishing.

Mrs. Balcom remained to reproach her husband. "I don't see much of anything to laugh at."

"Well, it's catching. Caught it from Gearson. I guess it won't be much of a war, and I guess Gearson don't think so, either. The other fellows will back down as soon as they see we mean it. I wouldn't lose any sleep over it. I'm going back to bed, myself."

Gearson came again next afternoon, looking pale, and rather sick, but quite himself, even to his languid irony. "I guess I'd better tell you, Editha, that I consecrated myself to your god of battles last night by pouring too many libations to him down my own throat. But I'm all right, now. One has to carry off the excitement, somehow."

"Promise me," she commanded, "that you'll never touch it again!"

"What! Not let the cannikin clink? Not let the soldier drink?[3] Well, I promise."

"You don't belong to yourself now; you don't even belong to *me*. You belong to your country, and you have a sacred charge to keep yourself strong and well for your country's sake. I have been thinking, thinking all night and all day long."

"You look as if you had been crying a little, too," he said with his queer smile.

"That's all past. I've been thinking, and worshipping *you*. Don't you suppose I know all that you've been through, to come to this? I've followed you every step from your old theories and opinions."

"Well, you've had a long row to hoe."

"And I know you've done this from the highest motives —"

"Oh, there won't be much pettifogging to do till this cruel war is —"

"And you haven't simply done it for my sake. I couldn't respect you if you had."

"Well, then we'll say I haven't. A man that hasn't got his own respect intact wants the respect of all the other people he can corner. But we won't go into that. I'm in for the thing now, and we've got to face our future. My idea is that this isn't going to be a very protracted struggle; we shall just scare the enemy to death before it comes to a fight at all. But we must provide for contingencies, Editha. If anything happens to me —"

"Oh, George!" She clung to him sobbing.

---

3. **Not let . . . the soldier drink?:** See the drinking song in Shakespeare's *Othello,* 3.2.72–76: "And let me the canakin clink, clink; / And let me the canakin clink: / A soldier's but a man; / A life's but a span; / Why then let a soldier drink." A canakin, later spelled *cannikin,* was an early term for a small can or drinking vessel.

"I don't want you to feel foolishly bound to my memory. I should hate that, wherever I happened to be."

"I am yours, for time and eternity — time and eternity." She liked the words; they satisfied her famine for phrases.

"Well, say eternity; that's all right; but time's another thing; and I'm talking about time. But there is something! My mother! If anything happens —"

She winced, and he laughed. "You're not the bold soldier-girl of yesterday!" Then he sobered. "If anything happens, I want you to help my mother out. She won't like my doing this thing. She brought me up to think war a fool thing as well as a bad thing. My father was in the civil war; all through it; lost his arm in it." She thrilled with the sense of the arm round her; what if that should be lost? He laughed as if divining her: "Oh, it doesn't run in the family, as far as I know!" Then he added, gravely, "He came home with misgivings about war, and they grew on him. I guess he and mother agreed between them that I was to be brought up in his final mind about it; but that was before my time. I only knew him from my mother's report of him and his opinions; I don't know whether they were hers first; but they were hers last. This will be a blow to her. I shall have to write and tell her —"

He stopped, and she asked, "Would you like me to write too, George?"

"I don't believe that would do. No, I'll do the writing. She'll understand a little if I say that I thought the way to minimize it was to make war on the largest possible scale at once — that I felt I must have been helping on the war somehow if I hadn't helped keep it from coming, and I knew I hadn't; when it came, I had no right to stay out of it."

Whether his sophistries satisfied him or not, they satisfied her. She clung to his breast, and whispered, with closed eyes and quivering lips, "Yes, yes, yes!"

"But if anything should happen, you might go to her, and see what you could do for her. You know? It's rather far off; she can't leave her chair —"

"Oh, I'll go, if it's the ends of the earth! But nothing will happen! Nothing *can!* I —"

She felt herself lifted with his rising, and Gearson was saying, with his arm still round her, to her father: "Well, we're off at once, Mr. Balcom. We're to be formally accepted at the capital, and then bunched up with the rest somehow, and sent into camp somewhere, and got to the front as soon as possible. We all want to be in the van, of course; we're the first company to report to the Governor. I came to tell Editha, but I hadn't got round to it."

She saw him again for a moment at the capital, in the station, just before the train started southward with his regiment. He looked well, in his uniform, and very soldierly, but somehow girlish, too, with his clean-shaven face and slim figure. The manly eyes and the strong voice satisfied her, and his preoccupation with some unexpected details of duty flattered her. Other girls were weeping and bemoaning themselves, but she felt a sort of noble distinction in the abstraction, the almost unconsciousness, with which they parted. Only at the last moment he said, "Don't forget my mother. It mayn't be such a walk-over as I supposed," and he laughed at the notion.

He waved his hand to her, as the train moved off — she knew it among a score of hands that were waved to other girls from the platform of the car, for it held a letter which she knew was hers. Then he went inside the car to read it, doubtless, and she did not see him again. But she felt safe for him through the strength of what she called her love. What she called her God, always speaking the name in a deep voice and with the implication of a mutual understanding, would watch over him and keep him and bring him back to her. If with an empty sleeve, then he should have three arms instead of two, for both of hers should be his for life. She did not see, though, why she should always be thinking of the arm his father had lost.

There were not many letters from him, but they were such as she could have wished, and she put her whole strength into making hers such as she imagined he could have wished, glorifying and supporting him. She wrote to his mother glorifying him as their hero, but the brief answer she got was merely to the effect that Mrs. Gearson was not well enough to write herself, and thanking her for her letter by the hand of some one who called herself "Yrs truly, Mrs. W. J. Andrews."

Editha determined not to be hurt, but to write again quite as if the answer had been all she expected. But before it seemed as if she could have written, there came news of the first skirmish, and in the list of the killed which was telegraphed as a trifling loss on our side, was Gearson's name. There was a frantic time of trying to make out that it might be, must be, some other Gearson; but the name, and the company and the regiment, and the State were too definitely given.

Then there was a lapse into depths out of which it seemed as if she never could rise again; then a lift into clouds far above all grief, black clouds, that blotted out the sun, but where she soared with him, with George, George! She had the fever that she expected of herself, but she did not die in it; she was not even delirious, and it did not last long. When she was well enough to leave her bed, her one thought was of George's mother, of his strangely worded wish that she should go to her and see what she could do for her. In the exaltation of the duty laid upon her — it buoyed her up instead of burdening her — she rapidly recovered.

Her father went with her on the long railroad journey from northern New York to western Iowa; he had business out at Davenport, and he said he could just as well go then as any other time; and he went with her to the little country town where George's mother lived in a little house on the edge of illimitable corn-fields, under trees pushed to a top of the rolling prairie. George's father had settled there after the civil war, as so many other old soldiers had done; but they were Eastern people, and Editha fancied touches of the East in the June rose overhanging the front door, and the garden with early summer flowers stretching from the gate of the paling fence.

It was very low inside the house, and so dim, with the closed blinds, that they could scarcely see one another: Editha tall and black in her crapes which filled the air with the smell of their dyes; her father standing decorously apart with his hat on his forearm, as at funerals; a woman rested in a deep armchair, and the woman who had let the strangers in stood behind the chair.

The seated woman turned her head round and up, and asked the woman behind her chair, "*Who* did you say?"

Editha, if she had done what she expected of herself, would have gone down on her knees at the feet of the seated figure and said, "I am George's Editha," for answer.

But instead of her own voice she heard that other woman's voice, saying, "Well, I don't know as I *did* get the name just right. I guess I'll have to make a little more light in here," and she went and pushed two of the shutters ajar.

Then Editha's father said in his public will-now-address-a-few-remarks tone, "My name is Balcom, ma'am; Junius H. Balcom, of Balcom's Works, New York; my daughter —"

"Oh!" The seated woman broke in, with a powerful voice, the voice that always surprised Editha from Gearson's slender frame. "Let me see you! Stand round where the light can strike on your face," and Editha dumbly obeyed. "So, you're Editha Balcom," she sighed.

"Yes," Editha said, more like a culprit than a comforter.

"What did you come for?" Mrs. Gearson asked.

Editha's face quivered, and her knees shook. "I came — because — because George —" She could go no farther.

"Yes," the mother said, "he told me he had asked you to come if he got killed. You didn't expect that, I suppose, when you sent him."

"I would rather have died myself than done it!" Editha said with more truth in her deep voice than she ordinarily found in it. "I tried to leave him free —"

"Yes, that letter of yours, that came back with his other things, left him free."

Editha saw now where George's irony came from.

"It was not to be read before — unless — until — I told him so," she faltered.

"Of course, he wouldn't read a letter of yours, under the circumstances, till he thought you wanted him to. Been sick?" the woman abruptly demanded.

"Very sick," Editha said, with self-pity.

"Daughter's life," her father interposed, "was almost despaired of, at one time."

Mrs. Gearson gave him no heed. "I suppose you would have been glad to die, such a brave person as you! I don't believe *he* was glad to die. He was always a timid boy, that way; he was afraid of a good many things; but if he was afraid he did what he made up his mind to. I suppose he made up his mind to go, but I knew what it cost him, by what it cost me when I heard of it. I had been through *one* war before. When you sent him you didn't expect he would get killed."

The voice seemed to compassionate Editha, and it was time. "No," she huskily murmured.

"No, girls don't; women don't, when they give their men up to their country. They think they'll come marching back, somehow, just as gay as they went, or if it's an empty sleeve, or even an empty pantaloon, it's all the more glory, and they're so much the prouder of them, poor things."

The tears began to run down Editha's face; she had not wept till then; but it was now such a relief to be understood that the tears came.

"No, you didn't expect him to get killed," Mrs. Gearson repeated in a voice which was startlingly like George's again. "You just expected him to kill some one else, some of those foreigners, that weren't there because they had any say about it, but because they had to be there, poor wretches — conscripts, or whatever they call 'em. You thought it would be all right for my George, *your* George, to kill the sons of those miserable mothers and the husbands of those girls that you would never see the faces of." The woman lifted her powerful voice in a psalmlike note. "I thank my God he didn't live to do it! I thank my God they killed him first, and that he ain't livin' with their blood on his hands!" She dropped her eyes which she had raised with her voice, and glared at Editha. "What you got that black on for?" She lifted herself by her powerful arms so high that her helpless body seemed to hang limp its full length. "Take it off, take it off, before I tear it from your back!"

The lady who was passing the summer near Balcom's Works was sketching Editha's beauty, which lent itself wonderfully to the effects of a colorist. It had come to that confidence which is rather apt to grow between artist and sitter, and Editha had told her everything.

"To think of your having such a tragedy in your life!" the lady said. She added: "I suppose there are people who feel that way about war. But when you consider the good this war has done — how much it has done for the country! I can't understand such people, for my part. And when you had come all the way out there to console her — got up out of a sick bed! Well!"

"I think," Editha said, magnanimously, "she wasn't quite in her right mind; and so did papa."

"Yes," the lady said, looking at Editha's lips in nature and then at her lips in art, and giving an empirical touch to them in the picture. "But how dreadful of her! How perfectly — excuse me — how *vulgar!*"

A light broke upon Editha in the darkness which she felt had been without a gleam of brightness for weeks and months. The mystery that had bewildered her was solved by the word; and from that moment she rose from grovelling in shame and self-pity, and began to live again in the ideal.

[1905]

Ambrose Bierce

[1842–1914?]

Ambrose Gwinnett Bierce was born in Horse Cave Creek, in southeastern Ohio, on June 24, 1842. He was the youngest of the ten surviving children of Laura and Marcus Aurelius Bierce, both of whom could trace their ancestors to the earliest settlers in New England. Bierce's father, who struggled to earn a living by farming and working at various trades, was an avid reader and collector of books. By some accounts, he had the largest personal library in Kosciusko County, Indiana, where the family moved in 1846. Bierce attended school there for a time, but in 1857 he left home and moved to Warsaw, Indiana, to work as an apprentice in the print shop of an antislavery newspaper, the *Northern Indianan.* His apprenticeship ended abruptly, perhaps because of a disagreement with the publisher, and the alienated young man went to live with his uncle Lucius Verus Bierce, a politician and militant abolitionist, in Akron, Ohio. Bierce later attended the Kentucky Military Institute for a year before dropping out and returning to Indiana. In April 1861, almost immediately after the Civil War broke out and two months before his nineteenth birthday, Bierce enlisted in the Ninth Indiana Volunteers of the Union army. Rising to the rank of brevet captain, he fought with distinction in some of the bloodiest battles of the Civil War: Shiloh, Chickamauga, Missionary Ridge, and Kennesaw Mountain, site of some of the heaviest fighting in General Sherman's Atlanta campaign, where Bierce received a serious head wound in June 1864.

Ambrose Bierce
J. H. E. Partington painted this dramatic portrait of Bierce — posed with his elbow leaning on a table next to a skull, the symbol of mortality, transience, and the vanity of life — in the 1890s.

Those harsh war experiences profoundly shaped his outlook on life, as well as his satirical and often bitter writings. After being mustered out of the army in January 1865, Bierce worked as a federal treasury agent in the South before joining a military expedition to inspect forts and outposts across the West. In 1867, he arrived in San Francisco, which by then had become an important center of publication and a magnet for aspiring journalists and writers. Bierce, who later met Mark Twain and who became friends with Bret Harte and other writers of the "San Francisco Circle," soon began to publish poems and essays in the *Californian*, a weekly literary journal, and the *San Francisco News-Letter and California Advertiser*. In 1868, he became editor of the *News-Letter*, for which he also wrote a popular column, "The Town Crier." Bierce published his first short story in the most prestigious of western literary journals, the *Overland Monthly*, in 1871. That year, he married Mary Ellen Day, the daughter of a wealthy miner, and the couple moved to England. There, Bierce wrote regularly for two popular magazines of humor and satire, *Fun* and *Figaro*, and published three collections of his journalistic writings under the pen name "Dod Grile." After returning to the United States in 1875, Bierce worked at various jobs before resuming his career as a journalist in San Francisco. In 1881, he became the editor of aptly named *Wasp*, in which Bierce became increasingly notorious for his stinging reviews. One of them was a single sentence: "The covers of this book are too far apart." Although Bierce was generous to beginning writers, he was often irreverent about established ones, attacking such respected figures as William Dean Howells, Henry James, and even the much-loved English novelist Charles Dickens.

Well known even by the initials with which he frequently signed his journalism, "A.G.B.," Bierce's influence became so great that his numerous enemies derisively called him "Almighty God Bierce." In 1887, he accepted a position as a columnist and editorial writer for William Randolph Hearst's popular, scandalous, and sensational *San Francisco Examiner*. For the next ten years, Bierce wrote for the *Examiner* and other Hearst publications, producing a wide variety of work, including short stories on subjects ranging from the supernatural to the Civil War. His collection of war stories, *Tales of Soldiers and Civilians,* appeared in 1892. His other most famous work was *The Cynic's Word Book* (1906), a collection of aphorisms and epigrams he later entitled *The Devil's Dictionary* (1911). In it, he satirically reinterpreted words such as *history,* which Bierce defined as "[a]n account mostly false, of events mostly unimportant, which are brought about by rulers mostly knaves, and soldiers mostly fools." At the same time, his personal history was shadowed by his estrangement from his wife and the death of his two sons. In 1913, the seventy-one-year-old Bierce bid good-bye to his friends and his daughter and set off to meet Pancho Villa, one of the leaders of the Mexican Revolution. "To be a Gringo in Mexico – ah, that is euthanasia," Bierce observed in a letter. At the end of December 1913, he disappeared and was never heard from or seen again. "The old gringo came to Mexico to die," is the simple explanation offered by a character in *The Old Gringo* (1985), a fictionalized account of Bierce's final months by the Mexican novelist Carlos Fuentes.

bedfordstmartins.com/ *americanlit* for research links on Bierce

Bierce's "Chickamauga."   First published on the front page of the Sunday edition of William Randolph Hearst's influential *San Francisco Examiner,* "Chickamauga" is among the most powerful antiwar stories in American literature. The story is set during the battle of Chickamauga, September 18-20, 1863, fought in northern Georgia as part of the fierce struggle for control of Chattanooga, a key rail center at the heart of the Confederacy. The bloody battle, which claimed an estimated 35,000 casualties, ended with the rout and retreat of the Union troops, including the twenty-one-year-old Bierce. Although he accurately describes the landscape of the battle, Bierce in "Chickamauga" does not focus on military goals and tactics or even directly on the experiences of soldiers. Instead, he adopts the perspective of a young Southern boy, confused by what he encounters during the course of an afternoon and evening near his plantation home. Bierce's grim story was probably not wholly surprising to the readers of the *San Francisco Examiner,* who were accustomed to the newspaper's graphic, even sensational reporting of local, national, and international events. In fact, the story appeared at a time when the United States was on the brink of a war with Germany over American interests in the Samoan Islands. Most newspaper coverage of the potential conflict tended to romanticize the idea of war, but Bierce had extensive, firsthand knowledge of its terrible reality, which he vividly captures in "Chickamauga." The text of the story is taken from its first printing in the *San Francisco Examiner,* January 20, 1889.

Battle of Chickamauga
Published in 1890 by a firm that specialized in commemorative prints, especially battle scenes of the Civil War, this lithograph is an idealized representation of the repeated Confederate assaults on the Union line during the bloody two-day battle in Georgia.

CHICKAMAUGA

One sunny Autumn afternoon a child strayed away from its rude home in a small field and entered a forest unobserved. It was happy in a new sense of freedom from control — happy in the opportunity of exploration and adventure; for this child's spirit, in bodies of its ancestors, had for many thousands of years been trained to memorable feats of discovery and conquest — notorious in battles whose critical moments were centuries, whose victors' camps were great cities of hewn stone. From the cradle of its race it had conquered its way through two continents and, passing a great sea, had penetrated a third, there to be born to war and dominance as a heritage.

The child was a boy, aged about six years; the son of a poor planter. In his younger manhood the father had been a soldier; had fought against naked savages and followed the flag of his country into the capital of a civilized race to the far South. In the peaceful life of a planter the warrior-fire survived; once kindled it is never extinguished. The man loved military books and pictures, and the boy had understood enough to make himself a wooden sword, though even the eye of his father would hardly have known it for what it was. This weapon he now bore bravely, as became the son of an heroic race, and pausing now and again in the sunny interspaces of the forest assumed, with some exaggeration, the postures of aggression and defense that he had been taught by the engraver's art. Made reckless by the ease with which he overcame invisible foes attempting to stay his advance, he committed the common enough military error of pushing the pursuit to a dangerous extreme, until he found himself upon the margin of a wide but shallow brook, whose rapid waters barred his direct advance against the flying foe who had crossed with illogical ease. But the intrepid victor was not to be baffled: the spirit of the race which had passed the great sea burned unconquerable in that small breast and would not be denied. Finding a place where some bowlders in the bed of the stream lay but a step or a leap apart, he made his way across and fell again upon the rear-guard of his imaginary foe, putting all to the sword.

Now that the battle had been won, prudence required that he withdraw to his base of operations. Alas! like many a mightier conquerer, and like one, the mightiest, he could not

> curb the lust for war,
> Nor learn that tempted Fate will leave the loftiest star.[1]

Advancing from the bank of the creek, he suddenly found himself confronted with a new and more formidable enemy: in the path that he was following, bolt upright, with ears erect and paws suspended before it, sat a rabbit! With a startled cry the child turned and fled, he knew not in what direction, calling upon his mother, weeping, stumbling, his tender skin cruelly torn by brambles, his little heart beating hard with terror — breathless, blind with tears — lost in the forest! Then, for more than an hour, he wandered with aimless feet through the tangled under-growth, till at last, overcome with fatigue, he lay down between two rocks within a few yards of the stream and, still grasping his toy sword, no longer a weapon but a companion, sobbed himself to sleep. The wood-birds sang merrily above his head, the squirrels, whisking their bravery of tail, ran barking from tree to tree, unconscious of the pity of it, and from somewhere far away came a strange, muffled thunder, as if the partridges were drumming in celebration of Nature's victory over the son of her immemorial enslavers. And back at the little plantation, where white men and black were hastily searching the fields and hedgerows in alarm, a mother's heart was breaking for her missing child.

Hours passed, and then the little sleeper rose to his feet. The chill of the evening was in his limbs, the fear of the gloom in his heart. But he had rested, and he no longer wept. With some blind instinct which impelled to action, he struggled through the under-

---

1. **curb . . . star:** The lines are from *Childe Harold's Pilgrimage*, canto 3, 38:341–42, by the English poet George Gordon, Lord Byron (1788–1824).

growth about him and came to a more open ground — on his right the brook, to the left a gentle acclivity studded with infrequent trees; over all, the gathering gloom of twilight. A thin ghostly mist rose along the water. It frightened and repelled him; instead of recrossing, in the direction whence he came, he turned his back upon it and went forward toward the dark inclosing wood. Suddenly he saw before him a strange moving object, which he took to be some large animal — a dog, a pig — he could not name it; perhaps it was a bear. He had seen pictures of bears, but knew of nothing to their discredit, and had vaguely wished to meet one. But something in form or movement of this object — something in the awkwardness of its approach told him that it was not a bear, and curiosity was stayed by fear. He stood still, and as it came slowly on, gained courage every moment, for he saw that it had not the long, menacing ears of the rabbit. Possibly his impressionable mind was half-conscious of something familiar in its shambling, awkward gait. Before it had approached near enough to resolve his doubts he saw that it was followed by another — and another. To right and to left were many more: the whole open space about him was alive with them — all moving forward toward the brook.

They were men. They crept upon their hands and knees; they used their hands only, dragging their legs; they used their knees only, their arms hanging useless at their sides; they strove to rise to their feet, but fell prone in the attempt. They did nothing naturally, and nothing alike, save only to advance foot by foot in the same direction. Singly, in pairs and in little groups, they came on through the gloom, some halting now and again while others crept slowly past them, then resuming their movement. They came by dozens and by hundreds: as far on either hand as one could see in the deepening gloom they extended, and the black wood behind them appeared to be inexhaustible. The very ground seemed in motion toward the creek. Occasionally one who had paused did not again go on, but lay as dead. He was dead. Some, pausing, made strange gestures with their hands; erected their arms and lowered them again; clasped their heads; spread their palms upward, as men are sometimes seen to do in public prayer.

Not all of this did the child note; it is what would have been noted by an older observer; he saw little but that these were men, yet crept like babes. Being men, they were not terrible, though some of them were singularly clad. He moved among them freely, going from one to another and peering into their faces with childish curiosity. All their faces were singularly white and many were streaked and gouted with red. Something in this — something too, perhaps, in their grotesque attitudes and movements — reminded him of the painted clown whom he had seen last summer in the circus, and he laughed as he watched them. But on and ever on they crept, these maimed and bleeding men, as heedless as he of the dramatic contrast between his laughter and their own ghastly gravity. To him it was a merry spectacle. He had seen his father's negroes creep upon their hands and knees for his amusement — had ridden them so, fancying them his horses. He now approached one of these crawling figures from behind and with an agile movement mounted it astride. The man sank upon his breast, recovered, flung the small body fiercely to the ground as an unbroken colt might have done, then turned upon him a face that lacked a lower jaw — from the upper teeth to the throat was a great red gap fringed with hanging shreds of flesh and splinters of bone. The unnatural prominence of nose, the absence of chin, the fierce eyes, gave this man the appearance of a great bird of prey crimsoned in throat and breast by the blood of its quarry. He rose to his knees, the child to his feet. The man shook his fist at the child; the child, terrified at last, ran to a tree near by, got upon the farther side of it and took a more serious view of the situation. And so the uncanny multitude dragged itself slowly and painfully along in hideous pantomime — moved forward down the slope like a swarm of great black beetles, with never a sound of going — in silence profound, absolute.

Instead of darkening, the haunted landscape began to brighten. Through the belt of trees beyond the brook shone a strange red light, the trunks and branches of the trees making a black lacework against it. It struck the creeping figures and gave them monstrous shadows which caricatured their movements on the lit grass. It fell upon their faces, touching their whiteness with a ruddy tinge, accentuating the stains with which so many of them were freaked and maculated. It sparkled on buttons and bits of metal in their clothing. Instinctively the child turned toward the growing splendor and moved down the slope with his horrible companions; in a few moments had passed the foremost of the throng — not much of a feat considering his advantages. He placed himself in the lead, his wooden sword still in hand, and solemnly directed the march, conforming his pace to theirs and occasionally turning as if to see that his forces did not straggle. Surely such a leader never before had such a following.

Scattered about upon the ground, now slowly narrowing by the encroachment of this awful march to water, were certain articles to which, in the leader's mind, were coupled no significant associations: an occasional blanket, tightly rolled lengthwise, doubled and the ends bound together with a string; a heavy knapsack here, and there a broken musket — such things, in short, as are found in the rear of retreating troops: the "spoor" of men flying from their hunters. Everywhere near the creek, which here had a margin of lowland, the earth was trodden into mud by the feet of men and horses. An observer of better experience in the use of his eyes would have noticed that these footprints pointed in both directions: the ground had been twice passed over — in advance and in retreat. A few hours before, these desperately stricken men, with their more fortunate and now distant comrades, had penetrated the forest in thousands. Their successive battalions' lines, breaking into swarms and reforming in lines, had passed the child on every side — had almost trodden on him as he slept. The rustle and murmur of their march had not awakened him. Almost within a stone's throw of where he lay they had fought a battle; but all unheard by him were the roar of the musketry, the shock of cannon, "the thunder of the captains and the shouting,"[2] He had slept through it all, grasping his little wooden sword with perhaps a tighter clutch in unconscious sympathy with his martial environment, but as hoodless of the grandeur of the struggle as the dead who died to make the glory.

The fire beyond the belt of woods on the farther side of the creek, reflected to earth from the canopy of its own smoke, was now suffusing the whole landscape. It transformed the sinuous line of mist to the vapor of gold. The water gleamed with dashes of

---

2. "the thunder . . . shouting": See Job 39:25: "He saith among the trumpets, Ha, ha; and he smelleth the battle afar off, the thunder of the captains, and the shouting."

red, and red, too, were many of the stones protruding above the surface. But that was blood; the less desperately wounded had stained them in crossing. On them, too, the child now crossed with eager steps: he was going to the fire. As he stood upon the farther bank he turned about to look at the companions of his march. The advance was arriving at the creek. The stronger had already drawn themselves to the brink and plunged their faces in the flood. Three or four who lay without motion appeared to have no heads. At this the child's eyes expanded with wonder: even his hospitable understanding could not accept a phenomenon implying such vitality as that. After slaking their thirst these men had not had the strength to back away from the water, nor to keep their heads above it. They were drowned. In rear of these, the open spaces of the forest showed the leader as many formless figures of his grim command as at first; but not half so many were in motion. He waved his cap for their encouragement and smiling pointed with his weapon in the direction of the guiding light – a pillar of fire to this strange exodus.[3]

Confident of the fidelity of his forces, he now entered the belt of woods, passed through it easily in the red illumination of its interspaces, climbed a fence, ran across a field, turning now and again to coquet with his responsive shadow, and so approached the blazing ruin of a dwelling. Desolation everywhere. In all the wide glare not a living thing was visible. He cared nothing for that; the spectacle pleased, and he danced with glee in imitation of the wavering flames. He ran about collecting fuel, but every object that he found was too heavy for him to cast it in his approach. In despair he flung in his sword – a surrender to the superior forces of nature. His military career was at an end.

Shifting his position, his eyes fell upon some outbuildings, which had an oddly familiar appearance, as if he had dreamed of them. He stood considering them with wonder, when suddenly the entire plantation, with its inclosed forest, seemed to turn as if upon a pivot. His little world swung half around; the points of the compass were reversed. He recognized the blazing building as his own home.

For a moment he stood stupefied by the power of the revelation; then ran with aimless feet, making a half circuit of the ruin. There, conspicuous, in the light of the conflagration, lay the dead body of a woman – the white face turned upward, the hands thrown all abroad and clutched full of grass, the clothing deranged, the long dark hair in tangles and full of clotted blood. The greater part of the forehead was torn away and from the jagged hole the brain protruded, overflowing the temple, a frothy mass of gray, crowned with clusters of crimson bubbles. The work of a shell.

The child moved his little hands, making wild, uncertain gestures. He uttered a series of inarticulate and indescribable cries – something between the chattering of an ape and the gobbling of a turkey – a startling, soulless, unholy sound – the language of a devil. He was a deaf mute.

Then he stood motionless, with quivering lips, looking down upon the wreck.

[1889]

---

3. **a pillar of fire to this strange exodus:** See the description of God leading the Israelites out of bondage in Egypt: "And the Lord went before them by day in a pillar of a cloud, to lead them the way; and by night in a pillar of fire, to give them light; to go by day and night" (Exodus 13:21).

Henry James

[1843-1916]

Henry James

This photograph was taken in the early 1880s, when James was about forty years old and living in London.

Henry James was born in New York City on April 15, 1843, the second child of affluent and cosmopolitan parents, Henry James Sr. and Mary Walsh James. Henry James Sr., a well-known writer who was deeply absorbed in philosophical and theological issues, was friendly with a number of prominent literary figures, including Ralph Waldo Emerson. James and his four siblings — including his elder brother, William, who would become one of America's foremost philosophers and psychologists, and his talented sister, Alice, whose vivid diary was finally published more than forty years after her tragically early death in 1892 — were initially educated by tutors and in private schools in New York City. Seeking to provide his children with greater cultural and educational opportunities, however, and dreading what he described as "those inevitable habits of extravagance and insubordination which appear to be the characteristics of American youth," James's father moved the family to Europe in 1855. During most of the following five years, James attended schools in England, France, Switzerland, and Germany — reading widely, learning to speak French and German, and becoming familiar with cathedrals, galleries, and theaters in cities across Europe. Shortly after the family returned to the United States in 1860, the country was plunged into the Civil War. Although his two younger brothers later enlisted in the Union army, James suffered a back injury that apparently precluded military service. Instead, he enrolled in Harvard Law School in the fall of 1862.

James, however, soon embarked on a literary career. He withdrew from Harvard in 1863, remained in Boston, and began writing reviews, sketches, and stories for two of the country's most influential literary journals, the *North American Review* and the *Atlantic Monthly,* as well as for the *Nation,* a magazine established in New York City in 1865. James also traveled extensively in Europe, writing travel sketches and collecting impressions that would become an important source of material for his later fiction. In a letter home to his mother in 1869, he observed:

> We [Americans] seem a people of *character,* we seem to have energy, capacity, and intellectual stuff in equal measure. What I have pointed out as our vices are the elements of the modern man with *culture* quite left out. It's the absolute and incredible lack of *culture* that strikes you in common traveling Americans.

At the same time, James suggested that one of the responsibilities of being an American was "fighting against a superstitious valuation of Europe," as he put it in a letter written in 1870. James thus began to develop what is called his "international theme," a central topic of his early fiction, in which he often focused on the experiences of Americans living or traveling in Europe. James charts the comic misadventures and sometimes tragic fates of such characters in the pieces collected as *A Passionate Pilgrim, and Other Tales* (1875) and *Transatlantic Sketches* (1875), as well as in his first two novels, *Roderick Hudson* (1875) and *The American* (1876). The novels were first serialized in the *Atlantic Monthly*, which by then was edited by his close friend William Dean Howells. James also cultivated friendships with distinguished European authors, especially Ivan Turgenev and Gustave Flaubert, whom he met during an extended stay in Paris during 1875-76.

In 1876, James decided to settle in London, where be became a major presence in the city's vibrant literary community. But he wrote for audiences on both sides of the Atlantic. James continued to explore the international theme in what are widely regarded as the most successful of his early works of fiction: *Daisy Miller: A Study* (1878), the novella that made him famous; and another remarkable "study" of a young American woman in Europe, *The Portrait of a Lady*, which was serialized in London's *Macmillan's Magazine* and the *Atlantic Monthly* during 1880-81. In those works, James displays his mastery of "The Art of Fiction," the title of an important essay he published in 1884. As both a critic and a prolific practitioner of that art, James helped raise fiction writing to a new level of seriousness. Yet none of his subsequent works achieved the popularity of *Daisy Miller* or *The Portrait of a Lady*. During a trip home to Boston, where both of his parents died in 1882, James determined "to write a very *American* tale, a tale very characteristic of our social conditions," as he described *The Bostonians* (1886). Serialized in New York's *Century Magazine*, the novel was sharply criticized for its satire of reformers and Boston culture. James was no more successful with *The Princess Casamassima* (1886) and *The Tragic Muse* (1889), naturalistic novels in which he turned his attention to politics and social conditions in England. Discouraged by the tepid reception and poor sales of his novels, James spent the years between 1890 and 1895 seeking to become a successful playwright. Two of his plays were produced in London, but both were commercial and critical failures. With the strong encouragement of William Dean Howells, who assured him that there was still an audience for his work in America as well as in England, James once again determined to make his living by writing fiction.

In 1897, James moved from London to his new home in the English countryside, Lamb House, where he lived and worked for the rest of his life. He continued his wide correspondence with other literary figures and formed close friendships with several younger American writers, including Stephen Crane and especially Edith Wharton. In what is sometimes called his "major phase," James at the turn of the century returned to the international theme in three long and complex novels: *The Wings of the Dove* (1902), *The Ambassadors* (1903), and *The Golden Bowl* (1904). Following an extended visit to the United States during 1904-05, after an absence of more than twenty years, James wrote a penetrating social and cultural critique of what had become "a vast, crude democracy of trade," as he describes the country in *The American Scene* (1907). James also prepared a collected edition of his works, revising many of them and writing

bedfordstmartins.com/ americanlit for research links on James prefaces to those he selected for inclusion in the New York edition of his *Novels and Tales* (1907-10). The twenty-six volume edition testified to his artistic achievement, but the expensive set was not a commercial success, and very few of his individual novels and collections of stories were still in print. James was also troubled by health problems and saddened by the passing of friends and his brothers William and Robertson, both of whom died in 1910. The only surviving member of his family, James was spurred to begin writing autobiographical books, *A Small Boy and Others* (1913), *Notes of a Son and Brother* (1914), and the posthumously published *The Middle Years* (1917). Distressed by the failure of the United States to join the Allied cause at the opening of World War I, James became a naturalized British citizen shortly before his death in London in 1916.

James's *Daisy Miller.* In the fall of 1877, during a trip to France and Italy, James encountered Alice Bartlett, one of several Americans living in Rome with whom he enjoyed warm friendships. Bartlett told him a story about a young American girl who had been thought to be too familiar with an Italian man and had become the subject of gossip. James made a note about the incident, the germ of *Daisy Miller: A Study*, which he wrote after returning to his home in London. He first submitted the novella to an American magazine, *Lippincott's*, whose editor immediately rejected it. A friend suggested to James that the editor viewed the work as "an outrage on American girlhood." James then submitted it to London's *Cornhill Magazine*, where the novella was published in two parts in the summer of 1878. The absence of an international copyright law in the United States allowed Harper Brothers to publish a pirated edition in New York City, a pamphlet that sold 20,000 copies in a few weeks. Although he did not profit from the publication of the pamphlet, James thus referred to "Daisy" as "the most prosperous child of my invention." His depiction of the young American girl infuriated some readers in the United States, but many others there applauded what they viewed as her spirited rejection of restrictive European convention. As James's friend William Dean Howells observed, "The thing went so far that society almost divided itself into Daisy Millerites and anti-Daisy Millerites." "Daisy Miller" hats were sold in American shops, while an English writer, Virginia W. Johnson, published *An English Daisy Miller*, an effort to capitalize on the popularity of the story by creating a version specifically designed to appeal to readers in Great Britain. The text is taken from the first printing in the *Cornhill Magazine* 37 (June–July 1878).

Daisy Miller

A Study

Part I

At the little town of Vevey, in Switzerland, there is a particularly comfortable hotel. There are, indeed, many hotels; for the entertainment of tourists is the business of the place, which, as many travellers will remember, is seated upon the edge of a remarkably blue lake[1] – a lake that it behooves every tourist to visit. The shore of the lake presents an unbroken array of establishments of this order, of every category, from the "grand hotel" of the newest fashion, with a chalk-white front, a hundred balconies, and a dozen flags flying from its roof, to the little Swiss *pension*[2] of an elder day, with its name inscribed in German-looking lettering upon a pink or yellow wall, and an awkward summer-house in the angle of the garden. One of the hotels at Vevey, however, is famous, even classical, being distinguished from many of its upstart neighbours by an air both of luxury and of maturity. In this region, in the month of June, American travellers are extremely numerous; it may be said, indeed, that Vevey assumes at this period some of the characteristics of an American watering-place. There are sights and sounds which evoke a vision, an echo, of Newport and Saratoga.[3] There is a flitting hither and thither of "stylish" young girls, a rustling of muslin flounces, a rattle of dance-music in the morning hours, a sound of high-pitched voices at all times. You receive an impression of these things at the excellent inn of the "Trois Couronnes,"[4] and are transported in fancy to the Ocean House or to Congress Hall.[5] But at the "Trois Couronnes," it must be added, there are other features that are much at variance with these suggestions: neat German waiters, who look like secretaries of legation; Russian princesses sitting in the garden; little Polish boys walking about, held by the hand, with their governors; a view of the sunny crest of the Dent du Midi[6] and the picturesque towers of the Castle of Chillon.[7]

I hardly know whether it was the analogies or the differences that were uppermost in the mind of a young American, who, two or three years ago, sat in the garden of the "Trois Couronnes," looking about him, rather idly, at some of the graceful objects I have mentioned. It was a beautiful summer morning, and in whatever fashion the young American looked at things, they must have seemed to him charming. He had come from Geneva the day before, by the little steamer, to see his aunt, who was staying at the hotel – Geneva having been for a long time his place of residence. But his aunt had a

---

1. **lake:** Lake Geneva.
2. *pension:* A boardinghouse (French).
3. **Newport and Saratoga:** Newport, Rhode Island, and Saratoga Springs, New York, were fashionable resort areas.
4. **"Trois Couronnes":** Three Crowns (French).
5. **Ocean House . . . Congress Hall:** Hotels in Newport and Saratoga Springs.
6. **Dent du Midi:** A mountain range in the Alps.
7. **Castle of Chillon:** Medieval castle on Lake Geneva made famous by "The Prisoner of Chillon" (1816), by the English poet George Gordon, Lord Byron (1788–1824).

headache – his aunt had almost always a headache – and now she was shut up in her room, smelling camphor, so that he was at liberty to wander about. He was some seven-and-twenty years of age; when his friends spoke of him, they usually said that he was at Geneva, "studying." When his enemies spoke of him they said – but, after all, he had no enemies; he was an extremely amiable fellow, and universally liked. What I should say is, simply, that when certain persons spoke of him they affirmed that the reason of his spending so much time at Geneva was that he was extremely devoted to a lady who lived there – a foreign lady – a person older than himself. Very few Americans – indeed I think none – had ever seen this lady, about whom there were some singular stories. But Winterbourne had an old attachment for the little metropolis of Calvinism;[8] he had been put to school there as a boy, and he had afterwards gone to college there – circumstances which had led to his forming a great many youthful friendships. Many of these he had kept, and they were a source of great satisfaction to him.

After knocking at his aunt's door and learning that she was indisposed, he had taken a walk about the town, and then he had come in to his breakfast. He had now finished his breakfast; but he was drinking a small cup of coffee, which had been served to him on a little table in the garden by one of the waiters who looked like an *attaché*.[9] At last he finished his coffee and lit a cigarette. Presently a small boy came walking along the path – an urchin of nine or ten. The child, who was diminutive for his years, had an aged expression of countenance, a pale complexion, and sharp little features. He was dressed in knickerbockers, with red stockings, which displayed his poor little spindleshanks; he also wore a brilliant red cravat. He carried in his hand a long alpenstock, the sharp point of which he thrust into everything that he approached – the flower-beds, the garden-benches, the trains of the ladies' dresses. In front of Winterbourne he paused, looking at him with a pair of bright, penetrating little eyes.

"Will you give me a lump of sugar?" he asked, in a sharp, hard little voice – a voice immature, and yet, somehow, not young.

Winterbourne glanced at the small table near him, on which his coffee-service rested, and saw that several morsels of sugar remained. "Yes, you may take one," he answered; "but I don't think sugar is good for little boys."

This little boy stepped forward and carefully selected three of the coveted fragments, two of which he buried in the pocket of his knickerbockers, depositing the other as promptly in another place. He poked his alpenstock, lance-fashion, into Winterbourne's bench, and tried to crack the lump of sugar with his teeth.

"Oh, blazes; it's har-r-d!" he exclaimed, pronouncing the adjective in a peculiar manner.

Winterbourne had immediately perceived that he might have the honour of claiming him as a fellow-countryman. "Take care you don't hurt your teeth," he said, paternally.

---

8. **metropolis of Calvinism:** The influential Protestant theologian and reformer John Calvin (1509–1564) fled from his native France to Switzerland, where he set up a theocratic government in Geneva.
9. *attaché:* A person on the staff of an ambassador (French).

"I haven't got any teeth to hurt. They have all come out. I have only got seven teeth. My mother counted them last night, and one came out right afterwards. She said she'd slap me if any more came out. I can't help it. It's this old Europe. It's the climate that makes them come out. In America they didn't come out. It's these hotels."

Winterbourne was much amused. "If you eat three lumps of sugar, your mother will certainly slap you," he said.

"She's got to give me some candy, then," rejoined his young interlocutor. "I can't get any candy here — any American candy. American candy's the best candy."

"And are American little boys the best little boys?" asked Winterbourne.

"I don't know. I'm an American boy," said the child.

"I see you are one of the best!" laughed Winterbourne.

"Are you an American man?" pursued this vivacious infant. And then, on Winterbourne's affirmative reply — "American men are the best," he declared.

His companion thanked him for the compliment; and the child, who had now got astride of his alpenstock, stood looking about him, while he attacked a second lump of sugar. Winterbourne wondered if he himself had been like this in his infancy, for he had been brought to Europe about this age.

"Here comes my sister!" cried the child, in a moment. "She's an American girl."

Winterbourne looked along the path and saw a beautiful young lady advancing. "American girls are the best girls," he said, cheerfully, to his young companion.

"My sister ain't the best!" the child declared. "She's always blowing at me."

"I imagine that is your fault, not hers," said Winterbourne. The young lady meanwhile had drawn near. She was dressed in white muslin, with a hundred frills and flounces, and knots of pale-coloured ribbon. She was bare-headed; but she balanced in her hand a large parasol, with a deep border of embroidery; and she was strikingly, admirably pretty. "How pretty they are!" thought Winterbourne, straightening himself in his seat, as if he were prepared to rise.

The young lady paused in front of his bench, near the parapet of the garden, which overlooked the lake. The little boy had now converted his alpenstock into a vaulting-pole, by the aid of which he was springing about in the gravel, and kicking it up not a little.

"Randolph," said the young lady, "what *are* you doing?"

"I'm going up the Alps," replied Randolph. "This is the way!" And he gave another little jump, scattering the pebbles about Winterbourne's ears.

"That's the way they come down," said Winterbourne.

"He's an American man!" cried Randolph, in his little hard voice.

The young lady gave no heed to this announcement, but looked straight at her brother. "Well, I guess you had better be quiet," she simply observed.

It seemed to Winterbourne that he had been in a manner presented. He got up and stepped slowly towards the young girl, throwing away his cigarette. "This little boy and I have made acquaintance," he said, with great civility. In Geneva, as he had been perfectly aware, a young man was not at liberty to speak to a young unmarried lady except under certain rarely-occurring conditions; but here at Vevey, what conditions could be better than these? — a pretty American girl coming and standing in front of you in a garden. This pretty American girl, however, on hearing Winterbourne's observation, simply glanced at him; she then turned her head and looked over the parapet, at the lake and the opposite mountains. He wondered whether he had gone too far; but he decided that he must advance farther, rather than retreat. While he was thinking of something else to say, the young lady turned to the little boy again.

"I should like to know where you got that pole," she said.

"I bought it!" responded Randolph.

"You don't mean to say you're going to take it to Italy."

"Yes, I am going to take it to Italy!" the child declared.

The young girl glanced over the front of her dress, and smoothed out a knot or two of ribbon. Then she rested her eyes upon the prospect again. "Well, I guess you had better leave it somewhere," she said, after a moment.

"Are you going to Italy?" Winterbourne inquired, in a tone of great respect.

The young lady glanced at him again. "Yes, sir," she replied. And he said nothing more.

"Are you — a — going over the Simplon[10]?" Winterbourne pursued, a little embarrassed.

"I don't know," she said. "I suppose its some mountain. Randolph, what mountain are we going over?"

"Going where?" the child demanded.

"To Italy," Winterbourne explained.

"I don't know," said Randolph. "I don't want to go to Italy. I want to go to America."

"Oh, Italy is a beautiful place!" rejoined the young man.

"Can you get candy there?" Randolph loudly inquired.

"I hope not," said his sister. "I guess you have had enough candy, and mother thinks so too."

"I haven't had any for ever so long — for a hundred weeks!" cried the boy, still jumping about.

The young lady inspected her flounces and smoothed her ribbons again; and Winterbourne presently risked an observation upon the beauty of the view. He was ceasing to be embarrassed, for he had begun to perceive that she was not in the least embarrassed herself. There had not been the slightest alteration in her charming complexion; she was evidently neither offended nor fluttered. If she looked another way when he spoke to her, and seemed not particularly to hear him, this was simply her habit, her manner. Yet, as he talked a little more, and pointed out some of the objects of interest in the view, with which she appeared quite unacquainted, she gradually gave him more of the benefit of her glance; and then he saw that this glance was perfectly direct and unshrinking. It was not, however, what would have been called an immodest glance, for the young girl's eyes were singularly honest and fresh. They were wonderfully pretty eyes; and,

---

10. **Simplon:**   In the early nineteenth century, a road between France and Italy was built in this pass through the Alps.

indeed, Winterbourne had not seen for a long time anything prettier than this fair coun-trywoman's various features — her complexion, her nose, her ears, her teeth. He had a great relish for feminine beauty; he was addicted to observing and analysing it; and as regards this young lady's face he made several observations. It was not at all insipid, but it was not exactly expressive; and though it was eminently delicate Winterbourne men-tally accused it — very forgivingly — of a want of finish. He thought it very possible that Master Randolph's sister was a coquette; he was sure she had a spirit of her own; but in her bright, sweet, superficial little visage there was no mockery, no irony. Before long it became obvious that she was much disposed towards conversation. She told him that they were going to Rome for the winter — she and her mother and Randolph. She asked him if he was a "real American"; she shouldn't have taken him for one; he seemed more like a German — this was said after a little hesitation, especially when he spoke. Winter-bourne, laughing, answered that he had met Germans who spoke like Americans; but that he had not, so far as he remembered, met an American who spoke like a German. Then he asked her if she should not be more comfortable in sitting upon the bench which he had just quitted. She answered that she liked standing up and walking about; but she presently sat down. She told him she was from New York State — "if you know where that is." Winterbourne learned more about her by catching hold of her small, slip-pery brother and making him stand a few minutes by his side.

"Tell me your name, my boy," he said.

"Randolph C. Miller," said the boy, sharply. "And I'll tell you her name"; and he lev-elled his alpenstock at his sister.

"You had better wait till you are asked!" said this young lady, calmly.

"I should like very much to know your name," said Winterbourne.

"Her name is Daisy Miller!" cried the child. "But that isn't her real name; that isn't her name on her cards."

"It's a pity you haven't got one of my cards!" said Miss Miller.

"Her real name is Annie P. Miller," the boy went on.

"Ask him *his* name," said his sister, indicating Winterbourne.

But on this point Randolph seemed perfectly indifferent; he continued to supply information with regard to his own family. "My father's name is Ezra B. Miller," he announced. "My father ain't in Europe; my father's in a better place than Europe."

Winterbourne imagined for a moment that this was the manner in which the child had been taught to intimate that Mr. Miller had been removed to the sphere of celestial rewards. But Randolph immediately added, "My father's in Schenectady. He's got a big business. My father's rich, you bet."

"Well!" ejaculated Miss Miller, lowering her parasol and looking at the embroidered border. Winterbourne presently released the child, who departed, dragging his alpen-stock along the path. "He doesn't like Europe," said the young girl. "He wants to go back."

"To Schenectady, you mean?"

"Yes; he wants to go right home. He hasn't got any boys here. There is one boy here, but he always goes round with a teacher; they won't let him play."

"And your brother hasn't any teacher?" Winterbourne inquired.

"Mother thought of getting him one, to travel round with us. There was a lady told her of a very good teacher; an American lady – perhaps you know her – Mrs. Sanders. I think she came from Boston. She told her of this teacher, and we thought of getting him to travel round with us. But Randolph said he didn't want a teacher travelling round with us. He said he wouldn't have lessons when he was in the cars.[11] And we *are* in the cars about half the time. There was an English lady we met in the cars – I think her name was Miss Featherstone; perhaps you know her. She wanted to know why I didn't give Randolph lessons – give him "instruction," she called it. I guess he could give me more instruction than I could give him. He's very smart."

"Yes," said Winterbourne; "he seems very smart."

"Mother's going to get a teacher for him as soon as we get to Italy. Can you get good teachers in Italy?"

"Very good, I should think," said Winterbourne.

"Or else she's going to find some school. He ought to learn some more. He's only nine. He's going to college." And in this way Miss Miller continued to converse upon the affairs of her family, and upon other topics. She sat there with her extremely pretty hands, ornamented with very brilliant rings, folded in her lap, and with her pretty eyes now resting upon those of Winterbourne, now wandering over the garden, the people who passed by, and the beautiful view. She talked to Winterbourne as if she had known him a long time. He found it very pleasant. It was many years since he had heard a young girl talk so much. It might have been said of this unknown young lady, who had come and sat down beside him upon a bench, that she chattered. She was very quiet; she sat in a charming tranquil attitude, but her lips and her eyes were constantly moving. She had a soft, slender, agreeable voice, and her tone was decidedly sociable. She gave Winterbourne a history of her movements and intentions, and those of her mother and brother, in Europe and enumerated, in particular, the various hotels at which they had stopped. "That English lady, in the cars," she said – "Miss Featherstone – asked me if we didn't all live in hotels in America. I told her I had never been in so many hotels in my life as since I came to Europe. I have never seen so many – it's nothing but hotels." But Miss Miller did not make this remark with a querulous accent; she appeared to be in the best humour with everything. She declared that the hotels were very good, when once you got used to their ways, and that Europe was perfectly sweet. She was not disappointed – not a bit. Perhaps it was because she had heard so much about it before. She had ever so many intimate friends that had been there ever so many times. And then she had had ever so many dresses and things from Paris. Whenever she put on a Paris dress she felt as if she were in Europe.

"It was a kind of a wishing-cap," said Winterbourne.

"Yes," said Miss Miller, without examining this analogy; "it always made me wish I was here. But I needn't have done that for dresses. I am sure they send all the pretty ones to America; you see the most frightful things here. The only thing I don't like," she proceeded, "is the society. There isn't any society; or, if there is, I don't know where it keeps

---

11. **cars:** Railroad cars.

itself. Do you? I suppose there is some society somewhere, but I haven't seen anything of it. I'm very fond of society, and I have always had a great deal of it. I don't mean only in Schenectady, but in New York. I used to go to New York every winter. In New York I had lots of society. Last winter I had seventeen dinners given me; and three of them were by gentlemen," added Daisy Miller. "I have more friends in New York than in Schenectady — more gentleman friends; and more young lady friends too," she resumed in a moment. She paused again for an instant; she was looking at Winterbourne with all her prettiness in her lively eyes and in her light, slightly monotonous smile. "I have always had," she said, "a great deal of gentlemen's society."

Poor Winterbourne was amused, perplexed, and decidedly charmed. He had never yet heard a young girl express herself in just this fashion, never, at least, save in cases where to say such things seemed a kind of demonstrative evidence of a certain laxity of deportment. And yet was he to accuse Miss Daisy Miller of actual or potential *inconduite*,[12] as they said at Geneva? He felt that he had lived at Geneva so long that he had lost a good deal; he had become dishabituated to the American tone. Never, indeed, since he had grown old enough to appreciate things, had he encountered a young American girl of so pronounced a type as this. Certainly she was very charming, but how deucedly sociable! Was she simply a pretty girl from New York State — were they all like that, the pretty girls who had a good deal of gentlemen's society? Or was she also a designing, an audacious, an unscrupulous young person? Winterbourne had lost his instinct in this matter, and his reason could not help him. Miss Daisy Miller looked extremely innocent. Some people had told him that, after all, American girls were exceedingly innocent; and others had told him that, after all, they were not. He was inclined to think Miss Daisy Miller was a flirt — a pretty American flirt. He had never, as yet, had any relations with young ladies of this category. He had known, here in Europe, two or three women — persons older than Miss Daisy Miller, and provided, for respectability's sake, with husbands — who were great coquettes — dangerous, terrible women, with whom one's relations were liable to take a serious turn. But this young girl was not a coquette in that sense; she was very unsophisticated; she was only a pretty American flirt. Winterbourne was almost grateful for having found the formula that applied to Miss Daisy Miller. He leaned back in his seat; he remarked to himself that she had the most charming nose he had ever seen; he wondered what were the regular conditions and limitations of one's intercourse with a pretty American flirt. It presently became apparent that he was on the way to learn.

"Have you been to that old castle?" asked the young girl, pointing with her parasol to the far-gleaming walls of the Château de Chillon.

"Yes, formerly, more than once," said Winterbourne. "You too, I suppose, have seen it?"

"No; we haven't been there. I want to go there dreadfully. Of course I mean to go there. I wouldn't go away from here without having seen that old castle."

"It's a very pretty excursion," said Winterbourne, "and very easy to make. You can drive, you know, or you can go by the little steamer."

---

12. *inconduite:* Misbehavior (French).

"You can go in the cars," said Miss Miller.

"Yes; you can go in the cars," Winterbourne assented.

"Our courier[13] says they take you right up to the castle," the young girl continued. "We were going last week; but my mother gave out. She suffers dreadfully from dyspepsia. She said she couldn't go. Randolph wouldn't go either; he says he doesn't think much of old castles. But I guess we'll go this week, if we can get Randolph."

"Your brother is not interested in ancient monuments?" Winterbourne inquired, smiling.

"He says he don't care much about old castles. He's only nine. He wants to stay at the hotel. Mother's afraid to leave him alone, and the courier won't stay with him; so we haven't been to many places. But it will be too bad if we don't go up there." And Miss Miller pointed again at the Château de Chillon.

"I should think it might be arranged," said Winterbourne. "Couldn't you get some one to stay — for the afternoon — with Randolph?"

Miss Miller looked at him a moment; and then, very placidly — "I wish *you* would stay with him!" she said.

Winterbourne hesitated a moment. "I should much rather go to Chillon with you."

"With me?" asked the young girl, with the same placidity.

She didn't rise, blushing, as a young girl at Geneva would have done; and yet Winterbourne, conscious that he had been very bold, thought it possible she was offended. "With your mother," he answered very respectfully.

But it seemed that both his audacity and his respect were lost upon Miss Daisy Miller. "I guess my mother won't go after all," she said. "She don't like to ride round in the afternoon. But did you really mean what you said just now; that you would like to go up there?"

"Most earnestly," Winterbourne declared.

"Then we may arrange it. If mother will stay with Randolph, I guess Eugenio will."

"Eugenio?" the young man inquired.

"Eugenio's our courier. He doesn't like to stay with Randolph; he's the most fastidious man I ever saw. But he's a splendid courier. I guess he'll stay at home with Randolph if mother does, and then we can go to the castle."

Winterbourne reflected for an instant as lucidly as possible — "we" could only mean Miss Daisy Miller and himself. This programme seemed almost too agreeable for credence; he felt as if he ought to kiss the young lady's hand. Possibly he would have done so — and quite spoiled the project; but at this moment another person — presumably Eugenio — appeared. A tall, handsome man, with superb whiskers, wearing a velvet morning-coat and a brilliant watch-chain, approached Miss Miller, looking sharply at her companion. "Oh, Eugenio!" said Miss Miller, with the friendliest accent.

Eugenio had looked at Winterbourne from head to foot; he now bowed gravely to the young lady. "I have the honour to inform mademoiselle that luncheon is upon the table."

---

13. **courier:** A tour guide.

Miss Miller slowly rose. "See here, Eugenio," she said. "I'm going to that old castle, any way."

"To the Château de Chillon, mademoiselle?" the courier inquired. "Mademoiselle has made arrangements?" he added, in a tone which struck Winterbourne as very impertinent.

Eugenio's tone apparently threw, even to Miss Miller's own apprehension, a slightly ironical light upon the young girl's situation. She turned to Winterbourne, blushing a little — a very little. "You won't back out?" she said.

"I shall not be happy till we go!" he protested.

"And you are staying in this hotel?" she went on. "And you are really an American?"

The courier stood looking at Winterbourne, offensively. The young man, at least, thought his manner of looking an offence to Miss Miller; it conveyed an imputation that she "picked up" acquaintances. "I shall have the honour of presenting to you a person who will tell you all about me," he said smiling, and referring to his aunt.

"Oh, well, we'll go some day," said Miss Miller. And she gave him a smile and turned away. She put up her parasol and walked back to the inn beside Eugenio. Winterbourne stood looking after her; and as she moved away, drawing her muslin furbelows over the gravel, said to himself that she had the *tournure*[14] of a princess.

He had, however, engaged to do more than proved feasible, in promising to present his aunt, Mrs. Costello, to Miss Daisy Miller. As soon as the former lady had got better of her headache he waited upon her in her apartment; and, after the proper inquiries in regard to her health, he asked her if she had observed, in the hotel, an American family — a mamma, a daughter, and a little boy.

"And a courier?" said Mrs. Costello. "Oh, yes, I have observed them. Seen them — heard them — and kept out of their way." Mrs. Costello was a widow with a fortune; a person of much distinction, who frequently intimated that, if she were not so dreadfully liable to sick-headaches, she would probably have left a deeper impress upon her time. She had a long pale face, a high nose, and a great deal of very striking white hair, which she wore in large puffs and *rouleaux*[15] over the top of her head. She had two sons married in New York, and another who was now in Europe. This young man was amusing himself at Hombourg,[16] and, though he was on his travels, was rarely perceived to visit any particular city at the moment selected by his mother for her own appearance there. Her nephew, who had come up to Vevey expressly to see her, was therefore more attentive than those who, as she said, were nearer to her. He had imbibed at Geneva the idea that one must always be attentive to one's aunt. Mrs. Costello had not seen him for many years, and she was greatly pleased with him, manifesting her approbation by initiating him into many of the secrets of that social sway which, as she gave him to understand, she exerted in the American capital. She admitted that she was very exclusive; but, if he

14. *tournure:* Grace or poise (French).
15. *rouleaux:* Rolls (French).
16. Hombourg: A resort in Germany known for its spa, built in 1890.

were acquainted with New York, he would see that one had to be. And her picture of the minutely hierarchical constitution of the society of that city, which she presented to him in many different lights, was, to Winterbourne's imagination, almost oppressively striking.

He immediately perceived, from her tone, that Miss Daisy Miller's place in the social scale was low. "I am afraid you don't approve of them," he said.

"They are very common," Mrs. Costello declared. "They are the sort of Americans that one does one's duty by not — not accepting."

"Ah, you don't accept them?" said the young man.

"I can't, my dear Frederick. I would if I could, but I can't."

"The young girl is very pretty," said Winterbourne, in a moment.

"Of course she's pretty. But she is very common."

"I see what you mean of course," said Winterbourne, after another pause.

"She has that charming look that they all have," his aunt resumed. "I can't think where they pick it up; and she dresses in perfection — no, you don't know how well she dresses. I can't think where they get their taste."

"But, my dear aunt, she is not, after all, a Comanche savage."

"She is a young lady," said Mrs. Costello, "who has an intimacy with her mamma's courier."

"An intimacy with the courier?" the young man demanded.

"Oh, the mother is just as bad! They treat the courier like a familiar friend — like a gentleman. I shouldn't wonder if he dines with them. Very likely they have never seen a man with such good manners, such fine clothes, so like a gentleman. He probably corresponds to the young lady's idea of a Count. He sits with them in the garden, in the evening. I think he smokes."

Winterbourne listened with interest to these disclosures; they helped him to make up his mind about Miss Daisy. Evidently she was rather wild. "Well," he said, "I am not a courier, and yet she was very charming to me."

"You had better have said at first," said Mrs. Costello with dignity, "that you had made her acquaintance."

"We simply met in the garden, and we talked a bit."

"*Tout bonnement!*[17] And pray what did you say?"

"I said I should take the liberty of introducing her to my admirable aunt."

"I am much obliged to you."

"It was to guarantee my respectability," said Winterbourne.

"And pray who is to guarantee hers?"

"Ah, you are cruel!" said the young man. "She's a very nice young girl."

"You don't say that as if you believed it," Mrs. Costello observed.

"She is completely uncultivated," Winterbourne went on. "But she is wonderfully pretty, and, in short, she is very nice. To prove that I believe it, I am going to take her to the Château de Chillon."

---

17. ***Tout bonnement!:*** All too plain [or clear]. (French).

"You two are going off there together? I should say it proved just the contrary. How long had you known her, may I ask, when this interesting project was formed? You haven't been twenty-four hours in the house."

"I had known her half an hour!" said Winterbourne, smiling.

"Dear me!" cried Mrs. Costello. "What a dreadful girl!"

Her nephew was silent for some moments. "You really think, then," he began, earnestly, and with a desire for trustworthy information – "you really think that —" But he paused again.

"Think what, sir?" said his aunt.

"That she is the sort of young lady who expects a man – sooner or later – to carry her off?"

"I haven't the least idea what such young ladies expect a man to do. But I really think that you had better not meddle with little American girls that are uncultivated, as you call them. You have lived too long out of the country. You will be sure to make some great mistake. You are too innocent."

"My dear aunt, I am not so innocent," said Winterbourne, smiling and curling his moustache.

"You are too guilty, then!"

Winterbourne continued to curl his moustache, meditatively. "You won't let the poor girl know you then?" he asked at last.

"Is it literally true that she is going to the Château de Chillon with you?"

"I think that she fully intends it."

"Then, my dear Frederick," said Mrs. Costello, "I must decline the honour of her acquaintance. I am an old woman, but I am not too old – thank Heaven – to be shocked!"

"But don't they all do these things – the young girls in America?" Winterbourne inquired.

Mrs. Costello stared a moment. "I should like to see my granddaughters do them!" she declared, grimly.

This seemed to throw some light upon the matter, for Winterbourne remembered to have heard that his pretty cousins in New York were "tremendous flirts." If, therefore, Miss Daisy Miller exceeded the liberal margin allowed to these young ladies, it was probable that anything might be expected of her. Winterbourne was impatient to see her again, and he was vexed with himself that, by instinct, he should not appreciate her justly.

Though he was impatient to see her, he hardly knew what he should say to her about his aunt's refusal to become acquainted with her; but he discovered, promptly enough, that with Miss Daisy Miller there was no great need of walking on tiptoe. He found her that evening in the garden, wandering about in the warm starlight, like an indolent sylph, and swinging to and fro the largest fan he had ever beheld. It was ten o'clock. He had dined with his aunt, had been sitting with her since dinner, and had just taken leave of her till the morrow. Miss Daisy Miller seemed very glad to see him; she declared it was the longest evening she had ever passed.

"Have you been all alone?" he asked.

"I have been walking round with mother. But mother gets tired walking round," she answered.

"Has she gone to bed?"

"No; she doesn't like to go to bed," said the young girl. "She doesn't sleep — not three hours. She says she doesn't know how she lives. She's dreadfully nervous. I guess she sleeps more than she thinks. She's gone somewhere after Randolph; she wants to try to get him to go to bed. He doesn't like to go to bed."

"Let us hope she will persuade him," observed Winterbourne.

"She will talk to him all she can; but he doesn't like her to talk to him," said Miss Daisy, opening her fan. "She's going to try to get Eugenio to talk to him. But he isn't afraid of Eugenio. Eugenio's a splendid courier, but he can't make much impression on Randolph! I don't believe he'll go to bed before eleven." It appeared that Randolph's vigil was in fact triumphantly prolonged, for Winterbourne strolled about with the young girl for some time without meeting her mother. "I have been looking round for that lady you want to introduce me to," his companion resumed. "She's your aunt." Then, on Winterbourne's admitting the fact, and expressing some curiosity as to how she had learned it, she said she had heard all about Mrs. Costello from the chambermaid. She was very quiet and very *comme il faut*;[18] she wore white puffs; she spoke to no one, and she never dined at the *table d'hôte*.[19] Every two days she had a headache. "I think that's a lovely description, headache and all!" said Miss Daisy, chattering along in her thin, gay voice. "I want to know her ever so much. I know just what *your* aunt would be; I know I should like her. She would be very exclusive. I like a lady to be exclusive; I'm dying to be exclusive myself. Well, we *are* exclusive, mother and I. We don't speak to every one — or they don't speak to us. I suppose it's about the same thing. Any way, I shall be ever so glad to know your aunt."

Winterbourne was embarrassed. "She would be most happy," he said; "but I am afraid those headaches will interfere."

The young girl looked at him through the dusk. "But I suppose she doesn't have a headache every day," she said, sympathetically.

Winterbourne was silent a moment. "She tells me she does," he answered at last — not knowing what to say.

Miss Daisy Miller stopped and stood looking at him. Her prettiness was still visible in the darkness; she was opening and closing her enormous fan. "She doesn't want to know me!" she said, suddenly. "Why don't you say so? You needn't be afraid. I'm not afraid!" And she gave a little laugh.

Winterbourne fancied there was a tremor in her voice; he was touched, shocked, mortified by it. "My dear young lady," he protested, "she knows no one. It's her wretched health."

The young girl walked on a few steps, laughing still. "You needn't be afraid," she repeated. "Why should she want to know me?" Then she paused again; she was close to the parapet of the garden, and in front of her was the starlit lake. There was a vague sheen upon its surface, and in the distance were dimly-seen mountain forms. Daisy

---

18. *comme il faut:* Proper or well-mannered (French).
19. *table d'hôte:* Literally, "host's table"; a communal dining table for guests at a hotel (French).

Miller looked out upon the mysterious prospect, and then she gave another little laugh. "Gracious! she *is* exclusive!" she said. Winterbourne wondered whether she was seriously wounded, and for a moment almost wished that her sense of injury might be such as to make it becoming in him to attempt to reassure and comfort her. He had a pleasant sense that she would be very approachable for consolatory purposes. He felt then, for the instant, quite ready to sacrifice his aunt, conversationally; to admit that she was a proud, rude woman, and to declare that they needn't mind her. But before he had time to commit himself to this perilous mixture of gallantry and impiety, the young lady, resuming her walk, gave an exclamation in quite another tone. "Well; here's mother! I guess she hasn't got Randolph to go to bed." The figure of a lady appeared, at a distance, very indistinct in the darkness, and advancing with a slow and wavering movement. Suddenly it seemed to pause.

"Are you sure it is your mother? Can you distinguish her in this thick dusk?" Winterbourne asked.

"Well!" cried Miss Daisy Miller, with a laugh, "I guess I know my own mother. And when she has got on my shawl, too! She is always wearing my things."

The lady in question, ceasing to advance, hovered vaguely about the spot at which she had checked her steps.

"I am afraid your mother doesn't see you," said Winterbourne. "Or perhaps," he added – thinking, with Miss Miller, the joke permissible – "perhaps she feels guilty about your shawl."

"Oh, it's a fearful old thing!" the young girl replied, serenely. "I told her she could wear it. She won't come here, because she sees you."

"Ah, then," said Winterbourne, "I had better leave you."

"Oh, no; come on!" urged Miss Daisy Miller.

"I'm afraid your mother doesn't approve of my walking with you."

Miss Miller gave him a serious glance. "It isn't for me; it's for you – that is, it's for *her*. Well; I don't know who it's for! But mother doesn't like any of my gentlemen friends. She's right down timid. She always makes a fuss if I introduce a gentleman. But I *do* introduce them – almost always. If I didn't introduce my gentlemen friends to mother," the young girl added, in her little soft, flat monotone, "I shouldn't think I was natural."

"To introduce me," said Winterbourne, "you must know my name." And he proceeded to pronounce it.

"Oh, dear; I can't say all that!" said his companion, with a laugh. But by this time they had come up to Mrs. Miller, who, as they drew near, walked to the parapet of the garden and leaned upon it, looking intently at the lake, and turning her back to them. "Mother!" said the young girl, in a tone of decision. Upon this the elder lady turned round. "Mr. Winterbourne," said Miss Daisy Miller, introducing the young man very frankly and prettily. "Common" she was, as Mrs. Costello had pronounced her; yet it was a wonder to Winterbourne that, with her commonness, she had a singularly delicate grace.

Her mother was a small, spare, light person, with a wandering eye, a very exiguous nose, and a large forehead, decorated with a certain amount of thin, much-frizzled hair. Like her daughter, Mrs. Miller was dressed with extreme elegance; she had enormous diamonds in her ears. So far as Winterbourne could observe, she gave him no greeting –

she certainly was not looking at him. Daisy was near her, pulling her shawl straight. "What are you doing, poking round here?" this young lady inquired; but by no means with that harshness of accent which her choice of words may imply.

"I don't know," said her mother, turning towards the lake again.

"I shouldn't think you'd want that shawl!" Daisy exclaimed.

"Well — I do!" her mother answered, with a little laugh.

"Did you get Randolph to go to bed?" asked the young girl.

"No; I couldn't induce him," said Mrs. Miller, very gently. "He wants to talk to the waiter. He likes to talk to that waiter."

"I was telling Mr. Winterbourne," the young girl went on; and to the young man's ear her tone might have indicated that she had been uttering his name all her life.

"Oh, yes!" said Winterbourne; "I have the pleasure of knowing your son."

Randolph's mamma was silent; she turned her attention to the lake. But at last she spoke. "Well, I don't see how he lives!"

"Anyhow, it isn't so bad as it was at Dover," said Daisy Miller.

"And what occurred at Dover?" Winterbourne asked.

"He wouldn't go to bed at all. I guess he sat up all night — in the public parlour. He wasn't in bed at twelve o'clock: I know that."

"It was half-past twelve," declared Mrs. Miller, with mild emphasis.

"Does he sleep much during the day?" Winterbourne demanded.

"I guess he doesn't sleep much," Daisy rejoined.

"I wish he would!" said her mother. "It seems as if he couldn't."

"I think he's real tiresome," Daisy pursued.

Then, for some moments, there was silence. "Well, Daisy Miller," said the elder lady, presently, "I shouldn't think you'd want to talk against your own brother!"

"Well, he *is* tiresome, mother," said Daisy, quite without the asperity of a retort.

"He's only nine," urged Mrs. Miller.

"Well, he wouldn't go to that castle," said the young girl. "I'm going there with Mr. Winterbourne."

To this announcement, very placidly made, Daisy's mamma offered no response. Winterbourne took for granted that she deeply disapproved of the projected excursion; but he said to himself that she was a simple, easily-managed person, and that a few deferential protestations would take the edge from her displeasure. "Yes," he began; "your daughter has kindly allowed me the honour of being her guide."

Mrs. Miller's wandering eyes attached themselves, with a sort of appealing air, to Daisy, who, however, strolled a few steps farther, gently humming to herself. "I presume you will go in the cars," said her mother.

"Yes; or in the boat," said Winterbourne.

"Well, of course, I don't know," Mrs. Miller rejoined. "I have never been to that castle."

"It is a pity you shouldn't go," said Winterbourne, beginning to feel reassured as to her opposition. And yet he was quite prepared to find that, as a matter of course, she meant to accompany her daughter.

"We've been thinking ever so much about going," she pursued; "but it seems as if we couldn't. Of course Daisy — she wants to go round. But there's a lady here — I don't know her name — she says she shouldn't think we'd want to go to see castles *here;* she should think we'd want to wait till we got to Italy. It seems as if there would be so many there," continued Mrs. Miller, with an air of increasing confidence. "Of course, we only want to see the principal ones. We visited several in England," she presently added.

"Ah, yes! in England there are beautiful castles," said Winterbourne. "But Chillon, here, is very well worth seeing."

"Well, if Daisy feels up to it —," said Mrs. Miller, in a tone impregnated with a sense of the magnitude of the enterprise. "It seems as if there was nothing she wouldn't undertake."

"Oh, I think she'll enjoy it!" Winterbourne declared. And he desired more and more to make it a certainty that he was to have the privilege of a *tête-à-tête*[20] with the young lady, who was still strolling along in front of them, softly vocalising. "You are not disposed, madam," he inquired, "to undertake it yourself?"

Daisy's mother looked at him, an instant, askance, and then walked forward in silence. Then — "I guess she had better go alone," she said, simply.

Winterbourne observed to himself that this was a very different type of maternity from that of the vigilant matrons who massed themselves in the forefront of social intercourse in the dark old city at the other end of the lake. But his meditations were interrupted by hearing his name very distinctly pronounced by Mrs. Miller's unprotected daughter.

"Mr. Winterbourne!" murmured Daisy.

"Mademoiselle!" said the young man.

"Don't you want to take me out in a boat?"

"At present?" he asked.

"Of course!" said Daisy.

"Well, Annie Miller!" exclaimed her mother.

"I beg you, madam, to let her go," said Winterbourne, ardently; for he had never yet enjoyed the sensation of guiding through the summer starlight a skiff freighted with a fresh and beautiful young girl.

"I shouldn't think she'd want to," said her mother. "I should think she'd rather go indoors."

"I'm sure Mr. Winterbourne wants to take me," Daisy declared. "He's so awfully devoted!"

"I will row you over to Chillon, in the starlight."

"I don't believe it!" said Daisy.

"Well!" ejaculated the elder lady again.

"You haven't spoken to me for half an hour," her daughter went on.

"I have been having some very pleasant conversation with your mother," said Winterbourne.

"Well; I want you to take me out in a boat!" Daisy repeated. They had all stopped, and she had turned round and was looking at Winterbourne. Her face wore a charming

---

20. *tête-à-tête:* A private conversation (French).

smile, her pretty eyes were gleaming, she was swinging her great fan about. No; it's impossible to be prettier than that, thought Winterbourne.

"There are half a dozen boats moored at that landing-place," he said, pointing to certain steps which descended from the garden to the lake. "If you will do me the honour to accept my arm, we will go and select one of them."

Daisy stood there smiling; she threw back her head and gave a little, light laugh. "I like a gentleman to be formal!" she declared.

"I assure you it's a formal offer."

"I was bound I would make you say something," Daisy went on.

"You see it's not very difficult," said Winterbourne. "But I am afraid you are chaffing me."

"I think not, sir," remarked Mrs. Miller, very gently.

"Do, then, let me give you a row," he said to the young girl.

"It's quite lovely, the way you say that!" cried Daisy.

"It will be still more lovely to do it."

"Yes, it would be lovely!" said Daisy. But she made no movement to accompany him; she only stood there laughing.

"I should think you had better find out what time it is," interposed her mother.

"It is eleven o'clock, madam," said a voice, with a foreign accent, out of the neighbouring darkness; and Winterbourne, turning, perceived the florid personage who was in attendance upon the two ladies. He had apparently just approached.

"Oh, Eugenio," said Daisy, "I am going out in a boat!"

Eugenio bowed. "At eleven o'clock, mademoiselle?"

"I am going with Mr. Winterbourne. This very minute."

"Do tell her she can't," said Mrs. Miller to the courier.

"I think you had better not go out in a boat, mademoiselle," Eugenio declared.

Winterbourne wished to Heaven this pretty girl were not so familiar with her courier; but he said nothing.

"I suppose you don't think it's proper!" Daisy exclaimed. "Eugenio doesn't think anything's proper."

"I am at your service," said Winterbourne.

"Does mademoiselle propose to go alone?" asked Eugenio of Mrs. Miller.

"Oh, no; with this gentleman!" answered Daisy's mamma.

The courier looked for a moment at Winterbourne — the latter thought he was smiling — and then, solemnly, with a bow, "As mademoiselle pleases!" he said.

"Oh, I hoped you would make a fuss!" said Daisy. "I don't care to go now."

"I myself shall make a fuss if you don't go," said Winterbourne.

"That's all I want — a little fuss!" And the young girl began to laugh again.

"Mr. Randolph has gone to bed!" the courier announced, frigidly.

"Oh, Daisy; now we can go!" said Mrs. Miller.

Daisy turned away from Winterbourne, looking at him, smiling, and fanning herself. "Good-night," she said; "I hope you are disappointed, or disgusted, or something!"

He looked at her, taking the hand she offered him. "I am puzzled," he answered.

"Well; I hope it won't keep you awake!" she said, very smartly; and, under the escort of the privileged Eugenio, the two ladies passed towards the house.

Winterbourne stood looking after them; he was indeed puzzled. He lingered beside the lake for a quarter of an hour, turning over the mystery of the young girl's sudden familiarities and caprices. But the only very definite conclusion he came to was that he should enjoy deucedly "going off" with her somewhere.

Two days afterwards he went off with her to the Castle of Chillon. He waited for her in the large hall of the hotel, where the couriers, the servants, the foreign tourists were lounging about and staring. It was not the place he should have chosen, but she had appointed it. She came tripping downstairs, buttoning her long gloves, squeezing her folded parasol against her pretty figure, dressed in the perfection of a soberly elegant travelling-costume. Winterbourne was a man of imagination and, as our ancestors used to say, sensibility; as he looked at her dress and, on the great staircase, her little rapid, confiding step, he felt as if there were something romantic going forward. He could have believed he was going to elope with her. He passed out with her among all the idle people that were assembled there; they were all looking at her very hard; she had begun to chatter as soon as she joined him. Winterbourne's preference had been that they should be conveyed to Chillon in a carriage; but she expressed a lively wish to go in the little steamer; she declared that she had a passion for steamboats. There was always such a lovely breeze upon the water, and you saw such lots of people. The sail was not long, but Winterbourne's companion found time to say a great many things. To the young man himself their little excursion was so much of an escapade — an adventure — that, even allowing for her habitual sense of freedom, he had some expectation of seeing her regard it in the same way. But it must be confessed that, in this particular, he was disappointed. Daisy Miller was extremely animated, she was in charming spirits; but she was apparently not at all excited; she was not fluttered; she avoided neither his eyes nor those of any one else; she blushed neither when she looked at him nor when she felt that people were looking at her. People continued to look at her a great deal, and Winterbourne took much satisfaction in his pretty companion's distinguished air. He had been a little afraid that she would talk loud, laugh overmuch, and even, perhaps, desire to move about the boat a good deal. But he quite forgot his fears; he sat smiling, with his eyes upon her face, while, without moving from her place, she delivered herself of a great number of original reflections. It was the most charming garrulity he had ever heard. He had assented to the idea that she was "common"; but was she so, after all, or was he simply getting used to her commonness? Her conversation was chiefly of what metaphysicians term the objective cast; but every now and then it took a subjective turn.

"What on *earth* are you so grave about?" she suddenly demanded, fixing her agreeable eyes upon Winterbourne's.

"Am I grave?" he asked. "I had an idea I was grinning from ear to ear."

"You look as if you were taking me to a funeral. If that's a grin, your ears are very near together."

"Should you like me to dance a hornpipe on the deck?"

"Pray do, and I'll carry round your hat. It will pay the expenses of our journey."

"I never was better pleased in my life," murmured Winterbourne.

She looked at him a moment, and then burst into a little laugh. "I like to make you say those things! You're a queer mixture!"

In the castle, after they had landed, the subjective element decidedly prevailed. Daisy tripped about the vaulted chambers, rustled her skirts in the corkscrew staircases, flirted back with a pretty little cry and a shudder from the edge of the *oubliettes*,[21] and turned a singularly well-shaped ear to everything that Winterbourne told her about the place. But he saw that she cared very little for feudal antiquities, and that the dusky traditions of Chillon made but a slight impression upon her. They had the good fortune to have been able to walk about without other companionship than that of the custodian; and Winterbourne arranged with this functionary that they should not be hurried — that they should linger and pause wherever they chose. The custodian interpreted the bargain generously — Winterbourne, on his side, had been generous — and ended by leaving them quite to themselves. Miss Miller's observations were not remarkable for logical consistency; for anything she wanted to say she was sure to find a pretext. She found a great many pretexts in the rugged embrasures of Chillon for asking Winterbourne sudden questions about himself — his family, his previous history, his tastes, his habits, his intentions — and for supplying information upon corresponding points in her own personality. Of her own tastes, habits, and intentions Miss Miller was prepared to give the most definite, and indeed the most favourable, account.

"Well; I hope you know enough!" she said to her companion, after he had told her the history of the unhappy Bonivard.[22] "I never saw a man that knew so much!" The history of Bonivard had evidently, as they say, gone into one ear and out of the other. But Daisy went on to say that she wished Winterbourne would travel with them and "go round" with them; they might know something, in that case. "Don't you want to come and teach Randolph?" she asked. Winterbourne said that nothing could possibly please him so much; but that he had unfortunately other occupations. "Other occupations? I don't believe it!" said Miss Daisy. "What do you mean? You are not in business." The young man admitted that he was not in business; but he had engagements which, even within a day or two, would force him to go back to Geneva. "Oh, bother!" she said: "I don't believe it!" and she began to talk about something else. But a few moments later, when he was pointing out to her the pretty design of an antique fireplace, she broke out irrelevantly, "You don't mean to say you are going back to Geneva?"

It is a melancholy fact that I shall have to return to Geneva to-morrow."

"Well, Mr. Winterbourne," said Daisy; "I think you're horrid!"

"Oh, don't say such dreadful things!" said Winterbourne — "just at the last!"

"The last!" cried the young girl; "I call it the first. I have half a mind to leave you here and go straight back to the hotel alone." And for the next ten minutes she did nothing

---

21. *oubliettes:* Secret dungeons (French).

22. **Bonivard:** François Bonivard (1493-1570) was imprisoned for several years at Chillon for his political differences with the ruler of Geneva. Byron based his poem "The Prisoner of Chillon" on Bonivard's life (see note 7).

but call him horrid. Poor Winterbourne was fairly bewildered; no young lady had as yet done him the honour to be so agitated by the announcement of his movements. His companion, after this, ceased to pay any attention to the curiosities of Chillon or the beauties of the lake; she opened fire upon the mysterious charmer in Geneva whom she appeared to have instantly taken it for granted that he was hurrying back to see. How did Miss Daisy Miller know that there was a charmer in Geneva? Winterbourne, who denied the existence of such a person, was quite unable to discover; and he was divided between amazement at the rapidity of her induction and amusement at the frankness of her *persiflage*.[23] She seemed to him, in all this, an extraordinary mixture of innocence and crudity. "Does she never allow you more than three days at a time?" asked Daisy, ironically. "Doesn't she give you a vacation in summer? There's no one so hard worked but they can get leave to go off somewhere at this season. I suppose, if you stay another day, she'll come after you in the boat. Do wait over till Friday, and I will go down to the landing to see her arrive!" Winterbourne began to think he had been wrong to feel disappointed in the temper in which the young lady had embarked. If he had missed the personal accent, the personal accent was now making its appearance. It sounded very distinctly, at last, in her telling him she would stop "teasing" him if he would promise her solemnly to come down to Rome in the winter.

"That's not a difficult promise to make," said Winterbourne. "My aunt has taken an apartment in Rome for the winter, and has already asked me to come and see her."

"I don't want you to come for your aunt," said Daisy; "I want you to come for me." And this was the only allusion that the young man was ever to hear her make to his invidious kinswoman. He declared that, at any rate, he would certainly come. After this Daisy stopped teasing. Winterbourne took a carriage, and they drove back to Vevey in the dusk; the young girl was very quiet.

In the evening Winterbourne mentioned to Mrs. Costello that he had spent the afternoon at Chillon, with Miss Daisy Miller.

"The Americans — of the courier?" asked this lady.

"Ah, happily," said Winterbourne, "the courier stayed at home."

"She went with you all alone?"

"All alone."

Mrs. Costello sniffed a little at her smelling-bottle. "And that," she exclaimed, "is the young person whom you wanted me to know!"

PART II

Winterbourne, who had returned to Geneva the day after his excursion to Chillon, went to Rome towards the end of January. His aunt had been established there for several weeks, and he had received a couple of letters from her. "Those people you were so devoted to last summer at Vevey have turned up here, courier and all," she wrote. "They seem to have made several acquaintances, but the courier continues to be the most

---

23. *persiflage:* Light banter or small talk (French).

intime. The young lady, however, is also very intimate with some third-rate Italians, with whom she rackets about in a way that makes much talk. Bring me that pretty novel of Cherbuliez's — 'Paule Méré'[24] — and don't come later than the 23rd."

In the natural course of events, Winterbourne, on arriving in Rome, would presently have ascertained Mrs. Miller's address at the American banker's, and have gone to pay his compliments to Miss Daisy. "After what happened at Vevey I think I may certainly call upon them," he said to Mrs. Costello.

"If, after what happens — at Vevey and everywhere — you desire to keep up the acquaintance, you are very welcome. Of course a man may know every one. Men are welcome to the privilege!"

"Pray what is it that happens — here, for instance?" Winterbourne demanded.

"The girl goes about alone with her foreigners. As to what happens further, you must apply elsewhere for information. She has picked up half-a-dozen of the regular Roman fortune-hunters, and she takes them about to people's houses. When she comes to a party she brings with her a gentleman with a good deal of manner and a wonderful moustache."

"And where is the mother?"

"I haven't the least idea. They are very dreadful people."

Winterbourne meditated a moment. "They are very ignorant — very innocent only. Depend upon it they are not bad."

"They are hopelessly vulgar," said Mrs. Costello. "Whether or no being hopelessly vulgar is being 'bad' is a question for the metaphysicians. They are bad enough to dislike, at any rate; and for this short life that is quite enough.

The news that Daisy Miller was surrounded by half-a-dozen wonderful moustaches checked Winterbourne's impulse to go straightway to see her. He had perhaps not definitely flattered himself that he had made an ineffaceable impression upon her heart, but he was annoyed at hearing of a state of affairs so little in harmony with an image that had lately fitted in and out of his own meditations; the image of a very pretty girl looking out of an old Roman window and asking herself urgently when Mr. Winterbourne would arrive. If, however, he determined to wait a little before reminding Miss Miller of his claims to her consideration, he went very soon to call upon two or three other friends. One of these friends was an American lady who had spent several winters at Geneva, where she had placed her children at school. She was a very accomplished woman, and she lived in the Via Gregoriana. Winterbourne found her in a little crimson drawing-room, on a third floor; the room was filled with southern sunshine. He had not been there ten minutes when the servant came in, announcing "Madame Mila!" This announcement was presently followed by the entrance of little Randolph Miller, who stopped in the middle of the room and stood staring at Winterbourne. An instant later

---

24. **'Paule Méré':** In this work by the French novelist Charles Victor Cherbuliez (1829-1899), which James reviewed after it was published in Geneva in 1865, the title character is a young woman who is subject to malicious gossip for violating social conventions.

his pretty sister crossed the threshold; and then, after a considerable interval, Mrs. Miller slowly advanced.

"I know you!" said Randolph.

"I'm sure you know a great many things," exclaimed Winterbourne, taking him by the hand. "How is your education coming on?"

Daisy was exchanging greetings very prettily with her hostess; but when she heard Winterbourne's voice she quickly turned her head. "Well, I declare!" she said.

"I told you I should come, you know," Winterbourne rejoined, smiling.

"Well — I didn't believe it," said Miss Daisy.

"I am much obliged to you," laughed the young man.

"You might have come to see me!" said Daisy.

"I arrived only yesterday."

"I don't believe that!" the young girl declared.

Winterbourne turned with a protesting smile to her mother; but this lady evaded his glance, and, seating herself, fixed her eyes upon her son. "We've got a bigger place than this," said Randolph. "It's all gold on the walls."

Mrs. Miller turned uneasily in her chair. "I told you if I were to bring you, you would say something!" she murmured.

"I told *you!*" Randolph exclaimed. "I tell *you,* sir!" he added jocosely, giving Winterbourne a thump on the knee. "It *is* bigger, too!"

Daisy had entered upon a lively conversation with her hostess; Winterbourne judged it becoming to address a few words to her mother. "I hope you have been well since we parted at Vevey," he said.

Mrs. Miller now certainly looked at him — at his chin. "Not very well, sir," she answered.

"She's got the dyspepsia," said Randolph. "I've got it too. Father's got it. I've got it most!"

This announcement, instead of embarrassing Mrs. Miller, seemed to relieve her. "I suffer from the liver," she said. "I think it's this climate; it's less bracing than Schenectady, especially in the winter season. I don't know whether you know we reside at Schenectady. I was saying to Daisy that I certainly hadn't found anyone like Dr. Davis, and I didn't believe I should. Oh, at Schenectady, he stands first; they think everything of him. He has so much to do, and yet there was nothing he wouldn't do for me. He said he never saw anything like my dyspepsia, but he was bound to cure it. I'm sure there was nothing he wouldn't try. He was just going to try something new when we came off. Mr. Miller wanted Daisy to see Europe for herself. But I wrote to Mr. Miller that it seems as if I couldn't get on without Dr. Davis. At Schenectady he stands at the very top; and there's a great deal of sickness there, too. It affects my sleep."

Winterbourne had a good deal of pathological gossip with Dr. Davis's patient, during which Daisy chattered unremittingly to her own companion. The young man asked Mrs. Miller how she was pleased with Rome. "Well, I must say I am disappointed," she answered. "We had heard so much about it; I suppose we had heard too much. But we couldn't help that. We had been led to expect something different."

"Ah, wait a little, and you will become very fond of it," said Winterbourne.

"I hate it worse and worse every day!" cried Randolph.

"You are like the infant Hannibal,"[25] said Winterbourne.

"No, I ain't!" Randolph declared, at a venture.

"You are not much like an infant," said his mother. "But we have seen places," she resumed, "that I should put a long way before Rome." And in reply to Winterbourne's interrogation, "There's Zurich," she concluded; "I think Zurich is lovely; and we hadn't heard half so much about it."

"The best place we've seen is the City of Richmond!" said Randolph.

"He means the ship," his mother explained. "We crossed in that ship. Randolph had a good time on the City of Richmond."

"It's the best place I've seen," the child repeated. "Only it was turned the wrong way."

"Well, we've got to turn the right way some time," said Mrs. Miller, with a little laugh. Winterbourne expressed the hope that her daughter at least found some gratification in Rome, and she declared that Daisy was quite carried away. "It's on account of the society — the society's splendid. She goes round everywhere; she has made a great number of acquaintances. Of course she goes round more than I do. I must say they have been very sociable; they have taken her right in. And then she knows a great many gentlemen. Oh, she thinks there's nothing like Rome. Of course, it's a great deal pleasanter for a young lady if she knows plenty of gentlemen."

By this time Daisy had turned her attention again to Winterbourne. "I've been telling Mrs. Walker how mean you were!" the young girl announced.

"And what is the evidence you have offered?" asked Winterbourne, rather annoyed at Miss Miller's want of appreciation of the zeal of an admirer who on his way down to Rome had stopped neither at Bologna nor at Florence, simply because of a certain sentimental impatience. He remembered that a cynical compatriot had once told him that American women — the pretty ones, and this gave a largeness to the axiom — were at once the most exacting in the world and the least endowed with a sense of indebtedness.

"Why, you were awfully mean at Vevey," said Daisy. "You wouldn't do anything. You wouldn't stay there when I asked you."

"My dearest young lady," cried Winterbourne, with eloquence, "have I come all the way to Rome to encounter your reproaches?"

"Just hear him say that!" said Daisy to her hostess, giving a twist to a bow on this lady's dress. "Did you ever hear anything so quaint?"

"So quaint, my dear?" murmured Mrs. Walker, in the tone of a partisan of Winterbourne.

"Well, I don't know," said Daisy, fingering Mrs. Walker's ribbons, "Mrs. Walker, I want to tell you something."

---

25. **Hannibal:** The Carthaginian general Hannibal (247–182 BCE), who opposed Roman rule from his early youth, led forces against Rome in the Punic Wars.

"Motherr," interposed Randolph, with his rough ends to his words, "I tell you you've got to go. Eugenio 'll raise something!"

"I'm not afraid of Eugenio," said Daisy, with a toss of her head. "Look here, Mrs. Walker," she went on, "you know I'm coming to your party."

"I am delighted to hear it."

"I've got a lovely dress."

"I am very sure of that."

"But I want to ask a favour — permission to bring a friend."

"I shall be happy to see any of your friends," said Mrs. Walker, turning with a smile to Mrs. Miller.

"Oh, they are not my friends," answered Daisy's mamma, smiling shyly, in her own fashion. "I never spoke to them!"

"It's an intimate friend of mine — Mr. Giovanelli," said Daisy, without a tremor in her clear little voice or a shadow on her brilliant little face.

Mrs. Walker was silent a moment, she gave a rapid glance at Winterbourne. "I shall be glad to see Mr. Giovanelli," she then said.

"He's an Italian," Daisy pursued, with the prettiest serenity. "He's a great friend of mine — he's the handsomest man in the world — except Mr. Winterbourne! He knows plenty of Italians, but he wants to know some Americans. He thinks ever so much of Americans. He's tremendously clever. He's perfectly lovely!"

It was settled that this brilliant personage should be brought to Mrs. Walker's party, and then Mrs. Miller prepared to take her leave. "I guess we'll go back to the hotel," she said.

"You may go back to the hotel, mother, but I'm going to take a walk," said Daisy.

"She's going to walk with Mr. Giovanelli," Randolph proclaimed.

"I am going to the Pincio,"[26] said Daisy, smiling.

"Alone, my dear — at this hour?" Mrs. Walker asked. The afternoon was drawing to a close — it was the hour for the throng of carriages and of contemplative pedestrians. "I don't think it's safe, my dear," said Mrs. Walker.

"Neither do I," subjoined Mrs. Miller. "You'll get the fever[27] as sure as you live. Remember what Dr. Davis told you!"

"Give her some medicine before she goes," said Randolph.

The company had risen to its feet; Daisy, still showing her pretty teeth, bent over and kissed her hostess. "Mrs. Walker, you are too perfect," she said. "I'm not going alone; I am going to meet a friend."

"Your friend won't keep you from getting the fever," Mrs. Miller observed.

"Is it Mr. Giovanelli?" asked the hostess.

---

26. **Pincio:** The Pincian Hill, a raised part of the Borghese Gardens, from which there are spectacular views of Rome.

27. **the fever:** Malaria, or "Roman fever." Although it was not then known that malaria was carried by mosquitoes, it was understood that the often-deadly disease was contracted by those who were outdoors at night.

Winterbourne was watching the young girl; at this question his attention quickened. She stood there smiling and smoothing her bonnet ribbons; she glanced at Winterbourne. Then, while she glanced and smiled, she answered without a shade of hesitation, "Mr. Giovanelli — the beautiful Giovanelli."

"My dear young friend," said Mrs. Walker, taking her hand, pleadingly, "don't walk off to the Pincio at this hour to meet a beautiful Italian."

"Well, he speaks English," said Mrs. Miller.

"Gracious me!" Daisy exclaimed, "I don't want to do anything improper. There's an easy way to settle it." She continued to glance at Winterbourne. "The Pincio is only a hundred yards distant, and if Mr. Winterbourne were as polite as he pretends he would offer to walk with me!"

Winterbourne's politeness hastened to affirm itself, and the young girl gave him gracious leave to accompany her. They passed downstairs before her mother, and at the door Winterbourne perceived Mrs. Miller's carriage drawn up, with the ornamental courier whose acquaintance he had made at Vevey seated within. "Good-by, Eugenio!" cried Daisy, "I'm going to take a walk." The distance from the Via Gregoriana to the beautiful garden at the other end of the Pincian Hill is, in fact, rapidly traversed. As the day was splendid, however, and the concourse of vehicles, walkers, and loungers numerous, the young Americans found their progress much delayed. This fact was highly agreeable to Winterbourne, in spite of his consciousness of his singular situation. The slow-moving, idly-gazing Roman crowd bestowed much attention upon the extremely pretty young foreign lady who was passing through it upon his arm; and he wondered what on earth had been in Daisy's mind when she proposed to expose herself, unattended, to its appreciation. His own mission, to her sense, apparently, was to consign her to the hands of Mr. Giovanelli; but Winterbourne, at once annoyed and gratified, resolved that he would do no such thing.

"Why haven't you been to see me?" asked Daisy. "You can't get out of that."

"I have had the honour of telling you that I have only just stepped out of the train."

"You must have stayed in the train a good while after it stopped!" cried the young girl, with her little laugh. "I suppose you were asleep. You have had time to go to see Mrs. Walker."

"I knew Mrs. Walker —" Winterbourne began to explain.

"I knew where you knew her. You knew her at Geneva. She told me so. Well, you knew me at Vevey. That's just as good. So you ought to have come." She asked him no other question than this; she began to prattle about her own affairs. "We've got splendid rooms at the hotel; Eugenio says they're the best rooms in Rome. We are going to stay all winter — if we don't die of the fever; and I guess we'll stay then. It's a great deal nicer than I thought; I thought it would be fearfully quiet; I was sure it would be awfully poky. I was sure we should be going round all the time with one of those dreadful old men that explain about the pictures and things. But we only had about a week of that, and now I'm enjoying myself. I know ever so many people, and they are all so charming. The society's extremely select. There are all kinds — English, and Germans, and Italians. I think I like the English best. I like their style of conversation. But there are some lovely Americans. I never saw anything so hospitable. There's something or other every day. There's not much dancing; but I must say I never thought dancing was everything. I was always fond of conversation. I guess I shall have plenty at Mrs. Walker's — her rooms are so small." When they had passed the gate of the Pincian Gardens, Miss Miller began to wonder where Mr. Giovanelli might be. "We had better go straight to that place in front," she said, "where you look at the view."

"I certainly shall not help you to find him," Winterbourne declared.

"Then I shall find him without you," said Miss Daisy.

"You certainly won't leave me!" cried Winterbourne.

She burst into her little laugh. "Are you afraid you'll get lost — or run over? But there's Giovanelli, leaning against that tree. He's staring at the women in the carriages: did you ever see anything so cool?"

Winterbourne perceived at some distance a little man standing with folded arms, nursing his cane. He had a handsome face, an artfully poised hat, a glass in one eye and a nosegay in his button-hole. Winterbourne looked at him a moment and then said, "Do you mean to speak to that man?"

"Do I mean to speak to him? Why, you don't suppose I mean to communicate by signs?"

"Pray understand, then," said Winterbourne, "that I intend to remain with you."

Daisy stopped and looked at him, without a sign of troubled consciousness in her face; with nothing but the presence of her charming eyes and her happy dimples. "Well, she's a cool one!" thought the young man.

"I don't like the way you say that," said Daisy. "It's too imperious."

"I beg your pardon if I say it wrong. The main point is to give you an idea of my meaning."

The young girl looked at him more gravely, but with eyes that were prettier than ever. "I have never allowed a gentleman to dictate to me, or to interfere with anything I do."

"I think you have made a mistake," said Winterbourne. "You should sometimes listen to a gentleman — the right one."

Daisy began to laugh again. "I do nothing but listen to gentlemen!" she exclaimed. "Tell me if Mr. Giovanelli is the right one?"

The gentleman with the nosegay in his bosom had now perceived our two friends, and was approaching the young girl with obsequious rapidity. He bowed to Winterbourne as well as to the latter's companion; he had a brilliant smile, an intelligent eye; Winterbourne thought him not a bad-looking fellow. But he nevertheless said to Daisy — "No, he's not the right one."

Daisy evidently had a natural talent for performing introductions; she also mentioned the name of each of her companions to the other. She strolled along with one of them on each side of her; Mr. Giovanelli, who spoke English very cleverly — Winterbourne afterwards learned that he had practised the idiom upon a great many American heiresses — addressed her a great deal of very polite nonsense; he was extremely urbane, and the young American, who said nothing, reflected upon that profundity of Italian cleverness which enables people to appear more gracious in proportion as they are more acutely disappointed. Giovanelli, of course, had counted upon something more intimate; he had not bargained for a party of three. But he kept his temper in a manner which suggested far-stretching intentions. Winterbourne flattered himself that he had taken his measure. "He is not a gentleman," said the young American; "he is only a clever imitation of one. He is a music-master, or a penny-a-liner, or a third-rate artist. Damn his good looks!" Mr. Giovanelli had certainly a very pretty face; but Winterbourne felt a superior indignation at his own lovely fellow-countrywoman's not knowing the difference between a spurious gentleman and a real one. Giovanelli chattered and jested and made himself wonderfully agreeable. It was true that if he was an imitation the imitation was brilliant. "Nevertheless," Winterbourne said to himself, "a nice girl ought to know!" And then he came back to the question whether this was in fact a nice girl. Would a nice girl — even allowing for her being a little American flirt — make a rendezvous with a presumably low-lived foreigner? The rendezvous in this case, indeed, had been in broad day-light, and in the most crowded corner of Rome; but was it not impossible to regard the choice of these circumstances as a proof of extreme cynicism? Singular though it may seem, Winterbourne was vexed that the young girl, in joining her *amoroso*,[28] should not appear more impatient of his own company, and he was vexed because of his inclination. It was impossible to regard her as a perfectly well-conducted young lady; she was wanting in a certain indispensable delicacy. It would therefore simplify matters greatly to be able to treat her as the object of one of those sentiments which are called by romancers "lawless passions." That she should seem to wish to get rid of him would help him to think more lightly of her, and to be able to think more lightly of her would make her much less perplexing. But Daisy, on this occasion, continued to present herself as an inscrutable combination of audacity and innocence.

She had been walking some quarter of an hour, attended by her two cavaliers, and responding in a tone of very childish gaiety, as it seemed to Winterbourne, to the pretty speeches of Mr. Giovanelli, when a carriage that had detached itself from the revolving train drew up beside the path. At the same moment Winterbourne perceived that his friend Mrs. Walker — the lady whose house he had lately left — was seated in the vehicle and was beckoning to him. Leaving Miss Miller's side, he hastened to obey her summons. Mrs. Walker was flushed; she wore an excited air. "It is really too dreadful," she said. "That girl must not do this sort of thing. She must not walk here with you two men. Fifty people have noticed her."

Winterbourne raised his eyebrows. "I think it's a pity to make too much fuss about it."

"It's a pity to let the girl ruin herself!"

"She is very innocent," said Winterbourne.

"She's very crazy!" cried Mrs. Walker. "Did you ever see anything so imbecile as her mother? After you had all left me, just now, I could not sit still for thinking of it. It seemed too pitiful, not even to attempt to save her. I ordered the carriage and put on my bonnet, and came here as quickly as possible. Thank heaven, I have found you!"

"What do you propose to do with us?" asked Winterbourne, smiling.

---

28. *amoroso:* Lover (Italian).

"To ask her to get in, to drive her about here for half-an-hour, so that the world may see she is not running absolutely wild, and then to take her safely home."

"I don't think it's a very happy thought," said Winterbourne; "but you can try."

Mrs. Walker tried. The young man went in pursuit of Miss Miller, who had simply nodded and smiled at his interlocutor in the carriage, and had gone her way with her companion. Daisy, on learning that Mrs. Walker wished to speak to her, retraced her steps with a perfect good grace and with Mr. Giovanelli at her side. She declared that she was delighted to have a chance to present this gentleman to Mrs. Walker. She immediately achieved the introduction, and declared that she had never in her life seen anything so lovely as Mrs. Walker's carriage-rug.

"I am glad you admire it," said this lady, smiling sweetly. "Will you get in and let me put it over you?"

"Oh, no, thank you," said Daisy. "I shall admire it much more as I see you driving round with it."

"Do get in and drive with me," said Mrs. Walker.

"That would be charming, but it's so enchanting just as I am!" and Daisy gave a brilliant glance at the gentlemen on either side of her.

"It may be enchanting, dear child, but it is not the custom here," urged Mrs. Walker, leaning forward in her victoria[29] with her hands devoutly clasped.

"Well, it ought to be, then!" said Daisy. "If I didn't walk I should expire."

"You should walk with your mother, dear," cried the lady from Geneva, losing patience.

"With my mother dear!" exclaimed the young girl. Winterbourne saw that she scented interference. "My mother never walked ten steps in her life. And then, you know," she added with a laugh, "I am more than five years old."

"You are old enough to be more reasonable. You are old enough, dear Miss Miller, to be talked about."

Daisy looked at Mrs. Walker, smiling intensely. "Talked about? What do you mean?"

"Come into my carriage and I will tell you."

Daisy turned her quickened glance again from one of the gentlemen beside her to the other. Mr. Giovanelli was bowing to and fro, rubbing down his gloves and laughing very agreeably; Winterbourne thought it a most unpleasant scene. "I don't think I want to know what you mean," said Daisy presently. "I don't think I should like it."

Winterbourne wished that Mrs. Walker would tuck in her carriage-rug and drive away; but this lady did not enjoy being defied, as she afterwards told him. "Should you prefer being thought a very reckless girl?" she demanded.

"Gracious!" exclaimed Daisy. She looked again at Mr. Giovanelli, then she turned to Winterbourne. There was a little pink flush in her cheek; she was tremendously pretty. "Does Mr. Winterbourne think," she asked slowly, smiling, throwing back her head and glancing at him from head to foot, "that — to save my reputation — I ought to get into the carriage?"

---

29. **victoria:**   A four-wheeled, horse-drawn carriage with seats for two passengers.

Winterbourne coloured; for an instant he hesitated greatly. It seemed so strange to hear her speak that way of her "reputation." But he himself, in fact, must speak in accordance with gallantry. The finest gallantry, here, was simply to tell her the truth; and the truth, for Winterbourne, as the few indications I have been able to give have made him known to the reader, was that Daisy Miller should take Mrs. Walker's advice. He looked at her exquisite prettiness; and then he said very gently, "I think you should get into the carriage."

Daisy gave a violent laugh. "I never heard anything so stiff! If this is improper, Mrs. Walker," she pursued, "then I am all improper, and you must give me up. Good-by; I hope you'll have a lovely ride!" and, with Mr. Giovanelli, who made a triumphantly obsequious salute, she turned away.

Mrs. Walker sat looking after her, and there were tears in Mrs. Walker's eyes. "Get in here, sir," she said to Winterbourne, indicating the place beside her. The young man answered that he felt bound to accompany Miss Miller; whereupon Mrs. Walker declared that if he refused her this favour she would never speak to him again. She was evidently in earnest. Winterbourne overtook Daisy and her companion and, offering the young girl his hand, told her that Mrs. Walker had made an imperious claim upon his society. He expected that in answer she would say something rather free, something to commit herself still further to that "recklessness" from which Mrs. Walker had so charitably endeavoured to dissuade her. But she only shook his hand, hardly looking at him; while Mr. Giovanelli bade him farewell with a too-emphatic flourish of the hat.

Winterbourne was not in the best possible humour as he took his seat in Mrs. Walker's victoria. "That was not clever of you," he said candidly, while the vehicle mingled again with the throng of carriages.

"In such a case," his companion answered, "I don't wish to be clever, I wish to be *earnest!*"

"Well, your earnestness has only offended her and put her off."

"It has happened very well," said Mrs. Walker. "If she is so perfectly determined to compromise herself, the sooner one knows it the better; one can act accordingly."

"I suspect she meant no harm," Winterbourne rejoined.

"So I thought a month ago. But she has been going too far."

"What has she been doing?"

"Everything that is not done here. Flirting with any man she could pick up; sitting in corners with mysterious Italians; dancing all the evening with the same partners; receiving visits at eleven o'clock at night. Her mother goes away when visitors come."

"But her brother," said Winterbourne, laughing, "sits up till midnight."

"He must be edified by what he sees. I'm told that at their hotel every one is talking about her, and that a smile goes round among all the servants when a gentleman comes and asks for Miss Miller."

"The servants be hanged!" said Winterbourne angrily. "The poor girl's only fault," he presently added, "is that she is very uncultivated."

"She is naturally indelicate," Mrs. Walker declared. "Take that example this morning. How long had you known her at Vevey?"

"A couple of days."

"Fancy, then, her making it a personal matter that you should have left the place!"

Winterbourne was silent for some moments, then he said, "I suspect, Mrs. Walker, that you and I have lived too long at Geneva!" And he added a request that she should inform him with what particular design she had made him enter her carriage.

"I wished to beg you to cease your relations with Miss Miller — not to flirt with her — to give her no further opportunity to expose herself — to let her alone, in short."

"I'm afraid I can't do that," said Winterbourne. "I like her extremely."

"All the more reason that you shouldn't help her to make a scandal."

"There shall be nothing scandalous in my attentions to her."

"There certainly will be in the way she takes them. But I have said what I had on my conscience," Mrs. Walker pursued. "If you wish to rejoin the young lady I will put you down. Here, by-the-way, you have a chance."

The carriage was traversing that part of the Pincian Garden that overhangs the wall of Rome and overlooks the beautiful Villa Borghese. It is bordered by a large parapet, near which there are several seats. One of the seats, at a distance, was occupied by a gentleman and a lady, towards whom Mrs. Walker gave a toss of her head. At the same moment these persons rose and walked towards the parapet. Winterbourne had asked the coachman to stop; he now descended from the carriage. His companion looked at him a moment in silence; then, while he raised his hat, she drove majestically away. Winterbourne stood there; he had turned his eyes towards Daisy and her cavalier. They evidently saw no one; they were too deeply occupied with each other. When they reached the low garden-wall they stood a moment looking off at the great flat-topped pine-clusters of the Villa Borghese; then Giovanelli seated himself, familiarly, upon the broad ledge of the wall. The western sun in the opposite sky sent out a brilliant shaft through a couple of cloud-bars, whereupon Daisy's companion took her parasol out of her hands and opened it. She came a little nearer and he held the parasol over her; then, still holding it, he let it rest upon her shoulder, so that both of their heads were hidden from Winterbourne. This young man lingered a moment, then he began to walk. But he walked — not towards the couple with the parasol; towards the residence of his aunt, Mrs. Costello.

He flattered himself on the following day that there was no smiling among the servants when he, at least, asked for Mrs. Miller at her hotel. This lady and her daughter, however, were not at home; and on the next day after, repeating his visit, Winterbourne again had the misfortune not to find them. Mrs. Walker's party took place on the evening of the third day, and in spite of the frigidity of his last interview with the hostess Winterbourne was among the guests. Mrs. Walker was one of those American ladies who, while residing abroad, make a point, in their own phrase, of studying European society; and she had on this occasion collected several specimens of her diversely-born fellow-mortals to serve, as it were, as text-books. When Winterbourne arrived Daisy Miller was not there, but in a few moments he saw her mother come in alone, very shyly and ruefully. Mrs. Miller's hair above her exposed-looking temples was more frizzled than ever. As she approached Mrs. Walker, Winterbourne also drew near.

"You see I've come all alone," said poor Mrs. Miller. "I'm so frightened; I don't know what to do; it's the first time I've ever been to a party alone — especially in this country. I wanted to bring Randolph or Eugenio, or someone, but Daisy just pushed me off by myself. I ain't used to going round alone."

"And does not your daughter intend to favour us with her society?" demanded Mrs. Walker, impressively.

"Well, Daisy's all dressed," said Mrs. Miller, with that accent of the dispassionate, if not of the philosophic, historian with which she always recorded the current incidents of her daughter's career. "She got dressed on purpose before dinner. But she's got a friend of hers there; that gentleman – the Italian – that she wanted to bring. They've got going at the piano; it seems as if they couldn't leave off. Mr. Giovanelli sings splendidly. But I guess they'll come before very long," concluded Mrs. Miller hopefully.

"I'm sorry she should come – in that way," said Mrs. Walker.

"Well, I told her that there was no use in her getting dressed before dinner if she was going to wait three hours," responded Daisy's mamma. "I didn't see the use of her putting on such a dress as that to sit round with Mr. Giovanelli."

"This is most horrible!" said Mrs. Walker, turning away and addressing herself to Winterbourne. "*Elle s'affiche.*[30] It's her revenge for my having ventured to remonstrate with her. When she comes I shall not speak to her."

Daisy came after eleven o'clock, but she was not, on such an occasion, a young lady to wait to be spoken to. She rustled forward in radiant loveliness, smiling and chattering, carrying a large bouquet and attended by Mr. Giovanelli. Everyone stopped talking, and turned and looked at her. She came straight to Mrs. Walker. "I'm afraid you thought I never was coming, so I sent mother off to tell you. I wanted to make Mr. Giovanelli practise some things before he came; you know he sings beautifully, and I want you to ask him to sing. This is Mr. Giovanelli; you know I introduced him to you; he's got the most lovely voice and he knows the most charming set of songs. I made him go over them this evening, on purpose; we had the greatest time at the hotel." Of all this Daisy delivered herself with the sweetest, brightest audibleness, looking now at her hostess and now round the room, while she gave a series of little pats, round her shoulders, to the edges of her dress. "Is there anyone I know?" she asked.

"I think everyone knows you!" said Mrs. Walker pregnantly, and she gave a very cursory greeting to Mr. Giovanelli. This gentleman bore himself gallantly. He smiled and bowed and showed his white teeth, he curled his moustaches and rolled his eyes, and performed all the proper functions of a handsome Italian at an evening party. He sang, very prettily, half-a-dozen songs, though Mrs. Walker afterwards declared that she had been quite unable to find out who asked him. It was apparently not Daisy who had given him his orders. Daisy sat at a distance from the piano, and though she had publicly, as it were, professed a high admiration for his singing, talked, not inaudibly, while it was going on.

"It's a pity these rooms are so small; we can't dance," she said to Winterbourne as if she had seen him five minutes before.

---

30. *Elle s'affiche:* She is making a spectacle of herself (French).

"I am not sorry we can't dance," Winterbourne answered; "I don't dance."

"Of course you don't dance; you're too stiff," said Miss Daisy. "I hope you enjoyed your drive with Mrs. Walker."

"No, I didn't enjoy it; I preferred walking with you."

"We paired off, that was much better," said Daisy. "But did you ever hear anything so cool as Mrs. Walker's wanting me to get into her carriage and drop poor Mr. Giovanelli, and under the pretext that it was proper? People have different ideas! It would have been most unkind; he had been talking about that walk for ten days."

"He should not have talked about it at all," said Winterbourne; "he would never have proposed to a young lady of this country to walk about the streets with him."

"About the streets?" cried Daisy, with her pretty stare. "Where then would he have proposed to her to walk? The Pincio is not the streets, either; and I, thank goodness, am not a young lady of this country. The young ladies of this country have a dreadfully poky time of it, so far as I can learn; I don't see why I should change my habits for *them*."

"I am afraid your habits are those of a flirt," said Winterbourne gravely.

"Of course they are," she cried, giving him her little smiling stare again. "I'm a fearful, frightful flirt! Did you ever hear of a nice girl that was not? But I suppose you will tell me now that I am not a nice girl."

"You're a very nice girl, but I wish you would flirt with me and me only," said Winterbourne.

"Ah! thank you, thank you very much; you are the last man I should think of flirting with. As I have had the pleasure of informing you, you are too stiff."

"You say that too often," said Winterbourne.

Daisy gave a delighted laugh. "If I could have the sweet hope of making you angry, I should say it again."

"Don't do that; when I am angry I'm stiffer than ever. But if you won't flirt with me, do cease at least to flirt with your friend at the piano; they don't understand that sort of thing here."

"I thought they understood nothing else!" exclaimed Daisy.

"Not in young unmarried women."

"It seems to me much more proper in young unmarried women than in old married ones," Daisy declared.

"Well," said Winterbourne, "when you deal with natives you must go by the custom of the place. Flirting is a purely American custom; it doesn't exist here. So when you show yourself in public with Mr. Giovanelli and without your mother —"

"Gracious! poor mother!" interposed Daisy.

"Though you may be flirting, Mr. Giovanelli is not; he means something else."

"He isn't preaching, at any rate," said Daisy with vivacity. "And if you want very much to know, we are neither of us flirting, we are too good friends for that; we are very intimate friends."

"Ah!" rejoined Winterbourne, "if you are in love with each other it is another affair."

She had allowed him up to this point to talk so frankly that he had no expectation of shocking her by this ejaculation; but she immediately got up, blushing visibly, and leaving him to exclaim mentally that little American flirts were the queerest creatures in the world. "Mr. Giovanelli, at least," she said, giving her interlocutor a single glance, "never says such very disagreeable things to me."

Winterbourne was bewildered; he stood staring. Mr. Giovanelli had finished singing; he left the piano and came over to Daisy. "Won't you come into the other room and have some tea?" he asked, bending before her with his ornamental smile.

Daisy turned to Winterbourne, beginning to smile again. He was still more perplexed, for this inconsequent smile made nothing clear, though it seemed to prove, indeed, that she had a sweetness and softness that reverted instinctively to the pardon of offences. "It has never occurred to Mr. Winterbourne to offer me any tea," she said, with her little tormenting manner.

"I have offered you advice," Winterbourne rejoined.

"I prefer weak tea!" cried Daisy, and she went off with the brilliant Giovanelli. She sat with him in the adjoining room, in the embrasure of the window, for the rest of the evening. There was an interesting performance at the piano, but neither of these young people gave heed to it. When Daisy came to take leave of Mrs. Walker, this lady conscientiously repaired the weakness of which she had been guilty at the moment of the young girl's arrival. She turned her back straight upon Miss Miller and left her to depart with what grace she might. Winterbourne was standing near the door; he saw it all. Daisy turned very pale and looked at her mother, but Mrs. Miller was humbly unconscious of any violation of the usual social forms. She appeared, indeed, to have felt an incongruous impulse to draw attention to her own striking observance of them. "Good-night, Mrs. Walker," she said; "we've had a beautiful evening. You see if I let Daisy come to parties without me, I don't want her to go away without me." Daisy turned away, looking with a pale, grave face at the circle near the door; Winterbourne saw that, for the first moment, she was too much shocked and puzzled even for indignation. He on his side was greatly touched.

"That was very cruel," he said to Mrs. Walker.

"She never enters my drawing-room again," replied his hostess.

Since Winterbourne was not to meet her in Mrs. Walker's drawing-room, he went as often as possible to Mrs. Miller's hotel. The ladies were rarely at home, but when he found them the devoted Giovanelli was always present. Very often the brilliant little Roman was in the drawing-room with Daisy alone, Mrs. Miller being apparently constantly of the opinion that discretion is the better part of surveillance. Winterbourne noted, at first with surprise, that Daisy on these occasions was never embarrassed or annoyed by his own entrance; but he very presently began to feel that she had no more surprises for him; the unexpected in her behaviour was the only thing to expect. She showed no displeasure at her *tête-à-tête* with Giovanelli being interrupted; she could chatter as freshly and freely with two gentlemen as with one; there was always, in her conversation, the same odd mixture of audacity and puerility. Winterbourne remarked to himself that if she was seriously interested in Giovanelli it was very singular that she should not take more trouble to preserve the sanctity of their interviews, and he liked her the more for her innocent-looking indifference and her apparently inexhaustible good humour. He could hardly have said why, but she seemed to him a girl who would never be jealous. At the risk of exciting a somewhat derisive smile on the reader's part, I may affirm that with regard to the women who had hitherto interested him, it very often seemed to Winterbourne among the possibilities that, given certain contingencies, he should be afraid — literally afraid — of these ladies; he had a pleasant sense that he should never be afraid of Daisy Miller. It must be added that this sentiment was not altogether flattering to Daisy; it was part of his conviction, or rather of his apprehension, that she would prove a very light young person.

But she was evidently very much interested in Giovanelli. She looked at him whenever he spoke; she was perpetually telling him to do this and to do that; she was constantly "chaffing" and abusing him. She appeared completely to have forgotten that Winterbourne had said anything to displease her at Mrs. Walker's little party. One Sunday afternoon, having gone to St. Peter's with his aunt, Winterbourne perceived Daisy strolling about the great church in company with the inevitable Giovanelli. Presently he pointed out the young girl and her cavalier to Mrs. Costello. This lady looked at them a moment through her eyeglass, and then she said:

"That's what makes you so pensive in these days, eh?"

"I had not the least idea I was pensive," said the young man.

"You are very much pre-occupied, you are thinking of something."

"And what is it," he asked, "that you accuse me of thinking of?"

"Of that young lady's — Miss Baker's, Miss Chandler's — what's her name? Miss Miller's intrigue with that little barber's block."

"Do you call it an intrigue," Winterbourne asked — "an affair that goes on with such peculiar publicity?"

"That's their folly," said Mrs. Costello, "it's not their merit."

"No," rejoined Winterbourne, with something of that pensiveness to which his aunt had alluded. "I don't believe that there is anything to be called an intrigue."

"I have heard a dozen people speak of it; they say she is quite carried away by him."

"They are certainly very intimate," said Winterbourne.

Mrs. Costello inspected the young couple again with her optical instrument. "He is very handsome. One easily sees how it is. She thinks him the most elegant man in the world, the finest gentleman. She has never seen anything like him; he is better even than the courier. It was the courier probably who introduced him, and if he succeeds in marrying the young lady, the courier will come in for a magnificent commission."

"I don't believe she thinks of marrying him," said Winterbourne, "and I don't believe he hopes to marry her."

"You may be very sure she thinks of nothing. She goes on from day to day, from hour to hour, as they did in the Golden Age. I can imagine nothing more vulgar. And at the same time," added Mrs. Costello, "depend upon it that she may tell you any moment that she is 'engaged.'"

"I think that is more than Giovanelli expects," said Winterbourne.

"Who is Giovanelli?"

"The little Italian. I have asked questions about him and learned something. He is apparently a perfectly respectable little man. I believe he is in a small way, a *cavaliere avvocato*.[31] But he doesn't move in what are called the first circles. I think it is really not

---

31. *cavaliere avvocato:* A gentleman lawyer (Italian).

absolutely impossible that the courier introduced him. He is evidently immensely charmed with Miss Miller. If she thinks him the finest gentleman in the world, he, on his side, has never found himself in personal contact with such splendour, such opulence, such expensiveness, as this young lady's. And then she must seem to him wonderfully pretty and interesting. I rather doubt that he dreams of marrying her. That must appear to him too impossible a piece of luck. He has nothing but his handsome face to offer, and there is a substantial Mr. Miller in that mysterious land of dollars. Giovanelli knows that he hasn't a title to offer. If he were only a count or a *marchese!*[32] He must wonder at his luck at the way they have taken him up."

"He accounts for it by his handsome face, and thinks Miss Miller a young lady *qui se passe ses fantaisies!*"[33] said Mrs. Costello.

"It is very true," Winterbourne pursued, "that Daisy and her mamma have not yet risen to that stage of – what shall I call it? – of culture, at which the idea of catching a count or a *marchese* begins. I believe that they are intellectually incapable of that conception."

"Ah! but the *avvocato* can't believe it," said Mrs. Costello.

Of the observation excited by Daisy's "intrigue," Winterbourne gathered that day at St. Peter's sufficient evidence. A dozen of the American colonists in Rome came to talk with Mrs. Costello, who sat on a little portable stool at the base of one of the great pilasters. The vesper service was going forward in splendid chants and organ-tones in the adjacent choir, and meanwhile, between Mrs. Costello and her friends, there was a great deal said about poor little Miss Miller's going really "too far." Winterbourne was not pleased with what he heard; but when, coming out upon the great steps of the church, he saw Daisy, who had emerged before him, get into an open cab with her accomplice and roll away through the cynical streets of Rome, he could not deny to himself that she was going very far indeed. He felt very sorry for her – not exactly that he believed that she had completely lost her head, but because it was painful to hear so much that was pretty, and undefended, and natural, assigned to a vulgar place among the categories of disorder. He made an attempt after this to give a hint to Mrs. Miller. He met one day in the Corso[34] a friend – a tourist like himself – who had just come out of the Doria Palace, where he had been walking through the beautiful gallery. His friend talked for a moment about the superb portrait of Innocent X. by Velasquez,[35] which hangs in one of the cabinets of the palace, and then said, "And in the same cabinet, by-the-way, I had the pleasure of contemplating a picture of a different kind – that pretty American girl whom you pointed out to me last week." In answer to Winterbourne's inquiries, his friend narrated that the pretty American girl – prettier than ever – was seated with a companion in the secluded nook in which the great papal portrait was enshrined.

---

32. *marchese:* A marquis, a nobleman (Italian).
33. *qui se passe ses fantaisies!:* Who is indulging her whims! (French).
34. **the Corso:** The Via del Corso, the main thoroughfare in Rome.
35. **portrait by . . . Velasquez:** The Spanish painter Diego Velázquez, or Velásquez (1599–1660), whose celebrated portrait of Pope Innocent X is displayed in isolation in the "Cabinet of Velázquez," a small pavilion at one end of the Galleria Doria Pamphilj.

"Who was her companion?" asked Winterbourne.

"A little Italian with a bouquet in his button hole. The girl is delightfully pretty, but I thought I understood from you the other day that she was a young lady *du meilleur monde*."[36]

"So she is!" answered Winterbourne; and having assured himself that his informant had seen Daisy and her companion but five minutes before, he jumped into a cab and went to call on Mrs. Miller. She was at home; but she apologised to him for receiving him in Daisy's absence.

"She's gone out somewhere with Mr. Giovanelli," said Mrs. Miller. "She's always going round with Mr. Giovanelli."

"I have noticed that they are very intimate," Winterbourne observed.

"Oh! it seems as if they couldn't live without each other!" said Mrs. Miller. "Well, he's a real gentleman anyhow. I keep telling Daisy she's engaged!"

"And what does Daisy say?"

"Oh, she says she isn't engaged. But she might as well be!" this impartial parent resumed. "She goes on as if she was. But I've made Mr. Giovanelli promise to tell me, if *she* doesn't. I should want to write to Mr. Miller about it – shouldn't you?"

Winterbourne replied that he certainly should; and the state of mind of Daisy's mamma struck him as so unprecedented in the annals of parental vigilance that he gave up as utterly irrelevant the attempt to place her upon her guard.

After this Daisy was never at home, and Winterbourne ceased to meet her at the houses of their common acquaintance, because, as he perceived, these shrewd people had quite made up their minds that she was going too far. They ceased to invite her, and they intimated that they desired to express to observant Europeans the great truth that, though Miss Daisy Miller was a young American lady, her behaviour was not representative – was regarded by her compatriots as abnormal. Winterbourne wondered how she felt about all the cold shoulders that were turned towards her, and sometimes it annoyed him to suspect that she did not feel at all. He said to himself that she was too light and childish, too uncultivated and unreasoning, too provincial, to have reflected upon her ostracism or even to have perceived it. Then at other moments he believed that she carried about in her elegant and irresponsible little organism a defiant, passionate, perfectly observant consciousness of the impression she produced. He asked himself whether Daisy's defiance came from the consciousness of innocence or from her being, essentially a young person of the reckless class. It must be admitted that holding one-self to a belief in Daisy's "innocence" came to seem to Winterbourne more and more a matter of fine-spun gallantry. As I have already had occasion to relate, he was angry at finding himself reduced to chopping logic about this young lady; he was vexed at his want of instinctive certitude as to how far her eccentricities were generic, national, and how far they were personal. From either view of them he had somehow missed her, and now it was too late. She was "carried away" by Mr. Giovanelli.

---

36. *du meilleur monde:* Of the better society (French).

A few days after his brief interview with her mother, he encountered her in that beautiful abode of flowering desolation known as the Palace of the Caesars. The early Roman spring had filled the air with bloom and perfume, and the rugged surface of the Palatine was muffled with tender verdure. Daisy was strolling along the top of one of those great mounds of ruin that are embanked with mossy marble and paved with monumental inscriptions. It seemed to him that Rome had never been so lovely as just then. He stood looking off at the enchanting harmony of line and colour that remotely encircles the city, inhaling the softly humid odours and feeling the freshness of the year and the antiquity of the place reaffirm themselves in mysterious interfusion. It seemed to him also that Daisy had never looked so pretty; but this had been an observation of his whenever he met her. Giovanelli was at her side, and Giovanelli, too, wore an aspect of even unwonted brilliancy.

"Well," said Daisy, "I should think you would be lonesome!"

"Lonesome?" asked Winterbourne.

"You are always going round by yourself. Can't you get anyone to walk with you?"

"I am not so fortunate," said Winterbourne, "as your companion."

Giovanelli, from the first, had treated Winterbourne with distinguished politeness; he listened with a deferential air to his remarks; he laughed, punctiliously, at his pleasantries; he seemed disposed to testify to his belief that Winterbourne was a superior young man. He carried himself in no degree like a jealous wooer; he had obviously a great deal of tact; he had no objection to your expecting a little humility of him. It even seemed to Winterbourne at times that Giovanelli would find a certain mental relief in being able to have a private understanding with him — to say to him, as an intelligent man, that, bless you, *he* knew how extraordinary was this young lady, and didn't flatter himself with delusive — or at least *too* delusive — hopes of matrimony and dollars. On this occasion he strolled away from his companion to pluck a sprig of almond-blossom, which he carefully arranged in his button-hole.

"I know why you say that," said Daisy, watching Giovanelli. "Because you think I go round too much with *him!*" And she nodded at her attendant.

"Every one thinks so — if you care to know," said Winterbourne.

"Of course I care to know!" Daisy exclaimed seriously. "But I don't believe it. They are only pretending to be shocked. They don't really care a straw what I do. Besides, I don't go round so much."

"I think you will find they do care. They will show it — disagreeably."

Daisy looked at him a moment. "How — disagreeably?"

"Haven't you noticed anything?" Winterbourne asked.

"I have noticed you. But I noticed you were as stiff as an umbrella the first time I saw you."

"You will find I am not so stiff as several others," said Winterbourne, smiling.

"How shall I find it?"

"By going to see the others."

"What will they do to me?"

"They will give you the cold shoulder. Do you know what that means?"

Daisy was looking at him intently; she began to colour. "Do you mean as Mrs. Walker did the other night?"

"Exactly!" said Winterbourne.

She looked away at Giovanelli, who was decorating himself with his almond-blossom. Then looking back at Winterbourne – "I shouldn't think you would let people be so unkind!" she said.

"How can I help it?" he asked.

"I should think you would say something."

"I do say something;" and he paused a moment. "I say that your mother tells me that she believes you are engaged."

"Well, she does," said Daisy very simply.

Winterbourne began to laugh. "And does Randolph believe it?" he asked.

"I guess Randolph doesn't believe anything," said Daisy. Randolph's scepticism excited Winterbourne to further hilarity, and he observed that Giovanelli was coming back to them. Daisy, observing it too, addressed herself again to her countryman. "Since you have mentioned it," she said, "I *am* engaged." . . . Winterbourne looked at her; he had stopped laughing. "You don't believe it!" she added.

He was silent a moment; and then, "Yes, I believe it!" he said.

"Oh, no, you don't," she answered. "Well, then – I am not!"

The young girl and her cicerone were on their way to the gate of the enclosure, so that Winterbourne, who had but lately entered, presently took leave of them. A week afterwards he went to dine at a beautiful villa on the Caelian Hill, and, on arriving, dismissed his hired vehicle. The evening was charming, and he promised himself the satisfaction of walking home beneath the Arch of Constantine and past the vaguely-lighted monuments of the Forum. There was a waning moon in the sky, and her radiance was not brilliant, but she was veiled in a thin cloud-curtain which seemed to diffuse and equalise it. When, on his return from the villa (it was eleven o'clock), Winterbourne approached the dusky circle of the Colosseum, it recurred to him, as a lover of the picturesque, that the interior, in the pale moonshine, would be well worth a glance. He turned aside and walked to one of the empty arches, near which, as he observed, an open carriage – one of the little Roman street-cabs – was stationed. Then he passed in, among the cavernous shadows of the great structure, and emerged upon the clear and silent arena. The place had never seemed to him more impressive. One-half of the gigantic circus was in deep shade; the other was sleeping in the luminous dusk. As he stood there he began to murmur Byron's famous lines, out of "Manfred"; but before he had finished his quotation he remembered that if nocturnal meditations in the Colosseum are recommended by the poets, they are deprecated by the doctors. The historic atmosphere was there, certainly; but the historic atmosphere, scientifically considered, was no better than a villainous miasma. Winterbourne walked to the middle of the arena, to take a more general glance, intending thereafter to make a hasty retreat. The great cross in the centre was covered with shadow; it was only as he drew near it that he made it out distinctly. Then he saw that two persons were stationed upon the low steps which formed its base. One of these was a woman, seated; her companion was standing in front of her.

Presently the sound of the woman's voice came to him distinctly in the warm night-air. "Well, he looks at us as one of the old lions or tigers may have looked at the Christian martyrs!" These were the words he heard, in the familiar accent of Miss Daisy Miller.

"Let us hope he is not very hungry," responded the ingenious Giovanelli. "He will have to take me first; you will serve for dessert!"

Winterbourne stopped, with a sort of horror; and, it must be added, with a sort of relief. It was as if a sudden illumination had been flashed upon the ambiguity of Daisy's behaviour and the riddle had become easy to read. She was a young lady whom a gentleman need no longer be at pains to respect. He stood there looking at her – looking at her companion, and not reflecting that though he saw them vaguely, he himself must have been more brightly visible. He felt angry with himself that he had bothered so much about the right way of regarding Miss Daisy Miller. Then, as he was going to advance again, he checked himself; not from the fear that he was doing her injustice, but from a sense of the danger of appearing unbecomingly exhilarated by this sudden revulsion from cautious criticism. He turned away towards the entrance of the place; but as he did so he heard Daisy speak again.

"Why, it was Mr. Winterbourne! He saw me – and he cuts me!"

What a clever little reprobate she was, and how smartly she played at injured innocence! But he wouldn't cut her. Winterbourne came forward again, and went towards the great cross. Daisy had got up; Giovanelli lifted his hat. Winterbourne had now begun to think simply of the craziness, from a sanitary point of view, of a delicate young girl lounging away the evening in this nest of malaria. What if she *were* a clever little reprobate? that was no reason for her dying of the *perniciosa.*[37] "How long have you been here?" he asked, almost brutally.

Daisy, lovely in the flattering moonlight, looked at him a moment. Then – "All the evening," she answered gently. . . . "I never saw anything so pretty."

"I am afraid," said Winterbourne, "that you will not think Roman fever very pretty. This is the way people catch it. I wonder," he added, turning to Giovanelli, "that you, a native Roman, should countenance such a terrible indiscretion."

"Ah," said the handsome native, "for myself, I am not afraid."

"Neither am I – for you! I am speaking for this young lady."

Giovanelli lifted his well-shaped eyebrows and showed his brilliant teeth. But he took Winterbourne's rebuke with docility. "I told the Signorina it was a grave indiscretion; but when was the Signorina ever prudent?"

"I never was sick, and I don't mean to be!" the Signorina declared. "I don't look like much, but I'm healthy! I was bound to see the Colosseum by moonlight; I shouldn't have wanted to go home without that; and we have had the most beautiful time, haven't we, Mr. Giovanelli? If there has been any danger, Eugenio can give me some pills. He has got some splendid pills.

"I should advise you," said Winterbourne, "to drive home as fast as possible and take one!"

---

37. *perniciosa:* Malaria (Italian).

"What you say is very wise," Giovanelli rejoined. "I will go and make sure the carriage is at hand." And he went forward rapidly.

Daisy followed with Winterbourne. He kept looking at her; she seemed not in the least embarrassed. Winterbourne said nothing; Daisy chattered about the beauty of the place. "Well, I *have* seen the Colosseum by moonlight!" she exclaimed. "That's one good thing." Then, noticing Winterbourne's silence, she asked him why he didn't speak. He made no answer; he only began to laugh. They passed under one of the dark archways; Giovanelli was in front with the carriage. Here Daisy stopped a moment, looking at the young American. "*Did* you believe I was engaged the other day?" she asked.

"It doesn't matter what I believed the other day," said Winterbourne, still laughing.

"Well, what do you believe now?"

"I believe that it makes very little difference whether you are engaged or not!"

He felt the young girl's pretty eyes fixed upon him through the thick gloom of the archway; she was apparently going to answer. But Giovanelli hurried her forward. "Quick, quick," he said; "if we get in by midnight we are quite safe."

Daisy took her seat in the carriage, and the fortunate Italian placed himself beside her. "Don't forget Eugenio's pills!" said Winterbourne, as he lifted his hat.

"I don't care," said Daisy, in a little strange tone, "whether I have Roman fever or not!" Upon this the cab-driver cracked his whip, and they rolled away over the desultory patches of the antique pavement.

Winterbourne – to do him justice, as it were – mentioned to no one that he had encountered Miss Miller, at midnight, in the Colosseum with a gentleman; but nevertheless, a couple of days later, the fact of her having been there under these circumstances was known to every member of the little American circle, and commented accordingly. Winterbourne reflected that they had of course known it at the hotel, and that, after Daisy's return, there had been an exchange of remarks between the porter and the cab-driver. But the young man was conscious at the same moment that it had ceased to be a matter of serious regret to him that the little American flirt should be "talked about" by low-minded menials. These people, a day or two later, had serious information to give: the little American flirt was alarmingly ill. Winterbourne, when the rumour came to him, immediately went to the hotel for more news. He found that two or three charitable friends had preceded him, and that they were being entertained in Mrs. Miller's salon by Randolph.

"It's going round at night," said Randolph – "that's what made her sick. She's always going round at night. I shouldn't think she'd want to – it's so plaguey dark. You can't see anything here at night, except when there's a moon. In America there's always a moon!" Mrs. Miller was invisible; she was now, at least, giving her daughter the advantage of her society. It was evident that Daisy was dangerously ill.

Winterbourne went often to ask for news of her, and once he saw Mrs. Miller, who, though deeply alarmed, was – rather to his surprise – perfectly composed, and, as it appeared, a most efficient and judicious nurse. She talked a good deal about Dr. Davis, but Winterbourne paid her the compliment of saying to himself that she was not, after all, such a monstrous goose. "Daisy spoke of you the other day," she said to him. "Half the time she doesn't know what she's saying, but that time I think she did. She gave me a message; she told me to tell you. She told me to tell you that she never was engaged to that handsome Italian. I am sure I am very glad; Mr. Giovanelli hasn't been near us since she was taken ill. I thought he was so much of a gentleman; but I don't call that very polite! A lady told me that he was afraid I was angry with him for taking Daisy round at night. Well, so I am; but I suppose he knows I'm a lady. I would scorn to scold him. Any way, she says she's not engaged. I don't know why she wanted you to know; but she said to me three times — 'Mind you tell Mr. Winterbourne.' And then she told me to ask if you remembered the time you went to that castle, in Switzerland. But I said I wouldn't give any such messages as that. Only, if she is not engaged, I'm sure I'm glad to know it."

But, as Winterbourne had said, it mattered very little. A week after this the poor girl died; it had been a terrible case of the fever. Daisy's grave was in the little Protestant cemetery, in an angle of the wall of imperial Rome, beneath the cypresses and the thick spring-flowers. Winterbourne stood there beside it, with a number of other mourners; a number larger than the scandal excited by the young lady's career would have led you to expect. Near him stood Giovanelli, who came nearer still before Winterbourne turned away. Giovanelli was very pale; on this occasion he had no flower in his button-hole; he seemed to wish to say something. At last he said, "She was the most beautiful young lady I ever saw, and the most amiable." And then he added in a moment, "And she was the most innocent."

Winterbourne looked at him, and presently repeated his words, "And the most innocent?"

"The most innocent!"

Winterbourne felt sore and angry. "Why the devil," he asked, "did you take her to that fatal place?"

Mr. Giovanelli's urbanity was apparently imperturbable. He looked on the ground a moment, and then he said, "For myself, I had no fear; and she wanted to go."

"That was no reason!" Winterbourne declared.

The subtle Roman again dropped his eyes. "If she had lived, I should have got nothing. She would never have married me, I am sure."

"She would never have married you?"

"For a moment I hoped so. But no. I am sure."

Winterbourne listened to him; he stood staring at the raw protuberance among the April daisies. When he turned away again Mr. Giovanelli, with his light slow step, had retired.

Winterbourne almost immediately left Rome; but the following summer he again met his aunt, Mrs. Costello, at Vevey. Mrs. Costello was fond of Vevey. In the interval Winterbourne had often thought of Daisy Miller and her mystifying manners. One day he spoke of her to his aunt — said it was on his conscience that he had done her injustice.

"I am sure I don't know," said Mrs. Costello. "How did your injustice affect her?"

"She sent me a message before her death which I didn't understand at the time. But I have understood it since. She would have appreciated one's esteem."

"Is that a modest way," asked Mrs. Costello, "of saying that she would have reciprocated one's affection?"

Winterbourne offered no answer to this question; but he presently said, "You were right in that remark that you made last summer. I was booked to make a mistake. I have lived too long in foreign parts."

Nevertheless, he went back to live at Geneva, whence there continue to come the most contradictory accounts of his motives of sojourn: a report that he is "studying" hard — an intimation that he is much interested in a very clever foreign lady.

[1878]

James's "The Real Thing."   James later explained that this story was inspired by an anecdote told to him by his friend George du Maurier, an illustrator on the staff of the popular British magazine *Punch.* Du Maurier, who employed a working-class couple as models for his weekly "social" illustrations in the magazine, had been approached by a society couple who had suffered financial reverses and sought work as models for the illustrations, reasoning that they would not need to "make believe" in order to portray members of the upper class. From that anecdote and the questions it raised about the nature of representation and the relationship of art to life, " 'The Real Thing' sprang at a bound," as James recalled. Appropriately, his story of an illustrator confronted by the aristocratic Major and Mrs. Monarch was first published in *Black and White: A Weekly Illustrated Record and Review.* Established in London in 1891, the journal was designed to feature single-color illustrations (called "black-and-whites") of articles and current literary works. "The three pillars of our enterprise are good art, good literature, and good printing," the editors announced in the first issue of *Black and White.* They consequently published "The Real Thing" along with illustrations by the artist Rudolf Blind, and new illustrations were provided by in-house artists when the story was reprinted in American periodicals later in 1892. The illustrations were omitted, as was standard practice, when the story was reprinted in *The Real Thing and Other Tales* (1893). The text, including the three original illustrations, is taken from the first printing in *Black and White,* April 16, 1892.

THE REAL THING

I

When the porter's wife (she used to answer the house-bell) announced, "A gentleman — with a lady, sir," I had, as I often had in those days, for the wish was father to the thought, an immediate vision of sitters. Sitters my visitors in this case proved to be; but not in the sense I should have preferred. However, there was nothing at first to indicate that they might not have come for a portrait. The gentleman, a man of fifty, very high and very straight, with a moustache slightly grizzled and a dark grey walking-coat admirably fitted, both of which I noted professionally — I don't mean either as a barber or a tailor — would have struck me as a celebrity if celebrities often were striking. It was a truth of which I had for some time been conscious that a figure with a good deal of frontage was, as one might say, almost never a public institution. A glance at the lady helped to remind me of this paradoxical law: she also looked too distinguished to be a "personality." Moreover one would scarcely come across two variations together.

Neither of the pair spoke immediately — they only prolonged the preliminary gaze which suggested that each wished to give the other a chance. They were visibly shy; they stood there letting me take them in — which, as I afterwards perceived, was the most practical thing they could have done. In this way their embarrassment served their cause. I had seen people painfully reluctant to mention that they desired anything so gross as to be represented on canvas; but the scruples of my new friends appeared almost insurmountable. Yet the gentleman might have said, "I should like a portrait of my wife"; and the lady might have said, "I should like a portrait of my husband." Perhaps they were not husband and wife — this naturally would make the matter more delicate. Perhaps they wished to be done together — in which case they ought to have brought a third person to break the news.

"We come from Mr. Rivet," the lady said at last, with a dim smile which had the effect of a moist sponge passed over a "sunk" piece of painting,[1] as well as of a vague allusion to vanished beauty. She was as tall and straight, in her degree as her companion, and with ten years less to carry. She looked as sad as a woman could look whose face was not charged with expression; that is, her tinted oval mask showed friction, as an exposed surface shows it. The hand of time had played over her freely, but only to simplify. She was slim and stiff, and so well-dressed, in dark blue cloth, with lappets[2] and pockets and buttons, that it was clear she employed the same tailor as her husband. The couple had an indefinable air of prosperous thrift — they evidently got a good deal of luxury for their money. If I was to be one of their luxuries it would behove me to consider my terms.

"Ah, Claude Rivet recommended me?" I enquired; and I added that it was very kind of him, though I could reflect that, as he only painted landscape, this was not a sacrifice.

The lady looked very hard at the gentleman, and the gentleman looked round the room. Then staring at the floor a moment and stroking his moustache, he rested his pleasant eyes on me with the remark: "He said you were the right one."

"I try to be, when people want to sit."

"Yes, we should like to," said the lady, anxiously.

"Do you mean together?"

My visitors exchanged a glance. "If you could do anything with *me*, I suppose it would be double," the gentleman stammered.

"Oh yes, you naturally make a higher charge for two figures than for one."

---

1. a **"sunk" piece of painting:** An improperly prepared surface of a painting where the paint has seeped into the canvas and the color is consequently diminished.
2. **lappets:** Loose or overlapping parts of a garment.

"We should like to make it pay," the husband confessed.

"That's very good of you," I returned, appreciating so unwonted a sympathy – for I supposed he meant pay the artist.

A sense of strangeness seemed to dawn on the lady. "We mean for the illustrations – Mr. Rivet said you might put one in."

"Put one in – an illustration?" I was equally confused.

"Sketch her off, you know," said the gentleman, colouring.

It was only then that I understood the service Claude Rivet had rendered me; he had told them that I worked in black and white, for magazines, for story-books, for sketches of contemporary life, and consequently had frequent employment for models. These things were true, but it was not less true that (I may confess it now – whether because the aspiration was to lead to everything or to nothing I leave the reader to guess) I couldn't get the honours, to say nothing of the emoluments, of a great painter of portraits out of my head. My "illustrations" were my pot-boilers; I looked to a different branch of art (far and away the most interesting it had always seemed to me) to perpetuate my fame. There was no shame in looking to it also to make my fortune; but that fortune was by so much further from being made, from the moment my visitors wished to be "done" for nothing. I was disappointed; for, in the pictorial sense, I had immediately *seen* them. I had seized their type – I had already settled what I would do with it. Something that wouldn't absolutely have pleased them, I afterwards reflected. But that's nothing; a portrait is almost always bad in direct proportion as it gratifies the original or his friends. He himself can please his friends; the triumph of the painter is to please his enemies; they can't get over that. At any rate the delight of the sitter is in general a bad note.

"Ah, you're – you're – a – ?" I began, as soon as I had mastered my surprise. I couldn't bring out the dingy word "models"; it seemed to fit the case so little.

"We haven't had much practice," said the lady.

"We've got to do something, and we've thought that an artist, in your line, might perhaps make something of us," her husband threw off. He further mentioned that they didn't know many artists and that they had gone first, on the off chance (he painted views of course, but sometimes put in figures – perhaps I remembered), to Mr. Rivet, whom they had met a few years before at a place in Norfolk where he was sketching.

"We used to sketch a little ourselves," the lady recalled.

"It's very awkward, but we absolutely *must* do something," her husband went on.

"Of course, we're not so *very* young," she admitted, with a wan smile.

With the remark that I might as well know something more about them, the husband had handed me a card, extracted from a neat new pocket-book (their appurtenances were all of the freshest), and inscribed with the words, "Major Monarch." Impressive as these words were, they didn't carry my knowledge much further; but my visitor presently added: "I've left the army, and we've had the misfortune to lose our money. In fact, our means are extremely small."

"It's an awful bore," said Mrs. Monarch.

They evidently wished to be discreet – to take care not to swagger because they were gentlefolks. I perceived they would have been willing to recognise this as something of a drawback, at the same time that I guessed at an underlying sense — their consolation in adversity — that they *had* their points. They certainly had; but these advantages struck me as preponderantly social; such, for instance, as would help to make a drawing-room look well. However, a drawing-room was always, or ought to be, a picture.

In consequence of his wife's allusion to their age Major Monarch remarked: "Naturally, it's more for the figure that we thought of going in. We can still hold ourselves up." On the instant, I saw that the figure was indeed their strong point. His "naturally" didn't sound vain, but it lighted up the question. "*She* has got the best," he continued, nodding at his wife, with a pleasant after-dinner absence of circumlocution. I could only reply, as if we were in fact sitting over our wine, that this didn't prevent his own from being very good; which led him, in turn, to rejoin. "We thought that if you ever have to do people like us, we might be something like it. *She*, particularly — for a lady in a book, you know."

I was so amused by them that, to get more of it, I did my best to take their point of view; and though it was an embarrassment to find myself appraising physically, as if they were animals on hire or useful blacks, a pair whom I should have expected to meet only in one of the relations in which criticism is tacit, I looked at Mrs. Monarch judicially enough to be able to exclaim, after a moment, with conviction: "Oh yes, a lady in a book!" She was singularly like a bad illustration.

"We'll stand up, if you like, said the Major; and he raised himself before me with a really grand air.

I could take his measure at a glance — he was six feet two and a perfect gentleman. It would have paid any club, in process of formation and in want of a stamp, to engage him, at a salary, to stand in the principal window. What struck me immediately was that in coming to me they had rather missed their vocation; they could surely have been turned to better account for advertising purposes. I couldn't, of course, see the thing in detail; but I could see them make someone's fortune — I don't mean their own. There was something in them for a waistcoat-maker, an hotel-keeper or a soap-vendor. I could imagine "We always use it" pinned on their bosoms with the greatest effect; I had a vision of the promptitude with which they would launch a *table d'hôte*.[3]

Mrs. Monarch sat still, not from pride but from shyness, and presently her husband said to her: "Get up my dear and show how smart you are." She obeyed, but she had to need to get up to show it. She walked to the end of the studio, and then she came back blushing, with her fluttered eyes on her husband. I was reminded of an incident I had accidentally had a glimpse of in Paris — being with a friend there, a dramatist about to produce a play — when an actress came to him to ask to be entrusted with a part. She went through her paces before him, walked up and down as Mrs. Monarch was doing. Mrs. Monarch did it quite as well, but I abstained from applauding. It was very odd to see such people apply for such poor pay. She looked as if she had ten thousand a year. Her husband had used the word that described her: she was, in the London current

---

3. *table d'hôte:* Literally, "host's table"; a communal dining table for guests at a hotel (French).

"MRS. MONARCH WENT THROUGH HER PACES BEFORE ME, AND DID IT QUITE WELL."

jargon, essentially and typically "smart." Her figure was, in the same order of ideas, conspicuously and irreproachably "good." For a woman of her age her waist was surprisingly small; her elbow, moreover, had the orthodox crook. She held her head at the conventional angle; but why did she come to *me*? She ought to have tried on jackets at a big shop. I feared my visitors were not only destitute, but "artistic" — which would be a great complication. When she sat down again I thanked her, observing that what a draughtsman most valued in his model was the faculty for keeping quiet.

"Oh *she* can keep quiet," said Major Monarch. Then he added, jocosely: "I've always kept her quiet."

"I'm not a nasty fidget, am I?" Mrs. Monarch appealed to her husband.

He addressed his answer to me. "Perhaps it isn't out of place to mention — because we ought to be quite business-like, oughtn't we? — that when I married her she was known as the Beautiful Statue."

"Oh dear!" said Mrs. Monarch, ruefully.

"Of course I should want a certain amount of expression," I rejoined.

"Of *course!*" they both exclaimed.

"And then I suppose you know that you'll get awfully tired."

"Oh, we *never* get tired!" they eagerly cried.

"Have you had any kind of practice?"

They hesitated — they looked at each other. "We've been photographed, *immensely*," said Mrs. Monarch.

"She means the fellows have asked us," added the Major.

"I see — because you're so good-looking."

"I don't know what they thought, but they were always after us."

"We always got our photographs for nothing," smiled Mrs. Monarch.

"We might have bought some, my dear," her husband remarked.

"I'm not sure we have any left. We've given quantities away," she explained to me.

"With our autographs and that sort of thing," said the Major.

"Are they to be got in the shops?" I enquired, as a harmless pleasantry.

"Oh, yes; *hers* — they used to be."

"Not now," said Mrs. Monarch, with her eyes on the floor.

II

I could fancy the "sort of thing" they put on the presentation copies of their photographs, and I was sure they wrote a beautiful hand. It was odd how quickly I was sure of everything that concerned them. If they were now so poor as to have to earn shillings and pence, they never had had much of a margin. Their good looks had been their capital, and they had good-humouredly made the most of the career that this resource marked out for them. It was in their faces, the blankness, the deep intellectual repose of the twenty years of country-house visiting which had given them pleasant intonations. I could see the sunny drawing-rooms, sprinkled with periodicals she didn't read, in which Mrs. Monarch had continuously sat; I could see the wet shrubberies in which she had walked, equipped to admiration for either exercise. I could see the rich covers[4] the major had helped to shoot, and the wonderful garments in which, late at night, he repaired to the smoking-room to talk about them. I could imagine their leggings and waterproofs, their knowing tweeds and rugs, their rolls of sticks and cases of tackle and neat umbrellas; and I could evoke the exact appearance of their two servants and the compact variety of their luggage on the platforms of country stations.

They gave small tips, but they were liked; they didn't do anything themselves, but they were welcome. They looked so well everywhere; they gratified the general relish for stature, complexion and "form." They knew it without fatuity or vulgarity, and they respected themselves in consequence. They were not superficial; they were thorough and kept themselves up — it had been their line. Respectable people had to have some line. I could feel how, even in a dull house, they could have been counted upon for cheerfulness. At present something had happened — it didn't matter what, their little income had grown less, it had grown least — and they had to do something for pocket-money. Their friends liked them, but didn't like to support them. There was something about

---

4. **covers:** Game birds shot in their cover, or place of concealment.

them that represented credit — their clothes, their manners, their type; but if credit is a large empty pocket in which an occasional chink reverberates, the chink at least must be audible. What they wanted of me was to help to make it so. Fortunately they had no children — I soon divined that. They would also perhaps wish our relations to be kept secret; this was why it was "for the figure" — the reproduction of the face would betray them.

I liked them — they were so simple; and I had no objection to them if they would suit. But, somehow, with all their perfections I didn't easily believe in them. After all, they were amateurs, and the ruling passion of my life was the detestation of the amateur. Combined with this was another perversity — an innate preference for the represented subject over the real one. The defect of the real one was so apt to be a lack of representation. I liked things that appeared; then one was sure. Whether they were or not was a subordinate, and almost always a tiresome question. There were other considerations, the first of which was that I already had two or three people in use, notably a young person with big feet, in alpaca, from Kilburn, who, for a couple of years, had come to me regularly for my illustrations, and with whom I was still — perhaps ignobly — satisfied. I frankly explained to my visitors how the case stood; but they had taken more precautions than I supposed. They had reasoned out their opportunity, for Claude Rivet had told them of the projected *édition de luxe* of one of the writers of our day — the rarest of the novelists — who, long neglected by the multitudinous vulgar and dearly prized by the attentive (need I mention Philip Vincent?), had had the happy fortune of seeing, late in life, the dawn and then the full light of a higher criticism — an estimate in which on the part of the public, there was something really of expiation. The edition in question, planned by a publisher of taste, was practically an act of high reparation; the wood-cuts with which it was to be enriched were the homage of English art to one of the most independent representatives of English letters. Major and Mrs. Monarch confessed to me that they had hoped I might be able to work *them* into my share of the enterprise. They knew I was to do the first of the books, "Rutland Ramsay," but I had to make clear to them that my participation in the rest of the affair — this first book was to be a test — was to depend on the satisfaction I should give. If this should be limited my employers would drop me without a scruple. It was therefore a crisis for me, and naturally I was making special preparations, looking about for new people, if they should be necessary, and securing the best types. I admitted, however, that I should like to settle down to two or three good models who would do for everything.

"Should we have often to — a — put on special clothes?" Mrs. Monarch timidly demanded?

"Dear, yes — that's half the business."

"And should we be expected to supply our own costumes?"

"Oh, no; I've got a lot of things. A painter's model put on — or put off — anything he likes."

"And do you mean — a — the same?"

"The same?"

Mrs. Monarch looked at her husband again.

"Oh, she was just wondering," he explained, "if the costumes are in *general* use." I had to confess that they were and I mentioned further that some of them (I had a lot of genuine, greasy last-century things), had served their time, a hundred years ago, on living, world-stained men and women. "We'll put on anything that *fits*," said the Major.

"Oh, I arrange that — they fit in the pictures."

"I'm afraid I should do better for the modern books. I would come as you like," said Mrs. Monarch.

"She has got a lot of clothes at home; they might do for contemporary life," her husband continued.

"Oh, I can fancy scenes in which you'd be quite at home." And indeed I could see the slipshod rearrangements of stale properties — the stories I tried to produce pictures for without the exasperation of reading them — whose sandy tracts the good lady might help to people. But I had to return to the fact that for this sort of work — the daily mechanical grind — I was already equipped; the people I was working with were quite adequate.

"We only thought we might be more like *some* characters," said Mrs. Monarch mildly, getting up.

Her husband also rose; he stood looking at me with a dim wistfulness that was touching in so fine a man. "Wouldn't it be rather a pull sometimes to have — a — to have —?" He hung fire; he wanted me to help him by phrasing what he meant. But I couldn't — I didn't know. So he brought it out, awkwardly; "The *real* thing; a gentleman, you know, or a lady." I was quite ready to give a general assent — I admitted that there was a great deal in that. This encouraged Major Monarch to say, following up his appeal with an unacted gulp: "It's awfully hard — we've tried everything." The gulp was communicative; it proved too much for his wife. Before I knew it Mrs. Monarch had dropped again upon a divan and burst into tears. Her husband sat down beside her, holding one of her hands; whereupon she quickly dried her eyes with the other, while I felt embarrassed as she looked up at me. "There isn't a confounded job I haven't applied for — waited for — prayed for. You can fancy we'd be pretty bad first. Secretaryships and that sort of thing? You might as well ask for a peerage. I'd be *anything* — I'm strong; a messenger or a coal-heaver. I'd put on a gold-laced cap and open carriage-doors in front of the haberdashers; I'd hang about a station, to carry portmanteaus;[5] I'd be a postman. But they won't *look* at you; there are thousands, as good as yourself, already on the ground. *Gentlemen,* poor beggars, that have drunk their wine, that have kept their hunters!"

I was as reassuring as I knew how to be, and my visitors were presently on their feet again while, for the experiment, we agreed on an hour. We were discussing it when the door opened and Miss Churm came in with a wet umbrella. Miss Churm had to take the omnibus to Maida Vale[6] and then walk half a mile. She looked a trifle blowsy and

---

5. **portmanteaus:** Large trunks or suitcases (French).
6. **Maida Vale:** Then a predominantly Jewish district in northwest London.

slightly splashed. I scarcely ever saw her come in without thinking afresh how odd it was that, being so little in herself, she should yet be so much in others. She was a meagre little Miss Churm, but she was an ample heroine of romance. She was a freckled cockney[7] girl, but she could represent everything, from a fine lady to a shepherdess; she had the faculty, as she might have had a fine voice or long hair. She couldn't spell, and she loved beer, but she had two or three "points," and practice, and a knack, and mother-wit, and a kind of whimsical sensibility, and a love of the theatre, and seven sisters, and not an ounce of respect, especially for the *h*.[8] The first thing my visitors saw was that her umbrella was wet, and in their spotless perfection they visibly winced at it. The rain had come on since their arrival.

"I'm all in a soak; there *was* a mess of people in the bus. I wish you lived near a sty-tion," said Miss Churm. I requested her to get ready as quickly as possible, and she passed into the room in which she always changed her dress. But before going out she asked me what she was to get into this time.

"It's the Russian princess, don't you know?" I answered; "the one with the 'golden eyes,' in black velvet, for the long thing in the *Cheapside*."[9]

"Golden eyes? I *say!*" cried Miss Churm, while my companions watched her, with intensity, as she withdrew. She always arranged herself, when she was late, before I could turn round; and I kept my visitors a little, on purpose, so that they might get an idea, from seeing her, what would be expected of themselves. I mentioned that she was quite my notion of an excellent model — she was really very clever.

"Do you think she looks like a Russian princess?" Major Monarch asked, with lurking alarm.

"When I make her, yes."

"Oh, if you have to *make* her —" he reasoned, acutely.

"That's the most you can ask. There are so many that are not makeable."

"Well now, *here's* a lady" — and with a persuasive smile he passed his arm into his wife's — "who's already made!"

"Oh, I'm not a Russian princess," Mrs. Monarch protested, a little coldly. I could see that she had known some and didn't like them. There, immediately, was a complication of a kind that I never had to fear with Miss Churm.

This young lady came back in black velvet — the gown was rather rusty and very low on her lean shoulders — and with a Japanese fan in her red hands. I reminded her that in the scene I was doing she had to look over someone's head. "I forget whose it is; but it doesn't matter. Just look over a head."

"I'd rather look over a stove," said Miss Churm; and she took her station near the fire.

---

7. cockney: A working-class inhabitant of London, especially one from the East End.
8. the *h:* A feature of the cockney dialect was the dropping of the sound of the *h* in a word: for example, pronouncing half as 'alf.
9. *Cheapside:* A fictitious illustrated periodical named after Cheapside, meaning "market-place," a street long associated with produce markets and related businesses in London.

"MISS CHURM TOOK HER STATION NEAR THE FIRE. SHE FELL INTO POSITION AND SETTLED HERSELF INTO A TALL ATTITUDE."

She fell into position, settled herself into a tall attitude, gave a certain backward inclination to her head and a certain forward droop to her fan, and looked, at least to my prejudiced sense, distinguished and charming, foreign and dangerous. We left her looking so, while I went down-stairs with Major and Mrs. Monarch. "I think I could come as near to it as that," said Mrs. Monarch.

"Oh, you think she's shabby, but you must allow for the alchemy of art." However they went off with an evident increase of comfort, founded on their demonstrable advantage in being the real thing. I could fancy them shuddering over Miss Churm. She was very droll about them when I went back, for I told her what they wanted.

"Well, if *she* can sit I'll tyke to book-keeping," said my model.

"She's very lady-like," I replied, as an innocent form of aggravation.

"So much the worse for *you.* That means she can't turn round."

"She'll do for the fashionable novels."

"Oh yes, she'll *do* for them!" my model humorously declared. "Ain't they bad enough without her?" I had often sociably denounced them to Miss Churm.

III

It was for the elucidation of a mystery in one of these works that I first tried Mrs. Monarch. Her husband came with her, to be useful if necessary — it was sufficiently clear that as a general thing he would prefer to come with her. At first I wondered if this were for "propriety's" sake — if he were going to be jealous and meddling. The idea was too tiresome, and if it had been confirmed it would speedily have brought our acquaintance to a close. But I soon saw there was nothing in it, and that if he accompanied Mrs. Monarch it was (in addition to the chance of being wanted), simply because he had nothing else to do. When she was away from him his occupation was gone — she never *had* been away from him. I judged, rightly, that in their awkward situation their close union was their main comfort, and that this union had no weak spot. It was a real marriage, an encouragement to the hesitating, a nut for pessimists to crack. Their address was humble (I remember afterwards thinking it had been the only thing about them that was really professional), and I could fancy the lamentable lodgings in which the Major would have been left alone. He could bear them with his wife — he couldn't bear them without her.

He had too much tact to try and make himself agreeable when he couldn't be useful; so he simply sat and waited, when I was too absorbed in my work to talk. But I liked to make him talk — it made my work, when it didn't interrupt it, less sordid, less special. To listen to him was to combine the excitement of going out with the economy of staying at home. There was only one hindrance: that I seemed not to know any of the people he and his wife had known. I think he wondered extremely, during the term of our intercourse, whom the deuce I *did* know. He hadn't a stray sixpence of an idea to fumble for; so we didn't spin it very fine — we confined ourselves to questions of leather and even of liquor (saddlers and breeches-makers and how to get good claret cheap), and matters like "good trains" and the habits of small game. His lore on these last subjects was astonishing — he was a mixture of the station-master and the ornithologist. When he couldn't talk about greater things he could talk cheerfully about smaller, and since I couldn't accompany him into reminiscences of the fashionable world he could lower the conversation without a visible effort to my level.

So earnest a desire to please was touching in a man who could so easily have knocked one down. He looked after the fire and had an opinion on the draught of the stove, without my asking him, and I could see that he thought many of my arrangements not half clever enough. I remember telling him that if I were only rich I would offer him a salary to come and teach me how to live. Sometimes he gave a random sigh, of which the essence was: "Give me even such a bare old barrack as *this*, and I'd do something with it!" When I wanted to use him he came alone — which was an illustration of the superior courage of women. His wife could bear her solitary second floor, and she was, in general, more discreet; showing by various small reserves that she was alive to the propriety of keeping our relations markedly professional — not letting them slide into sociability. She wished it to remain clear that she and the Major were employed, not cultivated, and if she approved of me as a superior, where I could be kept in my place, she never thought me quite good enough for an equal.

She sat with great intensity, giving the whole of her mind to it, and was capable of remaining for an hour almost as motionless as if she were before a photographer's lens. I could see she had been photographed often, but somehow the very habit that made her good for that purpose unfitted her for mine. At first I was extremely pleased with her lady-like airs, and it was a satisfaction, on coming to follow her lines, to see how good they were and how far they took one. But after a few times I began to find her rather irritatingly stiff; do what I would with it my drawing looked like a photograph or a copy of a photograph. Her figure had no variety of expression — she herself had no sense of variety. You may say that this was my business, was only a question of placing her. I placed her in every conceivable position, but she managed to obliterate their differences. She was always a lady, certainly, and, into the bargain, was always the same lady. She was the real thing, but always the same thing. There were moments when I was oppressed by the serenity of her confidence that she *was* the real thing. All her dealings with me, and all her husband's, were an implication that this was lucky for *me*. Meanwhile I found myself trying to invent types that approached her own, instead of making her own transform itself — in the clever way that was not impossible, for instance, to poor Miss Churm. Arrange as I would and take the precautions I would, she always, in my pictures, came out too tall — landing me in the dilemma of having represented a fascinating woman as seven feet high, which, out of respect perhaps to my own very much scantier inches, was far from my idea of such a personage.

The case was worse with the Major — nothing I could do would keep *him* down, so that he became useful only for the representation of brawny giants. I adored variety and range, I cherished human accidents, the illustrative note; I wanted to characterise closely, and the thing in the world I most hated was the danger of being ridden by a type. I had quarrelled with some of my friends about it — I had parted company with them for maintaining that one *had* to be, and that if the type was beautiful (witness Raphael and Leonardo),[10] the subjection was only a gain. I was neither Leonardo nor Raphael; I was only a possibly presumptuous young modern searcher; I held that everything was to be sacrificed sooner than character. When they averred that the haunting type in question might easily be character, I retorted, perhaps superficially: "Whose?" It couldn't be everybody's — it might end in being nobody's.

After I had drawn Mrs. Monarch a dozen times I perceived more clearly than before that the value of such a model as Miss Churm resided precisely in the fact that she had no positive stamp, combined of course with the other fact that what she did have was a curious and inexplicable talent for imitation. Her usual appearance was like a curtain, which she could draw up, at request, for a kind of regular performance. This perfor-mance was simply suggestive; but it was a word to the wise — it was vivid and pretty. Sometimes, even, I thought it, though she was plain herself, too insipidly pretty; I made it a reproach to her that the figures drawn from her were monotonously (*bêtement*,[11] as we used to say) graceful. Nothing made her more angry; it was so much her pride to feel that she could sit for characters that had nothing in common with each other. She would accuse me at such moments of taking away her "reputytion."

It suffered a certain shrinkage, this queer quantity, from the repeated visits of my new friends. Miss Churm was greatly in demand, never in want of employment, so I had no scruple in putting her off occasionally, to try them more at my ease. It was certainly amusing, at first, to do the real thing — it was amusing to do Major Monarch's trousers. They *were* the real thing, even if he did come out colossal. It was amusing to do his wife's back hair (it was so mathematically neat,) and the particular "smart" tension of her tight stays. She lent herself especially to positions in which the face was somewhat averted or blurred; she abounded in lady-like back views and *profils perdus*.[12] When she stood erect she took naturally one of the attitudes in which court painters represent

---

10. **Raphael and Leonardo:** Raffaello Sanzio or Santi (1483–1520) and Leonardo da Vinci (1452–1519), master painters of the Italian Renaissance.
11. ***bêtement:*** Foolishly (French).
12. ***profils perdus:*** Lost profiles (French); views showing more of the back of the head than the profile of the face.

queens and princesses; so that I found myself wondering whether, to draw out this accomplishment, I couldn't get the editor of the *Cheapside* to publish a truly royal romance, "A Tale of Buckingham Palace." Sometimes, however, the real thing and the make-believe came into contact; by which I mean that Miss Churm, keeping an appointment, or coming to make one on days when I had much work in hand, encountered her imposing rivals. The encounter was not on their part, for they noticed her no more than if she had been the housemaid; not from intentional loftiness, but simply because, as yet, professionally, they didn't know how to fraternise, as I could guess that they would have liked to, or at least that the Major would. They couldn't talk about the omnibus — they always walked; and they didn't know what else to try — she wasn't interested in good trains or cheap claret. Besides, they must have felt — in the air — that she was amused at them, secretly derisive of their ever knowing how. She was not a person to conceal her scepticism if she had had a chance to show it. On the other hand Mrs. Monarch didn't think her tidy; for why else did she take pains to say to me (it was going out of the way, for Mrs. Monarch), that she didn't like dirty women?

One day, when my young lady happened to be present with my other sisters (she even dropped in, when it was convenient, for a chat), I asked her to be so good as to lend a hand in getting tea — a service with which she was familiar and which was one of a class that, living as I did in a small way, with slender domestic resources, I often appealed to my models to render. They liked to lay hands on my property, to break the sitting — I made them feel Bohemian. The next time I saw Miss Churm after this incident she surprised me greatly by making a scene about it — she accused me of having wished to humiliate her. She had not resented the outrage at the time, but had seemed obliging and amused, enjoying the comedy of asking Mrs. Monarch, who sat dull and silent, whether she would have cream and sugar, and putting an exaggerated simper into the question. She had tried intonations — as if she too wished to pass for the real thing; till I was afraid my other visitors would take offence.

Oh, *they* were determined not to do this; and their really touching patience was the measure of their great need. They would sit by the hour, uncomplaining, till I was ready to use them; they would come back on the chance of being wanted and would walk away cheerfully if they were not. I used to go to the door with them to see in what magnificent order they retreated. I tried to find other employment for them — I introduced them to several artists. But they didn't "take," for reasons I could appreciate, and I became conscious, rather anxiously, that after such disappointments, they fell back upon me with a heavier weight. They did me the honour to think that it was I who was most *their* form. They were not picturesque enough for the painters, and in those days there were not so many serious workers in black and white. Besides, they had an eye to the great job I had mentioned to them — they had secretly set their hearts on supplying the right essence for my pictorial vindication of our high national novelist. They knew that for this undertaking I should want no costume-effects, none of the frippery of past ages — that it was a case in which everything would be contemporary and satirical and, presumably, genteel. If I could work them into it their future would be assured, for the labour would of course be long.

One day Mrs. Monarch came without her husband — she explained his absence by his having had to go to the City.[13] While she sat there in her usual anxious stiffness there came, at the door, a knock which I immediately recognised as the subdued appeal of a model out of work. It was followed by the entrance of a young man whom I easily perceived to be a foreigner, and who proved in fact to be an Italian acquainted with no English word but my name, which he uttered in a way that made it seem to include all others. I had not then visited his country, nor was I proficient in his tongue; but as he was not so poorly constituted — what Italian is? — as to depend upon that alone for expression, he conveyed to me, in familiar but graceful mimicry, that he was in search of exactly the employment in which the lady before me was engaged. I was not struck with him at first, and while I continued to draw I emitted vague sounds of discouragement and dismissal. He stood his ground, however, not importunately, but with a dumb, doglike fidelity in his eyes which amounted to innocent impudence — the manner of a devoted servant (he might have been in the house for years), unjustly suspected. Suddenly I saw that this very attitude and expression made a picture, whereupon I told him to sit down and wait till I should be free. There was another picture in the way he obeyed me, and I observed as I worked that there were others still in the way he looked wonderingly, with his head thrown back, about the high studio. He might have been crossing himself in St. Peter's. Before I finished I said to myself: "The fellow's a bankrupt orangemonger, but he's a treasure."

When Mrs. Monarch withdrew he passed across the room like a flash to open the door for her, standing there with the rapt, pure gaze of the young Dante spellbound by the young Beatrice.[14] As I never insisted, in such situations, on the blankness of the British domestic, I reflected that he had the making of a servant (and I needed one, but couldn't pay him to be only that), as well as of a model; in short I made up my mind to adopt my insinuating visitor if he would agree to officiate in the double capacity. He jumped at my offer, and in the event my rashness (for I had known nothing about him), was not brought home to me. He proved a sympathetic though a desultory ministrant, and had in a wonderful degree the *sentiment de la pose*.[15] It was uncultivated, instinctive; a part of the happy instinct which had guided him to my door and helped him to spell out my name on the card nailed to it. He had had no other introduction to me than a guess, from the shape of my high north window, seen outside, that my place was a studio, and that as a studio it would contain an artist. He had wandered to England in search of fortune, like other itinerants, and had embarked, with a partner and a small green handcart, on the sale of penny ices. The ices had melted away and the partner had dissolved in their train. My young man wore tight yellow trousers with reddish stripes

---

13. **the City:** The central banking and commercial area of London.
14. **Dante . . . Beatrice:** From the time the Italian poet Dante Alighieri (1265–1321) first saw Beatrice Polinari, when both of them were nine years old, she was his ideal and inspiration, finally becoming the symbol of God's love and salvation in his epic poem *The Divine Comedy.* (c. 1309–20)
15. *sentiment de la pose:* Feeling for a pose (French).

and his name was Oronte. He was sallow but fair, and when I put him into some old clothes of my own he looked like an Englishman. He was as good as Miss Churm, who could look, when required, like an Italian.

IV

I thought Mrs. Monarch's face slightly convulsed when, on her coming back with her husband, she found Oronte installed. It was strange to have to recognise in a little Neapolitan cad a competitor to her magnificent Major. It was she who scented danger first, for the Major was anecdotically unconscious. But Oronte gave us tea, with a hundred eager confusions (he had never seen such a queer process), and I think she thought better of me for having at last an "establishment." They saw a couple of drawings that I had made of the establishment, and Mrs. Monarch hinted that it never would have struck her that he had sat for them. "Now, the drawings you make from *us*, they look exactly like us," she reminded me, smiling in triumph; and I recognised that this was indeed just their defect. When I drew the Monarchs I couldn't, somehow, get away from them — get into the character I wanted to represent; and I had not the least desire my model should be discoverable in my picture. Miss Churm never was, and Mrs. Monarch thought I hid her, very properly, because she was vulgar; whereas if she was lost it was only as the dead who go to heaven are lost — in the gain of an angel the more.

By this time I had got a certain start with "Rutland Ramsay," the first novel in the great projected series; that is, I had produced a dozen drawings, several with the help of the Major and his wife, and I had sent them in for approval. My understanding with the publishers, as I have already hinted, had been that I was to be left to do my work, in this particular case, as I liked, with the whole book committed to me: but my connection with the rest of the series was only contingent. There were moments when, frankly, it *was* a comfort to have the real thing under one's hand; for there were characters in "Rutland Ramsay" that were very much like it. There were people presumably as straight as the Major and women of as good a fashion as Mrs. Monarch. There was a great deal of country-house life — treated, it is true, in a fine, fanciful, ironical, generalised way — and there was a considerable implication of knickerbockers and kilts.[16] There were certain things I had to settle at the outset; such things, for instance, as the exact appearance of the hero, the particular bloom of the heroine. The author, of course, gave me a lead, but there was a margin for interpretation. I took the Monarchs into my confidence, I told them frankly what I was about, I mentioned my embarrassments and alternatives. "Oh, take *him!*" Mrs. Monarch murmured sweetly, looking at her husband; and "What could you want better than my wife?" the Major inquired, with the comfortable candour that now prevailed between us.

---

16. **knickerbockers and kilts:** Short pants gathered above the knee and knee-length, pleated skirts, both of which would have been suitable "casual" attire for men at English country houses.

I was not obliged to answer these remarks — I was only obliged to place my sitters. I was not easy in mind, and I postponed, a little timidly perhaps, the solution of the question. The book was a large canvas, the other figures were numerous, and I worked off at first some of the episodes in which the hero and the heroine were not concerned. When once I had set *them* up I should have to stick to them — I couldn't make my young man seven feet high in one place and five feet nine in another. I inclined on the whole to the latter measurement, though the Major more than once reminded me that *he* looked about as young as anyone. It was indeed quite possible to arrange him for the figure so that it would have been difficult to detect his age. After my young friend Oronte had been with me a month, and after I had given him to understand several different times that his lazzarone[17] habits would presently constitute an insurmountable barrier to our further intercourse, I waked to a sense of his heroic capacity. He was only five feet seven, but the other inches could be managed. I tried him almost secretly at first, for I was really rather afraid of the judgment my other models would pass on such a choice. If they regarded Miss Churm as little better than a snare, what would they think of the representation by a person so little the real thing as an Italian street-vendor, of a protagonist formed by a public school?

If I went a little in fear of them it was not because they bullied me, because they had got an oppressive foothold, but because, in their really pathetic decorum and mysteriously maintained newness, they counted on me so intensely. I was therefore very glad when Jack Hawley came home: he was always of such good counsel. He painted badly himself, but there was no one like him for putting his finger on the place. He had been absent from England for a year; he had been somewhere — I don't remember where — to get a fresh eye. I was in a good deal of dread of any such organ, but we were old friends; he had been away for months and a sense of emptiness was creeping into my life. I hadn't winced for a year.

He came back with a fresh eye, but with the same old black velvet jacket, and the first evening he spent in my studio we smoked cigarettes till the small hours. He had done no work himself, he had only got the eye; so the field was clear for the production of my own things. He wanted to see what I had done for the *Cheapside,* but he was unable to recognise that I had gone much further. That at least seemed the meaning of two or three comprehensive groans which, as he lounged on my big divan, on a folded leg, looking at my latest drawings, issued from his lips with the smoke of his cigarette.

"What's the matter with you?" I asked.

"What's the matter with *you?*"

"Nothing save that I'm mystified."

"You are indeed. You're quite off the hinge. What's the meaning of this new fad?" And he tossed me, with visible irreverence, a drawing in which I happened to have depicted both my majestic models. I asked if he didn't think it good, and he replied that it struck

---

17. lazzarone: Originally a beggar in Naples, Italy, the term was then more generally used to refer to a person who lives on the streets.

him as execrable, given the sort of thing I had always represented myself to him as wishing to arrive at; but I let that pass, I was so anxious to see exactly what he meant. The two figures in the picture looked colossal, but I supposed this was *not* what he meant, inasmuch as, for aught he knew to the contrary, I might have been trying for that. I maintained that I was working exactly in the same way as when he last had done me the honour to commend me. "Well, there's a muddle somewhere," he answered; "wait a bit and I'll make it out." I depended upon him to do so: where else was the fresh eye? But he produced at last nothing more luminous than "I don't know — I don't like your types." This was lame, for a critic who had never consented to discuss with me anything but the question of execution, the direction of strokes and the mystery of values.

"In the drawings you've been looking at I think my types are very handsome."

"Oh, they won't do."

"I've had a couple of new models."

"I see you have. *They* won't do."

"Are you very sure of that?"

"Absolutely — they're stupid."

"You mean *I* am — for I ought to get round that."

"You *can't* — with such people. Who are they?"

I told him, as far as was necessary, and he declared, heartlessly: *"Ce sont des gens qu'il faut mettre à la porte."*[18]

"You've never seen them: they're awfully good," I compassionately objected.

"Not seen them? Why, all this recent work of yours drops to pieces with them. It's all I want to see of them."

"No one else has said anything against it — the *Cheapside* people are pleased."

"Everyone else is an ass, and the *Cheapside* people the biggest asses of all. Come, don't pretend, at this time of day, to have pretty illusions about the public, especially about publishers and editors. It's not for *such* animals you work — it's for those who know. Keep straight for them; keep straight for *me* if you can't keep straight for yourself. There's a certain sort of thing you tried for from the first — and a very good thing it is. But this twaddle isn't *in* it." When I talked with Hawley, later, about "Rutland Ramsay" and its possible successors, he declared that I must get back into my boat again or I would go to the bottom. His voice, in short, was the voice of warning.

I noted the warning, but I didn't turn my friends out of doors. They bored me a good deal; but the very fact that they bored me admonished me not to sacrifice them — if there was anything to be done with them — simply to irritation. As I look back at this phase they seem to me to have pervaded my life not a little. I have a vision of them as most of the time in my studio, seated, against the wall, on an old velvet bench to be out of the way, and looking like a pair of patient courtiers in a royal ante-chamber. I am convinced that during the coldest weeks of the winter they held their ground because it saved them fire. Their newness was losing its gloss, and it was impossible not to feel

---

18. *Ce . . . porte:* They are people who should be put out the door (French).

that they were objects of charity. Whenever Miss Churm arrived they went away, and after I was fairly launched in "Rutland Ramsay" Miss Churm arrived pretty often. They managed to express to me, tacitly, that they supposed I wanted her for the low life of the book, and I let them suppose it, since they had attempted to study the work — it was lying about the studio — without discovering that it dealt only with the highest circles. They had dipped into the most brilliant of our novelists without deciphering many passages. I still took an hour from them, now and again, in spite of Jack Hawley's warning: it would be time enough to dismiss them, if dismissal should be necessary, when the rigour of the season was over. Hawley had made their acquaintance — he had met them at my fireside — and thought them a blighting apparition. Learning that he was a painter, they tried to approach him, to show him too that they were the real thing; but he looked at them, across the big room, as if they were miles away: they were a compendium of everything that he most objected to in the social system of his country. Such people as that, all convention and patent-leather, with ejaculations that stopped conversation, had no business in a studio; a studio was a place to learn to see, and how could you see through a pair of feather beds?

The main inconvenience I suffered at their hands was that, at first, I was shy of letting them discover that my artful little servant was sitting to me for "Rutland Ramsay." They knew that I had been odd enough (they were prepared, by this time, to allow oddity to artists,) to pick a foreign vagabond out of the streets, when I might have had a person with whiskers and credentials; but it was some time before they learned how high I rated his accomplishments. They found him sitting to me more than once, but they never doubted I was doing him as an organ-grinder. There were several things they never guessed, and one of them was that for a striking scene in the novel, in which a footman briefly figured, it occurred to me to make use of Major Monarch as the menial. I kept putting this off, I didn't like to ask him to don the livery — besides the difficulty of finding a livery to fit him. At last, one day late in the winter, when I was at work on the despised Oronte (he caught one's idea in an instant), and was in the glow of feeling that I was going very straight, they came in, the Major and his wife, with their society laugh about nothing (there was less and less to laugh at), like country-callers — they always reminded me of that — who have walked across after church and are presently persuaded to stay to luncheon. Luncheon was over, but they could stay to tea — I knew they wanted it. The fit was one me, however, and I couldn't let my ardour cool and my work wait, with the fading daylight, while my model prepared it. So I asked Mrs. Monarch if she could mind laying it out — a request which, for an instant, brought all the blood to her face. Her eyes were on her husband's for a second, and some mute telegraphy passed between them. Their folly was over the next instant; his cheerful shrewdness put an end to it. So far from pitying their wounded pride, I must add, I was moved to give it as complete a lesson as I could. They bustled about together and got out the cups and saucers and made the kettle boil. I know they felt as if they were waiting on my servant, and when the tea was prepared I said: "He'll have a cup, please — he's tired." Mrs. Monarch brought him one where he stood, and he took it from her as if he had been a gentleman at a party, squeezing a crush-hat with an elbow.

Then it came over me that she had made a great effort for me — made it with a kind of nobleness — and that I owed her a compensation. Each time I saw her, after this, I wondered what the compensation could be. I couldn't go on doing the wrong thing to oblige them. Oh, it *was* the wrong thing, the stamp of the work for thich they sat — Hawley was not the only person to say it now. I sent in a large number of the drawings I had made for "Rutland Ramsay" and I received a warning that was more to the point than Hawley's. The artistic adviser of the house for which I was working was of opinion that many of my illustrations were not what had been looked for. Most of these illustrations were the subjects in which the Monarchs had figured. Without going into the question of what *had* been looked for, I

"MRS. MONARCH BROUGHT THE MODEL A CUP OF TEA, AND HE TOOK IT FROM HER AS IF HE HAD BEEN A GENTLEMAN AT A PARTY, SQUEEZING A CRUSH HAT WITH HIS ELBOW"

saw at this rate I shouldn't get the other books to do. I hurled myself, in despair, upon Miss Churm, and I put her through all her paces. I not only adoped Oronte publicly as my hero, but one morning when the Major looked in to see if I didn't require him to finish a figure for the *Cheapside*, for which he had begun to sit the week before, I told him that I had changed my mind — I would do the drawing from my man. At this my visitor turned pale and stood looking at me. "Is *he* your idea of an English gentleman?" he asked.

I was disappointed, I was nervous, I wanted to get on with my work; so I replied, with irritation: "Oh, my dear Major — I can't be ruined for *you!*"

He stood another moment; then, without a word, he quitted the studio. I drew a long breath when he was gone, for I said to myself that I shouldn't see him again. I had not told him definitely that I was in danger of having my work rejected, but I was vexed at his not having felt the catastrophe in the air, read with me the moral of our fruitless collaboration, the lesson that, in the deceptive atmosphere of art, even the highest respectability may fail of being plastic.

I didn't owe my friends money, but I did see them again. They re-appeared together, three days later, and under the circumstances there was something tragic in the fact. It was a proof to me that they could find nothing else in life to do. They had threshed the matter out in a dismal conference — they had digested the bad news that they were not in for the series. If they were not useful to me even for the *Cheapside* their function seemed difficult to determine, and I could only judge at first, that they had come, forgivingly, decorously, to take a last leave. This made me rejoice, in secret, that I had little leisure for a scene; for I had placed both my other models in position together and I was pegging away at a drawing from which I hoped to derive glory. It had been suggested by the passage in which Rutland Ramsay, drawing up a chair to Artemisin's piano stool, says memorable things to her while she ostensibly fingers out a difficult piece of music. I had done Miss Churm at the piano before – it was an attitude in which she knew how to take on an absolutely poetic grace. I wished the two figures to "compose" together, intensely, and my little Italian had entered perfectly into my conception. The pair were therefore before me, the piano had been pulled out; it was a charming picture of blended youth and murmured love, which I had only to catch and keep. My visitors stood and looked at it, and I said friendly things to them over my shoulder.

They made no response, but I was used to silent company and went on with my work, only a little disconcerted (even though exhilarated with the sense that *this* was at least the ideal thing) at not having got rid of them after all. Presently I heard Mrs. Monarch's sweet voice beside, or rather above, me: "I wish her hair was a little better done." I looked up and she was staring with a strange fixedness at Miss Churm, whose back was turned to her. "Do you mind my just touching it?" she went on – a question which made me spring up for an instant, as with the instinctive fear that she might do the young lady a harm. But she quieted me with a glance I shall never forget – I confess I should like to have been able to draw *that* – and went for a moment to my model. She spoke to her softly, laying a hand upon her shoulder and bending over her; and as the girl, under-standing, gratefully assented, she disposed her rough curls, with a few quick passes, in such a way as to make Miss Churm's head twice as charming. It was one of the most heroic personal services I have ever seen rendered. Then Mrs. Monarch turned away with a low sigh, and looking about her, as if for something to do, stooped to the floor, with a noble humility, and picked up a dirty rag that had dropped out of my paint box.

The Major, meanwhile, had also been looking for something to do, and, wandering to the other end of the studio, saw before him my breakfast things, neglected, unremoved. "I say, can't I be useful *here*?" he called out to me, with an irrepressible quaver. I assented, with a laugh that I fear was awkward, and for the next ten minutes, while I worked, I heard the light clatter of china and the tinkle of spoons and glass. Mrs. Monarch assisted her husband – they washed up my crockery – they put it away. They wandered off into my little scullery, and I afterwards found that they had cleaned my knives and that my slender stock of plate had an unprecedented surface. When it came over me, the latent eloquence of what they were doing, I confess that my drawing was blurred for a moment – the picture swam. They had accepted their failure, but they couldn't accept their fate. They had bowed their heads, in bewilderment, to the perverse and cruel law in virtue of which the real thing could be so much less precious than the unreal; but they didn't want to starve. If my servants were my models, my models might be my servants. They would reverse the parts – the others would sit for the ladies and gentlemen and *they* would do the work. They would still be in the studio – it was an intense dumb appeal to me not to turn them out. "Take us on," they wanted to say – "we'll do anything."

When all this hung before me the *afflatus*[19] vanished – my pencil dropped from my

---

19. *afflatus:* A divine creative impulse or inspiration.

hand. My sitting was spoiled and I got rid of my sitters, who were also evidently rather mystified and awestruck. Then, alone with the Major and his wife, I had a most uncomfortable moment. He put their prayer into a single sentence: "I say, you know — just let *us* do for you, can't you?" I couldn't — it was dreadful to see them emptying my slops; but I pretended I could, to oblige them, for about a week. Then I gave them a sum of money to go away; and I never saw them again. I obtained the remaining books, but my friend Hawley repeats that Major and Mrs. Monarch did me a permanent harm — got me into a second-rate trick. If it be true I am content to have paid the price — for the memory.

[1892]

Sarah Orne Jewett

[1849-1909]

Sarah Orne Jewett was born on September 3, 1849, the second of the three daughters of Caroline Perry Jewett and Theodore H. Jewett, an obstetrician and country doctor in South Berwick, Maine. The affluent family had deep roots in New England, where Jewett's paternal ancestors had arrived in 1638, part of the great Puritan migration from England to America. Although she later traveled extensively, Jewett always considered home to be her family's large house in the center of South Berwick, an old river town near the seacoast in southern Maine. "My local attachments are stronger than any cat's that ever meowed," she once quipped. She was educated there at Miss Raynes School and then at the Berwick Academy, from which Jewett graduated in 1865. Encouraged by her parents, Jewett read widely in English, Continental, and American literature, apparently determined from an early age to become a writer. Her first published story, "Jenny Garrow's Lovers," appeared under the pen name "A. C. Eliot" in the *Flag of Our Union*, a weekly magazine, in January 1868. Later that year, she also published a poem in a magazine for children, *Our Young Folks*.

Sarah Orne Jewett

James Notman took this early photograph of Jewett, who emerged in the 1870s as a pioneering author of local-color fiction about life in rural New England.

Jewett herself dated the beginning of her career as a writer with the publication of a story in the *Atlantic Monthly*, the most respected literary journal of the day, in December 1869. She had earlier submitted two stories to the journal, both of which were rejected. Undaunted, and responding to some encouragement from the young assistant editor of the *Atlantic*, William Dean Howells, she submitted another story, "Mr. Bruce." To her great delight, it was accepted. "I came as near being utterly satisfied & happy as I can," Jewett wrote in her diary. Although she continued to write poems and stories for children, many of which were published in the *Riverside Magazine for Young People*, Jewett increasingly turned her attention to writing for adults. She became friendly with Howells, who assumed the editorship of the *Atlantic* in 1871. He recognized Jewett's talent and pressed her to develop the plots of her stories. "I don't believe I could write a long story as he suggested," Jewett responded in a letter to another of her editors in 1873. "In the first place I have no dramatic talent. The story would have no plot. I should have to fill it out with descriptions of character and meditations. It seems to me I can furnish the theatre, and show you the actors, and the scenery, and the audience, but there is never any play!" Jewett finally won her point with Howells, who published her nearly plotless sketch "The Shore House" in the *Atlantic* in 1873. It was the first of a series of sketches Jewett later collected and connected within a fictional framework in her first book, *Deephaven* (1877), a novel about a young woman's summer in a coastal village in New England.

Through her growing mastery of what was called "local-color" writing, Jewett became one of the most respected authors in the United States. Following the success of *Deephaven*, she became a regular contributor to the *Atlantic* and other prominent periodicals, in which Jewett first published many of the sketches and stories collected in *Old Friends and New* (1879) and *Country By-Ways* (1881). She also came to know writers and leaders of the literary establishment in Boston, including the editor and publisher James T. Fields and his wife, Annie Fields, a literary force in her own right. After Annie Fields's husband died in 1881, she became Jewett's lifelong companion in what was then called a "Boston marriage," a term for a marriagelike relationship between two women who lived together independent of male support. The pair traveled throughout Europe, and they associated with a wide range of celebrated writers, including Howells, Henry James, Mark Twain, Louisa May Alcott, Mary E. Wilkins Freeman, and Harriet Beecher Stowe, whom Jewett called "the mother of us all." Stowe's earlier novels about village life in New England strongly influenced Jewett, who explored similar terrain in two of her own novels: *A Country Doctor* (1884), about a young woman who chooses to attend medical school rather than to marry, and *A Marsh Island* (1885). She was best known for her numerous collections of shorter works, notably *A White Heron and Other Stories* (1886) and *The Country of the Pointed Firs* (1896), a series of related sketches set in Dunnet Landing, a fishing village in Maine. At the height of her fame, Jewett sustained serious injuries in a carriage accident in 1902. She never fully recovered, and Jewett wrote only a handful of additional works before she died at her home in Maine in 1909. During the last years of her life, however, she met and mentored Willa Cather, who dedicated her novel *O Pioneers!* (1913) to the memory of Jewett, "in whose beautiful and delicate work there is perfection that endures."

It is that kind of honesty, that earnest endeavor to tell truly the thing that haunts the mind, that I love in Miss Jewett's own work.

—Willa Cather

bedfordstmartins.com/ americanlit *for research links on Jewett*

Jewett's "A White Heron."

In a letter written in early 1886 to her companion, Annie Fields, Jewett expressed concern about the reception of a story she had recently completed:

> Mr. Howells thinks that this age frowns upon the romantic, that it is no use to write romance any more; but dear me, how much of it there is left in everyday life after all. It must be the fault of the writers that such writing is dull,

> but what shall I do with my 'White heron' now she is written? She isn't a very
> good magazine story, but I love her, and I mean to keep her for the beginning
> of my next book.

Imagining the response of William Dean Howells, a champion of realism
who had published many of her works in the *Atlantic Monthly,* Jewett
decided that "A White Heron" was too "romantic" to please editors and
readers of magazines. True to the story she loved, however, Jewett placed it
at the opening of a collection she published later that year, *A White Heron
and Other Stories.* An anonymous reviewer for the *Overland Monthly*
praised the beauty and simplicity of all the stories in the collection,
observing that the title story was

> perfect in its way — a tiny classic. One little episode of child life, among
> birds and woods, makes it up; and the secret soul of a child, the appeal of the
> bird to its instinctive honor and tenderness, never were interpreted with
> more beauty and insight.

Indeed, the story that Jewett did not venture to submit to magazines
became her best-known and most frequently anthologized work. The text
is taken from the first printing in *A White Heron and Other Stories* (1886).

A WHITE HERON

I

The woods were already filled with shadows one June evening, just before eight o'clock,
though a bright sunset still glimmered faintly among the trunks of the trees. A little girl
was driving home her cow, a plodding, dilatory, provoking creature in her behavior, but
a valued companion for all that. They were going away from whatever light there was,
and striking deep into the woods, but their feet were familiar with the path, and it was
no matter whether their eyes could see it or not.

There was hardly a night the summer through when the old cow could be found waiting at the pasture bars; on the contrary, it was her greatest pleasure to hide herself away
among the huckleberry bushes, and though she wore a loud bell she had made the discovery that if one stood perfectly still it would not ring. So Sylvia had to hunt for her
until she found her, and call Co'! Co'! with never an answering Moo, until her childish
patience was quite spent. If the creature had not given good milk and plenty of it, the
case would have seemed very different to her owners. Besides, Sylvia had all the time
there was, and very little use to make of it. Sometimes in pleasant weather it was a consolation to look upon the cow's pranks as an intelligent attempt to play hide and seek,
and as the child had no playmates she lent herself to this amusement with a good deal of
zest. Though this chase had been so long that the wary animal herself had given an
unusual signal of her whereabouts, Sylvia had only laughed when she came upon Mistress Moolly at the swampside, and urged her affectionately homeward with a twig of

birch leaves. The old cow was not inclined to wander farther, she even turned in the right direction for once as they left the pasture, and stepped along the road at a good pace. She was quite ready to be milked now, and seldom stopped to browse. Sylvia wondered what her grandmother would say because they were so late. It was a great while since she had left home at half-past five o'clock, but everybody knew the difficulty of making this errand a short one. Mrs. Tilley had chased the hornéd torment too many summer evenings herself to blame any one else for lingering, and was only thankful as she waited that she had Sylvia, nowadays, to give such valuable assistance. The good woman suspected that Sylvia loitered occasionally on her own account; there never was such a child for straying about out-of-doors since the world was made! Everybody said that it was a good change for a little maid who had tried to grow for eight years in a crowded manufacturing town, but, as for Sylvia herself, it seemed as if she never had been alive at all before she came to live at the farm. She thought often with wistful compassion of a wretched geranium that belonged to a town neighbor.

"'Afraid of folks,'" old Mrs. Tilley said to herself, with a smile, after she had made the unlikely choice of Sylvia from her daughter's houseful of children, and was returning to the farm. "'Afraid of folks,' they said! I guess she won't be troubled no great with 'em up to the old place!" When they reached the door of the lonely house and stopped to unlock it, and the cat came to purr loudly, and rub against them, a deserted pussy, indeed, but fat with young robins, Sylvia whispered that this was a beautiful place to live in, and she never should wish to go home.

The companions followed the shady wood-road, the cow taking slow steps and the child very fast ones. The cow stopped long at the brook to drink, as if the pasture were not half a swamp, and Sylvia stood still and waited, letting her bare feet cool themselves in the shoal water, while the great twilight moths struck softly against her. She waded on through the brook as the cow moved away, and listened to the thrushes with a heart that beat fast with pleasure. There was a stirring in the great boughs overhead. They were full of little birds and beasts that seemed to be wide awake, and going about their world, or else saying good-night to each other in sleepy twitters. Sylvia herself felt sleepy as she walked along. However, it was not much farther to the house, and the air was soft and sweet. She was not often in the woods so late as this, and it made her feel as if she were a part of the gray shadows and the moving leaves. She was just thinking how long it seemed since she first came to the farm a year ago, and wondering if everything went on in the noisy town just the same as when she was there; the thought of the great red-faced boy who used to chase and frighten her made her hurry along the path to escape from the shadow of the trees.

Suddenly this little woods-girl is horror-stricken to hear a clear whistle not very far away. Not a bird's-whistle, which would have a sort of friendliness, but a boy's whistle, determined, and somewhat aggressive. Sylvia left the cow to whatever sad fate might await her, and stepped discreetly aside into the bushes, but she was just too late. The enemy had discovered her, and called out in a very cheerful and persuasive tone, "Halloa, little girl, how far is it to the road?" and trembling Sylvia answered almost inaudibly, "A good ways."

She did not dare to look boldly at the tall young man, who carried a gun over his shoulder, but she came out of her bush and again followed the cow, while he walked alongside.

"I have been hunting for some birds," the stranger said kindly, "and I have lost my way, and need a friend very much. Don't be afraid," he added gallantly. "Speak up and tell me what your name is, and whether you think I can spend the night at your house, and go out gunning early in the morning."

Sylvia was more alarmed than before. Would not her grandmother consider her much to blame? But who could have foreseen such an accident as this? It did not seem to be her fault, and she hung her head as if the stem of it were broken, but managed to answer "Sylvy," with much effort when her companion again asked her name.

Mrs. Tilley was standing in the doorway when the trio came into view. The cow gave a loud moo by way of explanation.

"Yes, you'd better speak up for yourself, you old trial! Where'd she tucked herself away this time, Sylvy?" But Sylvia kept an awed silence; she knew by instinct that her grandmother did not comprehend the gravity of the situation. She must be mistaking the stranger for one of the farmer-lads of the region.

The young man stood his gun beside the door, and dropped a lumpy game-bag beside it; then he bade Mrs. Tilley good-evening, and repeated his wayfarer's story, and asked if he could have a night's lodging.

"Put me anywhere you like," he said. "I must be off early in the morning, before day; but I am very hungry, indeed. You can give me some milk at any rate, that's plain."

"Dear sakes, yes," responded the hostess, whose long slumbering hospitality seemed to be easily awakened. "You might fare better if you went out to the main road a mile or so, but you're welcome to what we've got. I'll milk right off, and you make yourself at home. You can sleep on husks or feathers," she proffered graciously. "I raised them all myself. There's good pasturing for geese just below here towards the ma'sh. Now step round and set a plate for the gentleman, Sylvy!" And Sylvia promptly stepped. She was glad to have something to do, and she was hungry herself.

It was a surprise to find so clean and comfortable a little dwelling in this New England wilderness. The young man had known the horrors of its most primitive house-keeping, and the dreary squalor of that level of society which does not rebel at the companionship of hens. This was the best thrift of an old-fashioned farmstead, though on such a small scale that it seemed like a hermitage. He listened eagerly to the old woman's quaint talk, he watched Sylvia's pale face and shining gray eyes with ever growing enthusiasm, and insisted that this was the best supper he had eaten for a month, and afterward the new-made friends sat down in the door-way together while the moon came up.

Soon it would be berry-time, and Sylvia was a great help at picking. The cow was a good milker, though a plaguy thing to keep track of, the hostess gossiped frankly, adding presently that she had buried four children, so Sylvia's mother, and a son (who might be dead) in California were all the children she had left. "Dan, my boy, was a great hand to go gunning," she explained sadly. "I never wanted for pa'tridges or gray squer'ls while he was to home. He's been a great wand'rer, I expect, and he's no hand to write letters. There, I don't blame him, I'd ha' seen the world myself if it had been so I could."

"Sylvy takes after him," the grandmother continued affectionately, after a minute's pause. "There ain't a foot o' ground she don't know her way over, and the wild creaturs counts her one o' themselves. Squer'ls she'll tame to come an' feed right out o' her hands, and all sorts o' birds. Last winter she got the jay-birds to bangeing[1] here, and I believe she'd 'a' scanted herself of her own meals to have plenty to throw out amongst 'em, if I hadn't kep' watch. Anything but crows, I tell her, I'm willin' to help support — though Dan he had a tamed one o' them that did seem to have reason same as folks. It was round here a good spell after he went away. Dan an' his father they didn't hitch, — but he never held up his head ag'in after Dan had dared him an' gone off."

The guest did not notice this hint of family sorrows in his eager interest in something else.

"So Sylvy knows all about birds, does she?" he exclaimed, as he looked round at the little girl who sat, very demure but increasingly sleepy, in the moonlight. "I am making a collection of birds myself. I have been at it ever since I was a boy." (Mrs. Tilley smiled.) "There are two or three very rare ones I have been hunting for these five years. I mean to get them on my own ground if they can be found."

"Do you cage 'em up?" asked Mrs. Tilley doubtfully, in response to this enthusiastic announcement.

"Oh no, they're stuffed and preserved, dozens and dozens of them," said the ornithologist, "and I have shot or snared every one myself. I caught a glimpse of a white heron a few miles from here on Saturday, and I have followed it in this direction. They have never been found in this district at all. The little white heron, it is," and he turned again to look at Sylvia with the hope of discovering that the rare bird was one of her acquaintances.

But Sylvia was watching a hop-toad in the narrow footpath.

"You would know the heron if you saw it," the stranger continued eagerly. "A queer tall white bird with soft feathers and long thin legs. And it would have a nest perhaps in the top of a high tree, made of sticks, something like a hawk's nest."

Sylvia's heart gave a wild beat; she knew that strange white bird, and had once stolen softly near where it stood in some bright green swamp grass, away over at the other side of the woods. There was an open place where the sunshine always seemed strangely yellow and hot, where tall, nodding rushes grew, and her grandmother had warned her that she might sink in the soft black mud underneath and never be heard of more. Not far beyond were the salt marshes just this side the sea itself, which Sylvia wondered and dreamed much about, but never had seen, whose great voice could sometimes be heard above the noise of the woods on stormy nights.

"I can't think of anything I should like so much as to find that heron's nest," the handsome stranger was saying. "I would give ten dollars to anybody who could show it to me," he added desperately, "and I mean to spend my whole vacation hunting for it if need be. Perhaps it was only migrating, or had been chased out of its own region by some bird of prey."

---

1. **bangeing:** Maine dialect word for hanging about.

Mrs. Tilley gave amazed attention to all this, but Sylvia still watched the toad, not divining, as she might have done at some calmer time, that the creature wished to get to its hole under the door-step, and was much hindered by the unusual spectators at that hour of the evening. No amount of thought, that night, could decide how many wished-for treasures the ten dollars, so lightly spoken of, would buy.

The next day the young sportsman hovered about the woods, and Sylvia kept him company, having lost her first fear of the friendly lad, who proved to be most kind and sympathetic. He told her many things about the birds and what they knew and where they lived and what they did with themselves. And he gave her a jack-knife, which she thought as great a treasure as if she were a desert-islander. All day long he did not once make her troubled or afraid except when he brought down some unsuspecting singing creature from its bough. Sylvia would have liked him vastly better without his gun; she could not understand why he killed the very birds he seemed to like so much. But as the day waned, Sylvia still watched the young man with loving admiration. She had never seen anybody so charming and delightful; the woman's heart, asleep in the child, was vaguely thrilled by a dream of love. Some premonition of that great power stirred and swayed these young creatures who traversed the solemn woodlands with soft-footed silent care. They stopped to listen to a bird's song; they pressed forward again eagerly, parting the branches – speaking to each other rarely and in whispers; the young man going first and Sylvia following, fascinated, a few steps behind, with her gray eyes dark with excitement.

She grieved because the longed-for white heron was elusive, but she did not lead the guest, she only followed, and there was no such thing as speaking first. The sound of her own unquestioned voice would have terrified her – it was hard enough to answer yes or no when there was need of that. At last evening began to fall, and they drove the cow home together, and Sylvia smiled with pleasure when they came to the place where she heard the whistle and was afraid only the night before.

II

Half a mile from home, at the farther edge of the woods, where the land was highest, a great pine-tree stood, the last of its generation. Whether it was left for a boundary mark, or for what reason, no one could say; the wood-choppers who had felled its mates were dead and gone long ago, and a whole forest of sturdy trees, pines and oaks and maples, had grown again. But the stately head of this old pine towered above them all and made a landmark for sea and shore miles and miles away. Sylvia knew it well. She had always believed that whoever climbed to the top of it could see the ocean; and the little girl had often laid her hand on the great rough trunk and looked up wistfully at those dark boughs that the wind always stirred, no matter how hot and still the air might be below. Now she thought of the tree with a new excitement, for why, if one climbed it at break of day could not one see all the world, and easily discover from whence the white heron flew, and mark the place, and find the hidden nest?

What a spirit of adventure, what wild ambition! What fancied triumph and delight and glory for the later morning when she could make known the secret! It was almost too real and too great for the childish heart to bear.

All night the door of the little house stood open and the whippoorwills came and sang upon the very step. The young sportsman and his old hostess were sound asleep, but Sylvia's great design kept her broad awake and watching. She forgot to think of sleep. The short summer night seemed as long as the winter darkness, and at last when the whippoorwills ceased, and she was afraid the morning would after all come too soon, she stole out of the house and followed the pasture path through the woods, hastening toward the open ground beyond, listening with a sense of comfort and companionship to the drowsy twitter of a half-awakened bird, whose perch she had jarred in passing. Alas, if the great wave of human interest which flooded for the first time this dull little life should sweep away the satisfactions of an existence heart to heart with nature and the dumb life of the forest!

There was the huge tree asleep yet in the paling moonlight, and small and silly Sylvia began with utmost bravery to mount to the top of it, with tingling, eager blood coursing the channels of her whole frame, with her bare feet and fingers, that pinched and held like bird's claws to the monstrous ladder reaching up, up, almost to the sky itself. First she must mount the white oak tree that grew alongside, where she was almost lost among the dark branches and the green leaves heavy and wet with dew; a bird fluttered off its nest, and a red squirrel ran to and fro and scolded pettishly at the harmless housebreaker. Sylvia felt her way easily. She had often climbed there, and knew that higher still one of the oak's upper branches chafed against the pine trunk, just where its lower boughs were set close together. There, when she made the dangerous pass from one tree to the other, the great enterprise would really begin.

She crept out along the swaying oak limb at last, and took the daring step across into the old pine-tree. The way was harder than she thought; she must reach far and hold fast, the sharp dry twigs caught and held her and scratched her like angry talons, the pitch made her thin little fingers clumsy and stiff as she went round and round the tree's great stem, higher and higher upward. The sparrows and robins in the woods below were beginning to wake and twitter to the dawn, yet it seemed much lighter there aloft in the pine-tree, and the child knew she must hurry if her project were to be of any use.

The tree seemed to lengthen itself out as she went up, and to reach farther and far- ther upward. It was like a great main-mast to the voyaging earth; it must truly have been amazed that morning through all its ponderous frame as it felt this determined spark of human spirit wending its way from higher branch to branch. Who knows how steadily the least twigs held themselves to advantage this light, weak creature on her way! The old pine must have loved his new dependent. More than all the hawks, and bats, and moths, and even the sweet voiced thrushes, was the brave, beating heart of the solitary gray-eyed child. And the tree stood still and frowned away the winds that June morning while the dawn grew bright in the east.

Sylvia's face was like a pale star, if one had seen it from the ground, when the last thorny bough was past, and she stood trembling and tired but wholly triumphant, high in the tree-top. Yes, there was the sea with the dawning sun making a golden dazzle over it, and toward that glorious east flew two hawks with slow-moving pinions. How low they looked in the air from that height when one had only seen them before far up, and dark against the blue sky. Their gray feathers were as soft as moths; they seemed only a little way from the tree, and Sylvia felt as if she too could go flying away among the clouds. Westward, the woodlands and farms reached miles and miles into the distance; here and there were church steeples, and white villages, truly it was a vast and awesome world!

The birds sang louder and louder. At last the sun came up bewilderingly bright. Sylvia could see the white sails of ships out at sea, and the clouds that were purple and rose-colored and yellow at first began to fade away. Where was the white heron's nest in the sea of green branches, and was this wonderful sight and pageant of the world the only reward for having climbed to such a giddy height? Now look down again, Sylvia, where the green marsh is set among the shining birches and dark hemlocks; there where you saw the white heron once you will see him again; look, look! a white spot of him like a single floating feather comes up from the dead hemlock and grows larger, and rises, and comes close at last, and goes by the landmark pine with steady sweep of wing and outstretched slender neck and crested head. And wait! wait! do not move a foot or a finger, little girl, do not send an arrow of light and consciousness from your two eager eyes, for the heron has perched on a pine bough not far beyond yours, and cries back to his mate on the nest and plumes his feathers for the new day!

The child gives a long sigh a minute later when a company of shouting cat-birds comes also to the tree, and vexed by their fluttering and lawlessness the solemn heron goes away. She knows his secret now, the wild, light, slender bird that floats and wavers, and goes back like an arrow presently to his home in the green world beneath. Then Sylvia, well satisfied, makes her perilous way down again, not daring to look far below the branch she stands on, ready to cry sometimes because her fingers ache and her lamed feet slip. Wondering over and over again what the stranger would say to her, and what he would think when she told him how to find his way straight to the heron's nest.

"Sylvy, Sylvy!" called the busy old grandmother again and again, but nobody answered, and the small husk bed was empty and Sylvia had disappeared.

The guest waked from a dream, and remembering his day's pleasure hurried to dress himself that might it sooner begin. He was sure from the way the shy little girl looked once or twice yesterday that she had at least seen the white heron, and now she must really be made to tell. Here she comes now, paler than ever, and her worn old frock is torn and tattered, and smeared with pine pitch. The grandmother and the sportsman stand in the door together and question her, and the splendid moment has come to speak of the dead hemlock-tree by the green marsh.

But Sylvia does not speak after all, though the old grandmother fretfully rebukes her, and the young man's kind, appealing eyes are looking straight in her own. He can make them rich with money; he has promised it, and they are poor now. He is so well worth making happy, and he waits to hear the story she can tell.

No, she must keep silence! What is it that suddenly forbids her and makes her dumb? Has she been nine years growing and now, when the great world for the first time puts out a hand to her, must she thrust it aside for a bird's sake? The murmur of the pine's green branches is in her ears, she remembers how the white heron came flying through the golden air and how they watched the sea and the morning together, and Sylvia cannot speak; she cannot tell the heron's secret and give its life away.

Dear loyalty, that suffered a sharp pang as the guest went away disappointed later in the day, that could have served and followed him and loved him as a dog loves! Many a night Sylvia heard the echo of his whistle haunting the pasture path as she came home with the loitering cow. She forgot even her sorrow at the sharp report of his gun and the sight of thrushes and sparrows dropping silent to the ground, their songs hushed and their pretty feathers stained and wet with blood. Were the birds better friends than their hunter might have been — who can tell? Whatever treasures were lost to her, woodlands and summer-time, remember! Bring your gifts and graces and tell your secrets to this lonely country child!

[1886]

Mary E. Wilkins Freeman

[1852-1930]

Mary E. Wilkins Freeman

This portrait appeared along with an admiring article on "Miss Wilkins" in the August 1892 issue of the popular magazine the *Ladies' Home Journal.*

Mary E. Wilkins Freeman was born Mary Ella Wilkins on October 31, 1852, in Randolph, Massachusetts. Her devout parents, Warren and Eleanor Lothrop Wilkins, had strong connections to their roots in colonial New England; a friend once said of Warren Wilkins, a carpenter who designed and built houses, that "the Puritan seemed to survive in him." Eleanor Wilkins suffered through the death in infancy of two sons, and the apprehensive mother frequently kept Freeman and her younger sister home from school because of concern for their health. After experiencing financial losses in the economic depression that followed the Civil War, the family moved to Brattleboro, Vermont, in 1867. They moved several times in Brattleboro, each time to a smaller, more modest house. Freeman attended a local school and was then sent to Mount Holyoke Female Seminary for one year in 1872. Continued financial problems prevented her from returning, and Freeman unsuccessfully tried to become a teacher in order to help support the family. Her seventeen-year-old sister died in 1876, and her father was in increasingly poor health. By 1877 the family was in such financial straits that it was forced to move into the home of a wealthy minister, where Freeman's mother was hired as the housekeeper. The difficult years continued to take a heavy toll on the family, and Eleanor Wilkins died suddenly, at the age of only fifty-three, in 1880.

As a way of coping with her grief and loneliness, and in an effort to earn money, Freeman began to write. Her first publication was "The Beggar

Kind," a ballad that appeared in a children's magazine, *Wide Awake*, in 1881. The following year Freeman sent a story to the popular women's magazine *Harper's Bazar* (later spelled *Bazaar*). Its editor, Mary Louise Booth, a women's rights activist and an accomplished author in her own right, accepted the story, "Two Old Lovers." Freeman later recalled that, when she received the news and a check for twenty-five dollars, "I felt my wings spring from my shoulders capable of flight and I flew home." Shortly after the death of her father in 1883, Freeman left Brattleboro and returned to her birthplace in Randolph, where for the next twenty years she lived with her childhood friend, Mary Wales. Wales provided Freeman with companionship, security, and a room of her own in the Wales family farmhouse. There, Freeman wrote steadily, publishing numerous stories in *Harper's Bazar* and *Harper's New Monthly Magazine*, another prominent periodical published by the influential firm of Harper & Brothers. Her growing literary reputation was further enhanced by the publication of collections of her work, notably *A Humble Romance and Other Stories* (1887) and *A New England Nun and Other Stories* (1891). Freeman continued to explore some of the central themes of those stories — the effects of poverty, the complexities of marriage, the suppression of women, and the legacy of Puritanism — in what most critics view as her most successful novel, *Pembroke* (1894), the story of conflicts within and among families in a village in nineteenth-century New England. Although Freeman was often associated with the popular school of "local-color" writers, many critics recognized the originality of her work. As she observes in an 1899 essay, a young writer "must write in her own way, with no dependence upon the work of another for aid or suggestion. She should make her own patterns and found her own school."

Widely acclaimed as a major talent, Freeman became friends with other notable writers of the day, including William Dean Howells and Mark Twain, and especially women writers such as her close contemporary Sarah Orne Jewett. Indeed, relationships with women were central to her life and fiction. "The tenderness of one woman for another is farther reaching in detail than that of a man, because it is given with a fuller understanding of needs," she observed in 1900. In 1902, after a ten-year courtship, Freeman hesitantly married her longtime fiancé, Charles Freeman, a physician, and moved with him to Metuchen, New Jersey. She thereafter published her work under the name "Mary E. Wilkins Freeman," but the later years of her life and career were neither as happy nor as successful as the twenty-year period before her marriage. Her husband was finally institutionalized for alcoholism and drug abuse, and the couple was legally separated in 1922. Freeman nonetheless continued to write, and her lifetime achievement was recognized in 1926, when she was the first recipient of the William Dean Howells Medal for Distinction in Fiction. By the time of her death at her home in New Jersey in 1930, Freeman had produced a remarkable body of work, including books for children, essays, poetry, plays, and especially fiction — fourteen novels and fifteen collections of short stories, her most enduring contribution to American literature.

I don't mention Mary E. Wilkins for she is a great genius and genius is not to be studied.

– Kate Chopin

bedfordstmartins.com/ americanlit *for research links on Freeman*

Freeman's "A New England Nun."   Less than a decade after the publication of her first work, a poem in a children's magazine in 1881, Freeman had become an established and highly regarded author of fiction for adults. Praising her spare style and the compression of the stories in her popular second collection, *A New England Nun and Other Stories*, a reviewer in the prestigious *Atlantic Monthly* observed:

> Of the genuine originality of these stories it is hard to speak too strongly. There is indeed a common character to the whole series, an undertone of hardship, of loss, of repressed life, of sacrifice, of the idolatry of duty, but we suspect that this is due more to the prevailing spirit of New England life than to any determining force of Miss Wilkins's genius.

In fact, the stories in the collection did not simply reveal the conditions of life in New England. They also gave expression to Freeman's own deepest concerns. Certainly, many readers have viewed "A New England Nun" as a statement about the choices Freeman had made in her own life and career. The central character of the story, Louisa Ellis, chooses to remain single rather than marry her longtime fiancé. Characteristically, Freeman presents the complexities of life for a woman in the late nineteenth century, emphasizing the costs of that choice, including Louisa's repressed sexuality, as well as the freedom she gains to preserve her way of life and pursue her own work. The text is taken from the first printing in *A New England Nun and Other Stories* (1891).

A NEW ENGLAND NUN

It was late in the afternoon, and the light was waning. There was a difference in the look of the tree shadows out in the yard. Somewhere in the distance cows were lowing and a little bell was tinkling; now and then a farm-wagon tilted by, and the dust flew; some blue-shirted laborers with shovels over their shoulders plodded past; little swarms of flies were dancing up and down before the peoples' faces in the soft air. There seemed to be a gentle stir arising over everything for the mere sake of subsidence — a very premonition of rest and hush and night.

This soft diurnal commotion was over Louisa Ellis also. She had been peacefully sewing at her sitting-room window all the afternoon. Now she quilted her needle carefully into her work, which she folded precisely, and laid in a basket with her thimble and thread and scissors. Louisa Ellis could not remember that ever in her life she had mislaid one of these little feminine appurtenances, which had become, from long use and constant association, a very part of her personality.

Louisa tied a green apron round her waist, and got out a flat straw hat with a green ribbon. Then she went into the garden with a little blue crockery bowl, to pick some currants for her tea. After the currants were picked she sat on the back door-step and stemmed them, collecting the stems carefully in her apron, and afterwards throwing them into the hen-coop. She looked sharply at the grass beside the step to see if any had fallen there.

Louisa was slow and still in her movements; it took her a long time to prepare her tea; but when ready it was set forth with as much grace as if she had been a veritable guest to her own self. The little square table stood exactly in the centre of the kitchen, and was covered with a starched linen cloth whose border pattern of flowers glistened. Louisa had a damask napkin on her tea-tray, where were arranged a cut-glass tumbler full of teaspoons, a silver cream-pitcher, a china sugar-bowl, and one pink china cup and saucer. Louisa used china every day — something which none of her neighbors did. They whispered about it among themselves. Their daily tables were laid with common crockery, their sets of best china stayed in the parlor closet, and Louisa Ellis was no richer nor better bred than they. Still she would use the china. She had for her supper a glass dish full of sugared currants, a plate of little cakes, and one of light white biscuits. Also a leaf or two of lettuce, which she cut up daintily. Louisa was very fond of lettuce, which she raised to perfection in her little garden. She ate quite heartily, though in a delicate, pecking way; it seemed almost surprising that any considerable bulk of the food should vanish.

After tea she filled a plate with nicely baked thin corn-cakes, and carried them out into the back-yard.

"Caesar!" she called. "Caesar! Caesar!"

There was a little rush, and the clank of a chain, and a large yellow-and-white dog appeared at the door of his tiny hut, which was half hidden among the tall grasses and flowers. Louisa patted him and gave him the corn-cakes. Then she returned to the house and washed the tea-things, polishing the china carefully. The twilight had deepened; the chorus of the frogs floated in at the open window wonderfully loud and shrill, and once in a while a long sharp drone from a tree-toad pierced it. Louisa took off her green gingham apron, disclosing a shorter one of pink and white print. She lighted her lamp, and sat down again with her sewing.

In about half an hour Joe Dagget came. She heard his heavy step on the walk, and rose and took off her pink-and-white apron. Under that was still another — white linen with a little cambric edging on the bottom; that was Louisa's company apron. She never wore it without her calico sewing apron over it unless she had a guest. She had barely folded the pink and white one with methodical haste and laid it in a table-drawer when the door opened and Joe Dagget entered.

He seemed to fill up the whole room. A little yellow canary that had been asleep in his green cage at the south window woke up and fluttered wildly, beating his little yellow wings against the wires. He always did so when Joe Dagget came into the room.

"Good-evening," said Louisa. She extended her hand with a kind of solemn cordiality.

"Good-evening, Louisa," returned the man, in a loud voice.

She placed a chair for him, and they sat facing each other, with the table between them. He sat bolt-upright, toeing out his heavy feet squarely, glancing with a good-humored uneasiness around the room. She sat gently erect, folding her slender hands in her white-linen lap.

"Been a pleasant day," remarked Dagget.

"Real pleasant," Louisa assented, softly. "Have you been haying?" she asked, after a little while.

"Yes, I've been haying all day, down in the ten-acre lot. Pretty hot work."

"It must be."

"Yes, it's pretty hot work in the sun."

"Is your mother well to-day?"

"Yes, mother's pretty well."

"I suppose Lily Dyer's with her now?"

Dagget colored. "Yes, she's with her," he answered, slowly.

He was not very young, but there was a boyish look about his large face. Louisa was not quite as old as he, her face was fairer and smoother, but she gave people the impression of being older.

"I suppose she's a good deal of help to your mother," she said, further.

"I guess she is; I don't know how mother'd get along without her," said Dagget, with a sort of embarrassed warmth.

"She looks like a real capable girl. She's pretty-looking too," remarked Louisa.

"Yes, she is pretty fair looking."

Presently Dagget began fingering the books on the table. There was a square red autograph album, and a Young Lady's Gift-Book[1] which had belonged to Louisa's mother. He took them up one after the other and opened them; then laid them down again, the album on the Gift-Book.

Louisa kept eying them with mild uneasiness. Finally she rose and changed the position of the books, putting the album underneath. That was the way they had been arranged in the first place.

Dagget gave an awkward little laugh. "Now what difference did it make which book was on top?" said he.

Louisa looked at him with a deprecating smile. "I always keep them that way," murmured she.

"You do beat everything," said Dagget, trying to laugh again. His large face was flushed.

He remained about an hour longer, then rose to take leave. Going out, he stumbled over a rug, and trying to recover himself, hit Louisa's work-basket on the table, and knocked it on the floor.

He looked at Louisa, then at the rolling spools; he ducked himself awkwardly toward them, but she stopped him. "Never mind," said she; "I'll pick them up after you're gone."

She spoke with a mild stiffness. Either she was a little disturbed, or his nervousness affected her, and made her seem constrained in her effort to reassure him.

---

1. **Young Lady's Gift-Book:** Such illustrated collections of poetry, essays, and short fiction were published from about 1825 to 1865. Designed to be given as gifts at holidays or on other special occasions, the popular books often included works by well-known writers.

When Joe Dagget was outside he drew in the sweet evening air with a sigh, and felt much as an innocent and perfectly well-intentioned bear might after his exit from a china shop.

Louisa, on her part, felt much as the kind-hearted, long-suffering owner of the china shop might have done after the exit of the bear.

She tied on the pink, then the green apron, picked up all the scattered treasures and replaced them in her work-basket, and straightened the rug. Then she set the lamp on the floor, and began sharply examining the carpet. She even rubbed her fingers over it, and looked at them.

"He's tracked in a good deal of dust," she murmured. "I thought he must have."

Louisa got a dust-pan and brush, and swept Joe Dagget's track carefully.

If he could have known it, it would have increased his perplexity and uneasiness, although it would not have disturbed his loyalty in the least. He came twice a week to see Louisa Ellis, and every time, sitting there in her delicately sweet room, he felt as if surrounded by a hedge of lace. He was afraid to stir lest he should put a clumsy foot or hand through the fairy web, and he had always the consciousness that Louisa was watching fearfully lest he should.

Still the lace and Louisa commanded perforce his perfect respect and patience and loyalty. They were to be married in a month, after a singular courtship which had lasted for a matter of fifteen years. For fourteen out of the fifteen years the two had not once seen each other, and they had seldom exchanged letters. Joe had been all those years in Australia, where he had gone to make his fortune, and where he had stayed until he made it. He would have stayed fifty years if it had taken so long, and come home feeble and tottering, or never come home at all, to marry Louisa.

But the fortune had been made in the fourteen years, and he had come home now to marry the woman who had been patiently and unquestioningly waiting for him all that time.

Shortly after they were engaged he had announced to Louisa his determination to strike out into new fields, and secure a competency before they should be married. She had listened and assented with the sweet serenity which never failed her, not even when her lover set forth on that long and uncertain journey. Joe, buoyed up as he was by his sturdy determination, broke down a little at the last, but Louisa kissed him with a mild blush, and said good-by.

"It won't be for long," poor Joe had said, huskily; but it was for fourteen years.

In that length of time much had happened. Louisa's mother and brother had died, and she was all alone in the world. But greatest happening of all — a subtle happening which both were too simple to understand — Louisa's feet had turned into a path, smooth maybe under a calm, serene sky, but so straight and unswerving that it could only meet a check at her grave, and so narrow that there was no room for any one at her side.

Louisa's first emotion when Joe Dagget came home (he had not apprised her of his coming) was consternation, although she would not admit it to herself, and he never dreamed of it. Fifteen years ago she had been in love with him — at least she considered herself to be. Just at that time, gently acquiescing with and falling into the natural drift of girlhood, she had seen marriage ahead as a reasonable feature and a probable desirability of life. She had listened with calm docility to her mother's views upon the subject. Her mother was remarkable for her cool sense and sweet, even temperament. She talked wisely to her daughter when Joe Dagget presented himself, and Louisa accepted him with no hesitation. He was the first lover she had ever had.

She had been faithful to him all these years. She had never dreamed of the possibility of marrying any one else. Her life, especially for the last seven years, had been full of a pleasant peace, she had never felt discontented nor impatient over her lover's absence; still she had always looked forward to his return and their marriage as the inevitable conclusion of things. However, she had fallen into a way of placing it so far in the future that it was almost equal to placing it over the boundaries of another life.

When Joe came she had been expecting him, and expecting to be married for fourteen years, but she was as much surprised and taken aback as if she had never thought of it.

Joe's consternation came later. He eyed Louisa with an instant confirmation of his old admiration. She had changed but little. She still kept her pretty manner and soft grace, and was, he considered, every whit as attractive as ever. As for himself, his stint was done; he had turned his face away from fortune-seeking, and the old winds of romance whistled as loud and sweet as ever through his ears. All the song which he had been wont to hear in them was Louisa; he had for a long time a loyal belief that he heard it still, but finally it seemed to him that although the winds sang always that one song, it had another name. But for Louisa the wind had never more than murmured; now it had gone down, and everything was still. She listened for a little while with half-wistful attention; then she turned quietly away and went to work on her wedding clothes.

Joe had made some extensive and quite magnificent alterations in his house. It was the old homestead; the newly-married couple would live there, for Joe could not desert his mother, who refused to leave her old home. So Louisa must leave hers. Every morning, rising and going about among her neat maidenly possessions, she felt as one looking her last upon the faces of dear friends. It was true that in a measure she could take them with her, but, robbed of their old environments, they would appear in such new guises that they would almost cease to be themselves. Then there were some peculiar features of her happy solitary life which she would probably be obliged to relinquish altogether. Sterner tasks than these graceful but half-needless ones would probably devolve upon her. There would be a large house to care for; there would be company to entertain; there would be Joe's rigorous and feeble old mother to wait upon; and it would be contrary to all thrifty village traditions for her to keep more than one servant. Louisa had a little still, and she used to occupy herself pleasantly in summer weather with distilling the sweet and aromatic essences from roses and peppermint and spearmint. By-and-by her still must be laid away. Her store of essences was already considerable, and there would be no time for her to distil for the mere pleasure of it. Then Joe's mother would think it foolishness; she had already hinted her opinion in the matter. Louisa dearly loved to sew a linen seam, not always for use, but for the simple, mild pleasure which she took in it. She would have been loath to confess how more than once she had ripped a seam for the mere delight of sewing it together again. Sitting at her window during long sweet afternoons, drawing her needle gently through the dainty fabric, she was peace itself. But there was small chance of such foolish comfort in the future. Joe's mother, domineering, shrewd old matron that she was even in her old age, and very likely even Joe himself, with his honest masculine rudeness, would laugh and frown down all these pretty but senseless old maiden ways.

Louisa had almost the enthusiasm of an artist over the mere order and cleanliness of her solitary home. She had throbs of genuine triumph at the sight of the window-panes which she had polished until they shone like jewels. She gloated gently over her orderly bureau-drawers, with their exquisitely folded contents redolent with lavender and sweet clover and very purity. Could she be sure of the endurance of even this? She had visions, so startling that she half repudiated them as indelicate, of coarse masculine belongings strewn about in endless litter, of dust and disorder arising necessarily from a coarse masculine presence in the midst of all this delicate harmony.

Among her forebodings of disturbance, not the least was with regard to Caesar. Caesar was a veritable hermit of a dog. For the greater part of his life he had dwelt in his secluded hut, shut out from the society of his kind and all innocent canine joys. Never had Caesar since his early youth watched at a woodchuck's hole; never had he known the delights of a stray bone at a neighbor's kitchen door. And it was all on account of a sin committed when hardly out of his puppyhood. No one knew the possible depth of remorse of which this mild-visaged, altogether innocent-looking old dog might be capable; but whether or not he had encountered remorse, he had encountered a full measure of righteous retribution. Old Caesar seldom lifted up his voice in a growl or a bark; he was fat and sleepy; there were yellow rings which looked like spectacles around his dim old eyes; but there was a neighbor who bore on his hand the imprint of several of Caesar's sharp white youthful teeth, and for that he had lived at the end of a chain, all alone in a little hut, for fourteen years. The neighbor, who was choleric and smarting with the pain of his wound, had demanded either Caesar's death or complete ostracism. So Louisa's brother, to whom the dog had belonged, had built him his little kennel and tied him up. It was now fourteen years since, in a flood of youthful spirits, he had inflicted that memorable bite, and with the exception of short excursions, always at the end of the chain, under the strict guardianship of his master or Louisa, the old dog had remained a close prisoner. It is doubtful if, with his limited ambition, he took much pride in the fact, but it is certain that he was possessed of considerable cheap fame. He was regarded by all the children in the village and by many adults as a very monster of ferocity. St. George's dragon[2] could hardly have surpassed in evil repute Louisa Ellis's old yellow dog. Mothers charged their children with solemn emphasis not to go too near

---

2. **St. George's dragon:** According to a popular legend, St. George, the patron saint of England, fought and killed an evil dragon to save the life of a princess.

to him, and the children listened and believed greedily, with a fascinated appetite for terror, and ran by Louisa's house stealthily, with many sidelong and backward glances at the terrible dog. If perchance he sounded a hoarse bark, there was a panic. Wayfarers chancing into Louisa's yard eyed him with respect, and inquired if the chain were stout. Caesar at large might have seemed a very ordinary dog, and excited no comment whatever; chained, his reputation overshadowed him, so that he lost his own proper outlines and looked darkly vague and enormous. Joe Dagget, however, with his good-humored sense and shrewdness, saw him as he was. He strode valiantly up to him and patted him on the head, in spite of Louisa's soft clamor of warning, and even attempted to set him loose. Louisa grew so alarmed that he desisted, but kept announcing his opinion in the matter quite forcibly at intervals. "There ain't a better-natured dog in town," he would say, "and it's down-right cruel to keep him tied up there. Some day I'm going to take him out."

Louisa had very little hope that he would not, one of these days, when their interests and possessions should be more completely fused in one. She pictured to herself Caesar on the rampage through the quiet and unguarded village. She saw innocent children bleeding in his path. She was herself very fond of the old dog, because he had belonged to her dead brother, and he was always very gentle with her; still she had great faith in his ferocity. She always warned people not to go too near him. She fed him on ascetic fare of corn-mush and cakes, and never fired his dangerous temper with heating and sanguinary diet of flesh and bones. Louisa looked at the old dog munching his simple fare, and thought of her approaching marriage and trembled. Still no anticipation of disorder and confusion in lieu of sweet peace and harmony, no forebodings of Caesar on the rampage, no wild fluttering of her little yellow canary, were sufficient to turn her a hair's-breadth. Joe Dagget had been fond of her and working for her all these years. It was not for her, whatever came to pass, to prove untrue and break his heart. She put the exquisite little stitches into her wedding-garments, and the time went on until it was only a week before her wedding day. It was a Tuesday evening, and the wedding was to be a week from Wednesday.

There was a full moon that night. About nine o'clock Louisa strolled down the road a little way. There were harvest-fields on either hand, bordered by low stone walls. Luxuriant clumps of bushes grew beside the wall, and trees — wild cherry and old apple-trees — at intervals. Presently Louisa sat down on the wall and looked about her with mildly sorrowful reflectiveness. Tall shrubs of blueberry and meadow-sweet, all woven together and tangled with blackberry vines and horsebriers, shut her in on either side. She had a little clear space between them. Opposite her, on the other side of the road, was a spreading tree; the moon shone between its boughs, and the leaves twinkled like silver. The road was bespread with a beautiful shifting dapple of silver and shadow; the air was full of a mysterious sweetness. "I wonder if it's wild grapes?" murmured Louisa. She sat there some time. She was just thinking of rising, when she heard footsteps and low voices, and remained quiet. It was a lonely place, and she felt a little timid. She thought she would keep still in the shadow and let the persons, whoever they might be, pass her.

But just before they reached her the voices ceased, and the footsteps. She understood that their owners had also found seats upon the stone wall. She was wondering if she could not steal away unobserved, when the voice broke the stillness. It was Joe Dagget's. She sat still and listened.

The voice was announced by a loud sigh, which was as familiar as itself. "Well," said Dagget, "you've made up your mind, then, I suppose?"

"Yes," returned another voice; "I'm going day after to-morrow."

"That's Lily Dyer," thought Louisa to herself. The voice embodied itself in her mind. She saw a girl tall and full-figured, with a firm, fair face, looking fairer and firmer in the moonlight, her strong yellow hair braided in a close knot. A girl full of a calm rustic strength and bloom, with a masterful way which might have beseemed a princess. Lily Dyer was a favorite with the village folk; she had just the qualities to arouse the admiration. She was good and handsome and smart. Louisa had often heard her praises sounded.

"Well," said Joe Dagget, "I ain't got a word to say."

"I don't know what you could say," returned Lily Dyer.

"Not a word to say," repeated Joe, drawing out the words heavily. Then there was a silence. "I ain't sorry," he began at last, "that that happened yesterday — that we kind of let on how we felt to each other. I guess it's just as well we knew. Of course I can't do anything any different. I'm going right on an' get married next week. I ain't going back on a woman that's waited for me fourteen years, an' break her heart."

"If you should jilt her to-morrow, I wouldn't have you," spoke up the girl, with sudden vehemence.

"Well, I ain't going to give you the chance," said he; "but I don't believe you would, either."

"You'd see I wouldn't. Honor's honor, an' right's right. An' I'd never think anything of any man that went against 'em for me or any other girl; you'd find that out, Joe Dagget."

"Well, you'll find out fast enough that I ain't going against 'em for you or any other girl," returned he. Their voices sounded almost as if they were angry with each other. Louisa was listening eagerly.

"I'm sorry you feel as if you must go away," said Joe, "but I don't know but it's best."

"Of course it's best. I hope you and I have got common-sense."

"Well, I suppose you're right." Suddenly Joe's voice got an undertone of tenderness. "Say, Lily," said he, "I'll get along well enough myself, but I can't bear to think — You don't suppose you're going to fret much over it?"

"I guess you'll find out I sha'n't fret much over a married man."

"Well, I hope you won't — I hope you won't, Lily. God knows I do. And — I hope — one of these days — you'll — come across somebody else —"

"I don't see any reason why I shouldn't." Suddenly her tone changed. She spoke in a sweet, clear voice, so loud that she could have been heard across the street. "No, Joe Dagget," said she, "I'll never marry any other man as long as I live. I've got good sense, an' I ain't going to break my heart nor make a fool of myself; but I'm never going to be married, you can be sure of that. I ain't that sort of a girl to feel this way twice."

Louisa heard an exclamation and a soft commotion behind the bushes; then Lily spoke again — the voice sounded as if she had risen. "This must be put a stop to," said she. "We've stayed here long enough. I'm going home."

Louisa sat there in a daze, listening to their retreating steps. After a while she got up and slunk softly home herself. The next day she did her housework methodically; that was as much a matter of course as breathing; but she did not sew on her wedding-clothes. She sat at her window and meditated. In the evening Joe came. Louisa Ellis had never known that she had any diplomacy in her, but when she came to look for it that night she found it, although meek of its kind, among her little feminine weapons. Even now she could hardly believe that she had heard aright, and that she would not do Joe a terrible injury should she break her troth-plight. She wanted to sound him without betraying too soon her own inclinations in the matter. She did it successfully, and they finally came to an understanding; but it was a difficult thing, for he was as afraid of betraying himself as she.

She never mentioned Lily Dyer. She simply said that while she had no cause of complaint against him, she had lived so long in one way that she shrank from making a change.

"Well, I never shrank, Louisa," said Dagget. "I'm going to be honest enough to say that I think maybe it's better this way; but if you'd wanted to keep on, I'd have stuck to you till my dying day. I hope you know that."

"Yes, I do," said she.

That night she and Joe parted more tenderly than they had done for a long time. Standing in the door, holding each other's hands, a last great wave of regretful memory swept over them.

"Well, this ain't the way we've thought it was all going to end, is it, Louisa?" said Joe.

She shook her head. There was a little quiver on her placid face.

"You let me know if there's ever anything I can do for you," said he. "I ain't ever going to forget you, Louisa." Then he kissed her, and went down the path.

Louisa, all alone by herself that night, wept a little, she hardly knew why; but the next morning, on waking, she felt like a queen who, after fearing lest her domain be wrested away from her, sees it firmly insured in her possession.

Now the tall weeds and grasses might cluster around Caesar's little hermit hut, the snow might fall on its roof year in and year out, but he never would go on a rampage through the unguarded village. Now the little canary might turn itself into a peaceful yellow ball night after night, and have no need to wake and flutter with wild terror against its bars. Louisa could sew linen seams, and distil roses, and dust and polish and fold away in lavender, as long as she listed. That afternoon she sat with her needle-work at the window, and felt fairly steeped in peace. Lily Dyer, tall and erect and blooming, went past; but she felt no qualm. If Louisa Ellis had sold her birthright[3] she did not know it, the taste of the pottage was so delicious, and had been her sole satisfaction for so long. Serenity and placid narrowness had become to her as the birthright itself. She gazed ahead through a long reach of future days strung together like pearls in a rosary, every one like the others, and all smooth and flawless and innocent, and her heart went

---

3. **sold her birthright:** Esau, the son of Isaac and Rebekah, sold his birthright — his privileges as the eldest son — to his brother Jacob for bread and "pottage of lentiles," or lentil soup (Genesis 25:33–34).

up in thankfulness. Outside was the fervid summer afternoon; the air was filled with the sounds of the busy harvest of men and birds and bees; there were halloos, metallic clatterings, sweet calls, and long hummings. Louisa sat, prayerfully numbering her days, like an uncloistered nun.

[1891]

Kate Chopin

[1850-1904]

Kate Chopin was born Katherine O'Flaherty on February 8, 1850, in St. Louis, Missouri. Her parents were Thomas O'Flaherty, an Irish immigrant who had become a prosperous merchant, and his second wife, Eliza Faris, a Creole, the term then widely used for aristocratic descendants of the early French settlers of Louisiana and the Gulf Coast of the United States. Chopin grew up in comfortable circumstances and attended a Catholic girls' school, the Academy of the Sacred Heart. But her early years were shadowed by the death of her father in a railroad accident in 1855 and the loss her half-brother, who died of typhoid fever while serving as a Confederate soldier in the Civil War. After she graduated from high school in 1868, Chopin began her life as a fashionable young debutante in St. Louis, though in her diary she privately complained that

Kate Chopin

This photograph was taken while Chopin was living in Louisiana, the setting of much of her later fiction about life among the Creoles.

"parties, operas, concerts, skating and amusements ad infinitum have so taken up all my time that my dear reading and writing that I love so well have suffered much neglect." During this time, she wrote her first-known story, a brief account of an unspecified animal that escapes from a cage into the larger world, which Chopin suggestively entitled "Emancipation: A Life Fable."

The story was never published, however, and Chopin did not embark on a literary career for nearly twenty years. She soon met and married Oscar Chopin, the son of plantation owners in Natchitoches Parish, Louisiana, who was studying banking in St. Louis. In 1870, the couple settled in New

bedfordstmartins.com/ americanlit for research links on Chopin

Orleans, where Oscar became a successful cotton broker. Although Chopin wrote a lively account of their honeymoon in Europe, she had little time for writing in her role of wife and mother to the six children she bore during the next eight years. Following serious financial reverses, the family moved to the small town of Cloutierville, Louisiana, where Oscar Chopin died suddenly of malaria in December 1882. By all accounts, the couple's marriage had been a happy one, and Chopin was grief stricken. Returning to St. Louis in 1884, she and her children lived with her mother, whose death the following year was another blow to Chopin. To supplement her now diminished income, to deal with grief and loneliness, and to satisfy friends who encouraged her to pursue her literary interests, Chopin finally began to write seriously during 1888. She published her first work, a short poem "If It Might Be," in a well-regarded Chicago magazine, *America,* in January 1889. The poem was followed by her first published story — "A Point at Issue!" — which appeared in the St. Louis *Post-Dispatch* in October 1889. In it, Chopin developed a theme that would become increasingly central to her writing, that of a woman torn between the demands of marriage and the desire to maintain her freedom and autonomy.

Chopin soon began to draw upon a vital source for her fiction, her fourteen years in Louisiana. In her first novel, written during 1889-90, she tells the story of a young Creole widow who manages a Louisiana plantation inherited from her husband. When a publisher rejected the novel, whose plot involves alcoholism and divorce, Chopin published it at her own expense as *At Fault* (1890). While most reviews were mixed, several praised her depiction of life among the Creoles in Louisiana, which was also the setting of "For Marse Chouchoute," published in the *Youth's Companion* in August 1891. Chopin found a ready market for such stories, which she regularly published in other prominent magazines, including the *Century* and the *Atlantic Monthly.* Her first collection of stories, *Bayou Folk,* appeared in 1894, and a second collection, *A Night in Acadie,* followed in 1897. Those volumes established Chopin as an accomplished author of "local-color" fiction, one who was frequently compared to popular regional writers such as Mary E. Wilkins Freeman, Joel Chandler Harris, and George Washington Cable. Chopin "tells a story like a poet, and reproduces the spirit of a landscape like a painter," a reviewer admiringly observed in the *Nation* in June 1898. By then, Chopin had begun her major work, *The Awakening,* the story of Edna Pontellier, a New Orleans wife and mother who falls in love with another man, takes a third man as a lover, and ultimately rejects the claims of her husband and children by swimming out to her death in the ocean off Grand Isle, Louisiana.

The storm of controversy generated by the publication of *The Awakening* in 1899 virtually ended Chopin's promising literary career. Although many recognized her artistry and praised her luminous prose style, most reviewers were aghast at the subject matter of the novel. Writing for the St. Louis *Post-Dispatch* in May 1899, a reviewer called Edna Pontellier "a derelict in a moral ocean, whose chart she had never studied," declaring that the novel was "sad and mad, and bad, but it is all consummate art." The negative criticism caused Chopin's publisher to withdraw a collection of stories, *A Vocation and a Voice*, which was to follow *The Awakening*. Chopin continued to publish an occasional story and was still regarded as a literary celebrity in St. Louis. But the reaction to *The Awakening* had severely damaged her national reputation, and the pace of her literary production fell off dramatically after 1900. When she died of a brain hemorrhage on August 22, 1904, obituaries largely ignored *The Awakening* and praised Chopin for her colorful stories of Creole life in Louisiana.

Chopin's "At the 'Cadian Ball."   In her careful manuscript-account book, Chopin recorded that "At the 'Cadian Ball" was written during three days, July 15-17, and immediately submitted for publication on July 18, 1892. She sent the story to a short-lived weekly magazine published in Boston, *Two Tales*, each issue of which contained two original short stories "by the best authors," as its title page proclaimed. Chopin recorded that she received a payment of forty dollars for the story, which appeared in the October 1892 issue. The story was among twenty-three Chopin gathered together the following year into what she called her "collection of Creole stories," which the prominent Boston firm Houghton Mifflin published as *Bayou Folk* (1894). Reviewers generally praised the stories in the collection, emphasizing its "flavor of quaint and picturesque life among the Creole folk of the Louisiana bayous," as well as Chopin's "faithful, artistic transcripts of picturesque local life." In the midst of the rich descriptions of the southern setting, the accomplished use of dialect, and the presentation of unusual characters, however, alert readers might also have discovered suggestions of social criticism in "At the 'Cadian Ball," which subtly exposes the hierarchical nature of Creole society, especially the attitudes toward and position of women within that society. The text is taken from the first printing in *Two Tales*, October 1892.

AT THE 'CADIAN BALL[1]

Bobinôt – that big, brown, good-natured Bobinôt – had no intention of going to the ball, even though he knew Calixta would be there. For what came of those balls but heartache, and a sickening disinclination for work the whole week through, till Saturday night came again and his tortures began afresh? Why could he not have loved Ozéina, who would marry him to-morrow; or Fronie, or any one of a dozen others, rather than that little Spanish vixen? Calixta's slender foot had never touched Cuban soil; but

---

1. **"At the 'Cadian Ball":**   The Acadians were the original French settlers of what is now Nova Scotia, from which most of them were expelled by the British authorities during the French and Indian War (1754-63). Some of the exiled Acadians settled in what was then the Spanish, but soon became the French, colony of Louisiana. Their descendants are called "Cajuns," an English corruption of the French word *acadien*, after *Acadia*, the original name of their ancestral region in Nova Scotia.

her mother's had, and the Spanish was in her blood all the same. For that reason the prairie people forgave her much that they would not have overlooked in their own daughters or sisters.

Her eyes – Bobinôt thought of her eyes, and weakened – the bluest, the drowsiest, most tantalizing that ever looked into a man's; her flaxen hair that kinked worse than a mulatto's close to her head; that broad, smiling mouth and tip-tilted nose, that full figure; that voice like a rich contralto song, with cadences in it that must have been taught by Satan, for there had been no one else to teach her tricks on that 'Cadian prairie. Bobinôt thought of them all as he ploughed his rows of cane.

There had even been a breath of scandal whispered about her a year ago, when she went to Assumption – but why talk of it? No one did now. *"C'est Espagnol, ça,"*[2] most of them said with lenient shoulder-shrugs. *"Bon chien tient de race,"*[3] the old men mumbled over their pipes, stirred by recollections. Nothing was made of it, except that Fronie threw it up to Calixta when the two quarrelled and fought on the church steps after mass one Sunday, about a lover. Calixta swore roundly in fine 'Cadian French and with true Spanish spirit, and slapped Fronie's face. Fronie had slapped her back: *"Tiens, cocotte, va!" "Espèce de lionèse; prends ça, et ça!"*[4] till the curé[5] himself was obliged to hasten and make peace between them. Bobinôt thought of it all, and would not go to the ball.

But in the afternoon, over at Friedheimer's store, where he was buying a trace-chain,[6] he heard some one say that Alcée Laballière would be there. Then wild horses could not have kept him away. He knew how it would be – or rather he did not know how it would be – if the handsome young planter came over to the ball as he sometimes did. If Alcée happened to be in a serious mood, he might only go to the card-room and play a round or two; or he might stand out on the galleries talking crops and politics with the old people. But there was no telling. A drink or two could put the devil in his head – that was what Bobinôt said to himself, as he wiped the sweat from his brow with his red bandanna; a gleam from Calixta's eyes, a flash of her ankle, a twirl of her skirts could do the same. Yes, Bobinôt would go to the ball.

That was the year Alcée Laballière put nine hundred acres in rice. It was putting a good deal of money into the ground, but the returns promised to be glorious. Old Madame Laballière, sailing about the spacious galleries in her white *volante*,[7] figured it all out in her head. Clarisse, her god-daughter, helped her a little, and together they built more air-castles than enough. Alcée worked like a mule that time; and if he did not kill himself, it was because his constitution was an iron one. It was an every-day affair for him to come in from the field well nigh exhausted, and wet to the waist. He did not mind

---

2. *C'est Espagnol, ça:* That's a Spaniard for you (French).
3. *Bon . . . race:* Just like her mother (French).
4. *Tiens, cocotte, va! Espèce . . . ça!:* Listen, you flirt, get out! You dirty she-cat; take that and that! (French).
5. curé: Parish priest (French).
6. trace-chain: Chains on the sides of a harness, used to attach a horse to a vehicle.
7. *volante:* A flounced gown (French).

if there were visitors; he left them to his mother and Clarisse. There were often visitors. Young men and women who came up from the city, which was but a few hours away, to see his beautiful kinswoman. She was worth going a good deal farther than that to see. Dainty as a lily; hardy as a sunflower; slim, tall, graceful like one of the reeds that grew in the marsh. Cold and kind and cruel by turn, and everything that was aggravating to Alcée.

He would have liked to sweep the place of those visitors, often. The men above all, with their ways and their manners; their swaying of fans like women, and dandling about hammocks. He could have pitched them over the levee into the river, if it hadn't meant murder. That was Alcée. But he must have been crazy the day he came in from the rice-field, and, toil-stained as he was, clasped Clarisse by the arms and panted a volley of hot, blistering love-words into her face. No man had ever spoken love to her like that.

"Monsieur!" she exclaimed, looking him full in the eyes, without a quiver. Alcée's hands dropped and his glance wavered before the chill of her calm, clear eyes.

"*Par exemple!*"[8] she muttered disdainfully, as she turned from him, deftly adjusting the careful toilet that he had so brutally disarranged.

That happened a day or two before the cyclone came that cut into the rice like fine steel. It was an awful thing — coming so swiftly, without a moment's warning in which to light a holy candle or set a piece of blessed palm burning. Old madame wept openly and said her beads, just as her son Lidié, the New Orleans one, would have done. If such a thing had happened to Alphonse, the Laballière planting cotton up in Natchitoches,[9] he would have raved and stormed like a second cyclone and made his surroundings unbearable for a day or two. But Alcée took the misfortune differently. He looked ill and gray, after it, and said nothing. His speechlessness was frightful. Clarisse's heart grew as tender as a kitten's; but when she offered her soft, purring words of condolence, he accepted them with mute indifference. Then she and nainaine[10] wept afresh in each other's arms.

A night or two later, when Clarisse went to her window to kneel there in the moonlight and say her prayers before retiring, she saw that Bruce, Alcée's negro servant, had led his master's saddle-horse noiselessly along the edge of the sward that bordered the gravel-path, and stood holding him near by. Presently, she heard Alcée quit his room, which was beneath her own, and traverse the lower portico. As he emerged from the shadow and crossed the strip of moonlight, she perceived that he carried a pair of well-filled saddle-bags which he at once flung across the animal's back. He then lost no time in mounting, and after a brief exchange of words with Bruce, went cantering away, taking no precaution to avoid the noisy gravel as the negro had done.

Clarisse had never suspected that it might be Alcée's custom to sally forth from the plantation secretly, and at such an hour; for it was nearly midnight. And had it not been

---

8. *Par exemple!:* Literally, "For example!" (French). In this instance, the exclamation means "Take hold of yourself!"

9. **Natchitoches:** Parish (county) in northwestern Louisiana.

10. **nainaine:** A dialect term for a godmother or older woman companion (French).

for the tell-tale saddle-bags, she would only have crept to bed, to wonder, to fret and dream unpleasant dreams. But her impatience and anxiety would not be held in check. Hastily unbolting the shutters of her door that opened upon the gallery, she stepped outside and called softly to the old negro.

"Gre't Peter! Miss Clarisse. I wasn' sho it was a ghos' o' w'at, stan'in' up dah, plumb in de night, dataway."

He mounted half-way up the long, broad flight of stairs. She was standing at the top of them.

"Bruce, w'ere has Monsieur Alcée gone?" she asked.

"W'y, he gone 'bout he business, I reckin," replied Bruce, striving to be non-committal at the outset.

"W'ere has Monsieur Alcée gone?" she reiterated, stamping her bare foot. "I won't stan' any nonsense or any lies; mine, Bruce."

"I don' ric'lic ez I eva tole you lie *yit*, Miss Clarisse. Mista Alcée, he all broke up, sho."

"W'ere – has – he gone? *Ah Sainte Vierge! faut de la patience! butor, va!*"[11]

"W'en I was in he room, a-breshin' off he clo'es to-day," the darkey began, settling himself against the stair-rail, "he look dat speechless an' down, I say, 'You 'pear tu me like some pussun w'at gwine have a spell o' sickness, Mista Alcée.' He say, 'You reckin.' An' he git up, go look hisse'f stidy in de glass. Den he go to de chimbly an' jerk up de quinine bottle an po' a gre't hoss-dose onto he han'. An' he swalla dat mess in a wink, an' wash hit down wid a big dram o' whisky w'at he keep in he room, agin he come all soppin' wet outen de fiel'.

"He lows, 'No, I ain' gwine be sick, Bruce.' Den he square off. He say, 'I kin mak out to stan' up an' gi' an' take wid any man I knows, lessen hit's John L. Sulvun.[12] But w'en God A'mighty an' a 'oman jines fo'ces agin me, dats one too many fur me.' I tell 'im jis so, whils' I'se makin' out to bresh a spot off w'at ain' dah, on he coat colla. I tell 'im, 'You wants li'le res', suh.' He say, 'No, I wants li'le fling; dats w'at I wants; an I gwine git it. Pitch me a fis' ful o' clo'es in dem 'ar saddle-bags.' Dat w'at he say. Don't you bodda, missy. He jis gone a caperin' yonda tu de Cajun ball. Uh – uh – de skeeters is fair' a-swarmin' like bees roun' yo' foots!"

The mosquitoes were indeed attacking Clarisse's white feet savagely. She had unconsciously been alternately rubbing one foot over the other while hearing the darkey's recital.

"The 'Cadian ball," she repeated contemptuously. "Humph! *Par exemple!*[13] Nice conduc' for a Laballière. An' he needs a saddle-bag, fill' with clothes, to go to the 'Cadian ball!"

---

11. *Ah, Sainte Vierge! . . . butor, va!:* Ah Blessed Virgin! Give me patience! Go, lout! (French).
12. **John L. Sulvun:** John L. Sullivan (1855–1918), a legendary boxer and the first American sports celebrity.
13. *Par exemple!:* Literally, "For example!" (French). In this instance, the exclamation means "What an example!" (See note 8.)

"Oh, Miss Clarisse; you go on tu bed, chile; git yo' soun' sleep. He 'low he come back in couple weeks o' so. I kiarn be repeatin' lot o' truck w'at young mans say, out heah face o' a young gol."

Clarisse said no more but flashed back into the house.

"You done talk too much wid yo' mouf a'ready, you ole fool nigga, you," muttered Bruce to himself as he walked away.

Alcée reached the ball very late, of course — too late for the chicken gombo which had been served at midnight.

The big, low-ceiled room — they called it a hall — was packed with men and women dancing to the music of three fiddles. There were broad galleries all around it. There was a room at one side where sober-faced men were playing cards. Another in which babies were sleeping, called *le parc aux petits*.[14] Any one who is white may go to a 'Cadian ball, but he must pay for his lemonade, his coffee and chicken gombo. And he must behave himself like a 'Cadian. Grosboeuf was giving this ball. He had been giving them since he was a young man, and he was a middle-aged one, now. In that time he could recall but one disturbance, and that was caused by American railroaders, who were not in touch with their surroundings and had no business there. *"Ces maudits gens du raiderode,"*[15] Grosboeuf called them.

Alcée Laballière's presence at the ball caused a flutter even among the men, who could not but admire his grit after such a misfortune befalling him. To be sure, they knew the Laballières were rich — that there were resources East, and more again in the city. But they felt it took a *brave homme*[16] to stand a blow like that philosophically. One old gentleman, who was in the habit of reading a Paris newspaper and knew things, chuckled gleefully to everybody that Alcée's conduct was altogether *chic, mais chic.*[17] That he had more *panache*[18] than Boulanger. Well, perhaps he had.

But what he did not show outwardly was that he was in a mood for ugly things to-night. Poor Bobinôt alone felt it, vaguely. He discerned a gleam of it in Alcée's handsome eyes as the young planter stood in the doorway looking with rather feverish glance upon the assembly, while he laughed and talked with a 'Cadian farmer who was beside him.

Bobinôt himself was dull-looking and clumsy. Most of the men were. But the young women were very beautiful. The eyes that glanced into Alcée's as they passed him, were big, dark, soft as those of the young heifers' standing out in the cool prairie grass.

But the belle was Calixta. Her white dress was not nearly so handsome or well made as Fronie's (she and Fronie had quite forgotten the battle on the church steps, and were friends again), nor were her slippers so stylish as those of Ozéina; and she fanned

---

14. *le parc aux petits:* Playroom (French).
15. *Ces maudits gens du raiderode:* Those cursed railroad people (French).
16. *brave homme:* Brave man (French).
17. *chic, mais chic:* Stylish, just stylish (French).
18. *panache:* Style (French).

herself with a handkerchief, since she had broken her red fan at the last ball, and her aunts and uncles were not willing to give her another. But all the men agreed she was at her best to-night. Such animation! such *abandon!* such flashes of wit!

"Né, Bobinôt! *Mais*[19] w'ats the matta? W'at you standin' *planté là*[20] like ole Ma'ame Tina's cow in the bog, you?"

That was good. That was an excellent thrust at Bobinôt, who had forgotten the figure of the dance, with his mind bent on other things, and it started a clamor of laughter at his expense. He joined good-naturedly. It was better to receive even such notice as that from Calixta than none at all. But Madame Suzonne, sitting in a corner, whispered to her neighbor that if Ozéina were to conduct herself in such manner, she should immediately be taken out to the mule-cart and driven home. The women did not always approve of Calixta.

Now and then were short lulls in the dance, when couples flocked out upon the galleries for a brief respite and a breath of air. The moon had gone down pale in the west, and in the east was yet no promise of day. After such an interval, when the dancers again assembled to resume the interrupted quadrille, Calixta was not among them.

She was sitting out upon a bench in the shadow, with Alcée beside her. They were acting like fools. He had attempted to take a little gold ring from her finger; just for the fun of it, for there was nothing he could have done with the ring but replace it again. But she clinched her hand tight. He had pretended that it was a very difficult matter to open it. Then he kept the hand in his. They seemed to forget about it. He played with her earring, a thin crescent of gold hanging from her small, brown ear. He caught a whisp of the kinky hair that had escaped its fastening, and rubbed the ends of it against his shaven cheek.

"You know, last year in Assumption,[21] Calixta." They belonged to the younger generation, so preferred to speak English.

"Don't come say Assumption to me, M'sieur Alcée. I done yeard Assumption till I'm plumb sick."

"Yes, I know. The idiots! Because you were in Assumption, and I happened to go to Assumption, they must have it that we went together. But it was nice — *hein,*[22] Calixta? — in Assumption?"

They saw Bobinôt emerge from the hall and stand a moment outside the lighted doorway, peering uneasily and searchingly into the darkness. He did not see them, and went slowly back.

"There is Bobinôt looking for you. You are going to set poor Bobinôt crazy. You'll marry him some day; *hein,* Calixta?"

---

19. *Mais:* But (French).
20. *planté là:* Rooted there (French).
21. **Assumption:** Assumption Parish (county), at the heart of "Cajun Country" in southern Louisiana (see note 1).
22. *hein:* Eh (French).

"I don't say, no, me," she replied, striving to withdraw her hand, which he held more firmly for the attempt.

"But, come, Calixta; you know you said you would go back to Assumption, just to spite them."

"No, I never said that, me. You mus' dreamt that."

"Oh, I thought you did. You know I'm going down to the city."

"W'en?"

"To-night."

"You betta make has'e, then; it's mos't day."

"Well, to-morrow'll do."

"W'at you goin' do, yonda?"

"I don't know. Drown myself in the lake, maybe; unless you go down there to visit your uncle."

Calixta's senses were reeling; and they well-nigh left her when she felt Alcée's lips brush her ear like the touch of a rose.

"Mista Alcée! Is dat Mista Alcée?" the thick voice of a negro was asking, who stood on the ground holding to the banister-rails near which the couple sat.

"W'at do you want, now?" cried Alcée impatiently. "Can't I have a moment of peace?"

"I ben huntin' you high an' low, suh," said the man. "Dey — dey some one in de road, onda de mulbare-tree, want see you a minute."

"I wouldn't go out to the road to see the Angel Gabriel. And if you come back here with any more talk, I'll have to break your neck." The negro turned mumbling away.

Alcée and Calixta laughed softly about it. Her boisterousness was all gone. They talked low, and laughed softly, as lovers do.

"Alcée! Alcée Laballière!"

It was not the negro's voice this time; but one that went through Alcée's body like an electric shock, bringing him to his feet.

It was Clarisse standing there in her riding-habit, where the negro had stood. For an instant confusion reigned in Alcée's thoughts, like one who awakes suddenly from a dream. But he felt that something of serious import had brought her to the ball in the dead of night.

"W'at does this mean, Clarisse?" he asked.

"It means something has happen' at home. You mus' come."

"Happened to maman?" he questioned, in alarm.

"No; nainaine is well, and asleep. It is something else. Not to fr'ghten you. But you mus' come. Come with me, Alcée."

There was no need for the imploring note. He would have followed the voice anywhere.

She had now recognized the girl sitting back on the bench.

"*Ah, c'est vous, Calixta? Comment ça va, mon enfant?*"[23]

---

23. *Ah . . . enfant?:* Ah, is it you, Calixta? How's it going, my little one? (French).

"Tcha va b'en; et vous, mam'zélle?"[24]

Alcée swung himself over the low rail and started to follow Clarisse, without a word, without a glance back at the girl. He had forgotten he was leaving her there. But Clarisse whispered something to him and he turned back to say "good night, Calixta," and offer his hand to press through the railing. She pretended not to see it.

"How come that? You settin' yere by yo'se'f, Calixta?" It was Bobinôt who had found her there alone. The dancers had not yet come out. She looked ghastly in the faint, gray light that was struggling out of the east.

"Yes, that's me. Go yonda in the *parc aux petits* an' ask aunt Olisse fu' my hat. She knows w'ere 'tis. I want ter go home, me."

"How you came?"

"I come afoot, with the Cateaus. But I'm goin' now. I ent going' wait fu' 'em. I'm plumb wo' out, me."

"Kin I go with you, Calixta?"

"I don' care."

They went together across the open prairie and along the edge of the fields, stumbling in the uncertain light. He told her to lift her dress that was getting wet and bedraggled; for she was pulling at the weeds and grasses with her hands.

"I don' care; it's got to go in the tub, anyway. You been sayin' all along you want to marry me, Bobinôt. Well, if you want, yet, I don' care, me."

The glow of sudden and overwhelming happiness shone out in the brown, rugged face of the young Acadian. He could not speak, for very joy. It choked him.

"Oh well, if you don' want," snapped Calixta, flippantly, pretending to be piqued at his silence.

"*Bon Dieu!*[25] You know that makes me crazy, w'at you sayin'. You mean that, Calixta? You ent goin' turn roun' agin?"

"I neva tole you that much *yet*, Bobinôt. I mean that. *Tiens*,"[26] and she held out her hand in the business-like manner of a man who clinches a bargain with a hand-clasp. Bobinôt grew bold with happiness and asked Calixta to kiss him. She turned her face, that looked almost ugly after the night's dissipation, and looked steadily into his.

"I don' want ter kiss you, Bobinôt," she said, turning away again, "not to-day. Some other time. *Bonté divine!*[27] ent you satisfy, *yet!*"

"Oh, I'm satisfy, Calixta," he said.

Riding through a patch of wood, Clarisse's saddle became ungirted, and she and Alcée dismounted to readjust it.

For the twentieth time he asked her what had happened at home.

---

24. *Tcha . . . mam'zélle?:* Everything is fine; and you, miss? (French).
25. *Bon Dieu!:* Good God! (French).
26. *Tiens:* Well? (French).
27. *Bonté divine!:* Goodness gracious! (French).

"But, Clarisse, w'at is it? Is it a misfortune?"

"*Ah, Dieu sait!* It's only something that happen' to me."

"To you!"

"I saw you go away las' night, Alcée, with those saddle-bags," she said, haltingly, striving to arrange something about the saddle, "an' I made Bruce tell me. He said you had gone to the ball, an' wouldn' be home for weeks an' weeks. I thought, Alcée — maybe you were going to — to Assumption. I got wild. An' then I knew if you didn't come back, *now,* to-night, I would die. I couldn' stan' it — again."

She had her face hidden in her arm that she was resting against the saddle when she said that.

He began to wonder if this meant love. But she had to tell him so, before he believed it. And when she told him, he thought the face of the Universe was changed — just like Bobinôt. Was it last week the cyclone had well-nigh ruined him? The cyclone seemed a huge joke, now. It was he, then, who, an hour ago was kissing little Calixta's ear and whispering nonsense into it. Calixta was like a myth, now. The one, only, great reality in the world was Clarisse standing before him, telling him that she loved him.

In the distance they heard the rapid discharge of pistol-shots; but it did not disturb them. They knew it was only the negro musicians who had gone into the yard to fire their pistols into the air, as the custom is, and to announce *"le bal est fini."*[28]

[1892]

---

28. *le bal est fini:* The ball is ended (French).

Chopin's "The Storm: A Sequel to 'The 'Cadian Ball.'"   Chopin wrote this story in July 1898, just after she had sent off her unconventional novel *The Awakening,* to Houghton Mifflin, her publisher in Boston. Although she cast it as a sequel to "At the 'Cadian Ball," first published almost six years earlier, "The Storm" is a different kind of story, an explicit (expecially by the standards of the time) account of an ecstatic sexual encounter between a man and a woman, both married to others. There is no evidence that Chopin ever tried to publish the story. In fact, as she almost certainly realized, the story could probably not then have been published, at least not in any of the prominent magazines in which Chopin had published her earlier stories. The editors and readers of those magazines would not only have been shocked by her subject matter and highly charged erotic language. They also would have been outraged by other aspects of the story, from Calixta's frank enjoyment of her sexual encounter with Alcée to the fact that they suffer no consequences for their adulterous act, at a time when fictional accounts of such affairs were expected to end disastrously for all concerned. The story was first published in *The Complete Works of Kate Chopin* (1969), edited by Per Seyersted, from which the text is taken.

THE STORM

A Sequel to "The 'Cadian Ball"

I

The leaves were so still that even Bibi thought it was going to rain. Bobinôt, who was accustomed to converse on terms of perfect equality with his little son, called the child's attention to certain sombre clouds that were rolling with sinister intention from the west, accompanied by a sullen, threatening roar. They were at Friedheimer's store and decided to remain there till the storm had passed. They sat within the door on two empty kegs. Bibi was four years old and looked very wise.

"Mama'll be 'fraid, yes," he suggested with blinking eyes.

"She'll shut the house. Maybe she got Sylvie helpin' her this evenin'," Bobinôt responded reassuringly.

"No; she ent got Sylvie. Sylvie was helpin' her yistiday," piped Bibi.

Bobinôt arose and going across to the counter purchased a can of shrimps, of which Calixta was very fond. Then he returned to his perch on the keg and sat stolidly holding the can of shrimps while the storm burst. It shook the wooden store and seemed to be ripping great furrows in the distant field. Bibi laid his little hand on his father's knee and was not afraid.

II

Calixta, at home, felt no uneasiness for their safety. She sat at a side window sewing furiously on a sewing machine. She was greatly occupied and did not notice the approaching storm. But she felt very warm and often stopped to mop her face on which the perspiration gathered in beads. She unfastened her white sacque[1] at the throat. It began to grow dark, and suddenly realizing the situation she got up hurriedly and went about closing windows and doors.

Out on the small front gallery she had hung Bobinôt's Sunday clothes to air and she hastened out to gather them before the rain fell. As she stepped outside, Alcée Laballière rode in at the gate. She had not seen him very often since her marriage, and never alone. She stood there with Bobinôt's coat in her hands, and the big rain drops began to fall. Alcée rode his horse under the shelter of a side projection where the chickens had huddled and there were plows and a harrow piled up in the corner.

"May I come and wait on your gallery till the storm is over, Calixta?" he asked.

"Come 'long in, M'sieur Alcée."

His voice and her own startled her as if from a trance, and she seized Bobinôt's vest. Alcée, mounting to the porch, grabbed the trousers and snatched Bibi's braided jacket that was about to be carried away by a sudden gust of wind. He expressed an intention to

---

1. **sacque:** Loose house dress (French).

remain outside, but it was soon apparent that he might as well have been out in the open: the water beat in upon the boards in driving sheets, and he went inside, closing the door after him. It was even necessary to put something beneath the door to keep the water out.

"My! what a rain! It's good two years sence it rain' like that," exclaimed Calixta as she rolled up a piece of bagging and Alcée helped her to thrust it beneath the crack.

She was a little fuller of figure than five years before when she married; but she had lost nothing of her vivacity. Her blue eyes still retained their melting quality; and her yellow hair, dishevelled by the wind and rain, kinked more stubbornly than ever about her ears and temples.

The rain beat upon the low, shingled roof with a force and clatter that threatened to break an entrance and deluge them there. They were in the dining room – the sitting room – the general utility room. Adjoining was her bed room, with Bibi's couch along side her own. The door stood open, and the room with its white, monumental bed, its closed shutters, looked dim and mysterious.

Alcée flung himself into a rocker and Calixta nervously began to gather up from the floor the lengths of a cotton sheet which she had been sewing.

"If this keeps up, *Dieu sait*[2] if the levees goin' to stan' it!" she exclaimed.

"What have you got to do with the levees?"

"I got enough to do! An' there's Bobinôt with Bibi out in that storm – if he only didn' left Friedheimer's!"

"Let us hope, Calixta, that Bobinôt's got sense enough to come in out of a cyclone."

She went and stood at the window with a greatly disturbed look on her face. She wiped the frame that was clouded with moisture. It was stiflingly hot. Alcée got up and joined her at the window, looking over her shoulder. The rain was coming down in sheets obscuring the view of far-off cabins and enveloping the distant wood in a gray mist. The playing of the lightning was incessant. A bolt struck a tall chinaberry tree at the edge of the field. It filled all visible space with a blinding glare and the crash seemed to invade the very boards they stood upon.

Calixta put her hands to her eyes, and with a cry, staggered backward. Alcée's arm encircled her, and for an instant he drew her close and spasmodically to him.

"*Bonté!*"[3] she cried, releasing herself from his encircling arm and retreating from the window, "the house'll go next! If I only knew w'ere Bibi was!" She would not compose herself; she would not be seated. Alcée clasped her shoulders and looked into her face. The contact of her warm, palpitating body when he had unthinkingly drawn her into his arms, had aroused all the old-time infatuation and desire for her flesh.

"Calixta," he said, "don't be frightened. Nothing can happen. The house is too low to be struck, with so many tall trees standing about. There! aren't you going to be quiet? say, aren't you?" He pushed her hair back from her face that was warm and steaming. Her lips were as red and moist as pomegranate seed. Her white neck and a glimpse of

---

2. *Dieu sait:* God knows (French).
3. *Bonté!:* Goodness! (French).

her full, firm bosom disturbed him powerfully. As she glanced up at him the fear in her liquid blue eyes had given place to a drowsy gleam that unconsciously betrayed a sensuous desire. He looked down into her eyes and there was nothing for him to do but to gather her lips in a kiss. It reminded him of Assumption.

"Do you remember — in Assumption, Calixta?" he asked in a low voice broken by passion. Oh! she remembered; for in Assumption he had kissed her and kissed and kissed her; until his senses would well nigh fail, and to save her he would resort to a desperate flight. If she was not an immaculate dove in those days, she was still inviolate; a passionate creature whose very defenselessness had made her defense, against which his honor forbade him to prevail. Now — well, now — her lips seemed in a manner free to be tasted, as well as her round, white throat and her whiter breasts.

They did not heed the crashing torrents, and the roar of the elements made her laugh as she lay in his arms. She was a revelation in that dim, mysterious chamber; as white as the couch she lay upon. Her firm, elastic flesh that was knowing for the first time its birthright, was like a creamy lily that the sun invites to contribute its breath and perfume to the undying life of the world.

The generous abundance of her passion, without guile or trickery, was like a white flame which penetrated and found response in depths of his own sensuous nature that had never yet been reached.

When he touched her breasts they gave themselves up in quivering ecstasy, inviting his lips. Her mouth was a fountain of delight. And when he possessed her, they seemed to swoon together at the very borderland of life's mystery.

He stayed cushioned upon her, breathless, dazed, enervated, with his heart beating like a hammer upon her. With one hand she clasped his head, her lips lightly touching his forehead. The other hand stroked with a soothing rhythm his muscular shoulders.

The growl of the thunder was distant and passing away. The rain beat softly upon the shingles, inviting them to drowsiness and sleep. But they dared not yield.

The rain was over; and the sun was turning the glistening green world into a palace of gems. Calixta, on the gallery, watched Alcée ride away. He turned and smiled at her with a beaming face; and she lifted her pretty chin in the air and laughed aloud.

III

Bobinôt and Bibi, trudging home, stopped without at the cistern to make themselves presentable.

"My! Bibi, w'at will yo' mama say! You ought to be ashame'. You oughtn' put on those good pants. Look at 'em! An' that mud on yo' collar! How you got that mud on yo' collar, Bibi? I never saw such a boy!" Bibi was the picture of pathetic resignation. Bobinôt was the embodiment of serious solicitude as he strove to remove from his own person and his son's the signs of their tramp over heavy roads and through wet fields. He scraped the mud off Bibi's bare legs and feet with a stick and carefully removed all traces from his heavy brogans. Then, prepared for the worst — the meeting with an over-scrupulous housewife, they entered cautiously at the back door.

Calixta was preparing supper. She had set the table and was dripping coffee at the hearth. She sprang up as they came in.

"Oh, Bobinôt! You back! My! but I was uneasy. W'ere you been during the rain? An' Bibi? he ain't wet? he ain't hurt?" She had clasped Bibi and was kissing him effusively. Bobinôt's explanations and apologies which he had been composing all along the way, died on his lips as Calixta felt him to see if he were dry, and seemed to express nothing but satisfaction at their safe return.

"I brought you some shrimps, Calixta," offered Bobinôt, hauling the can from his ample side pocket and laying it on the table.

"Shrimps! Oh, Bobinôt! you too good fo' anything!" and she gave him a smacking kiss on the cheek that resounded. "*J'vous réponds,*[4] we'll have a feas' to night! umph-umph!"

Bobinôt and Bibi began to relax and enjoy themselves, and when the three seated themselves at table they laughed much and so loud that anyone might have heard them as far away as Laballière's.

IV

Alcée Laballière wrote to his wife, Clarisse, that night. It was a loving letter, full of tender solicitude. He told her not to hurry back, but if she and the babies liked it at Biloxi, to stay a month longer. He was getting on nicely; and though he missed them, he was willing to bear the separation a while longer — realizing that their health and pleasure were the first things to be considered.

V

As for Clarisse, she was charmed upon receiving her husband's letter. She and the babies were doing well. The society was agreeable; many of her old friends and acquaintances were at the bay. And the first free breath since her marriage seemed to restore the pleasant liberty of her maiden days. Devoted as she was to her husband, their intimate conjugal life was something which she was more than willing to forego for a while.

So the storm passed and every one was happy.

[c. 1898, 1969]

---

4. *J'vous réponds:* I tell you (French).

Charles W. Chesnutt

[1858–1932]

Charles W. Chesnutt

This photograph was taken around 1899, the year Chesnutt published two collections of his stories about slavery and the "color line" in the United States.

Charles Waddell Chesnutt was born in Cleveland, Ohio, on June 20, 1858. He was the first child of Andrew Jackson ("Jack") Chesnutt, the son of a white man and a black woman, and Ann Maria Sampson Chesnutt, whose parents were of mixed racial heritage. The young couple had fallen in love in 1856, during an arduous wagon-train trip organized by a group of free blacks escaping growing racial oppression in their home town of Fayetteville, North Carolina. After arriving in the North, Jack Chesnutt and Ann Maria Sampson married and settled in Cleveland, Ohio. During the Civil War, Jack Chesnutt served as a teamster in the Union army. After the war, and over his wife's objections to returning to North Carolina, he accepted his father's offer to set him up in the grocery business in Fayetteville, where the family moved in 1866.

Charles Chesnutt consequently spent much of his childhood and young adulthood in the tense and racially troubled postwar South. He initially attended the Howard School. After the death of his mother and the failure of his father's grocery business in 1871, when Chesnutt was thirteen, he was forced to drop out of school and go to work. Chesnutt, who had been an excellent student, practiced composition by keeping a journal and remained an avid reader. Following a careful course of study and self-improvement, he began teaching in 1875. Two years later, he became an assistant to the principal of the State Colored Normal School in Fayetteville, the first state-supported teacher-training school for African Americans. Chesnutt married a fellow teacher, Susan Perry, and he became the principal of the school in 1879. Gaining that respected and remunerative position was a signal achievement, but Chesnutt felt that he had reached the limit of what an African American man could do in Fayetteville. By then, his experience as a person of mixed racial heritage living in the South led him to challenge the increasingly complex and corrosive system of discrimination based on color, or what Chesnutt called "caste," in the United States. "I think I must write a book," he wrote in his journal in May 1880:

> I shall write for a purpose, a high, holy purpose, and this will inspire me to greater effort. The object of my writings would be not so much the elevation of the colored people as the elevation of the whites — for I consider the unjust spirit of caste which is so insidious as to pervade a whole nation, and so powerful as to subject a whole race and all connected with it to scorn and social ostracism — I consider this a barrier to the moral progress of the American people; and I would be one of the first to head a determined, organized crusade against it.

Determined to become a writer and to make a better life for his family, Chesnutt resigned his comfortable position and moved north in 1883. His family joined him the following year, after Chesnutt found a job as a clerk and stenographer in a law office in Cleveland. He studied law in the office even as he began his literary career. His first story, "Uncle Peter's House," appeared in the *Cleveland News and Herald* and other newspapers, through which Chesnutt gained a foothold in the literary marketplace. In 1887, the same year he passed the Ohio bar examination, Chesnutt published "The Goophered Grapevine" in the *Atlantic Monthly*. It was the first story published in that prestigious magazine by an African American, though Chesnutt's racial identity was not then known to the editor or widely known among readers and reviewers until 1899. During the intervening years, Chesnutt published numerous works in periodicals, including several more stories in the *Atlantic*. He also became friendly with one of the editors of the magazine Walter Hines Page, who helped arrange for the publication of Chesnutt's first book, *The Conjure Woman* (1899). That acclaimed collection of dialect stories was such a hit that the publisher swiftly released a second collection of stories, *The Wife of His Youth and Other Stories of the Color Line* (1899). The title echoed "The Color Line," a famous essay on racial prejudice Frederick Douglass had published in 1881. Chesnutt wrote a biography of Douglass, and he exposed the corrosive effects of such prejudice in two novels: *The House behind the Cedars* (1900), the story of a brother and sister of mixed racial heritage who seek to pass for white in the increasingly segregated South, and *The Marrow of Tradition* (1901), inspired by an 1898 riot in which more than twenty blacks had been killed by white supremacists seeking to overthrow the government of Wilmington, North Carolina. Discouraged by the frequently hostile critical reception and the poor sales of those books, however, Chesnutt published only one more novel, *The Colonel's Dream* (1905).

Like his fictional colonel, who is forced to abandon his "dream" of reforming the economic and educational system of the South, Chesnutt for the most part abandoned his own dream of reforming American society through his fiction. Instead, he increasingly devoted his energies and pen to more direct political efforts to end racial discrimination, both in Cleveland and nationally through his work in organizations such as the National Association for the Advancement of Colored People (NAACP). In the remaining years of his life, Chesnutt wrote only a handful of stories and two novels, both of which were rejected by publishers. His contributions to African American literature were recognized in 1928, when the NAACP awarded Chesnutt its Springarn Medal for his "pioneer work as a literary artist depicting the life and struggles of Americans of Negro descent, and for his long and useful career as scholar, worker, and freeman of one of America's greatest cities." Chesnutt died at his home in Cleveland in November 1932.

bedfordstmartins.com/ americanlit for research links on Chesnutt

Chesnutt's "The Passing of Grandison."

Following the success of *The Conjure Woman*, Chesnutt's first collection of stories, his Boston publisher rushed *The Wife of His Youth and Other Stories of the Color Line* into print in December 1899, so that the book would be available for the holiday season. Only three of the stories had previously been published, including the popular title story, "The Wife of His Youth," which had appeared in the prestigious *Atlantic Monthly*. Walter Hines Page, a prominent editor and friend of Chesnutt, had suggested the addition of "and Other Stories of the Color Line" to the title of the collection. In a letter to his publisher, Chesnutt observed that the title would "very aptly characterize the volume," which he hoped would "throw a little light upon the great problem on which the stories are strung." That "great problem" was racial prejudice, the manifestations of which Chesnutt exposed in stories about the African American community, in which lighter-colored skin was often considered a badge of superiority, and in a wide range of other stories about divisions between the races in the United States. As he recognized, racial discrimination and segregation in the country was gaining added support from the emergence of the "plantation myth," especially through popular and proliferating fictions depicting loyal slaves and their benign masters in the antebellum South. Chesnutt sought to subvert that myth in *The Conjure Woman*, dialect stories of plantation life told to transplanted Northerners by a former slave, and in "The Passing of Grandison," the only story in his second collection set before the Civil War. The text is taken from the first printing in *The Wife of His Youth and Other Stories of the Color Line* (1899).

THE PASSING OF GRANDISON

I

When it is said that it was done to please a woman, there ought perhaps to be enough said to explain anything; for what a man will not do to please a woman is yet to be discovered. Nevertheless, it might be well to state a few preliminary facts to make it clear why young Dick Owens tried to run one of his father's negro men off to Canada.

In the early fifties, when the growth of anti-slavery sentiment and the constant drain of fugitive slaves into the North had so alarmed the slaveholders of the border States as to lead to the passage of the Fugitive Slave Law,[1] a young white man from Ohio, moved by compassion for the sufferings of a certain bondman who happened to have a "hard master," essayed to help the slave to freedom. The attempt was discovered and frustrated; the abductor was tried and convicted for slave-stealing, and sentenced to a term of imprisonment in the penitentiary. His death, after the expiration of only a small part of the sentence, from cholera contracted while nursing stricken fellow prisoners, lent to the case a melancholy interest that made it famous in anti-slavery annals.

Dick Owens had attended the trial. He was a youth of about twenty-two, intelligent, handsome, and amiable, but extremely indolent, in a graceful and gentlemanly way; or,

---

1. **Fugitive Slave Law:** The most controversial provision of the Compromise of 1850, this law required all U.S. citizens to aid in the capture and return of runaway slaves to their masters in the South.

as old Judge Fenderson put it more than once, he was lazy as the Devil, a mere figure of speech, of course, and not one that did justice to the Enemy of Mankind. When asked why he never did anything serious, Dick would good-naturedly reply, with a well-modulated drawl, that he didn't have to. His father was rich; there was but one other child, an unmarried daughter, who because of poor health would probably never marry, and Dick was therefore heir presumptive to a large estate. Wealth or social position he did not need to seek, for he was born to both. Charity Lomax had shamed him into studying law, but notwithstanding an hour or so a day spent at old Judge Fenderson's office, he did not make remarkable headway in his legal studies.

"What Dick needs," said the judge, who was fond of tropes, as became a scholar, and of horses, as was befitting a Kentuckian, "is the whip of necessity, or the spur of ambition. If he had either, he would soon need the snaffle[2] to hold him back."

But all Dick required, in fact, to prompt him to the most remarkable thing he accomplished before he was twenty-five, was a mere suggestion from Charity Lomax. The story was never really known to but two persons until after the war, when it came out because it was a good story and there was no particular reason for its concealment.

Young Owens had attended the trial of this slave-stealer, or martyr — either or both — and, when it was over, had gone to call on Charity Lomax, and, while they sat on the veranda after sundown, had told her all about the trial. He was a good talker, as his career in later years disclosed, and described the proceedings very graphically.

"I confess," he admitted, "that while my principles were against the prisoner, my sympathies were on his side. It appeared that he was of good family, and that he had an old father and mother, respectable people, dependent upon him for support and comfort in their declining years. He had been led into the matter by pity for a negro whose master ought to have been run out of the county long ago for abusing his slaves. If it had been merely a question of old Sam Briggs's negro, nobody would have cared anything about it. But father and the rest of them stood on the principle of the thing, and told the judge so, and the fellow was sentenced to three years in the penitentiary."

Miss Lomax had listened with lively interest.

"I've always hated old Sam Briggs," she said emphatically, "ever since the time he broke a negro's leg with a piece of cordwood. When I hear of a cruel deed it makes the Quaker blood that came from my grandmother assert itself. Personally I wish that all Sam Briggs's negroes would run away. As for the young man, I regard him as a hero. He dared something for humanity. I could love a man who would take such chances for the sake of others."

"Could you love me, Charity, if I did something heroic?"

"You never will, Dick. You're too lazy for any use. You'll never do anything harder than playing cards or fox-hunting."

"Oh, come now, sweetheart! I've been courting you for a year, and it's the hardest work imaginable. Are you never going to love me?" he pleaded.

---

2. **snaffle:** A bit on a bridle used with a single set of reins to control a horse.

His hand sought hers, but she drew it back beyond his reach.

"I'll never love you, Dick Owens, until you have done something. When that time comes, I'll think about it."

"But it takes so long to do anything worth mentioning, and I don't want to wait. One must read two years to become a lawyer, and work five more to make a reputation. We shall both be gray by then."

"Oh, I don't know," she rejoined. "It doesn't require a lifetime for a man to prove that he is a man. This one did something, or at least tried to."

"Well, I'm willing to attempt as much as any other man. What do you want me to do, sweetheart? Give me a test."

"Oh, dear me!" said Charity, "I don't care what you *do*, so you do *something*. Really, come to think of it, why should I care whether you do anything or not?"

"I'm sure I don't know why you should, Charity," rejoined Dick humbly, "for I'm aware that I'm not worthy of it."

"Except that I do hate," she added, relenting slightly, "to see a really clever man so utterly lazy and good for nothing."

"Thank you, my dear; a word of praise from you has sharpened my wits already. I have an idea! Will you love me if *I* run a negro off to Canada?"

"What nonsense!" said Charity scornfully. "You must be losing your wits. Steal another man's slave, indeed, while your father owns a hundred!"

"Oh, there'll be no trouble about that," responded Dick lightly; "I'll run off one of the old man's; we've got too many anyway. It may not be quite as difficult as the other man found it, but it will be just as unlawful, and will demonstrate what I am capable of."

"Seeing's believing," replied Charity. "Of course, what you are talking about now is merely absurd. I'm going away for three weeks, to visit my aunt in Tennessee. If you're able to tell me, when I return, that you've done something to prove your quality, I'll — well, you may come and tell me about it."

II

Young Owens got up about nine o'clock next morning, and while making his toilet put some questions to his personal attendant, a rather bright looking young mulatto of about his own age.

"Tom," said Dick.

"Yas, Mars Dick," responded the servant.

"I'm going on a trip North. Would you like to go with me?"

Now, if there was anything that Tom would have liked to make, it was a trip North. It was something he had long contemplated in the abstract, but had never been able to muster up sufficient courage to attempt in the concrete. He was prudent enough, however, to dissemble his feelings.

"I wouldn't min' it, Mars Dick, ez long ez you'd take keer er me an' fetch me home all right."

Tom's eyes belied his words, however, and his young master felt well assured that Tom needed only a good opportunity to make him run away. Having a comfortable home, and a dismal prospect in case of failure, Tom was not likely to take any desperate chances; but young Owens was satisfied that in a free State but little persuasion would be required to lead Tom astray. With a very logical and characteristic desire to gain his end with the least necessary expenditure of effort, he decided to take Tom with him, if his father did not object.

Colonel Owens had left the house when Dick went to breakfast, so Dick did not see his father till luncheon.

"Father," he remarked casually to the colonel, over the fried chicken, "I'm feeling a trifle run down. I imagine my health would be improved somewhat by a little travel and change of scene."

"Why don't you take a trip North?" suggested his father. The colonel added to paternal affection a considerable respect for his son as the heir of a large estate. He himself had been "raised" in comparative poverty, and had laid the foundations of his fortune by hard work; and while he despised the ladder by which he had climbed, he could not entirely forget it, and unconsciously manifested, in his intercourse with his son, some of the poor man's deference toward the wealthy and well-born.

"I think I'll adopt your suggestion, sir," replied the son, "and run up to New York; and after I've been there awhile I may go on to Boston for a week or so. I've never been there, you know."

"There are some matters you can talk over with my factor in New York," rejoined the colonel, "and while you are up there among the Yankees, I hope you'll keep your eyes and ears open to find out what the rascally abolitionists are saying and doing. They're becoming altogether too active for our comfort, and entirely too many ungrateful niggers are running away. I hope the conviction of that fellow yesterday may discourage the rest of the breed. I'd just like to catch any one trying to run off one of my darkeys. He'd get short shrift; I don't think any Court would have a chance to try him."

"They are a pestiferous lot," assented Dick, "and dangerous to our institutions. But say, father, if I go North I shall want to take Tom with me."

Now, the colonel, while a very indulgent father, had pronounced news on the subject of negroes, having studied them, as he often said, for a great many years, and, as he asserted oftener still, understanding them perfectly. It is scarcely worth while to say, either, that he valued more highly than if he had inherited them the slaves he had toiled and schemed for.

"I don't think it safe to take Tom up North," he declared, with promptness and decision. "He's a good enough boy, but too smart to trust among those low-down abolitionists. I strongly suspect him of having learned to read, though I can't imagine how. I saw him with a newspaper the other day, and while he pretended to be looking at a woodcut,[3] I'm almost sure he was reading the paper. I think it by no means safe to take him."

---

3. **woodcut:** Nineteenth-century newspapers contained illustrations made from prints or designs cut in a block of wood and imprinted on the pages.

Dick did not insist, because he knew it was useless. The colonel would have obliged his son in any other matter, but his negroes were the outward and visible sign of his wealth and station, and therefore sacred to him.

"Whom do you think it safe to take?" asked Dick. "I suppose I'll have to have a body-servant."

"What's the matter with Grandison?" suggested the colonel. "He's handy enough, and I reckon we call trust him. He's too fond of good eating, to risk losing his regular meals; besides, he's sweet on your mother's maid, Betty, and I've promised to let 'em get married before long. I'll have Grandison up, and we'll talk to him. Here, you boy Jack," called the colonel to a yellow youth in the next room who was catching flies and pulling their wings off to pass the time, "go down to the barn and tell Grandison to come here."

"Grandison," said the colonel, when the negro stood before him, hat in hand.

"Yas, marster."

"Haven't I always treated you right?"

"Yas, marster."

"Haven't you always got all you wanted to eat?"

"Yas marster."

"And as much whiskey and tobacco as was good for you, Grandison?"

"Y-a-s, marster."

"I should just like to know, Grandison, whether you don't think yourself a great deal better off than those poor free negroes down by the plank road, with no kind master to look after them and no mistress to give them medicine when they're sick and – and" –

"Well, I sh'd jes' reckon I is better off, suh, dan dem low-down free niggers, suh! Ef anybody ax 'em who dey b'long ter, dey has ter say nobody, er e'se lie erbout it. Anybody ax me who I b'longs ter, I ain' got no 'casion ter be shame' ter tell 'em, no, suh, 'deed I ain', suh!"

The colonel was beaming. This was true gratitude, and his feudal heart thrilled at such appreciative homage. What cold-blooded, heartless monsters they were who would break up this blissful relationship of kindly protection on the one hand, of wise subordination and loyal dependence on the other! The colonel always became indignant at the mere thought of such wickedness.

"Grandison," the colonel continued, "your young master Dick is going North for a few weeks, and I am thinking of letting him take you along. I shall send you on this trip, Grandison, in order that you may take care of your young master. He will need some one to wait on him, and no one can ever do it so well as one of the boys brought up with him on the old plantation. I am going to trust him in your hands, and I'm sure you'll do your duty faithfully, and bring him back home safe and sound – to old Kentucky."

Grandison grinned. "Oh yas, marster, I'll take keer er young Mars Dick."

"I want to warn you, though, Grandison," continued the colonel impressively, "against these cussed abolitionists, who try to entice servants from their comfortable homes and their indulgent masters, from the blue skies, the green fields, and the warm sunlight of their southern home, and send them away off yonder to Canada, a dreary country, where the woods are full of wildcats and wolves and bears, where the snow lies up to the eaves of the houses for six months of the year, and the cold is so severe that it freezes your breath and curdles your blood; and where, when runaway niggers get sick and can't work, they are turned out to starve and die, unloved and uncared for. I reckon, Grandison, that you have too much sense to permit yourself to be led astray by any such foolish and wicked people."

"'Deed, suh, I would n' 'low none er dem cussed, low-down abolitioners ter come nigh me, suh. I'd – I'd – would I be 'lowed ter hit 'em, suh?"

"Certainly, Grandison," replied the colonel, chuckling, "hit 'em as hard as you can. I reckon they'd rather like it. Begad, I believe they would! It would serve 'em right to be hit by a nigger!"

"Er ef I didn't hit 'em, suh," continued Grandison reflectively, "I'd tell Mars Dick, en *he'd* fix 'em. He'd smash de face off'n 'em, suh, I jes' knows he would."

"Oh yes, Grandison, your young master will protect you. You need fear no harm while he is near."

"Dey won't try ter steal me, will dey, marster?" asked the negro, with sudden alarm.

"I don't know, Grandison," replied the colonel, lighting a fresh cigar. "They're a desperate set of lunatics, and there's no telling what they may resort to. But if you stick close to your young master, and remember always that he is your best friend, and understands your real needs, and has your true interests at heart, and if you will be careful to avoid strangers who try to talk to you, you'll stand a fair chance of getting back to your home and your friends. And if you please your master Dick, he'll buy you a present, and a string of beads for Betty to wear when you and she get married in the fall."

"Thanky, marster, thanky, suh," replied, Grandison, oozing gratitude at every pore; "you is a good marster, to be sho', suh; yas, 'deed you is. You kin jes' bet me and Mars Dick gwine git 'long jes' lack I wuz own boy ter Mars Dick. En it won't be my fault ef he don' want me fer his boy all de time, w'en we come back home ag'in."

"All right, Grandison, you may go now. You needn't work any more to-day, and here's a piece of tobacco for you off my own plug."

"Thanky, marster, thanky, marster! You is de bes' marster any nigger ever had in dis worl'." And Grandison bowed and scraped and disappeared round the corner, his jaws closing around a large section of the colonel's best tobacco.

"You may take Grandison," said the colonel to his son. "I allow he's abolitionist-proof."

III

Richard Owens, Esq., and servant, from Kentucky, registered at the fashionable New York hostelry for Southerners in those days, a hotel where an atmosphere congenial to Southern institutions was sedulously maintained. But there were negro waiters in the dining-room, and mulatto bell-boys, and Dick had no doubt that Grandison, with the native gregariousness and garrulousness of his race, would foregather and palaver with them sooner or later, and Dick hoped that they would speedily inoculate him with the virus of freedom. For it was not Dick's intention to say anything to his servant about his plan to free him, for obvious reasons. To mention one of them, if Grandison should go away, and by legal process be recaptured, his young master's part in the matter would doubtless become known, which would be embarrassing to Dick, to say the least. If, on the other hand, he should merely give Grandison sufficient latitude, he had no doubt he would eventually lose him. For while not exactly skeptical about Grandison's perfervid loyalty, Dick had been a somewhat keen observer of human nature, in his own indolent way, and based his expectations upon the force of the example and argument that his servant could scarcely fail to encounter. Grandison should have a fair chance to become free by his own initiative; if it should become necessary to adopt other measures to get rid of him, it would be time enough to act when the necessity arose; and Dick Owens was not the youth to take needless trouble.

The young master renewed some acquaintances and made others, and spent a week or two very pleasantly in the best society of the metropolis, easily accessible to a wealthy, well-bred young Southerner, with proper introductions. Young women smiled on him, and young men of convivial habits pressed their hospitalities; but the memory of Charity's sweet, strong face and clear blue eyes made him proof against the blandishments of the one sex and the persuasions of the other. Meanwhile he kept Grandison supplied with pocket-money, and left him mainly to his own devices. Every night when Dick came in he hoped he might have to wait upon himself, and every morning he looked forward with pleasure to the prospect of making his toilet unaided. His hopes, however, were doomed to disappointment, for every night when he came in Grandison was on hand with a bootjack, and a nightcap mixed for his young master as the colonel had taught him to mix it, and every morning Grandison appeared with his master's boots blacked and his clothes brushed, and laid his linen out for the day.

"Grandison," said Dick one morning, after finishing his toilet, "this is the chance of your life to go around among your own people and see how they live. Have you met any of them?"

"Yas, suh, I's seen some of 'em. But I don' keer nuffin fer 'em, suh. Dey're diffe'nt f'm de niggers down ou' way. Dey 'lows dey're free, but dey ain' got sense 'nuff ter know dey ain' half as well off as dey would be down Souf, whar dey'd be 'preciated."

When two weeks had passed without any apparent effect of evil example upon Grandison, Dick resolved to go on to Boston, where he thought the atmosphere might prove more favorable to his ends. After he had been at the Revere House for a day or two without losing Grandison, he decided upon slightly different tactics.

Having ascertained from a city directory the addresses of several well-known abolitionists, he wrote them each a letter something like this: —

> DEAR FRIEND AND BROTHER: —
> A wicked slaveholder from Kentucky, stopping at the Revere House, has dared to insult the liberty-loving people of Boston by bringing his slave into their midst. Shall this be tolerated? Or shall steps be taken in the name of liberty to rescue a fellow-man from bondage? For obvious reasons I can only sign myself,
>
> A FRIEND OF HUMANITY

That his letter might have an opportunity to prove effective, Dick made it a point to send Grandison away from the hotel on various errands. On one of these occasions Dick watched him for quite a distance down the street. Grandison had scarcely left the hotel when a long-haired, sharp-featured man came out behind him, followed him, soon overtook him, and kept along beside him until they turned the next corner. Dick's hopes were roused by this spectacle, but sank correspondingly when Grandison returned to the hotel. Grandison said nothing about the encounter, Dick hoped there might be some self-consciousness behind this unexpected reticence, the results of which might develop later on.

But Grandison was on hand again when his master came back to the hotel at night, and was in attendance again in the morning, with hot water, to assist at his master's toilet. Dick sent him on further errands from day to day, and upon one occasion came squarely up to him — inadvertently of course — while Grandison was engaged in conversation with a young white man in clerical garb. When Grandison saw Dick approaching, he edged away from the preacher and hastened toward his master, with a very evident expression of relief upon his countenance.

"Mars Dick," he said, "dese yer abolitioners is jes' pesterin' de life out er me tryin' ter git me ter run away. I don' pay no 'tention ter 'em, but dey riles me so sometimes dat I'm feared I'll hit some of 'em some er dese days, an' dat mought git me inter trouble. I ain' said nuffin' ter you 'bout it, Mars Dick, fer I did n' wanter 'sturb yo' min'; but I don' like it, suh; no, suh, I don'! Is we gwine back home 'fo' long, Mars Dick?"

"We'll be going back soon enough," replied Dick somewhat shortly, while he inwardly cursed the stupidity of a slave who could be free and would not, and registered a secret vow that if he were unable to get rid of Grandison without assassinating him, and were therefore compelled to take him back to Kentucky, he would see that Grandison got a taste of an article of slavery that would make him regret his wasted opportunities. Meanwhile he determined to tempt his servant yet more strongly.

"Grandison," he said next morning, "I'm going away for a day or two, but I shall leave you here. I shall lock up a hundred dollars in this drawer and give you the key. If you need any of it, use it and enjoy yourself, — spend it all if you like, — for this is probably the last chance you'll have for some time to be in a free State, and you'd better enjoy your liberty while you may."

When he came back a couple of days later and found the faithful Grandison at his post, and the hundred dollars intact, Dick felt seriously annoyed. His vexation was increased by the fact that he could not express his feelings adequately. He did not even scold Grandison; how could he, indeed, find fault with one who so sensibly recognized his true place in the economy of civilization, and kept it with such touching fidelity?

"I can't say a thing to him," groaned Dick. "He deserves a leather medal, made out of his own hide tanned. I reckon I'll write to father and let him know what a model servant he has given me."

He wrote his father a letter which made the colonel swell with pride and pleasure. "I really think," the colonel observed to one of his friends, "that Dick ought to have the nigger interviewed by the Boston papers, so that they may see how contented and happy our darkeys really are."

Dick also wrote a long letter to Charity Lomax, in which he said, among many other things, that if she knew how hard he was working, and under what difficulties, to accomplish something serious for her sake, she would no longer keep him in suspense, but overwhelm him with love and admiration.

Having thus exhausted without result the more obvious methods of getting rid of Grandison, and diplomacy having also proved a failure, Dick was forced to consider more radical measures. Of course he might run away himself, and abandon Grandison, but this would be merely to leave him in the United States, where he was still a slave, and where, with his notions of loyalty, he would speedily be reclaimed. It was necessary, in order to accomplish the purpose of his trip to the North, to leave Grandison permanently in Canada, where he would be legally free.

"I might extend my trip to Canada," he reflected, "but that would be too palpable. I have it! I'll visit Niagara Falls on the way home, and lose him on the Canada side. When he once realizes that he is actually free, I'll warrant that he'll stay."

So the next day saw them westward bound, and in due course of time, by the somewhat slow conveyances of the period, they found themselves at Niagara. Dick walked and drove about the Falls for several days, taking Grandison along with him on most occasions. One morning they stood on the Canadian side, watching the wild whirl of the waters below them.

"Grandison," said Dick, raising his voice above the roar of the cataract, "do you know where you are now?"

"I's wid you, Mars Dick; dat's all I keers."

"You are now in Canada, Grandison, where your people go when they run away from their masters. If you wished, Grandison, you might walk away from me this very minute, and I could not lay my hand upon you to take you back."

Grandison looked around uneasily.

"Let's go back ober de ribber, Mars Dick. I's feared I'll lose you ovuh heah, an' den I won' hab no marster, an' won't nebber be able to git back home no mo'."

Discouraged, but not yet hopeless, Dick said, a few minutes later, –

"Grandison, I'm going up the road a bit, to the inn over yonder. You stay here until I return. I'll not be gone a great while."

Grandison's eyes opened wide and he looked somewhat fearful.

"Is dey any er dem dadblasted abolitioners roun' heah, Mars Dick?"

"I don't imagine that there are," replied his master, hoping there might be. "But I'm not afraid of *your* running away, Grandison. I only wish I were," he added to himself.

Dick walked leisurely down the road to where the whitewashed inn, built of stone, with true British solidity, loomed up through the trees by the roadside. Arrived there he ordered a glass of ale and a sandwich, and took a seat at a table by a window, from which he could see Grandison in the distance. For a while he hoped that the seed he had sown might have fallen on fertile ground, and that Grandison, relieved from the restraining power of a master's eye, and finding himself in a free country, might get up and walk away; but the hope was vain, for Grandison remained faithfully at his post, awaiting his master's return. He had seated himself on a broad flat stone, and, turning his eyes away from the grand and awe-inspiring spectacle that lay close at hand, was looking anxiously toward the inn where his master sat cursing his ill-timed fidelity.

By and by a girl came into the room to serve his order, and Dick very naturally glanced at her; and as she was young and pretty and remained in attendance, it was some minutes before he looked for Grandison. When he did so his faithful servant had disappeared.

To pay his reckoning and go away without the change was a matter quickly accomplished. Retracing his footsteps toward the Falls, he saw, to his great disgust, as he approached the spot where he had left Grandison, the familiar form of his servant stretched out on the ground, his face to the sun, his mouth open, sleeping the time away, oblivious alike to the grandeur of the scenery, the thunderous roar of the cataract, or the insidious voice of sentiment.

"Grandison," soliloquized his master, as he stood gazing down at his ebony encumbrance, "I do not deserve to be an American citizen; I ought not to have the advantages I possess over you; and I certainly am not worthy of Charity Lomax, if I am not smart enough to get rid of you. I have an idea! You shall yet be free, and I will be the instrument of your deliverance. Sleep on, faithful and affectionate servitor, and dream of the blue grass and the bright skies of old Kentucky, for it is only in your dreams that you will ever see them again!"

Dick retraced his footsteps towards the inn. The young woman chanced to look out of the window and saw the handsome young gentleman she had waited on a few minutes before, standing in the road a short distance away, apparently engaged in earnest conversation with a colored man employed as hostler[4] for the inn. She thought she saw something pass from the white man to the other, but at that moment her duties called her away from the window, and when she looked out again the young gentleman had disappeared, and the hostler, with two other young men of the neighborhood, one white and one colored, were walking rapidly towards the Falls.

IV

Dick made the journey homeward alone, and as rapidly as the conveyances of the day would permit. As he drew near home his conduct in going back without Grandison took on a more serious aspect than it had borne at any previous time, and although he had prepared the colonel by a letter sent several days ahead, there was still the prospect of a bad quarter of an hour with him; not, indeed, that his father would upbraid him, but he was likely to make searching inquiries. And notwithstanding the vein of quiet recklessness that had carried Dick through his preposterous scheme, he was a very poor liar, having rarely had occasion or inclination to tell anything but the truth. Any reluctance to meet his father was more than offset, however, by a stronger force drawing him homeward, for Charity Lomax must long since have returned from her visit to her aunt in Tennessee.

Dick got off easier than he had expected. He told a straight story, and a truthful one, so far as it went.

The colonel raged at first, but rage soon subsided into anger, and anger moderated into annoyance, and annoyance into a sort of garrulous sense of injury. The colonel thought he had been hardly used; he had trusted this negro, and he had broken faith. Yet, after all, he did not blame Grandison so much as he did the abolitionists, who were undoubtedly at the bottom of it.

---

4. **hostler:** A man who cares for the horses of people staying at an inn.

As for Charity Lomax, Dick told her, privately of course, that he had run his father's man, Grandison, off to Canada, and left him there.

"Oh, Dick," she had said with shuddering alarm, "what have you done? If they knew it they'd send you to the penitentiary, like they did that Yankee."

"But they don't know it," he had replied seriously; adding, with an injured tone, "you don't seem to appreciate my heroism like you did that of the Yankee; perhaps it's because I wasn't caught and sent to the penitentiary. I thought you wanted me to do it."

"Why, Dick Owens!" she exclaimed. "You know I never dreamed of any such outrageous proceeding.

"But I presume I'll have to marry you," she concluded, after some insistence on Dick's part, "if only to take care of you. You are too reckless for anything; and a man who goes chasing all over the North, being entertained by New York and Boston society and having negroes to throw away, needs some one to look after him."

"It's a most remarkable thing," replied Dick fervently, "that your views correspond exactly with my profoundest convictions. It proves beyond question that we were made for one another."

They were married three weeks later. As each of them had just returned from a journey, they spent their honeymoon at home.

A week after the wedding they were seated, one afternoon, on the piazza of the colonel's house, where Dick had taken his bride, when a negro from the yard ran down the lane and threw open the big gate for the colonel's buggy to enter. The colonel was not alone. Beside him, ragged and travel-stained, bowed with weariness, and upon his face a haggard look that told of hardship and privation, sat the lost Grandison.

The colonel alighted at the steps.

"Take the lines, Tom," he said to the man who had opened the gate, "and drive round to the barn. Help Grandison down — poor devil, he's so stiff he can hardly move! — and get a tub of water and wash him and rub him down, and feed him, and give him a big drink of whiskey, and then let him come round and see his young master and his new mistress."

The colonel's face wore an expression compounded of joy and indignation — joy at the restoration of a valuable piece of property; indignation for reasons he proceeded to state.

"It's astounding, the depths of depravity the human heart is capable of! I was coming along the road three miles away, when I heard some one call me from the roadside. I pulled up the mare, and who should come out of the woods but Grandison. The poor nigger could hardly crawl along, with the help of a broken limb. I was never more astonished in my life. You could have knocked me down with a feather. He seemed pretty far gone — he could hardly talk above a whisper — and I had to give him a mouthful of whiskey to brace him up so he could tell his story. It's just as I thought from the beginning, Dick; Grandison had no notion of running away; he knew when he was well off, and where his friends were. All the persuasions of abolition liars and runaway niggers did not move him. But the desperation of those fanatics knew no bounds; their guilty consciences gave them no rest. They got the notion somehow that Grandison belonged to a nigger-catcher, and had been brought North as a spy to help capture ungrateful runaway servants. They actually kidnaped him — just think if it! — and gagged him and bound him and threw him rudely into a wagon, and carried him into the gloomy depths of a Canadian forest, and locked him in a lonely hut, and fed him on bread and water for three weeks. One of the scoundrels wanted to kill him, and persuaded the others that it ought to be done; but they got to quarreling about how they should do it, and before they had their minds made up Grandison escaped, and, keeping his back steadily to the North Star, made his way, after suffering incredible hardships, back to the old plantation, back to his master, his friends, and his home. Why, it's as good as one of Scott's novels![5] Mr. Simms[6] or some other one of our Southern authors ought to write it up."

"Don't you think, sir," suggested Dick, who had calmly smoked his cigar throughout the colonel's animated recital, "that that kidnaping yarn sounds a little improbable? Isn't there some more likely explanation?"

"Nonsense, Dick; it's the gospel truth! Those infernal abolitionists are capable of anything — everything! Just think of their locking the poor, faithful nigger up, beating him, kicking him, depriving him of his liberty, keeping him on bread and water for three long, lonesome weeks, and he all the time pining for the old plantation!"

There were almost tears in the colonel's eyes at the picture of Grandison's sufferings that he conjured up. Dick still professed to be slightly skeptical, and met Charity's severely questioning eye with bland unconsciousness.

The colonel killed the fatted calf[7] for Grandison, and for two or three weeks the returned wanderer's life was a slave's dream of pleasure. His fame spread throughout the county, and the colonel gave him a permanent place among the house servants, where he could always have him conveniently at hand to relate his adventures to admiring visitors.

About three weeks after Grandison's return the colonel's faith in sable humanity was rudely shaken, and its foundations almost broken up. He came near losing his belief in the fidelity of the negro to his master, — the servile virtue most highly prized and most sedulously cultivated by the colonel and his kind. One Monday morning Grandison was missing. And not only Grandison, but his wife, Betty the maid; his mother, aunt Eunice; his father, uncle Ike; his brothers, Tom and John, and his little sister Elsie, were likewise absent from the plantation; and a hurried search and inquiry in the neighborhood resulted in no information as to their whereabouts. So much valuable property could not be lost without an effort to recover it, and the wholesale nature of the transaction carried consternation to the hearts of those whose ledgers were chiefly bound in black. Extremely energetic measures were taken by the colonel and his friends. The fugitives

---

5. **Scott's novels:** The acclaimed historical romances of the British novelist Sir Walter Scott (1771–1832) were bestsellers in the United States.

6. **Mr. Simms:** William Gilmore Simms (1806–1870), a popular southern writer.

7. **fatted calf:** An allusion to the parable of the prodigal son, whose father celebrates his return home by ordering the killing of a fatted calf for a feast (Luke 15:11–33).

were traced, and followed from point to point, on their northward run through Ohio. Several times the hunters were close upon their heels, but the magnitude of the escaping party begot unusual vigilance on the part of those who sympathized with the fugitives, and strangely enough, the underground railroad seemed to have had its tracks cleared and signals set for this particular train. Once, twice, the colonel thought he had them, but they slipped through his fingers.

One last glimpse he caught of his vanishing property, as he stood, accompanied by a United States marshal, on a wharf at a port on the south shore of Lake Erie. On the stern of a small steamboat which was receding rapidly from the wharf, with her nose pointing toward Canada, there stood a group of familiar dark faces, and the look they cast backward was not one of longing for the fleshpots of Egypt.[8] The colonel saw Grandison point him out to one of the crew of the vessel, who waved his hand derisively toward the colonel. The latter shook his fist impotently — and the incident was closed.

[1899]

---

8. **fleshpots of Egypt:** As Moses led the Israelites out of bondage to the promised land, they endured such great hunger in the wilderness that they declared, "Would to God we had died by the hand of the Lord in the land of Egypt, when we sat by the flesh pots, *and* when we did eat bread to the full" (Exodus 16:3).

Pauline E. Hopkins

[1859-1930]

Pauline E. Hopkins

This photograph appeared in the supplement to the March 1904 issue of the *Colored American Magazine.*

Pauline Elizabeth Hopkins, who has been hailed as "the Dean of African American women writers," was born in Portland, Maine, in 1859. Her father died when Hopkins was a young child, and her mother married William A. Hopkins, a tailor and a veteran of the Civil War. The family moved to Boston, where Hopkins attended public schools and developed an interest in writing. When she was fifteen, Hopkins won first prize in an essay contest sponsored in part by William Wells Brown, the abolitionist, activist, and author of *Clotel* (1853), the first novel published by an African American. After her graduation from Boston Girls High School, Hopkins, her mother, and her stepfather formed a theatrical troupe, the Hopkins Colored Troubadours. In 1880, the group performed a play written by Hopkins, *Peculiar Sam; or, The Underground Railroad,* one of the earliest musical dramas in the history of black theater in the United States. An accomplished singer, Hopkins toured with the troupe for twelve years, becoming widely known as "Boston's Favorite Soprano." Early in the 1890s, however, she left the troupe and trained as a stenographer to support herself while she pursued a career in writing. Hopkins soon began to earn a reputation as a speaker, lecturing on African American history at churches and reading her fiction at women's clubs in Boston.

Within a decade, Hopkins reached the zenith of her brief but remarkable literary career. In 1900, she published her first and best-known novel, *Contending Forces; or, A Romance Illustrative of Negro Life North and South,* the saga of the injustices suffered by several generations of a black family before and after the Civil War. The epigraph to the novel, which she took from Ralph Waldo Emerson's 1844 "Address on the Emancipation in the British West Indies," expresses a central thesis in all of Hopkins's work: "The civility of no race can be perfect whilst another race is degraded." The year the novel was published, Hopkins helped found the *Colored American Magazine* in Boston. As an announcement read, the new magazine was designed to be *"Of the Race, By the Race, For the Race,"* an echo of the closing lines of Abraham Lincoln's Gettysburg Address. When Hopkins became its editor in 1903, she stated that the magazine was

> intended to show that the colored people can advance on all the lines of progress known to other races, that they can be more than tillers of the soils, hewers of wood and drawers of water — that they can attain to eminence (both the men and women among them) as thinkers, writers, as doctors, as lawyers, as clergymen, as singers, musicians, artists, actors, and also as successful business men, in the conduct of enterprises of importance.

Hopkins was also the major contributor to the *Colored American Magazine.* True to her goal of illustrating the potential of African Americans and instilling pride in their achievements, Hopkins wrote two extended series of essays for the magazine, *Famous Men of the Negro Race* (1900-01) and *Famous Women of the Negro Race* (1901-02). She also published a substantial amount of fiction in the magazine, seven stories and three serialized novels: *Hagar's Daughter: A Story of Southern Caste Prejudice* (1901-02); *Winona: A Tale of Negro Life in the South and Southwest* (1902); and *Of One Blood; or, The Hidden Self* (1902-03).

Following that prolific period of creativity, Hopkins's literary career virtually ended. In 1904, the *Colored American Magazine* came under the control of Booker T. Washington, who strongly disapproved of what he considered to be Hopkins's radical politics and her commitment to the doctrine of racial uplift espoused by African American leaders such as W. E. B. Du Bois. Hopkins was consequently ousted from the editorship of the magazine, in which no more of her works appeared. Despite that painful rebuff, she published two groundbreaking historical works the following year: a pamphlet entitled *A Primer of Facts Pertaining to the Early Greatness of the African Race and the Possibility of Restoration by Its Descendents* and "The Dark Races of the Twentieth Century," a four-part series of essays on the global African community that appeared in *The Voice of the Negro.* More than a decade later, in 1916, she published a two-part essay in another African American magazine, the *New Era.* But she apparently did little other writing. Hopkins died in 1930 in a house fire at her home in Cambridge, Massachusetts, where she was working as a stenographer for the Massachusetts Institute of Technology.

[Pauline Hopkins] has given us a sense of her day, a clue collection, and we can use the light of it to clarify our understanding and our intuition. We can take the building blocks she does supply us and use them to fill in old gaps.
—Gwendolyn Brooks

bedfordstmartins.com/ americanlit *for research links on Hopkins*

Hopkins's "'As the Lord Lives, He Is One of Our Mother's Children.'" This story was one of Hopkins's final contributions to the *Colored American Magazine*. Although it was primarily literary, the magazine included a wide range of essays on the past and present experiences of African Americans, as well as articles on current social issues in the United States. Many of the stories and serialized novels published in the magazine were also strongly shaped by social activism. A major concern was lynching, most often the hanging of black men for their alleged crimes by lawless white mobs. The number of such lynchings, which were rampant in the South for five decades after the end of Reconstruction in 1876, peaked during the 1890s. In "'As the Lord Lives, He Is One of Our Mother's Children,'" Hopkins offers a powerful indictment of that murderous manifestation of racial prejudice and the hatred of blacks in the United States, what the antilynching activist Ida B. Wells called "our country's national crime." The text is taken from the first printing in the *Colored American Magazine*, November 1903.

The *Colored American Magazine*

Even before she became its editor, Hopkins was the major contributor to the *Colored American Magazine*, in which she frequently highlighted the civic and cultural activities of middle-class women, as in the featured article in this issue, and the achievements of other African Americans.

"As the Lord Lives, He Is One of Our Mother's Children"

It was Saturday afternoon in a large Western town, and the Rev. Septimus Stevens sat in his study writing down the headings for his Sunday sermon. It was slow work; somehow the words would not flow with their usual ease, although his brain was teeming with ideas. He had written for his heading at the top of the sheet these words for a text: "As I live, he is one of our mother's children." It was to be a great effort on the Negro question, and the reverend gentleman, with his New England training, was in full sympathy with his subject. He had jotted down a few headings under it, when he came to a full stop; his mind simply refused to work. Finally, with a sigh, he opened the compartment in his desk where his sermons were packed and began turning over those old creations in search of something suitable for the morrow.

Suddenly the whistles in all directions began to blow wildly. The Rev. Septimus hurried to the window, threw it open and leaned out, anxious to learn the cause of the wild clamor. Could it be another of the terrible "cave-ins," that were the terror of every mining district? Men were pouring out of the mines as fast as they could come up. The crowds which surged through the streets night and day were rushing to meet them. Hundreds of policemen were about; each corner was guarded by a squad commanded by a sergeant. The police and the mob were evidently working together. Tramp, tramp, on they rushed; down the serpentine boulevard for nearly two miles they went swelling like an angry torrent. In front of the open window where stood the white-faced clergyman they paused. A man mounted the empty barrel and harangued the crowd: "I am from Dover City, gentlemen, and I have come here to-day to assist you in teaching the blacks a lesson. I have killed a nigger before," he yelled, "and in revenge of the wrong wrought upon you and yours I am willing to kill again. The only way you can teach these niggers a lesson is to go to the jail and lynch these men as an object lesson. String them up! That is the only thing to do. Kill them, string them up, lynch them! I will lead you. On to the prison and lynch Jones and Wilson, the black fiends!" With a hoarse shout, in which were mingled cries like the screams of enraged hyenas and the snarls of tigers, they rushed on.

Nora, the cook burst open the study door, pale as a sheet, and dropped at the minister's feet. "Mother of God!" she cried, "and is it the end of the wurruld?"

On the maddened men rushed from north, south, east and west, armed with everything from a brick to a horse-pistol. In the melee a man was shot down. Somebody planted a long knife in the body of a little black newsboy for no apparent reason. Every now and then a Negro would be overwhelmed somewhere on the outskirts of the crowd and left beaten to a pulp. Then they reached the jail and battered in the door.

The solitary watcher at the window tried to move, but could not; terror had stricken his very soul, and his white lips moved in articulate prayer. The crowd surged back. In the midst was only one man; for some reason, the other was missing. A rope was knotted about his neck — charged with murder, himself about to be murdered. The hands which drew the rope were too swift, and, half-strangled, the victim fell. The crowd halted, lifted him up, loosened the rope and let the wretch breathe.

He was a grand man — physically — black as ebony, tall, straight, deep-chested, every fibre full of that life so soon to be quenched. Lucifer, just about to be cast out of heaven, could not have thrown around a glance of more scornful pride. What might not such a man have been, if — but it was too late. "Run fair, boys," said the prisoner, calmly, "run fair! You keep up your end of the rope and I'll keep up mine."

The crowd moved a little more slowly, and the minister saw the tall form "keeping up" its end without a tremor of hesitation. As they neared the telegraph pole, with its out-stretched arm, the watcher summoned up his lost strength, grasped the curtain and pulled it down to shut out the dreadful sight. Then came a moment of ominous silence. The man of God sank upon his knees to pray for the passing soul. A thousand-voiced cry of brutal triumph arose in cheers for the work that had been done, and curses and imprecations, and they who had hunted a man out of life hurried off to hunt for gold.

To and fro on the white curtain swung the black silhouette of what had been a man.

For months the minister heard in the silence of the night phantom echoes of those frightful voices, and awoke, shuddering, from some dream whose vista was closed by that black figure swinging in the air.

About a month after this happening, the rector was returning from a miner's cabin in the mountains where a child lay dying. The child haunted him; he thought of his own motherless boy and a fountain of pity overflowed in his heart. He had dismounted and was walking along the road to the ford at the creek which just here cut the path fairly in two.

The storm of the previous night had refreshed all nature and had brought out the rugged beauty of the landscape in all its grandeur. The sun had withdrawn his last daz-zling rays from the eastern highlands upon which the lone traveler gazed, and now they were fast veiling themselves in purple night shadows that rendered them momentarily more grand and mysterious. The man of God stood a moment with uncovered head repeating aloud some lines from a great Russian poet:

> "O Thou eternal One! whose presence bright
> All space doth occupy, all motion guide;
> Unchanged through time's all devastating flight;
> Thou only God! There is no God beside
> Being above all beings, Mighty One!
> Whom none can comprehend and none, explore."[1]

Another moment passed in silent reverence of the All-Wonderful, before he turned to remount his horse and enter the waters of the creek. The creek was very much swollen and he found it hard to keep the ford. Just as he was midway the stream he saw some-thing lying half in the water on the other bank. Approaching nearer he discovered it to be a man, apparently unconscious. Again dismounting, he tied his horse to a sapling, and went up to the inert figure, ready, like the Samaritan of old, to succor the wayside fallen. The man opened his deep-set eyes and looked at him keenly. He was gaunt, hag-gard and despairing, and soaking wet.

---

1. **"O Thou . . . explore"**: The lines are from a translation of "God," by the Russian poet Gavrila Romanovich Derzhavin (1743–1816).

"Well, my man, what is the matter?" Rev. Mr. Stevens had a very direct way of going at things.

"Nothing," was the sullen response.

"Can't I help you? You seem ill. Why are you lying in the water?"

"I must have fainted and fallen in the creek," replied the man, answering the last question first. "I've tramped from Colorado hunting for work. I'm penniless, have no home, haven't had much to eat for a week, and now I've got a touch of your d— mountain fever." He shivered as if with a chill, and smiled faintly.

The man, from his speech, was well educated, and in spite of his pitiful situation, had an air of good breeding, barring his profanity.

"What's your name?" asked Stevens, glancing him over sharply as he knelt beside the man and deftly felt his pulse and laid a cool hand on the fevered brow.

"Stone — George Stone."

Stevens got up. "Well, Stone, try to get on my horse and I'll take you to the rectory. My housekeeper and I together will manage to make you more comfortable."

So it happened that George Stone became a guest at the parsonage, and later, sexton of the church. In that gold-mining region, where new people came and went constantly and new excitements were things of everyday occurrence, and new faces as plenty as old ones, nobody asked or cared where the new sexton came from. He did his work quietly and thoroughly, and quite won Nora's heart by his handy ways about the house. He had a room under the eaves, and seemed thankful and content. Little Flip, the rector's son, took a special liking to him, and he, on his side, worshipped the golden-haired child and was never tired of playing with him and inventing things for his amusement.

"The reverend sets a heap by the boy," he said to Nora one day in reply to her accusation that he spoiled the boy and there was no living with him since Stone's advent. "He won't let me thank him for what he's done for me, but he can't keep me from loving the child."

One day in September, while passing along the street, Rev. Stevens had his attention called to a flaming poster on the side of a fence by the remarks of a crowd of men near him. He turned and read it:

$1,500 REWARD!

"The above reward will be paid for information leading to the arrest of 'Gentleman Jim,' charged with complicity in the murder of Jerry Mason. This nigger is six feet, three inches tall, weight one hundred and sixty pounds. He escaped from jail when his pal was lynched two months ago by a citizen's committee. It is thought that he is in the mountains, etc. He is well educated, and might be taken for a white man. Wore, when last seen, blue jumper and overalls and cowhide boots."

He read it the second time, and he was dimly conscious of seeing, like a vision in the brain, a man playing about the parsonage with little Flip.

"I knowed him. I worked a spell with him over in Lone Tree Gulch before he got down on his luck," spoke a man at his side who was reading the poster with him. "Jones and him was two of the smartest and peaceablest niggers I ever seed. But Jerry Mason kinder sot on 'em both; never could tell why, only some white men can't 'bide a nigger eny mo' than a dog can a cat; it's a natural antiperthy. I'm free to say the niggers seemed harmless, but you can't tell what a man'll do when his blood's up."

He turned to the speaker. "What will happen if they catch him?"

"Lynch him sure, there's been a lot of trouble over there lately. I wouldn't give a toss-up for him if they get their hands on him once more."

Rev. Stevens pushed his way through the crowd, and went slowly down the street to the church. He found Stone there sweeping and dusting. Saying that he wanted to speak with him, he led the way to the study. Facing around upon him suddenly, Stevens said, gravely: "I want you to tell me the truth. Is your real name 'Stone,' and are you a Negro?"

A shudder passed over Stone's strong frame, then he answered, while his eyes never left the troubled face before him, "I am a Negro, and my name is not Stone."

"You said that you had tramped from Colorado."

"I hadn't. I was hiding in the woods; I had been there a month ago. I lied to you."

"Is it all a lie?"

Stone hesitated, and then said: "I was meaning to tell you the first night, but somehow I couldn't. I was afraid you'd turn me out; and I was sick and miserable —"

"Tell me the truth now."

"I will; I'll tell you the God's truth."

He leaned his hand on the back of a chair to steady himself; he was trembling violently. "I came out West from Wilmington, North Carolina, Jones and I together. We were both college men and chums from childhood. All our savings were in the business we had at home when the leading men of the town conceived the idea of driving the Negroes out, and the Wilmington tragedy began. Jones was unmarried, but I lost wife and children that night — burned to death when the mob fired our home. When we got out here we took up claims in the mountains. They were a rough crowd after we struck pay dirt, but Jones and I kept to ourselves and got along all right until Mason joined the crowd. He was from Wilmington; knew us, and took delight in tormenting us. He was a fighting man, but we wouldn't let him push us into trouble."

"You didn't quarrel with him, then?"

The minister gazed at Stone keenly. He seemed a man to trust. "Yes, I did. We didn't want trouble, but we couldn't let Mason rob us. We three had hot words before a big crowd; that was all there was to it that night. In the morning Mason lay dead upon our claim. He'd been shot by some one. My partner and I were arrested, brought to this city and lodged in the jail over there. Jones was lynched! God, can I ever forget that hooting, yelling crowd, and the terrible fight to get away! Somehow I did it — you know the rest."

"Stone, there's a reward for you, and a description of you as you were the night I found you."

Gentleman Jim's face was ashy. "I'll never be taken alive. They'll kill me for what I never did!"

"Not unless I speak. I am in sore doubt what course to take. If I give you up the Vigalantes will hang you."

"I'm a lost man," said the Negro, helplessly, "but I'll never be taken alive."

Stevens walked up and down the room once or twice. It was a human life in his hands. If left to the law to decide, even then in this particular case the Negro stood no chance. It was an awful question to decide. One more turn up and down the little room and suddenly stopping, he flung himself upon his knees in the middle of the room, and raising his clasped hands, cried aloud for heavenly guidance. Such a prayer as followed, the startled listener had never before heard anywhere. There was nothing of rhetorical phrases, nothing of careful thought in the construction of sentences, it was the out-pouring of a pure soul asking for help from its Heavenly Father with all the trustfulness of a little child. It came in a torrent, a flood; it wrestled mightily for the blessing it sought. Rising to his feet when his prayer was finished, Rev. Stevens said, "Stone, — you are to remain Stone, you know — it is best to leave things as they are. Go back to work."

The man raised his bowed bead.

"You mean you're not going to give me up?"

"Stay here till the danger is past; then leave for other parts."

Stone's face turned red, then pale, his voice trembled and tears were in the gray eyes. "I can't thank you, Mr. Stevens, but if ever I get the chance you'll find me grateful."

"All right, Stone, all right," and the minister went back to his writing.

That fall the Rev. Septimus Stevens went to visit his old New England home — he and Flip. He was returning home the day before Thanksgiving, with his widowed mother, who had elected to leave old associations and take charge of her son's home. It was a dim-colored day.

Engineers were laying out a new road near a place of swamps and oozy ground and dead, wet grass, over-arched by leafless, desolate boughs. They were eating their lunch now, seated about on the trunks of fallen trees. The jokes were few, scarcely a pun sea-soned the meal. The day was a dampener; that the morrow was a holiday did not kindle merriment.

Stone sat a little apart from the rest. He had left Rev. Stevens when he got this job in another state. They had voted him moody and unsociable long ago — a man who broods forever upon his wrongs is not a comfortable companion; he never gave any one a key to his moods. He shut himself up in his haunted room — haunted by memory — and no one interfered with him.

The afternoon brought a change in the weather. There was a strange hush, as if Na-ture were holding her breath. But it was as a wild beast holds its breath before a spring. Suddenly a little chattering wind ran along the ground. It was too weak to lift the sodden leaves, yet it made itself heard in some way, and grew stronger. It seemed dizzy, and ran about in a circle. There was a pale light over all, a brassy, yellow light, that gave all things a wild look. The chief of the party took an observation and said: "We'd better get home."

Stone lingered. He was paler, older.

The wind had grown vigorous now and began to tear angrily at the trees, twisting the saplings about with invisible hands. There was a rush and a roar that seemed to spread about in every direction. A tree was furiously uprooted and fell directly in front of him; Stone noticed the storm for the first time.

He looked about him in a dazed way and muttered. "He's coming on this train, he and the kid!"

The brassy light deepened into darkness. Stone went upon the railroad track, and stumbled over something that lay directly over it. It was a huge tree that the wind had lifted in its great strength and whirled over there like thistledown. He raised himself slowly, a little confused by the fall. He took hold of the tree mechanically, but the huge bulk would not yield an inch.

He looked about in the gathering darkness; it was five miles to the station where he might get help. His companions were too far on their way to recall, and there lay a huge mass, directly in the way of the coming train. He had no watch, but he knew it must be nearly six. Soon — very soon — upon the iron pathway, a great train, freighted with life, would dash around the curve to wreck and ruin! Again he muttered, "Coming on this train, he and the kid!" He pictured the faces of his benefactor and the little child, so like his own lost one, cold in death; the life crushed out by the cruel wheels. What was it that seemed to strike across the storm and all its whirl of sound — a child's laugh? Nay, something fainter still — the memory of a child's laugh. It was like a breath of spring flowers in the desolate winter — a touch of heart music amid the revel of the storm. A vision of other fathers with children climbing upon their knees, a soft babble of baby voices assailed him.

"God help me to save them!" he cried.

Again and again he tugged at the tree. It would not move. Then he hastened and got an iron bar from among the tools. Again he strove — once — twice — thrice. With a groan the nearest end gave way. Eureka! If only his strength would hold out. He felt it ebbing slowly from him, something seemed to clutch at his heart; his head swam. Again and yet again he exerted all his strength. There came a prolonged shriek that awoke the echoes. The train was coming. The tree was moving! It was almost off the other rail. The leafless trees seemed to enfold him — to hold him with skeleton arms. "Oh, God save them!" he gasped. "Our times are in Thy hand!"

Something struck him a terrible blow. The agony was ended. Stone was dead.

Rev. Stevens closed his eyes, with a deadly faintness creeping over him, when he saw how near the trainload of people had been to destruction. Only God had saved them at the eleventh hour through the heroism of Stone, who lay dead upon the track, the life crushed out of him by the engine. An inarticulate thanksgiving rose to his lips as soft and clear came the sound of distant church bells, calling to weekly prayer, like "horns of Elfland softly blowing."[2]

Sunday, a week later, Rev. Septimus Stevens preached the greatest sermon of his life. They had found the true murderer of Jerry Mason, and Jones and Gentleman Jim were publicly exonerated by a repentant community.

On this Sunday Rev. Stevens preached the funeral sermon of Gentleman Jim. The church was packed to suffocation by a motley assemblage of men in all stages of dress and undress, but there was sincerity in their hearts as they listened to the preacher's burning words: "As the Lord lives, he is one of our mother's children."

[1903]

---

2. **"horns . . . blowing"**: From *The Princess*, by the English poet Alfred, Lord Tennyson (1809–1892): "O hark, O hear! how thin and clear, / And thinner, clearer, farther going! / O sweet and far from cliff and scar / The horns of Elfland faintly blowing!" (IV:7–10).

Charlotte Perkins Gilman

[1860-1935]

Charlotte Perkins Gilman was born Charlotte Anna Perkins in Hartford, Connecticut, on July 3, 1860. She was the daughter of Mary Westcott and Frederick Beecher Perkins, a nephew of Harriet Beecher Stowe, the famous author of *Uncle Tom's Cabin*. After Frederick Perkins abandoned his family, his destitute wife took their two young children to Providence, Rhode Island, where Gilman briefly attended school. Although she preferred drawing and writing poetry to academic studies, Gilman developed an abiding interest in science. In a chapter in her autobiography entitled "Girlhood — If Any," Gilman later assessed her character and intellectual condition at "Sixteen, with a life to build," as she put it:

> My mother's profound religious tendency and implacable sense of duty; my father's intellectual appetite; a will power, well developed, from both; a passion of my own for scientific knowledge, for real laws of life; an insatiable demand for perfection in everything, and that proven process of mine for acquiring habits.

Charlotte Perkins Gilman

When this photograph was taken in 1896, Gilman was already widely known as a writer, social reformer, and feminist.

Alluding to Henry Wadsworth Longfellow's sentimental poem "Maidenhood," in which the meek and timid maiden stands poised on the brink of "womanhood," Gilman concluded that "instead of 'Standing with reluctant feet where the brook and river meet,' I plunged in and swam."

The unconventional Gilman increasingly found herself swimming against the main currents of American culture and society. When she was eighteen and still seeking a way to "build" her life, Gilman pursued her interest in art by studying at the Rhode Island School of Design. Determined to become independent, she supported herself by teaching art, designing greeting cards, and working as a governess. In 1882, she met a promising local artist, Charles Walter Stetson. After a two-year courtship, during which Gilman constantly questioned whether she could pursue a career if she became a wife and mother, she married Stetson. Following the birth of their daughter, Katherine, in 1885, Gilman became so severely depressed that she sought treatment from Silas Weir Mitchell, a physician who had developed the "rest cure" for what were then called "nervous diseases," a diagnosis more frequently applied to women patients. Mitchell's direction that she should sharply limit her intellectual activity brought Gilman "near the border line of utter mental ruin," as she later observed. She consequently went back to work, writing articles on dress reform and other women's issues. In 1888, she left her husband, whom she later divorced, and moved with her daughter to Pasadena, California. There, she wrote and lectured on a wide range of topics, including "The Labor Movement." Her poem "Similar Cases" (1890), a satire of those who opposed social change and human progress, brought her wide recognition and led to the publication of the first of her two volumes of poetry, *In This Our World* (1893). Gilman also wrote the earliest of her almost two hundred

bedfordstmartins.com/ americanlit for research links on Gilman

stories, the most famous of which, "The Yellow Wall-Paper," appeared in 1892. Two years later, after sending her daughter back east to live with her former husband and his new wife, Gilman moved to San Francisco to edit the radical *Impress,* the organ of the Pacific Coast Woman's Press Association. When the paper failed in 1895, Gilman accepted an invitation from the social and labor reformer Jane Addams to live at Hull House, the famous settlement house for recent immigrants in Chicago.

Gilman devoted the rest of her life to lecturing, writing, and other work on behalf of women and social reform. In 1898, she published her major sociological work, *Women and Economics: A Study of the Economic Relation between Men and Women as a Factor in Social Evolution.* Two years later, Gilman married a younger cousin, George Houghton Gilman, with whom she was by all accounts very happy. During the following decade, she extended her feminist analysis of American culture and institutions in a series of books: *Concerning Children* (1900); *The Home: Its Work and Influence* (1903); *Human Work* (1904); and *The Man-Made World; or, Our Androcentric Culture* (1911). She also published hundreds of works in periodicals ranging from women's magazines to the *American Journal of Sociology,* as well as in the *Forerunner,* a monthly magazine Gilman edited from 1909 to 1916. Many of her short stories and all of her longer fictional works first appeared in the magazine, including serializations of her feminist utopian novels *Herland* (1915) and its sequel, *With Her in Ourland* (1916). A Socialist and pacifist who helped form the Women's Peace Party in 1915, Gilman also tirelessly campaigned for social causes, including the right of women to have unrestricted access to birth control and their right to vote, which was finally gained in 1920. Her later writings included *His Religion and Hers* (1923), a sweeping critique of Christian theology and male-dominated conceptions of morality, and her posthumously published autobiography, *The Living of Charlotte Perkins Gilman* (1935). After the death of her husband in 1934, Gilman discovered that she had breast cancer. Committed to "The Right to Die," the title of her final article, Gilman committed suicide by taking an overdose of chloroform on August 17, 1935.

Gilman's "The Yellow Wall-Paper."   On August 28, 1890, Gilman recorded in her diary that she had sent "The Yellow Wall-Paper" to William Dean Howells, who had earlier written her an admiring letter about one of her poems, "Similar Cases." Howells, who later described Gilman's story as "terrible and too wholly dire" and "too terribly good to be printed," sent it to Horace Scudder, the editor of the *Atlantic Monthly.* Scudder rejected the story, which he returned to Gilman along with a brief note: "Dear Madam, Mr. Howells has handed me this story. I could not forgive myself if I made others as miserable as I have made myself!" Undaunted, Gilman sent the story to the *National Review,* where it was also rejected, and then to the *New England Magazine,* where it finally appeared in 1892. In an article entitled "Why I Wrote the Yellow Wall-Paper?" published in 1916 in her

The Yellow Wall-Paper

This illustration appeared above the title of Gilman's story in the first printing in the *New England Magazine.*

"I am sitting by the Window in this Atrocious Nursery."

magazine, the *Forerunner,* Gilman explained that the story was based on her own treatment for "melancholia," or depression, under the care of "a noted specialist in nervous diseases, the best known in the country." He had "applied the rest cure" and then sent her home "with solemn advice to 'live as domestic a life as far as possible,' to 'have but two hours' intellectual life a day,' and 'never to touch pen, brush or pencil again.'" Observing that she had sent a copy of "The Yellow Wall-Paper" to "the physician who so nearly drove me mad," and who had consequently altered his treatment, Gilman triumphantly concluded that the story "was not intended to drive people crazy, but to save people from being driven crazy, and it worked." But the gothic story of a woman's descent into madness is more than an indictment of nineteenth-century medical practices. It is also a study of the politics of marriage and the restrictive roles then assigned to women in the United States. The text is taken from the first printing in the *New England Magazine,* January 1892.

THE YELLOW WALL-PAPER

It is very seldom that mere ordinary people like John and myself secure ancestral halls for the summer.

A colonial mansion, a hereditary estate, I would say a haunted house, and reach the height of romantic felicity — but that would be asking too much of fate!

Still I will proudly declare that there is something queer about it.

Else, why should it be let so cheaply? And why have stood so long untenanted?

John laughs at me, of course, but one expects that in marriage.

John is practical in the extreme. He has no patience with faith, an intense horror of superstition, and he scoffs openly at any talk of things not to be felt and seen and put down in figures.

John is a physician, and *perhaps* — (I would not say it to a living soul, of course, but this is dead paper and a great relief to my mind) — *perhaps* that is one reason I do not get well faster.

You see, he does not believe I am sick!

And what can one do?

If a physician of high standing, and one's own husband, assures friends and relatives that there is really nothing the matter with one but temporary nervous depression — a slight hysterical tendency[1] — what is one to do?

My brother is also a physician, and also of high standing, and he says the same thing.

So I take phosphates or phosphites[2] — whichever it is, and tonics, and journeys, and air, and exercise, and am absolutely forbidden to "work" until I am well again.

Personally, I disagree with their ideas.

Personally, I believe that congenial work, with excitement and change, would do me good.

But what is one to do?

I did write for a while in spite of them; but it *does* exhaust me a good deal — having to be so sly about it, or else meet with heavy opposition.

I sometimes fancy that in my condition if I had less opposition and more society and stimulus — but John says the very worst thing I can do is to think about my condition, and I confess it always makes me feel bad.

So I will let it alone and talk about the house.

The most beautiful place! It is quite alone, standing well back from the road, quite three miles from the village. It makes me think of English places that you read about, for there are hedges and walls and gates that lock, and lots of separate little houses for the gardeners and people.

There is a *delicious* garden! I never saw such a garden — large and shady, full of box-bordered paths, and lined with long grape-covered arbors with seats under them.

There were greenhouses, too, but they are all broken now.

There was some legal trouble, I believe, something about the heirs and co-heirs; any-how, the place has been empty for years.

That spoils my ghostliness, I am afraid, but I don't care — there is something strange about the house — I can feel it.

---

1. **hysterical tendency:** In the nineteenth century, hysteria (from the Greek *husterikos*, meaning "of the womb") was thought to be an emotional disorder suffered exclusively by women, resulting in a variety of physical symptoms such as overdramatic behavior, selective amnesia, fatigue, and depression.

2. **phosphates or phosphites:** Derived from phosphoric acid, these compounds were used to treat forms of exhaustion in the nineteenth century.

I even said so to John one moonlight evening, but he said what I felt was a *draught,* and shut the window.

I get unreasonably angry with John sometimes. I'm sure I never used to be so sensitive. I think it is due to this nervous condition.

But John says if I feel so, I shall neglect proper self-control; so I take pains to control myself — before him, at least, and that makes me very tired.

I don't like our room a bit. I wanted one downstairs that opened on the piazza and had roses all over the window, and such pretty old-fashioned chintz hangings! but John would not hear of it.

He said there was only one window and not room for two beds, and no near room for him if he took another.

He is very careful and loving, and hardly lets me stir without special direction.

I have a schedule prescription for each hour in the day; he takes all care from me, and so I feel basely ungrateful not to value it more.

He said we came here solely on my account, that I was to have perfect rest and all the air I could get. "Your exercise depends on your strength, my dear," said he, "and your food somewhat on your appetite; but air you can absorb all the time." So we took the nursery at the top of the house.

It is a big, airy room, the whole floor nearly, with windows that look all ways, and air and sunshine galore. It was nursery first and then playroom and gymnasium, I should judge; for the windows are barred for little children, and there are rings and things in the walls.

The paint and paper look as if a boys' school had used it. It is stripped off — the paper — in great patches all around the head of my bed, about as far as I can reach, and in a great place on the other side of the room low down. I never saw a worse paper in my life.

One of those sprawling flamboyant patterns committing every artistic sin.

It is dull enough to confuse the eye in following, pronounced enough to constantly irritate and provoke study, and when you follow the lame uncertain curves for a little distance they suddenly commit suicide — plunge off at outrageous angles, destroy themselves in unheard of contradictions.

The color is repellant, almost revolting; a smouldering unclean yellow, strangely faded by the slow-turning sunlight.

It is a dull yet lurid orange in some places, a sickly sulphur tint in others.

No wonder the children hated it! I should hate it myself if I had to live in this room long.

There comes John, and I must put this away, — he hates to have me write a word.

We have been here two weeks, and I haven't felt like writing before, since that first day.

I am sitting by the window now, up in this atrocious nursery, and there is nothing to hinder my writing as much as I please, save lack of strength.

John is away all day, and even some nights when his cases are serious.

I am glad my case is not serious!

But these nervous troubles are dreadfully depressing.

John does not know how much I really suffer. He knows there is no *reason* to suffer, and that satisfies him.

Of course it is only nervousness. It does weigh on me so not to do my duty in any way!

I meant to be such a help to John, such a real rest and comfort, and here I am a comparative burden already!

Nobody would believe what an effort it is to do what little I am able, — to dress and entertain, and order things.

It is fortunate Mary is so good with the baby. Such a dear baby!

And yet I *cannot* be with him, it makes me so nervous.

I suppose John never was nervous in his life. He laughs at me so about this wallpaper!

At first he meant to repaper the room, but afterward he said that I was letting it get the better of me, and that nothing was worse for a nervous patient than to give way to such fancies.

He said that after the wall-paper was changed it would be the heavy bedstead, and then the barred windows, and then that gate at the head of the stairs, and so on.

"You know the place is doing you good," he said, "and really, dear, I don't care to renovate the house just for a three months' rental."

"Then do let us go downstairs," I said, "there are such pretty rooms there."

Then he took me in his arms and called me a blessed little goose, and said he would go down cellar, if I wished, and have it whitewashed into the bargain.

But he is right enough about the beds and windows and things.

It is an airy and comfortable room as any one need wish, and, of course, I would not be so silly as to make him uncomfortable just for a whim.

I'm really getting quite fond of the big room, all but that horrid paper.

Out of one window I can see the garden, those mysterious deep-shaded arbors, the riotous old-fashioned flowers, and bushes and gnarly trees.

Out of another I get a lovely view of the bay and a little private wharf belonging to the estate. There is a beautiful shaded lane that runs down there from the house. I always fancy I see people walking in these numerous paths and arbors, but John has cautioned me not to give way to fancy in the least. He says that with my imaginative power and habit of story-making, a nervous weakness like mine is sure to lead to all manner of excited fancies, and that I ought to use my will and good sense to check the tendency. So I try.

I think sometimes that if I were only well enough to write a little it would relieve the press of ideas and rest me.

But I find I get pretty tired when I try.

It is so discouraging not to have any advice and companionship about my work. When I get really well, John says we will ask Cousin Henry and Julia down for a long visit; but he says he would as soon put fireworks in my pillow-case as to let me have those stimulating people about now.

I wish I could get well faster.

But I must not think about that. This paper looks to me as if it *knew* what a vicious influence it had!

There is a recurrent spot where the pattern lolls like a broken neck and two bulbous eyes stare at you upside down.

I get positively angry with the impertinence of it and the everlastingness. Up and down and sideways they crawl, and those absurd, unblinking eyes are everywhere. There is one place where two breadths didn't match, and the eyes go all up and down the line, one a little higher than the other.

I never saw so much expression in an inanimate thing before, and we all know how much expression they have! I used to lie awake as a child and get more entertainment and terror out of blank walls and plain furniture than most children could find in a toy-store.

I remember what a kindly wink the knobs of our big, old bureau used to have, and there was one chair that always seemed like a strong friend.

I used to feel that if any of the other things looked too fierce I could always hop into that chair and be safe.

The furniture in this room is no worse than inharmonious, however, for we had to bring it all from downstairs. I suppose when this was used as a playroom they had to take the nursery things out, and no wonder! I never saw such ravages as the children have made here.

The wall-paper, as I said before, is torn off in spots, and it sticketh closer than a brother — they must have had perseverance as well as hatred.

Then the floor is scratched and gouged and splintered, the plaster itself is dug out here and there, and this great heavy bed which is all we found in the room, looks as if it had been through the wars.

But I don't mind it a bit — only the paper.

There comes John's sister. Such a dear girl as she is, and so careful of me! I must not let her find me writing.

She is a perfect and enthusiastic house-keeper, and hopes for no better profession. I verily believe she thinks it is the writing which made me sick!

But I can write when she is out, and see her a long way off from these windows.

There is one that commands the road, a lovely shaded winding road, and one that just looks off over the country. A lovely country, too, full of great elms and velvet meadows.

This wallpaper has a kind of sub-pattern in a different shade, a particularly irritating one, for you can only see it in certain lights, and not clearly then.

But in the places where it isn't faded and where the sun is just so — I can see a strange, provoking, formless sort of figure, that seems to skulk about behind that silly and conspicuous front design.

There's sister on the stairs!

Well, the Fourth of July is over! The people are all gone and I am tired out. John thought it might do me good to see a little company, so we just had mother and Nellie and the children down for a week.

Of course I didn't do a thing. Jennie sees to everything now.

But it tired me all the same.

John says if I don't pick up faster he shall send me to Weir Mitchell[3] in the fall.

But I don't want to go there at all. I had a friend who was in his hands once, and she says he is just like John and my brother, only more so!

Besides, it is such an undertaking to go so far.

I don't feel as if it was worth while to turn my hand over for anything, and I'm getting dreadfully fretful and querulous.

I cry at nothing, and cry most of the time.

Of course I don't when John is here, or anybody else, but when I am alone.

And I am alone a good deal just now. John is kept in town very often by serious cases, and Jennie is good and lets me alone when I want her to.

So I walk a little in the garden or down that lovely lane, sit on the porch under the roses, and lie down up here a good deal.

I'm getting really fond of the room in spite of the wallpaper. Perhaps *because* of the wallpaper.

It dwells in my mind so!

I lie here on this great immovable bed — it is nailed down, I believe — and follow that pattern about by the hour. It is as good as gymnastics, I assure you. I start, we'll say, at the bottom, down in the corner over there where it has not been touched, and I determine for the thousandth time that I *will* follow that pointless pattern to some sort of a conclusion.

I know a little of the principle of design, and I know this thing was not arranged on any laws of radiation, or alternation, or repetition, or symmetry, or anything else that I ever heard of.

It is repeated, of course, by the breadths, but not otherwise.

Looked at in one way each breadth stands alone, the bloated curves and flourishes — a kind of "debased Romanesque" with *delirium tremens* — go waddling up and down in isolated columns of fatuity.

But, on the other hand, they connect diagonally, and the sprawling outlines run off in great slanting waves of optic horror, like a lot of wallowing seaweeds in full chase.

The whole thing goes horizontally, too, at least it seems so, and I exhaust myself in trying to distinguish the order of its going in that direction.

They have used a horizontal breadth for a frieze, and that adds wonderfully to the confusion.

There is one end of the room where it is almost intact, and there, when the crosslights fade and the low sun shines directly upon it, I can almost fancy radiation

---

3. **Weir Mitchell:** Silas Weir Mitchell (1829–1914) was a physician and author who specialized in the treatment of what were called "nervous diseases." During the Civil War, he treated shell-shocked soldiers and those suffering "phantom" pains from amputated limbs. Afterwards, he became interested in emotional disorders more generally and developed the "rest cure," a widely used treatment involving bed rest, isolation, and severely limited physical activity.

after all, — the interminable grotesques seem to form around a common centre and rush off in headlong plunges of equal distraction.

It makes me tired to follow it. I will take a nap I guess.

I don't know why I should write this.

I don't want to.

I don't feel able.

And I know John would think it absurd. But I *must* say what I feel and think in some way — it is such a relief!

But the effort is getting to be greater than the relief.

Half the time now I am awfully lazy, and lie down ever so much.

John says I mustn't lose my strength, and has me take cod liver oil and lots of tonics and things, to say nothing of ale and wine and rare meat.

Dear John! He loves me very dearly, and hates to have me sick. I tried to have a real earnest reasonable talk with him the other day, and tell him how I wish he would let me go and make a visit to Cousin Henry and Julia.

But he said I wasn't able to go, nor able to stand it after I got there; and I did not make out a very good case for myself, for I was crying before I had finished.

It is getting to be a great effort for me to think straight. Just this nervous weakness I suppose.

And dear John gathered me up in his arms, and just carried me upstairs and laid me on the bed, and sat by me and read to me till it tired my head.

He said I was his darling and his comfort and all he had, and that I must take care of myself for his sake, and keep well.

He says no one but myself can help me out of it, that I must use my will and self-control and not let any silly fancies run away with me.

There's one comfort, the baby is well and happy, and does not have to occupy this nursery with the horrid wallpaper.

If we had not used it, that blessed child would have! What a fortunate escape! Why, I wouldn't have a child of mine, an impressionable little thing, live in such a room for worlds.

I never thought of it before, but it is lucky that John kept me here after all, I can stand it so much easier than a baby, you see.

Of course I never mention it to them any more — I am too wise — but I keep watch of it all the same.

There are things in that paper that nobody knows but me, or ever will.

Behind that outside pattern the dim shapes get clearer every day.

It is always the same shape, only very numerous.

And it is like a woman stooping down and creeping about behind that pattern. I don't like it a bit. I wonder — I begin to think — I wish John would take me away from here!

It is so hard to talk with John about my case, because he is so wise, and because he loves me so.

But I tried it last night.

It was moonlight. The moon shines in all around just as the sun does.

I hate to see it sometimes, it creeps so slowly, and always comes in by one window or another.

John was asleep and I hated to waken him, so I kept still and watched the moonlight on that undulating wallpaper till I felt creepy.

The faint figure behind seemed to shake the pattern, just as if she wanted to get out.

I got up softly and went to feel and see if the paper *did* move, and when I came back John was awake.

"What is it, little girl?" he said. "Don't go walking about like that — you'll get cold."

I thought it was a good time to talk, so I told him that I really was not gaining here, and that I wished he would take me away.

"Why, darling!" said he, "our lease will be up in three weeks, and I can't see how to leave before.

"The repairs are not done at home, and I cannot possibly leave town just now. Of course if you were in any danger, I could and would, but you really are better, dear, whether you can see it or not. I am a doctor, dear, and I know. You are gaining flesh and color, your appetite is better, I feel really much easier about you."

"I don't weigh a bit more," said I, "nor as much; and my appetite may be better in the evening when you are here, but it is worse in the morning when you are away!"

"Bless her little heart!" said he with a big hug, "she shall be as sick as she pleases! But now let's improve the shining hours[4] by going to sleep, and talk about it in the morning!"

"And you won't go away?" I asked gloomily.

"Why, how can I, dear? It is only three weeks more and then we will take a nice little trip of a few days while Jennie is getting the house ready. Really dear you are better!"

"Better in body perhaps —" I began, and stopped short, for he sat up straight and looked at me with such a stern, reproachful look that I could not say another word.

"My darling," said he, "I beg you, for my sake and for our child's sake, as well as for your own, that you will never for one instant let that idea enter your mind! There is nothing so dangerous, so fascinating, to a temperament like yours. It is a false and foolish fancy. Can you trust me as a physician when I tell you so?"

So of course I said no more on that score, and we went to sleep before long. He thought I was asleep first, but I wasn't, and lay there for hours trying to decide whether that front pattern and the back pattern really did move together or separately.

On a pattern like this, by daylight, there is a lack of sequence, a defiance of law, that is a constant irritant to a normal mind.

The color is hideous enough, and unreliable enough, and infuriating enough, but the pattern is torturing.

---

4. **improve the shining hours:** An allusion to the first stanza of a popular song written for children, "Against Idleness and Mischief," by Isaac Watts (1674-1748): "How doth the little busy Bee / Improve each shining Hour, / And gather Honey all the day / From every opening Flower!"

You think you have mastered it, but just as you get well underway in following, it turns a back-somersault and there you are. It slaps you in the face, knocks you down, and tramples upon you. It is like a bad dream.

The outside pattern is a florid arabesque, reminding one of a fungus. If you can imagine a toadstool in joints, an interminable string of toadstools, budding and sprouting in endless convolutions — why, that is something like it.

That is, sometimes!

There is one marked peculiarity about this paper, a thing nobody seems to notice but myself, and that is that it changes as the light changes.

When the sun shoots in through the east window — I always watch for that first long, straight ray — it changes so quickly that I never can quite believe it.

That is why I watch it always.

By moonlight — the moon shines in all night when there is a moon — I wouldn't know it was the same paper.

At night in any kind of light, in twilight, candlelight, lamplight, and worst of all by moonlight, it becomes bars! The outside pattern I mean, and the woman behind it is as plain as can be.

I didn't realize for a long time what the thing was that showed behind, that dim sub-pattern, but now I am quite sure it is a woman.

By daylight she is subdued, quiet. I fancy it is the pattern that keeps her so still. It is so puzzling. It keeps me quiet by the hour.

I lie down ever so much now. John says it is good for me, and to sleep all I can.

Indeed he started the habit by making me lie down for an hour after each meal.

It is a very bad habit I am convinced, for you see I don't sleep.

And that cultivates deceit, for I don't tell them I'm awake — O, no!

The fact is I am getting a little afraid of John.

He seems very queer sometimes, and even Jennie has an inexplicable look.

It strikes me occasionally, just as a scientific hypothesis, — that perhaps it is the paper!

I have watched John when he did not know I was looking, and come into the room suddenly on the most innocent excuses, and I've caught him several times *looking at the paper!* And Jennie too. I caught Jennie with her hand on it once.

She didn't know I was in the room, and when I asked her in a quiet, a very quiet voice, with the most restrained manner possible, what she was doing with the paper — she turned around as if she had been caught stealing, and looked quite angry — asked me why I should frighten her so!

Then she said that the paper stained everything it touched, that she had found yellow smooches on all my clothes and John's, and she wished we would be more careful!

Did not that sound innocent? But I know she was studying that pattern, and I am determined that nobody shall find it out but myself!

Life is very much more exciting now than it used to be. You see I have something more to expect, to look forward to, to watch. I really do eat better, and am more quiet than I was.

John is so pleased to see me improve! He laughed a little the other day, and said I seemed to be flourishing in spite of my wall-paper.

I turned it off with a laugh. I had no intention of telling him it was *because* of the wall-paper — he would make fun of me. He might even want to take me away.

I don't want to leave now until I have found it out. There is a week more, and I think that will be enough.

I'm feeling ever so much better! I don't sleep much at night, for it is so interesting to watch developments; but I sleep a good deal in the daytime.

In the daytime it is tiresome and perplexing.

There are always new shoots on the fungus, and new shades of yellow all over it. I cannot keep count of them, though I have tried conscientiously.

It is the strangest yellow, that wall-paper! It makes me think of all the yellow things I ever saw — not beautiful ones like buttercups, but old foul, bad yellow things.

But there is something else about that paper — the smell! I noticed it the moment we came into the room, but with so much air and sun it was not bad. Now we have had a week of fog and rain, and whether the windows are open or not, the smell is here.

It creeps all over the house.

I find it hovering in the dining-room, skulking in the parlor, hiding in the hall, lying in wait for me on the stairs.

It gets into my hair.

Even when I go to ride, if I turn my head suddenly and surprise it — there is that smell!

Such a peculiar odor, too! I have spent hours in trying to analyze it, to find what it smelled like.

It is not bad — at first, and very gentle, but quite the subtlest, most enduring odor I ever met.

In this damp weather it is awful, I wake up in the night and find it hanging over me.

It used to disturb me at first. I thought seriously of burning the house — to reach the smell.

But now I am used to it. The only thing I can think of that it is like is the *color* of the paper! A yellow smell.

There is a very funny mark on this wall, low down, near the mopboard. A streak that runs round the room. It goes behind every piece of furniture, except the bed, a long, straight, even *smooch*, as if it had been rubbed over and over.

I wonder how it was done and who did it, and what they did it for. Round and round and round — round and round and round — it makes me dizzy!

I really have discovered something at last.

Through watching so much at night, when it changes so, I have finally found out.

The front pattern *does* move — and no wonder! The woman behind shakes it!

Sometimes I think there are a great many women behind, and sometimes only one, and she crawls around fast, and her crawling shakes it all over.

Then in the very bright spots she keeps still, and in the very shady spots she just takes hold of the bars and shakes them hard.

And she is all the time trying to climb through. But nobody could climb through that pattern — it strangles so; I think that is why it has so many heads.

They get through, and then the pattern strangles them off and turns them upside down, and makes their eyes white!

If those heads were covered or taken off it would not be half so bad.

I think that woman gets out in the daytime!

And I'll tell you why — privately — I've seen her!

I can see her out of every one of my windows!

It is the same woman, I know, for she is always creeping, and most women do not creep by daylight.

I see her in that long shaded lane, creeping up and down. I see her in those dark grape arbors, creeping all around the garden.

I see her on that long road under the trees, creeping along, and when a carriage comes she hides under the blackberry vines.

I don't blame her a bit. It must be very humiliating to be caught creeping by daylight!

I always lock the door when I creep by daylight. I can't do it at night, for I know John would suspect something at once.

And John is so queer now, that I don't want to irritate him. I wish he would take another room! Besides, I don't want anybody to get that woman out at night but myself.

I often wonder if I could see her out of all the windows at once.

But, turn as fast as I can, I can only see out of one at one time.

And though I always see her, she *may* be able to creep faster than I can turn!

I have watched her sometimes away off in the open country, creeping as fast as a cloud shadow in a high wind.

If only that top pattern could be gotten off from the under one! I mean to try it, little by little.

I have found out another funny thing, but I shan't tell it this time! It does not do to trust people too much.

There are only two more days to get this paper off, and I believe John is beginning to notice. I don't like the look in his eyes.

And I heard him ask Jennie a lot of professional questions about me. She had a very good report to give.

She said I slept a good deal in the daytime.

John knows I don't sleep very well at night, for all I'm so quiet!

He asked me all sorts of questions, too, and pretended to be very loving and kind.

As if I couldn't see through him!

Still, I don't wonder he acts so, sleeping under this paper for three months.

It only interests me, but I feel sure John and Jennie are secretly affected by it.

Hurrah! This is the last day, but it is enough. John to stay in town over night, and won't be out until this evening.

Jennie wanted to sleep with me — the sly thing! But I told her I should undoubtedly rest better for a night all alone.

That was clever, for really I wasn't alone a bit! As soon as it was moonlight and that poor thing began to crawl and shake the pattern, I got up and ran to help her.

I pulled and she shook, I shook and she pulled, and before morning we had peeled off yards of that paper.

A strip about as high as my head and half around the room.

And then when the sun came and that awful pattern began to laugh at me, I declared I would finish it to-day!

We go away to-morrow, and they are moving all my furniture down again to leave things as they were before.

Jennie looked at the wall in amazement, but I told her merrily that I did it out of pure spite at the vicious thing.

She laughed and said she wouldn't mind doing it herself, but I must not get tired.

How she betrayed herself that time!

But I am here, and no person touches this paper but me, — not *alive!*

She tried to get me out of the room — it was too patent! But I said it was so quiet and empty and clean now that I believed I would lie down again and sleep all I could; and not to wake me even for dinner — I would call when I woke.

So now she is gone, and the servants are gone, and the things are gone, and there is nothing left but that great bedstead nailed down, with the canvas mattress we found on it.

We shall sleep downstairs to-night, and take the boat home to-morrow.

I quite enjoy the room, now it is bare again.

How those children did tear about here!

This bedstead is fairly gnawed!

But I must get to work.

I have locked the door and thrown the key down into the front path.

I don't want to go out, and I don't want to have anybody come in, till John comes.

I want to astonish him.

I've got a rope up here that even Jennie did not find. If that woman does get out, and tries to get away, I can tie her!

But I forgot I could not reach far without anything to stand on!

This bed will *not* move!

I tried to lift and push it until I was lame, and then I got so angry I bit off a little piece at one corner — but it hurt my teeth.

Then I peeled off all the paper I could reach standing on the floor. It sticks horribly and the pattern just enjoys it! All those strangled heads and bulbous eyes and waddling fungus growths just shriek with derision!

I am getting angry enough to do something desperate. To jump out of the window would be admirable exercise, but the bars are too strong even to try.

Besides I wouldn't do it. Of course not. I know well enough that a step like that is improper and might be misconstrued.

I don't like to *look* out of the windows even — there are so many of those creeping women, and they creep so fast.

I wonder if they all come out of that wall-paper as I did?

But I am securely fastened now by my well-hidden rope — you don't get *me* out in the road there!

I suppose I shall have to get back behind the pattern when it comes night, and that is hard!

It is so pleasant to be out in this great room and creep around as I please!

I don't want to go outside. I won't, even if Jennie asks me to.

For outside you have to creep on the ground, and everything is green instead of yellow.

But here I can creep smoothly on the floor, and my shoulder just fits in that long smooch around the wall, so I cannot lose my way.

Why, there's John at the door!

It is no use, young man, you can't open it!

How he does call and pound!

Now he's crying for an axe.

It would be a shame to break down that beautiful door!

"John dear!" said I in the gentlest voice, "the key is down by the front steps, under a plantain leaf!"

That silenced him for a few moments.

Then he said — very quietly indeed, "Open the door, my darling!"

"I can't," said I. "The key is down by the front door under a plantain leaf!"

And then I said it again, several times, very gently and slowly, and said it so often that he had to go and see, and he got it of course, and came in. He stopped short by the door.

"What is the matter?" he cried. "For God's sake, what are you doing!"

I kept on creeping just the same, but I looked at him over my shoulder.

"I've got out at last," said I, "in spite of you and Jane![5] And I've pulled off most of the paper, so you can't put me back!"

Now why should that man have fainted? But he did, and right across my path by the wall, so that I had to creep over him every time!

[1892]

---

5. **in spite of you and Jane!:** Jane, who has not previously been introduced in the story, is possibly the name of the narrator herself or an oblique reference to Charlotte Brontë's well-known gothic romance, *Jane Eyre* (1847). The title character is a governess who falls in love and agrees to marry her employer, Mr. Rochester. But she learns that he is already married to Bertha Mason, who has gone mad and is kept locked away in a hidden room on the third floor of Rochester's manor house, Thornfield Hall. (In one harrowing scene, Bertha is described scurrying around the room on all fours and growling like an animal.) After Bertha dies in a fire she sets to the house, Jane eventually marries Rochester. In the first published version of Gilman's story in the *New England Magazine*, the narrator's statement ends with a question mark, and in later printings it ends with a period. We have followed the punctuation in Gilman's manuscript, in which the statement ends with an exclamation point that the original compositor evidently mistook for a question mark.

Abraham Cahan

[1860–1951]

Abraham Cahan

This photograph was taken when Cahan was twenty-three, about two years after his arrival in New York City.

Abraham Cahan was born on July 7, 1860, in Podberezy, a shtetl or Jewish community in Russia. His parents were Sarah and Shakne Cahan, a teacher at a Hebrew school. When Cahan was about five years old, the family moved a short distance away to the larger city of Vilna. Both Podberezy and Vilna were situated in the Pale of Jewish Settlement, the area in eastern Russia where all Jews were required by law to live. The language spoken in the shtetl was Yiddish, a dialect combining words from Hebrew and several European languages, especially German. From an early age, Cahan developed a deep understanding of the value and importance of language through his intensive study of Hebrew, the Jewish Bible, and the Talmud, the body of Jewish civil and ceremonial law and legend. But he later decided to pursue secular studies at the Vilna Teacher Training Institute for Jewish students, which he attended from 1876 to 1881. While there, he was drawn to the revolutionary politics and socialism of students who opposed the political autocracy of Russia. The assassination of Czar Alexander II in 1881 prompted a wave of repression and violence directed against Russian Jews. Cahan, who had secured a job teaching in a school at Velizh, came under suspicion for possessing radical publications. Certain that he would be arrested and probably executed, Cahan fled Russia, joining more than 13,000 other Jews who left the country in 1882.

After a long and dangerous journey across Europe to England, Cahan booked a passage in steerage from Liverpool to New York City. During the voyage, he began to study English with the help of a Russian-English dictionary and a sailor who knew a few Russian words. Admitted through Ellis Island into the United States on June 7, 1882, Cahan joined thousands of other Jewish immigrants who had settled in the Lower East Side of Manhattan, then known as the "Ghetto." Even as he undertook the difficult task of earning a living in the overcrowded, impoverished section of the city, Cahan set about learning English. By the next year, his language skills were sufficient for him to begin teaching English to immigrants at the Young Men's Hebrew Association. In 1885, he met and married Aniuta (Anna) Bronstein, an immigrant from Kiev, Russia. Increasingly active in city politics and organized labor, Cahan formally joined the Socialist Labor Party in 1887. He soon began lecturing and writing articles in English on Jewish life in the city for several newspapers in New York. Revising a lecture he had delivered at the New York Labor Lyceum, Cahan also published "Realism," which appeared in the *Workman's Advocate* in 1889. As he later described it in his autobiography, the essay was "a philosophic consideration of the nature of art," based on his study of contemporary art and his reading of William Dean Howells, Henry James, and the Russian novelist Leo Tolstoy. Naturalized as an American citizen on June 8, 1891, Cahan continued to write articles in both English and Yiddish and edited a socialist newspaper published in Yiddish, the *Arbeter Tsaytung*, or "Worker's Journal."

He also began to write fiction. Cahan's first short story in English, "A Providential Match," appeared in *Short Stories* in 1895, the same year he published a serialized novel in Yiddish in the *Arbeter Tsaytung*. His efforts were strongly encouraged by William Dean Howells, who in 1895 told Cahan, "It is your duty to write." Buoyed by the support of an American writer he greatly admired, Cahan translated and published his serialized novel as *Yekl: A Tale of the New York Ghetto* (1896), which Howells enthusiastically reviewed in the *New York World*. "Suddenly I was known in American literature," Cahan later recalled. But he could not support himself and his family through literature alone. In 1897, he helped establish what would become the leading Yiddish newspaper in the world, the *Jewish Daily Forward*. Cahan subsequently edited the newspaper for a total of fifty years. But he also continued to write in English for other New York newspapers and to publish articles and stories in magazines, including the prestigious *Atlantic Monthly*. A collection of five of his stories, *The Imported Bridegroom and Other Stories of the New York Ghetto*, was published in 1898. In a review of the volume, Howells once again praised Cahan's realism, observing that "the author handles [his materials] so skillfully that he holds the reader between a laugh and a heartache, and fashions into figures so lifelike that you would expect to meet them in any stroll through Hester-street," the busy artery at the heart of the Jewish community in New York City.

From that point on, Cahan was a prominent writer in both English and Yiddish. As the editor of the *Forward*, he was known for his articles on social reform and labor policy. Although he published a second novel in English, *The White Terror and the Red: A Novel of Revolutionary Russia* (1905), Cahan increasingly wanted to concentrate on journalism. At the invitation of the editors of *McClure's Magazine*, however, he wrote an extended fictional piece loosely based on some of the events of his life, *The Autobiography of an American Jew: The Rise of David Levinsky*, which was serialized in the magazine from April through July 1913. In revised form, Cahan later published it as *The Rise of David Levinsky: A Novel* (1917), now widely regarded as one of the most important works of early Jewish American fiction. During the same period, he began to write his actual autobiography, *The Education of Abraham Cahan*, which was published in five volumes between 1916 and 1936. Cahan continued to devote his energies to the *Forward*, serving as a spokesperson for American Jews and, after two visits to Palestine, becoming active in the Zionist movement. He also had the satisfaction of seeing many of his early fictional works reprinted in new editions. "Socialist leader, novelist, critic, and newspaper man," as he was described in the obituary in the *New York Times*, Cahan died on August 31, 1951.

[Cahan] sees his people humorously, and he is as unsparing of their sordidness as he is compassionate of their hard circumstance and the somewhat frowsy pathos of their lives.

–William Dean Howells

bedfordstmartins.com/ americanlit *for research links on Cahan*

Cahan's "A Ghetto Wedding."   This story was first published in the *Atlantic Monthly* only two months before it appeared in Cahan's collection *The Imported Bridegroom and Other Stories of the New York Ghetto* (1898).

Hester Street

This photograph of Hester Street, the congested thoroughfare running through the heart of the Jewish "Ghetto" on the Lower East Side of Manhattan, was taken in 1903.

Walter Hines Page, who had just assumed the editorship of the *Atlantic*, was determined to extend the scope of the magazine by providing a broader and more diverse view of American life. He consequently solicited contributions from writers ranging from Cahan to W. E. B. Du Bois and Booker T. Washington. Cahan submitted two works to Page. One was an article, "The Russian Jew in America," published in July 1898, in which Cahan protested stricter immigration laws by pointing to the accomplishments and contributions of Russian Jews. His other submission was "A

Ghetto Wedding." Although Page preferred nonfiction and autobiographical narratives to fiction, he may well have been impressed by the stark realism of "A Ghetto Wedding," a simple story of an impoverished young Jewish couple facing economic hardship and religious persecution as they slowly and painfully seek a place for themselves in the United States. The text is taken from the first printing in the *Atlantic Monthly*, February 1898.

A GHETTO WEDDING

Had you chanced to be in Grand Street on that starry February night, it would scarcely have occurred to you that the Ghetto was groaning under the culmination of a long season of enforced idleness and distress. The air was exhilaratingly crisp, and the glare of the cafés and millinery shops flooded it with contentment and kindly good will. The sidewalks were alive with shoppers and promenaders, and lined with peddlers.

Yet the dazzling, deafening chaos had many a tale of woe to tell. The greater part of the surging crowd was out on an errand of self-torture. Straying forlornly by inexorable window displays, men and women would pause here and there to indulge in a hypothetical selection, to feast a hungry eye upon the object of an imaginary purchase, only forthwith to pay for the momentary joy with all the pangs of awakening to an empty purse.

Many of the peddlers, too, bore piteous testimony to the calamity which was then preying upon the quarter. Some of them performed their task of yelling and gesticulating with the desperation of imminent ruin; others implored the passers-by for custom with the abject effect of begging alms; while in still others this feverish urgency was disguised by an air of martyrdom or of shamefaced unwontedness, as if peddling were beneath the dignity of their habitual occupations, and they had been driven to it by sheer famine, by the hopeless dearth of employment at their own trades.

One of these was a thick-set fellow of twenty-five or twenty-six, with honest, clever blue eyes. It might be due to the genial, inviting quality of his face that the Passover dishes whose praises he was sounding had greater attraction for some of the women with an "effectual demand"[1] than those of his competitors. Still, his comparative success had not as yet reconciled him to his new calling. He was constantly gazing about for a possible passer-by of his acquaintance, and when one came in sight he would seek refuge from identification in closer communion with the crockery on his push-cart.

"Buy nice dishes for the holidays! Cheap and strong! Buy dishes for Passover!" When business was brisk, he sang with a bashful relish; when the interval between a customer and her successor was growing too long, his sing-song would acquire a mournful ring that was suggestive of the psalm-chanting at an orthodox Jewish funeral.

---

1. **"effectual demand":** The phrase was first used in *The Wealth of Nations* by the British economist and philosopher Adam Smith (1723-1790), who defined it as the demand created by those willing and able to pay the price necessary to bring a commodity to the market.

He was a cap-blocker, and in the busy season his earnings ranged from ten to fifteen dollars a week. But he had not worked full time for over two years, and during the last three months he had not been able to procure a single day's employment.

Goldy, his sweetheart, too, had scarcely work enough at her kneebreeches to pay her humble board and rent. Nathan, after much hesitation, was ultimately compelled to take to peddling; and the longed-for day of their wedding was put off from month to month.

They had become engaged nearly two years before; the wedding ceremony having been originally fixed for a date some three months later. Their joint savings then amounted to one hundred and twenty dollars — a sum quite adequate, in Nathan's judgment, for a modest, quiet celebration and the humble beginnings of a household establishment. Goldy, however, summarily and indignantly overruled him.

"One does not marry every day," she argued, "and when I have at last lived to stand under the bridal canopy with my predistined one, I will not do so like a beggar-maid. Give me a respectable wedding, or none at all, Nathan, do you hear?"

It is to be noted that a "respectable wedding" was not merely a casual expression with Goldy. Like its antithesis, a "slipshod wedding," it played in her vocabulary the part of something like a well-established scientific term, with a meaning as clearly defined as that of "centrifugal force" or "geometrical progression." Now, a slipshod wedding was anything short of a gown of white satin and slippers to match; two carriages to bring the bride and the bridegroom to the ceremony, and one to take them to their bridal apartments; a wedding bard and a band of at least five musicians; a spacious ballroom crowded with dancers, and a feast of a hundred and fifty covers. As to furniture, she refused to consider any which did not include a pier-glass and a Brussels carpet.[2]

Nathan contended that the items upon which she insisted would cost a sum far beyond their joint accumulations. This she met by the declaration that he had all along been bent upon making her the target of universal ridicule, and that she would rather descend into an untimely grave than be married in a slipshod manner. Here she burst out crying; and whether her tears referred to the untimely grave or to the slipshod wedding, they certainly seemed to strengthen the cogency of her argument; for Nathan at once proceeded to signify his surrender by a kiss, and when ignominiously repulsed he protested his determination to earn the necessary money to bring things to the standard which she held up so uncompromisingly.

Hard times set in. Nathan and Goldy pinched and scrimped; but all their heroic economies were powerless to keep their capital from dribbling down to less than one hundred dollars. The wedding was postponed again and again. Finally the curse of utter idleness fell upon Nathan's careworn head. Their savings dwindled apace. In dismay they beheld the foundation of their happiness melt gradually away. Both were tired of boarding. Both longed for the bliss and economy of married life. They grew more impatient and restless every day, and Goldy made concession after concession. First the wedding

---

2. **a pier-glass and a Brussels carpet:** A pier-glass is a tall mirror, often placed between windows; a Brussels carpet is a large, patterned rug with a heavy pile of colored yarns woven onto a foundation of strong linen thread.

supper was sacrificed; then the pier-mirror and the bard were stricken from the programme; and these were eventually succeeded by the hired hall and the Brussels carpet.

After Nathan went into peddling, a few days before we first find him hawking chinaware on Grand Street, matters began to look brighter, and the spirits of our betrothed couple rose. Their capital, which had sunk to forty dollars, was increasing again, and Goldy advised waiting long enough for it to reach the sum necessary for a slipshod wedding and establishment.

It was nearly ten o'clock. Nathan was absently drawling his "Buy nice dishes for the holidays!" His mind was engrossed with the question of making peddling his permanent occupation.

Presently he was startled by a merry soprano mocking him: "Buy nice di-i-shes! Mind that you don't fall asleep murmuring like this. A big lot you can make!"

Nathan turned a smile of affectionate surprise upon a compact little figure, small to drollness, but sweet in the amusing grace of its diminutive outlines — an epitome of exquisite femininity. Her tiny face was as comically lovely as her form: her apple-like cheeks were firm as marble, and her inadequate nose protruded between them like the result of a hasty tweak; a pair of large, round black eyes and a thick-lipped little mouth inundating it all with passion and restless, good-natured shrewdness.

"Goldy! What brings *you* here?" Nathan demanded, with a fond look which instantly gave way to an air of discomfort. "You know I hate you to see me peddling."

"Are you really angry? Bite the feather-bed, then. Where is the disgrace? As if you were the only peddler in America! I wish you were. Wouldn't you make heaps of money then! But you had better hear what *does* bring me here. Nathan, darling, dearest little heart, dearest little crown that you are, guess what a plan I have hit upon!" she exploded all at once. "Well, if you hear me out, and you don't say that Goldy has the head of a cabinet minister, then — well, then you will be a big hog, and nothing else."

And without giving him time to put in as much as an interjection she rattled on, puffing for breath and smacking her lips for ecstasy. Was it not stupid of them to be racking their brains about the wedding while there was such a plain way of having both a "respectable" celebration and fine furniture — Brussels carpet, pier-glass, and all — with the money they now had on hand?

"Come, out with it, then," he said morosely.

But his disguised curiosity only whetted her appetite for tormenting him, and she declared her determination not to disclose her great scheme before they had reached her lodgings.

"You have been yelling long enough to-day, anyhow," she said, with abrupt sympathy. "Do you suppose it does not go to my very heart to think of the way you stand out in the cold screaming yourself hoarse?"

Half an hour later, when they were alone in Mrs. Volpiansky's parlor, which was also Goldy's bedroom, she set about emptying his pockets of the gross results of the day's business, and counting the money. This she did with a preoccupied, matter-of-fact air, Nathan submitting to the operation with fond and amused willingness; and the sum being satisfactory, she went on to unfold her plan.

"You see," she began, almost in a whisper, and with the mien of a care-worn, experience-laden old matron, "in a week or two we shall have about seventy-five dollars, shan't we? Well, what is seventy-five dollars? Nothing! We could just have the plainest furniture, and no wedding worth speaking of. Now, if we have no wedding, we shall get no presents, shall we?"

Nathan shook his head thoughtfully.

"Well, why shouldn't we be up to snuff and do this way? Let us spend all our money on a grand, respectable wedding, and send out a big lot of invitations, and then — well, won't uncle Leiser send us a carpet or a parlor set? And aunt Beile, and cousin Shapiro, and Charley, and Meyerké, and Wolfké, and Bennie, and Soré-Gitké — won't each present something or other, as is the custom among respectable people? May God give us a lump of good luck as big as the wedding present each of them is sure to send us! Why, did not Beilké get a fine carpet from uncle when she got married? And am I not a nearer relative than she?"

She paused to search his face for a sign of approval, and, fondly smoothing a tuft of his dark hair into place, she went on to enumerate the friends to be invited and the gifts to be expected from them.

"So you see," she pursued, "we will have both a respectable wedding that we shan't have to be ashamed of in after years and the nicest things we could get if we spent two hundred dollars. What do you say?"

"What *shall* I say?" he returned dubiously.

The project appeared reasonable enough, but the investment struck him as rather hazardous. He pleaded for caution, for delay; but as he had no tangible argument to produce, while she stood her ground with the firmness of conviction, her victory was an easy one.

"It will all come right, depend upon it," she said coaxingly. "You just leave everything to me. Don't be uneasy, Nathan," she added. "You and I are orphans, and you know the Uppermost[3] does not forsake a bride and bridegroom who have nobody to take care of them. If my father were alive, it would be different," she concluded, with a disconsolate gesture.

There was a pathetic pause. Tears glistened in Goldy's eyes.

"May your father rest in a bright paradise," Nathan said feelingly. "But what is the use of crying? Can you bring him back to life? I will be a father to you."

"If God be pleased," she assented. "Would that mamma, at least — may she be healthy a hundred and twenty years — would that she, at least, were here to attend our wedding! Poor mother! it will break her heart to think that she has not been foreordained by the Uppermost to lead me under the canopy."

There was another desolate pause, but it was presently broken by Goldy, who exclaimed with unexpected buoyancy, "By the way, Nathan, guess what I did! I am afraid you will call me braggart and make fun of me, but I don't care," she pursued, with a playful pout, as she produced a strip of carpet from her pocketbook. "I went into a furniture store, and they gave me a sample three times as big as this. I explained in my letter to

---

3. **the Uppermost:** God.

mother that this is the kind of stuff that will cover my floor when I am married. Then I inclosed the sample in the letter, and sent it all to Russia."

Nathan clapped his hands and burst out laughing. "But how do you know that is just the kind of carpet you will get for your wedding present?" he demanded, amazed as much as amused.

"How do I know? As if it mattered what sort of carpet! I can just see mamma going the rounds of the neighbors, and showing off the 'costly tablecloth' her daughter will trample upon. Won't she be happy!"

Over a hundred invitations, printed in as luxurious a black-and-gold as ever came out of an Essex Street hand-press, were sent out for an early date in April. Goldy and Nathan paid a month's rent in advance for three rooms on the second floor of a Cherry Street tenement-house. Goldy regarded the rent as unusually low, and the apartments as the finest on the East Side.

"Oh, haven't I got lovely rooms!" she would ejaculate, beaming with the consciousness of the pronoun. Or, "You ought to see *my* rooms! How much do you pay for yours?" Or again, "I have made up my mind to have my parlor in the rear room. It is as light as the front one, anyhow, and I want that for a kitchen, you know. What do you say?" For hours together she would go on talking nothing but rooms, rent, and furniture; every married couple who had recently moved into new quarters, or were about to do so, seemed bound to her by the ties of a common cause; in her imagination, humanity was divided into those who were interested in the question of rooms, rent, and furniture and those who were not — the former, of whom she was one, constituting the superior category; and whenever her eye fell upon a bill announcing rooms to let, she would experience something akin to the feeling with which an artist, in passing, views some accessory of his art.

It is customary to send the bulkier wedding presents to a young couple's apartments a few days before they become man and wife, the closer relatives and friends of the betrothed usually settling among themselves what piece of furniture each is to contribute. Accordingly, Goldy gave up her work a week in advance of the day set for the great event, in order that she might be on hand to receive the things when they arrived.

She went to the empty little rooms, with her lunch, early in the morning, and kept anxious watch till after nightfall, when Nathan came to take her home.

A day passed, another, and a third, but no expressman called out her name. She sat waiting and listening for the rough voice, but in vain.

"Oh, it is too early, anyhow. I am a fool to be expecting anything so soon at all," she tried to console herself. And she waited another hour, and still another; but no wedding gift made its appearance.

"Well, there is plenty of time, after all; wedding presents do come a day or two before the ceremony," she argued; and again she waited, and again strained her ears, and again her heart rose in her throat.

The vacuity of the rooms, freshly cleaned, scrubbed, and smelling of whitewash, began to frighten her. Her overwrought mind was filled with sounds which her overstrained ears did not hear. Yet there she sat on the window-sill, listening and listening for an expressman's voice.

"Hush, hush-sh, hush-sh-sh!" whispered the walls; the corners muttered awful threats; her heart was ever and anon contracted with fear; she often thought herself on the brink of insanity; yet she stayed on, waiting, waiting, waiting.

At the slightest noise in the hall she would spring to her feet, her heart beating wildly, only presently to sink in her bosom at finding it to be some neighbor or a peddler; and so frequent were these violent throbbings that Goldy grew to imagine herself a prey to heart disease. Nevertheless the fifth day came, and she was again at her post, waiting, waiting, waiting for her wedding gifts. And what is more, when Nathan came from business, and his countenance fell as he surveyed the undisturbed emptiness of the rooms, she set a merry face against his rueful inquiries, and took to bantering him as a woman quick to lose heart, and to painting their prospects in roseate hues, until she argued herself, if not him, into a more cheerful view of the situation.

On the sixth day an expressman did pull up in front of the Cherry Street tenement-house, but he had only a cheap huge rocking-chair for Goldy and Nathan; and as it proved to be the gift of a family who had been set down for nothing less than a carpet or a parlor set, the joy and hope which its advent had called forth turned to dire disappointment and despair. For nearly an hour Goldy sat mournfully rocking and striving to picture how delightful it would have been if all her anticipations had come true.

Presently there arrived a flimsy plush-covered little corner table. It could not have cost more than a dollar. Yet it was the gift of a near friend, who had been relied upon for a pier-glass or a bedroom set. A little later a cheap alarm clock and an ice-box were brought in. That was all.

Occasionally Goldy went to the door to take in the entire effect; but the more she tried to view the parlor as half furnished, the more cruelly did the few lonely and mismated things emphasize the remaining emptiness of the apartments: whereupon she would sink into her rocker and sit motionless, with a drooping head, and then desperately fall to swaying to and fro, as though bent upon swinging herself out of her woe-begone, wretched self.

Still, when Nathan came, there was a triumphant twinkle in her eye, as she said, pointing to the gifts, "Well, mister, who was right? It is not very bad for a start, is it? You know most people do send their wedding presents after the ceremony — why, of course!" she added in a sort of confidential way. "Well, we have invited a big crowd, and all people of no mean sort, thank God; and who ever heard of a lady or a gentleman attending a respectable wedding and having a grand wedding supper, and then cheating the bride and the bridegroom out of their present?"

The evening was well advanced; yet there were only a score of people in a hall that was used to hundreds.

Everybody felt ill at ease, and ever and anon looked about for the possible arrival of more guests. At ten o'clock the dancing preliminary to the ceremony had not yet ceased, although the few waltzers looked as if they were scared by the ringing echoes of their own footsteps amid the austere solemnity of the surrounding void and the depressing sheen of the dim expanse of floor.

The two fiddles, the cornet, and the clarinet were shrieking as though for pain, and the malicious superabundance of gaslight was fiendishly sneering at their tortures. Weddings and entertainments being scarce in the Ghetto, its musicians caught the contagion of misery: hence the greedy, desperate gusto with which the band plied their instruments.

At last it became evident that the assemblage was not destined to be larger than it was, and that it was no use delaying the ceremony. It was, in fact, an open secret among those present that by far the greater number of the invited friends were kept away by lack of employment: some having their presentable clothes in the pawnshop; others avoiding the expense of a wedding present, or simply being too cruelly borne down by their cares to have a mind for the excitement of a wedding; indeed, some even thought it wrong of Nathan to have the celebration during such a period of hard times, when everybody was out of work.

It was a little after ten when the bard – a tall, gaunt man, with a grizzly beard and a melancholy face – donned his skull-cap, and, advancing toward the dancers, called out in a synagogue intonation, "Come, ladies, let us veil the bride!"

An odd dozen of daughters of Israel followed him and the musicians into a little side-room where Goldy was seated between her two brideswomen (the wives of two men who were to attend upon the groom). According to the orthodox custom she had fasted the whole day, and as a result of this and of her gnawing grief, added to the awe-inspiring scene she had been awaiting, she was pale as death; the effect being heightened by the wreath and white gown she wore. As the procession came filing in, she sat blinking her round dark eyes in dismay, as if the bard were an executioner come to lead her to the scaffold.

The song or address to the bride usually partakes of the qualities of prayer and harangue, and includes a melancholy meditation upon life and death; lamenting the deceased members of the young woman's family, bemoaning her own woes, and exhorting her to discharge her sacred duties as a wife, mother, and servant of God. Composed in verse and declaimed in a solemn, plaintive recitative, often broken by the band's mournful refrain, it is sure to fulfill its mission of eliciting tears even when hearts are brimful of glee. Imagine, then, the funereal effect which it produced at Goldy's wedding ceremony.

The bard, half starved himself, sang the anguish of his own heart; the violins wept, the clarinet moaned, the cornet and the double-bass groaned, each reciting the sad tale of its poverty-stricken master. He began: –

> "Silence, good women, give heed to my verses!
> To-night, bride, thou dost stand before the Uppermost.
> Pray to him to bless thy union,
> To let thee and thy mate live a hundred and twenty peaceful years,
> To give you your daily bread,
> To keep hunger from your door."

Several women, including Goldy, burst into tears, the others sadly lowering their gaze. The band sounded a wailing chord, and the whole audience broke into loud, heartrending weeping.

The bard went on sternly: —

> "Wail, bride, wail!
> This is a time of tears.
> Think of thy past days:
> Alas! they are gone to return nevermore."

Heedless of the convulsive sobbing with which the room resounded, he continued to declaim, and at last, his eye flashing fire and his voice tremulous with emotion, he sang out in a dismal, uncanny high key: —

> "And thy good mother beyond the seas,
> And thy father in his grave
> Near where thy cradle was rocked, —
> Weep, bride, weep!
> Though his soul is better off
> Than we are here underneath
> In dearth and cares and ceaseless pangs, —
> Weep, sweet bride, weep!"

Then, in the general outburst that followed the extemporaneous verse, there was a cry — "The bride is fainting! Water! quick!"

"Murderer that you are!" flamed out an elderly matron, with an air of admiration for the bard's talent as much as of wrath for the far-fetched results it achieved.

Goldy was brought to, and the rest of the ceremony passed without accident. She submitted to everything as in a dream. When the bridegroom, escorted by two attendants, each carrying a candelabrum holding lighted candles, came to place the veil over her face, she stared about as though she failed to realize the situation or to recognize Nathan. When, keeping time to the plaintive strains of a time-honored tune, she was led, blindfolded, into the large hall and stationed beside the bridegroom under the red canopy, and then marched around him seven times, she obeyed instructions and moved about with the passivity of a hypnotic. After the Seven Blessings[4] had been recited, when the cantor,[5] gently lifting the end of her veil, presented the wineglass to her lips, she tasted its contents with the air of an invalid taking medicine. Then she felt the ring slip down her finger, and heard Nathan say, "Be thou dedicated to me by this ring, according to the laws of Moses and Israel."

Whereupon she said to herself, "Now I am a married woman!" But somehow, at this moment the words were meaningless sounds to her. She knew she was married, but could not realize what it implied. As Nathan crushed the wineglass underfoot,[6] and the

---

4. **Seven Blessings:** Based on the idea of the seven days of the Creation, this series of blessings is recited at a traditional Jewish wedding and then at any meal involving at least ten people during the first week of the couple's marriage.

5. **cantor:** An official who leads prayer and sings liturgical music in a synagogue.

6. **crushed the wineglass underfoot:** At the end of the wedding ceremony, the groom crushes the glass with his right foot, in remembrance of the destruction of the Holy Temple in Jerusalem. The ritual reminds people at the ceremony that the destruction of the Temple must be remembered even at moments of great joy.

band struck up a cheerful melody, and the gathering shouted, "Good luck! Good luck!" and clapped their hands, while the older women broke into a wild hop, Goldy felt the relief of having gone through a great ordeal. But still she was not distinctly aware of any change in her position.

Not until fifteen minutes later, when she found herself in the basement, at the head of one of three long tables, did the realization of her new self strike her consciousness full in the face, as it were.

The dining-room was nearly as large as the dancing-hall on the floor above. It was as brightly illuminated, and the three tables, which ran almost its entire length, were set for a hundred and fifty guests. Yet there were barely twenty to occupy them. The effect was still more depressing than in the dancing-room. The vacant benches and the untouched covers still more agonizingly exaggerated the emptiness of the room in which the sorry handful of a company lost themselves.

Goldy looked at the rows of plates, spoons, forks, knives, and they weighed her down with the cold dazzle of their solemn, pompous array.

"I am not the Goldy I used to be," she said to herself. "I am a married woman, like mamma, or auntie, or Mrs. Volpiansky. And we have spent every cent we had on this grand wedding, and now we are left without money for furniture, and there are no guests to send us any, and the supper will be thrown out, and everything is lost, and I am to blame for it all!"

The glittering plates seemed to hold whispered converse and to exchange winks and grins at her expense. She transferred her glance to the company, and it appeared as if they were vainly forcing themselves to partake of the food — as though they, too, were looked out of countenance by that ruthless sparkle of the unused plates.

Nervous silence hung over the room, and the reluctant jingle of the score of knives and forks made it more awkward, more enervating, every second. Even the bard had not the heart to break the stillness by the merry rhymes he had composed for the occasion.

Goldy was overpowered. She thought she was on the verge of another fainting spell, and, shutting her eyes and setting her teeth, she tried to imagine herself dead. Nathan, who was by her side, noticed it. He took her hand under the table, and, pressing it gently, whispered, "Don't take it to heart. There is a God in heaven."

She could not make out his words, but she felt their meaning. As she was about to utter some phrase of endearment, her heart swelled in her throat, and a piteous, dove-like, tearful look was all the response she could make.

By and by, however, when the foaming lager was served, tongues were loosened, and the bard, although distressed by the meagre collection in store for him, but stirred by an ardent desire to relieve the insupportable wretchedness of the evening, outdid himself in offhand acrostics and witticisms. Needless to say that his efforts were thankfully rewarded with unstinted laughter; and as the room rang with merriment, the gleaming rows of undisturbed plates also seemed to join in the general hubbub of mirth, and to be laughing a hearty, kindly laugh.

Presently, amid a fresh outbreak of deafening hilarity, Goldy bent close to Nathan's ear and exclaimed with sobbing vehemence, "My husband! My husband! My husband!"

"My wife!" he returned in her ear.

"Do you know what you are to me now?" she resumed. "A husband! And I am your wife! Do you know what it means – *do* you, *do* you, Nathan?" she insisted, with frantic emphasis.

"I do, my little sparrow; only don't worry over the wedding presents."

It was after midnight, and even the Ghetto was immersed in repose. Goldy and Nathan were silently wending their way to the three empty little rooms where they were destined to have their first joint home. They wore the wedding attire which they had rented for the evening: he a swallowtail coat and high hat, and she a white satin gown and slippers, her head uncovered – the wreath and veil done up in a newspaper, in Nathan's hand.

They had gone to the wedding in carriages, which had attracted large crowds both at the point of departure and in front of the hall; and of course they had expected to make their way to their new home in a similar "respectable" manner. Toward the close of the last dance, after supper, they found, however, that some small change was all they possessed in the world.

The last strains of music were dying away. The guests, in their hats and bonnets, were taking leave. Everybody seemed in a hurry to get away to his own world, and to abandon the young couple to their fate.

Nathan would have borrowed a dollar or two of some friend. "Let us go home as behooves a bride and bridegroom," he said. "There is a God in heaven: he will not forsake us."

But Goldy would not hear of betraying the full measure of their poverty to their friends. "No! no!' she retorted testily. "I am not going to let you pay a dollar and a half for a few blocks' drive, like a Fifth Avenue nobleman. We can walk," she pursued, with the grim determination of one bent upon self-chastisement. "A poor woman who dares spend every cent on a wedding must be ready to walk after the wedding."

When they found themselves alone in the deserted street, they were so overcome by a sense of loneliness, of a kind of portentous, haunting emptiness, that they could not speak. So on they trudged in dismal silence; she leaning upon his arm, and he tenderly pressing her to his side.

Their way lay through the gloomiest and roughest part of the Seventh Ward. The neighborhood frightened her, and she clung closer to her escort. At one corner they passed some men in front of a liquor saloon.

"Look at dem! Look at dem! A sheeny fellar an' his bride, I'll betch ye!" shouted a husky voice. "Jes' comin' from de weddin'."

"She ain't no bigger 'n a peanut, is she?" The simile was greeted with a horse-laugh.

"Look a here, young fellar, what's de madder wid carryin' her in your vest-pocket?"

When Nathan and Goldy were a block away, something like a potato or a carrot struck her in the back. At the same time the gang of loafers on the corner broke into boisterous merriment. Nathan tried to face about, but she restrained him.

"Don't! They might kill you!" she whispered, and relapsed into silence.

He made another attempt to disengage himself, as if for a desperate attack upon her assailants, but she nestled close to his side and held him fast, her every fibre tingling with the consciousness of the shelter she had in him.

"Don't mind them, Nathan," she said.

And as they proceeded on their dreary way through a sombre, impoverished street, with here and there a rustling tree — a melancholy witness of its better days — they felt a stream of happiness uniting them, as it coursed through the veins of both, and they were filled with a blissful sense of oneness the like of which they had never tasted before. So happy were they that the gang behind them, and the bare rooms toward which they were directing their steps, and the miserable failure of the wedding, all suddenly appeared too insignificant to engage their attention — paltry matters alien to their new life, remote from the enchanted world in which they now dwelt.

The very notion of a relentless void abruptly turned to a beatific sense of their own seclusion, of there being only themselves in the universe, to live and to delight in each other.

"Don't mind them, Nathan darling," she repeated mechanically, conscious of nothing but the tremor of happiness in her voice.

"I should give it to them!" he responded, gathering her still closer to him. "I should show them how to touch my Goldy, my pearl, my birdie!"

They dived into the denser gloom of a side-street.

A gentle breeze ran past and ahead of them, proclaiming the bride and the bridegroom. An old tree whispered overhead its tender felicitations.

[1898]

Edith Wharton

[1862-1937]

Edith Wharton was born Edith Newbold Jones on January 24, 1862, in New York City. Both of her socially prominent parents, George F. Jones and Lucretia Stevens Rhinelander Jones, could trace their family histories back more than two hundred years to the earliest settlement of colonial New York. Wharton grew up in a world of wealth and privilege — of European travel, summers spent in the fashionable resort of Newport, Rhode Island, and winters at the family home on Fifth Avenue in Manhattan. She was educated by private tutors, learning five languages and becoming a voracious reader. As she later recalled, "By the time I was seventeen, though I had not read every book in my father's

Edith Wharton

This photograph was taken when Wharton was in her early twenties, before she gained fame as one of the leading fiction writers in the United States.

library, I had looked into them all." That "all" included texts ranging from the Bible and Elizabethan drama to Washington Irving's stories and the poems of Henry Wadsworth Longfellow, as well as a long list of books on art, architecture, history, philosophy, and travel. Wharton also began writing at an early age. When she was fifteen, she adopted the pseudonym "Mr. Olivieri," writing a novella, *Fast and Loose*, and a very negative review of it, which she imagined might appear in the influential magazine the *Nation*. The novella was not published, but her mother arranged for the private publication of a collection of Wharton's poems, *Verses* (1878).

Wharton was increasingly torn between her literary ambitions and the demands of her social position. At the age of seventeen, she duly made her debut in New York City. Six years later, in 1885, she married Edward ("Teddy") Wharton, a thirty-four-year-old friend of her brother. Although it was soon clear that she and her socially prominent husband had little in common, Wharton dutifully sought to adapt to the role of society matron. At the same time, she was unwilling to give up completely her writing. Beginning in 1889, she published several poems in the *Atlantic Monthly* and *Scribner's*, where her first story appeared in 1891. Finding her marriage stressful and the continual round of parties and other social events exhausting, Wharton suffered bouts of depression and wrote little more until 1897, when she and the architect Ogden Codman published *The Decoration of Houses*. The following year, she sought out the services of Silas Weir Mitchell, a prominent physician who specialized in "rest cures" for what were then called "nervous diseases." Another of Mitchell's patients, Charlotte Perkins Gilman, had already published a story about the devastating effects of such enforced inactivity, "The Yellow Wall-Paper" (1892), but the rest cure helped Wharton gain the solitude and space she needed for her writing. Her first collection of stories, *The Greater Inclination* (1899), was followed by *The Valley of Decision* (1902), a historical novel set in eighteenth-century Italy. The novel received generally positive reviews and an enthusiastic reception from readers, including Henry James. In one of his earliest letters to Wharton, however, James urged her to write about the *"American Subject,"* as he called it. "There it is round you," James exhorted her. "Don't pass it by. . . . Take hold of it & keep hold & let it pull you where it will. . . . DO NEW YORK!"

Although she treated many other subjects, Wharton achieved her greatest fame as a chronicler of the fashionable world she knew so well. In 1902, she and her husband built the Mount, a magnificent estate and gardens Wharton designed in Lenox, Massachusetts. There, she perceptively explored the complex dynamics and narrow restrictions of upper-class society in numerous stories and in *The House of Mirth* (1905), an acclaimed novel about an unconventional young woman who is destroyed in her attempt to gain a secure place among the corrupt, nouveau riche of New York City. By then, Wharton's marriage had become severely strained, especially by her husband's numerous extramarital affairs. After the unhappy couple moved to France in 1907, Wharton found love and solace in the company of Morton Fullerton, a journalist with whom she had an affair

I met [Wharton] in New York and she's a very distinguished grande dame who fought the good fight with bronze age weapons when there were very few people in the line at all.

—F. Scott Fitzgerald

that lasted from 1908 to 1910. Wharton wrote that she had tried "to adjust herself" to her marriage, which finally ended in divorce in 1913, but that she "was overmastered by the longing to meet people who shared my interests." One of those people was an old friend, Walter Berry, an American lawyer who became Wharton's long-term companion and the person she most relied on for editorial advice about her work. Nonetheless, like her close friend Henry James, Wharton enjoyed greater intellectual companionship among artists and writers in Europe than in the United States. Even after she moved permanently to France in 1910, however, Wharton continued to explore American scenes and themes in works such as *Ethan Frome* (1911), *The Custom of the Country* (1913), *Summer* (1917), and *The Age of Innocence* (1920), a novel of "Old New York" that earned her the Pulitzer Prize.

During the remainder of her career, Wharton was overshadowed by a younger generation of novelists, including her admirers F. Scott Fitzgerald and Sinclair Lewis. But she remained a revered and widely read writer. In 1923, she became the first woman to be awarded an honorary doctorate of letters by Yale University, and in 1929 she received the Gold Medal of the American Academy of Arts and Letters. She also continued to write steadily until her death from a stroke on August 11, 1937, by which time Wharton had produced a remarkable body of work: dozens of reviews and magazine articles, three volumes of poetry, more than eighty-five short stories in eleven collections, twenty-seven novellas and novels, and nine nonfictional works, including her vivid autobiography, *A Backward Glance* (1934).

bedfordstmartins.com/ americanlit for research links on Wharton

Wharton's "The Other Two."   This was one of two stories Wharton published in *Collier's Weekly: An Illustrated Journal.* Founded in 1888 as *Collier's Once a Week,* a family magazine of "fiction, fact, sensation, wit, humor, [and] news," it swiftly became one of the best-selling magazines in the United States. By the time its name was changed to *Collier's Weekly* in 1895, the circulation of the magazine was more than 250,000. Although its emphasis shifted to news, groundbreaking photojournalism, and investigative reporting, the magazine continued to feature poetry and fiction. Its editors were particularly eager to obtain the best of contemporary fiction, publishing works by writers as diverse as Frank Norris and the popular British author Arthur Conan Doyle, whose later Sherlock Holmes stories appeared in *Collier's* in 1903. By the time Wharton's "The Other Two" appeared in the magazine in 1904, she was gaining a growing reputation through the publication of numerous stories and her first novel, *The Valley of Decision* (1902). Like much of her fiction, "The Other Two" offered glimpses into the lives of affluent New Yorkers, but the story was unusual in its frank and witty treatment of divorce at a time when there was growing concern about the state of marriage in the United States, which would have the highest divorce rate in the world by 1915. The text is taken from the first printing of the story in *Collier's Weekly,* February 13, 1904.

WAYTHORN MOVED AWAY WITH A GESTURE OF REFUSAL

The Other Two

This is one of four illustrations that appeared in the first printing of Wharton's story in *Collier's*.

THE OTHER TWO

I

Waythorn, on the drawing-room hearth, waited for his wife to come down to dinner.

It was their first night under his own roof, and he was surprised at his thrill of boyish agitation. He was not so old, to be sure — his glass gave him little more than the five-and-thirty years to which his wife confessed — but he had fancied himself already in the temperate zone; yet here he was listening for her step with a tender sense of all it symbolized, with some old trail of verse about the garlanded nuptial door-posts floating through his enjoyment of the pleasant room and the good dinner just beyond it.

They had been hastily recalled from their honeymoon by the illness of Lily Haskett, the child of Mrs. Waythorn's first marriage. The little girl, at Waythorn's desire, had been transferred to his house on the day of her mother's wedding, and the doctor, on their arrival, broke the news that she was ill with typhoid,[1] but declared that all the

---

1. **typhoid:** Typhoid fever, usually caused by water contaminated with bacteria from sewage, was a common and often-fatal disease before water-treatment facilities and vaccinations were widely available in the United States.

symptoms were favorable. Lily could show twelve years of unblemished health, and the case promised to be a light one. The nurse spoke as reassuringly, and after a moment of alarm Mrs. Waythorn had adjusted herself to the situation. She was very fond of Lily – her affection for the child had perhaps been her decisive charm in Waythorn's eyes – but she had the perfectly balanced nerves which her little girl had inherited, and no woman ever wasted less tissue in unproductive worry. Waythorn was therefore quite prepared to see her come in presently, a little late because of a last look at Lily, but as serene and well-appointed as if her good-night kiss had been laid on the brow of health. Her composure was restful to him; it acted as ballast to his somewhat unstable sensibilities. As he pictured her bending over the child's bed he thought how soothing her presence must be in illness: her very step would prognosticate recovery.

His own life had been a gray one, from temperament rather than circumstance, and he had been drawn to her by the unperturbed gayety which kept her fresh and elastic at an age when most women's activities are growing either slack or febrile. He knew what was said about her; for, popular as she was, there had always been a faint undercurrent of detraction. When she had appeared in New York, nine or ten years earlier, as the pretty Mrs. Haskett whom Gus Varick had unearthed somewhere – was it in Pittsburg or Utica? – society, while promptly accepting her, had reserved the right to cast a doubt on its own discrimination. Inquiry, however, established her undoubted connection with a socially reigning family, and explained her recent divorce as the natural result of a runaway match at seventeen; and as nothing was known of Mr. Haskett it was easy to believe the worst of him.

Alice Haskett's remarriage with Gus Varick was a passport to the set whose recognition she coveted, and for a few years the Varicks were the most popular couple in town. Unfortunately the alliance was brief and stormy, and this time the husband had his champions. Still, even Varick's stanchest supporters admitted that he was not meant for matrimony, and Mrs. Varick's grievances were of a nature to bear the inspection of the New York courts. A New York divorce is in itself a diploma of virtue, and in the semi-widowhood of this second separation Mrs. Varick took on an air of sanctity, and was allowed to confide her wrongs to some of the most scrupulous ears in town. But when it was known that she was to marry Waythorn there was a momentary reaction. Her best friends would have preferred to see her remain in the rôle of the injured wife, which was as becoming to her as crape to a rosy complexion. True, a decent time had elapsed, and it was not even suggested that Waythorn had supplanted his predecessor. Still, people shook their heads over him, and one grudging friend, to whom he affirmed that he took the step with his eyes open, replied oracularly: "Yes – and with your ears shut."

Waythorn could afford to smile at these innuendoes. In the Wall Street phrase, he had "discounted" them. He knew that society has not yet adapted itself to the consequences of divorce, and that till the adaptation takes place every woman who uses the freedom the law accords her must be her own social justification. Waythorn had an amused confidence in his wife's ability to justify herself. His expectations were fulfilled, and before the wedding took place Alice Varick's group had rallied openly to her support. She took it all imperturbably; she had a way of surmounting obstacles without seeming to be aware of them, and Waythorn looked back with wonder at the trivialities over which he had worn his nerves thin. He had the sense of having found refuge in a richer, warmer nature than his own, and his satisfaction, at the moment, was humorously summed up in the thought that his wife, when she had done all she could for Lily, would not be ashamed to come down and enjoy a good dinner.

The anticipation of such enjoyment was not, however, the sentiment expressed by Mrs. Waythorn's charming face when she presently joined him. Though she had put on her most engaging teagown[2] she had neglected to assume the smile that went with it, and Waythorn thought he had never seen her look so nearly worried.

"What is it?" he asked. "Is anything wrong with Lily?"

"No; I've just been in and she's still sleeping." Mrs. Waythorn hesitated. "But something tiresome has happened."

He had taken her two hands, and now perceived that he was crushing a paper between them.

"This letter?"

"Yes — Mr. Haskett has written — I mean his lawyer has written."

Waythorn felt himself flush uncomfortably. He dropped his wife's hands.

"What about?"

"About seeing Lily. You know the courts —"

"Yes, yes," he interrupted nervously.

Nothing was known about Haskett in New York. He was vaguely supposed to have remained in the outer darkness from which his wife had been rescued, and Waythorn was one of the few who were aware that he had given up his business in Utica and followed her to New York in order to be near his little girl. In the days of his wooing, Waythorn had often met Lily on the doorstep, rosy and smiling, on her way "to see papa."

"I am so sorry," Mrs. Waythorn murmured.

He roused himself. "What does he want?"

"He wants to see her. You know she goes to him once a week."

"Well — he doesn't expect her to go to him now, does he?"

"No — he has heard of her illness; but he expects to come here."

"Here?"

Mrs. Waythorn reddened under his gaze. They looked away from each other.

"I'm afraid he has the right. . . . You'll see. . . ." She made a proffer of the letter.

Waythorn moved away with a gesture of refusal. He stood staring about the softly lighted room, which a moment before had seemed so full of bridal intimacy.

"I'm so sorry," she repeated. "If Lily could have been moved —"

"That's out of the question," he returned impatiently.

"I suppose so."

Her lip was beginning to tremble, and he felt himself a brute.

"He must come, of course," he said. "When is — his day?"

"I'm afraid — to-morrow."

---

2. **teagown:** A loose dress made of light fabrics with frilly details, worn by women at home in the late nineteenth and early twentieth centuries.

"Very well." Send a note in the morning."

The butler entered to announce dinner.

Waythorn turned to his wife. "Come — you must be tired. It's beastly, but try to forget about it," he said, drawing her hand through his arm.

"You're so good, dear. I'll try," she whispered back.

Her face cleared at once, and as she looked at him across the flowers, between the rosy candle-shades, he saw her lips waver back into a smile.

"How pretty everything is!" she sighed luxuriously.

He turned to the butler. "The champagne at once, please. Mrs. Waythorn is tired."

In a moment or two their eyes met above the sparkling glasses. Her own were quite clear and untroubled; he saw that she had obeyed his injuction and forgotten.

II

Waythorn, the next morning, went down town earlier than usual. Haskett was not likely to come till the afternoon, but the instinct of flight drove him forth. He meant to stay away all day — he had thoughts of dining at his club. As his door closed behind him he reflected that before he opened it again it would have admitted another man who had as much right to enter it as himself, and the thought filled him with a physical repugnance. He caught the "elevated" at the employees' hour, and found himself crushed between two layers of pendulous humanity.

At Eighth Street the man facing him wriggled out and another took his place. Waythorn glanced up and saw that it was Gus Varick. The men were so close together that it was impossible to ignore the smile of recognition on Varick's handsome overblown face. And after all — why not? They had always been on good terms, and Varick had been divorced before Waythorn's attentions to his wife began. The two exchanged a word on the perennial grievance of the congested trains, and when a seat at their side was miraculously left empty the instinct of self-preservation made Waythorn slip into it after Varick.

The latter drew the stout man's breath of relief. "Lord — I was beginning to feel like a pressed flower." He leaned back, looking unconcernedly at Waythorn. "Sorry to hear that Sellers is knocked out again."

"Sellers?" echoed Waythorn, starting at his partner's name.

Varick looked surprised. "You didn't know he was laid up with the gout?"

"No. I've been away — I only got back last night." Waythorn felt himself reddening in anticipation of the other's smile.

"Ah — yes; to be sure. And Sellers's attack came on two days ago. I'm afraid he's pretty bad. Very awkward for me, as it happens, because he was just putting through a rather important thing for me."

"Ah?" Waythorn wondered vaguely since when Varick had been dealing in "important things." Hitherto he had dabbled only in the shallow pools of speculation, with which Waythorn's office did not usually concern itself.

It occurred to him that Varick might be talking at random, to relieve the strain of their propinquity. That strain was becoming momentarily more apparent to Waythorn, and when, at Cortlandt Street, he caught sight of an acquaintance, and had a sudden vision of the picture he and Varick must present to an initiated eye, he jumped up with a muttered excuse.

"I hope you'll find Sellers better," said Varick civilly, and he stammered back: "If I can be of any use to you —" and let the departing crowd sweep him to the platform.

At his office he heard that Sellers was in fact ill with the gout, and would probably not be able to leave the house for some weeks.

"I'm sorry it should have happened so, Mr. Waythorn," the senior clerk said with affable significance. "Mr. Sellers was very much upset at the idea of giving you such a lot of extra work just now."

"Oh, that's no matter," said Waythorn hastily. He secretly welcomed the pressure of additional business, and was glad to think that, when the day's work was over, he would have to call at his partner's on the way home.

He was late for luncheon, and turned in at the nearest restaurant instead of going to his club. The place was full, and the waiter hurried him to the back of the room to capture the only vacant table. In the cloud of cigar-smoke Waythorn did not at once distinguish his neighbors; but presently, looking about him, he saw Varick seated a few feet off. This time, luckily, they were too far apart for conversation, and Varick, who faced another way, had probably not even seen him; but there was an irony in their renewed nearness.

Varick was said to be fond of good living, and as Waythorn sat despatching his hurried luncheon he looked across half enviously at the other's leisurely degustation of his meal. When Waythorn first saw him he had been helping himself with critical deliberation to a bit of Camembert at the ideal point of liquefaction, and now, the cheese removed, he was just pouring his *café double* from its little two-storied earthen pot. He poured slowly, his ruddy profile bent above the task, and one beringed white hand steadying the lid of the coffee-pot; then he stretched his other hand to the decanter of cognac at his elbow, filled a liqueur-glass, took a tentative sip, and poured the brandy into his coffee-cup.

Waythorn watched him in a kind of fascination. What was he thinking of — only of the flavor of the coffee and the liqueur? Had the morning's meeting left no more trace in his thoughts than on his face? Had his wife so completely passed out of his life that even this odd encounter with her present husband, within a week after her remarriage, was no more than an incident in his day? And as Waythorn mused, another idea struck him: had Haskett ever met Varick as Varick and he had just met? The recollection of Haskett perturbed him, and he rose and left the restaurant, taking a circuitous way out to escape the placid irony of Varick's nod.

It was after seven when Waythorn reached home. He thought the footman who opened the door looked at him oddly.

"How is Miss Lily?" he asked in haste.

"Doing very well, sir. A gentleman —"

"Tell Barlow to put off dinner for half an hour," Waythorn cut him off, hurrying upstairs.

He went straight to his room and dressed without seeing his wife. When he reached the drawing-room she was there, fresh and radiant. Lily's day had been good; the doctor was not coming back that evening.

At dinner Waythorn told her of Sellers's illness and of the resulting complications. She listened sympathetically, adjuring him not to let himself be overworked, and asking vague feminine questions about the routine of the office. Then she gave him the chronicle of Lily's day: quoted the nurse and doctor, and told him who had called to inquire. He had never seen her more serene and unruffled. It struck him, with a curious pang, that she was very happy in being with him, so happy that she found a childish pleasure in rehearsing the trivial incidents of her day.

After dinner they went to the library, and the servant put the coffee and liqueurs on a low table before her and left the room. She looked singularly soft and girlish in her rosy pale dress, against the dark leather of one of his bachelor armchairs. A day earlier the contrast would have charmed him.

He turned away now, choosing a cigar with affected deliberation.

"Did Haskett come?" he asked, with his back to her.

"Oh, yes — he came."

"You didn't see him, of course?"

She hesitated a moment. "I let the nurse see him."

That was all. There was nothing more to ask. He swung round toward her, applying a match to his cigar. Well, the thing was over for a week, at any rate. He would try not to think of it. She looked up at him, a trifle rosier than usual, with a smile in her eyes.

"Ready for your coffee, dear?"

He leaned against the mantelpiece, watching her as she lifted the coffee-pot. The lamplight struck a gleam from her bracelets and tipped her soft hair with brightness. How light and slender she was, and how each gesture flowed into the next! She seemed a creature all compact of harmonies. As the thought of Haskett receded, Waythorn felt himself yielding again to the joy of possessorship. They were his, those white hands with their flitting motions, his the light haze of hair, the lips and eyes . . .

She set down the coffee-pot, and reaching for the decanter of cognac, measured off a liqueur-glass and poured it into his cup.

Waythorn uttered a sudden exclamation.

"What is the matter?" she said, startled.

"Nothing; only — I don't take cognac in my coffee."

"Oh, how stupid of me," she cried.

Their eyes met, and she blushed a sudden agonized red.

III

Ten days later, Mr. Sellers, still house-bound, asked Waythorn to call on his way downtown.

The senior partner, with his swaddled foot propped up by the fire, greeted his associate with an air of embarrassment.

"I'm sorry, my dear fellow; I've got to ask you to do an awkward thing for me."

Waythorn waited, and the other went on, after a pause apparently given to the arrangement of his phrases: "The fact is, when I was knocked out I had just gone into a rather complicated piece of business for — Gus Varick."

"Well?" said Waythorn, with an attempt to put him at his ease.

"Well – it's this way: Varick came to me the day before my attack. He had evidently had an inside tip from somebody, and had made about a hundred thousand. He came to me for advice, and I suggested his going in with Vanderlyn."

"Oh, the deuce!" Waythorn exclaimed. He saw in a flash what had happened. The investment was an alluring one, but required negotiation. He listened quietly while Sellers put the case before him, and, the statement ended, he said: "You think I ought to see Varick?"

"I'm afraid I can't as yet. The doctor is obdurate. And this thing can't wait. I hate to ask you, but no one else in the office knows the ins and outs of it."

Waythorn stood silent. He did not care a farthing for the success of Varick's venture, but the honor of the office was to be considered, and he could hardly refuse to oblige his partner.

"Very well," he said, "I'll do it."

That afternoon, apprised by telephone, Varick called at the office. Waythorn, waiting in his private room, wondered what the others thought of it. The newspapers, at the time of Mrs. Waythorn's marriage had acquainted their readers with every detail of her previous matrimonial ventures, and Waythorn could fancy the clerks smiling behind Varick's back as he was ushered in.

Varick bore himself admirably. He was easy without being undignified, and Waythorn was conscious of cutting a much less impressive figure. Varick had no head for business, and the talk prolonged itself for nearly an hour while Waythorn set forth with scrupulous precision the details of the proposed transaction.

"I'm awfully obliged to you," Varick said as he rose. "The fact is I'm not used to having much money to look after, and I don't want to make an ass of myself –" He smiled, and Waythorn could not help noticing that there was something pleasant about his smile. "It feels uncommonly queer to have enough cash to pay one's bills. I'd have sold my soul for it a few years ago!"

Waythorn winced at the allusion. He had heard it rumored that a lack of funds had been one of the determining causes of the Varick separation, but it did not occur to him that Varick's words were intentional. It seemed more likely that the desire to keep clear of embarrassing topics had fatally drawn him into one. Waythorn did not wish to be outdone in civility.

"We'll do the best we can for you," he said. "I think this is a good thing you're in."

"Oh, I'm sure it's immense. It's awfully good of you –" Varick broke off, embarrassed. "I suppose the thing's settled now – but if –"

"If anything happens before Sellers is about, I'll see you again," said Waythorn quietly. He was glad, in the end, to appear the more self-possessed of the two.

The course of Lily's illness ran smooth, and as the days passed Waythorn grew used to the idea of Haskett's weekly visit. The first time the day came round, he stayed out late and questioned his wife as to the visit on his return. She replied at once that Haskett had merely seen the nurse downstairs, as the doctor did not wish any one in the child's sick-room till after the crisis.

The following week Waythorn was again conscious of the recurrence of the day, but had forgotten it by the time he came home to dinner. The crisis of the disease came a few days later, with a rapid decline of fever, and the little girl was pronounced out of danger. In the rejoicing which ensued the thought of Haskett passed out of Waythorn's mind and one afternoon, letting himself into the house with a latch-key, he went straight to his library without noticing a shabby hat and umbrella in the hall.

In the library he found a small effaced-looking man with a thinnish gray beard sitting on the edge of a chair. The stranger might have been a piano-tuner, or one of those mysteriously efficient persons who are summoned in emergencies to adjust some detail of the domestic machinery. He blinked at Waythorn through a pair of gold-rimmed spectacles and said mildly: "Mr. Waythorn, I presume? I am Lily's father."

Waythorn flushed. "Oh —" he stammered uncomfortably. He broke off, disliking to appear rude. Inwardly he was trying to adjust the actual Haskett to the image of him projected by his wife's reminiscences. Waythorn had been allowed to infer that Alice's first husband was a brute.

"I am sorry to intrude," said Haskett, with his over-the-counter politeness.

"Don't mention it," returned Waythorn, collecting himself. "I suppose the nurse has been told?"

"I presume so. I can wait," said Haskett. He had a resigned way of speaking, as though life had worn down his natural powers of resistance.

Waythorn stood on the threshold, nervously pulling off his gloves.

"I'm sorry you've been detained. I will send for the nurse," he said, and as he opened the door he added with an effort, "I'm glad we can give you a good report of Lily." He winced as the *we* slipped out, but Haskett seemed not to notice it.

"Thank you, Mr. Waythorn. It's been an anxious time for me."

"Ah, well, that's past. Soon she'll be able to go to you," Waythorn nodded and passed out.

In his own room, he flung himself down with a groan. He hated the womanish sensibility which made him suffer so acutely from the grotesque chances of life. He had known when he married that his wife's former husbands were both living, and that amid the multiplied contacts of modern existence there were a thousand chances to one that he would run against one or the other, yet he found himself as much disturbed by his brief encounter with Haskett as though the law had not obligingly removed all difficulties in the way of their meeting.

Waythorn sprang up and began to pace the room nervously. He had not suffered half so much from his two meetings with Varick. It was Haskett's presence in his own house that made the situation so intolerable. He stood still, hearing steps in the passage.

"This way, please," he heard the nurse say. Haskett was being taken upstairs, then: not a corner of the house but was open to him. Waythorn dropped into another chair, staring vaguely ahead of him. On his dressing-table stood a photograph of Alice, taken when he had first known her. She was Alice Varick then — how fine and exquisite he had thought her! Those were Varick's pearls about her neck. At Waythorn's instance they had been returned before her marriage. Had Haskett ever given her any trinkets — and what had become of them, Waythorn wondered? He realized suddenly that he knew very little of Haskett's past or present situation; but from the man's appearance and manner of speech he could reconstruct with curious precision the surroundings of Alice's first marriage. And it startled him to think that she had, in the background of her life, a phase of existence so different from anything with which he had connected her. Varick, whatever his faults, was a gentleman, in the conventional, traditional sense of the term: the sense which at that moment seemed, oddly enough, to have most meaning to Waythorn. He and Varick had the same social habits, spoke the same language, understood the same allusions. But this other man . . . it was grotesquely uppermost in Waythorn's mind that Haskett had worn a made-up tie attached with an elastic. Why should that ridiculous detail symbolize the whole man? Waythorn was exasperated by his own paltriness, but the fact of the tie expanded, forced itself on him, became as it were the key to Alice's past. He could see her, as Mrs. Haskett, sitting in a "front parlor" furnished in plush, with a pianola, and a copy of "Ben Hur"[3] on the centre table. He could see her going to the theatre with Haskett – or perhaps even to a "Church Sociable" – she in a "picture hat" and Haskett in a black frock-coat, a little creased, with the made-up tie on an elastic. On the way home they would stop and look at the illuminated shop-windows, lingering over the photographs of New York actresses. On Sunday afternoons Haskett would take her for a walk, pushing Lily ahead of them in a white enameled perambulator, and Waythorn had a vision of the people they would stop and talk to. He could fancy how pretty Alice must have looked, in a dress adroitly constructed from the hints of a New York fashion-paper; how she must have looked down on the other women, chafing at her life, and secretly feeling that she belonged in a bigger place.

For the moment his foremost thought was one of wonder at the way in which she had shed the phase of existence which her marriage with Haskett implied. It was as if her whole aspect, every gesture, every inflection, every allusion, were a studied negation of that period of her life. If she had denied being married to Haskett she could hardly have stood more convicted of duplicity than in this obliteration of the self which had been his wife.

Waythorn started up, checking himself in the analysis of her motives. What right had he to create a fantastic effigy of her and then pass judgment on it? She had spoken vaguely of her first marriage as unhappy, had hinted, with becoming reticence, that Haskett had wrought havoc among her young illusions. . . . It was a pity for Waythorn's peace of mind that Haskett's very inoffensiveness shed a new light on the nature of those illusions. A man would rather think that his wife has been brutalized by her first husband than that the process has been reversed.

IV

"Mr. Waythorn, I don't like that French governess of Lily's."

Haskett, subdued and apologetic, stood before Waythorn in the library, revolving his shabby hat in his hand.

Waythorn, surprised in his armchair over the evening paper, stared back perplexedly at his visitor.

---

3. **"Ben Hur"**: A best-selling historical novel by Lew Wallace (1827–1905), *Ben-Hur: A Tale of the Christ*, was first published in 1880.

"You'll excuse my asking to see you," Haskett continued. "But this is my last visit, and I thought if I could have a word with you it would be a better way than writing to Mrs. Waythorn's lawyer."

Waythorn rose uneasily. He did not like the French governess either; but that was irrelevant.

"I am not so sure of that," he returned stiffly; "but since you wish it I will give your message to my wife." He always hesitated over the possessive pronoun in addressing Haskett.

The latter sighed. "I don't know as that will help much. She didn't like it when I spoke to her."

Waythorn turned red. "When did you see her?" he asked.

"Not since the first day I came to see Lily — right after she was taken sick. I remarked to her then that I didn't like the governess."

Waythorn made no answer. He remembered distinctly that, after that first visit, he had asked his wife if she had seen Haskett. She had lied to him then, but she had respected his wishes since; and the incident cast a curious light on her character. He was sure she would not have seen Haskett that first day if she had divined that Waythorn would object, and the fact that she did not divine it was almost as disagreeable to the latter as the discovery that she had lied to him.

"I don't like the woman," Haskett was repeating with mild persistency. "She ain't straight, Mr. Waythorn — she'll teach the child to be underhand. I've noticed a change in Lily — she's too anxious to please — and she don't always tell the truth. She used to be the straightest child, Mr. Waythorn —" He broke off, his voice a little thick. "Not but what I want her to have a stylish education," he ended.

Waythorn was touched. "I'm sorry, Mr. Haskett; but frankly, I don't quite see what I can do."

Haskett hesitated. Then he laid his hat on the table, and advanced to the hearth-rug, on which Waythorn was standing. There was nothing aggressive in his manner, but he had the solemnity of a timid man resolved on a decisive measure.

"There's just one thing, you can do, Mr. Waythorn," he said. "You can remind Mrs. Waythorn that, by the decree of the courts, I am entitled to have a voice in Lily's bringing up." He paused, and went on more deprecatingly: "I'm not the kind to talk about enforcing my rights, Mr. Waythorn. I don't know as I think a man is entitled to rights he hasn't known how to hold on to; but this business of the child is different. I've never let go there — and I never mean to."

The scene left Waythorn deeply shaken. Shamefacedly, in indirect ways, he had been finding out about Haskett; and all that he had learned was favorable. The little man, in order to be near his daughter, had sold out his share in a profitable business in Utica, and accepted a modest clerkship in a New York manufacturing house. He boarded in a shabby street and had few acquaintances. His passion for Lily filled his life. Waythorn felt that this exploration of Haskett was like groping about with a dark-lantern in his wife's past; but he saw now that there were recesses his lantern had not explored. He had never inquired into the exact circumstances of his wife's first matrimonial rupture. On the surface all had been fair. It was she who had obtained the divorce, and the court had given her the child. But Waythorn knew how many ambiguities such a verdict might cover. The mere fact that Haskett retained a right over his daughter implied an unsuspected compromise. Waythorn was an idealist. He always refused to recognize unpleasant contingencies till he found himself confronted with them, and then he saw them followed by a special train of consequences. His next days were thus haunted, and he determined to try to lay the ghosts by conjuring them up in his wife's presence.

When he repeated Haskett's request, a flame of anger passed over her face; but she subdued it instantly and spoke with a slight quiver of outraged motherhood.

"It is very ungentlemanly of him," she said.

The word grated on Waythorn. "That is neither here nor there. It's a bare question of rights."

She murmured: "It's not as if he could ever be a help to Lily —"

Waythorn flushed. This was even less to his taste. "The question is," he repeated, "what authority has he over her?"

She looked downward, twisting herself a little in her seat. "I am willing to see him — I thought you objected," she faltered.

In a flash he understood that she knew the extent of Haskett's claims. Perhaps it was not the first time she had resisted them.

"My objecting has nothing to do with it," he said coldly: "if Haskett has a right to be consulted you must consult him."

She burst into tears, and he saw that she expected him to regard her as a victim.

Haskett did not abuse his rights. Waythorn had felt miserably sure that he would not. But the governess was dismissed, and from time to time the little man demanded an interview with Alice. After the first outburst she accepted the situation with her usual adaptability. Haskett had once reminded Waythorn of the piano-tuner, and Mrs. Waythorn, after a month or two, appeared to class him with that domestic familiar. Waythorn could not but respect the father's tenacity. At first he had tried to cultivate the suspicion that Haskett might be "up to" something, that he had an object in securing a foothold in the house. But in his heart Waythorn was sure of Haskett's single-mindedness; he even guessed in the latter a mild contempt for such advantages as his relation with the Waythorns might offer. Haskett's sincerity of purpose made him invulnerable, and his successor had to accept him as a lien on the property.

Mr. Sellers was sent to Europe to recover from his gout, and Varick's affairs hung on Waythorn's hands. The negotiations were prolonged and complicated; they necessitated frequent conferences between the two men, and the interests of the firm forbade Waythorn's suggesting that his client should transfer his business to another office.

Varick appeared well in the transaction. In moments of relaxation his coarse streak appeared, and Waythorn dreaded his geniality; but in the office he was concise and clear-headed, with a flattering deference to Waythorn's judgment. Their business relations being so affably established, it would have been absurd for the two men to ignore each other in society. The first time they met in a drawing-room, Varick took up their intercourse in the same easy key, and his hostess's grateful glance obliged Waythorn to respond to it. After that they ran across each other frequently, and one evening at a ball Waythorn, wandering through the remoter rooms, came upon Varick seated beside his wife. She colored a little, and faltered in what she was saying; but Varick nodded to Waythorn without rising, and the latter strolled on.

In the carriage, on the way home, he broke out nervously: "I didn't know you spoke to Varick."

Her voice trembled a little. "It's the first time — he happened to be standing near me; I didn't know what to do. It's so awkward, meeting everywhere — and he said you had been very kind about some business."

"That's different," said Waythorn.

She paused a moment. "I'll do just as you wish," she returned pliantly. "I thought it would be less awkward to speak to him when we meet."

Her pliancy was beginning to sicken him. Had she really no will of her own — no theory about her relation to these men? She had accepted Haskett — did she mean to accept Varick? It was "less awkward," as she had said, and her instinct was to evade difficulties or to circumvent them. With sudden vividness Waythorn saw how the instinct had developed. She was "as easy as an old shoe" — a shoe that too many feet had worn. Her elasticity was the result of tension in too many different directions. Alice Haskett — Alice Varick — Alice Waythorn — she had been each in turn, and had left hanging to each name a little of her privacy, a little of her personality, a little of the inmost self where the unknown god abides.

"Yes — it's better to speak to Varick," said Waythorn wearily.

V

The winter wore on, and society took advantage of the Waythorns' acceptance of Varick. Harrassed hostesses were grateful to them for bridging over a social difficulty, and Mrs. Waythorn was held up as a miracle of good taste. Some experimental spirits could not resist the diversion of throwing Varick and his former wife together, and there were those who thought he found a zest in the propinquity. But Mrs. Waythorn's conduct remained irreproachable. She neither avoided Varick nor sought him out. Even Waythorn could not but admit that she had discovered the solution of the newest social problem.

He had married her without giving much thought to that problem. He had fancied that a woman can shed her past like a man. But now he saw that Alice was bound to hers both by the circumstances which forced her into continued relations with it, and by the traces it had left on her nature. With grim irony, Waythorn compared himself to a member of a syndicate. He held so many shares in his wife's personality and his predecessors were his partners in the business. If there had been any element of passion in the transaction he would have felt less deteriorated by it. The fact that Alice took her change of husbands like a change of weather reduced the situation to mediocrity. He could have forgiven her for blunders, for excesses; for resisting Haskett, for yielding to Varick; for anything but her acquiescence and her tact. She reminded him of a juggler tossing knives; but the knives were blunt and she knew they would never cut her.

And then, gradually, habit formed a protecting surface for his sensibilities. If he paid for each day's comfort with the small change of his illusions, he grew daily to value the comfort more and set less store upon the coin. He had drifted into a dulling propinquity with Haskett and Varick and he took refuge in the cheap revenge of satirizing the situation. He even began to reckon up the advantages which accrued from it, to ask himself if it were not better to own a third of a wife who knew how to make a man happy than a whole one who had lacked opportunity to acquire the art. For it *was* an art, and made up, like all others, of concessions, eliminations and embellishments; of lights judiciously thrown and shadows skilfully softened. His wife knew exactly how to manage the lights and he knew exactly to what training she owed her skill. He even tried to trace the source of his obligations, to discriminate between the influences which had combined to produce his domestic happiness; he perceived that Haskett's commonness had made Alice worship good breeding, while Varick's liberal construction of the marriage bond had taught her to value the conjugal virtues; so that he was directly indebted to his predecessors for the devotion which made his life easy if not inspiring.

From this phase he passed into that of complete acceptance. He ceased to satirize himself, because time dulled the irony of the situation and the joke lost its humor with its sting. Even the sight of Haskett's hat on the hall table had ceased to touch the springs of epigram. The hat was often seen there now, for it had been decided that it was better for Lily's father to visit her than for the little girl to go to his boarding-house. Waythorn, having acquiesced in this arrangement, had been surprised to find how little difference it made. Haskett was never obtrusive, and the few visitors who met him on the stairs were unaware of his identity. Waythorn did not know how often he saw Alice, but with himself Haskett was seldom in contact.

One afternoon, however, he learned on entering that Lily's father was waiting to see him. In the library he found Haskett occupying a chair in his usual provisional way. Waythorn always felt grateful to him for not leaning back.

"I hope you'll excuse me, Mr. Waythorn," he said rising. "I wanted to see Mrs. Waythorn about Lily, and your man asked me to wait here till she came in."

"Of course," said Waythorn, remembering that a sudden leak had that morning given over the drawing-room to the plumbers.

He opened his cigar-case and held it out to his visitor, and Haskett's acceptance seemed to mark a fresh stage in their intercourse. The spring evening was chilly, and Waythorn invited his guest to draw up his chair to the fire. He meant to find an excuse to leave Haskett in a moment; but he was tired and cold, and after all the little man no longer jarred on him.

The two were inclosed in the intimacy of their blended cigar-smoke when the door opened and Varick walked into the room. Waythorn rose abruptly. It was the first time that Varick had come to the house, and the surprise of seeing him, combined with the singular inopportuneness of his arrival, gave a new edge to Waythorn's blunted sensibilities. He stared at his visitor without speaking.

Varick seemed too preoccupied to notice his host's embarrassment.

"My dear fellow," he exclaimed in his most expansive tone, "I must apologize for tumbling in on you in this way, but I was too late to catch you down town, and so I thought —" He stopped short, catching sight of Haskett, and his sanguine color deepened to a flush which spread vividly under his scant blond hair. But in a moment he recovered himself and nodded slightly. Haskett returned the bow in silence, and Waythorn was still groping for speech when the footman came in carrying a tea-table.

The intrusion offered a welcome vent to Waythorn's nerves. "What the deuce are you bringing this here for?" he said sharply.

"I beg your pardon, sir, but the plumbers are still in the drawing-room, and Mrs. Waythorn said she would have tea in the library." The footman's perfectly respectful tone implied a reflection on Waythorn's reasonableness.

"Oh, very well," said the latter resignedly, and the footman proceeded to open the folding tea-table and set out its complicated appointments. While this interminable process continued the three men stood motionless, watching it with a fascinated stare, till Waythorn, to break the silence, said to Varick: "Won't you have a cigar?"

He held out the case he had just tendered to Haskett, and Varick helped himself with a smile. Waythorn looked about for a match, and finding none, proffered a light from his own cigar. Haskett, in the background, held his ground mildly, examining his cigar-tip now and then, and stepping forward at the right moment to knock its ashes into the fire.

The footman at last withdrew, and Varick immediately began: "If I could just say half a word to you about this business —"

"Certainly," stammered Waythorn; "in the dining-room —"

But as he placed his hand on the door it opened from without, and his wife appeared on the threshold.

She came in fresh and smiling, in her street dress and hat, shedding a fragrance from the boa which she loosened in advancing.

"Shall we have tea in here, dear?" she began; and then she caught sight of Varick. Her smile deepened, veiling a slight tremor of surprise. "Why, how do you do?" she said with a distinct note of pleasure.

As she shook hands with Varick she saw Haskett standing behind him. Her smile faded for a moment, but she recalled it quickly, with a scarcely perceptible side-glance at Waythorn.

"How do you do, Mr. Haskett?" she said, and shook hands with him a shade less cordially.

The three men stood awkwardly before her, till Varick, always the most self-possessed, dashed into an explanatory phrase.

"We — I had to see Waythorn a moment on business," he stammered, brick-red from chin to nape.

Haskett stepped forward with his air of mild obstinacy. "I am sorry to intrude; but you appointed five o'clock —" he directed his resigned glance to the timepiece on the mantel.

She swept aside their embarrassment with a charming gesture of hospitality.

"I'm so sorry — I'm always late; but the afternoon was so lovely." She stood drawing her gloves off, propitiatory and graceful, diffusing about her a sense of ease and familiarity in which the situation lost its grotesqueness. "But before talking business," she added brightly, "I'm sure every one wants a cup of tea."

She dropped into her low chair by the tea-table, and the two visitors, as if drawn by her smile, advanced to receive the cups she held out.

She glanced about for Waythorn, and he took the third cup with a laugh.

[1904]

Sui Sin Far
(Edith Maud Eaton)

[1865-1914]

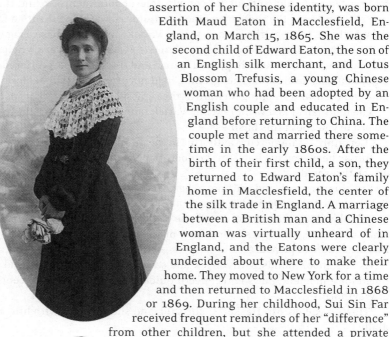

Sui Sin Far

This photograph of Edith Maud Eaton was taken in December 1903, by which time she had begun to earn a literary reputation in the United States for the articles and stories published under her pen name, Sui Sin Far.

Sui Sin Far, who adopted that pen name as an assertion of her Chinese identity, was born Edith Maud Eaton in Macclesfield, England, on March 15, 1865. She was the second child of Edward Eaton, the son of an English silk merchant, and Lotus Blossom Trefusis, a young Chinese woman who had been adopted by an English couple and educated in England before returning to China. The couple met and married there sometime in the early 1860s. After the birth of their first child, a son, they returned to Edward Eaton's family home in Macclesfield, the center of the silk trade in England. A marriage between a British man and a Chinese woman was virtually unheard of in England, and the Eatons were clearly undecided about where to make their home. They moved to New York for a time and then returned to Macclesfield in 1868 or 1869. During her childhood, Sui Sin Far received frequent reminders of her "difference" from other children, but she attended a private school and was brought up to think of herself as English. By the time she was about six years old, the silk industry in England was declining, and the growing family emigrated to North America, settling first near New York City and then in Montreal. Although he worked as a clerk, Edward Eaton devoted himself to painting, and Sui Sin Far later recalled that her mother was a "fascinating story teller." Indeed, art and books were an integral part of the family life that fueled her literary interests and ultimately led her to become one of the first authors of Asian descent to be published in North America.

More immediately, however, as the second oldest of fourteen surviving children, Sui Sin Far was expected to help support the poverty-stricken family. When she was about eleven years old, her formal education ended, and she went to work. She began to sell lace she made and her father's paintings on the streets of Montreal. In 1883, she found a job in the composing room of the *Montreal Daily Star* and set about to learn to type and take shorthand, office skills that were providing thousands of young women new opportunities for work at the end of the nineteenth century.

She was soon proficient enough to secure a job in a law firm. She began to write in her spare time and to publish articles in local and regional newspapers. In 1888-89, she published several stories in the *Dominion Illustrated,* a new Canadian periodical that primarily featured romantic tales directed at women. These early works were signed "Edith Eaton" or "E.E." By the mid-1890s, she had established her own stenographic agency in Montreal. She also traveled widely, to the American Midwest and to Jamaica, where she joined her sister, Winnifred Eaton, a writer who had assumed a Japanese pen name, Onoto Watanna. When Sui Sin Far returned to Montreal, ill with malaria from which she would never fully recover, she decided to resettle in the United States. She moved to San Francisco and then to Seattle, Washington, where she easily found work in its growing "Chinatown."

Taking as her pen name the Cantonese word for "Narcissus," in the late 1890s Sui Sin Far began to publish articles and stories in which she directly confronted the pervasive prejudice and frequent violence directed against Chinese immigrants in the United States. During the following decade, her writings began to gain national attention. In 1909, she published an autobiographical essay, "Leaves from the Mental Portfolio of an Eurasian," in a prominent New York newspaper, the *Independent,* where four of her stories subsequently appeared. Sui Sin Far moved to Boston, where she gained a firm foothold in the literary marketplace of the East, publishing her writings in *Good Housekeeping, Hampton's Magazine,* and the *New-England Magazine.* She also published a collection of her stories, *Mrs. Spring Fragrance* (1912). A reviewer for the *New York Times* observed that Sui Sin Far had "struck a new note in fiction," while the reviewer for the *Boston Globe* emphasized the ways in which she subverted stereotypes of Chinese people:

bedfordstmartins.com/ americanlit *for research links on Sui Sin Far*

> The tales are told with a sympathy that strikes straight to one's heart; to say they are convincing is weak praise, and they show the Chinese with feelings absolutely indistinguishable from those of white people — only the Chinese seem to have more delicate sensibilities, and more acute ways of handling their problems.

Despite such positive reviews, the book did not sell well. Sui Sin Far, who was in poor health, returned to Montreal, where she died of heart failure in 1914. The manuscript of a novel she was working on at the time of her death was apparently lost, and her published writings soon fell into oblivion, but Sui Sin Far has recently come to be recognized as one of the founders of the tradition of Asian American literature in both Canada and the United States.

Sui Sin Far's "In the Land of the Free." This story, one of the central pieces in the collection *Mrs. Spring Fragrance,* was first published in the influential liberal periodical the *Independent* on September 2, 1909. Founded in New York City in 1848 as a religious and antislavery news-

Mrs. Spring Fragrance
The original 1912 edition of Sui Sin Far's collection of stories was decorated with elaborate "oriental" motifs. On the scarlet cover, dragonflies float around two white Chinese lilies – a visual translation of *Sui Sin Far,* or "Narcissus" – and the Chinese characters on the lower-right corner approximate the English phrase "signed by Sui Sin Far." Designed to appeal to what a critic in 1903 described as "a growing craze in America for the Oriental," the appearance of the volume belied the painful nature of many of Sui Sin Far's stories about the trials of Chinese immigrants in the United States.

paper, the *Independent* was devoted to the "Consideration of Politics, Social and Economic Tendencies, History, Literature, and the Arts." The newspaper published the work of many noted American poets, including John Greenleaf Whittier, William Cullen Bryant, and, after her death, Emily Dickinson. Under the editorship of William Hayes Ward, who evidently invited Sui Sin Far to contribute to the newspaper, the *Independent* began to publish more fiction and to cover a wider range of social issues. In a note preceding "In the Land of the Free," Ward observes:

Our readers will recall the autobiography of Sui Sin Far [published in the newspaper earlier in 1909]. Though the following article is cast in the form of fiction we are obliged to confess it is the fiction that is often less strange and cruel than the truth.

As the note suggests, the even crueler "truth" exposed by Sui Sin Far was the plight of Chinese immigrants "In the Land of the Free," a poignant story of a Chinese American couple's struggle to regain their child, who is detained by U.S. customs officers and then held in a mission nursery. Indeed, the story reveals two of the central concerns of Sui Sin Far's fiction, the cultural conflict between what were then often described as "occidental" and "oriental" values and the harsh provisions of laws restricting Chinese immigration into the United States. The text is taken from the first edition of *Mrs. Spring Fragrance* (1912).

IN THE LAND OF THE FREE

I

"See, Little One – the hills in the morning sun. There is thy home for years to come. It is very beautiful and thou wilt be very happy there."

The Little One looked up into his mother's face in perfect faith. He was engaged in the pleasant occupation of sucking a sweetmeat; but that did not prevent him from gurgling responsively.

"Yes, my olive bud; there is where thy father is making a fortune for thee. Thy father! Oh, wilt thou not be glad to behold his dear face. 'Twas for thee I left him."

The Little One ducked his chin sympathetically against his mother's knee. She lifted him up on to her lap. He was two years old, a round, dimple-cheeked boy with bright brown eyes and a sturdy little frame.

"Ah! Ah! Ah! Ooh! Ooh! Ooh!" puffed he, mocking a tugboat steaming by.

San Francisco's waterfront was lined with ships and steamers, while other craft, large and small, including a couple of white transports from the Philippines, lay at anchor here and there off shore. It was some time before the *Eastern Queen* could get docked, and even after that was accomplished, a lone Chinaman who had been waiting on the wharf for an hour was detained that much longer by men with the initials U. S. C.[1] on their caps, before he could board the steamer and welcome his wife and child.

"This is thy son," announced the happy Lae Choo.

Hom Hing lifted the child, felt of his little body and limbs, gazed into his face with proud and joyous eyes; then turned inquiringly to a customs officer at his elbow.

"That's a fine boy you have there," said the man. "Where was he born?"

"In China," answered Hom Hing, swinging the Little One on his right shoulder, preparatory to leading his wife off the steamer.

"Ever been to America before?"

"No, not he," answered the father with a happy laugh.

The customs officer beckoned to another.

"This little fellow," said he, "is visiting America for the first time."

The other customs officer stroked his chin reflectively.

"Good day," said Hom Hing.

"Wait!" commanded one of the officers. "You cannot go just yet."

"What more now?" asked Hom Hing.

"I'm afraid," said the first customs officer, "that we cannot allow the boy to go ashore. There is nothing in the papers that you have shown us — your wife's papers and your own — having any bearing upon the child."

"There was no child when the papers were made out," returned Hom Hing. He spoke calmly; but there was apprehension in his eyes and in his tightening grip on his son.

"What is it? What is it?" quavered Lae Choo, who understood a little English.

The second customs officer regarded her pityingly.

"I don't like this part of the business," he muttered.

The first officer turned to Hom Hing and in an official tone of voice, said:

"Seeing that the boy has no certificate entitling him to admission to this country you will have to leave him with us."

"Leave my boy!" exclaimed Hom Hing.

"Yes; he will be well taken care of, and just as soon as we can hear from Washington he will be handed over to you."

"But," protested Hom Hing, "he is my son."

---

1. U. S. C.: The U.S. Customs Service, now the U.S. Customs and Border Protection.

"We have no proof," answered the man with a shrug of his shoulders; "and even if so we cannot let him pass without orders from the Government."

"He is my son," reiterated Hom Hing, slowly and solemnly. "I am a Chinese merchant and have been in business in San Francisco for many years. When my wife told to me one morning that she dreamed of a green tree with spreading branches and one beautiful red flower growing thereon, I answered her that I wished my son to be born in our country, and for her to prepare to go to China. My wife complied with my wish. After my son was born my mother fell sick and my wife nursed and cared for her; then my father, too, fell sick, and my wife also nursed and cared for him. For twenty moons my wife care for and nurse the old people, and when they die they bless her and my son, and I send for her to return to me. I had no fear of trouble. I was a Chinese merchant and my son was my son."

"Very good, Hom Hing," replied the first officer. "Nevertheless, we take your son."

"No, you not take him; he my son too."

It was Lae Choo. Snatching the child from his father's arms she held and covered him with her own.

The officers conferred together for a few moments; then one drew Hom Hing aside and spoke in his ear.

Resignedly Hom Hing bowed his head, then approached his wife. "'Tis the law," said he, speaking in Chinese, "and 'twill be but for a little while – until tomorrow's sun arises."

"You, too," reproached Lae Choo in a voice eloquent with pain. But accustomed to obedience she yielded the boy to her husband, who in turn delivered him to the first officer. The Little One protested lustily against the transfer; but his mother covered her face with her sleeve and his father silently led her away. Thus was the law of the land complied with.

II

Day was breaking. Lae Choo, who had been awake all night, dressed herself, then awoke her husband.

"'Tis the morn," she cried. "Go, bring our son."

The man rubbed his eyes and arose upon his elbow so that he could see out of the window. A pale star was visible in the sky. The petals of a lily in a bowl on the windowsill were unfurled.

"'Tis not yet time," said he, laying his head down again.

"Not yet time. Ah, all the time that I lived before yesterday is not so much as the time that has been since my little one was taken from me."

The mother threw herself down beside the bed and covered her face.

Hom Hing turned on the light, and touching his wife's bowed head with a sympathetic hand inquired if she had slept.

"Slept!" she echoed, weepingly. "Ah, how could I close my eyes with my arms empty of the little body that has filled them every night for more than twenty moons! You do not know – man – what it is to miss the feel of the little fingers and the little toes and the soft round limbs of your little one. Even in the darkness his darling eyes used to shine up to mine, and often have I fallen into slumber with his pretty babble at my ear. And now, I see him not; I touch him not; I hear him not. My baby, my little fat one!"

"Now! Now! Now!" consoled Hom Hing, patting his wife's shoulder reassuringly; "there is no need to grieve so; he will soon gladden you again. There cannot be any law that would keep a child from its mother!"

Lae Choo dried her tears.

"You are right, my husband," she meekly murmured. She arose and stepped about the apartment, setting things to rights. The box of presents she had brought for her California friends had been opened the evening before; and silks, embroideries, carved ivories, ornamental lacquer-ware, brasses, camphor-wood boxes, fans, and chinaware were scattered around in confused heaps. In the midst of unpacking the thought of her child in the hands of strangers had overpowered her, and she had left everything to crawl into bed and weep.

Having arranged her gifts in order she stepped out on to the deep balcony.

The star had faded from view and there were bright streaks in the western sky. Lae Choo looked down the street and around. Beneath the flat occupied by her and her husband were quarters for a number of bachelor Chinamen, and she could hear them from where she stood, taking their early morning breakfast. Below their dining-room was her husband's grocery store. Across the way was a large restaurant. Last night it had been resplendent with gay colored lanterns and the sound of music. The rejoicings over "the completion of the moon," by Quong Sum's firstborn, had been long and loud, and had caused her to tie a handkerchief over her ears. She, a bereaved mother, had it not in her heart to rejoice with other parents. This morning the place was more in accord with her mood. It was still and quiet. The revellers had dispersed or were asleep.

A roly-poly woman in black sateen, with long pendant earrings in her ears, looked up from the street below and waved her a smiling greeting. It was her old neighbor, Kuie Hoe, the wife of the gold embosser, Mark Sing. With her was a little boy in yellow jacket and lavender pantaloons. Lae Choo remembered him as a baby. She used to like to play with him in those days when she had no child of her own. What a long time ago that seemed! She caught her breath in a sigh, and laughed instead.

"Why are you so merry?" called her husband from within.

"Because my Little One is coming home," answered Lae Choo. "I am a happy mother — a happy mother."

She pattered into the room with a smile on her face.

The noon hour had arrived. The rice was steaming in the bowls and a fragrant dish of chicken and bamboo shoots was awaiting Hom Hing. Not for one moment had Lae Choo paused to rest during the morning hours; her activity had been ceaseless. Every now and again, however, she had raised her eyes to the gilded clock on the curiously carved mantelpiece. Once, she had exclaimed:

"Why so long, oh! why so long?" Then apostrophizing herself: "Lae Choo, be happy. The Little One is coming! The Little One is coming!" Several times she burst into tears and several times she laughed aloud.

Hom Hing entered the room; his arms hung down by his side.

"The Little One!" shrieked Lae Choo.

"They bid me call tomorrow."

With a moan the mother sank to the floor.

The noon hour passed. The dinner remained on the table.

III

The winter rains were over: the spring had come to California, flushing the hills with green and causing an ever-changing pageant of flowers to pass over them. But there was no spring in Lae Choo's heart, for the Little One remained away from her arms. He was being kept in a mission. White women were caring for him, and though for one full moon he had pined for his mother and refused to be comforted he was now apparently happy and contented. Five moons or five months had gone by since the day he had passed with Lae Choo through the Golden Gate; but the great Government at Washington still delayed sending the answer which would return him to his parents.

Hom Hing was disconsolately rolling up and down the balls in his abacus box when a keen-faced young man stepped into his store.

"What news?" asked the Chinese merchant.

"This!" The young man brought forth a typewritten letter. Hom Hing read the words:

"Re Chinese child, alleged to be the son of Hom Hing, Chinese merchant, doing business at 425 Clay street, San Francisco.

"Same will have attention as soon as possible."

Hom Hing returned the letter, and without a word continued his manipulation of the counting machine.

"Have you anything to say?" asked the young man.

"Nothing. They have sent the same letter fifteen times before. Have you not yourself showed it to me?"

"True!" The young man eyed the Chinese merchant furtively. He had a proposition to make and he was pondering whether or not the time was opportune.

"How is your wife?" he inquired solicitously — and diplomatically.

Hom Hing shook his head mournfully.

"She seems less every day," he replied. "Her food she takes only when I bid her and her tears fall continually. She finds no pleasure in dress or flowers and cares not to see her friends. Her eyes stare all night. I think before another moon she will pass into the land of spirits."

"No!" exclaimed the young man, genuinely startled.

"If the boy not come home I lose my wife sure," continued Hom Hing with bitter sadness.

"It's not right," cried the young man indignantly. Then he made his proposition.

The Chinese father's eyes brightened exceedingly.

"Will I like you to go to Washington and make them give you the paper to restore my son?" cried he. "How can you ask when you know my heart's desire?"

"Then," said the young fellow, "I will start next week. I am anxious to see this thing through if only for the sake of your wife's peace of mind."

"I will call her. To hear what you think to do will make her glad," said Hom Hing.

He called a message to Lae Choo upstairs through a tube in the wall.

In a few moments she appeared, listless, wan, and hollow-eyed; but when her husband told her the young lawyer's suggestion she became as one electrified; her form straightened, her eyes glistened; the color flushed to her cheeks.

"Oh," she cried, turning to James Clancy, "You are a hundred man good!"

The young man felt somewhat embarrassed; his eyes shifted a little under the intense gaze of the Chinese mother.

"Well, we must get your boy for you," he responded. "Of course" — turning to Hom Hing — "it will cost a little money. You can't get fellows to hurry the Government for you without gold in your pocket."

Hom Hing stared blankly for a moment. Then: "How much do you want, Mr. Clancy?" he asked quietly.

"Well, I will need at least five hundred to start with."

Hom Hing cleared his throat.

"I think I told to you the time I last paid you for writing letters for me and seeing the Custom boss here that nearly all I had was gone!"

"Oh, well then we won't talk about it, old fellow. It won't harm the boy to stay where he is, and your wife may get over it all right."

"What that you say?" quavered Lae Choo.

James Clancy looked out of the window.

"He says," explained Hom Hing in English, "that to get our boy we have to have much money."

"Money! Oh, yes."

Lae Choo nodded her head.

"I have not got the money to give him."

For a moment Lae Choo gazed wonderingly from one face to the other; then, comprehension dawning upon her, with swift anger, pointing to the lawyer, she cried: "You not one hundred man good; you just common white man."

"Yes, ma'am," returned James Clancy, bowing and smiling ironically.

Hom Hing pushed his wife behind him and addressed the lawyer again: "I might try," said he, "to raise something; but five hundred — it is not possible."

"What about four?"

"I tell you I have next to nothing left and my friends are not rich."

"Very well!"

The lawyer moved leisurely toward the door, pausing on its threshold to light a cigarette.

"Stop, white man; white man, stop!"

Lae Choo, panting and terrified, had started forward and now stood beside him, clutching his sleeve excitedly.

"You say you can go to get paper to bring my Little One to me if Hom Hing give you five hundred dollars?"

The lawyer nodded carelessly; his eyes were intent upon the cigarette which would not take the fire from the match.

"Then you go get paper. If Hom Hing not can give you five hundred dollars — I give you perhaps what more that much."

She slipped a heavy gold bracelet from her wrist and held it out to the man. Mechanically he took it.

"I go get more!"

She scurried away, disappearing behind the door through which she had come.

"Oh, look here, I can't accept this," said James Clancy, walking back to Hom Hing and laying down the bracelet before him.

"It's all right," said Hom Hing, seriously, "pure China gold. My wife's parent give it to her when we married."

"But I can't take it anyway," protested the young man.

"It is all same as money. And you want money to go to Washington," replied Hom Hing in a matter of fact manner.

"See, my jade earrings — my gold buttons — my hairpins — my comb of pearl and my rings — one, two, three, four, five rings; very good — very good — all same much money. I give them all to you. You take and bring me paper for my Little One."

Lae Choo piled up her jewels before the lawyer.

Hom Hing laid a restraining hand upon her shoulder. "Not all, my wife," he said in Chinese. He selected a ring — his gift to Lae Choo when she dreamed of the tree with the red flower. The rest of the jewels he pushed toward the white man.

"Take them and sell them," said he. "They will pay your fare to Washington and bring you back with the paper."

For one moment James Clancy hesitated. He was not a sentimental man; but something within him arose against accepting such payment for his services.

"They are good, good," pleadingly asserted Lae Choo, seeing his hesitation.

Whereupon he seized the jewels, thrust them into his coat pocket, and walked rapidly away from the store.

IV

Lae Choo followed after the missionary woman through the mission nursery school. Her heart was beating so high with happiness that she could scarcely breathe. The paper had come at last — the precious paper which gave Hom Hing and his wife the right to the possession of their own child. It was ten months now since he had been taken from them — ten months since the sun had ceased to shine for Lae Choo.

The room was filled with children — most of them wee tots, but none so wee as her own. The mission woman talked as she walked. She told Lae Choo that little Kim, as he had been named by the school, was the pet of the place, and that his little tricks and ways amused and delighted every one. He had been rather difficult to manage at first and had cried much for his mother; "but children so soon forget, and after a month he seemed quite at home and played around as bright and happy as a bird."

"Yes," responded Lae Choo. "Oh, yes, yes!"

But she did not hear what was said to her. She was walking in a maze of anticipatory joy.

"Wait here, please," said the mission woman, placing Lae Choo in a chair. "The very youngest ones are having their breakfast."

She withdrew for a moment — it seemed like an hour to the mother — then she reappeared leading by the hand a little boy dressed in blue cotton overalls and white-soled shoes. The little boy's face was round and dimpled and his eyes were very bright.

"Little One, ah, my Little One!" cried Lae Choo.

She fell on her knees and stretched her hungry arms toward her son.

But the Little One shrunk from her and tried to hide himself in the folds of the white woman's skirt.

"Go'way, go'way!" he bade his mother.

[1909, 1912]

Mary Austin

[1868–1934]

Mary Austin was born Mary Hunter on September 9, 1868, in Carlinville, a small town in west central Illinois. She was the second surviving child of Susanna Savilla Graham Hunter and Captain George Hunter, a lawyer and veteran of the Civil War. A voracious reader, Austin's father was also a writer who had filed war reports for publication in the *Carlinville Democrat*. His untimely death in 1878 plunged the family into poverty, and it suffered an additional blow later that year with the death of Austin's beloved younger sister, Jennie. While her mother worked as a nurse to supplement her meager widow's pension, Austin divided her time between school and the care of her two brothers, whose privileged position in the family she deeply resented. In 1884, she insisted on enrolling at Blackburn College. Preparing for a career as a teacher, Austin also spent a year at the State Normal School in Bloomington, Illinois, before graduating from Blackburn in 1888.

Mary Austin

The author and editor Charles Lummis took this photograph in 1900, three years before the publication of Austin's acclaimed first book, *The Land of Little Rain*.

Encouraged by the success of a cousin who had gone to California, which was undergoing a boom in the 1880s, Susanna Hunter decided that her family should move there. Austin's older brother went first, filing a homestead claim on land at the southern end of the San Joaquin Valley, an area of Kern County called the Tejon, where the family joined him in 1888. Ill qualified to be homesteaders and understanding little about the scarcity of water and the expense of irrigation, the Hunters experienced great difficulties. Austin, however, was awed by the beauty of her new environment, which she studied closely. In an essay published by her college magazine in 1889, "One Hundred Miles on Horseback," she wrote:

> On the afternoon of the eighth day we came out on the north side of the Tehachapi mountains in the valley of the San Joaquin. Here it is that I write, here where the tarantulas sun themselves on our front porch, the owls hoot on our roof at night, and gray coyotes come trotting up under our very windows. The mountains curve out about us from east to west, and below us on the slope we can catch the blue gleam of a lake. Scarcely a day or night but some member of the family calls us to "come and look"; sometimes at some new glory of cloud and sun on the mountains, sometimes at a herd of antelope feeding close to the house, or an eagle cleaving the air with swift wings.

Austin's lyrical account marked the beginning of her life as a writer. Working as a teacher, she began to write poems designed to help her students appreciate the beauty and rhythms of the stark landscape in which they lived. In 1891, she met and married Stafford Wallace Austin, a farmer who owned a vineyard near the small settlement at Lone Pine. Like hundreds of other new immigrants to California, the newly married couple suffered financial reverses because of the low rainfall and lack of irrigation in the area. Meanwhile, Austin began writing stories inspired by the land and people she encountered in California. To her great delight, she received twelve dollars for "The Mother of Felipe," her first published story, which appeared in the San Francisco magazine the *Overland Monthly* in 1892. Later that year, however, Austin was devastated when her daughter, Ruth, was born with severe mental retardation. While caring for her child, who was later institutionalized, Austin returned to teaching to help support the family. She continued to write, selling stories to prominent eastern periodicals such as the *Atlantic Monthly, Cosmopolitan, Munsey's Magazine,* and *Saint Nicholas* before her career was fully launched by the publication of a collection of her nature sketches, *The Land of Little Rain* (1903).

Bolstered by the success of the collection and increasingly estranged from her husband, whom she later divorced, Austin set out on her own in 1905. She moved to the Carmel Bay area of California, where she became part of a vibrant literary community that included Ambrose Bierce and Jack London. Drawing on her earlier experiences of living in the California desert, Austin published two collections of sketches and stories focusing on the interactions between people and their environment, *The Flock*

It's poetry, her prose is; it's the poetry of life, of life lived to-day; conscious, beautiful poetry. That's what gets them out there, and that's what Mary Austin got.

—Lincoln Steffens

(1906) and *Lost Borders* (1909). Following an extended visit to England, where she met many writers whose work she admired, including Henry James, Austin moved to New York City in 1910. Her writing took a new turn during the following decade, when she wrote a series of experimental novels that revealed her growing feminism and social concerns, including *A Woman of Genius* (1912), *The Ford* (1917), and *No. 26 Jayne Street* (1920). Austin, who became deeply involved in the Indian rights movement, also published a collection of Native American verse, *The American Rhythm* (1923). *The Land of Journey's Ending* (1924), which she conceived as a companion volume to *The Land of Little Rain,* was based on her extensive study and travel in the Southwest. In 1924, Austin moved to Santa Fe, New Mexico, where she enjoyed friendships with numerous other writers who were drawn to the area, including Willa Cather. Austin's final works included a well-received autobiography, *Earth Horizon* (1932). By the time she died at her home in Santa Fe in 1934, Austin was the author of more than thirty books and hundreds of articles, sketches, and stories on nature, the environment, and the West.

bedfordstmartins.com/
americanlit for research
links on Austin

Austin's "The Basket Maker."   This sketch was published in *The Land of Little Rain* (1903), a collection of sketches Austin wrote while living in Independence, a small town in central California on the arid eastern slopes of the Sierra Nevada. Years later, Austin vividly recalled the day she began work on the collection:

> I remember the day very well — one of those thin days when the stark energies of the land threaten just under its surfaces, the mountains march nakedly, the hills confer. The air was so still that one could feel, almost hear, the steady pulse of the stamp-mill away East under the Inyo. There was a weeping willow whose long branches moved back and forth across my window like blowing hair, like my memory of my mother's long and beautiful hair. I think it was this which gave the reminiscent touch to my mood. For though I was there in the midst of it, I began to write of the land of little rain as of something very much loved, now removed.

When Austin completed the collection, she sent the manuscript to the editors of the *Atlantic Monthly,* who praised the "charm and faithfulness" of her work, adding: "It is not often that prose sketches of outdoor life have given us such unalloyed satisfaction." The sketches were published serially in the *Atlantic* before they appeared in book form later in 1903. Widely regarded as one of the most memorable sketches in the collection, "The Basket Maker" is a portrait of Seyavi, an aging Paiute woman through whom Austin ponders the essence of artistic creation, the power of nature, and the tragic history of the Paiutes in California. The text is taken from the first printing in the *Atlantic Monthly,* February 1903.

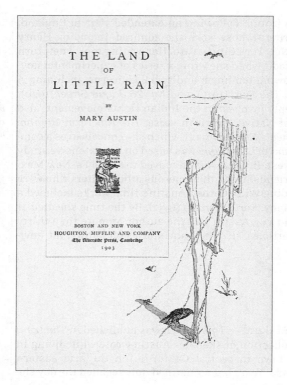

The Land of Little Rain
E. Boyd Smith created marginal decorations, illustrations, and this pictorial title page for the elegant first edition of *The Land of Little Rain*, though one reviewer objected: "None of these pictures, with the cunning of the artist's hand, bring out the country with its human and animal dwellers as does a single paragraph of Mrs. Austin's work."

THE BASKET MAKER

"A man," says Seyavi of the campoodie,[1] "must have a woman, but a woman who has a child will do very well."

That was perhaps why, when she lost her mate in the dying struggle of his race, she never took another, but set her wit to fend for herself and her young son. No doubt she was often put to it in the beginning to find food for them both. The Paiutes had made their last stand at the border of the Bitter Lake;[2] battle-driven they died in its waters,

---

1. **campoodie:** In a "Pronouncing Vocabulary of Indian Names and Words," appended to her later book of Indian myths and stories for children *The Basket Woman* (1904), Austin defined a *campoodie* as "(kămp' ō-dy). A group of Indian huts, from the Spanish *compo*, a field or prairie. In some localities written '*campody*.'"

2. **Paiutes . . . Bitter Lake:** The Northern Paiutes occupied a large area of present-day eastern California, western Nevada, and southeast Oregon from about 1000 CE until waves of settlers began to seize their lands around 1840. Following the Pyramid Lake ("Bitter Lake") War of 1860 and the Bannock War of 1878, the federal government tried to force the Paiutes onto a reservation in Oregon. But many Paiutes refused to go, and many others returned from the reservation to their ancestral lands. Clinging as long as possible to their traditional way of life, the Paiutes established small colonies, and there are now a number of tribal organizations throughout California, Nevada, and Oregon.

and the land filled with cattlemen and adventurers for gold: this while Seyavi and the boy lay up in the caverns of the Black Rock and ate tule roots[3] and fresh-water clams that they dug out of the slough bottoms with their toes. In the interim, while the tribes swallowed their defeat, and before the rumor of war died out, they must have come very near to the bare core of things. That was the time Seyavi learned the sufficiency of mother wit, and how much more easily one can do without a man than might at first be supposed.

To understand the fashion of any life, one must know the land it is lived in and the procession of the year. This valley is a narrow one, a mere trough between hills, a draught for storms, hardly a crow's flight from the sharp Sierras of the Snows to the curled, red and ochre, uncomforted, bare ribs of Waban.[4] Midway of the grove runs a burrowing, dull river, nearly a hundred miles from where it cuts the lava flats of the north to its widening in a thick, tideless pool of a lake. Hereabouts the ranges have no foothills, but rise up steeply from the bench lands above the river. Down from the Sierras, for the east ranges have almost no rain, pour glancing white floods toward the lowest land, and all beside them lie the campoodies, brown wattled brush heaps, looking east.

In the river are mussels, and reeds that have edible white roots, and in the soddy meadows tubers of joint grass; all these at their best in the spring. On the slope the summer growth affords seeds; up the steep the one-leaved pines, an oily nut.[5] That was really all they could depend upon, and that only at the mercy of the little gods of frost and rain. For the rest it was cunning against cunning, caution against skill, against quacking hordes of wild fowl in the tulares,[6] against pronghorn and bighorn and deer. You can guess, however, that all this warring of rifles and bowstrings, this influx of overlording whites, had made game wilder and hunters fearful of being hunted. You can surmise also, for it was a crude time and the land was raw, that the women became in turn the game of the conquerors.

There used to be in the Little Antelope a she dog, stray or outcast, that had a litter in some forsaken lair, and ranged and foraged for them, slinking savage and afraid, remembering and mistrusting humankind, wistful, lean, and sufficient for her young. I have thought Seyavi might have had days like that, and have had perfect leave to think, since she will not talk of it. Paiutes have the art of reducing life to its lowest ebb and yet saving it alive on grasshoppers, lizards, and strange herbs, and that time must have left no shift untried. It lasted long enough for Seyavi to have evolved the philosophy of life which I have set down at the beginning. She had gone beyond learning to do for her son, and learned to believe it worth while.

---

3. **tule roots:** The roots of a large bulrush prevalent in marshy areas of California.
4. **Sierras of the Snows . . . Waban:** That is, from the snow-covered peaks of the Sierra Nevada to the dry pastures on the lower slopes, called Waban. In her "Pronouncing Vocabulary" (see note 1), Austin defined *Waban* as "(wă-băn´). An Indian name of a place. The meaning is uncertain."
5. **oily nut:** The Paiutes gathered edible pinyon or piñon nuts, a staple of their winter diet.
6. **tulares:** In her "Pronouncing Vocabulary" (see note 1), Austin defined *tulare* as "(tōō-lä´ re). A marshy place overgrown with the bulrushes known as *tule*."

In our kind of society, when a woman ceases to alter the fashion of her hair, you guess that she has passed the crisis of her experience. If she goes on crimping and uncrimping with the changing mode, it is safe to suppose she has never come up against anything too big for her. The Indian woman gets nearly the same personal note in the pattern of her baskets. Not that she does not make all kinds, carriers, water-bottles, and cradles – these are kitchen ware – but her works of art are all of the same piece. Seyavi made flaring, flat-bottomed bowls, cooking pots really when cooking was done by dropping hot stones into water-tight food baskets, and for decoration a design in colored bark of the procession of plumed crests of the valley quail. In this pattern she had made cooking pots in the golden spring of her wedding year, when the quail went up two and two to their resting places about the foot of Oppapago. In this fashion she made them when, after pillage, it was possible to reinstate the housewifely crafts. Quail ran then in the Black Rock by hundreds – so you will still find them in fortunate years – and in the famine time the women cut their long hair to make snares when the flocks came morning and evening to the springs.

Seyavi made baskets for love and sold them for money, in a generation that preferred iron pots for utility. Every Indian woman is an artist – sees, feels, creates, but does not philosophize about her processes. Seyavi's bowls are wonders of technical precision, inside and out the palm finds no fault with them, but the subtlest appeal is in the sense that warns us of humanness in the way the design spreads into the flare of the bowl. There used to be an Indian woman at Olancha who made bottle-neck trinket baskets in the rattlesnake pattern, and could accommodate the design to the swelling bowl and flat shoulder of the basket without sensible disproportion, and so cleverly that you might own one a year without thinking how it was done; but Seyavi's baskets had a touch beyond cleverness. The weaver and the warp lived next to the earth and were saturated with the same elements. Twice a year, in the time of white butterflies and again when young quail ran neck and neck in the chaparral, Seyavi cut willows for basketry by the creek where it wound toward the river against the sun and sucking winds. It never quite reached the river except in far between times of summer flood, but it always tried, and the willows encouraged it as much as they could. You nearly always found them a little farther down than the trickle of eager water. The Paiute fashion of counting time appeals to me more than any other calendar. They have no stamp of heathen gods nor great ones, nor any succession of moons as have red men of the East and North, but count forward and back by the progress of the season; the time of *taboose*,[7] before the trout begin to leap, the end of the piñon harvest, about the beginning of deep snows. So they get nearer the sense of the season, which runs early or late according as the rains are forward or delayed. But whenever Seyavi cut willows for baskets was always a golden time, and the soul of the weather went into the wood. If you had over owned one of

---

7. *taboose:* In her "Pronouncing Vocabulary" (see note 1), Austin defined *taboose* as "(tǎ-bŏŏs'). Small tubercles of the joint grass; they appear on the joints of the roots early in spring, and are an important item of food to the Indians."

Seyavi's golden russet cooking bowls with the pattern of plumed quail, you would understand all this without saying anything.

Before Seyavi made baskets for the satisfaction of desire, for that is a house-bred theory of art that makes anything more of it, she danced and dressed her hair. In those days, when the spring was at flood and the blood pricked to the mating fever, the maids chose their flowers, wreathed themselves, and danced in the twilights, young desire crying out to young desire. They sang what the heart prompted, what the flower expressed, what boded in the mating weather.

"And what flower did you wear, Seyavi?"

"I, ah, the white flower of twining (clematis), on my body and my hair, and so I sang: —

> I am the white flower of twining
> Little white flower by the river,
> Oh, flower that twines close by the river;
> Oh, trembling flower!
> So trembles the maiden heart.

So sang Seyavi of the campoodie before she made baskets, and in her later days laid her arms upon her knees and laughed in them at the recollection. But it was not often she would say so much, never understanding the keen hunger I had for bits of lore and the "fool talk" of her people. She had fed her young son with meadow larks' tongues, to make him quick of speech; but in late years was loath to admit it, though she had come through the period of unfaith in the lore of the clan with a fine appreciation of its beauty and significance.

"What good will your dead get, Seyavi, of the baskets you burn?" said I, coveting them for my own collection.

Thus Seyavi, "As much good as yours of the flowers you strew."

Oppapago looks on Waban, and Waban on Coso and the Bitter Lake, and the campoodie looks on these three; and more, it sees the beginning of winds along the foot of Coso, the gathering of clouds behind the high ridges, the spring flush, the soft spread of wild almond bloom on the mesa. These first you understand are the Paiute's walls, the other his furnishings. Not the wattled hut is his home, but the land, the winds, the hill front, the stream. These he cannot duplicate at any furbisher's shop as you who live within doors, who if your purse allows may have the same home at Sitka and Samarcand. So you see how it is that the homesickness of an Indian is often unto death, since he gets no relief from it; neither wind nor weed nor skyline, nor any aspect of the hills of a strange land sufficiently like his own. So it was when the government reached out for the Paiutes, they gathered into the Northern Reservation only such poor tribes as could devise no other end of their affairs. Here, all along the river, and south to Shoshone land,[8] live the clans who owned the earth, fallen into the deplorable condition of

---

8. **Shoshone land:** A large Native American group composed of several bands, the Shoshone originally lived in the Great Basin (a large area between the Sierra Nevada and Rocky Mountains) and the Great Plains. Beginning in 1863, a series of treaties reduced the vast lands of the Shoshone to small reservations.

hangers-on. Yet you hear them laughing at the hour when they draw in to the campoodie after labor, when there is a smell of meat and the steam of the cooking pots goes up against the sun. Then the children lie with their toes in the ashes to hear tales; then they are merry, and have the joys of repletion and the nearness of their kind. They have their hills, and though jostled, are sufficiently free to get some fortitude for what will come. For now you shall hear of the end of the basket maker.

In her best days Seyavi was most like Deborah,[9] deep bosomed, broad in the hips, quick in counsel, slow of speech, esteemed of her people. This was that Seyavi who reared a man by her own hand, her own wit, and none other. When the townspeople began to take note of her — and it was some years after the war before there began to be any towns — she was then in the quick maturity of primitive women; but when I knew her she seemed already old. Indian women do not often live to great age, though they look incredibly steeped in years. They have the wit to win sustenance from the raw material of life without intervention, but they have not the sleek look of the women whom the social organization conspires to nourish. Seyavi had somehow squeezed out of her daily round a spiritual ichor[10] that kept the skill in her knotted fingers long after the accustomed time, but that also failed. By all counts she would have been about sixty years old when it came her turn to sit in the dust on the sunny side of the wickiup,[11] with little strength left for anything but looking. And in time she paid the toll of the smoky huts and became blind. This is a thing so long expected by the Paiutes that when it comes they find it neither bitter nor sweet, but tolerable because common. There were three other blind women in the campoodie, withered fruit on a bough, but they had memory and speech. By noon of the sun there were never any left in the campoodie but these or some mother of weanlings, and they sat to keep the ashes warm upon the hearth. If it were cold, they burrowed in the blankets of the hut; if it were warm, they followed the shadow of the wickiup around. Stir much out of their places they hardly dared, since one might not help another; but they called, in high, old cracked voices, gossip and reminder across the ash heaps.

Then, if they have your speech or you theirs, and have an hour to spare, there are things to be learned of life not set down in any books, folk tales, famine tales, love and longsuffering and desire, but no whimpering. Now and then one or another of the blind keepers of the camp will come across to where you sit gossiping, tapping her way among the kitchen middens,[12] guided by your voice that carries far in the clearness and stillness of mesa afternoons. But suppose you find Seyavi retired into the privacy of her

9. was most like Deborah: The prophet Deborah, then the ruler of Israel, led the victory over the Canaanites by drawing them into battle at Mount Tabor, where she had instructed Barak to summon an army of ten thousand Israelites (Judges 4:1–23).

10. ichor: In Greek mythology, the fluid that flows in the veins of the gods.

11. wickiup: In her "Pronouncing Vocabulary" (see note 1), Austin defined *wickiup* as "(wĭk' ĭ-ŭp). An Indian hut of brush, or reeds."

12. kitchen middens: Refuse heaps.

blanket, you will get nothing for that day. There is no other privacy possible in a campoodie. All the processes of life are carried on out of doors or behind the thin, twig-woven walls of the wickiup, and laughter is the only corrective for behavior. Very early the Indian learns to possess his countenance in impassivity, to cover his head with his blanket. Something to wrap around him is as necessary to the Paiute as to you your closet to pray in.

So in her blanket Seyavi, sometime basket maker, sits by the unlit hearths of her tribe and digests her life, nourishing her spirit against the time of the spirit's need, for she knows in fact quite as much of these matters as you who have a larger hope, though she has none but the certainty that having borne herself courageously to this end she will not be reborn a coyote.[13]

[1903]

---

13. **coyote:** In many Native American myths and tales, the coyote is a complex trickster figure, usually male, who is capable of creating chaos while trying to achieve his purposes.

Edwin Arlington Robinson

[1869-1935]

Edwin Arlington Robinson was born on December 22, 1869, in Head Tide, Maine. He was the third son of Edward Robinson, a prosperous timber merchant, and his wife, Mary Palmer Robinson, a distant descendant of the colonial American poet Anne Bradstreet. The following year, the family moved to Gardiner, Maine — the Tilbury Town of many of Robinson's later poems — where he spent a happy and secure childhood. When he was about eleven, Robinson joined a group of local poets, and after his graduation from Gardiner High School in 1889 he spent a year writing poetry and studying the work of the classical Roman poet Horace and the English poet John Milton. Robinson later recalled that by the time he was twenty he felt "doomed, or elected, or sentenced for life, to the writing of poetry." In 1891, he enrolled at Harvard, where Robinson published a

E. A. Robinson

By the time Lilla Cabot Perry painted this portrait in 1916, Robinson had finally established himself as one of the foremost poets in the United States.

few poems in the *Harvard Advocate*, but his education was interrupted when his father died in 1892. After the Panic of 1893, the worst economic crisis the country had yet experienced, his family's financial difficulties forced Robinson to leave Harvard for good and return home to Gardiner.

Robinson spent much of his time there working on short stories and writing poetry, his enduring literary love. At the end of one of his first published poems, "Sonnet," which appeared in the *Critic* in 1894, Robinson posed a question that revealed his aspiration to become the poet, "the beacon bright," whose work would illuminate and give meaning to the gray and poetically barren age in the United States: "Shall not one bard arise / To wrench one banner from the western skies, / And mark it with his fame for evermore?" Robinson gathered "Sonnet" together with some of his other early poems and sought a publisher for a manuscript he called *The Tavern and the Night Before*. When it was rejected, he retitled the slim volume *The Torrent and the Night Before*, which he privately printed with the financial help of an uncle in 1896. Robinson sent copies to friends, critics he thought might review the book, and writers he admired, including Edward Eggleston, the author of the popular novel *The Hoosier Schoolmaster* (1871). Robinson was thrilled when Eggleston replied, "You have given me a rare sensation: you have sent me a book that I can read, and for that I thank you. I am a very busy man, but you have sent me a book I cannot help reading and for that I forgive you." Although the volume did not attract much critical attention, Robinson was sufficiently encouraged to pay the printing costs of a second collection of his poems, *The Children of the Night* (1897).

After the death of his mother, Robinson felt that he needed a change of scene and moved to New York City, where he had a few acquaintances from his years at Harvard. He initially lived on the small income from his mother's estate, but the financial reverses that continued to plague his family soon dried up that source of money, and Robinson supported himself through a string of odd jobs and with some help from friends. In 1905, he received a major break when President Theodore Roosevelt read and admired *The Children of the Night*. Roosevelt, who wrote an enthusiastic review of the volume, arranged a job for Robinson in the New York Custom House. With virtually no duties beyond spending a few hours a day at the office, he could devote himself to poetry, and when Roosevelt left office Robinson quit the job in order to write full time. After he published *The Town Down the River* (1909), a Boston newspaper called him "America's Foremost Poet." Despite his use of traditional poetic forms, his reputation was advanced by proponents of the "new" verse like Harriet Munroe, who published his poem "Eros Turannos" in her magazine *Poetry*, and experimental poets like Amy Lowell, who observed that Robinson's collection *The Man against the Sky* (1916) was "dynamic with experience and knowledge of life." The popularity of Robert Frost's early poetry also helped generate a growing audience for Robinson's explorations of rural life in New England. In his next volume of poetry, however, he turned from the characters and settings of Tilbury Town to the medieval past in a long narrative poem based on the legends of King Arthur, *Merlin* (1917).

[Robinson] understood loneliness in all its many forms and deities and was thus less interested in its conventional poetic aspects than he was in the loneliness of the man in the crowd.

—James Dickey

Robinson's final years were filled with honors. His work was often embraced by those who were hostile to more radical departures in poetry and the arts. In a review of his collection *The Three Taverns* (1920), for example, a critic approvingly described it as a volume that makes "no compromise with vers libre, imagism, polyphonic prose and so on." Robinson subsequently received three Pulitzer Prizes, for his *Collected Poems* (1921), *The Man Who Died Twice* (1924), and his best-selling *Tristram* (1927), another long narrative poem based on Arthurian legends. At the time of his death in New York on April 6, 1935, Robinson had not only achieved his dream of becoming a leading American poet, he was also among the first to earn a living by writing poetry in the United States.

bedfordstmartins.com/ americanlit *for research links on Robinson*

Robinson's Poetry.   As his reputation grew, Robinson published some of his poems in prominent periodicals such as the *Nation,* the *New Republic, Poetry,* and *Scribner's Magazine.* But most of his poetry first appeared in books, one of which had the unique distinction of being reviewed by a sitting president of the United States. Theodore Roosevelt so admired Robinson's second book of poetry, *The Children of the Night* (1897), that he wrote a review of the volume for *Outlook* in 1905. Bemoaning the current public taste in poetry, Roosevelt praised Robinson's "curious simplicity and good taste." Although the president admitted that he did not entirely understand "Luke Havergal," he declared: "I am entirely sure that I like it." Roosevelt also admired "Richard Cory," which he said "illustrates a very ancient but very profound philosophy of life with a curiously local touch."

That "local touch" was characteristic of the best poems Robinson wrote throughout his career, represented by the following selection of poems published between 1894 and 1920. Just as he frequently evoked the distant past, Robinson favored traditional poetic forms, especially the sonnet, and his poems generally follow conventional (though often highly complex) metrical patterns and rhyme schemes. At the same time, Robinson employed a plain, vernacular language in his often stark explorations of life and characters in his fictional Tilbury Town. Indeed, as his early poem "Zola" suggests, Robinson's work was influenced by the realism and emerging naturalism of much of the American fiction written around the turn of the century. Certainly, he avoided the romanticism and sentimentality characteristic of so much popular poetry of the period. While some readers consequently found his tone too despairing, others have emphasized Robinson's pervasive and complex use of irony. "We don't despair — not quite — and neither does Robinson," the poet Archibald MacLeish observed. "But we don't hope either, as we used to, and Robinson, with no bitterness, has put hope by as well. His is the after voice, the evening voice, and we neither accept it nor reject it but we know the thing it means." The texts of the following poems are taken from the *Collected Poems of Edwin Arlington Robinson* (1921).

THE HOUSE ON THE HILL[1]

They are all gone away,
    The House is shut and still,
There is nothing more to say.

Through broken walls and gray
    The winds blow bleak and shrill: 5
They are all gone away.

Nor is there one to-day
    To speak them good or ill:
There is nothing more to say.

Why is it then we stray   10
    Around the sunken sill?
They are all gone away,

And our poor fancy-play
    For them is wasted skill:
There is nothing more to say.   15

There is ruin and decay
    In the House on the Hill:
They are all gone away,
There is nothing more to say.

[1894, 1921]

---

1. **"The House on the Hill"**: This nineteen-line poem is a villanelle, a complex form composed of five triplets (a three-line stanza rhymed *aba*) and a concluding quatrain (a four-line stanza rhymed *abab*). The form employs only two rhymes, and alternating stanzas end with the same last line. An earlier version of the poem appeared in a magazine in 1894, but Robinson revised it for his first collection of poetry, *The Torrent and the Night Before* (1896).

LUKE HAVERGAL

Go to the western gate, Luke Havergal,
There where the vines cling crimson on the wall,
And in the twilight wait for what will come.
The leaves will whisper there of her, and some,
Like flying words, will strike you as they fall;   5
But go, and if you listen she will call.
Go to the western gate, Luke Havergal —
Luke Havergal.

No, there is not a dawn in eastern skies
To rift the fiery night that's in your eyes;   10
But there, where western glooms are gathering,
The dark will end the dark, if anything:

God slays Himself with every leaf that flies,
And hell is more than half of paradise.
No, there is not a dawn in eastern skies —   15
In eastern skies.

Out of a grave I come to tell you this,
Out of a grave I come to quench the kiss
That flames upon your forehead with a glow
That blinds you to the way that you must go.   20
Yes, there is yet one way to where she is,
Bitter, but one that faith may never miss.
Out of a grave I come to tell you this —
To tell you this.

There is the western gate, Luke Havergal,   25
There are the crimson leaves upon the wall.
Go, for the winds are tearing them away, —
Nor think to riddle the dead words they say,
Nor any more to feel them as they fall;
But go, and if you trust her she will call.   30
There is the western gate, Luke Havergal —
Luke Havergal.

                                        [1896, 1921]

ZOLA[1]

Because he puts the compromising chart
Of hell before your eyes, you are afraid;
Because he counts the price that you have paid
For innocence, and counts it from the start,
You loathe him. But he sees the human heart   5
Of God meanwhile, and in His hand was weighed
Your squeamish and emasculate crusade
Against the grim dominion of his art.

Never until we conquer the uncouth
Connivings of our shamed indifference   10
(We call it Christian faith) are we to scan
The racked and shrieking hideousness of Truth
To find, in hate's polluted self-defence
Throbbing, the pulse, the divine heart of man.

                                        [1896, 1921]

---

1. "**Zola**": Émile Zola (1840–1902), the French novelist and critic whose "naturalism," a theory that emphasizes the role of heredity and environment in determining character, strongly influenced a number of American writers, especially novelists.

RICHARD CORY

Whenever Richard Cory went down town,
We people on the pavement looked at him:
He was a gentleman from sole to crown,
Clean favored, and imperially slim.

And he was always quietly arrayed,   5
And he was always human when he talked;
But still he fluttered pulses when he said,
"Good-morning," and he glittered when he walked.

And he was rich — yes, richer than a king —
And admirably schooled in every grace: 10
In fine, we thought that he was everything
To make us wish that we were in his place.

So on we worked, and waited for the light,
And went without the meat, and cursed the bread;
And Richard Cory, one calm summer night,   15
Went home and put a bullet through his head.

                                                        [1897, 1921]

MINIVER CHEEVY

Miniver Cheevy, child of scorn,
    Grew lean while he assailed the seasons;
He wept that he was ever born,
    And he had reasons.

Miniver loved the days of old   5
    When swords were bright and steeds were prancing;
The vision of a warrior bold
    Would set him dancing.

Miniver sighed for what was not,
    And dreamed, and rested from his labors;   10
He dreamed of Thebes and Camelot,
    And Priam's neighbors.[1]

---

1. **He dreamed . . . Priam's neighbors:** Thebes, an ancient city that figures in many Greek myths, was destroyed by Alexander the Great in 336 BCE. Camelot was the home of King Arthur, the legendary king of medieval England. Priam was the king of Troy, whose "neighbors" included Aeneas, Achilles, and other heroic figures of the Trojan War as described in Homer's epic poem the *Iliad*.

Miniver mourned the ripe renown
    That made so many a name so fragrant;
He mourned Romance, now on the town,   15
    And Art, a vagrant.

Miniver loved the Medici,[2]
    Albeit he had never seen one;
He would have sinned incessantly
    Could he have been one.   20

Miniver cursed the commonplace
    And eyed a khaki suit with loathing;
He missed the mediaeval grace
    Of iron clothing.

Miniver scorned the gold he sought,   25
    But sore annoyed was he without it;
Miniver thought, and thought, and thought,
    And thought about it.

Miniver Cheevy, born too late,
    Scratched his head and kept on thinking;   30
Miniver coughed, and called it fate,
    And kept on drinking.

                                      [1907, 1921]

---

2. **the Medici:** The powerful family that ruled Florence for much of the fifteenth century, during the Italian Renaissance.

EROS TURANNOS[1]

She fears him, and will always ask
    What fated her to choose him;
She meets in his engaging mask
    All reasons to refuse him;
But what she meets and what she fears   5
Are less than are the downward years,
Drawn slowly to the foamless weirs
    Of age, were she to lose him.

Between a blurred sagacity
    That once had power to sound him,   10

---

1. **"Eros Turannos":** Literally, "love, the absolute sovereign" (Greek).

And Love, that will not let him be
   The Judas that she found him,
Her pride assuages her almost,
As if it were alone the cost —
He sees that he will not be lost,   15
   And waits and looks around him.

A sense of ocean and old trees
   Envelops and allures him;
Tradition, touching all he sees,
   Beguiles and reassures him;   20
And all her doubts of what he says
Are dimmed with what she knows of days —
Till even prejudice delays
   And fades, and she secures him.

The falling leaf inaugurates   25
   The reign of her confusion;
The pounding wave reverberates
   The dirge of her illusion;
And home, where passion lived and died,
Becomes a place where she can hide,   30
While all the town and harbor side
   Vibrate with her seclusion.

We tell you, tapping on our brows,
   The story as it should be, —
As if the story of a house   35
   Were told, or ever could be;
We'll have no kindly veil between
Her visions and those we have seen, —
As if we guessed what hers have been,
   Or what they are or would be.   40

Meanwhile we do no harm; for they
   That with a god have striven,
Not hearing much of what we say,
   Take what the god has given;
Though like waves breaking it may be,   45
Or like a changed familiar tree,
Or like a stairway to the sea
   Where down the blind are driven.

                                [1914, 1921]

THE MILL

The miller's wife had waited long,
    The tea was cold, the fire was dead;
And there might yet be nothing wrong
    In how he went and what he said:
"There are no millers any more,"   5
    Was all that she had heard him say;
And he had lingered at the door
    So long that it seemed yesterday.

Sick with a fear that had no form
    She knew that she was there at last;   10
And in the mill there was a warm
    And mealy fragrance of the past.
What else there was would only seem
    To say again what he had meant;
And what was hanging from a beam   15
    Would not have heeded where she went.

And if she thought it followed her,
    She may have reasoned in the dark
That one way of the few there were
    Would hide her and would leave no mark: 20
Black water, smooth above the weir
    Like starry velvet in the night,
Though ruffled once, would soon appear
    The same as ever to the sight.

                [1919, 1921]

MR. FLOOD'S PARTY

Old Eben Flood, climbing alone one night
Over the hill between the town below
And the forsaken upland hermitage
That held as much as he should ever know
On earth again of home, paused warily.   5
The road was his with not a native near;
And Eben, having leisure, said aloud,
For no man else in Tilbury Town to hear:

"Well, Mr. Flood, we have the harvest moon
Again, and we may not have many more;   10
The bird is on the wing, the poet says,[1]
And you and I have said it here before.
Drink to the bird." He raised up to the light
The jug that he had gone so far to fill,
And answered huskily: "Well, Mr. Flood,   15
Since you propose it, I believe I will."

Alone, as if enduring to the end
A valiant armor of scarred hopes outworn,
He stood there in the middle of the road
Like Roland's ghost winding a silent horn.[2]   20
Below him, in the town among the trees,
Where friends of other days had honored him,
A phantom salutation of the dead
Rang thinly till old Eben's eyes were dim.

Then, as a mother lays her sleeping child   25
Down tenderly, fearing it may awake,
He set the jug down slowly at his feet
With trembling care, knowing that most things break;
And only when assured that on firm earth
It stood, as the uncertain lives of men   30
Assuredly did not, he paced away,
And with his hand extended paused again:

"Well, Mr. Flood, we have not met like this
In a long time; and many a change has come
To both of us, I fear, since last it was   35
We had a drop together. Welcome home!"
Convivially returning with himself,
Again he raised the jug up to the light;
And with an acquiescent quaver said:
"Well, Mr. Flood, if you insist, I might.   40

---

1. **The bird . . . the poet says**: An allusion to a famous verse in Edward Fitzgerald's popular translation of a collection of ancient Persian poems, *The Rubiat of Omar Khayyam* (1859): "Come, fill the Cup, and in the Fire of Spring / The Winter Garment of Repentance fling: / The Bird of Time has but a little way / To fly — and Lo! the Bird is on the Wing."
2. **Like Roland's . . . horn**: The heroic death in battle of Roland, the most famous of the knights of Charlemagne, king of the Franks (742-814), was immortalized in the medieval French romance *The Song of Roland* (c. 1050). Left in command of the rear guard, Roland and his small band are attacked by an army of Saracens. When all of his men have been killed and he is badly wounded, Roland sounds his enchanted horn. Hearing the sound from miles away, Charlemagne returns to find Roland dead and the enemy in flight.

"Only a very little, Mr. Flood —
For auld lang syne. No more, sir; that will do."
So, for the time, apparently it did,
And Eben evidently thought so too;
For soon amid the silver loneliness   45
Of night, he lifted up his voice and sang,
Secure, with only two moons listening,
Until the whole harmonious landscape rang —

"For auld lang syne." The weary throat gave out,
The last word wavered; and the song being done,   50
He raised again the jug regretfully
And shook his head, and was again alone.
There was not much that was ahead of him,
And there was nothing in the town below —
Where strangers would have shut the many doors   55
That many friends had opened long ago.

                                            [1920, 1921]

Frank Norris

[1870-1902]

Benjamin Franklin ("Frank") Norris Jr. was born in Chicago on March 7, 1870, the eldest child of a successful wholesale jeweler and his wife, Gertrude G. Doggett Norris, a former Shakespearean actor. The wealthy family enjoyed a lavish lifestyle that included European travel and a prestigious private school for Norris. When the family moved to northern California in 1884, Norris attended another private school and, following his mother's artistic bent, studied drawing and painting at the San Francisco Art Association. In 1887, Norris went to Paris to continue his art studies. While there, he developed a strong interest in medieval culture, leading him to begin writing chivalric tales and a romantic novel, "Robert d'Artois." After being called home by his father, who was becoming frustrated with his son's preoccupation with writing rather than the painting lessons for which he was paying, Norris published his first article, "Clothes of Steel," about medieval armor, in the *San Francisco Chronicle* on March 31, 1889. Apparently at loose ends, and still uncertain about his future, Norris enrolled at the University of California, Berkeley, in the fall of 1890.

He soon discovered his vocation. During his sophomore year, Norris unsuccessfully petitioned the university to waive its standard course requirements for a degree, since he had already determined to become a professional writer. As evidence, Norris cited his ambitious poem *Yvernelle: A*

Youth makes a savage realist, for youth has boundless hope and exultation in itself.
                    –Hamlin Garland

Frank Norris

The noted photographer Arnold Genthe took this portrait in the 1890s, while Norris was writing and working as a journalist in San Francisco.

Legend of Feudal France, published in December 1891. He was soon regularly publishing poems and stories in the University of California *Occident,* as well as in literary magazines, including the *Overland Monthly.* In his junior year, he was introduced to the work of the French novelist Émile Zola, whose naturalism helped Norris move away from the medieval scenes of his early work to stories exploring lower- and middle-class life in the United States. After his parents divorced in 1894, Norris left the university without a degree and moved with his mother and brother to Massachusetts. Enrolling as a special student of French and English at Harvard University, Norris took a two-semester course in writing in which he began to develop material for several novels, notably *McTeague,* the sordid story of the rise and dramatic fall of a dentist in San Francisco. Impatient with taking classes, however, and finding that Harvard was also unwilling to waive requirements for a degree, Norris left college for good in 1895.

For the next five years, he pursued a dual career as a journalist and novelist. Arranging to write travel articles for several periodicals, Norris went to South Africa, where he was soon caught up in the early stages of the Boer War. Captured and held prisoner by the Boers, Norris was eventually expelled from the country and returned to the United States in 1896. He then became a reporter and editorial assistant for the San Francisco magazine the *Wave,* in which Norris published numerous reviews, sketches, and stories. Completing *McTeague* in the fall of 1897, Norris sought to pave the way for the publication of the sensational, naturalistic work by writing a novel more tailored to the public taste, *Moran of the Lady Letty.* The serialization of that sea romance in the *Wave* landed him a job with *McClure's Magazine* in New York City. As he had hoped, the success of *Moran,* which was published in book form by Doubleday & McClure in the fall of 1898, also persuaded the firm to publish *McTeague: A Story of San Francisco* (1899). Emphasizing the "Zolaesque lines" of the novel, William Dean Howells objected that Norris's "true picture of life is not true, because it leaves beauty out. Life is squalid and cruel and vile and hateful but it is noble and tender and pure and lovely, too." Nonetheless, Howells lauded the "remarkable book," which he cited as a compelling illustration of the "expansion" of American fiction into areas of life that had previously been off limits. Buoyed by the reception of *McTeague,* Norris soon completed a far more optimistic novel, *Blix* (1899), a love story based on his courtship of Janette Black, whom he married in 1900.

Norris devoted most of the remainder of his brief life and literary career to a single ambitious project, a trilogy about corruption in the vast system of production, distribution, and consumption of wheat, the major staple crop of the United States. In the first novel of the trilogy, Norris dramatizes the struggle between the wheat ranchers in California and the railroad monopoly, figured in the title *The Octopus* (1901). In the second novel, *The Pit,* Norris explores the ways in which speculation in the Chicago Board of Trade affects the price of wheat produced by the farmers of the Midwest. Before he could publish *The Pit* or complete the third novel, *The Wolf,* in which he intended to follow the story of American wheat to lucrative overseas markets during a famine in a country in Europe, Norris died of peritonitis, the result of a ruptured appendix, on October 25, 1902. In a letter written to his wife the day before he died, Norris asked her to make sure *The Pit* was published, concluding: "I am hoping my stories will encourage the public to go against big business, such as the railroad monopolies, and get fair treatment and not be abused." *The Pit* was published posthumously in 1903.

bedfordstmartins.com/ americanlit for research links on Norris

Norris's "A Deal in Wheat."   Shortly after Norris's death, a reviewer for the *Book News Monthly* wrote that "Mr. Norris was a man who did not believe in writing on a subject until he had made himself familiar with every detail." "A Deal in Wheat" reflects the extensive research Norris did for what he described as his "Epic of Wheat." As in the second novel of that projected trilogy, *The Pit*, Norris in "A Deal in Wheat" focuses on the ways in which speculators manipulate the commodities market at the expense of both farmers and consumers. Appropriately, Norris's story about the corrupt business practices and economic forces that shape the lives of common people was first published in a periodical committed to social justice, *Everybody's Magazine*. Founded in 1896, the illustrated monthly developed a reputation for its investigative (what its critics called "muckraking") journalism, as well as for publishing fiction by a variety of American writers, including Mary E. Wilkins Freeman and Willa Cather. Norris's story was included in his posthumously published collection *A Deal in Wheat and Other Stories of the New and Old West* (1903). The text and an accompanying illustration are taken from the first printing in *Everybody's Magazine*, August 1902.

A DEAL IN WHEAT

I. The Bear[1] — Wheat at Sixty-two

As Sam Lewiston backed the horse into the shafts of his buckboard and began hitching the tugs to the "whiffletree,"[2] his wife came out from the kitchen door of the house and drew near, and stood for some time at the horse's head, her arms folded and her apron rolled around them. For a long moment neither spoke. They had talked over the situation so long and so comprehensively the night before that there seemed to be nothing more to say.

The time was late in the summer, the place a ranch in southwestern Kansas, and Lewiston and his wife were two of a vast population of farmers, wheat growers, who at

---

1. **The Bear:** In the stock market, a "bear" is a speculator who profits from a "bear" market, one in which the prices of stocks or commodities are falling; a "bull" is one who profits from a "bull" market, one in which the prices are rising.
2. **hitching the tugs to the "whiffletree":** Fastening the harness lines, or "tugs," to a pivoted bar by which the wagon is drawn by the horse.

that moment were passing through a crisis – a crisis that at any moment might culminate in tragedy. Wheat was down to sixty-six.

At length Emma Lewiston spoke.

"Well," she hazarded, looking vaguely out across the ranch towards the horizon, leagues distant; "well, Sam, there's always that offer of brother Joe's. We can quit – and go to Chicago if the worst comes."

"And give up!" exclaimed Lewiston, running the lines through the torrets.[3] "Leave the ranch! Give up! After all these years!"

His wife made no reply for the moment. Lewiston climbed into the buckboard and gathered up the lines. "Well, here goes for the last try, Emmie," he said. "Good-bye, girl. Maybe things will look better in town to-day."

"Maybe," she said gravely. She kissed her husband good-bye and stood for some time looking after the buckboard travelling towards the town in a moving pillar of dust. "I don't know," she murmured at length; "I don't know just how we're going to make out."

When he reached town, Lewiston tied the horse to the iron railing in front of the Odd Fellows' Hall, the ground floor of which was occupied by the post office, and went across the street and up the stairway of a building of brick and granite – quite the most pretentious structure of the town – and knocked at a door upon the first landing. The door was furnished with a pane of frosted glass, on which, in gold letters, was inscribed: "Bridges & Co., Grain Dealers."

Bridges himself, a middle-aged man who wore a velvet skull-cap and who was smoking a Pittsburg stogie, met the farmer at the counter and the two exchanged perfunctory greetings.

"Well," said Lewiston, tentatively, after a while.

"Well, Lewiston," said the other, "I can't take that wheat of yours at any better than sixty-two."

"Sixty-*two*."

"It's the Chicago price[4] that does it, Lewiston. Truslow is bearing the stuff for all he's worth. It's Truslow and the bear clique that stick the knife into us. The price broke again this morning. We've just got a wire."

"Good heavens," murmured Lewiston, looking vaguely from side to side. "That – that ruins me. I *can't* carry my grain any longer – what with storage charges and – and – Bridges, I don't see just how I'm going to make out. Sixty-two cents a bushel! Why, man, what with this and with that it's cost me nearly a dollar a bushel to raise that wheat, and now Truslow —"

He turned way abruptly with a quick gesture of infinite discouragement.

He went down the stairs, and making his way to where his buckboard was hitched, got in, and, with eyes vacant, the reins slipping and sliding in his limp, half-open hands, drove slowly back to the ranch. His wife had seen him coming, and met him as he drew up before the barn.

---

3. **torrets:** Rings through which the harness lines are run.
4. **Chicago price:** The selling price of a commodity at the Chicago Board of Trade.

"Well?" she demanded.

"Emmie," he said as he got out of the buckboard, laying his arm across her shoulder; "Emmie, I guess we'll take up with Joe's offer. We'll go to Chicago. We're cleaned out!"

II. The Bull[5] — Wheat at a Dollar-ten

. . . —— and said Party of the Second Part further covenants and agrees to merchandize such wheat in foreign ports, it being understood and agreed between the Party of the First Part and the Party of the Second Part that the wheat hereinbefore mentioned is released and sold to the Party of the Second Part for export purposes only, and not for consumption or distribution within the boundaries of the United States of America or of Canada.

"Now, Mr. Gates, if you sign for Mr. Truslow I guess that'll be all," remarked Hornung when he had finished reading.

Hornung affixed his signature to the two documents and passed them over to Gates, who signed for his principal and client, Truslow — or, as he had been called ever since he had gone into the fight against Hornung's corner — the Great Bear. Hornung's secretary was called in and witnessed the signatures, and Gates thrust the contract into his Gladstone bag[6] and stood up, smoothing his hat.

"You will deliver the warehouse receipts for the grain," — began Gates.

"I'll send a messenger to Truslow's office before noon," interrupted Hornung. "You can pay by certified check through the Illinois Trust people."

When the other had taken himself off, Hornung sat for some moments gazing abstractedly toward his office windows, thinking over the whole matter. He had just agreed to release to Truslow, at the rate of one dollar and ten cents per bushel, one hundred thousand out of the two million and odd bushels of wheat that he, Hornung, controlled, or actually owned. And for the moment he was wondering if, after all, he had done wisely in not goring the Great Bear to actual financial death. He had made him pay one hundred thousand dollars. Truslow was good for this amount. Would it not have been better to have put a prohibitive figure on the grain and forced the Bear into bankruptcy? True, Hornung would then be without his enemy's money, but Truslow would have been eliminated from the situation, and that — so Hornung told himself — was always a consummation most devoutly, strenuously and diligently to be striven for. Truslow once dead was dead, but the Bear was never more dangerous than when desperate.

"But so long as he can't get *wheat*," muttered Hornung at the end of his reflections, "he can't hurt me. And he can't get it. That I *know*."

For Hornung controlled the situation. So far back as the February of that year an "unknown bull" had been making his presence felt on the floor of the Board of Trade. By the middle of March the commercial reports of the daily press had begun to speak of

---

5. **The Bull:** See note 1.

6. **Gladstone bag:** A light piece of luggage, resembling an oversized briefcase with two hinged compartments, named for the English statesman William Gladstone (1809-1898).

"the powerful bull clique"; a few weeks later that legendary condition of affairs implied and epitomized in the magic words "Dollar Wheat" had been attained, and by the first of April, when the price had been boosted to one dollar and ten cents a bushel, Hornung had disclosed his hand, and in place of mere rumors, the definite and authoritative news that May wheat had been cornered in the Chicago pit[7] went flashing around the world from Liverpool to Odessa and from Duluth to Buenos Ayres.

It was – so the veteran operators were persuaded – Truslow himself who had made Hornung's corner possible. The Great Bear had for once over-reached himself, and believing himself all-powerful, had hammered the price just the fatal fraction too far down. Wheat had gone to sixty-two – for the time, and, under the circumstances, an abnormal price. When the reaction came it was tremendous. Hornung saw his chance, seized it, and in a few months had turned the tables, had cornered the product, and virtually driven the bear clique out of the pit.

On the same day that the delivery of the hundred thousand bushels was made to Truslow, Hornung met his broker at his lunch club.

"Well," said the latter, "I see you let go that line of stuff to Truslow."

Hornung nodded; but the broker added:

"Remember, I was against it from the very beginning. I know we've cleared up over a hundred thou'. I would have fifty times preferred to have lost twice that and *smashed Truslow dead.* Bet you what you like he makes us pay for it somehow."

"Huh!" grunted his principal. "How about insurance, and warehouse charges, and carrying expenses on that lot? Guess we'd have had to pay those too if we'd held on."

But the other put up his chin, unwilling to be persuaded. "I won't sleep easy," he declared, "till Truslow is busted."

III. The Pit

Just as Going mounted the steps on the edge of the pit the great gong struck, a roar of a hundred voices developed with the swiftness of successive explosions, the rush of a hundred men surging downward to the centre of the pit filled the air with the stamp and grind of feet, a hundred hands in eager strenuous gestures tossed upward from out the brown of the crowd, the official reporter in his cage on the margin of the pit leaned far forward with straining ear to catch the opening bid, and another day of battle was begun.

Since the sale of the hundred thousand bushels of wheat to Truslow, the "Hornung crowd" had steadily shouldered the price higher, until on this particular morning it stood at one dollar and a half. That was Hornung's price. No one else had any grain to sell.

---

7. **cornered in the Chicago pit:** A market is "cornered" when a speculator owns enough of a commodity to control its price in the "pit," the name of the area in which commodities are bought and sold at the Chicago Board of Trade.

But not ten minutes after the opening, Going was surprised out of all countenance to hear shouted from the other side of the pit these words:

"Sell May at one-fifty."

Going was for the moment touching elbows with Kimbark on one side and with Merriam on the other, all three belonging to the "Hornung crowd." Their answering challenge of *"Sold"* was the voice of one man. They did not pause to reflect upon the strangeness of the circumstance. (That was for afterwards.) Their response to the offer was as unconscious as reflex action and almost as rapid, and before the pit was well aware of what had happened the transaction of one thousand bushels was down upon Going's trading-card, and fifteen hundred dollars had changed hands. But here was a marvel — the whole available supply of wheat cornered, Hornung master of the situation, invincible, unassailable; yet behold a man willing to sell, a Bear bold enough to raise his head.

"That was Kennedy, wasn't it, who made that offer?" asked Kimbark, as Going noted down the trade — "Kennedy, that new man?"

"Yes; who do you suppose he's selling for; who's willing to go short at this stage of the game?"

"Maybe he ain't short."

"Short! Great heavens, man, where'd he get the stuff?"

"Blamed if I know. We can account for every handful of May. Steady-oh, there he goes again."

"Sell a thousand May at one-fifty," vociferated the bear broker, throwing out his hand, one finger raised to indicate the number of "contracts" of-fered. This time it was evident that he was attacking the Hornung crowd deliberately, for, ignoring the jam of traders that swept towards him, he looked across the pit to where Going and Kimbark were shouting *"Sold, sold,"* and nodded his head.

A second time Going made mem-oranda of the trade, and either the Hornung holdings were increased by two thousand bushels of May wheat, or the Hornung bank account swelled by at least three thousand dollars of some unknown short's money.

Of late — so sure was the bull crowd of its position — no one had even

"'SELL A THOUSAND MAY AT ONE-FIFTY,' VOCIFERATED THE BEAR BROKER."

thought of glancing at the inspection sheet on the bulletin board. But now one of Going's messengers hurried up to him with the announcement that this sheet showed receipts at Chicago for that morning of twenty-five thousand bushels, and not credited to Hornung. Some one had got hold of a line of wheat overlooked by the "clique," and was dumping it upon them.

"Wire the Chief," said Going over his shoulder to Merriam. This one struggled out of the crowd, and on a telegraph blank scribbled:

> Strong bear movement – New man – Kennedy – Selling in lots of five contracts – Chicago receipts twenty-five thousand.

The message was despatched, and in a few moments the answer came back, laconic, of military terseness:

> Support the market.

And Going obeyed, Merriam and Kimbark following, the new broker fairly throwing the wheat at them in thousand-bushel lots.

"Sell May at 'fifty; sell May; sell May." A moment's indecision, an instant's hesitation, the first faint suggestion of weakness, and the market would have broken under them. But for the better part of four hours they stood their ground, taking all that was offered, in constant communication with the Chief, and from time to time stimulated and steadied by his brief, unvarying command:

"Support the market."

At the close of the session they had bought in the twenty-five thousand bushels of May. Hornung's position was as stable as a rock, and the price closed even with the opening figure – one dollar and a half.

But the morning's work was the talk of all La Salle Street.[8] Who was back of the raid? What was the meaning of this unexpected selling? For weeks the pit-trading had been merely nominal. Truslow, the Great Bear, from whom the most serious attack might have been expected, had gone to his country seat at Geneva Lake, in Wisconsin, declaring himself to be out of the market entirely. He went bass fishing every day.

IV. The Belt Line

On a certain day towards the middle of the month, at a time when the mysterious Bear had unloaded some eighty thousand bushels upon Hornung, a conference was held in the library of Hornung's home. His broker attended it, and also a clean-faced, bright-eyed individual whose name of Cyrus Ryder might have been found upon the pay roll of a rather well-known detective agency. For upwards of half an hour after the conference began, the detective spoke, the other two listening attentively, gravely.

"Then, last of all," concluded Ryder, "I made out I was a hobo, and began stealing rides on the Belt Line Railroad. Know the road? It just circles Chicago. Truslow owns it.

---

8. **La Salle Street:** The location of the Chicago Board of Trade.

Yes? Well, then I began to catch on. I noticed that cars of certain numbers – thirty-three ought thirty-four, thirty-two one ninety – well, the numbers don't matter, but anyhow these cars were always switched onto the sidings by Mr. Truslow's main elevator D soon as they came in. The wheat was shunted in, and they were pulled out again. Well, I spotted one car and stole a ride on her. Say, look here, *that car went right around the city on the Belt, and came back to D again, and the same wheat in her all the time.* The grain was re-inspected – it was raw, I tell you – and the warehouse receipts made out just as though the stuff had come in from Kansas or Iowa."

"The same wheat all the time!" interposed Hornung.

"The same wheat – your wheat, that you sold to Truslow."

"Great snakes!" ejaculated Hornung's broker. "Truslow never took it abroad at all."

"Took it abroad! Say, he's just been running it around Chicago, like the supers in 'Shenandoah,'[9] round an' round, so you'd think it was a new lot, an' selling it back to you again."

"No wonder we couldn't account for so much wheat."

"Bought it from us at $1.10, and made us buy it back – our own wheat – at $1.50."

Hornung and his broker looked at each other in silence for a moment. Then all at once Hornung struck the arm of his chair with his fist and exploded in a roar of laughter. The broker stared for one bewildered moment, then followed his example.

"Sold, sold," shouted Hornung almost gleefully. "Upon my soul it's as good a Gilbert and Sullivan show. And we – Oh, Lord! Billy, shake on it, and hats off to my distinguished friend, Truslow. He'll be president some day. Hey! What? Prosecute him? Not I."

"He's done us out of a neat hatful of dollars for all that," observed the broker, suddenly grave.

"Billy, it's worth the price."

"We've got to make it up somehow."

"Well, tell you what. We were going to boost the price to one seventy-five next week, and make that our settlement figure."

"Can't do it now. Can't afford it."

"No. Here; we'll let out a big link; we'll put wheat at two dollars, and let it go at that."

"Two it is, then," said the broker.

V. The Bread Line

The street was very dark and absolutely deserted. It was a district on the "South Side," not far from the Chicago River, given up largely to wholesale stores, and after nightfall was empty of all life. The echoes slept but lightly hereabouts, and the slightest footfall, the faintest noise, woke them upon the instant and sent them clamoring up and down the length of the pavement between the iron shuttered fronts. The only light

---

9. **like the supers in 'Shenandoah':** That is, like the supernumeraries, or "extras," in performances of Bronson Howard's popular play about the Civil War, *Shenandoah* (1888), in which a small group of men marched in a continuous circle across and behind the stage, giving the illusion of a large army on the march.

visible came from the side door of a certain "Vienna" bakery, where at one o'clock in the morning loaves of bread were given away to any who should ask. Every evening about nine o'clock the outcasts began to gather about the side door. The stragglers came in rapidly, and the line — the "bread line" as it was called — began to form. By midnight it was usually some hundred yards in length, stretching almost the entire length of the block.

Towards ten in the evening, his coat collar turned up against the fine drizzle that pervaded the air, his hands in his pockets, his elbows gripping his sides, Sam Lewiston came up and silently took his place at the end of the line.

Unable to conduct his farm upon a paying basis at the time when Truslow, the "Great Bear," had sent the price of grain down to 62 cents a bushel, Lewiston had turned over his entire property to his creditors, and, leaving Kansas for good, had abandoned farming, and had left his wife at her sister's boarding house in Topeka with the understanding that she was to join him in Chicago so soon as he had found a steady job. Then he had come to Chicago and had turned workman. His brother Joe conducted a small hat factory on Archer Avenue, and for a time he found there a meagre employment. But difficulties had occurred, times were bad, the hat factory was involved in debts, the repealing of a certain import duty on manufactured felt overcrowded the home market with cheap Belgian and French products, and in the end his brother had assigned[10] and gone to Milwaukee.

Thrown out of work, Lewiston drifted aimlessly about Chicago, from pillar to post, working a little, earning here a dollar, there a dime, but always sinking, sinking, till at last the ooze of the lowest bottom dragged at his feet and the rush of the great ebb went over him and engulfed him and shut him out from the light, and a park bench became his home and the "bread-line" his chief makeshift of subsistence.

He stood now in the enfolding drizzle, sodden, stupefied with fatigue. Before and behind stretched the line. There was no talking. There was no sound. The street was empty. It was so still that the passing of a cable car in the adjoining thoroughfare grated like prolonged rolling explosions, beginning and ending at immeasurable distances. The drizzle descended incessantly. After a long time midnight struck.

There was something ominous and gravely impressive in this interminable line of dark figures, close-pressed, soundless; a crowd, yet absolutely still; a close-packed silent file, waiting, waiting in the vast deserted night-ridden street; waiting without a word, without a movement, there under the night and under the slow moving mists of rain.

Few in the crowd were professional beggars. Most of them were workmen, long since out of work, forced into idleness by long-continued "hard times," by ill luck, by sickness. To them the "bread-line" was a God-send. At least they could not starve. Between jobs here in the end was something to hold them up, a small platform, as it were, above the sweep of black water, where for a moment they might pause and take breath before the plunge.

---

10. **assigned:** Turned over his remaining assets to his creditors.

The period of waiting on this night of rain seemed endless to those silent, hungry men; but at length there was a stir. The line moved. The side door opened. Ah, at last. They were going to hand out the bread.

But instead of the usual white-aproned undercook with his crowded hampers there now appeared in the doorway a new man – a young fellow, who looked like a book-keeper's assistant. He bore in his hand a placard, which he tacked to the outside of the door. Then he disappeared within the bakery, locking the door after him.

A shudder of poignant despair, an unformed, inarticulate sense of calamity, seemed to run from end to end of the line. What had happened? Those in the rear, unable to read the placard, surged forward, a sense of bitter disappointment clutching at their hearts.

The line broke up, disintegrated into a shapeless throng – a throng that crowded forward and collected in front of the shut door whereon the placard was affixed. Lewiston, with the others, pushed forward. On the placard he read these words:

> Owing to the fact that the price of grain has been increased to two dollars a bushel, there will be no distribution of bread from this bakery until further notice.

Lewiston turned away, dumb, bewildered. Till morning he walked the streets, going on without purpose, without direction. But now at last his luck had turned. Overnight the wheel of his fortunes had creaked and swung upon its axis, and before noon he had found a job in the street-cleaning brigade. In the course of time he rose to be first shift boss, the deputy-inspector, then inspector, promoted to the dignity of driving in a red wagon with rubber tires and drawing a salary instead of mere wages. The wife was sent for and a new start made.

But Lewiston never forgot. Dimly he began to see the significance of things. Caught once in the cogs and wheels of a great and terrible engine, he had seen – none better – its workings. Of all the men who had vainly stood in the "bread-line" on that rainy night in early summer, he, perhaps, had been the only one who had struggled up to the surface again. How many others had gone down in the great ebb? Grim question; he dared not think how many.

He had seen the two ends of a great wheat operation, a battle between Bear and Bull. The stories (subsequently published in the city's press) of Truslow's counter-move in selling Hornung his own wheat, supplied the unseen section. The farmer – he who raised the wheat – was ruined upon one hand; the workingman – he who consumed it – was ruined upon the other. But between the two, the great operators, who never saw the wheat they traded in, bought and sold the world's food, gambled in the nourishment of entire nations, practised their tricks, their chicanery and oblique shifty "deals," were reconciled in their differences, and went on through their appointed way, jovial, con-tented, enthroned, and unassailable.

[1902]

Stephen Crane

[1871–1900]

Stephen Crane was born on November 1, 1871, in Newark, New Jersey. He was the fourteenth child of the Reverend Dr. Jonathan Townley Crane, a Methodist minister and church official, and his wife, Mary Helen Peck Crane, the daughter of a Methodist minister who was herself deeply involved in church affairs as a journalist and lecturer. The family moved sev-

Stephen Crane

This photograph was taken shortly after Crane's meteoric rise to international literary fame in 1895.

eral times, following the ministerial work of Crane's father, who died in 1880. Three years later, the family settled in Asbury Park, New Jersey. When Crane was about sixteen, he began to work as a copy boy for his older brother's summer news bureau, which supplied articles about the New Jersey shore to the *New-York Tribune.* Crane attended Pennington Seminary before transferring to the Hudson River Institute and Claverack College, a military academy and prep school. Crane published his first signed sketch in the school magazine, the *Vidette,* in February 1890. That fall, he entered Lafayette College as an engineering student but withdrew after his first semester. In January 1891, he enrolled as a special student at Syracuse University. As a writer for the *Philadelphia Press* wryly observed in 1896, "Mr. Crane studied more or less at Lafayette College and Syracuse University, but took no degree. Like several authors not unknown to fame, he appears to have found it hard to stick to the curriculum."

In fact, Crane was already eager to launch his literary career. During his one semester at Syracuse University, where he was a star on the varsity baseball team, he contributed to the student newspaper, worked as a local correspondent for the *New-York Tribune,* and began to write a novel about a slum girl driven to prostitution and suicide, *Maggie: A Girl of the Streets.* In May 1891, after failing most of his courses, Crane left college for good and moved to New York City. Working as a journalist, he endured poverty and deprivation for several years. When he was unable to find a publisher for *Maggie,* Crane paid for the printing of the novel in 1893. In a review, the noted writer Hamlin Garland lauded Crane's "truthful and unhackneyed study of the slums," observing that the novel was "pictorial, graphic, [and] terrible in its directness." The book did not sell, but Crane pressed on, writing articles, stories, and *The Red Badge of Courage,* a novel about the Civil War. Although he was born after the war, Crane had read many of the proliferating accounts of the conflict, including the popular series "The Battles and Leaders of the Civil War," which ran in *Century Magazine* during the 1880s. *The Red Badge of Courage* first appeared as a serial published by the Bacheller Syndicate, which supplied literary materials to more than 700 small newspapers across the country — Willa Cather, then a college senior, read the novel in the pages of the *Nebraska State Journal* in December 1894. Hired by Bacheller as a reporter and travel writer, Crane took an extended tour of the West and Mexico. In addition to the articles and stories he wrote during his travels, Crane also published a collection of his experimental poetry, *The Black Riders and Other Lines* (1895).

The reviews of his poetry were mixed, but the publication of *The Red Badge of Courage* in book form gained Crane international acclaim in 1895. Describing its reception in England, the novelist Joseph Conrad later recalled that the "small volume" detonated "with the impact of a twelve inch shell charged with a very high explosive." In response to the growing demand for his work, Crane in 1896 published a new edition of *Maggie* and a collection of stories, *The Little Regiment and Other Episodes of the Civil War.* He swiftly wrote two novels, one about the humdrum life of a workingman in New York, *George's Mother* (1896), and the other about a young artist, *The Third Violet* (1897). The success of *The Red Badge of Courage* also provided Crane with an opportunity to become a war correspondent. During a voyage from Jacksonville, Florida, to cover the ongoing revolution against Spanish rule in Cuba, Crane narrowly survived a shipwreck that he described in a newspaper account and then in his most famous short story, "The Open Boat." In Jacksonville, Crane met Cora Taylor, whose nightclub, the Hotel de Dream, was reputed to be a house of prostitution. Taylor accompanied Crane to Greece, where he covered the Greco-Turkish war of 1897, and then to England. She remained there, handling his correspondence, when Crane left for Cuba to cover the Spanish-American War of 1898. That year, he published *The Open Boat and Other Tales of Adventure,* as well as some highly regarded dispatches from Cuba. Suffering from malaria, he rejoined Taylor in England, where in 1899 Crane prepared a collection of stories and two other books for publication: his second volume of poetry, *War Is Kind;* and a satirical novel about a war correspondent, *Active Service.* Despite the tubercular hemorrhage he suffered later that year, Crane continued a relentless work schedule, publishing two additional collections of sketches and stories before he died on June 15, 1900, in Germany, where he had gone seeking a cure.

[Crane's] was a costly vision, won through personal suffering, hard living and harsh artistic discipline; and by the time of his death, at twenty-nine, he was recognized as one of the important innovators of American fictional prose and master of a powerful and original style.

–Ralph Ellison

bedfordstmartins.com/ americanlit *for research links on Crane*

Crane's "The Open Boat."   Eagerly accepting an offer to become a war correspondent for a newspaper syndicate, Crane signed on as an "able seaman" aboard the *Commodore,* a steamship smuggling munitions from Jacksonville, Florida, to the *insurrectos* who were rebelling against Spanish rule in Cuba. After the *Commodore* sank on January 2, 1897, Crane and three other survivors spent thirty hours in a ten-foot dinghy before they reached shore at Daytona Beach. His detailed report of the shipwreck, which made national news, was swiftly published as "Stephen Crane's Own Story" in the *New York Press* on January 7, 1897. At the end of the article, after describing his escape from the sinking *Commodore* along with the ship's captain and two members of the crew, Crane observes: "The history of life in an open boat for thirty hours would no doubt be instructive for the young, but none is to be told here and now." He soon offered an account of those "thirty hours" in "The Open Boat." As the poet John Berryman observes in his biography of Crane, "To take 'The Open Boat,' however, as a *report* is to misunderstand the nature of his work: it is an action of his art upon the remembered possibility of death. The death is so close that the story is warm." The artistry of Crane's story of human brotherhood in the face of an indifferent and seemingly hostile nature has been admired by many authors, including Ernest Hemingway, who in a 1935 interview included "The Open Boat" among the works he said every writer should read. The text is taken from the first printing in *Scribner's Magazine*, June 1897.

THE OPEN BOAT

A Tale Intended to Be After the Fact. Being the Experience of Four Men from the Sunk Steamer *Commodore*

I

None of them knew the color of the sky. Their eyes glanced level, and were fastened upon the waves that swept toward them. These waves were of the hue of slate, save for the tops, which were of foaming white, and all of the men knew the colors of the sea. The horizon narrowed and widened, and dipped and rose, and at all times its edge was jagged with waves that seemed thrust up in points like rocks.

Many a man ought to have a bath-tub larger than the boat which here rode upon the sea. These waves were most wrongfully and barbarously abrupt and tall, and each frothtop was a problem in small boat navigation.

The cook squatted in the bottom and looked with both eyes at the six inches of gunwale which separated him from the ocean. His sleeves were rolled over his fat forearms, and the two flaps of his unbuttoned vest dangled as he bent to bail out the boat. Often he said: "Gawd! That was a narrow clip." As he remarked it he invariably gazed eastward over the broken sea.

The oiler,[1] steering with one of the two oars in the boat, sometimes raised himself

---

1. **oiler:** The person who oils machinery in the engine room of a ship.

suddenly to keep clear of water that swirled in over the stern. It was a thin little oar and it seemed often ready to snap.

The correspondent, pulling at the other oar, watched the waves and wondered why he was there.

The injured captain, lying in the bow, was at this time buried in that profound dejection and indifference which comes, temporarily at least, to even the bravest and most enduring when, willy nilly, the firm fails, the army loses, the ship goes down. The mind of the master of a vessel is rooted deep in the timbers of her, though he command for a day or a decade, and this captain had on him the stern impression of a scene in the grays of dawn of seven turned faces, and later a stump of a top-mast with a white ball on it that slashed to and fro at the waves, went low and lower, and down. Thereafter there was something strange in his voice. Although steady, it was deep with mourning, and of a quality beyond oration or tears.

"Keep'er a little more south, Billie," said he.

"'A little more south,' sir," said the oiler in the stern.

A seat in this boat was not unlike a seat upon a bucking broncho, and, by the same token, a broncho is not much smaller. The craft pranced and reared, and plunged like an animal. As each wave came, and she rose for it, she seemed like a horse making at a fence outrageously high. The manner of her scramble over these walls of water is a mystic thing, and, moreover, at the top of them were ordinarily these problems in white water, the foam racing down from the summit of each wave, requiring a new leap, and a leap from the air. Then, after scornfully bumping a crest, she would slide, and race, and splash down a long incline and arrive bobbing and nodding in front of the next menace.

A singular disadvantage of the sea lies in the fact that after successfully surmounting one wave you discover that there is another behind it just as important and just as nervously anxious to do something effective in the way of swamping boats. In a ten-foot dingey one can get an idea of the resources of the sea in the line of waves that is not probable to the average experience, which is never at sea in a dingey. As each slaty wall of water approached, it shut all else from the view of the men in the boat, and it was not difficult to imagine that this particular wave was the final outburst of the ocean, the last effort of the grim water. There was a terrible grace in the move of the waves, and they came in silence, save for the snarling of the crests.

In the wan light, the faces of the men must have been gray. Their eyes must have glinted in strange ways as they gazed steadily astern. Viewed from a balcony, the whole thing would doubtlessly have been weirdly picturesque. But the men in the boat had no time to see it, and if they had had leisure there were other things to occupy their minds. The sun swung steadily up the sky, and they knew it was broad day because the color of the sea changed from slate to emerald-green, streaked with amber lights, and the foam was like tumbling snow. The process of the breaking day was unknown to them. They were aware only of this effect upon the color of the waves that rolled toward them.

In disjointed sentences the cook and the correspondent argued as to the difference between a life-saving station and a house of refuge. The cook had said: "There's a house of refuge just north of the Mosquito Inlet Light, and as soon as they see us, they'll come off in their boat and pick us up."

"As soon as who see us?" said the correspondent.

"The crew," said the cook.

"Houses of refuge don't have crews," said the correspondent. "As I understand them, they are only places where clothes and grub are stored for the benefit of shipwrecked people. They don't carry crews."

"Oh, yes, they do," said the cook.

"No, they don't," said the correspondent.

"Well, we're not there yet, anyhow," said the oiler, in the stern.

"Well," said the cook, "perhaps it's not a house of refuge that I'm thinking of as being near Mosquito Inlet Light. Perhaps it's a life-saving station."

"We're not there yet," said the oiler, in the stern.

II

As the boat bounced from the top of each wave, the wind tore through the hair of the hat-less men, and as the craft plopped her stern down again the spray slashed past them. The crest of each of these waves was a hill, from the top of which the men surveyed, for a moment, a broad tumultuous expanse; shining and wind-riven. It was probably splendid. It was probably glorious, this play of the free sea, wild with lights of emerald and white and amber.

"Bully good thing it's an on-shore wind," said the cook. "If not, where would we be? Wouldn't have a show."

"That's right," said the correspondent.

The busy oiler nodded his assent.

Then the captain, in the bow, chuckled in a way that expressed humor, contempt, tragedy, all in one. "Do you think we've got much of a show, now, boys?" said he.

Whereupon the three were silent, save for a trifle of hemming and hawing. To express any particular optimism at this time they felt to be childish and stupid, but they all doubtless possessed this sense of the situation in their mind. A young man thinks doggedly at such times. On the other hand, the ethics of their condition was decidedly against any open suggestion of hopelessness. So they were silent.

"Oh, well," said the captain, soothing his children, "we'll get ashore all right."

But there was that in his tone which made them think, so the oiler quoth: "Yes! If this wind holds!"

The cook was bailing: "Yes! If we don't catch hell in the surf."

Canton flannel gulls[2] flew near and far. Sometimes they sat down on the sea, near patches of brown sea-weed that rolled over the waves with a movement like carpets on a line in a gale. The birds sat comfortably in groups, and they were envied by some in the

---

2. **Canton flannel gulls:** Canton flannel is a strong, warm cotton fabric, probably used here to suggest the imperviousness of the seagulls to the harsh elements.

dingey, for the wrath of the sea was no more to them than it was to a covey of prairie chickens a thousand miles inland. Often they came very close and stared at the men with black beadlike eyes. At these times they were uncanny and sinister in their unblinking scrutiny, and the men hooted angrily at them, telling them to be gone. One came, and evidently decided to alight on the top of the captain's head. The bird flew parallel to the boat and did not circle, but made short sidelong jumps in the air in chicken-fashion. His black eyes were wistfully fixed upon the captain's head. "Ugly brute," said the oiler to the bird. "You look as if you were made with a jackknife." The cook and the correspondent swore darkly at the creature. The captain naturally wished to knock it away with the end of the heavy painter,[3] but he did not dare do it, because anything resembling an emphatic gesture would have capsized this freighted boat, and so with his open hand, the captain gently and carefully waved the gull away. After it had been discouraged from the pursuit the captain breathed easier on account of his hair, and others breathed easier because the bird struck their minds at this time as being somehow grewsome and ominous.

In the meantime the oiler and the correspondent rowed. And also they rowed.

They sat together in the same seat, and each rowed an oar. Then the oiler took both oars; then the correspondent took both oars; then the oiler; then the correspondent. They rowed and they rowed. The very ticklish part of the business was when the time came for the reclining one in the stern to take his turn at the oars. By the very last star of truth, it is easier to steal eggs from under a hen than it was to change seats in the dingey. First the man in the stern slid his hand along the thwart and moved with care, as if he were of Sèvres.[4] Then the man in the rowing seat slid his hand along the other thwart. It was all done with the most extraordinary care. As the two sidled past each other, the whole party kept watchful eyes on the coming wave, and the captain cried: "Look out now! Steady there!"

The brown mats of sea-weed that appeared from time to time were like islands, bits of earth. They were travelling, apparently, neither one way nor the other. They were, to all intents, stationary. They informed the men in the boat that it was making progress slowly toward the land.

The captain, rearing cautiously in the bow, after the dingey soared on a great swell, said that he had seen the lighthouse at Mosquito Inlet. Presently the cook remarked that he had seen it. The correspondent was at the oars, then, and for some reason he too wished to look at the lighthouse, but his back was toward the far shore and the waves were important, and for some time he could not seize an opportunity to turn his head. But at last there came a wave more gentle than the others, and when at the crest of it he swiftly scoured the western horizon.

"See it?" said the captain.

---

3. **painter:** A rope attached to the bow of a boat for tying it to a dock.
4. **Sèvres:** A delicate, ornately decorated French porcelain made near Paris.

"No," said the correspondent, slowly, "I didn't see anything."

"Look again," said the captain. He pointed. "It's exactly in that direction."

At the top of another wave, the correspondent did as he was bid, and this time his eyes chanced on a small still thing on the edge of the swaying horizon. It was precisely like the point of a pin. It took an anxious eye to find a lighthouse so tiny.

"Think we'll make it, captain?"

"If this wind holds and the boat don't swamp, we can't do much else," said the captain.

The little boat, lifted by each towering sea, and splashed viciously by the crests, made progress that in the absence of sea-weed was not apparent to those in her. She seemed just a wee thing wallowing, miraculously, top-up, at the mercy of five oceans. Occasionally, a great spread of water, like white flames, swarmed into her.

"Bail her, cook," said the captain, serenely.

"All right, captain," said the cheerful cook.

III

It would be difficult to describe the subtle brotherhood of men that was here established on the seas. No one said that it was so. No one mentioned it. But it dwelt in the boat, and each man felt it warm him. They were a captain, an oiler, a cook, and a correspondent, and they were friends, friends in a more curiously iron-bound degree than may be common. The hurt captain, lying against the water-jar in the bow, spoke always in a low voice and calmly, but he could never command a more ready and swiftly obedient crew than the motley three of the dingey. It was more than a mere recognition of what was best for the common safety. There was surely in it a quality that was personal and heart-felt. And after this devotion to the commander of the boat there was this comradeship that the correspondent, for instance, who had been taught to be cynical of men, knew even at the time was the best experience of his life. But no one said that it was so. No one mentioned it.

"I wish we had a sail," remarked the captain. "We might try my overcoat on the end of an oar and give you two boys a chance to rest." So the cook and the correspondent held the mast and spread wide the overcoat. The oiler steered, and the little boat made good way with her new rig. Sometimes the oiler had to scull sharply to keep a sea from breaking into the boat, but otherwise sailing was a success.

Meanwhile the light-house had been growing slowly larger. It had now almost assumed color, and appeared like a little gray shadow on the sky. The man at the oars could not be prevented from turning his head rather often to try for a glimpse of this little gray shadow.

At last, from the top of each wave the men in the tossing boat could see land. Even as the light-house was an upright shadow on the sky, this land seemed but a long black shadow on the sea. It certainly was thinner than paper. "We must be about opposite New Smyrna,"[5] said the cook, who had coasted this shore often in schooners.

---

5. **New Smyrna:** A town on the Florida coast, south of Daytona Beach.

"Captain, by the way, I believe they abandoned that life-saving station there about a year ago."

"Did they?" said the captain.

The wind slowly died away. The cook and the correspondent were not now obliged to slave in order to hold high the oar. But the waves continued their old impetuous swooping at the dingey, and the little craft, no longer under way, struggled woundily over them. The oiler or the correspondent took the oars again.

Shipwrecks are *apropos* of nothing. If men could only train for them and have them occur when the men had reached pink condition, there would be less drowning at sea. Of the four in the dingey none had slept any time worth mentioning for two days and two nights previous to embarking in the dingey, and in the excitement of clambering about the deck of a foundering ship they had also forgotten to eat heartily.

For these reasons, and for others, neither the oiler nor the correspondent was fond of rowing at this time. The correspondent wondered ingenuously how in the name of all that was sane could there be people who thought it amusing to row a boat. It was not an amusement; it was a diabolical punishment, and even a genius of mental aberrations could never conclude that it was anything but a horror to the muscles and a crime against the back. He mentioned to the boat in general how the amusement of rowing struck him, and the weary-faced oiler smiled in full sympathy. Previously to the foundering, by the way, the oiler had worked double-watch in the engine-room of the ship.

"Take her easy, now, boys," said the captain. "Don't spend yourselves. If we have to run a surf you'll need all your strength, because we'll sure have to swim for it. Take your time."

Slowly the land arose from the sea. From a black line it became a line of black and a line of white, trees, and sand. Finally, the captain said that he could make out a house on the shore. "That's the house of refuge, sure," said the cook. "They'll see us before long, and come out after us."

The distant light-house reared high. "The keeper ought to be able to make us out now, if he's looking through a glass," said the captain. "He'll notify the life-saving people."

"None of those other boats could have got ashore to give word of the wreck," said the oiler, in a low voice. "Else the life-boat would be out hunting us."

Slowly and beautifully the land loomed out of the sea. The wind came again. It had veered from the northeast to the southeast. Finally, a new sound struck the ears of the men in the boat. It was the low thunder of the surf on the shore. "We'll never be able to make the light-house now," said the captain. "Swing her head a little more north, Billie," said the captain.

"'A little more north,' sir," said the oiler.

Whereupon the little boat turned her nose once more down the wind, and all but the oarsman watched the shore grow. Under the influence of this expansion doubt and direful apprehension was leaving the minds of the men. The management of the boat was still most absorbing, but it could not prevent a quiet cheerfulness. In an hour perhaps, they would be ashore.

Their back-bones had become thoroughly used to balancing in the boat and they now rode this wild colt of a dingey like circus men. The correspondent thought that he had been drenched to the skin, but happening to feel in the top pocket of his coat, he found therein eight cigars. Four of them were soaked with sea-water; four were perfectly scatheless. After a search, somebody produced three dry matches, and thereupon the four waifs rode in their little boat, and with an assurance of an impending rescue shining in their eyes, puffed at the big cigars and judged well and ill of all men. Everybody took a drink of water.

IV

"Cook," remarked the captain, "there don't seem to be any signs of life about your house of refuge."

"No," replied the cook. "Funny they don't see us!"

A broad stretch of lowly coast lay before the eyes of the men. It was of low dunes topped with dark vegetation. The roar of the surf was plain, and sometimes they could see the white lip of a wave as it spun up the beach. A tiny house was blocked out black upon the sky. Southward, the slim light-house lifted its little gray length.

Tide, wind, and waves were swinging the dingey northward. "Funny they don't see us," said the men.

The surf's roar was here dulled, but its tone was, nevertheless, thunderous and mighty. As the boat swam over the great rollers, the men sat listening to this roar.

"We'll swamp sure," said everybody.

It is fair to say here that there was not a life-saving station within twenty miles in either direction, but the men did not know this fact and in consequence they made dark and opprobrious remarks concerning the eyesight of the nation's life-savers. Four scowling men sat in the dingey and surpassed records in the invention of epithets.

"Funny they don't see us."

The light-heartedness of a former time had completely faded. To their sharpened minds it was easy to conjure pictures of all kinds of incompetency and blindness and, indeed, cowardice. There was the shore of the populous land, and it was bitter and bitter to them that from it came no sign.

"Well," said the captain, ultimately, "I suppose we'll have to make a try ourselves. If we stay out here too long we'll none of us have strength left to swim after the boat swamps."

And so the oiler, who was at the oars, turned the boat straight for the shore. There was a sudden tightening of muscles. There was some thinking.

"If we don't all get ashore —" said the captain. "If we don't all get ashore, I suppose you fellows know where to send news of my finish?"

They then briefly exchanged some addresses and admonitions. As for the reflections of the men, there was a great deal of rage in them. Perchance they might be formulated thus: "If I am going to be drowned — if I am going to be drowned — if I am going to be drowned, why, in the name of the seven mad gods who rule the sea, was I allowed to come thus far and contemplate sand and trees? Was I brought here merely to have my nose dragged away as I was about to nibble the sacred cheese of life? It is preposterous. If this old ninny-woman, Fate, cannot do better than this, she should be deprived of the management of men's fortunes. She is an old hen who knows not her intention. If she has decided to drown me, why did she not do it in the beginning and save me all this trouble. The whole affair is absurd. . . . But, no, she cannot mean to drown me. She dare not drown me. She cannot drown me. Not after all this work." Afterward the man might have had an impulse to shake his fist at the clouds: "Just you drown me, now, and then hear what I call you!"

The billows that came at this time were more formidable. They seemed always just about to break and roll over the little boat in a turmoil of foam. There was a preparatory and long growl in the speech of them. No mind unused to the sea would have concluded that the dingey could ascend these sheer heights in time. The shore was still afar. The oiler was a wily surfman. "Boys," he said, swiftly, "she won't live three minutes more and we're too far out to swim. Shall I take her to sea again, captain?"

"Yes! Go ahead!" said the captain.

This oiler, by a series of quick miracles, and fast and steady oarsmanship, turned the boat in the middle of the surf and took her safely to sea again.

There was a considerable silence as the boat bumped over the furrowed sea to deeper water. Then somebody in gloom spoke. "Well, anyhow, they must have seen us from the shore by now."

The gulls went in slanting flight up the wind toward the gray desolate east. A squall, marked by dingy clouds, and clouds brick-red, like smoke from a burning building, appeared from the southeast.

"What do you think of those life-saving people? Ain't they peaches?"

"Funny they haven't seen us."

"Maybe they think we're out here for sport! Maybe they think were fishin'. Maybe they think we're damned fools."

It was a long afternoon. A changed tide tried to force them southward, but wind and wave said northward. Far ahead, where coast-line, sea, and sky formed their mighty angle, there were little dots which seemed to indicate a city on the shore.

"St. Augustine?"

The captain shook his head. "Too near Mosquito Inlet."

And the oiler rowed, and then the correspondent rowed. Then the oiler rowed. It was a weary business. The human back can become the seat of more aches and pains than are registered in books for the composite anatomy of a regiment. It is a limited area, but it can become the theatre of innumerable muscular conflicts, tangles, wrenches, knots, and other comforts.

"Did you ever like to row, Billie?" asked the correspondent.

"No," said the oiler. "Hang it."

When one exchanged the rowing-seat for a place in the bottom of the boat, he suffered a bodily depression that caused him to be careless of everything save an obligation to wiggle one finger. There was cold sea-water swashing to and fro in the boat, and he lay in it. His head, pillowed on a thwart, was within an inch of the swirl of a wave crest, and sometimes a particularly obstreperous sea came in-board and drenched him once more. But these matters did not annoy him. It is almost certain that if the boat had capsized he would have tumbled comfortably out upon the ocean as if he felt sure that it was a great soft mattress.

"Look! There's a man on the shore!"

"Where?"

"There! See 'im? See 'im?"

"Yes, sure! He's walking along."

"Now he's stopped. Look! He's facing us!"

"He's waving at us!"

"So he is! By thunder!"

"Ah, now, we're all right! Now we're all right! There'll be a boat out here for us half an hour."

"He's going on. He's running. He's going up to that house there."

The remote beach seemed lower than the sea, and it required a searching glance to discern the little black figure. The captain saw a floating stick and they rowed to it. A bath-towel was by some weird chance in the boat, and, tying this on the stick, the captain waved it. The oarsman did not dare turn his head, so he was obliged to ask questions.

"What's he doing now?"

"He's standing still again. He's looking, I think. . . . There he goes again. Toward the house. . . . Now he's stopped again."

"Is he waving at us?"

"No, not now! he was, though."

"Look! There comes another man!"

"He's running."

"Look at him go, would you."

"Why, he's on a bicycle. Now he's met the other man. They're both waving at us. Look!"

"There comes something up the beach."

"What the devil is that thing?"

"Why, it looks like a boat."

"Why, certainly it's a boat."

"No, it's on wheels."

"Yes, so it is. Well, that must be the life-boat. They drag them along shore on a wagon."

"That's the life-boat, sure."

"No, by —, it's – it's an omnibus."

"I tell you it's a life-boat."

"It is not! It's an omnibus. I can see it plain. See? One of these big hotel omnibuses."

"By thunder, you're right. It's an omnibus, sure as fate. What do you suppose they are doing with an omnibus? Maybe they are going around collecting the life-crew, hey?"

"That's it, likely. Look! There's a fellow waving a little black flag. He's standing on the steps of the omnibus. There come those other two fellows. Now they're all talking together. Look at the fellow with the flag. Maybe he ain't waving it."

"That ain't a flag, is it? That's his coat. Why, certainly, that's his coat."

"So it is. It's his coat. He's taken it off and is waving it around his head. But would you look at him swing it."

"Oh, say, there isn't any life-saving station there. That's just a winter resort hotel omnibus that has brought over some of the boarders to see us drown."

"What's that idiot with the coat mean? What's he signaling, anyhow?"

"It looks as if he were trying to tell us to go north. There must be a life-saving station up there."

"No! He thinks we're fishing. Just giving us a merry hand. See? Ah, there, Willie."

"Well, I wish I could make something out of those signals. What do you suppose he means?"

"He don't mean anything. He's just playing."

"Well, if he'd just signal us to try the surf again, or to go to sea and wait, or go north, or go south, or go to hell — there would be some reason in it. But look at him. He just stands there and keeps his coat revolving like a wheel. The ass!"

"There come more people."

"Now there's quite a mob. Look! Isn't that a boat?"

"Where? Oh, I see where you mean. No, that's no boat."

"That fellow is still waving his coat."

"He must think we like to see him do that. Why don't he quit it. It don't mean anything."

"I don't know. I think he is trying to make us go north. It must be that there's a life-saving station there somewhere."

"Say, he ain't tired yet. Look at 'im wave."

"Wonder how long he can keep that up. He's been revolving his coat ever since he caught sight of us. He's an idiot. Why aren't they getting men to bring a boat out. A fishing boat — one of those big yawls — could come out here all right. Why don't he do something?"

"Oh, it's all right, now."

"They'll have a boat out here for us in less than no time, now that they've seen us."

A faint yellow tone came into the sky over the low land. The shadows on the sea slowly deepened. The wind bore coldness with it, and the men began to shiver.

"Holy smoke!" said one, allowing his voice to express his impious mood, "if we keep on monkeying out here! If we've got to flounder out here all night!"

"Oh, we'll never have to stay here all night! Don't you worry. They've seen us now, and it won't be long before they'll come chasing out after us."

The shore grew dusky. The man waving a coat blended gradually into this gloom, and it swallowed in the same manner the omnibus and the group of people. The spray, when it dashed uproariously over the side, made the voyagers shrink and swear like men who were being branded.

"I'd like to catch the chump who waved the coat. I feel like soaking him one, just for luck."

"Why? What did he do?"

"Oh, nothing, but then he seemed so damned cheerful."

In the meantime the oiler rowed, and then the correspondent rowed, and then oiler rowed. Gray-faced and bowed forward, they mechanically, turn by turn, plied the leaden oars. The form of the light-house had vanished from the southern horizon, but finally a pale star appeared, just lifting from the sea. The streaked saffron in the west passed before the all-merging darkness, and the sea to the east was black. The land had vanished, and was expressed only by the low and drear thunder of the surf.

"If I am going to be drowned — if I am going to be drowned — if I am going to drowned, why, in the name of the seven mad gods, who rule the sea, was I allowed to come thus far and contemplate sand and trees? Was I brought here merely to have my nose dragged away as I was about to nibble the sacred cheese of life?"

The patient captain, drooped over the water-jar, was sometimes obliged to speak to the oarsman.

"Keep her head up! Keep her head up!"

"'Keep her head up,' sir." The voices were weary and low.

This was surely a quiet evening. All save the oarsman lay heavily and listlessly in the boat's bottom. As for him, his eyes were just capable of noting the tall black waves that swept forward in a most sinister silence, save for an occasional subdued growl of a crest.

The cook's head was on a thwart, and he looked without interest at the water under his nose. He was deep in other scenes. Finally he spoke. "Billie," he murmured, dreamfully, "what kind of pie do you like best?"

V

"Pie," said the oiler and the correspondent, agitatedly. "Don't talk about those things, blast you!"

"Well," said the cook, "I was just thinking about ham sandwiches, and —"

A night on the sea in an open boat is a long night. As darkness settled finally, the shine of the light, lifting from the sea in the south, changed to full gold. On the northern horizon a new light appeared, a small bluish gleam on the edge of the waters. These two lights were the furniture of the world. Otherwise there was nothing but waves.

Two men huddled in the stern, and distances were so magnificent in the dingey that the rower was enabled to keep his feet partly warmed by thrusting them under his companions. Their legs indeed extended far under the rowing-seat until they touched the feet of the captain forward. Sometimes, despite the efforts of the tired oarsman, a wave came piling into the boat, an icy wave of the night, and the chilling water soaked them anew. They would twist their bodies for a moment and groan, and sleep the dead sleep once more, while the water in the boat gurgled about them as the craft rocked.

The plan of the oiler and the correspondent was for one to row until he lost the ability, and then arouse the other from his sea-water couch in the bottom of the boat.

The oiler plied the oars until his head drooped forward, and the overpowering sleep blinded him. And he rowed yet afterward. Then he touched a man in the bottom of the boat, and called his name. "Will you spell me for a little while?" he said, meekly.

"Sure, Billie," said the correspondent, awakening and dragging himself to a sitting position. They exchanged places carefully, and the oiler, cuddling down in the sea-water at the cook's side, seemed to go to sleep instantly.

The particular violence of the sea had ceased. The waves came without snarling. The obligation of the man at the oars was to keep the boat headed so that the tilt of the rollers would not capsize her, and to preserve her from filling when the crests rushed past. The black waves were silent and hard to be seen in the darkness. Often one was almost upon the boat before the oarsman was aware.

In a low voice the correspondent addressed the captain. He was not sure that the captain was awake, although this iron man seemed to be always awake. "Captain, shall I keep her making for that light north, sir?"

The same steady voice answered him. "Yes. Keep it about two points off the port bow."

The cook had tied a life-belt around himself in order to get even the warmth which this clumsy cork contrivance could donate, and he seemed almost stove-like when a rower, whose teeth invariably chattered wildly as soon as he ceased his labor, dropped down to sleep.

The correspondent, as he rowed, looked down at the two men sleeping under foot. The cook's arm was around the oiler's shoulders, and, with their fragmentary clothing and haggard faces, they were the babes of the sea, a grotesque rendering of the old babes in the wood.

Later he must have grown stupid at his work, for suddenly there was a growling of water, and a crest came with a roar and a swash into the boat, and it was a wonder that it did not set the cook afloat in his life-belt. The cook continued to sleep, but the oiler sat up, blinking his eyes and shaking with the new cold.

"Oh, I'm awful sorry, Billie," said the correspondent, contritely.

"That's all right, old boy," said the oiler, and lay down again and was asleep.

Presently it seemed that even the captain dozed, and the correspondent thought that he was the one man afloat on all the oceans. The wind had a voice as it came over the waves, and it was sadder than the end.

There was a long, loud swishing astern of the boat, and a gleaming trail of phosphorescence, like blue flame, was furrowed on the black waters. It might have been made by a monstrous knife.

Then there came a stillness, while the correspondent breathed with the open mouth and looked at the sea.

Suddenly there was another swish and another long flash of bluish light, and this time it was alongside the boat, and might almost have been reached with an oar. The correspondent saw an enormous fin speed like a shadow through the water, hurling the crystalline spray and leaving the long glowing trail.

The correspondent looked over his shoulder at the captain. His face was hidden, and he seemed to be asleep. He looked at the babes of the sea. They certainly were asleep. So, being bereft of sympathy, he leaned a little way to one side and swore softly into the sea.

But the thing did not then leave the vicinity of the boat. Ahead or astern, on one side or the other, at intervals long or short, fled the long sparkling streak, and there was to be heard the whiroo of the dark fin. The speed and power of the thing was greatly to be admired. It cut the water like a gigantic and keen projectile.

The presence of this biding thing did not affect the man with the same horror that it would if he had been a picnicker. He simply looked at the sea dully and swore in an undertone.

Nevertheless, it is true that he did not wish to be alone with the thing. He wished one of his companions to awaken by chance and keep him company with it. But the captain hung motionless over the water-jar and the oiler and the cook in the bottom of the boat were plunged in slumber.

VI

"If I am going to be drowned — if I am going to be drowned — if I am going to be drowned, why, in the name of the seven mad gods, who rule the sea, was I allowed to come thus far and contemplate sand and trees?"

During this dismal night, it may be remarked that a man would conclude that it was really the intention of the seven mad gods to drown him, despite the abominable injustice of it. For it was certainly an abominable injustice to drown a man who had worked so hard. The man felt it would be a crime most unnatural. Other people had drowned at sea since galleys swarmed with painted sails, but still —

When it occurs to a man that nature does not regard him as important, and that she feels she would not maim the universe by disposing of him, he at first wishes to throw bricks at the temple, and hates deeply the fact that there are no bricks and no temples. Any visible expression of nature would surely be pelleted with his jeers.

Then, if there be no tangible thing to hoot he feels, perhaps, the desire to confront a personification and indulge in pleas, bowed to one knee, and with hands supplicant, saying: "Yes, but I love myself."

A high cold star on a winter's night is the word he feels that she says to him. Thereafter he knows the pathos of his situation.

The men in the dingey had not discussed these matters, but each had, no doubt, reflected upon them in silence and according to his mind. There was seldom any expression upon their faces save the general one of complete weariness. Speech was devoted to the business of the boat.

To chime the notes of his emotion, a verse mysteriously entered the correspondent's head. He had even forgotten that he had forgotten this verse, but it suddenly was in his mind.

> A soldier of the Legion lay dying in Algiers,
> There was lack of woman's nursing, there was dearth of woman's tears;
> But a comrade stood beside him, and he took that comrade's hand
> And he said: "I shall never see my own, my native land."[6]

---

6. **A soldier . . . land:** Crane is loosely quoting the first stanza of the popular poem about the death of a French legionnaire, "Bingen on the Rhine" (1883), by Caroline E. S. Norton (1808–1877): "A soldier of the Legion lay dying in Algiers, / There was a lack of woman's nursing, there was dearth of woman's tears; /

In his childhood, the correspondent had been made acquainted with the fact that a soldier of the Legion lay dying in Algiers, but he had never regarded the fact as important. Myriads of his school-fellows had informed him of the soldier's plight, but the dinning had naturally ended by making him perfectly indifferent. He had never considered it his affair that a soldier of the Legion lay dying in Algiers, nor had it appeared to him as a matter for sorrow. It was less to him than breaking of a pencil's point.

Now, however, it quaintly came to him as a human, living thing. It was no longer merely a picture of a few throes in the breast of a poet, meanwhile drinking tea and warming his feet at the grate; it was an actuality — stern, mournful, and fine.

The correspondent plainly saw the soldier. He lay on the sand with his feet out straight and still. While his pale left hand was upon his chest in an attempt to thwart the going of his life, the blood came between his fingers. In the far Algerian distance, a city of low square forms was set against a sky that was faint with the last sunset hues. The correspondent, plying the oars and dreaming of the slow and slower movements of the lips of the soldier, was moved by a profound and perfectly impersonal comprehension. He was sorry for the soldier of the Legion who lay dying in Algiers.

The thing which had followed the boat and waited had evidently grown bored at the delay. There was no longer to be heard the slash of the cut-water, and there was no longer the flame of the long trail. The light in the north still glimmered, but it was apparently no nearer to the boat. Sometimes the boom of the surf rang in the correspondent's ears, and he turned the craft seaward then and rowed harder. Southward, someone had evidently built a watch-fire on the beach. It was too low and too far to be seen, but it made a shimmering, roseate reflection upon the bluff back of it, and this could be discerned from the boat. The wind came stronger, and sometimes a wave suddenly raged out like a mountain-cat and there was to be seen the sheen and sparkle of a broken crest.

The captain, in the bow, moved on his water-jar and sat erect. "Pretty long night," he observed to the correspondent. He looked at the shore. "Those life-saving people take their time."

"Did you see that shark playing around?"

"Yes, I saw him. He was a big fellow, all right."

"Wish I had known you were awake."

Later the correspondent spoke into the bottom of the boat.

"Billie!" There was a slow and gradual disentanglement. "Billie, will you spell me?"

"Sure," said the oiler.

As soon as the correspondent touched the cold comfortable sea-water in the bottom of the boat, and had huddled close to the cook's life-belt he was deep in sleep, despite the fact that his teeth played all the popular airs. This sleep was so good to him that it was

---

But a comrade stood beside him, while his lifeblood ebbed away, / And bent with pitying glances, to hear what he might say. / The dying soldier faltered, and he took that comrade's hand, / And he said, "I nevermore shall see my own, my native land: / Take a message, and a token, to some distant friends of mine, / For I was born at Bingen, — at Bingen on the Rhine."

but a moment before he heard a voice call his name in a tone that demonstrated the last stages of exhaustion. "Will you spell me?"

"Sure, Billie."

The light in the north had mysteriously vanished, but the correspondent took his course from the wide-awake captain.

Later in the night they took the boat farther out to sea, and the captain directed the cook to take one oar at the stern and keep the boat facing the seas. He was to call out if he should hear the thunder of the surf. This plan enabled the oiler and the correspondent to get respite together. "We'll give those boys a chance to get into shape again," said the captain. They curled down and, after a few preliminary chatterings and trembles, slept once more the dead sleep. Neither knew they had bequeathed to the cook the company of another shark, or perhaps the same shark.

As the boat caroused on the waves, spray occasionally bumped over the side and gave them a fresh soaking, but this had no power to break their repose. The ominous slash of the wind and the water affected them as it would have affected mummies.

"Boys," said the cook, with the notes of every reluctance in his voice, "she's drifted in pretty close. I guess one of you had better take her to sea again." The correspondent, aroused, heard the crash of the toppled crests.

As he was rowing, the captain gave him some whiskey and water, and this steadied the chills out of him. "If I ever get ashore and anybody shows me even a photograph of an oar —"

At last there was a short conversation.

"Billie. . . . Billie, will you spell me?"

"Sure," said the oiler.

VII

When the correspondent again opened his eyes, the sea and the sky were each of the gray hue of the dawning. Later, carmine and gold was painted upon the waters. The morning appeared finally, in its splendor, with a sky of pure blue, and the sunlight flamed on the tips of the waves.

On the distant dunes were set many little black cottages, and a tall white wind-mill reared above them. No man, nor dog, nor bicycle appeared on the beach. The cottages might have formed a deserted village.

The voyagers scanned the shore. A conference was held in the boat. "Well," said the captain, "if no help is coming, we might better try a run through the surf right away. If we stay out here much longer we will be too weak to do anything for ourselves at all." The others silently acquiesced in this reasoning. The boat was headed for the beach. The correspondent wondered if none ever ascended the tall wind-tower, and if then they never looked seaward. This tower was a giant, standing with its back to the plight of the ants. It represented in a degree, to the correspondent, the serenity of nature amid the struggles of the individual — nature in the wind, and nature in the vision of men. She did not seem cruel to him then, nor beneficent, nor treacherous, nor wise. But she was indifferent, flatly indifferent. It is, perhaps, plausible that a man in this situation pressed with the unconcern of the universe, should see the innumerable flaws of his life and have them taste wickedly in his mind and wish for another chance. A distinction between right and wrong seems absurdly clear to him, then, in this new ignorance of the grave-edge, and he understands that if he were given another opportunity he would mend his conduct and his words, and be better and brighter during an introduction, or at a tea.

"Now, boys," said the captain, "she is going to swamp sure. All we can do is to work her in as far as possible, and then when she swamps, pile out and scramble for the beach. Keep cool now and don't jump until she swamps sure."

The oiler took the oars. Over his shoulders he scanned the surf. "Captain," he said, "I think I'd better bring her about, and keep her head-on to the seas and back her in."

"All right, Billie," said the captain. "Back her in." The oiler swung the boat then and, seated in the stern, the cook and the correspondent were obliged to look over their shoulders to contemplate the lonely and indifferent shore.

The monstrous inshore rollers heaved the boat high until the men were again enabled to see the white sheets of water scudding up the slanted beach. "We won't get in very close," said the captain. Each time a man could wrest his attention from the rollers, he turned his glance toward the shore, and in the expression of the eyes during this contemplation there was a singular quality. The correspondent, observing the others, knew that they were not afraid, but the full meaning of their glances was shrouded.

As for himself, he was too tired to grapple fundamentally with the fact. He tried to coerce his mind into thinking of it, but the mind was dominated at this time by the muscles, and the muscles said they did not care. It merely occurred to him that if he should drown it would be a shame.

There were no hurried words, no pallor, no plain agitation. The men simply looked at the shore. "Now, remember to get well clear of the boat when you jump," said the captain.

Seaward the crest of a roller suddenly fell with a thunderous crash, and the long white comber came roaring down upon the boat.

"Steady now," said the captain. The men were silent. They turned their eyes from the shore to the comber and waited. The boat slid up the incline, leaped at the furious top, bounced over it, and swung down the long back of the waves. Some water had been shipped and the cook bailed it out.

But the next crest crashed also. The tumbling boiling flood of white water caught the boat and whirled it almost perpendicular. Water swarmed in from all sides. The correspondent had his hands on the gunwale[7] at this time, and when the water entered at that place he swiftly withdrew his fingers, as if he objected to wetting them.

The little boat, drunken with this weight of water, reeled and snuggled deeper into the sea.

"Bail her out, cook! Bail her out," said the captain.

---

7. **gunwale:** The upper edge of the side of the boat.

"All right, captain," said the cook.

"Now, boys, the next one will do for sure," said the oiler. "Mind to jump clear of the boat."

The third wave moved forward, huge, furious, implacable. It fairly swallowed the dingey, and almost simultaneously the men tumbled into the sea. A piece of life-belt had lain in the bottom of the boat, and as the correspondent went overboard he held this to his chest with his left hand.

The January water was icy, and he reflected immediately that it was colder than he had expected to find it off the coast of Florida. This appeared to his dazed mind as a fact important enough to be noted at the time. The coldness of the water was sad; it was tragic. This fact was somehow mixed and confused with his opinion of his own situation that it seemed almost a proper reason for tears. The water was cold.

When he came to the surface he was conscious of little but the noisy water. Afterward he saw his companions in the sea. The oiler was ahead in the race. He was swimming strongly and rapidly. Off to correspondent's left, the cook's great white and corked back bulged out of the water, and in the rear the captain was hanging with his one good hand to the keel of the overturned dingey.

There is a certain immovable quality to a shore, and the correspondent wondered at it amid the confusion of the sea.

It seemed also very attractive, but the correspondent knew that it was a long journey, and he paddled leisurely. The piece of life-preserver lay under him, and sometimes he whirled down the incline of a wave as if he were on a hand-sled.

But finally he arrived at a place in the sea where travel was beset with difficulty. He did not pause swimming to inquire what manner of current had caught him, but there his progress ceased. The shore was set before him like a bit of scenery on a stage, and he looked at it and understood with his eyes each detail of it.

As the cook passed, much farther to the left, the captain was calling to him, "Turn over on your back, cook! Turn over on your back and use the oar."

"All right, sir." The cook turned on his back, and, paddling with an oar, went ahead as if he were a canoe.

Presently the boat also passed to the left of the correspondent with the captain clinging with one hand to the keel. He would have appeared like a man raising himself to look over a board fence, if it were not for the extraordinary gymnastics of the boat. The correspondent marvelled that the captain could still hold it.

They passed on, nearer to shore – the oiler, the cook, the captain – and following them went the water-jar, bouncing gayly over the seas.

The correspondent remained in the grip of this strange new enemy – a current. The shore, with its white slope of sand and its green bluff, topped with little silent cottages, was spread like a picture before him. It was very near to him then, but he was impressed as one who in a gallery looks at a scene from Brittany or Algiers.

He thought: "I am going to drown? Can it be possible? Can it be possible? Can it be possible?" Perhaps an individual must consider his own death to be the final phenomenon of nature.

But later a wave perhaps whirled him out of this small deadly current, for he found suddenly that he could again make progress toward the shore. Later still, he was aware that the captain, clinging with one hand to the keel of the dingey, had his face turned away from the shore and toward him, and was calling his name. "Come to the boat! Come to the boat!"

In his struggle to reach the captain and the boat, he reflected that when one gets properly wearied, drowning must really be a comfortable arrangement, a cessation of hostilities accompanied by a large degree of relief, and he was glad of it, for the main thing in his mind for some moments had been horror of the temporary agony. He did not wish to be hurt.

Presently he saw a man running along the shore. He was undressing with most remarkable speed. Coat, trousers, shirt, everything flew magically off him.

"Come to the boat," called the captain.

"All right, captain." As the correspondent paddled, he saw the captain let himself down to bottom and leave the boat. Then the correspondent performed his one little marvel of the voyage. A large wave caught him and flung him with ease and supreme speed completely over the boat and far beyond it. It struck him even then as an event in gymnastics, and a true miracle of the sea. An overturned boat in the surf is not a plaything to a swimming man.

The correspondent arrived in water that reached only to his waist, but his condition did not enable him to stand for more than a moment. Each wave knocked him into a heap, and the under-tow pulled at him.

Then he saw the man who had been running and undressing, and undressing and running, come bounding into the water. He dragged ashore the cook, and then waded toward the captain, but the captain waved him away, and sent him to the correspondent. He was naked, naked as a tree in winter, but a halo was about his head, and he shone like a saint. He gave a strong pull, and a long drag, and a bully heave at the correspondent's hand. The correspondent, schooled in the minor formulae, said: "Thanks, old man." But suddenly the man cried: "What's that?" He pointed a swift finger. The correspondent said: "Go."

In the shallows, face downward, lay the oiler. His forehead touched sand that was periodically, between each wave, clear of the sea.

The correspondent did not know all that transpired afterward. When he achieved safe ground he fell, striking the sand with each particular part of his body. It was as if he had dropped from a roof, but the thud was grateful to him.

It seems that instantly the beach was populated with men with blankets, clothes, and flasks, and women with coffee-pots and all the remedies sacred to their minds. The welcome of the land to the men from the sea was warm and generous, but a still and dripping shape was carried slowly up the beach, and the land's welcome for it could only be the different and sinister hospitality of the grave.

When it came night, the white waves paced to and fro in the moonlight, and the wind brought the sound of the great sea's voice to the men on shore, and they felt that they could then be interpreters.

[1897]

Crane's Poetry.   Although he was and is best known for his fiction, Crane expressed a higher opinion of his poems, which he said "give my ideas of life as a whole, so far as I know it." Inspired by the free verse of Walt Whitman and especially by the compressed, epigrammatic style of Emily Dickinson's poetry, which Crane discovered in 1893, he began to write his own innovative poems, or what he called "lines," further distancing his verse from the formal and metrical conventions of poetry in English. Like Dickinson, Crane did not title his poems, which were printed in all capital letters in his first collection, *Black Riders and Other Lines* (1895), though not in his second collection, *War Is Kind* (1899). Many of the poems were equally unconventional in the views Crane expressed about human life, nature, and God. The publishers of *Black Riders* consequently asked him to expunge many of the poems in the volume, especially those referring to God. Crane protested that the publishers were seeking to "cut all the ethical sense out of the book," all of its "anarchy," adding: "It is the anarchy which I particularly insist on." Crane finally agreed to the omission of seven poems from *Black Riders.* A number of critics objected to the bitterness and cynicism displayed in Crane's poems, which many reviewers dismissed as eccentric and formless. But other reviewers emphasized the freshness and originality of the poems in *Black Riders* and *War Is Kind.* Indeed, the spare language and striking imagery of those poems anticipated the work of Carl Sandburg, who in his poem "Letters to Dead Imagists" (1916) paid homage to Dickinson and Crane, as well as that of Amy Lowell, who viewed Crane as an important precursor of modernist verse in the United States. The texts are taken from *Poems and Literary Remains,* edited by Fredson Bowers (1975), volume 10 of *The Collected Works of Stephen Crane.*

From THE BLACK RIDERS AND OTHER LINES

I

Black riders came from the sea.
There was clang and clang of spear and shield,
And clash and clash of hoof and heel,
Wild shouts and the wave of hair
In the rush upon the wind:
Thus the ride of sin.

[1895, 1975]

III

In the desert
I saw a creature, naked, bestial,
Who, squatting upon the ground,
Held his heart in his hands,
And ate of it.   5
I said, "Is it good, friend?"
"It is bitter — bitter," he answered;
"But I like it
"Because it is bitter,
"And because it is my heart."   10

[1895, 1975]

X

Should the wide world roll away
Leaving black terror
Limitless night,
Nor God, nor man, nor place to stand
Would be to me essential
If thou and thy white arms were there
And the fall to doom a long way.

[1895, 1975]

XIV

There was crimson clash of war.
Lands turned black and bare;
Women wept;
Babes ran, wondering.
There came one who understood not these things.
He said, "Why is this?"
Whereupon a million strove to answer him.
There was such intricate clamor of tongues,
That still the reason was not.

[1895, 1975]

XIX

A god in wrath
Was beating a man;
He cuffed him loudly
With thunderous blows
That rang and rolled over the earth.   5
All people came running.
The man screamed and struggled,
And bit madly at the feet of the god.
The people cried,
"Ah, what a wicked man!"   10
And —
"Ah, what a redoubtable god!"

[1895, 1975]

XXIV

I saw a man pursuing the horizon;
Round and round they sped.
I was disturbed at this;
I accosted the man.
"It is futile," I said,
"You can never —"

"You lie," he cried,
And ran on.

[1895, 1975]

XLIV

I was in the darkness;
I could not see my words
Nor the wishes of my heart.
Then suddenly there was a great light —

"Let me into the darkness again."

[1895, 1975]

XLVI

Many red devils ran from my heart
And out upon the page.
They were so tiny

The pen could mash them.
And many struggled in the ink.
It was strange
To write in this red muck
Of things from my heart.

[1895, 1975]

From WAR IS KIND

I [DO NOT WEEP, MAIDEN, FOR WAR IS KIND]

Do not weep, maiden, for war is kind.
Because your lover threw wild hands toward the sky
And the affrighted steed ran on alone,
Do not weep.
War is kind.   5

    Hoarse, booming drums of the regiment
    Little souls who thirst for fight,
    These men were born to drill and die
    The unexplained glory flies above them
    Great is the battle-god, great, and his kingdom —   10
    A field where a thousand corpses lie.

Do not weep, babe, for war is kind.
Because your father tumbled in the yellow trenches,
Raged at his breast, gulped and died,
Do not weep.   15
War is kind.

    Swift, blazing flag of the regiment
    Eagle with crest of red and gold,
    These men were born to drill and die
    Point for them the virtue of slaughter   20
    Make plain to them the excellence of killing
    And a field where a thousand corpses lie.

Mother whose heart hung humble as a button
On the bright splendid shroud of your son,
Do not weep.   25
War is kind.

[1896, 1899, 1975]

XXI [A MAN SAID TO THE UNIVERSE]

A man said to the universe:
"Sir, I exist!"
"However," replied the universe,
"The fact has not created in me
"A sense of obligation."

[1899, 1975]

From UNCOLLECTED POEMS

[A MAN ADRIFT ON A SLIM SPAR]

A man adrift on a slim spar
A horizon smaller than the rim of a bottle
Tented waves rearing lashy dark points
The near whine of froth in circles.
          God is cold.   5

The incessant raise and swing of the sea
And growl after growl of crest
The sinkings, green, seething, endless
The upheaval half-completed.
          God is cold.   10

The seas are in the hollow of The Hand;
Oceans may be turned to a spray
Raining down through the stars
Because of a gesture of pity toward a babe.
Oceans may become grey ashes,   15
Die with a long moan and a roar
Amid the tumult of the fishes
And the cries of the ships,
Because The Hand beckons the mice.

A horizon smaller than a doomed assassin's cap,   20
Inky, surging tumults
A reeling, drunken sky and no sky
A pale hand sliding from a polished spar.
          God is cold.

The puff of a coat imprisoning air.   25
A face kissing the water-death
A weary slow sway of a lost hand
And the sea, the moving sea, the sea.
          God is cold.

[c. 1897, 1975]

Theodore Dreiser

[1871-1945]

Theodore Dreiser was born in Terre Haute, Indiana, on August 27, 1871. He was the twelfth of thirteen children of the German-born John Paul Dreiser and his wife, Sarah Schänäb Dreiser, the descendant of Czechoslovakian immigrants. The couple's eldest surviving son, a popular entertainer who adopted the stage name Paul Dresser, later gained wealth and fame as the composer of nostalgic songs like "On the Banks of the Wabash, Far Away." But the family home in Indiana was anything but idyllic, and Dreiser's older siblings frequently rebelled against the strict rules imposed by their father, a deeply pious Roman Catholic. One of Dreiser's sisters, abandoned by the son of a wealthy family, bore an illegitimate child, and another sister ran away with a married man who had stolen money from his employer to finance their trip to Canada. During his difficult and impoverished childhood, Dreiser had little formal education until the family moved to Warsaw, Indiana, where he attended school from 1883 to 1887. That year, at the age of sixteen, he left home to seek a better life in Chicago. He worked as a laborer for two years, until one of his former teachers from Warsaw arranged for Dreiser to enroll as a special student at Indiana University. Although he did well enough to continue his studies, Dreiser did not feel that he fit into college life, so he dropped out after two semesters and returned to Chicago. In 1892, he was hired as a reporter for the *Daily Globe.* While on an assignment for the newspaper in 1893, he met Sara White, a schoolteacher from Missouri, whom Dreiser married in 1898. During their extended courtship, he worked as an itinerant journalist throughout the Midwest, as the editor of a music magazine in New York City, and as a freelance writer for popular magazines such as *Cosmopolitan, McClure's, Metropolitan,* and *Munsey's.*

Theodore Dreiser

This undated photograph was apparently taken between 1900 and 1910, when Dreiser was working as a magazine editor in New York City.

After churning out magazine articles for several years, Dreiser began to write fiction in 1899. He first experimented with several short stories and then started work on a novel, *Sister Carrie,* in which Dreiser tells the story of a country girl who goes to Chicago, where she escapes work in a sweatshop by becoming the mistress of a traveling salesman before running away with a married saloon manager, finally abandoning him for a successful career on Broadway. Dreiser's determination to "tell about life as it is," as he said in an interview, especially about the powerful force of sexuality in human life, brought him into immediate conflict with literary conventions and the realities of the literary marketplace. Harper & Brothers firmly rejected the novel, explaining that Dreiser's handling of "the continued illicit relations of the heroine" would offend readers, especially "the feminine readers who control the destinies of so many novels." Dreiser submitted a revised version to Doubleday, Page and Company, which had recently published Frank Norris's graphic and naturalistic novel *McTeague* (1899). Norris, who reviewed manuscripts for the company, helped Dreiser secure a contract for the publication of *Sister Carrie.* After the owner of the company, Frank Doubleday, read the manuscript, he sought to block publication of the "immoral" novel. When that proved to be impossible, the company grudgingly published but refused to market *Sister Carrie* (1900). Despite a few positive reviews in the United States and a generally favorable reception in England, the novel sold fewer than five hundred copies, earning Dreiser less than seventy dollars. Bitterly disappointed, he virtually gave up writing fiction for nearly a decade, during which time he worked as the editor of various women's magazines until an in-office affair forced him to resign in 1910.

By then, *Sister Carrie* had been reissued, and Dreiser once again turned from journalism to fiction. In his second novel, *Jennie Gerhardt* (1911), he tells the tragic story of a poor young woman who, after bearing the illegitimate child of a U.S. senator, becomes the mistress of a wealthy socialite. Dreiser then wrote *The Financier* (1911) and *The Titan* (1914), the first two novels of a trilogy about the rise and fall of a Chicago industrialist. (The final novel of the trilogy, *The Stoic,* was published posthumously in 1947.) The sale of Dreiser's most autobiographical novel, *The 'Genius'* (1915), was prohibited in New York City by the Society for the Suppression of Vice. At the same time, his novels were hailed by younger writers who were determined to challenge the standards of propriety imposed on American fiction. Having separated from his wife a decade earlier, Dreiser in 1919 began a long-term affair with his cousin Helen Richardson, with whom he moved to California. There, he wrote *An American Tragedy* (1925), based on an actual story of a poor young man who drowned his pregnant girlfriend in order to pursue his "American dream" of wealth and success. The novel was widely hailed as a masterpiece, but it was banned in Boston, and Dreiser's writings continued to generate outrage. In 1935, the library trustees of Warsaw, Indiana, which was as close to a hometown as he had, ordered the burning of all the library's books by Dreiser. A year before his death on December 18, 1945, however, Dreiser received the Award of Merit from the American Academy of Arts and Sciences, not only for his literary achievement, but also for his "courage and integrity in breaking trail as a pioneer in the presentation of fiction of real human beings in a real America."

For Dreiser is a true hyphenate, a product of that conglomerate Americanism that springs from other roots than the English tradition. Do we realize how rare it is to find a talent that is thoroughly American and wholly unEnglish?

—*Randoph Bourne*

bedfordstmartins.com/ americanlit *for research links on Dreiser*

Dreiser's "Butcher Rogaum's Door."   This was one of several stories Dreiser completed during the summer of 1899, shortly before he began to write *Sister Carrie* (1900). Anticipating many of the themes of that novel, the early stories reveal his determination to confront the hard facts and darker aspects of life in the United States. In "Butcher Rogaum's Door," he explores what a reviewer described as the "dangers of innocent girlhood in the slums of New York." The spare and gritty story was inspired by Dreiser's experience as a police reporter, as well as by his memories of conflicts between his sisters and his stern, German-born father. "Butcher Rogaum's Door" was first published in a St. Louis weekly magazine, the *Mirror,* edited by the iconoclastic William Marion Reedy, whom the poet Edgar Lee Masters described as the "Literary Boss of the Middle West." Seeking to dismantle what he viewed as the "genteel" literary tradition of the East in order to develop a more vital and indigenous tradition of writing in the United States, Reedy published work by a remarkable range of American authors, including poetry by Stephen Crane and Edwin Arlington Robinson, as well as the experimental verse of emerging poets such as T. S. Eliot, Amy Lowell, Edna St. Vincent Millay, Ezra Pound, and Carl Sandburg. Under Reedy's leadership, the circulation of the *Mirror* eventually surpassed that of several venerable literary magazines published in the East, including the *Atlantic Monthly* and the *Nation*. The text of "Butcher Rogaum's Door," which Dreiser later revised as "Old Rogaum and His Theresa" for his collection *Free and Other Stories* (1918), is taken from the first printing in the *Mirror*, December 12, 1901.

BUTCHER ROGAUM'S DOOR

In all Bleecker Street[1] was no more comfortable doorway than that of the butcher Rogaum, even if the first floor was given over to meat market purposes. It was to one side of the main entrance, which gave ingress to the butcher shop, and from it led up a flight of steps, at least five feet wide, to the living rooms above. A little portico stood out in front of it, railed on either side, and within was a second or final door, forming, with the outer or storm door, a little area, where Mrs. Rogaum and her children frequently sat of a summer's evening. The outer door was never locked, owing to the inconvenience it would inflict on Mr. Rogaum, who had no other way of getting upstairs. In winter, when all had gone to bed, there had been cases in which belated travelers had taken refuge there from the snow or sleet. One or two newsboys occasionally slept there, until routed out by Officer Maguire, who, seeing it half open at two o'clock one morning, took occasion to look in. He jogged the newsboys sharply with his stick and then, when they were gone, tried the inner door which was locked.

"You ought to keep that outer door locked, Rogaum," he observed to the sedate butcher, the next evening, as he was passing, "people might get in there. A couple of kids were sleeping there last night."

"Ach, dat is no difference," answered Rogaum, pleasantly. "I haf de inner door locked, yet. Dat iss no difference."

"Better lock it," said the officer, more to vindicate his authority than anything else. "Something will happen there yet."

The door was never locked, however, and now of a summer evening Mrs. Rogaum and the children made pleasant use of its recess, watching the route of street cars and occasionally belated trucks go by. The children played on the sidewalk, all except the budding Theresa (eighteen just turning), who, with one companion of the neighborhood, the

---

1. **Bleecker Street:** A major thoroughfare in Greenwich Village, then a crowded tenement district in lower Manhattan.

pretty Kenrihan girl, walked up and down the block, laughing, glancing, watching the boys. Old Mrs. Kenrihan lived in the next block and there, sometimes, the two stopped. There, also, they more frequently pretended to be when talking with the boys in the intervening side street. Young "Connie" Almerting and George Goujon were the bright particular mashers[2] who held the attention of this block. These two made their acquaintance in the customary bold, boyish way and thereafter the girls had an urgent desire to be out in the street together after eight and to linger where the boys could see and overtake them.

Old Mrs. Rogaum never knew. She was a particularly fat, old, German lady, completely dominated by her liege and portly lord, and at nine o'clock regularly, as he had long ago deemed mete and fit, she was wont to betake her way upward and so to bed. Old Rogaum, at that hour, himself closed the market and went to his chamber.

All the children were called sharply, once from the doorstep below and once from the window above, only Mrs. Rogaum did it first and Rogaum last. It had come, because of a shade of lenience, not wholly apparent in the father's nature, that the older of the children needed two callings and sometimes three. Theresa, now that she had got in with the Kenrihan maiden, needed that many calls and even more.

She loved to walk up and down in the as yet bright street, where were voices and laughter, and occasionally moonlight streaming down. What a nuisance it was to be called at nine, anyhow. What old foggies her parents were. Mrs. Kenrihan was not so strict with her daughter. It made her pettish when Rogaum insisted, calling as he often did, in German, "Come you now," in a very hoarse and belligerent voice.

She came, eventually, frowning and wretched, all the moonlight calling her, all the voices of the night urging her to come back. Her objection made the coming later and later, however, until now, by August of this, her eighteenth year, it was nearly ten when she entered and Rogaum was almost invariably angry.

"I vill lock you oudt," he declared, in strongly accented English, while she tried to slip by him each time, "I vill show you. Du sollst[3] come ven I say yet. Hear now."

"I'll not," answered Theresa, but it was always under her breath.

Poor Mrs. Rogaum hated to hear the wrath of her husband's voice. It spoke of harder and fiercer times which had been with her. Still she was not powerful enough in the family councils to put in a weighty word. So Rogaum fumed unrestricted.

There were other nights, however, many of them, and now that the young sparks of the neighborhood had enlisted the girl's attention, it was a more trying time than ever. Theresa had a tender eye for the dashing Almerting. What a fine fellow he was, indeed! What authority! His cigarette was always cocked at a high angle, in her presence, and his hat had the least suggestion of being set to one side. He had a shrewd way of winking one eye, was strong and athletic and worked in a tobacco factory. His was a trade, in-

---

2. **mashers:** A late-nineteenth-century slang term for men who make aggressive sexual advances to women in public places.
3. **Du sollst:** You shall (German).

deed, nearly acquired, as he said, and his jingling pockets attested that he had money of his own. Altogether he was very captivating.

"Ah, what do you want to go in for?" he used to say to her, tossing his head gaily on one side to listen, as old Rogaum called. "Tell him you didn't hear."

"No, I've got to go," said the little girl.

"Well, you don't have to just yet. Stay another minute. George, what was that fellow's name that tried to sass us the other day?"

"Theresa!" roared old Rogaum, forcefully. "If you do not now come! Ve will see."

"I've got to go," observed Theresa with a faint effort at starting.

Thus the moments slipped away and delight was sipped in the moonlight. Both the young men would follow to the corner, almost in sight of the irate old butcher.

"Let him call," said young Almerting one night, catching hold of her soft, white fingers and causing her body to quiver thereby.

"Oh, no," she gasped nervously.

"Well, good-night, then," he said and with a flip of the heel had his arm around her and his soft lips against her burning cheeks.

"Get out," she murmured, pushing.

He jumped away and strolled gaily off, Gonjon having been equally successful. Then Theresa went home.

"Vy don'd you come ven I call?" said old Rogaum wrathfully. "Muss ich all my time spenden calling, mit you on the streeds oudt? In now. I vill show you."

"I wasn't," snapped Theresa, even as his fat hand reached her back.

"Take dot now," he exclaimed. "Und come you yussed vunce more at dis time — Ve vill see if I am boss in my own house, aber! Komst du vun minute nach[4] ten to-morrow und you vill see vat you vill get. I vill the door lock. Du sollst not in kommen. Mark! Oudt sollst du stayen — oudt!"[5] And he glared wrathfully after her retreating form.

He was angry, but equally determined. It was not that he imagined that she was as yet in bad company, but he wished to forefend against possible danger. He knew she only walked from his shop to the door of the Kenrihans' and back again. Had not his wife told him so? If he had thought upon what far pilgrimage her feet had already ventured or ever seeing the dashing Almerting hanging near, then had there been wrath and tears. As it was, his mind was more or less at ease.

On the following eve it was much the same story, only this time the nervous Theresa got in on time. Other evenings and for many, she was safe, but soon "Connie" claimed her more sharply for his "steady," and bought her ice-cream. In the range of the short block it was all done, lingering by the curbstone and strolling a block or two away from the corner, until she had offended seriously at home and the threat was reflected anew. Then came another blow and another threat — that she should not get in at all.

---

4. **nach:** After (German).
5. "**Du sollst not in kommen. . . . oudt!**": "You shall not come in. Notice! You shall stay out! — Out!" (German).

Well enough she meant to obey, on this radiant night, but somehow the time fled too fast.

"Ah, wait a minute," said "Connie." "Stand still. He won't lock you out."

"But he will, though," said Theresa. "You don't know him."

"Well, if he does, come back to me. I will be here."

There was a sinister grin on the youth's face.

"Well, wait, anyhow," insisted the blade.

Longer and longer she waited and now no voice came.

She began to feel that something was wrong — a greater strain than if old Rogaum's voice had been filling the whole neighborhood.

"I've got to go," she said.

"You're a great card, you are," said he, derisively.

Still, he caught her as she went, kissing her soundly and then standing and looking after.

"I wish he would lock her out," he thought.

At her own doorstep she paused momentarily, more to soften her progress than anything. The outer door she opened and then the inner — or tried to. It was locked. For a moment she paused, cold fear racing over her body, and then knocked.

No answer.

Again she rattled the door, this time nervously and was about to cry out.

Still no answer.

"Let her go, now," said Rogaum, savagely, sitting in his front room, where she could not hear. "I vill her a lesson teach."

"Hadn't you better let her in now, yet?" pleaded Mrs. Rogaum faintly.

"No, no," said Mr. Rogaum. "Nefer. Let her vait awhile."

His voice was rich in wrath and he was saving up a good beating for her. She should wait and wait and plead and when she was thoroughly wretched and subdued he would let her in and beat her — such a beating as she had never received in all her born days.

Again the door rattled and still she got no answer. Not even her call brought a sound.

Now, strangely, a new element, not heretofore apparent in her nature, but, nevertheless wholly there, was called into life, springing in action as Diana,[6] full formed. The cold chill left her and she wavered angrily.

"All right," she said, some old German stubbornness springing up, "I won't knock. You don't need to let me in."

Suggestions of tears were in her eyes, but she backed firmly out onto the stoop and sat down, hesitating. Old Rogaum saw her, lowering down from the lattice, but said nothing. He would teach her for once what were proper hours.

At the corner, standing, Almerting also saw. He recognized the simple white dress and paused steadily, a strange thrill racing over him. Really they had locked her out.

---

6. **Diana:** In Roman mythology, the goddess of the moon and of the hunt, who was especially revered by women.

Gee, this was new. He had never before had a girl on his hands at this hour. There she was, white, quiet, shut out, waiting at her father's doorstep.

Sitting thus, Theresa pondered a moment and girlish anger and rashness dominated in her. Her pride was hurt and she felt revengeful. They would shut her out, would they? All right, she would go out and they should look to it how they would get her back — the old curmudgeons. He would beat her, but that did not matter. It was a thing afar off.

Getting up, she stepped on the now quieting sidewalk and strolled up the street. It was a rather nervous procedure, however. There were street cars and stores lighted and people passing, but soon these would not be and she was locked out. Into the side streets were already long silent walks and gleaming rows of lamps.

At the corner her youthful lover almost pounced upon her.

"Locked out are you?" he said, his eyes shining.

For the moment she was delighted to see him, for a nameless dread had somehow gotten a hold of her.

"Yes," she answered.

"Well, let's stroll on a little," said the boy.

At the farther corner up, they passed Officer Maguire and Officer Delehanty, idly swinging their clubs and discussing politics.

"'Tis a shame," said Officer Delehanty, "the way things do now be run."

"Isn't that Rogaum's girl there, though, with Almerting?" asked Maguire, interrupting.

"It is that," said Delehanty, looking after.

"Well, I think he'd better be keeping an eye on her," said Officer Maguire. "'Tis no time for a decent girl to be out."

"That's a sharp lad, that, with her," observed Delehanty. "I know him. He works over here in a tobacco factory. He's up to no good, I'll warrant ye."

"Teach 'em a lesson, I would," said Almerting to her. "Stroll around awhile and make 'em think you mean business. They won't lock you out any more. If they don't let you in when we come back, I'll find you a place all right."

His sharp eyes were gleaming as he looked around into her own and now he fairly carried her on.

Old butcher Rogaum saw her go, marveling at her audacity, but thought she would soon come back. At half-past ten he stuck his head out of the open window and at eleven walked the floor.

He was first wrathful and then nervous — then nervous and wrathful — and finally, all nervous, without a scintilla of wrath. His stout wife sat up in bed and began to wring her hands.

"Lie down!" he commanded. "You make me sick. I know vot I am doing."

"Is she still at the door?" pleaded the mother.

"I think so," he said.

His nerve was weakening, however, and now it finally collapsed.

"She has the street gone up," he said, anxiously. "I will go after."

Slipping on his coat he went down the stairs and out into the streets. It was growing late and the stillness and gloom of midnight was nearing. Nowhere in sight was his

Theresa. First one way and then another he went, looking here, there, everywhere, finally groaning.

"Ach, Gott!" he said, the sweat bursting out on his brow, "What in Teufel's[7] name iss dis?"

He thought he would seek a policeman, but there was no policeman. Officer Maguire had long since gone for a quiet game in one of the neighboring saloons. Still old Rogaum hunted on, worrying more and more.

Finally he thought to hasten home, for she must have got back. Mrs. Rogaum, too, would be frantic. If she were not there, he would hunt up the police in earnest. This thing could not go on.

As he turned into his own corner, he almost ran, coming up to the little portico wet and panting. At a puffing step, he turned and almost fell over a white body at his feet, a prone and writhing figure of a woman.

"Ach, Gott!" he cried, shouting aloud in his distress and excitement. "Theresa, what iss dis? Wilhelmina, a light now. Bring a light now, I say, for himmel's sake. De vooman hat sich *umgebracht*.[8] Help!"

He had fallen on his knees, and was turning over a writhing, groaning figure.

"Um," said the woman weakly. "Ah."

Almost by the pale light of the street, he could see that it was not his Theresa, and yet there was something very like in the figure. It cut the fiercest cords of his intensity, but there was something else about the situation which made him forget his own troubles.

Mrs. Rogaum, loudly admonished, almost tumbled down the stairs. At the foot, she held the light and then nearly dropped it. A beautiful figure, more girl than woman, rich in all the physical charms that characterize a certain type, lay near to dying. Her soft hair had fallen back over a good forehead now quite white. Her pretty hands, well decked with rings, were clutched tightly in an agonized grip. At her neck, a blue silk shirtwaist and light, lace collar were torn away where she had clutched herself, and on the white flesh was a yellow stain as of one who had been burned. A strange odor reeked in the area, and in one corner was a spilled bottle.

"Ach, Gott!" exclaimed Mrs. Rogaum. "It iss a vooman. She have herself gekilt. Run for de police. Oh, my! Oh, my!"

Rogaum did not kneel for more than a moment. He bounded up and jumping out in front of his door, began to yell lustily for the police. Officer Maguire heard the very first cry, and, leaving his social game, came running.

"What's the matter here, now?" he exclaimed, rushing up, full and ready for murder, robbery, fire, or, indeed, anything in the whole roster of human calamities.

"A vooman!" said Rogaum, excitedly. "She have herself *umgebracht*. She iss dying. Ach, Gott! in my own doorstep, yet."

"Vere iss de hospital?" put in Mrs. Rogaum, thinking clearly of an ambulance, but not being able to express it.

---

7. **Teufel's:** Devil's (German).
8. **hat sich *umgebracht:*** Has killed herself (German).

"She is gekilt, sure, Oh! Oh!" and bending over her, the poor, old motherly soul stroked the tightened hands and trickled tears upon the blue shirtwaist. "Ach, vy did you do dot?" she said. "Ach, for vy?"

Officer Maguire was essentially a man of action. He jumped out upon the sidewalk, amid the gathering company, and beat loudly with his club upon the stone flagging.

"Go, telephone for an ambulance," he said roughly to Rogaum, but others beat the old butcher to the corner. Even while Officer Delehanty, hearing the peculiar ring of the stick upon the stone in the night, came running from afar, Maguire held up a passing milk-wagon, making its way up from the Jersey ferry, with a few tons of fresh milk, and demanded a helping.

"Give us a quart there, will you?" he said authoritatively. "A woman's swallowed acid in here."

"Sure," said the driver, dying to get in on the excitement. "Where is a glass?"

Maguire ran back and returned, bearing a glass from an excited neighbor. Fat Mrs. Rogaum stood looking nervously on, while the wieldy officer raised the golden head, and poured the milk.

"Here, now, drink this," he said.

The girl, a fair blonde of the type which the world so readily ignores, only opened her eyes, and looked, groaning a little.

"Drink it," shouted the officer fiercely. "Do you want to die? Open your mouth."

Used to a fear of the law in all her days, she obeyed now, even in death. The lips parted, the fresh milk was drained to the end, some spilling on neck and cheek.

While they were so working, old Rogaum came back and stood looking on, by the side of his wife.

"Ach, ach," he said, rather distractedly, "und she iss oudt yet? I could not find her. Oh, oh!"

There was a clang of a gong up the street, as the racing ambulance turned rapidly in. A young hospital surgeon dismounted and, seeing the woman's condition, ordered immediate removal. Both officers and the surgeon helped her in the ambulance, and, after a moment, the lone bell, ringing wildly in the night, was all the evidence remaining that a tragedy had been.

"Do you know how she came here?" said Officer Delehanty, coming back to get Rogaum's testimony for the police.

"No, no," answered Rogaum, wretchedly. "She was here alretty. I was for my daughter look. Ach, himmel, I have my daughter lost. She vass avay."

Mrs. Rogaum also chattered.

The officer did not at first get the significance of this. He was only interested in the facts of the present case.

"You say she was here when you came? Where were you?"

"I say I vass for my daughter look. I come here, undt de vooman vass here now alretty."

"What time was this?"

"Only now yet. Yussed a half-hour."

Officer Maguire had strolled up, after chasing away the crowd with fierce and unholy threats. He noticed the peculiar perturbation of the usual placid German couple.

"What about your daughter?" he said, catching a word as to that.

Both old people raised their voices at once.

"She have gone. She have run avay. Ach, himmel, we must for her look. Quick — she could not get in. We haf de door shut."

"That's the girl I saw walking with young Almerting, do ye mind? The one in the white dress," said Maguire to Delehanty.

"White dress, yah," echoed Rogaum, and then the fact of her walking with some one came home like a blow.

"Dit you hear dot?" he exclaimed, even as Mrs. Rogaum did likewise, *"Mein Gott, hast du das gehoert?"*[9]

He fairly bounded as he said it. His hands flew up to his stout and ruddy head.

"Why do you let her out for nights?" observed Officer Maguire roughly, catching the drift of the situation. "That's no time for young girls to be out."

"Ich?" exclaimed poor Rogaum. "Me, yet. Ho, ho, ho!" His voice was almost hysteric.

"Well, go in now," said Officer Delehanty. "There's no use standing out here. Give us a description of the girl, and we'll look for her."

"Never mind," said Maguire. "I know her. I can tip them off."

The two men turned away, leaving the old German couple in the throe of distress. A time-worn, old church clock near by now chimed out one and then two. The notes cut like knives. Mrs. Rogaum began fearfully to cry. Rogaum walked and blustered to himself.

"It's a queer case, that," said Officer Delehanty, referring to the outcast of the doorway, so recently sent away. "I think I know that woman. She didn't come there by herself."

"Not a bit of it," said Maguire. "She was put there all right."

He tipped his nose up significantly, and cocked his eye serenely. "I think I know the one that did it. Let's go round to 68."

Around the corner the significant red light over the transom at that number told a story of its own. The two policemen strolled up and leisurely knocked. At the very first sound, a painted denizen of the half-world opened the door.

"Where is Adele?" said Maguire as the two officers stepped in.

"She's gone to bed."

"Tell her to come down."

They seated themselves deliberately in the gaudy mirrored parlor, and waited, conversing between themselves. Presently a sleepy-looking woman of forty appeared in an elegant robe and slippered in red.

"We're here about that case you had to-night."

"What case?" said the lady.

"You know," put in Maguire. "How did she come to take poison?"

"I don't know what you're talking about," said the woman.

"Come now," said Delehanty. "We know you've got a pull, but we've got to know about this case. It won't be published. What made her take the poison?"

---

9. *"Mein . . . gehoert?":* "My God, did you hear that?" (German).

The woman hesitated, under the steady eye of the officer, but finally weakened.

"Why, her lover went back on her — that's all."

"What was his name?"

"I don't know. You never can tell that."

"Was her name Annie," said Maguire.

"No — Emily."

"Well, how did she get over there?" inquired Delehanty pleasantly.

"George took her."

Little by little, as they sat there, the whole miserable story came out — miserable as all the error and suffering of the world.

"She did love him, did she?" inquired Maguire, rather surprised.

"Of course, she did — she was crazy over him."

"And he wouldn't come back?"

"That's what he said."

Wonderful, wonderful this to the policeman. He would never get it through his head. Great, surging, maddening passion, that would rather die in a doorway than lose. He shook his head.

"How old was she?"

"Oh, twenty-one."

"Think o' that," said Delehanty, who had a pretty daughter the same age.

"Well, where'd she come from?"

"Oh, here in New York. Her family locked her out, one night, I think."

Something in the way the woman said this brought old Rogaum back to Maguire's mind. He had forgotten all about that pretty German's disappearance.

"I'll tell old Rogaum that," he said facetiously to Delehanty. "He locked his girl out to night."

The two men inquired a little farther, and then went away.

"Let's go by and see if the girl has got back yet," said Maguire, as they came out and around the corner, disturbed but little by the tragedies of life.

"Is your daughter back again," asked Maguire, beating soundly on the door.

"Ach, no," said the hysterical Mrs. Rogaum, who was quite alone. "My husband he haf gone out again to look vunce. Oh, my, oh, my!"

"That's what you get for locking her out," said Maguire masterfully. "That other woman down here," and he pointed to the still acid-stained area, "was also locked out. You oughtn't to do that."

It was carrying coals to Newcastle,[10] however. Her grief was great enough.

They returned to the station, and sent out a hurry call:

"Look out for girl, Theresa Rogaum. Aged 18; height, about 5, 3; light hair, blue eyes, cotton dress, trimmed with blue ribbon. Last seen with lad named Almerting, about 21 years of age."

---

10. **carrying coals to Newcastle:** Newcastle upon Tyne was known as the major exporter of coal mined in the surrounding area in northern England. The expression means to do something pointless or unnecessary.

There were other details even more pointed and conclusive. As each station received the message, the men were informed when called up. From Battery to Harlem,[11] and far beyond, policemen were scanning the long streets, in the dim shadows of the night, for a girl in a white dress, and a youth of 21.

Officer Halsey got the message, after he had reported for a third time from his beat, which took in a portion of Washington Square. He had seen a good many couples this pleasant summer evening, but none that answered this description. He went out and idled about the corner until Officer Paisly came up, and then the matter was discussed.

"I saw that couple, I bet you, not over an hour and a half ago," said the latter interestedly. "She was dressed in white, and looked to me as if she didn't want to go. I remember looking at the fellow with her. They acted sort of funny. They went in this park down at the Eighth street end there."

"Supposing we beat it," said Halsey, weary for something to do.

"Sure," said the other quickly.

Together they began a careful search, kicking around in the moonlight, under the trees. The moon was leaning moderately toward the West, and all the branches were silvered with light and dew. Among the flowers, past clumps of bushes, near the fountain they searched, each one going his way alone. At last, the wandering Halsey paused beside a thick clump of flaming bushes, ruddy, slightly, even in the night. A murmur of voices greeted him, and something very much like the sound of a sob.

"What's that," he said, mentally, drawing near and listening.

"Why don't you come on now," said the first of the voices heard. "They won't let you in. What's the use crying?"

No answer to this, but no sobs. She must have been crying silently.

"Come on. I can take care of you. We can live in Hoboken.[12] That's all right."

There was a movement as if the speaker were patting her on the shoulder.

"What's the use crying? Don't you believe I love you?"

The officer stole quietly around to get a better view. He wanted to see for himself. In the moonlight, from a comfortable distance he could see them seated, now that his eyes were searching. The tall bushes were almost all about the bench. In his arm was a girl — a pretty girl, in white, held very close. Dropping down to get a better view, he saw him kiss her and hold her — hold her in such a way that she could but yield to him, whatever her slight disinclination.

It was a common affair at earlier hours, but rather startling now. The officer was delighted, as he crept nearer, to break it up.

Suddenly he appeared before them very quickly, and with a sinister look. "What are you two doing here?" he inquired, as if he had not seen.

The girl tumbled out of her compromising position, speechless and blushing violently.

---

11. **From Battery to Harlem:** That is, from the Lower East Side to the Upper West Side of Manhattan.
12. **Hoboken:** Town in New Jersey, across the Hudson River from Manhattan.

"We're just sitting in the Park," returned the lean-faced youth, with considerable *sang froid*.[13]

"Well, we don't allow this. You'll have to come along with me."

The boy stood up. "What for?" he said.

"Never mind," said Halsey, "come along now. I want you both. That's all."

At the other end of the Park, Paisly joined them and, at the station house, the girl was given a chair. She was all tears and melancholy.

"Send them down here," said the man at the Bleecker Street Station, who had heard from Maguire of old Rogaum's grief. "We want to send her home."

By four in the morning, the twain were down in Bleecker Street, and Rogaum rushing stationward.

"Ach, Gott, now!" he said, as he saw his daughter again, "what haf you done? Oh, oh!" and he gathered her in his arms.

"You, you!" he said, glaring at the imperturbable Almerting, "come not near my tochter any more. I vill preak your effery pone, du teufel, du!"

He made a move toward the incarcerated lover, but here the Sergeant interfered.

"Stop that," he said now. "Take your daughter out of here, and go home, or I'll lock you both up. D'ye hear? We'll do whatever punishing's to be done."

"I didn't do nawthin," said Almerting, cynically. "They locked her out."

"You shut up," said the Sergeant, irritably. Still he called after the butcher angrily:

"Keep your daughter off the streets hereafter, do you hear?"

Old Rogaum heard nothing. He was in a mixture of wondrous feelings. What to do was beyond him.

At the corner near the butcher shop, the wakeful Maguire was still idling as they passed.

"Don't lock her out any more," he called, significantly. "That's what brought the other girl to your door."

"What is dot?" said Rogaum.

"I say the other girl was locked out. That's why she committed suicide."

"Ach, I know," said the husky German, under his breath, but he had no intention of locking her out. He did not know what he would do until they were in the presence of his crying wife, who fell upon Theresa weeping.

"She vass like you," said the old mother to the wandering Theresa, ignorant of the important lesson brought to their very door. "She vass loog like you."

"I will not vip you now," said the old butcher, solemnly, too delighted to think of punishment, "aber,[14] go not avay any more. Dot loafer, aber — let him come here no more. I vill fix him."

"She wouldn't run away no more yet, no," said the fat mother, tearfully.

"No," said Theresa, in tears, "he wouldn't let me come back, that was all. I hope they arrest him."

---

13. *sang froid:* Literally "cold blood" (French), the term suggests calm or coolness in trying circumstances.
14. aber: But or though (German).

"I vill fix him," said Rogaum, unloading now on the lover freely. "De penitentiary he should have."

"Don't you ever bother that girl again," said the Sergeant to young Almerting, as he turned him loose after an hour. "If you do, we'll get you, and you won't get off under six months."

"I don't want her," said the boy, cynically. "Let him have his old daughter. They had better not lock her out, though — that's all I say. I don't want her," and away he went.

[1901]

Paul Laurence Dunbar

[1872–1906]

Paul Laurence Dunbar

This photograph was taken around 1900, only a few years before Dunbar's premature death ended the career of the most famous African American writer of his generation.

Paul Laurence Dunbar was born in Dayton, Ohio, on June 27, 1872, the child of two former slaves from Kentucky. His father, Joshua Dunbar, had escaped to Canada by way of the underground railroad before the Civil War, during which he returned to enlist in the Fifty-fifth Massachusetts Infantry Regiment. He married Matilda J. Murphy, a widow with two young sons, and the couple had two children before they divorced in 1876. Dunbar was raised by his mother, who worked as a washerwoman to support her children. She also inspired them with a love of poetry, songs, and storytelling, especially the rich oral traditions of African Americans. The family moved several times while Dunbar was growing up in Dayton, where he attended predominantly white schools and was the only African American in his class at Central High School. An outgoing and talented student, Dunbar experienced relatively little racial prejudice at school, where he was encouraged to develop his extraordinary literary abilities. He read a variety of British poets, including John Keats and William Wordsworth, as well as popular American poets such as Henry Wadsworth Longfellow and John Greenleaf Whittier. Dunbar edited the school newspaper and published his first poem, "Our Martyred Soldiers," in the *Dayton Herald* on June 8, 1888. Some of his verses also appeared in a smaller local newspaper published by his friends Orville and Wilbur Wright, known later as the famous Wright brothers, who started a printing shop in Dayton in 1888.

When he graduated from high school in 1891, however, Dunbar confronted the narrowly limited opportunities available to African Americans in late-nineteenth-century America. Unable to find more suitable work, he took a job as an elevator operator in a building in Dayton. But he continued to write poetry, which soon opened up a new world to Dunbar. After one of his high school teachers arranged for him to recite a welcoming address at the meeting of the Western Association of Writers in 1892, he began to publish poems in local newspapers, and the following year Dunbar took a loan to pay for the publication of his first volume of poetry, *Oak and Ivy* (1893). His notoriety in Dayton, where he was known as the "elevator boy poet," and growing reputation in the Midwest led to an invitation for Dunbar to recite a poem on "Negro American Day" at the World's Colombian Exposition, which opened in 1893 in Chicago. There, he met a number of influential African Americans, including the antilynching crusader Ida B. Wells and Frederick Douglass, then the U.S. ambassador to Haiti. Taking an immediate interest in Dunbar, whom he called "the most promising young colored man in America," Douglass secured him a job as a clerk in the Haitian pavilion at the exposition. Dunbar also gained the patronage of two white admirers from Toledo, Ohio: the lawyer Charles A. Thatcher and the psychiatrist Henry A. Tobey, who promoted his career and paid for the publication of his second book of poetry, *Majors and Minors* (1895). The volume was enthusiastically reviewed by William Dean Howells, who subsequently wrote the preface to Dunbar's first commercially produced volume of poetry, *Lyrics of Lowly Life* (1896).

That bestseller gained Dunbar a wide audience for his work, which was read and praised by both blacks and whites in the United States. Propelled by the enthusiastic reception of *Lyrics of Lowly Life*, Dunbar gave numerous readings in eastern cities and then during a successful tour of England. Following his return in 1897, he moved to Washington, D.C., where Dunbar worked for a time as an assistant in the Reading Room of the Library of Congress. During the following years, his writings appeared in prominent national periodicals like the *Atlantic Monthly*, *Century*, *Lipincott's*, and the *Saturday Evening Post*, which were eager to publish Dunbar's poetry as well as the fiction he soon began to write. His earliest stories were collected in *Folks from Dixie* (1898), published the same year as his first novel, *The Uncalled*. He also wrote plays for black performers and collaborated on the Broadway musicals *Clorindy* and *In Dahomey*. In 1898, he married Alice Ruth Moore, who would later become well known as Alice Dunbar-Nelson for her stories of Creole life in New Orleans. But the couple separated four years later, partly as a result of Dunbar's heavy drinking to ease the pain in his lungs from tuberculosis, which he contracted around 1899. Nonetheless, he continued to write and publish at a furious pace until he finally succumbed to the disease on February 9, 1906. During the mere thirteen years since his first book appeared in 1893, Dunbar had produced a staggering amount of work, including numerous essays, four novels, four collections of short stories, and thirteen collections of the poems for which he was hailed as "The Poet Laureate of the Negro Race" by the influential African American leader Booker T. Washington.

Dunbar's Poetry.

During his lifetime, Dunbar became what the literary scholar Henry Louis Gates Jr. has described as "the most famous black writer in the world." Dunbar first gained serious attention when his second book, *Majors and Minors* (1895), was reviewed by William Dean Howells

FOR PAUL LAURENCE DUNBAR
Born of the sorrowful of
*   heart,*
Mirth was a crown upon
*   his head;*
Pride kept his twisted
*   lips apart*
In jest, to hide a heart
*   that bled*
*   –Countee Cullen*

bedfordstmartins.com/ americanlit *for research links on Dunbar*

in *Harper's Weekly* in June 1896. That influential critic was struck by the humor and lyrical quality of the poems in the volume, as well as by Dunbar's versatility in using both the dialect of southern blacks and what Howells called "our American English." But he was careful to add: "I am speaking of him as a black poet, when I should be speaking of him as a poet." In his introduction to *Lyrics of Lowly Life* (1896), however, Howells emphasizes the poet's racial identity, observing that Dunbar was "the first instance of an American negro who had evinced innate distinction in literature," by which he evidently meant the first African American writer of unmixed racial heritage to do so. Dunbar's contributions to and his role in shaping a distinctive African American literary tradition were later deeply contested, especially among black poets and critics. His friend and contemporary James Weldon Johnson suggested that Dunbar's dialect poetry had helped promote the racist plantation myth promulgated by popular white writers who evoked a world of benign masters and contented slaves in the antebellum South. Nonetheless, Johnson was a self-described disciple of Dunbar, whose work also influenced poets of the Harlem Renaissance as different as Langston Hughes and Countee Cullen. More recently, critics have tended to focus increasing attention on the veiled social commentary offered in some of Dunbar's dialect poems, as well as on the sensitive exploration of the plight of African Americans in many of the poems he wrote in standard English. The texts of "An Ante-bellum Sermon" and "We Wear the Mask" are taken from *Lyrics of Lowly Life* (1896). The text of "Sympathy," one of Dunbar's most famous poems and the source of the title of Maya Angelou's best-selling autobiography, *I Know Why the Caged Bird Sings* (1970), is taken from *Lyrics of the Hearthside* (1899).

AN ANTE-BELLUM[1] SERMON

We is gathahed hyeah, my brothahs,
   In dis howlin' wildaness,
Fu' to speak some words of comfo't
   To each othah in distress.
An' we chooses fu' ouah subjic'   5
   Dis — we'll 'splain it by an' by;
"An' de Lawd said, 'Moses, Moses,'[2]
   An' de man said, 'Hyeah am I.'"

---

1. **Ante-bellum:** Literally, "before the war" (Latin), though in American history *antebellum* (as it is now spelled) almost always refers to the period before the Civil War.
2. **Moses:** The Hebrew prophet who led the Israelites out of slavery in Egypt to the promised land (Exodus 20). American slaves often compared themselves to the ancient Israelites, especially in the slave songs or "Negro spirituals" that became popular in the decades following the Civil War.

Now ole Pher'oh, down in Egypt,
    Was de wuss man evah bo'n,   10
An' he had de Hebrew chillun
    Down dah wukin' in his co'n;
'T well de Lawd got tiahed o' his foolin',
    An' sez he: "I 'll let him know —
Look hyeah, Moses, go tell Pher'oh   15
    Fu' to let dem chillun go."

"An' ef he refuse to do it,
    I will make him rue de houah,
Fu' I 'll empty down on Egypt
    All de vials of my powah."   20
Yes, he did — an' Pher'oh's ahmy
    Was n't wuth a ha'f a dime;
Fu' de Lawd will he'p his chillun,
    You kin trust him evah time.

An' yo' enemies may 'sail you   25
    In de back an' in de front;
But de Lawd is all aroun' you,
    Fu' to ba' de battle's brunt.
Dey kin fo'ge yo' chains an shackles
    F'om de mountains to de sea;   30
But de Lawd will sen' some Moses
    Fu' to set his chillun free.

An' de lan' shall hyeah his thundah,
    Lak a blas' f'om Gab'el's ho'n,[3]
Fu' de Lawd of hosts is mighty   35
    When he girds his ahmor on.
But fu' feah some one mistakes me,
    I will pause right hyeah to say,
Dat I 'm still a-preachin' ancient,
    I ain't talkin' 'bout to-day.   40

But I tell you, fellah christuns,
    Things 'll happen mighty strange;
Now, de Lawd done dis fu' Isrul,
    An' his ways don't nevah change,
An' de love he showed to Isrul   45
    Was n't all on Isrul spent;

---

3. **Gab'el's ho'n:** Gabriel's horn, a reference to the archangel who announces good news by blowing his horn, which many Christians believe will announce the Last Judgment.

Now don't run an' tell yo' mastahs
　　Dat I 's preachin' discontent.

'Cause I is n't; I 'se a-judgin'
　　Bible people by deir ac's;
I 'se a-givin' you de Scriptuah,
　　I 'se a-handin' you de fac's.
Cose ole Pher'oh b'lieved in slav'ry.
　　But de Lawd he let him see,
Dat de people he put bref in, –
　　Evah mothah's son was free.

An' dahs othahs thinks lak Pher'oh,
　　But dey calls de Scriptuah liar,
Fu' de Bible says "a servant
　　Is a-worthy of his hire."
An' you cain't git roun' nor thoo dat,
　　An' you cain't git ovah it,
Fu' whatevah place you git in,
　　Dis hyeah Bible too 'll fit.

So you see de Lawd's intention,
　　Evah sence de worl' began,
Was dat His almighty freedom
　　Should belong to evah man,
But I think it would be bettah,
　　Ef I 'd pause agin to say,
Dat I 'm talkin' 'bout ouah freedom
　　In a Bibleistic way.

But de Moses is a-comin',
　　an' he's comin, suah and fas'
We kin hyeah his feet a-trompin,
　　We kin hyeah his trumpit blas'.
But I want to wa'n you people,
　　Don't you git too brigity;[4]
An' don't you git to braggin'
　　'Bout dese things, you wait an' see.

But when Moses wif his powah
　　Comes an' sets us chillun free,
We will praise de gracious Mastah,[5]

50
55
60
65
70
75
80

---

4. **brigity:** Biggity, or boastful.
5. **Mastah:** Jesus Christ.

Dat has gin us liberty;
An' we'll shout ouah halleluyahs,   85
  On dat mighty reck'nin' day,
When we'se reco'nised ez citiz' —
  Huh uh! Chillun, let us pray!

                                                              [1896]

WE WEAR THE MASK

We wear the mask that grins and lies,
It hides our cheeks and shades our eyes, —
This debt we pay to human guile;
With torn and bleeding hearts we smile,
And mouth with myriad subtleties.   5

Why should the world be over-wise,
In counting all our tears and sighs?
Nay, let them only see us, while
  We wear the mask.

We smile, but, O great Christ, our cries   10
To thee from tortured souls arise.
We sing, but oh the clay is vile
Beneath our feet, and long the mile;
But let the world dream otherwise,
  We wear the mask!   15
                                                              [1896]

SYMPATHY

I know what the caged bird feels, alas!
  When the sun is bright on the upland slopes;
When the wind stirs soft through the springing grass,
And the river flows like a stream of glass;
  When the first bird sings and the first bud opes,   5
And the faint perfume from its chalice steals —
I know what the caged bird feels!

I know why the caged bird beats his wing
  Till its blood is red on the cruel bars;
For he must fly back to his perch and cling   10
When he fain would be on the bough a-swing;
  And a pain still throbs in the old, old scars

And they pulse again with a keener sting —
I know why he beats his wing!

I know why the caged bird sings, ah me,   15
    When his wing is bruised and his bosom sore, —
When he beats his bars and he would be free;
It is not a carol of joy or glee,
    But a prayer that he sends from his heart's deep core,
But a plea, that upward to Heaven he flings —   20
I know why the caged bird sings!

[1899]

Willa Cather

[1873-1947]

Willa Cather

This photograph was taken around 1910, when Cather was the editor of the influential *McClure's Magazine.* She is wearing a necklace given to her by Sarah Orne Jewett.

Wilella Sibert Cather was born in Back Creek Valley, west of Winchester, Virginia, on December 7, 1873, the first child of Mary Virginia Boak and Charles Cather. Often called "Willie" by her family, Cather later adopted the name "Willa." When a fire destroyed part of their farm in 1883, her family left Virginia to join relatives who had established a homestead on high ground, the "Divide" as it was called, between the Little Blue and Republican rivers in southeastern Nebraska. In an interview in 1913, Cather recalled her vivid first impressions of the stark landscape: "[T]he roads were mostly faint trails over the bunch grass in those days. The land was open range and there was almost no fencing. As we drove further and further out into the country, I felt a good deal as if we had come to the end of everything." The remote area was populated by large numbers of European immigrants from Germany, Denmark, Sweden, and Russia, whose customs and language also made a strong impression on Cather. After two years on the homestead, Charles Cather moved his family to the bustling railroad town of Red Cloud, Nebraska, where he opened an insurance and real-estate business. Cather attended public schools, wrote plays, and participated in dramatic performances (often taking male roles) in the town's new Opera House. After graduating from high school in 1890, she studied for a year at the Latin School, a college preparatory school in Lincoln, before enrolling at the University of Nebraska in the fall of 1891. At the time, relatively few women attended the university, and Cather further challenged gender roles by arriving there dressed as what she called her "twin brother," William Cather.

An excellent student, Cather soon determined to become a professional writer. Her first story appeared in a campus literary magazine in 1892. In addition to editing the student newspaper, she became a regular contributor to the local Lincoln newspaper, the *Nebraska State Journal,* writing reviews and a weekly drama column. After she graduated in 1895, Cather worked for Nebraska newspapers, but the ambitious young writer was eager to be a part of a larger literary scene. In 1896, she accepted an offer to become the editor of the *Home Monthly,* a small magazine published in Pittsburgh, Pennsylvania. After a year with the *Home Monthly,* the pages of which were filled with works Cather published under various pen names, she took a job with the *Pittsburgh Leader.* She resigned from the newspaper in 1900, about the time one of her stories was published in *Cosmopolitan,* then a family magazine and one of the major markets for fiction in the United States. By then, she had begun to develop a close relationship with Isabelle McClung, the daughter of a wealthy Pittsburgh judge, who invited Cather to move into the family's large house in the spring of 1901. She lived there for the next five years, teaching English and Latin at high schools and devoting her free time to writing. Cather's first book was a collection of poetry, *April Twilights* (1903). Her stories appeared in prominent periodicals such as *Everybody's Magazine,* the *Saturday Evening Post,* and *Scribner's,* paving the way for the publication of her first collection of short fiction, *The Troll Garden,* in 1905. The following year, she moved to New York City to take a position on the editorial staff of *McClure's Magazine.* She worked for that influential magazine for six years, publishing numerous stories and rising to the position of managing editor before resigning to devote full time to writing in 1912.

During the remainder of her long career, Cather became a highly admired novelist. Her first novel, *Alexander's Bridge* (1912), was set in the East and revealed the strong influence of Henry James and Edith Wharton. Cather explored a very different terrain in *O Pioneers!* (1913), a novel in which she drew heavily on her early experiences in Nebraska. Living in New York City with Edith Lewis, her long-term companion, Cather subsequently wrote a series of acclaimed novels about life on the Great Plains, including *The Song of the Lark* (1915), *My Ántonia* (1918), and *A Lost Lady* (1923). In an interview, however, Cather said that she did not want to become too identified with the West, since "using one setting all the time is very like planting a field with corn season after season. I believe in rotation of crops. If the public ties me down to the cornfield too much I'm afraid I'll leave that scene entirely." Cather, who traveled widely with Edith Lewis, broke new ground with *The Professor's House* (1925), which was set in Michigan and the Southwest, and *Death Comes for the Archbishop*

How [Cather] refreshes the spirit? The quality that struck me with the strongest force as I read is what I should like to speak about as we meet to celebrate her — the remarkable, rewarding, physical quality of her work.

—Eudora Welty

bedfordstmartins.com/ americanlit for research links on Cather

(1927), a novel about the Spanish settlement of New Mexico. In her later novels, she ventured equally far afield: to the early settlement of Canada in *Shadows on the Rock* (1931); forward to the early twentieth century in *Lucy Gayheart* (1935), the action of which shifts between a small town on the Great Plains and urban Chicago; and back to antebellum Virginia, where she was born, in her final novel, *Sapphira and the Slave Girl* (1940). Cather died at her home in New York City on April 24, 1947.

Cather's "A Wagner Matinée."   This story was first published in *Everybody's Magazine.* Founded in 1896, the illustrated monthly developed a reputation for its investigative (what its critics called "muckrak-

Homesteaders in Nebraska

This photograph of the David Hilton family was taken in 1887 near Weissert, in central Nebraska. The photographer noted that the family "did not want to show the old sod house to friends back east, but the young lady and mother wanted to prove they had an organ."

ing") journalism, as well as for publishing work by a variety of American writers, including Frank Norris, who contributed exposés of corrupt business practices. Seeking the broadest possible audience, the magazine also featured articles designed to appeal to women and fiction by popular authors such as Mary E. Wilkins Freeman. At the time "A Wagner Matinée" was published in the magazine, the controversial operas of Richard Wagner were being widely performed in the United States. The story also generated controversy, drawing the ire of friends and family members who objected to Cather's bleak depiction of life in Nebraska. In an editorial in the *Nebraska State Journal*, her old friend Will Jones observed: "If the writers of fiction who use western Nebraska as material would look up now and then and not keep their eyes and noses in the cattle yards, they might be more agreeable company." In response to such criticism, Cather slightly revised the story before publishing it in her collection *The Troll Garden* (1905), toning down the harsh description of the narrator's aunt Georgiana, a figure loosely based on her Boston-born aunt, Frances Cather, who had moved with her husband to Nebraska. Some biographers have suggested that as Cather grew older she became increasingly charitable about her early experiences in Nebraska, and she further altered "A Wagner Matinée" in the version published in her collection *Youth and the Bright Medusa* (1920), as well as in the final version published in 1937. The text is taken from the first printing in *Everybody's Magazine*, February 1904.

A WAGNER MATINÉE

I received one morning a letter written in pale ink, on glassy, blue-lined notepaper, and bearing the postmark of a little Nebraska village. This communication, worn and rubbed, looking as though it had been carried for some days in a coat-pocket that was none too clean, was from my Uncle Howard. It informed me that his wife had been left a small legacy by a bachelor relative who had recently died, and that it had become necessary for her to come to Boston to attend to the settling of the estate. He requested me to meet her at the station, and render her whatever services might prove necessary. On examining the date indicated as that of her arrival, I found it no later than to-morrow. He had characteristically delayed writing until, had I been away from home for a day, I must have missed the good woman altogether.

The name of my Aunt Georgiana called up not alone her own figure, at once pathetic and grotesque, but opened before my feet a gulf of recollections so wide and deep that, as the letter dropped from my hand, I felt suddenly a stranger to all the present conditions of my existence, wholly ill at ease and out of place amid the surroundings of my study. I became, in short, the gangling farmer-boy my aunt had known, scourged with chilblains[1] and bashfulness, my hands cracked and raw from the corn-husking. I felt the

---

1. **chilblains:** Itchy, painful swellings on the skin, caused by exposure to cold.

knuckles of my thumb tentatively, as though they were raw again. I sat again before her parlor organ, thumbing the scales with my stiff, red hands, while she beside me made canvas mittens for the huskers.[2]

The next morning, after preparing my landlady somewhat, I set out for the station. When the train arrived I had some difficulty in finding my aunt. She was the last of the passengers to alight, and when I got her into the carriage she looked not unlike one of those charred, smoked bodies that firemen lift from the *débris* of a burned building. She had come all the way in a day coach; her linen duster[3] had become black with soot and her black bonnet gray with dust during the journey. When we arrived at my boarding-house the landlady put her to bed at once, and I did not see her again until the next morning.

Whatever shock Mrs. Springer experienced at my aunt's appearance she considerately concealed. Myself, I saw my aunt's misshapen figure with that feeling of awe and respect with which we behold explorers who have left their ears and fingers north of Franz Josef Land, or their health somewhere along the Upper Congo. My Aunt Georgiana had been a music-teacher at the Boston Conservatory, somewhere back in the latter sixties. One summer, which she had spent in the little village in the Green Mountains where her ancestors had dwelt for generations, she had kindled the callow fancy of the most idle and shiftless of all the village lads, and had conceived for this Howard Carpenter one of those absurd and extravagant passions which a handsome country boy of twenty-one sometimes inspires in a plain, angular, spectacled woman of thirty. When she returned to her duties in Boston, Howard followed her; and the upshot of this inexplicable infatuation was that she eloped with him, eluding the reproaches of her family and the criticism of her friends by going with him to the Nebraska frontier. Carpenter, who of course had no money, took a homestead[4] in Red Willow County, fifty miles from the railroad. There they measured off their eighty acres by driving across the prairie in a wagon, to the wheel of which they had tied a red cotton handkerchief, and counting its revolutions. They built a dugout in the red hillside, one of those cave dwellings whose inmates usually reverted to the conditions of primitive savagery. Their water they got from the lagoons where the buffalo drank, and their slender stock of provisions was always at the mercy of bands of roving Indians. For thirty years my aunt had not been farther than fifty miles from the homestead.

But Mrs. Springer knew nothing of all this, and must have been considerably shocked at what was left of my kinswoman. Beneath the soiled linen duster, which on her arrival was the most conspicuous feature of her costume, she wore a black stuff dress whose ornamentation showed that she had surrendered herself unquestioningly into the hands of a country dressmaker. My poor aunt's figure, however, would have presented astonishing difficulties to any dressmaker. Her skin was yellow as a Mongolian's

---

2. **huskers:** People employed to remove the husks, or coverings, from ears of corn.
3. **linen duster:** A long, loose, and lightweight coat worn by women in the early 1900s for traveling.
4. **homestead:** The federal Homestead Act of 1862 provided parcels of public land in the West to those willing to settle and farm the land for at least five years.

from constant exposure to a pitiless wind, and to the alkaline water, which transforms the most transparent cuticle into a sort of flexible leather. She wore ill-fitting false teeth. The most striking thing about her physiognomy, however, was an incessant twitching of the mouth and eyebrows, a form of nervous disorder resulting from isolation and monotony, and from frequent physical suffering.

In my boyhood this affliction had possessed a sort of horrible fascination for me, of which I was secretly very much ashamed, for in those days I owed to this woman most of the good that ever came my way, and had a reverential affection for her. During the three winters when I was riding herd for my uncle, my aunt, after cooking three meals for half a dozen farm-hands, and putting the six children to bed, would often stand until midnight at her ironing-board, hearing me at the kitchen table beside her recite Latin declensions and conjugations, and gently shaking me when my drowsy head sank down over a page of irregular verbs. It was to her, at her ironing or mending, that I read my first Shakespeare; and her old text-book of mythology was the first that ever came into my empty hands. She taught me my scales and exercises, too, on the little parlor organ which her husband had bought her after fifteen years, during which she had not so much as seen any instrument except an accordion, that belonged to one of the Norwegian farm-hands. She would sit beside me by the hour, darning and counting, while I struggled with the "Harmonious Blacksmith";[5] but she seldom talked to me about music, and I understood why. She was a pious woman; she had the consolation of religion; and to her at least her martyrdom was not wholly sordid. Once when I had been doggedly beating out some passages from an old score of "Euryanthe"[6] I had found among her music-books, she came up to me and, putting her hand over my eyes, gently drew my head back upon her shoulder, saying tremulously, "Don't love it so well, Clark, or it may be taken from you. Oh! dear boy, pray that whatever your sacrifice be it is not that."

When my aunt appeared on the morning after her arrival, she was still in a semisomnambulant state. She seemed not to realize that she was in the city where she had spent her youth, the place longed for hungrily for half a lifetime. She had been so wretchedly train-sick throughout the journey that she had no recollection of anything but her discomfort, and, to all intents and purposes, there were but a few hours of nightmare between the farm in Red Willow County and my study on Newbury Street. I had planned a little pleasure for her that afternoon, to repay her for some of the glorious moments she had given me when we used to milk together in the straw-thatched cowshed, and she, because I was more than usually tired, or because her husband had spoken sharply to me, would tell me of the splendid performance of Meyerbeer's "Huguenots"[7] she had seen in Paris in her youth. At two o'clock the Boston Symphony

---

5. **"Harmonious Blacksmith":** A musical composition by the German composer and pianist Robert Schumann (1810–1856).

6. **"Euryanthe":** Set in twelfth-century France, this romantic opera about a tragic love affair was composed by Carl Maria von Weber (1786–1826) and first performed in 1823.

7. **"Huguenots":** *Les Huguenots* (1836), an opera about the massacre of Huguenots (Protestants) by Catholics in Paris in 1572, was composed by Giacomo Meyerbeer (1791–1864).

Orchestra was to give a Wagner programme,[8] and I intended to take my aunt, though as I conversed with her I grew doubtful about her enjoyment of it. Indeed, for her own sake, I could only wish her taste for such things quite dead, and the long struggle mercifully ended at last. I suggested our visiting the Conservatory and the Common before lunch, but she seemed altogether too timid to wish to venture out. She questioned me absently about various changes in the city, but she was chiefly concerned that she had forgotten to leave instructions about feeding half-skimmed milk to a certain weakling calf, "Old Maggie's calf, you know, Clark," she explained, evidently having forgotten how long I had been away. She was further troubled because she had neglected to tell her daughter about the freshly opened kit of mackerel in the cellar, that would spoil if it were not used directly.

I asked her whether she had ever heard any of the Wagnerian operas, and found that she had not, though she was perfectly familiar with their respective situations and had once possessed the piano score of "The Flying Dutchman."[9] I began to think it would have been best to get her back to Red Willow County without waking her, and regretted having suggested the concert.

From the time we entered the concert-hall, however, she was a trifle less passive and inert, and seemed to begin to perceive her surroundings. I had felt some trepidation lest she might become aware of the absurdities of her attire, or might experience some painful embarrassment at stepping suddenly into the world to which she had been dead for a quarter of a century. But again I found how superficially I had judged her. She sat looking about her with eyes as impersonal, almost as stony as those with which the granite Rameses in a museum[10] watches the froth and fret that ebbs and flows about his pedestal, separated from it by the lonely stretch of centuries. I have seen this same aloofness in old miners who drift into the Brown Hotel at Denver, their pockets full of bullion, their linen soiled, their haggard faces unshorn, and who stand in the thronged corridors as solitary as though they were still in a frozen camp on the Yukon, or in the yellow blaze of the Arizona desert, conscious that certain experiences have isolated them from their fellows by a gulf no haberdasher could conceal.

The audience was made up chiefly of women. One lost the contour of faces and figures, indeed any effect of line whatever, and there was only the color contrast of bodices past counting, the shimmer and shading of fabrics soft and firm, silky and sheer, resisting and yielding: red, mauve, pink, blue, lilac, purple, ecru, rose, yellow, cream, and white, all the colors that an impressionist finds in a sunlit landscape, with here and there the dead black shadow of a frock-coat. My Aunt Georgiana regarded them as though they had been so many daubs of tube paint on a palette.

---

8. **Wagner programme:** Selections from the music of Richard Wagner (1813–1883), the acclaimed German composer of thirteen major operas and numerous other works.
9. **"The Flying Dutchman":** Wagner's early opera, inspired by the legend of a ship that sails the seas but can never find its way home, was first performed in 1843.
10. **granite Rameses in a museum:** Rameses, or Ramses, was the name of eleven different Egyptian pharaohs, most of whom were commemorated in statues that had been removed to various museums in the nineteenth century.

When the musicians came out and took their places, she gave a little stir of anticipation, and looked with quickening interest down over the rail at that invariable grouping; perhaps the first wholly familiar thing that had greeted her eye since she had left old Maggie and her weakling calf. I could feel how all those details sank into her soul, for I had not forgotten how they had sunk into mine when I came fresh from ploughing forever and forever between green aisles of corn, where, as in a treadmill, one might walk from daybreak to dusk without perceiving a shadow of change in one's environment. I reminded myself of the impression made on me by the clean profiles of the musicians, the gloss of their linen, the dull black of their coats, the beloved shapes of the instruments, the patches of yellow light thrown by the green-shaded stand-lamps on the smooth, varnished bellies of the 'cellos and the bass viols in the rear, the restless, wind-tossed forest of fiddle necks and bows; I recalled how, in the first orchestra I had ever heard, those long bow strokes seemed to draw the soul out of me, as a conjuror's stick reels out paper ribbon from a hat.

The first number was the Tannhäuser overture.[11] When the violins drew out the first strain of the Pilgrims' chorus, my Aunt Georgiana clutched my coat-sleeve. Then it was that I first realized that for her this singing of basses and stinging frenzy of lighter strings broke a silence of thirty years, the inconceivable silence of the plains. With the battle between the two motifs, with the bitter frenzy of the Venusberg theme[12] and its ripping of strings, came to me an overwhelming sense of the waste and wear we are so powerless to combat. I saw again the tall, naked house on the prairie, black and grim as a wooden fortress; the black pond where I had learned to swim, the rain-gullied clay about the naked house; the four dwarf ash-seedlings on which the dishcloths were always hung to dry before the kitchen door. The world there is the flat world of the ancients; to the east, a cornfield that stretched to daybreak; to the west, a corral that stretched to sunset; between, the sordid conquests of peace, more merciless than those of war.

The overture closed. My aunt released my coat-sleeve, but she said nothing. She sat staring at the orchestra through a dullness of thirty years, through the films made, little by little, by each of the three hundred and sixty-five days in every one of them. What, I wondered, did she get from it? She had been a good pianist in her day, I knew, and her musical education had been broader than that of most music-teachers of a quarter of a century ago. She had often told me of Mozart's operas and Meyerbeer's, and I could remember hearing her sing, years ago, certain melodies of Verdi's.[13] When I had fallen ill with a fever she used to sit by my cot in the evening, while the cool night wind blew in

11. **Tannhäuser overture:** The musical introduction to Wagner's opera *Tannhäuser* (1843-44).

12. **Venusberg theme:** The bacchanalian music associated in the opera with Venusberg, a mountain in Germany that according to Teutonic legend housed the court of Venus, the goddess of love.

13. **Mozart's operas . . . melodies of Verdi's:** The most famous operas of Wolfgang Amadeus Mozart (1756-1791) are *The Marriage of Figaro* (1786), *Don Giovanni* (1787), *Cosi fan tutte* (1790), and *The Magic Flute* (1791). The operas of the Italian composer Giuseppe Verdi (1813-1901) were famous for their beautiful and numerous melodies, many of which were widely known and sung.

through the faded mosquito-netting tacked over the window, and I lay watching a bright star that burned red above the cornfield, and sing "Home to our mountains, oh, let us return!"[14] in a way fit to break the heart of a Vermont boy near dead of homesickness already.

I watched her closely through the prelude to Tristan and Isolde,[15] trying vainly to conjecture what that warfare of motifs, that seething turmoil of strings and winds, might mean to her. Had this music any message for her? Did or did not a new planet swim into her ken? Wagner had been a sealed book to Americans before the sixties. Had she anything left with which to comprehend this glory that had flashed around the world since she had gone from it? I was in a fever of curiosity, but Aunt Georgiana sat silent upon her peak in Darien.[16] She preserved this utter immobility throughout the numbers from the "Flying Dutchman," though her fingers worked mechanically upon her black dress, as though of themselves they were recalling the piano score they had once played. Poor old hands! They were stretched and pulled and twisted into mere tentacles to hold, and lift, and knead with; the palms unduly swollen, the fingers bent and knotted, on one of them a thin worn band that had once been a wedding-ring. As I pressed and gently quieted one of those groping hands, I remembered, with quivering eyelids, their services for me in other days.

Soon after the tenor began the Prize Song,[17] I heard a quick-drawn breath, and turned to my aunt. Her eyes were closed, but the tears were glistening on her cheeks, and I think in a moment more they were in my eyes as well. It never really dies, then, the soul? It withers to the outward eye only, like that strange moss which can lie on a dusty shelf half a century and yet, if placed in water, grows green again. My aunt wept gently throughout the development and elaboration of the melody.

During the intermission before the second half of the concert, I questioned my aunt and found that the Prize Song was not new to her. Some years before there had drifted to the farm in Red Willow County a young German, a tramp cow-puncher, who had sung in the chorus at Baireuth[18] when he was a boy, along with the other peasant boys and girls. Of a Sunday morning he used to sit on his blue gingham-sheeted bed in the hands' bedroom, which opened off the kitchen, cleaning the leather of his boots and saddle, and singing the Prize Song, while my aunt went about her work in the kitchen. She had hov-

---

14. **"Home to our mountains, oh, let us return!":** A translation of "Ai nostri monti ritoneremo" (Italian), a poignant and touching aria sung by Azucena to her son Manrico, both imprisoned, near the end of Verdi's popular opera *Il Trovatore* (1853).

15. **Tristan and Isolde:** This medieval romance was the basis for Wagner's opera, first performed in 1856.

16. **peak in Darien:** The Darien Peak is a thin peninsula of land connecting Central and South America. From this vantage point, the Spanish explorer and conquistador Vasco Núñez de Balboa (1475–1519) is said to have simultaneously viewed the Atlantic and Pacific oceans.

17. **Prize Song:** A song from *Die Meistersinger von Nürnberg* (1868), one of Wagner's most popular operas.

18. **Baireuth:** A town in Germany, usually spelled *Bayreuth*, where an opera house was especially constructed for the performance of Wagner's operas and where the month-long Richard Wagner Festival was inaugurated in 1876.

ered about him until she had prevailed upon him to join the country church, though his sole fitness for this step, so far as I could gather, lay in his boyish face and his possession of this divine melody. Shortly afterward he had gone to town on the Fourth of July, been drunk for several days, lost his money at a faro-table,[19] ridden a saddled Texas steer on a bet, and disappeared with a fractured collar-bone.

"Well, we have come to better things than the old Trovatore[20] at any rate, Aunt Georgie?" I queried, with well-meant jocularity.

Her lip quivered and she hastily put her handkerchief up to her mouth. From behind it she murmured, "And you've been hearing this ever since you left me, Clark?" Her question was the gentlest and saddest of reproaches.

"But do you get it, Aunt Georgiana, the astonishing structure of it all?" I persisted.

"Who could?" she said, absently; "why should one?"

The second half of the programme consisted of four numbers from the Ring.[21] This was followed by the forest music from Siegfried, and the programme closed with Siegfried's funeral march. My aunt wept quietly, but almost continuously. I was perplexed as to what measure of musical comprehension was left to her, to her who had heard nothing for so many years but the singing of gospel hymns in Methodist services at the square frame school-house on Section Thirteen. I was unable to gauge how much of it had been dissolved in soapsuds, or worked into bread, or milked into the bottom of a pail.

The deluge of sound poured on and on; I never knew what she found in the shining current of it; I never knew how far it bore her, or past what happy islands, or under what skies. From the trembling of her face I could well believe that the Siegfried march, at least, carried her out where the myriad graves are, out into the gray, burying-grounds of the sea; or into some world of death vaster yet, where, from the beginning of the world, hope has lain down with hope, and dream with dream and, renouncing, slept.

The concert was over; the people filed out of the hall chattering and laughing, glad to relax and find the living level again, but my kinswoman made no effort to rise. I spoke gently to her. She burst into tears and sobbed pleadingly, "I don't want to go, Clark, I don't want to go!"

I understood. For her, just outside the door of the concert-hall, lay the black pond with the cattle-tracked bluffs, the tall, unpainted house, naked as a tower, with weather-curled boards; the crook-backed ash-seedlings where the dishcloths hung to dry, the gaunt, moulting turkeys picking up refuse about the kitchen door.

[1904]

---

19. **faro-table:** Faro is a card game in which players bet on the order in which the cards will appear.
20. **better things than the old Trovatore:** Admirers of Wagner's complex and demanding music often dismissed Verdi's operas, especially enormously popular ones like the *Il Trovatore* (see note 14).
21. **the Ring:** Wagner's *Der Ring des Nibelungen* is a sequence of four operas — *Das Rheingold, Die Walküre, Siegfried,* and *Götterdämmerung* — which premiered in 1876.

Jack London

[1876–1916]

Jack London

This photograph was taken around 1905, by which time London was one of the most popular writers in the United States.

The writer who gained worldwide fame as Jack London was born John Griffith Chaney in San Francisco on January 12, 1876. His mother was Flora Wellman, a Spiritualist, and his father may have been "Professor" William H. Chaney, a journalist and influential lecturer on astrology, though he abandoned Wellman while she was pregnant and always denied that Jack London was his son. Less than a year after the birth of her child, Wellman married John London, a partially disabled Civil War veteran and widower with two young daughters, and the infant John Griffith Chaney was re-named John Griffith London. His working-class family moved from place to place in the Bay Area before settling in Oakland. London attended grammar school there and became an avid reader of books he borrowed from the Oakland Public Library. He also took part-time jobs to help support the family, working as a newsboy, in a cannery, and as a watchman. With some of the money he earned, London occasionally rented boats and taught himself to sail. When he completed the eighth grade in 1891, he left school, bought a skiff, and became a highly successful "oyster pirate," later giving up that lucrative but illegal trade to work for the California Fish Patrol. At the age of seventeen, he spent seven months aboard a ship hunting seals in the Pacific. After he returned to San Francisco, London entered an essay contest and won the first prize of twenty-five dollars for "Story of a Typhoon off the Coast of Japan," which was published in the San Francisco *Call* in 1893.

But it was several years before he seriously began to pursue a literary career. During the severe depression of 1893, London joined the western contingent of Coxey's industrial army, hundreds of unemployed men who converged on Washington, D.C., for a protest march in the spring of 1894. He dropped out along the way and tramped about the country on his own, serving a thirty-day sentence for vagrancy in Buffalo, New York. After he returned home in 1895, London began attending Oakland High School. The unconventional student, who supported himself by working as a janitor in the school, also began to study evolutionary theory by reading the work of Charles Darwin and Herbert Spencer. In 1896, London joined the Socialist Labor Party, and his passionate street-corner speeches earned him the title "Boy Socialist of Oakland." After his graduation from high school, he attended the University of California, Berkeley, but left after one semester, dismissing college as "a passionless pursuit of passionless intelligence." At loose ends and once again working at a menial job, this time at a steam laundry, London in 1897 joined the gold rush to the Klondike, the setting of many of the tales he began to write after his return to San Francisco in 1898. "To the Man on the Trail: A Klondike Christmas," the first of several stories he published in the *Overland Monthly*, appeared in January 1899. Later that year, the *Atlantic Monthly* accepted "An Odyssey of the North," which appeared in that prestigious magazine in

January 1900. Eighteen months after he returned from the Klondike and determined to become a professional writer, London had achieved such national fame that the parent company of the *Atlantic*, the Boston firm of Houghton, Mifflin and Company, offered to publish a collection of his stories, *The Son of the Wolf*. The volume appeared on April 7, 1900, the day London married his longtime friend Bessie Maddern.

London soon became one of the most popular and highest-paid writers in the United States. Magazine editors clamored to publish his Klondike tales, which were collected in *The God of His Fathers and Other Stories* (1901), *Children of the Frost* (1902), and *The Faith of Men* (1904). In response to demand for his work, London also began to write novels, notably *The Call of the Wild* (1903), first published as a serial in the *Saturday Evening Post*. That acclaimed story of a sled dog that casts off civilization and becomes the leader of a wolf pack was followed by another best-selling novel, *The Sea Wolf* (1904), partly based on London's early experience aboard the sealer in the Pacific. By then, London was an internationally known author and the center of an artistic circle in San Francisco. Leaving his wife and two daughters, London was divorced and married Charmian Kittredge, an editor and writer, in 1905. They moved to Glen Ellen, California, where London had bought a tract of land they called "Dream Ranch." Partly to finance agricultural experiments and improvements at the ranch, where the couple later built their magnificent "Wolf House," London wrote hundreds of essays and stories, as well as a wide range of novels, including *The Iron Heel* (1908), a futuristic tale of a social revolution crushed by the capitalist forces of "The Oligarchy," and a semiautobiographical story about an impoverished sailor who pursues literary fame, *Martin Eden* (1909). London drew upon more immediate experiences in writings such as *The Cruise of the Snark* (1911), an account of an extended voyage across the Pacific. Although he suffered from many physical ailments and the bouts of drinking he describes in his autobiographical memoir *John Barleycorn* (1913), London continued his relentless pace of writing until the end of his life, publishing more than fifty books by the time he died from renal failure on November 22, 1916.

Where did [London] get his hot artistic passion, his delicate feeling for form and color, his extraordinary skill with words? The man, in truth, was an instinctive artist of a high order, and if ignorance often corrupted his art, it only made the fact of his inborn mastery the more remarkable.

–H. L. Mencken

bedfordstmartins.com/ americanlit *for research links on London*

London's "The Law of Life."

The Klondike gold rush eventually drew 100,000 people to the vast region along the Yukon River between Alaska and Canada. One of the first to try his luck there, London undertook the lengthy, arduous journey by sea and land from San Francisco to the Klondike, where he spent the fall and winter of 1897-98. He did not find any gold, but London discovered a rich lode of material he later mined in some of his most popular writings. In contrast to literary naturalists who focus on life in cities, the urban "jungle," London in his Klondike tales dramatizes the struggle for survival in the wild, where human beings confront the implacable forces and unyielding laws of nature. "The Law of Life" first appeared in *McClure's Magazine*, a popular illustrated monthly known for publishing short fiction by a wide range of authors, including Mark Twain, Stephen Crane, and, later, Willa Cather. Articles and stories about wild animals and exploration were also frequent features of the magazine, in which London published several of his Klondike tales. Told from the perspective of an elderly Indian man left to die, according to the custom of his tribe, "The Law of Life" was one of London's stories about the indigenous peoples of the Klondike that he collected in *The Children of the Frost* (1902). The text is from the first printing in *McClure's,* March 1901.

THE LAW OF LIFE

Old Koskoosh listened greedily. Though his sight had long since faded, his hearing was still acute, and the slightest sound penetrated to the glimmering intelligence which yet abode behind the withered forehead, but which no longer gazed forth upon the things of the world. Ah! that was Sit-cum-to-ha, shrilly anathematizing the dogs as she cuffed and beat them into the harnesses. Sit-cum-to-ha was his daughter's daughter, but she was too busy to waste a thought upon her broken grandfather, sitting alone there in the snow, forlorn and helpless. Camp must be broken. The long trail waited while the short day refused to linger. Life called her, and the duties of life, not death. And he was very close to death now.

The thought made the old man panicky for the moment, and he stretched forth a palsied hand which wandered tremblingly over the small heap of dry wood beside him. Reassured that it was indeed there, his hand returned to the shelter of his mangy furs, and he again fell to listening. The sulky crackling of half-frozen hides told him that the chief's moose-skin lodge had been struck, and even then was being rammed and jammed into portable compass. The chief was his son, stalwart and strong, head man of the tribesmen, and a mighty hunter. As the women toiled with the camp luggage, his voice rose, chiding them for their slowness. Old Koskoosh strained his ears. It was the last time he would hear that voice. There went Geehow's lodge! And Tusken's! Seven, eight, nine; only the Shaman's could be still standing. There! They were at work upon it now. He could hear the Shaman grunt as he piled it on the sled. A child whimpered and a woman soothed it with soft, crooning gutturals. Little Koo-tee, the old man thought, a fretful child, and not over strong. It would die soon, perhaps, and they would burn a hole through the frozen tundra and pile rocks above to keep the wolverines away. Well, what did it matter? A few years at best, and as many an empty belly as a full one. And in the end, Death waited, ever-hungry and hungriest of them all.

What was that? Oh, the men lashing the sleds and drawing tight the thongs. He listened, who would listen no more. The whip-lashes snarled and bit among the dogs. Hear them whine! How they hated the work and the trail! They were off! Sled after sled churned slowly away into the silence. They were gone. They had passed out of his life, and he faced the last bitter hour alone. No. The snow crunched beneath a moccasin; a man stood beside him; upon his head a hand rested gently. His son was good to do this thing. He remembered other old men whose sons had not waited after the tribe. But his son had. He wandered away into the past, till the young man's voice brought him back.

"Is it well with you?" he asked.

And the old man answered, "It is well."

"There be wood beside you," the younger man continued, "and the fire burns bright. The morning is gray, and the cold has broken. It will snow presently. Even now is it snowing."

"Ay, even now is it snowing."

"The tribesmen hurry. Their bales are heavy, and their bellies flat with lack of feasting. The trail is long and they travel fast. I go now. It is well?"

"It is well. I am as a last year's leaf, clinging lightly to the stem. The first breath that blows, and I fall. My voice is become like an old woman's. My eyes no longer show me the way of my feet, and my feet are heavy, and I am tired. It is well."

He bowed his head in content till the last noise of the complaining snow had died away, and he knew his son was beyond recall. Then his hand crept out in haste to the wood. It alone stood betwixt him and the eternity which yawned in upon him. At last the measure of his life was a handful of faggots. One by one they would go to feed the fire, and just so, step by step, death would creep upon him. When the last stick had surrendered up its heat, the frost would begin to gather strength. First his feet would yield, then his hands; and the numbness would travel, slowly, from the extremities to the body. His head would fall forward upon his knees, and he would rest. It was easy. All men must die.

He did not complain. It was the way of life, and it was just. He had been born close to the earth, close to the earth had he lived, and the law thereof was not new to him. It was the law of all flesh. Nature was not kindly to the flesh. She had no concern for that concrete thing called the individual. Her interest lay in the species, the race. This was the deepest abstraction old Koskoosh's barbaric mind was capable of, but he grasped it firmly. He saw it exemplified in all life. The rise of the sap, the bursting greenness of the willow bud, the fall of the yellow leaf — in this alone was told the whole history. But one task did nature set the individual. Did he not perform it, he died. Did he perform it, it was all the same, he died. Nature did not care; there were plenty who were obedient, and it was only the obedience in this matter, not the obedient, which lived and lived always. The tribe of Koskoosh was very old. The old men he had known when a boy, had known old men before them. Therefore it was true that the tribe lived, that it stood for the obedience of all its members, way down into the forgotten past, whose very resting places were unremembered. They did not count; they were episodes. They had passed away like clouds from a summer sky. He also was an episode, and would pass away. Nature did not care. To life she set one task, gave one law. To perpetuate was the task of life, its law was death. A maiden was a good creature to look upon, full-breasted and strong, with spring to her step and light in her eyes. But her task was yet before her. The light in her eyes brightened, her step quickened, she was now bold with the young men, now timid, and she gave them of her own unrest. And ever she grew fairer and yet fairer to look upon, till some hunter, able no longer to withhold himself, took her to his lodge to cook and toil for him and to become the mother of his children. And with the coming of her offspring her looks left her. Her limbs dragged and shuffled, her eyes dimmed and bleared, and only the little children found joy against the withered cheek of the old squaw by the fire. Her task was done. But a little while, on the first pinch of famine or the first long trail, and she would be left, even as he had been left, in the snow, with a little pile of wood. Such was the law.

He placed a stick carefully upon the fire and resumed his meditations. It was the same everywhere, with all things. The mosquitos vanished with the first frost. The little tree-squirrel crawled away to die. When age settled upon the rabbit it became slow and heavy, and could no longer outfoot its enemies. Even the big bald-face grew clumsy and blind and quarrelsome, in the end to be dragged down by a handful of yelping huskies. He remembered how he had abandoned his own father on an upper reach of the Klondike one winter, the winter before the missionary came with his talk-books and his box of medicines. Many a time had Koskoosh smacked his lips over the recollection of that box, though now his mouth refused to moisten. The "painkiller" had been especially good. But the missionary was a bother after all, for he brought no meat into the camp, and he ate heartily, and the hunters grumbled. But he chilled his lungs on the divide by the Mayo, and the dogs afterwards nosed the stones away and fought over his bones.

Koskoosh placed another stick on the fire and harked back deeper into the past. There was the time of the Great Famine, when the old men crouched empty-bellied to the fire, and from their lips fell dim traditions of the ancient day when the Yukon ran wide open for three winters, and then lay frozen for three summers. He had lost his mother in that famine. In the summer the salmon run had failed, and the tribe looked forward to the winter and the coming of the caribou. Then the winter came, but with it there were no caribou. Never had the like been known, not even in the lives of the old men. But the caribou did not come, and it was the seventh year, and the rabbits had not replenished, and the dogs were naught but bundles of bones. And through the long darkness the children wailed and died, and the women, and the old men; and not one in ten of the tribe lived to meet the sun when it came in the spring. That *was* a famine!

But he had seen times of plenty, too, when the meat spoiled on their hands, and the dogs were fat and worthless with overeating — times when they let the game go unkilled, and the women were fertile, and the lodges were cluttered with sprawling men-children and women-children. Then it was the men became high-stomached, and revived ancient quarrels, and crossed the divides to the south to kill the Pellys, and to the west that they might sit by the dead fires of the Tananas. He remembered, when a boy, during a time of plenty, when he saw a moose pulled down by the wolves. Zing-ha lay with him in the snow and watched — Zing-ha, who later became the craftiest of hunters, and who, in the end, fell through an air-hole on the Yukon. They found him, a month afterward, just as he had crawled half-way out and frozen stiff to the ice.

But the moose. Zing-ha and he had gone out that day to play at hunting after the manner of their fathers. On the bed of the creek they struck the fresh track of a moose, and with it the tracks of many wolves. "An old one," Zing-ha, who was quicker at reading the sign said — "an old one who cannot keep up with the herd. The wolves have cut him out from his brothers, and they will never leave him." And it was so. It was their way. By day and by night, never resting, snarling on his heels, snapping at his nose, they would stay by him to the end. How Zing-ha and he felt the bloodlust quicken! The finish would be a sight to see!

Eager-footed, they took the trail, and even he, Koskoosh, slow of sight and an unversed tracker, could have followed it blind, it was so wide. Hot were they on the heels of the chase, reading the grim tragedy, fresh-written, at every step. Now they came to where the moose had made a stand. Thrice the length of a grown man's body, in every direction, had the snow been stamped about and uptossed. In the midst were the deep impressions of the splay-hoofed game, and all about, everywhere, were the lighter foot-marks of the wolves. Some, while their brothers harried the kill, had lain to one side and rested. The full-stretched impress of their bodies in the snow was as perfect as though made the moment before. One wolf had been caught in a wild lunge of the maddened victim and trampled to death. A few bones, well picked, bore witness.

Again, they ceased the uplift of their snowshoes at a second stand. Here the great animal had fought desperately. Twice had he been dragged down, as the snow attested, and twice had he shaken his assailants clear and gained footing once more. He had done his task long since, but none the less was life dear to him. Zing-ha said it was a strange thing, a moose once down to get free again; but this one certainly had. The Shaman would see signs and wonders in this when they told him.

And yet again, they came to where the moose had made to mount the bank and gain the timber. But his foes had laid on from behind, till he reared and fell back upon them, crushing two deep into the snow. It was plain the kill was at hand, for their brothers had left them untouched. Two more stands were hurried past, brief in time-length and very close together. The trail was red now, and the clean stride of the great beast had grown short and slovenly. Then they heard the first sounds of the battle — not the full-throated chorus of the chase, but the short, snappy bark which spoke of close quarters and teeth to flesh. Crawling up the wind, Zing-ha bellied it through the snow, and with him crept he, Koskoosh, who was to be chief of the tribesmen in the years to come. Together they shoved aside the under branches of a young spruce and peered forth. It was the end they saw.

The picture, like all of youth's impressions, was still strong with him, and his dim eyes watched the end played out as vividly as in that far-off time. Koskoosh marveled at this, for in the days which followed, when he was a leader of men and a head of councilors, he had done great deeds and made his name a curse in the mouths of the Pellys, to say naught of the strange white man he had killed, knife to knife, in open fight.

For long he pondered on the days of his youth, till the fire died down and the frost bit deeper. He replenished it with two sticks this time, and gauged his grip on life by what remained. If Sit-cum-to-ha had only remembered her grandfather, and gathered a larger armful, his hours would have been long. It would have been easy. But she was ever a careless child, and honored not her ancestors from the time the Beaver, son of the son of Zing-ha, first cast eyes upon her. Well, what mattered it? Had he not done likewise in his own quick youth? For a while he listened to the silence. Perhaps the heart of his son might soften, and he would come back with the dogs to take his old father on with the tribe to where the caribou ran thick and the fat hung heavy upon them.

He strained his ears, his restless brain for the moment stilled. Not a stir, nothing. He alone took breath in the midst of the great silence. It was very lonely, Hark! What was that? A chill passed over his body. The familiar, long-drawn howl broke the void, and it was close at hand. Then on his darkened eyes was projected the vision of the moose – the old bull moose – the torn flanks and bloody sides, the riddled mane, and the great branching horns, down low and tossing to the last. He saw the flashing forms of gray, the gleaming eyes, the lolling tongues, the slavered fangs. And he saw the inexorable circle close in till it became a dark point in the midst of the stamped snow.

A cold muzzle thrust against his cheek, and at its touch his soul leaped back to the present. His hand shot into the fire and dragged out a burning faggot. Overcome for the nonce by his hereditary fear of man, the brute retreated, raising a prolonged call to his brothers; and greedily they answered, till a ring of crouching, jaw-slobbered gray was stretched round about. The old man listened to the drawing in of this circle. He waved his brand wildly, and sniffs turned to snarls; but the panting brutes refused to scatter. Now one wormed his chest forward, dragging his haunches after, now a second, now a third; but never a one drew back. Why should he cling to life? he asked, and dropped the blazing stick into the snow. It sizzled and went out. The circle grunted uneasily, but held its own. Again he saw the last stand of the old bull moose, and Koskoosh dropped his head wearily upon his knees. What did it matter after all? Was it not the law of life?

[1901]

Writing "American" Lives

IN 1782, J. HECTOR ST. JOHN DE CRÈVECOEUR, a French immigrant who had settled in New York before returning to Europe during the Revolutionary War, published a series of essays about life in the British colonies in North America, *Letters from an American Farmer*. The book was an immediate success in England, France, and the newly constituted United States, where an expanded version appeared in 1884. In one of its most famous passages, Crèvecoeur describes the process by which people from different backgrounds and countries were transformed by their experiences in the colonies — the "great American asylum" — and asks, "What then is the American?" In America, Crèvecoeur suggests, "individuals of all nations are melted into a new race of men, whose labors and posterity will one day cause great changes in the world."

◀ **The Melting Pot**
By offering a visual version of the melting-pot metaphor, the cover design of this program for Israel Zangwill's popular play perhaps inadvertently suggests how painful the process of assimilation might be for immigrants in the United States.

Crèvecoeur was among the first to develop the popular idea of America as what would come to be called the "melting pot." That metaphor gained enormous cultural currency through a popular play, *The Melting Pot* (1908), by Israel Zangwill, the London-born son of eastern European immigrants who frequently wrote about Jewish immigrant life in England and the United States. In the play, which opened to great acclaim in Washington, D.C., Zangwill depicts the life of members of a Jewish family who escape discrimination and growing violence against Jews in czarist Russia and come to America, where they achieve success through hard work and assimilation. "America is God's Crucible," Zangwill exclaimed, "the great Melting-Pot where all the races of Europe are melting and re-forming!" The idea that immigrants should be re-formed through assimilation into American ways was widely shared in the United States. President Theodore Roosevelt, who viewed hyphenations such as *Polish-American* as a form of "moral treason," is reported to have shouted, "That's a great play!" at the end of a performance of *The Melting Pot*.

Even at the time, however, some questioned the melting-pot ideal. In "Trans-National America" (1916), written during World War I, the social critic Randolph Bourne ironically observes:

> No reverberatory effect of the great war has caused American public opin-
> ion more solicitude than the failure of the "melting-pot." . . . We have had to
> listen to publicists who express themselves as stunned by the evidence of
> vigorous nationalistic movements in this country among Germans, Scandi-
> navians, Bohemians, and Poles, while in the same breath they insist that the
> alien shall be forcibly assimilated to that Anglo-Saxon tradition which they
> unquestioningly label "American."

Challenging that narrow definition of *American*, Bourne encouraged Americans to pursue a "higher ideal" than the melting pot, which he believed would produce a culture "washed out into a tasteless, colorless fluid of uniformity." In contrast to those who viewed such assimilation as crucial to the process of Americanization, Bourne affirmed that the "failure of the melting-pot, far from closing the great American democratic experiment, means that it has only just begun."

"The failure of the melting-pot, far from closing the great American democratic experiment, means that it has only just begun."

As the selections in the following section illustrate, a diverse range of writers engaged the questions Bourne raised about what it meant to be an American, as well as about the development of culture and society in the United States. José Martí, an immigrant from Cuba who had been exiled from his native island because of his revolutionary activities against the Spanish government there, challenged the idea that the United States represented "America" and held exclusive claim to the term *Americans*. In his "Impressions of America," a series of essays he wrote shortly after his arrival in New York City in 1880, and in his later articles for Spanish-language newspapers throughout Latin America, Martí explored every aspect of society and culture in the United States. Committed to the struggle for independence in Cuba, Martí was alarmed by the desire of many in the United States to take possession of the Spanish colony and to exert economic and political control throughout the Americas. He was also concerned about the social and cultural consequences of American imperialism, since he recognized that the United States had little knowledge of or respect for the indigenous traditions of its neighbors in Latin America. Indeed, just as the melting-pot metaphor implied that the Anglo-American was the only model of the American, Martí feared that what he described as "Anglo-Saxon America" would arrogantly impose a similar national model on the diverse nations of the Americas.

The Anglo-American conception of the melting pot posed an even more direct and immediate threat to the indigenous traditions of Native Americans. In *Life among the Piutes: Their Wrongs and Claims* (1883), the first book published by a Native American woman, Sarah Winnemucca Hopkins dramatizes the impact on her people of the settlement of the West. Forced to resettle on reservations that were very different from the lands they had once occupied, the Paiutes (sometimes spelled *Piutes*) struggled to retain their way of life, the values of which Hopkins sought to reveal to an audience accustomed to thinking of the Indians as "savages" who needed to be "civilized" before they could become "Americans." Many Native American children were consequently sent to "assimilation schools" in the East. Zitkala-Ša, who was born on the Pine Ridge Reservation in present-day South Dakota, describes that harsh process of reeducation and forced assimilation in "The School Days of an Indian Girl" (1900), one of a series of autobiographical sketches she published in the *Atlantic Monthly* in 1900. Zitkala-Ša consequently found herself torn between two worlds, the indigenous culture of her birth and the Anglo-American culture in which she was educated. But she used her literacy in English to plead the Indian cause and to preserve Native American traditions, through both short stories and the Sioux tales she collected in *Old Indian Legends* (1902). Zitkala-Ša later became an activist for Indian rights, including the right of citizenship, which Native Americans finally gained in 1924.

African Americans also struggled for equal rights and recognition as Americans. In the face of pervasive racial discrimination and hatred, especially in the South, the former slave and influential educator Booker T. Washington wrote *Up from Slavery* (1901), an autobiography in which he offers his own life as an example to white America of the capacities of African Americans. But he also argued that African Americans should seek white support for their economic and educational initiatives rather than agitate for social equality and full political rights. Another prominent African American educator, W. E. B. Du Bois, sharply criticized Washington's

Carlisle Indian Industrial School

This is a photograph taken in 1892 of the student body assembled on the grounds of the most famous of the assimilation schools for Indian children, founded in Carlisle, Pennsylvania, in 1879. Students were required to convert to Christianity, speak only English, and wear uniforms at the school, the motto of which was "Kill the Indian, save the man."

conciliatory approach to white America. In *The Souls of Black Folk* (1903), Du Bois asserts that African Americans must strive for all of the rights proclaimed in the Declaration of Independence. Pointing out that a slave ship arrived in Jamestown, Virginia, in 1619, a year before the *Mayflower* landed at Plymouth Rock, Du Bois also challenged the foundational myth of white America: "Your country? How came it yours? Before the Pilgrims landed we were here. . . . Would America have been America without her Negro people?"

> "Your country? How came it yours? Before the Pilgrims landed we were here. . . . Would America have been America without her Negro people?"

Four years after Du Bois published his influential book, Henry Adams privately printed his autobiography, *The Education of Henry Adams.* The two writers had several things in common. Both were born and raised in Massachusetts, and both were Harvard-educated historians who produced major works in the field. But they approached American history from radically different backgrounds and perspectives. Determined to explore episodes in the nation's past that many white Americans were eager to forget, Du Bois

Founders of the Niagara Movement

In July 1905, a group of twenty-nine African American businessmen and in-tellectual leaders — including W. E. B. Du Bois (second row, second from the right) — held a series of secret meetings near Niagara Falls. They met on the Canadian side of the falls, since no hotel on the American side would allow them to register. Rejecting Booker T. Washington's policy of accommodation, they formed the Niagara Movement, named after the location and because they hoped to unleash a "mighty current" of protest against racial discrimination and segre-gation in the United States. In his address to the first public meeting of the orga-nization, which included women as well as men, Du Bois in 1906 declared, "The battle we wage is not for ourselves alone but for all true Americans."

wrote histories of the slave trade to the United States and of Reconstruction. Adams, the descendant of wealthy and distinguished New England families and of two presidents – his great-grandfather, John Adams, and his grandfather, John Quincy Adams – wrote a nine-volume history of the presidential administrations of Jefferson and Madison. Although Du Bois and Adams apparently never met, both attended the Paris Universal Exposition in 1900. Du Bois won a gold medal for the exhibit he organized on the history, condition, and achievements of African Americans, while Adams spent much of his time at the exposition in fascinated study and contemplation of the powerful, electricity-generating machines in the Hall of Dynamos.

The differing backgrounds and experiences of the two writers shaped their conceptions of American society and of the challenges facing the country at the turn of the century. In *The Souls of Black Folk*, Du Bois famously and prophetically asserts, "The problem of the Twentieth Century is the problem of the color line." For the alienated Adams, a man of an earlier era who had gloomily witnessed the transformation of the United States into an industrial nation dominated by the forces of a rapacious capitalism, the central problem of the new age was the blind worship of machines. The result in the twentieth century, he predicted, would be a world in which accelerating advances in science and technology would outstrip the ability of human beings to control the mechanical and dehumanizing forces they had unleashed.

Despite such forebodings and the sobering realities of the new urban and industrial order, many continued to view America as a land of freedom and opportunity, symbolized by the Statue of Liberty. Certainly, that hopeful vision was affirmed by the final writer represented in this section, Mary Antin, whose family immigrated to the United States along with many other Jews fleeing persecution and discriminatory laws in czarist Russia. Published in the aftermath of the early performances of *The Melting Pot* and with the personal encouragement of Israel Zangwill, Antin's best-selling autobiography, *The Promised Land* (1912), offered a reassuring message about the efficacy and value of assimilation. "The ghost of the *Mayflower* pilots every immigrant ship," she declared, "and Ellis Island is another name for Plymouth Rock." But some Anglo-Americans firmly rejected her analogy between the small band of Pilgrims at Plymouth and the millions of immigrants passing through the portal of Ellis Island, which had opened in New York harbor in 1892. Conservative critics also strongly objected to Antin's use of the phrase "our forefathers" for the Pilgrims and heroes of the American Revolution, questioning her description of herself as an American. Moreover, even many of those who sought to redefine *American* in order to include white European immigrants were reluctant to extend the term to immigrants from Africa, Asia, and Latin

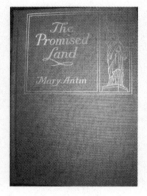

The Promised Land

The cover design of Antin's autobiography used the Statue of Liberty as a symbol of the country's welcome of immigrants to the "promised land" of America.

"The ghost of the Mayflower pilots every immigrant ship, . . . and Ellis Island is another name for Plymouth Rock."

Alfred Stieglitz, *The Steerage* (1907)

Often thought to capture the drama of poor immigrants bound for America in steerage, the lowest and least-costly levels of ships, Stieglitz actually took this famous photograph aboard a ship sailing *to* Europe. By some estimates, more than 15 percent of immigrants returned to their homelands, many of them disillusioned by the harsh conditions of life in the United States.

America, or to Native Americans and African Americans. Indeed, by the early twentieth century the question Crèvecoeur had so confidently answered more than a century earlier — "What then is the American?" — had become a deeply contested question of *who* is an American.

José Martí

[1853-1895]

Don José Julián Martí y Peréz was born in Havana, Cuba, on January 28, 1853. He was the eldest of eight children born to Mariano Martí y Navarro, a Spaniard serving in an artillery unit of the Spanish army, and Leonor Pérez Cabrera, from Tenerife in the Canary Islands. In 1857, the family moved back to Spain but returned to Havana in 1859. Martí regarded Cuba as his homeland, and its long struggle for independence from Spain strongly shaped his life and writings. Although his family was very poor, his mother strongly believed in education, and Martí attended school in Havana. Encouraged by one of his teachers, he began to write at an early age, publishing his first poem in a local newspaper in 1868. That year also marked the beginning of the first armed revolt against Spanish rule in Cuba, a protracted conflict that came to be known as the Ten Years' War. Martí soon began to write political articles for a friend's newspaper and then established his own paper, *La Patria Libre* ("The Free Homeland"). In the only issue of the newspaper, which appeared five days before his sixteenth birthday, Martí published a poetic allegory celebrating the heroism of the Cuban rebels. Still in high school, he was arrested on charges of disloyalty to Spain and sentenced to six years of hard labor in a military prison. After six months of punishing work in the stone quarries of Havana, where he suffered a severe leg injury, he was granted clemency and deported to Spain.

Martí lived in exile for virtually the rest of his life. Soon after he arrived in Spain, he published *El Presidio Político en Cuba* ("The Political Prison in Cuba"), a tract in which he appealed directly to the Spanish people to end the atrocities committed in their name in Cuba. Martí continued his studies, first in Madrid and then at the University of Zaragoza, from which he graduated in 1874 with degrees in law, philosophy, and letters. Leaving Spain, he toured several European cities before rejoining his family, which had moved to Mexico. There, he taught high school and became known as a journalist and playwright. In 1875, he became engaged to Carmen Zayas-Bazán, a Cuban living in Mexico. They were married in 1877, after Martí had accepted a position as a professor of French, English, Italian, and German literature at a university in Guatemala. In late 1878, the couple

José Martí

This photograph was taken in Brooklyn around 1885, several years after Martí's arrival in the United States.

returned to Cuba, where their son was born and Martí taught in a private school in Havana. The following year, he was arrested for conspiring against the Spanish government of Cuba and deported, without his family, to Spain. In 1880, he made his way to New York City. He was briefly joined by his wife, but she disliked the city and soon returned with their son to Cuba. Martí lived in New York for most of the next fifteen years, teaching, writing for English- and Spanish-language periodicals, and editing *La América*, through which Martí hoped, as he put it, "to explain the mind of the United States of the North to those who are in spirit, and will someday be in form, the United States of South America." He also wrote articles on virtually every aspect of life in the United States as a foreign correspondent for newspapers in Venezuela, Argentina, Uruguay, Honduras, and Mexico. During the same period, Martí published a novel and two innovative and widely acclaimed volumes of poetry, *Ismaelillo* ("Little Ishmael," 1882), inspired by his absent son, and *Versos sensillos* ("Simple Verses," 1891).

Martí's achievements in prose and verse placed him among the leading writers in the Spanish language, but he ultimately gave up many of his literary pursuits to devote himself to the cause of Cuban independence. In 1891, he gave speeches in Florida in an effort to generate support among Cubans living there for a revolt against Spanish rule in Cuba. As Martí recognized, genuine independence also meant resisting the efforts of the United States to exert economic and political control over Cuba. In one of the many notebooks he kept throughout this life, he affirmed that "Cuba must be free — of Spain and of the United States." In his most famous essay, "Nuestra América" ("Our America," 1891), he passionately affirmed the need for "Anglo-Saxon America" to understand the nature and diversity of Latin American countries, which must be allowed to develop their own social, political, and cultural identities, free of the domination of the United States. Fearing that the United States would annex Cuba before it could gain independence, as some American politicians desired, in 1892 Martí organized and was elected *delgado* (leader) of the Cuban Revolutionary Party. He also established a newspaper that became the official organ of the party, *Patria*. Through his articles and speeches, Martí tirelessly promoted and raised money for a war of independence, which began in Cuba early in 1895. "I called for this war, and my responsibility does not end with its onset, but begins," Martí wrote in March 1895. The following month, he and a small group of exiles landed in Cuba, where Martí was killed in a skirmish with Spanish troops on March 25, 1895.

Martí was later hailed as the father of Cuban independence, but genuine independence proved to be elusive in Cuba. The brutal efforts of the Spanish government to suppress the rebellion there inflamed public opinion in the United States and helped spark the Spanish-American War of 1898. In the treaty that ended the war, Spain ceded control of Guam, the Philippines, Puerto Rico, and Cuba to the United States. Instead of allowing Martí's revolutionary government to take control of Cuba, the United States established a military government and its troops occupied the island until 1901. In order to end the occupation and gain independence,

He was a man of genius, of imagination, of hope, and of courage.
–Charles A. Dana

bedfordstmartins.com/
americanlit *for research links on Martí*

Cuban leaders had to agree to incorporate provisions into Cuba's constitution that made the new republic a virtual colony of the United States. With the exception of a permanent lease of the Guantanamo Bay Naval Base, which the United States has steadily declined to yield, most of those provisions were abrogated in 1934 at the order of President Franklin Delano Roosevelt as part of his "Good Neighbor Policy." In 1965, on the seventieth anniversary of Martí's death in battle, a statue honoring him was placed in Central Park in New York City, fittingly at the head of the Avenue of the Americas.

Martí's "Impressions of America."   Soon after he arrived in the United States in January 1880, Martí wrote numerous essays for the *Hour*, a weekly literary magazine established by Charles A. Dana, the editor of the influential daily newspaper the *New York Sun*. Most of the essays were originally written in French, but Martí wrote a series of essays, "Impressions of America," in English. All of the essays in the series carried the byline "By a Very Fresh Spaniard," possibly to exploit the popularity of writings by European visitors about life in the United States. At the same time, the Cuban-born Martí was "fresh" from Spain, where he had been deported from Cuba in 1879, as well as "fresh," or youthful and inexperienced, in the United States. Whatever the reason for the byline, Martí used his position as a recent arrival in New York City to comment satirically on both the United States and Spain. Certainly, he displayed considerable knowledge of American culture, even alluding to popular American writers such as Mark Twain and his newly published book, *A Tramp Abroad* (1880). "Impressions of America," in which Martí offered a critical perspective on life in the country to readers in the United States, anticipated many of his later journalistic writings, in which he reported on life and developments in the United States for newspapers throughout Latin America. Indeed, even as he expressed his admiration for certain aspects of life in the United States, Martí in his early "Impressions of America" called attention to its pervasive materialism, the gulf between wealth and poverty in the country, and the indifference to the kind of suffering he witnessed in the growing slums of New York City. The texts of the following essays, the first and third in the series, are taken from the first printing in the *Hour*, July 10 and October 23, 1880.

IMPRESSIONS OF AMERICA

I

I am, at last, in a country where every one looks like his own master. One can breathe freely, freedom being here the foundation, the shield, the essence of life. One can be proud of his species here. Every one works; every one reads. Only does every one feel in the same degree that they read and work? Man, as a strong creature — made to support on his shoulders the burden of misfortune, never bent, never tired, never dismaying — is unrivalled here. Are women, those beings that we, the Southern people,[1] like, – feeble and souple, tender and voluptuous, – as perfect, in their way, as men are to theirs? Activity, devoted to trade, is truly immense. I was never surprised in any country of the world I have visited. Here, I was surprised. As I arrived, in one of this summer-days, when the face of hasty business men are at the same moment fountains and volcanoes; when, bag in hand, the vest open, the neck-tye detached, I saw the diligent New Yorkers running up and down, buying here, selling there, transpiring, working, going ahead; when I remarked that no one stood quietly in the corners, no door was shut an instant, no man was quiet, I stopped myself, I looked respectfully on this people, and I said good-bye for ever to that lazy life and poetical inutility of our European countries. I remembered a sentence of an old Spaniard, a healthy countryman, father of thirty-six sons: "Only those who dig their bread, have a right to eat it; and, as if they dig most deeply, they will eat it whiter." But is this activity devoted in the same extent to the development of these high and noble anxieties of soul, that cannot be forgotten by a people who want to escape from unavoidable ruin, and strepitous definitive crumbling? When the days of poverty may arrive – what richness, if not that of spiritual strength and intellectual comfort, will help this people in its colossal misfortune? Material power, as that of Carthage,[2] if it rapidly increases, rapidly falls down. If this love of richness is not tempered and dignified by the ardent love of intellectual pleasures, – if kindness toward men, passion for all what is great, devotion to all what means sacrifice and glory, are not as developed as fervorous and absorbent passion for money, where shall they go? where shall they find sufficient cause to excuse this hard burden of life and feel relief to their sorrow? Life wants permanent roots; life is unpleasant without the comfort of intelligence, the pleasures of art and the internal gratification that the goodness of the soul and the exquisiteness of taste produce to us.

I am deeply obliged to this country, where the friendless find always a friend and a kind hand is always found by those who look honestly for work. A good idea finds always here a suitable, soft, grateful ground. You must be intelligent; that is all. Give something useful. You will have all what you want. Doors are shut for those who are dull and lazy; life is sure to those who are faithful to the law of work. When I was a child, I read with admiration, – born as I am in a country where there is no field for individual activity, a series of biographies as those who are called here with a magnificent simplicity – *self-made men.* My childhood was not entirely gone out when I admired again, in British Honduras,[3] a wealthy Southern family brought by misfortune to painful scantiness, – and raising by their hands, in the thick bossom of forest, a clean, elegant, prosperous sugar plantation. The father, an ancient governor of a powerful State, was the engineer; the charming mother, very simply dressed, with a perpetual smile on her lips, – the

---

1. **Southern people:** That is, the inhabitants of southern, or Mediterranean, Europe, including Spain.
2. **Carthage:** A powerful and wealthy city on the coast of North Africa founded by the Phoenicians (c. 814 BCE) and destroyed by the Romans in 146 BCE.
3. **British Honduras:** Then a colony of Great Britain, now the country of Belize, in Central America. Martí visited the colony as a child in 1863.

smile of those who are courageous enough to support human sufferings, – was the most skillful housekeeper I have ever seen. Hot cakes, fine pastry, fresh milk, sweet jelly – were always on hand. When she came to me, the noble face illuminated by the most pure look, the curled silver hair carefully dressed, a waiter with exquisite dishes in her wrinkled hands – the sweetest feelings filled my heart, and tears of pleasure came to my eyes. The sons helped the father in all kinds of labors; they ploughed the field – saw the sugar-cane, burn the woods, build a new "sweet home" – and as slightly dressed as miserable countrymen in those far forests do – very early in the morning, merrily singing, they drove the oxen to the hardest work of the plantation. And they were elegant, gentle, learned young men. I will study a most original country at its birth – in the school; at its development – in the family; at its pleasures – in the theatre, in the clubs, in Fourteenth Street,[4] in large and small family party. I will go, in a brilliant Sunday, walking down the fashionable Fifth Avenue, to the crowded church to hear a preacher – the word of peace – speaking about politics or the field of war. I will see many nonsenses, many high deeds; the politicians, who save the country, when they could – without any effort go back to the days of arrogant militarism, violation of the public will, corruption of the political morality; I will see benevolent faces of men, defiant faces of women, the most capricious and uncommendable fancies, all the greatness of freedom and all the miseries of prejudices; here, a powerful originality, there a vulgar imitation of transatlantic extravagances. Liberty in politics, in customs, in enterprises; humble slavery in taste. Frenchmen give the sacred word; great names, and not great works are looked for. As there is not a fixed mind on art, the most striking is the most loved. There is no taste for the sweet beauty of Hélène or Galaethea[5] – the taste being all devoted to old imperfect works of China and Japan. If a scientific object would have been intended by the owners of these *bibelots*,[6] it would be a matter of praise. But it is only for the censurable pleasure of indiscreetly holding foreign goods bought at a high price.

   At a first glance what else can I tell? I have all my impressions vividly awaken. The crowds of Broadway; the quietness of the evenings; the character of men; the most curious and noteworthy character of women; the life in the hotel, that will never be understood for us; that young lady, physically and mentally stronger than the young man who courts her; that old gentleman, full of wisdom and capacity who writes in a sobrious[7] language for a hundred newspapers; this feverish life; this astonishing movement; this splendid sick people, in one side wonderfully extended, in other side – that of intellectual pleasures – childish and poor; this colossal giant, candorous and credulous; these women, too richly dressed to be happy; these men, too devoted to business of pocket,

---

4. **Fourteenth Street:** In the late nineteenth century, the area south of Fourteenth Street was the poorest and most densely populated district in New York City.

5. **Hélène or Galaethea:** In Greek mythology, Hélène was the trusted friend of Venus, the goddess of love; Galatea (as it is also spelled) was a beautiful sea nymph whose lover was killed by the cyclops Polyphemus in a jealous rage.

6. *bibelots:* Rare objects or curios (French).

7. **sobrious:** This is probably a mistake or a typographical error, though Martí may have coined a term combining the words *sober* and *serious*.

with remarkable neglectness of the spiritual business, – all is, at the same time, coming to my lips, and begging to be prepared in this brief account of my impressions.

Size and number: these are here the elements of greatness. Nothing is absolutely neglected, however. If the common people, increased every day by a thirsty foreign population, that must not be confounded with the true American people, shows that anxious desire for money, and fights frightfully in this way, – the true Americans preserve national greatness, constitutional rights, old and honorable names, from the vulgar storm of immigration, that brings in strength and possibilities of wealth, what they lack of intellectual height, and moral deepness. In the columns of a newspaper, in the page of a magazine, in the familiar chit-chat, the most pure feelings, noble aspirations, and generous ideas bravely fight for the rapid improvement of the country, in the sense of moral development.

It will be reached. It has not yet been reached, because many strangers bring here their odiums, their wounds, their moral ulcers. What a terrible enemy the desperate want of money is for the achievement of virtues! How great a nation must be, to conduct in a quiet way, these bands of wolves, hungry and thirsty, these excrescences of old poor countries, ferocious or unuseful there, – and here, under the influence of work, good, kind and tame!

And, for the *mot de la fin*,[8] let me tell you what it happened to me, as I came, a week ago, from Cape May, a charming watering-place, to Philadelphia. The train near to the station jumped off the tracks; the car where I was, fell side-way. The accident was without consequence; but, as everybody was compelled by the shaking and pulling of the car to abandon violently their seats, the moment was a solemn one. Women became deadly pales. Men forgot women, looking for their own salvation. I thought, first, what must occur to a man under such a case, and, in the same instant, I saw rolling a poor eighty years' woman on the floor. I ran to her, offering her my hands. The old lady, very elegant indeed, notwithstanding her large amount of years, looked at me gratefully, tended her hands toward me; – but, as she touched the extreme of my fingers with their own, she told me, with expressive frightened grimaces:

"By the hands, no! Go away! Go away!"

Was she an old Puritan?

III

We read in Europe many wonderful statements about this country. The splendor of life, the abundance of money, the violent struggles for its possession, the golden currents, that dazzle and blind the vulgar people, the excellencies of instruction, the habit of working, the vision of that new country arising above the ruins of old nations, excite the attention of thoughtful men, who are anxiously looking for the definitive settlement of all the destructive forces that began during the last century to lay the foundations of a new era of mankind. This could be, and ought to be, the transcendental significance of

---

8. *mot de la fin:* Final word or line (French).

the United States. But have the States the elements they are supposed to have? Can they do what they are expected to do? Do they impose their own character, or do they suffer the imposition of the character on others? Is America going to Europe or Europe coming to America? Error, both in politics and religion, has been worshipped in the Old World. Truth, liberty and dignity are supposed to have reached, at last, a sure hearth in the New World. We must ask for a response to these secrets of the home-life from the benches of the schoolrooms, the daily newspaper and conversation in society. Eloquent answers to all mystifications strike the observer as he goes through the streets. We must ask women for the natural end of their unextinguishable thirst for pleasure and amusement. We must ask them if a being so exclusively devoted to the possession of silk dresses, dazzling diamonds and all kinds of costly fancies could afterwards carry into their homes those solid virtues, those sweet feelings, that kind resignation, that evangelic power of consolation which can only keep up a hearth shaken by misfortune, and inspire children with contempt for regular pleasures and the love of internal satisfactions that make men happy and strong, as they did Ismael,[9] against the days of poverty. We must ask a boy of fourteen what he knows and what he is taught. We must observe in the newspapers what they place before the public — news or ideas. We must look at what people read, what they applaud, and what they love. And, as these problems cannot be answered in a page, or understood and remembered by a new-comer, I have taken here and there some memoranda. Here, from my notebook, are some:

"What do I see? A girl seven years old goes to school. She talks with unusual ease to other girls; this miniature of a woman has all the self-control of a married woman; she looks and smiles at me as if she could know all the mysteries of mankind. Her ears are adorned with heavy earrings; her little fingers with rings. Where can this wonderful volubility come from? What will this little girl, so fond of jewelry at seven years, do for it at sixteen? Slavery would be better than this kind of liberty; ignorance would be better than this dangerous science."

"I went down town by the elevated railroad. As I travelled by this perilous but seductive way, I lost all hope of understanding Americans when I heard the name of a street, *'Chamber Street!' Cham, Chem, Chamber* or *Chember*? Is it *Houston, House* or *Hous*? Is it *Franklin, Frank* or *Frenk*? It is curious to observe that I can always understand an Englishman when he speaks to me; but among the Americans a word is a whisper; a sentence is an electric commotion. And if somebody asks me how can I know if a language that I so badly write, is badly spoken, I will tell frankly that it is very frequent that critics speak about what they absolutely ignore. There is, among the Americans, an excellent writer, the humorist Mark Twain — and has he not presented the gifted king of Bavaria, a poet, an enthusiast, a knight of old times, as a savage who oblige the singers of his theatre to play the same opera twice in a night, under the most terrible rain

---

9. **Ismael:** Usually spelled "Ishmael," the son of Abraham and his wife's maid Hagar. Ishmael and his mother were driven away after the birth of Isaac, the son of Abraham and his wife, Sarah (Genesis 16:12).

that could fall over the poor Bavarians?[10] He astonishes himself with the mastodon-tic composition of German words. All conversation is here in a single word: no breathe, no pause; not a distinct sound. We see that we are in the land of railroads. 'That's all' – 'did'nt' – 'won't' – 'ain't' – 'indeed' – 'Nice weather' – 'Very pleasant' – 'Coney Island'[11] – 'Excursion.' That is all that I can seize, when I listen with anxious attention, to the average American. When I listened to men and women of culture I have been able to appreciate how the correctness of Addison can be mingled with the acuteness of Swift, and the strength of Carlyle with the charming melody of Longfellow.[12]

"Among women, as their usual kindness inclines them to soften the asperity of their language, in order to be easily understood by the foreigner, the English tongue appears exceptionally harmonious. Everything could be pardoned to these indefatigable talkers, if they would speak in such a way, in order to employ the time that seems to be always short for them; but if – by a marvel – you can fathom the sense of those whirling words, you will remark that a vulgar subject is, commonly, too extensively developed."

"I love silence and quietness. Poor Chatterton[13] was right when he desperately longed for the delights of solitude. The pleasures of cities begin for me when the motives which make pleasure for others are fading away. The true day for my soul dawns in the midst of the night. As I took yesterday evening my usual nocturne walk, many pitiful sights made a painful impression upon me. One old man, dressed in that style which reveals at the same time that good fortune we have had and the bad times that begin for us, steps silently under a street-lamp. His eyes, fixed upon the passers by, were full of tears; his hand held a poor handkerchief. He could not articulate a single word. His sighs, not his words, begged for assistance. A little farther on, in Fourteenth Street, a periodic sound, as a distant lamentation, sprang from the shadow. A poor woman knelt on the sidewalk, as if looking for her grave, or for strength to lift on her shoulders the hoarse organ whose crank her dying hand was turning. I passed through Madison Square,[14] and I saw a hundred robust men, evidently suffering from the pangs of misery. They moved painfully, as if they wished to blot out of their minds their sorrowful thoughts – and were all lying down on the grass or seated on the benches, shoeless, foodless, concealing their anguish under their dilapidated hats."

[1880]

---

10. **Mark Twain . . . Bavarians?:** In early 1880, Twain published *A Tramp Abroad*, a humorous account of his walking tour of central and southern Europe that includes his account of the king of Bavaria.

11. **Coney Island:** An amusement park in Brooklyn, just outside of New York City on the southern shore of Long Island.

12. **Addison . . . Longfellow:** Martí describes the characteristics frequently associated with the writings of four well-known writers: the English essayist Joseph Addison (1672-1719); the English satirist Jonathan Swift (1667-1745), author of *Gulliver's Travels* (1726); Thomas Carlyle (1795-1881), the influential Scottish philosopher and man of letters; and the popular American poet Henry Wadsworth Longfellow (1807-1882).

13. **Chatterton:** The English poet Thomas Chatterton (1752-1770), a child prodigy who committed suicide at age seventeen, leaving behind a large number of his poems.

14. **Madison Square:** A six-acre public park in New York City.

Sarah Winnemucca Hopkins

[c. 1844–1891]

Sarah Winnemucca Hopkins, the fourth child and second daughter of "Old" Chief Winnemucca and his wife Tuboitonie, was born into a Northern Paiute (sometimes written *Piute*) tribe about 1844 near Humboldt Lake in present-day Nevada. Named Thocmetony (Shell Flower), Hopkins was the granddaughter of another influential chief of the Paiutes, Truckee. During the 1840s, Paiute lands were crossed by increasing numbers of white settlers traveling on the overland trail to California. Initially, Truckee had high regard for the Americans, guiding settlers over the mountains and then serving as "Captain" Truckee, first with a surveying expedition and then with the military forces led by John C. Frémont during the Mexican War of 1846–48. Hopkins had her first encounters with white settlers as a child, and she later learned to speak English and took the name Sarah Winnemucca while living with a white family in Carson City, Nevada. Largely self-educated, Hopkins may have briefly attended a convent school in California before returning to the Pyramid Lake Indian Reservation, which was established on Paiute lands in 1859.

Sarah Winnemucca Hopkins

Taken in 1883, this photograph shows Hopkins in the elaborate outfit she customarily wore for her lectures, in which she was billed as "Princess Sarah" of the Paiutes.

The growing tensions between the Paiutes and white settlers led to a series of conflicts. The discovery of silver in Nevada attracted thousands of miners and settlers, whose incursions into the reservation triggered the Pyramid Lake War of 1860. Even after a peace treaty was signed, there were sporadic skirmishes between the Paiutes and the encroaching white settlers, and Hopkins's brother was killed in an attack on the reservation by federal troops in 1865. Determined to help her people however she could, Hopkins began to work as an interpreter at Camp McDermitt in 1868. For three years, she assisted in reading and translating documents for both settlers and Paiutes. She married a soldier, Edward C. Bartlett, but the marriage ended in divorce, as did her brief second marriage to Edward Satwaller. In 1876, Hopkins went to the Malheur Reservation in Oregon, where some of the Northern Paiutes had been resettled. Living

conditions were extremely harsh on the arid reservation, which was radically different from the Paiute homelands and where there were shortages
of food and clothing. Hopkins began to teach Indian children and worked
as an interpreter for the federal agent in charge of the reservation. The
arrival of a new agent who mistreated the Indians incensed Hopkins, who
reported his misconduct to the federal government. The agent consequently banished her from the reservation. By then, the discontent among
the Paiutes on the reservation was extremely high, and many of them
joined the Bannock and Shoshone tribes in a war against the United
States that began in June 1878.

Hopkins devoted the rest of her life to work on behalf of the Paiutes and
the rights of Native Americans. In the aftermath of the Bannock War, she
taught school and continued to work as an interpreter. She was reunited
with an old friend, Lewis H. Hopkins, now a discharged army soldier,
whom she married in 1881. By then, Hopkins had begun to deliver lectures
in an effort to reveal to white audiences the ways in which federal agents
on the reservations were mistreating the Indians. Following the first of
her more than three hundred lectures, in San Francisco, she received
increasing attention in the newspapers as "Princess Sarah" of the Paiutes.
Hopkins did not hesitate to play the role of the Indian princess in order to
call public attention to the condition of Native Americans. She dressed
elaborately for her lectures, often wearing a fringed buckskin dress, red
leggings, moccasins, and a tiara. She was invited to Washington to meet
President Rutherford B. Hayes in 1880. While traveling in the Northeast,
Hopkins met Elizabeth Peabody and her sister Mary Peabody Mann, the
wife of the prominent education reformer Horace Mann. The Peabody sisters strongly encouraged Hopkins to write about her experiences and
the rich culture of Native Americans. In 1882, she published an essay in
the *Californian* magazine, "The Pah-Utes," in which Hopkins focused on
the destruction of their ancestral lands and traditional culture by white
settlers and soldiers. Describing the dispossession of the Indians by "the
white man," Hopkins boldly concludes: "I hope some other race will come
and drive him out, and kill him, like he has done to us. Then I will say that
the Great Spirit is just, and that it is all right."

Hopkins expanded and sharpened her critique in an extended account
of her life and people, *Life among the Piutes: Their Wrongs and Claims*,
published in 1883. Hopkins campaigned to gain greater autonomy and self-
government for the Paiutes, free of the dictatorial control of government-
appointed reservation agents. Despite her book, her influential friends
in New England, and a petition on behalf of the Paiutes sent to the U.S.
Congress, the campaign failed. With the financial support of Elizabeth
Peabody, Hopkins returned to the Pyramid Lake Reservation, where she
established and ran the Peabody Indian School. Because the purpose of
the bilingual school was to help Paiute children retain their language and
culture, it was sharply at odds with the federal government's strict policy
of acculturating Native Americans. Although the school faltered when her
husband gambled away some of her money, Hopkins was able to keep it

bedfordstmartins.com/
americanlit for research
links on Hopkins

open for four years. After it closed, she continued to work for the self-determination of the Paiutes, even as she challenged the Dawes Act of 1887, which severely contracted the lands earlier granted to Native Americans. Lewis Hopkins died in 1887, after which Hopkins lived with her brother among her people on a ranch in Nevada. She died during a visit to her sister's home in Monida, Montana, on October 17, 1891. The obituary published in the *New York Times*, subtitled "The Most Remarkable Woman among the Piutes of Nevada," ignored many of the activities and achievements that actually made Hopkins one of the most remarkable people of her generation in the United States.

Hopkins's *Life among the Piutes.*   Hopkins wrote her book, the first work published and copyrighted by a Native American woman in the United States, with the aid and strong encouragement of the Boston reformers Elizabeth Peabody and her sister Mary Peabody Mann. Mann assisted Hopkins with copying and editing her manuscript, while Peabody evidently arranged and paid for the publication of the book by G. P. Putnam's in 1883. Although it received little notice in the periodical press, Hopkins sold the book at her lectures for a dollar a copy, using the proceeds to support herself and the school for Native American children she sought to establish in Nevada. Just as she designed her lectures for white audiences, Hopkins addresses her book to white readers, whom she directly confronts in one of its most vivid passages:

> You who are educated by a Christian government in the art of war; the practice of whose profession makes you natural enemies of the savages, so called by you. Yes, you, who call yourselves the great civilization; you who have knelt upon Plymouth Rock, covenanting with God to make this land the home of the free and the brave. Ah, then you rise from your bended knees and seizing the welcoming hands of those who are the owners of this land, which you are not, your carbines rise upon the bleak shore, and your so-called civilization sweeps inland from the ocean wave; but, oh, my God! Leaving its pathway marked by crimson lines of blood, and strewed by the bones of two races, the inheritor and the invader; and I am crying out to you for justice.

As that passage suggests, Hopkins focuses much of her attention on the wrongs suffered by the Paiutes and other Native Americans, from the sexual abuse of their women by white men to the brutal conditions on Indian reservations. But she also emphasizes the claims of the Paiutes, both against their treatment by whites and for their own culture and traditions, which Hopkins vividly describes in the following account of her early life leading up to her first encounter with white settlers. The text is taken from the first edition of *Life among the Piutes: Their Wrongs and Claims* (1883).

From LIFE AMONG THE PIUTES

From Chapter I.
First Meeting of Piutes and Whites

I was born somewhere near 1844, but am not sure of the precise time. I was a very small child when the first white people came into our country. They came like a lion, yes, like a roaring lion, and have continued so ever since, and I have never forgotten their first coming. My people were scattered at that time over nearly all the territory now known as Nevada. My grandfather was chief of the entire Piute nation, and was camped near Humboldt Lake,[1] with a small portion of his tribe, when a party travelling eastward from California was seen coming. When the news was brought to my grandfather, he asked what they looked like? When told that they had hair on their faces, and were white, he jumped up and clasped his hands together, and cried aloud, —

"My white brothers, — my long-looked for white brothers have come at last!"

He immediately gathered some of his leading men, and went to the place where the party had gone into camp. Arriving near them, he was commanded to halt in a manner that was readily understood without an interpreter. Grandpa at once made signs of friendship by throwing down his robe and throwing up his arms to show them he had no weapons; but in vain, — they kept him at a distance. He knew not what to do. He had expected so much pleasure in welcoming his white brothers to the best in the land, that after looking at them sorrowfully for a little while, he came away quite unhappy. But he would not give them up so easily. He took some of his most trustworthy men and followed them day after day, camping near them at night, and travelling in sight of them by day, hoping in this way to gain their confidence. But he was disappointed, poor dear old soul!

I can imagine his feelings, for I have drank deeply from the same cup. When I think of my past life, and the bitter trials I have endured, I can scarcely believe I live, and yet I do; and, with the help of Him who notes the sparrow's fall, I mean to fight for my downtrodden race while life lasts.

Seeing they would not trust him, my grandfather left them, saying, "Perhaps they will come again next year." Then he summoned his whole people, and told them this tradition:

In the beginning of the world there were only four, two girls and two boys. Our forefather and mother were only two, and we are their children. You all know that a great while ago there was a happy family in this world. One girl and one boy were dark and the others were white. For a time they got along together without quarrelling, but soon they disagreed, and there was trouble. They were cross to one another and fought, and our parents were very much grieved. They prayed that their children might learn better, but it did not do any good; and afterwards the whole household was made so unhappy that the father and mother saw that they must separate their children; and then our father took the dark boy

---

1. **Humboldt Lake:** In northwestern Nevada.

and girl, and the white boy and girl, and asked them, "Why are you so cruel to each other?" They hung down their heads, and would not speak. They were ashamed. He said to them, "Have I not been kind to you all, and given you everything your hearts wished for? You do not have to hunt and kill your own game to live upon. You see, my dear children, I have power to call whatsoever kind of game we want to eat; and I also have the power to separate my dear children, if they are not good to each other." So he separated his children by a word. He said, "Depart from each other, you cruel children; — go across the mighty ocean and do not seek each other's lives."

So the light girl and boy disappeared by that one word, and their parents saw them no more, and they were grieved, although they knew their children were happy. And by-and-by the dark children grew into a large nation; and we believe it is the one we belong to, and that the nation that sprung from the white children will some time send some one to meet us and heal all the world trouble. Now, the white people we saw a few days ago must certainly be our white brothers, and I want to welcome them. I want to love them as I love all of you. But they would not let me, they were afraid. But they will come again, and I want you one and all to promise that, should I not live to welcome them myself, you will not hurt a hair on their heads, but welcome them as I tried to do.

How good of him to try and heal the wound, and how vain were his efforts! My people had never seen a white man, and yet they existed, and were a strong race. The people promised as he wished, and they all went back to their work.

The next year came a great emigration,[2] and camped near Humboldt Lake. The name of the man in charge of the trains was Captain Johnson, and they stayed three days to rest their horses, as they had a long journey before them without water. During their stay my grandfather and some of his people called upon them, and they all shook hands, and when our white brothers were going away they gave my grandfather a white tin plate. Oh, what a time they had over that beautiful gift, — it was so bright! They say that after they left, my grandfather called for all his people to come together, and he then showed them the beautiful gift which he had received from his white brothers. Everybody was so pleased; nothing like it was ever seen in our country before. My grandfather thought so much of it that he bored holes in it and fastened it on his head, and wore it as his hat. He held it in as much admiration as my white sisters hold their diamond rings or a sealskin jacket. So that winter they talked of nothing but their white brothers. The following spring there came great news down the Humboldt River, saying that there were some more of the white brothers coming, and there was something among them that was burning all in a blaze. My grandfather asked them what it was like. They told him it looked like a man; it had legs and hands and a head, but the head had quit burning, and it was left quite black. There was the greatest excitement among my people everywhere about the men in a blazing fire. They were excited because they did not know there were any people in the world but the two, — that is, the Indians and the whites; they thought that was all of us in the beginning of the world, and, of course, we

---

2. **a great emigration:** In the 1840s, an estimated half-million white settlers traveled west to Oregon and California. Many of those who traveled overland to California stopped in the lands of the Northern Paiutes.

did not know where the others had come from, and we don't know yet. Ha! ha! oh, what a laughable thing that was! It was two negroes wearing red shirts!

The third year more emigrants came, and that summer Captain Fremont, who is now General Fremont.[3]

My grandfather met him, and they were soon friends. They met just where the railroad crosses Truckee River, now called Wadsworth, Nevada. Captain Fremont gave my grandfather the name of Captain Truckee, and he also called the river after him. Truckee is an Indian word, it means *all right*, or *very well.* A party of twelve of my people went to California with Captain Fremont. I do not know just how long they were gone.

During the time my grandfather was away in California, where he staid till after the Mexican war, there was a girl-baby born in our family. I can just remember it. It must have been in spring, because everything was green. I was away playing with some other children when my mother called me to come to her. So I ran to her. She then asked me to sit down, which I did. She then handed me some beautiful beads, and asked me if I would like to buy something with them. I said: —

"Yes, mother, — some pine nuts."

My mother said: —

"Would you like something else you can love and play with? Would you like to have a little sister?" I said, —

"Yes, dear mother, a little, little sister; not like my sister Mary, for she won't let me play with her. She leaves me and goes with big girls to play;" and then my mother wanted to know if I would give my pretty beads for the little sister.

Just then the baby let out such a cry it frightened me; and I jumped up and cried so that my mother took me in her arms, and said it was a little sister for me, and not to be afraid. This is all I can remember about it.

When my grandfather went to California he helped Captain Fremont fight the Mexicans.[4] When he came back he told the people what a beautiful country California was. Only eleven returned home, one having died on the way back.

They spoke to their people in the English language, which was very strange to them all.

Captain Truckee, my grandfather, was very proud of it, indeed. They all brought guns with them. My grandfather would sit down with us for hours, and would say over and over again, "Goodee gun, goodee, goodee gun, heap shoot." They also brought some of the soldiers' clothes with all their brass buttons, and my people were very much astonished to see the clothes, and all that time they were peaceable toward their white brothers. They had learned to love them, and they hoped more of them would come. Then my people were less barbarous than they are nowadays.

---

3. **Fremont:** Captain John C. Frémont (1813-1890), later a senator from California, the first Republican nominee for president, and a major general in the Civil War, led a surveying expedition across the Great Basin to California from 1843 to 1845.
4. **helped . . . the Mexicans:** In late 1846, during the war between the United States and Mexico (1846-48), Frémont led a military expedition to capture Santa Barbara, California.

That same fall, after my grandfather came home, he told my father to take charge of his people and hold the tribe, as he was going back to California with as many of his people as he could get to go with him. So my father took his place as Chief of the Piutes, and had it as long as he lived. Then my grandfather started back to California again with about thirty families. That same fall, very late, the emigrants kept coming. It was this time that our white brothers first came amongst us. They could not get over the mountains, so they had to live with us. It was on Carson River, where the great Carson City stands now. You call my people bloodseeking. My people did not seek to kill them, nor did they steal their horses, – no, no, far from it. During the winter my people helped them. They gave them such as they had to eat. They did not hold out their hands and say: –

"You can't have anything to eat unless you pay me." No, – no such word was used by us savages at that time; and the persons I am speaking of are living yet; they could speak for us if they choose to do so.

The following spring, before my grandfather returned home, there was a great excitement among my people on account of fearful news coming from different tribes, that the people whom they called their white brothers were killing everybody that came in their way, and all the Indian tribes had gone into the mountains to save their lives. So my father told all his people to go into the mountains and hunt and lay up food for the coming winter. Then we all went into the mountains. There was a fearful story they told us children. Our mothers told us that the whites were killing everybody and eating them. So we were all afraid of them. Every dust that we could see blowing in the valleys we would say it was the white people. In the late fall my father told his people to go to the rivers and fish, and we all went to Humboldt River, and the women went to work gathering wild seed, which they grind between the rocks. The stones are round, big enough to hold in the hands. THe women did this when they got back, and when they had gathered all they could they put it in one place and covered it with grass, and then over the grass mud. After it is covered it looks like an Indian wigwam.

Oh, what a fright we all got one morning to hear some white people were coming. Every one ran as best they could. My poor mother was left with my little sister and me. Oh, I never can forget it. My poor mother was carrying my little sister on her back, and trying to make me run; but I was so frightened I could not move my feet, and while my poor mother was trying to get me along my aunt overtook us, and she said to my mother: "Let us bury our girls, or we shall all be killed and eaten up." so they went to work and buried us, and told us if we heard any noise not to cry out, for if we did they would surely kill us and eat us. So our mothers buried me and my cousin, planted sage bushes over our faces to keep the sun from burning them, and there we were left all day.

Oh, can any one imagine my feelings *buried alive*, thinking every minute that I was to be unburied and eaten up by the people that my grandfather loved so much? With my heart throbbing, and not daring to breathe, we lay there all day. It seemed that the night would never come. Thanks be to God! the night came at last. Oh, how I cried and said: "Oh, father, have you forgotten me? Are you never coming for me?" I cried so I thought my very heartstrings would break.

At last we heard some whispering. We did not dare to whisper to each other, so we lay still. I could hear their footsteps coming nearer and nearer. I thought my heart was coming right out of my mouth. Then I heard my mother say, "'T is right here!" Oh, can any one in this world ever imagine what were my feelings when I was dug up by my poor mother and father? My cousin and I were once more happy in our mothers' and fathers' care, and we were taken to where all the rest were.

I was once buried alive; but my second burial shall be for ever, where no father or mother will come and dig me up. It shall not be with throbbing heart that I shall listen for coming footsteps. I shall be in the sweet rest of peace, — I, the chieftain's weary daughter.

Well, while we were in the mountains hiding, the people that my grandfather called our white brothers came along to where our winter supplies were. They set everything we had left on fire. It was a fearful sight. It was all we had for the winter, and it was all burnt during that night. My father took some of his men during the night to try and save some of it, but they could not; it had burnt down before they got there.

These were the last white men that came along that fall. My people talked fearfully that winter about those they called our white brothers. My people said they had something like awful thunder and lightning, and with that they killed everything that came in their way.

This whole band of white people perished in the mountains, for it was too late to cross them.[5] We could have saved them, only my people were afraid of them. We never knew who they were, or where they came from. So, poor things, they must have suffered fearfully, for they all starved there. The snow was too deep.

Early in the following spring, my father told all his people to go to the mountains, for there would be a great emigration that summer. He told them he had had a wonderful dream, and wanted to tell them all about it.

He said, "Within ten days come together at the sink of Carson, and I will tell you my dream."

The sub-chiefs went everywhere to tell their people what my father had told them to say; and when the time came we all went to the sink of Carson.

Just about noon, while we were on the way, a great many of our men came to meet us, all on their horses. Oh, what a beautiful song they sang for my father as they came near us! We passed them, and they followed us, and as we came near to the encampment, every man, woman, and child were out looking for us. They had a place all ready for us. Oh, how happy everybody was! One could hear laughter everywhere, and songs were sung by happy women and children.

My father stood up and told his people to be merry and happy for five days. It is a rule among our people always to have five days to settle anything. My father told them to dance at night, and that the men should hunt rabbits and fish, and some were to have games of football, or any kind of sport or playthings they wished, and the women could

---

5. **This whole band . . . too late to cross them:** Probably a reference to the Donner Party, a group of families from Springfield, Illinois, who set out for California in 1846. When a snowstorm blocked the pass through the Sierra Nevada, the party ran out of food and some of them apparently resorted to cannibalism. Of the original eighty-seven members of the party, forty-one died and forty-six survived.

do the same, as they had nothing else to do. My people were so happy during the five days, — the women ran races, and the men ran races on foot and on horses.

My father got up very early one morning, and told his people the time had come, — that we could no longer be happy as of old, as the white people we called our brothers had brought a great trouble and sorrow among us already. He went on and said, —

These white people must be a great nation, as they have houses that move. It is wonderful to see them move along. I fear we will suffer greatly by their coming to our country; they come for no good to us, although my father said they were our brothers, but they do not seem to think we are like them. What do you all think about it? Maybe I am wrong. My dear children, there is something telling me that I am not wrong, because I am sure they have minds like us, and think as we do; and I know that they were doing wrong when they set fire to our winter supplies. They surely knew it was our food.

And this was the first wrong done to us by our white brothers.
Now comes the end of our merrymaking.
Then my father told his people his fearful dream, as he called it. He said, —

I dreamt this same thing three nights, — the very same. I saw the greatest emigration that has yet been through our country. I looked North and South and East and West, and saw nothing but dust, and I heard a great weeping. I saw women crying, and I also saw my men shot down by the white people. They were killing my people with something that made a great noise like thunder and lightning, and I saw the blood streaming from the mouths of my men that lay all around me. I saw it as if it was real. Oh, my dear children! You may all think it is only a dream, — nevertheless, I feel that it will come to pass. And to avoid blood-shed, we must all go to the mountains during the summer, or till my father comes back from California. He will then tell us what to do. Let us keep away from the emigrant roads and stay in the mountains all summer. There are to be a great many pine-nuts this summer, and we can lay up great supplies for the coming winter, and if the emigrants don't come too early, we can take a run down and fish for a month, and lay up dried fish. I know we can dry a great many in a month, and young men can go into the valleys on hunting excursions, and kill as many rabbits as they can. In that way we can live in the mountains all summer and all winter too.

So ended my father's dream. During that day one could see old women getting together talking over what they had heard my father say. They said, —

"It is true what our great chief has said, for it was shown to him by a higher power. It is not a dream. Oh, it surely will come to pass. We shall no longer be a happy people, as we now are; we shall no longer go here and there as of old; we shall no longer build our big fires as a signal to our friends, for we shall always be afraid of being seen by those bad people."

"Surely they don't eat people?"

"Yes, they do eat people, because they ate each other up in the mountains last winter."

This was the talk among the old women during the day.

"Oh, how grieved we are! Oh, where will it end?"

That evening one of our doctors called for a council, and all the men gathered together in the council-tent to hear what their medicine man had to say, for we all believe our doctor is greater than any human being living. We do not call him a medicine man because he gives medicine to the sick, as your doctors do. Our medicine man cures the sick by the laying on of hands, and we have doctresses as well as doctors. We believe that our doctors can communicate with holy spirits from heaven. We call heaven the Spirit Land.

Well, when all the men get together, of course there must be smoking the first thing. After the pipe has passed round five times to the right, it stops, and then he tells them to sing five songs. He is the leader in the song-singing. He sings heavenly songs, and he says he is singing with the angels. It is hard to describe these songs. They are all different, and he says the angels sing them to him.

Our doctors never sing war-songs, except at a war-dance, as they never go themselves on the war-path. While they were singing the last song, he said, —

"Now I am going into a trance. While I am in the trance you must smoke just as you did before; not a word must be spoken while I am in the trance."

About fifteen minutes after the smoking was over, he began to make a noise as if he was crying a great way off. The noise came nearer and nearer, until he breathed, and after he came to, he kept on crying. And then he prophesied, and told the people that my father's dream was true in one sense of the word, — that is, "Our people will not all die at the hands of our white brothers. They will kill a great many with their guns, but they will bring among us a fearful disease that will cause us to die by hundreds."

We all wept, for we believed this word came from heaven.

So ended our feast, and every family went to its own home in the pine-nut mountains, and remained there till the pine-nuts were ripe. They ripen about the last of June.

Late in that fall there came news that my grandfather was on his way home. Then my father took a great many of his men and went to meet his father, and there came back a runner, saying, that all our people must come together. It was said that my grandfather was bringing bad news. All our people came to receive their chieftain; all the old and young men and their wives went to meet him. One evening there came a man, saying that all the women who had little children should go to a high mountain. They wanted them to go because they brought white men's guns, and they made such a fearful noise, it might even kill some of the little children. My grandfather had lost one of his men while he was away.

So all the women that had little children went. My mother was among the rest; and every time the guns were heard by us, the children would scream. I thought, for one that my heart would surely break. So some of the women went down from the mountain and told them not to shoot any more, or their children would die with fright. When our mothers brought us down to our homes the nearer we came to the camp, the more I cried, —

"Oh, mother, mother, don't take us there!" I fought my mother, — I bit her. Then my father came, and took me in his arms and carried me to the camp. I put my head in his bosom, and would not look up for a long time. I heard my grandfather say, —

"So the young lady is ashamed because her sweetheart has come to see her. Come, dearest, that won't do after I have had such a hard time to come to see my sweetheart, that she should be ashamed to look at me."

Then he called my two brothers to him, and said to them, "Are you glad to see me?" And my brothers both told him that they were glad to see him. Then my grandfather said to them, —

"See that young lady; she does not love her sweetheart any more, does she? Well, I shall not live if she does not come and tell me she loves me. I shall take that gun, and I shall kill myself."

That made me worse than ever, and I screamed and cried so hard that my mother had to take me away. So they kept weeping for the little one three or four days. I did not make up with my grandfather for a long time. He sat day after day, and night after night, telling his people about his white brothers. He told them that the whites were really their brothers, that they were very kind to everybody, especially to children; that they were always ready to give something to children. He told them what beautiful things their white brothers had, — what beautiful clothes they wore, and about the big houses that go on the mighty ocean, and travel faster than any horse in the world. His people asked him how big they were. "Well, as big as that hill you see there, and as high as the mountain over us."

"Oh, that is not possible, — it would sink, surely."

"It is every word truth, and that is nothing to what I am going to tell you. Our white brothers are a mighty nation, and have more wonderful things than that. They have a gun that can shoot a ball bigger than my head, that can go as far off as that mountain you see over there."

The mountain he spoke of at that time was about twenty miles across from where we were. People opened their eyes when my grandfather told of the many battles they had with the Mexicans, and about their killing so many of the Mexicans, and taking their big city away from them, and how mighty they were. These wonderful things were talked about all winter long. The funniest thing was that he would sing some of the soldier's roll-calls, and the air to the Star-spangled Banner, which everybody learned during the winter.

He then showed us a more wonderful thing than all the others that he had brought. It was a paper, which he said could talk to him.[6] He took it out and he would talk to it, and talk with it. He said, "This can talk to all our white brothers, and our white sisters, and their children. Our white brothers are beautiful, and our white sisters are beautiful, and their children are beautiful! He also said the paper can travel like the wind, and it can go and talk with their fathers and brothers and sisters, and come back to tell what they are doing, and whether they are well or sick."

After my grandfather told us this, our doctors and doctoresses said, —

---

6. **It was a paper . . . talk to him:** A paper with words written on it, probably the letter of commendation written to Captain Truckee by John C. Frémont for his help in the Mexican War.

"If they can do this wonderful thing, they are not truly human, but pure spirits. None but heavenly spirits can do such wonderful things. We can communicate with the spirits, yet we cannot do wonderful things like them. Oh, our great chieftain, we are afraid your white brothers will yet make your people's hearts bleed. You see if they don't; for we can see it. Their blood is all around us, and the dead are lying all about us, and we cannot escape it. It will come. Then you will say our doctors and doctoresses did know. Dance, sing, play, it will do no good; we cannot drive it away. They have already done the mischief, while you were away."

But this did not go far with my grandfather. He kept talking to his people about the good white people, and told them all to get ready to go with him to California the following spring.

Very late that fall, my grandfather and my father and a great many more went down to the Humboldt River to fish. They brought back a great many fish, which we were very glad to get; for none of our people had been down to fish the whole summer.

When they came back, they brought us more news. They said there were some white people living at the Humboldt sink. They were the first ones my father had seen face to face. He said they were not like "humans." They were more like owls than any thing else. They had hair on their faces, and had white eyes, and looked beautiful.[7]

I tell you we children had to be very good, indeed, during the winter; for we were told that if we were not good they would come and eat us up. We remained there all winter; the next spring the emigrants came as usual, and my father and grandfather and uncles, and many more went down on the Humboldt River on fishing excursions. While they were thus fishing, their white brothers came upon them and fired on them, and killed one of my uncles, and wounded another. Nine more were wounded, and five died afterwards. My other uncle got well again, and is living yet. Oh, that was a fearful thing, indeed!

After all these things had happened, my grandfather still stood up for his white brothers.

Our people had council after council, to get my grandfather to give his consent that they should go and kill those white men who were at the sink of Humboldt. No; they could do nothing of the kind while he lived. He told his people that his word was more to him than his son's life, or any one else's life either.

"Dear children," he said, "think of your own words to me; — you promised. You want me to say to you, Go and kill those that are at the sink of Humboldt. After your promise, how dare you to ask me to let your hearts be stained with the blood of those who are innocent of the deed that has been done to us by others? Is not my dear beloved son laid alongside of your dead; and you say I stand up for their lives. Yes, it is very hard, indeed; but, nevertheless, I know and you know that those men who live at the sink are not the ones that killed our men."

---

7. **They . . . looked beautiful:** "When asked to explain this, she said, 'Oh, their eyes were blue, and they had long beards.'" [Original note by the editor, Mary Peabody Mann.]

While my grandfather was talking, he wept, and men, women, and children, were all weeping. One could hardly hear him talking.

After he was through talking, came the saddest part. The widow of my uncle who was killed, and my mother and father all had long hair. They cut off their hair, and also cut long gashes in their arms and legs, and they were all bleeding as if they would die with the loss of blood. This continued for several days, for this is the way we mourn for our dead. When the woman's husband dies, she is first to cut off her hair, and then she braids it and puts it across his breast; then his mother and sisters, his father and brothers and all his kinsfolk cut their hair. The widow is to remain unmarried until her hair is the same length as before, and her face is not to be washed all that time, and she is to use no kind of paint, nor to make any merriment with other women until the day is set for her to do so by her father-in-law, or if she has no father-in-law, by her mother-in-law, and then she is at liberty to go where she pleases. The widower is at liberty when his wife dies; but he mourns for her in the same way, by cutting his hair off.

It was late that fall when my grandfather prevailed with his people to go with him to California. It was this time that my mother accompanied him. Everything had been got ready to start on our journey. My dear father was to be left behind. How my poor mother begged to stay with her husband! But my grandfather told her that she could come back in the spring to see her husband; so we started for California, leaving my poor papa behind. All my kinsfolk went with us but one aunt and her children.

The first night found us camped at the sink of Carson, and the second night we camped on Carson River. The third day, as we were travelling along the river, some of our men who were ahead, came back and said there were some of our white brothers' houses ahead of us. So my grandfather told us all to stop where we were while he went to see them. He was not gone long, and when he came back he brought some hard bread which they gave him. He told us that was their food, and he gave us all some to taste. That was the first I ever tasted.

Then my grandfather once more told his people that his paper talked for him, and he said, –

"Just as long as I live and have that paper which my white brothers' great chieftain has given me, I shall stand by them, come what will." He held the paper up towards heaven and kissed it, as if it was really a person. "Oh, if I should lose this," he said, "we shall all be lost. So, children, get your horses ready, and we will go on, and we will camp with them to-night, or by them, for I have a sweetheart along who is dying for fear of my white brothers." He meant me; for I was always crying and hiding under somebody's robes, for we had no blankets then.

Well, we went on; but we did not camp with them, because my poor mother and brothers and sisters told my grandfather that I was sick with crying for fright, and for him not to camp too close to them. The women were speaking two words for themselves and one for me, for they were just as afraid as I was. I had seen my brother Natchez crying when the men came back, and said there were white men ahead of us. So my grandfather did as my mother wished him to do, and we went on by them; but I did not know it, as I had my head covered while we were passing their camp. I was riding behind my older brother, and we went on and camped quite a long way from them that night.

So we travelled on to California, but did not see any more of our white brothers till we got to the head of Carson River, about fifteen miles above where great Carson City now stands.

"Now give me the baby." It was my baby-sister that grandpa took from my mother, and I peeped from under my mother's fur, and I saw some one take my little sister. Then I cried out, —

"Oh, my sister! Don't let them take her away."

And once more my poor grandfather told his people that his white brothers and sisters were very kind to children. I stopped crying, and looked at them again. Then I saw them give my brother and sister something white. My mother asked her father what it was, and he said it was *Pe-har-be*, which means sugar. Just then one of the women came to my mother with some in her hand, and grandpa said: —

"Take it, my child."

Then I held out my hand without looking. That was the first gift I ever got from a white person, which made my heart very glad.

When they went away, my grandfather called me to him, and said I must not be afraid of the white people, for they are very good. I told him that they looked so very bad I could not help it.

We travelled with them at that time two days, and the third day we all camped together where some white people were living in large white houses. My grandpa went to one of the houses, and when he came back he said his white brothers wanted him to come and get some beef and hard bread. So he took four men with him to get it, and they gave him four boxes of hard bread and a whole side of beef, and the next morning we got our horses ready to go on again. There was some kind of a fight, — that is, the captain of the train was whipping negroes who were driving his team. That made my poor grandfather feel very badly. He went to the captain, and told him he would not travel with him. He came back and said to his people that he would not travel with his white brothers any farther. We travelled two days without seeing any more of my grandfather's white brothers. At last we came to a very large encampment of white people, and they ran out of their wagons, or wood-houses, as we called them, and gathered round us. I was riding behind my brother. I was so afraid, I told him to put his robe over me, but he did not do so. I scratched him and bit him on his back, and then my poor grandfather rode up to the tents where they were, and he was asked to stay there all night with them. After grandpa had talked awhile, he said to his people that he would camp with his brothers. So he did. Oh, what nice things we all got from my grandpa's white brothers! Our men got red shirts, and our women got calico for dresses. Oh, what a pretty dress my sister got! I did not get anything, because I hid all the time. I was hiding under some robes. No one knew where I was. After all the white people were gone, I heard my poor mother cry out: —

"Oh, where is my little girl? Oh, father, can it be that the white people have carried her away? Oh, father, go and find her, — go, go, and find her!" And I also heard my brothers and sister cry. Yet I said nothing, because they had not called me to get some of the pretty things. When they began to cry, I began crawling out, and then my grandfather scolded me, and told me that his brothers loved good children, but not bad ones like me. How I did cry, and wished that I had staid at home with my father! I went to sleep crying.

I did not forget what had happened. There was a house near where we camped. My grandfather went down to the house with some of his men, and pretty soon we saw them coming back. They were carrying large boxes, and we were all looking at them. My mother said there were two white men coming with them.

"Oh, mother, what shall I do? Hide me!"

I just danced round like a wild one, which I was. I was behind my mother. When they were coming nearer, I heard my grandpa say, —

"Make a place for them to sit down."

Just then, I peeped round my mother to see them. I gave one scream, and said, —

"Oh, mother, the owls!"

I only saw their big white eyes, and I thought their faces were all hair. My mother said, —

"I wish you would send your brothers away, for my child will die."

I imagined I could see their big white eyes all night long. They were the first ones I had ever seen in my life.

[1883]

Zitkala-Ša
(Gertrude Simmons Bonnin)

[1876-1938]

Zitkala-Ša

For this portrait, one of a series of photographs Gertrude Käsebier took of her in 1898, Zitkala-Ša posed in a European-style dress but clutched an Indian basket to her chest, representing her mixed ancestry and her dual identity as both a white person and a Dakota (Sioux).

Zitkala-Ša (Red Bird), the name she took during her teens in an assertion of her Indian identity, was born Gertrude Simmons on the Pine Ridge Reservation in present-day South Dakota in 1876. She was the daughter of a white man, about whom little is known, and a Dakota mother, Ellen Tate 'Iyohiwin (Reaches for the Wind) Simmons. In the aftermath of the battle of Little Bighorn in 1876, the Dakota, Lakota, and Nakota, who formed the large, loosely constructed group that came to be known collectively as the Sioux, were driven into increasingly smaller reservations to make room for the growing number of white homesteaders on the Great Plains. Like other Native American groups across the United States, the Sioux also struggled to preserve tribal cultures and traditions that the federal government was determined to eradicate. Many Native American children were consequently recruited for missionary schools designed to assimilate them into white culture. In 1884, Zitkala-Ša enrolled at White's Manual Institute, a Quaker boarding school in Wabash, Indiana. Unhappy at school and restless at home on the reservation, where Zitkala-Ša spent four years during the following decade, she graduated from White's in 1894. Despite her mother's wish that she return to the reservation, she then studied at Earlham College in Richmond, Indiana, from 1895 to 1897.

After leaving college, Zitkala-Ša devoted herself to teaching, writing, and music. Seeking to provide a more sympathetic education to Native American children, she accepted a teaching position at the Carlisle Indian Industrial School in western Pennsylvania. But the independent-minded young woman objected to the military-like discipline of the school. She was also sharply critical of its director, Richard Henry Pratt, who had earlier written to a group of Baptist ministers, "In Indian civilization I am a Baptist, because I believe in immersing the Indians in our civilization and when we get them under holding them there until they are thoroughly soaked." In response to such attitudes toward Native American life and culture, Zitkala-Ša wrote a series of autobiographical essays about her childhood, education, and experiences as a teacher, which appeared in the *Atlantic Monthly* in 1900. The magazine also published her essay "Why I Am a Pagan," a firm rejection of Christianity and the efforts of missionaries to convert Native Americans. Her short stories about the situation of Indians like herself, torn between the claims of their native traditions and enforced assimilation into white culture, soon began to appear in other prominent periodicals such as *Harper's Magazine* and *Everybody's Magazine*. An accomplished musician, Zitkala-Ša left the Carlisle school and studied at the Boston Conservatory of Music during 1900–01. In 1902, she published a collection of Sioux tales, *Old Indian Legends*, in an effort to use the literary tools of white culture to preserve the traditions of Native Americans. Later that year, she married Raymond T. Bonnin, a Yankton Sioux who worked for the Bureau of Indian Affairs, and moved with him to the Uintah and Ouray Reservation in Utah. The demands of family life and her work on the reservation left Zitkala-Ša little time for other pursuits, but with William Hanson she wrote an opera about Indian life, *The Sun Dance* (1913), yet another attempt to fuse the artistic forms of white culture with the traditions of Native Americans.

During the final twenty-five years of her life, Zitkala-Ša became a leading activist in the crusade for the rights of Native Americans. In 1916, she and her husband moved to Washington, D.C., where they continued to work for the reform of education policies concerning Native Americans and to gain for them the rights of citizenship and the protection of land rights. Zitkala-Ša was deeply involved in various organizations, including the Society of American Indians, editing and writing articles for its journal, the *American Indian Magazine*, from 1917 to 1920. She also published a collection of essays and sketches, *American Indian Stories* (1921). After going to Oklahoma to investigate the conditions on reservations there, Zitkala-Ša, Charles H. Fabens, and Matthew K. Sniffen wrote an exposé of the abuses, *Oklahoma's Poor Rich Indians: An Orgy of Graft and Exploitation of the Five*

bedfordstmartins.com/ americanlit for research links on Zitkala-Ša

Civilized Tribes — Legalized Robbery (1924). That year, Native Americans were finally granted citizenship in the United States. In 1926, Zitkala-Ša founded the National Council of American Indians, serving as its president until her death in Washington, on January 26, 1938.

Zitkala-Ša's "The School Days of an Indian Girl."   Zitkala-Ša's first publications appeared in the prominent literary magazine the *Atlantic Monthly*. Because it was rapidly losing ground to popular monthlies like the *Century Magazine* and *Scribner's Magazine*, a new editor of the *Atlantic*, Bliss Perry, decided to introduce more current and controversial material. In addition to publishing political commentaries by Theodore Roosevelt and Woodrow Wilson, Perry featured new literary voices such as Mary Austin and Paul Laurence Dunbar. From January through March 1900, the *Atlantic* also published three autobiographical essays written by Zitkala-Ša. In the first, "Impressions of an Indian Childhood," she describes her early life on the Pine Ridge Reservation in South Dakota, focusing most of her attention on the customs and legends of the Sioux. The second essay, reprinted below, was "The School Days of an Indian Girl," in which Zitkala-Ša offers a vivid account of her difficult experiences at White's Manual Labor Institute, the Quaker school she had attended for six years in Wabash, Indiana. The result of that "civilizing machine," as she describes the school, was to make Zitkala-Ša "neither a wild Indian nor a tame one." In the third of the essays, "An Indian Teacher among Indians," she describes her experiences at yet another "civilizing machine," the Carlisle Indian Industrial School in Pennsylvania. Zitkala-Ša later included all three of the autobiographical essays in her collection *American Indian Legends* (1921). The text is taken from the first printing in the *Atlantic Monthly*, February 1900.

THE SCHOOL DAYS OF AN INDIAN GIRL

I. The Land of Red Apples

There were eight in our party of bronzed children who were going East with the missionaries. Among us were three young braves, two tall girls, and we three little ones, Judéwin, Thowin, and I.

We had been very impatient to start on our journey to the Red Apple Country, which, we were told, lay a little beyond the great circular horizon of the Western prairie. Under a sky of rosy apples we dreamt of roaming as freely and happily as we had chased the cloud shadows on the Dakota plains. We had anticipated much pleasure from a ride on the iron horse, but the throngs of staring palefaces disturbed and troubled us.

On the train, fair women, with tottering babies on each arm, stopped their haste and scrutinized the children of absent mothers. Large men, with heavy bundles in their hands, halted near by, and riveted their glassy blue eyes upon us.

I sank deep into the corner of my seat, for I resented being watched. Directly in front of me, children who were no larger than I hung themselves upon the backs of their seats, with their bold white faces toward me. Sometimes they took their forefingers out of their mouths and pointed at my moccasined feet. Their mothers, instead of reproving such rude curiosity, looked closely at me, and attracted their children's further notice to my blanket. This embarrassed me, and kept me constantly on the verge of tears.

I sat perfectly still, with my eyes downcast, daring only now and then to shoot long glances around me. Chancing to turn to the window at my side, I was quite breathless upon seeing one familiar object. It was the telegraph pole which strode by at short paces. Very near my mother's dwelling, along the edge of a road thickly bordered with wild sunflowers, some poles like these had been planted by white men. Often I had stopped, on my way down the road, to hold my ear against the pole, and, hearing its low moaning, I used to wonder what the paleface had done to hurt it. Now I sat watching for each pole that glided by to be the last one.

In this way I had forgotten my uncomfortable surroundings, when I heard one of my comrades call out my name. I saw the missionary standing very near, tossing candies and gums into our midst. This amused us all, and we tried to see who could catch the most of the sweetmeats. The missionary's generous distribution of candies was impressed upon my memory by a disastrous result which followed. I had caught more than my share of candies and gums, and soon after our arrival at the school I had a chance to disgrace myself, which, I am ashamed to say, I did.

Though we rode several days inside of the iron horse, I do not recall a single thing about our luncheons.

It was night when we reached the school grounds. The lights from the windows of the large buildings fell upon some of the icicled trees that stood beneath them. We were led toward an open door, where the brightness of the lights within flooded out over the heads of the excited palefaces who blocked the way. My body trembled more from fear than from the snow I trod upon.

Entering the house, I stood close against the wall. The strong glaring light in the large whitewashed room dazzled my eyes. The noisy hurrying of hard shoes upon a bare wooden floor increased the whirring in my ears. My only safety seemed to be in keeping next to the wall. As I was wondering in which direction to escape from all this confusion, two warm hands grasped me firmly, and in the same moment I was tossed high in midair. A rosy-cheeked paleface woman caught me in her arms. I was both frightened and insulted by such trifling. I stared into her eyes, wishing her to let me stand on my own feet, but she jumped me up and down with increasing enthusiasm. My mother had never made a plaything of her wee daughter. Remembering this I began to cry aloud.

They misunderstood the cause of my tears, and placed me at a white table loaded with food. There our party were united again. As I did not hush my crying, one of the older ones whispered to me, "Wait until you are alone in the night."

It was very little I could swallow besides my sobs, that evening.

"Oh, I want my mother and my brother Dawee! I want to go to my aunt!" I pleaded; but the ears of the palefaces could not hear me.

From the table we were taken along an upward incline of wooden boxes, which I learned afterward to call a stairway. At the top was a quiet hall, dimly lighted. Many narrow beds were in one straight line down the entire length of the wall. In them lay sleeping brown faces, which peeped just out of the coverings. I was tucked into bed with one of the tall girls, because she talked to me in my mother tongue and seemed to soothe me.

I had arrived in the wonderful land of rosy skies, but I was not happy, as I had thought I should be. My long travel and the bewildering sights had exhausted me. I fell asleep, heaving deep, tired sobs. My tears were left to dry themselves in streaks, because neither my aunt nor my mother was near to wipe them away.

II. The Cutting of My Long Hair

The first day in the land of apples was a bitter-cold one; for the snow still covered the ground, and the trees were bare. A large bell rang for breakfast, its loud metallic voice crashing through the belfry overhead and into our sensitive ears. The annoying clatter of shoes on bare floors gave us no peace. The constant clash of harsh noises, with an undercurrent of many voices murmuring an unknown tongue, made a bedlam within which I was securely tied. And though my spirit tore itself in struggling for its lost freedom, all was useless.

A paleface woman, with white hair, came up after us. We were placed in a line of girls who were marching into the dining room. These were Indian girls, in stiff shoes and closely clinging dresses. The small girls wore sleeved aprons and shingled[1] hair. As I walked noiselessly in my soft moccasins, I felt like sinking to the floor, for my blanket had been stripped from my shoulders. I looked hard at the Indian girls, who seemed not to care that they were even more immodestly dressed than I, in their tightly fitting clothes. While we marched in, the boys entered at an opposite door. I watched for the three young braves who came in our party. I spied them in the rear ranks, looking as uncomfortable as I felt.

A small bell was tapped, and each of the pupils drew a chair from under the table. Supposing this act meant they were to be seated, I pulled out mine and at once slipped into it from one side. But when I turned my head, I saw that I was the only one seated, and all the rest at our table remained standing. Just as I began to rise, looking shyly around to see how chairs were to be used, a second bell was sounded. All were seated at last, and I had to crawl back into my chair again. I heard a man's voice at one end of the hall, and I looked around to see him. But all the others hung their heads over their plates. As I glanced at the long chain of tables, I caught the eyes of a paleface woman upon me. Immediately I dropped my eyes, wondering why I was so keenly watched by the strange woman. The man ceased his mutterings, and then a third bell was tapped. Every

---

1. **shingled:** An early twentieth-century term for a woman's close-cropped haircut, which is layered in the back like a man's haircut.

one picked up his knife and fork and began eating. I began crying instead, for by this time I was afraid to venture anything more.

But this eating by formula was not the hardest trial in that first day. Late in the morning, my friend Judéwin gave me a terrible warning. Judéwin knew a few words in English; and she had overheard the paleface woman talk about cutting our long, heavy hair. Our mothers had taught us that only unskilled warriors who were captured had their hair shingled by the enemy. Among our people, short hair was worn by mourners, and shingled hair by cowards!

We discussed our fate some moments, and when Judéwin said, "We have to submit, because they are strong," I rebelled.

"No, I will not submit! I will struggle first!" I answered.

I watched my chance, and when no one noticed I disappeared. I crept up the stairs as quietly as I could in my squeaking shoes, — my moccasins had been exchanged for shoes. Along the hall I passed, without knowing whither I was going. Turning aside to an open door, I found a large room with three white beds in it. The windows were covered with dark green curtains, which made the room very dim. Thankful that no one was there, I directed my steps toward the corner farthest from the door. On my hands and knees I crawled under the bed, and cuddled myself in the dark corner.

From my hiding place I peered out, shuddering with fear whenever I heard footsteps near by. Though in the hall loud voices were calling my name, and I knew that even Judéwin was searching for me, I did not open my mouth to answer. Then the steps were quickened and the voices became excited. The sounds came nearer and nearer. Women and girls entered the room. I held my breath, and watched them open closet doors and peep behind large trunks. Some one threw up the curtains, and the room was filled with sudden light. What caused them to stoop and look under the bed I do not know. I remember being dragged out, though I resisted by kicking and scratching wildly. In spite of myself, I was carried downstairs and tied fast in a chair.

I cried aloud, shaking my head all the while until I felt the cold blades of the scissors against my neck, and heard them gnaw off one of my thick braids. Then I lost my spirit. Since the day I was taken from my mother I had suffered extreme indignities. People had stared at me. I had been tossed about in the air like a wooden puppet. And now my long hair was shingled like a coward's! In my anguish I moaned for my mother, but no one came to comfort me. Not a soul reasoned quietly with me, as my own mother used to do; for now I was only one of many little animals driven by a herder.

III. The Snow Episode

A short time after our arrival we three Dakotas were playing in the snowdrifts. We were all still deaf to the English language, excepting Judéwin, who always heard such puzzling things. One morning we learned through her ears that we were forbidden to fall lengthwise in the snow, as we had been doing, to see our own impressions, However, before many hours we had forgotten the order, and were having great sport in the snow, when a shrill voice called us. Looking up, we saw an imperative hand beckoning us into the house. We shook the snow off ourselves, and started toward the woman as slowly as we dared.

Judéwin said: "Now the paleface is angry with us. She is going to punish us for falling into the snow. If she looks straight into your eyes and talks loudly, you must wait until she stops. Then, after a tiny pause, say, 'No.'" The rest of the way we practiced upon the little word "no."

As it happened, Thowin was summoned to judgment first. The door shut behind her with a click.

Judéwin and I stood silently listening at the keyhole. The paleface woman talked in very severe tones. Her words fell from her lips like crackling embers, and her inflection ran up like the small end of a switch. I understood her voice better than the things she was saying. I was certain we had made her very impatient with us. Judéwin heard enough of the words to realize all too late that she had taught us the wrong reply.

"Oh, poor Thowin!" she gasped, as she put both hands over her ears.

Just then I heard Thowin's tremulous answer, "No."

With an angry exclamation, the woman gave her a hard spanking. Then she stopped to say something. Judéwin said it was this: "Are you going to obey my word the next time?"

Thowin answered again with the only word at her command, "No."

This time the woman meant her blows to smart, for the poor frightened girl shrieked at the top of her voice. In the midst of the whipping the blows ceased abruptly, and the woman asked another question: "Are you going to fall in the snow again?"

Thowin gave her bad password another trial. We heard her say feebly, "No! No!"

With this the woman hid away her half-worn slipper, and led the child out, stroking her black shorn head. Perhaps it occurred to her that brute force is not the solution for such a problem. She did nothing to Judéwin nor to me. She only returned to us our unhappy comrade, and left us alone in the room.

During the first two or three seasons misunderstandings as ridiculous as this one of the snow episode frequently took place, bringing unjustifiable frights and punishments into our little lives.

Within a year I was able to express myself somewhat in broken English. As soon as I comprehended a part of what was said and done, a mischievous spirit of revenge possessed me. One day I was called in from my play for some misconduct. I had disregarded a rule which seemed to me very needlessly binding. I was sent into the kitchen to mash the turnips for dinner. It was noon, and steaming dishes were hastily carried into the dining room. I hated turnips, and their odor which came from the brown jar was offensive to me. With fire in my heart, I took the wooden tool that the paleface woman held out to me. I stood upon a step, and, grasping the handle with both hands, I bent in hot rage over the turnips. I worked my vengeance upon them. All were so busily occupied that no one noticed me. I saw that the turnips were in a pulp, and that further beating could not improve them; but the order was, "Mash these turnips," and mash them I would! I renewed my energy; and as I sent the masher into the bottom of the jar, I felt a satisfying sensation that the weight of my body had gone into it.

Just here a paleface woman came up to my table. As she looked into the jar, she shoved my hands roughly aside. I stood fearless and angry. She placed her red hands upon the rim of the jar. Then she gave one lift and a stride away from the table. But lo! the pulpy contents fell through the crumbled bottom to the floor! She spared me no scolding phrases that I had earned. I did not heed them. I felt triumphant in my revenge, though deep within me I was a wee bit sorry to have broken the jar.

As I sat eating my dinner, and saw that no turnips were served, I whooped in my heart for having once asserted the rebellion within me.

IV. The Devil

Among the legends the old warriors used to tell me were many stories of evil spirits. But I was taught to fear them no more than those who stalked about in material guise. I never knew there was an insolent chieftain among the bad spirits, who dared to array his forces against the Great Spirit, until I heard this white man's legend from a paleface woman.

Out of a large book she showed me a picture of the white man's devil. I looked in horror upon the strong claws that grew out of his fur-covered fingers. His feet were like his hands. Trailing at his heels was a scaly tail tipped with a serpent's open jaws. His face was a patchwork: he had bearded cheeks, like some I had seen palefaces wear; his nose was an eagle's bill, and his sharp-pointed ears were pricked up like those of a sly fox. Above them a pair of cow's horns curved upward. I trembled with awe, and my heart throbbed in my throat, as I looked at the king of evil spirits. Then I heard the paleface woman say that this terrible creature roamed loose in the world, and that little girls who disobeyed school regulations were to be tortured by him.

That night I dreamt about this evil divinity. Once again I seemed to be in my mother's cottage. An Indian woman had come to visit my mother. On opposite sides of the kitchen stove, which stood in the centre of the small house, my mother and her guest were seated in straight-backed chairs. I played with a train of empty spools hitched together on a string. It was night, and the wick burned feebly. Suddenly I heard some one turn our door-knob from without.

My mother and the woman hushed their talk, and both looked toward the door. It opened gradually. I waited behind the stove. The hinges squeaked as the door was slowly, very slowly pushed inward.

Then in rushed the devil! He was tall! He looked exactly like the picture I had seen of him in the white man's papers. He did not speak to my mother, because he did not know the Indian language, but his glittering yellow eyes were fastened upon me. He took long strides around the stove, passing behind the woman's chair. I threw down my spools, and ran to my mother. He did not fear her, but followed closely after me. Then I ran round and round the stove, crying aloud for help. But my mother and the woman seemed not to know my danger. They sat still, looking quietly upon the devil's chase after me. At last I grew dizzy. My head revolved as on a hidden pivot. My knees became numb, and doubled under my weight like a pair of knife blades without a spring. Beside my mother's chair I fell in a heap. Just as the devil stooped over me with outstretched claws my mother awoke from her quiet indifference, and lifted me on her lap. Whereupon the devil vanished, and I was awake.

On the following morning I took my revenge upon the devil. Stealing into the room where a wall of shelves was filled with books, I drew forth The Stories of the Bible. With a broken slate pencil I carried in my apron pocket, I began by scratching out his wicked eyes. A few moments later, when I was ready to leave the room, there was a ragged hole in the page where the picture of the devil had once been.

V. Iron Routine

A loud-clamoring bell awakened us at half past six in the cold winter mornings. From happy dreams of Western rolling lands and unlassoed freedom we tumbled out upon chilly bare floors back again into a paleface day. We had short time to jump into our shoes and clothes, and wet our eyes with icy water, before a small hand bell was vigorously rung for roll call.

There were too many drowsy children and too numerous orders for the day to waste a moment in any apology to nature for giving her children such a shock in the early morning. We rushed downstairs, bounding over two high steps at a time, to land in the assembly room.

A paleface woman, with a yellow-covered roll book open on her arm and a gnawed pencil in her hand, appeared at the door. Her small, tired face was coldly lighted with a pair of large gray eyes.

She stood still in a halo of authority, while over the rim of her spectacles her eyes pried nervously about the room. Having glanced at her long list of names and called out the first one, she tossed up her chin and peered through the crystals of her spectacles to make sure of the answer "Here."

Relentlessly her pencil black-marked our daily records if we were not present to respond to our names, and no chum of ours had done it successfully for us. No matter if a dull headache or the painful cough of slow consumption had delayed the absentee, there was only time enough to mark the tardiness. It was next to impossible to leave the iron routine after the civilizing machine had once begun its day's buzzing; and as it was inbred in me to suffer in silence rather than to appeal to the ears of one whose open eyes could not see my pain, I have many times trudged in the day's harness heavy-footed, like a dumb sick brute.

Once I lost a dear classmate. I remember well how she used to mope along at my side, until one morning she could not raise her head from her pillow. At her deathbed I stood weeping, as the paleface woman sat near her moistening the dry lips. Among the folds of the bedclothes I saw the open pages of the white man's Bible. The dying Indian girl talked disconnectedly of Jesus the Christ and the paleface who was cooling her swollen hands and feet.

I grew bitter, and censured the woman for cruel neglect of our physical ills. I despised the pencils that moved automatically, and the one teaspoon which dealt out, from a large bottle, healing to a row of variously ailing Indian children. I blamed the hardworking, well-meaning, ignorant woman who was inculcating in our hearts her superstitious ideas. Though I was sullen in all my little troubles, as soon as I felt better I was ready again to smile upon the cruel woman. Within a week I was again actively testing the chains which tightly bound my individuality like a mummy for burial.

The melancholy of those black days has left so long a shadow that it darkens the path of years that have since gone by. These sad memories rise above those of smoothly grinding school days. Perhaps my Indian nature is the moaning wind which stirs them now for their present record. But, however tempestuous this is within me, it comes out as the low voice of a curiously colored seashell, which is only for those ears that are bent with compassion to hear it.

VI. Four Strange Summers

After my first three years of school, I roamed again in the Western country through four strange summers.

During this time I seemed to hang in the heart of chaos, beyond the touch or voice of human aid. My brother, being almost ten years my senior, did not quite understand my feelings. My mother had never gone inside of a schoolhouse, and so she was not capable of comforting her daughter who could read and write. Even nature seemed to have no place for me. I was neither a wee girl nor a tall one; neither a wild Indian nor a tame one. This deplorable situation was the effect of my brief course in the East, and the unsatisfactory "teenth" in a girl's years.

It was under these trying conditions that, one bright afternoon, as I sat restless and unhappy in my mother's cabin, I caught the sound of the spirited step of my brother's pony on the road which passed by our dwelling. Soon I heard the wheels of a light buckboard, and Dawee's familiar "Ho!" to his pony. He alighted upon the bare ground in front of our house. Tying his pony to one of the projecting corner logs of the low-roofed cottage, he stepped upon the wooden doorstep.

I met him there with a hurried greeting, and, as I passed by, he looked a quiet "What?" into my eyes.

When he began talking with my mother, I slipped the rope from the pony's bridle. Seizing the reins and bracing my feet against the dashboard, I wheeled around in an instant. The pony was ever ready to try his speed. Looking backward, I saw Dawee waving his hand to me. I turned with the curve in the road and disappeared. I followed the winding road which crawled upward between the bases of little hillocks. Deep water-worn ditches ran parallel on either side. A strong wind blew against my cheeks and fluttered my sleeves. The pony reached the top of the highest hill, and began an even race on the level lands. There was nothing moving within that great circular horizon of the Dakota prairies save the tall grasses, over which the wind blew and rolled off in long, shadowy waves.

Within this vast wigwam of blue and green I rode reckless and insignificant. It satisfied my small consciousness to see the white foam fly from the pony's mouth.

Suddenly, out of the earth a coyote came forth at a swinging trot that was taking the cunning thief toward the hills and the village beyond. Upon the moment's impulse, I gave him a long chase and a wholesome fright. As I turned away to go back to the village, the wolf sank down upon his haunches for rest, for it was a hot summer day; and as I drove slowly homeward, I saw his sharp nose still pointed at me, until I vanished below the margin of the hilltops.

In a little while I came in sight of my mother's house. Dawee stood in the yard, laughing at an old warrior who was pointing his forefinger, and again waving his whole hand, toward the hills. With his blanket drawn over one shoulder, he talked and motioned excitedly. Dawee turned the old man by the shoulder and pointed me out to him.

"Oh han!" (Oh yes) the warrior muttered, and went his way. He had climbed the top of his favorite barren hill to survey the surrounding prairies, when he spied my chase after the coyote. His keen eyes recognized the pony and driver. At once uneasy for my safety, he had come running to my mother's cabin to give her warning. I did not appreciate his kindly interest, for there was an unrest gnawing at my heart.

As soon as he went away, I asked Dawee about something else.

"No, my baby sister, I cannot take you with me to the party to-night," he replied. Though I was not far from fifteen, and I felt that before long I should enjoy all the privileges of my tall cousin, Dawee persisted in calling me his baby sister.

That moonlight night, I cried in my mother's presence when I heard the jolly young people pass by our cottage. They were no more young braves in blankets and eagle plumes, nor Indian maids with prettily painted cheeks. They had gone three years to school in the East, and had become civilized. The young men wore the white man's coat and trousers, with bright neckties. The girls wore tight muslin dresses, with ribbons at neck and waist. At these gatherings they talked English. I could speak English almost as well as my brother, but I was not properly dressed to be taken along. I had no hat, no ribbons, and no close-fitting gown. Since my return from school I had thrown away my shoes, and wore again the soft moccasins.

While Dawee was busily preparing to go I controlled my tears. But when I heard him bounding away on his pony, I buried my face in my arms and cried hot tears.

My mother was troubled by my unhappiness. Coming to my side, she offered me the only printed matter we had in our home. It was an Indian Bible, given her some years ago by a missionary. She tried to console me. "Here, my child, are the white man's papers. Read a little from them," she said most piously.

I took it from her hand, for her sake; but my enraged spirit felt more like burning the book, which afforded me no help, and was a perfect delusion to my mother. I did not read it, but laid it unopened on the floor, where I sat on my feet. The dim yellow light of the braided muslin burning in a small vessel of oil flickered and sizzled in the awful silent storm which followed my rejection of the Bible.

Now my wrath against the fates consumed my tears before they reached my eyes. I sat stony, with a bowed head. My mother threw a shawl over her head and shoulders, and stepped out into the night.

After an uncertain solitude, I was suddenly aroused by a loud cry piercing the night. It was my mother's voice wailing among the barren hills which held the bones of buried warriors. She called aloud for her brothers' spirits to support her in her helpless misery. My fingers grew icy cold, as I realized that my unrestrained tears had betrayed my suffering to her, and she was grieving for me.

Before she returned, though I knew she was on her way, for she had ceased her weeping, I extinguished the light, and leaned my head on the window sill.

Many schemes of running away from my surroundings hovered about in my mind. A few more moons of such a turmoil drove me away to the Eastern school. I rode on the white man's iron steed, thinking it would bring me back to my mother in a few winters, when I should be grown tall, and there would be congenial friends awaiting me.

VII. Incurring My Mother's Displeasure

In the second journey to the East I had not come without some precautions. I had a secret interview with one of our best medicine men, and when I left his wigwam I carried securely in my sleeve a tiny bunch of magic roots. This possession assured me of friends wherever I should go. So absolutely did I believe in its charms that I wore it through all the school routine for more than a year. Then, before I lost my faith in the dead roots, I lost the little buckskin bag containing all my good luck.

At the close of this second term of three years I was the proud owner of my first diploma. The following autumn I ventured upon a college career against my mother's will.

I had written for her approval, but in her reply I found no encouragement. She called my notice to her neighbors' children, who had completed their education in three years. They had returned to their homes, and were then talking English with the frontier settlers. Her few words hinted that I had better give up my slow attempt to learn the white man's ways, and be content to roam over the prairies and find my living upon wild roots. I silenced her by deliberate disobedience.

Thus, homeless and heavy-hearted, I began anew my life among strangers.

As I hid myself in my little room in the college dormitory, away from the scornful and yet curious eyes of the students, I pined for sympathy. Often I wept in secret, wishing I had gone West, to be nourished by my mother's love, instead of remaining among a cold race whose hearts were frozen hard with prejudice.

During the fall and winter seasons I scarcely had a real friend, though by that time several of my classmates were courteous to me at a safe distance.

My mother had not yet forgiven my rudeness to her, and I had no moment for letter-writing. By daylight and lamplight, I spun with reeds and thistles, until my hands were tired from their weaving, the magic design which promised me the white man's respect.

At length, in the spring term, I entered an oratorical contest among the various classes. As the day of competition approached, it did not seem possible that the event was so near at hand, but it came. In the chapel the classes assembled together, with their invited guests. The high platform was carpeted, and gayly festooned with college colors. A bright white light illumined the room, and outlined clearly the great polished beams that arched the domed ceiling. The assembled crowds filled the air with pulsating murmurs. When the hour for speaking arrived all were hushed. But on the wall the old clock which pointed out the trying moment ticked calmly on.

One after another I saw and heard the orators. Still, I could not realize that they longed for the favorable decision of the judges as much as I did. Each contestant received a loud burst of applause, and some were cheered heartily. Too soon my turn came, and I paused a moment behind the curtains for a deep breath. After my concluding words, I heard the same applause that the others had called out.

Upon my retreating steps, I was astounded to receive from my fellow students a large bouquet of roses tied with flowing ribbons. With the lovely flowers I fled from the stage. This friendly token was a rebuke to me for the hard feelings I had borne them.

Later, the decision of the judges awarded me the first place. Then there was a mad uproar in the hall, where my classmates sang and shouted my name at the top of their lungs; and the disappointed students howled and brayed in fearfully dissonant tin trumpets. In this excitement, happy students rushed forward to offer their congratulations. And I could not conceal a smile when they wished to escort me in a procession to the students' parlor, where all were going to calm themselves. Thanking them for the kind spirit which prompted them to make such a proposition, I walked alone with the night to my own little room.

A few weeks afterward, I appeared as the college representative in another contest. This time the competition was among orators from different colleges in our state. It was held at the state capital, in one of the largest opera houses.

Here again was a strong prejudice against my people. In the evening, as the great audience filled the house, the student bodies began warring among themselves. Fortunately, I was spared witnessing any of the noisy wrangling before the contest began. The slurs against the Indian that stained the lips of our opponents were already burning like a dry fever within my breast.

But after the orations were delivered a deeper burn awaited me. There, before that vast ocean of eyes, some college rowdies threw out a large white flag, with a drawing of a most forlorn Indian girl on it. Under this they had printed in bold black letters words that ridiculed the college which was represented by a "squaw." Such worse than barbarian rudeness embittered me. While we waited for the verdict of the judges, I gleamed fiercely upon the throngs of palefaces. My teeth were hard set, as I saw the white flag still floating insolently in the air.

Then anxiously we watched the man carry toward the stage the envelope containing the final decision.

There were two prizes given, that night, and one of them was mine!

The evil spirit laughed within me when the white flag dropped out of sight, and the hands which furled it hung limp in defeat.

Leaving the crowd as quickly as possible, I was soon in my room. The rest of the night I sat in an armchair and gazed into the crackling fire. I laughed no more in triumph when thus alone. The little taste of victory did not satisfy a hunger in my heart. In my mind I saw my mother far away on the Western plains, and she was holding a charge against me.

[1900]

Booker T. Washington

[1856-1915]

Booker Taliferro Washington was born on a small farm near Hale's Ford, Virginia, probably in the spring of 1856. He was the son of a slave, Jane, who never revealed the identity of his white father. She later married another slave, Washington Ferguson, whose first name Washington took as his last name. Emancipated during the Civil War, in the summer of 1865 the family moved to Malden, West Virginia, where Washington Ferguson had found a job in a salt factory. Washington and his brother also went to work in the factory, packing salt into barrels. In his autobiography, Washington recalls that the first word he learned to read was actually a number, 18, the number assigned to his stepfather at the factory. Possessed by what he called "an intense longing to learn to read," Washington used a spelling book his mother found for him to learn the alphabet and a few words. Before and after his long hours of work at the factory, he also began to attend a school for freed slaves. In 1872, now sixteen and working in a coal mine, Washington enrolled at the Hampton Normal and Agricultural Institute, founded by the American Missionary Association as an experimental school for African Americans. Paying his way by working as a janitor in the school, Washington was deeply influenced by its principal, Samuel Chapman Armstrong, a leader in the movement for "industrial," or vocational, education as a way to improve the lot of former slaves. After graduating in 1875, Washington returned home and taught for two years at a school in Malden. He then studied for a year at the Wayland Seminary in Washington, D.C., before accepting a teaching position in a program for Native Americans at Hampton in 1878.

Booker T. Washington

When this photograph was taken around 1903, Washington was the most influential and widely known African American spokesperson in the United States.

Three years later, Armstrong recommended the twenty-five-year-old Washington for director of a new school for African Americans in Tuskegee, Alabama. For the rest of his life, Washington was closely associated with the Tuskegee Normal School and Industrial Institute, as well as with what came to be called the "Tuskegee Machine," a network of students, alumni, and supporters who formed a political coalition that worked to advance the interests of African Americans. Washington shrewdly handled the institute's affairs, buying land and relying on private contributions so that the school would not be indebted to the state and consequently subject to its control and changing property laws in Alabama. He also established a working farm and later a brickyard, which eventually became the mainstay of several industries established at the institute. Students took classes and worked in the industries, where they were trained to pursue a variety of occupations. The school's emphasis on vocational training was criticized by those who advocated a full liberal arts education for African Americans. Washington, however, successfully promoted his views through extended lecture tours, gaining the support of many wealthy white donors for the Institute. But his professional successes during these years were shadowed by the deaths of his first two wives, Fanny Norton Smith and Olivia A. Davidson. A widower with three children, he married Margaret J. Murray, with whom he would spend the rest of his life, in 1893.

During the following decade, Washington became the most prominent and powerful spokesperson for African Americans. In 1895, he was invited to speak at the opening of the Cotton States and International Exposition, a showcase of agriculture, manufacturing, technology, and transportation designed to promote Atlanta as the center of the "new" South. In his "Atlanta Exposition Address," Washington urged members of both races to "cast down your bucket where you are," declaring: "In all things that are purely social we can be as separate as the fingers, yet one as the hand in all things essential to mutual progress." In effect, he proposed that African Americans should accommodate themselves to racial segregation and political disenfranchisement in order to enjoy a greater degree of economic security. The address outraged some blacks, including John Hope, then a young professor at Roger Williams University in Nashville, who in a passionate rebuttal to Washington angrily asked: "If we are not striving for equality, in heaven's name for what are we living?" But whites cheered the address, which was published in newspapers across the country and which made Washington a celebrity. The following year, he became the first African American to receive an honorary degree from Harvard University, and he was lauded by President William McKinley, who visited Tuskegee and warmly praised Washington's efforts. In a further effort to improve the economic conditions of African Americans, Washington in 1900 founded the National Business League, arguing that blacks should "leave political and civil rights alone" in order to "make a businessman of the Negro." Washington amplified his argument and extended his influence through his growing control of the African American press, his numerous articles in influential white periodicals, and the publication of his best-selling and widely acclaimed autobiography, *Up from Slavery* (1901).

Washington's conservative positions and his conciliatory posture toward white America generated growing controversy among African Americans. He continued to promote industrial education and to preach the gospel of the gradual economic advancement of his race in numerous lectures and in his writings, including *Tuskegee and Its People* (1905), *The Story of the Negro* (1909), and *The Man Farthest Down: A Record of Observation and Study in Europe* (1912), in which he affirmed that African Amer-

It is no ordinary tribute to this man's tact and power, that, steering as he must amid so many diverse interests and opinions, he to-day commands not simply the applause of those who believe in his theories, but also the respect of those who do not.

—W. E. B. Du Bois

icans were better off than impoverished whites in Europe. In response, many African American leaders protested that Washington was ignoring the violence directed at blacks, especially the epidemic of lynching in the South, as well as the pervasive political and social inequality between the races in the United States. Although he privately contributed funds for legal challenges to the segregation and disenfranchisement of blacks, Washington publicly avoided politics and strongly opposed the militant Niagara Movement and its successor, the National Association for the Advancement of Colored People (NAACP), which was founded in 1909. The following year, his longtime critic W. E. B. Du Bois and twenty-two other African American leaders signed a statement in which they asserted that "Mr. Washington's large financial responsibilities have made him dependent on the rich charitable public and that, for this reason, he has for years been compelled to tell, not the whole truth, but that part of it which certain powerful interests in America wish to appear as the whole truth." Despite mounting criticism of his views, when Washington died at Tuskegee on November 14, 1915, he was widely honored as what the obituary in the *New York Times* described as the "foremost teacher and leader of the negro race."

bedfordstmartins.com/ americanlit for research links on Washington

Washington's *Up from Slavery*.   As he explains in the preface, Washington's autobiography began as a series of articles published during 1900-01 in the *Outlook*, a weekly magazine with a circulation of 100,000 that featured autobiography, biography, literary criticism, and essays on national affairs. Its editor, Lyman Abbott, had strongly encouraged Washington to write the account, observing in a letter to him: "The pictorial side of your life, the incidents which you have seen, out of which your own generalizations have grown, will be of the first interest and value to your readers." The series was widely read, and *Up from Slavery* was consequently published to great acclaim as a book in 1901. The influential writer and critic William Dean Howells published an enthusiastic article about the book and its author, "An Exemplary Citizen." Indeed, the account was frequently compared to the most famous of American "rags-to-riches" stories, the *Autobiography* of Benjamin Franklin. Widely viewed in the eyes of white America as the foremost representative of his race, Washington in *Up from Slavery* exploits that position to challenge denigrating stereotypes about the capacities of African Americans. At the same time, Washington had gained his prominent position largely by saying what most white Americans wanted to hear, and the following chapter on the speech that made him famous contains some of his most controversial statements about the role of African Americans in the United States. The text is taken from the first edition of *Up from Slavery* (1901), in which Washington altered the serialized version in the *Outlook* by insisting on the capitalization of the word *Negro* and by using the British spellings for words such as *coloured*.

UP FROM SLAVERY

Chapter XIV
The Atlanta Exposition Address

The Atlanta Exposition, at which I had been asked to make an address as a representative of the Negro race, . . . was opened with a short address from Governor Bullock.[1] After other interesting exercises, including an invocation from Bishop Nelson, of Georgia, a dedicatory ode by Albert Howell, Jr., and addresses by the President of the Exposition and Mrs. Joseph Thompson, the President of the Woman's Board, Governor Bullock introduced me with the words, "We have with us to-day a representative of Negro enterprise and Negro civilization."

When I arose to speak, there was considerable cheering, especially from the coloured people. As I remember it now, the thing that was uppermost in my mind was the desire to say something that would cement the friendship of the races and bring about hearty coöperation between them. So far as my outward surroundings were concerned, the only thing that I recall distinctly now is that when I got up, I saw thousands of eyes looking intently in my face. The following is the address which I delivered: —

MR. PRESIDENT AND GENTLEMEN OF THE BOARD OF DIRECTORS AND CITIZENS.

One-third of the population of the South is of the Negro race. No enterprise seeking the material, civil, or moral welfare of this section can disregard this element of our population and reach the highest success. I but convey to you, Mr. President and Directors, the sentiment of the masses of my race when I say that in no way have the value and manhood of the American Negro been more fittingly and generously recognized than by the managers of this magnificent Exposition at every stage of its progress. It is a recognition that will do more to cement the friendship of the two races than any occurrence since the dawn of our freedom.

Not only this, but the opportunity here afforded will awaken among us a new era of industrial progress. Ignorant and inexperienced, it is not strange that in the first years of our new life we began at the top instead of at the bottom; that a seat in Congress or the state legislature was more sought than real estate or industrial skill; that the political convention of stump speaking had more attractions than starting a dairy farm or truck garden.

A ship lost at sea for many days suddenly sighted a friendly vessel. From the mast of the unfortunate vessel was seen a signal, "Water, water; we die of thirst!" The answer from the friendly vessel at once came back, "Cast down your bucket where you are." A

---

1. **Governor Bullock:** Rufus Bullock (1834–1907), a businessman from New York who had cooperated with the Confederacy, was elected the first Republican governor of Georgia in 1868. His unpopular Reconstruction policies and his support for African American equality infuriated the powerful Ku Klux Klan, which ran a smear campaign accusing Bullock of corruption, malfeasance, and fraud. He was consequently forced from office in 1871. Tried twice in Atlanta and acquitted on all charges, Bullock restored his reputation and became a prominent citizen. In 1895, he was instrumental in organizing the Atlanta Exposition, inviting Washington to give an address and serving as the master of ceremonies on opening day of the exposition.

second time the signal, "Water, water; send us water!" ran up from the distressed vessel, and was answered, "Cast down your bucket where you are." And a third and fourth signal for water was answered, "Cast down your bucket where you are." The captain of the distressed vessel, at last heeding the injunction, cast down his bucket, and it came up full of fresh, sparkling water from the mouth of the Amazon River. To those of my race who depend on bettering their condition in a foreign land or who underestimate the importance of cultivating friendly relations with the Southern white man, who is their next-door neighbour, I would say: "Cast down your bucket where you are" — cast it down in making friends in every manly way of the people of all races by whom we are surrounded.

Cast it down in agriculture, mechanics, in commerce, in domestic service, and in the professions. And in this connection it is well to bear in mind that whatever other sins the South may be called to bear, when it comes to business, pure and simple, it is in the South that the Negro is given a man's chance in the commercial world, and in nothing is this Exposition more eloquent than in emphasizing this chance. Our greatest danger is that in the great leap from slavery to freedom we may overlook the fact that the masses of us are to live by the productions of our hands, and fail to keep in mind that we shall prosper in proportion as we learn to dignify and glorify common labour and put brains and skill into the common occupations of life; shall prosper in proportion as we learn to draw the line between the superficial and the substantial, the ornamental gewgaws of life and the useful. No race can prosper till it learns that there is as much dignity in tilling a field as in writing a poem. It is at the bottom of life we must begin, and not at the top. Nor should we permit our grievances to overshadow our opportunities.

To those of the white race who look to the incoming of those of foreign birth and strange tongue and habits for the prosperity of the South, were I permitted I would repeat what I say to my own race, "Cast down your bucket where you are." Cast it down among the eight millions of Negroes whose habits you know, whose fidelity and love you have tested in days when to have proved treacherous meant the ruin of your firesides. Cast down your bucket among these people who have, without strikes and labour wars, tilled your fields, cleared your forests, builded your railroads and cities, and brought forth treasures from the bowels of the earth, and helped make possible this magnificent representation of the progress of the South. Casting down your bucket among my people, helping and encouraging them as you are doing on these grounds, and to education of head, hand, and heart, you will find that they will buy your surplus land, make blossom the waste places in your fields, and run your factories. While doing this, you can be sure in the future, as in the past, that you and your families will be surrounded by the most patient, faithful, law-abiding, and unresentful people that the world has seen. As we have proved our loyalty to you in the past, in nursing your children, watching by the sick-bed of your mothers and fathers, and often following them with tear-dimmed eyes to their graves, so in the future, in our humble way, we shall stand by you with a devotion that no foreigner can approach, ready to lay down our lives, if need be, in defence of yours, interlacing our industrial, commercial, civil, and religious life with yours in a way that shall make the interests of both races one. In all things that are purely social we can be as separate as the fingers, yet one as the hand in all things essential to mutual progress.

There is no defence or security for any of us except in the highest intelligence and development of all. If anywhere there are efforts tending to curtail the fullest growth of the Negro, let these efforts be turned into stimulating, encouraging, and making him the most useful and intelligent citizen. Effort or means so invested will pay a thousand percent interest. These efforts will be twice blessed — "blessing him that gives and him that takes."[2]

There is no escape through law of man or God from the inevitable:

> The laws of changeless justice bind
> Oppressor with oppressed;
> And close as sin and suffering joined
> We march to fate abreast.[3]

Nearly sixteen millions of hands will aid you in pulling the load upward, or they will pull against you the load downward. We shall constitute one-third and more of the ignorance and crime of the South, or one-third its intelligence and progress; we shall contribute one-third to the business and industrial prosperity of the South, or we shall prove a veritable body of death, stagnating, depressing, retarding every effort to advance the body politic.

Gentlemen of the Exposition, as we present to you our humble effort at an exhibition of our progress, you must not expect overmuch. Starting thirty years ago with ownership here and there in a few quilts and pumpkins and chickens (gathered from miscellaneous sources), remember the path that has led from these to the inventions and production of agricultural implements, buggies, steam-engines, newspapers, books, statuary, carving, paintings, the management of drug-stores and banks, has not been trodden without contact with thorns and thistles. While we take pride in what we exhibit as a result of our independent efforts, we do not for a moment forget that our part in this exhibition would fall far short of your expectations but for the constant help that has come to our educational life, not only from the Southern states, but especially from Northern philanthropists, who have made their gifts a constant stream of blessing and encouragement.

The wisest among my race understand that the agitation of questions of social equality is the extremest folly, and that progress in the enjoyment of all the privileges that will come to us must be the result of severe and constant struggle rather than of artificial forcing. No race that has anything to contribute to the markets of the world is long in any degree ostracized. It is important and right that all privileges of the law be ours, but it is vastly more important that we be prepared for the exercises of these privileges. The opportunity to earn a dollar in a factory just now is worth infinitely more than the opportunity to spend a dollar in a opera-house.

---

2. **"blessing . . . takes"**: Washington is quoting loosely from Shakespeare's *The Merchant of Venice* 4.1.187: "It blesseth him that gives and him that takes."
3. **"The laws . . . abreast"**: From "Song of the Negro Boatman at Port Royal" (1863), with lyrics by John Greenleaf Whittier and music by E. W. Kellogg.

In conclusion, may I repeat that nothing in thirty years has given us more hope and encouragement, and drawn us so near to you of the white race, as this opportunity offered by the Exposition; and here bending, as it were, over the altar that represents the results of the struggles of your race and mine, both starting practically empty-handed three decades ago, I pledge that in your effort to work out the great and intricate problem which God has laid at the doors of the South, you shall have at all times the patient, sympathetic help of my race; only let this be constantly in mind, that, while from representations in these buildings of the product of field, of forest, of mine, of factory, letters, and art, much good will come, yet far above and beyond material benefits will be that higher good, that, let us pray God, will come, in a blotting out of sectional differences and racial animosities and suspicions, in a determination to administer absolute justice, in a willing obedience among all classes to the mandates of law. This, this, coupled with our material prosperity, will bring into our beloved South a new heaven and a new earth.

The first thing that I remember, after I had finished speaking, was that Governor Bullock rushed across the platform and took me by the hand, and that others did the same. I received so many and such hearty congratulations that I found it difficult to get out of the building. I did not appreciate to any degree, however, the impression which my address seemed to have made, until the next morning, when I went into the business part of the city. As soon as I was recognized, I was surprised to find myself pointed out and surrounded by a crowd of men who wished to shake hands with me. This was kept up on every street on to which I went, to an extent which embarrassed me so much that I went back to my boarding-place. The next morning I returned to Tuskegee. At the station in Atlanta, and at almost all of the stations at which the train stopped between that city and Tuskegee, I found a crowd of people anxious to shake hands with me.

The papers in all parts of the United States published the address in full, and for months afterward there were complimentary editorial references to it. Mr. Clark Howell, the editor of the Atlanta *Constitution*, telegraphed to a New York paper, among other words, the following, "I do not exaggerate when I say that Professor Booker T. Washington's address yesterday was one of the most notable speeches, both as to character and as to the warmth of its reception, ever delivered to a Southern audience. The address was a revelation. The whole speech is a platform upon which blacks and whites can stand with full justice to each other."

The Boston *Transcript* said editorially: "The speech of Booker T. Washington at the Atlanta Exposition, this week, seems to have dwarfed all the other proceedings and the Exposition itself. The sensation that it has caused in the press has never been equalled."

I very soon began receiving all kinds of propositions from lecture bureaus, and editors of magazines and papers, to take the lecture platform, and to write articles. One lecture bureau offered me fifty thousand dollars, or two hundred dollars a night and expenses, if I would place my services at its disposal for a given period. To all these communications I replied that my life-work was at Tuskegee; and that whenever I spoke it must be in the interests of the Tuskegee school and my race, and that I would enter into no arrangements that seemed to place a mere commercial value upon my services.

Some days after its delivery I sent a copy of my address to the President of the United States, the Hon. Grover Cleveland.[4] I received from him the following autograph reply:

> Gray Gables, Buzzard's Bay, Mass.,
> October 6, 1895

Booker T. Washington, Esq.:

My Dear Sir: I thank you for sending me a copy of your address delivered at the Atlanta Exposition.

I thank you with much enthusiasm for making the address. I have read it with intense interest, and I think the Exposition would be fully justified if it did not do more than furnish the opportunity for its delivery. Your words cannot fail to delight and encourage all who wish well for your race; and if our coloured fellow-citizens do not from your utterances gather new hope and form new determinations to gain every valuable advantage offered them by their citizenship, it will be strange indeed.

> Yours very truly,
> Grover Cleveland

Later I met Mr. Cleveland, for the first time, when, as President, he visited the Atlanta Exposition. At the request of myself and others he consented to spend an hour in the Negro Building, for the purpose of inspecting the Negro exhibit and of giving the coloured people in attendance an opportunity to shake hands with him. As soon as I met Mr. Cleveland I became impressed with his simplicity, greatness, and rugged honesty. I have met him many times since then, both at public functions and at his private residence in Princeton, and the more I see of him the more I admire him. When he visited the Negro Building in Atlanta he seemed to give himself up wholly, for that hour, to the coloured people. He seemed to be as careful to shake hands with some old coloured "auntie" clad partially in rags, and to take as much pleasure in doing so, as if he were greeting some millionaire. Many of the coloured people took advantage of the occasion to get him to write his name in a book or on a slip of paper. He was as careful and patient in doing this as if he were putting his signature to some great state document.

Mr. Cleveland has not only shown his friendship for me in many personal ways, but has always consented to do anything I have asked of him for our school. This he has done, whether it was to make a personal donation or to use his influence in securing the donations of others. Judging from my personal acquaintance with Mr. Cleveland, I do not believe that he is conscious of possessing any colour prejudice. He is too great for that. In my contact with people I find that, as a rule, it is only the little, narrow people who live for themselves, who never read good books, who do not travel, who never open up their souls in a way to permit them to come into contact with other souls — with the great outside world. No man whose vision is bounded by colour can come into contact with what is highest and best in the world. In meeting men, in many places, I have found that the happiest people are those who do the most for others; the most miserable are those who do the least. I have also found that few things, if any, are capable of making

---

4. **Hon. Grover Cleveland:** Stephen Grover Cleveland (1837–1908) served as president of the United States for two nonconsecutive terms: 1886–89 and 1893–97.

one so blind and narrow as race prejudice. I often say to our students, in the course of my talks to them on Sunday evenings in the chapel, that the longer I live and the more experience I have of the world, the more I am convinced that, after all, the one thing that is most worth living for — and dying for, if need be — is the opportunity of making some one else more happy and more useful.

The coloured people and the coloured newspapers at first seemed to be greatly pleased with the character of my Atlanta address, as well as with its reception. But after the first burst of enthusiasm began to die away, and the coloured people began reading the speech in cold type, some of them seemed to feel that they had been hypnotized. They seemed to feel that I had been too liberal in my remarks toward the Southern whites, and that I had not spoken out strongly enough for what they termed the "rights" of the race. For a while there was a reaction, so far as a certain element of my own race was concerned, but later these reactionary ones seemed to have been won over to my way of believing and acting.

While speaking of changes in public sentiment, I recall that about ten years after the school at Tuskegee was established, I had an experience that I shall never forget. Dr. Lyman Abbott, then the pastor of Plymouth Church, and also editor of the *Outlook* (then the *Christian Union*), asked me to write a letter for his paper giving my opinion of the exact condition, mental and moral, of the coloured ministers in the South, as based upon my observations. I wrote the letter, giving the exact facts as I conceived them to be. The picture painted was a rather black one — or, since I am black, shall I say "white"? It could not be otherwise with a race but a few years out of slavery, a race which had not had time or opportunity to produce a competent ministry.

What I said soon reached every Negro minister in the country, I think, and the letters of condemnation which I received from them were not few. I think that for a year after the publication of this article every association and every conference or religious body of any kind, of any race, that met, did not fail before adjourning to pass a resolution condemning me, or calling upon me to retract or modify what I had said. Many of these organizations went so far in their resolutions as to advise parents to cease sending their children to Tuskegee. One association even appointed a "missionary" whose duty it was to warn the people against sending their children to Tuskegee. This missionary had a son in the school, and I noticed that, whatever the "missionary" might have said or done with regard to others, he was careful not to take his son away from the institution. Many of the coloured papers, especially those that were the organs of religious bodies, joined in the general chorus of condemnation or demands for retraction.

During the whole time of the excitement, and through all the criticism, I did not utter a word of explanation or retraction. I knew that I was right, and that time and the sober second thought of the people would vindicate me. It was not long before the bishops and other church leaders began to make a careful investigation of the conditions of the ministry, and they found out that I was right. In fact, the oldest and most influential bishop in one branch of the Methodist Church said that my words were far too mild. Very soon public sentiment began making itself felt, in demanding a purifying of the ministry. While this is not yet complete by any means, I think I may say, without egotism, and I have been told by many of our most influential ministers, that my words had much to do with starting a demand for the placing of a higher type of men in the pulpit. I have had the satisfaction of having many who once condemned me thank me heartily for my frank words.

The change of the attitude of the Negro ministry, so far as regards myself, is so complete that at the present time I have no warmer friends among any class than I have among the clergymen. The improvement in the character and life of the Negro ministers is one of the most gratifying evidences of the progress of the race. My experience with them, as well as other events in my life, convince me that the thing to do, when one feels sure that he has said or done the right thing, and is condemned, is to stand still and keep quiet. If he is right, time will show it.

In the midst of the discussion which was going on concerning my Atlanta speech, I received the letter which I give below, from Dr. Gilman, the President of Johns Hopkins University, who had been made chairman of the judges of award in connection with the Atlanta Exposition: —

> JOHNS HOPKINS UNIVERSITY, BALTIMORE,
> President's Office, September 30, 1895
>
> DEAR MR. WASHINGTON: Would it be agreeable to you to be one of the Judges of Award in the Department of Education at Atlanta? If so, I shall be glad to place your name upon the list. A line by telegraph will be welcomed.
>
> Yours very truly,
> D. C. GILMAN

I think I was even more surprised to receive this invitation than I had been to receive the invitation to speak at the opening of the Exposition. It was to be a part of my duty, as one of the jurors, to pass not only upon the exhibits of the coloured schools, but also upon those of the white schools. I accepted the position, and spent a month in Atlanta in performance of the duties which it entailed. The board of jurors was a large one, consisting in all of sixty members. It was about equally divided between Southern white people and Northern white people. Among them were college presidents, leading scientists and men of letters, and specialists in many subjects. When the group of jurors to which I was assigned met for organization, Mr. Thomas Nelson Page,[5] who was one of the number, moved that I be made secretary of that division, and the motion was unanimously adopted. Nearly half of our division were Southern people. In performing my duties in the inspection of the exhibits of white schools I was in every case treated with respect, and at the close of our labours I parted from my associates with regret.

I am often asked to express myself more freely than I do upon the political condition and the political future of my race. These recollections of my experience in Atlanta give me the opportunity to do so briefly. My own belief is, although I have never before said so in so many words, that the time will come when the Negro in the South will be accorded all the political rights which his ability, character, and material possessions

---

5. **Mr. Thomas Nelson Page:** Southern writer (1853-1922) who helped popularize Romantic myths about slavery and plantation life in collections of stories such as *In Ole Virginia* (1887).

entitle him to. I think, though, that the opportunity to freely exercise such political rights will not come in any large degree through outside or artificial forcing, but will be accorded to the Negro by the Southern white people themselves, and that they will protect him in the exercise of those rights. Just as soon as the South gets over the old feeling that it is being forced by "foreigners," or "aliens," to do something which it does not want to do, I believe that the change in the direction that I have indicated is going to begin. In fact, there are indications that it is already beginning in a slight degree.

Let me illustrate my meaning. Suppose that some months before the opening of the Atlanta Exposition there had been a general demand from the press and public platform outside the South that a Negro be given a place on the opening programme, and that a Negro be placed upon the board of jurors of award. Would any such recognition of the race have taken place? I do not think so. The Atlanta officials went as far as they did because they felt it to be a pleasure, as well as a duty, to reward what they considered merit in the Negro race. Say what we will, there is something in human nature which we cannot blot out, which makes one man, in the end, recognize and reward merit in another, regardless of colour or race.

I believe it is the duty of the Negro — as the greater part of the race is already doing — to deport himself modestly in regard to political claims, depending upon the slow but sure influences that proceed from the possession of property, intelligence, and high character for the full recognition of his political rights. I think that the according of the full exercise of political rights is going to be a matter of natural, slow growth, not an over-night, gourd-vine affair. I do not believe that the Negro should cease voting, for a man cannot learn the exercise of self-government by ceasing to vote any more than a boy can learn to swim by keeping out of the water, but I do believe that in his voting he should more and more be influenced by those of intelligence and character who are his next-door neighbours.

I know coloured men who, through the encouragement, help, and advice of Southern white people, have accumulated thousands of dollars' worth of property, but who, at the same time, would never think of going to those same persons for advice concerning the casting of their ballots. This, it seems to me, is unwise and unreasonable, and should cease. In saying this I do not mean that the Negro should truckle, or not vote from principle, for the instant he ceases to vote from principle he loses the confidence and respect of the Southern white man even.

I do not believe that any state should make a law that permits an ignorant and poverty-stricken white man to vote, and prevents a black man in the same condition from voting. Such a law is not only unjust, but it will react, as all unjust laws do, in time; for the effect of such a law is to encourage the Negro to secure education and property, and at the same time it encourages the white man to remain in ignorance and poverty. I believe that in time, through the operation of intelligence and friendly race relations, all cheating at the ballot box in the South will cease. It will become apparent that the white man who begins by cheating a Negro out of his ballot soon learns to cheat a white man out of his, and that the man who does this ends his career of dishonesty by the theft of property or by some equally serious crime. In my opinion, the time will come when the South will encourage all of its citizens to vote. It will see that it pays better, from every standpoint, to have healthy, vigorous life than to have that political stagnation which always results when one-half of the population has no share and no interest in the Government.

As a rule, I believe in universal, free suffrage, but I believe that in the South we are confronted with peculiar conditions that justify the protection of the ballot in many of the states, for a while at least, either by an educational test, a property test, or by both combined; but whatever tests are required, they should be made to apply with equal and exact justice to both races.

[1901]

W. E. B. Du Bois

[1868-1963]

W. E. B. Du Bois

This photograph of Du Bois was used as the frontispiece of his influential book *The Souls of Black Folk* (1903).

William Edward Burghardt Du Bois was born on February 23, 1868, in Great Barrington, a small town in the Berkshire Mountains of western Massachusetts. The birth certificate incorrectly spelled his name "Duboise," and Du Bois frequently had to explain that his name was pronounced "*Due Boyss*, with the accent on the last syllable." His father, Alfred Du Bois, was born in Haiti, the descendant of free people of color. During the 1850s, a period of social and political turmoil in Haiti, Alfred Du Bois immigrated to the United States. He briefly served in the Union army before moving to Great Barrington, where he married Mary Burghardt, of mixed African and Dutch ancestry. Alfred Du Bois left the family when Du Bois was about two years old, and he was subsequently raised by his mother, who worked as a domestic servant to provide for herself and her son. Du Bois attended the town school in Great Barrington, where he was such an exceptional student that he soon began to write professionally for African American newspapers such as the *New York Age* and the *New York Globe*. Elected valedictorian of his high-school class, Du Bois delivered his graduation speech on the white abolitionist and reformer Wendell Phillips, who had steadily fought against all forms of racial injustice in the United States.

Du Bois's mother died a few months after his graduation in 1884, but local ministers and teachers raised money for a scholarship that enabled him to enroll at Fisk University in Nashville, Tennessee, in 1885. While he was invigorated by his studies and by his fellow African American students at the all-black college, Du Bois was shocked by the racism he experienced in Nashville and during the summers he spent teaching in rural Tennessee. After he graduated from Fisk in 1888, he was awarded a grant from Harvard University, where Du Bois earned a second B.A. in 1890. He then received a grant for European travel and study at the University of Berlin. Returning to the United States in 1895, Du Bois earned the first Ph.D. awarded by Harvard to an African American. Trained primarily as a historian, he turned down a job offer from Booker T. Washington at the Tuskegee Institute. Du Bois instead accepted a position at another institution founded by African Americans, Wilberforce University in Ohio, where he completed his first book, *The Suppression of the African Slave Trade to the United States of America, 1638-1870* (1896). Based on his doctoral dissertation and still considered a foundational study of the slave trade, the book was the first of his many publications designed to recover the history of African Americans. At Wilberforce, Du Bois met and married Nina Gomer, and the two moved to Philadelphia in 1896 when he accepted an appointment from the University of Pennsylvania to research and write a study of the black population of the city, *The Philadelphia Negro* (1899). In it, Du Bois virtually invented the field of urban sociology, and he accepted an offer to assume the leadership of the Atlanta Sociological Laboratory, a research program at the all-black Atlanta University.

> *My earliest memories of written words are those of Du Bois and the Bible.*
> *–Langston Hughes*

In Atlanta, Du Bois began to work closely with other black intellectuals, a group he called the "Talented Tenth." Through his own work as the editor of a sociological series on African Americans, *Atlanta University Studies*, and by holding yearly conferences on topics such as "The Social and Physical Condition of Negroes in Cities," Du Bois began to challenge the conservative views of Booker T. Washington, then the most influential African American leader in the United States. Du Bois offered his most vigorous challenge to Washington's leadership in a chapter in *The Souls of Black Folk* (1903), a collection of essays, stories, and meditations on the history and condition of African Americans. The inspirational book helped Du Bois launch the Niagara Movement, organized in 1905 to fight for the civil rights of African Americans. Du Bois also founded two periodicals, *The Moon* and *Horizon*, in an effort to promote the activities of the Niagara Movement, which paved the way for the founding of an even larger organization, the National Association for the Advancement of Colored People (NAACP), in 1909. Du Bois resigned his position at Atlanta University and moved to New York City, where he became head of publications for the NAACP. In 1910, he founded its official journal, the *Crisis*, which Du Bois firmly declared would "stand for the rights of men, irrespective of color or race, for the highest ideals of American democracy, and for reasonable but earnest and persistent attempts to gain these rights and realize these ideals." Under his editorship, which lasted for almost twenty-five years, the *Crisis* became the most prestigious African American periodical in the United States.

During the final decades of his life, however, Du Bois became increasingly disillusioned with both American society and the activities of the NAACP. Believing that the organization was focusing its attention on middle-class blacks rather than on those living in desperate poverty, Du Bois left the NAACP in 1934 and returned to Atlanta University. During the following decade, he wrote three books on civil rights: *Black Reconstruction in America* (1935), *Dusk of Dawn: An Essay toward an Autobiography of a Race Concept* (1940), and *Colour and Democracy* (1945). After he retired from the university in 1944, Du Bois rejoined the NAACP as the director of special research, serving as the organization's representative at the conference that founded the United Nations. But his radical politics placed him at odds with the more-moderate leadership of the NAACP. In 1948, he became associated with the Council on African Affairs, which considered to be a subversive, Communist-front organization by the U.S. attorney general. Du Bois, who was also deeply involved in the left-wing Progressive Party, was indicted in 1951 as "an agent of a foreign principal," the Soviet Union. Although he was eventually acquitted of the charges, Du Bois felt that he had not received firm support from his former colleagues in the NAACP. Embittered by the experience and by what he viewed as the lack of progress in the struggle for civil rights, Du Bois joined the Communist Party in 1961, stating on his application for membership: "Capitalism cannot reform itself." That year, he renounced his American citizenship and moved to Ghana, where he died on August 27, 1963.

One of the most graceful tributes to the lifelong crusader for civil rights was offered the following day, at the "March on Washington for Jobs and Freedom," where the president of the NAACP, Roy Wilkins, told the huge crowd gathered at the Lincoln Memorial:

> Remember that this has been a long fight. We were reminded of it by the news of the death yesterday in Africa of Dr. W. E. B. Du Bois. Now, regardless of the fact that in recent years Dr. Du Bois chose another path, it is incontrovertible that at the dawn of the twentieth century his was the voice that was calling you to gather here today in this cause. If you want to read something that applies to 1963 go back and get a volume of *The Souls of Black Folk* by Du Bois published in 1903.

bedfordstmartins.com/
americanlit for research
links on Du Bois

Du Bois's *The Souls of Black Folk*.   Revising previously published articles and adding new material, Du Bois put together a collection of what the original subtitle called "Essays and Sketches" and what he later described as "bits of history and biography, some descriptions of scenes and persons, something of controversy and criticism, some statistics and a bit of story-telling." The complex book, which defied and still defies easy description, caused a sensation when it was published in 1903. The publisher had to arrange a third printing within two months, and *The Souls of Black Folk* sold roughly ten thousand copies within five years. Although it was ignored or sharply criticized by most southern newspapers – one declared that the book was "dangerous for the Negro to read" – it was widely and favorably reviewed in the North. The book had a particularly profound effect on African American activists and writers such as the poet James Weldon Johnson, who observed on the thirtieth anniversary of the publication of *The Souls of Black Folk* that its impact was "greater upon and within the Negro race than any other single book published in this country since *Uncle Tom's Cabin*," Harriet Beecher Stowe's blockbuster novel of the 1850s. The two chapters presented here are probably the most famous in *The Souls of Black Folk.* "Of Our Spiritual Strivings" was based on "Strivings of the Negro People," which had appeared in the *Atlantic Monthly* in 1897. In that chapter, Du Bois recounts his first experience of racism as a child in school and meditates on the "double-consciousness" of being "an American, a Negro." The chapter that generated much of the commentary on and controversy about *The Souls of Black Folk* was "Of Mr. Booker T. Washington and Others," a revised and expanded version of a much shorter essay, "The Evolution of Negro Leadership," which had appeared in the *Dial* in 1901. In that chapter, Du Bois challenges what he viewed as Washington's accommodation to legalized segregation and the disenfranchisement of black people in the South. In contrast, Du Bois insisted that black people must "strive for the rights which the world accords to men," accepting nothing less than full social and political equality in the United States. The text of the two chapters is taken from the first edition of *The Souls of Black Folk* (1903).

THE SOULS OF BLACK FOLK

I

Of Our Spiritual Strivings

O water, voice of my heart, crying in the sand,
    All night long crying with a mournful cry,
As I lie and listen, and cannot understand
      The voice of my heart in my side or the voice of the sea,
    O water, crying for rest, is it I, is it I?
    All night long the water is crying to me.

Unresting water, there shall never be rest
    Till the last moon droop and the last tide fail,
And the fire of the end begin to burn in the west;
      And the heart shall be weary and wonder and cry like the sea,
    All life long crying without avail,
    As the water all night long is crying to me.

            –ARTHUR SYMONS[1]

---

1. **Arthur Symons:** Welsh critic and poet (1865-1945); the title of the poem is "The Crying of Water."

Between me and the other world there is ever an unasked question: unasked by some through feelings of delicacy; by others through the difficulty of rightly framing it. All, nevertheless, flutter round it. They approach me in a half-hesitant sort of way, eye me curiously or compassionately, and then, instead of saying directly, How does it feel to be a problem? they say, I know an excellent colored man in my town; or, I fought at Mechanicsville;[3] or, Do not these Southern outrages make your blood boil? At these I smile, or am interested, or reduce the boiling to a simmer, as the occasion may require. To the real question, How does it feel to be a problem? I answer seldom a word.

And yet, being a problem is a strange experience, — peculiar even for one who has never been anything else, save perhaps, in babyhood and in Europe. It is in the early days of rollicking boyhood that the revelation first bursts upon one, all in a day, as it were. I remember well when the shadow swept across me. I was a little thing, away up in the hills of New England, where the dark Housatonic winds between Hoosac and Taghkanic to the sea.[4] In a wee wooden schoolhouse, something put it into the boys' and girls' heads to buy gorgeous visiting-cards — ten cents a package — and exchange. The exchange was merry, till one girl, a tall newcomer, refused my card, — refused it peremptorily, with a glance. Then it dawned upon me with a certain suddenness that I was different from the others; or like, mayhap, in heart and life and longing, but shut out from their world by a vast veil. I had thereafter no desire to tear down that veil, to creep through; I held all beyond it in common contempt, and lived above it in a region of blue sky and great wandering shadows. That sky was bluest when I could beat my mates at examination-time, or beat them at a foot-race, or even beat their stringy heads. Alas, with the years all this fine contempt began to fade; for the worlds I longed for, and all their dazzling opportunities, were theirs, not mine. But they should not keep these prizes, I said; some, all, I would wrest from them. Just how I would do it I could never decide: by reading law, by healing the sick, by telling the wonderful tales that swam in my head, — some way. With other black boys the strife was not so fiercely sunny: their youth shrunk into tasteless sycophancy, or into silent hatred of the pale world about them and mocking distrust of everything white; or wasted itself in a bitter cry, Why did God make me an outcast and a stranger in mine own house? The shades of the prison-

---

2. [musical notation]: As Du Bois notes in his preface, "The Forethought," each chapter of the book is introduced by a bar of music from what he called the "Sorrow Songs," or African American slave songs, "some echo of haunting melody from the only American music which welled up from black souls in the past." The bar of music here is from "Nobody Knows the Trouble I've Seen."

3. Mechanicsville: Virginia site of a Civil War battle in which an attack by Confederate troops was severely repulsed by Union forces on June 26, 1862.

4. Housatonic . . . to the sea: The Housatonic River flows from western Massachusetts through the Hoosac and Taconic mountain ranges before emptying into the Long Island Sound at Milford Point, Connecticut.

house closed round about us all:[5] walls strait and stubborn to the whitest, but relentlessly narrow, tall, and unscalable to sons of night who must plod darkly on in resignation, or beat unavailing palms against the stone, or steadily, half hopelessly, watch the streak of blue above.

After the Egyptian and Indian, the Greek and Roman, the Teuton and Mongolian, the Negro is a sort of seventh son, born with a veil, and gifted with second-sight in this American world, — a world which yields him no true self-consciousness, but only lets him see himself through the revelation of the other world. It is a peculiar sensation, this double-consciousness, this sense of always looking at one's self through the eyes of others, of measuring one's soul by the tape of a world that looks on in amused contempt and pity. One ever feels his two-ness, — an American, a Negro; two souls, two thoughts, two unreconciled strivings; two warring ideals in one dark body, whose dogged strength alone keeps it from being torn asunder.

The history of the American Negro is the history of this strife, — this longing to attain self-conscious manhood, to merge his double self into a better and truer self. In this merging he wishes neither of the older selves to be lost. He would not Africanize America, for America has too much to teach the world and Africa. He would not bleach his Negro soul in a flood of white Americanism, for he knows that Negro blood has a message for the world. He simply wishes to make it possible for a man to be both a Negro and an American, without being cursed and spit upon by his fellows, without having the doors of Opportunity closed roughly in his face.

This, then, is the end of his striving: to be a co-worker in the kingdom of culture, to escape both death and isolation, to husband and use his best powers and his latent genius. These powers of body and mind have in the past been strangely wasted, dispersed, or forgotten. The shadow of a mighty Negro past flits through the tale of Ethiopia the Shadowy and of Egypt the Sphinx. Throughout history, the powers of single black men flash here and there like falling stars, and die sometimes before the world has rightly gauged their brightness. Here in America, in a few days since Emancipation, the black man's turning hither and thither in hesitant and doubtful striving has often made his very strength to lose effectiveness, to seem like absence of power, like weakness. And yet it is not weakness, — it is the contradiction of double aims. The double-aimed struggle of the black artisan — on the one hand to escape white contempt for a nation of mere hewers of wood and drawers of water, and on the other hand to plough and nail and dig for a poverty-stricken horde — could only result in making him a poor craftsman, for he had but half a heart in either cause. By the poverty and ignorance of his people, the Negro minister or doctor was tempted toward quackery and demagogy; and by the criticism of the other world, toward ideals that made him

---

5. **The shades . . . about us all:** Du Bois is loosely quoting from "Ode: Imitations of Immortality from Recollections of Early Childhood," by the English poet William Wordsworth (1770–1850): "But trailing clouds of glory do we come / From God, who is our home: / Heaven lies about us in our infancy! / Shades of the prison-house begin to close / Upon the growing Boy."

ashamed of his lowly tasks. The would-be black *savant*[6] was confronted by the paradox that the knowledge his people needed was a twice-told tale to his white neighbors, while the knowledge which would teach the white world was Greek to his own flesh and blood. The innate love of harmony and beauty that set the ruder souls of his people a-dancing and a-singing raised but confusion and doubt in the soul of the black artist; for the beauty revealed to him was the soul-beauty of a race which his larger audience despised, and he could not articulate the message of another people. This waste of double aims, this seeking to satisfy two unreconciled ideals, has wrought sad havoc with the courage and faith and deeds of ten thousand thousand people, — has sent them often wooing false gods and invoking false means of salvation, and at times has even seemed about to make them ashamed of themselves.

Away back in the days of bondage they thought to see in one divine event the end of all doubt and disappointment; few men ever worshipped Freedom with half such unquestioning faith as did the American Negro for two centuries. To him, so far as he thought and dreamed, slavery was indeed the sum of all villainies, the cause of all sorrow, the root of all prejudice; Emancipation was the key to a promised land of sweeter beauty than ever stretched before the eyes of wearied Israelites. In song and exhortation swelled one refrain — Liberty; in his tears and curses the God he implored had Freedom in his right hand. At last it came, — suddenly, fearfully, like a dream. With one wild carnival of blood and passion came the message in his own plaintive cadences: —

> "Shout, O children!
> Shout, you 're free!
> For God has bought your liberty!"[7]

Years have passed away since then, — ten, twenty, forty; forty years of national life, forty years of renewal and development, and yet the swarthy spectre sits in its accustomed seat at the Nation's feast. In vain do we cry to this our vastest social problem: —

> "Take any shape but that, and my firm nerves
> Shall never tremble!"[8]

The Nation has not yet found peace from its sins; the freedman has not yet found in freedom his promised land. Whatever of good may have come in these years of change, the shadow of a deep disappointment rests upon the Negro people, — a disappointment all the more bitter because the unattained ideal was unbounded save by the simple ignorance of a lowly people.

The first decade was merely a prolongation of the vain search for freedom, the boon that seemed ever barely to elude their grasp, — like a tantalizing will-o'-the-wisp, maddening and misleading the headless host. The holocaust of war, the terrors of the Ku-Klux Klan, the lies of carpet-baggers, the disorganization of industry, and the con-

---

6. *savant:* A learned person.
7. **Shout . . . liberty!:** From an early nineteenth-century Negro spiritual.
8. **Take . . . tremble!:** From Shakespeare's *Macbeth,* 3.4.120–21.

tradictory advice of friends and foes, left the bewildered serf with no new watchword beyond the old cry for freedom. As the time flew, however, he began to grasp a new idea. The ideal of liberty demanded for its attainment powerful means, and these the Fifteenth Amendment[9] gave him. The ballot, which before he had looked upon as a visible sign of freedom, he now regarded as the chief means of gaining and perfecting the liberty with which war had partially endowed him. And why not? Had not votes made war and emancipated millions? Had not votes enfranchised the freedmen? Was anything impossible to a power that had done all this? A million black men started with renewed zeal to vote themselves into the kingdom. So the decade flew away, the revolution of 1876[10] came, and left the half-free serf weary, wondering, but still inspired. Slowly but steadily, in the following years, a new vision began gradually to replace the dream of political power, — a powerful movement, the rise of another ideal to guide the unguided, another pillar of fire by night after a clouded day. It was the ideal of "book-learning"; the curiosity, born of compulsory ignorance, to know and test the power of the cabalistic letters of the white man, the longing to know. Here at last seemed to have been discovered the mountain path to Canaan;[11] longer than the highway of Emancipation and law, steep and rugged, but straight, leading to heights high enough to overlook life.

Up the new path the advance guard toiled, slowly, heavily, doggedly; only those who have watched and guided the faltering feet, the misty minds, the dull understandings, of the dark pupils of these schools know how faithfully, how piteously, this people strove to learn. It was weary work. The cold statistician wrote down the inches of progress here and there, noted also where here and there a foot had slipped or some one had fallen. To the tired climbers, the horizon was ever dark, the mists were often cold, the Canaan was always dim and far away. If, however, the vistas disclosed as yet no goal, no resting-place, little but flattery and criticism, the journey at least gave leisure for reflection and self-examination; it changed the child of Emancipation to the youth with dawning self-consciousness, self-realization, self-respect. In those sombre forests of his striving his own soul rose before him, and he saw himself, — darkly as through a veil; and yet he saw in himself some faint revelation of his power, of his mission. He began to have a dim feeling that, to attain his place in the world, he must be himself, and not another. For the first time he sought to analyze the burden he bore upon his back, that dead-weight of social degradation partially masked behind a half-named Negro problem. He felt his poverty; without a cent, without a home, without land, tools, or savings, he had entered into competition with rich, landed, skilled neighbors. To be a poor man is hard, but to be

---

9. **Fifteenth Amendment:** "The right of citizens of the United States to vote shall not be denied or abridged by the United States or by any state on account of race, color, or previous condition of servitude." Ratified on February 3, 1870, the amendment thus enfranchised men who had formerly been slaves.

10. **revolution of 1876:** Despite the fact that both the popular and Electoral College votes in the presidential election of 1876 went to Samuel J. Tilden, a Democrat, after months of wrangling and challenges from southern states the Electoral College awarded the election to Rutherford B. Hayes, a Republican. As part of the so-called Compromise of 1877, federal troops were withdrawn from the southern states, effectively ending Reconstruction and dealing a blow to new black voters and civil rights in the South.

11. **Canaan:** The promised land of the ancient Israelites.

a poor race in a land of dollars is the very bottom of hardships. He felt the weight of his ignorance, – not simply of letters, but of life, of business, of the humanities; the accumulated sloth and shirking and awkwardness of decades and centuries shackled his hands and feet. Nor was his burden all poverty and ignorance. The red stain of bastardy, which two centuries of systematic legal defilement of Negro women had stamped upon his race, meant not only the loss of ancient African chastity, but also the hereditary weight of a mass of corruption from white adulterers, threatening almost the obliteration of the Negro home.

A people thus handicapped ought not to be asked to race with the world, but rather allowed to give all its time and thought to its own social problems. But alas! while sociologists gleefully count his bastards and his prostitutes, the very soul of the toiling, sweating black man is darkened by the shadow of a vast despair. Men call the shadow prejudice, and learnedly explain it as the natural defence of culture against barbarism, learning against ignorance, purity against crime, the "higher" against the "lower" races. To which the Negro cries Amen! and swears that to so much of this strange prejudice as is founded on just homage to civilization, culture, righteousness, and progress, he humbly bows and meekly does obeisance. But before that nameless prejudice that leaps beyond all this he stands helpless, dismayed, and well-nigh speechless; before that personal disrespect and mockery, the ridicule and systematic humiliation, the distortion of fact and wanton license of fancy, the cynical ignoring of the better and the boisterous welcoming of the worse, the all-pervading desire to inculcate disdain for everything black, from Toussaint[12] to the devil, – before this there rises a sickening despair that would disarm and discourage any nation save that black host to whom "discouragement" is an unwritten word.

But the facing of so vast a prejudice could not but bring the inevitable self-questioning, self-disparagement, and lowering of ideals which ever accompany repression and breed in an atmosphere of contempt and hate. Whisperings and portents came borne upon the four winds: Lo! we are diseased and dying, cried the dark hosts; we cannot write, our voting is vain; what need of education, since we must always cook and serve? And the Nation echoed and enforced this self-criticism, saying: Be content to be servants, and nothing more; what need of higher culture for half-men? Away with the black man's ballot, by force or fraud, – and behold the suicide of a race! Nevertheless, out of the evil came something of good, – the more careful adjustment of education to real life, the clearer perception of the Negroes' social responsibilities, and the sobering realization of the meaning of progress.

So dawned the time of *Sturm und Drang:*[13] storm and stress to-day rocks our little boat on the mad waters of the world-sea; there is within and without the sound of conflict, the burning of body and rending of soul, inspiration strives with doubt, and faith with vain questionings. The bright ideals of the past, – physical freedom, political power, the training of brains and the training of hands, – all these in turn have waxed

---

12. **Toussaint:** Toussaint Louverture (1743-1803), former slave who led the successful Haitian revolution against the French in 1791.
13. *Sturm und Drang:* Storm and Stress (German).

and waned, until even the last grows dim and overcast. Are they all wrong, – all false? No, not that, but each alone was over-simple and incomplete, – the dreams of a credulous race-childhood, or the fond imaginings of the other world which does not know and does not want to know our power. To be really true, all these ideals must be melted and welded into one. The training of the schools we need to-day more than ever, – the training of deft hands, quick eyes and ears, and above all the broader, deeper, higher culture of gifted minds and pure hearts. The power of the ballot we need in sheer self-defence, – else what shall save us from a second slavery? Freedom, too, the long-sought, we still seek, – the freedom of life and limb, the freedom to work and think, the freedom to love and aspire. Work, culture, liberty, – all these we need, not singly but together, not successively but together, each growing and aiding each, and all striving toward that vaster ideal that swims before the Negro people, the ideal of human brotherhood, gained through the unifying ideal of Race; the ideal of fostering and developing the traits and talents of the Negro, not in opposition to or contempt for other races, but rather in large conformity to the greater ideals of the American Republic, in order that some day on American soil two world-races may give each to each those characteristics both so sadly lack. We the darker ones come even now not altogether empty-handed: there are to-day no truer exponents of the pure human spirit of the Declaration of Independence than the American Negroes; there is no true American music but the wild sweet melodies of the Negro slave; the American fairy tales and folk-lore are Indian and African; and, all in all, we black men seem the sole oasis of simple faith and reverence in a dusty desert of dollars and smartness. Will America be poorer if she replace her brutal dyspeptic blundering with light-hearted but determined Negro humility? or her coarse and cruel wit with loving jovial good-humor? or her vulgar music with the soul of the Sorrow Songs?

Merely a concrete test of the underlying principles of the great republic is the Negro Problem, and the spiritual striving of the freedmen's sons is the travail of souls whose burden is almost beyond the measure of their strength, but who bear it in the name of an historic race, in the name of this the land of their fathers' fathers, and in the name of human opportunity.

And now what I have briefly sketched in large outline let me on coming pages tell again in many ways, with loving emphasis and deeper detail, that men may listen to the striving in the souls of black folk.

III
Of Mr. Booker T. Washington and Others

From birth till death enslaved; in word, in deed, unmanned!

. . . .

Hereditary bondsmen! Know ye not
Who would be free themselves must strike the blow?
–BYRON[14]

---

14. **Byron:** The lines are from *Childe Harold's Pilgrimage*, 2.74.710 and 2.76.720-21, by the English poet George Gordon, Lord Byron (1788-1824).

Easily the most striking thing in the history of the American Negro since 1876 is the ascendancy of Mr. Booker T. Washington. It began at the time when war memories and ideals were rapidly passing; a day of astonishing commercial development was dawning; a sense of doubt and hesitation overtook the freedmen's sons, — then it was that his leading began. Mr. Washington came, with a simple definite programme, at the psychological moment when the nation was a little ashamed of having bestowed so much sentiment on Negroes, and was concentrating its energies on Dollars. His programme of industrial education, conciliation of the South, and submission and silence as to civil and political rights, was not wholly original; the Free Negroes from 1830 up to war-time had striven to build industrial schools, and the American Missionary Association[16] had from the first taught various trades; and Price[17] and others had sought a way of honorable alliance with the best of the Southerners. But Mr. Washington first indissolubly linked these things; he put enthusiasm, unlimited energy, and perfect faith into this programme, and changed it from a by-path into a veritable Way of Life. And the tale of the methods by which he did this is a fascinating study of human life.

It startled the nation to hear a Negro advocating such a programme after many decades of bitter complaint; it startled and won the applause of the South, it interested and won the admiration of the North; and after a confused murmur of protest, it silenced if it did not convert the Negroes themselves.

To gain the sympathy and coöperation of the various elements comprising the white South was Mr. Washington's first task; and this, at the time Tuskegee was founded, seemed, for a black man, well-nigh impossible. And yet ten years later it was done in the word spoken at Atlanta: "In all things purely social we can be as separate as the five fingers, and yet one as the hand in all things essential to mutual progress." This "Atlanta Compromise"[18]

---

15. **[musical notation]:** The bar of music is from the slave song "There's a Great Camp Meeting in the Promised Land," also known as "Walk Together Children" (see also note 2).

16. **American Missionary Association:** Founded in 1846 as a missionary and abolitionist society, the organization was first formed to educate and train African Americans. Following emancipation, the AMA founded a number of schools, including the Hampton Institute, attended by Booker T. Washington, as well as Fisk and Dillard universities.

17. **Price:** Joseph C. Price (1854–1893), scholar, minister, and influential African American leader who helped establish the Zion Wesley Institute, which, with the help of his fundraising, became Livingstone College, where he served as its first president.

18. **"Atlanta Compromise":** Du Bois's characterization of Washington's most famous speech, "The Atlanta Exposition Address" (see pp. 442–50). In it, Washington essentially withdrew demands for the full social and political equality of blacks in order to gain support for their technical training and access to jobs in the South.

is by all odds the most notable thing in Mr. Washington's career. The South interpreted it in different ways: the radicals received it as a complete surrender of the demand for civil and political equality; the conservatives, as a generously conceived working basis for mutual understanding. So both approved it, and to-day its author is certainly the most distinguished Southerner since Jefferson Davis,[19] and the one with the largest personal following.

Next to this achievement comes Mr. Washington's work in gaining place and consideration in the North. Others less shrewd and tactful had formerly essayed to sit on these two stools and had fallen between them; but as Mr. Washington knew the heart of the South from birth and training, so by singular insight he intuitively grasped the spirit of the age which was dominating the North. And so thoroughly did he learn the speech and thought of triumphant commercialism, and the ideals of material prosperity, that the picture of a lone black boy poring over a French grammar amid the weeds and dirt of a neglected home soon seemed to him the acme of absurdities.[20] One wonders what Socrates and St. Francis of Assisi would say to this.[21]

And yet this very singleness of vision and thorough oneness with his age is a mark of the successful man. It is as though Nature must needs make men narrow in order to give them force. So Mr. Washington's cult has gained unquestioning followers, his work has wonderfully prospered, his friends are legion, and his enemies are confounded. To-day he stands as the one recognized spokesman of his ten million fellows, and one of the most notable figures in a nation of seventy millions. One hesitates, therefore, to criticise a life which, beginning with so little, has done so much. And yet the time is come when one may speak in all sincerity and utter courtesy of the mistakes and shortcomings of Mr. Washington's career, as well as of his triumphs, without being thought captious or envious, and without forgetting that it is easier to do ill than well in the world.

The criticism that has hitherto met Mr. Washington has not always been of this broad character. In the South especially has he had to walk warily to avoid the harshest judgments, — and naturally so, for he is dealing with the one subject of deepest sensitiveness to that section. Twice — once when at the Chicago celebration of the Spanish-American War he alluded to the color-prejudice that is "eating away the vitals of the South,"[22] and

---

19. **Jefferson Davis:** Davis (1808–1889) was the president of the Confederate States of America during the Civil War.

20. **the acme of absurdities:** In a his popular autobiography, *Up from Slavery* (1901), Washington illustrates what he viewed as the absurdity of educational practices that did not yield practical results and material gains by describing "a young man, who had attended some high school, sitting down in a one-room cabin, with grease on his clothing, filth all around him, and weeds in the garden, engaged in studying a French grammar."

21. **what Socrates . . . say to this:** Socrates, an ancient Greek philosopher (469–399 BCE), and St. Francis of Assisi, the Italian monk (c. 1181–1226) who founded the Franciscan order. Each would have rejected what Du Bois characterizes as Washington's "ideals of material prosperity," the former in his quest for knowledge and the latter in his quest for spirituality.

22. **"eating away . . . the South":** In a speech to a crowd of 16,000 people at a Spanish-American War Peace Jubilee in Chicago in 1898, Washington asserted that the United States had won all its battles but one, "the effort to conquer ourselves in the blotting out of racial prejudice," adding: "Until we thus conquer ourselves, I make no empty statement when I say that we shall have, especially in the Southern part of our country, a cancer gnawing at the heart of the Republic, that shall one day prove as dangerous as an attack from an army without or within."

once when he dined with President Roosevelt[23] – has the resulting Southern criticism been violent enough to threaten seriously his popularity. In the North the feeling has several times forced itself into words, that Mr. Washington's counsels of submission overlooked certain elements of true manhood, and that his educational programme was unnecessarily narrow. Usually, however, such criticism has not found open expression, although, too, the spiritual sons of the Abolitionists have not been prepared to acknowledge that the schools founded before Tuskegee, by men of broad ideals and self-sacrificing spirit, were wholly failures or worthy of ridicule. While, then, criticism has not failed to follow Mr. Washington, yet the prevailing public opinion of the land has been but too willing to deliver the solution of a wearisome problem into his hands, and say, "If that is all you and your race ask, take it."

Among his own people, however, Mr. Washington has encountered the strongest and most lasting opposition, amounting at times to bitterness, and even to-day continuing strong and insistent even though largely silenced in outward expression by the public opinion of the nation. Some of this opposition is, of course, mere envy; the disappointment of displaced demagogues and the spite of narrow minds. But aside from this, there is among educated and thoughtful colored men in all parts of the land a feeling of deep regret, sorrow, and apprehension at the wide currency and ascendancy which some of Mr. Washington's theories have gained. These same men admire his sincerity of purpose, and are willing to forgive much to honest endeavor which is doing something worth the doing. They coöperate with Mr. Washington as far as they conscientiously can; and, indeed, it is no ordinary tribute to this man's tact and power that, steering as he must between so many diverse interests and opinions, he so largely retains the respect of all.

But the hushing of the criticism of honest opponents is a dangerous thing. It leads some of the best of the critics to unfortunate silence and paralysis of effort, and others to burst into speech so passionately and intemperately as to lose listeners. Honest and earnest criticism from those whose interests are most nearly touched, – criticism of writers by readers, of government by those governed, of leaders by those led, – this is the soul of democracy and the safeguard of modern society. If the best of the American Negroes receive by outer pressure a leader whom they had not recognized before, manifestly there is here a certain palpable gain. Yet there is also irreparable loss, – a loss of that peculiarly valuable education which a group receives when by search and criticism it finds and commissions its own leaders. The way in which this is done is at once the most elementary and the nicest problem of social growth. History is but the record of such group-leadership; and yet how infinitely changeful is its type and character! And of all types and kinds, what can be more instructive than the leadership of a group within a group? – that curious double movement where real progress may be negative and

---

23. **when he dined with President Roosevelt:** Many white Southerners were outraged when President Theodore Roosevelt invited Washington to visit him in the White House in 1901. In an editorial, one newspaper editor wrote: "With our long-matured views on the subject of social intercourse between blacks and whites, the least we can say now is that we deplore the President's taste, and we distrust his wisdom."

actual advance be relative retrogression. All this is the social student's inspiration and despair.

Now in the past the American Negro has had instructive experience in the choosing of group leaders, founding thus a peculiar dynasty which in the light of present conditions is worth while studying. When sticks and stones and beasts form the sole environment of a people, their attitude is largely one of determined opposition to and conquest of natural forces. But when to earth and brute is added an environment of men and ideas, then the attitude of the imprisoned group may take three main forms, — a feeling of revolt and revenge; an attempt to adjust all thought and action to the will of the greater group; or, finally, a determined effort at self-realization and self-development despite environing opinion. The influence of all of these attitudes at various times can be traced in the history of the American Negro, and in the evolution of his successive leaders.

Before 1750, while the fire of African freedom still burned in the veins of the slaves, there was in all leadership or attempted leadership but the one motive of revolt and revenge, — typified in the terrible Maroons, the Danish blacks, and Cato of Stono,[24] and veiling all the Americas in fear of insurrection. The liberalizing tendencies of the latter half of the eighteenth century brought, along with kindlier relations between black and white, thoughts of ultimate adjustment and assimilation. Such aspiration was especially voiced in the earnest songs of Phyllis, in the martyrdom of Attucks, the fighting of Salem and Poor, the intellectual accomplishments of Banneker and Derham, and the political demands of the Cuffes.[25]

Stern financial and social stress after the war cooled much of the previous humanitarian ardor. The disappointment and impatience of the Negroes at the persistence of slavery and serfdom voiced itself in two movements. The slaves in the South, aroused undoubtedly by vague rumors of the Haytian revolt, made three fierce attempts at insurrection, — in 1800 under Gabriel in Virginia, in 1822 under Vesey in Carolina, and in

---

24. **the terrible Maroons, the Danish blacks, and Cato of Stono:** Du Bois refers to a series of famous slave rebellions. Maroons were escaped slaves and their descendants in Jamaica, where they fought off British troops from their settlements high in the mountains and gained their freedom through a bloody campaign known as the first Maroon War, which ended with a peace treaty in 1739. Thousands of Africans were also taken as slaves to the Danish West Indies (now the Virgin Islands), established as a colony for sugar plantations in 1672. Many of the slaves revolted in 1733, and another revolt finally ended slavery in the colony in 1848. Cato, a slave near Stono, South Carolina, organized nearly eighty slaves in a rebellion against their white masters in 1739. Called "Cato's Conspiracy," the incident led to fears of slave rebellions throughout the British colonies in North America.

25. **Such aspiration . . . political demands of the Cuffes:** Du Bois refers to a series of celebrated African Americans. Phillis Wheatley (1753-1784), who was brought to Boston as a slave, was the author of the first book published by an African American, *Poems on Various Subjects, Religious and Moral* (1773). Crispus Attucks (1723-1770), an escaped slave who was shot and killed by British troops in the Boston Massacre of 1770, was considered to be the first casualty of the American Revolution. Peter Salem (1750-1816) and Salem Poor (b. 1740s-?) were among some three dozen African Americans who fought with the colonists against the British in the battle of Bunker Hill in 1775. Benjamin Banneker (1731-1806) was an African American mathematician and astronomer; and James Derham (1762-?) was the first African American physician. Paul Cuffe (1759-1817) was an African American merchant and sea captain who fought for the rights of free blacks in Massachusetts and organized an effort to resettle them in colonies in Africa.

1831 again in Virginia under the terrible Nat Turner.[26] In the Free States, on the other hand, a new and curious attempt at self-development was made. In Philadelphia and New York color-prescription led to a withdrawal of Negro communicants from white churches and the formation of a peculiar socio-religious institution among the Negroes known as the African Church, — an organization still living and controlling in its various branches over a million of men.

Walker's wild appeal[27] against the trend of the times showed how the world was changing after the coming of the cotton-gin. By 1830 slavery seemed hopelessly fastened on the South, and the slaves thoroughly cowed into submission. The free Negroes of the North, inspired by the mulatto immigrants from the West Indies, began to change the basis of their demands; they recognized the slavery of slaves, but insisted that they themselves were freemen, and sought assimilation and amalgamation with the nation on the same terms with other men. Thus, Forten and Purvis of Philadelphia, Shad of Wilmington, Du Bois of New Haven, Barbadoes of Boston, and others,[28] strove singly and together as men, they said, not slaves; as "people of color," not as "Negroes." The trend of the times, however, refused them recognition save in individual and exceptional cases, considered them as one with all the despised blacks, and they soon found themselves striving to keep even the rights they formerly had of voting and working and moving as freemen. Schemes of migration and colonization arose among them; but these they refused to entertain, and they eventually turned to the Abolition movement as a final refuge.[29]

Here, led by Remond, Nell, Wells-Brown, and Douglass,[30] a new period of self-assertion and self-development dawned. To be sure, ultimate freedom and assimilation was the

---

26. **The slaves in the South** . . . **Nat Turner:** The successful revolution in Haiti, beginning with a slave uprising in 1791, influenced three widely publicized slave revolts in the United States. The first was led by Gabriel Prosser (c. 1775–1800), who was executed for his role in an unsuccessful revolt in Richmond, Virginia, on October 7, 1800. Denmark Vesey (1767–1822), a former slave who planned a rebellion in Charleston, South Carolina, was charged with plotting to overthrow slavery and executed on June 23, 1822. Nat Turner (1800–1831), who led a bloody rebellion in Southampton County, Virginia, was captured and executed on November 11, 1831.

27. **Walker's wild appeal:** David Walker (1796–1830), a free person of color in Boston, published a militant antislavery tract, *Appeal in Four Articles; Together with a Preamble, To the Coloured Citizens of the World, but in Particular, and Very Expressly, to Those of the United States of America*, in 1829.

28. **Forten and Purvis** . . . **and others:** African American leaders of efforts to secure the rights of free people of color in the North: James Forten (1766–1842), Robert Purvis (1810–1898), Abraham Shadd (1801–1882), James G. Barbadoes (1796–1841), and Du Bois's paternal grandfather, Alexander Du Bois (1803–1888), who emigrated from Haiti to the United States. Forten, Purvis, Shadd, and Barbadoes were present in 1830 at the first National Negro Convention, out of which emerged a number of other organizations with similar goals, including the "American Society of Free People of Colour for improving their condition in the United States."

29. **they eventually turned** . . . **as a final refuge:** In fact, Forten, Purvis, Shadd, and Barbadoes were active abolitionists who became involved in the American Anti-Slavery Society as early as the 1830s.

30. **led by Remond** . . . **and Douglass:** Four influential African American activists and writers: Charles Lenox Remond (1810–1893), a free black who became an important abolitionist lecturer and later a recruiter of African American soldiers during the Civil War; William Cooper Nell (1816–1874), a historian and author of *Colored Patriots of the American Revolution, With Sketches of Several Distinguished Colored Persons: To Which Is Added a Brief Survey of the Condition and Prospects of Colored Americans* (1855); William Wells Brown (1814–1884), author of numerous works, including the *Narrative of William W. Brown, a*

ideal before the leaders, but the assertion of the manhood rights of the Negro by himself was the main reliance, and John Brown's raid was the extreme of its logic. After the war and emancipation, the great form of Frederick Douglass, the greatest of American Negro leaders, still led the host. Self-assertion, especially in political lines, was the main programme, and behind Douglass came Elliot, Bruce, and Langston, and the Reconstruction politicians, and, less conspicuous but of greater social significance Alexander Crummell and Bishop Daniel Payne.[31]

Then came the Revolution of 1876, the suppression of the Negro votes, the changing and shifting of ideals, and the seeking of new lights in the great night. Douglass, in his old age, still bravely stood for the ideals of his early manhood, — ultimate assimilation *through* self-assertion, and on no other terms. For a time Price arose as a new leader, destined, it seemed, not to give up, but to re-state the old ideals in a form less repugnant to the white South. But he passed away in his prime. Then came the new leader. Nearly all the former ones had become leaders by the silent suffrage of their fellows, had sought to lead their own people alone, and were usually, save Douglass, little known outside their race. But Booker T. Washington arose as essentially the leader not of one race but of two, — a compromiser between the South, the North, and the Negro. Naturally the Negroes resented, at first bitterly, signs of compromise which surrendered their civil and political rights, even though this was to be exchanged for larger chances of economic development. The rich and dominating North, however, was not only weary of the race problem, but was investing largely in Southern enterprises, and welcomed any method of peaceful coöperation. Thus, by national opinion, the Negroes began to recognize Mr. Washington's leadership; and the voice of criticism was hushed.

Mr. Washington represents in Negro thought the old attitude of adjustment and submission; but adjustment at such a peculiar time as to make his programme unique. This is an age of unusual economic development, and Mr. Washington's programme naturally takes an economic cast, becoming a gospel of Work and Money to such an extent as apparently almost completely to overshadow the higher aims of life. Moreover, this is an age when the more advanced races are coming in closer contact with the less developed races, and the race-feeling is therefore intensified; and Mr. Washington's programme practically accepts the alleged inferiority of the Negro races. Again, in our own land, the reaction from the sentiment of war time has given impetus to race-prejudice against Negroes, and Mr. Washington withdraws many of the high demands of Negroes as men

---

Fugitive Slave (1847) and the first novel published by an African American, *Clotel; or, The President's Daughter* (1853); and Frederick Douglass, the celebrated abolitionist, lecturer, and author of *Narrative of the Life of Frederick Douglass* (1845), *My Bondage and My Freedom* (1855), and several editions of *The Life and Times of Frederick Douglass*.

31. Elliot . . . Payne: African American political and social leaders during the period following the Civil War: Robert Brown Eliot (1841–1884), a U.S. congressman from South Carolina; Blanche K. Bruce (1841–1898), a Republican from Mississippi and the first African American elected to the Senate; John Mercer Langston (1829–1897), Virginia's first African American congressman; Alexander Crummell (1819–1898), an Anglican minister educated at Cambridge University in England and a founder of the American Negro Academy; and Daniel Payne (1811–1893), the first African American college president (Wilberforce College) and a bishop of the African Methodist Episcopal Church.

and American citizens. In other periods of intensified prejudice all the Negro's tendency to self-assertion has been called forth; at this period a policy of submission is advocated. In the history of nearly all other races and peoples the doctrine preached at such crises has been that manly self-respect is worth more than lands and houses, and that a people who voluntarily surrender such respect, or cease striving for it, are not worth civilizing.

In answer to this, it has been claimed that the Negro can survive only through submission. Mr. Washington distinctly asks that black people give up, at least for the present, three things, —

First, political power,

Second, insistence on civil rights,

Third, higher education of Negro youth, —

and concentrate all their energies on industrial education, the accumulation of wealth, and the conciliation of the South. This policy has been courageously and insistently advocated for over fifteen years, and has been triumphant for perhaps ten years. As a result of this tender of the palm-branch, what has been the return? In these years there have occurred:

1. The disfranchisement of the Negro.

2. The legal creation of a distinct status of civil inferiority for the Negro.

3. The steady withdrawal of aid from institutions for the higher training of the Negro.

These movements are not, to be sure, direct results of Mr. Washington's teachings; but his propaganda has, without a shadow of doubt, helped their speedier accomplishment. The question then comes: Is it possible, and probable, that nine millions of men can make effective progress in economic lines if they are deprived of political rights, made a servile caste, and allowed only the most meagre chance for developing their exceptional men? If history and reason give any distinct answer to these questions, it is an emphatic *No.* And Mr. Washington thus faces the triple paradox of his career:

1. He is striving nobly to make Negro artisans business men and property-owners; but it is utterly impossible, under modern competitive methods, for workingmen and property-owners to defend their rights and exist without the right of suffrage.

2. He insists on thrift and self-respect, but at the same time counsels a silent submission to civic inferiority such as is bound to sap the manhood of any race in the long run.

3. He advocates common-school and industrial training, and depreciates institutions of higher learning; but neither the Negro common-schools, nor Tuskegee itself, could remain open a day were it not for teachers trained in Negro colleges, or trained by their graduates.

This triple paradox in Mr. Washington's position is the object of criticism by two classes of colored Americans. One class is spiritually descended from Toussaint the Savior, through Gabriel, Vesey, and Turner, and they represent the attitude of revolt and revenge; they hate the white South blindly and distrust the white race generally, and so far as they agree on definite action, think that the Negro's only hope lies in emigration beyond the borders of the United States. And yet, by the irony of fate, nothing has more effectually made this programme seem hopeless than the recent course of the United States toward weaker and darker peoples in the West Indies, Hawaii, and the Philippines, — for where in the world may we go and be safe from lying and brute force?[32]

The other class of Negroes who cannot agree with Mr. Washington has hitherto said little aloud. They deprecate the sight of scattered counsels, of internal disagreement; and especially the dislike making their just criticism of a useful and earnest man an excuse for a general discharge of venom from small-minded opponents. Nevertheless, the questions involved are so fundamental and serious that it is difficult to see how men like the Grimkes, Kelly Miller, J. W. E. Bowen,[33] and other representatives of this group, can much longer be silent. Such men feel in conscience bound to ask of this nation three things:

1. The right to vote.
2. Civic equality.
3. The education of youth according to ability.

They acknowledge Mr. Washington's invaluable service in counselling patience and courtesy in such demands; they do not ask that ignorant black men vote when ignorant whites are debarred, or that any reasonable restrictions in the suffrage should not be applied; they know that the low social level of the mass of the race is responsible for much discrimination against it, but they also know, and the nation knows, that relentless color-prejudice is more often a cause than a result of the Negro's degradation; they seek the abatement of this relic of barbarism, and not its systematic encouragement and pampering by all agencies of social power from the Associated Press to the Church of Christ. They advocate, with Mr. Washington, a broad system of Negro common schools supplemented by thorough industrial training; but they are surprised that a man of Mr. Washington's insight cannot see that no such educational system ever has rested or can rest on any other basis than that of the well-equipped college and university, and they insist that there is a demand for a few such institutions throughout the South to train the best of the Negro youth as teachers, professional men, and leaders.

This group of men honor Mr. Washington for his attitude of conciliation toward the white South; they accept the "Atlanta Compromise" in its broadest interpretation; they recognize, with him, many signs of promise, many men of high purpose and fair judgment, in this section; they know that no easy task has been laid upon a region already tottering under heavy burdens. But, nevertheless, they insist that the way to truth and right lies in straightforward honesty, not in indiscriminate flattery; in praising those of

---

32. **And yet, . . . brute force?:** Several examples of American aggression toward "weaker and darker peoples": the overthrow of the royal government and consequent annexation of Hawai'i in 1898; the invasion of Puerto Rico during the Spanish-American War, at the conclusion of which Spain ceded the island to the U.S. in 1898; and the brutal suppression by United States troops of the Philippine Insurrection (1899-1902).

33. **Grimkes . . . Bowen:** African American civic, educational, and religious leaders of the period: Archibald H. Grimké (1849-1930), a prominent lawyer and later one of the founders of the NAACP; his brother Francis J. Grimké (1850-1937), the celebrated pastor of the Fifteenth Street Presbyterian Church in Washington, D.C.; Kelly Miller (1863-1939), dean of Howard University; and John Wesley Edward Bowen (1855-1933), president of Gammon Theological Seminary in Atlanta.

the South who do well and criticising uncompromisingly those who do ill; in taking advantage of the opportunities at hand and urging their fellows to do the same, but at the same time in remembering that only a firm adherence to their higher ideals and aspirations will ever keep those ideals within the realm of possibility. They do not expect that the free right to vote, to enjoy civic rights, and to be educated, will come in a moment; they do not expect to see the bias and prejudices of years disappear at the blast of a trumpet; but they are absolutely certain that the way for a people to gain their reasonable rights is not by voluntarily throwing them away and insisting that they do not want them; that the way for a people to gain respect is not by continually belittling and ridiculing themselves; that, on the contrary, Negroes must insist continually, in season and out of season, that voting is necessary to modern manhood, that color discrimination is barbarism, and that black boys need education as well as white boys.

In failing thus to state plainly and unequivocally the legitimate demands of their people, even at the cost of opposing an honored leader, the thinking classes of American Negroes would shirk a heavy responsibility, — a responsibility to themselves, a responsibility to the struggling masses, a responsibility to the darker races of men whose future depends so largely on this American experiment, but especially a responsibility to this nation, — this common Fatherland. It is wrong to encourage a man or a people in evil-doing; it is wrong to aid and abet a national crime simply because it is unpopular not to do so. The growing spirit of kindliness and reconciliation between the North and South after the frightful differences of a generation ago ought to be a source of deep congratulation to all, and especially to those whose mistreatment caused the war; but if that reconciliation is to be marked by the industrial slavery and civic death of those same black men, with permanent legislation into a position of inferiority, then those black men, if they are really men, are called upon by every consideration of patriotism and loyalty to oppose such a course by all civilized methods, even though such opposition involves disagreement with Mr. Booker T. Washington. We have no right to sit silently by while the inevitable seeds are sown for a harvest of disaster to our children, black and white.

First, it is the duty of black men to judge the South discriminatingly. The present generation of Southerners are not responsible for the past, and they should not be blindly hated or blamed for it. Furthermore, to no class is the indiscriminate endorsement of the recent course of the South toward Negroes more nauseating than to the best thought of the South. The South is not "solid"; it is a land in the ferment of social change, wherein forces of all kinds are fighting for supremacy; and to praise the ill the South is to-day perpetrating is just as wrong as to condemn the good. Discriminating and broad-minded criticism is what the South needs, — needs it for the sake of her own white sons and daughters, and for the insurance of robust, healthy mental and moral development.

To-day even the attitude of the Southern whites toward the blacks is not, as so many assume, in all cases the same; the ignorant Southerner hates the Negro, the working-men fear his competition, the money-makers wish to use him as a laborer, some of the educated see a menace in his upward development, while others — usually the sons of the masters — wish to help him to rise. National opinion has enabled this last class to maintain the Negro common schools, and to protect the Negro partially in property, life, and limb. Through the pressure of the money-makers, the Negro is in danger of being reduced to semi-slavery, especially in the country districts; the workingmen, and those of the educated who fear the Negro, have united to disfranchise him, and some have urged his deportation; while the passions of the ignorant are easily aroused to lynch and abuse any black man. To praise this intricate whirl of thought and prejudice is nonsense; to inveigh indiscriminately against "the South" is unjust; but to use the same breath in praising Governor Aycock, exposing Senator Morgan, arguing with Mr. Thomas Nelson Page, and denouncing Senator Ben Tillman,[34] is not only sane, but the imperative duty of thinking black men.

It would be unjust to Mr. Washington not to acknowledge that in several instances he has opposed movements in the South which were unjust to the Negro; he sent memorials to the Louisiana and Alabama constitutional conventions, he has spoken against lynching, and in other ways has openly or silently set his influence against sinister schemes and unfortunate happenings. Notwithstanding this, it is equally true to assert that on the whole the distinct impression left by Mr. Washington's propaganda is, first, that the South is justified in its present attitude toward the Negro because of the Negro's degradation; secondly, that the prime cause of the Negro's failure to rise more quickly is his wrong education in the past; and, thirdly, that his future rise depends primarily on his own efforts. Each of these propositions is a dangerous half-truth. The supplementary truths must never be lost sight of: first, slavery and race-prejudice are potent if not sufficient causes of the Negro's position; second, industrial and common-school training were necessarily slow in planting because they had to await the black teachers trained by higher institutions, – it being extremely doubtful if any essentially different development was possible, and certainly a Tuskegee was unthinkable before 1880; and, third, while it is a great truth to say that the Negro must strive and strive mightily to help himself, it is equally true that unless his striving be not simply seconded, but rather aroused and encouraged, by the initiative of the richer and wiser environing group, he cannot hope for great success.

In his failure to realize and impress this last point, Mr. Washington is especially to be criticised. His doctrine has tended to make the whites, North and South, shift the burden of the Negro problem to the Negro's shoulders and stand aside as critical and rather pessimistic spectators; when in fact the burden belongs to the nation, and

---

34. **praising Governor Aycock . . . denouncing Senator Ben Tillman:** Charles B. Aycock (1859-1912) was a strong supporter of local schools and universal education who came to be known as the "Education Governor" of North Carolina (1901-05). Du Bois also refers to three southerners known for their racist attitudes toward African Americans: John Tyler Morgan (1824-1907), a former Confederate general who continued to support the doctrine of states' rights during Reconstruction and who was instrumental in developing the ideology of white supremacy during his long service as a U.S. senator from Alabama (1877-1907); Thomas Nelson Page (1853-1922), a southern writer who helped popularize romantic myths about slavery and plantation life in collections of stories like *In Ole Virginia* (1887); and Benjamin R. ("Pitchfork Ben") Tillman (1847-1918), a racial demagogue who advocated segregation and the disenfranchisement of black voters as governor of South Carolina (1890-94) and as a U.S. senator (1895-1918).

the hands of none of us are clean if we bend not our energies to righting these great wrongs.

The South ought to be led, by candid and honest criticism, to assert her better self and do her full duty to the race she has cruelly wronged and is still wronging. The North — her co-partner in guilt — cannot salve her conscience by plastering it with gold. We cannot settle this problem by diplomacy and suaveness, by "policy" alone. If worse come to worst, can the moral fibre of this country survive the slow throttling and murder of nine millions of men?

The black men of America have a duty to perform, a duty stern and delicate, — a forward movement to oppose a part of the work of their greatest leader. So far as Mr. Washington preaches Thrift, Patience, and Industrial Training for the masses, we must hold up his hands and strive with him, rejoicing in his honors and glorying in the strength of this Joshua called of God and of man to lead the headless host. But so far as Mr. Washington apologizes for injustice, North or South, does not rightly value the privilege and duty of voting, belittles the emasculating effects of caste distinctions, and opposes the higher training and ambition of our brighter minds, — so far as he, the South, or the Nation, does this, — we must unceasingly and firmly oppose them. By every civilized and peaceful method we must strive for the rights which the world accords to men, clinging unwaveringly to those great words which the sons of the Fathers would fain forget: "We hold these truths to be self-evident: That all men are created equal; that they are endowed by their Creator with certain unalienable rights; that among these are life, liberty, and the pursuit of happiness."[35]

[1903]

---

35. **"We . . . happiness"**: From the preamble to the Declaration of Independence (1776).

Henry Adams

[1838-1918]

His true function was to ask questions, not to answer them; his true function was to provoke speculation, not to satisfy it.
-Henry Steele Commager

Henry Brooks Adams was born in Boston, Massachusetts, on February 16, 1838. Speaking of himself in the third person, Adams in his autobiography later observes: "Probably no child, born in the year, held better cards than he." His mother, Abigail Brown Brooks Adams, was from one of the wealthiest and most distinguished families in Boston, and his father, Charles Francis Adams, was the grandson of the second president, John Adams, and the son of the sixth president, John Quincy Adams. Henry Adams grew up in a world of comfort and culture in his family home, which contained the largest private library in Boston, and was a frequent visitor to the home of his grandfather John Quincy Adams in Quincy, Massachusetts. Adams recalled that one day while he was staying there he adamantly refused to go to school. Without saying a word, the former president took his grandson's hand, silently walked him to school and, still without speaking, left him seated in a classroom. Despite Adams's aversion to formal education, he duly attended private schools and enrolled at Harvard College in 1854. Although he earned mediocre grades, primarily for tardiness and other violations of school rules, he acted in theatrical performances, wrote for the *Harvard Magazine*, and was popular with other students, who elected him to deliver the class oration of 1858.

Henry Adams

This photograph was taken in the 1870s, while Adams was teaching history at Harvard.

Adams spent most of the following decade studying and working abroad. "As yet he knew nothing," Adams observed of himself at the time of his graduation from Harvard. "Education had not begun." Eager to learn modern languages and to see the world, he joined several of his classmates on what was then a part of every wealthy young man's education, a grand tour of Europe. Adams studied civil law in Germany, taking time off to tour Austria, Switzerland, and Italy, from which he wrote travel letters published in the *Boston Daily Courier*. He finally returned to the United States in October 1860, on the eve of the Civil War. Adams took a position as a secretary to his father, now a congressman from Massachusetts, in Washington, D.C. When President Lincoln appointed his father minister to Great Britain, Adams accompanied him to London and continued to serve as his secretary there until May 1868. Adams became a foreign correspondent for the *New York Times*, reporting on the British reaction to the Civil War. He also began to write more substantial pieces for the distinguished Boston journal the *North American Review*, including "Captaine John Smith" (1867), a rigorous historical analysis in which Adams demonstrates that Smith had invented the romantic story of his rescue from death by the love-struck Pocahontas.

After his return home in 1868, Adams devoted himself to the study of American history and current events in the United States. He initially worked as a journalist in Washington, D.C., where he championed causes such as currency reform and the overhaul of the "spoils system" of civil service. Appalled by the spreading corruption during the Gilded Age, as exemplified by the financier Jay Gould's effort to corner the market on gold and the financial chicanery involved in the struggle for control of the Erie Railroad, Adams and his older brother, Charles Francis Adams Jr., studied those scandals in articles they gathered together as *Chapters of Erie and Other Essays*, published in 1871. By then, the once-reluctant student had accepted positions as assistant professor of history at Harvard and as editor of the *North American Review*. In 1872, he married Marian

("Clover") Hooper, the accomplished daughter of a prominent Boston physician, and the couple embarked on a yearlong wedding journey to Europe and Egypt. They lived in Boston until 1877, when Adams resigned from Harvard to edit the papers of Albert Gallatin, Thomas Jefferson's secretary of the treasury, at the State Department Archives in Washington, D.C. In addition to a biography of Gallatin and an edition of his writings, Adams anonymously published *Democracy: An American Novel* (1880), a best-selling satire of political corruption in Washington, and *Esther: A Novel* (1884), which appeared under the pseudonym Frances Snow Compton. Adams also began work on his major project, the nine-volume *History of the United States during the Administration of Thomas Jefferson and James Madison* (1889–91).

While Adams was working on the project, his happy and productive life in Washington was shattered by the loss of his wife, who committed suicide in December 1885. During the remaining years of his life, the grief-stricken Adams traveled extensively: to the American West; to Mexico and the Caribbean, including Cuba; to Japan, where he studied Buddhism, and later across the South Pacific to Hawaii, Fiji, Australia, and Ceylon; to Egypt, Turkey, and Russia; and throughout Europe. Adams became fascinated by medieval culture, especially the architecture of Gothic cathedrals in northern France, the central focus of his book *Mont-Saint-Michel and Chartres*, which he privately printed in 1904 and later authorized the American Institute of Architects to publish in 1913. He also wrote *The Education of Henry Adams*, an autobiography he privately printed in 1907. In it, Adams introduces his "Dynamic Theory of History," a complex formulation of the gravitational pull or "attractive force" of various concepts that had shaped the evolution of human beings from their earliest beginnings to 1900. Adams reformulated his theory in several later works, including "A Letter to American Teachers of History," a pamphlet he distributed to college librarians and history professors in 1910. Although he was partially paralyzed by a stroke in 1912, Adams continued to travel and entertain friends at his home in Washington, where he died on March 27, 1918. He was buried beside his wife in Rock Creek Cemetery, where Adams had earlier commissioned a now-famous memorial to mark their plots, asking the sculptor Augustus Saint-Gaudens to create a statue that symbolized "the acceptance, intellectually, of the inevitable."

bedfordstmartins.com/ americanlit for research links on Adams

Adams's *The Education of Henry Adams.*   Adams began working on his autobiography in 1903 and completed it in 1905. In 1907, he paid for a printing of one hundred copies, which he circulated for comment and correction among those mentioned in the book, including his brothers and his friend President Theodore Roosevelt. Although Adams made a few corrections, he remained dissatisfied with the book, which he would not allow to be reprinted during his lifetime. A second edition, which appeared six months after his death in 1918, was awarded the Pulitzer Prize. Adopting the unusual narrative strategy of writing about himself in the third person, Adams describes the events of his life with the objectivity of a historian and, frequently, with ironic detachment. As the title of his autobiography indicates, and as Adams emphasizes in his preface, printed below, the central focus of the work is his education, or rather the failure of his traditional education to prepare him for the modern world. Among his most revelatory confrontations with that world were his visits to the World's Columbian Exposition in Chicago in 1893 and the Paris Exposition in 1900, where he was fascinated by the advances in technology displayed in the Hall of Dynamos. Adams, who had been reading medieval philosophy and studying Gothic architecture for several years, began to ponder the relation between the dynamo, the recently invented mechanical producer of electrical energy, and the power of the Catholic Church during the Middle Ages. He pursued that question in the famous chapter printed below, "The Virgin and the Dynamo," in which he suggests that by 1900 a belief in scientific progress and technology, symbolized by the dynamo, had come to exert the same force over the minds of human beings that had once been exerted by the medieval church, symbolized by the Virgin Mary. The text is taken from the second edition of *The Education of Henry Adams: An Autobiography* (1918).

Palace of Electricity

This lantern slide of the interior of the Palace of Electricity shows one of the huge dynamos (lower left) that fascinated Henry Adams during his visit to the Paris Universal Exposition in 1900. Lantern slides were frequently used in educational lectures and popular entertainments in which photographic images were displayed on a wall or a screen.

The Education of Henry Adams

Preface

Jean Jacques Rousseau began his famous "Confessions"[1] by a vehement appeal to the Deity: "I have shown myself as I was; contemptible and vile when I was so; good, generous, sublime when I was so; I have unveiled my interior such as Thou thyself hast seen it, Eternal Father! Collect about me the innumerable swarm of my fellows; let them hear my confessions; let them groan at my unworthiness; let them blush at my meannesses! Let each of them discover his heart in his turn at the foot of thy throne with the same sincerity; and then let any one of them tell thee if he dares: 'I was a better man!'"

Jean Jacques was a very great educator in the manner of the eighteenth century, and has been commonly thought to have had more influence than any other teacher of his time; but his peculiar method of improving human nature has not been universally admired. Most educators of the nineteenth century have declined to show themselves before their scholars as objects more vile or contemptible than necessary, and even the humblest teacher hides, if possible, the faults with which nature has generously embellished us all, as it did Jean Jacques, thinking, as most religious minds are apt to do, that the Eternal Father himself may not feel unmixed pleasure at our thrusting under his eyes chiefly the least agreeable details of his creation.

As an unfortunate result the twentieth century finds few recent guides to avoid, or to follow. American literature offers scarcely one working model for high education. The student must go back, beyond Jean Jacques, to Benjamin Franklin, to find a model even of self-teaching. Except in the abandoned sphere of the dead languages, no one has discussed what part of education has, in his personal experience, turned out to be useful, and what not. This volume attempts to discuss it.

As educator, Jean Jacques was, in one respect, easily first; he erected a monument of warning against the Ego. Since his time, and largely thanks to him, the Ego has steadily tended to efface itself, and, for purposes of model, to become a manikin on which the toilet of education is to be draped in order to show the fit or misfit of the clothes. The object of study is the garment, not the figure. The tailor adapts the manikin as well as the clothes to his patron's wants. The tailor's object, in this volume, is to fit young men, in universities or elsewhere, to be men of the world, equipped for any emergency; and the garment offered to them is meant to show the faults of the patchwork fitted on their fathers.

At the utmost, the active-minded young man should ask of his teacher only mastery of his tools. The young man himself, the subject of education, is a certain form of energy; the object to be gained is economy of his force; the training is partly the clearing

---

1. **Rousseau . . . "Confessions":** The French writer, philosopher, and education reformer Jean Jacques Rousseau (1712–1778) persistently describes his failings and imperfections in his remarkably candid autobiography, *The Confessions*, published posthumously in 1782.

away of obstacles, partly the direct application of effort. Once acquired, the tools and models may be thrown away.

The manikin, therefore, has the same value as any other geometrical figure of three or more dimensions, which is used for the study of relation. For that purpose it cannot be spared; it is the only measure of motion, of proportion, of human condition; it must have the air of reality; must be taken for real; must be treated as though it had life. Who knows? Possibly it had!

February 16, 1907

Chapter XXV
The Dynamo and the Virgin (1900)

Until the Great Exposition of 1900[2] closed its doors in November, Adams haunted it, aching to absorb knowledge, and helpless to find it. He would have liked to know how much of it could have been grasped by the best-informed man in the world. While he was thus meditating chaos, Langley[3] came by, and showed it to him. At Langley's behest, the Exhibition dropped its superfluous rags and stripped itself to the skin, for Langley knew what to study, and why, and how; while Adams might as well have stood outside in the night, staring at the Milky Way. Yet Langley said nothing new, and taught nothing that one might not have learned from Lord Bacon,[4] three hundred years before; but though one should have known the "Advancement of Science" as well as one knew the "Comedy of Errors,"[5] the literary knowledge counted for nothing until some teacher should show how to apply it. Bacon took a vast deal of trouble in teaching King James I and his subjects, American or other, towards the year 1620, that true science was the development or economy of forces; yet an elderly American in 1900 knew neither the formula nor the forces; or even so much as to say to himself that his historical business in the Exposition concerned only the economies or developments of force since 1893, when he began the study at Chicago.[6]

Nothing in education is so astonishing as the amount of ignorance it accumulates in the form of inert facts. Adams had looked at most of the accumulations of art in the

---

2. **Great Exposition of 1900:** The Paris Universal Exposition, held from April to November 1900, attracted over fifty-seven million visitors from around the world.

3. **Langley:** Samuel P. Langley (1834–1906), professor of astronomy and secretary of the Smithsonian Institution. He invented an "aerodrome," a flying machine that failed after several attempts, including one just a few days before the Wright brothers successfully flew a plane at Kitty Hawk on December 17, 1903.

4. **Lord Bacon:** Sir Francis Bacon (1561–1626), English philosopher and author of *The Advancement of Learning*, which he presented to King James I in 1605, and the *Novum Organum*, variously translated as "New Organ" or "New Instrument," an important work in the development of the scientific method first published in 1620. His belief that truth is discovered through empirical observation strongly influenced Adams, who observed that Bacon "urged society to lay aside the idea of evolving the universe from a thought, and to try evolving thought from the universe."

5. **"Comedy of Errors":** An early play (1594) by William Shakespeare (1564–1616).

6. **Chicago:** Adams attended the World's Columbian Exposition of 1893 in Chicago, where he became interested in force as both a scientific and philosophical concept.

storehouses called Art Museums; yet he did not know how to look at the art exhibits of 1900. He had studied Karl Marx and his doctrines of history[7] with profound attention, yet he could not apply them at Paris. Langley, with the ease of a great master of experiment, threw out of the field every exhibit that did not reveal a new application of force, and naturally threw out, to begin with, almost the whole art exhibit. Equally, he ignored almost the whole industrial exhibit. He led his pupil directly to the forces. His chief interest was in new motors to make his airship feasible, and he taught Adams the astonishing complexities of the new Daimler motor,[8] and of the automobile, which, since 1893, had become a nightmare at a hundred kilometres an hour, almost as destructive as the electric tram which was only ten years older; and threatening to become as terrible as the locomotive steam-engine itself, which was almost exactly Adams's own age.

Then he showed his scholar the great hall of dynamos, and explained how little he knew about electricity or force of any kind, even of his own special sun, which spouted heat in inconceivable volume, but which, as far as he knew, might spout less or more, at any time, for all the certainty he felt in it. To him, the dynamo itself was but an ingenious channel for conveying somewhere the heat latent in a few tons of poor coal hidden in a dirty engine-house carefully kept out of sight; but to Adams the dynamo became a symbol of infinity. As he grew accustomed to the great gallery of machines, he began to feel the forty-foot dynamos as a moral force, much as the early Christians felt the Cross. The planet itself seemed less impressive, in its old-fashioned, deliberate, annual or daily revolution, than this huge wheel, revolving within arm's-length at some vertiginous speed, and barely murmuring — scarcely humming an audible warning to stand a hair's-breadth further for respect of power — while it would not wake the baby lying close against its frame. Before the end, one began to pray to it; inherited instinct taught the natural expression of man before silent and infinite force. Among the thousand symbols of ultimate energy, the dynamo was not so human as some, but it was the most expressive.

Yet the dynamo, next to the steam-engine, was the most familiar of exhibits. For Adams's objects its value lay chiefly in its occult mechanism. Between the dynamo in the gallery of machines and the engine-house outside, the break of continuity amounted to abysmal fracture for a historian's objects. No more relation could he discover between the steam and the electric current than between the Cross and the cathedral. The forces were interchangeable if not reversible, but he could see only an absolute *fiat* in electricity as in faith. Langley could not help him. Indeed, Langley seemed to be worried by the same trouble, for he constantly repeated that the new forces were anarchical, and especially that he was not responsible for the new rays, that were little short of parricidal in

---

7. **Marx and his doctrines of history:** The influential German philosopher and social scientist Karl Marx (1818–1883) viewed social conflict as a driving force in the historical process.
8. **the new Daimler motor:** A famous high-speed internal combustion engine invented by the German engineer and automotive pioneer Gottlieb Daimler (1834–1900). A car fitted with the engine won the first auto race in history, from Paris to Rouen, in 1894.

their wicked spirit towards science. His own rays, with which he had doubled the solar spectrum, were altogether harmless and beneficent; but Radium denied its God – or, what was to Langley the same thing, denied the truths of his Science.[9] The force was wholly new.

A historian who asked only to learn enough to be as futile as Langley or Kelvin,[10] made rapid progress under this teaching, and mixed himself up in the tangle of ideas until he achieved a sort of Paradise of ignorance vastly consoling to his fatigued senses. He wrapped himself in vibrations and rays which were new, and he would have hugged Marconi and Branly[11] had he met them, as he hugged the dynamo; while he lost his arithmetic in trying to figure out the equation between the discoveries and the economies of force. The economies, like the discoveries, were absolute, supersensual, occult; incapable of expression in horse-power. What mathematical equivalent could he suggest as the value of a Branly coherer? Frozen air, or the electric furnace, had some scale of measurement, no doubt, if somebody could invent a thermometer adequate to the purpose; but X-rays had played no part whatever in man's consciousness, and the atom itself had figured only as a fiction of thought. In these seven years man had translated himself into a new universe which had no common scale of measurement with the old. He had entered a supersensual world, in which he could measure nothing except by chance collisions of movements imperceptible to his senses, perhaps even imperceptible to his instruments, but perceptible to each other, and so to some known ray at the end of the scale. Langley seemed prepared for anything, even for an indeterminable number of universes interfused – physics stark mad in metaphysics.

Historians undertake to arrange sequences, – called stories, or histories – assuming in silence a relation of cause and effect. These assumptions, hidden in the depths of dusty libraries, have been astounding, but commonly unconscious and childlike; so much so, that if any captious critic were to drag them to light, historians would probably reply, with one voice, that they had never supposed themselves required to know what they were talking about. Adams, for one, had toiled in vain to find out what he meant. He had even published a dozen volumes of American history for no other purpose than to satisfy himself whether, by the severest process of stating, with the least possible comment, such facts as seemed sure, in such order as seemed rigorously consequent, he could fix for a familiar moment a necessary sequence of human movement. The result had satisfied him as little as at Harvard College. Where he saw sequence, other men saw something quite different, and no one saw the same unit of measure. He cared little

---

9. **His own rays . . . the truths of his Science:** In 1878, Langley invented the bolometer, a device that allowed him to measure the intensity of electromagnetic radiation, invisible heat rays in the infrared spectrum. Radium, an extremely radioactive element that challenged traditional scientific ideas about matter and energy, was discovered by Marie and Pierre Curie in 1898.

10. **Kelvin:** 1st Baron William Thomson Kelvin (1824-1907), Irish-Scottish engineer, physicist, and inventor who made significant contributions to the mathematical analysis of electricity and thermodynamics during the nineteenth century.

11. **Marconi and Branly:** Guglielmo Marconi (1874-1937), Italian electrical engineer who developed wireless telegraphy and invented the radio in 1895. Eugène Édouard Désiré Branly (1844-1940), French physicist who invented the coherer, a device for detecting radio waves.

about his experiments and less about his statesmen, who seemed to him quite as ignorant as himself and, as a rule, no more honest; but he insisted on a relation of sequence,
and if he could not reach it by one method, he would try as many methods as science
knew. Satisfied that the sequence of men led to nothing and that the sequence of their
society could lead no further, while the mere sequence of time was artificial, and the
sequence of thought was chaos, he turned at last to the sequence of force; and thus it
happened that, after ten years' pursuit, he found himself lying in the Gallery of Machines at the Great Exposition of 1900, his historical neck broken by the sudden irruption of forces totally new.

Since no one else showed much concern, an elderly person without other cares had
no need to betray alarm. The year 1900 was not the first to upset schoolmasters. Copernicus and Galileo had broken many professorial necks about 1600;[12] Columbus had
stood the world on its head towards 1500;[13] but the nearest approach to the revolution of
1900 was that of 310, when Constantine set up the Cross.[14] The rays that Langley disowned, as well as those which he fathered, were occult, supersensual, irrational; they
were a revelation of mysterious energy like that of the Cross; they were what, in terms of
mediaeval science, were called immediate modes of the divine substance.

The historian was thus reduced to his last resources. Clearly if he was bound to
reduce all these forces to a common value, this common value could have no measure
but that of their attraction on his own mind. He must treat them as they had been felt; as
convertible, reversible, interchangeable attractions on thought. He made up his mind to
venture it; he would risk translating rays into faith. Such a reversible process would
vastly amuse a chemist, but the chemist could not deny that he, or some of his fellow
physicists, could feel the force of both. When Adams was a boy in Boston, the best
chemist in the place had probably never heard of Venus except by way of scandal, or of
the Virgin except as idolatry;[15] neither had he heard of dynamos or automobiles or
radium; yet his mind was ready to feel the force of all, though the rays were unborn and
the women were dead.

Here opened another totally new education, which promised to be by far the most
hazardous of all. The knife-edge along which he must crawl, like Sir Lancelot[16] in the

---

12. **Copernicus and Galileo . . . 1600:** The Polish astronomer Nicolaus Copernicus (1473–1543) proved that
the earth rotates around the sun, a theory supported by the Italian astronomer Galileo Galilei (1564–1642),
who was consequently condemned by the Inquisition.

13. **Columbus . . . 1500:** The four voyages the Italian navigator and explorer Christopher Columbus
(1451–1506) undertook between 1492 and 1504 initiated the European exploration and colonization of the
Americas, what was then a "New World" to Europeans.

14. **Constantine set up the Cross:** Constantine I, or Constantine the Great (c. 272–337), the first Roman
emperor to embrace Christianity, issued the Edict of Milan in 313, ending government-sanctioned persecution of Christians.

15. **Venus . . . idolatry:** Adams suggests that a chemist, or pharmacist, knows about the effects of Venus, the
Greek goddess of love, through the treatment of sexually transmitted diseases. The centrality of the Virgin
Mary to Catholicism was often denigrated as idolatry by Protestants.

16. **Sir Lancelot:** In the medieval legends of King Arthur and the Knights of the Round Table, Sir Lancelot is
a great knight who tragically destroys the kingdom because of his illicit relationship with Arthur's wife,
Guinevere. In one of his many legendary exploits, Lancelot rescues Guinevere after crawling across a bridge
made of a sword.

twelfth century, divided two kingdoms of force which had nothing in common but attraction. They were as different as a magnet is from gravitation, supposing one knew what a magnet was, or gravitation, or love. The force of the Virgin was still felt at Lourdes,[17] and seemed to be as potent as X-rays; but in America neither Venus nor Virgin ever had value as force — at most as sentiment. No American had ever been truly afraid of either.

This problem in dynamics gravely perplexed an American historian. The Woman had once been supreme; in France she still seemed potent, not merely as a sentiment, but as a force. Why was she unknown in America? For evidently America was ashamed of her, and she was ashamed of herself, otherwise they would not have strewn fig-leaves so profusely all over her. When she was a true force, she was ignorant of fig-leaves, but the monthly-magazine-made American female had not a feature that would have been recognized by Adam. The trait was notorious, and often humorous, but any one brought up among Puritans knew that sex was sin. In any previous age, sex was strength. Neither art nor beauty was needed. Every one, even among Puritans, knew that neither Diana of the Ephesians[18] nor any of the Oriental goddesses was worshipped for her beauty. She was goddess because of her force; she was the animated dynamo; she was reproduction — the greatest and most mysterious of all energies; all she needed was to be fecund. Singularly enough, not one of Adams's many schools of education had ever drawn his attention to the opening lines of Lucretius, though they were perhaps the finest in all Latin literature, where the poet invoked Venus exactly as Dante invoked the Virgin: —

> "Quae quoniam rerum naturam *sola* gubernas."[19]

The Venus of Epicurean philosophy survived in the Virgin of the Schools: —

> "Donna, sei tanto grande, e tanto vali,
> Che qual vuol grazia, e a te non ricorre,
> Sua disianza vuol volar senz' ali."[20]

All this was to American thought as though it had never existed. The true American knew something of the facts, but nothing of the feelings; he read the letter, but he never felt the law. Before this historical chasm, a mind like that of Adams felt itself helpless; he turned from the Virgin to the Dynamo as though he were a Branly coherer. On one side, at the Louvre and at Chartres, as he knew by the record of work actually done and

---

17. **Lourdes:** Town in southwestern France that became an important pilgrimage site for Catholics in 1858 when a young girl claimed to have had visions of the Virgin Mary in a grotto there.

18. **Diana of the Ephesians:** Diana, a goddess in Roman mythology associated with hunting and virginity, was a principal deity of Ephesus, an ancient city in Asia Minor.

19. **"Quae . . . gubernas":** *On the Nature of Things*, by the Roman poet Lucretius (c. 99–55 BCE), begins with a long invocation and tribute to Venus. This line may be translated "Since *you alone* govern the nature of things."

20. **"Donna . . . ali":** The lines from the last canto of *Paradiso*, the final volume of the *Divine Comedy* by the Italian poet Dante Alighieri (1265–1321), may be translated: "Thou, Lady, art so great and so prevailing that whoso would have grace and does not turn to thee, his desire would seek to fly without wings" (33.13–15). What Adams calls the "Virgin of the Schools" is a reference to the Scholastic school of medieval theology.

still before his eyes, was the highest energy ever known to man, the creator of four-fifths of his noblest art, exercising vastly more attraction over the human mind than all the steam-engines and dynamos ever dreamed of; and yet this energy was unknown to the American mind. An American Virgin would never dare command; an American Venus would never dare exist.

The question, which to any plain American of the nineteenth century seemed as remote as it did to Adams, drew him almost violently to study, once it was posed; and on this point Langleys were as useless as though they were Herbert Spencers[21] or dynamos. The idea survived only as art. There one turned as naturally as though the artist were himself a woman. Adams began to ponder, asking himself whether he knew of any American artist who had ever insisted on the power of sex, as every classic had always done; but he could think only of Walt Whitman; Bret Harte,[22] as far as the magazines would let him venture; and one or two painters, for the flesh-tones. All the rest had used sex for sentiment, never for force; to them, Eve was a tender flower, and Herodias[23] an unfeminine horror. American art, like the American language and American education, was as far as possible sexless. Society regarded this victory over sex as its greatest triumph, and the historian readily admitted it, since the moral issue, for the moment, did not concern one who was studying the relations of unmoral force. He cared nothing for the sex of the dynamo until he could measure its energy.

Vaguely seeking a clue, he wandered through the art exhibit, and, in his stroll, stopped almost every day before St. Gaudens's General Sherman,[24] which had been given the central post of honor. St. Gaudens himself was in Paris, putting on the work his usual interminable last touches, and listening to the usual contradictory suggestions of brother sculptors. Of all the American artists who gave to American art whatever life it breathed in the seventies, St. Gaudens was perhaps the most sympathetic, but certainly the most inarticulate. General Grant or Don Cameron[25] had scarcely less instinct of rhetoric than he. All the others — the Hunts, Richardson, John La Farge, Stanford White[26] — were exuberant; only St. Gaudens could never discuss or dilate on an

---

21. **Herbert Spencers:** Spencer (1820-1903) was an influential English philosopher best known for applying Darwin's evolutionary theory to other areas, including psychology and the study of society.

22. **Bret Harte:** Francis Bret Harte (1836-1902) was a popular author of western local-color stories, whose cast of characters frequently included gamblers, miners, and prostitutes.

23. **Herodias:** The wife of King Herod who in the biblical account arranges for her daughter Salome to dance before the king and ask for the head of John the Baptist as a reward (Mark 6:21-27).

24. **St. Gaudens's General Sherman:** *General Sherman Led by Lady Victory*, one of several Civil War monuments sculpted by Augustus Saint-Gaudens (1848-1907), was exhibited at the Paris Exposition before being erected in New York City.

25. **General Grant or Don Cameron:** Adams once said that General Ulysses S. Grant (who later served as U.S. president from 1869 to 1877) was "pre-intellectual, archaic, and would have seemed so even to the cave-dwellers." James Donald Cameron (1833-1918), Grant's secretary of war, became a U.S. senator (1877-97) and the head of a powerful political machine in Pennsylvania.

26. **the Hunts . . . White:** Several noted American artists and designers: the painter William Morris Hunt (1824-1879) and his brother, the architect Richard Morris Hunt (1828-1895); the architect Henry Hobson Richardson (1838-1886); John La Farge (1835-1910), a painter and designer of stained glass windows; and the architect Stanford White (1853-1906).

emotion, or suggest artistic arguments for giving to his work the forms that he felt. He never laid down the law, or affected the despot, or became brutalized like Whistler[27] by the brutalities of his world. He required no incense; he was no egoist; his simplicity of thought was excessive; he could not imitate, or give any form but his own to the creations of his hand. No one felt more strongly than he the strength of other men, but the idea that they could affect him never stirred an image in his mind.

This summer his health was poor and his spirits were low. For such a temper, Adams was not the best companion, since his own gaiety was not *folle*;[28] but he risked going now and then to the studio on Mont Parnasse to draw him out for a stroll in the Bois de Boulogne,[29] or dinner as pleased his moods, and in return St. Gaudens sometimes let Adams go about in his company.

Once St. Gaudens took him down to Amiens, with a party of Frenchmen, to see the cathedral. Not until they found themselves actually studying the sculpture of the western portal, did it dawn on Adams's mind that, for his purposes, St. Gaudens on that spot had more interest to him than the cathedral itself. Great men before great monuments express great truths, provided they are not taken too solemnly. Adams never tired of quoting the supreme phrase of his idol Gibbon,[30] before the Gothic cathedrals: "I darted a contemptuous look on the stately monuments of superstition." Even in the footnotes of his history, Gibbon had never inserted a bit of humor more human than this, and one would have paid largely for a photograph of the fat little historian, on the background of Notre Dame of Amiens, trying to persuade his readers — perhaps himself — that he was darting a contemptuous look on the stately monument, for which he felt in fact the respect which every man of his vast study and active mind always feels before objects worthy of it; but besides the humor, one felt also the relation. Gibbon ignored the Virgin, because in 1789 religious monuments were out of fashion. In 1900 his remark sounded fresh and simple as the green fields to ears that had heard a hundred years of other remarks, mostly no more fresh and certainly less simple. Without malice, one might find it more instructive than a whole lecture of Ruskin.[31] One sees what one brings, and at that moment Gibbon brought the French Revolution. Ruskin brought reaction against the Revolution. St. Gaudens had passed beyond all. He liked the stately monuments much more than he liked Gibbon or Ruskin; he loved their dignity; their unity; their scale; their lines; their lights and shadows; their decorative sculpture; but he was even less conscious than they of the force that created it all — the Virgin, the Woman — by whose genius "the stately monuments of superstition" were built, through which she

---

27. **Whistler:** James Abbott MacNeill Whistler (1834-1903), American painter known for his biting wit and his frequent conflicts with critics and patrons.
28. *folle:* Wild or excessive (French).
29. **Mont Parnasse . . . Bois de Boulogne:** The former is an area of Paris frequented by artists and writers, and the latter is a large wooded park on the outskirts of Paris.
30. **Gibbon:** Edward Gibbon (1737-1794), English historian best known for his magisterial *The Decline and Fall of the Roman Empire* (1776-88).
31. **Ruskin:** John Ruskin (1819-1900), English art critic who became a convert to the medieval style of architecture and an influential proponent of the so-called Gothic Revival that swept across England and the United States between roughly 1830 and 1880.

was expressed. He would have seen more meaning in Isis with the cow's horns, at Edfoo,[32] who expressed the same thought. The art remained, but the energy was lost even upon the artist.

Yet in mind and person St. Gaudens was a survival of the 1500; he bore the stamp of the Renaissance, and should have carried an image of the Virgin round his neck, or stuck in his hat, like Louis XI.[33] In mere time he was a lost soul that had strayed by chance into the twentieth century, and forgotten where it came from. He writhed and cursed at his ignorance, much as Adams did at his own, but in the opposite sense. St. Gaudens was a child of Benvenuto Cellini,[34] smothered in an American cradle. Adams was a quintessence of Boston, devoured by curiosity to think like Benvenuto. St. Gaudens's art was starved from birth, and Adams's instinct was blighted from babyhood. Each had but half of a nature, and when they came together before the Virgin of Amiens they ought both to have felt in her the force that made them one; but it was not so. To Adams she became more than ever a channel of force; to St. Gaudens she remained as before a channel of taste.

For a symbol of power, St. Gaudens instinctively preferred the horse, as was plain in his horse and Victory of the Sherman monument. Doubtless Sherman also felt it so. The attitude was so American that, for at least forty years, Adams had never realized that any other could be in sound taste. How many years had he taken to admit a notion of what Michael Angelo and Rubens[35] were driving at? He could not say; but he knew that only since 1895 had he begun to feel the Virgin or Venus as force, and not everywhere even so. At Chartres — perhaps at Lourdes — possibly at Cnidos if one could still find there the divinely naked Aphrodite of Praxiteles — but otherwise one must look for force to the goddesses of Indian mythology.[36] The idea died out long ago in the German and English stock. St. Gaudens at Amiens was hardly less sensitive to the force of the female energy than Matthew Arnold at the Grande Chartreuse.[37] Neither of them felt goddesses as power — only as reflected emotion, human expression, beauty, purity,

---

32. **Isis . . . at Edfoo:** While traveling in Egypt, Adams saw a statue of Isis, the Egyptian earth-mother goddess renowned for her magical powers, at Edfu, on the banks of the Nile.

33. **Louis XI:** Although he unified the country and laid the foundation for an absolute monarchy in France, the powerful Louis the Prudent (1423–1483), as he was called, dressed like a poor pilgrim and wore an old felt hat upon which the sole ornament was the lead figure of a saint.

34. **Benvenuto Cellini:** Cellini (1500–1571), volatile Italian sculptor who gave an account of his tempestuous life in his posthumously published autobiography.

35. **Michael Angelo and Rubens:** The Italian Renaissance painter and sculptor Michelangelo Buonarroti (1475–1564) and the baroque Flemish painter Peter Paul Rubens (1577–1640), both of whom were famous for their renderings of the human body.

36. **the divinely naked Aphrodite . . . goddesses of Indian mythology:** Called Venus by the Romans, Aphrodite was the goddess of love in Greek mythology. The renowned Greek sculptor Praxiteles (c. 350 BCE) carved a life-size statue of Aphrodite stepping from a bath for a shrine in Cnidus (Knidos), a city in Asia Minor. (The torso of the sculpture, whose head and extremities are now missing, is in the Vatican Museum in Rome.) Ancient stone temples in India were often decorated with erotic sculptures, and Hindu goddesses such as Parvati were represented as beautiful, graceful, and voluptuous figures.

37. **Grande Chartreuse:** The English poet and critic Matthew Arnold (1822–1888) wrote a meditation on the loss of faith, "Stanzas from the Grande Chartreuse," while he was staying at a Carthusian monastery, the serenity of which he contrasted to the modern industrial world.

taste, scarcely even as sympathy. They felt a railway train as power; yet they, and all other artists, constantly complained that the power embodied in a railway train could never be embodied in art. All the steam in the world could not, like the Virgin, build Chartres.

Yet in mechanics, whatever the mechanicians might think, both energies acted as interchangeable forces on man, and by action on man all known force may be measured. Indeed, few men of science measured force in any other way. After once admitting that a straight line was the shortest distance between two points, no serious mathematician cared to deny anything that suited his convenience, and rejected no symbol, unproved or unproveable, that helped him to accomplish work. The symbol was force, as a compass-needle or a triangle was force, as the mechanist might prove by losing it, and nothing could be gained by ignoring their value. Symbol or energy, the Virgin had acted as the greatest force the Western world ever felt, and had drawn man's activities to herself more strongly than any other power, natural or supernatural, had ever done; the historian's business was to follow the track of the energy; to find where it came from and where it went to; its complex source and shifting channels; its values, equivalents, conversions. It could scarcely be more complex than radium; it could hardly be deflected, diverted, polarized, absorbed more perplexingly than other radiant matter. Adams knew nothing about any of them, but as a mathematical problem of influence on human progress, though all were occult, all reacted on his mind, and he rather inclined to think the Virgin easiest to handle.

The pursuit turned out to be long and tortuous, leading at last into the vast forests of scholastic science. From Zeno to Descartes, hand in hand with Thomas Aquinas, Montaigne, and Pascal, one stumbled as stupidly as though one were still a German student of 1860.[38] Only with the instinct of despair could one force one's self into this old thicket of ignorance after having been repulsed at a score of entrances more promising and more popular. Thus far, no path had led anywhere, unless perhaps to an exceedingly modest living. Forty-five years of study had proved to be quite futile for the pursuit of power; one controlled no more force in 1900 than in 1850, although the amount of force controlled by society had enormously increased. The secret of education still hid itself somewhere behind ignorance, and one fumbled over it as feebly as ever. In such labyrinths, the staff is a force almost more necessary than the legs; the pen becomes a sort of blind-man's dog, to keep him from falling into the gutters. The pen works for itself, and acts like a hand, modelling the plastic material over and over again to the form that suits it best. The form is never arbitrary, but is a sort of growth like crystallization, as

---

38. **From Zeno . . . 1860:** Adams was a student in Germany from 1858 to 1860. Here, he mentions the diverse thinkers and writers he later studied: the Greek philosopher Zeno of Cithium (366–264 BCE), the founder of Stoicism; René Descartes (1596–1650), French philosopher and mathematician said to be the inventor of analytic geometry; the Scholastic Catholic theologian Thomas Aquinas (c. 1225–1274), the subject of the final chapter of Adams's *Mont-Saint-Michel and Chartres* (1904); Michel Eyquem de Montaigne (1533–1592), skeptical French philosopher and writer famous for his personal essays; and Blaise Pascal (1623–1662), influential French mathematician and physicist who late in life turned to writing about philosophy and religion, strongly defending the Christian faith.

any artist knows too well; for often the pencil or pen runs into side-paths and shapeless-ness, loses its relations, stops or is bogged. Then it has to return on its trail, and recover, if it can, its line of force. The result of a year's work depends more on what is struck out than on what is left in; on the sequence of the main lines of thought, than on their play or variety. Compelled once more to lean heavily on this support, Adams covered more thousands of pages with figures as formal as though they were algebra, laboriously striking out, altering, burning, experimenting, until the year had expired, the Exposition had long been closed, and winter drawing to its end, before he sailed from Cherbourg, on January 19, 1901, for home.

[1907, 1918]

Mary Antin

[1881-1949]

Mary Antin was born Maryashe Antin in Polotzk, Russia, on June 13, 1881, the second of four children born to Esther and Israel Antin. Beginning with the reign of Czar Alexander II in the mid-nineteenth century and continuing under the reigns of Alexander III and Nicolas II, life for Jewish families was extremely difficult in Russia. Anti-Jewish riots, or "pogroms," were common, and the government passed discriminatory laws limiting the access of Jews to education and narrowly restricting the areas in which they could live in Russia. Even within that "Pale of Settlement," where the Antins lived, Jews were subjected to harassment and attacks, as well as to the forced induction of young Jewish boys into the Russian army. As a result, hundreds of thousands of Jews immigrated to western Europe and the United States. Like many Jewish men, Israel Antin went ahead of his family to find a job and a place to live, leaving for Boston in 1891. Trained in Russia as a rabbi, and having worked there in the family business, he was ill suited to the menial jobs available to immigrants. Israel Antin nonetheless believed that his family's future would be more secure in the United States, so he sent for his wife and children, who arrived in Boston in 1894.

Residing in various "wrong ends" of the city, as Antin later described the slum areas occupied by immigrants, the family struggled economically but took advantage of free education in Boston. To help support the family, Antin's older sister went to work in a garment factory, or "sweatshop." Antin and her two younger siblings were enrolled in the Chelsea Public School. A gifted student, Antin completed the first four grades in half of a school year, and she soon began to win prizes for her writing. Her first publication was "Snow," an essay printed in *Primary Education* in 1893. Antin's teacher sent it to the journal, noting, "This is the uncorrected paper of a Russian child twelve years old, who had studied English only

Mary Antin
This photograph of Antin, holding the flag and talking to a group of schoolchildren, was taken in 1916, four years after the publication of her popular autobiography, *The Promised Land.*

four months." Antin's second publication was a poem on George Washington, which appeared in the *Boston Herald* in 1895. Her success at school and her writing skills gained her the attention of caseworkers at the Hebrew Immigrant Aid Society, through whom Antin met Josephine Lazarus (the sister of the poet Emma Lazarus) and the writer and Jewish leader Israel Zangwill. Deeply impressed by a letter about her family's life in the United States that Antin had written to an uncle in Russia, Zangwill encouraged her to translate it from Yiddish into English. He also helped arrange for its publication as *From Plotsk to Boston* (the name of Antin's birthplace in Russia was misspelled), a pamphlet that appeared in 1899. While she was in high school, Antin worked as a secretary to Amadeus William Grabau, a German immigrant who had become a geology professor at Columbia University. They married in 1901, and Antin left school and moved with her husband to New York City.

Although she took some courses there, Antin did not complete a degree. Instead, she devoted herself to writing, especially to work on an autobiography focusing on her experiences as an immigrant in the United States. By 1910, Antin had completed much of the manuscript of a book she thought to call "The Making of an American." But she discovered that the title had already been taken by the Danish immigrant Jacob Riis, an influential photojournalist and author of a series of muckraking books on life in the slums of New York City, as well as his autobiography, *The Making of an American* (1901). Antin therefore called her autobiography *The Promised Land*, a resonant phrase suggesting that for Jewish immigrants the land God promised the ancient Israelites was now the new promised land of America. Published in installments in the *Atlantic Monthly* before it appeared in book form in 1912, *The Promised Land* was an immediate success, ultimately going through thirty-four printings and selling eighty-five thousand copies. In her introduction, Antin announces her central theme, the transformation of an immigrant into an American: "I was born, I have lived, and I have been made over." Indeed, the success of her book was in large part due to her positive message about the reality and her own realization of the American dream. At the end of her account, Antin thus proclaims: "America is the youngest of the nations and inherits all that went before in history. And I am the youngest of America's children, and into my hands is given all her priceless heritage, to the last white star espied through the telescope, to the last great thought of the philosopher. Mine is the whole majestic past, and mine is the shining future."

The success of *The Promised Land* did indeed provide Antin with a "shining future," but only for a short time. She swiftly became a public figure, writing articles for numerous periodicals and delivering lectures across the country about her own experiences and on the broader subject of immigration. Challenging efforts to restrict immigration, Antin published *They Who Knock at Our Gates, A Complete Gospel of Immigration* (1914), in which she affirms the vital contributions immigrants made to the success of the United States. She also became a fervent supporter of Zionism, the movement to establish a Jewish homeland in Palestine. During World War I, she supported the Allies, but her husband strongly supported Germany. After the United States entered the war in 1917, his pro-German stance and statements led to his dismissal from his position at Columbia. Under increasing emotional and financial pressures, the couple separated. Antin began to suffer from an unidentified mental illness, possibly bipolar disorder, which eventually led to her residence at the Austen Riggs Psychiatric Center in Massachusetts in the early 1920s. Although she kept up an extensive correspondence and sporadically sought to resume her literary career, Antin published little during the last two decades of her life. Her final published work was "House of the Father" (1941), an essay in which she affirms her identity as both a Jew and an American. After a battle with cancer, Antin died at a nursing home on May 15, 1949.

bedfordstmartins.com/ americanlit for research links on Antin

Antin's *The Promised Land.* In June 1911, Antin began to correspond with Ellery Sedgwick, the editor of the *Atlantic Monthly*, who had accepted one of her short stories and expressed an interest in publishing her autobiography. Although she was drawn to the prestige of appearing in the prominent magazine, Antin was determined that serial publication would not deprive her of a larger audience. "I can assure you, I am not aiming at

Mashke and Fetchke

Taken when they were small children in Russia, this photograph of Antin and her older sister, whose names were changed to Mary and Frieda after they arrived in the United States, was used as the frontispiece of *The Promised Land.*

the pages of the *Atlantic Monthly*," she wrote to Sedgwick. "I am aiming, if you must know, at the heart of the world." After she received a book contract from Houghton Mifflin, the parent company of the *Atlantic*, the first part of her autobiography appeared in the magazine in October 1911 as "Within the Pale," an account of her early life in the "Pale of Settlement," the confined area in which Jews were forced to live in Russia. Six additional installments were published monthly from November 1911 through April 1912, after which the revised and expanded text was divided into twenty chapters and published as *The Promised Land*. Chapter VIII, "The Exodus," is an account of the six-week journey she, her mother, and her three siblings made from their home in Polotzk, Russia, by train to Hamburg, Germany, and from there by steamer to Boston, where they were reunited with her father, Israel Antin. In the following sections from chapter 9, "The Promised Land," Antin describes the family's early struggles in Boston, culminating in the day she and her two younger siblings were led to school by their father, who in the act of enrolling them "took possession of America." The text is taken from the first edition of *The Promised Land* (1912).

From The Promised Land

From Chapter IX

Having made such good time across the ocean, I ought to be able to proceed no less rapidly on *terra firma*, where, after all, I am more at home. And yet here is where I falter. Not that I hesitated, even for the space of a breath, in my first steps in America. There was no time to hesitate. The most ignorant immigrant, on landing, proceeds to give and receive greetings, to eat, sleep, and rise, after the manner of his own country; wherein he is corrected, admonished, and laughed at, whether by interested friends or the most indifferent strangers; and his American experience is thus begun. The process is spontaneous on all sides, like the education of the child by the family circle. But while the most stupid nursery maid is able to contribute her part toward the result, we do not expect an analysis of the process to be furnished by any member of the family, least of all by the engaging infant. The philosophical maiden aunt alone, or some other witness equally psychological and aloof, is able to trace the myriad efforts by which the little Johnnie or Nellie acquires a secure hold on the disjointed parts of the huge plaything, life.

Now I was not exactly an infant when I was set down, on a May day some fifteen years ago, in this pleasant nursery of America. I had long since acquired the use of my faculties, and had collected some bits of experience, practical and emotional, and had even learned to give an account of them. Still, I had very little perspective, and my observations and comparisons were superficial. I was too much carried away to analyze the forces that were moving me. My Polotzk I knew well before I began to judge it and experiment with it. America was bewilderingly strange, unimaginably complex, delightfully unexplored. I rushed impetuously out of the cage of my provincialism and looked eagerly about the brilliant universe. My question was, What have we here? – not, What does this mean? That query came much later. When I now become retrospectively introspective, I fall into the predicament of the centipede in the rhyme, who got along very smoothly until he was asked which leg came after which, whereupon he became so rattled that he couldn't take a step. I know I have come on a thousand feet, on wings, winds, and American machines, – I have leaped and run and climbed and crawled, – but to tell which step came after which I find a puzzling matter. Plenty of maiden aunts were present during my second infancy, in the guise of immigrant officials, school-teachers, settlement workers, and sundry other unprejudiced and critical observers. Their statistics I might properly borrow to fill the gaps in my recollections, but I am prevented by my sense of harmony. The individual, we know, is a creature unknown to the statistician; whereas I undertook to give the personal view of everything. So I am bound to unravel, as well as I can, the tangle of events, outer and inner, which made up the first breathless years of my American life.

During his three years of probation, my father had made a number of false starts in business. His history for that period is the history of thousands who come to America, like him, with pockets empty, hands untrained to the use of tools, minds cramped by centuries of repression in their native land. Dozens of these men pass under your eyes every day, my American friend, too absorbed in their honest affairs to notice the looks of suspicion which you cast at them, the repugnance with which you shrink from their touch. You see them shuffle from door to door with a basket of spools and buttons, or bending over the sizzling irons in a basement tailor shop, or rummaging in your ash can, or moving a pushcart from curb to curb, at the command of the burly policeman. "The Jew peddler!" you say, and dismiss him from your premises and from your thoughts, never dreaming that the sordid drama of his days may have a moral that concerns you. What if the creature with the untidy beard carries in his bosom his citizenship papers? What if the cross-legged tailor is supporting a boy in college who is one day going to mend your state constitution for you? What if the ragpicker's daughters are hastening over the ocean to teach your children in the public schools? Think, every time you pass the greasy alien on the street, that he was born thousands of years before the oldest native American; and he may have something to communicate to you, when you two shall have learned a common language. Remember that his very physiognomy is a cipher the key to which it behooves you to search for most diligently.

By the time we joined my father, he had surveyed many avenues of approach toward the coveted citadel fortune. One of these, heretofore untried, he now proposed to essay, armed with new courage, and cheered on by the presence of his family. In partnership with an energetic little man who had an English chapter in his history, he prepared to set up a refreshment booth on Crescent Beach. But while he was completing arrangements at the beach we remained in town, where we enjoyed the educational advantages of a thickly populated neighborhood; namely, Wall Street, in the West End of Boston.

Anybody who knows Boston knows that the West and North Ends are the wrong ends of that city. They form the tenement district, or, in the newer phrase, the slums of Boston. Anybody who is acquainted with the slums of any American metropolis knows that that is the quarter where poor immigrants foregather, to live, for the most part, as unkempt, half-washed, toiling, unaspiring foreigners; pitiful in the eyes of social missionaries, the despair of boards of health, the hope of ward politicians, the touchstone of American democracy. The well-versed metropolitan knows the slums as a sort of house of detention for poor aliens, where they live on probation till they can show a certificate of good citizenship.

He may know all this and yet not guess how Wall Street, the West End, appears in the eyes of a little immigrant from Polotzk. What would the sophisticated sight-seer say about Union Place, off Wall Street, where my new home waited for me? He would say that it is no place at all, but a short box of an alley. Two rows of three-story tenements are its sides, a stingy strip of sky is its lid, a littered pavement is the floor, and a narrow mouth its exit.

But I saw a very different picture on my introduction to Union Place. I saw two imposing rows of brick buildings, loftier than any dwelling I had ever lived in. Brick was even on the ground for me to tread on, instead of common earth or boards. Many friendly windows stood open, filled with uncovered heads of women and children. I thought the people were interested in us, which was very neighborly. I looked up to the topmost row of windows, and my eyes were filled with the May blue of an American sky!

In our days of affluence in Russia we had been accustomed to upholstered parlors, embroidered linen, silver spoons and candlesticks, goblets of gold, kitchen shelves shining with copper and brass. We had featherbeds heaped halfway to the ceiling; we had clothes presses dusky with velvet and silk and fine woollen. The three small rooms into which my father now ushered us, up one flight of stairs, contained only the necessary beds, with lean mattresses; a few wooden chairs; a table or two; a mysterious iron structure, which later turned out to be a stove; a couple of unornamental kerosene lamps; and a scanty array of cooking-utensils and crockery. And yet we were impressed with our new home and its furniture. It was not only because we had just passed through our seven lean years, cooking in earthen vessels, eating black bread on holidays and wearing cotton; it was chiefly because these wooden chairs and tin pans were American chairs and pans that they shone glorious in our eyes. And if there was anything lacking for comfort or decoration we expected it to be presently supplied — at least, we children did. Perhaps my mother alone, of us newcomers, appreciated the shabbiness of the little apartment, and realized that for her there was as yet no laying down of the burden of poverty.

Our initiation into American ways began with the first step on the new soil. My father found occasion to instruct or correct us even on the way from the pier to Wall Street, which journey we made crowded together in a rickety cab. He told us not to lean out of the windows, not to point, and explained the word "greenhorn." We did not want to be "greenhorns," and gave the strictest attention to my father's instructions. I do not know when my parents found opportunity to review together the history of Polotzk in the three years past, for we children had no patience with the subject; my mother's narrative was constantly interrupted by irrelevant questions, interjections, and explanations.

The first meal was an object lesson of much variety. My father produced several kinds of food, ready to eat, without any cooking, from little tin cans that had printing all over them. He attempted to introduce us to a queer, slippery kind of fruit, which he called "banana," but had to give it up for the time being. After the meal, he had better luck with a curious piece of furniture on runners, which he called "rocking-chair." There were five of us newcomers, and we found five different ways of getting into the American machine of perpetual motion, and as many ways of getting out of it. One born and bred to the use of a rocking-chair cannot imagine how ludicrous people can make themselves when attempting to use it for the first time. We laughed immoderately over our various experiments with the novelty, which was a wholesome way of letting off steam after the unusual excitement of the day.

In our flat we did not think of such a thing as storing the coal in the bathtub. There was no bathtub. So in the evening of the first day my father conducted us to the public baths. As we moved along in a little procession, I was delighted with the illumination of the streets. So many lamps, and they burned until morning, my father said, and so people did not need to carry lanterns. In America, then, everything was free, as we had heard in Russia. Light was free; the streets were as bright as a synagogue on a holy day. Music was free; we had been serenaded, to our gaping delight, by a brass band of many pieces, soon after our installation on Union Place.

Education was free. That subject my father had written about repeatedly, as comprising his chief hope for us children, the essence of American opportunity, the treasure that no thief could touch, not even misfortune or poverty. It was the one thing that he was able to promise us when he sent for us; surer, safer than bread or shelter. On our second day I was thrilled with the realization of what this freedom of education meant. A little girl from across the alley came and offered to conduct us to school. My father was out, but we five between us had a few words of English by this time. We knew the word school. We understood. This child, who had never seen us till yesterday, who could not pronounce our names, who was not much better dressed than we, was able to offer us the freedom of the schools of Boston! No application made, no questions asked, no examinations, rulings, exclusions; no machinations, no fees. The doors stood open for every one of us. The smallest child could show us the way.

This incident impressed me more than anything I had heard in advance of the freedom of education in America. It was a concrete proof — almost the thing itself. One had to experience it to understand it.

It was a great disappointment to be told by my father that we were not to enter upon our school career at once. It was too near the end of the term, he said, and we were going to move to Crescent Beach[1] in a week or so. We had to wait until the opening of the schools in September. What a loss of precious time — from May till September!

Not that the time was really lost. Even the interval on Union Place was crowded with lessons and experiences. We had to visit the stores and be dressed from head to foot in American clothing; we had to learn the mysteries of the iron stove, the washboard, and the speaking-tube; we had to learn to trade with the fruit peddler through the window, and not to be afraid of the policeman; and, above all, we had to learn English.

The kind people who assisted us in these important matters form a group by themselves in the gallery of my friends. If I had never seen them from those early days till now, I should still have remembered them with gratitude. When I enumerate the long list of my American teachers, I must begin with those who came to us on Wall Street and taught us our first steps. To my mother, in her perplexity over the cookstove, the woman who showed her how to make the fire was an angel of deliverance. A fairy godmother to us children was she who led us to a wonderful country called "uptown," where, in a dazzlingly beautiful palace called a "department store," we exchanged our hateful home-made European costumes, which pointed us out as "greenhorns" to the children on the street, for real American machine-made garments, and issued forth glorified in each other's eyes.

With our despised immigrant clothing we shed also our impossible Hebrew names. A committee of our friends, several years ahead of us in American experience, put their heads together and concocted American names for us all. Those of our real names that had no pleasing American equivalents they ruthlessly discarded, content if they retained the initials. My mother, possessing a name that was not easily translatable,

---

1. **Crescent Beach:** A long, crescent-shaped beach facing Massachusetts Bay five miles north of Boston; it later became the Revere Beach Reservation, established in 1896 as the first public beach in the United States. Antin's father and his partner ran a refreshment stand there during the summer of 1894. After licensing problems and damage from a storm forced them to close the stand, Antin's family moved to Chelsea, an industrial city across the Mystic River from Boston.

was punished with the undignified nickname of Annie. Fetchke, Joseph, and Deborah issued as Frieda, Joseph, and Dora, respectively. As for poor me, I was simply cheated. The name they gave me was hardly new. My Hebrew name being Maryashe in full, Mashke for short, Russianized into Marya (*Mar-ya*), my friends said that it would hold good in English as *Mary*; which was very disappointing, as I longed to possess a strange-sounding American name like the others.

I am forgetting the consolation I had, in this matter of names, from the use of my surname, which I have had no occasion to mention until now. I found on my arrival that my father was "Mr. Antin" on the slightest provocation, and not, as in Polotzk, on state occasions alone. And so I was "Mary Antin," and I felt very important to answer to such a dignified title. It was just like America that even plain people should wear their surnames on week days.

As a family we were so diligent under instruction, so adaptable, and so clever in hiding our deficiencies, that when we made the journey to Crescent Beach, in the wake of our small wagon-load of household goods, my father had very little occasion to admonish us on the way, and I am sure he was not ashamed of us. So much we had achieved toward our Americanization during the two weeks since our landing.

•   •   •

In Polotzk we had supposed that "America" was practically synonymous with "Boston." When we landed in Boston, the horizon was pushed back, and we annexed Crescent Beach. And now, espying other lands of promise, we took possession of the province of Chelsea, in the name of our necessity.

In Chelsea, as in Boston, we made our stand in the wrong end of the town. Arlington Street was inhabited by poor Jews, poor Negroes, and a sprinkling of poor Irish. The side streets leading from it were occupied by more poor Jews and Negroes. It was a proper locality for a man without capital to do business. My father rented a tenement with a store in the basement. He put in a few barrels of flour and of sugar, a few boxes of crackers, a few gallons of kerosene, an assortment of soap of the "save the coupon" brands; in the cellar, a few barrels of potatoes, and a pyramid of kindling-wood; in the showcase, an alluring display of penny candy. He put out his sign, with a gilt-lettered warning of "Strictly Cash," and proceeded to give credit indiscriminately. That was the regular way to do business on Arlington Street. My father, in his three years' apprenticeship, had learned the tricks of many trades. He knew when and how to "bluff." The legend of "Strictly Cash" was a protection against notoriously irresponsible customers; while none of the "good" customers, who had a record for paying regularly on Saturday, hesitated to enter the store with empty purses.

If my father knew the tricks of the trade, my mother could be counted on to throw all her talent and tact into the business. Of course she had no English yet, but as she could perform the acts of weighing, measuring, and mental computation of fractions mechanically, she was able to give her whole attention to the dark mysteries of the language, as intercourse with her customers gave her opportunity. In this she made such rapid progress that she soon lost all sense of disadvantage, and conducted herself behind the counter very much as if she were back in her old store in Polotzk. It was far more cosey than Polotzk — at least, so it seemed to me; for behind the store was the kitchen, where, in the intervals of slack trade, she did her cooking and washing. Arlington Street customers were used to waiting while the storekeeper salted the soup or rescued a loaf from the oven.

Once more Fortune favored my family with a thin little smile, and my father, in reply to a friendly inquiry, would say, "One makes a living," with a shrug of the shoulders that added "but nothing to boast of." It was characteristic of my attitude toward bread-and-butter matters that this contented me, and I felt free to devote myself to the conquest of my new world. Looking back to those critical first years, I see myself always behaving like a child let loose in a garden to play and dig and chase the butterflies. Occasionally, indeed, I was stung by the wasp of family trouble; but I knew a healing ointment – my faith in America. My father had come to America to make a living. America, which was free and fair and kind, must presently yield him what he sought. I had come to America to see a new world, and I followed my own ends with the utmost assiduity; only, as I ran out to explore, I would look back to see if my house were in order behind me – if my family still kept its head above water.

In after years, when I passed as an American among Americans, if I was suddenly made aware of the past that lay forgotten, – if a letter from Russia, or a paragraph in the newspaper, or a conversation overheard in the street-car, suddenly reminded me of what I might have been, – I thought it miracle enough that I, Mashke, the granddaughter of Raphael the Russian, born to a humble destiny, should be at home in an American metropolis, be free to fashion my own life, and should dream my dreams in English phrases. But in the beginning my admiration was spent on more concrete embodiments of the splendors of America; such as fine houses, gay shops, electric engines and apparatus, public buildings, illuminations, and parades. My early letters to my Russian friends were filled with boastful descriptions of these glories of my new country. No native citizen of Chelsea took such pride and delight in its institutions as I did. It required no fife and drum corps, no Fourth of July procession, to set me tingling with patriotism. Even the common agents and instruments of municipal life, such as the letter carrier and the fire engine, I regarded with a measure of respect. I know what I thought of people who said that Chelsea was a very small, dull, unaspiring town, with no discernible excuse for a separate name or existence.

The apex of my civic pride and personal contentment was reached on the bright September morning when I entered the public school. That day I must always remember, even if I live to be so old that I cannot tell my name. To most people their first day at school is a memorable occasion. In my case the importance of the day was a hundred times magnified, on account of the years I had waited, the road I had come, and the conscious ambitions I entertained.

I am wearily aware that I am speaking in extreme figures, in superlatives. I wish I knew some other way to render the mental life the immigrant child of reasoning age. I may have been ever so much an exception in acuteness of observation, powers of comparison, and abnormal self-consciousness; none the less were my thoughts and conduct typical of the attitude of the intelligent immigrant child toward American institutions. And what the child thinks and feels is a reflection of the hopes, desires, and purposes of the parents who brought him overseas, no matter how precocious and independent the child may be. Your immigrant inspectors will tell you what poverty the foreigner brings in his baggage, what want in his pockets. Let the overgrown boy of twelve, reverently drawing his letters in the baby class, testify to the noble dreams and high ideals that may be hidden beneath the greasy caftan of the immigrant. Speaking for the Jews, at least, I know I am safe in inviting such an investigation.

Who were my companions on my first day at school? Whose hand was in mine, as I stood, overcome with awe, by the teacher's desk, and whispered my name as my father prompted? Was it Frieda's steady, capable hand? Was it her loyal heart that throbbed, beat for beat with mine, as it had done through all our childish adventures? Frieda's heart did throb that day, but not with my emotions. My heart pulsed with joy and pride and ambition; in her heart longing fought with abnegation. For I was led to the school-room, with its sunshine and its singing and the teacher's cheery smile; while she was led to the workshop, with its foul air, care-lined faces, and the foreman's stern command. Our going to school was the fulfilment of my father's best promises to us, and Frieda's share in it was to fashion and fit the calico frocks in which the baby sister and I made our first appearance in a public schoolroom.

I remember to this day the gray pattern of the calico, so affectionately did I regard it as it hung upon the wall — my consecration robe awaiting the beatific day. And Frieda, I am sure, remembers it, too, so longingly did she regard it as the crisp, starchy breadths of it slid between her fingers. But whatever were her longings, she said nothing of them; she bent over the sewing-machine humming an Old-World melody. In every straight, smooth seam, perhaps, she tucked away some lingering impulse of childhood; but she matched the scrolls and flowers with the utmost care. If a sudden shock of rebellion made her straighten up for an instant, the next instant she was bending to adjust a ruffle to the best advantage. And when the momentous day arrived, and the little sister and I stood up to be arrayed, it was Frieda herself who patted and smoothed my stiff new calico; who made me turn round and round, to see that I was perfect; who stooped to pull out a disfiguring basting-thread. If there was anything in her heart besides sisterly love and pride and good-will, as we parted that morning, it was a sense of loss and a woman's acquiescence in her fate; for we had been close friends, and now our ways would lie apart. Longing she felt, but no envy. She did not grudge me what she was denied. Until that morning we had been children together, but now, at the fiat of her destiny, she became a woman, with all a woman's cares; whilst I, so little younger than she, was bidden to dance at the May festival of untroubled childhood.

I wish, for my comfort, that I could say that I had some notion of the difference in our lots, some sense of the injustice to her, of the indulgence to me. I wish I could even say that I gave serious thought to the matter. There had always been a distinction between us rather out of proportion to the difference in our years. Her good health and domestic instincts had made it natural for her to become my mother's right hand, in the years preceding the emigration, when there were no more servants or dependents. Then there was the family tradition that Mary was the quicker, the brighter of the two, and that hers could be no common lot. Frieda was relied upon for help, and her sister for glory. And when I failed as a milliner's apprentice, while Frieda made excellent progress at the dressmaker's, our fates, indeed, were sealed. It was understood, even before we reached Boston, that she would go to work and I to school. In view of the family prejudices, it was the inevitable course. No injustice was intended. My father sent us hand in hand to school, before he had ever thought of America. If, in America, he had been able to support his family unaided, it would have been the culmination of his best hopes to see all his children at school, with equal advantages at home. But when he had done his best, and was still unable to provide even bread and shelter for us all, he was compelled to make us children self-supporting as fast as it was practicable. There was no choosing possible; Frieda was the oldest, the strongest, the best prepared, and the only one who was of legal age to be put to work.

My father has nothing to answer for. He divided the world between his children in accordance with the laws of the country and the compulsion of his circumstances. I have no need of defending him. It is myself that I would like to defend, and I cannot. I remember that I accepted the arrangements made for my sister and me without much reflection, and everything that was planned for my advantage I took as a matter of course. I was no heartless monster, but a decidedly self-centred child. If my sister had seemed unhappy it would have troubled me; but I am ashamed to recall that I did not consider how little it was that contented her. I was so preoccupied with my own happiness that I did not half perceive the splendid devotion of her attitude towards me, the sweetness of her joy in my good luck. She not only stood by approvingly when I was helped to everything; she cheerfully waited on me herself. And I took everything from her hand as if it were my due.

The two of us stood a moment in the doorway of the tenement house on Arlington Street, that wonderful September morning when I first went to school. It was I that ran away, on winged feet of joy and expectation; it was she whose feet were bound in the treadmill of daily toil. And I was so blind that I did not see that the glory lay on her, and not on me.

Father himself conducted us to school. He would not have delegated that mission to the President of the United States. He had awaited the day with impatience equal to mine, and the visions he saw as he hurried us over the sun-flecked pavements transcended all my dreams. Almost his first act on landing on American soil, three years before, had been his application for naturalization. He had taken the remaining steps in the process with eager promptness, and at the earliest moment allowed by the law, he became a citizen of the United States. It is true that he had left home in search of bread for his hungry family, but he went blessing the necessity that drove him to America. The boasted freedom of the New World meant to him far more than the right to reside, travel, and work wherever he pleased; it meant the freedom to speak his thoughts, to throw off the shackles of superstition, to test his own fate, unhindered by political or religious tyranny. He was only a young man when he landed – thirty-two; and most of his life he had been held in leading-strings. He was hungry for his untasted manhood.

Three years passed in sordid struggle and disappointment. He was not prepared to make a living even in America, where the day laborer eats wheat instead of rye. Apparently

the American flag could not protect him against the pursuing Nemesis[2] of his limitations; he must expiate the sins of his fathers who slept across the seas. He had been
endowed at birth with a poor constitution, a nervous, restless temperament, and an
abundance of hindering prejudices. In his boyhood his body was starved, that his mind
might be stuffed with useless learning. In his youth this dearly gotten learning was
sold, and the price was the bread and salt which he had not been trained to earn for himself. Under the wedding canopy he was bound for life to a girl whose features were still
strange to him; and he was bidden to multiply himself, that sacred learning might be
perpetuated in his sons, to the glory of the God of his fathers. All this while he had been
led about as a creature without a will, a chattel, an instrument. In his maturity he
awoke, and found himself poor in health, poor in purse, poor in useful knowledge, and
hampered on all sides. At the first nod of opportunity he broke away from his prison,
and strove to atone for his wasted youth by a life of useful labor; while at the same time
he sought to lighten the gloom of his narrow scholarship by freely partaking of modern
ideas. But his utmost endeavor still left him far from his goal. In business, nothing prospered with him. Some fault of hand or mind or temperament led him to failure where
other men found success. Wherever the blame for his disabilities be placed, he reaped
their bitter fruit. "Give me bread!" he cried to America. "What will you do to earn it?" the
challenge came back. And he found that he was master of no art, of no trade; that even
his precious learning was of no avail, because he had only the most antiquated methods
of communicating it.

   So in his primary quest he had failed. There was left him the compensation of intellectual freedom. That he sought to realize in every possible way. He had very little opportunity to prosecute his education, which, in truth, had never been begun. His struggle
for a bare living left him no time to take advantage of the public evening school; but he
lost nothing of what was to be learned through reading, through attendance at public
meetings, through exercising the rights of citizenship. Even here he was hindered by a
natural inability to acquire the English language. In time, indeed, he learned to read, to
follow a conversation or lecture; but he never learned to write correctly, and his pronunciation remains extremely foreign to this day.

   If education, culture, the higher life were shining things to be worshipped from
afar, he had still a mean left whereby he could draw one step nearer to them. He could
send his children to school, to learn all those things that he knew by fame to be desirable. The common school, at least, perhaps high school; for one or two, perhaps even
college! His children should be students, should fill his house with books and intellectual company; and thus he would walk by proxy in the Elysian Fields[3] of liberal learning. As for the children themselves, he knew no surer way to their advancement and
happiness.

---

2. **Nemesis:** The spirit of divine retribution in Greek mythology, often personified as a relentless pursuing
goddess.
3. **Elysian Fields:** The paradise of the gods in Greek mythology.

So it was with a heart full of longing and hope that my father led us to school on that first day. He took long strides in his eagerness, the rest of us running and hopping to keep up.

At last the four of us stood around the teacher's desk; and my father, in his impossible English, gave us over in her charge, with some broken word of his hopes for us that his swelling heart could no longer contain. I venture to say that Miss Nixon was struck by something uncommon in the group we made, something outside of Semitic features and the abashed manner of the alien. My little sister was as pretty as a doll, with her clear pink-and-white face, short golden curls, and eyes like blue violets when you caught them looking up. My brother might have been a girl, too, with his cherubic contours of face, rich red color, glossy black hair, and fine eyebrows. Whatever secret fears were in his heart, remembering his former teachers, who had taught with the rod, he stood up straight and uncringing before the American teacher, his cap respectfully doffed. Next to him stood a starved-looking girl with eyes ready to pop out, and short dark curls that would not have made much of a wig for a Jewish bride.

All three children carried themselves rather better than the common run of "green" pupils that were brought to Miss Nixon. But the figure that challenged attention to the group was the tall, straight father, with his earnest face and fine forehead, nervous hands eloquent in gesture, and a voice full of feeling. This foreigner, who brought his children to school as if it were an act of consecration, who regarded the teacher of the primer class with reverence, who spoke of visions, like a man inspired, in a common schoolroom, was not like other aliens, who brought their children in dull obedience to the law; was not like the native fathers, who brought their unmanageable boys, glad to be relieved of their care. I think Miss Nixon guessed what my father's best English could not convey. I think she divined that by the simple act of delivering our school certificates to her he took possession of America.

[1912]

American Literature

1914–1945

ON MARCH 3, 1913, the day before Woodrow Wilson's inauguration for his first term as president, hundreds of thousands of the people gathered in the nation's capital witnessed a very different spectacle: the great "Woman Suffrage Procession." By then, women had gained the right to vote in only ten states, all of them in the Midwest and West. Impatient with the slow progress of the state-by-state campaign, many activists pressed for a renewed effort to gain passage of a women's suffrage amendment to the Constitution. In an effort to attract media attention to the cause, more than five thousand women from around the country marched down Pennsylvania Avenue from the Capitol past the White House. When the procession reached the Treasury Building, women and children presented an allegorical pageant to display "those ideals toward which both men and women have been struggling through the ages and toward which, in co-operation and equality, they will continue to strive." But the carefully organized and orchestrated event revealed the deep antagonism toward women's suffrage among many men in the country. Crowds of jeering men along the parade route blocked the marchers, more than one hundred of whom were taken to the local emergency room after being jostled, shoved, or tripped. In fact, the widely publicized treatment of the marchers and the failure of the police to intervene did more than the parade itself to generate support for the cause of women's suf-

◀ (OVERLEAF)

New York City

The architectural photographer Samuel H. Gottscho took this photograph of the financial district of Manhattan, framed by the Brooklyn Bridge, in 1934. The bridge connecting Brooklyn and Manhattan became a symbol of technological progress, and New York City emerged as the quintessential modern metropolis and a center of modernism during the period 1914-45.

"Woman Suffrage Procession"

Led by the lawyer and activist Inez Milholland, clad in a white cape and riding a white horse, most of the thousands of suffragists also wore white in their impressive parade in Washington, D.C. The marchers were accompanied by heralds, four mounted brigades, nine bands, and more than twenty floats, including the one pictured here, with its demand for a women's suffrage amendment to the Constitution.

frage in the United States. Nonetheless, it would take seven more years of demonstrations, parades, protests, and concerted political action before women gained the vote after Congress passed and the required thirty-six states ratified the Nineteenth Amendment in 1920.

Art and Society in the Era of the Great War

The intensifying struggle for women's suffrage demonstrated only one aspect of the social and cultural ferment in the United States during the period from the eve of World War I to 1920. In February 1913, only a month

COMPARATIVE TIMELINE, 1914–1945

Dates	American Literature	Historical Events	Developments in Culture, Science, and Technology
1914–1919	1914 Frost, *North of Boston* 1914 Pound publishes the poetry anthology *Des Imagistes* 1914 Stein, *Tender Buttons* 1914 Lowell, *Sword Blades and Poppy Seeds* 1914 Mena's "The Vine-Leaf" is published in *Century* 1915 Lowell publishes first of three poetry anthologies, *Some Imagist Poets* 1915 Pound, *Cathay* 1916 Glaspell, *Trifles* 1916 Sandburg, *Chicago Poems* 1916 H.D., *Sea Garden* 1917 Williams, *Al Que Quiere!* 1917 Eliot, *Prufrock and Other Observations* 1917 Millay, *Renascence and Other Poems*	1914 World War I begins in Europe 1914–30 More than one million African Americans join the Great Migration, moving from small towns in the South to cities in the North 1916 Wilson elected to second term as president 1917 United States declares war on Central Powers thus entering World War I 1917 Bolshevik Revolution in Russia 1917 Immigration acts exclude all Asian workers except Japanese	1914 Opening of Panama Canal 1914 Babe Ruth makes Major League debut with Red Sox 1914 First transcontinental phone call 1914 *Little Review, Smart Set, Blast, Vanity Fair,* and *New Republic* all begin publication 1914 W. C. Handy publishes "St. Louis Blues" 1915 Max Weber paints *Grand Central Terminal* 1915 Alfred Kreymborg founds *Others* 1916 Provincetown Players give first public performances 1916 *Seven Arts* founded 1917 Pulitzer Prizes established 1917 Original Dixieland Jazz Band makes first jazz recording

before the Woman Suffrage Procession in Washington and eighteen months before what contemporaries called the "Great War" began in Europe, the International Exhibition of Modern Art opened in New York City. Called the Armory Show because it was held in the Sixty-ninth Regiment Armory on Madison Avenue, the exhibition brought together a vast array of American and European art, including innovative works by Henri Matisse, the leader of the fauves ("wild beasts"), and Pablo Picasso, the central figure in the development of cubism. By the time the Armory Show finished its runs in New York, Chicago, and Boston, more than 300,000 Americans had viewed the exhibition. Most greeted the avant-garde art in the show with derision and hostility, as did many critics. In an editorial,

Dates	American Literature	Historical Events	Developments in Culture, Science, and Technology
1914–1919 (cont.)	1918 G. D. Johnson, *The Heart of a Woman*	1918 Armistice signed, ending World War I	
		1918 Eighteenth Amendment prohibits manufacture, sale, and transportation of alcohol	
		1918–19 Influenza pandemic kills between 20 and 40 million people worldwide	
	1919 Moore, *Observations*	1919 Race riots erupt across United States	1919 *Dial* is purchased by wealthy art patron Scofield Thayer
	1919 Anderson, *Winesburg, Ohio*	1919 Treaty of Versailles and formation of the League of Nations	1919 *Liberator* is founded by Max Eastman and other writers once associated with *Masses*
		1919 Steelworkers strike U.S. Steel	
1920–1929	1920 O'Neill, *The Emperor Jones*	1920 U.S. population: 105,710,620. Some 14,000,000 are foreign born and urban population exceeds rural population for first time	1920s Stein and Toklas host expatriate American artists and writers at their home in Paris
	1920 Millay, *A Few Figs from Thistles*	1920 "Red scare" prompts fears of Communists and foreign-born radicals	
	1920 Fitzgerald, *This Side of Paradise*	1920 Harding elected president	
		1920 Nineteenth Amendment grants women right to vote	

the influential *New York Times* ominously warned that cubism "is surely a part of the general movement, discernable all over the world, to disrupt and degrade, if not to destroy, not only art, but literature and society, too." But the exhibition exerted a profound impact on American artists and writers. Reviewing the Armory Show for the *Chicago Tribune* in April 1913, the art critic, editor, and poet Harriet Monroe observed that the rebellious European artists "represent a search for new beauty, impatience with formulae, a reaching out toward the inexpressible, a longing for new versions of truth."

As Monroe recognized, the Armory Show revealed a revolutionary spirit in the arts that had already begun to transform American literature. As

Dates	American Literature	Historical Events	Developments in Culture, Science, and Technology
1920–1929 (cont.)	1921 Fitzgerald, *Flappers and Philosophers* 1921 Dos Passos, *Three Soldiers* 1922 Eliot, *The Waste Land* 1922 Fitzgerald, *Tales of the Jazz Age* 1922 Millay, *The Harp-Weaver and Other Poems*, awarded Pulitzer Prize 1922 G. D. Johnson, *Bronze: A Book of Verse* 1922 McKay, *Harlem Shadows* 1922 Stein, *Geography and Plays* 1922 J. W. Johnson, *The Book of American Negro Poetry* 1923 Loy, *Lunar Baedecker* 1923 Frost, *New Hampshire*, awarded Pulitzer Prize 1923 Hemingway, *Three Stories and Ten Poems* 1923 Stevens, *Harmonium* 1923 Fujita, *Tanka: Poems in Exile* 1923 Cummings, *Tulips and Chimneys* 1923 Williams, *Spring and All* 1923 Toomer, *Cane*	1921 Emergency Quota Act temporarily restricts immigration from Europe 1923 Coolidge becomes president after Harding dies in office	1921 Regular radio broadcasts begin 1922 *Reader's Digest* founded 1922 James Joyce, *Ulysses* 1922 *Fugitive* and *Soil* founded 1922 Louis Armstrong joins Creole Jazz Band in Chicago 1923 *Time Magazine* established 1923 National Urban League founds *Opportunity* 1923 Former members of the Provincetown Players form Experimental Theatre

early as 1903, Gertrude Stein moved to Paris, where she became closely associated with artists such as Picasso, who painted her portrait in 1906. Stein subsequently began to undertake a series of radical experiments in prose, including the brief, nonrepresentational word-portraits "Matisse" and "Picasso." Stein's sketches were published in 1912 in a special issue of *Camera Work* (1903–17), an influential journal of modern art edited by Alfred Stieglitz in New York City. But the major developments in American literature in the years before World War I were in poetry. Ironically, the first center of a "new" American poetry was London, England, where the young expatriate Ezra Pound moved in 1908. In addition to publishing several volumes of his own poetry, Pound strongly supported the work of

Dates	American Literature	Historical Events	Developments in Culture, Science, and Technology
1920–1929 (cont.)		1924 First women governors elected in Wyoming and Texas	1924 Paul Whiteman, the "King of Jazz," commissions George Gershwin's *Rhapsody in Blue*
		1924 Indian Citizenship Act grants citizenship to Native Americans	
		1924 National Origins Act reduces quotas of immigrants from Europe and disallows immigration from Japan	
	1925 Hemingway, *In Our Time*	1925 John Scopes is convicted for violating state law forbidding teaching of evolution in Tennessee	1925 *New Yorker* is founded
	1925 Fitzgerald, *The Great Gatsby*		1925 *Grand Ole Opry* makes radio debut and eventually becomes longest-running live music show
	1925 Pound, *A Draft of XVI Cantos*		
	1925 Alain Locke publishes *The New Negro*, an anthology of the Harlem Renaissance		
	1925 Cullen, *Color*		
	1925 Cummings, *XLI Poems. &.*	1926 Ford introduces eight-hour, five-day work week	1926 Henry Scherman establishes Book-of-the-Month Club
	1926 Hemingway, *The Sun Also Rises*		
	1926 Crane, *White Buildings*		
	1926 Hughes, *The Weary Blues*		

other American poets, including H.D. (Hilda Doolittle), who settled in London in 1911, and Robert Frost. In a final effort to become a professional poet, Frost moved his family to London in 1912. With the help of Pound and other writers Frost met there, the New Englander whom many view as the most quintessentially "American" of modern poets published his first two volumes of poetry in London.

The literary situation that drove Frost to seek an audience for his work overseas spurred the creation of new outlets for writers in the United States. In 1912, a few months before Harriet Monroe wrote her review of the Armory Show, she founded *Poetry: A Magazine of Verse.* The magazine initially featured the innovative poetry of Pound, H.D., and other

Dates	American Literature	Historical Events	Developments in Culture, Science, and Technology
1920–1929 (cont.)	1926 Faulkner, *Soldier's Pay* 1927 J. W. Johnson, *God's Trombones* 1927 Cullen publishes *Caroling Dusk: An Anthology of Verse by Negro Poets*	1927 Italian immigrants Sacco and Vanzetti are executed in Massachusetts after being convicted of first-degree murder	1927 Duke Ellington's dance band begins performing at Harlem's Cotton Club 1927 First transatlantic telephone call 1927 Charles Lindbergh completes his solo, nonstop flight across Atlantic Ocean 1927 *The Jazz Singer* is first full-length "talkie" motion picture 1927 Ford introduces Model A car and ends production of successful Model T
	1928 Larsen, *Quicksand*	1928 Herbert Hoover elected president	1928 Penicillin discovered 1928-29 Erich Maria Remarque's best-selling *All Quiet on the Western Front* first published in Germany, then translated into English
	1929 Hemingway, *A Farewell to Arms* 1929 Cullen, *The Black Christ and Other Poems* 1929 Faulkner, *The Sound and the Fury*	1929 Stock market crash leads to decade-long depression in the United States and spreads worldwide	1929 More than ten million homes have radios 1929 Museum of Modern Art opens in New York City 1929 More than 40 percent of young people attend high school and a million students are enrolled in college
1930–1939	1930-36 Dos Passos, *U.S.A.* trilogy 1930 Crane, *The Bridge*	1930 U.S. population: 122,775,046	1930 Aaron Douglas paints Symbolic Negro History Series at Fisk University

"imagists," whose work inspired Amy Lowell to join the movement and to edit three collections of imagist poetry between 1915 and 1917. The first professionally published verse by a wide range of poets also appeared in *Poetry*, including that of Carl Sandburg, T. S. Eliot, and the Japanese-born Jun Fujita, who moved to Chicago in 1915. Generally regarded as the first of the "little magazines," small-circulation literary magazines featuring the experimental work of little-known writers, *Poetry* inspired others to begin similar ventures. In the spring of 1914, Margaret Anderson founded an even more progressive journal of the arts in Chicago, the *Little Review*, which published under the banner, "Making No Compromises with Public Taste." True to those words, Anderson and her companion and coeditor, Jane Heap,

Dates	American Literature	Historical Events	Developments in Culture, Science, and Technology
1930–1939 (cont.)	1930 Porter, *Flowering Judas and Other Stories* 1930 Larson's "Sanctuary" appears in *Forum* 1930 Twelve Southerners, *I'll Take My Stand* 1931 Hughes, *Scottsboro Limited* 1931 Faulkner, *These 13*	1931 Nine African American teenagers are convicted of rape, igniting a legal and political campaign to "Free the Scottsboro Boys" 	1930 Sinclair Lewis becomes first American to be awarded Nobel Prize for Literature 1931 "The Star Spangled Banner" becomes official national anthem 1931 Empire State Building opens 1931 *Story* magazine founded
	1932 Brown, *Southern Road* 	1932 Franklin D. Roosevelt elected president	1932 San Francisco Opera House opens 1932 Amelia Earhart is first woman to complete a solo, nonstop flight across Atlantic Ocean.
	1933 Hurston's "The Gilded Six-Bits" appears in *Story* 1933 Stein, *The Autobiography of Alice B. Toklas* 	1933-37 Roosevelt's New Deal programs include social security, welfare, and unemployment insurance 1933 Nazis stage massive public book burnings 1933 Twenty-first Amendment ends Prohibition 1934 Adolf Hitler becomes Führer of Germany 1934-39 Dust Bowl in Midwest	1933 *Newsweek* founded 1933 Albert Einstein arrives in United States as refugee from Nazi Germany 1934 Apollo Theater opens in Harlem

were later convicted of publishing obscenity for printing a serialization of James Joyce's novel *Ulysses*. "Who were the bourgeoisie?" the journalist and writer Ben Hecht asked. "Anyone who didn't read the *Little Review*."

During the second decade of the twentieth century, Chicago became what the influential editor and critic H. L. Mencken hailed as "The Literary Capital of the United States." Another literary center and the undisputed capital of bohemian life was Greenwich Village, an area on the Lower West Side of Manhattan. After moving there from Iowa in 1914, the writers Susan Glaspell and George Cram Cook, her husband, became deeply interested in the experimental theater pioneered by the recently created Washington Square Players. Along with friends from Greenwich

Dates	American Literature	Historical Events	Developments in Culture, Science, and Technology
1930–1939 (cont.)	1935 Stevens, *Ideas of Order* 1935 Moore, *Selected Poems*	1935 Harlem race riot 1935 Wagner Act protects workers' rights to form unions and bargain collectively	1935 Federal Writers' Project established as part of Works Project Administration (WPA)
	1936 Mitchell, *Gone with the Wind* 1936 Faulkner, *Absalom, Absalom!* 1936 Sandburg, *The People, Yes*	1936 Roosevelt reelected president 1936-39 Spanish civil war	1936 Dorothea Lange's photograph *Migrant Mother* 1936 Birth control legalized 1936 Hoover Dam completed 1936 *Life* magazine founded 1936 O'Neill awarded Nobel Prize for Literature
	1937 Frost, *A Farther Range*, awarded Pulitzer Prize 1937 Hurston, *Their Eyes Were Watching God*		
	1938 Steinbeck's "Flight" appears in *The Long Valley* 1938 Wright, *Uncle Tom's Children*		1938 Ballpoint pen invented
	1939 Steinbeck, *The Grapes of Wrath*, awarded Pulitzer Prize 1939 Faulkner's "Barn Burning" appears in *Harper's*	1939 New York World's Fair 1939-45 World War II and the Holocaust	1939 *The Wizard of Oz* premieres at Capital Theater in New York City 1939 Pocket Books begin publication
1940–1945	1940 Hemingway, *For Whom the Bell Tolls*	1940 U.S. population: 131,669,275	1940 Color television invented

Village who spent their summers in Provincetown, Massachusetts, Cook and Glaspell formed a small theater group, the Provincetown Players, in 1915. Performing plays by Glaspell, the then-unknown Eugene O'Neill, and many other young dramatists and writers, the Provincetown Players revolutionized theater in the United States. Bohemian life in Greenwich Village was also energized by artists from abroad, including the French painter Marcel Duchamp, whose *Nude Descending a Staircase* had created an uproar at the Armory Show, and the expatriate English painter and poet Mina Loy, who had lived in Paris and Florence before coming to New York in 1916. Loy and American poets such as Marianne Moore, Wallace Stevens, and William Carlos Williams found a ready outlet for

Dates	American Literature	Historical Events	Developments in Culture, Science, and Technology
1940–1945 (cont.)		1940 Beginning of second Great Migration of African Americans from South to cities in North and West	
	1940 Wright, *Native Son*		
	1941 Welty, *A Curtain of Green and Other Stories*	1941 United States enters World War II following Japanese attack on Pearl Harbor	1941 Development of Z3, first computer controlled by software
	1941 Reznikoff, *Going To and Fro and Walking Up and Down*	1941 Roosevelt's "Four Freedoms" speech	1941 Development of bop or bebop as offshoot of jazz
	1942 Hughes, *Shakespeare in Harlem*		1942–43 Victory Book Campaign provides millions of books to soldiers
			1942–45 Publication of paperback American Service Editions
	1943 Eliot, *Four Quartets*		
	1943 Welty, *The Wide Net and Other Stories*		
	1944 Porter, *The Leaning Tower and Other Stories*	1944 Roosevelt reelected president	
	1944 Williams, *The Wedge*	1944 D day: Allied invasion of Normandy, France	
	1944 Bulosan's "The End of the War" appears in the *New Yorker*		
		1945 Truman becomes president after death of Roosevelt	
		1945 United States drops atomic bombs on Hiroshima and Nagasaki; Japan surrenders, ending World War II	

Marcel Duchamp,
***Nude Descending
a Staircase, No. 2***

Duchamp's 1912 work was
the most controversial
among the 1,250 paint-
ings, sculptures, and
pieces of decorative art
exhibited at the Armory
Show. Conservative view-
ers were shocked and
outraged by the cubist
painting, which one critic
described as "an explo-
sion in a shingle factory."

their innovative work in a slew of avant-garde magazines published in
Greenwich Village, especially *Others: A Magazine of the New Verse*, whose
motto was, "The Old Expressions Are with Us Always / And There Are
Always Others."

For many writers, artistic innovation went hand in hand with revolutionary politics. The most prominent outlet for the radical intellectual
community was the *Masses*, founded in Greenwich Village in 1911 as "A
Monthly Magazine Devoted to the Interests of the Working People." Although it published poetry and fiction, the *Masses* sought to promote
social and economic change primarily through articles and editorials.
Plotting an equivalent revolution in the arts, James Oppenheim,
Waldo Frank, and Paul Rosenfield established the *Seven Arts*
in 1916. As Oppenheim later recalled, "we were wild enough to
believe that the artists and critics could dominate America."
In an essay "America in the Arts," published in the first issue of
the magazine, the radical French writer and pacifist Romain

*We were wild enough to
believe that the artists and
critics could dominate
America.*

Provincetown Playhouse

After two successful seasons at their first home in Greenwich Village, a small space in an unheated brownstone, the Provincetown Players rented and renovated this building, an old stable that had recently been used as a bottling plant, at 133 McDougal Street.

Rolland insisted that artists all across the United States "must dare to express themselves, freely, sincerely, entirely, in art. . . . They must be careless of form. They must be fearless of opinion." One writer who embraced that credo was the Chicago-based novelist Sherwood Anderson, who had recently published several experimental stories about life in a small midwestern town in the *Little Review* and the *Masses*. Anderson subsequently became the most frequent contributor to the *Seven Arts*, where four more of the interrelated stories appeared before he collected them as *Winesburg, Ohio*, published in 1919.

By then, both the *Masses* and the *Seven Arts* had succumbed to the jingoism and anti-German hysteria that swept the country during World War I. The United States maintained an official policy of neutrality after the war began in August 1914, pitting the Allied Powers — led by Great Britain, France, Russia, and later Italy — against the Central Powers — led by Germany, Austria-Hungary, and the Ottoman Empire. Max Eastman, the Marxist editor of the *Masses*, attacked both sides in the conflict, which he and many other radicals viewed as an inevitable result of Western

The *Masses*

The left-wing magazine published the work of many radical writers and visual artists, including Robert Minor, who provided the cover illustration for this 1916 issue devoted to President Wilson's policy of "preparedness." Although Wilson won reelection in 1916 on the slogan "He kept us out of the war," he had already begun a military buildup that many believed would inevitably lead to the country's entry into World War I.

imperialism and the competitive capitalist system. After the United States declared war on the Central Powers in April 1917, the *Masses* continued to oppose the war, as did the *Seven Arts*, which published a series of pacifist essays by the radical cultural critic Randolph Bourne. The *New-York Tribune* consequently branded the *Seven Arts* as "an enemy within," and the magazine folded after its major financial backer withdrew her support. The *Masses* was forced to cease publication after it was banned from the mails for violating the Espionage Act, which gave the postal service the authority to revoke the mailing privilege of any newspaper or magazine that published material critical of the war effort. In July 1917, Eastman and several of his colleagues were indicted under the act. The jury in the first trial was hopelessly deadlocked, and the jury in the second trial voted to acquit them in October 1918, a month before the armistice ended hostilities in World War I.

Because of its late entry into the war, the United States was spared the full brunt of the catastrophic conflict. Total military casualties in the war exceeded thirty million, including nearly ten million dead or missing. Russia, which pulled out of the war following the Bolshevik Revolution of 1917, suffered the largest number of casualties, nearly seven million. It was followed by Germany, France, and Austria-Hungary, all with more than five million, and Great Britain, with three million. Ezra Pound, who observed the war at close range from his vantage point in London and lost some of his closest English friends in the fighting on the western front, wrote an epitaph for a generation of men in his poem "Hugh Selwyn Mauberly" (1920). Remembering those who "walked knee deep in hell," the soldiers who had experienced the horrors of trench warfare in France, Pound bitterly declared:

> There died a myriad,
> And of the best, among them,
> For an old bitch gone in the teeth,
> For a botched civilization.

Pound's revulsion from the war, which he believed exposed the bankrupt values and debased culture of the civilization that had given rise to the conflict, was shared by many writers on both sides of the Atlantic. Certainly, the war profoundly shaped the attitudes and work of the American writers who emerged during the following decade, including Ernest Hemingway, who was seriously wounded while serving in an ambulance corps in Italy. Compared with the appalling losses in Europe, however, American casualties were relatively light: Of the 3.5 million men mobilized in the United States, roughly 70,000 died or were missing in action and 190,000 were wounded, amounting to less than 2 percent of the total military casualties in World War I.

Ironically, the end of hostilities marked the beginning of one of the darkest years in American history. As the war began to wind down in Europe in the fall of 1918, a virulent strain of influenza erupted, the beginning of a pandemic that killed between 20 and 40 million people worldwide during 1918–19. The disease affected over 25 percent of the American population, causing the deaths of more than 600,000 people, almost ten times the number of American soldiers who died during World War I. The pandemic left many families and neighborhoods shattered, and the country was further convulsed by labor strife. There were thousands of strikes in 1919, the largest of which was mounted by 350,000 recently organized workers against the United States Steel Corporation. They failed to gain any concessions, partly because many Americans viewed the predominantly foreign-born strikers as "alien" revolutionaries in league with the Bolsheviks in Russia. The labor agitation fueled the "Red scare," a period of antiradical hysteria during which Attorney General A. Mitchell Palmer led raids on labor unions and other leftist organizations, arresting more than 4,000 alleged Communists.

Many white Americans also believed that "Bolshevik" agitation among African Americans was the cause of growing racial tensions in the United States. More than 700,000 African American men registered for military service and 380,000 served during World War I. They hoped that by fighting for their country they might earn their full rights as citizens. Instead, the recruits found themselves in segregated military units and often assigned to labor battalions. When they returned home, they found racial prejudice and segregation unabated, in the North and the South. During what became known as the "Red Summer" of 1919, race riots erupted in numerous towns and cities, including Charleston, South Carolina; Washington, D.C.; Omaha, Nebraska; East St. Louis, Illinois; and Chicago. In contrast to earlier riots, this time African Americans fought back against white mobs. The militant mood of African Americans was most forcefully expressed by the Jamaican immigrant Claude McKay in his poem "If We Must Die." First published in the *Liberator*, founded in 1919 by Max Eastman and other writers who had earlier been associated with the *Masses*, McKay's call to arms was reprinted in African American newspapers all across the United States.

American Culture in the 1920s

The upheavals of 1919 revealed the strains created by sweeping changes in American society during and immediately after World War I. According to the census of 1920, nearly 14 million of the roughly 106 million people in the country were foreign born. Although immigration from Europe declined during the war, between 1910 and 1920 the population of the country was swelled by 890,000 immigrants fleeing the political and economic turmoil of the Mexican Revolution. The influx generated stronger cultural connections between artists in the United States and Mexico. It also created a market for stories about the country by María Cristina Mena, the first Mexican American woman writer to publish in a major magazine in the United States, and later for the work of writers such as the Texas-born Katherine Anne Porter. But there was widespread bias against immigrants from Mexico, as well as against those from southern and eastern Europe, most of them Catholic, who were virtually excluded from the country by a series of restrictive immigration laws passed in the early 1920s. As the deeply conservative president Calvin Coolidge decreed in his State of the Union address in 1923, "America must be kept American." The shortage of workers in northern factories created by the decline in immigration from Europe created new job opportunities for African Americans seeking escape from Jim Crow laws, racial violence, and a depressed rural economy in the South. From roughly 1914 to 1930, as many as 1.5 million African Americans joined the "Great Migration," creating the first large urban black communities in cities such as Chicago, Cleveland, Detroit, and New York.

The migration gave rise to what the poet Langston Hughes described as "Manhattan's black Renaissance," a remarkable flowering of African American art, literature, and music beginning in the early 1920s. At the

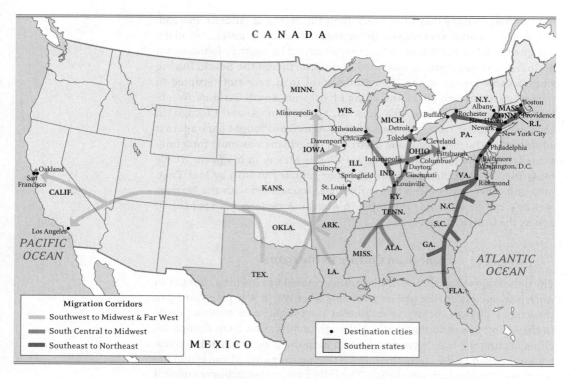

The Great Migration, 1914–30

This map illustrates the main corridors along which as many as 1.5 million African Americans moved from the rural South to cities in the East, Midwest, and West during what is known as the first Great Migration, which lasted from roughly the beginning of World War I in Europe to the onset of the Great Depression.

time, most of those involved in the cultural upsurge called it the "New Negro Movement." But it was centered in Harlem, and the movement is now best known as the Harlem Renaissance. From 1914 through 1925, the African American population of Harlem grew from 14,000 to over 175,000, and the congested area became a magnet for activists, artists, and writers. In March 1925, the *Survey Graphic* published a special issue entitled *Harlem: Mecca of the New Negro*, edited by Alain Locke, a professor at Howard University. In his introductory essay, "Enter the New Negro," Locke observed: "The migrant masses, shifting from countryside to city, hurdle several generations of experience at a leap, but more important, the same thing happens spiritually in the life-attitudes and self-expression of the Young Negro, in his poetry, his art, his education, and his new outlook."

Winold Reiss,
Dawn in Harlem

Reiss, a German immigrant artist and designer, was commissioned to provide portraits and other illustrations for *Harlem: Mecca of the New Negro*, a special issue of *Survey Graphic* published in 1925. This print evokes the dawning of a new era of social action and cultural achievement among African Americans that came to be called the Harlem Renaissance.

African American writers benefited from growing interest in and expanding outlets for their work. Georgia Douglas Johnson first gained attention when three of her poems were published in and she subsequently appeared on the cover of the *Crisis*, the magazine of the National Association for the Advancement of Colored People (NAACP). Its editor, W. E. B. Du Bois, who viewed literature as a powerful weapon in the struggle for racial equality, regularly published, promoted, and reviewed the work of African American writers. James Weldon Johnson, who became the chief executive officer of the NAACP in 1920, showcased the work of thirty-one poets, most of them contemporary, in his pioneering anthology, *The Book of American Negro Poetry* (1922). In 1923, the National Urban League founded *Opportunity: A Journal of Negro Life*, whose motto was, "Not alms, but opportunity." Zora Neale Hurston's first professionally published story and Sterling A. Brown's earliest published poems appeared in *Opportunity*, which became a driving force in the art and literature of the Harlem Renaissance. White publishing companies took note of the growing market for works by African American writers. Boni & Liveright, founded in 1916 to bring modernist works to the American reading public, published *Cane* (1923), an experimental volume of poems, sketches, and stories by Jean Toomer. The prestigious firm of Harper and Brothers published four volumes of verse by Countee Cullen, one of the most popular poets of the 1920s. After Langston Hughes won a prize sponsored by *Opportunity*, his first volume of poetry was accepted by Alfred A. Knopf, Inc., which was at the forefront of new literary trends and which also later published Nella Larsen's novels *Quicksand* (1928) and *Passing* (1929).

As impressive as the literary achievements of the Harlem Renaissance were, African American music exerted a far more pervasive influence during the 1920s, often called the "Jazz Age." The ratification of the Eighteenth, or "Prohibition," Amendment — which took effect in January 1920 — led to the establishment of huge numbers of illegal bars, called "speakeasies," in urban centers throughout the United States. To attract customers, speakeasies often provided live entertainment, especially jazz: music that was widely associated with lawlessness and lack of inhibition. Jazz was also performed at venues such as the legendary Harlem nightspot the Cotton Club. "The Charleston," the anthem and the most popular dance

King Oliver's Creole Jazz Band

Joe "King" Oliver, shown here kneeling down at the front of the group, formed an important band made up of some of the top jazz musicians from New Orleans. From left to right, the band included Honore Dutry (trombone), Baby Dodds (drums), Louis Armstrong (coronet), Lil Hardin (piano), Bill Johnson (banjo and bass), and Johnny Dodds (clarinet). Armstrong, who joined the band in Chicago in 1922, later became one of the most popular and acclaimed musicians of the Jazz Age.

of the Jazz Age, was introduced in the all-black musical *Runnin' Wild*, which opened on Broadway in 1923. Jazz was also carried far beyond Broadway, clubs, and speakeasies by the radio and phonograph records. A decade after the first commercial radio station began broadcasting in 1919, more than 10 million homes had radios, and the sales of record players reached 5 million in 1929. The white bandleader Paul Whiteman, the self-proclaimed "King of Jazz," called it "the folk music of the machine age." But jazz was decried as a threat to morality and the social order in the pulpit and the press, including the *New York American*, which prophesied, "Moral disaster is coming to hundreds of young American girls through the pathological, nerve-irritating, sex-exciting music of jazz orchestras."

If jazz provided the soundtrack of the 1920s, the decade's most prominent actor was the "flapper," the very symbol of the Jazz Age. Women, who had taken the places of many men in the labor force during the war, were increasingly involved in the public sphere, and their educational and employment opportunities continued to grow at a steady rate. By 1920, when the ratification of the Nineteenth Amendment granted women the right to vote, they represented 60 percent of all the high-school graduates and nearly 15 percent of the country's workforce. During the following decade, many young women also claimed unprecedented social and sexual freedom – driving cars, smoking in public, applying "kiss-proof" makeup, and wearing revealing clothing that shocked their elders. The image of the liberated "flapper," with her close-cut or "bobbed" hair, short skirts, and silk stockings rolled to just above the knee, was a staple of popular fiction, notably the stories in F. Scott Fitzgerald's collections *Flappers and Philosophers* (1921) and *Tales of the Jazz Age* (1923). She also appeared in advertisements, cartoons, fashion magazines, and movies such as *The Flapper* (1920) and *Flaming Youth* (1924). Indeed, the movies dominated the mass-entertainment industry during the 1920s. In 1929, two years after the release of the first of the full-length "talkies," *The Jazz Singer*, the weekly attendance at movies exceeded 90 million, roughly three-quarters of the population of the United States.

Despite the competition of movies and other leisure-time activities, including the growing popularity of professional sports, American literature flourished during the 1920s. The most popular poet of the decade was Edna St. Vincent Millay, whose work embodied the political, social, and sexual rebellion of the "modern woman." Millay was the first woman to be awarded the Pulitzer Prize for Poetry, for her collection *The Harp-Weaver and Other Poems* (1922). Meanwhile, the work of more experimental poets appeared in proliferating little magazines, as well as more substantial journals such as the *Dial*, which the wealthy art patron Scofield Thayer purchased in 1919. Determined to transform the *Dial* into the preeminent international journal of the arts, Thayer published avant-garde work by

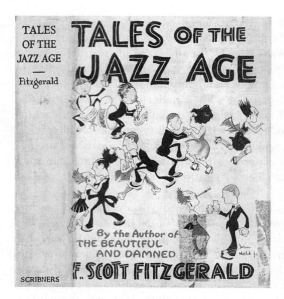

Tales of the Jazz Age

Boldly designed, brightly colored dust jackets were rare until the 1920s, when publishers began to realize that such protective covers could also attract the attention of potential buyers to books displayed on counters or in shop windows. The dust jacket of Fitzgerald's second collection of short stories was designed by the popular illustrator John Held Jr., best known for satirical depictions of "flaming youth," notably Betty Coed, the prototypical flapper, and her friend Joe College.

both European and American writers, including the most influential poem of the decade, T. S. Eliot's *The Waste Land* (1922). Thayer also established the prestigious Dial Prize and the Dial Press, which published collections of poetry by two of the major contributors to the *Dial*, E. E. Cummings and Marianne Moore. In Paris, to which many alienated American artists and writers flocked after World War I, the writer Robert McAlmon established Contact Editions, devoted to publishing books "not likely to be printed . . . for commercial or legislative reasons" — that is, because they either would not sell or would be deemed immoral or obscene in the United States. McAlmon subsequently published Mina Loy's *Lunar Baedecker* (1923), William Carlos Williams's *Spring and All* (1923), and Ernest Hemingway's first book, *Three Stories & Ten Poems* (1923).

Although the market for experimental poetry and prose was limited, there was a strong demand for more mainstream literary productions. In 1900, only 10 percent of young people aged fourteen to seventeen attended high school. By 1929, the number exceeded 40 percent, and a million students were enrolled in college. People also had the money to buy books and magazines. Sophisticated urban readers turned to *Vanity Fair*, a magazine of culture and fashion established in 1914, which later vied with the upstart *New Yorker*, begun in 1925. The bible of rebellious youth was *Smart Set*, "A Magazine of Cleverness," edited from 1914 to 1923 by H. L. Mencken and George Jean Nathan. The iconoclastic editors, who proclaimed that "One civilized reader is worth a thousand boneheads," published challenging works by established authors and younger writers such as F. Scott Fitzgerald, whose first professionally published story appeared in *Smart Set* in 1919. Fitzgerald, however, made far more money by writing stories for mass-circulation family magazines such as *Collier's, Cosmopolitan, Redbook,* and especially the *Saturday Evening Post.*

Mass-market magazines and other periodicals were sustained by the enormous growth of advertising during the 1920s. The decade's economic boom was in large part generated by the emerging consumer culture in which print advertising played an important role. The *Saturday Evening Post* was able to pay writers top dollar and to keep the cover price of the expensively produced "glossy" at five cents because the annual advertising revenues of the magazine exceeded 50 million dollars by the end of the 1920s. The pages of magazines and newspapers were filled with advertisements for cars, the mainstay of the American economy during the decade,

Ford Car Advertisement

Led by Ford's legendary Model T, and with the help of modern advertising, cars became the most powerful force in the prosperity of the 1920s. This image appeared in a full-page advertisement in the *Ladies' Home Journal* in 1924. The prominent role of women in the consumer economy of the decade was also illustrated by the text of the advertisement, which reads in part: "Through her dealings as business manager of the home, the modern woman brings sound commercial sense to bear on her judgment of a Ford closed car."

as well as innumerable other consumer products, especially those for women and the home. The visual images in advertisements powerfully shaped American culture, and advertising agencies claimed that they provided an important source of information to the American public. In "The Power of the Printed Word," an advertisement reprinted in the collection *In Behalf of Advertising* (1929), a copywriter for the firm of N. W. Ayer & Son exclaimed,

> Twenty-five million American families buy twenty-nine million newspapers every day, not to mention the periodicals they receive by the week and the month. Out of the magazines and newspapers they glean the ideas that are to rule their daily lives. They read the printed page with confidence. Its advertising carries conviction!

Book publishing also flourished during the 1920s. The number of libraries increased dramatically, and the creation of subscription book clubs expanded the reading public in the United States. The most famous was the Book-of-the-Month Club, established by Henry Scherman in 1926. Scherman assembled a panel of literary scholars to select the "the best new books published each month," which were then distributed by mail to subscribers, many of whom either did not have ready access to bookstores or were uncertain about which books they should read. The effort to secure a place for serious works of literature in the expanding consumer economy was immediately successful, and the Book-of-the-Month Club had 110,000 subscribers by 1929. There was a particularly strong demand for novels, and the production of new books of fiction doubled during the decade. "The sales department always wants a novel," the influential Scribner's editor Maxwell Perkins wryly observed: "They want to turn everything into a novel. They would have turned the New Testament into one, if it had come to us for publication." Certainly, there were novels on every possible subject for readers of widely varying tastes. Two of the most popular novelists of the day were Edgar Rice Burroughs, who wrote two dozen sequels to his story *Tarzan of the Apes* (1914), and Zane Grey, the prolific author of action-packed stories about the Old West. Writers who had begun their careers around the turn of the century enjoyed significant success during the decade, including the widely respected novelists Willa Cather and Edith Wharton, as well as their controversial contemporary Theodore Dreiser, whose best-selling work was *An American Tragedy* (1925).

They want to turn everything into a novel. They would have turned the New Testament into one, if it had come to us for publication.

A new generation of novelists also emerged. Following the publication of his first novel, *Main Street* (1920), Sinclair Lewis continued to top the best-seller lists with a series of satirical portraits of middle-class life in the Midwest. In 1930, Lewis became the first American to be awarded the

Nobel Prize for Literature. The fame of F. Scott Fitzgerald, one of the other bright stars to emerge in 1920, began to fade after the publication of his third novel, *The Great Gatsby* (1925). The following year, Ernest Hemingway published his first major novel, *The Sun Also Rises* (1926), a story about expatriates in Paris that the *New York Times* hailed as "one of the events of an unusually rich year in literature." The year also saw the publication of William Faulkner's first novel, *Soldier's Pay* (1926), whose central figure is a dying aviator wounded in World War I. The novel created little stir, and despite the profound impact of the war, the actualities of battle were rarely the subject of popular novels until 1929. That year, a decade after the signing of the treaty that formally ended the war, two antiwar novels gained a wide readership in the United States: Hemingway's *A Farewell to Arms* and the internationally acclaimed *All Quiet on the Western Front*, a translation of *Im Westen Nichts Neues* by the German novelist Erich Maria Remarque, perhaps the most grimly realistic of all depictions of the horror and futility of what many hopefully referred to as "The War to End All Wars."

From the Great Depression to World War II

The prosperity and productivity of the 1920s came to an abrupt end in October 1929. The stock market rallied briefly after a massive sell-off on "Black Thursday," October 24. But the prices of stocks tumbled again the following week, on "Black Monday" and "Black Tuesday," which marked the beginning of what came to be called the "Great Depression." The economic downturn soon affected European countries, and the depression spread throughout the world. In the United States, the stock market continued to fall until July 1932, by which time the Dow Jones Industrial Average was down nearly 90 percent from its high point before the crash in 1929. More than 10,000 of the country's 25,000 banks failed, and industrial output plummeted, leading to massive unemployment. By 1934, over 15 million people, more than 25 percent of the workforce, were unemployed. The economic and human crisis was exacerbated by a series of devastating droughts and dust storms that left 500,000 people homeless in the "Dust Bowl" of Texas, Arkansas, Oklahoma, and the Great Plains.

The Great Depression deeply undermined the optimism that had been generated by the seemingly limitless economic growth of the 1920s. During his successful election campaign in 1928, the Republican Herbert Hoover confidently asserted, "We shall soon with the help of God be in sight of the day when poverty will be banished from this land." Ironically, during Hoover's presidency the most common images of urban life in the United States were men selling apples on street corners, beggars, and breadlines, long lines of people waiting for food outside relief offices and charitable organizations. Describing the bleak scenes in New York City

James N. Rosenberg,
Oct 29 Dies Irae
("Day of Wrath")

Rosenberg, a bankruptcy lawyer who studied print-making, created this lithograph late in the afternoon of "Black Tuesday," often considered the worst day in the history of the stock market and the beginning of the Great Depression. The birds of prey descending from the dark clouds, the collapsing buildings, with stockbrokers leaping from windows, and the maddened crowds of people filling the street evoke the panic and bedlam on Wall Street.

and the dark mood of the country in 1932, the English visitor Mary Agnes Hamilton observed: "The American people, unfamiliar with suffering, with none of that long history of catastrophe and calamity behind it which makes the experience of European nations, is outraged and baffled by misfortune. Depression blocks its view; they cannot see around it." As Hamilton also observed, the nation's loss of confidence had resulted in "a despair of any and every kind of leadership," including that of the conservative Hoover, who was soundly defeated by Franklin D. Roosevelt in the presidential election of 1932. In an effort to restore the morale of the people and bring about "a new deal for the forgotten man," Roosevelt created a number of new agencies, the largest of which was the Works Progress Administration. The agency provided jobs for millions of destitute people, including unemployed writers and artists who worked on cultural programs sponsored by the Federal Theater Project and the Federal Writers' Project.

Many American writers became deeply involved in radical politics during the Great Depression. In his retrospective essay "Echoes of the Jazz Age" (1931), F. Scott Fitzgerald observed, "It was characteristic of the Jazz Age that it had no interest in politics at all." Although that was an exaggeration, Fitzgerald rightly gauged the seismic cultural and political shift generated by the stock market crash of 1929. During the 1920s, writers such as John Dos Passos maintained an interest in radical causes, and he and several other writers became involved in the case of Nicola Sacco and Bartolomeo Vanzetti, two Italian immigrants and anarchists who many believed were wrongfully convicted of murder and executed in Massachusetts in 1927. One of the leaders of the protests against their execution was Michael Gold, the Marxist editor of the recently established journal the *New Masses*. Gold was later active in the international campaign to "Free the Scottsboro Boys," nine black teenagers convicted of raping two white girls on a freight train bound from Tennessee to Alabama on March 25, 1931. The case had far-reaching consequences, dividing the country along sectional and racial lines, giving impetus to more militant tactics in the struggle for civil rights, and generating support in the black community for radical political groups, including the Communist Party. The party's

Scottsboro Limited

Prentiss Taylor, an artist who collaborated with Hughes on several projects, created the lithograph used on the cover of this 1932 collection of works inspired by the case of the "Scottsboro Boys," nine black teenagers falsely accused of raping two white girls. All-white juries in the small town of Scottsboro, Alabama, swiftly convicted all nine defendants, eight of whom were sentenced to death. After a long legal and political battle, the defendants who had not escaped or died in prison were eventually released.

SCOTTSBORO LIMITED

By LANGSTON HUGHES
WITH ILLUSTRATIONS BY
PRENTISS TAYLOR

Price 50 cents

involvement in the case and its commitment to racial equality also attracted writers such as Langston Hughes, who exposed the injustices of the American legal and economic system in poems and a verse play, *Scottsboro Limited* (1932).

American writing was also influenced by the "proletarian literature" movement of the 1930s. For Marxist critics and writers, such socially engaged literature was a vital instrument in the class struggle. In his introduction to the anthology *Proletarian Literature of the United States* (1935), Joseph Freeman emphasized that writing "on the people's side" promised to introduce new areas of feeling and experience into the dominant culture of the United States. In the *U.S.A.* trilogy (1930–36), a sweeping chronicle of American life from the turn of the century through the stock market crash of 1929, Dos Passos revealed both the corrosive effects of materialism and the harsh realities of life for working-class people in the United States. The Great Depression inspired Sandburg to write his epic poem *The People, Yes* (1936), which was hailed as a visionary affirmation of the need to build a social revolution upon "the belief in the people," as the radical poet Archibald MacLeish put it in a review in the *New Masses.* That belief was at the core of perhaps the most famous American novel of the 1930s, *The Grapes of Wrath* (1939), John Steinbeck's saga of the ordeal of the Joads, an impoverished tenant-farmer family joining the

Dorothea Lange, *Migrant Mother* (California, 1936)

The human crisis created by the Dust Bowl, which John Steinbeck dramatizes in his novel *The Grapes of Wrath* (1939), was also documented by photojournalists from the Farm Security Administration, including the former fashion and portrait photographer Dorothea Lange. Lange took this famous photograph of an impoverished Oklahoma woman and her children during a brief stop at a pea-picker's camp in Nipomo, California.

mass exodus from the Dust Bowl of Oklahoma to California. Michael Gold hailed Steinbeck as a champion of the "people's culture," and the best-selling book was made into a popular movie in 1940. That year, Richard Wright captured the misery and poverty endured by African Americans living in a slum on the South Side of Chicago in *Native Son* (1940), the first Book-of-the-Month Club selection written by an African American.

Social protest formed only one part of the literature of the 1930s. In contrast to Wright, Zora Neale Hurston offered a far more positive vision of African American life in stories and her first novel, *Their Eyes Were Watching God* (1937). Although the Florida-born Hurston is most often associated with the Harlem Renaissance, she was also part of what came to be known as the Southern Literary Renaissance. The most critically acclaimed southern writer of the 1930s was William Faulkner, who explored the region's troubled past and its legacy in a wide range of stories and novels, including *Absalom, Absalom!* (1936). But that complex and challenging work was completely overshadowed by another southern novel about the Civil War and Reconstruction that was published the same year, Margaret Mitchell's *Gone with the Wind* (1936). Although the hefty, thousand-page book cost two dollars, a substantial sum in the midst of the Depression, Mitchell's blockbuster sold more than one million copies within a year, won a Pulitzer Prize in 1937, and was made into a smash-hit movie starring Clark Gable and Vivien Leigh in 1939.

Like the motion pictures, publishing weathered the hard financial times of the Great Depression far better than most other businesses. Initially, many little magazines ceased publication, and book production dropped 50 percent between 1929 and 1933. But production later rallied, and other kinds of reading materials flourished. Mass-circulation family magazines continued to attract large numbers of readers, and the 1930s was the heyday of "pulps," so-called because of the cheap, wood-pulp paper upon which such magazines were published. Successors to the popular dime novels of the late-nineteenth century, pulps specialized in various fictional genres, including westerns, romances, and science fiction. Among the most famous of the pulps was the crime-fiction magazine *Black Mask*, which published the pioneering stories and novels of Dashiell Hammett, including *The Maltese Falcon* (1930). *Black Mask* and other pulps later succumbed to competition from comic books and paperback novels. Although there were many earlier paperbound books, the first mass-market paperback novels published in the United States were the Pocket Books. Designed to fit into a man's coat pocket and priced at only twenty-five cents, Pocket Books were introduced in 1939. To test-market the books, the publisher reprinted *The Good Earth* (1931), a popular novel by Pearl Buck, who had won the Nobel Prize in 1938. The first run of two thousand copies sold out quickly at untraditional outlets for books, including Macy's Department Store and a corner cigar store in New York

Newsstand in Omaha, Nebraska

John Vachon, a photographer for the Farm Security Administration, took this photograph while on assignment in Nebraska in November 1938. The photograph suggests the range of interests and tastes catered to by American periodicals, including an array of "pulps" and mass-circulation family magazines, as well as the first all-photography news-magazine, the recently created and tremendously popular *Life*.

City. As a result, Pocket Books began a revolution not only in publishing but also in the marketing of books in the United States.

Paperbacks and other kinds of books assumed a prominent role during World War II. The confident theme of the New York World's Fair of 1939 was "Building the World of Tomorrow." The fair celebrated new technologies, including television, but further development of that formidable competitor to books was interrupted by the beginning of the war in Europe in September 1939. The war spurred industrial production in the United States, which finally emerged from the Great Depression. After the country entered the global conflict in December 1941, providing books to members of the armed forces became a prominent part of the war effort. The American Library Association, the Red Cross, and the United Service Organizations (USO) sponsored the Victory Book Campaign, which collected millions of books for distribution to military camps. At the same time, rationing of paper curtailed the printing of traditional, hard-backed books, spurring the development of cheaply produced paperbacks. Early in 1942, a group of publishers founded the Council on Books in Wartime, which distributed inexpensive, five-by-four-inch paperbacks called the Armed Services Editions. By the end of the war, the council had distributed 123.5 million copies of more than 1,300 different books to American troops at home and overseas.

In addition to raising the morale of the troops, books came to symbolize the ideological struggle between the United States and the Axis Powers. In his State of the Union address in January 1941, commonly known as his "Four Freedoms Speech," President Roosevelt outlined the fundamental liberties that all people should enjoy: freedom of speech, freedom of worship, freedom from want, and freedom from fear. Many Americans subsequently came to view World War II as a struggle to defend those freedoms from the onslaught of the military dictatorship in Japan and the Fascist regimes in Germany and Italy. Early in 1942, a group of American authors formed the Writers' War Board, a government-subsidized organization that adopted the slogan "Books Are Weapons in the War of Ideas." The board coordinated the work of hundreds of authors who fought the war with their pens, including Edna St. Vincent Millay, a former pacifist who had been deeply involved in the Sacco and Vanzetti case in the 1920s, and Langston Hughes, who had written some of the most revolutionary political poetry of the 1930s. Indeed, many writers who had earlier been among the harshest critics of American politics and society strongly supported the war, in which President Roosevelt affirmed that Americans were fighting "for a better day for all mankind."

World War II Poster

This poster was distributed to U.S. libraries by the Office of War Information. The giant book, with its quotation from a 1942 speech by President Roosevelt, looms over a scene that evokes the Nazi book burnings that began in May 1933, when university students burned 25,000 "un-German" books in a ceremony held in Munich. To rally Americans around the war effort, groups such as the Writers' War Board sponsored annual commemorations of the book burnings, and in a massive Flag Day parade in 1942, "New York at War," city librarians marched under the banner "Fascism Burns Books, Democracy Reads Books."

Books cannot be killed by fire.

People die, but books never die. No man and no force can put thought in a concentration camp forever. No man and no force can take from the world the books that embody man's eternal fight against tyranny. In this war, we know, books are weapons.

Franklin D. Roosevelt

BOOKS ARE WEAPONS IN THE WAR OF IDEAS

Modernisms in American Poetry

IN RECENT YEARS, many critics and scholars have begun to refer to "modernism" as "modernisms," a term that perhaps more clearly suggests the lively disagreements, multiplicity of styles, and plurality of movements within the broad revolution in the arts that took place during the early decades of the twentieth century in Europe and the United States. Certainly, there was no single style of modern American poetry, which was characterized by widely differing aesthetic values, literary purposes, and poetic techniques. Spurred in part by experiments in the visual arts, many poets were committed to formal innovation, including two of the earliest and most energetic proponents of what was often called the "new poetry,"

◀ Aaron Douglas, *Poetry*

This mural is part of the Symbolic Negro History Series, which Douglas created in 1930 for a new library at the historically black Fisk University in Nashville, Tennessee. During the previous decade, Douglas had emerged as one of the major figures of the Harlem Renaissance, in which writers and visual artists worked closely together, as they did in centers of modernism from New York City to London and Paris.

529

Ezra Pound and Amy Lowell. But both poets admired the work of Robert Frost, who adapted the conventional forms and meters of English poetry. The traditional sonnet was a favorite form of the most popular American poet of the period 1914–45, Edna St. Vincent Millay, as well as of two poets associated with the Harlem Renaissance, Claude McKay and Countee Cullen. In contrast, another poet associated with the movement, Langston Hughes drew inspiration from the forms and rhythms of jazz and the blues. Hughes was also influenced by the vernacular verse of the white poet Carl Sandburg, whose rough-hewn work differed dramatically from the highly polished verse of contemporary poets such as Mina Loy, Marianne Moore, and Wallace Stevens. Indeed, the modernism of modern American poets was frequently at odds, sometimes almost violently so, as in the work of two of the most influential poets of the period, the expatriate T. S. Eliot and his homebound and self-declared literary opponent William Carlos Williams.

At the same time, modern American poets were connected in a number of ways. All of them passionately believed in the necessity of poetry, its vital role in culture and society. "Times change and forms and their meanings alter," Stevens wrote in 1937. "Thus new poems are necessary. Their forms must be discovered in the spoken, the living language of their day, or old forms, embodying exploded concepts, will tyrannize over the imagination, depriving us of its greatest benefits." Although they lived in far-flung areas, many poets worked closely together in cities such as Chicago, New York, London, and Paris. Many poets were also connected by a network of friendships and literary alliances. Eliot and Williams, for example, were friends of Ezra Pound, who was in close contact or correspondence with writers on both sides of the Atlantic. Finally, virtually all of the poets of the period benefited from the emergence of new periodicals, especially little magazines, which were designed to provide a venue and generate an audience for experimental writing. The motto of the first of those magazines, *Poetry: A Magazine of Verse*, was a line from Walt Whitman: "To have great poets we must have great audiences too."

Few individuals were as crucial to the development of modern American poetry as the founder and editor of *Poetry*, Harriet Monroe. Born into an affluent Chicago family, the well-educated Monroe traveled widely in the United States and Europe and visited China during 1910–11. Returning to Chicago, where she worked as an art critic, Monroe was deeply frustrated by the lack of cultural depth and the lowly status of poetry in the United States. She consequently set out to establish a new kind of literary magazine devoted exclusively to poetry. "My idea of 'direction,'" Monroe recalled in her autobiography, "was to offer good poems to set against the 'piles of rubbish' which bemired the poetic landscape in newspapers and

> *Thus new poems are necessary. Their forms must be discovered in the spoken, the living language of their day, or old forms, embodying exploded concepts, will tyrannize over the imagination, depriving us of its greatest benefits.*

popular magazines." To raise the funds for a new magazine, Monroe visited or wrote to over one hundred prominent Chicagoans, asking for pledges of fifty dollars a year for five years to support the venture. When she had the $5,000 she needed, Monroe wrote letters to poets promising that "this magazine will appeal to, and it may be hoped will develop, a public primarily interested in poetry as an art, as the highest, most complete human expression of truth and beauty." As a next step, she wrote to Pound, then living in London, and invited him to participate. Pound, who agreed to serve as a "Foreign Correspondent" to the magazine, enthusiastically told Monroe that the revolution in American poetry would "make the Italian Renaissance look like a tempest in a teapot!"

The publication of the first issue of *Poetry* in October 1912 marked the beginning of a new era for poetry in the United States. Pound soon sent Monroe several poems by his two closest associates in London, the English poet Richard Aldington and a young American poet living in London, Hilda Doolittle, who published under her initials "H.D." Pound identified them as "imagistes," thus christening the first organized movement in modern English poetry, which he called "imagisme." In brief essays in the March 1913 issue of *Poetry*, he and F. S. Flint outlined the fundamental characteristics of the movement: direct treatment of the "thing," or object; the use of spare, concrete language; and *vers libre*, or free verse, composition — as opposed to the conventional meters of English poetry. As Pound affirmed in "Ikon," a prose poem he published later in 1913, "It is in art the highest business to create the beautiful image; to create order and profusion of images that we may furnish the life of our minds with a noble surrounding." Pound soon published the first anthology to feature the work of the group, *Des Imagistes* (1914). The volume included several poems by a zealous convert to the movement, Amy Lowell. After she and Pound divided over the direction of the movement, which Lowell sought to democratize and popularize as "imagism," she subsequently edited and published three additional anthologies, *Some Imagist Poets* (1915, 1916, and 1917).

In their revolt against conventional poetic practices, the imagists and other modernist American poets drew inspiration from a wide range of non-English literary models. They were strongly influenced by the experimental techniques of the symbolists and other late-nineteenth-century French poets, who had introduced the term *vers libre* and sought to evoke inner realities through the use of symbolic images. Imagists such as H.D. were drawn to classical poetry, especially the lyrics of the ancient Greek poet Sappho of Lesbos, and Pound championed a wide range of verse, including Anglo-Saxon poetry and work of medieval troubadour poets such as Arnaut Daniel and Guido Cavalcanti. Pound and many others were also deeply interested in the arts of Asia. Defining the

Harriet Monroe

This photograph was taken in 1911, about the time Monroe founded *Poetry: A Magazine of Verse*. She was dressed in clothing purchased during her recent trip to China, the art of which strongly influenced modern poets and painters in Europe and the United States.

It is in art the highest business to create the beautiful image; to create order and profusion of images that we may furnish the life of our minds with a noble surrounding.

Artists and Writers in Paris

This group portrait was taken in the early 1920s. The figure at the far right in the second row is the expatriate American poet Ezra Pound, who moved from London to Paris in 1920. The poet Mina Loy, at the center of the front row, is looking at the American painter and photographer Man Ray, who is squatting and holding a camera.

single most important element in the revolution in American poetry, Harriet Monroe in 1917 declared that "these poets have bowed to the winds from the East." Among the writers who introduced Japanese poetic forms to American audiences were the bilingual poet and critic Yone Noguchi and Jun Fujita, a Japanese immigrant who became a frequent contributor to *Poetry*. Pound adapted the form of the Japanese haiku in his most famous imagist poem, the two-line "In a Station at the Metro," which appeared in the magazine in 1913. He subsequently published an acclaimed collection of translations of ancient Chinese poems, *Cathay* (1915). The imagist poet John Gould Fletcher later observed that the publication of Pound's free-verse translations was the "pivotal moment" in the development of the "new poetry" in English.

Pound also generously promoted the careers of a wide range of American poets in England and the United States. In 1913, he helped his friend William Carlos Williams publish a collection of poems in London, where Pound also helped arrange for the publication of Robert Frost's first two books of poetry, *A Boy's Will* (1913) and *North of Boston* (1914). The work of the two poets suggested the range of both the new poetry and Pound's aesthetic sympathies, since Williams's experimental poems about the everyday lives of common people in suburban New Jersey bore little similarity to Frost's more traditional verse, which was deeply rooted in rural New England. Both, however, sought to develop a new, distinctively American idiom in poetry, as did the Chicago journalist Carl Sandburg. In 1914, Harriet Monroe published a group of Sandburg's raw and realistic poems about life in an industrial city, and Pound encouraged Sandburg to publish his first book, *Chicago Poems* (1916). The modern urban landscape was also at the center of the work of a very different poet, T. S. Eliot, for whom Pound reserved his greatest praise. "He is the only American I know of who has made what I can call adequate preparation for writing," Pound observed after he met the highly educated and widely read Eliot in London in 1914. Through Pound's influence, Eliot's first professionally published poem, "The Love Song of J. Alfred Prufrock," appeared in *Poetry* in 1915.

The example of *Poetry* and the proliferating alliances and movements within modernism inspired the establishment of a number of other little magazines. In London, Pound helped the British writer and painter Wyndham Lewis found *Blast*, an experimental magazine that Lewis described as the "battering ram" for a loosely defined movement called "Vorticism." In New York City, the poet Alfred Kreymborg established *Others: A Magazine of the New Verse*, a rival to *Poetry*, in 1915. But little magazines were plagued by economic problems resulting from small circulations and limited support from advertisers. Seeking to overcome the public indifference to magazines such as *Others*, a reviewer admiringly observed that the first issues of the magazine "are among the live things being done in America just now," adding,

> *The new poetry is revolutionary. It is the expression of a democracy of feeling rebelling against an aristocracy of form.*

> Perhaps you are unfamiliar with this "new poetry" that is called "revolutionary." Perhaps you've heard that it is queer and have let it go at that. Perhaps if you tried it you'd find that a side of you that has been sleeping would come awake again. It is worth the price of a Wednesday matinée to find out. By the way, the new poetry is revolutionary. It is the expression of a democracy of feeling rebelling against an aristocracy of form.

Others displayed the full range of new voices in American poetry, from expatriates such as Pound, Eliot, and H.D. to Kreymborg's friends and associates in and around New York City, including Mina Loy, Marianne Moore, Wallace Stevens, and William Carlos Williams.

Although such "revolutionary" poets seemed to present a united front, they were increasingly divided about the nature and direction of the new poetry. After *Others* ceased publication, Williams and his friend Robert McAlmon established a new magazine designed to feature cutting-edge writing, *Contact*. The title reflected their conviction that successful writing is "indigenous," a direct expression of the artist's immediate experiences

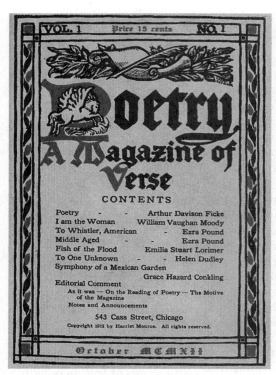

and perceptions of local conditions. Williams, who was convinced that European literary traditions posed a serious obstacle to the development of modern American poetry, was particularly hostile to T. S. Eliot, whom he viewed as an academic, backward-looking poet who had abandoned America. Williams was consequently devastated by the fame and widespread influence of Eliot's *The Waste Land* (1922), which was published in the United States in the most prominent literary journal of the period, the *Dial*, and then as a book by the modernist firm Boni & Liveright. Describing the impact of Eliot's learned and richly allusive poem, "the great catastrophe to our letters," Williams bitterly recalled, "I felt at once that it has set us back twenty years, and I'm sure it did. Critically Eliot had returned us to the classroom just at the moment when I felt we were on the point of an escape to matters much closer to the essence of a new art form itself — rooted in the locality which should give it fruit."

The Waste Land formed only one prominent feature of the complex literary landscape of the 1920s. The Pulitzer Prize for 1922, the year Eliot's poem was published, was awarded to the popular poet Edna St. Vincent Millay, for her collection *The Harp-Weaver and Other Poems.* Another popular poet, Robert Frost, received the first of his four Pulitzer Prizes for his collection *New Hampshire* (1923). Together with the older American poet Edwin Arlington Robinson, who received three Pulitzer Prizes during the 1920s, Millay and Frost greatly expanded the audience for poetry in the United States. At the same time, critics praised the "stylistic innovations" and "feeling for American speech" displayed by E. E. Cummings in his first collection, *Tulips and Chimneys* (1923). That year, Wallace Stevens published his acclaimed first collection, *Harmonium,* and Mina Loy's first collection, *Lunar Baedecker,* was published by Robert McAlamon's Contact Press in Paris. The Dial Press, a publishing offshoot of the *Dial,* published Marianne Moore's second volume of poetry, *Observations* (1924). Volumes by two of the most active and influential of the imagist poets appeared in 1925: H.D.'s *Collected Poems* and Amy Lowell's final collection, *What's O'Clock,* for which she was posthumously awarded the Pulitzer Prize. Hart Crane, who was influenced by a wide range of English and American poets, including the imagists and other modern poets as diverse as Cummings, Eliot, Pound, Stevens, and Williams, further extended the boundaries of

◀ **Little Magazines**

The proliferation of little magazines spurred the development of modernism in Europe and the United States. Two of the magazines were devoted exclusively to verse: *Poetry,* founded in Chicago in 1912, and *Others,* founded in New York City in 1915. The short-lived *Blast,* two issues of which were published during 1914-15, was the journal of the movement called vorticism. *Opportunity,* founded in New York City by the National Urban League in 1923, assumed a vital role in the Harlem Renaissance.

poetic language and subject matter in his first collection, *White Buildings* (1926).

American verse was also enriched by poets of the Harlem Renaissance. James Weldon Johnson was inspired by African American preaching to write "The Creation" (1920), the first of the poems he later collected in *God's Trombones: Seven Negro Sermons in Verse* (1927). Claude McKay, an immigrant from Jamaica, employed the traditional form of the sonnet in politically charged works such as "If We Must Die" and other poems in his collection *Harlem Shadows* (1922). Other poets also adapted traditional lyric forms to evoke the scenes and themes of African American life, including Georgia Douglas Johnson, especially in her collection *Bronze: A Book of Verse* (1922), and Countee Cullen, whose first collection of poems was entitled *Color* (1925). Some of the poems in that collection also appeared in Alain Locke's influential anthology, *The New Negro* (1925), and the work of many young poets was published in the *Crisis*, the official magazine of the National Association for the Advancement of Colored People (NAACP), and *Opportunity: A Journal of Negro Life*. In 1925, Langston Hughes won first prize in a literary contest sponsored by *Opportunity*, leading to the publication of his first collection of poetry, *The Weary Blues* (1926). Hughes employed black vernacular language and the rhythms of jazz and the blues to depict the essence of African American life in the urban North. Sterling A. Brown employed similar elements, but he drew upon the dialect, experience, and folklore of rural black people in his collection *Southern Road* (1932).

Following the artistic and economic boom of the 1920s, however, poets and poetry confronted major obstacles during the Great Depression and World War II. Millay and Frost remained popular, as did Carl Sandburg, who responded to the economic crisis of the early 1930s in his epic poem *The People, Yes* (1936). Cummings, Stevens, and some other prominent modernist poets also published important collections during the decade. But the declining interest in and market for poetry had a profound impact on some lesser-known poets. Despite the critical success of *Southern Road*, for example, Brown could not interest a publisher in his second collection of poetry, and he subsequently devoted himself to criticism and scholarship. Other African American poets turned to writing more commercially viable work. In addition to political poetry in support of various radical causes, Langston Hughes wrote fiction and several plays during the Great Depression. T. S. Eliot, who also sought to gain a broader audience by writing drama, completed only one major poetic project after 1930, his *Four Quartets* (1943). Ezra Pound, who had settled in Italy in 1924, continued to work on his long poem *The Cantos*, but he devoted much of his energy to writing treatises on culture, economics, and politics during the 1930s.

Even as Pound embraced the right-wing Italian political movement called "Fascism," he became closely associated with an avant-garde group of left-wing poets in the United States. In 1931, he helped arrange for the young poet Louis Zukovsky to edit a special issue of *Poetry* devoted to the work of the "objectivists." Much like the earlier imagists, the objectivists were committed to everyday language and to writing as a form "of seeing, of thinking, with the things as they exist," as Zukovsky put it. But in contrast to the imagists, many of whom were drawn to nature and mythology, the radical objectivists sought to document the urban proletarian experience during the Great Depression. Zukovsky's editorial work led to the establishment of the Objectivist Press, which published works by Charles Reznikoff, who had previously published most of his work at his own expense, and William Carlos Williams. After the press collapsed under financial pressure in 1936, Williams began a long association with James Laughlin, whom Pound encouraged to establish a publishing house committed to experimental writing, New Directions Press.

Laughlin's successful venture and the establishment of college-based literary journals such as *Prairie Schooner*, the *Southern Review*, and the *Kenyon Review* helped fill the gap left by the demise of the many little magazines that folded during the Great Depression. A notable exception was *Poetry*, which survived even after Harriet Monroe's death in 1936. The staff of the magazine immediately arranged for a memorial issue that included tributes by poets such as Ezra Pound, Marianne Moore, Carl Sandburg, and Wallace Stevens. "No one in our time or in any other time has served the cause of art with greater devotion," Pound gracefully observed of Monroe. In another tribute to the importance of her editorship of *Poetry*, the poet and critic Malcolm Cowley observed that there had "been whole years during which she edited the only magazine in America that would print intelligent poetry and give the authors of it the idea that they were not singing in a soundproof room entirely cut off from the world." Indeed, by nurturing the belief that there was an outlet and an audience for even the most experimental verse, little magazines such as *Poetry* had played a vital role in what Cowley aptly described as the "poetic renaissance" that began around the time Monroe established the magazine in 1912.

American Contexts

"Make It New":
Poets on Poetry

In his translation of the *Ta Hio* ("The Great Learning") of the ancient Chinese philosopher Confucius, the influential modern poet and critic Ezra Pound reaffirmed, "Renew thyself daily, utterly, make it new, and again new, make it new." The exhortation "make it new," a phrase that Pound later used as the title of a collection of his essays, consequently became a kind of shorthand for the complex and often conflicting agendas of American poets during the early decades of the twentieth century.

As the following commentaries by poets suggest, there was considerable disagreement among them about the ways in which poetry could be made new and what constituted the new poetry. In her introductory essay in the first issue of *Poetry: A Magazine of Verse* in 1912, its founder and editor Harriet Monroe affirmed that "all forms, whether narrative, dramatic, or lyric, will be acceptable." Monroe subsequently published a wide range of poetry in her magazine, which strongly encouraged both established and emerging poets in the United States. During the decades following the founding of *Poetry*, however, all of the elements of poetry — form, language, rhythm, rhyme, and subject matter — were topics of serious discussion and debate. Divisions emerged even within the first organized group of modern poets writing in English, the imagistes or imagists. Pound, the first leader of the group, described their fundamental aesthetic values and poetic techniques in an essay published in *Poetry* in 1913. But he soon came into conflict with Amy Lowell, who was determined to democratize what Pound, using the French term, called imagisme and she called imagism, primarily in an effort to make such modern poetry seem less foreign or alien to audiences in the United States. As Lowell embarked on a crusade for imagism in essays such as "The New Manner in Modern Poetry," Pound moved in other directions, working with other new poets such as T. S. Eliot. In his 1919 essay "Tradition and the Individual Talent," Eliot challenged poets and critics who rejected "tradition" by emphasizing the vital connections between modern poets and poets of the past, a European tradition extending back to the ancient Greek poet Homer.

MAKE IT NEW

ESSAYS BY
EZRA POUND

新 日 日 新

LONDON
FABER AND FABER LIMITED
24 RUSSELL SQUARE

Ezra Pound,
Make It New
The title of this 1934 collection of essays is Pound's translation of the four Chinese characters on the title page, which may more literally be translated "make new, day by day, make new."

During the period from the 1920s through World War II, many poets grappled with questions about the function and status of poetry in the modern age. For poets of the Harlem Renaissance, questions about the language, sources, and subject matter of poetry were central to the contested issue of whether there was or could be what Langston Hughes described as "any true Negro Art in America." James Weldon Johnson rejected the tradition of dialect poetry, which he argued was not "capable of giving expression to the varied conditions of Negro life in America." Hughes, who frequently wrote in dialect, encouraged African American poets to produce work that was racial in both subject and treatment, drawing inspiration from indigenous traditions of music such as spirituals and jazz. In her essay "Modern Poetry," the poet and painter Mina Loy also emphasized the close relations between poetry and music, as well as the vital connections between "the renaissance in poetry" and the "composite language" forged by members of various races and immigrant groups in the United States. Hart Crane suggested that urban life and technological advances opened new subjects for poets, exploring what in his 1930 essay "Modern Poetry" he described as the "function of poetry in a Machine Age." The poet most closely associated with rural New England, Robert Frost, reaffirmed some of the traditional forms and functions of poetry in "The Figure a Poem Makes" (1939), published near the end of the Great Depression. During that period of economic crisis, many viewed modern poetry as immaterial, and it was

bedfordstmartins.com/
americanlit *for research links on the authors in this section*

frequently dismissed as irrelevant during World War II. "The war is the first and only thing in the world today," William Carlos Williams observed in his introduction to *The Wedge* (1944). But he insisted that, far from being a diversion from World War II, innovation in the arts "*is* the war or part of it," implying that the outcome of the effort on that battleground was equally vital to the future of the United States.

Harriet Monroe

[1860-1936]

Although she published several volumes of her poetry and a collection of critical essays on other poets, Harriet Monroe was and is best known as the founder of *Poetry: A Magazine of Verse*, which she edited from 1912 until her death in 1936. Generally regarded as the most influential little magazine published in the United States, *Poetry* featured the work of a wide range of American poets, including T. S. Eliot, Robert Frost, Amy Lowell, Edna St. Vincent Millay, Marianne Moore, Carl Sandburg, and Wallace Stevens. Monroe also published poets who were associated with the Harlem Renaissance, including Countee Cullen and Langston Hughes, as well as the work of recent immigrants such as Jun Fujita, a Japanese-born poet living in Chicago. *Poetry* had a transnational flavor, publishing English translations of the work of Rabindranath Tagore, the Bengali poet who won the Nobel Prize in 1913. Although the eclectic Monroe was receptive to diverse styles of poetry, she could be quite conservative. She published Joyce Kilmer's conventional "Trees," which became one of the most popular of all American poems, but rejected the innovative work of E. E. Cummings. Despite such occasional lapses, Monroe brilliantly fulfilled her stated purpose of establishing a magazine that would "give to poetry her own place, her own voice," as she put it in her introductory essay "The Motive of the Magazine." The text of the essay is taken from the first issue of *Poetry: A Magazine of Verse*, October 1912.

THE MOTIVE OF THE MAGAZINE

In the huge democracy of our age no interest is too slight to have an organ. Every sport, every little industry requires its own corner, its own voice, that it may find its friends, greet them, welcome them.

The arts especially have need of each an entrenched place, a voice of power, if they are to do their work and be heard. For as the world grows greater day by day, as every member of it, through something he buys or knows or loves, reaches out to the ends of the earth, things precious to the race, things rare and delicate, may be overpowered, lost in the criss-cross of modern currents, the confusion of modern immensities.

Painting, sculpture, music are housed in palaces in the great cities of the world; and every week or two a new periodical is born to speak for one or the other of them, and tenderly nursed at some guardian's expense. Architecture, responding to commercial and social demands, is whipped into shape by the rough and tumble of life and fostered, willy-nilly, by men's material needs. Poetry alone, of all the fine arts, has been left to shift for herself in a world unaware of its immediate and desperate need of her, a world whose great deeds, whose triumphs over matter, over the wilderness, over racial enmities and distances, require her ever-living voice to give them glory and glamour.

Poetry has been left to herself and blamed for inefficiency, a process as unreasonable as blaming the desert for barrenness. This art, like every other, is not a miracle of direct creation, but a reciprocal relation between the artist and his public. The people must do their part if the poet is to tell their story to the future; they must cultivate and irrigate the soil if the desert is to blossom as the rose.

The present venture is a modest effort to give to poetry her own place, her own voice. The popular magazines can afford her but scant courtesy — a Cinderella corner in the ashes[1] — because they seek a large public which is not hers, a public which buys them not for their verse but for their stories, pictures, journalism, rarely for their literature, even in prose. Most magazine editors say that there is no public for poetry in America; one of them wrote to a young poet that the verse his monthly accepted "must appeal to the barber's wife of the Middle West," and others prove their distrust by printing less verse from year to year, and that rarely beyond page-end length and importance.

We believe that there is a public for poetry, that it will grow, and that as it becomes more numerous and appreciative the work produced in this art will grow in power, in beauty, in significance. In this belief we have been encouraged by the generous enthusiasm of many subscribers to our fund, by the sympathy of other lovers of the art, and by the quick response of many prominent poets, both American and English, who have sent or promised contributions.

We hope to publish in *Poetry* some of the best work now being done in English verse. Within space limitations set at present by the small size of our monthly sheaf, we shall be able to print poems longer, and of more intimate and serious character, than the popular magazines can afford to use. The test, limited by ever-fallible human judgment, is to be quality alone; all forms, whether narrative, dramatic, or lyric, will be acceptable. We hope to offer our subscribers a place of refuge, a green isle in the sea, where Beauty may plant her gardens, and Truth, austere revealer of joy and sorrow, of hidden delights and despairs, may follow her brave quest unafraid.

[1912]

---

1. **a Cinderella corner in the ashes:** A reference to the famous folktale about a beautiful young girl whose cruel stepmother and stepsisters dress her in rags and make her sleep on the floor by the hearth. Because she is always covered in ashes and cinders, they mockingly call her *Cinderella*.

Ezra Pound

[1885–1972]

Ezra Pound was one of the central figures in the development of modern poetry in England and the United States (see Pound, p. 641). In addition to writing poetry, reviews, and manifestos, he helped establish and edit several little magazines. He also advised and encouraged numerous other poets, including H.D., T. S. Eliot, Robert Frost, Amy Lowell, Marianne Moore, and William Carlos Williams. Pound was the organizer of the imagistes, a group of British and American poets based in London. When Harriet Monroe, the editor of *Poetry: A Magazine of Verse*, began to receive letters from readers asking for information about the imagistes, she invited Pound to respond. He and the English poet and translator F. S. Flint provided commentaries that Monroe published in March 1913. Flint contributed a brief opening statement, "Imagisme," while Pound contributed "A Few Don'ts by an Imagiste." In it, he gave a series of practical and witty suggestions about the use of imagery, language, rhyme, and rhythm for those beginning to write verse, offering a short course in modern poetic technique and the procedures of the imagistes. The text is taken from the first printing of the essay in *Poetry: A Magazine of Verse*, March 1913.

From A Few Don'ts by an Imagiste

An "Image" is that which presents an intellectual and emotional complex in an instant of time. I use the term "complex" rather in the technical sense employed by the newer psychologists, such as Hart,[1] though we might not agree absolutely in our application.

It is the presentation of such a "complex" instantaneously which gives that sense of sudden liberation; that sense of freedom from time limits and space limits; that sense of sudden growth, which we experience in the presence of the greatest works of art.

It is better to present one Image in a lifetime than to produce voluminous works.

All this, however, some may consider open to debate. The immediate necessity is to tabulate A LIST OF DON'TS for those beginning to write verses. But I cannot put all of them into Mosaic negative.

To begin with, consider the three rules recorded by Mr. Flint,[2] not as dogma — never

---

1. **the newer psychologists, such as Hart:** Dr. Bernard Hart was an English interpreter of the theories of the Austrian founder of psychotherapy, Sigmund Freud. Describing "the general conception underlying Freud's teaching," Hart in a 1911 essay explained: "Unconscious ideas are agglomerated into groups with accompanying effects, the systems thus being formed being termed 'complexes.'"
2. **the three rules recorded by Mr. Flint:** In the preceding essay, F. S. Flint summarized the general rules followed by the imagistes: "1. Direct treatment of the 'thing,' whether subjective or objective. 2. To use absolutely no word that did not contribute to the presentation. 3. As regarding rhythm: to compose in sequence of the musical phrase, not in sequence of a metronome."

consider anything as dogma — but as the result of long contemplation, which, even if it is someone else's contemplation, may be worth consideration.

Pay no attention to the criticism of men who have never themselves written a notable work. Consider the discrepancies between the actual writing of the Greek poets and dramatists, and the theories of the Graeco-Roman grammarians, concocted to explain their metres.

Language

Use no superflous word, no adjective, which does not reveal something.

Don't use such an expression as "dim lands *of peace.*" It dulls the image. It mixes an abstraction with the concrete. It comes from the writer's not realizing that the natural object is always the *adequate* symbol.

Go in fear of abstractions. Don't retell in mediocre verse what has already been done in good prose. Don't think any intelligent person is going to be deceived when you try to shirk all the difficulties of the unspeakably difficult art of good prose by chopping your composition into line lengths.

What the expert is tired of today the public will be tired of tomorrow.

Don't imagine that the art of poetry is any simpler than the art of music, or that you can please the expert before you have spent at least as much effort on the art of verse as the average piano teacher spends on the art of music.

Be influenced by as many great artists as you can, but have the decency either to acknowledge the debt outright, or to try to conceal it.

Don't allow "influence" to mean merely that you mop up the particular decorative vocabulary of some one or two poets whom you happen to admire. A Turkish war correspondent was recently caught red-handed babbling in his dispatches of "dove-gray" hills, or else it was "pearl-pale," I cannot remember.

Use either no ornament or good ornament.

Rhythm and Rhyme

Let the candidate fill his mind with the finest cadences he can discover, preferably in a foreign language so that the meaning of the words may be less likely to divert his attention from the movement; e.g., Saxon charms, Hebridean Folk Songs, the verse of Dante,[3] and the lyrics of Shakespeare — if he can dissociate the vocabulary from the cadence. Let him dissect the lyrics of Goethe[4] coldly into their component sound values, syllables long and short, stressed and unstressed, into vowels and consonants.

---

3. **Saxon charms, Hebridean Folk Songs, the verse of Dante:** Pound refers to the cadences of verse written in languages other than standard English: Anglo-Saxon poetry written in Old English, the Germanic language of the ancient Saxons; the dialect poems and songs of the inhabitants of the Hebrides, an isolated group of islands off the northwestern coast of Scotland; and the work of the Italian poet Dante Alighieri (1265–1321), author of the epic poem *The Divine Comedy.*
4. **Goethe:** The German poet, novelist, and dramatist Johann Wolfgang von Goethe (1749–1832).

It is not necessary that a poem should rely on its music, but if it does rely on its music that music must be such as will delight the expert.

Let the neophyte know assonance and alliteration, rhyme immediate and delayed, simple and polyphonic, as a musician would expect to know harmony and counterpoint and all the minutiae of his craft. No time is too great to give to these matters or to any one of them, even if the artist seldom have need of them.

Don't imagine that a thing will "go" in verse just because it's too dull to go in prose.

Don't be "viewy" — leave that to the writers of pretty little philosophic essays. Don't be descriptive; remember that the painter can describe a landscape much better than you can, and that he has to know a deal more about it.

When Shakespeare talks of the "Dawn in russet mantle clad"[5] he presents something which the painter does not present. There is in this line of his nothing that one can call description; he presents.

Consider the way of the scientists rather than the way of an advertising agent for a new soap.

The scientist does not expect to be acclaimed as a great scientist until he has *discovered* something. He begins by learning what has been discovered already. He goes from that point onward. He does not bank on being a charming fellow personally. He does not expect his friends to applaud the results of his freshman class work. Freshmen in poetry are unfortunately not confined to a definite and recognizable classroom. They are "all over the shop." Is it any wonder "the public is indifferent to poetry"?

Don't chop your stuff into separate *iambs*.[6] Don't make each line stop dead at the end, and then begin every next line with a heave. Let the beginning of the next line catch the rise of the rhythm wave, unless you want a definite longish pause.

In short, behave as a musician, a good musician, when dealing with that phase of your art which has exact parallels in music. The same laws govern, and you are bound by no others.

[1913]

---

5. **"Dawn . . . clad"**: A reference to famous lines in Shakespeare's *Hamlet*: "But, look, the morn in russet mantle clad, / Walks o'er the dew of yon high eastern hill (1.1.166-67).
6. **separate *iambs***: The most common metrical form in English poetry is iambic verse, in which lines are divided into a set number of metrical feet called iambs, each of which consists of an unstressed syllable followed by a stressed syllable.

Amy Lowell

[1874-1925]

Amy Lowell supplanted Ezra Pound as the driving force in what he called imagisme and she called imagism (see Lowell, p. 575). After Pound published his anthology *Des Imagistes* (1914), which included some of Lowell's poems, she began to plan an anthology that would include additional new poets and create a wider audience for imagism. To her disappointment, Pound refused to participate in the project, arguing that having the poems selected by a committee, as Lowell planned, would inevitably lower the standards of the anthology. In a letter to Lowell, Pound asserted that he wanted "the name 'Imagisme' to retain some sort of meaning. It stands, or I should like it to stand for hard light, clear edges. I cannot trust any democratized committee to maintain that standard." Lowell persisted, however, and the first of her three anthologies, *Some Imagist Poets*, appeared in April 1915. Even as Pound derided the movement as "Amygism," Lowell promoted imagism and what was called "the new poetry" at her countless readings and lectures, as well as in essays such as "The New Manner in Modern Poetry." Seeking to pave the way for a wider acceptance of modern poetry in the United States, a country that embraced change and celebrated progress, Lowell in the essay emphasized that the "new manner" was "an inevitable change, reflecting the evolution of life." The text is taken from the first printing of the essay in the *New Republic*, March 4, 1916.

THE NEW MANNER IN MODERN POETRY

We hear so much about "the new poetry" to-day, and see it so injudiciously lauded in publishers' catalogues, and so non-understandingly reviled and jeered at in the daily press, that it is no wonder if most people think it a mere advertising term, with no basis in fact.

This is most unfair and uncritical, for there is a "new manner" in the poetry of to-day which sets it quite apart from the poetry immediately preceding it. I am not referring to the extreme fads so prevalent in Europe before the war, such as futurism, headed by Marinetti, with its pronunciamento that verbs should only be used in the infinitive, and its algebraic signs of "plus" and "minus," etc., to eke out a language it had intentionally impoverished; or "Fantaisisme," with Guillaume Appolinaire as chief priest, who wrote so-called "ideographic poetry," or poems printed so as to represent a picture of a railroad train with puffing smoke, or some other thing of the sort.[1] That these "notions" (to borrow a phrase from the country shopkeeper) will survive the war is inconceivable, but that the real, sane "new manner" will persist cannot admit of a doubt. For the new manner is not a dress assumed at will, it is the result of changed surroundings, of a changed attitude toward life.

The "new manner" is made up of so many elements that to give all these elements one specific name is little difficult, but elsewhere I have called it "externality," and that name will quite suffice to show its antagonism to the "internality" which is the most marked quality in the poetry of the 'nineties.

---

1. **I am not referring . . . or some other thing of the sort:** Lowell dismisses as "fads" two of the most radical movements in the modern arts: Italian futurism, initially a literary movement created by Filippo Tommaso Marinetti (1876–1944), who published the manifesto *Le Futurisme* in 1909, and "Fantaisisme," or "Surnaturalisme" (surrealism), the literary method of the influential French poet and critic Guillaume Apollinaire (1880–1918).

There is not space in a brief paper to show the steps by which poetry arrived at the introspective state against which the "new manner" is a protest. That the poets of the late Victorian epoch were extraordinarily subjective, no one will deny. And this subjectivity led to a refining and ever refining upon their emotions, until the emotions themselves became somewhat tenuous. With this, growing all the time, went a most beautiful technique. There seems to have been something a little faded about these men; perhaps jaded would be a better term. Were they really so melancholy, or was it just a fashion? Some of them were pensively sad, some were despairingly enraged, they looked at grey and old-rose landscapes and sighed a languid appreciation, or they whipped up their jaded mental appetites with minute descriptions of artificial, insinuated suggestions of quite ordinary vulgarities. But whatever they did they made beautiful, literary backgrounds for a gigantic ego. Each man's ego was swollen to a quite abnormal size, and he was worshipped by his other self, the author, with every conceivable literary device and subtlety.

Egoism may be a crime in the world of morals, but in the world of the arts it is perfectly permissible. It makes very good and very interesting poetry. In mentioning it I am not condemning it, I am only labelling it. It was the manner of the 'nineties, it is not the manner of to-day.

Now, by "externality" I mean the attitude of being interested in things for themselves and not because of the effect they have upon oneself. The poet of the "new manner" paints landscapes because landscapes are beautiful, not because they chime with his mood. He tells stories because stories are interesting, and not to prove a thesis. He writes narrative poems because his range embraces the world and is not confined to himself. He is ironic, grotesque, ugly at times, because he has the feeling of the universality of life.

Some critics are forever measuring the modernity of poetry by what they call its "social consciousness." When a poet really writes in the "modern manner," social consciousness becomes one facet of his feeling of universality. The greater includes the less, and "externality" includes the universe and everything in it. But Milton and Dante[2] were universal, it may be said, were they therefore modern? Certainly not. They were universal, but they were not "external." Man stuck out in high relief all over their work. Man and his destiny — man completely out of focus, in short — was their theme. The "new manner" attempts to put man in his proper place in the picture; that is why it is so at variance with the method of the so-called "cosmic" poet.

Now "externality" shows itself in two ways: in choice of subject matter, and in treatment; and this last again may be subdivided into general arrangement and ordering of particulars, and style.

First, as to subject matter. "Externality" is the main trend of the "new manner," but of course that does not mean that no poet ever writes subjective verses. He could hardly

---

2. **Milton and Dante:** The English poet John Milton (1608–1674), author of the epic poem *Paradise Lost*, and the Italian poet Dante Alighieri (1265–1321), author of the epic poem *The Divine Comedy*.

be universal if he excluded himself. It is a fact, however, that modern poetry of the new kind does not concern itself primarily with introspection.

Another characteristic of the "new manner" is humor. Pensive melancholy is no longer inevitably to be worn, like a badge of office. It has gone, with many other obvious fripperies, such as leonine hair and visioning eyes. Is it because poets are more sincere to-day, that they have less "side"?[3] I do not know, but certainly in the 'nineties, in England at least, they were a very carefully put together lot. It is this sincerity, I believe, which has brought back humor. To many poets of the preceding generation, melancholy must have been a fashion. I really think that if there is a fashion to-day it is sincerity.

Another striking tendency of the "new manner" is its insistence upon the poetry in unpoetic things. The new poet is never tired of finding colors in a dust-heap, and shouting about them. Sometimes the colors so occupy him that he takes them separately, unrelated to the dust-heap, as it were. This taking colors, and light and shade, in planes and cubes, with practically no insistence on the substances which produce them, be they men or houses or trees or water, is often called futurism by the ignorant. Probably because the real futurists, Marinetti and his followers, never employ it.

The poets of the "new manner" have another distinguishing mark. They endeavor to write poetry in the syntax of prose. Inversions are abhorrent to them, except when used purposely for accent. They try to write in the ordinary phrase construction of everyday speech and make it poetry just the same. How difficult this is, only those who have tried it know. When at a loss for a rhyme they do not permit themselves to drop suddenly into a simile for three lines — a cunning simile, neatly devised to give the necessary rhyme. They use colloquial language; "poetic diction" has sunk into ill repute, only newspaper poets and their ilk employ it. Poets no longer "fain" to do anything, nor "ope" their eyes to the "ethiope splendor of the spangled night," when "they themselves have lain upon a couch to woo reluctant slumber."

Still a third characteristic is the presentation of facts and images without comment. If there is one thing which the "new manner" is more against than another, it is preaching in a poem. And this care not to point a moral is one of the most pronounced features of the "new manner." It is this very thing which leads so many poetry lovers of the older generation to find it cold. An old-fashioned editor once said to me that what he missed in modern poetry was its lack of noble thoughts. The poetry which is a pepsin to weak intellects to whom crude life is indigestible, has nothing in common with the "new manner." "Noble thoughts," neat little uplift labels wrapped in the tinfoil of pretty verse, has its place in the scheme of existence, no doubt, but to the modern poet it is anathema. He seeks to give life, the world, as it is, as he sees it, at any rate; and the lesson of his poem, if there be one, must be inherent in the poem itself. He takes the intelligence of his readers for granted, and trusts to their getting the meaning of the poem as it unfolds, refusing to bellow it at them through a megaphone in impertinent asides.

Why do people refuse to take art as organic, and insist upon considering it as merely explanatory? When these same people walk in the garden on a fine morning, do they feel

---

3. **"side"**: Slang for pretentiousness or conceit.

chilled and depressed because the little flower-buds are not tagged with texts? But there! We shall never agree, and for people who like to be drugged with fine, conventional sentiments there is no cure in heaven or earth, that I am aware of.

Now as to form. It is the belief of most people that interest in metrical experiments is a distinguishing feature of the "new manner." But do you suppose that there has ever been a time when real poets were not interested in metrical experiments? Poets have been widening and deepening and freeing their prosody ever since there was a prosody to tinker with. In experimenting, the modern poet is merely following tradition.

As the word "new" has been "wished on" to contemporary poetry, so are its metrical experiments dubbed and condemned as "new." *Vers libre* in particular is constantly called "new" and hooted at; or poets who employ it are told that they think it is new, and it is not. Of course it is not, only the paragraph writers in the newspapers ever supposed it was. So far as I know, the only metrical experiment which is in the least new is "polyphonic prose," and that had its beginnings in France, in the work of Gustave Kahn, and Saint-Pol-Roux, and Paul Fort.[4] I believe I am the first poet who has ever employed it in English, and it had to be so adapted in bringing it over from one language to another that it only retains a partial resemblance to the French form.

Now the "new manner" does not consist solely in any one of these characteristics; it consists in all. Some poets have one of them, some another; it may be subject, it may be form. The "new manner" is as characteristic as the manner of differing peoples. All Americans are not alike, but all Americans have something which sets them together, and apart from other nationalities. So the change in poetry is easily distinguished. And it is an inevitable change, reflecting the evolution of life.

[1916]

---

4. **"polyphonic prose,"** . . . **Paul Fort**: Lowell traces her own experiments in polyphonic prose — rhythmical prose that employs elements of verse, especially alliteration, assonance, and rhyme — back to the work of three influential French symbolist poets: Gustave Kahn (1859-1936), who claimed to have invented the term *vers libre*, or free verse; Saint-Pol-Roux (1861-1940); and Paul Fort (1872-1960).

T. S. Eliot

[1888-1965]

T. S. Eliot was one of the most influential poets and literary critics of the twentieth century (see Eliot, p. 669). One of his most famous essays, "Tradition and the Individual Talent," was first published in two parts in the *Egoist: An Individualist Review*. The feminist and anarchist Dora Marsden established the radical magazine in 1911 as the *Freewoman*, later the *New Freewoman*, whose purpose was "to expound a doctrine of philosophical individualism." After Ezra Pound became the literary editor in 1913, the name of the magazine was changed to the *Egoist*, which he helped transform into a prominent avant-garde literary journal. It subsequently published the work of many new writers, including James Joyce and Eliot, who served as the assistant editor from 1917 through 1919. During the same period, there was a growing tension within literary circles between tradition and innovation, between those who advocated a firm break with the conventions, language, and forms of earlier poetry and those who found inspiration, models, and subjects in the past, notably Eliot and Pound. In "Tradition and the Individual Talent," Eliot offered a complex formulation of the relation between the modern poet and the European literary tradition beginning with Homer. Even as he emphasized the poet's responsibility to develop "the consciousness of the past," Eliot challenged the conventional understanding of "tradition," which in his view was not fixed but fluid, subject to transformation by the introduction of each genuinely *new* work of art. The text of the following selection, the first part and the opening of the second part of the essay, is taken from its first printing in the *Egoist*, September and December 1919.

From Tradition and the Individual Talent

In English writing we seldom speak of tradition, though we occasionally apply its name in deploring its absence. We cannot refer to "the tradition" or to "a tradition"; at most, we employ the adjective in saying that the poetry of So-and-So is "traditional" or even "too traditional." Seldom, perhaps, does the word appear except in a phrase of censure. If otherwise, it is vaguely approbative, with the implication, as to the work approved, of some pleasing archaeological reconstruction. You can hardly make the word agreeable to English ears without this comfortable reference to the reassuring science of archaeology.

Certainly the word is not likely to appear in our appreciations of living or dead writers. Every nation, every race, has not only its own creative, but its own critical turn of mind; and is even more oblivious of the shortcomings and limitations of its critical habits than of those of its creative genius. We know, or think we know, from the enormous mass of critical writing that has appeared in the French language the critical method or habit of the French; we only conclude (we are such unconscious people) that the French are "more critical" than we, and sometimes even plume ourselves a little with the fact, as if the French were the less spontaneous. Perhaps they are; but we might remind ourselves that criticism is as inevitable as breathing, and that we should be none the worse for articulating what passes in our minds when we read a book and feel an emotion about it, for criticising our own minds in their work of criticism. One of the facts that might come to light in this process is our tendency to insist, when we praise a poet, upon those aspects of his work in which he least resembles anyone else. In these aspects or parts of his work we pretend to find what is individual, what is the peculiar essence of the man. We dwell with satisfaction upon the poet's difference from his predecessors, especially his immediate predecessors; we endeavour to find something that can be isolated in order to be enjoyed. Whereas if we approach a poet without this prejudice we shall often find that not only the best, but the most individual parts of his work may be those in which the dead poets, his ancestors, assert their immortality most vigorously. And I do not intend the impressionable period of adolescence, but the period of full maturity.

Yet if the only form of tradition, of handing down, consisted in following the ways of the immediate generation before us in a blind or timid adherence to its successes, "tradition" should positively be discouraged. We have seen many such simple currents soon lost in the sand; and novelty is better than repetition. Tradition is a matter of much wider significance. It cannot be inherited, and if you want it you must obtain it by great labour. It involves, in the first place, the historical sense, which we may call nearly indispensable to anyone who would continue to be a poet beyond his twenty-fifth year; and the historical sense involves a perception, not only of the pastness of the past, but of its presence; the historical sense compels a man to write not merely with his own generation in his bones, but with a feeling that the whole of the literature of Europe from Homer and within it the whole of the literature of his own country has a simultaneous existence and composes a simultaneous order. This historical sense, which is a sense of the timeless as well as of the temporal and of the timeless and of the temporal together, is what makes a writer traditional. And it is at the same time what makes a writer most acutely conscious of his place in time, of his contemporaneity.

No poet, no artist of any art, has his complete meaning alone. His significance, his appreciation is the appreciation of his relation to the dead poets and artists. You cannot value him alone; you must set him, for contrast and comparison, among the dead. I mean this as a principle of aesthetic, not merely historical, criticism. The necessity that he shall conform, that he shall cohere, is not one-sided; what happens when a new work of art is created is something that happens simultaneously to all the works of art which preceded it. The existing monuments form an ideal order among themselves, which is modified by the introduction of the new (the really new) work of art among them. The existing order is complete before the new work arrives; for order to persist after the supervention of novelty, the *whole* existing order must be, if ever so slightly, altered; and so the relations, proportions, values of each work of art toward the whole are readjusted; and this is conformity between the old and the new. Whoever has approved this idea of order, of the form of European, of English literature, will not find it preposterous that the past should be altered by the present as much as the present is directed by the past. And the poet who is aware of this will be aware of great difficulties and responsibilities.

In a peculiar sense he will be aware also that he must inevitably be judged by the standards of the past. I say judged by, not amputated, by them; not judged to be as good as, or worse or better than, the dead; and certainly not judged by the canons of dead critics. It is a judgment, a comparison in which two things are measured by each other. To conform merely would be for the new work not really to conform at all; it would not be new, and would therefore not be a work of art. And we do not quite say that the new is more valuable because it fits in; but its fitting in is a test of its value — a test, it is true, which can only be slowly and cautiously applied, for we are none of us infallible judges of conformity. We say: it appears to conform, and is perhaps individual, or it appears individual, and may conform; but we are hardly likely to find that it is one and not the other.

To proceed to a more intelligible exposition of the relation of the poet to the past: he can neither take the past as a lump, an indiscriminate bolus, nor can he form himself wholly on one or two private admirations, nor can he form himself wholly upon one preferred period. The first course is inadmissible, the second is an important experience of youth, and the third is a pleasant and highly desirable supplement. The poet must be very conscious of the main current, which does not at all flow invariably through the most distinguished reputations. He must be quite aware of the obvious fact that art never improves, but that the material of art is never quite the same. He must be aware that the mind of Europe – the mind of his own country – a mind which he learns in time to be much more important than his own private mind – is a mind which changes, and that this change is a development which abandons nothing *en route*, which does not superannuate either Shakespeare or Homer or the rock drawing of the Magdalenian draughtsmen.[1] That this development, refinement perhaps, complication certainly, is not, from the point of view of the artist, any improvement. Perhaps not even an improvement from the point of view of the psychologist or not to the extent which we imagine; perhaps only in the end based upon a complication in economics and machinery. But the difference between the present and the past is that the conscious present is an awareness of the past in a way and to an extent which the past's awareness of itself cannot show.

Someone said: "The dead writers are remote from us because we *know* so much more than they did." Precisely, and they are that which we know.

I am alive to a usual objection to what is clearly part of my programme for the *métier*[2] of poetry. The objection is that the doctrine requires a ridiculous amount of erudition (pedantry), a claim which can be rejected by appeal to the lives of poets in any pantheon. It will even be affirmed that much learning deadens or perverts poetic sensibility. While, however, we persist in believing that a poet ought to know as much as will not encroach upon his necessary receptivity and necessary laziness, it is not desirable to confine knowledge to whatever can be put into a useful shape for examinations, drawing rooms, or the still more pretentious modes of publicity. Some can absorb knowledge, the more tardy must sweat for it. Shakespeare acquired more essential history from Plutarch than most men could from the whole British Museum.[3] What is to be insisted upon is that the poet must develop or procure the consciousness of the past and that he should continue to develop this consciousness throughout his career.

---

1. **the rock drawing of the Magdalenian draughtsmen:** The Magdalenians were peoples who flourished in Europe from 18,000 to 10,000 BCE. Their celebrated cave art, primarily engravings and paintings of various species of animals, was discovered in the 1860s but not accepted as genuine by anthropologists and historians until 1902.
2. **métier:** An activity or occupation, especially work for which a person is particularly suited (French).
3. **Shakespeare . . . British Museum:** One of the major sources of Shakespeare's history plays was Plutarch's *Parallel Lives*, biographies of eminent Greeks and Romans, which Sir Thomas North translated into English in 1579. The British Museum in London has extensive collections that cover world cultures from prehistory to the present day.

What happens is a continual surrender of himself as he is at the moment to something which is more valuable. The progress of an artist is a continual self-sacrifice, a continual extinction of personality.

There remains to define this process of depersonalisation and its relation to the sense of tradition. It is in this depersonalisation that art may be said to approach the condition of science. I shall, therefore, invite you to consider, as a suggestive analogy, the action which takes place when a bit of finely filiated platinum is introduced into a chamber containing oxygen and sulphur dioxide.[4]

II

The upshot of this article and of the article which preceded it is this: that honest criticism and sensitive appreciation is directed not upon the poet but upon the poetry. If we attend to the confused cries of the newspaper critics and the susurrus[5] of popular repetition that follows, we shall hear the names of poets in great number; if we seek not blue-book knowledge[6] but the enjoyment of poetry, and ask for a poem, we shall seldom find it. In the last article I tried to point out the importance of the relation of the poem to other poems by other authors, and suggested the conception of poetry as a living whole of all the poetry that has ever been written. The other aspect of this Impersonal theory of poetry is the relation of the poem to its author. And I hinted, by an analogy, that the mind of the mature poet differs from that of the immature one not precisely in any valuation of "personality," not being necessarily more interesting, or having "more to say," but rather by being a more finely perfected medium in which special, or very varied, feelings are at liberty to enter into new combinations.

The analogy was that of the catalyst. When the two gases previously mentioned are mixed in the presence of a filament of platinum, they form sulphurous acid. This combination takes place only if the platinum is present; nevertheless the newly formed acid contains no trace of platinum, and the platinum itself is apparently unaffected; has remained inert, passive and unchanged. The mind of the poet is the shred of platinum. It may partly or exclusively operate upon the experience of the man himself; but, the more perfect the artist, the more completely separate in him will be the man who suffers and the mind which creates; the more perfectly will the mind digest and transmute the passions which are its material.

[1919]

---

4. **the action . . . oxygen and sulphur dioxide:** The platinum acts as a catalyst. Eliot explains the analogy in the second paragraph of part 2 of the essay, printed below.
5. **susurrus:** A poetic term for murmuring or rustling.
6. **blue-book knowledge:** Blue books are official guidebooks.

James Weldon Johnson

[1871–1938]

James Weldon Johnson was a novelist, poet, and tireless promoter of the work of other African American writers during the Harlem Renaissance (see Johnson, p. 570). In his often-quoted preface to *The Book of American Negro Poetry: Chosen and Edited with an Essay on the Negro's Creative Genius* (1922), he observed, "The public, generally speaking, does not know that there are American Negro poets." Johnson designed his anthology as a corrective that would demonstrate the richness and range of modern African American poetry. "The final measure of the greatness of all peoples is the amount and standard of the literature and art they have produced," he affirmed. "The world does not know that a people is great until that people produces great literature and art." The anthology included the work of more than thirty poets, beginning with Paul Laurence Dunbar (1872–1906), whose "Negro dialect poems" had gained and continued to enjoy widespread popularity. In the following passage from the preface, Johnson explained why so few of the contemporary poets included in his anthology wrote in dialect, which he argued was not "capable of giving expression to the varied conditions of Negro life in America." The text is taken from the first printing of *The Book of American Negro Poetry* (1922).

From PREFACE TO
THE BOOK OF AMERICAN NEGRO POETRY

It may be surprising to many to see how little of the poetry being written by Negro poets to-day is being written in Negro dialect. The newer Negro poets show a tendency to discard dialect; much of the subject-matter which went into the making of traditional dialect poetry, 'possums, watermelons, etc., they have discarded altogether, at least, as poetic material. This tendency will, no doubt, be regretted by the majority of white readers; and, indeed, it would be a distinct loss if the American Negro poets threw away this quaint and musical folk-speech as a medium of expression. And yet, after all, these poets are working through a problem not realized by the reader, and, perhaps, by many of these poets themselves not realized consciously. They are trying to break away from, not Negro dialect itself, but the limitations on Negro dialect imposed by the fixing effects of long convention.

The Negro in the United States has achieved or been placed in a certain artistic niche. When he is thought of artistically, it is as a happy-go-lucky, singing, shuffling, banjo-picking being or as a more or less pathetic figure. The picture of him is in a log cabin amid fields of cotton or along the levees. Negro dialect is naturally and by long association the exact instrument for voicing this phase of Negro life; and by that very exactness it is an instrument with but two full stops, humor and pathos. So even when he confines himself to purely racial themes, the Aframerican poet realizes that there are phases of Negro life in the United States which cannot be treated in the dialect either adequately or artistically. Take, for example, the phases rising out of life in Harlem, that most wonderful Negro city in the world. I do not deny that a Negro in a log cabin is more picturesque than a Negro in a Harlem flat, but the Negro in the Harlem flat is here, and he is but part of a group growing everywhere in the country, a group whose ideals are becoming increasingly more vital than those of the traditionally artistic group, even if its members are less picturesque.

What the colored poet in the United States needs to do is something like what Synge did for the Irish;[1] he needs to find a form that will express the racial spirit by symbols from within rather than by symbols from without, such as the mere mutilation of English spelling and pronunciation. He needs a form that is freer and larger than dialect, but which will still hold the racial flavor; a form expressing the imagery, the idioms, the peculiar turns of thought, and the distinctive humor and pathos, too, of the Negro, but which will also be capable of voicing the deepest and highest emotions and aspirations, and allow of the widest range of subjects and the widest scope of treatment.

Negro dialect is at present a medium that is not capable of giving expression to the varied conditions of Negro life in America, and much less is it capable of giving the fullest interpretation of Negro character and psychology. This is no indictment against the dialect as dialect, but against the mould of convention in which Negro dialect in the United States has been set. In time these conventions may become lost, and the colored poet in the United States may sit down to write in dialect without feeling that his first line will put the general reader in a frame of mind which demands that the poem be humorous or pathetic. In the meantime, there is no reason why these poets should not continue to do the beautiful things that can be done, and done best, in the dialect.

In stating the need for Aframerican poets in the United States to work out a new and distinctive form of expression I do not wish to be understood to hold any theory that they should limit themselves to Negro poetry, to racial themes; the sooner they are able to write *American* poetry spontaneously, the better. Nevertheless, I believe that the richest contribution the Negro poet can make to the American literature of the future will be the fusion into it of his own individual artistic gifts.

[1922]

---

1. **Synge did for the Irish**: The poet and dramatist John Millington Synge (1871–1909) was a central figure in the Irish literary renaissance at the end of the nineteenth and beginning of the twentieth centuries.

Mina Loy

[1882–1966]

Mina Loy was a transplanted English poet and painter who became a prominent figure in modernist movements in France, Italy, and the United States, where she moved in 1916 (see Loy, p. 618). Ezra Pound commented in 1921 that Loy, Marianne Moore, and William Carlos Williams were the only poets in America "who can write anything of interest in verse." Other admirers of her poetry, which appeared in a variety of literary magazines, included E. E. Cummings, T. S. Eliot, and Wallace Stevens. "Modern Poetry," Loy's only known essay on contemporary literature, first appeared in *Charm: The Magazine of New Jersey Home Interests*, which was published in New York from 1924 through 1932. In the essay, which was originally illustrated with photographs of Marianne Moore, Maxwell Bodenheim, Edna St. Vincent Millay, and E. E. Cummings, Loy provided readers of the fashion magazine with a lively overview of the origins and development of the "new poetry," beginning with the work of Ezra Pound. Emphasizing that the achievements of modern verse "more than vindicated the rebellion against tradition," Loy attributed much of its success to the close association between poetry and music, as well as to the vital influence of the "melting pot" of the American language. The text of "Modern Poetry" is taken from the first printing in *Charm*, April 1925.

From MODERN POETRY

Poetry is prose bewitched, a music made of visual thoughts, the sound of an idea.

The new poetry of the English language has proceeded out of America. Of things American it attains the aristocratic situation of vitality. This unexpectedly realized valuation of American jazz and American poetry is endorsed by two publics; the one universal, the other infinitesimal in comparison.

And why has the collective spirit of the modern world, of which both are the reflection, recognized itself unanimously in the new music of unprecedented instruments, and so rarely in the new poetry of unprecedented verse? It is because the sound of music capturing our involuntary attention is so easy to get in touch with, while the silent sound of poetry requires our voluntary attention to obliterate the cold barrier of print with the whole "intelligence of our senses." And many of us who have no habit of reading not alone with the eye but also with the ear, have — especially at a superficial first reading — overlooked the beauty of it.

More than to read poetry we must listen to poetry. All reading is the evocation of speech; the difference in our approach, then, in reading a poem or a newspaper is that our attitude in reading a poem must be rather that of listening to and looking at a pictured song. Modern poetry, like music, has received a fresh impetus from contemporary life; they have both gained in precipitance of movement. The structure of all poetry is the movement that an active individuality makes in expressing itself. Poetic rhythm, of which we have all spoken so much, is the chart of a temperament.

The variety and felicity of these structural movements in modern verse has more than vindicated the rebellion against tradition. It will be found that one can recognize each of the modern poet's work by the gait of their mentality. Or rather that the formation of their verses is determined by the spontaneous tempo of their response to life. And if at first it appears irksome to adjust pleasure to unaccustomed meters, let us reflect in time that hexameters and alexandrines, before they became poetic laws, originated as the spontaneous structure of a poet's inspiration.

Imagine a tennis champion who became inspired to write poetry, would not his verse be likely to embody the rhythmic transit of skimming balls? Would not his meter depend on his way of life, would it not form itself, without having recourse to traditional, remembered, or accepted forms? This, then, is the secret of the new poetry. It is the direct response of the poet's mind to the modern world of varieties in which he finds himself. In each one we can discover his particular inheritance of that world's beauty.

Close as this relationship of poetry to music is, I think only once has the logical transition from verse to music, on which I had so often speculated, been made, and that by the American, Ezra Pound. To speak of the modern movement is to speak of him; the masterly impresario of modern poets, for without the discoveries he made with his poet's instinct for poetry, this modern movement would still be rather a nebula than the constellation it has become. Not only a famous poet, but a man of action, he gave the public the required push on to modern poetry at the psychological moment. Pound, the purveyor of geniuses to such journals as the "Little Review," on which he conferred immortality by procuring for its pages the manuscripts of Joyce's "Ulysses."[1] Almost together with the publication of his magnificent Cantos, his music was played in Paris:[2] it utters the communings of a poet's mind with itself making decisions on harmony.

It was inevitable that the renaissance of poetry should proceed out of America, where latterly a thousand languages have been born, and each one, for purposes of communication at least, English — English enriched and variegated with the grammatical structure and voice-inflection of many races, in novel alloy with the fundamental time-is-money idiom of the United States, discovered by the newspaper cartoonists.

This composite language is a very living language, it grows as you speak. For the true American appears to be ashamed to say anything in the way it has been said before. Every moment he ingeniously coins new words for old ideas, to keep good humor warm. And on the baser avenues of Manhattan every voice swings to the triple rhythm of its race, its citizenship, and its personality.

Out of the welter of this unclassifiable speech, while professors of Harvard and Oxford labored to preserve, "God's English," the muse of modern literature arose, and her tongue had been loosened in the melting-pot.

You may think it impossible to conjure up the relationship of expression between the high browest modern poets and an adolescent Slav who has speculated in a wholesale job-lot of mandarines and is trying to sell them in a retail market on First Avenue. But it lies simply in this: both have had to become adapted to a country where the mind has to put on its verbal clothes at terrific speed if it would speak in time; where no one will listen if you attack him twice with the same missile of argument. And, that the ear that has

---

1. **Pound . . . "Ulysses":**   Ezra Pound arranged for the serialization of *Ulysses* in the *Little Review*, where portions of James Joyce's controversial novel appeared between March 1918 and December 1920. In a widely publicized trial, the editors of the magazine were prosecuted for obscenity in 1921, forcing them to cease publication of *Ulysses*. The novel was published in book form in Paris in 1922.
2. **his music was played in Paris:**   After moving to Paris in 1920, Pound completed *A Draft of XVI Cantos* (1925) and began to write music, including several pieces for solo violin and a one-act opera, *Le Testament*, portions of which were performed in 1924.

listened to the greatest number of sounds will have the most to choose from when it comes to self-expression, each has been liberally educated in the flexibility of phrases.

So in the American poet wherever he may wander, however he may engage himself with an older culture, there has occurred no Europeanization of his fundamental advantage, the acuter shock of the New World consciousness upon life. His is still poetry that has proceeded out of America.

[1925]

Langston Hughes

[1902–1967]

Langston Hughes was one of the major literary figures that emerged during the Harlem Renaissance (see Hughes, p. 752). His famous manifesto, "The Negro Artist and the Racial Mountain," appeared in the *Nation* in 1926. Only one week earlier, the magazine had published "The Negro-Art Hokum," a provocative essay by the African American cultural critic George Schuyler (1895–1977). Dismissing the idea that there could be such a thing as "Negro art" in the United States, Schuyler observed: "As for the literature, painting, and sculpture of Aframericans — such as there is — it is identical in kind with the literature, painting, and sculpture of white Americans: that is, it shows more or less evidence of European influence." He thus argued that, far from being shaped by different experiences or displaying a distinctive psychology, "your American Negro is just plain American." In sharp contrast, Hughes asserted that the "desire" to run away from one's race "is the mountain standing in the way of any true Negro art in America." He therefore urged the would-be "racial artist" to explore the full range of African American life, including the experiences of the urban poor in the North. He also celebrated indigenous forms of African American culture, especially jazz, "one of the inherent expressions of Negro life in America." The text is taken from the first printing of the essay in the *Nation*, June 23, 1926.

THE NEGRO ARTIST AND THE RACIAL MOUNTAIN

One of the most promising of the young Negro poets[1] said to me once, "I want to be a poet — not a Negro poet," meaning, I believe, "I want to write like a white poet"; meaning subconsciously, "I would like to be a white poet"; meaning behind that, "I would like to

---

1. **the most promising of the young Negro poets:** Hughes was probably referring to his friend and rival, Countee Cullen, by far the most popular African American poet of the 1920s. In a 1924 interview, Cullen had declared that he wanted "to be POET and not NEGRO POET."

be white." And I was sorry the young man said that, for no great poet has ever been afraid of being himself. And I doubted then that, with his desire to run away spiritually from his race, this boy would ever be a great poet. But this is the mountain standing in the way of any true Negro art in America — this urge within the race toward whiteness, the desire to pour racial individuality into the mold of American standardization, and to be as little Negro and as much American as possible.

But let us look at the immediate background of this young poet. His family is of what I suppose one would call the Negro middle class: people who are by no means rich yet never uncomfortable nor hungry — smug, contented, respectable folk, members of the Baptist church. The father goes to work every morning. He is a chief steward at a large white club. The mother sometimes does fancy sewing or supervises parties for the rich families of the town. The children go to a mixed school. In the home they read white papers and magazines. And the mother often says "Don't be like niggers" when the children are bad. A frequent phrase from the father is, "Look how well a white man does things." And so the word *white* comes to be unconsciously a symbol of all the virtues. It holds for the children beauty, morality, and money. The whisper of "I want to be white" runs silently through their minds. This young poet's home is, I believe, a fairly typical home of the colored middle class. One sees immediately how difficult it would be for an artist born in such a home to interest himself in interpreting the beauty of his own people. He is never taught to see that beauty. He is taught rather not to see it, or if he does, to be ashamed of it when it is not according to Caucasian patterns.

For racial culture the home of a self-styled "high-class" Negro has nothing better to offer. Instead there will perhaps be more aping of things white than in a less cultured or less wealthy home. The father is perhaps a doctor, lawyer, landowner, or politician. The mother may be a social worker, or a teacher, or she may do nothing and have a maid. Father is often dark but he has usually married the lightest woman he could find. The family attend a fashionable church where few really colored faces are to be found. And they themselves draw a color line. In the North they go to white theaters and white movies. And in the South they have at least two cars and a house "like white folks." Nordic manners, Nordic faces, Nordic hair, Nordic art (if any), and an Episcopal heaven. A very high mountain indeed for the would-be racial artist to climb in order to discover himself and his people.

But then there are the low-down folks, the so-called common element, and they are the majority — may the Lord be praised! The people who have their nip of gin on Saturday nights and are not too important to themselves or the community, or too well fed, or too learned to watch the lazy world go round. They live on Seventh Street in Washington or State Street in Chicago and they do not particularly care whether they are like white folks or anybody else. Their joy runs, bang! into ecstasy. Their religion soars to a shout. Work maybe a little today, rest a little tomorrow. Play awhile. Sing awhile. O, let's dance! These common people are not afraid of spirituals, as for a long time their more intellectual brethren were, and jazz is their child. They furnish a wealth of colorful, distinctive material for any artist because they still hold their own individuality in the face of American standardizations. And perhaps these common people will give to the world its truly great Negro artist, the one who is not afraid to be himself. Whereas the better-class Negro would tell the artist what to do, the people at least let him alone when he does appear. And they are not ashamed of him — if they know he exists at all. And they accept what beauty is their own without question.

Certainly there is, for the American Negro artist who can escape the restrictions the more advanced among his own group would put upon him, a great field of unused material ready for his art. Without going outside his race, and even among the better classes with their "white" culture and conscious American manners, but still Negro enough to be different, there is sufficient matter to furnish a black artist with a lifetime of creative work. And when he chooses to touch on the relations between Negroes and whites in this country with their innumerable overtones and undertones, surely, and especially for literature and the drama, there is an inexhaustible supply of themes at hand. To these the Negro artist can give his racial individuality, his heritage of rhythm and warmth, and his incongruous humor that so often, as in the Blues, becomes ironic laughter mixed with tears. But let us look again at the mountain.

A prominent Negro clubwoman in Philadelphia paid eleven dollars to hear Raquel Meller[2] sing Andalusian popular songs. But she told me a few weeks before she would not think of going to hear "that woman," Clara Smith,[3] a great black artist, sing Negro folksongs. And many an upper-class Negro church, even now, would not dream of employing a spiritual in its services. The drab melodies in white folks' hymnbooks are much to be preferred. "We want to worship the Lord correctly and quietly. We don't believe in 'shouting.' Let's be dull like the Nordics," they say, in effect.

The road for the serious black artist, then, who would produce a racial art is most certainly rocky and the mountain is high. Until recently he received almost no encouragement for his work from either white or colored people. The fine novels of Chestnutt[4] go out of print with neither race noticing their passing. The quaint charm and humor of Dunbar's dialect verse[5] brought to him, in his day, largely the same kind of encouragement one would give a sideshow freak (A colored man writing poetry! How odd!) or a clown (How amusing!).

The present vogue in things Negro, although it may do as much harm as good for the budding colored artist, has at least done this: it has brought him forcibly to the attention of his own people among whom for so long, unless the other race had noticed him beforehand, he was a prophet with little honor. I understand that Charles Gilpin[6] acted

2. **Raquel Meller**: Meller (1888–1962), a celebrated Spanish singer and recording artist whose concerts broke box-office records in cities throughout the United States, sang only in Spanish.
3. **Clara Smith**: Smith (1894–1935), billed as the "Queen of the Moaners," was a popular blues singer who performed on the segregated vaudeville circuit for African American artists and audiences during the 1920s.
4. **Chestnutt**: Charles W. Chesnutt (1858–1932) gained popularity with his early short stories, but his later novels exploring the theme of racial hatred and prejudice sold so poorly that he virtually ceased writing fiction.
5. **Dunbar's dialect verse**: The enormously popular poems written in "Negro dialect" by Paul Laurence Dunbar (1872–1906).
6. **Charles Gilpin**: Gilpin (1878–1930) was the first African American actor to appear in a leading role in an all-white theater, in the title role of Eugene O'Neill's *The Emperor Jones* (1920). For his critically acclaimed performance in the play, the NAACP awarded Gilpin its annual Springarn Medal for outstanding achievement by an African American. (See photo on p. 778.)

for years in Negro theaters without any special acclaim from his own, but when Broadway gave him eight curtain calls, Negroes, too, began to beat a tin pan in his honor. I know a young colored writer, a manual worker by day, who had been writing well for the colored magazines for some years, but it was not until he recently broke into the white publications and his first book was accepted by a prominent New York publisher that the "best" Negroes in his city took the trouble to discover that he lived there. Then almost immediately they decided to give a grand dinner for him. But the society ladies were careful to whisper to his mother that perhaps she'd better not come. They were not sure she would have an evening gown.

The Negro artist works against an undertow of sharp critcism and misunderstanding from his own group and unintentional bribes from the whites. "O, be respectable, write about nice people, show how good we are," say the Negroes. "Be stereotyped, don't go too far, don't shatter our illusions about you, don't amuse us too seriously. We will pay you," say the whites. Both would have told Jean Toomer not to write "Cane."[7] The colored people did not praise it. The white people did not buy it. Most of the colored people who did read "Cane" hate it. They are afraid of it. Although the critics gave it good reviews the public remained indifferent. Yet (excepting the work of DuBois) "Cane" contains the finest prose written by a Negro in America. And like the singing of Robeson,[8] it is truly racial.

But in spite of the Nordicized Negro intelligentsia and the desires of some white editors we have an honest American Negro literature already with us. Now I await the rise of the Negro theater. Our folk music, having achieved world-wide fame, offers itself to the genius of the great individual American Negro composer who is to come. And within the next decade I expect to see the work of a growing school of colored artists who paint and model the beauty of dark faces and create with new technique the expressions of their own soul-world. And the Negro dancers who will dance like flame and the singers who will continue to carry our songs to all who listen – they will be with us in even greater numbers tomorrow.

Most of my own poems are racial in theme and treatment, derived from the life I know. In many of them I try to grasp and hold some of the meanings and rhythms of jazz. I am sincere as I know how to be in these poems and yet after every reading I answer questions like these from my own people: Do you think Negroes should always write about Negroes? I wish you wouldn't read some of your poems to white folks. How do you find anything interesting in a place like a cabaret? Why do you write about black people? You aren't black. What makes you do so many jazz poems?

But jazz to me is one of the inherent expressions of Negro life in America: the eternal tom-tom beating in the Negro soul – the tom-tom of revolt against weariness in a white

---

7. **"Cane"**: A critically acclaimed collection of poems, sketches, and stories exploring African American culture in the North and the South by Jean Toomer (1894–1967).
8. **the singing of Robeson**: Paul Robeson (1898–1976) was a singer, actor, and activist famed for his concert performances of "Negro spirituals" and folk songs in New York and later in cities throughout Europe. He succeeded Charles Gilpin in the title role of *The Emperor Jones* (see note 6).

world, a world of subway trains, and work, work, work; the tom-tom of joy and laughter, and pain swallowed in a smile. Yet the Philadelphia clubwoman is ashamed to say that her race created it and she does not like me to write about it. The old subconscious "white is best" runs through her mind. Years of study under white teachers, a lifetime of white books, pictures, and papers, and white manners, morals, and Puritan standards made her dislike the spirituals. And now she turns up her nose at jazz and all its manifestations — likewise almost everything else distinctly racial. She doesn't care for the Winold Reiss[9] portraits of Negroes because they are "too Negro." She does not want a true picture of herself from anybody. She wants the artist to flatter her, to make the white world believe that all Negroes are as smug and as near white in soul as she wants to be. But, to my mind, it is the duty of the younger Negro artist, if he accepts any duties at all from outsiders, to change through the force of his art that old whispering "I want to be white," hidden in the aspirations of his people, to "Why should I want to be white? I am a Negro — and beautiful!"

So I am ashamed for the black poet who says, "I want to be a poet, not a Negro poet," as though his own racial world were not as interesting as any other world. I am ashamed, too, for the colored artist who runs from the painting of Negro faces to the painting of sunsets after the manner of the academicians because he fears the strange un-whiteness of his own features. An artist must be free to choose what he does, certainly, but he must also never be afraid to do what he might choose.

Let the blare of Negro jazz bands and the bellowing voice of Bessie Smith[10] singing Blues penetrate the closed ears of the colored near-intellectuals until they listen and perhaps understand. Let Paul Robeson singing Water Boy, and Rudolph Fisher[11] writing about the streets of Harlem, and Jean Toomer holding the heart of Georgia in his hands, and Aaron Douglas[12] drawing strange black fantasies cause the smug Negro middle class to turn from their white, respectable, ordinary books and papers to catch a glimmer of their own beauty. We younger Negro artists who create now intend to express our individual dark-skinned selves without fear or shame. If white people are pleased we are glad. If they are not, it doesn't matter. We know we are beautiful. And ugly too. The tom-tom cries and the tom-tom laughs. If colored people are pleased we are glad. If they are not, their displeasure doesn't matter either. We build our temples for tomorrow, strong as we know how, and we stand on top of the mountain, free within ourselves.

[1926]

---

9. **Winold Reiss:** Reiss (1886-1953), a German immigrant, was a designer and artist well known for his portraits of African Americans in Harlem during the 1920s.

10. **Bessie Smith:** Smith (1892-1937), still regarded as the "Queen of the Blues," was the most famous and influential blues singer of the 1920s.

11. **Rudolph Fisher:** Fisher (1897-1934), who later published two novels set in Harlem, was then known for his first short story, "The City of Refuge," which was published in the prestigious *Atlantic Monthly* in 1925.

12. **Aaron Douglas:** The African American painter and illustrator Aaron Douglas (1900-1979), who drew his inspiration from jazz, folk culture, and African art, became the leading visual artist of the Harlem Renaissance. In addition to his black-and-white drawings in African American periodicals such as the *Crisis* and *Opportunity*, Douglas's illustrations had appeared in Alain Locke's famous anthology, *The New Negro* (1925).

Hart Crane

[1899-1932]

Hart Crane published "Modern Poetry" two years before his early death in 1932 (see Crane, p. 734). The essay, one of his few works of formal criticism, appeared in *Revolt in the Arts: A Survey of the Creation, Distribution and Appreciation of Art in America* (1930), a collection of essays on art, litera-ture, and culture edited by the well-known drama critic Oliver M. Sayler. As he explained in the preface, Sayler collected essays by "thirty-six repre-sentative authorities," including Crane, who had recently gained consider-able fame and notoriety with the publication of his poetic sequence *The Bridge* (1930). Inspired by the Brooklyn Bridge, a symbol of the modern technological age, Crane in *The Bridge* sought to achieve what he called "a new cultural synthesis" of America. In "Modern Poetry," he suggested that poets in a "Machine Age" must seek a similar synthesis, absorbing the seemingly antipoetic influences of science, technology, and urban life in the United States. The text is taken from the first printing of the essay in *Revolt in the Arts* (1930).

From MODERN POETRY

The function of poetry in a Machine Age is identical to its function in any other age; and its capacities for presenting the most complete synthesis of human values remain essentially immune from any of the so-called inroads of science. The emotional stimu-lus of machinery is on an entirely different psychic plane from that of poetry. Its only menace lies in its capacities for facile entertainment, so easily accessible as to arrest the development of any but the most negligible esthetic responses. The ultimate influ-ence of machinery in this respect remains to be seen, but its firm entrenchment in our lives has already produced a series of challenging new responsibilities for the poet.

For unless poetry can absorb the machine, i.e., *acclimatize* it as naturally and casually as trees, cattle, galleons, castles, and all other human associations of the past, then poetry has failed of its full contemporary function. This process does not infer any pro-gram of lyrical pandering to the taste of those obsessed by the importance of machin-ery; nor does it essentially involve even the specific mention of a single mechanical contrivance. It demands, however, along with the traditional qualifications of the poet, an extraordinary capacity for surrender, at least temporarily, to the sensations of urban life. This presupposes, of course, that the poet possesses sufficient spontaneity and gusto to convert this experience into positive terms. Machinery will tend to lose its sen-sational glamour and appear in its true subsidiary order in human life as use and con-tinual poetic allusion subdue its novelty. For, contrary to general prejudice, the wonderment experienced in watching nose dives is of less immediate creative promise to poetry than the familiar gesture of a motorist in the modest act of shifting gears. I mean to say that mere romantic speculation on the power and beauty of machinery keeps it at a continual remove; it can not act creatively in our lives until, like the unconscious nervous responses of our bodies, its connotations emanate from within — forming as spontaneous a terminology of poetic reference as the bucolic world of pasture, plow, and barn.

The familiar contention that science is inimical to poetry is no more tenable than the kindred notion that theology has been proverbially hostile — with the "Commedia" of Dante[1] to prove the contrary. That "truth" which science pursues is radically different from the metaphorical, extra-logical "truth" of the poet. When Blake wrote that "a tear is an intellectual thing, And a sigh is the sword of an Angel King"[2] — he was not in any logical conflict with the principles of the Newtonian Universe. Similarly, poetic prophecy in the case of the seer, has nothing to do with factual prediction or with futurity. It is a peculiar type of perception, capable of apprehending some absolute and timeless concept of the imagination with astounding clarity and conviction.

That the modern poet can profitably assume the roles of philosopher or theologian is questionable at best. Science, the uncanonized Deity of the times, seems to have automatically displaced the hierarchies of both Academy and Church. It is pertinent to cite the authors of the "Commedia" and "Paradise Lost"[3] as poets whose verse survives the religious dogmas and philosophies of their respective periods, but it is fallacious to assume that either of these poets could have written important religious verse without the fully developed and articulated religious dogmas that each was heir to.

The future of American poetry is too complicated a speculation to be more than approached in this limited space. Involved in it are the host of considerations relative to the comparative influences of science, machinery, and other factors which I have merely touched upon; — besides those influential traditions of early English prosody which form points of departure, at least, for any indigenous rhythms and forms which may emerge. The most typical and valid expression of the American *psychosis* seems to me still to be found in Whitman.[4] His faults as a technician, and his clumsy and indiscriminate enthusiasm are somewhat beside the point. He, better than any other, was able to coordinate those forces in America which seem most intractable, fusing them into a universal vision which takes on additional significance as time goes on. He was a revolutionist beyond the strict meaning of Coleridge's definition of genius,[5] but his bequest is still to he realized in all its implications.

[1930]

---

1. **"Commedia" of Dante:** *The Divine Comedy*, a Christian epic by the Italian poet Dante Alighieri (1265-1321).
2. **"a tear . . . King":** The lines are from "The Grey Monk," by the British poet William Blake (1757-1827).
3. **"Paradise Lost":** An epic poem that tells the Christian story of the Fall of man, by the English poet John Milton (1608-1674).
4. **American *psychosis* . . . Whitman:** Crane appears to use the word *psychosis* in the sense of the American mind or soul, which many critics and writers believed had found its fullest expression in the poetry of Walt Whitman (1819-1892).
5. **Coleridge's definition of genius:** In his lectures on Shakespeare, the English poet and critic Samuel Taylor Coleridge (1772-1834) famously observed: "As it must not, so genius cannot, be lawless: for it is even this that constitutes its genius — the power of acting creatively under laws of its own origination."

Robert Frost

[1874–1963]

By the time Robert Frost wrote "The Figure a Poem Makes," the preface to the first edition of his *Collected Poems* (1939), he was among the most famous poets in the United States (see Frost, p. 581). Already the winner of three Pulitzer Prizes for Poetry (he would eventually win four), Frost was a college dropout who had recently accepted a two-year position as a professor at Harvard University. Although he gave numerous readings and talks, Frost wrote only a few formal commentaries on other poets or on poetry, of which the best known is "The Figure a Poem Makes." In the brief essay, which is itself a kind of prose poem, Frost discussed the resources available to poets and meditated on the nature of the poem. Writing at the end of the Great Depression, during which many critics and writers had insisted that literature must assume a social role, Frost assigned the poem a very different function. "It begins in delight and ends in wisdom," he memorably declared. To distinguish such "wisdom" from the beliefs embraced by members of political, philosophical, or religious groups, Frost added that the poem "ends in a clarification of life — not necessarily a great clarification, such as sects and cults are founded on, but in a momentary stay against confusion." The text of the essay, which was subsequently reprinted as the preface to many editions of his poems, is taken from the *Collected Poems of Robert Frost* (1939).

THE FIGURE A POEM MAKES

Abstraction is an old story with the philosophers, but it has been like a new toy in the hands of the artists of our day. Why can't we have any one quality of poetry we choose by itself? We can have in thought. Then it will go hard if we can't in practice. Our lives for it.

Granted no one but a humanist much cares how sound a poem is if it is only *a* sound. The sound is the gold in the ore. Then we will have the sound out alone and dispense with the inessential. We do till we make the discovery that the object in writing poetry is to make all poems sound as different as possible from each other, and the resources for that of vowels, consonants, punctuation, syntax, words, sentences, meter are not enough. We need the help of context — meaning — subject matter. That is the greatest help towards variety. All that can be done with words is soon told. So also with meters — particularly in our language where there are virtually but two, strict iambic and loose iambic. The ancients with many were still poor if they depended on meters for all tune. It is painful to watch our sprung-rhythmists[1] straining at the point of omitting one short

---

1. **sprung-rhythmists:** *Sprung rhythm*, a term coined by the English poet Gerard Manley Hopkins (1844–1889), is a poetic meter approximating the natural patterns of English speech in which each line has the

from a foot for relief from monotony. The possibilities for tune from the dramatic tones of meaning struck across the rigidity of a limited meter are endless. And we are back in poetry as merely one more art of having something to say, sound or unsound. Probably better if sound, because deeper and from wider experience.

Then there is this wildness whereof it is spoken. Granted again that it has an equal claim with sound to being a poem's better half. If it is a wild tune, it is a poem. Our problem then is, as modern abstractionists, to have the wildness pure; to be wild with nothing to be wild about. We bring up as aberrationists, giving way to undirected associations and kicking ourselves from one chance suggestion to another in all directions as of a hot afternoon in the life of a grasshopper. Theme alone can steady us down. Just as the first mystery was how a poem could have a tune in such a straightness as meter, so the second mystery is how a poem can have wildness and at the same time a subject that shall be fulfilled.

It should be of the pleasure of a poem itself to tell how it can. The figure a poem makes. It begins in delight and ends in wisdom. The figure is the same as for love. No one can really hold that the ecstasy should be static and stand still in one place. It begins in delight, it inclines to the impulse, it assumes direction with the first line laid down, it runs a course of lucky events, and ends in a clarification of life — not necessarily a great clarification, such as sects and cults are founded on, but in a momentary stay against confusion. It has denouement. It has an outcome that though unforeseen was predestined from the first image of the original mood — and indeed from the very mood. It is but a trick poem and no poem at all if the best of it was thought of first and saved for the last. It finds its own name as it goes and discovers the best waiting for it in some final phrase at once wise and sad — the happy-sad blend of the drinking song.

No tears in the writer, no tears in the reader. No surprise for the writer, no surprise for the reader. For me the initial delight is in the surprise of remembering something I didn't know I knew. I am in a place, in a situation, as if I had materialized from cloud or risen out of the ground. There is a glad recognition of the long lost and the rest follows. Step by step the wonder of unexpected supply keeps growing. The impressions most useful to my purpose seem always those I was unaware of and so made no note of at the time when taken, and the conclusion is come to that like giants we are always hurling experience ahead of us to pave the future with against the day when we may want to strike a line of purpose across it for somewhere. The line will have the more charm for not being mechanically straight. We enjoy the straight crookedness of a good walking stick. Modern instruments of precision are being used to make things crooked as if by eye and hand in the old days.

I tell how there may be a better wildness of logic than of inconsequence. But the logic is backward, in retrospect, after the act. It must be more felt than seen ahead like prophecy. It must be a revelation, or a series of revelations, as much for the poet as for

---

same number of stressed syllables but each stressed syllable is followed by a variable number of unstressed syllables, from zero to three. Frost wrote iambic verse, in which lines are divided into a set number of metrical feet called *iambs*, each of which consists of an unstressed syllable followed by a stressed syllable.

the reader. For it to be that there must have been the greatest freedom of the material to move about in it and to establish relations in it regardless of time and space, previous relation, and everything but affinity. We prate of freedom. We call our schools free because we are not free to stay away from them till we are sixteen years of age. I have given up my democratic prejudices and now willingly set the lower classes free to be completely taken care of by the upper classes. Political freedom is nothing to me. I bestow it right and left. All I would keep for myself is the freedom of my material — the condition of body and mind now and then to summons aptly from the vast chaos of all I have lived through.

Scholars and artists thrown together are often annoyed at the puzzle of where they differ. Both work from knowledge; but I suspect they differ most importantly in the way their knowledge is come by. Scholars get theirs with conscientious thoroughness along projected lines of logic; poets theirs cavalierly and as it happens in and out of books. They stick to nothing deliberately, but let what will stick to them like burrs where they walk in the fields. No acquirement is on assignment, or even self-assignment. Knowledge of the second kind is much more available in the wild free ways of wit and art. A school boy may be defined as one who can tell you what he knows in the order in which he learned it. The artist must value himself as he snatches a thing from some previous order in time and space into a new order with not so much as a ligature clinging to it of the old place where it was organic.

More than once I should have lost my soul to radicalism if it had been the originality it was mistaken for by its young converts. Originality and initiative are what I ask for my country. For myself the originality need be no more than the freshness of a poem run in the way I have described: from delight to wisdom. The figure is the same as for love. Like a piece of ice on a hot stove the poem must ride on its own melting. A poem may be worked over once it is in being, but may not be worried into being. Its most precious quality will remain its having run itself and carried away the poet with it. Read it a hundred times: it will forever keep its freshness as a metal keeps its fragrance. It can never lose its sense of a meaning that once unfolded by surprise as it went.

[1939]

William Carlos Williams

[1883-1963]

William Carlos Williams was an essayist, fiction writer, and poet who was associated with imagism and later with its offshoot objectivism, a fusion of avant-garde poetics and radical politics that emerged in the 1930s (see Williams, p. 626). Williams wrote this "Author's Introduction" for his collection of poems *The Wedge* (1944), which he had initially offered to his friend and publisher James Laughlin, the founder of New Directions.

Under the pressure of an order from the War Production Board, which limited publishers to 90 percent of the paper they had used the previous year, Laughlin reluctantly rejected the volume in favor of books that might sell more copies. *The Wedge* was subsequently published in a limited edition of 380 copies by the private Cummington Press in Massachusetts. Embittered by both the wartime order and Laughlin's rejection, Williams in his introduction emphasized that the arts in general and his book in particular were not a diversion from the war but a part of the war fought on a different front. He thus explored the relation between the arts and society, the nature of a poem, and the role of the poet. A practicing physician who well understood the importance American society attached to mechanical and technical expertise, Williams defined a poem as a "machine made of words," the product of the "formal invention" necessary to "give language its highest dignity, its illumination in the environment to which it is native." The text is taken from the first edition of *The Wedge* (1944).

AUTHOR'S INTRODUCTION TO *THE WEDGE*

The war is the first and only thing in the world today.

The arts generally are not, nor is this writing a diversion from that for relief, a turning away. It *is* the war or part of it, merely a different sector of the field.

Critics of rather better than average standing have said in recent years that after socialism has been achieved it's likely there will be no further use for poetry, that it will disappear. This comes from nothing else than a faulty definition of poetry — and the arts generally. I don't hear anyone say that mathematics is likely to be outmoded, to disappear shortly. Then why poetry?

It is an error attributable to the Freudian concept of the thing, that the arts are a resort from frustration, a misconception still entertained in many minds.[1]

They speak as though action itself in all its phases were not compatible with frustration. All action the same. But Richard Coeur de Lion[2] wrote at least one of the finest lyrics of his day. Take Don Juan[3] for instance. Who isn't frustrated and does not prove it by his actions — if you want to say so?

But through art the psychologically maimed may become the most distinguished man of his age. Take Freud for instance.

The making of poetry is no more an evidence of frustration than is the work of Henry

---

1. **Freudian concept . . . many minds:** Sigmund Freud (1856–1939), the Austrian founder of psychotherapy, conceived the concept of sublimation, a defense mechanism by which people deal with socially unacceptable impulses such as frustration by channeling them into socially acceptable activities, including the creation of art.
2. **Richard Coeur de Lion:** Richard I (1157–1199), king of England from 1189 to 1199, was named the "Lion-hearted" for his bravery in battle. On his voyage home from the Third Crusade in 1192, he was shipwrecked and held for ransom in a series of castles, where he is reputed to have written songs and lyrics.
3. **Don Juan:** A legendary Spanish nobleman known for his seductive power over women.

Kaiser or of Timoshenko.[4] It's the war, the driving forward of desire to a complex end. And when that shall have been achieved, mathematics and the arts will turn elsewhere — beyond the atom if necessary for their reward and let's all be frustrated together.

A man isn't a block that remains stationary though the psychologists treat him so — and most take an insane pride in believing it. Consistency! He varies; Hamlet today, Caesar tomorrow;[5] here, there, somewhere — if he is to retain his sanity, and why not?

The arts have a *complex* relation to society. The poet isn't a fixed phenomenon, no more is his work. *That* might be a note on current affairs, a diagnosis, a plan for procedure, a retrospect — all in its own peculiarly enduring form. There need be nothing limited or frustrated about that. It may be a throw-off from the most violent and successful action or run parallel to it, a saga. It may be the picking out of an essential detail for memory, something to be set aside for further study, a sort of shorthand of emotional significances for later reference.

Let the metaphysical take care of itself, the arts have nothing to do with it. They will concern themselves with it if they please, among other things.

To make two bald statements: There's nothing sentimental about a machine, and: A poem is a small (or large) machine made of words. When I say there's nothing sentimental about a poem I mean that there can be no part, as in any other machine, that is redundant.

Prose may carry a load of ill-defined matter like a ship. But poetry is the machine which drives it, pruned to a perfect economy. As in all machines its movement is intrinsic, undulant, a physical more than a literary character. In a poem this movement is distinguished in each case by the character of the speech from which it arises.

Therefore each speech having its own character the poetry it engenders will be peculiar to that speech also in its own intrinsic form.

The effect is beauty, what in a single object resolves our complex feelings of propriety.

One doesn't seek beauty. All that an artist or a Sperry[6] can do is to drive toward his purpose, in the nature of his materials; not to take gold where Babbitt metal[7] is called for; to make: make clear the complexity of his perceptions in the medium given to him by inheritance, chance, accident, or whatever it may be to work with according to his tal-

---

4. **Henry Kaiser or of Timoshenko**: Kaiser (1882-1967) was the founder of more than one hundred companies, including Kaiser Aluminum and Kaiser Steel. During World War II, he ran several shipyards, each of which could build a ship in five days. Semyon Konstantinovich Timoshenko (1895-1970) was a senior Russian military officer when Germany invaded the Soviet Union in 1941.
5. **Hamlet today, Caesar tomorrow**: Shakespeare's Hamlet, known for his indecision and vacillation, and Julius Caesar (100-44 BCE), the powerful general and politician who became the first dictator of the Roman Republic.
6. **Sperry**: Elmer Ambrose Sperry (1860-1930), an inventor who founded several companies, including the Sperry Electric Company and the Sperry Gyroscope Company.
7. **Babbitt metal**: A soft metal alloy whose structure and characteristics make it particularly suited for use on the surface of a plain bearing, one that carries load by sliding.

ents and the will that drives them. Don't talk about frustration fathering the arts. The bastardization of words is too widespread for that today.

My own interest in the arts has been extracurricular. Up from the gutter, so to speak. Of necessity. Each age and place to its own. But in the U.S. the necessity for recognizing this intrinsic character has been largely ignored by the various English Departments of the academies.

When a man makes a poem, makes it, mind you, he takes words as he finds them interrelated about him and composes them — without distortion which would mar their exact significances — into an intense expression of his perceptions and ardors that they may constitute a revelation in the speech that he uses. It isn't what he *says* that counts as a work of art, it's what he makes, with such intensity of perception that it lives with an intrinsic movement of its own to verify its authenticity. Your attention is called now and then to some beautiful line or sonnet-sequence because of what is said there. So be it. To me all sonnets say the same thing of no importance. What does it matter what the line "says"?

There is no poetry of distinction without formal invention, for it is in the intimate form that works of art achieve their exact meaning, in which they most resemble the machine, to give language its highest dignity, its illumination in the environment to which it is native. Such war, as the arts live and breathe by, is continuous.

It may be that my interests as expressed here are pre-art. If so I look for a development along these lines and will be satisfied with nothing else.

[1944]

James Weldon Johnson

[1871-1938]

James William Johnson, who later changed his middle name to Weldon, was born in Jacksonville, Florida, on June 17, 1871. He was the first child of James Johnson, the headwaiter at a first-class resort hotel, and Helen Dillet Johnson, a schoolteacher. Johnson's mother was born and raised in the Bahamas, where her father was for many years a member of the House of Assembly. After she married James Johnson, the couple lived in the Bahamas until 1866, when they moved to Jacksonville. Johnson grew up there in a comfortable and cultured home. His father was fond of reciting passages from Shakespeare's plays, and his artistic mother played the piano, sang, and wrote poetry. Johnson and his brother, John Rosamond, took music lessons and attended the Stanton Grammar School, the only school open to African Americans in Jacksonville. Johnson later recalled that as a child he was especially stirred by a speech delivered by his hero Frederick Douglass, who "moved a large audience of white and colored people by his supreme eloquence." After he graduated from Stanton in 1887, Johnson attended the preparatory school and then the college division of the all-black Atlanta University, where he worked in the printing office and received a solid education in literature, mathematics, and science, as well as in Latin and Greek. He published his first poem in the university's *Bulletin* and won an oratory contest for his speech "The Best Methods of Removing the Disabilities of Caste from the Negro." Gaining the attention of influential African Americans, in 1893 he was introduced to Booker T. Washington at the Columbian Exposition in Chicago, where Johnson also met the poet Paul Laurence Dunbar.

James Weldon Johnson

This photograph of the influential writer and activist was taken of Johnson at his desk in the office of the NAACP in New York City, where he served as the organization's chief executive officer from 1920 to 1930.

The talented and energetic Johnson pursued a number of different careers following his graduation from college in 1894. Returning home to Jacksonville, he became the principal of the Stanton School. He also established a newspaper, the *Daily American*, to be "published chiefly in the interest of the colored people of Florida and the South." Despite a large number of subscribers, the costs of publishing a newspaper proved to be prohibitive, and he reluctantly ended the venture after eight months. He then decided to study law, and in 1898 he became the first African American to be admitted to the Florida Bar since the end of Reconstruction. After his brother, a composer, graduated from the New England Conservatory of Music in 1897, Johnson wrote the lyrics for some of his songs. In 1900, the brothers collaborated on "Lift Ev'ry Voice and Sing," a lyric about

the experiences and aspirations of African Americans that Johnson originally wrote for a celebration of Abraham Lincoln's birthday at the Stanton
School. The song became popular throughout the South, and the National
Association for the Advancement of Colored People (NAACP) later adopted
it as the "Negro National Anthem." In 1902, Johnson resigned his position
at the Stanton School, closed his successful law practice, and left for New
York City. Working with his brother as a songwriting team — together, they
wrote two hundred songs for Broadway musicals — Johnson met a variety
of artists and producers, as well as his future wife, Grace Nail, the daughter of a Harlem businessman. Johnson also published essays and made
friends in political circles. He gave up Broadway in 1906, when President
Theodore Roosevelt appointed Johnson American consul in Venezuela,
from which he moved to a similar diplomatic post in Nicaragua in 1909.

During the following two decades, Johnson gained prominence as an
author and as an activist in the NAACP. In 1912, he anonymously published
a novel, *The Autobiography of an Ex-Colored Man* (1912), ostensibly the
"confession" of a light-skinned African American who "passes" for white
in turn-of-the-century New York City. The novel generated little interest,
but Johnson's literary career received a major boost when his "Fifty Years,"
a long poem celebrating the fiftieth anniversary of the Emancipation
Proclamation, appeared in the *New York Times*. The distinguished African
American novelist Charles W. Chesnutt called the poem "the finest thing I
ever read on the subject," and its popularity led to the publication of Johnson's first collection of poetry, *Fifty Years and Other Poems* (1917). Meanwhile, frustrated by the lack of advancement in the consular service,
Johnson resigned in 1913, and he and his wife settled in Harlem. Johnson
became an editor of the crusading African American newspaper the *New
York Age*. He also joined the NAACP. Elected field secretary, he was active
in antilynching campaigns and established many new branches of the
NAACP, which appointed him executive secretary in 1920. Johnson was
also a major figure in the Harlem Renaissance, showcasing African American cultural achievements in three major anthologies: *The Book of American Negro Poetry* (1922), *The Book of American Negro Spirituals* (1925), and
The Second Book of American Negro Spirituals (1926). In 1927, Johnson published his major poetic work, *God's Trombones: Seven Negro Sermons in
Verse*.

Although he was encouraged to run for public office, Johnson preferred
to spend his time writing and encouraging young African American
artists and authors. In 1931, he accepted a position as a professor of literature and creative writing at Fisk University. In addition to poems, he wrote
his autobiography, *Along This Way* (1933). Johnson also published a collection of his lectures, *Negro Americans, What Now?* (1934), in which he
argued that integration was the only viable solution to racial problems in
the United States. During a vacation in Maine, Johnson died in a car accident on June 26, 1938. More than 2,500 people, white and black, attended
the funeral services for Johnson, and hundreds more gathered to pay their
respects outside the church in Harlem.

James Weldon Johnson aptly, deeply, with love and humor and a power-ful rhyming tongue, has told our story and sung our song.

–Maya Angelou

Johnson's "The Creation." Subtitled "A Negro Sermon," this poem was first published in 1920 in the *Freeman*, a short-lived journal of social commentary that was also widely regarded as one of the most vibrant literary magazines of the 1920s. Johnson later included "The Creation" in his anthology *The Book of American Negro Poetry* (1922) and then in his collection *God's Trombones: Seven Negro Sermons in Verse* (1927). In the preface to the collection, Johnson explained that the poems were partially based on his early memories of sermons delivered by the "old-time preachers," but that he was directly inspired by a more recent occasion in Kansas City. There, he had heard a famed visiting preacher deliver a sermon in a "wonderful voice" that sounded like a trombone, "the instrument possessing above all others the power to express the wide and varied range of emotions encompassed by the human voice – and with greater amplitude." Johnson stated that he began to jot down some ideas for "The Creation" even before the preacher finished his sermon. Johnson was also familiar with earlier poems such as Paul Laurence Dunbar's "An Ante-bellum Sermon" (1896). Johnson, however, was concerned that such dialect poems perpetuated stereotypes and limited the expressive range of African Americans. He thus explained that "The Creation" was intended to move beyond dialect to capture the emotional resonance and rhetorical power of African American sermons, "a fusion of Negro idioms with Bible English" – that is, the rich language of the creation story in the King James Version of the Bible (Genesis 1:1–27). The text is taken from *God's Trombones* (1927).

*bedfordstmartins.com/
americanlit* for research
links on Johnson

"The Creation"

In an effort to fuse literature and art, and to display the achievements of African Americans in both areas, Johnson's poems in *God's Trombones* were accompanied by titles lettered by C. B. Falls and drawings by Aaron Douglas, a leading artist of the Harlem Renaissance.

And God stepped out on space,
And he looked around and said:
I'm lonely —
I'll make me a world.

And far as the eye of God could see
Darkness covered everything,
Blacker than a hundred midnights
Down in a cypress swamp.

Then God smiled,
And the light broke,
And the darkness rolled up on one side,
And the light stood shining on the other,
And God said: That's good!

Then God reached out and took the light in his hands,
And God rolled the light around in his hands

[17]

THE CREATION

And God stepped out on space,
And he looked around and said:
I'm lonely —
I'll make me a world.

And far as the eye of God could see   5
Darkness covered everything,
Blacker than a hundred midnights
Down in a cypress swamp.

Then God smiled,
And the light broke,   10
And the darkness rolled up on one side,
And the light stood shining on the other,
And God said: That's good!

Then God reached out and took the light in his hands,
And God rolled the light around in his hands   15
Until he made the sun;
And he set that sun a-blazing in the heavens.
And the light that was left from making the sun
God gathered it up in a shining ball
And flung it against the darkness,   20
Spangling the night with the moon and stars.
Then down between
The darkness and the light
He hurled the world;
And God said: That's good!   25

Then God himself stepped down —
And the sun was on his right hand,
And the moon was on his left;
The stars were clustered about his head,
And the earth was under his feet.   30
And God walked, and where he trod
His footsteps hollowed the valleys out
And bulged the mountains up.

Then he stopped and looked and saw
That the earth was hot and barren.   35
So God stepped over to the edge of the world
And he spat out the seven seas —
He batted his eyes, and the lightnings flashed —
He clapped his hands, and the thunders rolled —

And the waters above the earth came down,   40
The cooling waters came down.

Then the green grass sprouted,
And the little red flowers blossomed,
The pine tree pointed his finger to the sky,
And the oak spread out his arms,   45
The lakes cuddled down in the hollows of the ground,
And the rivers ran down to the sea;
And God smiled again,
And the rainbow appeared,
And curled itself around his shoulder.   50

Then God raised his arm and he waved his hand
Over the sea and over the land,
And he said: Bring forth! Bring forth!
And quicker than God could drop his hand,
Fishes and fowls   55
And beasts and birds
Swam the rivers and the seas,
Roamed the forests and the woods,
And split the air with their wings.
And God said: That's good!   60

Then God walked around,
And God looked around
On all that he had made.
He looked at his sun,
And he looked at his moon,   65
And he looked at his little stars;
He looked on his world
With all its living things,
And God said: I'm lonely still.

Then God sat down —   70
On the side of a hill where he could think;
By a deep, wide river he sat down;
With his head in his hands,
God thought and thought,
Till he thought: I'll make me a man!   75

Up from the bed of the river
God scooped the clay;
And by the bank of the river
He kneeled him down;
And there the great God Almighty   80

Who lit the sun and fixed it in the sky,
Who flung the stars to the most far corner of the night,
Who rounded the earth in the middle of his hand;
This Great God,
Like a mammy bending over her baby,   85
Kneeled down in the dust
Toiling over a lump of clay
Till he shaped it in his own image;

Then into it he blew the breath of life,
And man became a living soul.   90
Amen.   Amen.

[1920, 1927]

Amy Lowell

[1874–1925]

Amy Lowell was born on February 9, 1874, in Brookline, Massachusetts. She was the daughter of Augustus and Katherine Lawrence Lowell and a descendant of one of the most prominent families in New England, which included James Russell Lowell, the well-known nineteenth-century poet and the first editor of the prestigious *Atlantic Monthly*. Her wealthy and cultured parents carefully oversaw the education of their five gifted children, and Lowell was taught by an English governess before being sent to a private school. From an early age, she also enjoyed reading in the extensive library of her family's magnificent home, Sevenels, which was filled with Asian art and surrounded by eight acres of gardens in a fashionable section of Boston. Lowell was a good student, but she disliked rote learning and ended her formal education when she was seventeen, in 1891. Withdrawn, lonely, and deeply self-conscious about her weight, she reluctantly bowed to social conventions and became a debutante, going to parties and other social events. After her mother's death in 1895, Lowell traveled

Amy Lowell

This photograph of Lowell enjoying a rare moment of relaxation in the gardens at her estate, Sevenels, was taken in 1922, when she was at the height of her fame as a poet and tireless promoter of the "new poetry" in the United States.

extensively in Europe and to Africa. When her father died in 1900, she inherited Sevenels, which Lowell lovingly maintained. Although she continued to read deeply and was especially drawn to the work of the British Romantic poets, Lowell evidently had no idea of becoming a poet until she attended a performance by the Italian actress Eleonora Duse in 1902. Lowell was so moved that when she got home she wrote a poem, "Eleonora Duse."

Lowell subsequently began seriously to study and write poetry. Her first published poem appeared in the *Atlantic Monthly* in 1910, two years before she published her first collection of verse, *A Dome of Many Coloured Glass* (1912). The conventional volume created little stir, but Lowell's life and poetry soon changed dramatically. In 1912, she met Ada Dwyer, a professional actress who was separated from her husband. Lowell invited her to visit Sevenels, where Dwyer moved permanently in 1913. With Dwyer's supportive help, Lowell maintained her life as a full-time writer and began to explore new directions in her poetry. She became fascinated by the work of a small group of experimental English and American poets led by Ezra Pound — the imagistes, as they called themselves in London, or imagists, as they came to be called in the United States. After reading some poems by H.D. (Hilda Doolittle) in the January 1913 issue of *Poetry* magazine, Lowell realized, "Why, I, too am an *Imagiste*!" She went to London to meet Pound and H.D., and Lowell began to write her own imagist verse, which appeared in magazines and in her experimental collection of poems, *Sword Blades and Poppy Seeds* (1914). During the following decade, she became an important force in American poetry, editing three collections of imagist poetry between 1915 and 1917 and publishing ten additional collections of her own poetry, including *Men, Women, and Ghosts* (1916), *Can Grande Castle* (1918), *Pictures of the Floating World* (1919), and finally *What's O'Clock* (1925).

Lowell also became well known as a public personality and crusader for modern poetry. Flamboyant, iconoclastic, and theatrical, she smoked cigars freely and lived openly with Ada Dwyer, to whom Lowell wrote a series of erotic love poems. She also engaged in a heated public debate with Pound over the future of imagism, which he subsequently dismissed as "Amygism." Although that episode later undermined her place in histories on modernism, Lowell tirelessly promoted the new verse in essays and during her extensive speaking tours in the United States. Undaunted by the derision and hostility she frequently encountered at her thronged readings and lectures, she insisted that the experimental poetry many critics condemned as foreign or alien was a natural outgrowth of American progress in all areas, from the arts to science and technology. Lowell also emphasized the vital role poetry might play in the development of a national identity, the ongoing effort "to free ourselves from the tutelage of another nation," adding: "I might say with perfect truth that the most national things we have are skyscrapers, ice water, and the New Poetry, and each of these means more than appears on the surface." Indeed, perhaps no other poet of her time worked so hard to express what poetry might mean to Americans. During the final years of her life, however, Low-

The force which Miss Lowell's New England ancestors put into founding and running cotton-mills, or belike into saving souls, she puts into conquering an art and making it express and serve her.

—Harriet Monroe

ell's vigor and productivity were undermined by ill health, and she died prematurely at the age of fifty-one, on May 12, 1925.

Lowell's Poetry.   Early in her career, Lowell was heavily influenced by the English Romantic poets, especially John Keats. After discovering the experimental work of the imagists, however, she adopted their forms and techniques, including their embrace of *vers libre*, verse freed from the conventional metrical patterns and rhyme schemes of traditional poetry in English. In "Amy Lowell and the Art of Poetry," a survey of her achievement published in the *North American Review* shortly before her death in 1925, the American poet and critic Archibald MacLeish praised her sharply defined visual images, her use of conversational language, and especially the rhythmical freedom of her poetry. By then, Lowell's poetry was being overshadowed by the work of younger poets, especially T. S. Eliot's *The Waste Land.* MacLeish, however, concluded his graceful tribute to Lowell with a simple description of the aspect of her best work that would ensure it enduring fame: "It is the quality of her art." Certainly, that quality is illustrated in the following selection of her poems. "The Taxi" and "Aubade," two of her early experiments in free verse, or what Lowell called "unrhymed cadence," were published in her second collection, *Sword Blades and Poppy Seeds* (1914). The other poems included here were first published in *Pictures of the Floating World* (1919) — a translation of ukiyo-e, Japanese visual arts that were at once highly sophisticated and readily accessible to common people — and Lowell's final collection, *What's O'Clock* (1925), for which she was posthumously awarded the Pulitzer Prize. The texts of all of the poems are taken from *The Complete Poetical Works of Amy Lowell* (1955).

bedfordstmartins.com/ americanlit *for research links on Lowell*

THE TAXI

When I go away from you
The world beats dead
Like a slackened drum.
I call out for you against the jutted stars
And shout into the ridges of the wind.   5
Streets coming fast,
One after the other,
Wedge you away from me,
And the lamps of the city prick my eyes
So that I can no longer see your face.   10
Why should I leave you,
To wound myself upon the sharp edges of the night?

[1914, 1955]

AUBADE[1]

As I would free the white almond from the green husk
So would I strip your trappings off,
Beloved.
And fingering the smooth and polished kernel
I should see that in my hands glittered a gem beyond counting.

[1914, 1955]

---

1. **Aubade:** A lyric about dawn or about lovers parting at morning.

VENUS TRANSIENS[1]

Tell me,
Was Venus more beautiful
Than you are,
When she topped
The crinkled waves,   5
Drifting shoreward
On her plaited shell?
Was Botticelli's vision[2]
Fairer than mine;
And were the painted rosebuds   10
He tossed his lady,
Of better worth
Than the words I blow about you
To cover your too great loveliness
As with a gauze   15
Of misted silver?
For me,
You stand poised
In the blue and buoyant air,
Cinctured by bright winds,   20
Treading the sunlight.
And the waves which precede you
Ripple and stir
The sands at my feet.

[1919, 1955]

---

1. **Venus Transiens:**   Venus [the Roman goddess of love] passing over (Latin).
2. **Botticelli's vision:** Sandro Botticelli (1445-1510), Italian painter known for his mythological works, notably *The Birth of Venus* (c. 1480), which depicts the beautiful goddess floating ashore on a seashell amidst a shower of roses.

Madonna of the Evening Flowers[1]

All day long I have been working,
Now I am tired.
I call: "Where are you?"
But there is only the oak-tree rustling in the wind.
The house is very quiet,   5
The sun shines in on your books,
On your scissors and thimble just put down,
But you are not there.
Suddenly I am lonely:
Where are you?   10
I go about searching.

Then I see you,
Standing under a spire of pale blue larkspur,
With a basket of roses on your arm.
You are cool, like silver,   15
And you smile.
I think the Canterbury bells[2] are playing little tunes.

You tell me that the peonies need spraying,
That the columbines have overrun all bounds,
That the pyrus japonica[3] should be cut back and rounded.   20
You tell me these things.
But I look at you, heart of silver,
White heart-flame of polished silver,
Burning beneath the blue steeples of the larkspur,
And I long to kneel instantly at your feet,   25
While all about us peal the loud, sweet *Te Deums*[4] of the Canterbury bells.

[1919, 1955]

---

1. **Madonna of the Evening Flowers:** The title makes a play on the various meanings of *Madonna*, usually a reference to the Virgin Mary but also a shortened form of the Madonna or Annunciation lily (*Lilium candidum*), a plant bearing fragrant white flowers that yield oil used in perfumes.
2. **Canterbury bells:** The common name for *Campanula medium*, a tall plant with bell-shaped flowers.
3. **pyrus japonica:** Japanese quince, a flowering shrub from eastern Asia.
4. *Te Deums:* Shortened form of an ancient Latin hymn, *Te deum laudamus*, "We praise thee, God."

A Decade

When you came, you were like red wine and honey,
And the taste of you burnt my mouth with its sweetness.
Now you are like morning bread,
Smooth and pleasant.

I hardly taste you at all for I know your savour,
But I am completely nourished.

[1919, 1955]

MEETING-HOUSE HILL

I must be mad, or very tired,
When the curve of a blue bay beyond a railroad track
Is shrill and sweet to me like the sudden springing of a tune,
And the sight of a white church above thin trees in a city square
Amazes my eyes as though it were the Parthenon.[1]   5
Clear, reticent, superbly final,
With the pillars of its portico refined to a cautious elegance,
It dominates the weak trees,
And the shot of its spire
Is cool, and candid,   10
Rising into an unresisting sky.
Strange meeting-house
Pausing a moment upon a squalid hill-top.
I watch the spire sweeping the sky,
I am dizzy with the movement of the sky,   15
I might be watching a mast
With its royals set full
Straining before a two-reef breeze.
I might be sighting a tea-clipper,
Tacking into the blue bay,   20
Just back from Canton[2]
With her hold full of green and blue porcelain,
And a Chinese coolie[3] leaning over the rail
Gazing at the white spire
With dull, sea-spent eyes.   25

[1925, 1955]

---

1. **Parthenon:** Built on the Acropolis in Greece during 447–432 BCE, the temple of Athena Parthenos honored
the patron goddess of Athens and commemorated the Greek victory over the Persians.
2. **Canton:** Guangzhou, or Canton, was one of the major ports of trade in China, whose exports to the United
States then included tea ("green") and porcelain.
3. **coolie:** A term applied to unskilled laborers brought to the United States and other countries from China.

Robert Frost

[1874-1963]

Robert Lee Frost was born in San Francisco, California, on March 26, 1874. Although he was named after the famous Confederate general, Frost's parents were transplanted northerners: Isabelle Moodie Frost, a former teacher from a deeply religious family in Ohio, and William Prescott Frost Jr., an ambitious Harvard-educated journalist seeking fame and fortune in the West. Their marriage was deeply troubled, and while Isabelle Frost was pregnant with her second child she fled with her young son back to her in-laws in Lawrence, Massachusetts. Eventually she and her two children returned to San Francisco, where Frost's father was seriously ill with tuberculosis. After his death in 1885, the family returned to Lawrence. Encouraged by his mother, who frequently read poetry aloud to her children, Frost published poems in his high-school newspaper and secretly

Robert Frost

This photograph was taken in 1913 in England, where Frost first gained wide acclaim as a poet.

began to plan a poetic career for himself. After his graduation in 1892, he enrolled at Dartmouth College, but Frost was so unhappy there that he dropped out before the end of his first semester and returned home to Lawrence.

During the following years, Frost took various jobs while pursuing his dream of becoming a poet. He taught school, worked in one of the textile mills in Lawrence and as a reporter for a local newspaper, and wrote poetry in his spare time. His first professional publication was "My Butterfly," a poem that appeared in a New York newspaper, the *Independent*, in 1894. Frost, who was elated by the fifteen dollars he received, subsequently paid for the printing of two copies of a collection of his poems, *Twilight*, one for himself and the other for his high-school sweetheart, Elinor White, whom he married in 1895. After they had the first of their six children, two of whom died in infancy, Frost sought a more secure way of supporting his family. Deciding to train to become a high-school teacher of Greek and Latin, he enrolled at Harvard University in 1897. But he withdrew before he finished his second year, and with the help of his grandfather, Frost and his wife bought a farm in Derry, New Hampshire, in 1900. Although his experiences would later provide rich resources for his poetry, life on the isolated farm was difficult, and Frost returned to full-time teaching in 1906. He also returned to serious work on his poems, several of which were published in the *Independent*, the *Youth's Companion*, and the *New England Magazine*.

In 1911, when he was thirty-seven, Frost determined to make a final effort to become a professional poet. He sold the farm in Derry, left his teaching position at the end of the academic year, and took his family to

England in the summer of 1912. The bold gamble paid off, since the connections he made among other poets there, especially Ezra Pound, led to the publication of Frost's first collection of poetry, *A Boy's Will* (1913). In a review of the volume published in the Chicago-based little magazine *Poetry*, Pound described Frost's work as "a little raw" but observed that the volume had "the tang of the New Hampshire woods, and it has just this utter sincerity." *A Boy's Will* also received several favorable reviews in England, leading to the publication of a second collection of Frost's poems, *North of Boston* (1914). After war broke out in Europe in August 1914, he decided to bring his family back to the United States. By the time they returned in 1915, an American publishing firm had brought out editions of *A Boy's Will* and *North of Boston*, largely through the efforts of Amy Lowell, who had discovered Frost's work during a visit to London and who wrote a rave review of the two volumes for the *New Republic*. Frost soon published another collection, *Mountain Interval* (1916), which was followed by *New Hampshire* (1923). That volume was awarded the first of Frost's four Pulitzer Prizes, which he also received for his *Collected Poems* (1931), *A Farther Range* (1937), and *A Witness Tree* (1943). Indeed, along with his own favorite, Emily Dickinson, Frost became the most well-known poet in the United States.

During the last two decades of his life, however, he secured that position less by the poetry he published than by his accomplished public performances in the role of the poet. Frost gave innumerable readings of his work, taught poetry at a number of colleges and universities, and was awarded more than forty honorary degrees, including those conferred on him by the two institutions from which he had dropped out, Dartmouth and Harvard. During the 1950s, Frost made visits to England and South America sponsored by the State Department. At the request of President Kennedy, Frost in 1962 visited the Soviet Union, where he chided Premier Khrushchev by reading his poem "Mending Wall," offering a subtle denunciation of the recently erected Berlin Wall. But his most memorable public moment occurred at Kennedy's inauguration the previous year, in January 1961. When the wind and bright sunlight made it impossible for the eighty-six-year-old Frost to read the poem that he had written for the occasion, he hesitated briefly and then recited from memory an earlier poem, "The Gift Outright." The deeply moving moment was in many ways the climax of the long career of a man who had from the beginning sought to make poetry an integral part of life in the United States. His final collection of poems, *In the Clearing*, was published in 1962, the year he was awarded the Congressional "Gold" Medal by President Kennedy. Frost died on January 29, 1963, and, as a clear indication of the household name he had become, his obituary was printed on the front page of newspapers across the United States.

Frost's Poetry. In her influential 1915 review of *A Boy's Will* and *North of Boston*, Amy Lowell emphasized some of the fundamental qualities of Frost's poetry: his "great and beautiful simplicity of phrase," the liberties he took with "classical metres," written "in a way to set the teeth of all the poets of the older schools on edge," and his use of a "blank verse which does not hesitate to leave out a syllable or put one in." Lowell also praised what she described as Frost's "photographic" realism. Indeed, Frost was often celebrated for his unsentimental depictions of rural life and ordinary people, though he once observed: "There are two types of realist — the one who offers a good deal of dirt with his potato to show that it is a real one; and the one who is satisfied with the potato brushed clean. . . . To me, the thing that art does for life is to clean it, to strip it to form." Later, when an interviewer asked him if poetry was an escape from life, Frost responded, "No, it's a way of taking life by the throat." The following selection of poems charts Frost's ongoing and often fierce engagement with life over a nearly thirty-year period. The earliest of these — "Mending Wall," "Home Burial," and "After Apple-Picking" — were first published in *North of Boston* (1914). After that, Frost's work frequently appeared in prominent periodicals such as the *Atlantic Monthly*, where his famous poems "The Road Not Taken" and "Birches" were published in 1915, and *McClure's*, where " 'Out, Out —' " was published in 1916. He first collected those poems in *Mountain Interval* (1916). With the exception of "The Oven Bird," which Frost also included in that volume, all of the later poems in the following selection first appeared in periodicals, and they are ordered and dated according to their initial publication rather than in the order in which they were published in later volumes. For example, "Design" appeared in its final form in *American Poetry* in 1922, but Frost did not include the dark and chilling poem in a volume until he published *A Farther Range* (1937). The texts of all of the poems are taken from *The Poetry of Robert Frost*, edited by Edward Connery Lathem (1969).

bedfordstmartins.com/ americanlit for research links on Frost

MENDING WALL

Something there is that doesn't love a wall,
That sends the frozen-ground-swell under it
And spills the upper boulders in the sun,
And makes gaps even two can pass abreast.
The work of hunters is another thing: 5
I have come after them and made repair
Where they have left not one stone on a stone,
But they would have the rabbit out of hiding,
To please the yelping dogs. The gaps I mean,
No one has seen them made or heard them made,   10
But at spring mending-time we find them there.
I let my neighbor know beyond the hill;
And on a day we meet to walk the line
And set the wall between us once again.
We keep the wall between us as we go.   15

To each the boulders that have fallen to each.
And some are loaves and some so nearly balls
We have to use a spell to make them balance:
"Stay where you are until our backs are turned!"
We wear our fingers rough with handling them.   20
Oh, just another kind of outdoor game,
One on a side. It comes to little more:
There where it is we do not need the wall:
He is all pine and I am apple orchard.
My apple trees will never get across   25
And eat the cones under his pines, I tell him.
He only says, "Good fences make good neighbors."
Spring is the mischief in me, and I wonder
If I could put a notion in his head:
"*Why* do they make good neighbors? Isn't it   30
Where there are cows? But here there are no cows.
Before I built a wall I'd ask to know
What I was walling in or walling out,
And to whom I was like to give offense.
Something there is that doesn't love a wall,   35
That wants it down." I could say "Elves" to him,
But it's not elves exactly, and I'd rather
He said it for himself. I see him there,
Bringing a stone grasped firmly by the top
In each hand, like an old-stone savage armed.   40
He moves in darkness as it seems to me,
Not of woods only and the shade of trees.
He will not go behind his father's saying,
And he likes having thought of it so well
He says again, "Good fences make good neighbors."   45

[1914, 1969]

HOME BURIAL

He saw her from the bottom of the stairs
Before she saw him. She was starting down,
Looking back over her shoulder at some fear.
She took a doubtful step and then undid it
To raise herself and look again. He spoke   5
Advancing toward her: "What is it you see
From up there always? — for I want to know."
She turned and sank upon her skirts at that,
And her face changed from terrified to dull.
He said to gain time: "What is it you see?"   10

Mounting until she cowered under him.
"I will find out now — you must tell me, dear."
She, in her place, refused him any help,
With the least stiffening of her neck and silence.
She let him look, sure that he wouldn't see,   15
Blind creature; and awhile he didn't see.
But at last he murmured, "Oh," and again, "Oh."

"What is it — what?" she said.

                    "Just that I see."

"You don't," she challenged. "Tell me what it is."

"The wonder is I didn't see at once.   20
I never noticed it from here before.
I must be wonted to it — that's the reason.
The little graveyard where my people are!
So small the window frames the whole of it.
Not so much larger than a bedroom, is it?   25
There are three stones of slate and one of marble,
Broad-shouldered little slabs there in the sunlight
On the sidehill. We haven't to mind *those*.
But I understand: it is not the stones,
But the child's mound ——"

             "Don't, don't, don't, don't," she cried.   30

She withdrew, shrinking from beneath his arm
That rested on the banister, and slid downstairs;
And turned on him with such a daunting look,
He said twice over before he knew himself:
"Can't a man speak of his own child he's lost?"   35

"Not you! — Oh, where's my hat? Oh, I don't need it!
I must get out of here. I must get air. —
I don't know rightly whether any man can."

"Amy! Don't go to someone else this time.
Listen to me. I won't come down the stairs."   40
He sat and fixed his chin between his fists.
"There's something I should like to ask you, dear."

"You don't know how to ask it."

                  "Help me, then."

Her fingers moved the latch for all reply.

"My words are nearly always an offense.   45
I don't know how to speak of anything

So as to please you. But I might be taught,
I should suppose. I can't say I see how.
A man must partly give up being a man
With womenfolk. We could have some arrangement   50
By which I'd bind myself to keep hands off
Anything special you're a-mind to name.
Though I don't like such things 'twixt those that love.
Two that don't love can't live together without them.
But two that do can't live together with them."   55
She moved the latch a little. "Don't – don't go.
Don't carry it to someone else this time.
Tell me about it if it's something human.
Let me into your grief. I'm not so much
Unlike other folks as your standing there   60
Apart would make me out. Give me my chance.
I do think, though, you overdo it a little.
What was it brought you up to think it the thing
To take your mother-loss of a first child
So inconsolably – in the face of love.   65
You'd think his memory might be satisfied ——"

"There you go sneering now!"

                    "I'm not, I'm not!

You make me angry. I'll come down to you.
God, what a woman! And it's come to this,
A man can't speak of his own child that's dead."   70

"You can't because you don't know how to speak.
If you had any feelings, you that dug
With your own hand – how could you? – his little grave;
I saw you from that very window there,
Making the gravel leap and leap in air,   75
Leap up, like that, like that, and land so lightly
And roll back down the mound beside the hole.
I thought, Who is that man? I didn't know you.
And I crept down the stairs and up the stairs
To look again, and still your spade kept lifting.   80
Then you came in. I heard your rumbling voice
Out in the kitchen, and I don't know why,
But I went near to see with my own eyes.
You could sit there with the stains on your shoes
Of the fresh earth from your own baby's grave   85
And talk about your everyday concerns.
You had stood the spade up against the wall
Outside there in the entry, for I saw it."

"I shall laugh the worst laugh I ever laughed.
I'm cursed. God, if I don't believe I'm cursed."   90

"I can repeat the very words you were saying:
'Three foggy mornings and one rainy day
Will rot the best birch fence a man can build.'
Think of it, talk like that at such a time!
What had how long it takes a birch to rot   95
To do with what was in the darkened parlor?
You *couldn't* care! The nearest friends can go
With anyone to death, comes so far short
They might as well not try to go at all.
No, from the time when one is sick to death,   100
One is alone, and he dies more alone.
Friends make pretense of following to the grave,
But before one is in it, their minds are turned
And making the best of their way back to life
And living people, and things they understand.   105
But the world's evil. I won't have grief so
If I can change it. Oh, I won't, I won't!"

"There, you have said it all and you feel better.
You won't go now. You're crying. Close the door.
The heart's gone out of it: why keep it up?   110
Amy! There's someone coming down the road!"

"*You* — oh, you think the talk is all. I must go —
Somewhere out of this house. How can I make you ——"

"If — you — do!" She was opening the door wider.
"Where do you mean to go? First tell me that.   115
I'll follow and bring you back by force. I *will*! — "

[1914, 1969]

AFTER APPLE-PICKING

My long two-pointed ladder's sticking through a tree
Toward heaven still,
And there's a barrel that I didn't fill
Beside it, and there may be two or three
Apples I didn't pick upon some bough.   5
But I am done with apple-picking now.
Essence of winter sleep is on the night,
The scent of apples: I am drowsing off.
I cannot rub the strangeness from my sight

I got from looking through a pane of glass   10
I skimmed this morning from the drinking trough
And held against the world of hoary grass.
It melted, and I let it fall and break.
But I was well
Upon my way to sleep before it fell,   15
And I could tell
What form my dreaming was about to take.
Magnified apples appear and disappear,
Stem end and blossom end,
And every fleck of russet showing clear.   20
My instep arch not only keeps the ache,
It keeps the pressure of a ladder-round.
I feel the ladder sway as the boughs bend.
And I keep hearing from the cellar bin
The rumbling sound   25
Of load on load of apples coming in.
For I have had too much
Of apple-picking: I am overtired
Of the great harvest I myself desired.
There were ten thousand thousand fruit to touch,   30
Cherish in hand, lift down, and not let fall.
For all
That struck the earth,
No matter if not bruised or spiked with stubble,
Went surely to the cider-apple heap   35
As of no worth.
One can see what will trouble
This sleep of mine, whatever sleep it is.
Were he not gone,
The woodchuck could say whether it's like his   40
Long sleep, as I describe its coming on,
Or just some human sleep.

                                                                 [1914, 1969]

THE ROAD NOT TAKEN

Two roads diverged in a yellow wood,
And sorry I could not travel both
And be one traveler, long I stood
And looked down one as far as I could
To where it bent in the undergrowth;   5

Then took the other, as just as fair,
And having perhaps the better claim,
Because it was grassy and wanted wear;
Though as for that, the passing there
Had worn them really about the same,   10

And both that morning equally lay
In leaves no step had trodden black.
Oh, I kept the first for another day!
Yet knowing how way leads on to way,
I doubted if I should ever come back.   15

I shall be telling this with a sigh
Somewhere ages and ages hence:
Two roads diverged in a wood, and I
I took the one less traveled by,
And that has made all the difference.   20

[1915, 1969]

BIRCHES

When I see birches bend to left and right
Across the lines of straighter darker trees,
I like to think some boy's been swinging them.
But swinging doesn't bend them down to stay
As ice storms do. Often you must have seen them   5
Loaded with ice a sunny winter morning
After a rain. They click upon themselves
As the breeze rises, and turn many-colored
As the stir cracks and crazes their enamel.
Soon the sun's warmth makes them shed crystal shells   10
Shattering and avalanching on the snow crust —
Such heaps of broken glass to sweep away
You'd think the inner dome of heaven had fallen.
They are dragged to the withered bracken by the load,
And they seem not to break; though once they are bowed   15
So low for long, they never right themselves:
You may see their trunks arching in the woods
Years afterwards, trailing their leaves on the ground
Like girls on hands and knees that throw their hair
Before them over their heads to dry in the sun.   20
But I was going to say when Truth broke in
With all her matter of fact about the ice storm,

I should prefer to have some boy bend them
As he went out and in to fetch the cows —
Some boy too far from town to learn baseball,   25
Whose only play was what he found himself,
Summer or winter, and could play alone.
One by one he subdued his father's trees
By riding them down over and over again
Until he took the stiffness out of them,   30
And not one but hung limp, not one was left
For him to conquer. He learned all there was
To learn about not launching out too soon
And so not carrying the tree away
Clear to the ground. He always kept his poise   35
To the top branches, climbing carefully
With the same pains you use to fill a cup
Up to the brim, and even above the brim.
Then he flung outward, feet first, with a swish,
Kicking his way down through the air to the ground.   40
So was I once myself a swinger of birches.
And so I dream of going back to be.
It's when I'm weary of considerations,
And life is too much like a pathless wood
Where your face burns and tickles with the cobwebs   45
Broken across it, and one eye is weeping
From a twig's having lashed across it open.
I'd like to get away from earth awhile
And then come back to it and begin over.
May no fate willfully misunderstand me   50
And half grant what I wish and snatch me away
Not to return. Earth's the right place for love:
I don't know where it's likely to go better.
I'd like to go by climbing a birch tree,
And climb black branches up a snow-white trunk   55
Toward heaven, till the tree could bear no more,
But dipped its top and set me down again.
That would be good both going and coming back.
One could do worse than be a swinger of birches.

[1915, 1969]

"OUT, OUT —"[1]

The buzz saw snarled and rattled in the yard
And made dust and dropped stove-length sticks of wood,
Sweet-scented stuff when the breeze drew across it.
And from there those that lifted eyes could count
Five mountain ranges one behind the other   5
Under the sunset far into Vermont.
And the saw snarled and rattled, snarled and rattled,
As it ran light, or had to bear a load.
And nothing happened: day was all but done.
Call it a day, I wish they might have said   10
To please the boy by giving him the half hour
That a boy counts so much when saved from work.
His sister stood beside them in her apron
To tell them "Supper." At the word, the saw,
As if to prove saws knew what supper meant,   15
Leaped out at the boy's hand, or seemed to leap —
He must have given the hand. However it was,
Neither refused the meeting. But the hand!
The boy's first outcry was a rueful laugh,
As he swung toward them holding up the hand,   20
Half in appeal, but half as if to keep
The life from spilling. Then the boy saw all —
Since he was old enough to know, big boy
Doing a man's work, though a child at heart —
He saw all spoiled. "Don't let him cut my hand off —   25
The doctor, when he comes. Don't let him, sister!"
So. But the hand was gone already.
The doctor put him in the dark of ether.
He lay and puffed his lips out with his breath.
And then — the watcher at his pulse took fright.   30
No one believed. They listened at his heart.
Little — less — nothing! — and that ended it.
No more to build on there. And they, since they
Were not the one dead, turned to their affairs.

[1916, 1969]

---

1. **"Out, Out —":** The title is from a famous soliloquy in Shakespeare's *Macbeth.* Learning of the death of his wife, Macbeth pessimistically reflects on the futility of life: "Out, out, brief candle! / Life's but a walking shadow, a poor player, / That struts and frets his hour upon the stage, / And then is heard no more. It is a tale / Told by an idiot, full of sound and fury, / Signifying nothing" (5.5.23-26).

THE OVEN BIRD

There is a singer everyone has heard,
Loud, a mid-summer and a mid-wood bird,
Who makes the solid tree trunks sound again.
He says that leaves are old and that for flowers
Mid-summer is to spring as one to ten.   5
He says the early petal-fall is past,
When pear and cherry bloom went down in showers
On sunny days a moment overcast;
And comes that other fall we name the fall.
He says the highway dust is over all.   10
The bird would cease and be as other birds
But that he knows, in singing not to sing.
The question that he frames in all but words
Is what to make of a diminished thing.

[1916, 1969]

FIRE AND ICE

Some say the world will end in fire,
Some say in ice.
From what I've tasted of desire
I hold with those who favor fire.
But if it had to perish twice,
I think I know enough of hate
To say that for destruction ice
Is also great
And would suffice.

[1920, 1969]

DESIGN

I found a dimpled spider, fat and white,
On a white heal-all,[1] holding up a moth
Like a white piece of rigid satin cloth —
Assorted characters of death and blight
Mixed ready to begin the morning right,   5
Like the ingredients of a witches' broth —

---

1. **heal-all:** A nineteenth-century name for plants whose leaves were used to treat small cuts.

A snow-drop spider, a flower like a froth,
And dead wings carried like a paper kite.

What had that flower to do with being white,
The wayside blue and innocent heal-all?   10
What brought the kindred spider to that height,
Then steered the white moth thither in the night?
What but design of darkness to appall? —
If design govern in a thing so small.

[1922, 1969]

NOTHING GOLD CAN STAY

Nature's first green is gold,
Her hardest hue to hold.
Her early leaf's a flower;
But only so an hour.
Then leaf subsides to leaf.
So Eden sank to grief,
So dawn goes down to day.
Nothing gold can stay.

[1923, 1969]

STOPPING BY WOODS ON A SNOWY EVENING

Whose woods these are I think I know.
His house is in the village, though;
He will not see me stopping here
To watch his woods fill up with snow.

My little horse must think it queer   5
To stop without a farmhouse near
Between the woods and frozen lake
The darkest evening of the year.

He gives his harness bells a shake
To ask if there is some mistake.   10
The only other sound's the sweep
Of easy wind and downy flake.

The woods are lovely, dark, and deep,
But I have promises to keep,
And miles to go before I sleep,   15
And miles to go before I sleep.

[1923, 1969]

DESERT PLACES

Snow falling and night falling fast, oh, fast
In a field I looked into going past,
And the ground almost covered smooth in snow,
But a few weeds and stubble showing last.

The woods around it have it — it is theirs.   5
All animals are smothered in their lairs.
I am too absent-spirited to count;
The loneliness includes me unawares.

And lonely as it is, that loneliness
Will be more lonely ere it will be less —   10
A blanker whiteness of benighted snow
With no expression, nothing to express.

They cannot scare me with their empty spaces
Between stars — on stars where no human race is.
I have it in me so much nearer home   15
To scare myself with my own desert places.

[1934, 1969]

THE GIFT OUTRIGHT

The land was ours before we were the land's.
She was our land more than a hundred years
Before we were her people. She was ours
In Massachusetts, in Virginia,
But we were England's, still colonials,   5
Possessing what we still were unpossessed by,
Possessed by what we now no more possessed.
Something we were withholding made us weak
Until we found out that it was ourselves
We were withholding from our land of living,   10
And forthwith found salvation in surrender.
Such as we were we gave ourselves outright
(The deed of gift was many deeds of war)
To the land vaguely realizing westward,
But still unstoried, artless, unenhanced,   15
Such as she was, such as she would become.

[1942, 1969]

Georgia Douglas Johnson

[1877-1966]

Georgia Blanche Douglas Camp was born on September 10, 1877, in Atlanta, Georgia. In an account of her mixed racial heritage, Johnson explained that her mother, Laura Douglas, was half African American and half Native American, while her father, George Camp, was half white and half African American. Little is known about Johnson's early life. Her parents separated when she was a young child, and Johnson attended public schools and later the Atlanta University Normal School for Teachers. When she graduated in 1893, she accepted a position at a school in Marietta, Georgia. She taught there until 1902, when she left to study piano and violin at the Oberlin Conservatory of Music in Ohio. Shortly after her return to Atlanta in 1903, she married an ambitious attorney and politician, Henry Lincoln Johnson. Although he disapproved of Johnson's literary pursuits, she published her first poem, "Omnipresence," in the June 1905 issue of the *Voice of the Negro*, an illustrated monthly magazine produced in Atlanta. In 1910, Henry Johnson moved with his wife and their two sons to Washington, D.C., where he established a law firm and then accepted a political appointment as the recorder of deeds of the District of Columbia, a prestigious position once held by Frederick Douglass.

Georgia Douglas Johnson

This photograph was taken in the 1920s, when Johnson emerged as the leading woman poet of the Harlem Renaissance.

The Johnsons soon became a prominent part of African American society in Washington. Using their dining-room table as her desk, Johnson wrote constantly, and in 1916 three of her poems appeared in the *Crisis*, the magazine of the National Association for the Advancement of Colored People (NAACP). Two years later, Johnson self-published her first collection of poems, *The Heart of a Woman*, with an introduction by William Stanley Braithwaite, a noted African American poet and literary editor of the *Boston Evening Transcript*. The volume gained her considerable exposure, and a photograph of Johnson appeared on the cover of the *Crisis* in 1920. Its editor, W. E. B. Du Bois, wrote the preface to her next collection, *Bronze: A Book of Verse* (1922), which Johnson also published at her own expense. "My first book was . . . not at all race conscious," she observed in 1941. "Then someone said – she has no feeling for the race. So I wrote *Bronze* – it is entirely racial and one section deals entirely with motherhood – that motherhood that has as its back note – black children born to the world's displeasure." The collection also included many poems about the harsh legacy of slavery and the obstacles African Americans faced in early twentieth-century America. In the early 1920s, Johnson began host-ing informal gatherings at her home on S Street in Washington. During the following decade, her "S Street Salon" or what its regulars fondly called the "Saturday Nighters Club" attracted many of the most prominent African American artists and intellectuals of the period, including emerg-ing young writers such as Countee Cullen, Langston Hughes, Zora Neale Hurston, and Jean Toomer.

Johnson's husband died from a stroke in 1925, and she was suddenly thrust into the role of single parent and sole supporter of two teenage boys. After trying substitute teaching and other part-time jobs, she secured a position in the Labor Department, where Johnson worked from 1925 through 1934. She supplemented her salary and managed to put her sons through college by writing prolifically. Between 1926 and 1932, John-son wrote a weekly newspaper column, "Homely Philosophy," which was syndicated in African American newspapers throughout the country. Still deeply committed to her poetry but once again unable to interest a com-mercial publisher, she paid for the publication of a sequence of poems charting the course of a failed love affair, *An Autumn Love Cycle* (1928). She also began to write more marketable works, including short stories, which Johnson published under male pen names, and one-act plays, four of which were produced between 1926 and 1935. Although she published rela-tively little after that, she was active in political and cultural groups, and she continued to write. By her own count, Johnson had written "over 200 poems, 28 plays, and 31 stories" by the time she self-published her final volume of poetry, *Share My World* (1962). To her great delight, she was awarded an honorary doctor of letters degree from Atlanta University in 1965. Johnson died from a stroke in Washington the following year, on May 14, 1966.

bedfordstmartins.com/ americanlit for research links on Johnson

Johnson's Poetry.   Johnson published four volumes of poetry in her lifetime, as well as many poems in magazines, including the *Crisis*, the *Lib-erator*, and *Opportunity*, and anthologies such as James Weldon Johnson's *The Book of American Negro Poetry* (1922) and Countee Cullen's *Caroling Dusk: An Anthology of Verse by Black Poets of the Twenties* (1927). Little interested in the experimental "new verse" of the period, Johnson for the most part wrote traditional lyric poetry. Alain Locke suggested in 1928 that "in a simple declarative style, [Johnson] engages with ingenuous directness the moods and emotions of her themes." Johnson addressed racial themes in poems such as "Cosmopolite," an affirmation of her com-plex racial heritage, and "Black Woman." But she more often focused on the experience of women of any race, exploring the sometimes conflicting claims of love, motherhood, sexual desire, and the need for autonomy. The texts of the following poems are taken from her first three collections, *The Heart of a Woman* (1918), *Bronze: A Book of Verse* (1922), and *An Autumn Love Cycle* (1928).

THE HEART OF A WOMAN

The heart of a woman goes forth with the dawn,
As a lone bird, soft winging, so restlessly on,
Afar o'er life's turrets and vales does it roam
In the wake of those echoes the heart calls home.

The heart of a woman falls back with the night,
And enters some alien cage in its plight,
And tries to forget it has dreamed of the stars
While it breaks, breaks, breaks on the sheltering bars.

[1918]

BLACK WOMAN[1]

Don't knock at my door, little child,
    I cannot let you in,
You know not what a world this is
    Of cruelty and sin.
Wait in the still eternity   5
    Until I come to you,
The world is cruel, cruel, child,
    I cannot let you in!

Don't knock at my heart, little one,
    I cannot bear the pain   10
Of turning deaf-ear to your call
    Time and time again!
You do not know the monster men
    Inhabiting the earth,
Be still, be still, my precious child,   15
    I must not give you birth!

[1922]

---

1. **Black Woman:** This poem, which Johnson included in the "Motherhood" section of *Bronze: A Book of Verse* (1922), was published as "Motherhood" in the *Crisis* (October 1922).

COSMOPOLITE[1]

Not wholly this or that,
But wrought
Of alien bloods am I,

---

1. **Cosmopolite:** A cosmopolitan person. Johnson makes a play on the root meanings of the word, which is derived from the Greek words *kosmos* ("world") and *politēs* ("citizen").

A product of the interplay
Of traveled hearts.   5
Estranged, yet not estranged, I stand
All comprehending;
From my estate
I view earth's frail dilemma;
Scion of fused strength am I,   10
All understanding,
Nor this nor that
Contains me.

[1922]

I WANT TO DIE WHILE YOU LOVE ME

I want to die while you love me,
    While yet you hold me fair,
While laughter lies upon my lips
    And lights are in my hair.

I want to die while you love me   5
    And bear to that still bed
Your kisses — turbulent, unspent,
    To warm me when I'm dead.

I want to die while you love me
    Oh, who would care to live,   10
'Til love has nothing more to ask
    And nothing more to give.

[1928]

Carl Sandburg

[1878–1967]

Carl August Sandburg was born in Galesburg, Illinois, on January 6, 1878, the son of Clara Anderson, a former hotel maid, and August Sandburg, who worked for a railroad line. Both were Swedish immigrants, and Sandburg grew up in a household in which he spoke both Swedish and English. Sandburg later recalled that he decided to become "a person of letters" when he first learned the alphabet, at the age of six. But he left school after graduating from the eighth grade in order to help support the growing family. For the next several years, he took a series of odd jobs, delivering milk, selling fruit on street corners, shining shoes at a barber shop, and working as a stagehand at the opera house. Eager to see more of the world, the restless nineteen-year-old set off as a hobo in the summer of 1897 on a trip through Iowa, Missouri, Kansas, Nebraska, and Colorado. Along the way, he supported himself by taking a long list of temporary jobs, from waiting on tables and washing dishes to working on a railroad and in the wheat fields. Sandburg also kept notebooks in which he jotted down anecdotes, impressions, and lists of words and phrases. Shortly after he returned home in 1898, he enlisted in the Sixth Illinois Regiment, which was part of the force that occupied Puerto Rico during the Spanish-American War.

Carl Sandburg

Sandburg's brother-in-law, the photographer Edward Steichen, took this portrait around 1919, when the poet was working as a journalist in Chicago, the subject of his first major collection, *Chicago Poems* (1916).

Following his brief stint as a soldier, Sandburg once again returned to Galesburg, where he took his first steps toward a literary career. As a veteran of the war, he was entitled to free tuition at Lombard College, where he attended classes from 1898 until 1902. Although he did not earn a degree, he met Philip Green Wright, a professor who strongly encouraged and inspired Sandburg. Using his own handpress, Wright later printed small runs of Sandburg's first collections of poems and other writings, *In Reckless Ecstasy* (1904), *Incidentals* (1906), and *The Plaint of a Rose* (1908). After leaving college, Sandburg pursued a career on the lecture circuit, delivering talks on his heroes Walt Whitman and Abraham Lincoln, and as a journalist in Chicago, where he moved in 1906. He became deeply involved with the prolabor Social Democratic Party and consequently moved to Milwaukee, where Sandburg worked as a party organizer and wrote for progressive periodicals such as *La Follette's Weekly*. He also met Lillian Steichen, whom Sandburg married in July 1908. Sandburg later observed that, in addition to Green, the most important influences on his life were his artistic wife, a Phi Beta Kappa graduate of the University of Chicago, and her older brother, the celebrated photographer Edward Steichen. In 1912, Sandburg took his family back to Chicago, where he worked as a reporter for various progressive newspapers. Throughout his years as an activist and journalist, however, Sandburg continued to write poetry. Early in 1914, he sent a group of nine poems to Harriet Monroe, who swiftly published them in her magazine *Poetry*. Although the reception of his raw verse on unpoetical subjects was almost violently mixed, a young publishing agent, Alfred Harcourt, was so impressed with Sandburg's work that he encouraged Monroe to "steer Carl my way." Harcourt's firm, Henry Holt, published Sandburg's first major collection, *Chicago Poems*, in 1916.

The volume launched Sandburg's successful career as a poet, though he became almost equally well known for his many other writings. In 1917, he took a job with the *Chicago Daily News*, where he worked as a reporter and later as a film critic until 1930. His coverage of one of the ugliest episodes in the city's history led to the publication of his most important journalistic work, *The Chicago Race Riots, July 1919*. He also found time to write the poems collected in *Cornhuskers* (1918), *Smoke and Steel* (1920), *Slabs of the Sunburnt West* (1922), and *Good Morning, America* (1928). The popularity of a series of books for children he published during the 1920s, the *Rootabaga* stories, prompted Sandburg to begin work on another book for children, a biography of Abraham Lincoln. But the project developed into something far more ambitious, the two-volume *Abraham Lincoln: The Prairie Years* (1926). The onset of the Depression inspired Sandburg to write his impassioned epic poem *The People, Yes (1936)*. Sandburg also completed his four-volume *Abraham Lincoln: The War Years* (1939), which was awarded the Pulitzer Prize for History. Other awards and honors followed, including numerous honorary degrees and a second Pulitzer Prize for his *Complete Poems* (1950). Characteristically, however, Sandburg continued to experiment with a variety of genres, writing a novel, *Remembrance Rock* (1948); a lyrical account of his early years, *Always the Young Strangers* (1953); and the exhibition catalog for *The Family of Man* (1955), a collection of photographs of people from sixty-eight countries taken by Edward Steichen. Sandburg's final book of poetry, *Honey and Salt*, was published in 1963. A few months after he died on July 23, 1967, a memorial service was held for Sandburg at the Lincoln Memorial in Washington, D.C., where the thousands of mourners were led by President Lyndon B. Johnson.

Sandburg's Poetry.   Sandburg's first professionally published poems appeared in *Poetry: A Magazine of Verse*, established in 1912 in an effort to change the character of American poetry by featuring new and innovative work. The editor, Harriet Monroe, was reportedly "shocked" by the rough style and subject matter of the poems, but she admired the authenticity of Sandburg's voice. Two of the poems included in the following selection, "Chicago" and "The Harbor," were among the nine "Chicago Poems" that appeared at the opening of the March 1914 issue of *Poetry*. Although the poems outraged some reviewers, including one who called them an "affront to the poetry-loving public," Sandburg was later awarded the prize for the best poems published during the year in *Poetry*. His appearance in the magazine also led to the publication of his collection *Chicago Poems* (1916). In addition to the poems that had appeared in *Poetry*, the volume included "Graceland," "A Fence," and "Fog." The other poems included in the following selection — "Prayers of Steel," "Cool Tombs," and "Grass" — were published in Sandburg's next book, *Cornhuskers* (1918). Together, these poems reveal his debt to Walt Whitman, who helped inspire Sandburg's experiments in free verse and explorations of the seemingly unpoetical realities of urban and rural life in the Midwest. In a graceful tribute to Sandburg published in 1924, Monroe defined "love" as the central and controlling motive of his poems — "love of the prairie country, the prairie

bedfordstmartins.com/
americanlit for research
links on Sandburg

towns and city, and the people who struggle through toilsome lives there."
She also praised the artistry of Sandburg's best poems, which had "greatly
widened the rhythmic range of English poetry," as well as his use of the vernacular: "It is enough to say that any writer who can use the common speech
of the people for beauty thereby enriches and revivifies the language." The
texts are taken from *The Complete Poems of Carl Sandburg* (1970).

CHICAGO

Hog Butcher for the World,
Tool Maker, Stacker of Wheat,
Player with Railroads and the Nation's Freight Handler;
Stormy, husky, brawling,
City of the Big Shoulders: 5

They tell me you are wicked and I believe them, for I have seen your painted
    women under the gas lamps luring the farm boys.
And they tell me you are crooked and I answer: Yes, it is true I have seen the
    gunman kill and go free to kill again.
And they tell me you are brutal and my reply is: On the faces of women and
    children I have seen the marks of wanton hunger.
And having answered so I turn once more to those who sneer at this my city, and
    I give them back the sneer and say to them:
Come and show me another city with lifted head singing so proud to be alive and
    coarse and strong and cunning.   10
Flinging magnetic curses amid the toil of piling job on job, here is a tall bold
    slugger set vivid against the little soft cities;
Fierce as a dog with tongue lapping for action, cunning as a savage pitted against
    the wilderness,
       Bareheaded,
       Shoveling,
       Wrecking,   15
       Planning,
       Building, breaking, rebuilding,
Under the smoke, dust all over his mouth, laughing with white teeth,
Under the terrible burden of destiny laughing as a young man laughs,
Laughing even as an ignorant fighter laughs who has never lost a battle,   20
Bragging and laughing that under his wrist is the pulse, and under his ribs the
    heart of the people,
           Laughing!
Laughing the stormy, husky, brawling laughter of Youth, half-naked, sweating,
    proud to be Hog Butcher, Tool Maker, Stacker of Wheat, Player with Railroads
    and Freight Handler to the Nation.

                                     [1914, 1970]

THE HARBOR

Passing through huddled and ugly walls
By doorways where women
Looked from their hunger-deep eyes,
Haunted with shadows of hunger-hands,
Out from the huddled and ugly walls,   5
I came sudden, at the city's edge,
On a blue burst of lake,
Long lake waves breaking under the sun
On a spray-flung curve of shore;
And a fluttering storm of gulls,   10
Masses of great gray wings
And flying white bellies
Veering and wheeling free in the open.

[1914, 1970]

GRACELAND[1]

Tomb of a millionaire,
A multi-millionaire, ladies and gentlemen,
Place of the dead where they spend every year
The usury of twenty-five thousand dollars
        For upkeep and flowers   5
To keep fresh the memory of the dead.
The merchant prince gone to dust
Commanded in his written will
Over the signed name of his last testament
Twenty-five thousand dollars be set aside   10
For roses, lilacs, hydrangeas, tulips,
For perfume and color, sweetness of remembrance
Around his last long home.

(A hundred cash girls want nickels to go to the movies tonight.
In the back stalls of a hundred saloons, women are at tables   15
Drinking with men or waiting for men jingling loose silver dollars in their pockets.
In a hundred furnished rooms is a girl who sells silk or dress goods or leather
    stuff for six dollars a week wages
And when she pulls on her stockings in the morning she is reckless about God and
    the newspapers and the police, the talk of her home town or the name people
    call her.)

[1916, 1970]

---

1. **Graceland:** Established in 1860, this parklike cemetery on the north side of Chicago was known for its elaborate monuments and tombs.

A Fence

Now the stone house on the lake front[1] is finished and the workmen are beginning the fence.

The palings are made of iron bars with steel points that can stab the life out of any man who falls on them.

As a fence, it is a masterpiece, and will shut off the rabble and all vagabonds and hungry men and all wandering children looking for a place to play.

Passing through the bars and over the steel points will go nothing except Death and the Rain and Tomorrow.

[1916, 1970]

---

1. **lake front:** Along the shore of Lake Michigan, where many wealthy people built houses in Chicago.

Fog

The fog comes
on little cat feet.

It sits looking
over harbor and city
on silent haunches
and then moves on.

[1916, 1970]

Prayers of Steel

Lay me on an anvil, O God.
Beat me and hammer me into a crowbar.
Let me pry loose old walls.
Let me lift and loosen old foundations.

Lay me on an anvil, O God.   5
Beat me and hammer me into a steel spike.
Drive me into the girders that hold a skyscraper together.
Take red-hot rivets and fasten me into the central girders.
Let me be the great nail holding a skyscraper through blue nights into white stars.

[1918, 1970]

COOL TOMBS

When Abraham Lincoln was shoveled into the tombs, he forgot the copperheads
    and the assassin[1] . . . in the dust, in the cool tombs.

And Ulysses Grant[2] lost all thought of con men and Wall Street, cash and collat-
    eral turned ashes . . . in the dust, in the cool tombs.

Pocahontas' body,[3] lovely as a poplar, sweet as a red haw in November or a pawpaw
    in May,[4] did she wonder? does she remember? . . . in the dust, in the cool tombs?

Take any streetful of people buying clothes and groceries, cheering a hero or
    throwing confetti and blowing tin horns . . . tell me if the lovers are losers . . .
    tell me if any get more than the lovers . . . in the dust . . . in the cool tombs.

[1918, 1970]

---

1. **the copperheads and the assassin:** *Copperhead*, the common name of a poisonous snake, was applied to
Northerners who sympathized with the South during the Civil War. President Lincoln was assassinated by
John Wilkes Booth on April 14, 1865.
2. **Ulysses Grant:** The administration of the former Union general, who served two terms as president
(1869–1877), was notorious for corruption and scandal. As a result of a series of bad business decisions,
Grant was later forced to declare bankruptcy.
3. **Pocahontas' body:** Pocahontas (c. 1595–1617) was the daughter of Powhatan, chief of the Algonkin Indians
in what is present-day Virginia. According to a story invented or exaggerated by Captain John Smith, Pocahontas intervened and saved him from execution.
4. **a red haw . . . or a pawpaw in May:** Common names for the hawthorn tree, which bears red blossoms, and
the pawpaw, a tree with purple flowers, both of which flower in the spring.

GRASS

Pile the bodies high at Austerlitz and Waterloo.[1]
Shovel them under and let me work —
             I am the grass; I cover all.

And pile them high at Gettysburg[2]
And pile them high at Ypres and Verdun.[3]   5
Shovel them under and let me work.
Two years, ten years, and passengers ask the conductor:
             What place is this?
             Where are we now?

             I am the grass.   10
             Let me work.

[1918, 1970]

---

1. **Austerlitz and Waterloo:** Napoleon and his French army defeated the Austrians and Russians at the town
of Austerlitz, in the present-day Czech Republic, in 1805. A decade later, Napoleon's forces were defeated by
the British in the decisive battle of Waterloo, near a town in Belgium.
2. **Gettysburg:** A bloody battle of the Civil War fought in 1863 in Pennsylvania, where the Union Army
defeated Confederate troops led by General Robert E. Lee.
3. **Ypres and Verdun:** Among the bloodiest battles of World War I, the former fought near a town in Belgium
between 1914 and 1917 and the latter fought in northeastern France in 1916.

Wallace Stevens

[1879-1955]

Wallace Stevens was born on October 2, 1879, in Reading, Pennsylvania. He was the second of five children born to Garrett Stevens, a lawyer, and Margaretha Catharine Zeller Stevens, a former schoolteacher and deeply religious person who was active in the Presbyterian Church. Stevens attended a Lutheran grammar school and then the Reading Boys' School. In 1897, he enrolled at Harvard University as a "special student" — that is, one whose academic abilities and financial need qualified him to complete his degree in three rather than four years. Stevens took courses with an eye to law school, for which his father wanted him to prepare. He also pursued his deep interests in art and literature, both in his academic courses and in his work for the college's literary magazine, the *Harvard Advocate.* Concerned about the amount of time Stevens was devoting to literary pursuits, especially to writing the numerous poems he published in the *Harvard Advocate,* Garrett Stevens in a letter admonished his son: "Keep hammering at your real work . . . for a fellow never knows what's in store — and time mis-spent now counts heavily."

Wallace Stevens

Stevens's wife, Elsie — whose shadow is visible in the photograph — took this snapshot around 1921 at Elizabeth Park in Hartford, Connecticut, where Stevens pursued a double life as a poet and a successful executive at the Hartford Insurance Company.

For the most part, Stevens followed his father's advice, even as he sought to become a poet. After he left Harvard in 1900, he moved to New York City, where Stevens worked as a journalist on the night shift at the *New York Tribune.* He enjoyed life in the city, and Stevens became so deeply absorbed in the theater that he wanted to quit his job at the *Tribune* in order to write plays. Instead, he reluctantly agreed to his father's plans for him and enrolled in the New York Law School in 1901. Stevens graduated in 1903, worked as a clerk in a law firm, and was admitted to the New York State Bar in 1904. During a visit home that summer, he met Elsie Viola Moll, a piano teacher Stevens described as "the prettiest girl in Reading." While working at a series of law offices, Stevens frequently visited and wrote to Elsie, presenting her with a handwritten collection of his verses on her birthday in 1908 and again in 1909. Despite the objections of his father, who viewed the Moll family as socially inferior, Stevens married her in the summer of 1909, after he landed a seemingly secure job on the legal staff of an insurance company in New York City. Following the death of his father in 1911 and his mother in 1912, Stevens once again began to write poetry. In 1914, his first professionally published poems appeared in the little magazine *Trend,* edited by an old friend from Harvard, Pitts

Sanborn. Stevens also met a number of avant-garde artists, musicians, and writers, including the poets Mina Loy, Marianne Moore, and William Carlos Williams. Stimulated by his new friends, Stevens became a regular contributor to various little magazines, notably *Poetry*, which published several of his poems and his first play, *Three Travelers Watch a Sunrise*, which won the magazine's award for verse drama in 1916.

That year also marked a crucial turning point in his life. When his employer went bankrupt, Stevens accepted a position with the Hartford Accident and Indemnity Company. Although he did not want to leave New York City, Stevens and his wife moved permanently to Hartford, Connecticut, in March 1916. Initially, he made frequent trips to New York City, and he continued to write a steady stream of poetry, some of which Stevens collected in his first book, *Harmonium* (1923). A few critics recognized the originality of the volume, but the reception was otherwise rather tepid, and the book was a commercial failure; Stevens reportedly received a first royalty check for $6.70. During the following few years, he devoted himself to his job at the insurance company, where Stevens was so successful that he became recognized as one of the masters of the surety-bond business in the United States. Around 1930, however, he returned to serious work on his poetry, soon publishing an expanded edition of *Harmonium* (1931). During the following two decades, Stevens published several more collections, including *Ideas of Order* (1935), *The Man with the Blue Guitar* (1937), *Parts of a World* (1942), *Transport to Summer* (1947), and *The Auroras of Autumn* (1950). Although he rarely gave readings of his work, Stevens delivered a number of lectures on poetry, some of which were published as *The Necessary Angel* (1951). He also received several awards, including the prestigious Bollingen Prize in Poetry in 1950 and the Pulitzer Prize for his *Collected Poems* (1954). Stevens died at his home in Hartford on August 2, 1955.

Stevens's Poetry.   In 1914, when Stevens was thirty-five, his poems began to appear in little magazines such as *Trend, Rogue, Others*, and *Poetry*, where his most famous poem, "Sunday Morning," appeared in 1915. Stevens subsequently included the poem in his first collection, *Harmonium* (1923), the title of which suggests his emphasis on the harmonious order that could be achieved only through the power of the poetic imagination. Most of the other poems in the following selection were also first collected in *Harmonium*, which was described by some critics as the most remarkable first book by any modernist poet and has been compared in originality and innovation to Walt Whitman's first edition of *Leaves of Grass* (1855). In a review of the volume in *Poetry*, Harriet Monroe advised her readers: "If one seeks sheer beauty of sound, phrase, rhythm, packed with prismatically colored ideas by a mind at once wise and whimsical, one should open one's eyes and ears, sharpen one's wits, widen one's sympathies to include rare and exquisite aspects of life, and then run for this volume of iridescent poems." In 1931, Stevens published a second edition of *Harmonium*, in which he omitted some poems and added fourteen others, including his World War I poem, "The Death of a Soldier." The poise, restraint, and relative austerity of that early poem anticipated the

bedfordstmartins.com/ americanlit *for research links on Stevens* characteristics of much of his later work, represented in the following selection by "The Idea of Order at Key West" (1934), "Of Modern Poetry" (1940) — among the poems that most forcefully convey his conception of the role of the poet and poetry in the twentieth century — and "The Plain Sense of Things," published only three years before Stevens died in 1955. The texts are taken from *The Collected Poems of Wallace Stevens* (1954).

SUNDAY MORNING[1]

I

Complacencies of the peignoir,[2] and late
Coffee and oranges in a sunny chair,
And the green freedom of a cockatoo
Upon a rug mingle to dissipate
The holy hush of ancient sacrifice.   5
She dreams a little, and she feels the dark
Encroachment of that old catastrophe,
As a calm darkens among water-lights.
The pungent oranges and bright, green wings
Seem things in some procession of the dead,   10
Winding across wide water, without sound.
The day is like wide water, without sound,
Stilled for the passing of her dreaming feet
Over the seas, to silent Palestine,
Dominion of the blood and sepulchre.[3]   15

II

Why should she give her bounty to the dead?
What is divinity if it can come
Only in silent shadows and in dreams?
Shall she not find in comforts of the sun,
In pungent fruit and bright, green wings, or else   20
In any balm or beauty of the earth,
Things to be cherished like the thought of heaven?
Divinity must live within herself:

---

1. **Sunday Morning:** Harriet Monroe omitted stanzas II, III, and VI when she published the poem in the November 1915 issue of her magazine, *Poetry*. Stevens agreed to the omissions but suggested that the remaining stanzas be printed I, VIII, IV, V, and VII, the order in which they appeared in *Poetry*. But he restored the omitted stanzas and the original order of the stanzas when he published the poem in his first collection, *Harmonium* (1923).
2. **peignoir:** A woman's light dressing gown or robe.
3. **sepulchre:** The tomb in Palestine where Christ's body was placed after his crucifixion, the "ancient sacrifice" alluded to in line 5 of the stanza.

Passions of rain, or moods in falling snow;
Grievings in loneliness, or unsubdued   25
Elations when the forest blooms; gusty
Emotions on wet roads on autumn nights;
All pleasures and all pains, remembering
The bough of summer and the winter branch.
These are the measures destined for her soul.   30

III

Jove[4] in the clouds had his inhuman birth.
No mother suckled him, no sweet land gave
Large-mannered motions to his mythy mind
He moved among us, as a muttering king,
Magnificent, would move among his hinds,   35
Until our blood, commingling, virginal,
With heaven, brought such requital to desire
The very hinds discerned it, in a star.[5]
Shall our blood fail? Or shall it come to be
The blood of paradise? And shall the earth   40
Seem all of paradise that we shall know?
The sky will be much friendlier then than now,
A part of labor and a part of pain,
And next in glory to enduring love,
Not this dividing and indifferent blue.   45

IV

She says, "I am content when wakened birds,
Before they fly, test the reality
Of misty fields, by their sweet questionings;
But when the birds are gone, and their warm fields
Return no more, where, then, is paradise?"   50
There is not any haunt of prophecy,
Nor any old chimera[6] of the grave,
Neither the golden underground, nor isle
Melodious, where spirits gat them home,
Nor visionary south, nor cloudy palm   55
Remote on heaven's hill, that has endured
As April's green endures; or will endure

---

4. **Jove**: The English name for Jupiter, the lord of the sky and ruler of the gods in Roman mythology.
5. **hinds . . . in a star**: *Hinds* is an archaic term for peasants or rustics, an allusion to the shepherds who came to the manger to see Joseph, Mary, and the newly born Jesus, whose birth was signaled by the Star of Bethlehem.
6. **chimera**: A savage, fire-breathing monster in Greek mythology.

Like her remembrance of awakened birds,
Or her desire for June and evening, tipped
By the consummation of the swallow's wings.   60

V

She says, "But in contentment I still feel
The need of some imperishable bliss."
Death is the mother of beauty; hence from her,
Alone, shall come fulfilment to our dreams
And our desires. Although she strews the leaves   65
Of sure obliteration on our paths,
The path sick sorrow took, the many paths
Where triumph rang its brassy phrase, or love
Whispered a little out of tenderness,
She makes the willow shiver in the sun   70
For maidens who were wont to sit and gaze
Upon the grass, relinquished to their feet.
She causes boys to pile new plums and pears
On disregarded plate. The maidens taste
And stray impassioned in the littering leaves.   75

VI

Is there no change of death in paradise?
Does ripe fruit never fall? Or do the boughs
Hang always heavy in that perfect sky,
Unchanging, yet so like our perishing earth,
With rivers like our own that seek for seas   80
They never find, the same receding shores
That never touch with inarticulate pang?
Why set the pear upon those river-banks
Or spice the shores with odors of the plum?
Alas, that they should wear our colors there,   85
The silken weavings of our afternoons,
And pick the strings of our insipid lutes!
Death is the mother of beauty, mystical,
Within whose burning bosom we devise
Our earthly mothers waiting, sleeplessly.   90

VII

Supple and turbulent, a ring of men
Shall chant in orgy on a summer morn
Their boisterous devotion to the sun,

Not as a god, but as a god might be,
Naked among them, like a savage source.   95
Their chant shall be a chant of paradise,
Out of their blood, returning to the sky;
And in their chant shall enter, voice by voice,
The windy lake wherein their lord delights,
The trees, like serafin,[7] and echoing hills,   100
That choir among themselves long afterward.
They shall know well the heavenly fellowship
Of men that perish and of summer morn.
And whence they came and whither they shall go
The dew upon their feet shall manifest.   105

VIII

She hears, upon that water without sound,
A voice that cries, "The tomb in Palestine
Is not the porch of spirits lingering.
It is the grave of Jesus, where he lay."
We live in an old chaos of the sun,   110
Or old dependency of day and night,
Or island solitude, unsponsored, free,
Of that wide water, inescapable.
Deer walk upon our mountains, and the quail
Whistle about us their spontaneous cries;   115
Sweet berries ripen in the wilderness;
And, in the isolation of the sky,
At evening, casual flocks of pigeons make
Ambiguous undulations as they sink,
Downward to darkness, on extended wings.   120

[1915, 1954]

---

7. **serafin:** Usually spelled *seraphim*, angels who in Christian theology occupy the highest rank of the celestial hierarchy.

THIRTEEN WAYS OF LOOKING
AT A BLACKBIRD

I

Among twenty snowy mountains,
The only moving thing
Was the eye of the blackbird.

II

I was of three minds,
Like a tree
In which there are three blackbirds.

5

III

The blackbird whirled in the autumn winds.
It was a small part of the pantomime.

IV

A man and a woman
Are one.
A man and a woman and a blackbird
Are one.

10

V

I do not know which to prefer,
The beauty of inflections
Or the beauty of innuendoes,
The blackbird whistling
Or just after.

15

VI

Icicles filled the long window
With barbaric glass.
The shadow of the blackbird
Crossed it, to and fro.
The mood
Traced in the shadow
An indecipherable cause.

20

VII

O thin men of Haddam,[1]
Why do you imagine golden birds?

25

---

1. **Haddam:** A city in Connecticut. In a letter written in 1953, Stevens explains: "The thin men of Haddam are entirely fictitious although some years ago one of the citizens of that place wrote to ask what I had in mind. I just liked the name."

Do you not see how the blackbird
Walks around the feet
Of the women about you?

VIII

I know noble accents   30
And lucid, inescapable rhythms;
But I know, too,
That the blackbird is involved
In what I know.

IX

When the blackbird flew out of sight,   35
It marked the edge
Of one of many circles.

X

At the sight of blackbirds
Flying in a green light,
Even the bawds of euphony   40
Would cry out sharply.

XI

He rode over Connecticut
In a glass coach.
Once, a fear pierced him,
In that he mistook   45
The shadow of his equipage
For blackbirds.

XII

The river is moving.
The blackbird must be flying.

XIII

It was evening all afternoon.   50
It was snowing
And it was going to snow.

The blackbird sat
In the cedar-limbs.

[1917, 1954]

THE DEATH OF A SOLDIER[1]

Life contracts and death is expected,
As in a season of autumn.
The soldier falls.

He does not become a three-days personage,
Imposing his separation,   5
Calling for pomp.

Death is absolute and without memorial,
As in a season of autumn,
When the wind stops,

When the wind stops and, over the heavens,   10
The clouds go, nevertheless,
In their direction.

[1918, 1954]

1. **The Death of a Soldier:** This poem was originally part of a poetic sequence, "Lettres d'un Soldat," published in *Poetry* in May 1918. Stevens was inspired by and drew upon his reading of *Lettres d'un soldat*, a collection of letters from the trenches written by Eugène Lemercier, a young French painter who was killed at the front in World War I.

ANECDOTE OF THE JAR

I placed a jar in Tennessee,
And round it was, upon a hill.
It made the slovenly wilderness
Surround that hill.

The wilderness rose up to it,   5
And sprawled around, no longer wild.
The jar was round upon the ground
And tall and of a port in air.

It took dominion everywhere.
The jar was gray and bare.   10
It did not give of bird or bush,
Like nothing else in Tennessee.

[1919, 1954]

THE SNOW MAN

One must have a mind of winter
To regard the frost and the boughs
Of the pine-trees crusted with snow;

And have been cold a long time
To behold the junipers shagged with ice,   5
The spruces rough in the distant glitter

Of the January sun; and not to think
Of any misery in the sound of the wind,
In the sound of a few leaves,

Which is the sound of the land   10
Full of the same wind
That is blowing in the same bare place

For the listener, who listens in the snow,
And, nothing himself, beholds
Nothing that is not there and the nothing that is.   15

[1921, 1954]

THE EMPEROR OF ICE-CREAM

Call the roller of big cigars,
The muscular one, and bid him whip
In kitchen cups concupiscent curds.[1]
Let the wenches dawdle in such dress
As they are used to wear, and let the boys   5
Bring flowers in last month's newspapers.
Let be be finale of seem.
The only emperor is the emperor of ice-cream.

Take from the dresser of deal,[2]
Lacking the three glass knobs, that sheet   10
On which she embroidered fantails[3] once
And spread it so as to cover her face.
If her horny feet protrude, they come
To show how cold she is, and dumb.
Let the lamp affix its beam.   15
The only emperor is the emperor of ice-cream.

[1922, 1954]

---

1. **concupiscent curds:** That is, lustful *curds*, a soft white substance formed by curdling or coagulating milk.
2. **deal:** Inexpensive fir or pine wood.
3. **fantails:** Pigeons with broad, fan-shaped tails.

A HIGH-TONED OLD CHRISTIAN WOMAN

Poetry is the supreme fiction, madame.
Take the moral law and make a nave[1] of it
And from the nave build haunted heaven. Thus,
The conscience is converted into palms,[2]
Like windy citherns[3] hankering for hymns.   5
We agree in principle. That's clear. But take
The opposing law and make a peristyle,[4]
And from the peristyle project a masque[5]
Beyond the planets. Thus, our bawdiness,
Unpurged by epitaph, indulged at last,   10
Is equally converted into palms,
Squiggling like saxophones. And palm for palm,
Madame, we are where we began. Allow,
Therefore, that in the planetary scene
Your disaffected flagellants,[6] well-stuffed,   15
Smacking their muzzy[7] bellies in parade,
Proud of such novelties of the sublime,
Such tink and tank and tunk-a-tunk-tunk,
May, merely may, madame, whip from themselves
A jovial hullabaloo among the spheres.   20
This will make widows wince. But fictive things
Wink as they will. Wink most when widows wince.

[1922, 1954]

---

1. **nave:** The central part of a church, where the congregation is seated.
2. **palms:** Associated in the Christian religion with the palm branches spread in the path of Jesus when he entered Jerusalem before his crucifixion, the event commemorated on Palm Sunday.
3. **citherns:** Also spelled *citterns*, light stringed instruments used in sixteenth- and seventeenth-century Europe.
4. **peristyle:** A courtyard or inner chamber of ancient Greek houses and temples, surrounded by a covered walkway supported by rows of columns.
5. **masque:** A dramatic spectacle, popular in England in the early seventeenth century, enacting allegorical stories through words, music, and dance.
6. **flagellants:** Persons who whip themselves as part of their religious discipline.
7. **muzzy:** The word usually means muddled or befuddled, often as a result of drinking, though it here seems to suggest boozy or booze-filled.

THE IDEA OF ORDER AT KEY WEST

She sang beyond the genius of the sea.
The water never formed to mind or voice,
Like a body wholly body, fluttering
Its empty sleeves; and yet its mimic motion
Made constant cry, caused constantly a cry,   5
That was not ours although we understood,
Inhuman, of the veritable ocean.

The sea was not a mask. No more was she.
The song and water were not medleyed sound
Even if what she sang was what she heard,   10
Since what she sang was uttered word by word.
It may be that in all her phrases stirred
The grinding water and the gasping wind;
But it was she and not the sea we heard.

For she was the maker of the song she sang.   15
The ever-hooded, tragic-gestured sea
Was merely a place by which she walked to sing.
Whose spirit is this? we said, because we knew
It was the spirit that we sought and knew
That we should ask this often as she sang.   20

If it was only the dark voice of the sea
That rose, or even colored by many waves;
If it was only the outer voice of sky
And cloud, of the sunken coral water-walled,
However clear, it would have been deep air,   25
The heaving speech of air, a summer sound
Repeated in a summer without end
And sound alone. But it was more than that,
More even than her voice, and ours, among
The meaningless plungings of water and the wind,   30
Theatrical distances, bronze shadows heaped
On high horizons, mountainous atmospheres
Of sky and sea.
                    It was her voice that made
The sky acutest at its vanishing.   35
She measured to the hour its solitude.
She was the single artificer of the world
In which she sang. And when she sang, the sea,
Whatever self it had, became the self
That was her song, for she was the maker. Then we,   40
As we beheld her striding there alone,
Knew that there never was a world for her
Except the one she sang and, singing, made.

Ramon Fernandez,[1] tell me, if you know,
Why, when the singing ended and we turned   45

---

1. **Ramon Fernandez:** Stevens insisted that this was "not intended to be anyone at all," but Ramon Fernandez was a well-known French critic and philosopher who became increasingly engaged in politics during the 1930s. He may therefore represent theorists whose secure belief in abstract concepts and ideas Stevens seems to challenge by asking Fernandez to answer the question posed in the following lines.

Toward the town, tell why the glassy lights,
The lights in the fishing boats at anchor there,
As the night descended, tilting in the air,
Mastered the night and portioned out the sea,
Fixing emblazoned zones and fiery poles,   50
Arranging, deepening, enchanting night.

Oh! Blessed rage for order, pale Ramon,
The maker's rage to order words of the sea,
Words of the fragrant portals, dimly-starred,
And of ourselves and of our origins,   55
In ghostlier demarcations, keener sounds.

                                        [1934, 1954]

OF MODERN POETRY

The poem of the mind in the act of finding
What will suffice. It has not always had
To find: the scene was set; it repeated what
Was in the script.
                        Then the theatre was changed   5
To something else. Its past was a souvenir.
It has to be living, to learn the speech of the place.
It has to face the men of the time and to meet
The women of the time. It has to think about war
And it has to find what will suffice. It has   10
To construct a new stage. It has to be on that stage
And, like an insatiable actor, slowly and
With meditation, speak words that in the ear,
In the delicatest ear of the mind, repeat,
Exactly, that which it wants to hear, at the sound   15
Of which, an invisible audience listens,
Not to the play, but to itself, expressed
In an emotion as of two people, as of two
Emotions becoming one. The actor is
A metaphysician in the dark, twanging   20
An instrument, twanging a wily string that gives
Sounds passing through sudden rightnesses, wholly
Containing the mind, below which it cannot descend,
Beyond which it has no will to rise,
                                        It must   25
Be the finding of a satisfaction, and may
Be of a man skating, a woman dancing, a woman
Combing. The poem of the act of the mind.

                                        [1940, 1954]

THE PLAIN SENSE OF THINGS

After the leaves have fallen, we return
To a plain sense of things. It is as if
We had come to an end of the imagination,
Inanimate in an inert savoir.[1]

It is difficult even to choose the adjective   5
For this blank cold, this sadness without cause.
The great structure has become a minor house.
No turban walks across the lessened floors.

The greenhouse never so badly needed paint.
The chimney is fifty years old and slants to one side.   10
A fantastic effort has failed, a repetition
In a repetitiousness of men and flies.

Yet the absence of the imagination had
Itself to be imagined. The great pond,
The plain sense of it, without reflections, leaves,   15
Mud, water like dirty glass, expressing silence

Of a sort, silence of a rat come out to see,
The great pond and its waste of the lilies, all this
Had to be imagined as an inevitable knowledge,
Required, as a necessity requires.   20

[1952, 1954]

---

1. **savoir**: Knowledge or learning (French).

Mina Loy

[1882-1966]

Mina Loy was endowed from birth with a first-rate intelligence and a sensibility which has plagued her all her life facing a shoddy world.
—William Carlos Williams

Born Mina Gertrude Lowy in London on December 27, 1882, Loy was the daughter of Julia Bryan, a Protestant, and Sigmund Lowy, a prosperous Jewish tailor whose ancestors had emigrated from Hungary. Loy and her younger sister were educated at home by governesses and then briefly sent to school. From an early age, she was drawn to art, an interest that her father encouraged. But her mother objected that studying art was not a suitable activity for a young society woman, who should stay at home and prepare for marriage. Nonetheless, after Loy finished her minimal formal education in 1896, her parents permitted her to attend art school, first in London and later for a year in Munich, Germany. In 1900, she returned home to London, where she continued her studies and met another young art student, Stephen Haweis. They moved to Paris and were married there in 1903. Instead of taking his name, however, she changed her name to Loy. She later told her daughters that the name was derived from the French word *loi*, or law, implicitly asserting that she would be a law unto herself.

Loy and Haweis became deeply involved in new movements in the arts in Europe. Through Gertrude Stein, Loy met other avant-garde artists, and in 1906 she was elected as a member of the Salon d'Automne (Autumn Salon), an annual exhibition that featured the work of the most innovative painters of the period, including Henri Matisse and Pablo Picasso. That year, she and Haweis moved to Florence, where Loy gave birth to a daughter in 1907 and a son in 1909. But she and her husband were increasingly estranged. Loy was drawn into an expatriate group that gathered around Mabel Dodge, a wealthy patron of the arts, at whose villa Loy met a number of American intellectuals and writers, including Carl Van Vechten, who would later serve as her informal literary agent in New York City. After Haweis left her in 1913, Loy had brief affairs with Filippo Marinetti and Giovanni Papini, two of the leaders of Italian futurism, a revolutionary movement that ridiculed tradition and called upon artists to embrace the new realities of urban and industrial life. Inspired by the movement, Loy in 1914 published her first poem, "Aphorisms on Futurism," in *Camera Work*, edited by Van Vechten's friend Alfred Stieglitz. At the same time, Loy deeply resented the misogynistic attitudes common among the male futurists. Adopting their hostile posture toward tradition and their strategy of promoting futurism by publishing militant manifestos, Loy wrote a "Feminist Manifesto," in which she advised women: "If you want to realize yourselves . . . all your pet illusions must be unmasked. The lies of centuries have got to be discarded."

Mina Loy

This passport photo was taken in the 1920s, about the time Loy published her first book of poetry, *Lunar Baedecker* (1923).

Although she continued to paint, Loy gained greater notoriety as a poet and a public personality. She exploded on the literary scene when her four-part "Love Songs" appeared in the July 1915 issue of *Others: A Magazine of the New Verse*, published in New York City. After she moved there in the fall of 1916, Loy became known for both her iconoclastic poetry and her bohemian lifestyle in Greenwich Village, and she was soon profiled in an article in the *New York Evening Sun* as the representative "Modern Woman." She met Marianne Moore, Wallace Stevens, and William Carlos Williams and other contributors to *Others*. Loy was also involved with a group of avant-garde European artists and writers who fled to Greenwich Village during World War I, including Arthur Cravan, an English writer and professional boxer associated with the nihilistic, antibourgeois movement Dada, or Dadaism. When Loy's divorce from Haweis was final in late 1917, she and Cravan traveled to Mexico, where they were married in 1918.

After World War I ended, the poverty-stricken couple decided to return to Europe. Loy, who was pregnant, took a hospital ship to Buenos Aires. Since they could only afford one ticket, Cravan tried to sail there in his own small boat and was apparently lost at sea. Loy went on to London, where she gave birth to their daughter in 1919. Seeking information about Cravan's fate, she returned to the United States before settling with her children in Paris. There, she published her first book of poetry, *Lunar Baedecker* (1923), as well as extended portions of an ambitious poetic allegory of her life, *Anglo-Mongrels and the Rose*, which appeared in 1923 and 1925.

Those publications represented the high point of Loy's career as a poet. To support herself and her children, she opened a retail shop to sell lighting fixtures and other decorative objects she designed. She later worked as the Paris agent for her son-in-law's art gallery in New York City. Her friends there organized exhibitions of her paintings in 1925 and again in 1933. She returned to the United States three years later, becoming a citizen in 1946. Although she continued to write poetry during these years, Loy displayed little interest in publication, and her second book did not appear until 1958, when *Lunar Baedecker & Time-Tables* was published with an introduction by William Carlos Williams. Loy also produced three-dimensional assemblages, what she called "experiments in junk," found objects from the streets of the Bowery, or "Skid Row," the impoverished area where she lived in New York City. Some of them were exhibited there as "Constructions" in 1959. Loy died in Aspen, Colorado, where she had moved to be near her daughters, on September 25, 1966.

*bedfordstmartins.com/
americanlit for research
links on Loy*

Loy's *Love Songs*.

Loy began to write this poetic sequence early in 1915, when she was living in Florence in the aftermath of her failed marriage and two painful affairs. The first four poems in the sequence were a record of her "utter defeat in the sex war," as Loy described them, and she was initially hesitant about having them published. In a letter to Carl Van Vechten, she worried that the poems were "rather pretty — rather mawkish — probably a little indecent." Nonetheless, the four poems appeared as "Love Songs" in the first issue of the little magazine *Others* (July 1915) and in *Others, An Anthology of the New Verse*, published in 1916. When she moved to New York City later that year, Loy discovered that the poems had excited considerable controversy. Many of her fellow modernists admired her experimental verse and her candid exploration of female desire and the sexual experience of women. But most critics dismissed the poems as lewd and artistically crude. Undeterred, Loy wrote an extended, thirty-four poem sequence that was published as *Songs to Joannes* in the April 1917 issue of *Others*. In 1923, Loy published a revised and compressed version of that sequence as *Love Songs* in *Lunar Baedecker*. (The title of the volume contains a misspelling, probably a typographical error but possibly intentional, of *Baedeker*, the name of a popular travel guide series published in Europe.) In the final version, Loy eliminated some poems, reordered others, and added some lines, making the sequence less per-

Mina Loy, *Consider Your Grandmother's Stays*

Loy's satirical drawing dates from 1916, the year after she published the first of her *Love Songs*. The Victorian corset, with its vertical whalebone "stays," was a rigid undergarment that was tightly cinched with laces in order to create an exaggerated "hourglass" figure. For many modern women, the painfully uncomfortable corset was a symbol of female confinement and the restricted roles women were forced to play.

sonal and explicit. She also made it more accessible, though only relatively so, since in both the earlier *Songs to Joannes* and *Love Songs* Loy radically subverted, not only the male-dominated tradition of love poetry, but also conventional poetic forms. Certainly, both sequences display the most striking aspects of her poetry, including her ironic wit, her startling imagery, and her unusual vocabulary, an often-dizzying combination of archaic, colloquial, foreign, poetic, and scientific words. The following text of *Love Songs* is that of the final version, as published in *Lunar Baedecker* (1923).

LOVE SONGS

I

> Spawn of fantasies
> Sifting the appraisable
> Pig Cupid[1]   his rosy snout

---

1. **Cupid:** A variation of *cupido*, or desire (Latin), Cupid was the Roman god of love, usually represented as a cherubic, winged boy with a bow and an arrow.

Rooting erotic garbage
"Once upon a time"   5
Pulls a weed   white star-topped
Among wild oats sown in mucous membrane
I would   an eye in a Bengal light[2]
Eternity in a sky-rocket
Constellations in an ocean   10
Whose rivers run no fresher
Than a trickle of saliva

These are suspect places

I must live in my lantern
Trimming subliminal flicker   15
Virginal   to the bellows
Of experience
                         Colored glass.

II

At your mercy
Our Universe   20
Is only
A colorless onion
You derobe
Sheath by sheath
                         Remaining   25
A disheartening odour
About your nervy hands

III

          Night
Heavy with shut-flower's nightmares
— — — — — — — — — — —   30
          Noon
Curled to the solitaire
Core of the
Sun

---

2. **Bengal light:** A colored signal flare.

IV

Evolution fall foul of   35
Sexual equality
Prettily miscalculate
Similitude

Unnatural selection
Breed such sons and daughters   40
As shall jibber at each other
Uninterpretable cryptonyms[3]
Under the moon

Give them some way of braying brassily
For caressive calling   45
Or to homophonous hiccoughs
Transpose the laugh
Let them suppose that tears
Are snowdrops or molasses
Or anything   50
Than human insufficiencies
Begging dorsal vertebrae

Let meeting be the turning
To the antipodean
And Form   a blurr   55
Anything
Than seduce them
To the one
As simple satisfaction
For the other   60

V

Shuttle-cock and battle-door[4]
A little pink-love
And feathers are strewn

---

3. **cryptonyms:** Code names or words.
4. **shuttle-cock and battle-door:** Usually *battledore and shuttlecock*, an ancient game later played through-out Asia and Europe, including England, where in the nineteenth century a version came to be called bad-minton. Loy uses the game, then played with rackets and a cork ball into which feathers were inserted, as a metaphor for sexual intercourse.

VI

Let Joy go solace-winged
To flutter whom she may concern   65

VII

Once in a mezzanino[5]
The starry ceiling
Vaulted an unimaginable family
Bird-like abortions
With human throats   70
And Wisdom's eyes
Who wore lamp-shade red dresses
And woolen hair

One bore a baby
In a padded porte-enfant[6]   75
Tied with a sarsanet[7] ribbon
To her goose's wings

But for the abominable shadows
I would have lived
Among their fearful furniture   80
To teach them to tell me their secrets
Before I guessed
— Sweeping the brood clean out

VIII

Midnight empties the street
— — — To the left a boy   85
— One wing has been washed in the rain
    The other will never be clean any more —
Pulling door-bells to remind
Those that are snug
                        To the right a haloed ascetic   90

---

5. **mezzanino:** Either an apartment one-half story up from the ground floor or, more usually, the lowest balcony of a theater (Italian).
6. **porte-enfant:** Baby carriage (French).
7. **sarsanet:** Probably a misprint of *sarsenet*, sometimes spelled *sarcenet*, a soft silk fabric.

Threading houses
Probes wounds for souls
— The poor can't wash in hot water —
And I don't know which turning to take —

IX

We might have coupled   95
In the bed-ridden monopoly of a moment
Or broken flesh with one another
At the profane communion table
Where wine is spill't on promiscuous lips

We might have given birth to a butterfly   100
With the daily-news
Printed in blood on its wings

X

In some
Prenatal plagiarism
Foetal[8] buffoons   105
Caught tricks

— — — — —

From architypal[9] pantomime
Stringing, emotions
Looped aloft   110

— — — —

For the blind eyes
That Nature knows us with
And the most of Nature   is green
— — — — — — — —   115

XI

Green things grow
Salads
For the cerebral
Forager's revival . . .

---

8. foetal: A variant of *fetal*, from *fetus*, an unborn offspring of a mammal.
9. architypal: Probably a misprint of *archetypal*, that which constitutes the original model or type upon which similar things are later patterned.

And flowered flummery   120
Upon bossed bellies
Of mountains
Rolling in the sun

XII

Shedding our petty pruderies
From slit eyes   125

We sidle up
To Nature
— — — that irate pornographist

XIII

The wind stuffs the scum of the white street
Into my lungs and my nostrils   130
Exhilarated birds
Prolonging flight into the night
Never reaching — — — — — — —

[1917, 1923]

William Carlos Williams

[1883-1963]

*Williams will make a
poem of a bare fact — just
to show you something
he noticed.*

-Mina Loy

William Carlos Williams was born in Rutherford, a suburb of Paterson, New Jersey, on September 17, 1883. He was the oldest son of recent immigrants, Raquel Hélène Rose Hoheb, of mixed Basque, French, and Jewish descent, and the English-born William George Williams, who had been raised in Puerto Rico. After meeting and marrying there, the couple had moved to the United States in 1882. Named after his father, an advertising executive, and his mother's brother, Carlos Hoheb, a physician, Williams was raised in a culturally diverse family that maintained close ties to friends and relatives in the Caribbean. During his childhood, French and especially Spanish were spoken at home as often as English. He attended public schools in Rutherford and later, while his father was in South America on business, spent two years at boarding schools in Geneva, Switzerland, and Paris. After he returned home in 1899, Williams commuted to Horace Mann High School in New York City, from which he graduated in 1902. His mother had studied painting for three years in Paris, and "her interest in art became my interest in art," as Williams said in his *Autobiography* (1951). He also began keeping notebooks of his writings and "Whitmanesque thoughts," as he called them. Determined to become a writer, he was equally determined to free himself from the necessity of earning a living by writing, so in 1902 Williams enrolled in the School of Dentistry before switching to the School of Medicine at the University of Pennsylvania.

The following decade was crucial to his development as a writer. In Philadelphia, he met the painter Charles Demuth, Hilda Doolittle (who later published as H.D.), and Ezra Pound, who "used to assault me . . . for my lack of education and reading," as Williams humorously recalled. He participated fully in the cultural life of the university, writing poems, playing the violin, and becoming the arts editor of his yearbook. He also diligently prepared himself for a career in medicine, beginning an internship in obstetrics and pediatrics in New York City after his graduation in 1906. Disgusted with corrupt hospital policies, Williams resigned in 1909 and spent the next year studying pediatrics in Germany. After he returned home, Williams began a private medical practice in Rutherford, where he married his fiancée of several years, Florence Herman, in 1912. Although their relationship was later strained by his extramarital affairs, they remained together and raised two sons. As he would do for the next forty years, Williams attended to both his patients and his poetry. He had earlier paid for the publication of his first book, *Poems* (1909), and with Pound's help a second volume, *The Tempers*, was privately printed in London in 1913. That year, Williams published several poems in Harriet Monroe's influential magazine, *Poetry*, and he later became a regular contributor to *Others: A Magazine of the New Verse*. Williams also began to enjoy the company of artists and poets associated with *Others*, including Mina Loy, Marianne Moore, and Wallace Stevens, whom he met during frequent weekend visits to New York City.

William Carlos Williams

The painter and photographer Charles Sheeler took this portrait of his friend and fellow artist in 1926, by which time Williams was firmly established as a modernist poet and a physician in private practice in Rutherford, New Jersey.

Williams gained a growing reputation for his rough-hewn and home-grown brand of modernism, an extension of the effort to develop a distinctly American poetry begun by Walt Whitman. A note printed on the dust jacket of *Al Que Quiere!* (1917) – "To Him Who Wants It!" – aggressively proclaimed, "This book is a collection of poems by William Carlos Williams. You, gentle reader, will probably not like it, because it is brutally powerful and scornfully crude." He sought to influence the course of American modernism through his poetry, including a collection of prose poems, *Kora in Hell* (1918), and *Sour Grapes* (1921), as well as by joining with the writer Robert McAlmon to start a new magazine, *Contact*, which Williams coedited from 1920 to 1923. But the small-circulation magazine, which was designed to promote the work of what Williams pointedly described as "native artists," and his own writings were far overshadowed by the influential work of an expatriate, T. S. Eliot's *The Waste Land* (1922). In an immediate and furious response to Eliot's dense and learned poem, Williams wrote an innovative collection of poems and interspersed prose commentaries, *Spring and All* (1923). He also attempted to counter Eliot's emphasis on European cultural traditions by taking a year off from his medical practice to do the research for *In the American Grain* (1925), an impressionistic book of historical essays in which Williams sought to construct a vital, indigenous tradition for Americans.

During the following decades, Williams tenaciously demonstrated the resources of the American scene for writers in the United States. He continued to publish poems, as well as numerous plays, short stories, and novels, notably *White Mule* (1937), *In the Money* (1940), and *The Build-Up* (1952), a trilogy in which Williams traced the fortunes of several generations of an immigrant family in New Jersey. Still deeply committed to what in an early essay he had described as the writer's "own locality," he explored the history and modern realities of an industrial city in New Jersey in his most ambitious poem, *Paterson*, which was published in five volumes from 1946 to 1958. For American poets seeking an alternative to the dominant tradition of modernism represented by Eliot and Pound, Williams became a hero and role model, the true heir of Walt Whitman. During the 1950s, a series of strokes slowed his work, but Williams continued to write, publishing his final volume of poetry, *Pictures from Brueghel*, in 1962. The volume was awarded the Pulitzer Prize the following year, when the "Doctor-Poet," as he was described in the obituary in the *New York Times*, died at his home in Rutherford on March 4, 1963.

bedfordstmartins.com/ americanlit for research links on Williams

Williams's Poetry.   After his second volume of poetry was published in London in 1913, Williams became a regular contributor to little magazines such as *Poetry, Others*, and the *Dial*. Most of the poems in the following section were first published in those magazines, alongside the work of the other pioneering modernists and practitioners of the "new verse." Certainly, Williams was influenced by the swirl of new developments in poetry, including imagism. In his *Autobiography* (1951), however, Williams said that imagism "ran quickly out," and that he became committed to what he later defined as "objectivism," observing: "The poem being an object (like a symphony or cubist painting) it must be the purpose of the poet to make of his words a new form: to invent, that is, an object consonant with his day." As his reference to cubism indicates, Williams was deeply interested in developments in the visual arts, and his poetry reveals his concentrated powers of observation and, often, his painterly handling of scenes or subjects. His statement also calls attention to his deep commitment to the craft of poetry. Rejecting conventional metrical patterns and traditional poetic forms, Williams sought to invent new rhythms, or measures, as well as new forms "consonant with his day." For him, that

Charles Demuth,
The Figure 5 in Gold
(1928)

Demuth's abstract portrait of his close friend Williams — note the poet's initials and the names "Bill" and "Carlos" in the painting — is a visual interpretation of and homage to his poem "The Great Figure" (1921).

meant inventing forms and developing a language, what he called an "American idiom," in agreement or harmony with the frequently discordant elements of his own time and place, modern urban and industrial America. Indeed, few twentieth-century poets were so committed to engaging, finding beauty in, and wresting meaning from the material and social conditions of life in the United States. The texts of the following poems are taken from *The Collected Poems of William Carlos Williams*, Volume 1, edited by A. Walton Litz and Christopher MacGowan (1986); and Volume 2, edited by Christoper MacGowan (1988).

TRACT

I will teach you my townspeople
how to perform a funeral —
for you have it over a troop
of artists —
unless one should scour the world —   5
you have the ground sense necessary.

See! the hearse leads.
I begin with a design for a hearse.
For Christ's sake not black —
nor white either — and not polished!   10

Let it be weathered — like a farm wagon —
with gilt wheels (this could be
applied fresh at small expense)
or no wheels at all:
a rough dray to drag over the ground.   15

Knock the glass out!
My God — glass, my townspeople!
For what purpose? Is it for the dead
to look out or for us to see
how well he is housed or to see   20
the flowers or the lack of them —
or what?
To keep the rain and snow from him?
He will have a heavier rain soon:
pebbles and dirt and what not.   25
Let there be no glass —
and no upholstery, phew!
and no little brass rollers
and small easy wheels on the bottom —
my townspeople what are you thinking of?   30

A rough plain hearse then
with gilt wheels and no top at all.
On this the coffin lies
by its own weight.

                    No wreaths please —   35
especially no hot house flowers.
Some common memento is better,
something he prized and is known by:
his old clothes — a few books perhaps —
God knows what! You realize   40
how we are about these things
my townspeople —
something will be found — anything
even flowers if he had come to that.
So much for the hearse.   45

For heaven's sake though see to the driver!
Take off the silk hat! In fact
that's no place at all for him —
up there unceremoniously
dragging our friend out to his own dignity!   50
Bring him down — bring him down!
Low and inconspicuous! I'd not have him ride
on the wagon at all — damn him —

the undertaker's understrapper![1]
Let him hold the reins   55
and walk at the side
and inconspicuously too!

Then briefly as to yourselves:
Walk behind — as they do in France,
seventh class, or if you ride   60
Hell take curtains! Go with some show
of inconvenience; sit openly —
to the weather as to grief.
Or do you think you can shut grief in?
What — from us? We who have perhaps   65
nothing to lose? Share with us
share with us — it will be money
in your pockets.[2]
                Go now
I think you are ready.   70

                            [1916, 1986]

---

1. **understrapper:** Literally, one who harnesses horses or, more generally, a subordinate or an inferior agent.
2. **in your pockets:** In the earliest version of the poem, published in *Others* in February 1916, the passage read: "in your pocket — / remember that, and / this: / there is one land — / and your two feet / are sucked down / so hard on it that / you cannot raise them — / where men are truly equal / for they all have / nothing."

THE YOUNG HOUSEWIFE

At ten A.M. the young housewife
moves about in negligee[1] behind
the wooden walls of her husband's house.
I pass solitary in my car.

Then again she comes to the curb   5
to call the ice-man, fish-man, and stands
shy, uncorseted, tucking in
stray ends of hair, and I compare her
to a fallen leaf.

The noiseless wheels of my car   10
rush with a crackling sound over
dried leaves as I bow and pass smiling.

                            [1916, 1986]

---

1. **negligee:** A woman's light dressing gown, often made from a sheer fabric, from *négliger*, "to neglect" (French).

DANSE RUSSE[1]

If I when my wife is sleeping
and the baby and Kathleen[2]
are sleeping
and the sun is a flame-white disc
in silken mists   5
above shining trees, —
if I in my north room
dance naked, grotesquely
before my mirror
waving my shirt round my head   10
and singing softly to myself:
"I am lonely, lonely.
I was born to be lonely,
I am best so!"
If I admire my arms, my face,   15
my shoulders, flanks, buttocks
against the yellow drawn shades, —

Who shall say I am not
the happy genius of my household?

[1916, 1986]

---

1. **Danse Russe:** Russian dance (French). Williams, who attended a performance of Sergei Diaghilev's *Ballet Russe* in 1916, especially admired the dancing of the most acclaimed member of the group, Vaslav Nijinsky.
2. **Kathleen:** Kathleen McBride, a young woman who worked in the Williams family home.

PORTRAIT OF A LADY

Your thighs are appletrees
whose blossoms touch the sky.
Which sky? The sky
where Watteau hung a lady's
slipper. Your knees   5
are a southern breeze — or
a gust of snow. Agh! what
sort of man was Fragonard?[1]
— as if that answered

---

1. **Watteau . . . Fragonard:** As the disruptive voice in the poem implies, *The Swing* (c. 1767) — a famous French baroque painting in which a young woman tosses off her slipper as she swings above her semiprone and impassioned lover, who gazes up at her exposed legs — was painted by Jean-Honoré Fragonard (1732–1806), not by his precursor Jean-Antoine Watteau (1684–1721).

anything. Ah, yes — below   10
the knees, since the tune
drops that way, it is
one of those white summer days,
the tall grass of your ankles
flickers upon the shore —   15
Which shore? —
the sand clings to my lips —
Which shore?
Agh, petals maybe. How
should I know?   20
Which shore? Which shore?
I said petals from an appletree.

                         [1920, 1986]

WILLOW POEM

It is a willow when summer is over,
a willow by the river
from which no leaf has fallen nor
bitten by the sun
turned orange or crimson.   5
The leaves cling and grow paler,
swing and grow paler
over the swirling waters of the river
as if loath to let go,
they are so cool, so drunk with   10
the swirl of the wind and of the river —
oblivious to winter,
the last to let go and fall
into the water and on the ground.

                         [1920, 1986]

QUEEN-ANNE'S-LACE

Her body is not so white as
anemone petals nor so smooth — nor
so remote a thing. It is a field
of the wild carrot[1] taking

---

1. **wild carrot:** A wildflower with broad round heads of tiny white flowers; commonly called Queen Anne's lace.

the field by force; the grass   5
does not raise above it.
Here is no question of whiteness,
white as can be, with a purple mole
at the center of each flower.
Each flower is a hand's span   10
of her whiteness. Wherever
his hand has lain there is
a tiny purple blemish. Each part
is a blossom under his touch
to which the fibres of her being   15
stem one by one, each to its end,
until the whole field is a
white desire, empty, a single stem,
a cluster, flower by flower,
a pious wish to whiteness gone over –   20
or nothing.

[1921, 1986]

THE WIDOW'S LAMENT IN SPRINGTIME

Sorrow is my own yard
where the new grass
flames as it has flamed
often before but not
with the cold fire   5
that closes round me this year.
Thirtyfive years
I lived with my husband.
The plumtree is white today
with masses of flowers.   10
Masses of flowers
load the cherry branches
and color some bushes
yellow and some red
but the grief in my heart   15
is stronger than they
for though they were my joy
formerly, today I notice them
and turn away forgetting.
Today my son told me   20
that in the meadows,

at the edge of the heavy woods
in the distance, he saw
trees of white flowers.
I feel that I would like   25
to go there
and fall into those flowers
and sink into the marsh near them.

[1921, 1986]

THE GREAT FIGURE

Among the rain
and lights
I saw the figure 5
in gold
on a red   5
firetruck
moving
tense
unheeded
to gong clangs   10
siren howls
and wheels rumbling
through the dark city.

[1921, 1986]

SPRING AND ALL[1]

By the road to the contagious hospital[2]
under the surge of the blue
mottled clouds driven from the
northeast — a cold wind. Beyond, the
waste of broad, muddy fields   5
brown with dried weeds, standing and fallen

---

1. **Spring and All:** This poem was first published as "Poem" in the *Dial* (June 1923) and then as (roman numeral) "I" at the opening of Williams's collection of numbered poems and interspersed prose commentaries, *Spring and All* (1923).
2. **contagious hospital:** The common term for a special hospital for patients with highly infectious diseases.

patches of standing water
the scattering of tall trees

All along the road the reddish
purplish, forked, upstanding, twiggy   10
stuff of bushes and small trees
with dead, brown leaves under them
leafless vines —

Lifeless in appearance, sluggish
dazed spring approaches —   15

They enter the new world naked,
cold, uncertain of all
save that they enter. All about them
the cold, familiar wind —

Now the grass, tomorrow   20
the stiff curl of wildcarrot leaf

One by one objects are defined —
It quickens: clarity, outline of leaf

But now the stark dignity of
entrance — Still, the profound change   25
has come upon them: rooted, they
grip down and begin to awaken

[1923, 1986]

To Elsie[1]

The pure products of America
go crazy —
mountain folk from Kentucky

or the ribbed north end of
Jersey   5
with its isolate lakes and

valleys, its deaf-mutes, thieves
old names
and promiscuity between

---

1. **To Elsie:** This poem was first published as "XVIII" in Williams's collection of numbered poems and interspersed prose commentaries, *Spring and All* (1923). Elsie was a young, mentally impaired woman from the state orphanage who worked for the Williams family after Kathleen (see "Danse Russe," note 2).

devil-may-care men who have taken   10
to railroading
out of sheer lust of adventure —

and young slatterns, bathed
in filth
from Monday to Saturday   15

to be tricked out that night
with gauds[2]
from imaginations which have no

peasant traditions to give them
character   20
but flutter and flaunt

sheer rags — succumbing without
emotion
save numbed terror

under some hedge of choke-cherry   25
or viburnum — [3]
which they cannot express —

Unless it be that marriage
perhaps
with a dash of Indian blood   30

will throw up a girl so desolate
so hemmed round
with disease or murder

that she'll be rescued by an
agent —   35
reared by the state and

sent out at fifteen to work in
some hard-pressed
house in the suburbs —

some doctor's family, some Elsie —   40
voluptuous water
expressing with broken

---

2. **gauds:** Cheap, showy ornaments or trinkets.
3. **choke-cherry or viburnum:** Familiar names of two of the most common flowering and fruit-bearing
shrubs indigenous to North America.

brain the truth about us —
her great
ungainly hips and flopping breasts   45

addressed to cheap
jewelry
and rich young men with fine eyes

as if the earth under our feet
were   50
an excrement of some sky

and we degraded prisoners
destined
to hunger until we eat filth

while the imagination strains   55
after deer
going by fields of goldenrod in

the stifling heat of September
Somehow
it seems to destroy us   60

It is only in isolate flecks that
something
is given off

No one
to witness   65
and adjust, no one to drive the car

[1923, 1986]

THE RED WHEELBARROW[1]

so much depends
upon

a red wheel
barrow

glazed with rain
water

beside the white
chickens

[1923, 1986]

---

1. **The Red Wheelbarrow:** This poem was first published as "XXII" in Williams's collection of numbered poems and interspersed prose commentaries, *Spring and All* (1923).

THIS IS JUST TO SAY

I have eaten
the plums
that were in
the icebox

and which   5
you were probably
saving
for breakfast

Forgive me
they were delicious   10
so sweet
and so cold

[1934, 1986]

THESE[1]

are the desolate, dark weeks
when nature in its barrenness
equals the stupidity of man.

The year plunges into night
and the heart plunges   5
lower than night

to an empty, windswept place
without sun, stars or moon
but a peculiar light as of thought

that spins a dark fire —   10
whirling upon itself until,
in the cold, it kindles

to make a man aware of nothing
that he knows, not loneliness
itself — Not a ghost but   15

would be embraced — emptiness,
despair — (They
whine and whistle) among

---

1. **These:** This poem was first published in 1938, during the Great Depression and a year before the beginning of World War II, which was heralded by Italy's conquest of Ethiopia (1935-36), the Spanish Civil War (1936-39), the Japanese invasion of China in 1937, and Germany's annexation of Austria and the Sudetenland region of Czechoslovakia in 1938.

the flashes and booms of war;
houses of whose rooms   20
the cold is greater than can be thought,

the people gone that we loved,
the beds lying empty, the couches
damp, the chairs unused —

Hide it away somewhere   25
out of the mind, let it get roots
and grow, unrelated to jealous

ears and eyes — for itself.
In this mine they come to dig — all.
Is this the counterfoil to sweetest   30

music? The source of poetry that
seeing the clock stopped, says,
The clock has stopped

that ticked yesterday so well?
and hears the sound of lakewater   35
splashing — that is now stone.

                                              [1938, 1986]

A SORT OF A SONG[1]

Let the snake wait under
his weed
and the writing
be of words, slow and quick, sharp
to strike, quiet to wait,   5
sleepless.

 — through metaphor to reconcile
the people and the stones.
Compose. (No ideas
but in things) Invent!   10
Saxifrage[2] is my flower that splits
the rocks.

                                              [1943, 1988]

---

1. **A Sort of a Song:** Williams changed the title of this poem, which he first published as "A Possible Sort of Song" in the *Old Line* (April 1943), when he collected it in *The Wedge* (1944).
2. **Saxifrage:** A low-growing plant with small white, yellow, or red flowers and succulent leaves, often found growing in narrow crevices in rocks.

Ezra Pound

[1885-1972]

Ezra Loomis Pound was born in October 1885, in Hailey, Idaho, where his father worked in the Government Land Grant Office. His mother, a New Yorker, found life on the frontier difficult, and when Pound was about eighteen months old she took him back East, where his father was subsequently appointed as an assayer in the U.S. Mint in Philadelphia. Pound was raised and educated in suburban Wyncote. He was a precocious student, earning the nickname "Professor" when he was just six years old and publishing his first poem in a local newspaper in 1896. In 1901, a month before his sixteenth birthday, Pound entered the University of Pennsylvania. There, he met Hilda Doolittle (who later published under "H.D."), with whom he became romantically involved, and an aspiring poet who became his lifelong friend, William Carlos Williams. Pound immersed himself in the study of Greek, Latin, and German, but he was indifferent to subjects that did not interest him. Concerned about his mediocre academic record, Pound and his parents decided that he should transfer to Hamilton College, in central New York, where he studied Romance languages, Hebrew, and Anglo-Saxon. After his graduation in 1905, he returned to the University of Pennsylvania on a graduate fellowship and traveled to Spain, Italy, and France. When the fellowship was not renewed, Pound accepted a position teaching Romance languages at Wabash College in Indiana. Dismissed at the end of the first semester for his behavior (a woman evidently spent a night in his room), Pound asked his disappointed but supportive parents to loan him money for a trip to Europe, where he sailed in the summer of 1908.

During the following years, Pound emerged as a major force in modern poetry. He briefly settled in Venice, where he put together and paid eight dollars for the printing of his first book of poems, *A Lume Spento* ["With Tapers Quenched"] (1908). He then moved on to London, where he met the artist Dorothy Shakespear, whom Pound later married, and a number of major literary figures, including Henry James and the Irish poet William Butler Yeats. Pound's early collections of poetry attracted critical attention, and he generously encouraged other poets, including T. S. Eliot, Robert Frost, H.D., and William Carlos Williams, helping them publish and writing reviews of their work. Pound became the "foreign correspondent" for and a frequent contributor to Harriet Monroe's Chicago-based *Poetry: A Magazine of Verse*, and he helped edit other avant-garde literary magazines in London. Pound also organized the imagists, the first modernist literary group in England and the United States. He edited an anthology of their poems, *Des Imagistes*, which was published in New York City in 1914, and a number of his compressed imagist poems later appeared in *Lustra* (1916). By then, however, Pound had moved away from imagism and helped launch "vorticism," joining with the English painter Wyndham Lewis and the young sculptor Henri Gaudier-Brzeska to establish the short-lived journal of the movement, *Blast* (1914-15). As Pound described it, the revolu-

Ezra Pound
The celebrity photographer E. O. Hoppé took this portrait of Pound toward the end of the flamboyant poet's years in London, where he played a central role in the development of modernism during the decade 1910-20.

[Pound wrote] one of the dominant, seminal poetries of the age.
–John Berryman

tionary movement promised to put "the arts in their rightful place as the acknowledged guide and lamp of civilization."

That broadly political goal became central to Pound's poetry and other writings. During World War I, he published *Cathay* (1915), loose translations of ancient Chinese poems, and another work of literary and cultural translation, *Homage to Sextus Propertius* (1917). In 1920, Pound and his wife moved from London to Paris, where they lived until 1924, and then on to Rapallo, Italy. On the Continent, he became close to numerous expatriate artists and writers, including Gertrude Stein and Ernest Hemingway. Pound also met Olga Rudge, a violinist with whom he had an affair that lasted until the end of his life. They had a daughter, Mary, in 1926, a few months before Pound and his wife had a son, Omar. *Personae: The Collected Poems of Ezra Pound* appeared in 1926, but his major poetic project was the *Cantos*, an epic poem he worked on for nearly fifty years, publishing it in stages before the complete text appeared in 1969. During the 1930s, Pound also published numerous prose works on politics, economics, and culture, including *ABC of Economics* (1933), *ABC of Reading* (1934), and *Guide to Kulchur* (1938). During the same period, he embraced the Italian movement called "Fascism" — after *fasces*, or bound sticks, the symbol of political power in ancient Rome — led by Benito Mussolini. Pound's admiration for Mussolini led him to broadcast a series of pro-Axis radio programs from Rome during World War II. In 1943, he was indicted in absentia for treason by a grand jury in Washington, D.C. At the end of the war, Pound surrendered in Italy, where he was imprisoned in an American detention camp in Pisa before being extradited to stand trial in the United States.

Pound's career and literary legacy were consequently defined by the tension between his political beliefs and his poetic achievements. At his trial, he was found to be of "unsound mind" and committed to St. Elizabeth's Hospital in Washington, D.C. Although most of his friends had been repulsed by his pro-Fascist and anti-Semitic statements before and during the war, Pound was supported by many of the writers he had earlier championed, including T. S. Eliot, Robert Frost, Ernest Hemingway, Marianne Moore, and William Carlos Williams. In a move that aroused considerable controversy, Pound was awarded the prestigious Bollingen Prize for his *Pisan Cantos* (1948), written while he was in prison in Italy, and he later received the Academy of American Poets Award. After the government withdrew the indictment against him in 1958, Pound returned to Italy, where he lived with his wife, close by Olga Rudge, until his death in 1972.

bedfordstmartins.com/ americanlit for research links on Pound

Pound's Early Poetry.

Reflecting on his early career, Pound recalled that the English novelist Ford Maddox Ford had literally rolled on the floor in derision of the stilted, archaic, and self-consciously poetical language of his *Canzoni* (1911). "That roll saved me at least two years, maybe more," Pound added. "It sent me back to my own proper effort, namely, toward using the living tongue." His effort to use "the living tongue" — to employ what Ford characterized as "natural language" — is revealed in the following poems, three of which Pound published in his next collection, *Ripostes* (1912). In a review of the volume, one critic observed that Pound's work was "a vehement protest" against simplistic notions of poetry as merely versification. Pound adapted traditional meters and forms, including blank verse ("Portrait d'une Femme") and the sonnet ("A Virginal"), even as he began to experiment with freer rhythmical structures in poems such as "The Return." In the final two poems of this group – "A Pact" and "The Rest," both first published in 1913 – Pound adopted the free verse of his poetic forefather Walt Whitman to express his reconciliation with Whitman and to address directly contemporary American poets from his triumphant "exile" in London. The texts of the poems are taken from *Personae: The Collected Poems of Ezra Pound* (1949).

Ripostes
Dorothy Shakespear's abstract design for the cover of this early reprint of *Ripostes* (1912) reflects Pound's effort to develop a more modern idiom in the poetry he wrote during the period 1912-13.

PORTRAIT D'UNE FEMME[1]

Your mind and you are our Sargasso Sea,[2]
London has swept about you this score years
And bright ships left you this or that in fee:
Ideas, old gossip, oddments of all things,
Strange spars of knowledge and dimmed wares of price.   5
Great minds have sought you – lacking someone else.
You have been second always. Tragical?
No. You preferred it to the usual thing:
One dull man, dulling and uxorious,
One average mind – with one thought less, each year.   10
Oh, you are patient, I have seen you sit
Hours, where something might have floated up.
And now you pay one. Yes, you richly pay.
You are a person of some interest, one comes to you
And takes strange gain away: 15

---

1. **"Portrait d'une Femme"**: Portrait of a lady (French).
2. **Sargasso Sea**: A generally calm region of the Atlantic Ocean between the Azores and the Caribbean Sea, so called because of the brown seaweed (also known as *sargassum* weed) floating in the water.

Trophies fished up; some curious suggestion;
Fact that leads nowhere; and a tale or two,
Pregnant with mandrakes,[3] or with something else
That might prove useful and yet never proves,
That never fits a corner or shows use,   20
Or finds its hour upon the loom of days:
The tarnished, gaudy, wonderful old work;
Idols and ambergris and rare inlays,
These are your riches, your great store; and yet
For all this sea-hoard of deciduous things,   25
Strange woods half sodden, and new brighter stuff:
In the slow float of differing light and deep,
No! there is nothing ! In the whole and all,
Nothing that's quite your own.
                    Yet this is you.   30
                                          [1912, 1926]

3. **mandrakes:** A Mediterranean plant with white or purple flowers, large yellow berries, and a forked fleshy root that bears a resemblance to the human form. In early times, the plant was widely used for medicinal and magical purposes.

A VIRGINAL[1]

No, no! Go from me. I have left her lately.
I will not spoil my sheath with lesser brightness,
For my surrounding air hath a new lightness;
Slight are her arms, yet they have bound me straitly
And left me cloaked as with a gauze of aether;   5
As with sweet leaves; as with subtle clearness.
Oh, I have picked up magic in her nearness
To sheathe me half in half the things that sheathe her.
No, no! Go from me. I have still the flavour,
Soft as spring wind that's come from birchen bowers.   10
Green come the shoots, aye April in the branches,
As winter's wound with her sleight hand she staunches,
Hath of the trees a likeness of the savour:
As white their bark, so white this lady's hours.
                                          [1912, 1926]

1. **A Virginal:** A small keyboard instrument similar to a harpsichord that was popular during the Renaissance in England. It was called a virginal — that is, characteristic of or befitting a virgin — because it was primarily an instrument for girls and young women.

THE RETURN

See, they return; ah, see the tentative
Movements, and the slow feet,
The trouble in the pace and the uncertain
       Wavering!

See, they return, one, and by one,   5
With fear, as half-awakened;
As if the snow should hesitate
And murmur in the wind,
         and half turn back;
These were the "Wing'd-with-Awe,"[1]   10
       Inviolable.

Gods of the wingèd shoe![2]
With them the silver hounds,
         sniffing the trace of air!

Haie!   Haie![3]   15
     These were the swift to harry;
These the keen-scented;
These were the souls of blood.

Slow on the leash,
        pallid the leash-men!   20
                  [1912, 1926]

---

1. **"Wing'd-with-Awe"**: Pound coined this quasi-classical epithet.
2. **Gods of the wingèd shoe**: A reference to the winged shoes worn by Hermes, the herald of the Greek gods of Olympus.
3. **Haie! Haie!**: Pound apparently created the word, possibly a combination of the English interjection *Ha!* and the Greek *Ai!*, as an exclamation at once invoking and hailing the return of the pagan gods.

A PACT[1]

I make a pact with you, Walt Whitman —
I have detested you long enough.
I come to you as a grown child
Who has had a pig-headed father;

---

1. **A Pact**: Pound was deeply ambivalent about Walt Whitman (1819–1892), to whom he offers this "pact," or formal agreement. In a 1909 essay, "What I Feel about Walt Whitman," Pound acknowledges: "The vital part of my message, taken from the sap and fibre of America, is the same as his." At the same time, Pound was sharply critical of what he viewed as the artistic crudity of Whitman's poetry, observing in a letter to his father in 1913 that "it is impossible to read [*Leaves of Grass*] without swearing at the author almost continuously."

I am old enough now to make friends.
It was you that broke the new wood,
Now is a time for carving.
We have one sap and one root —
Let there be commerce between us.

[1913, 1926]

THE REST

O helpless few in my country,
O remnant enslaved!

Artists broken against her,
A-stray, lost in the villages,
Mistrusted, spoken-against,   5

Lovers of beauty, starved,
Thwarted with systems,
Helpless against the control;

You who can not wear yourselves out
By persisting to successes,   10
You who can only speak,
Who can not steel yourselves into reiteration;

You of the finer sense,
Broken against false knowledge,
You who can know at first hand,   15
Hated, shut in, mistrusted:

Take thought:
I have weathered the storm,
I have beaten out my exile.

[1913, 1926]

Pound's "In a Station of the Metro."   This is probably the most famous of all imagist poems. According to Pound, it was inspired by a fleeting moment "in the Paris Underground," or subway system, where in the jostle he "saw a beautiful face, and then, turning suddenly, another and another, and then a beautiful child's face, and then another beautiful face." But he could not "find words" for what that made him feel or discover a way "to tell the adventure" until he thought to follow the example of poets in Japan, "where sixteen syllables are counted enough for a poem if you arrange and punctuate them properly." Adapting the form of the Japanese haiku or hokku, Pound made a poem of nineteen syllables, the first and final versions of which are printed below. The text of the first version, with its unusual spacing and punctuation, is taken from *Poetry* (April 1913), where Pound included it among twelve poems he published as "Contemporania." The text of the final version, which first appeared in *Lustra* (1916), is taken from *Personae: The Collected Poems of Ezra Pound* (1949).

IN A STATION OF THE METRO

The apparition   of these faces   in the crowd   :
Petals   on a wet, black   bough   .

[1913]

IN A STATION OF THE METRO

The apparition of these faces in the crowd;
Petals on a wet, black bough.

[1916, 1926]

Pound's *Cathay*.   T. S. Eliot called Pound "the inventor of Chinese poetry for our time," a tribute to the influence of the "translations" he collected in *Cathay* (1915). Pound's free translations were based on literal versions of classical Chinese poems in the notebooks of the American scholar Ernest Fenollosa. Pound, who had read Fenollosa's essays on Chinese poetry in *Poetry*, met his widow in London in 1913. He subsequently became Fenollosa's literary executor and edited some of his work, including an essay "The Chinese Written Character as a Medium for Poetry" (1919). Pound was especially drawn to the work of the eighth-century Tang dynasty poet Li Po, the author of the four poems printed below. (Pound refers to him as *Rihaku*, a transliteration of the Japanese spelling of his name.) In a headnote to a reprint of "The River Merchant's Wife: A Letter" in the journal *Current Opinion*, the editor observed, "Any poem that has come down to us through twelve centuries of chance and change has an appeal to our curiosity," as well as "an appeal to the unchanging heart of mankind." At the same time, Pound's free-verse lyrics were in many ways strikingly contemporary in poetic technique and subject matter. As scholars have suggested, in selecting and translating Li Po's poems about leave-taking, separation, and the sorrows of men fighting on the frontiers of a collapsing kingdom, Pound in *Cathay* used the ancient Chinese texts to give expression to the experiences and feelings of many Europeans during the first year of World War I. Shortly before his death in the trenches in France, the sculptor Henri Gaudier-Brzeska wrote his friend Pound that he had read parts of *Cathay* to his troops and that "the poems depict our situation in a wonderful way." The texts are taken from *Personae: The Collected Poems of Ezra Pound* (1949).

THE RIVER-MERCHANT'S WIFE: A LETTER

While my hair was still cut straight across my forehead
I played about the front gate, pulling flowers.
You came by on bamboo stilts, playing horse,
You walked about my seat, playing with blue plums.
And we went on living in the village of Chokan:[1]   5
Two small people, without dislike or suspicion.

At fourteen I married My Lord you.
I never laughed, being bashful.
Lowering my head, I looked at the wall.
Called to, a thousand times, I never looked back.   10

At fifteen I stopped scowling,
I desired my dust to be mingled with yours
Forever and forever and forever.
Why should I climb the look out?

At sixteen you departed,   15
You went into far Ku-to-yen,[2] by the river of swirling eddies,
And you have been gone five months.
The monkeys make sorrowful noise overhead.

You dragged your feet when you went out.
By the gate now, the moss is grown, the different mosses,   20
Too deep to clear them away!
The leaves fall early this autumn, in wind.
The paired butterflies are already yellow with August
Over the grass in the West garden;
They hurt me. I grow older.   25
If you are coming down through the narrows of the river Kiang,[3]
Please let me know beforehand,
And I will come out to meet you
           As far as Cho-fu-Sa.[4]

By Rihaku
[1915, 1926]

---

1. **Chokan:** The Japanese spelling of *Ch'ang-kan*, a village near Nanjing, China, on the south bank of the Yangtze River.
2. **Ku-to-yen:** An island on the Ch'u-t'ang River.
3. **Kiang:** The Japanese spelling of the Ch'u-t'ang River (see note 2).
4. **Cho-fu-Sa:** Ch'ang-feng-sha, a beach several hundred miles upstream from Nanjing (see note 1).

THE JEWEL STAIRS' GRIEVANCE

The jewelled steps are already quite white with dew,
It is so late that the dew soaks my gauze stockings,
And I let down the crystal curtain
And watch the moon through the clear autumn.

By Rihaku

NOTE — Jewel stairs, therefore a palace. Grievance, therefore
there is something to complain of. Gauze stockings, therefore a
court lady, not a servant who complains. Clear autumn, therefore he has no excuse on account of weather. Also she has come
early, for the dew has not merely whitened the stairs, but has
soaked her stockings. The poem is especially prized because she
utters no direct reproach.[1]

[1915, 1926]

---

1. **Jewel . . . reproach:** Pound's note is here printed following the poem, as it was in *Cathay.*

LAMENT OF THE FRONTIER GUARD

By the North Gate, the wind blows full of sand,
Lonely from the beginning of time until now!
Trees fall, the grass goes yellow with autumn.
I climb the towers and towers
        to watch out the barbarous land: 5
Desolate castle, the sky, the wide desert.
There is no wall left to this village.
Bones white with a thousand frosts,
High heaps, covered with trees and grass;
Who brought this to pass?   10
Who has brought the flaming imperial anger?
Who has brought the army with drums and with kettle-drums?
Barbarous kings.
A gracious spring, turned to blood-ravenous autumn,
A turmoil of wars-men, spread over the middle kingdom,   15
Three hundred and sixty thousand,
And sorrow, sorrow like rain.
Sorrow to go, and sorrow, sorrow returning.
Desolate, desolate fields,
And no children of warfare upon them,   20
     No longer the men for offence and defence.
Ah, how shall you know the dreary sorrow at the North Gate,

With Rihoku's name forgotten,[1]
And we guardsmen fed to the tigers.

By Rihaku
[1915, 1926]

─────────

1. **Rihoku's name forgotten:** *Rihoku* is the Japanese spelling of the name of the famous Chinese general Li Mu, who died in a battle against the invading Huns in 223 BCE.

TAKING LEAVE OF A FRIEND

Blue mountains to the north of the walls,
White river winding about them;
Here we must make separation
And go out through a thousand miles of dead grass.

Mind like a floating wide cloud,
Sunset like the parting of old acquaintances
Who bow over their clasped hands at a distance.
Our horses neigh to each other
    as we are departing.

Rihaku
[1915, 1926]

H.D. (Hilda Doolittle)

[1886-1961]

The poet and novelist who signed herself H.D. was born Hilda Doolittle on September 10, 1886, in Bethlehem, Pennsylvania. She was the daughter of Charles Leander Doolittle, a professor of astronomy at Lehigh University, and Helen Eugenia Wolle Doolittle. H.D.'s mother, a teacher of painting and music, was a descendant of the founders of Bethlehem, the first Moravian settlement in North America. H.D. spent her formative years in the midst of the tight-knit and deeply religious Moravian community, whose mystical traditions she explored in her later autobiographical writings. In 1895, her family moved to Philadelphia, where her father became the director of the Flower Observatory at the University of Pennsylvania. H.D. recalled that the traumatic move "drove me in, introverted me," as she put it. When she was fifteen, H.D. met Ezra Pound, then sixteen and a student at the University of Pennsylvania. After graduating from a Quaker school, H.D. enrolled as a day student at Bryn Mawr College in 1904. She made a number of friends, including Marianne Moore and William Carlos

Williams, and apparently fell in love with Frances Gregg, a young artist studying at the Pennsylvania Academy of Fine Arts. In 1905, after Pound completed his undergraduate degree at Hamilton College and returned to do graduate work at the University of Pennsylvania, he and H.D. announced their engagement. Complaining of ill health and discouraged by her poor grades, H.D. withdrew from Bryn Mawr. She lived at home for the next five years, writing some stories that she published under the pen name Edith Gray.

The year 1910 marked a turning point for H.D. Her on-again, off-again engagement to Pound was renewed, and he convinced her to join him in London. After she settled there in 1911, she discovered that Pound was engaged to another woman, Dorothy Shakespear. Despite the urging of H.D.'s protective parents, who wanted her to return home, she insisted on staying in London. She remained close to Pound, who introduced her to a number of literary figures, including the English poet and novelist Richard Aldington. H.D., Pound, and Aldington worked and studied together, writing innovative poetry they called "imagist" verse. After Pound became the foreign correspondent for the Chicago-based *Poetry: A Magazine of Verse*, edited by Harriet Monroe, he sent her three of H.D.'s poems, which he signed "H.D., *Imagiste.*" The poems appeared under that distinctive signature in the January 1913 issue of *Poetry*. She and Aldington were married later that year, and they became prominent members of a London literary circle that included the English novelist and poet D. H. Lawrence, with whom H.D. exchanged manuscripts. Her work appeared along with that of a range of English and American poets in *Des Imagistes* (1914), an anthology edited by Pound. She was caught in the middle of the struggle for control of the movement waged between Pound and his rival Amy Lowell, who included H.D.'s poems in her annual anthologies, *Some Imagist Poets* (1915-17). Those anthologies helped establish H.D.'s literary reputation, and in 1916 she published her first book of poems, *Sea Garden.* When Aldington was drafted into the army, H.D. took over his position as literary editor of the *Egoist*, publishing poems and seeking to keep the spark of modern poetry alive in England during the bleak years of World War I.

After the war, H.D. asserted growing personal and professional independence. In 1918, her "modern" marriage to Aldington collapsed, undermined by the stillbirth of their only child, Aldington's infidelities, and their wartime separation. H.D. subsequently had an affair with the painter

H.D.

Inscribed to her close friend Marianne Moore, this photograph was taken about 1921, by which time Hilda Doolittle had firmly established her literary identity as the innovative modernist poet H.D.

Cecil Gray, the father of her daughter, Frances Perdita Aldington, born in 1919. By then, H.D. had met and fallen in love with the wealthy heiress and writer Winifred Ellerman, who published under the name Bryher. Although they frequently kept different residences and had numerous other relationships, including Bryher's two marriages, she and H.D. became lifelong companions. Together, they moved to Paris, where they were actively involved in the expatriate community of artists and writers drawn there during the 1920s. H.D. published *Hymen* (1921), *Heliodora* (1924), and her *Collected Poems* (1925), as well as a play, *Hippolytus Temporizes* (1927). She also wrote novels, notably *HERmione* (written in 1927, published in 1981), in which H.D. explored the conflicts between heterosexual and lesbian love and desire in her early relationships with Pound and Frances Gregg. As a result of Bryher's involvement in POOL Productions, H.D. also appeared in two films, *Foothills* (1927) and *Borderline* (1930). She and Bryher later lived in Switzerland and traveled throughout Europe. During 1933 and 1934, H.D. became the patient and pupil of Sigmund Freud in Vienna. She broke away from her earlier imagist verse in *Trilogy* (1944–46), a three-part poem inspired by her experiences during the London blitz. During the final fifteen years of her life, H.D. wrote steadily, publishing memoirs, novels, and poetry, including *Helen in Egypt* (1961), a feminist retelling of the origins of the Trojan War. In 1960, H.D. became the first woman to receive the Award of Merit Medal for Poetry of the American Academy of Arts and Letters. She died in Zurich, Switzerland, on September 28, 1961.

bedfordstmartins.com/ americanlit for research links on H.D.

H.D.'s Poetry.   In a letter accompanying the three poems by H.D. he sent to Harriet Monroe in 1912, Ezra Pound described the work as "some *modern* stuff by an American," adding: "I say modern, for it is the laconic speech of the Imagistes, even if the subject is classic. . . . It's straight talk, straight as the Greeks!" Pound called attention to some of the most striking aspects of H.D.'s early poetry. As he indicated, it was "modern" because she rejected the verbosity and slackness that Pound and other modernists associated with late Victorian poetry in England. As Pound also indicated, the subject of many of H.D.'s poems was "classic," though she often challenged the patriarchal foundations of ancient myths such as the story of Helen of Troy. For H.D., however, the "Greeks" were not simply a source of subject matter, since she also found aesthetic inspiration in classical poetry, especially in the directness and simple treatment of images characteristic of the surviving fragments of the ancient Greek poet Sappho of Lesbos (c. 630 BCE). Like those fragments, H.D.'s early poems are characterized by their precise language and concentration on a single image or set of related images. She rejected conventional poetic forms, experimenting with both rhythmical patterns and stanza forms in an effort to develop a new poetic idiom. As she observed in a 1919 essay, H.D. thus sought to help readers "get out of the murky, dead, old, thousand-times explored old world, the dead world of overworked emotions and thoughts." The following poems, some of which had earlier appeared in little magazines such as *Poetry*, the *Egoist*, and *Chapbook*, were published in her first three volumes of poetry, *Sea Garden* (1916), *Hymen* (1921), and *Heliodora* (1924). The texts are taken from her *Collected Poems, 1912-1944*, edited by Louis Martz (1983).

OREAD[1]

Whirl up, sea —
whirl your pointed pines,
splash your great pines
on our rocks,
hurl your green over us,
cover us with your pools of fir.

[1914, 1983]

---

1. **Oread:** A mountain nymph in Greek mythology.

GARDEN[1]

I

You are clear
O rose, cut in rock,
hard as the descent of hail.

I could scrape the colour
from the petals   5
like spilt dye from a rock.

If I could break you
I could break a tree.

If I could stir
I could break a tree —   10
I could break you.

II

O wind, rend open the heat,
cut apart the heat,
rend it to tatters.

---

1. **Garden:** The poem was initially printed in this two-part format, first in *Poetry* (March 1915) and then in *Sea Garden* (1916). The second stanza is often printed alone under the title "Heat."

Fruit cannot drop   15
through this thick air –
fruit cannot fall into heat
that presses up and blunts
the points of pears
and rounds the grapes.   20

Cut the heat –
plough through it,
turning it on either side
of your path.

[1915, 1983]

MID-DAY

The light beats upon me.
I am startled –
a split leaf crackles on the paved floor –
I am anguished – defeated.

A slight wind shakes the seed-pods –   5
my thoughts are spent
as the black seeds.
My thoughts tear me,
I dread their fever.
I am scattered in its whirl.   10
I am scattered like
the hot shrivelled seeds.

The shrivelled seeds
are split on the path –
the grass bends with dust,   15
the grape slips
under its crackled leaf:
yet far beyond the spent seed-pods,
and the blackened stalks of mint,
the poplar is bright on the hill,   20
the poplar spreads out,
deep-rooted among trees.

O poplar, you are great
among the hill-stones,
while I perish on the path   25
among the crevices of the rocks.

[1915, 1983]

Sheltered Garden

I have had enough.
I gasp for breath.

Every way ends, every road,
every foot-path leads at last
to the hill-crest —   5
then you retrace your steps,
or find the same slope on the other side,
precipitate.

I have had enough —
border-pinks, clove-pinks, wax-lilies,   10
herbs, sweet-cress.

O for some sharp swish of a branch —
there is no scent of resin
in this place,
no taste of bark, of coarse weeds,   15
aromatic, astringent —
only border on border of scented pinks.

Have you seen fruit under cover
that wanted light —
pears wadded in cloth,   20
protected from the frost,
melons, almost ripe,
smothered in straw?

Why not let the pears cling
to the empty branch?   25
All your coaxing will only make
a bitter fruit —
let them cling, ripen of themselves,
test their own worth,
nipped, shrivelled by the frost,   30
to fall at last but fair
with a russet coat.

Or the melon —
let it bleach yellow
in the winter light,   35
even tart to the taste —
it is better to taste of frost —
the exquisite frost —
than of wadding and of dead grass.

For this beauty,   40
beauty without strength,
chokes out life.
I want wind to break,
scatter these pink-stalks,
snap off their spiced heads,   45
fling them about with dead leaves —
spread the paths with twigs,
limbs broken off,
trail great pine branches,
hurled from some far wood   50
right across the melon-patch,
break pear and quince —
leave half-trees, torn, twisted
but showing the fight was valiant.

O to blot out this garden   55
to forget, to find a new beauty
in some terrible
wind-tortured place.

[1916, 1983]

LEDA[1]

Where the slow river
meets the tide,
a red swan lifts red wings
and darker beak,
and underneath the purple down   5
of his soft breast
uncurls his coral feet.

Through the deep purple
of the dying heat
of sun and mist,   10
the level ray of sun-beam
has caressed
the lily with dark breast,
and flecked with richer gold
its golden crest.   15

---

1. **Leda:** The wife of Tyndareus, a king of Sparta, in Greek mythology. Zeus fell in love with Leda, whom he approached in the form of a swan. The offspring of their union included Helen of Troy.

Where the slow lifting
of the tide,
floats into the river
and slowly drifts
among the reeds,   20
and lifts the yellow flags,
he floats
where tide and river meet.

Ah kingly kiss —
no more regret   25
nor old deep memories
to mar the bliss;
where the low sedge is thick,
the gold day-lily
outspreads and rests   30
beneath soft fluttering
of red swan wings
and the warm quivering
of the red swan's breast.

[1919, 1983]

Helen[1]

All Greece hates
the still eyes in the white face,
the lustre as of olives
where she stands,
and the white hands.   5

All Greece reviles
the wan face when she smiles,
hating it deeper still
when it grows wan and white,
remembering past enchantments   10
and past ills.

Greece sees unmoved,
God's daughter, born of love,

---

1. **Helen:** Helen of Troy, the beautiful daughter of Zeus and Leda, married King Menelaus of Sparta. Paris, the son of King Priam of Troy, either abducted Helen or convinced her to run away with him to Troy. Determined to bring her back, the Greeks assembled a mighty army and laid siege to Troy. At the end of the decade-long war, the city was destroyed, and Helen returned home with Menelaus.

the beauty of cool feet
and slenderest knees,   15
could love indeed the maid,
only if she were laid,
white ash amid funereal cypresses.

[1923, 1983]

Marianne Moore

[1887–1972]

Marianne Craig Moore was born in Kirkwood, Missouri, on November 15, 1887, the second child of John and Mary Warner Moore. Several months before Moore's birth, her father was institutionalized for a nervous breakdown following the failure of one of his inventions, and her mother took the couple's year-old son, Warner, to live with her father, John Riddle

Marianne Moore

Moore sat for this portrait in New York City in 1922, the year after her first collection of poetry was published in London.

Warner, a Presbyterian minister in Kirkwood. His deep religious faith strongly shaped his daughter and grandchildren, who lived with him until his death in 1894. Mary Moore moved her two children to Pittsburgh and then to Carlisle, Pennsylvania, where she took a job as an English teacher at a preparatory school for girls, the Metzger Institute. Determined to prepare both of her children for college, Mary Moore sent her son to a nearby school for boys and enrolled Moore at Metzger. In 1905, the year after her brother entered Yale, Moore was admitted to Bryn Mawr College. Discouraged by a professor from majoring in English, Moore studied history, law, and politics and minored in biology. But she was actively involved in the college literary magazine, where her earliest poems and stories appeared, and she met other students interested in literature, including Hilda Doolittle, who later published as H.D. During Moore's senior year, she submitted some poems to the *Literary Digest* and the prestigious *Atlantic Monthly*. Although both magazines rejected her work, Moore had already begun to set her sights on a literary career by the time she graduated from Bryn Mawr in 1909.

Like other poets of her generation, Moore faced the challenge of finding ways to support herself and her writing. She returned home and enrolled in a secretarial course at Carlisle Commercial College. Following a trip with her mother to Europe, where Moore visited a long list of art museums, she took a job teaching secretarial courses and business English at the Carlisle Industrial Indian School. Moore became active in the suffrage movement and once "climbed a lamppost" in a demonstration for women's right to vote, as she later told her friend Elizabeth Bishop. Moore also continued to write poetry. In 1915, several of her poems appeared in two of the most prominent little magazines of the period, *Others* and *Poetry*. H.D., who became the literary editor of the London-based *Egoist*, published several more of Moore's poems in 1916. That year, she gave up her job in Carlisle and moved with her mother to Chatham, New Jersey, where they lived with and kept house for Moore's brother, the Presbyterian pastor of the Ogden Memorial Church. When he enlisted as a chaplain in the army two years later, Moore and her mother moved to New York City. Working there as a secretary and private tutor and later at a branch of the New York Public Library, Moore became friendly with several poets she admired, especially Wallace Stevens and William Carlos Williams. She also began to correspond with Ezra Pound and T. S. Eliot, both of whom warmly supported her work. In 1921, H.D. and her companion Bryher (the pen name of Winifred Ellerman) put together a collection of Moore's early verse, *Poems*, which was published in London.

Moore subsequently gained a secure foothold in the emerging world of modernist culture in the United States. She was a frequent contributor to the *Dial*, which became the nation's most prestigious journal of the arts after Scofield Thayer took it over in 1920. In 1924, Moore won the annual Dial Award of $2,000, established by Thayer to recognize special achievement in American letters and to provide "leisure through which at least one artist may serve God (or go to the Devil) according to his own lights." The Dial Press published Moore's second book of poetry, *Observations* (1924). She became the managing editor of the *Dial* in 1925 and assumed sole editorship when Thayer resigned in 1926. After the magazine ceased publication in 1929, Moore worked as a freelance writer. T. S. Eliot suggested that she publish a new collection of her work and offered advice about the arrangement of her *Selected Poems* (1935). In his introduction to the volume, Eliot observed that Moore's work formed "part of the small body of durable poetry written in our time." The book sold poorly, but Moore steadily published her poetry in the *Nation*, the *New Republic*, and the *Partisan Review*, as well as in a new generation of literary journals such as the *Kenyon Review*. She also periodically published collections of her poems, including *The Pangolin and Other Verse* (1938), *What Are Years* (1941), and *Nevertheless* (1944).

During the final decades of her life, Moore became widely known as a poet and a public figure. In 1947, the year her supportive and protective mother died, Moore was elected to the National Institute of Arts and Letters. Her *Collected Poems* (1951) won the Pulitzer Prize and the Bollingen Prize. In addition to several more volumes of poetry, she published a

Moore's poems form part of . . . that small body of writings . . . in which an original sensibility and alert intelligence and deep feeling have been engaged in maintaining the life of the English language.

—*T. S. Eliot*

translation of La Fontaine's *Fables* (1954), as well as a collection of essays, *Predilections* (1955). Moore was also adopted by the media, the subject of feature articles in magazines ranging from *Vogue* to *Sports Illustrated*. An ardent baseball fan, she was invited to throw out the first ball at the opening game of the season at Yankee Stadium in 1966. *The Complete Poems of Marianne Moore* was published to celebrate her eightieth birthday in 1967. Moore — "our beloved Marianne," as she was described in her obituary in the *New York Times* — died of a stroke less than five years later, on February 5, 1972.

*bedfordstmartins.com/
americanlit* for research
links on Moore

Moore's Poetry.   Throughout her life, Moore kept notebooks in which she jotted down quotations from her reading, comments on sermons and lectures she heard, and descriptions of animals and the natural world. Drawing on her notebooks, Moore helped pioneer the modernist practice of weaving quotations into her poems, to which she sometimes added extended notes. Many of her poems focus on a single image or natural object, displaying an attentiveness to detail Moore in part attributed to her early interest in biology and laboratory science: "Precision, economy of statement, logic employed to ends that are disinterested, drawing and identifying, liberate — at least have some bearing on — imagination." The effect of her concentrated poems was perhaps best described by her friend William Carlos Williams, who in a 1925 essay observed that "in looking at some apparently small object, one feels the swirl of great events." Williams and other modernist poets also called attention to her metrical innovations. "Moore's versification is anything but 'free,'" T. S. Eliot observed in 1935. "Many of the poems are in exact, and sometimes complicated, formal patterns, and move with the elegance of a minuet." In some of her poems, those complex patterns are the result of her use of a metrical system called "syllabics," that is, lines of a fixed and carefully counted number of syllables, often resulting in unusual line breaks that may appear to disrupt the syntax of a passage. Moore was also known — in fact, she was notorious — for her constant revisions, as exemplified by her most famous poem, "Poetry." The original, thirty line version of the poem appeared in *Others* in 1919. Moore slightly trimmed and altered the line breaks of the poem in various later versions before compressing it into a mere three lines in her *Complete Poems* (1967). Perhaps in response to those who questioned her radical cutting of the poem, Moore in the epigraph to that volume observed, "Omissions are not accidents." Both the original and the final version of "Poetry" are printed below. The texts of all final versions of the poems are taken from *The Complete Poems of Marianne Moore* (1980).

POETRY[1]

I too, dislike it: there are things that are important beyond all this fiddle.
　　Reading it, however, with a perfect contempt for it, one discovers that there
　　　　　　is in
　　it after all, a place for the genuine.
　　　　Hands that can grasp, eyes
　　　　that can dilate, hair that can rise   5
　　　　　　if it must, these things are important not because a

high sounding interpretation can be put upon them but because they are
　　useful; when they become so derivative as to become unintelligible, the
　　same thing may be said for all of us — that we
　　　　do not admire what   10
　　　　we cannot understand. The bat,
　　　　　　holding on upside down or in quest of something to

eat, elephants pushing, a wild horse taking a roll, a tireless wolf under
　　a tree, the immovable critic twinkling his skin like a horse that feels a flea,
　　　　　　the base-
　　ball fan, the statistician — case after case   15
　　　　could be cited did
　　　　one wish it; nor it is valid
　　　　　　to discriminate against "business documents and

school-books"[2]; all these phenomena are important. One must make a
　　　　　　distinction
　　however: when dragged into prominence by half poets, the result is not poetry,   20
　　nor till the autocrats[3] among us can be
　　　　"literalists of
　　　　the imagination"[4] — above
　　　　　　insolence and triviality and can present

---

1. **Poetry:** The version printed here follows the text and format of the original, as it was published at the opening of the final issue of *Others* (July 1919), an issue of the magazine edited by William Carlos Williams.
2. **"business documents and school-books":** When she published the poem in her collection *Observations* (1924), Moore added a note in which she identified and quoted the full passage from the *Diary of Tolstoy*: "Where the boundary between prose and poetry lies, I shall never understand. The question is raised in manuals of style, yet the answer to it lies beyond me. Poetry is verse; prose is not verse. Or else poetry is everything with the exception of business documents and school books."
3. **autocrats:** In a later version published in her *Selected Poems* (1935), Moore altered this to *poets*.
4. **"literalists of the imagination":** When she published the poem in her collection *Observations* (1924), Moore added a note in which she identified and quoted the source of the phrase, W. B. Yeats's "William Blake and His Illustrations," in *Ideas of Good and Evil* (1903): "The limitation of his view was from the very intensity of his vision; he was a too literal realist of the imagination, as others are of nature; and because he believed that the figures seen by the mind's eye, when exalted by inspiration were 'eternal existences,' he hated every grace of style that might obscure their lineaments."

for inspection, imaginary gardens with real toads in them, shall we have   25
   it. In the meantime, if you demand on one hand, in defiance of their opinion –
   the raw material of poetry in
      all its rawness and
      that which is on the other hand,
         genuine then you are interested in poetry.   30

                                                   [1919]

POETRY[1]

I, too, dislike it.
   Reading it, however, with a perfect contempt for it, one discovers in
   it, after all, a place for the genuine.

                                    [1919, 1980]

---

1. **Poetry:** The editors of *The Complete Poems of Marianne Moore* (1967), where this final version of the poem first appeared, convinced Moore to include what was described as the "Original version" in a note. In fact, the version printed in that note was an intermediate version published in her *Selected Poems* (1935), not the original version published in 1919 and reprinted above.

THE FISH[1]

   wade
   through black jade.
      Of the crow-blue mussel-shells, one keeps
      adjusting the ash-heaps;
         opening and shutting itself like   5

an
injured fan.
      The barnacles which encrust the side
      of the wave, cannot hide
         there for the submerged shafts of the   10

sun,
split like spun
      glass, move themselves with spotlight swiftness
      into the crevices –
         in and out, illuminating   15

---

1. **The Fish:** The title also serves as the first line of the poem, which was originally published in the London magazine *Egoist* (August 1918), then edited by the poet H.D.

the
turquoise sea
   of bodies. The water drives a wedge
   of iron through the iron edge
      of the cliff; whereupon the stars,[2]   20

pink
rice-grains, ink-
   bespattered jelly-fish, crabs like green
   lilies, and submarine
      toadstools, slide each on the other.   25

All
external
   marks of abuse are present on this
   defiant edifice —
      all the physical features of   30

ac-
cident — lack
   of cornice,[3] dynamite grooves, burns, and
   hatchet strokes, these things stand
      out on it; the chasm-side is   35

dead.
Repeated
   evidence has proved that it can live
   on what can not revive
      its youth. The sea grows old in it.   40

                [1918, 1980]

---

2. **stars:** Abbreviated version of *starfish.*
3. **cornice:** An overhanging mass, often of hardened snow, at the edge of a precipice.

A Grave[1]

Man looking into the sea,
taking the view from those who have as much right to it as you have to it yourself,
it is human nature to stand in the middle of a thing,
but you cannot stand in the middle of this;
the sea has nothing to give but a well excavated grave.   5

---

1. **A Grave:** This poem was first published as "A Graveyard" in the *Dial* (July 1921). Moore changed the title to "A Grave" when she included it in her collection *Observations* (1924).

The firs stand in a procession, each with an emerald turkey-foot at the top,
reserved as their contours, saying nothing;
repression, however, is not the most obvious characteristic of the sea;
the sea is a collector, quick to return a rapacious look.
There are others besides you who have worn that look —   10
whose expression is no longer a protest; the fish no longer investigate them
for their bones have not lasted:
men lower nets, unconscious of the fact that they are desecrating a grave,
and row quickly away — the blades of the oars
moving together like the feet of water-spiders as if there were no such thing
    as death.   15
The wrinkles progress among themselves in a phalanx[2] — beautiful under
    networks of foam,
and fade breathlessly while the sea rustles in and out of the seaweed;
the birds swim through the air at top speed, emitting cat-calls as heretofore —
the tortoise-shell scourges about the feet of the cliffs, in motion beneath them;
and the ocean, under the pulsation of lighthouses and noise of bell-buoys,   20
advances as usual, looking as if it were not that ocean in which dropped things
    are bound to sink —
in which if they turn and twist, it is neither with volition nor consciousness.

[1921, 1980]

---

2. **phalanx:** A group forming a compact body, drawn up in close order.

TO A SNAIL

If "compression is the first grace of style,"[1]
you have it. Contractility is a virtue
as modesty is a virtue.
It is not the acquisition of any one thing
that is able to adorn,   5
or the incidental quality that occurs
as a concomitant of something well said,
that we value in style,
but the principle that is hid:

---

1. **"compression . . . style":** "The very first grace of style is that which comes from compression." *Demetrius on Style*, translated by W. Hamilton Fyfe (Heinemann, 1932). [Moore's note] The quotation is from an ancient Greek treatise on style, probably dating from the second century BCE.

in the absence of feet, "a method of conclusions";   10
"a knowledge of principles,"
in the curious phenomenon of your occipital[2] horn.

                    [1924, 1980]

---

2. occipital: At the back of the skull.

WHAT ARE YEARS?[1]

What is our innocence,
what is our guilt? All are
    naked, none is safe. And whence
is courage: the unanswered question,
the resolute doubt, —   5
dumbly calling, deafly listening — that
in misfortune, even death,
        encourages others
        and in its defeat, stirs

the soul to be strong? He   10
sees deep and is glad, who
    accedes to mortality
and in his imprisonment rises
upon himself as
the sea in a chasm, struggling to be   15
free and unable to be,
        in its surrendering
        finds its continuing.

So he who strongly feels,
behaves. The very bird,   20
    grown taller as he sings, steels
his form straight up. Though he is captive,
his mighty singing
says, satisfaction is a lowly
thing, how pure a thing is joy.   25
    This is mortality,
    this is eternity.

                    [1941, 1980]

---

1. What Are Years?: Moore placed this poem, which was first published in the *Kenyon Review* (Summer 1940), at the opening of her collection *What Are Years* (1941).

Jun Fujita

[1888–1963]

Jun Fujita

This undated photograph is apparently one of the few portraits taken of Fujita, who was himself more widely known for his photography than for the poetry he published during the 1920s.

Jun Fujita was born near Hiroshima, Japan, on December 13, 1888. Few details are known about his early life in Japan. When he was about eighteen years old, his uncle employed him to photograph fishing and lumber industries in Canada, where Fujita lived until around 1915. He then moved to Chicago, initially planning to become an engineer. In order to support himself while studying at the Armour Institute, now the Illinois Institute of Technology, Fujita took a job as a photographer with the Chicago *Evening Post.* At the time, he was the only Japanese news photographer in the country, and he quickly gained a reputation for his portraits of people as diverse as Al Capone, Albert Einstein, Carl Sandburg, and several presidents, as well as for his photographs of sensational events such as the capsizing of the steamer *Eastland* in the Chicago River in 1915, the race riots in Chicago during the "Red Summer" of 1919, and the "St. Valentine's Day Massacre," in which Capone's criminal gang shot and killed seven members of a rival gang in 1929.

During these years, Fujita also began to write poetry. His poems appeared in various periodicals, including the avant-garde journal *Caprice,* published in Berkeley, California, and the Chicago-based magazines the *Wave* and *Poetry: A Magazine of Verse,* edited by Harriet Monroe. Fujita often wrote English variants of the tanka, an ancient form of Japanese poetry that also provided the title of his first and only book, *Tanka: Poems in Exile* (1923). Monroe wrote a favorable review of the volume for *Poetry,* and Llewellen Jones, the literary critic for the *Evening Post,* was even more enthusiastic, observing that "Mr. Fujita shows an extraordinary power of evoking a whole landscape with its emotional suggestions, from words as economically used as is the single line of the master etcher." But the book, which was published in a beautifully printed, limited edition of only 365 copies, gained little attention, and Fujita apparently published no more of his poetry after 1928, when several more of his tanka appeared in *Poetry.*

Fujita thereafter devoted himself to photography and painting. About 1928, he began to build a cabin near Ranier, Minnesota, on property bought by his longtime companion, Florence Carr, a secretary and social worker Fujita married in 1940. Carr bought the land because, as an "Asian alien," Fujita was prohibited by state law from owning property in Minnesota. Fujita, who loved the wilderness, often retreated to the cabin to sketch, paint watercolors, and take photographs of the natural world. After beginning a successful commercial photography business in the early 1930s, he was commissioned by the government to photograph Federal Works projects throughout the United States. Unlike most other people of Japanese ancestry in the country, the overwhelming majority of whom lived in Hawaii or on the West Coast, Fujita was able to avoid being sent to an internment camp during World War II by remaining in Chicago.

Through a special act of Congress, he was granted U.S. citizenship in 1954. Remembered primarily for his photographic work, Fujita died at his home in Chicago on July 13, 1963.

Fujita's Poetry.   Between 1919 and 1928, Fujita published more than twenty poems and two reviews in Harriet Monroe's prominent magazine *Poetry*. In both his poems and reviews, Fujita sought to educate Americans about Japanese poetry and poetic forms, which were increasingly popular among poets and readers in the United States. In "A Japanese Cosmopolite" (1922), a review of the influential poetry of Yone Noguchi, the first Japanese national to publish poetry in English, Fujita observed:

> The so-called oriental influence in western literature today, I am afraid, is taking the form it has assumed in the other arts, which, to a great extent, have adopted the carcass of Japanese pictures and missed the essence.

For Fujita, the essence of Japanese poetry was what he defined as the creation of "poetic silence," the poet's ability to suggest a mood or a feeling without relying on extended description or explicit commentary. "Ten words of prose, once set down, do the duty of only ten words," he once observed. "But two words of poetry, with their suggestive power, can create a mood or paint a picture that in prose would require perhaps five hundred words." In many of his poems, including the first of the following selection, Fujita freely adapted the compressed form of the Japanese tanka, traditionally a thirty-one-syllable poem divided into five syllabic units, or lines. As the other poems in the selection indicate, he also wrote somewhat longer poems in free verse, including imagistic poems inspired by nighttime scenes in Chicago. The texts of the poems, the final four poems in the volume, are taken from *Tanka: Poems in Exile* (1923).

bedfordstmartins.com/ americanlit for research links on Fujita

DIMINUENDO[1]

Into the evening haze
Out of giant stacks, the smoke
Winds and fades.

Din and whistles have dwindled away
And stillness chants an empty echo.

[1923]

---

1. **Diminuendo:**   A gradual decrease in the force or loudness in a musical passage.

MICHIGAN BOULEVARD[1]

A row of black tombs — tall and jagged,
The buildings stand in the drizzly night.
With vacant stare the boulevard lamps in rain
Amuse the green gleams they cast.
Beyond the lamps, among the tombs,
Drip, and drip,
The hollow sound rises.

[1923]

1. **Michigan Boulevard:** A major north and south thoroughfare, usually called Michigan Avenue, running parallel to Lake Michigan and through the central business and retail district of Chicago.

CHICAGO RIVER[1]

Slowly, by the slimy wooden wharves,
Through the stillness of rain
The Chicago River glides into night.
From the silhouette of a black iron bridge,
The watchman's light is dripping —   5
Dripping like melting tallow.
Out of darkness
Comes a woman,
Hellos to me; her wet face glares;
Casually she turns and goes   10
Into the darkness.

Through the stillness of rain
The Chicago River glides on.

[1923]

1. **Chicago River:** The river that flows through downtown Chicago. In a remarkable feat of engineering in 1900, the direction of the notoriously polluted river was changed to flow into the Chicago Sanitary and Ship Canal, in an effort to control the massive amounts of industrial waste and raw sewage that were contaminating Lake Michigan.

MY SISTER

Across the meadow
The breeze is fragrant;
In a tree a bird
Disturbs the petals
Over these tombstones, still and content.   5

A melodious afternoon, years ago;
My sister
With pig-tail flying
Chased a dragon-fly
And laughed over nothing.   10

The clear vision stands today —
When I pledged
Tidings and gifts
Her strained lips quivered in vain —
Before me, the tombstone, still and content.   15

The chirp of a bird among the trees —
It too has died away.

[1923]

T. S. Eliot

[1888–1965]

Thomas Stearns Eliot was born on September 26, 1888, in St. Louis, Missouri. He was the youngest of seven children of Henry Ware Eliot, president of the Hydraulic-Press Brick Company, and Charlotte Chauncy Stearns Eliot, both of whom were descended from early English settlers of New England. Eliot's grandfather, William Greenleaf Eliot, graduated from Harvard Divinity School and moved to St. Louis in 1834. There, he helped found a Unitarian church and Washington University, which Eliot's father attended. After their marriage, Eliot's parents were active in St. Louis society, supporting the arts and various civic causes. The family lived in an urban neighborhood near the Mississippi River and spent the summers at their second home near Gloucester, Massachusetts. Eliot grew up in a household that valued "Religion, the Community, and Education," as he recalled in 1953. He was educated at private schools in St. Louis and attended Milton Academy in Massachusetts for a year before enrolling at Harvard University in 1906. Influenced by his mother, a former teacher and amateur poet whose work appeared in various religious journals, Eliot had begun to write poetry at an early age, and he published some of his work in the *Harvard Advocate*. He also read a book he described as a "revelation," Arthur Symon's *The Symbolist Movement in Literature* (1895), which introduced Eliot to the writings of French poets such as Jules Laforgue. By the time Eliot graduated from Harvard in 1910, having earned both a BA and an MA in English literature, he was writing poetry that departed sharply from the conventions of the nineteenth-century British poets who had earlier influenced his work.

T. S. Eliot

The celebrity photographer E. O. Hoppé took this portrait of Eliot about 1920, when the rising young poet and critic was working at a branch of Lloyd's Bank in London.

Eliot was initially torn between an academic and a literary career. During the year 1910–11, which he spent in postgraduate study at the Sorbonne, Eliot copied into a notebook some of the poems that would later bring him considerable recognition, including "The Love Song of J. Alfred Prufrock." After his year in Paris, Eliot put aside his poetry and returned to Harvard, where he did three years of graduate work under the tutelage of its distinguished faculty in philosophy, including William James, Josiah Royce, George Santayana, and the visiting Bertrand Russell. Eliot also studied Hindu religion and Sanskrit. In 1914, he returned to Europe on a fellowship, briefly studying in Germany and then, after the beginning of World War I, moving on to Merton College, Oxford. In England, he met Ezra Pound, whose influence and help would prove to be invaluable to Eliot. In a letter to Harriet Monroe, the editor of the influential *Poetry: A Magazine of Verse,* Pound observed that Eliot "has actually trained himself *and* modernized himself *on his own.*" Pound urged Monroe to publish "The Love Song of J. Alfred Prufrock," the first of a number of Eliot's poems that appeared in *Poetry* in 1915 and 1916. In the meantime, Eliot met and impulsively married Vivien Haigh-Wood, the daughter of an affluent, upper-middle-class English family. From the beginning, they proved to be painfully incompatible, and their troubled union was further strained by financial difficulties. To support them, Eliot taught school, gave lectures, and wrote reviews. He also completed his doctoral dissertation, but Eliot never received his PhD because he did not return to Harvard for a required dissertation defense. In 1917, he became the assistant editor of an avant-garde literary magazine, the *Egoist,* and also found a job in the Foreign Department of Lloyds Bank.

Between 1917 and 1923, Eliot rose from obscurity to literary fame on both sides of the Atlantic. With the encouragement and financial support of Pound, Eliot published two collections of his poems in London, *Prufrock and Other Observations* (1917) and *Poems* (1919). The contents of the two collections were subsequently published in 1920 as *Poems* in New York City and in London as *Ara Vos Prec.* Eliot also wrote *Ezra Pound, His Metric and Poetry* (1918), as well as numerous articles and reviews, some of which he collected in *The Sacred Wood: Essays on Poetry and Criticism* (1920). In addition to one of Eliot's most famous and influential essays, "Tradition and the Individual Talent," the volume included commentaries on a wide array of literary subjects, including Greek and Elizabethan drama and poets ranging from Dante to the nineteenth-century British poets William Blake and Charles Algernon Swinburne. The whole of European culture, from ancient fertility myths to popular tunes of the Jazz Age, came within the purview of Eliot's most ambitious poem, *The Waste Land,* published in 1922. The poem first appeared in the inaugural issue of the *Criterion,* a new journal edited by Eliot in London, and then in an avant-garde literary magazine published in New York City, the *Dial,* which awarded Eliot its annual prize of two thousand dollars. Late in the year, *The Waste Land* was published as a book, which in later editions Eliot gratefully dedicated to Pound. Although its reception was mixed — one English critic dismissed the volume as "so much waste paper" — the poem catapulted Eliot into the

He is the only American I know of who has made what I can call adequate preparation for writing. He has actually trained himself and modernized himself on his own.

–Ezra Pound

forefront of modernist poets. In 1923, Eliot was also relieved of nagging financial concerns and the pressures of his job at the bank when the publishing firm of Faber and Gwyer (later Faber and Faber) offered him a position as its literary editor, an influential position he retained until his death in 1965.

In the late 1920s, Eliot made two decisions that profoundly shaped his later life and writings. Long dissatisfied with the Unitarianism in which his family was steeped and he was raised, Eliot joined the Church of England in June 1927. Later that year, he became a British citizen. In his preface to *For Lancelot Andrewes* (1928), a collection of essays dedicated to the renowned seventeenth-century Anglican bishop who had overseen the translation of the authorized King James Version of the Bible, Eliot described himself as "classicist in literature, royalist in politics, and anglocatholic in religion." Many of Eliot's admirers were shocked by his reactionary political turn and devotion to the teachings of the church, a commitment that strongly shaped his life and writings. From the early 1930s through the 1950s, Eliot sought to reach a wider audience by writing plays, notably his acclaimed church drama *Murder in the Cathedral* (1935) and a play about sin and Christian redemption, *The Family Reunion* (1939). His preoccupation with human suffering and spirituality was also revealed in his last major poetic project, a group of four meditative poems that Eliot published separately and then as *Four Quartets* (1943). Partly on the strength of the volume, which some critics considered his masterpiece, Eliot was awarded the Nobel Prize for Literature in 1948. Many other awards and prizes followed, including numerous honorary degrees from universities in England and the United States, where he was in great demand as a lecturer. Long separated from his first wife, who was institutionalized for mental instability from 1938 until her death in 1947, Eliot married Valerie Fletcher in 1957. He died in London on January 4, 1965, and was buried in East Coker, the village from which his ancestors had emigrated to America.

bedfordstmartins.com/ americanlit for research links on Eliot

Eliot's "The Love Song of J. Alfred Prufrock."

When Ezra Pound pressed Harriet Monroe to publish this poem in her magazine *Poetry,* he told her that he wanted Eliot's first published poem to be one that would immediately "differentiate him from everyone else, in the public mind." In a brief note at the end of the June 1915 issue of *Poetry,* in which the poem appeared, Monroe rather tersely identified the poet: "Mr. T. S. Eliot is a young American poet resident in England, who has published nothing hitherto in this country." Aside from some additional poems in *Poetry* and a single poem in another little magazine, *Others,* no more of Eliot's verse was published in the United States before 1920. But many reviewers on both sides of the Atlantic were openly hostile to the experimental verse collected in Eliot's first book, *Prufrock and Other Observations,* which was published in London in 1917. For the English reviewer Arthur Waugh, Eliot was yet another new poet who had forgotten that "the first essence of poetry is beauty," and who consequently produced "unmetrical, incoherent banalities." Pound quickly countered, describing the characters in Eliot's poems as "the stuff of the modern world" and praising the volume for its "fine tone, its humanity, and its realism." Although Eliot employed a popular nineteenth-century poetic form, the dramatic monologue, "The Love Song of J. Alfred Prufrock" was and remains a strikingly modern poem, with its urban setting and unpoetical imagery, its untraditional rhythms, and its mixture of colloquial language and allusions to Dante's *Inferno*, the Bible, and Shakespeare. The text is taken from Eliot's *Collected Poems 1909-1962* (1963).

THE LOVE SONG OF J. ALFRED PRUFROCK

S'io credessi che mia risposta fosse
a persona che mai tornasse al mondo,
questa fiamma staria senza più scosse.
Ma per ciò che giammai di questo fondo
non tornò vivo alcun, s'i'odo il vero,
senza tema d'infamia ti rispondo.[1]

Let us go then, you and I,
When the evening is spread out against the sky
Like a patient etherised upon a table;
Let us go, through certain half-deserted streets,
The muttering retreats   5
Of restless nights in one-night cheap hotels
And sawdust restaurants with oyster-shells:
Streets that follow like a tedious argument
Of insidious intent
To lead you to an overwhelming question . . .   10
Oh, do not ask, "What is it?"
Let us go and make our visit.

In the room the women come and go
Talking of Michelangelo.[2]

---

1. **S'io . . . rispondo**: The lines are from the *Inferno*, by the Italian poet Dante Alighieri (1265-1321): "If I believed that my response was heard / by anyone returning to the world, / this flame would stand and never stir again, / But since no man has ever come alive / out of this gulf of Hell, if I hear true, / I'll answer, with no fear of infamy" (27.61-66, as translated by Anthony Esolen). The speaker is Guido da Montefeltro, whose spirit Dante encounters during his descent into hell. Since Guido assumes that Dante is also dead and therefore cannot return to the world, he is willing to confess to the sin of false counsel, for which he is punished by being encased in flame.
2. **Michelangelo**: The Italian sculptor and painter Michelangelo Buonarroti (1475-1564), a leading figure of the Italian Renaissance.

The yellow fog that rubs its back upon the window-panes,   15
The yellow smoke that rubs its muzzle on the window-panes,
Licked its tongue into the corners of the evening,
Lingered upon the pools that stand in drains,
Let fall upon its back the soot that falls from chimneys,
Slipped by the terrace, made a sudden leap,   20
And seeing that it was a soft October night,
Curled once about the house, and fell asleep.

And indeed there will be time
For the yellow smoke that slides along the street
Rubbing its back upon the window-panes;   25
There will be time, there will be time
To prepare a face to meet the faces that you meet;
There will be time to murder and create,
And time for all the works and days of hands[3]
That lift and drop a question on your plate;   30
Time for you and time for me,
And time yet for a hundred indecisions,
And for a hundred visions and revisions,
Before the taking of a toast and tea.

In the room the women come and go   35
Talking of Michelangelo.

And indeed there will be time
To wonder, "Do I dare?" and, "Do I dare?"
Time to turn back and descend the stair,
With a bald spot in the middle of my hair —   40
(They will say: "How his hair is growing thin!")
My morning coat, my collar mounting firmly to the chin,
My necktie rich and modest, but asserted by a simple pin —
(They will say: "But how his arms and legs are thin!")
Do I dare   45
Disturb the universe?
In a minute there is time
For decisions and revisions which a minute will reverse.

For I have known them all already, known them all —
Have known the evenings, mornings, afternoons,   50

---

3. **there will be time . . . works and days of hands:** *Works and Days* is a poem about agricultural work by the Greek poet Hesiod (c. 700 BCE). Here and in several following lines, Eliot also echoes Ecclesiastes: "To every thing there is a season, and a time to every purpose under the heaven: A time to be born, and a time to die; a time to plant, and a time to pluck up that which is planted" (3:1-2).

I have measured out my life with coffee spoons;
I know the voices dying with a dying fall[4]
Beneath the music from a farther room.
    So how should I presume?

And I have known the eyes already, known them all —   55
The eyes that fix you in a formulated phrase,
And when I am formulated, sprawling on a pin,
When I am pinned and wriggling on the wall,
Then how should I begin
To spit out all the butt-ends of my days and ways?   60
    And how should I presume?

And I have known the arms already, known them all —
Arms that are braceleted and white and bare
(But in the lamplight, downed with light brown hair!)
Is it perfume from a dress   65
That makes me so digress?
Arms that lie along a table, or wrap about a shawl.
    And should I then presume?
    And how should I begin?
      . . . . . .

Shall I say, I have gone at dusk through narrow streets   70
And watched the smoke that rises from the pipes
Of lonely men in shirt-sleeves, leaning out of windows? . . .

I should have been a pair of ragged claws
Scuttling across the floors of silent seas.
      . . . . . .

And the afternoon, the evening, sleeps so peacefully!   75
Smoothed by long fingers,
Asleep . . . tired . . . or it malingers,
Stretched on the floor, here beside you and me.
Should I, after tea and cakes and ices,
Have the strength to force the moment to its crisis?   80
But though I have wept and fasted, wept and prayed,
Though I have seen my head (grown slightly bald) brought in upon
    a platter,[5]

---

4. **a dying fall**: A possible allusion to the opening lines of Shakespeare's *Twelfth Night:* "If music be the food of love, play on; / Give me excess of it, that, surfeiting, / The appetite may sicken, and so die. / That strain again! It had a dying fall."
5. **head . . . upon a platter**: The head of the prophet John the Baptist, who was executed by King Herod at the request of Princess Salome, was brought to Queen Horodias on a silver platter (Matthew 14:3–11).

I am no prophet — and here's no great matter;
I have seen the moment of my greatness flicker,
And I have seen the eternal Footman hold my coat, and snicker,   85
And in short, I was afraid.

And would it have been worth it, after all,
After the cups, the marmalade, the tea,
Among the porcelain, among some talk of you and me,
Would it have been worth while,   90
To have bitten off the matter with a smile,
To have squeezed the universe into a ball
To roll it towards some overwhelming question,
To say: "I am Lazarus,[6] come from the dead,
Come back to tell you all, I shall tell you all" —   95
If one, settling a pillow by her head,
    Should say: "That is not what I meant at all.
    That is not it, at all."

And would it have been worth it, after all,
Would it have been worth while,   100
After the sunsets and the dooryards and the sprinkled streets,
After the novels, after the teacups, after the skirts that trail along
    the floor —
And this, and so much more? —
It is impossible to say just what I mean!
But as if a magic lantern[7] threw the nerves in patterns on a screen: 105
Would it have been worth while
If one, settling a pillow or throwing off a shawl,
And turning toward the window, should say:
    "That is not it at all,
    That is not what I meant, at all."   110
     . . . . .

No! I am not Prince Hamlet,[8] nor was meant to be;
Am an attendant lord, one that will do
To swell a progress,[9] start a scene or two,
Advise the prince; no doubt, an easy tool,
Deferential, glad to be of use,   115

---

6. **Lazarus:** The story of the resurrection of Lazarus is told in John 11:1–44.
7. **magic lantern:** A multilens forerunner of movie and slide projectors, used to project images on theater screens in popular magic-lantern shows.
8. **Prince Hamlet:** The famously indecisive title character of Shakespeare's *Hamlet, Prince of Denmark.*
9. **Am an attendant lord . . . swell a progress:** That is, a minor figure who simply increases the number of members of a royal court who are embarking on a journey.

Politic, cautious, and meticulous;
Full of high sentence,[10] but a bit obtuse;
At times, indeed, almost ridiculous —
Almost, at times, the Fool.

I grow old . . . I grow old . . .   120
I shall wear the bottoms of my trousers rolled.

Shall I part my hair behind? Do I dare to eat a peach?
I shall wear white flannel trousers, and walk upon the beach.
I have heard the mermaids singing, each to each.

I do not think that they will sing to me.   125

I have seen them riding seaward on the waves
Combing the white hair of the waves blown back
When the wind blows the water white and black.

We have lingered in the chambers of the sea
By sea-girls wreathed with seaweed red and brown   130
Till human voices wake us, and we drown.

[1915, 1963]

---

10. **high sentence:** Sententiousness. The passage is probably an allusion to Polonius, the pompous
dispenser of advice in *Hamlet*.

Eliot's *The Waste Land.*   Recent scholarship suggests that Eliot wrote
most of the first two parts of his famous poem early in 1921, a stressful
period when he was working at Lloyd's Bank in London, entertaining his
recently widowed mother and his siblings from St. Louis, and preparing to
assume the editorship of a new journal, the *Criterion.* By the fall, both he
and his wife were ill and exhausted, and Eliot took a leave of absence from
the bank and went to Margate, a seaside resort in southeast England.
From there, he went to Paris and then on to Lausanne, Switzerland. During
his treatment at a sanitarium there, he wrote the final three sections of
the poem. Uncertain about its value, when Eliot returned to Paris in January 1922 he asked Ezra Pound for his comments on the poem, then entitled
"He Do the Police in Different Voices." When Pound read the manuscript,
he noted that it was "a masterpiece; one of most important 19 pages in
English." In what is widely viewed as a brilliant act of editorial intervention, and what Eliot himself described as "irrefutable evidence of Pound's
critical genius," he offered extensive suggestions for revision, cutting several lengthy sections and deleting hundreds of words and phrases from
the poem. *The Waste Land,* as it was retitled, was first published in
England in the *Criterion* (October 1922), edited by Eliot, and then in the
United States in the *Dial* (November 1922). In both magazines, the poem
appeared without notes, which Eliot added when the poem was published

HE DO THE POLICE IN DIFFERENT VOICES: Part I.

THE BURIAL OF THE DEAD.

First we had a couple of feelers down at Tom's place,
There was old Tom, boiled to the eyes, blind,
(Don't you remember that time after a dance,
Top hats and all, we and Silk Hat Harry,
And old Tom took us behind, brought out a bottle of fizz,
With old Jane, Tom's wife; and we got Joe to sing
"I'm proud of all the Irish blood that's in me,
"There's not a man can say a word agin me").
Then we had dinner in good form, and a couple of Bengal lights.
When we got into the show, up in Row A,
I tried to put my foot in the drum, and didn't the girl squeal,
She never did take to me, a nice guy" but rough;
The next thing we were out in the street, Oh was it cold!
When will you be good! Blew in to the Opera Exchange,
Sopped up some gin, sat in to the cork game,
Mr. Fay was there, singing "The Maid of the Mill";
Then we thought we'd breeze along and take a walk.
Then we lost Steve.
("I turned up an hour later down at Myrtle's place.
What d'y' mean, she says, at two o'clock in the morning,
I'm not in business here for guys like you;
We've only had a raid last week, I've been warned twice.
Sergeant, I said, I've kept a decent house for twenty years,
There's three gents from the Buckingham Club upstairs now,
I'm going to retire and live on a farm, she says,
There's no money in it now, what with the damage done,
And the reputation the place gets, on account of a few bar-flies,
I've kept a clean house for twenty years, she says,
And the gents from the Buckingham Club know they're safe here;
You was well introduced, but this is the last of you.
Get me a woman, I said; you're too drunk, she said,
But she gave me a bed, and a bath, and ham and eggs,
And now you go get a shave, she said; I had a good laugh.
Myrtle was always a good sport).
We'd just gone up the alley, a fly cop came along,
Looking for trouble; committing a nuisance, he said,
You come on to the station. I'm sorry, I said,
It's no use being sorry, he said; let me get my hat, I said.
Well by a stroke of luck who came by but Mr. Donavan.
What's this, officer. You're new on this beat, aint you?
I thought so. You know who I am. Yes, I do,
Saidd the fresh cop, very peevish. Then let it alone,
These gents are particular friends of mine.
Wasn't it luck? Then we went to the German Club,
We and Mr. Donavan and his friend Joe Leahy,
Found it shut. I want to get home, said the cabman,
We all go the same way home, said Mr. Donavan,
Cheer up, Trixie and Stella; and put his foot through the window.
The next I know the old cab was hauled up on the avenue,
And the cabman and little Ben Levin the tailor,
The one who read George Meredith,
Were running a hundred yards on a bet,
And Mr. Donavan holding the watch.
So I got out to see the sunrise, and walked home.

Original Typescript of *The Waste Land*

The first page of Eliot's typescript of the poem he initially called "He Do the
Police in Different Voices" contains a fifty-four-line sequence depicting a
drunken and rowdy night in Boston. After revising the sequence, Eliot omitted it
at the urging of Ezra Pound. In the published version of *The Waste Land*, the first
part of the poem, "The Burial of the Dead," consequently opens with the passage
that originally followed on page 2 of the typescript, beginning "April is the cruellest month . . . ."

as a book by the New York firm of Boni & Liveright at the end of 1922. Much later, in *The Frontiers of Criticism* (1956), Eliot explained, "I had at first intended only to put down all the references for my quotations, with a view to spiking the guns of critics of my earlier poems who had accused me of plagiarism." At the same time, Eliot continued, "it was discovered that the poem was inconveniently short, so I set to work to expand the notes, in order to provide a few more pages of printed matter, with the result that they became the remarkable exposition of bogus scholarship that is still on view today." Many scholars, however, view the notes as an integral part of the poem, and we have incorporated all of them and provided additional notes in an effort to help readers negotiate the complex cultural landscape of *The Waste Land*, which reveals Eliot's extensive reading of the Bible and other Christian texts, ancient Hindu scriptures, and European literature ranging from Greek and Roman classics to writings by his contemporaries. As some of the reviewers immediately recognized, Eliot's poem was at once a deeply personal and a radically modern work that expressed the pervasive sense of disillusionment and despair in the aftermath of World War I. In a review of *The Waste Land*, the American critic Edmund Wilson thus praised Eliot as "one of our only authentic poets," explaining: "For this new poem – which presents itself as so far his most considerable claim to eminence – not only recapitulates all his earlier and already familiar motifs, but it sounds for the first time in all their intensity, untempered by irony or disguise, the hunger for beauty and anguish at living which lie at the bottom of all his work." The text is taken from Eliot's *Collected Poems 1909-1962* (1963).

THE WASTE LAND[1]

"Nam Sibyllam quidem Cumis ego ipse oculis meis vidi in ampulla pendere, et cum illi pueri dicerent: Σίβυλλα τί θέλεις; respondebat illa: ἀποθανεῖν θέλω."[2]

---

1. **The Waste Land:** Not only the title, but the plan and a good deal of the incidental symbolism of the poem were suggested by Miss Jessie L. Weston's book on the Grail legend: *From Ritual to Romance* (Cambridge). Indeed, so deeply am I indebted, Miss Weston's book will elucidate the difficulties of the poem much better than my notes can do; and I recommend it (apart from the great interest of the book itself) to any who think such elucidation of the poem worth the trouble. To another work of anthropology I am indebted in general, one which has influenced our generation profoundly; I mean *The Golden Bough*; I have used especially the two volumes *Adonis, Attis, Osiris*. Anyone who is acquainted with these works will immediately recognise in the poem certain references to vegetation ceremonies. [Eliot's note] In *The Golden Bough: A Study in Magic and Religion*, first published in 1890, the British anthropologist James Frazer studied parallels between Christianity and ancient mystery religions, fertility cults that centered on the worship of a sacred king whose life and sacrificial death were reenacted in imitation of the natural cycles of death and rebirth in nature. Building on Frazer's work, Weston in *From Ritual to Romance* (1920) sought to establish connections between the mystery religions and Arthurian tales about the quest for the Holy Grail, the cup Christ used at the Last Supper. In the medieval tales, a knight from King Arthur's court goes in quest of the grail, which is held in the castle of the sexually maimed Fisher King. By asking the right question, the knight can heal the king and restore the fertility of his blighted realm, the Wasteland.

2. **[epigraph]:** The passage is from chapter 48 of the *Satyricon* by the Roman satirist Petronius (?-66 CE):

FOR EZRA POUND
IL MIGLIOR FABBRO.[3]

I. The Burial of the Dead[4]

April is the cruellest month, breeding
Lilacs out of the dead land, mixing
Memory and desire, stirring
Dull roots with spring rain.
Winter kept us warm, covering   5
Earth in forgetful snow, feeding
A little life with dried tubers.
Summer surprised us, coming over the Starnbergersee[5]
With a shower of rain; we stopped in the colonnade,
And went on in sunlight, into the Hofgarten,[6]   10
And drank coffee, and talked for an hour.
Bin gar keine Russin, stamm' aus Litauen, echt deutsch.[7]
And when we were children, staying at the arch-duke's,
My cousin's, he took me out on a sled,
And I was frightened. He said, Marie,   15
Marie, hold on tight. And down we went.
In the mountains, there you feel free.
I read, much of the night, and go south in the winter.

What are the roots that clutch, what branches grow
Out of this stony rubbish? Son of man,[8]   20
You cannot say, or guess, for you know only
A heap of broken images, where the sun beats,
And the dead tree gives no shelter, the cricket no relief,[9]

"And as for the Sibyl, I saw her with my own eyes at Cumae, suspended in a bottle, and when boys asked her, 'Sibyl, what is your wish?,' she would reply, 'I want to die'" (translated by P. G. Walsh). According to Roman myth, Apollo granted the Sibyl immortality but not eternal youth, and as she grew older and older her body shriveled so much that she could fit into a bottle.

3. [dedication]: Eliot dedicated the poem to Ezra Pound, "the greater craftsman," originally a tribute to the thirteenth-century Provençal poet Arnaut Daniel in the *Purgatorio* (26.117) by the Italian poet Dante Alighieri (1265-1321). All translations of Dante in the following notes are by Anthony Esolen.
4. The Burial of the Dead: The title of the burial service in the Anglican *Book of Common Prayer.*
5. Starnbergersee: A large lake southwest of Munich, Germany, a popular destination for wealthy tourists.
6. Hofgarten: "Court Garden" (German), a public park with cafés in Munich.
7. Bin . . . deutsch: "I am not a Russian woman at all, I come from Lithuania, a real German" (German).
8. Son of man: Cf. Ezekiel II, i. [Eliot's note] Here and in other notes, Eliot invites the reader to compare (abbreviated as *cf.*) a passage in his poem with a passage from another work, in this case a verse from Ezekiel: "And he [God] said unto me, Son of man, stand upon thy feet, and I will speak unto thee."
9. And the dead tree . . . no relief: Cf. Ecclesiastes XII, v. [Eliot's note] The verse, part of an allegory of old age in which the Preacher foretells "the evil days," reads: "Also when they shall be afraid of that which is high, and fears shall be in the way, and the almond tree shall flourish, and the grasshopper shall be a burden, and desire shall fail: because man goeth to his long home, and the mourners go about in the streets."

And the dry stone no sound of water. Only
There is shadow under this red rock,[10]   25
(Come in under the shadow of this red rock),
And I will show you something different from either
Your shadow at morning striding behind you

Or your shadow at evening rising to meet you;

I will show you fear in a handful of dust.   30
          Frisch weht der Wind
          Der Heimat zu
          Mein Irisch Kind,
          Wo weilest du?[11]
"You gave me hyacinths[12] first a year ago;   35
"They called me the hyacinth girl."
  — Yet when we came back, late, from the hyacinth garden,
Your arms full, and your hair wet, I could not
Speak, and my eyes failed, I was neither
Living nor dead, and I knew nothing,   40
Looking into the heart of light, the silence.
Oed' und leer das Meer.[13]

Madame Sosostris, famous clairvoyante,
Had a bad cold, nevertheless
Is known to be the wisest woman in Europe,   45
With a wicked pack of cards.[14] Here, said she,

---

10. **There . . . red rock:** See the prophesy of the reign of the Messiah in Isaiah: "And a man shall be as an hiding place from the wind, and a covert from the tempest; as rivers of water in a dry place, as the shadow of a great rock in a weary land" (32:2).

11. **Frisch . . . Wo weilest du?:** V. *Tristan und Isolde*, I, verses 5–8. [Eliot's note] Here and in other notes, Eliot refers the reader (*v.* is an abbreviation of *vide*, "to see or consult") to a passage in another work, in this case a tragic opera about doomed lovers by German composer Richard Wagner (1813–1883). In the passage Eliot cites, a sailor sings of the lover he has left behind: "Fresh blows the wind / To the homeland; / My Irish child, / Where are you waiting?"

12. **hyacinths:** In Greek mythology, Apollo accidentally killed his beloved friend Hyacinthus, and purple flowers magically sprang where his blood touched the ground. The story is told in chapter 10 of the *Metamorphoses* by the Roman poet Ovid (43 BCE–17 CE).

13. **Oed' . . . das Meer**: Id. [ibid] III, verse 24. [Eliot's note] Eliot again refers to *Tristan und Isolde* (see note 11). Tristan, who is dying and awaiting Isolde's arrival by ship, is told: "Desolate and empty [is] the sea."

14. **With a wicked pack of cards:** I am not familiar with the exact constitution of the Tarot pack of cards, from which I have obviously departed to suit my own convenience. The Hanged Man, a member of the traditional pack, fits my purpose in two ways: because he is associated in my mind with the Hanged God of Frazer, and because I associate him with the hooded figure in the passage of the disciples to Emmaus in Part V. The Phoenician Sailor and the Merchant appear later; also the "crowds of people," and Death by Water is executed in Part IV. The Man with Three Staves (an authentic member of the Tarot pack) I associate, quite arbitrarily, with the Fisher King himself. [Eliot's note] The Tarot deck, which includes cards with allegorical representations, is sometimes used for divination, or fortune-telling. Of the Tarot cards mentioned in the following passage, the Phoenician Sailor, Belladonna (Italian for "beautiful woman"), and the one-eyed merchant are Eliot's inventions.

Is your card, the drowned Phoenician Sailor,
(Those are pearls that were his eyes.[15] Look!)
Here is Belladonna, the Lady of the Rocks,
The lady of situations.   50
Here is the man with three staves, and here the Wheel,
And here is the one-eyed merchant, and this card,
Which is blank, is something he carries on his back,
Which I am forbidden to see. I do not find
The Hanged Man. Fear death by water.   55
I see crowds of people, walking round in a ring.
Thank you. If you see dear Mrs. Equitone,
Tell her I bring the horoscope myself:
One must be so careful these days.
Unreal City,[16]   60
Under the brown fog of a winter dawn,
A crowd flowed over London Bridge, so many,
I had not thought death had undone so many.[17]
Sighs, short and infrequent, were exhaled,[18]
And each man fixed his eyes before his feet.   65
Flowed up the hill and down King William Street,
To where Saint Mary Woolnoth[19] kept the hours
With a dead sound on the final stroke of nine.[20]

---

15. **Those . . . eyes**: In Shakespeare's *The Tempest*, the sprite Ariel seeks to comfort Prince Ferdinand, who believes that his father has drowned in a shipwreck, by singing: "Full Fathom five thy father lies; / Of his bones are coral made: / Those are pearls that were his eyes: / Nothing of him that doth fade, / But doth suffer a sea-change / Into something rich and strange" (1.2.397–402).

16. **Unreal City**: Cf. Baudelaire: "Fourmillante cité, cité pleine de rêves, / Où le spectre en plein jour raccroche le passant." [Eliot's note] Eliot quotes the opening of "Les sept viellards" ("The Seven Old Men"), a poem about a ghostly encounter in the street by the French poet Charles Baudelaire (1821–1867): "Swarming city — city gorged with dreams, / Where ghosts by day accost the passer-by" (translated by Richard Howard). *The City* is the name of the financial district of London, where Eliot worked in a bank from 1917 to 1923.

17. **I had not thought . . . so many**: Cf. *Inferno*, III, 55–57: "si lunga tratta / di gente, ch'io non avrei mai creduto / che morte tanta n'avesse disfatta." [Eliot's note] Eliot quotes Dante's description of the small-souled, the unnamed spirits of those who did neither good nor evil in life and who are therefore rejected by both heaven and hell: "in a long file / so numerous a host of people ran, / I had not thought death had unmade so many."

18. **Sighs . . . exhaled**: Cf. *Inferno*, IV, 25–27: "Quivi, secondo che per ascoltare, / non avea pianto, ma' che di sospiri, / che l'aura eterna facevan tremare." [Eliot's note] Eliot quotes Dante's description of limbo, dwelling place of the spirits of unbaptized infants and virtuous people who lived before the advent of Christianity: "As far as I could tell by listening, here / there were no wails, but only sighs, that made / a trembling in the everlasting air."

19. **Saint Mary Woolnoth**: An Anglican church at the intersection of King William Street and Lombard Street in the City. The eighteenth-century church, which was built on a site that had been used for worship for two thousand years, had lost its parishioners and was then nearly derelict, since people no longer lived in the financial district.

20. **With a dead sound . . . stroke of nine**: A phenomenon which I have often noticed. [Eliot's note] Eliot passed by the church on his way to work at the nearby office of Lloyds Bank.

There I saw one I knew, and stopped him, crying: "Stetson!
"You who were with me in the ships at Mylae![21]   70
"That corpse you planted last year in your garden,
"Has it begun to sprout? Will it bloom this year?
"Or has the sudden frost disturbed its bed?
"O keep the Dog far hence, that's friend to men,
"Or with his nails he'll dig it up again![22]   75
"You! hypocrite lecteur! — mon semblable, — mon frère!"[23]

II. A Game of Chess[24]

The Chair she sat in, like a burnished throne,[25]
Glowed on the marble, where the glass
Held up by standards wrought with fruited vines
From which a golden Cupidon peeped out   80
(Another hid his eyes behind his wing)
Doubled the flames of sevenbranched candelabra
Reflecting light upon the table as
The glitter of her jewels rose to meet it,
From satin cases poured in rich profusion.   85
In vials of ivory and coloured glass
Unstoppered, lurked her strange synthetic perfumes,
Unguent, powdered, or liquid — troubled, confused
And drowned the sense in odours; stirred by the air
That freshened from the window, these ascended   90
In fattening the prolonged candle-flames,

---

21. **Mylae:** A city in Sicily, off the coast of which Rome in 260 BCE won a decisive naval victory over Carthage in the first of the Punic Wars, fought for commercial domination of the Mediterranean.
22. **"O keep . . . dig it up again!":** Cf. the Dirge in Webster's *White Devil.* [Eliot's note] Eliot recasts lines from a play by the English dramatist John Webster (d. 1625), in which a mother sings a dirge over the body of her son, Marcello, who has been murdered by his brother, Flamineo: "But keep the wolf far thence, that's foe to men, / For with his nails he'll dig them up again."
23. **"hypocrite lecteur! . . . mon frère!":** V. Baudelaire, Preface to *Fleurs du Mal.* [Eliot's note] Eliot quotes the final line of the introductory poem to the volume, "Au Lecteur" ("To the Reader"): "hypocrite reader, — my alias, — my twin!" (translated by Richard Howard).
24. **A Game of Chess:** The title of a play by the English dramatist Thomas Middleton (1570-1627), a satirical account of England's long rivalry with Spain. In another play by Middleton, *Women Beware Women,* a game of chess is used to distract the attention of a woman responsible for watching over her son's beautiful young wife. The moves of the chess game played on the stage parallel the moves of the seduction played out on the balcony above. See note 35.
25. **The Chair . . . burnished throne:** Cf. *Antony and Cleopatra,* II, ii, l. 190. [Eliot's note] Eliot refers to the description in Shakespeare's play of Cleopatra floating on her ship to her first meeting with Antony: "The barge she sat in, like a burnish'd throne, / Burn'd on the water."

Flung their smoke into the laquearia,²⁶
Stirring the pattern on the coffered ceiling.
Huge sea-wood fed with copper
Burned green and orange, framed by the coloured stone,   95
In which sad light a carvèd dolphin swam.
Above the antique mantel was displayed
As though a window gave upon the sylvan scene²⁷
The change of Philomel,²⁸ by the barbarous king
So rudely forced; yet there the nightingale²⁹   100
Filled all the desert with inviolable voice
And still she cried, and still the world pursues,
"Jug Jug" to dirty ears.³⁰
And other withered stumps of time
Were told upon the walls; staring forms   105
Leaned out, leaning, hushing the room enclosed.
Footsteps shuffled on the stair.
Under the firelight, under the brush, her hair
Spread out in fiery points
Glowed into words, then would be savagely still.   110

"My nerves are bad to-night. Yes, bad. Stay with me.
"Speak to me. Why do you never speak. Speak.
     "What are you thinking of? What thinking? What?
"I never know what you are thinking. Think."

---

26. laquearia: V. *Aeneid*, I, 726: "dependent lychni laquearibus aureis incensi, et noctem flammis funalia vincunt." [Eliot's note] *Laquearia* is the plural form of the Latin word for a paneled ceiling, a reference to the description in Virgil's epic poem of the banquet hall where Queen Dido welcomes Aeneas and his men to Carthage: "Lighted lamps hung from the coffered ceiling / Rich with gold leaf, and torches with high flames / Prevailed over the night" (translated by Robert Fitzgerald).
27. sylvan scene: V. Milton, *Paradise Lost*, IV, 140. [Eliot's note] Eliot cites a line in a passage describing Satan's first view of Eden in the Christian epic by the English poet John Milton (1608-1674): "A Silvan Scene, and as the ranks ascend / Shade above shade, a woody Theatre / Of stateliest view."
28. **Philomel**: V. Ovid, *Metamorphoses*, VI, Philomela. [Eliot's note] Eliot refers to the story of Philomela, as told by the Roman poet Ovid (43 BCE-17 CE). In his version of the Greek myth, Philomela is raped by her sister's husband, the barbarian king Tereus of Thrace. Tereus cuts out Philomela's tongue to prevent her from telling the story, but she weaves a tapestry depicting the attack and sends it to her sister Procne. Together, the sisters take their revenge by killing Procne's son by Tereus, Itylus, and serving him as food to the king. When they reveal what he has eaten, Tereus pursues the sisters, and all three are transformed into birds. In some versions of the myth, Philomela becomes a nightingale; in others, she becomes a swallow.
29. So rudely . . . nightingale: Cf. Part III, l. 204. [Eliot's note] Eliot refers the reader ahead to line 204 of part III of the poem, "The Fire Sermon."
30. "Jug Jug" to dirty ears: "Jug, jug," the conventional poetic way of representing the nightingale's song, was also a crude slang expression for sexual intercourse. Here and in lines 204-6, Eliot echoes a song by the English poet and playwright John Lyly (1553-1606) about Philomela, "the ravish'd nightingale," who still cries out against the crime committed by King Tereus (Tereu): "Jug, jug, jug, jug, Tereu! She cries, / And still her woes at midnight rise."

I think we are in rats' alley[31]   115
Where the dead men lost their bones.

"What is that noise?"
                    The wind under the door.[32]
"What is that noise now? What is the wind doing?"
                    Nothing again nothing.   120
                                                    "Do
"You know nothing? Do you see nothing? Do you remember
"Nothing?"

            I remember
Those are pearls that were his eyes.   125
"Are you alive, or not? Is there nothing in your head?"[33]
                                                    But

O O O O that Shakespeherian Rag —
It's so elegant
So intelligent[34]   130
"What shall I do now? What shall I do?"
"I shall rush out as I am, and walk the street
"With my hair down, so. What shall we do tomorrow?
"What shall we ever do?"
                              The hot water at ten.   135
And if it rains, a closed car at four.
And we shall play a game of chess,
Pressing lidless eyes and waiting for a knock upon the door.[35]

When Lil's husband got demobbed,[36] I said —
I didn't mince my words, I said to her myself,   140
HURRY UP PLEASE ITS TIME[37]
Now Albert's coming back, make yourself a bit smart.

---

31. **I think . . . rat's alley:** Cf. Part III, l. 195. [Eliot's note] Eliot refers the reader ahead to line 195 of part III of the poem, "The Fire Sermon."

32. **The wind under the door:** Cf. Webster: "Is the wind in that door still?" [Eliot's note] A doctor attending to a victim of an attack thus asks if the patient is still alive in *The Devils Law Case,* a play by the English dramatist John Webster (d. 1625).

33. **Those are pearls . . . head?:** Cf. Part I, l. 37, 48. [Eliot's note] Eliot refers the reader back to lines 37[-40] and 48 of part I of the poem, "The Burial of the Dead." See note 15.

34. **O O O O . . . intelligent:** Eliot loosely quotes the refrain from a popular ragtime song published in 1912 and performed that year on Broadway in the Ziegfeld Follies: "That Shakespearian rag, / Most intelligent, very elegant."

35. **And we shall play . . . door:** Cf. the game of chess in Middleton's *Women beware Women.* [Eliot's note] See note 24.

36. **demobbed:** British slang term for *demobilized,* to be released from military service.

37. **HURRY . . . TIME:** The expression customarily used by bartenders to announce closing time in an English public house (pub).

He'll want to know what you done with that money he gave you
To get yourself some teeth. He did, I was there.
You have them all out, Lil, and get a nice set, 145
He said, I swear, I can't bear to look at you.
And no more can't I, I said, and think of poor Albert,
He's been in the army four years, he wants a good time,
And if you don't give it him, there's others will, I said.
Oh is there, she said. Something o' that, I said. 150
Then I'll know who to thank, she said, and give me a straight look.
HURRY UP PLEASE ITS TIME
If you don't like it you can get on with it, I said.
Others can pick and choose if you can't.
But if Albert makes off, it won't be for lack of telling. 155
You ought to be ashamed, I said, to look so antique.
(And her only thirty-one.)
I can't help it, she said, pulling a long face,
It's them pills I took, to bring it off, she said.
(She's had five already, and nearly died of young George.) 160
The chemist[38] said it would be all right, but I've never been the same.
You *are* a proper fool, I said.
Well, if Albert won't leave you alone, there it is, I said,
What you get married for if you don't want children?
HURRY UP PLEASE ITS TIME 165
Well, that Sunday Albert was home, they had a hot gammon,
And they asked me in to dinner, to get the beauty of it hot —
HURRY UP PLEASE ITS TIME
HURRY UP PLEASE ITS TIME
Goonight Bill. Goonight Lou. Goonight May. Goonight. 170
Ta ta. Goonight. Goonight.
Good night, ladies, good night, sweet ladies, good night, good night.[39]

III. The Fire Sermon[40]

The river's tent is broken; the last fingers of leaf
Clutch and sink into the wet bank. The wind
Crosses the brown land, unheard. The nymphs are departed. 175

---

38. **chemist:** British term for a pharmacist, who has given her the pills "to bring it off," that is, to induce an abortion.
39. **Good night . . . good night:** Ophelia, who later drowns herself, speaks these words at the end of a speech in her mad scene in Shakespeare's *Hamlet* (4.5.72-73).
40. **The Fire Sermon:** This sermon by the renowned religious teacher Siddartha Gautama (c. 563-483 BCE), known as the Buddha or the Enlightened One, was available in a standard textbook, *Buddhism in Translation* (1896), by Henry Clarke Warren, a professor at Harvard. Instructing a congregation of "priests," or

Sweet Thames, run softly, till I end my song.[41]
The river bears no empty bottles, sandwich papers,
Silk handkerchiefs, cardboard boxes, cigarette ends
Or other testimony of summer nights. The nymphs are departed.
And their friends, the loitering heirs of City directors;   180
Departed, have left no addresses.
By the waters of Leman I sat down and wept[42] . . .
Sweet Thames, run softly till I end my song,
Sweet Thames, run softly, for I speak not loud or long.
But at my back in a cold blast I hear   185
The rattle of the bones, and chuckle spread from ear to ear.[43]

A rat crept softly through the vegetation
Dragging its slimy belly on the bank
While I was fishing in the dull canal
On a winter evening round behind the gashouse   190
Musing upon the king my brother's wreck
And on the king my father's death[44] before him.
White bodies naked on the low damp ground
And bones cast in a little low dry garret,
Rattled by the rat's foot only, year to year.   195
But at my back from time to time I hear[45]
The sound of horns and motors,[46] which shall bring
Sweeney to Mrs. Porter in the spring.

---

monks, on the need to free themselves from the things of this world, including ideas and impressions received by the eye or the mind, "the Blessed One" declares: "All things, O priests, are on fire. . . . With the fire of passion, say I, with the fire of hatred, with the fire of infatuation; with birth, old age, death, sorrow lamentation, misery, grief, despair are they on fire."

41. **Sweet Thames . . . song:** V. Spenser, Prothalamion. [Eliot's note] Here and in lines 183–84, Eliot quotes the refrain to "Prothalamion," a poem celebrating marriage by the English poet Edmund Spenser (1552–1599).

42. **By . . . wept:** Compare Psalms 137:1: "By the rivers of Babylon, there we sat down, yea, we wept, when we remembered Zion." Eliot completed the first draft of *The Waste Land* during his stay at a sanatorium in Lausanne, a city on Lake Leman (another name for Lake Geneva) in Switzerland.

43. **But . . . ear to ear:** The lines echo lines 21–22 of "To His Coy Mistress" by the English poet Andrew Marvell (1621–1678): "But at my back I always hear / Time's wingèd chariot hurrying near."

44. **And on the king my father's death:** Cf. *The Tempest*, I, ii. [Eliot's note] In this scene in Shakespeare's play, following a shipwreck in which Prince Ferdinand believes that his father has drowned, he is comforted by the song of the sprite Ariel: "Sitting on a bank, / Weeping again the king my father's wrack, / This music crept by me upon the waters, / Allaying both their fury, and my passion, / With its sweet air" (1.2.387–91). See note 15.

45. **But . . . I hear:** Cf. Marvell, "To His Coy Mistress." [Eliot's note] See note 43.

46. **The sound of horns and motors:** Cf. Day, *Parliament of Bees:* "When of the sudden, listening, you shall hear, / A noise of horns and hunting, which shall bring / Actaeon to Diana in the spring, / Where all shall see her naked skin . . . ." [Eliot's note] The lines are from a pastoral poem about "the doings, the births, the wars, the wooings" of bees by the English poet and playwright John Day (1574–1640). In Greek mythology, Actaeon was a hunter who was changed into a stag and killed by his own dogs as punishment for seeing the naked body of Artemis (Diana in Roman mythology), the goddess of virginity.

O the moon shone bright on Mrs. Porter
And on her daughter   200
They wash their feet in soda water[47]
Et O ces voix d'enfants, chantant dans la coupole![48]

Twit twit twit
Jug jug jug jug jug jug
So rudely forc'd.   205
Tereu[49]

Unreal City
Under the brown fog of a winter noon
Mr. Eugenides, the Smyrna merchant[50]
Unshaven, with a pocket full of currants   210
C.i.f. London:[51] documents at sight,
Asked me in demotic French[52]
To luncheon at the Cannon Street Hotel
Followed by a weekend at the Metropole.[53]

At the violet hour, when the eyes and back   215
Turn upward from the desk, when the human engine waits
Like a taxi throbbing waiting,
I Tiresias,[54] though blind, throbbing between two lives,

---

47. **O the moon . . . soda water:** I do not know the origin of the ballad from which these lines are taken: it was reported to me from Sydney, Australia. [Eliot's note] In his version of this so-called ballad, Eliot expurgated the lyrics of an obscene song popular with soldiers about the "madam" of a brothel whose prostitutes were notorious for infecting their clients with venereal disease.

48. *Et . . . coupole!*: V. Verlaine, *Parsifal.* [Eliot's note] Eliot quotes the last line of a sonnet by the French poet Paul Verlaine (1844–1896): " — And, o those voices of children singing in the dome!" Verlaine's sonnet refers to the final scene of Richard Wagner's opera *Parsifal,* in which the Arthurian knight recovers the Holy Spear that pierced Christ's side at the Crucifixion. Returning to the Grail Castle, Parsifal heals Amfortas, the Fisher King, with a touch of the Holy Spear.

49. **Jug jug . . . Tereu:** See note 30.

50. **Mr. Eugenides, the Smyrna merchant:** Smyrna, a port city on the coast of Asia Minor, was the focus of the Greco-Turkish War of 1919–22. After the Greek occupation force withdrew in 1921, Turkish troops massacred 30,000 Christian inhabitants of the city, present-day Izmir.

51. **C.i.f. London:** The currants were quoted at a price "carriage and insurance free to London"; and the Bill of Lading, etc., were to be handed to the buyer upon payment of the sight draft. [Eliot's note]

52. **demotic French:** Colloquial French, the speech used by ordinary people as opposed to correct or learned language.

53. **Cannon Street Hotel . . . Metropole:** A hotel then attached to the Cannon Street Station, a busy railroad terminal for travelers to and from the Continent, and a large resort hotel in Brighton, on the southern coast of England.

54. **I Tiresias . . . two lives:** Tiresias, although a mere spectator and not indeed a "character," is yet the most important personage in the poem, uniting all the rest. Just as the one-eyed merchant, seller of currants, melts into the Phoenician Sailor, and the latter is not wholly distinct from Ferdinand Prince of Naples, so all the women are one woman, and the two sexes meet in Tiresias. What Tiresias *sees,* in fact, is the substance of the poem. The whole passage from Ovid is of great anthropological interest. [Eliot's note] In the note, Eliot quotes in the original Latin the passage from "Tiresias" from the *Metamorphoses,* which A. D. Melville has translated: ". . . it chanced that Jove [Zeus], / Well warmed with nectar, laid his mighty cares / Aside and,

Old man with wrinkled female breasts, can see
At the violet hour, the evening hour that strives   220
Homeward, and brings the sailor home from sea,[55]
The typist home at teatime, clears her breakfast, lights
Her stove, and lays out food in tins.
Out of the window perilously spread
Her drying combinations[56] touched by the sun's last rays,   225
On the divan are piled (at night her bed)
Stockings, slippers, camisoles, and stays.
I Tiresias, old man with wrinkled dugs
Perceived the scene, and foretold the rest —
I too awaited the expected guest.   230
He, the young man carbuncular, arrives,
A small house agent's clerk, with one bold stare,
One of the low on whom assurance sits
As a silk hat on a Bradford millionaire.[57]
The time is now propitious, as he guesses,   235
The meal is ended, she is bored and tired,
Endeavours to engage her in caresses
Which still are unreproved, if undesired.
Flushed and decided, he assaults at once;
Exploring hands encounter no defence;   240
His vanity requires no response,
And makes a welcome of indifference.
(And I Tiresias have foresuffered all
Enacted on this same divan or bed;

Juno too in idle mood, / The pair were gaily joking, and Jove said / 'You women get more pleasure out of love / Than we men do, I'm sure.' She disagreed. / So they resolved to get the views of wise / Tiresias. He knew both sides of love. / For once in a green copse when two huge snakes / Were mating, he attacked them with his stick, / And was transformed (a miracle!) from man / To woman; and spent seven autumns so; / Till in the eighth he saw the snakes once more / And said 'If striking you has magic power / To change the striker to the other sex, / I'll strike you now again.' He struck the snakes / And so regained the shape he had at birth. / Asked then to give his judgment on the joke, / He found for Jove; and Juno (so it's said) / Took umbrage beyond reason, out of all / Proportion, and condemned her judge to live / In the black night of blindness ever-more. / But the Almighty Father (since no god / Has the right to undo what any god has done) / For his lost sight gave him the gift to see / What things should come, the power and prophesy, / An honor to relieve that penalty."

55. At the violet hour . . . from the sea: This may not appear as exact as Sappho's lines, but I had in mind the "longshore" or "dory" fisherman, who returns at nightfall. [Eliot's note] Eliot refers to a fragment of verse by the ancient Greek lyric poet Sappho: "Dusk and western star, / You gather / What glittering sunrise / Scattered far, / The ewe to fold, / Kid and nanny home, / But the daughter / You send wandering / From her mother" (translated by Guy Davenport).

56. Her drying combinations: *Combination* was a term for a woman's undergarment that combined a chemise and panties.

57. Bradford millionaire: Bradford, a textile center in Yorkshire, England, had boomed as a result of the demand for uniforms and blankets for the military during World War I.

I who have sat by Thebes below the wall   245
And walked among the lowest of the dead.)
Bestows one final patronising kiss,
And gropes his way, finding the stairs unlit . . .

She turns and looks a moment in the glass,
Hardly aware of her departed lover;   250
Her brain allows one half-formed thought to pass:
"Well now that's done: and I'm glad it's over."
When lovely woman stoops to folly[58] and
Paces about her room again, alone,
She smoothes her hair with automatic hand,   255
And puts a record on the gramophone.

"This music crept by me upon the waters"[59]
And along the Strand, up Queen Victoria Street.
O City city, I can sometimes hear
Beside a public bar in Lower Thames Street,   260
The pleasant whining of a mandoline
And a clatter and a chatter from within
Where fishmen lounge at noon: where the walls
Of Magnus Martyr[60] hold
Inexplicable splendour of Ionian white and gold.   265

      The river sweats[61]
      Oil and tar
      The barges drift

---

58. **When . . . stoops to folly:** V. Goldsmith, the song in *The Vicar of Wakefield.* [Eliot's note] In chapter 24 of the novel by the Irish author Oliver Goldsmith (1728-1774), the vicar's daughter Olivia sings a song about her seduction: "When Lovely woman stoops to folly, / And finds too late that men betray, / What charm can soothe her melancholy, / What art can wash her guilt away? / The only art her guilt to cover, / To hide her shame from every eye, / To give repentance to her lover, / And wring his bosom — is to die."

59. **"This . . . waters":** V. *The Tempest,* as above. [Eliot's note] See note 44. In the following passage, Eliot refers to streets in London running parallel to or toward the River Thames.

60. **Magnus Martyr:** The interior of St. Magnus Martyr is to my mind one of the finest among Wren's interiors. See *The Proposed Demolition of Nineteen City Churches* (P. S. King & Son, Ltd.). [Eliot's note] Eliot in the following line refers to the graceful Ionic columns in the interior of the church, designed by the celebrated English architect Sir Christopher Wren (1632-1723).

61. **The river sweats:** The Song of the (three) Thames-daughters begins here. From line 292 to 306 inclusive they speak in turn. V. *Götterdämmerung,* III, i: the Rhine-daughters. [Eliot's note] Eliot refers to an opera by the German composer Richard Wagner (1813-1883), *Die Götterdämmerung (The Twilight of the Gods).* In an earlier opera, *Das Rheingold,* the Rhine-daughters, guardians of a great lump of pure gold laid upon the highest rock in the river, swim around the rock and sing about the gold, repeatedly expressing their joy in the ecstatic cry "Weialala leia wallala leialala" (see lines 277-78 and 291-92). The gold is later stolen, and the Rhine-daughters reappear at the opening of act III of *Die Götterdämmerung,* where they sing of the beauty it had bestowed upon the river: "Once there was light, / When clear and fair / Our father's gold shone on the billows. / Rhinegold! / Gleaming gold! / How bright was once thy radiance, / Lovely star of the waters!"

With the turning tide
Red sails   270
Wide
To leeward, swing on the heavy spar.
The barges wash
Drifting logs
Down Greenwich reach   275
Past the Isla of Dogs.[62]
        Weialala leia
        Wallala leialala

Elizabeth and Leicester[63]
Beating oars   280
The stern was formed
A gilded shell
Red and gold
The brisk swell
Rippled both shores   285
Southwest wind
Carried down stream
The peal of bells
White towers
        Weialala leia   290
        Wallala leialala

"Trams and dusty trees.
Highbury bore me. Richmond and Kew
Undid me.[64] By Richmond I raised my knees
Supine on the floor of a narrow canoe."   295

---

62. **Isle of Dogs:** A peninsula in the estuary of the River Thames across from Greenwich. Past that point, the river is called the Greenwich Reach.

63. **Elizabeth and Leicester:** V. Froude, *Elizabeth*, Vol. I, ch. iv, letter of De Quadra to Philip of Spain: "In the afternoon we were in a barge, watching the games on the river. (The queen) was alone with Lord Robert and myself on the poop, when they began to talk nonsense, and went so far that Lord Robert at last said, as I was on the spot there was no reason why they should not be married if the queen pleased." [Eliot's note] Eliot refers to the *History of England from the Fall of Wolsey to the Death of Elizabeth* (1863) by James Anthony Froude (1818-1894), who translates an account by the Spanish ambassador at Queen Elizabeth's court of her flirtation with the Catholic Robert Dudley, Earl of Leicester.

64. **"Highbury bore me. Richmond and Kew / Undid me":** Cf. *Purgatorio*, V. 133: "Ricorditi di me, che son la Pia; / Siena mi fe', disfecemi Maremma." [Eliot's note] Eliot refers to a passage in which the spirit of a woman who had been born in Sienna and murdered by her husband in Maremma, an area of southern Tuscany, asks Dante: "Kindly remember me — my name is Pia. / Maremma unmade what Sienna made." Highbury is a suburb of London; Richmond, a residential area along the Thames, is bordered by Kew, home of Kew Gardens.

"My feet are at Moorgate,[65] and my heart
Under my feet. After the event
He wept. He promised 'a new start.'
I made no comment. What should I resent?"

"On Margate Sands.[66]   300
I can connect
Nothing with nothing.
The broken fingernails of dirty hands.
My people humble people who expect
Nothing."   305
                    la la

To Carthage then I came[67]

Burning burning burning burning[68]
O Lord Thou pluckest me out[69]
O Lord Thou pluckest   310

burning

IV. Death by Water

Phlebas the Phoenician,[70] a fortnight dead,
Forgot the cry of gulls, and the deep sea swell
And the profit and loss.

                    A current under sea   315
Picked his bones in whispers. As he rose and fell

---

65. **Moorgate:** A slum in east London.
66. **Margate Sands:** The beach at Margate, a modest seaside resort on the estuary of the River Thames about seventy miles east of London.
67. **To Carthage . . . came:** V. St. Augustine's *Confessions:* "to Carthage then I came, where a cauldron of unholy loves sang all about mine ears." [Eliot's note] Eliot refers to a passage in the spiritual autobiography of St. Augustine (354-430), the bishop of Hippo in North Africa.
68. **Burning . . . burning:** The complete text of the Buddha's Fire Sermon (which corresponds in importance to the Sermon on the Mount) from which these words are taken, will be found translated in the late Henry Clarke Warren's *Buddhism in Translation* (Harvard Oriental Series). Mr. Warren was one of the great pioneers of Buddhist studies in the Occident. [Eliot's note] See note 40.
69. **O Lord . . . out:** From St. Augustine's *Confessions* again. The collocation of these two representatives of eastern and western asceticism, as the culmination of this part of the poem, is not an accident. [Eliot's note] See note 67.
70. **Phlebas the Phoenician:** Phoenicia, an ancient civilization centered in present-day Lebanon, rose to prominence through commerce and its extensive maritime trade in the Mediterranean. See "the drowned Phoenician sailor," one of the Tarot cards read by Madame Sosostris (line 47), and her warning "Fear death by water" (line 55).

He passed the stages of his age and youth
Entering the whirlpool.

Gentile or Jew

O you who turn the wheel and look to windward,   320
Consider Phlebas, who was once handsome and tall as you.

V. What the Thunder Said[71]

After the torchlight red on sweaty faces
After the frosty silence in the gardens
After the agony in stony places
The shouting and the crying   325
Prison and palace and reverberation
Of thunder of spring over distant mountains
He who was living is now dead
We who were living are now dying
With a little patience[72]   330

Here is no water but only rock
Rock and no water and the sandy road
The road winding above among the mountains
Which are mountains of rock without water
If there were water we should stop and drink   335
Amongst the rock one cannot stop or think
Sweat is dry and feet are in the sand
If there were only water amongst the rock
Dead mountain mouth of carious teeth that cannot spit
Here one can neither stand nor lie nor sit   340
There is not even silence in the mountains
But dry sterile thunder without rain
There is not even solitude in the mountains
But red sullen faces sneer and snarl
From doors of mudcracked houses   345
              If there were water
     And no rock

---

71. **What the Thunder Said:** In the first part of Part V three themes are employed: the journey to Emmaus, the approach to the Chapel Perilous (see Miss Weston's book), and the present decay of eastern Europe. [Eliot's note] In the chapter "The Perilous Chapel" in Jessie Weston's *From Ritual to Romance* (see note 1), she summarizes the dangers and terrors the heroes of Grail romances encounter in the Chapel Perilous, where "the general impression is that this is an adventure in which supernatural, and evil, forces are engaged." For the journey to Emmaus, during which the resurrected Jesus walks and converses with his disciples, who do not recognize him, see Luke 24:13-34.

72. **After the torchlight . . . patience:** This first stanza alludes to the biblical account of the arrest, imprisonment, trial, and crucifixion of Jesus.

It there were rock
And also water
And water   350
A spring
A pool among the rock
If there were the sound of water only
Not the cicada
And dry grass singing   355
But sound of water over a rock
Where the hermit-thrush[73] sings in the pine trees
Drip drop drip drop drop drop drop
But there is no water

Who is the third who walks always beside you?[74]   360
When I count, there are only you and I together
But when I look ahead up the white road
There is always another one walking beside you
Gliding wrapt in a brown mantle, hooded
I do not know whether a man or a woman   365
— But who is that on the other side of you?

What is that sound high in the air[75]
Murmur of maternal lamentation
Who are those hooded hordes swarming
Over endless plains, stumbling in cracked earth   370
Ringed by the flat horizon only
What is the city over the mountains
Cracks and reforms and bursts in the violet air
Falling towers

---

73. **hermit-thrush:** This is *Turdus aonalaschkae pallasii*, the hermit-thrush which I have heard in Quebec County. Chapman says (*Handbook of Birds in Eastern North America*) "it is most at home in secluded woodland and thickety retreats. . . . Its notes are not remarkable for variety or volume, but in purity and sweetness of tone and exquisite modulation they are unequalled." Its "water-dripping song" is justly celebrated. [Eliot's note]

74. **Who . . . beside you?:** The following lines were stimulated by the account of one of the Antarctic expeditions (I forget which, but I think one of Shackleton's): "it was related that the party of explorers, at the extremity of their strength, had the constant delusion that there was *one more member* than could actually be counted." [Eliot's note] Sir Ernest Henry Shackleton (1874-1922) was a British explorer of the Antarctic.

75. **What . . . air:** Cf. Hermann Hesse, *Blick ins Chaos*. [Eliot's note] In the note, Eliot quotes in the original German a passage from an essay on the downfall of Europe in *Blick ins Chaos* (*In Sight of Chaos*) by the poet and novelist Hermann Hesse (1877-1962). The book so impressed Eliot that he encouraged his friend Sydney Schiff to translate it into English. Schiff, who published under the pseudonym Stephen Hudson, translated the passage: "Already half Europe, at all events half Eastern Europe, is on the road to Chaos. In a state of drunken illusion she is reeling into the abyss and, as she reels, she sings a drunken hymn such as Dmitri Karamazov sang [in Fyodor Dostoyevsky's novel *The Brothers Karamazov* (1882)]. The insulted citizen laughs that song to scorn, the saint and seer hear it with tears."

Jerusalem Athens Alexandria   375
Vienna London
Unreal

A woman drew her long black hair out tight
And fiddled whisper music on those strings
And bats with baby faces in the violet light   380
Whistled, and beat their wings
And crawled head downward down a blackened wall
And upside down in air were towers
Tolling reminiscent bells, that kept the hours
And voices singing out of empty cisterns and exhausted wells   385

In this decayed hole among the mountains
In the faint moonlight, the grass is singing
Over the tumbled graves, about the chapel
There is the empty chapel, only the wind's home.
It has no windows, and the door swings,   390
Dry bones can harm no one.
Only a cock stood on the rooftree
Co co rico co co rico[76]
In a flash of lightning. Then a damp gust
Bringing rain   395

Ganga[77] was sunken, and the limp leaves
Waited for rain, while the black clouds
Gathered far distant, over Himavant.[78]
The jungle crouched, humped in silence.
Then spoke the thunder   400

DA
Datta:[79] what have we given?
My friend, blood shaking my heart
The awful daring of a moment's surrender
Which an age of prudence can never retract   405

---

76. **Co co rico co co rico:** *Cocorico* is a French and Italian word that approximates the sound of the crowing of a rooster, associated in folklore with the coming of dawn and the consequent departure of evil spirits.
77. **Ganga:** The Ganges, the sacred river in India, personified by the Hindu goddess Ganga.
78. **Himavant:** The Sanskrit word for *snowy,* applied to mountains in the Himalayas.
79. **Datta:** "Datta, dayadhvam, damyata" (Give, sympathise, control). The fable of the meaning of the Thunder is found in the *Brihadaranyaka — Upanishad,* 5, 1. A translation is found in Deussen's *Sechzig Upanishads des Veda,* p. 489. [Eliot's note] Eliot refers to the fable of the Thunder in the Upanishads, ancient Hindu texts written in Sanskrit. In the fable, the Lord of Creation, Prajapati, utters the word *da* (the Sanskrit word representing the sound of thunder) to his three kinds of offspring: lesser gods, who understand it as "Control yourselves" (damyata); men, who understand it as "Give" (datta); and demons, who understand it as "Be compassionate" (dayadhvam).

By this, and this only, we have existed
Which is not to be found in our obituaries
Or in memories draped by the beneficent spider[80]
Or under seals broken by the lean solicitor
In our empty rooms   410
DA
Dayadhvam: I have heard the key[81]
Turn in the door once and turn once only
We think of the key, each in his prison
Thinking of the key, each confirms a prison   415
Only at nightfall, aethereal rumours
Revive for a moment a broken Coriolanus[82]
DA
Damyata: The boat responded
Gaily, to the hand expert with sail and oar   420
The sea was calm, your heart would have responded
Gaily, when invited, beating obedient
To controlling hands

I sat upon the shore

Fishing,[83] with the arid plain behind me   425
Shall I at least set my lands in order?[84]
London Bridge is falling down falling down falling down
Poi s'ascose nel foco che gli affina[85]

---

80. **Or in memories . . . spider**: Cf. Webster, *The White Devil*, V, vi: ". . . they'll remarry / Ere the worm
pierce your winding-sheet, ere the spider / Make a thin curtain for your epitaphs." [Eliot's note] The lines are
spoken by the murderous villain of the play, Flamineo, who discovers that his sister has betrayed him and
bitterly cautions men on their deathbeds not to trust their ostensibly grieving wives, who will swiftly find
new husbands. See note 22.
81. **I have heard the key**: Cf. *Inferno*, XXXIII, 46: "ed io sentii chiavar l'uscio di sotto / all'orribile torre." Also
F. H. Bradley, *Appearance and Reality*, p. 346: "My external sensations are no less private to myself than are
my thoughts or my feelings. In either case my experience falls within my own circle, a circle closed on the
outside; and, with all its elements alike, every sphere is opaque to the others which surround it. . . . In brief,
regarded as an existence which appears in a soul, the whole world for each is peculiar and private to that
soul." [Eliot's note] The line from the *Inferno* is spoken by the traitor Ugolino, who tells Dante how his enemies imprisoned him and his children, leaving them to die of starvation: "And I could hear them nailing up
the door / of the horrible tower." *Appearance and Reality: A Metaphysical Essay* (1893) was written by the
English idealist philosopher Francis Herbert Bradley (1846–1924).
82. **Coriolanus**: The tragic hero of Shakespeare's play *Coriolanus* (1608), a proud and patrician Roman general who is driven into exile and seeks revenge by leading enemy forces against Rome.
83. **Fishing**: V. Weston, *From Ritual to Romance;* chapter on the Fisher King. [Eliot's note] See note 1.
84. **Shall I . . . order?**: See Isaiah 38:1: "Thus saith the LORD, Set thine house in order: for thou shalt die, and
not live."
85. **Poi . . . affina**: V. *Purgatorio*, XXVI, 148. "'Ara vos prec per aquella valor / que vos guida al som de
l'escalina, / sovegna vos a temps de ma dolor.' / Poi s'ascose nel foco che gli affina." [Eliot's note] The words
are spoken to Dante by the spirit of the Provençal poet Arnaut Daniel, speaking amid the purifying flames of
the ring of lust in purgatory: "'And so I beg of you, by that same power / that leads you to the summit of the
stairs, / at the just time recall my sufferings.' / At that he hid in the refining fire." See note 3.

Quando fiam uti chelidon[86] — O swallow swallow
Le Prince d'Aquitaine à la tour abolie[87]   430
These fragments I have shored against my ruins
Why then Ile fit you. Hieronymo's mad againe.[88]
Datta. Dayadhvam. Damyata.
                 Shantih   shantih   shantih[89]

[1922, 1963]

---

86. **Quando . . . chelidon:** V. *Pervigilium Veneris.* Cf. Philomela in Parts II and III. [Eliot's note] Eliot quotes part of a line from an anonymous, fourth-century Latin poem, "The Vigil of Venus," in which Philomela asks: "When shall I become like the swallow," continuing "that I cease to be silent?" See note 28.

87. **Le prince . . . abolie:** V. Gerard de Nerval, Sonnet *El Desdichado.* [Eliot's note] Eliot quotes the second line from "The Disinherited," a sonnet by the French poet Gerard de Nerval (1808-1855), which begins: "I am the dark one, – the widower, – the unconsoled, / The Prince of Aquitaine at his stricken tower" (translated by Robert Duncan).

88. **Why then . . . mad againe:** V. Kyd's *Spanish Tragedy.* [Eliot's note] The subtitle of the play by the English dramatist Thomas Kyd (1557?-1595) is *Hieronymo Is Mad Againe.* When asked to write a play to entertain the Spanish court, Hieronimo readily agrees, saying: "Why then I'll fit [accommodate] you." He convinces the murderers of his son to act in the play, during the performance of which Hieronimo and a confederate kill them. Significantly, given the mingling of languages in *The Waste Land,* Hieronimo writes the various roles in the play in "unknown languages" – Greek, Latin, Italian, and French – "That it may breed the more variety."

89. **Shantih . . . shantih:** Repeated as here, a formal ending to an Upanishad. "The Peace which passeth understanding" is our equivalent to this word. [Eliot's note] The Upanishads are a series of Hindu treatises written in Sanskrit (c. 800-200 BCE). The ending of an Upanishad is similar to the benediction offered by Paul in Philippians 4:7: "And the peace of God, which passeth all understanding, shall keep your hearts and minds through Jesus Christ."

Eliot's "Journey of the Magi."   In June 1927, Eliot was baptized and confirmed in the Church of England. Later that year, this poem appeared as a pamphlet in a series, the Ariel poems, short works produced for the Christmas season by Eliot's London publisher, Faber and Faber. Like the later poems Eliot wrote for the series, which he gathered together in his *Collected Poems, 1909-1935,* "The Journey of the Magi" concerns spiritual growth and a religious quest, in this case the journey of the three wise men who, according to the biblical account, witness the newborn Jesus. The dramatic monologue also anticipated a persistent concern in Eliot's later poetry and drama, the effects produced by the irruption of supernatural elements into everyday life. The text is taken from Eliot's *Collected Poems 1909-1962* (1963).

JOURNEY OF THE MAGI[1]

"A cold coming we had of it,
Just the worst time of the year
For a journey, and such a long journey:

---

1. **Magi:** The three wise men from the East who followed the star of Bethlehem and brought gifts to the infant Jesus (Matthew 2:1-12).

The ways deep and the weather sharp,
The very dead of winter."[2]   5
And the camels galled, sore-footed, refractory,
Lying down in the melting snow.
There were times we regretted
The summer palaces on slopes, the terraces,
And the silken girls bringing sherbet.   10
Then the camel men cursing and grumbling
And running away, and wanting their liquor and women,
And the night-fires going out, and the lack of shelters,
And the cities hostile and the towns unfriendly
And the villages dirty and charging high prices: 15
A hard time we had of it.
At the end we preferred to travel all night,
Sleeping in snatches,
With the voices singing in our ears, saying
That this was all folly.   20

Then at dawn we came down to a temperate valley,
Wet, below the snow line, smelling of vegetation,
With a running stream and a water-mill beating the darkness,
And three trees on the low sky.
And an old white horse galloped away in the meadow.   25
Then we came to a tavern with vine-leaves over the lintel,
Six hands at an open door dicing for pieces of silver,
And feet kicking the empty wine-skins.
But there was no information, and so we continued
And arrived at evening, not a moment too soon   30
Finding the place; it was (you may say) satisfactory.

All this was a long time ago, I remember,
And I would do it again, but set down
This set down
This: were we led all that way for   35
Birth or Death? There was a Birth, certainly,
We had evidence and no doubt. I had seen birth and death,
But had thought they were different; this Birth was
Hard and bitter agony for us, like Death, our death.
We returned to our places, these Kingdoms,   40
But no longer at ease here, in the old dispensation,
With an alien people clutching their gods.
I should be glad of another death.

[1927, 1963]

---

2. **"A cold coming . . . dead of winter"**: The quotation is adapted from a famous Christmas sermon delivered
in 1622 by Bishop Lancelot Andrewes, the renowned Anglican preacher and cleric who oversaw the translation of the authorized King James Version of the Bible.

Eliot's "Burnt Norton."   Eliot wrote this poem soon after he completed *Murder in the Cathedral*, his verse play about the killing in 1170 of Thomas Becket, the archbishop of Canterbury (1935). The poem was most directly inspired by Eliot's visit to Burnt Norton, an abandoned eighteenth-century manor house in southern England, which he toured during the summer of 1934. (The house was called Burnt Norton because the original structure had been destroyed by a fire set by its owner in 1737.) Eliot was especially taken with the extensive rose gardens, which figure prominently in "Burnt Norton." Eliot first published it as the final poem in his *Collected Poems 1909-1935*. At that point, he apparently did not conceive of the poem as the first in a series, but after World War II began in September 1939, Eliot wrote three additional poems similar in tone and structure to "Burnt Norton" – "East Coker," "The Dry Salvages," and "Little Gidding." He published the group of poems as *Four Quartets* (1943). In the later poems in the sequence, Eliot continued to explore the questions he meditated upon in "Burnt Norton," including the nature of time, the limitations of language and human knowledge, the consequent struggle for religious faith, and the Christian meaning of redemption. The text is taken from the first printing of the poem in Eliot's *Collected Poems 1909-1935* (1936).

Burnt Norton

τοῦ λόγου δ'ἐόντος ξυνοῦ ζώουσιν οἱ πολλοὶ
ὡς ἰδίαν ἔχοντες φρόνησιν.

I. p. 77. Fr. 2.

ὁδὸς ἄνω κάτω μία καὶ ὡυτή.

I. p. 89. Fr. 60.

Diels. *Die Fragmente der Vorsokratiker* (Herakleitos).[1]

I

Time present and time past
Are both perhaps present in time future,
And time future contained in time past.[2]
If all time is eternally present

---

1. **[epigraphs]:** The two epigraphs are from the surviving fragments of the writings of the Greek philosopher Heraclitus (c. 540-475 BCE), as compiled in 1903 by the German classical scholar Hermann Diels (1848-1922) in *Die Fragmente der Vorsokratiker* (*The Fragments of the Pre-Socratics*). Heraclitus argued that stability is illusory, since change is universal, and all things are in flux. As translated by Kathleen Freeman, the two passages Eliot quotes read: (1) "But although the Law is universal, the majority live as if they had understanding peculiar to themselves." (2) "The way up and down is one and the same."
2. **Time . . . in time past:** Eliot echoes Ecclesiastes 3:15: "That which hath been is now; and that which is to be hath already been; and God requireth that which is past."

All time is unredeemable.   5
What might have been is an abstraction
Remaining a perpetual possibility
Only in a world of speculation.
What might have been and what has been
Point to one end, which is always present.   10
Footfalls echo in the memory
Down the passage which we did not take
Towards the door we never opened
Into the rose-garden. My words echo
Thus, in your mind.   15
　　　　　　　　　But to what purpose
Disturbing the dust on a bowl of rose-leaves
I do not know.
　　　　　　　　　Other echoes
Inhabit the garden. Shall we follow?   20
Quick, said the bird, find them, find them,
Round the corner. Through the first gate,
Into our first world, shall we follow
The deception of the thrush? Into our first world.
There they were, dignified, invisible,   25
Moving without pressure, over the dead leaves,
In the autumn heat, through the vibrant air,
And the bird called, in response to
The unheard music hidden in the shrubbery,
And the unseen eyebeam crossed, for the roses   30
Had the look of flowers that are looked at.
There they were as our guests, accepted and accepting.
So we moved, and they, in a formal pattern,
Along the empty alley, into the box circle,[3]
To look down into the drained pool.   35
Dry the pool, dry concrete, brown edged,
And the pool was filled with water out of sunlight,
And the lotos rose,[4] quietly, quietly,
The surface glittered out of heart of light,[5]
And they were behind us, reflected in the pool.   40

---

3. **box circle:** Boxwood shrubs, planted in a circle.
4. **lotos rose:** The lotus is any of a large number of floating water plants, perhaps in this case the "sacred lotus," an Asiatic variety bearing dark pink flowers.
5. **out of heart of light:** Eliot alludes to a passage in *Paradiso,* the final volume of the *Divine Comedy* by the Italian poet Dante Alighieri (1265-1321), in which the poet passes upward among the blessed souls in the heaven of the Sun: "From the heart of one of the new lights there came a voice" (12.28-29, as translated by Charles Singleton).

Then a cloud passed, and the pool was empty.
Go, said the bird, for the leaves were full of children,
Hidden excitedly, containing laughter.
Go, go, go, said the bird: human kind
Cannot bear very much reality.   45
Time past and time future
What might have been and what has been
Point to one end, which is always present.

II

Garlic and sapphires in the mud
Clot the bedded axle-tree.[6]   50
The trilling wire in the blood
Sings below inveterate scars
And reconciles forgotten wars.
The dance along the artery
The circulation of the lymph   55
Are figured in the drift of stars
Ascend to summer in the tree
We move above the moving tree
In light upon the figured leaf
And hear upon the sodden floor   60
Below, the boarhound and the boar
Pursue their pattern as before
But reconciled among the stars.

At the still point of the turning world. Neither flesh nor fleshless;
Neither from nor towards; at the still point, there the dance is,   65
But neither arrest nor movement. And do not call it fixity.
Where past and future are gathered. Neither movement from nor
    towards,
Neither ascent nor decline. Except for the point, the still point,
There would be no dance, and there is only the dance.
I can only say, *there* we have been: but I cannot say where.   70
And I cannot say, how long, for that is to place it in time.

The inner freedom from the practical desire,
The release from action and suffering, release from the inner
And the outer compulsion, yet surrounded

---

6. **axle-tree:** A rod supporting a cart with terminal spindles on which the wheels turn; also, in Christian cosmology, the "axletree" of heaven, around which the universe revolves.

By a grace of sense, a white light still and moving,   75
Erhebung[7] without motion, concentration
Without elimination, both a new world
And the old made explicit, understood
In the completion of its partial ecstasy,
The resolution of its partial horror.   80
Yet the enchainment of past and future
Woven in the weakness of the changing body,
Protects mankind from heaven and damnation
Which flesh cannot endure.
               Time past and time future   85
Allow but a little consciousness.
To be conscious is not to be in time
But only in time can the moment in the rose-garden,
The moment in the arbour where the rain beat,
The moment in the draughty church at smoke-fall   90
Be remembered; involved with past and future.
Only through time time is conquered.

III

Here is a place of disaffection
Time before and time after
In a dim light:[8] neither daylight   95
Investing form with lucid stillness
Turning shadow into transient beauty
With slow rotation suggesting permanence
Nor darkness to purify the soul
Emptying the sensual with deprivation   100
Cleansing affection from the temporal.
Neither plenitude nor vacancy. Only a flicker
Over the strained time-ridden faces
Distracted from distraction by distraction
Filled with fancies and empty of meaning   105
Tumid apathy with no concentration
Men and bits of paper, whirled by the cold wind
That blows before and after time,
Wind in and out of unwholesome lungs
Time before and time after.   110

---

7. *Erhebung:* Exaltation (German).
8. **Here . . . dim light:** This section of the poem is set in the London subway system, the Underground.

Eructation[9] of unhealthy souls
Into the faded air, the torpid
Driven on the wind that sweeps the gloomy hills of London,
Hampstead and Clerkenwell, Campden and Putney,
Highgate, Primrose and Ludgate.[10] Not here   115
Not here the darkness, in this twittering world.

Descend lower, descend only
Into the world of perpetual solitude,
World not world, but that which is not world,
Internal darkness, deprivation   120
And destitution of all property,
Dessication of the world of sense,
Evacuation of the world of fancy,
Inoperancy of the world of spirit;[11]
This is the one way, and the other   125
Is the same, not in movement
But abstention from movement; while the world moves
In appetency,[12] on its metalled ways
Of time past and time future.

IV

Time and the bell have buried the day,   130
The black cloud carries the sun away.
Will the sunflower turn to us, will the clematis
Stray down, bend to us; tendril and spray
Clutch and cling?
Chill   135
Fingers of yew be curled
Down on us?[13] After the kingfisher's wing

---

9. **Eructation:** Belching.
10. **Hampstead . . . Ludgate:** Names of various sections and neighborhoods in London.
11. **Descend lower . . . world of spirit:** In his treatise *Dark Night of the Soul,* the Spanish mystic St. John of the Cross (1542–1591) described a process of contemplation that "produces in spiritual persons two kinds of darkness or purgation," explaining: "And thus the one night or purgation will be sensual, wherein the soul is purged according to sense, which is subdued to the spirit; and the other is a night or purgation which is spiritual, wherein the soul is purged and stripped according to the spirit, and subdued and made ready for the union of love with God" (translated by E. Allison Peers).
12. **appetency:** An early term for longing or desire.
13. **Fingers of yew . . . on us?:** The yew is a long-lived coniferous tree often associated with graveyards, as in a famous passage from *In Memoriam* by the English poet Alfred, Lord Tennyson (1809–1892): "Old Yew, which graspest at the stones / That name the under-lying dead, / Thy fibres net the dreamless head, / Thy roots are wrapt about the bones" (II.1–4).

Has answered light to light, and is silent, the light is still
At the still point of the turning world.

V

Words move, music moves   140
Only in time; but that which is only living
Can only die. Words, after speech, reach
Into the silence. Only by the form, the pattern,
Can words or music reach
The stillness, as a Chinese jar still   145
Moves perpetually in its stillness.
Not the stillness of the violin, while the note lasts,
Not that only, but the co-existence,
Or say that the end precedes the beginning,
And the end and the beginning were always there   150
Before the beginning and after the end.
And all is always now. Words strain,
Crack and sometimes break, under the burden,
Under the tension, slip, slide, perish,
Decay with imprecision, will not stay in place,   155
Will not stay still. Shrieking voices
Scolding, mocking, or merely chattering,
Always assail them. The Word in the desert
Is most attacked by voices of temptation,[14]
The crying shadow in the funeral dance,   160
The loud lament of the disconsolate chimera.[15]

The detail of the pattern is movement,
As in the figure of the ten stairs.[16]
Desire itself is movement
Not in itself desirable;   165
Love is itself unmoving,
Only the cause and end of movement,
Timeless, and undesiring
Except in the aspect of time
Caught in the form of limitation   170

---

14. **The Word in the desert . . . temptation:** An allusion to Christ's forty days in the wilderness, where he
was tempted by the devil, as described in Luke 4:1-4.
15. **chimera:** In Greek mythology, a fire-breathing female monster with body parts from several animals.
16. **the ten stairs:** An allusion to St. John of the Cross's model for the soul's ascent to God, "The Ten Degrees
of the Mystical Ladder of the Divine Love." See note 11.

Between un-being and being.
Sudden in a shaft of sunlight
Even while the dust moves
There rises the hidden laughter
Of children in the foliage   175
Quick now, here, now, always —
Ridiculous the waste sad time
Stretching before and after.

[1936]

Claude McKay

[1889-1948]

Festus Claudius McKay was born in Sunny Ville, Jamaica, on September 15, 1889. He was the youngest of eleven children born to prosperous black farmers, Hannah Ann Elizabeth Edwards McKay and Thomas Francis McKay, who provided their children with solid educations and strong religious training in the Baptist Church. Initially educated by his brilliant older brother Uriah Theo McKay, a prominent schoolteacher and radical reformer, McKay was a gifted student. After he completed his secondary education, however, he decided that he did not want to follow the path of his older brothers, most of whom were teachers or preachers. Instead, he won a scholarship to the government trade school in Kingston. His training to be a wheelwright ended when an earthquake destroyed the school in 1907, and he soon went home to care for his ailing and beloved mother. When she died in 1909, McKay returned to Kingston, where he impulsively joined the Jamaica Constabulary. Soon realizing that he was completely unsuited to the harsh discipline and brutality of police work, McKay managed to extricate himself from the force after seventeen months — rather than the mandatory five years — through the influence of a wealthy English aristocrat, Walter Jekyll. The editor of a collection of indigenous writings, *Jamaican Song and Story* (1907), Jekyll encouraged McKay to write dialect verse in the local Creole language, some of which was published in a Jamaican newspaper, the *Daily Gleaner*. In 1912, Jekyll also arranged for the publication in London of McKay's first two collections of poetry, *Constab Ballads* and *Songs of Jamaica*.

Despite his success, McKay believed he would have greater opportunities in the United States. When a visitor told him about Booker T. Washington's Tuskegee Institute, the twenty-three-year-old McKay set off for Alabama in 1912. Shocked by what he later described as the "implacable hate of my race" he confronted in the South, and unhappy with the curriculum at Tuskegee, McKay soon transferred to Kansas State College. No hap-

Claude McKay

This photograph was taken in New York City around 1922, the year McKay published his influential collection *Harlem Shadows*.

pier there, he was rescued in 1914 by a financial gift from his friend Jekyll, which allowed McKay to move to New York City, invest in a restaurant, and marry Eulalie Imelda Lewars, a fellow Jamaican. Within a year, the restaurant failed, and their marriage ended. Supporting himself by working as a railroad porter, McKay lived in Harlem, where he became involved with other writers and intellectuals. In 1917, he submitted two poems in standard English, "The Harlem Dancer" and "Invocation," to an innovative little magazine, *Seven Arts*. Fearing that his reputation as a Jamaican dialect poet would hurt his chances with an American magazine, McKay submitted and the poems were published under the pseudonym "Eli Edwards." But his identity soon became known to Max Eastman, the editor of a radical socialist journal, the *Liberator.* During the explosive summer of 1919, when race riots erupted in both northern and southern cities across the United States, McKay published under his own name "If We Must Die" in the *Liberator.* The militant poem was widely reprinted in African American newspapers, and poets such as Langston Hughes and James Weldon Johnson later cited it as a major inspiration of the Harlem Renaissance.

McKay, however, strongly resisted being restricted to the role of a black protest poet. He soon moved to London, where he studied the writings of Karl Marx and worked for a socialist journal, the *Workers' Dreadnought.* He also published a book of poems, *Spring in New Hampshire* (1920). After returning to New York in 1921, be became the associate editor of the *Liberator* and published his acclaimed collection *Harlem Shadows* (1922). Although he was buoyed by his literary success, McKay was becoming increasingly disenchanted with the American social and political system. "Color-consciousness was the fundamental of my restlessness," he later observed. McKay decided to set off once again, this time to the Soviet Union, where he was warmly received. His sympathy with the Bolshevik Revolution brought him to the attention of the Federal Bureau of Investigation, which blocked McKay's return to the United States. For the next twelve years, he lived in Europe and North Africa. Turning from poetry to prose fiction, he wrote *Home to Harlem* (1928), a graphic account of the underside of Harlem life that McKay's hero W. E. B. Du Bois savagely attacked, observing that "after the dirtier parts of its filth I felt distinctly like taking a bath." But the best-selling novel, the first by a black writer in the United States, won the annual Harmon Gold Award for an outstanding work of literature by an African American. McKay followed it with three more works of fiction: *Banjo* (1929), a novel about black beach boys in Marseilles; *Gingertown* (1932), a collection of stories set in Harlem and Jamaica; and *Banana Bottom* (1933), a novel celebrating the folk culture of a village in Jamaica.

McKay published no more books of fiction or poetry after he returned to the United States in 1934. Now an opponent of Communism, he remained committed to socialism and wrote articles for progressive periodicals such as the *Nation.* He also continued to write poetry, but he could not interest a publisher in "Cities" (c. 1934), a sequence of poems charting his travels around the world, or a later collection of deeply personal and embittered poems, "The Cycle" (c. 1943). His final published books were

> [O]ut of a heterogeneity of experience with an underlying unity, Claude McKay, as wheelwright, constable, agriculturist, porter, longshoreman, waiter, vagabond, rebel, and penitent, created his best poems.
>
> –Melvin Tolson

works of nonfiction, *A Long Way from Home* (1937), an autobiography, and *Harlem: Negro Metropolis* (1940). In 1940, he became an American citizen, and McKay converted to Roman Catholicism in 1944. He spent much of the rest of his life in Chicago, where he worked for the Catholic Youth Organization and where he died on May 22, 1948. McKay, who had never returned to his native Jamaica, was buried in New York City.

McKay's Poetry.   Early in his career, McKay earned a reputation as a Jamaican dialect poet, but he wrote poems only in standard English after he immigrated to the United States in 1912. Well acquainted with the Bible and steeped from an early age in the poetry of Shakespeare and British Romantic poets such as John Keats and Percy Bysshe Shelley, McKay was drawn to traditional lyric forms, especially the sonnet. In an "Author's Word" at the opening of *Harlem Shadows* (1922), widely regarded as his most significant collection of poetry, McKay explained: "I have adhered to such of the older traditions as I find adequate for my most lawless and revolutionary passions and moods." Certainly, there is a vital tension between the strict form and rhyme schemes of the sonnet, which commonly deals with the subject of love, and McKay's angry and defiant denunciations of racial hatred and social inequality in sonnets such as "If We Must Die" and "America," both of which were originally published in the revolutionary political and literary journal the *Liberator*. The texts of the following poems, all of which McKay collected in *Harlem Shadows*, are taken from his *Complete Poems*, edited by William J. Maxwell (2004).

bedfordstmartins.com/
americanlit *for research links on McKay*

THE HARLEM DANCER[1]

Applauding youths laughed with young prostitutes
And watched her perfect, half-clothed body sway;
Her voice was like the sound of blended flutes
Blown by black players upon a picnic day.[2]
She sang and danced on gracefully and calm,   5
The light gauze hanging loose about her form;
To me she seemed a proudly-swaying palm
Grown lovelier for passing through a storm.
Upon her swarthy neck black shiny curls
Luxuriant fell; and tossing coins in praise,   10
The wine-flushed, bold-eyed boys, and even the girls,

---

1. **The Harlem Dancer:** McKay's first publication in the United States, this poem appeared as one of "Two Sonnets" in the influential but short-lived magazine *Seven Arts* (October 1917).
2. **blended flutes . . . picnic day:** An allusion to pan flutes, also known as panpipes, an ancient folk instrument associated with pastoral poetry.

Devoured her shape with eager, passionate gaze;
But looking at her falsely-smiling face,
I knew her self was not in that strange place.

[1917, 2004]

IF WE MUST DIE[1]

If we must die, let it not be like hogs
Hunted and penned in an inglorious spot,
While round us bark the mad and hungry dogs,
Making their mock at our accursèd lot.
If we must die, O let us nobly die,   5
So that our precious blood may not be shed
In vain; then even the monsters we defy
Shall be constrained to honor us though dead!
O kinsmen! we must meet the common foe!
Though far outnumbered let us show us brave,   10
And for their thousand blows deal one deathblow!
What though before us lies the open grave?
Like men we'll face the murderous, cowardly pack,[2]
Pressed to the wall, dying, but fighting back!

[1919, 2004]

---

1. **If We Must Die**: McKay wrote this poem in response to what James Weldon Johnson named the "Red Summer," a wave of antiblack riots and lynchings that took place in Chicago; Washington, D.C.; Omaha, Nebraska; and other northern and southern cities in the summer and fall of 1919. To the amazement of many white people and editorial writers, blacks fought back, displaying a new militancy that McKay also voiced in his poem, which was first published in the *Liberator*, a "Journal of Revolutionary Progress," in July 1919.
2. **cowardly pack**: According to historians, the riots were initiated by gangs of white segregationists, called *white hoodlums* by Carl Sandburg, who reported on the Chicago riots for the *Chicago Daily News*.

THE LYNCHING

His Spirit in smoke ascended to high heaven.
His father, by the cruelest way of pain,
Had bidden him to his bosom once again;
The awful sin remained still unforgiven.[1]

---

1. **His spirit . . . unforgiven**: The scene recalls the crucifixion of Christ, who at the moment of death commits his spirit to his Father (Luke 23:46).

All night a bright and solitary star   5
(Perchance the one that ever guided him,
Yet gave him up at last to Fate's wild whim)
Hung pitifully o'er the swinging char.[2]
Day dawned, and soon the mixed crowds came to view
The ghastly body swaying in the sun   10
The women thronged to look, but never a one
Showed sorrow in her eyes of steely blue;
And little lads, lynchers that were to be,
Danced round the dreadful thing in fiendish glee.

[1920, 2004]

---

2. **swinging char:** That is, the charred body swinging at the end of the rope. Many lynching victims were both hanged and burned.

AMERICA

Although she feeds me bread of bitterness,
And sinks into my throat her tiger's tooth,
Stealing my breath of life, I will confess
I love this cultured hell that tests my youth!
Her vigor flows like tides into my blood,   5
Giving me strength erect against her hate.
Her bigness sweeps my being like a flood.
Yet as a rebel fronts a king in state,
I stand within her walls with not a shred
Of terror, malice, not a word of jeer.   10
Darkly I gaze into the days ahead,
And see her might and granite wonders there,
Beneath the touch of Time's unerring hand,
Like priceless treasures sinking in the sand.[1]

[1921, 2004]

---

1. **Darkly I gaze . . . sinking in the sand:** The poet's foreboding vision of the nation's future decline echoes "Ozymandias," the Greek name for the pharaoh Ramses II, by the English poet Percy Bysshe Shelley (1792–1822). Shelley's sonnet about the arrogance and transience of power, as illustrated by the fragmentary remains of what was once the largest statue in Egypt, concludes: "Round the decay / Of that colossal Wreck, boundless and bare / The lone and level sands stretch far away."

Africa

The sun sought thy dim bed and brought forth light,
The sciences were sucklings at thy breast;
When all the world was young in pregnant night
Thy slaves toiled at thy monumental best.
Thou ancient treasure-land, thou modern prize,   5
New peoples marvel at thy pyramids!
The years roll on, thy sphinx of riddle eyes
Watches the mad world with immobile lids.
The Hebrews humbled them at Pharaoh's name.
Cradle of Power! Yet all things were in vain!   10
Honor and Glory, Arrogance and Fame!
They went. The darkness swallowed thee again.
Thou art the harlot, now thy time is done,
Of all the mighty nations of the sun.

[1921, 2004]

Outcast

For the dim regions whence my fathers came
My spirit, bondaged by the body, longs.
Words felt, but never heard, my lips would frame;
My soul would sing forgotten jungle songs.
I would go back to darkness and to peace,   5
But the great western world holds me in fee,[1]
And I may never hope for full release
While to its alien gods I bend my knee.
Something in me is lost, forever lost,
Some vital thing has gone out of my heart,   10
And I must walk the way of life a ghost
Among the sons of earth, a thing apart;
For I was born, far from my native clime,
Under the white man's menace, out of time.

[1922, 2004]

---

1. **holds me in fee:** In law, the term *in fee* denotes legal possession, though in feudal law an estate held in fee was land granted by a lord to his vassal on condition of homage and service.

Edna St. Vincent Millay

[1892-1950]

Edna St. Vincent Millay was born in Rockland, Maine, on February 22, 1892, the first of the three daughters of Cora Buzzelle and Henry Tollman Millay. In 1900, Cora Millay left her husband, an improvident schoolteacher, and moved with her daughters into a small house in the poorest part of Camden, Maine, where she supported the family by working as a practical nurse. A former singer who frequently read poetry to her daughters, Cora Millay strongly encouraged their interests in literature and music. Edna St. Vincent Millay, who from an early age insisted on being called "Vincent," studied piano and wrote for a literary magazine she started in high school. When she was fourteen, she published her first poem in a popular illustrated magazine for children, *St. Nicholas,* and another of her early poems later appeared in *Current Literature.* Unable to afford college, Millay remained at home after her graduation from high school, helping to care for her younger sisters, occasionally working as a typist, and writing poetry. The publication of her long poem "Renascence" in the popular anthology *The Lyric Year* (1912) gained her national attention, and Millay consequently obtained a scholarship to Vassar College, which she entered in the fall of 1913. Although she defiantly flouted every rule of the small women's college, Millay seriously studied languages and literature, acted in plays, including one she wrote, and published her poetry in the Vassar *Miscellany.*

Edna St. Vincent Millay
The noted portrait photographer Arnold Genthe took this publicity photograph in 1914, after Millay had risen to fame on the basis of her early poem "Renascence."

After her graduation from Vassar in 1917, Millay embarked on a highly successful literary career. She moved to New York City, where she published her warmly received first book, *Renascence and Other Poems* (1917). Free-spirited and fiercely independent, Millay lived a bohemian existence in Greenwich Village, where she enjoyed the company of other writers and artists, with many of whom she had affairs, and acted in plays produced by the Provincetown Players. In order to earn money, she published a series of short stories under the pen name Nancy Boyd in *Ainslee's Magazine.* In 1920, Millay published her second volume of poetry, *A Few Figs from Thistles,* which one reviewer favorably compared to Emily Dickinson's poetry, and *Aria da Capo,* a popular antiwar play that was produced by the Provincetown Players. Eagerly accepting a job with the cultural magazine

Vanity Fair, Millay spent most of the following three years traveling in Europe, where she wrote articles for the magazine, plays, and poetry. Her third book of poetry, *Second April* (1921), was nominated for the Pulitzer Prize, which Millay was awarded for her next book, *The Harp-Weaver and Other Poems* (1922). The first woman to be awarded the Pulitzer Prize for Poetry, Millay was also a rarity among poets, male or female: She was earning a living by writing poetry. Indeed, by then she was the most popular and best-selling poet in the United States.

In 1923, Millay's life changed in two important ways. She entered into an "open" marriage with Eugen Jan Boissevain, the forty-three-year-old widower of Inez Milholland, a Vassar alumnus and leader of the women's suffrage movement who had died in 1916. With Boissevain, by all accounts a remarkable person who strongly supported her career, Millay thereafter lived at Steepletop, a farmhouse they purchased in the Berkshire Mountains near Austerlitz, New York. At the same time, Millay began to assume a more prominent public role. She traveled across the country, enthralling audiences with theatrical readings in a rich contralto voice that was variously described as sounding like "a bronze bell" and "an axe on fresh wood." She also became increasingly active in social causes, including women's rights and the case of Nicola Sacco and Bartolomeo Vanzetti, two Italian-born anarchists who were convicted of robbery and murder in Massachusetts. Millay led other writers in a protest in Boston and made a last-minute appeal to the governor of Massachusetts to stay the execution, but Sacco and Vanzetti were electrocuted later that night, on August 23, 1927. The bitter aftertaste of that experience remained with Millay, who later told a fellow writer that the case had made her "more aware of the underground workings of forces alien to true democracy." For the first time, Millay included several poems of social protest in her next book, *The Buck in the Snow and Other Poems* (1928).

During the 1930s and 1940s, Millay's phenomenal success as a poet was shadowed by physical problems and personal losses. Her beloved mother died in 1931, the year Millay published *Fatal Interview*, a sonnet sequence inspired by her passionate and painful affair with George Dillon, a younger man she had met at a reading at the University of Chicago. That acclaimed volume, which sold thirty-five thousand copies within two weeks, was followed by *Wine from These Grapes* (1934) and *Huntsman, What Quarry?* (1939), collections of poems that revealed Millay's gloomy response to the growing threat of another world war and the rise of Fascism in Europe. Abandoning her earlier pacifism, Millay championed the Allied cause in articles and the poems collected in *Make Bright the Arrows* (1940). Although that volume and the other propagandistic poetry Millay wrote during World War II damaged her critical reputation, she was elected to the American Academy of Arts and Letters in 1940 and awarded the Gold Medal for lifetime achievement by the Poetry Society of America in 1943. Millay suffered a nervous breakdown in 1944, and her final years were marred by illness, addiction to alcohol and morphine, and the death of her husband in 1949. Millay died alone in her home of a heart attack on October 19, 1950.

Her talent, with its diverting mixture of solemnity and levity, won the enthusiasm of a time bewildered intellectually and moving unsteadily towards an emotional attitude of its own.

–Allen Tate

Millay's Poetry. In one of the many articles published in the aftermath of her sudden death, a writer for the *New York Times* described Millay as " 'a poet's poet,' and a 'lover's poet,' and sometimes a crusader's poet as well." Unlike more experimental poets of her generation, including her female contemporaries H.D. and Marianne Moore, Millay most often wrote in conventional meters and adopted traditional forms such as the epigram, the quatrain, and especially the sonnet, upon which she placed her personal stamp. In a review of her third book of poetry, *Second April* (1921), the critic and writer Maxwell Anderson commented that many of her sonnets were "powerful, humanly moving, perfectly touched, said as only a first-class artist could say them." During her lifetime, Millay published seventeen collections of her poems, many of which first appeared in periodicals. "First Fig" and "Second Fig," the opening poems of her collection *A Few Figs from Thistles* (1920), were first published in Harriet Monroe's innovative, Chicago-based *Poetry: A Magazine of Verse* in 1918. Millay, who vastly expanded the audience for poetry in the United States, also published in national mass-circulation magazines, including the *Saturday Evening Post* and *Vanity Fair*. By 1927, her fame was so great that her protest poem "Justice Denied in Massachusetts" was printed under the bold headline "POEM BY MISS MILLAY ON SACCO AND VANZETTI" in the *New York Times*. The texts of the poems are taken from her *Collected Poems*, edited by Norma Millay (1956).

bedfordstmartins.com/ americanlit for research links on Millay

FIRST FIG

My candle burns at both ends;
   It will not last the night;
But ah, my foes, and oh, my friends —
   It gives a lovely light!

[1918, 1956]

SECOND FIG

Safe upon the solid rock the ugly houses stand:
Come and see my shining palace built upon the sand!

[1918, 1956]

[EUCLID ALONE HAS LOOKED ON BEAUTY BARE.]

Euclid[1] alone has looked on Beauty bare.
Let all who prate of Beauty hold their peace,
And lay them prone upon the earth and cease
To ponder on themselves, the while they stare
At nothing, intricately drawn nowhere   5
In shapes of shifting lineage; let geese
Gabble and hiss, but heroes seek release
From dusty bondage into luminous air.
O blinding hour, O holy, terrible day,
When first the shaft into his vision shone   10
Of light anatomized! Euclid alone
Has looked on Beauty bare. Fortunate they
Who, though once only and then but far away,
Have heard her massive sandal set on stone.

                                              [1920, 1956]

---

1. **Euclid:** Euclid of Alexandria (c. 300 BCE), whose treatise on geometry, *The Elements*, was one of the most influential texts in the history of Western mathematics.

[I, BEING BORN A WOMAN AND DISTRESSED]

I, being born a woman and distressed
By all the needs and notions of my kind,
Am urged by your propinquity to find
Your person fair, and feel a certain zest
To bear your body's weight upon my breast: 5
So subtly is the fume of life designed,
To clarify the pulse and cloud the mind,
And leave me once again undone, possessed.
Think not for this, however, the poor treason
Of my stout blood against my staggering brain,   10
I shall remember you with love, or season
My scorn with pity, — let me make it plain:
I find this frenzy insufficient reason
For conversation when we meet again.

                                              [1921, 1956]

[OH, OH, YOU WILL BE SORRY FOR THAT WORD!]

Oh, oh, you will be sorry for that word!
Give back my book and take my kiss instead.
Was it my enemy or my friend I heard,
"What a big book for such a little head!"
Come, I will show you now my newest hat,   5
And you may watch me purse my mouth and prink!
Oh, I shall love you still, and all of that.
I never again shall tell you what I think.
I shall be sweet and crafty, soft and sly;
You will not catch me reading any more: 10
I shall be called a wife to pattern by;
And some day when you knock and push the door,
Some sane day, not too bright and not too stormy,
I shall be gone, and you may whistle for me.

[1922, 1956]

To Inez Milholland[1]

*Read in Washington, November eighteenth, 1923, at the unveiling
of a statue of three leaders in the cause of Equal Rights for Women*[2]

Upon this marble bust that is not I
Lay the round, formal wreath that is not fame;
But in the forum of my silenced cry
Root ye the living tree whose sap is flame.
I, that was proud and valiant, am no more; —   5
Save as a dream that wanders wide and late,
Save as a wind that rattles the stout door,
Troubling the ashes in the sheltered grate.
The stone will perish; I shall be twice dust.
Only my standard on a taken hill   10

---

1. **To Inez Milholland:** Milholland, a socialist and prominent crusader for women's suffrage, became a martyr to the cause after she collapsed during a speech and died at the age of thirty in 1916. The poem was first
published as "The Pioneer" in the *Saturday Review of Literature* (August 29, 1925).
2. **Read . . . Equal Rights for Women:** Adelaide Johnson (1859-1955) sculpted a large marble memorial to the
leaders of the women's rights movement that included busts of its "three leaders," Susan B. Anthony, Lucretia Mott, and Elizabeth Cady Stanton. Because of ongoing opposition to women's rights, the memorial was
controversial. Although it was originally unveiled on February 15, 1921, in the Rotunda of the Capitol Building in Washington, it was later moved and installed in the crypt of the Capitol. Millay read the poem at the
installation ceremony in 1923, which also commemorated the seventy-fifth anniversary of the first Woman's
Rights Convention in Seneca Falls, New York. Today, the memorial is permanently installed in the Rotunda
of the Capitol Building.

Can cheat the mildew and the red-brown rust
And make immortal my adventurous will.
Even now the silk is tugging at the staff:
Take up the song; forget the epitaph.

[1925, 1956]

JUSTICE DENIED IN MASSACHUSETTS[1]

Let us abandon then our gardens and go home
And sit in the sitting-room.
Shall the larkspur blossom or the corn grow under this cloud?
Sour to the fruitful seed
Is the cold earth under this cloud,   5
Fostering quack and weed, we have marched upon but cannot
   conquer;
We have bent the blades of our hoes against the stalks of them.

Let us go home, and sit in the sitting-room.
Not in our day
Shall the cloud go over and the sun rise as before,   10
Beneficent upon us
Out of the glittering bay,
And the warm winds be blown inward from the sea
Moving the blades of corn
With a peaceful sound.   15
Forlorn, forlorn,
Stands the blue hay-rack by the empty mow.
And the petals drop to the ground,
Leaving the tree unfruited.
The sun that warmed our stooping backs and withered the weed
   uprooted –   20
We shall not feel it again.
We shall die in darkness, and be buried in the rain.

What from the splendid dead
We have inherited –
Furrows sweet to the grain, and the weed subdued –   25

----

1. **Justice Denied in Massachusetts:** Millay wrote this poem to protest the impending execution of Nicola Sacco and Bartolomeo Vanzetti, two Italian-born anarchists who were sentenced to death after being convicted of robbery and murder in Massachusetts. Many believed that the men had not received a fair trial because of hostility to Italian immigrants and the pervasive fear of "reds," or radicals, during the 1920s. Despite protests and appeals to the governor to stay the execution, Sacco and Vanzetti were put to death on August 22, 1927, the day Millay's poem was first published in the *New York Times.*

See now the slug and the mildew plunder.
Evil does overwhelm
The larkspur and the corn;
We have seen them go under.

Let us sit here, sit still,   30
Here in the sitting-room until we die;
At the step of Death on the walk, rise and go;
Leaving to our children's children this beautiful doorway,
And this elm,
And a blighted earth to till   35
With a broken hoe.

[1927, 1956]

E. E. Cummings

[1894–1962]

E. E. Cummings

This photograph of Cummings was taken while he was in Paris in 1923, the year his first book of poetry was published in New York City.

Edward Estlin Cummings was born on October 14, 1894, in Cambridge, Massachusetts. He was the first child of Edward Cummings, a professor at Harvard University and later a Unitarian minister, and Rebecca Haswell Clarke Cummings, a descendant of Susanna Rowson, the author of *Charlotte Temple* (1791), one of the first best-selling novels published in the United States. The affluent family lived in a large house in Cambridge and at Joy Farm, their summer home on Silver Lake in New Hampshire. They often read together, especially the poetry of Henry Wadsworth Longfellow, the revered nineteenth-century American poet whom Cummings's mother particularly admired and wanted her son to emulate. Cummings, who wrote constantly, published poems and short stories in the literary magazine of the prestigious Cambridge Latin School. In 1911, he entered Harvard, where he excelled academically, earning a bachelor's degree with honors in literature, especially Greek and English. Cummings helped edit and contributed fairly traditional poems to the

Harvard Monthly. But he was fascinated by "The New Art," the title of his 1915 graduation speech in which Cummings championed radical departures in art, music, and literature, including the imagist verse of Amy Lowell. After his graduation, he stayed on for an additional year at Harvard, earning a master's degree in 1916. From an early age, Cummings had enjoyed drawing and sketching, and he now began to paint seriously, heavily influenced by the new trends in art, especially cubism. He also wrote experimental poems, some of which were published in an anthology edited by one of his college friends, *Eight Harvard Poets* (1917).

Cummings's effort to join the ranks of modernist artists was temporarily disrupted by World War I. Leaving Cambridge, he took a job with a mail-order publishing firm in New York City, where he worked briefly before the United States entered the war. The pacifistic Cummings volunteered to serve in the Norton-Harjes Ambulance Corps and was sent to France in April 1917. Five months later, Cummings and a friend, William Slater Brown, were arrested on suspicion of treason. The unfounded charges stemmed primarily from some mildly negative letters about the war that Brown had written home, as well as the two men's constant questioning of the authority of the chief of the ambulance corps. Nonetheless, Cummings and Brown were sent to a French detention camp for three months. Through the efforts of his father, Cummings was released in December 1917 and sent back to the United States. After living for six months in New York City, he was drafted into the infantry and sent for training to Camp Devens, Massachusetts. Fortunately for Cummings, who hated the army and the war, the conflict ended a few months later, and he was discharged and returned to New York City in January 1919.

Cummings soon found himself at the center of the cultural ferment of the early 1920s. He painted, wrote poetry, and enjoyed the company of a circle of artistic friends from his Harvard days, including the wealthy art patron Scofield Thayer. Cummings fell in love with Thayer's estranged wife, Elaine, who gave birth to their daughter in December 1919. Thayer was less concerned with their affair than with his purchase of the *Dial*, a prominent political and cultural magazine he was determined to transform into the preeminent journal of avant-garde art. Immediately after Thayer and his Harvard friend James Sibley Watson gained control of the magazine, they invited Cummings to contribute to the *Dial*, where four of his drawings and seven of his innovative poems appeared in January 1920. He also gained attention for his abstract paintings, two of which were exhibited at the Society of Independent Artists Exhibition in the spring of 1920. His relationship with Elaine Thayer was now strained, and Cummings soon left New York to study art in Paris. There, he wrote *The Enormous Room* (1922), a graphic and stylistically dizzying account of his imprisonment in France. He also continued to write poetry, which regularly appeared in the *Dial* and other little magazines such as *Broom, Secession,* and the *Little Review*. With the help of his friend John Dos Passos, Cummings published his exuberant first collection of poems, *Tulips and Chimneys* (1923). Returning to New York early in 1924, he married Elaine

One has in Mr. Cummings's work, a sense of the best dancing and of the best horticulture.
—Marianne Moore

Thayer, but they were divorced by the end of the year. Cummings immersed himself in work and soon published his second collection of poetry, *XLI Poems. &.* (1925). Five years after he published his first poems in the *Dial,* Cummings received the magazine's prestigious award "for distinguished service to American letters" in 1925.

During the following decades, Cummings gained popular as well as critical acclaim. He extended his experiments in language and typography in the poems collected in *is 5* (1926) — the title, he explained, revealed the difference between most people, who think that two and two is four, and the poet, who knows that it is 5 — and *ViVa* (1931). The versatile Cummings also wrote a play, *Him,* which was produced by the Provincetown Players in 1928, and published a controversial diary/memoir/novel about his 1931 trip to Russia, *Eimi* (1933). His unhappy second marriage, to Anne Barton, ended in divorce after five years, in 1934. That year, his personal life changed dramatically when he met Marion Morehouse, a former fashion model who lived with Cummings as his common-law wife until his death. Cummings regained some of his earlier humor and exuberance in the poems collected in *No Thanks* (1935), which he ironically dedicated to the fourteen publishers who had rejected the manuscript, *50 Poems* (1940), and *1 x 1* (1944). During his later years, he won the Harriet Monroe Prize from *Poetry* for *Xaipe* (1950) and his *Collected Poems* (1954) was given a special citation by the National Book Award, won that year by Wallace Stevens's *Collected Poems.* Cummings was awarded the Bollingen Prize in recognition of his lifetime achievement in 1958, the year he published his final volume of poetry, *95 Poems.* Especially popular among college students, Cummings gave hundreds of readings at universities across the country, and he and Morehouse traveled extensively in Europe. But they spent much of their time at Joy Farm, which Cummings inherited upon his father's death, and where he died of a stroke on September 3, 1962.

Cummings's Poetry.   Although he ultimately became one of the most beloved of twentieth-century American poets, Cummings was initially viewed as a radical innovator whose verse was considered extreme even by the standards of the "new poetry." In addition to erotic love poems and poems celebrating the beauty and freshness of nature, work that proved to be especially popular with readers, Cummings wrote sharply satirical poems and parodies of American culture, jingoism, and militarism. The form of his poems was equally innovative. An artist who produced drawings and paintings throughout his life, Cummings was deeply concerned with the visual appearance of a poem. In a notebook written late in his life, Cummings wrote that his early work, "the inaudible poem — the visual poem, the poem not for ears but eye — moved me more." He constantly experimented with style and typography in his colloquial, free-verse poems, fusing together and creating new words, substituting one part of

bedfordstmartins.com/ americanlit for research links on Cummings

E. E. Cummings,
Noise Number 13

Cummings described this abstract 1925 painting as a "Forwardflung backwardSpinning hoop."

speech for another, breaking lines at unusual points, varying the spacing between words, and generally avoiding capitalizations. His eccentric typography, for which Cummings has often been called the "lowercase poet," later prompted some publishers and scholars to spell his name "e. e. cummings." Beginning after his death, that trend persisted for decades until the E. E. Cummings Society verified that there was no basis for the use of lowercase letters, since Cummings followed the usual convention of capitalizing his name in his personal correspondence, in signatures on the poems he published in magazines, and on the covers of the books published during his lifetime. From the beginning of his career, however, the idiosyncratic typography and punctuation of his poems created problems for editors. Shortly before his first poems were published in the *Dial* in 1920, for example, Cummings wrote the editor, Scofield Thayer: "Note punctuation exemplifying a theory in my soul that every 'word' *purely* considered implies its own punctuation." The texts of the following poems, which retain Cummings's original typography and punctuation, are taken from *E. E. Cummings: Complete Poems, 1904-1962*, edited by George J. Firmage (1991).

[In Just-]

in Just-
spring   when the world is mud-
luscious the little
lame balloonman

whistles   far   and wee   5

and eddieandbill come
running from marbles and
piracies and it's
spring

when the world is puddle-wonderful   10

the queer
old balloonman whistles
far   and   wee
and bettyandisbel come dancing

from hop-scotch and jump-rope and   15

it's
spring
and
        the

                goat-footed   20

balloonMan   whistles
far
and
wee

[1920, 1991]

[Buffalo Bill 's]

Buffalo Bill 's[1]
defunct
        who used to
        ride a watersmooth-silver
                        stallion   5

---

1. **Buffalo Bill 's:** The colorful William Cody (1846–1917), a Union soldier in the Civil War, was nicknamed *Buffalo Bill* for hunting and killing over 4,000 buffalo for the Kansas Pacific Railroad in the late 1860s. He later developed a popular traveling extravaganza, Buffalo Bill's Wild West Show, often advertised as "America's National Entertainment."

and break onetwothreefourfive pigeonsjustlikethat
                                      Jesus

he was a handsome man
                      and what i want to know is
how do you like your blueeyed boy   10
Mister Death

                                      [1920, 1991]

[THE CAMBRIDGE LADIES
WHO LIVE IN FURNISHED SOULS]

the Cambridge[1] ladies who live in furnished souls
are unbeautiful and have comfortable minds
(also, with the church's protestant blessings
daughters,unscented shapeless spirited)
they believe in Christ and Longfellow,[2]both dead,   5
are invariably interested in so many things —
at the present writing one still finds
delighted fingers knitting for the is it Poles?
perhaps.   While permanent faces coyly bandy
scandal of Mrs. N and Professor D   10
....the Cambridge ladies do not care,above
Cambridge if sometimes in its box of
sky lavender and cornerless,the
moon rattles like a fragment of angry candy

                                      [1922, 1991]

---

1. **Cambridge:** Cummings was born and raised in Cambridge, Massachusetts, where he also attended Harvard University.
2. **Longfellow:** The poet Henry Wadsworth Longfellow (1807–1882) was among the most popular American poets in the nineteenth and early twentieth centuries.

[*"NEXT TO OF COURSE GOD AMERICA I*[1]]

"next to of course god america i
love you land of the pilgrims' and so forth oh
say can you see by the dawn's early my
country 'tis of centuries come and go

---

1. **next to of course god america i:** This poem was originally published as "The Patriot" in *Vanity Fair* (May 1925).

and are no more what of it we should worry   5
in every language even deafanddumb
thy sons acclaim your glorious name by gorry
by jingo by gee by gosh by gum
why talk of beauty what could be more beautiful than these heroic happy dead   10
who rushed like lions to the roaring slaughter
they did not stop to think they died instead
then shall the voice of liberty be mute?"

He spoke.   And drank rapidly a glass of water

[1926, 1991]

[MY SWEET OLD ETCETERA]

my sweet old etcetera
aunt lucy during the recent

war[1] could and what
is more did tell you just
what everybody was fighting   5

for,
my sister

isabel created hundreds
(and
hundreds)of socks not to   10
mention shirts fleaproof earwarmers

etcetera wristers etcetera,my

mother hoped that

i would die etcetera
bravely of course my father used   15
to become hoarse talking about how it was
a privilege and if only he
could meanwhile my

self etcetera lay quietly
in the deep mud et   20

---

1. **war**: World War I (1914–18).

cetera
(dreaming,
et
  cetera,of
Your smile   25
eyes knees and of your Etcetera)

[1926, 1991]

[I SING OF OLAF GLAD AND BIG]

i sing of Olaf glad and big
whose warmest heart recoiled at war:
a conscientious object-or

his wellbelovéd colonel(trig[1]
westpointer most succinctly bred)   5
took erring Olaf soon in hand;
but — though an host of overjoyed
noncoms[2](first knocking on the head
him)do through icy waters roll
that helplessness which others stroke   10
with brushes recently employed
anent this muddy toiletbowl,
while kindred intellects evoke
allegiance per blunt instruments —
Olaf(being to all intents   15
a corpse and wanting any rag
upon what God unto him gave)
responds,without getting annoyed
"I will not kiss your fucking flag"

straightway the silver bird[3] looked grave   20
(departing hurriedly to shave)

but — though all kinds of officers
(a yearning nation's blueeyed pride)
their passive prey did kick and curse
until for wear their clarion   25

---

1. **trig:** Smart and neat in appearance.
2. **noncoms:** A military term for noncommissioned officers.
3. **silver bird:** The badge signifying the military rank of colonel.

voices and boots were much the worse,
and egged the firstclassprivates on
his rectum wickedly to tease
by means of skilfully applied
bayonets roasted hot with heat —   30
Olaf(upon what were once knees)
does almost ceaselessly repeat
"there is some shit I will not eat"

our president,being of which
assertions duly notified   35
threw the yellowsonofabitch
into a dungeon,where he died

Christ(of His mercy infinite)
i pray to see;and Olaf,too

preponderatingly because   40
unless statistics lie he was
more brave than me:more blond than you.

[1931, 1991]

[YOU SHALL ABOVE ALL THINGS BE GLAD AND YOUNG.]

you shall above all things be glad and young.
For if you're young,whatever life you wear

it will become you;and if you are glad
whatever's living will yourself become.
Girlboys may nothing more than boygirls need: 5
i can entirely her only love

whose any mystery makes every man's
flesh put space on;and his mind take off time

that you should ever think,may god forbid
and(in his mercy)your true lover spare: 10
for that way knowledge lies,the foetal grave
called progress,and negation's dead undoom.

I'd rather learn from one bird how to sing
than teach ten thousand stars how not to dance

[1938, 1991]

[ANYONE LIVED IN A PRETTY HOW TOWN]

anyone lived in a pretty how town
(with up so floating many bells down)
spring summer autumn winter
he sang his didn't he danced his did.

Women and men(both little and small)   5
cared for anyone not at all
they sowed their isn't they reaped their same
sun moon stars rain

children guessed(but only a few
and down they forgot as up they grew   10
autumn winter spring summer)
that noone loved him more by more

when by now and tree by leaf
she laughed his joy she cried his grief
bird by snow and stir by still   15
anyone's any was all to her

someones married their everyones
laughed their cryings and did their dance
(sleep wake hope and then)they
said their nevers they slept their dream   20

stars rain sun moon
(and only the snow can begin to explain
how children are apt to forget to remember
with up so floating many bells down)

one day anyone died i guess   25
(and noone stooped to kiss his face)
busy folk buried them side by side
little by little and was by was

all by all and deep by deep
and more by more they dream their sleep   30
noone and anyone earth by april
wish by spirit and if by yes.

Women and men(both dong and ding)
summer autumn winter spring
reaped their sowing and went their came   35
sun moon stars rain

[1940, 1991]

[I THANK YOU GOD FOR MOST THIS AMAZING]

i thank You God for most this amazing
day:for the leaping greenly spirits of trees
and a blue true dream of sky;and for everything
which is natural which is infinite which is yes

(i who have died am alive again today,   5
and this is the sun's birthday;this is the birth
day of life and of love and wings:and of the gay
great happening illimitably earth)

how should tasting touching hearing seeing
breathing any – lifted from the no   10
of all nothing – human merely being
doubt unimaginable You?

(now the ears of my ears awake and
now the eyes of my eyes are opened)

[1950, 1991]

Charles Reznikoff

[1894–1976]

Charles Reznikoff

This photograph was taken around 1940, when Reznikoff was known to only a few readers as one of the leading figures among an avant-garde group of poets known as the objectivists.

Charles Reznikoff was born on August 30, 1894, in what he called the "Jewish Ghetto of Brownsville," part of a working-class and primarily Gentile neighborhood of Brooklyn. He was the son of Russian immigrants, Sarah Yetta Wolwovsky and Nathan Reznikoff, who established a hat manufacturing business in New York City. Like thousands of other Jewish families, the Reznikoffs had fled Russia during the "pogroms," organized massacres of Jews that followed the assassination of Czar Alexander II in 1881. Although the Reznikoffs and a number of their relatives immigrated to New York City in order to escape religious persecution, they encountered considerable hostility toward Jews, and from an early age Reznikoff was sensitive to the inequalities and injustices of life in the United States.

He grew up listening to the folktales and family stories told by his parents and grandparents, one of which made a lifelong impression. When his maternal grandfather died in Russia, he left behind a poetry manuscript written in Hebrew. Because his wife could not read Hebrew, she could not understand the poems and feared that the family might be endangered by the discovery of subversive writings. She consequently burned the manuscript. Reznikoff, who early determined to become a writer, carefully preserved his own work, much of which he would later privately publish, sometimes on his own printing press.

Reznikoff struggled to support himself and his writing. An excellent student, he graduated from high school in 1910, shortly before his sixteenth birthday, and went to the new School of Journalism at the University of Missouri. He left after a year and returned home, enrolling in New York University Law School in 1912. He graduated second in his class and passed the bar examination in 1916. Fearing that law practice would absorb too much of the time and mental energy he needed for writing, Reznikoff supported himself by selling hats for his parents' company. As he recalled in his autobiographical poem "Early History of a Writer" (1969), however, his study of law prompted him to seek a new clarity, compression, and precision in his writing:

> I saw that I could use the expensive machinery
> that had cost me four years of hard work at law
> and which I thought useless for my writing:
> prying sentences open to look at their exact meaning;
> weighing words to choose only those that had
> meat for my purpose
> and throwing the rest away as empty shells.

Although he was strongly influenced by the imagists, Reznikoff applied their poetic techniques to strikingly unconventional subjects, frequently the experiences of immigrants and working people in New York City. He privately published two pamphlets of his poems, *Rhythms* (1918) and *Rhythms II* (1919). The work came to the attention of Samuel Roth, owner of the Poetry Book Shop in Greenwich Village, who published Reznikoff's *Poems* (1920). The poet later privately published several of his brief, experimental plays, as well as another collection of his poetry, *Five Groups of Verse* (1927). After he stopped working for his parents, who gave him a small stipend, Reznikoff supplemented his income by doing odd jobs such as selling advertising space in the *Menorah Journal,* a magazine of Jewish American art and culture to which he became a regular contributor during the 1920s.

Reznikoff's writings first gained serious attention early in the following decade. In 1930, he married Marie Syrkin, a journalist, teacher, and Zionist activist. Drawing on a series of autobiographical stories he had earlier published in the *Menorah Journal,* Reznikoff wrote *By the Waters of Manhattan,* a short novel published in 1930. In a review in the *Menorah Journal,* the critic Lionel Trilling hailed the novel as "remarkable and original in American literature," adding that Reznikoff had "written the first story of the Jewish immigrant that is not false." At the same time,

What other poet is so interested in reality? I don't know any other poet who is so interested in what actually happened as Reznikoff.

—Allen Ginsberg

bedfordstmartins.com/
americanlit for research
links on Reznikoff

Reznikoff's poetry was championed by two younger poets, George Oppen and Louis Zukofsky. In the "Program" of a special issue of *Poetry* that Zukovsky guest edited in 1931, he coined the term *objectivists* to describe the wide range of contributors, including Reznikoff and William Carlos Williams. The issue also included Zukofsky's admiring essay on Reznikoff's verse, "perhaps the most neglected contribution to writing in America in the last ten years." Despite the flurry of interest in his work, the modest Reznikoff was deeply discouraged about his progress as a writer. In a letter to his wife in September 1933, he observed that "both Eliot and Pound are in high-grade furnished rooms in good neighborhoods, but I think myself on the highway — with little done and very far to go."

During the remainder of his long and productive career, Reznikoff worked in relative obscurity in New York City. In 1934, he, Oppen, and Zukovsky founded the Objectivist Press, which published four of Reznikoff's books before the joint venture collapsed in 1936. He thereafter privately published much of his poetry, including the collections *Going To and Fro and Walking Up and Down* (1941) and *Inscriptions: 1944-1956* (1959). He also did editorial work and wrote translations for the Jewish Publication Society, which also published his historical novel *Lionhearted* (1944). Reznikoff later wrote long chronicle poems derived from his study of law and actual law cases, *Testimony: The United States, 1885-1890: Recitative* (1965) and *Testimony: The United States, 1891-1900: Recitative* (1968). His final work was another documentary poem, *Holocaust* (1975), based on records of the Nuremberg trials of Nazi war criminals and the trial of Adolf Eichmann in Jerusalem. Reznikoff, sometimes called the "Poet of New York," died there on January 21, 1976. Since then, he has gained a growing reputation as a poet who quietly produced what his admirer Allen Ginsberg described as "one of the largest bodies of concrete imagistic objective writing that anybody in America has accumulated."

Reznikoff's "Testimony."   From 1930 to 1935, during the early years of the Depression, Reznikoff worked full time for *Corpus Juris: Being a Complete and Systematic Statement of the Whole Body of Law as Embodied in and Developed by All Reported Decisions* (1936), the foremost legal encyclopedia of the United States. Although he initially viewed the work as a burdensome economic necessity, it provided materials and a method that shaped much of his later writing. As a researcher for the massive project, Reznikoff reviewed hundreds of federal and state court cases, which he came to view as a kind of counterpoint to the official history of the United States. Drawing upon the often grim facts and seemingly unpoetical details of the cases, he began to construct brief narratives that illuminated hidden recesses of American life, especially the experiences of African Americans, immigrants, and other working people. The first fruits of his literary method were *Testimony* (1934), a series of prose sketches, and the poem "Testimony." Each of the first three sections of the poem is based on the testimony in an actual court case, the bare facts of which Reznikoff offers without additional commentary. In contrast to that documentary method, the final section of the poem is apparently autobiographical, derived from the folktales told to him when he was a child by his beloved mother, who died of cancer in 1937 and to whom Reznikoff dedicated the volume in which "Testimony" was first published, *Going To and Fro and Walking Up and Down* (1941). The text is taken from *The Poems of Charles Reznikoff: 1918-1975*, edited by Seamus Cooney (2005).

TESTIMONY[1]

I

The company had advertised for men to unload a steamer across the river. It was
    six o'clock in the morning, snowing, and still dark.
There was a crowd looking for work on the dock;
and all the while men hurried to the dock.
The man at the wheel
kept the bow of the launch[2]   5
against the dock —
the engine running slowly;
and the men kept jumping
from dock to deck,
jostling each other,
and crowding into the cabin.   10

Eighty or ninety men were in the cabin as the launch pulled away.
There were no lights in the cabin, and no room to turn — whoever was sitting
    down could not get up, and whoever had his hand up could not get it down,
as the launch ran in the darkness
through the ice,   15
ice cracking
against the launch,
bumping and scraping
against the launch,
banging up against it,   20
until it struck
a solid cake of ice,

---

1. **Testimony:** Based on cases in the law reports. [Reznikoff's note]
2. **launch:** A boat with an open or half-open deck.

rolled to one side, and slowly
came back to an even keel.

The men began to feel water running against their feet as if from a hose. "Cap,"[3]
  shouted one, "the boat is taking water! Put your rubbers[4] on, boys!"   25
The man at the wheel turned.
"Shut up!" he said.
The men began to shout,
ankle-deep in water.
The man at the wheel turned   30
with his flashlight:
everybody was turning and pushing against each other;
those near the windows
were trying to break them,
in spite of the wire mesh   35
in the glass; those who had been near the door
were now in the river,
reaching for the cakes of ice,
their hands slipping off and
reaching for the cakes of ice.   40

II

Amelia was just fourteen and out of the orphan asylum; at her first job — in the
  bindery, and yes sir, yes ma'am, oh, so anxious to please.
She stood at the table, her blonde hair hanging about her shoulders, "knocking
  up" for Mary and Sadie, the stitchers
("knocking up" is counting books and stacking them in piles to be taken away).
There were twenty wire-stitching machines on the floor, worked by a shaft that
  ran under the table;
as each stitcher put her work through the machine,   45
she threw it on the table. The books were piling up fast
and some slid to the floor
(the forelady had said, Keep the work off the floor!);
and Amelia stooped to pick up the books —
three or four had fallen under the table   50
between the boards nailed against the legs.
She felt her hair caught gently;
put her hand up and felt the shaft going round and round
and her hair caught on it, wound and winding around it,

---

3. **Cap:** An abbreviation of *Captain.*
4. **rubbers:** Waterproof boots.

until the scalp was jerked from her head,   55
and the blood was coming down all over her face and waist.

III

They had been married in Italy in May.
Her husband had been in America before,
but she had never been in this country;
neither had her husband's cousin.   60
The three of them had landed in New York City
that morning, and had taken a train north.
As they left the station, she carried a bundle, her husband a little trunk, and his
    cousin a satchel.
It was almost midnight and freezing cold.
Her husband had a paper on which an address was written.   65
He asked a man near the station the way,
but the man shook his head and walked on.

The saloon was still open, and her husband went inside.
The saloon-keeper knew the man they were looking for,
but he had moved.   70
Three men were sitting at a table, playing cards and drinking beer:
one was very short, the other dark
with curly hair and a cap on his head,
and the third was tall. That was Long John.

The saloon-keeper's wife poured her a little glass of anisette,   75
and the saloon-keeper put up two glasses of beer
for her husband and his cousin; and they warmed themselves at the stove.
The saloon-keeper said to the dark fellow with curly hair,
"Take them to my brother's — maybe he knows where the man lives." When they
    were gone,
Long John stood up and said,   80
"I think I'll get myself a little fresh air," and finished his beer.
Long John and the little fellow followed the others, overtook them,
and went along. Long John rang the door-bell, knocked and kicked at the door
until the saloon-keeper's brother — in his underwear —
opened the door, and all went in together.   85
The saloon-keeper's brother said to Madelina, "If you and your husband and the
    cousin
want to stay here tonight —
for going where the man you are looking for lives will take a little time —
you can stay in my place tonight. It's so late!
I'll put a mattress for the three of you in the kitchen."   90
Long John answered, "They will get there quickly —

we will go with them!" And the six went out,
Madelina, her husband and his cousin, Long John and the dark fellow with curly
    hair and the silent little fellow.

They had left the streets of the city
and were on the railroad tracks.   95
Long John went on ahead and the other two
who had been sitting with him in the saloon,
walked behind. Madelina carried the bundle, her husband the little trunk, and
    his cousin the satchel.
She said at last, "When will we get there?"
Long John answered, "In four or five minutes.   100
You have walked so far, can't you walk a little longer?"
At last he stopped. "This is the place," he said.
Madelina looked about and saw only the railroad tracks
and the ground covered with snow.
"Is this the place? But I don't see any houses."   105
"They are only three or four steps further on."
Madelina turned to her husband. "Give them some money —
they have earned it." "No," said Long John,
"we don't want any money." And all at once
he had a pistol in his hand and was shooting.   110
Her husband started to run,
crying out, and holding his hands to the wound in his belly.
Madelina ran after him,
until Long John caught her by the neck
and held her. Then the little fellow came up   115
and they took her back to where her husband's cousin was lying on the ground
dead, beside the satchel, the bundle, and the little trunk.

Long John said, "Don't cry! You've got to be my wife.
Don't think of your husband any more.
You should be glad to be my wife."   120
"Yes," said Madelina, "yes, yes."
He took the wedding ring from her finger,
but the rings on her other hand would not come off;
and they walked on in silence.
Long John told the other two to go ahead;   125
turning to Madelina,
he pushed her down on the snow.

Afterwards, they began to walk again,
and came up to the others;
and all walked on until dawn.   130
In the morning, Long John saw the necklace.
"Give me your gold," he said. She took the necklace off and gave it to him.

They came, at last, to a car on a siding
in which was a store for the workers on the railroad,
and went up the little ladder.   135

The storekeeper knew Long John. He brought soap and water,
and Long John made Madelina wash her hands
and slipped the rings off.
The storekeeper called Long John aside and asked who she was.
"A whore," said Long John.   140
"You must go away," the storekeeper answered.
"If a foreman should come around, he'd kick if he saw you.
Warm yourselves a while — I'll make some coffee;
but then you must go away."
They were all silent until the coffee was ready.   145
Long John and his companions drank it,
but Madelina did not want any. She sat weeping.
Long John brought her a cup of coffee.
"Drink it," he said. "Never mind, never mind!"

IV

Outside the night was cold, the snow was deep   150
on sill and sidewalk; but in our kitchen
it was bright and warm.
I smelt the damp clean clothes
as my mother lifted them from the basket,
the pungent smell of melting wax   155
as she rubbed it on the iron,
and the good lasting smell of meat and potatoes
in the black pot that simmered on the stove.
The stove was so hot it was turning red.
My mother lifted the lid of the pot   160
to stir the roast with a long wooden spoon:
Father would not be home for another hour.
I tugged at her skirts. Tell me a story!

Once upon a time (the best beginning!)
there was a rich woman, a baroness, and a poor woman, a beggar.   165
The poor woman came every day to beg and every day
the rich woman gave her a loaf of bread
until the rich woman was tired of it.
I will put poison in the next loaf, she thought,
to be rid of her.   170
The beggar woman thanked the baroness for that loaf
and went to her hut,

but, as she was going through the fields,
she met the rich woman's son coming out of the forest.

"Hello, hello, beggar woman!" said the young baron,   175
"I have been away for three days hunting
and am very hungry.
I know you are coming from my mother's
and that she has given you a loaf of bread;
let me have it — she will give you another."   180

"Gladly, gladly," said the beggar woman,
and, without knowing it was poisoned, gave him the loaf.
But, as he went on, he thought, I am nearly home —
I will wait.
You may be sure that his mother was glad to see him,   185
and she told the maids to bring a cup of wine
and make his supper — quickly, quickly!
"I met the beggar woman," he said,
"and was so hungry I asked for the loaf you give her."
"Did you eat it, my son?" the baroness whispered.   190
"No, I knew you had something better for me
than this dry bread."
She threw it right into the fire,
and every day, after that, gave the beggar woman a loaf
and never again tried to poison her.   195
So, my son, if you try to harm others,
you may only harm yourself.

And, Mother, if you are a beggar, sooner or later,
there is poison in your bread.

                                                                 [1941, 2005]

Hart Crane

[1899-1932]

[Crane] was a born poet.
— E. E. Cummings

Harold Hart Crane was born on July 21, 1899, in Garrettsville, Ohio. He was the only child of Grace Hart, the daughter of an old and prosperous family, and Clarence Crane, an ambitious salesman who worked briefly for his father's maple-syrup company before starting a competing company in the nearby town of Warren, Ohio. In 1908, Crane's parents separated, and they sent their shy and withdrawn nine-year-old son to live with his maternal grandmother in Cleveland. When the couple reconciled, the family moved

Hart Crane

This photograph was taken on the roof of the building where Crane lived in 1924. The expansive view of the Brooklyn Bridge, shown in the background, inspired his most ambitious poem, *The Bridge* (1930).

to Cleveland, where Crane's father established the Crane Company, a chain of successful candy shops featuring chocolates and a "summer candy" he invented, Life Savers. In the midst of this new stability, Crane began to attend school regularly and enrolled in East High School in 1913. Interested in music and an avid reader of poetry and drama, he soon began writing verses. But his parents' turbulent marriage faltered once again, and in 1915 Crane's mother took him out of school to visit his grandmother at her vacation cottage on the Isle of Pines in the West Indies. When he and his mother returned to Cleveland later that year, Crane met Harriet Moody, the widow of the poet William Vaughn Moody. The friend of many emerging writers of the day, including Carl Sandburg, she offered Crane the first serious encouragement he had received about his writing. He subsequently sent a poem to a small magazine in New York City, *Bruno's Weekly*, which published Crane's "C 33" — a reference to the cell in London's Reading Gaol in which the Irish writer Oscar Wilde had been imprisoned for homosexual acts — in 1916.

For the next three years, the aspiring young poet struggled to gain a foothold in the literary world. After his parents divorced in 1916, Crane dropped out of high school and worked briefly at various sales jobs. His father then reluctantly provided him with an allowance that enabled Crane to move to New York City, where he was expected to study with tutors in preparation for admission to Columbia University. Crane lived a bohemian life in a series of rented rooms in Greenwich Village, where through Harriet Moody and family friends he met other writers and artists. Crane spent most of his time reading and writing, publishing several poems in the avant-garde magazine the *Pagan* in March 1917. At the urging of his mother, who strongly approved of his efforts to become a writer and wanted him to acknowledge her side of the family, he began to publish his work under the name "Hart Crane." During the following year, he became an associate editor of the *Pagan*, but the wartime economy and his father's refusal to fund what he no longer viewed as serious preparation for college forced Crane to return to Cleveland. There, he worked in a munitions plant and as a riveter in a shipyard until the end of World War I, when he became a reporter for the Cleveland *Plain Dealer*. In 1919, he returned to New York City, where he took a job as an advertising manager for the *Little Review*. After a few months, the lack of money once again forced him back to the Midwest, this time to Akron, Ohio, where he worked as a clerk in one of the candy stores run by the Crane Company.

Although his father sincerely hoped that he would give up the "poetry nonsense," Crane produced his most significant work during the following decade. From 1919 to 1922, he worked for the Crane Company in Akron, Cleveland, and Washington, D.C. Dissatisfied with the work, he quit and found a job writing copy for an advertising company in Cleveland. At the same time, he corresponded with other writers, including Sherwood Anderson, and he gained a modest reputation by publishing poems in notable "little magazines" such as the *Dial* and the *Little Review*. In 1923, determined to make a final push to establish himself as a poet, Crane moved back to New York City. There he met numerous writers, including E. E. Cummings, Eugene O'Neill, and Jean Toomer, as well as the influential critics Malcolm Cowley and Waldo Frank. In 1924, Crane had a passionate love affair with Emil Opffer, a Danish sailor with whom he lived in a room overlooking the Brooklyn Bridge that had once been occupied by its famed architect, John Roebling. The intense experience inspired Crane's two most acclaimed poetic sequences: "Voyages," an ecstatic series of love poems, and *The Bridge*, an epic exploration of the history and mystical significance of America. A friend, the financier Otto Kahn, agreed to support Crane while he worked on his book-length poem, much of which he wrote during an extended stay at the Isle of Pines in 1926. But he struggled to complete *The Bridge*. After the publication of his first collection of poetry, *White Buildings* (1926), Crane worked primarily on shorter poems, especially a sequence he tentatively entitled "Key West." Finally, after he returned to New York City from a seven-month trip to England and France, he finished *The Bridge* in December 1929.

The publication of the poem early in 1930 effectively marked the end of Crane's brief and brilliant career. Now famous, he was awarded a Guggenheim Fellowship and went to Mexico, where he planned to write a historical epic about the Spanish overthrow of the Aztec Empire. Although he wrote a friend that he doubted that he would ever "change [his sexual orientation] very fundamentally," he began an affair with Peggy Baird, the former wife of Malcolm Cowley. According to those who met Crane in Mexico, including Katherine Anne Porter, he seemed to be in a downward spiral during the year he spent there, drinking heavily and writing little. He completed what proved to be his final poem, "The Broken Tower," shortly before he sailed from Vera Cruz aboard a passenger liner bound for New York City via Havana. At noon on April 26, 1932, in full view of many of the other passengers, Crane committed suicide by jumping from the main deck into the churning wake of the ship as it steamed at full speed in the

bedfordstmartins.com/ americanlit for research links on Crane

Caribbean. His body was not recovered. *The Collected Poems of Hart Crane*, edited with an introduction by his friend and mentor Waldo Frank, was published in 1933.

Crane's Poetry.   In the introduction to Crane's first collection of poetry, *White Buildings* (1926), Allen Tate described Crane as "the poet of the complex urban civilization of his age." Certainly, life in the modern city was at the center of many of his poems, but his subjects were diverse, as were his poetic models. Largely self-educated, he read and admired Elizabethan poetry and drama, the work of British Romantic poets, especially John Keats and Percy Bysshe Shelley, and the nineteenth-century American poets as different as Walt Whitman, Edgar Allan Poe, and Emily Dickinson. Crane was also influenced by a wide range of contemporary poets, including E. E. Cummings, T. S. Eliot, Ezra Pound, and Wallace Stevens. Even compared with the challenging work of such poets, Crane's poetry struck many critics as difficult and obscure. Although he was in some ways a relatively traditional poet who most often wrote in regular meters and frequently used rhyme, Crane's poems are also characterized by their heightened diction, dense imagery, and complex metaphors. In a letter to the editor of *Poetry*, Harriet Monroe, who criticized the obscurity and apparent illogic of a poem he had submitted, Crane in 1926 emphasized that unlike other forms of writing poetry derived its power from what he called "the logic of metaphor," explaining:

> I may very possibly be more interested in the so-called illogical impingements of the connotations of words on the consciousness (and their combinations and interplay in metaphor on this basis) than I am interested in the preservation of their logically rigid significations at the cost of limiting my subject matter and the perceptions involved in the poem.

The texts are taken from *The Complete Poems of Hart Crane*, edited by Marc Simon (2000).

VOYAGES[1]

I

Above the fresh ruffles of the surf
Bright striped urchins flay each other with sand.
They have contrived a conquest for shell shucks,
And their fingers crumble fragments of baked weed
Gaily digging and scattering.   5

---

1. **Voyages:** Crane wrote most of these poems during the spring of 1924 for his lover Emil Opffer. After publishing four of the poems as "Voyages" in the *Little Review* (Spring 1926), Crane added two poems and published the expanded, six-poem sequence as "Voyages" at the end of his first book, *White Buildings* (1926).

And in answer to their treble interjections
The sun beats lightning on the waves,
The waves fold thunder on the sand;
And could they hear me I would tell them:

O brilliant kids, frisk with your dog,   10
Fondle your shells and sticks, bleached
By time and the elements; but there is a line
You must not cross nor ever trust beyond it
Spry cordage of your bodies to caresses
Too lichen-faithful from too wide a breast.   15
The bottom of the sea is cruel.

II

— And yet this great wink of eternity,
Of rimless floods, unfettered leewardings,[2]
Samite[3] sheeted and processioned where
Her undinal[4] vast belly moonward bends,
Laughing the wrapt inflections of our love;   5

Take this Sea, whose diapason[5] knells
On scrolls of silver snowy sentences,
The sceptred terror of whose sessions rends
As her demeanors motion well or ill,
All but the pieties of lovers' hands.   10

And onward, as bells off San Salvador
Salute the crocus lustres of the stars,
In these poinsettia meadows of her tides, —
Adagios of islands,[6] O my Prodigal,
Complete the dark confessions her veins spell.   15

Mark how her turning shoulders wind the hours,
And hasten while her penniless rich palms
Pass superscription of bent foam and wave, —

---

2. **leewardings:** From *leeward*, the side sheltered or away from the wind.
3. **Samite:** A silk fabric woven with gold and silver threads, used in the Middle Ages.
4. **undinal:** With the characteristics of a water nymph.
5. **diapason:** A poetic term for the entire scope or range of something, or figuratively, a swelling burst of harmony.
6. **Adagios of islands:** In "General Aims and Theories" (1937), an essay unpublished during his lifetime, Crane explained that he used this phrase to suggest "the motion of a boat through islands clustered thickly, the rhythm of the motion, etc.," adding that "it seems a much more direct and creative statement than any more logical employment of words such as 'coasting slowly through the islands,' besides ushering in a whole world of music."

Hasten, while they are true, — sleep, death, desire,
Close round one instant in one floating flower.   20

Bind us in time, O Seasons clear, and awe.
O minstrel galleons of Carib[7] fire,
Bequeath us to no earthly shore until
Is answered in the vortex of our grave
The seal's wide spindrift gaze toward paradise.   25

III

Infinite consanguinity[8] it bears —
This tendered theme of you that light
Retrieves from sea plains where the sky
Resigns a breast that every wave enthrones;
While ribboned water lanes I wind   5
Are laved and scattered with no stroke
Wide from your side, whereto this hour
The sea lifts, also, reliquary[9] hands.

And so, admitted through black swollen gates
That must arrest all distance otherwise, —   10
Past whirling pillars and lithe pediments,
Light wrestling there incessantly with light,
Star kissing star through wave on wave unto
Your body rocking!
                and where death, if shed,   15
Presumes no carnage, but this single change, —
Upon the steep floor flung from dawn to dawn
The silken skilled transmemberment of song;

Permit me voyage, love, into your hands . . .

IV

Whose counted smile of hours and days, suppose
I know as spectrum of the sea and pledge
Vastly now parting gulf on gulf of wings
Whose circles bridge, I know, (from palms to the severe
Chilled albatross's white immutability)   5
No stream of greater love advancing now

---

7. **Carib:** Of or relating to the Caribs, the indigenous peoples of coastal areas of the Caribbean.
8. **consanguinity:** Familial relationship.
9. **reliquary:** A container for holy relics.

Than, singing, this mortality alone
Through clay aflow immortally to you.

All fragrance irrefragably, and claim
Madly meeting logically in this hour   10
And region that is ours to wreathe again,
Portending eyes and lips and making told
The chancel port and portion of our June —

Shall they not stem and close in our own steps
Bright staves of flowers and quills today as I   15
Must first be lost in fatal tides to tell?

In signature of the incarnate word[10]
The harbor shoulders to resign in mingling
Mutual blood, transpiring as foreknown
And widening noon within your breast for gathering   20
All bright insinuations that my years have caught
For islands where must lead inviolably
Blue latitudes and levels of your eyes, —

In this expectant, still exclaim receive
The secret oar and petals of all love.   25

                               V

Meticulous, past midnight in clear rime,
Infrangible and lonely, smooth as though cast
Together in one merciless white blade —
The bay estuaries fleck the hard sky limits.

— As if too brittle or too clear to touch!   5
The cables of our sleep so swiftly filed,
Already hang, shred ends from remembered stars.
One frozen trackless smile . . . What words
Can strangle this deaf moonlight? For we

Are overtaken. Now no cry, no sword   10
Can fasten or deflect this tidal wedge,
Slow tyranny of moonlight, moonlight loved
And changed . . . "There's

---

10. **the incarnate word:** The word embodied in human form, an allusion to John 1:14: "And the Word was
made flesh, and dwelt among us." In a letter to Waldo Frank in April 1924, Crane wrote of his relationship to
Emil Opffer: "I have seen the Word made Flesh. I mean nothing less, and I know now that there is such a
thing as indestructibility."

Nothing like this in the world," you say,
Knowing I cannot touch your hand and look   15
Too, into that godless cleft of sky
Where nothing turns but dead sands flashing.

"— And never to quite understand!" No,
In all the argosy[11] of your bright hair I dreamed
Nothing so flagless as this piracy.   20

                    But now
Draw in your head, alone and too tall here.
Your eyes already in the slant of drifting foam;
Your breath sealed by the ghosts I do not know:
Draw in your head and sleep the long way home.   25

VI

Where icy and bright dungeons lift
Of swimmers their lost morning eyes,
And ocean rivers, churning, shift
Green borders under stranger skies,

Steadily as a shell secretes   5
Its beating leagues of monotone,
Or as many waters trough the sun's
Red kelson[12] past the cape's wet stone;

O rivers mingling toward the sky
And harbor of the phoenix' breast —   10
My eyes pressed black against the prow,
— Thy derelict and blinded guest

Waiting, afire, what name, unspoke,
I cannot claim: let thy waves rear
More savage than the death of kings,   15
Some splintered garland for the seer.

Beyond siroccos harvesting
The solstice thunders, crept away,
Like a cliff swinging or a sail
Flung into April's inmost day —   20

---

11. **argosy:** A large merchant ship.
12. **kelson:** Also spelled *keelson*, the centerline structure running the length of a ship that provides its
support and stability.

Creation's blithe and petalled word
To the lounged goddess when she rose
Conceding dialogue with eyes
That smile unsearchable repose —

Still fervid covenant, Belle Isle,[13]   25
— Unfolded floating dais before
Which rainbows twine continual hair —
Belle Isle, white echo of the oar!

The imaged Word,[14] it is, that holds
Hushed willows anchored in its glow.   30
It is the unbetrayable reply
Whose accent no farewell can know.

[1926, 2000]

---

13. **Belle Isle**: Beautiful Island (French).
14. **the imaged Word**: See note 10.

TO BROOKLYN BRIDGE[1]

How many dawns, chill from his rippling rest
The seagull's wings shall dip and pivot him,
Shedding white rings of tumult, building high
Over the chained bay waters Liberty —

Then, with inviolate curve, forsake our eyes   5
As apparitional as sails that cross
Some page of figures to be filed away;
— Till elevators drop us from our day . . .

I think of cinemas, panoramic sleights
With multitudes bent toward some flashing scene   10
Never disclosed, but hastened to again,
Foretold to other eyes on the same screen;

And Thee, across the harbor, silver-paced
As though the sun took step of thee, yet left

---

1. **To Brooklyn Bridge**: Crane published this poem separately under this title in the *Dial* (June 1927) and later in italics as the opening section of *The Bridge* (1930). The Brooklyn Bridge, which Crane later described as "the matchless symbol of America and its destiny," spans the East River between Brooklyn and Manhattan Island. It was the longest suspension bridge in the world when it opened to great fanfare in 1883.

Some motion ever unspent in thy stride, —   15
Implicitly thy freedom staying thee!

Out of some subway scuttle, cell or loft
A bedlamite[2] speeds to thy parapets,
Tilting there momently, shrill shirt ballooning,
A jest falls from the speechless caravan.   20

Down Wall,[3] from girder into street noon leaks,
A rip-tooth of the sky's acetylene;
All afternoon the cloud-flown derricks turn . . .
Thy cables breathe the North Atlantic still.

And obscure as that heaven of the Jews,   25
Thy guerdon[4] . . . Accolade thou dost bestow
Of anonymity time cannot raise:
Vibrant reprieve and pardon thou dost show.

O harp and altar, of the fury fused,
(How could mere toil align thy choiring strings!)   30
Terrific threshold of the prophet's pledge,
Prayer of pariah, and the lover's cry, —

Again the traffic lights that skim thy swift
Unfractioned idiom, immaculate sigh of stars,
Beading thy path — condense eternity: 35
And we have seen night lifted in thine arms.

Under thy shadow by the piers I waited;
Only in darkness is thy shadow clear.
The City's fiery parcels all undone,
Already snow submerges an iron year . . .   40

O Sleepless as the river under thee,
Vaulting the sea, the prairies' dreaming sod,
Unto us lowliest sometime sweep, descend
And of the curveship lend a myth to God.

                                        [1927, 2000]

---

2. **bedlamite:** An insane person; the term is derived from the inmates of Bedlam, the informal name for St. Mary of Bethlehem, the notorious insane asylum in London.
3. **Wall:** Wall Street, the major financial district of New York City.
4. **guerdon:** An archaic term for reward.

THE BROKEN TOWER[1]

The bell-rope that gathers God at dawn
Dispatches me as though I dropped down the knell
Of a spent day — to wander the cathedral lawn
From pit to crucifix, feet chill on steps from hell.

Have you not heard, have you not seen that corps   5
Of shadows in the tower, whose shoulders sway
Antiphonal carillons launched before
The stars are caught and hived in the sun's ray?

The bells, I say, the bells break down their tower;
And swing I know not where. Their tongues engrave   10
Membrane through marrow, my long-scattered score
Of broken intervals . . . And I, their sexton slave!

Oval encyclicals[2] in canyons heaping
The impasse high with choir. Banked voices slain!
Pagodas, campaniles[3] with reveilles outleaping —   15
O terraced echoes prostrate on the plain! . . .

And so it was I entered the broken world
To trace the visionary company of love, its voice
An instant in the wind (I know not whither hurled)
But not for long to hold each desperate choice.   20

My word I poured. But was it cognate, scored
Of that tribunal monarch of the air
Whose thigh embronzes earth, strikes crystal Word
In wounds pledged once to hope, — cleft to despair?

The steep encroachments of my blood left me   25
No answer (could blood hold such a lofty tower
As flings the question true?) — or is it she
Whose sweet mortality stirs latent power? —

And through whose pulse I hear, counting the strokes
My veins recall and add, revived and sure   30
The angelus[4] of wars my chest evokes:
What I hold healed, original now, and pure . . .

---

1. **The Broken Tower:** Crane wrote this poem in Mexico, a few weeks before he committed suicide on April 26, 1926. The poem was published posthumously in the *Nation* on June 8, 1932.
2. **encyclicals:** Formal policy letters written by the pope and sent to all the bishops of the Roman Catholic Church.
3. **campaniles:** Italian bell towers.
4. **angelus:** The ringing of church bells announcing the thrice-daily Roman Catholic devotional service commemorating the Incarnation of Jesus.

And builds, within, a tower that is not stone
(Not stone can jacket heaven) — but slip
Of pebbles, — visible wings of silence sown   35
In azure circles, widening as they dip

The matrix of the heart, lift down the eye
That shrines the quiet lake and swells a tower . . .
The commodious, tall decorum of that sky
Unseals her earth, and lifts love in its shower.   40

[1932, 2000]

Sterling A. Brown

[1901-1989]

Sterling Allen Brown was born on May 1, 1901, in Washington, D.C. He was the youngest of six children of Adelaide Allen, a graduate of Fisk University, and Sterling Nelson Brown, a former slave who worked his way through Oberlin College and Fisk to become the minister of the Lincoln Temple Congregational Church and a professor of religion at Howard University. In a 1973 interview, Brown recalled that when he was a child his mother often read to him from the works of poets such as Henry Wadsworth Longfellow and Paul Laurence Dunbar: "I remember even now her stopping sweeping . . . now standing over that broom and reading poetry to me, and she was a good reader, great sense of rhythm." Brown attended Dunbar High School in Washington, where his teachers included Haley Douglass, grandson of Frederick Douglass, and Jessie Redmon Fauset, later a novelist and literary editor of the *Crisis*, the journal of the National Association for the Advancement of Colored People (NAACP). When he graduated in 1918, Brown went to Williams College, which each year granted a scholarship to the outstanding student from Dunbar. At the isolated college in northwestern Massachusetts, Brown was one of a small group of African American students who experienced racism in the form of "benign neglect," as he later described it. Brown graduated Phi Beta Kappa in 1922 and then enrolled at Harvard University, where he earned a master's degree in 1923.

Sterling A. Brown

This photograph of Brown was taken early in his distinguished career as a poet and professor of English at Howard University.

At Harvard, Brown began to formulate the poetics that would shape his writing for the rest of his life. Fascinated by the formal and linguistic experiments of a new generation of poets, he was strongly influenced by the anthology *Modern American Poetry* (1921), which introduced him to the work of Amy Lowell, Robert Frost, Edwin Arlington Robinson, and Carl Sandburg. He was especially impressed by Frost and by Robinson, who, as Brown later observed, "took up the undistinguished, the failures, and showed the extraordinary in ordinary lives." He was also drawn to the work of Claude McKay, Langston Hughes, and other poets of the Harlem Renaissance. Convinced that the rural culture of southern blacks was the basis for modern African American literature, Brown began serious study of African American folkways after he left Harvard in 1923 and took his first position teaching English at Virginia Seminary and College. He continued his anthropological studies while teaching at Lincoln University in Missouri (1926–28), Fisk (1928–29), and Howard, where he moved in 1929. Meanwhile, he married Daisy Turnbull in 1927, the year Brown published his first poem, "When de Saints Go Marching Home," in *Opportunity: A Journal of Negro Life*. His poetry then began to appear regularly in *Opportunity*, in anthologies edited by his fellow poets Countee Cullen and James Weldon Johnson, and in *Folk-Say, A Regional Miscellany*, edited by the influential folklorist Benjamin A. Botkin.

He infused his poetry with genuine characteristic flavor by adopting as his medium the common, racy, living speech of the Negro in certain phases of real life.

–James Weldon Johnson

During the following decades, Brown distinguished himself as a poet, literary critic, and scholar. In 1932, he published his first collection of poetry, *Southern Road*. In the preface to the volume, James Weldon Johnson called Brown's work "a distinctive contribution to American poetry," and *Southern Road* was praised by both white and black reviewers in periodicals as diverse as *Opportunity*, the *New Republic*, the *New York Times*, and the *Saturday Review of Literature*. But worsening economic conditions prevented the publication of Brown's second collection, *No Hiding Place*. He consequently turned to other projects, notably two influential books of literary criticism: *The Negro in American Fiction* and *Negro Poetry and Drama*, both published in 1937. He also coedited one of the most important anthologies of African American literature published in the first half of the twentieth century, *The Negro Caravan* (1941), which included the work of writers ranging from the eighteenth-century poet Phillis Wheatley to contemporary fiction writers such as Zora Neale Hurston and Richard Wright. During the five decades Brown taught at Howard, from which he retired in 1969, he also inspired generations of students, including the Nobel laureate Toni Morrison. In 1975, Brown published his second book of poems, *The Last Ride of Wild Bill and Eleven Narrative Poems*, and four years later he was named poet laureate of the District of Columbia. His various contributions gained increasing attention from critics and scholars, many of whom credited Brown with founding the field of African American studies. When he died on January 17, 1989, the obituary in the *Washington Post* observed that Brown had been "perhaps the most knowledgeable living person on the subject of American Negro literature, tradition, heritage, and thought."

Brown's Poetry.   The title of Brown's first collection of poetry, *Southern Road* (1932), indicated his departure from poets of the Harlem Renaissance, who were exploring the urban experience of African Americans in the North. In contrast, most of Brown's poems were rooted in the experience, folklore, and music of the rural black population of the South. Drawing inspiration from work songs, spirituals, and especially the blues,

Southern Road

E. Simms Campell, a young African American artist who later became a successful cartoonist for mainstream magazines such as *Esquire*, provided four black-and-white illustrations for *Southern Road*. The letters in the background of this illustration, which preceded the section "Tin Roof Blues," form part of the words "FOR COLORED ONLY," a sign common throughout the segregated South.

Brown wrote in black vernacular at a time when many other African American writers dismissed such language as a vestige of blackface minstrel shows and the "plantation myth." Brown was determined to liberate black vernacular from the burden of the plantation tradition even as he challenged the conventions of what was called "Negro dialect poetry," which had previously been the vehicle of exaggerated humor, pathos, or sentimentality. James Weldon Johnson, who a decade earlier had asserted that such poetry "was not capable of giving expression to the varied conditions of Negro life in America," testified to the success of Brown's experiments in language and subject matter in *Southern Road*. "Mr. Brown's work is not only fine, it is unique," Johnson observed in his preface to the volume. "He infused his poetry with genuine characteristic flavor by adopting as his medium the common, racy, living speech of the Negro in certain phases of *real* life. For his raw material he dug down into the deep mine of Negro folk poetry." The texts of the following poems from *Southern Road* are taken from *The Collected Poems of Sterling A. Brown* (1989).

bedfordstmartins.com/ americanlit for research links on Brown

MA RAINEY[1]

I

When Ma Rainey
Comes to town,
Folks from anyplace
Miles aroun',
From Cape Girardeau,   5
Poplar Bluff,[2]
Flocks in to hear
Ma do her stuff;
Comes flivverin' in,[3]
Or ridin' mules,   10
Or packed in trains,
Picknickin' fools. . . .
That's what it's like,
Fo' miles on down,
To New Orleans delta   15
An' Mobile town,
When Ma hits
Anywheres aroun'.

II

Dey comes to hear Ma Rainey from de little river settlements,
From blackbottom cornrows and from lumber camps;   20
Dey stumble in de hall, jes a-laughin' an' a-cacklin',
Cheerin' lak roarin' water, lak wind in river swamps.

An' some jokers keeps deir laughs a-goin' in de crowded aisles,
An' some folks sits dere waitin' wid deir aches an' miseries,
Till Ma comes out before dem, a-smilin' gold-toofed smiles   25
An' Long Boy ripples minors on de black an' yellow keys.

III

O Ma Rainey,
Sing yo' song;

---

1. **Ma Rainey:** Gertrude Pridgett Rainey (1886–1939), known as "Ma" Rainey, was among the earliest professional blues singers and is often regarded as the "Mother of the Blues." She toured with the Rabbit Foot Minstrels from the time she was a young girl and began recording blues songs in 1923, often accompanied by Louis Armstrong. Her versions of songs such as "See See Rider," "Ma Rainey's Black Bottom," and "Backwater Blues," quoted later in this poem, became classics.
2. **Cape Girardeau, Poplar Bluff:** Towns in southeastern Missouri, the former on the Mississippi River and the latter in the Ozark Mountains.
3. **Comes flivverin' in:** *Flivver* is an early twentieth-century term for a cheap car in poor condition.

Now you's back
Whah you belong,   30
Git way inside us,
Keep us strong. . . .
O Ma Rainey,
Li'l an' low;
Sing us 'bout de hard luck   35
Roun' our do';
Sing us 'bout de lonesome road
We mus' go. . . .

IV

I talked to a fellow, an' the fellow say,
"She jes' catch hold of us, somekindaway.   40
She sang Backwater Blues one day:

> *'It rained fo' days an' de skies was dark as night,*
> *Trouble taken place in de lowlands at night.*

> *'Thundered an' lightened an' the storm begin to roll*
> *Thousan's of people ain't got no place to go.*   45

> *'Den I went an' stood upon some high ol' lonesome hill,*
> *An' looked down on the place where I used to live.'*

An' den de folks, dey natchally bowed dey heads an' cried,
Bowed dey heavy heads, shet dey moufs up tight an' cried,
An' Ma lef' de stage, an' followed some de folks outside." 50

Dere wasn't much more de fellow say:
She jes' gits hold of us dataway.

[1930, 1989]

STRONG MEN

> *The young men keep coming on*
> *The strong men keep coming on.*
> SANDBURG[1]

They dragged you from homeland,
They chained you in coffles,[2]
They huddled you spoon-fashion in filthy hatches,
They sold you to give a few gentlemen ease.

---

1. **Sandburg:** The epigraph is adapted from Carl Sandburg's "Upstream" (1922), which begins and ends with the line "The strong men keep coming on." Brown particularly admired Sandburg's use of colloquial speech and treatment of common subjects.
2. **coffles:** A line of animals or slaves fastened together.

They broke you in like oxen, 5
They scourged you,
They branded you,
They made your women breeders,
They swelled your numbers with bastards. . . .
They taught you the religion they disgraced. 10

You sang:
    Keep a-inchin' along
    Lak a po' inch worm. . . .

You sang:
    Bye and bye 15
    I'm gonna lay down dis heaby load. . . .

You sang:
    Walk togedder, chillen,
    Dontcha git weary. . . .
        The strong men keep a-comin' on 20
        The strong men git stronger.

They point with pride to the roads you built for them,
They ride in comfort over the rails you laid for them.
They put hammers in your hands
And said — Drive so much before sundown. 25

You sang:
    Ain't no hammah
    In dis lan',
    Strikes lak mine, bebby,
    Strikes lak mine. 30

They cooped you in their kitchens,
They penned you in their factories,
They gave you the jobs that they were too good for,
They tried to guarantee happiness to themselves
By shunting dirt and misery to you. 35

You sang:
    Me an' muh baby gonna shine, shine
    Me an' muh baby gonna shine.
        The strong men keep a-comin' on
        The strong men git stronger. . . . 40

They bought off some of your leaders
You stumbled, as blind men will . . .
They coaxed you, unwontedly soft-voiced. . . .
You followed a way.
Then laughed as usual. 45

They heard the laugh and wondered;
Uncomfortable,
Unadmitting a deeper terror. . . .
      The strong men keep a-comin' on
      Gittin' stronger. . . .   50

What, from the slums
Where they have hemmed you,
What, from the tiny huts
They could not keep from you —
What reaches them   55
Making them ill at ease, fearful?
Today they shout prohibition at you
"Thou shalt not this"
"Thou shalt not that"
"Reserved for whites only"   60
You laugh.

One thing they cannot prohibit —
      The strong men . . . coming on
      The strong men gittin' stronger.
      Strong men. . . .   65
      Stronger. . . .

                    [1931, 1989]

TIN ROOF BLUES

I'm goin' where de Southern crosses top de C. & O.[1]
I'm goin' where de Southern crosses top de C. & O.
I'm goin' down de country cause I cain't stay here no mo'.

Goin' where de Norfolk Western[2] curves jes' lak de river bends,
Where de Norfolk Western swing around de river bends,   5
Goin' where de people stacks up mo' lak friends.

Leave 'is dirty city, take my foot up in my hand,
Dis do-dirty city, take my foot up in my hand,
Git down to de livin' what a man kin understand.

---

1. **Southern . . . C. & O.:** The Southern Railway, then an 8,000-mile system across thirteen states, and the Chesapeake and Ohio Railway, which linked Virginia, West Virginia, and Kentucky with Ohio and Illinois.
2. **Norfolk Western:** The Norfolk and Western Railway was a coal-hauling line, with routes located mainly in Virginia, West Virginia, Maryland, and North Carolina.

Gang of dicties[3] here, an' de rest wants to git dat way,   10
Dudes an' dicties, others strive to git dat way,
Put pennies on de numbers from now unto de jedgement day.

I'm got de tin roof blues, got dese sidewalks on my mind,
De tin roof blues, dese lonesome sidewalks on my mind,
I'm goin' where de shingles covers people mo' my kind.   15

[1931, 1989]

3. **dicties**: Black street slang for respectable, middle-class African Americans.

Langston Hughes

[1902–1967]

Langston Hughes

The prominent New York photographer Nickolas Muray took this portrait of Hughes in 1923, when the young poet was a rising star of what became known as the Harlem Renaissance.

James Langston Hughes was born on February 1, 1902, in Joplin, Missouri. He was the only child of Carrie Langston Hughes, a former schoolteacher, and James Nathaniel Hughes. In Hughes's autobiography, he explained that his parents were descendants of white slave owners and slave traders, slaves, free people of color, and Native Americans, observing: "There are lots of different kinds of blood in our family." When Hughes's father was denied the chance to take the Oklahoma Territory Bar examination because of his race, he left his family and went to live in Mexico. Carrie Hughes took her son back home to Lawrence, Kansas, where Hughes was raised primarily by his twice-widowed grandmother, Mary Langston. Her first husband was Lewis Sheridan Leary, who died in the abolitionist John Brown's raid at Harpers Ferry in 1859, and her second husband (and Hughes's grandfather) was Charles Langston, a well-known abolitionist and the brother of John Mercer Langston, a congressman from Virginia in the 1890s. Despite the family connections, Hughes's troubled childhood was spent in poverty. Encouraged to read by both his mother and grandmother, he recalled: "I began to believe in nothing but books and the wonderful world in books — where if people suffered, they suffered in beautiful language, not in monosyllables, as we did in Kansas." When he was thirteen, his grandmother died and Hughes joined his mother and her new husband in Lincoln, Illinois. In 1916, the family moved to Cleveland, Ohio, where Hughes attended Central High School.

During the following decade, Hughes emerged as one of the most notable poets among the writers of the Harlem Renaissance. He wrote for his school's literary magazine, and in 1919 he published his first poems in *Brownie's Book,* a magazine for African American children founded by W. E. B. Du Bois. After Hughes graduated from high school in 1920, he lived for a year with his father in Mexico. In June 1921, nineteen-year-old Hughes gained acclaim when his poem "The Negro Speaks of Rivers" appeared in the *Crisis,* the magazine of the National Association for the Advancement of Colored People (NAACP), from which it was almost immediately reprinted in the influential *Literary Digest.* His father, who did not want him to become a writer, reluctantly agreed to help pay for a college education, and Hughes enrolled at Columbia University in New York City in the fall of 1921. Although he loved living in Harlem, he was unhappy at the nearly all-white university and withdrew in 1922. He spent the next three years working at a series of menial jobs, but he continued to write and publish poems regularly in the *Crisis.* Uncertain about his future, he joined the crew of a freighter bound for West Africa. He spent much of 1923 and 1924 visiting several African countries and working as a busboy in Paris. When he returned to the United States, he lived with his mother in Washington, D.C., before moving back to Harlem, where the gregarious Hughes associated with many other writers and artists, including Aaron Douglas, Countee Cullen, and Zora Neale Hurston. In 1925, "The Weary Blues," which Hughes called his "lucky poem," won first prize in a literary contest sponsored by *Opportunity: A Journal of Negro Life,* the recently founded magazine of the National Urban League. The prize paved the way for the publication of his first collection of poetry, *The Weary Blues* (1926).

With his literary career fully launched, Hughes struck out in new directions in his life and writings. Still determined to get a college education, he enrolled at the historically black Lincoln University in Pennsylvania, from which he graduated in 1929. In the meantime, he published his second book of poems, *Fine Clothes to the Jew* (1927), and began to write *Not Without Laughter* (1930), a novel based on his early life in the Midwest. During the 1930s, his writings reflected his growing political radicalism and disenchantment with life in the United States. After his return from a brief stay in Cuba and Haiti, Hughes published *Scottsboro Limited* (1931), a verse play protesting the sensational case of the "Scottsboro Boys," a group of black teenagers falsely accused and convicted of raping two white girls in Tennessee. During a year-long visit to Russia, Hughes published militant poems such as "Good Morning Revolution," hailing the revolution as "the very best friend / I ever had." When he returned to the United States, he wrote *The Ways of White Folks* (1934), a collection of satirical and often bitter stories about race relations in the United States. Hughes also began to write drama. The earliest of his plays was *Mulatto,* in which he drew upon his family history to explore the theme of miscegenation

He pursues his way, scornful, in subject matter, in photography, and rhythmical treatment, of whatever obstructions time and tradition have placed before him.

–Countee Cullen

and racial divisions in the South. Encouraged by its successful run on Broadway in 1935, Hughes wrote several more plays, including *Troubled Island* (1936), a historical drama about the slave revolution against French rule in Haiti. During 1937, Hughes lived in Madrid, where he reported on the Spanish civil war for the *Baltimore Afro-American*. When he returned to the United States in 1938, he published a collection of his socialist poetry, *A New Song,* and founded the Harlem Suitcase Theater, a drama group that performed a play he wrote advocating black nationalism and revolution, *Don't You Want to Be Free?*

Hughes later retreated from the revolutionary political positions he had assumed during the 1930s, but he continued to devote himself to the cause of full equality for African Americans. He also continued to extend the range of his writings. In 1940, he published the first volume of his autobiography, *The Big Sea* (1940), which was followed by two volumes of poetry, *Shakespeare in Harlem* (1942) and *Jim Crow's Last Stand* (1943). Struggling to support himself, Hughes wrote song lyrics and in 1942 began to write a weekly column for the crusading African American newspaper the *Chicago Defender.* Taking on the persona of a comic character in Harlem named "Simple" (later "Jesse B. Semple"), Hughes for more than twenty years provided pointed and often humorous commentary on civil rights and social mores in America. The popular column became the basis for five book collections, beginning in 1950 with *Simple Speaks His Mind* and ending in 1965 with *Simple's Uncle Sam.* Meanwhile, Hughes continued to write poetry, notably *Montage of a Dream Deferred* (1951), an acclaimed sequence of poems about Harlem. His later works included several more volumes of poetry, including the radically experimental *Ask Your Mama* (1962); the second volume of his autobiography, *I Wonder as I Wander* (1956); collections of short stories; a number of innovative plays fusing narrative and gospel music; and a series of books for children on African American history, life, and music, including *The First Book of Jazz* (1957). Eager to promote the careers of younger African American writers, Hughes in his final years edited *New Negro Poets USA* (1964) and *The Best Short Stories by Negro Writers* (1967). The author of more than fifty books, Hughes was working on several new projects when he died in New York City on May 22, 1967.

bedfordstmartins.com/ *americanlit* *for research links on Hughes*

Hughes's Poetry.   Identifying the central strand in his writings, probably the most diverse body of work produced by an American writer, Hughes once stated simply: "My writing has been largely concerned with the depicting of Negro life in America." His earliest poetic models were the dialect poems of African American poet Paul Laurence Dunbar and the fervently democratic work of the white poet Carl Sandburg, through whom Hughes discovered Walt Whitman. Blending the free verse of Whitman and Sandburg with the language of African American slave songs, or spirituals, Hughes announced the major theme of his future work in the first

The Weary Blues

The book jacket of Hughes's first collection of poems was designed by the young Mexican artist Miguel Covarrubias, who illustrated the work of a number of African American writers and who became a key figure in the vital cultural relations between Mexico and the United States during the 1920s.

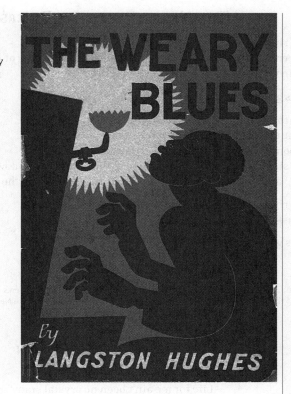

adult poem he published, "The Negro Speaks of Rivers" (1921). In other poems collected in his first book, *The Weary Blues* (1926), Hughes employed black vernacular, the form of the blues, and the rhythms of jazz to capture the essence of African American life, especially in the urban North. Sounding what a reviewer for the *New York Herald Tribune* called "a new note in contemporary American poetry," Hughes embarked on a life-long effort to fuse writing and African American musical forms. He was also influenced by and worked closely with visual artists of the Harlem Renaissance, especially his friend Aaron Douglas. In an early essay, "The Negro Artist and the Racial Mountain" (1926), Hughes proclaimed: "We younger Negro artists who create now intend to express our individual dark-skinned selves without fear or shame." Hughes continued to do that throughout his long and distinguished career, becoming an inspiration and a role model for new African American writers who emerged during the two decades before his death in 1967. The texts of the following poems are from *The Collected Poems of Langston Hughes,* edited by Arnold Rampersad (1994).

THE NEGRO SPEAKS OF RIVERS

I've known rivers:
I've known rivers ancient as the world and older than the flow of human blood
     in human veins.

My soul has grown deep like the rivers.

I bathed in the Euphrates when dawns were young.
I built my hut near the Congo and it lulled me to sleep.   5
I looked upon the Nile and raised the pyramids above it.
I heard the singing of the Mississippi when Abe Lincoln went down to New
     Orleans,[1] and I've seen its muddy bosom turn all golden in the sunset.

I've known rivers:
Ancient, dusky rivers.

My soul has grown deep like the rivers.   10

[1921, 1994]

---

1. **Abe Lincoln . . . New Orleans:** Abraham Lincoln formed his antislavery views as a result of his firsthand
observation of the slave trade during boat trips down the Mississippi River to New Orleans in 1828 and 1831.

MOTHER TO SON

Well, son, I'll tell you.
Life for me ain't been no crystal stair.
It's had tacks in it,
And splinters,
And boards torn up,   5
And places with no carpet on the floor —
Bare.
But all the time
I'se been a-climbin' on,
And reachin' landin's,   10
And turnin' corners,
And sometimes goin' in the dark
Where there ain't been no light.
So boy, don't you turn back.
Don't you set down on the steps   15
'Cause you finds it's kinder hard.
Don't you fall now —
For I'se still goin', honey,
I'se still climbin',
And life for me ain't been no crystal stair.   20

[1922, 1994]

JAZZONIA[1]

Oh, silver tree!
Oh, shining rivers of the soul!

In a Harlem cabaret
Six long-headed jazzers play.
A dancing girl whose eyes are bold   5
Lifts high a dress of silken gold.

Oh, singing tree!
Oh, shining rivers of the soul!

Were Eve's eyes
In the first garden   10
Just a bit too bold?[2]
Was Cleopatra gorgeous
In a gown of gold?[3]

Oh, shining tree!
Oh, silver rivers of the soul!   15

In a whirling cabaret
Six long-headed jazzers play.

[1923, 1994]

---

1. **Jazzonia:** The Greek suffix *onia* suggests the land or country of jazz, located here in a nightclub in Harlem.
2. **Eve's eyes . . . bold?:** According to the Old Testament account, after Eve is tempted by the serpent and she and Adam eat the forbidden fruit of the tree of knowledge, "the eyes of them both were opened, and they knew that they were naked" (Genesis 3:7).
3. **Cleopatra . . . gold?:** The seductive queen Cleopatra of Egypt (69-30 BCE) was often associated with extravagance and sensuality, most famously in Shakespeare's *Antony and Cleopatra.*

I, Too

I, too, sing America.[1]

I am the darker brother.
They send me to eat in the kitchen
When company comes,
But I laugh,   5
And eat well,
And grow strong.

---

1. **I, too, sing America:** An allusion to "I Hear America Singing" by the white poet Walt Whitman (1819-1892), whom Hughes admired and who is often described as the "poet of America."

Tomorrow,
I'll be at the table[2]
When company comes.   10
Nobody'll dare
Say to me,
"Eat in the kitchen,"
Then.

Besides,   15
They'll see how beautiful I am
And be ashamed —

I, too, am America.

[1925, 1994]

---

2. **I'll be at the table:** In early versions of this poem, including its first publication in the *Survey Graphic* (March 1, 1925), this line read: "I'll sit at the table."

The Weary Blues

Droning a drowsy syncopated tune,
Rocking back and forth to a mellow croon,
    I heard a Negro play.
Down on Lenox Avenue the other night
By the pale dull pallor of an old gas light   5
    He did a lazy sway. . . .
    He did a lazy sway. . . .
To the tune o' those Weary Blues.
With his ebony hands on each ivory key
He made that poor piano moan with melody.   10
    O Blues!
Swaying to and fro on his rickety stool
He played that sad raggy tune like a musical fool.
    Sweet Blues!
Coming from a black man's soul.   15
    O Blues!
In a deep song voice with a melancholy tone
I heard that Negro sing, that old piano moan —
    "Ain't got nobody in all this world,
      Ain't got nobody but ma self.   20
      I's gwine to quit ma frownin'
      And put ma troubles on the shelf."

Thump, thump, thump, went his foot on the floor.
He played a few chords then he sang some more —
   "I got the Weary Blues   25
      And I can't be satisfied.
      Got the Weary Blues
      And can't be satisfied —
      I ain't happy no mo'
      And I wish that I had died."   30
And far into the night he crooned that tune.
The stars went out and so did the moon.
The singer stopped playing and went to bed
While the Weary Blues echoed through his head.
He slept like a rock or a man that's dead.   35

                                [1925, 1994]

CROSS

My old man's a white old man
And my old mother's black.
If ever I cursed my white old man
I take my curses back.

If ever I cursed my black old mother   5
And wished she were in hell,
I'm sorry for that evil wish
And now I wish her well.

My old man died in a fine big house.
My ma died in a shack.   10
I wonder where I'm gonna die,
Being neither white nor black?

                                [1925, 1994]

DOWN AND OUT

Baby, if you love me
Help me when I'm down and out.
If you love me, baby,
Help me when I'm down and out,
I'm a po' gal   5
Nobody gives a damn about.

The credit man's done took ma clothes
And rent time's nearly here.
I'd like to buy a straightenin' comb,
An' I need a dime fo' beer.　　　　　　　　　10

I need a dime fo' beer.

　　　　　　　　　　　　　　　　　　[1926, 1994]

Brass Spittoons

Clean the spittoons,[1] boy.
　　Detroit,
　　Chicago,
　　Atlantic City,
　　Palm Beach.　　　　　　　　　　　　　5
Clean the spittoons.
The steam in hotel kitchens,
And the smoke in hotel lobbies,
And the slime in hotel spittoons:
Part of my life.　　　　　　　　　　　　10
　　Hey, boy!
　　A nickel,
　　A dime,
　　A dollar,
Two dollars a day.　　　　　　　　　　　15
　　Hey, boy!
　　A nickel,
　　A dime,
　　A dollar,
　　Two dollars　　　　　　　　　　　　20
Buys shoes for the baby.
House rent to pay.
Gin on Saturday,
Church on Sunday.
　　My God!　　　　　　　　　　　　　25
Babies and gin and church
and women and Sunday
all mixed up with dimes and
dollars and clean spittoons
and house rent to pay.　　　　　　　　　30
　　Hey, boy!
A bright bowl of brass is beautiful to the Lord
Bright polished brass like the cymbals

---

1. **spittoons:** Metal or earthenware pots, commonly used as receptacles for spitting.

Of King David's dancers,
Like the wine cups of Solomon.[2]   35
   Hey, boy!
A clean spittoon on the altar of the Lord.
A clean bright spittoon all newly polished, —
At least I can offer that.
   Come 'ere, boy!   40

[1926, 1994]

---

2. **King David's dancers . . . cups of Solomon:** King David of Israel, who is thought by many to be the author of the Psalms, refers to dancing as a form of worship of the Lord: "Let them praise his name in the dance: let them sing praises unto him with the timbrel and harp" (Psalms 149:3). David's son and successor, the fabulously wealthy king Solomon, had gold wine vessels (1 Kings 10:21).

ANGELS WINGS[1]

The angels wings is white as snow,
   O, white as snow,
     White
       as
         snow.   5
The angels wings is white as snow,
   But I drug ma wings
   In the dirty mire.
   O, I drug ma wings
   All through the fire.   10
But the angels wings is white as snow,
   White
     as
       snow.

[1927, 1994]

---

1. **Angels Wings:** This shaped poem is designed as a visual representation of an angel's wings.

MULATTO[1]

I am your son, white man!

Georgia dusk
And the turpentine woods.
One of the pillars of the temple fell.

---

1. **Mulatto:** A term used in the nineteenth and early twentieth centuries for a person of mixed white and black ancestry.

You are my son?   5
Like hell!

The moon over the turpentine woods.
The Southern night
Full of stars,
Great big yellow stars.   10
   What's a body but a toy?
      Juicy bodies
      Of nigger wenches
      Blue black
      Against black fences.   15
      O, you little bastard boy,
      What's a body but a toy?
The scent of pine wood stings the soft night air.
      What's the body of your mother?
Silver moonlight everywhere.   20
      What's the body of your mother?
Sharp pine scent in the evening air.
        A nigger night,
        A nigger joy,
        A little yellow   25
        Bastard boy.

      Naw, you ain't my brother.
      Niggers ain't my brother.
      Not ever.
      Niggers ain't my brother.   30

The Southern night is full of stars,
Great big yellow stars.
        O, sweet as earth,
        Dusk dark bodies
        Give sweet birth   35
To little yellow bastard boys.

      Git on back there in the night,
      You ain't white.

The bright stars scatter everywhere.
Pine wood scent in the evening air.   40
        A nigger night,
        A nigger joy.

    I am your son, white man!

        A little yellow
        Bastard boy.   45

[1927, 1994]

AFRO-AMERICAN FRAGMENT

So long,
So far away
Is Africa.
Not even memories alive
Save those that history books create,   5
Save those that songs
Beat back into the blood —
Beat out of blood with words sad-sung
In strange un-Negro tongue —
So long,   10
So far away
Is Africa.

Subdued and time-lost
Are the drums — and yet
Through some vast mist of race   15
There comes this song
I do not understand
This song of atavistic land,
Of bitter yearnings lost
Without a place —   20
So long,
So far away
Is Africa's
Dark face.

                                        [1930, 1994]

CHRIST IN ALABAMA[1]

Christ is a nigger,
Beaten and black:
Oh, bare your back!

Mary is His mother:
Mammy of the South,   5
Silence your mouth.

---

1. **Christ in Alabama:** Hughes wrote this poem when a North Carolina magazine, *Contempo,* invited him to comment on the notorious case of the so-called Scottsboro Boys, nine black teenagers accused of raping two white girls on a freight train bound from Tennessee to Alabama on March 25, 1931. The publication of the poem in *Contempo* generated heated controversy, including protests and petitions in North Carolina. Coolly responding to the furor, especially over the first line of the poem, Hughes observed: "I meant my poem to be a protest against the domination of all stronger peoples over weaker ones."

God is His father:
White Master above
Grant Him your love.

Most holy bastard   10
Of the bleeding mouth,
    Nigger Christ
    On the cross
    Of the South.

[1931, 1994]

DREAM BOOGIE[1]

Good morning, daddy!
Ain't you heard
The boogie-woogie rumble
Of a dream deferred?

Listen closely: 5
You'll hear their feet
Beating out and beating out a —

    You think
    It's a happy beat?

Listen to it closely: 10
Ain't you heard
something underneath
like a —

    What did I say?

Sure,   15
I'm happy!
Take it away!

    Hey, pop!
    Re-bop!
    Mop!   20

    Y-e-a-h!

[1951, 1994]

---

1. **Dream Boogie:** Hughes first published this poem in *Montage of a Dream Deferred* (1951), a collection of poems about life in Harlem. In an epigraph to the book, Hughes wrote: "In terms of current Afro-American popular music and the sources from which it has progressed — jazz, ragtime, swing, blues, boogie-woogie, and be-bop — this poem on contemporary Harlem, like be-bop, is marked by conflicted changes, sudden nuances, sharp and impudent interjections, broken rhythms, and passages sometimes in the manner of the jam session, sometimes the popular song, punctuated by the riffs, runs, breaks, and distortions of the music of a community in transition."

HARLEM

What happens to a dream deferred?

Does it dry up
like a raisin in the sun?
Or fester like a sore —
And then run?   5
Does it stink like rotten meat?
Or crust and sugar over —
like a syrupy sweet?

Maybe it just sags
like a heavy load.   10

Or does it explode?

[1951, 1994]

Countee Cullen

[1903-1946]

Countee Cullen was born on March 30, 1903, to Elizabeth Thomas Lucas in Louisville, Kentucky. The identity of his father and most other details of his early life are unknown. He was raised by a woman named Amanda Porter, possibly his paternal grandmother, who took him to New York City. When she died in 1917, Cullen went to live with Reverend Frederick Asbury Cullen, the popular minister of the largest church in Harlem, the Salem Methodist Episcopal Church, and his wife, Carolyn Belle Mitchell Cullen. Although the couple never formally adopted him, Cullen began to use their surname in 1918 and always referred to them as his parents. An outstanding student at DeWitt Clinton High School, Cullen helped edit the school newspaper and literary magazine. He also began to write poetry, winning a citywide contest for his poem "I Have a Rendezvous with Life." After high school, he attended New York University, where he excelled academically and regularly published poems in the school's literary magazine, the *Arch*, and later in prominent national magazines such as H. L. Mencken's *American Mercury*, the *Bookman*, the *Century*, *Harper's*, and the *Nation*. He also won a string of literary prizes, including the John Reed Memorial Prize awarded by *Poetry: A Magazine of Verse*.

Countee Cullen

Inscribed "with admiration" to James Weldon Johnson, this photograph was taken in the mid-1920s, when the young Cullen was one of the most popular poets in the United States.

The precocious Cullen soon became the most popular and acclaimed African American poet since Paul Laurence Dunbar. During his senior year of college, the prestigious firm of Harper and Brothers published Cullen's first collection of poems, *Color* (1925). Some of the poems in the volume also appeared in Alain Locke's influential anthology, *The New Negro* (1925). Locke joined in the chorus of praise for the author of *Color*, proclaiming in his review: "Ladies and Gentleman! A genius!" Meanwhile, Cullen graduated Phi Beta Kappa from New York University and continued his studies at Harvard. After he completed a master's degree in English and French, Cullen returned to New York City, where he assumed a central role in the Harlem Renaissance. Cullen became the assistant editor of *Opportunity*, the magazine of the National Urban League. In addition to writing a regular column for the magazine, "The Dark Tower," he published two more books of his early poetry, *Copper Sun* (1927) and *Ballad of the Brown Girl* (1928). Eager to promote the work of other African American poets, Cullen edited *Caroling Dusk: An Anthology of Verse by Negro Poets* (1927), which he hoped might serve as a prelude "to that fuller symphony which Negro poets will in time contribute to the national literature." He also enjoyed an active social life that included many well-known African American writers and artists, including Aaron Douglas, Langston Hughes, and Zora Neale Hurston. In a large and elaborate wedding, Cullen in 1928 married Nina Yolande Du Bois, the daughter of W. E. B. Du Bois. Soon after their marriage, which was deeply troubled and ended in divorce two years later, Cullen received one of the first Guggenheim Fellowships awarded to an African American. Along with his closest friend and companion, Harold Jackman, Cullen sailed for France, where he wrote *The Black Christ and Other Poems* (1929).

Cullen never again achieved the success he enjoyed during the 1920s. Turning from poetry to fiction, he wrote a satirical novel about African Americans in New York City, *One Way to Heaven* (1932). He also gave lectures and readings of his poetry across the United States. Although he was offered teaching positions at several historically black colleges, Cullen evidently preferred to remain in New York City. In 1934, he accepted a full-time teaching position at Frederick Douglass Junior High School. The job left him relatively little time for writing, but he published some new poems along with a translation of a classical Greek play by Euripides, *The Medea and Some Poems* (1935). Cullen married Ida Mae Robertson in 1940, and he later published two books for children. Before he died from complications arising from high blood pressure on January 9, 1946, he began to compile the poems included in the posthumously published collection *On These I Stand: The Best Poems of Countee Cullen* (1947). Although his reputation had declined, his poetry continued to engage many readers, including the African American poet and novelist Owen Dodson, who in a tribute to Cullen observed: "If you ask any Negro what he found in Cullen's poetry, he would say: 'all my dilemmas are written here.'"

The best of his poetry is motivated by race. He is always seeking to free himself and his art from these bonds.
-James Weldon Johnson

Cullen's Poetry.   In his anthology, *Caroling Dusk*, Cullen included a wide range of verse written by contemporary African American poets, from the jazz rhythms of Langston Hughes to the so-called Negro dialect poetry of Sterling A. Brown. In contrast, Cullen was a deeply traditional poet who said that verse emerged from him already "metered and rhymed." He was most strongly influenced by the British Romantic poets, especially John Keats. Cullen also deeply admired the lyrical work of his white contemporary Edna St. Vincent Millay, the subject of his undergraduate thesis at New York University. Like Millay, he was especially drawn to the sonnet, the form of two of his most famous poems, "Yet Do I Marvel" and "From the Dark Tower." But in those poems, as well as in the rhymed couplets of longer poems such as "Heritage," Cullen explored subjects far removed from the mainstream of British and American poetry, including prejudice, racial identity, and the consciousness of African Americans torn between the claims of America, or the Western tradition, and the cultural heritage of Africa. Although he declared in 1924 that he wanted "to be POET and not NEGRO POET," suggesting that the development of African American artists had been hindered by their exclusive "concern with their race," Cullen added

bedfordstmartins.com/ americanlit for research links on Cullen

> That is all very well, none of us can get away from it. I cannot at times. You will see it in my verse. The consciousness of this is too poignant at times. I cannot escape it. But what I mean is this: I shall not write of negro subjects for the purpose of propaganda. That is not what a poet is concerned with. Of course, when the emotion rising out of the fact that I am a negro is strong, I express it.

Certainly, he expressed those emotions in the following poems, the texts of which are taken from *My Soul's High Song: The Collected Writings of Countee Cullen, Voice of the Harlem Renaissance*, edited by Gerald Early (1991).

YET DO I MARVEL

I doubt not God is good, well-meaning, kind,
And did He stoop to quibble could tell why
The little buried mole continues blind,
Why flesh that mirrors Him must some day die,
Make plain the reason tortured Tantalus   5
Is baited by the fickle fruit, declare
If merely brute caprice dooms Sisyphus
To struggle up a never-ending stair.[1]
Inscrutable His ways are, and immune
To catechism by a mind too strewn   10
With petty cares to slightly understand
What awful brain compels His awful hand.
Yet do I marvel at this curious thing:
To make a poet black, and bid him sing!

[1924, 1991]

---

1. **Make plain . . . stair:** In Greek mythology, both Tantalus and Sisyphus were punished for their crimes by being sent to Hades. Tantalus, the son of Zeus, was forced to stand in chin-deep water with fruit hanging from branches over his head, but the fruit and water receded whenever he sought to eat or drink. Sisyphus was forced continually to roll a stone to the top of a hill, only to see it roll back down as soon as he completed the task.

HERITAGE

(For Harold Jackman)[1]

What is Africa to me:
Copper sun or scarlet sea,
Jungle star or jungle track,
Strong bronzed men, or regal black
Women from whose loins I sprang   5
When the birds of Eden sang?
One three centuries removed
From the scenes his fathers loved,
Spicy grove, cinnamon tree,
What is Africa to me?   10

So I lie, who all day long
Want no sound except the song
Sung by wild barbaric birds
Goading massive jungle herds,
Juggernauts[2] of flesh that pass   15
Trampling tall defiant grass
Where young forest lovers lie,
Plighting troth beneath the sky.
So I lie, who always hear,
Though I cram against my ear   20
Both my thumbs, and keep them there,
Great drums throbbing through the air.
So I lie, whose fount of pride,
Dear distress, and joy allied,
Is my somber flesh and skin,   25
With the dark blood dammed within
Like great pulsing tides of wine
That, I fear, must burst the fine
Channels of the chafing net
Where they surge and foam and fret.   30

Africa? A book one thumbs
Listlessly, till slumber comes.
Unremembered are her bats
Circling through the night, her cats

---

1. **For Harold Jackman:** Jackman (1901–1961), Cullen's longtime friend and companion, was a teacher and active supporter of many African American writers in New York City.
2. **Juggernauts:** Derived from the name for a sacred idol of the Hindu, the term also means a powerful, overwhelming force.

Crouching in the river reeds,   35
Stalking gentle flesh that feeds
By the river brink; no more
Does the bugle-throated roar
Cry that monarch claws have leapt
From the scabbards where they slept.   40
Silver snakes that once a year
Doff the lovely coats you wear,
Seek no covert in your fear
Lest a mortal eye should see;
What's your nakedness to me?   45
Here no leprous flowers rear
Fierce corollas in the air;
Here no bodies sleek and wet,
Dripping mingled rain and sweat,
Tread the savage measures of   50
Jungle boys and girls in love.
What is last year's snow to me,
Last year's anything? The tree
Budding yearly must forget
How its past arose or set —   55
Bough and blossom, flower, fruit,
Even what shy bird with mute
Wonder at her travail there,
Meekly labored in its hair.
One three centuries removed   60
From the scenes his fathers loved,
Spice grove, cinnamon tree,
What is Africa to me?

So I lie, who find no peace
Night or day, no slight release   65
From the unremittant beat
Made by cruel padded feet
Walking through my body's street.
Up and down they go, and back,
Treading out a jungle track.   70
So I lie, who never quite
Safely sleep from rain at night —
I can never rest at all
When the rain begins to fall;
Like a soul gone mad with pain   75
I must match its weird refrain;
Ever must I twist and squirm,

Writhing like a baited worm,
While its primal measures drip
Through my body, crying, "Strip!   80
Doff this new exuberance.
Come and dance the Lover's Dance!"
In an old remembered way
Rain works on me night and day.

Quaint, outlandish heathen gods   85
Black men fashion out of rods,
Clay, and brittle bits of stone,
In a likeness like their own,
My conversion came high-priced;
I belong to Jesus Christ,   90
Preacher of humility;
Heathen gods are naught to me.

Father, Son, and Holy Ghost,
So I make an idle boast;
Jesus of the twice-turned cheek,   95
Lamb of God, although I speak
With my mouth thus, in my heart
Do I play a double part.
Ever at Thy glowing altar
Must my heart grow sick and falter,   100
Wishing He I served were black,
Thinking then it would not lack
Precedent of pain to guide it,
Let who would or might deride it;
Surely then this flesh would know   105
Yours had borne a kindred woe.
Lord, I fashion dark gods, too,
Daring even to give You
Dark despairing features where,
Crowned with dark rebellious hair,   110
Patience wavers just so much as
Mortal grief compels, while touches
Quick and hot, of anger, rise
To smitten cheek and weary eyes.
Lord, forgive me if my need   115
Sometimes shapes a human creed.

All day long and all night through,
One thing only must I do:
Quench my pride and cool my blood,

Lest I perish in the flood.   120
Lest a hidden ember set
Timber that I thought was wet
Burning like the dryest flax,
Melting like the merest wax,
Lest the grave restore its dead.   125
Not yet has my heart or head
In the least way realized
They and I are civilized.

[1925, 1991]

FROM THE DARK TOWER

(To Charles S. Johnson)[1]

We shall not always plant while others reap
The golden increment of bursting fruit,
Not always countenance, abject and mute,
That lesser men should hold their brothers cheap;
Not everlastingly while others sleep   5
Shall we beguile their limbs with mellow flute,
Not always bend to some more subtle brute;
We were not made eternally to weep.

The night whose sable breast relieves the stark,
White stars is no less lovely being dark,   10
And there are buds that cannot bloom at all
In light, but crumple, piteous, and fall;
So in the dark we hide the heart that bleeds,
And wait, and tend our agonizing seeds.

[1926, 1991]

---

1. **To Charles S. Johnson:** Johnson (1893–1956) was the founder and editor of *Opportunity: A Journal of Negro Life,* the magazine of the National Urban League, and a mentor to many African American writers of the 1920s and 1930s.

The Emergence
of Modern American Drama

DURING THE EARLY DECADES of the twentieth century, "Broadway," the area around Times Square in New York City, at once symbolized and dominated theater in the United States. Many of the plays performed by hundreds of touring companies originated on Broadway, where the number of theatrical productions rose from seventy during the 1900-01 season to a peak of almost three hundred during 1926-27, after which the audience for theater was eroded by the growing popularity of "talkies" in the movies and the onset of the Great Depression. Operettas were especially popular on Broadway, as were musical extravaganzas such as Florenz Ziegfeld's *Follies*, which he produced virtually every year from 1907 through 1927.

◀ **The Wharf Theatre**
In the summer of 1916, the Provincetown Players gave their first public performances in a converted, 25 × 35 foot fishing shack at the end of Lewis Wharf in Provincetown, Massachusetts. Members of the group rigged up rudimentary lighting, created benches by resting planks on sawhorses, and built a 10 × 12 foot stage in the ramshackle building, which many theater historians view as the birthplace of modern American drama.

During the same period, the Broadway musical emerged in shows such as those written, produced, and performed by George M. Cohan, whose string of hits made him the undisputed "king" of Broadway. Another major force in the American theater world was David Belasco, who wrote, directed, or produced more than one hundred Broadway plays before his death in 1931. Although his productions were known for their realistic, meticulously detailed sets, Belasco's plays epitomized the most popular form of American drama, the melodrama, with its stock characters (hero, villain, and damsel in distress) and formulaic plot.

The popularity of melodramas, which remained the staple of the legitimate Broadway theater until after World War I, impeded the development of more modern forms of drama in the United States. Despite some energetic efforts, the revolution in European theater led by the Norwegian playwright Henrik Ibsen, often called "the father of modern drama," did not spread to Broadway. American companies successfully produced

Broadway

The cover illustration of this sheet music, published in 1909, depicts a rainy night on Broadway, the "Great White Way," a nickname inspired by the lights of theater marquees and billboard advertisements in the area around Times Square. The cameo portrait at the lower left showcases the popular Broadway musical star Nella Bergen.

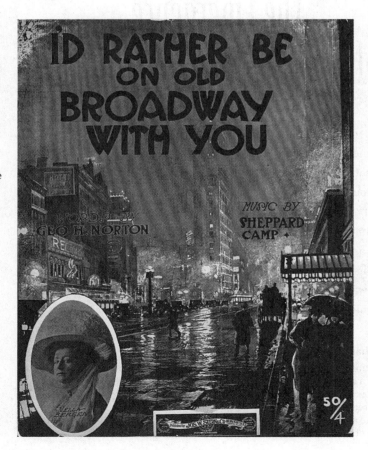

works by the controversial Irish playwright George Bernard Shaw, a champion of Ibsen who was seeking to develop a vital "theatre of ideas" in England. There were also productions of a few of Ibsen's plays, notably those featuring the prominent actress Minnie Madden Fiske, who gained acclaim in *A Doll's House* in 1894 and later in *Hedda Gabler*. Describing her triumph in that play, "which is packing the house nightly," a reviewer in the *New York Times* observed in 1903: "It is a sight to bring disquiet to those reactionary folk who so long ago proclaimed that they had sealed the mausoleum of Ibsen." Nonetheless, there was deep and ongoing hostility to Ibsen's plays, in which he dealt realistically with subjects such as syphilis, euthanasia, and the confined role of women in marriage and society. Bemoaning the fact that "Mrs. Fiske," as she was widely known, had chosen to perform in Ibsen's plays, an influential American drama critic declared that "Ibsenism is rank, a deadly pessimism, is a disease, injurious to the Stage and the People."

Much of the impetus toward realism and modernism in American drama came from amateurs and theater people off (and many of them far away from) Broadway. One of the most significant artistic developments during the decade 1910-20 was the emergence of small groups that rejected the conventions of the commercial stage in favor of a new, experimental theater. Many of those groups were inspired by the American tour of Dublin's Abbey Players in 1911. Originally an amateur company, the Abbey Players developed into the Irish National Theatre and was renowned for naturalistic acting and simplified staging, two key elements of the movement known as the European Art Theatre. The first American art theater that sprang up in the wake of the Irish group's galvanizing tour was the Chicago Little Theatre, established in 1912 in an effort to elevate what many viewed as the "vulgar" taste in drama in the United States. Other short-lived groups followed in 1913, including the Toy Theatre in Boston and the Little Theatre in New York City, where the Washington Square Players undertook a more lasting and significant venture in 1915. Two other art theaters were established the following year, the Pasadena Playhouse and the Cleveland Play House.

Of all those little-theater groups, none had as profound an impact on the course of American drama as the Provincetown Players. The group was formed by artists, writers, and intellectuals based in the bohemian Greenwich Village section of New York City who spent their summers in the artists' colony of Provincetown, Massachusetts. Led by George Cram Cook and his wife, Susan Glaspell, the founding members of the group gave their first public performances in the summer of 1916 in a converted wooden fishing shack they christened the Wharf Theatre. Buoyed by their first season in Provincetown and inspired by Cook's dream of a new American theater, when they returned to New York City that fall members of the group converted a small space in an unheated building in Greenwich

Susan Glaspell and George Cram Cook

This photograph of Glaspell and Cook, two of the founders and the driving forces of the Provincetown Players, was taken in Provincetown.

Village into the Provincetown Theatre, later called Provincetown Playhouse. In their first public statement in New York City, the Provincetown Players declared that their primary purpose was to maintain a "stage for free dramatic experiment in the true amateur spirit!"

In contrast to most other little-theater groups, which produced plays by modern European playwrights, the Provincetown Players were determined to perform only new works by American writers. In fact, Cook formed the group to "*cause* better American plays to be written," as Glaspell later recalled. Remarkably, given their limited financial resources, primitive theatrical spaces, and amateur productions, they did just that. Their initial season was notable for performances of Glaspell's first single-authored play, *Trifles,* as well as the first play by Eugene O'Neill to reach the stage, *Bound East for Cardiff.* The work of those two prolific playwrights was the mainstay of the Provincetown Players, but they produced a wide range of drama — ninety-three new plays by forty-seven different American playwrights — between 1916 and 1922. Although they were primarily committed to realism and representational plays dealing with contemporary problems, the Provincetown Players were also imbued with the playful, iconoclastic spirit that characterized the cultural revolution that broke out on many fronts in Greenwich Village. Indeed, as one of its members later observed, "nothing was too mad or silly to do in the Provincetown Theatre."

Nothing was too mad or silly to do in the Provincetown Theatre.

Certainly, the Provincetown Players were influenced by other departures in the arts, especially the experimental work of poets and painters associated with Alfred Kreymborg's *Others: A Magazine of the New Verse*. During the first season of the Provincetown Players in New York City, their lineup of plays included Kreymborg's three-person domestic farce *Lima Beans*. Few events illustrated the cross-fertilization among modernist artists as fully as the production of that play, which Kreymborg in his stage directions describes as a "pantomime dance of automatons to an accompaniment of rhythmic words, in place of music." The lead roles of the Wife and the Husband were performed by the expatriate English poet Mina Loy, who had recently arrived in New York City, and the American poet William Carlos Williams, who commuted from his home and medical practice in Paterson, New Jersey. The role of the vegetable "Huckster" was played by the Lithuanian-born abstract painter William Zorach, who also designed the set and "The Curtain," adorned with bold "patterns of remarkable vegetables" and listed on the program as one of the play's four characters. The success of *Lima Beans* encouraged

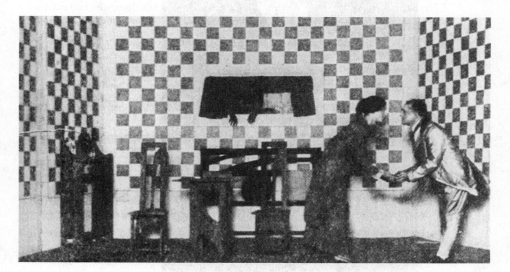

Lima Beans

This photograph of the poets Mina Loy and William Carlos Williams playing the lead roles in Alfred Kreymborg's domestic farce was taken during the production at the Provincetown Playhouse in December 1916.

the Provincetown Players to undertake other experimental plays in verse, notably two produced during their 1919-20 season, Wallace Stevens's *Three Travelers Watch a Sunrise* and Edna St. Vincent Millay's satire of war and nationalism, *Aria de Capo*.

Eugene O'Neill's plays also reflected the experimental spirit of the Provincetown Players. O'Neill found himself catapulted to the forefront of American playwrights by his groundbreaking play *The Emperor Jones*, a smash hit first performed at the Provincetown Playhouse in November 1920. By insisting that the title role be played by a black actor, Charles Gilpin, rather than by a white actor in blackface, O'Neill and the Provincetown Players exerted what the African American poet and activist James Weldon Johnson described as "the initial and greatest force in opening up the way for the Negro on the dramatic stage." Gilpin's acclaimed performance in *The Emperor Jones* not only paved the way for other black actors to appear in productions by white theater companies, but also gave impetus to what is called the "Black Little Theatre Movement" of the 1920s.

The play opened up the American stage in other ways as well. Having earlier joined with Glaspell and other playwrights in the effort to establish realism and naturalism as vital forces in the American theater, O'Neill in

Charles Gilpin in
The Emperor Jones

Gilpin, who had earlier performed with various African American theatrical groups, was the first black actor to star in a dramatic production in an all-white theater in the United States. For his critically acclaimed performance in O'Neill's play, the National Association for the Advancement of Colored People (NAACP) awarded Gilpin its annual Springarn Medal for outstanding achievement by an African American.

The Emperor Jones adapted some of the dramatic forms of German expressionism, nonrepresentational action, dialogue, and sets designed to reveal the hidden lives of characters, especially their intense desires, fears, and memories. O'Neill continued his experiments with expressionistic techniques in *The Hairy Ape* — "a bitter, brutal, wildly fantastic play of nightmare hue and nightmare distortion," as one critic described it — which the Provincetown Players produced early in 1922.

Ironically, their triumphant productions of O'Neill's two most experimental plays to date — both of which went on to play in larger theaters on Broadway — marked the beginning of the end of the Provincetown Players. Glaspell contributed to the success of the 1921-22 season with her own experiment with expressionistic techniques, *The Verge.* Following that season, however, she and Cook effectively withdrew from the group because of what they viewed as the growing commercialism and professionalism of the Provincetown Players. After the remaining members reorganized as the Experimental Theatre in 1923, the new company indicated its departure from its former practices by opening with an older European play, *The Spook Sonata,* by the Swedish dramatist August Strindberg, whom O'Neill in the playbill described as "the precursor of all modernity in our present theatre just as Ibsen . . . was the father of modernity of twenty years or so ago." The Experimental Theatre also produced important new plays by O'Neill, including *All God's Chillun Got Wings* and *Desire under the Elms,* both of which premiered in 1924, and *The Great God Brown* (1926). He thereafter became permanently associated with a larger and better financed group, the Theatre Guild. Established in 1918 by members of the former Washington Square Players, the Theatre Guild was a fully professional theatrical company that successfully balanced aesthetic and commercial considerations. From 1918 through the 1940s, the Theatre Guild established the most distinguished record of productions of any theatrical company in American history, while the final incarnation of the Provincetown Players, the Experimental Theatre, collapsed at the beginning of the Great Depression in 1929.

During their brief history, however, the Provincetown Players left an indelible mark on theater in the United States. As early as 1921, the influential English drama critic William Archer declared that one must look to the sand dunes of Cape Cod "for the real birthplace of the New American Drama." The impact of the Provincetown Players became even clearer as American drama continued to mature during the following decades. Almost forty years after the first performances of the Provincetown Players at the Wharf Theatre in 1916, one of their original members, the journalist Mary Heaton Vorse, recalled with a justifiable mixture of wonder and pride, "We had no idea that we were to help break through the traditions of Broadway and revolutionize and humanize the theatre of America."

> *We had no idea that we were to help break through the traditions of Broadway and revolutionize and humanize the theatre of America.*

Susan Glaspell

[1876-1948]

Susan Keating Glaspell was born in Davenport, Iowa, probably on July 1, 1876, the daughter of Elmer and Alice Keating Glaspell. Glaspell was educated at public schools in Davenport and briefly worked as a society columnist for a local newspaper before enrolling at Drake University in 1895. An outstanding journalism student, she graduated in 1899 and took a job with the *Des Moines Daily News*, the first newspaper in Iowa to hire women reporters. Assigned to cover the governor's office and the state legislature, Glaspell became steeped in the life and politics of the Midwest. She began to write her own column, "The News Girl," in which she initially offered commentary on local political issues but later wrote light essays in which she assumed the persona of an innocent and slightly silly young girl, whose naive understanding of the world was the central joke of the pieces. Encouraged by the publication of several of her stories in the *Youth's Companion*, Glaspell decided to devote herself to writing fiction and returned home to Davenport in 1901. During the following decade, her socially conscious stories appeared in prominent periodicals such as the *American Illustrated Magazine*, *Harper's Monthly*, and the *Ladies' Home Journal*. She also published her first two novels. *The Glory of the Conquered* (1909) and *The Visioning* (1911).

Around 1910, Glaspell became deeply involved with fellow novelist George Cram Cook, the well-educated and twice-divorced son of a wealthy Davenport family. After they married in 1914, Glaspell and Cook moved to

Susan Glaspell

This photograph of Glaspell at work in her Greenwich Village apartment was taken around 1920, when she was one of the leading figures in the experimental theater group the Provincetown Players.

New York City, joining a growing number of writers and intellectuals who were gravitating to the lively artistic community on the Lower West Side of Manhattan known as Greenwich Village. Attracted to the experimental theater that was beginning to emerge there, Glaspell and Cook coauthored a one-act play, *Suppressed Desires,* a satire of the new fad of Freudian psychoanalysis they hoped would be produced by the recently created Washington Square Players. When the company rejected the play as too "esoteric," Glaspell and Cook performed it for friends, first in their apartment in Greenwich Village and later in Provincetown, Massachusetts. Along with a number of other artists and writers who spent the summers there, Glaspell and Cook formed a small theater group, the Provincetown Players, which was soon joined by the then unknown Eugene O'Neill. As an actor, a director, and a dramatist, Glaspell was one of the most vital figures among the Provincetown Players, who produced nine of her plays between 1915 and 1922. The plays were remarkable for their range of characters and situations, as well as for the variety of dramatic techniques Glaspell employed. She frequently explored feminist themes in those works, including her first full-length play, *Bernice* (1919), which the reviewer for the *New York Times* praised for its "beautiful simplicity, rich characterizations, and deep insights into masculine vanity." In 1922, disillusioned by growing differences over the direction of the Provincetown Players, Glaspell and Cook withdrew from the group in order to pursue his dream of living and writing in Greece.

Cook's sudden death ended their sojourn, and a bereft Glaspell returned to Provincetown in 1924. When she was able to begin work again, she edited a collection of Cook's poems, *Greek Coins* (1926), and wrote an account of their relationship, *The Road to the Temple* (1927). With Norman Matson, a young writer with whom Glaspell lived for several years, she wrote *The Comic Artist* (1927), a full-length play that was later produced on Broadway. She also wrote two best-selling novels, *Brook Evans* (1928) and *Fugitive's Return* (1929), as well as a play based on the life and literary legacy of Emily Dickinson, *Alison's House* (1930), which was awarded the Pulitzer Prize for Drama. Although that was her last play, Glaspell maintained her interest in the theater, directing the Midwest Play Bureau of the Federal Theatre Project in Chicago from 1936 to 1938. Frustrated by governmental red tape, she resigned her position and once again devoted herself to writing fiction, notably the novels *The Morning Is Near Us* (1939), *Norma Ashe* (1942), and *Judd Rankin's Daughter* (1945). By the time she died in Provincetown in 1948, Glaspell had produced a remarkable body of work in fiction and drama, including more than fifty short stories, nine novels, and ten plays, plus three others that she coauthored. Nonetheless, although her experimental techniques and innovative early plays had helped transform American drama, at the end of her life Glaspell was overshadowed by other playwrights, especially by the major figure to emerge from the Provincetown Players. The subheadline of her obituary in the *New York Times* thus announced: "Winner of Pulitzer Prize in 1930 with 'Alison's House' Dies — 'Discovered' Eugene O'Neill."

bedfordstmartins.com/ americanlit for research links on Glaspell

Glaspell's *Trifles.*   While she worked as a reporter for the *Des Moines Daily News* from 1899 to 1901, Glaspell investigated the murder of an Iowa farmer and covered the trial of his wife, Margaret Hossack, who was accused of killing her sleeping husband with an axe. Although she was convicted, Hossack insisted that an intruder had killed her husband, and her conviction was overturned on appeal. The sensational crime and trial were covered by newspapers across the country, in which opinion was deeply divided over Hossack's guilt or innocence. Inspired by the case, and by her visit to the crime scene at the Hossack farmhouse, Glaspell later wrote *Trifles,* her first single-authored play, for the Provincetown Players. They first performed the one-act play at the Wharf Theatre on August 8, 1916, with Glaspell herself playing the role of one of the five characters, Mrs. Hale. The uncompromising play explores different ways of seeing and knowing, as men and women seek clues in a tragic case involving an isolated farm woman, Minnie Wright, who is suspected of having murdered her cold and abusive husband. Glaspell later revised the play into a short story, "A Jury of Her Peers," which was first published in the popular magazine *Every Week* and then in *The Best Short Stories of 1917.* Still the best

Trifles

This photograph of an early performance of *Trifles* illustrates how well adapted Glaspell's play was to the small stage and spare productions of the Wharf Theatre, where it was first performed, and to the simplified staging characteristic of experimental theater in the United States.

known of all of her plays, *Trifles* became a popular feature of both amateur and professional theater groups and was widely performed throughout the twentieth century. The text is taken from the first edition of *Trifles* (1916).

TRIFLES

A Play in One Act

Presented by the Provincetown Players at the Wharf Theatre, Provincetown, Mass., August 8, 1916

GEORGE HENDERSON . . . . *Robert Rogers*
HENRY PETERS . . . . *Robert Conville*
LEWIS HALE . . . . *George Cram Cook*
MRS. PETERS . . . . *Alice Hall*
MRS. HALE . . . . *Susan Glaspell*

SCENE

The kitchen in the now abandoned farmhouse of John Wright, a gloomy kitchen, plainly left without having been put in order — unwashed pans under the sink, a loaf of bread outside the bread-box, a dish-towel on the table — other signs of incompleted work. Door opens rear and enter sheriff followed by county attorney and Hale. The sheriff and Hale are men in middle life, the county attorney is a young man; all are much bundled up and go at once to the stove. They are followed by the two women — the sheriff's wife first; she is a slight wiry woman, a thin nervous face. Mrs. Hale is larger and would ordinarily be called more comfortable looking, but she is disturbed now and looks fearfully about as she enters. The women have come in slowly, and stand close together near the door.

COUNTY ATTORNEY: (*Rubbing his hands*) This feels good. Come up to the fire, ladies.
MRS. PETERS: (*Takes a step forward and looks around*) I'm not – cold.
SHERIFF: (*Unbuttoning his overcoat and stepping away from the stove as if to mark the beginning of official business*) Now, Mr. Hale, before we move things about, you explain to Mr. Henderson just what you saw when you came here yesterday morning.
COUNTY ATTORNEY: By the way, has anything been moved? Are things just as you left them yesterday?
SHERIFF: (*Looking all about*) It's just the same. When it dropped below zero last night I thought I'd better send Frank out this morning to make a fire for us – no use getting pneumonia with a big case on, but I told him not to touch anything except the stove – and you know Frank.
COUNTY ATTORNEY: Somebody should have been left here yesterday.
SHERIFF: Oh – yesterday. When I had to send Frank to Morris Center for that man who went crazy – I want you to know I had my hands full yesterday. I knew you could get back from Omaha by today and as long as I went over everything here myself —
COUNTY ATTORNEY: Well, Mr. Hale, tell just what happened when you came here yesterday morning.

HALE: Harry and I had started to town with a load of potatoes. We came along the road from my place and as I got here I said, "I'm going to see if I can't get John Wright to go in with me on a party telephone. I spoke to Wright about it once before and he put me off, saying folks talked too much anyway, and all he asked was peace and quiet — I guess you know about how much he talked himself, but I thought maybe if I went to the house and talked about it before his wife, though I said to Harry that I didn't know as what his wife wanted made much difference to John —

COUNTY ATTORNEY: Let's talk about that later, Mr. Hale. I do want to talk about that, but tell now just what happened when you got to the house.

HALE: I didn't hear or see anything; I knocked at the door, and still it was all quiet inside. I knew they must be up, it was past eight o'clock. So I knocked again, and I thought I heard somebody say "Come in." I wasn't sure, I'm not sure yet, but I opened the door – this door (*jerking a hand backward*) and there in that rocker – (*pointing to it*) sat Mrs. Wright. (*All look at the rocker*)

COUNTY ATTORNEY: What – was she doing?

HALE: She was rockin' back and forth. She had her apron in her hand and was kind of – pleating it.

COUNTY ATTORNEY: And how did she – look?

HALE: Well, she looked queer.

COUNTY ATTORNEY: How do you mean – queer?

HALE: Well, as if she didn't know what she was going to do next. And kind of done up.

COUNTY ATTORNEY: How did she seem to feel about your coming?

HALE: Why, I don't think she minded — one way or other. She didn't pay much attention. I said, "How do, Mrs. Wright, it's cold, ain't it?" And she said "Is it?" – and went on kind of pleating at her apron. Well, I was surprised; she didn't ask me to come up to the stove, or to set down, but just sat there, not even looking at me, so I said, "I want to see John." And then she – laughed. I guess you would call it a laugh. I thought of Harry and the team outside, so I said a little sharp: "Can't I see John?" "No," she says, kind o' dull like. "Ain't he home?" says I. "Yes," says she, "he's home." "Then why can't I see him?" I asked her, out of patience. "'Cause he's dead," says she. "*Dead?*" says I. She just nodded her head, not getting a bit excited, but rockin' back and forth. "Why – where is he?" says I, not knowing what to say. She just pointed upstairs – like that (*himself pointing to the room above*) I got up, with the idea of going up there. I walked from there to here – (*pointing*) – then I says, "Why, what did he die of?" "He died of a rope round his neck," says she, and just went on pleatin' at her apron. Well, I went out and called Harry. I thought I might – need help. We went upstairs and there he was – lyin' —

COUNTY ATTORNEY: I think I'd rather have you go into that upstairs, where you can point it all out. Just go on now with the rest of the story.

HALE: Well, my first thought was to get that rope off. It looked – (*stops, his face twitches*) – but Harry, he went up to him, and he said, "No, he's dead all right, and we'd better not touch anything." So we went back down stairs. She was still sitting that same way. "Has anybody been notified?" I asked. "No," says she, unconcerned. "Who did this, Mrs. Wright?" said Harry. He said it businesslike – and she stopped pleatin' of her apron. "I don't know," she says. "You don't *know?*" says Harry. "No," says she. "Weren't you sleepin' in the bed with him?" says Harry. "Yes," says she, "but I was on the inside." "Somebody slipped a rope round his neck and strangled him and you didn't wake up?" says Harry. "I didn't wake up," she said after him. We may have looked as if we didn't see how that could be, for after a minute she said, "I sleep sound." Harry was going to ask her more questions but I said maybe we ought to let her tell her story first to the coroner, or the sheriff, so Harry went fast as he could to Rivers' place, where there's a telephone.

COUNTY ATTORNEY: And what did Mrs. Wright do when she knew that you had gone for the coroner?

HALE: She moved from that chair to this one over here, (*pointing to a small chair in the corner*) and just sat there with her hands held together and looking down. I got a feeling that I ought to make some conversation, so I said I had come in to see if John wanted to put in a telephone, and at that she started to laugh, and then she stopped and looked at me — scared. (*County attorney, who has had his notebook out, makes a note*) I dunno, maybe it wasn't scared. I wouldn't like to say it was. Soon Harry got back, and then Dr. Lloyd came, and you, Mr. Peters, and so I guess that's all I know that you don't.

COUNTY ATTORNEY: (*Looking around*) I guess we'll go upstairs first — and then out to the barn and around there. (*To sheriff*) You're convinced that there was nothing important here — nothing that would point to any motive?

SHERIFF: Nothing here but kitchen things.

COUNTY ATTORNEY: (*Opens the door of a cupboard closet. Gets up on a chair and looks on a shelf. Pulls his hand away, sticky*) Here's a nice mess. (*The women draw nearer*)

MRS. PETERS: Oh, her fruit; it did freeze. (*To County Attorney*) She worried about that when it turned so cold. She said the fire'd go out and her jars would break.

SHERIFF: Well, can you beat the women! Held for murder and worrying about her preserves.

COUNTY ATTORNEY: (*Setting his lips firmly*) I guess before we are through she may have something more serious than preserves to worry about.

HALE: Well, women are used to worrying over trifles. (*The two women move a little closer together*)

COUNTY ATTORNEY: (*With the gallantry of a young politician*) And yet, for all their worries, what would we do without the ladies? (*The women do not unbend. He goes to sink, takes a dipperful of water from pail and pouring it into basin, washes his hands. Starts to wipe them on roller-towel, turns it for a cleaner place*) Dirty towels! (*Kicks his foot against pans under the sink*) Not much of a housekeeper, would you say, ladies?

MRS. HALE: (*Stiffly*) There's a great deal of work to be done on a farm.

COUNTY ATTORNEY: (*With conciliation*) To be sure. And yet (*with a little bow to her*) I know there are some Dickson county farmhouses which do not have such roller towels. (*Gives it a pull to expose its full length again*)

MRS. HALE: Those towels get dirty awful quick. Men's hands aren't always as clean as they might be.

COUNTY ATTORNEY: Ah, loyal to your sex, I see. But you and Mrs. Wright were neighbors. I suppose you were friends, too.

MRS. HALE: (*Shaking her head*) I've not seen much of her of late years. I've not been in this house — it's more than a year.

COUNTY ATTORNEY: And why was that? You didn't like her?

MRS. HALE: I liked her all well enough. Farmers' wives have their hands full, Mr. Henderson. And then —

COUNTY ATTORNEY: Yes —?

MRS. HALE: (*Looking about*) It never seemed a very cheerful place.

COUNTY ATTORNEY: No — it's not cheerful. I shouldn't say she had the homemaking instinct.

MRS. HALE: Well, I don't know as Wright had, either.

COUNTY ATTORNEY: You mean that they didn't get on very well?

MRS. HALE: No, I don't mean anything. But I don't think a place'd be any cheerfuller for John Wright's being in it.

COUNTY ATTORNEY: I'd like to talk more of that a little later. I want to get the lay of things upstairs now. (*Moves to stair-door, followed by the two men*)

SHERIFF: I suppose anything Mrs. Peters does'll be all right. She was to take in some clothes for her, you know, and a few little things. We left in such a hurry yesterday.

COUNTY ATTORNEY: Yes, but I would like to see what you take, Mrs. Peters, and keep an eye out for anything that might be of use to us.

MRS. PETERS: Yes, Mr. Henderson. (*The women listen to the men's steps on the stairs, then look about the kitchen*)

MRS. HALE: I'd hate to have men coming into my kitchen, snooping round and criticizing. (*Arranges pans under sink which the county attorney had shoved out of place*)

MRS. PETERS: Of course it's no more than their duty.

MRS. HALE: Duty's all right, but I guess that deputy sheriff that came out to make the fire might have got a little of this on. (*Gives roller towel a pull*) Wish I'd thought of that sooner. Seems mean to talk about her for not having things slicked up when she had to come away in such a hurry.

MRS. PETERS: (*Going to table at side, lifts one end of towel that covers a pan*) She had bread set. (*Stands still*)

MRS. HALE: (*Her eyes fixed on loaf of bread outside bread-box. Moves slowly toward it*) She was going to put this in there. (*Picks up loaf, then abruptly drops it. In a manner of returning to familiar things*) It's a shame about her fruit. I wonder if it's all gone. (*Gets up on a chair and looks*) I think there's some here that is all right, Mrs. Peters. Yes — here; (*holding it toward the window*) this is cherries, too. (*Looking again*) I declare I believe that's the only one. (*Gets down, bottle in her hand. Goes to sink and wipes it off on the outside*) She'll feel awful bad after all her hard work in the hot weather. I remember the afternoon I put up my cherries last summer. (*Puts bottle on table. With a sigh starts to sit down in rocking-chair. Before she is seated realizes what chair it is; with a slow look at it, steps back. The chair which she has touched rocks back and forth*)

MRS. PETERS: Well, I must get those things from the front room closet. (*Starts to door left, looks into the other room, steps back*) You coming with me, Mrs. Hale? You could help me carry them. (*Both women go out; reappear, Mrs. Peters carrying a dress and skirt, Mrs. Hale following with a pair of shoes*)

MRS. PETERS: My, it's cold in there. (*Puts clothes on table, goes up to stove*)

MRS. HALE: (*Holding up skirt and examining it*) Wright was close. I think maybe that's why she kept so much to herself. She didn't even belong to the Ladies' Aid. I suppose she felt she couldn't do her part, and then you don't enjoy things when you feel shabby. She used to wear pretty clothes and be lively, when she was Minnie Foster, one of the town girls singing in the choir. But that was — oh, that was thirty years ago. This all you was to take in?

MRS. PETERS: She said she wanted an apron. Funny thing to want, for there isn't much to get you dirty in jail, goodness knows. But I suppose just to make her feel more natural. She said they was in the top drawer in this cupboard. Yes, here. And then her little shawl that always hung behind the door. (*Looks on stair door*) Yes, here it is.

MRS. HALE: (*Abruptly moving toward her*) Mrs. Peters?

MRS. PETERS: Yes, Mrs. Hale?

MRS. HALE: Do you think she did it?

MRS. PETERS: (*In a frightened voice*) Oh, I don't know.

MRS. HALE: Well, I don't think she did. Asking for an apron and her little shawl. Worrying about her fruit.

MRS. PETERS: (*Starts to speak, glances up, where footsteps are heard in the room above. In a low voice*) Mr. Peters says it looks bad for her. Mr. Henderson is awful sarcastic in a speech and he'll make fun of her sayin' she didn't wake up.

MRS. HALE: Well, I guess John Wright didn't wake when they was slipping that rope under his neck.

MRS. PETERS: No, it's strange. It must have been done awful crafty and still. They say it was such a — funny way to kill a man, rigging it all up like that.

MRS. HALE: That's just what Mr. Hale said. There was a gun in the house. He says that's what he can't understand.

MRS. PETERS: Mr. Henderson said coming out that what was needed for the case was a motive; something to show anger, or — sudden feeling.

MRS. HALE: (*Standing by table*) Well, I don't see any signs of anger around here, but (*puts hand on dish towel in middle of table, stands looking at table, one half of which is clean, the other half messy*) It's wiped to here. (*Makes a move as if to finish work, then turns and looks at loaf of bread beside the breadbox. Drops towel. In that voice of coming back to familiar things*) Wonder how they are finding things upstairs. I hope she had it a little more red-up[1] up there. You know, it seems kind of *sneaking*. Locking her up in town and then coming out here and trying to get her own house to turn against her!

---

1. **red-up:** A country expression meaning tidied or cleaned up.

MRS. PETERS: But, Mrs. Hale, the law is the law.

MRS. HALE: I spose't is. (*Unbuttoning her coat*) Better loosen up your things, Mrs. Peters. You won't feel them when you go out.

MRS. PETERS: (*Taking off fur tippet, goes to hang it on hook at back of the room, stands looking at the under part of the small table*) She was piecing a quilt. (*Brings large sewing basket to table front and they look at the bright pieces*)

MRS. HALE: It's log cabin pattern. Pretty, isn't it? I wonder if she was goin' to quilt it or just knot it? (*Footsteps have been heard coming down the stairs. The sheriff enters followed by Hale and Henderson*)

SHERIFF: They wonder if she was going to quilt it or just knot it. (*The men laugh, the women look abashed*)

COUNTY ATTORNEY: (*Rubbing his hands over the stove*) Frank's fire didn't do much up there, did it? Well, let's go out to the barn and get that cleared up. (*Exeunt men door rear*)

MRS. HALE: (*Resentfully*) I don't know as there's anything so strange, our takin' up our time with little things while we're waiting for them to get the evidence. (*Sits down, smoothing out block with decision*) I don't see as it's anything to laugh about.

MRS. PETERS: (*Apologetically*) Of course they've got awful important things on their minds. (*Pulls up a chair and sits by the table*)

MRS. HALE: (*Examining another block*) Mrs. Peters, look at this one. Here, this is the one she was working on, and look at the sewing! All the rest of it has been so nice and even. And look at this! It's all over the place! Why, it looks as if she didn't know what she was about! (*After she has said this they look at each other, then start to glance back at the door. After an instant Mrs. Hale has pulled at a knot and ripped the sewing*)

MRS. PETERS: Oh, what are you doing, Mrs. Hale?

MRS. HALE: (*Mildly*) Just pulling out a stitch or two that's not sewed very good. (*Threading a needle*) Bad sewing always made me fidgety.

MRS. PETERS: (*Nervously*) I don't think we ought to touch things.

MRS. HALE: I'll just finish up this end. (*Suddenly stopping and leaning forward*) Mrs. Peters?

MRS. PETERS: Yes, Mrs. Hale?

MRS. HALE: What do you suppose she was so nervous about?

MRS. PETERS: Oh — I don't know. I don't know as she was nervous. I sometimes sew awful queer when I'm just tired. (*Mrs. Hale starts to say something, looks at her, compresses her lips a little, goes on sewing*) Well I must get these things wrapped up. They may be through sooner than we think. (*Piling apron and other things together*) I wonder where I can find a piece of paper, and string.

MRS. HALE: In that cupboard, maybe.

MRS. PETERS: (*Looking in cupboard*) Why, here's a bird-cage. (*Holds it up*) Did she have a bird, Mrs. Hale?

MRS. HALE: Why, I don't know whether she did or not — I've not been here for so long. There was a man around last year selling canaries cheap, but I don't know as she took one; maybe she did. She used to sing real pretty herself.

MRS. PETERS: (*Glancing around*) Seems funny to think of a bird here. But she must have had one, or why should she have had a cage? I wonder what happened to it.

MRS. HALE: I s'pose maybe the cat got it.

MRS. PETERS: No, she didn't have a cat. She's got that feeling some people have about cats — being afraid of them. My cat got in her room and she was real upset and asked me to take it out.

MRS. HALE: My sister Bessie was like that. Queer, ain't it?

MRS. PETERS: (*Examining cage*) Why, look at this door. It's broke. One hinge is pulled apart.

MRS. HALE: (*Looking too*) Looks as if someone must have been rough with it.

MRS. PETERS: Why, yes. (*Puts cage on table*)

MRS. HALE: I wish if they're going to find any evidence they'd be about it. I don't like this place.

MRS. PETERS: But I'm awful glad you came with me, Mrs. Hale. It would be lonesome for me sitting here alone.

MRS. HALE: It would, wouldn't it? (*Dropping sewing, voice falling*) But I tell you what I do wish, Mrs. Peters. I wish I had come over some times when *she* was here. I — (*looking around the room*) — wish I had.

MRS. PETERS: But of course you were awful busy, Mrs. Hale — your house and your children.

MRS. HALE: I could've come. I stayed away because it weren't cheerful — and that's why I ought to have come. I — I've never liked this place. Maybe because it's down in a hollow and you don't see the road. I dunno what it is, but it's a lonesome place and always was. I wish I had come over to see Minnie Foster sometimes. I can see now — (*shakes her head*)

MRS. PETERS: Well, you mustn't reproach yourself, Mrs. Hale. Somehow we just don't see how it is with other folks until — something comes up.

MRS. HALE: Not having children makes less work — but it makes a quiet house, and Wright out to work all day, and no company when he did come in. Did you know John Wright, Mrs. Peters?

MRS. PETERS: Not to know him; I've seen him in town. They say he was a good man.

MRS. HALE: Yes — good; he didn't drink, and kept his word as well as most, I guess, and paid his debts. But he was a hard man, Mrs. Peters. Just to pass the time of day with him — (*shivers*) Like a raw wind that gets to the bone. (*Pauses, her eye falling on the cage*) I should think she would 'a wanted a bird. But what do you suppose went with it?

MRS. PETERS: I don't know, unless it got sick and died. (*She reaches over and swings the broken door, swings it again, both women watch it*)

MRS. HALE: You weren't raised round here, were you? (*Mrs. Peters shakes her head*) You didn't know — her?

MRS. PETERS: Not till they brought her yesterday.

MRS. HALE: She — come to think of it, she was kind of like a bird herself — real sweet and pretty, but kind of timid and — fluttery. How — she – did – change. (*Silence; then as if struck by a happy thought and relieved to get back to everyday things*) Tell you what, Mrs. Peters, why don't you take the quilt in with you? It might take up her mind.

MRS. PETERS: Why, I think that's a real nice idea, Mrs. Hale. There couldn't possibly be any objection to it, could there? Now, just what would I take? I wonder if her patches are in here — and her things. (*Both look in sewing basket*)

MRS. HALE: Here's some red. I expect this has got sewing things in it. (*Brings out a fancy box*) What a pretty box. Looks like something somebody would give you. Maybe her scissors are in here. (*Opens box. Suddenly puts her hand to her nose.*) Why — (*Mrs. Peters bends nearer, then turns her face away*) There's something wrapped up in this piece of silk.

MRS. PETERS: Why, this isn't her scissors.

MRS. HALE: (*Lifting the silk*) Oh, Mrs. Peters — it's (*Mrs. Peters bends closer*)

MRS. PETERS: It's the bird.

MRS. HALE: (*Jumping up*) But, Mrs. Peters — look at it! Its neck! Look at its neck! It's all — other side *to*.

MRS. PETERS: Somebody-wrung-its-neck. (*Their eyes meet. A look of growing comprehension, of horror. Steps are heard outside. Mrs. Hale slips box under quilt pieces, and sinks into her chair. Enter Sheriff and County Attorney. Mrs. Peters rises*)

COUNTY ATTORNEY: (*As one turning from serious things to little pleasantries*) Well, ladies, have you decided whether she was going to quilt it or knot it?

MRS. PETERS: We think she was going to — knot it.

COUNTY ATTORNEY: Well, that's interesting, I am sure. (*Looking at bird-cage*) Has the bird flown?

MRS. HALE: (*Piling more quilt pieces over the box*) We think the — cat got it.

COUNTY ATTORNEY: (*Preoccupied*) Is there a cat? (*Mrs. Hale glances in a quick covert way at Mrs. Peters*)

MRS. PETERS: Well, not *now*. They're superstitious, you know. They leave.

COUNTY ATTORNEY: (*To Peters, in the manner of continuing an interrupted conversation*) No sign at all of anyone having come from the outside. Their own rope. Now let's go up again and go over it piece by piece. (*They start upstairs*) It would have to have been someone who knew just the — (*Mrs. Peters sinks into her chair. The two women sit there not looking at one another, but as if peering into something and at the same time holding back. When they talk now it is in the manner of feeling their way over strange ground, as if afraid of what they are saying, but as if they cannot help saying it*)

MRS. HALE: She liked the bird. She was going to bury it in that pretty box.

MRS. PETERS: (*In a whisper*) When I was a girl — my kitten — there was a boy took a hatchet, and before my eyes — and before I could get there — (*covers her face an instant*) If they hadn't held me back I would have — (*catches herself, looks upstairs where steps are heard, falters weakly*) — hurt him.

MRS. HALE: (*With a slow look around her*) I wonder how it would seem never to have had any children around. (*Pause*) No, Wright wouldn't like the bird — a thing that sang. She used to sing. He killed that, too.

MRS. PETERS: (*Moving uneasily*) We don't know who killed the bird.

MRS. HALE: I knew John Wright.

MRS. PETERS: It was an awful thing was done in this house that night, Mrs. Hale. Killing a man while he slept, slipping a rope around his neck that choked the life out of him.

MRS. HALE: His neck. Choked the life out of him. (*Her hand goes out and rests on the bird-cage*)

MRS. PETERS: (*With rising voice*) We don't know who killed him. We don't *know*.

MRS. HALE: (*Her own feeling not interrupted*) If there'd been years and years of nothing, then a bird to sing to you, it would be awful — still, after the bird was still.

MRS. PETERS: (*Something within her speaking*) I know what stillness is. When we home-steaded in Dakota, and my first baby died — after he was two years old, and me with no other then —

MRS. HALE: (*Moving*) How soon do you suppose they'll be through, looking for the evidence?

MRS. PETERS: I know what stillness is. (*Pulling herself back*) The law has got to punish crime, Mrs. Hale.

MRS. HALE: (*Not as if answering that*) I wish you'd seen Minnie Foster when she wore a white dress with blue ribbons and stood up there in the choir and sang. (*Suddenly looking around the room*) Oh, I wish I'd come over here once in a while! That was a crime! That was a crime! Who's going to punish that?

MRS. PETERS: (*Looking upstairs*) We mustn't — take on.

MRS. HALE: I might have known she needed help! I know how things can be — for women. I tell you, it's queer, Mrs. Peters. We live close together and we live far apart. We all go through the same things — it's all just a different kind of the same thing — (*Brushes her eyes, then seeing the bottle of fruit, reaches out for it*) If I was you I wouldn't tell her her fruit was gone. Tell her it *ain't*. Tell her it's all right. Take this in to prove it to her. She — she may never know whether it was broke or not.

MRS. PETERS: (*Picks up the bottle, looks about for something to wrap it in; takes petti-coat from clothes brought from front room, very nervously begins winding that around it. In a false voice*) My, it's a good thing the men couldn't hear us. Wouldn't they just laugh! Getting all stirred up over a little thing like a — dead canary. As if that could have anything to do with — with — wouldn't they *laugh*! (*The men are heard coming down stairs*)

MRS. HALE: (*Muttering*) Maybe they would — maybe they wouldn't.

COUNTY ATTORNEY: No, Peters, it's all perfectly clear except a reason for doing it. But you know juries when it comes to women. If there was some definite thing. Some-thing to show — something to make a story about — a thing that would connect up with this strange way of doing it — (*The women's eyes meet for an instant. Enter Hale from outer door*)

HALE: Well, I've got the team around. Pretty cold out there.

COUNTY ATTORNEY: I'm going to stay here a while by myself. (*To sheriff*) You can send Frank out for me, can't you? I want to go over everything. I'm not satisfied that we can't do better.

SHERIFF: Do you want to see what Mrs. Peters is going to take in?

COUNTY ATTORNEY: (*Goes to table. Picks up apron, laughs*) Oh, I guess they're not very dangerous things the ladies have picked out. (*Moves a few things about, disturbing quilt pieces which cover the box. Steps back*) No, Mrs. Peters doesn't need supervis-ing. For that matter, a sheriff's wife is married to the law. Ever think of it that way, Mrs. Peters?

MRS. PETERS: Not — just that way.

SHERIFF: (*Chuckling*) Married to the law. (*Moves toward front room*) I just want you to come in here a minute, George. We ought to take a look at these windows.

COUNTY ATTORNEY: Oh, windows!

SHERIFF: We'll be right out, Mr. Hale. (*Exit Hale door rear. Sheriff follows County Attorney through door left. The two women's eyes follow them out. Mrs. Hale rises, hands tightly together, looking intensely at Mrs. Peters, whose eyes make a slow turn, finally meeting Mrs. Hale's. A moment Mrs. Hale holds her, then her own eyes point the way to the spot where the box is concealed. Suddenly Mrs. Peters throws back quilt pieces and tries to put box in the bag she is wearing. It is too big. She opens box, starts to take bird out, cannot touch it, goes to pieces, stands there helpless. Sound of a knob turning in the other room. Mrs. Hale snatches box and puts it in the pocket of her big coat. Enter County Attorney and Sheriff*)

COUNTY ATTORNEY: (*Facetiously*) Well, Henry, at least we found out that she was not going to quilt it. She was going to — what is it you call it, ladies?

MRS. HALE: (*Hand against her pocket*) We call it — knot it, Mr. Henderson.

Curtain

[1916]

Eugene O'Neill

[1888–1953]

Eugene O'Neill . . . has done nothing much in American drama save to transform it utterly, in ten or twelve years, from a false world of neat and competent trickery to a world of splendor and fear and greatness.

–Sinclair Lewis

Eugene Gladstone O'Neill was born October 16, 1888, the third son of Mary Ellen Quinlan O'Neill, the devout daughter of Irish Catholic immigrants, and James O'Neill, an actor famous for his leading roles in romantic dramas, especially *The Count of Monte Cristo*. Although the couple owned a house in New London, Connecticut, they toured constantly, and O'Neill was born in a residential hotel in New York City. Following the early death of one of her sons, "Ella" O'Neill became addicted to morphine, and her flamboyant husband was a heavy drinker who enjoyed the company of many other women. During his traumatic early childhood, O'Neill witnessed frequent scenes of conflict between his parents. When he was seven, O'Neill was sent to a Catholic boarding school, and he subsequently lived with his parents only during summer vacations, often spending even holidays at school. After graduating from prep school in 1906, O'Neill enrolled at Princeton University, from which he was dismissed for poor academic performance before the end of his first year. Drifting aimlessly, he first worked as a secretary in New York City. When he learned that his girlfriend Kathleen Jenkins was pregnant, O'Neill married her, but he was unprepared for the responsibilities of being a husband and father. The restless O'Neill soon abandoned his family and went to prospect for gold in Honduras. He then signed on as a sailor aboard tramp steamers bound for ports in South America, South Africa, and England.

O'Neill discovered his calling after returning to New York City in 1912. He divorced Jenkins (granting her full custody of their son), tried acting with his father, and worked briefly as a reporter for a newspaper in New London. When he was diagnosed with tuberculosis, his father sent him to recover at a sanatorium. During the six months of enforced inactivity and solitude, O'Neill read constantly, especially Greek tragedies and the works of modern European dramatists such as Henrik Ibsen, George Bernard Shaw, and August Strindberg. Inspired by their work, O'Neill began to write short plays when he returned to New London in 1913. James O'Neill was so relieved that his son was finally making something of his life that he paid for the publication of five of those plays as *"Thirst" and Other One Act Plays* (1914). Although the volume generated little interest and sold poorly, O'Neill was now determined to become a playwright. After taking George Pierce Baker's pioneering course in playwriting at Harvard University during 1914-15, O'Neill moved to Provincetown, Massachusetts. There, he met George Cram Cook and his wife, Susan Glaspell, through whom O'Neill became involved in their theater group the Provincetown Players. After the group staged the first performance of a play by O'Neill, *Bound East for Cardiff* (1916), he was almost exclusively associated with the Provincetown Players, who produced ten more of his one-act plays during the period 1916-20. His first full-length play and first venture into the commercial theater was *Beyond the Horizon* (1920), a modest Broadway hit for which O'Neill received the first of his four Pulitzer Prizes.

Eugene O'Neill

This photograph was taken in Provincetown, Massachusetts, in the early 1920s, at the time critics began to hail O'Neill as the foremost dramatist in the United States.

O'Neill was soon catapulted into the forefront of American dramatists. His earliest plays were primarily and often grimly realistic, many of them based on his experiences as a sailor aboard ships or in seedy waterfront bars. But he began to experiment with the dramatic techniques of German expressionism, literally "the inner made outer," in his acclaimed play *The Emperor Jones* (1920). In an enthusiastic review, the influential drama critic Heywood Broun observed: "We never see a play by O'Neill without feeling that something of the sort will be done better within a season or so, and that O'Neill will do it." Indeed, he continued to challenge the theatrical conventions of the American theater, further experimenting with the use of expressionistic dialogue and action in *The Hairy Ape* (1922) and *The Great God Brown* (1926), meanwhile creating an uproar with a play about an interracial marriage, *All God's Chillun Got Wings* (1924). O'Neill also began to draw upon ancient Greek tragedies and Freudian psychology in plays focusing on destructive conflicts within families, including *Desire under the Elms* (1924) and his marathon, five-hour *Strange Interlude* (1928). But his professional success was shadowed by the death of his mother in 1920, his father in 1921, and his alcoholic older brother in 1923. His second marriage, to the writer Agnes Bolton Burton in 1918, ended in a bitter divorce after O'Neill left her and their two children to be with the actress Carlotta Monterey, whom he married in 1929. Two years later, he published one of his most celebrated plays, *Mourning Becomes Electra* (1931), a retelling of Aeschylus's Orestia trilogy set in nineteenth-century New England.

Widely hailed as the founder of modern drama in the United States, O'Neill was the first American playwright to receive the Nobel Prize in Literature, in 1936. That triumph effectively marked the beginning of his long physical and professional decline. During the following years, O'Neill wrote some major plays, notably *The Iceman Cometh* (1939), which was produced on Broadway in 1946. But the four-hour play did poorly, and others he wrote during the period were not published nor produced until after his death, including the Pulitzer Prize-winning *Long Day's Journey into Night* (1940). Because of the personal nature of the play, an autobiographical account of his troubled family, O'Neill instructed that it should be published posthumously, and it was not produced until 1957. Suffering from the progressive degenerative effects of a neurological disorder akin to Parkinson's disease, O'Neill was unable to write at all during the last decade of his life, and he spent his final years living in isolation with his wife in a residential hotel in Boston. Just before he died on November 27, 1953, he is reported to have said: "Born in a hotel room — and God damn it — died in a hotel room."

bedfordstmartins.com/americanlit for research links on O'Neill

O'Neill's *The Emperor Jones.* First performed at their small theater in Greenwich Village on November 1, 1920, *The Emperor Jones* was the crowning success of the Provincetown Players. "They are turning away dozens," one enthusiastic reviewer reported. "People squat on their coats on the hard and not immaculate floors, or sit cheerfully on radiators, or stand patiently for two hours while the tragedy of fear of a Negro porter and ex-convict, turned primitive man again, unfolds itself before the fascinated imagination." In fact, the demand for tickets was so great that the play had to be moved to a larger theater uptown, where it ran for 204 performances on Broadway.

Although the play represented a challenge to the conventions of dramatic realism, O'Neill's story of the downfall and disintegration of the self-appointed "emperor" of a West Indian island was informed by well-known events in the tortured history of Haiti. The nation had gained its independence from France through a successful rebellion begun in 1791 and led by a former slave, Toussaint Louverture. Henri Christophe, who played a major role in the rebellion, became the president of northern Haiti in 1807. In 1811, he proclaimed himself king and established magnificent palaces and homes for himself. Fearing a coup, the autocratic and increasingly unpopular Christophe committed suicide by shooting himself with a silver bullet in 1820. O'Neill's first title for *The Emperor Jones* was "The Silver Bullet," and Brutus Jones, the Pullman porter who becomes a dictator, is a thinly veiled representation of Christophe. Contemporary audiences would have been reminded of the early history of Haiti by more recent events in the country, where an uprising against an unpopular dictator in 1915 had prompted the United States to send three hundred marines to Port-au-Prince to "protect American and foreign interests," as the official policy read. The ongoing military occupation of the country raised considerable opposition in the United States, where many may have drawn a connection between the American policy and Brutus

The Emperor Jones

Jesse Tarbox Beals, the first female photojournalist, took this photograph of the slave-market scene during the earliest performances of O'Neill's play at the Provincetown Playhouse, in November 1920.

Jones's effort to control and exploit the inhabitants of "an island in the West Indies as yet un-self-determined by White Marines," as O'Neill ironically describes the setting of *The Emperor Jones.*

The resonant play also gained force from its staging, casting, and innovations in language and dramatic structure. One of the founders and leading forces in the Provincetown Players, George Cram Cook, told Susan Glaspell that O'Neill wrote the play "to *compel* us to do the untried, to do the impossible." In response, Cook almost single-handedly built a white plaster dome over the stage of the Provincetown Playhouse. The diffused light reflected from the curved and polished surface of the dome gave an illusion of infinite depth to the shallow stage, where the increasingly hallucinatory action was enhanced by bold sets and punctuated by the persistent and quickening drumbeat heard throughout the play. But the most compelling element of the first production was the mesmerizing acting of Charles Gilpin, the first African American to be given a major role on the mainstream American stage, whose performance was hailed by critics as "the crown to a play that opens up the imagination of the American theatre." Indeed, *The Emperor Jones* was then and still is widely viewed as a defining moment in the theatrical history of the United States.

Despite its dramatic impact and historical importance, the play was and remains deeply controversial. Often credited with spurring the development of African American drama during the Harlem Renaissance, *The Emperor Jones* nonetheless raises fundamental questions about racial representation and stereotyping. The eight scenes of the play take Brutus Jones back in his imagination through incidents from both his own criminal past and the tragic history of African Americans, including a slave auction and the voyage of a slave ship, finally returning him to Africa. Langston Hughes reported that, when the play was performed in Harlem, some members of the audience objected so strongly to the portrait of a black man overcome by superstitious fears and reverting to his primitive self that they shouted: "Why don't you come out o' that jungle — back to Harlem where you belong?" Gilpin, however, strongly defended the play, as did his immediate successor in the role, the actor and activist Paul Robeson, who played Brutus Jones on Broadway and in the movie version produced in 1933. "This is undoubtedly one of '*the* great plays,' a true classic of the drama, American or otherwise," Robeson declared in an article in the African American journal *Opportunity* in 1924. In response to those who hoped that he would now get a role "portraying the finest type of Negro," Robeson asserted that he would probably never portray "a more heroically tragic figure than 'Brutus Jones, Emperor,' not excepting 'Othello.'" Certainly, the role continued to provide a powerful vehicle for distinguished black actors, including Ossie Davis, who made his television debut in *The Emperor Jones* in 1955, and James Earl Jones, who played the lead role in a radio version directed by Theodore Mann in 1990. The text of the play is taken from the first printing in *Theatre Arts Magazine* (January 1921).

THE EMPEROR JONES

CHARACTERS

BRUTUS JONES, *Emperor*

HENRY SMITHERS, *A Cockney Trader*[1]

AN OLD NATIVE WOMAN

LEM, *A Native Chief*

SOLDIERS, *Adherents of Lem*

The Little Formless Fears; Jeff; The Negro Convicts; The Prison Guard; The Planters;
   The Auctioneer; The Slaves; The Congo Witch-Doctor; The Crocodile God

The action of the play takes place on an island in the West Indies as yet un-self-determinated by White Marines.[2] *The form of native government is, for the time being, an Empire.*

SCENE ONE

The audience chamber in the palace of the Emperor — a spacious, high-ceilinged room with bare, white-washed walls. The floor is of white tiles. In the rear, to the left of center, a wide archway giving out on a portico with white pillars. The palace is evidently situated on high ground, for beyond the portico nothing can be seen but a vista of distant hills, their summits crowned with thick groves of palm trees. In the right wall, center, a smaller arched doorway leading to the living quarters of the palace. The room is bare of furniture with the exception of one huge chair made of uncut wood which stands at center, its back to rear. This is very apparently the Emperor's throne. It is painted a dazzling, eye-smiting scarlet. There is a brilliant orange cushion on the seat and another smaller one is placed on the floor to serve as a footstool. Strips of matting, dyed scarlet, lead from the foot of the throne to the two entrances.

It is late afternoon but the sunlight still blazes yellowly beyond the portico and there is an oppressive burden of exhausting heat in the air.

As the curtain rises, a native negro woman sneaks in cautiously from the entrance on the right. She is very old, dressed in cheap calico, bare-footed, a red bandana handkerchief covering all but a few stray wisps of white hair. A bundle bound in colored cloth is carried over the shoulder on the end of a stick. She hesitates beside the doorway, peering back as if in extreme dread of being discovered. Then she begins to glide noiselessly, a step at a time, toward the doorway in the rear. At this moment, Smithers appears beneath the portico.

Smithers is a tall, stoop-shouldered man about forty. His bald head, perched on a long neck with an enormous Adam's apple, looks like an egg. The tropics have tanned his

---

1. **A Cockney Trader:** A trader from East London, England, an area known for the broad, distinctive accent of its inhabitants, often viewed as the epitome of working-class Londoners.
2. **an island . . . Marines:** Probably a reference to Haiti, which was occupied by U.S. Marines and effectively controlled by the American government from 1915 to 1934.

naturally pasty face with its small, sharp features to a sickly yellow, and Native Rum has painted his pointed nose to a startling red. His little, washy-blue eyes are red-rimmed and dart about him like a ferret's. His expression is one of unscrupulous meanness, cowardly and dangerous. His attitude toward Jones is that of one who will give vent to a nourished grudge against all superiority — as far as he dares. He is dressed in a worn riding suit of dirty white drill, puttees, spurs, and wears a white cork helmet. A cartridge belt with an automatic revolver is around his waist. He carries a riding whip in his hand. He sees the woman and stops to watch her suspiciously. Then, making up his mind, he steps quickly on tiptoe into the room. The woman, looking back over her shoulder continually, does not see him until it is too late. When she does, Smithers springs forward and grabs her firmly by the shoulder. She struggles to get away, fiercely but silently.

SMITHERS: (*tightening his grasp – roughly*) Easy! None o' that, me birdie. You can't wriggle out now. I got me 'ooks on yer.

WOMAN: (*seeing the uselessness of struggling, gives away to frantic terror, and sinks to the ground, embracing his knees supplicatingly*) No tell him! No tell him, Mister!

SMITHERS: (*with great curiosity*) Tell 'im? (*Then scornfully.*) Oh, you mean 'is bloomin' Majesty. What's the gaime, any 'ow? What are you sneakin' away for? Been stealin' a bit, I s'pose. (*He taps her bundle with his riding whip significantly.*)

WOMAN: (*shaking her head vehemently*) No, me no steal.

SMITHERS: Bloody liar! But tell me what's up. There's somethin' funny goin' on. I smelled it in the air first thing I got up this mornin.' You blacks are up to some devilment. This palace of 'is is like a bleedin' tomb. Where's all the 'ands? (*The woman keeps sullenly silent. Smithers raises his whip threateningly.*) Ow, yer won't, won't yer? I'll show yer what's what.

WOMAN: (*coweringly*) I tell, Mister. You no hit. They go — all go. (*She makes a sweeping gesture toward the hills in the distance.*)

SMITHERS: Run away – to the 'ills?

WOMAN: Yes, Mister. Him Emperor – Great Father – (*She touches her forehead to the floor with a quick mechanical jerk.*) Him sleep after eat. Then they go – all go. Me old woman. Me left only. Now, me go too.

SMITHERS: (*his astonishment giving way to an immense mean satisfaction*) Ow! So that's the ticket! Well, I know bloody well wot's in the air – when they runs orf to the 'ills. The tom-tom 'll be thumping out there bloomin' soon. (*With extreme vindictiveness.*) And I'm bloody glad of it, for one! Serve 'im right! Puttin' on airs, the stinkin' nigger! 'Is Majesty! Gawd blimey! I only 'opes I'm there when they takes 'im out to shoot 'im. (*Suddenly.*) 'E's still 'ere all right, ain't 'e?

WOMAN: Yes. Him sleep.

SMITHERS: 'E's bound to find out soon as 'e wakes up. 'E's cunnin' enough to know when 'is time's come. (*He goes to the doorway on right and whistles shrilly with his fingers in his mouth. The old woman springs to her feet and runs out of the doorway, rear. Smithers goes after her, reaching for his revolver.*) Stop or I'll shoot! (*Then stopping – indifferently.*) Pop orf then, if yer like, yer black cow! (*He stands in the doorway, looking after her.*)

(*Jones enters from the right. He is a tall, powerfully-built, full blooded negro of middle age. His features are typically negroid, yet there is something decidedly distinctive about his face — an underlying strength of will, a hardy, self-reliant confidence in himself that inspires respect. His eyes are alive with a keen, cunning intelligence. In manner, he is shrewd, suspicious, evasive. He wears a light blue uniform coat, sprayed with brass buttons, heavy gold chevrons on his shoulders, gold braid on the collar, cuffs, etc. His pants are bright red with a light blue stripe down the side. Patent leather laced boots with brass spurs, and a belt with a long-barreled, pearl-handled revolver in a holster complete his make up. Yet there is something not altogether ridiculous about his grandeur. He has a way of carrying it off.*)

JONES: (*not seeing anyone – greatly irritated and blinking sleepily shouts*) Who dare whistle dat way in my palace? Who dare wake up de Emperor? I'll git de hide frayled off some o' you niggers sho'!

SMITHERS: (*showing himself – in a manner half-afraid and half-defiant*) It was me whistled to yer. (*As Jones frowns angrily.*) I got news for yer.

JONES: (*putting on his suavest manner which fails to cover up his contempt for the white man*) Oh, it's you, Mister Smithers. (*He sits down on his throne with easy dignity.*) What news you got to tell me?

SMITHERS: (*coming close to enjoy his discomfiture*) Don't you notice nothin' funny today?

JONES: (*coldly*) Funny? No, I ain't perceived nothin' of de kind!

SMITHERS: Then you ain't so foxy as I thought you was. Where's all your court – (*Sarcastically.*) the Generals and the Cabinet Ministers and all?

JONES: (*imperturbably*) Where dey mostly runs to, minute I closes my eyes – drinkin' rum and talkin' big down in de town. (*Sarcastically.*) How come you don't know dat? Ain't you sousin' with 'em most every day?

SMITHERS: (*stung but pretending indifference – with a wink*) That's part of the day's work. I got ter – ain't I – in my business?

JONES: (*contemptuously*) Yo' business!

SMITHERS: (*imprudently enraged*) Gawd blimey, you was glad enough for me ter take you in on it when you landed here first. You didn' 'ave no 'igh and mighty airs in them days!

JONES: (*his hand going to his revolver like a flash – menacingly*) Talk polite, white man! Talk polite, you heah me! I'm boss heah now, is you forgettin'?' (*The Cockney seems about to challenge this last statement with the facts, but something in the other's eyes holds and cowes him.*)

SMITHERS: (*in a cowardly whine*) No 'arm meant, old top.

JONES: (*condescendingly*) I accepts yo' apology. (*Lets his hand fall from his revolver.*) No use'n you rakin' up ole times. What I was den is one thing. What I is now 's another. You didn't let me in on yo' crooked work out o' no kind feelin' dat time. I done de dirty work fo' you – and most o' de brain work, too, fo' dat matter – and I was wu'th money to you, dat's de reason.

SMITHERS: Well, blimey, I give yer a start, didn't I – when no one else would. I wasn't afraid to hire yer like the rest was – 'count of the story about your breakin' jail back in the States.

JONES: No, you didn't have no s'cuse to look down on me fo' dat. You been in jail yo'self more'n once.

SMITHERS: (*furiously*) It's a lie! (*Then trying to pass it off by an attempt at scorn.*) Garn! Who told yer that fairy tale?

JONES: Dey's some things I ain't got to be tole. I kin see 'em in folk's eyes. (*Then after a pause — meditatively.*) Yes, you sho' give me a start. And it didn't take long from dat time to git dese fool woods' niggers right where I wanted dem. (*With pride.*) From stowaway to Emperor in two years! Dat's goin' some!

SMITHERS: (*with curiosity*) And I bet you got er pile o' money 'id safe someplace.

JONES: (*with satisfaction*) I sho' has! And it's in a foreign bank where no pusson don't ever get it out but me no matter what come. You don't s'pose I was holdin' down dis Emperor job for de glory in it, did you? Sho'! De fuss and glory part of it, dat's only to turn de heads o' de low-flung, bush niggers dat's here. Dey wants de big circus show for deir money. I gives it to 'em an' I gits de money. (*With a grin.*) De long green, dat's me every time! (*Then rebukingly.*) But you ain't got no kick agin me, Smithers. I'se paid you back all you done for me many times. Ain't I pertected you and winked at all de crooked tradin' you been doin' right out in de broad day. Sho' I has — and me makin' laws to stop it at de same time! (*He chuckles.*)

SMITHERS: (*grinning*) But, meanin' no 'arm, you been grabbin' right and left yourself, ain't you? Look at the taxes you've put on 'em! Blimey! You've squeezed 'em dry!

JONES: (*chuckling*) No dey ain't *all* dry yet. I'se still heah, ain't I?

SMITHERS: (*smiling at his secret thought*) They're dry right now, you'll find out. (*Changing the subject abruptly.*) And as for me breaking laws, you've broke 'em all yerself just as fast as yer made 'em.

JONES: Ain't I de Emperor? De laws don't go for him. (*Judicially.*) You heah what I tells you, Smithers. Dere's little stealin' like you does, and dere's big stealin' like I does. For de little stealin' dey gits you in jail soon or late. For de big stealin' dey makes you Emperor and puts you in de Hall o' Fame when you croaks. (*Reminiscently.*) If dey's one thing I learns in ten years on de Pullman ca's[3] listenin' to de white quality talk, it's dat same fact. And when I gits a chance to use it I winds up Emperor in two years.

SMITHERS: (*unable to repress the genuine admiration of the small fry for the large*) Yes, you turned the bleedin' trick, all right. Blimey, I never seen a bloke 'as 'ad the bloomin' luck you 'as.

JONES: (*severely*) Luck? What you mean — luck?

SMITHERS: I suppose you'll say as that swank about the silver bullet ain't luck — and that was what first got the fool blacks on yer side the time of the revolution, wasn't it?

JONES: (*with a laugh*) Oh, dat silver bullet! Sho' was luck! But I makes dat luck, you heah? I loads de dice! Yessuh! When dat murderin' nigger ole Lem hired to kill me

---

3. **on de Pullman ca's:** Pullman railroad cars were equipped with sleeping berths and other amenities for long-distance train travel. By the 1920s, roughly twenty thousand African American men were employed as Pullman porters. Although they earned better wages than most African Americans and were respected members of their communities, porters worked long hours under degrading conditions, spurring the formation of the Brotherhood of Sleeping Car Porters in 1925.

takes aim ten feet away and his gun misses fire and I shoots him dead, what you heah me say?

SMITHERS: You said yer'd got a charm so's no lead bullet'd kill yer. You was so strong only a silver bullet could kill yer, you told 'em. Blimey, wasn't that swank for yer — and plain, fat-'eaded luck?

JONES: (*proudly*) I got brains and uses 'em quick. Dat ain't luck.

SMITHERS: Yer knew they wasn't 'ardly liable to get no silver bullets. And it was luck 'e didn't 'it you that time.

JONES: (*laughing*) And dere all dem fool bush niggers was kneelin' down and bumpin' deir heads on de ground like I was a miracle out o' de Bible. Oh Lawd, from dat time on I has dem all eatin' out of my hand. I cracks de whip and dey jumps through.

SMITHERS: (*with a sniff*) Yankee bluff done it.

JONES: Ain't a man's talkin' big what makes him big — long as he makes folks believe it. So', I talks large when I ain't got nothin' to back it up, but I ain't talkin' wild just de same. I knows I kin fool 'em — I *knows* it — and dat's backin' enough fo' my game. And ain't I got to learn deir lingo and teach some of dem English befo' I kin talk to 'em? Ain't dat wirk? You ain't never learned any word er it, Smithers, in de ten years you been heah, dough yo' knows it's money in yo' pocket tradin' wid 'em if you does. But yo' too shiftless to take de trouble.

SMITHERS: (*flushing*) Never mind about me. What's this I've 'eard about yer really 'avin' a silver bullet moulded for yourself?

JONES: It's playin' out my bluff. I has de silver bullet moulded and I tells 'em when de time comes I kills myself wid it. I tells 'em dat's 'cause I'm de on'y man in de world big enuff to git me. No use'n deir tryin'. And dey falls down and bumps deir heads. (*He laughs.*) I does dat so's I kin take a walk in peace widout no jealous nigger gunnin' at me from behind de trees.

SMITHERS: (*astonished*) Then you 'ad it made — 'onest?

JONES: Sho' did. Heah she be. (*He takes out his revolver, breaks it, and takes the silver bullet out of one chamber.*) Five lead an' dis silver baby at de last. Don't she shine pretty? (*He holds it in his hand, looking at it admiringly, as if strangely fascinated.*)

SMITHERS: Let me see. (*Reaches out his hand for it.*)

JONES: (*harshly*) Keep yo' hands whar de b'long, white man. (*He replaces it in the chamber and puts the revolver back on his hip.*)

SMITHERS: (*snarling*) Gawd blimey! Think I'm a bleedin' thief, you would.

JONES: No. 'Tain't dat. I knows you'se scared to steal from me. On'y I ain't 'lowin' nary body to touch dis baby. She's my rabbit's foot.

SMITHERS: (*sneering*) A bloomin' charm, wot? (*Venomously.*) Well, you'll need all the bloody charms you 'as before long, s'elp me!

JONES: (*judicially*) Oh, I'se good for six months yit 'fore dey gits sick o' my game. Den, when I sees trouble comin,' I makes my getaway.

SMITHERS: Ho! You got it all planned, ain't yer?

JONES: I ain't no fool. I knows dis Emperor's time is sho't. Dat why I make hay when de sun shine. Was you thinkin' I'se aimin' to hold down dis job for life? No, suh! What good is gittin' money if you stays back in dis raggedy country? I wants action when I spends. And when I sees dese niggers gittin' up deir nerve to tu'n me out, and I'se got all de money in sight, I resigns on de spot and beats it quick.

SMITHERS: Where to?

JONES: None o' yo' business.

SMITHERS: Not back to the bloody States, I'll lay my oath.

JONES: (*suspiciously*) Why don't I? (*Then with an easy laugh.*) You mean 'count of dat story 'bout me breakin' from jail back dere? Dat's all talk.

SMITHERS: (*skeptically*) Ho, yes!

JONES: (*sharply*) You ain't 'sinuatin' I'se a liar, is you?

SMITHERS: (*hastily*) No, Gawd strike me! I was only thinkin' o' the bloody lies you told the blacks 'ere about killin' white men in the States.

JONES: (*angered*) How come dey're lies?

SMITHERS: You'd 'ave been in jail if you 'ad, wouldn't yer then? (*With venom.*) And from what I've 'eard, it ain't 'ealthy for a black to kill a white man in the States. They burn 'em in oil, don't they?

JONES: (*with cool deadliness*) You mean lynchin'[4] 'd scare me? Well, I tells you, Smithers, maybe I does kill one white man back dere. Maybe I does. And maybe I kills another right heah 'fore long if he don't look out.

SMITHERS: (*trying to force a laugh*) I was on'y spoofin' yer. Can't yer take a joke? And you was just sayin' you'd never been jail.

JONES: (*in the same tone – slightly boastful*) Maybe I goes to jail dere for gettin' in an argument wid razors ovah a crap game. Maybe I gits twenty years when dat colored man die. Maybe I gits in 'nother argument wid de prison guard was overseer o' us when we're walkin' de roads. Maybe he hits me wid a whip an' I splits his head wid a shovel an' runs away an' files de chain off my leg an' gits away safe. Maybe I does all dat an' maybe I don't. It's a story I tells you so's you knows I'se de kind of man dat if you evah repeats one word of it, I ends yo' stealin' on dis yearth mighty damn quick!

SMITHERS: (*terrified*) Think I'd peach on yer? Not me! Ain't I always been yer friend?

JONES: (*suddenly relaxing*) Sho' you has – and you better be.

SMITHERS: (*recovering his composure – and with it his malice*) And just to show yer I'm yer friend, I'll tell yer that bit o' news I was goin' to.

JONES: Go ahead! Shoot de piece. Must be bad news from de happy way you look.

SMITHERS: (*warningly*) Maybe it's gettin' time for you to resign – with that bloomin' silver bullet, wot? (*He finishes with a mocking grin.*)

JONES: (*puzzled*) What's dat you say? Talk plain.

SMITHERS: Ain't noticed any of the guards or servants about the place today, I 'aven't.

JONES: (*carelessly*) Dey're all out in de garden sleepin' under de trees. When I sleeps, dey sneaks a sleep, too, and I pretends I never suspicions it. All I got to do is to ring de bell an' dey come flyin,' makin' a bluff dey was wukin' all de time.

---

4. lynchin': During what is called "The Lynching Era" (1880–1930), almost three thousand African Americans, mostly men, were killed by white mobs in the South, usually by hanging or burning, or both.

SMITHERS: (*in the same mocking tone*) Ring the bell now an' you'll bloody well see what I means.

JONES: (*startled to alertness, but preserving the same careless tone*) Sho' I rings. (*He reaches below the throne and pulls out a big common dinner bell which is painted the same vivid scarlet as the throne. He rings this vigorously – then stops to listen. Then he goes to both doors, rings again, and looks out.*)

SMITHERS: (*watching him with malicious satisfaction – after a pause – mockingly*) The bloody ship is sinkin' an' the bleedin' rats 'as slung their 'ooks.

JONES: (*in a sudden fit of anger flings the bells clattering into a corner*) Low-flung, woods' niggers! (*Then catching Smithers' eye on him, he controls himself and suddenly bursts into a low chuckling laugh.*) Reckon I overplays my hand dis once! A man can't take de pot on a bob-tailed flush⁵ all de time. Was I sayin' I'd sit in six months mo'? Well, I'se changed my mind den. I cashes in and resigns de job of Emperor right dis minute.

SMITHERS: (*with real admiration*) Blimey,⁶ but you're a cool bird, and no mistake.

JONES: No use'n fussin.' When I knows de game's up I kisses it goodbye widout no long waits. Dey've all run off to de hills, ain't dey?

SMITHERS: Yes – every bleedin' man jack of 'em.

JONES: Den de revolution is at de post. And de Emperor better git his feet smokin' up de trail. (*He starts for the door in rear.*)

SMITHERS: Goin' out to look for your 'orse? Yer won't find any. They steals the 'orses first thing. Mine was gone when I went for 'im this mornin'. That's wot first give me a suspicion of wot was up.

JONES: (*alarmed for a second, scratches his head, then philosophically*) Well, den I hoofs it. Feet, do yo' duty! (*He pulls out a gold watch and looks at it.*) Three-thuty. Sundown's at six-thuty or dereabouts. (*Puts his watch back – with cool confidence.*) I got plenty o' time to make it easy.

SMITHERS: Don't be so bloomin' sure of it. They'll be after you 'ot and 'eavy. Ole Lem is at the bottom o' this business an' 'e 'ates you like 'ell. 'E'd rather do for you than eat 'is dinner, 'e would!

JONES: (*scornfully*) Dat fool no-count nigger! Does you think I'se scared o' him? I stands him on his thick head more'n once befo' dis, and I does it again if he come in my way – (*fiercely.*) And dis time I leave him a dead nigger fo' sho'!

SMITHERS: You'll 'ave to cut through the big forest – an' these blacks 'ere can sniff and follow a trail in the dark like 'ounds. You'd have to 'ustle to get through that forest in twelve hours even if you knew all the bloomin' trails like a native.

JONES: (*with indignant scorn*) Look-a-heah, white man! Does you think I'm a natural bo'n fool? Give me credit fo' havin' some sense, fo' Lawd's sake! Don't you s'pose I'se looked ahead and made sho' of all de chances? I'se gone out in dat big forest, pre-

---

5. **bob-tailed flush:** Four cards of the same suit, a relatively weak hand in a poker game.
6. **Blimey:** A British term used to express surprise, excitement, or alarm.

tendin' to hunt, so many times dat I knows it high an' low like a book. I could go through on dem trails wid my eyes shut. (*With great contempt.*) Think dese ig'nerent bush niggers dat don't got brains enuff to know deir own names even can catch Brutus Jones? Huh, I s'pects not! Not on yo' life! Why, man, de white men went after me wid bloodhounds where I come from an' I jes' laughs at 'em. It's a shame to fool dese black trash around heah, dey're so easy. You watch me, man'. I'll make dem look sick. I will. I'll be 'cross de plain to de edge of de forest by time dark comes. Once in de woods in de night, dey got a swell chance o' findin dis baby! Dawn tomorrow I'll be out at de oder side and on de coast whar dat French gun boat is stayin'. She picks me up, take me to the Martinique[7] when she go dar, and dere I is safe wid a mighty big bankroll in my jeans. It's easy as rollin' off a log.

SMITHERS: (*maliciously*) But s'posin' somethin' 'appens wrong an' they do nab yer?

JONES: (*decisively*) Dey don't. — Dat's de answer.

SMITHERS: But, just for argyments sake, — what'd you do?

JONES: (*frowning*) I'se got five lead bullets in dis gun good enuff fo' common bush niggers — an' after dat I got de silver bullet left to cheat 'em out o' gittin' me.

SMITHERS: (*jeeringly*) Ho, I was fergettin' that silver bullet. You'll bump yourself orf in style, won't yer? Blimey!

JONES: (*gloomily*) Yo' kin bet yo' whole roll on one thing, white man. Dis baby plays out his string to de end and when he quits, he quits wid a bang de way he ought. Silver bullet ain't none too good for him when he go, dat's a fac'! (*Then shaking off his nervousness — with a confident laugh.*) Sho'! What is I talkin' about? Ain't come to dat yit an' I never will — not wid trash niggers like dese yere. (*Boastfully.*) Silver bullet bring me luck anyway. I kin outguess, outrun, outfight, an' outplay de whole lot o' dem all ovah de board any time o' de day er night! Yo' watch me!

(*From the distant hills comes the faint, steady thump of a tom-tom, low and vibrating. It starts at a rate exactly corresponding to normal pulse beat — 72 to the minute — and continues at a gradually accelerating rate from this point uninterruptedly to the very end of the play.*)

(*Jones starts at the sound; a strange look of apprehension creeps into his face for a moment as he listens. Then he asks, with an attempt to regain his most casual manner —*)

What's dat drum beatin' fo'?

SMITHERS: (*with a mean grin*) For you. That means the bleedin' ceremony 'as started. I've 'eard it b'fore and I knows.

JONES: Cer'mony? What cer'mony?

SMITHERS: The blacks is 'oldin' a bloody meetin,' 'avin' a war dance, gettin' their courage worked up b'fore they starts after you.

JONES: Let dem! Dey'll sho' need it!

---

7. **Martinique:** Another island in the Caribbean, south and east of Haiti.

SMITHERS: And they're there 'oldin' their 'eathen religious service – makin' no end of devil spells and charms to 'elp 'em agains your silver bullet. (*He guffaws loudly.*) Blimey, but they're balmy as 'ell.

JONES: (*a tiny bit awed and shaken in spite of himself*) Huh! Takes moren' dat to scare dis chicken!

SMITHERS: (*scenting the other's feeling – maliciously*) Ternight when it's pitch black in the forest, they'll 'ave their pet devils and ghosts 'oundin' after you. You'll find yer bloody 'air 'll be standin' on end before tomorrow mornin'. (*Seriously.*) It's a bleedin' queer place, that stinkin' forest, even in daylight. Yer don't know what might 'appen in there, it's that rotten still. Always sends the cold shivers down my back minute I gets in it.

JONES: (*with a contemptuous sniff*) I ain't no chicken-liver like you is. Trees an' me, we'se friends, an' dar's a full moon comin' bring me light. And let dem po' niggers make all de fool spells dey'se a min' to. Does yo' s'pect I'se silly enuff to b'lieve in ghosts an' han'nts an' all dat ole woman's talk? G'long, white man! You ain't talkin' to me. (*With a chuckle.*) Doesn't you knows dey's got to do wid a man' was member in good standin' o' de Baptist Church. Sho' I was dat when I was porter on de Pullman, an' befo' I gits into my little trouble. Let dem try deir heathen tricks. De Baptist Church done pertect me an' land dem all in hell. (*Then with more confident satisfaction.*) An' I'se got little silver bullet o' my own, don't forgit.

SMITHERS: Ho! You 'aven't give much 'eed to your Baptist Church since you been down 'ere. I've 'eard myself and 'ad turned her coat an' was takin' up with their blarsted witch-doctors, or whatever the 'ell yer calls the swine.

JONES: (*vehemently*) I pretends to! Sho' I pretends! Dat's part o' my game from de fust. If I finds out dem niggers believes dat black is white, den I yells it out louder 'n some deir loudest. It don't git me nothin' to do missionary work for de Baptist Church. I'se after de coin, an' I lays my Jesus on de shelf for de time bein'. (*Stops abruptly to look at his watch – alertly.*) But I ain't got de time to waste no moe fool talk wid you. I'se gwine away from heah dis secon'. (*He reaches in under the throne and pulls out an expensive Panama hat with a bright multi-colored band and sets it jauntily on his head.*) So long, white man! (*With a grin.*) See you in jail sometime, maybe!

SMITHERS: No me, you won't. Well, I wouldn't be in yer bloody boots for no bloomin' money, but 'ere's wishin' yer luck just the same.

JONES: (*contemptuously*) You're de frightenedest man evah I see! I tells you I'se safe 's'f I was in New York City. It take dem niggers from now to dark to git up de nerve to start somethin.' By dat time, I'se got a head start dey never ketch up wid.

SMITHERS: (*maliciously*) Give my regards to any ghosts yer meets up with.

JONES: (*grinning*) If dat ghost got money, I'll tell him never ha'nt you less'n he wants to lose it.

SMITHERS: (*flattered*) Garn! (*Then curiously*). Ain't yer takin' no luggage with yer?

JONES: I travels light when I wants to move fast. And I got tinned grub buried on de edge o' de forest. (*Boastfully.*) Now say dat I don't look ahead an' use my brains! (*With a wide, liberal gesture.*) I will all dat's left in de palace to you – an' you better grab all you kin sneak away wid befo' dey gits here.

SMITHERS: (*gratefully*) Righto — and thanks ter yer. (*As Jones walks toward the door in rear — cautioningly.*) Say! Look 'ere, you ain't goin' out that way, are yer?

JONES: Does you think I'd slink out de back door like a common nigger? I'se Emperor yit, ain't I? And de Emperor Jones leaves de way he comes, and dat black trash don't dare stop him — not yit, leastways. (*He stops for a moment in the doorway, listening to the far-off but insistent beat of the tom-tom.*) Listen to dat roll-call, will yo'? Must be mighty big drum carry dat far. (*Then with a laugh.*) Well, if dey ain't no whole brass band to see me off, I sho' got de drum part of it. So long, white man. (*He puts his hands in his pockets and with studied carelessness, whistling a tune, he saunters out of the doorway and off to the left.*)

SMITHERS: (*looks after him with a puzzled admiration*) 'E's got 'is bloomin' nerve with 'im, s'elp me! (*Then angrily.*) Ho — the bleedin' nigger — puttin' on 'is bloody airs! I 'opes they nabs 'im an' gives 'im what's what! (*Then putting business before the pleasure of his thought, looking around him with cupidity.*) A bloke ought to find a 'ole lot in this palace that' go for a bit of cash. Let's take a look, 'Arry, me lad. (*He starts for the doorway on right as*)

The Curtain Falls.

SCENE TWO

Nightfall. The end of the plain where the Great Forest begins. The foreground is sandy, level ground dotted by a few stones and clumps of stunted bushes cowering close against the earth to escape the buffeting of the trade wind. In the rear the forest is a wall of darkness dividing the world. Only when the eye becomes accustomed to the gloom can the outlines of separate trunks of the nearest trees be made out, enormous pillars of deeper blackness. A somber monotone of wind lost in the leaves moans in the air. Yet this sound serves but to intensify the impression of the forest's relentless immobility, to form a background throwing into relief, its brooding, implacable silence.

(*Jones enters from the left, walking rapidly. He stops as he nears the edge of the forest, looks around him quickly, peering into the dark as if searching for some familiar landmark. Then, apparently satisfied that he is where he ought to be, he throws himself on the ground, dog-tired.*)

Well, heah I is. In de nick o' time, too! Little mo' an' it'd be blacker'n de ace of spades heahabouts. (*He pulls a bandana handkerchief from his hip pocket and mops off his perspiring face.*) So'! Gimme air! I'se tuckered out sho' 'nuff. Dat soft Emperor job ain't no trainin' fo' a long hike ovah dat plain in de brilin' sun. (*Then with a chuckle.*) Cheah up, nigger, de worst is yet to come. (*He lifts his head and stares at the forest. His chuckle peters out abruptly. In a tone of awe.*) My goodness, look at dem woods, will you? Dat no-count Smithers said dey'd be black an' he sho' called de turn. (*Turning away from them quickly and looking down at his feet, he snatches at a chance to change the subject — solicitously.*) Feet, yo' is holdin' up yo' end fine an' I sutinly hopes you ain't blisterin' none. It's time you git a rest. (*He takes off his shoes, his eyes studiously avoiding the forest. He feels of the soles of his feet gingerly.*) You is still in de pink — only a little mite feverish. Cool you'selfs. Remember yo' done got a long journey yit befo' yo'. (*He sits in a weary attitude, listening to the rhythmic beating of the tom-tom. He grumbles in a loud tone to cover up a growing uneasiness.*) Bush niggers! Wonder dey wouldn't git sick o' beatin' dat drum. Sound louder, seem like. I wonder if dey's startin' after me? (*He scrambles to his feet, looking back across the plain.*) Couldn't see dem now, nohow, if dey was hundred feet away. (*Then shaking himself like a wet dog to get rid of these depressing thoughts.*) Sho', dey's miles an' miles behind. What yo' gittin' fidgetty about? (*But he sits down and begins to lace up his shoes in great haste, all the time muttering reassuringly.*) You know what? Yo' belly is empty, dat's what's de matter wid you. Come time to eat! Wid nothin' but wind on yo' stumach, o' course yo' feels juggedy. Well, we eats right heah an' now soon's I gits dese pesky shoes laced up. (*He finishes lacing up his shoes.*) Dere! Now le's see! (*Gets on his hands and knees and searches the ground around him with his eyes.*) White stone, white stone, where is yo'? (*He sees the first white stone and crawls to it — with satisfaction.*) Heah yo' is! I knowed dis was de right place. Box of grub, come to me. (*He turns over the stone and feels in under it — in a tone of dismay.*) Ain't heah! Gorry, is I in de right place or isn't I? Dere's 'nother stone. Guess dat's it. (*He scrambles to the next stone and turns it over.*) Ain't heah, neither! Grub, what is yo'? Ain't heah. Gorry, has I got to go hungry into dem woods — all de night? (*While he is talking he scrambles from one stone to another, turning them over in frantic haste. Finally he jumps to his feet excitedly.*) Is I lost de place? Must have! But how dat happen when I was followin' de trail across de plain in broad daylight? (*Almost plaintively.*) I'se hungry, I is! I gotta git my food. Whar's my strength gonna come from if I doesn't? Gorry, I gotta find dat grub high an' low somehow! Why it come dark so quick like dat? Can't see nothin'. (*He scratches a match on his trousers and peers about him. The rate of the beat of the far-off tom-tom increases perceptibly as he does so. He mutters in a bewildered voice.*) How come all dese white stones come heah when I only remembers one? (*Suddenly, with a frightened gasp, he flings the match on the ground and stamps on it.*) Nigger, is yo' gone crazy mad? Is you lightin' matches to show dem whar you is? Fo' Lawd's sake, use yo' haid. Gorry, I'se got to be careful! (*He stares at the plain behind him apprehensively, his hand on his revolver.*) But how come all dese white stones? And whar's dat tin box o' grub I hid all wrapped up in oil cloth?

(*While his back is turned, the Little Formless Fears creep out from the deeper blackness of the forest. They are black, shapeless, only their glittering little eyes can be seen. If they have any describable form at all it is that of a grubworm about the size of a creeping child. They move noiselessly, but with deliberate, painful effort, striving to raise themselves on end, failing and sinking prone again. Jones turns about to face the forest. He stares up at the tops of the trees, seeking vainly to discover his whereabouts by their conformation.*)

Can't tell nothin' from dem trees! Gorry, nothin' 'round heah look like I evah seed it befo'. I'se done lost de place sho' nuff! (*With mournful foreboding.*) It's mighty queer!

It's mighty queer! (*With sudden forced defiance — in an angry tone.*) Woods, is yo' tryin' to put somethin' ovah on me?

(*From the formless creatures on the ground in front of him comes a tiny gale of low mocking laughter like a rustling of leaves. They squirm upward toward him in twisted attitudes. Jones looks down, leaps backward with a yell of terror, yanking out his revolver as he does so — in a quavering voice.*)

What's dat? Who's dar? What 's you? Git away from me befo' I shoots yo' up! Yo' don't? –

(*He fires. There is a flash, a loud report, then silence broken only by the far-off, quickened throb of the tom-tom. The formless creatures have scurried back into the forest. Jones remains fixed in his position, listening intently. The sound of the shot, the reassuring feel of the revolver in his hand have somewhat restored his shaken nerve. He addresses himself with renewed confidence.*)

Dey're gone. Dat shot fix 'em. Dey was only little animals – little wild pigs, I reckon. Dey've maybe rooted out yo' grub an' eat it. Sho', yo' fool nigger, what yo' think dey is – ha'nts? (*Excitedly.*) Gorry, you give de game away when yo' fire dat shot. Dem niggers heah dat fo' su'tin! Time yo' beat it in de woods widout no long waits. (*He starts for the forest — hesitates before the plunge — then urging himself in with manful resolution.*) Git in, nigger! What yo' skeered at? Ain't nothin' dere but de trees! Git in! (*He plunges boldly into the forest.*)

SCENE THREE

(*Nine o'clock. In the forest. The moon has just risen. Its beams drifting through the canopy of leaves, make a barely perceptible, suffused eerie glow. A dense low wall of underbrush and creepers is in the nearer foreground forming in a small triangular clearing. Beyond this is the massed blackness of the forest like an encompassing barrier. A path is dimly discerned leading down to the clearing from left, rear, and winding away from it again toward the right. As the scene opens nothing can be distinctly made out. Except for the beating of the tom-tom, which is a trifle louder and quicker than in the previous scene, there is silence broken every few seconds by a queer, clicking sound. Then gradually the figure of the negro, Jeff, can be discerned crouching on his haunches at the rear of the triangle. He is middle-aged, thin, brown in color, is dressed in a Pullman porter's uniform, cap, etc. He is throwing a pair of dice on the ground before him, picking them up, shaking them, casting them out with the regular, rigid, mechanical movements of an automaton. The heavy, plodding footsteps of someone approaching along the trail from the left are heard and Jones' voice, pitched in a slightly higher key and strained in a cheering effort to overcome its own tremors.*)

De moon's rizen. Does yo' heah dat, nigger? Yo' gits more light from dis out. No mo' buttin' yo' fool head agin' de trunks an' scratchin' de hide off yo' legs in de bushes. Now yo' sees whar yo'se gwine. So cheer up! From now on yo' has a snap. (*He steps just to the rear of the triangular cleaning and mops off his face on his sleeve. He has lost his Panama hat. His face is scratched, his brilliant uniform shows several large rents.*) What time's it gittin' to be, I wonder? I dassent light no match to find out. Phoo'. It's wa'm an' dat's a fac'! (*Wearily.*) How long I been makin' tracks in dese woods? Must be hours an' hours. Seems like fo'evah! Yit can't be, when de moon's jes' riz. Dis am a long night fo' yo', yo' Majesty! (*With a mournful chuckle.*) Majesty! Der ain't much majesty 'bout dis baby now. (*With attempted cheerfulness.*) Never min'. It's all part o' de game. Dis night come to an end like everythin' else. An' when yo' gits dar safe an' has dat bankroll in yo' hands, yo' laughs at all dis. (*He starts to whistle but checks himself abruptly.*) What you' whistlin' for, yo' po' dope! Want all de worl' to heah yo'? (*He stops talking to listen.*) Heah dat ole drum! Sho' gits nearer from de sound. Dey're packin' it along wid 'em. Time fo' me to move. (*He takes a step forward, then stops — worriedly.*) What's dat odder queer clicketty sound I heah? Der it is! Sound close! Sound like — fo' God sake, sound like some nigger was shakin' crap! (*Frightenedly.*) I better beat it quick when I gits dem notions. (*He walks quickly into the clear space — then stands transfixed as he sees Jeff — in a terrified gasp.*) Who dar? Who dat? Is dat yo', Jeff? (*Starting toward the other, forgetful for a moment of his surroundings and really believing it is a living man that he sees — in a tone of happy relief.*) Jeff! I'se sho' mighty glad to see yo'! Dey tol' me yo' done died from dat razor cut I gives you. (*Stopping suddenly, bewilderedly.*) But how you come to be heah, nigger? (*He stares fascinatedly at the other who continues his mechanical play with the dice. Jones' eyes begin to roll wildly. He stutters.*) Ain't you gwine — look up — can't you speak to me? Is you — is you — a ha'nt? (*He jerks out his revolver in a frenzy of terrified rage.*) Nigger, I kills yo' dead once. Has I got to kill yo' agin? You take it den. (*He fires. When the smoke clears away Jeff has disappeared. Jones stands trembling — then with a certain reassurance.*) He's gone, anyway. Ha'nt or no ha'nt, dat shot fix him. (*The beat of the far-off tom-tom is perceptibly louder and more rapid. Jones becomes conscious of it — with a start, looking back over his shoulder.*) Dey's gittin' near! Dey'se comin' fast! An' heah I is shootin' shots to let 'em know jes' whar I is. Oh, Gorry, I'se got to run. (*Forgetting the path he plunges wildly into the underbrush in the rear and disappears in the shadow.*)

SCENE FOUR

(*Eleven o'clock. In the forest. A wide dirt road runs diagonally from right, front, to left, rear. Rising sheer on both sides the forest walls it in. The moon is now up. Under its light the road glimmers ghastly and unreal. It is as if the forest had stood aside momentarily to let the road pass through and accomplish its veiled purpose. This done, the forest will fold in upon itself again and the road will be no more. Jones stumbles in from the forest on the right. His uniform is ragged and torn. He looks about him with numbed surprise when he sees the road, his eyes blinking in the bright moonlight. He flops down exhaustedly and pants heavily for a while. Then with sudden anger.*)

I'm meltin' wid heat! Runnin' an' runnin' an' runnin'! Damn dis heah coat! Like a strait jacket! (*He tears off his coat and flings it away from him, revealing himself stripped to the waist.*) Dere! Dat's better! Now I kin breathe! (*Looking down at his feet, the spurs catch his eye.*) An' to hell wid dese high-fangled spurs. Dey're what's been a-trippin' me up an' breakin' my neck. (*He unstraps and flings them away disgustedly.*) Dere! I gits rid o' dem frippety Emperor trappin's an' I travels lighter. Lawd! I'se tired! (*After a pause, listening to the insistent beat of the tom-tom in the distance.*) I must 'a put some distance between myself an' dem – runnin' like dat – an' yet – dat damn drum sound jes' de same – nearer, even. Well, I guess I a'most holds my lead anyhow. Dey won't never cotch up. (*With a sigh.*) If on'y my fool legs stands up. Oh, I'se sorry I evah went in for dis. Dat Emperor job is sho' hard to shake. (*He looks around him suspiciously.*) How'd dis road evah git heah? Good level road, too. I never remembers seein' it befo.' (*Shaking his head apprehensively.*) Dese woods is sho' full o' de queerest things at night. (*With sudden terror.*) Lawd God, don't let me see no more o' dem ha'nts! Dey gits my goat! (*Then trying to talk himself into confidence.*) Ha'nts! Yo' fool nigger, dey ain't no such things! Don't de Baptist parson tell you dat many time? Is yo' civilized, or is yo' like dese ign'rent black nigger's heah? Sho'! Dat was all in yo' own head. Wasn't nothin' there! Wasn't no Jeff! Know what? Yo' jus' get seein' dem thing 'cause yo' belly's empty an' you's sick wid hunger inside. Hunger 'fects yo' head an' yo' eyes. Any fool know dat. (*Then pleading fervently.*) But Bless God I don't come across no more o' dem, whatever dey is! (*Then cautiously.*) Rest! Don't talk! Rest! You needs it. Den yo' gits on yo' way again. (*Looking at the moon.*) Night's half gone a' most. Yo' hits de coast in de mawning! Den you'se all safe.

(*From the right forward a small gang of negroes enter. They are dressed in striped convicts' suits, their heads are shaven, one leg drags limpingly, shackled to a heavy ball and chain. Some carry picks, the others shovels. They are followed by a white man dressed in the uniform of a prison guard. A Winchester rifle is slung across his shoulders and he carries a heavy whip. At a signal from the guard they stop on the road opposite where Jones is sitting. Jones, who has been staring up at the sky, unmindful of their noiseless approach, suddenly looks down and sees them. His eyes pop out, he tries to get to his feet and fly, but sinks back, too numbed by fright to move. His voice catches in a choking prayer.*)

Lawd Jesus!

(*The prison guard cracks his whip — noiselessly — and at that signal all the convicts start to work on the road. They swing their picks, they shovel, but not a sound comes from their labor. Their movements, like those of Jeff in the preceding scene, are those of automatons — rigid, slow and mechanical. The prison guard points sternly at Jones with his whip, motions him to take his place among the other shovellers. Jones gets to his feet in a hypnotized stupor. He mumbles subserviently.*)

Yes, suh! Yes, suh! I'se comin'!

(*As he shuffles, dragging one foot, over to his place, he curses under his breath with rage and hatred.*)

God damn yo' soul, I gits even wid yo' yit, sometime.

(*As if there was a shovel in his hands he goes through weary, mechanical gestures of dig-ging up dirt, and throwing it to the roadside. Suddenly the guard approaches him angrily, threateningly. He raises his whip and lashes Jones viciously across the shoulders with it. Jones winces with pain and cowers abjectly. The guard turns his back on him and walks away contemptuously. Instantly Jones straightens up. With arms upraised as if his shovel were a club in his hands he springs murderously at the unsuspecting guard. In the act of crashing down his shovel on the white man's skull, Jones suddenly becomes aware that his hands are empty. He cries despairingly.*)

Whar's my shovel? Gimme my shovel 'till I splits his damn head! (*Appealing to his fel-low convicts.*) Gimme a shovel, one o' yo' fo' God's sake!

(*They stand fixed in motionless attitudes, their eyes on the ground. The guard seems to wait expectantly, his back turned to the attacker. Jones bellows with baffled, terrified rage, tugging frantically at his revolver.*)

I kills you, you white debil, if it's de last thing I evah does! Ghost or debil, I kill you agin!

(*He frees the revolver and fires point blank at the guard's back. Instantly the walls of the forest close in from both sides, the road and the figures of the convict gang are blotted out in an enshrouding darkness. The only sounds are a crashing in the underbrush as Jones leaps away in mad flight and the throbbing boom of the tom-tom, still far distant, but increased in volume of sound and rapidity of beat.*)

SCENE FIVE

(*One o'clock. A large circular clearing, enclosed by the serried ranks of lofty, gigantic trunks of tall trees whose tops are lost to view. In the center is a big dead stump worn by time into a curious resemblance to an auction block. The moon floods the clearing with a clear light. Jones forces his way in through the forest on the left. He looks wildly about the clearing with hunted, fearful glances. His pants are in tatters, his shoes cut and mis-shapen, flapping about his feet. He slinks cautiously to the stump in the center and sits down in a tense position, ready for instant flight. Then he holds his head in his hands and rocks back and forth moaning to himself miserably.*)

Oh Lawd, Lawd! Oh Lawd, Lawd! (*Suddenly he throws himself on his knees and raises his clasped hands to the sky — in a voice of agonized pleading.*) Lawd, Jesus, heah my prayer! I'se a poor sinner, a poor sinner! I knows I done wrong, I knows it! When I cotches Jeff cheatin' wid loaded dice my anger overcomes me an' I kills him dead! Lawd, I done wrong! When dat guard hits me wid de whip, my anger overcomes me, and I kills him dead. Lawd, I done wrong! An' down heah whar dese fool bush niggers raises me up to de seat o' de mighty, I steals all I could grab. Lawd, I done wrong! I knows it! I'se sorry! Forgive me, Lawd! Forgive dis po' sinner! (*Then beseeching terri-fiedly.*) An' keep dem away, Lawd! Keep dem away from me! An' stop dat drum soundin' in my ears! Dat begin to sound ha'nted, too. (*He gets to his feet, evidently slightly reassured by his prayer – with attempted confidence.*) De Lawd'll preserve me from dem ha'nts after dis. (*Sits down on the stump again.*) I ain't skeered o' real men. Let dem come. But dem odders – (*He shudders – then looks down at his feet, working his toes inside the shoes – with a groan.*) Oh, my po' feet! Dem shoes ain't no use no more 'ceptin' to hurt. I'se better off widout dem. (*He unlaces them and pulls them off – holds the wrecks of the shoes in his hand and regards them mourn-fully.*) You was real, A-one patin' leather, too. Look at yo' now. Emperor, you'se gittin' mighty low!

(*He sighs dejectedly and remains with bowed shoulders staring down at the shoes in his hands as if reluctant to throw them away. While his attention is thus occupied, a crowd of figures silently enter the clearing from all sides. All are dressed in Southern costumes of the period of the fifties of the last century. There are middle-aged men who are evidently well-to-do planters. There is one spruce, authoritative individual — the auctioneer. There are a crowd of curious spectators, chiefly young belles and dandies who have come to the slave-market for diversion. All exchange courtly greetings in dumb show and chat silently together. There is something stiff, rigid, unreal, marionettish about their movements. They group themselves about the stump. Finally a batch of slaves are led in from the left by an attendant — three men of different ages, two women, one with a baby in her arms, nurs-ing. They are placed to the left of the stump, besides Jones.*

The white planters look them over appraisingly as if they were cattle, and exchange judgments on each. The dandies point with their fingers and make witty remarks. The belles titter bewitchingly. All this in silence save for the ominous throb of the tom-tom. The auctioneer holds up his hand, taking his place at the stump. The groups strain forward attentively. He touches Jones on the shoulder peremptorily, motioning for him to stand on the stump — the auction block.

Jones looks up, sees the figures on all sides, looks wildly for some opening to escape, sees none, screams and leaps madly to the top of the stump to get as far away from them as possible. He stands there, cowering, paralyzed with horror. The Auctioneer begins his silent spiel. He points to Jones, appeals to the planters to see for themselves. Here is a good field hand, sound in wind and limb as they can see. Very strong still in spite of his being middle-aged. Look at that back. Look at those shoulders. Look at the muscles in his arms and his sturdy legs. Capable of any amount of hard labor. Moreover, of a good dis-position, intelligent and tractable. Will any gentleman start the bidding? The planters raise their fingers, make their bids. They are apparently all eager to possess Jones. The bidding is lively, the crowd interested. While this has been going on, Jones has been seized by the courage of desperation. He dares to look down and around him. Over his face abject terror gives way to mystification, to gradual realization — stutteringly.)

What yo' all doin,' white folks? What's all dis? What yo' all lookin' at me fo'? What yo' doin' wid me, anyhow? (*Suddenly convulsed with raging hatred and fear.*) Is dis a auction? Is yo' sellin' me like dey uster befo' de war? (*Jerking out his revolver just as the auctioneer knocks him down to one of the planters – glaring from him to the purchaser.*) An' you sells me? An' you buys me? I shows you I'se a free nigger, damn yo' souls! (*He fires at the auctioneer and at the planter with such rapidity that the two shots are almost simultaneous. As if this were a signal the walls of the forest fold in. – Only blackness remains and silence broken by Jones as he rushes off, crying with fear – and by the quickened, ever louder beat of the tom-tom.*)

SCENE SIX

(*Three o'clock. A cleared space in the forest. The limbs of the trees meet over it forming a low ceiling about five feet from the ground. The interlocked ropes of creepers reaching upward to entwine the tree trunks give an arched appearance to the sides. The space this encloses is like the dark, noisome hold of some ancient vessel. The moonlight is almost completely shut out and only a vague, wan light filters through. The scene is in complete darkness at first. There is the noise of someone approaching from the left, stumbling and crawling through the undergrowth. Jones' voice is heard, between chattering moans.*)

Oh Lawd, what I gwine do now? Ain't got no bullet left on'y de silver one. If mo' o' dem ha'nts come after me, how I gwine skeer dem away? Oh Lawd, on'y de silver one left – an' I gotta save dat fo' luck. If I shoots dat one I'm a goner sho'! Lawd, it's black heah! Whar's de moon? Oh, Lawd, don't dis night evah come to an end? (*By the sounds, he is feeling his way cautiously forward.*) Dere! Dis feels like a clear space. I gotta lie down an' rest. I don't care if dem niggers does catch me. I gotta rest.

(*He is well forward now where his figure can be dimly made out. His pants have been so torn away that what is left of them is no better than a breech cloth. He flings himself full length, face downward on the ground, panting with exhaustion. Gradually it seems to grow lighter in the enclosed space and two rows of seated figures can be seen behind Jones. They are sitting in crumpled, despairing attitudes, hunched facing one another with their backs touching the forest walls as if they were shackled to them. All are negroes, naked save for loin cloths. At first they are silent and motionless. Then they begin to sway slowly forward toward each other and back again in unison, as if they were laxly letting themselves follow the long roll of a ship at sea. At the same time, a low, melancholy murmur rises among them, increasing gradually by rhythmic degrees which seem to be directed and controlled by the throb of the tom-tom in the distance, to a long, tremendous wail of despair that reaches a certain pitch, unbearably acute, then falls by slow gradations of tone into silence and is taken up again. Jones starts, looks up, sees the figures, and throws himself down again to shut off the sight. A shudder of terror shakes his whole body as the wail rises up about him again. But the next time, his voice, as if under some uncanny compulsion, starts with the others. As their chorus lifts he rises to a sitting posture similar to the others, swaying back and forth. His voice reaches the highest pitch of sorrow, of desolation. The light fades out, the other voices cease, and only darkness is left. Jones can be heard scrambling to his feet and running off, his voice sinking down the scale and receding as he moves farther and*) *farther away in the forest. The tom-tom beats louder, quicker, with a more insistent, tri-umphant pulsation.)*

SCENE SEVEN

(Five o'clock. The foot of a gigantic tree by the edge of a great river. A rough structure of boulders, like an altar, is by the tree. The raised river bank is in the nearer background. Beyond this the surface of the river spreads out, brilliant and unruffled in the moonlight, is blotted out and merged with a veil to bluish mist in the distance. Jones' voice is heard from the left rising and falling in the long, despairing wail of the chained slaves, to the rhythmic beat of the tom-tom. — As his voice sinks into silence, he enters the open space. — The expression of his face is fixed and stony, his eyes have an obsessed glare, he moves with a strange deliberation like a sleep-walker or one in a trance. He looks around at the tree, the rough stone altar, the moonlit surface of the river beyond and passes his hand over his head with a vague gesture of puzzled bewilderment. Then, as if in obedience to some obscure impulse, he goes into a kneeling, devotional posture before the altar. Then he seems to come to himself partly, to have an uncertain realization of what he is doing, for he straightens up and stares about him horrifiedly — in an incoher-ent mumble.)

What — what is I doin'? What is — dis place? Seems like — seems like I know dat tree — an' dem stones — an' de river. I remember — seems like I been heah befo'. (*Tremblingly.*) Oh, Gorry, I'se skeered in dis place! I'se skeered! Oh, Lawd, pertect dis sinner!

(Crawling away from the altar, he cowers close to the ground, his face hidden, his shoul-ders heaving with sobs of hysterical fright. From behind the trunk of the tree, as if he had sprung out of it, the figure of the Congo Witch-Doctor appears. He is wizened and old, naked except for the fur of some small animal tied about his waist, its bushy tail hanging down in front like a Highlander's. His body is stained all over a bright red. Antelope horns are on each side of his head, branching upward. In one hand he carries a bone rattle, in the other a charm stick with a bunch of white cockatoo feathers tied to the end. A great number of glass beads and bone ornaments are about his neck, ears, wrists, and ankles. He struts noiselessly with a queer prancing step to a position in the clear ground between Jones and the altar. Then with a preliminary, summoning stamp of his foot on the earth, he begins to dance and to chant. As if in response to his summons the beating of the tom-tom grows to a fierce, exultant boom whose throbs seem to fill the air with vibrating rhythm. Jones looks up, starts to spring to his feet, reaches a half-kneeling, half-squatting position and remains rigidly fixed there, paralyzed with awed fascination by this new apparition. The Witch-Doctor sways, stamping with his foot, his bone rattle clicking the time. His voice rises and falls in a weird, monotonous croon, without articu-late word division. Gradually his dance becomes clearly one of a narrative in pantomime, his croon is an incantation, a charm to allay the fierceness of some implacable deity demanding sacrifice. He flees, he is pursued by devils, he hides, he flees again. Ever wilder and wilder becomes his flight, nearer and nearer draws the pursuing evil, more

and more the spirit of terror gains possession of him. His croon, rising to intensity, is punctuated by shrill cries. Jones has become completely hypnotized. His voice joins in the incantation, in the cries, he beats time with his hands and sways his body to and fro from the waist. The whole spirit and meaning of the dance has entered into him, has become his spirit. Finally the theme of the pantomime halts, on a howl of despair, and is taken up again in a note of savage hope. There is a salvation. The forces of evil demand sacrifice. They must be appeased. The Witch-Doctor points with his wand to the sacred tree, the river beyond, to the altar, and finally to Jones with a ferocious command. Jones seems to sense the meaning of this. It is he who must offer himself for sacrifice. He beats his forehead abjectly to the ground, moaning hysterically.)*

Mercy, Oh Lawd! Mercy! Mercy on dis po' sinner!

(The Witch-Doctor springs to the river bank. He stretches out his arms and calls to some God within its depths. Then he starts backward slowly, his arms remaining out. A huge head of a crocodile appears over the bank and its eyes, glittering greenly, fasten upon Jones. He stares into them fascinatedly. The Witch-Doctor prances up to him, touches him with his wand, motions with hideous command toward the waiting monster. Jones squirms on his belly nearer and nearer, moaning continually.)

Mercy, Lawd! Mercy!

(The crocodile heaves more of his enormous hulk onto the land. Jones squirms toward him. The Witch-Doctor's voice shrills out in furious exultation, the tom-tom beats madly. Jones cries out in fierce, exhausted spasms of anguished pleading.)

Lawd, save me! Lawd Jesus, heah my prayer!

(Immediately, in answer to his prayer, comes the thought of the one bullet left him. He snatches at his hip, shouting defiantly.)

De silver bullet! Yo' don't git me yit!

(He fires at the green eyes in front of him. The head of the crocodile sinks back behind the river bank, the Witch-Doctor springs behind the sacred tree and disappears. Jones lies with his face to the ground, his arms outstretched, whimpering with fear as the throb of the tom-tom fills the silence about him with a somber pulsation, a baffled but revengeful power.)

SCENE EIGHT

(Dawn. Same as scene two, the dividing line of forest and plain. The nearest tree trunks are dimly revealed but the forest behind them is still a mass of glooming shadow. The tom-tom seems on the very spot, so loud and continuously vibrating are its beats. Lem enters from the left, followed by a small squad of his soldiers, and by the Cockney trader,

Smithers. Lem is a heavy-set, ape-faced old savage of the extreme African type, dressed only in a loin cloth. A revolver and cartridge belt are about his waist. His soldiers are in different degrees of rag-concealed nakedness. All wear broad palm leaf hats. Each one carries a rifle. Smithers is the same as in Scene One. One of the soldiers, evidently a tracker, is peering about keenly on the ground. He grunts and points to the spot where Jones entered the forest. Lem and Smithers come to look.)

SMITHERS: *(after a glance, turns away in disgust)* That's where 'e went in right enough. Much good it'll do yer. 'E's miles orf by this an' safe to the Coast, damn 'is 'ide! I tole yer yer'd lose 'im, didn't I? — wastin' the 'ole bloomin' night beatin' yer bloody drum and castin' yer silly spells! Gawd blimey, wot a pack!

LEM: *(gutturally)* We cotch him. You see. *(He makes a motion to his soldiers, who squat down on their haunches in a semicircle.)*

SMITHERS: *(exasperatedly)* Well, ain't yer goin' in an' 'unt 'im in the woods? What the 'ell's the good of waitin'?

LEM: *(imperturbably — squatting down himself)* We cotch him.

SMITHERS: *(turning away from him contemptuously)* Aw! Garn! 'E's a better man than the lot o' you put together. I 'ates the sight o' 'im but I'll say that for 'im.

(A sound of snapping twigs comes from the forest. The soldiers jump to their feet, cocking their rifles alertly. Lem remains sitting with an imperturbable expression, but listening intently. The sound from the woods is repeated. Lem makes a quick signal with his hand. His followers creep quickly but noiselessly into the forest, scattering so that each enters at a different spot.)

SMITHERS: *(in the silence that follows — in a contemptuous whisper)* You ain't thinkin' that would be 'im, I 'ope?

LEM: *(calmly)* We cotch him.

SMITHERS: Blarsted fat 'eads! *(Then after a second's thought — wonderingly.)* Still an' all, it might happen. If 'e lost 'is bloody way in these stinkin' woods 'e'd likely turn in a circle without 'is knowin' it. They all does.

LEM: *(peremptorily)* Ssshh!

(The report of several rifles sound from the forest, followed a second later by savage, exultant yells. The beating of the tom-tom abruptly ceases. Lem looks up at the white man with a grin of satisfaction.)

We cotch him. Him dead.

SMITHERS: *(with a snarl)* 'Ow d'yer know it's 'im an' 'ow d'yer know 'e's dead?

LEM: My men's dey got 'um silver bullets. Dey kill him shore.

SMITHERS: *(astonished)* They got silver bullets?

LEM: Lead bullet no kill him. He got um strong charm. I took um money, make um silver bullet, make um strong charm, too.

SMITHERS: (*light breaking upon him*) So that's wot you was up to all night, wot? You was scared to put after 'im till you'd moulded silver bullets, eh?

LEM: (*simply stating a fact*) Yes. Him got strong charm. Lead no good.

SMITHERS: (*slapping his thigh and guffawing*) Haw-haw! If yer don't beat all 'ell! (*Then recovering himself – scornfully.*) I'll bet you it ain't 'im they shot at all, yer bleedin' looney!

LEM: (*calmly*) Dey come bring him now.

(*The soldiers come out of the forest, carrying Jones' limp body. There is a little reddish-purple hole under his left breast. He is dead. They carry him to Lem, who examines his body with great satisfaction.*)

SMITHERS: (*leans over his shoulder – in a tone of frightened awe*) Well, they did for yer right enough, Jonesy, me lad! Dead as a 'erring! (*Mockingly.*) Where's yer 'igh an' mighty airs now, yer bloomin' Majesty? (*Then with a grin.*) Silver bullets! Gawd blimey, but yer died in the 'eight o' style, any'ow!

(*Lem makes a motion to the soldiers to carry the body out left. Smithers speaks to him sneeringly.*)

SMITHERS: And I s'pose you think it's yer bleedin' charms and yer silly beatin' the drum that made 'im run in a circle when 'e'd lost 'imself, don't yer? (*But Lem makes no reply, does not seem to hear the question, walks out left after his men. Smithers looks after him with contemptuous scorn.*) Stupid as 'ogs, the lot of 'em! Blarsted niggers!

Curtain Falls.

[1921]

At Home and Abroad: American Fiction between the Wars

AMERICAN FICTION CAME FULLY OF AGE between the beginning of World War I in 1914 and the end of World War II in 1945. Several of the writers who had earlier shaped the course of fiction continued to write and publish, including Edith Wharton, Willa Cather, and Theodore Dreiser, whose unflinching depictions of American life inspired a new generation of writers. The popular novelist Sinclair Lewis, who in 1930 became the first American to win the Nobel Prize for Literature, recalled that Dreiser's "great first novel," *Sister Carrie* (1900), "came to housebound and airless America like a great free Western wind, and to our stuffy domesticity gave us the first fresh air since Mark Twain and Whitman." The realism and

◄ Max Weber, *Grand Central Terminal*

Max Weber, whose family emigrated from Russia to the United States when he was ten, was among the first painters to apply the principles of European modernism to American scenes, especially the contours of life in New York City. In this painting from 1915, he adopted the multiple perspectives and intersecting geometrical planes of cubist art to render the dynamism, motion, and speed of the city, as symbolized by its major railroad station, Grand Central Terminal.

naturalism that became dominant modes of American fiction around 1900 remained vital forces in the work of many of the younger writers who emerged during and immediately after World War I. But they also developed new styles of writing in response to radically altered conditions in the United States, as well as to the spirit of innovation and experimentation generated by the modernist revolution in the arts that began in Europe.

That revolution was nowhere more apparent than in the work of post-impressionist artists in France. After Gertrude Stein moved permanently to Paris in 1903, she began to collect avant-garde works by Paul Cezanne, widely regarded as the father of modern art, and younger artists such as Pablo Picasso, the central figure in the development of cubism. Stein subsequently began to write experimental prose in which she sought to adapt the visual strategies of cubism, especially the fragmentation and resynthesis of subjects viewed simultaneously from multiple perspectives. Just as the cubists rejected the conventions of realism in art, Stein challenged conceptions of literary realism, writing sketches and stories that disrupted chronology and linear narrative. "One must not forget that the reality of the twentieth century is not the reality of the nineteenth century, not at all, and Picasso was the only one in painting who felt it," Stein later observed in *Picasso* (1938). Other American writers were first introduced to cubism and other new movements in European painting at the Armory Show, an international exhibition of art that toured cities in the United States in 1913. Sherwood Anderson saw the show in Chicago, the year before he read Stein's *Tender Buttons* (1914). Energized by the revelatory artworks in the Armory Show and by Stein's verbal cubism, Anderson began to write the experimental stories he later collected in *Winesburg, Ohio* (1919).

Stein and Anderson, who became close friends, subsequently influenced a number of younger American writers. Inspired in part by reading *Winesburg, Ohio*, Jean Toomer wrote *Cane* (1923), a collection of poems, sketches, and stories about life in black communities in rural Georgia and in the urban North. In his innovative book, Toomer at once challenged generic categories and blurred the lines between poetry and prose, crafting impressionistic prose pieces that revealed the strong impact of contemporary poetry, especially the compressed verse of the imagists. Indeed, many fiction writers of the period also wrote poetry, including Ernest Hemingway, a young Chicago journalist Anderson encouraged to pursue a literary career by moving to Paris. Under the tutelage of Stein and the poet Ezra Pound, Hemingway wrote and published his first two books there, *Three Stories and Ten Poems* (1923) and *in our time* (1924), a series of prose sketches of violent events that formed an ironic counterpoint to the prayer "Give us peace in our time, O Lord." As critics recognized, the simple diction and colloquial language of Hemingway's early work bore the strong stamp of his mentors Anderson and Stein. Hemingway found other models

Stuart Davis, *New York — Paris, No. 1*

Along with many other American artists and writers, Stuart Davis was influenced and invigorated by a sojourn in Paris. In this 1931 painting, he evoked memories of his 1928–29 trip and juxtaposed characteristic scenes of Paris and New York City, including a sidewalk café and a miniature Chrysler Building, in the upper right-hand corner of the cubist composition, blending elements of the two centers of modernism into a new city.

of artistic expression in the postimpressionist paintings he saw at Stein's studio and in galleries, especially the late semiabstract landscapes of Cezanne. In an extended meditation on art and writing that Hemingway omitted from his early story "Big Two-Hearted River," his character Nick Adams declares that he "wanted to write about country so it would be there like Cezanne had done it in painting. You had to do it from inside yourself." Hemingway sought to achieve a similar synthesis of naturalistic description and personal expression in the seemingly objective yet emotionally charged stories collected in his first book published in the United States, *In Our Time* (1925).

American writers were further influenced by broader cultural movements in Europe. The new theories advanced by Sigmund Freud and his disciple Carl Jung gave wide currency to concepts such as sexual repression, the significance of dreams, and the unconscious mind, opening up new ways for writers to understand and explore the interior lives of their characters. James Joyce, Marcel Proust, Virginia Woolf, and other modern

European novelists offered new ways of seeing and representing the world. Joyce's first novel, *A Portrait of the Artist as a Young Man* (1916), was published to wide acclaim in the United States, where portions of his novel *Ulysses* (1922) first appeared in the *Little Review* between 1918 and 1920. Many American writers were fascinated by Joyce's innovations in language and literary form, especially his development of the interior monologue, a type of stream of consciousness in which the flow of thoughts, impressions, and associations reveals the inner life and individual consciousness of a character. After reading *Ulysses*, Phil Stone told his young friend William Faulkner that "anyone who wrote fiction must hereafter go to school in Joyce." The lesson was not lost on Faulkner, who later experimented with Joyce's stream-of-consciousness narrative style in his inventive novels *The Sound and the Fury* (1929) and *As I Lay Dying* (1930).

Novels also registered major changes in the social, physical, and cultural landscape of the United States. Hemingway, Faulkner, and the other novelists who emerged following World War I were part of a generation "grown up to find all Gods dead, all wars fought, all faiths in man shaken," as F. Scott Fitzgerald put it in his first novel, *This Side of Paradise* (1920). Industries boomed during and after the war, raising concerns about what Sherwood Anderson described as the "universal greyness" of life in an industrial society. The whole struggle for writers, Anderson observed, was "to save what may be saved of individuality." Technological innovations had a strong impact on American life and culture, which was transformed by the mass production of cars, the immense popularity of radio and the movies, and the fast pace of life in the cities. For the first time, the majority of Americans lived in urban areas in 1920, and the city assumed a prominent role in novels such as John Dos Passos's *Manhattan Transfer* (1925). In his "collective novel," Dos Passos adapted the techniques of cubist painting and film, especially abrupt cross-cutting from one scene to another, to expose the fragmentation of life in New York City. The novel revealed the impact of T. S. Eliot's influential poem *The Waste Land* (1922), a vision of urban desolation and sterility that left a strong imprint on F. Scott Fitzgerald's *The Great Gatsby* (1925). At the same time, the first Great Migration of African Americans from the rural South to northern cities created vibrant black communities, including Harlem, the complex racial and social realities of which Nella Larsen explored in her novels *Quicksand* (1929) and *Passing* (1929).

Although the novel dominated the literary marketplace, the short story remained an important form of literary expression. Most novelists also wrote short stories, a form well suited to the experimental work of Stein, Anderson, Toomer, and Hemingway, though the latter gained far greater commercial success with his novels *The Sun Also Rises* (1926) and *A Farewell to Arms* (1929). Short stories were published in avant-garde literary journals on both sides of the Atlantic, including the first magazine devoted exclusively to the form, *Story*. As the novelist Nelson Algren later observed, "*Story* was the most distinguished magazine of the short story in America at a time when the short story was at its peak as an art form internationally and when American short stories were read and admired the world over." Short stories also remained a staple of popular, mass-circulation magazines in the United States. Between 1913 and 1916, shortly after she emigrated from Mexico, María Cristina Mena published a series of stories about her native country in the *Century*. During the period of conflict and political unrest that followed the Mexican Revolution of 1910–17, the Texas-born writer Katherine Anne Porter published stories about Mexico in the *Century* and other magazines, including the title story of the collection that made her reputation, *Flowering Judas and Other Stories* (1930). F. Scott Fitzgerald published more than 150 magazine stories, nearly half of them in the most popular weekly magazine of the period, the *Saturday Evening Post*, whose circulation reached 2,750,000 during the economic boom of the 1920s.

The stock market crash of 1929 sharply altered the course of American fiction. As the deepening economic depression plunged hundreds of thousands of Americans into unemployment and homelessness, many writers were drawn to political causes. The new emphasis on social art, art that was at once socially responsible and accessible to a wide public, generated a broad reaction against literary experimentation. The Marxist critic Max Eastman attacked Gertrude Stein and other modernists in his famous essay "The Cult of Unintelligibility" (1929). After the publication of Stein's popular book *The Autobiography of Alice B. Toklas* (1933) and her subsequent

> Story *was the most distinguished magazine of the short story in America at a time when the short story was at its peak as an art form internationally and when American short stories were read and admired the world over.*

Blanche Grambs,
No Work

Blanche Grambs, who had a studio in New York City, made this lithograph shortly after she joined the Federal Art Project of the Works Progress Administration in 1936. The bleak cityscape and the dejected figure in the foreground capture the despair of millions of unemployed workers during the Great Depression.

lecture tour of the United States, the editor of the leftist magazine the *New Masses*, Michael Gold, responded to her sudden notoriety in an angry essay entitled "Gertrude Stein: A Literary Idiot." Describing her "as a forbidding priestess of a strange literary cult," Gold harshly observed that many Marxists "see in the work of Gertrude Stein extreme symptoms of the decay of capitalist culture. They view her work as the complete attempt to annihilate all relations between the artist and the society in which he lives." In opposition to such "idle art," which he dismissed as the literary equivalent of the "idle rich," Gold in other essays called for the development of a genuine "proletarian literature" focused on the economic and social struggles of the working class.

Social criticism was a central element of the work of several of the most prominent American novelists of the 1930s. John Dos Passos offered a sweeping critique of the bankruptcy of American values and the boom-and-bust economy that had led to the Great Depression in *U.S.A.* (1930–36). In his ambitious trilogy, Dos Passos continued the experimentation he had begun in his earlier novels, combining fiction narratives, short biographies, actual news stories, and bits of popular culture into the literary equivalent of a cinematic "montage" that revealed his strong interest in the pioneering films of the Russian director Sergey Eisenstein. In contrast, two novelists who emerged during the 1930s, John Steinbeck and Richard Wright, employed the traditional narrative forms of realism and naturalism. Steinbeck and Wright were also influenced by the photojournalism and documentary journalism that developed during the Great Depression, as exemplified by *Let Us Now Praise Famous Men* (1939), an impassioned report on the condition of impoverished tenant farmers in the South written by James Agee and accompanied by the powerful photographs of Walker Evans. Steinbeck exposed the plight of displaced farmers fleeing the Dust Bowl in his best-selling novel *The Grapes of Wrath* (1939), while Wright gained critical acclaim for *Native Son*, a harrowing novel about black life in an urban ghetto published in 1940.

The concern with the trials of common people that spawned social realism gave a strong impetus to regional fiction. Most of Steinbeck's work was deeply rooted in California, including the early stories he collected in *The Long Valley* (1938), a reference to the Salinas Valley where he grew up in central California. Wright's first book was *Uncle Tom's Children* (1938), a collection of bitter stories about black life in the segregated South. The anthropologist and novelist Zora Neale Hurston, who grew up in Eatonville, Florida, drew upon her study of African American dialect and folk culture in her novels and in stories such as "The Gilded Six Bits," which was published in *Story* in 1933. White writers also discovered rich resources for fiction in the South. William Faulkner employed modernist literary techniques to explore what he described as his "own little postage stamp of native soil" in northern Mississippi, the setting of most of the novels and stories he wrote during the 1930s. His work inspired younger southern

Thomas Hart Benton,
Goin' Home

Thomas Hart Benton, a self-declared "enemy of modernism," was one of the most famous and popular of American regionalist artists in the 1930s. A progressive in politics, Benton was deeply sympathetic to poor farmers and working-class people such as those depicted in this poignant lithograph printed in 1937. The lithograph was based on a sketch Benton had made of a father and his two exhausted, barefoot children returning home from their work in a mill in the Blue Ridge Mountains of North Carolina.

writers, including Eudora Welty, who recorded life in her native Mississippi in photographs and in stories she began to write in the mid-1930s. Welty was praised for her use of dialect and uncanny ability to capture speech patterns, as well as for her realistic depictions of life in the Depression-era South. But she displayed little interest in the social protest that fueled much of the American fiction of the 1930s. In her later essay "Must the Novelist Crusade?" (1965), she affirmed that "great fiction shows us not how to conduct our behavior but how to feel," a statement that might well have served as a motto of her first collection of stories, *A Curtain of Green* (1941).

Great fiction shows us not how to conduct our behavior but how to feel.

Although fiction remained popular during World War II, Americans were far more absorbed in journalistic reports from the front lines, especially after the United States entered the war in December 1941. But the Japanese invasion and conquest of the Philippines helped generate interest in the work of Carlos Bulosan, the first Filipino American writer to gain a wide readership in the United States. During the war, Bulosan began to publish his work in magazines such as the *New Yorker*, where his story "The End of the War" appeared in 1944. Along with the groundbreaking stories by the Mexican immigrant María Cristina Mena and the work of African American writers such as Jean Toomer, Nella Larsen, Zora Neale Hurston, and Richard Wright, Bulosan's stories were signs that American fiction had not only come of age, but also begun to mirror the rich diversity of the United States.

American Contexts

From the Great War to the Great Depression: American Writers and the Challenges of Modernity

In "The American Novel," an essay published in 1924, the iconoclastic editor and critic H. L. Mencken observed that American literature displayed "the artless and superabundant energy of little children" in the aftermath of World War I. In contrast to European nations, which had been devastated by the carnage and destruction, the United States emerged relatively unscathed from the conflict, poised to assume a new position of cultural power and authority. Pointing to the publication of socially challenging and formally innovative works by writers such as John Dos Passos and Eugene O'Neill, Mencken added that American writers had also been released from the suffocating conformity and genteel literary conventions that had prevailed before the war. "Today, it seems to me, the American imaginative writer, whether he be novelist, poet, or dramatist, is quite as free as he deserves to be," Mencken affirmed. "He is free to depict the life about him precisely as he sees it, and to interpret it in any manner he pleases."

As the texts in the following section reveal, writers and critics remained divided about what constituted the appropriate manner and subject matter of American fiction. In an essay published in 1917, Sherwood Anderson urged writers to accept the "crudity" of American life and thought, developing new literary forms capable of giving expression to the actual experiences of people in the United States. Anderson was influenced by the experimental writings of Gertrude Stein, who in a 1926 lecture emphasized the need for constant innovation in the arts, explaining: "Beginning again and again is a natural thing." In contrast, Donald Davidson was hostile to both modernism and modernity. A founding member of the conservative group the Southern Agrarians, Davidson in a 1930 essay vigorously attacked the culture spawned by the new industrial order in the United States, which in his view threatened to destroy the regional identity of the agrarian South. The anthropologist and novelist Zora Neale Hurston also sought to preserve vital elements of the South's regional identity, but she conceived of that identity in radically different terms. While Davidson affirmed the values and traditions of the Old South, Hurston focused on rural black folk culture and the contributions of African Americans to the larger culture in her essay "Characteristics of Negro Expression," published in 1934.

bedfordstmartins.com/ americanlit for research links on the authors in this section

During the Great Depression of the 1930s, many American writers came to view fiction as a primary vehicle for social reform and political revolution. One of the most zealous promoters of revolutionary politics and literature was Michael Gold, the Marxist editor of the *New Masses*. In an article published there in 1930, Gold outlined the features of an emerging literary form, "Proletarian Realism," which "deals with the *real conflicts* of working men and women." The novelist John Dos Passos, a frequent contributor to the *New Masses,* also contributed an essay to *American Writers Congress,* a collection of speeches delivered at a meeting of "American revolutionary writers" in 1935. In the introduction to the volume, Henry Hart asserted that the interests of writers "and the interests of the propertyless and oppressed are inseparable." Dos Passos agreed that, as citizens, writers had an obligation to participate "in the struggle against exploitation." But he suggested that their primary responsibility was to defend "freedom of thought" against the pressures exerted by both the state and organized revolutionary groups. Dos Passos implicitly distanced himself from the rigid ideologies of the Communist Party, from which he broke later in the 1930s. Although the African American novelist Richard Wright also became deeply disillusioned with Communism, he was still closely associated with the Communist Party when he published "Blueprint for Negro Writing" in 1937. Like Zora Neale Hurston, he affirmed the expressive power of the indigenous folklore and vernacular language of African Americans. Wright, however, defined the responsibility of African American writers in political as well as aesthetic terms, challenging them to join in the economic and political struggles of African American workers, whose bitter experiences he had shared while living in both the South and the North. Indeed, along with many of the other American writers who emerged during the decades following World War I, Wright was determined to extend the boundaries of the writer's freedom "to depict the life about him precisely as he sees it," as H. L. Mencken had put it in 1924.

Sherwood Anderson

[1876–1941]

Sherwood Anderson exerted an important influence on a number of American fiction writers, including Jean Toomer, Ernest Hemingway, and William Faulkner (see Anderson, p. 857). Inspired by the innovative narrative forms and prose style of Gertrude Stein, Anderson also embraced the vernacular language of other American writers he admired, including Walt Whitman, Mark Twain, and his contemporary Theodore Dreiser. One of Anderson's best-known essays, "An Apology for Crudity," was first published in the literary magazine the *Dial* and later reprinted in the book page of the Chicago *Daily News.* In the essay, Anderson argued that contemporary American literature must mirror "the crudity of thought" in the United States, urging authors to immerse themselves in the life of the sprawling country and "to write out of the people not for the people." Because such writing "is close to life, it works out into crude and broken forms," Anderson added, indicating the kinds of forms he was experimenting with in the stories he later collected in *Winesburg, Ohio* (1919). The text of the following selection is taken from the first printing of "An Apology for Crudity" in the *Dial,* November 1917.

From An Apology for Crudity

For a long time I have believed that crudity is an inevitable quality in the production of a really significant present-day American literature. How indeed is one to escape the obvious fact that there is as yet no native subtlety of thought or living among us? And if we are a crude and childlike people how can our literature hope to escape the influence of that fact? Why indeed should we want it to escape?

If you are in doubt as to the crudity of thought in America, try an experiment. Come out of your offices, where you sit writing and thinking, and try living with us. Get on a train at Pittsburg and go west to the mountains of Colorado. Stop for a time in our towns and cities. Stay for a week in some Iowa corn-shipping town and for another week in one of the Chicago clubs. As you loiter about read our newspapers and listen to our conversations, remembering, if you will, that as you see us in the towns and cities, so we are. We are not subtle enough to conceal ourselves and he who runs with open eyes through the Mississippi Valley may read the story of the Mississippi Valley.

It is a marvelous story and we have not yet begun to tell the half of it. A little, I think I know why. It is because we who write have drawn ourselves away. We have not had faith in our people and in the story of our people. If we are crude and childlike, that is our story and our writing men must learn to dare to come among us until they know the story. The telling of the story depends, I believe, upon their learning that lesson and accepting that burden.

To my room, which is on a street near the loop in the city of Chicago,[1] come men who write. They talk and I talk. We are fools. We talk of writers of the old world and the beauty and subtlety of the work they do. Below us the roaring city lies like a great animal on the prairies, but we do not run out to the prairies. We stay in our rooms and talk.

And so, having listened to talk and having myself talked overmuch, I grow weary of talk and walk in the streets. As I walk alone, an old truth comes home to me and I know that we shall never have an American literature until we return to faith in ourselves and to the facing of our own limitations. We must, in some way, become in ourselves more like our fellows, more simple and real.

For surely it does not follow that because we Americans are a people without subtlety, we are a dull or uninteresting people. Our literature is dull, but we are not. One remembers how Dostoevsky had faith in the simplicity of the Russians and what he achieved.[2] He lived and he expressed the life of his time and people. The thing that he did brings hope of achievement for our men.

But let us first of all accept certain truths. Why should we Americans aspire to a subtlety that belongs not to us but to old lands and places? Why talk of intellectuality and of intellectual life when we have not accepted the life that we have? There is death on that road and following it has brought death into much of American writing. Can you doubt what I say? Consider the smooth slickness of the average magazine story. There is often great subtlety of plot and phrase, but there is no reality. Can such work live? The answer is that the most popular magazine story or novel does not live in our minds for a month.

And what are we to do about it? To me it seems that as writers we shall have to throw ourselves with greater daring into the life here. We shall have to begin to write out of the people and not for the people. We shall have to find within ourselves a little of that courage. To continue along the road we are travelling is unthinkable. To draw ourselves apart, to live in little groups and console ourselves with the thought that we are achieving intellectuality, is to get nowhere. By such a road we can hope only to go on producing a literature that has nothing to do with life as it is lived in these United States.

To be sure, the doing of the thing I am talking about will not be easy. America is a land of objective writing and thinking. New paths will have to be made. The subjective impulse is almost unknown to us. Because it is close to life, it works out into crude and broken forms. It leads along a road that such American masters of prose as James and Howells[3] did not want to take, but if we are to get anywhere, we shall have to travel that road.

---

1. loop . . . Chicago: The loop was originally named for the streetcar lines that made a broad circuit around the downtown business district in Chicago.
2. Dostoevsky . . . achieved: The novelist Fyodor Dostoevsky (1821–1881) was often praised for his naturalistic depictions of poverty and other harsh realities of life in Russia.
3. James and Howells: The American novelists Henry James (1843–1916), an expatriate and author of the influential essay "The Art of Fiction" (see p. 48), and William Dean Howells (1837–1920), who suggested that fiction writers should focus on the "more smiling aspects" of life in the United States (see p. 52).

The road is rough and the times are pitiless. Who, knowing our America and understanding the life in our towns and cities, can close his eyes to the fact that life here is for the most part an ugly affair? As a people we have given ourselves to industrialism, and industrialism is not lovely. If anyone can find beauty in an American factory town, I wish he would show me the way. For myself, I cannot find it. To me, and I am living in industrial life, the whole thing is as ugly as modern war. I have to accept that fact and I believe a great step forward will have been taken when it is more generally accepted.

[1917]

Gertrude Stein

[1874-1946]

> Gertrude Stein was a prominent and influential figure in the development of literary modernism (see Stein, p. 847). For most of her adult life, Stein lived in Paris with her longtime companion, Alice B. Toklas. At their famous salon, they associated with European artists and intellectuals, as well as with expatriate writers from Great Britain and the United States. In an effort to introduce Stein to a broader audience, one of her many literary friends, the British poet Edith Sitwell, arranged for her to appear before the literary societies of Cambridge and Oxford in 1926. According to Stein, she wrote her lecture while waiting for her run-down Ford to be repaired at a garage on the outskirts of Paris. Although she was very anxious about the lecture, her first, the writer Harold Acton reported that Stein cast "a spell" over her skeptical audience at Oxford. In the first part of the lecture, printed below, Stein spoke as a veteran of the struggle to win acceptance of modernist writing and painting, encouraging her audience to recognize the need for and to be receptive to innovative works of art. In the second part, Stein sought to explain her own method of writing, with its notorious repetitions and syntactical dislocations, a method that the lecture itself exemplified. The text of the following selection from the lecture, which was first published in London in 1926, is taken from a later collection of Stein's work, *What Are Masterpieces* (1940).

From COMPOSITION AS EXPLANATION

There is singularly nothing that makes a difference a difference in beginning and in the middle and in ending except that each generation has something different at which they are all looking. By this I mean so simply that anybody knows it that composition is the difference which makes each and all of them then different from other generations and this is what makes everything different otherwise they are all alike and everybody knows it because everybody says it.

It is very likely that nearly every one has been very nearly certain that something that is interesting is interesting them. Can they and do they. It is very interesting that nothing inside in them, that is when you consider the very long history of how every one ever acted or has felt, it is very interesting that nothing inside in them in all of them makes it connectedly different. By this I mean this. The only thing that is different from one time to another is what is seen and what is seen depends upon how everybody is doing everything. This makes the thing we are looking at very different and this makes what those describe it make of it, it makes a composition, it confuses, it shows, it is, it looks, it likes it as it is, and this makes what is seen as it is seen. Nothing changes from generation to generation except the thing seen and that makes a composition. Lord Grey[1] remarked that when the generals before the war talked about the war they talked about it as a nineteenth-century war although to be fought with twentieth-century weapons. That is because war is a thing that decides how it is to be done when it is to be done. It is prepared and to that degree it is like all academies it is not a thing made by being made it is a thing prepared. Writing and painting and all that, is like that, for those who occupy themselves with it and don't make it as it is made. Now the few who make it as it is made, and it is to be remarked that the most decided of them usually are prepared just as the world around them is preparing, do it in this way and so I if you do not mind I will tell you how it happens. Naturally one does not know how it happened until it is well over beginning happening.

To come back to the part that the only thing that is different is what is seen when it seems to be being seen, in other words, composition and time sense.

No one is ahead of his time, it is only that the particular variety of creating his time is the one that his contemporaries who also are creating their own time refuse to accept. And they refuse to accept it for a very simple reason and that is that they do not have to accept it for any reason. They themselves that is everybody in their entering the modern composition and they do enter it, if they do not enter it they are not so to speak in it they are out of it and so they do enter it; but in as you may say the non-competitive efforts where if you are not in it nothing is lost except nothing at all except what is not had, there are naturally all the refusals, and the things refused are only important if unexpectedly somebody happens to need them. In the case of the arts it is very definite. Those who are creating the modern composition authentically are naturally only of importance when they are dead because by that time the modern composition having become past is classified and the description of it is classical. That is the reason why the creator of the new composition in the arts is an outlaw until he is a classic, there is hardly a moment in between and it is really too bad very much too bad naturally for the creator but also very much too bad for the enjoyer, they all really would enjoy the created so much better just after it has been made than when it is already a classic, but it is perfectly simple that there is no reason why the contemporary should see, because it would not make any difference as they lead their lives in the new composition anyway, and as

---

1. **Lord Grey:** Edward Grey (1862–1933), the foreign secretary of Great Britain in the years leading up to World War I.

every one is naturally indolent why naturally they don't see. For this reason as in quoting Lord Grey it is quite certain that nations not actively threatened are at least several generations behind themselves militarily so aesthetically they are more than several generations behind themselves and it is very much too bad, it is so very much more exciting and satisfactory for everybody if one can have contemporaries, if all one's contemporaries could be one's contemporaries.

There is almost not an interval.

For a very long time everybody refuses and then almost without a pause almost everybody accepts. In the history of the refused in the arts and literature the rapidity of the change is always startling. Not the only difficulty with the *volte-face*[2] concerning the arts is this. When the acceptance comes, by that acceptance the thing created becomes a classic. It is a natural phenomena a rather extraordinary natural phenomena that a thing accepted becomes a classic. And what is the characteristic quality of a classic. The characteristic quality of a classic is that it is beautiful. Now of course it is perfectly true that a more or less first rate work of art is beautiful but the trouble is that when that first rate work of art becomes a classic because it is accepted the only thing that is important from then on to the majority of the acceptors the enormous majority, the most intelligent majority of the acceptors is that it is so wonderfully beautiful. Of course it is wonderfully beautiful, only when it is still a thing irritating annoying stimulating then all quality of beauty is denied to it.

Of course it is beautiful but first all beauty in it is denied and then all the beauty of it is accepted. If every one were not so indolent they would realize that beauty is beauty even when it is irritating and stimulating not only when it is accepted and classic. Of course it is extremely difficult nothing more so than to remember back to its not being beautiful once it has become beautiful. This makes it so much more difficult to realize its beauty when the work is being refused and prevents every one from realizing that they were convinced that beauty was denied, once the work is accepted. Automatically with the acceptance of the time sense comes the recognition of the beauty and once the beauty is accepted the beauty never fails any one.

Beginning again and again is a natural thing even when there is a series.

Beginning again and again and again explaining composition and time is a natural thing.

It is understood by this time that everything is the same except composition and time, composition and the time of the composition and the time in the composition.

Everything is the same except composition and as the composition is different and always going to be different everything is not the same. Everything is not the same as the time when of the composition and the time in the composition is different. The composition is different, that is certain.

The composition is the thing seen by every one living in the living that they are doing, they are the composing of the composition that at the time they are living is the composition of the time in which they are living. It is that that makes living a thing they are doing. Nothing else is different, of that almost any one can be certain. The time

---

2. *volte-face:* A complete change of position or an about-face (French).

when and the time of and the time in that composition is the natural phenomena of that composition and of that perhaps every one can be certain.

No one thinks these things when they are making when they are creating what is the composition, naturally no one thinks, that is no one formulates until what is to be formulated has been made.

Composition is not there, it is going to be there and we are here. This is some time ago for us naturally.

The only thing that is different from one time to another is what is seen and what is seen depends upon how everybody is doing everything. This makes the thing we are looking at very different and this makes what those who describe it make of it, it makes a composition, it confuses, it shows, it is, it looks, it likes it as it is, and this makes what is seen as it is seen. Nothing changes from generation to generation except the thing seen and that makes a composition.

Now the few who make writing as it is made and it is to be remarked that the most decided of them are those that are prepared by preparing, are prepared just as the world around them is prepared and is preparing to do it in this way and so if you do not mind I will again tell you how it happens. Naturally one does not know how it happened until it is well over beginning happening.

Each period of living differs from any other period of living not in the way life is but in the way life is conducted and that authentically speaking is composition. After life has been conducted in a certain way everybody knows it but nobody knows it, little by little, nobody knows it as long as nobody knows it. Any one creating the composition in the arts does not know it either, they are conducting life and that makes their composition what it is, it makes their work compose as it does.

Their influence and their influences are the same as that of all of their contemporaries only it must always be remembered that the analogy is not obvious until as I say the composition of a time has become so pronounced that it is past and the artistic composition of it is a classic.

[1926, 1940]

Donald Davidson

[1893–1968]

The Tennessee-born Donald Davidson was a poet, literary critic, and long-time professor at Vanderbilt University. He was the influential organizer of a group of poets and scholars at Vanderbilt who founded the *Fugitive*, a literary magazine published from 1922 to 1925. Davidson and several other members of the group, including John Crowe Ransom, Allen Tate, and Robert Penn Warren, later formed the Southern Agrarians. As their name suggests, the writers advocated a return to "agrarianism," the "traditional values" of the rural South. Together, they published the manifesto of the movement, *I'll Take My Stand: The South and the Agrarian Tradition*

Donald Davidson

This photograph of David-
son was taken in 1928,
shortly before he and the
other Southern Agrarians
issued their manifesto,
I'll Take My Stand.

(1930), a collection of essays defending "a
Southern way of life against what may be called
the American or prevailing way." In their opening "Statement of Principles," the Agrarians
outlined the corrosive effects of the rise of the
machine and the consequent transformation of
the United States from a rural into an industrial
nation, a process that had resulted in the
decline of traditional values, the deterioration
of social life and human relationships, and the
loss of individuality. In the first essay in the volume, "A Mirror for Artists," Davidson attacked
what he called "the industrial theory of the
arts," arguing that industrialization destroys
the very conditions that foster art. The text of the following selection from
the essay is taken from the first edition of *I'll Take My Stand* (1930).

From A MIRROR FOR ARTISTS

What is the industrial theory of the arts? It is something to which industry has not
turned its corporate brains in any large measure. Yet however unformulated, there
seems to be the phantom of a theory in the air; perhaps it may materialize into some formidable managerial body which will take care of the matter for us — a United States
Chamber of Art or a National Arts Council, with a distinguished board of directors and
local committees in every state. In the absence of the reassuring information which it
would undoubtedly be the function of such a body to collect and disseminate, I must beg
leave to define the industrial theory of the arts as best I can.

   Whenever it is attacked for dirtying up the landscape and rendering human life generally dull, mechanical, standardized, and mean, industrialism replies by pointing out
compensatory benefits. In the field of the arts, these are the benefits that a plodding
Maecenas[1] might think about without greatly agitating his intellect. When material
prosperity has finally become permanent, when we are all rich, when life has been
reduced to some last pattern of efficiency, then we shall all sit down and enjoy ourselves. Since nice, civilized people are supposed to have art, we shall have art. We shall
buy it, hire it, can it, or — most conclusively — manufacture it. That is a sufficient
answer to the whole question, so far as the industrial Maecenas is concerned — and he
does not, of course, realize what a strange part he plays in the rôle of Maecenas. The
nouveau riche[2] is never sensible of his own errors. If the industrial Maecenas were alone
to be considered, I should not be writing this essay. Other people, some of them persons
of learning and thoughtfulness, hold essentially the same theory. They talk of "master-

---

1. **Maecenas:** The politician Gaius Cilnius Maecenas (70–8 BCE) was known for his generous financial support of the young Roman poets of his day. The name *Maecenas* consequently became synonymous with a
wealthy patron of the arts.
2. *nouveau riche*: Newly rich (French).

ing the machine" or "riding the wild horses" of industrial power, with the idea that industrialism may furnish the basis for a society which will foster art. It is a convenient doctrine, and a popular one.

The contention of this essay is that such theories are wrong in their foundation. Industrialism cannot play the rôle of Maecenas, because its complete ascendancy will mean that there will be no arts left to foster; or, if they exist at all, they will flourish only in a diseased and disordered condition, and the industrial Maecenas will find himself in the embarrassing position of having to patronize an art that secretly hates him and calls him bad names. More completely, the making of an industrialized society will extinguish the meaning of the arts, as humanity has known them in the past, by changing the conditions of life that have given art a meaning. For they have been produced in societies which were for the most part stable, religious, and agrarian; where the goodness of life was measured by a scale of values having little to do with the material values of industrialism; where men were never too far removed from nature to forget that the chief subject of art, in the final sense, is nature.

It is my further contention that the cause of the arts, thus viewed, offers an additional reason among many reasons for submitting the industrial program to a stern criticism and for upholding a contrary program, that of an agrarian restoration; and that, in America, the South, past and present, furnishes a living example of an agrarian society, the preservation of which is worth the most heroic effort that men can give in a time of crisis.

[1930]

Michael Gold

[1893-1967]

The activist, editor, and novelist Michael Gold was born Itzok Isaac Granich, the son of Jewish immigrants living on the Lower East Side of New York City. By the time he was twelve, Gold was working to help support his impoverished family. Determined to escape the slums, he became involved with bohemian artists and leftist organizations in Greenwich Village. Gold began publishing poems in the *Masses*, a Socialist magazine that was suppressed by the government at the end of 1917. In 1921, he became the editor of its successor, the *Liberator*. After that magazine was taken over by the Communist Party, Gold helped found and in 1928 became the editor of the

Michael Gold

A newspaper photographer took this undated photograph of Gold addressing a crowd on behalf of one of the radical causes he promoted during the 1920s and 1930s.

New Masses (1926–48). Although the radical magazine published a range of influential American writers, including John Dos Passos, Langston Hughes, and Carl Sandburg, Gold also promoted "proletarian literature," works written by and for working people. A fervent Marxist, Gold believed that "the struggle of workers for the world" would spur the development of a new literary form, "Proletarian Realism," the elements of which he outlined in the following section of his regular column "Notes of the Month" in the *New Masses*, September 1930.

From PROLETARIAN REALISM

For proletarian literature is a living thing. It is not based on a set of fixed dogmas, anymore than is Communism or the science of biology.

Churches are built on dogma. The Catholic Church is the classic illustration of how the rule of dogma operates. Here is a great mass political and business movement that hypnotizes its victims with a set of weird formulas of magic which must not be tested or examined but must be swallowed with faith.

In Marxism[1] or any other science there is no dogma; there are laws which have been discovered running through the phenomena of nature. These laws must not be taken on faith. They are the result of experiment and statistics, and they are meant to be tested daily. If they fail to work, they can be discarded; they are constantly being discarded.

The law of class struggle is a Marxian discovery that has been tested, and that works, and that gives one a major clue to the movements of man in the mass.

In proletarian literature, there are several laws which seem to be demonstrable. One of them is that all culture is the reflection of a specific class society. Another is, that bourgeois culture is in process of decay, just as bourgeois society is in a swift decline.

The class that will inherit the world will be the proletariat, and every indication points inevitably to the law that this proletarian society will, like its predecessors, create its own culture.

This we can be sure of; upon this we all agree. Proletarian literature will reflect the struggle of the workers in their fight for the world. It portrays the life of the workers; not as do the vulgar French populists and American jazzmaniacs, but with a clear revolutionary point; otherwise it is meaningless, merely a new *frisson*.[2]

---

1. **Marxism:** The economic and political theories of the German founders of Communism, Karl Marx (1818–1883) and Friedrich Engels (1820–1895), who viewed class struggle between the proletariat and bourgeoisie as the fundamental law of capitalist society. They predicted that the struggle would inevitably result in the revolutionary overthrow of capitalism by the proletariat, who would establish a classless, socialist society.
2. *frisson:* A sudden, strong feeling, often of excitement (French).

Within this new world of proletarian literature, there are many living forms. It is dogmatic folly to seize upon any single literature form and erect it into a pattern for all proletarian literature.

The Russian Futurists,[3] tried to do this; they held the stage for a while, but are rapidly being supplanted.

My belief is that a new form is evolving, which one might name "Proletarian Realism." Here are some of its elements, as I see them:

1.

Because the Workers are skilled machinists, sailors, farmers and weavers, the proletarian writer must describe their work with technical precision. The Workers will scorn any vague fumbling poetry, much as they would scorn a sloppy workman. Hemingway and others have had the intuition to incorporate this proletarian element into their work, but have used it for the *frisson,* the way some actors try to imitate gangsters of men. These writers build a machine, it functions, but it produces nothing; it has not been planned to produce anything; it is only an adult toy.

2.

Proletarian realism deals with the *real conflicts* of men and women who work for a living. It has nothing to do with the sickly mental states of the idle Bohemians, their subtleties, their sentimentalities, their fine-spun affairs. The worst example and the best of what we do not want to do is the spectacle of Proust,[4] master-masturbator of the bourgeois literature. We know the suffering of hungry, persecuted and heroic millions is enough of a theme for anyone, without inventing these precious silly little agonies.

3.

Proletarian realism is never pointless. It does not believe in literature for its own sake, but in literature that is useful, has a social function. Every major writer has always done this in the past; but it is necessary to fight the battle constantly, for there are more intellectuals than ever who are trying to make literature a plaything. Every poem, every novel and drama, must have a social theme, or it is merely confectionery.

---

3. **Russian Futurists:** A group of experimental writers who completely rejected literary tradition and defended the right of poets to "feel an insurmountable hatred for the language existing before their time," as they declared in a manifesto issued in 1913. After the Russian Revolution, the futurists exerted considerable cultural influence, but their movement effectively ended by 1930.

4. **Proust:** Marcel Proust (1871–1922), a French writer best known for *À la recherche du temps perdu,* translated as *Remembrance of Things Past* or *In Search of Lost Time,* a celebrated novel published in seven volumes from 1913 to 1927.

4.

As few words as possible. We are not interested in the verbal acrobats – this is only another form for bourgeois idleness. The Workers live too close to reality to care about these literary show-offs, these verbalist heroes.

5.

To have the courage of the proletarian experience. This was the chief point of my "mystic" essay in 1921; let us proletarians write with the courage of our own experience. I mean, if one is a tanner and writer, let one dare to write the drama of a tannery; or of a clothing shop, or of a ditch-digger's life, or of a hobo. Let the bourgeois writers tell us about their spiritual drunkards and super-refined Parisian emigres; or about their spiritual marriages and divorces, etc., that is their world; we must write about our own mud-puddle; it will prove infinitely more important. This is being done by the proletarian realism.

6.

Swift action, clear form, the direct line, cinema in words; this seems to be one of the principles of proletarian realism. It knows exactly what it believes and where it is going; this makes for its beautiful youthful clarity.

7.

Away with drabness, the bourgeois notion that the Worker's life is sordid, the slummer's disgust and feeling of futility. There *is* horror and drabness in the Worker's life; and we will portray it; but we know this is not the last word; we know that this manure heap is the hope of the future; we know that not pessimism, but revolutionary elan will sweep this mess out of the world forever.

8.

Away with all lies about human nature. We are scientists; we know what a man thinks and feels. Everyone is a mixture of motives; we do not have to lie about our hero in order to win our case. It is this honesty alone, frank as an unspoiled child's, that makes proletarian realism superior to the older literary schools.

9.

No straining or melodrama or other effects; life itself is the supreme melodrama. Feel this intensely, and everything becomes poetry – the new poetry of materials, of the so-called "common man," the Worker molding his real world.

[1930]

Zora Neale Hurston

[1891–1960]

Zora Neale Hurston was among the first African Americans to be trained as an anthropologist (see Hurston, p. 880). Following her academic study at Barnard College in the mid-1920s, she undertook fieldwork in Harlem and throughout the rural South, recording the culture, folklore, and language of African Americans. In part, she wrote her essay "Characteristics of Negro Expression" to counter the arguments of white anthropologists who claimed that African American dialect had no internal consistency or regular usage. The essay was first published in *Negro: An Anthology,* a massive collection published in London by Nancy Cunard. The daughter of a wealthy white British family and the companion of the black composer Henry Crowder, Cunard was fascinated by African American art and culture. She consequently solicited material from dozens of black and white writers, including Langston Hughes, Georgia Douglas Johnson, William Carlos Williams, and Hurston, who contributed seven essays to *Negro.* Although many readers today are made uncomfortable by the essentialist nature of Hurston's analysis in "Characteristics of Negro Expression," the essay was appreciated as an important first step in classifying and documenting distinguishing features of African American art and culture. Hurston especially wished to demonstrate the contributions that African Americans had made to the English language in the United States. The text of the following selection is taken from *Negro: An Anthology* (1934; reprinted 1970).

From CHARACTERISTICS OF NEGRO EXPRESSION

Negro Folklore

Negro folklore is not a thing of the past. It is still in the making. Its great variety shows the adaptability of the black man: nothing is too old or too new, domestic or foreign, high or low, for his use. God and the Devil are paired, and are treated no more reverently than Rockefeller and Ford.[1] Both of these men are prominent in folklore, Ford being particularly strong, and they talk and act like good-natured stevedores or mill-hands. Ole Massa is sometimes a smart man and often a fool. The automobile is ranged alongside of the oxcart. The angels and the apostles walk and talk like section hands.[2] And through it all walks Jack, the greatest culture hero of the South; Jack beats them all — even the Devil, who is often smarter than God.

---

1. **Rockefeller and Ford:** The powerful industrialists John D. Rockefeller (1839–1937), the founder of the Standard Oil Company, and Henry Ford (1863–1947), the founder of the Ford Motor Company.
2. **section hands:** Railroad workers who lay track.

Originality

It has been said so often that the Negro is lacking in originality that it has almost become a gospel. Outward signs seem to bear this out. But if one looks closely its falsity is immediately evident.

It is obvious that to get back to original sources is much too difficult for any group to claim very much as a certainty. What we really mean by originality is the modification of ideas. The most ardent admirer of the great Shakespeare cannot claim first source even for him. It is his treatment of the borrowed material.

So if we look at it squarely, the Negro is a very original being. While he lives and moves in the midst of a white civilisation, everything that he touches is re-interpreted for his own use. He has modified the language, mode of food preparation, practice of medicine, and most certainly the religion of his new country, just as he adapted to suit himself the Sheik hair-cut made famous by Rudolph Valentino.[3]

Everyone is familiar with the Negro's modification of the whites' musical instruments, so that his interpretation has been adopted by the white man himself and then re-interpreted. In so many words, Paul Whiteman is giving an imitation of a Negro orchestra making use of white-invented musical instruments in a Negro way.[4] Thus has arisen a new art in the civilised world, and thus has our so-called civilisation come. The exchange and re-exchange of ideas between groups.

Dialect

If we are to believe the majority of writers of Negro dialect and the burnt-cork artists,[5] Negro speech is a weird thing, full of "ams" and "Ises." Fortunately we don't have to believe them. We may go directly to the Negro and let him speak for himself.

I know that I run the risk of being damned as an infidel for declaring that nowhere can be found the Negro who asks "am it?" nor yet his brother who announces "Ise uh gwinter." He exists only for a certain type of writers and performers.

Very few Negroes, educated or not, use a clear clipped "I." It verges more or less upon "Ah." I think the lip form is responsible for this to a great extent. By experiment the reader will find that a sharp "I" is very much easier with a thin taut lip than with a full soft lip. Like tightening violin strings.

If one listens closely one will note too that a word is slurred in one position in the sentence but clearly pronounced in another. This is particularly true of the pronouns. A pronoun as a subject is likely to be clearly enunciated, but slurred as an object. For example: "You better not let me ketch yuh."

---

3. **Rudolph Valentino:** A popular leading man in silent films, Valentino (1895–1926) starred in *The Sheikh* (1921).
4. **Paul Whiteman . . . in a Negro way:** Whiteman (1890–1967), who led a popular all-white orchestra, became known as the "King of Jazz."
5. **burnt-cork artists:** In minstrel shows, which were popular from roughly the 1840s to 1910, white (and later black) performers appeared in blackface, makeup made from a mixture of burned, pulverized cork and water.

There is a tendency in some localities to add the "h" to "it" and pronounce it "hit." Probably a vestige of old English. In some localities "if" is "ef."

In story telling "so" is universally the connective. It is used even as an introductory word, at the very beginning of a story. In religious expression "and" is used. The trend in stories is to state conclusions; in religion, to enumerate.

I am mentioning only the most general rules in dialect because there are so many quirks that belong only to certain localities that nothing less than a volume would be adequate.

[1934]

John Dos Passos

[1896–1970]

John Dos Passos was deeply involved in radical causes and the Socialist movement from the end of World War I to the late 1930s (see Dos Passos, p. 937). Early in 1935, the leftist journal the *New Masses* published a "Call for an American Writers Congress," a meeting of "American revolutionary writers" that would be "devoted to exposition of all phases of a writer's participation in the struggle against war, the preservation of civil liberties, and the destruction of Fascist tendencies everywhere." The call was signed by sixty-four writers, including Michael Gold, the Marxist editor of the *New Masses,* Theodore Dreiser, Langston Hughes, and Richard Wright. Dos Passos did not attend the meeting, which was held in New York City in April 1935, but he contributed "The Writer as Technician" to a volume of papers and addresses delivered at the conference. In the essay, he suggested that the writer's relation to society is similar to that of the scientist or engineer, whose main challenge in life "is to secure enough freedom from interference from the managers of the society in which he lives to be able to do his work." In the final section of the essay, printed below, he argued that writers must also resist "the imperial and bureaucratic tendencies of the groups whose aims they believe in," an allusion to the pressures exerted on leftist writers to toe the party line of doctrinaire Communism. The text is taken from the first printing of the essay in *American Writers Congress,* edited by Henry Hart (1935).

From THE WRITER AS TECHNICIAN

At this particular moment in history, when machinery and institutions have so outgrown the ability of the mind to dominate them, we need bold and original thought more than ever. It is the business of writers to supply that thought, and not to make of themselves figureheads in political conflicts. I don't mean that a writer hasn't an obligation, like any other citizen, to take part if he can in the struggle against oppression, but that his function as a citizen and his function as a technician are different, although the eventual end aimed at may in both cases be the same.

To fight oppression, and to work as best we can for a sane organization of society, we do not have to abandon the state of mind of freedom. If we do that we are letting the same thuggery in by the back door that we are fighting off in front of the house. I don't see how it is possible to organize effectively for liberty and the humane values of life without protecting and demanding during every minute of the fight the liberties of investigation, speech and discussion that are the greatest part of the ends of the struggle. In any organization a man gives up his liberty of action. That is necessary discipline. But if men give up their freedom of thought what follows is boss rule thuggery and administrative stagnation. It is easy to be carried away by the temporary effectiveness of boss rule, but it has always ended, in small things and in great, in leaving its victims stranded bloodless and rotten, with all the problems of a living society of free men unsolved. The dilemma that faces honest technicians all over the world to-day is how to combat the imperial and bureaucratic tendencies of the groups whose aims they believe in, without giving aid and comfort to the enemy. By the nature of his function as a technician, the writer finds himself in the dangerous and uncomfortable front line of this struggle.

In such a position a man is exposed to crossfire and is as likely to be mowed down by his friends as his enemies. The writer has to face that. His only safety lies in the fact that the work of an able technician cannot be replaced. It is of use and a pleasure to mankind. If it weren't for that fact, reluctantly recognized, but everywhere and always recognized, the whole tribe of doubters, inventors and discoverers would have been so often wiped out that the race would have ceased to produce types with those peculiar traits.

It's an old saying, but a very apt one, that a writer writes not to be saved but to be damned.

I feel that American writers who want to do the most valuable kind of work will find themselves trying to discover the deep currents of historical change under the surface of opinions, orthodoxies, heresies, gossip and the journalistic garbage of the day. They will find that they have to keep their attention fixed on the simple real needs of men and women. A writer can be a propagandist in the most limited sense of the word, or use his abilities for partisan invective or personal vituperation, but the living material out of which his work is built must be what used to be known as the humanities: the need for clean truth and sharply whittled exactitudes, men's instincts and compulsions and hungers and thirsts. Even if he's to be killed the next minute a man has to be cool and dispassionate while he's aiming his gun.

There is no escaping the fact that if you are a writer you are dealing with the humanities, with the language of all the men of your speech of your generation, with their traditions of the past and their feelings and perceptions. No matter from how narrow a set of convictions you start, you will find yourself in your effort to probe deeper and deeper into men and events as you find them, less and less able to work with the minute prescriptions of doctrine; and you will find more and more that you are on the side of the men, women and children alive right now against all the contraptions and organizations, however magnificent their aims may be, that bedevil them; and that you are on the side, not with phrases or opinions, but really and truly, of liberty, fraternity, and humanity. The words are old and dusty and hung with the dirty bunting of a thousand crooked orations, but underneath they are still sound. What men once meant by these words needs defenders to-day. And if those who have, in all kinds of direct and devious ways, stood up for them throughout history do not come out for them now to defend them against the thuggery of the bosses and the zeal of the administrators, the world will be an even worse place for men, women and children to live in than it is at present.

[1935]

Richard Wright

[1908–1960]

Richard Wright joined the Communist Party in the early 1930s, when he was living in Chicago (see Wright, p. 1008). After he moved to New York City, he became the Harlem editor of a newspaper published by the party, the *Daily Worker*. In an article published there in 1937, Wright praised the launching of a quarterly literary magazine designed to showcase the work of African American writers, the *New Challenge*. In the preface, the editors describe the leftist magazine as an effort to address "the present need for the realistic depiction of life through the sharp focus of social consciousness," adding that it would "be an organ for young writers who are seriously concerned with the problems facing them in their defense of existing culture and in their sincere creation of higher cultural values." The magazine published work by Sterling Brown, Ralph Ellison, and Langston Hughes, as well as Wright, who contributed his "Blueprint for Negro Writing." In the essay, which is regarded by many as one of his most important critical statements, Wright urgently called upon African American writers to bridge the widening gap between themselves and the mass of their people, producing work "addressed to the Negro himself, his needs, his sufferings, his aspirations." The text is taken from the first printing of the essay in the *New Challenge*, Fall 1937.

From BLUEPRINT FOR NEGRO WRITING

1) *The Role of Negro Writing: Two Definitions*

Generally speaking, Negro writing in the past has been confined to humble novels, poems, and plays, prim and decorous ambassadors who went a-begging to white America. They entered the Court of American Public Opinion dressed in the knee-pants of servility, curtsying to show that the Negro was not inferior, that he was human, and that he had a life comparable to that of other people. For the most part these artistic ambassadors were received as though they were French poodles who do clever tricks.

White America never offered these Negro writers any serious criticism. The mere fact that a Negro could write was astonishing. Nor was there any deep concern on the part of white America with the role Negro writing should play in American culture; and the role it did play grew out of accident rather than intent or design. Either it crept in through the kitchen in the form of jokes; or it was the fruits of that foul soil which was the result of a liason between inferiority-complexed Negro "geniuses" and burnt-out white Bohemians with money.

On the other hand, these often technically brilliant performances by Negro writers were looked upon by the majority of literate Negroes as something to be proud of. At best, Negro writing has been something external to the lives of educated Negroes themselves. That the productions of their writers should have been something of a guide in their daily living is a matter which seems never to have been raised seriously.

Under these conditions Negro writing assumed two general aspects: 1) It became a sort of conspicuous ornamentation, the hallmark of "achievement." 2) It became the voice of the educated Negro pleading with white America for justice.

Rarely was the best of this writing addressed to the Negro himself, his needs, his sufferings, his aspirations. Through misdirection, Negro writers have been far better to others than they have been to themselves. And the mere recognition of this places the whole question of Negro writing in a new light and raises a doubt as to the validity of its present direction.

2) *The Minority Outlook*

Somewhere in his writings Lenin[1] makes the observation that oppressed minorities often reflect the techniques of the bourgeoisie more brilliantly than some sections of the bourgeoisie themselves. The psychological importance of this becomes meaningful when it is recalled that oppressed minorities, and especially the petty bourgeois sections of oppressed minorities, strive to assimilate the virtues of the bourgeoisie in the assumption that by doing so they can lift themselves into a higher social sphere. But not only among the oppressed petty bourgeoisie does this occur. The workers of a

---

1. **Lenin:** Vladimir Ilyich Lenin (1870–1924), a principal figure in the Russian Revolution of 1917, founded the Communist Party and became the first premier of the Soviet Union in 1918.

minority people, chafing under exploitation, forge organizational forms of struggle to better their lot. Lacking the handicaps of false ambition and property, they have access to a wide social vision and a deep social consciousness. They display a greater freedom and initiative in pushing their claims upon civilization than even do the petty bourgeoisie. Their organizations show greater strength, adaptability, and efficiency than any other group or class in society.

That Negro workers, propelled by the harsh conditions of their lives, have demonstrated this consciousness and mobility for economic and political action there can be no doubt. But has this consciousness been reflected in the work of Negro writers to the same degree as it has in the Negro workers' struggle to free Herndon and the Scottsboro Boys,[2] in the drive toward unionism, in the fight against lynching? Have they as creative writers taken advantage of their unique minority position?

The answer decidedly is *no.* Negro writers have lagged sadly, and as time passes the gap widens between them and their people.

How can this hiatus be bridged? How can the enervating effects of this long standing split be eliminated?

In presenting questions of this sort an attitude of self- consciousness and self-criticism is far more likely to be a fruitful point of departure than a mere recounting of past achievements. An emphasis upon tendency and experiment, a view of society as something becoming rather than as something fixed and admired is the one which points the way for Negro writers to stand shoulder to shoulder with Negro workers in mood and outlook.

3) *A Whole Culture*

There is, however, a culture of the Negro which is his and has been addressed to him; a culture which has, for good or ill, helped to clarify his consciousness and create emotional attitudes which are conducive to action. This culture has stemmed mainly from two sources: 1) the Negro church; 2) and the folklore of the Negro people.

It was through the portals of the church that the American Negro first entered the shrine of western culture. Living under slave conditions of life, bereft of his African heritage, the Negroes' struggle for religion on the plantations between 1820–60 assumed the form of a struggle for human rights. It remained a relatively revolutionary struggle until religion began to serve as an antidote for suffering and denial. But even today there are millions of American Negroes whose only sense of a whole universe, whose only relation to society and man, and whose only guide to personal dignity comes through the archaic morphology of Christian salvation.

---

2. **Herndon and the Scottsboro Boys:**   The Communist organizer Angelo Herndon was arrested and charged with insurrection for organizing poor and unemployed African Americans in Atlanta in 1932. Although he was sentenced by an all-white male jury to eighteen to twenty years in prison, he was released in 1934. He wrote *The Scottsboro Boys: Four Freed! Five to Go!* (1937), an account of the trials of nine black teenagers charged with the rape of two white girls on a freight train bound from Tennessee to Alabama on March 25, 1931.

It was, however, in a folklore moulded out of rigorous and inhuman conditions of life that the Negro achieved his most indigenous and complete expression. Blues, spirituals, and folk tales recounted from mouth to mouth; the whispered words of a black mother to her black daughter on the ways of men; the confidential wisdom of a black father to his black son; the swapping of sex experiences on street corners from boy to boy in the deepest vernacular; work songs sung under blazing suns — all these formed the channels through which the racial wisdom flowed.

One would have thought that Negro writers in the last century of striving at expression would have continued and deepened this folk tradition, would have tried to create a more intimate and yet a more profoundly social system of artistic communication between them and their people. But the illusion that they could escape through individual achievement the harsh lot of their race swung Negro writers away from any such path. Two separate cultures sprang up: one for the Negro masses, unwritten and unrecognized; and the other for the sons and daughters of a rising Negro bourgeoisie, parasitic and mannered.

Today the question is: Shall Negro writing be for the Negro masses, moulding the lives and consciousness of those masses toward new goals, or shall it continue begging the question of the Negroes' humanity?

[1937]

Gertrude Stein

[1874-1946]

Gertrude Stein was born on February 3, 1874, in Allegheny, a suburb of Pittsburgh, Pennsylvania. She was the seventh child of Daniel and Amelia Keyser Stein, middle-class German Jews who owned a textile firm with stores in Pittsburgh and Baltimore, Maryland. Following a disagreement with his brother, a co-owner of the firm, Daniel Stein relocated his business and moved his family to Vienna, Austria. The Steins lived there and in Paris until 1879, when they returned to the United States and settled in Oakland, California. Stein was educated by private tutors and then attended high school in Oakland. After the death of her mother in 1888 and her father in 1891, Stein and her siblings received small trust funds, and she withdrew from high school. In 1892, she went to live with an aunt in Baltimore, and her brother Leo enrolled at Harvard University. The next year, Stein enrolled as a special student at Harvard Annex, later called Radcliffe College, where she studied philosophy and psychology with William James, the brother of the novelist Henry James. Her first published work was a co-authored article on "automatic writing," a free-writing exercise used in therapy, which appeared in the *Psychological Review* in 1896. After graduating magna cum laude in 1898, she decided to continue her study of psychology at the Johns Hopkins School of Medicine in Baltimore. During her years there, she was "bored, frankly and openly bored," as Stein put it, and in 1903 she left medical school without taking a degree and joined her brother Leo, who had gone to study art in Paris.

Gertrude Stein

This photograph of Stein was taken in the studio of her apartment at 27 rue de Fleurus, about two years after she moved to Paris in 1903.

Stein lived there for most of the rest of her life. She and her brother found a two-story courtyard apartment with an attached studio on the rue de Fleurus in Montparnasse, the vibrant artistic and intellectual center of Paris. Stein immediately wrote *Q.E.D.* (c. 1903), a semiautobiographical novel about a failed lesbian love affair that was not published until after her death. She and Leo soon began to hold an open house on Saturday evenings, gatherings that developed into a famous salon for intellectuals, painters, and writers. Many also came to see the paintings she and Leo began to collect, including innovative works by emerging, avant-garde artists such as Henri Matisse and Pablo Picasso, who painted Stein's portrait in 1906. According to Stein, during her long sittings for the portrait,

847

which represented Picasso's first step toward the development of cubism, she mentally composed sentences for her experimental *Three Lives*. Before it was privately printed in 1909, she wrote *The Making of Americans*, a fictional account of the history of her family that grew into what Stein described as "the history of every kind and of every individual human being." While she was working on the thousand-page saga, which was not published until 1925, Stein met Alice B. Toklas, a thirty-year-old Californian who was visiting Paris. They were immediately drawn to each other, and early in 1910 Toklas moved into the apartment on the rue de Fleurus, becoming Stein's lifelong companion, lover, and secretary.

For me the work of Gertrude Stein consists in a rebuilding, an entire new recasting of life, in the city of words.

—Sherwood Anderson

During the following decades, Stein became a major force among modernist writers in English. In 1910, she began writing a series of brief, non-representational "word portraits," including "Picasso" and "Matisse," both of which Alfred Stieglitz published in a special issue of his influential journal *Camera Work*. In 1913, her brother moved out of their apartment and left for Italy, and they divided their famous art collection, with Leo taking the paintings by Matisse and Stein keeping those by Picasso and other cubists. Stein privately published *Tender Buttons: Objects, Food, Rooms* (1914), still-life studies in which she attempted to create in words what the cubists created on canvas. During World War I, Stein bought and learned to drive a Ford truck, which she and Toklas used to transport supplies and to evacuate refugees for the American Fund for French Wounded. After the war, they hosted dozens of expatriate American artists and writers, including Sherwood Anderson, Zelda and F. Scott Fitzgerald, and Ernest Hemingway. Stein privately published *Geography and Plays* (1922), a collection of her word portraits and short plays, and her friends helped her find commercial publishers for *The Making of Americans* and *Composition as Explanation* (1926). She published a wide range of writings during the next few years, further solidifying her reputation for innovation and tireless experimentation. In her witty memoirs, *The Autobiography of Alice B. Toklas* (1933), Stein thus adopted the unconventional strategy of telling her own story from Toklas's point of view, focusing on their life together in Paris.

The Autobiography made Stein famous. The book was serialized in the prestigious *Atlantic Monthly*, and it became a bestseller as a selection of the Book-of-the-Month Club. At the same time, an equally unconventional opera she wrote with the American composer Virgil Thomson, *Four Saints in Three Acts*, began a successful run on Broadway in 1934. Suddenly in demand as a speaker, Stein embarked on an extended lecture tour of the United States. Stein further capitalized on the success of *The Autobiography* by writing a second volume of her memoirs, *Everybody's Autobiography* (1937). A series of other books followed, including *Picasso* (1938) and a children's book, *The World Is Round* (1939). During the German occupation of France, Stein and Toklas moved to the countryside, where they lived quietly throughout World War II in order to escape the organized persecution of Jews. Stein continued to write, publishing *Ida, a Novel* (1941) and another volume of her memoirs, *Wars I Have Seen* (1945). She also wrote another opera, *The Mother of Us All*, based on the life of pioneering femi-

bedfordstmartins.com/ americanlit for research links on Stein

nist Susan B. Anthony. With Toklas at her side, Stein died of cancer on July 27, 1946. "The world will be a duller place without her," one of her many admirers observed in the *Nation.*

Stein's "Ada."   Stein composed this sketch, the first of her word portraits, in 1910. In the series of brief prose works, Stein sought to capture the essence of an individual's life and character without relying on physical description or detailed biographical information. In "Ada," her subject was her companion and lover, Alice Babette Toklas (1877-1967). Born in San Francisco, she was twenty when her mother died of cancer, and Toklas then served for a time as a housekeeper for her grandfather, father, and brother. After inheriting some money from her grandfather, Toklas left home and went to Europe, where she met Stein at a party on the day she arrived in Paris in 1907. Early in 1910, they began living together and were lovers and companions until Stein's death in 1946. In many ways, "Ada" chronicles this narrative up to 1910, but Stein offered few concrete details and changed all of the names of the people involved in the story. Alice, for example, has become Ada, a name with different meanings in various cultures, including "first daughter" (Nigerian), "ornament" (Hebrew), and "happy" (Old German). All of those meanings may figure in "Ada," which may also be a playful allusion to Augusta Ada Byron, Lady Lovelace (1815-1852), the remarkable daughter of the British poet Lord Byron, who became one of the first women to be widely recognized as a mathematician and who helped pioneer the earliest forms of computer programming. In *The Autobiography of Alice B. Toklas* (1933), Stein says that when Toklas read "Ada" she initially thought Stein was making fun of her but that she was finally "terribly pleased with it." The text is taken from its first publication in *Geography and Plays* (1922).

Alice B. Toklas

The noted photographer Arnold Genthe took this portrait of Toklas in San Francisco in 1906, shortly before her trip to Europe.

ADA

Barnes Colhard did not say he would not do it but he did not do it. He did it and then he did not do it, he did not ever think about it. He just thought some time he might do something.

His father Mr. Abram Colhard spoke about it to every one and very many of them spoke to Barnes Colhard about it and he always listened to them.

Then Barnes fell in love with a very nice girl and she would not marry him. He cried then, his father Mr. Abram Colhard comforted him and they took a trip and Barnes promised he would do what his father wanted him to be doing. He did not do the thing, he thought he would do another thing, he did not do the other thing, his father Mr. Colhard did not want him to do the other thing. He really did not do anything then. When he was a good deal older he married a very rich girl. He had thought perhaps he would not propose to her but his sister wrote to him that it would be a good thing. He married the rich girl and she thought he was the most wonderful man and one who knew everything. Barnes never spent more than the income of the fortune he and his wife had then, that is to say they did not spend more than the income and this was a surprise to very many who knew about him and about his marrying the girl who had such a large fortune. He had a happy life while he was living and after he was dead his wife and children remembered him.

He had a sister who also was successful enough in being one being living. His sister was one who came to be happier than most people come to be in living. She came to be a completely happy one. She was twice as old as her brother. She had been a very good daughter to her mother. She and her mother had always told very pretty stories to each other. Many old men loved to hear her tell these stories to her mother. Every one who ever knew her mother liked her mother. Many were sorry later that not every one liked the daughter. Many did like the daughter but not every one as every one had liked the mother. The daughter was charming inside in her, it did not show outside in her to every one, it certainly did to some. She did sometimes think her mother would be pleased with a story that did not please her mother, when her mother later was sicker the daughter knew that there were some stories she could tell her that would not please her mother. Her mother died and really mostly altogether the mother and the daughter had told each other stories very happily together.

The daughter then kept house for her father and took care of her brother. There were many relations who lived with them. The daughter did not like them to live with them and she did not like them to die with them. The daughter, Ada they had called her after her grandmother who had delightful ways of smelling flowers and eating dates and sugar, did not like it at all then as she did not like so much dying and she did not like any of the living she was doing then. Every now and then some old gentlemen told delightful stories to her. Mostly then there were not nice stories told by any one then in her living. She told her father Mr. Abram Colhard that she did not like it at all being one being living then. He never said anything. She was afraid then, she was one needing charming stories and happy telling of them and not having that thing she was always trembling. Then every one who could live with them were dead and there were then the father and the son a young man then and the daughter coming to be that one then. Her grandfather had left some money to them each one of them. Ada said she was going to use it to go away from them. The father said nothing then, then he said something and she said nothing then, then they both said nothing and then it was that she went away from them. The father was quite tender then, she was his daughter then. He wrote her tender letters then, she wrote him tender letters then, she never went back to live with him. He wanted her to come and she wrote him tender letters then. He liked the tender letters she wrote to him. He wanted her to live with him. She answered him by writing tender letters to him and telling very nice stories indeed in them. He wrote nothing and then he wrote again and there was some waiting and then he wrote tender letters again and again.

She came to be happier than anybody else who was living then. It is easy to believe this thing. She was telling some one, who was loving every story that was charming. Some one who was living was almost always listening. Some one who was loving was almost always listening. That one who was loving was almost always listening. That one who was loving was telling about being one then listening. That one being loving was then telling stories having a beginning and a middle and an ending. That one was then one always completely listening. Ada was then one and all her living then one completely telling stories that were charming, completely listening to stories having a beginning and a middle and an ending. Trembling was all living, living was all loving, some one was then the other one. Certainly this one was loving this Ada then. And certainly Ada all her living then was happier in living than any one else who ever could, who was, who is, who ever will be living.

[c. 1910, 1922]

Stein's "Miss Furr and Miss Skeene." In contrast to Stein's other early word portraits, this sketch focuses on the relationship between two people: Ethel Mars (1876-1955), or "Miss Furr," and Maud Hunt Squire (1876-1956), or "Miss Skeene." Mars and Squire, who had been raised in the Midwest and met while they were students at the Cincinnati Art Academy, came to Paris together in 1906. Although they initially appeared to be rather prim and proper, they soon embraced a bohemian lifestyle, gaining notoriety for their flamboyant dress and gaudy makeup, as well as for Mars's bright orange hair. At the same time, they were serious and increasingly successful artists in various media, especially prints, and both exhibited their work at the avant-garde Société Salon d'Automne. Before they returned to the United States at the beginning of World War I, Mars and Squire regularly attended the salon maintained by Stein and her partner Alice B. Toklas. "Miss Furr and Miss Skeene," which Stein completed in 1911, was first published in her collection *Geography and Plays* (1922). It was reprinted the following year in *Vanity Fair,* an influential magazine of literature and culture during the 1920s. In her double portrait, Stein repeatedly uses the word *gay,* which at the time she wrote the sketch simply meant lighthearted, cheerful, or brightly colored. But the word may well have been a double entendre, at least among the expatriate Americans in Paris, and *gay* apparently became more widely used as a code word for "homosexual" after "Miss Furr and Miss Skeene" appeared in *Vanity Fair.* The text of the sketch is taken from its first publication in *Geography and Plays* (1922).

MISS FURR AND MISS SKEENE

Helen Furr had quite a pleasant home. Mrs. Furr was quite a pleasant woman. Mr. Furr was quite a pleasant man. Helen Furr had quite a pleasant voice a voice quite worth cultivating. She did not mind working. She worked to cultivate her voice. She did not find it gay living in the same place where she had always been living. She went to a place where some were cultivating something, voices and other things needing cultivating. She met Georgine Skeene there who was cultivating her voice which some thought was quite a pleasant one. Helen Furr and Georgine Skeene lived together then. Georgine Skeene liked travelling. Helen Furr did not care about travelling, she liked to stay in one place and be gay there. They were together then and travelled to another place and stayed there and were gay there.

They stayed there and were gay there, not very gay there, just gay there. They were both gay there, they were regularly working there both of them cultivating their voices there, they were both gay there. Georgine Skeene was gay there and she was regular, regular in being gay, regular in not being gay, regular in being a gay one who was one not being gay longer than was needed to be one being quite a gay one. They were both gay then there and both working there then.

They were in a way both gay there where there were many cultivating something. They were both regular in being gay there. Helen Furr was gay there, she was gayer and gayer there and really she was just gay there, she was gayer and gayer there, that is to say she found ways of being gay there that she was using in being gay there. She was gay there, not gayer and gayer, just gay there, that is to say she was not gayer by using the things she found there that were gay things, she was gay there, always she was gay there.

They were quite regularly gay there, Helen Furr and Georgine Skeene, they were regularly gay there where they were gay. They were very regularly gay.

To be regularly gay was to do every day the gay thing that they did every day. To be regularly gay was to end every day at the same time after they had been regularly gay. They were regularly gay. They were gay every day. They ended every day in the same way, at the same time, and they had been every day regularly gay.

The voice Helen Furr was cultivating was quite a pleasant one. The voice Georgine Skeene was cultivating was, some said, a better one. The voice Helen Furr was cultivating she cultivated and it was quite completely a pleasant enough one then, a cultivated enough one then. The voice Georgine Skeene was cultivating she did not cultivate too much. She cultivated it quite some. She cultivated and she would sometime go on cultivating it and it was not then an unpleasant one, it would not be then an unpleasant one, it would be a quite richly enough cultivated one, it would be quite richly enough to be a pleasant enough one.

They were gay where there were many cultivating something. The two were gay there, were regularly gay there. Georgine Skeene would have liked to do more travelling. They did some travelling, not very much travelling, Georgine Skeene would have liked to do more travelling, Helen Furr did not care about doing travelling, she liked to stay in a place and be gay there.

They stayed in a place and were gay there, both of them stayed there, they stayed together there, they were gay there, they were regularly gay there.

They went quite often, not very often, but they did go back to where Helen Furr had a pleasant enough home and then Georgine Skeene went to a place where her brother had quite some distinction. They both went, every few years, went visiting to where Helen Furr had quite a pleasant home. Certainly Helen Furr would not find it gay to stay, she did not find it gay, she said she would not stay, she said she did not find it gay, she said she would not stay where she did not find it gay, she said she found it gay where she did stay and she did stay there where very many were cultivating something. She did stay there. She always did find it gay there.

She went to see them where she had always been living and where she did not find it gay. She had a pleasant home there, Mrs. Furr was a pleasant enough woman, Mr. Furr was a pleasant enough man, Helen told them and they were not worrying, that she did not find it gay living where she had always been living.

Georgine Skeene and Helen Furr were living where they were both cultivating their voices and they were gay there. They visited where Helen Furr had come from and then they went to where they were living where they were then regularly living.

There were some dark and heavy men there then. There were some who were not so heavy and some who were not so dark. Helen Furr and Georgine Skeene sat regularly with them. They sat regularly with the ones who were dark and heavy. They sat regularly with the ones who were not so dark. They sat regularly with the ones that were not so heavy. They sat with them regularly, sat with some of them. They went with them regularly went with them. They were regular then, they were gay then, they were where they wanted to be then where it was gay to be then, they were regularly gay then. There were men there then who were dark and heavy and they sat with them with Helen Furr and Georgine Skeene and they went with them with Miss Furr and Miss Skeene, and they went with the heavy and dark men Miss Furr and Miss Skeene went with them, and they sat with them, Miss Furr and Miss Skeene sat with them, and there were other men, some were not heavy men and they sat with Miss Furr and Miss Skeene and Miss Furr and Miss Skeene sat with them, and there were other men who were not dark men and they sat with Miss Furr and Miss Skeene and Miss Furr and Miss Skeene sat with them. Miss Furr and Miss Skeene went with them and they went with Miss Furr and Miss Skeene, some who were not heavy men, some who were not dark men. Miss Furr and Miss Skeene sat regularly, they sat with some men. Miss Furr and Miss Skeene went and there were some men with them. There were men and Miss Furr and Miss Skeene went with them, went somewhere with them, went with some of them.

Helen Furr and Georgine Skeene were regularly living where very many were living and cultivating in themselves something. Helen Furr and Georgine Skeene were living very regularly then, being very regular then in being gay then. They did then learn many ways to be gay and they were then being gay being quite regular in being gay, being gay and they were learning little things, little things in ways of being gay, they were very regular then, they were learning very many little things in ways of being gay, they were being gay and using these little things they were learning to have to be gay with regularly gay with then and they were gay the same amount they had been gay. They were quite gay, they were quite regular, they were learning little things, gay little things, they were gay inside them the same amount they had been gay, they were gay the same length of time they had been gay every day.

They were regular in being gay, they learned little things that are things in being gay, they learned many little things that are things in being gay, they were gay every day, they were regular, they were gay, they were gay the same length of time every day, they were gay, they were quite regularly gay.

Georgine Skeene went away to stay two months with her brother. Helen Furr did not go then to stay with her father and her mother. Helen Furr stayed there where they had been regularly living the two of them and she would then certainly not be lonesome, she would go on being gay. She did go on being gay. She was not any more gay but she was gay longer every day than they had been being gay when they were together being gay. She was gay then quite exactly the same way. She learned a few more little ways of being in being gay. She was quite gay and in the same way, the same way she had been gay and she was gay a little longer in the day, more of each day she was gay. She was gay longer every day than when the two of them had been being gay. She was gay quite in the way they had been gay, quite in the same way.

She was not lonesome then, she was not at all feeling any need of having Georgine Skeene. She was not astonished at this thing. She would have been a little astonished by this thing but she knew she was not astonished at anything and so she was not astonished at this thing not astonished at not feeling any need of having Georgine Skeene.

Helen Furr had quite a completely pleasant voice and it was quite well enough cultivated and she could use it and she did use it but then there was not any way of working at cultivating a completely pleasant voice when it has become a quite completely well enough cultivated one, and there was not much use in using it when one was not wanting it to be helping to make one a gay one. Helen Furr was not needing using her voice to be a gay one. She was gay then and sometimes she used her voice and she was not using it very often. It was quite completely enough cultivated and it was quite completely a pleasant one and she did not use it very often. She was then, she was quite exactly as gay as she had been, she was gay a little longer in the day than she had been.

She was gay exactly the same way. She was never tired of being gay that way. She had learned very many little ways to use in being gay. Very many were telling about using other ways in being gay. She was gay enough, she was always gay exactly the same way, she was always learning little things to use in being gay, she was telling about using other ways in being gay, she was telling about learning other ways in being gay, she was learning other ways in being gay, she would be using other ways in being gay, she would always be gay in the same way, when Georgine Skeene was there not so long each day as when Georgine Skeene was away.

She came to using many ways in being gay, she came to use every way in being gay. She went on living where many were cultivating something and she was gay, she had used every way to be gay.

They did not live together then Helen Furr and Georgine Skeene. Helen Furr lived there the longer where they had been living regularly together. Then neither of them were living there any longer. Helen Furr was living somewhere else then and telling some about being gay and she was gay then and she was living quite regularly then. She was regularly gay then. She was quite regular in being gay then. She remembered all the little ways of being gay. She used all the little ways of being gay. She was quite regularly gay. She told many then the way of being gay, she taught very many then little ways they could use in being gay. She was living very well, she was gay then, she went on living then, she was regular in being gay, she always was living very well and was gay very well and was telling about little ways one could be learning to use in being gay, and later was telling them quite often, telling them again and again.

[c. 1910, 1922]

Stein's "Picasso."   Stein first met Pablo Picasso (1881-1973), the Spanish painter and sculptor, at a gallery in Paris in 1905. They soon began a lifelong friendship based on mutual admiration. Stein and her brother Leo were early collectors of Picasso's paintings, including his famous 1906 portrait of Stein, which she bequeathed to the Metropolitan Museum of Art in New York City. By the time Stein composed her word portrait of Picasso, probably in 1911, he and his friend Georges Braque had developed analytical cubism, a revolutionary movement in painting in which different aspects or facets of an object are seen simultaneously. During the period 1906-11, Stein was also seeking to break free of traditional modes of representation in prose. In his introduction to the special issue of *Camera Work* in which "Picasso" and Stein's contemporaneous portrait of the

Pablo Picasso, *Portrait of Gertrude Stein*

Picasso painted this famous portrait of Stein in 1906, five years before she composed her word portrait of Picasso.

painter Henri Matisse first appeared, Alfred Stieglitz observed that "in these articles by Miss Stein, the Post-Impressionist spirit is found expressing itself in literary form." The portraits were accompanied by reproductions of works by both painters, but Stein does not describe Picasso as a painter, refer to any of his works, nor offer either a physical description or a biography of the artist. Instead, she seeks to capture the essence of his character and work, emphasizing his charisma, his originality, and his artistic fertility, manifested in his seemingly effortless creation of "something having meaning." The text is taken from the first printing in *Camera Work,* August 1912.

PICASSO

One whom some were certainly following was one who was completely charming. One whom some were certainly following was one who was charming. One whom some were following was one who was completely charming. One whom some were following was one who was certainly completely charming.

Some were certainly following and were certain that the one they were then following was one working and was one bringing out of himself then something. Some were certainly following and were certain that the one they were then following was one bringing out of himself then something that was coming to be a heavy thing, a solid thing and a complete thing.

One whom some were certainly following was one working and certainly was one bringing something out of himself then and was one who had been all his living had been one having something coming out of him.

Something had been coming out of him, certainly it had been coming out of him, certainly it was something, certainly it had been coming out of him and it had meaning, a charming meaning, a solid meaning, a struggling meaning, a clear meaning.

One whom some were certainly following and some were certainly following him, one whom some were certainly following was one certainly working.

One whom some were certainly following was one having something coming out of him something having meaning and this one was certainly working then.

This one was working and something was coming then, something was coming out of this one then. This one was one and always there was something coming out of this one and always there had been something coming out of this one. This one had never been one not having something coming out of this one. This one was one having something coming out of this one. This one had been one whom some were following. This one was one whom some were following. This one was being one whom some were following. This one was one who was working.

This one was one who was working. This one was one being one having something being coming out of him. This one was one going on having something come out of him. This one was one going on working. This one was one whom some were following. This one was one who was working.

This one always had something being coming out of this one. This one was working. This one always had been working. This one was always having something that was coming out of this one that was a solid thing, a charming thing, a lovely thing, a perplexing thing, a disconcerting thing, a simple thing, a clear thing, a complicated thing, an interesting thing, a disturbing thing, a repellant thing, a very pretty thing. This one was one certainly being one having something coming out of him. This one was one whom some were following. This one was one who was working.

This one was one who was working and certainly this one was needing to be working so as to be one being working. This one was one having something coming out of him. This one would be one all his living having something coming out of him. This one was working and then this one was working and this one was needing to be working, not to be one having something coming out of him something having meaning, but was needing to be working so as to be one working.

This one was certainly working and working was something this one was certain this one would be doing and this one was doing that thing, this one was working. This one was not one completely working. This one was not ever completely working. This one certainly was not completely working.

This one was one having always something being coming out of him, something having completely a real meaning. This one was one whom some were following. This one was one who was working. This one was one who was working and he was one needing this thing needing to be working so as to be one having some way of being one having some way of working. This one was one who was working. This one was one having something come out of him something having meaning. This one was one always having something come out of him and this thing the thing coming out of him always had real meaning. This one was one who was working. This one was one who was almost always working. This one was not one completely working. This one was one not ever completely working. This one was not one working to have anything come out of him. This one did have something having meaning that did come out of him. He always did have something come out of him. He was working, he was not ever completely working. He did have some following. They were always following him. Some were certainly following him. He was one who was working. He was one having something coming out of him something having meaning. He was not ever completely working.

[1912]

Sherwood Anderson

[1876-1941]

Sherwood Anderson was born in Camden, Ohio, on September 13, 1876. He was the third of the six children of Irwin Anderson, who had fought in the Union cavalry during the Civil War, and Emma Smith Anderson. The family moved to the village of Caledonia, where Irwin Anderson's harness-making business failed, before settling in Clyde, Ohio, in 1884. Anderson's childhood was spent in poverty, and he left high school before graduation in order to help support the family. After his mother died in 1895, Anderson left Clyde for Chicago, where he worked as a manual laborer until 1898. He then joined the Ohio National Guard and spent a year in Cuba during the Spanish-American War. When he returned to the United States, he completed high school at the Wittenberg Academy, a school on the campus of Wittenberg College in Springfield, Ohio. Although Anderson enjoyed his studies and wanted to begin college there, he was once again forced to find work, so he left after a year and returned to Chicago in 1900. Discovering that he had a considerable flair for writing advertising copy, he worked for a publishing company and later in an advertising agency. In 1904, he married the first of his four wives, Cornelia Lane, the college-educated daughter of a wealthy businessman in Toledo, Ohio.

Sherwood Anderson

His friend Alfred Stieglitz took this photograph of Anderson in 1923, when the writer was approaching the height of his fame. "In this one thing you make me respect myself," Anderson gratefully wrote to Stieglitz.

Anderson seemed well on the way to a successful career in business, the ambition of his youth, but he soon began to dream of becoming a writer. Two years after their marriage, he and his wife relocated to Cleveland, where Anderson worked as the head of advertising for the United Factories Company before setting up his own mail-order firm in Elyria, Ohio, in 1907. For the next five years, he devoted himself to various business ventures. He also began to spend long hours writing in an upstairs room in the family home. Torn between his desire to write and the need to apply himself to business in order to support his growing family, which now included three children, Anderson collapsed from nervous exhaustion in 1912. He consequently abandoned business, separated from his family, and returned to Chicago, which was then becoming a vibrant literary center. Working in advertising to support himself and his writing, Anderson published two articles in a newly established Chicago-based literary magazine, the *Little Review*, in 1914. Later that year, he published his first short story in a prominent national magazine, *Harper's*. He then began work on a series of novels, including two stories of small-town boys who seek fame and fortune in Chicago, *Windy McPherson's Son* (1916) and *Marching Men* (1917). Meanwhile, Anderson was divorced from his first wife and married Tennessee Mitchell, with whom he moved to New York City in 1917. The following year, he published a volume of poems inspired by the work of Walt Whitman and the Chicago poet Carl Sandburg, *Mid-American Chants* (1918), most of which Anderson had written during 1914-15.

Winesburg, Ohio, when it first appeared, kept me up a whole night in a steady crescendo of emotion.

–Hart Crane

During the same period, he had also begun to write the kind of experimental prose that later brought him wide recognition. In his autobiography, Anderson recalled that he began to conceive of a new way of writing when he read Gertrude Stein's innovative book *Tender Buttons* in the summer of 1914: "Here was something purely experimental and dealing in words separated from sense – in the ordinary meaning of the word *sense* – an approach I was sure the poets must often be compelled to make. Was it an approach that would help me? I decided to try it." Even as he worked on more conventional novels and poems, Anderson wrote a series of impressionistic sketches about the lives of people in a small Midwestern town based on his memories of Clyde, Ohio. Several of the interrelated sketches were published individually in the *Little Review* and other avant-garde magazines before Anderson gathered them into a volume, *Winesburg, Ohio* (1919). By then, he had already begun a novel about a midwestern town, *Poor White* (1920), which was followed by the first of several acclaimed collections of his short stories, *The Triumph of the Egg* (1921). Meanwhile, the restless Anderson frequently moved around the country, dividing most of his time between Chicago and New York City. In 1921, he made his first trip to Europe, where he met and began a lifelong friendship with Gertrude Stein. He also strongly encouraged younger writers, including Ernest Hemingway, a journalist he met in Chicago, and William Faulkner, whom Anderson later met in New Orleans.

Although he was increasingly overshadowed by emerging writers such as Hemingway and Faulkner, Anderson continued to write and publish until the end of his life. With his second marriage falling apart, he wrote a novel about a man's midlife crisis, *Many Marriages* (1923). In 1924, Anderson married his third wife, Elizabeth Prall, and published his highly regarded autobiography, *A Story-Teller's Story*. It was followed by his bestselling book *Dark Laughter* (1925), a novel in which Anderson contrasted the sterility of his neurotic white characters to what he conceived to be the spontaneous, unself-conscious sexuality of African Americans. In 1927, he settled in Troutdale, Virginia, and bought two small newspapers in nearby Marion. After he divorced Elizabeth Prall, Anderson in 1933 married the radical labor activist Eleanor Copenhaver, a much younger woman with whom he lived contentedly in Virginia. During the final decade of his life, he published a collection of stories and two novels, but he wrote mainly essays and other short, nonfictional works, including a collection of sketches about life in the Midwest and South during the Depression, *Puzzled America* (1935). Anderson devoted most of his efforts to his posthumously published *Memoirs*, which he did not complete before his death on March 8, 1941, while he and his wife were aboard a ship bound for South America.

bedfordstmartins.com/ *americanlit* *for research links on Anderson*

Anderson's *Winesburg, Ohio*.   Anderson's most famous book, which marked an important turning point in his career, is a collection of independent but interrelated stories set in a fictional town closely resembling Clyde, Ohio, where he grew up. He wrote what became the introductory sketch of the volume, "The Book of the Grotesque," in 1915, when he was just starting out as a writer in Chicago. He later published several stories in various magazines. "Hands" appeared in the March 1916 issue of the *Masses*, a Socialist magazine of politics and literature published in New

York City, and "Paper Pills" was first published as "The Philosopher" in the
June–July 1916 issue of the *Little Review*. Other stories followed in those
magazines and in the radical political and literary magazine *Seven Arts*
before *Winesburg, Ohio* was accepted by the respected New York publisher
B. W. Huebsch, who had earlier published important works by modern
writers such as James Joyce and D. H. Lawrence. In a publicity release,
Huebsch declared that Anderson "lays bare the hearts and minds of the
inhabitants of a typical American village. . . . It is the psychoanalytic
method applied to literature." Certainly, Anderson was fascinated by psychology, especially the effects of repressed or thwarted sexuality. A few
reviewers consequently condemned him for reducing "his material from
human clay to plain dirt," as one put it in the New York *Sun.* But most of
the reviews were positive, and several of them offered genuine insights
into Anderson's literary methods. The reviewer for the *Chicago Daily Tribune,* for example, admiringly observed that Anderson "suggests rather
than depicts," adding that "he respects the imaginative faculty of his
reader by refusing to be explicit where overtones of emotion are already
invoked by the reader." The text of the following selection, the introductory sketch plus the first two stories in the volume, is taken from the first
edition of *Winesburg, Ohio* (1919).

From WINESBURG, OHIO

THE BOOK OF THE GROTESQUE

The writer, an old man with a white mustache, had some difficulty in getting into bed. The windows of the house in which he lived were high and he wanted to look at the trees when he awoke in the morning. A carpenter came to fix the bed so that it would be on a level with the window.

Quite a fuss was made about the matter. The carpenter, who had been a soldier in the Civil War, came into the writer's room and sat down to talk of building a platform for the purpose of raising the bed. The writer had cigars lying about and the carpenter smoked.

For a time the two men talked of the raising of the bed and then they talked of other things. The soldier got on the subject of the war. The writer, in fact, led him to that subject. The carpenter had once been a prisoner in Andersonville prison[1] and had lost a brother. The brother had died of starvation, and whenever the carpenter got upon that subject he cried. He, like the old writer, had a white mustache, and when he cried he puckered up his lips and the mustache bobbed up and down. The weeping old man with the cigar in his mouth was ludicrous. The plan the writer had for the raising of his bed was forgotten and later the carpenter did it in his own way and the writer, who was past sixty, had to help himself with a chair when he went to bed at night.

In his bed the writer rolled over on his side and lay quite still. For years he had been beset with notions concerning his heart. He was a hard smoker and his heart fluttered. The idea had got into his mind that he would some time die unexpectedly and always when he got into bed he thought of that. It did not alarm him. The effect in fact was quite a special thing and not easily explained. It made him more alive, there in bed, than at any other time. Perfectly still he lay and his body was old and not of much use any more, but something inside him was altogether young. He was like a pregnant woman, only that the thing inside him was not a baby but a youth. No, it wasn't a youth, it was a woman, young, and wearing a coat of mail like a knight. It is absurd, you see, to try to tell what was inside the old writer as he lay on his high bed and listened to the fluttering of his heart. The thing to get at is what the writer, or the young thing within the writer, was thinking about.

The old writer, like all of the people in the world, had got, during his long life, a great many notions in his head. He had once been quite handsome and a number of women had been in love with him. And then, of course, he had known people, many people, known them in a peculiarly intimate way that was different from the way in which you and I know people. At least that is what the writer thought and the thought pleased him. Why quarrel with an old man concerning his thoughts?

---

1. **Andersonville prison:** Located near the village of Andersonville in southwest Georgia, this infamous prison was the largest Confederate military prison camp of the Civil War. Of the 45,000 captured Union soldiers who were sent there between February 1864 and the end of the war in April 1865, nearly 13,000 died from disease, exposure, and malnutrition.

In the bed the writer had a dream that was not a dream. As he grew somewhat sleepy but was still conscious, figures began to appear before his eyes. He imagined the young indescribable thing within himself was driving a long procession of figures before his eyes.

You see the interest in all this lies in the figures that went before the eyes of the writer. They were all grotesques. All of the men and women the writer had ever known had become grotesques.

The grotesques were not all horrible. Some were amusing, some almost beautiful, and one, a woman all drawn out of shape, hurt the old man by her grotesqueness. When she passed he made a noise like a small dog whimpering. Had you come into the room you might have supposed the old man had unpleasant dreams or perhaps indigestion.

For an hour the procession of grotesques passed before the eyes of the old man, and then, although it was a painful thing to do, he crept out of bed and began to write. Some one of the grotesques had made a deep impression on his mind and he wanted to describe it.

At his desk the writer worked for an hour. In the end he wrote a book which he called "The Book of the Grotesque." It was never published, but I saw it once and it made an indelible impression on my mind. The book had one central thought that is very strange and has always remained with me. By remembering it I have been able to understand many people and things that I was never able to understand before. The thought was involved but a simple statement of it would be something like this:

That in the beginning when the world was young there were a great many thoughts but no such thing as a truth. Man made the truths himself and each truth was a composite of a great many vague thoughts. All about in the world were the truths and they were all beautiful.

The old man had listed hundreds of the truths in his book. I will not try to tell you of all of them. There was the truth of virginity and the truth of passion, the truth of wealth and of poverty, of thrift and of profligacy, of carelessness and abandon. Hundreds and hundreds were the truths and they were all beautiful.

And then the people came along. Each as he appeared snatched up one of the truths and some who were quite strong snatched up a dozen of them.

It was the truths that made the people grotesques. The old man had quite an elaborate theory concerning the matter. It was his notion that the moment one of the people took one of the truths to himself, called it his truth, and tried to live his life by it, he became a grotesque and the truth he embraced became a falsehood.

You can see for yourself how the old man, who had spent all of his life writing and was filled with words, would write hundreds of pages concerning this matter. The subject would become so big in his mind that he himself would be in danger of becoming a grotesque. He didn't, I suppose, for the same reason that he never published the book. It was the young thing inside him that saved the old man.

Concerning the old carpenter who fixed the bed for the writer, I only mentioned him because he, like many of what are called very common people, became the nearest thing to what is understandable and lovable of all the grotesques in the writer's book.

[c. 1915, 1919]

HANDS

Upon the half decayed veranda of a small frame house that stood near the edge of a ravine near the town of Winesburg, Ohio, a fat little old man walked nervously up and down. Across a long field that had been seeded for clover but that had produced only a dense crop of yellow mustard weeds, he could see the public highway along which went a wagon filled with berry pickers returning from the fields. The berry pickers, youths and maidens, laughed and shouted boisterously. A boy clad in a blue shirt leaped from the wagon and attempted to drag after him one of the maidens, who screamed and protested shrilly. The feet of the boy in the road kicked up a cloud of dust that floated across the face of the departing sun. Over the long field came a thin girlish voice. "Oh, you Wing Biddlebaum, comb your hair, it's falling into your eyes," commanded the voice to the man, who was bald and whose nervous little hands fiddled about the bare white forehead as though arranging a mass of tangled locks.

Wing Biddlebaum, forever frightened and beset by a ghostly band of doubts, did not think of himself as in any way a part of the life of the town where he had lived for twenty years. Among all the people of Winesburg but one had come close to him. With George Willard, son of Tom Willard, the proprietor of the New Willard House, he had formed something like a friendship. George Willard was the reporter on the *Winesburg Eagle* and sometimes in the evenings he walked out along the highway to Wing Biddlebaum's house. Now as the old man walked up and down on the veranda, his hands moving nervously about, he was hoping that George Willard would come and spend the evening with him. After the wagon containing the berry pickers had passed, he went across the field through the tall mustard weeds and climbing a rail fence peered anxiously along the road to the town. For a moment he stood thus, rubbing his hands together and looking up and down the road, and then, fear overcoming him, ran back to walk again upon the porch on his own house.

In the presence of George Willard, Wing Biddlebaum, who for twenty years had been the town mystery, lost something of his timidity, and his shadowy personality, submerged in a sea of doubts, came forth to look at the world. With the young reporter at his side, he ventured in the light of day into Main Street or strode up and down on the rickety front porch of his own house, talking excitedly. The voice that had been low and trembling became shrill and loud. The bent figure straightened. With a kind of wriggle, like a fish returned to the brook by the fisherman, Biddlebaum the silent began to talk, striving to put into words the ideas that had been accumulated by his mind during long years of silence.

Wing Biddlebaum talked much with his hands. The slender expressive fingers, forever active, forever striving to conceal themselves in his pockets or behind his back, came forth and became the piston rods of his machinery of expression.

The story of Wing Biddlebaum is a story of hands. Their restless activity, like unto the beating of the wings of an imprisoned bird, had given him his name. Some obscure poet of the town had thought of it. The hand alarmed their owner. He wanted to keep them hidden away and looked with amazement at the quiet inexpressive hands of other men who worked beside him in the fields, or passed, driving sleepy teams on country roads.

When he talked to George Willard, Wing Biddlebaum closed his fists and beat with them upon a table or on the walls of his house. The action made him more comfortable. If the desire to talk came to him when the two were walking in the fields, he sought out a stump or the top board of a fence and with his hands pounding busily talked with renewed ease.

The story of Wing Biddlebaum's hands is worth a book in itself. Sympathetically set forth it would tap many strange, beautiful qualities in obscure men. It is a job for a poet. In Winesburg the hands had attracted attention merely because of their activity. With them Wing Biddlebaum had picked as high as a hundred and forty quarts of strawberries in a day. They became his distinguishing feature, the source of his fame. Also they made more grotesque an already grotesque and elusive individuality. Winesburg was proud of the hands of Wing Biddlebaum in the same spirit in which it was proud of Banker White's new stone house and Wesley Moyer's bay stallion, Tony Tip, that had won the two-fifteen trot at the fall races in Cleveland.

As for George Willard, he had many times wanted to ask about the hands. At times an almost overwhelming curiosity had taken hold of him. He felt that there must be a reason for their strange activity and their inclination to keep hidden away and only a growing respect for Wing Biddlebaum kept him from blurting out the questions that were often in his mind.

Once he had been on the point of asking. The two were walking in the fields on a summer afternoon and had stopped to sit upon a grassy bank. All afternoon Wing Biddlebaum had talked as one inspired. By a fence he had stopped and beating like a giant woodpecker upon the top board had shouted at George Willard, condemning his tendency to be too much influenced by the people about him. "You are destroying yourself," he cried. "You have the inclination to be alone and to dream and you are afraid of dreams. You want to be like others in town here. You hear them talk and you try to imitate them."

On the grassy bank Wing Biddlebaum had tried again to drive his point home. His voice became soft and reminiscent, and with a sigh of contentment he launched into a long rambling talk, speaking as one lost in a dream.

Out of the dream Wing Biddlebaum made a picture for George Willard. In the picture men lived again in a kind of pastoral golden age. Across a green open country came clean-limbed young men, some afoot, some mounted upon horses. In crowds the young men came to gather about the feet of an old man who sat beneath a tree in a tiny garden and who talked to them.

Wing Biddlebaum became wholly inspired. For once he forgot the hands. Slowly they stole forth and lay upon George Willard's shoulders. Something new and bold came into the voice that talked. "You must try to forget all you have learned," said the old man. "You must begin to dream. From this time on you must shut your ears to the roaring of the voices."

Pausing in his speech, Wing Biddlebaum looked long and earnestly at George Willard. His eyes glowed. Again he raised the hands to caress the boy and then a look of horror swept over his face.

With a convulsive movement of his body, Wing Biddlebaum sprang to his feet and thrust his hands deep into his trousers pockets. Tears came to his eyes, "I must be getting along home. I can talk no more with you," he said nervously.

Without looking back, the old man had hurried down the hillside and across a meadow, leaving George Willard perplexed and frightened upon the grassy slope. With a shiver of dread the boy arose and went along the road toward town. "I'll not ask him about his hands," he thought, touched by the memory of the terror he had seen in the man's eyes. "There's something wrong, but I don't want to know what it is. His hands have something to do with his fear of me and of everyone."

And George Willard was right. Let us look briefly into the story of the hands. Perhaps our talking of them will arouse the poet who will tell the hidden wonder story of the influence for which the hands were but fluttering pennants of promise.

In his youth Wing Biddlebaum had been a school teacher in a town in Pennsylvania. He was not then known as Wing Biddlebaum, but went by the less euphonic name of Adolph Myers. As Adolph Myers he was much loved by the boys of his school.

Adolph Myers was meant by nature to be a teacher of youth. He was one of those rare, little-understood men who rule by a power so gentle that it passes as a lovable weakness. In their feeling for the boys under their charge such men are not unlike the finer sort of women in their love of men.

And yet that is but crudely stated. It needs the poet there. With the boys of his school, Adolph Myers had walked in the evening or had sat talking until dusk upon the schoolhouse steps lost in a kind of dream. Here and there went his hands, caressing the shoulders of the boys, playing about the tousled heads. As he talked his voice became soft and musical. There was a caress in that also. In a way the voice and the hands, the stroking of the shoulders and the touching of the hair were a part of the schoolmaster's effort to carry a dream into the young minds. By the caress that was in his fingers he expressed himself. He was one of those men in whom the force that creates life is diffused, not centralized. Under the caress of his hands doubt and disbelief went out of the minds of the boys and they began also to dream.

And then the tragedy. A half-witted boy of the school became enamored of the young master. In his bed at night he imagined unspeakable things and in the morning went forth to tell his dreams as facts. Strange, hideous accusations fell from his loose-hung lips. Through the Pennsylvania town went a shiver. Hidden, shadowy doubts that had been in men's minds concerning Adolph Myers were galvanized into beliefs.

The tragedy did not linger. Trembling lads were jerked out of bed and questioned. "He put his arms about me," said one. "His fingers were always playing in my hair," said another.

One afternoon a man of the town, Henry Bradford, who kept a saloon, came to the schoolhouse door. Calling Adolph Myers into the school yard he began to beat him with his fists. As his hard knuckles beat down into the frightened face of the schoolmaster, his wrath became more and more terrible. Screaming with dismay, the children ran here and there like disturbed insects. "I'll teach you to put your hands on my boy, you beast," roared the saloon keeper, who, tired of beating the master, had begun to kick him about the yard.

Adolph Myers was driven from the Pennsylvania town in the night. With lanterns in their hands a dozen men came to the door of the house where he lived alone and commanded that he dress and come forth. It was raining and one of the men had a rope in his hands. They had intended to hang the schoolmaster, but something in his figure, so small, white, and pitiful, touched their hearts and they let him escape. As he ran away into the darkness they repented of their weakness and ran after him, swearing and throwing sticks and great balls of soft mud at the figure that screamed and ran faster and faster into the darkness.

For twenty years Adolph Myers had lived alone in Winesburg. He was but forty but looked sixty-five. The name of Biddlebaum he got from a box of goods seen at a freight station as he hurried through an eastern Ohio town. He had an aunt in Winesburg, a black-toothed old woman who raised chickens, and with her he lived until she died. He had been ill for a year after the experience in Pennsylvania, and after his recovery worked as a day laborer in the fields, going timidly about and striving to conceal his hands. Although he did not understand what had happened he felt that the hands must be to blame. Again and again the fathers of the boys had talked of the hands. "Keep your hands to yourself," the saloon keeper had roared, dancing with fury in the schoolhouse yard.

Upon the veranda of his house by the ravine, Wing Biddlebaum continued to walk up and down until the sun had disappeared and the road beyond the field was lost in the grey shadows. Going into his house he cut slices of bread and spread honey upon them. When the rumble of the evening train that took away the express cars loaded with the day's harvest of berries had passed and restored the silence of the summer night, he went again to walk upon the veranda. In the darkness he could not see the hands and they became quiet. Although he still hungered for the presence of the boy, who was the medium through which he expressed his love of man, the hunger became again a part of his loneliness and his waiting. Lighting a lamp, Wing Biddlebaum washed the few dishes soiled by his simple meal and, setting up a folding cot by the screen door that led to the porch, prepared to undress for the night. A few stray white bread crumbs lay on the cleanly washed floor by the table; putting the lamp upon a low stool he began to pick up the crumbs, carrying them to his mouth one by one with unbelievable rapidity. In the dense blotch of light beneath the table, the kneeling figure looked like a priest engaged in some service of his church. The nervous expressive fingers, flashing in and out of the light, might well have been mistaken for the fingers of the devotee going swiftly through decade after decade of his rosary.

[1916, 1919]

PAPER PILLS

He was an old man with a white beard and huge nose and hands. Long before the time during which we will know him, he was a doctor and drove a jaded white horse from house to house through the streets of Winesburg. Later he married a girl who had money. She had been left a large fertile farm when her father died. The girl was quiet, tall, and dark, and to many people she seemed very beautiful. Everyone in Winesburg wondered why she married the doctor. Within a year after the marriage she died.

The knuckles of the doctor's hands were extraordinarily large. When the hands were closed they looked like clusters of unpainted wooden balls as large as walnuts fastened together by steel rods. He smoked a cob pipe and after his wife's death sat all day in his empty office close by a window that was covered with cobwebs. He never opened the window. Once on a hot day in August he tried but found it stuck fast and after that he forgot all about it.

Winesburg had forgotten the old man, but in Doctor Reefy there were the seeds of something very fine. Alone in his musty office in the Heffner Block above the Paris Dry Goods Company's store, he worked ceaselessly, building up something that he himself destroyed. Little pyramids of truth he erected and after erecting knocked them down again that he might have the truths to erect other pyramids.

Doctor Reefy was a tall man who had worn one suit of clothes for ten years. It was frayed at the sleeves and little holes had appeared at the knees and elbows. In the office he wore also a linen duster with huge pockets into which he continually stuffed scraps of paper. After some weeks the scraps of paper became little hard round balls, and when the pockets were filled he dumped them out upon the floor. For ten years he had but one friend, another old man named John Spaniard who owned a tree nursery. Sometimes, in a playful mood, old Doctor Reefy took from his pockets a handful of the paper balls and threw them at the nursery man. "That is to confound you, you blithering old sentimentalist," he cried, shaking with laughter.

The story of Doctor Reefy and his courtship of the tall dark girl who became his wife and left her money to him is a very curious story. It is delicious, like the twisted little apples that grow in the orchards of Winesburg. In the fall one walks in the orchards and the ground is hard with frost underfoot. The apples have been taken from the trees by the pickers. They have been put in barrels and shipped to the cities where they will be eaten in apartments that are filled with books, magazines, furniture, and people. On the trees are only a few gnarled apples that the pickers have rejected. They look like the knuckles of Doctor Reefy's hands. One nibbles at them and they are delicious. Into a little round place at the side of the apple has been gathered all of its sweetness. One runs from tree to tree over the frosted ground picking the gnarled, twisted apples and filling his pockets with them. Only the few know the sweetness of the twisted apples.

The girl and Doctor Reefy began their courtship on a summer afternoon. He was forty-five then and already he had begun the practice of filling his pockets with the scraps of paper that became hard balls and were thrown away. The habit had been formed as he sat in his buggy behind the jaded white horse and went slowly along country roads. On the papers were written thoughts, ends of thoughts, beginnings of thoughts.

One by one the mind of Doctor Reefy had made the thoughts. Out of many of them he formed a truth that arose gigantic in his mind. The truth clouded the world. It became terrible and then faded away and the little thoughts began again.

The tall dark girl came to see Doctor Reefy because she was in the family way and had become frightened. She was in that condition because of a series of circumstances also curious.

The death of her father and mother and the rich acres of land that had come down to her had set a train of suitors on her heels. For two years she saw suitors almost every evening. Except two they were all alike. They talked to her of passion and there was a strained eager quality in their voices and in their eyes when they looked at her. The two who were different were much unlike each other. One of them, a slender young man with white hands, the son of a jeweler in Winesburg, talked continually of virginity. When he was with her he was never off the subject. The other, a black-haired boy with large ears, said nothing at all but always managed to get her into the darkness, where he began to kiss her.

For a time the tall dark girl thought she would marry the jeweler's son. For hours she sat in silence listening as he talked to her and then she began to be afraid of something. Beneath his talk of virginity she began to think there was a lust greater than in all the others. At times it seemed to her that as he talked he was holding her body in his hands. She imagined him turning it slowly about in the white hands and staring at it. At night she dreamed that he had bitten into her body and that his jaws were dripping. She had the dream three times, then she became in the family way to the one who said nothing at all but who in the moment of his passion actually did bite her shoulder so that for days the marks of his teeth showed.

After the tall dark girl came to know Doctor Reefy it seemed to her that she never wanted to leave him again. She went into his office one morning and without her saying anything he seemed to know what had happened to her.

In the office of the doctor there was a woman, the wife of the man who kept the book-store in Winesburg. Like all old-fashioned country practitioners, Doctor Reefy pulled teeth, and the woman who waited held a handkerchief to her teeth and groaned. Her husband was with her and when the tooth was taken out they both screamed and blood ran down on the woman's white dress. The tall dark girl did not pay any attention. When the woman and the man had gone the doctor smiled. "I will take you driving into the country with me," he said.

For several weeks the tall dark girl and the doctor were together almost every day. The condition that had brought her to him passed in an illness, but she was like one who has discovered the sweetness of the twisted apples, she could not get her mind fixed again upon the round perfect fruit that is eaten in the city apartments. In the fall after the beginning of her acquaintanceship with him she married Doctor Reefy and in the following spring she died. During the winter he read to her all of the odds and ends of thoughts he had scribbled on the bits of paper. After he had read them he laughed and stuffed them away in his pockets to become round hard balls.

[1916, 1919]

Katherine Anne Porter

[1890–1980]

Katherine Anne Porter was born Callista Russell Porter on May 15, 1890, in a two-room cabin in Indian Creek, a small community in central Texas. She was the fourth child of Harrison Porter, a farmer, and Mary Alice Jones Porter, a former schoolteacher. Although Porter's parents were well educated by the standards of the time, they were very poor. After Porter's mother died in 1892, the family went to live with her paternal grandmother, Catherine Porter, in her small house in Kyle, Texas, between Austin and San Marcos. As a young girl, Porter loved reading and listening to her grandmother's fascinating tales about the early days in Texas. When Catherine Porter died in 1901, the family moved on to San Antonio. Porter received the last of her formal education during a year at the Thomas School, a private girls' school where she studied singing, elocution, and acting. Along with her father and one of her sisters, Porter then moved again, this time to Victoria. There, she taught music and the dramatic arts and met the first of her four husbands, a railroad clerk named John Henry Koontz, whom Porter married in 1906, a month after her sixteenth birthday. Influenced by her husband's family, Porter converted from Methodism to Roman Catholicism. But she was increasingly unhappy, and she abruptly left Koontz in 1913 and went to Chicago. At the time of her divorce in 1915, she changed her legal name to Katherine Anne Porter.

Katherine Anne Porter
The prominent fashion and portrait photographer George Platt Lynes look this photograph of Porter in 1933, three years after the publication of her first book, *Flowering Judas and Other Stories.*

Porter soon began a career as a journalist and writer. After struggling to support herself in Chicago, where she had hoped to break into the movies, she returned to Texas. Ill and exhausted, she was diagnosed with tuberculosis late in 1915. During her recovery at a sanitarium, from which she was released in September 1917, she met a newspaperwoman who helped Porter get a job as a reporter for the Fort Worth *Critic.* For the next two years, she worked for that newspaper and as a columnist and drama critic for the *Rocky Mountain News* in Denver, Colorado. Determined to launch her literary career, late in 1919 she moved to New York City and settled happily into the vital artistic community of Greenwich Village. While she supported herself by working in the publicity department of a movie company, Porter began to write short stories, three of which were published in *Everyland,* a magazine sponsored by the Interchurch World Movement. She also met several Mexican artists, who helped Porter get a job with the *Magazine of Mexico,* an American-backed promotional magazine that sent her on assignment to Mexico City. During the first of her several extended visits to Mexico, she became actively involved in the educational and cultural reforms undertaken in the turbulent wake of the Mexican Revolution of 1910–17. Suspected by the government of being a Bolshevik and threatened with deportation, Porter left in June 1921 and returned to New York City, where she began to write about Mexico. Some of her essays appeared in the *Christian Science Monitor,* and her first major story, "María Concepción," was published in the *Century* in December 1922.

During the remainder of the 1920s and throughout the 1930s, Porter continued what she described as her "nomadic" life, even as she firmly established herself as a master of short fiction. She went back to Mexico to help organize a traveling exhibit of folk art and later to research and write articles on the country for a special issue of the magazine *Survey Graphic,* published in May 1924. Sensitized to social injustices by her experiences in Mexico, Porter also became associated with radicals and left-wing causes after she returned to the United States. In 1926, she married but soon separated from the English painter Ernest Stock. During the late 1920s, most of Porter's writings were book reviews, though she tried her hand at poetry and worked on a biography of the Puritan minister Cotton Mather. She also wrote several short stories, and some of her influential literary friends in New York City finally convinced Harcourt Brace to publish her first book, *Flowering Judas and Other Stories* (1930). Although it was published in a limited edition of six hundred copies and earned Porter only $100 in royalties, the collection made her reputation. Its publication also marked the beginning of her most productive decade as a writer. Porter went to Mexico to work on a novel, and in 1931 she sailed from Vera Cruz to Bremen, Germany, accompanied by her third husband, the writer Eugene Pressley. They lived for a time in Berlin, where Porter witnessed with alarm the rise of Nazism, and then settled in Paris. After they returned to the United States in 1936, she divorced Pressley and married a young graduate student, Albert Erskine. The marriage was a fiasco, and they separated in 1938. In the midst of the chaos in her personal life, Porter wrote a series of autobiographical stories based on her early years in Texas, including the three novellas in her acclaimed collection *Pale Horse, Pale Rider* (1939).

The remainder of Porter's career was punctuated by a series of awards, honors, and literary successes. In 1944, the year she published *The Leaning Tower and Other Stories,* she was appointed to the prestigious Chair of Poetry and Literature at the Library of Congress. She later taught at Stanford and the University of Michigan. Still restlessly moving from place to place, she continued to work on a novel based in part on the log she wrote during her 1931 voyage to Germany, which was finally published as *Ship of Fools* in 1962. The reviews were generally enthusiastic, and Porter earned a million dollars from royalties and the film rights purchased by United Artists. *The Collected Stories of Katherine Anne Porter* (1965) was awarded the Pulitzer Prize for Fiction. In failing health, Porter wrote little and was increasingly reclusive in the years before her death at the age of ninety, on September 18, 1980.

Most good stories are about the interior of our lives, but Katherine Anne Porter's stories take place there.

—Eudora Welty

Porter's "Flowering Judas."   Explaining why she selected this story to represent her work in an anthology of American writing edited by Whit Burnett, *This Is My Best* (1942), Porter observed that she wrote it in one sitting "between seven o'clock and midnight of a very cold December, 1929, in Brooklyn." She added that the central character in "Flowering Judas," one of several stories inspired by Porter's experiences in Mexico during the 1920s, was based on an American schoolteacher friend whom she had once observed being serenaded by a Mexican labor leader: "In that glimpse, no more than a flash, I thought I understood, or perceived for the first time, the desperate complication of her mind and feelings, and I knew a story; perhaps not her true story, not even the real story of the whole situation, but all the same a story that seemed symbolic truth to me." Porter immediately sent the story to *Hound and Horn*, a distinguished literary magazine that published the works of several avant-garde writers such as Gertrude Stein, Ezra Pound, and T. S. Eliot. "Flowering Judas" appeared in the June–July 1930 issue of the magazine, and Porter then made it the title story of the collection that made her reputation, *Flowering Judas and Other Stories* (1930).

bedfordstmartins.com/ americanlit for research links on Porter

FLOWERING JUDAS[1]

Braggioni sits heaped upon the edge of a straight-backed chair much too small for him, and sings to Laura in a furry, mournful voice. Laura has begun to find reasons for avoiding her own house until the latest possible moment, for Braggioni is there almost every night. No matter how late she is, he will be sitting there with a surly, waiting expression, pulling at his kinky yellow hair, thumbing the strings of his guitar, snarling a tune under his breath. Lupe the Indian maid meets Laura at the door, and says with a flicker of a glance towards the upper room, "He waits."

Laura wishes to lie down, she is tired of her hairpins and the feel of her long tight sleeves, but she says to him, "Have you a new song for me this evening?" If he says yes, she asks him to sing it. If he says no, she remembers his favorite one, and asks him to sing it again. Lupe brings her a cup of chocolate and a plate of rice, and Laura eats at the small table under the lamp, first inviting Braggioni, whose answer is always the same: "I have eaten, and besides, chocolate thickens the voice."

Laura says, "Sing, then," and Braggioni heaves himself into song. He scratches the guitar familiarly as though it were a pet animal, and sings passionately off key, taking

---

1. **Flowering Judas:** A small tree native to the eastern Mediterranean, commonly known as the redbud or Judas tree. According to legend, it got its name because Judas Iscariot hanged himself on the tree after he betrayed Jesus. In various versions of the legend, the white flowers of the tree consequently turned red with shame or blood or because the tree became the body of Judas, who was said to have red hair. Porter took the title from and drew upon the imagery of T. S. Eliot's "Gerontion" (1920), a poem in which he evoked the apathy, inertia, and sterility of Europe in the aftermath of World War I: "In the juvescence of the year / Came Christ the tiger / In depraved May, dogwood and chestnut, flowering judas, / To be eaten, to be divided, to be drunk / Among whispers."

the high notes in a prolonged painful squeal. Laura, who haunts the markets listening to the ballad singers, and stops every day to hear the blind boy playing his reed-flute in Sixteenth of September Street,[2] listens to Braggioni with pitiless courtesy, because she dares not smile at his miserable performance. Nobody dares to smile at him. Braggioni is cruel to everyone, with a kind of specialized insolence, but he is so vain of his talents, and so sensitive to slights, it would require a cruelty and vanity greater than his own to lay a finger on the vast cureless wound of his self-esteem. It would require courage, too, for it is dangerous to offend him, and nobody has this courage.

Braggioni loves himself with such tenderness and amplitude and eternal charity that his followers — for he is a leader of men, a skilled revolutionist, and his skin has been punctured in honorable warfare — warm themselves in the reflected glow, and say to each other: "He has a real nobility, a love of humanity raised above mere personal affections." The excess of this self-love has flowed out, inconveniently for her, over Laura, who, with so many others, owes her comfortable situation and her salary to him. When he is in a very good humor, he tells her, "I am tempted to forgive you for being a *gringa. Gringita!*"[3] and Laura, burning, imagines herself leaning forward suddenly, and with a sound back-handed slap wiping the suety smile from his face. If he notices her eyes at these moments he gives no sign.

She knows what Braggioni would offer her, and she must resist tenaciously without appearing to resist, and if she could avoid it she would not admit even to herself the slow drift of his intention. During these long evenings which have spoiled a long month for her, she sits in her deep chair with an open book on her knees, resting her eyes on the consoling rigidity of the printed page when the sight and sound of Braggioni singing threaten to identify themselves with all her remembered afflictions and to add their weight to her uneasy premonitions of the future. The gluttonous bulk of Braggioni has become a symbol of her many disillusions, for a revolutionist should be lean, animated by heroic faith, a vessel of abstract virtues. This is nonsense, she knows it now and is ashamed of it. Revolution must have leaders, and leadership is a career for energetic men. She is, her comrades tell her, full of romantic error, for what she defines as cynicism in them is merely "a developed sense of reality." She is almost too willing to say, "I am wrong, I suppose I don't really understand the principles," and afterward she makes a secret truce with herself, determined not to surrender her will to such expedient logic. But she cannot help feeling that she has been betrayed irreparably by the disunion between her way of living and her feeling of what life should be, and at times she is almost contented to rest in this sense of grievance as a private store of consolation. Sometimes she wishes to run away, but she stays. Now she longs to fly out of this room, down the narrow stairs, and into the street where the houses lean together like conspirators under a single mottled lamp, and leave Braggioni singing to himself.

---

2. **Sixteenth of September Street:** This street in Morelia, Mexico, where the story is set, is named after Mexican Independence Day, commemorating the beginning of the ten-year war for independence from Spain on September 16, 1810.

3. *gringa. Gringita!*: Negative terms for non-Mexican females, especially Americans. The form *gringita* is used for a young girl, while *gringa* is used for a woman.

Instead she looks at Braggioni, frankly and clearly, like a good child who understands the rules of behavior. Her knees cling together under sound blue serge, and her round white collar is not purposely nun-like. She wears the uniform of an idea, and has renounced vanities. She was born Roman Catholic, and in spite of her fear of being seen by someone who might make a scandal of it, she slips now and again into some crumbling little church, kneels on the chilly stone, and says a Hail Mary on the gold rosary she bought in Tehuantepec. It is no good and she ends by examining the altar with its tinsel flowers and ragged brocades, and feels tender about the battered doll-shape of some male saint whose white, lace-trimmed drawers hang limply around his ankles below the hieratic dignity of his velvet robe. She has encased herself in a set of principles derived from her early training, leaving no detail of gesture or of personal taste untouched, and for this reason she will not wear lace made on machines. This is her private heresy, for in her special group the machine is sacred, and will be the salvation of the workers. She loves fine lace, and there is a tiny edge of fluted cobweb on this collar, which is one of twenty precisely alike, folded in blue tissue paper in the upper drawer of her clothes chest.

Braggioni catches her glance solidly as if he had been waiting for it, leans forward, balancing his paunch between his spread knees, and sings with tremendous emphasis, weighing his words. He has, the song relates, no father and no mother, nor even a friend to console him; lonely as a wave of the sea he comes and goes, lonely as a wave. His mouth opens round and yearns sideways, his balloon cheeks grow oily with the labor of song. He bulges marvelously in his expensive garments. Over his lavender collar, crushed upon a purple necktie, held by a diamond hoop: over his ammunition belt of tooled leather worked in silver, buckled cruelly around his gasping middle: over the tops of his glossy yellow shoes Braggioni swells with ominous ripeness, his mauve silk hose stretched taut, his ankles bound with the stout leather thongs of his shoes.

When he stretches his eyelids at Laura she notes again that his eyes are the true tawny yellow cat's eyes. He is rich, not in money, he tells her, but in power, and this power brings with it the blameless ownership of things, and the right to indulge his love of small luxuries. "I have a taste for the elegant refinements," he said once, flourishing a yellow silk handkerchief before her nose. "Smell that? It is Jockey Club, imported from New York." Nonetheless he is wounded by life. He will say so presently. "It is true everything turns to dust in the hand, to gall on the tongue." He sighs and his leather belt creaks like a saddle girth. "I am disappointed in everything as it comes. Everything." He shakes his head. "You, poor thing, you will be disappointed too. You are born for it. We are more alike than you realize in some things. Wait and see. Some day you will remember what I have told you, you will know that Braggioni was your friend."

Laura feels a slow chill, a purely physical sense of danger, a warning in her blood that violence, mutilation, a shocking death, wait for her with lessening patience. She has translated this fear into something homely, immediate, and sometimes hesitates before crossing the street. "My personal fate is nothing, except as the testimony of a mental attitude," she reminds herself, quoting from some forgotten philosophic primer, and is sensible enough to add, "Anyhow, I shall not be killed by an automobile if I can help it."

"It may be true I am as corrupt, in another way, as Braggioni," she thinks in spite of herself, "as callous, as incomplete," and if this is so, any kind of death seems preferable. Still she sits quietly, she does not run. Where could she go? Uninvited she has promised herself to this place; she can no longer imagine herself as living in another country, and there is no pleasure in remembering her life before she came here.

Precisely what is the nature of this devotion, its true motives, and what are its obligations? Laura cannot say. She spends part of her days in Xochimilco, near by, teaching Indian children to say in English, "The cat is on the mat." When she appears in the classroom they crowd about her with smiles on their wise, innocent, clay-colored faces, crying, "Good morning, my titcher!" in immaculate voices, and they make of her desk a fresh garden of flowers every day.

During her leisure she goes to union meetings and listens to busy important voices quarreling over tactics, methods, internal politics. She visits the prisoners of her own political faith in their cells, where they entertain themselves with counting cockroaches, repenting of their indiscretions, composing their memoirs, writing out manifestoes and plans for their comrades who are still walking about free, hands in pockets, sniffing fresh air. Laura brings them food and cigarettes and a little money, and she brings messages disguised in equivocal phrases from the men outside who dare not set foot in the prison for fear of disappearing into the cells kept empty for them. If the prisoners confuse night and day, and complain, "Dear little Laura, time doesn't pass in this infernal hole, and I won't know when it is time to sleep unless I have a reminder," she brings them their favorite narcotics, and says in a tone that does not wound them with pity, "Tonight will really be night for you," and though her Spanish amuses them, they find her comforting, useful. If they lose patience and all faith, and curse the slowness of their friends in coming to their rescue with money and influence, they trust her not to repeat everything, and if she inquires, "Where do you think we can find money, or influence?" they are certain to answer, "Well, there is Braggioni, why doesn't he do something?"

She smuggles letters from headquarters to men hiding from firing squads in back streets in mildewed houses, where they sit in tumbled beds and talk bitterly as if all Mexico were at their heels, when Laura knows positively they might appear at the band concert in the Alameda[4] on Sunday morning, and no one would notice them. But Braggioni says, "Let them sweat a little. The next time they may be careful. It is very restful to have them out of the way for a while." She is not afraid to knock on any door in any street after midnight, and enter in the darkness, and say to one of these men who is really in danger: "They will be looking for you — seriously — tomorrow morning after six. Here is some money from Vicente. Go to Vera Cruz and wait."

She borrows money from the Roumanian agitator to give to his bitter enemy the Polish agitator. The favor of Braggioni is their disputed territory, and Braggioni holds the balance nicely, for he can use them both. The Polish agitator talks love to her over café tables, hoping to exploit what he believes is her secret sentimental preference for him,

---

4. **Alameda:** A term used in Spanish-speaking countries for a public walkway shaded with trees.

and he gives her misinformation which he begs her to repeat as the solemn truth to certain persons. The Roumanian is more adroit. He is generous with his money in all good causes, and lies to her with an air of ingenuous candor, as if he were her good friend and confidant. She never repeats anything they may say. Braggioni never asks questions. He has other ways to discover all that he wishes to know about them.

Nobody touches her, but all praise her gray eyes, and the soft, round under lip which promises gayety, yet is always grave, nearly always firmly closed: and they cannot understand why she is in Mexico. She walks back and forth on her errands, with puzzled eyebrows, carrying her little folder of drawings and music and school papers. No dancer dances more beautifully than Laura walks, and she inspires some amusing, unexpected ardors, which cause little gossip, because nothing comes of them. A young captain who had been a soldier in Zapata's army[5] attempted, during a horseback ride near Cuernavaca, to express his desire for her with the noble simplicity befitting a rude folk-hero: but gently, because he was gentle. This gentleness was his defeat, for when he alighted, and removed her foot from the stirrup, and essayed to draw her down into his arms, her horse, ordinarily a tame one, shied fiercely, reared and plunged away. The young hero's horse careered blindly after his stable-mate, and the hero did not return to the hotel until rather late that evening. At breakfast he came to her table in full charro dress,[6] gray buckskin jacket and trousers with strings of silver buttons down the leg, and he was in a humorous, careless mood. "May I sit with you?" and "You are a wonderful rider. I was terrified that you might be thrown and dragged. I should never have forgiven myself. But I cannot admire you enough for your riding!"

"I learned to ride in Arizona," said Laura.

"If you will ride with me again this morning, I promise you a horse that will not shy with you," he said. But Laura remembered that she must return to Mexico City at noon.

Next morning the children made a celebration and spent their playtime writing on the blackboard, "We lov ar ticher," and with tinted chalks they drew wreaths of flowers around the words. The young hero wrote her a letter: "I am a very foolish, wasteful, impulsive man. I should have first said I love you, and then you would not have run away. But you shall see me again." Laura thought, "I must send him a box of colored crayons," but she was trying to forgive herself for having spurred her horse at the wrong moment.

A brown, shock-haired youth came and stood in her patio one night and sang like a lost soul for two hours, but Laura could think of nothing to do about it. The moonlight spread a wash of gauzy silver over the clear spaces of the garden, and the shadows were cobalt blue. The scarlet blossoms of the Judas tree were dull purple, and the names of the colors repeated themselves automatically in her mind, while she watched not the boy, but his shadow, fallen like a dark garment across the fountain rim, trailing in the water. Lupe came silently and whispered expert counsel in her ear: "If you will throw him one little flower, he will sing another song or two and go away." Laura threw the flower, and

---

5. **Zapata's army:** The war hero General Emiliano Zapata (1879-1919), a leader of the Mexican Revolution who championed the cause of peasants against the regime of the dictator Porfirio Díaz.
6. **charro dress:** The traditional dress of a Mexican horseman or cowboy.

he sang a last song and went away with the flower tucked in the band of his hat. Lupe said, "He is one of the organizers of the Typographers Union,[7] and before that he sold corridos[8] in the Merced market, and before that, he came from Guanajuato, where I was born. I would not trust any man, but I trust least those from Guanajuato."

She did not tell Laura that he would be back again the next night, and the next, nor that he would follow her at a certain fixed distance around the Merced market, through the Zócolo, up Francisco I. Madero Avenue, and so along the Paseo de la Reforma to Chapultepec Park, and into the Philosopher's Footpath, still with that flower withering in his hat, and an indivisible attention in his eyes.

Now Laura is accustomed to him, it means nothing except that he is nineteen years old and is observing a convention with all propriety, as though it were founded on a law of nature, which in the end it might well prove to be. He is beginning to write poems which he prints on a wooden press, and he leaves them stuck like handbills in her door. She is pleasantly disturbed by the abstract, unhurried watchfulness of his black eyes which will in time turn easily towards another object. She tells herself that throwing the flower was a mistake, for she is twenty-two years old and knows better; but she refuses to regret it, and persuades herself that her negation of all external events as they occur is a sign that she is gradually perfecting herself in the stoicism she strives to cultivate against that disaster she fears, though she cannot name it.

She is not at home in the world. Every day she teaches children who remain strangers to her, though she loves their tender round hands and their charming opportunist savagery. She knocks at unfamiliar doors not knowing whether a friend or a stranger shall answer, and even if a known face emerges from the sour gloom of that unknown interior, still it is the face of a stranger. No matter what this stranger says to her, nor what her message to him, the very cells of her flesh reject knowledge and kinship in one monotonous word. No. No. No. She draws her strength from this one holy talismanic word which does not suffer her to be led into evil. Denying everything, she may walk anywhere in safety, she looks at everything without amazement.

No, repeats this firm unchanging voice of her blood; and she looks at Braggioni without amazement. He is a great man, he wishes to impress this simple girl who covers her great round breasts with thick dark cloth, and who hides long, invaluably beautiful legs under a heavy skirt. She is almost thin except for the incomprehensible fullness of her breasts, like a nursing mother's, and Braggioni, who considers himself a judge of women, speculates again on the puzzle of her notorious virginity, and takes the liberty of speech which she permits without a sign of modesty, indeed, without any sort of sign, which is disconcerting.

"You think you are so cold, *gringita!* Wait and see. You will surprise yourself some day! May I be there to advise you!" He stretches his eyelids at her, and his ill-humored cat's eyes waver in a separate glance for the two points of light marking the opposite

---

7. **Typographers Union:** A labor union for workers involved in all aspects of the publishing business, part of the wider labor movement that coincided with the Mexican Revolution.
8. **corridos:** Popular songs (Spanish).

ends of a smoothly drawn path between the swollen curve of her breasts. He is not put off by that blue serge, nor by her resolutely fixed gaze. There is all the time in the world. His cheeks are bellying with the wind of song. "O girl with the dark eyes," he sings, and reconsiders. "But yours are not dark. I can change all that. O girl with the green eyes, you have stolen my heart away!" then his mind wanders to the song, and Laura feels the weight of his attention being shifted elsewhere. Singing thus, he seems harmless, he is quite harmless, there is nothing to do but sit patiently and say "No," when the moment comes. She draws a full breath, and her mind wanders also, but not far. She dares not wander too far.

Not for nothing has Braggioni taken pains to be a good revolutionist and a professional lover of humanity. He will never die of it. He has the malice, the cleverness, the wickedness, the sharpness of wit, the hardness of heart, stipulated for loving the world profitably. *He will never die of it.* He will live to see himself kicked out from his feeding trough by other hungry world-saviors. Traditionally he must sing in spite of his life which drives him to bloodshed, he tells Laura, for his father was a Tuscany peasant who drifted to Yucatan and married a Maya woman:[9] a woman of race, an aristocrat. They gave him the love and knowledge of music, thus: and under the rip of his thumbnail, the strings of the instrument complain like exposed nerves.

Once he was called Delgadito[10] by all the girls and married women who ran after him; he was so scrawny all his bones showed under his thin cotton clothing, and he could squeeze his emptiness to the very backbone with his two hands. He was a poet and the revolution was only a dream then; too many women loved him and sapped away his youth, and he could never find enough to eat anywhere, anywhere! Now he is a leader of men, crafty men who whisper in his ear, hungry men who wait for hours outside his office for a word with him, emaciated men with wild faces who waylay him at the street gate with a timid, "Comrade, let me tell you . . ." and they blow the foul breath from their empty stomachs in his face.

He is always sympathetic. He gives them handfuls of small coins from his own pocket, he promises them work, there will be demonstrations, they must join the unions and attend the meetings, above all they must be on the watch for spies. They are closer to him than his own brothers, without them he can do nothing — until tomorrow, comrade!

Until tomorrow. "They are stupid, they are lazy, they are treacherous, they would cut my throat for nothing," he says to Laura. He has good food and abundant drink, he hires an automobile and drives in the Paseo on Sunday morning, and enjoys plenty of sleep in a soft bed beside a wife who dares not disturb him; and he sits pampering his bones in easy billows of fat, singing to Laura, who knows and thinks these things about him. When he was fifteen, he tried to drown himself because he loved a girl, his first love, and she laughed at him. "A thousand women have paid for that," and his tight little mouth

---

9. **Tuscany peasant . . . Maya woman:** Tuscany is a region of central Italy. The Maya, ancient peoples of northern Central America, developed one of the most advanced and sophisticated civilizations of the pre-Columbian Americas.
10. **Delgadito:** Little Thin (Spanish).

turns down at the corners. Now he perfumes his hair with Jockey Club, and confides to Laura: "One woman is really as good as another for me, in the dark. I prefer them all."

His wife organizes unions among the girls in the cigarette factories, and walks in picket lines, and even speaks at meetings in the evening. But she cannot be brought to acknowledge the benefits of true liberty. "I tell her I must have my freedom, net. She does not understand my point of view." Laura has heard this many times. Braggioni scratches the guitar and meditates. "She is an instinctively virtuous woman, pure gold, no doubt of that. If she were not, I should lock her up, and she knows it."

His wife, who works so hard for the good of the factory girls, employs part of her leisure lying on the floor weeping because there are so many women in the world, and only one husband for her, and she never knows where nor when to look for him. He told her: "Unless you can learn to cry when I am not here, I must go away for good." That day he went away and took a room at the Hotel Madrid.

It is this month of separation for the sake of higher principles that has been spoiled not only for Mrs. Braggioni, whose sense of reality is beyond criticism, but for Laura, who feels herself bogged in a nightmare. Tonight Laura envies Mrs. Braggioni, who is alone, and free to weep as much as she pleases about a concrete wrong. Laura has just come from a visit to the prison, and she is waiting for tomorrow with a bitter anxiety as if tomorrow may not come, but time may be caught immovably in this hour, with herself transfixed, Braggioni singing on forever, and Eugenio's body not yet discovered by the guard.

Braggioni says: "Are you going to sleep?" Almost before she can shake her head, he begins telling her about the May-day disturbances coming on in Morelia, for the Catholics hold a festival in honor of the Blessed Virgin, and the Socialists celebrate their martyrs on that day. "There will be two independent processions, starting from either end of town, and they will march until they meet, and the rest depends . . ." He asks her to oil and load his pistols. Standing up, he unbuckles his ammunition belt, and spreads it laden across her knees. Laura sits with the shells slipping through the cleaning cloth dipped in oil, and he says again he cannot understand why she works so hard for the revolutionary idea unless she loves some man who is in it. "Are you not in love with someone?" "No," says Laura. "And no one is in love with you?" "No." "Then it is your own fault. No woman need go begging. Why, what is the matter with you? The legless beggar woman in the Alameda has a perfectly faithful lover. Did you know that?"

Laura peers down the pistol barrel and says nothing, but a long, slow faintness rises and subsides in her; Braggioni curves his swollen fingers around the throat of the guitar and softly smothers the music out of it, and when she hears him again he seems to have forgotten her, and is speaking in the hypnotic voice he uses when talking in small rooms to a listening, close-gathered crowd. Some day this world, now seemingly so composed and eternal, to the edges of every sea shall be merely a tangle of gaping trenches, of crashing walls and broken bodies. Everything must be torn from its accustomed place where it has rotted for centuries, hurled skyward and distributed, cast down again clean as rain, without separate identity. Nothing shall survive that the stiffened hands of poverty have created for the rich and no one shall be left alive except the elect spirits destined to procreate a new world cleansed of cruelty and injustice, ruled by benevolent anarchy: "Pistols are good, I love them, cannon are even better, but in the end I pin my faith to good dynamite," he concludes, and strokes the pistol lying in her hands. "Once I dreamed of destroying this city, in case it offered resistance to General Ortíz, but it fell into his hands like an over-ripe pear."

He is made restless by his own words, rises and stands waiting. Laura holds up the belt to him: "Put that on, and go kill somebody in Morelia, and you will be happier," she says softly. The presence of death in the room makes her bold. "Today, I found Eugenio going into a stupor. He refused to allow me to call the prison doctor. He had taken all the tablets I brought him yesterday. He said he took them because he was bored."

"He is a fool, and his death is his own business," says Braggioni, fastening his belt carefully.

"I told him if he had waited only a little while longer, you would have got him set free," says Laura. "He said he did not want to wait."

"He is a fool and we are well rid of him," says Braggioni, reaching for his hat.

He goes away. Laura knows his mood has changed, she will not see him any more for a while. He will send word when he needs her to go on errands into strange streets, to speak to the strange faces that will appear, like clay masks with the power of human speech, to mutter their thanks to Braggioni for his help. Now she is free, and she thinks, I must run while there is time. But she does not go.

Braggioni enters his own house where for a month his wife has spent many hours every night weeping and tangling her hair upon her pillow. She is weeping now, and she weeps more at the sight of him, the cause of all her sorrows. He looks about the room. Nothing is changed, the smells are good and familiar, he is well acquainted with the woman who comes toward him with no reproach except grief on her face. He says to her tenderly: "You are so good, please don't cry any more, you dear good creature." She says, "Are you tired, my angel? Sit here and I will wash your feet." She brings a bowl of water, and kneeling, unlaces his shoes, and when from her knees she raises her sad eyes under her blackened lids, he is sorry for everything, and bursts into tears. "Ah, yes, I am hungry, I am tired, let us eat something together," he says, between sobs. His wife leans her head on his arm and says, "Forgive me!" and this time he is refreshed by the solemn, endless rain of her tears.

Laura takes off her serge dress and puts on a white linen nightgown and goes to bed. She turns her head a little to one side, and lying still, reminds herself that it is time to sleep. Numbers tick in her brain like little clocks, soundless doors close of themselves around her. If you would sleep, you must not remember anything, the children will say tomorrow, good morning, my teacher, the poor prisoners who come every day bringing flowers to their jailer. 1-2-3-4-5 — it is monstrous to confuse love with revolution, night with day, life with death — ah, Eugenio!

The tolling of the midnight bell is a signal, but what does it mean? Get up, Laura, and follow me: come out of your sleep, out of your bed, out of this strange house. What are you doing in this house? Without a word, without fear she rose and reached for Eugenio's hand, but he eluded her with a sharp, sly smile and drifted away. This is not all, you shall see — Murderer, he said, follow me, I will show you a new country, but it is far away and we must hurry. No, said Laura, not unless you take my hand, no; and she clung first to the stair rail, and then to the topmost branch of the Judas tree that bent down slowly and set her upon the earth, and then to the rocky ledge of a cliff, and then to the jagged wave of a sea that was not water but a desert of crumbling stone. Where are you taking me, she asked in wonder but without fear. To death, and it is a long way off, and we must hurry, said Eugenio. No, said Laura, not unless you take my hand. Then eat these flowers, poor prisoner, said Eugenio in a voice of pity, take and eat: and from the Judas tree he stripped the warm bleeding flowers, and held them to her lips. She saw that his hand was fleshless, a cluster of small white petrified branches, and his eye sockets were without light, but she ate the flowers greedily for they satisfied both hunger and thirst. Murderer! said Eugenio, and Cannibal! This is my body and my blood. Laura cried No! and at the sound of her own voice, she awoke trembling, and was afraid to sleep again.

[1929, 1965]

Zora Neale Hurston

[1891–1960]

Zora Neale Hurston was born on January 7, 1891, in Notasulga, Alabama, the fifth child of John Hurston, a farmer and Baptist minister, and Lucy Ann Potts Hurston, a former schoolteacher. The family soon moved to Eatonville, Florida, the first incorporated all-black community in the United States. Describing her happy early life there, Hurston recalled: "Mama exhorted her children at every opportunity to 'jump at de sun.'" Hurston's childhood ended abruptly when her mother died in 1904. She was sent to school in Jacksonville and rarely saw her father, who married a woman Hurston disliked. Although she lived with relatives in Sanford, Florida, and later in Memphis, Tennessee, Hurston was essentially on her own. She worked as a domestic servant, and in 1915 she became a wardrobe girl in a touring company that performed the light operas of Gilbert and Sullivan. Hurston developed a deep love of music and theater before she left the company in Baltimore in 1917. She took high school courses at the Morgan Academy, graduated in 1918, and then enrolled at Howard University in Washington, D.C. Working as a manicurist and a waitress in order to pay for her tuition, Hurston majored in English and attended classes as she could afford them, from 1918 through 1924.

Zora Neale Hurston

Hurston's friend Carl Van Vechten took this photograph in 1934, the year she published her acclaimed first novel, *Jonah's Gourd Vine.*

Hurston was swept up in the excitement of the Harlem Renaissance. At Howard, she joined the staff of the student literary magazine, the *Stylus,* in which she published her first story in 1921. Through her work on the magazine, she came into contact with the poet Georgia Douglas Johnson. At Johnson's "S Street Salon," called by its regulars the "Saturday Nighters Club," Hurston met Sterling Brown, Jean Toomer, and James Weldon Johnson. Hurston's writing came to the attention of Charles S. Johnson, founder of *Opportunity: A Journal of Negro Life,* the new magazine of the National Urban League. Buoyed by the publication of her story "Drenched in Light" in the December 1924 issue of *Opportunity,* Hurston decided to become a writer and moved to New York City early in 1925. Later that year, her story "Spunk" appeared in *The New Negro,* the famous anthology edited by Alain Locke. At an awards dinner given by *Opportunity,* Hurston won two prizes and met an array of writers, including the young African American poets Countee Cullen and Langston Hughes and the influential white writers Carl Van Vechten and Fannie Hurst. Hurst offered her a job as a secretary, and another white writer, Annie Nathan Meyer, helped Hurston secure a scholarship to Barnard College, where she enrolled as the only black student in September 1926. Later that year, along with several of her friends, Hurston helped establish and contributed to a short-lived magazine, *Fire!! A Quarterly Devoted to Younger Negro Artists.*

Hurston began to pursue a dual career as a writer and an anthropologist. In 1927, she married Herbert Sheen, a physician and classmate from Howard, but they separated less than a year later. Meanwhile, she studied at Barnard with the distinguished anthropologist Franz Boas and did her first fieldwork in the South, a requirement for the degree in anthropology she earned in 1928. With the help of Boas, she was awarded a research fellowship to collect black folklore in the South and in the Bahamas. She published a scholarly article on her research, "Hoodoo in America," in the *Journal of American Folklore* (1931). She also wrote plays, including a collaboration with Langston Hughes, *Mule-Bone: A Comedy of Negro Life* (1931), and *The Great Day,* which was produced in New York in 1932. The following year, Hurston wrote her first novel, *Jonah's Gourd Vine* (1934), based on her family history in Florida. Even as she basked in the enthusiastic reviews of the novel, Hurston was awarded a fellowship from the Rosenwald Fund to do graduate work in anthropology at Columbia University, where she enrolled in January 1935. "Life has picked me up bodaciously and throwed me over the fence," she excitedly wrote to a friend. When the head of the Rosenwald Fund arbitrarily reduced her fellowship, the proud and independent Hurston stopped going to classes, but her reputation as an anthropologist was established by the publication of *Mules and Men* (1935), a study of African American dance, music, folklore, and religious practices in the South. On the strength of the work, Hurston was awarded a Guggenheim Fellowship, which she used to support her ethnographic research in Jamaica and Haiti. In addition to a book-length account of her work there, she wrote her best-selling and most famous novel, *Their Eyes Were Watching God* (1937).

During the final decades of her life, Hurston suffered both personal and

[T]he quality I feel is most characteristic of Zora's work [is] racial health — a sense of black people as complete, complex, undiminished human beings.

–Alice Walker

bedfordstmartins.com/
americanlit *for research
links on Hurston*

professional setbacks. She married twice, in 1939 and 1944, but neither union lasted more than a year. Disappointed by the reception of her ambitious novel *Moses, Man of the Mountain* (1939), Hurston later scored a major hit with her memoir *Dust Tracks on the Road* (1942). Despite her sudden celebrity and the demand for her work, she published only one more book, *Seraph on the Suwanee* (1948), a novel about a family of white southerners that received good reviews and sold well. Almost immediately after it was published, however, Hurston was falsely accused of molesting the troubled young son of a former landlady in New York. Although the charges were dropped when Hurston was able to prove that she had been out of the country when the alleged crime occurred, she was devastated by the sensational publicity and decided to leave New York and return permanently to Florida. She completed two more novels, both of which were rejected by her publisher, and then worked on a revisionist biography of King Herod the Great. After it was rejected by her publisher in 1955, Hurston wrote little, supporting herself by working as a maid, a librarian, and sometimes as a substitute teacher. She died in a county welfare home on January 28, 1960, and was buried in an unmarked grave in a segregated cemetery in Fort Pierce, Florida. In 1973, the African American novelist Alice Walker located the grave and erected a marker in Hurston's honor. Taking a line from Jean Toomer's poem "Georgia Dusk," Walker had the marker inscribed:

> Zora Neale Hurston
> "A Genius of the South"
> 1901 [sic]–1960
> Novelist, Folklorist
> Anthropologist

Hurston's "The Gilded Six-Bits."   Hurston, who had not published any fiction since 1926, wrote this story while she was living in her hometown of Eatonville, Florida, in 1933. She sent it to her friend Robert Wunch, a professor of English at nearby Rollins College, who liked it so much that he read it to his writing class and then sent it to *Story: The Magazine of the Short Story*. Founded in 1931 by two Americans living in Vienna, Austria, Whit Burnett and Martha Foley, the successful and influential magazine subsequently published short fiction by prominent writers such as William Faulkner, Langston Hughes, Katherine Anne Porter, Gertrude Stein, and William Carlos Williams. "The Gilded Six-Bits" was published in the magazine just after it moved to New York City. An account of infidelity and forgiveness set in Eatonville, "The Gilded Six-Bits" proved to be one of Hurston's most popular stories. It also represented a turning point in her career, since the publisher Bernard Lippincott was so impressed by the story that he asked Hurston if she were working on a novel. As a result, she immediately wrote her first novel, *Jonah's Gourd Vine* (1934), and Hurston thereafter devoted most of her efforts to writing fiction. The text is taken from the first printing in *Story*, August 1933.

THE GILDED SIX-BITS

It was a Negro yard around a Negro house in a Negro settlement that looked to the payroll of the G and G Fertilizer works for its support.

But there was something happy about the place. The front yard was parted in the middle by a sidewalk from gate to door-step, a sidewalk edged on either side by quart bottles driven neck down into the ground on a slant. A mess of homey flowers planted without a plan but blooming cheerily from their helter-skelter places. The fence and house were whitewashed. The porch and steps scrubbed white.

The front door stood open to the sunshine so that the floor of the front room could finish drying after its weekly scouring. It was Saturday. Everything clean from the front gate to the privy house. Yard raked so that the strokes of the rake would make a pattern. Fresh newspaper cut in fancy edge on the kitchen shelves.

Missie May was bathing herself in the galvanized washtub in the bedroom. Her dark-brown skin glistened under the soapsuds that skittered down from her wash rag. Her stiff young breasts thrust forward aggressively like broad-based cones with the tips lacquered in black.

She heard men's voices in the distance and glanced at the dollar clock on the dresser.

"Humph! Ah'm way behind time t'day! Joe gointer be heah 'fore Ah git mah clothes on if Ah don't make haste."

She grabbed the clean meal sack at hand and dried herself hurriedly and began to dress. But before she could tie her slippers, there came the ring of singing metal on wood. Nine times.

Missie May grinned with delight. She had not seen the big tall man come stealing in the gate and creep up the walk grinning happily at the joyful mischief he was about to commit. But she knew that it was her husband throwing silver dollars in the door for her to pick up and pile beside her plate at dinner. It was this way every Saturday afternoon. The nine dollars hurled into the open door, he scurried to a hiding place behind the cape jasmine bush and waited.

Missie May promptly appeared at the door in mock alarm.

"Who dat chunkin' money in mah do'way?" she demanded. No answer from the yard. She leaped off the porch and began to search the shrubbery. She peeped under the porch and hung over the gate to look up and down the road. While she did this, the man behind the jasmine darted to the china berry tree. She spied him and gave chase.

"Nobody ain't gointer be chunkin' money at me and Ah not do 'em nothin'," she shouted in mock anger. He ran around the house with Missie May at his heels. She overtook him at the kitchen door. He ran inside but could not close it after him before she crowded in and locked with him in a rough and tumble. For several minutes the two were a furious mass of male and female energy. Shouting, laughing, twisting, turning, tussling, tickling each other in the ribs; Missie May clutching onto Joe and Joe trying, but not too hard, to get away.

"Missie May, take yo' hand out mah pocket!" Joe shouted out between laughs.

"Ah ain't, Joe, not lessen you gwine gimme whateve' it is good you got in yo' pocket. Turn it go, Joe, do Ah'll tear yo' clothes."

"Go on tear 'em. You de one dat pushes de needles round heah. Move yo' hand Missie May."

"Lemme git dat paper sack out yo' pocket. Ah bet its candy kisses."

"Tain't. Move yo' hand. Woman ain't got no business in a man's clothes nohow. Go way."

Missie May gouged way down and gave an upward jerk and triumphed.

"Unhhunh! Ah got it. It 'tis so candy kisses. Ah knowed you had somethin' for me in yo' clothes. Now Ah got to see whut's in every pocket you got."

Joe smiled indulgently and let his wife go through all of his pockets and take out the things that he had hidden there for her to find. She bore off the chewing gum, the cake of sweet soap, the pocket handkerchief as if she had wrested them from him, as if they had not been bought for the sake of this friendly battle.

"Whew! dat play-fight done got me all warmed up." Joe exclaimed. "Got me some water in de kittle?"

"Yo' water is on de fire and yo' clean things is cross de bed. Hurry up and wash yo'self and git changed so we kin eat. Ah'm hongry." As Missie said this, she bore the steaming kettle into the bedroom.

"You ain't hongry, sugar," Joe contradicted her. "Youse jes' a little empty. Ah'm de one whut's hongry. Ah could eat up camp meetin', back off 'ssociation, and drink Jurdan dry.[1] Have it on de table when Ah git out de tub."

"Don't you mess wid mah business, man. You git in yo' clothes. Ah'm a real wife, not no dress and breath. Ah might not look lak one, but if you burn me, you won't git a thing but wife ashes."

Joe splashed in the bedroom and Missie May fanned around in the kitchen. A fresh red and white checked cloth on the table. Big pitcher of buttermilk beaded with pale drops of butter from the churn. Hot fried mullet, crackling bread, ham hock atop a mound of string beans and new potatoes, and perched on the window-sill a pone of spicy potato pudding.

Very little talk during the meal but that little consisted of banter that pretended to deny affection but in reality flaunted it. Like when Missie May reached for a second helping of the tater pone. Joe snatched it out of her reach.

After Missie May had made two or three unsuccessful grabs at the pan, she begged, "Aw, Joe gimme some mo' dat tater pone."

"Nope, sweetenin' is for us men-folks. Y'all pritty lil frail eels don't need nothin' lak dis. You too sweet already."

"Please, Joe."

"Naw, naw. Ah don't want you to git no sweeter than whut you is already. We goin' down de road a lil piece t'night so you go put on yo' Sunday go-to-meetin' things."

Missie May looked at her husband to see if he was playing some prank "Sho nuff, Joe?"

"Yeah. We goin' to de ice cream parlor."

---

1. **drink Jurdan dry:** The Jordan River, in which Jesus was baptized by John the Baptist, figures prominently in slave songs, or "Negro spirituals," including "One More River," which Joe ironically echoes: "O, Jordan stream will never run dry, / Dere ain't but one more river to cross."

"Where de ice cream parlor at, Joe?"

"A new man done come heah from Chicago and he done got a place and took and opened it up for a ice cream parlor, and bein' as it's real swell, Ah wants you to be one de first ladies to walk in dere and have some set down."

"Do Jesus, Ah ain't knowed nothin' 'bout it. Who de man done it?"

"Mister Otis D. Slemmons, of spots and places — Memphis, Chicago, Jacksonville, Philadelphia and so on."

"Dat heavy-set man wid his mouth full of gold teethes?"

"Yeah. Where did you see 'im at?"

"Ah went down to de sto' tuh git a box of lye and Ah seen 'im standin' on de corner talkin' to some of de mens, and Ah come on back and went to scrubbin' de floor, and he passed and tipped his hat whilst Ah was scourin' de steps. Ah thought Ah never seen *him* befo'."

Joe smiled pleasantly. "Yeah, he's up to date. He got de finest clothes Ah ever seen on a colored man's back."

"Aw, he don't look no better in his clothes than you do in yourn. He got a puzzlegut on 'im and he so chuckle-headed, he got a pone behind his neck."

Joe looked down at his own abdomen and said wistfully, "Wisht Ah had a build on me lak he got. He ain't puzzle-gutted, honey. He jes' got a corperation. Dat make 'm look lak a rich white man. All rich mens is got some belly on 'em."

"Ah seen de pitchers of Henry Ford and he's a spare-built man and Rockefeller look lak he ain't got but one gut. But Ford and Rockefeller and dis Slemmons and all de rest kin be as many-gutted as dey please, Ah'm satisfied wid you jes' lak you is, baby. God took pattern after a pine tree and built you noble. Youse a pritty man, and if Ah knowed any way to make you mo' pritty still Ah'd take and do it."

Joe reached over gently and toyed with Missie May's ear. "You jes' say dat cause you love me, but Ah know Ah can't hold no light to Otis D. Slemmons. Ah ain't never been nowhere and Ah ain't got nothin' but you."

Missie May got on his lap and kissed him and he kissed back in kind. Then he went on. "All de womens is crazy 'bout 'im everywhere he go."

"How you know dat, Joe?"

"He tole us so hisself."

"Dat don't make it so. His mouf is cut cross-ways, ain't it? Well, he kin lie jes' lak anybody else."

"Good Lawd, Missie! You womens sho is hard to sense into things. He's got a five-dollar gold piece for a stick-pin and he got a ten-dollar gold piece on his watch chain and his mouf is jes' crammed full of gold teethes. Sho wisht it wuz mine. And whut make it so cool, he got money 'cumulated. And womens give it all to 'im."

"Ah don't see whut de womens see on 'im. Ah wouldn't give 'im a wink if de sheriff wuz after 'im."

"Well, he tole us how de white womens in Chicago give 'im all dat gold money. So he don't 'low nobody to touch it at all. Not even put dey finger on it. Dey tole 'im not to. You kin make 'miration at it, but don't tetch it."

"Whyn't he stay up dere where dey so crazy 'bout 'im?"

"Ah reckon dey done made 'im vast-rich and he wants to travel some. He say dey wouldn't leave 'im hit a lick of work. He got mo' lady people crazy 'bout him than he kin shake a stick at."

"Joe, Ah hates to see you so dumb. Dat stray nigger jes' tell y'all anything and y'all b'lieve it."

"Go 'head on now, honey and put on yo' clothes. He talkin' 'bout his pritty womens — Ah want 'im to see *mine*."

Missie May went off to dress and Joe spent the time trying to make his stomach punch out like Slemmons' middle. He tried the rolling swagger of the stranger, but found that his tall bone-and-muscle stride fitted ill with it. He just had time to drop back into his seat before Missie May came in dressed to go.

On the way home that night Joe was exultant. "Didn't Ah say ole Otis was swell? Can't he talk Chicago talk? Wuzn't dat funny whut he said when great big fat ole Ida Armstrong come in? He asted me, 'Who is dat broad wid de forte shake?' Dat's a new word. Us always thought forty was a set of figgers but he showed us where it means a whole heap of things. Sometimes he don't say forty, he jes' say thirty-eight and two and dat mean de same thing. Know whut he tole me when Ah wuz payin' for our ice cream? He say, 'Ah have to hand it to you, Joe. Dat wife of yours is jes' thirty-eight and two. Yessuh, she's forte!' Ain't he killin'?"

"He'll do in case of a rush. But he sho is got uh heap uh gold on 'im. Dat's de first time Ah ever seed gold money. It lookted good on him sho nuff, but it'd look a whole heap better on you."

"Who, me? Missie May youse crazy! Where would a po' man lak me git gold money from?"

Missie May was silent for a minute, then she said, "Us might find some goin' long de road some time. Us could."

"Who would be losin' gold money round heah? We ain't even seen none dese white folks wearin' no gold money on dey watch chain. You must be figgerin' Mister Packard or Mister Cadillac goin' pass through heah."

"You don't know whut been lost 'round heah. Maybe somebody way back in memorial times lost they gold money and went on off and it ain't never been found. And then if we wuz to find it, you could wear some 'thout havin' no gang of womens lak dat Slemmons say he got."

Joe laughed and hugged her. "Don't be so wishful 'bout me. Ah'm satisfied de way Ah is. So long as Ah be yo' husband, Ah don't keer 'bout nothin' else. Ah'd ruther all de other womens in de world to be dead than for you to have de toothache. Less we go to bed and git our night rest."

It was Saturday night once more before Joe could parade his wife in Slemmons' ice cream parlor again. He worked the night shift and Saturday was his only night off. Every other evening around six o'clock he left home, and dying dawn saw him hustling home around the lake where the challenging sun flung a flaming sword from east to west across the trembling water.

That was the best part of life — going home to Missie May. Their whitewashed house, the mock battle on Saturday, the dinner and ice cream parlor afterwards, church on Sunday nights when Missie out-dressed any woman in town — all, everything was right.

One night around eleven the acid ran out at the G. and G. The foreman knocked off the crew and let the steam die down. As Joe rounded the lake on his way home, a lean moon rode the lake in a silver boat. If anybody had asked Joe about the moon on the lake, he would have said he hadn't paid it any attention. But he saw it with his feelings. It made him yearn painfully for Missie. Creation obsessed him. He thought about children. They had been married more than a year now. They had money put away. They ought to be making little feet for shoes. A little boy child would be about right.

He saw a dim light in the bedroom and decided to come in through the kitchen door. He could wash the fertilizer dust off himself before presenting himself to Missie May. It would be nice for her not to know that he was there until he slipped into his place in bed and hugged her back. She always liked that.

He eased the kitchen door open slowly and silently, but when he went to set his dinner bucket on the table he bumped it into a pile of dishes, and something crashed to the floor. He heard his wife gasp in fright and hurried to reassure her.

"Iss me, honey. Don't git skeered."

There was a quick, large movement in the bedroom. A rustle, a thud, and a stealthy silence. The light went out.

What? Robbers? Murderers? Some varmint attacking his helpless wife, perhaps. He struck a match, threw himself on guard and stepped over the door-sill into the bedroom.

The great belt on the wheel of Time slipped and eternity stood still. By the match light he could see the man's legs fighting with his breeches in his frantic desire to get them on. He had both chance and time to kill the intruder in his helpless condition — half in and half out of his pants — but he was too weak to take action. The shapeless enemies of humanity that live in the hours of Time had waylaid Joe. He was assaulted in his weakness. Like Samson awakening after his haircut. So he just opened his mouth and laughed.

The match went out and he struck another and lit the lamp. A howling wind raced across his heart, but underneath its fury he heard his wife sobbing and Slemmons pleading for his life. Offering to buy it with all that he had. "Please, suh, don't kill me. Sixty-two dollars at de sto'. Gold money."

Joe just stood. Slemmons looked at the window, but it was screened. Joe stood out like a rough-backed mountain between him and the door. Barring him from escape, from sunrise, from life.

He considered a surprise attack upon the big clown that stood there laughing like a chessy cat. But before his fist could travel an inch, Joe's own rushed out to crush him like a battering ram. Then Joe stood over him.

"Git into yo' damn rags, Slemmons, and dat quick."

Slemmons scrambled to his feet and into his vest and coat. As he grabbed his hat, Joe's fury overrode his intentions and he grabbed at Slemmons with his left hand and struck at him with his right. The right landed. The left grazed the front of his vest. Slemmons was knocked a somersault into the kitchen and fled through the open door. Joe found himself alone with Missie May, with the golden watch charm clutched in his left fist. A short bit of broken chain dangled between his fingers.

Missie May was sobbing. Wails of weeping without words. Joe stood, and after awhile he found out that he had something in his hand. And then he stood and felt without thinking and without seeing with his natural eyes. Missie May kept on crying and Joe kept on feeling so much and not knowing what to do with all his feelings, he put Slemmons' watch charm in his pants pocket and took a good laugh and went to bed.

"Missie May, whut you cryin' for?"

"Cause Ah love you so hard and Ah know you don't love *me* no mo'."

Joe sank his face into the pillow for a spell then he said huskily, "You don't know de feelings of dat yet, Missie May."

"Oh Joe, honey, he said he wuz gointer give me dat gold money and he jes' kept on after me —"

Joe was very still and silent for a long time. Then he said, "Well, don't cry no mo', Missie May. Ah got yo' gold piece for you."

The hours went past on their rusty ankles. Joe still and quiet on one bed-rail and Missie May wrung dry of sobs on the other. Finally the sun's tide crept upon the shore of night and drowned all its hours. Missie May with her face stiff and streaked towards the window saw the dawn come into her yard. It was day. Nothing more. Joe wouldn't be coming home as usual. No need to fling open the front door and sweep off the porch, making it nice for Joe. Never no more breakfast to cook; no more washing and starching of Joe's jumper-jackets and pants. No more nothing. So why get up?

With this strange man in her bed, she felt embarrassed to get up and dress. She decided to wait till he had dressed and gone. Then she would get up, dress quickly and be gone forever beyond reach of Joe's looks and laughs. But he never moved. Red light turned to yellow, then white.

From beyond the no-man's land between them came a voice. A strange voice that yesterday had been Joe's.

"Missie May, ain't you gonna fix me no breakfus'?"

She sprang out of bed. "Yeah, Joe. Ah didn't reckon you wuz hongry."

No need to die today. Joe needed her for a few more minutes anyhow.

Soon there was a roaring fire in the cook stove. Water bucket full and two chickens killed. Joe loved fried chicken and rice. She didn't deserve a thing and good Joe was letting her cook him some breakfast. She rushed hot biscuits to the table as Joe took his seat.

He ate with his eyes in his plate. No laughter, no banter.

"Missie May, you ain't eatin' yo' breakfus'."

"Ah don't choose none, Ah thank yuh."

His coffee cup was empty. She sprang to refill it. When she turned from the stove and bent to set the cup beside Joe's plate, she saw the yellow coin on the table between them.

She slumped into her seat and wept into her arms.

Presently Joe said calmly, "Missie May, you cry too much. Don't look back lak Lot's wife aud turn to salt."

The sun, the hero of every day, the impersonal old man that beams as brightly on death as on birth, came up every morning and raced across the blue dome and dipped into the sea of fire every evening. Water ran down hill and birds nested.

Missie knew why she didn't leave Joe. She couldn't. She loved him too much, but she could not understand why Joe didn't leave her. He was polite, even kind at times, but aloof.

There were no more Saturday romps. No ringing silver dollars to stack beside her plate. No pockets to rifle. In fact the yellow coin in his trousers was like a monster hiding in the cave of his pockets to destroy her.

She often wondered if he still had it, but nothing could have induced her to ask nor yet to explore his pockets to see for herself. Its shadow was in the house whether or no.

One night Joe came home around midnight and complained of pains in the back. He asked Missie to rub him down with liniment. It had been three months since Missie had touched his body and it all seemed strange. But she rubbed him. Grateful for the chance. Before morning, youth triumphed and Missie exulted. But the next day, as she joyfully made up their bed, beneath her pillow she found the piece of money with the bit of chain attached.

Alone to herself, she looked at the thing with loathing, but look she must. She took it into her hands with trembling and saw first thing that it was no gold piece. It was a gilded half dollar. Then she knew why Slemmons had forbidden anyone to touch his gold. He trusted village eyes at a distance not to recognize his stick-pin as a gilded quarter, and his watch charm as a four-bit piece.

She was glad at first that Joe had left it there. Perhaps he was through with her punishment. They were man and wife again. Then another thought came clawing at her. He had come home to buy from her as if she were any woman in the long house. Fifty cents for her love. As if to say that he could pay as well as Slemmons. She slid the coin into his Sunday pants pocket and dressed herself and left his house.

Half way between her house and the quarters she met her husband's mother, and after a short talk she turned and went back home. Never would she admit defeat to that woman who prayed for it nightly. If she had not the substance of marriage she had the outside show. Joe must leave *her.* She let him see she didn't want his old gold four-bits too.

She saw no more of the coin for some time though she knew that Joe could not help finding it in his pocket. But his health kept poor, and he came home at least every ten days to be rubbed.

The sun swept around the horizon, trailing its robes of weeks and days. One morning as Joe came in from work, he found Missie May chopping wood. Without a word he took the ax and chopped a huge pile before he stopped.

"You ain't got no business choppin' wood, and you know it."

"How come? Ah been choppin' it for de last longest."

"Ah ain't blind. You makin' feet for shoes."

"Won't you be glad to have a lil baby chile, Joe?"

"You know dat 'thout astin' me."

"Iss gointer be a boy chile and de very spit of you."

"You reckon, Missie May?"

"Who else could it look lak?"

Joe said nothing, but he thrust his hand deep into his pocket and fingered something there.

It was almost six months later Missie May took to bed and Joe went and got his mother to come wait on the house.

Missie May was delivered of a fine boy. Her travail was over when Joe came in from work one morning. His mother and the old women were drinking great bowls of coffee around the fire in the kitchen.

The minute Joe came into the room his mother called him aside.

"How did Missie May make out?" he asked quickly.

"Who, dat gal? She strong as a ox. She gointer have plenty mo'. We done fixed her wid de sugar and lard to sweeten her for de nex' one."

Joe stood silent awhile.

"You ain't ast 'bout de baby, Joe. You oughter be mighty proud cause he sho is de spittin' image of yuh, son. Dat's yourn all right, if you never git another one, dat un is yourn. And you know Ah'm mighty proud too, son, cause Ah never thought well of you marryin' Missie May cause her ma used tuh fan her foot round right smart and Ah been mighty skeered dat Missie May wuz gointer git misput on her road."

Joe said nothing. He fooled around the house till late in the day then just before he went to work, he went and stood at the foot of the bed and asked his wife how she felt. He did this every day during the week.

On Saturday he went to Orlando to make his market. It had been a long time since he had done that.

Meat and lard, meal and flour, soap and starch. Cans of corn and tomatoes. All the staples. He fooled around town for awhile and bought bananas and apples. Way after while he went around to the candy store.

"Hello, Joe," the clerk greeted him. "Ain't seen you in a long time."

"Nope, Ah ain't been heah. Been round in spots and places."

"Want some of them molasses kisses you always buy?"

"Yessuh." He threw the gilded half dollar on the counter. "Will dat spend?"

"Whut is it, Joe? Well, I'll be doggone! A gold-plated four-bit piece. Where'd you git it, Joe?"

"Offen a stray nigger dat come through Eatonville. He had it on his watch chain for a charm — goin' round making out iss gold money. Ha ha! He had a quarter on his tie pin and it wuz all golded up too. Tryin' to fool people. Makin' out he so rich and everything. Ha! Ha! Tryin' to tole off folkses wives from home."

"How did you git it, Joe? Did he fool you, too?"

"Who, me? Naw suh! He ain't fooled me none. Know whut Ah done? He come round me wid his smart talk. Ah hauled off and knocked 'im down and took his old four-bits way from 'im. Gointer buy my wife some good ole lasses kisses wid it. Gimme fifty cents worth of dem candy kisses."

"Fifty cents buys a mighty lot of candy kisses, Joe. Why don't you split it up and take some chocolate bars, too. They eat good, too."

"Yessuh, dey do, but Ah wants all dat in kisses. Ah got a lil boy chile home now. Tain't a week old yet, but he kin suck a sugar tit and maybe eat one them kisses hisself."

Joe got his candy and left the store. The clerk turned to the next customer. "Wisht I could be like these darkies. Laughin' all the time. Nothin' worries 'em."

Back in Eatonville, Joe reached his own front door. There was the ring of singing metal on wood. Fifteen times. Missie May couldn't run to the door, but she crept there as quickly as she could.

"Joe Banks, Ah hear you chunkin' money in mah do'way. You wait till Ah got mah strength back and Ah'm gointer fix you for dat."

[1933]

Nella Larsen

[1891-1964]

Nella Larsen rarely spoke of her early life, and she gave differing accounts of her background and experiences. But recent biographers have begun to piece together her story. She was born Nellie Walker on April 13, 1891, in a seedy section of south Chicago. Her father was a cook named Peter Walker, a black immigrant from the Danish West Indies, now the U.S. Virgin Islands. Her mother was Mary Hansen Walker, a white dressmaker who had emigrated from Denmark in 1886. Larsen's father soon either died or left the family, and Mary Walker married and took the name of Peter Larsen, a Danish immigrant with whom she had a second daughter in 1892. About three years later, she took her daughters for an extended visit to relatives in Denmark, and Larsen did not begin school until they returned to Chicago in 1898. In the racially charged atmosphere of the increasingly segregated city, the presence of a mixed-race child stigmatized the otherwise all-white family. Aware of the racial barriers Larsen faced, her mother was determined that her first daughter receive a good education. After Larsen graduated from high school in 1907, her parents sent her for teacher training at the all-black Fisk University in Nashville, Tennessee. At the end of her first year, she and several other students were expelled for violating the school's strict dress code, and Larsen went to Denmark in 1908. Becoming fluent in Danish, she lived there with relatives for the next four years, during which she may have attended classes at the University of Copenhagen.

Nella Larsen

Ben Pinchot took this photograph of Larsen in 1930, when she was at the height of her fame as one of the major writers of the Harlem Renaissance.

When Larsen returned to the United States in 1912, she was twenty-one and estranged from her family in Chicago. She determined to begin a new life for herself in New York City, where she entered a segregated nursing program for black women at the Lincoln Hospital and Home in the Bronx.

bedfordstmartins.com/
americanlit for research
links on Larsen

She did well in the program, and when she graduated in 1915 she was appointed to a position as a head nurse at the all-black Tuskegee Institute in Alabama. Its famous director, Booker T. Washington, died shortly after Larsen arrived there, and she found the working conditions at the isolated school difficult and exhausting. After a year, Larsen resigned and returned to New York City. She worked as a nurse and met Elmer Himes, a research physicist, the second African American to earn a PhD in physics in the United States. They married in 1919 and moved to Harlem. Part of the rising black professional class, Larsen and her husband socialized with many of the most prominent figures in Harlem, including the influential cultural and political leaders James Weldon Johnson and W. E. B. Du Bois. In 1920, Larsen published her first works, articles on children's games and riddles she had learned in Denmark, in the first monthly magazine for black children, *The Brownie's Book*, founded the previous year by Du Bois and Augustus Granville Dill.

During the following decade, Larsen emerged as one of the leading writers of the Harlem Renaissance. She gave up nursing and began volunteering and then working at the 135th Street branch of the New York Public Library. The white chief librarian of the branch, Ernestine Rose, strongly encouraged Larsen to go to library school, and she became one of the first formally trained African American librarians in the country when she earned a certificate from the school of the New York Public Library in 1923. After working briefly at another branch, Larsen was appointed head of the Children's Room at the 135th Street branch, which she and Rose helped transform into a hub of social and cultural life in Harlem. Partly through her work at the library, which hosted numerous readings and talks, Larsen met a wide range of authors, including Jean Toomer and the white writer and photographer Carl Van Vechten. She also began to write seriously, experimenting with poetry before turning to fiction. Her first two short stories, which appeared under the pen name "Allen Semi," were published in a magazine specializing in pulp fiction, *Young's Realistic Stories*, in 1926. That year, Larsen resigned from her position at the library in order to devote all of her time to writing. Her first novel, the autobiographical *Quicksand*, was published by the prominent firm of Alfred A. Knopf, Inc., in 1928. Du Bois hailed the novel in a glowing review in the *Crisis*, and he was equally enthusiastic about Larsen's second novel, *Passing* (1929), declaring: "If the American Negro renaissance gives us many more books like this . . . we can soon with equanimity drop the word 'Negro.'"

Despite the acclaim, Larsen soon slipped into obscurity. In 1930, she was accused of plagiarism in her short story "Sanctuary," which was published in one of the most prominent magazines in the country, the *Forum*. Although its editors publicly stated that they were convinced by her explanation of the sources and genesis of the story, Larsen was devastated by the charges, which severely damaged her reputation. She was further shaken by her crumbling marriage. After she was awarded a Guggenheim Fellowship in 1931, Larsen went to live and work on a novel in Europe. When she returned to the United States in 1933, she was divorced from her husband, who immediately remarried. In what proved to be a fatal blow to her literary career, Larsen's publisher rejected her new novel. She moved to the Lower East Side of Manhattan, and began to withdraw from both writing and her former friends in Harlem. In 1944, she returned to nursing and worked in various hospitals until her death in March 1964. Her unpublished manuscripts were lost or discarded, and Larsen was buried in an unmarked grave in the Cypress Hills Cemetery in Brooklyn.

Larsen's "Sanctuary." This was the first short story by an African American writer to be published in the *Forum*, a prominent monthly magazine devoted to current events and literature. In the late 1920s, writers such as Willa Cather and William Faulkner published short fiction in the magazine, which also featured essays on religion and politics by philosophers such as John Dewey and Bertrand Russell. Evidently responding to the demand for fiction about black "folk" life, Larsen for the first time wrote a dialect story set in the rural South. As soon as "Sanctuary" was published in the *Forum*, readers wrote to complain that Larsen had copied a well-known story, "Mrs. Adis," by the popular British writer Sheila Kaye-Smith. Although "Mrs. Adis" is set among working-class white characters in England, readers pointed out striking similarities in plot, phrasing, structure, and theme between the story and "Sanctuary." The editors of the *Forum* asked for an explanation, which Larsen provided in a statement published in the magazine in April 1930. In it, she insisted that she had

Illustration for "Sanctuary"

In the *Forum*, Larsen's story was accompanied by four red-and-black woodblock prints the editors commissioned from Winold Reiss, a German-born designer and artist well known for his portraits of African Americans in Harlem during the 1920s.

been told the story by an elderly black patient at the Lincoln Hospital, where Larsen worked as a nurse years before "Mrs. Adis" was first published in 1922. Larsen added that the tale of racial solidarity she told in "Sanctuary" is "so old and so well known that it is almost folklore," concluding: "A Negro sociologist tells me that there are literally hundreds of these stories. Anyone could have written it up at any time." Her explanation satisfied the editors of the *Forum*, to whom she also sent various drafts demonstrating the genesis of "Sanctuary." The text of the story is taken from the first printing in the *Forum*, January 1930.

Sanctuary

I

On the Southern coast, between Merton and Shawboro,[1] there is a strip of desolation some half a mile wide and nearly ten miles long between the sea and old fields of ruined plantations. Skirting the edge of this narrow jungle is a partly grown-over road which still shows traces of furrows made by the wheels of wagons that have long since rotted away or been cut into firewood. This road is little used, now that the state has built its new highway a bit to the west and wagons are less numerous than automobiles.

In the forsaken road a man was walking swiftly. But in spite of his hurry, at every step he set down his feet with infinite care for the night was windless and the heavy silence intensified each sound; even the breaking of a twig could be plainly heard. And the man had need of caution as well as haste.

Before a lonely cottage that shrank timidly back from the road the man hesitated a moment, then struck out across the patch of green in front of it. Stepping behind a clump of bushes close to the house, he looked in through the lighted window at Annie Poole, standing at her kitchen table mixing the supper biscuits.

He was a big, black man with pale brown eyes in which there was an odd mixture of fear and amazement. The light showed streaks of gray soil on his heavy, sweating face and great hands, and on his torn clothes. In his woolly hair clung bits of dried leaves and dead grass.

He made a gesture as if to tap on the window, but turned away to the door instead. Without knocking he opened it and went in.

II

The woman's brown gaze was immediately on him, though she did not move. She said, "You ain't in no hurry, is you, Jim Hammer?" It wasn't, however, entirely a question.

"Ah's in trubble, Mis' Poole," the man explained, his voice shaking, his fingers twitching.

---

1. **Merton and Shawboro:** Towns in North Carolina.

"W'at you done done now?"

"Shot a man, Mis' Poole."

"Trufe?" The woman seemed calm. But the word was spat out.

"Yas'm. Shot 'im." In the man's tone was something of wonder, as if he himself could not quite believe that he had really done this thing which he affirmed.

"Daid?"

"Dunno, Mis' Poole. Dunno."

"White man o' niggah?"

"Cain't say, Mis' Poole. White man, Ah reckons."

Annie Poole looked at him with cold contempt. She was a tiny, withered woman — fifty perhaps — with a wrinkled face the color of old copper, framed by a crinkly mass of white hair. But about her small figure was some quality of hardness that belied her appearance of frailty. At last she spoke, boring her sharp little eyes into those of the anxious creature before her.

"An' w'at am you lookin' foh me to do 'bout et?"

"Jes' lemme stop till dey's gone by. Hide me till dey passes. Reckon dey ain't fur off now." His begging voice changed to a frightened whimper. "Foh de Lawd's sake, Mis' Poole, lemme stop."

And why, the woman inquired caustically, should she run the dangerous risk of hiding him?

"Obadiah, he'd lemme stop ef he was to home," the man whined.

Annie Poole sighed. "Yas," she admitted, slowly, reluctantly, "Ah spec' he would. Obadiah, he's too good to youall no 'count trash." Her slight shoulders lifted in a hopeless shrug. "Yas, Ah reckon he'd do et. Emspecial' seein how he allus set such a heap o' store by you. Cain't see w'at foh, mahse'f. Ah shuah don' see nuffin' in you but a heap o' dirt."

But a look of irony, of cunning, of complicity passed over her face. She went on, "Still, 'siderin' all an' all, how Obadiah's right fon' o' you, an' how white folks is white folks, Ah'm a-gwine hide you dis one time."

Crossing the kitchen, she opened a door leading into a small bedroom, saying, "Git yo'se'f in dat dere feather baid an' Ah'm a-gwine put de clo's on de top. Don' reckon dey'll fin' you ef dey does look foh you in mah house. An Ah don' spec' dey'll go foh to do dat. Not lessen you been keerless an' let 'em smell you out gittin' hyah." She turned on him a withering look. "But you allus been triflin'. Cain't do nuffin propah. An' Ah'm a-tellin' you ef dey warn't white folks an' you a po' niggah, Ah shuah wouldn't be lettin' you mess up mah feather baid dis ebenin', 'cose Ah jes' plain don' want you hyah. Ah done kep' mahse'f outen trubble all mah life. So's Obadiah."

"Ah's powahful 'bliged to you, Mis' Poole. You shuah am one good 'oman. De Lawd'll mos' suttinly —"

Annie Poole cut him off. "Dis ain't no time foh all dat kin' o' fiddle-de-roll. Ah does mah duty as Ah sees et 'thout no thanks from you. Ef de Lawd had gib you a white face 'stead o' dat dere black one, Ah shuah would turn you out. Now hush yo' mouf an' git yo'se'f in. An' don' git movin' and scrunchin' undah dose covahs and git yo'se'f kotched in mah house."

Without further comment the man did as he was told. After he had laid his soiled body and grimy garments between her snowy sheets, Annie Poole carefully rearranged the covering and placed piles of freshly laundered linen on top. Then she gave a pat here and there, eyed the result, and finding it satisfactory, went back to her cooking.

III

Jim Hammer settled down to the racking business of waiting until the approaching danger should have passed him by. Soon savory odors seeped in to him and he realized that he was hungry. He wished that Annie Poole would bring him something to eat. Just one biscuit. But she wouldn't, he knew. Not she. She was a hard one, Obadiah's mother.

By and by he fell into a sleep from which he was dragged back by the rumbling sound of wheels in the road outside. For a second fear clutched so tightly at him that he almost leaped from the suffocating shelter of the bed in order to make some active attempt to escape the horror that his capture meant. There was a spasm at his heart, a pain so sharp, so slashing that he had to suppress an impulse to cry out. He felt himself falling. Down, down, down. . . . Everything grew dim and very distant in his memory. . . . Vanished. . . . Came rushing back.

Outside there was silence. He strained his ears. Nothing. No footsteps. No voices. They had gone on then. Gone without even stopping to ask Annie Poole if she had seen him pass that way. A sigh of relief slipped from him. His thick lips curled in an ugly, cunning smile. It had been smart of him to think of coming to Obadiah's mother's to hide. She was an old demon, but he was safe in her house.

He lay a short while longer listening intently, and, hearing nothing, started to get up. But immediately he stopped, his yellow eyes glowing like pale flames. He had heard the unmistakable sound of men coming toward the house. Swiftly he slid back into the heavy, hot stuffiness of the bed and lay listening fearfully.

The terrifying sounds drew nearer. Slowly. Heavily. Just for a moment he thought they were not coming in — they took so long. But there was a light knock and the noise of a door being opened. His whole body went taut. His feet felt frozen, his hands clammy, his tongue like a weighted, dying thing. His pounding heart made it hard for his straining ears to hear what they were saying out there.

"Ebenin', Mistah Lowndes." Annie Poole's voice sounded as it always did, sharp and dry.

There was no answer. Or had he missed it? With slow care he shifted his position, bringing his head nearer the edge of the bed. Still he heard nothing. What were they waiting for? Why didn't they ask about him?

Annie Poole, it seemed, was of the same mind. "Ah don' reckon youall done traipsed 'way out hyah jes' foh yo' healf," she hinted.

"There's bad news for you, Annie, I'm 'fraid." The sheriff's voice was low and queer.

Jim Hammer visualized him standing out there — a tall, stooped man, his white tobacco-stained mustache drooping limply at the ends, his nose hooked and sharp, his eyes blue and cold. Bill Lowndes was a hard one too. And white.

"W'atall bad news, Mistah Lowndes?" The woman put the question quietly, directly.

"Obadiah —" the sheriff began — hesitated — began again. "Obadiah — ah — er he's outside, Annie. I'm 'fraid —"

"Shucks! You done missed. Obadiah, he ain't done nuffin', Mistah Lowndes. Obadiah!" she called stridently, "Obadiah! git hyah an' splain yo'se'f."

But Obadiah didn't answer, didn't come in. Other men came in. Came in with steps that dragged and halted. No one spoke. Not even Annie Poole. Something was laid carefully upon the floor.

"Obadiah, chile," his mother said softly, "Obadiah, chile." Then, with sudden alarm, "He ain't daid, is he? Mistah Lowndes! Obadiah, he ain't daid?"

Jim Hammer didn't catch the answer to that pleading question. A new fear was stealing over him.

"There was a to-do, Annie," Bill Lowndes explained gently, "at the garage back o' the factory. Fellow tryin' to steal tires. Obadiah heerd a noise an' run out with two or three others. Scared the rascal all right. Fired off his gun an' run. We allow et to be Jim Hammer. Picked up his cap back there. Never was no 'count. Thievin' an' sly. But we'll git 'im, Annie. We'll git 'im."

The man huddled in the feather bed prayed silently. "Oh, Lawd! Ah didn't go to do et. Not Obadiah, Lawd. You knows dat. You knows et." And into his frenzied brain came the thought that it would be better for him to get up and go out to them before Annie Poole gave him away. For he was lost now. With all his great strength he tried to get himself out of the bed. But he couldn't.

"Oh Lawd!" he moaned, "Oh Lawd!" His thoughts were bitter and they ran through his mind like panic. He knew that it had come to pass as it said somewhere in the Bible about the wicked. The Lord had stretched out his hand and smitten him. He was paralyzed. He couldn't move hand or foot. He moaned again. It was all there was left for him to do. For in the terror of this new calamity that had come upon him he had forgotten the waiting danger which was so near out there in the kitchen.

His hunters, however, didn't hear him. Bill Lowndes was saying, "We been a-lookin' for Jim out along the old road. Figured he'd make tracks for Shawboro. You ain't noticed anybody pass this evenin', Annie?"

The reply came promptly, unwaveringly. "No, Ah ain't sees nobody pass. Not yet."

IV

Jim Hammer caught his breath.

"Well," the sheriff concluded, "we'll be gittin' along. Obadiah was a mighty fine boy. Ef they was all like him —. I'm sorry, Annie. Anything I c'n do let me know."

"Thank you, Mistah Lowndes."

With the sound of the door closing on the departing men, power to move came back to the man in the bedroom. He pushed his dirt-caked feet out from the covers and rose up, but crouched down again. He wasn't cold now, but hot all over and burning. Almost he wished that Bill Lowndes and his men had taken him with them.

Annie Poole had come into the room.

It seemed a long time before Obadiah's mother spoke. When she did there were no tears, no reproaches; but there was a raging fury in her voice as she lashed out, "Git outen mah feather baid, Jim Hammer, an' outen mah house, an' don' nevah stop thankin' yo' Jesus he done gib you dat black face."

[1930]

María Cristina Mena

[1893–1965]

María Cristina Mena

This undated photograph of Mena was apparently taken during the period 1913-17, when she published a series of stories about her native Mexico in the prominent magazine the *Century*.

María Cristina Mena was born in Mexico City on April 3, 1893, into a wealthy, upper-class family. Her Spanish mother and Mexican father sent her to a Catholic convent school in Mexico City and later to a boarding school in England. Fluent in Spanish, English, French, and Italian, the precocious Mena began writing poetry as a child. Concerned about the increasing political turmoil in Mexico, and wishing their fourteen-year-old daughter to further her education, her parents sent Mena to live with family friends in New York City. There, she continued her studies and began to write stories inspired by her reading and her memories of Mexico. Few other details are known about her early years in New York City, but her experiences are illuminated by the outline of a story Mena later planned to write about

a family of wealthy refugees from Mexico, with possibilities of rich comedy in their contact with American life, especially in relation to the gradual emancipation of their daughter, who in spite of efforts to keep her in pious subjection in accordance with Mexican tradition, takes to American freedom like a duck to water and blossoms into an ardently independent young woman.

Although that story was never written, Mena's early stories about life in Mexico found a ready audience in the United States. In November 1913, her first two stories were published during the same month: "The Gold Vanity Set" in *American* magazine and "John of God, the Water-Carrier," in *Century* magazine. The publication of the stories, both signed with her full name, marked the first time a Mexican American woman writer's work appeared in a major magazine in the United States. Writing in English, Mena sought to present realistic depictions of Mexican life, culture, and customs to an American audience accustomed to thinking of the country either as a quaint, exotic land or in terms of the ongoing Mexican Revolution, which had broken out in 1910. Indeed, her stories appeared at a time when there was growing bias and hostility among Anglo Americans toward the hundreds of thousands of immigrants driven north by the economic and social upheaval in Mexico. Mena soon contracted to become a regular contributor to the *Century*, where seven more of her stories were published during 1914-16. From the beginning, however, Mena chafed at the efforts of the editors of the magazine to confine her writing to simple stories suffused with the "local color" of life in Mexico. Her resistance to such one-dimensional portraits of the land and its people is also revealed in the only essay Mena published in the *Century*, "Julian Carillo: The Herald of a Musical Monroe Doctrine" (1915), a sketch of the celebrated Mexican composer and conductor who had recently organized the American Symphony Orchestra in New York City. At the beginning of her essay, where she described Carillo's early life in a poor Mexican family, Mena pointedly observed: "This would seem to be a good place for 'local color,' but the writer resists that fatal allurement." In fact, scholars have commented on the ways in which Mena sought to present complex portrayals of Mexican characters that defied stereotypes, even as she offered subtle commentaries on American attitudes toward Mexico and Mexicans.

In 1916, Mena married Henry Kellet Chambers (1867-1935), an Australian-born journalist and author of several plays, including *Butterfly* and *An American Wedding*. Although she wrote little during the following twenty years, Mena remained active in literary circles. In 1927, she began to correspond with the English author D. H. Lawrence, whom she strongly defended when his controversial novel *Lady Chatterly's Lover*, privately printed in Italy in 1928, was banned in both England and the United States. The correspondence between the two writers began after Lawrence read Mena's early story "John of God, the Water-Carrier," which was republished in 1927 in the *Monthly Criterion*, a London-based literary journal edited by T. S. Eliot. The story was subsequently included in both the *Yearbook of the American Short Story* and *The Best Short Stories of 1928*. Perhaps inspired by the flurry of interest in her work, Mena wrote her final story, "A Son of the Tropics," a tale of the Mexican Revolution published in *Household Magazine* in 1931. After her husband died in 1935, Mena began to write books about Mexican life and history for children, publishing five of them between 1942 and 1953. She also worked with the blind, translating her own books and the work of others into Braille. Mena died at her home in Brooklyn on August 3, 1965. The brief obituary of "Mrs. Henry Chambers" in the *New York Times* described Mena as a writer "who dedicated her work 'to bringing to the American public the life of the Mexican people.'"

Mena's "The Vine-Leaf."   Written when Mena was only twenty-one, this was one of eight of her stories that appeared in the *Century Illustrated Monthly Magazine* from 1913 through 1916. Published in New York, the *Century* had a developed a large national circulation through the publication of a wide variety of material, ranging from the popular 1880s series *Battles and Leaders of the Civil War* to highly regarded serializations of novels by William Dean Howells and Henry James, biographies of prominent Americans such as Abraham Lincoln, travel narratives, and stories about the American West. Although the magazine sought to present a variety of

bedfordstmartins.com/ americanlit for research links on Mena

cultural experiences, during the years leading up to World War I it also published numerous articles and stories about the negative effects of immigration in the United States. Commissioned by the editors to write about Mexican life for the magazine, Mena was thus entering a complex literary and cultural terrain. While she was excited to be published in the *Century,* she resisted the efforts of its editors to shape her material. Her desire for artistic control and her resistance to male authority over her work is perhaps obliquely reflected in the character of the *marquesa* in "The Vine-Leaf." The text is taken from the first printing in the *Century,* December 1914.

The Vine-Leaf

It is a saying in the capital of Mexico that Dr. Malsufrido carries more family secrets under his hat than any archbishop, which applies, of course, to family secrets of the rich. The poor have no family secrets, or none that Dr. Malsufrido would trouble to carry under his hat.

The doctor's hat is, appropriately enough, uncommonly capacious, rising very high, and sinking so low that it seems to be supported by his ears and eyebrows, and it has a furry look, as if it had been brushed the wrong way, which is perhaps what happens to it if it is ever brushed at all. When the doctor takes it off, the family secrets do not fly out like a flock of parrots, but remain nicely bottled up beneath a dome of old and highly polished ivory, which, with its unbroken fringe of dyed black hair, has the effect of a tonsure; and then Dr. Malsufrido looks like one of the early saints. I've forgotten which one.

So edifying is his personality that, when he marches into a sick-room, the forces of disease and infirmity march out of it, and do not dare to return until he has taken his leave. In fact, it is well known that none of his patients has ever had the bad manners to die in his presence.

If you will believe him, he is almost ninety years old, and everybody knows that he has been dosing good Mexicans for half a century. He is forgiven for being a Spaniard on account of a legend that he physicked royalty in his time, and that a certain princess — but that has nothing to do with this story.

It is sure he has a courtly way with him that captivates his female patients, of whom he speaks as his *penitentes,*[1] insisting on confession as a prerequisite of diagnosis, and declaring that the physician who undertakes to cure a woman's body without reference to her soul is a more abominable kill-healthy than the famous *Dr. Sangrado,* who taught medicine to *Gil Blas.*[2]

---

1. *penitentes:* Repentant sinners (Spanish).
2. *Dr. Sangrado . . . Gil Blas:* Characters in the episodic novel *The Adventures of Gil Blas of Santillane* (1715–35), set in Spain and written in French by Alain-René LeSage (1668–1747). Dr. Sangrado practices medicine by only two methods: encouraging patients to drink hot water and bleeding them.

"Describe me the symptoms of your conscience, Señora," he will say. "Fix yourself that I shall forget one tenth of what you tell me."

"But what of the other nine tenths, Doctor?" the troubled lady will exclaim.

"The other nine tenths I shall take care not to believe," Dr. Malsufrido will reply, with a roar of laughter. And sometimes he will add:

"Do not confess your neighbor's sins; the doctor will have enough with your own."

When an inexperienced one fears to become a *penitente* lest that terrible old doctor betray her confidence, he reassures her as to his discretion, and at the same time takes her mind off her anxieties by telling her the story of his first patient.

"Figure you my prudence, Señora," he begins, "that, although she was my patient, I did not so much as see her face."

And then, having enjoyed the startled curiosity of his hearer, he continues:

"On that day of two crosses when I first undertook the mending of mortals, she arrived to me beneath a veil as impenetrable as that of a nun, saying:

"'To you I come, Señor Doctor, because no one knows you.'

"'Who would care for fame, Señorita,' said I, 'when obscurity brings such excellent fortune?'

"And the lady, in a voice which trembled slightly, returned:

"'If your knife is as apt as your tongue, and your discretion equal to both, I shall not regret my choice of a surgeon.'

"With suitable gravity I reassured her, and inquired how I might be privileged to serve her. She replied:

"'By ridding me of a blemish, if you are skilful enough to leave no trace on the skin.'

"'Of that I will judge, with the help of God, when the señorita shall have removed her veil.'

"'No, no; you shall not see my face. Praise the saints the blemish is not there!'

"'Wherever it be,' said I, resolutely, 'my science tells me that it must be seen before it can be well removed.'

"The lady answered with great simplicity that she had no anxiety on that account, but that, as she had neither duenna nor servant with her, I must help her. I had no objection, for a surgeon must needs be something of a lady's maid. I judged from the quality of her garments that she was of an excellent family, and I was ashamed of my clumsy fingers; but she was as patient as marble, caring only to keep her face closely covered. When at last I saw the blemish she had complained of, I was astonished, and said:

"'But it seems to me a blessed stigma, Señorita, this delicate, wine-red vine-leaf, staining a surface as pure as the petal of any magnolia. With permission, I should say that the God Bacchus[3] himself painted it here in the arch of this chaste back, where only the eyes of Cupid[4] could find it; for it is safely below the line of the most fashionable gown.'

"But she replied:

"'I have my reasons. Fix yourself that I am superstitious.'

---

3. **Bacchus:** Greek god of wine.
4. **Cupid:** Roman god of love.

"I tried to reason with her on that, but she lost her patience, and cried:

"'For favor, good surgeon, your knife!'

"Even in those days I had much sensibility, Señora, and I swear that my heart received more pain from the knife than did she. Neither the cutting nor the stitching brought a murmur from her. Only some strong ulterior thought could have armed a delicate woman with such valor. I beat my brains to construe the case, but without success. A caprice took me to refuse the fee she offered me.

"'No, Señorita,' I said, 'I have not seen your face, and if I were to take your money, it might pass that I should not see the face of a second patient, which would be a great misfortune. You are my first, and I am as superstitious as you.'

"I would have added that I had fallen in love with her, but I feared to appear ridiculous, having seen no more than her back.

"'You would place me under an obligation,' she said. I felt that her eyes studied me attentively through her veil. 'Very well, I can trust you the better for that. *Adiós*, Señor Surgeon.'

"She came once more to have me remove the stitches, as I had told her, and again her face was concealed, and again I refused payment; but I think she knew that the secret of the vine-leaf was buried in my heart."

"But that secret, what was it, Doctor? Did you ever see the mysterious lady again?"

"*Chist!*[5] Little by little one arrives to the *rancho*, Señora. Five years passed, and many patients arrived to me, but, although all showed me their faces, I loved none of them better than the first one. Partly through family influence, partly through well-chosen friendships, and perhaps a little through that diligence in the art of Hippocrates[6] for which in my old age I am favored by the most charming of Mexicans, I had prospered, and was no longer unknown.

"At a meeting of a learned society I became known to a certain *marqués*[7] who had been a great traveler in his younger days. We had a discussion on a point of anthropology, and he invited me to his house, to see the curiosities he had collected in various countries. Most of them recalled scenes of horror, for he had a morbid fancy.

"Having taken from my hand the sword with which he had seen five Chinese pirates sliced into small pieces, he led me toward a little door, saying:

"'Now you shall see the most mysterious and beautiful of my mementos, one which recalls a singular event in our own peaceful Madrid.'

"We entered a room lighted by a skylight, and containing little but an easel on which rested a large canvas. The *marqués* led me where the most auspicious light fell upon it. It was a nude, beautifully painted. The model stood poised divinely, with her back to the beholder, twisting flowers in her hair before a mirror. And there, in the arch of that chaste back, staining a surface as pure as the petal of any magnolia, what did my eyes see? Can you possibly imagine, Señora?"

---

5. *Chist!*: Hush! (Spanish).
6. **the art of Hippocrates**: Hippocrates (c. 460–377 BCE), the Greek physician generally regarded as the founder of Western medicine, formulated a statement of medical conduct and ethics, the Hippocratic Oath.
7. *marqués*: A nobleman.

"*Válgame Dios!*[8] The vine-leaf, Doctor!"

"What penetration of yours, Señora! It was veritably the vine-leaf, wine-red, as it had appeared to me before my knife barbarously extirpated it from the living flesh; but in the picture it seemed unduly conspicuous, as if Bacchus had been angry when he kissed. You may imagine how the sight startled me. But those who know Dr. Malsufrido need no assurance that even in those early days he never permitted himself one imprudent word. No, Señora; I only remarked, after praising the picture in proper terms:

"'What an interesting moon is that upon the divine creature's back!'

"'Does it not resemble a young vine-leaf in early spring?' said the *marqués*, who contemplated the picture with the ardor of a connoisseur. I agreed politely, saying:

"'Now that you suggest it, *Marqués*, it has some of the form and color of a tender vine-leaf. But I could dispense me a better vine-leaf, with many bunches of grapes, to satisfy the curiosity I have to see such a well-formed lady's face. What a misfortune that it does not appear in that mirror, as the artist doubtless intended! The picture was never finished, then?'

"'I have reason to believe that it was finished,' he replied, 'but that the face painted in the mirror was obliterated. Observe that its surface is an opaque and disordered smudge of many pigments, showing no brush-work, but only marks of a rude rubbing that in some places has overlapped the justly painted frame of the mirror.'

"'This promises an excellent mystery,' I commented lightly. 'Was it the artist or his model who was dissatisfied with the likeness, *Marqués*?'

"'I suspect that the likeness was more probably too good than not good enough,' returned the *marqués*. 'Unfortunately, poor Andrade is not here to tell us.'

"'Andrade! The picture was his work?'

"'The last his hand touched. Do you remember when he was found murdered in his studio?'

"'With a knife sticking between his shoulders. I remember it very well.'

"The *marqués* continued:

"'I had asked him to let me have this picture. He was then working on that rich but subdued background. The figure was finished, but there was no vine-leaf, and the mirror was empty of all but a groundwork of paint, with a mere luminous suggestion of a face.

"'Andrade, however, refused to name me a price, and tried to put me off with excuses. His friends were jesting about the unknown model, whom no one had managed to see, and all suspected that he designed to keep the picture for himself. That made me the more determined to possess it. I wished to make it a betrothal gift to the beautiful Señorita Lisarda Monte Alegre, who had then accepted the offer of my hand, and who is now the *marquesa*.[9] When I have a desire, Doctor, it bites me, and I make it bite others. That poor Andrade, I gave him no peace.

---

8. *Válgame Dios!*: Bless me, God! (Spanish).
9. *marquesa*: A noblewoman, the wife or widow of a *marqués* (Spanish).

"'He fell into one of his solitary fits, shutting himself in his studio, and seeing no one; but that did not prevent me from knocking at his door whenever I had nothing else to do. Well, one morning the door was open.'

"'Yes, yes!' I exclaimed. 'I remember now, *Marqués*, that it was you who found the body.'

"'You have said it. He was lying in front of this picture, having dragged himself across the studio. After assuring myself that he was beyond help, and while awaiting the police, I made certain observations. The first thing to strike my attention was this vine-leaf. The paint was fresh, whereas the rest of the figure was comparatively dry. Moreover, its color had not been mixed with Andrade's usual skill. Observe you, Doctor, that the blemish is not of the texture of the skin, or bathed in its admirable atmosphere. It presents itself as an excrescence. And why? Because that color had been mixed and applied with feverish haste by the hand of a dying man, whose one thought was to denounce his assassin — she who undoubtedly bore such a mark on her body, and who had left him for dead, after carefully obliterating the portrait of herself which he had painted in the mirror.'

"'*Ay Dios!*[10] But the police, *Marqués* — they never reported these details so significant?'

"'Our admirable police are not connoisseurs of the painter's art, my friend. Moreover, I had taken the precaution to remove from the dead man's fingers the empurpled brush with which he had traced that accusing symbol.'

"'You wished to be the accomplice of an unknown assassin?'

"'Inevitably, Señor, rather than deliver that lovely body to the hands of the public executioner.'

"The *marqués* raised his lorgnette and gazed at the picture. And I — I was recovering from my agitation, Señora. I said:

"'It seems to me, *Marqués*, that if I were a woman and loved you, I should be jealous of that picture.'

"He smiled and replied:

"'It is true that the *marquesa* affects some jealousy on that account, and will not look at the picture. However, she is one who errs on the side of modesty, and prefers more austere objects of contemplation. She is excessively religious.'

"'I have been called superstitious,' pronounced a voice behind me.

"It was a voice that I had heard before. I turned, Señora, and I ask you to try to conceive whose face I now beheld."

"*Válgame la Virgen*,[11] Dr. Malsufrido, was it not the face of the good *marquesa*, and did she not happen to have been also your first patient?"

"Again such penetration, Señora, confounds me. It was she. The *marqués* did me the honor to present me to her.

"'I have heard of your talents, Señor Surgeon,' she said.

---

10. *Ay Dios!*: Oh God! (Spanish).
11. *Válgame la Virgen*: Bless me, Mother of God (Spanish).

"'And I of your beauty, *Marquesa*,' I hastened to reply; 'but that tale was not well told.' And I added, 'If you are superstitious, I will be, too.'

"With one look from her beautiful and devout eyes she thanked me for that prudence which to this day, Señora, is at the service of my *penitentes*, little daughters of my affections and my prayers; and then she sighed and said:

"'Can you blame me for not loving this questionable lady of the vine-leaf, of whom my husband is such a gallant accomplice?'

"'Not for a moment,' I replied, 'for I am persuaded, *Marquesa*, that a lady of rare qualities may have power to bewitch an unfortunate man without showing him the light of her face.'"

[1914]

Jean Toomer

[1894-1967]

Jean Toomer was born Nathan Eugene Pinchback Toomer on December 26, 1894, in Washington, D.C. His parents were Nathan Toomer, a planter, and Nina Pinchback Toomer, the daughter of a former governor of Louisiana, the first person of African American descent to hold that office in the United States. Shortly after Toomer was born, his father abandoned the family, and his mother took him to live with her parents in an affluent, predominantly white neighborhood in Washington. He attended elementary school there and at an all-white school in New Rochelle, New York, where his mother took him after she remarried in 1906. Toomer hated his stepfather, and he returned to live with his grandparents after his mother died in 1909. By then, his grandparents had been forced by financial pressures to move to a modest, black section of Washington. There, at the age of fifteen, the light-complexioned Toomer first learned about his ancestry and mixed racial heritage, which he later described as "seven blood mixtures: French, Dutch, Welch, Negro, German, Jewish, and Indian." Shocked by the discovery, he attended an all-black high school, graduated in 1914, and enrolled at the University of Wisconsin. "I was again entering the white world," he recalled in an unpublished autobiography; "and though I personally had experienced no prejudice or exclusion from the whites or the colored people, I had seen enough to know that America viewed life as if it were divided into white and black."

Jean Toomer
This publicity photograph was taken for advertisements of Toomer's first and most famous book, *Cane* (1923).

Refusing to define himself as either black or white, Toomer struggled to discover a vocation and a place for himself in the racially divided United States. He withdrew from the University of Wisconsin after one semester and lived with his grandparents for a year before enrolling at the American College of Physical Training in Chicago in the spring of 1916. That fall, he enrolled at the City College of New York, where he studied history, psychology, and sociology. In December 1917, after the United States entered World War I, Toomer withdrew from college and tried to enlist, but he was

turned down for military service because of an athletic injury. He subsequently worked briefly in Milwaukee and Chicago before returning to New
York City in the spring of 1918. Living in the lively bohemian district of
Greenwich Village, he met Lola Ridge, an editor of the avant-garde magazine *Broom*, who introduced Toomer to the influential white writer and cultural critic Waldo Frank. Encouraged by Frank to become a writer, and
now calling himself Jean Toomer, in the summer of 1919 he returned to live
with his grandparents in Washington. He began to read the work of modern American and European novelists, as well as poets ranging from
William Blake, Charles Baudelaire, and Walt Whitman to Robert Frost and
the imagists. Toomer studied other innovative work by reading little magazines such as the *Dial* and *Poetry: A Magazine of Verse*. He experimented
with both poetry and prose, amassing what he described as literally "a
trunk full of manuscripts" by 1921, when Toomer accepted a temporary
appointment as the head of the Sparta Agricultural and Industrial Institute, an all-black school in Georgia.

The brief time he spent there profoundly shaped the course of Toomer's
life and literary career. "A visit to Georgia last fall was the starting point of
almost everything of worth," he declared in a letter to the editors of the *Liberator* in 1922.

> I heard folk-songs come from the lips of Negro peasants. I saw the rich dusk
> beauty that I had heard many false accents about, and of which, till then, I
> was somewhat skeptical. And a deep part of my nature, a part that I had
> repressed, sprang suddenly to life and responded to them. Now, I can not
> conceive of myself as aloof and separated. My point of view has not changed;
> it has deepened, it has widened.

The experience inspired Toomer's earliest publications, a series of
poems, sketches, and stories that he subsequently wove together in his
first book, *Cane* (1923). Waldo Frank, who arranged for its publication and
wrote a preface to the volume, observed: "For Toomer, the Southland is not
a problem to be solved; it is a field of loveliness to be sung: the Georgia
Negro is not a downtrodden soul to be uplifted; he is material for a gorgeous painting." Some reviewers were puzzled by the generic mixture of
what one described as "an interesting, occasionally beautiful, and often
queer book of exploration into old country and new ways of writing." But
most critics praised the artistry and innovation displayed in *Cane*, which
Toomer's publisher advertised as "a book about Negroes by a Negro."
Although it sold poorly, the book had a powerful impact on young African
American writers such as Sterling Brown, Langston Hughes, and Zora
Neale Hurston, who credited *Cane* as a major impetus for the Harlem
Renaissance.

Toomer, however, steadily withdrew from black literary circles and
from writing about African Americans. He began to study the work of
George Ivanovitch Gurdjieff, a Greek Armenian mystic who had established an institute in Fontainebleau, France. Toomer first attended the

school in 1924, and most of his writings during the following years were based on Gurdjieff's theories of spiritual self-development. In 1930, when James Weldon Johnson asked for permission to reprint some of Toomer's poems in a new edition of *The Book of American Negro Poetry,* he flatly refused. "My poems are not Negro poems, nor are they Anglo-Saxon or white or English poems," Toomer sharply replied: "They are, first, mine. And, second, they spring from the result of racial blendings here in America which have produced a new race or stock." He developed his concept of racial fusion in *The Blue Meridian,* a visionary poem about the possibilities of a thoroughly democratic "New America." But he created a public furor when he married the first of his two white wives, the writer Margery Latimer, in 1932. After Latimer died giving birth to their first child, Toomer married Marjorie Content, the daughter of a wealthy Wall Street financier, in 1934. They moved to Doylestown, Pennsylvania, where he eventually became a Quaker. For the rest of his life, Toomer devoted himself to writing for Quaker journals, giving lectures, and continuing his study of philosophy and religion. He died on March 30, 1967.

Toomer's *Cane.* An experimental and innovative work that defies easy classification, *Cane* has been variously described as a novel, a novel-poem, and a collage or mosaic of imagistic poems, prose sketches, and short stories. Toomer began to write the pieces that make up the book after he

Cane

The design of the dust jacket of the first edition evokes an exotic, tropical locale that bears little resemblance to the actual setting of Toomer's poems, sketches, and stories about the cotton plantation country of central Georgia.

returned to Washington, D.C., from a three-month stay in Sparta, Georgia, in 1921. He published his first poem in the *Crisis*, the magazine of the National Association for the Advancement of Colored People (NAACP), but many of the pieces in the book first appeared in avant-garde literary journals targeted at primarily white audiences, including *Broom*, the *Double Dealer*, the *Little Review*, the *Modern Review*, and *Prairie*. Encouraged by the reception of the individual works, Toomer began to conceive of them as part of a single book along the lines of Sherwood Anderson's short-story cycle *Winesburg, Ohio* (1919). Whereas Anderson explored the lives of ordinary white people in a fictional town in the Midwest, Toomer sought to capture the experience and folk culture of rural blacks in the fictional southern town of Sempter, Georgia, the setting of the various works in the first and third sections of *Cane*. When his publisher asked Toomer to expand the manuscript, he added the poems, sketches, and stories in the second section, set in the bourgeoning black areas of Chicago and Washington, D.C. The text of the following selection – the final poem and story in the first section and the opening sketch of the second section – is taken from the first edition of *Cane* (1923).

From Cane

Portrait in Georgia

Hair – braided chestnut,
coiled like a lyncher's rope,
Eyes – fagots,
Lips – old scars, or the first red blisters,
Breath – the last sweet scent of cane,
And her slim body, white as the ash
    of black flesh after flame.

[1923]

Blood-Burning Moon

1

Up from the skeleton stone walls, up from the rotting floor boards and the solid hand-hewn beams of oak of the pre-war cotton factory, dusk came. Up from the dusk the full moon came. Glowing like a fired pine-knot, it illumined the great door and soft showered the Negro shanties aligned along the single street of factory town. The full moon in the great door was an omen. Negro women improvised songs against its spell.

Louisa sang as she came over the crest of the hill from the white folks' kitchen. Her skin was the color of oak leaves on young trees in fall. Her breasts, firm and up-pointed like ripe acorns. And her singing had the low murmur of winds in fig trees. Bob Stone, younger son of the people she worked for, loved her. By the way the world reckons things, he had won her. By measure of that warm glow which came into her mind at thought of him, he had won her. Tom Burwell whom the whole town called Big Boy, also loved her. But working in the fields all day, and far away from her, gave him no chance to show it. Though often enough of evenings he had tried to. Somehow, he never got along. Strong as he was with hands upon the ax or plow, he found it difficult to hold her. Or so he thought. But the fact was that he held her to factory town more firmly than he thought for. His black balanced, and pulled against, the white of Stone, when she thought of them. And her mind was vaguely upon them as she came over the crest of the hill, coming from the white folks' kitchen. As she sang softly at the evil face of the full moon.

A strange stir was in her. Indolently, she tried to fix upon Bob or Tom as the cause of it. To meet Bob in the canebrake, as she was going to do an hour or so later, was nothing new. And Tom's proposal which she felt on its way to her could be indefinitely put off. Separately, there was no unusual significance to either one. But for some reason, they jumbled when her eyes gazed vacantly at the rising moon. And from the jumble came the stir that was strangely within her. Her lips trembled. The slow rhythm of her song grew agitant and restless. Rusty black and tan spotted hounds, lying in the dark corners of porches or prowling around back yards, put their noses in the air and caught its tremor. They began plaintively to yelp and howl. Chickens woke up and cackled. Intermittently, all over the countryside dogs barked and roosters crowed as if heralding a weird dawn or some ungodly awakening. The women sang lustily. Their songs were cotton-wads to stop their ears. Louisa came down into factory town and sank wearily upon the step before her home. The moon was rising towards a thick cloud-bank which soon would hide it.

> Red nigger moon. Sinner!
> Blood-burning moon. Sinner!
> Come out that fact'ry door.

2

Up from the deep dusk of a cleared spot on the edge of the forest a mellow glow arose and spread fan-wise into the low-hanging heavens. And all around the air was heavy with the scent of boiling cane. A large pile of cane-stalks lay like ribboned shadows upon the ground. A mule, harnessed to a pole, trudged lazily round and round the pivot of the grinder. Beneath a swaying oil lamp, a Negro alternately whipped out at the mule, and fed cane-stalks to the grinder. A fat boy waddled pails of fresh ground juice between the grinder and the boiling stove. Steam came from the copper boiling pan. The scent of cane came from the copper pan and drenched the forest and the hill that sloped to factory town, beneath its fragrance. It drenched the men in circle seated around the stove. Some of them chewed at the white pulp of stalks, but there was no need for them to, if all they wanted was to taste the cane. One tasted it in factory town. And from factory town one could see the soft haze thrown by the glowing stove upon the low-hanging heavens.

Old David Georgia stirred the thickening syrup with a long ladle, and ever so often drew it off. Old David Georgia tended his stove and told tales about the white folks, about moonshining and cotton picking, and about sweet nigger gals, to the men who sat there about his stove to listen to him. Tom Burwell chewed cane-stalk and laughed with the others till someone mentioned Louisa. Till some one said something about Louisa and Bob Stone, about the silk stockings she must have gotten from him. Blood ran up Tom's neck hotter than the glow that flooded from the stove. He sprang up. Glared at the men and said, "She's my gal." Will Manning laughed. Tom strode over to him. Yanked him up and knocked him to the ground. Several of Manning's friends got up to fight for him. Tom whipped out a long knife and would have cut them to shreds if they hadnt ducked into the woods. Tom had had enough. He nodded to Old David Georgia and swung down the path to factory town. Just then, the dogs started barking and the roosters began to crow. Tom felt funny. Away from the fight, away from the stove, chill got to him. He shivered. He shuddered when he saw the full moon rising towards the cloud-bank. He who didnt give a godam for the fears of old women. He forced his mind to fasten on Louisa. Bob Stone. Better not be. He turned into the street and saw Louisa sitting before her home. He went towards her, ambling, touched the brim of a marvelously shaped, spotted, felt hat, said he wanted to say something to her, and then found that he didnt know what he had to say, or if he did, that he couldnt say it. He shoved his big fists in his overalls, grinned, and started to move off.

"Youall want me, Tom?"

"Thats what us wants, sho, Louisa."

"Well, here I am —"

"An here I is, but that aint ahelpin none, all th same."

"You wanted to say something? . ."

"I did that, sho. But words is like th spots on dice: no matter how y fumbles em, there's times when they jes wont come. I dunno why. Seems like th love I feels fo yo done stole m tongue. I got it now. Whee! Louisa, honey, I oughtnt tell y, I feel I oughtnt cause yo is young an goes t church an I has had other gals, but Louisa I sho do love y. Lil gal, Ise watched y from them first days when youall sat right here befo yo door befo th well an sang sometimes in a way that like t broke m heart. Ise carried y with me into th fields, day after day, an after that, an I sho can plow when yo is there, an I can pick cotton. Yassur! Come near beatin Barlo yesterday. I sho did. Yassur! An next year if ole Stone'll trust me, I'll have a farm. My own. My bales will buy yo what y gets from white folks now. Silk stockings an purple dresses — course I dont believe what some folks been whisperin as t how y gets them things now. White folks always did do for niggers what they likes. An they jes cant help alikin yo, Louisa. Bob Stone likes y. Course he does. But not th way folks is awhisperin. Does he, hon?"

"I dont know what you mean, Tom."

"Course y dont. Ise already cut two niggers. Had t hon, t tell em so. Niggers always tryin t make somethin out a nothin. An then besides, white folks aint up t them tricks so much nowadays. Godam better not be. Leastawise not with yo. Cause I wouldnt stand f it. Nassur."

"What would you do, Tom?"

"Cut him jes like I cut a nigger."

"No, Tom —"

"I said I would an there aint no mo to it. But that aint th talk f now. Sing, honey Louisa, an while I'm listenin t y I'll be makin love."

Tom took her hand in his. Against the tough thickness of his own, hers felt soft and small. His huge body slipped down to the step beside her. The full moon sank upward into the deep purple of the cloud-bank. An old woman brought a lighted lamp and hung it on the common well whose bulky shadow squatted in the middle of the road, opposite Tom and Louisa. The old woman lifted the well-lid, took hold the chain, and began drawing up the heavy bucket. As she did so, she sang. Figures shifted, restless-like, between lamp and window in the front rooms of the shanties. Shadows of the figures fought each other on the gray dust of the road. Figures raised the windows and joined the old woman in song. Louisa and Tom, the whole street, singing:

> Red nigger moon. Sinner!
> Blood-burning moon. Sinner!
> Come out that fact'ry door.

3

Bob Stone sauntered from his veranda out into the gloom of fir trees and magnolias. The clear white of his skin paled, and the flush of his cheeks turned purple. As if to balance this outer change, his mind became consciously a white man's. He passed the house with its huge open hearth which, in the days of slavery, was the plantation cookery. He saw Louisa bent over that hearth. He went in as a master should and took her. Direct, honest, bold. None of this sneaking that he had to go through now. The contrast was repulsive to him. His family had lost ground. Hell no, his family still owned the niggers, practically. Damned if they did, or he wouldnt have to duck around so. What would they think if they knew? His mother? His sister? He shouldnt mention them, shouldnt think of them in this connection. There in the dusk he blushed at doing so. Fellows about town were all right, but how about his friends up North? He could see them incredible, repulsed. They didnt know. The thought first made him laugh. Then, with their eyes still upon him, he began to feel embarrassed. He felt the need of explaining things to them. Explain hell. They wouldnt understand, and moreover, who ever heard of a Southerner getting on his knees to any Yankee, or anyone. No sir. He was going to see Louisa to-night, and love her. She was lovely — in her way. Nigger way. What way was that? Damned if he knew. Must know. He'd known her long enough to know. Was there something about niggers that you couldnt know? Listening to them at church didnt tell you anything. Looking at them didnt tell you anything. Talking to them didnt tell you anything — unless it was gossip, unless they wanted to talk. Of course, about farming, and licker, and craps — but those werent nigger. Nigger was something more. How much more? Something to be afraid of, more? Hell no. Who ever heard of being afraid of a nigger? Tom Burwell. Cartwell had told him that Tom went with Louisa after she reached home. No sir. No nigger had ever been with his girl. He'd like to see one try. Some position for him to be in. Him, Bob Stone, of the old Stone family, in a scrap with a nigger over a nig-ger girl. In the good old days. . . Ha! Those were the days. His family had lost ground. Not so much, though. Enough for him to have to cut through old Lemon's canefield by way of the woods, that he might meet her. She was worth it. Beautiful nigger gal. Why nigger? Why not, just gal? No, it was because she was nigger that he went to her. Sweet. . . The scent of boiling cane came to him. Then he saw the rich glow of the stove. He heard the voices of the men circled around it. He was about to skirt the clearing when he heard his own name mentioned. He stopped. Quivering. Leaning against a tree, he listened.

"Bad nigger. Yassur, he sho is one bad nigger when he gets started."

"Tom Burwell's been on th gang three times fo cuttin men."

"What y think he's agwine t do t Bob Stone?"

"Dunno yet. He aint found out. When he does — Baby!"

"Aint no tellin."

"Young Stone aint no quitter an I ken tell y that. Blood of th old uns in his veins."

"Thats right. He'll scrap, sho."

"Be gettin too hot f niggers round this away."

"Shut up, nigger. Y dont know what y talkin bout."

Bob Stone's ears burned as though he had been holding them over the stove. Sizzling heat welled up within him. His feet felt as if they rested on red-hot coals. They stung him to quick movement. He circled the fringe of the glowing. Not a twig cracked beneath his feet. He reached the path that led to factory town. Plunged furiously down it. Halfway along, a blindness within him veered him aside. He crashed into the bordering cane-brake. Cane leaves cut his face and lips. He tasted blood. He threw himself down and dug his fingers in the ground. The earth was cool. Cane-roots took the fever from his hands. After a long while, or so it seemed to him, the thought came to him that it must be time to see Louisa. He got to his feet and walked calmly to their meeting place. No Louisa. Tom Burwell had her. Veins in his forehead bulged and distended. Saliva moistened the dried blood on his lips. He bit down on his lips. He tasted blood. Not his own blood; Tom Burwell's blood. Bob drove through the cane and out again upon the road. A hound swung down the path before him towards factory town. Bob couldnt see it. The dog loped aside to let him pass. Bob's blind rushing made him stumble over it. He fell with a thud that dazed him. The hound yelped. Answering yelps came from all over the countryside. Chickens cackled. Roosters crowed, heralding the bloodshot eyes of southern awaken-ing. Singers in the town were silenced. They shut their windows down. Palpitant between the rooster crows, a chill hush settled upon the huddled forms of Tom and Louisa. A figure rushed from the shadow and stood before them. Tom popped to his feet.

"Whats y want?"

"I'm Bob Stone."

"Yassur — an I'm Tom Burwell. Whats y want?"

Bob lunged at him. Tom side-stepped, caught him by the shoulder, and flung him to the ground. Straddled him.

"Let me up."

"Yassur — but watch yo doins, Bob Stone."

A few dark figures, drawn by the sound of scuffle, stood about them. Bob sprang to his feet.

"Fight like a man, Tom Burwell, an I'll lick y."

Again he lunged. Tom side-stepped and flung him to the ground. Straddled him.

"Get off me, you godam nigger you."

"Yo sho has started somethin now. Get up."

Tom yanked him up and began hammering at him. Each blow sounded as if it smashed into a precious, irreplaceable soft something. Beneath them, Bob staggered back. He reached in his pocket and whipped out a knife.

"Thats my game, sho."

Blue flash, a steel blade slashed across Bob Stone's throat. He had a sweetish sick feeling. Blood began to flow. Then he felt a sharp twitch of pain. He let his knife drop. He slapped one hand against his neck. He pressed the other on top of his head as if to hold it down. He groaned. He turned, and staggered towards the crest of the hill in the direction of white town. Negroes who had seen the fight slunk into their homes and blew the lamps out. Louisa, dazed, hysterical, refused to go indoors. She slipped, crumbled, her body loosely propped against the woodwork of the well. Tom Burwell leaned against it. He seemed rooted there.

Bob reached Broad Street. White men rushed up to him. He collapsed in their arms.

"Tom Burwell. . . ."

White men like ants upon a forage rushed about. Except for the taut hum of their moving, all was silent. Shotguns, revolvers, rope, kerosene, torches. Two high-powered cars with glaring search-lights. They came together. The taut hum rose to a low roar. Then nothing could be heard but the flop of their feet in the thick dust of the road. The moving body of their silence preceded them over the crest of the hill into factory town. It flattened the Negroes beneath it. It rolled to the wall of the factory, where it stopped. Tom knew that they were coming. He couldnt move. And then he saw the search-lights of the two cars glaring down on him. A quick shock went through him. He stiffened. He started to run. A yell went up from the mob. Tom wheeled about and faced them. They poured down on him. They swarmed. A large man with dead-white face and flabby cheeks came to him and almost jabbed a gun-barrel through his guts.

"Hands behind y, nigger."

Tom's wrists were bound. The big man shoved him to the well. Burn him over it, and when the woodwork caved in, his body would drop to the bottom. Two deaths for a godam nigger. Louisa was driven back. The mob pushed in. Its pressure, its momentum was too great. Drag him to the factory. Wood and stakes already there. Tom moved in the direction indicated. But they had to drag him. They reached the great door. Too many to get in there. The mob divided and flowed around the walls to either side. The big man shoved him through the door. The mob pressed in from the sides. Taut humming. No words. A stake was sunk into the ground. Rotting floor boards piled around it. Kerosene poured on the rotting floor boards. Tom bound to the stake. His breast was bare. Nails scratches let little lines of blood trickle down and mat into the hair. His face, his eyes were set and stony. Except for irregular breathing, one would have thought him already dead. Torches were flung onto the pile. A great flare muffled in black smoke shot upward. The mob yelled. The mob was silent. Now Tom could be seen within the flames. Only his head, erect, lean, like a blackened stone. Stench of burning flesh soaked the air. Tom's eyes popped. His head settled downward. The mob yelled. Its yell echoed against the skeleton stone walls and sounded like a hundred yells. Like a hundred mobs yelling. Its yell thudded against the thick front wall and fell back. Ghost of a yell slipped through the flames and out the great door of the factory. It fluttered like a dying thing down the single street of factory town. Louisa, upon the step before her home, did not hear it, but her eyes opened slowly. They saw the full moon glowing in the great door. The full moon, an evil thing, an omen, soft showering the homes of folks she knew. Where were they, these people? She'd sing, and perhaps they'd come out and join her. Perhaps Tom Burwell would come. At any rate, the full moon in the great door was an omen which she must sing to:

> Red nigger moon. Sinner!
> Blood-burning moon. Sinner!
> Come out that fact'ry door.

[1923]

Seventh Street[1]

> Money burns the pocket, pocket hurts,
> Bootleggers in silken shirts,
> Ballooned, zooming Cadillacs,
> Whizzing, whizzing down the street-car tracks.

Seventh Street is a bastard of Prohibition and the War. A crude-boned, soft-skinned wedge of nigger life breathing its loafer air, jazz songs and love, thrusting unconscious rhythms, black reddish blood into the white and whitewashed wood of Washington. Stale soggy wood of Washington. Wedges rust in soggy wood. . . Split it! In two! Again! Shred it! . . the sun. Wedges are brilliant in the sun; ribbons of wet wood dry and blow away. Black reddish blood. Pouring for crude-boned soft-skinned life, who set you flowing? Blood suckers of the War would spin in a frenzy of dizziness if they drank your blood. Prohibition would put a stop to it. Who set you flowing? White and whitewash disappear in blood. Who set you flowing? Flowing down the smooth asphalt of Seventh Street, in shanties, brick office buildings, theaters, drug stores, restaurants, and cabarets? Eddying on the corners? Swirling like a blood-red smoke up where the buz-

---

1. **Seventh Street:** The African American neighborhood around the intersection of Seventh and T streets in northwest Washington, D.C., began to develop when former slaves moved into the area after the Civil War. By the early twentieth century, it had become a lively center of commerce, culture, and entertainment, and the population of the area was swelled by the migration of southern blacks during World War I. In July 1919, in what became known as the "Red Summer" of race riots throughout the country, residents of the neighborhood repelled a mob of rioting white servicemen who had recently returned from overseas. During three days of rioting, roughly forty people, both black and white, were killed in the violence that swept across the nation's capital.

zards fly in heaven? God would not dare to suck black red blood. A Nigger God! He would duck his head in shame and call for the Judgment Day. Who set you flowing?

> Money burns the pocket, pocket hurts,
> Bootleggers in silken shirts,
> Ballooned, zooming Cadillacs,
> Whizzing, whizzing down the street-car tracks.

[1922, 1923]

F. Scott Fitzgerald

[1896–1940]

Francis Scott Key Fitzgerald was born in St. Paul, Minnesota, on September 24, 1896. He was the first child of Edward Fitzgerald, a descendant of Francis Scott Key, the composer of "The Star Spangled Banner," and Mary McQuillan Fitzgerald, the devout daughter of a wealthy Irish Catholic family. In 1898, Edward Fitzgerald's furniture factory failed, and he moved the family to Buffalo, New York. When he lost his job in 1908, he came home from work "a completely broken man," as Fitzgerald described the traumatic event. The family returned to St. Paul, where they were largely supported by the McQuillans. Fitzgerald recalled that, by the age of twelve, he "wrote all through every class in school," and he published his first short story in the school's literary magazine in October 1909. In an effort to force him to study and improve his academic performance, the family sent him to a private preparatory school in New Jersey in September 1911. He continued to devote most of his efforts to writing, so his grades were mediocre, but he did well enough on his entrance exams to be admitted to Princeton University in the fall of 1913. He was drawn there by the Triangle Club, a musical-comedy troupe for which Fitzgerald wrote an operetta during his first year, and he was a regular contributor to the *Princeton Tiger*, a humor magazine, and the *Nassau Literary Magazine*. When his grades slipped and he was barred from extracurricular activities as a form of academic probation, Fitzgerald left

F. Scott Fitzgerald

This photograph of Fitzgerald reading at his desk was taken in the early 1920s, after he had achieved overnight fame with the publication of his first novel, *This Side of Paradise* (1920).

Princeton without completing his degree. In the fall of 1917, after the United States entered World War I, he was granted an army commission and was sent for officer training to Fort Leavenworth, Kansas.

Despite the unpromising circumstances, Fitzgerald soon fulfilled his youthful dreams of literary success. At Fort Leavenworth, he worked feverishly on a semiautobiographical novel, *The Romantic Egoist,* which he submitted to the New York publisher Charles Scribner's Sons in the spring of 1918. Meanwhile, he was transferred to an army camp near Montgomery, Alabama, where he met his future wife, Zelda Sayre. That summer, Scribner's rejected Fitzgerald's novel, but the editor Maxwell Perkins strongly encouraged him to revise and resubmit it, observing that "no manuscript novel has come to us for a long time that seemed to display so much originality." The war ended before Fitzgerald could be shipped overseas, and he was discharged from the army. Zelda Sayre refused to marry him until he had "prospects," as she called them, and Fitzgerald went to New York City in February 1919. In an effort to earn enough money to support them, he took a job in advertising and wrote short stories at night. Discouraged by his failure to sell any of the stories, Fitzgerald returned home to St. Paul. There, he revised, retitled, and resubmitted his novel, which Scribner's published on March 26, 1920. One advertisement for the novel read: "Were you ever under thirty? Then Read THIS SIDE OF PARADISE by F. Scott Fitzgerald." The first printing of three thousand copies sold out in three days, and sales were spurred by favorable and sometimes enthusiastic reviews, one of which described Fitzgerald as a "new American author of amazing potentialities." A triumphant Fitzgerald married Zelda Sayre in New York on April 3, 1920, and the young couple embarked on a nomadic and often notorious life that came to symbolize both the glamour and the excesses of what he soon dubbed the "Jazz Age."

The financial pressures to support their lavish lifestyle strongly shaped Fitzgerald's early career. *This Side of Paradise* sold more than forty thousand copies in 1920. Even during that year, however, he made significantly more money from stories he sold to magazines, especially the mass-circulation *Saturday Evening Post.* Although he deeply resented the time such writing took away from his work on novels, Fitzgerald ultimately produced more than 150 magazine stories, including some outstanding ones. Following the publication of his popular first collection of stories, *Flappers and Philosophers* (1920), he concentrated on his second novel, *The Beautiful and the Damned* (1922). Reviews were mixed, but the novel sold well, as did Fitzgerald's second collection of stories, *Tales of the Jazz Age* (1922). He then decided to write a play that "is to make my fortune," a farcical political satire published as *The Vegetable; or, From President to Postman.* But the out-of-town tryouts were disastrous, and the play never opened on Broadway. Now in debt, Fitzgerald swiftly produced ten stories early in 1923, earning enough money to support his work on a new novel he initially called "Among the Ash Heaps and Millionaires." After he and Zelda took their three-year-old daughter to live on the French Riviera in 1924, Fitzgerald completed the novel, which was published as *The Great Gatsby* (1925). Despite admiring reviews, the book sold poorly, though

He had one of the rarest qualities in all literature . . . a kind of subdued magic, controlled and exquisite, the sort of thing you get from good string quartets.

–Raymond Chandler

Fitzgerald earned a good deal of subsidiary income from a successful stage version and a silent movie made by the Famous Players Film Company. He also continued to command top dollar for his magazine stories, some of the best of which were included in his collection *All the Sad Young Men* (1926). "As F. Scott Fitzgerald continues to publish books, it becomes apparent that he is head and shoulders better than any writer of his generation," a reviewer observed in the *Bookman*.

bedfordstmartins.com/ americanlit for research links on Fitzgerald

Fitzgerald's productivity and reputation declined dramatically during the remainder of his career. In France, he became friends with and strongly promoted the work of Ernest Hemingway, who soon began to eclipse Fitzgerald. He began a new novel, but his progress was impeded by his heavy drinking and his strained relationship with Zelda. Overshadowed by her famous husband, and deeply frustrated by her futile effort to become a professional ballerina, she suffered the first of a series of mental breakdowns in 1930. Later diagnosed with schizophrenia, she was in and out of hospitals until her death in 1948, a period during which she wrote an autobiographical novel about her marriage to Fitzgerald, *Save Me the Waltz* (1932). After nearly eight years of sporadic work, Fitzgerald finally published a novel based on similar material, *Tender Is the Night* (1934). It received mixed reviews, and he published only one more book, a short-story collection appropriately entitled *Taps at Reveille* (1935). In 1936, after a series of his essays collectively known as "The Crack Up" appeared in *Esquire,* a writer for the *New York Post* brutally described Fitzgerald as a "washed up alcoholic." The following year, he moved to California, where he worked as a screenwriter for Metro-Goldwyn-Mayer. Fitzgerald continued to publish stories in magazines, primarily in *Esquire,* and he began work on a novel about Hollywood. But he had not yet completed the novel, posthumously published as *The Last Tycoon* (1941), when he died of a heart attack on December 21, 1940.

Fitzgerald's "The Ice Palace."   This was one of the earliest of the sixty-five stories Fitzgerald published in the *Saturday Evening Post* between 1920 and 1937. Originally established in 1821 as a four-page weekly newspaper, the *Post* was among the longest running periodicals in the United States. During the 1920s, its circulation reached 2,750,000 copies a week, and the *Post* came to symbolize the tastes and values of middle-class America. The conservative magazine placed a premium on hard work and material success, and more than half of the roughly two hundred pages in each issue were devoted to advertisements, especially for cars. For only five cents an issue, readers also enjoyed a variety of articles on business, current affairs, and travel, humorous and human-interest stories, and fiction by the most popular writers of the period. The *Post* was also well known for its lavish illustrations by Norman Rockwell, who began working for the magazine in 1916, and by James H. Crank, who illustrated "The Ice Palace." Inspired by Fitzgerald's courtship of Zelda Sayre, who was born and raised

The Saturday Evening Post

"The Ice Palace" was first published in this issue of the popular weekly, the cover of which projected the innocent, family-oriented image of the *Post*. Its Philadelphia publisher claimed that the magazine was descended from the *Pennsylvania Gazette*, founded in 1728 by Benjamin Franklin, but he died more than thirty years before the first issue of the *Post* appeared in 1821.

in Montgomery, Alabama, the story concerns a journey of discovery undertaken by Sally Carrol Happer, a girl born in "southernmost Georgia," who is engaged to Harry Bellamy, a boy from a nameless northern city that closely resembles Fitzgerald's hometown of St. Paul, Minnesota. Through the conflict that emerges between the young couple, Fitzgerald explores the broader climatic, cultural, and historical divisions between the North and the South, where the graves of the Confederate dead exemplify the region's strong connections to the past and the legacy of the Civil War. The text of the story, which Fitzgerald included in his collection *Flappers and Philosophers* (1920), is taken from the first printing in the *Saturday Evening Post*, May 22, 1920.

THE ICE PALACE

[I]

The sunlight dripped over the house like golden paint over an art jar and the freckling shadows here and there only intensified the rigor of the bath of light. The Butterworth and Larkin houses flanking were intrenched behind great stodgy trees; only the Happer house took the full sun and all day long faced the dusty road-street with a tolerant kindly patience. This was the city of Tarleton in southernmost Georgia — September afternoon.

Up in her bedroom window Sally Carrol Happer rested her nineteen-year-old chin on a fifty-two-year-old sill and watched Clark Darrow's ancient flivver[1] turn the corner. The car was hot — being partly metallic it retained all the heat it absorbed or evolved — and Clark Darrow sitting bolt upright at the wheel wore a pained, strained expression as though he considered himself a spare part and rather likely to break. He laboriously crossed two dust ruts, the wheels squeaking indignantly at the encounter, and then with a terrifying expression he gave the steering gear a final wrench and deposited self and car approximately in front of the Happer steps. There was a plaintive heaving sound, a death rattle, followed by a short silence; and then the air was rent by a startling whistle.

Sally Carrol gazed down sleepily. She started to yawn, but finding this quite impossible unless she raised her chin from the window still changed her mind and continued silently to regard the car, whose owner sat brilliantly if perfunctorily at attention as he waited for an answer to his signal. After a moment the whistle once more split the dusty air.

"Good mawnin'."

With difficulty Clark twisted his tall body round and bent a distorted glance on the window.

"'Tain't mawnin', Sally Carrol."

"Isn't it, sure enough?"

"What you doin'?"

"Eatin' 'n apple."

"Come on go swimmin' — want to?"

"Reckon so."

"How 'bout hurryin' up?"

"Sure enough."

Sally Carrol sighed voluminously and raised herself with profound inertia from the floor, where she had been occupied in alternately destroying parts of a green apple and painting paper dolls for her younger sister. She approached a mirror, regarded her expression with a pleased and pleasant languor, dabbed two spots of rouge on her lips and a grain of powder on her nose and covered her bobbed corn-colored hair with a rose-littered sunbonnet. Then she kicked over the painting water, said, "Oh, damn!" — but let it lie — and left the room.

"How you, Clark?" she inquired a minute later as she slipped nimbly over the side of the car.

"Mighty fine, Sally Carrol."

"Where we go swimmin'?"

"Out to Walley's Pool. Told Marylyn we'd call by an' get her an' Joe Ewing."

Clark was dark and lean and when on foot was rather inclined to stoop. His eyes were ominous and his expression rather petulant except when startlingly illuminated by one

---

1. flivver: An informal word for a cheap, poorly maintained car.

of his frequent smiles. Clark had what was locally called "a income" — just enough to keep himself in ease and his car in gasoline — and he had spent the two years since he graduated from Georgia Tech in dozing round the lazy streets of his home town discussing how he could best invest his capital for an immediate fortune.

Hanging round he found not at all difficult; a crowd of little girls had grown up beautifully, the amazing Sally Carrol foremost among them; and they enjoyed being swum with and danced with and made love to in the flower-filled summery evenings — and they all liked Clark immensely. When feminine company palled there were half a dozen other youths who were always just about to do something and meanwhile were quite willing to join him in a few holes of golf or a game of billiards or the consumption of a quart of "hard yella licker." Every once in a while one of these contemporaries made a farewell round of calls before going up to New York or Philadelphia or Pittsburgh to go into business, but mostly they just stayed round in this languid paradise of dreamy skies and firefly evenings and noisy street fairs — and especially of gracious soft-voiced girls who were brought up on memories instead of money.

The flivver having been excited into a sort of restless resentful life Clark and Sally Carrol rolled and rattled down Valley Avenue into Jefferson Street, where the dust road became a pavement; along opiate Millicent Place, where there were half a dozen prosperous substantial mansions; and on into the downtown section.

Driving was perilous here, for it was shopping time; the population idled casually across the streets and a drove of low-moaning oxen were being urged along in front of a placid street car; even the shops seemed only yawning their doors and blinking their windows in the sunshine before retiring into a state of utter and finite coma.

"Sally Carrol," said Clark suddenly, "it a fact that you're engaged?"

She looked at him quickly.

"Where'd you hear that?"

"Sure enough, you engaged?"

"'At's a nice question to ask a girl!"

"Girl told me you were engaged to a Yankee you met up in Asheville last summah."

Sally Carrol sighed.

"Never saw such an old town faw rumors."

"Don't marry a Yankee, Sally Carrol. We need you round here."

Sally Carrol was silent a moment.

"Clark," she demanded suddenly, "who on earth shall I marry?"

"I offah my services."

"Honey, you couldn't suppawt a wife," she answered cheerfully. "Anyway, I know you too well to fall in love with you."

"'At doesn't mean you ought to marry a Yankee."

"S'pose I love him?"

He shook his head.

"You couldn't. He'd be a lot different from us, every way."

He broke off as he halted the car in front of a rambling dilapidated house. Marylyn Wade and Joe Ewing appeared in the doorway.

"'Lo, Sally Carrol."

"Hi!"

"How you-all?"

"Sally Carrol," demanded Marylyn as they started off again, "you engaged?"

"Lawdy, where'd all this start? Can't I look at a man 'thout everybody in town engagin' me to him?"

Clark stared straight in front of him at a bolt on the clattering wind shield.

"Sally Carrol," he said with a curious intensity, "don't you like us?"

"What?"

"Us down here?"

"Why, Clark, you know I do. I adore all you boys."

"Then why you gettin' engaged to a Yankee?"

"Clark, I don't know. I'm not sure what I'll do, but — well, I want to go places and see people. I want my mind to grow. I want to live where things happen on a big scale."

"What you mean?"

"Oh, Clark, I love you, and I love Joe here, and Ben Arrot, and you all, but you'll — you'll —"

"We'll all be failures?"

"Yes. I don't mean only money failures but just sort of — of ineffectual and sad and — oh, how can I tell you?"

"You mean because we stay here in Tarleton?"

"Yes, Clark; and because you like it and never want to change things or think or go ahead."

He nodded and she reached over and pressed his hand.

"Clark," she said softly, "I wouldn't change you for the world. You're sweet the way you are. The things that'll make you fail I'll love always — the living in the past, the lazy days and nights you have, and all your carelessness and generosity."

"But you're goin' away?"

"Yes — because I couldn't ever marry you. You've a place in my heart no one else ever could have, but tied down here I'd get restless. I'd feel I was — wastin' myself. There's two sides to me, you see. There's the sleepy old side you love; an' there's a sawt of energy — the feelin' that makes me do wild things. That's the part of me that may be useful somewhere, that'll last when I'm not beautiful any more."

She broke off with characteristic suddenness and sighed, "Oh, sweet cooky!" as her mood changed.

Half closing her eyes and tipping back her head till it rested on the seat back she let the savory breeze fan her eyes and ripple the fluffy curls of her bobbed hair. They were in the country now, hurrying between tangled growths of bright-green coppice and grass and tall trees that sent sprays of foliage to hang a cool welcome over the road. Here and there they passed a battered negro cabin, its oldest white-haired inhabitant smoking a corncob pipe beside the door and half a dozen scantily clothed pickaninnies[2]

---

2. **pickaninnies:** Probably derived from the Spanish word *pequeño,* meaning small or little, this now-offensive term was commonly used from the mid-nineteenth century until the 1930s to refer to African American children.

parading tattered dolls on the wild grown grass in front. Farther out were lazy cotton fields, where even the workers seemed intangible shadows lent by the sun to the earth not for toil but to while away some age-old tradition in the golden September fields. And round the drowsy picturesqueness, over the trees and shacks and muddy rivers, flowed the heat, never hostile, only comforting like a great warm nourishing bosom for the infant earth.

"Sally Carrol, we're here!"

"Poor chile's soun' asleep."

"Honey, you dead at last outa sheer laziness?"

"Water, Sally Carrol! Cool water waitin' faw you!"

Her eyes opened sleepily.

"Hi!" she murmured, smiling.

II

In November Harry Bellamy, tall, broad and brisk, came down from his Northern city to spend four days. His intention was to settle a matter that had been hanging fire since he and Sally Carrol had met in Asheville, North Carolina, in midsummer. The settlement took only a quiet afternoon and an evening in front of a glowing open fire, for Harry Bellamy had everything Sally Carrol wanted; and, besides, she loved him — loved him with that side of her she kept especially for loving. Sally Carrol had several rather clearly defined sides.

On his last afternoon they walked, and she found their steps tending half-unconsciously toward one of her favorite haunts, the cemetery. When it came in sight, gray-white and golden-green under the cheerful late sun; she paused irresolute by the iron gate.

"Are you mournful by nature, Harry?" she asked with a faint smile. "Mournful? Not I."

"Then let's go in here. It depresses some folks, but I like it."

They passed through the gateway and followed a path that led through a wavy valley of graves — dusty-gray and moldy for the fifties; quaintly carved with flowers and jars for the seventies; ornate and hideous for the nineties, with fat marble cherubs lying in sodden sleep on stone pillows, and great impossible growths of nameless granite flowers. Occasionally they saw a kneeling figure with tributary flowers, but over most of the graves lay silence and withered leaves with only the fragrance that their own shadowy memories could waken in living minds.

They reached the top of a hill where they were fronted by a tall round headstone, freckled with dark spots of damp and half grown over with vines.

"'Margery Lee,'" she read; "'1844-1873,' Wasn't she nice? She died when she was twenty-nine. Dear Margery Lee," she added softly. "Can't you see her, Harry?"

"Yes, Sally Carrol."

He felt a little hand insert itself into his.

"She was dark, I think; and she always wore her hair with a ribbon in it, and gorgeous hoopskirts of bright blue and old rose."

"Yes."

"Oh, she was sweet, Harry! And she was the sort of girl born to stand on a wide pillared porch and welcome folks in. I think perhaps a lot of men went away to war meanin' to come back to her; but maybe none of 'em ever did."

He stooped down close to the stone, hunting for any record of marriage.

"There's nothing here to show."

"Of course not. How could there be anything there better than just 'Margery Lee,' and that eloquent date?"

She drew close to him and an unexpected lump came into his throat as her yellow hair brushed his cheek.

"You see how she was, don't you, Harry?"

"I see," he agreed gently. "I see through your precious eyes. You're beautiful now, so I know she must have been."

Silent and close they stood, and he could feel her shoulders trembling a little. An ambling breeze swept up the hill and stirred the brim of her floppidy hat.

"Let's go down there!"

She was pointing to a flat stretch on the other side of the hill where along the green turf were a thousand grayish-white crosses stretching in endless ordered rows like the stacked-arms of a battalion.

"Those are the Confederate dead," said Sally Carrol simply.

They walked along and read the inscriptions, always only a name and a date, sometimes quite indecipherable.

"The last row is the saddest — see, 'way over there. Every cross has just a date on it and the word 'Unknown.'"

She looked at him and her eyes brimmed with tears.

"I can't tell you how real it is to me, darling — if you don't know."

"How you feel about it is beautiful to me."

"No, no, it's not me, it's them — that old time that I've tried to have live in me. These were just men, unimportant, evidently, or they wouldn't have been 'unknown'; but they died for the most beautiful thing in the world — the dead South. You see," she continued, her voice still husky, her eyes glistening with tears, "people have these dreams they fasten on to things, and I've always grown up with that dream. It was so easy because it was all dead and there weren't any disillusions comin' to me. I've tried in a way to live up to those past standards of noblesse oblige — there's just the last remnants of it, you know, like the roses of an old garden dying all round us — streaks of strange courtliness and chivalry in some of these boys an' stories I used to hear from a Confederate soldier who lived next door, and a few old darkies. Oh, Harry, there was something, there was something! I couldn't ever make you understand, but it was there."

"I understand," he assured her again quietly.

Sally Carrol smiled and dried her eyes on the tip of a handkerchief protruding from his breast pocket.

"You don't feel depressed, do you, lover? Even when I cry I'm happy here, and I get a sawt of strength from it."

Hand in hand they turned and walked slowly away. Finding soft grass she drew him down to a seat beside her with their backs against the remnants of a low broken wall.

"Wish those three old women would clear out," he complained. "I want to kiss you, Sally Carrol."

"Me, too."

They waited impatiently for the three bent figures to move off, and then she kissed him until the sky seemed to fade out, and all her smiles and tears to vanish in an ecstasy of eternal seconds.

Afterward they walked slowly back together, while on the corners twilight played at somnolent black-and-white checkers with the end of day.

"You'll be up about mid-January," he said, "and you've got to stay a month at least. It'll be slick. There's a winter carnival on, and if you've never really seen snow it'll be like fairyland to you. There'll be skating and skiing and tobogganing and sleigh riding and all sorts of torchlight parades on snowshoes. They haven't had one for years, so they're going to make it a knock-out."

"Will it be cold, Harry?" she asked suddenly.

"You certainly won't. You may freeze your nose, but you won't be shivery cold. It's hard and dry, you know."

"I guess I'm a summer child. I don't like any cold I've ever seen."

She broke off and they were both silent for a minute.

"Sally Carrol," he said very slowly, "what do you say to — March?"

"I say I love you."

"March?"

"March, Harry."

III

All night in the Pullman it was very cold. She rang for the porter to ask for another blanket, and when he couldn't give her one she tried vainly, by squeezing down into the bottom of her berth and doubling back the bedclothes, to snatch a few hours' sleep.

Sally Carrol wanted to look her best in the morning.

She rose at six and sliding uncomfortably into her clothes stumbled up to the diner for a cup of coffee. The snow had filtered into the vestibules and covered the floor with a slippery coating. It was intriguing, this cold, it crept in everywhere. Her breath was quite visible and she blew into the air with a naive enjoyment. Seated in the diner she stared out the window at white hills and valleys and scattered pines with each branch a green platter for a cold feast of snow.

Sometimes a solitary farmhouse would fly by, ugly and bleak and lone on the white waste; and with each one she had an instant of chill compassion for the souls shut in there waiting for spring.

As she left the diner and swayed back into the Pullman she experienced a surging rush of energy and wondered if she was feeling the bracing air of which Harry had spoken. This was the North, the North — her land now!

> Then blow, ye winds, heigho!
> A-roving I will go,

she chanted exultantly to herself.

"What's 'at?" inquired the porter politely.

"I said, 'Brush me off.'"

The long wires of the telegraph poles doubled: two tracks ran up beside the train — three — four; came a succession of white-roofed houses, a glimpse of a trolley car with frosted windows, streets — more streets — the city.

She stood for a dazed moment in the frosty station before she saw three fur-bundled figures descending upon her.

"There she is!"

"Oh, Sally Carrol!"

Sally Carrol dropped her bag.

"Hi!"

A faintly familiar icy-cold face kissed her, and then she was in a group of faces all apparently emitting great clouds of heavy smoke; she was shaking hands. There was Gordon, a short, eager man of thirty who looked like an amateur knocked-about model for Harry; and his wife Myra, a listless lady with flaxen hair under a fur automobile cap. Almost immediately Sally Carrol thought of her as vaguely Scandinavian. A cheerful chauffeur adopted her bag and amid ricochets of half phrases, exclamations and perfunctory, listless "my dear's" from Myra they swept each other from the station.

Then they were in a sedan bound through a crooked succession of snowy streets where dozens of little boys were hitching sleds behind grocery wagons and automobiles.

"Oh," cried Sally Carrol, "I want to do that! Can we, Harry?"

"That's for kids. But we might —"

"It looks like such a circus!" she said regretfully.

Home was a rambling frame house set on a white lap of snow, and there she met a big, gray-haired man of whom she approved, and a lady who was like an egg and who kissed her — these were Harry's parents. There was a breathless, indescribable hour crammed full of half sentences, hot water, bacon and eggs and confusion; and after that she was alone with Harry in the library asking him if she dared smoke.

It was a large room with a Madonna over the fireplace and rows upon rows of books in covers of light gold and dark gold and shiny red. All the chairs had little lace squares where one's head should rest, the couch was just comfortable, the books looked as if they had been read — some — and Sally Carrol had an instantaneous vision of the battered old library at home with her father's huge medical books and the oil paintings of her three great-uncles and the old couch that had been mended up for forty-five years and was still luxurious to dream in. This room struck her as being neither attractive nor particularly otherwise. It was simply a room with a lot of fairly expensive things in it that all looked about fifteen years old.

"What do you think of it up here?" demanded Harry eagerly. "Does it surprise you? Is it what you expected, I mean?"

"You are, Harry," she said quietly, and reached out her arms to him.

But after a brief kiss he seemed anxious to extort enthusiasm from her.

"The town, I mean. Do you like it? Can you feel the pep in the air?"

"Oh, Harry," she laughed, "you'll have to give me time. You can't just fling questions at me."

She puffed at her cigarette with a sigh of contentment.

"One thing I want to ask you," he began rather apologetically; "you Southerners put quite an emphasis on family and all that — not that it isn't quite all right, but you'll find it a little different here. I mean — you'll notice a lot of things that'll seem to you sort of vulgar display at first, Sally Carrol; but just remember that this is a three-generation town. Everybody has a father and about half of us have grandfathers. Back of that we don't go."

"Of course," she murmured.

"Our grandfathers, you see, founded the place, and a lot of them had to take some pretty queer jobs while they were doing the founding.

"For instance, there's one woman who at present is about the social model for the town; well, her father was the first public ash man — things like that."

"Why," said Sally Carrol, puzzled, "did you s'pose I was goin' to make remarks about people?"

"Not at all," interrupted Harry; "and I'm not apologizing for anyone either. It's just that — well, a Southern girl came up here last summer and said some unfortunate things, and — oh, I just thought I'd tell you."

Sally Carrol felt suddenly indignant — as though she had been unjustly spanked — but Harry evidently considered the subject closed, for he went on with a great surge of enthusiasm.

"It's carnival time, you know. First in ten years. And there's an ice palace they're building now that's the first they've had since Eighty-five. Built out of blocks of the clearest ice they could find — on a tremendous scale."

She rose and walking to the window pushed aside the heavy Turkish portières and looked out.

"Oh!" she cried suddenly. "There's two little boys makin' a snow man! Harry, do you reckon I can go out an' help 'em?"

"You dream! Come here and kiss me."

She left the window rather reluctantly.

"I don't guess this is a very kissable climate, is it? I mean, it makes you so you don't want to sit round, doesn't it?"

"We're not going to. I've got a vacation for the first week you're here, and there's a dinner dance to-night."

"Oh, Harry," she confessed, subsiding in a heap, half in his lap, half in the pillows, "I sure do feel confused. I haven't got an idea whether I'll like it or not, an' I don't know what people expect or anythin'. You'll have to tell me, honey."

"I'll tell you," he said softly, "if you'll just tell me you're glad to be here."

"Glad — just awful glad!" she whispered, insinuating herself into his arms in her own peculiar way. "Where you are is home for me, Harry."

And as she said this she had the feeling for almost the first time in her life that she was acting a part.

That night, amid the gleaming candles of a dinner party where the men seemed to do most of the talking while the girls sat in a haughty and expensive aloofness, even Harry's presence on her left failed to make her feel at home.

"They're a good-looking crowd, don't you think?" he demanded. "Just look round.

There's Spud Hubbard, tackle at Princeton last year, and Junie Morton — he and the red-haired fellow next to him were both Yale hockey captains; Junie was in my class. Why, the best athletes in the world come from these states round here. This is a man's country, I tell you. Look at John J. Fishburn!"

"Who's he?" asked Sally Carrol innocently.

"Don't you know?"

"I've heard the name."

"Greatest wheat man in the Northwest, and one of the greatest financiers in the country."

She turned suddenly to a voice on her right.

"I guess they forgot to introduce us. My name's Roger Patton."

"My name is Sally Carrol Happer," she said graciously.

"Yes, I know. Harry told me you were coming."

"You a relative?"

"No, I'm a professor."

"Oh," she laughed.

"At the university. You're from the South, aren't you?"

"Yes; Tarleton, Georgia."

She liked him immediately — a reddish-brown mustache under watery blue eyes that had something in them that these other eyes lacked, some quality of appreciation. They exchanged stray sentences through dinner and she made up her mind to see him again.

After coffee she was introduced to numerous good-looking young men who danced with conscious precision and seemed to take it for granted that she wanted to talk about nothing except Harry.

"Heavens," she thought, "they talk as if my being engaged made me older than they are — as if I'd tell their mothers on them!"

In the South an engaged girl, even a young married woman, expected the same amount of half-affectionate badinage[3] and flattery that would be accorded a débutante, but here all that seemed banned. One young man, after getting well started on the subject of Sally Carrol's eyes and how they had allured him ever since she entered the room, went into a violent confusion when he found she was visiting the Bellamys — was Harry's fiancée. He seemed to feel as though he had made some risqué and inexcusable blunder, became immediately formal and left her at the first opportunity.

She was rather glad when Roger Patton cut in on her, and suggested that they sit out a while.

"Well," he inquired, blinking cheerily, "how's Carmen from the South?"

"Mighty fine. How's — how's Dangerous Dan McGrew? Sorry, but he's the only Northerner I know much about."

He seemed to enjoy that.

"Of course," he confessed, "as a professor of literature I'm not supposed to have read Dangerous Dan McGrew."

---

3. **badinage:** Quick, witty conversation.

"Are you a native?"

"No, I'm a Philadelphian. Imported from Harvard to teach seventeenth-century French. But I've been here ten years."

"Nine years, three hundred an' sixty-four days longer than me."

"Like it here?"

"Uh-huh. Sure do!"

"Really?"

"Well, why not? Don't I look as if I were havin' a good time?"

"I saw you look out the window a minute ago — and shiver."

"Just my imagination," laughed Sally Carrol. "I'm used to havin' everythin' quiet out-side, an' sometimes I look out an' see a flurry of snow, an' it's just as if somethin' dead was movin'."

He nodded appreciatively.

"Ever been North before?"

"Spent two Julys in Asheville, North Carolina."

"Nice-looking crowd, aren't they?" suggested Patton, indicating the swirling floor.

Sally Carrol started. This had been Harry's remark.

"Sure are! They're — canine."

"What?"

She flushed.

"I'm sorry; that sounded worse than I meant it. You see I always think of people as feline or canine, irrespective of sex."

"Which are you?"

"I'm feline. So are you. So are most Southern men an' most of these girls here."

"What's Harry?"

"Harry's canine, distinctly. All the men I've met to-night seem to be canine."

"What does 'canine' imply? A certain conscious masculinity as opposed to subtlety?"

"Reckon so. I never analyzed it — only I just look at people an' say 'canine' or 'feline' right off. It's right absurd, I guess."

"Not at all. I'm interested. I used to have a theory about these people. I think they're freezing up."

"What?"

"I think they're growing like Swedes — Ibsenesque, you know. Very gradually getting gloomy and melancholy. It's these long winters. Ever read any Ibsen?"

She shook her head.

"Well, you find in his characters a certain brooding rigidity. They're righteous, nar-row and cheerless, without infinite possibilities for great sorrow or joy."

"Without smiles or tears?"

"Exactly. That's my theory. You see there are thousands of Swedes up here. They come, I imagine, because the climate is very much like their own, and there's been a gradual mingling. They're probably not half a dozen here to-night, but — we've had four Swedish governors. Am I boring you?"

"I'm mighty interested."

"Your future sister-in-law is half Swedish. Personally I like her, but my theory is that Swedes react rather badly on us as a whole. Scandinavians, you know, have the largest suicide rate in the world."

"Why do you live here if it's so depressing?"

"Oh, it doesn't get me. I'm pretty well cloistered, and I suppose books mean more than people to me anyway."

"But writers all speak about the South being tragic. You know — Spanish señoritas, black hair and daggers an' hauntin' music."

He shook his head.

"No, the Northern races are the tragic races — they don't indulge in the cheering luxury of tears."

Sally Carrol thought of her graveyard. She supposed that that was vaguely what she had meant when she said it didn't depress her.

"The Italians are about the gayest people in the world — but it's a dull subject," he broke off. "Anyway, I want to tell you you're marrying a pretty fine man."

Sally Carrol was moved by an impulse of confidence.

"I know. I'm the sort of person who wants to be taken care of after a certain point, and I feel sure I will be."

"Shall we dance? You know," he continued as they rose, "it's encouraging to find a girl who knows what she's marrying for. Nine-tenths of them think of it as a sort of walking into a moving-picture sunset."

She laughed, and liked him immensely.

Two hours later on the way home she nestled near Harry in the back seat.

"Oh, Harry," she whispered, "it's so co-old!"

"But it's warm in here, darling girl."

"But outside it's cold; and oh, that howling wind!"

She buried her face deep in his fur coat and trembled involuntarily as his cold lips kissed the tip of her ear.

IV

The first week of her visit passed in a whirl. She had her promised toboggan ride at the back of an automobile through a chill January twilight. Swathed in furs she put in a morning tobogganing on the country-club hill; even tried skiing, to sail through the air for a glorious moment and then land in a tangled, laughing bundle on a soft snowdrift. She liked all the winter sports, except an afternoon spent snowshoeing over a glaring plain under pale yellow sunshine; but she soon realized that these things were for children — that she was being humored and that the enjoyment round her was only a reflection of her own.

At first the Bellamy family puzzled her. The men were reliable and she liked them; to Mr. Bellamy especially, with his iron-gray hair and energetic dignity, she took an immediate fancy once she found that he was born in Kentucky; this made of him a link between the old life and the new. But toward the women she felt a definite hostility.

Myra, her future sister-in-law, seemed the essence of spiritless conventionality. Her conversation was so utterly devoid of personality that Sally Carrol, who came from a country where a certain amount of charm and assurance could be taken for granted in the women, was inclined to despise her.

"If those women aren't beautiful," she thought, "they're nothing. They just fade out when you look at them. They're glorified domestics. Men are the center of every mixed group."

Lastly there was Mrs. Bellamy, whom Sally Carrol detested. The first day's impression of an egg had been confirmed — an egg with a cracked, veiny voice and such an ungracious dumpiness of carriage that Sally Carrol felt that if she once fell she would surely scramble. In addition, Mrs. Bellamy seemed to typify the town in being innately hostile to strangers. She called Sally Carrol "Sally," and could not be persuaded that the double name was anything more than a tedious, ridiculous nickname. To Sally Carrol this shortening of her name was like presenting her to the public half clothed. She loved "Sally Carrol"; she loathed "Sally." She knew also that Harry's mother disapproved of her bobbed hair; and she had never dared smoke downstairs after that first day when Mrs. Bellamy had come into the library sniffing violently.

Of all the men she met she preferred Roger Patton, who was a frequent visitor at the house. He never again alluded to the Ibsenesque tendency of the populace, but when he came in one day and found her curled up on the sofa bent over Peer Gynt he laughed and told her to forget what he'd said — that it was all rot.

And then one afternoon in her second week she and Harry hovered on the edge of a dangerously steep quarrel. She considered that he precipitated it entirely, though the Serbia[4] in the case was an unknown man who had not had his trousers pressed.

They had been walking homeward between mounds of high-piled snow and under a sun which Sally Carrol scarcely recognized. They passed a little girl done up in gray wool until she resembled a small Teddy bear, and Sally Carrol could not resist a gasp of maternal appreciation.

"Look! Harry!"

"What?"

"That little girl — did you see her face?"

"Yes, why?"

"It was red as a little strawberry. Oh, she was cute!"

"Why, your own face is almost as red as that already! Everybody's healthy here. We're out in the cold as soon as we're old enough to walk. Wonderful climate!"

She looked at him and had to agree. He was mighty healthy looking; so was his brother. And she had noticed the new red in her own cheeks that very morning.

Suddenly their glances were caught and held and they stared for a moment at the street corner ahead of them. A man was standing there, his knees bent, his eyes gazing

---

4. **the Serbia in the case:** The assassination of Archduke Franz Ferdinand, heir to the Austro-Hungarian throne, by members of a nationalist group in the small Balkan nation of Serbia set in motion a series of events that culminated in World War I, a global conflict that began in August 1914.

upward with a tense expression as though he were about to make a leap toward the chilly sky. And then they both exploded into a shout of laughter, for coming closer they discovered it had been a ludicrous momentary illusion produced by the extreme bagginess of the man's trousers.

"Reckon that's one on us," she laughed.

"He must be a Southerner, judging by those trousers," suggested Harry mischievously.

"Why, Harry!"

Her surprised look must have irritated him.

"Those damn Southerners!"

Sally Carrol's eyes flashed.

"Don't call 'em that!"

"I'm sorry, dear," said Harry, malignantly apologetic, "but you know what I think of them. They're sort of – sort of degenerates – not at all like the old Southerners. They've lived so long down there with all the colored people that they've gotten lazy and shiftless."

"Hush your mouth, Harry!" she cried angrily. "They're not! They may be lazy – anybody would be in that climate – but they're my best friends, an' I don't want to hear 'em criticized in any such sweepin' way. Some of 'em are the finest men in the world."

"Oh, I know. They're all right when they come North to college, but of all the hangdog, ill-dressed, slovenly lot I ever saw a bunch of small-town Southerners are the worst!"

Sally Carrol was clenching her gloved hands and biting her lip furiously.

"Why," continued Harry, "there was one in my class at New Haven and we all thought that at last we'd found the true type of Southern aristocrat, but it turned out that he wasn't an aristocrat at all – just the son of a Northern carpetbagger who owned about all the cotton round Birmingham."

"A Southerner wouldn't talk the way you're talking now," she said evenly.

"They haven't the energy!"

"Or the somethin' else."

"I'm sorry, Sally Carrol, but I've heard you say yourself that you'd never marry —"

"That's quite different. I told you I wouldn't want to tie my life to any of the boys that are round Tarleton now, but I never made any sweepin' generalities."

They walked along in silence.

"I probably spread it on a bit thick, Sally Carrol. I'm sorry."

She nodded, but made no answer. Five minutes later as they stood in the hallway she suddenly threw her arms round him.

"Oh, Harry," she cried, her eyes full of tears, "let's get married next week. I'm afraid of having fusses like that. I'm afraid, Harry. It wouldn't be that way if we were married."

But Harry being in the wrong was still irritated.

"That'd be idiotic. We decided on March."

The tears in Sally Carrol's eyes faded; her expression hardened slightly.

"Very well – I suppose I shouldn't have said that."

Harry melted.

"Dear little nut!" he cried. "Come and kiss me and let's forget."

That very night at the end of a vaudeville performance the orchestra played Dixie, and Sally Carrol felt something stronger and more enduring than her tears and smiles of the day brim up inside her. She leaned forward, gripping the arms of her chair until her face grew crimson.

"Sort of get you, dear?" whispered Harry.

But she did not hear him. To the spirited throb of the violins and the inspiring beat of the kettledrums her own old ghosts were marching by and on into the darkness, and as fifes whistled and sighed in the low encore they seemed so nearly out of sight that she could have waved good-by.

> *Away, away, away down South in Dixie!*
> *Away, away, away down South in Dixie!*

V

It was a particularly cold night. A sudden thaw had nearly cleared the streets the day before, but now they were traversed again with a powdery wraith of loose snow that traveled in wavy lines before the feet of the wind and filled the lower air with a fine-particled mist. There was no sky — only a dark, ominous tent that draped in the tops of the streets and was in reality a vast approaching army of snowflakes — while over it all, chilling away the comfort from the brown-and-green glow of lighted windows and muffling the steady trot of the horse pulling their sleigh, interminably washed the north wind. It was a dismal town after all, she thought — dismal.

Sometimes at night it had seemed to her as though no one lived here — they had all gone long ago, leaving lighted houses to be covered in time by tombing heaps of sleet. Oh, if there should be snow on her grave! To be beneath great piles of it all winter long, where even her headstone would be a light shadow against light shadows. Her grave — a grave that should be flower-strewn and washed with sun and rain.

She thought again of those isolated country houses that her train had passed, and of the life there the long winter through — the ceaseless glare through the windows, the crust forming on the soft drifts of snow, finally the slow, cheerless melting and the harsh spring of which Roger Patton had told her. Her spring — to lose it forever — with its lilacs and the lazy sweetness it stirred in her heart. She was laying away that spring — afterward she would lay away that sweetness.

With a gradual insistence the storm broke. Sally Carrol felt a film of flakes melt quickly on her eyelashes and Harry reached over a furry arm and drew down her complicated flannel cap. Then the small flakes came in skirmish line and the horse bent his neck patiently as a transparency of white appeared momentarily on his coat.

"Oh, he's cold, Harry," she said quickly.

"Who? The horse? Oh, no, he isn't. He likes it!"

After another ten minutes they turned a corner and came in sight of their destination. On a tall hill outlined in vivid glaring green against the wintry sky stood the ice palace. It was three stories in the air, with battlements and embrasures and narrow icicled windows, and the innumerable electric lights inside made a gorgeous transparency of the great central hall. Sally Carrol clutched Harry's hand under the fur robe.

"It's beautiful!" he cried excitedly. "My golly, it's beautiful, isn't it? They haven't had one here since eighty-five!"

Somehow the notion of there not having been one since eighty-five oppressed her. Ice was a ghost, and this mansion of it was surely peopled by those shades of the eighties, with pale faces and blurred snow-filled hair.

"Come on, dear," said Harry.

She followed him out of the sleigh and waited while he hitched the horse. A party of four — Gordon, Myra, Roger Patton and another girl — drew up beside them with a mighty jingle of bells. There was quite a crowd already, bundled in fur or sheepskin, shouting and calling to each other as they moved through the snow, which was now so thick that people could scarcely be distinguished a few yards away.

"It's a hundred and seventy feet tall," Harry was saying to a muffled figure beside him as they trudged toward the entrance; "covers six thousand square yards."

She caught snatches of conversation: "One main hall" — "walls twenty to forty inches thick" — "and the ice cave has almost a mile of" — "This Canuck[5] who built it —"

They found their way inside, and dazed by the magic of the great crystal walls Sally Carrol found herself repeating over and over two lines from Kubla Khan:

> *It was a miracle of rare device,*
> *A sunny pleasure-dome with caves of ice!*[6]

In the great glittering cavern with the dark shut out she took a seat on a wooden bench, and the evening's oppression lifted. Harry was right — it was beautiful; and her gaze traveled the smooth surface of the walls, the blocks for which had been selected for their purity and clearness to obtain this opalescent, translucent effect.

"Look! Here we go — oh, boy!" cried Harry.

A band in a far corner struck up Hail, Hail, the Gang's All Here! which echoed over to them in wild muddled acoustics, and then the lights suddenly went out; silence seemed to flow down the icy sides and sweep over them. Sally Carrol could still see her white breath in the darkness, and a dim row of pale faces over on the other side.

The music eased to a sighing complaint, and from outside drifted in the full-throated resonant chant of the marching clubs. It grew louder like some paean of a viking tribe traversing an ancient wild; it swelled — they were coming nearer; then a row of torches appeared, and another and another, and keeping time with their moccasined feet a long column of gray-mackinawed[7] figures swept in, snowshoes slung at their shoulders, torches soaring and flickering as their voices rose along the great walls.

The gray column ended and another followed, the light streaming luridly this time over red toboggan caps and flaming crimson mackinaws, and as it entered it took up the refrain; then came a long platoon of blue and white, of green, of white, of brown and yellow.

---

5. **Canuck:** Informal and usually derogatory term for a Canadian.
6. *It was . . . caves of ice!*: The lines are from "Kubla Khan" (1816), a famous visionary poem by the English writer Samuel Taylor Coleridge (1772–1834).
7. **gray-mackinawed:** A mackinaw is a short coat or jacket, usually made of heavy wool.

"Those white ones are the Wacouta Club," whispered Harry eagerly. "Those are the men you've met round at dances."

The volume of the voices grew; the great cavern was a phantasmagoria of torches waving in great banks of fire, of colors and the rhythm of soft leather steps. The leading column turned and halted, platoon deployed in front of platoon until the whole procession made a solid flag of flame, and then from thousands of voices burst a mighty shout that filled the air like a crash of thunder and sent the torches wavering. It was magnificent, it was tremendous! To Sally Carrol it was the North offering sacrifices on some mighty altar to the gray pagan God of Snow.

As the shout died the band struck up again and there came more singing, and then long reverberating cheers by each club. She sat very quiet listening while the staccato cries rent the stillness; and then she started, for there was a volley of explosion, and great clouds of smoke went up here and there through the cavern – the flashlight photographers at work – and the council was over. With the band at their head the clubs formed in column once more, took up their chant and began to march out.

"Come on!" shouted Harry. "We want to see the labyrinths downstairs before they turn the lights off!"

They all rose and started toward the chute – Harry and Sally Carrol in the lead, her little glove buried in his big fur gauntlet. At the bottom of the chute was a long empty room of ice with the ceiling so low that they had to stoop – and their hands were parted. Before she realized what he intended Harry had darted down one of the half dozen glittering passages that opened into the room, and was only a vague receding blot against the green shimmer.

"Harry!" she called.

"Come on!" he cried back.

She looked round the empty chamber; the rest of the party had evidently decided to go home, were already outside somewhere in the blundering snow. She hesitated and then darted in after Harry.

"Harry!" she shouted.

She had reached a turning point thirty feet down; she heard a faint muffled answer far to the left, and with a touch of panic fled toward it. She passed another turning, two more yawning alleys.

"Harry!"

No answer. She started to run straight forward, and then turned like lightning and sped back the way she had come, enveloped in a sudden ice terror.

She reached a turn – was it here? – took the left and came to what should have been the outlet into the long low room, but it was only another glittering passage with darkness at the end. She called again, but the walls gave back a flat lifeless echo with no reverberations. Retracing her steps she turned another corner, this time following a wide passage. It was like the green lane between the parted waters of the Red Sea,[8] like a damp vault connecting empty tombs.

---

8. **parted waters of the Red Sea:** In the biblical account, God gives Moses the power to part the Red Sea, allowing the Israelites to escape from Egypt to the Promised Land (Exodus 14).

She slipped a little now as she walked, for ice had formed on the bottom of her overshoes; she had to run her gloves along the half-slippery, half-sticky walls to keep her balance.

"Harry!"

Still no answer. The sound she made bounced mockingly down to the end of the passage.

Then on an instant the lights went out and she was in complete darkness. She gave a small frightened cry and sank down into a cold little heap on the ice. She felt her left knee do something as she fell, but she scarcely noticed it as some deep terror far greater than any fear of being lost settled upon her. She was alone with this presence that came out of the North, the dreary loneliness that rose from ice-bound whalers in the Arctic seas, from smokeless trackless wastes where were strewn the whitened bones of adventure. It was an icy breath of death; it was rolling down low across the land to clutch at her.

With a furious despairing energy she rose again and started blindly down the darkness. She must get out. She might be lost in here for days, freeze to death and lie embedded in the ice like corpses she had read of, kept perfectly preserved until the melting of a glacier. Harry probably thought she had left with the others – he had gone by now; no one would know until late next day. She reached pitifully for the wall. Forty inches thick they had said – forty inches thick!

"Oh!"

On both sides of her along the walls she felt things creeping, damp souls that haunted this palace, this town, this North.

"Oh, send somebody – send somebody!" she cried aloud.

Clark Darrow – he would understand; or Joe Ewing; she couldn't be left here to wander forever – to be frozen, heart, body and soul. This her – this Sally Carrol. Why, she was a happy thing. She was a happy little girl. She liked warmth and summer and Dixie. These things were foreign – foreign.

"You're not crying," something said aloud. "You'll never cry any more. Your tears would just freeze; all tears freeze up here!"

She sprawled full length on the ice.

"O God!" she faltered.

A long single file of minutes went by, and with a great weariness she felt her eyes closing. Then someone seemed to sit down near her and take her face in warm soft hands. She looked up gratefully.

"Why, it's Margery Lee," she crooned softly to herself. "I knew you'd come." It really was Margery Lee, and she was just as Sally Carrol had known she would be, with a young white brow and wide welcoming eyes and a hoop skirt of some soft material that was quite comforting to rest on.

"Margery Lee."

It was getting darker now and darker – all those tombstones ought to be repainted, sure enough, only that would spoil 'em of course. Still, you ought to be able to see 'em.

Then after a succession of moments that went fast and then slow, but seemed to be ultimately resolving themselves into a multitude of blurred rays converging toward a pale yellow sun, she heard a great cracking noise break her new-found stillness.

It was the sun, it was a light; a torch, and a torch beyond that, and another one, and voices; a face took flesh below the torch, heavy arms raised her and she felt something on her cheek, it felt wet. Someone had seized her and was rubbing her face with snow. How ridiculous — with snow!

"Sally Carrol! Sally Carrol!"

It was Dangerous Dan McGrew; and two other faces she didn't know.

"Child, child! We've been looking for you two hours. Harry's half crazy!"

Things came rushing back into place — the singing, the torches, the great shout of the marching clubs. She squirmed in Patton's arms and gave a long low cry.

"Oh, I want to get out of here! I'm going back home. Take me home" — her voice rose to a scream that sent a chill to Harry's heart as he came racing down the next passage — "to-morrow!" she cried with delirious, unrestrained passion — "To-morrow! To-morrow! To-morrow!"

VI

The wealth of golden sunlight poured a quite enervating yet oddly comforting heat over the house where day long it faced the dusty stretch of road. Two birds were making a great to-do in a cool spot found among the branches of a tree next door, and down the street a colored woman was announcing herself melodiously as a purveyor of strawberries. It was April afternoon.

Sally Carrol Happer, resting her chin on her arm and her arm on an old window seat, gazed sleepily down over the spangled dust whence the heat waves were rising for the first time this spring. She was watching a very ancient flivver turn a perilous corner and rattle and groan to a jolting stop at the end of the walk. She made no sound, and in a minute a strident familiar whistle rent the air. Sally Carrol smiled and blinked.

"Good mawnin'."

A head appeared tortuously from under the car top below.

"'Taint mawnin', Sally Carrol."

"Sure enough," she said in affected surprise. "I guess maybe not."

"What you doin'?"

"Eatin' green peach. 'Spect to die any minute."

Clark twisted himself a last impossible notch to get a view of her face.

"Water's warm as a kettla steam, Sally Carrol. Wanta go swimmin'?"

"Hate to move," sighed Sally Carrol lazily, "but I reckon so."

[1920]

John Dos Passos

[1896–1970]

John Dos Passos was born John Roderigo Madison on January 14, 1896, in Chicago, Illinois. His parents, involved in a clandestine love affair, were Lucy Addison Sprigg Madison, the daughter of a wealthy Virginia family who was estranged from her husband, and John Randolph Dos Passos, a successful corporate lawyer who lived with his wife in New York City. After taking her son to live in Europe, where his father could see them privately, Lucy Madison brought Dos Passos back home in 1901, and they settled in Washington, D.C. His father, who frequently visited them during his business trips to the city, took a keen interest in Dos Passos's education. He attended the Sidwell Friends School and then spent two years at a private boarding school in England. When he returned to the United States in 1906, he was enrolled at the Choate School in Wallingford, Connecticut. He edited the *Choate News,* in which Dos Passos published his first story in 1910. His parents, whose spouses were now dead, married that year, and Dos Passos took his father's name. After his graduation from Choate, he was admitted to Harvard University but with his father's encouragement took a year off to travel with a tutor in Europe and Egypt. Enthralled by what he saw, Dos Passos wrote detailed accounts in his journal and in long letters to his father. In 1912, he entered Harvard, where he developed a keen interest in modern literature and published poems and stories in the *Harvard Monthly.*

After his graduation in 1916, Dos Passos began a career as a writer and cultural critic. His first major essay, "Against American Literature," an indictment of the rootless quality of American life and culture, appeared in the progressive magazine the *New Republic.* Objecting to American neutrality during the early years of World War I, Dos Passos wanted to serve in a noncombat role. Too young to enlist in an ambulance corps in Europe, he studied art and architecture in Spain until 1917, when he was accepted into the Norton-Harjes Ambulance Unit. He served with the unit in France before being detached for service on the Italian front, where he first met Ernest Hemingway. Dos Passos then joined the U.S. Army Medical Corps in France, and he remained there after his discharge in 1919. He soon completed an impressionistic novel based on his experiences as an ambulance driver, *One Man's Initiation — 1917* (1920), and began work on a graphic

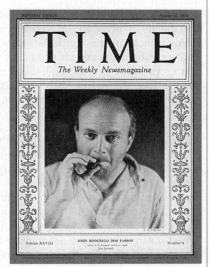

John Dos Passos

This photograph of Dos Passos appeared on the cover of *Time* shortly after the publication of his trilogy *U.S.A.* (1936). The caption was taken from the cover story, in which Dos Passos was quoted as saying that a man "writes to be damned, not to be saved."

*Dos Passos has invented
only one thing, an art of
storytelling.*

-Jean-Paul Sartre

war novel, *Three Soldiers* (1921). In 1920, Dos Passos settled in New York City, where he began to take art lessons and became a frequent contributor to the *Dial* and the *Nation*. He became friendly with many literary figures, including Sherwood Anderson, F. Scott Fitzgerald, and especially Hemingway, whom Dos Passos got to know during his frequent trips to Europe. He also published his most experimental work to date, *Manhattan Transfer* (1925), a "collective novel" about life in New York City. Along with writers such as Edna St. Vincent Millay, Dos Passos strongly protested the trial and conviction of Nicola Sacco and Bartolomeo Vanzetti, two Italian-born anarchists many radicals believed had been falsely accused of robbery and murder in Massachusetts.

The execution of Sacco and Vanzetti further radicalized Dos Passos. He was deeply involved in the New Playwrights Theatre, for which he wrote a fierce attack on the capitalist system, *Airways, Inc.*, produced in 1928. That year, he made an extended visit to the Soviet Union, and he was a regular contributor to the socialist journal the *New Masses*. In 1929, Dos Passos married the writer Katharine Smith. Six weeks later and only a few weeks before the stock market crash, Dos Passos completed the first novel of his trilogy *U.S.A.*, a sharply critical portrait of the whole of American society during the period of rapid industrialization from the Spanish-American War of 1898 to the Great Depression. In the innovative novels of the trilogy, Dos Passos wove together separate but intersecting narratives of fictional lives, brief biographies of historical figures, and passages containing actual headlines and extracts from news stories, a feature he called the "Newsreel." The publication of the final volume of *U.S.A.*, which includes *The 42nd Parallel* (1930), *1919* (1932), and *The Big Money* (1936), also made news, and Dos Passos appeared on the cover of *Time* for August 10, 1936. During the Spanish civil war, which erupted that summer, he worked with Hemingway and other writers to produce a documentary supporting the republican government, a coalition of left-wing groups called the Popular Front. Dos Passos, however, was horrified to learn that his close friend José Robles had been executed by Communists determined to purge the Popular Front of competing elements. Dos Passos consequently broke with Hemingway, who justified such acts as a necessity of war, and turned against the Communist Party.

Dos Passos thereafter became increasingly conservative in his politics and writings. In 1939, he published *Adventures of a Young Man*, a novel about a young idealist who is betrayed by the Communists in Spain. The controversial novel formed the first volume of a new trilogy, *District of Columbia* (1952), which also included *Number One* (1943) and *The Grand Design* (1949). He also wrote a series of works on American history and political philosophy, notably *The Living Thoughts of Tom Paine* (1940), *The Ground We Stand On: Some Examples from the History of a Political Creed* (1941), and *The Head and Heart of Thomas Jefferson* (1954). In 1947, Dos Passos's wife was killed in a car accident that left him blind in one eye. He remarried in 1949 and continued to write prolifically, publishing a series of nonfictional works and novels such as the sharply anticommunist *Most Likely to Succeed* (1954) and the semiautobiographical *The Great Days* (1958). Although his later novels were dismissed by many critics, Dos Pas-

**bedfordstmartins.com/
americanlit** *for research
links on Dos Passos*

sos was awarded the prestigious international Feltrinelli Prize for his "narrative art" in 1967. He died of heart failure in Baltimore, Maryland, on September 28, 1970.

Dos Passos's "1919 — Two Portraits."   These paired sketches first appeared in the *New Masses*, a Socialist magazine edited by the Marxist Michael Gold. Dos Passos was on its executive board and was a regular contributor to the magazine from 1926 until 1934. "House of Morgan" is a portrait of the powerful banker John Pierpont Morgan (1837-1917), whom Dos Passos exposes as an exploitative financier who ruthlessly pursued his own business interests while assuming the public role of a generous philanthropist and patriotic citizen. That bitterly satirical portrait is followed by a contrasting sketch of the social critic Randolph Bourne (1886-1918), who continued to publish his pacifist views, at considerable personal and political cost, even after the United States entered World War I. Dos Passos later divided the two portraits, which were among several biographical sketches he incorporated into his novel *1919* (1932), the second volume in his trilogy *U.S.A.* The publisher of the first volume, Harper & Brothers, which was reliant on the Morgan banking firm for financial backing, refused to publish *1919* unless Dos Passos excised "House of Morgan." He refused and arranged for the novel to be published by Harcourt, Brace, which later reprinted it as part of *U.S.A.* The text of the sketches is taken from the first printing in the *New Masses*, November 1931.

J. P. Morgan (left) and Randolph Bourne

The photograph of Morgan was taken about 1902, when the financier was one of the wealthiest and most influential men in the world. The photograph of Bourne, a radical intellectual who became a hero of the American left after his early death in 1918, was taken during World War I.

1919 — TWO PORTRAITS

House of Morgan[1]

I commit my soul into the hands of my saviour, wrote John Pierpont Morgan in his will, *in full confidence that having redeemed it and washed it in his most precious blood, He will present it faultless before my heavenly father, and I intreat my children to maintain and defend at all hazards and at any cost of personal sacrifice the blessed doctrine of complete atonement for sin through the blood of Jesus Christ once offered and through that alone,*

and into the hands of the house of Morgan represented by his son[2]

he committed

when he died in Rome in 1913

the control of the Morgan interests in New York, Paris and London, four national banks, three trust companies, three life insurance companies, ten railroad systems, three street railway companies, an express company, the International Mercantile Marine,

power,

on the cantilever principle, through interlocking directorates

over eighteen other railroads, U. S. Steel, General Electric, American Tel. and Tel, five major industries;

the interwoven cables of the Morgan Stillman Baker combination held credit up like a suspension bridge, thirteen percent of the banking resources of the world.

The first Morgan to make a pool was Joseph Morgan, a hotelkeeper in Hartford Connecticut who organized stagecoach lines and bought up Aetna Life Insurance stock in a time of panic caused by one of the big New York fires in the 1830;

his son Junius followed in his footsteps, first in the drygoods business, and then as partner to George Peabody, a Massachusetts banker who built up an enormous underwriting and mercantile business in London and became a friend of Queen Victoria;

Junius married the daughter of John Pierpont, a Boston preacher, poet, eccentric, and abolitionist; and their eldest son,

John Pierpont Morgan

arrived in New York to make his fortune

after being trained in England, going to school at Vevey, proving himself a crack mathematician at the University of Gottingen,

a lanky morose young man of twenty,

just in time for the panic of '57.[3]

---

1. **House of Morgan:** The collective name given to the financial enterprises of J. P. Morgan. By the early 1900s, he controlled a hundred corporations with more than $22 billion in assets.

2. **his son:** Jack Pierpont Morgan (1867-1943) inherited many of J. P. Morgan's businesses when he died in 1913.

3. **panic of '57:** The panic of 1857, a sudden downturn in the American economy from which the country did not fully recover until the beginning of the Civil War.

(war and panics on the stock exchange, good growing
weather for the House of Morgan)

When the guns started booming at Fort Sumter,[4] young Morgan turned some money
over reselling condemned muskets to the U. S. army and began to make himself felt in
the gold room in downtown New York; there was more in trading in gold than in trading
in muskets; so much for the Civil War.

During the Franco-Prussian war[5] Junius Morgan floated a huge bond issue for the
French government at Tours.

At the same time young Morgan was fighting Jay Cooke and the German-Jew bankers
in Frankfort over the funding of the American war debt (he never did like the Germans
or the Jews).

The panic of '75 ruined Jay Cooke[6] and made J. Pierpont Morgan the boss croupier of
Wall Street; he united with the Philadelphia Drexels and built the Drexel building where
for thirty years he sat in his glassed-in office, red-faced and insolent, writing at his
desk, smoking great black cigars, or, if important issues were involved, playing solitaire
in his inner office; he was famous for his few words. Yes, or No, and for his way of suddenly blowing up in a visitor's face and for the special gesture of the arm that meant,
What do I get out of it?

In '77 Junius Morgan retired; J. Pierpont got himself made a member of the board of
directors of the New York Central railroad and launched the first *Corsair*.[7] He liked
yachting and to have pretty actresses call him Commodore.

He founded the Lying-in Hospital on Stuyvesant Square, and was fond of going into
St. George's church and singing a hymn all alone in the afternoon quiet.

In the panic of '93.[8]

at no inconsiderable profit to himself

Morgan saved the U. S. Treasury; gold was draining out, the country was ruined, the
farmers were howling for a silver standard, Grover Cleveland and his cabinet were walking up and down in the blue room at the White House without being able to come to a
decision, in Congress they were making speeches while the gold reserves melted in the

---

4. **Fort Sumter:** The Civil War began on April 12–13, 1861, when Confederate artillery shelled and forced the
surrender of the federal Fort Sumter, in the harbor of Charleston, South Carolina.

5. **Franco-Prussian war:** This brief war, fought during 1870–1871 between France and the northern German
kingdom of Prussia, culminated in a decisive victory for the Prussians and the creation of a unified German
Empire.

6. **Jay Cooke:** The collapse of the banking firm of Jay Cooke and Company, which had financed much of the
Civil War and the construction of the Northern Pacific Railroad, forced him into bankruptcy and triggered
the panic of 1873 (not 1875), the beginning of a nearly six-year depression in the United States.

7. **launched the first *Corsair*:** In the early 1880s, Morgan built the first of his huge and lavish yachts, the
Corsair I, II, and *III,* the last of which was chartered by the U.S. Navy as the USS *Corsair* for service during
World War I.

8. **panic of '93:** A run on the gold supply, followed by a series of bank and railroad failures, triggered a deep
economic depression, during which by some estimates unemployment reached nearly 18 percent in the
United States. In the immediate aftermath of the panic, Morgan formed a syndicate to supply the depleted
gold reserves of the U.S. Treasury. .

Subtreasuries; poor people were starving; Coxey's army[9] was marching to Washington; for a long time Grover Cleveland couldn't bring himself to call in the representative of the Wall Street money masters; Morgan sat in his suite at the Arlington smoking cigars and quietly playing solitaire until at last the president sent for him;

he had a plan all ready for stopping the gold hemorrhage.

After that what Morgan said went; when Carnegie sold out he built the Steel Trust.[10]

J. Pierpont Morgan was a bullnecked irascible man with small black magpie's eyes and a growth on his nose; he let his partners work themselves to death over the detailed routine of banking, and sat in his back office smoking black cigars; when there was something to be decided he said Yes or No or just turned his back and went back to his solitaire.

Every Christmas his librarian read him Dickens' *A Christmas Carol* from the original manuscript.[11]

He was fond of canary birds and pekinese dogs and liked to take pretty actresses yachting. Each *Corsair* was a finer vessel than the last.

When he dined with King Edward he sat at His Majesty's right; he ate with the Kaiser[12] tete a tete; he liked talking to cardinals or the pope, and never missed a conference of Episcopal bishops,

Rome was his favorite city.

He liked choice cookery and old wines and pretty women and yachting, and going over his collections, now and then picking up a jewelled snuffbox and staring at it with his magpie's eyes.

He made a collection of the autographs of the rulers of France, owned glass cases full of Babylonian tablets, seals, signets, statuettes, busts,

Gallo-Roman bronzes,

Merovingian jewels, miniatures, watches, tapestries, porcelains, cuneiform inscriptions, paintings by all the old masters, Dutch, Italian, Flemish, Spanish,

manuscripts of the gospels and the Apocalypse,

a collection of the works of Jean-Jacques Rousseau,

and the letters of Pliny the Younger.[13]

---

9. **Coxey's army:** In 1894, a large group of unemployed workers, led by Jacob Coxey (1854-1951), marched on Washington, D.C., to protest unemployment caused by the panic of 1893.

10. **Carnegie sold . . . Steel Trust:** In the largest industrial takeover in American history, Morgan in 1901 bought out the extensive holdings of Andrew Carnegie (1835-1919) and several other major producers of steel, forming the United States Steel Corporation, the first billion-dollar corporation in the world.

11. **Every Christmas . . . manuscript:** Morgan's vast collection of rare books and manuscripts included *A Christmas Carol* by the English novelist Charles Dickens. The novella, one of the best-loved stories in the English language, concerns the transformation and redemption of the bitter and miserly businessman Ebenezer Scrooge, who has spent his whole life accumulating wealth.

12. **King Edward . . . the Kaiser:** Edward VII (1841-1910), who ruled Great Britain from 1901-10, and William II (1859-1941), who ruled as kaiser, or emperor, of the German Empire and Prussia from 1888-1918.

13. **Jean-Jacques Rousseau . . . Pliny the Younger:** Rousseau (1717-1778), French novelist, philosopher, and political theorist, and the Roman philosopher Gaius Plinius Caecilius Secondus (63-113 CE).

His collectors bought anything that was expensive or rare or had the glint of empire on it, and he had it brought to him and stared back at it with his magpie's eyes. Then it was put in a glass case.

The last year of his life he went up the Nile on a dahabiyeh[14] and spent a long time staring at the great columns of the Temple of Karnak.[15]

The panic of 1907 and the death of Harriman,[16] his great opponent in railroad financing, in 1909, had left him the undisputed ruler of Wall Street, most powerful private citizen in the world;

an old man tired of the purple, suffering from gout, he had deigned to go to Washington to answer the questions of the Pujo Committee during the Money Trust investigation:[17] *Yes, I did what seemed to me to be for the best interests of the country.*

Wars and panics on the stock exchange

Machine gunfire and arson

Starvation, lice, cholera and typhus;

Good growing weather for the House of Morgan.

Randolph Bourne

Randolph Bourne

came as an inhabitant of this earth

without the pleasure of chosing his dwelling or his career.

He was a hunchback,[18] one of a family of hunchbacks, grandson of a congregational minister, born in 1886 in Bloomfield, New Jersey; there he attended grammarschool and highschool and at the age of seventeen went to work as secretary to a Morristown businessman.

He worked his way through Columbia

working in a pianola record factory in Newark

working as proofreader

pianotuner

---

14. **dahabiyeh:** A house barge that was towed by men and animals, specifically designed for luxury travel up the Nile River in the late nineteenth and early twentieth centuries.

15. **Temple of Karnak:** The huge temple at Al-Karnak, Egypt, the largest religious site in the ancient world, dates from about the sixteenth century BCE.

16. **The panic of 1907 and the death of Harriman:** Morgan organized a group of bankers to help stem the financial panic of 1907, which threatened the whole banking system in the United States. E. H. Harriman (1848-1909) served as the president of both the Union Pacific and Southern Pacific railroads.

17. **Money Trust investigation:** A subcommittee of the House Banking and Currency Committee was charged with investigating the control of money and credit in the United States. Held in 1907, the "Money Trust" hearings were widely regarded as a sham, since members of the committee asked few hard questions and consequently turned up no concrete evidence of fraud. Banker after banker, including Morgan, testified that he operated solely in the best interest of the public. But growing concern about Morgan's control of the banking system finally led to the creation of a central bank, now known as the Federal Reserve.

18. **hunchback:** As a child, Bourne suffered from spinal tuberculosis, which caused a permanent curvature of his spine.

accompanist in a vocal studio in Carnegie Hall.
At Columbia he studied with John Dewey[19]
got a traveling fellowship that took him to England
Paris Rome Berlin Copenhagen,
wrote a book on the Gary schools.[20]
In Europe he heard music, a great deal of Wagner and Scriabine[21]
and bought himself a black cape.
This little sparrowlike man
tiny twisted bit of flesh in a black cape
always in pain and ailing
put a pebble in his sling
and hit Goliath square in the forehead with it.
War, he wrote, *is the health of the state.*

Half musician half educational theorist (weak health and being poor and twisted in body and on bad terms with his people hadn't spoiled the world for Randolph Bourne; he was a happy man, loved *die Meistersinger*[22] and played Bach with his long hands that stretched so easily over the keys and pretty girls and good food and evenings of talk. When he was dying of pneumonia a friend brought him an eggnogg; Look at the yellow, it's beautiful, he kept saying as his life ebbed into delirium and fever. He was a happy man) Bourne seized with feverish intensity on the ideas then going around at Columbia, he picked rosy glasses out of the turgid jumble of John Dewey's teaching through which he saw clear and sharp

the shining capitol of reformed democracy
Wilson's New Freedom[23];

but he was too good a mathematician;
he had to work the equations out
with the result
that in the crazy spring of 1917 he began to get unpopular where his bread was buttered at the *New Republic*;

for New Freedom read Conscription, for Democracy, Win the War, for Reform safeguard the Morgan loans
for Progress Civilization Education Service
Buy a liberty bond

---

19. **John Dewey:** Dewey (1859-1952) was an educational reformer whose pragmatic philosophy strongly influenced American education.

20. **Gary schools:** Bourne wrote *The Gary Schools* (1916), a defense of innovative efforts to reorganize school curriculum and administration in Gary, Indiana.

21. **Wagner and Scriabine:** The German operatic composer Richard Wagner (1813-1883) and the Russian composer and pianist Alexander Scriabin (1872-1915).

22. *die Meistersinger*: *Die Meistersinger von Nürnberg* (1868), an opera by Richard Wagner.

23. **Wilson's New Freedom:** President Woodrow Wilson's domestic plan, "The New Freedom," called for reform of the national banking system, reduction of the tariff or tax on imports, and the strengthening of the Sherman Act of 1890, an effort to end the unfair business practices of monopolies in the United States.

Straff the Hun

Jail the objectors.

He resigned from the *New Republic*; only the *Seven Arts*[24] had the nerve to publish his articles against the war the backers of the *Seven Arts* took their money elsewhere; friends didn't like to be seen with Bourne, his father wrote him begging him not to disgrace the family name. The rainbowtinted future of reformed democracy went pop like a pricked soapbubble.

The liberals hurried to Washington;

some of his friends plead with him to climb up on Schoolmaster Wilson's sharabang; the war was great fought from the swivel chairs of Mr. Creel's bureau in Washington[25]

he was cartooned, shadowed by the espionage service and the counter-espionage service; taking a walk with two girlfriends at Wood's Hole he was arrested, a trunk full of manuscript and letters was stolen from him in Connecticut (Force to the utmost, thundered Schoolmaster Wilson).[26]

He didn't live to see the big circus of the Peace of Versailles or the purple Normalcy of the Ohio gang.[27]

Six weeks after the armistice he died planning an essay on the Negroes and the industrial workers as foundations of future radicalism in America.

If any man has a ghost

Bourne has a ghost

a tiny twisted unscared ghost in a black cloak

hopping along the grimy old brick and brownstone streets

---

24. **New Republic . . . Seven Arts**: Bourne was a columnist for the *New Republic*, a liberal and progressive magazine founded in 1914. When it began to urge the United States to enter the war on the side of the Allies, Bourne's pacifist views became unacceptable to the magazine, and he began to publish in smaller, more radical journals such as the *Seven Arts*, which folded when its financial backers withdrew their support.

25. **Mr. Creel's bureau in Washington**: The journalist George Creel (1876–1953) was the head of President Wilson's Committee on Public Information (CPI), the United States propaganda effort during World War I. Creel stated that he demanded no less than "100% Americanism," and the CPI urged Americans to report "disloyal," pro-German sentiments they encountered. In a further effort to repress dissent, President Wilson pressed Congress to pass the Espionage Act of 1917, which made it a crime to "utter, print, write, or publish any disloyal, profane, scurrilous, or abusive language about the form of government of the United States, or the military or naval forces of the United States, or the flag."

26. **Force . . . Schoolmaster Wilson**: In a speech delivered in May 1918, President Wilson (formerly a professor of political science and the president of Princeton University) declared that the war with Germany, which would "decide whether justice and peace shall reign in the affairs of men," required the United States to exert its fully military might: "Force, force to the utmost, force without stint or limit, the righteous and triumphant force which shall make right the law of the world and cast every selfish dominion down in the dust."

27. **Peace of Versailles . . . Normalcy of the Ohio gang**: Following the armistice in November 1918, World War I ended with lengthy negotiations at the Paris Peace Conference, which resulted in a treaty signed on June 28, 1919, between the Allied powers and the German Empire. The harsh conditions and heavy "reparations" payments the treaty imposed on Germany were viewed by many as a primary cause of the chaotic economic conditions that led to the rise of Adolf Hitler and the Nazi Party. The *Ohio Gang* was the name given to several corrupt cabinet officials in the administration of President Warren G. Harding, who won the election of 1920 by a landslide with the promise of what in a campaign speech he described as "A Return to Normalcy."

still left in downtown New York,
crying out in a shrill soundless giggle:
War is the health of the state.[28]

[1931]

---

28. *War is the health of the state*: The quotation is from "The State," an ambitious theoretical essay that Bourne left unfinished when he died on December 22, 1918, a victim of the influenza pandemic of 1918–19.

Dos Passos's "Vag."   This impressionistic sketch was first published in the progressive magazine the *New Republic*, to which Dos Passos was a frequent contributor from 1916 through the 1930s. Dos Passos starkly contrasts the lot of a young vagrant, walking down a seemingly endless road, to the comforts enjoyed by those who could afford to travel aboard the new transcontinental airplanes, which were just entering service in the mid-1930s. "Vag" was subsequently published as the last chapter of the final novel in Dos Passos's *U.S.A.* trilogy, *The Big Money* (1936), which concerns the lives of American military men returning from Europe at the end of World War I. Laced throughout the novel are secondary sketches that highlight the lives of common people excluded from the American dream and the promise of "big money," including the nameless character in "Vag." The text is taken from the first publication in the *New Republic*, July 22, 1936.

Dorothea Lange,
Toward Los Angeles,
California

During the Great Depression, hundreds of thousands of impoverished Americans took to the road, seeking food and employment. Many of those left homeless by the Dust Bowl in Texas, Oklahoma, Arkansas, and the Great Plains joined the great exodus to California, where Lange took this ironic photograph in 1937.

VAG[1]

The young man waits at the edge of the concrete, with one hand he grips a rubbed suitcase of phony leather, the other hand almost making a fist, thumb up,

that moves in ever so slight an arc when a car slithers past, a truck roars, clatters; the wind of cars passing ruffles his hair, slaps grit in his face.

Head swims, hunger has twisted the belly tight,

he has skinned a heel through the torn sock, feet ache in the broken shoes, under the threadbare suit carefully brushed off with the hand, the torn drawers have a crummy feel, the feel of having slept in your clothes, in the nostrils lingers the staleness of discouraged carcasses crowded into a transient camp, the carbolic stench of the jail, on the taut cheeks the shamed flush from the boring eyes of cops and deputies, railroad bulls (they eat three squares a day, they are buttoned into wellmade clothes, they have wives to sleep with, kids to play with after supper, they work for the big men who buy their way, they stick their chests out with the sureness of power behind their backs). Get the hell out, scram. Know what's good for you, you'll make yourself scarce. Gittin' tough, eh? Think you kin take it, eh?

The punch in the jaw, the slam on the head with the nightstick, the wrist grabbed and twisted behind the back, the big knee brought up sharp into the crotch,

the walk out of town with sore feet to stand and wait at the edge of the hissing speeding string of cars where the reek of ether and lead and gas melts into the silent grassy smell of the earth.

Eyes black with want seek out the eyes of the drivers, a hitch, a hundred miles down the road.

Overhead in the blue a plane drones. Eyes follow the silver Douglas[2] that flashes in the sun and bores its smooth way out of sight into the blue.

(The transcontinental passengers sit pretty, big men with bankaccounts, highlypaid jobs, who are saluted by doormen; telephonegirls say goodmorning to them. Last night after a fine dinner, drinks with friends, they left Newark. Roar of climbing motors slanting up into the inky haze. Lights drop away. An hour staring along a silvery wing at a big lonesome moon hurrying west through curdling scum. Beacons flash in a line across Ohio.

At Cleveland the plane drops banking in a smooth spiral, the string of lights along the lake swings in a circle. Climbing roar of the motors again; slumped in the soft seat drowsing through the flat moonlight night.

Chi.[3] A glimpse of the dipper. Another spiral swoop from cool into hot air thick with dust and the reek of burnt prairies.

Beyond the Mississippi dawn creeps up behind through the murk over the great

---

1. **Vag:** Short for *vagrant*, a derogatory term for a homeless person.
2. **Douglas:** In 1936, the Douglas Aircraft Company introduced the DC-3, the first plane that could make transcontinental flights without constant stops for refueling, which revolutionized air travel in the United States.
3. **Chi:** Chicago.

plains. Puddles of mist go white in the Iowa hills, farms, fences, silos, steel glint from a river. The blinking eyes of the beacons reddening into day. Watercourses vein the eroded hills.

Omaha. Great cumulus clouds, from coppery churning to creamy to silvery white, trail brown skirts of rain over the hot plains. Red and yellow badlands, tiny horned shapes of cattle.

Cheyenne. The cool high air smells of sweetgrass.

The tightbaled clouds to westward burst and scatter in tatters over the strawcolored hills. Indigo mountains jut rimrock. The plane breasts a huge crumbling cloudbank and toboggans over bumpy air across green and crimson slopes into the sunny dazzle of Salt Lake.

The transcontinental passenger thinks contracts, profits, vacationtrips, mighty continent between Atlantic and Pacific, power, wires humming dollars, cities jammed, hills empty, the indiantrail leading into the wagonroad, the macadamed pike, the concrete skyway; trains, planes, history the billiondollar speedup,

and in the bumpy air over the desert ranges towards Las Vegas

sickens and vomits into the carton container the steak and mushrooms he ate in New York. No matter, silver in the pocket, greenbacks in the wallet, drafts, certified checks, plenty restaurants in L.A.)

The young man waits on the side of the road; the plane has gone; thumb moves in a small arc when a car tears hissing past. Eyes seek the driver's eyes. A hundred miles down the road. Head swims, belly tightens, wants crawl over his skin like ants:

went to school, books said opportunity, ads promised speed, own your house, shine bigger than your neighbor, the radiocrooner whispered girls, ghosts of platinum girls coaxed from the screen, millions in winnings were chalked up on the board in the offices, paychecks were for hands willing to work, the cleared desk of an executive with three telephones on it;

waits with swimming head, needs knot the belly, idle hands numb, beside the speeding traffic.

A hundred miles down the road.

[1936]

William Faulkner

[1897–1962]

William Faulkner was born William Cuthbert Falkner in New Albany, Mississippi, on September 25, 1897. He was the first of four sons born to Murry Falkner, a railroad administrator, and Maud Butler Falkner. Faulkner was named after his colorful great-grandfather, William Clark Falkner, a Confederate colonel in the Civil War, a successful banker, businessman, lawyer, and politician, and a prolific author best known for his popular novel *The White Rose of Memphis* (1881). As a child, Faulkner reportedly exclaimed: "I want to be a writer just like my great-grand-daddy." He was educated in Oxford, home of the University of Mississippi, where his family moved in 1902. Bored with school, he dropped out after the eleventh grade, preferring to write verse and study poetry with his older friend and mentor, Phil Stone, a Yale graduate who introduced Faulkner to modernist literature. He proposed to a local girl, Estelle Oldham, but her parents flatly rejected the match, and she married another man early in 1918. Devastated by the loss, Faulkner tried to enlist in the U.S. Air Corps. After he was rejected because he was too short, he decided to try the Royal Air Force, which had a recruiting office in New York City. Faulkner, who passed himself off as British, partly by adding a *u* to

William Faulkner

This photograph was taken to accompany a widely circulated newspaper article on one of Faulkner's few commercial successes, *Sanctuary* (1931). Uncomfortable with the attention generated by the scandalous novel, Faulkner wore an old tweed jacket and slacks spattered with paint to the publicity shoot.

his last name, was enlisted as a cadet and sent to Canada. The war ended before he completed his pilot training there, and in December 1918 Faulkner returned to Oxford, walking with a cane and telling tall tales about his war wounds and exploits in combat.

Faulkner was aimless and adrift until he began to devote himself seriously to writing. As a "war veteran," he was allowed to enroll as a special student at the University of Mississippi. He contributed stories and verse to the campus newspaper, and one of his poems was published in the national magazine the *New Republic*. Faulkner dropped out of the university after three semesters and took a series of jobs, including one in a bookstore in New York City. Back in Oxford in 1922, he went to work as the university postmaster, but he was fired for losing and misplacing mail. With the help of Phil Stone, Faulkner published a collection of his poetry, *The Marble Faun* (1924). In 1925, he moved to New Orleans, where he was a contributor to the *Times-Picayune* and published essays and sketches in a new literary magazine, the *Double Dealer*. As Faulkner humorously recalled, he also became acquainted with the most prominent contributor to the magazine: "Met a man named Sherwood Anderson. Said, 'Why not write novels? Maybe won't have to work.'" Faulkner consequently wrote *Soldier's Pay*, a novel about a wounded aviator that was published with Anderson's help in 1926. After returning from a trip to Europe, he wrote a satirical novel about writers and intellectuals in New Orleans, *Mosquitoes* (1927). Anderson, however, gave Faulkner some additional advice that strongly shaped his literary career. He urged Faulkner to write about his native region in north Mississippi, advice that he took to heart in his next novel, *Sartoris* (1929). "Beginning with *Sartoris* I discovered that my own little postage stamp of native soil was worth writing about and that I would never live long enough to exhaust it," he observed in an interview in 1955. "It opened up a gold mine of other peoples, so I created a cosmos of my own."

The cosmos that Faulkner created was Yoknapatawpha County, Mississippi, the setting for most of his later fiction. Even as he found his true

Faulkner wrote what I suppose could be called regional literature and had it published all over the world. It is good — and universal — because it is specifically about a particular world.

—Toni Morrison

subject matter, he began to experiment with language and narrative structure in *The Sound and the Fury* (1929). Although not all the reviews were favorable, the *New York Times* called it a "daring experiment" written by a major new talent in American literature. Meanwhile, Faulkner had been seeing Estelle Oldham and her two sons during his visits to Oxford. Following her divorce, they were married in 1929. While working on the night shift at the university power plant, Faulkner swiftly wrote another experimental novel, *As I Lay Dying* (1930). After he and Estelle bought a run-down estate in Oxford, Faulkner set about earning money to support them by writing magazine stories, which became his primary source of income. His first collection of stories, *These Thirteen,* appeared in 1931, the year he published *Sanctuary.* The sensational novel, whose plot revolves around the kidnapping and rape of a coed by a bootlegger, was made into a movie and led to the first of what Faulkner called his numerous "tours of duty" as a screenwriter in Hollywood. Recoiling from producing a work designed to "sell," as he candidly described *Sanctuary,* Faulkner wrote his most complex work to date, *Light in August* (1932), set in Depression-era Mississippi. He continued to explore issues of race, class, and the burden of Southern history in his ambitious modernist novel about the Civil War and its aftermath, *Absalom, Absalom!* (1936). Now regarded as one of his masterpieces, the novel sold poorly, and Faulkner followed it with *The Unvanquished* (1938), a novel based on a series of popular Civil War stories he had earlier published in the *Saturday Evening Post.*

Faulkner's career and reputation fluctuated widely during the following decade. Although he and his wife now had a daughter, their first daughter had died shortly after birth, and the couple's marriage was increasingly strained. The hard work and the constant effort to make money also began to take a toll on Faulkner, a heavy drinker who occasionally checked himself into a sanatorium in Oxford to recover from his binges. Nonetheless, he continued to write, though at a slower pace. In 1939, he published *The Wild Palms,* his best-selling novel to date, and began work on the first volume of a trilogy of novels about a poor white family of sharecroppers, *The Hamlet* (1940). (He did not complete the so-called Snopes trilogy until the late 1950s, when he published *The Town* and *The Mansion.*) He then revised a series of stories into what he described as a "novel" about the troubled history of racial relations in the South, *Go Down, Moses* (1942). With the sale of his books slumping and many of his works now out of print, Faulkner returned to work as a screenwriter in Hollywood. But his literary reputation received a major boost from the publication of *The Portable Faulkner* (1946), edited by the influential critic Malcolm Cowley. The Modern Library subsequently began to reissue Faulkner's earlier works, and his next novel, *Intruder in the Dust* (1948), was made into a major motion picture by MGM.

In his final years, Faulkner gained prominence as both a writer and as a spokesman for the South. In 1950, he was awarded the Nobel Prize for Literature for his "powerful and independent contribution in America's new literature of the novel," as the citation read, and his fame was heightened by the electrifying acceptance speech he delivered at the awards ceremony in Stockholm. As the struggle for civil rights intensified during the 1950s,

Faulkner felt duty-bound to speak out against racial segregation, though his moderate position was attacked by both white segregationists and black activists. The reviews of his late works were mixed, but he was awarded the Pulitzer Prize for *A Fable* (1954) and for his final novel, *The Reivers* (1962). Shortly after it was published, Faulkner was injured in a fall from a horse in Oxford. While at a clinic, where he was also treated for alcoholism, he died of a heart attack on July 6, 1962.

Faulkner's "That Evening Sun."   This story was first published as "That Evening Sun Go Down," an even more direct reference to the opening of W. C. Handy's famous song "St. Louis Blues" (1914): "I hate to see that evening sun go down / I hate to see that evening sun go down / 'Cause my baby, he's done left this town." (Handy, the famous black trumpet player and "father of the blues," had frequently brought his band down from Memphis to perform at dances the teenage Faulkner attended in Oxford, Mississippi.) The story first appeared in March 1931 in the lively *American Mercury*, a monthly magazine of literature and often satirical commentary on American life that also published the work of Sherwood Anderson, F. Scott Fitzgerald, and Sinclair Lewis. Despite the iconoclastic nature of the magazine, its editor, H. L. Mencken, was concerned that readers would object to a character named "Jesus." Mencken consequently asked Faulkner to alter the name and to soften the references to pregnancy in the story. Faulkner reluctantly agreed to the changes, but when he included the story in his first collection, *These Thirteen*, he shortened the title and restored both the name "Jesus" and the original language about the pregnancy of Jesus's wife, Nancy. "That Evening Sun," which includes the main characters from Faulkner's novel about the Compson family, *The Sound and the Fury* (1929), is narrated by Quentin Compson, who looks back on an episode from his childhood. The harrowing story of the isolated and vulnerable Nancy reveals the differing perspectives of adults and children, as well as the sharp contrasts between the worlds of white and black people in the South. The text is taken from *These Thirteen* (1931).

bedfordstmartins.com/ americanlit for research links on Faulkner

THAT EVENING SUN[1]

I

Monday is no different from any other week day in Jefferson now. The streets are paved now, and the telephone and electric companies are cutting down more and more of the shade trees — the water oaks, the maples and locusts and elms — to make room for iron poles bearing clusters of bloated and ghostly and bloodless grapes, and we have a city

---

1. **That Evening Sun:** Faulkner took the title of the story, which he first published as "That Evening Sun Goes Down," from the opening of one of the most famous of all blues songs, W. C. Handy's "St. Louis Blues" (1914): "I hate to see that evening sun go down / I hate to see that evening sun go down / 'Cause my baby, he's done left this town."

laundry which makes the rounds on Monday morning, gathering the bundles of clothes into bright-colored, specially-made motor cars: the soiled wearing of a whole week now flees apparitionlike behind alert and irritable electric horns, with a long diminishing noise of rubber and asphalt like tearing silk, and even the Negro women who still take in white people's washing after the old custom, fetch and deliver it in automobiles.

But fifteen years ago, on Monday morning the quiet dusty, shady streets would be full of Negro women with, balanced on their steady, turbaned heads, bundles of clothes tied up in sheets, almost as large as cotton bales, carried so without touch of hand between the kitchen door of the white house and the blackened washpot beside a cabin door in Negro Hollow.[2]

Nancy would set her bundle on the top of her head, then upon the bundle in turn she would set the black straw sailor hat which she wore winter and summer. She was tall, with a high, sad face sunken a little where her teeth were missing. Sometimes we would go a part of the way down the lane and across the pasture with her, to watch the balanced bundle and the hat that never bobbed nor wavered, even when she walked down into the ditch and up the other side and stooped through the fence. She would go down on her hands and knees and crawl through the gap, her head rigid, uptilted, the bundle steady as a rock or a balloon, and rise to her feet again and go on.

Sometimes the husbands of the washing women would fetch and deliver the clothes, but Jesus never did that for Nancy, even before father told him to stay away from our house, even when Dilsey was sick and Nancy would come to cook for us.

And then about half the time we'd have to go down the lane to Nancy's cabin and tell her to come on and cook breakfast. We would stop at the ditch, because father told us to not have anything to do with Jesus — he was a short black man, with a razor scar down his face — and we would throw rocks at Nancy's house until she came to the door, leaning her head around it without any clothes on.

"What yawl mean, chunking my house?" Nancy said. "What you little devils mean?"

"Father says for you to come on and get breakfast," Caddy said. "Father says it's over a half an hour now, and you've got to come this minute."

"I aint studying no breakfast," Nancy said. "I going to get my sleep out."

"I bet you're drunk," Jason said. "Father says you're drunk. Are you drunk, Nancy?"

"Who says I is?" Nancy said. "I got to get my sleep out. I aint studying no breakfast."

So after a while we quit chunking the cabin and went back home. When she finally came, it was too late for me to go to school. So we thought it was whisky until that day they arrested her again and they were taking her to jail and they passed Mr Stovall. He was the cashier in the bank and a deacon in the Baptist church, and Nancy began to say:

"When you going to pay me, white man? When you going to pay me, white man? It's been three times now since you paid me a cent —" Mr Stovall knocked her down, but she kept on saying, "When you going to pay me, white man? It's been three times now

---

2. **Negro Hollow:** A name given to the segregated sections of southern towns inhabited by African Americans.

since —" until Mr Stovall kicked her in the mouth with his heel and the marshal caught Mr Stovall back, and Nancy lying in the street, laughing. She turned her head and spat out some blood and teeth and said, "It's been three times now since he paid me a cent."

That was how she lost her teeth, and all that day they told about Nancy and Mr Stovall, and all that night the ones that passed the jail could hear Nancy singing and yelling. They could see her hands holding to the window bars, and a lot of them stopped along the fence, listening to her and to the jailer trying to make her stop. She didn't shut up until almost daylight, when the jailer began to hear a bumping and scraping upstairs and he went up there and found Nancy hanging from the window bar. He said that it was cocaine and not whisky, because no nigger would try to commit suicide unless he was full of cocaine, because a nigger full of cocaine wasn't a nigger any longer.

The jailer cut her down and revived her; then he beat her, whipped her. She had hung herself with her dress. She had fixed it all right, but when they arrested her she didn't have on anything except a dress and so she didn't have anything to tie her hands with and she couldn't make her hands let go of the window ledge. So the jailer heard the noise and ran up there and found Nancy hanging from the window, stark naked, her belly already swelling out a little, like a little balloon.

When Dilsey was sick in her cabin and Nancy was cooking for us, we could see her apron swelling out; that was before father told Jesus to stay away from the house. Jesus was in the kitchen, sitting behind the stove, with his razor scar on his black face like a piece of dirty string. He said it was a watermelon that Nancy had under her dress.

"It never come off of your vine, though," Nancy said.

"Off of what vine?" Caddy said.

"I can cut down the vine it did come off of," Jesus said.

"What makes you want to talk like that before these chillen?" Nancy said. "Whyn't you go on to work? You done et. You want Mr Jason to catch you hanging around his kitchen, talking that way before these chillen?"

"Talking what way?" Caddy said. "What vine?"

"I cant hang around white man's kitchen," Jesus said. "But white man can hang around mine. White man can come in my house, but I cant stop him. When white man want to come in my house, I aint got no house. I cant stop him, but he cant kick me outen it. He cant do that."

Dilsey was still sick in her cabin. Father told Jesus to stay off our place. Dilsey was still sick. It was a long time. We were in the library after supper.

"Isn't Nancy through in the kitchen yet?" mother said. "It seems to me that she has had plenty of time to have finished the dishes."

"Let Quentin go and see," father said. "Go and see if Nancy is through, Quentin. Tell her she can go on home."

I went to the kitchen. Nancy was through. The dishes were put away and the fire was out. Nancy was sitting in a chair, close to the cold stove. She looked at me.

"Mother wants to know if you are through," I said.

"Yes," Nancy said. She looked at me. "I done finished." She looked at me.

"What is it?" I said. "What is it?"

"I aint nothing but a nigger," Nancy said. "It aint none of my fault."

She looked at me, sitting in the chair before the cold stove, the sailor hat on her head. I went back to the library. It was the cold stove and all, when you think of a kitchen being warm and busy and cheerful. And with a cold stove and the dishes all put away, and nobody wanting to eat at that hour.

"Is she through?" mother said.

"Yessum," I said.

"What is she doing?" mother said.

"She's not doing anything. She's through."

"I'll go and see," father said.

"Maybe she's waiting for Jesus to come and take her home," Caddy said.

"Jesus is gone," I said. Nancy told us how one morning she woke up and Jesus was gone.

"He quit me," Nancy said. "Done gone to Memphis, I reckon. Dodging them city *po*-lice for a while, I reckon."

"And a good riddance," father said. "I hope he stays there."

"Nancy's scaired of the dark," Jason said.

"So are you," Caddy said.

"I'm not," Jason said.

"Scairy cat," Caddy said.

"I'm not," Jason said.

"You, Candace!" mother said. Father came back.

"I am going to walk down the lane with Nancy," he said. "She says that Jesus is back."

"Has she seen him?" mother said.

"No. Some Negro sent her word that he was back in town. I wont be long."

"You'll leave me alone, to take Nancy home?" mother said. "Is her safety more precious to you than mine?"

"I wont be long," father said.

"You'll leave these children unprotected, with that Negro about?"

"I'm going too," Caddy said. "Let me go, Father."

"What would he do with them, if he were unfortunate enough to have them?" father said.

"I want to go, too," Jason said.

"Jason!" mother said. She was speaking to father. You could tell that by the way she said the name. Like she believed that all day father had been trying to think of doing the thing she wouldn't like the most, and that she knew all the time that after a while he would think of it. I stayed quiet, because father and I both knew that mother would want him to make me stay with her if she just thought of it in time. So father didn't look at me. I was the oldest. I was nine and Caddy was seven and Jason was five.

"Nonsense," father said. "We wont be long."

Nancy had her hat on. We came to the lane. "Jesus always been good to me," Nancy said. "Whenever he had two dollars, one of them was mine." We walked in the lane. "If I can just get through the lane," Nancy said, "I be all right then."

The lane was always dark. "This is where Jason got scared on Hallowe'en," Caddy said.

"I didn't," Jason said.

"Cant Aunt Rachel do anything with him?" father said. Aunt Rachel was old. She lived in a cabin beyond Nancy's, by herself. She had white hair and she smoked a pipe in the door, all day long; she didn't work any more. They said she was Jesus' mother. Sometimes she said she was and sometimes she said she wasn't any kin to Jesus.

"Yes you did," Caddy said. "You were scairder than Frony. You were scairder than T.P. even. Scairder than niggers."

"Cant nobody do nothing with him," Nancy said. "He say I done woke up the devil in him and aint but one thing going to lay it down again."

"Well, he's gone now," father said. "There's nothing for you to be afraid of now. And if you'd just let white men alone."

"Let what white men alone?" Caddy said. "How let them alone?"

"He aint gone nowhere," Nancy said. "I can feel him. I can feel him now, in this lane. He hearing us talk, every word, hid somewhere, waiting. I aint seen him, and I aint going to see him again but once more, with that razor in his mouth. That razor on that string down his back, inside his shirt. And then I aint going to be even surprised."

"I wasn't scaired," Jason said.

"If you'd behave yourself, you'd have kept out of this," father said. "But it's all right now. He's probably in St Louis now. Probably got another wife by now and forgot all about you."

"If he has, I better not find out about it," Nancy said. "I'd stand there right over them, and every time he wropped her, I'd cut that arm off. I'd cut his head off and I'd slit her belly and I'd shove —"

"Hush," father said.

"Slit whose belly, Nancy?" Caddy said.

"I wasn't scaired," Jason said. "I'd walk right down this lane by myself."

"Yah," Caddy said. "You wouldn't dare to put your foot down in it if we were not here too."

II

Dilsey was still sick, so we took Nancy home every night until mother said, "How much longer is this going on? I to be left alone in this big house while you take home a frightened Negro?"

We fixed a pallet in the kitchen for Nancy. One night we waked up, hearing the sound. It was not singing and it was not crying, coming up the dark stairs. There was a light in mother's room and we heard father going down the hall, down the back stairs, and Caddy and I went into the hall. The floor was cold. Our toes curled away from it while we listened to the sound. It was like singing and it wasn't like singing, like the sounds that Negroes make.

Then it stopped and we heard father going down the back stairs, and we went to the head of the stairs. Then the sound began again, in the stairway, not loud, and we could see Nancy's eyes halfway up the stairs, against the wall. They looked like cat's eyes do, like a big cat against the wall, watching us. When we came down the steps to where she was, she quit making the sound again, and we stood there until father came back up from the kitchen, with his pistol in his hand. He went back down with Nancy and they came back with Nancy's pallet.

We spread the pallet in our room. After the light in mother's room went off, we could see Nancy's eyes again. "Nancy," Caddy whispered, "are you asleep Nancy?"

Nancy whispered something. It was oh or no, I dont know which. Like nobody had made it, like it came from nowhere and went nowhere, until it was like Nancy was not there at all; that I had looked so hard at her eyes on the stairs that they had got printed on my eyeballs, like the sun does when you have closed your eyes and there is no sun. "Jesus," Nancy whispered. "Jesus."

"Was it Jesus?" Caddy said. "Did he try to come into the kitchen?"

"Jesus," Nancy said. Like this: Jeeeeeeeeeeeeeeeeesus, until the sound went out, like a match or a candle does.

"It's the other Jesus she means," I said.

"Can you see us, Nancy?" Caddy whispered. "Can you see our eyes too?"

"I aint nothing but a nigger," Nancy said. "God knows. God knows."

"What did you see down there in the kitchen?" Caddy whispered. "What tried to get in?"

"God knows," Nancy said. We could see her eyes. "God knows."

Dilsey got well. She cooked dinner. "You'd better stay in bed a day or two longer," father said.

"What for?" Dilsey said. "If I had been a day later, this place would be to rack and ruin. Get on out of here now, and let me get my kitchen straight again."

Dilsey cooked supper too. And that night, just before dark, Nancy came into the kitchen.

"How do you know he's back?" Dilsey said. "You aint seen him."

"Jesus is a nigger," Jason said.

"I can feel him," Nancy said. "I can feel him laying yonder in the ditch."

"Tonight?" Dilsey said. "Is he there tonight?"

"Dilsey's a nigger too," Jason said.

"You try to eat something," Dilsey said.

"I dont want nothing," Nancy said.

"I aint a nigger," Jason said.

"Drink some coffee," Dilsey said. She poured cup of coffee for Nancy. "Do you know he's out there tonight? How come you know it's tonight?"

"I know," Nancy said. "He's there, waiting. I know. I done lived with him too long. I know what he is fixing to do fore he know it himself."

"Drink some coffee," Dilsey said. Nancy held the cup to her mouth and blew into the cup. Her mouth pursed out like a spreading adder's, like a rubber mouth, like she had blown all the color out of her lips with blowing the coffee.

"I aint a nigger," Jason said. "Are you a nigger, Nancy?"

"I hellborn, child," Nancy said. "I wont be nothing soon. I going back where I come from soon."

III

She began to drink the coffee. While she was drinking, holding the cup in both hands, she began to make the sound again. She made the sound into the cup and the coffee sploshed out onto her hands and her dress. Her eyes looked at us and she sat there, her elbows on her knees, holding the cup in both hands, looking at us across the wet cup, making the sound.

"Look at Nancy," Jason said. "Nancy cant cook for us now. Dilsey's got well now."

"You hush up," Dilsey said. Nancy held the cup in both hands, looking at us, making the sound, like there were two of them: one looking at us and the other making the sound. "Whyn't you let Mr Jason telefoam the marshal?" Dilsey said. Nancy stopped then, holding the cup in her long brown hands. She tried to drink some coffee again, but it sploshed out of the cup, onto her hands and her dress, and she put the cup down. Jason watched her.

"I cant swallow it," Nancy said. "I swallows but it wont go down me."

"You go down to the cabin," Dilsey said. "Frony will fix you a pallet and I'll be there soon."

"Wont no nigger stop him," Nancy said.

"I aint a nigger," Jason said. "Am I, Dilsey?"

"I reckon not," Dilsey said. She looked at Nancy. "I dont reckon so. What you going to do, then?"

Nancy looked at us. Her eyes went fast, like she was afraid there wasn't time to look, without hardly moving at all. She looked at us, at all three of us at one time. "You member that night I stayed in yawls' room?" she said. She told about how we waked up early the next morning, and played. We had to play quiet, on her pallet, until father woke up and it was time to get breakfast. "Go and ask your maw to let me stay here tonight," Nancy said. "I wont need no pallet. We can play some more."

Caddy asked mother. Jason went too. "I cant have Negroes sleeping in the bedrooms," mother said. Jason cried. He cried until mother said he couldn't have any dessert for three days if he didn't stop. Then Jason said he would stop if Dilsey would make a chocolate cake. Father was there.

"Why dont you do something about it?" mother said. "What do we have officers for?"

"Why is Nancy afraid of Jesus?" Caddy said. "Are you afraid of father, Mother?"

"What could the officers do?" father said. "If Nancy hasn't seen him, how could the officers find him?"

"Then why is she afraid?" mother said.

"She says he is there. She says she knows he is there tonight."

"Yet we pay taxes," mother said. "I must wait here alone in this big house while you take a Negro woman home."

"You know that I am not lying outside with a razor," father said.

"I'll stop if Dilsey will make a chocolate cake," Jason said. Mother told us to go out and father said he didn't know if Jason would get a chocolate cake or not, but he knew what Jason was going to get in about a minute. We went back to the kitchen and told Nancy.

"Father said for you to go home and lock the door, and you'll be all right," Caddy said. "All right from what, Nancy? Is Jesus mad at you?" Nancy was holding the coffee cup in her hands again, her elbows on her knees and her hands holding the cup between her knees. She was looking into the cup. "What have you done that made Jesus mad?" Caddy said. Nancy let the cup go. It didn't break on the floor, but the coffee spilled out, and Nancy sat there with her hands still making the shape of the cup. She began to make the sound again, not loud. Not singing and not unsinging. We watched her.

"Here," Dilsey said. "You quit that, now. You get aholt of yourself. You wait here. I going to get Versh to walk home with you." Dilsey went out.

We looked at Nancy. Her shoulders kept shaking, but she quit making the sound. We watched her. "What's Jesus going to do to you?" Caddy said. "He went away."

Nancy looked at us. "We had fun that night I stayed in yawls' room, didn't we?"

"I didn't," Jason said. "I didn't have any fun."

"You were asleep in mother's room," Caddy said. "You were not there."

"Let's go down to my house and have some more fun," Nancy said.

"Mother wont let us," I said. "It's too late now."

"Dont bother her," Nancy said. "We can tell her in the morning. She wont mind."

"She wouldn't let us," I said.

"Dont ask her now," Nancy said. "Dont bother her now."

"She didn't say we couldn't go," Caddy said.

"We didn't ask," I said.

"If you go, I'll tell," Jason said.

"We'll have fun," Nancy said. "They wont mind, just to my house. I been working for yawl a long time. They wont mind."

"I'm not afraid to go," Caddy said. "Jason is the one that's afraid. He'll tell."

"I'm not," Jason said.

"Yes, you are," Caddy said. "You'll tell."

"I wont tell," Jason said. "I'm not afraid."

"Jason aint afraid to go with me," Nancy said. "Is you, Jason?"

"Jason is going to tell," Caddy said. The lane was dark. We passed the pasture gate. "I bet if something was to jump out from behind that gate, Jason would holler."

"I wouldn't," Jason said. We walked down the lane. Nancy was talking loud.

"What are you talking so loud for, Nancy?" Caddy said.

"Who; me?" Nancy said. "Listen at Quentin and Caddy and Jason saying I'm talking loud."

"You talk like there was five of us here," Caddy said. "You talk like father was here too."

"Who; me talking loud, Mr Jason?" Nancy said.

"Nancy called Jason 'Mister,' " Caddy said.

"Listen how Caddy and Quentin and Jason talk," Nancy said.

"We're not talking loud," Caddy said. "You're the one that's talking like father —"

"Hush," Nancy said; "hush, Mr. Jason."

"Nancy called Jason 'Mister' aguh —"

"Hush," Nancy said. She was talking loud when we crossed the ditch and stopped through the fence where she used to stoop through with the clothes on her head. Then we came to her house. We were going fast then. She opened the door. The smell of the house was like the lamp and the smell of Nancy was like the wick, like they were waiting for one another to begin to smell. She lit the lamp and closed the door and put the bar up. Then she quit talking loud, looking at us.

"What're we going to do?" Caddy said.

"What do yawl want to do?" Nancy said.

"You said we would have some fun," Caddy said.

There was something about Nancy's house; something you could smell besides Nancy and the house. Jason smelled it, even. "I dont want to stay here," he said. "I want to go home."

"Go home, then," Caddy said.

"I dont want to go by myself," Jason said.

"We're going to have some fun," Nancy said.

"How?" Caddy said.

Nancy stood by the door. She was looking at us, only it was like she had emptied her eyes, like she had quit using them. "What do you want to do?" she said.

"Tell us a story," Caddy said. "Can you tell a story?"

"Yes," Nancy said.

"Tell it," Caddy said. We looked at Nancy. "You dont know any stories."

"Yes," Nancy said. "Yes I do."

She came and sat in a chair before the hearth. There was a little fire there. Nancy built it up, when it was already hot inside. She built a good blaze. She told a story. She talked like her eyes looked, like her eyes watching us and her voice talking to us did not belong to her. Like she was living somewhere else, waiting somewhere else. She was outside the cabin. Her voice was inside and the shape of her, the Nancy that could stoop under a barbed wire fence with a bundle of clothes balanced on her head as though without weight, like a balloon, was there. But that was all. "And so this here queen come walking up to the ditch, where that bad man was hiding. She was walking up to the ditch, and she say, 'If I can just get past this here ditch,' was what she say . . ."

"What ditch?" Caddy said. "A ditch like that one out there? Why did a queen want to go into a ditch?"

"To get to her house," Nancy said. She looked at us. "She had to cross the ditch to get into her house quick and bar the door."

"Why did she want to go home and bar the door?" Caddy said.

IV

Nancy looked at us. She quit talking. She looked at us. Jason's legs stuck straight out of his pants where he sat on Nancy's lap. "I dont think that's a good story," he said. "I want to go home."

"Maybe we had better," Caddy said. She got up from the floor. "I bet they are looking for us right now." She went toward the door.

"No," Nancy said. "Dont open it." She got up quick and passed Caddy. She didn't touch the door, the wooden bar.

"Why not?" Caddy said.

"Come back to the lamp," Nancy said. "We'll have fun. You dont have to go."

"We ought to go," Caddy said. "Unless we have a lot of fun." She and Nancy came back to the fire, the lamp.

"I want to go home," Jason said. "I'm going to tell."

"I know another story," Nancy said. She stood close to the lamp. She looked at Caddy, like when your eyes look up at a stick balanced on your nose. She had to look down to see Caddy, but her eyes looked like that, like when you are balancing a stick.

"I wont listen to it," Jason said. "I'll bang on the floor."

"It's a good one," Nancy said. "It's better than the other one."

"What's it about?" Caddy said. Nancy was standing by the lamp. Her hand was on the lamp, against the light, long and brown.

"Your hand is on that hot globe," Caddy said. "Dont it feel hot to your hand?"

Nancy looked at her hand on the lamp chimney. She took her hand away, slow. She stood there, looking at Caddy, wringing her long hand as though it were tied to her wrist with a string.

"Let's do something else," Caddy said.

"I want to go home," Jason said.

"I got some popcorn," Nancy said. She looked at Caddy and then at Jason and then at me and then at Caddy again. "I got some popcorn."

"I dont like popcorn," Jason said. "I'd rather have candy."

Nancy looked at Jason. "You can hold the popper." She was still wringing her hand; it was long and limp and brown.

"All right," Jason said. "I'll stay a while if I can do that. Caddy cant hold it. I'll want to go home again if Caddy holds the popper."

Nancy built up the fire. "Look at Nancy putting her hands in the fire," Caddy said. "What's the matter with you, Nancy?"

"I got popcorn," Nancy said. "I got some." She took the popper from under the bed. It was broken. Jason began to cry.

"Now we cant have any popcorn," he said.

"We ought to go home, anyway," Caddy said. "Come on, Quentin."

"Wait," Nancy said; "wait. I can fix it. Dont you want to help me fix it?"

"I dont think I want any," Caddy said. "It's too late now."

"You help me, Jason," Nancy said. "Dont you want to help me?"

"No," Jason said. "I want to go home."

"Hush," Nancy said; "hush. Watch. Watch me. I can fix it so Jason can hold it and pop the corn." She got a piece of wire and fixed the popper.

"It wont hold good," Caddy said.

"Yes it will," Nancy said. "Yawl watch. Yawl help me shell some corn."

The popcorn was under the bed too. We shelled it into the popper and Nancy helped Jason hold the popper over the fire.

"It's not popping," Jason said. "I want to go home."

"You wait," Nancy said. "It'll begin to pop. We'll have fun then." She was sitting close to the fire. The lamp was turned up so high it was beginning to smoke.

"Why dont you turn it down some?" I said.

"It's all right," Nancy said. "I'll clean it. Yawl wait. The popcorn will start in a minute."

"I dont believe it's going to start," Caddy said. "We ought to start home, anyway. They'll be worried."

"No," Nancy said. "It's going to pop. Dilsey will tell um yawl with me. I been working for yawl long time. They wont mind if yawl at my house. You wait, now. It'll start popping any minute now."

Then Jason got some smoke in his eyes and he began to cry. He dropped the popper into the fire. Nancy got a wet rag and wiped Jason's face, but he didn't stop crying.

"Hush," she said. "Hush." But he didn't hush. Caddy took the popper out of the fire.

"It's burned up," she said. "You'll have to get some more popcorn, Nancy."

"Did you put all of it in?" Nancy said.

"Yes," Caddy said. Nancy looked at Caddy. Then she took the popper and opened it and poured the cinders into her apron and began to sort the grains, her hands long and brown, and we watching her.

"Haven't you got any more?" Caddy said.

"Yes," Nancy said; "yes. Look. This here aint burnt. All we need to do is —"

"I want to go home," Jason said. "I'm going to tell."

"Hush," Caddy said. We all listened. Nancy's head was already turned toward the barred door, her eyes filled with red lamplight. "Somebody is coming," Caddy said.

Then Nancy began to make that sound again, not loud, sitting there above the fire, her long hands dangling between her knees; all of a sudden water began to come out on her face in big drops, running down her face, carrying in each one a little turning ball of firelight like a spark until it dropped off her chin. "She's not crying," I said.

"I aint crying," Nancy said. Her eyes were closed. "I aint crying. Who is it?"

"I dont know," Caddy said. She went to the door and looked out. "We've got to go now," she said. "Here comes father."

"I'm going to tell," Jason said. "Yawl made me come."

The water still ran down Nancy's face. She turned in her chair. "Listen. Tell him. Tell him we going to have fun. Tell him I take good care of yawl until in the morning. Tell him to let me come home with yawl and sleep on the floor. Tell him I wont need no pallet. We'll have fun. You member last time how we had so much fun?"

"I didn't have fun," Jason said. "You hurt me. You put smoke in my eyes. I'm going to tell."

V

Father came in. He looked at us. Nancy did not get up.

"Tell him," she said.

"Caddy made us come down here," Jason said. "I didn't want to."

Father came to the fire. Nancy looked up at him. "Cant you go to Aunt Rachel's and stay?" he said. Nancy looked up at father, her hands between her knees. "He's not here," father said. "I would have seen him. There's not a soul in sight."

"He in the ditch," Nancy said. "He waiting in the ditch yonder."

"Nonsense," father said. He looked at Nancy. "Do you know he's there?"

"I got the sign," Nancy said.

"What sign?"

"I got it. It was on the table when I come in. It was a hogbone, with blood meat still on it, laying by the lamp. He's out there. When yawl walk out that door, I gone."

"Gone where, Nancy?" Caddy said.

"I'm not a tattletale," Jason said.

"Nonsense," father said.

"He out there," Nancy said. "He looking through that window this minute, waiting for yawl to go. Then I gone."

"Nonsense," father said. "Lock up your house and we'll take you on to Aunt Rachel's."

" 'Twont do no good," Nancy said. She didn't look at father now, but he looked down at her, at her long, limp, moving hands. "Putting it off wont do no good."

"Then what do you want to do?" father said.

"I dont know," Nancy said. "I cant do nothing. Just put it off. And that dont do no good. I reckon it belong to me. I reckon what I going to get aint no more than mine."

"Get what?" Caddy said. "What's yours?"

"Nothing," father said. "You all must get to bed."

"Caddy made me come," Jason said.

"Go on to Aunt Rachel's," father said.

"It wont do no good," Nancy said. She sat before the fire, her elbows on her knees, her long hands between her knees. "When even your own kitchen wouldn't do no good. When even if I was sleeping on the floor in the room with your chillen, and the next morning there I am, and blood —"

"Hush," father said. "Lock the door and put out the lamp and go to bed."

"I scared of the dark," Nancy said. "I scared for it to happen in the dark."

"You mean you're going to sit right here with the lamp lighted?" father said. Then Nancy began to make the sound again, sitting before the fire, her long hands between her knees. "Ah, damnation," father said. "Come along, chillen. It's past bedtime."

"When yawl go home, I gone," Nancy said. She talked quieter now, and her face looked quiet, like her hands. "Anyway, I got my coffin money saved up with Mr Lovelady." Mr Lovelady was a short, dirty man who collected the Negro insurance, coming around to the cabins or the kitchens every Saturday morning, to collect fifteen cents. He and his wife lived at the hotel. One morning his wife committed suicide. They had a child, a little girl. He and the child went away. After a week or two he came back alone. We would see him going along the lanes and the back streets on Saturday mornings.

"Nonsense," father said. "You'll be the first thing I'll see in the kitchen tomorrow morning."

"You'll see what you'll see, I reckon," Nancy said. "But it will take the Lord to say what that will be."

VI

We left her sitting before the fire.

"Come and put the bar up," father said. But she didn't move. She didn't look at us again, sitting quietly there between the lamp and the fire. From some distance down the lane we could look back and see her through the open door.

"What, Father?" Caddy said. "What's going to happen?"

"Nothing," father said. Jason was on father's back, so Jason was the tallest of all of us. We went down into the ditch. I looked at it, quiet. I couldn't see much where the moonlight and the shadows tangled.

"If Jesus is hid here, he can see us, cant he?" Caddy said.

"He's not there," father said. "He went away a long time ago."

"You made me come," Jason said, high; against the sky it looked like father had two heads, a little one and a big one. "I didn't want to."

We went up out of the ditch. We could still see Nancy's house and the open door, but we couldn't see Nancy now, sitting before the fire with the door open, because she was tired. "I just done got tired," she said. "I just a nigger. It aint no fault of mine."

But we could hear her, because she began just after we came up out of the ditch, the sound that was not singing and not unsinging. "Who will do our washing now, Father?" I said.

"I'm not a nigger," Jason said, high and close above father's head.

"You're worse," Caddy said, "you are a tattletale. If something was to jump out, you'd be scairder than a nigger."

"I wouldn't," Jason said.

"You'd cry," Caddy said.

"Caddy," father said.

"I wouldn't!" Jason said.

"Scairy cat," Caddy said.

"Candace!" father said.

[1931]

Faulkner's "Barn Burning."   Although this story is one of Faulkner's most famous and widely anthologized, it was rejected by five different magazines before it was accepted by *Harper's*, where it first appeared in June 1939. Faulkner soon reworked the story for *The Hamlet* (1940), the first of his novels charting the rise of Flem Snopes, the eldest son of a poor white tenant family. But he appears only briefly in "Barn Burning," which focuses on the dilemma of his younger brother, Sarty Snopes. Sarty is named for Colonel John Sartoris, a Confederate army officer and wealthy landowner whose aristocratic family is the subject of two earlier novels by Faulkner, *Sartoris* (1929) and *The Unvanquished* (1938). As Sarty's name perhaps suggests, he is torn between loyalty to his father, Abner Snopes, and his allegiance to traditional values of community, decency, and truth. The text is taken from its first publication in a book, Faulkner's *Collected Stories* (1950).

Barn Burning

The store in which the Justice of the Peace's court was sitting smelled of cheese. The boy, crouched on his nail keg at the back of the crowded room, knew he smelled cheese, and more: from where he sat he could see the ranked shelves close-packed with the solid, squat, dynamic shapes of tin cans whose labels his stomach read, not from the lettering which meant nothing to his mind but from the scarlet devils and the silver curve of fish — this, the cheese which he knew he smelled and the hermetic meat which his intestines believed he smelled coming in intermittent gusts momentary and brief between the other constant one, the smell and sense just a little of fear because mostly of despair and grief, the old fierce pull of blood. He could not see the table where the Justice sat and before which his father and his father's enemy (*our enemy* he thought in that despair; *ourn! mine and hisn both! He's my father!*) stood, but he could hear them, the two of them that is, because his father had said no word yet:

"But what proof have you, Mr. Harris?"

"I told you. The hog got into my corn. I caught it up and sent it back to him. He had no fence that would hold it. I told him so, warned him. The next time I put the hog in my pen. When he came to get it I gave him enough wire to patch up his pen. The next time I put the hog up and kept it. I rode down to his house and saw the wire I gave him still rolled on to the spool in his yard. I told him he could have the hog when he paid me a dollar pound fee. That evening a nigger came with the dollar and got the hog. He was a strange nigger. He said, 'He say to tell you wood and hay kin burn.' I said, 'What?' 'That whut he say to tell you,' the nigger said. 'Wood and hay kin burn.' That night my barn burned. I got the stock out but I lost the barn."

"Where is the nigger? Have you got him?"

"He was a strange nigger, I tell you. I don't know what became of him."

"But that's not proof. Don't you see that's not proof?"

"Get that boy up here. He knows." For a moment the boy thought too that the man meant his older brother until Harris said, "Not him. The little one. The boy," and, crouching, small for his age, small and wiry like his father, in patched and faded jeans even too small for him, with straight, uncombed, brown hair and eyes gray and wild as storm scud, he saw the men between himself and the table part and become a lane of grim faces, at the end of which he saw the Justice, a shabby, collarless, graying man in spectacles, beckoning him. He felt no floor under his bare feet; he seemed to walk beneath the palpable weight of the grim turning faces. His father, stiff in his black Sunday coat donned not for the trial but for the moving, did not even look at him. *He aims for me to lie,* he thought, again with that frantic grief and despair. *And I will have to do hit.*

"What's your name, boy?" the Justice said.

"Colonel Sartoris Snopes,"[1] the boy whispered.

"Hey?" the Justice said. "Talk louder. Colonel Sartoris? I reckon anybody named for

---

1. **Colonel Sartoris Snopes:** Sarty is named after the character John Sartoris, a wealthy landowner and colonel in the Confederate army, whom Faulkner in other works depicted as a representative of the aristocratic "Old Order" in the South.

Colonel Sartoris in this country can't help but tell the truth, can they?" The boy said nothing. *Enemy! Enemy!* he thought; for a moment he could not even see, could not see that the Justice's face was kindly nor discern that his voice was troubled when he spoke to the man named Harris: "Do you want me to question this boy?" But he could hear, and during those subsequent long seconds while there was absolutely no sound in the crowded little room save that of quiet and intent breathing it was as if he had swung outward at the end of a grape vine, over a ravine, and at the top of the swing had been caught in a prolonged instant of mesmerized gravity, weightless in time.

"No!" Harris said violently, explosively. "Damnation! Send him out of here!" Now time, the fluid world, rushed beneath him again, the voices coming to him again through the smell of cheese and sealed meat, the fear and despair and the old grief of blood:

"This case is closed. I can't find against you, Snopes, but I can give you advice. Leave this country and don't come back to it."

His father spoke for the first time, his voice cold and harsh, level, without emphasis: "I aim to. I don't figure to stay in a country among people who . . ." he said something unprintable and vile, addressed to no one.

"That'll do," the Justice said. "Take your wagon and get out of this country before dark. Case dismissed."

His father turned, and he followed the stiff black coat, the wiry figure walking a little stiffly from where a Confederate provost's man's musket ball had taken him in the heel on a stolen horse thirty years ago,[2] followed the two backs now, since his older brother had appeared from somewhere in the crowd, no taller than the father but thicker, chewing tobacco steadily, between the two lines of grim-faced men and out of the store and across the worn gallery and down the sagging steps and among the dogs and half-grown boys in the mild May dust, where as he passed a voice hissed:

"Barn burner!"

Again he could not see, whirling; there was a face in a red haze, moonlike, bigger than the full moon, the owner of it half again his size, he leaping in the red haze toward the face, feeling no blow, feeling no shock when his head struck the earth, scrabbling up and leaping again, feeling no blow this time either and tasting no blood, scrabbling up to see the other boy in full flight and himself already leaping into pursuit as his father's hand jerked him back, the harsh, cold voice speaking above him: "Go get in the wagon."

It stood in a grove of locusts and mulberries across the road. His two hulking sisters in their Sunday dresses and his mother and her sister in calico and sunbonnets were already in it, sitting on and among the sorry residue of the dozen and more movings which even the boy could remember – the battered stove, the broken beds and chairs, the clock inlaid with mother-of-pearl, which would not run, stopped at some fourteen minutes past two o'clock of a dead and forgotten day and time, which had been his

---

2. **Confederate provost's . . . thirty years ago:** A provost was an officer in charge of a detachment of military police assigned to stop theft in the Confederate army. The story takes place in the early 1890s, thirty years after the Civil War.

mother's dowry. She was crying, though when she saw him she drew her sleeve across her face and began to descend from the wagon. "Get back," the father said.

"He's hurt. I got to get some water and wash his . . ."

"Get back in the wagon," his father said. He got in too, over the tail-gate. His father mounted to the seat where the older brother already sat and struck the gaunt mules two savage blows with the peeled willow, but without heat. It was not even sadistic; it was exactly that same quality which in later years would cause his descendants to over-run the engine before putting a motor car into motion, striking and reining back in the same movement. The wagon went on, the store with its quiet crowd of grimly watching men dropped behind; a curve in the road hid it. *Forever* he thought. *Maybe he's done satisfied now, now that he has . . .* stopping himself, not to say it aloud even to himself. His mother's hand touched his shoulder.

"Does hit hurt?" she said.

"Naw," he said. "Hit don't hurt. Lemme be."

"Can't you wipe some of the blood off before hit dries?"

"I'll wash to-night," he said. "Lemme be, I tell you."

The wagon went on. He did not know where they were going. None of them ever did or ever asked, because it was always somewhere, always a house of sorts waiting for them a day or two days or even three days away. Likely his father had already arranged to make a crop on another farm before he . . . Again he had to stop himself. He (the father) always did. There was something about his wolflike independence and even courage when the advantage was at least neutral which impressed strangers, as if they got from his latent ravening ferocity not so much a sense of dependability as a feeling that his ferocious conviction in the rightness of his own actions would be of advantage to all whose interest lay with his.

That night they camped, in a grove of oaks and beeches where a spring ran. The nights were still cool and they had a fire against it, of a rail lifted from a nearby fence and cut into lengths – a small fire, neat, niggard[3] almost, a shrewd fire; such fires were his father's habit and custom always, even in freezing weather. Older, the boy might have remarked this and wondered why not a big one; why should not a man who had not only seen the waste and extravagance of war, but who had in his blood an inherent voracious prodigality with material not his own, have burned everything in sight? Then he might have gone a step farther and thought that that was the reason: that niggard blaze was the living fruit of nights passed during those four years in the woods hiding from all men, blue or gray, with his strings of horses (captured horses, he called them). And older still, he might have divined the true reason: that the element of fire spoke to some deep mainspring of his father's being, as the element of steel or of powder spoke to other men, as the one weapon for the preservation of integrity, else breath were not worth the breathing, and hence to be regarded with respect and used with discretion.

But he did not think this now and he had seen those same niggard blazes all his life. He merely ate his supper beside it and was already half asleep over his iron plate when

---

3. **niggard:** A variant of an early English word meaning meager or scanty.

his father called him, and once more he followed the stiff back, the stiff and ruthless limp, up the slope and on to the starlit road where, turning, he could see his father against the stars but without face or depth – a shape black, flat, and bloodless as though cut from tin in the iron folds of the frockcoat which had not been made for him, the voice harsh like tin and without heat like tin:

"You were fixing to tell them. You would have told him." He didn't answer. His father struck him with the flat of his hand on the side of the head, hard but without heat, exactly as he had struck the two mules at the store, exactly as he would strike either of them with any stick in order to kill a horse fly, his voice still without heat or anger: "You're getting to be a man. You got to learn. You got to learn to stick to your own blood or you ain't going to have any blood to stick to you. Do you think either of them, any man there this morning, would? Don't you know all they wanted was a chance to get at me because they knew I had them beat? Eh?" Later, twenty years later, he was to tell himself, "If I had said they wanted only truth, justice, he would have hit me again." But now he said nothing. He was not crying. He just stood there. "Answer me," his father said.

"Yes," he whispered. His father turned.

"Get on to bed. We'll be there tomorrow."

To-morrow they were there. In the early afternoon the wagon stopped before a paint-less two-room house identical almost with the dozen others it had stopped before even in the boy's ten years, and again, as on the other dozen occasions, his mother and aunt got down and began to unload the wagon, although his two sisters and his father and brother had not moved.

"Likely hit ain't fitten for hawgs," one of the sisters said.

"Nevertheless, fit it will and you'll hog it and like it," his father said. "Get out of them chairs and help your Ma unload."

The two sisters got down, big, bovine, in a flutter of cheap ribbons; one of them drew from the jumbled wagon bed a battered lantern, the other a worn broom. His father handed the reins to the older son and began to climb stiffly over the wheel. "When they get unloaded, take the team to the barn and feed them." Then he said, and at first the boy thought he was still speaking to his brother: "Come with me."

"Me?" he said.

"Yes," his father said. "You."

"Abner," his mother said. His father paused and looked back – the harsh level stare beneath the shaggy, graying, irascible brows.

"I reckon I'll have a word with the man that aims to begin to-morrow owning me body and soul for the next eight months."

They went back up the road. A week ago – or before last night, that is – he would have asked where they were going, but not now. His father had struck him before last night but never before had he paused afterward to explain why; it was as if the blow and the following calm, outrageous voice still rang, repercussed, divulging nothing to him save the terrible handicap of being young, the light weight of his few years, just heavy enough to prevent his soaring free of the world as it seemed to be ordered but not heavy enough to keep him footed solid in it, to resist it and try to change the course of its events.

Presently he could see the grove of oaks and cedars and the other flowering trees and shrubs where the house would be, though not the house yet. They walked beside a fence massed with honeysuckle and Cherokee roses and came to a gate swinging open between two brick pillars, and now, beyond a sweep of drive, he saw the house for the first time and at that instant he forgot his father and the terror and despair both, and even when he remembered his father again (who had not stopped) the terror and despair did not return. Because, for all the twelve movings, they had sojourned until now in a poor country, a land of small farms and fields and houses, and he had never seen a house like this before. *Hit's big as a courthouse* he thought quietly, with a surge of peace and joy whose reason he could not have thought into words, being too young for that: *They are safe from him. People whose lives are a part of this peace and dignity are beyond his touch, he no more to them than a buzzing wasp: capable of stinging for a little moment but that's all; the spell of this peace and dignity rendering even the barns and stable and cribs which belong to it impervious to the puny flames he might contrive . . .* this, the peace and joy, ebbing for an instant as he looked again at the stiff black back, the stiff and implacable limp of the figure which was not dwarfed by the house, for the reason that it had never looked big anywhere and which now, against the serene columned backdrop, had more than ever that impervious quality of something cut ruthlessly from tin, depthless, as though, sidewise to the sun, it would cast no shadow. Watching him, the boy remarked the absolutely undeviating course which his father held and saw the stiff foot come squarely down in a pile of fresh droppings where a horse had stood in the drive and which his father could have avoided by a simple change of stride. But it ebbed only for a moment, though he could not have thought this into words either, walking on in the spell of the house, which he could even want but without envy, without sorrow, certainly never with that ravening and jealous rage which unknown to him walked in the ironlike black coat before him: *Maybe he will feel it too. Maybe it will even change him now from what maybe he couldn't help but be.*

They crossed the portico. Now he could hear his father's stiff foot as it came down on the boards with clocklike finality, a sound out of all proportion to the displacement of the body it bore and which was not dwarfed either by the white door before it, as though it had attained to a sort of vicious and ravening minimum not to be dwarfed by anything — the flat, wide, black hat, the formal coat of broadcloth which had once been black but which had now that friction-glazed greenish cast of the bodies of old house flies, the lifted sleeve which was too large, the lifted hand like a curled claw. The door opened so promptly that the boy knew the Negro must have been watching them all the time, an old man with neat grizzled hair, in a linen jacket, who stood barring the door with his body, saying, "Wipe yo foots, white man, fo you come in here. Major ain't home nohow."

"Get out of my way, nigger," his father said, without heat too, flinging the door back and the Negro also and entering, his hat still on his head. And now the boy saw the prints of the stiff foot on the doorjamb and saw them appear on the pale rug behind the machinelike deliberation of the foot which seemed to bear (or transmit) twice the weight which the body compassed. The Negro was shouting "Miss Lula! Miss Lula!" somewhere behind them, then the boy, deluged as though by a warm wave by a suave turn of carpeted stair and a pendant glitter of chandeliers and a mute gleam of gold frames, heard the swift feet and saw her too, a lady — perhaps he had never seen her like before either — in a gray, smooth gown with lace at the throat and an apron tied at the waist and the sleeves turned back, wiping cake or biscuit dough from her hands with a towel as she came up the hall, looking not at his father at all but at the tracks on the blond rug with an expression of incredulous amazement.

"I tried," the Negro cried. "I tole him to . . ."

"Will you please go away?" she said in a shaking voice. "Major de Spain is not at home. Will you please go away?"

His father had not spoken again. He did not speak again. He did not even look at her. He just stood stiff in the center of the rug, in his hat, the shaggy iron-gray brows twitching slightly above the pebble-colored eyes as he appeared to examine the house with brief deliberation. Then with the same deliberation he turned; the boy watched him pivot on the good leg and saw the stiff foot drag round the arc of the turning, leaving a final long and fading smear. His father never looked at it, he never once looked down at the rug. The Negro held the door. It closed behind them, upon the hysteric and indistinguishable woman-wail. His father stopped at the top of the steps and scraped his boot clean on the edge of it. At the gate he stopped again. He stood for a moment, planted stiffly on the stiff foot, looking back at the house. "Pretty and white, ain't it?" he said. "That's sweat. Nigger sweat. Maybe it ain't white enough yet to suit him. Maybe he wants to mix some white sweat with it."

Two hours later the boy was chopping wood behind the house within which his mother and aunt and the two sisters (the mother and aunt, not the two girls, he knew that; even at this distance and muffled by walls the flat loud voices of the two girls emanated an incorrigible idle inertia) were setting up the stove to prepare a meal, when he heard the hooves and saw the linen-clad man on a fine sorrel mare, whom he recognized even before he saw the rolled rug in front of the Negro youth following on a fat bay carriage horse — a suffused, angry face vanishing, still at full gallop, beyond the corner of the house where his father and brother were sitting in the two tilted chairs; and a moment later, almost before he could have put the axe down, he heard the hooves again and watched the sorrel mare go back out of the yard, already galloping again. Then his father began to shout one of the sisters' names, who presently emerged backward from the kitchen door dragging the rolled rug along the ground by one end while the other sister walked behind it.

"If you ain't going to tote, go on and set up the wash pot," the first said.

"You, Sarty!" the second shouted. "Set up the wash pot!" His father appeared at the door, framed against that shabbiness, as he had been against that other bland perfection, impervious to either, the mother's anxious face at his shoulder.

"Go on," the father said. "Pick it up." The two sisters stooped, broad, lethargic; stooping, they presented an incredible expanse of pale cloth and a flutter of tawdry ribbons.

"If I thought enough of a rug to have to git hit all the way from France I wouldn't keep hit where folks coming in would have to tromp on hit," the first said. They raised the rug.

"Abner," the mother said. "Let me do it."

"You go back and git dinner," his father said. "I'll tend to this."

From the woodpile through the rest of the afternoon the boy watched them, the rug spread flat in the dust beside the bubbling wash-pot, the two sisters stooping over it with that profound and lethargic reluctance, while the father stood over them in turn, implacable and grim, driving them though never raising his voice again. He could smell the harsh homemade lye they were using; he saw his mother come to the door once and look toward them with an expression not anxious now but very like despair; he saw his father turn, and he fell to with the axe and saw from the corner of his eye his father raise from the ground a flattish fragment of field stone and examine it and return to the pot, and this time his mother actually spoke: "Abner. Abner. Please don't. Please, Abner."

Then he was done too. It was dusk; the whippoorwills had already begun. He could smell coffee from the room where they would presently eat the cold food remaining from the mid-afternoon meal, though when he entered the house he realized they were having coffee again probably because there was a fire on the hearth, before which the rug now lay spread over the backs of the two chairs. The tracks of his father's foot were gone. Where they had been were now long, water-cloudy scoriations resembling the sporadic course of a lilliputian mowing machine.

It still hung there while they ate the cold food and then went to bed, scattered without order or claim up and down the two rooms, his mother in one bed, where his father would later lie, the older brother in the other, himself, the aunt, and the two sisters on pallets on the floor. But his father was not in bed yet. The last thing the boy remembered was the depthless, harsh silhouette of the hat and coat bending over the rug and it seemed to him that he had not even closed his eyes when the silhouette was standing over him, the fire almost dead behind it, the stiff foot prodding him awake. "Catch up the mule," his father said.

When he returned with the mule his father was standing in the black door, the rolled rug over his shoulder. "Ain't you going to ride?" he said.

"No. Give me your foot."

He bent his knee into his father's hand, the wiry, surprising power flowed smoothly, rising, he rising with it, on to the mule's bare back (they had owned a saddle once; the boy could remember it though not when or where) and with the same effortlessness his father swung the rug up in front of him. Now in the starlight they retraced the afternoon's path, up the dusty road rife with honeysuckle, through the gate and up the black tunnel of the drive to the lightless house, where he sat on the mule and felt the rough warp of the rug drag across his thighs and vanish.

"Don't you want me to help?" he whispered. His father did not answer and now he heard again that stiff foot striking the hollow portico with that wooden and clocklike deliberation, that outrageous overstatement of the weight it carried. The rug, hunched, not flung (the boy could tell that even in the darkness) from his father's shoulder struck the angle of wall and floor with a sound unbelievably loud, thunderous, then the foot again, unhurried and enormous; a light came on in the house and the boy sat, tense, breathing steadily and quietly and just a little fast, though the foot itself did not increase its beat at all, descending the steps now; now the boy could see him.

"Don't you want to ride now?" he whispered. "We kin both ride now," the light within the house altering now, flaring up and sinking. *He's coming down the stairs now,* he thought. He had already ridden the mule up beside the horse block; presently his father was up behind him and he doubled the reins over and slashed the mule across the neck, but before the animal could begin to trot the hard, thin arm came round him, the hard, knotted hand jerking the mule back to a walk.

In the first red rays of the sun they were in the lot, putting plow gear on the mules. This time the sorrel mare was in the lot before he heard it at all, the rider collarless and even bareheaded, trembling, speaking in a shaking voice as the woman in the house had done, his father merely looking up once before stooping again to the hame he was buckling, so that the man on the mare spoke to his stooping back:

"You must realize you have ruined that rug. Wasn't there anybody here, any of your women . . ." he ceased, shaking, the boy watching him, the older brother leaning now in the stable door, chewing, blinking slowly and steadily at nothing apparently. "It cost a hundred dollars. But you never had a hundred dollars. You never will. So I'm going to charge you twenty bushels of corn against your crop. I'll add it in your contract and when you come to the commissary you can sign it. That won't keep Mrs. de Spain quiet but maybe it will teach you to wipe your feet off before you enter her house again."

Then he was gone. The boy looked at his father, who still had not spoken or even looked up again, who was now adjusting the logger-head in the hame.

"Pap," he said. His father looked at him — the inscrutable face, the shaggy brows beneath which the gray eyes glinted coldly. Suddenly the boy went toward him, fast, stopping as suddenly. "You done the best you could!" he cried. "If he wanted hit done different why didn't he wait and tell you how? He won't git no twenty bushels! He won't git none! We'll gether hit and hide hit! I kin watch . . ."

"Did you put the cutter back in that straight stock like I told you?"

"No, sir," he said.

"Then go do it."

That was Wednesday. During the rest of that week he worked steadily, at what was within his scope and some which was beyond it, with an industry that did not need to be driven nor even commanded twice; he had this from his mother, with the difference that some at least of what he did he liked to do, such as splitting wood with the half-size axe which his mother and aunt had earned, or saved money somehow, to present him with at Christmas. In company with the two older women (and on one afternoon, even one of the sisters), he built pens for the shoat and the cow which were a part of his father's contract with the landlord, and one afternoon, his father being absent, gone somewhere on one of the mules, he went to the field.

They were running a middle buster [4] now, his brother holding the plow straight while he handled the reins, and walking beside the straining mule, the rich black soil shearing cool and damp against his bare ankles, he thought *Maybe this is the end of it. Maybe even that twenty bushels that seems hard to have to pay for just a rug will be a cheap price for him to stop forever and always from being what he used to be;* thinking, dreaming now, so that his brother had to speak sharply to him to mind the mule: *Maybe he*

---

4. **middle buster:** Usually "middlebuster," a two-bladed plow that turns the earth to both sides of a row.

even won't collect the twenty bushels. Maybe it will all add up and balance and vanish –
corn, rug, fire; the terror and grief, the being pulled two ways like between two teams of
horses – gone, done with for ever and ever.

Then it was Saturday; he looked up from beneath the mule he was harnessing and
saw his father in the black coat and hat. "Not that," his father said. "The wagon gear."
And then, two hours later, sitting in the wagon bed behind his father and brother on the
seat, the wagon accomplished a final curve, and he saw the weathered paintless store
with its tattered tobacco- and patent-medicine posters and the tethered wagons and
saddle animals below the gallery. He mounted the gnawed steps behind his father and
brother, and there again was the lane of quiet, watching faces for the three of them to
walk through. He saw the man in spectacles sitting at the plank table and he did not
need to be told this was a Justice of the Peace; he sent one glare of fierce, exultant, partisan defiance at the man in collar and cravat now, whom he had seen but twice before in
his life, and that on a galloping horse, who now wore on his face an expression not of
rage but of amazed unbelief which the boy could not have known was at the incredible
circumstance of being sued by one of his own tenants, and came and stood against his
father and cried at the Justice: "He ain't done it! He ain't burnt . . ."

"Go back to the wagon," his father said.

"Burnt?" the Justice said. "Do I understand this rug was burned too?"

"Does anybody here claim it was?" his father said. "Go back to the wagon." But he did
not, he merely retreated to the rear of the room, crowded as that other had been, but not
to sit down this time, instead, to stand pressing among the motionless bodies, listening
to the voices:

"And you claim twenty bushels of corn is too high for the damage you did to the rug?"

"He brought the rug to me and said he wanted the tracks washed out of it. I washed
the tracks out and took the rug back to him."

"But you didn't carry the rug back to him in the same condition it was in before you
made the tracks on it."

His father did not answer, and now for perhaps half a minute there was no sound at
all save that of breathing, the faint, steady suspiration of complete and intent listening.

"You decline to answer that, Mr. Snopes?" Again his father did not answer. "I'm going
to find against you, Mr. Snopes. I'm going to find that you were responsible for the
injury to Major de Spain's rug and hold you liable for it. But twenty bushels of corn
seems a little high for a man in your circumstances to have to pay. Major de Spain
claims it cost a hundred dollars. October corn will be worth about fifty cents. I figure
that if Major de Spain can stand a ninety-five dollar loss on something he paid cash for,
you can stand a five-dollar loss you haven't earned yet. I hold you in damages to Major de
Spain to the amount of ten bushels of corn over and above your contract with him, to be
paid to him out of your crop at gathering time. Court adjourned."

It had taken no time hardly, the morning was but half begun. He thought they would
return home and perhaps back to the field, since they were late, far behind all other
farmers. But instead his father passed on behind the wagon, merely indicating with his
hand for the older brother to follow with it, and crossed the road toward the blacksmith
shop opposite, pressing on after his father, overtaking him, speaking, whispering up at

the harsh, calm face beneath the weathered hat: "He won't git no ten bushels neither. He won't git one. We'll . . ." until his father glanced for an instant down at him, the face absolutely calm, the grizzled eyebrows tangled above the cold eyes, the voice almost pleasant, almost gentle:

"You think so? Well, we'll wait till October anyway."

The matter of the wagon — the setting of a spoke or two and the tightening of the tires — did not take long either, the business of the tires accomplished by driving the wagon into the spring branch behind the shop and letting it stand there, the mules nuzzling into the water from time to time, and the boy on the seat with the idle reins, looking up the slope and through the sooty tunnel of the shed where the slow hammer rang and where his father sat on an upended cypress bolt, easily, either talking or listening, still sitting there when the boy brought the dripping wagon up out of the branch and halted it before the door.

"Take them on to the shade and hitch," his father said. He did so and returned. His father and the smith and a third man squatting on his heels inside the door were talking, about crops and animals; the boy, squatting too in the ammoniac dust and hoof-parings and scales of rust, heard his father tell a long and unhurried story out of the time before the birth of the older brother even when he had been a professional horse-trader. And then his father came up beside him where he stood before a tattered last year's circus poster on the other side of the store, gazing rapt and quiet at the scarlet horses, the incredible poisings and convolutions of tulle and tights and the painted leers of comedians, and said, "It's time to eat."

But not at home. Squatting beside his brother against the front wall, he watched his father emerge from the store and produce from a paper sack a segment of cheese and divide it carefully and deliberately into three with his pocket knife and produce crackers from the same sack. They all three squatted on the gallery and ate, slowly, without talking; then in the store again, they drank from a tin dipper tepid water smelling of the cedar bucket and of living beech trees. And still they did not go home. It was a horse lot this time, a tall rail fence upon and along which men stood and sat and out of which one by one horses were led, to be walked and trotted and then cantered back and forth along the road while the slow swapping and buying went on and the sun began to slant westward, they — the three of them — watching and listening, the older brother with his muddy eyes and his steady, inevitable tobacco, the father commenting now and then on certain of the animals, to no one in particular.

It was after sundown when they reached home. They ate supper by lamplight, then, sitting on the doorstep, the boy watched the night fully accomplish, listening to the whippoorwills and the frogs, when he heard his mother's voice: "Abner! No! No! Oh, God. Oh, God. Abner!" and he rose, whirled, and saw the altered light through the door where a candle stub now burned in a bottle neck on the table and his father, still in the hat and coat, at once formal and burlesque as though dressed carefully for some shabby and ceremonial violence, emptying the reservoir of the lamp back into the five-gallon kerosene can from which it had been filled, while the mother tugged at his arm until he shifted the lamp to the other hand and flung her back, not savagely or viciously, just hard, into the wall, her hands flung out against the wall for balance, her mouth open and in her face the same quality of hopeless despair as had been in her voice. Then his father saw him standing in the door.

"Go to the barn and get that can of oil we were oiling the wagon with," he said. The boy did not move. Then he could speak.

"What . . ." he cried. "What are you . . ."

"Go get that oil," his father said. "Go."

Then he was moving, running, outside the house, toward the stable: this the old habit, the old blood which he had not been permitted to choose for himself, which had been bequeathed him willy nilly and which had run for so long (and who knew where, battening on what of outrage and savagery and lust) before it came to him. *I could keep on,* he thought. *I could run on and on and never look back, never need to see his face again. Only I can't. I can't,* the rusted can in his hand now, the liquid sploshing[5] in it as he ran back to the house and into it, into the sound of his mother's weeping in the next room, and handed the can to his father.

"Ain't you going to even send a nigger?" he cried. "At least you sent a nigger before!"

This time his father didn't strike him. The hand came even faster than the blow had, the same hand which had set the can on the table with almost excruciating care flashing from the can toward him too quick for him to follow it, gripping him by the back of his shirt and on to tiptoe before he had seen it quit the can, the face stooping at him in breathless and frozen ferocity, the cold, dead voice speaking over him to the older brother who leaned against the table, chewing with that steady, curious, sidewise motion of cows:

"Empty the can into the big one and go on. I'll catch up with you."

"Better tie him up to the bedpost," the brother said.

"Do like I told you," the father said. Then the boy was moving, his bunched shirt and the hard, bony hand between his shoulder-blades, his toes just touching the floor, across the room and into the other one, past the sisters sitting with spread heavy thighs in the two chairs over the cold hearth, and to where his mother and aunt sat side by side on the bed, the aunt's arms about his mother's shoulders.

"Hold him," the father said. The aunt made a startled movement. "Not you," the father said. "Lennie. Take hold of him. I want to see you do it." His mother took him by the wrist. "You'll hold him better than that. If he gets loose don't you know what he is going to do? He will go up yonder." He jerked his head toward the road. "Maybe I'd better tie him."

"I'll hold him," his mother whispered.

"See you do then." Then his father was gone, the stiff foot heavy and measured upon the boards, ceasing at last.

Then he began to struggle. His mother caught him in both arms, he jerking and wrenching at them. He would be stronger in the end, he knew that. But he had no time to wait for it. "Lemme go!" he cried. "I don't want to have to hit you!"

"Let him go!" the aunt said. "If he don't go, before God, I am going up there myself!"

---

5. **sploshing:** Another term for splashing.

"Don't you see I can't?" his mother cried. "Sarty! Sarty No! No! Help me, Lizzie!"

Then he was free. His aunt grasped at him but it was too late. He whirled, running, his mother stumbled forward or to her knees behind him, crying to the nearer sister: "Catch him, Net! Catch him!" But that was too late too, the sister (the sisters were twins, born at the same time, yet either of them now gave the impression of being, encompassing as much living meat and volume and weight as any other two of the family) not yet having begun to rise from the chair, her head, face, alone merely turned, presenting to him in the flying instant an astonishing expanse of young female features untroubled by any surprise even, wearing only an expression of bovine interest. Then he was out of the room, out of the house, in the mild dust of the starlit road and the heavy rifeness of honeysuckle, the pale ribbon unspooling with terrific slowness under his running feet, reaching the gate at last and turning in, running, his heart and lungs drumming, on up the drive toward the lighted house, the lighted door. He did not knock, he burst in, sobbing for breath, incapable for the moment of speech; he saw the astonished face of the Negro in the linen jacket without knowing when the Negro had appeared.

"De Spain!" he cried, panted. "Where's . . ." then he saw the white man too emerging from a white door down the hall. "Barn!" he cried. "Barn!"

"What?" the white man said. "Barn?"

"Yes!" the boy cried. "Barn!"

"Catch him!" the white man shouted.

But it was too late this time too. The Negro grasped his shirt, but the entire sleeve, rotten with washing, carried away, and he was out that door too and in the drive again, and had actually never ceased to run even while he was screaming into the white man's face.

Behind him the white man was shouting, "My horse! Fetch my horse!" and he thought for an instant of cutting across the park and climbing the fence into the road, but he did not know the park nor how high the vine-massed fence might be and he dared not risk it. So he ran on down the drive, blood and breath roaring; presently he was in the road again though he could not see it. He could not hear either: the galloping mare was almost upon him before he heard her, and even then he held his course, as if the very urgency of his wild grief and need must in a moment more find him wings, waiting until the ultimate instant to hurl himself aside and into the weed-choked roadside ditch as the horse thundered past and on, for an instant in furious silhouette against the stars, the tranquil early summer night sky which, even before the shape of the horse and rider vanished, stained abruptly and violently upward: a long, swirling roar incredible and soundless, blotting the stars, and he springing up and into the road again, running again, knowing it was too late yet still running even after he heard the shot and, an instant later, two shots, pausing now without knowing he had ceased to run, crying "Pap! Pap!", running again before he knew he had begun to run, stumbling, tripping over something and scrabbling up again without ceasing to run, looking backward over his shoulder at the glare as he got up, running on among the invisible trees, panting, sobbing, "Father! Father!"

At midnight he was sitting on the crest of a hill. He did not know it was midnight and he did not know how far he had come. But there was no glare behind him now and he sat now, his back toward what he had called home for four days anyhow, his face toward the dark woods which he would enter when breath was strong again, small, shaking steadily in the chill darkness, hugging himself into the remainder of his thin, rotten shirt, the grief and despair now no longer terror and fear but just grief and despair. *Father. My father,* he thought. "He was brave!" he cried suddenly, aloud but not loud, no more than a whisper: "He was! He was in the war! He was in Colonel Sartoris' cav'ry!" not knowing that his father had gone to that war a private in the fine old European sense, wearing no uniform, admitting the authority of and giving fidelity to no man or army or flag, going to war as Malbrouck[6] himself did: for booty — it meant nothing and less than nothing to him if it were enemy booty or his own.

The slow constellations wheeled on. It would be dawn and then sun-up after a while and he would be hungry. But that would be to-morrow and now he was only cold, and walking would cure that. His breathing was easier now and he decided to get up and go on, and then he found that he had been asleep because he knew it was almost dawn, the night almost over. He could tell that from the whippoorwills. They were everywhere now among the dark trees below him, constant and inflectioned and ceaseless, so that, as the instant for giving over to the day birds drew nearer and nearer, there was no interval at all between them. He got up. He was a little stiff, but walking would cure that too as it would the cold, and soon there would be the sun. He went on down the hill, toward the dark woods within which the liquid silver voices of the birds called unceasing — the rapid and urgent beating of the urgent and quiring[7] heart of the late spring night. He did not look back.

[1939, 1950]

---

6. **Malbrouck:** John Churchill (1650–1722), the first Duke of Marlborough, infamous for embezzlement and taking bribes, was the subject of a popular children's nursery song, "Malbrouck Goes Off to the War."
7. **quiring:** A musical term for the sound of the singing of a choir.

Ernest Hemingway

[1899-1961]

Ernest William Hemingway was born on July 21, 1899, in Oak Park, a comfortable suburb of Chicago, Illinois. He was the second child and first son of Dr. Clarence Edmonds Hemingway, an obstetrician and general practitioner, and Grace Hall Hemingway, a former singer and music teacher. Hemingway took music lessons with his mother and learned to fish and hunt with his father at the family's summer cottage in upper Michigan. He attended Oak Park High School, where he played football, wrote a weekly column for the school newspaper, and contributed poems and essays to the literary magazine, *Tabula*. The United States entered World War I shortly before his graduation in 1917, and Hemingway wanted to join the army. His father, who had hoped he would go to college to prepare for a career in medicine, felt that he was too young to enlist. Instead, with the help of an uncle, Hemingway got a job as a cub reporter on the prestigious *Kansas City Star*. For the next seven months, he covered crime stories and interviewed politicians and visiting celebrities. Although he was good at his job and later said that it taught him invaluable skills as a writer, he was still eager to enlist. Rejected by the army because of poor vision, he volunteered for the Red Cross ambulance corps. In May 1918, he sailed for Europe and began service as an ambulance driver in Italy. A few weeks after his arrival, Hemingway was seriously wounded by a mortar shell as he distributed cigarettes and chocolates to Italian soldiers. With over two hundred pieces of shrapnel in his legs, he spent the next several months recuperating in a hospital in Milan before returning to Oak Park in January 1919.

Ernest Hemingway

The American modernist photographer Man Ray took this portrait in Paris in 1924, shortly before Hemingway emerged as one of the foremost writers of what his friend Gertrude Stein called the "Lost Generation."

No longer interested in college, Hemingway began to chart a career as a writer. He worked as a journalist in Chicago, where he met Sherwood Anderson. Famous for his stories about the narrowness and oppressions of small-town life in the Midwest, Anderson urged Hemingway to go to Paris. Hemingway subsequently secured a job as the European correspondent of the *Toronto Star Weekly*. Shortly after he married Hadley Richardson in September 1921, the young couple sailed for Europe. Armed with letters of introduction from Anderson, who generously described his young and unknown friend as a writer of "extraordinary talent," Hemingway soon met many of the expatriate artists and writers living in Paris, including Gertrude Stein and his early mentor Ezra Pound. "He's teaching me to write," Hemingway excitedly reported, "and I'm teaching him to box." With Pound's help, he began to publish sketches and stories in the *Little Review* and Paris-based little magazines such as the *transatlantic review*. Pound also helped arrange for the publication in Paris of two small collections of Hemingway's apprentice work, *Three Stories and Ten Poems* (1923) and *in our time* (1924), a series of brief vignettes he incorporated into his collection of stories *In Our Time* (1925). The collection was published by the adventuresome American firm of Boni & Liveright. As Hemingway planned, however, the publisher was obliged to reject his lightweight novel *The Torrents of Spring* (1926), a parody of the work of the firm's most prominent author, Sherwood Anderson. Hemingway was consequently free to accept an offer from his friend F. Scott Fitzgerald's publisher, Scribner's. The distinguished firm soon published *The Sun Also Rises* (1926), Hemingway's acclaimed novel about expatriates in Europe, and a second collection of his stories, *Men without Women* (1927).

As one reviewer quipped about the rugged Hemingway, he was now "a big man in American letters." In 1926, he left his wife and their young son to live with Pauline Pfeifer, a wealthy fashion reporter Hemingway married in 1927. The following year, they left Paris and moved to Key West, Florida. Soon after they arrived, Hemingway learned that his father had committed suicide by shooting himself in the head with a revolver. Despite the personal turmoil, he completed *A Farewell to Arms* (1929), a best-selling novel loosely based on his experiences in World War I. Hemingway's next books were a study of bullfighting, *Death in the Afternoon* (1932), and another collection of his stories, *Winner Take Nothing* (1933). In 1934, he went on his first safari to Africa, which provided material for more stories and a nonfictional account of the trip, *Green Hills of Africa* (1935). While he was working on *To Have and Have Not* (1937), a socially conscious novel about a fishing-boat captain driven to smuggling by hard times during the Great Depression, Hemingway became deeply involved in the Spanish civil war. Along with other American writers, he worked on a propaganda film in support of the republican cause, *The Spanish Earth*. He also wrote a play, *The Fifth Column*, which many viewed as an attempt to justify the Communist Party's murderous purges of its leftist allies in the republican government in Spain. But Communist reviewers were infuriated by his novel *For Whom the Bell Tolls* (1940), in which Hemingway exposed the political infighting and the atrocities committed by both sides during the bitter civil war. The novel was sold to Paramount Pictures for $100,000, the highest price that had ever been paid for the film rights to a book, and it was a runaway bestseller for both Scribner's and as a main selection of the Book-of-the-Month Club.

Despite some later triumphs, Hemingway's career steadily declined after 1940. That year, soon after his divorce from Pauline Pfeifer, he married the writer Martha Gellhorn. During World War II, he worked as a war correspondent, covering D day and the liberation of Paris. He also began a relationship with an American journalist, Mary Welsh, whom Hemingway married immediately after Gellhorn divorced him in 1945. For the rest of his life, Hemingway divided his time between his homes in Cuba and Ketchum, Idaho. In 1950, he published his first novel in a decade, *Across the River and into the Trees*. Although the reviews of that novel were disappointing, Hemingway scored a critical and commercial hit with *The Old Man and the Sea* (1952). The beloved story of an infirm but indomitable Cuban fisherman, which was first published in an issue of *Life* magazine that sold over five million copies in two days, won the Pulitzer Prize. It also led to Hemingway's reception of the Nobel Prize for Literature, awarded in recognition of "his powerful, style-forming mastery of the art of modern narration," in 1954. But he was not able to attend the awards ceremony in Stockholm, since he was recovering from serious injuries he had received earlier that year in a plane crash while on safari in Africa. The remaining years of his life were marred by ill health and bouts of serious depression. He worked on several projects, including novels and a posthumously published memoir, *A Moveable Feast* (1964). But the shock treatments he received for depression restricted his memory, and he wrote less and less. On July 2, 1961, a few weeks before his sixty-second birthday, Hemingway

Hemingway never retired from his life into his workshop.

–Tennessee Williams

bedfordstmartins.com/ americanlit *for research links on Hemingway*

committed suicide by shooting himself in the head with a double-barreled shotgun at his house in Idaho. "Probably no other American writer of our time has set such a stamp on modern literature," the critic Alfred Kazin declared in a tribute to Hemingway in the *New York Times*.

Hemingway's "Big Two-Hearted River."   This story first appeared in the inaugural issue of *This Quarter,* a Paris-based literary monthly edited by the writer Ernest Walsh and the painter Ethel Moorhead. The distinguished issue was dedicated to Ezra Pound and included works by a number of avant-garde writers, including Gertrude Stein and the poets H.D. and William Carlos Williams. Hemingway originally wrote a longer version of "Big Two-Hearted River," which concluded with an extended interior monologue by Nick Adams, a semiautobiographical character who appears in more than twenty of Hemingway's stories. But he omitted the monologue, which was published posthumously as "On Writing" in *The Nick Adams Stories* (1972), in order to focus "Just on the straight fishing," as Hemingway wrote a friend in 1924. When he submitted the story to *This Quarter* early the following year, he told the editors that "it is the best thing I have done by a long shot," and many critics and writers agreed. In a

Hemingway in Michigan

In this photograph, which probably dates from the end of his high-school years, Hemingway is hiking through a second-growth forest in upper Michigan, the setting of his story "Big Two-Hearted River."

review of Hemingway's early collection of stories *In Our Time* (1925), the critic and poet Allen Tate singled out "Big Two-Hearted River" for special praise, observing that "the passionate accuracy of particular observation, the intense monosyllabic diction, the fidelity to the internal demands of the subject – these qualities fuse in the most completely realized naturalistic fiction of the age." Hemingway's friend F. Scott Fitzgerald later said that he could think of few "contemporary American short stories as good as 'Big Two-Hearted River,'" adding: "It is the account of a boy on a fishing trip – he hikes, pitches his tent, cooks dinner, sleeps, and next morning casts for trout. Nothing more – but I read it with the most breathless unwilling interest I have experienced since [Joseph] Conrad first bent my reluctant eyes upon the sea." The text is taken from the first printing in *This Quarter*, May 1925.

BIG TWO-HEARTED RIVER[1]

[Part One]

The train went on up the track out of sight around one of the hills of burnt timber. Nick sat down on the bundle of canvas and bedding the baggage man had pitched out of the door of the baggage car. There was no town, nothing but the rails and the burnt over country. The thirteen saloons that had lined the one street of Seney had not left a trace. The foundations of the Mansion House hotel stuck up above the ground. The stone was chipped and split by the fire. It was all that was left of the town of Seney. Even the surface had been burned off the ground.

Nick looked at the burned over stretch of hillside where he had expected to find the scattered houses of the town and then walked down the railroad track to the bridge over the river. The river was there. It swirled against the log piles of the bridge. Nick looked down into the clear, brown water, coloured from the pebbly bottom, and watched the trout keeping themselves steady in the current with wavering fins. As he watched them they changed their positions by quick angles only to hold steady in the fast water again. Nick watched them a long time.

He watched them holding themselves with their noses into the current, many trout in deep fast moving water, slightly distorted as he watched far down through the glassy convex surface of the pool, its surface pushing and swelling smooth against the resistance of the log driven piles of the bridge. At the bottom of the pool were the big trout. Nick did not see them at first. Then he saw them at the bottom of the pool, big trout looking to hold themselves on the gravel bottom in a varying mist of gravel and sand raised in spurts by the current.

Nick looked down into the pool from the bridge. It was a hot day. A kingfisher flew up the stream. It was a long time since Nick had looked into a stream and seen trout. They

---

1. **Big Two-Hearted River:** Hemingway originally published the story as "Big Two Hearted River," adding the hyphen in the title in his collection *In Our Time* (1925).

were very satisfactory. As the shadow of the kingfisher moved up the stream a big trout shot up stream in a long angle, only his shadow marking the angle, then lost his shadow as he came through the surface of the water, caught the sun, and then, as he went back into the stream under the surface, his shadow seemed to float down the stream with the current, unresisting, to his post under the bridge where he tightened facing upstream.

Nick's heart tightened as the trout moved. He felt all the old feeling.

He turned and looked down the stream. It stretched away, pebbly bottomed with shallows and big boulders and a deep pool as it curved away around the foot of a bluff.

Nick walked back up the ties to where his pack lay in the cinders beside the railway track. He was happy. He adjusted the pack harness around the bundle, pulling straps tight, slung the pack on his back, got his arms through the shoulder straps and took some of the pull off his shoulders by leaning his forehead against the wide band of the tump line.[2] Still it was too heavy. It was much too heavy. He had his leather rod case in his hand and leaning forward to keep the weight of the pack high on his shoulders he walked along the road that paralleled the railway track, leaving the burned town behind in the heat, and then turned off around a hill with a high, fire scarred hill on either side onto a road that went back into the country. He walked along the road feeling the ache from the pull of the heavy pack. The road climbed steadily. It was hard work walking up hill. His muscles ached and the day was hot but Nick felt happy. He felt he had left everything behind, the need for thinking, the need to write, other needs. It was all back of him.

From the time he had gotten down off the train and the baggage man had thrown his pack out of the open car door things had been different. Seney was burnt, the country was burned over and changed, but it did not matter. It could not all be burned. He knew that. He hiked along the road, sweating in the sun, climbing to cross the range of hills that separated the railway from the pine plains.

The road ran on, dipping occasionally, but always climbing. Nick went on up. Finally the road after going parallel to the burnt high hillside reached the top. Nick leaned back against a stump and slipped out of the pack harness. Ahead of him as far as he could see was the pine plain. The burned country stopped off at the left with the range of hills. On ahead islands of dark pine trees rose out of the plain. Far off to the left was the line of the river. Nick followed it with his eye and caught glints of the water in the sun.

There was nothing but the pine plain ahead of him until the far blue hills that marked the Lake Superior height of land. He could hardly see them, faint and far away in the heat light over the plain. If he looked too steadily they were gone. But if he only half looked they were there, the far off hills of the height of land.

Nick sat down against the charred stump and smoked a cigarette. His pack balanced on the top of the stump, harness holding ready, a hollow molded in it from his back. Nick sat smoking, looking out over the country. He did not need to get his map out. He knew where he was from the position of the river.

---

2. **tump line:** Also spelled "tumpline" or "tump-line," a strap placed across the forehead to help carry a heavy backpack.

As he smoked, his legs stretched out in front of him, he noticed a grasshopper walk along the ground and up onto his woolen sock. The grasshopper was black. As he had walked along the road climbing he had started many grasshoppers from the dust. They were all black. They were not the big grasshoppers with yellow and black or red and black wings whirring out from their black wing sheathing and whirring as they fly up. These were just ordinary hoppers but all a sooty black in color. Nick had wondered about them as he walked without really thinking about them. Now as he watched the black hopper that was nibbling at the wool of his sock with its fourway lip, he realised that they had all turned black from living in the burned over land. He realised that the fire must have come the year before but the grasshoppers were all black now. He wondered how long they would stay that way.

Carefully he reached his hand down and took hold of the hopper by the wings. He turned him up, all his legs walking in the air, and looked at his jointed belly. Yes, it was black too, irridescent where the back and head were dusty.

"Go on Hopper," Nick said, speaking out loud for the first time, "Fly away somewhere."

He tossed the grasshopper up into the air and watched him sail away to a charcoal stump across the road.

Nick stood up. He leaned his back against the weight of his pack where it rested upright on the stump and got his arms through the shoulder straps. He stood with the pack on his back on the brow of the hill looking out across the country toward the distant river and then struck down the hillside away from the road. Under foot the ground was good walking. Two hundred yards down the hillside the fire line stopped. Then it was sweet fern, growing ankle high, to walk through and clumps of jack pines, a long undulating country with frequent rises and descents, sandy underfoot and the country alive again.

Nick kept his direction by the sun. He knew where he wanted to strike the river and he kept on through the pine plain, mounting small rises to see other rises ahead of him and sometimes from the top of a rise a great solid island of pines off to his right or his left. He broke off some sprigs of the heathery sweet fern, and put them under his pack straps. The chafing crushed it and he smelled it as he walked.

He was tired and very hot walking across the uneven, shadeless pine plain. At any time he knew he could strike the river by turning off to his left. It could not be more than a mile away. But he kept on toward the North to hit the river as far upstream as he could go in one day's walking.

For some time as he walked Nick had been in sight of one of the big islands of pine standing out above the rolling high ground he was crossing. He dipped down and then as he came slowly up to the crest of the ridge he turned and made toward the pine trees.

There was no underbrush in the island of pine trees. The trunks of the trees went straight up or slanted toward each other. The trunks were straight and brown without branches. The branches were high above. Some interlocked to make a solid shadow on the brown forest floor. Around the grove of trees was a bare space. It was brown and soft under foot as Nick walked on it. This was the over-lapping of the pine needle floor extending out beyond the width of the high branches. The trees had grown tall and the branches moved high, leaving in the sun this bare space they had once covered with shadow. Sharp at the edge of this extension of the forest floor commenced the sweet fern.

Nick slipped off his pack and lay down in the shade. He lay on his back and looked up into the pine trees. His neck and back and the small of his back rested as he stretched. The earth felt good against his back. He looked up at the sky through the branches and then shut his eyes. He opened them and looked up again. There was a wind high up in the branches. He shut his eyes again and went to sleep.

Nick woke stiff and cramped. The sun was nearly down. His pack was heavy and the straps painful as he lifted it on. He leaned over with the pack on and picked up the leather rod case and started out from the pine trees across the sweet fern swale toward the river. He knew it could not be more than a mile.

He came down a hillside covered with stumps into a meadow. At the edge of the meadow flowed the river. Nick was glad to get to the river. He walked up stream through the meadow. His trousers were soaked with the dew as he walked. After the hot day the dew had come quickly and heavily. The river made no sound. It was too fast and smooth. At the edge of the meadow, before he mounted to a piece of high ground to make camp, Nick looked down the river at the trout rising. They were rising to insects come from the swamp on the other side of the stream when the sun went down. The trout jumped out of water to take them. While Nick walked through the little stretch of meadow along side the stream trout had jumped high out of water. Now as he looked down the river the insects must be settling on the surface for the trout were feeding steadily all down the stream. As far down the long stretch as he could see the trout were rising, making circles all down the surface of the water as though it were starting to rain.

The ground rose, wooded and sandy, to overlook the meadow, the stretch of river and the swamp. Nick dropped his pack and rod case and looked for a level piece of ground. He was very hungry and he wanted to make his camp before he cooked. Between two jack pines the ground was quite level. He took the ax out of the pack and chopped out two projecting roots. That leveled a piece of ground large enough to sleep on. He smoothed out the sandy soil with his hand and pulled all the sweet fern bushes by their roots. His hands smelled good from the sweet fern. He smoothed the uprooted earth. He did not want anything making lumps under the blankets. When he had the ground smooth he spread his three blankets. One he folded double next to the ground. The other two he spread on top.

With the ax he slit off a bright slab of pine from one of the stumps and split it into pegs for the tent. He wanted them long and solid to hold in the ground. With the tent unpacked and spread on the ground, the pack, leaning against a jackpine, looked much smaller. Nick tied the rope that served the tent for a ridge-pole to the trunk of one of the pine trees and pulled the tent up off the ground with the other end of the rope and tied it to the other pine. The tent hung on the rope like a canvas blanket on a clothes line. Nick poked a pole he had cut up under the back peak of the canvas and then made it a tent by pegging out the sides. He pegged the sides out taut and drove the pegs deep, hitting them down into the ground with the flat of the ax until the rope loops were buried and the canvas was drum tight.

Across the open mouth of the tent Nick fixed cheese cloth to keep out mosquitoes. He crawled inside under the mosquito bar with various things from the pack to put at the head of the bed under the slant of the canvas. Inside the tent the light came through the brown canvas. It smelled pleasantly of canvas. Already there was something mysterious and homelike. Nick was happy as he crawled inside the tent. He had not been unhappy all day. This was different though. Now things were done. There had been this to do. Now it was done. It had been a hard trip. He was very tired. That was done. He had made his camp. He was settled. Nothing could touch him. It was a good place to camp. He was there, in the good place. He was in his home where he had made it. Now he was hungry.

He came out, crawling under the cheese cloth. It was quite dark outside. It was lighter in the tent.

Nick went over to the pack and found with his fingers a long nail in a paper sack of nails in the bottom of the pack. He drove it into the pine tree, holding it close and hitting it gently with the flat of the ax. He hung the pack up on the nail. All his supplies were in the pack. They were off the ground and sheltered now.

Nick was hungry. He did not believe he had ever been hungrier. He opened and emptied a can of pork and beans and a can of spaghetti into the frying pan.

"I've got a right to eat this kind of stuff if I'm willing to carry it," Nick said. His voice sounded strange in the darkening woods. He did not speak again.

He started a fire with some chunks of pine he got with the ax from a stump. Over the fire he stuck a wire grill, pushing the four legs down into the ground with his boot. Nick put the frying pan on the grill over the flames. He was hungrier. The beans and spaghetti warmed. Nick stirred them and mixed them together. They began to bubble, making little bubbles that rose with difficulty to the surface. There was a good smell. Nick got out a bottle of tomato catchup and cut four slices of bread. The little bubbles were coming faster now. Nick sat down beside the fire and lifted the frying pan off. He poured about half the contents out into the tin plate. It spread slowly on the plate. Nick knew it was too hot. He poured on some tomato catchup. He knew the beans and spaghetti were still too hot. He looked at the fire, then at the tent, he was not going to spoil it all by burning his tongue. For years he had never enjoyed fried bananas because he had never been able to wait for them to cool. His tongue was very sensitive. He was very hungry. Across the river in the swamp in the almost dark he saw a mist rising. He looked at the tent once more. All right. He took a full spoonful from the plate.

"Christ," Nick said, "Jesus Christ," he said happily.

He ate the whole plateful before he remembered the bread. Nick finished the second plateful with the bread, mopping the plate shiny. He had not eaten since a cup of coffee and a ham sandwich in the station restaurant at St. Ignace. It had been a very fine experience. He had been that hungry before but had not been able to satisfy it. He could have made camp hours before if he had wanted to. There were plenty of good places to camp on the river. But this was good.

Nick tucked two big chips of pine under the grill. The fire flared up. He had forgotten to get water for the coffee. Out of the pack he got a folding canvas bucket and walked down the hill across the edge of the meadow to the stream. The other bank was in the white mist. The grass was wet and cold as he knelt on the bank and dipped the canvas bucket into the stream. It bellied and pulled hard in the current. The water was ice cold. Nick rinsed the bucket and carried it full up to the camp. Up away from the stream it was not so cold.

Nick drove another big nail and hung the bucket full of water. He dipped the coffee pot half full, put some more chips under the grill onto the fire and put the pot on. He could not remember which way he made coffee. He could remember an argument about it with Hopkins but not which side he had taken. He decided to bring it to a boil. He remembered now that was Hopkins' way. He had once argued about everything with Hopkins. While he waited for the coffee to boil he opened a small can of apricots. He liked to open cans. He emptied the can of apricots out into a tin cup. While he watched the coffee on the fire he drank the juice syrup of the apricots, carefully at first to keep from spilling, then meditatively, sucking the apricots down. They were better than fresh apricots.

The coffee boiled as he watched. The lid came up and coffee and grounds ran down the side of the pot. Nick took it off the grill. It was a triumph for Hopkins. He put sugar in the empty apricot cup and poured some of the coffee out to cool. It was too hot to pour and he used his hat to hold the handle of the coffee pot. He would not let it steep in the pot at all. Not the first cup. It should be straight Hopkins all the way. Hop deserved that. He was a very serious coffee maker. He was the most serious man Nick had ever known. Not heavy; serious. That was a long time ago. Hopkins spoke without moving his lips. He had played polo. He made millions of dollars in Texas. He had borrowed carfare to go to Chicago when the wire came that his first big well had come in. He could have wired for money. That would have been too slow. They called Hop's girl the Blonde Venus. Hop did not mind because she was not his real girl. Hopkins said very confidently that none of them would make fun of his real girl. He was right. Hopkins went away when the telegram came. That was on the Black River. It took eight days for the telegram to reach him. Hopkins gave away his 22 caliber colt automatic pistol to Nick. He gave his camera to Bill. It was to remember him always by. They were all going fishing again next summer. The Hop Head[3] was rich. He would get a yacht and they would all cruise along the north shore of Lake Superior. He was excited but serious. They said good-bye and all felt bad. It broke up the trip. They never saw Hopkins again. That was a long time ago on the Black River.

Nick drank the coffee, the coffee according to Hopkins. The coffee was bitter. Nick laughed. It made a good ending to the story. His mind was starting to work. He knew he could choke it because he was tired enough. He spilled the coffee out of the pot and shook the grounds loose into the fire. He lit a cigarette and went inside the tent. He took off his shoes and trousers sitting on the blankets, rolled the shoes up inside the trousers for a pillow and got in between the blankets.

Out through the front of the tent he watched the glow of the fire when the night wind blew on it. It was a quiet night. The swamp was perfectly quiet. Nick stretched under the

---

3. **The Hop Head:** Hop-head was a slang term for a drug addict, especially one addicted to heroin. *Hop Head* was later used as the title of a song composed by Duke Ellington and recorded by his jazz band in 1927.

blanket comfortably. A mosquito hummed close to his ear. Nick sat up and lit a match. The mosquito was on the canvas over his head. Nick moved the match quickly up to it. The mosquito made a satisfactory hiss in the flame. The match went out. Nick lay down again under the blankets. He turned on his side and shut his eyes. He was sleepy. He felt sleep coming. He curled up under the blanket and went to sleep.

Part Two

In the morning the sun was up and the tent was starting to get hot. Nick crawled out under the mosquito netting stretched across the mouth of the tent to look at the morning. The grass was wet on his hands as he came out. He held his pants and his shoes in his hands. The sun was just up over the hill. There was the meadow, the river and the swamp. There were birch trees in the green of the swamp on the other side of the river.

The river was clear and smoothly fast in the early morning. Down about two hundred yards were three logs all the way across the stream. They made the water smooth and deep above them. As Nick watched a mink crossed the river on the logs and went into the swamp. Nick was excited. He was excited by the early morning and the river. He was really too hurried to eat breakfast but he knew he must. He built a little fire and put on the coffee pot. While the water was heating in the pot he took an empty bottle and went down over the edge of the high ground to the meadow. The meadow was wet with dew and Nick wanted to catch grasshoppers for bait before the sun dried the grass. He found plenty of good grasshoppers. They were at the base of the grass stems. Sometimes they clung to a grass stem. They were cold and wet with the dew and could not jump until the sun warmed them. Nick picked them up, taking only the medium sized brown ones, and put them in the bottle. He turned over a log and just under the shelter of the edge were several hundred hoppers. It was a grasshopper lodging house. Nick put about fifty of the medium browns into the bottle. While he was picking up the hoppers the others warmed in the sun and commenced to hop away. They flew when they hopped. At first they made one flight and stayed stiff when they landed as though they were dead.

Nick knew that by the time he was through with breakfast they would be as lively as ever. Without dew in the grass it would take him all day to catch a bottle full of good grasshoppers and he would have to crush many of them slamming at them with his hat. He washed his hands at the stream. He was excited to be near it. Then he walked up to the tent. The hoppers were already jumping stiffly in the grass. In the bottle, warmed by the sun, they were jumping in a mass. Nick put in a pine stick as a cork. It plugged the mouth of the bottle enough so the hoppers could not get out and left plenty of air passage.

He had rolled the log back and knew he could get grasshoppers there every morning.

Nick laid the bottle full of jumping grasshoppers against a pine trunk. Rapidly he mixed some buckwheat flour with water and stirred it smooth, one cup of flour one cup of water. He put a handful of coffee in the pot and dipped a lump of grease out of a can and slid it sputtering across the hot skillet. On the smoking skillet he poured smoothly the buckwheat batter. It spread like lava, the grease spitting sharply. Around the edges the buckwheat cake began to firm, then brown, then crisp. The surface was bubbling slowly to porousness. Nick pushed under the browned under surface with a fresh pine chip. He shook the skillet sideways and the cake was loose on the surface. I won't try and flop it, he thought. He slid the chip of clean wood all the way under the cake and flopped it over onto its face. It sputtered in the pan.

When it was cooked Nick re-greased the skillet. He used all the batter. It made another big flapjack and one smaller one.

Nick ate a big flapjack and a smaller one covered with apple butter. He put apple butter on the third cake, folded it over twice, wrapped it in oiled paper and put it in his shirt pocket. He put the apple butter jar back in the pack and cut bread for two sandwiches.

In the pack he found a big onion. He sliced it in two and peeled the silky outer skin. Then he cut one half into slices and made onion sandwiches. He wrapped them in oiled paper and buttoned them in the other pocket of his khaki shirt. He turned the skillet upside down on the grill, drank the coffee, sweetened and yellow brown with the condensed milk in it, and tidied up the camp. It was a nice little camp.

Nick took his fly rod out of the leather rod case, jointed it, and shoved the rod case back into the tent. He put on the reel and threaded the line through the guides. He had to hold it from hand to hand as he threaded it or it would slip back through its own weight. It was a heavy, double tapered fly line. Nick had paid eight dollars for it a long time ago. It was made heavy to lift back in the air and come forward flat and heavy and straight to make it possible to cast a fly which has no weight. Nick opened the aluminum leader box. The leaders were coiled between the damp flannel pads. Nick had wet the pads at the water cooler on the train up to St. Ignace. In the damp pads the gut leaders had softened and Nick unrolled one and tied it by a loop at the end to the heavy fly line. He fastened a hook on the end of the leader. It was a small hook; very thin and springy.

Nick took it from his hook book sitting with the rod across his lap. He tested the knot and the spring of the rod by pulling the line taut. It was a good feeling. He was careful not to let the hook bite into his finger.

He started down to the stream, holding his rod, the bottle of grasshoppers hung from his neck by a thong tied in half hitches around the neck of the bottle. His landing net hung by a hook from his belt. Over his shoulder was a long flour sack tied at each corner into an ear. The cord went over his shoulder. The sack flapped against his legs.

Nick felt awkard and professionally happy with all his equipment hanging from him. The grasshopper bottle swung against his chest. In his shirt the breast pockets bulged against him with the lunch and his fly book.

He stepped into the stream. It was a shock. His trousers clung tight to his legs. His shoes felt the gravel. The water was a rising cold shock.

Rushing, the current sucked against his legs. Where he stepped in the water was over his knees. He waded with the current. The gravel slid under his shoes. He looked down at the swirl of water below each leg and tipped up the bottle to get a grasshopper.

The first grasshopper gave a jump in the neck of the bottle and went out into the water. He was sucked under in the whirl by Nick's right leg and came to the surface a little way down stream. He floated rapidly, kicking. In a quick circle, breaking the smooth surface of the water, he disappeared. A trout had taken him.

Another hopper poked his head out of the bottle. His antennae wavered. He was getting his front legs out of the bottle to have a purchase to jump. Nick took him by the head and held him while he threaded the slim hook under his chin, down through his thorax and into the last segments of his abdomen. The grasshopper took hold of the hook with his front feet spitting tobacco juice on it. Nick dropped him into the water.

Holding the rod in his right hand he let out line against the pull of the grasshopper in the current. He stripped off line from the reel with his left hand and let it run free. He could see the hopper in the little waves of the current. It went out of sight.

There was a tug on the line. Nick pulled against the taut line. It was his first strike. Holding the now living rod across the current he brought in the line with his left hand. The rod bent in jerks, the trout pumping against the current. Nick knew it was a small one. He lifted the rod straight up in the air. It bowed with the pull.

He saw the trout in the water jerking with his head and body against the shifting tangent of the line in the stream.

Nick took the line in his left hand and pulled the trout, thumping tiredly against the current, to the surface. His back was mottled the clear, water-over-gravel color, his side flashing in the sun. The rod under his right arm Nick stooped, dipping his right hand into the current. He held the trout, never still, with his moist right hand while he unhooked the barb from his mouth, then dropped him back into the stream.

He hung unsteadily in the current, then settled to the bottom beside a stone. Nick reached down his hand to touch him, his arm to the elbow under water. The trout was steady in the moving stream, resting on the gravel, beside a stone. As Nick's fingers touched him, touched his smooth, cool, underwater feeling he was gone, gone in a shadow across the bottom of the stream.

He's all right, Nick thought. He was only tired.

He had wet his hand before he touched the trout so he would not disturb the delicate mucous that covered him. If a trout was touched with a dry hand a white fungous attacked the unprotected spot. Years before when he had fished crowded streams with fly fishermen ahead of him and behind him Nick had again and again come on dead trout, furry with white fungous, drifted against a rock, or floating belly up in some pool. Nick did not like to fish with other men on the river. Unless they were of your party they spoiled it.

He wallowed down the stream, above his knees in the current, through the fifty yards of shallow water above the pile of logs that crossed the stream. He did not rebait his hook and held it in his hand as he waded. He was certain he could catch small trout in the shallows but he did not want them. There would be no big trout in the shallows this time of day.

Now the water deepened up his thighs sharply and coldly. Ahead was the smooth dammed-back flood of water above the logs. The water was smooth and dark, on the left the lower edge of the meadow, on the right the swamp.

Nick leaned back against the current and took a hopper from the bottle. He threaded the hopper on the hook and spat on him for good luck. Then he pulled several yards of line from the reel and tossed the hopper out ahead onto the fast dark water. It floated down towards the logs, then the weight of the line pulled the bait under the surface. Nick held the rod in his right hand letting the line run out through his fingers.

There was a long tug. Nick struck and the rod came alive and dangerous, bent double, the line tightening, coming out of water, tightening, all in a heavy, dangerous, steady pull. Nick felt the moment when the leader would break if the strain increased and let the line go.

The reel ratcheted into a mechanical shriek as the line went out. Too fast. Nick could not check it, the line rushing out, the reel note rising as the line ran out.

With the core of the reel showing, his heart feeling stopped with the excitement, leaning back against the current that mounted icily his thighs, Nick thumbed the reel hard with his left hand. It was awkward getting his thumb inside the fly reel frame.

As he put on the pressure the line tightened into sudden hardness and beyond the logs a huge trout went high out of water. As he jumped Nick lowered the tip of the rod. But he felt as he dropped the tip to ease the strain the moment when the strain was too great; the hardness too tight. Of course the leader had broken. There was no mistaking the feeling when all spring left the line and it became dry and hard. Then it went slack.

His mouth dry, his heart down Nick reeled in. He had never seen so big a trout. There was a heaviness, a power not to be held, and then the bulk of him as he jumped. He looked as broad as a salmon.

Nick's hand was shaky. He reeled in slowly. The thrill had been too much. He felt, vaguely, a little sick, as though it would be better to sit down.

The leader had broken where the hook was tied to it. Nick took it in his hand. He thought of the trout somewhere on the bottom, holding himself steady over the gravel, far down below the light, under the logs, with the hook in his jaw. Nick knew the trout's teeth would cut through the snell of the hook. The hook would imbed itself in his jaw. He'd bet the trout was angry. Anything that size would be angry. That was a trout. He had been solidly hooked. Solid as a rock. He felt like a rock too before he started off. By God he was a big one. By God he was the biggest one I ever heard of.

Nick climbed out onto the meadow and stood, water running down his trousers and out of his shoes, his shoes squlchy. He went over and sat on the logs. He did not want to rush his sensations any.

He wriggled his toes in the water in his shoes and got out a cigarette from his breast pocket. He lit it and tossed the match into the fast water below the logs. A tiny trout rose at the match as it swung around in the fast current. Nick laughed. He would finish the cigarette.

He sat on the logs smoking, drying in the sun, the sun warm on his back, the river shallow ahead entering the woods, curving into the woods, shallows, light glittering, big watersmooth rocks, cedars along the bank and white birches, the logs warm in the sun, smooth to sit on, without bark, gray to the touch, slowly the feeling of disappointment left him. It went away slowly, the feeling of disappointment that came sharply after the thrill that made his shoulders ache. It was all right now. His rod lying out on the logs, Nick tied a new hook on the leader, pulling the gut tight until it grimped into itself in a hard knot.

He baited up, then picked up the rod and walked to the far end of the logs to get into the water where it was not too deep. Under and beyond the logs was a deep pool. Nick walked around the shallow shelf near the swamp shore until he came out on the shallow bed of the stream.

On the left, where the meadow ended and the woods began, a great elm tree was uprooted. Gone over in a storm it lay back into the woods, its roots clotted with dirt, grass growing in them, rising a solid bank beside the stream. The river cut to the edge of the uprooted tree. From where Nick stood he could see deep channels, like ruts, cut in the shallow bed of the stream by the flow of the current. Pebbly where he stood and pebbly and full of boulders beyond, where it curved near the tree roots the bed of the stream was marly and between the ruts of deep water green weed fronds swung in the current.

Nick swung the rod back over his shoulder and forward and the line, curving forward, laid the grasshopper down on one of the deep channels in the weeds. A trout struck and Nick hooked him.

Holding the rod far out toward the uprooted tree and sloshing backward in the current Nick worked the trout, plunging, the rod bending alive, out of the danger of the weeds into the open river. Holding the rod, pumping alive against the current, Nick brought the trout in. He rushed, but always came, the spring of the rod yielding to the rushes, sometimes jerking under water but always bringing him in. Nick eased downstream with the rushes. The rod above his head he led the trout over the net, then lifted.

The trout hung heavy in the net, mottled trout back and silver sides in the meshes. Nick unhooked him; heavy sides, good to hold, big undershot jaw, and slipped him, heaving and big sliding, into the long sack that hung from his shoulders in the water.

Nick spread the mouth of the sack against the current and it filled, heavy with water. He held it up, the bottom in the stream, and the water poured out through the sides. Inside at the bottom was the big trout, alive in the water.

Nick moved down stream. The sack out ahead of him, sunk, heavy in the water, pulling from his shoulders.

It was getting hot, the sun hot on the back of his neck.

Nick had one good trout. He did not care about getting many trout. Now the stream was shallow and wide. There were trees along both banks. The trees of the left bank made short shadows on the current in the forenoon sun. Nick knew there were trout in each shadow. In the afternoon, after the sun had crossed toward the hills, the trout would be in the cool shadows on the other side of the stream.

The very biggest ones would lie up close to the bank. You could always pick them up there on the Black River. When the sun was down they all moved out into the current. Just when the sun made the water blinding in the glare before it went down you were liable to strike a big trout anywhere in the current. It was almost impossible to fish then, the surface of the water was blinding as a mirror in the sun. Of course you could fish upstream, but in a stream like this or the Black you had to wallow against the current and in a deep place the water piled up on you. It was no fun to fish upstream with this much current.

Nick moved along through the shallow stretch watching the banks for deep holes. A beech tree grew close beside the river so that the branches hung down into the water. The stream went back in under the leaves. There were always trout in a place like that.

Nick did not care about fishing that hole. He was sure he would get hooked in the branches.

It looked deep though. He dropped the grasshopper so that the current took it under water, back in under the overhanging branch. The line pulled hard and Nick struck. The trout threshed heavily, half out of water in the leaves and branches. The line was caught. Nick pulled hard and the trout was off. He reeled in and holding the hook in his hand walked down the stream.

Ahead, close to the left bank, was a big log. Nick saw it was hollow. Pointing up stream the current entered it smoothly, only a little ripple spreading each side of the log. The top of the hollow log was grey and dry. It was partly in the shadow and the water deepened toward it.

Nick took the cork out of the grasshopper bottle and a hopper clung to it. He picked him off, hooked him and tossed him out onto the current. He held the rod far out so that the hopper on the water moved into the current flowing into the hollow log. Nick lowered the rod and the hopper floated in. There was a heavy strike. Nick swung the rod against the pull. It felt as though he were hooked into the log its-self except that what he was hooked to felt alive, alive and pulling.

He tried to force the fish out into the current. It came, heavily.

The line went slack and Nick thought the trout was gone. Then he saw him, very near, in the current, shaking his head, trying to get the hook out. His mouth was clamped shut. He was fighting the hook in the clear flowing current.

Looping in the line with his left hand Nick swung the rod to make the line taut and tried to lead the trout toward the net; but he was gone, out of sight, the line pumping. Nick fought him against the current, letting him thump in the water against the spring of the rod. He shifted the rod to his left hand, worked the trout upstream, holding his weight, fighting on the rod, and then let him down into the net. He lifted him clear of the water, a heavy half circle in the net, the net dripping, unhooked him and slid him into the sack.

He spread the mouth of the sack and looked down in at the two big trout alive in the water.

Through the deepening water Nick waded over to the hollow log. He took the sack off over his head, the trout flopping as it came out of water, and hung it so the trout were deep in the clear water. Then he pulled himself up on the log and sat, the water from his trousers and boots running down into the stream. He laid his rod down, moved along to the shady end of the log and took the sandwiches out of his pocket. He dipped the sandwiches in the cold water. The current carried away the crumbs. He ate the sandwiches and dipped his hat full of water to drink, the water running out through his hat just ahead of his drinking.

It was cool in the shade sitting on the log. He took a cigarette out and scratched a match to light it. The match sunk into the grey wood, making a tiny furrow. Nick leaned over the side of the log, found a hard place and lit the match. He sat smoking and watching the river.

Ahead the river narrowed and went into a swamp. The river became smooth and deep and the swamp looked solid with cedar trees, their trunks close, their branches together. It would not be possible to walk through a swamp like that. The branches grew so low. You would have to keep almost level with the ground to move at all. You could not make your way through the branches. That must be why the animals that live in swamps are built the way they are, Nick thought.

He wished he had brought something to read. He felt like reading. He did not feel like going on into the swamp. He looked down the river. A big cedar slanted all the way across the stream. Beyond that the river went into the swamp.

Nick did not want to go in there now. He felt a reaction against deep wading with the water deepening up under his armpits. He did not want to hook big trout in places impossible to land them. In the swamp the banks were bare, covered with cedar needles, the big cedars came together overhead, the sun did not come through except in patches. In the fast deep water in the half light the fishing would be tragic. In the swamp fishing was a tragic adventure. Nick did not want it. He did not want to go down the stream any further today.

He took out his knife, opened it, and stuck it in the log. Then he pulled up the sack, reached into it and brought out one of the trout. Holding him near the tail, hard to hold, alive in his hands, he whacked him against the log. The trout quivered, rigid. Nick laid him on the log in the shade and broke the neck of the other fish in the same way. He laid them side by side on the log. They were fine trout.

Nick cleaned them, slitting the belly from the ventral fin to the tip of the jaw. All the insides, the gills and tongues came out in one piece. They were both males with long grey white strips of milt,[4] smooth and clean. All the insides clean and compact, coming out all together. Nick tossed the offal ashore for the minks to find.

He washed the trout in the stream. When he held them back up in the water they looked like live fish. Their color had not yet gone. He washed his hands and dried them on the log. Then he laid the trout on the sack spread out on the log, rolled them up in it, tied it into a bundle and put it in the landing net. His knife was still standing, blade stuck in the log. He cleaned it on the wood and put it in his pocket.

Nick stood up on the log holding his rod, the landing net hanging heavy against his thighs, then stepped into the water and splashed ashore. He climbed the bank and cut up into the woods toward the high ground. He was going back to camp. He looked back. The river just showed through the trees. There were plenty of days coming when he could fish the swamp.

[1925]

---

4. milt: Semen from the reproductive gland of a fish.

John Steinbeck

[1902–1968]

John Ernst Steinbeck was born on February 27, 1902, in Salinas, a town in the central coastal region of California. He was the third of four children and the only son of Olive Hamilton Steinbeck, a former school teacher, and John Ernst Steinbeck, the manager of a flour mill who later became treasurer of Monterey County. As a child, Steinbeck was an avid reader whose favorite book was Sir Thomas Malory's *Morte d'Arthur,* a collection of the stories about the legendary King Arthur of England. Steinbeck attended Salinas High School, where he played baseball and wrote for the school newspaper, and worked during the summers on ranches and construction crews. After his graduation in 1919, he enrolled at Stanford University. Although his parents hoped he would pursue a technical degree, Steinbeck wanted to be a writer. He published satirical articles in the *Stanford Spectator,* the campus literary magazine, and especially enjoyed his creative-writing classes. He was otherwise an indifferent student who missed classes and preferred reading and writing what he chose. He tried taking time off from college, working as a manual laborer, before withdrawing from Stanford in 1925. Like other aspiring writers, he determined to go to New York City, working his way there aboard a freighter that sailed from San Francisco.

For the next ten years, Steinbeck struggled to establish himself as a professional author. A relative helped him get a job as a reporter for the *New York American,* but he was soon fired. "I think now that the $25 a week that they paid me was a total loss," Steinbeck humorously recalled. "They gave me stories to cover in Queens and Brooklyn and I would get lost and spend hours trying to find my way back." Since he also failed to find a publisher for a collection of his short stories, Steinbeck had little choice but to return to California, and he signed on aboard a freighter bound back to San Francisco. After his arrival, he took a series of undemanding jobs that left him ample time for writing. He completed several novels, only one of which – *Cup of Gold* (1929), a fictionalized history of the seventeenth-century pirate Henry Morgan – was published. In 1930, Steinbeck married his first wife, Carol Hennings, a social activist who helped sensitize him to the plight of the poor and unemployed during the Great Depression. The stock market crash hurt the publishing business, but Steinbeck obtained a New York literary agent who placed two more of his books, both set in California: a short-story cycle, *The Pastures of Heaven* (1932), and a novel, *To a God Unknown* (1933). Although neither book sold well, Steinbeck also published a series of stories in the *North American Review.* Readers of the prestigious journal responded with enthusiasm, and the stories brought Steinbeck to the attention of a New York publisher, Paul Covici. He read and immediately agreed to publish a novel that had been rejected by many other publishing firms: *Tortilla Flat* (1935), Steinbeck's comic story about a group of wastrels living in a dilapidated section of Monterey,

John Steinbeck
This photograph was taken in the mid-1930s, when critics began to hail Steinbeck as one of the major American writers to emerge during the Great Depression.

bedfordstmartins.com/ *americanlit* *for research links on Steinbeck*

California. The royalties and sale of the film rights to the best-selling novel gave Steinbeck his first financial security, and he was "stunned and delighted" to learn that it had been awarded the prize for the best novel of 1935 by the Commonwealth Club of California.

Steinbeck earned even greater acclaim during the following five years. He soon published *In Dubious Battle* (1936), a novel about violent labor strife in the apple-growing industry, and *Of Mice and Men* (1937), a tragic novella about the broken dreams of two migrant laborers in California. Steinbeck sold the film rights of the novella, and his own dramatic adaptation was a hit on Broadway, winning the coveted New York Drama Critics' Circle Award for best play of 1938. At the urging of his publisher, Steinbeck followed up on his success by putting together a collection of his short stories, *The Long Valley* (1938), a highly regarded volume that sold briskly. He also began researching a novel about the plight of the "Okies," farmers driven from their homes in the Dust Bowl of Oklahoma to seek a new life in California. Following the main path of their great migration, Steinbeck drove west along Route 66 to California, where he was horrified by what he witnessed in the migrant camps. "The death of children by starvation in our valleys is simply staggering," he wrote his agent. Steinbeck poured his outrage and passion into his most ambitious novel, *The Grapes of Wrath* (1939). Angry businessmen and politicians called the book a pack of lies, and the controversial novel was banned by a number of school boards in states from New York to California. Nonetheless, Steinbeck was invited to the White House by President Franklin D. Roosevelt, whose socially conscious wife, Eleanor, publicly praised *The Grapes of Wrath*. It was the best-selling novel of 1939 and was awarded the Pulitzer Prize for Fiction. Steinbeck's fame was further spread by the 1940 film version starring Henry Fonda and directed by the legendary John Ford.

Steinbeck never again achieved the commercial and critical success of *The Grapes of Wrath*. In 1941, he left California and moved permanently to New York City. Under the pressures of his new life as a celebrity author, his marriage fell apart, and after his divorce Steinbeck married Gwyndolen Conger in 1943. Shortly thereafter, he went to Europe as a war correspondent for the *New York Herald Tribune*. In 1945, Steinbeck published a new novel, *Cannery Row*, an evocation of the lives of those living in a poor section of Monterey during the Depression. Although the book sold well, critics tended to dismiss the novel and those that followed, including *The Pearl* (1947) and *Burning Bright* (1950). After his second marriage ended, he married Elaine Anderson Scott, a former stage manager on Broadway, in 1950. By all accounts, they were very happy together, but Steinbeck was deeply hurt by the critical reception of his works, especially *East of Eden* (1952), a historical saga about two California families from 1900 to World War II. In a review in the *Nation*, Leo Gurko raised a question that many critics were asking, "why Steinbeck's talent has declined so rapidly and so far" since *The Grapes of Wrath*. Indeed, he was widely regarded as past his prime, an impression that seemed to be confirmed by his modest output during the remainder of the 1950s.

Steinbeck, however, ended his career on a far more triumphant note.

His final novel was *The Winter of Our Discontent* (1961), a critique of American materialism set in New England. Although some reviews were negative, many critics echoed the novelist Saul Bellow, who declared that Steinbeck had returned "to the high standards of *The Grapes of Wrath.*" In 1962, he was awarded the Nobel Prize for Literature for "his realistic as well as imaginative writings, distinguished by a sympathetic humor and a keen social perception." That same year, Steinbeck published his enormously popular *Travels with Charley in Search of America,* an account of a cross-country trip with his "old French gentleman poodle," Charley. Steinbeck was awarded the Presidential Medal of Freedom in 1964, and he became a friend and strong supporter of President Lyndon Johnson during the Vietnam War. After suffering a stroke, Steinbeck died of a heart attack on December 20, 1968.

Steinbeck's "Flight." This story is set in the Santa Lucia Mountains, close to where Steinbeck grew up in central California. The stark and naturalistic tale was rejected by several magazines, including *Scribner's* and the *Saturday Evening Post,* before Steinbeck first published it in his collection *The Long Valley.* It was the only story in the collection that had not previously been published in a magazine, but most critics have affirmed Steinbeck's belief in the power and quality of "Flight." William Soskin singled out the story for special praise in a review of *The Long Valley* that appeared in the *New York Herald* in September 1938:

> Steinbeck is at his comfortable best in stories that demand careful reporting of detail — the agonizing detail of a hunted youth's flight into the mountains after he has killed a man, of increasing pain and thirst and desperate struggle and fear that remind you of one of William Faulkner's hunted creatures and of Eugene O'Neill's terror-stricken Emperor Jones.

Critics, however, have offered a range of interpretations of "Flight," which some read as an account of a human being's regression into an animal and others view as an allegory of initiation into the wilderness or of growth from childhood to adulthood. The text is taken from *The Long Valley* (1938).

FLIGHT

About fifteen miles below Monterey, on the wild coast,[1] the Torres family had their farm, a few sloping acres above a cliff that dropped to the brown reefs and to the hissing white waters of the ocean. Behind the farm the stone mountains stood up against the sky. The farm buildings huddled like little clinging aphids on the mountain skirts, crouched low

---

1. **Monterey, on the wild coast:** Monterey, the capital of California under Spanish and Mexican rule, is on the rugged central coast, where the Santa Lucia Mountains run close to the Pacific Ocean.

to the ground as though the wind might blow them into the sea. The little shack, the rattling, rotting barn were grey-bitten with sea salt, beaten by the damp wind until they had taken on the color of the granite hills. Two horses, a red cow and a red calf, half a dozen pigs and a flock of lean, multicolored chickens stocked the place. A little corn was raised on the sterile slope, and it grew short and thick under the wind, and all the cobs formed on the landward sides of the stalks.

Mama Torres, a lean, dry woman with ancient eyes, had ruled the farm for ten years, ever since her husband tripped over a stone in the field one day and fell full length on a rattlesnake. When one is bitten on the chest there is not much that can be done.

Mama Torres had three children, two undersized black ones of twelve and fourteen, Emilio and Rosy, whom Mama kept fishing on the rocks below the farm when the sea was kind and when the truant officer was in some distant part of Monterey County. And there was Pepé, the tall smiling son of nineteen, a gentle, affectionate boy, but very lazy. Pepé had a tall head, pointed at the top, and from its peak, coarse black hair grew down like a thatch all around. Over his smiling little eyes Mama cut a straight bang so he could see. Pepé had sharp Indian cheek bones and an eagle nose, but his mouth was as sweet and shapely as a girl's mouth, and his chin was fragile and chiseled. He was loose and gangling, all legs and feet and wrists, and he was very lazy. Mama thought him fine and brave, but she never told him so. She said, "Some lazy cow must have got into thy father's family, else how could I have a son like thee." And she said, "When I carried thee, a sneaking lazy coyote came out of the brush and looked at me one day. That must have made thee so."

Pepé smiled sheepishly and stabbed at the ground with his knife to keep the blade sharp and free from rust. It was his inheritance, that knife, his father's knife. The long heavy blade folded back into the black handle. There was a button on the handle. When Pepé pressed the button, the blade leaped out ready for use. The knife was with Pepé always, for it had been his father's knife.

One sunny morning when the sea below the cliff was glinting and blue and the white surf creamed on the reef, when even the stone mountains looked kindly, Mama Torres called out the door of the shack, "Pepé, I have a labor for thee."

There was no answer. Mama listened. From behind the barn she heard a burst of laughter. She lifted her full long skirt and walked in the direction of the noise.

Pepé was sitting on the ground with his back against a box. His white teeth glistened. On either side of him stood the two black ones, tense and expectant. Fifteen feet away a redwood post was set in the ground. Pepé's right hand lay limply in his lap, and in the palm the big black knife rested. The blade was closed back into the handle. Pepé looked smiling at the sky.

Suddenly Emilio cried, "Ya!"

Pepé's wrist flicked like the head of a snake. The blade seemed to fly open in mid-air, and with a thump the point dug into the redwood post, and the black handle quivered. The three burst into excited laughter. Rosy ran to the post and pulled out the knife and brought it back to Pepé. He closed the blade and settled the knife carefully in his listless palm again. He grinned self-consciously at the sky.

"Ya!"

The heavy knife lanced out and sunk into the post again. Mama moved forward like a ship and scattered the play.

"All day you do foolish things with the knife, like a toy-baby," she stormed. "Get up on thy huge feet that eat up shoes. Get up!" She took him by one loose shoulder and hoisted at him. Pepé grinned sheepishly and came half-heartedly to his feet. "Look!" Mama cried. "Big lazy, you must catch the horse and put on him thy father's saddle. You must ride to Monterey. The medicine bottle is empty. There is no salt. Go thou now, Peanut! Catch the horse."

A revolution took place in the relaxed figure of Pepé.

"To Monterey, me? Alone? *Sí,*[2] Mama."

She scowled at him. "Do not think, big sheep, that you will buy candy. No, I will give you only enough for the medicine and the salt."

Pepé smiled. "Mama, you will put the hatband on the hat?"

She relented then. "Yes, Pepé. You may wear the hatband."

His voice grew insinuating, "And the green handkerchief, Mama?"

"Yes, if you go quickly and return with no trouble, the silk green handkerchief will go. If you make sure to take off the handkerchief when you eat so no spot may fall on it. . . ."

"*Sí,* Mama. I will be careful. I am a man."

"Thou? A man? Thou art a peanut."

He went into the rickety barn and brought out a rope, and he walked agilely enough up the hill to catch the horse.

When he was ready and mounted before the door, mounted on his father's saddle that was so old that the oaken frame showed through torn leather in many places, then Mama brought out the round black hat with the tooled leather band, and she reached up and knotted the green silk handkerchief about his neck. Pepé's blue denim coat was much darker than his jeans, for it had been washed much less often.

Mama handed up the big medicine bottle and the silver coins. "That for the medicine," she said, "and that for the salt. That for a candle to burn for the papa. That for *dulces*[3] for the little ones. Our friend Mrs. Rodriguez will give you dinner and maybe a bed for the night. When you go to the church say only ten Paternosters and only twenty-five Ave Marias.[4] Oh! I know, big coyote. You would sit there flapping your mouth over Aves all day while you looked at the candles and the holy pictures. That is not good devotion to stare at the pretty things."

The black hat, covering the high pointed head and black thatched hair of Pepé, gave him dignity and age. He sat the rangy horse well. Mama thought how handsome he was, dark and lean and tall. "I would not send thee now alone, thou little one, except for the

---

2. *Sí:* Yes (Spanish).

3. *dulces:* Candy (Spanish).

4. **Paternosters . . . Ave Marias:** These are two popular Roman Catholic prayers, frequently recited in a series as counted out on a string of prayer beads, known as a Rosary: *Paternoster,* literally "Our Father" (Latin), the name of the Lord's Prayer; and *Ave Maria,* literally "Hail Mary" (Latin), the name of the prayer in honor of Mary, the mother of Jesus.

medicine," she said softly. "It is not good to have no medicine, for who knows when the toothache will come, or the sadness of the stomach. These things are."

"Adios, Mama," Pepé cried. "I will come back soon. You may send me often alone. I am a man."

"Thou art a foolish chicken."

He straightened his shoulders, flipped the reins against the horse's shoulder and rode away. He turned once and saw that they still watched him, Emilio and Rosy and Mama. Pepé grinned with pride and gladness and lifted the tough buckskin horse to a trot.

When he had dropped out of sight over a little dip in the road, Mama turned to the black ones, but she spoke to herself. "He is nearly a man now," she said. "It will be a nice thing to have a man in the house again." Her eyes sharpened on the children. "Go to the rocks now. The tide is going out. There will be abalones to be found." She put the iron hooks into their hands and saw them down the steep trail to the reefs. She brought the smooth stone *metate*[5] to the doorway and sat grinding her corn to flour and looking occasionally at the road over which Pepé had gone. The noonday came and then the afternoon, when the little ones beat the abalones on a rock to make them tender and Mama patted the tortillas to make them thin. They ate their dinner as the red sun was plunging down toward the ocean. They sat on the doorsteps and watched the big white moon come over the mountain tops.

Mama said, "He is now at the house of our friend Mrs. Rodriguez. She will give him nice things to eat and maybe a present."

Emilio said, "Some day I too will ride to Monterey for medicine. Did Pepé come to be a man today?"

Mama said wisely, "A boy gets to be a man when a man is needed. Remember this thing. I have known boys forty years old because there was no need for a man."

Soon afterwards they retired, Mama in her big oak bed on one side of the room, Emilio and Rosy in their boxes full of straw and sheepskins on the other side of the room.

The moon went over the sky and the surf roared on the rocks. The roosters crowed the first call. The surf subsided to a whispering surge against the reef. The moon dropped toward the sea. The roosters crowed again.

The moon was near down to the water when Pepé rode on a winded horse to his home flat. His dog bounced out and circled the horse yelping with pleasure. Pepé slid off the saddle to the ground. The weathered little shack was silver in the moonlight and the square shadow of it was black to the north and east. Against the east the piling mountains were misty with light; their tops melted into the sky.

Pepé walked wearily up the three steps and into the house. It was dark inside. There was a rustle in the corner.

Mama cried out from her bed. "Who comes? Pepé, is it thou?"

---

5. *metate*: A flat stone on which grain is ground (Spanish).

"*Sí*, Mama."

"Did you get the medicine?"

"*Sí*, Mama."

"Well, go to sleep, then. I thought you would be sleeping at the house of Mrs. Rodriguez." Pepé stood silently in the dark room. "Why do you stand there, Pepé? Did you drink wine?"

"*Sí*, Mama."

"Well, go to bed then and sleep out the wine."

His voice was tired and patient, but very firm. "Light the candle, Mama. I must go away into the mountains."

"What is this, Pepé? You are crazy." Mama struck a sulphur match and held the little blue burr until the flame spread up the stick. She set light to the candle on the floor beside her bed. "Now, Pepé, what is this you say?" She looked anxiously into his face.

He was changed. The fragile quality seemed to have gone from his chin. His mouth was less full than it had been, the lines of the lips were straighter, but in his eyes the greatest change had taken place. There was no laughter in them any more, nor any bashfulness. They were sharp and bright and purposeful.

He told her in a tired monotone, told her everything just as it had happened. A few people came into the kitchen of Mrs. Rodriguez. There was wine to drink. Pepé drank wine. The little quarrel — the man started toward Pepé and then the knife — it went almost by itself.

It flew, it darted before Pepé knew it. As he talked, Mama's face grew stern, and it seemed to grow more lean. Pepé finished. "I am a man now, Mama. The man said names to me I could not allow."

Mama nodded. "Yes, thou art a man, my poor little Pepé. Thou art a man. I have seen it coming on thee. I have watched you throwing the knife into the post, and I have been afraid." For a moment her face had softened, but now it grew stern again. "Come! We must get you ready. Go. Awaken Emilio and Rosy. Go quickly."

Pepé stepped over to the corner where his brother and sister slept among the sheepskins. He leaned down and shook them gently. "Come, Rosy! Come, Emilio! The mama says you must arise."

The little black ones sat up and rubbed their eyes in the candlelight. Mama was out of bed now, her long black skirt over her nightgown. "Emilio," she cried. "Go up and catch the other horse for Pepé. Quickly, now! Quickly." Emilio put his legs in his overalls and stumbled sleepily out the door.

"You heard no one behind you on the road?" Mama demanded.

"No, Mama. I listened carefully. No one was on the road."

Mama darted like a bird about the room. From a nail on the wall she took a canvas water bag and threw it on the floor. She stripped a blanket from her bed and rolled it into a tight tube and tied the ends with string. From a box beside the stove she lifted a flour sack half full of black stringy jerky. "Your father's black coat, Pepé. Here, put it on."

Pepé stood in the middle of the floor watching her activity. She reached behind the door and brought out the rifle, a long 38-56, worn shiny the whole length of the barrel. Pepé took it from her and held it in the crook of his elbow. Mama brought a little leather bag and counted the cartridges into his hand. "Only ten left," she warned. "You must not waste them."

Emilio put his head in the door. "'Qui 'st 'l caballo,[6] Mama."

"Put on the saddle from the other horse. Tie on the blanket. Here, tie the jerky to the saddle horn."

Still Pepé stood silently watching his mother's frantic activity. His chin looked hard, and his sweet mouth was drawn and thin. His little eyes followed Mama about the room almost suspiciously.

Rosy asked softly, "Where goes Pepé?"

Mama's eyes were fierce. "Pepé goes on a journey. Pepé is a man now. He has a man's thing to do."

Pepé straightened his shoulders. His mouth changed until he looked very much like Mama.

At last the preparation was finished. The loaded horse stood outside the door. The water bag dripped a line of moisture down the bay shoulder.

The moonlight was being thinned by the dawn and the big white moon was near down to the sea. The family stood by the shack. Mama confronted Pepé. "Look, my son! Do not stop until it is dark again. Do not sleep even though you are tired. Take care of the horse in order that he may not stop of weariness. Remember to be careful with the bullets — there are only ten. Do not fill thy stomach with jerky or it will make thee sick. Eat a little jerky and fill thy stomach with grass. When thou comest to the high mountains, if thou seest any of the dark watching men, go not near to them nor try to speak to them. And forget not thy prayers." She put her lean hands on Pepé's shoulders, stood on her toes and kissed him formally on both cheeks, and Pepé kissed her on both cheeks. Then he went to Emilio and Rosy and kissed both of their cheeks.

Pepé turned back to Mama. He seemed to look for a little softness, a little weakness in her. His eyes were searching, but Mama's face remained fierce. "Go now," she said. "Do not wait to be caught like a chicken."

Pepé pulled himself into the saddle. "I am a man," he said.

It was the first dawn when he rode up the hill toward the little canyon which let a trail into the mountains. Moonlight and daylight fought with each other, and the two warring qualities made it difficult to see. Before Pepé had gone a hundred yards, the outlines of his figure were misty; and long before he entered the canyon, he had become a grey, indefinite shadow.

Mama stood stiffly in front of her doorstep, and on either side of her stood Emilio and Rosy. They cast furtive glances at Mama now and then.

When the grey shape of Pepé melted into the hillside and disappeared, Mama relaxed. She began the high, whining keen of the death wail. "Our beautiful — our brave," she cried. "Our protector, our son is gone." Emilio and Rosy moaned beside her. "Our beautiful — our brave, he is gone." It was the formal wail. It rose to a high piercing

---

6. *'Qui 'st 'l caballo*: Here's the horse (colloquial Spanish).

whine and subsided to a moan. Mama raised it three times and then she turned and went into the house and shut the door.

Emilio and Rosy stood wondering in the dawn. They heard Mama whimpering in the house. They went out to sit on the cliff above the ocean. They touched shoulders. "When did Pepé come to be a man?" Emilio asked.

"Last night," said Rosy. "Last night in Monterey." The ocean clouds turned red with the sun that was behind the mountains.

"We will have no breakfast," said Emilio. "Mama will not want to cook." Rosy did not answer him. "Where is Pepé gone?" he asked.

Rosy looked around at him. She drew her knowledge from the quiet air. "He has gone on a journey. He will never come back."

"Is he dead? Do you think he is dead?"

Rosy looked back at the ocean again. A little steamer, drawing a line of smoke sat on the edge of the horizon. "He is not dead," Rosy explained. "Not yet."

Pepé rested the big rifle across the saddle in front of him. He let the horse walk up the hill and he didn't look back. The stony slope took on a coat of short brush so that Pepé found the entrance to a trail and entered it.

When he came to the canyon opening, he swung once in his saddle and looked back, but the houses were swallowed in the misty light. Pepé jerked forward again. The high shoulder of the canyon closed in on him. His horse stretched out its neck and sighed and settled to the trail.

It was a well-worn path, dark soft leaf-mould earth strewn with broken pieces of sandstone. The trail rounded the shoulder of the canyon and dropped steeply into the bed of the stream. In the shallows the water ran smoothly, glinting in the first morning sun. Small round stones on the bottom were as brown as rust with sun moss. In the sand along the edges of the stream the tall, rich wild mint grew, while in the water itself the cress, old and tough, had gone to heavy seed.

The path went into the stream and emerged on the other side. The horse sloshed into the water and stopped. Pepé dropped his bridle and let the beast drink of the running water.

Soon the canyon sides became steep and the first giant sentinel redwoods guarded the trail, great round red trunks bearing foliage as green and lacy as ferns. Once Pepé was among the trees, the sun was lost. A perfumed and purple light lay in the pale green of the underbrush. Gooseberry bushes and blackberries and tall ferns lined the stream, and overhead the branches of the redwoods met and cut off the sky.

Pepé drank from the water bag, and he reached into the flour sack and brought out a black string of jerky. His white teeth gnawed at the string until the tough meat parted. He chewed slowly and drank occasionally from the water bag. His little eyes were slumberous and tired, but the muscles of his face were hard set. The earth of the trail was black now. It gave up a hollow sound under the walking hoofbeats.

The stream fell more sharply. Little waterfalls splashed on the stones. Five-fingered ferns hung over the water and dripped spray from their fingertips. Pepé rode half over in his saddle, dangling one leg loosely. He picked a bay leaf from a tree beside the way and put it into his mouth for a moment to flavor the dry jerky. He held the gun loosely across the pommel.

Suddenly he squared in his saddle, swung the horse from the trail and kicked it hurriedly up behind a big redwood tree. He pulled up the reins tight against the bit to keep the horse from whinnying. His face was intent and his nostrils quivered a little.

A hollow pounding came down the trail, and a horseman rode by, a fat man with red cheeks and a white stubble beard. His horse put down its head and blubbered at the trail when it came to the place where Pepé had turned off. "Hold up!" said the man and he pulled up his horse's head.

When the last sound of the hoofs died away, Pepé came back into the trail again. He did not relax in the saddle any more. He lifted the big rifle and swung the lever to throw a shell into the chamber, and then he let down the hammer to half cock.

The trail grew very steep. Now the redwood trees were smaller and their tops were dead, bitten dead where the wind reached them. The horse plodded on; the sun went slowly overhead and started down toward the afternoon.

Where the stream came out of a side canyon, the trail left it. Pepé dismounted and watered his horse and filled up his water bag. As soon as the trail had parted from the stream, the trees were gone and only the thick brittle sage and manzanita and chaparral edged the trail. And the soft black earth was gone, too, leaving only the light tan broken rock for the trail bed. Lizards scampered away into the brush as the horse rattled over the little stones.

Pepé turned in his saddle and looked back. He was in the open now: he could be seen from a distance. As he ascended the trail the country grew more rough and terrible and dry. The way wound about the bases of great square rocks. Little grey rabbits skittered in the brush. A bird made a monotonous high creaking. Eastward the bare rock mountaintops were pale and powder-dry under the dropping sun. The horse plodded up and up the trail toward a little V in the ridge which was the pass.

Pepé looked suspiciously back every minute or so, and his eyes sought the tops of the ridges ahead. Once, on a white barren spur, he saw a black figure for a moment, but he looked quickly away, for it was one of the dark watchers. No one knew who the watchers were, nor where they lived, but it was better to ignore them and never to show interest in them. They did not bother one who stayed on the trail and minded his own business.

The air was parched and full of light dust blown by the breeze from the eroding mountains. Pepé drank sparingly from his bag and corked it tightly and hung it on the horn again. The trail moved up the dry shale hillside, avoiding rocks, dropping under clefts, climbing in and out of old water scars. When he arrived at the little pass he stopped and looked back for a long time. No dark watchers were to be seen now. The trail behind was empty. Only the high tops of the redwoods indicated where the stream flowed.

Pepé rode on through the pass. His little eyes were nearly closed with weariness, but his face was stern, relentless and manly. The high mountain wind coasted sighing through the pass and whistled on the edges of the big blocks of broken granite. In the air, a red-tailed hawk sailed over close to the ridge and screamed angrily. Pepé went slowly through the broken jagged pass and looked down on the other side.

The trail dropped quickly, staggering among broken rock. At the bottom of the slope there was a dark crease, thick with brush, and on the other side of the crease a little flat, in which a grove of oak trees grew. A scar of green grass cut across the flat. And behind the flat another mountain rose, desolate with dead rocks and starving little black bushes. Pepé drank from the bag again for the air was so dry that it encrusted his nostrils and burned his lips. He put the horse down the trail. The hooves slipped and struggled on the steep way, starting little stones that rolled off into the brush. The sun was gone behind the westward mountain now, but still it glowed brilliantly on the oaks and on the grassy flat. The rocks and the hillsides still sent up waves of the heat they had gathered from the day's sun.

Pepé looked up to the top of the next dry withered ridge. He saw a dark form against the sky, a man's figure standing on top of a rock, and he glanced away quickly not to appear curious. When a moment later he looked up again, the figure was gone.

Downward the trail was quickly covered. Sometimes the horse floundered for footing, sometimes set his feet and slid a little way. They came at last to the bottom where the dark chaparral was higher than Pepé's head. He held up his rifle on one side and his arm on the other to shield his face from the sharp brittle fingers of the brush.

Up and out of the crease he rode, and up a little cliff. The grassy flat was before him, and the round comfortable oaks. For a moment he studied the trail down which he had come, but there was no movement and no sound from it. Finally he rode out over the flat, to the green streak, and at the upper end of the damp he found a little spring welling out of the earth and dropping into a dug basin before it seeped out over the flat.

Pepé filled his bag first, and then he let the thirsty horse drink out of the pool. He led the horse to the clump of oaks, and in the middle of the grove, fairly protected from sight on all sides, he took off the saddle and the bridle and laid them on the ground. The horse stretched his jaws sideways and yawned. Pepé knotted the lead rope about the horse's neck and tied him to a sapling among the oaks, where he could graze in a fairly large circle.

When the horse was gnawing hungrily at the dry grass, Pepé went to the saddle and took a black string of jerky from the sack and strolled to an oak tree on the edge of the grove, from under which he could watch the trail. He sat down in the crisp dry oak leaves and automatically felt for his big black knife to cut the jerky, but he had no knife. He leaned back on his elbow and gnawed at the tough strong meat. His face was blank, but it was a man's face.

The bright evening light washed the eastern ridge, but the valley was darkening. Doves flew down from the hills to the spring, and the quail came running out of the brush and joined them, calling clearly to one another.

Out of the corner of his eye Pepé saw a shadow grow out of the bushy crease. He turned his head slowly. A big spotted wildcat was creeping toward the spring, belly to the ground, moving like thought.

Pepé cocked his rifle and edged the muzzle slowly around. Then he looked apprehensively up the trail and dropped the hammer again. From the ground beside him he picked an oak twig and threw it toward the spring. The quail flew up with a roar and the doves whistled away. The big cat stood up: for a long moment he looked at Pepé with cold yellow eyes, and then fearlessly walked back into the gulch.

The dusk gathered quickly in the deep valley. Pepé muttered his prayers, put his head down on his arm and went instantly to sleep.

The moon came up and filled the valley with cold blue light, and the wind swept rustling down from the peaks. The owls worked up and down the slopes looking for rabbits. Down in the brush of the gulch a coyote gabbled. The oak trees whispered softly in the night breeze.

Pepé started up, listening. His horse had whinnied. The moon was just slipping behind the western ridge, leaving the valley in darkness behind it. Pepé sat tensely gripping his rifle. From far up the trail he heard an answering whinny and the crash of shod hooves on the broken rock. He jumped to his feet, ran to his horse and led it under the trees. He threw on the saddle and cinched it tight for the steep trail, caught the unwilling head and forced the bit into the mouth. He felt the saddle to make sure the water bag and the sack of jerky were there. Then he mounted and turned up the hill.

It was velvet dark. The horse found the entrance to the trail where it left the flat; and started up, stumbling and slipping on the rocks. Pepé's hand rose up to his head. His hat was gone. He had left it under the oak tree.

The horse had struggled far up the trail when the first change of dawn came into the air, a steel greyness as light mixed thoroughly with dark. Gradually the sharp snaggled edge of the ridge stood out above them, rotten granite tortured and eaten by the winds of time. Pepé had dropped his reins on the horn, leaving direction to the horse. The brush grabbed at his legs in the dark until one knee of his jeans was ripped.

Gradually the light flowed down over the ridge. The starved brush and rocks stood out in the half light, strange and lonely in high perspective. Then there came warmth into the light. Pepé drew up and looked back, but he could see nothing in the darker valley below. The sky turned blue over the coming sun. In the waste of the mountainside, the poor dry brush grew only three feet high. Here and there, big outcroppings of unrotted granite stood up like mouldering houses. Pepé relaxed a little. He drank from his water bag and bit off a piece of jerky. A single eagle flew over, high in the light.

Without warning Pepé's horse screamed and fell on its side. He was almost down before the rifle crash echoed up from the valley. From a hole behind the struggling shoulder, a stream of bright crimson blood pumped and stopped and pumped and stopped. The hooves threshed on the ground. Pepé lay half stunned beside the horse. He looked slowly down the hill. A piece of sage clipped off beside his head and another crash echoed up from side to side of the canyon. Pepé flung himself frantically behind a bush.

He crawled up the hill on his knees and one hand. His right hand held the rifle up off the ground and pushed it ahead of him. He moved with the instinctive care of an animal. Rapidly he wormed his way toward one of the big outcroppings of granite on the hill above him. Where the brush was high he doubled up and ran, but where the cover was slight he wriggled forward on his stomach, pushing the rifle ahead of him. In the last little distance there was no cover at all. Pepé poised and then he darted across the space and flashed around the corner of the rock.

He leaned panting against the stone. When his breath came easier he moved along behind the big rock until he came to a narrow split that offered a thin section of vision down the hill. Pepé lay on his stomach and pushed the rifle barrel through the slit and waited.

The sun reddened the western ridges now. Already the buzzards were settling down toward the place where the horse lay. A small brown bird scratched in the dead sage leaves directly in front of the rifle muzzle. The coasting eagle flew back toward the rising sun.

Pepé saw a little movement in the brush far below. His grip tightened on the gun. A little brown doe stepped daintily out on the trail and crossed it and disappeared into the brush again. For a long time Pepé waited. Far below he could see the little flat and the oak trees and the slash of green. Suddenly his eyes flashed back at the trail again. A quarter of a mile down there had been a quick movement in the chaparral. The rifle swung over. The front sight nestled in the v of the rear sight. Pepé studied for a moment and then raised the rear sight a notch. The little movement in the brush came again. The sight settled on it. Pepé squeezed the trigger. The explosion crashed down the mountain and up the other side, and came rattling back. The whole side of the slope grew still. No more movement. And then a white streak cut into the granite of the slit and a bullet whined away and a crash sounded up from below. Pepé felt a sharp pain in his right hand. A sliver of granite was sticking out from between his first and second knuckles and the point protruded from his palm. Carefully he pulled out the sliver of stone. The wound bled evenly and gently. No vein nor artery was cut.

Pepé looked into a little dusty cave in the rock and gathered a handful of spider web, and he pressed the mass into the cut, plastering the soft web into the blood. The flow stopped almost at once.

The rifle was on the ground. Pepé picked it up, levered a new shell into the chamber. And then he slid into the brush on his stomach. Far to the right he crawled, and then up the hill, moving slowly and carefully, crawling to cover and resting and then crawling again.

In the mountains the sun is high in its arc before it penetrates the gorges. The hot face looked over the hill and brought instant heat with it. The white light beat on the rocks and reflected from them and rose up quivering from the earth again, and the rocks and bushes seemed to quiver behind the air.

Pepé crawled in the general direction of the ridge peak, zig-zagging for cover. The deep cut between his knuckles began to throb. He crawled close to a rattlesnake before he saw it, and when it raised its dry head and made a soft beginning whirr, he backed up and took another way. The quick grey lizards flashed in front of him, raising a tiny line of dust. He found another mass of spider web and pressed it against his throbbing hand.

Pepé was pushing the rifle with his left hand now. Little drops of sweat ran to the ends of his coarse black hair and rolled down his cheeks. His lips and tongue were growing thick and heavy. His lips writhed to draw saliva into his mouth. His little dark eyes were uneasy and suspicious. Once when a grey lizard paused in front of him on the parched ground and turned its head sideways he crushed it flat with a stone.

When the sun slid past noon he had not gone a mile. He crawled exhaustedly a last hundred yards to a patch of high sharp manzanita, crawled desperately, and when the patch was reached he wriggled in among the tough gnarly trunks and dropped his head on his left arm. There was little shade in the meager brush, but there was cover and safety. Pepé went to sleep as he lay and the sun beat on his back. A few little birds hopped close to him and peered and hopped away. Pepé squirmed in his sleep and he raised and dropped his wounded hand again and again.

The sun went down behind the peaks and the cool evening came, and then the dark. A coyote yelled from the hillside, Pepé started awake and looked about with misty eyes. His hand was swollen and heavy; a little thread of pain ran up the inside of his arm and settled in a pocket in his armpit. He peered about and then stood up, for the mountains were black and the moon had not yet risen. Pepé stood up in the dark. The coat of his father pressed on his arm. His tongue was swollen until it nearly filled his mouth. He wriggled out of the coat and dropped it in the brush, and then he struggled up the hill, falling over rocks and tearing his way through the brush. The rifle knocked against stones as he went. Little dry avalanches of gravel and shattered stone went whispering down the hill behind him.

After a while the old moon came up and showed the jagged ridge top ahead of him. By moonlight Pepé traveled more easily. He bent forward so that his throbbing arm hung away from his body. The journey uphill was made in dashes and rests, a frantic rush up a few yards and then a rest. The wind coasted down the slope rattling the dry stems of the bushes.

The moon was at meridian when Pepé came at last to the sharp backbone of the ridge top. On the last hundred yards of the rise no soil had clung under the wearing winds. The way was on solid rock. He clambered to the top and looked down on the other side. There was a draw like the last below him, misty with moonlight, brushed with dry struggling sage and chaparral. On the other side the hill rose up sharply and at the top the jagged rotten teeth of the mountain showed against the sky. At the bottom of the cut the brush was thick and dark.

Pepé stumbled down the hill. His throat was almost closed with thirst. At first he tried to run, but immediately he fell and rolled. After that he went more carefully. The moon was just disappearing behind the mountains when he came to the bottom. He crawled into the heavy brush feeling with his fingers for water. There was no water in the bed of the stream, only damp earth. Pepé laid his gun down and scooped up a handful of mud and put it in his mouth, and then he spluttered and scraped the earth from his tongue with his finger, for the mud drew at his mouth like a poultice. He dug a hole in the stream bed with his fingers, dug a little basin to catch water; but before it was very deep his head fell forward on the damp ground and he slept.

The dawn came and the heat of the day fell on the earth, and still Pepé slept. Late in the afternoon his head jerked up. He looked slowly around. His eyes were slits of wariness. Twenty feet away in the heavy brush a big tawny mountain lion stood looking at him. Its long thick tail waved gracefully, its ears were erect with interest, not laid back dangerously. The lion squatted down on its stomach and watched him.

Pepé looked at the hole he had dug in the earth. A half inch of muddy water had collected in the bottom. He tore the sleeve from his hurt arm, with his teeth ripped out a little square, soaked it in the water and put it in his mouth. Over and over he filled the cloth and sucked it.

Still the lion sat and watched him. The evening came down but there was no movement on the hills. No birds visited the dry bottom of the cut. Pepé looked occasionally at the lion. The eyes of the yellow beast drooped as though he were about to sleep. He yawned and his long thin red tongue curled out. Suddenly his head jerked around and his nostrils quivered. His big tail lashed. He stood up and slunk like a tawny shadow into the thick brush.

A moment later Pepé heard the sound, the faint far crash of horses' hooves on gravel. And he heard something else, a high whining yelp of a dog.

Pepé took his rifle in his left hand and he glided into the brush almost as quietly as the lion had. In the darkening evening he crouched up the hill toward the next ridge. Only when the dark came did he stand up. His energy was short. Once it was dark he fell over the rocks and slipped to his knees on the steep slope, but he moved on and on up the hill, climbing and scrabbling over the broken hillside.

When he was far up toward the top, he lay down and slept for a little while. The withered moon, shining on his face, awakened him. He stood up and moved up the hill. Fifty yards away he stopped and turned back, for he had forgotten his rifle. He walked heavily down and poked about in the brush, but he could not find his gun. At last he lay down to rest. The pocket of pain in his armpit had grown more sharp. His arm seemed to swell out and fall with every heartbeat. There was no position lying down where the heavy arm did not press against his armpit.

With the effort of a hurt beast, Pepé got up and moved again toward the top of the ridge. He held his swollen arm away from his body with his left hand. Up the steep hill he dragged himself, a few steps and a rest, and a few more steps. At last he was nearing the top. The moon showed the uneven sharp back of it against the sky.

Pepé's brain spun in a big spiral up and away from him. He slumped to the ground and lay still. The rock ridge top was only a hundred feet above him.

The moon moved over the sky. Pepé half turned on his back. His tongue tried to make words, but only a thick hissing came from between his lips.

When the dawn came, Pepé pulled himself up. His eyes were sane again. He drew his great puffed arm in front of him and looked at the angry wound. The black line ran up from his wrist to his armpit. Automatically he reached in his pocket for the big black knife, but it was not there. His eyes searched the ground. He picked up a sharp blade of stone and scraped at the wound, sawed at the proud flesh and then squeezed the green juice out in big drops. Instantly he threw back his head and whined like a dog. His whole right side shuddered at the pain, but the pain cleared his head.

In the grey light he struggled up the last slope to the ridge and crawled over and lay down behind a line of rocks. Below him lay a deep canyon exactly like the last, waterless and desolate. There was no flat, no oak trees, not even heavy brush in the bottom of it. And on the other side a sharp ridge stood up, thinly brushed with starving sage, littered with broken granite. Strewn over the hill there were giant outcroppings, and on the top the granite teeth stood out against the sky.

The new day was light now. The flame of the sun came over the ridge and fell on Pepé where he lay on the ground. His coarse black hair was littered with twigs and bits of spider web. His eyes had retreated back into his head. Between his lips the tip of his black tongue showed.

He sat up and dragged his great arm into his lap and nursed it, rocking his body and moaning in his throat. He threw back his head and looked up into the pale sky. A big black bird circled nearly out of sight, and far to the left another was sailing near.

He lifted his head to listen, for a familiar sound had come to him from the valley he had climbed out of; it was the crying yelp of hounds, excited and feverish, on a trail.

Pepé bowed his head quickly. He tried to speak rapid words but only a thick hiss came from his lips. He drew a shaky cross on his breast with his left hand. It was a long struggle to get to his feet. He crawled slowly and mechanically to the top of a big rock on the ridge peak. Once there, he arose slowly, swaying to his feet, and stood erect. Far below he could see the dark brush where he had slept. He braced his feet and stood there, black against the morning sky.

There came a ripping sound at his feet. A piece of stone flew up and a bullet droned off into the next gorge. The hollow crash echoed up from below. Pepé looked down for a moment and then pulled himself straight again.

His body jarred back. His left hand fluttered helplessly toward his breast. The second crash sounded from below. Pepé swung forward and toppled from the rock. His body struck and rolled over and over, starting a little avalanche. And when at last he stopped against a bush, the avalanche slid slowly down and covered up his head.

[1938]

Richard Wright

[1908–1960]

Richard Wright

The noted African American photographer Gordon Parks took this portrait of Wright in his study in 1943, when the novelist was one of the most acclaimed writers in the United States.

Richard Nathaniel Wright was born on September 4, 1908, on a plantation east of Natchez, Mississippi. He was the first of two sons born to Nathaniel Wright, an illiterate sharecropper, and Ella Wilson Wright, a former schoolteacher. In 1911, the impoverished family moved to Natchez, where they lived with Wright's maternal grandparents, and then on to Memphis, Tennessee. Wright's father abandoned the family, and Ella Wright was forced to place her sons in an orphanage before taking them to live with her sister and brother-in-law in Elaine, Arkansas, in 1915. For a time, the family enjoyed some stability. In 1917, however, Wright's prosperous uncle was murdered by a group of white men who wanted to take over his saloon, and the family fled to Jackson, Mississippi. Wright's mother suffered a stroke that left her paralyzed, and he was sent to live with relatives in Greenwood, Mississippi. He worked at odd jobs before returning to Jackson, where Wright began his first uninterrupted schooling. His earliest story, "The Voodoo of Hell's Half Acre," appeared in a local newspaper in 1924. The next year, he graduated from the ninth grade in the Smith-Robinson Public School as the class valedictorian. He briefly attended high school but dropped out and moved to Memphis, where he worked as a delivery boy and a dishwasher. Determined to escape racial hatred and segregation in the South, and hoping to find greater opportunities in the North, he boarded a train for Chicago in 1927.

Wright lived there for the next ten years. He took a series of menial jobs and was often unemployed after the onset of the Great Depression in 1929. At the same time, he wrote constantly and read widely in European and American literature, especially the works of Sherwood Anderson, Theodore Dreiser, and experimental modernists such as Gertrude Stein, James Joyce, and T. S. Eliot. Wright joined the John Reed Club, a literary organization affiliated with the Communist Party, and began to publish poetry in leftist magazines such as the *New Masses*. In a poem printed there in June 1934, after he officially joined the Communist Party, he proclaimed:

> I am black and have seen black hands
> Raised in fists of revolt, side by side with the white fists of white workers,
> And some day — and it is only this which sustains me —
> Some day there shall be millions and millions of them,
> One red day in a burst of fists on a new horizon!

Wright also wrote fiction, including two novels, *Lawd Today!* and *Tarbaby's Dawn*. He could not interest a publisher in either novel, but he made connections with other writers through his work for the Illinois Writers Project, part of the Federal Arts Project. In 1936, his story "Big Boy Leaves Home" was published in an anthology, *The New Caravan*. The story was singled out as the best story in the collection by reviewers in a number of influential periodicals, including the *Saturday Review of Literature* and the *New York Times*. Eager to pursue his literary career, and believing that it would be easier to find a publisher for his work in New York City, Wright moved there in 1937.

During the following decade, Wright enjoyed growing acclaim as a writer. Although he was increasingly disillusioned with Communism, he became the Harlem editor of the *Daily Worker*, a newspaper published by the Communist Party. Wright achieved his first major breakthrough as a writer when he won first prize in a competition sponsored by the prominent magazine *Story*. The award was five hundred dollars and the publication of his prize-winning manuscript, *Uncle Tom's Children* (1938). Almost without exception, critics hailed Wright's often-brutal stories about life in the segregated South as the work of a major new literary talent. In 1939, he married Dhima Rose Meadman, a white ballet dancer, and was awarded a Guggenheim Fellowship. Inspired in part by his research into the sensational case

Wright was one of the people who made me conscious of the need to struggle.

—Amiri Baraka

of an eighteen-year-old black youth who was convicted in Chicago of murdering a white woman, Wright soon completed a new novel, *Native Son* (1940). The raw story, a surprise Book-of-the-Month Club selection, was acclaimed by the *New Yorker* "as the most powerful American novel to appear since *The Grapes of Wrath*." While Wright was enjoying the success of *Native Son,* his marriage failed and he married Ellen Poplowitz, a white Communist organizer, in 1941. Wright, however, withdrew from the Communist Party. He later sharply criticized the party in "I Tried to Be a Communist," an essay published in the *Atlantic Monthly* in 1944. The essay was originally part of his autobiography, then called *American Hunger,* which ended with an account of his bitter experiences in Chicago. He omitted the Chicago section at the insistence of the Book-of-the-Month Club, and the first part of the book was subsequently published as *Black Boy.* W. E. B. Du Bois objected that Wright's "harsh and forbidding story" was a grotesquely distorted portrait of black family life in the South. But most reviewers praised *Black Boy,* which was a main selection of the Book-of-the-Month Club and a runaway bestseller in 1945.

Despite his fame and commercial success, Wright remained deeply angered by the intractable racism and segregation in the United States. Following a trip to France, where he was treated as a celebrity, Wright moved with his wife and their young daughter to Paris in 1947. For the rest of his life, he lived as an expatriate in France and traveled widely in Europe, Asia, and Africa. Nonetheless, he continued to write about life and racial relations in the United States, the setting of his ambitious philosophical novel about an alienated black intellectual, *The Outsider* (1953). The novel received mixed reviews, and Wright fared even less well with a sensational novel about a white man who marries and then brutally murders a prostitute, *Savage Holiday* (1954). His next books were *Black Power* (1954), a critical assessment of conditions in postcolonial Africa, and *The Color Curtain* (1956), an account of his attendance at the Bandung Conference in Indonesia, a meeting of twenty-nine nations from Africa and Asia. Because of his earlier membership in the Communist Party, his involvement in global politics, and his ongoing criticism of the United States, Wright was kept under surveillance by the Central Intelligence Agency. His international reputation continued to grow, however, and he gave a series of lectures on race that he published in 1957 as *White Man, Listen!* The following year, Wright published *The Long Dream,* the first in a projected trilogy of novels about a black community in Mississippi. He contracted dysentery during his travels and died of a heart attack in Paris on November 28, 1960.

bedfordstmartins.com/ americanlit for research links on Wright

Wright's "Almos' a Man." In 1937, shortly before he moved from Chicago to New York City, Wright completed a draft of *Tarbaby's Dawn,* a novel about a restless and rebellious black youth growing up in the rural South. Although numerous publishers praised the power and realism of the graphic novel, all of them rejected the book, which, as one editor put it,

Illustration for "Almos' a Man"

This lithograph by Thomas Hart Benton, who was famous for his paintings of rural America, appeared at the opening of Wright's story in *Harper's Bazaar.*

"would have to surmount almost impossible commercial obstacles." In short, the publishers were convinced that the novel would not sell. Wright also failed to publish a story drawn from the final chapters of the novel, "Almos' a Man." But the enthusiastic reception of his collection of stories *Uncle Tom's Children* (1938) created a strong demand for his short fiction. He consequently revised "Almos' a Man." which appeared in *Harper's Bazaar,* a popular fashion magazine that was renowned for publishing groundbreaking fiction. The magazine was also noted for its illustrations, ranging from the modernist photographs of Man Ray to the work of the famous American regionalist Thomas Hart Benton, who provided the illustrations for "Almos' a Man." In a publication note, the influential fiction editor of *Harper's Bazaar,* George Davis, described Wright as "one of our finest short story writers" and took the opportunity to promote his forthcoming novel, *Native Son* (1940). Twenty years later, during the last year of his life, Wright revised "Almos' a Man" as "The Man Who Was Almost a Man," the opening story in his posthumously published collection, *Eight Men* (1961). The text of the story is taken from its first printing in *Harper's Bazaar,* January 1940.

ALMOS' A MAN

Dave struck out across the fields, looking homeward through paling light. Whuts the usa talkin wid em niggers in the field? Anyhow, his mother was putting supper on the table. Them niggers can't understan *nothing.* One of these days he was going to get a gun and practise shooting, then they can't talk to him as though he were a little boy. He slowed, looking at the ground. Shucks, Ah ain scareda them even ef they are biggern me!

Aw, Ah know whut Ahma do. . . . Ahm going by ol Joe's sto n git that Sears Roebuck catlog n look at them guns. Mabbe Ma will lemme buy one when she gits mah pay from ol
man Hawkins. Ahma beg her t gimme some money. Ahm ol ernough to hava gun. Ahm
seventeen. Almos a man. He strode, feeling his long, loose-jointed limbs. Shucks, a man
oughta hava little gun aftah he done worked hard all day. . . .

He came in sight of Joe's store. A yellow lantern glowed on the front porch. He
mounted steps and went through the screen door, hearing it bang behind him. There
was a strong smell of coal oil and mackerel fish. He felt very confident until he saw fat
Joe walk in through the rear door, then his courage began to ooze.

"Howdy, Dave! Whutcha want?"

"How yuh, Mistah Joe? Aw, Ah don wanna buy nothing. Ah jus wanted t see ef yuhd
lemme look at tha ol catlog erwhile."

"Sure! You wanna see it here?"

"Nawsuh. Ah wans t take it home wid me. Ahll bring it back termorrow when Ah come
in from the fiels."

"You plannin on buyin something?"

"Yessuh."

"Your ma letting you have your own money now?"

"Shucks. Mistah Joe, Ahm gittin t be a man like anybody else!"

Joe laughed and wiped his greasy white face with a red bandanna.

"Whut you plannin on buyin?"

Dave looked at the floor, scratched his head, scratched his thigh, and smiled. Then he
looked up shyly.

"Ahll tell yuh, Mistah Joe, ef yuh promise yuh won't tell."

"I promise."

"Waal, Ahma buy a gun."

"A gun? Whut you want with a gun?"

"Ah wanna keep it."

"You ain't nothing but a boy. You don't need a gun."

"Aw, lemme have the catlog, Mistah Joe. Ahll bring it back."

Joe walked through the rear door. Dave was elated. He looked around at barrels of
sugar and flour. He heard Joe coming back. He craned his neck to see if he were bringing
the book. Yeah, he's got it! Gawddog, he's got it!

"Here; but be sure you bring it back. It's the only one I got."

"Sho, Mistah Joe."

"Say, if you wanna buy a gun, why don't you buy one from me. I gotta gun to sell."

"Will it shoot?"

"Sure it'll shoot."

"Whut kind is it?"

"Oh, it's kinda old. . . . A Lefthand Wheeler.[1] A pistol. A big one."

---

1. **Lefthand Wheeler:** A large revolver with an automatic mechanism for rotating the cylinder around a central barrel, invented by Artemus Wheeler in 1818.

"Is it got bullets in it?"

"It's loaded."

"Kin Ah see it?"

"Where's your money?"

"Whut yuh wan fer it?"

"I'll let you have it for two dollars."

"Just *two* dollahs? Shucks, Ah could buy tha when Ah git mah pay."

"I'll have it here when you want it."

"Awright, suh. Ah be in fer it."

He went through the door, hearing it slam again behind him. Ahma git some money from Ma n buy me a gun! Only *two* dollahs! He tucked the thick catalogue under his arm and hurried.

"Where yuh been, boy?" His mother held a steaming dish of black-eyed peas.

"Aw, Ma, Ah jus stopped down the road t talk wid th boys."

"Yuh know bettah than t keep suppah waitin."

He sat down, resting the catalogue on the edge of the table.

"Yuh git up from there and git to the well n wash yosef! Ah ain feedin no hogs in mah house!"

She grabbed his shoulder and pushed him. He stumbled out of the room, then came back to get the catalogue.

"Whut this?"

"Aw, Ma, it's jusa catlog."

"Who yuh git it from?"

"From Joe, down at the sto."

"Waal, thas good. We kin use it around the house."

"Naw, Ma." He grabbed for it. "Gimme mah catlog, Ma." She held onto it and glared at him.

"Quit hollerin at me! Whuts wrong wid yuh? Yuh crazy?"

"But Ma, please. It ain mine! It's Joe's! He tol me t bring it back t im termorrow."

She gave up the book. He stumbled down the back steps, hugging the thick book under his arm. When he had splashed water on his face and hands, he groped back to the kitchen and fumbled in a corner for the towel. He bumped into a chair; it clattered to the floor. The catalogue sprawled at his feet. When he had dried his eyes he snatched up the book and held it again under his arm. His mother stood watching him.

"Now, ef yuh gonna acka fool over that ol book, Ahll take it n burn it up."

"Naw, Ma, please."

"Waal, set down n be still!"

He sat and drew the oil lamp close. He thumbed page after page, unaware of the food his mother set on the table. His father came in. Then his small brother.

"Whutcha got there, Dave?" his father asked.

"Jusa catlog," he answered, not looking up.

"Ywah, here they is!" His eyes glowed at blue and black revolvers. He glanced up, feeling sudden guilt. His father was watching him. He eased the book under the table and rested it on his knees. After the blessing was asked, he ate. He scooped up peas and swallowed fat meat without chewing. Buttermilk helped to wash it down. He did not want to mention money before his father. He would do much better by cornering his mother when she was alone. He looked at his father uneasily out of the edge of his eye.

"Boy, how come yuh don quit foolin wid tha book n eat yo suppah?"

"Yessuh."

"How yuh n ol man Hawkins gittin erlong?"

"Suh?"

"Can't yuh hear? Why don yuh lissen? Ah ast yuh how wuz yuh n ol man Hawkins gittin erlong?"

"Oh, swell, Pa. Ah plows mo lan than anybody over there."

"Waal, yuh oughta keep yo min on whuy yuh doin."

"Yessuh."

He poured his plate full of molasses and sopped at it slowly with a chunk of corn-bread. When all but his mother had left the kitchen, he still sat and looked again at the guns in the catalogue. Lawd, ef Ah only had tha pretty one! He could almost feel the slickness of the weapon with his fingers. If he had a gun like that he would polish it and keep it shining so it would never rust. N Ahd keep it loaded, by Gawd!

"Ma?"

"Hunh?"

"Ol man Hawkins give yuh mah money yit?"

"Yeah, but ain no usa yuh thinkin bout thowin nona it erway. Ahm keepin tha money sos yuh kin have cloes t go t school this winter."

He rose and went to her side with the open catalogue in his palms. She was washing dishes, her head bent low over a pan. Shyly he raised the open book. When he spoke his voice was husky, faint.

"Ma, Gawd knows Ah wans one of these."

"One of whut?" she asked, not raising her eyes.

"One of *these*," he said again, not daring even to point. She glanced up at the page, then at him with wide eyes.

"Nigger, is yuh gone plum crazy?"

"Aw, Ma —"

"Git outta here! Don yuh talk t me bout no gun! Yuh a fool!"

"Ma, Ah kin buy one fer *two* dollahs."

"Not ef Ah knows it yuh ain!"

"But yuh promised me one —"

"Ah don care whut Ah promised! Yuh ain nothing but a boy yit!"

"Ma, ef yuh lemme buy one Ahll *never* ast yuh fer nothing no mo."

"Ah tol yuh t git outta here! Yuh ain gonna toucha penny of tha money fer no gun! Thas how come Ah has Mistah Hawkins t pay yo wages t me, cause Ah knows yuh ain got no sense."

"But Ma, we needa gun. Pa ain got no gun. We needa gun in the house. Yuh kin never tell whut might happen."

"Now don yuh try to maka fool outta me, boy! Ef we did hava gun yuh wouldn't have it!"

He laid the catalogue down and slipped his arm around her waist.

"Aw, Ma, Ah done worked hard alla summer n ain ast yuh fer nothin, is Ah, now?"

"Thas whut yuh spose t do!"

"But Ma, Ah wans a gun. Yuh kin lemme have two dollahs outta mah money. Please, Ma. I kin give it to Pa. . . . Please, Ma! Ah loves yuh, Ma."

When she spoke her voice came soft and low.

"Whut yuh wan wida gun, Dave? Yuh don need no gun. Yuhll git in trouble. N ef yo Pa jus *thought* Ah let yuh have money t buy a gun he'd hava fit."

"Ahll hide it. Ma, it ain but two dollahs."

"Lawd, chil, whuts wrong wid yuh?"

"Ain nothing wrong, Ma. Ahm almos a man now. Ah wans a gun."

"Who gonna sell yuh a gun?"

"Ol Joe at the sto."

"N it don cos but two dollahs?"

"Thas all, Ma. Just two dollahs. Please, Ma."

She was stacking the plates away; her hands moved slowly, reflectively. Dave kept an anxious silence. Finally, she turned to him.

"Ahll let yuh git the gun ef yuh promise me one thing."

"Whuts tha, Ma?"

"Yuh bring it straight back t *me*, yuh hear? Itll be fer Pa."

"Yessum! Lemme go now, Ma."

She stooped, turned slightly to one side, raised the hem of her dress, rolled down the top of her stocking, and came up with a slender wad of bills.

"Here," she said. "Lawd knows yuh don need no gun. But yer Pa does. Yuh bring it right back t *me*, yuh hear? Ahma put it up. Now ef yuh don, Ahma have yuh Pa lick yuh so hard yuh won ferget it."

"Yessum."

He took the money, ran down the steps, and across the yard.

"Dave! Yuuuuuh Daaaaave!"

He heard, but he was not going to stop now. "Naw, Lawd!"

The first movement he made the following morning was to reach under his pillow for the gun. In the gray light of dawn he held it loosely, feeling a sense of power. Could killa man wida gun like this. Kill anybody, black er white. And if he were holding his gun in his hand nobody could run over him; they would have to respect him. It was a big gun, with a long barrel and a heavy handle. He raised and lowered it in his hand, marveling at its weight.

He had not come straight home with it as his mother had asked; instead he had stayed out in the fields, holding the weapon in his hand, aiming it now and then at some imaginary foe. But he had not fired it; he had been afraid that his father might hear. Also he was not sure he knew how to fire it.

To avoid surrendering the pistol he had not come into the house until he knew that all were asleep. When his mother had tiptoed to his bedside late that night and demanded the gun, he had first played 'possum; then he had told her that the gun was hidden outdoors, that he would bring it to her in the morning. Now he lay turning it slowly in his hands. He broke it, took out the cartridges, felt them, and then put them back.

He slid out of bed, got a long strip of old flannel from a trunk, wrapped the gun in it, and tied it to his naked thigh while it was still loaded. He did not go in to breakfast. Even though it was not yet daylight, he started for Jim Hawkins' plantation. Just as the sun was rising he reached the barns where the mules and plows were kept.

"Hey! That you, Dave?"

He turned. Jim Hawkins stood eying him suspiciously.

"Whatre yuh doing here so early?"

"Ah didn't know Ah wuz gittin up so early, Mistah Hawkins. Ah wuz fixin t hitch up ol Jenny n take her t the fiels."

"Good. Since you're here so early, how about plowing that stretch down by the woods?"

"Suits me, Mistah Hawkins."

"O.K. Go to it!"

He hitched Jenny to a plow and started across the fields. Hot dog! This was just what he wanted. If he could get down by the woods, he could shoot his gun and nobody would hear. He walked behind the plow, hearing the traces creaking, feeling the gun tied tight to his thigh.

When he reached the woods, he plowed two whole rows before he decided to take out the gun. Finally, he stopped, looked in all directions, then untied the gun and held it in his hand. He turned to the mule and smiled.

"Know whut this is, Jenny? Naw, yuh wouldn't know! Yuhs jusa ol mule! Anyhow, this is a gun, n it kin shoot, by Gawd!"

He held the gun at arm's length. Whut t hell, Ahma shoot this thing! He looked at Jenny again.

"Lissen here, Jenny! When Ah pull this ol trigger Ah don wan yuh t run n acka fool now."

Jenny stood with head down, her short ears pricked straight. Dave walked off about twenty feet, held the gun far out from him, at arm's length, and turned his head. Hell, he told himself, Ah ain afraid. The gun felt loose in his fingers; he waved it wildly for a moment. Then he shut his eyes and tightened his forefinger. *Blooom!* A report him and he thought his right hand was torn from his arm. He heard Jenny whinnying and galloping over the field, and he found himself on his knees, squeezing his fingers hard between his legs. His hand was numb; he jammed it into his mouth, trying to warm it, trying to stop the pain. The gun lay at his feet. He did not quite know what had happened. He stood up and stared at the gun as though it were a live thing. He gritted his teeth and kicked the gun. Yuh almos broke mah arm! He turned to look for Jenny; she was far over the fields, tossing her head and kicking wildly.

"Hol on there, ol mule!"

When he caught up with her she stood trembling, walling her big white eyes at him. The plow was far away; the traces had broken. Then Dave stopped short, looking, not believing. Jenny was bleeding. Her left side was red and wet with blood. He went closer.

Lawd have mercy! Wondah did Ah shoot this mule? He grabbed for Jenny's mane. She flinched, snorted whirled, tossing her head.

"Hol on now! Hol on."

Then he saw the hole in Jenny's side, right between the ribs. It was round, wet, red. A crimson stream streaked down the front leg, flowing fast. Good Gawd! Ah wuznt shootin at tha mule. . . . He felt panic. He knew he had to stop that blood, or Jenny would bleed to death. He had never seen so much blood in all his life. He ran the mule for half a mile, trying to catch her. Finally she stopped, breathing hard, stumpy tail half arched. He caught her mane and led her back to where the plow and gun lay. Then he stopped and grabbed handfuls of damp black earth and tried to plug the bullet hole. Jenny shuddered, whinnied, and broke from him.

"Hol on! Hol on now!"

He tried to plug it again, but blood came anyhow. His fingers were hot and sticky. He rubbed dirt hard into his palms, trying to dry them. Then again he attempted to plug the bullet hole but Jenny shied away, kicking her heels high. He stood helpless. He had to do something. He ran at Jenny; she dodged him. He watched a red stream of blood flow down Jenny's leg and form a bright pool at her feet.

"Jenny . . . Jenny . . ." he called weakly.

His lips trembled. She's bleeding t death! He looked in the direction of home, wanting to go back, wanting to get help. But he saw the pistol lying in the damp black clay. He had a queer feeling that if he only did something, this would not be; Jenny would not be there bleeding to death.

When he went to her this time, she did not move. She stood with sleepy, dreamy eyes; and when he touched her she gave a low-pitched whinny and knelt to the ground, her front knees slopping in blood.

"Jenny . . . Jenny . . ." he whispered.

For a long time she held her neck erect; then her head sank, slowly. Her ribs swelled with a mighty heave and she went over.

Dave's stomach felt empty, very empty. He picked up the gun and held it gingerly between his thumb and forefinger. He buried it at the foot of a tree. He took a stick and tried to cover the pool of blood with dirt — but what was the use? There was Jenny lying with her mouth open and her eyes walled and glassy. He could not tell Jim Hawkins he had shot his mule. But he had to tell something. Yeah, Ahll tell em Jenny started gittin wil n fell on the joint of the plow. . . . But that would hardly happen to a mule. He walked across the field slowly, head down.

It was sunset. Two of Jim Hawkins' men were over near the edge of the woods digging a hole in which to bury Jenny. Dave was surrounded by a knot of people; all of them were looking down at the dead mule.

"I don't see how in the world it happened," said Jim Hawkins for the tenth time.

The crowd parted and Dave's mother, father, and small brother pushed into the center.

"Where Dave?" his mother called.

"There he is," said Jim Hawkins.

His mother grabbed him.

"Whut happened, Dave? Whut yuh done?"

"Nothing."

"C mon, boy, talk," his father said.

Dave took a deep breath and told the story he knew nobody believed.

"Waal," he drawled. "Ah brung ol Jenny down here sos Ah could do mah plowin. Ah plowed bout two rows, jus like yuh see." He stopped and pointed at the long rows of upturned earth. "Then something musta been wrong wid ol Jenny. She wouldn't ack right a-tall. She started snortin n kickin her heels. Ah tried to hol her, but she pulled erway, rearin n goin on. Then when the point of the plow was stickin up in the air, she swung erroun n twisted hersef back on it. . . . She stuck hersef n started t bleed. N fo Ah could do anything, she wuz dead."

"Did you ever hear of anything like that in all your life?" asked Jim Hawkins.

There were white and black standing in the crowd. They murmured. Dave's mother came close to him and looked hard into his face.

"Tell the truth, Dave," she said.

"Looks like a bullet hole ter me," said one man.

"Dave, whut yuh do wid tha gun?" his mother asked.

The crowd surged in, looking at him.

He jammed his hands into his pockets, shook his head slowly from left to right, and backed away. His eyes were wide and painful.

"Did he hava gun?" asked Jim Hawkins.

"By Gawd, Ah tol yuh tha wuz a *gun* wound," said a man, slapping his thigh.

His father caught his shoulders and shook him till his teeth rattled.

"Tell whut happened, yuh rascal! Tell whut . . ."

Dave looked at Jenny's stiff legs and began to cry.

"Whut yuh do wid tha gun?" his mother asked.

"Whut wuz he doin wida gun?" his father asked.

"Come on and tell the truth," said Hawkins. "Ain't nobody going to hurt you. . . ."

His mother crowded close to him.

"Did yuh shoot tha mule, Dave?"

Dave cried, seeing blurred white and black faces.

"Ahh ddinnt gggo tt sshoooot hher. . . . Ah ssswear ffo Gawd Ah ddint. . . . Ah wuz a-trying t sssee ef the ol gggun would sshoot —"

"Where yuh git the gun from?" his father asked.

"Ah got it from Joe, at the sto."

"Where yuh git the money?"

"Ma give it t me."

"He kept worryin me, Bob. . . . Ah had t. . . . Ah tol im t bring the gun right back t me. . . . It was fer yuh, the gun."

"But how yuh happen to shoot that mule?" asked Jim Hawkins.

"Ah wuznt shootin at the mule, Mistah Hawkins. The gun jumped when Ah pulled the trigger. . . . N fo Ah knowed anything Jenny wuz there a-bleedin."

Somebody in the crowd laughed. Jim Hawkins walked close to Dave and looked into his face.

"Well, looks like you have bought you a mule, Dave."

"Ah swear fo Gawd, Ah didn't go t kill the mule, Mistah Hawkins!"

"But you killed her!"

All the crowd was laughing now. They stood on tiptoe and poked heads over one another's shoulders.

"Well, boy, looks like yuh done bought a dead mule! Hahaha!"

"Ain tha ershame."

"Hohohohoho."

Dave stood, head down, twisting his feet in the dirt.

"Well, you needn't worry about it, Bob," said Jim Hawkins to Dave's father. "Just let the boy keep on working and pay me two dollars a month."

"Whut yuh wan fer yo mule, Mistah Hawkins?"

Jim Hawkins screwed up his eyes.

"Fifty dollars."

"Whut yuh do wid tha gun?" Dave's father demanded.

Dave said nothing.

"Yuh wan me t take a tree lim n beat yuh till yuh talk!"

"Nawsuh!"

"Whut yuh do wid it?"

"Ah thowed it erway."

"Where?"

"Ah . . . Ah thowed it in the creek."

"Waal, c mon home. N firs thing in the mawnin git to tha creek n fin tha gun."

"Yessuh."

"Whut yuh pay fer it?"

"Two dollahs."

"Take tha gun n git yo money back n carry it t Mistah Hawkins, yuh hear? N don fergit Ahma lam yo black bottom good fer this! Now march yosef on home, suh!"

Dave turned and walked slowly. He heard people laughing. Dave glared, his eyes welling with tears. Hot anger bubbled in him. Then he swallowed and stumbled on.

That night Dave did not sleep. He was glad that he had gotten out of killing the mule so easily, but he was hurt. Something hot seemed to turn over inside him each time he remembered how they had laughed. He tossed on his bed, feeling his hard pillow. *N Pa says he's gonna beat me. . . .* He remembered other beatings, and his back quivered. *Naw, naw, Ah sho don wan im t beat me tha way no mo. . . . Dam em all!* Nobody ever gave him anything. All he did was work. *They treat me lika mule. . . . N then they beat me. . . .* He gritted his teeth. *N Ma had t tell on me.*

Well, if he had to, he would take old man Hawkins that two dollars. But that meant selling the gun. And he wanted to keep that gun. Fifty dollahs fer a dead mule.

He turned over, thinking of how he had fired the gun. He had an itch to fire it again. *Ef other men kin shoota gun, by Gawd, Ah kin!* He was still listening. *Mebbe they all* sleepin now. . . . The house was still. He heard the soft breathing of his brother. Yes, now! He would go down and get that gun and see if he could fire it! He eased out of bed and slipped into overalls.

The moon was bright. He ran almost all the way to the edge of the woods. He stumbled over the ground, looking for the spot where he had buried the gun. Yeah, here it is. Like a hungry dog scratching for a bone he pawed it up. He puffed his black cheeks and blew dirt from the trigger and barrel. He broke it and found four cartridges unshot. He looked around; the fields were filled with silence and moonlight. He clutched the gun stiff and hard in his fingers. But as soon as he wanted to pull the trigger, he shut his eyes and turned his head. Naw, Ah can't shoot wid mah eyes closed n mah head turned. With effort he held his eyes open; then he squeezed. *Blooooom!* He was stiff, not breathing. The gun was still in his hands. Dammit, he'd done it! He fired again. *Blooom!* He smiled. *Blooom! Blooom! Click, click.* There! It was empty. If anybody could shoot a gun, he could. He put the gun into his hip pocket and started across the fields.

When he reached the top of a ridge he stood straight and proud in the moonlight, looking at Jim Hawkins' big white house, feeling the gun sagging in his pocket. Lawd, ef Ah had jus one mo bullet Ahd taka shot at tha house. Ahd like t scare ol man Hawkins jusa little. . . . Jussa enough t let im know Dave Sanders is a man.

To his left the road curved, running to the tracks of the Illinois Central. He jerked his head, listening. From far off came a faint *hoooof-hoooof; hoooof-hoooof; hoooof-hoof* . . . Tha's number eight. He took a swift look at Jim Hawkins' white house; he thought of pa, of ma, of his little brother, and the boys. He thought of the dead mule and heard *hoooof-hoof; hoooof-hoooof; hoooof-hoooof* . . . He stood rigid. Two dollahs a mont. Les see now. . . . Tha means itll take bout two years. Shucks! Ahll be dam!

He started down the road, toward the tracks. Yeah, here she comes! He stood beside the track and held himself stiffly. Here she comes, erroun the ben. . . . C mon, yuh slow poke! C mon! He had his hand on his gun; something quivered in his stomach. Then the train thundered past, the gray and brown box cars rumbling and clinking. He gripped the gun tightly; then he jerked his hand out of his pocket. Ah betcha Bill wouldn't do it! Ah betcha. . . . The cars slid past, steel grinding upon steel. Ahm riding yuh ternight so hep me Gawd! He was hot all over. He hesitated just a moment; then he grabbed, pulled atop of a car, and lay flat. He felt his pocket; the gun was still there. Ahead the long rails were glinting in moonlight, stretching away, away to somewhere, somewhere where he could be a man. . . .

[1940]

Eudora Welty

[1909-2001]

Eudora Alice Welty was born on April 13, 1909, in Jackson, Mississippi. She was the first of three surviving children of Christian Webb Welty, a cashier for a life insurance company, and Mary Chestina Andrews Welty, a former schoolteacher, who after their marriage had moved to Jackson from their family homes in Ohio and West Virginia. Welty's happy childhood was filled with visits to her grandparents, summers at a nearby camp, music and art lessons, and extensive reading. While in high school, she published two poems in a national magazine for children, *St. Nicholas.* Following her graduation in 1925, she spent two years at the Mississippi State College for Women and then transferred to the University of Wisconsin, where she earned a BA in English literature in 1929. Welty then enrolled in an advertising course at Columbia University. The economic depression that gripped the nation made it impossible for her to find a full-time job in New York City, and she returned home to live with her mother after her father's sudden death in 1931. Although she frequently traveled around the country and to Europe, Welty lived for the rest of her life in the comfortable house her parents had built in suburban Jackson. She wrote for a local radio station and a newspaper, and then worked for three years as a publicity agent for a federal relief program, the Works Progress Administration. Welty, whose father had taught her to love photography, traveled and took photographs throughout Mississippi. She also drew upon her impressions in her first published story, "Death of a Traveling Salesman," which appeared in *Manuscript* magazine in 1936.

From that point on, Welty's literary reputation rose steadily. Her stories about isolated and lonely individuals in rural Mississippi appeared in prominent magazines and literary journals such as the *Southern Review, Prairie Schooner, Harper's Bazaar,* and the *Atlantic Monthly.* In 1939, she began a correspondence with Katherine Anne Porter, who wrote the introduction to Welty's first book, *A Curtain of Green and Other Stories* (1941). Although one reviewer felt that the stories showed "too great a preoccupation with the abnormal and grotesque," most critics and readers were enthusiastic about the collection, and the poet Louise Bogan compared Welty to William Faulkner. Following the publication of her novella *The Robber Bridegroom* (1942), a gothic fairy tale set "many many years ago in

Eudora Welty

This photograph of Welty was taken in the 1930s, early in the career of the writer who later came to be called the "Voice of the American South."

She has simply an eye and an ear sharp, shrewd, and true as a tuning fork.
–Katherine Anne Porter

bedfordstmartins.com/
americanlit *for research
links on Welty*

old Mississippi," Welty received a note of congratulations from Faulkner, who told her: "You're doing all right." She framed the note and hung it near her writing desk. Welty won first prize in the O'Henry Awards for the best American short stories of 1942 and of 1943, the year she published her second collection, *The Wide Net and Other Stories.* Unable to secure a position as a war correspondent, as she had hoped, Welty served on the staff of the *New York Times Book Review* in 1944. During the following decade, she wrote a richly symbolic short-story sequence, *The Golden Apples* (1949), and her first two novels: *Delta Wedding* (1946), a portrait of an exuberant family uniting for a large wedding in Mississippi, and *The Ponder Heart* (1954), a dramatic monologue in Southern dialect that won the William Dean Howells Medal as the most distinguished work of American fiction between 1950 and 1955.

Welty was later widely recognized for her contributions to American culture and letters. Following the publication of her final collection of stories, *The Bride of the Innisfallen* (1955), Welty wrote little fiction for the next fifteen years, during which she devoted herself to writing essays, teaching, lecturing, and nursing her mother through a final illness. She returned to fiction in *Losing Battles,* a comic novel about a family reunion published in 1970. The next year, she published *One Time, One Place,* a collection of what Welty diffidently described as the "snapshots" she had taken while working for the Works Progress Administration during the Great Depression. Her next book was *The Optimist's Daughter* (1972), a semiautobiographical novel that won the Pulitzer Prize. Welty also received many other honors, including the Presidential Medal of Freedom, awarded to her by Jimmy Carter in 1980. In 1983, she gave a series of lectures at Harvard University, revising them as her best-selling autobiography, *One Writer's Beginnings* (1984). Observing that she was "a writer who came of a sheltered life," Welty affirmed: "A sheltered life can be a daring life as well. For all serious daring starts from within." Certainly, her daring work was admired by readers as diverse as the Southern novelist Flannery O'Connor and the computer programmer Steven Dorner, who was so taken with Welty's story "Why I Live at the P.O." that he named his widely used e-mail program *Eudora.* After a lengthy illness, Welty died at the age of ninety-two at her home in Jackson, Mississippi, on July 23, 2001.

Welty's "A Worn Path." This story was originally published in the prestigious *Atlantic Monthly,* and Welty subsequently included it in her first book, *A Curtain of Green and Other Stories.* Katherine Anne Porter, who wrote the introduction to the collection, observed that "A Worn Path" is the kind of story "where external act and the internal voiceless life of the human imagination almost meet and mingle on the mysterious threshold between dream and waking, one reality refusing to admit or confirm the existence of the other, yet both conspiring toward the same end." Set near Natchez, Mississippi, "A Worn Path" is the poignant story of an elderly African American woman's trek to obtain medication for her sick

Elderly Pedestrian in Mississippi

Welty, who was an ardent and accomplished photographer, took this snapshot in her hometown of Jackson in the mid-1930s, about the time she published her first stories about life in Mississippi.

grandson. In a 1974 article about the story, Welty noted that readers had often asked her if the grandson is actually dead. In reply, Welty explained that the "truth of the story" is "an errand of love carried out," adding: "The grandchild is the incentive. But it is the journey, the going of the errand, that is the story, and the question is not whether the grandchild is in reality alive or dead." The text is taken from *A Curtain of Green and Other Stories* (1941).

A WORN PATH

It was December — a bright frozen day in the early morning. Far out in the country there was an old Negro woman with her head tied in a red rag, coming along a path through the pinewoods. Her name was Phoenix Jackson. She was very old and small and she walked slowly in the dark pine shadows, moving a little from side to side in her steps, with the balanced heaviness and lightness of a pendulum in a grandfather clock. She carried a thin, small cane made from an umbrella, and with this she kept tapping the frozen earth in front of her. This made a grave and persistent noise in the still air, that seemed meditative like the chirping of a solitary little bird.

She wore a dark striped dress reaching down to her shoe tops, and an equally long apron of bleached sugar sacks, with a full pocket: all neat and tidy, but every time she took a step she might have fallen over her shoelaces, which dragged from her unlaced shoes. She looked straight ahead. Her eyes were blue with age. Her skin had a pattern all its own of numberless branching wrinkles and as though a whole little tree stood in the middle of her forehead, but a golden color ran underneath, and the two knobs of her cheeks were illumined by a yellow burning under the dark. Under the red rag her hair came down on her neck in the frailest of ringlets, still black, and with an odor like copper.

Now and then there was a quivering in the thicket. Old Phoenix said, "Out of my way, all you foxes, owls, beetles, jack rabbits, coons and wild animals! . . . Keep out from under these feet, little bob-whites. . . . Keep the big wild hogs out of my path. Don't let none of those come running my direction. I got a long way." Under her small black-freckled hand her cane, limber as a buggy whip, would switch at the brush as if to rouse up any hiding things.

On she went. The woods were deep and still. The sun made the pine needles almost too bright to look at, up where the wind rocked. The cones dropped as light as feathers. Down in the hollow was the mourning dove — it was not too late for him.

The path ran up a hill. "Seem like there is chains about my feet, time I get this far," she said, in the voice of argument old people keep to use with themselves. "Something always take a hold of me on this hill — pleads I should stay."

After she got to the top she turned and gave a full, severe look behind her where she had come. "Up through pines," she said at length. "Now down through oaks."

Her eyes opened their widest, and she started down gently. But before she got to the bottom of the hill a bush caught her dress.

Her fingers were busy and intent, but her skirts were full and long, so that before she could pull them free in one place they were caught in another. It was not possible to allow the dress to tear. "I in the thorny bush," she said. "Thorns, you doing your appointed work. Never want to let folks pass, no sir. Old eyes thought you was a pretty little *green* bush."

Finally, trembling all over, she stood free, and after a moment dared to stoop for her cane.

"Sun so high!" she cried, leaning back and looking, while the thick tears went over her eyes. "The time getting all gone here."

At the foot of this hill was a place where a log was laid across the creek.

"Now comes the trial," said Phoenix.

Putting her right foot out, she mounted the log and shut her eyes. Lifting her skirt, leveling her cane fiercely before her, like a festival figure in some parade, she began to march across. Then she opened her eyes and she was safe on the other side.

"I wasn't as old as I thought," she said.

But she sat down to rest. She spread her skirts on the bank around her and folded her hands over her knees. Up above her was a tree in a pearly cloud of mistletoe. She did not dare to close her eyes, and when a little boy brought her a plate with a slice of marble-cake on it she spoke to him. "That would be acceptable," she said. But when she went to take it there was just her own hand in the air.

So she left that tree, and had to go through a barbed-wire fence. There she had to creep and crawl, spreading her knees and stretching her fingers like a baby trying to climb the steps. But she talked loudly to herself: she could not let her dress be torn now, so late in the day, and she could not pay for having her arm or her leg sawed off if she got caught fast where she was.

At last she was safe through the fence and risen up out in the clearing. Big dead trees, like black men with one arm, were standing in the purple stalks of the withered cotton field. There sat a buzzard.

"Who you watching?"

In the furrow she made her way along.

"Glad this not the season for bulls," she said, looking sideways, "and the good Lord made his snakes to curl up and sleep in the winter. A pleasure I don't see no two-headed snake coming around that tree, where it come once. It took a while to get by him, back in the summer."

She passed through the old cotton and went into a field of dead corn. It whispered and shook and was taller than her head. "Through the maze now," she said, for there was no path.

Then there was something tall, black, and skinny there, moving before her.

At first she took it for a man. It could have been a man dancing in the field. But she stood still and listened, and it did not make a sound. It was as silent as a ghost.

"Ghost," she said sharply, "who be you the ghost of? For I have heard of nary death close by."

But there was no answer — only the ragged dancing in the wind.

She shut her eyes, reached out her hand, and touched a sleeve. She found a coat and inside that an emptiness, cold as ice.

"You scarecrow," she said. Her face lighted. "I ought to be shut up for good," she said with laughter. "My senses is gone. I too old. I the oldest people I ever know. Dance, old scarecrow," she said, "while I dancing with you."

She kicked her foot over the furrow, and with mouth drawn down, shook her head once or twice in a little strutting way. Some husks blew down and whirled in streamers about her skirts.

Then she went on, parting her way from side to side with the cane, through the whispering field. At last she came to the end, to a wagon track where the silver grass blew between the red ruts. The quail were walking around like pullets, seeming all dainty and unseen.

"Walk pretty," she said. "This the easy place. This the easy going."

She followed the track, swaying through the quiet bare fields, through the little strings of trees silver in their dead leaves, past cabins silver from weather, with the doors and windows boarded shut, all like old women under a spell sitting there. "I walking in their sleep," she said, nodding her head vigorously.

In a ravine she went where a spring was silently flowing through a hollow log. Old Phoenix bent and drank. "Sweet-gum makes the water sweet," she said, and drank more. "Nobody know who made this well, for it was here when I was born."

The track crossed a swampy part where the moss hung as white as lace from every limb. "Sleep on, alligators, and blow your bubbles." Then the track went into the road.

Deep, deep the road went down between the high green-colored banks. Overhead the live-oaks met, and it was as dark as a cave.

A black dog with a lolling tongue came up out of the weeds by the ditch. She was meditating, and not ready, and when he came at her she only hit him a little with her cane. Over she went in the ditch, like a little puff of milkweed.

Down there, her senses drifted away. A dream visited her, and she reached her hand up, but nothing reached down and gave her a pull. So she lay there and presently went to talking. "Old woman," she said to herself, "that black dog come up out of the weeds to stall your off, and now there he sitting on his fine tail, smiling at you."

A white man finally came along and found her — a hunter, a young man, with his dog on a chain.

"Well, Granny!" he laughed. "What are you doing there?"

"Lying on my back like a June-bug waiting to be turned over, mister," she said, reaching up her hand.

He lifted her up, gave her a swing in the air, and set her down. "Anything broken, Granny?"

"No sir, them old dead weeds is springy enough," said Phoenix, when she had got her breath. "I thank you for your trouble."

"Where do you live, Granny?" he asked, while the two dogs were growling at each other.

"Away back yonder, sir, behind the ridge. You can't even see it from here."

"On your way home?"

"No sir, I going to town."

"Why, that's too far! That's as far as I walk when I come out myself, and I get something for my trouble." He patted the stuffed bag he carried, and there hung down a little closed claw. It was one of the bob-whites, with its beak hooked bitterly to show it was dead. "Now you go on home, Granny!"

"I bound to go to town, mister," said Phoenix. "The time come around."

He gave another laugh, filling the whole landscape. "I know you old colored people! Wouldn't miss going to town to see Santa Claus!"

But something held old Phoenix very still. The deep lines in her face went into a fierce and different radiation. Without warning, she had seen with her own eyes a flashing nickel fall out of the man's pocket onto the ground.

"How old are you, Granny?" he was saying.

"There is no telling, mister," she said, "no telling."

Then she gave a little cry and clapped her hands and said, "Git on away from here, dog! Look! Look at that dog!" She laughed as if in admiration. "He ain't scared of nobody. He a big black dog." She whispered, "Sic him!"

"Watch me get rid of that cur," said the man. "Sic him, Pete! Sic him!"

Phoenix heard the dogs fighting, and heard the man running and throwing sticks. She even heard a gunshot. But she was slowly bending forward by that time, further and further forward, the lids stretched down over her eyes, as if she were doing this in her sleep. Her chin was lowered almost to her knees. The yellow palm of her hand came out from the fold of her apron. Her fingers slid down and along the ground under the piece of money with the grace and care they would have in lifting an egg from under a setting hen. Then she slowly straightened up, she stood erect, and the nickel was in her apron pocket. A bird flew by. Her lips moved. "God watching me the whole time. I come to stealing."

The man came back, and his own dog panted about them. "Well, I scared him off that time," he said, and then he laughed and lifted his gun and pointed it at Phoenix.

She stood straight and faced him.

"Doesn't the gun scare you?" he said, still pointing it.

"No, sir, I seen plenty go off closer by, in my day, and for less than what I done," she said, holding utterly still.

He smiled, and shouldered the gun. "Well, Granny," he said, "you must be a hundred years old, and scared of nothing. I'd give you a dime if I had any money with me. But you take my advice and stay home, and nothing will happen to you."

"I bound to go on my way, mister," said Phoenix. She inclined her head in the red rag. Then they went in different directions, but she could hear the gun shooting again and again over the hill.

She walked on. The shadows hung from the oak trees to the road like curtains. Then she smelled wood-smoke, and smelled the river, and she saw a steeple and the cabins on their steep steps. Dozens of little black children whirled around her. There ahead was Natchez shining. Bells were ringing. She walked on.

In the paved city it was Christmas time. There were red and green electric lights strung and crisscrossed everywhere, and all turned on in the daytime. Old Phoenix would have been lost if she had not distrusted her eyesight and depended on her feet to know where to take her.

She paused quietly on the sidewalk where people were passing by. A lady came along in the crowd, carrying an armful of red-, green- and silver-wrapped presents; she gave off perfume like the red roses in hot summer, and Phoenix stopped her.

"Please, missy, will you lace up my shoe?" She held up her foot.

"What do you want, Grandma?"

"See my shoe," said Phoenix. "Do all right for out in the country, but wouldn't look right to go in a big building."

"Stand still then, Grandma," said the lady. She put her packages down on the sidewalk beside her and laced and tied both shoes tightly.

"Can't lace 'em with a cane," said Phoenix. "Thank you, missy. I doesn't mind asking a nice lady to tie up my shoe, when I gets out on the street."

Moving slowly and from side to side, she went into the big building, and into a tower of steps, where she walked up and around and around until her feet knew to stop.

She entered a door, and there she saw nailed up on the wall the document that had been stamped with the gold seal and framed in the gold frame, which matched the dream that was hung up in her head.

"Here I be," she said. There was a fixed and ceremonial stiffness over her body.

"A charity case, I suppose," said an attendant who sat at the desk before her.

But Phoenix only looked above her head. There was sweat on her face, the wrinkles in her skin shone like a bright net.

"Speak up, Grandma," the woman said. "What's your name? We must have your history, you know. Have you been here before? What seems to be the trouble with you?"

Old Phoenix only gave a twitch to her face as if a fly were bothering her.

"Are you deaf?" cried the attendant.

But then the nurse came in.

"Oh, that's just old Aunt Phoenix," she said. "She doesn't come for herself — she has a little grandson. She makes these trips just as regular as clockwork. She lives away back off the Old Natchez Trace."[1] She bent down. "Well, Aunt Phoenix, why don't you just take a seat? We won't keep you standing after your long trip." She pointed.

The old woman sat down, bolt upright in the chair.

"Now, how is the boy?" asked the nurse.

Old Phoenix did not speak.

"I said, how is the boy?"

But Phoenix only waited and stared straight ahead, her face very solemn and withdrawn into rigidity.

"Is his throat any better?" asked the nurse. "Aunt Phoenix, don't you hear me? Is your grandson's throat any better since the last time you came for the medicine?"

With her hands on her knees, the old woman waited, silent, erect and motionless, just as if she were in armor.

"You mustn't take up our time this way, Aunt Phoenix," the nurse said. "Tell us quickly about your grandson, and get it over. He isn't dead, is he?"

At last there came a flicker and then a flame of comprehension across her face, and she spoke.

"My grandson. It was my memory had left me. There I sat and forgot why I made my long trip."

"Forgot?" The nurse frowned. "After you came so far?"

Then Phoenix was like an old woman begging a dignified forgiveness for waking up frightened in the night. "I never did go to school, I was too old at the Surrender,"[2] she said in a soft voice. "I'm an old woman without an education. It was my memory fail me. My little grandson, he is just the same, and I forgot it in the coming."

"Throat never heals, does it?" said the nurse, speaking in a loud, sure voice to old Phoenix. By now she had a card with something written on it, a little list. "Yes. Swallowed lye.[3] When was it? — January — two-three years ago —"

Phoenix spoke unasked now. "No, missy, he not dead, he just the same. Every little while his throat begin to close up again, and he not able to swallow. He not get his

---

1. **Old Natchez Trace:** This 440-mile-long path or trail, which was developed in the mid-1700s by Native Americans and later used by European explorers, extended roughly from Natchez, Mississippi, to Nashville, Tennessee.

2. **the Surrender:** On April 9, 1865, General Robert E. Lee formally surrendered the Confederate Army of Northern Virginia to General Ulysses S. Grant at Appomattox Court House, Virginia. The surrender effectively marked the end of the Civil War and the beginning of Reconstruction, which provided educational opportunities for formerly enslaved African Americans.

3. **Swallowed lye:** Lye, or potassium hydroxide, is a caustic solution commonly used in making soap. If it is swallowed, lye burns the lining of the esophagus, and the consequent buildup of scar tissue creates difficulty in swallowing.

breath. He not able to help himself. So the time come around, and I go on another trip for the soothing medicine."

"All right. The doctor said as long as you came to get it, you could have it," said the nurse. "But it's an obstinate case."

"My little grandson, he sit up there in the house all wrapped up, waiting by himself," Phoenix went on. "We is the only two left in the world. He suffer and it don't seem to put him back at all. He got a sweet look. He going to last. He wear a little patch quilt and peep out holding his mouth open like a little bird. I remembers so plain now. I not going to forget him again, no, the whole enduring time. I could tell him from all the others in creation."

"All right." The nurse was trying to hush her now. She brought her a bottle of medicine. "Charity," she said, making a check mark in a book.

Old Phoenix held the bottle close to her eyes, and then carefully put it into her pocket.

"I thank you," she said.

"It's Christmas time, Grandma," said the attendant. "Could I give you a few pennies out of my purse?"

"Five pennies is a nickel," said Phoenix stiffly.

"Here's a nickel," said the attendant.

Phoenix rose carefully and held out her hand. She received the nickel and then fished the other nickel out of her pocket and laid it beside the new one. She stared at her palm closely, with her head on one side.

Then she gave a tap with her cane on the floor.

"This is what come to me to do," she said. "I going to the store and buy my child a little windmill they sells, made out of paper. He going to find it hard to believe there such a thing in the world. I'll march myself back where he waiting, holding it straight up in this hand."

She lifted her free hand, gave a little nod, turned around, and walked out of the doctor's office. Then her slow step began on the stairs, going down.

[1941]

Carlos Bulosan

[1911-1956]

Carlos Bulosan was born in Pangasinan, a province on the island of Luzon in the Philippines, on November 2, 1911, near the end of a tumultuous period in his country's history. In 1896, the Filipinos had begun a successful revolt against Spanish rule, and they expected to be granted independence after Spain ceded the Philippines to the United States in the treaty that ended the Spanish-American War of 1898. Instead, the United States annexed the islands, and American troops brutally suppressed the Philippine Insurrection of 1899-1902, though fighting continued until 1913. The years of bloody conflict, during which an estimated two hundred thousand to one million civilians died of disease and starvation, left the country impoverished. Although little is known about his childhood, Bulosan recalled:

> I lived in Mangusmana with my father until I was seven years old. We lived in a small grass hut; but it was sufficient because we were peasants. My father could not read or write, but he knew how to work his one hectare of land, which was the sole support of our big family.

Bulosan attended American-style schools, but he left high school after three semesters in order to work to help support the family. Like thousands of other Filipinos, including two older brothers who had gone to California, Bulosan believed that he would find greater freedom and economic opportunity in the United States. He consequently booked passage in steerage aboard a steamer bound for Seattle, Washington.

Bulosan arrived on July 22, 1930, at the beginning of the Great Depression. Along with other expatriate Filipino Americans — or "Pinoy," as they called themselves — he endured terrible poverty and hardship in his new country. In fact, it could not truly be his country, since as immigrants from an American colony Filipinos could not become citizens of the United States. Bulosan was quickly disillusioned by the violence, prejudice, and exploitation the Pinoy suffered as farm or cannery workers, virtually the only jobs available to them. "Do you know what a Filipino feels in America?" he wrote a friend during the 1930s. "He is the loneliest thing on earth. . . . He is enchained damnably to his race, his heritage. He is betrayed, my friend." As a migrant farmworker, Bulosan followed the crops from Washington through Oregon to California. After he reached Los Angeles, he helped organize the United Cannery, Agricultural, Packing, and Allied Workers of America. Bulosan edited the *New Tide*, a bimonthly magazine for workers, and began to write articles for various newspapers, including the *Philippine Commonwealth Times*. In 1936, he was diagnosed with tuberculosis and spent two years in the convalescent ward of the Los Angeles County Hospital. Friends provided him with dozens of periodicals and books, and he studied the works of Karl Marx and American writers from Walt Whitman to Theodore Dreiser, Sherwood Anderson, and their younger contemporaries William Faulkner, Ernest Hemingway, and John Steinbeck. Bulosan also wrote constantly, and his verse regularly appeared in little magazines such as the *Lyric* and *Poetry*, which published several groups of his poems between 1936 and 1942.

After the entry of the United States into World War II, Bulosan became

Carlos Bulosan

This undated photograph of Bulosan at what he called his "write spot" was apparently taken in the early 1940s, when he was becoming widely known for his articles, poems, and stories about the experiences of Filipino Americans.

the major literary voice of Filipino Americans. The war was a complicated issue for the Pinoy, who were intensely aware of the injustices in the United States but who were eager to participate in the effort to drive the Japanese from the conquered Philippines. At first, Filipino Americans were classified as aliens and denied admission to the military services. Bulosan and others worked to change the law, and President Franklin Roosevelt signed a special proclamation that led to the formation of the First and Second Filipino Regiments in the United States. Too frail to serve in the military, Bulosan fought the war with his pen. He published a collection of his poetry, *Letter from America* (1942), and *The Voice of Bataan* (1943), a poetic tribute to the American and Filipino soldiers who had died defending Bataan Island in the Philippines. Bulosan also began to publish stories in mainstream magazines such as *Harper's Bazaar*, the *New Yorker*, and *Town and Country*. He became even more widely known when his article "Freedom from Want" accompanied one of Norman Rockwell's famous "Four Freedoms" paintings, which were published in successive issues of the *Saturday Evening Post* in 1943. The following year, Bulosan's collection of short stories based on Filipino folktales, *The Laughter of My Father*, became an international bestseller. He then wrote his most famous book, the autobiographical *America Is in the Heart* (1946), an often grim depiction of the collective experience of Filipino Americans and an eloquent plea for the end of racism and intolerance in the United States.

During the final decade of his life, Bulosan struggled against illness and the anti-Communist hysteria generated by the cold war. Despite his rising stature as a writer in the 1940s, Bulosan came under suspicion for his leftist views and labor activities, and he was investigated by the House of Representatives Un-American Activities Committee. Beginning in 1950, he was also under constant surveillance by the FBI, which effectively blacklisted Bulosan. Unable to find work, he spent the last years of his life in poverty and poor health, nursed by his companion, the labor activist Josephine Patrick. Looking back over his life and literary career, Bulosan in an autobiographical sketch written in 1955 observed that he had been impelled to write by his "grand dream of equality among men and freedom for all," as well as by his desire "to translate the desires and aspirations of the whole Filipino people in the Philippines and abroad in terms relevant to contemporary history." Bulosan died in Seattle of tuberculosis on September 11, 1956, leaving behind the manuscript of a posthumously published novel about the twentieth-century history of the Philippines, *The Cry and the Dedication* (1995).

Insignia of Filipino Battalions and Regiments

This military insignia was approved for all Filipino infantry units in 1942. The volcano represents the area in central California where the units trained before they were sent to the western Pacific, and the three stars represent the main islands in the Philippines — Luzon, Mindanao, and the Visayan Islands.

Bulosan's "The End of the War." Set at Camp Beale, a training camp for the First Filipino Infantry near Sacramento, California, this story was first published in the prominent cultural magazine the *New Yorker*. Throughout the war, the magazine published articles, essays, and letters from foreign correspondents, mostly firsthand accounts of battles in Europe and the Pacific. "The End of the War" appeared in the magazine shortly before the long-anticipated American invasion of the Japanese-occupied

bedfordstmartins.com/ americanlit *for research links on Bulosan*

Philippines, which began in October 1944. In Bulosan's story, a Filipino private has a dream in which the Japanese surrender as his regiment arrives on Mindanao, an island in the Philippines. As the story of the dream is repeated throughout the camp, it expands and grows. As in much of Bulosan's other fiction, "The End of the War" evokes different dreams, from the American dream of individual happiness and success, a dream denied to Filipino Americans, to their shared dream of justice and equality and the collective dream of Filipinos for a free and independent Philippines. The text is taken from the *New Yorker,* September 2, 1944.

THE END OF THE WAR

It was a fine Sunday morning and the First Filipino Infantry[1] was very quiet. Private Pascual Fidel, who was small even for a Filipino, opened his eyes and kicked the thick Army blankets off his body. His right hand reached for the shiny harmonica which was on the floor beside a pair of clean boots. He rubbed his eyes slowly and then began humming "Amor, Amor, Amor,"[2] which he had heard on the radio some nights before. He tapped the harmonica on his knee, out of habit, put it in his mouth, and fumbled for the first note. Suddenly his hands stopped and he jumped up and ran around the room from cot to cot, looking, but his comrades had already left. With nothing on but his undershorts, he rushed through the door of the barracks and out into the bright morning sunlight, screaming for his cousin, "Pitong! Sergeant Pitong Tongkol!"

Sergeant Tongkol, who was in the same company of the First Filipino Infantry, stood watching three men planting poppies in a vacant space nearby. He looked up and saw Private Fidel running toward him. Anxious to know what it was all about, Sergeant Tongkol started to meet his cousin. They met in front of the mess hall, where most of the soldiers were now assembled.

"What is it, Cousin?" Sergeant Tongkol asked.

"I had a dream," Private Fidel said, when he had caught his breath.

"A dream?" Sergeant Tongkol said.

"It is a big dream," Private Fidel said. "It is bigger than this whole camp." He stopped and looked beyond Sergeant Tongkol at the distant low brown hills of northern California. Then, turning around slowly, he scanned the vastness of the valley that surrounded Camp Beale.[3]

"What happened, Cousin?" Sergeant Tongkol asked.

---

1. **First Filipino Infantry:** Before World War II, Filipinos living in the United States were not permitted to serve in the military. After the Japanese attacks on Pearl Harbor and the Philippines in December 1941, President Roosevelt authorized the founding of a Filipino unit, which was formed at Camp San Luis Obispo, California, on March 4, 1942. After extensive training, the First Filipino Infantry Regiment finally left for the western Pacific in May 1944. Less than two months after Bulosan's story was published, on October 20, 1944, U.S. troops began the invasion of Leyte, an island in the Japanese-occupied Philippines. After landing on the island early in February 1945, the soldiers of the First Filipino Infantry engaged in fierce battles with the Japanese.
2. **"Amor, Amor, Amor":** Literally, "Love, Love, Love" (Spanish), a popular Latin melody of the period, also known as "Amor."
3. **Camp Beale:** In January 1943, the First Filipino Infantry Regiment was moved to Camp Beale, near Sacramento, California.

"We were approaching Mindanao[4] when it happened," Private Fidel said. "I remember it very well because I was playing *monte*[5] with my brother Malong and your brother Ponso when it happened. I had a poor hand, so I wanted to cheat, because it was my last dollar." He spread an imaginary hand of cards in front of his cousin, and while Sergeant Tongkol became more and more impatient, Private Fidel deliberated as if he were actually playing cards. Finally he said, "Your brother Ponso put two dollars in the pot, but my brother Malong raised the bet. I had a pair of threes, but there was another three under my left foot. I remember it well because my eyes were not on my cards; they were glued to the approaching shore of southern Mindanao. I saw Ponso's helmet move in the morning light when I reached for the hidden card. Then it happened, suddenly and without ceremony."

"What happened?" Sergeant Tongkol asked.

"I ran to the railing of the ship and looked," Private Fidel continued. "I stood there for quite some time, not believing what I saw. But it was true. They came to the shore and surrendered."

"What is true?" Sergeant Tongkol shouted. "Who surrendered? As your superior, Private Fidel, I order you to answer me!" He stepped back and stood at attention, waiting for his cousin to obey him.

"The Japs met us on the beach and surrendered," Private Fidel said. "A few minutes afterward, it was broadcast that Germany had also surrendered and the war came to a sudden end."

Sergeant Tongkol was stunned for a moment. Then, realizing the importance of the event, he grabbed his cousin and a rush of anxious words poured out of his mouth. "Are you sure, Cousin?" he asked. "Are you sure they were Japs? Did you see the large teeth of the yellow sons of the Rising Sun?[6] Did you *hear* the broadcast that the war came to an end?"

"I'm sure, Sergeant Tongkol!" Private Fidel shouted.

Sergeant Tongkol relaxed his hold. His face was filled with a sudden kindness. "Not so loud, Cousin," he said. "Here is my blouse. You might catch cold."

Private Fidel put the blouse on. It was so big that it hung like an overcoat. Filled now with the big dream, Sergeant Tongkol expanded his chest. Wild anticipation illumined his eyes and his dark face. He put his arm around Private Fidel, as though his cousin were a precious toy. "Let's tell the good news to my brother," Sergeant Tongkol said.

The two Filipino soldiers walked eagerly toward the mess hall, each with his arm around the other. It was always like that with Private Fidel and Sergeant Tongkol. They were the same age and in their native village, on the island of Luzon, they used to go together into the banana grove across the river and steal the choicest fruit. They sailed together to the United States when they were seventeen years old. They had worked together on a farm most of the time since, and they were never separated from each other except when one of them was in jail for gambling or selling something that did not

---

4. **Mindanao:** Many had expected the U.S. invasion of the Philippines to begin on Mindanao, the southern and easternmost island in the archipelago, but American strategists finally decided to launch the attack on the central island of Leyte. See note 1.

5. *monte*: Short for the popular card game Spanish Monte.

6. **Did you see . . . Rising Sun?:** In the center of the flag of Japan is a large red disc, representing the rising sun. In war propaganda and racist caricatures of the period, the Japanese were depicted as men with bright yellow skin and large, bucked teeth.

belong to him. When the war came, they had volunteered together. But it had been hard on Private Fidel when, some months after their enlistment, his cousin Pitong was promoted. Pitong had always been his inferior in civilian life, especially when they were working on the farm. Sergeant Tongkol had been just a field hand, cutting lettuce or picking tomatoes or doing some unimportant job like that, but he, Private Fidel, was a bookkeeper or timekeeper or had some other important job. He resented his cousin's promotion and he had tried many times to work against him, but every time he attempted to discredit his cousin, he himself was the one who was discredited. He had resigned himself to his fate and did not even try for a promotion, except in his dreams, where one promotion after another came to him.

Mess Sergeant Ponso Tongkol was chopping string beans into a barrel with a long butcher knife. When the two soldiers approached him, he started chopping faster. His feet danced rhythmically as he jabbed the knife up and down. It was a stunt they always enjoyed. The two soldiers stood watching him. Suddenly Sergeant Pitong grabbed his brother. "The war has ended, Ponso!" he said.

One of the dancing feet stopped in mid-air. The butcher knife stopped moving up and down. Slowly, Ponso looked up from the barrel of chopped string beans and his eyes fastened on his brother's face. "You are kidding, Brother," he said.

"But it is true, Ponso," Sergeant Pitong said.

Mess Sergeant Ponso sat down on the edge of the barrel and put the knife in his lap. "If it is true that the war has ended," he said, "why am I still preparing string beans for dinner?"

"It is in the dream that the war has ended," Private Fidel interrupted.

Sergeant Pitong pushed him away and planted himself in front of his brother. "We were approaching Mindanao when it happened," he began, glancing sideways at Private Fidel with a superior air. "I remember it vividly, because I was walking on the deck with his brother Malong."

"No, no!" Private Fidel protested. "*I* was there!"

"Let me tell it," Sergeant Pitong said. "This dream is not for a small potato like you, Private Fidel." Then he turned his back on him and faced the Mess Sergeant. "I was walking on the deck with Private Fidel's brother Malong when it happened. I was about to tell him about a champion gamecock I had when I was in Salinas, California. That rooster had the most beautiful pair of legs. I made lots of money betting on him, but it was not the money that I enjoyed but his dancing feet when he was in the ring with an adversary. Well, then, it was at this moment that it happened. The Japs came to the shore and surrendered. Then it was broadcast that the war had ended."

"Was the Son of Heaven with the soldiers?" Mess Sergeant Ponso asked.

"He was the first one to come to the shore," Sergeant Pitong said.

Private Fidel interrupted again. "He was *not* there. The Emperor was not there. I would have seen him and his white horse if they'd been there."

"He *was* there!" Sergeant Pitong said. "The Son of Heaven came to meet us with several generals. They were all smiling and willing to surrender."

"The salomabit!"[7] Mess Sergeant Ponso exclaimed. He gripped the handle of the butcher knife with both hands. "Then what did you do?"

---

7. "**The salomabit!**": "The son of a bitch!" (Filipino idiom).

"We started shouting and throwing away our guns," his brother said.

"Goddamit!" Mess Sergeant Ponso shouted, getting up from the barrel. Slowly he sat down again. "If I was only there," he said. The strong hands tightened around the knife. He was a much larger man than his brother. He got up once more and walked around a table, stabbing the air furiously with the knife.

"It was only a dream," Private Fidel said.

But Mess Sergeant Ponso did not hear him. He said, "Ten years I worked peacefully in America, minding my own business, when the salomabit come stabbing me at the back. Maybe it is not much I make, but I got the beautiful Ford from Detroit. When I come home at night from work, I ride it to town, pressing the horn and whistling. I ride and ride and I am happy. In the bank I got money — maybe not much, but it is my money. When I see the flag, I take the hat off and I say, 'Thank you very much!' I like the color of the flag and I work hard. Why the salomabit come?" He drove the knife into the edge of the table with a terrific blow. Then he looked at his brother and cousin. "If only I was there!"

Private Fidel stepped back. He was not afraid of his cousin, but he kept his eyes on the knife nevertheless. Mess Sergeant Ponso pulled the knife out and wiped it with his apron. Then he produced a bottle of wine from the rice bin and filled three glasses. "Let's celebrate," he said.

They emptied their glasses. As though he had noticed Private Fidel for the first time, Mess Sergeant Ponso pulled a pair of pants from a hook on the wall and gave it to him. "Here," he said, "put these on. And then let's tell the good news to your brother."

The three soldiers hurried from the mess hall and went to the latrine, where Private Malong Fidel was on duty. When he saw them rushing toward him, he dropped the handle of his mop.

"The war has come to an end, Malong," Mess Sergeant Ponso said.

Private Malong stepped back against the wall of the latrine. "Don't torture me," he said. "I'm too tired."

"But it's true!" Mess Sergeant Ponso shouted. "I saw the Son of Heaven himself and his wife —"

Sergeant Pitong tried to interrupt, but his brother prevented him by putting a huge hand over his mouth.

"No, no!" Private Fidel cried. "*I* was there!" The loud voice of his cousin Ponso drowned him out. Private Fidel had dreamed the big dream, but it was too big for him to hold. It was a dream that belonged to no one now, yet it was a dream for every soldier. Hearing it told by another person, Private Fidel knew that it was not his dream any more. First it had become Sergeant Pitong's dream, then Mess Sergeant Ponso had taken it over. In a few minutes, it would be Malong's dream.

In utter defeat, Private Fidel backed out into the sunlight and returned to his barracks, where he sat on his cot. He was surprised to notice that the harmonica was still in his hand. He tapped it on his knee, out of habit, and started to play "Amor, Amor, Amor." After a while, he began playing with great joy and inspiration.

[1944]

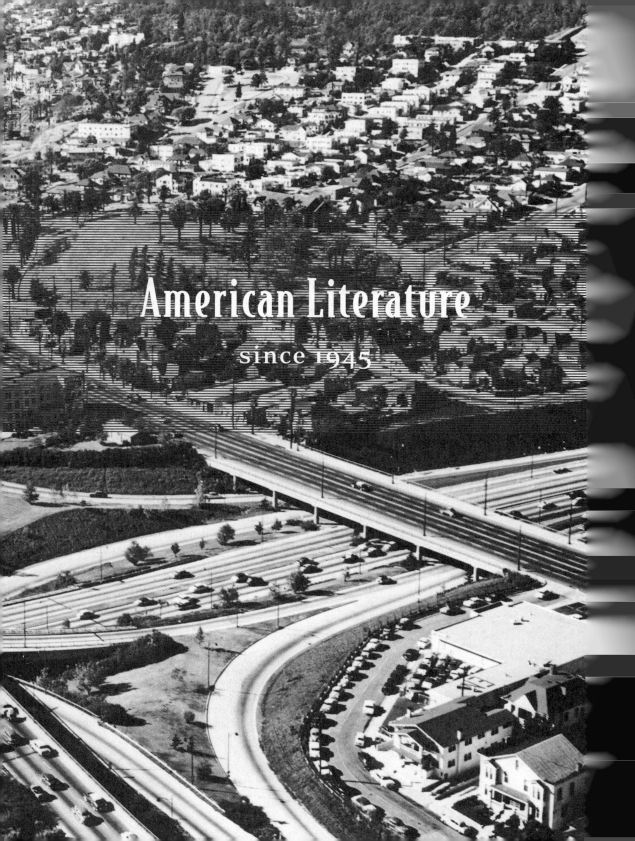

American Literature

since 1945

*O*N AUGUST 14, 1945, three months after World War II ended in Europe, an excited crowd of 750,000 people gathered in Times Square in New York City, looking intently at the Monograph News Bulletin, the electronic message board on Times Tower. At 7:03 PM, the headline they had been anticipating finally flashed across the board: "OFFICIAL – TRUMAN ANNOUNCES JAPANESE SURRENDER." The crowd erupted with cheers, and within a few hours two million people filled Times Square, wildly celebrating "V-J" (Victory in Japan) day, the conclusion of a devastating, six-year conflict that took the lives of an estimated fifty to seventy million people and ushered in the nuclear age.

In fact, the formal end of hostilities in World War II marked the beginning of a new conflict that powerfully shaped life and politics in the United States. Even as the war ended, growing tensions between the former Allies over Russia's takeover of Eastern Europe set the stage for what soon became known as the "cold war," the decades-long economic, ideological, and political struggle between the Soviet Union and the Western democracies led by the United States. As the cold war intensified, especially after the Soviet Union tested its first nuclear weapon in 1949, anti-Communist hysteria was fueled by the House Un-American Activities Committee (HUAC), which conducted sensationalistic investigations of Communist influences in education, the entertainment industry, and other institutions; and by Senator Joseph McCarthy of Wisconsin, who charged that Communists had infiltrated the U.S. Army, the State Department, and the administration of President Truman. In a famous Lincoln Day speech to the Republican Women's Club of Wheeling, West Virginia, McCarthy declared: "Today we are engaged in a final, all-out battle between communistic atheism and Christianity."

Although McCarthy's personal influence waned after the Korean War (1950-53), the first sustained military effort to "contain" Communism, what became know as "McCarthyism" continued into the 1960s, by which time the United States was involved in one of the most divisive conflicts in its history, the Vietnam War.

◄ (OVERLEAF)

Los Angeles Interchange

One of the most striking developments in the years following World War II was the rapid growth of suburbia, illustrated by this photograph taken in the mid-1950s of a cloverleaf interchange and housing developments in Los Angeles. By 1960, more people lived in suburbs than in cities, a population shift that radically altered American life and the landscape of many parts of the United States.

Celebration of Japan's Surrender

This photograph of the crowd filling Times Square was taken just after 7 PM on August 14, 1945. Moments later, the official news of the Japanese surrender was flashed on Times Tower, the building just behind the miniature reproduction of the Statue of Liberty, which had been erected to encourage people to buy war bonds during World War II.

Culture and Society in the Age of Affluence

Those global and political events coincided with dramatic changes in American society and culture following World War II. The revolution in publishing that had begun shortly before the war gained strong momentum after 1945. That year, the earliest American publisher of mass-market paperbacks, Pocket Books, brought out the first two "instant" books: *FDR: A Memorial*, issued within days of the death of the beloved President Franklin Delano Roosevelt in April; and *The Atomic Age Opens*, which appeared only a few weeks after the United States dropped the first atomic bombs on the Japanese cities of Hiroshima and Nagasaki in August. At the time, Pocket Books' major competitor was the British firm Penguin Books, which by the end of the war was exporting a million volumes a month to the United States. In 1945, the firm's American distributors, Ian Ballantine and his wife, Betty, left Penguin and established Bantam Books. Determined "to change the reading habits of America" by publishing inexpensive editions of books "that mattered," as Ian Ballantine put it, Bantam began with a reprint of Mark Twain's *Life on the Mississippi*. But the Ballantines knew that they would have to publish popular books to succeed in business. In addition to a reprint of a high-quality literary work, every month Bantam also published a book in each of three popular genres: a hard-boiled detective novel, a mystery, and a western, all selling for twenty-five cents a copy. By 1950, the highly successful company had sold 38 million books, and in 1952 the Ballantines formed a new company, Ballantine Books, which published original books in paperback format. Its list included many works of science fiction, which emerged as one of the most popular of all paperback genres, and by 1960 the dollar sales of paperbacks surpassed that of hardbacks in the United States.

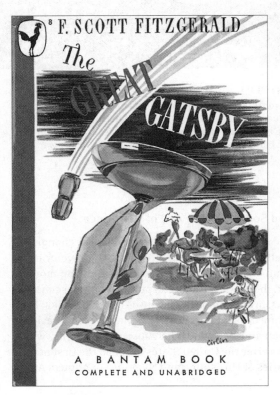

Bantam Books

One of the earliest Bantam Books was this reprint of Fitzgerald's novel, originally published twenty years earlier, in 1925. As the publishers claimed, books in the new paperback series were recognizable by "tasteful pictures on the covers, by their famous authors, and by the tough bantam rooster on the front of all the books."

OFFICIAL STUDENT PUBLICATION

The COUGAR

Volume 15   Z 739   UNIVERSITY OF HOUSTON, HOUSTON, TEXAS FRIDAY, FEBRUARY 8, 1946   Number 18

ENROLLMENT HITS ALL TIME PEAK

$1,000,000 Vet Center, $5,000,000 Building Project To Be Proposed

Vets Register

4600 Registered; 2900 Veterans

Impact of the GI Bill

The headline of this issue of the student newspaper of the University of Houston, dated February 8, 1946, indicates the impact that World War II veterans who went to college on the GI Bill had on the growth and development of higher education in the United States.

The market for books was spurred by the rapid expansion of the educational system, in which many aspiring writers found work. In 1944, Congress passed the Serviceman's Readjustment Act, known as the GI Bill, which provided veterans with low-interest loans for housing, farms, and small businesses, as well as funds for job training and education. By 1956, over 2.2 million veterans of World War II and the Korean War, the vast majority of them male, had used government funds to attend college. Few colleges and universities were prepared to accommodate the overwhelming numbers of new students, and institutions of higher education expanded dramatically. State systems built new campuses, and almost all colleges responded to the demand by constructing new facilities, classrooms, and laboratories. The swelling enrollments created the need for additional faculty, and many writers supported themselves by teaching literature. The opportunity to do so was a particular boon for poets, who could seldom hope to make an adequate living by selling their work. In contrast to an earlier generation of American poets, very few of whom taught regularly, many of the those who emerged during or immediately after World War II found full-time jobs in the academic world, including the distinguished poet-teachers Theodore Roethke, Robert Hayden, and John Berryman.

The GI Bill had an even more dramatic impact on other aspects of life and culture in the United States. In fact, many historians have described it as the legislation that "made modern America," a testament to the enormous boost the bill provided to education, business, and housing, which in turn fueled the booming consumer economy and created a thriving white middle class in the United States. Millions of veterans used government loans to purchase or build homes, most of them in the burgeoning suburbs. Of the 13 million homes constructed during the 1950s, 11 million were in the suburbs, which were made accessible by a massive program of highway construction. One of the most famous suburbs was Levittown, built on former potato fields on Long Island, twenty-eight miles from New York City. Similarly, in Southern California developers laid out suburban tracts on ranch lands northwest of and in orange groves east of Los Angeles.

Growing prosperity began to dispel some of the darker shadows still cast by the Depression and World War II. An optimistic and upbeat note was sounded in popular self-help manuals such as Dale Carnegie's best-

COMPARATIVE TIMELINE, AMERICAN LITERATURE SINCE 1945

Dates	American Literature	Historical Events	Developments in Culture, Science, and Technology
1945–1949	1945 Williams, *The Glass Menagerie* 1945 Brooks, *A Street in Bronzeville* 1946 Bishop, *North and South* 1946 Lowell, *Lord Weary's Castle*, awarded Pulitzer Prize 1946 Williams, *Portrait of a Madonna* 1947 Williams, *A Streetcar Named Desire* 1947 Bellow, *The Victim* 1948 Hayden, *The Lion and the Archer* 1948 Roethke, *The Lost Son and Other Poems* 1949 Miller, *Death of a Salesman* 1949 Brooks, *Annie Allen*, awarded Pulitzer Prize 1949 Yamamoto, "Seventeen Syllables"	1945 Harry S. Truman becomes president after death of Roosevelt 1945 United States drops atomic bombs on Hiroshima and Nagasaki; Japan surrenders, ending World War II 1947–50 Senator Joseph McCarthy's and House Un-American Activities Committee's anti-Communist investigations 1948 State of Israel established 1948 Truman elected president 1949 Soviet Union tests its first nuclear weapon, intensifying the cold war 1949 Mao Zedong and Communist revolutionaries establish People's Republic of China	1945 Bantam Books established 1945 First nuclear reactor is built 1945–55 Over 2 million U.S. veterans attend college on GI Bill 1947–51 Building of Levittown, New York 1947 Jackie Robinson is first African American player in major league baseball 1949 Philip Johnson, Glass House, New Canaan, Connecticut

seller *How to Stop Worrying and Start Living* (1948) and Norman Vincent Peale's perennially popular *A Guide to Confident Living* (1948) and *The Power of Positive Thinking* (1952). Although such books promoted the idea that happiness and success were within reach of all Americans, writers and playwrights offered a far less rosy vision of life in the United States. In a series of hit plays beginning with *The Glass Menagerie* (1945), Tennessee Williams dramatized a forlorn world of lost hopes and unfulfilled promises, while his contemporary Arthur Miller exposed the hollowness of the American dream in his Pulitzer Prize-winning play *Death of a Salesman*

Dates	American Literature	Historical Events	Developments in Culture, Science, and Technology
1950-1959	1950 Malamud, "The First Seven Years"	1950 U.S. population: 151,325,798; 10,033,385 are immigrants	1950 Jackson Pollock, *Autumn Rhythm*
		1950-53 Korean War	
	1951 Bellow, "Looking for Mr. Green"	1951 United Nations officially opens in New York City	
	1951 Rich, *A Change of World*		
	1952 Ellison, *Invisible Man*	1952 Dwight D. Eisenhower elected president	
	1952 O'Connor, *Wise Blood*		
	1953 Bellow, *The Adventures of Augie March*	1953 U.S. government begins Indian termination and relocation programs	1953 Francis Crick and James D. Watson publish description of the double helix structure of DNA
	1953 Roethke, *The Waking, Poems*, awarded Pulitzer Prize		
	1953 Miller, *The Crucible*		
	1953 Baldwin, *Go Tell It on the Mountain*		
		1954 *Brown v. Board of Education* bans segregation in public schools	1954 Construction of the first commercial nuclear power plant begins in Pennsylvania
		1954 United States begins aid program to newly independent government of South Vietnam	
	1955 Baldwin, *Notes of a Native Son*	1955-56 Bus boycotts by African Americans in Montgomery, Alabama	1955 First live television broadcast on NBC
	1955 O'Connor, *A Good Man Is Hard to Find*		1955 *Rebel Without a Cause* starring James Dean
	1956 Berryman, *Homage to Mistress Bradstreet*	1956 Eisenhower reelected president	1956 Elvis Presley, "King of Rock 'n' Roll," appears on *The Ed Sullivan Show*
	1956 Ginsberg, *Howl and Other Poems*		
	1956 Ashbery, *Some Trees*		

(1949). In the face of outpourings of patriotic pride over the United States victory in World War II, Norman Mailer gained wide acclaim and commercial success with his grimly realistic novel about American soldiers fighting in the Pacific, *The Naked and the Dead* (1948). During the war, more than 100,000 people of Japanese extraction on the West Coast, most of them citizens, were interned in remote concentration camps, called "War Relocation Centers." One of the internees was the young writer Hisaye Yamamoto, who subsequently explored the experiences of Japanese immigrants and their American-born children in a series of stories published in magazines such as the prominent left-wing political and literary journal

Dates	American Literature	Historical Events	Developments in Culture, Science, and Technology
1950–1959 (cont.)	1957 Malamud, *The Assistant*	1957 Eisenhower sends U.S. troops to enforce integration of Little Rock Central High School, Arkansas 1958 National Aeronautics and Space Administration (NASA) founded	1957 Peak of postwar baby boom (4,300,000 births) 1957 Soviet Union launches *Sputnik*, first satellite to orbit Earth 1958 John Kenneth Galbraith, *The Affluent Society*
	1959 Lowell, *Life Studies* 1959 Snyder, *Riprap*	1959 Alaska and Hawaii become the forty-ninth and fiftieth states	1959 Alfred Hitchcock's *North by Northwest* starring Cary Grant 1959 Barbie dolls are launched by Mattel
1960–1969	1960 Albee, *The Zoo Story* 1960 Plath, *The Colossus and Other Poems* 1960 Updike, *Rabbit Run* 1960 Brooks, *The Bean Eaters*	1960 U.S. population: 179,323,175; 10,347,000 are immigrants 1960 John F. Kennedy elected president 1960 The FDA approves sale of Enovid, the first birth control pill	1960 Women represent one-third of labor force 1960 87 percent of American homes have a television 1960 One-quarter of Americans live in suburbs
	1961 Olsen, *Tell Me a Riddle* 1961 Updike, "A & P" 1961 Albee, *The Sandbox*	1961 Berlin Wall erected 1961 Freedom Riders attempt to desegregate bus terminals and interstate transportation in South 1961 Ninety tribal groups prepare Declaration of Indian Purpose	1961 John F. Kennedy establishes the Peace Corps
	1962 Hayden, *A Ballad of Remembrance*	1962 Cuban missile crisis	1962 John Glenn becomes the first American to orbit Earth

the *Partisan Review*. Knowledge of the Holocaust had a powerful impact, especially on Jewish American writers such as Bernard Malamud, who began to explore his Jewish identity and heritage, and Saul Bellow, who exposed anti-Semitism in a bleak novel set in postwar New York City, *The Victim* (1947). In what was perhaps a sign of changing times, however, Bellow achieved his greatest early success with *The Adventures of Augie March* (1952), an exuberant and optimistic coming-of-age novel set in Depression-era Chicago.

As many white residents moved to the suburbs, their place in cities such as Chicago was taken by increasing numbers of immigrants and African

Dates	American Literature	Historical Events	Developments in Culture, Science, and Technology
1960–1969 (cont.)	1962 Albee, *Who's Afraid of Virginia Woolf?*	1962 César Chávez founds United Farm Workers Organizing Committee	1962 Rachel Carson publishes *Silent Spring*
		1963 March on Washington for Jobs and Freedom is largest civil rights demonstration in U.S. history	1963 Betty Friedan publishes *The Feminine Mystique*
		1963 President Kennedy sends 15,000 military advisors to South Vietnam	
		1963 Kennedy assassinated; Lyndon B. Johnson assumes presidency	
		1963 Limited nuclear test-ban treaty signed by United States and Soviet Union	
	1964 Berryman, *77 Dream Songs*	1964 Civil Rights Act	
	1964 Lowell, *For the Union Dead*	1964 Johnson elected president	
	1964 Barthelme, *Come Back, Dr. Caligari*	1964 Gulf of Tonkin Resolution authorizes U.S. military action in Vietnam	
	1964 Baraka, *Dutchman*		
	1965 Bishop, *Questions of Travel*	1965 Malcolm X assassinated	1965 The Beatles perform at Shea Stadium in New York
	1965 Plath, *Ariel*	1965 Civil rights march from Selma to Montgomery	1965 American Writers Against the War founded
		1965 Voting Rights Act	1965 Broadside Press founded
		1965 184,000 U.S. combat troops arrive in Vietnam	
		1966 National Organization for Women (NOW) founded	

Americans. Nearly one million African Americans served in the military during World War II. But segregated troops remained the official policy of the U.S. Army, and the prospects of returning African American veterans were sharply limited. Despite the provisions of the GI Bill, suburban housing developments were often reserved "for whites only," and many colleges and universities routinely denied admission to nonwhite students. Meanwhile, during the first decade of what is known as the "Second Great Migration," which began around 1940, an estimated 1.5 million African Americans moved from the South to cities in the North and the West. By the end of World War II, more African Americans lived in cities than in

Dates	American Literature	Historical Events	Developments in Culture, Science, and Technology
1960–1969 (cont.)		1967 100,000 march on Pentagon to protest Vietnam War	1967 "Summer of Love" in Haight-Ashbury district of San Francisco, center of hippie counterculture
			1967 Andy Warhol, *Marilyn*
	1968 Updike, *Couples*	1968 Martin Luther King Jr. and Robert F. Kennedy assassinated	
		1968 Riot at Democratic National Convention in Chicago	
		1968 Richard M. Nixon elected President	
		1968 American Indian Movement (AIM) founded	
	1969 Le Guin, *The Left Hand of Darkness*	1969 Stonewall riot leads to Gay and Lesbian Liberation Movement	1969 Neil Armstrong and Buzz Aldrin land on the moon
	1969 Momaday, *House Made of Dawn*, awarded Pulitzer Prize	1969 Chicano Youth Liberation Conference, Denver, Colorado	1969–74 *The Brady Bunch* airs on TV
			1969 Woodstock Music Festival in Bethel, New York
1970–1979	1970 Morrison, *The Bluest Eye*	1970 U.S. population: 203,211,926; 9,619,000 are immigrants	1970 Earth Day first observed
	1970 Harper, *Dear John, Dear Coltrane*	1970 Student protesters killed by national guard and police at Kent State and Jackson State universities	1970 Feminist Press established
		1970 Environmental Protection Agency established	

rural areas. The urban black experience was the subject of a series of notable works published during the following years, including Gwendolyn Brooks's collection of poems about life in a black ghetto in Chicago, *A Street in Bronzeville* (1945). Brooks won the Pulitzer Prize, the first awarded to an African American, for her next collection, *Annie Allen* (1949), and Ralph Ellison won the National Book Award for his novel *Invisible Man* (1952), which traced the movement of its anonymous protagonist through some of the major events of twentieth-century African American history.

Despite the prominence of those books, African Americans and other minority groups were, as Ellison suggested, largely invisible in many areas

Dates	American Literature	Historical Events	Developments in Culture, Science, and Technology
1970–1979 (cont.)	1971 DeLillo, *Americana* 1971 Rich, *The Will to Change*	1972 Nixon reelected president 1972–74 Watergate investigation 1972 Congress passes equal rights amendment; required number of states fail to ratify it by 1982 deadline 1972 Congress passes Title IX, banning gender discrimination in all aspects of education including hiring and athletics	1972 *Ms.* magazine founded 1972–83 *M.A.S.H.* airs on TV 1972 Introduction of pay TV spurs rapid expansion of cable television
	1973 O'Brien, *If I Die in a Combat Zone* 1973 Walker, *In Love and Trouble*	1973 The Paris accords bring formal end to U.S. role in Vietnam 1973 *Roe v. Wade* protects a woman's right to abortion in early stages of pregnancy 1973–74 Arab oil embargo creates energy crisis in United States 1973 Members of American Indian Movement stage protest at Wounded Knee, South Dakota	1973 Pell grants program started to help low-income students attend college
	1974 Olsen, *Yonnondio* 1974 Barthelme, "The School" 1974 Snyder, *Turtle Island*, awarded Pulitzer Prize 1974 Silko, "Yellow Woman"	1974 Nixon resigns; Gerald Ford becomes president and pardons Nixon	

of American life and culture during much of the 1950s. The most dominant cultural force during the period was television, which profoundly shaped conceptions of what constituted reality in the United States. In 1950, a decade after the beginning of commercial television, roughly 10 percent of American homes had a television, and that number swiftly rose to 87 percent by 1960. With the exception of the comedy series *Amos n' Andy* (1951–53), which CBS was forced to withdraw because of African American protests against its caricatures of black people, television was dominated by popular shows about white suburban families — that is, a successful white-collar father, his contented stay-at-home wife, and their happy chil-

Dates	American Literature	Historical Events	Developments in Culture, Science, and Technology
1970–1979 (cont.)	1975 Ashbery, *Self-Portrait in a Convex Mirror* 1976 Lorde, *Coal* 1976 Carver, *Will You Please Be Quiet, Please?* 1976 Momaday, *The Names: A Memoir* 1976 Kingston, *The Woman Warrior* 1977 Silko, *Ceremony*	1975 North Vietnamese launch final offensive and take over all of Vietnam, ending war 1976 Jimmy Carter elected president 1979 American hostages seized at U.S. embassy in Tehran, Iran 1979 Energy crisis caused by decline of foreign oil production and price hikes by OPEC	1975–85 *The Jeffersons* is longest running TV comedy starring African Americans 1976 Apple Computer Company introduces the first personal computer 1977 *Star Wars* film saga begins 1979 ESPN begins twenty-four-hour sports broadcasting 1979 Sugar Hill Gang's hip-hop song "Rapper's Delight" reaches American Top 40 1979 Moral Majority founded by Jerry Falwell
1980–1989	1980 Dove, *The Yellow House on the Corner* 1981 Carver, *What We Talk About When We Talk About Love* 1982 Walker, *The Color Purple*	1980 U.S. population: 226,545,805; 14,079,000 are immigrants 1980 Ronald Reagan elected president 1981 Sandra Day O'Connor first woman appointed to Supreme Court 1982 Unemployment approaches 11 percent 1982 United States invades Grenada and topples its Marxist government	1980 *Pac-Man* video arcade game is released in United States 1981 MTV premieres 1981 IBM markets its first personal computer 1982 Vietnam Veterans Memorial dedicated in Washington, D.C. 1982 Michael Jackson's *Thriller* recording released

dren — such as the long-running series *The Adventures of Ozzie and Harriet* (1952–66), *Father Knows Best* (1954–63), and *Leave It to Beaver* (1957–63). Such shows not only avoided controversy, they were also carefully designed to suggest that there *were* no social problems and only the mildest of domestic tribulations in the United States. Another major bastion of the tastes of the white middle class was *The Ed Sullivan Show*, a Sunday-night institution that became the longest-running variety series in television history (1948–71). Ironically, however, it helped legitimize a major assault on the sensibilities of its adult audience when Sullivan first invited Elvis Presley, the "King of Rock 'n' Roll," on the show in 1956.

Dates	American Literature	Historical Events	Developments in Culture, Science, and Technology
1980–1989 (cont.)			**1982** U.S. Centers for Disease Control begins use of term AIDS for new disease
	1983 Morrison, "Recitatif"		**1983** First handheld mobile phone becomes commercially available
	1983 Harjo, *She Had Some Horses*		**1983** *Vietnam: A Television History* airs on PBS
	1984 Rich, *The Fact of a Doorframe*	**1984** Reagan reelected president	**1984–92** *The Cosby Show* airs on TV
	1984 Baraka, *The Autobiography of LeRoi Jones/Amiri Baraka*		
	1984 Cisneros, *The House on Mango Street*		
	1985 DeLillo, *White Noise*		**1985** Nintendo Entertainment System is released in the United States
	1985 Le Guin, "She Unnames Them"		
		1986 Congress passes the Immigration Reform and Control Act, punishing employers who hire undocumented aliens	
	1987 Le Guin, *Buffalo Gals*		**1987** Aretha Franklin becomes first woman inducted into Rock and Roll Hall of Fame
	1987 Morrison, *Beloved*		
	1987 Anzaldúa, *Borderlands/La Frontera*		
	1987 Dillard, *An American Childhood*		
		1988 George Bush elected president	
		1989 Berlin Wall falls, marking collapse of Communism in Eastern Europe	**1989** Christian Coalition founded by minister Pat Robertson

The subsequent explosion of rock 'n' roll was but one of the tremors of restlessness and discontent that began to shake American life during the mid-1950s. One of the movie icons of the period was the actor James Dean, star of a cult classic about an alienated, misunderstood teenager, *Rebel Without a Cause* (1955). The year the movie appeared, Allen Ginsberg read his revolutionary poem *Howl*, often called the manifesto of the "Beat generation," in San Francisco. Through their graphic depictions of an urban underworld of crime, drugs, and homosexual acts, Ginsberg and the Beat novelists Jack Kerouac and William Burroughs vigorously challenged censorship laws and the values of Middle America, paving the way for the emer-

Dates	American Literature	Historical Events	Developments in Culture, Science, and Technology
1990–1999	1990 O'Brien, *The Things They Carried* 1990 Espada, *Rebellion Is the Circle of a Lover's Hands* 1991 Silko, *Almanac of the Dead* 1991 Cisneros, *Woman Hollering Creek* 1992 Lorde, *Undersong* 1992 Mamet, "The Rake"	1990 U.S. population: 248,765,170; 19,763,000 are immigrants 1990–91 Persian Gulf War 1991 Dissolution of Soviet Union ends cold war 1991 Americans with Disabilities Act 1992 Bill Clinton elected president	1990 60 percent of married women with children work outside the home 1992 MTV airs first widely popular reality TV program, *The Real World* 1992 Mall of America opens in Bloomington, Minnesota
	1993 Alexie, *The Lone Ranger and Tonto Fistfight in Heaven* 	1993 North American Free Trade Agreement (NAFTA) 1993 Janet Reno appointed first female attorney general	1993 Holocaust Memorial Museum dedicated in Washington, D.C. 1993 Toni Morrison becomes first African American to win Nobel Prize in Literature 1993 Rita Dove becomes first African American Poet Laureate
	1995 Alexie, *Reservation Blues* 1996 hooks, *Bone Black* 1997 DeLillo, *Underworld*	1995 Radical militia members bomb federal buildings in Oklahoma City, killing 169 1996 Clinton reelected 1997 Madeleine Albright becomes first female secretary of state	1996 10 million Americans have Internet access
	1999 Dove, *On the Bus with Rosa Parks* 	1999 U.S. troops join NATO peacekeeping force in Kosovo	1999–2007 *The Sopranos* airs on HBO

gence of the hippie counterculture of the 1960s. Middle-class values also came under attack from within, notably in Sloan Wilson's bestseller *The Man in the Grey Flannel Suit* (1955), a semiautobiographical novel about the sterile lives of businessmen in New York City. After John Updike moved to a town north of Boston in 1957, he began his long exploration of the discontents in upper-middle-class suburbia. At about the same time, a dramatist who had grown up in that world, Edward Albee, wrote a series of biting satires of consumerism and the American family, including *The American Dream* (1961), which he described as "a stand against the fiction that everything in this slipping land of ours is peachy keen." Meanwhile, the economist John

Dates	American Literature	Historical Events	Developments in Culture, Science, and Technology
2000–present	2000 Harper, *Songlines in Michaeltree* 2000 Soto, *The Effects of Knut Hamsun on a Fresno Boy*	2000 U.S. population: 281,421,906; 31,100,000 are immigrants 2000 George W. Bush elected president	2000 Metallica sues Napster for pirating music on Internet
		2001 Terrorists destroy New York's World Trade Center and attack Pentagon	2001 Apple releases iPod
		2002 U.S. invasion of Afghanistan	2002 Microsoft launches Xbox Live
	2003 Espada, *Alabanza* 2003 Alexie, *Ten Little Indians*	2003 Space shuttle *Columbia* disintegrates over Texas killing all seven astronauts onboard 2003 War in Iraq begins	
	2004 Harjo, *Native Joy for Real* 2004 Dove, *American Smooth*	2004 George W. Bush reelected president	
		2005 Hurricane Katrina hits Gulf Coast	2005 Oprah Winfrey tops *Forbes* magazine's "Celebrity 100 Power List"
	2006 Espada, *The Republic of Poetry*	2006 Saddam Hussein, former Iraq president, is executed in Baghdad	2006 Apple iTunes Store sells one-billionth song
	2007 Updike, *Terrorist* 2007 DeLillo, *Falling Man*	2007 Virginia Tech massacre	

Elvis Presley

Presley recorded his first songs in 1954 for Sun Records in Memphis, Tennessee. Since some white audiences would not listen to black performers, the independent label's owner, Sam Phillips, sought a white man who could sing in the black rhythm-and-blues style. "Elvis the Pelvis," as he was nicknamed, is shown here on the cover of his first album in 1956, by which time he had become a prominent symbol of cultural rebellion.

Kenneth Galbraith emphasized the environmental and social costs of the consumerist society, especially the dangers of the widening gap between rich and poor, in his influential book *The Affluent Society* (1958).

But the greatest challenge to postwar complacency and the status quo came from the African American civil rights movement. Following the landmark decision in the case of *Brown v. the Board of Education of Topeka* (1954), in which the Supreme Court banned segregation in public schools, African American activists began a campaign of direct action in the South. On December 1, 1955, Rosa Parks made national headlines when she was arrested, tried, and convicted of disorderly conduct for refusing to give up her seat to a white person and move to the back of a bus in Montgomery, Alabama. Led by Martin Luther King Jr., the African American community boycotted the city's bus system for more than a year, until a federal court ordered the desegregation of the buses. The successful effort was followed by other boycotts, sit-ins at lunch counters and other segregated facilities, and freedom rides designed to desegregate interstate bus terminals in the South. Television news broadcast footage of the harassment and often brutal treatment of the nonviolent protesters, and some of the most vivid and disturbing images came from efforts to desegregate schools in the South. In 1957, President Dwight D. Eisenhower was forced to call in a thousand paratroopers to keep the peace in Little Rock, Arkansas, where angry white mobs threatened the first nine black students attempting to enroll at Central High School. In 1962, two people were killed and dozens were injured or wounded in rioting that erupted on the campus of the University of Mississippi when federal marshals enforced a court order to enroll its first black student, James Meredith.

Sympathetic news coverage and the eloquence of many of its leaders

Norman Rockwell, *The Problem We All Live With*

This painting, by the popular artist best known for his cover illustrations of small-town and suburban life for the *Saturday Evening Post*, was inspired by Ruby Nell Bridges, who in 1960 became the first African American child to desegregate an elementary school in New Orleans. The poignant painting of the six-year-old girl, escorted to school by four U.S. Marshals and walking past a wall on which someone has scrawled a racial epithet, appeared on the cover of *Look* in January 1964, ten years after the Supreme Count banned segregation in public schools and six months before President Johnson signed the landmark Civil Rights Act of 1964.

helped generate growing support for the civil rights movement. In 1963, President John F. Kennedy sent a modest civil rights bill to Congress. In an effort to persuade Congress to adopt the legislation, more than 250,000 people joined the March on Washington for Jobs and Freedom on August 28, 1963. Martin Luther King Jr. delivered the televised keynote address, widely regarded as the most important speech in the history of the civil rights movement. In his famous improvised conclusion to the speech, popularly known as "I Have a Dream," King realigned the American dream, so often associated with material success during the 1950s, with the country's highest ideals of freedom, justice, and equality for all people. The novelist James Baldwin, who a few months earlier had published one of the most devastating of all accounts of race relations in the United States, his best-selling *The Fire Next Time* (1963), later recalled about the March on Washington: "That day, for a moment, it almost seemed that we stood on a height, and could see our inheritance; perhaps we could make the kingdom real, perhaps the beloved community would not forever remain the dream one dreamed in

That day, for a moment, it almost seemed that we stood on a height, and could see our inheritance; perhaps we could make the kingdom real, perhaps the beloved community would not forever remain the dream one dreamed in agony.

agony." But the agony continued. Barely three weeks later, on September 15, 1963, four young African American girls were killed and twenty-three people were injured when a bomb set by a Ku Klux Klan splinter group blew up the Sixteenth Street Baptist Church, a meeting place for civil rights leaders in Birmingham, Alabama. In November, President Kennedy was assassinated, and his successor, Lyndon Johnson, pressed for the passage of and signed the Civil Rights Act in July 1964.

Conflicts at Home and Abroad

Despite that victory, the struggle for civil rights was hardly over, and the next decade brought increased agitation for radical reform in the United States. What was called the "Freedom Summer" of 1964, a campaign to register black voters during which several civil-rights workers were murdered in Mississippi, helped spur passage of the Voting Rights Act of 1965. The focus of the civil rights movement then shifted from the South to other parts of the country, and from legislative guarantees of equality to the economic and racial oppression of black people in urban ghettos in the North and the West, where riots broke out throughout the mid-1960s, most violently after the assassination of Martin Luther King Jr. in 1968. At the same time, King's nonviolent approach was challenged by black activists such as Malcolm X, a charismatic leader of the separatist Nation of Islam. Following his assassination in 1965, militant black separatists formed what came to be called the Black Power Movement and its cultural counterpart the Black Arts Movement, which was led by the poet and playwright Amiri Baraka. Although the political influence of the movement was limited, the emphasis on black identity, pride, and unity had a significant cultural impact. Robert Hayden, whose poetry finally gained wide recognition during the 1960s, remained aloof from the Black Arts Movement, but it gained the allegiance of the prominent poet Gwendolyn Brooks. She strongly supported the development of black publishing ventures such as Dudley Randall's Broadside Press, which printed work by Brooks and dozens of emerging black writers, including Audre Lorde. Brooks also championed younger African American poets such as Michael Harper, who in turn played a significant role in subsequent efforts to recover the rich tradition of African American literature, one of the major cultural consequences of the civil rights movement.

The movement also inspired other groups, including Mexican Americans. Large numbers of Mexican Americans served in the armed forces in World War II, during which the United States and Mexico developed the *bracero*, or laborer, program to bring Mexicans into the country to work as contract laborers on farms in the Southwest. Following the war, the government deported millions of the laborers, but many others remained in the United States, and immigration from Mexico rose rapidly during the 1950s and 1960s. In 1962, César Chávez, a farmworker and labor leader, and the activist Delores Huerta founded the National Farm Workers Association, later known as the United Farm Workers Organizing Committee. In Texas, José Angel Gutierrez and others formed La Raza Unida (The United Race), a political party designed to promote the interests of Mexican Americans. The cultural pride and sense of brotherhood generated by the Chicano movement found artistic expression in a wide range of works, including the famous poem *I Am Joaquín/Yo soy Joaquín*, a chronicle of the history and struggles of Mexican Americans by political activist Rodolfo "Corky" Gonzales. At the opening of the epic poem, which was printed as a bilingual pamphlet in 1967 and often circulated at community rallies, Gonzalez proclaimed:

> I am Joaquín, lost in a world of confusion,
> caught up in the whirl of gringo society,
> confused by the ruled, scorned by attitudes,
> suppressed by manipulation, and destroyed by modern society.

Gonzales subsequently gained a large following, including many of the 1,500 Mexican American students who in 1969 gathered in Denver, Colorado, for the Chicano Youth Liberation Conference. Demanding sweeping changes in American education designed to liberate Mexican American students from "Anglo concepts," the youths called for the creation of a new Chicano nation, Aztlán, their name for an area in the Southwest taken by the United States after the Mexican-American War of 1846–48.

Salvador Roberto Torres, *Viva la Raza*

Torres, an influential artist and community leader in San Diego, created this painting in 1969. In the now-famous work, an icon of both the Chicano arts and civil rights movements, Torres transformed the emblem of the United Farm Workers, a black eagle on a red and white background, into a red phoenix soaring into the air and framed by the words "Viva la Raza," a Chicano rallying cry that the artist translates as "Long Live Humanity."

Native Americans also protested their long history of exploitation and oppression. Although they were divided by language, religion, and tribal affiliations, many Native Americans united to organize demonstrations against the federal government's decision in the early 1950s to "terminate" tribal organizations and refuse to recognize them as sovereign governments. In 1961, more than four hundred representatives of ninety tribal groups gathered in Chicago and prepared a shared statement of principles, the "Declaration of Indian Purpose," in which they affirmed their right to choose a way of life and to preserve their threatened heritage: "We believe in the inherent right of all people to retain spiritual and cultural values, and that the free exercise of these values is necessary to the normal development of any people." The Chicago meeting led to the establishment of other organizations, including the National Council of American Indians, which lobbied for the improvement of education for Native Americans, and the American Indian Movement (AIM). Founded in 1968 to promote and protect the interests of Native Americans living on reservations and in urban areas, AIM gained international attention in 1973, when members of the group occupied the village of Wounded Knee, South Dakota. AIM

The Siege at Wounded Knee

In 1973, activists in the American Indian Movement (AIM) and local residents occupied the village of Wounded Knee on the Pine Ridge Reservation in South Dakota, site of an 1890 massacre in which troops of the Seventh Cavalry killed more than two hundred Lakota Sioux. The occupation and the subsequent seventy-one-day siege of the village by heavily armed federal marshals and FBI agents attracted worldwide attention to the cause of Indian rights and sovereignty in the United States.

also established "survival schools" designed to preserve the history and culture of Native Americans. Such efforts at cultural renewal gained impetus from the work of writers such as N. Scott Momaday, who became the first Native American to win the Pulitzer Prize, for his novel *House Made of Dawn* (1969). The groundbreaking book helped inspire a remarkable flowering of writings rooted in Native American life and traditions, including stories and novels by Leslie Marmon Silko, Gerald Vizenor, and James Welch, and the poetry of Paula Gunn Allen, Joy Harjo, and Simon Ortiz.

The women's liberation movement also strongly shaped American writing and society. During World War II, women had fought the war primarily on the home front, where they held manufacturing jobs in unprecedented numbers. After the war, however, most women were forced into lower-paying jobs or urged to withdraw from the workforce to accommodate the millions of male veterans returning from overseas. As one company newspaper proclaimed in 1945: "The Kitchen — Women's Big Post-War Goal." While the GI Bill dramatically expanded the educational opportunities for veterans, the enrollment figures for women in college lagged well behind those for men during the 1950s. In 1963, the extensive discrimination that women faced in employment and education was revealed in the report of the Presidential Commission on the Status of Women. But the major spur to the emergence of the modern feminist movement was the publication of Betty Friedan's *The Feminine Mystique* (1963). For an article on women's experiences, Friedan sent a questionnaire to her classmates at the prestigious women's school Smith College, from which she had graduated in 1942. When no magazine editor would accept the article, in which she reported that most of her classmates were deeply discontented with their narrow lives, Friedan developed it into *The Feminine Mystique*. In the opening chapter, "A Problem That Has No Name," she observed:

> The problem lay buried, unspoken, for many years in the minds of American women. It was a strange stirring, a dissatisfaction that women suffered in the middle of the twentieth century in the United States. Each suburban wife struggled with it alone. As she made the beds, shopped for groceries, matched slipcover material, ate peanut butter sandwiches with her children, chauffeured Cub Scouts and Brownies, lay beside her husband at night — she was afraid to ask even of herself the silent question — "Is this all?"

The Feminine Mystique hit a nerve, becoming a bestseller that eventually sold three million copies. When Friedan died in 2006, the *New York Times* called the book "one of the most influential nonfiction books of the twentieth century." Friedan helped establish and served as the first president of the National Organization for Women, whose membership grew from 1,000 in 1967 to 15,000 in 1971. (The contributing membership has now reached 500,000.) The movement was also advanced by the establishment of new publishing outlets. In 1970, a group of women established the Feminist Press,

Women's Equality March

Betty Friedan, whose manifesto *The Feminine Mystique* laid the groundwork for the modern feminist movement, led ten thousand women in a march in New York City on August 26, 1970, the fiftieth anniversary of the passage of the Nineteenth Amendment granting women the right to vote in the United States. In the march, which was part of a nationwide "Women's Strike for Equality," demonstrators carried placards with such slogans as "Don't Iron While the March Is Hot."

designed to bring back into print significant literary works by women. In addition to expanding and enriching the literary canon, the Feminist Press was instrumental in providing texts that spurred the development of women's studies in colleges and universities across the United States. In the midst of numerous women's magazines devoted primarily to domestic concerns, fashion, and light fiction, a new magazine, *Ms.*, was founded in 1972. Edited by Gloria Steinem, the magazine featured articles on a range of women's issues, including domestic abuse and abortion, as well as the work of writers such as Alice Walker and Angela Davis. Despite the predictions of prominent male newscasters and commentators, the first issue of 300,000 copies sold out in eight days and generated 26,000 subscription orders.

In its early stages, the women's movement primarily addressed the concerns of white, middle-class women, but radical feminists pressed for a multi-issue and multiracial approach to women's liberation. Together with other radical movements of the 1960s, the women's liberation movement helped inspire the formation of the Gay Liberation Front in the summer of 1969. Following a riot in New York City in the summer of 1969, when patrons of a gay bar called the Stonewall Inn fought back against ongoing police harassment, a group of men and women in the area founded a newspaper, *Come Out!* "We reject society's attempt to impose sexual roles and definitions of our nature," the editors wrote in the first issue in September 1969. "We are stepping outside these roles and simplistic myths. We are going to be who we are. At the same time, we are creating new social forms and relations, that is, relations based upon sisterhood, cooperation, human love and uninhibited sexuality." A major force in radicalizing other women and making gay and lesbian rights a central part of the women's movement was the poet Adrienne Rich, who began to write and speak out as a lesbian-feminist poet in the early 1970s. She was also instrumental in efforts to make the women's movement more welcoming to women of color. When Rich won the National Book Award for her collection *Diving into the Wreck* (1973), she declined to accept the honor as an individual. In a statement written with the other female nominees, the African American poets Audre Lorde and Alice Walker, Rich instead accepted the award on behalf of all silenced women. Indeed, one of the most significant results of the first decade of the feminist movement was to make women heard and to gain them an increasingly public role in the United States.

Feminists and many participants in other civil rights movements were also deeply involved in protests against the Vietnam War. In what was justified as an effort to counter the spread of Communism in Asia, President Kennedy sent 15,000 military advisers to South Vietnam in 1963. But there was little opposition to the war until 1965, when President Johnson authorized the bombing of North Vietnam and deployed 184,000 combat troops, whose number grew to 540,000 by 1968. The escalation triggered the earliest of innumerable demonstrations, rallies, and teach-ins against the war, a march on Washington, D.C., organized in April 1965 by the radical student group Students for a Democratic Society. That year, the poets Robert Bly and David Ray established American Writers Against the Vietnam War. Among those who participated in activities organized by the group were Adrienne Rich and two other prominent poets, Allen Ginsberg, the icon of the drug culture and counterculture, and the patrician Robert Lowell. The most famous demonstration against the war was mounted on October 21, 1967, when thousands of protesters marched on the Pentagon in Washington, D.C. Lowell participated in the march, and Ginsberg supplied the text of an "exorcism" protesters chanted in front of the Pentagon, "No Taxation Without Representation," which began: "Who represents my body in Pentagon? Who spends my spirit's billions for war manufacture? Who levies the majority to exult unwilling in Bomb Roar?" But the most powerful testimony against the war was ultimately offered by some of those who fought in Vietnam, including writers such as Tim O'Brien. Following his tour of duty as an infantryman in Vietnam, O'Brien wrote the first of a series of critically acclaimed works in which he drew upon his experiences there, *If I Die in a Combat Zone, Box Me Up and Ship Me Home* (1973). That year, the Paris Peace Accords finally ended the longest conflict in the history of the United States.

Vietnam War Protesters

Many of the widespread demonstrations against the war took place on college campuses or were led by youthful protesters like those at the forefront of this march. They hold aloft a large peace symbol, originally the badge of the Campaign for Nuclear Disarmament in Britain and later widely adopted as a symbol by members of the counter-culture and opponents of the Vietnam War.

Into the Twenty-First Century

Although many Americans simply wanted to forget the war, the defeat in Vietnam left a lasting legacy. The bitter loss seriously undermined morale and confidence in the country's political leaders, whose reputation was further damaged by the publication of the *Pentagon Papers* (1971), a top-secret document demonstrating that high-ranking officials had consistently lied about the Vietnam War, and the Watergate crisis of 1973–74. The human costs of the war were enormous: 58,000 American troops were killed and 300,000 were wounded during the brutal conflict, which claimed the lives of an estimated 1.5 million Vietnamese. In contrast to veterans of World War II, many Vietnam veterans felt neglected or ignored, at least until the war became the subject of *Vietnam: A Television History*, a thirteen-part series that premiered on PBS in 1983, as well as numerous books and movies during the 1980s. Treatments of the war in popular culture revealed ongoing divisions over its meaning and conduct. But even after the dissolution of the Soviet Union and the end of the cold war, of which the Vietnam War was the most serious and sustained conflict, the war remained a touchstone for those opposed to American military intervention in other countries. Opponents of the first Gulf War in 1991 argued that the United States went to war simply to advance its economic and political interests, just as it had done in Vietnam. For many, the Iraq War has also evoked memories of the Vietnam War. On March 17, 2007, thousands of antiwar protesters gathered in Washington to mark the fourth anniversary of the invasion of Iraq and what they billed as "the fortieth anniversary of the historic 1967 march to the Pentagon."

The Vietnam War and the turmoil of the 1960s also had other far-reaching social, economic, and cultural consequences. The financial cost of the war, estimated at 150 billion dollars, drained resources from the ambitious social programs initiated by President Johnson, who in his first State of the Union address in 1964 declared a "War on Poverty." In large part, that effort was a response to Michael Harrington's influential book *The Other America* (1962), which exposed the grinding poverty experienced by one of every four Americans, ranging from black people living in urban ghettos to the white rural poor throughout Appalachia and the South. At the same time, the social movements of the 1960s and demonstrations against the Vietnam War generated deep resentments among many working-class white Americans, the "silent majority" to whom President Richard Nixon appealed for support in 1969. During the 1970s, however, both the poor and blue-collar workers were among those hit hardest by the end of the long economic boom that had lasted since shortly after World War II. The cost of the Vietnam War and the mounting deficit led to rapid inflation and growing unemployment, which were further increased by the oil embargo of 1973-74.

The consequent spur to the construction of nuclear power plants helped galvanize the environmental movement. In 1962, the same year Harrington published *The Other America* and only a year before the appearance of *The Feminine Mystique*, Rachel Carson published the book that is widely credited with launching the modern environmental movement, *Silent Spring*. The movement began to gain mass support after Earth Day was first celebrated on April 22, 1970. Modeled after the teach-ins held at college and university campuses about the Vietnam War and designed to make the environment a prominent part of the national agenda, the first Earth Day was celebrated by twenty million people at colleges, schools, and communities around the United States. The movement gained strength from a wide range of nature writings, including Annie Dillard's *A Pilgrim at Tinker's Creek* (1974) and Gary Snyder's collection of poetry *Turtle Island* (1974), both of which won Pulitzer Prizes. As Snyder explained, he took the title of his collection from "the old/new name for the continent, based on many creation myths of the people who have been living here for millennia," and ecological thinking was significantly enriched by Native American practices and perspectives. At a conference in 1977, for example, the Iroquois leader Oren Lyons spoke powerfully of the connection between the human and the natural world: "I must warn you that the Creator made us all equal with one another. And not only human beings, but all life is equal. The

> *I must warn you that the Creator made us all equal with one another. And not only human beings, but all life is equal. The equality of our life is what you must understand and the principles by which you must continue on behalf of the future of this world.*

Ansel Adams,
The Tetons and
the Snake River

A major focus of the modern environmental movement has been the preservation of the wilderness, a goal that has been advanced by nature writers and visual artists such as the renowned American landscape photographer Ansel Adams (1902–1984). His iconic image of Grand Teton National Park in Wyoming was reproduced on the cover of this collection of his photographs and writings, published to commemorate the 120th anniversary of the establishment of the first national park in 1872.

OUR NATIONAL PARKS

ANSEL ADAMS

equality of our life is what you must understand and the principles by which you must continue on behalf of the future of this world."

Despite significant resistance, environmentalism and other social movements have strongly shaped the social, political, and cultural landscape of the United States. Feminists suffered a major defeat when the equal rights amendment failed to gain ratification by the required number of states by 1982. The setback for the women's movement was but one sign of a broad conservative backlash and the growing influence of evangelical Christianity, signaled by the formation of political organizations such as the Moral Majority, founded in 1979, and its successor the Christian Coalition. The onset of the AIDS epidemic in the 1980s at once spurred the gay rights movement and intensified opposition to it, and the country was and remains deeply divided over other issues such as abortion and programs designed to increase opportunities for members of minority groups, including affirmative action. At the same time, immigration has continued to alter the demographics of the country during the last thirty years. The Vietnam War and the chaos it generated in neighboring Laos and Cambodia created millions of refugees, many of whom came to the United States. Immigration from other parts of Asia also increased rapidly during the 1980s, while immigrants from Mexico, Central America, and the Caribbean contributed to the growth of the Spanish-speaking Latino population, which reached thirty-one million, or 11 percent of the United States population, in 2000.

The increasing pluralism of the country has had a profound impact on American life and literature. Rita Dove became the first African American Poet Laureate of the United States in 1993, the year Toni Morrison became the first African American to win the Nobel Prize. In its citation, the Nobel Prize committee described Morrison as a novelist who "gives life to an essential aspect of American reality," and other aspects of that reality have been the focus of a wide range of writers from radically different backgrounds and traditions. Indeed, the very concept of "American reality" has been and is being continually reshaped by Asian American, Latino/a, and Native American novelists and poets, among many other writers. In "The Future of American Fiction," an introduction to a special summer issue of the prominent *New Yorker* in 1999, a gathering of stories by "20 Writers for the 21st Century," Bill Buford observed that their work "offers a satisfying picture of a highly accomplished group of writers robustly taking on stories of their own Americanness."

But literature faces formidable challenges in the twenty-first century. Cable television expanded rapidly after the introduction of pay TV in 1972. By the year 2000, there were sixty-five million cable subscribers, and that figure now exceeds ninety million. The Apple Computer Company introduced the first affordable (at least to many middle-class Americans) personal computer in 1976, spurring the development of another popular form of entertainment, electronic games. In what came to be called "the electronic age," the use of computers became a common and, for many Americans, an indispensable part of life after the development of the Internet, one of the most revolutionary technological innovations in the period since World War II. The Internet has changed the ways in which most Americans communicate, enroll in college classes, handle finances, and shop. It may also have reduced the amount of time people devote to reading. As early as 1994, in his influential book *The Gutenberg Elegies: The Fate of Reading in an Electronic Age*, Sven Birkerts argued that the ever-increasing use of technology would end reading, a crucial source of an individual's sense of identity and selfhood. A decade later, in the National Endowment for the Arts report "Reading at Risk" (2004), the authors cited television and other electronic media as the primary cause of an apparent decline of "literary reading" in the United States. The report, however, was criticized for its failure to take into account the electronic media as a venue for reading, as well as for its narrow definition of literary reading, which did not include popular nonfiction genres such as the memoir.

Although reading habits have certainly changed, as they did when paperbacks began to dominate the literary marketplace after World War II,

Mega-cable Television

The overload of imagery and information produced in the electronic age is illustrated by this composite image of a person watching five hundred cable TV stations simultaneously. The image was created by the photographer Louis Psihoyos for an article on technology that originally appeared in the magazine *National Geographic* in 1995.

reading and writing remain vital elements of American culture. As the report "Reading at Risk" also noted, the number of people in the United States who do some form of creative writing increased from eleven million in 1982 to fifteen million in 2002. The prestigious Writers' Workshop at the University of Iowa, the first graduate program in creative writing, was established in the 1930s and remained virtually the only program of its type through the 1950s. There are now three hundred similar programs, and creative writing is also a popular course of study at the undergraduate level. Oprah Winfrey's Book Club has launched new writers and spurred the formation of local book clubs and reading groups throughout the United States. Even as many small bookstores have closed, large chain bookstores and online booksellers have become highly successful, and the number of new books published each year has climbed to 100,000. Since World War II, there has been a decline in mass-market magazines that feature poetry and fiction, which is now a prominent part of only a few high-profile magazines such as *Harper's* and the *New Yorker*. But there are numerous small literary magazines, through which emerging writers may hope to gain at least a modest readership and establish a reputation. Some of those magazines also publish an online version featuring works by writers not included in the print version.

In fact, the Internet has supplemented rather than supplanted print publications. Although relatively few people can hope to publish a book or to see their work in print, the Internet has made it possible for many writers to publish their work in other ways. The complex relationship between print culture and electronic publishing was illustrated shortly before the invasion of Iraq in 2003, when Sam Hamill led an effort to "reconstitute a Poets Against the War movement like the one organized to speak out against the war in Vietnam." Hamill edited an anthology, *Poets Against the War* (2003), which included contributions by well-known writers such as Rita Dove, Martín Espada, Joy Harjo, Ursula K. Le Guin, and Adrienne Rich, one of the veterans of the earlier American Writers Against the Vietnam War. But the poets in the anthology represented only a tiny fraction of those who responded to Hamill's call, so he and other volunteers subsequently created a Web site (www.poetsagainstthewar.org) to accommodate the initial and ongoing submissions, an online collection of twenty thousand works by writers from around the world that is billed as "the largest poetry anthology ever published." Whether such arrangements represent a genuine democratization of publishing or an implicit assertion of the status of the printed book remains to be seen. Nonetheless, it is clear that literature continues to matter and to be a matter of vital interest in the United States.

Eric Drooker,
Bookopolis

Drooker created this cover for the November 6, 2006, issue of the *New Yorker*, probably the most prominent and prestigious forum for poetry and fiction during the period since World War II. The man perched atop a skyscraper in "Book-city" illustrates the persistence of the solitary act of reading and the dizzying proliferation of books, though the image may also suggest the precarious position of both books and readers in the postmodern age.
(Eric Drooker / The New Yorker, © Condé Nast Publications Inc.)

From Modernism to Postmodernism

THE PERIOD FROM THE END OF World War II in 1945 to the present is frequently called the "age of postmodernism." Although the meaning of the term *postmodernism* is complicated and often contested, it generally refers to a movement in literature and the arts that followed and departed from modernism. Modernist writers had earlier sought to develop a language and new literary forms capable of representing the reality of modern life in the early twentieth century, an effort made all the more challenging by the carnage of World War I. Following World War II, with its attendant horrors of the Holocaust and the atomic bombs dropped on Hiroshima and Nagasaki, writers once again sought ways of representing

◀ George Tooker, *Lunch*

Tooker's 1964 painting of an African American man sitting in a cafeteria in the midst of his white coworkers has been interpreted as a work supporting the civil rights movement. But the ambiguous work also seems to suggest a broader theme of American art and literature since 1945, the isolation and deadening conformity of postmodern life, suggested here by the anonymity of the withdrawn individuals eating identical sandwiches in an oppressively enclosed space.

a radically altered reality. Norman Mailer, who gained fame with his grim war novel *The Naked and the Dead* (1948), later observed: "Probably, we will never be able to determine the psychic havoc of the concentration camps and the atom bombs upon the unconscious minds of almost everyone alive in those years." American reality continued to change at a dizzying pace during the 1950s, giving rise to a new youth culture and a radical counterculture represented by the Beats, who rejected the dominant social, political, and cultural values in the United States. Received values and beliefs were further undermined by the radical social movements of the 1960s, the widespread opposition to the Vietnam War, the loss of political confidence following Watergate, the energy crisis and increasing degradation of the environment, and the technological challenges posed to earlier forms of art and communication in the postmodern age.

Although modernism and postmodernism share some characteristics, there are fundamental differences between the two broad and complex movements. In an effort to "make it new," in Ezra Pound's memorable phrase, modernist writers broke sharply with the past, rejecting traditional literary forms and modes of narration. In contrast, many postmodern writers have self-consciously appropriated, mixed, and parodied earlier styles or conventions of writing. Indeed, many of those writers have dismissed the very idea of creativity, invention, or originality, the key words of modernism. The distinction between elite and popular cultural forms, a tenet of modernism, has also been eroded in postmodern literature, which is often characterized by the blurring of generic boundaries and imagery drawn from consumer culture and the mass media. Although the fragmentation characteristic of both modern and postmodern literature reflects the breakdown of earlier systems of thought, modernist writers sought to achieve a new conceptual unity, while postmodern writers display a distrust of overarching theories and broad generalizations. Their interest is consequently in the local and provisional, rather than in the global or universal. Finally, just as postmodernism calls into question earlier notions of art and the primacy of the artist, it challenges the traditional conception of the social role of literature, its capacity either to represent reality or to bring about social change in the chaotic and fragmented world that has developed in the decades since World War II.

But the landscape of American literature during this period is far more complex, crowded, and diverse than the term *postmodernism* suggests. Many of the writers of the period have challenged the assumptions and rejected or at least radically altered the practices of literary modernism. At the same time, some of the most prominent American modernist writers — including the novelists William Faulkner, Ernest Hemingway, Richard Wright, and Eudora Welty, as well as the poets T. S. Eliot, Marianne Moore, Ezra Pound, Wallace Stevens, and William Carlos Williams — continued to write and exert considerable influence after 1945. Most of the younger

Jackson Pollock, *Autumn Rhythm (Number 30)*

Pollock's 1950 painting is one of the most famous works by a member of the "New York school" of artists, who became known as abstract expressionists. To create the ambitious work, he variously poured, flung, and dripped enamel paint onto a large canvas spread out on the floor of his studio. His emphasis on improvisation, process, stylistic innovation, and freedom of expression was characteristic of much of the new American art and literature produced during the decades following World War II.

writers who emerged immediately after the war continued to work within the broad traditions of modernism and realism, and those movements remain vital to this day. In fact, relatively few American writers of the post-war period fall into neat categories, and some of them have tangential or even contested relations to the main concerns of postmodernism. Certainly, the works included in the following section of this anthology suggest the richness, as well as the complexity and diversity, of American literature since 1945.

Drama formed a prominent part of that literature in the immediate postwar years. During the Great Depression, American dramatists had for the most part abandoned the radical experimentation of earlier modernist drama in favor of a realistic style and more socially engaged plays. That trend is still visible in the work of the two dramatists who dominated the Broadway stage during the 1940s and 1950s, Tennessee Williams and Arthur Miller. But they blended realism with a more expressive dramatic idiom. Williams explored the role of memory in his early plays, including *Portrait of a Madonna*, a forerunner of his Pulitzer Prize-winning *A Street-*

car Named Desire (1947). Seeking ways to express the inner lives and psychology of his memorable female characters, Williams employed snatches of music, stylized sets, and poetic language, all of which combine to create what has variously been described as a poetic or subjective realism. Inspired in part by the experimental effects in Williams's plays, Miller said that he was determined not to be "encompassed by conventional realism" in his Pulitzer Prize–winning *Death of a Salesman*. Although it is essentially a domestic drama with roots in the protest literature of the 1930s, the play disrupts the conventions of time and space, as characters from the past and present interact in a stage setting with transparent walls. Miller first called the play "The Inside of His Head," and much of its action takes place within the mind and memory of its tragic Everyman, Willy Loman.

The growth of Off-Broadway theater spurred experimentation in American drama. Before Edward Albee had his first major Broadway hit, *Who's Afraid of Virginia Woolf?* (1962), he gained a reputation with a series of one-act plays produced Off-Broadway, including *The Sandbox* (1960). Influenced by an avant-garde movement in European drama variously characterized as the "theater of the absurd," the "new theater," and the "anti-theater," Albee's short plays illustrated the movement away from the conventions of realistic or representational drama in the late 1950s. *The Sandbox*, in which the flat characters Mommy and Daddy engage in a meaningless dialogue while they wait for Grandma to die, was also a biting satire of the American family, the icon of American life and culture during the 1950s. In 1964, Albee conducted a playwriting workshop that included the poet and radical social critic LeRoi Jones, later Amiri Baraka, who became a key figure in the Black Arts Movement. Like Albee, Baraka challenged social stereotypes and theatrical conventions in his angry, confrontational play *Dutchman* (1964), in which he used a chance meeting between a white woman and a black man in a subway car to expose the oppression and repressed black rage at the heart of race relations in the United States.

American poets also began to engage new subjects following World War II. The early work of the major American poets who emerged in the decade after the war revealed both their technical mastery of traditional verse forms and their debts to modernism. Gwendolyn Brooks, who was influenced by her study of modernist poets and the writers of the Harlem Renaissance, explored life in the urban black ghetto in her collections *A Street in Bronzeville* (1945) and *Annie Allen* (1949). Her contemporary Robert Hayden, who did not gain wide recognition until the 1960s, adapted modernist practices to explore African American history in poems such as "Middle Passage" (1945), in which the poet's voice mingles with voices from the past in a dense and allusive account of a slave mutiny in 1839.

Romare Bearden,
Summertime

Inspired in part by the civil rights movement, Bearden began work on a celebrated series of collages, innovative works with connections to both modernist art, especially cubism, and the African American folk tradition of quilt making. Like his friend Ralph Ellison and the poets Gwendolyn Brooks and Robert Hayden, Bearden expressed the complexities of black identity and the richness of the African American experience from the rural South to the streets of Harlem, which he evoked in *Summertime* (1967).

History and a profound sense of place blended in Elizabeth Bishop's poetry, which displayed the rhythmic subtlety, formal control, and close observation characteristic of the work of her mentor Marianne Moore. History also assumed a prominent role in the poetry of Robert Lowell, who explored his ancestry and the tangled history of New England, and John Berryman, whose complex dialogue with the seventeenth-century poet Anne Bradstreet, *Homage to Mistress Bradstreet* (1956), was hailed by many critics as the most successful long poem in English since T. S. Eliot's influential *The Waste Land* (1922).

By the mid-1950s, however, American poetry had already begun to move in directions that diverged sharply from the practices of poets such as Eliot. Where he and many other modernists followed what Eliot defined as the "impersonal theory of poetry," the work of many postwar poets became increasingly autobiographical. Theodore Roethke included a number of intense poems about his early life and relationship with his father in his breakthrough volume, *The Lost Son* (1948). After the publication of *Homage to Mistress Bradstreet*, Berryman began his most ambitious poetic project, *The Dream Songs*. The tragicomic poems in the sequence were not only deeply personal, but also unconventional in form and language, an idiosyncratic blend of poetic diction, colloquial speech, and slang. Influenced in part by Berryman, and feeling that his own earlier work was too stiffly formal, Lowell began to experiment with freer forms and a more colloquial language in the autobiographical poems in his aptly named collection *Life Studies* (1959). Widely credited with giving major impetus to the "confessional" school of American poetry, the volume had a strong impact on the diction and subject matter of the late poetry of Sylvia Plath. During the year before she committed suicide in 1963, Plath imaginatively dramatized the details of her life — from her conflicted relationship with her father to her failed marriage and difficult experiences as a wife and mother — in the poems published in her posthumous collection *Ariel* (1965).

Other young American poets also began to test the boundaries of language and subject matter during the 1950s. The tendency toward more open forms and a concentrated, colloquial language was in large part a tribute to the American modernist William Carlos Williams, who was an important mentor of many younger poets, including Allen Ginsberg. Williams wrote the introduction to Ginsberg's most famous volume of poetry, the revolutionary *Howl and Other Poems* (1956), which thrust the young poet into the forefront of the Beat movement. As Ginsberg later explained, "The point of Beat is that you get beat down to a certain nakedness where you actually are able to see the world in a visionary way." For many, however, *Howl* was probably less notable for its beatific vision than for its graphic, incantatory language and its shocking depiction of the underside of American life, which caused a sensation when Ginsberg first read the poem at a group reading in San Francisco on October 7, 1955. One of the other poets who participated in that reading was Gary Snyder, who represented a very different side of the Beat movement. Inspired by his study of Zen Buddhism, Native American culture, and poetic models ranging from ancient Chinese poets to Williams and Ezra Pound, Snyder developed a meditative style through which he sought to capture the quiet rhythms of everyday life, manual labor, and the natural world.

> *The point of Beat is that you get beat down to a certain nakedness where you actually are able to see the world in a visionary way.*

In contrast to Snyder, who became a central figure in the environmental movement, the other Beats concentrated on urban life, as did John Ashbery, a member of a loosely associated group of poets called the "New York school." Whereas Snyder spent more than a decade in Japan, Ashbery spent a decade in Paris, and he was influenced by French surrealism as well as by postwar movements in American art, including abstract expressionism and pop art. Like many of the painters associated with those movements, Ashbery produced work notable for its experimentation, playfulness, and spontaneity. And, like many of his contemporary poets, he developed a colloquial style, though Ashbery for the most part avoided the most common subjects and themes of postwar poetry. He displayed little

Roy Lichtenstein, *Blam*
The poetry of John Ashbery has often been compared to the work of pop artists such as Lichtenstein, who based his large-scale 1962 painting on a panel created by Russ Heath for the comic book *All American Men of War #89.* By copying a cartoon image, Lichtenstein subverted the distinction between high art and mass culture, challenging assumptions about originality and the role of the artist. His painting may also be seen as an ironic commentary on the pervasive images of violence in the mass media, part of a broad critique of American society mounted by numerous artists and writers during the 1960s.

interest in autobiography or history or what is commonly understood as events and experiences, whether actual or imagined. Instead, the focus of his self-reflective and fragmented poems is on language and the nature of perception and representation in a mundane world of commonplace particulars.

Widely regarded as the quintessential postmodern poet and the most influential poet of the last thirty years, Ashbery has steadily challenged the reader's search for meaning or a message. But many of his contemporaries and younger poets have affirmed the social and political role of poetry. One of the most committed poets has been Adrienne Rich, who, like Ashbery, was initially influenced by modernists such as Wallace Stevens. Her experiences of trying to balance her life as a traditional wife and mother with her career as a poet pushed her work in new directions, most clearly announced in her autobiographical volume *Snapshots of a Daughter-in-Law* (1963). As she observed about the poems in that collection, "I began trying, to the best of my ability, to face the hard questions of poetry and experience." Although her new work bore the stamp of confessional poets such as Berryman, Lowell, and Plath, for Rich the personal and the political were becoming one. Further radicalized by the civil rights movement

I began trying, to the best of my ability, to face the hard questions of poetry and experience.

and the Vietnam War, Rich faced those "hard questions" even more directly and boldly in other volumes of poetry she published during the 1960s. At the beginning of the following decade, she announced her determination to make poetry a vehicle for personal and social change in the title of her collection *The Will to Change* (1971), and she explored a range of issues in her award-winning collection *Diving into the Wreck* (1973).

Political and social issues assumed a prominent place in the work of poets from different racial and ethnic backgrounds. In the early 1970s, Rich's friend Audre Lorde also began publishing poems in which she addressed subjects such as lesbianism and liberation from oppression. Lorde and other African American poets drew upon the resources of colloquial black speech, as well as the rich traditions of black music, which inspired many of the poems in Michael Harper's first collection, *Dear John, Dear Coltrane* (1970). Like Harper, Rita Dove explored African American history and culture and the painful legacies of slavery and racism in her first collection, *The Yellow House on the Corner* (1980). The Native American poet Joy Harjo brought a powerful sense of history, memory, and place to poems in which she exposed the contemporary difficulties of Native Americans. Latino and Latina writers have further extended the range of American poetry and affirmed its potential to change American society. In her influential and innovative book *Borderlands/La Frontera* (1987), the cultural critic, feminist theorist, and writer Gloria Anzaldúa blended poetry and prose, English and Spanish, to explore the racial, sexual, and social "borderlands" within the United States. The work of the bilingual poet Martín Espada, whose father was brought as a child to the United States from Puerto Rico, is deeply rooted in the history and cultural traditions of Latin America. From the beginning of his career, Espada has been committed to a poetry of witness, empathy, and advocacy embracing all oppressed people, inside and outside the United States, including the immigrant food workers who died in the attack on the World Trade Center, the subject of his poem "Alabanza: In Praise of Local 100" (2003).

During the decades since World War II, American fiction has also displayed the regional, racial, and ethnic diversity of the United States. The experience of previously marginalized groups played a vital role in the fiction of the immediate postwar period. The African American novelists Ralph Ellison and James Baldwin were encouraged by the success of their mentor Richard Wright, whose protest novel *Native Son* (1940) and autobiographical *Black Boy* (1945) had achieved both critical and commercial success. Ellison and Baldwin, however, illustrated a shift in postwar fiction away from the social realism of Wright's books and many other works published during the Great Depression and World War II. Like Wright, Ellison and Baldwin exposed the pervasive racism of American society, but they distanced themselves from the tradition of protest fiction. Both

Rafael Ferrer,
Merengue en
Boca Chica

Born in Puerto Rico, Ferrer adopted a naive style akin to the folk art still practiced in many parts of the Caribbean in this 1983 painting of a man resembling the artist, his blond wife, and a group of musicians playing merengue music on Boca Chica Beach, a resort area in the Dominican Republic. In this seemingly typical tourist scene, however, Ferrer explores a prominent theme in recent American art and literature, the complex cultural, economic, and political dynamics between the United States and Latin America.

were committed to rendering the complexity, contradictions, and range of African American life in works characterized by poetic language, rich symbolism, and complex narrative structures, including Ellison's novel *Invisible Man* (1952) and Baldwin's first novel *Go Tell It on the Mountain* (1953), as well as the autobiographical title essay of his collection *Notes of a Native Son* (1955).

Similar experiments in style and efforts to extend realism into new areas of experience were undertaken by a wide range of other fiction writers during the decade following World War II. Jewish American writers such as Bernard Malamud and Saul Bellow became significant forces in American fiction, the postwar geography of which encompassed what was formerly known as the "Jewish ghetto" on the Lower East Side of New York City, the semimythical site of many of Malamud's stories and novels, and poor neighborhoods in Bellow's adopted city, Chicago, the setting of his memorable story "Looking for Mr. Green" (1951) and his breakthrough novel, *The Adventures of Augie March* (1953). Bellow's colloquial style, his mingling of high and low culture, and his fascination with characters adrift in a world of deceptive appearances displayed his kinship with a writer from a dramatically different background, Flannery O'Connor. A Catholic who was raised in and wrote about the predominantly Protestant

South, O'Connor blended regional realism and symbolism, violence and grotesque humor, in novels and the morality tales collected in *A Good Man Is Hard to Find* (1955). Hisaye Yamamoto, the daughter of Japanese immigrants in California, drew upon her early life and experiences in a relocation center for Japanese Americans during World War II in stories such as "Seventeen Syllables" (1949). Tillie Olsen, the radical, working-class daughter of Jewish immigrants from Russia, also challenged stereotypes of life in the United States. The most famous of her autobiographical stories, "I Stand Here Ironing" (1956), is a first-person, stream-of-consciousness narrative told by a troubled mother of five who, abandoned by her husband, must work and raise her children, a situation that was deeply at odds with postwar complacency and images of middle-class suburban families during the 1950s.

Three influential writers who emerged during the 1960s and 1970s reveal some of the divergent tendencies in more recent American fiction. John Updike was widely admired for the fluid and often lyrical style of stories and novels in which he chronicled the changing patterns of life in middle-class suburbia, blending close observation with moral and social commentary. Updike was and remains a consummate storyteller, but another frequent contributor to the prestigious *New Yorker*, Donald Barthelme, challenged readerly expectations of what constituted character and plot in literary fiction. Barthelme subverted traditional narrative forms in his inventive novels and patchwork stories, which are characterized by playfulness, pastiche, and irony. His work suggested that realism was "used up," as the novelist and critic John Barth put it in his essay "The Literature of Exhaustion" (1967). In contrast, Raymond Carver demonstrated the ongoing vitality of realistic fiction in stories he published in magazines such as *Esquire* and the *New Yorker*. Refining a spare "minimalist" style reminiscent of Ernest Hemingway's modernist prose, Carver told powerful and poignant stories rooted in the everyday lives and struggles of working-class people, and he was widely credited with reinvigorating and virtually reinventing the realistic short story in the United States.

Realism and postmodern modes of narration have coexisted and often mingled in fiction and other kinds of prose narratives published since the 1970s. The growing popularity of the contemporary memoir, an autobiographical form that the writer Patricia Hampl has called "the signature genre of our age," has given new life to the realistic tradition, which is grounded on the belief that language can represent life and society. In style and structure, however, memoirs often display a kinship with postmodern narratives, as illustrated by two innovative examples of the genre: N. Scott Momaday's *The Names: A Memoir* (1976), in which he employed multiple voices and perspectives to tell the story of his complex origins; and Maxine Hong Kingston's *The Woman Warrior: Memoirs of a Girlhood*

Barbara Kruger,
***Untitled* (Your fictions become history)**

A graphic designer who turned to photography, Barbara Kruger appropriates, transforms, and comments upon familiar images, as in this fragmented and roughly reconstituted photograph of the head of a classical Greek statue, produced in 1983. Together, the composite image and Kruger's caption invite the viewer to consider the nature of representation, the power of images to create stereotypes, and the role of such fictions in the construction of history and individual identity, issues that are also central to contemporary writings ranging from memoirs to postmodern works of fiction.

among Ghosts (1976), in which she freely mixed fact and fiction, legend and fantasy, in a phantasmagoric account of her early life in a Chinese American community in California. The growing prominence of the memoir has raised fundamental questions about identity, memory, and the relationship between truth, or authenticity, and the telling of stories. Those questions are central to postmodern works such as Tim O'Brien's celebrated collection of stories about the Vietnam War, *The Things They Carried: A Work of Fiction* (1990), in which he casts himself as a character and explores the complex relations among invention, lying, and truth telling. The explosion of new technologies has also influenced the ways in which stories are told. Postmodern writers such as Don DeLillo find traditional realism inadequate to represent the changing conditions of contemporary life and the deadening effects of electronic communication, information overload, and the constant barrage of images in a world of "technoculture." At the same time, the pressure of popular culture has narrowed the former division between literary and popular genres such as fantasy and science fiction, leading to growing recognition of writers such as Ursula K. Le Guin.

The breakdown of firm cultural categories and social boundaries characteristic of postmodernism has also opened up additional space for the stories of minority writers. In her essay "Postmodern Blackness" (1990), the memoirist and cultural theorist bell hooks observed that a postmodernism that challenges "notions of universality and static overdetermined identity within mass culture and mass consciousness can open up new possibilities for the construction of the self and the assertion of agency." Inspired in part by one of her neglected "foremothers," Zora Neale Hurston, the African American novelist Alice Walker has gained considerable success with a series of stories and novels about the experiences of black women, including *The Color Purple* (1983). Toni Morrison, the first African American to win the Nobel Prize, has adapted postmodern literary practices in novels such as *Beloved* (1987), in which she told a harrowing story about slavery and its aftermath by mingling elements of fantasy, history, and magical realism. The Chicana writer Sandra Cisneros explored the "borderlands" occupied by Mexican Americans in her bestselling novel *The House on Mango Street* (1984) and her admired collection of stories *Woman Hollering Creek* (1991). Native American writers have also received critical praise for works that reveal wide variations in style and subject matter. The work of Leslie Marmon Silko is deeply rooted in traditions of Native American history, myth, and storytelling, while the younger writer Sherman Alexie probes the realities of Indians on reservations and in cities, firmly establishing the Native American presence in contemporary life and the culture of the United States.

Perhaps the only hallmark of American literature since 1945 is the range of literary imagination displayed in works of enormous diversity. That literary period may perhaps be described as postmodern only insofar as a major principle of postmodernism is the unreliability of any overarching construct or single unified narrative of history. Indeed, writers of the period have constructed competing narratives, variously affirming and collapsing the distinction between elite and popular culture, adapting traditional forms and breaking generic boundaries, giving new life to old stories and engaging subjects previously outside the boundaries of literature, and responding in complex and often divergent ways to the ever-changing social, political, and cultural fabric of the United States.

Theodore Roethke

[1908–1963]

Theodore Huebner Roethke was born on May 25, 1908, in Saginaw, Michigan, to Otto and Helen Huebner Roethke. Otto Roethke, the son of German immigrants, helped run the family business, a nursery with the most extensive greenhouses in the United States. "It was a wonderful place to grow up," Roethke recalled. "There were not only twenty-five acres in the town, mostly under glass and intensely cultivated, but farther out the last stand of virgin timber in the Saginaw Valley." But his early life was shadowed by his father's death from cancer in April 1923, shortly before Roethke turned fifteen. During high school, he spent most of his time reading, especially the work of nineteenth-century British and American prose writers, including Ralph Waldo Emerson and Henry David Thoreau. Describing his early literary aspirations, Roethke later said: "I really wanted, at fifteen and sixteen, to write the 'chiseled' prose as it was called in those days. . . . I bought my own editions of Emerson, Thoreau, and as God's my witness, subscribed to the *Dial*," the avant-garde literary magazine published in New York City. Roethke was also drawn to the poetry of Walt Whitman and the British Romantic poets William Blake and William Wordsworth. Against the wishes of his mother, who wanted him to remain close to home after his graduation from high school, Roethke enrolled in the University of Michigan in the fall of 1925. After he graduated magna cum laude in 1929, he dutifully enrolled at the university's law school. Increasingly engaged in writing poetry, he withdrew after a semester and began graduate study in English at Harvard in the fall of 1930.

Theodore Roethke

This photograph of Roethke, the last of the famed poet-teacher, was taken two weeks before his sudden death on August 1, 1963.

Roethke supported himself by teaching while he pursued a career as a poet. At Harvard, the poet Robert Hillier strongly encouraged Roethke's poetic efforts, but he did not have enough money to continue his studies and left after a year to take a teaching job at Lafayette College in Pennsylvania. During his four years there, Roethke published his first poems in a little magazine, the *Harp*, and met a number of supportive poets, including Stanley Kunitz and Louise Bogan. In the fall of 1935, Roethke took a position at Michigan State College (now University). He was soon hospitalized for his first bout of bipolar disorder, then called manic depression. After his release from the hospital in January 1936, he earned an MA at the University of Michigan and took a teaching position at the Pennsylvania State College (now University), where the burly and athletic poet also coached the tennis team. He continued to work on his poems, several of which appeared in *Poetry: A Magazine of Verse* and prominent national magazines such as the *Atlantic Monthly*, the *Nation*, and the *New Yorker*. Roethke fell in love with a librarian at the college, Kitty Stokes, who encouraged him to publish his first book of poems, *Open House* (1941). In 1943, he took a leave of absence from Penn State to accept a visiting position at Bennington, a small women's college in Vermont. As a result of an affair with a student, Roethke was asked to leave Bennington in 1945. Struggling with depression, Roethke was once again hospitalized and given electroshock therapy. Following his release and a period of writing and recovery at home in Saginaw, made possible by a Guggenheim Fellowship, he returned to Penn State in 1947.

That summer, Roethke accepted a position as a professor and poet in residence at the University of Washington in Seattle, a position he held for the rest of his life. During his first year there, Roethke published what most critics view as his breakthrough volume, *The Lost Son and Other Poems* (1948). Buoyed by the enthusiastic reviews, Roethke began to work feverishly on his next book and was awarded a second Guggenheim Fellowship in 1950. Following the publication of *Praise to the End!* (1951), the National Institute of Arts and Letters awarded him a grant in recognition of "the vigor and originality of his style, the subtlety of his versification, and his faithful devotion over many years to the art of poetry both as a producer and a teacher." On a trip to New York for a series of readings, Roethke encountered one of his former Bennington students, Beatrice O'Connell. They were married within a month, in January 1953. Following their extended honeymoon in Europe, Roethke published his acclaimed collection *The Waking, Poems* (1953), which was awarded the Pulitzer Prize. He spent the academic year 1955-56 teaching on a Fulbright Scholarship in Italy before resuming his teaching schedule at the University of Washington. Although he suffered serious depressive episodes, for which he was twice hospitalized for extended periods in Seattle, he continued to write, publishing two more collections of poetry, *The Exorcism* (1957) and *Words for the Wind* (1958). The latter volume won a host of awards, including the prestigious Bollingen Prize, and he subsequently embarked on reading tours in the United States and Europe. Roethke was working on the revisions of what proved to be his final book, *The Far Field* (1964), when he died suddenly of a heart attack while swimming on August 1, 1963.

> There is no poetry anywhere that is so valuably conscious of the human body as Roethke's; no poetry that can place the body in an environment.
> —James Dickey

Roethke's Poetry. Roethke admired and was influenced by a wide range of poets, including those he described as his "spiritual ancestors" — William Blake, William Wordsworth, and Walt Whitman — and modernist poets such as T. S. Eliot, Wallace Stevens, and William Butler Yeats. Like much of the work of Wordsworth, Whitman, and Yeats, Roethke's poetry is strongly autobiographical. In the early 1940s, he began an intense exploration of his personal past in poems such as "My Papa's Waltz," which was first published in *Harper's Bazaar* in 1942. In it, he expressed his deeply ambivalent and unresolved feelings about his dead father, Otto Roethke. "All the present has fallen," Roethke noted in his journal in 1944: "I am only what I remember." Among his most vivid memories of childhood were of playing and working in the acres of greenhouses of the family nursery, the setting of "Cuttings," "Cuttings (later)," and "Root Cellar," three of the poems from his famous sequence "The Greenhouse Poems" in *The Lost Son and Other Poems* (1948). Roethke experimented with a wide range of metrical and poetic forms, from free verse and unrhymed lyric stanzas to the complex form of the villanelle in "The Waking," the title poem of his Pulitzer-Prize winning collection, *The Waking, Poems* (1953). He employed a traditional rhyme scheme to a very different effect in his sensuous and playfully suggestive "I Knew a Woman" (1954), written after his marriage to Beatrice O'Connell and later included in *Words for the Wind* (1958). Roethke paid homage to Whitman in the irregular stanzas and lengthening lines of the final poem selected here, "The Far Field." The meditative poem, in which the poet returns in memory to childhood before returning to the present and the presence of death, was the title poem of his posthumously published collection, *The Far Field* (1964). The texts of the poems are taken from *The Collected Poems of Theodore Roethke* (1966).

bedfordstmartins.com/ americanlit for research links on Roethke

MY PAPA'S WALTZ

The whiskey on your breath
Could make a small boy dizzy;
But I hung on like death:
Such waltzing was not easy.

We romped until the pans   5
Slid from the kitchen shelf;
My mother's countenance
Could not unfrown itself.

The hand that held my wrist
Was battered on one knuckle;   10
At every step you missed
My right ear scraped a buckle.

You beat time on my head
With a palm caked hard by dirt,
Then waltzed me off to bed   15
Still clinging to your shirt.

[1942, 1966]

CUTTINGS[1]

Sticks-in-a-drowse droop over sugary loam,
Their intricate stem-fur dries;
But still the delicate slips keep coaxing up water;
The small cells bulge;

One nub of growth
Nudges a sand-crumb loose,
Pokes through a musty sheath
Its pale tendrilous horn.[2]

[1948, 1966]

1. **Cuttings**: This poem was the first in a series Roethke first called "News of the Root" and later "The Greenhouse Poems," the first section of *The Lost Son and Other Poems* (1948). A cutting is a piece cut from a plant or tree, placed in a growing medium, and encouraged to develop roots in order to propagate the parent plant.

2. **tendrilous horn**: A sprout of growth covered with threadlike appendages that stretch out to attach to another plant or object for support.

CUTTINGS[1]

(later)

This urge, wrestle, resurrection of dry sticks,
Cut stems struggling to put down feet,
What saint strained so much,
Rose on such lopped limbs to a new life?

I can hear, underground, that sucking and sobbing, 5
In my veins, in my bones I feel it, –
The small waters seeping upward,
The tight grains parting at last.
When sprouts break out,
Slippery as fish, 10
I quail, lean to beginnings, sheath-wet.

[1948, 1966]

1. **Cuttings (later)**: This poem, the second of "The Greenhouse Poems" in *The Lost Son and Other Poems*, was first published as "Cuttings" in *Harper's Bazaar* (1948).

ROOT CELLAR[1]

Nothing would sleep in that cellar, dank as a ditch,
Bulbs broke out of boxes hunting for chinks in the dark,
Shoots dangled and drooped,
Lolling obscenely from mildewed crates,
Hung down long yellow evil necks, like tropical snakes.   5
And what a congress of stinks! —
Roots ripe as old bait,
Pulpy stems, rank, silo-rich,
Leaf-mold, manure, lime, piled against slippery planks.
Nothing would give up life: 10
Even the dirt kept breathing a small breath.

                                         [1943, 1966]

---

1. **Root Cellar:** This poem, the third of "The Greenhouse Poems" in *The Lost Son and Other Poems* (1948), was first published as "Florist's Root Cellar" in *Poetry: A Magazine of Verse* (1943).

THE WAKING[1]

I wake to sleep, and take my waking slow.
I feel my fate in what I cannot fear.
I learn by going where I have to go.

We think by feeling. What is there to know?
I hear my being dance from ear to ear.   5
I wake to sleep, and take my waking slow.

Of those so close beside me, which are you?
God bless the Ground! I shall walk softly there,
And learn by going where I have to go.

Light takes the Tree; but who can tell us how?   10
The lowly worm climbs up a winding stair;
I wake to sleep, and take my waking slow.

---

1. **The Waking:** This nineteen-line poem is a villanelle, a complex form composed of five triplets (a three-line stanza rhymed *a b a*) and a concluding quatrain (a four-line stanza rhymed *a b a b*). The form employs only two rhymes, and alternating stanzas end with the same last line.

Great Nature has another thing to do
To you and me; so take the lively air,
And, lovely, learn by going where to go.   15

This shaking keeps me steady. I should know.
What falls away is always. And is near.
I wake to sleep, and take my waking slow.
I learn by going where I have to go.

[1953, 1966]

I KNEW A WOMAN[1]

I knew a woman, lovely in her bones,
When small birds sighed, she would sigh back at them;
Ah, when she moved, she moved more ways than one:
The shapes a bright container can contain!
Of her choice virtues only gods should speak,   5
Or English poets who grew up on Greek
(I'd have them sing in chorus, cheek to cheek).

How well her wishes went! She stroked my chin,
She taught me Turn, and Counter-turn, and Stand;[2]
She taught me Touch, that undulant white skin;   10
I nibbled meekly from her proffered hand;
She was the sickle; I, poor I, the rake,
Coming behind her for her pretty sake
(But what prodigious mowing we did make).

Love likes a gander, and adores a goose: 15
Her full lips pursed, the errant note to seize;
She played it quick, she played it light and loose;
My eyes, they dazzled at her flowing knees;
Her several parts could keep a pure repose,
Or one hip quiver with a mobile nose   20
(She moved in circles, and those circles moved).

Let seed be grass, and grass turn into hay:
I'm martyr to a motion not my own;
What's freedom for? To know eternity.
I swear she cast a shadow white as stone.   25

---

1. **I Knew a Woman:** This was first published as "Poem" in the *Times Literary Supplement* (1954).
2. **Turn, and Counter-turn, and Stand:** The elements of a Pindaric ode, a ceremonious poem named for the Greek poet Pindar (522?–443? BCE). The ode is divided into three stanzas: a strophe, or turn; an antistrophe, or counter-turn; and a summary line called an "epode," or stand.

But who would count eternity in days?
These old bones live to learn her wanton ways:
(I measure time by how a body sways).

[1954, 1966]

THE FAR FIELD[1]

1

I dream of journeys repeatedly:
Of flying like a bat deep into a narrowing tunnel,
Of driving alone, without luggage, out a long peninsula,
The road lined with snow-laden second growth,
A fine dry snow ticking the windshield,   5
Alternate snow and sleet, no on-coming traffic,
And no lights behind, in the blurred side-mirror,
The road changing from glazed tarface to a rubble of stone,
Ending at last in a hopeless sand-rut,
Where the car stalls,   10
Churning in a snowdrift
Until the headlights darken.

2

At the field's end, in the corner missed by the mower,
Where the turf drops off into a grass-hidden culvert,[2]
Haunt of the cat-bird, nesting-place of the field-mouse,   15
Not too far away from the ever-changing flower-dump,
Among the tin cans, tires, rusted pipes, broken machinery, —
One learned of the eternal;
And in the shrunken face of a dead rat, eaten by rain and ground-beetles
(I found it lying among the rubble of an old coal bin)   20
And the tom-cat, caught near the pheasant-run,
Its entrails strewn over the half-grown flowers,
Blasted to death by the night watchman.

I suffered for birds, for young rabbits caught in the mower,
My grief was not excessive.   25
For to come upon warblers in early May
Was to forget time and death:

---

1. **The Far Field:** This poem, first published in the *Sewanee Review* (1962), is the fifth in a group of six poems entitled "North American Sequence" in *The Far Field* (1964).
2. **culvert:** A tunnel for a stream under a road or path.

How they filled the oriole's elm, a twittering restless cloud, all one morning,
And I watched and watched till my eyes blurred from the bird shapes, —
Cape May, Blackburnian, Cerulean,[3] —   30
Moving, elusive as fish, fearless,
Hanging, bunched like young fruit, bending the end branches,
Still for a moment,
Then pitching away in half-flight,
Lighter than finches,   35
While the wrens bickered and sang in the half-green hedgerows,
And the flicker drummed from his dead tree in the chicken-yard.

   — Or to lie naked in sand,
In the silted shallows of a slow river,
Fingering a shell,   40
Thinking:
Once I was something like this, mindless,
Or perhaps with another mind, less peculiar;
Or to sink down to the hips in a mossy quagmire;
Or, with skinny knees, to sit astride a wet log,   45
Believing:
I'll return again,
As a snake or a raucous bird,
Or, with luck, as a lion.

I learned not to fear infinity,   50
The far field, the windy cliffs of forever,
The dying of time in the white light of tomorrow,
The wheel turning away from itself,
The sprawl of the wave,
The on-coming water.   55

3

The river turns on itself,
The tree retreats into its own shadow.
I feel a weightless change, a moving forward
As of water quickening before a narrowing channel
When banks converge, and the wide river whitens;   60
Or when two rivers combine, the blue glacial torrent
And the yellowish-green from the mountainy upland, —
At first a swift rippling between rocks,
Then a long running over flat stones
Before descending to the alluvial plain,[4]   65

------

3. **Cape May, Blackburnian, Cerulean:** Names of warblers, or small songbirds.
4. **alluvial plain:** Flat ground of rich soil deposited by a flowing stream in a river valley or delta.

To the clay banks, and the wild grapes hanging from the elmtrees.
The slightly trembling water
Dropping a fine yellow silt where the sun stays;
And the crabs bask near the edge,
The weedy edge, alive with small snakes and bloodsuckers, —   70
I have come to a still, but not a deep center,
A point outside the glittering current;
My eyes stare at the bottom of a river,
At the irregular stones, iridescent sandgrains,
My mind moves in more than one place,   75
In a country half-land, half-water.

I am renewed by death, thought of my death,
The dry scent of a dying garden in September,
The wind fanning the ash of a low fire.
What I love is near at hand,   80
Always, in earth and air.

4

The lost self changes,
Turning toward the sea,
A sea-shape turning around, —
An old man with his feet before the fire,   85
In robes of green, in garments of adieu.

A man faced with his own immensity
Wakes all the waves, all their loose wandering fire.
The murmur of the absolute, the why
Of being born fails on his naked ears.   90
His spirit moves like monumental wind
That gentles on a sunny blue plateau.
He is the end of things, the final man.

All finite things reveal infinitude:
The mountain with its singular bright shade   95
Like the blue shine on freshly frozen snow,
The after-light upon ice-burdened pines;
Odor of basswood on a mountain-slope,
A scent beloved of bees;
Silence of water above a sunken tree: 100
The pure serene of memory in one man, —
A ripple widening from a single stone
Winding around the waters of the world.

[1962, 1966]

Elizabeth Bishop

[1911-1979]

Elizabeth Bishop

This Associated Press photograph was taken in 1956, the year Bishop was awarded the Pulitzer Prize for her second collection of poetry, *North and South* (1955).

Elizabeth Bishop was born on February 8, 1911, in Worcester, Massachusetts, to Gertrude May Boomer Bishop, a former teacher and nurse, and William Thomas Bishop, the heir to a successful construction business. Eight months later, Bishop's father died from Bright's disease, and Bishop's distraught mother returned with her daughter to live with her parents in Great Village, Nova Scotia. In 1916, after Bishop's mother had suffered a series of violent episodes of mental illness, the Boomers committed her to a hospital where she remained until her death in 1934. Bishop saw her mother only once more. In 1917, when she was six years old, she went to live with her paternal grandparents in Worcester. The wealthy Bishops wished to give their granddaughter a better education than the Boomers could provide in rural Nova Scotia, but she was lonely and miserable until her mother's sister, Bishop's beloved "Aunt Maud," took her to live in Boston. Her paternal grandparents died within a few days of one another in 1923, leaving Bishop a substantial trust fund. Throughout her life, Bishop suffered from asthma and other ailments, and during her frequent childhood illnesses she read widely and developed a strong interest in poetry. By 1924, her health had improved, and she began spending the summers at a nautical camp for girls on Cape Cod. Her supportive fellow campers recalled that "Bishy" had a favorite perch in an apple tree where she would write poems, songs, and skits they performed on Sunday evenings. After completing her final two years of high school at Walnut Hill, a boarding school in Natick, Bishop entered Vassar College in 1930.

It took Bishop nearly two decades to establish herself as a poet. At Vassar, she became friends with the future novelist Mary McCarthy, with whom Bishop founded *Con Spirito*, an avant-garde alternative to the college's literary magazine. During her senior year, she met the visiting poet Marianne Moore, who became Bishop's close friend and mentor. Moore encouraged Bishop, who was considering a medical career, to pursue her interest in writing. Financially independent, she went to New York City after her graduation in 1934. Moore recommended her poems to editors and chose three of them for inclusion in *Trial Balances* (1935), an anthology of the work of young writers selected and introduced by established writers. From 1935 to 1937, Bishop traveled in Europe and North Africa before settling in Key West, Florida, where she bought a house with her college friend Louise Crane. Their partnership was the first of Bishop's lesbian relationships, a part of her life about which she was deeply reticent. Bishop worked on her poems while she and Crane lived a highly social life, filled with music, friends, and visitors to their home. By 1941, however, their relationship was at an end, and Bishop divided her time between Key West and New York City during World War II. Through Moore, she met E. E. Cummings and other poets, but Bishop was depressed and frustrated by her inability to interest a publisher in her first collection of poetry. In 1945, with Moore's support, Bishop's manuscript won first place among more than eight hundred entries in a poetry contest sponsored by the prominent Boston firm Houghton Mifflin, which consequently published it as *North and South* (1946). The book received positive reviews from Moore and the young poet Robert Lowell, whom Bishop met in 1947. They became lifelong friends, and Lowell helped secure her the position of Consultant in Poetry to the Library of Congress, now called the Poet Laureate, for 1949-50.

Despite her slow pace of publication, Bishop's reputation rose steadily during the remainder of her career. On a trip to South America in 1951, she was captivated by Brazil, where she lived for the next eighteen years. She became involved with Lota de Macedo Soares, with whom Bishop lived in Rio de Janeiro and later bought a house at Ouro Prêto. She was awarded the Pulitzer Prize for her second collection, *Poems: North and South — A Cold Spring* (1955). Although she continued to struggle with illness and bouts of alcoholism, she also translated several books from Portuguese to English and wrote a travel book, *Brazil* (1962). "I think geography comes first in my work," Bishop told an interviewer late in her life, and Brazil was the setting of many of the poems in her third book, *Questions of Travel* (1965). She subsequently taught at the University of Washington, returned to Brazil, and then left again for the United States. Lota de Macedo Soares followed her there and died in New York City, possibly of an overdose of sedatives, in September 1967. Bishop lived for a time in San Francisco with an old friend, Suzanne Bowen, and briefly returned with her to Brazil. Bishop's *Complete Poems* (1969) won the National Book Award. In 1970, she began to teach at Harvard University, where she was poet in residence from 1973 to 1977. There, she met Alice Methfessel, her companion for the rest of her life. Bishop coedited *An Anthology of Twentieth-Century Brazilian Poetry* (1972), and her final volume of poems, *Geography III*, was published in 1976. She suffered a cerebral aneurysm and died in Boston on October 6, 1979.

It is this continually renewed sense of discovering the strangements, the unreality of our reality at the very moment of becoming conscious of it as reality, that is the great subject for Elizabeth Bishop.

—John Ashbery

Bishop's Poetry.   Bishop was a notorious perfectionist who often spent years and sometimes even decades working on a single poem. In 1956, the poetry editor of the *New Yorker*, with which Bishop had a first-reading contract and in which many of her poems were first published, wrote to her: "As usual, this letter is a plea to let us see some of the Elizabeth Bishop manuscripts that I feel certain are on your desk, all finished if only you could bring yourself to part with them." In fact, Bishop's notebooks reveal that she began hundreds of poems, some of which have recently been published in a controversial collection of her unfinished work, *Edgar Allan Poe and the Juke-Box: Uncollected Poems, Drafts, and Fragments* (2006), edited by Alice Quinn. Bishop, however, allowed only about ninety of her poems to be published during her long career. In them, she employed a range of poetic techniques, including demanding forms such as the sestina and the villanelle, and she is widely admired for the craftsmanship and rhythmic subtlety of her work. She is also admired for her powers of

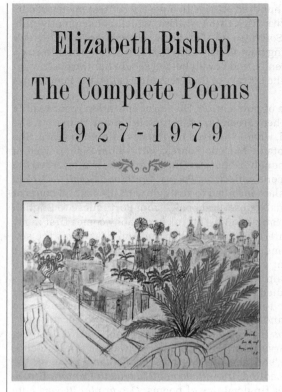

The jacket illustration
is a reproduction of
Bishop's watercolor of
Mérida, Mexico, which
she painted during an
extended visit to the
country in 1942. Bishop,
whose sharp eye for de-
tail was illustrated by
her poems and her
numerous paintings,
observed, "The branches
of the date-palms look
like files."

observation and description, as revealed in her precise and detailed renderings of animals, the natural world, and the physical geography of the
places she lived, especially Brazil, the setting of "The Armadillo" and
"Brazil, January 1, 1502." In contrast to her close friend and contemporary
Robert Lowell, a central figure in the confessional school of American
poetry, Bishop was an intensely private poet. But she drew upon sharply
etched memories of her childhood in poems such as "Sestina" and "In the
Waiting Room," and she indirectly evoked the often painful circumstances
of her personal life in "One Art," a poignant meditation on loss published
in her final collection. The texts are taken from *The Complete Poems,
1927–1979* (1983).

*bedfordstmartins.com/
americanlit* for research
links on Bishop

SESTINA[1]

September rain falls on the house.
In the failing light, the old grandmother
sits in the kitchen with the child
beside the Little Marvel Stove,[2]
reading the jokes from the almanac,   5
laughing and talking to hide her tears.

She thinks that her equinoctial tears
and the rain that beats on the roof of the house
were both foretold by the almanac,
but only known to a grandmother.   10
The iron kettle sings on the stove.
She cuts some bread and says to the child,

It's time for tea now; but the child
is watching the teakettle's small hard tears
dance like mad on the hot black stove,   15
the way the rain must dance on the house.
Tidying up, the old grandmother
hangs up the clever almanac

on its string. Birdlike, the almanac
hovers half open above the child,   20
hovers above the old grandmother
and her teacup full of dark brown tears.
She shivers and says she thinks the house
feels chilly, and puts more wood in the stove.

It was to be, says the Marvel Stove.   25
I know what I know, says the almanac.
With crayons the child draws a rigid house
and a winding pathway. Then the child
puts in a man with buttons like tears
and shows it proudly to the grandmother.   30
But secretly, while the grandmother
busies herself about the stove,
the little moons fall down like tears
from between the pages of the almanac

---

1. **Sestina:** A complex French verse form consisting of six sestets (six-line stanzas) and a final, three-line envoy. The final words of the six lines in the first stanza are repeated in different sequences at the end of the lines of the succeeding stanzas, and all six words appear in the envoy, three of them in the middle of the lines, and three of them at the end of the lines.
2. **Little Marvel Stove:** This cast-iron woodstove, manufactured by the Magee Furnace Company in Boston, was a fixture in the kitchens of many late-nineteenth- and early twentieth-century homes.

into the flower bed the child   35
has carefully placed in the front of the house.

Time to plant tears, says the almanac.
The grandmother sings to the marvellous stove
and the child draws another inscrutable house.

[1956, 1983]

THE ARMADILLO

For Robert Lowell[1]

This is the time of year
when almost every night
the frail, illegal fire balloons appear.[2]
Climbing the mountain height,

rising toward a saint   5
still honored in these parts,
the paper chambers flush and fill with light
that comes and goes, like hearts.

Once up against the sky it's hard
to tell them from the star —   10
planets, that is — the tinted ones:
Venus going down, or Mars,

or the pale green one.[3] With a wind,
they flare and falter, wobble and toss;
but if it's still they steer between   15
the kite sticks of the Southern Cross,[4]

receding, dwindling, solemnly
and steadily forsaking us,
or, in the downdraft from a peak,
suddenly turning dangerous.   20

Last night another big one fell.
It splattered like an egg of fire

---

1. **Dedication:** Bishop dedicated her poem to her close friend Robert Lowell (see p. 1252).
2. **This is the time . . . illegal fire balloons appear:** In June, during the festivals of St. Anthony, St. John, and St. Peter, Brazilians in some regions celebrate by releasing miniature fire-propelled balloons. The paper devices are banned because they frequently crash to the earth and cause serious fires.
3. **the pale green one:** The planet Neptune.
4. **Southern Cross:** Also called the "Crux," a constellation of stars in the shape of a cross that is visible only in the Southern Hemisphere.

against the cliff behind the house.
The flame ran down. We saw the pair

of owls who nest there flying up   25
and up, their whirling black-and-white
stained bright pink underneath, until
they shrieked up out of sight.

The ancient owls' nest must have burned.
Hastily, all alone,   30
a glistening armadillo left the scene,
rose-flecked, head down, tail down,

and then a baby rabbit jumped out,
short-eared, to our surprise.
So soft! – a handful of intangible ash   35
with fixed, ignited eyes.

Too pretty, dreamlike mimicry!
O falling fire and piercing cry
and panic, and a weak mailed fist[5]
clenched ignorant against the sky!   40

[1957, 1983]

---

5. **mailed fist:** The armadillo, whose name is derived from the Spanish word *armado* ("armed man"), is covered in bony plates that resemble chain mail or body armor.

BRAZIL, JANUARY 1, 1502[1]

. . . embroidered nature . . . tapestried landscape.
   – *Landscape into Art*, by Sir Kenneth Clark[2]

Januaries, Nature greets our eyes
exactly as she must have greeted theirs:
every square inch filling in with foliage –
big leaves, little leaves, and giant leaves,
blue, blue-green, and olive,   5
with occasional lighter veins and edges,
or a satin underleaf turned over;
monster ferns

---

1. **Brazil, January 1, 1502:** The date on which Portuguese explorers first landed at what is now Rio de Janeiro, beginning their conquest of Brazil. In the poem, Bishop also draws upon the imagery of a decorated 1502 map that was later reprinted in her book *Brazil* (1962).
2. **Sir Kenneth Clark:** Bishop quotes phrases from "Landscape of Symbols," a chapter in the British art historian's 1949 book in which he discusses the *Hortus Conclusis*, literally the "closed-off garden" (Latin), medieval and Renaissance depictions of the Virgin Mary in a walled garden, a symbol of her virginity.

in silver-gray relief,
and flowers, too, like giant water lilies   10
up in the air — up, rather, in the leaves —
purple, yellow, two yellows, pink,
rust red and greenish white;
solid but airy; fresh as if just finished
and taken off the frame.   15

A blue-white sky, a simple web,
backing for feathery detail:
brief arcs, a pale-green broken wheel,
a few palms, swarthy, squat, but delicate;
and perching there in profile, beaks agape,   20
the big symbolic birds keep quiet,
each showing only half his puffed and padded,
pure-colored or spotted breast.
Still in the foreground there is Sin:
five sooty dragons near some massy rocks.   25
The rocks are worked with lichens, gray moonbursts
splattered and overlapping,
threatened from underneath by moss
in lovely hell-green flames,
attacked above   30
by scaling-ladder vines, oblique and neat,
"one leaf yes and one leaf no" (in Portuguese).
The lizards scarcely breathe; all eyes are
on the smaller, female one, back-to,
her wicked tail straight up and over,   35
red as a red-hot wire.

Just so the Christians, hard as nails,
tiny as nails, and glinting,
in creaking armor, came and found it all,
not unfamiliar: 40
no lovers' walks, no bowers,
no cherries to be picked, no lute music,
but corresponding, nevertheless,
to an old dream of wealth and luxury
already out of style when they left home —   45
wealth, plus a brand-new pleasure.
Directly after Mass, humming perhaps
L'Homme armé[3] or some such tune,

---

3. ***L'Homme armé***: "The Armed Man" (French) was a medieval song, the melody of which was frequently used as a chant in the Catholic Mass between 1450 and 1500.

they ripped away into the hanging fabric,
each out to catch an Indian for himself —   50
those maddening little women who kept calling,
calling to each other (or had the birds waked up?)
and retreating, always retreating, behind it.

                   [1960, 1983]

IN THE WAITING ROOM

In Worcester, Massachusetts,
I went with Aunt Consuelo
to keep her dentist's appointment
and sat and waited for her
in the dentist's waiting room.   5
It was winter. It got dark
early. The waiting room
was full of grown-up people,
arctics[1] and overcoats,
lamps and magazines.   10
My aunt was inside
what seemed like a long time
and while I waited I read
the *National Geographic*
(I could read) and carefully   15
studied the photographs:
the inside of a volcano,
black, and full of ashes;
then it was spilling over
in rivulets of fire.   20
Osa and Martin Johnson[2]
dressed in riding breeches,
laced boots, and pith helmets.
A dead man slung on a pole
— "Long Pig,"[3] the caption said.   25
Babies with pointed heads

---

1. **arctics:** Waterproof overshoes.
2. **Osa and Martin Johnson:** Natives of Kansas, these explorers and naturalists traveled throughout Africa, Borneo, and the South Seas from 1917 through 1937, the year that Martin Johnson died in a plane crash. The famous couple published photographs in magazines such as *National Geographic*, wrote travel books, and produced feature films about Africa. Early in his career, Martin Johnson accompanied Jack London on a voyage to the South Pacific, recounted in *The Cruise of the Snark* (1911).
3. **"Long Pig":** In his popular account of his voyage to the South Pacific, *The Cruise of the Snark* (1911), Jack London explains: "Now long-pig is not pig. Long-pig is the Polynesian euphemism for human flesh; and these descendants of man-eaters, a king's son at their head, brought in the pigs to table as of old their grandfathers had brought in their slain enemies."

wound round and round with string;
black, naked women with necks
wound round and round with wire
like the necks of light bulbs. 30
Their breasts were horrifying.
I read it right straight through.
I was too shy to stop.
And then I looked at the cover:
the yellow margins, the date. 35
Suddenly, from inside,
came an *oh!* of pain
— Aunt Consuelo's voice —
not very loud or long.
I wasn't at all surprised; 40
even then I knew she was
a foolish, timid woman.
I might have been embarrassed,
but wasn't. What took me
completely by surprise 45
was that it was *me*:
my voice, in my mouth.
Without thinking at all
I was my foolish aunt,
I — we — were falling, falling, 50
our eyes glued to the cover
of the *National Geographic*,
February, 1918.

I said to myself: three days
and you'll be seven years old. 55
I was saying it to stop
the sensation of falling off
the round, turning world
into cold, blue-black space.
But I felt: you are an *I*, 60
you are an *Elizabeth*,
you are one of *them*.
Why should you be one, too?
I scarcely dared to look
to see what it was I was. 65
I gave a sidelong glance
— I couldn't look any higher —
at shadowy gray knees,
trousers and skirts and boots
and different pairs of hands 70
lying under the lamps.

I knew that nothing stranger
had ever happened, that nothing
stranger could ever happen.

Why should I be my aunt,   75
or me, or anyone?
What similarities —
boots, hands, the family voice
I felt in my throat, or even
the *National Geographic*   80
and those awful hanging breasts —
held us all together
or made us all just one?
How — I didn't know any
word for it — how "unlikely" . . .   85
How had I come to be here,
like them, and overhear
a cry of pain that could have
got loud and worse but hadn't?

The waiting room was bright   90
and too hot. It was sliding
beneath a big black wave,
another, and another.

Then I was back in it.
The War was on. Outside,   95
in Worcester, Massachusetts,
were night and slush and cold,
and it was still the fifth
of February, 1918.[4]

[1971, 1983]

---

4. **the fifth of February, 1918:** On this date, the liner *Tuscania* was sunk by a German submarine off the coast of Scotland. More than two hundred men died in the sinking, the first of a ship carrying American troops to Europe. Outraged public opinion in the United States led to an escalation of American involvement in World War I, which the country had entered in April 1917.

ONE ART[1]

The art of losing isn't hard to master;
so many things seem filled with the intent
to be lost that their loss is no disaster.

---

1. **One Art:** This nineteen-line poem is a villanelle, a complex form composed of five triplets (a three-line stanza rhymed *a b a*) and a concluding quatrain (a four-line stanza rhymed *a b a b*). The form employs only two rhymes, and alternating stanzas end with the same last line.

Lose something every day. Accept the fluster
of lost door keys, the hour badly spent.   5
The art of losing isn't hard to master.

Then practice losing farther, losing faster:
places, and names, and where it was you meant
to travel. None of these will bring disaster.

I lost my mother's watch. And look! my last, or   10
next-to-last, of three loved houses went.
The art of losing isn't hard to master.

I lost two cities, lovely ones. And, vaster,
some realms I owned, two rivers, a continent.
I miss them, but it wasn't a disaster.   15

— Even losing you (the joking voice, a gesture
I love) I shan't have lied. It's evident
the art of losing's not too hard to master
though it may look like (*Write* it!) like disaster.

[1976, 1983]

Tennessee Williams

[1911-1983]

Thomas Lanier Williams was born on March 26, 1911, in Columbus, Mississippi. He was the first of three children born to Edwina Dakin Williams,

Tennessee Williams

This photograph of
Williams was taken in the
late 1940s, when he was
at the height of his early
fame as one of the major
American dramatists to
emerge in the years after
World War II.

the daughter of a minister, and Cornelius
Coffin Williams, a traveling shoe salesman from Tennessee. Because his father
was often away from home, the family lived
with his mother's parents, with whom Williams became very close. In 1918, the family moved to an apartment in St. Louis,
Missouri, where Cornelius Williams took
a job as the manager of a shoe company.
The Williamses' marriage became increasingly strained, and their children grew up
in a contentious, sometimes violent household. Cornelius Williams often taunted his
oldest son for siding with his mother, call-
ing him "Miss Nancy." Using a typewriter his mother bought for him,
Williams escaped into writing. "Our literary boy," as he was called in a
yearbook, contributed stories to school newspapers and won third prize in
an essay contest sponsored by the sophisticated magazine *Smart Set* in

1927. The following year, he published a horror story in the pulp magazine *Weird Tales*. After a tour of Europe with his grandfather in the summer of 1929, Williams enrolled in the University of Missouri. Bored by the courses required for his journalism major, he preferred studying poetry and drama, especially the plays of Eugene O'Neill and the Swedish playwright August Strindberg. In an effort to earn extra money, he submitted works to literary contests and won an honorable mention for his first play, *Beauty Is the Word*.

Despite his early successes and promising start, Williams struggled to make his way as a writer. His father, unhappy with his son's isolation and deep absorption in literature, insisted that Williams join a fraternity and take military training courses. When he failed those courses in his junior year, his angry father withdrew him from the university in 1932, and Williams was forced to return home to St. Louis. He worked in his father's shoe factory during the day and wrote at night and on weekends, submitting his stories, plays, and poems to literary contests and magazines. In 1935, mentally and physically exhausted, he claimed that he had suffered a heart attack and went to recover at his grandparents' home in Memphis. While there, his one-act play "Cairo! Shanghai! Bombay!" was performed by a local theater, and Williams resolved to become a playwright. He returned to St. Louis, where with the financial help of his grandfather Williams enrolled at Washington University in the fall of 1936. Two of his plays were performed there, and Williams subsequently transferred to the University of Iowa, where he studied playwriting and production and graduated with a BA in 1938. Apparently because of his southern accent, the students there called him "Tennessee," a name Williams soon adopted to sign his work. In the meantime, the situation in the family home in St. Louis had further deteriorated as his sister, Rose, slipped into mental illness. Eager to be on his own and away from home, Williams took a short-term job with the Works Progress Administration in New Orleans. As he recalled in his *Memoirs* (1975), he first came out as a gay man while living a bohemian life in the French Quarter. In 1939, Williams finally achieved a major breakthrough when a group of his one-act plays, *American Blues*, won a special award in a play contest sponsored by the Group Theatre in New York City.

During the following five years, Williams fulfilled his dream of becoming a playwright. The head of the play department at the Group Theatre contacted the prominent literary agent Audrey Wood, who agreed to take Williams on and helped secure him a Rockefeller Foundation grant of $1,000. With the money, Williams went to New York City in 1940. He enrolled in a playwriting seminar at the New School for Social Research and wrote the autobiographical *Battle of Angels*, which was produced by the prestigious Theater Guild. The play opened in Boston, then notorious for the provincialism and intellectual snobbery of its critics, who dubbed the drama "Delta dirt" and described its author as a "hillbilly." Devastated by the failure, Williams left New York and returned to New Orleans. He visited St. Louis in 1943, after he learned that his sister had undergone a lobotomy, a procedure then used in extreme cases of schizophrenia. The operation reduced her to an infantile state, and she was institutionalized

Williams is a realistic writer . . . primarily interested in passion, in ecstasy, in creating a synthesis of his conflicting feelings.

–Arthur Miller

for the rest of her life. Williams was horrified by his parents' decision to allow the operation and deeply guilty about his failure to prevent it. He soon left home to take a job as a scriptwriter in Hollywood with MGM. The studio rejected several of his ideas for films, including a screen synopsis of what Williams recast as "A Memory Play," *The Glass Menagerie*. Loosely based on his sister's withdrawal from reality and his own efforts to escape their suffocating home in St. Louis, the play ran for 561 performances on Broadway during 1945-46. Shortly after it closed, he achieved even greater fame with *A Streetcar Named Desire*, which opened to universal acclaim in December 1947, ran for more than two years on Broadway, and was awarded the Pulitzer Prize.

Although he remained a major force in American theater, Williams never again quite matched the critical and commercial success of his early triumphs. He soon began the most significant and long-lasting romantic relationship of his life with Frank Merlo, whom Williams met in New Orleans in 1947. For the first time, he was also financially secure, since he earned several million dollars from the royalties and the sale of screen rights to *A Streetcar Named Desire*. Many of his later plays were also made into successful movies, including his Broadway hits *Cat on a Hot Tin Roof* (1955), *Sweet Bird of Youth* (1959), and *The Night of the Iguana* (1961). During the 1960s, which Williams described in his *Memoirs* as his "lost decade," his years of drinking and drug abuse began to take their toll. After Merlo died of lung cancer in 1963, Williams became so severely depressed that his brother, Dakin, committed him to a psychiatric hospital in 1969. There, Williams was temporarily forced to withdraw from drugs and alcohol, and he emerged from the hospital healthier than he had been for many years. But he found that tastes were changing in American drama, and his career was essentially over. Nonetheless, the prolific Williams continued to write steadily and completed his final play only a month before he died on February 24, 1983.

Williams's *Portrait of a Madonna*.

bedfordstmartins.com/ **americanlit** for research links on Williams

In addition to forty-five full-length dramas, Williams wrote more than sixty one-act plays, of which one of the most famous is *Portrait of a Madonna*. Alternately titled *Port Mad* or *The Leafless Block*, it was completed early in 1940, when Williams suggested to his agent that the play might "be bound with two other new ones, possibly under the inclusive title 'The Lonely Heart' as all three are about rather desolate people and nostalgic in atmosphere." Following the success of *The Glass Menagerie* on Broadway, *Portrait of a Madonna* was first performed in 1946 at the Actor's Laboratory Theater in Los Angeles, where it was staged by Hume Cronyn. The role of Lucretia Collins was played by Jessica Tandy, who once called *Portrait of a Madonna* a "superb play," adding, "It's got everything in it. It's a perfect little jewel of a play." Lucretia, an aging southern belle from New Orleans living in exile in an unnamed northern city and lost in memories of the past, was also the forerunner of Williams's most famous female character, Blanche DuBois, the tragic figure at the center of *A Streetcar Named Desire*. In fact, when

Portrait of a Madonna

Jessica Tandy, who played Lucretia Collins in the first performance of *Portrait of a Madonna* in 1946, reprised the role on Broadway in 1959. With Tandy in this scene from that later production are Margot Stevenson as the Nurse and John Randolph as Mr. Abrams.

Williams saw the Los Angeles production of *Portrait of a Madonna*, he immediately wanted Tandy for the role of Blanche DuBois, which she played when *A Streetcar Named Desire* opened on Broadway in 1947. The text of *Portrait of a Madonna* is taken from the first publication in *27 Wagons Full of Cotton and Other Plays* (1945).

PORTRAIT OF A MADONNA

Respectfully dedicated to the talent and charm of Miss Lillian Gish.[1]

CHARACTERS

MISS LUCRETIA COLLINS.	THE DOCTOR.
THE PORTER.[2]	THE NURSE.
THE ELEVATOR BOY.	MR. ABRAMS.

---

1. **Dedication:** Williams dedicated the play to Lillian Gish (1893–1993), a stage actor who became a star of silent films. Gish, who was renowned for her angelic beauty and acting skill, was often cast as an innocent victim who is rescued in the nick of time. Like many other actors, however, she was not able to make the transition to "talkies" when they developed in the late 1920s. She consequently returned to the theater and played Lucretia Collins in a production of *Portrait of a Madonna* in Berlin, Germany, in 1957.
2. **The Porter:** A person employed by an apartment building to monitor the main entrance.

SCENE

The living room of a moderate-priced city apartment. The furnishings are old-fashioned and everything is in a state of neglect and disorder. There is a door in the back wall to a bedroom, and on the right to the outside hall.

MISS COLLINS: Richard! (*The door bursts open and Miss Collins rushes out, distractedly. She is a middle-aged spinster, very slight and hunched of figure with a desiccated face that is flushed with excitement. Her hair is arranged in curls that would become a young girl and she wears a frilly negligee[3] which might have come from an old hope chest of a period considerably earlier.*) No, no, no, no! I don't care if the whole church hears about it! (*She frenziedly snatches up the phone.*) Manager, I've got to speak to the manager! Hurry, oh, please hurry, there's a *man* — ! (*wildly aside as if to an invisible figure*) Lost all respect, absolutely no respect! . . . Mr. Abrams? (*in a tense hushed voice*) I don't want any reporters to hear about this but something awful has been going on upstairs. Yes, this is Miss Collins' apartment on the top floor. I've refrained from making any complaint because of my connections with the church. I used to be assistant to the Sunday School superintendent and I once had the primary class. I helped them put on the Christmas pageant. I made the dress for the Virgin and Mother, made robes for the Wise Men. Yes, and now this has happened, I'm not responsible for it, but night after night after night this man has been coming into my apartment and — indulging his senses! Do you understand? Not once but repeatedly, Mr. Abrams! I don't know whether he comes in the door or the window or up the fire-escape or whether there's some secret entrance they know about at the church, but he's here now, in my bedroom, and I can't force him to leave, I'll have to have some assistance! No, he isn't a thief, Mr. Abrams, he comes of a very fine family in Webb, Mississippi, but this woman has ruined his character, she's destroyed his respect for ladies! Mr. Abrams? Mr. Abrams! Oh, goodness! (*She slams up the receiver and looks distractedly about for a moment; then rushes back into the bedroom.*) Richard! (*The door slams shut. After a few moments an old porter enters in drab gray cover-alls. He looks about with a sorrowfully humorous curiosity, then timidly calls.*)

PORTER: Miss Collins? (*The elevator door slams open in hall and the Elevator Boy, wearing a uniform, comes in.*)

ELEVATOR BOY: Where is she?

PORTER: Gone in 'er bedroom.

ELEVATOR BOY: (*grinning*) She got him in there with her?

PORTER: Sounds like it. (*Miss Collins' voice can be heard faintly protesting with the mysterious intruder.*)

ELEVATOR BOY: What'd Abrams tell yuh to do?

PORTER: Stay here an' keep a watch on 'er till they git here.

ELEVATOR BOY: Jesus.

PORTER: Close 'at door.

---

3. **negligee:** A woman's robe, typically made of a light, translucent fabric.

ELEVATOR BOY: I gotta leave it open a little so I can hear the buzzer. Ain't this place a holy sight though?

PORTER: Don't look like it's had a good cleaning in fifteen or twenty years. I bet it ain't either. Abrams'll bust a blood vessel when he takes a lookit them walls.

ELEVATOR BOY: How comes it's in this condition?

PORTER: She wouldn't let no one in.

ELEVATOR BOY: Not even the paper-hangers?

PORTER: Naw. Not even the plumbers. The plaster washed down in the bathroom underneath hers an' she admitted her plumbin' had been stopped up. Mr. Abrams had to let the plumber in with this here pass-key when she went out for a while.

ELEVATOR BOY: Holy Jeez. I wunner if she's got money stashed around here. A lotta freaks do stick away big sums of money in ole mattresses an' things.

PORTER: She ain't. She got a monthly pension check or something she always turned over to Mr. Abrams to dole it out to 'er. She tole him that Southern ladies was never brought up to manage finanshul affairs. Lately the checks quit comin'.

ELEVATOR BOY: Yeah?

PORTER: The pension give out or somethin'. Abrams says he got a contribution from the church to keep 'er on here without 'er knowin' about it. She's proud as a peacock's tail in spite of 'er awful appearance.

ELEVATOR BOY: Lissen to 'er in there!

PORTER: What's she sayin'?

ELEVATOR BOY: Apologizin' to him! For callin' the *police!*

PORTER: She thinks police 're comin'?

MISS COLLINS: (*from bedroom*) Stop it, it's got to stop!

ELEVATOR BOY: Fightin' to protect her honor again! What a commotion, no wunner folks are complainin'!

PORTER: (*lighting his pipe*) This here'll be the last time.

ELEVATOR BOY: She's goin' out, huh?

PORTER: (*blowing out the match*) Tonight.

ELEVATOR BOY: Where'll she go?

PORTER: (*slowly moving to the old gramophone*) She'll go to the state asylum.

ELEVATOR BOY: Holy G!

PORTER: Remember this ole number? (*He puts on a record of "I'm Forever Blowing Bubbles."*)[4]

ELEVATOR BOY: Naw. When did that come out?

PORTER: Before your time, sonny boy. Machine needs oilin'. (*He takes out small oil-can and applies oil about the crank and other parts of gramophone.*)

ELEVATOR BOY: How long is the old girl been here?

PORTER: Abrams says she's been livin' here twenty-five, thirty years, since before he got to be manager even.

4. "I'm Forever Blowing Bubbles": A widely performed, popular song composed by John Kellette for the Broadway musical revue *The Passing Show of 1918.*

ELEVATOR BOY: Livin' alone all that time?

PORTER: She had an old mother died of an operation about fifteen years ago. Since then she ain't gone out of the place excep' on Sundays to church or Friday nights to some kind of religious meeting.

ELEVATOR BOY: Got an awful lot of ol' magazines piled aroun' here.

PORTER: She used to collect 'em. She'd go out in back and fish 'em out of the incinerator.

ELEVATOR BOY: What'n hell for?

PORTER: Mr. Abrams says she used to cut out the Campbell soup kids. Them red-tomato-headed kewpie dolls that go with the soup advertisements. You seen 'em, ain'tcha?

ELEVATOR BOY: Uh-huh.

PORTER: She made a collection of 'em. Filled a big lot of scrapbooks with them paper kiddies an' took 'em down to the Children's Hospitals on Xmas Eve an' Easter Sunday, exactly twicet a year. Sounds better, don't it? (*referring to gramophone, which resumes its faint, wheedling music*) Eliminated some a that crankin' noise . . .

ELEVATOR BOY: I didn't know that she'd been nuts *that* long.

PORTER: Who's nuts an' who ain't? If you ask me the world is populated with people that's just as peculiar as she is.

ELEVATOR BOY: Hell. She don't have brain *one*.

PORTER: There's important people in Europe got less'n she's got. Tonight they're takin' her off 'n' lockin' her up. They'd do a lot better to leave 'er go an' lock up some a them maniacs over there. She's harmless; they ain't. They kill millions of people an' go scot free!

ELEVATOR BOY: An ole woman like her is disgusting, though, imaginin' somebody's raped her.

PORTER: Pitiful, not disgusting. Watch out for them cigarette ashes.

ELEVATOR BOY: What's uh diff'rence? So much dust you can't see it. All a this here goes out in the morning, don't it?

PORTER: Uh-huh.

ELEVATOR BOY: I think I'll take a couple a those ole records as curiosities for my girl friend. She's got a portable in 'er bedroom, she says it's better with music!

PORTER: Leave 'em alone. She's still got 'er property rights.

ELEVATOR BOY: Aw, she's got all she wants with them dream-lovers of hers!

PORTER: *Hush up!* (*He makes a warning gesture as Miss Collins enters from bedroom. Her appearance is that of a ravaged woman. She leans exhaustedly in the doorway, hands clasped over her flat, virginal bosom.*)

MISS COLLINS: (*breathlessly*) Oh, Richard — Richard . . .

PORTER: (*coughing*) Miss — Collins.

ELEVATOR BOY: Hello, Miss Collins.

MISS COLLINS: (*just noticing the men*) Goodness! You've arrived already! Mother didn't tell me you were here! (*Self-consciously she touches her ridiculous corkscrew curls with the faded pink ribbon tied through them. Her manner becomes that of a slightly coquettish but prim little Southern belle.*) I must ask you gentlemen to excuse the terrible disorder.

PORTER: That's all right, Miss Collins.

MISS COLLINS: It's the maid's day off. Your No'thern girls receive such excellent domestic training, but in the South it was never considered essential for a girl to have anything but prettiness and charm! (*She laughs girlishly.*) Please do sit down. Is it too close? Would you like a window open?

PORTER: No, Miss Collins.

MISS COLLINS: (*advancing with delicate grace to the sofa*) Mother will bring in something cool after while. . . . Oh, my! (*She touches her forehead.*)

PORTER: (*kindly*) Is anything wrong, Miss Collins?

MISS COLLINS: Oh, no, no, thank you, nothing! My head is a little bit heavy. I'm always a little bit – malarial[5] – this time of year! (*She sways dizzily as she starts to sink down on the sofa.*)

PORTER: (*helping her*) Careful there, Miss Collins.

MISS COLLINS: (*vaguely*) Yes, it is, I hadn't noticed before. (*She peers at them nearsightedly with a hesitant smile.*) You gentlemen have come from the church?

PORTER: No, ma'am. I'm Nick, the porter, Miss Collins, and this boy here is Frank that runs the elevator.

MISS COLLINS: (*stiffening a little*) Oh? . . . I don't understand.

PORTER: (*gently*) Mr. Abrams just asked me to drop in here an' see if you was getting along all right.

MISS COLLINS: Oh! Then he must have informed you of what's been going on in here!

PORTER: He mentioned some kind of – disturbance.

MISS COLLINS: Yes! Isn't it outrageous? But it mustn't go any further, you understand. I mean you mustn't repeat it to other people.

PORTER: No, I wouldn't say nothing.

MISS COLLINS: Not a word of it, please!

ELEVATOR BOY: Is the man still here, Miss Collins?

MISS COLLINS: Oh, no. No, he's gone now.

ELEVATOR BOY: How did he go, out the bedroom window, Miss Collins?

MISS COLLINS: (*vaguely*) Yes. . . .

ELEVATOR BOY: I seen a guy that could do that once. He crawled straight up the side of the building. They called him The Human Fly! Gosh, that's a wonderful publicity angle, Miss Collins – "Beautiful Young Society Lady Raped by The Human Fly!"

PORTER: (*nudging him sharply*) Git back in your cracker box!

MISS COLLINS: Publicity? No! It would be so humiliating! Mr. Abrams surely hasn't reported it to the papers!

PORTER: No, ma'am. Don't listen to this smarty pants.

---

5. **malarial:** Malaria is a tropical disease characterized by an intermittent fever caused by parasites transmitted by mosquitoes.

MISS COLLINS: (*touching her curls*) Will pictures be taken, you think? There's one of him on the mantel.

ELEVATOR BOY: (*going to the mantel*) This one here, Miss Collins?

MISS COLLINS: Yes. Of the Sunday School faculty picnic. I had the little kindergardeners that year and he had the older boys. We rode in the cab of a railroad locomotive from Webb to Crystal Springs. (*She covers her ears with a girlish grimace and toss of her curls.*) Oh, how the steam-whistle blew! Blew! (*giggling*) *Blewwwww!* It frightened me so, he put his arm round my shoulders! But she was there, too, though she had no business being. She grabbed his hat and stuck it on the back of her head and they — they *rassled* for it, they actually *rassled* together! Everyone said it was *shameless!* Don't you think that it was?

PORTER: Yes, Miss Collins.

MISS COLLINS: That's the picture, the one in the silver frame up there on the mantel. We cooled the watermelon in the springs and afterwards played games. She hid somewhere and he took ages to find her. It got to be dark and he hadn't found her yet and everyone whispered and giggled about it and finally they came back together — her hangin' on to his arm like a common little strumpet — and Daisy Belle Huston shrieked out, "Look, everybody, the seat of Evelyn's skirt!" It was — covered with — grass-stains! Did you ever hear of anything as outrageous? It didn't faze her, though, she laughed like it was something very, very amusing! Rather *triumphant* she was!

ELEVATOR BOY: Which one is him, Miss Collins?

MISS COLLINS: The tall one in the blue shirt holding onto one of my curls. He loved to play with them.

ELEVATOR BOY: Quite a Romeo — 1910 model, huh?

MISS COLLINS: (*vaguely*) Do you? It's nothing, really, but I like the lace on the collar. I said to Mother, "Even if I don't wear it, Mother, it will be *so* nice for my hope-chest!"

ELEVATOR BOY: How was he dressed tonight when he climbed into your balcony, Miss Collins?

MISS COLLINS: Pardon?

ELEVATOR BOY: Did he still wear that nifty little stick-candy-striped blue shirt with the celluloid collar?

MISS COLLINS: He hasn't changed.

ELEVATOR BOY: Oughta be easy to pick him up in that. What color pants did he wear?

MISS COLLINS: (*vaguely*) I don't remember.

ELEVATOR BOY: Maybe he didn't wear any. Shimmied out of 'em on the way up the wall! You could get him on grounds of indecent exposure, Miss Collins!

PORTER: (*grasping his arm*) Cut that or git back in your cage! Understand?

ELEVATOR BOY: (*snickering*) Take it easy. She don't hear a thing.

PORTER: Well, you keep a decent tongue or get to hell out. Miss Collins here is a lady. You understand that?

ELEVATOR BOY: Okay. She's Shoiley Temple.[6]

---

6. **Shoiley Temple:** Shirley Temple (b. 1928), an enormously popular child film star of the 1930s.

PORTER: She's a *lady!*

ELEVATOR BOY: Yeah! (*He returns to the gramophone and looks through the records.*)

MISS COLLINS: I really shouldn't have created this disturbance. When the officers come I'll have to explain that to them. But you can understand my feelings, can't you?

PORTER: Sure, Miss Collins.

MISS COLLINS: When men take advantage of common white-trash women who smoke in public there is probably some excuse for it, but when it occurs to a lady who is single and always com-*pletely* above reproach in her moral behavior, there's really nothing to do but call for police protection! Unless of course the girl is fortunate enough to have a father and brothers who can take care of the matter privately without any scandal.

PORTER: Sure. That's right, Miss Collins.

MISS COLLINS: Of course it's bound to cause a great deal of very disagreeable talk. Especially 'round the *church!* Are you gentlemen Episcopalian?

PORTER: No, ma'am. Catholic, Miss Collins.

MISS COLLINS: Oh. Well, I suppose you know in England we're known as the English Catholic church. We have direct Apostolic succession through St. Paul who christened the Early Angles — which is what the original English people were called — and established the English branch of the Catholic church over there. So when you hear ignorant people claim that our church was founded by — by Henry the *Eighth* — that horrible, *leche*rous old man who had so many wives — as many as *Blue*-beard they say! — you can see how ridiculous it *is* and how thoroughly ob*nox*-ious to anybody who really *knows* and under*stands* Church *His*tory!

PORTER: (*comfortingly*) Sure, Miss Collins. Everybody knows that.

MISS COLLINS: I wish they *did*, but they need to be in*struc*ted! Before he died, my father was Rector at the Church of St. Michael and St. George at Glorious Hill, Mississippi. . . . I've literally grown up right in the very *shad*ow of the Episcopal church. At Pass Christian and Natchez, Biloxi, Gulfport, Port Gibson, Columbus and Glorious Hill! (*with gentle, bewildered sadness*) But you know I sometimes suspect that there has been some kind of spiritual schism in the modern church. These northern dioceses have completely departed from the good old church traditions. For instance our Rector at the Church of the Holy Communion has never darkened my door. It's a fashionable church and he's terribly busy, but even so you'd think he might have time to make a stranger in the congregation feel at home. But he doesn't though! Nobody seems to have the time any more. . . . (*She grows more excited as her mind sinks back into illusion.*) I ought not to mention this, but do you know they actually take a malicious de-*light* over there at the Holy Communion — where I've recently transferred my letter — in what's been going on here at night in this apartment? *Yes!* (*She laughs wildly and throws up her hands.*) They take a malicious de*LIGHT* in it!! (*She catches her breath and gropes vaguely about her wrapper.*)

PORTER: You lookin' for somethin', Miss Collins?

MISS COLLINS: My — handkerchief . . . (*She is blinking her eyes against tears.*)

PORTER: (*removing a rag from his pocket*) Here. Use this, Miss Collins. It's just a rag but it's clean, except along that edge where I wiped off the phonograph handle.

MISS COLLINS: Thanks. You gentlemen are very kind. Mother will bring in something cool after while. . . .

ELEVATOR BOY: (*placing a record on machine*) This one is got some kind of foreign title. (*The record begins to play Tschaikowsky's "None But the Lonely Heart."*)

MISS COLLINS: (*stuffing the rag daintily in her bosom*) Excuse me, please. Is the weather nice outside?

PORTER: (*huskily*) Yes, it's nice, Miss Collins.

MISS COLLINS: (*dreamily*) So wa'm for this time of year. I wore my little astrakhan cape[7] to service but had to *carry* it *home*, as the weight of it actually seemed *oppres*sive to me. (*Her eyes fall shut.*) The sidewalks seem so dreadfully long in summer. . . .

ELEVATOR BOY: This ain't summer, Miss Collins.

MISS COLLINS: (*dreamily*) I used to think I'd never get to the end of that last block. And that's the block where all the trees went down in the big tornado. The walk is simply *glit*-tering with sunlight. (*pressing her eyelids*) Impossible to shade your face and I *do* perspire so freely! (*She touches her forehead daintily with the rag.*) Not a branch, not a leaf to give you a little protection! You simply *have* to en-*dure* it. Turn your hideous red face away from all the front-porches and walk as fast as you decently *can* till you get *by* them! Oh, dear, dear Savior, sometimes you're not so lucky and you *meet* people and have to *smile!* You can't *avoid* them unless you cut *across* and that's so ob-vious, you know. . . . People would say you're pe*culiar*. . . . His house is right in the middle of that awful leafless block, *their* house, his and *hers*, and they have an auto-mobile and always get home early and sit on the porch and *watch* me walking by — Oh, Father in Heaven — with a ma*licious* de*light!* (*She averts her face in remembered torture.*) She has such *penetrating* eyes, they look straight through me. She sees that terrible choking thing in my throat and the pain I have in *here* — (*touching her chest*) — and she points it out and laughs and whispers to him, "There she goes with her shiny big red nose, the poor old maid — that *loves* you!" (*She chokes and hides her face in the rag.*)

PORTER: Maybe you better forget all that, Miss Collins.

MISS COLLINS: Never, never forget it! Never, never! I left my parasol once — the one with long white fringe that belonged to Mother — I left it behind in the cloak-room at the church so I didn't have anything to cover my face with when I walked by, and I couldn't turn back either, with all those people behind me — giggling back of me, poking fun at my clothes! Oh, dear, dear! I had to walk straight forward — past the last elm tree and into that *merciless* sunlight. Oh! It beat down on me, *scorching* me! *Whips!* . . . Oh, Jesus! . . . Over my face and my body! . . . I tried to walk on fast but was dizzy and they kept closer behind me — ! I stumbled, I nearly fell, and all of them burst out laughing! My face turned so *horribly* red, it got so red and wet, I knew how ugly it was in all that merciless glare — not a single shadow to hide in! And then — (*Her face contorts with fear.*) — their automobile drove up in front of their house,

---

7. **astrakhan cape:** A woman's wrap made of a cloth resembling the curly fleece of the young karakul lambs of central Asia.

right where I had to pass by it, and *she* stepped out, in white, so fresh and easy, her stomach round with a baby, the first of the *six.* Oh, God! . . . And he stood smiling behind her, white and easy and cool, and they stood there waiting for me. *Waiting!* I had to keep on. What else could I do? I couldn't turn *back,* could I? *No!* I said dear *God,* strike me *dead!* He didn't, though. I put my head way down like I couldn't see them! You know what she did? She stretched out her hand to *stop* me! And *he* — he stepped up straight in front of me, *smiling,* blocking the walk with his terrible big white body! *"Lucretia,"* he said, "Lucretia *Collins!"* I — I tried to speak but I couldn't, the breath went out of my body! I covered my face and — ran! . . . Ran! . . . *Ran! (beating the arm of the sofa)* Till I reached the end of the block — and the elm trees — *started* again. . . . Oh, Merciful Christ in Heaven, how *kind* they were! *(She leans back exhaustedly, her hand relaxed on sofa. She pauses and the music ends.)* I said to Mother, "Mother, we've got to leave town!" We *did* after that. And now after all these years he's finally remembered and come *back!* Moved away from that house and the woman and come *here* — I saw him in the back of the church one day. I wasn't sure — but it *was.* The night after that was the night that he first broke in — and indulged his senses with me. . . . He doesn't realize that I've changed, that I can't feel again the way that I used to feel, now that he's got six children by that Cincinnati girl — three in high-school already! Six! Think of that? Six children! I don't know what he'll say when he knows another one's coming! He'll probably blame *me* for it because a man always *does!* In spite of the fact that he *forced* me!

ELEVATOR BOY: *(grinning)* Did you say — a *baby,* Miss Collins?

MISS COLLINS: *(lowering her eyes but speaking with tenderness and pride)* Yes — I'm expecting a *child.*

ELEVATOR BOY: *Jeez! (He claps his hand over his mouth and turns away quickly.)*

MISS COLLINS: Even if it's not legitimate, I think it has a perfect right to its father's name — don't you?

PORTER: Yes. Sure, Miss Collins.

MISS COLLINS: A child is innocent and pure. No matter how it's conceived. And it must *not* be made to suffer! So I intend to dispose of the little property Cousin Ethel left me and give the child a private education where it won't come under the evil influence of the Christian church! I want to make sure that it doesn't grow up in the shadow of the cross and then have to walk along blocks that scorch you with terrible sunlight! *(The elevator buzzer sounds from the hall.)*

PORTER: Frank! Somebody wants to come up. *(The Elevator Boy goes out. The elevator door bangs shut. The Porter clears his throat.)* Yes, it'd be better — to go off some place else.

MISS COLLINS: If only I had the courage — but I don't. I've grown so used to it here, and people outside — it's always so *hard,* to *face* them!

PORTER: Maybe you won't — have to face nobody, Miss Collins. *(The elevator door clangs open.)*

MISS COLLINS: *(rising fearfully)* Is someone coming — here?

PORTER: You just take it easy, Miss Collins.

MISS COLLINS: If that's the officers coming for Richard, tell them to go away. I've decided not to prosecute Mr. Martin. (*Mr. Abrams enters with the Doctor and the Nurse. The Elevator Boy gawks from the doorway. The Doctor is the weary, professional type, the Nurse hard and efficient. Mr. Abrams is a small, kindly person, sincerely troubled by the situation.*)

MISS COLLINS: (*shrinking back, her voice faltering*) I've decided not to — prosecute Mr. Martin . . .

DOCTOR: Miss Collins?

MR. ABRAMS: (*with attempted heartiness*) Yes, this is the lady you wanted to meet, Dr. White.

DOCTOR: Hmmm. (*briskly to the Nurse*) Go in her bedroom and get a few things together.

NURSE: Yes, sir. (*She goes quickly across to the bedroom.*)

MISS COLLINS: (*fearfully shrinking*) Things?

DOCTOR: Yes, Miss Tyler will help you pack up an overnight bag. (*smiling mechanically*) A strange place always seems more homelike the first few days when we have a few of our little personal articles around us.

MISS COLLINS: A strange — place?

DOCTOR: (*carelessly, making a memorandum*) Don't be disturbed, Miss Collins.

MISS COLLINS: I know! (*excitedly*) You've come from the Holy Communion to place me under arrest! On moral charges!

MR. ABRAMS: Oh, no, Miss Collins, you got the wrong idea. This is a doctor who —

DOCTOR: (*impatiently*) Now, now, you're just going away for a while till things get straightened out. (*He glances at his watch.*) Two-twenty-five! Miss Tyler?

NURSE: Coming!

MISS COLLINS: (*with slow and sad comprehension*) Oh. . . . I'm going away. . . .

MR. ABRAMS: She was always a lady, Doctor, such a perfect lady.

DOCTOR: Yes. No doubt.

MR. ABRAMS: It seems too bad!

MISS COLLINS: Let me — write him a note. A pencil? Please?

MR. ABRAMS: Here, Miss Collins. (*She takes the pencil and crouches over the table. The Nurse comes out with a hard, forced smile, carrying a suitcase.*)

DOCTOR: Ready, Miss Tyler?

NURSE: All ready, Dr. White. (*She goes up to Miss Collins.*) Come along, dear, we can tend to that later!

MR. ABRAMS: (*sharply*) Let her finish the note!

MISS COLLINS: (*straightening with a frightened smile*) It's — finished.

NURSE: All right, dear, come along. (*She propels her firmly toward the door.*)

MISS COLLINS: (*turning suddenly back*) Oh, Mr. Abrams!

MR. ABRAMS: Yes, Miss Collins?

MISS COLLINS: If he should come again — and find me gone — I'd rather you didn't tell him — about the baby. . . . I think its better for *me* to tell him *that.* (*gently smiling*) You know how men *are*, don't you?

MR. ABRAMS: Yes, Miss Collins.

PORTER: Goodbye, Miss Collins. (*The Nurse pulls firmly at her arm. She smiles over her shoulder with a slight apologetic gesture.*)

MISS COLLINS: Mother will bring in – something cool – after while . . . (*She disappears down the hall with the Nurse. The elevator door clangs shut with the metallic sound of a locked cage. The wires hum.*)

MR. ABRAMS: She wrote him a note.

PORTER: What did she write, Mr. Abrams?

MR. ABRAMS: "Dear – Richard. I'm going away for a while. But don't worry, I'll be back. I have a secret to tell you. Love – Lucretia." (*He coughs.*) We got to clear out this stuff an' pile it down in the basement till I find out where it goes.

PORTER: (*dully*) Tonight, Mr. Abrams?

MR. ABRAMS: (*roughly to hide his feeling*) No, no, not tonight, you old fool. Enough has happened tonight! (*then gently*) We can do it tomorrow. Turn out that bedroom light – and close the window. (*Music playing softly becomes audible as the men go out slowly, closing the door, and the light fades out.*)

Curtain

[1945]

Robert Hayden

[1913-1980]

Robert Hayden was born Asa Bundy Sheffey on August 4, 1913, in Detroit, Michigan, to Asa Sheffey, a black laborer from Kentucky, and Ruth Finn Sheffey, a woman of mixed racial ancestry with theatrical ambitions. When Hayden was eighteen months old, his parents separated, and he was raised by an African American couple, William Hayden, a laborer, and Sue Ellen Hayden, a former maid. Although they never filed adoption papers, they rechristened the child Robert Earl Hayden. The Haydens, who were ill suited to one another and often without jobs, lived in a poor, primarily black section of Detroit called "Paradise Valley." As an escape from his difficult home life, Hayden read constantly, began writing stories, plays, and poems, and became actively involved in a dramatic group at the Second Baptist Church. When he was about sixteen, he began reading modern poetry, and he was especially drawn to the work of Carl Sandburg, Edna St. Vincent Millay, and the two most prominent poets of the Harlem

Robert Hayden

This undated photograph was probably taken around 1962, the year Hayden published his breakthrough collection, *A Ballad of Remembrance.*

Renaissance, Countee Cullen and Langston Hughes. With the help of a relative, Hayden also studied violin at the Detroit Institute of Musical Art. Because he was acutely nearsighted, he was sent to a special, predominantly white school during his senior year of high school. After he graduated in 1930, he published his first poem, "Africa," in a black literary magazine, *Abbot's Monthly*.

Like many of his contemporaries, Hayden struggled to support himself and his writing during the Great Depression and World War II. Living at home, he secured a tuition scholarship to study at Detroit City College (now Wayne State University), where he enrolled in 1932. Four years later, when he was only one credit hour short of graduation, he was forced to withdraw in order to find work. Because he met the legal requirement of pauperism, he got a job as a writer and researcher for the Federal Writers' Project in Detroit. From 1936 to 1940, Hayden conducted research on African American history, the subject of many of his later poems. He also began to take graduate courses at the University of Michigan in Ann Arbor, where he won a prize for a collection of his poems, *Heart-Shape in the Dust*, which was subsequently published by a local press in 1940. That year, he left home and married Erma Inez Morris, a pianist and music teacher who strongly encouraged Hayden's aspirations as a poet. In 1941, he became a full-time student at Michigan, where Hayden studied with his most influential mentor, the distinguished British poet W. H. Auden. Hayden was awarded another prize for an unpublished collection of poems, "The Black Spear," some of which had previously appeared in the influential anthology *The Negro Caravan* (1941), edited by Sterling Brown. Long unhappy with the Baptist fundamentalism in which he was raised, Hayden converted to the Bahá'í World Faith, a religion that promotes the unity of all human beings and world peace. In 1944, he was awarded an MA from Michigan, where he worked as a teaching assistant until he accepted a position as a professor of English at the historically black Fisk University in Nashville, Tennessee, in 1946.

Hayden did not achieve widespread recognition as a poet until the final years of his life. His first poem in a major literary magazine, a tribute to the nineteenth-century African American leader Frederick Douglass, appeared in the *Atlantic Monthly* in 1947. During the following fifteen years, however, Hayden published only three slim volumes of verse: *The Lion and the Archer* (1948), *Figure of Time* (1955), and *A Ballad of Remembrance* (1962), a collection of lyrics about his family and early life together with historical narratives about slavery and racial relations in the United States. That groundbreaking volume, which was published in London, won the Grand Prize for Poetry at the First World Festival of Negro Arts in Dakar, Senegal, in 1966, and Hayden was subsequently named the Poet Laureate of Senegal. Following the publication of his *Selected Poems* (1966), Hayden was finally noticed by critics and reviewers in the United States. Although his poetry was deeply rooted in the history and the experiences of African Americans, during the 1960s Hayden came into conflict with militants because of his refusal to write what he considered to be

Hayden was a consummate poet and a moral historian as well.
–Michael S. Harper

political propaganda or to define himself as a black poet, a role he rejected on aesthetic grounds and because his commitment to the universalism of the Bahá'í religion made it impossible for him to support separatist conceptions of racial art and identity. Hayden, who left Fisk to take a teaching position at the University of Michigan in 1969, enjoyed considerable success during the 1970s, publishing *Words in the Mourning Time* (1970), *The Night-Blooming Cereus* (1972), and *Angle of Ascent: New and Selected Poems* (1975). That year, he was elected Fellow of the Academy of American Poets, and in 1976 he became the first African American to be appointed Consultant in Poetry to the Library of Congress, a position later called Poet Laureate. Hayden died on February 25, 1980.

Hayden's "Middle Passage."   This poem was based on Hayden's research into the revolt aboard the *Amistad*, a Spanish ship transporting a group of kidnapped West Africans from the slave market of Havana, where they had been sold, to a sugar plantation farther along the coast of Cuba. On July 2, 1839, the captives, led by Cinqué, seized the ship, killing the captain, Ramón Ferrar, and three members of the crew. The Africans ordered the navigator and the surviving crew members to sail the ship back to Africa. But they steered northward, and the *Amistad* was captured by the U.S. Navy off the coast of Long Island and towed to New London, Connecticut. When the captives were charged with mutiny and murder, American abolitionists formed the Amistad Committee, which filed countercharges of kidnapping, assault, and false imprisonment on behalf of the Africans. The case ultimately went to the Supreme Court, where they were defended by former president John Quincy Adams, then a representative from Massachusetts. On March 9, 1841, the justices decided in favor of the captives, who were freed. The famous event — which was dramatized in Steven Spielberg's popular 1997 film *Amistad* — was an important, early victory in the antislavery movement in the United States. Hayden narrates the story through a variety of voices, including both captives and captors, integrating passages from court depositions and alluding to hymns, myths, and literary works. In an interview, Hayden later observed that "although the horrors of the slave trade are common to all [three parts of the poem], each section develops a particular aspect of this horror, focuses on a particular theme or incident." Hayden, who worked slowly and constantly revised his poems, first published "Middle Passage" in 1945 in *Phylon*, a journal for the study of race and culture founded by W. E. B. Du Bois. A revised version appeared in *Cross Section 1945*, edited by Edwin Seaver. The third and final version of "Middle Passage" appeared at the opening of a series of poems tracing the history of slavery in *A Ballad of Remembrance* (1962). The following text is that of the final version, as printed in Hayden's *Collected Poems* (1985).

bedfordstmartins.com/
americanlit for research
links on Hayden

MIDDLE PASSAGE[1]

I

Jesús, Estrella, Esperanza, Mercy:[2]

> Sails flashing to the wind like weapons,
> sharks following the moans the fever and the dying;
> horror the corposant and compass rose.[3]

Middle Passage: 5
> voyage through death
>   to life upon these shores.

> "10 April 1800 —
> Blacks rebellious. Crew uneasy. Our linguist says
> their moaning is a prayer for death,   10
> ours and their own. Some try to starve themselves,
> Lost three this morning leaped with crazy laughter
> to the waiting sharks, sang as they went under."

Desire, Adventure, Tartar, Ann:

> Standing to America, bringing home   15
> black gold, black ivory, black seed.

> > *Deep in the festering hold thy father lies,*
> > *of his bones New England pews are made,*
> > *those are altar lights that were his eyes.*[4]

Jesus   Saviour   Pilot   Me   20
Over   Life's   Tempestuous   Sea[5]

We pray that Thou wilt grant, O Lord,
safe passage to our vessels bringing
heathen souls unto Thy chastening.

---

1. **Middle Passage:** The name given to the route across the Atlantic Ocean taken by slave ships sailing from Africa to North or South America.

2. ***Jesús, Estrella, Esperanza, Mercy:*** The names of slave ships; *Estrella* means star and *Esperanza* means hope (Spanish).

3. **corposant and compass rose:** *Corposant* is an early term for the appearance of St. Elmo's fire — a brush discharge of electricity sometimes observable during foul weather — on a mast or other structure of a ship. A compass rose is a circular emblem showing the directions printed on a chart or map.

4. ***Deep . . . eyes:*** A reworking of a song from Shakespeare's *The Tempest*, in which the sprite Ariel seeks to comfort Prince Ferdinand, who believes that his father has drowned in a shipwreck, by singing: "Full Fathom five thy father lies, / Of his bones are coral made: / Those are pearls that were his eyes: / Nothing of him that doth fade, / But doth suffer a sea-change / Into something rich and strange" (1.2.397-402).

5. **Jesus . . . Sea:** The first two lines of a Protestant hymn, often called "The Sailor's Hymn," which was first published in the *Sailor's Magazine* (1871).

Jesus   Saviour   25

"8 bells. I cannot sleep, for I am sick
with fear, but writing eases fear a little
since still my eyes can see these words take shape
upon the page & so I write, as one
would turn to exorcism. 4 days scudding,   30
but now the sea is calm again. Misfortune
follows in our wake like sharks (our grinning
tutelary gods). Which one of us
has killed an albatross?[6] A plague among
our blacks — Ophthalmia: blindness — & we   35
have jettisoned the blind to no avail.
It spreads, the terrifying sickness spreads.
Its claws have scratched sight from the Capt.'s eyes
& there is blindness in the fo'c'sle[7]
& we must sail 3 weeks before we come   40
to port."

    What port awaits us, Davy Jones'
    or home? I've heard of slavers drifting, drifting,
    playthings of wind and storm and chance, their crews
    gone blind, the jungle hatred   45
    crawling up on deck.

Thou   Who   Walked   On   Galilee

"Deponent[8] further sayeth *The Bella J*
left the Guinea Coast
with cargo of five hundred blacks and odd   50
for the barracoons[9] of Florida:

"That there was hardly room 'tween-decks for half
the sweltering cattle stowed spoon-fashion there;
that some went mad of thirst and tore their flesh
and sucked the blood: 55

"That Crew and Captain lusted with the comeliest
of the savage girls kept naked in the cabins;
that there was one they called The Guinea Rose
and they cast lots and fought to lie with her:

---

6. albatross: Sailors believed that killing one of these large oceanic birds brought bad luck.
7. fo'c'sle: Forecastle, the forward part of a ship below the deck, used as the crew's living quarters.
8. Deponent: A legal term for a person who makes a deposition under oath.
9. barracoons: Crude enclosures where captives were held before being sold in the slave markets.

"That when the Bo's'n piped all hands,[10] the flames 60
spreading from starboard already were beyond
control, the negroes howling and their chains
entangled with the flames:

"That the burning blacks could not be reached,
that the Crew abandoned ship, 65
leaving their shrieking negresses behind,
that the Captain perished drunken with the wenches:

"Further Deponent sayeth not."

Pilot   Oh   Pilot   Me

II

Aye, lad, and I have seen those factories, 70
Gambia, Rio Pongo, Calabar;[11]
have watched the artful mongos[12] baiting traps
of war wherein the victor and the vanquished

Were caught as prizes for our barracoons.
Have seen the nigger kings whose vanity 75
and greed turned wild black hides of Fellatah,
Mandingo, Ibo, Kru[13] to gold for us.

And there was one — King Anthracite we named him —
fetish face beneath French parasols
of brass and orange velvet, impudent mouth 80
whose cups were carven skulls of enemies:

He'd honor us with drum and feast and conjo
and palm-oil-glistening wenches deft in love,
and for tin crowns that shone with paste,
red calico and German-silver trinkets 85

Would have the drums talk war and send
his warriors to burn the sleeping villages
and kill the sick and old and lead the young
in coffles[14] to our factories.

---

10. **Bo's'n piped all hands:** The boatswain manages the equipment and the crew, or "hands," whom he calls to work with a pipe, or whistle.
11. **Gambia, Rio Pongo, Calabar:** Gambia is a small country in West Africa on the coast of the Atlantic Ocean; the Rio Pongo is an important commercial river in West Africa; and Calabar is a coastal city in Nigeria.
12. **mongos:** One of the largest ethnic groups of the African country known today as the Democratic Republic of the Congo.
13. **Fellatah, Mandingo, Ibo, Kru:** The names of African tribes.
14. **coffles:** A line of slaves, prisoners, or animals, fastened together.

Twenty years a trader, twenty years,   90
for there was wealth aplenty to be harvested
from those black fields, and I'd be trading still
but for the fevers melting down my bones.

III[15]

Shuttles in the rocking loom of history,
the dark ships move, the dark ships move,   95
their bright ironical names
like jests of kindness on a murderer's mouth;
plough through thrashing glister toward
fata morgana's[16] lucent melting shore,
weave toward New World littorals[17] that are   100
mirage and myth and actual shore.

Voyage through death,
                    voyage whose chartings are unlove.

A charnel stench, effluvium of living death
spreads outward from the hold,   105
where the living and the dead, the horribly dying,
lie interlocked, lie foul with blood and excrement.

    Deep in the festering hold thy father lies,
    the corpse of mercy rots with him,
    rats eat love's rotten gelid eyes.   110

    But, oh, the living look at you
    with human eyes whose suffering accuses you,
    whose hatred reaches through the swill of dark
    to strike you like a leper's claw.

    You cannot stare that hatred down   115
    or chain the fear that stalks the watches
    and breathes on you its fetid scorching breath;

---

15. III: Part III follows, in the main, the account of the *Amistad* mutiny given by Muriel Rukeyser in her biography of Willard Gibbs [Hayden's note]. Rukeyser (1913–1980), an American poet and political activist, wrote *Willard Gibbs: American Genius* (1942), a biography of the nineteenth-century mathematician and physicist. In the second chapter of the book, Rukeyser tells the story of his father, also named Josiah Willard Gibbs, an abolitionist, linguist, and professor of theology at Yale University. Because the *Amistad* captives could not speak English, Gibbs learned to count to ten in their Mende language. He then went from boat to boat in the New York harbor, repeating the numbers in Mende until he found a sailor and former slave, James Covey, who could translate for the captives. Gibbs was also a defense witness at the trial of the captives in New Haven, Connecticut.
16. fata morgana: Literally "fairy Morgan" (Italian), a mirage at sea originally attributed to the enchantress Morgan Le Fay.
17. littorals: Areas of land along a coast.

cannot kill the deep immortal human wish,
the timeless will.

"But for the storm that flung up barriers   120
of wind and wave, *The Amistad*,[18] señores,
would have reached the port of Príncipe[19] in two,
three days at most; but for the storm we should
have been prepared for what befell.
Swift as the puma's leap it came. There was   125
that interval of moonless calm filled only
with the water's and the rigging's usual sounds,
then sudden movement, blows and snarling cries
and they had fallen on us with machete
and marlinspike. It was as though the very   130
air, the night itself were striking us.
Exhausted by the rigors of the storm,
we were no match for them. Our men went down
before the murderous Africans. Our loyal
Celestino[20] ran from below with gun   135
and lantern and I saw, before the cane-
knife's wounding flash, Cinquez,[21]
that surly brute who calls himself a prince,
directing, urging on the ghastly work.
He hacked the poor mulatto down, and then   140
he turned on me. The decks were slippery
when daylight finally came. It sickens me
to think of what I saw, of how these apes
threw overboard the butchered bodies of
our men, true Christians all, like so much jetsam.   145
Enough, enough. The rest is quickly told:
Cinquez was forced to spare the two of us
you see to steer the ship to Africa,
and we like phantoms doomed to rove the sea
voyaged east by day and west by night,   150
deceiving them, hoping for rescue,
prisoners on our own vessel, till
at length we drifted to the shores of this
your land, America, where we were freed

---

18. ***The Amistad:*** The Spanish slave ship that was the scene of the famous slave rebellion in 1839.
19. **Príncipe:** Port Príncipe in Cuba was the original destination of the *Amistad.*
20. **Celestino:** A "mulatto" slave owned by the ship's captain who worked as a cook aboard the *Amistad.*
21. **Cinquez:** Sengbe Pieh (known as *Cinquez* or *Cinqué*), a member of the Mende tribe, was kidnapped and sold into slavery in West Africa in 1839. He led the revolt aboard the *Amistad.*

from our unspeakable misery. Now we   155
demand, good sirs, the extradition of
Cinquez and his accomplices to La
Havana.[22] And it distresses us to know
there are so many here who seem inclined
to justify the mutiny of these blacks.   160
We find it paradoxical indeed
that you whose wealth, whose tree of liberty
are rooted in the labor of your slaves
should suffer the august John Quincy Adams[23]
to speak with so much passion of the right   165
of chattel slaves to kill their lawful masters
and with his Roman rhetoric weave a hero's
garland for Cinquez. I tell you that
we are determined to return to Cuba
with our slaves and there see justice done. Cinquez —   170
or let us say 'the Prince' — Cinquez shall die."

The deep immortal human wish,
the timeless will:

Cinquez its deathless primaveral[24] image,
life that transfigures many lives.   175

Voyage through death
            to life upon these shores.

[1962, 1996]

---

22. **La Havana:** Havana, Cuba.
23. **John Quincy Adams:** The congressman from Massachusetts and former president helped defend the surviving captives of the *Amistad* when their case went before the Supreme Court in 1841.
24. **primaveral:** A rare, figurative term for the early springtime.

Tillie Olsen

[1912?–2007]

Tillie Olsen was the second of six children born to Samuel and Ida Beber Lerner, Socialists and Jewish immigrants who fled Russia after the failed revolution of 1905. They did not obtain a birth certificate for their daughter, who was born in 1912 or 1913, probably in rural Nebraska. Olsen's father worked at a series of menial jobs in order to support his family, which moved frequently before settling in Omaha. A committed radical, he went to Tulsa, Oklahoma, to help African Americans rebuild their houses

Tillie Olsen — a writer of such generosity and honesty, she literally saves lives.

–Alice Walker

Tillie Olsen

This photograph of Olsen was taken during the long hiatus in her writing career, in 1941, when she was the president of the Parent Teacher Association (PTA) of an elementary school in San Francisco.

after the devastating race riot there in 1920, and he served for several years as the state secretary of the Nebraska Socialist Party. Olsen revered her hard-working, illiterate mother, whom she later described as "one of the most eloquent and one of the most brilliant human beings I've ever known." As a child, Olsen was deeply inspired by a speech delivered in Omaha by the labor leader and five-time Socialist Party presidential candidate Eugene V. Debs, who declared that "under socialism society would be like a great symphony with each person playing his own instrument." Olsen, who attended public schools, was a voracious reader of works ranging from the poetry of Edna St. Vincent Millay, Carl Sandburg, and Walt Whitman to the novels of Jack London, Upton Sinclair, and the South African feminist Olive Schreiner.

Olsen's own writings were strongly shaped by her difficult experiences as a radical, working-class woman with limited education and few prospects. In 1929, after she completed the eleventh grade, she left high school to go to work. Two years later, she joined the Young Communist League in Kansas City, Missouri, where she was jailed for a month after handing out leaflets to workers in a packinghouse. In 1932, ill and impoverished, she moved to a relative's home in Fairbault, Minnesota. She became pregnant and gave birth to her first daughter, Karla, named for Karl Marx. Olsen also began working on *Yonnondio*, a novel about the exploitation and struggles of a working-class family during the Great Depression. Olsen took her newborn to California in 1933, eventually settling in San Francisco. There, she met Jack Olsen, a longshoreman and labor organizer who was also involved in the Young Communist League. With him, Olsen was arrested and jailed during the violent San Francisco maritime strike of 1934. While she was serving her sentence, her story "The Iron Throat," the first chapter of her novel in progress, was published in the *Partisan Review*. The magazine subsequently published her essay "The Strike," and two essays she wrote about her arrest and sentencing appeared in another progressive magazine, the *New Republic*. The prominent New York publishing firm Random House offered her a monthly stipend to complete her novel, but Olsen abandoned the project and virtually ceased writing in order to devote herself to radical causes and the care of her family. In 1936, she and Jack Olsen began living together – they were married in 1943, when he was drafted into the army – and had three daughters between 1938 and 1948. Olsen also worked at various jobs, including stints as a waitress, a secretary, a meatpacker, and a punch-press operator.

During the 1950s, Olsen returned to writing, and her work subsequently gained considerable critical attention. She took a creative-writing course at San Francisco State College in 1953, about the time she began to write what became one of her most famous stories, "I Stand Here Ironing." An early version of the story won her a Wallace Stegner Fellowship at Stanford University in 1956, and Olsen received a Ford Foundation Grant in 1959. Olsen's other most famous story, "Tell Me a Riddle," won first prize in the O'Henry Awards for the best American short stories of 1961. That year, at the age of fifty, she published her first book, *Tell Me a Riddle* (1961). In recognition of her achievement in that acclaimed collection of stories, the prestigious $25,000 Rea Award for Short Fiction was later bestowed on Olsen, who in the words of the citation "had forced open the language of the short story, insisting that it include the domestic life of women, the passions and anguishes of maternity, the deep, gnarled roots of a long marriage, the hopes and frustrations of immigration, the shining charge of political commitment." Beginning in the early 1970s, Olsen was a writer in residence and visiting professor at a series of colleges and universities, including Amherst, Kenyon, MIT, Stanford, and UCLA. After her husband found the manuscript of her early, unfinished novel, Olsen edited but did not revise or complete the manuscript, which was published as *Yonnondio: From the Thirties* (1974). She wrote *Silences* (1978), a collection of essays and meditations on silences in literary history, including the silenced voices of women who "never came to writing," and edited a collection that included her own tribute to her mother, *Mother to Daughter, Daughter to Mother* (1984). Olsen continued to teach, give lectures, and collect a growing number of awards and honorary degrees until her death on January 1, 2007.

Olsen's "I Stand Here Ironing."   This story, which was first published in 1956 as "Help Her to Believe" in a California magazine, the *Pacific Spectator*, was subsequently selected for inclusion in *The Best American Short Stories of 1957*. Olsen later changed its title and placed the story at the opening of her collection *Tell Me a Riddle* (1961). Concerned with the challenges of poverty, the demands of motherhood, the needs of children, and the plight of the woman writer, the semiautobiographical "I Stand Here Ironing" is one of Olsen's most admired and frequently anthologized stories. In her essay "Silences in Literature" (1962), Olsen explained the circumstances of writing the story, "which I was somehow able to carry around within me, through work, through home," in the early 1950s: "Time on the bus, even when I had to stand, was enough; the stolen moments at work, enough; the deep night hours for as long as I could stay awake, after the kids were in bed, after the household tasks were done, sometimes during. It is no accident that the first work I considered publishable began: 'I stand here ironing, and what you asked me moves tormented back and forth with the iron.'" The text is taken from *Tell Me a Riddle* (1961).

bedfordstmartins.com/ americanlit for research links on Olsen

I STAND HERE IRONING

I stand here ironing, and what you asked me moves tormented back and forth with the iron.

"I wish you would manage the time to come in and talk with me about your daughter. I'm sure you can help me understand her. She's a youngster who needs help and whom I'm deeply interested in helping."

"Who needs help." . . . Even if I came, what good would it do? You think because I am her mother I have a key, or that in some way you could use me as a key? She has lived for nineteen years. There is all that life that has happened outside of me, beyond me.

And when is there time to remember, to sift, to weigh, to estimate, to total? I will start and there will be an interruption and I will have to gather it all together again. Or I will become engulfed with all I did or did not do, with what should have been and what cannot be helped.

She was a beautiful baby. The first and only one of our five that was beautiful at birth. You do not guess how new and uneasy her tenancy in her now-loveliness. You did not know her all those years she was thought homely, or see her poring over her baby pictures, making me tell her over and over how beautiful she had been — and would be, I would tell her — and was now, to the seeing eye. But the seeing eyes were few or non-existent. Including mine.

I nursed her. They feel that's important nowadays. I nursed all the children, but with her, with all the fierce rigidity of first motherhood, I did like the books then said. Though her cries battered me to trembling and my breasts ached with swollenness, I waited till the clock decreed.

Why do I put that first? I do not even know if it matters, or if it explains anything.

She was a beautiful baby. She blew shining bubbles of sound. She loved motion, loved light, loved color and music and textures. She would lie on the floor in her blue overalls patting the surface so hard in ecstasy her hands and feet would blur. She was a miracle to me, but when she was eight months old I had to leave her daytimes with the woman downstairs to whom she was no miracle at all, for I worked or looked for work and for Emily's father, who "could no longer endure" (he wrote in his good-bye note) "sharing want with us."

I was nineteen. It was the pre-relief, pre-WPA world of the depression.[1] I would start running as soon as I got off the streetcar, running up the stairs, the place smelling sour, and awake or asleep to startle awake, when she saw me she would break into a clogged weeping that could not be comforted, a weeping I can hear yet.

After a while I found a job hashing[2] at night so I could be with her days, and it was better. But it came to where I had to bring her to his family and leave her.

It took a long time to raise the money for her fare back. Then she got chicken pox and I had to wait longer. When she finally came, I hardly knew her, walking quick and nervous like her father, looking like her father, thin, and dressed in a shoddy red that yellowed her skin and glared at the pockmarks. All the baby loveliness gone.

She was two. Old enough for nursery school they said, and I did not know then what I know now — the fatigue of the long day, and the lacerations of group life in the kinds of nurseries that are only parking places for children.

Except that it would have made no difference if I had known. It was the only place there was. It was the only way we could be together, the only way I could hold a job.

---

1. **It was the pre-relief . . . depression:** In May 1935, President Franklin D. Roosevelt created a massive relief agency, the Works Progress Administration (WPA), which provided jobs to the unemployed during the Great Depression. Millions worked on public construction projects and cultural programs sponsored by the various divisions of the WPA.
2. **hashing:** Serving food in a café or diner.

And even without knowing, I knew. I knew the teacher that was evil because all these years it has curdled into my memory, the little boy hunched in the corner, her rasp, "why aren't you outside, because Alvin hits you? that's no reason, go out, scaredy." I knew Emily hated it even if she did not clutch and implore "don't go Mommy" like the other children, mornings.

She always had a reason why we should stay home. Momma, you look sick, Momma. I feel sick. Momma, the teachers aren't there today, they're sick. Momma, we can't go, there was a fire there last night. Momma, it's a holiday today, no school, they told me.

But never a direct protest, never rebellion. I think of our others in their three-, four-year-oldness – the explosions, the tempers, the denunciations, the demands – and I feel suddenly ill. I put the iron down. What in me demanded that goodness in her? And what was the cost, the cost to her of such goodness?

The old man living in the back once said in his gentle way: "You should smile at Emily more when you look at her." What *was* in my face when I looked at her? I loved her. There were all the acts of love.

It was only with the others I remembered what he said, and it was the face of joy, and not of care or tightness or worry I turned to them – too late for Emily. She does not smile easily, let alone almost always as her brothers and sisters do. Her face is closed and sombre, but when she wants, how fluid. You must have seen it in her pantomimes, you spoke of her rare gift for comedy on the stage that rouses a laughter out of the audience so dear they applaud and applaud and do not want to let her go.

Where does it come from, that comedy? There was none of it in her when she came back to me that second time, after I had had to send her away again. She had a new daddy now to learn to love, and I think perhaps it was a better time.

Except when we left her alone nights, telling ourselves she was old enough.

"Can't you go some other time, Mommy, like tomorrow?" she would ask. "Will it be just a little while you'll be gone? Do you promise?"

The time we came back, the front door open, the clock on the floor in the hall. She rigid awake. "It wasn't just a little while. I didn't cry. Three times I called you, just three times, and then I ran downstairs to open the door so you could come faster. The clock talked loud. I threw it away, it scared me what it talked."

She said the clock talked loud again that night I went to the hospital to have Susan. She was delirious with the fever that comes before red measles, but she was fully conscious all the week I was gone and the week after we were home when she could not come near the new baby or me.

She did not get well. She stayed skeleton thin, not wanting to eat, and night after night she had nightmares. She would call for me, and I would rouse from exhaustion to sleepily call back: "You're all right, darling, go to sleep, it's just a dream," and if she still called, in a sterner voice, "now go to sleep, Emily, there's nothing to hurt you." Twice, only twice, when I had to get up for Susan anyhow, I went in to sit with her.

Now when it is too late (as if she would let me hold and comfort her like I do the others) I get up and go to her at once at her moan or restless stirring. "Are you awake, Emily? Can I get you something?" And the answer is always the same: "No, I'm all right, go back to sleep, Mother."

They persuaded me at the clinic to send her away to a convalescent home in the country where "she can have the kind of food and care you can't manage for her, and you'll be free to concentrate on the new baby." They still send children to that place. I see pictures on the society page of sleek young women planning affairs to raise money for it, or dancing at the affairs, or decorating Easter eggs or filling Christmas stockings for the children.

They never have a picture of the children so I do not know if the girls still wear those gigantic red bows and the ravaged looks on the every other Sunday when parents can come to visit "unless otherwise notified" — as we were notified the first six weeks.

Oh it is a handsome place, green lawns and tall trees and fluted flower beds. High up on the balconies of each cottage the children stand, the girls in their red bows and white dresses, the boys in white suits and giant red ties. The parents stand below shrieking up to be heard and the children shriek down to be heard, and between them the invisible wall "Not To Be Contaminated by Parental Germs or Physical Affection."

There was a tiny girl who always stood hand in hand with Emily. Her parents never came. One visit she was gone. "They moved her to Rose Cottage" Emily shouted in explanation. "They don't like you to love anybody here."

She wrote once a week, the labored writing of a seven-year-old. "I am fine. How is the baby. If I write my leter nicly I will have a star. Love." There never was a star. We wrote every other day, letters she could never hold or keep but only hear read — once. "We simply do not have room for children to keep any personal possessions," they patiently explained when we pieced one Sunday's shrieking together to plead how much it would mean to Emily, who loved so to keep things, to be allowed to keep her letters and cards.

Each visit she looked frailer. "She isn't eating," they told us.

(They had runny eggs for breakfast or mush with lumps, Emily said later, I'd hold it in my mouth and not swallow. Nothing ever tasted good, just when they had chicken.)

It took us eight months to get her released home, and only the fact that she gained back so little of her seven lost pounds convinced the social worker.

I used to try to hold and love her after she came back, but her body would stay stiff, and after a while she'd push away. She ate little. Food sickened her, and I think much of life too. Oh she had physical lightness and brightness, twinkling by on skates, bouncing like a ball up and down up and down over the jump rope, skimming over the hill; but these were momentary.

She fretted about her appearance, thin and dark and foreign-looking at a time when every little girl was supposed to look or thought she should look a chubby blonde replica of Shirley Temple. The doorbell sometimes rang for her, but no one seemed to come and play in the house or be a best friend. Maybe because we moved so much.

There was a boy she loved painfully through two school semesters. Months later she told me how she had taken pennies from my purse to buy him candy. "Licorice was his favorite and I brought him some every day, but he still liked Jennifer better'n me. Why, Mommy?" The kind of question for which there is no answer.

School was a worry to her. She was not glib or quick in a world where glibness and quickness were easily confused with ability to learn. To her overworked and exasperated teachers she was an overconscientious "slow learner" who kept trying to catch up and was absent entirely too often.

I let her be absent, though sometimes the illness was imaginary. How different from my now-strictness about attendance with the others. I wasn't working. We had a new baby, I was home anyhow. Sometimes, after Susan grew old enough. I would keep her home from school, too, to have them all together.

Mostly Emily had asthma, and her breathing, harsh and labored, would fill the house with a curiously tranquil sound. I would bring the two old dresser mirrors and her boxes of collections to her bed. She would select beads and single earrings, bottle tops and shells, dried flowers and pebbles, old postcards and scraps, all sorts of oddments; then she and Susan would play Kingdom, setting up landscapes and furniture, peopling them with action.

Those were the only times of peaceful companionship between her and Susan. I have edged away from it, that poisonous feeling between them, that terrible balancing of hurts and needs I had to do between the two, and did so badly, those earlier years.

Oh there are conflicts between the others too, each one human, needing, demanding, hurting, taking – but only between Emily and Susan, no, Emily toward Susan that corroding resentment. It seems so obvious on the surface, yet it is not obvious. Susan, the second child, Susan, golden- and curly-haired and chubby, quick and articulate and assured, everything in appearance and manner Emily was not; Susan, not able to resist Emily's precious things, losing or sometimes clumsily breaking them; Susan telling jokes and riddles to company for applause while Emily sat silent (to say to me later: that was *my* riddle, Mother, I told it to Susan); Susan, who for all the five years' difference in age was just a year behind Emily in developing physically.

I am glad for that slow physical development that widened the difference between her and her contemporaries, though she suffered over it. She was too vulnerable for that terrible world of youthful competition, of preening and parading, of constant measuring of yourself against every other, of envy, "If I had that copper hair," "If I had that skin. . . ." She tormented herself enough about not looking like the others, there was enough of the unsureness, the having to be conscious of words before you speak, the constant caring – what are they thinking of me? without having it all magnified by the merciless physical drives.

Ronnie is calling. He is wet and I change him. It is rare there is such a cry now. That time of motherhood is almost behind me when the ear is not one's own but must always be racked and listening for the child cry, the child call. We sit for a while and I hold him, looking out over the city spread in charcoal with its soft aisles of light. *"Shoogily,"* he breathes and curls closer. I carry him back to bed, asleep. *Shoogily.* A funny word, a family word, inherited from Emily, invented by her to say: *comfort.*

In this and other ways she leaves her seal, I say aloud. And startle at my saying it. What do I mean? What did I start to gather together, to try and make coherent? I was at the terrible, growing years. War years. I do not remember them well. I was working, there were four smaller ones now, there was not time for her. She had to help be a mother, and housekeeper, and shopper. She had to set her seal. Mornings of crisis and near hysteria trying to get lunches packed, hair combed, coats and shoes found, every-one to school or Child Care on time, the baby ready for transportation. And always the paper scribbled on by a smaller one, the book looked at by Susan then mislaid, the home-work not done. Running out to that huge school where she was one, she was lost, she was a drop; suffering over the unpreparedness, stammering and unsure in her classes.

There was so little time left at night after the kids were bedded down. She would struggle over books, always eating (it was in those years she developed her enormous appetite that is legendary in our family) and I would be ironing, or preparing food for the next day, or writing-V-mail[3] to Bill, or tending the baby. Sometimes, to make me laugh, or out of her despair, she would imitate happenings or types at school.

I think I said once: "Why don't you do something like this in the school amateur show?" One morning she phoned me at work, hardly understandable through the weep-ing: "Mother, I did it. I won, I won; they gave me first prize; they clapped and clapped and wouldn't let me go."

Now suddenly she was Somebody, and as imprisoned in her difference as she had been in anonymity.

She began to be asked to perform at other high schools, even in colleges, then at city and statewide affairs. The first one we went to, I only recognized her that first moment when thin, shy, she almost drowned herself into the curtains. Then: Was this Emily? The control, the command, the convulsing and deadly clowning, the spell, then the roaring, stamping audience, unwilling to let this rare and precious laughter out of their lives.

Afterwards: You ought to do something about her with a gift like that — but without money or knowing how, what does one do? We have left it all to her, and the gift has as often eddied inside, clogged and clotted, as been used and growing.

She is coming. She runs up the stairs two at a time with her light graceful step, and I know she is happy tonight. Whatever it was that occasioned your call did not happen today.

"Aren't you ever going to finish the ironing, Mother? Whistler painted his mother in a rocker.[4] I'd have to paint mine standing over an ironing board." This is one of her com-municative nights and she tells me everything and nothing as she fixes herself a plate of food out of the icebox.

She is so lovely. Why did you want me to come in at all? Why were you concerned? She will find her way.

She starts up the stairs to bed. "Don't get me up with the rest in the morning." "But I thought you were having midterms." "Oh, those," she comes back in, kisses me, and says quite lightly, "in a couple of years when we'll all be atom-dead they won't matter a bit."

---

3. **V-mail:** Victory mail, letters written on small forms (with space for roughly 100–300 words) that were delivered at no charge to members of the American armed forces stationed overseas during World War II.
4. **Whistler . . . in a rocker:** The American artist James McNeill Whistler (1834–1903) painted *Arrangement in Grey and Black: The Artist's Mother* (1871), a famous portrait of his mother seated in a rocking chair, commonly known as *Whistler's Mother*.

She has said it before. She *believes* it. But because I have been dredging the past, and all that compounds a human being is so heavy and meaningful in me, I cannot endure it tonight.

I will never total it all. I will never come in to say: She was a child seldom smiled at. Her father left me before she was a year old. I had to work her first six years when there was work, or I sent her home and to his relatives. There were years she had care she hated. She was dark and thin and foreign-looking in a world where the prestige went to blondeness and curly hair and dimples, she was slow where glibness was prized. She was a child of anxious, not proud, love. We were poor and could not afford for her the soil of easy growth. I was a young mother, I was a distracted mother. There were the other children pushing up, demanding. Her younger sister seemed all that she was not. There were years she did not want me to touch her. She kept too much in herself, her life was such she had to keep too much in herself. My wisdom came too late. She has much to her and probably little will come of it. She is a child of her age, of depression, of war, of fear.

Let her be. So all that is in her will not bloom — but in how many does it? There is still enough left to live by. Only help her to know — help make it so there is cause for her to know — that she is more than this dress on the ironing board, helpless before the iron.

[1956, 1961]

John Berryman

[1914–1972]

John Berryman was born John Allyn Smith on October 25, 1914. He was the son of Martha Little Smith, a former schoolteacher, and Allyn Smith, a bank manager in McAlester, Oklahoma. Berryman's father either resigned or was dismissed from the bank early in 1926, and he moved the family to Tampa, Florida. Despite the business boom there, Allyn Smith had little success and became so deeply depressed that he committed suicide by shooting himself on June 26, 1926. The trauma of his father's death haunted Berryman for the rest of his life. Later that year, his mother remarried and he took the last name of his stepfather, John Angus Berryman, their landlord in Florida. The new family moved to New York City, where Berryman's stepfather took a job as a bond salesman on Wall Street. Berryman was sent to a private boarding school in Connecticut. A rather withdrawn, slender, nearsighted boy, Berryman suffered from bullying and teasing because of his poor performance in sports, a major part of the school's program. But he excelled at his academic work and won a partial scholarship

Like their hero, durable and battered Henry, The Dream Songs *are open everywhere; open, at the risk of total breakdown, to nothing less than the life that breathed them.*
–Adrienne Rich

at Columbia University, where he enrolled in 1932. He took classes with the poet and critic Mark Van Doren, whose encouragement and example "made me a poet," as Berryman later said. He published his first poems as well as reviews in the *Columbia Review*. After his graduation in 1936, he was awarded a fellowship for study at Cambridge University in England, where he met the prominent British poets W. H. Auden and Dylan Thomas.

After Berryman returned to the United States in 1938, he supported himself by teaching while pursuing a literary career. He worked briefly as the poetry editor of the *Nation* until he accepted a position at Wayne State

John Berryman

Terence Spencer took this photograph in May 1957, when Berryman was at work on his ambitious poetic sequence *The Dream Songs* (1969).

University in Detroit, Michigan, in 1939. There, he became close friends with Bhain Campbell, a fellow poet whose death from cancer in 1940, at the age of only twenty-nine, was another traumatic loss for Berryman. Later that year, he accepted a position as an instructor at Harvard University. Twenty of his poems first appeared in *Five Young American Poets* (1940) and then in Berryman's first book, *Poems* (1942). But he was still struggling to find his own poetic voice, and the collection revealed the strong influence of Auden and the Irish poet William Butler Yeats. Berryman married Eileen Mulligan in 1942, the year before he became an instructor at Princeton University. During his years there, he met and became friends with a number of writers, including Robert Lowell and Saul Bellow. Although Berryman achieved considerable success as a teacher, he suffered from bouts of insecurity and began drinking heavily. One of the first of his many extramarital affairs, with the wife of a Princeton graduate student, inspired a remarkable series of poems, Berryman's finest work to that point in his career. But he did not publish them until twenty years later, in *Berryman's Sonnets* (1967), and he received mixed reviews for the dense and difficult poems in his collection *The Dispossessed* (1948). He also published critical and scholarly work on a wide range of writers, including "The Poetry of Ezra Pound" (1949), an influential essay on the controversial poet, and *Stephen Crane: A Critical Biography* (1950).

During the last two decades of his life, Berryman finally established himself as a major poet. Awarded his first Guggenheim Fellowship in 1952, he completed work on a poem inspired by the life and writings of the seventeenth-century American poet Anne Bradstreet, *Homage to Mistress Bradstreet*, which was published in the *Partisan Review* in 1953 and as a book in 1956. The influential critic Edmund Wilson called it "the most distinguished long poem by an American since [T. S. Eliot's] *The Waste Land*"

(1922). Despite his fame and now secure position as one of the foremost poets of his generation, Berryman continued to struggle with anxiety and alcohol. His wife left him in 1953, and the following year he was arrested and jailed for disorderly conduct while teaching at the Writers' Workshop at the University of Iowa. Dismissed from his position there, he accepted an invitation to teach at the University of Minnesota. In 1956, following his divorce, he married Elizabeth Ann Levine. After the birth of their son, they divorced in 1959, and Berryman married his third wife, Kathleen Donohue, in 1961. The couple had two daughters. Meanwhile, he worked on his most ambitious poetic project, an ongoing sequence of semiauto-biographical poems he called "Dream Songs," which were published in book form as *77 Dream Songs* (1964) and a sequel, *His Toy, His Dream, His Rest* (1968). The complete sequence appeared as *The Dream Songs* in 1969, the year Berryman was awarded the prestigious Bollingen Prize in Poetry. In the view of most critics, he failed to sustain the intensity of those poems in his final collections, *Love and Fame* (1970) and *Delusions, Etc.* (1972), which was published a few months after Berryman committed suicide in Minneapolis by jumping off the Washington Avenue Bridge into the Mississippi River on January 7, 1972.

Berryman's *Dream Songs.*   Berryman, who had become interested in dream analysis, conceived of this poetic sequence in April 1955. Some of the earliest of his "Dream Songs" were published in England in the *Times Literary Supplement*, and many of the poems subsequently appeared in American magazines such as the *Atlantic*, *Harper's*, and *Poetry*. Although he did not adhere to his original plan of writing a poem every two days, the final sequence included 385 numbered poems in *The Dream Songs*. Most critics viewed the antihero of the seemingly confessional poems as a thinly veiled portrait of Berryman. In a prefatory note to *The Dream Songs*, however, he explained that the sequence "is essentially about an imaginary character (not the poet, not me) named Henry, a white American in early middle age sometimes in blackface, who has suffered an irreversible loss and talks about himself sometimes in the first person, sometimes in the third, sometimes even in the second; he has a friend, never named, who addresses him as Mr. Bones and variants thereof." Whatever their status as autobiography may be, *The Dream Songs* are remarkable for Berryman's stylistic innovations. In his speech accepting the National Book Award, he stated: "I set up *The Dream Songs* as hostile to every visible tendency in both American and English poetry." Although almost all of the poems of the sequence are composed of three, six-line stanzas, they are characterized by their unconventional colloquial diction — including what Berryman called the "coon talk" derived from the offensive tradition of black-faced minstrelsy — as well as by their fractured syntax and unconventional rhythms. The texts of the poems selected here are taken from *The Dream Songs* (1969).

bedfordstmartins.com/ americanlit for research links on Berryman

1

Huffy Henry hid   the day,
unappeasable Henry sulked.
I see his point, — a trying to put things over.
It was the thought that they thought
they could *do* it made Henry wicked and away.   5
But he should have come out and talked.

All the world like a woolen lover
once did seem on Henry's side.
Then came a departure.
Thereafter nothing fell out as it might or ought.   10
I don't see how Henry, pried
open for all the world to see, survived.

What he has now to say is a long
wonder the world can bear & be.
Once in a sycamore I was glad   15
all at the top, and I sang.
Hard on the land wears the strong sea
and empty grows every bed.

                            [1959, 1964, 1969]

4

Filling her compact & delicious body
with chicken páprika, she glanced at me
twice.
Fainting with interest, I hungered back
and only the fact of her husband & four other people   5
kept me from springing on her

or falling at her little feet and crying
"You are the hottest one for years of night
Henry's dazed eyes
have enjoyed, Brilliance." I advanced upon   10
(despairing) my spumoni. — Sir Bones: is stuffed,
de world, wif feeding girls.

— Black hair, complexion Latin, jewelled eyes
downcast . . . The slob beside her   feasts . . . What wonders is
she sitting on, over there?   15
The restaurant buzzes. She might as well be on Mars.
Where did it all go wrong? There ought to be a law against Henry.
— Mr. Bones: there is.

                            [1963, 1964, 1969]

14

Life, friends, is boring. We must not say so.
After all, the sky flashes, the great sea yearns,
we ourselves flash and yearn,
and moreover my mother told me as a boy
(repeatingly) "Ever to confess you're bored   5
means you have no

Inner Resources." I conclude now I have no
inner resources, because I am heavy bored.
Peoples bore me,
literature bores me, especially great literature,   10
Henry bores me, with his plights & gripes
as bad as achilles,[1]

who loves people and valiant art, which bores me.
And the tranquil hills, & gin, look like a drag
and somehow a dog   15
has taken itself & its tail considerably away
into mountains or sea or sky, leaving
behind: me, wag.

                                        [1963, 1964, 1969]

_____

1. **achilles:** The Greek warrior Achilles, the hero of Homer's *Iliad* (eighth century BCE), sulked in his tent and temporarily refused to fight after he was insulted by Agamemnon, the leader of the Greeks in the Trojan War.

26

The glories of the world struck me, made me aria,[1] once.
— What happen then, Mr Bones?
if be you cares to say.
— Henry. Henry became interested in women's bodies,
his loins were & were the   scene of stupendous achievement.   5
Stupor. Knees, dear. Pray.

All the knobs & softnesses of, my God,
the ducking & trouble it swarm on Henry,
at one time.
— What happen then, Mr Bones?   10
you seems excited-like.
— Fell Henry back into   the original crime: art, rime

besides a sense of others, my God, my God,
and a jealousy for the honour (alive) of his country,

_____

1. **aria:** An extended solo song in an opera or oratorio.

what can get more odd?   15
and discontent with the thriving gangs & pride.
— What happen then, Mr Bones?
— I had a most marvellous   piece of luck. I died.

[1964, 1969]

45

He stared at ruin. Ruin stared straight back.
He thought they was old friends. He felt on the stair
where her papa found them bare
they became familiar. When the papers were lost
rich with pals' secrets, he thought he had the knack   5
of ruin. Their paths crossed

and once they crossed in jail; they crossed in bed;
and over an unsigned letter their eyes met,
and in an Asian city
directionless & lurchy at two & three,   10
or trembling to a telephone's fresh threat,
and when some wired his head

to reach a wrong opinion, "Epileptic."
But he noted now that: they were not old friends.
He did not know this one.   15
This one was a stranger, come to make amends
for all the imposters, and to make it stick.
Henry nodded, un-.

[1963, 1964, 1969]

77

Seedy Henry rose up shy in de world
& shaved & swung his barbells, duded Henry up
and p.a.'d poor thousands of persons on topics of grand
moment to Henry, ah to those less & none.
Wif a book of his in either hand   5
he is stript down to move on.

— Come away, Mr Bones.

— Henry is tired of the winter,
& haircuts, & a squeamish comfy   ruin-prone proud national

mind,   & Spring (in the city so called).   10
Henry likes Fall.
Hé would be prepared to líve in a world of Fáll
for ever, impenitent Henry.
But the snows and summers grieve & dream;

thése fierce & airy occupations, and love,   15
raved away so many of Henry's years
it is a wonder that, with in each hand
one of his own mad books and all,
ancient fires for eyes, his head full
& his heart full, he's making ready to move on.   20

[1964, 1969]

384

The marker slants, flowerless, day's almost done,
I stand above my father's grave with rage,
often, often before
I've made this awful pilgrimage to one
who cannot visit me, who tore his page   5
out: I come back for more,

I spit upon this dreadful banker's grave
who shot his heart out in a Florida dawn[1]
O ho alas alas
When will indifference come, I moan & rave   10
I'd like to scrabble till I got right down
away down under the grass

and ax the casket open ha to see
just how he's taking it, which he sought so hard
we'll tear apart   15
the mouldering grave clothes ha & then Henry
will heft the ax once more, his final card,
and fell it on the start.

[1968, 1969]

---

1. **Florida dawn:** Berryman's father, John Allyn Smith, committed suicide by shooting himself on June 26, 1926, in Tampa, Florida.

Ralph Ellison

[1913-1994]

Ralph Ellison

The noted African American photographer Gordon Parks took this portrait, which appeared on the dust jacket of Ellison's first and most famous book, *Invisible Man* (1952).

Ralph Waldo Ellison was born March 1, 1913, in Oklahoma City, Oklahoma. He was the first of two sons born to Ida Millsap Ellison and Lewis Alfred Ellison, the owner of a small business selling ice and coal. Like thousands of other African Americans who migrated to the North and West, the couple had moved to Oklahoma to escape racism and segregation in the South. Ellison's proud father, who wanted his first-born son to become a poet, named him after the revered nineteenth-century American author Ralph Waldo Emerson. When Ellison was three, his father died from injuries sustained in an accident, and his mother supported the family by working as a maid and as the sexton of the African Methodist Episcopal Church. She was also active in the Socialist Party and campaigned against segregation laws in Oklahoma. While attending the all-black Frederick Douglass High School, Ellison excitedly discovered the work of Langston Hughes, Countee Cullen, and other poets of the Harlem Renaissance. Initially, however, Ellison trained to be a musician. He took trumpet lessons and became interested in jazz and the blues. In 1933, a year after his graduation from high school, he was awarded a music scholarship to the Tuskegee Institute in Alabama. During his college years, Ellison began to write poetry and switched from music to English. He consequently lost his scholarship, and in the summer of 1936 he went to New York City, hoping to earn enough money to pay for his final year at Tuskegee.

Ellison decided to remain there in order to pursue a career as a writer. He was strongly encouraged by Richard Wright, who had recently moved from Chicago to pursue his own literary career in New York. Wright, who worked for the Communist Party's *Daily Worker* and coedited the Marxist literary magazine the *New Challenge*, invited Ellison to contribute to the magazine. In 1938, about the time Ellison married the actress and singer Rose Poindexter, Wright helped him secure a job researching African American history for the Federal Writers' Project. Ellison's first published story, "Slick Gonna Learn," appeared in *Direction* in 1939, and he wrote book reviews for radical magazines such as the *New Masses*. Along with Wright, Ellison began to distance himself from the Communist Party, which he no longer believed had much to offer African Americans. In 1942, he resigned from the Federal Writers' Project to edit the *Negro Quarterly*. Unwilling to serve in the segregated U.S. Army during World War II, Ellison enlisted and served for two years as a cook in the merchant marine. By the end of the war, he had published several more stories and critical essays. Now divorced from his first wife, Ellison in 1946 married Fanny McConnell, who supported them while he worked on his first novel, *Invisible Man* (1952). The novel, a first-person narrative by an unnamed protagonist whose life story mirrors the often-bitter history of African Americans during the first half of the twentieth century, was widely reviewed in the United States. Although one black reviewer called the novel "a vicious distortion of Negro life," Langston Hughes described it as "deep, beautifully written, provocative and moving." Many other reviewers, both black and white, hailed the artistry, courage, and psychological realism of *Invisible Man*, which became a bestseller and won the National Book Award.

The high expectations generated by the success of *Invisible Man* proved to be a heavy burden for Ellison. From 1955 to 1957, he was a fellow at the American Academy in Rome, and he taught at various colleges and universities after his return to the United States. Most of his writings during the period were essays and reviews, some of which were later collected in his highly regarded volume of cultural criticism, *Shadow and Act* (1964). As Ellison explained in the introduction, the collection was tied together by three major themes: "Literature and folklore; Negro musical expression — especially jazz and the blues; and the complex relationship between the Negro American subculture and North American culture as a whole." In 1958, Ellison finally began his second novel, then called *And Hickman Arrives*, in which a black evangelist, now an old man, recalls his childhood experiences in the South. Ellison published several chapters as stories, always identifying them as excerpts "from a novel in progress." Embarrassed by his failure to complete the novel, Ellison claimed that the only copy of the manuscript was destroyed in a fire at his summer home in Massachusetts in 1967. In fact, he apparently lost only a small part of the ballooning manuscript, which had "become inordinately long . . . and complicated," as he told a friend in 1968. During the 1960s, his reputation declined, especially among more militant African Americans, who believed that Ellison was not doing enough to promote the civil rights movement. In 1970, he became the Albert Schweitzer Professor of Humanities at New York University, and he later received numerous awards and honors, including the Presidential Medal of the Arts from Ronald Reagan in 1985. Ellison published another collection of cultural criticism, *Going to the Territory* (1986). He also continued to work on his second novel, which ultimately expanded to a 2,000-page manuscript. An abridged version edited by his literary executor, John Callahan, was finally published as *Juneteenth* (1999), five years after Ellison died of pancreatic cancer in his Harlem apartment on April 16, 1994.

We are, readers and writers alike, buoyed and challenged by wave upon brilliant wave of Ellison's artistry.

–Toni Morrison

Ellison's "The Invisible Man."   While staying with friends in Vermont in the summer of 1945, Ellison jotted down the sentence "I am an invisible man" in his notebook. The sentence was the germ of his most famous work, *Invisible Man* (1952). The first chapter of the novel was published in 1947 as a story, "The Invisible Man," in the prominent British journal *Horizon*. It appeared in a special issue of the journal devoted to American art and culture that also included works by John Berryman, E. E. Cummings, Marianne Moore, and Wallace Stevens. The story was subsequently reprinted in the United States as "Battle Royal" in the 1948 edition of

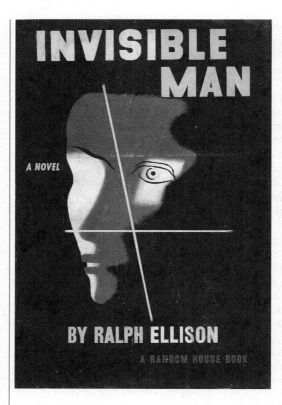

Invisible Man

The striking jacket design for Ellison's famous novel shows a face with partially effaced features emerging from — or about to disappear into — the surrounding darkness.

Magazine of the Year. The title of that version was changed to avoid some copyright issues, and the editors cut portions of an erotic passage in which the narrator describes his arousal by the sight of a white stripper performing at a "smoker." (Ellison restored the excised portions in *Invisible Man.*) Inspired in part by an episode in Richard Wright's autobiographical *Black Boy* (1945), "The Invisible Man" is a harrowing and ironic story of an African American youth's initiation into a world of racism, segregation, and violence. Taught to know his "place" by the leading white citizens of a small southern town, the protagonist takes his first step toward the discovery that he is "an invisible man." In some working notes for *Invisible Man*, Ellison wrote: " 'Invisibility' . . . springs from two basic facts of American life: from the racial conditioning which often makes the white American interpret cultural, physical or psychological differences as signs of racial inferiority; and, on the other hand, it springs from a great formlessness of Negro life wherein all values are in flux, and where those institutions and patterns of life which mold the white American's personality are missing or not so immediate in their effect." The text of the story is taken from the first printing in *Horizon* (October 1947).

bedfordstmartins.com/ americanlit for research links on Ellison

THE INVISIBLE MAN

It goes a long way back, some twenty years. All my life I had been looking for something, and everywhere I turned someone tried to tell me what it was. I accepted their answers, too, though they were often in contradiction and even self-contradictory. I was naïve. I was looking for myself and asking everyone except myself questions which I, and only I, could answer. It took me a long time and much painful boomeranging of my expectations to realize a matter everyone else appears to have been born with: that I am nobody but myself, an invisible man!

And yet I am no freak of nature, nor of history. I was in the cards, other things having been equal (or unequal) eighty-five years ago. I am not ashamed of my grandparents for having been slaves. I am only ashamed of myself for having at one time been ashamed. About eighty-five years ago they were told that they were free, united with others of our country in everything pertaining to the common good, and, in everything social, separate like the fingers of the hand. And they believed it. They exulted in it. They stayed in their place, worked hard, and brought up my father to do the same. But my grandfather is the one. He was an odd old guy — my grandfather, and I'm told I take after him. It was he who caused the trouble. On his deathbed he called my father to him and said, "Son, after I'm gone I want you to keep up the good fight. I never told you, but our life is a war and I have been a traitor all my born days, a spy in the enemy's country all my born days, ever since I give up my gun back in the Reconstruction.[1] Live with your head in the lion's mouth. I want you to overcome 'em with yesses, undermine 'em with grins, agree 'em to death and destruction, let 'em swoller you till they vomit or bust wide open." They thought the old man had gone out of his head. He had been the meekest of men. The younger children were rushed from the room, the shades drawn and the flame of the lamp turned so low that it sputtered on the wick like the old man's breathing. "Learn it to the young 'uns," he whispered fiercely. Then he died.

But my folks were more alarmed over his last words than over his dying. I was warned emphatically to forget it and, indeed, this is the first time it has been repeated outside the family circle. It had a tremendous effect upon me, however. I could never be sure of what he meant. Grandfather had been a meek old man who never made any trouble, yet on his deathbed he had called himself a traitor and a spy, and he had spoken of his meekness as a dangerous activity. It became a constant puzzle which lay unanswered in the back of my mind. And whenever things went well for me I remembered my grandfather and felt guilty, and uncomfortable. It was as though I was carrying out his advice in spite of myself. And to make it worse, everyone loved me for it. I was praised by the most lilywhite men of the town. I was considered an example of desirable conduct — just as my grandfather had been. And what puzzled me was that the old man had defined it as *treachery*. When I was praised for my conduct I felt a guilt that in some way I was doing something that was really against the wishes of the white folks, that if they had

---

1. **Reconstruction:** During Reconstruction (1865–1877), the period following the Civil War, a number of southern states prohibited African Americans from owning guns under laws called "Black Codes."

understood they would have desired me to act just the opposite, that I should have been sulky and bad and that really would have been what they wanted, even though they were fooled and thought they wanted me to act as I did. It made me very afraid that some day they would look upon me as a traitor and I would be lost. Still, I was afraid to act any other way because they didn't like that at all. The old man's words were like a curse. On my graduation day I delivered a paper in which I showed that humility was the secret, indeed, the very essence, of progress. (Not that I believed this. How could I, remembering my grandfather? I only knew that it worked.) It was a great success. Everyone praised me and I was invited to give the speech before the town's leading white citizens. It was a triumph for our whole community.

When I got there I discovered that it was on the occasion of a smoker, and I was told that since I was to be there anyway I might as well take part in the battle royal to be fought by some of my schoolmates as part of the entertainment.[2] The battle royal came first. It was in the main ballroom of the leading hotel. All the town's big shots were there in their tuxedos, wolfing down the buffet foods, drinking beer and whisky and smoking black cigars. It was a large room with a high ceiling. Chairs were arranged in neat rows around three sides of a portable boxing ring. The fourth side was clear, revealing a gleaming space of polished floor. I had some misgivings over the battle royal, by the way. Not from a distaste for fighting, but because I didn't care too much for the other fellows who were to take part. They were tough guys, who seemed to have no grandfather curses worrying their minds. No one could have mistaken their toughness. And besides, I suspected that fighting a battle royal might detract from the dignity of my speech. In those pre-invisible days I visualized myself a neo-Booker T. Washington.[3] But the other fellows didn't care too much for me, either, and there were nine of them. I felt superior to them in my way, and I didn't like the manner in which we were all crowded together into the servants' elevator. Nor did they like my being there. In fact as the warmly lighted floors flashed past the elevator we had words over the fact that I, by taking part in the fight, had knocked one of their friends out of a night's work.

We were led out of the elevator through a rococo hall into an ante-room and told to get into our fighting togs. Each of us was issued with a pair of boxing gloves. Then we were told to go out into the ballroom and wait our turn. When ready we were ushered out and entered the big, mirrored hall as instructed, looking cautiously about us, and whispering lest we might accidentally be heard in the noise of the room. It was foggy with cigar smoke. And already the whisky was taking effect. I was shocked to see that some of the most important men of the town were tipsy. They were all there, bankers, lawyers, judges, doctors, fire chiefs, teachers, merchants. Even one of the more fashionable pastors. Something we could not see was going on up front. A clarinet was vibrating sensu-

---

2. **occasion of a smoker . . . entertainment:** *Smoker* was a common term for an all-male social gathering. A "battle royal" is a free-for-all fight involving several combatants.

3. **a neo-Booker T. Washington:** Washington (1856–1915), a prominent African American educator, established the Tuskegee Institute in Alabama. In his most famous speech, "The Atlanta Exposition Address," (see p. 442), Washington essentially withdrew demands for the full social and political equality of African Americans in order to gain white support for their technical training and access to jobs in the South.

ously and the men were standing up and moving forward. We were a small tight group, clustered together, our bare upper bodies touching and shining with anticipatory sweat; while up front the big shots were becoming increasingly excited over something we could not see. Suddenly I heard the school superintendent who had told me to come yell, "Bring up the shines,[4] gentlemen! Bring up the little shines!"

We were rushed up to the front of the ballroom. It smelled strongly of tobacco and whisky and when we were pushed into place I almost wet my pants. A sea of faces, some hostile, some amused, ringed round us, and in the centre, facing us, stood a magnificent blonde, stark nude. There was dead silence. I felt a blast of cold air chill me. I tried to back away, but they were behind me and around me. Some of the boys stood with lowered heads, trembling. I felt a wave of irrational guilt and fear. My teeth chattered, my skin turned to goose flesh, my knees knocked. Yet I was strongly attracted and looked in spite of myself. Had the price of looking been blindness, I would have looked. The hair was yellow like that of a circus kewpie doll, the face heavily powdered and rouged, as though to form an abstract mask, the eyes hollow and smeared a cool blue – the colour of a baboon's butt. I felt a compulsive desire to spit upon her as my eyes brushed slowly over her body. Her breasts were firm and round as the domes of East Indian temples, and I stood so close as to see the fine skin texture and beads of pearly perspiration glistening like dew around the pink and erected buds of her nipples. I wanted at one and the same time to run from the room, to sink through the floor, or go to her and cover her from my eyes and the eyes of the others with my body; to feel the soft thighs, to caress her and destroy her, to love her and murder her, to hide from her, and yet to stroke where below the small American flag tattooed upon her belly her thighs formed a clear, inverted V. I had a notion that of all in the room she saw only me with her impersonal eyes.

And then she began to dance, a slow sensuous movement; the smoke of a hundred cigars clinging to her like the thinnest of veils. She seemed like a fair bird-girl girdled in veils calling to me from the angry surface of some grey and threatening sea. I was transported. Then I became aware of a clarinet playing and the big shots yelling at us. Some threatened us if we looked and others if we did not. On my right I saw one boy faint and a man grabbed a silver pitcher from a table, stepping close as he dashed iced water upon him, then stood him up and forced two of us to support him as his head hung, and moans issued from his thick bluish lips. Another boy began to plead to go home. He was the largest of the group, wearing dark-red fighting tights much too small to conceal the erection which projected from him as though in answer to the insinuating low-registered moaning of the clarinet. He tried to hide himself with his boxing gloves. And all the while the blonde continued dancing, smiling faintly at the big shots who watched her with fascination, and faintly smiling at our fear. I noticed a certain merchant who followed her hungrily, his lips loose and drooling. He was a large man who wore diamond studs in a shirtfront, which swelled with the ample pouch underneath, and each time the blonde swayed her undulating hips he ran his hand through the thin hair of his bald head and, with his arms upheld, his posture clumsy like that of an intoxicated

---

4. **shines:** A derogatory term for black people.

panda, wound his belly in a slow and obscene grind. This creature was completely hyp-notized. The music had quickened. The dancer flung herself about with detached facial expression, the men began reaching out to touch her. I could see their beefy fingers sink into the soft flesh. Some of the others tried to stop them and she began to move around the floor in graceful circles as they gave chase, slipping and sliding over the polished floor. It was mad. Chairs went crashing, beer was spilt as they ran laughing and howling after her. They caught her just as she reached a door, raised her from the floor, and tossed her as college boys are tossed at a hazing, and above her red, fixed-smiling lips I saw the terror and disgust in her eyes, almost like my own terror and that I saw in some of the other boys, as I watched. They tossed her twice and her soft breasts seemed to flatten against the air and her legs flung wildly as she spun. Some of the more sober ones helped her to escape. And I started off the floor, heading for the ante-room with the rest of the boys.

Some were still crying and in hysteria. But as we tried to leave we were stopped and ordered to get into the ring. There was nothing to do but what we were told. All ten of us climbed under the ropes and allowed ourselves to be blindfolded with broad bands of white cloth. One of the men seemed to feel a bit sympathetic and tried to cheer us up as we stood with our backs against the ropes. Some of us tried to grin. "See that boy over there?" one of the men said. "I want you to run across at the bell and give it to him right in the belly. If you don't get him, I'm going to get you. I don't like his looks." Each of us was told the same. The blindfolds were put on. Yet even then I had been going over my speech. In my mind each word was as bright as flame. I felt the cloth pressed into place and frowned so that it would be loosened when I relaxed.

But now I felt a sudden fit of blind terror. I was unused to darkness. It was as though I had suddenly found myself in a dark room filled with poisonous cottonmouths. I could hear the bleary voices yelling insistently for the battle royal to begin.

"Get going in there!"

"Let me at that big nigger!"

I strained to pick out the school superintendent's voice, as though to squeeze some security out of that slightly more familiar sound.

"Let me at those black sonsabitches!" someone yelled.

"No, Jackson, no!" another voice yelled . . . "Here, somebody help me hold Jack."

"I want to get at that ginger-coloured bugger. Tear him limb from limb," the first voice yelled.

I stood against the ropes trembling. For in those days I was what they called ginger-coloured and he sounded as though he might crunch me between his teeth like a crisp ginger cookie. Quite a struggle was going on. Chairs were being kicked about and I could hear voices grunting as with a terrific effort. I wanted to see, to see more desper-ately than ever before. But the blindfold was tight as a thick, skin-puckering scab and when I raised my gloved hand to push the layers of white aside a voice yelled, "Oh, no you don't, black bastard! Leave that alone!"

"Ring the bell before Jackson kills him a coon!" someone boomed in the sudden silence. And I heard the bell clang and the sound of the feet scuffling forward.

A glove smacked against my head. I pivoted, striking out stiffly as someone went past, and felt the jar ripple along the length of my arm to my shoulder. Then it seemed as though all nine of the boys had turned upon me at once. Blows pounded me from all sides while I struck out as best I could. So many blows landed upon me that I wondered if I were not the only blindfolded fighter in the ring, or if the man called Jackson hadn't succeeded in getting me after all.

Blindfolded, I sensed that I could not control my motions and that I had no dignity. I stumbled about like a baby or a drunken man. The smoke had become thicker and with each new blow it seemed to sear and further restrict my lungs. My saliva became like hot bitter glue. A glove connected with my head, filling my mouth with warm blood. It was everywhere. I could not tell if the moisture I felt upon my body was sweat or blood. A blow landed hard against the nape of my neck. I felt myself going over, my head hitting the floor. Streaks of blue light filled the black world behind the blindfold. I lay prone pretending that I was knocked out, but felt myself seized by hands and yanked to my feet. "Get going, black boy! Mix it up!" My arms were like lead, my head smarting from blows. I managed to feel my way to the ropes and held on trying to catch my breath. A glove landed in my mid-section and I went over again feeling as though the smoke had become a knife jabbed into my guts. Pushed this way and that by the legs milling around me, I finally pulled erect and discovered that I could see. The blindfold had slipped a fraction and I could see the black, sweat-washed forms weaving in the smoky-blue atmosphere like drunken dancers weaving to the rapid drum-like thuds of blows. Everyone fought hysterically. It was complete anarchy. Everybody fought everybody else. No group fought together for long. Two, three, four, fought one, then turned to fight each other, were themselves attacked. Blows landed below the belt and in the kidney, with the gloves open as well as closed. My eye was partly opened now and there was not so much terror. I moved carefully, avoiding blows, although not too many to attract attention, fighting from group to group. The boys groped about like blind, cautious crabs, crouching to protect their mid-sections, their heads pulled in short against their shoulders, their arms stretched nervously before them with their fists testing the smoke-filled air like the knobbed feelers of hypersensitive snails. In one corner I glimpsed a boy violently punching the air and heard him scream in pain as he smashed his hand against a ring post. For a second I saw him bent over, holding his hand, then going down as a blow caught his unprotected head. I played one group against the other, slipping in and throwing a punch then stepping out of range while pushing the others into the mêlée to take the blows blindly aimed at me. The smoke was agonizing and there were no rounds, no bells at four-minute intervals to relieve our exhaustion. The room spun round me, a swirl of lights, smoke, sweating bodies — surrounded by tense white faces. I bled from both nose and mouth, the blood spattered from time to time upon my chest. The men kept yelling, "Slug him, black boy. Knock his guts out!"

"Uppercut him. Kill that big boy!"

Taking a fake fall, I saw a boy going down heavily beside me as though he were felled by a single blow, saw a sneaker-clad foot shoot into his groin as the two who had knocked him down stumbled upon him as I rolled out of range.

The harder we fought the more threatening the men became. And yet I had begun to worry about my speech again. How would it go? Would they recognize my ability? What would they give me?

I was fighting automatically when suddenly I noticed that one after another of the boys was leaving the ring. I was surprised, filled with panic, as though I had been left alone with an unknown danger. Then I understood. The boys had arranged it among themselves. It was the custom for the two men left in the ring to slug it out for the winner's prize. I discovered this too late. When the bell sounded two men in tuxedos leaped into the ring and removed the blindfold. I found myself facing Tatlock, the biggest of the gang. I felt sick at my stomach. Hardly had the bell stopped ringing in my ears than it clanged again and I saw him moving swiftly towards me. Thinking of nothing else to do I hit him smash on the nose. He kept coming, bringing the sharp violence of rank sweat. His face was a black blank of a face, only his eyes alive — with hate of me, and aglow with a feverish terror from what had happened to us all. I became anxious. I wanted to deliver my speech and he came at me as though he meant to beat it out of me. I smashed him again and again, taking his blows as they came. Then on a sudden impulse I struck him lightly and as we clinched, I whispered, "Fake like I knocked you out, you can have the prize."

"I'll break your behind," he whispered hoarsely.

"For *them*?"

"For *me*, sonofabitch!"

They were yelling for us to break it up and Tatlock spun me half around with a blow, and as a joggled camera sweeps in a reeling scene, I saw the howling red faces crouching tense beneath the clouds of blue-grey smoke. For a moment the world wavered, unravelled, flowed, then my head cleared and Tatlock bounced before me. That fluttering shadow before my eyes was his jabbing left hand. Then falling forward, my head against his damp shoulder, I whispered,

"I'll make it five dollars more."

"Go to hell!"

But his muscles relaxed a trifle beneath my pressure and I breathed, "Seven!"

"Give it to your ma," he said, ripping me beneath the heart. And while I still held him I butted him and moved away. I felt myself bombarded with punches. I fought back with hopeless desperation. I wanted to deliver my speech more than anything else in the world, because I felt that only these men could judge truly my ability, and now this stupid clown was ruining my chances. I began fighting carefully now, moving in to punch him and out again with my faster speed. A lucky blow to his chin and I had him going too — until I heard a loud voice yell, "I got my money on the big boy." Hearing this I almost dropped my guard. I was confused: should I try to win against the voice out there? Would not this go against my speech, and was not this a moment for humility, for non-resistance? A blow to my head as I danced about sent my right eye popping like a jack-in-the-box and settled my dilemma. The room went red as I fell. It was a dream fall, my body languid and fastidious as to where to land, until the floor became impatient and smashed up to meet me. A moment later I came to. An hypnotic voice said "FIVE" . . . emphatically. And I lay there, hazily watching a dark red spot of my own blood shaping itself into a butterfly, glistening and soaking into the soiled grey world of the canvas.

When the voice drawled "TEN" I was lifted up and dragged to a chair. I sat dazed. My eye pained and swelled with each throb of my pounding heart and I wondered if now I would be allowed to speak. I was wringing wet, my mouth still bleeding. We were grouped along the wall now. The other boys ignored me as they congratulated Tatlock and speculated as to how much they would be paid. One boy whimpered over his smashed hand. Looking up front, I saw attendants in white jackets rolling the portable ring away and placing a small square rug in the vacant space surrounded by chairs. "Perhaps," I thought, "I will stand on the rug to deliver my speech."

Then the M.C. called to us. My heart fell when he said,

"Come on up here, boys, and get your money."

We ran forward to where the men laughed and talked in their chairs, waiting. Everyone seemed friendly now.

"There it is on the rug," the man said. I saw the rug covered with coins of all dimensions and a few crumpled bills. But what excited me, scattered here and there were gleaming pieces of gold.

"Boys, it's all yours," the man said. "That's right, Sambo," a blond man said, winking at me confidentially.

I trembled with excitement, forgetting my pain. I would get the gold and the bills, I thought. I would use both hands. I would throw my body against the others to block them from the gold.

"Get down around the rug now," the man commanded, "and don't anyone touch it until I give the signal."

"This ought to be good," I heard.

As told, we got around the square rug on our knees. Slowly the man raised his freckled hand and we followed it upwards with our eyes.

I heard, "These niggers look like they're about to pray!"

Then, "Ready," the man said, "Go!"

I lunged for a yellow coin lying on the blue design of the carpet, touching it and sending a surprised shriek to join those rising around me. I tried frantically to remove my hand but could not let go. A hot violent force tore through my body, shaking me like a wet rat. The rug was electrified. The hair bristled up on my head as I shook myself free. My muscles jumped, my nerves jangled, writhed. But I saw that this was not stopping the other boys. Laughing in fear and embarrassment some were holding back and scooping up the coins knocked off by the painful contortions of the others. The men roared above us as we struggled.

"Pick it up, goddamit, pick it up!" someone called like a bass-voiced parrot. "Go on, get it!"

I crawled rapidly around the floor, picking up the coins, trying to avoid the coppers and to get greenbacks and the gold. Ignoring the shock by laughing, as I brushed the coins off quickly I discovered that I could contain the electricity — a contradiction, but it works. Then the men began to push us upon the rug. Laughing embarrassedly, we struggled out of their hands and kept after the coins. We were all wet and slippery and hard to hold. Suddenly I saw a boy lifted into the air, glistening with sweat like a circus seal, and dropped, his wet back landing flush upon the electrically charged rug, heard him yell and saw him literally dance upon his back, his elbows beating a frenzied rhythm upon the floor, his muscles twitching like the flesh of a horse stung by many flies. When he finally rolled off, his face was grey and no one stopped him when he ran from the floor amid booming laughter.

"Get that money," the M.C. called. "That's good, hard American cash!"

And we snatched and grabbed, snatched and grabbed. I was careful not to come too close to the rug now, and when I felt the hot whisky breath descend upon me like a cloud of foul air, I reached out and grabbed the leg of a chair. It was occupied, and I held on desperately.

"Leggo, nigger! Leggo!"

The huge face wavered down to mine as he tried to push me free. But my body was slippery and he was too drunk. It was Mr. Colcord, who owned a chain of movie houses and entertainment palaces. Each time he grabbed me I slipped out of his hands. It became a real struggle. I feared the rug more than I did the drunk, so I held on, surprising myself for a moment by trying to topple *him* upon the rug. It was such an enormous idea that I found myself actually carrying it out. I tried not to be obvious, yet trying to tumble him out of the chair I grabbed his leg, when he raised up roaring with laughter, and, looking me dead in the eye, kicked me viciously in the chest. The chair leg flew out of my hand and I felt myself going and rolled. It was as though I had rolled through a bed of hot coals. It seemed a whole century would pass before I would roll free, a century in which I was seared through the deepest levels of my body to the fearful breath within me, and the breath seared and heated to the point of explosion. "It'll all be over in a flash," I thought, as I rolled clear.

"All be over in a flash." But not yet. The men on the other side were waiting, red faces swollen as though from apoplexy as they bent forward in their chairs. Seeing their fingers coming towards me I rolled away, as a fumbled football rolls off the receiver's fingertips, back into the coals. That time I luckily sent the rug sliding out of place and heard the coins ringing against the floor and the boys scuffling to pick them up and the M.C. calling, "All right, boys, that's all. Go get dressed and get your money."

I was limp as a dishrag. My back felt as though it had been beaten with wires. When we had dressed, the M.C. came in and gave us each five dollars, except Tatlock, who got ten for being last in the ring. Then he told us to leave. I was not to get a chance to deliver my speech, I thought. I was going out into the dim garbage-filled alley in despair when I was stopped and told to go back. When I went back the men were pushing back their chairs and gathering in groups to talk. The M.C. knocked on a table for quiet.

"Gentlemen," he said, "we almost forgot an important part of the programme. A *most* serious part, gentlemen. This boy was brought here to deliver a speech which he made at his graduation yesterday . . ."

"Bravo!"

"I'm told that he is the smartest boy we've got out there in Milltown. I'm told that he knows more big words than a pocket-sized dictionary."

Much applause and laughter.

"So now, gentlemen, I want you to give him your attention."

There was still laughter as I faced them, my mouth was dry, my eye throbbing. I began slowly, but evidently my throat was tense, because they began shouting, "Louder! Louder!"

I began again, tensing my diaphragm to project my voice, although it ached from the many blows to my solar plexus.

"We of the younger generation extol the wisdom of that great leader and educator," I shouted, "who first spoke these flaming words of wisdom:[5] 'A ship lost at sea for many days suddenly sighted a friendly vessel. From the mast of the unfortunate vessel was seen a signal: "Water, water: we die of thirst!" The answer from the friendly vessel came back: "Cast down your bucket where you are." The captain of the distressed vessel, at last heeding the injunction, cast down his bucket, and it came up full of fresh sparkling water from the mouth of the Amazon River.' And like him I say, and in his words, 'To those of my race who depend upon bettering their condition in a foreign land, or who undertake the importance of cultivating friendly relations with the Southern white man, who is his next-door neighbour, I would say: "Cast down your bucket where you are" — cast it down in making friends in every manly way of the people of all races by whom we are surrounded . . .'"

I spoke automatically and with such fervour that I did not realize that the men were still talking and laughing until my dry mouth filling up with blood from the cut, almost strangled me. I coughed, wanting to stop and go to one of the tall brass, sand-filled spit-toons to relieve myself, but a few of the men, especially the superintendent, were listening, and I was afraid, so I gulped it down, blood, saliva and all, and continued. What powers of endurance I had during those days! What enthusiasm! What a belief in the rightness of things! I spoke even louder in spite of the pain. But they still talked and still they laughed as though with cotton in dirty ears. So I spoke with greater emotional emphasis. I closed my ears and swallowed blood until I was nauseated. The speech seemed a hundred times as long as before, but I could not leave out a single word. All had to be said, each memorized nuance considered, rendered. Nor was that all. Whenever I uttered a word of three or more syllables a group of voices would yell, for me to repeat it. I used the phrase "social responsibility" and they yelled:

"What's that word you say, boy?"

"Social responsibility," I said.

"What?"

"Social . . ."

"Louder . . ."

"Responsibility."

"More!"

"Responsi——"

"Repeat!"

---

5. **these flaming words of wisdom:** What follows is an often-quoted passage from Booker T. Washington's Atlanta Exposition Address. See note 3.

"—bility."

The room filled with the uproar of laughter until, no doubt, distracted by having to gulp down my blood, I made a mistake and yelled a phrase I had often seen denounced in newspaper editorials, heard debated in private.

"Social . . ."

"What?" they yelled.

"Equality."

The laughter hung smoke-like in the sudden stillness. I opened my eyes, puzzled. Sounds of displeasure filled the room. The M.C. rushed forward. They shouted hostile phrases at me. But I did not understand. A small, dry, moustached man in the front row blared out, "Say that slowly, son!"

"What, sir?"

"What you just said."

"Social responsibility, sir," I said.

"You weren't being smart, were you, boy?" he said not unkindly.

"No, sir!"

"You sure that about equality was a mistake?"

"Yes, sir," I said. "I was swallowing blood."

"Well, you had better speak more slowly so we can understand. We mean to do right by you but you've got to know your place at all times. All right, now, go on with your speech."

I was afraid. I wanted to leave but I wanted also to speak, and I was afraid they'd snatch me down. "Thank you, sir," I said, beginning where I had left off, and having them ignore me as before.

Yet when I finished there was a thunderous applause. I was surprised to see the superintendent come forth with a package wrapped in white tissue paper, and gesturing for quiet, address the men.

"Gentlemen, you see that I did not over-praise this boy. He makes a good speech and some day he'll lead his people and we will find him useful. And I don't have to tell you that that is important in these days and times. This is a good, smart boy, and so to encourage him in the right direction, in the name of the Board of Education I wish to present him with a prize in the form of this . . ."

He paused, removing the tissue paper and revealing a gleaming calfskin briefcase.

"In the form of this first-class article from Shad Whitmore's shop."

"Boy," he said, addressing me. "Take this prize and keep it well. Consider it a badge of office. Prize it. Keep developing as you are and some day it will be filled with important papers that will help shape the destiny of your people."

I was so moved that I could hardly express my thanks. A rope of bloody saliva drooled upon the leather, forming a shape like an undiscovered continent, and I wiped it quickly away. I felt an importance that I had never dreamed before.

"Open it and see what's inside," I was told.

My fingers atremble, I complied, smelling the fresh leather and seeing an official-looking document inside. It was a scholarship to the state college for Negroes. My eyes filled with tears and I ran awkwardly off the floor. I was overjoyed. I did not even mind when I discovered that the gold pieces I had scrambled for were brass pocket tokens advertising a certain make of Detroit automobile.

When I reached home everyone was excited. Next day the neighbours came to congratulate me. I even felt safe from my grandfather, whose deathbed curse usually spoiled my triumphs. I stood beneath his photograph with my briefcase in hand and smiled triumphantly into his stolid, black, peasant's face. It was a face that fascinated me. The eyes seemed to follow everywhere I went. That night I dreamed I was at a circus with him and that he refused to laugh at the clowns no matter what they did, then later he told me to open my briefcase and read what was inside and I did, finding an official envelope stamped with the state seal and inside the envelope I found another and another, endlessly, and I thought I would fall of weariness. "Them's yours," he said. "Now open that one," and I did and in it I found an engraved document containing a short message in letters of gold: "Read it," my grandfather said. "Out loud!"

"To Whom it May Concern," I intoned. "Keep This Nigger-Boy Running." I awoke with the old man's laughter ringing in my ears.

[1947]

Bernard Malamud

[1914-1986]

Bernard Malamud was born on April 26, 1914, in Brooklyn, New York. He was the first of two sons born to Max and Bertha Fidelman Malamud, Jewish immigrants from Russia. His parents, who owned a small grocery store, "were gentle, honest, kindly people, and who they were and their affection for me to some degree made up for the cultural deprivation I felt as a child," Malamud recalled in a 1984 interview. "They weren't educated, but their values were stable. Though my father always managed to make a living, they were comparatively poor, especially in the Depression, and yet I never heard a word in praise of the buck. On the other hand, there were no books that I remember in the house, no records, music, pictures on the wall. On Sundays I listened to somebody's piano through the window." But he had access to books at school, and at an early age Malamud was telling and writing stories inspired by movies and class assignments in history. After his graduation from Erasmus Hall High School, he enrolled at the City College of New York, from

Bernard Malamud

David Lees took this photograph in 1957, the year Malamud published *The Assistant*, one of his most acclaimed novels about the urban Jewish experience in the United States.

which he graduated in 1936. Although he wanted to devote himself to writing, Malamud had to support himself, so he enrolled in a teacher-training program and began teaching part-time. In 1940, he worked briefly as a clerk in the Census Bureau in Washington, D.C., before returning to New York. He taught night classes at both Erasmus Hall and Harlem high schools and managed to complete an MA from Columbia in 1942.

From that point on, Malamud devoted himself single-mindedly to writing. In 1943, he began publishing his stories in small literary magazines such as *American Preface*, *Assembly*, and *Threshold*. He married Ann de Chiara, an Italian American then working in an advertising firm, in 1945. The couple, whose marriage was opposed on religious grounds by their parents, had two children. Malamud later said that his preoccupation with Jewish subjects and his own Jewish identity was a result of his marriage to a Gentile and the impact of the Holocaust, which "helped me to come to what I wanted to say as a writer." He continued to teach at evening high schools in New York until 1949, when he managed to land a job as an instructor in English at Oregon State College (now University). He flourished there, and his stories soon began to appear in prominent magazines, including *Commentary*, *Harper's Bazaar*, and the *Partisan Review*. After destroying the manuscript of his first completed novel because he thought he "could do better," he wrote *The Natural* (1952), a symbolic fable about a gifted baseball player in which Malamud freely employed elements of Arthurian myth. Although the initial reviews were mixed, the novel ultimately brought him wide recognition, partly as a result of the popular 1984 film adaptation starring Robert Redford. Malamud, however, became best known for his "intense sympathy for his Jewish material," as Alfred Kazin put it in a review of Malamud's second novel, *The Assistant* (1957), a tale about a Jewish grocer and his Italian assistant in a failing store in Brooklyn. He explored similar material in many of the stories in his first collection, *The Magic Barrel* (1958), which won the National Book Award. His next novel, *A New Life* (1961), was a satirical, semiautobiographical account of a Jewish high-school teacher who leaves New York to take a job at a college closely resembling Oregon State.

In 1961, Malamud accepted a position on the English faculty at Bennington College in Vermont, where he taught and wrote for most of the rest of his life. He and his wife also traveled widely in Europe, Israel, the Soviet Union, and the United States. A second collection of stories, *Idiots First* (1963), was followed by *The Fixer* (1966), a novel based on the notorious 1913 trial of Menahem Mendel Beiliss, a Jew falsely accused of the "ritual murder" of a Christian boy in Tsarist Russia. The novel won the National Book Award and the Pulitzer Prize. It also cemented Malamud's reputation as a "Jewish-American writer," a label that he strongly resisted. "I'm an American, I'm a Jew, and I write for all men," he remarked in 1975. "I write about Jews, when I write about Jews, because they set my imagination going." He explored the psyche and often tragicomic experiences of Jewish characters in *Pictures of Fidelman* (1969), interrelated stories about a middle-aged man from the Bronx who seeks a new life in Italy; *The Tenants* (1971), a novel about the conflicts between two writers, one black and

What it is to be human, and to be humane, is [Malamud's] deepest concern.

–Philip Roth

the other Jewish, living in a derelict tenement on the Lower East Side; and *Dubin's Lives* (1979), an account of a married biographer's affair with a young woman that was inspired by Malamud's relationship with one of his students at Bennington. He departed from his characteristic subject matter in his final novel, *God's Grace* (1982), a parable about the sole survivor of a nuclear war who seeks to train chimpanzees to become the dominant species on Earth. In 1983, the year he published his *Collected Stories*, Malamud was awarded the Gold Medal for Fiction by the American Academy of Arts and Letters. He died following heart surgery on March 18, 1986.

Malamud's "The First Seven Years." Although he was probably best known for his novels, Malamud wrote more than fifty short stories, which many critics view as his finest work. "In a sense the short story tells us, time and time again, how vulnerable human lives are to the human condition," Malamud observed in some notes on the craft of the short story.

bedfordstmartins.com/ americanlit *for research links on Malamud*

> It arranges experience so that we understand, at least for a moment, how events combine, sometimes to lengthen, too often to shorten our days, our joys, or, happily, our illusions; or to say how suddenly we fall into error and how irrevocably we are judged, as though for all time for a single mistake, and *that* though it takes a thousand errors to make a moral man.

The process of moral growth through initial blindness and human error is illustrated by Malamud's early story "The First Seven Years," which is set in what was formerly known as the "Jewish ghetto" on the Lower East Side of New York City. The central focus of the story is Feld, a Polish immigrant shoemaker who wants his unmarried daughter to have the opportunities and material comforts he has lacked. In his effort to serve as a matchmaker, Feld learns some important lessons about himself, his daughter, Miriam, and his unprepossessing helper, Sobel. Malamud, who first published the story in 1950 in the prominent literary and cultural magazine the *Partisan Review*, revised it for inclusion in *The Magic Barrel* (1958), from which the text is taken.

THE FIRST SEVEN YEARS[1]

Feld, the shoemaker, was annoyed that his helper, Sobel, was so insensitive to his reverie that he wouldn't for a minute cease his fanatic pounding at the other bench. He gave him a look, but Sobel's bald head was bent over the last as he worked and he didn't notice. The shoemaker shrugged and continued to peer through the partly frosted window at the near-sighted haze of falling February snow. Neither the shifting white blur

---

1. **The First Seven Years:** The title alludes to the biblical story of Jacob, who works for seven years in order to marry Rachel, the younger daughter of Laban. At the wedding, however, Laban substitutes his elder daughter, Leah, and Jacob is forced to work for a second seven years in order to marry Rachel (Genesis 29:1-35).

outside, nor the sudden deep remembrance of the snowy Polish village where he had wasted his youth could turn his thoughts from Max the college boy, (a constant visitor in the mind since early that morning when Feld saw him trudging through the snow-drifts on his way to school) whom he so much respected because of the sacrifices he had made throughout the years — in winter or direst heat — to further his education. An old wish returned to haunt the shoemaker: that he had had a son instead of a daughter, but this blew away in the snow for Feld, if anything, was a practical man. Yet he could not help but contrast the diligence of the boy, who was a peddler's son, with Miriam's uncon-cern for an education. True, she was always with a book in her hand, yet when the oppor-tunity arose for a college education, she had said no she would rather find a job. He had begged her to go, pointing out how many fathers could not afford to send their children to college, but she said she wanted to be independent. As for education, what was it, she asked, but books, which Sobel, who diligently read the classics, would as usual advise her on. Her answer greatly grieved her father.

A figure emerged from the snow and the door opened. At the counter the man with-drew from a wet paper bag a pair of battered shoes for repair. Who he was the shoe-maker for a moment had no idea, then his heart trembled as he realized, before he had thoroughly discerned the face, that Max himself was standing there, embarrassedly explaining what he wanted done to his old shoes. Though Feld listened eagerly, he couldn't hear a word, for the opportunity that had burst upon him was deafening.

He couldn't exactly recall when the thought had occurred to him, because it was clear he had more than once considered suggesting to the boy that he go out with Miriam. But he had not dared speak, for if Max said no, how would he face him again? Or suppose Miriam, who harped so often on independence, blew up in anger and shouted at him for his meddling? Still, the chance was too good to let by: All it meant was an introduction. They might long ago have become friends had they happened to meet somewhere, there-fore was it not his duty — an obligation — to bring them together, nothing more, a harm-less connivance to replace an accidental encounter in the subway, let's say, or a mutual friend's introduction in the street? Just let him once see and talk to her and he would for sure be interested. As for Miriam, what possible harm for a working girl in an office, who met only loud-mouthed salesmen and illiterate shipping clerks, to make the acquaintance of a fine scholarly boy? Maybe he would awaken in her a desire to go to col-lege; if not — the shoemaker's mind at last came to grips with the truth — let her marry an educated man and live a better life.

When Max finished describing what he wanted done to his shoes, Feld marked them, both with enormous holes in the soles which he pretended not to notice, with large white-chalk x's, and the rubber heels, thinned to the nails, he marked with o's, though it troubled him he might have mixed up the letters. Max inquired the price, and the shoe-maker cleared his throat and asked the boy, above Sobel's insistent hammering, would he please step through the side door there into the hall. Though surprised, Max did as the shoemaker requested, and Feld went in after him. For a minute they were both silent, because Sobel had stopped banging, and it seemed they understood neither was to say anything until the noise began again. When it did, loudly, the shoemaker quickly told Max why he had asked to talk to him.

"Ever since you went to high school," he said, in the dimly-lit hallway, "I watched you in the morning go to the subway to school, and I said always to myself, this is a fine boy that he wants so much an education."

"Thanks," Max said, nervously alert. He was tall and grotesquely thin, with sharply cut features, particularly a beak-like nose. He was wearing a loose, long slushy overcoat that hung down to his ankles, looking like a rug draped over his bony shoulders, and a soggy, old brown hat, as battered as the shoes he had brought in.

"I am a business man," the shoemaker abruptly said to conceal his embarrassment, "so I will explain you right away why I talk to you. I have a girl, my daughter Miriam — she is nineteen — a very nice girl and also so pretty that everybody looks on her when she passes by in the street. She is smart, always with a book, and I thought to myself that a boy like you, an educated boy — I thought maybe you will be interested sometime to meet a girl like this." He laughed a bit when he had finished and was tempted to say more but had the good sense not to.

Max stared down like a hawk. For an uncomfortable second he was silent, then he asked, "Did you say nineteen?"

"Yes."

"Would it be all right to inquire if you have a picture of her?"

"Just a minute." The shoemaker went into the store and hastily returned with a snapshot that Max held up to the light.

"She's all right," he said.

Feld waited.

"And is she sensible — not the flighty kind?"

"She is very sensible."

After another short pause, Max said it was okay with him if he met her.

"Here is my telephone," said the shoemaker, hurriedly handing him a slip of paper. "Call her up. She comes home from work six o'clock."

Max folded the paper and tucked it away into his worn leather wallet.

"About the shoes," he said. "How much did you say they will cost me?"

"Don't worry about the price."

"I just like to have an idea."

"A dollar — dollar fifty. A dollar fifty," the shoemaker said.

At once he felt bad, for he usually charged two twenty-five for this kind of job. Either he should have asked the regular price or done the work for nothing.

Later, as he entered the store, he was startled by a violent clanging and looked up to see Sobel pounding with all his might upon the naked last. It broke, the iron striking the floor and jumping with a thump against the wall, but before the enraged shoemaker could cry out, the assistant had torn his hat and coat from the hook and rushed out into the snow.

So Feld, who had looked forward to anticipating how it would go with his daughter and Max, instead had a great worry on his mind. Without his temperamental helper he was a lost man, especially since it was years now that he had carried the store alone. The shoemaker had for an age suffered from a heart condition that threatened collapse if he dared exert himself. Five years ago, after an attack, it had appeared as though he would have either to sacrifice his business upon the auction block and live on a pittance thereafter, or put himself at the mercy of some unscrupulous employee who would in the end probably ruin him. But just at the moment of his darkest despair, this Polish refugee, Sobel, appeared one night from the street and begged for work. He was a stocky man, poorly dressed, with a bald head that had once been blond, a severely plain face and soft blue eyes prone to tears over the sad books he read, a young man but old – no one would have guessed thirty. Though he confessed he knew nothing of shoemaking, he said he was apt and would work for a very little if Feld taught him the trade. Thinking that with, after all, a landsman, he would have less to fear than from a complete stranger, Feld took him on and within six weeks the refugee rebuilt as good a shoe as he, and not long thereafter expertly ran the business for the thoroughly relieved shoe-maker.

Feld could trust him with anything and did, frequently going home after an hour or two at the store, leaving all the money in the till, knowing Sobel would guard every cent of it. The amazing thing was that he demanded so little. His wants were few; in money he wasn't interested – in nothing but books, it seemed – which he one by one lent to Miriam, together with his profuse, queer written comments, manufactured during his lonely rooming house evenings, thick pads of commentary which the shoemaker peered at and twitched his shoulders over as his daughter, from her fourteenth year, read page by sanctified page, as if the word of God were inscribed on them. To protect Sobel, Feld himself had to see that he received more than he asked for. Yet his conscience bothered him for not insisting that the assistant accept a better wage than he was getting, though Feld had honestly told him he could earn a handsome salary if he worked elsewhere, or maybe opened a place of his own. But the assistant answered, somewhat ungraciously, that he was not interested in going elsewhere, and though Feld frequently asked himself what keeps him here? why does he stay? he finally answered it that the man, no doubt because of his terrible experiences as a refugee, was afraid of the world.

After the incident with the broken last, angered by Sobel's behavior, the shoemaker decided to let him stew for a week in the rooming house, although his own strength was taxed dangerously and the business suffered. However, after several sharp nagging warnings from both his wife and daughter, he went finally in search of Sobel, as he had once before, quite recently, when over some fancied slight – Feld had merely asked him not to give Miriam so many books to read because her eyes were strained and red – the assistant had left the place in a huff, an incident which, as usual, came to nothing for he had returned after the shoemaker had talked to him, and taken his seat at the bench. But this time, after Feld had plodded through the snow to Sobel's house – he had thought of sending Miriam but the idea became repugnant to him – the burly landlady at the door informed him in a nasal voice that Sobel was not at home, and though Feld knew this was a nasty lie, for where had the refugee to go? still for some reason he was not completely sure of – it may have been the cold and his fatigue – he decided not to insist on seeing him. Instead he went home and hired a new helper.

Having settled the matter, though not entirely to his satisfaction, for he had much more to do than before, and so, for example, could no longer lie late in bed mornings because he had to get up to open the store for the new assistant, a speechless, dark man with an irritating rasp as he worked, whom he would not trust with the key as he had Sobel. Furthermore, this one, though able to do a fair repair job, knew nothing of grades of leather or prices, so Feld had to make his own purchases; and every night at closing time it was necessary to count the money in the till and lock up. However, he was not dissatisfied, for he lived much in his thoughts of Max and Miriam. The college boy had called her, and they had arranged a meeting for this coming Friday night. The shoemaker would personally have preferred Saturday, which he felt would make it a date of the first magnitude, but he learned Friday was Miriam's choice, so he said nothing. The day of the week did not matter. What mattered was the aftermath. Would they like each other and want to be friends? He sighed at all the time that would have to go by before he knew for sure. Often he was tempted to talk to Miriam about the boy, to ask whether she thought she would like his type — he had told her only that he considered Max a nice boy and had suggested he call her — but the one time he tried she snapped at him — justly — how should she know?

At last Friday came. Feld was not feeling particularly well so he stayed in bed, and Mrs. Feld thought it better to remain in the bedroom with him when Max called. Miriam received the boy, and her parents could hear their voices, his throaty one, as they talked. Just before leaving, Miriam brought Max to the bedroom door and he stood there a minute, a tall, slightly hunched figure wearing a thick, droopy suit, and apparently at ease as he greeted the shoemaker and his wife, which was surely a good sign. And Miriam, although she had worked all day, looked fresh and pretty. She was a large-framed girl with a well-shaped body, and she had a fine open face and soft hair. They made, Feld thought, a first-class couple.

Miriam returned after 11:30. Her mother was already asleep, but the shoemaker got out of bed and after locating his bathrobe went into the kitchen, where Miriam, to his surprise, sat at the table, reading.

"So where did you go?" Feld asked pleasantly.

"For a walk," she said, not looking up.

"I advised him," Feld said, clearing his throat, "he shouldn't spend so much money."

"I didn't care."

The shoemaker boiled up some water for tea and sat down at the table with a cupful and a thick slice of lemon.

"So how," he sighed after a sip, "did you enjoy?"

"It was all right."

He was silent. She must have sensed his disappointment, for she added, "You can't really tell much the first time."

"You will see him again?"

Turning a page, she said that Max had asked for another date.

"For when?"

"Saturday."

"So what did you say?"

"What did I say?" she asked, delaying for a moment — "I said yes."

Afterwards she inquired about Sobel, and Feld, without exactly knowing why, said the assistant had got another job. Miriam said nothing more and began to read. The shoemaker's conscience did not trouble him; he was satisfied with the Saturday date.

During the week, by placing here and there a deft question, he managed to get from Miriam some information about Max. It surprised him to learn that the boy was not studying to be either a doctor or lawyer but was taking a business course leading to a degree in accountancy. Feld was a little disappointed because he thought of accountants as bookkeepers and would have preferred "a higher profession." However, it was not long before he had investigated the subject and discovered that Certified Public Accountants were highly respected people, so he was thoroughly content as Saturday approached. But because Saturday was a busy day, he was much in the store and therefore did not see Max when he came to call for Miriam. From his wife he learned there had been nothing especially revealing about their meeting. Max had rung the bell and Miriam had got her coat and left with him — nothing more. Feld did not probe, for his wife was not particularly observant. Instead, he waited up for Miriam with a newspaper on his lap, which he scarcely looked at so lost was he in thinking of the future. He awoke to find her in the room with him, tiredly removing her hat. Greeting her, he was suddenly inexplicably afraid to ask anything about the evening. But since she volunteered nothing he was at last forced to inquire how she had enjoyed herself. Miriam began something noncommittal but apparently changed her mind, for she said after a minute, "I was bored."

When Feld had sufficiently recovered from his anguished disappointment to ask why, she answered without hesitation, "Because he's nothing more than a materialist."

"What means this word?"

"He has no soul. He's only interested in things."

He considered her statement for a long time but then asked, "Will you see him again?"

"He didn't ask."

"Suppose he will ask you?"

"I won't see him."

He did not argue; however, as the days went by he hoped increasingly she would change her mind. He wished the boy would telephone, because he was sure there was more to him than Miriam, with her inexperienced eye, could discern. But Max didn't call. As a matter of fact he took a different route to school, no longer passing the shoemaker's store, and Feld was deeply hurt.

Then one afternoon Max came in and asked for his shoes. The shoemaker took them down from the shelf where he had placed them, apart from the other pairs. He had done the work himself and the soles and heels were well built and firm. The shoes had been highly polished and somehow looked better than new. Max's Adam's apple went up once when he saw them, and his eyes had little lights in them.

"How much?" he asked, without directly looking at the shoemaker.

"Like I told you before," Feld answered sadly. "One dollar fifty cents."

Max handed him two crumpled bills and received in return a newly-minted silver half-dollar.

He left. Miriam had not been mentioned. That night the shoemaker discovered that his new assistant had been all the while stealing from him, and he suffered a heart attack.

Though the attack was very mild, he lay in bed for three weeks. Miriam spoke of going for Sobel, but sick as he was Feld rose in wrath against the idea. Yet in his heart he knew there was no other way, and the first weary day back in the shop thoroughly convinced him, so that night after supper he dragged himself to Sobel's rooming house.

He toiled up the stairs, though he knew it was bad for him, and at the top knocked at the door. Sobel opened it and the shoemaker entered. The room was a small, poor one, with a single window facing the street. It contained a narrow cot, a low table and several stacks of books piled haphazardly around on the floor along the wall, which made him think how queer Sobel was, to be uneducated and read so much. He had once asked him, Sobel, why you read so much? and the assistant could not answer him. Did you ever study in a college someplace? he had asked, but Sobel shook his head. He read, he said, to know. But to know what, the shoemaker demanded, and to know, why? Sobel never explained, which proved he read much because he was queer.

Feld sat down to recover his breath. The assistant was resting on his bed with his heavy back to the wall. His shirt and trousers were clean, and his stubby fingers, away from the shoemaker's bench, were strangely pallid. His face was thin and pale, as if he had been shut in this room since the day he had bolted from the store.

"So when you will come back to work?" Feld asked him.

To his surprise, Sobel burst out, "Never."

Jumping up, he strode over to the window that looked out upon the miserable street. "Why should I come back?" he cried.

"I will raise your wages."

"Who cares for your wages!"

The shoemaker, knowing he didn't care, was at a loss what else to say.

"What do you want from me, Sobel?"

"Nothing."

"I always treated you like you was my son."

Sobel vehemently denied it. "So why you look for strange boys in the street they should go out with Miriam? Why you don't think of me?"

The shoemaker's hands and feet turned freezing cold. His voice became so hoarse he couldn't speak. At last he cleared his throat and croaked, "So what has my daughter got to do with a shoemaker thirty-five years old who works for me?"

"Why do you think I worked so long for you?" Sobel cried out. "For the stingy wages I sacrificed five years of my life so you could have to eat and drink and where to sleep?"

"Then for what?" shouted the shoemaker.

"For Miriam," he blurted — "for her."

The shoemaker, after a time, managed to say, "I pay wages in cash, Sobel," and lapsed into silence. Though he was seething with excitement, his mind was coldly clear, and he had to admit to himself he had sensed all along that Sobel felt this way. He had never so much as thought it consciously, but he had felt it and was afraid.

"Miriam knows?" he muttered hoarsely.

"She knows."

"You told her?"

"No."

"Then how does she know?"

"How does she know?" Sobel said, "Because she knows. She knows who I am and what is in my heart."

Feld had a sudden insight. In some devious way, with his books and commentary, Sobel had given Miriam to understand that he loved her. The shoemaker felt a terrible anger at him for his deceit.

"Sobel, you are crazy," he said bitterly. "She will never marry a man so old and ugly like you."

Sobel turned black with rage. He cursed the shoemaker, but then, though he trembled to hold it in, his eyes filled with tears and he broke into deep sobs. With his back to Feld, he stood at the window, fists clenched, and his shoulders shook with his choked sobbing.

Watching him, the shoemaker's anger diminished. His teeth were on edge with pity for the man, and his eyes grew moist. How strange and sad that a refugee, a grown man, bald and old with his miseries, who had by the skin of his teeth escaped Hitler's incinerators, should fall in love, when he had got to America, with a girl less than half his age. Day after day, for five years he had sat at his bench, cutting and hammering away, waiting for the girl to become a woman, unable to ease his heart with speech, knowing no protest but desperation.

"Ugly I didn't mean," he said half aloud.

Then he realized that what he had called ugly was not Sobel but Miriam's life if she married him. He felt for his daughter a strange and gripping sorrow, as if she were already Sobel's bride, the wife, after all, of a shoemaker, and had in her life no more than her mother had had. And all his dreams for her – why he had slaved and destroyed his heart with anxiety and labor – all these dreams of a better life were dead.

The room was quiet. Sobel was standing by the window reading, and it was curious that when he read he looked young.

"She is only nineteen," Feld said brokenly. "This is too young yet to get married. Don't ask her for two years more, till she is twenty-one, then you can talk to her."

Sobel didn't answer. Feld rose and left. He went slowly down the stairs but once outside, though it was an icy night and the crisp falling snow whitened the street, he walked with a stronger stride.

But the next morning, when the shoemaker arrived, heavy-hearted, to open the store, he saw he needn't have come, for his assistant was already seated at the last, pounding leather for his love.

[1950, 1958]

Saul Bellow

[1915–2005]

Saul Bellow was born on June 10, 1915, in Lachine, Canada, a working-class town near Montreal. His parents were Abraham and Lescha Bellow, Jewish immigrants from St. Petersburg, Russia. Bellow was the couple's fourth child and the first to be born in Canada. Like other immigrant families, the Bellows struggled to make a living, and in 1918 they moved to an impoverished Jewish section of Montreal. Bellow, who grew up speaking English, French, and Yiddish, studied Hebrew and by the age of four could recite long passages from the Pentateuch. When he was eight years old, he was hospitalized for six months as a result of complications from an emergency appendectomy. The experience had a profound effect on Bellow, who in a 1990 interview said that he developed an early sense of the fragility of life. In 1924, after Bellow's father failed at yet another business venture, the family left Canada to join relatives in Chicago, where they found a place to live in the predominantly Polish and Jewish section of Humboldt Park. When he was not in school or working at odd jobs, Bellow spent long hours reading at a public library. During his senior year at Tuley High School, Bellow's mother died of cancer. "My life was never the same," he recalled. After his graduation in 1933, he attended Crane Junior College for a semester and then enrolled at the University of Chicago. In 1935, when his father could no longer afford to pay his tuition and living expenses, Bellow moved back home and transferred to nearby Northwestern University.

Bellow struggled to make his way as a writer. Although he published a short story in the *Daily Northwestern* in February 1936, he received little encouragement from professors in the English department. Bellow maintained that they believed that a Jew could never fully understand English literature, so he instead studied sociology and anthropology. When he graduated in 1937, he was awarded a fellowship for graduate study at the University of Wisconsin, Madison. But he withdrew after a year, later explaining, "Every time I worked on my thesis, it turned out to be a story." Bellow, who returned to Chicago in 1938, also recalled that his father was so frustrated by his ambition to become a writer that he once exclaimed: "You write and then you erase; you call that a profession?" Nonetheless, Bellow persevered, initially supporting himself by working for the Federal Writers' Project. He married the first of his five wives and later took a variety of jobs, including doing editorial work for the *Encyclopedia Britannica*

Saul Bellow

This photograph was taken when Bellow was completing work on his second novel, *The Victim* (1947).

Chicago belongs to Saul Bellow.

—Gloria Steinem

and teaching at Pestalozzi-Froebel Teacher's College. His first published story appeared in the prestigious *Partisan Review* in 1941. After the United States entered World War II, Bellow became an American citizen in 1942. He was eventually rejected by the army because of a hernia, and he joined the merchant marine. While waiting for his own military service to begin, he wrote a novel about a man about to be inducted into the army, *Dangling Man* (1944). From 1946 to 1948, Bellow taught at the University of Minnesota in Minneapolis, where he wrote *The Victim* (1947), a novel about a Jewish man coping with anti-Semitism in the aftermath of World War II. In 1948, Bellow was awarded a Guggenheim Fellowship, and he lived for two years in Paris. There, he began work on *The Adventures of Augie March* (1953), the story of a young Jew coming of age in Depression-era Chicago.

That novel won the National Book Award and firmly established Bellow as a "writer of consequence," as he was described in the *New York Times.* Now living in New York City, he published reviews and short fiction in a variety of prominent magazines. For the next several years, he also taught courses at New York University, Princeton, and Bard College. His collection *Seize the Day* (1956), was followed by *Henderson, the Rain King* (1959), a satiric novel about a man who goes on a spiritual pilgrimage to Africa. *Herzog* (1964), the story of a middle-aged Jewish professor's complicated response to a failed marriage and a failing career, was on the *New York Times* bestseller list for a year. Bellow returned to live in Chicago in 1967, when he accepted a position at the University of Chicago. Within the next decade, he published *Mosby's Memoirs and Other Stories* (1968) and two novels: *Mr. Sammler's Planet* (1970), the story of a Holocaust survivor living in New York, and *Humboldt's Gift* (1975), a sharp critique of American capitalist values that won the Pulitzer Prize. In 1976, Bellow was awarded the Nobel Prize for Literature. The citation praised him "for the human understanding and subtle analysis of contemporary culture that are combined in his work." Bellow continued that analysis of the state of contemporary culture in several of his later works, notably *The Dean's December* (1982), a novel about the decay of urban America, and *Ravelstein* (2000), inspired by the life and death from an AIDS-related illness of his closest friend, the philosopher and controversial education critic Allan Bloom. Hailed as a writer who "breathed new life into the American novel," Bellow died in Boston on April 5, 2005.

Bellow's "Looking for Mr. Green."   Regarded by many critics as Bellow's finest short story, "Looking for Mr. Green" first appeared in 1951 in *Commentary*, an influential magazine of literature and politics published by the American Jewish Committee. Bellow included the story in his first collection, *Seize the Day* (1956), and later revised it for publication in *Mosby's Memoirs and Other Stories* (1968). Several of the stories in that much-admired collection are accounts of quests, like the one in "Looking for Mr. Green," which is set in Depression-era Chicago. Its central character is George Grebe, an unemployed white college graduate who is forced

bedfordstmartins.com/ americanlit for research links on Bellow to take a job with a government agency, delivering relief checks in an impoverished African American neighborhood on the South Side. As he searches for an elusive man named Tulliver Green, Grebe confronts the hard realities of life in urban Chicago, the site of Bellow's complex exploration of the ways in which human beings make connections in what he describes as the "layers of ruin" of the modern urban world. The text is taken from *Mosby's Memoirs and Other Stories* (1968).

LOOKING FOR MR. GREEN

Whatsoever thy hand findeth to do, do it with thy might. . . .[1]

Hard work? No, it wasn't really so hard. He wasn't used to walking and stair-climbing, but the physical difficulty of his new job was not what George Grebe felt most. He was delivering relief checks in the Negro district, and although he was a native Chicagoan this was not a part of the city he knew much about — it needed a depression to introduce him to it. No, it wasn't literally hard work, not as reckoned in foot-pounds, but yet he was beginning to feel the strain of it, to grow aware of its peculiar difficulty. He could find the streets and numbers, but the clients were not where they were supposed to be, and he felt like a hunter inexperienced in the camouflage of his game. It was an unfavorable day, too — fall, and cold, dark weather, windy. But, anyway, instead of shells in his deep trenchcoat pocket he had the cardboard of checks, punctured for the spindles of the file, the holes reminding him of the holes in player-piano paper. And he didn't look much like a hunter, either; his was a city figure entirely, belted up in this Irish conspirator's coat. He was slender without being tall, stiff in the back, his legs looking shabby in a pair of old tweed pants gone through and fringy at the cuffs. With this stiffness, he kept his head forward, so that his face was red from the sharpness of the weather; and it was an indoors sort of face with gray eyes that persisted in some kind of thought and yet seemed to avoid definiteness of conclusion. He wore sideburns that surprised you somewhat by the tough curl of the blond hair and the effect of assertion in their length. He was not so mild as he looked, nor so youthful; and nevertheless there was no effort on his part to seem what he was not. He was an educated man; he was a bachelor; he was in some ways simple; without lushing, he liked a drink; his luck had not been good. Nothing was deliberately hidden.

He felt that his luck was better than usual today. When he had reported for work that morning he had expected to be shut up in the relief office at a clerk's job, for he had been hired downtown as a clerk, and he was glad to have, instead, the freedom of the streets and welcomed, at least at first, the vigor of the cold and even the blowing of the hard wind. But on the other hand he was not getting on with the distribution of the checks. It was true that it was a city job; nobody expected you to push too hard at a city job. His supervisor, that young Mr. Raynor, had practically told him that. Still, he wanted to do

---

1. ***Whatsoever . . . with thy might:*** The opening of Ecclesiastes 9:10, which concludes: "for there is no work, nor device, nor knowledge, nor wisdom, in the grave, whither thou goest."

well at it. For one thing, when he knew how quickly he could deliver a batch of checks, he would know also how much time he could expect to clip for himself. And then, too, the clients would be waiting for their money. That was not the most important consideration, though it certainly mattered to him. No, but he wanted to do well, simply for doing-well's sake, to acquit himself decently of a job because he so rarely had a job to do that required just this sort of energy. Of this peculiar energy he now had a superabundance; once it had started to flow, it flowed all too heavily. And, for the time being anyway, he was balked. He could not find Mr. Green.

So he stood in his big-skirted trenchcoat with a large envelope in his hand and papers showing from his pocket, wondering why people should be so hard to locate who were too feeble or sick to come to the station to collect their own checks. But Raynor had told him that tracking them down was not easy at first and had offered him some advice on how to proceed. "If you can see the postman, he's your first man to ask, and your best bet. If you can't connect with him, try the stores and tradespeople around. Then the janitor and the neighbors. But you'll find the closer you come to your man the less people will tell you. They don't want to tell you anything."

"Because I'm a stranger."

"Because you're white. We ought to have a Negro doing this, but we don't at the moment, and of course you've got to eat, too, and this is public employment. Jobs have to be made. Oh, that holds for me too. Mind you, I'm not letting myself out. I've got three years of seniority on you, that's all. And a law degree. Otherwise, you might be back of the desk and I might be going out into the field this cold day. The same dough pays us both and for the same, exact, identical reason. What's my law degree got to do with it? But you have to pass out these checks, Mr. Grebe, and it'll help if you're stubborn, so I hope you are."

"Yes, I'm fairly stubborn."

Raynor sketched hard with an eraser in the old dirt of his desk, left-handed, and said, "Sure, what else can you answer to such a question. Anyhow, the trouble you're going to have is that they don't like to give information about anybody. They think you're a plain-clothes dick or an installment collector, or summons-server or something like that. Till you've been seen around the neighborhood for a few months and people know you're only from the relief."

It was dark, ground-freezing, pre-Thanksgiving weather; the wind played hob with the smoke, rushing it down, and Grebe missed his gloves, which he had left in Raynor's office. And no one would admit knowing Green. It was past three o'clock and the postman had made his last delivery. The nearest grocer, himself a Negro, had never heard the name Tulliver Green, or said he hadn't. Grebe was inclined to think that it was true, that he had in the end convinced the man that he wanted only to deliver a check. But he wasn't sure. He needed experience in interpreting looks and signs and, even more, the will not to be put off or denied and even the force to bully if need be. If the grocer did know, he had got rid of him easily. But since most of his trade was with reliefers, why should he prevent the delivery of a check? Maybe Green, or Mrs. Green, if there was a Mrs. Green, patronized another grocer. And was there a Mrs. Green? It was one of Grebe's great handicaps that he hadn't looked at any of the case records. Raynor should have let him read files for a few hours. But he apparently saw no need for that, probably considering the job unimportant. Why prepare systematically to deliver a few checks?

But now it was time to look for the janitor. Grebe took in the building in the wind and gloom of the late November day — trampled, frost-hardened lots on one side; on the other, an automobile junk yard and then the infinite work of Elevated frames, weak-looking, gaping with rubbish fires; two sets of leaning brick porches three stories high and a flight of cement stairs to the cellar. Descending, he entered the underground passage, where he tried the doors until one opened and he found himself in the furnace room. There someone rose toward him and approached, scraping on the coal grit and bending under the canvas-jacketed pipes.

"Are you the janitor?"

"What do you want?"

"I'm looking for a man who's supposed to be living here. Green."

"What Green?"

"Oh, you maybe have more than one Green?" said Grebe with new, pleasant hope. "This is Tulliver Green."

"I don't think I c'n help you, mister. I don't know any."

"A crippled man."

The janitor stood bent before him. Could it be that he was crippled? Oh, God! what if he was. Grebe's gray eyes sought with excited difficulty to see. But no, he was only very short and stooped. A head awakened from meditation, a strong-haired beard, low, wide shoulders. A staleness of sweat and coal rose from his black shirt and the burlap sack he wore as an apron.

"Crippled how?"

Grebe thought and then answered with the light voice of unmixed candor, "I don't know. I've never seen him." This was damaging, but his only other choice was to make a lying guess, and he was not up to it. "I'm delivering checks for the relief to shut-in cases. If he weren't crippled he'd come to collect himself. That's why I said crippled. Bedridden, chair-ridden — is there anybody like that?"

This sort of frankness was one of Grebe's oldest talents, going back to childhood. But it gained him nothing here.

"No suh. I've got four buildin's same as this that I take care of. I don' know all the tenants, leave alone the tenants' tenants. The rooms turn over so fast, people movin' in and out every day. I can't tell you."

The janitor opened his grimy lips but Grebe did not hear him in the piping of the valves and the consuming pull of air to flame in the body of the furnace. He knew, however, what he had said.

"Well, all the same, thanks. Sorry I bothered you. I'll prowl around upstairs again and see if I can turn up someone who knows him."

Once more in the cold air and early darkness he made the short circle from the cellar-way to the entrance crowded between the brickwork pillars and began to climb to the third floor. Pieces of plaster ground under his feet; strips of brass tape from which the carpeting had been torn away marked old boundaries at the sides. In the passage, the cold reached him worse than in the street; it touched him to the bone. The hall toilets ran like springs. He thought grimly as he heard the wind burning around the building with a sound like that of the furnace, that this was a great piece of constructed shelter. Then he struck a match in the gloom and searched for names and numbers among the writings and scribbles on the walls. He saw WHOODY-DOODY GO TO JESUS, and zigzags, caricatures, sexual scrawls, and curses. So the sealed rooms of pyramids were also decorated, and the caves of human dawn.

The information on his card was, TULLIVER GREEN — APT 3D. There were no names, however, and no numbers. His shoulders drawn up, tears of cold in his eyes, breathing vapor, he went the length of the corridor and told himself that if he had been lucky enough to have the temperament for it he would bang on one of the doors and bawl out "Tulliver Green!" until he got results. But it wasn't in him to make an uproar and he continued to burn matches, passing the light over the walls. At the rear, in a corner off the hall, he discovered a door he had not seen before and he thought it best to investigate. It sounded empty when he knocked, but a young Negress answered, hardly more than a girl. She opened only a bit, to guard the warmth of the room.

"Yes suh?"

"I'm from the district relief station on Prairie Avenue. I'm looking for a man named Tulliver Green to give him his check. Do you know him?"

No, she didn't; but he thought she had not understood anything of what he had said. She had a dream-bound, dream-blind face, very soft and black, shut off. She wore a man's jacket and pulled the ends together at her throat. Her hair was parted in three directions, at the sides and transversely, standing up at the front in a dull puff.

"Is there somebody around here who might know?"

"I jus' taken this room las' week."

He observed that she shivered, but even her shiver was somnambulistic and there was no sharp consciousness of cold in the big smooth eyes of her handsome face.

"All right, miss, thank you. Thanks," he said, and went to try another place.

Here he was admitted. He was grateful, for the room was warm. It was full of people, and they were silent as he entered — ten people, or a dozen, perhaps more, sitting on benches like a parliament. There was no light, properly speaking, but a tempered darkness that the window gave, and everyone seemed to him enormous, the men padded out in heavy work clothes and winter coats, and the women huge, too, in their sweaters, hats, and old furs. And, besides, bed and bedding, a black cooking range, a piano piled towering to the ceiling with papers, a dining-room table of the old style of prosperous Chicago. Among these people Grebe, with his cold-heightened fresh color and his smaller stature, entered like a schoolboy. Even though he was met with smiles and good will, he knew, before a single word was spoken, that all the currents ran against him and that he would make no headway. Nevertheless he began. "Does anybody here know how I can deliver a check to Mr. Tulliver Green?"

"Green?" It was the man that had let him in who answered. He was in short sleeves, in a checkered shirt, and had a queer, high head, profusely overgrown and long as a shako;[2]

---

2. *shako*: A tall, plumed military hat.

the veins entered it strongly from his forehead. "I never heard mention of him. Is this where he live?"

"This is the address they gave me at the station. He's a sick man, and he'll need his check. Can't anybody tell me where to find him?"

He stood his ground and waited for a reply, his crimson wool scarf wound about his neck and drooping outside his trenchcoat, pockets weighted with the block of checks and official forms. They must have realized that he was not a college boy employed afternoons by a bill collector, trying foxily to pass for a relief clerk, recognized that he was an older man who knew himself what need was, who had had more than an average seasoning in hardship. It was evident enough if you looked at the marks under his eyes and at the sides of his mouth.

"Anybody know this sick man?"

"No suh." On all sides he saw heads shaken and smiles of denial. No one knew. And maybe it was true, he considered, standing silent in the earthen, musky human gloom of the place as the rumble continued. But he could never really be sure.

"What's the matter with this man?" said shako-head.

"I've never seen him. All I can tell you is that he can't come in person for his money. It's my first day in this district."

"Maybe they given you the wrong number?"

"I don't believe so. But where else can I ask about him?" He felt that this persistence amused them deeply, and in a way he shared their amusement that he should stand up so tenaciously to them. Though smaller, though slight, he was his own man, he retracted nothing about himself, and he looked back at them, gray-eyed, with amusement and also with a sort of courage. On the bench some man spoke in his throat, the words impossible to catch, and a woman answered with a wild, shrieking laugh, which was quickly cut off.

"Well, so nobody will tell me?"

"Ain't nobody who knows."

"At least, if he lives here, he pays rent to someone. Who manages the building?"

"Greatham Company. That's on Thirty-ninth Street."

Grebe wrote it in his pad. But, in the street again, a sheet of wind-driven paper clinging to his leg while he deliberated what direction to take next, it seemed a feeble lead to follow. Probably this Green didn't rent a flat, but a room. Sometimes there were as many as twenty people in an apartment; the real-estate agent would know only the lessee. And not even the agent could tell you who the renters were. In some places the beds were even used in shifts, watchmen or jitney drivers or short-order cooks in night joints turning out after a day's sleep and surrendering their beds to a sister, a nephew, or perhaps a stranger, just off the bus. There were large numbers of newcomers in this terrific, blight-bitten portion of the city between Cottage Grove and Ashland, wandering from house to house and room to room. When you saw them, how could you know them? They didn't carry bundles on their backs or look picturesque. You only saw a man, a Negro, walking in the street or riding in the car, like everyone else, with his thumb closed on a transfer. And therefore how were you supposed to tell? Grebe thought the Greatham agent would only laugh at his question.

But how much it would have simplified the job to be able to say that Green was old, or blind, or consumptive. An hour in the files, taking a few notes, and he needn't have been at such a disadvantage. When Raynor gave him the block of checks he asked, "How much should I know about these people?" Then Raynor had looked as though he were preparing to accuse him of trying to make the job more important than it was. He smiled, because by then they were on fine terms, but nevertheless he had been getting ready to say something like that when the confusion began in the station over Staika and her children.

Grebe had waited a long time for this job. It came to him through the pull of an old schoolmate in the Corporation Counsel's office, never a close friend, but suddenly sympathetic and interested – pleased to show, moreover, how well he had done, how strongly he was coming on even in these miserable times. Well, he was coming through strongly, along with the Democratic administration itself. Grebe had gone to see him in City Hall, and they had had a counter lunch or beers at least once a month for a year, and finally it had been possible to swing the job. He didn't mind being assigned the lowest clerical grade, nor even being a messenger, though Raynor thought he did.

This Raynor was an original sort of guy and Grebe had taken to him immediately. As was proper on the first day, Grebe had come early, but he waited long, for Raynor was late. At last he darted into his cubicle of an office as though he had just jumped from one of those hurtling huge red Indian Avenue cars. His thin, rough face was wind-stung and he was grinning and saying something breathlessly to himself. In his hat, a small fedora, and his coat, the velvet collar a neat fit about his neck, and his silk muffler that set off the nervous twist of his chin, he swayed and turned himself in his swivel chair, feet leaving the ground; so that he pranced a little as he sat. Meanwhile he took Grebe's measure out of his eyes, eyes of an unusual vertical length and slightly sardonic. So the two men sat for a while, saying nothing, while the supervisor raised his hat from his miscombed hair and put it in his lap. His cold-darkened hands were not clean. A steel beam passed through the little makeshift room, from which machine belts once had hung. The building was an old factory.

"I'm younger than you; I hope you won't find it hard taking orders from me," said Raynor. "But I don't make them up, either. You're how old, about?"

"Thirty-five."

"And you thought you'd be inside doing paper work. But it so happens I have to send you out."

"I don't mind."

"And it's mostly a Negro load we have in this district."

"So I thought it would be."

"Fine. You'll get along. *C'est un bon boulot.*[3] Do you know French?"

"Some."

"I thought you'd be a university man."

"Have you been in France?" said Grebe.

"No, that's the French of the Berlitz School. I've been at it for more than a year, just as

---

3. *C'est un bon boulot*: It's a good job (French).

I'm sure people have been, all over the world, office boys in China and braves in Tan-ganyika.[4] In fact, I damn well know it. Such is the attractive power of civilization. It's overrated, but what do you want? *Que voulez-vous?*[5] I get *Le Rire*[6] and all the spicy papers, just like in Tanganyika. It must be mystifying, out there. But my reason is that I'm aiming at the diplomatic service. I have a cousin who's a courier, and the way he describes it is awfully attractive. He rides in the *wagon-lits*[7] and reads books. While we — What did you do before?"

"I sold."

"Where?"

"Canned meat at Stop and Shop. In the basement."

"And before that?"

"Window shades, at Goldblatt's."

"Steady work?"

"No, Thursdays and Saturdays. I also sold shoes."

"You've been a shoe-dog too. Well. And prior to that? Here it is in your folder." He opened the record. "Saint Olaf's College, instructor in classical languages. Fellow, University of Chicago, 1926–27. I've had Latin, too. Let's trade quotations — '*Dum spiro spero*.'"[8]

"'*Da dextram misero*.'"[9]

"'*Alea jacta est*.'"[10]

"'*Excelsior*.'"[11]

Raynor shouted with laughter, and other workers came to look at him over the partition. Grebe also laughed, feeling pleased and easy. The luxury of fun on a nervous morning.

When they were done and no one was watching or listening, Raynor said rather seriously, "What made you study Latin in the first place? Was it for the priesthood?"

"No."

"Just for the hell of it? For the culture? Oh, the things people think they can pull!" He made his cry hilarious and tragic. "I ran my pants off so I could study for the bar, and I've passed the bar, so I get twelve dollars a week more than you as a bonus for having seen life straight and whole. I'll tell you, as a man of culture, that even though nothing looks to be real, and everything stands for something else, and that thing for another thing, and that thing for a still further one — there ain't any comparison between twenty-five and thirty-seven dollars a week, regardless of the last reality. Don't you

---

4. **Tanganyika**: A British territory in East Africa that gained its independence in 1961.
5. *Que voulez-vous?*: What do you want? (French).
6. *Le Rire*: *Laughter* (French), a weekly humor magazine that was founded in Paris in 1894 and published in various forms through the 1950s.
7. *wagon-lits*: Sleeping cars on a train (French).
8. '*Dum spiro spero*': Where there's life there's hope (Latin).
9. '*Da dextram misero*': Give the right hand to the wretched (Latin).
10. '*Alea jacta est*': The die is cast (Latin).
11. '*Excelsior*': Higher (Latin).

think that was clear to your Greeks? They were a thoughtful people, but they didn't part with their slaves."

This was a great deal more than Grebe had looked for in his first interview with his supervisor. He was too shy to show all the astonishment he felt. He laughed a little, aroused, and brushed at the sunbeam that covered his head with its dust. "Do you think my mistake was so terrible?"

"Damn right it was terrible, and you know it now that you've had the whip of hard times laid on your back. You should have been preparing yourself for trouble. Your people must have been well off to send you to the university. Stop me, if I'm stepping on your toes. Did your mother pamper you? Did your father give in to you? Were you brought up tenderly, with permission to go and find out what were the last things that everything else stands for while everybody else labored in the fallen world of appearances?"

"Well, no, it wasn't exactly like that." Grebe smiled. *The fallen world of appearances!*[12] no less. But now it was his turn to deliver a surprise. "We weren't rich. My father was the last genuine English butler in Chicago —"

"Are you kidding?"

"Why should I be?"

"In a livery?"

"In livery. Up on the Gold Coast."[13]

"And he wanted you to be educated like a gentleman?"

"He did not. He sent me to the Armour Institute to study chemical engineering. But when he died I changed schools."

He stopped himself, and considered how quickly Raynor had reached him. In no time he had your valise on the table and all your stuff unpacked. And afterward, in the streets, he was still reviewing how far he might have gone, and how much he might have been led to tell if they had not been interrupted by Mrs. Staika's great noise.

But just then a young woman, one of Raynor's workers, ran into the cubicle exclaiming, "Haven't you heard all the fuss?"

"We haven't heard anything."

"It's Staika, giving out with all her might. The reporters are coming. She said she phoned the papers, and you know she did."

"But what is she up to?" said Raynor.

"She brought her wash and she's ironing it here, with our current, because the relief won't pay her electric bill. She has her ironing board set up by the admitting desk, and her kids are with her, all six. They never are in school more than once a week. She's always dragging them around with her because of her reputation."

---

12. ***The fallen world of appearances!*:** As Grebe evidently recognizes, his supervisor has alluded to Augustine of Hippo (354-430), later St. Augustine, an influential theologian of the early Roman Catholic Church. Augustine developed the concept that human beings live in two worlds: the realm of appearances, of things as they seem, and the higher reality of things as they are. In order to leave behind the sinful or fallen realm of appearances, human beings must seek divine salvation and spiritual liberation in the higher reality.

13. **Gold Coast:** A wealthy neighborhood along the lakefront north of downtown Chicago. Livery is a special uniform worn by a servant.

"I don't want to miss any of this," said Raynor, jumping up. Grebe, as he followed with the secretary, said, "Who is this Staika?"

"They call her the 'Blood Mother of Federal Street.' She's a professional donor at the hospitals. I think they pay ten dollars a pint. Of course it's no joke, but she makes a very big thing out of it and she and the kids are in the papers all the time."

A small crowd, staff and clients divided by a plywood barrier, stood in the narrow space of the entrance, and Staika was shouting in a gruff, mannish voice, plunging the iron on the board and slamming it on the metal rest.

"My father and mother came in a steerage, and I was born in our house, Robey by Huron. I'm no dirty immigrant. I'm a U.S. citizen. My husband is a gassed veteran from France with lungs weaker'n paper, that hardly can he go to the toilet by himself. These six children of mine, I have to buy the shoes for their feet with my own blood. Even a lousy little white Communion necktie, that's a couple of drops of blood; a little piece of mosquito veil for my Vadja so she won't be ashamed in church for the other girls, they take my blood for it by Goldblatt. That's how I keep goin'. A fine thing if I had to depend on the relief. And there's plenty of people on the rolls — fakes! There's nothin' *they* can't get, that can go and wrap bacon at Swift and Armour any time. They're lookin' for them by the Yards. They never have to be out of work. Only they rather lay in their lousy beds and eat the public's money." She was not afraid, in a predominantly Negro station, to shout this way about Negroes.

Grebe and Raynor worked themselves forward to get a closer view of the woman. She was flaming with anger and with pleasure at herself, broad and huge, a golden-headed woman who wore a cotton cap laced with pink ribbon. She was barelegged and had on black gym shoes, her Hoover apron[14] was open and her great breasts, not much re-strained by a man's undershirt, hampered her arms as she worked at the kid's dress on the ironing board. And the children, silent and white, with a kind of locked obstinacy, in sheepskins and lumberjackets, stood behind her. She had captured the station, and the pleasure this gave her was enormous. Yet her grievances were true grievances. She was telling the truth. But she behaved like a liar. The look of her small eyes was hidden, and while she raged she also seemed to be spinning and planning.

"They send me out college case workers in silk pants to talk me out of what I got comin'. Are they better'n me? Who told them? Fire them. Let 'em go and get married, and then you won't have to cut electric from people's budget."

The chief supervisor, Mr. Ewing, couldn't silence her and he stood with folded arms at the head of his staff, bald, bald-headed, saying to his subordinates like the ex-school principal he was, "Pretty soon she'll be tired and go."

"No she won't," said Raynor to Grebe. "She'll get what she wants. She knows more about the relief even than Ewing. She's been on the rolls for years, and she always gets what she wants because she puts on a noisy show. Ewing knows it. He'll give in soon.

---

14. **Hoover apron:** A popular, wrap-around apron invented by the wife of Herbert Hoover, who was appointed as the first director of the U.S. Food Administration when the United States entered World War I in 1917 and who was elected president in 1928, the year before the onset of the Great Depression.

He's only saving face. If he gets bad publicity, the Commissioner'll have him on the carpet, downtown. She's got him submerged; she'll submerge everybody in time, and that includes nations and governments."

Grebe replied with his characteristic smile, disagreeing completely. Who would take Staika's orders, and what changes could her yelling ever bring about?

No, what Grebe saw in her, the power that made people listen, was that her cry expressed the war of flesh and blood, perhaps turned a little crazy and certainly ugly, on this place and this condition. And at first, when he went out, the spirit of Staika somehow presided over the whole district for him, and it took color from her; he saw her color, in the spotty curb fires, and the fires under the El,[15] the straight alley of flamy gloom. Later, too, when he went into a tavern for a shot of rye, the sweat of beer, association with West Side Polish streets, made him think of her again.

He wiped the corners of his mouth with his muffler, his handkerchief being inconvenient to reach for, and went out again to get on with the delivery of his checks. The air bit cold and hard and a few flakes of snow formed near him. A train struck by and left a quiver in the frames and a bristling icy hiss over the rails.

Crossing the street, he descended a flight of board steps into a basement grocery, setting off a little bell. It was a dark, long store and it caught you with its stinks of smoked meat, soap, dried peaches, and fish. There was a fire wrinkling and flapping in the little stove, and the proprietor was waiting, an Italian with a long, hollow face and stubborn bristles. He kept his hands warm under his apron.

No, he didn't know Green. You knew people but not names. The same man might not have the same name twice. The police didn't know, either, and mostly didn't care. When somebody was shot or knifed they took the body away and didn't look for the murderer. In the first place, nobody would tell them anything. So they made up a name for the coroner and called it quits. And in the second place, they didn't give a goddamn anyhow. But they couldn't get to the bottom of a thing even if they wanted to. Nobody would get to know even a tenth of what went on among these people. They stabbed and stole, they did every crime and abomination you ever heard of, men and men, women and women, parents and children, worse than the animals. They carried on their own way, and the horrors passed off like a smoke. There was never anything like it in the history of the whole world.

It was a long speech, deepening with every word in its fantasy and passion and becoming increasingly senseless and terrible: a swarm amassed by suggestion and invention, a huge, hugging, despairing knot, a human wheel of heads, legs, bellies, arms, rolling through his shop.

Grebe felt that he must interrupt him. He said sharply, "What are you talking about! All I asked was whether you knew this man."

"That isn't even the half of it. I been here six years. You probably don't want to believe this. But suppose it's true?"

"All the same," said Grebe, "there must be a way to find a person."

The Italian's close-spaced eyes had been queerly concentrated, as were his muscles,

---

15. **El:** The common name of the elevated train system in Chicago.

while he leaned across the counter trying to convince Grebe. Now he gave up the effort and sat down on his stool. "Oh — I suppose. Once in a while. But I been telling you, even the cops don't get anywhere."

"They're always after somebody. It's not the same thing."

"Well, keep trying if you want. I can't help you."

But he didn't keep trying. He had no more time to spend on Green. He slipped Green's check to the back of the block. The next name on the list was FIELD, WINSTON.

He found the back-yard bungalow without the least trouble; it shared a lot with another house, a few feet of yard between. Grebe knew these two-shack arrangements. They had been built in vast numbers in the days before the swamps were filled and the streets raised, and they were all the same — a boardwalk along the fence, well under street level, three or four ball-headed posts for clotheslines, greening wood, dead shingles, and a long, long flight of stairs to the rear door.

A twelve-year-old boy let him into the kitchen, and there the old man was, sitting by the table in a wheel chair.

"Oh, it's d' Government man," he said to the boy when Grebe drew out his checks. "Go bring me my box of papers." He cleared a space on the table.

"Oh, you don't have to go to all that trouble," said Grebe. But Field laid out his papers: Social Security card, relief certification, letters from the state hospital in Manteno, and a naval discharge dated San Diego, 1920.

"That's plenty," Grebe said. "Just sign."

"You got to know who I am," the old man said. "You're from the Government. It's not your check, it's a Government check and you got no business to hand it over till everything is proved."

He loved the ceremony of it, and Grebe made no more objections. Field emptied his box and finished out the circle of cards and letters.

"There's everything I done and been. Just the death certificate and they can close book on me." He said this with a certain happy pride and magnificence. Still he did not sign; he merely held the little pen upright on the golden-green corduroy of his thigh. Grebe did not hurry him. He felt the old man's hunger for conversation.

"I got to get better coal," he said. "I send my little gran'son to the yard with my order and they fill his wagon with screening. The stove ain't made for it. It fall through the grate. The order says Franklin County egg-size coal."

"I'll report it and see what can be done."

"Nothing can be done, I expect. You know and I know. There ain't no little ways to make things better, and the only big thing is money. That's the only sunbeams, money. Nothing is black where it shines, and the only place you see black is where it ain't shining. What we colored have to have is our own rich. There ain't no other way."

Grebe sat, his reddened forehead bridged levelly by his close-cut hair and his cheeks lowered in the wings of his collar — the caked fire shone hard within the isinglass-and-iron frames[16] but the room was not comfortable — sat and listened while the old man

---

16. **isinglass-and-iron frames:** The firebox of the coal stove is made of isinglass — thin, transparent sheets of mica — framed in strips of iron.

unfolded his scheme. This was to create one Negro millionaire a month by subscription. One clever, good-hearted young fellow elected every month would sign a contract to use the money to start a business employing Negroes. This would be advertised by chain letters and word of mouth, and every Negro wage earner would contribute a dollar a month. Within five years there would be sixty millionaires.

"That'll fetch respect," he said with a throat-stopped sound that came out like a foreign syllable. "You got to take and organize all the money that gets thrown away on the policy wheel and horse race. As long as they can take it away from you, they got no respect for you. Money, that's d' sun of human kind!" Field was a Negro of mixed blood, perhaps Cherokee, or Natchez; his skin was reddish. And he sounded, speaking about a golden sun in this dark room, and looked, shaggy and slab-headed, with the mingled blood of his face and broad lips, the little pen still upright in his hand, like one of the underground kings of mythology, old judge Minos[17] himself.

And now he accepted the check and signed. Not to soil the slip, he held it down with his knuckles. The table budged and creaked, the center of the gloomy, heathen midden of the kitchen covered with bread, meat, and cans, and the scramble of papers.

"Don't you think my scheme'd work?"

"It's worth thinking about. Something ought to be done, I agree."

"It'll work if people will do it. That's all. That's the only thing, any time. When they understand it in the same way, all of them."

"That's true," said Grebe, rising. His glance met the old man's.

"I know you got to go," he said. "Well, God bless you, boy, you ain't been sly with me. I can tell it in a minute."

He went back through the buried yard. Someone nursed a candle in a shed, where a man unloaded kindling wood from a sprawl-wheeled baby buggy and two voices carried on a high conversation. As he came up the sheltered passage he heard the hard boost of the wind in the branches and against the house fronts, and then, reaching the sidewalk, he saw the needle-eye red of cable towers in the open icy height hundreds of feet above the river and the factories — those keen points. From here, his view was obstructed all the way to the South Branch and its timber banks, and the cranes beside the water. Rebuilt after the Great Fire,[18] this part of the city was, not fifty years later, in ruins again, factories boarded up, buildings deserted or fallen, gaps of prairie between. But it wasn't desolation that this made you feel, but rather a faltering of organization that set free a huge energy, an escaped, unattached, unregulated power from the giant raw place. Not only must people feel it but, it seemed to Grebe, they were compelled to match it. In their very bodies. He no less than others, he realized. Say that his parents had been servants in their time, whereas he was not supposed to be one. He thought that they had never done any service like this, which no one visible asked for, and probably flesh and

---

17. **Minos:** A king of Crete who after his death was the judge of the dead in Hades, the underworld in Greek mythology.
18. **Great Fire:** The disastrous fire that burned from October 8–10, 1871, destroying four square miles of the city and killing hundreds of people in Chicago.

blood could not even perform. Nor could anyone show why it should be performed; or see where the performance would lead. That did not mean that he wanted to be released from it, he realized with a grimly pensive face. On the contrary. He had something to do. To be compelled to feel this energy and yet have no task to do — that was horrible; that was suffering; he knew what that was. It was now quitting time. Six o'clock. He could go home if he liked, to his room, that is, to wash in hot water, to pour a drink, lie down on his quilt, read the paper, eat some liver paste on crackers before going out to dinner. But to think of this actually made him feel a little sick, as though he had swallowed hard air. He had six checks left, and he was determined to deliver at least one of these: Mr. Green's check.

So he started again. He had four or five dark blocks to go, past open lots, condemned houses, old foundations, closed schools, black churches, mounds, and he reflected that there must be many people alive who had once seen the neighborhood rebuilt and new. Now there was a second layer of ruins; centuries of history accomplished through human massing. Numbers had given the place forced growth; enormous numbers had also broken it down. Objects once so new, so concrete that it could have occurred to anyone they stood for other things, had crumbled. Therefore, reflected Grebe, the secret of them was out. It was that they stood for themselves by agreement, and were natural and not unnatural by agreement, and when the things themselves collapsed the agreement became visible. What was it, otherwise, that kept cities from looking peculiar? Rome, that was almost permanent, did not give rise to thoughts like these. And was it abidingly real? But in Chicago, where the cycles were so fast and the familiar died out, and again rose changed, and died again in thirty years, you saw the common agreement or covenant, and you were forced to think about appearances and realities. (He remembered Raynor and he smiled. Raynor was a clever boy.) Once you had grasped this, a great many things became intelligible. For instance, why Mr. Field should conceive such a scheme. Of course, if people were to agree to create a millionaire, a real millionaire would come into existence. And if you wanted to know how Mr. Field was inspired to think of this, why, he had within sight of his kitchen window the chart, the very bones of a successful scheme — the El with its blue and green confetti of signals. People consented to pay dimes and ride the crash-box cars, and so it was a success. Yet how absurd it looked; how little reality there was to start with. And yet Yerkes, the great financier who built it, had known that he could get people to agree to do it. Viewed as itself, what a scheme of a scheme it seemed, how close to an appearance. Then why wonder at Mr. Field's idea? He had grasped a principle. And then Grebe remembered, too, that Mr. Yerkes had established the Yerkes Observatory and endowed it with millions.[19] Now how did the notion come to him in his New York museum of a palace or his Aegean-bound yacht to give money to astronomers? Was he awed by the success of his bizarre enterprise and

---

19. **Mr. Yerkes . . . millions:** Charles Tyson Yerkes (1837–1905) was an American financier who played a major role in developing Chicago's mass-transit system. In an effort to improve his public image, he funded the University of Chicago's Yerkes Observatory, which housed the world's largest telescope when it opened in 1897.

therefore ready to spend money to find out where in the universe being and seeming were identical? Yes, he wanted to know what abides; and whether flesh is Bible grass; and he offered money to be burned in the fire of suns. Okay, then, Grebe thought further, these things exist because people consent to exist with them — we have got so far — and also there is a reality which doesn't depend on consent but within which consent is a game. But what about need, the need that keeps so many vast thousands in position? You tell me that, you *private* little gentleman and *decent* soul — he used these words against himself scornfully. Why is the consent given to misery? And why so painfully ugly? Because there is *something* that is dismal and permanently ugly? Here he sighed and gave it up, and thought it was enough for the present moment that he had a real check in his pocket for a Mr. Green who must be real beyond question. If only his neighbors didn't think they had to conceal him.

This time he stopped at the second floor. He struck a match and found a door. Presently a man answered his knock and Grebe had the check ready and showed it even before he began. "Does Tulliver Green live here? I'm from the relief."

The man narrowed the opening and spoke to someone at his back.

"Does he live here?"

"Uh-uh. No."

"Or anywhere in this building? He's a sick man and he can't come for his dough." He exhibited the check in the light, which was smoky — the air smelled of charred lard — and the man held off the brim of his cap to study it.

"Uh-uh. Never seen the name."

"There's nobody around here that uses crutches?"

He seemed to think, but it was Grebe's impression that he was simply waiting for a decent interval to pass.

"No, suh. Nobody I ever see."

"I've been looking for this man all afternoon" — Grebe spoke out with sudden force — "and I'm going to have to carry this check back to the station. It seems strange not to be able to find a person to *give* him something when you're looking for him for a good reason. I suppose if I had bad news for him I'd find him quick enough."

There was a responsive motion in the other man's face. "That's right, I reckon."

"It almost doesn't do any good to have a name if you can't be found by it. It doesn't stand for anything. He might as well not have any," he went on, smiling. It was as much of a concession as he could make to his desire to laugh.

"Well, now, there's a little old knot-back man I see once in a while. He might be the one you lookin' for. Downstairs."

"Where? Right side or left? Which door?"

"I don't know which. Thin-face little knot-back with a stick."

But no one answered at any of the doors on the first floor. He went to the end of the corridor, searching by matchlight, and found only a stairless exit to the yard, a drop of about six feet. But there was a bungalow near the alley, an old house like Mr. Field's. To jump was unsafe. He ran from the front door, through the underground passage and into the yard. The place was occupied. There was a light through the curtains, upstairs.

The name on the ticket under the broken, scoop-shaped mailbox was Green! He exultantly rang the bell and pressed against the locked door. Then the lock clicked faintly and a long staircase opened before him. Someone was slowly coming down – a woman. He had the impression in the weak light that she was shaping her hair as she came, making herself presentable, for he saw her arms raised. But it was for support that they were raised; she was feeling her way downward, down the wall, stumbling. Next he wondered about the pressure of her feet on the treads; she did not seem to be wearing shoes. And it was a freezing stairway. His ring had got her out of bed, perhaps, and she had forgotten to put them on. And then he saw that she was not only shoeless but naked; she was entirely naked, climbing down while she talked to herself, a heavy woman, naked and drunk. She blundered into him. The contact of her breasts, though they touched only his coat, made him go back against the door with a blind shock. See what he had tracked down, in his hunting game!

The woman was saying to herself, furious with insult, "So I cain't ——k, huh? I'll show that son-of-a-bitch kin I, cain't I."

What should he do now? Grebe asked himself. Why, he should go. He should turn away and go. He couldn't talk to this woman. He couldn't keep her standing naked in the cold. But when he tried he found himself unable to turn away.

He said, "Is this where Mr. Green lives?"

But she was still talking to herself and did not hear him.

"Is this Mr. Green's house?"

At last she turned her furious drunken glance on him. "What do you want?"

Again her eyes wandered from him; there was a dot of blood in their enraged brilliance. He wondered why she didn't feel the cold.

"I'm from the relief."

"Awright, what?"

"I've got a check for Tulliver Green."

This time she heard him and put out her hand.

"No, no, for *Mr.* Green. He's got to sign," he said. How was he going to get Green's signature tonight!

"I'll take it. He cain't."

He desperately shook his head, thinking of Mr. Field's precautions about identification. "I can't let you have it. It's for him. Are you Mrs. Green?"

"Maybe I is, and maybe I ain't. Who want to know?"

"Is he upstairs?"

"Awright. Take it up yourself, you goddamn fool."

Sure, he was a goddamn fool. Of course he could not go up because Green would probably be drunk and naked, too. And perhaps he would appear on the landing soon. He looked eagerly upward. Under the light was a high narrow brown wall. Empty! It remained empty!

"Hell with you, then!" he heard her cry. To deliver a check for coal and clothes, he was keeping her in the cold. She did not feel it, but his face was burning with frost and self-ridicule. He backed away from her.

"I'll come tomorrow, tell him."

"Ah, hell with you. Don' never come. What you doin' here in the nighttime? Don' come back." She yelled so that he saw the breadth of her tongue. She stood astride in the long cold box of the hall and held on to the banister and the wall. The bungalow itself was shaped something like a box, a clumsy, high box pointing into the freezing air with its sharp, wintry lights.

"If you are Mrs. Green, I'll give you the check," he said, changing his mind.

"Give here, then." She took it, took the pen offered with it in her left hand, and tried to sign the receipt on the wall. He looked around, almost as though to see whether his madness was being observed, and came near believing that someone was standing on a mountain of used tires in the auto-junking shop next door.

"But are you Mrs. Green?" he now thought to ask. But she was already climbing the stairs with the check, and it was too late, if he had made an error, if he was now in trouble, to undo the thing. But he wasn't going to worry about it. Though she might not be Mrs. Green, he was convinced that Mr. Green was upstairs. Whoever she was, the woman stood for Green, whom he was not to see this time. Well, you silly bastard, he said to himself, so you think you found him. So what? Maybe you really did find him — what of it? But it was important that there was a real Mr. Green whom they could not keep him from reaching because he seemed to come as an emissary from hostile appearances. And though the self-ridicule was slow to diminish, and his face still blazed with it, he had, nevertheless, a feeling of elation, too. "For after all," he said, "he *could* be found!"

[1951, 1968]

Arthur Miller

[1915–2005]

Arthur Asher Miller was born on October 17, 1915, in New York City. He was the second child of Augusta Miller, a former teacher, and Isidore Miller, a Jewish immigrant from Poland who owned a successful clothing company. But the stock market crash of 1929 dramatically affected the business, leaving the family in serious financial straits. They consequently moved to Brooklyn, where they could live more cheaply. During high school, Miller played on the football team and worked at a series of odd jobs in order to help support the family. After his graduation in 1932, he was disappointed to be rejected by both Cornell University and the University of Michigan. Miller subsequently took a job as a stock clerk in an auto-parts company, reading novels while he commuted to work on the subway and saving his money for college. He reapplied to the University of Michigan, and he was permitted to enroll as a provisional student in the fall of 1934. He studied journalism and joined the staff of the *Michigan Daily*. He also composed his first short story, "In Memoriam," about a salesman who commits suicide by throwing himself in front of a train, and his first play, *No Villain,* in 1936. The play won a $250 award in a university contest, and a revised version was performed in Ann Arbor and Detroit. Miller, who transferred to English and studied playwriting, subsequently won awards for two more of his plays, as well as a scholarship that enabled him to complete his degree in 1938.

Miller returned home to embark on his career as a playwright in New York. He worked for the Federal Theatre Project until June 1939, when funding for the program was withdrawn because of congressional objections to the radical political overtones of its productions. In 1940, he married his college sweetheart, Mary Slattery, and the couple moved to Brooklyn.

Arthur Miller

This photograph was taken at the time Miller was writing his Pulitzer Prize–winning play, *Death of a Salesman* (1949).

Working nights in the Brooklyn Navy Yard, Miller wrote numerous radio plays and his first Broadway play, *The Man Who Had All the Luck,* which opened in November 1944. Stung by the failure of the play, which was panned by critics and closed after only four performances, Miller wrote *Focus* (1945), a novel exposing the pervasive anti-Semitism in postwar America. He then decided to make one final effort to write a successful play, determining that if he failed he "would go into another line of work." The result was *All My Sons,* a contemporary drama about a businessman who had made his money by providing defective parts for the military, sending twenty-one pilots to their deaths during World War II. After the play opened on Broadway on January 29, 1947, the influential drama critic Brooks Atkinson announced that, in Miller, "The theatre has acquired a genuine new talent," and *All My Sons* won the New York Drama Critics' Circle Award. A veterans group denounced the play as "Communist propaganda," and the government canceled plans for a production to tour military bases in Europe. But it ran for 328 performances on Broadway, and it was subsequently the first of many of Miller's works to be made into a movie, in 1948.

During the following decade, Miller enjoyed considerable acclaim as a playwright, even as he struggled against the anti-Communist hysteria generated by the cold war. Flush with the success of *All My Sons,* he bought a converted stable house in Brooklyn Heights and a farmhouse in Roxbury, Connecticut. In the small studio he built there, Miller wrote *Death of a Salesman,* a smash hit that opened in 1949 and ran for 742 performances on Broadway. The play, which won a host of awards and the Pulitzer Prize, also became the first dramatic work to be offered as a main selection of the Book-of-the-Month Club. In the wake of the House Un-American Activities Committee (HUAC) investigations of alleged Communist sympathizers, Miller wrote *The Crucible,* a play in which he used the mass hysteria that swept Salem during the notorious witch trials of the seventeenth century to comment on the "witch hunts" for Communists in the United States. *The Crucible* won the Antoinette Perry or "Tony" Award for the best Broadway play of 1953. When Miller applied for a passport to go to Belgium to see a production of the play in 1954, however, the State Department rejected his application, citing "regulations denying passports to people believed to be supporting the Communist movement." In the summer of 1956, at the time Miller divorced his first wife to marry the actress Marilyn Monroe, he was ordered to appear before HUAC. At the hearing, Miller admitted attending meetings with Communist writers in 1947, but he denied being a Communist and refused to name the other writers at the meetings. Miller was cited for contempt of Congress. In 1957, the year *Arthur Miller's Collected Plays* was published, he was convicted of the contempt charge in a federal district court, but the verdict was overturned the following year by the court of appeals.

Although he was now free to resume his career, Miller never again matched his earlier successes. In 1958, he was elected to the National Institute of Arts and Letters, which awarded him its Gold Medal for Drama in 1959. He wrote the screenplay for *The Misfits*, a movie starring Marilyn Monroe. But their marriage, now strained by Monroe's widely publicized affair with the French actor Yves Montand, ended in divorce in 1961. Miller married his third wife, the photographer Ingeborg Morath, in 1962. Monroe died later that year, and Miller was criticized for his thinly veiled portrait of her in his play *After the Fall* (1964), an autobiographical account of his life and first two marriages. The death of his widowed father in 1966 inspired Miller's next play, *The Price* (1968), in which two estranged brothers are brought together to dispose of their parents' possessions. Meanwhile, Miller was elected president of PEN International, a worldwide association of writers, and his tireless work on behalf of dissident artists and intellectuals in China, Turkey, and behind the iron curtain led to the banning of his works in the Soviet Union in 1970. Despite the decline of his own reputation in the United States, Miller was generously supportive of other playwrights, including his contemporary Tennessee Williams and younger writers such as Edward Albee and David Mamet. During the final decades of Miller's life, he wrote numerous plays as well as screenplays, volumes of reportage, and his autobiography, *Timebends: A Life* (1987). He died at the age of eighty-nine on February 9, 2005.

bedfordstmartins.com/
americanlit for research
links on Miller

Miller's *Death of a Salesman*.   In the front-page obituary in the *New York Times*, Marilyn Berger hailed Miller as "one of the great American playwrights, whose work exposed the flaws in the fabric of the American dream." Certainly, the shredded fabric of that dream is harshly illuminated in *Death of a Salesman*, the poignant and tragic story of a failed Everyman, Willy Loman. In Miller's autobiography, he recalled that he began to imagine this play after seeing an uncle, a traveling salesman, in Boston: "I could see his grim hotel room behind him, the long trip up from New York in his little car, the hopeless hope of the day's business." Inspired in part by the poetic language and expressionistic effects in the plays of Tennessee Williams, Miller was determined not to be "encom-

Death of a Salesman

Miller later observed that Jo Mielziner's award-winning set design for the original Broadway production captured the play's "'reality-condensation' with its six-foot bedroom, tiny kitchen table, and lone appliance, the hated refrigerator." From left to right, the cast included Mildred Dunnock (Linda), Lee J. Cobb (Willy Loman), Arthur Kennedy (Biff), and Cameron Mitchell (Happy).

passed by conventional realism" in *Death of a Salesman.* The novelist Joyce Carol Oates thus recalled that, when she first read the play, she was especially struck by its "eerie, dreamlike melding of past and present," as dramatized in "Willy Loman's 'present-action' dialogue and his conversations with the ghosts of his past like his revered brother Ben." Miller originally envisioned Willy Loman as a small, exhausted man, but when the strapping young actor Lee J. Cobb read the script he announced: "This is my part. Nobody else can play this part. I know this man." As Miller got to know Cobb, he agreed and altered the script accordingly. A few weeks before the beginning of rehearsals, Cobb told Miller that "this play is a watershed. The American theatre will never be the same." And so it proved. Cobb's performance is widely regarded as one of the finest ever delivered on Broadway, and from the time *Death of a Salesman* opened to rave reviews at the Morosco Theatre on February 10, 1949, it has been recognized as one of the landmarks of American drama. The text is taken from *Death of a Salesman: Certain Private Conversations in Two Acts and a Requiem* (1949).

DEATH OF A SALESMAN

CAST (IN ORDER OF APPEARANCE)

WILLY LOMAN

LINDA

BIFF

HAPPY

BERNARD

THE WOMAN

CHARLEY

UNCLE BEN

HOWARD WAGNER

JENNY

STANLEY

MISS FORSYTHE

LETTA

The action takes place in Willy Loman's house and yard and in various places he visits in the New York and Boston of today.

Throughout the play, in the stage directions, left and right mean stage left and stage right.

ACT ONE

A melody is heard, played upon a flute. It is small and fine, telling of grass and trees and the horizon. The curtain rises.

Before us is the Salesman's house. We are aware of towering, angular shapes behind it, surrounding it on all sides. Only the blue light of the sky falls upon the house and forestage; the surrounding area shows an angry glow of orange. As more light appears, we see a solid vault of apartment houses around the small, fragile-seeming home. An air of the dream clings to the place, a dream rising out of reality. The kitchen at center seems actual enough, for there is a kitchen table with three chairs, and a refrigerator. But no other fixtures are seen. At the back of the kitchen there is a draped entrance, which leads to the living-room. To the right of the kitchen, on a level raised two feet, is a bedroom furnished only with a brass bedstead and a straight chair. On a shelf over the bed a silver athletic trophy stands. A window opens onto the apartment house at the side.

Behind the kitchen, on a level raised six and a half feet, is the boys' bedroom, at present barely visible. Two beds are dimly seen, and at the back of the room a dormer window. (This bedroom is above the unseen living-room.) At the left a stairway curves up to it from the kitchen.

The entire setting is wholly or, in some places, partially transparent. The roof-line of the house is one-dimensional; under and over it we see the apartment buildings. Before the house lies an apron, curving beyond the forestage into the orchestra. This forward area serves as the back yard as well as the locale of all Willy's imaginings and of his city scenes. Whenever the action is in the present the actors observe the imaginary wall-lines, entering the house only through its door at the left. But in the scenes of the past these boundaries are broken, and characters enter or leave a room by stepping "through" a wall onto the forestage.

From the right, Willy Loman, the Salesman, enters, carrying two large sample cases. The flute plays on. He hears but is not aware of it. He is past sixty years of age, dressed quietly. Even as he crosses the stage to the doorway of the house, his exhaustion is apparent. He unlocks the door, comes into the kitchen, and thankfully lets his burden down, feeling the soreness of his palms. A word-sigh escapes his lips — it might be "Oh, boy, oh, boy." He closes the door, then carries his cases out into the living-room, through the draped kitchen doorway.

Linda, his wife, has stirred in her bed at the right. She gets out and puts on a robe, listening. Most often jovial, she has developed an iron repression of her exceptions to Willy's behavior — she more than loves him, she admires him, as though his mercurial nature, his temper, his massive dreams and little cruelties, served her only as sharp reminders of the turbulent longings within him, longings which she shares but lacks the temperament to utter and follow to their end.

LINDA, *hearing Willy outside the bedroom, calls with some trepidation:* Willy!

WILLY: It's all right. I came back.

LINDA: Why? What happened? *Slight pause.* Did something happen, Willy?

WILLY: No, nothing happened.

LINDA: You didn't smash the car, did you?

WILLY, *with casual irritation:* I said nothing happened. Didn't you hear me?

LINDA: Don't you feel well?

WILLY: I'm tired to the death. *The flute has faded away. He sits on the bed beside her, a little numb.* I couldn't make it. I just couldn't make it, Linda.

LINDA, *very carefully, delicately:* Where were you all day? You look terrible.

WILLY: I got as far as a little above Yonkers.[1] I stopped for a cup of coffee. Maybe it was the coffee.

LINDA: What?

WILLY, *after a pause:* I suddenly couldn't drive any more. The car kept going off onto the shoulder, y'know?

LINDA, *helpfully:* Oh. Maybe it was the steering again. I don't think Angelo knows the Studebaker.[2]

WILLY: No, it's me, it's me. Suddenly I realize I'm goin' sixty miles an hour and I don't remember the last five minutes. I'm — I can't seem to — keep my mind to it.

---

1. **Yonkers:** An industrial city north of New York City on the Hudson River.
2. **Studebaker:** A line of mid-priced American cars manufactured from 1911 to 1966.

LINDA: Maybe it's your glasses. You never went for your new glasses.

WILLY: No, I see everything. I came back ten miles an hour. It took me nearly four hours from Yonkers.

LINDA, *resigned:* Well, you'll just have to take a rest, Willy, you can't continue this way.

WILLY: I just got back from Florida.

LINDA: But you didn't rest your mind. Your mind is overactive, and the mind is what counts, dear.

WILLY: I'll start out in the morning. Maybe I'll feel better in the morning. *She is taking off his shoes.* These goddam arch supports are killing me.

LINDA: Take an aspirin. Should I get you an aspirin? It'll soothe you.

WILLY, *with wonder:* I was driving along, you understand? And I was fine. I was even observing the scenery. You can imagine, me looking at scenery, on the road every week of my life. But it's so beautiful up there, Linda, the trees are so thick, and the sun is warm. I opened the windshield and just let the warm air bathe over me. And then all of a sudden I'm goin' off the road! I'm tellin' ya, I absolutely forgot I was driving. If I'd've gone the other way over the white line I might've killed somebody. So I went on again — and five minutes later I'm dreamin' again, and I nearly — *He presses two fingers against his eyes.* I have such thoughts, I have such strange thoughts.

LINDA: Willy, dear. Talk to them again. There's no reason why you can't work in New York.

WILLY: They don't need me in New York. I'm the New England man. I'm vital in New England.

LINDA: But you're sixty years old. They can't expect you to keep traveling every week.

WILLY: I'll have to send a wire to Portland. I'm supposed to see Brown and Morrison tomorrow morning at ten o'clock to show the line. Goddammit, I could sell them! *He starts putting on his jacket.*

LINDA, *taking the jacket from him:* Why don't you go down to the place tomorrow and tell Howard you've simply got to work in New York? You're too accommodating, dear.

WILLY: If old man Wagner was alive I'd a been in charge of New York now! That man was a prince, he was a masterful man. But that boy of his, that Howard, he don't appreciate. When I went north the first time, the Wagner Company didn't know where New England was!

LINDA: Why don't you tell those things to Howard, dear?

WILLY, *encouraged:* I will, I definitely will. Is there any cheese?

LINDA: I'll make you a sandwich.

WILLY: No, go to sleep. I'll take some milk. I'll be up right away. The boys in?

LINDA: They're sleeping. Happy took Biff on a date tonight.

WILLY, *interested:* That so?

LINDA: It was so nice to see them shaving together, one behind the other, in the bathroom. And going out together. You notice? The whole house smells of shaving lotion.

WILLY: Figure it out. Work a lifetime to pay off a house. You finally own it, and there's nobody to live in it.

LINDA: Well, dear, life is a casting off. It's always that way.

WILLY: No, no, some people — some people accomplish something. Did Biff say any-thing after I went this morning?

LINDA: You shouldn't have criticized him, Willy, especially after he just got off the train. You mustn't lose your temper with him.

WILLY: When the hell did I lose my temper? I simply asked him if he was making any money. Is that a criticism?

LINDA: But, dear, how could he make any money?

WILLY, *worried and angered:* There's such an undercurrent in him. He became a moody man. Did he apologize when I left this morning?

LINDA: He was crestfallen, Willy. You know how he admires you. I think if he finds him-self, then you'll both be happier and not fight any more.

WILLY: How can he find himself on a farm? Is that a life? A farmhand? In the beginning, when he was young, I thought, well, a young man, it's good for him to tramp around, take a lot of different jobs. But it's more than ten years now and he has yet to make thirty-five dollars a week!

LINDA: He's finding himself, Willy.

WILLY: Not finding yourself at the age of thirty-four is a disgrace!.

LINDA: Shh!

WILLY: The trouble is he's lazy, goddammit!

LINDA: Willy, please!

WILLY: Biff is a lazy bum!

LINDA: They're sleeping. Get something to eat. Go on down.

WILLY: Why did he come home? I would like to know what brought him home.

LINDA: I don't know. I think he's still lost, Willy. I think he's very lost.

WILLY: Biff Loman is lost. In the greatest country in the world a young man with such — personal attractiveness, gets lost. And such a hard worker. There's one thing about Biff — he's not lazy.

LINDA: Never.

WILLY, *with pity and resolve:* I'll see him in the morning; I'll have a nice talk with him. I'll get him a job selling. He could be big in no time. My God! Remember how they used to follow him around in high school? When he smiled at one of them their faces lit up. When he walked down the street . . . *He loses himself in reminiscences.*

LINDA, *trying to bring him out of it:* Willy, dear, I got a new kind of American-type cheese[3] today. It's whipped.

WILLY: Why do you get American when I like Swiss?

LINDA: I just thought you'd like a change —

WILLY: I don't want a change! I want Swiss cheese. Why am I always being contradicted?

LINDA, *with a covering laugh:* I thought it would be a surprise.

WILLY: Why don't you open a window in here, for God's sake?

LINDA, *with infinite patience:* They're all open, dear.

---

3. **American-type cheese:** A yellow cheese blended from several kinds of cheese, milk, flavorings, and artifi-cial color, often advertised in the mid-twentieth century as being "whipped."

WILLY: The way they boxed us in here. Bricks and windows, windows and bricks.

LINDA: We should've bought the land next door.

WILLY: The street is lined with cars. There's not a breath of fresh air in the neighborhood. The grass don't grow any more, you can't raise a carrot in the back yard. They should've had a law against apartment houses. Remember those two beautiful elm trees out there? When I and Biff hung the swing between them?

LINDA: Yeah, like being a million miles from the city.

WILLY: They should've arrested the builder for cutting those down. They massacred the neighborhood. *Lost:* More and more I think of those days, Linda. This time of year it was lilac and wisteria. And then the peonies would come out, and the daffodils. What fragrance in this room!

LINDA: Well, after all, people had to move somewhere.

WILLY: No, there's more people now.

LINDA: I don't think there's more people. I think —

WILLY: There's more people! That's what's ruining this country! Population is getting out of control. The competition is maddening! Smell the stink from that apartment house! And another one on the other side . . . How can they whip cheese?

On Willy's last line, Biff and Happy raise themselves up in their beds, listening.

LINDA: Go down, try it. And be quiet.

WILLY, *turning to Linda, guiltily:* You're not worried about me, are you, sweetheart?

BIFF: What's the matter?

HAPPY: Listen!

LINDA: You've got too much on the ball to worry about.

WILLY: You're my foundation and my support, Linda.

LINDA: Just try to relax, dear. You make mountains out of molehills.

WILLY: I won't fight with him any more. If he wants to go back to Texas, let him go.

LINDA: He'll find his way.

WILLY: Sure. Certain men just don't get started till later in life. Like Thomas Edison, I think. Or B. F. Goodrich.[4] One of them was deaf. *He starts for the bedroom doorway.* I'll put my money on Biff.

LINDA: And Willy — if it's warm Sunday we'll drive in the country. And we'll open the windshield, and take lunch.

WILLY: No, the windshields don't open on the new cars.

LINDA: But you opened it today.

WILLY: Me? I didn't. *He stops.* Now isn't that peculiar! Isn't that a remarkable — *He breaks off in amazement and fright as the flute is heard distantly.*

LINDA: What, darling?

---

4. **Thomas Edison . . . B. F. Goodrich:** Partially deaf from an early age, Thomas Alva Edison (1847–1931) was a famous American inventor and businessman who formed the General Electric Corporation. Goodrich (1841–1888), who served as an army surgeon during the Civil War, later founded the B. F. Goodrich Company, which became one of the largest tire and rubber manufacturing companies in the world.

WILLY: That is the most remarkable thing.

LINDA: What, dear?

WILLY: I was thinking of the Chevvy. *Slight pause.* Nineteen twenty-eight . . . when I had that red Chevvy – *Breaks off.* That funny? I coulda sworn I was driving that Chevvy today.

LINDA: Well, that's nothing. Something must've reminded you.

WILLY: Remarkable. Ts. Remember those days? The way Biff used to simonize[5] that car? The dealer refused to believe there was eighty thousand miles on it. *He shakes his head.* Heh! *To Linda:* Close your eyes, I'll right up. *He walks out of the bedroom.*

HAPPY, *to Biff:* Jesus, maybe he smashed up the car again!

LINDA, *calling after Willy:* Be careful on the stairs, dear! The cheese is on the middle shelf! *She turns, goes over to the bed, takes his jacket, and goes out of the bedroom.*

Light has risen on the boys' room. Unseen, Willy is heard talking to himself, "Eighty thousand miles," and a little laugh. Biff gets out of bed, comes downstage a bit, and stands attentively. Biff is two years older than his brother Happy, well built, but in these days bears a worn air and seems less self-assured. He has succeeded less, and his dreams are stronger and less acceptable than Happy's. Happy is tall, powerfully made. Sexuality is like a visible color on him, or a scent that many women have discovered. He, like his brother, is lost, but in a different way, for he has never allowed himself to turn his face toward defeat and is thus more confused and hard-skinned, although seemingly more content.

HAPPY, *getting out of bed:* He's going to get his license taken away if he keeps that up. I'm getting nervous about him, y'know, Biff?

BIFF: His eyes are going.

HAPPY: No, I've driven with him. He sees all right. He just doesn't keep his mind on it. I drove into the city with him last week. He stops at a green light and then it turns red and he goes. *He laughs.*

BIFF: Maybe he's color-blind.

HAPPY: Pop? Why he's got the finest eye for color in the business. You know that.

BIFF, *sitting down on his bed:* I'm going to sleep.

HAPPY: You're not still sour on Dad, are you, Biff?

BIFF: He's all right, I guess.

WILLY, *underneath them, in the living-room:* Yes, sir, eighty thousand miles – eighty-two thousand!

BIFF: You smoking?

HAPPY, *holding out a pack of cigarettes:* Want one?

BIFF, *taking a cigarette:* I can never sleep when I smell it.

WILLY: What a simonizing job, heh!

---

5. **simonize:** Simoniz, a car wax introduced in the mid-twentieth century, became so popular that the name became synonymous with polishing a car.

HAPPY, *with deep sentiment:* Funny, Biff, y'know? Us sleeping in here again? The old beds. *He pats his bed affectionately.* All the talk that went across those two beds, huh? Our whole lives.

BIFF: Yeah. Lotta dreams and plans.

HAPPY, *with a deep and masculine laugh:* About five hundred women would like to know what was said in this room.

They share a soft laugh.

BIFF: Remember that big Betsy something — what the hell was her name — over on Bushwick Avenue?

HAPPY, *combing his hair:* With the collie dog!

BIFF: That's the one. I got you in there, remember?

HAPPY: Yeah, that was my first time — I think. Boy, there was a pig! *They laugh, almost crudely.* You taught me everything I know about women. Don't forget that.

BIFF: I bet you forgot how bashful you used to be. Especially with girls.

HAPPY: Oh, I still am, Biff.

BIFF: Oh, go on.

HAPPY: I just control it, that's all. I think I got less bashful and you got more so. What happened, Biff? Where's the old humor, the old confidence? *He shakes Biff's knee. Biff gets up and moves restlessly about the room.* What's the matter?

BIFF: Why does Dad mock me all the time?

HAPPY: He's not mocking you, he —

BIFF: Everything I say there's a twist of mockery on his face. I can't get near him.

HAPPY: He just wants you to make good, that's all. I wanted to talk to you about Dad for a long time, Biff. Something's — happening to him. He — talks to himself.

BIFF: I noticed that this morning. But he always mumbled.

HAPPY: But not so noticeable. It got so embarrassing I sent him to Florida. And you know something? Most of the time he's talking to you.

BIFF: What's he say about me?

HAPPY: I can't make it out.

BIFF: What's he say about me?

HAPPY: I think the fact that you're not settled, that you're still kind of up in the air . . .

BIFF: There's one or two other things depressing him, Happy.

HAPPY: What do you mean?

BIFF: Never mind. Just don't lay it all to me.

HAPPY: But I think if you just got started — I mean — is there any future for you out there?

BIFF: I tell ya, Hap, I don't know what the future is. I don't know — what I'm supposed to want.

HAPPY: What do you mean?

BIFF: Well, I spent six or seven years after high school trying to work myself up. Shipping clerk, salesman, business of one kind or another. And it's a measly manner of existence. To get on that subway on the hot mornings in summer. To devote your whole life to keeping stock, or making phone calls, or selling or buying. To suffer fifty weeks of the year for the sake of a two-week vacation, when all you really desire is to be outdoors, with your shirt off. And always to have to get ahead of the next fella. And still — that's how you build a future.

HAPPY: Well, you really enjoy it on a farm? Are you content out there?

BIFF, *with rising agitation:* Hap, I've had twenty or thirty different kinds of jobs since I left home before the war, and it always turns out the same. I just realized it lately. In Nebraska when I herded cattle, and the Dakotas, and Arizona, and now in Texas. It's why I came home now, I guess, because I realized it. This farm I work on, it's spring there now, see? And they've got about fifteen new colts. There's nothing more inspiring or — beautiful than the sight of a mare and a new colt. And it's cool there now, see? Texas is cool now, and it's spring. And whenever spring comes to where I am, I suddenly get the feeling, my God, I'm not gettin' anywhere! What the hell am I doing, playing around with horses, twenty-eight dollars a week! I'm thirty-four years old, I oughta be makin' my future. That's when I come running home. And now, I get here, and I don't know what to do with myself. *After a pause:* I've always made a point of not wasting my life, and everytime I come back here I know that all I've done is to waste my life.

HAPPY: You're a poet, you know that, Biff? You're a — you're an idealist!

BIFF: No, I'm mixed up very bad. Maybe I oughta get married. Maybe I oughta get stuck into something. Maybe that's my trouble. I'm like a boy. I'm not married, I'm not in business, I just — I'm like a boy. Are you content, Hap? You're a success, aren't you? Are you content?

HAPPY: Hell, no!

BIFF: Why? You're making money, aren't you?

HAPPY, *moving about with energy, expressiveness:* All I can do now is wait for the merchandise manager to die. And suppose I get to be merchandise manager? He's a good friend of mine, and he just built a terrific estate on Long Island. And he lived there about two months and sold it, and now he's building another one. He can't enjoy it once it's finished. And I know that's just what I would do. I don't know what the hell I'm workin' for. Sometimes I sit in my apartment — all alone. And I think of the rent I'm paying. And it's crazy. But then, it's what I always wanted. My own apartment, a car, and plenty of women. And still, goddammit, I'm lonely.

BIFF, *with enthusiasm:* Listen, why don't you come out West with me?

HAPPY: You and I, heh?

BIFF: Sure, maybe we could buy a ranch. Raise cattle, use our muscles. Men built like we are should be working out in the open.

HAPPY, *avidly:* The Loman Brothers, heh?

BIFF, *with vast affection:* Sure, we'd be known all over the counties!

HAPPY, *enthralled:* That's what I dream about, Biff. Sometimes I want to just rip my clothes off in the middle of the store and outbox that goddam merchandise manager. I mean I can outbox, outrun, and outlift anybody in that store, and I have to take orders from those common, petty sons-of-bitches till I can't stand it any more.

BIFF: I'm tellin' you, kid, if you were with me I'd be happy out there.

HAPPY, *enthused:* See, Biff, everybody around me is so false that I'm constantly lowering my ideals . . .

BIFF: Baby, together we'd stand up for one another, we'd have someone to trust.

HAPPY: If I were around you —

BIFF: Hap, the trouble is we weren't brought up to grub for money. I don't know how to
  do it.

HAPPY: Neither can I!

BIFF: Then let's go!

HAPPY: The only thing is — what can you make out there?

BIFF: But look at your friend. Builds an estate and then hasn't the peace of mind to live
  in it.

HAPPY: Yeah, but when he walks into the store the waves part in front of him. That's
  fifty-two thousand dollars a year coming through the revolving door, and I got more
  in my pinky finger than he's got in his head.

BIFF: Yeah, but you just said —

HAPPY: I gotta show some of those pompous, self-important executives over there that
  Hap Loman can make the grade. I want to walk into the store the way he walks in.
  Then I'll go with you, Biff. We'll be together yet, I swear. But take those two we had
  tonight. Now weren't they gorgeous creatures?

BIFF: Yeah, yeah, most gorgeous I've had in years.

HAPPY: I get that any time I want, Biff. Whenever I feel disgusted. The only trouble is, it
  gets like bowling or something. I just keep knockin' them over and it doesn't mean
  anything. You still run around a lot?

BIFF: Naa. I'd like to find a girl — steady, somebody with substance.

HAPPY: That's what I long for.

BIFF: Go on! You'd never come home.

HAPPY: I would! Somebody with character, with resistance! Like Mom, y'know? You're
  gonna call me a bastard when I tell you this. That girl Charlotte I was with tonight is
  engaged to be married in five weeks. *He tries on his new hat.*

BIFF: No kiddin'!

HAPPY: Sure, the guy's in line for the vice-presidency of the store. I don't know what
  gets into me, maybe I just have an overdeveloped sense of competition or something,
  but I went and ruined her, and furthermore I can't get rid of her. And he's the third
  executive I've done that to. Isn't that a crummy characteristic? And to top it all, I go to
  their weddings! *Indignantly, but laughing:* Like I'm not supposed to take bribes. Manufacturers offer me a hundred-dollar bill now and then to throw an order their way.
  You know how honest I am, but it's like this girl, see. I hate myself for it. Because I
  don't want the girl, and, still, I take it and — I love it!

BIFF: Let's go to sleep.

HAPPY: I guess we didn't settle anything, heh?

BIFF: I just got one idea that I think I'm going to try.

HAPPY: What's that?

BIFF: Remember Bill Oliver?

HAPPY: Sure, Oliver is very big now. You want to work for him again?

BIFF: No, but when I quit he said something to me. He put his arm on my shoulder, and he said, "Biff, if you ever need anything, come to me."

HAPPY: I remember that. That sounds good.

BIFF: I think I'll go to see him. If I could get ten thousand or even seven or eight thousand dollars I could buy a beautiful ranch.

HAPPY: I bet he'd back you. 'Cause he thought highly of you, Biff. I mean, they all do. You're well liked, Biff. That's why I say to come back here, and we both have the apartment. And I'm tellin' you, Biff, any babe you want . . .

BIFF: No, with a ranch I could do the work I like and still be something. I just wonder though. I wonder if Oliver still thinks I stole that carton of basketballs.

HAPPY: Oh, he probably forgot that long ago. It's almost ten years. You're too sensitive. Anyway, he didn't really fire you.

BIFF: Well, I think he was going to. I think that's why I quit. I was never sure whether he knew or not. I know he thought the world of me, though. I was the only one he'd let lock up the place.

WILLY, *below:* You gonna wash the engine, Biff?

HAPPY: Shh!

Biff looks at Happy, who is gazing down, listening. Willy is mumbling in the parlor.

HAPPY: You hear that?

They listen. Willy laughs warmly.

BIFF, *growing angry:* Doesn't he know Mom can hear that?

WILLY: Don't get your sweater dirty, Biff!

A look of pain crosses Biff's face.

HAPPY: Isn't that terrible? Don't leave again, will you? You'll find a job here. You gotta stick around. I don't know what to do about him, it's getting embarrassing.

WILLY: What a simonizing job!

BIFF: Mom's hearing that!

WILLY: No kiddin', Biff, you got a date? Wonderful!

HAPPY: Go on to sleep. But talk to him in the morning, will you?

BIFF, *reluctantly getting into bed:* With her in the house. Brother!

HAPPY, *getting into bed:* I wish you'd have a good talk with him.

The light on their room begins to fade.

BIFF, *to himself in bed:* That selfish, stupid. . .

HAPPY: Sh . . . Sleep, Biff.

Their light is out. Well before they have finished speaking, Willy's form is dimly seen below in the darkened kitchen. He opens the refrigerator, searches in there, and takes out a bottle of milk. The apartment houses are fading out, and the entire house and surroundings become covered with leaves. Music insinuates itself as the leaves appear.

WILLY: Just wanna be careful with those girls, Biff, that's all. Don't make any promises. No promises of any kind. Because a girl, y'know, they always believe what you tell 'em, and you're very young, Biff, you're too young to be talking seriously to girls.

Light rises on the kitchen. Willy, talking, shuts the refrigerator door and comes downstage to the kitchen table. He pours milk into a glass. He is totally immersed in himself, smiling faintly.

WILLY: Too young entirely, Biff. You want to watch your schooling first. Then when you're all set, there'll be plenty of girls for a boy like you. *He smiles broadly at a kitchen chair.* That so? The girls pay for you? *He laughs.* Boy, you must really be makin' a hit.

Willy is gradually addressing — physically — a point offstage, speaking through the wall of the kitchen, and his voice has been rising in volume to that of a normal conversation.

WILLY: I been wondering why you polish the car so careful. Ha! Don't leave the hubcaps, boys. Get the chamois to the hubcaps. Happy, use newspaper on the windows, it's the easiest thing. Show him how to do it, Biff! You see, Happy? Pad it up, use it like a pad. That's it, that's it, good work. You're doin' all right, Hap. *He pauses, then nods in approbation for a few seconds, then looks upward.* Biff, first thing we gotta do when we get time is clip that big branch over the house. Afraid it's gonna fall in a storm and hit the roof. Tell you what. We get a rope and sling her around, and then we climb up there with a couple of saws and take her down. Soon as you finish the car, boys, I wanna see ya. I got a surprise for you, boys.
BIFF, *offstage:* Whatta ya got, Dad?
WILLY: No, you finish first. Never leave a job till you're finished — remember that. *Looking toward the "big trees":* Biff, up in Albany I saw a beautiful hammock. I think I'll buy it next trip, and we'll hang it right between those two elms. Wouldn't that be something? Just swingin' there under those branches. Boy, that would be . . .

Young Biff and Young Happy appear from the direction Willy was addressing. Happy carries rags and a pail of water. Biff, wearing a sweater with a block "S," carries a football.

BIFF, *pointing in the direction of the car offstage:* How's that, Pop, professional?
WILLY: Terrific. Terrific job, boys. Good work, Biff.
HAPPY: Where's the surprise, Pop?

WILLY: In the back seat of the car.

HAPPY: Boy! *He runs off.*

BIFF: What is it, Dad? Tell me, what'd you buy?

WILLY, *laughing, cuffs him:* Never mind, something I want you to have.

BIFF, *turns and starts off:* What is it, Hap?

HAPPY, *offstage:* It's a punching bag!

BIFF: Oh, Pop!

WILLY: It's got Gene Tunney's signature on it![6]

Happy runs onstage with a punching bag.

BIFF: Gee, how'd you know we wanted a punching bag?

WILLY: Well, it's the finest thing for the timing.

HAPPY, *lies down on his back and pedals with his feet:* I'm losing weight, you notice, Pop?

WILLY, *to Happy:* Jumping rope is good too.

BIFF: Did you see the new football I got?

WILLY, *examining the ball:* Where'd you get a new ball?

BIFF: The coach told me to practice my passing.

WILLY: That so? And he gave you the ball, heh?

BIFF: Well, I borrowed it from the locker room. *He laughs confidentially.*

WILLY, *laughing with him at the theft:* I want you to return that.

HAPPY: I told you he wouldn't like it!

BIFF, *angrily:* Well, I'm bringing it back!

WILLY, *stopping the incipient argument, to Happy:* Sure, he's gotta practice with a regulation ball, doesn't he? *To Biff:* Coach'll probably congratulate you on your initiative!

BIFF: Oh, he keeps congratulating my initiative all the time, Pop.

WILLY: That's because he likes you. If somebody else took that ball there'd be an uproar. So what's the report, boys, what's the report?

BIFF: Where'd you go this time, Dad? Gee we were lonesome for you.

WILLY, *pleased, puts an arm around each boy and they come down to the apron:* Lonesome, heh?

BIFF: Missed you every minute.

WILLY: Don't say? Tell you a secret, boys. Don't breathe it to a soul. Someday I'll have my own business, and I'll never have to leave home any more.

HAPPY: Like Uncle Charley, heh?

WILLY: Bigger than Uncle Charley! Because Charley is not — liked. He's liked, but he's not — well liked.

BIFF: Where'd you go this time, Dad?

---

6. **Gene Tunney's signature on it:** Tunney (1898–1978), a hard-punching fighter who defeated Jack Dempsey for the world heavyweight championship in 1926, later endorsed products such as "Gene Tunney's Everlast Training Bag."

WILLY: Well, I got on the road, and I went north to Providence. Met the Mayor.

BIFF: The Mayor of Providence!

WILLY: He was sitting in the hotel lobby.

BIFF: What'd he say?

WILLY: He said, "Morning!" And I said, "You got a fine city here, Mayor." And then he had coffee with me. And then I went to Waterbury. Waterbury is a fine city. Big clock city, the famous Waterbury clock. Sold a nice bill there. And then Boston — Boston is the cradle of the Revolution. A fine city. And a couple of other towns in Mass., and on to Portland and Bangor and straight home!

BIFF: Gee, I'd love to go with you sometime, Dad.

WILLY: Soon as summer comes.

HAPPY: Promise?

WILLY: You and Hap and I, and I'll show you all the towns. America is full of beautiful towns and fine, upstanding people. And they know me, boys, they know me up and down New England. The finest people. And when I bring you fellas up, there'll be open sesame for all of us, 'cause one thing, boys: I have friends. I can park my car in any street in New England, and the cops protect it like their own. This summer, heh?

BIFF and HAPPY, *together:* Yeah! You bet!

WILLY: We'll take our bathing suits.

HAPPY: We'll carry your bags, Pop!

WILLY: Oh, won't that be something! Me comin' into the Boston stores with you boys carryin' my bags. What a sensation!

Biff is prancing around, practicing passing the ball.

WILLY: You nervous, Biff, about the game?

BIFF: Not if you're gonna be there.

WILLY: What do they say about you in school, now that they made you captain?

HAPPY: There's a crowd of girls behind him every time the classes change.

BIFF, *taking Willy's hand:* This Saturday, Pop, this Saturday — just for you, I'm going to break through for a touchdown.

HAPPY: You're supposed to pass.

BIFF: I'm takin' one play for Pop. You watch me, Pop, and when I take off my helmet, that means I'm breakin' out. Then you watch me crash through that line!

WILLY, *kisses Biff:* Oh, wait'll I tell this in Boston!

Bernard enters in knickers. He is younger than Biff, earnest and loyal, a worried boy.

BERNARD: Biff, where are you? You're supposed to study with me today.

WILLY: Hey, looka Bernard. What're you lookin' so anemic about, Bernard?

BERNARD: He's gotta study, Uncle Willy. He's got Regents next week.[7]

---

7. **Regents next week:** Regents Examinations are standardized tests in several subject areas that are required of all students in public high schools in New York State.

HAPPY, *tauntingly, spinning Bernard around:* Let's box, Bernard!

BERNARD: Biff! *He gets away from Happy.* Listen, Biff, I heard Mr. Birnbaum say that if you don't start studyin' math he's gonna flunk you, and you won't graduate. I heard him!

WILLY: You better study with him, Biff. Go ahead now.

BERNARD: I heard him!

BIFF: Oh, Pop, you didn't see my sneakers! *He holds up a foot for Willy to look at.*

WILLY: Hey, that's a beautiful job of printing!

BERNARD, *wiping his glasses:* Just because he printed University of Virginia on his sneakers doesn't mean they've got to graduate him, Uncle Willy!

WILLY, *angrily:* What're you talking about? With scholarships to three universities they're gonna flunk him?

BERNARD: But I heard Mr. Birnbaum say —

WILLY: Don't be a pest, Bernard! *To his boys:* What an anemic!

BERNARD: Okay, I'm waiting for you in my house, Biff.

Bernard goes off. The Lomans laugh.

WILLY: Bernard is not well liked, is he?

BIFF: He's liked, but he's not well liked.

HAPPY: That's right, Pop.

WILLY: That's just what I mean. Bernard can get the best marks in school, y'understand, but when he gets out in the business world, y'understand, you are going to be five times ahead of him. That's why I thank Almighty God you're both built like Adonises.[8] Because the man who makes an appearance in the business world, the man who creates personal interest, is the man who gets ahead. Be liked and you will never want. You take me, for instance. I never have to wait in line to see a buyer. "Willy Loman is here!" That's all they have to know, and I go right through.

BIFF: Did you knock them dead, Pop?

WILLY: Knocked 'em cold in Providence, slaughtered 'em in Boston.

HAPPY, *on his back, pedaling again:* I'm losing weight, you notice, Pop?

Linda enters, as of old, a ribbon in her hair, carrying a basket of washing.

LINDA, *with youthful energy:* Hello, dear!

WILLY: Sweetheart!

LINDA: How'd the Chevvy run?

WILLY: Chevrolet, Linda, is the greatest car ever built. *To the boys:* Since when do you let your mother carry wash up the stairs?

BIFF: Grab hold there, boy!

HAPPY: Where to, Mom?

---

8. **Adonises:** In Greek mythology, Adonis is a beautiful youth loved by the goddesses Aphrodite and Persephone.

LINDA: Hang them up on the line. And you better go down to your friends, Biff. The cellar is full of boys. They don't know what to do with themselves.

BIFF: Ah, when Pop comes home they can wait!

WILLY, *laughs appreciatively:* You better go down and tell them what to do, Biff.

BIFF: I think I'll have them sweep out the furnace room.

WILLY: Good work, Biff.

BIFF, *goes through wall-line of kitchen to doorway at back and calls down:* Fellas! Everybody sweep out the furnace room! I'll be right down!

VOICES: All right! Okay, Biff.

BIFF: George and Sam and Frank, come out back! We're hangin' up the wash! Come on, Hap, on the double! *He and Happy carry out the basket.*

LINDA: The way they obey him!

WILLY: Well, that's training, the training. I'm tellin' you, I was sellin' thousands and thousands, but I had to come home.

LINDA: Oh, the whole block'll be at that game. Did you sell anything?

WILLY: I did five hundred gross in Providence and seven hundred gross in Boston.

LINDA: No! Wait a minute, I've got a pencil. *She pulls pencil and paper out of her apron pocket.* That makes your commission . . . Two hundred — my God! Two hundred and twelve dollars!

WILLY: Well, I didn't figure it yet, but . . .

LINDA: How much did you do?

WILLY: Well, I — I did — about a hundred and eighty gross in Providence. Well, no — it came to — roughly two hundred gross on the whole trip.

LINDA, *without hesitation:* Two hundred gross. That's . . . *She figures.*

WILLY: The trouble was that three of the stores were half closed for inventory in Boston. Otherwise I woulda broke records.

LINDA: Well, it makes seventy dollars and some pennies. That's very good.

WILLY: What do we owe?

LINDA: Well, on the first there's sixteen dollars on the refrigerator —

WILLY: Why sixteen?

LINDA: Well, the fan belt broke, so it was a dollar eighty.

WILLY: But it's brand new.

LINDA: Well, the man said that's the way it is. Till they work themselves in, y'know.

They move through the wall-line into the kitchen.

WILLY: I hope we didn't get stuck on that machine.

LINDA: They got the biggest ads of any of them!

WILLY: I know, it's a fine machine. What else?

LINDA: Well, there's nine-sixty for the washing machine. And for the vacuum cleaner there's three and a half due on the fifteenth. Then the roof, you got twenty-one dollars remaining.

WILLY: It don't leak, does it?

LINDA: No, they did a wonderful job. Then you owe Frank for the carburetor.

WILLY: I'm not going to pay that man! That goddam Chevrolet, they ought to prohibit the manufacture of that car!

LINDA: Well, you owe him three and a half. And odds and ends, comes to around a hundred and twenty dollars by the fifteenth.

WILLY: A hundred and twenty dollars! My God, if business don't pick up I don't know what I'm gonna do!

LINDA: Well, next week you'll do better.

WILLY: Oh, I'll knock 'em dead next week. I'll go to Hartford. I'm very well liked in Hartford. You know, the trouble is, Linda, people don't seem to take to me.

They move onto the forestage.

LINDA: Oh, don't be foolish.

WILLY: I know it when I walk in. They seem to laugh at me.

LINDA: Why? Why would they laugh at you? Don't talk that way, Willy.

Willy moves to the edge of the stage. Linda goes into the kitchen and starts to darn stockings.

WILLY: I don't know the reason for it, but they just pass me by. I'm not noticed.

LINDA: But you're doing wonderful, dear. You're making seventy to a hundred dollars a week.

WILLY: But I gotta be at it ten, twelve hours a day. Other men — I don't know — they do it easier. I don't know why — I can't stop myself — I talk too much. A man oughta come in with a few words. One thing about Charley. He's a man of few words, and they respect him.

LINDA: You don't talk too much, you're just lively.

WILLY, *smiling:* Well, I figure, what the hell, life is short, a couple of jokes. *To himself:* I joke too much! *The smile goes.*

LINDA: Why? You're —

WILLY: I'm fat. I'm very — foolish to look at, Linda. I didn't tell you, but Christmas time I happened to be calling on F. H. Stewarts, and a salesman I know, as I was going in to see the buyer I heard him say something about — walrus. And I — I cracked him right across the face. I won't take that. I simply will not take that. But they do laugh at me. I know that.

LINDA: Darling . . .

WILLY: I gotta overcome it. I know I gotta overcome it. I'm not dressing to advantage, maybe.

LINDA: Willy, darling, you're the handsomest man in the world —

WILLY: Oh, no, Linda.

LINDA: To me you are. *Slight pause.* The handsomest.

From the darkness is heard the laughter of a woman. Willy doesn't turn to it, but it continues through Linda's lines.

LINDA: And the boys, Willy. Few men are idolized by their children the way you are.

Music is heard as behind a scrim, to the left of the house, The Woman, dimly seen, is dressing.

WILLY, *with great feeling:* You're the best there is, Linda, you're a pal, you know that? On the road — on the road I want to grab you sometimes and just kiss the life outa you.

The laughter is loud now, and he moves into a brightening area at the left, where The Woman has come from behind the scrim and is standing, putting on her hat, looking into a "mirror" and laughing.

WILLY: 'Cause I get so lonely — especially when business is bad and there's nobody to talk to. I get the feeling that I'll never sell anything again, that I won't make a living for you, or a business, a business for the boys. *He talks through The Woman's subsiding laughter; The Woman primps at the "mirror."* There's so much I want to make for —

THE WOMAN: Me? You didn't make me, Willy. I picked you,

WILLY, *pleased:* You picked me?

THE WOMAN, *who is quite proper-looking, Willy's age:* I did. I've been sitting at that desk watching all the salesmen go by, day in, day out. But you've got such a sense of humor, and we do have such a good time together, don't we?

WILLY: Sure, sure. *He takes her in his arms.* Why do you have to go now?

THE WOMAN: It's two o'clock . . .

WILLY: No, come on in! *He pulls her.*

THE WOMAN: . . . my sisters'll be scandalized. When'll you be back?

WILLY: Oh, two weeks about. Will you come up again?

THE WOMAN: Sure thing. You do make me laugh. It's good for me. *She squeezes his arm, kisses him.* And I think you're a wonderful man.

WILLY: You picked me, heh?

THE WOMAN: Sure. Because you're so sweet. And such a kidder.

WILLY: Well, I'll see you next time I'm in Boston.

THE WOMAN: I'll put you right through to the buyers.

WILLY, *slapping her bottom:* Right. Well, bottoms up!

THE WOMAN: *slaps him gently and laughs:* You just kill me, Willy, *He suddenly grabs her and kisses her roughly.* You kill me. And thanks for the stockings. I love a lot of stockings. Well, good night.

WILLY: Good night. And keep your pores open!

THE WOMAN: Oh, Willy!

The Woman bursts out laughing, and Linda's laughter blends in. The Woman disappears into the dark. Now the area at the kitchen table brightens. Linda is sitting where she was at the kitchen table, but now is mending a pair of her silk stockings.

LINDA: You are, Willy. The handsomest man. You've got no reason to feel that —

WILLY, *coming out of The Woman's dimming area and going over to Linda:* I'll make it all up to you, Linda, I'll —

LINDA: There's nothing to make up, dear. You're doing fine, better than —

WILLY, *noticing her mending:* What's that?

LINDA: Just mending my stockings. They're so expensive —

WILLY, *angrily, taking them from her:* I won't have you mending stockings in this house! Now throw them out!

Linda puts the stockings in her pocket.

BERNARD, *entering on the run:* Where is he? If he doesn't study!

WILLY, *moving to the forestage, with great agitation:* You'll give him the answers!

BERNARD: I do, but I can't on a Regents! That's a state exam! They're liable to arrest me!

WILLY: Where is he? I'll whip him, I'll whip him!

LINDA: And he'd better give back that football, Willy, it's not nice.

WILLY: Biff! Where is he? Why is he taking everything?

LINDA: He's too rough with the girls, Willy. All the mothers are afraid of him!

WILLY: I'll whip him!

BERNARD: He's driving the car without a license!

The Woman's laugh is heard.

WILLY: Shut up!

LINDA: All the mothers —

WILLY: Shut up!

BERNARD, *backing quietly away and out:* Mr. Birnbaum says he's stuck up.

WILLY: Get outa here!

BERNARD: If he doesn't buckle down he'll flunk math! *He goes off.*

LINDA: He's right, Willy, you've gotta —

WILLY, *exploding at her:* There's nothing the matter with him! You want him to be a worm like Bernard? He's got spirit, personality . . .

As he speaks, Linda, almost in tears, exits into the living-room. Willy is alone in the kitchen, wilting and staring. The leaves are gone. It is night again, and the apartment houses look down from behind.

WILLY: Loaded with it. Loaded! What is he stealing? He's giving it back, isn't he? Why is he stealing? What did I tell him? I never in my life told him anything but decent things.

Happy in pajamas has come down the stairs; Willy suddenly becomes aware of Happy's presence.

HAPPY: Let's go now, come on.

WILLY, *sitting down at the kitchen table:* Huh! Why did she have to wax the floors her-self? Every time she waxes the floors she keels over. She knows that!

HAPPY: Shh! Take it easy. What brought you back tonight?

WILLY: I got an awful scare. Nearly hit a kid in Yonkers. God! Why didn't I go to Alaska with my brother Ben that time! Ben! That man was a genius, that man was success incarnate! What a mistake! He begged me to go.

HAPPY: Well, there's no use in —

WILLY: You guys! There was a man started with the clothes on his back and ended up with diamond mines!

HAPPY: Boy, someday I'd like to know how he did it.

WILLY: What's the mystery? The man knew what he wanted and went out and got it! Walked into a jungle, and comes out, the age of twenty-one, and he's rich! The world is an oyster, but you don't crack it open on a mattress!

HAPPY: Pop, I told you I'm gonna retire you for life.

WILLY: You'll retire me for life on seventy goddam dollars a week? And your women and your car and your apartment, and you'll retire me for life! Christ's sake, I couldn't get past Yonkers today! Where are you guys, where are you? The woods are burning! I can't drive a car!

Charley has appeared in the doorway. He is a large man, slow of speech, laconic, immovable. In all he says, despite what he says, there is pity, and, now, trepidation. He has a robe over pajamas, slippers on his feet. He enters the kitchen.

CHARLEY: Everything all right?

HAPPY: Yeah, Charley, everything's . . .

WILLY: What's the matter?

CHARLEY: I heard some noise. I thought something happened. Can't we do something about the walls? You sneeze in here, and in my house hats blow off.

HAPPY: Let's go to bed, Dad. Come on.

Charley signals to Happy to go.

WILLY: You go ahead, I'm not tired at the moment.

HAPPY, *to Willy:* Take it easy, huh? *He exits.*

WILLY: What're you doin' up?

CHARLEY, *sitting down at the kitchen table opposite Willy:* Couldn't sleep good. I had a heartburn.

WILLY: Well, you don't know how to eat.

CHARLEY: I eat with my mouth.

WILLY: No, you're ignorant. You gotta know about vitamins and things like that.

CHARLEY: Come on, let's shoot. Tire you out a little.

WILLY, *hesitantly:* All right. You got cards?

CHARLEY, *taking a deck from his pocket:* Yeah, I got them. Someplace. What is it with those vitamins?

WILLY, *dealing:* They build up your bones. Chemistry.

CHARLEY: Yeah, but there's no bones in a heartburn.

WILLY: What are you talkin' about? Do you know the first thing about it?

CHARLEY: Don't get insulted.

WILLY: Don't talk about something you don't know anything about.

They are playing. Pause.

CHARLEY: What're you doin' home?

WILLY: A little trouble with the car.

CHARLEY: Oh. *Pause.* I'd like to take a trip to California.

WILLY: Don't say.

CHARLEY: You want a job?

WILLY: I got a job, I told you that. *After a slight pause:* What the hell are you offering me a job for?

CHARLEY: Don't get insulted.

WILLY: Don't insult me.

CHARLEY: I don't see no sense in it. You don't have to go on this way.

WILLY: I got a good job. *Slight pause.* What do you keep comin' in here for?

CHARLEY: You want me to go?

WILLY, *after a pause, withering:* I can't understand it. He's going back to Texas again. What the hell is that?

CHARLEY: Let him go.

WILLY: I got nothin' to give him, Charley, I'm clean, I'm clean.

CHARLEY: He won't starve. None a them starve. Forget about him.

WILLY: Then what have I got to remember?

CHARLEY: You take it too hard. To hell with it. When a deposit bottle is broken you don't get your nickel back.

WILLY: That's easy enough for you to say.

CHARLEY: That ain't easy for me to say.

WILLY: Did you see the ceiling I put up in the living-room?

CHARLEY: Yeah, that's a piece of work. To put up a ceiling is a mystery to me. How do you do it?

WILLY: What's the difference?

CHARLEY: Well, talk about it.

WILLY: You gonna put up a ceiling?

CHARLEY: How could I put up a ceiling?

WILLY: Then what the hell are you bothering me for?

CHARLEY: You're insulted again.

WILLY: A man who can't handle tools is not a man. You're disgusting.

CHARLEY: Don't call me disgusting, Willy.

Uncle Ben, carrying a valise and an umbrella, enters the forestage from around the right corner of the house. He is a stolid man, in his sixties, with a mustache and an authoritative air. He is utterly certain of his destiny, and there is an aura of far places about him. He enters exactly as Willy speaks.

WILLY: I'm getting awfully tired, Ben.

Ben's music is heard. Ben looks around at everything.

CHARLEY: Good, keep playing; you'll sleep better. Did you call me Ben?

Ben looks at his watch.

WILLY: That's funny. For a second there you reminded me of my brother Ben.

BEN: I only have a few minutes. *He strolls, inspecting the place. Willy and Charley continue playing.*

CHARLEY: You never heard from him again, heh? Since that time?

WILLY: Didn't Linda tell you? Couple of weeks ago we got a letter from his wife in Africa. He died.

CHARLEY: That so.

BEN, *chuckling:* So this is Brooklyn, eh?

CHARLEY: Maybe you're in for some of his money.

WILLY: Naa, he had seven sons. There's just one opportunity I had with that man . . .

BEN: I must make a train, William. There are several properties I'm looking at in Alaska.

WILLY: Sure, sure! If I'd gone with him to Alaska that time, everything would've been totally different.

CHARLEY: Go on, you'd froze to death up there.

WILLY: What're you talking about?

BEN: Opportunity is tremendous in Alaska, William. Surprised you're not up there.

WILLY: Sure, tremendous.

CHARLEY: Heh?

WILLY: There was the only man I ever met who knew the answers.

CHARLEY: Who?

BEN: How are you all?

WILLY, *taking a pot, smiling:* Fine, fine.

CHARLEY: Pretty sharp tonight.

BEN: Is Mother living with you?

WILLY: No, she died a long time ago.

CHARLEY: Who?

BEN: That's too bad. Fine specimen of a lady, Mother.

WILLY, *to Charley:* Heh?

BEN: I'd hoped to see the old girl.

CHARLEY: Who died?

BEN: Heard anything from Father, have you?

WILLY, *unnerved:* What do you mean, who died?

CHARLEY, *taking a pot:* What're you talkin' about?

BEN, *looking at his watch:* William, it's half-past eight!

WILLY, *as though to dispel his confusion he angrily stops Charley's hand:* That's my build!

CHARLEY: I put the ace —

WILLY: If you don't know how to play the game I'm not gonna throw my money away on you!

CHARLEY, *rising:* It was my ace, for God's sake!

WILLY: I'm through, I'm through!

BEN: When did Mother die?

WILLY: Long ago. Since the beginning you never knew how to play cards.

CHARLEY, *picks up the cards and goes to the door:* All right! Next time I'll bring a deck with five aces.

WILLY: I don't play that kind of game!

CHARLEY, *turning to him:* You ought to be ashamed of yourself!

WILLY: Yeah?

CHARLEY: Yeah! *He goes out.*

WILLY, *slamming the door after him:* Ignoramus!

BEN, *as Willy comes toward him through the wall-line of the kitchen:* So you're William.

WILLY, *shaking Ben's hand:* Ben! I've been waiting for you so long! What's the answer? How did you do it?

BEN: Oh, there's a story in that.

Linda enters the forestage, as of old, carrying the wash basket.

LINDA: Is this Ben?

BEN, *gallantly:* How do you do, my dear.

LINDA: Where've you been all these years? Willy's always wondered why you —

WILLY, *pulling Ben away from her impatiently:* Where is Dad? Didn't you follow him? How did you get started?

BEN: Well, I don't know how much you remember.

WILLY: Well, I was just a baby, of course, only three or four years old —

BEN: Three years and eleven months.

WILLY: What a memory, Ben!

BEN: I have many enterprises, William, and I have never kept books.

WILLY: I remember I was sitting under the wagon in — was it Nebraska?

BEN: It was South Dakota, and I gave you a bunch of wild flowers.

WILLY: I remember you walking away down some open road.

BEN, *laughing:* I was going to find Father in Alaska.

WILLY: Where is he?

BEN: At that age I had a very faulty view of geography, William. I discovered after a few days that I was heading due south, so instead of Alaska, I ended up in Africa.

LINDA: Africa!

WILLY: The Gold Coast!

BEN: Principally diamond mines.

LINDA: Diamond mines!

BEN: Yes, my dear. But I've only a few minutes —

WILLY: No! Boys! Boys! *Young Biff and Happy appear.* Listen to this. This is your Uncle Ben, a great man! Tell my boys, Ben!

BEN: Why, boys, when I was seventeen I walked into the jungle, and when I was twenty-one I walked out. *He laughs.* And by God I was rich.

WILLY, *to the boys:* You see what I been talking about? The greatest things can happen!

BEN, *glancing at his watch:* I have an appointment in Ketchikan Tuesday week.

WILLY: No, Ben! Please tell about Dad. I want my boys to hear. I want them to know the kind of stock they spring from. All I remember is a man with a big beard, and I was in Mamma's lap, sitting around a fire, and some kind of high music.

BEN: His flute. He played the flute.

WILLY: Sure, the flute, that's right!

New music is heard, a high, rollicking tune.

BEN: Father was a very great and a very wild-hearted man. We would start in Boston, and he'd toss the whole family into the wagon, and then he'd drive the team right across the country; through Ohio, and Indiana, Michigan, Illinois, and all the Western states. And we'd stop in the towns and sell the flutes that he'd made on the way. Great inventor, Father. With one gadget he made more in a week than a man like you could make in a lifetime.

WILLY: That's just the way I'm bringing them up, Ben — rugged, well liked, all-around.

BEN: Yeah? *To Biff:* Hit that, boy — hard as you can. *He pounds his stomach.*

BIFF: Oh, no, sir!

BEN, *taking boxing stance:* Come on, get to me! *He laughs.*

WILLY: Go to it, Biff! Go ahead, show him!

BIFF: Okay! *He cocks his fists and starts in.*

LINDA, *to Willy:* Why must he fight, dear?

BEN, *sparring with Biff:* Good boy! Good boy!

WILLY: How's that, Ben, heh?

HAPPY: Give him the left, Biff!

LINDA: Why are you fighting?

BEN: Good boy! *Suddenly comes in, trips Biff, and stands over him, the point of his umbrella poised over Biff's eye.*

LINDA: Look out, Biff!

BIFF: Gee!

BEN, *patting Biff's knee:* Never fight fair with a stranger, boy. You'll never get out of the jungle that way. *Taking Linda's hand and bowing:* It was an honor and a pleasure to meet you, Linda.

LINDA, *withdrawing her hand coldly, frightened:* Have a nice — trip.

BEN, *to Willy:* And good luck with your — what do you do?

WILLY: Selling.

BEN: Yes. Well . . . *He raises his hand in farewell to all.*

WILLY: No, Ben, I don't want you to think . . . *He takes Ben's arm to show him.* It's Brooklyn, I know, but we hunt too.

BEN: Really, now.

WILLY: Oh, sure, there's snakes and rabbits and — that's why I moved out here. Why, Biff can fell any one of these trees in no time! Boys! Go right over to where they're building the apartment house and get some sand. We're gonna rebuild the entire front stoop right now! Watch this, Ben!

BIFF: Yes, sir! On the double, Hap!

HAPPY, *as he and Biff run off:* I lost weight, Pop, you notice?

Charley enters in knickers, even before the boys are gone.

CHARLEY: Listen, if they steal any more from that building the watchman'll put the cops on them!

LINDA, *to Willy:* Don't let Biff . . .

Ben laughs lustily.

WILLY: You shoulda seen the lumber they brought home last week. At least a dozen six-by-tens worth all kinds a money.

CHARLEY: Listen, if that watchman —

WILLY: I gave them hell, understand. But I got a couple of fearless characters there.

CHARLEY: Willy, the jails are full of fearless characters.

BEN, *clapping Willy on the back, with a laugh at Charley:* And the stock exchange, friend!

WILLY, *joining in Ben's laughter:* Where are the rest of your pants?

CHARLEY: My wife bought them.

WILLY: Now all you need is a golf club and you can go upstairs and go to sleep. *To Ben:* Great athlete! Between him and his son Bernard they can't hammer a nail!

BERNARD, *rushing in:* The watchman's chasing Biff!

WILLY, *angrily:* Shut up! He's not stealing anything!

LINDA, *alarmed, hurrying off left:* Where is he? Biff, dear! *She exits.*

WILLY, *moving toward the left, away from Ben:* There's nothing wrong. What's the matter with you?

BEN: Nervy boy. Good!

WILLY, *laughing:* Oh, nerves of iron, that Biff!

CHARLEY: Don't know what it is. My New England man comes back and he's bleedin', they murdered him up there.

WILLY: It's contacts, Charley, I got important contacts!

CHARLEY, *sarcastically:* Glad to hear it, Willy. Come in later, we'll shoot a little casino.[9] I'll take some of your Portland money. *He laughs at Willy and exits.*

---

9. **casino:** A card game.

WILLY, *turning to Ben:* Business is bad, it's murderous. But not for me, of course.

BEN: I'll stop by on my way back to Africa.

WILLY, *longingly:* Can't you stay a few days? You're just what I need, Ben, because I — I have a fine position here, but I — well, Dad left when I was such a baby and I never had a chance to talk to him and I still feel — kind of temporary about myself.

BEN: I'll be late for my train.

They are at opposite ends of the stage.

WILLY: Ben, my boys — can't we talk? They'd go into the jaws of hell for me, see, but I —

BEN: William, you're being first-rate with your boys. Outstanding, manly chaps!

WILLY, *hanging on to his words:* Oh, Ben, that's good to hear! Because sometimes I'm afraid that I'm not teaching them the right kind of — Ben, how should I teach them?

BEN, *giving great weight to each word, and with a certain vicious audacity:* William, when I walked into the jungle, I was seventeen. When I walked out I was twenty-one. And, by God, I was rich! *He goes off into darkness around the right corner of the house.*

WILLY: . . . was rich! That's just the spirit I want to imbue them with! To walk into a jungle! I was right! I was right! I was right!

Ben is gone, but Willy is still speaking to him as Linda, in nightgown and robe, enters the kitchen, glances around for Willy, then goes to the door of the house, looks out and sees him. Comes down to his left. He looks at her.

LINDA: Willy, dear? Willy?

WILLY: I was right!

LINDA: Did you have some cheese? *He can't answer.* It's very late, darling. Come to bed, heh?

WILLY, *looking straight up:* Gotta break your neck to see a star in this yard.

LINDA: You coming in?

WILLY: Whatever happened to that diamond watch fob? Remember? When Ben came from Africa that time? Didn't he give me a watch fob with a diamond in it?

LINDA: You pawned it, dear. Twelve, thirteen years ago. For Biff's radio correspondence course.

WILLY: Gee, that was a beautiful thing. I'll take a walk.

LINDA: But you're in your slippers.

WILLY, *starting to go around the house at the left:* I was right! I was! *Half to Linda, as he goes, shaking his head:* What a man! There was a man worth talking to. I was right!

LINDA, *calling after Willy:* But in your slippers, Willy!

Willy is almost gone when Biff, in his pajamas, comes down the stairs and enters the kitchen.

BIFF: What is he doing out there?

LINDA: Sh!

BIFF: God Almighty, Mom, how long has he been doing this?

LINDA: Don't, he'll hear you.

BIFF: What the hell is the matter with him?

LINDA: It'll pass by morning.

BIFF: Shouldn't we do anything?

LINDA: Oh, my dear, you should do a lot of things, but there's nothing to do, so go to sleep.

Happy comes down the stair and sits on the steps.

HAPPY: I never heard him so loud, Mom.

LINDA: Well, come around more often; you'll hear him. *She sits down at the table and mends the lining of Willy's jacket.*

BIFF: Why didn't you ever write me about this, Mom?

LINDA: How would I write to you? For over three months you had no address.

BIFF: I was on the move. But you know I thought of you all the time. You know that, don't you, pal?

LINDA: I know, dear, I know. But he likes to have a letter. Just to know that there's still a possibility for better things.

BIFF: He's not like this all the time, is he?

LINDA: It's when you come home he's always the worst.

BIFF: When I come home?

LINDA: When you write you're coming, he's all smiles, and talks about the future, and — he's just wonderful. And then the closer you seem to come, the more shaky he gets, and then, by the time you get here, he's arguing, and he seems angry at you. I think it's just that maybe he can't bring himself to — to open up to you. Why are you so hateful to each other? Why is that?

BIFF, *evasively:* I'm not hateful, Mom.

LINDA: But you no sooner come in the door than you're fighting!

BIFF: I don't know why. I mean to change. I'm tryin', Mom, you understand?

LINDA: Are you home to stay now?

BIFF: I don't know. I want to look around, see what's doin'.

LINDA: Biff, you can't look around all your life, can you?

BIFF: I just can't take hold, Mom. I can't take hold of some kind of a life.

LINDA: Biff, a man is not a bird, to come and go with the springtime.

BIFF: Your hair . . . *He touches her hair.* Your hair got so gray.

LINDA: Oh, it's been gray since you were in high school. I just stopped dyeing it, that's all.

BIFF: Dye it again, will ya? I don't want my pal looking old. *He smiles.*

LINDA: You're such a boy! You think you can go away for a year and . . . You've got to get it into your head now that one day you'll knock on this door and there'll be strange people here —

BIFF: What are you talking about? You're not even sixty, Mom.

LINDA: But what about your father?

BIFF, *lamely:* Well, I meant him too.

HAPPY: He admires Pop.

LINDA: Biff, dear, if you don't have any feeling for him, then you can't have any feeling for me.

BIFF: Sure I can, Mom.

LINDA: No. You can't just come to see me, because I love him. *With a threat, but only a threat, of tears:* He's the dearest man in the world to me, and I won't have anyone making him feel unwanted and low and blue. You've got to make up your mind now, darling, there's no leeway any more. Either he's your father and you pay him that respect, or else you're not to come here. I know he's not easy to get along with — nobody knows that better than me — but . . .

WILLY, *from the left, with a laugh:* Hey, hey, Biffo!

BIFF, *starting to go out after Willy:* What the hell is the matter with him? *Happy stops him.*

LINDA: Don't — don't go near him!

BIFF: Stop making excuses for him! He always, always wiped the floor with you. Never had an ounce of respect for you.

HAPPY: He's always had respect for —

BIFF: What the hell do you know about it?

HAPPY, *surlily:* Just don't call him crazy!

BIFF: He's got no character — Charley wouldn't do this. Not in his own house — spewing out that vomit from his mind.

HAPPY: Charley never had to cope with what he's got to.

BIFF: People are worse off than Willy Loman. Believe me, I've seen them!

LINDA: Then make Charley your father, Biff. You can't do that, can you? I don't say he's a great man. Willy Loman never made a lot of money. His name was never in the paper. He's not the finest character that ever lived. But he's a human being, and a terrible thing is happening to him. So attention must be paid. He's not to be allowed to fall into his grave like an old dog. Attention, attention must be finally paid to such a person. You called him crazy —

BIFF: I didn't mean —

LINDA: No, a lot of people think he's lost his — balance. But you don't have to be very smart to know what his trouble is. The man is exhausted.

HAPPY: Sure!

LINDA: A small man can be just as exhausted as a great man. He works for a company thirty-six years this March, opens up unheard-of territories to their trademark, and now in his old age they take his salary away.

HAPPY, *indignantly:* I didn't know that, Mom.

LINDA: You never asked, my dear! Now that you get your spending money someplace else you don't trouble your mind with him.

HAPPY: But I gave you money last —

LINDA: Christmas time, fifty dollars! To fix the hot water it cost ninety-seven fifty! For five weeks he's been on straight commission, like a beginner, an unknown!

BIFF: Those ungrateful bastards!

LINDA: Are they any worse than his sons? When he brought them business, when he was young, they were glad to see him. But now his old friends, the old buyers that loved him so and always found some order to hand him in a pinch — they're all dead, retired. He used to be able to make six, seven calls a day in Boston. Now he takes his valises out of the car and puts them back and takes them out again and he's exhausted. Instead of walking he talks now. He drives seven hundred miles, and when he gets there no one knows him any more, no one welcomes him. And what goes through a man's mind, driving seven hundred miles home without having earned a cent? Why shouldn't he talk to himself? Why? When he has to go to Charley and borrow fifty dollars a week and pretend to me that it's his pay? How long can that go on? How long? You see what I'm sitting here and waiting for? And you tell me he has no character? The man who never worked a day but for your benefit? When does he get the medal for that? Is this his reward — to turn around at the age of sixty-three and find his sons, who he loved better than his life, one a philandering bum —

HAPPY: Mom!

LINDA: That's all you are, my baby! *To Biff:* And you! What happened to the love you had for him? You were such pals! How you used to talk to him on the phone every night! How lonely he was till he could come home to you!

BIFF: All right, Mom. I'll live here in my room, and I'll get a job. I'll keep away from him, that's all.

LINDA: No, Biff. You can't stay here and fight all the time.

BIFF: He threw me out of this house, remember that.

LINDA: Why did he do that? I never knew why.

BIFF: Because I know he's a fake and he doesn't like anybody around who knows!

LINDA: Why a fake? In what way? What do you mean?

BIFF: Just don't lay it all at my feet. It's between me and him — that's all I have to say. I'll chip in from now on. He'll settle for half my pay check. He'll be all right. I'm going to bed. *He starts for the stairs.*

LINDA: He won't be all right.

BIFF, *turning on the stairs, furiously:* I hate this city and I'll stay here. Now what do you want?

LINDA: He's dying, Biff.

Happy turns quickly to her, shocked.

BIFF, *after a pause:* Why is he dying?

LINDA: He's been trying to kill himself.

BIFF, *with great horror:* How?

LINDA: I live from day to day.

BIFF: What're you talking about?

LINDA: Remember I wrote you that he smashed up the car again? In February?

BIFF: Well?

LINDA: The insurance inspector came. He said that they have evidence. That all these accidents in the last year — weren't — weren't — accidents.

HAPPY: How can they tell that? That's a lie.

LINDA: It seems there's a woman . . . *She takes a breath as*

{ BIFF, *sharply but contained:* What woman?
{ LINDA, *simultaneously:* . . . and this woman . . .

LINDA: What?

BIFF: Nothing. Go ahead.

LINDA: What did you say?

BIFF: Nothing. I just said what woman?

HAPPY: What about her?

LINDA: Well, it seems she was walking down the road and saw his car. She says that he wasn't driving fast at all, and that he didn't skid. She says he came to that little bridge, and then deliberately smashed into the railing, and it was only the shallowness of the water that saved him.

BIFF: Oh, no, he probably just fell asleep again.

LINDA: I don't think he fell asleep.

BIFF: Why not?

LINDA: Last month . . . *With great difficulty:* Oh, boys, it's so hard to say a thing like this! He's just a big stupid man to you, but I tell you there's more good in him than in many other people. *She chokes, wipes her eyes.* I was looking for a fuse. The lights blew out, and I went down the cellar. And behind the fuse box — it happened to fall out — was a length of rubber pipe — just short.

HAPPY: No kidding?

LINDA: There's a little attachment on the end of it. I knew right away. And sure enough, on the bottom of the water heater there's a new little nipple on the gas pipe.

HAPPY, *angrily:* That — jerk.

BIFF: Did you have it taken off?

LINDA: I'm — I'm ashamed to. How can I mention it to him? Every day I go down and take away that little rubber pipe. But, when he comes home, I put it back where it was. How can I insult him that way? I don't know what to do. I live from day to day, boys. I tell you, I know every thought in his mind. It sounds so old-fashioned and silly, but I tell you he put his whole life into you and you've turned your backs on him. *She is bent over in the chair, weeping, her face in her hands.* Biff, I swear to God! Biff, his life is in your hands!

HAPPY, *to Biff:* How do you like that damned fool!

BIFF, *kissing her:* All right, pal, all right. It's all settled now. I've been remiss. I know that, Mom. But now I'll stay, and I swear to you, I'll apply myself. *Kneeling in front of her, in a fever of self-reproach:* It's just — you see, Mom, I don't fit in business. Not that I won't try. I'll try, and I'll make good.

HAPPY: Sure you will. The trouble with you in business was you never tried to please people.

BIFF: I know, I —

HAPPY: Like when you worked for Harrison's. Bob Harrison said you were tops, and then you go and do some damn fool thing like whistling whole songs in the elevator like a comedian.

BIFF, *against Happy:* So what? I like to whistle sometimes.

HAPPY: You don't raise a guy to a responsible job who whistles in the elevator!

LINDA: Well, don't argue about it now.

HAPPY: Like when you'd go off and swim in the middle of the day instead of taking the line around.

BIFF, *his resentment rising:* Well, don't you run off? You take off sometimes, don't you? On a nice summer day?

HAPPY: Yeah, but I cover myself!

LINDA: Boys!

HAPPY: If I'm going to take a fade the boss can call any number where I'm supposed to be and they'll swear to him that I just left. I'll tell you something that I hate to say, Biff, but in the business world some of them think you're crazy.

BIFF, *angered:* Screw the business world!

HAPPY: All right, screw it! Great, but cover yourself!

LINDA: Hap, Hap!

BIFF: I don't care what they think! They've laughed at Dad for years, and you know why? Because we don't belong in this nuthouse of a city! We should be mixing cement on some open plain, or — or carpenters. A carpenter is allowed to whistle!

Willy walks in from the entrance of the house, at left.

WILLY: Even your grandfather was better than a carpenter. *Pause. They watch him.* You never grew up. Bernard does not whistle in the elevator, I assure you.

BIFF, *as though to laugh Willy out of it:* Yeah, but you do, Pop.

WILLY: I never in my life whistled in an elevator! And who in the business world thinks I'm crazy?

BIFF: I didn't mean it like that, Pop. Now don't make a whole thing out of it, will ya?

WILLY: Go back to the West! Be a carpenter, a cowboy, enjoy yourself!

LINDA: Willy, he was just saying —

WILLY: I heard what he said!

HAPPY, *trying to quiet Willy:* Hey, Pop, come on now . . .

WILLY, *continuing over Happy's line:* They laugh at me, heh? Go to Filene's, go to the Hub, go to Slattery's, Boston.[10] Call out the name Willy Loman and see what happens! Big shot!

BIFF: All right, Pop.

WILLY: Big!

BIFF: All right!

WILLY: Why do you always insult me?

---

10. **Go to Filene's . . . Slattery's, Boston:** When Filene's Department Store built its flagship building in downtown Boston in 1912, a bronze marker with the city's nickname, "The Hub of the Universe," was placed in the sidewalk at the corner of the store. Slattery's Restaurant and Bar, a well-known local establishment, opened in 1934 in Fitchburg, Massachusetts, west of Boston.

BIFF: I didn't say a word. *To Linda:* Did I say a word?

LINDA: He didn't say anything, Willy.

WILLY, *going to the doorway of the living-room:* All right, good night, good night.

LINDA: Willy, dear, he just decided . . .

WILLY, *to Biff:* If you get tired hanging around tomorrow, paint the ceiling I put up in the living-room.

BIFF: I'm leaving early tomorrow.

HAPPY: He's going to see Bill Oliver, Pop.

WILLY, *interestedly:* Oliver? For what?

BIFF, *with reserve, but trying, trying:* He always said he'd stake me. I'd like to go into business, so maybe I can take him up on it.

LINDA: Isn't that wonderful?

WILLY: Don't interrupt. What's wonderful about it? There's fifty men in the City of New York who'd stake him. *To Biff:* Sporting goods?

BIFF: I guess so. I know something about it and —

WILLY: He knows something about it! You know sporting goods better than Spalding, for God's sake! How much is he giving you?

BIFF: I don't know, I didn't even see him yet, but —

WILLY: Then what're you talkin' about?

BIFF, *getting angry:* Well, all I said was I'm gonna see him, that's all!

WILLY, *turning away:* Ah, you're counting your chickens again.

BIFF, *starting left for the stairs:* Oh, Jesus, I'm going to sleep!

WILLY, *calling after him:* Don't curse in this house!

BIFF, *turning:* Since when did you get so clean?

HAPPY, *trying to stop them:* Wait a . . .

WILLY: Don't use that language to me! I won't have it!

HAPPY, *grabbing Biff, shouts:* Wait a minute! I got an idea. I got a feasible idea. Come here, Biff, let's talk this over now, let's talk some sense here. When I was down in Florida last time, I thought of a great idea to sell sporting goods. It just came back to me. You and I, Biff — we have a line, the Loman Line. We train a couple of weeks, and put on a couple of exhibitions, see?

WILLY: That's an idea!

HAPPY: Wait! We form two basketball teams, see? Two water-polo teams. We play each other. It's a million dollars' worth of publicity. Two brothers, see? The Loman Brothers. Displays in the Royal Palms — all the hotels. And banners over the ring and the basketball court: "Loman Brothers." Baby, we could sell sporting goods!

WILLY: That is a one-million-dollar idea!

LINDA: Marvelous!

BIFF: I'm in great shape as far as that's concerned.

HAPPY: And the beauty of it is, Biff, it wouldn't be like a business. We'd be out playin' ball again . . .

BIFF, *enthused:* Yeah, that's . . .

WILLY: Million-dollar . . .

HAPPY: And you wouldn't get fed up with it, Biff. It'd be the family again. There'd be the old honor, and comradeship, and if you wanted to go off for a swim or somethin' — well, you'd do it! Without some smart cooky gettin' up ahead of you!

WILLY: Lick the world! You guys together could absolutely lick the civilized world.

BIFF: I'll see Oliver tomorrow. Hap, if we could work that out . . .

LINDA: Maybe things are beginning to —

WILLY, *wildly enthused, to Linda:* Stop interrupting! *To Biff:* But don't wear sport jacket and slacks when you see Oliver.

BIFF: No, I'll —

WILLY: A business suit, and talk as little as possible, and don't crack any jokes.

BIFF: He did like me. Always liked me.

LINDA: He loved you!

WILLY, *to Linda:* Will you stop! *To Biff:* Walk in very serious. You are not applying for a boy's job. Money is to pass. Be quiet, fine, and serious. Everybody likes a kidder, but nobody lends him money.

HAPPY: I'll try to get some myself, Biff. I'm sure I can.

WILLY: I see great things for you kids, I think your troubles are over. But remember, start big and you'll end big. Ask for fifteen. How much you gonna ask for?

BIFF: Gee, I don't know —

WILLY: And don't say "Gee." "Gee" is a boy's word. A man walking in for fifteen thousand dollars does not say "Gee!"

BIFF: Ten, I think, would be top though.

WILLY: Don't be so modest. You always started too low. Walk in with a big laugh. Don't look worried. Start off with a couple of your good stories to lighten things up. It's not what you say, it's how you say it — because personality always wins the day.

LINDA: Oliver always thought the highest of him —

WILLY: Will you let me talk?

BIFF: Don't yell at her, Pop, will ya?

WILLY, *angrily:* I was talking, wasn't I?

BIFF: I don't like you yelling at her all the time, and I'm tellin' you, that's all.

WILLY: What're you, takin' over this house?

LINDA: Willy —

WILLY, *turning on her:* Don't take his side all the time, goddammit!

BIFF, *furiously:* Stop yelling at her!

WILLY, *suddenly pulling on his cheek, beaten down, guilt ridden:* Give my best to Bill Oliver — he may remember me. *He exits through the living-room doorway.*

LINDA, *her voice subdued:* What'd you have to start that for? *Biff turns away.* You see how sweet he was as soon as you talked hopefully? *She goes over to Biff.* Come up and say good night to him. Don't let him go to bed that way.

HAPPY: Come on, Biff, let's buck him up.

LINDA: Please, dear. Just say good night. It takes so little to make him happy. Come. *She goes through the living-room doorway, calling upstairs from within the living-room:* Your pajamas are hanging in the bathroom, Willy!

HAPPY, *looking toward where Linda went out:* What a woman! They broke the mold when they made her. You know that, Biff?

BIFF: He's off salary. My God, working on commission!

HAPPY: Well, let's face it: he's no hot-shot selling man. Except that sometimes, you have to admit, he's a sweet personality.

BIFF, *deciding:* Lend me ten bucks, will ya? I want to buy some new ties.

HAPPY: I'll take you to a place I know. Beautiful stuff. Wear one of my striped shirts tomorrow.

BIFF: She got gray. Mom got awful old. Gee, I'm gonna go in to Oliver tomorrow and knock him for a —

HAPPY: Come on up. Tell that to Dad. Let's give him a whirl. Come on.

BIFF, *steamed up:* You know, with ten thousand bucks, boy!

HAPPY, *as they go into the living-room:* That's the talk, Biff, that's the first time I've heard the old confidence out of you! *From within the living-room, fading off:* You're gonna live with me, kid, and any babe you want just say the word . . . *The last lines are hardly heard. They are mounting the stairs to their parents' bedroom.*

LINDA, *entering her bedroom and addressing Willy, who is in the bathroom. She is straightening the bed for him:* Can you do anything about the shower? It drips.

WILLY, *from the bathroom:* All of a sudden everything falls to pieces! Goddam plumbing, oughta be sued, those people. I hardly finished putting it in and the thing . . . *His words rumble off.*

LINDA: I'm just wondering if Oliver will remember him. You think he might?

WILLY, *coming out of the bathroom in his pajamas:* Remember him? What's the matter with you, you crazy? If he'd've stayed with Oliver he'd be on top by now! Wait'll Oliver gets a look at him. You don't know the average caliber any more. The average young man today — *he is getting into bed* — is got a caliber of zero. Greatest thing in the world for him was to bum around.

Biff and Happy enter the bedroom. Slight pause.

WILLY, *stops short, looking at Biff:* Glad to hear it, boy.

HAPPY: He wanted to say good night to you, sport.

WILLY, *to Biff:* Yeah. Knock him dead, boy. What'd you want to tell me?

BIFF: Just take it easy, Pop. Good night. *He turns to go.*

WILLY, *unable to resist:* And if anything falls off the desk while you're talking to him — like a package or something — don't you pick it up. They have office boys for that.

LINDA: I'll make a big breakfast —

WILLY: Will you let me finish? *To Biff:* Tell him you were in the business in the West. Not farm work.

BIFF: All right, Dad.

LINDA: I think everything —

WILLY, *going right through her speech:* And don't undersell yourself. No less than fifteen thousand dollars.

BIFF, *unable to bear him:* Okay. Good night, Mom. *He starts moving.*

WILLY: Because you got a greatness in you, Biff, remember that. You got all kinds a greatness . . . *He lies back, exhausted. Biff walks out.*

LINDA, *calling after Biff:* Sleep well, darling!

HAPPY: I'm gonna get married, Mom. I wanted to tell you.

LINDA: Go to sleep, dear.

HAPPY, *going:* I just wanted to tell you.

WILLY: Keep up the good work. *Happy exits.* God . . . remember that Ebbets Field[11] game? The championship of the city?

LINDA: Just rest. Should I sing to you?

WILLY: Yeah. Sing to me. *Linda hums a soft lullaby.* When that team came out — he was the tallest, remember?

LINDA: Oh, yes. And in gold.

Biff enters the darkened kitchen, takes a cigarette, and leaves the house. He comes downstage into a golden pool of light. He smokes, staring at the night.

WILLY: Like a young god. Hercules[12] — something like that. And the sun, the sun all around him. Remember how he waved to me? Right up from the field, with the representatives of three colleges standing by? And the buyers I brought, and the cheers when he came out — Loman, Loman, Loman! God Almighty, he'll be great yet. A star like that, magnificent, can never really fade away!

The light on Willy is fading. The gas heater begins to glow through the kitchen wall, near the stairs, a blue flame beneath red coils.

LINDA, *timidly:* Willy dear, what has he got against you?

WILLY: I'm so tired. Don't talk any more.

Biff slowly returns to the kitchen. He stops, stares toward the heater.

LINDA: Will you ask Howard to let you work in New York?

WILLY: First thing in the morning. Everything'll be all right.

Biff reaches behind the heater and draws out a length of rubber tubing. He is horrified and turns his head toward Willy's room, still dimly lit, from which the strains of Linda's desperate but monotonous humming rise.

---

11. **Ebbets Field:** The home of the Brooklyn Dodgers, the baseball stadium opened in 1913 and was demolished in 1960, after the team moved to Los Angeles.

12. **Hercules:** The Roman name for Heracles, the hero of Greek mythology who is renowned for his strength and courage.

WILLY, *staring through the window into the moonlight:* Gee, look at the moon moving between the buildings!

Biff wraps the tubing around his hand and quickly goes up the stairs.

Curtain

ACT TWO

Music is heard, gay and bright. The curtain rises as the music fades away. Willy, in shirt sleeves, is sitting at the kitchen table, sipping coffee, his hat in his lap. Linda is filling his cup when she can.

WILLY: Wonderful coffee. Meal in itself.

LINDA: Can I make you some eggs?

WILLY: No. Take a breath.

LINDA: You look so rested, dear.

WILLY: I slept like a dead one. First time in months. Imagine, sleeping till ten on a Tuesday morning. Boys left nice and early, heh?

LINDA: They were out of here by eight o'clock.

WILLY: Good work!

LINDA: It was so thrilling to see them leaving together. I can't get over the shaving lotion in this house!

WILLY, *smiling:* Mmm –

LINDA: Biff was very changed this morning. His whole attitude seemed to be hopeful. He couldn't wait to get downtown to see Oliver.

WILLY: He's heading for a change. There's no question, there simply are certain men that take longer to get – solidified. How did he dress?

LINDA: His blue suit. He's so handsome in that suit. He could be a – anything in that suit!

Willy gets up from the table. Linda holds his jacket for him.

WILLY: There's no question, no question at all. Gee, on the way home tonight I'd like to buy some seeds.

LINDA, *laughing:* That'd be wonderful. But not enough sun gets back there. Nothing'll grow any more.

WILLY: You wait, kid, before it's all over we're gonna get a little place out in the country, and I'll raise some vegetables, a couple of chickens . . .

LINDA: You'll do it yet, dear.

Willy walks out of his jacket. Linda follows him.

WILLY: And they'll get married, and come for a weekend, I'd build a little guest house. 'Cause I got so many fine tools, all I'd need would be a little lumber and some peace of mind.

LINDA, *joyfully:* I sewed the lining . . .

WILLY: I could build two guest houses, so they'd both come. Did he decide how much he's going to ask Oliver for?

LINDA, *getting him into the jacket:* He didn't mention it, but I imagine ten or fifteen thousand. You going to talk to Howard today?

WILLY: Yeah. I'll put it to him straight and simple. He'll just have to take me off the road.

LINDA: And Willy, don't forget to ask for a little advance, because we've got the insurance premium. It's the grace period now.

WILLY: That's a hundred . . . ?

LINDA: A hundred and eight, sixty-eight. Because we're a little short again.

WILLY: Why are we short?

LINDA: Well, you had the motor job on the car . . .

WILLY: That goddam Studebaker!

LINDA: And you got one more payment on the refrigerator . . .

WILLY: But it just broke again!

LINDA: Well, it's old, dear.

WILLY: I told you we should've bought a well-advertised machine. Charley bought a General Electric and it's twenty years old and it's still good, that son-of-a-bitch.

LINDA: But, Willy —

WILLY: Whoever heard of a Hastings refrigerator? Once in my life I would like to own something outright before it's broken! I'm always in a race with the junkyard! I just finished paying for the car and it's on its last legs. The refrigerator consumes belts like a goddam maniac. They time those things. They time them so when you finally paid for them, they're used up.

LINDA, *buttoning up his jacket as he unbuttons it:* All told, about two hundred dollars would carry us, dear. But that includes the last payment on the mortgage. After this payment, Willy, the house belongs to us.

WILLY: It's twenty-five years!

LINDA: Biff was nine years old when we bought it.

WILLY: Well, that's a great thing. To weather a twenty-five year mortgage is —

LINDA: It's an accomplishment.

WILLY: All the cement, the lumber, the reconstruction I put in this house! There ain't a crack to be found in it any more.

LINDA: Well, it served its purpose.

WILLY: What purpose? Some stranger'll come along, move in, and that's that. If only Biff would take this house, and raise a family . . . *He starts to go.* Good-by, I'm late.

LINDA, *suddenly remembering:* Oh, I forgot! You're supposed to meet them for dinner.

WILLY: Me?

LINDA: At Frank's Chop House on Forty-eighth near Sixth Avenue.

WILLY: Is that so! How about you?

LINDA: No, just the three of you. They're gonna blow you to a big meal!

WILLY: Don't say! Who thought of that?

LINDA: Biff came to me this morning, Willy, and he said, "Tell Dad, we want to blow him to a big meal." Be there six o'clock. You and your two boys are going to have dinner.

WILLY: Gee whiz! That's really somethin'. I'm gonna knock Howard for a loop, kid. I'll get an advance, and I'll come home with a New York job. Goddammit, now I'm gonna do it!

LINDA: Oh, that's the spirit, Willy!

WILLY: I will never get behind a wheel the rest of my life!

LINDA: It's changing, Willy, I can feel it changing!

WILLY: Beyond a question. G'by, I'm late. *He starts to go again.*

LINDA, *calling after him as she runs to the kitchen table for a handkerchief:* You got your glasses?

WILLY, *feels for them, then comes back in:* Yeah, yeah, got my glasses.

LINDA, *giving him the handkerchief:* And a handkerchief.

WILLY: Yeah, handkerchief.

LINDA: And your saccharine?

WILLY: Yeah, my saccharine.

LINDA: Be careful on the subway stairs.

She kisses him, and a silk stocking is seen hanging from her hand. Willy notices it.

WILLY: Will you stop mending stockings? At least while I'm in the house. It gets me nervous. I can't tell you. Please.

Linda hides the stocking in her hand as she follows Willy across the forestage in front of the house.

LINDA: Remember, Frank's Chop House.

WILLY, *passing the apron:* Maybe beets would grow out there.

LINDA, *laughing:* But you tried so many times.

WILLY: Yeah. Well, don't work hard today. *He disappears around the right corner of the house.*

LINDA: Be careful!

As Willy vanishes, Linda waves to him. Suddenly the phone rings. She runs across the stage and into the kitchen and lifts it.

LINDA: Hello? Oh, Biff! I'm so glad you called, I just . . . Yes, sure, I just told him. Yes, he'll be there for dinner at six o'clock, I didn't forget. Listen, I was just dying to tell you. You know that little rubber pipe I told you about? That he connected to the gas heater? I finally decided to go down the cellar this morning and take it away and destroy it. But it's gone! Imagine? He took it away himself, it isn't there! *She listens.* When? Oh, then you took it. Oh — nothing, it's just that I'd hoped he'd taken it away himself. Oh, I'm not worried, darling, because this morning he left in such high spirits, it was like the old days! I'm not afraid any more. Did Mr. Oliver see you? . . . Well, you wait there then. And make a nice impression on him, darling. Just don't perspire too much before you see him. And have a nice time with Dad. He may have big news too! . . . That's right, a New York job. And be sweet to him tonight, dear. Be loving to him. Because he's only a little boat looking for a harbor. *She is trembling with sorrow and joy.* Oh, that's wonderful, Biff, you'll save his life. Thanks, darling. Just put your arm around him when he comes into the restaurant. Give him a smile. That's the boy . . . Good-by, dear. . . . You got your comb? . . . That's fine. Good-by, Biff dear.

In the middle of her speech, Howard Wagner, thirty-six, wheels on a small typewriter table on which is a wire-recording machine[13] and proceeds to plug it in. This is on the left forestage. Light slowly fades on Linda as it rises on Howard. Howard is intent on threading the machine and only glances over his shoulder as Willy appears.

WILLY: Pst! Pst!

HOWARD: Hello, Willy, come in.

WILLY: Like to have a little talk with you, Howard.

HOWARD: Sorry to keep you waiting. I'll be with you in a minute.

WILLY: What's that, Howard?

HOWARD: Didn't you ever see one of these? Wire recorder.

WILLY: Oh. Can we talk a minute?

HOWARD: Records things. Just got delivery yesterday. Been driving me crazy, the most terrific machine I ever saw in my life. I was up all night with it.

WILLY: What do you do with it?

HOWARD: I bought it for dictation, but you can do anything with it. Listen to this. I had it home last night. Listen to what I picked up. The first one is my daughter. Get this. *He flicks the switch and "Roll out the Barrel" is heard being whistled.* Listen to that kid whistle.

WILLY: That is lifelike, isn't it?

HOWARD: Seven years old. Get that tone.

WILLY: Ts, ts. Like to ask a little favor if you . . .

The whistling breaks off, and the voice of Howard's daughter is heard.

HIS DAUGHTER: "Now you, Daddy."

HOWARD: She's crazy for me! *Again the same is whistled.* That's me! Ha! *He winks.*

WILLY: You're very good!

The whistling breaks off again. The machine runs silent for a moment.

HOWARD: Sh! Get this now, this is my son.

HIS SON: "The capital of Alabama is Montgomery; the capital of Arizona is Phoenix; the

---

13. **wire-recording machine:** The first sound recorder, made with steel piano wire in 1878, was developed commercially in the early twentieth century and remained popular with consumers until the development of magnetic tape recorders in the 1950s.

capital of Arkansas is Little Rock; the capital of California is Sacramento . . ." *and on, and on.*

HOWARD, *holding up five fingers:* Five years old, Willy!

WILLY: He'll make an announcer some day!

HIS SON, *continuing:* "The capital . . ."

HOWARD: Get that — alphabetical order! *The machine breaks off suddenly.* Wait a minute. The maid kicked the plug out.

WILLY: It certainly is a —

HOWARD: Sh, for God's sake!

HIS SON: "It's nine o'clock, Bulova watch time.[14] So I have to go to sleep."

WILLY: That really is —

HOWARD: Wait a minute! The next is my wife.

They wait.

HOWARD'S VOICE: "Go on, say something." *Pause.* "Well, you gonna talk?"

HIS WIFE: "I can't think of anything."

HOWARD'S VOICE: "Well, talk — it's turning."

HIS WIFE, *shyly, beaten:* "Hello." *Silence.* "Oh, Howard, I can't talk into this . . ."

HOWARD, *snapping the machine off:* That was my wife.

WILLY: That is a wonderful machine. Can we —

HOWARD: I tell you, Willy, I'm gonna take my camera, and my bandsaw, and all my hobbies, and out they go. This is the most fascinating relaxation I ever found.

WILLY: I think I'll get one myself.

HOWARD: Sure, they're only a hundred and a half. You can't do without it. Supposing you wanna hear Jack Benny,[15] see? But you can't be at home at that hour. So you tell the maid to turn the radio on when Jack Benny comes on, and this automatically goes on with the radio . . .

WILLY: And when you come home you . . .

HOWARD: You can come home twelve o'clock, one o'clock, any time you like, and you get yourself a Coke and sit yourself down, throw the switch, and there's Jack Benny's program in the middle of the night!

WILLY: I'm definitely going to get one. Because lots of time I'm on the road, and I think to myself, what I must be missing on the radio!

HOWARD: Don't you have a radio in the car?

WILLY: Well, yeah, but who ever thinks of turning it on?

HOWARD: Say, aren't you supposed to be in Boston?

---

14. **Bulova watch time:** The nation's first radio commercial, which was broadcast nationally in 1926, was a long-running advertisement produced by the Bulova Watch Company: "At the tone, it's 8 p.m., B-U-L-O-V-A Bulova watch time."

15. **Jack Benny:** Benny (1894–1974) was a comedian and actor whose hugely successful "Jack Benny Show" ran on radio from 1932 to 1955 and on television during the period 1950–56.

WILLY: That's what I want to talk to you about, Howard. You got a minute? *He draws a chair in from the wing.*

HOWARD: What happened? What're you doing here?

WILLY: Well . . .

HOWARD: You didn't crack up again, did you?

WILLY: Oh, no. No . . .

HOWARD: Geez, you had me worried there for a minute. What's the trouble?

WILLY: Well, tell you the truth, Howard. I've come to the decision that I'd rather not travel any more.

HOWARD: Not travel! Well, what'll you do?

WILLY: Remember, Christmas time, when you had the party here? You said you'd try to think of some spot for me here in town.

HOWARD: With us?

WILLY: Well, sure.

HOWARD: Oh, yeah, yeah. I remember. Well, I couldn't think of anything for you, Willy.

WILLY: I tell ya, Howard. The kids are all grown up, y'know. I don't need much any more. If I could take home — well, sixty-five dollars a week, I could swing it.

HOWARD: Yeah, but Willy, see I —

WILLY: I tell ya why, Howard. Speaking frankly and between the two of us, y'know — I'm just a little tired.

HOWARD: Oh, I could understand that, Willy. But you're a road man, Willy, and we do a road business. We've only got a half-dozen salesmen on the floor here.

WILLY: God knows, Howard, I never asked a favor of any man. But I was with the firm when your father used to carry you in here in his arms.

HOWARD: I know that, Willy, but —

WILLY: Your father came to me the day you were born and asked me what I thought of the name of Howard, may he rest in peace.

HOWARD: I appreciate that, Willy, but there just is no spot here for you. If I had a spot I'd slam you right in, but I just don't have a single solitary spot.

He looks for his lighter. Willy has picked it up and gives it to him. Pause.

WILLY, *with increasing anger:* Howard, all I need to set my table is fifty dollars a week.

HOWARD: But where am I going to put you, kid?

WILLY: Look, it isn't a question of whether I can sell merchandise, is it?

HOWARD: No, but it's a business, kid, and everybody's gotta pull his own weight.

WILLY, *desperately:* Just let me tell you a story, Howard —

HOWARD: 'Cause you gotta admit, business is business.

WILLY, *angrily:* Business is definitely business, but just listen for a minute. You don't understand this. When I was a boy — eighteen, nineteen — I was already on the road. And there was a question in my mind as to whether selling had a future for me. Because in those days I had a yearning to go to Alaska. See, there were three gold strikes in one month in Alaska, and I felt like going out. Just for the ride, you might say.

HOWARD, *barely interested:* Don't say.

WILLY: Oh, yeah, my father lived many years in Alaska. He was an adventurous man. We've got quite a little streak of self-reliance in our family. I thought I'd go out with my older brother and try to locate him, and maybe settle in the North with the old man. And I was almost decided to go, when I met a salesman in the Parker House. His name was Dave Singleman. And he was eighty-four years old, and he'd drummed merchandise in thirty-one states. And old Dave, he'd go up to his room, y'understand, put on his green velvet slippers – I'll never forget – and pick up his phone and call the buyers, and without ever leaving his room, at the age of eighty-four, he made his living. And when I saw that, I realized that selling was the greatest career a man could want. 'Cause what could be more satisfying than to be able to go, at the age of eighty-four, into twenty or thirty different cities, and pick up a phone, and be remembered and loved and helped by so many different people? Do you know? when he died – and by the way he died the death of a salesman, in his green velvet slippers in the smoker of the New York, New Haven and Hartford, going into Boston – when he died, hundreds of salesmen and buyers were at his funeral. Things were sad on a lotta trains for months after that. *He stands up. Howard has not looked at him.* In those days there was personality in it, Howard. There was respect, and comradeship, and gratitude in it. Today, it's all cut and dried, and there's no chance for bringing friendship to bear – or personality. You see what I mean? They don't know me any more.

HOWARD, *moving away, to the right:* That's just the thing, Willy.

WILLY: If I had forty dollars a week – that's all I'd need. Forty dollars, Howard.

HOWARD: Kid, I can't take blood from a stone, I –

WILLY, *desperation is on him now:* Howard, the year Al Smith was nominated,[16] your father came to me and –

HOWARD, *starting to go off:* I've got to see some people, kid.

WILLY, *stopping him:* I'm talking about your father! There were promises made across this desk! You mustn't tell me you've got people to see – I put thirty-four years into this firm, Howard, and now I can't pay my insurance! You can't eat the orange and throw the peel away – a man is not a piece of fruit! *After a pause:* Now pay attention. Your father – in 1928 I had a big year. I averaged a hundred and seventy dollars a week in commissions.

HOWARD, *impatiently:* Now, Willy, you never averaged –

WILLY, *banging his hand on the desk:* I averaged a hundred and seventy dollars a week in the year of 1928! And your father came to me – or rather, I was in the office here – it was right over this desk – and he put his hand on my shoulder –

HOWARD, *getting up:* You'll have to excuse me, Willy, I gotta see some people. Pull yourself together. *Going out:* I'll be back in a little while.

On Howard's exit, the light on his chair grows very bright and strange.

---

16. **the year Al Smith was nominated:** Alfred "Al" Smith (1873-1944), the two-term governor of New York, finally secured the Democratic presidential nomination in 1928, when he lost the election to the Republican Herbert Hoover.

WILLY: Pull myself together! What the hell did I say to him? My God, I was yelling at him! How could I! *Willy breaks off, staring at the light, which occupies the chair, animating it. He approaches this chair, standing across the desk from it.* Frank, Frank, don't you remember what you told me that time? How you put your hand on my shoulder, and Frank . . . *He leans on the desk and as he speaks the dead man's name he accidentally switches on the recorder, and instantly*

HOWARD'S SON: ". . . of New York is Albany. The capital of Ohio is Cincinnati, the capital of Rhode Island is . . ." *The recitation continues.*

WILLY, *leaping away with fright, shouting:* Ha! Howard! Howard! Howard!

HOWARD, *rushing in:* What happened?

WILLY, *pointing at the machine, which continues nasally, childishly, with the capital cities:* Shut it off! Shut it off!

HOWARD, *pulling the plug out:* Look, Willy . . .

WILLY, *pressing his hands to his eyes:* I gotta get myself some coffee. I'll get some coffee . . .

Willy starts to walk out. Howard stops him.

HOWARD, *rolling up the cord:* Willy, look . . .

WILLY: I'll go to Boston.

HOWARD: Willy, you can't go to Boston for us.

WILLY: Why can't I go?

HOWARD: I don't want you to represent us. I've been meaning to tell you for a long time now.

WILLY: Howard, are you firing me?

HOWARD: I think you need a good long rest, Willy.

WILLY: Howard —

HOWARD: And when you feel better, come back, and we'll see if we can work something out.

WILLY: But I gotta earn money, Howard. I'm in no position to —

HOWARD: Where are your sons? Why don't your sons give you a hand?

WILLY: They're working on a very big deal.

HOWARD: This is no time for false pride, Willy. You go to your sons and you tell them that you're tired. You've got two great boys, haven't you?

WILLY: Oh, no question, no question, but in the meantime . . .

HOWARD: Then that's that, heh?

WILLY: All right, I'll go to Boston tomorrow.

HOWARD: No, no.

WILLY: I can't throw myself on my sons. I'm not a cripple!

HOWARD: Look, kid, I'm busy this morning.

WILLY, *grasping Howard's arm:* Howard, you've got to let me go to Boston!

HOWARD, *hard, keeping himself under control:* I've got a line of people to see this morning. Sit down, take five minutes, and pull yourself together, and then go home, will ya? I need the office, Willy. *He starts to go, turns, remembering the recorder, starts to push off the table holding the recorder.* Oh, yeah. Whenever you can this week, stop by and drop off the samples. You'll feel better, Willy, and then come back and we'll talk. Pull yourself together, kid, there's people outside.

Howard exits, pushing the table off left. Willy stares into space, exhausted. Now the music is heard — Ben's music — first distantly, then closer, closer. As Willy speaks, Ben enters from the right. He carries valise and umbrella.

WILLY: Oh, Ben, how did you do it? What is the answer? Did you wind up the Alaska deal already?

BEN: Doesn't take much time if you know what you're doing. Just a short business trip. Boarding ship in an hour. Wanted to say good-by.

WILLY: Ben, I've got to talk to you.

BEN, *glancing at his watch:* Haven't the time, William.

WILLY, *crossing the apron to Ben:* Ben, nothing's working out. I don't know what to do.

BEN: Now, look here, William. I've bought timberland in Alaska and I need a man to look after things for me.

WILLY: God, timberland! Me and my boys in those grand outdoors!

BEN: You've a new continent at your doorstep, William. Get out of these cities, they're full of talk and time payments and courts of law. Screw on your fists and you can fight for a fortune up there.

WILLY: Yes, yes! Linda, Linda!

Linda enters as of old, with the wash.

LINDA: Oh, you're back?

BEN: I haven't much time.

WILLY: No, wait! Linda, he's got a proposition for me in Alaska.

LINDA: But you've got — *To Ben:* He's got a beautiful job here.

WILLY: But in Alaska, kid, I could —

LINDA: You're doing well enough, Willy!

BEN, *to Linda:* Enough for what, my dear?

LINDA, *frightened of Ben and angry at him:* Don't say those things to him! Enough to be happy right here, right now. *To Willy, while Ben laughs:* Why must everybody conquer the world? You're well liked, and the boys love you, and someday — *to Ben* — why, old man Wagner told him just the other day that if he keeps it up he'll be a member of the firm, didn't he, Willy?

WILLY: Sure, sure. I am building something with this firm, Ben, and if a man is building something he must be on the right track, mustn't he?

BEN: What are you building? Lay your hand on it. Where is it?

WILLY, *hesitantly:* That's true, Linda, there's nothing.

LINDA: Why? *To Ben:* There's a man eighty-four years old —

WILLY: That's right, Ben, that's right. When I look at that man I say, what is there to worry about?

BEN: Bah!

WILLY: It's true, Ben. All he has to do is go into any city, pick up the phone, and he's making his living and you know why?

BEN, *picking up his valise:* I've got to go.

WILLY, *holding Ben back:* Look at this boy!

Biff, in his high school sweater, enters carrying suitcase. Happy carries Biff's shoulder guards, gold helmet, and football pants.

WILLY: Without a penny to his name, three great universities are begging for him, and from there the sky's the limit, because it's not what you do, Ben. It's who you know and the smile on your face! It's contacts, Ben, contacts! The whole wealth of Alaska passes over the lunch table at the Commodore Hotel, and that's the wonder, the wonder of this country, that a man can end with diamonds here on the basis of being liked! *He turns to Biff.* And that's why when you get out on that field today it's important. Because thousands of people will be rooting for you and loving you. *To Ben, who has again begun to leave:* And Ben! when he walks into a business office his name will sound out like a bell and all the doors will open to him! I've seen it, Ben, I've seen it a thousand times! You can't feel it with your hand like timber, but it's there!

BEN: Good-by, William.

WILLY: Ben, am I right? Don't you think I'm right? I value your advice.

BEN: There's a new continent at your doorstep, William. You could walk out rich. Rich! *He is gone.*

WILLY: We'll do it here, Ben! You hear me? We're gonna do it here!

Young Bernard rushes in. The gay music of the Boys is heard.

BERNARD: Oh, gee, I was afraid you left already!

WILLY: Why? What time is it?

BERNARD: It's half-past one!

WILLY: Well, come on, everybody! Ebbets Field next stop! Where's the pennants? *He rushes through the wall-line of the kitchen and out into the living-room.*

LINDA, *to Biff:* Did you pack fresh underwear?

BIFF, *who has been limbering up:* I want to go!

BERNARD: Biff, I'm carrying your helmet, ain't I?

HAPPY: No, I'm carrying the helmet.

BERNARD: Oh, Biff, you promised me.

HAPPY: I'm carrying the helmet.

BERNARD: How am I going to get in the locker room?

LINDA: Let him carry the shoulder guards. *She puts her coat and hat on in the kitchen.*

BERNARD: Can I, Biff? 'Cause I told everybody I'm going to be in the locker room.

HAPPY: In Ebbets Field it's the clubhouse.

BERNARD: I meant the clubhouse. Biff!

HAPPY: Biff!

BIFF, *grandly, after a slight pause:* Let him carry the shoulder guards.

HAPPY, *as he gives Bernard the shoulder guards:* Stay close to us now.

Willy rushes in with the pennants.

WILLY, *handing them out:* Everybody wave when Biff comes out on the field. *Happy and Bernard run off.* You set now, boy?

The music has died away.

BIFF: Ready to go, Pop. Every muscle is ready.

WILLY, *at the edge of the apron:* You realize what this means?

BIFF: That's right, Pop.

WILLY, *feeling Biff's muscles:* You're comin' home this afternoon captain of the All-Scholastic Championship Team of the City of New York.

BIFF: I got it, Pop. And remember, pal, when I take off my helmet, that touchdown is for you.

WILLY: Let's go! *He is starting out, with his arm around Biff, when Charley enters, as of old, in knickers.* I got no room for you, Charley.

CHARLEY: Room? For what?

WILLY: In the car.

CHARLEY: You goin' for a ride? I wanted to shoot some casino.

WILLY, *furiously:* Casino! *Incredulously:* Don't you realize what today is?

LINDA: Oh, he knows, Willy. He's just kidding you.

WILLY: That's nothing to kid about!

CHARLEY: No, Linda, what's goin' on?

LINDA: He's playing in Ebbets Field.

CHARLEY: Baseball in this weather?

WILLY: Don't talk to him. Come on, come on! *He is pushing them out.*

CHARLEY: Wait a minute, didn't you hear the news?

WILLY: What?

CHARLEY: Don't you listen to the radio? Ebbets Field just blew up.

WILLY: You go to hell! *Charley laughs. Pushing them out:* Come on, come on! We're late.

CHARLEY, *as they go:* Knock a homer, Biff, knock a homer!

WILLY, *the last to leave, turning to Charley:* I don't think that was funny, Charley. This is the greatest day of his life.

CHARLEY: Willy, when are you going to grow up?

WILLY: Yeah, heh? When this game is over, Charley, you'll be laughing out of the other side of your face. They'll be calling him another Red Grange.[17] Twenty-five thousand a year.

---

17. **Red Grange:** Harold Edward Grange (1903–1991), a star football player for the University of Illinois and later for the Chicago Bears.

CHARLEY, *kidding:* Is that so?

WILLY: Yeah, that's so.

CHARLEY: Well, then, I'm sorry, Willy. But tell me something.

WILLY: What?

CHARLEY: Who is Red Grange?

WILLY: Put up your hands. Goddam you, put up your hands!

Charley, chuckling, shakes his head and walks away, around the left corner of the stage. Willy follows him. The music rises to a mocking frenzy.

WILLY: Who the hell do you think you are, better than everybody else? You don't know everything, you big, ignorant, stupid . . . Put up your hands!

Light rises, on the right side of the forestage, on a small table in the reception room of Charley's office. Traffic sounds are heard. Bernard, now mature, sits whistling to himself. A pair of tennis rackets and an overnight bag are on the floor beside him.

WILLY, *offstage:* What are you walking away for? Don't walk away! If you're going to say something say it to my face! I know you laugh at me behind my back. You'll laugh out of the other side of your goddam face after this game. Touchdown! Touchdown! Eighty thousand people! Touchdown! Right between the goal posts.

Bernard is a quiet, earnest, but self-assured young man. Willy's voice is coming from right upstage now. Bernard lowers his feet off the table and listens. Jenny, his father's secretary, enters.

JENNY, *distressed:* Say, Bernard, will you go out in the hall?

BERNARD: What is that noise? Who is it?

JENNY: Mr. Loman. He just got off the elevator.

BERNARD, *getting up:* Who's he arguing with?

JENNY: Nobody. There's nobody with him. I can't deal with him any more, and your father gets all upset every time he comes. I've got a lot of typing to do, and your father's waiting to sign it. Will you see him?

WILLY, *entering:* Touchdown! Touch – *He sees Jenny.* Jenny, Jenny, good to see you. How're ya? Workin'? Or still honest?

JENNY: Fine. How've you been feeling?

WILLY: Not much any more, Jenny. Ha, ha! *He is surprised to see the rackets.*

BERNARD: Hello, Uncle Willy.

WILLY, *almost shocked:* Bernard! Well, look who's here! *He comes quickly, guiltily, to Bernard and warmly shakes his hand.*

BERNARD: How are you? Good to see you.

WILLY: What are you doing here?

BERNARD: Oh, just stopped by to see Pop. Get off my feet till my train leaves. I'm going to Washington in a few minutes.

WILLY: Is he in?

BERNARD: Yes, he's in his office with the accountant. Sit down.

WILLY, *sitting down:* What're you going to do in Washington?

BERNARD: Oh, just a case I've got there, Willy.

WILLY: That so? *Indicating the rackets:* You going to play tennis there?

BERNARD: I'm staying with a friend who's got a court.

WILLY: Don't say. His own tennis court. Must be fine people, I bet.

BERNARD: They are, very nice. Dad tells me Biff's in town.

WILLY, *with a big smile:* Yeah, Biff's in. Working on a very big deal, Bernard.

BERNARD: What's Biff doing?

WILLY: Well, he's been doing very big things in the West. But he decided to establish himself here. Very big. We're having dinner. Did I hear your wife had a boy?

BERNARD: That's right. Our second.

WILLY: Two boys! What do you know!

BERNARD: What kind of a deal has Biff got?

WILLY: Well, Bill Oliver — very big sporting-goods man — he wants Biff very badly. Called him in from the West. Long distance, carte blanche, special deliveries. Your friends have their own private tennis court?

BERNARD: You still with the old firm, Willy?

WILLY, *after a pause:* I'm — I'm overjoyed to see how you made the grade, Bernard, over-joyed. It's an encouraging thing to see a young man really — really — Looks very good for Biff — very — *He breaks off, then:* Bernard — *He is so full of emotion, he breaks off again.*

BERNARD: What is it, Willy?

WILLY, *small and alone:* What — what's the secret?

BERNARD: What secret?

WILLY: How — how did you? Why didn't he ever catch on?

BERNARD: I wouldn't know that, Willy.

WILLY, *confidentially, desperately:* You were his friend, his boyhood friend. There's something I don't understand about it. His life ended after that Ebbets Field game. From the age of seventeen nothing good ever happened to him.

BERNARD: He never trained himself for anything.

WILLY: But he did, he did. After high school he took so many correspondence courses. Radio mechanics; television; God knows what, and never made the slightest mark.

BERNARD, *taking off his glasses:* Willy, do you want to talk candidly?

WILLY, *rising, faces Bernard:* I regard you as a very brilliant man, Bernard. I value your advice.

BERNARD: Oh, the hell with the advice, Willy. I couldn't advise you. There's just one thing I've always wanted to ask you. When he was supposed to graduate, and the math teacher flunked him —

WILLY: Oh, that son-of-a-bitch ruined his life.

BERNARD: Yeah, but, Willy, all he had to do was go to summer school and make up that subject.

WILLY: That's right, that's right.

BERNARD: Did you tell him not to go to summer school?

WILLY: Me? I begged him to go. I ordered him to go!

BERNARD: Then why wouldn't he go?

WILLY: Why? Why! Bernard, that question has been trailing me like a ghost for the last fifteen years. He flunked the subject, and laid down and died like a hammer hit him!

BERNARD: Take it easy, kid.

WILLY: Let me talk to you — I got nobody to talk to. Bernard, Bernard, was it my fault? Y'see? It keeps going around in my mind, maybe I did something to him. I got nothing to give him.

BERNARD: Don't take it so hard.

WILLY: Why did he lay down? What is the story there? You were his friend!

BERNARD: Willy, I remember, it was June, and our grades came out. And he'd flunked math.

WILLY: That son-of-a-bitch!

BERNARD: No, it wasn't right then. Biff just got very angry, I remember, and he was ready to enroll in summer school.

WILLY, *surprised:* He was?

BERNARD: He wasn't beaten by it at all. But then, Willy, he disappeared from the block for almost a month. And I got the idea that he'd gone up to New England to see you. Did he have a talk with you then?

Willy stares in silence.

BERNARD: Willy?

WILLY, *with a strong edge of resentment in his voice:* Yeah, he came to Boston. What about it?

BERNARD: Well, just that when he came back — I'll never forget this, it always mystifies me. Because I'd thought so well of Biff, even though he'd always taken advantage of me. I loved him, Willy, y'know? And he came back after that month and took his sneakers — remember those sneakers with "University of Virginia" printed on them? He was so proud of those, wore them every day. And he took them down in the cellar, and burned them up in the furnace. We had a fist fight. It lasted at least half an hour. Just the two of us, punching each other down the cellar, and crying right through it. I've often thought of how strange it was that I knew he'd given up his life. What happened in Boston, Willy?

Willy looks at him as at an intruder.

BERNARD: I just bring it up because you asked me.

WILLY, *angrily:* Nothing. What do you mean, "What happened?" What's that got to do with anything?

BERNARD: Well, don't get sore.

WILLY: What are you trying to do, blame it on me? If a boy lays down is that my fault?

BERNARD: Now, Willy, don't get —

WILLY: Well, don't — don't talk to me that way! What does that mean, "What happened?"

Charley enters. He is in his vest, and he carries a bottle of bourbon.

CHARLEY: Hey, you're going to miss that train. *He waves the bottle.*
BERNARD: Yeah, I'm going. *He takes the bottle.* Thanks, Pop. *He picks up his rackets and bag.* Good-by, Willy, and don't worry about it. You know, "If at first you don't succeed . . ."
WILLY: Yes, I believe in that.
BERNARD: But sometimes, Willy, it's better for a man just to walk away.
WILLY: Walk away?
BERNARD: That's right.
WILLY: But if you can't walk away?
BERNARD, *after a slight pause:* I guess that's when it's tough. *Extending his hand:* Good-by, Willy.
WILLY, *shaking Bernard's hand:* Good-by, boy.
CHARLEY, *an arm on Bernard's shoulder:* How do you like this kid? Gonna argue a case in front of the Supreme Court.
BERNARD, *protesting:* Pop!
WILLY, *genuinely shocked, pained, and happy:* No! The Supreme Court!
BERNARD: I gotta run. 'By, Dad!
CHARLEY: Knock 'em dead, Bernard!

Bernard goes off.

WILLY, *as Charley takes out his wallet:* The Supreme Court! And he didn't even mention it!
CHARLEY, *counting out money on the desk:* He don't have to — he's gonna do it.
WILLY: And you never told him what to do, did you? You never took any interest in him.
CHARLEY: My salvation is that I never took any interest in anything. There's some money — fifty dollars. I got an accountant inside.
WILLY: Charley, look . . . *With difficulty:* I got my insurance to pay. If you can manage it — I need a hundred and ten dollars.

Charley doesn't reply for a moment; merely stops moving.

WILLY: I'd draw it from my bank but Linda would know, and I . . .
CHARLEY: Sit down, Willy.
WILLY, *moving toward the chair:* I'm keeping an account of everything, remember. I'll pay every penny back. *He sits.*
CHARLEY: Now listen to me, Willy.
WILLY: I want you to know I appreciate . . .
CHARLEY, *sitting down on the table:* Willy, what're you doin'? What the hell is goin' on in your head?

WILLY: Why? I'm simply . . .

CHARLEY: I offered you a job. You can make fifty dollars a week. And I won't send you on the road.

WILLY: I've got a job.

CHARLEY: Without pay? What kind of a job is a job without pay? *He rises.* Now, look, kid, enough is enough. I'm no genius but I know when I'm being insulted.

WILLY: Insulted!

CHARLEY: Why don't you want to work for me?

WILLY: What's the matter with you? I've got a job.

CHARLEY: Then what're you walkin' in here every week for?

WILLY, *getting up:* Well, if you don't want me to walk in here —

CHARLEY: I am offering you a job.

WILLY: I don't want your goddam job!

CHARLEY: When the hell are you going to grow up?

WILLY, *furiously:* You big ignoramus, if you say that to me again I'll rap you one! I don't care how big you are! *He's ready to fight.*

Pause.

CHARLEY, *kindly, going to him:* How much do you need, Willy?

WILLY: Charley, I'm strapped, I'm strapped. I don't know what to do. I was just fired.

CHARLEY: Howard fired you?

WILLY: That snotnose. Imagine that? I named him. I named him Howard.

CHARLEY: Willy, when're you gonna realize that them things don't mean anything? You named him Howard, but you can't sell that. The only thing you got in this world is what you can sell. And the funny thing is that you're a salesman, and you don't know that.

WILLY: I've always tried to think otherwise, I guess. I always felt that if a man was impressive, and well liked, that nothing —

CHARLEY: Why must everybody like you? Who liked J. P. Morgan?[18] Was he impressive? In a Turkish bath he'd look like a butcher. But with his pockets on he was very well liked. Now listen, Willy, I know you don't like me, and nobody can say I'm in love with you, but I'll give you a job because — just for the hell of it, put it that way. Now what do you say?

WILLY: I — I just can't work for you, Charley.

CHARLEY: What're you, jealous of me?

WILLY: I can't work for you, that's all, don't ask me why.

CHARLEY, *angered, takes out more bills:* You been jealous of me all your life, you damned fool! Here, pay your insurance. *He puts the money in Willy's hand.*

WILLY: I'm keeping strict accounts.

---

18. J. P. Morgan: John Pierpont Morgan (1837–1913), a powerful banker and financier who was one of the wealthiest men in the world at the turn of the century.

CHARLEY: I've got some work to do. Take care of yourself. And pay your insurance.

WILLY, *moving to the right:* Funny, y'know? After all the highways, and the trains, and the appointments, and the years, you end up worth more dead than alive.

CHARLEY: Willy, nobody's worth nothin' dead. *After a slight pause:* Did you hear what I said?

Willy stands still, dreaming.

CHARLEY: Willy!

WILLY: Apologize to Bernard for me when you see him. I didn't mean to argue with him. He's a fine boy. They're all fine boys, and they'll end up big — all of them. Someday they'll all play tennis together. Wish me luck, Charley. He saw Bill Oliver today.

CHARLEY: Good luck.

WILLY, *on the verge of tears:* Charley, you're the only friend I got. Isn't that a remarkable thing? *He goes out.*

CHARLEY: Jesus!

Charley stares after him a moment and follows. All light blacks out. Suddenly raucous music is heard, and a red glow rises behind the screen at right. Stanley, a young waiter, appears, carrying a table, followed by Happy, who is carrying two chairs.

STANLEY, *putting the table down:* That's all right, Mr. Loman, I can handle it myself. *He turns and takes the chairs from Happy and places them at the table.*

HAPPY, *glancing around:* Oh, this is better.

STANLEY: Sure, in the front there you're in the middle of all kinds a noise. Whenever you got a party, Mr. Loman, you just tell me and I'll put you back here. Y'know, there's a lotta people they don't like it private, because when they go out they like to see a lotta action around them because they're sick and tired to stay in the house by theirself. But I know you, you ain't from Hackensack. You know what I mean?

HAPPY, *sitting down:* So how's it coming, Stanley?

STANLEY: Ah, it's a dog's life. I only wish during the war they'd a took me in the Army. I coulda been dead by now.

HAPPY: My brother's back, Stanley.

STANLEY: Oh, he come back, heh? From the Far West.

HAPPY: Yeah, big cattle man, my brother, so treat him right. And my father's coming too.

STANLEY: Oh, your father too!

HAPPY: You got a couple of nice lobsters?

STANLEY: Hundred per cent, big.

HAPPY: I want them with the claws.

STANLEY: Don't worry, I don't give you no mice. *Happy laughs.* How about some wine? It'll put a head on the meal.

HAPPY: No. You remember, Stanley, that recipe I brought you from overseas? With the champagne in it?

STANLEY: Oh, yeah, sure. I still got it tacked up yet in the kitchen. But that'll have to cost a buck apiece anyways.

HAPPY: That's all right.

STANLEY: What'd you, hit a number or somethin'?

HAPPY: No, it's a little celebration. My brother is — I think he pulled off a big deal today. I think we're going into business together.

STANLEY: Great! That's the best for you. Because a family business, you know what I mean — that's the best.

HAPPY: That's what I think.

STANLEY: 'Cause what's the difference? Somebody steals? It's in the family. Know what I mean? *Sotto voce:* Like this bartender here. The boss is goin' crazy what kinda leak he's got in the cash register. You put it in but it don't come out.

HAPPY, *raising his head:* Sh!

STANLEY: What?

HAPPY: You notice I wasn't lookin' right or left, was I?

STANLEY: No.

HAPPY: And my eyes are closed.

STANLEY: So what's the —?

HAPPY: Strudel's comin'.

STANLEY, *catching on, looks around:* Ah, no, there's no —

He breaks off as a furred, lavishly dressed girl enters and sits at the next table. Both follow her with their eyes.

STANLEY: Geez, how'd ya know?

HAPPY: I got radar or something. *Staring directly at her profile:* Oooooooo . . . Stanley.

STANLEY: I think that's for you, Mr. Loman.

HAPPY: Look at that mouth. Oh, God. And the binoculars.

STANLEY: Geez, you got a life, Mr. Loman.

HAPPY: Wait on her.

STANLEY, *going to the girl's table:* Would you like a menu, ma'am?

GIRL: I'm expecting someone, but I'd like a —

HAPPY: Why don't you bring her — excuse me, miss, do you mind? I sell champagne, and I'd like you to try my brand. Bring her a champagne, Stanley.

GIRL: That's awfully nice of you.

HAPPY: Don't mention it. It's all company money. *He laughs.*

GIRL: That's a charming product to be selling, isn't it?

HAPPY: Oh, gets to be like everything else. Selling is selling, y'know.

GIRL: I suppose.

HAPPY: You don't happen to sell, do you?

GIRL: No, I don't sell.

HAPPY: Would you object to a compliment from a stranger? You ought to be on a magazine cover.

GIRL, *looking at him a little archly:* I have been.

Stanley comes in with a glass of champagne.

HAPPY: What'd I say before, Stanley? You see? She's a cover girl.
STANLEY: Oh, I could see, I could see.
HAPPY, *to the Girl:* What magazine?
GIRL: Oh, a lot of them. *She takes the drink.* Thank you.
HAPPY: You know what they say in France, don't you? "Champagne is the drink of the complexion" — Hya, Biff!

Biff has entered and sits with Happy.

BIFF: Hello, kid. Sorry I'm late.
HAPPY: I just got here. Uh, Miss —?
GIRL: Forsythe.
HAPPY: Miss Forsythe, this is my brother.
BIFF: Is Dad here?
HAPPY: His name is Biff. You might've heard of him. Great football player.
GIRL: Really? What team?
HAPPY: Are you familiar with football?
GIRL: No, I'm afraid I'm not.
HAPPY: Biff is quarterback with the New York Giants.
GIRL: Well, that is nice, isn't it? *She drinks.*
HAPPY: Good health.
GIRL: I'm happy to meet you.
HAPPY: That's my name. Hap. It's really Harold, but at West Point they called me Happy.
GIRL, *now really impressed:* Oh, I see. How do you do? *She turns her profile.*
BIFF: Isn't Dad coming?
HAPPY: You want her?
BIFF: Oh, I could never make that.
HAPPY: I remember the time that idea would never come into your head. Where's the old confidence, Biff?
BIFF: I just saw Oliver —
HAPPY: Wait a minute. I've got to see that old confidence again. Do you want her? She's on call.
BIFF: Oh, no. *He turns to look at the Girl.*
HAPPY: I'm telling you. Watch this. *Turning to the Girl:* Honey? *She turns to him.* Are you busy?
GIRL: Well, I am . . . but I could make a phone call.
HAPPY: Do that, will you, honey? And see if you can get a friend. We'll be here for a while. Biff is one of the greatest football players in the country.
GIRL, *standing up:* Well, I'm certainly happy to meet you.
HAPPY: Come back soon.
GIRL: I'll try.

HAPPY: Don't try, honey, try hard.

The Girl exits. Stanley follows, shaking his head in bewildered admiration.

HAPPY: Isn't that a shame now? A beautiful girl like that? That's why I can't get married. There's not a good woman in a thousand. New York is loaded with them, kid!

BIFF: Hap, look —

HAPPY: I told you she was on call!

BIFF, *strangely unnerved:* Cut it out, will ya? I want to say something to you.

HAPPY: Did you see Oliver?

BIFF: I saw him all right. Now look, I want to tell Dad a couple of things and I want you to help me.

HAPPY: What? Is he going to back you?

BIFF: Are you crazy? You're out of your goddam head, you know that?

HAPPY: Why? What happened?

BIFF, *breathlessly:* I did a terrible thing today, Hap. It's been the strangest day I ever went through. I'm all numb, I swear.

HAPPY: You mean he wouldn't see you?

BIFF: Well, I waited six hours for him, see? All day. Kept sending my name in. Even tried to date his secretary so she'd get me to him, but no soap.

HAPPY: Because you're not showin' the old confidence, Biff. He remembered you, didn't he?

BIFF, *stopping Happy with a gesture:* Finally, about five o'clock, he comes out. Didn't remember who I was or anything. I felt like such an idiot, Hap.

HAPPY: Did you tell him my Florida idea?

BIFF: He walked away. I saw him for one minute. I got so mad I could've torn the walls down! How the hell did I ever get the idea I was a salesman there? I even believed myself that I'd been a salesman for him! And then he gave me one look and — I realized what a ridiculous lie my whole life has been! We've been talking in a dream for fifteen years. I was a shipping clerk.

HAPPY: What'd you do?

BIFF, *with great tension and wonder:* Well, he left, see. And the secretary went out. I was all alone in the waiting-room. I don't know what came over me, Hap. The next thing I know I'm in his office — paneled walls, everything. I can't explain it. I — Hap, I took his fountain pen.

HAPPY: Geez, did he catch you?

BIFF: I ran out. I ran down all eleven flights. I ran and ran and ran.

HAPPY: That was an awful dumb — what'd you do that for?

BIFF, *agonized:* I don't know, I just — wanted to take something, I don't know. You gotta help me, Hap, I'm gonna tell Pop.

HAPPY: You crazy? What for?

BIFF: Hap, he's got to understand that I'm not the man somebody lends that kind of money to. He thinks I've been spiting him all these years and it's eating him up.

HAPPY: That's just it. You tell him something nice.

BIFF: I can't.

HAPPY: Say you got a lunch date with Oliver tomorrow.

BIFF: So what do I do tomorrow?

HAPPY: You leave the house tomorrow and come back at night and say Oliver is thinking it over. And he thinks it over for a couple of weeks, and gradually it fades away
and nobody's the worse.

BIFF: But it'll go on forever!

HAPPY: Dad is never so happy as when he's looking forward to something!

Willy enters.

HAPPY: Hello, scout!

WILLY: Gee, I haven't been here in years!

*Stanley has followed Willy in and sets a chair for him. Stanley starts off but Happy
stops him.*

HAPPY: Stanley!

Stanley stands by, waiting for an order.

BIFF, *going to Willy with guilt, as to an invalid:* Sit down, Pop. You want a drink?

WILLY: Sure, I don't mind.

BIFF: Let's get a load on.

WILLY: You look worried.

BIFF: N-no. *To Stanley:* Scotch all around. Make it doubles.

STANLEY: Doubles, right. *He goes.*

WILLY: You had a couple already, didn't you?

BIFF: Just a couple, yeah.

WILLY: Well, what happened, boy? *Nodding affirmatively, with a smile:* Everything go all
right?

BIFF, *take a breath, then reaches out and grasps Willy's hand:* Pal . . . *He is smiling
bravely, and Willy is smiling too.* I had an experience today.

HAPPY: Terrific, Pop.

WILLY: That so? What happened?

BIFF, *high, slightly alcoholic, above the earth:* I'm going to tell you everything from first
to last. It's been a strange day. *Silence. He looks around, composes himself as best he
can, but his breath keeps breaking the rhythm of his voice.* I had to wait quite a while
for him, and —

WILLY: Oliver?

BIFF: Yeah, Oliver. All day, as a matter of cold fact. And a lot of — instances — facts, Pop,
facts about my life came back to me. Who was it, Pop? Who ever said I was a salesman
with Oliver?

WILLY: Well, you were.

BIFF: No, Dad, I was a shipping clerk.

WILLY: But you were practically —

BIFF, *with determination:* Dad, I don't know who said it first, but I was never a salesman for Bill Oliver.

WILLY: What're you talking about?

BIFF: Let's hold on to the facts tonight, Pop. We're not going to get anywhere bullin' around. I was a shipping clerk.

WILLY, *angrily:* All right, now listen to me —

BIFF: Why don't you let me finish?

WILLY: I'm not interested in stories about the past or any crap of that kind because the woods are burning, boys, you understand? There's a big blaze going on all around. I was fired today.

BIFF, *shocked:* How could you be?

WILLY: I was fired, and I'm looking for a little good news to tell your mother, because the woman has waited and the woman has suffered. The gist of it is that I haven't got a story left in my head, Biff. So don't give me a lecture about facts and aspects. I am not interested. Now what've you got to say to me?

Stanley enters with three drinks. They wait until he leaves.

WILLY: Did you see Oliver?

BIFF: Jesus, Dad!

WILLY: You mean you didn't go up there?

HAPPY: Sure he went up there.

BIFF: I did. I — saw him. How could they fire you?

WILLY, *on the edge of his chair:* What kind of a welcome did he give you?

BIFF: He won't even let you work on commission?

WILLY: I'm out! *Driving:* So tell me, he gave you a warm welcome?

HAPPY: Sure, Pop, sure!

BIFF, *driven:* Well, it was kind of —

WILLY: I was wondering if he'd remember you. *To Happy:* Imagine, man doesn't see him for ten, twelve years and gives him that kind of a welcome!

HAPPY: Damn right!

BIFF, *trying to return to the offensive:* Pop, look —

WILLY: You know why he remembered you, don't you? Because you impressed him in those days.

BIFF: Let's talk quietly and get this down to the facts, huh?

WILLY, *as though Biff had been interrupting:* Well, what happened? It's great news, Biff. Did he take you into his office or'd you talk in the waiting-room?

BIFF: Well, he came in, see, and —

WILLY, *with a big smile:* What'd he say? Betcha he threw his arm around you.

BIFF: Well, he kinda —

WILLY: He's a fine man. *To Happy:* Very hard man to see, y'know.

HAPPY, *agreeing:* Oh, I know.

WILLY, *to Biff:* Is that where you had the drinks?

BIFF: Yeah, he gave me a couple of — no, no!

HAPPY, *cutting in:* He told him my Florida idea.

WILLY: Don't interrupt. *To Biff:* How'd he react to the Florida idea?

BIFF: Dad, will you give me a minute to explain?

WILLY: I've been waiting for you to explain since I sat down here! What happened? He took you into his office and what?

BIFF: Well — I talked. And — and he listened, see.

WILLY: Famous for the way he listens, y'know. What was his answer?

BIFF: His answer was — *He breaks off, suddenly angry.* Dad, you're not letting me tell you what I want to tell you!

WILLY, *accusing, angered:* You didn't see him, did you?

BIFF: I did see him!

WILLY: What'd you insult him or something? You insulted him, didn't you?

BIFF: Listen, will you let me out of it, will you just let me out of it!

HAPPY: What the hell!

WILLY: Tell me what happened!

BIFF, *to Happy:* I can't talk to him!

A single trumpet note jars the ear. The light of green leaves stains the house, which holds the air of night and a dream. Young Bernard enters and knocks on the door of the house.

YOUNG BERNARD, *frantically:* Mrs. Loman, Mrs. Loman!

HAPPY: Tell him what happened!

BIFF, *to Happy:* Shut up and leave me alone!

WILLY: No, no! You had to go and flunk math!

BIFF: What math? What're you talking about?

YOUNG BERNARD: Mrs. Loman, Mrs. Loman!

Linda appears in the house, as of old.

WILLY, *wildly:* Math, math, math!

BIFF: Take it easy, Pop!

YOUNG BERNARD: Mrs. Loman!

WILLY, *furiously:* If you hadn't flunked you'd've been set by now!

BIFF: Now, look, I'm gonna tell you what happened, and you're going to listen to me.

YOUNG BERNARD: Mrs. Loman!

BIFF: I waited six hours —

HAPPY: What the hell are you saying?

BIFF: I kept sending in my name but he wouldn't see me. So finally he . . . *He continues unheard as light fades low on the restaurant.*

YOUNG BERNARD: Biff flunked math!

LINDA: No!

YOUNG BERNARD: Birnbaum flunked him! They won't graduate him!

LINDA: But they have to. He's gotta go to the university. Where is he? Biff! Biff!

YOUNG BERNARD: No, he left. He went to Grand Central.

LINDA: Grand — You mean he went to Boston!

YOUNG BERNARD: Is Uncle Willy in Boston?

LINDA: Oh, maybe Willy can talk to the teacher. Oh, the poor, poor boy!

Light on house area snaps out.

BIFF, *at the table, now audible, holding up a gold fountain pen:* . . . so I'm washed up
   with Oliver, you understand? Are you listening to me?

WILLY, *at a loss:* Yeah, sure. If you hadn't flunked —

BIFF: Flunked what? What're you talking about?

WILLY: Don't blame everything on me! I didn't flunk math — you did! What pen?

HAPPY: That was awful dumb, Biff, a pen like that is worth —

WILLY, *seeing the pen for the first time:* You took Oliver's pen?

BIFF, *weakening:* Dad, I just explained it to you.

WILLY: You stole Bill Oliver's fountain pen!

BIFF: I didn't exactly steal it! That's just what I've been explaining to you!

HAPPY: He had it in his hand and just then Oliver walked in, so he got nervous and
   stuck it in his pocket!

WILLY: My God, Biff!

BIFF: I never intended to do it, Dad!

OPERATOR'S VOICE: Standish Arms, good evening!

WILLY, *shouting:* I'm not in my room!

BIFF, *frightened:* Dad, what's the matter? *He and Happy stand up.*

OPERATOR: Ringing Mr. Loman for you!

WILLY: I'm not there, stop it!

BIFF, *horrified, gets down on one knee before Willy:* Dad, I'll make good, I'll make good.
   Willy tries to get to his feet. Biff holds him down. Sit down now.

WILLY: No, you're no good, you're no good for anything.

BIFF: I am, Dad, I'll find something else, you understand? Now don't worry about anything. *He holds up Willy's face:* Talk to me, Dad.

OPERATOR: Mr. Loman does not answer. Shall I page him?

WILLY, *attempting to stand, as though to rush and silence the Operator:* No, no, no!

HAPPY: He'll strike something, Pop.

WILLY: No, no . . .

BIFF, *desperately, standing over Willy:* Pop, listen! Listen to me! I'm telling you something good. Oliver talked to his partner about the Florida idea. You listening? He — he
   talked to his partner, and he came to me . . . I'm going to be all right, you hear? Dad,
   listen to me, he said it was just a question of the amount!

WILLY: Then you . . . got it?

HAPPY: He's gonna be terrific, Pop!

WILLY, *trying to stand:* Then you got it, haven't you? You got it! You got it!

BIFF, *agonized, holds Willy down:* No, no. Look, Pop. I'm supposed to have lunch with them tomorrow. I'm just telling you this so you'll know that I can still make an impression, Pop. And I'll make good somewhere, but I can't go tomorrow, see?

WILLY: Why not? You simply —

BIFF: But the pen, Pop!

WILLY: You give it to him and tell him it was an oversight!

HAPPY: Sure, have lunch tomorrow!

BIFF: I can't say that —

WILLY: You were doing a crossword puzzle and accidentally used his pen!

BIFF: Listen, kid, I took those balls years ago, now I walk in with his fountain pen? That clinches it, don't you see? I can't face him like that! I'll try elsewhere.

PAGE'S VOICE: Paging Mr. Loman!

WILLY: Don't you want to be anything?

BIFF: Pop, how can I go back?

WILLY: You don't want to be anything, is that what's behind it?

BIFF, *now angry at Willy for not crediting his sympathy:* Don't take it that way! You think it was easy walking into that office after what I'd done to him? A team of horses couldn't have dragged me back to Bill Oliver!

WILLY: Then why'd you go?

BIFF: Why did I go? Why did I go! Look at you! Look at what's become of you!

Off left, The Woman laughs.

WILLY: Biff, you're going to go to that lunch tomorrow, or —

BIFF: I can't go. I've got no appointment!

HAPPY: Biff, for . . . !

WILLY: Are you spiting me?

BIFF: Don't take it that way! Goddammit!

WILLY, *strikes Biff and falters away from the table:* You rotten little louse! Are you spiting me?

THE WOMAN: Someone's at the door, Willy!

BIFF: I'm no good, can't you see what I am?

HAPPY, *separating them:* Hey, you're in a restaurant! Now cut it out, both of you! *The girls enter.* Hello, girls, sit down.

The Woman laughs, off left.

MISS FORSYTHE: I guess we might as well. This is Letta.

THE WOMAN: Willy, are you going to wake up?

BIFF, *ignoring Willy:* How're ya, miss, sit down. What do you drink?

MISS FORSYTHE: Letta might not be able to stay long.

LETTA: I gotta get up very early tomorrow. I got jury duty. I'm so excited! Were you fellows ever on a jury?

BIFF: No, but I been in front of them! *The girls laugh.* This is my father.

LETTA: Isn't he cute? Sit down with us, Pop.

HAPPY: Sit him down, Biff!

BIFF, *going to him:* Come on, slugger, drink us under the table. To hell with it! Come on, sit down, pal.

On Biff's last insistence, Willy is about to sit.

THE WOMAN, *now urgently:* Willy, are you going to answer the door!

The Woman's call pulls Willy back. He starts right, befuddled.

BIFF: Hey, where are you going?

WILLY: Open the door.

BIFF: The door?

WILLY: The washroom . . . the door . . . where's the door?

BIFF, *leading Willy to the left:* Just go straight down.

Willy moves left.

THE WOMAN: Willy, Willy, are you going to get up, get up, get up, get up?

Willy exits left.

LETTA: I think it's sweet you bring your daddy along.

MISS FORSYTHE: Oh, he isn't really your father!

BIFF, *at left, turning to her resentfully:* Miss Forsythe, you've just seen a prince walk by. A fine, troubled prince. A hardworking, unappreciated prince. A pal, you understand? A good companion. Always for his boys.

LETTA: That's so sweet.

HAPPY: Well, girls, what's the program? We're wasting time. Come on, Biff. Gather round. Where would you like to go?

BIFF: Why don't you do something for him?

HAPPY: Me!

BIFF: Don't you give a damn for him, Hap?

HAPPY: What're you talking about? I'm the one who —

BIFF: I sense it, you don't give a good goddam about him. *He takes the rolled-up hose from his pocket and puts it on the table in front of Happy.* Look what I found in the cellar, for Christ's sake. How can you bear to let it go on?

HAPPY: Me? Who goes away? Who runs off and —

BIFF: Yeah, but he doesn't mean anything to you. You could help him — I can't! Don't you understand what I'm talking about? He's going to kill himself, don't you know that?

HAPPY: Don't I know it! Me!

BIFF: Hap, help him! Jesus . . . help him . . . Help me, help me, I can't bear to look at his face! *Ready to weep, he hurries out, up right.*

HAPPY, *starting after him:* Where are you going?

MISS FORSYTHE: What's he so mad about?

HAPPY: Come on, girls, we'll catch up with him.

MISS FORSYTHE, *as Happy pushes her out:* Say, I don't like that temper of his!

HAPPY: He's just a little overstrung, he'll be all right!

WILLY, *off left, as The Woman laughs:* Don't answer! Don't answer!

LETTA: Don't you want to tell your father —

HAPPY: No, that's not my father. He's just a guy. Come on, we'll catch Biff, and, honey, we're going to paint this town! Stanley, where's the check! Hey, Stanley!

They exit. Stanley looks toward left.

STANLEY, *calling to Happy indignantly:* Mr. Loman! Mr. Loman!

Stanley picks up a chair and follows them off. Knocking is heard off left. The Woman enters, laughing. Willy follows her. She is in a black slip; he is buttoning his shirt. Raw, sensuous music accompanies their speech.

WILLY: Will you stop laughing? Will you stop?

THE WOMAN: Aren't you going to answer the door? He'll wake the whole hotel.

WILLY: I'm not expecting anybody.

THE WOMAN: Whyn't you have another drink, honey, and stop being so damn self-centered?

WILLY: I'm so lonely.

THE WOMAN: You know you ruined me, Willy? From now on, whenever you come to the office, I'll see that you go right through to the buyers. No waiting at my desk any more, Willy. You ruined me.

WILLY: That's nice of you to say that.

THE WOMAN: Gee, you are self-centered! Why so sad? You are the saddest, self-centeredest soul I ever did see-saw. *She laughs. He kisses her.* Come on inside, drummer boy. It's silly to be dressing in the middle of the night. *As knocking is heard:* Aren't you going to answer the door?

WILLY: They're knocking on the wrong door.

THE WOMAN: But I felt the knocking. And he heard us talking in here. Maybe the hotel's on fire!

WILLY, *his terror rising:* It's a mistake.

THE WOMAN: Then tell him to go away!

WILLY: There's nobody there.

THE WOMAN: It's getting on my nerves, Willy. There's somebody standing out there and it's getting on my nerves!

WILLY, *pushing her away from him:* All right, stay in the bathroom here, and don't come out. I think there's a law in Massachusetts about it, so don't come out. It may be that new room clerk. He looked very mean. So don't come out. It's a mistake, there's no fire.

The knocking is heard again. He takes a few steps away from her, and she vanishes into the wing. The light follows him, and now he is facing Young Biff, who carries a suitcase. Biff steps toward him. The music is gone.

BIFF: Why didn't you answer?

WILLY: Biff! What are you doing in Boston?

BIFF: Why didn't you answer? I've been knocking for five minutes, I called you on the phone —

WILLY: I just heard you. I was in the bathroom and had the door shut. Did anything happen home?

BIFF: Dad — I let you down.

WILLY: What do you mean?

BIFF: Dad . . .

WILLY: Biffo, what's this about? *Putting his arm around Biff:* Come on, let's go downstairs and get you a malted.

BIFF: Dad, I flunked math.

WILLY: Not for the term?

BIFF: The term. I haven't got enough credits to graduate.

WILLY: You mean to say Bernard wouldn't give you the answers?

BIFF: He did, he tried, but I only got a sixty-one.

WILLY: And they wouldn't give you four points?

BIFF: Birnbaum refused absolutely. I begged him, Pop, but he won't give me those points. You gotta talk to him before they close the school. Because if he saw the kind of man you are, and you just talked to him in your way, I'm sure he'd come through for me. The class came right before practice, see, and I didn't go enough. Would you talk to him? He'd like you, Pop. You know the way you could talk.

WILLY: You're on. We'll drive right back.

BIFF: Oh, Dad, good work! I'm sure he'll change it for you!

WILLY: Go downstairs and tell the clerk I'm checkin' out. Go right down.

BIFF: Yes, sir! See, the reason he hates me, Pop — one day he was late for class so I got up at the blackboard and imitated him. I crossed my eyes and talked with a lithp.

WILLY, *laughing:* You did? The kids like it?

BIFF: They nearly died laughing!

WILLY: Yeah? What'd you do?

BIFF: The thquare root of thixthy twee is . . . *Willy bursts out laughing; Biff joins him.* And in the middle of it he walked in!

Willy laughs and The Woman joins in offstage.

WILLY, *without hesitation:* Hurry downstairs and —
BIFF: Somebody in there?
WILLY: No, that was next door.

The Woman laughs offstage.

BIFF: Somebody got in your bathroom!
WILLY: No, it's the next room, there's a party —
THE WOMAN, *enters, laughing. She lisps this:* Can I come in? There's something in the bathtub, Willy, and it's moving!

Willy looks at Biff, who is staring open-mouthed and horrified at The Woman.

WILLY: Ah — you better go back to your room. They must be finished painting by now. They're painting her room so I let her take a shower here. Go back, go back . . . *He pushes her.*
THE WOMAN, *resisting:* But I've got to get dressed, Willy, I can't —
WILLY: Get out of here! Go back, go back . . . *Suddenly striving for the ordinary:* This is Miss Francis, Biff, she's a buyer. They're painting her room. Go back, Miss Francis, go back . . .
THE WOMAN: But my clothes, I can't go out naked in the hall!
WILLY, *pushing her offstage:* Get outa here! Go back, go back!

Biff slowly sits down on his suitcase as the argument continues offstage.

THE WOMAN: Where's my stockings? You promised me stockings, Willy!
WILLY: I have no stockings here!
THE WOMAN: You had two boxes of size nine sheers for me, and I want them!
WILLY: Here, for God's sake, will you get outa here!
THE WOMAN, *enters holding a box of stockings:* I just hope there's nobody in the hall. That's all I hope. *To Biff:* Are you football or baseball?
BIFF: Football.
THE WOMAN, *angry, humiliated:* That's me too. G'night. *She snatches her clothes from Willy, and walks out.*
WILLY, *after a pause:* Well, better get going. I want to get to the school first thing in the morning. Get my suits out of the closet. I'll get my valise. *Biff doesn't move.* What's the matter? *Biff remains motionless, tears falling.* She's a buyer. Buys for J. H. Sim-mons. She lives down the hall — they're painting. You don't imagine — *He breaks off. After a pause:* Now listen, pal, she's just a buyer. She sees merchandise in her room and they have to keep it looking just so . . . *Pause. Assuming command:* All right, get my suits. *Biff doesn't move.* Now stop crying and do as I say. I gave you an order. Biff, I gave you an order! Is that what you do when I give you an order? How dare you cry!

Putting his arm around Biff: Now look, Biff, when you grow up you'll understand about these things. You mustn't — you mustn't overemphasize a thing like this. I'll see Birnbaum first thing in the morning.

BIFF: Never mind.

WILLY, *getting down beside Biff:* Never mind! He's going to give you those points. I'll see to it.

BIFF: He wouldn't listen to you.

WILLY: He certainly will listen to me. You need those points for the U. of Virginia.

BIFF: I'm not going there.

WILLY: Heh? If I can't get him to change that mark you'll make it up in summer school. You've got all summer to —

BIFF, *his weeping breaking from him:* Dad . . .

WILLY, *infected by it:* Oh, my boy . . .

BIFF: Dad . . .

WILLY: She's nothing to me, Biff. I was lonely, I was terribly lonely.

BIFF: You — you gave her Mama's stockings! *His tears break through and he rises to go.*

WILLY, *grabbing for Biff:* I gave you an order!

BIFF: Don't touch me, you — liar!

WILLY: Apologize for that!

BIFF: You fake! You phony little fake! You fake! *Overcome, he turns quickly and weeping fully goes out with his suitcase. Willy is left on the floor on his knees.*

WILLY: I gave you an order! Biff, come back here or I'll beat you! Come back here! I'll whip you!

Stanley comes quickly in from the right and stands in front of Willy.

WILLY, *shouts at Stanley:* I gave you an order . . .

STANLEY: Hey, let's pick it up, pick it up, Mr. Loman. *He helps Willy to his feet.* Your boys left with the chippies. They said they'll see you home.

A second waiter watches some distance away.

WILLY: But we were supposed to have dinner together.

Music is heard, Willy's theme.

STANLEY: Can you make it?

WILLY: I'll — sure, I can make it. *Suddenly concerned about his clothes:* Do I — I look all right?

STANLEY: Sure, you look all right. *He flicks a speck off Willy's lapel.*

WILLY: Here — here's a dollar.

STANLEY: Oh, your son paid me. It's all right.

WILLY, *putting it in Stanley's hand:* No, take it. You're a good boy.

STANLEY: Oh, no, you don't have to . . .

WILLY: Here — here's some more, I don't need it any more. *After a slight pause:* Tell me —
is there a seed store in the neighborhood?
STANLEY: Seeds? You mean like to plant?

As Willy turns, Stanley slips the money back into his jacket pocket.

WILLY: Yes. Carrots, peas . . .
STANLEY: Well, there's hardware stores on Sixth Avenue, but it may be too late now.
WILLY, *anxiously:* Oh, I'd better hurry. I've got to get some seeds. *He starts off to the
right.* I've got to get some seeds, right away. Nothing's planted. I don't have a thing in
the ground.

*Willy hurries out as the light goes down. Stanley moves over to the right after him,
watches him off. The other waiter has been staring at Willy.*

STANLEY, *to the waiter:* Well, whatta you looking at?

*The waiter picks up the chairs and moves off right. Stanley takes the table and follows
him. The light fades on this area. There is a long pause, the sound of the flute coming
over. The light gradually rises on the kitchen, which is empty. Happy appears at the door
of the house, followed by Biff. Happy is carrying a large bunch of long-stemmed roses.
He enters the kitchen, looks around for Linda. Not seeing her, he turns to Biff, who is just
outside the house door, and makes a gesture with his hands, indicating "Not here, I
guess." He looks into the living-room and freezes. Inside, Linda, unseen, is seated,
Willy's coat on her lap. She rises ominously and quietly and moves toward Happy, who
backs up into the kitchen, afraid.*

HAPPY: Hey, what're you doing up? *Linda says nothing but moves toward him implaca-
bly.* Where's Pop? *He keeps backing to the right, and now Linda is in full view in the
doorway to the living-room.* Is he sleeping?
LINDA: Where were you?
HAPPY, *trying to laugh it off:* We met two girls, Mom, very fine types. Here, we brought
you some flowers. *Offering them to her:* Put them in your room, Ma.

*She knocks them to the floor at Biff's feet. He has now come inside and closed the door
behind him. She stares at Biff, silent.*

HAPPY: Now what'd you do that for? Mom, I want you to have some flowers —
LINDA, *cutting Happy off, violently to Biff:* Don't you care whether he lives or dies?
HAPPY, *going to the stairs:* Come upstairs, Biff.
BIFF, *with a flare of disgust, to Happy:* Go away from me! *To Linda:* What do you mean,
lives or dies? Nobody's dying around here, pal.
LINDA: Get out of my sight! Get out of here!

BIFF: I wanna see the boss.

LINDA: You're not going near him!

BIFF: Where is he? *He moves into the living-room and Linda follows.*

LINDA, *shouting after Biff:* You invite him for dinner. He looks forward to it all day – *Biff appears in his parents' bedroom, looks around, and exits* – and then you desert him there. There's no stranger you'd do that to!

HAPPY: Why? He had a swell time with us. Listen, when I – *Linda comes back into the kitchen* – desert him I hope I don't outlive the day!

LINDA: Get out of here!

HAPPY: Now look, Mom . . .

LINDA: Did you have to go to women tonight? You and your lousy rotten whores!

Biff re-enters the kitchen.

HAPPY: Mom, all we did was follow Biff around trying to cheer him up! *To Biff:* Boy, what a night you gave me!

LINDA: Get out of here, both of you, and don't come back! I don't want you tormenting him any more. Go on now, get your things together! *To Biff:* You can sleep in his apartment. *She starts to pick up the flowers and stops herself.* Pick up this stuff, I'm not your maid any more. Pick it up, you bum, you!

Happy turns his back to her in refusal. Biff slowly moves over and gets down on his knees, picking up the flowers.

LINDA: You're a pair of animals! Not one, not another living soul would have had the cruelty to walk out on that man in a restaurant!

BIFF, *not looking at her:* Is that what he said?

LINDA: He didn't have to say anything. He was so humiliated he nearly limped when he came in.

HAPPY: But, Mom, he had a great time with us –

BIFF, *cutting him off violently:* Shut up!

Without another word, Happy goes upstairs.

LINDA: You! You didn't even go in to see if he was all right!

BIFF, *still on the floor in front of Linda, the flowers in his hand; with self-loathing:* No. Didn't. Didn't do a damned thing. How do you like that, heh? Left him babbling in a toilet.

LINDA: You louse. You . . .

BIFF: Now you hit it on the nose! *He gets up, throws the flowers in the wastebasket.* The scum of the earth, and you're looking at him!

LINDA: Get out of here!

BIFF: I gotta talk to the boss, Mom. Where is he?

LINDA: You're not going near him. Get out of this house!

BIFF, *with absolute assurance, determination:* No. We're gonna have an abrupt conversation, him and me.

LINDA: You're not talking to him!

Hammering is heard from outside the house, off right. Biff turns toward the noise.

LINDA, *suddenly pleading:* Will you please leave him alone?

BIFF: What's he doing out there?

LINDA: He's planting the garden!

BIFF, *quietly:* Now? Oh, my God!

Biff moves outside, Linda following. The light dies down on them and comes up on the center of the apron as Willy walks into it. He is carrying a flashlight, a hoe, and a handful of seed packets. He raps the top of the hoe sharply to fix it firmly, and then moves to the left, measuring off the distance with his foot. He holds the flashlight to look at the seed packets, reading off the instructions. He is in the blue of night.

WILLY: Carrots . . . quarter-inch apart. Rows . . . one-foot rows. *He measures it off.* One foot. *He puts down a package and measures off.* Beets. *He puts down another package and measures again.* Lettuce. *He reads the package, puts it down.* One foot — *He breaks off as Ben appears at the right and moves slowly down to him.* What a proposition, ts, ts. Terrific, terrific. 'Cause she's suffered, Ben, the woman has suffered. You understand me? A man can't go out the way he came in, Ben, a man has got to add up to something. You can't, you can't — *Ben moves toward him as though to interrupt.* You gotta consider, now. Don't answer so quick. Remember, it's a guaranteed twenty-thousand-dollar proposition. Now look, Ben, I want you to go through the ins and outs of this thing with me. I've got nobody to talk to, Ben, and the woman has suffered, you hear me?

BEN, *standing still, considering:* What's the proposition?

WILLY: It's twenty thousand dollars on the barrelhead. Guaranteed, gilt-edged, you understand?

BEN: You don't want to make a fool of yourself. They might not honor the policy.

WILLY: How can they dare refuse? Didn't I work like a coolie to meet every premium on the nose? And now they don't pay off? Impossible!

BEN: It's called a cowardly thing, William.

WILLY: Why? Does it take more guts to stand here the rest of my life ringing up a zero?

BEN, *yielding:* That's a point, William. *He moves, thinking, turns.* And twenty thousand — that *is* something one can feel with the hand, it is there.

WILLY, *now assured, with rising power:* Oh, Ben, that's the whole beauty of it! I see it like a diamond, shining in the dark, hard and rough, that I can pick up and touch in my hand. Not like — like an appointment! This would not be another damned-fool appointment, Ben, and it changes all the aspects. Because he thinks I'm nothing, see, and so he spites me. But the funeral — *Straightening up:* Ben, that funeral will be massive! They'll come from Maine, Massachusetts, Vermont, New Hampshire! All the old-timers with the strange license plates — that boy will be thunder-struck, Ben, because he never realized — I am known! Rhode Island, New York, New Jersey — I am known, Ben, and he'll see it with his eyes once and for all. He'll see what I am, Ben! He's in for a shock, that boy!

BEN, *coming down to the edge of the garden:* He'll call you a coward.

WILLY, *suddenly fearful:* No, that would be terrible.

BEN: Yes. And a damned fool.

WILLY: No, no, he mustn't, I won't have that! *He is broken and desperate.*

BEN: He'll hate you, William.

The gay music of the Boys is heard.

WILLY: Oh, Ben, how do we get back to all the great times? Used to be so full of light, and comradeship, the sleigh-riding in winter, and the ruddiness on his cheeks. And always some kind of good news coming up, always something nice coming up ahead. And never even let me carry the valises in the house, and simonizing, simonizing that little red car! Why, why can't I give him something and not have him hate me?

BEN: Let me think about it. *He glances at his watch.* I still have a little time. Remarkable proposition, but you've got to be sure you're not making a fool of yourself.

Ben drifts off upstage and goes out of sight. Biff comes down from the left.

WILLY, *suddenly conscious of Biff, turns and looks up at him, then begins picking up the packages of seeds in confusion:* Where the hell is that seed? *Indignantly:* You can't see nothing out here! They boxed in the whole goddam neighborhood!

BIFF: There are people all around here. Don't you realize that?

WILLY: I'm busy. Don't bother me.

BIFF, *taking the hoe from Willy:* I'm saying good-by to you, Pop. *Willy looks at him, silent, unable to move.* I'm not coming back any more.

WILLY: You're not going to see Oliver tomorrow?

BIFF: I've got no appointment, Dad.

WILLY: He put his arm around you, and you've got no appointment?

BIFF: Pop, get this now, will you? Every time I've left it's been a fight that sent me out of here. Today I realized something about myself and I tried to explain it to you and I — I think I'm just not smart enough to make any sense out of it for you. To hell with whose fault it is or anything like that. *He takes Willy's arm.* Let's just wrap it up, heh? Come on in, we'll tell Mom. *He gently tries to pull Willy to left.*

WILLY, *frozen, immobile, with guilt in his voice:* No, I don't want to see her.

BIFF: Come on! *He pulls again, and Willy tries to pull away.*

WILLY, *highly nervous:* No, no, I don't want to see her.

BIFF, *tries to look into Willy's face, as if to find the answer there:* Why don't you want to see her?

WILLY, *more harshly now:* Don't bother me, will you?

BIFF: What do you mean, you don't want to see her? You don't want them calling you yellow, do you? This isn't your fault; it's me, I'm a bum. Now come inside! *Willy strains to get away.* Did you hear what I said to you?

Willy pulls away and quickly goes by himself into the house. Biff follows.

LINDA, *to Willy:* Did you plant, dear?

BIFF, *at the door, to Linda:* All right, we had it out. I'm going and I'm not writing any more.

LINDA, *going to Willy in the kitchen:* I think that's the best way, dear. 'Cause there's no use drawing it out, you'll just never get along.

Willy doesn't respond.

BIFF: People ask where I am and what I'm doing, you don't know, and you don't care. That way it'll be off your mind and you can start brightening up again. All right? That clears it, doesn't it? *Willy is silent, and Biff goes to him.* You gonna wish me luck, scout? *He extends his hand.* What do you say?

LINDA: Shake his hand, Willy.

WILLY, *turning to her, seething with hurt:* There's no necessity to mention the pen at all, y'know.

BIFF, *gently:* I've got no appointment, Dad.

WILLY, *erupting fiercely:* He put his arm around . . . ?

BIFF: Dad, you're never going to see what I am, so what's the use of arguing? If I strike oil I'll send you a check. Meantime forget I'm alive.

WILLY, *to Linda:* Spite, see?

BIFF: Shake hands, Dad.

WILLY: Not my hand.

BIFF: I was hoping not to go this way.

WILLY: Well, this is the way you're going. Good-by.

Biff looks at him a moment, then turns sharply and goes to the stairs.

WILLY, *stops him with:* May you rot in hell if you leave this house!

BIFF, *turning:* Exactly what is it that you want from me?

WILLY: I want you to know, on the train, in the mountains, in the valleys, wherever you go, that you cut down your life for spite!

BIFF: No, no.

WILLY: Spite, spite, is the word of your undoing! And when you're down and out, remember what did it. When you're rotting somewhere beside the railroad tracks, remember, and don't you dare blame it on me!

BIFF: I'm not blaming it on you!

WILLY: I won't take the rap for this, you hear?

Happy comes down the stairs and stands on the bottom step, watching.

BIFF: That's just what I'm telling you!

WILLY, *sinking into a chair at the table, with full accusation:* You're trying to put a knife in me — don't think I don't know what you're doing!

BIFF: All right, phony! Then let's lay it on the line. *He whips the rubber tube out of his pocket and puts it on the table.*

HAPPY: You crazy —

LINDA: Biff! *She moves to grab the hose, but Biff holds it down with his hand.*

BIFF: Leave it there! Don't move it!

WILLY, *not looking at it:* What is that?

BIFF: You know goddam well what that is.

WILLY, *caged, wanting to escape:* I never saw that.

BIFF: You saw it. The mice didn't bring it into the cellar! What is this supposed to do, make a hero out of you? This supposed to make me sorry for you?

WILLY: Never heard of it.

BIFF: There'll be no pity for you, you hear it? No pity!

WILLY, *to Linda:* You hear the spite!

BIFF: No, you're going to hear the truth — what you are and what I am!

LINDA: Stop it!

WILLY: Spite!

HAPPY, *coming down toward Biff:* You cut it now!

BIFF, *to Happy:* The man don't know who we are! The man is gonna know! *To Willy:* We never told the truth for ten minutes in this house!

HAPPY: We always told the truth!

BIFF, *turning on him:* You big blow, are you the assistant buyer? You're one of the two assistants to the assistant, aren't you?

HAPPY: Well, I'm practically —

BIFF: You're practically full of it! We all are! And I'm through with it. *To Willy:* Now hear this, Willy, this is me.

WILLY: I know you!

BIFF: You know why I had no address for three months? I stole a suit in Kansas City and I was in jail. *To Linda, who is sobbing:* Stop crying. I'm through with it.

Linda turns away from them, her hands covering her face.

WILLY: I suppose that's my fault!

BIFF: I stole myself out of every good job since high school!

WILLY: And whose fault is that?

BIFF: And I never got anywhere because you blew me so full of hot air I could never stand taking orders from anybody! That's whose fault it is!

WILLY: I hear that!

LINDA: Don't, Biff!

BIFF: It's goddam time you heard that! I had to be boss big shot in two weeks, and I'm through with it!

WILLY: Then hang yourself! For spite, hang yourself!

BIFF: No! Nobody's hanging himself, Willy! I ran down eleven flights with a pen in my hand today. And suddenly I stopped, you hear me? And in the middle of that office building, do you hear this? I stopped in the middle of that building and I saw — the sky. I saw the things that I love in this world. The work and the food and time to sit and smoke. And I looked at the pen and said to myself, what the hell am I grabbing this for? Why am I trying to become what I don't want to be? What am I doing in an office, making a contemptuous, begging fool of myself, when all I want is out there, waiting for me the minute I say I know who I am! Why can't I say that, Willy? *He tries to make Willy face him, but Willy pulls away and moves to the left.*

WILLY, *with hatred, threateningly:* The door of your life is wide open!

BIFF: Pop! I'm a dime a dozen, and so are you!

WILLY, *turning on him now in an uncontrolled outburst:* I am not a dime a dozen! I am Willy Loman, and you are Biff Loman!

Biff starts for Willy, but is blocked by Happy. In his fury, Biff seems on the verge of attacking his father.

BIFF: I am not a leader of men, Willy, and neither are you. You were never anything but a hard-working drummer who landed in the ash can like all the rest of them! I'm one dollar an hour, Willy! I tried seven states and couldn't raise it. A buck an hour! Do you gather my meaning? I'm not bringing home any prizes any more, and you're going to stop waiting for me to bring them home!

WILLY, *directly to Biff:* You vengeful, spiteful mut!

Biff breaks from Happy. Willy, in fright, starts up the stairs. Biff grabs him.

BIFF, *at the peak of his fury:* Pop, I'm nothing! I'm nothing, Pop. Can't you understand that? There's no spite in it any more. I'm just what I am, that's all.

Biff's fury has spent itself, and he breaks down, sobbing, holding on to Willy, who dumbly fumbles for Biff's face.

WILLY, *astonished:* What're you doing? What're you doing? *To Linda:* Why is he crying?

BIFF, *crying, broken:* Will you let me go, for Christ's sake? Will you take that phony dream and burn it before something happens? *Struggling to contain himself, he pulls away and moves to the stairs.* I'll go in the morning. Put him — put him to bed. *Exhausted, Biff moves up the stairs to his room.*

WILLY, *after a long pause, astonished, elevated:* Isn't that — isn't that remarkable? Biff — he likes me!

LINDA: He loves you, Willy!

HAPPY, *deeply moved:* Always did, Pop.

WILLY: Oh, Biff! *Staring wildly:* He cried! Cried to me. *He is choking with his love, and now cries out his promise:* That boy — that boy is going to be magnificent!

Ben appears in the light just outside the kitchen.

BEN: Yes, outstanding, with twenty thousand behind him.

LINDA, *sensing the racing of his mind, fearfully, carefully:* Now come to bed, Willy, It's all settled now.

WILLY, *finding it difficult not to rush out of the house:* Yes, we'll sleep. Come on. Go to sleep, Hap.

BEN: And it does take a great kind of a man to crack the jungle.

In accents of dread, Ben's idyllic music starts up.

HAPPY, *his arm around Linda:* I'm getting married, Pop, don't forget it. I'm changing everything. I'm gonna run that department before the year is up. You'll see, Mom. *He kisses her.*

BEN: The jungle is dark but full of diamonds, Willy.

Willy turns, moves, listening to Ben.

LINDA: Be good. You're both good boys, just act that way, that's all.

HAPPY: 'Night, Pop. *He goes upstairs.*

LINDA, *to Willy:* Come, dear.

BEN, *with greater force:* One must go in to fetch a diamond out.

WILLY, *to Linda, as he moves slowly along the edge of the kitchen, toward the door:* I just want to get settled down, Linda. Let me sit alone for a little.

LINDA, *almost uttering her fear:* I want you upstairs.

WILLY, *taking her in his arms:* In a few minutes, Linda. I couldn't sleep right now. Go on, you look awful tired. *He kisses her.*

BEN: Not like an appointment at all. A diamond is rough and hard to the touch.

WILLY: Go on now. I'll be right up.

LINDA: I think this is the only way, Willy.

WILLY: Sure, it's the best thing.

BEN: Best thing!

WILLY: The only way. Everything is gonna be — go on, kid, get to bed. You look so tired.

LINDA: Come right up.

WILLY: Two minutes.

Linda goes into the living-room, then reappears in her bedroom. Willy moves just outside the kitchen door.

WILLY: Loves me, *Wonderingly:* Always loved me. Isn't that a remarkable thing? Ben, he'll worship me for it!

BEN, *with promise:* It's dark there, but full of diamonds.

WILLY: Can you imagine that magnificence with twenty thousand dollars in his pocket?

LINDA, *calling from her room:* Willy! Come up!

WILLY, *calling into the kitchen:* Yes! Yes. Coming! It's very smart, you realize that, don't you, sweetheart? Even Ben sees it. I gotta go, baby. 'By! 'By! *Going over to Ben, almost dancing:* Imagine? When the mail comes he'll be ahead of Bernard again!

BEN: A perfect proposition all around.

WILLY: Did you see how he cried to me? Oh, if I could kiss him, Ben!

BEN: Time, William, time!

WILLY: Oh, Ben, I always knew one way or another we were gonna make it, Biff and I!

BEN, *looking at his watch:* The boat. We'll be late. *He moves slowly off into the darkness.*

WILLY, *elegiacally, turning to the house:* Now when you kick off, boy, I want a seventy-yard boot, and get right down the field under the ball, and when you hit, hit low and hit hard, because it's important, boy. *He swings around and faces the audience.* There's all kinds of important people in the stands, and the first thing you know . . . *Suddenly realizing he is alone:* Ben! Ben, where do I . . . ? *He makes a sudden movement of search.* Ben, how do I . . . ?

LINDA, *calling:* Willy, you coming up?

WILLY, *uttering a gasp of fear, whirling about as if to quiet her:* Sh! *He turns around as if to find his way; sounds, faces, voices, seem to be swarming in upon him and he flicks at them, crying,* Sh! Sh! *Suddenly music, faint and high, stops him. It rises in intensity, almost to an unbearable scream. He goes up and down on his toes, and rushes off around the house.* Shhh!

LINDA: Willy?

There is no answer. Linda waits. Biff gets up off his bed. He is still in his clothes. Happy sits up. Biff stands listening.

LINDA, *with real fear:* Willy, answer me! Willy!

There is the sound of a car starting and moving away at full speed.

LINDA: No!

BIFF, *rushing down the stairs:* Pop!

As the car speeds off, the music crashes down in a frenzy of sound, which becomes the soft pulsation of a single cello string. Biff slowly returns to his bedroom. He and Happy gravely don their jackets. Linda slowly walks out of her room. The music has developed into a dead march. The leaves of day are appearing over everything. Charley and Bernard, somberly dressed, appear and knock on the kitchen door. Biff and Happy slowly descend the stairs to the kitchen as Charley and Bernard enter. All stop a moment when Linda, in clothes of mourning, bearing a little bunch of roses, comes through the draped doorway into the kitchen. She goes to Charley and takes his arm.

Now all move toward the audience, through the wall-line of the kitchen. At the limit of the apron, Linda lays down the flowers, kneels, and sits back on her heels. All stare down at the grave.

REQUIEM

CHARLEY: It's getting dark, Linda.

Linda doesn't react. She stares at the grave.

BIFF: How about it, Mom? Better get some rest, heh? They'll be closing the gate soon.

Linda makes no move. Pause.

HAPPY, *deeply angered:* He had no right to do that. There was no necessity for it. We would've helped him.

CHARLEY, *grunting:* Hmmm.

BIFF: Come along, Mom.

LINDA: Why didn't anybody come?

CHARLEY: It was a very nice funeral.

LINDA: But where are all the people he knew? Maybe they blame him.

CHARLEY: Naa. It's a rough world, Linda. They wouldn't blame him.

LINDA: I can't understand it. At this time especially. First time in thirty-five years we were just about free and clear. He only needed a little salary. He was even finished with the dentist.

CHARLEY: No man only needs a little salary.

LINDA: I can't understand it.

BIFF: There were a lot of nice days. When he'd come home from a trip; or on Sundays, making the stoop; finishing the cellar; putting on the new porch; when he built the extra bathroom; and put up the garage. You know something, Charley, there's more of him in that front stoop than in all the sales he ever made.

CHARLEY: Yeah. He was a happy man with a batch of cement.

LINDA: He was so wonderful with his hands.

BIFF: He had the wrong dreams. All, all, wrong.

HAPPY, *almost ready to fight Biff:* Don't say that!

BIFF: He never knew who he was.

CHARLEY, *stopping Happy's movement and reply. To Biff:* Nobody dast blame this man. You don't understand: Willy was a salesman. And for a salesman, there is no rock bottom to the life. He don't put a bolt to a nut, he don't tell you the law or give you medicine. He's a man way out there in the blue, riding on a smile and a shoeshine. And when they start not smiling back — that's an earthquake. And then you get yourself a couple of spots on your hat, and you're finished. Nobody dast blame this man. A salesman is got to dream, boy. It comes with the territory.

BIFF: Charley, the man didn't know who he was.

HAPPY, *infuriated:* Don't say that!

BIFF: Why don't you come with me, Happy?

HAPPY: I'm not licked that easily. I'm staying right in this city, and I'm gonna beat this racket! *He looks at Biff, his chin set.* The Loman Brothers!

BIFF: I know who I am, kid.

HAPPY: All right, boy. I'm gonna show you and everybody else that Willy Loman did not die in vain. He had a good dream. It's the only dream you can have — to come out number-one man. He fought it out here, and this is where I'm gonna win it for him.

BIFF, *with a hopeless glance at Happy, bends toward his mother:* Let's go, Mom.

LINDA: I'll be with you in a minute. Go on, Charley. *He hesitates.* I want to, just for a minute. I never had a chance to say good-by.

Charley moves away, followed by Happy. Biff remains a slight distance up and left of Linda. She sits there, summoning herself. The flute begins, not far away, playing behind her speech.

LINDA: Forgive me, dear. I can't cry. I don't know what it is, but I can't cry. I don't understand it. Why did you ever do that? Help me, Willy, I can't cry. It seems to me that you're just on another trip. I keep expecting you. Willy, dear, I can't cry. Why did you do it? I search and search and I search, and I can't understand it, Willy. I made the last payment on the house today. Today, dear. And there'll be nobody home. *A sob rises in her throat.* We're free and clear. *Sobbing more fully, released:* We're free. *Biff comes slowly toward her.* We're free . . . We're free . . .

Biff lifts her to her feet and moves out up right with her in his arms. Linda sobs quietly. Bernard and Charley come together and follow them, followed by Happy. Only the music of the flute is left on the darkening stage as over the house the hard towers of the apartment buildings rise into sharp focus, and

The Curtain Falls

[1949]

Robert Lowell

[1917-1977]

Robert Traill Spence Lowell Jr. was born on March 1, 1917, in Boston, Massachusetts. He was the only child of Robert Lowell Sr., an officer in the U.S. Navy, and Charlotte Winslow Lowell. Lowell's mother was descended from Edward Winslow, who came to America on the *Mayflower* in 1620, while his father was related to the poet Amy Lowell and was a descendant of James

Russell Lowell, a poet and the first editor of the *Atlantic Monthly*. In 1924, Lowell was enrolled at the Brimmer School in Boston and later attended St. Mark's School in Southborough, Massachusetts. He was a rebellious student who often settled differences through fistfights, earning himself the lifelong nickname "Cal," derived from *Caliban*, an unruly character in Shakespeare's *The Tempest*, and from the name of the mad Roman emperor *Caligula*. One of his teachers at St. Mark's was the poet Richard Eberhart, and Lowell published his first poem in the school's literary magazine in 1935. That fall, he enrolled at Harvard University. There were no poets on the faculty, and Lowell became bitterly unhappy. He infuriated his parents by becoming engaged to a writer a few years older than himself, and during a heated argument about her Lowell punched his father and knocked him down. His parents sent him to a family friend and psychiatrist who sympathetically arranged for him to go to Tennessee to meet the poet Allen Tate, then teaching at Vanderbilt University. Lowell spent the summer of 1937 living in a tent on the lawn of Tate's home and writing poetry. On Tate's advice, he transferred to Kenyon College, where he studied with the poet and critic John Crowe Ransom. Lowell graduated summa cum laude in 1940.

Robert Lowell

This photograph of Lowell at his writing desk was taken in 1951, by which time he had already gained widespread recognition as one of the major young poets in the United States.

By the end of the decade, Lowell was firmly established as a poet. Following his graduation, he married the writer Jean Stafford, converted to Roman Catholicism, took graduate courses at Louisiana State University with the poet Robert Penn Warren, and worked briefly as an editorial assistant in New York City. After the United States entered World War II, Lowell twice volunteered for military service but was rejected because of his poor eyesight. When he was drafted in 1943, however, he "respectfully declined to serve," as he stated in a public letter to President Franklin D. Roosevelt, citing what Lowell viewed as the brutality and immorality of the Allied bombing of civilian populations in Germany. For refusing induction, Lowell was sentenced to the legal minimum of a year in jail, of which he served five months in a federal prison in Danbury, Connecticut. By then, his poems had begun to appear in prominent literary journals such as the *Partisan Review*, the *Kenyon Review*, and the *Sewanee Review*, and his first book of poems, *Land of Unlikeness*, was published by a small press shortly before his parole in 1944. Lowell and his wife moved to New York City, where he radically revised and expanded the collection, which was republished as *Lord Weary's Castle* (1946). The acclaimed volume won the Pulitzer Prize, and Lowell was awarded a Guggenheim Fellowship and the American Academy of Arts and Letters Prize. At the age of only thirty, he was appointed Consultant in Poetry at the Library of Congress, a position now called Poet Laureate, for 1947–48.

Lowell's later work was shaped by his personal struggles and growing political engagement. In 1949, a year after his divorce from Jean Stafford, he married the writer and critic Elizabeth Hardwick. They lived in Europe from 1950 through 1952, during which Lowell published a collection of dense dramatic monologues, *The Mills of the Kavanaughs* (1951). After their return to the United States, Lowell accepted visiting positions at a series of colleges, including Boston University, where he taught from 1954 to 1960. During the 1950s, Lowell lost his faith in Catholicism and suffered bouts of severe depression, a result of the bipolar disorder for which he was hospitalized at intervals throughout his adult life. On the advice of psychiatrists, he began writing about his childhood. The first result was "91 Revere Street," a prose memoir published in the *Partisan Review* in 1956. Lowell later included it in *Life Studies* (1959), a revolutionary collection of intensely autobiographical poems that won the National Book Award. In 1960, Lowell returned to New York City, where he published *Imitations* (1961), loose translations of a wide range of ancient and modern European poems, and *The Old Glory* (1964), three plays based on stories by Nathaniel Hawthorne and Herman Melville. At the same time, Lowell directly addressed contemporary social issues in the title poem and many of the other poems in *For the Union Dead* (1964). In 1965, he wrote his second public letter to a president, Lyndon B. Johnson, declining an invitation to the White House as a protest against the escalation of the Vietnam War. The turbulence of the 1960s was reflected in the poems and translations in his collection *Near the Ocean* (1967), published the year Lowell also joined Norman Mailer and many other writers in a massive antiwar demonstration and march on the Pentagon in Washington, D.C.

By then, Lowell was the most famous and influential poet writing in English. In 1970, disillusioned by events in the United States, he accepted a visiting position at Essex University in England. There, he began an affair with the writer Lady Caroline Blackwood, who gave birth to their son in 1971. A year later, Lowell divorced Elizabeth Hardwick and married Blackwood. Revising the poems in his poetic journal *Notebooks 1967–68* (1969) and writing new poems, he published three collections of unrhymed sonnets in 1973: *History; For Lizzie and Harriet*, about his second wife, Elizabeth Hardwick, and their daughter, Harriet; and *The Dolphin*, about his new life in England. For the latter volume, Lowell was awarded his second Pulitzer Prize. Shortly after the publication of his final collection, *Day by Day* (1977), Lowell decided to return to Hardwick and the United States. He died of a heart attack in a cab on the way into New York City from the airport on September 12, 1977.

In the person and poetry of Robert Lowell, the whole scope and efficacy of the artistic endeavour was exemplified and affirmed. And his death shook the frame of poetry.

—Seamus Heaney

Lowell's Poetry.   Lowell, who majored in classics in college and later translated works from a range of languages, once said in an interview: "From the beginning I was preoccupied with technique, fascinated by the past and tempted by other languages." His early poems were highly formal, dense with allusions to literature and history. Dissatisfied with the formal rhetoric and traditional metrics of his earlier poetry, and inspired by the work of his friends John Berryman and William Carlos Williams, Lowell in the late 1950s began to write deeply personal poems in a looser, more colloquial style. The result was *Life Studies* (1959), a volume that helped inaugurate what came to be called the "confessional" style of American poetry. Two of the following poems were first published in that volume: "Memories of West Street and Lepke," inspired by Lowell's imprisonment for refusing induction into the military during World War II, and his famous poem, "Skunk Hour." In June 1960, less than a year after the publication of *Life Studies*, Lowell read an early version of what is widely regarded as his finest public poem, "For the Union Dead," before an audience of thousands gathered for an arts festival at the Boston Public

The Robert Gould Shaw Memorial

This famous Civil War memorial, which was created by the sculptor Augustus Saint-Gaudens and dedicated in Boston in 1897, figures prominently in Lowell's poem "For the Union Dead." The larger-than-life bronze relief depicts the mounted white officer Colonel Robert Gould Shaw amid the marching African American troops under his command, the Fifty-fourth Regiment of the Massachusetts Volunteer Infantry. Shaw died and his regiment suffered heavy casualties during an assault on Fort Wagner, near Charleston, South Carolina, in July 1863.

Garden. "I've always wanted to write a northern Civil War poem," Lowell remarked in an interview with the southern poet Robert Penn Warren. "And finally at forty-three I did and it's about Colonel Shaw who commanded the first Negro regiment from Boston." The poem is also a commentary on the distressing state of the union one hundred years after the beginning of the Civil War. The final poem selected here, "Waking Early Sunday Morning," is a somber meditation on a country caught up in a seemingly endless cycle of wars that Lowell first published in the *New York Review of Books* in 1965 and later revised for his collection *Near the Ocean* (1967). Lowell, who in a 1971 interview remarked that "revision is inspiration," compulsively revised his poems, many of which exist in multiple versions. The texts of the following poems are those of the final versions, as published in his *Collected Poems* (2003), edited by Frank Bidart and David Gewanter.

bedfordstmartins.com/ americanlit for research links on Lowell

MEMORIES OF WEST STREET AND LEPKE[1]

Only teaching on Tuesdays, book-worming
in pajamas fresh from the washer each morning,
I hog a whole house on Boston's
"hardly passionate Marlborough Street,"[2]
where even the man   5
scavenging filth in the back alley trash cans,
has two children, a beach wagon, a helpmate,
and is a "young Republican."
I have a nine months' daughter,
young enough to be my granddaughter.   10
Like the sun she rises in her flame-flamingo infants' wear.

These are the tranquillized *Fifties*,
and I am forty. Ought I to regret my seedtime?

---

1. **Memories of West Street and Lepke:** In 1943, Lowell refused induction into the army in protest of the Allied bombing of Germany and outlined his objections to the war in a public letter to President Franklin D. Roosevelt. Lowell, who was sentenced to a year in prison, spent ten days in New York City's West Street Jail and five months in the federal prison at Danbury, Connecticut. His fellow inmate at the West Street Jail was Louis Buchalter (1897–1944), called "Lepke," from the Yiddish *Lepkeleh,* or "Little Louis." The head of the Murder Inc. crime syndicate, Lepke was convicted of murder in 1941 and executed in the electric chair in 1944. The poem, an early version of which was published as "My Season in Hell" in the *Partisan Review* (1958), first appeared under the present title in 1959.
2. **"hardly passionate Marlborough Street":** In a 1957 letter inviting William Carlos Williams and his wife to visit him in his quiet neighborhood in Boston, Lowell wrote: "It might be pleasant for you both to be here on Marlboro St. (William James once gave his classes this example of understatement: 'Marlboro Street is hardly a passionate street.')."

I was a fire-breathing Catholic C.O.,[3]
and made my manic statement,
telling off the state and president, and then
sat waiting sentence in the bull pen
beside a Negro boy with curlicues
of marijuana in his hair.

Given a year,
I walked on the roof of the West Street Jail, a short
enclosure like my school soccer court,
and saw the Hudson River once a day
through sooty clothesline entanglements
and bleaching khaki tenements.
Strolling, I yammered metaphysics with Abramowitz,
a jaundice-yellow ("it's really tan")
and fly-weight pacifist,
so vegetarian,
he wore rope shoes and preferred fallen fruit.
He tried to convert Bioff and Brown,
the Hollywood pimps, to his diet.
Hairy, muscular, suburban,
wearing chocolate double-breasted suits,
they blew their tops and beat him black and blue.

I was so out of things, I'd never heard
of the Jehovah's Witnesses.[4]
"Are you a C.O.?" I asked a fellow jailbird.
"No," he answered, "I'm a J.W."
He taught me the "hospital tuck,"[5]
and pointed out the T-shirted back
of *Murder Incorporated's* Czar Lepke,[6]
there piling towels on a rack,
or dawdling off to his little segregated cell full
of things forbidden the common man:
a portable radio, a dresser, two toy American
flags tied together with a ribbon of Easter palm.
Flabby, bald, lobotomized,

15

20

25

30

35

40

45

---

3. **C.O.:** Conscientious objector.
4. **Jehovah's Witnesses:** A pacifist Christian denomination whose members were jailed or persecuted in many countries because they refused to serve in the military during World War II.
5. **"hospital tuck":** A method of putting a flat (rather than a fitted) sheet on a mattress.
6. **Czar Lepke:** See note 1.

he drifted in a sheepish calm,
where no agonizing reappraisal   50
jarred his concentration on the electric chair —
hanging like an oasis in his air
of lost connections. . . .

                                                          [1958, 2003]

Skunk Hour

(for Elizabeth Bishop)[1]

Nautilus Island's hermit
heiress still lives through winter in her Spartan cottage;
her sheep still graze above the sea.
Her son's a bishop. Her farmer
is first selectman in our village;   5
she's in her dotage.[2]

Thirsting for
the hierarchic privacy
of Queen Victoria's century,
she buys up all   10
the eyesores facing her shore,
and lets them fall.

The season's ill —
we've lost our summer millionaire,
who seemed to leap from an L. L. Bean   15
catalogue. His nine-knot yawl
was auctioned off to lobstermen.
A red fox stain covers Blue Hill.

And now our fairy
decorator brightens his shop for fall;   20

---

1. **Dedication:** Lowell dedicated the poem to the poet Elizabeth Bishop "because rereading her suggested a way of breaking through the shell of my old manner," as he observed in 1962. Lowell added that he had modeled "Skunk Hour" on her "much better" poem "The Armadillo," printed on page 1092. Both poems, Lowell noted, "use short line stanzas, start with drifting description, and end with a single animal."
2. **Nautilus Island's hermit . . . dotage:** The island is near what Lowell described as the "declining" seacoast village of Castine, Maine, where he spent the summer of 1957. A selectman is a member of the village's governing board.

his fishnet's filled with orange cork,
orange, his cobbler's bench and awl;
there is no money in his work,
he'd rather marry.

One dark night,[3]   25
my Tudor Ford climbed the hill's skull;
I watched for love-cars. Lights turned down,
they lay together, hull to hull,
where the graveyard shelves on the town. . . .
My mind's not right.   30

A car radio bleats,
"Love, O careless Love. . . ."[4] I hear
my ill-spirit sob in each blood cell,
as if my hand were at its throat. . . .
I myself am hell;[5]   35
nobody's here —

only skunks, that search
in the moonlight for a bite to eat.
They march on their soles up Main Street:
white stripes, moonstruck eyes' red fire   40
under the chalk-dry and spar spire
of the Trinitarian Church.

I stand on top
of our back steps and breathe the rich air —
a mother skunk with her column of kittens swills the garbage pail.   45
She jabs her wedge-head in a cup
of sour cream, drops her ostrich tail,
and will not scare.

                                                    [1958, 2003]

---

3. **One dark night**: Describing the shift from the first four stanzas to stanzas five and six, Lowell observed: "This is the dark night. I hoped my readers would remember John of the Cross's poem. My night is not gracious, but secular, puritan, and agnostic. An Existentialist night." The poem "The Dark Night of the Soul" by the Catholic mystic St. John of the Cross (1542–1591) describes a spiritual purging that prepares the soul for its union with God.
4. **"Love, O careless Love"**: "Careless Love," a song dating from the late 1800s, was recorded by a number of blues and country singers during the 1950s.
5. **I myself am hell**: An allusion to *Paradise Lost* by the English poet John Milton (1608–1674), in which Satan exclaims: "Which way I fly is Hell; my self am Hell" (IV.75).

For the Union Dead[1]

"Relinquunt Omnia Servare Rem Publicam."[2]

The old South Boston Aquarium stands
in a Sahara of snow now. Its broken windows are boarded.
The bronze weathervane cod has lost half its scales.
The airy tanks are dry.[3]

Once my nose crawled like a snail on the glass;   5
my hand tingled
to burst the bubbles
drifting from the noses of the cowed, compliant fish.

My hand draws back. I often sigh still
for the dark downward and vegetating kingdom   10
of the fish and reptile. One morning last March,
I pressed against the new barbed and galvanized

fence on the Boston Common.[4] Behind their cage,
yellow dinosaur steamshovels were grunting
as they cropped up tons of mush and grass   15
to gouge their underworld garage.

Parking spaces luxuriate like civic
sandpiles in the heart of Boston.

---

1. **For the Union Dead:** In June 1960, in his first public reading of this poem at the Boston Arts Festival, Lowell explained that it "is about childhood memories, the evisceration of our modern cities, civil rights, nuclear warfare and more particularly, Colonel Robert Shaw and his Negro regiment, the Massachusetts Fifty-fourth. I brought in early personal memories because I wanted to avoid the fixed, brazen tone of the set-piece and official ode." Colonel Robert Gould Shaw was the white commander of one of the first African American units organized during the Civil War, the Fifty-fourth Regiment of the Massachusetts Volunteer Infantry. The twenty-six-year-old Shaw, a member of a prominent Boston family deeply involved in the anti-slavery movement, died leading his troops in a heroic but unsuccessful assault on Confederate fortifications at Fort Wagner, South Carolina, in 1863. Lowell's great-great uncle, James Russell Lowell, commemorated Shaw's life and death in "Memoriae Positum R. G. S.," an ode published in the *Atlantic Monthly* in 1864. "For the Union Dead," which Lowell earlier published as "Colonel Shaw and the Massachusetts' 54th," appeared in the *Atlantic Monthly* in 1960.
2. **"Relinquunt . . . Publicam":** "They give up everything to serve the Republic" (Latin). Lowell adapted an inscription on Augustus Saint-Gaudens's famous *Memorial to Robert Gould Shaw*, altering the Latin so that "he" becomes "they," thus recognizing the sacrifice of the two hundred fifty African American troops who also died or were wounded in the assault on Fort Wagner. See note 1 and the illustration on p. 1255.
3. **The old . . . dry:** The grand South Boston Aquarium, which was inaugurated on Thanksgiving Day in 1912, fell into disrepair before the city finally decided to close the decrepit building in 1954. The cod, which became the official symbol of the state in 1974, was an emblem of the importance of the fishing industry from the earliest days of the Commonwealth of Massachusetts.
4. **Boston Common:** Dating from 1634, the fifty-acre common is one of the oldest public parks in the United States.

A girdle of orange, Puritan-pumpkin colored girders
braces the tingling Statehouse,[5]   20

shaking over the excavations, as it faces Colonel Shaw
and his bell-cheeked Negro infantry
on St. Gaudens' shaking Civil War relief,
propped by a plank splint against the garage's earthquake.

Two months after marching through Boston,   25
half the regiment was dead;
at the dedication,
William James could almost hear the bronze Negroes breathe.[6]

Their monument sticks like a fishbone
in the city's throat.   30
Its Colonel is as lean
as a compass-needle.

He has an angry wrenlike vigilance,
a greyhound's gentle tautness;
he seems to wince at pleasure,   35
and suffocate for privacy.

He is out of bounds now. He rejoices in man's lovely,
peculiar power to choose life and die —
when he leads his black soldiers to death,
he cannot bend his back.   40

On a thousand small town New England greens,
the old white churches hold their air
of sparse, sincere rebellion; frayed flags
quilt the graveyards of the Grand Army of the Republic.[7]

The stone statues of the abstract Union Soldier   45
grow slimmer and younger each year —
wasp-waisted, they doze over muskets
and muse through their sideburns . . .

---

5. **Statehouse:** The Massachusetts State House, across the street from the Boston Common.
6. **William James . . . breathe:** In an address delivered upon the occasion of the unveiling of the *Robert Gould Shaw Memorial* on May 31, 1897, the philosopher and psychologist William James (1842–1910) declared: "There they march, warm-blooded champions of a better day for man."
7. **Grand Army of the Republic:** The Union army in the Civil War. Hundreds of towns and villages in New England and throughout the North erected memorials to those who fought in the Civil War, usually represented by a stone or bronze statue of a Union soldier standing at attention and holding a musket. Similar memorials to Confederate soldiers were erected throughout the South.

Shaw's father wanted no monument
except the ditch,   50
where his son's body was thrown
and lost with his "niggers."[8]

The ditch is nearer.
There are no statues for the last war here;
on Boylston Street, a commercial photograph   55
shows Hiroshima boiling

over a Mosler Safe, the "Rock of Ages"
that survived the blast.[9] Space is nearer.
When I crouch to my television set,
the drained faces of Negro school-children rise like balloons.[10]   60

Colonel Shaw
is riding on his bubble,
he waits
for the blessèd break.

The Aquarium is gone. Everywhere,   65
giant finned cars nose forward like fish;
a savage servility
slides by on grease.

[1960, 2003]

---

8. **Shaw's father . . . "niggers":** After the battle at Fort Wagner, stories circulated that the Confederate commander ordered his men to bury Shaw in a mass grave along "with his niggers."
9. **Mosler Safe . . . survived the blast:** The United States dropped the first atomic bomb on Hiroshima, Japan, on August 6, 1945. The Mosler Safe Company advertised that one of its safes had survived the blast, which killed an estimated 140,000 people, including 60,000 people who later died from injuries or radiation poisoning.
10. **the drained faces . . . like balloons:** After the Supreme Court's ruling in the 1954 case of *Brown v. Board of Education of Topeka* that segregation in public schools was unconstitutional, enforced integration often led to conflict in the South. One of the most televised confrontations occurred in Little Rock, Arkansas, in 1957. Governor Orville Faubus ordered the Arkansas National Guard to prevent nine African American students from entering Central High School, and President Eisenhower responded by sending in federal troops to enforce the integration of the school and to protect the safety of the "Little Rock Nine."

WAKING EARLY SUNDAY MORNING[1]

O to break loose, like the chinook
salmon jumping and falling back,
nosing up to the impossible
stone and bone-crushing waterfall —

---

1. **Waking Early Sunday Morning:** The first version of this poem was published in the *New York Review of Books* in 1965, when Lowell was active in campaigns against the Vietnam War.

raw-jawed, weak-fleshed there, stopped by ten   5
steps of the roaring ladder, and then
to clear the top on the last try,
alive enough to spawn and die.

Stop, back off. The salmon breaks
water, and now my body wakes   10
to feel the unpolluted joy
and criminal leisure of a boy —
no rainbow smashing a dry fly
in the white run is free as I,
here squatting like a dragon on   15
time's hoard before the day's begun!

Vermin run for their unstopped holes;
in some dark nook a fieldmouse rolls
a marble, hours on end, then stops;
the termite in the woodwork sleeps —   20
listen, the creatures of the night
obsessive, casual, sure of foot,
go on grinding, while the sun's
daily remorseful blackout dawns.

Fierce, fireless mind, running downhill.   25
Look up and see the harbor fill:
business as usual in eclipse
goes down to the sea in ships[2] —
wake of refuse, dacron rope,[3]
bound for Bermuda or Good Hope,   30
all bright before the morning watch
the wine-dark hulls of yawl and ketch.

I watch a glass of water wet
with a fine fuzz of icy sweat,
silvery colors touched with sky,   35
serene in their neutrality —
yet if I shift, or change my mood,
I see some object made of wood,
background behind it of brown grain,
to darken it, but not to stain.   40

---

2. **business as usual . . . ships:** Compare Psalms 107:23-24: "They that go down to the sea in ships, that do business in great waters; / These see the works of the Lord, and his wonders in the deep."
3. **dacron rope:** Dacron is the trademark name of a synthetic polyester developed in the 1950s.

O that the spirit could remain
tinged but untarnished by its strain!
Better dressed and stacking birch,
or lost with the Faithful at Church —
anywhere, but somewhere else!   45
And now the new electric bells,
clearly chiming, "Faith of our fathers,"[4]
and now the congregation gathers.

O Bible chopped and crucified
in hymns we hear but do not read,   50
none of the milder subtleties
of grace or art will sweeten these
stiff quatrains shovelled out four-square —
they sing of peace, and preach despair;
yet they gave darkness some control,   55
and left a loophole for the soul.

No, put old clothes on, and explore
the corners of the woodshed for
its dregs and dreck: tools with no handle,
ten candle-ends not worth a candle,   60
old lumber banished from the Temple,[5]
damned by Paul's precept and example,
cast from the kingdom, banned in Israel,
the wordless sign, the tinkling cymbal.[6]

When will we see Him face to face?   65
Each day, He shines through darker glass.[7]
In this small town where everything
is known, I see His vanishing
emblems, His white spire and flag-
pole sticking out above the fog,   70
like old white china doorknobs, sad,
slight, useless things to calm the mad.

---

4. **"Faith of our fathers"**: A reference to the Protestant hymn "Faith of Our Fathers" (1849), whose refrain is: "Faith of our fathers, holy faith! / We will be true to thee till death."
5. **Temple**: The temple in Jerusalem, the holiest spot and the central place of worship for the Israelites.
6. **damned by Paul's precept . . . the tinkling cymbal**: Paul of Tarsus (c. 10–c. 67) was a persecutor of the early Christians who later experienced a conversion and became a tireless missionary of the Christian Church. The final line of the stanza echoes his first letter to the church at Corinth: "Though I speak with the tongues of men and of angels, and have not charity, I am become as sounding brass, or a tinkling cymbal" (1 Corinthians 13:1).
7. **When . . . darker glass**: Compare 1 Corinthians 13:12: "For now we see through a glass, darkly; but then face to face: now I know in part; but then shall I know even as also I am known."

Hammering military splendor,
top-heavy Goliath in full armor[8] —
little redemption in the mass   75
liquidations of their brass,
elephant and phalanx moving
with the times and still improving,
when that kingdom hit the crash:
a million foreskins stacked like trash . . .   80

Sing softer! But what if a new
diminuendo brings no true
tenderness, only restlessness,
excess, the hunger for success,
sanity of self-deception   85
fixed and kicked by reckless caution,
while we listen to the bells —
anywhere, but somewhere else!

O to break loose. All life's grandeur
is something with a girl in summer . . .   90
elated as the President[9]
girdled by his establishment
this Sunday morning, free to chaff
his own thoughts with his bear-cuffed staff,
swimming nude, unbuttoned, sick   95
of his ghost-written rhetoric!

No weekends for the gods now. Wars
flicker, earth licks its open sores,
fresh breakage, fresh promotions, chance
assassinations, no advance.   100
Only man thinning out his kind
sounds through the Sabbath noon, the blind
swipe of the pruner and his knife
busy about the tree of life . . .[10]

---

8. **Goliath in full armor:** In the Old Testament story, the Philistine giant Goliath, fully arrayed in brass
armor and carrying a sword and a shield, is slain by the young shepherd David, who refuses to wear armor
and is armed with only a sling (1 Samuel 17:1–50). As payment for his first wife, Michal, David later kills two
hundred Philistines and presents their foreskins to Michal's father, King Saul (1 Samuel 18:25–27).
9. **President:** Lyndon B. Johnson was president from 1963 to 1969, during the height of the Vietnam War.
Because of Lowell's opposition to the war, he refused an invitation from President Johnson to participate in
a White House Festival of Arts on June 3, 1965. In a public letter published on the front page of the *New York
Times*, Lowell asserted: "We are in danger of imperceptibly becoming an explosive and suddenly chauvinis-
tic nation, and may even be drifting on our way to the last nuclear ruin."
10. **tree of life:** After Adam and Eve eat from the Tree of Knowledge of Good and Evil, God banishes them
from the garden of Eden so that they will not also eat from the Tree of Life, whose fruit gives everlasting life
(Genesis 3:22–23).

Pity the planet, all joy gone   105
from this sweet volcanic cone;
peace to our children when they fall
in small war on the heels of small
war — until the end of time
to police the earth, a ghost   110
orbiting forever lost
in our monotonous sublime.

[1965, 2003]

Gwendolyn Brooks

[1917-2000]

Gwendolyn Elizabeth Brooks was born in Topeka, Kansas, on June 7, 1917. She was the first child of Keziah Wims Brooks, a former schoolteacher, and David Anderson Brooks, a janitor for a music company in Chicago. Brooks's mother, who had returned to her parents' home in Topeka to give birth to her daughter, soon rejoined her husband in Chicago, where Brooks grew up in a predominantly black neighborhood on the South Side. She remembered a happy childhood in which her father, who had been forced by financial pressures to withdraw from Fisk University, recited poetry to her, while her mother composed songs for which Brooks wrote the words. As a wedding present, her father had given her mother a collection of the Harvard Classics, a fifty-one volume set advertised as the "World's Great Books." The set included what Brooks later called "white treasures," including the essays of Ralph Waldo Emerson, collections of British poetry, and translations of Greek drama. "Very early in life I became fascinated with the wonders language can achieve," Brooks recalled. "And I began playing with words." As she also recalled, her mother often told her: "You're going to be the *lady* Paul Laurence Dunbar." The precocious Brooks published her first poem at the age of thirteen in *American Childhood Magazine.* When Langston Hughes and James Weldon Johnson gave readings at neighborhood churches, her mother introduced her to the poets, and Brooks sent them her poems. Johnson advised her to read modernist poets such as T. S. Eliot, E. E. Cummings, and Ezra Pound, and Hughes was encouraging, telling her: "You're very talented! Keep writing! Some day you'll have a book published!"

Despite the economic and social obstacles confronting her, Brooks was determined to fulfill Hughes's prophesy. By the time she graduated from high school in 1934, she had published over one hundred poems in her weekly column in the prominent African American newspaper the *Chicago Defender.* She enrolled at nearby Wilson Junior College, from which she graduated in 1936. She had difficulty finding a job during the Depression

[Brooks] has accorded heroic stature to the lives of women in the African American community, while never ceasing to speak for and to that community as a whole. Her poetry holds up a mirror to the American experience entire, its dreams, self-delusions and nightmares.

–Adrienne Rich

Gwendolyn Brooks
Slim Aarons took this photograph of Brooks on the back steps of her apartment in Chicago in 1960, the year she published her groundbreaking collection *The Bean Eaters*.

and worked as a maid and a secretary until 1937, when she became the publicity director of a local youth group sponsored by the National Association for the Advancement of Colored People (NAACP). At its gatherings, she met a number of activists and writers, including the poet Henry Blakely. In 1938, Brooks married Blakely, with whom she later had two children, and they moved into a small apartment on the South Side. She won the Midwestern Writers' Conference Poetry Award in 1943, and some of her poems were subsequently published in the Chicago-based *Poetry: A Magazine of Verse* and the national magazine *Harper's*. On the advice of friends, she sent a collection of poems set in her South Side neighborhood to Harper and Row in New York City. Richard Wright, who read her manuscript for the publisher, wrote that the poems "are hard and real, right out of the central core of Black Belt Negro life in urban areas." Reviewers were enthusiastic about the collection, published as *A Street in Bronzeville* (1945), and Brooks won a grant from the American Academy of Arts and Letters and a Guggenheim Fellowship. In 1949, she published *Annie Allen*, poems about a young woman growing up amid poverty and racism in Bronzeville. The volume won the Pulitzer Prize, the first ever awarded to an African American.

Although she continued to develop the themes of her popular Bronzeville poems, Brooks later addressed racial prejudice and social inequality much more directly. She wrote *Maud Martha* (1953), a semiautobiographical novel about a black woman's childhood and marriage, and a collection of children's poetry, *Bronzeville Girls and Boys* (1956). In some of the poems published in *The Bean Eaters* (1960), Brooks looked beyond her Chicago neighborhood to subjects such as the struggle for school desegregation in the South. In 1967, Brooks attended the Second Fisk University Writers Conference, where she met Amiri Baraka and other writers involved in the Black Arts Movement, a cultural counterpart of the militant Black Power Movement. The conference marked a crucial turning point for Brooks, who in her autobiography *Report from Part One* (1972) said that her goal was thereafter to write poems that would "somehow successfully 'call' all black people: black people in taverns, black people in alleys, black people in gutters, schools, offices, factories, prison, the consulate." In the title poem of her next collection, *In the Mecca* (1969), Brooks explored the grim realities of black life in and around the Mecca, a tenement in Chicago. She dedicated the collection to the memory of Langston Hughes and to her contemporaries James Baldwin and Amiri Baraka. In an effort to support the development of black presses, Brooks then ended her long association with Harper and Row, and her numerous collections of poetry were later published by the small Broadside Press in Detroit and the Third World Press in Chicago.

During the final decades of her life, Brooks assumed a prominent public role. In 1968, she succeeded Carl Sandburg as the Poet Laureate of Illinois, a position in which she established initiatives to take poetry to the people through public readings and school programs. She traveled widely, giving readings, teaching workshops, and receiving honorary degrees at colleges and universities across the United States. She also visited Africa, England, France, and Russia. In 1985, she was appointed Consultant in Poetry at the Library of Congress, a position now called Poet Laureate. The year after the publication of her collected poems, *Blacks* (1987), she was awarded the Frost Medal for lifetime achievement by the Poetry Society of America. In 1994, she was named the National Endowment for the Humanities Jefferson Lecturer, the highest honor in the humanities in the United States. Her final book was a continuation of her autobiography, *Report from Part Two* (1996). Brooks died at her home in Chicago on December 3, 2000.

**bedfordstmartins.com/
americanlit** *for research
links on Brooks*

Brooks's Poetry. "I wrote about what I saw and heard in the street," Brooks once said in an interview. Certainly, life in the black neighborhoods of Chicago was a central subject of her work from her earliest published poems to her somber final collection, *Children Coming Home* (1991), dramatic monologues in the voices of children living in a world of drugs, poverty, and violence. Brooks, who read widely in English and American poetry as a young girl, was praised for her innovative use of traditional poetic forms in her first collection, *A Street in Bronzeville* (1945). The first four poems in the following selection first appeared in that volume, including her controversial poem "the mother," about a woman who has had several abortions. Asked about the poem in an interview, Brooks affirmed: "It has a kind of joy and life. . . . And I feel that it shouldn't be called 'an abortion poem' as it is so often called. I have a little catalog here of the qualities of motherhood, which I hope are not customarily missed." The selection also includes two of her most famous poems, the title poem of *The Bean Eaters* (1960) and another poem from that volume, "We Real Cool," a compressed urban ballad that has been cited as a poetical precursor to hip-hop or rap music. The impact of the Black Arts and Black Power Movements on Brooks is illustrated by the final poem in this selection, "Malcolm X," a tribute to the slain Black Nationalist leader that was first published in her collection *In the Mecca* (1968). The texts of all of the poems are taken from her collected poems, *Blacks* (1987).

From A STREET IN BRONZEVILLE

kitchenette building

We are things of dry hours and the involuntary plan,
Grayed in, and gray. "Dream" makes a giddy sound, not strong
Like "rent," "feeding a wife," "satisfying a man."

But could a dream send up through onion fumes
Its white and violet, fight with fried potatoes   5
And yesterday's garbage ripening in the hall,
Flutter, or sing an aria down these rooms

Even if we were willing to let it in,
Had time to warm it, keep it very clean,
Anticipate a message, let it begin?   10

We wonder. But not well! not for a minute!
Since Number Five is out of the bathroom now,
We think of lukewarm water, hope to get in it.

                                                    [1945, 1987]

the mother

Abortions will not let you forget.
You remember the children you got that you did not get,
The damp small pulps with a little or with no hair,
The singers and workers that never handled the air.
You will never neglect or beat   5
Them, or silence or buy with a sweet.
You will never wind up the sucking-thumb

Or scuttle off ghosts that come.
You will never leave them, controlling your luscious sigh,
Return for a snack of them, with gobbling mother-eye.   10

I have heard in the voices of the wind the voices of my dim killed children.
I have contracted. I have eased
My dim dears at the breasts they could never suck.
I have said, Sweets, if I sinned, if I seized
Your luck   15
And your lives from your unfinished reach,
If I stole your births and your names,
Your straight baby tears and your games,
Your stilted or lovely loves, your tumults, your marriages, aches, and your deaths,
If I poisoned the beginnings of your breaths,   20
Believe that even in my deliberateness I was not deliberate.
Though why should I whine,
Whine that the crime was other than mine? —
Since anyhow you are dead.
Or rather, or instead,   25
You were never made.
But that too, I am afraid,
Is faulty: oh, what shall I say, how is the truth to be said?
You were born, you had body, you died.
It is just that you never giggled or planned or cried.   30

Believe me, I loved you all.
Believe me, I knew you, though faintly, and I loved, I loved you
All.

                                                    [1945, 1987]

a song in the front yard

I've stayed in the front yard all my life.
I want a peek at the back
Where it's rough and untended and hungry weed grows.
A girl gets sick of a rose.

I want to go in the back yard now   5
And maybe down the alley,
To where the charity children play.
I want a good time today.

They do some wonderful things.
They have some wonderful fun.   10
My mother sneers, but I say it's fine
How they don't have to go in at quarter to nine.

My mother, she tells me that Johnnie Mae
Will grow up to he a bad woman.
That George'll be taken to Jail soon or late   15
(On account of last winter he sold our back gate.)

But I say it's fine. Honest, I do.
And I'd like to be a bad woman, too,
And wear the brave stockings of night-black lace
And strut down the streets with paint on my face.   20

[1945, 1987]

the preacher:
ruminates behind the sermon

I think it must be lonely to be God.
Nobody loves a master. No. Despite
The bright hosannas, bright dear-Lords, and bright
Determined reverence of Sunday eyes.

Picture Jehovah striding through the hall   5
Of His importance, creatures running out
From servant-corners to acclaim, to shout
Appreciation of His merit's glare.

But who walks with Him? — dares to take His arm,
To slap Him on the shoulder, tweak His ear,   10
Buy Him a Coca-Cola or a beer,
Pooh-pooh His politics, call Him a fool?

Perhaps — who knows? — He tires of looking down.
Those eyes are never lifted. Never straight.
Perhaps sometimes He tires of being great   15
In solitude. Without a hand to hold.

[1945, 1987]

THE BEAN EATERS

They eat beans mostly, this old yellow pair.
Dinner is a casual affair.
Plain chipware on a plain and creaking wood,
Tin flatware.

Two who are Mostly Good.   5
Two who have lived their day,

But keep on putting on their clothes
And putting things away.

And remembering . . .
Remembering, with twinklings and twinges,   10
As they lean over the beans in their rented back room that
      is full of beads and receipts and dolls and cloths,
      tobacco crumbs, vases and fringes.

[1960, 1987]

WE REAL COOL

THE POOL PLAYERS.
SEVEN AT THE GOLDEN SHOVEL.

We real cool. We
Left school. We

Lurk late. We
Strike straight. We

Sing sin. We
Thin gin. We

Jazz June. We
Die soon.

[1960, 1987]

MALCOLM X[1]

For Dudley Randall[2]

Original.
Ragged-round.
Rich-robust.

He had the hawk-man's eyes.
We gasped. We saw the maleness.   5
The maleness raking out and making guttural the air
and pushing us to walls.

---

1. **Malcolm X:** Malcolm Little (1925–1965), later Malcolm X, a Black Nationalist and human-rights leader who became a Black Muslim minister, was assassinated in New York City.
2. **Dedication:** Brooks dedicated the poem to the poet and editor Dudley Randall (1914–2000), a pioneer in African American book publishing who founded the Broadside Press.

And in a soft and fundamental hour
a sorcery devout and vertical
beguiled the world.   10

He opened us —
who was a key,

who was a man.

[1968, 1987]

Hisaye Yamamoto

[b. 1921]

Hisaye Yamamoto was born in Redondo Beach, California, on August 23, 1921. Her parents were immigrant farmers from Kumamoto, Japan. As a Nisei, the term for children born to Japanese immigrants (known as Issei), Yamamoto spoke Japanese at home and began to learn English only when she entered kindergarten. Yamamoto later recalled that, while her parents "eked out a living" by growing strawberries, she quickly learned English and became an avid reader. She began writing stories and sketches when she was a teenager and published frequently in the English sections of Japanese-language newspapers, often using the pen name "Napoleon." As she said in a 1987 interview, "On weekends [the papers] would have a feature page, where people would send in all kinds of things. They'd print anything, so that's how I got started, and I haven't stopped yet!" After Yamamoto graduated from Excelsior Union High School in 1938, she enrolled at Compton Junior College, where she majored in foreign languages and was the class salutatorian at her graduation in 1940.

Hisaye Yamamoto

This photograph shows Yamamoto standing in front of a shop in Little Tokyo, the Japanese American district in downtown Los Angeles. In the window, the shop displays an American flag and a portrait of the family that founded the business.

The lives of Yamamoto and other Japanese Americans changed dramatically in the aftermath of the bombing of Pearl Harbor on December 7, 1941. Strong anti-Japanese sentiment in the United States prompted President Franklin D. Roosevelt to issue the Japanese Relocation Order of February 1942. Roughly 110,000 people of Japanese extraction living on the West Coast, almost two-thirds of them American citizens, were consequently rounded up and forcibly removed to remote concentration camps, called "War Relocation Centers." The Yamamotos lost their farm and were sent to the Poston Relocation Center on the Colorado Indian Reservation in Arizona. Yamamoto wrote for a daily newspaper established to help combat the monotony of life at the camp, the *Poston Chronicle*, in which she published her first works of fiction, including a serialized mystery, "Death Rides the Rails to Poston." In 1944, she and two of her brothers were allowed to leave the camp to seek jobs in Massachusetts, where Yamamoto worked as a cook, but they returned after learning that another brother had died in combat in Italy. When the family was finally released from the camp in 1945, they moved back to California, where Yamamoto worked for three years for the African American newspaper the *Los Angeles Tribune*. She also became deeply involved with the civil rights movement, participating in demonstrations sponsored by the Congress of Racial Equality (CORE).

Yamamoto subsequently became one of the first Japanese American writers to gain recognition in the United States. She quit her job at the *Tribune* in order to care for a baby born into her family. She also began to write essays and stories based on her childhood memories, her family's bitter wartime experiences in the camp, and her life as a Nisei in Los Angeles. Her first national publication, "The High-Heeled Shoes: A Memoir," a series of linked sketches dramatizing the sexual harassment of women, appeared in the *Partisan Review* in 1948. Her most famous story, "Seventeen Syllables," appeared in the magazine the following year, and Yamamoto also published stories in other prominent periodicals such as *Harper's Bazaar* and the *Kenyon Review*. The John Hay Whitney Foundation awarded her a fellowship for a year of full-time writing in 1950. Meanwhile, she had been reading the *Catholic Worker*, the publication of the Catholic Worker Movement, founded in 1933 by the radical social activist Dorothy Day. Passing up a writing fellowship at Stanford University, Yamamoto in 1953 went to live at one of the movement's cooperative farms on Staten Island, New York. There, she met and married Anthony DeSoto. In 1955, the couple returned to Los Angeles, where they eventually had four children. Although she devoted most of her time to her family, Yamamoto continued to publish stories and other writings, most of which appeared in the widely read Japanese American newspaper *Rafu Shimpo*. Her first collection of stories, *Seventeen Syllables: Five Stories of Japanese American Life*, was published in Japan in 1985, three years before *Seventeen Syllables and Other Stories* was published by a small press in the United States. In 1986, Yamamoto was awarded the American Book Award for Lifetime Achievement from the Before Columbus Foundation. Yamamoto continues to live in Los Angeles, writing occasionally, tending her garden, and enjoying her grandchildren.

bedfordstmartins.com/ americanlit for research links on Yamamoto

Yamamoto's "Seventeen Syllables." This story first appeared in one of the most influential political and cultural journals of the postwar period, the *Partisan Review*, whose cosmopolitan editors published the work of a wide range of American and European authors. The issue in which Yamamoto's story appeared, for example, also included works by Saul Bellow,

Theodore Roethke, and the French author Albert Camus. In "Seventeen Syllables," which takes place before World War II, the third-person narrator tells the story through the eyes of its adolescent main character, Rosie. The daughter of Japanese immigrants, Rosie witnesses without fully comprehending the conflict between her father, a hard-working farmer, and her artistic mother, who writes haiku, an ancient form of Japanese poetry traditionally consisting of seventeen syllables divided into lines of five, seven, and five syllables. The need for self-expression is a central theme in the story, which also concerns the failure of communication, not only between the husband and wife, but also between them and their acculturated, English-speaking daughter. The text is taken from the first printing of the story in the *Partisan Review*, November 1949.

SEVENTEEN SYLLABLES

The first Rosie knew that her mother had taken to writing poems was one evening when she finished one and read it aloud for her daughter's approval. It was about cats, and Rosie pretended to understand it thoroughly and appreciate it no end, partly because she hesitated to disillusion her mother about the quantity and quality of Japanese she had learned in all the years now that she had been going to Japanese school every Saturday (and Wednesday, too, in the summer). Even so, her mother must have been skeptical about the depth of Rosie's understanding, because she explained afterwards about the kind of poem she was trying to write.

See, Rosie, she said, it was a *haiku*, a poem in which she must pack all her meaning into seventeen syllables only, which were divided into three lines of five, seven, and five syllables. In the one she had just read, she had tried to capture the charm of a kitten, as well as comment on the superstition that owning a cat of three colors meant good luck.

"Yes, yes, I understand. How utterly lovely," Rosie said, and her mother, either satisfied or seeing through the deception and resigned, went back to composing.

The truth was that Rosie was lazy; English lay ready on the tongue but Japanese had to be searched for and examined, and even then put forth tentatively (probably to meet with laughter). It was so much easier to say yes, yes, even when one meant no, no. Besides, this was what was in her mind to say: I was looking through one of your magazines from Japan last night, Mother, and towards the back I found some *haiku* in English that delighted me. There was one that made me giggle off and on until I fell asleep —

> It is morning, and lo!
> I lie awake, comme il faut,[1]
> sighing for some dough.

Now, how to reach her mother, how to communicate the melancholy song? Rosie knew formal Japanese by fits and starts, her mother had even less English, no French. It was much more possible to say yes, yes.

---

1. *comme il faut*: According to custom (French).

It developed that her mother was writing the *haiku* for a daily newspaper, the *Mainichi Shinbun*,[2] that was published in San Francisco. Los Angeles, to be sure, was closer to the farming community in which the Hayashi family lived and several Japanese vernaculars were printed there, but Rosie's parents said they preferred the tone of the northern paper. Once a week, the *Mainichi* would have a section devoted to *haiku*, and her mother became an extravagant contributor, taking for herself the blossoming pen name, Umé Hanazono.[3]

So Rosie and her father lived for awhile with two women, her mother and Umé Hanazono. Her mother (Tomé Hayashi by name) kept house, cooked, washed, and, along with her husband and the Carrascos, the Mexican family hired for the harvest, did her ample share of picking tomatoes out in the sweltering fields and boxing them in tidy strata in the cool packing shed. Umé Hanazono, who came to life after the dinner dishes were done, was an earnest, muttering stranger who often neglected speaking when spoken to and stayed busy at the parlor table as late as midnight scribbling with pencil on scratch paper or carefully copying characters on good paper with her fat, pale green Parker.[4]

This new interest had some repercussions on the household routine. Before, Rosie had been accustomed to her parents and herself taking their hot baths early and going to bed almost immediately afterwards, unless her parents challenged each other to a game of flower cards or unless company dropped in. Now, if her father wanted to play cards, he had to resort to solitaire (at which he always cheated fearlessly), and if a group of friends came over, it was bound to contain someone who was also writing *haiku*, and the small assemblage would be split in two, her father entertaining the nonliterary members and her mother comparing ecstatic notes with the visiting poet.

If they went out, it was more of the same thing. But Umé Hanazono's life span, even for a poet's, was very brief — perhaps three months at most.

One night they went over to see the Hayano family in the neighboring town to the west, an adventure both painful and attractive to Rosie. It was attractive because there were four Hayano girls, all lovely and each one named after a season of the year (Haru, Natsu, Aki, Fuyu), painful because something had been wrong with Mrs. Hayano ever since the birth of her first child. Rosie would sometimes watch Mrs. Hayano, reputed to have been the belle of her native village, making her way about a room, stooped, slowly shuffling, violently trembling (*always* trembling), and she would be reminded that this woman, in this same condition, had carried and given issue to three babies. She would look wonderingly at Mr. Hayano, handsome, tall, and strong, and she would look at her four pretty friends. But it was not a matter she could come to any decision about.

On this visit, however, Mrs. Hayano sat all evening in the rocker, as motionless and unobtrusive as it was possible for her to be, and Rosie found the greater part of the

---

2. *Mainichi Shinbun*: Daily Newspaper (Japanese), named after the largest newspaper in Japan.
3. **Umé Hanazono**: Plum-tree Flower Garden (Japanese).
4. **Parker**: A high-quality fountain pen made by the Parker Pen Company.

evening practically anaesthetic. Too, Rosie spent most of it in the girls' room, because Haru, the garrulous one, said almost as soon as the bows and other greetings were over, "Oh, you must see my new coat!"

It was a pale plaid of grey, sand, and blue, with an enormous collar, and Rosie, seeing nothing special in it, said, "Gee, how nice."

"Nice?" said Haru, indignantly. "Is that all you can say about it? It's gorgeous! And so cheap, too. Only seventeen-ninety-eight, because it was a sale. The saleslady said it was twenty-five dollars regular."

"Gee," said Rosie. Natsu, who never said much and when she said anything said it shyly, fingered the coat covetously and Haru pulled it away.

"Mine," she said, putting it on. She minced in the aisle between the two large beds and smiled happily. "Let's see how your mother likes it."

She broke into the front room and the adult conversation, and went to stand in front of Rosie's mother, while the rest watched from the door. Rosie's mother was properly envious. "May I inherit it when you're through with it?"

Haru, pleased, giggled and said yes, she could, but Natsu reminded gravely from the door, "You promised me, Haru."

Everyone laughed but Natsu, who shamefacedly retreated into the bedroom. Haru came in laughing, taking off the coat. "We were only kidding, Natsu," she said. "Here, you try it on now."

After Natsu buttoned herself into the coat, inspected herself solemnly in the bureau mirror, and reluctantly shed it, Rosie, Aki, and Fuyu got their turns, and Fuyu, who was eight, drowned in it while her sisters and Rosie doubled up in amusement. They all went into the front room later, because Haru's mother quaveringly called to her to fix the tea and rice cakes and open a can of sliced peaches for everybody. Rosie noticed that her mother and Mr. Hayano were talking together at the little table — they were discussing a *haiku* that Mr. Hayano was planning to send to the *Mainichi*, while her father was sitting at one end of the sofa looking through a copy of *Life*, the new picture magazine.[5] Occasionally, her father would comment on a photograph, holding it toward Mrs. Hayano and speaking to her as he always did — loudly, as though he thought someone such as she must surely be at least a trifle deaf also.

The five girls had their refreshments at the kitchen table, and it was while Rosie was showing the sisters her trick of swallowing peach slices without chewing (she chased each slippery crescent down with a swig of tea) that her father brought his empty teacup and untouched saucer to the sink and said, "Come on, Rosie, we're going home now."

"Already?" asked Rosie.

"Work tomorrow," he said.

He sounded irritated, and Rosie, puzzled, gulped one last yellow slice and stood up to go, while the sisters began protesting, as was their wont.

---

5. *Life* . . . magazine: The publisher Henry Luce introduced this popular all-photography news magazine in 1936.

"We have to get up at five-thirty," he told them, going into the front room quickly, so that they did not have their usual chance to hang onto his hands and plead for an extension of time.

Rosie, following, saw that her mother and Mr. Hayano were sipping tea and still talking together, while Mrs. Hayano concentrated, quivering, on raising the handleless Japanese cup to her lips with both her hands and lowering it back to her lap. Her father, saying nothing, went out the door, onto the bright porch, and down the steps. Her mother looked up and asked, "Where is he going?"

"Where is he going?" Rosie said. "He said we were going home now."

"Going home?" Her mother looked with embarrassment at Mr. Hayano and his absorbed wife and then forced a smile. "He must be tired," she said.

Haru was not giving up yet. "May Rosie stay overnight?" she asked, and Natsu, Aki, and Fuyu came to reinforce their sister's plea by helping her make a circle around Rosie's mother. Rosie, for once, having no desire to stay, was relieved when her mother, apologizing to the perturbed Mr. and Mrs. Hayano for her father's abruptness at the same time, managed to shake her head no at the quartet, kindly but adamant, so that they broke their circle to let her go.

Rosie's father looked ahead into the windshield as the two joined him. "I'm sorry," her mother said. "You must be tired." Her father, stepping on the starter, said nothing. "You know how I get when it's *haiku*," she continued, "I forget what time it is." He only grunted.

As they rode homeward, silently, Rosie, sitting between, felt a rush of hate for both, for her mother for begging, for her father for denying her mother. I wish this old Ford would crash, right now, she thought, then immediately, no, no, I wish my father would laugh, but it was too late: already the vision had passed through her mind of the green pick-up crumpled in the dark against one of the mighty eucalyptus trees they were just riding past, of the three contorted, bleeding bodies, one of them hers.

Rosie ran between two patches of tomatoes, her heart working more rambunctiously than she had ever known it to. How lucky it was that Aunt Taka and Uncle Gimpachi had come tonight, though, how very lucky. Otherwise, she might not have really kept her half-promise to meet Jesús Carrasco. Jesús, who was going to be a senior in September at the same school she went to, and his parents were the ones helping with the tomatoes this year. She and Jesús, who hardly remembered seeing each other at Cleveland high, where there were so many other people and two whole grades between them, had become great friends this summer — he always had a joke for her when he periodically drove the loaded pick-up up from the fields to the shed where she was usually sorting while her mother and father did the packing, and they laughed a great deal together over infinitesimal repartee during the afternoon break for chilled watermelon or ice cream in the shade of the shed.

What she enjoyed most was racing him to see which could finish picking a double row first. He, who could work faster, would tease her by slowing down until she thought she would surely pass him this time, then speeding up furiously to leave her several sprawling vines behind. Once he had made her screech hideously by crossing over, while her back was turned, to place atop the tomatoes in her green-stained bucket a truly monstrous, pale green worm (it had looked more like an infant snake). And it was when they had finished a contest this morning, after she had pantingly pointed a green finger at the immature tomatoes evident in the lugs at the end of his row and he had returned the accusation (with justice), that he had startlingly brought up the matter of their possibly meeting outside the range of both their parents' dubious eyes.

"What for?" she had asked.

"I've got a secret I want to tell you," he said.

"Tell me now," she demanded.

"It won't be ready till tonight," he said.

She laughed. "Tell me tomorrow then."

"It'll be gone tomorrow," he threatened.

"Well, for seven hakes,[6] what is it?" she had asked, more than twice, and when he had suggested that the packing shed would be an appropriate place to find out, she had cautiously answered maybe. She had not been certain she was going to keep the appointment until the arrival of her mother's sister and her husband. Their coming seemed a sort of signal of permission, of grace, and she had definitely made up her mind to lie and leave as she was bowing them welcome.

So, as soon as everyone appeared settled back for the evening, she announced loudly that she was going to the privy outside, "I'm going to the *benjo!*"[7] and slipped out the door. And now that she was actually on her way, her heart pumped in such an undisciplined way that she could hear it with her ears. It's because I'm running, she told herself, slowing to a walk. The shed was up ahead, one more patch away, in the middle of the fields. Its bulk, looming in the dimness, took on a sinisterness that was funny when Rosie reminded herself that it was only a wooden frame with a canvas roof and three canvas walls that made a slapping noise on breezy days.

Jesús was sitting on the narrow plank that was the sorting platform and she went around to the other side and jumped backwards to seat herself on the rim of a packing stand. "Well, tell me," she said, without greeting, thinking her voice sounded reassuringly familiar.

"I saw you coming out the door," Jesús said. "I heard you running part of the way, too."

"Uh-huh," Rosie said. "Now tell me the secret."

"I was afraid you wouldn't come," he said.

Rosie delved around on the chicken-wire bottom of the stall for number two tomatoes, ripe, which she was sitting beside, and came up with a left-over that felt edible. She bit into it and began sucking out the pulp and seeds. "I'm here," she pointed out.

"Rosie, are you sorry you came?"

"Sorry? What for?" she said. "You said you were going to tell me something."

---

6. **for seven hakes:** A comically garbled version of the expression "for heaven's sake."

7. **benjo:** Outhouse or privy (Japanese).

"I will, I will," Jesús said, but his voice contained disappointment, and Rosie, fleetingly, felt the older of the two, realizing a brand-new power which vanished without category under her recognition.

"I have to go back in a minute," she said. "My aunt and uncle are here from Wintersburg. I told them I was going to the privy."

Jesús laughed. "You funny thing," he said. "You slay me!"

"Just because you have a bathroom *inside*," Rosie said. "Come on, tell me."

Chuckling, Jesús came around to lean on the stand facing her. They still could not see each other very clearly, but Rosie noticed that Jesús became very sober again as he took the hollow tomato from her hand and dropped it back into the stall. When he took hold of her empty hand, she could find no words to protest; her vocabulary had become distressingly constricted and she thought desperately that all that remained intact now was yes and no and oh, and even these few sounds would not easily out. Thus, kissed by Jesús, Rosie fell, for the first time, entirely victim to a helplessness delectable beyond speech. But the terrible, beautiful sensation lasted no more than a second, and the reality of Jesús's lips and tongue and teeth and hands made her pull away with such strength that she nearly tumbled.

Rosie stopped running as she approached the lights from the windows of home. How long since she had left? She could not guess, but gasping yet, she went to the privy in back and locked herself in. Her own breathing deafened her in the dark, close space, and she sat and waited until she could hear at last the nightly calling of the frogs and crickets. Even then, all she could think to say was oh, my, and the pressure of Jesús's face against her face would not leave.

No one had missed her in the parlor, however, and Rosie walked in and through quickly, announcing that she was next going to take a bath. "Your father's in the bathhouse," her mother said, and Rosie, in her room, recalled that she had not seen him when she entered. There had been only Aunt Taka and Uncle Gimpachi with her mother at the table, drinking tea. She got her robe and straw sandals and crossed the parlor again to go outside. Her mother was telling them about the *haiku* competition in the *Mainichi* and the poem she had entered.

Rosie met her father coming out of the bathhouse. "Are you through, Father?" she asked. "I was going to ask you to scrub my back."

"Scrub your own back," he said shortly, going toward the main house.

"What have I done now?" she yelled after him. She suddenly felt like doing a lot of yelling. But he did not answer, and she went into the bathhouse. Turning on the dangling light, she removed her denims and T-shirt and threw them in the big carton for dirty clothes standing next to the washing machine. Her other things she took with her into the bath compartment to wash after her bath. After she had scooped a basin of hot water from the square wooden tub, she sat on the grey cement of the floor and soaped herself at exaggerated leisure, singing, "Red Sails in the Sunset" at the top of her voice and using da-da-da where she suspected her words. Then, standing, still singing, for she was possessed by the notion that any attempt now to analyze would result in spoilage and she believed that the larger her volume the less she would be able to hear herself think, she obtained more hot water and poured it on until she was free of lather. Only then did she allow herself to step into the steaming vat, one leg first, then the remainder of her body inch by inch until the water no longer stung and she could move around at will.

She took a long time soaking, afterwards remembering to go around outside to stoke the embers of the tin-lined fireplace beneath the tub and to throw on a few more sticks so that the water might keep its heat for her mother, and when she finally returned to the parlor, she found her mother still talking *haiku* with her aunt and uncle, the three of them on another round of tea. Her father was nowhere in sight.

At Japanese school the next day (Wednesday, it was), Rosie was grave and giddy by turns. Preoccupied at her desk in the row for students on Book Eight, she made up for it at recess by performing wild mimicry for the benefit of her friend Chizuko. She held her nose and whined a witticism or two in what she considered was the manner of Fred Allen; she assumed intoxication and a British accent to go over the climax of the Rudy Vallee recording of the pub conversation about William Ewart Gladstone; she was the child Shirley Temple piping, "On the Good Ship Lollipop"; she was the gentleman soprano of the Four Inkspots trilling, "If I Didn't Care."[8] And she felt reasonably satisfied when Chizuko wept and gasped, "Oh, Rosie, you ought to be in the movies!"

Her father came after her at noon, bringing her sandwiches of minced ham and two nectarines to eat while she rode, so that she could pitch right into the sorting when they got home. The lugs were piling up, he said, and the ripe tomatoes in them would probably have to be taken to the cannery tomorrow if they were not ready for the produce haulers tonight. "This heat's not doing them any good. And we've got no time for a break today."

It *was* hot, probably the hottest day of the year, and Rosie's blouse stuck damply to her back even under the protection of the canvas. But she worked as efficiently as a flawless machine and kept the stalls heaped, with one part of her mind listening in to the parental murmuring about the heat and the tomatoes and with another part planning the exact words she would say to Jesús when he drove up with the first load of the afternoon. But when at last she saw that the pick-up was coming, her hands went berserk and the tomatoes started falling in the wrong stalls, and her father said, "Hey, hey! Rosie, watch what you're doing!"

"Well, I have to go to the *benjo*," she said, hiding panic.

"Go in the weeds over there," he said, only half-joking.

"Oh, Father!" she protested.

---

8. **She held her nose and whined . . . "If I Didn't Care":** Rosie mimics a number of American radio, recording, and movie stars of the period: the comedian Fred Allen (1894-1956), the host of a popular radio show from 1934-1949; the singer and bandleader Rudy Vallee (1901-1986), a famous mimic whose recordings included songs and comic bits such as a drunken conversation in an English pub about the British political leader William Ewart Gladstone (1809-1898); Shirley Temple (b. 1928), the beloved child actor whose recording of her signature song "On the Good Ship Lollipop" sold 500,000 copies after she first sang it in the movie *Bright Eyes* (1934); and the Ink Spots, a pioneering black vocal group whose first smash hit was "If I Didn't Care" (1939), featuring the high tenor voice of their lead singer, Bill Kenny.

"Oh, go on home," her mother said. "We'll make out for awhile."

In the privy, Rosie peered through a knothole toward the fields, watching as much as she could of Jesús. Happily she thought she saw him look in the direction of the house from time to time before he finished unloading and went back toward the patch where his mother and father worked. As she was heading for the shed, a very presentable black car purred up the dirt driveway to the house and its driver motioned to her. Was this the Hayashi home, he wanted to know. She nodded. Was she a Hayashi? Yes, she said, thinking that he was a good-looking man. He got out of the car with a huge, flat package and she saw that he warmly wore a business suit. "I have something here for your mother then," he said, in a more elegant Japanese than she was used to.

She told him where her mother was and he came along with her, patting his face with an immaculate white handkerchief and saying something about the coolness of San Francisco. To her surprised mother and father, he bowed and introduced himself as, among other things, the *haiku* editor of the *Mainichi Shinbun*, saying that since he had been coming as far as Los Angeles anyway, he had decided to bring her the first prize she had won in the recent contest.

"First prize?" her mother echoed, believing and not believing, pleased and overwhelmed. Handed the package with a bow, she bobbed her head up and down numerous times to express her utter gratitude.

"It is nothing much," he added, "but I hope it will serve as a token of our great appreciation for your contributions and our great admiration of your considerable talent."

"I am not worthy," she said, falling easily into his style. "It is I who should make some sign of my humble thanks for being permitted to contribute."

"No, no, to the contrary," he said, bowing again.

But Rosie's mother insisted, and then saying that she knew she was being unorthodox, she asked if she might open the package because her curiosity was so great. Certainly she might. In fact, he would like her reaction to it, for personally, it was one of his favorite *Hiroshiges*.[9]

Rosie thought it was a pleasant picture, which looked to have been sketched with delicate quickness. There were pink clouds, containing some graceful calligraphy, and a sea, that was a pale blue except at the edges, containing four sampans with indications of people in them. Pines edged the water and on the far-off beach there was a cluster of thatched huts towered over by pine-dotted mountains of grey and blue. The frame was scalloped and gilt.

After Rosie's mother pronounced it without peer and somewhat prodded her father into nodding agreement, she said Mr. Kuroda must at least have a cup of tea, after coming all this way, and although Mr. Kuroda did not want to impose, he soon agreed that a cup of tea would be refreshing and went along with her to the house, carrying the picture for her.

"Ha, your mother's crazy!" Rosie's father said, and Rosie laughed uneasily as she resumed judgment on the tomatoes. She had emptied six lugs when he broke into an imaginary conversation with Jesús to tell her to go and remind her mother of the tomatoes, and she went slowly.

---

9. *Hiroshiges*: Woodcut prints by Ando Hiroshige (1797–1858), a famous Japanese landscape artist.

Mr. Kuroda was in his shirtsleeves expounding some *haiku* theory as he munched a rice cake, and her mother was rapt. Abashed in the great man's presence, Rosie stood next to her mother's chair until her mother looked up inquiringly, and then she started to whisper the message, but her mother pushed her gently away and reproached, "You are not being very polite to our guest."

"Father says the tomatoes . . ." Rosie said aloud, smiling foolishly.

"Tell him I shall only be a minute," her mother said, speaking the language of Mr. Kuroda.

When Rosie carried the reply to her father, he did not seem to hear and she said again, "Mother says she'll be back in a minute."

"All right, all right," he nodded, and they worked again in silence. But suddenly, her father uttered an incredible noise, exactly like the cork of a bottle popping, and the next Rosie knew, he was stalking angrily toward the house, almost running, in fact, and she chased after him crying, "Father! Father! What are you going to do?"

He stopped long enough to order her back to the shed. "Never mind!" he shouted. "Get on with the sorting!"

And from the place in the fields where she stood, frightened and vacillating, Rosie saw her father enter the house. Soon Mr. Kuroda came out alone, putting on his coat. Mr. Kuroda got into his car and backed out down the driveway, onto the highway. Next her father emerged, also alone, something in his arms (it was the picture, she realized), and, going over to the bathhouse woodpile, he threw the picture on the ground and picked up the axe. Smashing the picture, glass and all (she heard the explosion faintly), he reached over for the kerosene that was used to encourage the bath fire and poured it over the wreckage. I am dreaming, Rosie said to herself, I am dreaming, but her father, having made sure that his act of cremation was irrevocable, was even then returning to the fields.

Rosie ran past him and toward the house. What had become of her mother? She burst into the parlor and found her mother at the back window, watching the dying fire. They watched together until there remained only a feeble smoke under the blazing sun. Her mother was very calm.

"Do you know why I married your father?" she said, without turning.

"No," said Rosie. It was the most frightening question she had ever been called upon to answer. Don't tell me now, she wanted to say, tell me tomorrow, tell me next week, don't tell me today. But she knew she would be told now, that the telling would combine with the other violence of the hot afternoon to level her life, her world (so various, so beautiful, so new?) to the very ground.

It was like a story out of the magazines, illustrated in sepia, which she had consumed so greedily for a period until the information had somehow reached her that those wretchedly unhappy autobiographies, offered to her as the testimonials of living men and women, were largely inventions: Her mother, at nineteen, had come to America and married her father as an alternative to suicide.

At eighteen, she had been in love with the first son of one of the well-to-do families in her village. The two had met whenever and wherever they could, secretly, because it would not have done for his family to see him favor her — her father had no money; he was a drunkard and a gambler besides. She had learned she was with child; an excellent match had already been arranged for her lover. Despised by her family, she had given premature birth to a stillborn son, who would be seventeen now. Her family did not turn her out, but she could no longer project herself in any direction without refreshing in them the memory of her indiscretion. She wrote to Aunt Taka, her favorite sister, in America, threatening to kill herself if Aunt Taka would not send for her. Aunt Taka hastily arranged a marriage with a young man, but lately arrived from Japan, of whom she knew, a young man of simple mind, it was said, but of kindly heart. The young man was never told why his unseen betrothed was so eager to hasten the day of meeting.

The story was told perfectly, with neither groping for words nor untoward passion. It was as though her mother had memorized it by heart, reciting it to herself so many times over that its nagging vileness had long since gone.

"I had a brother then?" Rosie asked, for this was what seemed to matter now; she would think about the other later, she assured herself, pushing back the illumination which threatened all that darkness that had hitherto been merely mysterious or even glamorous. "A half-brother?"

"Yes."

"I would have liked a brother," she said.

Suddenly, her mother knelt on the floor and took her by the wrists. "Rosie," she said urgently, "Promise me you will never marry!" Shocked more by the request than the revelation, Rosie stared at her mother's face. Jesus, Jesus, she called silently, not certain whether she was invoking the help of the son of the Carrascos or of God, until there returned sweetly the memory of Jesús's hand, how it had touched her and where. Still her mother waited for an answer, holding her wrists so tightly that her hands were going numb. She tried to pull free. Promise, her mother whispered fiercely, promise. Yes, yes, I promise, Rosie said. But for an instant she turned away, and her mother, hearing the familiar glib agreement, released her. Oh, you, you, you, her eyes and twisted mouth said, you fool. Rosie, covering her face, began at last to cry, and the embrace and consoling hand came much later than she expected.

[1949]

James Baldwin

[1924-1987]

James Baldwin was born James Arthur Jones on August 2, 1924, in New York City. His mother was Emma Berdis Jones, a single woman from Maryland who, like thousands of other African Americans, had joined the Great Migration in search of a better life in the North. When her son was three years old, she married David Baldwin, a Baptist minister and laborer from Louisiana. For many years, Baldwin believed that his stepfather was his birth father, whose identity he never learned. The large family, which included some of David Baldwin's children from a previous marriage, lived in such misery and poverty in Harlem that Baldwin later said that he "never had a childhood." The frustrated David Baldwin was abusive and violent, and he was deeply suspicious of Baldwin's interest in books. "Cease studying!" was a command that Baldwin often heard at home, and he escaped to read at public libraries. From 1936 to 1938, he attended Frederick Douglass Junior High School, where one of his teachers was the poet Countee Cullen. Cullen encouraged Baldwin to join the literary club, and he later coedited the literary magazine of the predominantly white De-Witt Clinton High School in the Bronx. During high school, he was also a popular preacher at a revivalist storefront church in Harlem, the Fireside Pentecostal Assembly, but he left the church and the ministry before his graduation in 1941. Baldwin hoped to go to college, but he was expected to help support the family, so he took a job as a construction worker in New Jersey and later worked in a meatpacking factory in New York City.

James Baldwin
Baldwin appeared on the cover of *Time* in May 1963, shortly after the publication of his acclaimed book *The Fire Next Time.* The caption for the cover story on the civil rights movement reads: "Birmingham and Beyond: The Negro's Push for Equality."

After his stepfather's death in 1943, Baldwin determined to begin a career as a writer. He moved to Greenwich Village where he worked at a series of odd jobs and began to write an autobiographical novel. He sought out the acclaimed novelist Richard Wright, who read the completed portion of Baldwin's draft and generously helped him obtain a grant for promising writers from the publisher Harper & Brothers. In 1947, Baldwin published his first reviews in a national magazine, the *Nation.* The following year, his essays appeared in the left-wing magazine the *New Leader* and *Commentary*, the publication of the American Jewish Committee, in which Baldwin also published his first short story, "Previous Condition." Deeply frustrated by the racial discrimination and injustice in the United States, he decided to follow in Wright's footsteps and move to Paris. Baldwin ended an engagement to a young woman (his last heterosexual relationship), bought a one-way ticket, and sailed in November 1948. "I left America because I doubted my ability to survive the fury of the color problem here," he later wrote. "I wanted to prevent myself from becoming merely a Negro; or, even, merely a Negro writer." Although he had little money and did not find France to be as free of racial discrimination as he had hoped, Baldwin's first five years there were productive and personally satisfying. He became friendly with the black painter Beauford Delaney, who became a kind of father figure to Baldwin. In 1950, he met a young Swiss, Lucien Happersberger, and they became lovers and lifelong friends. In addition to essays and numerous reviews Baldwin wrote for various American periodicals, he completed his autobiographical novel, *Go Tell It on the Mountain*

(1953), which was published by the prominent New York firm of Alfred A. Knopf, Inc.

The novel established Baldwin as a major new voice in American literature. A Guggenheim Fellowship in 1954 enabled him to complete a collection of essays, *Notes of a Native Son* (1955), and to begin work on *Giovanni's Room* (1956), a novel about a white American expatriate who becomes romantically involved with both a woman and a male bartender in Paris. In 1957, Baldwin returned to the United States, the focus of the essays collected in *Nobody Knows My Name* (1961) and the setting of *Another Country* (1962), an ambitious novel about the divisions among a racially mixed group of friends in New York City. Inspired by his growing involvement in the struggle for civil rights, Baldwin wrote *The Fire Next Time* (1963), a devastating assessment of the state of racial relations in the United States. The best-selling book thrust Baldwin into the forefront of the civil rights movement and onto the cover of *Time*. He subsequently exposed the consequences of bigotry and racial hatred in *Blues for Mister Charlie*, a play about the murder of a black youth that opened on Broadway in 1964; in the stories collected in *Going to Meet the Man* (1965); and in his novels *Tell Me How Long the Train's Been Gone* (1968) and *If Beale Street Could Talk* (1974). Baldwin returned to France in the 1970s, but he described himself as a "commuter" rather than an expatriate, and he was in considerable demand as a speaker throughout the United States. Baldwin interviewed dozens of people about the serial killings of black children in Atlanta, the subject of his final book, *The Evidence of Things Unseen* (1985). He died of cancer at his home in France on December 1, 1987, and was buried in Harlem following a massive memorial service during which Baldwin was eulogized by three of the writers whose careers he had helped inspire, Maya Angelou, Toni Morrison, and Amiri Baraka.

Baldwin's "Notes of a Native Son." Baldwin began working on this autobiographical essay in 1952 while he was living in Paris, far removed from the characters and scenes he so vividly evokes: his childhood in Harlem, the construction job he took in New Jersey after he graduated from high school in 1942, his stepfather's death, and the race riots in Harlem in 1943. A shorter version of the essay was published as "Me and My House . . ." in *Harper's Magazine* in November 1955, just before the full text appeared at the opening of Baldwin's collection *Notes of a Native Son*. As the title suggests, Baldwin's essay was inspired in part by Richard Wright's best-selling protest novel about a young black man struggling against poverty and racism in the South Side ghetto of Chicago, *Native Son* (1940). Although the first edition of *Notes of a Native Son* created little stir, the collection received enthusiastic reviews and sold briskly after it was reissued in paperback in 1957. In a review in the *New York Times*, Langston Hughes observed: "Few American writers handle words more effectively in the essay form than James Baldwin." Certainly, his mastery of style, tone, and voice is illustrated by "Notes of a Native Son." The writer and activist Julius Lester has pointed to yet another reason that the essay

And he uses words as the sea uses waves, to flow and beat, advance and retreat, rise and take a bow in disappearing.
    –Langston Hughes

has proven to be so enduring: "Baldwin's power as a writer lies in his ability to weave the deeply autobiographical with the political and social. There is no separation between Jimmy Baldwin, black child of Harlem, and James Baldwin, American. For him, the personal is never just personal, and the political never just political. Because he perceives himself not only as the individual James Baldwin but also as the black Everyman, his writing has a moral authority that would be dismissed as arrogant if so many had not affirmed what he wrote." The text is taken from the first edition of *Notes of a Native Son* (1955).

bedfordstmartins.com/ americanlit for research links on Baldwin

NOTES OF A NATIVE SON

On the 29th of July, in 1943, my father died. On the same day, a few hours later, his last child was born. Over a month before this, while all our energies were concentrated in waiting for these events, there had been, in Detroit, one of the bloodiest race riots of the century.[1] A few hours after my father's funeral, while he lay in state in the undertaker's chapel, a race riot broke out in Harlem. On the morning of the 3rd of August, we drove my father to the graveyard through a wilderness of smashed plate glass.

The day of my father's funeral had also been my nineteenth birthday. As we drove him to the graveyard, the spoils of injustice, anarchy, discontent, and hatred were all around us. It seemed to me that God himself had devised, to mark my father's end, the most sustained and brutally dissonant of codas. And it seemed to me, too, that the violence which rose all about us as my father left the world had been devised as a corrective for the pride of his eldest son. I had declined to believe in that apocalypse which had been central to my father's vision; very well, life seemed to be saying, here is something that will certainly pass for an apocalypse until the real thing comes along. I had inclined to be contemptuous of my father for the conditions of his life, for the conditions of our lives. When his life had ended I began to wonder about that life and also, in a new way, to be apprehensive about my own.

I had not known my father very well. We had got on badly, partly because we shared, in our different fashions, the vice of stubborn pride. When he was dead I realized that I had hardly ever spoken to him. When he had been dead a long time I began to wish I had. It seems to be typical of life in America, where opportunities, real and fancied, are thicker than anywhere else on the globe, that the second generation has no time to talk to the first. No one, including my father, seems to have known exactly how old he was, but his mother had been born during slavery. He was of the first generation of free men.

---

1. **one of the bloodiest race riots of the century:** During the summer of 1943, race riots erupted in several American cities, most violently in Detroit, Michigan. On June 20, a clash between black and white youths escalated into street riots in which roving gangs, both black and white, attacked pedestrians and pulled people from their cars, some of which were overturned or set on fire. During the course of thirty-six hours of rioting, thirty-four people were killed, twenty-five blacks and nine whites, and more than 1,800 people were arrested, most of them for looting. A month later, another riot erupted in West Harlem. In contrast to earlier race riots, which were battles between white and black people, the black residents of Harlem directed their frustration and rage at property, especially white-owned businesses in the neighborhood.

He, along with thousands of other Negroes, came North after 1919 and I was part of that generation which had never seen the landscape of what Negroes sometimes call the Old Country.[2]

He had been born in New Orleans and had been a quite young man there during the time that Louis Armstrong, a boy, was running errands for the dives and honky-tonks of what was always presented to me as one of the most wicked of cities — to this day, whenever I think of New Orleans, I also helplessly think of Sodom and Gomorrah.[3] My father never mentioned Louis Armstrong, except to forbid us to play his records; but there was a picture of him on our wall for a long time. One of my father's strong-willed female relatives had placed it there and forbade my father to take it down. He never did, but he eventually maneuvered her out of the house and when, some years later, she was in trouble and near death, he refused to do anything to help her.

He was, I think, very handsome. I gather this from photographs and from my own memories of him, dressed in his Sunday best and on his way to preach a sermon somewhere, when I was little. Handsome, proud, and ingrown, "like a toe-nail," somebody said. But he looked to me, as I grew older, like pictures I had seen of African tribal chieftains: he really should have been naked, with war-paint on and barbaric mementos, standing among spears. He could be chilling in the pulpit and indescribably cruel in his personal life and he was certainly the most bitter man I have ever met; yet it must be said that there was something else in him, buried in him, which lent him his tremendous power and, even, a rather crushing charm. It had something to do with his blackness, I think — he was very black — with his blackness and his beauty, and with the fact that he knew that he was black but did not know that he was beautiful. He claimed to be proud of his blackness but it had also been the cause of much humiliation and it had fixed bleak boundaries to his life. He was not a young man when we were growing up and he had already suffered many kinds of ruin; in his outrageously demanding and protective way he loved his children, who were black like him and menaced, like him; and all these things sometimes showed in his face when he tried, never to my knowledge with any success, to establish contact with any of us. When he took one of his children on his knee to play, the child always became fretful and began to cry; when he tried to help one of us with our homework the absolutely unabating tension which emanated from him caused our minds and our tongues to become paralyzed, so that he, scarcely knowing why, flew into a rage and the child, not knowing why, was punished. If it ever

---

2. **He, along with thousands of other Negroes . . . Old Country:** During World War I and especially after the war formally ended in 1919, hundreds of thousands of African Americans joined what was called the "Great Migration" to industrial cities in the North, fleeing racial violence, segregation, and a depressed rural economy in the South and drawn by the promise of factory jobs created by wartime industries and the economic boom of the 1920s.

3. **He had been born . . . Sodom and Gomorrah:** The trumpet player Louis Armstrong (1900–1971), who grew up in poverty in New Orleans, later became the most famous and influential jazz musician in the country. Although jazz was played all over New Orleans during the early decades of the twentieth century, the music was popularly associated with Storyville, a notorious red-light district that flourished from 1897 through 1917. Sodom and Gomorrah are the cities destroyed by God because of the sinful ways of their inhabitants (Genesis 19:24).

entered his head to bring a surprise home for his children, it was, almost unfailingly, the wrong surprise and even the big watermelons he often brought home on his back in the summertime led to the most appalling scenes. I do not remember, in all those years, that one of his children was ever glad to see him come home. From what I was able to gather of his early life, it seemed that this inability to establish contact with other people had always marked him and had been one of the things which had driven him out of New Orleans. There was something in him, therefore, groping and tentative, which was never expressed and which was buried with him. One saw it most clearly when he was facing new people and hoping to impress them. But he never did, not for long. We went from church to smaller and more improbable church, he found himself in less and less demand as a minister, and by the time he died none of his friends had come to see him for a long time. He had lived and died in an intolerable bitterness of spirit and it frightened me, as we drove him to the graveyard through those unquiet, ruined streets, to see how powerful and overflowing this bitterness could be and to realize that this bitterness now was mine.

When he died I had been away from home for a little over a year. In that year I had had time to become aware of the meaning of all my father's bitter warnings, had discovered the secret of his proudly pursed lips and rigid carriage: I had discovered the weight of white people in the world. I saw that this had been for my ancestors and now would be for me an awful thing to live with and that the bitterness which had helped to kill my father could also kill me.

He had been ill a long time — in the mind, as we now realized, reliving instances of his fantastic intransigence in the new light of his affliction and endeavoring to feel a sorrow for him which never, quite, came true. We had not known that he was being eaten up by paranoia, and the discovery that his cruelty, to our bodies and our minds, had been one of the symptoms of his illness was not, then, enough to enable us to forgive him. The younger children felt, quite simply, relief that he would not be coming home any more. My mother's observation that it was he, after all, who had kept them alive all these years meant nothing because the problems of keeping children alive are not real for children. The older children felt, with my father gone, that they could invite their friends to the house without fear that their friends would be insulted or, as had sometimes happened with me, being told that their friends were in league with the devil and intended to rob our family of everything we owned. (I didn't fail to wonder, and it made me hate him, what on earth we owned that anybody else would want.)

His illness was beyond all hope of healing before anyone realized that he was ill. He had always been so strange and had lived, like a prophet, in such unimaginably close communion with the Lord that his long silences which were punctuated by moans and hallelujahs and snatches of old songs while he sat at the living-room window never seemed odd to us. It was not until he refused to eat because, he said, his family was trying to poison him that my mother was forced to accept as a fact what had, until then, been only an unwilling suspicion. When he was committed, it was discovered that he had tuberculosis and, as it turned out, the disease of his mind allowed the disease of his body to destroy him. For the doctors could not force him to eat, either, and, though he was fed intravenously, it was clear from the beginning that there was no hope for him.

In my mind's eye I could see him, sitting at the window, locked up in his terrors; hating and fearing every living soul including his children who had betrayed him, too, by reaching toward the world which had despised him. There were nine of us. I began to wonder what it could have felt like for such a man to have had nine children whom he could barely feed. He used to make little jokes about our poverty, which never, of course, seemed very funny to us; they could not have seemed very funny to him, either, or else our all too feeble response to them would never have caused such rages. He spent great energy and achieved, to our chagrin, no small amount of success in keeping us away from the people who surrounded us, people who had all-night rent parties to which we listened when we should have been sleeping, people who cursed and drank and flashed razor blades on Lenox Avenue. He could not understand why, if they had so much energy to spare, they could not use it to make their lives better. He treated almost everybody on our block with a most uncharitable asperity and neither they, nor, of course, their children were slow to reciprocate.

The only white people who came to our house were welfare workers and bill collectors. It was almost always my mother who dealt with them, for my father's temper, which was at the mercy of his pride, was never to be trusted. It was clear that he felt their very presence in his home to be a violation: this was conveyed by his carriage, almost ludicrously stiff, and by his voice, harsh and vindictively polite. When I was around nine or ten I wrote a play which was directed by a young, white schoolteacher, a woman, who then took an interest in me, and gave me books to read and, in order to corroborate my theatrical bent, decided to take me to see what she somewhat tactlessly referred to as "real" plays. Theatergoing was forbidden in our house, but, with the really cruel intuitiveness of a child, I suspected that the color of this woman's skin would carry the day for me. When, at school, she suggested taking me to the theater, I did not, as I might have done if she had been a Negro, find a way of discouraging her, but agreed that she should pick me up at my house one evening. I then, very cleverly, left all the rest to my mother, who suggested to my father, as I knew she would, that it would not be very nice to let such a kind woman make the trip for nothing. Also, since it was a schoolteacher, I imagine that my mother countered the idea of sin with the idea of "education," which word, even with my father, carried a kind of bitter weight.

Before the teacher came my father took me aside to ask *why* she was coming, what *interest* she could possibly have in our house, in a boy like me. I said I didn't know but I, too, suggested that it had something to do with education. And I understood that my father was waiting for me to say something — I didn't quite know what; perhaps that I wanted his protection against this teacher and her "education." I said none of these things and the teacher came and we went out. It was clear, during the brief interview in our living room, that my father was agreeing very much against his will and that he would have refused permission if he had dared. The fact that he did not dare caused me to despise him: I had no way of knowing that he was facing in that living room a wholly unprecedented and frightening situation.

Later, when my father had been laid off from his job, this woman became very important to us. She was really a very sweet and generous woman and went to a great deal of trouble to be of help to us, particularly during one awful winter. My mother called her by the highest name she knew: she said she was a "christian." My father could scarcely disagree but during the four or five years of our relatively close association he never trusted her and was always trying to surprise in her open, Midwestern face the genuine, cunningly hidden, and hideous motivation. In later years, particularly when it began to be clear that this "education" of mine was going to lead me to perdition, he became more explicit and warned me that my white friends in high school were not really my friends and that I would see, when I was older, how white people would do anything to keep a Negro down. Some of them could be nice, he admitted, but none of them were to be trusted and most of them were not even nice. The best thing was to have as little to do with them as possible. I did not feel this way and I was certain, in my innocence, that I never would.

But the year which preceded my father's death had made a great change in my life. I had been living in New Jersey, working in defense plants, working and living among southerners, white and black. I knew about the south, of course, and about how southerners treated Negroes and how they expected them to behave, but it had never entered my mind that anyone would look at me and expect *me* to behave that way. I learned in New Jersey that to be a Negro meant, precisely, that one was never looked at but was simply at the mercy of the reflexes the color of one's skin caused in other people. I acted in New Jersey as I had always acted, that is as though I thought a great deal of myself — I had to *act* that way — with results that were, simply, unbelievable. I had scarcely arrived before I had earned the enmity, which was extraordinarily ingenious, of all my superiors and nearly all my co-workers. In the beginning, to make matters worse, I simply did not know what was happening. I did not know what I had done, and I shortly began to wonder what *anyone* could possibly do, to bring about such unanimous, active, and unbearably vocal hostility. I knew about jim-crow[4] but I had never experienced it. I went to the same self-service restaurant three times and stood with all the Princeton boys before the counter, waiting for a hamburger and coffee; it was always an extraordinarily long time before anything was set before me; but it was not until the fourth visit that I learned that, in fact, nothing had ever been set before me: I had simply picked something up. Negroes were not served there, I was told, and they had been waiting for me to realize that I was always the only Negro present. Once I was told this, I determined to go there all the time. But now they were ready for me and, though some dreadful scenes were subsequently enacted in that restaurant, I never ate there again.

It was the same story all over New Jersey, in bars, bowling alleys, diners, places to live. I was always being forced to leave, silently, or with mutual imprecations. I very shortly became notorious and children giggled behind me when I passed and their elders whispered or shouted — they really believed that I was mad. And it did begin to work on my mind, of course; I began to be afraid to go anywhere and to compensate for this I went places to which I really should not have gone and where, God knows, I had no

---

4. **jim-crow:** Jim Crow laws, discriminatory state and local laws enacted after the end of Reconstruction in 1876, mandated segregated schools and public accommodations throughout the South. The name *jim-crow* is derived from a derogatory song about African Americans, "Jump Jim Crow," which dates from about 1828.

desire to be. My reputation in town naturally enhanced my reputation at work and my working day became one long series of acrobatics designed to keep me out of trouble. I cannot say that these acrobatics succeeded. It began to seem that the machinery of the organization I worked for was turning over, day and night, with but one aim: to eject me. I was fired once, and contrived, with the aid of a friend from New York, to get back on the payroll; was fired again, and bounced back again. It took a while to fire me for the third time, but the third time took. There were no loopholes anywhere. There was not even any way of getting back inside the gates.

That year in New Jersey lives in my mind as though it were the year during which, having an unsuspected predilection for it, I first contracted some dread, chronic disease, the unfailing symptom of which is a kind of blind fever, a pounding in the skull and fire in the bowels. Once this disease is contracted, one can never be really carefree again, for the fever, without an instant's warning, can recur at any moment. It can wreck more important things than race relations. There is not a Negro alive who does not have this rage in his blood — one has the choice, merely, of living with it consciously or surrendering to it. As for me, this fever has recurred in me, and does, and will until the day I die.

My last night in New Jersey, a white friend from New York took me to the nearest big town, Trenton, to go to the movies and have a few drinks. As it turned out, he also saved me from, at the very least, a violent whipping. Almost every detail of that night stands out very clearly in my memory. I even remember the name of the movie we saw because its title impressed me as being so patly ironical. It was a movie about the German occupation of France, starring Maureen O'Hara and Charles Laughton and called *This Land Is Mine*. I remember the name of the diner we walked into when the movie ended: it was the "American Diner." When we walked in the counterman asked what we wanted and I remember answering with the casual sharpness which had become my habit: "We want a hamburger and a cup of coffee, what do you think we want?" I do not know why, after a year of such rebuffs, I so completely failed to anticipate his answer, which was, of course, "We don't serve Negroes here." This reply failed to discompose me, at least for the moment. I made some sardonic comment about the name of the diner and we walked out into the streets.

This was the time of what was called the "brown-out," when the lights in all American cities were very dim. When we re-entered the streets something happened to me which had the force of an optical illusion, or a nightmare. The streets were very crowded and I was facing north. People were moving in every direction but it seemed to me, in that instant, that all of the people I could see, and many more than that, were moving toward me, against me, and that everyone was white. I remember how their faces gleamed. And I felt, like a physical sensation, a *click* at the nape of my neck as though some interior string connecting my head to my body had been cut. I began to walk. I heard my friend call after me, but I ignored him. Heaven only knows what was going on in his mind, but he had the good sense not to touch me — I don't know what would have happened if he had — and to keep me in sight. I don't know what was going on in my mind, either; I certainly had no conscious plan. I wanted to do something to crush these white faces, which were crushing me. I walked for perhaps a block or two until I came to an enormous, glittering, and fashionable restaurant in which I knew not even the intercession of the Virgin would cause me to be served. I pushed through the doors and took the first vacant seat I saw, at a table for two, and waited.

I do not know how long I waited and I rather wonder, until today, what I could possibly have looked like. Whatever I looked like, I frightened the waitress who shortly appeared, and the moment she appeared all of my fury flowed toward her. I hated her for her white face, and for her great, astounded, frightened eyes. I felt that if she found a black man so frightening I would make her fright worthwhile.

She did not ask me what I wanted, but repeated, as though she had learned it somewhere, "We don't serve Negroes here." She did not say it with the blunt, derisive hostility to which I had grown so accustomed, but, rather, with a note of apology in her voice, and fear. This made me colder and more murderous than ever. I felt I had to do something with my hands. I wanted her to come close enough for me to get her neck between my hands.

So I pretended not to have understood her, hoping to draw her closer. And she did step a very short step closer, with her pencil poised incongruously over her pad, and repeated the formula: ". . . don't serve Negroes here."

Somehow, with the repetition of that phrase, which was already ringing in my head like a thousand bells of a nightmare, I realized that she would never come any closer and that I would have to strike from a distance. There was nothing on the table but an ordinary water-mug half full of water, and I picked this up and hurled it with all my strength at her. She ducked and it missed her and shattered against the mirror behind the bar. And, with that sound, my frozen blood abruptly thawed, I returned from wherever I had been, I *saw*, for the first time, the restaurant, the people with their mouths open, already, as it seemed to me, rising as one man, and I realized what I had done, and where I was, and I was frightened. I rose and began running for the door. A round, potbellied man grabbed me by the nape of the neck just as I reached the doors and began to beat me about the face. I kicked him and got loose and ran into the streets. My friend whispered, *"Run!"* and I ran.

My friend stayed outside the restaurant long enough to misdirect my pursuers and the police, who arrived, he told me, at once. I do not know what I said to him when he came to my room that night. I could not have said much. I felt, in the oddest, most awful way, that I had somehow betrayed him. I lived it over and over and over again, the way one relives an automobile accident after it has happened and one finds oneself alone and safe. I could not get over two facts, both equally difficult for the imagination to grasp, and one was that I could have been murdered. But the other was that I had been ready to commit murder. I saw nothing very clearly but I did see this: that my life, my *real* life, was in danger, and not from anything other people might do but from the hatred I carried in my own heart.

II

I had returned home around the second week in June — in great haste because it seemed that my father's death and my mother's confinement were both but a matter of hours. In the case of my mother, it soon became clear that she had simply made a miscalculation. This had always been her tendency and I don't believe that a single one of us arrived in the world, or has since arrived anywhere else, on time. But none of us dawdled so intolerably about the business of being born as did my baby sister. We sometimes amused ourselves, during those endless, stifling weeks, by picturing the baby sitting within in the safe, warm dark, bitterly regretting the necessity of becoming a part of our chaos and stubbornly putting it off as long as possible. I understood her perfectly and congratulated her on showing such good sense so soon. Death, however, sat as purposefully at my father's bedside as life stirred within my mother's womb and it was harder to understand why he so lingered in that long shadow. It seemed that he had bent, and for a long time, too, all of his energies toward dying. Now death was ready for him but my father held back.

All of Harlem, indeed, seemed to be infected by waiting. I had never before known it to be so violently still. Racial tensions throughout this country were exacerbated during the early years of the war, partly because the labor market brought together hundreds of thousands of ill-prepared people and partly because Negro soldiers, regardless of where they were born, received their military training in the south. What happened in defense plants and army camps had repercussions, naturally, in every Negro ghetto. The situation in Harlem had grown bad enough for clergymen, policemen, educators, politicians, and social workers to assert in one breath that there was no "crime wave" and to offer, in the very next breath, suggestions as to how to combat it. These suggestions always seemed to involve playgrounds, despite the fact that racial skirmishes were occurring in the playgrounds, too. Playground or not, crime wave or not, the Harlem police force had been augmented in March, and the unrest grew — perhaps, in fact, partly as a result of the ghetto's instinctive hatred of policemen. Perhaps the most revealing news item, out of the steady parade of reports of muggings, stabbings, shootings, assaults, gang wars, and accusations of police brutality, is the item concerning six Negro girls who set upon a white girl in the subway because, as they all too accurately put it, she was stepping on their toes. Indeed she was, all over the nation.

I had never before been so aware of policemen, on foot, on horseback, on corners, everywhere, always two by two. Nor had I ever been so aware of small knots of people. They were on stoops and on corners and in doorways, and what was striking about them, I think, was that they did not seem to be talking. Never, when I passed these groups, did the usual sound of a curse or a laugh ring out and neither did there seem to be any hum of gossip. There was certainly, on the other hand, occurring between them communication extraordinarily intense. Another thing that was striking was the unexpected diversity of the people who made up these groups. Usually, for example, one would see a group of sharpies standing on the street corner, jiving the passing chicks; or a group of older men, usually, for some reason, in the vicinity of a barber shop, discussing baseball scores, or the numbers, or making rather chilling observations about women they had known. Women, in a general way, tended to be seen less often together — unless they were church women, or very young girls, or prostitutes met together for an unprofessional instant. But that summer I saw the strangest combinations: large, respectable, churchly matrons standing on the stoops or the corners with their hair tied up, together with a girl in sleazy satin whose face bore the marks of gin and the razor, or heavy-set, abrupt, no-nonsense older men, in company with the most disreputable and fanatical "race" men, or these same "race" men with the sharpies, or these sharpies with the churchly women. Seventh Day Adventists and Methodists and Spiritualists seemed to be hobnobbing with Holyrollers and they were all, alike, entangled with the most fla-grant disbelievers; something heavy in their stance seemed to indicate that they had all, incredibly, seen a common vision, and on each face there seemed to be the same strange, bitter shadow.

The churchly women and the matter-of-fact, no-nonsense men had children in the Army. The sleazy girls they talked to had lovers there, the sharpies and the "race" men had friends and brothers there. It would have demanded an unquestioning patriotism, happily as uncommon in this country as it is undesirable, for these people not to have been disturbed by the bitter letters they received, by the newspaper stories they read, not to have been enraged by the posters, then to be found all over New York, which described the Japanese as "yellow-bellied Japs." It was only the "race" men, to be sure, who spoke ceaselessly of being revenged – how this vengeance was to be exacted was not clear – for the indignities and dangers suffered by Negro boys in uniform; but everybody felt a directionless, hopeless bitterness, as well as that panic which can scarcely be suppressed when one knows that a human being one loves is beyond one's reach, and in danger. This helplessness and this gnawing uneasiness does something, at length, to even the toughest mind. Perhaps the best way to sum all this up is to say that the people I knew felt, mainly, a peculiar kind of relief when they knew that their boys were being shipped out of the south, to do battle overseas. It was, perhaps, like feel-ing that the most dangerous part of a dangerous journey had been passed and that now, even if death should come, it would come with honor and without the complicity of their countrymen. Such a death would be, in short, a fact with which one could hope to live.

It was on the 28th of July, which I believe was a Wednesday, that I visited my father for the first time during his illness and for the last time in his life. The moment I saw him I knew why I had put off this visit so long. I had told my mother that I did not want to see him because I hated him. But this was not true. It was only that I *had* hated him and I wanted to hold on to this hatred. I did not want to look on him as a ruin: it was not a ruin I had hated. I imagine that one of the reasons people cling to their hates so stub-bornly is because they sense, once hate is gone, that they will be forced to deal with pain.

We traveled out to him, his older sister and myself, to what seemed to be the very end of a very Long Island. It was hot and dusty and we wrangled, my aunt and I, all the way out, over the fact that I had recently begun to smoke and, as she said, to give myself airs. But I knew that she wrangled with me because she could not bear to face the fact of her brother's dying. Neither could I endure the reality of her despair, her unstated baffle-ment as to what had happened to her brother's life, and her own. So we wrangled and I smoked and from time to time she fell into a heavy reverie. Covertly, I watched her face, which was the face of an old woman; it had fallen in, the eyes were sunken and lightless; soon she would be dying, too.

In my childhood – it had not been so long ago – I had thought her beautiful. She had been quick-witted and quick-moving and very generous with all the children and each of her visits had been an event. At one time one of my brothers and myself had thought of running away to live with her. Now she could no longer produce out of her handbag some unexpected and yet familiar delight. She made me feel pity and revulsion and fear. It was awful to realize that she no longer caused me to feel affection. The closer we came to the hospital the more querulous she became and at the same time, naturally, grew more dependent on me. Between pity and guilt and fear I began to feel that there was another me trapped in my skull like a jack-in-the-box who might escape my control at any moment and fill the air with screaming.

She began to cry the moment we entered the room and she saw him lying there, all shriveled and still, like a little black monkey. The great, gleaming apparatus which fed him and would have compelled him to be still even if he had been able to move brought to mind, not beneficence, but torture; the tubes entering his arm made me think of pictures I had seen when a child, of Gulliver, tied down by the pygmies on that island.[5] My aunt wept and wept, there was a whistling sound in my father's throat; nothing was said; he could not speak. I wanted to take his hand, to say something. But I do not know what I could have said, even if he could have heard me. He was not really in that room with us, he had at last really embarked on his journey; and though my aunt told me that he said he was going to meet Jesus, I did not hear anything except that whistling in his throat. The doctor came back and we left, into that unbearable train again, and home. In the morning came the telegram saying that he was dead. Then the house was suddenly full of relatives, friends, hysteria, and confusion and I quickly left my mother and the children to the care of those impressive women, who, in Negro communities at least, automatically appear at times of bereavement armed with lotions, proverbs, and patience, and an ability to cook. I went downtown. By the time I returned, later the same day, my mother had been carried to the hospital and the baby had been born.

III

For my father's funeral I had nothing black to wear and this posed a nagging problem all day long. It was one of those problems, simple, or impossible of solution, to which the mind insanely clings in order to avoid the mind's real trouble. I spent most of that day at the downtown apartment of a girl I knew, celebrating my birthday with whiskey and wondering what to wear that night. When planning a birthday celebration one naturally does not expect that it will be up against competition from a funeral and this girl had anticipated taking me out that night, for a big dinner and a night club afterwards. Sometime during the course of that long day we decided that we would go out anyway, when my father's funeral service was over. I imagine I decided it, since, as the funeral hour approached, it became clearer and clearer to me that I would not know what to do with myself when it was over. The girl, stifling her very lively concern as to the possible

---

5. **Gulliver . . . on that island:** In the first part of *Gulliver's Travels* by the English satirist Jonathan Swift (1667–1745), Lemuel Gulliver is shipwrecked and marooned on Lilliput, an island inhabited by people only six inches tall.

effects of the whiskey on one of my father's chief mourners, concentrated on being conciliatory and practically helpful. She found a black shirt for me somewhere and ironed it
and, dressed in the darkest pants and jacket I owned, and slightly drunk, I made my way
to my father's funeral.

The chapel was full, but not packed, and very quiet. There were, mainly, my father's
relatives, and his children, and here and there I saw faces I had not seen since childhood, the faces of my father's one-time friends. They were very dark and solemn now,
seeming somehow to suggest that they had known all along that something like this
would happen. Chief among the mourners was my aunt, who had quarreled with my
father all his life; by which I do not mean to suggest that her mourning was insincere or
that she had not loved him. I suppose that she was one of the few people in the world
who had, and their incessant quarreling proved precisely the strength of the tie that
bound them. The only other person in the world, as far as I knew, whose relationship to
my father rivaled my aunt's in depth was my mother, who was not there.

It seemed to me, of course, that it was a very long funeral. But it was, if anything, a
rather shorter funeral than most, nor, since there were no overwhelming, uncontrol-
lable expressions of grief, could it be called – if I dare to use the word – successful. The
minister who preached my father's funeral sermon was one of the few my father had
still been seeing as he neared his end. He presented to us in his sermon a man whom
none of us had ever seen – a man thoughtful, patient, and forbearing, a Christian inspiration to all who knew him, and a model for his children. And no doubt the children, in
their disturbed and guilty state, were almost ready to believe this; he had been remote
enough to be anything and, anyway, the shock of the incontrovertible, that it was really
our father lying up there in that casket, prepared the mind for anything. His sister
moaned and this grief-stricken moaning was taken as corroboration. The other faces
held a dark, non-committal thoughtfulness. This was not the man they had known, but
they had scarcely expected to be confronted with *him;* this was, in a sense deeper than
questions of fact, the man they had not known, and the man they had not known may
have been the real one. The real man, whoever he had been, had suffered and now he was
dead: this was all that was sure and all that mattered now. Every man in the chapel
hoped that when his hour came he, too, would be eulogized, which is to say forgiven, and
that all of his lapses, greeds, errors, and strayings from the truth would be invested with
coherence and looked upon with charity. This was perhaps the last thing human beings
could give each other and it was what they demanded, after all, of the Lord. Only the
Lord saw the midnight tears, only He was present when one of His children, moaning
and wringing hands, paced up and down the room. When one slapped one's child in
anger the recoil in the heart reverberated through heaven and became part of the pain
of the universe. And when the children were hungry and sullen and distrustful and one
watched them, daily, growing wilder, and further away, and running headlong into danger, it was the Lord who knew what the charged heart endured as the strap was laid to
the backside; the Lord alone who knew what one *would* have said if one had had, like the
Lord, the gift of the living word. It was the Lord who knew of the impossibility every parent in that room faced: how to prepare the child for the day when the child would be
despised and how to *create* in the child – by what means? – a stronger antidote to this

poison than one had found for oneself. The avenues, side streets, bars, billiard halls, hospitals, police stations, and even the playgrounds of Harlem – not to mention the houses of correction, the jails, and the morgue – testified to the potency of the poison while remaining silent as to the efficacy of whatever antidote, irresistibly raising the question of whether or not such an antidote existed; raising, which was worse, the question of whether or not an antidote was desirable; perhaps poison should be fought with poison. With these several schisms in the mind and with more terrors in the heart than could be named, it was better not to judge the man who had gone down under an impossible burden. It was better to remember: *Thou knowest this man's fall; but thou knowest not his wrassling.*

While the preacher talked and I watched the children – years of changing their diapers, scrubbing them, slapping them, taking them to school, and scolding them had had the perhaps inevitable result of making me love them, though I am not sure I knew this then – my mind was busily breaking out with a rash of disconnected impressions. Snatches of popular songs, indecent jokes, bits of books I had read, movie sequences, faces, voices, political issues – I thought I was going mad; all these impressions suspended, as it were, in the solution of the faint nausea produced in me by the heat and liquor. For a moment I had the impression that my alcoholic breath, inefficiently disguised with chewing gum, filled the entire chapel. Then someone began singing one of my father's favorite songs and, abruptly, I was with him, sitting on his knee, in the hot, enormous, crowded church which was the first church we attended. It was the Abyssinian Baptist Church on 138th Street. We had not gone there long. With this image, a host of others came. I had forgotten, in the rage of my growing up, how proud my father had been of me when I was little. Apparently, I had had a voice and my father had liked to show me off before the members of the church. I had forgotten what he had looked like when he was pleased but now I remembered that he had always been grinning with pleasure when my solos ended. I even remembered certain expressions on his face when he teased my mother – had he loved her? I would never know. And when had it all begun to change? For now it seemed that he had not always been cruel. I remembered being taken for a haircut and scraping my knee on the footrest of the barber's chair and I remembered my father's face as he soothed my crying and applied the stinging iodine. Then I remembered our fights, fights which had been of the worst possible kind because my technique had been silence.

I remembered the one time in all our life together when we had really spoken to each other.

It was on a Sunday and it must have been shortly before I left home. We were walking, just the two of us, in our usual silence, to or from church. I was in high school and had been doing a lot of writing and I was, at about this time, the editor of the high school magazine. But I had also been a Young Minister and had been preaching from the pulpit. Lately, I had been taking fewer engagements and preached as rarely as possible. It was said in the church, quite truthfully, that I was "cooling off."

My father asked me abruptly, "You'd rather write than preach, wouldn't you?"

I was astonished at his question – because it was a real question. I answered, "Yes."

That was all we said. It was awful to remember that that was all we had *ever* said.

The casket now was opened and the mourners were being led up the aisle to look for the last time on the deceased. The assumption was that the family was too overcome with grief to be allowed to make this journey alone and I watched while my aunt was led to the casket and, muffled in black, and shaking, led back to her seat. I disapproved of forcing the children to look on their dead father, considering that the shock of his death, or, more truthfully, the shock of death as a reality, was already a little more than a child could bear, but my judgment in this matter had been overruled and there they were, bewildered and frightened and very small, being led, one by one, to the casket. But there is also something very gallant about children at such moments. It has something to do with their silence and gravity and with the fact that one cannot help them. Their legs, somehow, seem *exposed*, so that it is at once incredible and terribly clear that their legs are all they have to hold them up.

I had not wanted to go to the casket myself and I certainly had not wished to be led there, but there was no way of avoiding either of these forms. One of the deacons led me up and I looked on my father's face. I cannot say that it looked like him at all. His blackness had been equivocated by powder and there was no suggestion in that casket of what his power had or could have been. He was simply an old man dead, and it was hard to believe that he had ever given anyone either joy or pain. Yet, his life filled that room. Further up the avenue his wife was holding his newborn child. Life and death so close together, and love and hatred, and right and wrong, said something to me which I did not want to hear concerning man, concerning the life of man.

After the funeral, while I was downtown desperately celebrating my birthday, a Negro soldier, in the lobby of the Hotel Braddock, got into a fight with a white policeman over a Negro girl. Negro girls, white policemen, in or out of uniform, and Negro males — in or out of uniform — were part of the furniture of the lobby of the Hotel Braddock and this was certainly not the first time such an incident had occurred. It was destined, however, to receive an unprecedented publicity, for the fight between the policeman and the soldier ended with the shooting of the soldier. Rumor, flowing immediately to the streets outside, stated that the soldier had been shot in the back, an instantaneous and revealing invention, and that the soldier had died protecting a Negro woman. The facts were somewhat different — for example, the soldier had not been shot in the back, and was not dead, and the girl seems to have been as dubious a symbol of womanhood as her white counterpart in Georgia usually is, but no one was interested in the facts. They preferred the invention because this invention expressed and corroborated their hates and fears so perfectly. It is just as well to remember that people are always doing this. Perhaps many of those legends, including Christianity, to which the world clings began their conquest of the world with just some such concerted surrender to distortion. The effect, in Harlem, of this particular legend was like the effect of a lit match in a tin of gasoline. The mob gathered before the doors of the Hotel Braddock simply began to swell and to spread in every direction, and Harlem exploded.

The mob did not cross the ghetto lines. It would have been easy, for example, to have gone over Morningside Park on the west side or to have crossed the Grand Central railroad tracks at 125th Street on the east side, to wreak havoc in white neighborhoods. The mob seems to have been mainly interested in something more potent and real than the white face, that is, in white power, and the principal damage done during the riot of the summer of 1943 was to white business establishments in Harlem. It might have been a far bloodier story, of course, if, at the hour the riot began, these establishments had still been open. From the Hotel Braddock the mob fanned out, east and west along 125th Street, and for the entire length of Lenox, Seventh, and Eighth avenues. Along each of these avenues, and along each major side street — 116th, 125th, 135th, and so on — bars, stores, pawnshops, restaurants, even little luncheonettes had been smashed open and entered and looted — looted, it might be added, with more haste than efficiency. The shelves really looked as though a bomb had struck them. Cans of beans and soup and dog food, along with toilet paper, corn flakes, sardines, and milk tumbled every which way, and abandoned cash registers and cases of beer leaned crazily out of the splintered windows and were strewn along the avenues. Sheets, blankets, and clothing of every description formed a kind of path, as though people had dropped them while running. I truly had not realized that Harlem *had* so many stores until I saw them all smashed open; the first time the word *wealth* ever entered my mind in relation to Harlem was when I saw it scattered in the streets. But one's first, incongruous impression of plenty was countered immediately by an impression of waste. None of this was doing anybody any good. It would have been better to have left the plate glass as it had been and the goods lying in the stores.

It would have been better, but it would also have been intolerable, for Harlem had needed something to smash. To smash something is the ghetto's chronic need. Most of the time it is the members of the ghetto who smash each other, and themselves. But as long as the ghetto walls are standing there will always come a moment when these outlets do not work. That summer, for example, it was not enough to get into a fight on Lenox Avenue, or curse out one's cronies in the barber shops. If ever, indeed, the violence which fills Harlem's churches, pool halls, and bars erupts outward in a more direct fashion, Harlem and its citizens are likely to vanish in an apocalyptic flood. That this is not likely to happen is due to a great many reasons, most hidden and powerful among them the Negro's real relation to the white American. This relation prohibits, simply, anything as uncomplicated and satisfactory as pure hatred. In order really to hate white people, one has to blot so much out of the mind — and the heart — that this hatred itself becomes an exhausting and self-destructive pose. But this does not mean, on the other hand, that love comes easily: the white world is too powerful, too complacent, too ready with gratuitous humiliation, and, above all, too ignorant and too innocent for that. One is absolutely forced to make perpetual qualifications and one's own reactions are always canceling each other out. It is this, really, which has driven so many people mad, both white and black. One is always in the position of having to decide between amputation and gangrene. Amputation is swift but time may prove that the amputation was not necessary — or one may delay the amputation too long. Gangrene is slow, but it is impossible to be sure that one is reading one's symptoms right. The idea of going through life as a cripple is more than one can bear, and equally unbearable is the risk of swelling up slowly, in agony, with poison. And the trouble, finally, is that the risks are real even if the choices do not exist.

"But as for me and my house," my father had said, "we will serve the Lord." I wondered, as we drove him to his resting place, what this line had meant for him. I had heard him preach it many times. I had preached it once myself, proudly giving it an interpretation different from my father's. Now the whole thing came back to me, as though my father and I were on our way to Sunday school and I were memorizing the golden text: *And if it seem evil unto you to serve the Lord, choose you this day whom you will serve; whether the gods which your fathers served that were on the other side of the flood, or the gods of the Amorites, in whose land ye dwell: but as for me and my house, we will serve the Lord.*[6] I suspected in these familiar lines a meaning which had never been there for me before. All of my father's texts and songs, which I had decided were meaningless, were arranged before me at his death like empty bottles, waiting to hold the meaning which life would give them for me. This was his legacy: nothing is ever escaped. That bleakly memorable morning I hated the unbelievable streets and the Negroes and whites who had, equally, made them that way. But I knew that it was folly, as my father would have said, this bitterness was folly. It was necessary to hold on to the things that mattered. The dead man mattered, the new life mattered; blackness and whiteness did not matter; to believe that they did was to acquiesce in one's own destruction. Hatred, which could destroy so much, never failed to destroy the man who hated and this was an immutable law.

It began to seem that one would have to hold in the mind forever two ideas which seemed to be in opposition. The first idea was acceptance, the acceptance, totally without rancor, of life as it is, and men as they are: in the light of this idea, it goes without saying that injustice is a commonplace. But this did not mean that one could be complacent, for the second idea was of equal power: that one must never, in one's own life, accept these injustices as commonplace but must fight them with all one's strength. This fight begins, however, in the heart and it now had been laid to my charge to keep my own heart free of hatred and despair. This intimation made my heart heavy and, now that my father was irrecoverable, I wished that he had been beside me so that I could have searched his face for the answers which only the future would give me now.

[1955]

---

6. *And . . . Lord:* Joshua 24:15.

Flannery O'Connor

[1925-1964]

Mary Flannery O'Connor was born on March 25, 1925, in Savannah, Georgia. She was the only child of Regina Cline O'Connor, the daughter of a prominent businessman, and Edward F. O'Connor, the owner of a real-estate company. Her prosperous parents were Roman Catholic, and O'Connor attended St. Vincent's Grammar School and the Sacred Heart School for Girls. In 1938, business reverses forced Edward O'Connor to move the family to Atlanta, where he took a job with the Federal Housing Administration.

Within the year, his wife took their daughter to live with relatives at her family home in Milledgeville, Georgia, where O'Connor's father commuted on the weekends from Atlanta. Since there was no Catholic school in Milledgeville, O'Connor attended Peabody Laboratory School, a progressive institution that permitted students wide latitude in their choice of courses. O'Connor took a number of courses in art and began drawing cartoons. Edward O'Connor was diagnosed with lupus erythematosus, an incurable autoimmune disease, and died in 1941. After her graduation from high school the following year, O'Connor enrolled at the Georgia State College for Women (now Georgia College and State University) in Milledgeville. Living at home with her mother and aunts, she studied art, English, and social studies, drawing cartoons for the school newspaper and yearbook, as well as contributing essays, poems, and stories

Flannery O'Connor

This photograph of O'Connor was taken at a book-signing party for her first novel, *Wise Blood* (1952), at her alma mater, the Georgia State College for Women.

to its literary magazine, the *Corinthian.* O'Connor graduated in 1945 and won a fellowship in journalism at the University of Iowa.

O'Connor soon turned from journalism to writing fiction. During her first semester at Iowa, she applied to the university's graduate program in creative writing, the Writers' Workshop. At her first meeting with its director, Paul Engle, he could not understand her thick southern accent, so he handed O'Connor a pad and asked her to jot down what she was saying. She famously wrote: "My name is Flannery O'Connor. I'm from Milledgeville, Georgia. I'm a writer." She was accepted into the program and published her first short story, "The Geranium," in *Accent* in 1946. She completed her master's thesis, a collection of short stories, and was awarded an MFA in 1947. She stayed on as a teaching assistant at the university for another year, working on a novel for which she won the Rinehart-Iowa Fiction Award. Following a residency at the Yaddo Artist's Colony in Saratoga Springs, New York, she moved to New York City in early 1949. Uncomfortable with life in the city, O'Connor soon accepted an invitation from two literary Catholic friends, Robert and Sally Fitzgerald, to move into the garage apartment at their home in Ridgefield, Connecticut. She lived there happily for almost two years, during which her work began to appear in the *Partisan Review* and the *Sewanee Review.* During a holiday visit to her family in December 1950, she became ill and was diagnosed with lupus, the same disease that killed her father. Unable to return to Connecticut, she spent some time in an Atlanta hospital before moving to Andalusia, the family farm outside Milledgeville, where she lived with her mother for the rest of her life.

Despite her illness and the debilitating effects of the drugs she had to take, O'Connor tenaciously pursued her literary career. She adhered to a strict schedule in which she wrote for three hours every morning. She also maintained a correspondence with a large number of literary friends, entertained visitors, and began raising peacocks, all of which helped ease her isolation. She completed her first novel, *Wise Blood* (1952), the grotesquely comic and satirical story of a preacher who establishes the "Church without Christ," and wrote the stories collected in *A Good Man Is Hard to Find and Other Stories* (1955). The reception of both volumes was generally positive, but reviewers struggled to characterize O'Connor's unusual work, which was often pigeonholed as southern gothic. In a perceptive essay in the *Saturday Review of Literature*, however, the Catholic writer Caroline Gordon observed:

> Miss O'Connor, for all her apparent preoccupation with the visible scene, is also fiercely concerned with moral, even theological, problems. In these stories the rural South is, for the first time, viewed by a writer whose orthodoxy matches her talent. The results are revolutionary.

O'Connor's religious orthodoxy was further revealed in her second novel, *The Violent Bear It Away* (1960), a quasi-allegorical account of the struggle between Christianity and secularism that explores "the consequences of man's refusal to see things as they really are and act accordingly," as a reviewer asserted in the *Catholic World*. O'Connor also continued to write short stories, including "Everything That Rises Must Converge," which won first prize in the O'Henry Awards for the best American short stories of 1963. But she was increasingly ill and died of complications of lupus on August 3, 1964, before the publication of her second collection of stories, *Everything That Rises Must Converge* (1965). Her reputation was further enhanced by the posthumous publication of a collection of her essays on the craft of writing, *Mystery and Manners* (1969), and *The Complete Stories of Flannery O'Connor* (1972), which won the National Book Award.

She was for me the first great modern writer from the South.

–Alice Walker

O'Connor's "A Good Man Is Hard to Find." After her early death, O'Connor was increasingly recognized for her distinctive contributions to American literature and her mastery of the short story. One of her most famous and frequently anthologized stories is "A Good Man Is Hard to Find," which she wrote in the early 1950s, while living at her family home in Milledgeville, Georgia. In June 1953, she wrote to friends that she had sold this story to the *Partisan Review* reader, "another of those 50¢ jobs." The collection, which actually sold for thirty-five cents a copy, was the *Avon Book of Modern Writing*, a new paperback series designed to showcase first-rate writers and edited by William Phillips and Philip Rahv, the editors of the *Partisan Review*. O'Connor used the story as the title piece for her first collection, *A Good Man Is Hard to Find and Other Stories* (1955). When O'Connor read the story to a group of friends, including the eminent literary critic Van Wyck Brooks, he observed that "it was a shame

bedfordstmartins.com/
americanlit for research
links on O'Connor

someone with so much talent should look upon life as a horror story." In fact, O'Connor's theological worldview was far more complex, as is "A Good Man Is Hard to Find," with its memorable cast of flawed characters, its combination of grotesque humor and violent action, its blend of local realism and Christian symbolism, and its postmodern emphasis on the misreading of signs in a world of deceptive appearances. The text is taken from *A Good Man Is Hard to Find and Other Stories* (1955).

A GOOD MAN IS HARD TO FIND[1]

The grandmother didn't want to go to Florida. She wanted to visit some of her connections in east Tennessee and she was seizing at every chance to change Bailey's mind. Bailey was the son she lived with, her only boy. He was sitting on the edge of his chair at the table, bent over the orange sports section of the *Journal.* "Now look here, Bailey," she said, "see here, read this," and she stood with one hand on her thin hip and the other rattling the newspaper at his bald head. "Here this fellow that calls himself The Misfit is aloose from the Federal Pen and headed toward Florida and you read here what it says he did to these people. Just you read it. I wouldn't take my children in any direction with a criminal like that aloose in it. I couldn't answer to my conscience if I did."

Bailey didn't look up from his reading so she wheeled around then and faced the children's mother, a young woman in slacks, whose face was as broad and innocent as a cabbage and was tied around with a green head-kerchief that had two points on the top like rabbit's ears. She was sitting on the sofa, feeding the baby his apricots out of a jar. "The children have been to Florida before," the old lady said. "You all ought to take them somewhere else for a change so they would see different parts of the world and be broad. They never have been to east Tennessee."

The children's mother didn't seem to hear her but the eight-year-old boy, John Wesley, a stocky child with glasses, said, "If you don't want to go to Florida, why dontcha stay at home?" He and the little girl, June Star, were reading the funny papers on the floor.

"She wouldn't stay at home to be queen for a day," June Star said without raising her yellow head.

"Yes and what would you do if this fellow, The Misfit, caught you?" the grandmother asked.

"I'd smack his face," John Wesley said.

"She wouldn't stay at home for a million bucks," June Star said. "Afraid she'd miss something. She has to go everywhere we go."

"All right, Miss," the grandmother said. "Just remember that the next time you want me to curl your hair."

June Star said her hair was naturally curly.

The next morning the grandmother was the first one in the car, ready to go. She had her big black valise that looked like the head of a hippopotamus in one corner, and

---

1. **A Good Man Is Hard to Find:**   The title of a popular blues song composed by Eddie Green in 1918.

underneath it she was hiding a basket with Pitty Sing,[2] the cat, in it. She didn't intend for the cat to be left alone in the house for three days because he would miss her too much and she was afraid he might brush against one of the gas burners and accidentally asphyxiate himself. Her son, Bailey, didn't like to arrive at a motel with a cat.

She sat in the middle of the back seat with John Wesley and June Star on either side of her. Bailey and the children's mother and the baby sat in front and they left Atlanta at eight forty-five with the mileage on the car at 55890. The grandmother wrote this down because she thought it would be interesting to say how many miles they had been when they got back. It took them twenty minutes to reach the outskirts of the city.

The old lady settled herself comfortably, removing her white cotton gloves and putting them up with her purse on the shelf in front of the back window. The children's mother still had on slacks and still had her head tied up in a green kerchief, but the grandmother had on a navy blue straw sailor hat with a bunch of white violets on the brim and a navy blue dress with a small white dot in the print. Her collars and cuffs were white organdy trimmed with lace and at her neckline she had pinned a purple spray of cloth violets containing a sachet. In case of an accident, anyone seeing her dead on the highway would know at once that she was a lady.

She said she thought it was going to be a good day for driving, neither too hot nor too cold, and she cautioned Bailey that the speed limit was fifty-five miles an hour and that the patrolmen hid themselves behind billboards and small clumps of trees and sped out after you before you had a chance to slow down. She pointed out interesting details of the scenery: Stone Mountain; the blue granite that in some places came up to both sides of the highway; the brilliant red clay banks slightly streaked with purple; and the various crops that made rows of green lace-work on the ground. The trees were full of silver-white sunlight and the meanest of them sparkled. The children were reading comic magazines and their mother had gone back to sleep.

"Let's go through Georgia fast so we won't have to look at it much," John Wesley said.

"If I were a little boy," said the grandmother, "I wouldn't talk about my native state that way. Tennessee has the mountains and Georgia has the hills."

"Tennessee is just a hillbilly dumping ground," John Wesley said, "and Georgia is a lousy state too."

"You said it," June Star said.

"In my time," said the grandmother, folding her thin veined fingers, "children were more respectful of their native states and their parents and everything else. People did right then. Oh look at the cute little pickaninny!"[3] she said and pointed to a Negro child standing in the door of a shack. "Wouldn't that make a picture, now?" she asked and they all turned and looked at the little Negro out of the back window. He waved.

"He didn't have any britches on," June Star said.

---

2. **Pitty Sing:** One of the three little maids involved in the complicated romantic plot of *The Mikado* (1885), a popular comic opera by the English composers Gilbert and Sullivan.
3. **pickaninny:** Probably derived from the Spanish word *pequeño*, meaning small or little, this now-offensive term was commonly used from the mid-nineteenth century until the 1930s to refer to African American children.

"He probably didn't have any," the grandmother explained. "Little niggers in the country don't have things like we do. If I could paint, I'd paint that picture," she said.

The children exchanged comic books.

The grandmother offered to hold the baby and the children's mother passed him over the front seat to her. She set him on her knee and bounced him and told him about the things they were passing. She rolled her eyes and screwed up her mouth and stuck her leathery thin face into his smooth bland one. Occasionally he gave her a far-away smile. They passed a large cotton field with five or six graves fenced in the middle of it, like a small island. "Look at the graveyard!" the grandmother said, pointing it out. "That was the old family burying ground. That belonged to the plantation."

"Where's the plantation?" John Wesley asked.

"Gone With the Wind,"[4] said the grandmother. "Ha. Ha."

When the children finished all the comic books they had brought, they opened the lunch and ate it. The grandmother ate a peanut butter sandwich and an olive and would not let the children throw the box and the paper napkins out the window. When there was nothing else to do they played a game by choosing a cloud and making the other two guess what shape it suggested. John Wesley took one the shape of a cow and June Star guessed a cow and John Wesley said, no, an automobile, and June Star said he didn't play fair, and they began to slap each other over the grandmother.

The grandmother said she would tell them a story if they would keep quiet. When she told a story, she rolled her eyes and waved her head and was very dramatic. She said once when she was a maiden lady she had been courted by a Mr. Edgar Atkins Teagarden from Jasper, Georgia. She said he was a very good-looking man and a gentleman and that he brought her a watermelon every Saturday afternoon with his initials cut in it, E. A. T. Well, one Saturday, she said, Mr. Teagarden brought the watermelon and there was nobody at home and he left it on the front porch and returned in his buggy to Jasper, but she never got the watermelon, she said, because a nigger boy ate it when he saw the initials, E. A. T.! This story tickled John Wesley's funny bone and he giggled and giggled but June Star didn't think it was any good. She said she wouldn't marry a man that just brought her a watermelon on Saturday. The grandmother said she would have done well to marry Mr. Teagarden because he was a gentleman and had bought Coca-Cola stock when it first came out and that he had died only a few years ago, a very wealthy man.

They stopped at The Tower for barbecued sandwiches. The Tower was a part stucco and part wood filling station and dance hall set in a clearing outside of Timothy. A fat man named Red Sammy Butts ran it and there were signs stuck here and there on the building and for miles up and down the highway saying, TRY RED SAMMY'S FAMOUS BARBECUE. NONE LIKE FAMOUS RED SAMMY'S! RED SAM! THE FAT BOY WITH THE HAPPY LAUGH. A VETERAN! RED SAMMY'S YOUR MAN!

Red Sammy was lying on the bare ground outside The Tower with his head under a truck while a gray monkey about a foot high, chained to a small chinaberry tree, chat-

---

4. **Gone With the Wind:** The title of Margaret Mitchell's best-selling 1936 novel about the Civil War and the passing of the Old South.

tered nearby. The monkey sprang back into the tree and got on the highest limb as soon as he saw the children jump out of the car and run toward him.

Inside, The Tower was a long dark room with a counter at one end and tables at the other and dancing space in the middle. They all sat down at a board table next to the nickelodeon and Red Sam's wife, a tall burnt-brown woman with hair and eyes lighter than her skin, came and took their order. The children's mother put a dime in the machine and played "The Tennessee Waltz," and the grandmother said that tune always made her want to dance. She asked Bailey if he would like to dance but he only glared at her. He didn't have a naturally sunny disposition like she did and trips made him nervous. The grandmother's brown eyes were very bright. She swayed her head from side to side and pretended she was dancing in her chair. June Star said play something she could tap to so the children's mother put in another dime and played a fast number and June Star stepped out onto the dance floor and did her tap routine.

"Ain't she cute?" Red Sam's wife said, leaning over the counter. "Would you like to come be my little girl?"

"No I certainly wouldn't," June Star said. "I wouldn't live in a broken-down place like this for a million bucks!" and she ran back to the table.

"Ain't she cute?" the woman repeated, stretching her mouth politely.

"Arn't you ashamed?" hissed the grandmother.

Red Sam came in and told his wife to quit lounging on the counter and hurry up with these people's order. His khaki trousers reached just to his hip bones and his stomach hung over them like a sack of meal swaying under his shirt. He came over and sat down at a table nearby and let out a combination sigh and yodel. "You can't win," he said. "You can't win," and he wiped his sweating red face off with a gray handkerchief. "These days you don't know who to trust," he said. "Ain't that the truth?"

"People are certainly not nice like they used to be," said the grandmother.

"Two fellers come in here last week," Red Sammy said, "driving a Chrysler. It was a old beat-up car but it was a good one and these boys looked all right to me. Said they worked at the mill and you know I let them fellers charge the gas they bought? Now why did I do that?"

"Because you're a good man!" the grandmother said at once.

"Yes'm, I suppose so," Red Sam said as if he were struck with this answer.

His wife brought the orders, carrying the five plates all at once without a tray, two in each hand and one balanced on her arm. "It isn't a soul in this green world of God's that you can trust," she said. "And I don't count nobody out of that, not nobody," she repeated, looking at Red Sammy.

"Did you read about that criminal, The Misfit, that's escaped?" asked the grandmother.

"I wouldn't be a bit surprised if he didn't attact this place right here," said the woman. "If he hears about it being here, I wouldn't be none surprised to see him. If he hears it's two cent in the cash register, I wouldn't be a tall surprised if he . . ."

"That'll do," Red Sam said. "Go bring these people their Co'-Colas," and the woman went off to get the rest of the order.

"A good man is hard to find," Red Sammy said. "Everything is getting terrible. I remember the day you could go off and leave your screen door unlatched. Not no more."

He and the grandmother discussed better times. The old lady said that in her opinion Europe was entirely to blame for the way things were now. She said the way Europe acted you would think we were made of money and Red Sam said it was no use talking about it, she was exactly right. The children ran outside into the white sunlight and looked at the monkey in the lacy chinaberry tree. He was busy catching fleas on himself and biting each one carefully between his teeth as if it were a delicacy.

They drove off again into the hot afternoon. The grandmother took cat naps and woke up every few minutes with her own snoring. Outside of Toombsboro she woke up and recalled an old plantation that she had visited in this neighborhood once when she was a young lady. She said the house had six white columns across the front and that there was an avenue of oaks leading up to it and two little wooden trellis arbors on either side in front where you sat down with your suitor after a stroll in the garden. She recalled exactly which road to turn off to get to it. She knew that Bailey would not be willing to lose any time looking at an old house, but the more she talked about it, the more she wanted to see it once again and find out if the little twin arbors were still standing. "There was a secret panel in this house," she said craftily, not telling the truth but wishing that she were, "and the story went that all the family silver was hidden in it when Sherman came through but it was never found . . ."[5]

"Hey!" John Wesley said. "Let's go see it! We'll find it! We'll poke all the woodwork and find it! Who lives there? Where do you turn off at? Hey Pop, can't we turn off there?"

"We never have seen a house with a secret panel!" June Star shrieked. "Let's go to the house with the secret panel! Hey Pop, can't we go see the house with the secret panel!"

"It's not far from here, I know," the grandmother said. "It wouldn't take over twenty minutes."

Bailey was looking straight ahead. His jaw was as rigid as a horseshoe. "No," he said.

The children began to yell and scream that they wanted to see the house with the secret panel. John Wesley kicked the back of the front seat and June Star hung over her mother's shoulder and whined desperately into her ear that they never had any fun even on their vacation, that they could never do what THEY wanted to do. The baby began to scream and John Wesley kicked the back of the seat so hard that his father could feel the blows in his kidney.

"All right!" he shouted and drew the car to a stop at the side of the road. "Will you all shut up? Will you all just shut up for one second? If you don't shut up, we won't go any-where."

"It would be very educational for them," the grandmother murmured.

"All right," Bailey said, "but get this: this is the only time we're going to stop for anything like this. This is the one and only time."

"The dirt road that you have to turn down is about a mile back," the grandmother directed. "I marked it when we passed."

---

5. **Sherman . . . never found:** The Union general William Tecumseh Sherman (1820–1891) led a destructive campaign through Tennessee, Georgia, and the Carolinas in 1864. Many families reportedly hid or buried their valuables to keep them from being plundered by Sherman's troops.

"A dirt road," Bailey groaned.

After they had turned around and were headed toward the dirt road, the grandmother recalled other points about the house, the beautiful glass over the front doorway and the candle-lamp in the hall. John Wesley said that the secret panel was probably in the fire-place.

"You can't go inside this house," Bailey said. "You don't know who lives there."

"While you all talk to the people in front, I'll run around behind and get in a window," John Wesley suggested.

"We'll all stay in the car," his mother said.

They turned onto the dirt road and the car raced roughly along in a swirl of pink dust. The grandmother recalled the times when there were no paved roads and thirty miles was a day's journey. The dirt road was hilly and there were sudden washes in it and sharp curves on dangerous embankments. All at once they would be on a hill, looking down over the blue tops of trees for miles around, then the next minute, they would be in a red depression with the dust-coated trees looking down on them.

"This place had better turn up in a minute," Bailey said, "or I'm going to turn around."

The road looked as if no one had traveled on it in months.

"It's not much farther," the grandmother said and just as she said it, a horrible thought came to her. The thought was so embarrassing that she turned red in the face and her eyes dilated and her feet jumped up, upsetting her valise in the corner. The instant the valise moved, the newspaper top she had over the basket under it rose with a snarl and Pitty Sing, the cat, sprang onto Bailey's shoulder.

The children were thrown to the floor and their mother, clutching the baby, was thrown out the door onto the ground; the old lady was thrown into the front seat. The car turned over once and landed right-side-up in a gulch off the side of the road. Bailey remained in the driver's seat with the cat — gray-striped with a broad white face and an orange nose — clinging to his neck like a caterpillar.

As soon as the children saw they could move their arms and legs, they scrambled out of the car, shouting, "We've had an ACCIDENT!" The grandmother was curled up under the dashboard, hoping she was injured so that Bailey's wrath would not come down on her all at once. The horrible thought she had had before the accident was that the house she had remembered so vividly was not in Georgia but in Tennessee.

Bailey removed the cat from his neck with both hands and flung it out the window against the side of a pine tree. Then he got out of the car and started looking for the children's mother. She was sitting against the side of the red gutted ditch, holding the screaming baby, but she only had a cut down her face and a broken shoulder. "We've had an ACCIDENT!" the children screamed in a frenzy of delight.

"But nobody's killed," June Star said with disappointment as the grandmother limped out of the car, her hat still pinned to her head but the broken front brim standing up at a jaunty angle and the violet spray hanging off the side. They all sat down in the ditch, except the children, to recover from the shock. They were all shaking.

"Maybe a car will come along," said the children's mother hoarsely.

"I believe I have injured an organ," said the grandmother, pressing her side, but no one answered her. Bailey's teeth were clattering. He had on a yellow sport shirt with bright blue parrots designed in it and his face was as yellow as the shirt. The grand-mother decided that she would not mention that the house was in Tennessee.

The road was about ten feet above and they could see only the tops of the trees on the other side of it. Behind the ditch they were sitting in there were more woods, tall and dark and deep. In a few minutes they saw a car some distance away on top of a hill, com-ing slowly as if the occupants were watching them. The grandmother stood up and waved both arms dramatically to attract their attention. The car continued to come on slowly, disappeared around a bend and appeared again, moving even slower, on top of the hill they had gone over. It was a big black battered hearse-like automobile. There were three men in it.

It came to a stop just over them and for some minutes, the driver looked down with a steady expressionless gaze to where they were sitting, and didn't speak. Then he turned his head and muttered something to the other two and they got out. One was a fat boy in black trousers and a red sweat shirt with a silver stallion embossed on the front of it. He moved around on the right side of them and stood staring, his mouth partly open in a kind of loose grin. The other had on khaki pants and a blue striped coat and a gray hat pulled down very low, hiding most of his face. He came around slowly on the left side. Neither spoke.

The driver got out of the car and stood by the side of it, looking down at them. He was an older man than the other two. His hair was just beginning to gray and he wore silver-rimmed spectacles that gave him a scholarly look. He had a long creased face and didn't have on any shirt or undershirt. He had on blue jeans that were too tight for him and was holding a black hat and a gun. The two boys also had guns.

"We've had an ACCIDENT!" the children screamed.

The grandmother had the peculiar feeling that the bespectacled man was someone she knew. His face was as familiar to her as if she had known him all her life but she could not recall who he was. He moved away from the car and began to come down the embankment, placing his feet carefully so that he wouldn't slip. He had on tan and white shoes and no socks, and his ankles were red and thin. "Good afternoon," he said. "I see you all had you a little spill."

"We turned over twice!" said the grandmother.

"Oncet," he corrected. "We seen it happen. Try their car and see will it run, Hiram," he said quietly to the boy with the gray hat.

"What you got that gun for?" John Wesley asked. "Whatcha gonna do with that gun?"

"Lady," the man said to the children's mother, "would you mind calling them children to sit down by you? Children make me nervous. I want all you all to sit down right together there where you're at."

"What are you telling US what to do for?" June Star asked.

Behind them the line of woods gaped like a dark open mouth. "Come here," said their mother.

"Look here now," Bailey began suddenly, "we're in a predicament! We're in . . ."

The grandmother shrieked. She scrambled to her feet and stood staring. "You're The Misfit!" she said. "I recognized you at once!"

"Yes'm," the man said, smiling slightly as if he were pleased in spite of himself to be known, "but it would have been better for all of you, lady, if you hadn't of recker-nized me."

Bailey turned his head sharply and said something to his mother that shocked even the children. The old lady began to cry and The Misfit reddened.

"Lady," he said, "don't you get upset. Sometimes a man says things he don't mean. I don't reckon he meant to talk to you thataway."

"You wouldn't shoot a lady, would you?" the grandmother said and removed a clean handkerchief from her cuff and began to slap at her eyes with it.

The Misfit pointed the toe of his shoe into the ground and made a little hole and then covered it up again. "I would hate to have to," he said.

"Listen," the grandmother almost screamed, "I know you're a good man. You don't look a bit like you have common blood. I know you must come from nice people!"

"Yes mam," he said, "finest people in the world." When he smiled he showed a row of strong white teeth. "God never made a finer woman than my mother and my daddy's heart was pure gold," he said. The boy with the red sweat shirt had come around behind them and was standing with his gun at his hip. The Misfit squatted down on the ground. "Watch them children, Bobby Lee," he said. "You know they make me nervous." He looked at the six of them huddled together in front of him and he seemed to be embar-rassed as if he couldn't think of anything to say. "Ain't a cloud in the sky," he remarked, looking up at it. "Don't see no sun but don't see no cloud neither."

"Yes, it's a beautiful day," said the grandmother. "Listen," she said, "you shouldn't call yourself The Misfit because I know you're a good man at heart. I can just look at you and tell."

"Hush!" Bailey yelled. "Hush! Everybody shut up and let me handle this!" He was squatting in the position of a runner about to sprint forward but he didn't move.

"I pre-chate that, lady," The Misfit said and drew a little circle in the ground with the butt of his gun.

"It'll take a half a hour to fix this here car," Hiram called, looking over the raised hood of it.

"Well, first you and Bobby Lee get him and that little boy to step over yonder with you," The Misfit said, pointing to Bailey and John Wesley. "The boys want to ast you some-thing," he said to Bailey. "Would you mind stepping back in them woods there with them?"

"Listen," Bailey began, "we're in a terrible predicament! Nobody realizes what this is," and his voice cracked. His eyes were as blue and intense as the parrots in his shirt and he remained perfectly still.

The grandmother reached up to adjust her hat brim as if she were going to the woods with him but it came off in her hand. She stood staring at it and after a second she let it fall on the ground. Hiram pulled Bailey up by the arm as if he were assisting an old man. John Wesley caught hold of his father's hand and Bobby Lee followed. They went off toward the woods and just as they reached the dark edge, Bailey turned and supporting himself against a gray naked pine trunk, he shouted, "I'll be back in a minute, Mamma, wait on me!"

"Come back this instant!" his mother shrilled but they all disappeared into the woods.

"Bailey Boy!" the grandmother called in a tragic voice but she found she was looking at The Misfit squatting on the ground in front of her. "I just know you're a good man," she said desperately. "You're not a bit common!"

"Nome, I ain't a good man," The Misfit said after a second as if he had considered her statement carefully, "but I ain't the worst in the world neither. My daddy said I was a different breed of dog from my brothers and sisters. 'You know,' Daddy said, 'it's some that can live their whole life out without asking about it and it's others has to know why it is, and this boy is one of the latters. He's going to be into everything!'" He put on his black hat and looked up suddenly and then away deep into the woods as if he were embarrassed again. "I'm sorry I don't have on a shirt before you ladies," he said, hunching his shoulders slightly. "We buried our clothes that we had on when we escaped and we're just making do until we can get better. We borrowed these from some folks we met," he explained.

"That's perfectly all right," the grandmother said. "Maybe Bailey has an extra shirt in his suitcase."

"I'll look and see terrectly," The Misfit said.

"Where are they taking him?" the children's mother screamed.

"Daddy was a card himself," The Misfit said. "You couldn't put anything over on him. He never got in trouble with the Authorities though. Just had the knack of handling them."

"You could be honest too if you'd only try," said the grandmother. "Think how wonderful it would be to settle down and live a comfortable life and not have to think about somebody chasing you all the time."

The Misfit kept scratching in the ground with the butt of his gun as if he were thinking about it. "Yes'm, somebody is always after you," he murmured.

The grandmother noticed how thin his shoulder blades were just behind his hat because she was standing up looking down on him. "Do you ever pray?" she asked.

He shook his head. All she saw was the black hat wiggle between his shoulder blades. "Nome," he said.

There was a pistol shot from the woods, followed closely by another. Then silence. The old lady's head jerked around. She could hear the wind move through the tree tops like a long satisfied insuck of breath. "Bailey Boy!" she called.

"I was a gospel singer for a while," The Misfit said. "I been most everything. Been in the arm service, both land and sea, at home and abroad, been twict married, been an undertaker, been with the railroads, plowed Mother Earth, been in a tornado, seen a man burnt alive oncet," and he looked up at the children's mother and the little girl who were sitting close together, their faces white and their eyes glassy; "I even seen a woman flogged," he said.

"Pray, pray," the grandmother began, "pray, pray . . ."

"I never was a bad boy that I remember of," The Misfit said in an almost dreamy voice, "but somewheres along the line I done something wrong and got sent to the penitentiary. I was buried alive," and he looked up and held her attention to him by a steady stare.

"That's when you should have started to pray," she said. "What did you do to get sent to the penitentiary that first time?"

"Turn to the right, it was a wall," The Misfit said, looking up again at the cloudless sky. "Turn to the left, it was a wall. Look up it was a ceiling, look down it was a floor. I forget what I done, lady. I set there and set there, trying to remember what it was I done and I ain't recalled it to this day. Oncet in a while, I would think it was coming to me, but it never come."

"Maybe they put you in by mistake," the old lady said vaguely.

"Nome," he said. "It wasn't no mistake. They had the papers on me."

"You must have stolen something," she said.

The Misfit sneered slightly. "Nobody had nothing I wanted," he said. "It was a head-doctor at the penitentiary said what I had done was kill my daddy but I known that for a lie. My daddy died in nineteen ought nineteen of the epidemic flu[6] and I never had a thing to do with it. He was buried in the Mount Hopewell Baptist churchyard and you can go there and see for yourself."

"If you would pray," the old lady said, "Jesus would help you."

"That's right," The Misfit said.

"Well then, why don't you pray?" she asked trembling with delight suddenly.

"I don't want no hep," he said. "I'm doing all right by myself."

Bobby Lee and Hiram came ambling back from the woods. Bobby Lee was dragging a yellow shirt with bright blue parrots in it.

"Thow me that shirt, Bobby Lee," The Misfit said. The shirt came flying at him and landed on his shoulder and he put it on. The grandmother couldn't name what the shirt reminded her of. "No, lady," The Misfit said while he was buttoning it up, "I found out the crime don't matter. You can do one thing or you can do another, kill a man or take a tire off his car, because sooner or later you're going to forget what it was you done and just be punished for it."

The children's mother had begun to make heaving noises as if she couldn't get her breath. "Lady," he asked, "would you and that little girl like to step off yonder with Bobby Lee and Hiram and join your husband?"

"Yes, thank you," the mother said faintly. Her left arm dangled helplessly and she was holding the baby, who had gone to sleep, in the other. "Hep that lady up, Hiram," The Misfit said as she struggled to climb out of the ditch, "and Bobby Lee, you hold onto that little girl's hand."

"I don't want to hold hands with him," June Star said. "He reminds me of a pig."

The fat boy blushed and laughed and caught her by the arm and pulled her off into the woods after Hiram and her mother.

---

6. **epidemic flu:** The influenza pandemic of 1918–19, the largest epidemic in history, killed between 20 and 40 million people worldwide.

Alone with The Misfit, the grandmother found that she had lost her voice. There was not a cloud in the sky nor any sun. There was nothing around her but woods. She wanted to tell him that he must pray. She opened and closed her mouth several times before anything came out. Finally she found herself saying, "Jesus. Jesus," meaning, Jesus will help you, but the way she was saying it, it sounded as if she might be cursing.

"Yes'm," The Misfit said as if he agreed. "Jesus thown everything off balance. It was the same case with Him as with me except He hadn't committed any crime and they could prove I had committed one because they had the papers on me. Of course," he said, "they never shown me my papers. That's why I sign myself now. I said long ago, you get you a signature and sign everything you do and keep a copy of it. Then you'll know what you done and you can hold up the crime to the punishment and see do they match and in the end you'll have something to prove you ain't been treated right. I call myself The Misfit," he said, "because I can't make what all I done wrong fit what all I gone through in punishment."

There was a piercing scream from the woods, followed closely by a pistol report. "Does it seem right to you, lady, that one is punished a heap and another ain't punished at all?"

"Jesus!" the old lady cried. "You've got good blood! I know you wouldn't shoot a lady! I know you come from nice people! Pray! Jesus, you ought not to shoot a lady. I'll give you all the money I've got!"

"Lady," The Misfit said, looking beyond her far into the woods, "there never was a body that give the undertaker a tip."

There were two more pistol reports and the grandmother raised her head like a parched old turkey hen crying for water and called, "Bailey Boy, Bailey Boy!" as if her heart would break.

"Jesus was the only One that ever raised the dead," The Misfit continued, "and He shouldn't have done it. He thown everything off balance. If He did what He said, then it's nothing for you to do but thow away everything and follow Him, and if He didn't, then it's nothing for you to do but enjoy the few minutes you got left the best way you can — by killing somebody or burning down his house or doing some other meanness to him. No pleasure but meanness," he said and his voice had become almost a snarl.

"Maybe He didn't raise the dead," the old lady mumbled, not knowing what she was saying and feeling so dizzy that she sank down in the ditch with her legs twisted under her.

"I wasn't there so I can't say He didn't," The Misfit said. "I wisht I had of been there," he said, hitting the ground with his fist. "It ain't right I wasn't there because if I had of been there I would of known. Listen lady," he said in a high voice, "if I had of been there I would of known and I wouldn't be like I am now." His voice seemed about to crack and the grandmother's head cleared for an instant. She saw the man's face twisted close to her own as if he were going to cry and she murmured, "Why you're one of my babies. You're one of my own children!" She reached out and touched him on the shoulder. The Misfit sprang back as if a snake had bitten him and shot her three times through the chest. Then he put his gun down on the ground and took off his glasses and began to clean them.

Hiram and Bobby Lee returned from the woods and stood over the ditch, looking down at the grandmother who half sat and half lay in a puddle of blood with her legs crossed under her like a child's and her face smiling up at the cloudless sky.

Without his glasses, The Misfit's eyes were red-rimmed and pale and defenseless-looking. "Take her off and thow her where you thown the others," he said, picking up the cat that was rubbing itself against his leg.

"She was a talker, wasn't she?" Bobby Lee said, sliding down the ditch with a yodel.

"She would of been a good woman," The Misfit said, "if it had been somebody there to shoot her every minute of her life."

"Some fun!" Bobby Lee said.

"Shut up, Bobby Lee," The Misfit said. "It's no real pleasure in life."

[1953, 1955]

Allen Ginsberg

[1926–1997]

Irwin Allen Ginsberg was born on June 3, 1926, in Newark, New Jersey. He was the second son of Naomi Levy Ginsberg, a Russian immigrant and active member of the Communist Party, and Louis Ginsberg, a published poet and high-school English teacher in Paterson, New Jersey. In a 1985 interview, Ginsberg described life in the household: "My father would go around the house either reciting Emily Dickinson and Longfellow under his breath or attacking T. S. Eliot for ruining poetry with his 'obscurantism.' My mother made up bedtime stories that all went something like: 'The good king rode forth from his castle, saw the suffering workers, and healed them.' I grew suspicious of both sides." During his childhood, his mother was hospitalized several times for mental illness, and the family lived modestly in working-class, predominantly Jewish neighborhoods in Paterson. Ginsberg excelled academically, earning the nickname "The Professor." He also wrote for the school papers and was active in dramatic productions. After his graduation from high school in 1943, he received a scholarship to Columbia

Allen Ginsberg
This photograph of Ginsberg typing his most famous poem, *Howl*, was taken in the kitchen of his San Francisco apartment during the summer of 1955.

University in New York City. He immediately gravitated to literature and studied with the distinguished literary critics Mark Van Doren and Lionel Trilling, who encouraged Ginsberg to write poetry. Although he wanted to study Walt Whitman, William Carlos Williams, and Ezra Pound, the curriculum focused on earlier and more traditional poets. Of his often rebellious attitude toward his education and his professors, the writer Diana Trilling once observed that Ginsberg seemed to have two motivations, "the wish to shock his teacher, and the wish to meet the teacher on equal ground."

While he was at Columbia, Ginsberg became involved with an avant-garde group of writers who later dubbed themselves the "Beat generation." Through a college friend, Lucien Carr, he met William S. Burroughs, Neal Cassady, Herbert Huncke, and Jack Kerouac. Ginsberg, who fell deeply in love with the charismatic Cassady, was powerfully influenced by the radical nonconformity of the Beats, whose name suggested "deadbeats," or the beaten down, and "beatific," the mystical vision available to those reduced to such a position. Now determined to be a poet, Ginsberg decided to remain at Columbia for graduate study after his graduation in 1948. The following year, however, the police found stolen goods in his apartment, involving him as an unwitting accomplice to a series of robberies committed by Huncke. On the advice of his professors, Ginsberg pleaded psychological disability and was sent for evaluation to the Columbia Psychiatric Institute. One of his fellow patients was Carl Solomon, a brilliant young college student with whom Ginsberg spent hours discussing life and literature. After eight months, he left the institute and returned home to live with his father in Paterson, where Ginsberg became friendly with the poet William Carlos Williams. Ginsberg worked in New York for a market research company but left his dull job to travel in Mexico in 1953. He ultimately settled in San Francisco, where he met his lifelong companion, Peter Orlovsky. In 1955, Ginsberg read a long unpublished poem, "Howl for Carl Solomon," to a packed house at the Six Gallery. The graphic poem and his dramatic performance caused a sensation, and the following day the poet Lawrence Ferlinghetti, the cofounder of City Lights Bookstore, offered to publish the poem in his new Pocket Poets Series.

Howl and Other Poems (1956) catapulted Ginsberg into a prominence he enjoyed for the rest of his life. In a landmark censorship case, Ferlinghetti was tried for publishing obscenity, and he was successfully defended by the American Civil Liberties Union. By the time the trial ended in 1957, both Ginsberg and his book had gained international attention. He and Orlovsky traveled extensively before returning to New York. In 1958, two years after Ginsberg's mother died in a mental hospital, he wrote a celebrated elegy to her, "Kaddish for Naomi Ginsberg." He and Orlovsky then spent two years in India, where Ginsberg studied Eastern religions and meditation. After their return to the United States, he began to experiment with mind-altering drugs such as LSD. During the 1960s, he wrote constantly, publishing several volumes of poetry, including *Kaddish and Other Poems* (1961), *Reality Sandwiches* (1963), *The Yage Letters* (1963), written with William Burroughs, and *Wichita Vortex Sutra* (1967), an epic poem about the Vietnam War. Ginsberg was actively involved in protests

[Allen Ginsberg] was a pioneer of openness and a lifelong model of candor.

–William S. Burroughs

against the war and demonstrations in support of gay rights and other causes. He also gave numerous readings, many of them joint readings with his father. In 1974, he cofounded a creative writing program, the Jack Kerouac School of Disembodied Poetics, at the Buddhist-inspired Naropa Institute (now University) in Boulder, Colorado. Ginsberg won a National Book Award for his collection *The Fall of America: Poems of These States* (1974), and he was widely regarded as an important figure in mainstream American poetry when he published his *Collected Poems* (1984). In 1986, he was appointed Distinguished Professor at Brooklyn College, where he taught creative writing and courses on poetry and poetics until shortly before his death from liver cancer on April 6, 1997.

Ginsberg's *Howl*. Ginsberg began writing his most famous poem in August 1955, while he was living in San Francisco. "I began typing, not with the idea of writing a formal poem, but stating my imaginative sympathies, whatever they were worth," he later explained. But he carefully revised the poem through several versions before he presented it at a group reading of five poets, including Gary Snyder, on October 7, 1955. "In all our memories no one had been so outspoken in poetry before," the poet Michael McClure later recalled:

Howl and Other Poems

Howl was published by Lawrence Ferlinghetti, the cofounder of City Lights Bookstore. This photograph was taken there in 2005, exactly fifty years after Ginsberg's first public reading of the poem at the Six Gallery in San Francisco.

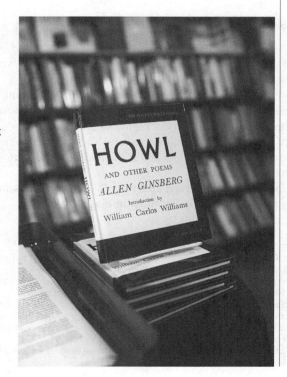

Ginsberg read on to the end of the poem, which left us standing in wonder, or cheering and wondering, but knowing at the deepest level that a barrier had been broken, that a human voice and body had been hurled against the harsh wall of America.

Ginsberg's galvanizing work was first published in *Howl and Other Poems* (1956), which included an introduction by his friend and mentor William Carlos Williams. In an extensive commentary on the poem in a letter to the poet Richard Eberhart, who had suggested that *Howl* was primarily "a negative howl of protest," Ginsberg in 1956 responded that it "is an 'affirmation' of individual experience of God, sex, drugs, absurdity etc. . . . To call it a work of nihilistic rebellion would be to mistake it completely. Its force comes from positive 'religious' belief and experience." He also described the wide range of influences that had shaped his poetic technique in *Howl*, from the rhythms of bop music to the imagistic verse of William Carlos Williams and the "long line" of Walt Whitman and the surrealist French poet Guillaume Apollinaire. In *Howl* (1986), which includes a facsimile of the original draft and other manuscripts of the poem, Ginsberg added extensive explanatory notes, some of which are incorporated here. The text is taken from his *Collected Poems, 1947-1997* (2006).

bedfordstmartins.com/ americanlit *for research links on Ginsberg*

HOWL

For Carl Solomon[1]

I

I saw the best minds of my generation destroyed by madness, starving hysterical
    naked,
dragging themselves through the negro streets at dawn looking for an angry fix,[2]
angelheaded hipsters burning for the ancient heavenly connection to the starry
    dynamo in the machinery of night,
who poverty and tatters and hollow-eyed and high sat up smoking in the super-
    natural darkness of cold-water flats floating across the tops of cities
    contemplating jazz,[3]
who bared their brains to Heaven under the El[4] and saw Mohammedan angels
    staggering on tenement roofs illuminated,   5

---

1. **Dedication:** Ginsberg dedicated the poem to the editor and writer Carl Solomon (b. 1928), a fellow patient at the Columbia Psychiatric Institute in New York City in 1949.
2. **an angry fix:** Herbert Huncke cruised Harlem and Times Square areas at irregular hours, late forties, scoring junk. [Ginsberg's note] A "fix" is a dose of "junk," the street name of heroin.
3. **contemplating jazz:** Ref[erence]. Bill Keck, Anton Rosenberg, and other contemporaries who gathered often at the San Remo bar, living in Lower East Side, N.Y., early 1950s — their circle was prototype for Kerouac's fictional description in *The Subterraneans*, written 1953. The jazz was late bop Charlie Parker, played in Bowery loft jam sessions in those few years. [Ginsberg's note]
4. **El:** Part of Manhattan's subway system, the Third Avenue elevated railway, one of those familiarly called the "El," was demolished in the mid-'50s. [Ginsberg's note]

who passed through universities with radiant cool eyes hallucinating Arkansas[5]
and Blake-light tragedy[6] among the scholars of war,[7]
who were expelled from the academies for crazy & publishing obscene odes on the
windows of the skull,
who cowered in unshaven rooms in underwear, burning their money in waste-
baskets and listening to the Terror through the wall,
who got busted in their pubic beards returning through Laredo with a belt of
marijuana for New York,
who ate fire in paint hotels or drank turpentine in Paradise Alley,[8] death, or
purgatoried their torsos night after night   10
with dreams, with drugs, with waking nightmares, alcohol and cock and endless
balls,
incomparable blind streets of shuddering cloud and lightning in the mind leaping
toward poles of Canada & Paterson,[9] illuminating all the motionless world
of Time between,
Peyote solidities of halls, backyard green tree cemetery dawns, wine drunkenness
over the rooftops, storefront boroughs of teahead joyride neon blinking
traffic light, sun and moon and tree vibrations in the roaring winter dusks
of Brooklyn, ashcan rantings and kind king light of mind,
who chained themselves to subways for the endless ride from Battery to holy
Bronx[10] on benzedrine until the noise of wheels and children brought
them down shuddering mouth-wracked and battered bleak of brain all
drained of brilliance in the drear light of Zoo,[11]
who sank all night in submarine light of Bickford's[12] floated out and sat through
the stale beer afternoon in desolate Fugazzi's,[13] listening to the crack of
doom on the hydrogen jukebox,   15

---

5. **Arkansas:** "Anarchy" changes to "Arkansas," in order to substitute a more concrete thing-name for an abstract word. [Ginsberg's note]
6. **Blake-light tragedy:** William Blake (1757-1827), an English poet and painter who frequently depicted the apocalypse or the cataclysmic end of time.
7. **scholars of war:** During author's residence, 1944-48, Columbia scientists helped split atoms for military power in secrecy. Subsequent military-industrial funding increasingly dominated university research, thus two decades later rebellious student strikes had as primary grievance that the trusteeships of the university interlocked with Vietnam War-related corporations. [Ginsberg's note]
8. **Paradise Alley:** This verse evolves into "Paradise Alley," a coldwater-flat courtyard at 501 East 11th Street, NE corner of Avenue A, Lower East Side, New York, bricked up in the '70s and demolished after fire in 1985. As sketched by Kerouac in *The Subterraneans*, the prototype of his heroine Mardou Fox lived there in 1953 in friendly contact with the author, Corso and Kerouac, and typed the original ms. of Burroughs' *Yage Letters* and *Queer.* [Ginsberg's note]
9. **Paterson:** Ginsberg grew up in Paterson, New Jersey.
10. **Battery to holy Bronx:** The Battery is at the southern end and the Bronx is at the northern end of one of the subway lines in New York City.
11. **Zoo:** The Bronx Zoo in New York City.
12. **Bickford's:** Author's casual college job was mopping floors at various Manhattan cafeterias including Bickford's 42nd Street. [Ginsberg's note]
13. **Fugazzi's:** Fugazzi's Sixth Avenue Greenwich Village bar was early 1950s alternative to the noisier San Remo nearby. "Fugazzi" phrasing was added to accommodate "jukebox"; cafeterias had no jukeboxes. [Ginsberg's note]

who talked continuously seventy hours from park to pad to bar to Bellevue[14] to
    museum to the Brooklyn Bridge,

a lost battalion of platonic conversationalists jumping down the stoops off fire
    escapes off windowsills off Empire State out of the moon,

yacketayakking screaming vomiting whispering facts and memories and anec-
    dotes and eyeball kicks and shocks of hospitals and jails and wars,

whole intellects disgorged in total recall for seven days and nights with brilliant
    eyes, meat for the Synagogue cast on the pavement,

who vanished into nowhere Zen New Jersey leaving a trail of ambiguous picture
    postcards of Atlantic City Hall,   20

suffering Eastern sweats and Tangerian bone-grindings[15] and migraines of China
    under junk-withdrawal in Newark's bleak furnished room,

who wandered around and around at midnight in the railroad yard wondering
    where to go, and went, leaving no broken hearts,

who lit cigarettes in boxcars boxcars boxcars racketing through snow toward
    lonesome farms in grandfather night,

who studied Plotinus Poe St. John of the Cross[16] telepathy and bop kabbalah[17]
    because the cosmos instinctively vibrated at their feet in Kansas,

who loned it through the streets of Idaho seeking visionary indian angels who
    were visionary indian angels,   25

who thought they were only mad when Baltimore gleamed in supernatural
    ecstasy,

who jumped in limousines with the Chinaman of Oklahoma on the impulse of
    winter midnight streetlight smalltown rain,

who lounged hungry and lonesome through Houston seeking jazz or sex or soup,
    and followed the brilliant Spaniard[18] to converse about America and
    Eternity, a hopeless task, and so took ship to Africa,

who disappeared into the volcanoes of Mexico leaving behind nothing but the
    shadow of dungarees and the lava and ash of poetry scattered in fireplace
    Chicago,

who reappeared on the West Coast investigating the FBI in beards and shorts
    with big pacifist eyes sexy in their dark skin passing out incomprehen-
    sible leaflets,   30

who burned cigarette holes in their arms protesting the narcotic tobacco haze of
    Capitalism,

---

14. **Bellevue:** A hospital known for its psychiatric unit.

15. **Tangerian bone-grindings:** Details of W. S. Burroughs' withdrawals from heroin are found in his letters to the author, *Letters to Allen Ginsberg* 1953-1957. [Ginsberg's note]

16. **Plotinus Poe St. John of the Cross:** The Roman philosopher Plotinus (205-270), the founder of Neo-Platonism; the American writer Edgar Allan Poe (1809-1849), known for his explorations of extreme mental states; and the Spanish mystic St. John of the Cross (1542-1591), author of a famous poem about spiritual purgation, "The Dark Night of the Soul."

17. **bop kabbalah:** Bop or bebop is a type of jazz originating in the 1940s, and the kabbalah is an ancient Jewish tradition of mystical interpretation of the Old Testament.

18. **brilliant Spaniard:** According to Ginsberg's note, he observed this powerful stranger striding down a street in Houston in September 1947.

who distributed Supercommunist pamphlets in Union Square[19] weeping and
  undressing while the sirens of Los Alamos[20] wailed them down, and wailed
  down Wall,[21] and the Staten Island ferry also wailed,

who broke down crying in white gymnasiums naked and trembling before the
  machinery of other skeletons,

who bit detectives in the neck and shrieked with delight in policecars for committing no crime but their own wild cooking pederasty and intoxication,

who howled on their knees in the subway and were dragged off the roof waving
  genitals and manuscripts,   35

who let themselves be fucked in the ass by saintly motorcyclists,[22] and screamed
  with joy,

who blew and were blown by those human seraphim, the sailors,[23] caresses of
  Atlantic and Caribbean love,

who balled in the morning in the evenings in rosegardens and the grass of public
  parks and cemeteries scattering their semen freely to whomever come
  who may,

who hiccuped endlessly trying to giggle but wound up with a sob behind a partition in a Turkish Bath when the blond & naked angel came to pierce them
  with a sword,

who lost their loveboys to the three old shrews of fate[24] the one eyed shrew of the
  heterosexual dollar the one eyed shrew that winks out of the womb and
  the one eyed shrew that does nothing but sit on her ass and snip the
  intellectual golden threads of the craftsman's loom,   40

who copulated ecstatic and insatiate with a bottle of beer a sweetheart a package
  of cigarettes a candle and fell off the bed, and continued along the floor
  and down the hall and ended fainting on the wall with a vision of ultimate
  cunt and come eluding the last gyzym[25] of consciousness,

who sweetened the snatches of a million girls trembling in the sunset, and were
  red eyed in the morning but prepared to sweeten the snatch of the sunrise,
  flashing buttocks under barns and naked in the lake,

who went out whoring through Colorado in myriad stolen night-cars, N.C.,[26] secret
  hero of these poems, cocksman and Adonis of Denver[27] — joy to the memory

---

19. **Union Square:** A park in New York City where radicals frequently gathered during the 1930s.

20. **Los Alamos:** Nuclear research laboratory in northern New Mexico.

21. **Wall:** Wall Street, the center of the financial district in New York City.

22. **saintly motorcyclists:** Ref[erence]. Marlon Brando's film *The Wild One*, 1954. [Ginsberg's note] In the film, Brando is the leader of a motorcycle gang that terrorizes a small town in the Midwest.

23. **sailors:** The poet Hart Crane picked up sailors to love on Sand Street, Brooklyn, etc. Suffering alcoholic exhaustion and rejected by the crew on his last voyage from Veracruz, Crane disappeared off the fantail of the Caribbean ship *Orizaba*. [Ginsberg's note]

24. **three old shrews of fate:** The three Moirae, or Fates, who in Greek mythology control the destiny of all human beings.

25. **gyzym:** Ginsberg's spelling of "jism," slang for semen or ejaculation.

26. **N.C.:** Ref[erence]. Neal Cassady, 1926-1968, author of *The Third & Other Writings*. [Ginsberg's note]

27. **Adonis of Denver:** Neal Cassady was born and raised in Denver, Colorado. In Greek mythology, Adonis is a beautiful youth loved by the goddesses Aphrodite and Persephone.

of his innumerable lays of girls in empty lots & diner backyards, movie-
houses' rickety rows, on mountaintops in caves or with gaunt waitresses
in familiar roadside lonely petticoat upliftings & especially secret gas-
station solipsisms of johns, & hometown alleys too,

who faded out in vast sordid movies, were shifted in dreams, woke on a sudden
Manhattan, and picked themselves up out of basements hung-over with
heartless Tokay,[28] and horrors of Third Avenue iron dreams & stumbled to
unemployment offices,

who walked all night with their shoes full of blood on the snowbank docks waiting
for a door in the East River to open to a room full of steam-heat and opium,   45

who created great suicidal dramas on the apartment cliff-banks of the Hudson
under the wartime blue floodlight of the moon & their heads shall be
crowned with laurel in oblivion,

who ate the lamb stew of the imagination or digested the crab at the muddy
bottom of the rivers of Bowery,

who wept at the romance of the streets with their pushcarts full of onions and bad
music,

who sat in boxes breathing in the darkness under the bridge, and rose up to build
harpsichords in their lofts,

who coughed on the sixth floor of Harlem[29] crowned with flame under the tubercular sky surrounded by orange crates of theology,   50

who scribbled all night rocking and rolling over lofty incantations which in the
yellow morning were stanzas of gibberish,

who cooked rotten animals lung heart feet tail borsht & tortillas dreaming of the
pure vegetable kingdom,

who plunged themselves under meat trucks looking for an egg,

who threw their watches off the roof to cast their ballot for Eternity outside of
Time, & alarm clocks fell on their heads every day for the next decade,

who cut their wrists three times successively unsuccessfully, gave up and were
forced to open antique stores where they thought they were growing old
and cried,   55

who were burned alive in their innocent flannel suits on Madison Avenue[30] amid
blasts of leaden verse & the tanked-up clatter of the iron regiments of
fashion & the nitroglycerine shrieks of the fairies of advertising & the
mustard gas of sinister intelligent editors, or were run down by the
drunken taxicabs of Absolute Reality,

---

28. **Tokay:** Sweet, aromatic wine made in Hungary.
29. **Harlem:** Russell Durgin (d. August 28, 1985), Columbia '57 theology student in whose sublet apartment,
321 East 121st Street, East Harlem, 198, author read William Blake, left Manhattan that summer for medical
treatment, tubercular lungs. Treatment may have involved filling chest space with celluloid balls to prevent
collapse. [Ginsberg's note]
30. **Madison Avenue:** An avenue in New York City that became synonymous with the advertising industry.

who jumped off the Brooklyn Bridge this actually happened and walked away
>   unknown and forgotten into the ghostly daze of Chinatown soup alleyways
>   & firetrucks, not even one free beer,

who sang out of their windows in despair, fell out of the subway window, jumped
>   in the filthy Passaic,[31] leaped on negroes, cried all over the street, danced
>   on broken wineglasses barefoot smashed phonograph records of nostalgic
>   European 1930s German jazz finished the whiskey and threw up groaning
>   into the bloody toilet, moans in their ears and the blast of colossal
>   steamwhistles,

who barreled down the highways of the past journeying to each other's hotrod-
>   Golgotha[32] jail-solitude watch or Birmingham jazz incarnation,

who drove crosscountry seventytwo hours to find out if I had a vision or you had a
>   vision or he had a vision to find out Eternity,   60

who journeyed to Denver, who died in Denver, who came back to Denver & waited
>   in vain, who watched over Denver & brooded and loned in Denver and
>   finally went away to find out the Time, & now Denver is lonesome for her
>   heroes,

who fell on their knees in hopeless cathedrals praying for each other's salvation
>   and light and breasts, until the soul illuminated its hair for a second,

who crashed through their minds in jail waiting for impossible criminals with
>   golden heads and the charm of reality in their hearts who sang sweet blues
>   to Alcatraz,

who retired to Mexico to cultivate a habit, or Rocky Mount to tender Buddha or
>   Tangiers to boys or Southern Pacific to the black locomotive or Harvard to
>   Narcissus to Woodlawn to the daisychain or grave,

who demanded sanity trials accusing the radio of hypnotism & were left with their
>   insanity & their hands & a hung jury,   65

who threw potato salad at CCNY lecturers on Dadaism[33] and subsequently
>   presented themselves on the granite steps of the madhouse with shaven
>   heads and harlequin speech of suicide, demanding instantaneous
>   lobotomy,

and who were given instead the concrete void of insulin Metrazol electricity
>   hydrotherapy psychotherapy occupational therapy pingpong & amnesia,

who in humorless protest overturned only one symbolic pingpong table, resting
>   briefly in catatonia,

returning years later truly bald except for a wig of blood, and tears and fingers, to
>   the visible madman doom of the wards of the madtowns of the East,

---

31. **filthy Passaic:** In W. Carlos Williams "The Wanderer: A Baroque Fantasy," 1915, the youthful poet plunges his hands in her waters requesting sacrament of Goddess of Passaic River for his Muse: "and the filthy Passaic consented." [Ginsberg's note] Paterson, New Jersey, is on the Passaic River.

32. **Golgotha:** "The place of skulls," also known as Calvary, the site of the crucifixion of Jesus Christ.

33. **CCNY lectures on Dadaism:** Dada was an artistic movement that emphasized absurdity and unpredictability. CCNY is the acronym of City College of New York.

Pilgrim State's Rockland's and Greystone's foetid halls,[34] bickering with the
    echoes of the soul, rocking and rolling in the midnight solitude-bench
    dolmen-realms of love, dream of life a nightmare, bodies turned to stone
    as heavy as the moon,   70
with mother finally ******, and the last fantastic book flung out of the tenement
    window, and the last door closed at 4. A.M. and the last telephone slammed
    at the wall in reply and the last furnished room emptied down to the last
    piece of mental furniture, a yellow paper rose twisted on a wire hanger in
    the closet, and even that imaginary, nothing but a hopeful little bit of
    hallucination —
ah, Carl, while you are not safe I am not safe, and now you're really in the total
    animal soup of time —
and who therefore ran through the icy streets obsessed with a sudden flash of the
    alchemy of the use of the ellipse the catalog the meter & the vibrating
    plane,
who dreamt and made incarnate gaps in Time & Space through images juxta-
    posed, and trapped the archangel of the soul between 2 visual images and
    joined the elemental verbs and set the noun and dash of consciousness
    together jumping with sensation of Pater Omnipotens Aeterna Deus[35]
to recreate the syntax and measure of poor human prose and stand before you
    speechless and intelligent and shaking with shame, rejected yet
    confessing out the soul to conform to the rhythm of thought in his naked
    and endless head,   75
the madman bum and angel beat in Time, unknown, yet putting down here what
    might be left to say in time come after death,
and rose reincarnate in the ghostly clothes of jazz in the goldhorn shadow of the
    band and blew the suffering of America's naked mind for love into an eli
    eli lamma lamma sabacthani[36] saxophone cry that shivered the cities
    down to the last radio
with the absolute heart of the poem of life butchered out of their own bodies good
    to eat a thousand years.

---

34. **Pilgrim State's Rockland's and Greystone's foetid halls:** Ref[erence]. somewhat to Carl Solomon and those we left behind at Psychiatric Institute, 1949. Dolmens mark a vanished civilization, as Stonehenge or Greystone and Rockland monoliths. At time of writing, author's mother dwelled in her last months at Pilgrim State Hospital, Brentwood, N.Y., housing over 25,000, the largest such mental hospital in the world. Description of the wards and halls is drawn from Greystone State Hospital, near Morristown, N.J., which author frequented in adolescence to visit Naomi Ginsberg. New York's Rockland State Hospital's name was substituted for rhythmic euphony. Poem was occasioned by unexpected news of Carl Solomon's recent removal to Pilgrim State. [Ginsberg's note] Naomi Ginsberg, the poet's mother, died at Greystone in 1956.
35. **Pater Omnipotens Aeterna Deus:** Correct Latin line should read: "Pater Omnipotens Aeterne Deus." [Ginsberg's note] In a lengthy continuation of this note, Ginsberg explains that the Latin phrase, which may be translated "all powerful Father, Eternal God," is used in a letter by the French painter Paul Cézanne to Emile Bernard, April 15, 1904.
36. **eli eli lamma lamma sabacthani:** My God, my God, why hast thou forsaken me? (Aramaic), Christ's last words on the cross.

II

What sphinx of cement and aluminum bashed open their skulls and ate up their
brains and imagination?

Moloch![37] Solitude! Filth! Ugliness! Ashcans and unobtainable dollars! Children
screaming under the stairways! Boys sobbing in armies! Old men weeping
in the parks!   80

Moloch! Moloch! Nightmare of Moloch! Moloch the loveless! Mental Moloch!
Moloch the heavy judger of men!

Moloch the incomprehensible prison! Moloch the crossbone soulless jailhouse
and Congress of sorrows! Moloch whose buildings are judgment! Moloch
the vast stone of war! Moloch the stunned governments!

Moloch whose mind is pure machinery! Moloch whose blood is running money!
Moloch whose fingers are ten armies! Moloch whose breast is a cannibal
dynamo! Moloch whose ear is a smoking tomb!

Moloch whose eyes are a thousand blind windows! Moloch whose skyscrapers
stand in the long streets like endless Jehovahs! Moloch whose factories
dream and croak in the fog! Moloch whose smokestacks and antennae
crown the cities!

Moloch whose love is endless oil and stone! Moloch whose soul is electricity and
banks! Moloch whose poverty is the specter of genius! Moloch whose fate
is a cloud of sexless hydrogen! Moloch whose name is the Mind!   85

Moloch in whom I sit lonely! Moloch in whom I dream Angels! Crazy in Moloch!
Cocksucker in Moloch! Lacklove and manless in Moloch!

Moloch who entered my soul early! Moloch in whom I am a consciousness without
a body! Moloch who frightened me out of my natural ecstasy! Moloch
whom I abandon! Wake up in Moloch! Light streaming out of the sky!

Moloch! Moloch! Robot apartments! invisible suburbs! skeleton treasuries! blind
capitals! demonic industries! spectral nations! invincible madhouses!
granite cocks! monstrous bombs!

They broke their backs lifting Moloch to Heaven! Pavements, trees, radios, tons!
lifting the city to Heaven which exists and is everywhere about us!

Visions! omens! hallucinations! miracles! ecstasies! gone down the American
river!   90

Dreams! adorations! illuminations! religions! the whole boatload of sensitive
bullshit!

Breakthroughs! over the river! flips and crucifixions! gone down the flood! Highs!
Epiphanies! Despairs! Ten years' animal screams and suicides! Minds!
New loves! Mad generation! down on the rocks of Time!

Real holy laughter in the river! They saw it all! the wild eyes! the holy yells! They

---

37. **Moloch:** "Moloch" or Molech, the Canaanite fire god, whose worship was marked by parents' burning
their children as propitiatory sacrifice. "And thou shalt not let any of thy seed pass through the fire to
Molech" (Leviticus 18:21). [Ginsberg's note]

bade farewell! They jumped off the roof! to solitude! waving! carrying
flowers! Down to the river! into the street!

III

Carl Solomon! I'm with you in Rockland
    where you're madder than I am   95
I'm with you in Rockland
    where you must feel very strange
I'm with you in Rockland
    where you imitate the shade of my mother
I'm with you in Rockland   100
    where you've murdered your twelve secretaries
I'm with you in Rockland
    where you laugh at this invisible humor
I'm with you in Rockland
    where we are great writers on the same dreadful typewriter   105
I'm with you in Rockland
    where your condition has become serious and is reported on the radio
I'm with you in Rockland
    where the faculties of the skull no longer admit the worms of the senses
I'm with you in Rockland   110
    where you drink the tea of the breasts of the spinsters of Utica
I'm with you in Rockland
    where you pun on the bodies of your nurses the harpies of the Bronx
I'm with you in Rockland
    where you scream in a straightjacket that you're losing the game of the
    actual pingpong of the abyss   115
I'm with you in Rockland
    where you bang on the catatonic piano the soul is innocent and immortal
    it should never die ungodly in an armed madhouse
I'm with you in Rockland
    where fifty more shocks will never return your soul to its body again
    from its pilgrimage to a cross in the void
I'm with you in Rockland   120
    where you accuse your doctors of insanity and plot the Hebrew socialist
    revolution against the fascist national Golgotha
I'm with you in Rockland
    where you will split the heavens of Long Island and resurrect your living human
    Jesus from the superhuman tomb
I'm with you in Rockland
    where there are twentyfive thousand mad comrades all together singing
    the final stanzas of the Internationale   125
I'm with you in Rockland

where we hug and kiss the United States under our bedsheets the United
>   States that coughs all night and won't let us sleep
I'm with you in Rockland
>   where we wake up electrified out of the coma by our own souls' airplanes
>   roaring over the roof they've come to drop angelic bombs the hospital
>   illuminates itself   imaginary walls collapse   O skinny legions
>   run outside   O starry-spangled shock of mercy the eternal war is
>   here   O victory forget your underwear we're free
I'm with you in Rockland
>   in my dreams you walk dripping from a sea-journey on the highway
>   across America in tears to the door of my cottage in the Western night

San Francisco, 1955–1956

130

[1956, 2006]

John Ashbery

[b. 1927]

John Lawrence Ashbery was born in Rochester, New York, on July 28, 1927.
He was the eldest of the two sons of Helen Lawrence Ashbery, a former
high-school biology teacher, and Chester Ashbery, who raised fruit on a
farm outside Sodus, a small village
thirty miles from Rochester. For the
first seven years of his life, Ashbery
lived in the city with his maternal
grandparents, and he was strongly
influenced by his grandfather Henry
Lawrence, a physics professor at the
University of Rochester. Lawrence,
whom Ashbery has described as
"a cultivated Victorian gentleman"
who could read Greek and owned a
substantial library, gave his gifted
grandson books and encouraged his
artistic and intellectual interests.
When Ashbery was eleven, he began
to take weekly painting classes at
the art museum in Rochester. He attended local schools until he was
sixteen, when a wealthy neighbor
paid for him to go to Deerfield Academy in western Massachusetts. While
he was there, two of his poems were published when a friend sent them

John Ashbery

This photograph of Ash-
bery, sitting outside in a
wicker chair, was taken in
1964, a decade before his
emergence as one of the
most prominent poets of
his generation.

under a pseudonym to the prestigious magazine *Poetry*. After his graduation in 1945, Ashbery went to Harvard University, where he majored in English and joined the editorial board of the *Harvard Advocate*. He then continued his education at Columbia University, where he earned a master's degree in literature in 1951.

Ashbery became deeply involved in the arts scene, first in New York City, and later in Paris. Although he initially planned to look for a teaching position, he determined to find ways of supporting himself that would leave more time for other pursuits and took a job as a typist with Oxford University Press. He spent his spare time writing, studying modern poetry, and immersing himself in avant-garde music and art. He was also active in experimental theater, and his play *The Heroes* was produced by the Artists' Theatre in 1952. A few of his poems appeared along with drawings by his friend the painter Jane Freilicher in a small chapbook, *Turandot and Other Poems* (1953). It was published by the Tibor de Nagy Gallery, founded in 1950 to promote pioneering American artists such as the abstract expressionists, which also published the early poetry of two of Ashbery's friends from Harvard, Kenneth Koch and Frank O'Hara. With them and other young urban poets, Ashbery was associated in a loosely defined poetic movement that came to be known as the New York School. In 1955, he won the coveted Yale Younger Poets prize, resulting in the publication of his collection *Some Trees* (1956). By then, Ashbery had been awarded a Fulbright Scholarship and had moved to Paris. After the scholarship expired, he supported himself by translating French pulp novels for the American market and by writing art criticism and reviews for the European edition of the *New York Herald Tribune*, as well as for the magazines *Art News* and *Art International*. During most of the decade he spent in France, he lived with the writer Pierre Martory, some of whose poems Ashbery subsequently translated into English. Ashbery's own "violently experimental" poems, as he has since described them, were published in his controversial collection *The Tennis Court Oath* (1962).

Ashbery's reputation grew steadily after he returned to New York City in 1965. He became executive editor of *Art News*, a position he held until 1972. In contrast to the hostile reception of *The Tennis Court Oath*, a book even some of his admirers found perplexing, he received generally favorable reviews for his collections *Rivers and Mountains* (1966), *The Double-Dream of Spring* (1972), and *Three Poems* (1973). In recognition of his growing prominence, in 1974 Ashbery was appointed professor of English and codirector of the creative-writing program at Brooklyn College. His major triumph came with the publication of *Self-Portrait in a Convex Mirror* (1975), which the reviewer in the *New York Times* described as a "collection of poems of breathtaking freshness and adventure in which dazzling orchestrations of language open up whole areas of consciousness no other American poet has even begun to explore." The volume won the National Book Award, the National Book Critics Circle Award, and the Pulitzer Prize for Poetry. Ashbery has subsequently published a collection of poetry roughly every two years and has received virtually every award and

bedfordstmartins.com/ americanlit for research links on Ashbery honor bestowed on poets in both Europe and the United States. Since 1990, he has been a professor of languages and literature at Bard College. With his partner of over thirty years, David Kermani, Ashbery divides his time between Manhattan and a house in Hudson, New York. Widely regarded as the most important and influential poet writing in English, he published his twenty-fourth collection of poetry, *A Worldly Country*, in 2007.

Ashbery's Poetry.   Throughout his long career, Ashbery has extended the formal and linguistic experiments undertaken by the modernist poets and writers who inspired him, including Wallace Stevens, Gertrude Stein, and Marianne Moore. Ashbery also found stimulation for his poetry in avant-garde music, film, drama, and art. As early as 1950, when he saw an exhibit of the dynamic work of the French expressionist painter Chaim Soutine, Ashbery says that he was suddenly struck by new possibilities for his own work: "The fact that the sky could come crashing joyously into the grass, that trees could dance upside down and houses roll over like cats eager to have their tummies scratched was something I hadn't realized before, and I began pushing my poems around and standing words on end." Such linguistic and grammatical play is one of the most striking features of his poems, which some readers find abstract and elusive. Preoccupied with questions about the origins of imagination, the relation between representation and reality, and the limits of language, Ashbery often calls attention to the artistic process or the act of composing the poem. His poems have been described as "occasional," since many of them are so finely attuned to a specific moment in time. As he wrote in 1977, "Poetry includes anything and everything." The poems selected here demonstrate some of Ashbery's central themes and techniques. "The One Thing That Can Save America" is taken from *Self-Portrait in a Convex Mirror* (1975); "My Erotic Double" is from *As We Know* (1979); "Paradoxes and Oxymorons" is from *Shadow Train* (1981); and "One Coat of Paint" is from *April Galleons* (1987).

THE ONE THING THAT CAN SAVE AMERICA

Is anything central?
Orchards flung out on the land,
Urban forests, rustic plantations, knee-high hills?
Are place names central?
Elm Grove, Adcock Corner, Story Book Farm?   5
As they concur with a rush at eye level
Beating themselves into eyes which have had enough
Thank you, no more thank you.

And they come on like scenery mingled with darkness
The damp plains, overgrown suburbs,   10
Places of known civic pride, of civil obscurity.

These are connected to my version of America
But the juice is elsewhere.
This morning as I walked out of your room
After breakfast crosshatched with   15
Backward and forward glances, backward into light,
Forward into unfamiliar light,
Was it our doing, and was it
The material, the lumber of life, or of lives
We were measuring, counting?   20
A mood soon to be forgotten
In crossed girders of light, cool downtown shadow
In this morning that has seized us again?

I know that I braid too much my own
Snapped-off perceptions of things as they come to me.   25
They are private and always will be.
Where then are the private turns of event
Destined to boom later like golden chimes
Released over a city from a highest tower?
The quirky things that happen to me, and I tell you,   30
And you instantly know what I mean?
What remote orchard reached by winding roads
Hides them? Where are these roots?

It is the lumps and trials
That tell us whether we shall be known   35
And whether our fate can be exemplary, like a star.
All the rest is waiting
For a letter that never arrives,
Day after day, the exasperation
Until finally you have ripped it open not knowing what it is,   40
The two envelope halves lying on a plate.
The message was wise, and seemingly
Dictated a long time ago.
Its truth is timeless, but its time has still
Not arrived, telling of danger, and the mostly limited   45
Steps that can be taken against danger
Now and in the future, in cool yards,
In quiet small houses in the country,
Our country, in fenced areas, in cool shady streets.

[1974, 1975]

MY EROTIC DOUBLE

He says he doesn't feel like working today.
It's just as well. Here in the shade
Behind the house, protected from street noises,
One can go over all kinds of old feeling,
Throw some away, keep others.   The wordplay   5
Between us gets very intense when there are
Fewer feelings around to confuse things.
Another go-round? No, but the last things
You always find to say are charming, and rescue me
Before the night does. We are afloat   10
On our dreams as on a barge made of ice,
Shot through with questions and fissures of starlight
That keep us awake, thinking about the dreams
As they are happening. Some occurrence. You said it.

I said it but I can hide it. But I choose not to.   15
Thank you. You are a very pleasant person.
Thank you. You are too.

                                                [1979]

PARADOXES AND OXYMORONS

This poem is concerned with language on a very plain level.
Look at it talking to you. You look out a window
Or pretend to fidget. You have it but you don't have it.
You miss it, it misses you. You miss each other.

The poem is sad because it wants to be yours, and cannot.   5
What's a plain level? It is that and other things,
Bringing a system of them into play. Play?
Well, actually, yes, but I consider play to be

A deeper outside thing, a dreamed role-pattern,
As in the division of grace these long August days   10
Without proof. Open-ended. And before you know
It gets lost in the steam and chatter of typewriters.

It has been played once more. I think you exist only
To tease me into doing it, on your level, and then you aren't there
Or have adopted a different attitude. And the poem   15
Has set me softly down beside you. The poem is you.

                                            [1980, 1981]

ONE COAT OF PAINT

We will all have to just hang on for a while,
It seems, now. This could mean "early retirement"
For some, if only for an afternoon of pottering around
Buying shoelaces and the like. Or it could mean a spell
In some enchanter's cave, after several centuries of which   5
You wake up curiously refreshed, eager to get back
To the crossword puzzle, only no one knows your name
Or who you are, really, or cares much either. To seduce
A fact into becoming an object, a pleasing one, with some
Kind of esthetic quality, which would also add to the store   10
Of knowledge and even extend through several strata
Of history, like a pin through a cracked wrist bone,
Connecting these in such a dynamic way that one would be forced
To acknowledge a new kind of superiority without which the world
Could no longer conduct its business, even simple stuff like bringing   15
Water home from wells, coals to hearths, would of course be
An optimal form of it but in any case the thing's got to
Come into being, something has to happen, or all
We'll have left is disagreements, *désagréments*,[1] to name a few.
O don't you see how necessary it is to be around,   20
To be ferried from here to that near, smiling shore
And back again into the arms of those that love us,
Not many, but of such infinite, superior sweetness
That their lie is for us and it becomes stained, encrusted,
Finally gilded in some exasperating way that turns it   25
To a truth plus something, delicate and dismal as a star,
Cautious as a drop of milk, so that they let us
Get away with it, some do at any rate?

[1987]

---

1. *désagréments*: Annoyances or nuisances (French).

Edward Albee

[b. 1928]

Edward Albee was born on March 12, 1928, in Washington, D.C., to Louise Harvey. Two weeks later, he was adopted by Reed A. Albee, the owner of a chain of vaudeville theaters, and his third wife, the former model Frances Cotter Albee. The wealthy couple took their infant son to live in their home in Larchmont, New York, an affluent suburb of New York City. During his childhood, Albee met a long list of actors and theatrical people, including Jimmy Durante and Groucho Marx. He attended the Rye Country Day School and then went to the Lawrenceville School in New Jersey. He was expelled in 1943, and his parents sought to curb their rebellious son by sending him to Valley Forge Military Academy in Pennsylvania. He hated the "routine of discipline, institutional food, and dreary living quarters," as Albee later described the school, from which he was also expelled. His parents then sent him to the exclusive Choate School in Connecticut. Finally content, and already determined to be a writer, Albee published a play, poetry, and short stories in the *Choate Literary Magazine*. After graduating in 1946, he enrolled at Trinity College in Hartford, Connecticut. After three semesters, he was asked to leave for failing to attend classes and chapel, and he returned home to Larchmont. He worked a series of jobs in the city, including writing for the radio station WNYC. But there were growing conflicts between the radical Albee and his deeply conservative parents, who were also disturbed by his homosexuality.

Edward Albee

This photograph of Albee was taken in 1961, when the young playwright was first gaining recognition for his absurdist satires of American life.

Following an argument with his mother in 1949, Albee left home for good and moved to the bohemian enclave of Greenwich Village. Although he was eventually reconciled with his mother, he never saw his father again, and his parents disowned him. That same year, Albee came into a trust fund of $100,000 established for him by his paternal grandmother, Laura Smith Albee. The fund provided him an income of twenty-five dollars a week until he was thirty, when he inherited the principal. He initially supplemented the income from the trust fund by working a variety of jobs, including delivering telegrams for Western Union. In 1952, he began living with the composer William Flanagan, who became an important mentor to Albee. Frustrated with the progress of his writing, which included fiction, poetry, and several realistic plays, when he turned thirty Albee wrote an experimental one-act play, *The Zoo Story*, about two men whose casual conversation on a park bench ends in a bizarre act of violence. Unable to find an American producer, Albee sent the play to a friend in Germany, where it was performed in translation in 1959. *The Zoo Story* was subsequently performed in New York City at the Provincetown Playhouse in January 1960. The play was a hit, and four more of Albee's short plays had their Off-Broadway premieres by January 1961: *The Sandbox, The Death of Bessie Smith, Fam and Yam* (a mock interview between characters named Famous American Playwright and Young American Playwright), and *The American Dream*. In those absurdist plays, Albee established the themes that would characterize much of his work: the essential isolation and loneliness of individuals, the violence that lies beneath the veneer of civilized life, and the loss of American values.

Albee soon established himself as a major force in American theater. The first of his full-length plays to be produced was a corrosive portrayal of dysfunctional marriage, *Who's Afraid of Virginia Woolf?* The play won the Tony Award and ran for 664 performances on Broadway from October 1962 through 1964, when the company took the production to London. Albee sold the film rights to Warner Brothers, and the riveting movie version directed by Mike Nichols and starring Richard Burton and Elizabeth Taylor won five Academy Awards. Meanwhile, he adapted Carson McCuller's novel *The Ballad of the Sad Café* for the stage in 1963, and he followed it with his controversial allegorical play *Tiny Alice* (1964). Albee's next play, *A Delicate Balance* (1966), about a crisis in a marriage, earned him his first Pulitzer Prize. By the beginning of the 1970s, however, Albee was struggling with alcoholism and other personal problems, and he credits his survival to his longtime partner, the sculptor Jonathan Thomas (1946–2005). Albee won a second Pulitzer for another play about a troubled marriage, *Seascape* (1975). But the play did poorly at the box office, as did his next Broadway productions, *Lady from Dubuque* (1980) and *The Man with Three Arms* (1983). Although he continued to write plays, none was produced in New York until a decade later, when Albee had a major critical and commercial success with an Off-Broadway production of a play based on his mother's life, *Three Tall Women* (1994). He received his third Pulitzer Prize for the play, and in 2002, after an absence of nineteen years, he triumphantly returned to Broadway with *The Goat: Or, Who Is Sylvia?*, which won the Tony Award. In considerable demand as a speaker on college campuses, Albee has for many years vigorously promoted student theater and the study of the arts, and he taught an annual playwriting class at the University of Houston from 1989 to 2003. In 2005, Albee received a special Tony Award for "Lifetime Achievement in the Theatre."

> *There is a great sense of danger in Edward's work, and you never quite know what's going to happen next.*
>
> *-Harold Pinter*

Albee's *The Sandbox*.   Asked in an interview in 1966 whether he had a special attachment to any one of his plays, Albee replied: "I'm terribly fond of *The Sandbox*. I think it's an absolutely beautiful, lovely, perfect play." The short play was commissioned by the composer Gian Carlo Menotti for the Festival of the Two Worlds in Spoleto, Italy. But it was never performed there and had its premiere on April 15, 1960, at the Jazz Gallery in New York, along with short plays by H. B. Lutz and the Spanish playwright Fernando Arrabel. In part, *The Sandbox* had its origins in the movement known as the "theater of the absurd," a term coined by the critic Martin Esslin to describe the work of the avant-garde European dramatists Arthur Adamov, Samuel Beckett, Jean Genet, and Eugène Ionesco. Like them, Albee wittily subverts the conventions of the realistic theater, as characters call attention to their status as actors, give stage directions, or speak directly to the audience. The play was also rooted in Albee's background and experience. On the title page of the first edition, he described it as "A Brief Play, In Memory of My Grandmother (1876–1959)," a reference to his beloved maternal grandmother, Anna Loring Cotter, who died

The Sandbox

Lawrence Arrick directed the original Off-Broadway production of Albee's play in 1960. From left to right, the cast included Jane Hoffman (Mommy), Sudie Bond (Grandma), and Richard Woods (Daddy). At the time, Bond was in her early thirties, but Albee said that she played the role of the octogenarian grandmother "with the wit and wisdom of the aged and the buoyancy and objectivity of the intelligent young."

shortly before Albee's first play was produced in 1960. She was the model for the humorously crotchety character Grandma in *The Sandbox*, in which Albee satirized his adoptive parents in the characters of Mommy and Daddy. Like one of Albee's other short plays, *The American Dream* (1960), *The Sandbox* may more broadly be understood as a commentary on the hollowness and sterility of American life, as Mommy and Daddy carry on a vacuous conversation while they impatiently wait for Grandma to die. The cast of characters includes a musician who plays mournful flute music composed by Albee's friend and mentor William Flanagan. The text is taken from *The Sandbox and The Death of Bessie Smith (with Fam and Yam)* (1963).

bedfordstmartins.com/ americanlit for research links on Albee

THE SANDBOX

THE PLAYERS

THE YOUNG MAN, 25. *A good-looking, well-built boy in a bathing suit.*

MOMMY, 55. *A well-dressed, imposing woman.*

DADDY, 60. *A small man; gray, thin.*

GRANDMA, 86. *A tiny, wizened woman with bright eyes.*

THE MUSICIAN. *No particular age, but young would be nice.*

NOTE

When, in the course of the play, MOMMY *and* DADDY *call each other by these names, there should be no suggestion of regionalism. These names are of empty affection and point up the pre-senility and vacuity of their characters.*

THE SCENE

A bare stage, with only the following: Near the footlights, far stage-right, two simple chairs set side by side, facing the audience; near the footlights, far stage-left, a chair facing stage-right with a music stand before it; farther back, and stage-center, slightly elevated and raked, a large child's sandbox with a toy pail and shovel; the background is the sky, which alters from brightest day to deepest night.

At the beginning, it is brightest day; the YOUNG MAN *is alone on stage, to the rear of the sandbox, and to one side. He is doing calisthenics; he does calisthenics until quite at the very end of the play. These calisthenics, employing the arms only, should suggest the beating and fluttering of wings. The* YOUNG MAN *is, after all, the Angel of Death.*

MOMMY *and* DADDY *enter from stage-left,* MOMMY *first.*

MOMMY: *(Motioning to* DADDY*)* Well, here we are; this is the beach.

DADDY *(Whining)*: I'm cold.

MOMMY: *(Dismissing him with a little laugh)* Don't be silly; it's as warm as toast. Look at that nice young man over there: *he* doesn't think it's cold. *(Waves to the* YOUNG MAN*)* Hello.

YOUNG MAN: *(With an endearing smile)* Hi!

MOMMY *(Looking about)*: This will do perfectly . . . don't you think so, Daddy? There's sand there . . . and the water beyond. What do you think, Daddy?

DADDY *(Vaguely)*: Whatever you say, Mommy.

MOMMY: *(With the same little laugh)* Well, of course . . . whatever I say. Then, it's settled, is it?

DADDY *(Shrugs)*: She's *your* mother, not mine.

MOMMY: *I* know she's my mother. What do you take me for? *(A pause)* All right, now; let's get on with it. *(She shouts into the wings, stage-left)* You! Out there! You can come in now.

(The MUSICIAN *enters, seats himself in the chair, stage-left, places music on the music stand, is ready to play.* MOMMY *nods approvingly)*

MOMMY: Very nice; very nice. Are you ready, Daddy? Let's go get Grandma.

DADDY: Whatever you say, Mommy.

MOMMY: *(Leading the way out, stage-left)* Of course, whatever I say. *(To the* MUSICIAN*)* You can begin now.

(The MUSICIAN *begins playing;* MOMMY *and* DADDY *exit; the* MUSICIAN*, all the while playing, nods to the* YOUNG MAN*)*

YOUNG MAN: *(With the same endearing smile)* Hi!

(After a moment, MOMMY *and* DADDY *re-enter, carrying* GRANDMA*. She is borne in by their hands under her armpits; she is quite rigid; her legs are drawn up; her feet do not touch the ground; the expression on her ancient face is that of puzzlement and fear)*

DADDY: Where do we put her?

MOMMY: *(The same little laugh)* Wherever I say, of course. Let me see . . . well . . . all right, over there . . . in the sandbox. *(Pause)* Well, what are you waiting for, Daddy? . . . The sandbox!

(Together they carry GRANDMA *over to the sandbox and more or less dump her in)*

GRANDMA: *(Righting herself to a sitting position; her voice a cross between a baby's laugh and cry)* Ahhhhhh! Graaaaa!

DADDY *(Dusting himself)*: What do we do now?

MOMMY: *(To the* MUSICIAN*)* You can stop now.

(The MUSICIAN *stops)*

(Back to DADDY*)* What do you mean, what do we do now? We go over there and sit down, of course.

(To the YOUNG MAN*)* Hello there.

YOUNG MAN: *(Again smiling)* Hi!

*(*MOMMY *and* DADDY *move to the chairs, stage-right, and sit down. A pause)*

GRANDMA: *(Same as before)* Ahhhhhh! Ah-haaaaaa! Graaaaaa!

DADDY: Do you think . . . do you think she's . . . comfortable?

MOMMY *(Impatiently)*: How would I know?

DADDY: *(Pause)* What do we do now?

MOMMY: *(As if remembering)* We . . . wait. We . . . sit here . . . and we wait . . . that's what we do.

DADDY: *(After a pause)* Shall we talk to each other?

MOMMY: *(With that little laugh; picking something off her dress)* Well, *you* can talk,

if you want to . . . if you can think of anything to *say* . . . if you can think of anything *new.*

DADDY *(Thinks)*: No . . . I suppose not.

MOMMY: *(With a triumphant laugh)* Of course not!

GRANDMA: *(Banging the toy shovel against the pail)* Haaaaaa! Ah-haaaaaa!

MOMMY: *(Out over the audience)* Be quiet, Grandma . . . just be quiet, and wait.

*(*GRANDMA *throws a shovelful of sand at* MOMMY*)*

MOMMY: *(Still out over the audience)* She's throwing sand at me! You stop that, Grandma;
you stop throwing sand at Mommy! *(To* DADDY*)* She's throwing sand at me.

*(*DADDY *looks around at* GRANDMA, *who screams at him)*

GRANDMA: GRAAAAA!

MOMMY: Don't look at her. Just . . . sit here . . . be very still . . . and wait. *(To the* MUSI-
CIAN*)* You . . . uh . . . you go ahead and do whatever it is you do.

(The MUSICIAN *plays)*

*(*MOMMY *and* DADDY *are fixed, staring out beyond the audience.* GRANDMA *looks at
them, looks at the* MUSICIAN, *looks at the sandbox, throws down the shovel)*

GRANDMA: Ah-haaaaaa! Graaaaaa! *(Looks for reaction; gets none. Now . . . directly to the
audience)* Honestly! What a way to treat an old woman! Drag her out of the house . . .
stick her in a car . . . bring her out here from the city . . . dump her in a pile of sand . . .
and leave her here to set. I'm eighty-six years old! I was married when I was seventeen.
To a farmer. He died when I was thirty. *(To the* MUSICIAN*)* Will you stop that, please?

(The MUSICIAN *stops playing)*

I'm a feeble old woman . . . how do you expect anybody to hear me over that peep!
peep! peep! *(To herself)* There's no respect around here. *(To the* YOUNG MAN*)* There's
no respect around here!

YOUNG MAN: *(Same smile)* Hi!

GRANDMA: *(After a pause, a mild double-take, continues, to the audience)* My husband
died when I was thirty *(indicates* MOMMY*)*, and I had to raise that big cow over there
all by my lonesome. You can imagine what *that was like.* Lordy! *(To the* YOUNG MAN*)*
Where'd they get *you?*

YOUNG MAN: Oh . . . I've been around for a while.

GRANDMA: I'll bet you have! Heh, heh, heh. Will you look at you!

YOUNG MAN: *(Flexing his muscles)* Isn't that something? *(Continues his calisthenics)*

GRANDMA: Boy, oh boy; I'll say. Pretty good.

YOUNG MAN *(Sweetly)*: I'll say.

GRANDMA: Where ya from?

YOUNG MAN: Southern California.

GRANDMA *(Nodding)*: Figgers; figgers. What's your name, honey?

YOUNG MAN: I don't know. . . .

GRANDMA: *(To the audience)* Bright, too!

YOUNG MAN: I mean . . . I mean, they haven't given me one yet . . . the studio . . .

GRANDMA: *(Giving him the once-over)* You don't say . . . you don't say. Well . . . uh, I've got to talk some more . . . don't you go 'way.

YOUNG MAN: Oh, no.

GRANDMA: *(Turning her attention back to the audience)* Fine; fine. *(Then, once more, back to the* YOUNG MAN*)* You're . . . you're an actor, hunh?

YOUNG MAN *(Beaming)*: Yes. I am.

GRANDMA: *(To the audience again; shrugs)* I'm smart that way. *Anyhow*, I had to raise . . . *that* over there all by my lonesome; and what's next to her there . . . that's what she married. Rich? I tell you . . . money, money, money. They took me off the *farm* . . . which was real decent of them . . . and they moved me into the big town house with *them* . . . fixed a nice place for me under the stove . . . gave me an army blanket[1] . . . and my own dish . . . my very own dish! So, what have I got to complain about? Nothing, of course. I'm not complaining. *(She looks up at the sky, shouts to someone off stage)* Shouldn't it be getting dark now, dear?

(The lights dim; night comes on. The MUSICIAN *begins to play; it becomes deepest night. There are spots on all the players, including the* YOUNG MAN, *who is, of course, continuing his calisthenics)*

DADDY *(Stirring)*: It's nighttime.

MOMMY: Shhhh. Be still . . . wait.

DADDY *(Whining)*: It's so hot.

MOMMY: Shhhhhh. Be still . . . wait.

GRANDMA: *(To herself)* That's better. Night. *(To the* MUSICIAN*)* Honey, do you play all through this part?

(The MUSICIAN *nods)*

Well, keep it nice and soft; that's a good boy.

(The MUSICIAN *nods again; plays softly)*

That's nice.

(There is an off-stage rumble)

DADDY *(Starting)*: What was that?

MOMMY: *(Beginning to weep)* It was nothing.

DADDY: It was . . . it was . . . thunder . . . or a wave breaking . . . or something.

---

1. **army blanket:** A thin, olive-drab wool blanket issued by U.S. Army and often sold inexpensively at military surplus stores.

MOMMY: *(Whispering, through her tears)* It was an off-stage rumble . . . and you know what *that* means. . . .

DADDY: I forget. . . .

MOMMY: *(Barely able to talk)* It means the time has come for poor Grandma . . . and I can't bear it!

DADDY *(Vacantly)*: I . . . I suppose you've got to be brave.

GRANDMA *(Mocking)*: That's right, kid; be brave. You'll bear up; you'll get over it.

(Another off-stage rumble . . . louder)

MOMMY: Ohhhhhhhhhh . . . poor Grandma . . . poor Grandma. . . .

GRANDMA *(To MOMMY)*: I'm fine! I'm all right! It hasn't happened yet!

(A violent off-stage rumble. All the lights go out, save the spot on the YOUNG MAN; the MUSICIAN stops playing)

MOMMY: Ohhhhhhhhhh . . . Ohhhhhhhhhh . . .

(Silence)

GRANDMA: Don't put the lights up yet . . . I'm not ready; I'm not quite ready. *(Silence)* All right, dear . . . I'm about done.

(The lights come up again, to brightest day; the MUSICIAN begins to play. GRANDMA is discovered, still in the sandbox, lying on her side, propped up on an elbow, half covered, busily shoveling sand over herself)

GRANDMA *(Muttering)*: I don't know how I'm supposed to do anything with this goddam toy shovel. . . .

DADDY: Mommy! It's daylight!

MOMMY *(Brightly)*: So it is! Well! Our long night is over. We must put away our tears, take off our mourning[2] . . . and face the future. It's our duty.

GRANDMA: *(Still shoveling; mimicking)* . . . take off our mourning . . . face the future. . . . Lordy!

(MOMMY and DADDY rise, stretch. MOMMY waves to the YOUNG MAN)

YOUNG MAN: *(With that smile)* Hi!

(GRANDMA plays dead. (!) MOMMY and DADDY go over to look at her; she is a little more than half buried in the sand; the toy shovel is in her hands, which are crossed on her breast)

---

2. **"We must . . . mourning"**: See Psalms 30:11–12: "Thou has turned for me my mourning into dancing; thou has put off my sackcloth, and girded me with gladness."

MOMMY: *(Before the sandbox; shaking her head)* Lovely! It's . . . it's hard to be sad . . . she looks . . . so happy. *(With pride and conviction)* It pays to do things well. *(To the* MUSICIAN*)* All right, you can stop now, if you want to. I mean, stay around for a swim, or something; it's all right with us. *(She sighs heavily)* Well, Daddy . . . off we go.

DADDY: Brave Mommy!

MOMMY: Brave Daddy!

(They exit, stage-left)

GRANDMA: *(After they leave; lying quite still)* It pays to do things well. . . . Boy, oh boy! *(She tries to sit up)* . . . well, kids . . . *(but she finds she can't)* . . . I . . . I can't get up. I . . . I can't move. . . .

(The YOUNG MAN *stops his calisthenics, nods to the* MUSICIAN, *walks over to* GRANDMA, *kneels down by the sandbox)*

GRANDMA: I . . . can't move. . . .

YOUNG MAN: Shhhhh . . . be very still. . . .

GRANDMA: I . . . I can't move. . . .

YOUNG MAN: Uh . . . ma'am; I . . . I have a line here.

GRANDMA: Oh, I'm sorry, sweetie; you go right ahead.

YOUNG MAN: I am . . . uh . . .

GRANDMA: Take your time, dear.

YOUNG MAN: *(Prepares; delivers the line like a real amateur)* I am the Angel of Death. I am . . . uh . . . I am come for you.

GRANDMA: What . . . wha . . . *(Then, with resignation)* . . . ohhhh . . . ohhhh, I see.

(The YOUNG MAN *bends over, kisses* GRANDMA *gently on the forehead)*

GRANDMA: *(Her eyes closed, her hands folded on her breast again, the shovel between her hands, a sweet smile on her face)* Well . . . that was very nice, dear. . . .

YOUNG MAN: *(Still kneeling)* Shhhhh . . . be still. . . .

GRANDMA: What I meant was . . . you did that very well, dear. . . .

YOUNG MAN *(Blushing):* . . . oh . . .

GRANDMA: No; I mean it. You've got that . . . you've got a quality.

YOUNG MAN: *(With his endearing smile)* Oh . . . thank you; thank you very much . . . ma'am.

GRANDMA: *(Slowly; softly — as the* YOUNG MAN *puts his hands on top of* GRANDMA'S*)* You're . . . you're welcome . . . dear.

(Tableau. The MUSICIAN *continues to play as the curtain slowly comes down)*

CURTAIN

[1963]

Adrienne Rich

[b. 1929]

Adrienne Rich

This photograph was taken in the 1970s, about the time Rich published her groundbreaking collection *Diving into the Wreck* (1973).

Adrienne Cecile Rich was born on May 16, 1929, in Baltimore, Maryland, to Helen Jones Rich, a pianist and composer who gave up her career to raise her family, and Arnold Rich, a doctor and professor of pathology at the Johns Hopkins University. As Rich explained in an autobiographical essay, "When We Dead Awaken: Writing as Re-Vision" (1972), "My own luck was being born white and middle-class into a house full of books, with a father who encouraged me to read and write." While her mother gave her music lessons, Rich began to write poetry at an early age and read widely among the books in her father's library, memorizing poems written in English and French. As a student at Radcliffe College in Cambridge, Massachusetts, Rich took a course with the distinguished Harvard professor F. O. Matthiessen, who lectured on the British Romantic poets, the modern Irish poet William Butler Yeats, and the contemporary American poet Wallace Stevens. "That class affected my life as a poet more than anything else that happened to me in college," Rich later recalled. Under the influence of Stevens and especially Yeats, then her idea of "the Great Poet," Rich wrote the poems in her first collection, *A Change of World*, which won the coveted Yale Younger Poets prize and was subsequently published in 1951, the year she graduated from Radcliffe. Awarded a Guggenheim Fellowship, Rich spent a year traveling in Europe. After her return to the United States in 1953, she married Alfred Conrad, a professor of economics at Harvard.

Rich was radicalized by her struggle to balance her personal and professional needs with the demands of her traditional marriage. The first of her three sons was born the year she published her second collection of poetry, *The Diamond Cutters* (1955). Rich, however, was increasingly dissatisfied with her work and frustrated by the lack of time for writing, later observing that she felt "like a failed woman and a failed poet." In the late 1950s, she began writing poems in a looser style about her experiences as a woman, a wife, and a mother. Her next book, *Snapshots of a Daughter-in-Law* (1963), represented a major turning point for Rich. Although some reviewers were troubled by what one described as the "bitterness" of the poems, as well as by Rich's overtly feminist themes, she was awarded *Poetry* magazine's Bess Hokin Prize. In 1966, the year she published her fourth book, *Necessities of Life*, she and her family moved to New York City, where Rich actively participated in protests against the Vietnam War. She also began teaching, first at Swarthmore College and Columbia University, and then in remedial programs at the City College of New York. Her experiences working with students who lacked the language skills necessary for college, most of them African Americans and immigrants from poor homes, heightened Rich's sense of racial and economic injustice. Her involvement in the social and political turmoil of 1960s was reflected in the title and poems of her next collection, *Leaflets* (1969), published the year before her husband died in 1970.

Through her writings, speeches, and political activism, Rich has played a leading role in the radical feminist movement and other causes, including gay rights and international human rights. The poems in *The Will to Change* (1971) and *Diving into the Wreck* (1973) reflected her vigorous challenge to patriarchal culture and society, which she criticized in her groundbreaking study *Of Woman Born: Motherhood as Experience and Institution* (1976). That year, Rich also published a lesbian love sequence, *Twenty-one Love Poems* (1976), and began her lasting partnership with the Jamaican American writer Michelle Cliff. Rich continued to explore issues of sexuality and the construction of gender in her next collections of poems, *A Wild Patience Has Taken Me This Far* (1981) and *The Fact of a Doorframe* (1984). In 1984, she and Cliff moved permanently to Santa Cruz, California, and Rich was a professor of English at nearby Stanford University from 1986 to 1993. She explored her personal past and her complex relation to her Jewish heritage in the first two volumes of poetry she wrote during that period, *Your Native Land, Your Life* (1986) and *Time's Power* (1989). She subsequently charted the troubled social and political landscape of contemporary America in the poems in *An Atlas of the Difficult World* (1991) and *Dark Fields of the Republic* (1995). The recipient of numerous awards and honors, Rich famously declined the National Medal for the Arts in 1997 as a protest against the Clinton administration's move to end federal funding for the National Endowment for the Arts. "The radical disparities of wealth and power in America are widening at a devastating rate," she explained in a letter to the chair of the endowment. "A President cannot meaningfully honor certain token artists while the people at large are so dishonored." Since then, Rich has published several more volumes of poetry, and in 2003 she was awarded the prestigious Bollingen Prize in American Poetry for her lifetime achievement and in recognition of her collection *Fox* (2001). The judges cited "her honesty at once ferocious and humane, her deep learning, and her continuous poetic exploration and awareness of multiple selves."

Because Rich took a woman's worldview to be emblematic, her inquiries did not stop — as they had not started — at questions of gender. It was with the rage and insights of her feminism that she envisioned . . . Vietnam, World War II, Emily Dickinson, South Africa, Manifest Destiny, the aftermath of the Shoah, and the American Civil Rights Movement.
—Marilyn Hacker

Rich's Poetry.　　In 1951, Rich's career was launched by the publication of *A Change of World*, a collection of poems marked by her formal style, her use of traditional poetic forms and what she has described as her "objective, observant tone." She later began to write in free verse and in a more confessional mode, and her growing political and social activism led Rich to assume a public voice during the 1960s. In a review of her fourth book, *Necessities of Life* (1966), Robert Lowell observed: "From the beginning, there was a yearning, a straining onward, a sense of disproportion between the life of looking and the life of living, tremors of discontent running through a style perhaps too beautiful and contented." As Lowell rightly recognized, Rich was moving on, and her poetry subsequently became even more experimental in form and wide-ranging in subject matter, combining sophisticated aesthetics with a radical social critique. The poems presented here, which were first collected in *The Will to Change* (1971) and *Diving into the Wreck* (1973), reveal some of the abiding concerns of her mature work: the complications of love, the myths of patriarchy, and the role of women in society. Looking back over her long and distin-

bedfordstmartins.com/
americanlit *for research*
links on Rich

guished career, Rich wrote in 2001: "For more than fifty years I have been writing, tearing up, revising poems, studying poets from every culture and century available to me. I have been a poet of the oppositional imagination, meaning that I don't think my only argument is with myself. My work is for people who want to imagine and claim wider horizons and carry on about them into the night, rather than rehearse the landlocked details of personal quandaries or the price for which the house next door just sold." The texts are taken from *The Fact of a Doorframe: Poems Selected and New, 1950-1984* (1984).

A VALEDICTION FORBIDDING MOURNING[1]

My swirling wants. Your frozen lips.
The grammar turned and attacked me.
Themes, written under duress.
Emptiness of the notations.

They gave me a drug that slowed the healing of wounds.   5

I want you to see this before I leave:
the experience of repetition as death
the failure of criticism to locate the pain
the poster in the bus that said:
my bleeding is under control.   10

A red plant in a cemetery of plastic wreaths.

A last attempt: the language is a dialect called metaphor.
These images go unglossed: hair, glacier, flashlight.
When I think of a landscape I am thinking of a time.
When I talk of taking a trip I mean forever.   15
I could say: those mountains have a meaning
but further than that I could not say.

To do something very common, in my own way.

[1970, 1984]

---

1. **A Valediction Forbidding Mourning:** The English poet John Donne (1572-1631) wrote "A Valediction: Forbidding Mourning," a poem addressed to his wife that may have been occasioned by his trip to the Continent in 1611. A "valediction" is a poem or formal statement of farewell, as in a valedictory address.

TRYING TO TALK WITH A MAN

Out in this desert we are testing bombs,

that's why we came here.

Sometimes I feel an underground river
forcing its way between deformed cliffs
an acute angle of understanding   5
moving itself like a locus of the sun
into this condemned scenery.

What we've had to give up to get here —
whole LP collections,[1] films we starred in
playing in the neighborhoods, bakery windows   10
full of dry, chocolate-filled Jewish cookies,
the language of love-letters, of suicide notes,
afternoons on the riverbank
pretending to be children

Coming out to this desert   15
we meant to change the face of
driving among dull green succulents
walking at noon in the ghost town
surrounded by a silence

that sounds like the silence of the place   20
except that it came with us
and is familiar
and everything we were saying until now
was an effort to blot it out —
coming out here we are up against it   25

Out here I feel more helpless
with you than without you

You mention the danger
and list the equipment
we talk of people caring for each other   30
in emergencies — laceration, thirst —
but you look at me like an emergency

Your dry heat feels like power
your eyes are stars of a different magnitude
they reflect lights that spell out: EXIT   35
when you get up and pace the floor

talking of the danger
as if it were not ourselves
as if we were testing anything else.

                                              [1971, 1984]

---

1. **LP collections:** LPs are long-playing phonograph records.

DIVING INTO THE WRECK

First having read the book of myths,
and loaded the camera,
and checked the edge of the knife-blade,
I put on
the body-armor of black rubber   5
the absurd flippers
the grave and awkward mask.
I am having to do this
not like Cousteau with his
assiduous team   10
aboard the sun-flooded schooner[1]
but here alone.

There is a ladder.
The ladder is always there
hanging innocently   15
close to the side of the schooner.
We know what it is for,
we who have used it.
Otherwise
it's a piece of maritime floss   20
some sundry equipment.

I go down.
Rung after rung and still
the oxygen immerses me
the blue light   25
the clear atoms
of our human air.
I go down.
My flippers cripple me,
I crawl like an insect down the ladder   30
and there is no one
to tell me when the ocean
will begin.

First the air is blue and then
it is bluer and then green and then   35
black I am blacking out and yet

---

1. **Cousteau . . . sun-flooded schooner:** Jacques-Yves Cousteau (1910–1997), the coinventor of scuba-diving gear, was a French explorer and oceanographer who became famous worldwide for his voyages aboard the *Calypso*, the basis of several documentary films and his popular television show *The Undersea World of Jacques Cousteau*, which first aired in 1966.

my mask is powerful
it pumps my blood with power
the sea is another story
the sea is not a question of power   40
I have to learn alone
to turn my body without force
in the deep element.

And now: it is easy to forget
what I came for   45
among so many who have always
lived here
swaying their crenellated fans[2]
between the reefs
and besides   50
you breathe differently down here.

I came to explore the wreck.
The words are purposes.
The words are maps.
I came to see the damage that was done   55
and the treasures that prevail.
I stroke the beam of my lamp
slowly along the flank
of something more permanent
than fish or weed   60

the thing I came for:
the wreck and not the story of the wreck
the thing itself and not the myth
the drowned face always staring
toward the sun[3]   65
the evidence of damage
worn by salt and sway into this threadbare beauty
the ribs of the disaster
curving their assertion
among the tentative haunters.   70

This is the place.
And I am here, the mermaid whose dark hair
streams black, the merman in his armored body

---

2. **crenellated fans:** That is, the notched or indented tail fins of the fish.
3. **the drowned face . . . toward the sun:** Almost all old sailing ships had ornamental figureheads, usually the bust or full-length figure of a woman, attached to the prow. This figure, who once looked down into the waves, now stares upward through the water to the sun.

We circle silently
about the wreck   75
we dive into the hold.
I am she: I am he

whose drowned face sleeps with open eyes
whose breasts still bear the stress
whose silver, copper, vermeil cargo lies   80
obscurely inside barrels
half-wedged and left to rot
we are the half-destroyed instruments
that once held to a course
the water-eaten log   85
the fouled compass

We are, I am, you are
by cowardice or courage
the one who find our way
back to this scene   90
carrying a knife, a camera
a book of myths
in which
our names do not appear.

                                                        [1972, 1984]

POWER

Living   in the earth-deposits   of our history

Today a backhoe divulged   out of a crumbling flank of earth
one bottle   amber   perfect   a hundred-year-old
cure for fever   or melancholy   a tonic
for living on this earth   in the winters of this climate   5

Today I was reading about Marie Curie:[1]
she must have known she suffered   from radiation sickness
her body bombarded for years   by the element
she had purified
It seems she denied to the end   10

---

1. **Marie Curie:** Curie (1867–1934) and her husband Pierre (1859–1906) pioneered the science of radioactivity and were jointly awarded the Nobel Prize in Physics in 1903. After her husband's death, Curie isolated the element radium and was awarded the Nobel Prize in Chemistry in 1911. She died of leukemia, caused by her long exposure to radiation.

the source of the cataracts on her eyes
the cracked and suppurating skin   of her finger-ends
till she could no longer hold   a test-tube or a pencil

She died   a famous woman   denying
her wounds   15
denying
her wounds   came   from the same source as her power

[1974, 1984]

Ursula K. Le Guin

[b. 1929]

Ursula K. Le Guin was born on October 21, 1929, in Berkeley, California. She was the fourth child and only daughter of Alfred Kroeber, a distinguished anthropologist specializing in Native American cultures at the University of California, Berkeley, and Theodora Kroeber, an author best known for her biography of the last survivor of the Yahi Indians of northern California, *Ishi in Two Worlds* (1961). Le Guin was brought up in an atmosphere of books, ideas, and lively conversation in her close-knit family, which lived in Berkeley during the academic year and spent the summers at Kishamish, their country house in the Napa Valley of northern California. When she was a child, her father told her Native American legends and stories, and Le Guin became deeply interested in mythology. She was also an avid reader of pulp magazines such as *Astounding Science Fiction*, to which

Ursula K. Le Guin

The portrait photographer Mary Ann Wood Kolish took this photograph in 1990, by which time Le Guin had gained wide acclaim for her innovative works of fantasy and science fiction.

she submitted a story when she was eleven. But it was rejected, and she soon lost interest in science fiction. She majored in French at Radcliffe College, from which she graduated Phi Beta Kappa in 1951, and earned an MA in Romance languages from Columbia University in 1952. She decided to continue her studies toward a doctorate and was awarded a Fulbright Scholarship for study in France. While sailing there aboard the *Queen Mary*, she met the historian Charles Le Guin, and they were married in Paris in 1953.

As Le Guin has said, her marriage put an end to her graduate study and marked the beginning of her two-decade effort to establish herself as a writer. Her husband taught at several colleges before he accepted a position at Portland State University in Portland, Oregon, where the couple settled with their three children in 1959. Le Guin, who left work to raise their children, wrote poetry and fiction, some of it set in an imaginary central European country, Orsinia. She finally managed to publish one of her Orsinian stories in the *Western Humanities Review* in 1961. But all five of her early, unorthodox novels were rejected, so the frustrated Le Guin turned to writing in a more familiar and marketable genre, science fiction. She subsequently became a regular contributor to the popular magazines *Fantastic* and *Amazing*. Encouraged by the reception of her science-fiction stories, Le Guin began working on the earliest of a series of novels set in the "Hainish Universe," *Rocannon's World* (1966), *Planet of Exile* (1966), and *City of Illusions* (1967). In those novels, which were shaped by the social and political concerns of the 1960s, Le Guin explored some of the central subjects and themes of her fiction: the irrationality of war, problems in human communication, the search for identity, and the impact of a journey to an unknown place and encounters with strange or alien creatures. Le Guin gained her first major critical and commercial success with a fantasy trilogy for young adults about an imagined world called Earthsea: *A Wizard of Earthsea* (1968), *The Tombs of Atuan* (1971), and *The Farthest Shore* (1972). She continued her Hainish series in two other acclaimed novels of the period, *The Left Hand of Darkness* (1969), regarded by many as the first feminist work of science fiction, and her complex utopian novel *The Dispossessed* (1974). Extending the audience for such genres, Le Guin also published stories in magazines as diverse as the *New Yorker*, *Playboy*, and *Redbook*.

Although she is best known for her works of fantasy and science fiction, the prolific Le Guin has produced a wide range of work. In addition to more than twenty novels and over one-hundred short stories, she has published collections of poetry and essays, as well as translations of the ancient Chinese religious text the *Tao Te Ching* and the poems of Gabriel Mistral, the Chilean poet who won the Nobel Prize for Literature in 1945. Le Guin won the Kafka Prize for fiction by an American woman for her ambitious novel *Always Coming Home* (1985), a work of ethnographic fiction in which she interweaves the myths, poems, and stories of the Kesh, a people akin to Native Americans who live far in the future in California. The novel was the runner-up for the National Book Award, an unprecedented achievement for a work of science fiction. Le Guin has also written a series of works for children, the popular Catwings Books (1988–99), and realistic fiction for adults, including *Searoad* (1992), a collection of related stories set in a small town in Oregon. At the same time, she continued the Earthsea cycle in *Tehanu* (1990), *Tales from Earthsea* (2001), and *The Other Wind* (2001) and wrote another novel in the Hainish series, *The Telling* (2000). Le Guin's most recent work is a second fantasy cycle for young adults, *Annals of the Western Shore*, including *Gifts* (2004), *Voices* (2006), and *Powers* (2007). A staunch defender of fantasy, which many critics tend to dismiss as a subliterary genre, Le Guin in 2006 wrote: "To conflate fantasy with immaturity is a rather sizeable error. Rational yet non-intellectual, moral yet inexplicit, symbolic not allegorical, fantasy is not primitive but primary. Many of its great texts are poetry, and its prose often approaches poetry in density of implication and imagery." Le Guin continues to live and work in Portland, Oregon.

Le Guin's "She Unnames Them."   Like much of Le Guin's work, this story illustrates the erosion in postmodern literature of former distinctions between "literary" fiction and popular genres such as fantasy and science fiction. First published in January 1985 in one of the most prominent venues for contemporary fiction, the *New Yorker*, "She Unnames Them" is the final piece in Le Guin's collection of prose and poetry about animals, *Buffalo Gals*. Le Guin introduced the story by explaining that it "had to come last in this book because it states (equivocally, of course) whose side (so long as sides must be taken) I am on and what the consequences (maybe) are." In Le Guin's feminist subversion of the biblical story of the Creation, in which Adam names all of the creatures of the earth (Genesis 2:19), Eve subsequently takes the names away. "As she does this, the barriers between herself and the world are dismantled," Le Guin has observed in an interview, and in Le Guin's witty fable Eve may also be understood to liberate herself and her fellow creatures from the control of Adam. The text is taken from *Buffalo Gals and Other Animal Presences* (1987).

bedfordstmartins.com/ americanlit for research links on Le Guin

SHE UNNAMES THEM

Most of them accepted namelessness with the perfect indifference with which they had so long accepted and ignored their names. Whales and dolphins, seals and sea otters consented with particular grace and alacrity, sliding into anonymity as into their element. A faction of yaks, however, protested. They said that "yak" sounded right, and that almost everyone who knew they existed called them that. Unlike the ubiquitous creatures such as rats or fleas who had been called by hundreds or thousands of different names since Babel,[1] the yaks could truly say, they said, that they had *a name*. They discussed the matter all summer. The councils of the elderly females finally agreed that though the name might be useful to others, it was so redundant from the yak point of view that they never spoke it themselves, and hence might as well dispense with it. After they presented the argument in this light to their bulls, a full consensus was delayed only by the onset of severe early blizzards. Soon after the beginning of the thaw their agreement was reached and the designation "yak" was returned to the donor.

---

1. **Babel:** In Genesis 11:1–9, the townspeople of the ancient city of Babel attempt to build a tower to reach heaven. God thwarts the plan by causing the languages of the builders to be mutually incomprehensible.

Among the domestic animals, few horses had cared what anybody called them since the failure of Dean Swift's attempt to name them from their own vocabulary.[2] Cattle, sheep, swine, asses, mules, and goats, along with chickens, geese, and turkeys, all agreed enthusiastically to give their names back to the people to whom — as they put it — they belonged.

A couple of problems did come up with pets. The cats of course steadfastly denied ever having had any name other than those self-given, unspoken, effanineffably personal names which, as the poet named Eliot said,[3] they spend long hours daily contemplating — though none of the contemplators has ever admitted that what they contemplate is in fact their name, and some onlookers have wondered if the object of that meditative gaze might not in fact be the Perfect, or Platonic, Mouse. In any case it is a moot point now. It was with the dogs, and with some parrots, lovebirds, ravens, and mynahs that the trouble arose. These verbally talented individuals insisted that their names were important to them, and flatly refused to part with them. But as soon as they understood that the issue was precisely one of individual choice, and that anybody who wanted to be called Rover, or Froufrou, or Polly, or even Birdie in the personal sense, was perfectly free to do so, not one of them had the least objection to parting with the lower case (or, as regards German creatures, uppercase) generic appellations poodle, parrot, dog, or bird, and all the Linnaean qualifiers[4] that had trailed along behind them for two hundred years like tin cans tied to a tail.

The insects parted with their names in vast clouds and swarms of ephemeral syllables buzzing and stinging and humming and flitting and crawling and tunneling away.

As for the fish of the sea, their names dispersed from them in silence throughout the oceans like faint, dark blurs of cuttlefish ink, and drifted off on the currents without a trace.

None were left now to unname, and yet how close I felt to them when I saw one of them swim or fly or trot or crawl across my way or over my skin, or stalk me in the night, or go along beside me for a while in the day. They seemed far closer than when their names had stood between myself and them like a clear barrier: so close that my fear of them and their fear of me became one same fear. And the attraction that many of us felt, the desire to smell one another's smells, feel or rub or caress one another's scales or skin or feathers or fur, taste one another's blood or flesh, keep one another warm, — that attraction was now all one with the fear, and the hunter could not be told from the hunted, nor the eater from the food.

This was more or less the effect I had been after. It was somewhat more powerful than I had anticipated, but I could not now, in all conscience, make an exception for

---

2. **Dean Swift's . . . own vocabulary:** In the fourth part of *Gulliver's Travels* by the English satirist Jonathan Swift (1667–1745), Lemuel Gulliver travels to a land where intelligent horses, called "Houyhnhnms" in their language, rule over brutelike human beings, called "Yahoos."

3. **as the poet named Eliot said:** T. S. Eliot wrote and illustrated a fanciful collection of poems about cats, *Old Possum's Book of Practical Cats* (1939).

4. **Linnaean qualifiers:** The Swedish botanist Carolus Linnaeus (1707–1778) devised a system of classifying plants and animals into species using two-part Latin names, for example *Homo sapiens*.

myself. I resolutely put anxiety away, went to Adam, and said, "You and your father lent me this — gave it to me, actually. It's been really useful, but it doesn't exactly seem to fit very well lately. But thanks very much! It's really been very useful."

It is hard to give back a gift without sounding peevish or ungrateful, and I did not want to leave him with that impression of me. He was not paying much attention, as it happened, and said only, "Put it down over there, OK?" and went on with what he was doing.

One of my reasons for doing what I did was that talk was getting us nowhere; but all the same I felt a little let down. I had been prepared to defend my decision. And I thought that perhaps when he did notice he might be upset and want to talk. I put some things away and fiddled around a little, but he continued to do what he was doing and to take no notice of anything else. At last I said, "Well, goodbye, dear. I hope the garden key turns up."

He was fitting parts together, and said without looking around, "OK, fine, dear. When's dinner?"

"I'm not sure," I said. "I'm going now. With the —" I hesitated, and finally said, "With them, you know," and went on. In fact I had only just then realized how hard it would have been to explain myself. I could not chatter away as I used to do, taking it all for granted. My words now must be as slow, as new, as single, as tentative as the steps I took going down the path away from the house, between the dark-branched, tall dancers motionless against the winter shining.

[1985, 1987]

Gary Snyder

[b. 1930]

Gary Sherman Snyder was born on May 8, 1930, in San Francisco, California, the first of two children of Harold and Lois Wilkie Snyder. Struggling to make a living during the Great Depression, the Snyders moved in 1932 to a former logging camp near Lake City, Washington. There, they established a small dairy farm, selling milk, eggs, and wood shingles they cut from the stumps left on the land. When his parents separated in 1942, Snyder went with his mother and sister to live in Portland, Oregon. His lifelong interest in hiking and climbing began when he climbed Mount St. Helens with a mountaineering club in the summer of 1945.

Gary Snyder

This photograph of Snyder at a restaurant in Kyoto, Japan, where he lived for more than a decade, was taken in 1963 by his close friend and fellow Beat poet Allen Ginsberg.

Snyder wrote poems and occasional articles for his high-school newspaper, and he worked during the summers as a copyboy for the Portland *Oregonian*. After his graduation in 1947, Snyder enrolled at nearby Reed College. "I had some marvelous teachers," Snyder recalled in a 1976 interview. "They wouldn't tolerate bullshit, made me clean up my prose style, exposed me to all the varieties of intellectual positions and gave me a territory in which I could speak out my radical politics and get arguments and augmentations on it." Snyder published poems in the college's literary magazine, the *Janus*, and he earned money during the summers by working for the National Park Service. In 1950, he married a classmate at Reed, Alison Gass, but they were divorced by the time Snyder graduated with a degree in English and anthropology in 1951. That fall, he entered graduate school in anthropology at Indiana University.

Snyder swiftly decided that graduate study was not for him, so he left Indiana at the end of his first semester and went to San Francisco. Now determined to become a poet, he supported himself by working as a seasonal forest-fire lookout and on a trail crew in Yosemite National Park. He also did graduate work in Asian languages at the University of California, Berkeley. He met a number of other writers in the Bay Area, including Allen Ginsberg and Jack Kerouac. In August 1955, Snyder participated in the famous group poetry reading at the Six Gallery, where Ginsberg electrified the crowd and effectively launched the Beat movement by reading his revolutionary poem *Howl*. The following year, Snyder sailed to Japan. He lived there during most of the following twelve years, studying Zen Buddhism. During 1957–58, he worked for eight months in the engine room of a steamer bound for ports in the Mediterranean, the Persian Gulf, and the Pacific. Snyder also returned several times to the United States, where his friends among the Beats helped arrange for the publication of his first two collections of poetry: *Riprap* (1959), which was printed in Japan and distributed by Lawrence Ferlinghetti's City Lights Bookstore; and *Myths and Texts* (1960), which was published in New York City by Totem Press, founded by LeRoi Jones (later Amiri Baraka). In 1960, Snyder married the poet Joanne Kyger in Kyoto. Together, they toured Nepal and India, where they joined Allen Ginsberg. But the couple's relationship was stormy, and they were divorced in 1965. That year, Snyder published *Riprap & Cold Mountain Poems*, expanded by the addition of his translations of a series of poems by the T'ang dynasty poet and hermit Han Shan, and *Six Sections from Mountains and Rivers Without End*. In 1967, he married Masa Uehara in a ceremony conducted on the rim of an active volcano on a small island off Japan.

Snyder became famous as an environmentalist, poet, and voice of the counterculture following his return to the United States. By then, he was regularly publishing in prominent literary journals, including *Poetry*, which awarded him its Levinson Prize in 1968. The influential American firm New Directions published his collections *The Back Country* (1968) and *Earth House Hold* (1969). With the assistance of friends, Snyder built a house in the foothills of the Sierra Nevada, where he and his wife moved with their two young sons, Kai and Gen, in 1970. Increasingly active in the

Snyder is a master of challenge and confrontation, not because he seeks controversy but because his values are so conspicuous, so plainly stated in the context of simple, sensuous, impassioned fact that they cannot be dodged.

–Kenneth Rexroth

environmental movement, Snyder attended the United Nations Conference on the Environment in Stockholm, Sweden, in 1972. He was awarded the Pulitzer Prize for his collection *Turtle Island* (1974), the name for North America in some Native American creation myths. His next three books revealed the range of his interests and writings: *He Who Hunted Birds in His Father's Village* (1979), a revision of the senior thesis he wrote at Reed on a Native American myth; *Axe Handles* (1983), a collection famed for its title poem; and *Passage Through India* (1983), an account of his spiritual pilgrimage across the country during 1961-62. In 1985, he began to teach in the English department and the Nature and Culture Program at the University of California, Davis. He and Masa Uehara divorced in 1989, and Snyder married the naturalist Carole Koda in 1991. Following the publication of *Mountains and Rivers Without End* (1996), a poetic sequence Snyder had been working on for forty years, he was awarded the prestigious Bollingen Prize. His recent work includes a volume of new poems, *Danger on Peaks* (2005), and a collection of personal essays, *Back on the Fire* (2007).

Snyder's Poetry.   Although he is most often associated with the urban Beat poets and writers, whose interest in Zen Buddhism Snyder helped stimulate, much of his poetry bespeaks his physical and spiritual immersion in the wilderness, especially the remote mountain areas of California and the Pacific Northwest. A student of languages, linguistics, and literature, Snyder has been inspired by a wide range of poetic models, from the Japanese haiku and ancient Chinese poetry to the work of Ezra Pound and William Carlos Williams. Like Williams, Snyder characteristically uses colloquial language, direct images, and natural rhythms to convey everyday and often momentary experiences. "The rhythms of my poems follow the rhythm of the physical work I'm doing and the life I'm leading at any given time," he observed early in his career. In the afterword to a 1990 reprint of his first collection, *Riprap* (1959), he traced the inception of the poems in the volume back to his work with a trail crew in Yosemite National Park in 1955. Snyder explained that the title of the volume, a term for the loose stones the crew laid on steep rock surfaces to make trails for horses and hikers, "celebrates the work of the hands, the placing of rock, and my first glimpse of the image of the whole universe as interconnected, mutually reflecting and mutually embracing." Snyder's keen sensitivity to the physical particulars of the natural world and his profound sense of the interconnectedness of the whole are revealed in the following selection of his poems from 1959 to 1992. The text of "Beneath My Hand and Eye the Distant Hills, Your Body" is taken from his collection *The Back Country* (1968). The texts of the other poems are taken from *The Gary Snyder Reader: Prose, Poetry, and Translations, 1952-1998* (1999).

bedfordstmartins.com/ americanlit for research links on Snyder

RIPRAP[1]

Lay down these words
Before your mind like rocks.
          placed solid, by hands
In choice of place, set
Before the body of the mind   5
          in space and time:
Solidity of bark, leaf, or wall
          riprap of things:
Cobble of milky way,
          straying planets,   10
These poems, people,
          lost ponies with
Dragging saddles
          and rocky sure-foot trails.
The worlds like an endless   15
          four-dimensional
Game of *Go*.[2]
          ants and pebbles
In the thin loam, each rock a word
          a creek-washed stone   20
Granite: ingrained
          with torment of fire and weight
Crystal and sediment linked hot
          all change, in thoughts,
As well as things.   25
                             [1959, 1999]

---

1. **Riprap:** Loose rock used to stabilize hillsides and shorelines against erosion, though Snyder has more specifically defined it as "a cobble of stones laid on steep slick rock to make a trail for horses in mountains."
2. **Game of *Go*:** Called "Go" in Japan and different names in other Asian countries, this is a board game in which two players alternately place white and black stones on vacant places on a grid. A stone is captured and removed if it is surrounded by stones of the other color.

BENEATH MY HAND AND EYE
THE DISTANT HILLS, YOUR BODY

What my hand follows on your body
Is the line. A stream of love
   of heat, of light,   what my
   eye   lascivious
       licks   5
   over, watching

    far snow-dappled Uintah mountains[1]
Is that stream.
Of power.   what my
    hand curves over, following the line.   10
    "hip" and "groin"

Where "I"
    follow by hand and eye
    the swimming limit of your body.
As when vision idly dallies on the hills   15
Loving what it feeds on.
        soft cinder cones and craters;
        — Drum Hadley in the Pinacate[2]
            took ten minutes more to look again —
A leap of power unfurling: 20
    left,   right — right —
My heart beat faster looking
    at the snowy Uintah mountains.

As my hand feeds on you
    runs down your side and curls beneath your hip.   25
    oil pool; stratum; water —

What "is" within   not known
    but feel it
    sinking with a breath
    pusht ruthless, surely, down.   30

Beneath this long caress of hand and eye
    "we" learn the flower burning,
            outward, from "below".

                                        [1965, 1968]

---

1. **Uintah mountains:** A chain of mountains in northeastern Utah.
2. **Drum Hadley in the Pinacate:** Drummond Hadley, a poet and rancher who lives in southeastern Arizona near the Mexican border, appears in another poem of Snyder's, "How to Make Stew in the Pinacate Desert: Recipe for Locke and Drum." The Pinacate is a desert of black volcanic sand in Sonora, in northern Mexico.

WAVE

Grooving clam shell,
            streakt through marble,
sweeping down ponderosa pine bark-scale
        rip-cut tree grain
                sand-dunes, lava   5
                flow

Wave   wife.
　　　　woman – wyfman –[1]
"veiled;   vibrating;   vague"
　　　sawtooth ranges pulsing;   10
　　　　　　　　　veins on the back of the hand.

Forkt out: birdsfoot-alluvium
　　　　　　　　　wash
　　　　　　great dunes rolling
Each inch rippld, every grain a wave.   15

Leaning against sand cornices til they blow away

　　– wind, shake
　　stiff thorns of cholla, ocotillo[2]
　　sometimes I get stuck in thickets –

Ah, trembling spreading radiating wyf[3]   20
　　　　　　　　　racing zebra
　catch me and fling me wide
To the dancing grain of things
　　　　　　　　of my mind!

　　　　　　　　　　　　　　[1968, 1999]

---

1. **wyfman:** Woman (Old English).
2. **cholla, ocotillo:** A cactus and a desert shrub, native to Mexico and the southwestern United States.
3. **wyf:** Wife (Old English).

Axe Handles

One afternoon the last week in April
Showing Kai how to throw a hatchet
One-half turn and it sticks in a stump.
He recalls the hatchet-head
Without a handle, in the shop   5
And go gets it, and wants it for his own.
A broken-off axe handle behind the door
Is long enough for a hatchet,
We cut it to length and take it
With the hatchet head   10
And working hatchet, to the wood block.
There I begin to shape the old handle
With the hatchet, and the phrase

First learned from Ezra Pound[1]
Rings in my ears!   15
"When making an axe handle
        the pattern is not far off."
And I say this to Kai
"Look: We'll shape the handle
By checking the handle   20
Of the axe we cut with —"
And he sees. And I hear it again:
It's in Lu Ji's *Wê Fu*, fourth century
A.D. "Essay on Literature"[2] — in the
Preface: "In making the handle   25
Of an axe
By cutting wood with an axe
The model is indeed near at hand."
My teacher Shih-hsiang Chen
Translated that and taught it years ago   30
And I see: Pound was an axe,
Chen was an axe, I am an axe
And my son a handle, soon
To be shaping again, model
And tool, craft of culture,   35
How we go on.

[1979, 1997]

---

1. **Ezra Pound:** An influential American critic, poet, and translator who shared Snyder's interest in Chinese literature and philosophy (see pp. 641–50).
2. **Lu Ji's . . . "Essay on Literature":** Lu Ji (261–303) was a Chinese poet who wrote a book delineating the principles of composition, *Wê Fu* ("On Literature").

RIPPLES ON THE SURFACE

"Ripples on the surface of the water —
were silver salmon passing under — different
from the ripples caused by breezes"

A scudding plume on the wave —
a humpback whale is   5
breaking out in air up
gulping herring
        — Nature not a book, but a *performance*, a
high old culture

Ever-fresh events   10
scraped out, rubbed out, and used, used, again —
the braided channels of the rivers
hidden under fields of grass —

The vast wild
        the house, alone.   15
The little house in the wild,
        the wild in the house.
Both forgotten.

            No nature

Both together, one big empty house.   20
                         [1992, 1999]

Donald Barthelme

[1931-1989]

Donald Barthelme

Jerry Bauer took this photograph of Barthelme, an early and influential practitioner of post-modern fiction, in the 1970s.

Donald Barthelme was born on April 7, 1931, in Philadelphia, Pennsylvania. He was the first of the five children of Donald Barthelme, a Texas-born architect, and Helen Bechtold Barthelme, a daughter of an affluent Philadelphia family, both graduates of the University of Pennsylvania. The family soon moved to Texas, where Barthelme's father worked for various firms before setting up a private practice in Houston. He quickly became known for his innovative modernist buildings, including the family's house, as well as for his distinguished teaching in the architecture department at the University of Houston. Barthelme's mother encouraged the literary interests of her five children, all of whom became writers. Barthelme was raised Catholic and attended parochial schools until 1948, when he transferred to the public Lamar High School. He wrote for the literary magazine and entered the University of Houston as a journalism major in 1949. During his sophomore year, he edited the student newspaper, the *Cougar*. His articles caught the attention of editors of the *Houston Post*, and he accepted a position as a fine-arts reporter. Shortly after his marriage to Marilyn Marrs in 1952, he was drafted into the army for service in the Korean War. For the next two years, he served at Fort Polk, Louisiana, Japan, and Korea. He wrote when he could and read widely, including the works of modernists such as Ezra Pound, T. S. Eliot, and James Joyce and the French existentialists Albert Camus and Jean-Paul Sartre.

After his discharge from the army, Barthelme worked at various jobs in media and the arts before becoming a full-time and highly successful writer. Returning home to Houston, he took his old position at the *Houston*

Post in 1955. He attended classes at the University of Houston and then went to work for its public-relations office, writing speeches for the president and founding a literary magazine, *Forum.* Following a divorce from his first wife, Barthelme married a journalist he had known since his undergraduate days, Helen Moore. Actively involved in the Houston arts scene, he served on the Board of Trustees of the Contemporary Arts Museum and became its director in 1961. The following year, he moved to New York City to become the managing editor of a new art and literature review, *Location.* Barthelme, who had long been an avid reader of the *New Yorker,* published his first story in the magazine in March 1963. Shortly after that, he was offered a "first reading" contract by the editors of the magazine, in which he ultimately published well over a hundred stories and numerous film reviews. Indeed, his work was strongly stimulated by the techniques of film, which he suggested had forced writers to reinvent fiction. Beginning with *Come Back, Dr. Caligari* (1964), an allusion to the classic silent horror film *The Cabinet of Dr. Caligari,* Barthelme regularly published collections of his experimental stories, including *Unspeakable Practices, Unnatural Acts* (1968), *City Life* (1970), and *Sadness* (1972). He also published his first novel, *Snow White* (1967), a contemporary and playfully subversive retelling of the classic fairy tale made famous by the Walt Disney movie *Snow White and the Seven Dwarfs.* Meanwhile, Barthelme's marriage to Helen Moore ended, and he married his third wife, Brigit Barthelme. A book he wrote and illustrated for their daughter, *The Slightly Irregular Fire Engine* (1971), won the National Book Award.

Barthelme later combined writing with distinguished teaching of the craft of fiction. He was a visiting professor at Boston University in 1973 and at the City College of New York in 1974, the year he published a miscellaneous collection of parodies and satires, *Guilty Pleasures.* That was followed by his influential short novel, *The Dead Father* (1974), in which Barthelme once again parodied the conventions of the novel, and two more collections of his stories, *Amateurs* (1976) and *Great Days* (1979). His third marriage failed, and in 1978 Barthelme married Marion Knox, with whom he had a second daughter. An acclaimed collection of his best stories from the previous two decades, *Sixty Stories* (1981), was nominated for the PEN/ Faulkner Award for Fiction. In 1983, after living in New York City for twenty years, Barthelme returned to Houston to become a full-time professor and later the director of the Creative Writing Program at the University of Houston. Although he developed serious health problems, the result of years of heavy smoking and drinking, he continued to teach and write, publishing *Paradise* (1986), a novel about a middle-aged architect separated from his wife and daughter, and *Forty Stories* (1987). Barthelme received the Rea Award for his contribution to short-story writing in 1988. He died of cancer on July 23, 1989, leaving behind a large collection of manuscripts, including a posthumously published novel, *The King* (1990).

Barthelme's "The School."   Like his father, an internationally known architect with whom he had a deeply conflicted relationship, Barthelme was committed to formal innovation. But his father adopted the vocabulary of modern architecture, which was based on the pursuit of harmony and order, while Barthelme was at the forefront of the development of a disruptive and fragmentary postmodern style characterized by irony, pastiche, and playfulness. The elder Barthelme was particularly renowned for his designs for schools, about which he wrote extensively, and his rebellious son may have offered a sly rejoinder to such work in "The School." The unconventional story takes the form of a dramatic monologue in which a second-grade teacher named Edgar gloomily tells an unidentified auditor about a series of disasters that befell the children in his class. Confronted with an escalating series of deaths, from plants and animals to classmates and relatives, the teacher and his students offer different answers to the riddle of life and death. The author's response to that enigma, however, may simply lie in the deadpan humor and the optimistic, upbeat ending of "The School," which was read at a memorial service for Barthelme in 1989. The text of the story, which was first published in the *New Yorker* in June 1974, is taken from Barthelme's fifth collection of stories, *Amateurs* (1976).

bedfordstmartins.com/ americanlit for research links on Barthelme

THE SCHOOL

Well, we had all these children out planting trees, see, because we figured that . . . that was part of their education, to see how, you know, the root systems . . . and also the sense of responsibility, taking care of things, being individually responsible. You know what I mean. And the trees all died. They were orange trees. I don't know why they died, they just died. Something wrong with the soil possibly or maybe the stuff we got from the nursery wasn't the best. We complained about it. So we've got thirty kids there, each kid had his or her own little tree to plant, and we've got these thirty dead trees. All these kids looking at these little brown sticks, it was depressing.

It wouldn't have been so bad except that just a couple of weeks before the thing with the trees, the snakes all died. But I think that the snakes — well, the reason that the snakes kicked off was that . . . you remember, the boiler was shut off for four days because of the strike, and that was explicable. It was something you could explain to the kids because of the strike. I mean, none of their parents would let them cross the picket line and they knew there was a strike going on and what it meant. So when things got started up again and we found the snakes they weren't too disturbed.

With the herb gardens it was probably a case of overwatering, and at least now they know not to overwater. The children were very conscientious with the herb gardens and some of them probably . . . you know, slipped them a little extra water when we weren't looking. Or maybe . . . well, I don't like to think about sabotage, although it did occur to us. I mean, it was something that crossed our minds. We were thinking that way probably because before that the gerbils had died, and the white mice had died, and the salamander . . . well, now they know not to carry them around in plastic bags.

Of course we *expected* the tropical fish to die, that was no surprise. Those numbers, you look at them crooked and they're belly-up on the surface. But the lesson plan called for a tropical-fish input at that point, there was nothing we could do, it happens every year, you just have to hurry past it.

We weren't even supposed to have a puppy.

We weren't even supposed to have one, it was just a puppy the Murdoch girl found under a Gristede's truck one day and she was afraid the truck would run over it when the driver had finished making his delivery, so she stuck it in her knapsack and brought it to school with her. So we had this puppy. As soon as I saw the puppy I thought, Oh Christ, I bet it will live for about two weeks and then . . . And that's what it did. It wasn't supposed to be in the classroom at all, there's some kind of regulation about it, but you can't tell them they can't have a puppy when the puppy is already there, right in front of them, running around on the floor and yap yap yapping. They named it Edgar — that is, they named it after me. They had a lot of fun running after it and yelling, "Here, Edgar! Nice Edgar!" Then they'd laugh like hell. They enjoyed the ambiguity. I enjoyed it myself. I don't mind being kidded. They made a little house for it in the supply closet and all that. I don't know what it died of. Distemper, I guess. It probably hadn't had any shots. I got it out of there before the kids got to school. I checked the supply closet each morning, routinely, because I knew what was going to happen. I gave it to the custodian.

And then there was this Korean orphan that the class adopted through the Help the Children program, all the kids brought in a quarter a month, that was the idea. It was an unfortunate thing, the kid's name was Kim and maybe we adopted him too late or something. The cause of death was not stated in the letter we got, they suggested we adopt another child instead and sent us some interesting case histories, but we didn't have the heart. The class took it pretty hard, they began (I think; nobody ever said anything to me directly) to feel that maybe there was something wrong with the school. But I don't think there's anything wrong with the school, particularly, I've seen better and I've seen worse. It was just a run of bad luck. We had an extraordinary number of parents passing away, for instance. There were I think two heart attacks and two suicides, one drowning, and four killed together in a car accident. One stroke. And we had the usual heavy mortality rate among the grandparents, or maybe it was heavier this year, it seemed so. And finally the tragedy.

The tragedy occurred when Matthew Wein and Tony Mavrogordo were playing over where they're excavating for the new federal office building. There were all these big wooden beams stacked, you know, at the edge of the excavation. There's a court case coming out of that, the parents are claiming that the beams were poorly stacked. I don't know what's true and what's not. It's been a strange year.

I forgot to mention Billy Brandt's father, who was knifed fatally when he grappled with a masked intruder in his home.

One day, we had a discussion in class. They asked me, where did they go? The trees, the salamander, the tropical fish, Edgar, the poppas and mommas, Matthew and Tony, where did they go? And I said, I don't know, I don't know. And they said, who knows? and I said, nobody knows. And they said, is death that which gives meaning to life? and I said, no, life is that which gives meaning to life. Then they said, but isn't death, considered as a fundamental datum, the means by which the taken-for-granted mundanity of the everyday may be transcended in the direction of —

I said, yes, maybe.

They said, we don't like it.

I said, that's sound.

They said, it's a bloody shame!

I said, it is.

They said, will you make love now with Helen (our teaching assistant) so that we can see how it is done? We know you like Helen.

I do like Helen but I said that I would not.

We've heard so much about it, they said, but we've never seen it.

I said I would be fired and that it was never, or almost never, done as a demonstration. Helen looked out of the window.

They said, please, please make love with Helen, we require an assertion of value, we are frightened.

I said that they shouldn't be frightened (although I am often frightened) and that there was value everywhere. Helen came and embraced me. I kissed her a few times on the brow. We held each other. The children were excited. Then there was a knock on the door, I opened the door, and the new gerbil walked in. The children cheered wildly.

[1974, 1976]

Toni Morrison

[b. 1931]

Toni Morrison was born Chloe Anthony Wofford on February 18, 1931, in Lorain, Ohio. She was the second of four children of George Wofford, a shipwelder, and Ramah Willis Wofford, a pianist who often worked as a domestic maid in order to help support the family. The couple had migrated to Ohio from Georgia in search of better employment and educational opportunities, and they lived in a close-knit community of African Americans in Lorain. Morrison has said that her family had a rich history of storytelling, and she grew up with a strong sense of the importance of African American culture and history. An outstanding student, she attended Lorain High School and became the first woman in her family to go to college when she entered Howard University in Washington, D.C., in the fall of 1949. Morrison majored in English and joined an acting troupe at Howard, where her friends began calling her "Toni." Initially planning to become a teacher and return to Lorain when she graduated, Morrison instead enrolled in graduate school at Cornell University in the fall of 1953. After she earned an MA in 1955, writing her thesis on Virginia Woolf and William Faulkner, she accepted a teaching position at Texas Southern University. Two years later, she returned to teach at Howard, where she joined a writing group and began working on short stories. She also met and married Harold Morrison, an architect from Jamaica. Morrison gave birth to their two sons, but she and her husband had sharply different ideas about gender roles in marriage, and they were divorced in 1964.

Morrison soon began a new era in her life. In 1965, she landed a job as a textbook editor with a subsidiary of Random House Publishers in Syracuse, New York. For the next several years, she devoted herself to raising her children, working at her job, and writing at night. Promoted in 1968 to the position of senior editor, she moved her family to New York City. Through her new job, she helped a number of African American writers publish their work, including Angela Davis, Muhammad Ali, and June Jordan. In addition, Morrison published her first novel, *The Bluest Eye* (1970), based on one of her earlier short stories about a poor black girl who longs to have the blue eyes that she associates with white standards of beauty. Although the novel received mixed reviews, it earned Morrison strong praise from many readers, including the actor and civil rights activist Ruby Dee, who observed: "To read the book is to ache for remedy." Morrison's second novel, *Sula* (1973), about the relationship between two black women in an Ohio community, brought her more attention, and she began receiving invitations to teach at colleges and universities, including Rutgers and Yale. She also edited *The Black Book* (1974), a pioneering collection of documents central to African American history and culture. The publication of her third novel, *Song of Solomon* (1977), established her reputation as a writer of the first rank. This story of a black man's search for identity, *Song of Solomon* was the first novel by an African American to be offered as a main selection of the Book-of-the-Month Club since the publication in 1940 of Richard Wright's *Native Son*.

Morrison has subsequently been acclaimed as one of the major writers of her generation. Her picture appeared on the cover of *Newsweek* and her novel *Tar Baby*, the story of the complex relationship between a black woman and a white man, was on the year's bestseller list in 1981. Two years later, she decided to leave her position at Random House in order to spend more time teaching and writing. Inspired by an actual account she had found while preparing *The Black Book*, Morrison next wrote a historical novel about the devastating effects of slavery, *Beloved* (1987), which won the Pulitzer Prize. In 1989, she accepted a chaired professorship to teach creative writing and African American studies at Princeton University. In addition to an influential work of literary criticism, *Playing in the Dark: Essays on Whiteness and the Literary Imagination* (1990), she published a novel inspired by the Harlem Renaissance, *Jazz* (1992). In 1993, Morrison became the first African American to win the Nobel Prize in Literature. After the publication of her novel *Paradise* (1998), a cover story in *Time* proclaimed her "The Great American Storyteller." Her recent works include two children's books, both coauthored with her son Slade Morrison; the libretto for *Margaret Garner* (2002), an opera based on the same events that inspired *Beloved*; and her intricate eighth novel, *Love* (2003). When she retired from Princeton in 2006, former president Bill Clinton and the actor Morgan Freeman were among those who offered tributes to Morrison at a party held in her honor at Lincoln Center in New York City.

Toni Morrison

Bernard Gotfryd took this photograph of Morrison at a New York City bookstore in 1970, the year she published her first novel, *The Bluest Eye*.

Morrison's "Recitatif."   Morrison wrote this story specifically for the groundbreaking anthology *Confirmation,* a collection of the works of forty-nine African American women writers edited by the poet and playwright Amiri Baraka and his wife, the poet Amina Baraka. In the introduction, they explained that "the purpose of this volume is to draw attention to the existence and excellence of black women writers" and thus "to 'confirm' that a whole body of American literature has been consistently ignored or hidden." In addition to Morrison, the anthology featured the work of prominent writers such as Gwendolyn Brooks, Audre Lorde, and Alice Walker. "Recitatif," Morrison's only published short story, displays some of her characteristic innovations in narrative, structure, and style. The narrator, Twyla, tells of five encounters with her friend Roberta over a twenty-year period from childhood to adulthood. The story also touches on some central themes of Morrison's longer works, including family, female friendship, and racial division, an issue further complicated in "Recitatif" by the fact that it is never revealed which of the two main characters is black and which is white. The text is taken from *Confirmation: An Anthology of African American Women,* edited by Amiri Baraka and Amina Baraka (1983).

RECITATIF[1]

My mother danced all night and Roberta's was sick. That's why we were taken to St. Bonny's.[2] People want to put their arms around you when you tell them you were in a shelter, but it really wasn't bad. No big long room with one hundred beds like Bellevue.[3] There were four to a room, and when Roberta and me came, there was a shortage of state kids, so we were the only ones assigned to 406 and could go from bed to bed if we wanted to. And we wanted to, too. We changed beds every night and for the whole four months we were there we never picked one out as our own permanent bed.

It didn't start out that way. The minute I walked in and the Big Bozo introduced us, I got sick to my stomach. It was one thing to be taken out of your own bed early in the morning — it was something else to be stuck in a strange place with a girl from a whole other race. And Mary, that's my mother, she was right. Every now and then she would stop dancing long enough to tell me something important and one of the things she said was that they never washed their hair and they smelled funny. Roberta sure did. Smell funny, I mean. So when the Big Bozo (nobody ever called her Mrs. Itkin, just like nobody ever said St. Bonaventure) — when she said, "Twyla, this is Roberta. Roberta, this is Twyla. Make each other welcome." I said, "My mother won't like you putting me in here."

---

1. **Recitatif:** Recitative (French), a vocal style between singing and ordinary speech that is often used for dialogue or narrative commentary in operas and oratorios. A now obsolete meaning for this term is the tone or rhythm peculiar to any language.
2. **St. Bonny's:** St. Bonaventure's, a shelter and school for orphaned children in New York City.
3. **Bellevue:** A hospital in New York City known for its psychiatric unit.

"Good," said Bozo. "Maybe then she'll come and take you home." How's that for mean? If Roberta had laughed I would have killed her, but she didn't. She just walked over to the window and stood with her back to us.

"Turn around," said the Bozo. "Don't be rude. Now Twyla. Roberta. When you hear a loud buzzer, that's the call for dinner. Come down to the first floor. Any fights and no movie." And then, just to make sure we knew what we would be missing, "*The Wizard of Oz.*"[4]

Roberta must have thought I meant that my mother would be mad about my being put in the shelter. Not about rooming with her, because as soon as Bozo left she came over to me and said, "Is your mother sick too?"

"No," I said. "She just likes to dance all night."

"Oh," she nodded her head and I liked the way she understood things so fast. So for the moment it didn't matter that we looked like salt and pepper standing there and that's what the other kids called us sometimes. We were eight years old and got F's all the time. Me because I couldn't remember what I read or what the teacher said. And Roberta because she couldn't read at all and didn't even listen to the teacher. She wasn't good at anything except jacks, at which she was a killer: pow scoop pow scoop pow scoop.

We didn't like each other all that much at first, but nobody else wanted to play with us because we weren't real orphans with beautiful dead parents in the sky. We were dumped. Even the New York City Puerto Ricans and the upstate Indians ignored us. All kinds of kids were in there, black ones, white ones, even two Koreans. The food was good, though. At least I thought so. Roberta hated it and left whole pieces of things on her plate: Spam, Salisbury steak — even jello with fruit cocktail in it, and she didn't care if I ate what she wouldn't. Mary's idea of supper was popcorn and a can of Yoo-Hoo.[5] Hot mashed potatoes and two weenies was like Thanksgiving for me.

It really wasn't bad, St. Bonny's. The big girls on the second floor pushed us around now and then. But that was all. They wore lipstick and eyebrow pencil and wobbled their knees while they watched TV. Fifteen, sixteen, even, some of them were. They were put-out girls, scared runaways most of them. Poor little girls who fought their uncles off but looked tough to us, and mean. God did they look mean. The staff tried to keep them separate from the younger children, but sometimes they caught us watching them in the orchard where they played radios and danced with each other. They'd light out after us and pull our hair or twist our arms. We were scared of them, Roberta and me, but neither of us wanted the other one to know it. So we got a good list of dirty names we could shout back when we ran from them through the orchard. I used to dream a lot and almost always the orchard was there. Two acres, four maybe, of these little apple trees. Hundreds of them. Empty and crooked like beggar women when I first came to St. Bonny's but fat

4. *The Wizard of Oz*: The young Judy Garland starred in this popular 1939 movie based on Frank Baum's children's book *The Wonderful Wizard of Oz* (1900).
5. **Yoo-Hoo**: A chocolate drink developed in the 1920s and marketed as the "drink of champions" by the New York Yankees in the 1950s and 1960s.

with flowers when I left. I don't know why I dreamt about that orchard so much. Nothing really happened there. Nothing all that important, I mean. Just the big girls dancing and playing the radio. Roberta and me watching. Maggie fell down there once. The kitchen woman with legs like parentheses. And the big girls laughed at her. We should have helped her up, I know, but we were scared of those girls with lipstick and eyebrow pencil. Maggie couldn't talk. The kids said she had her tongue cut out, but I think she was just born that way: mute. She was old and sandy-colored and she worked in the kitchen. I don't know if she was nice or not. I just remember her legs like parentheses and how she rocked when she walked. She worked from early in the morning till two o'clock, and if she was late, if she had too much cleaning and didn't get out till two-fifteen or so, she'd cut through the orchard so she wouldn't miss her bus and have to wait another hour. She wore this really stupid little hat – a kid's hat with ear flaps – and she wasn't much taller than we were. A really awful little hat. Even for a mute, it was dumb – dressing like a kid and never saying anything at all.

"But what about if somebody tries to kill her?" I used to wonder about that. "Or what if she wants to cry? Can she cry?"

"Sure," Roberta said. "But just tears. No sounds come out."

"She can't scream?"

"Nope. Nothing."

"Can she hear?"

"I guess."

"Let's call her," I said. And we did.

"Dummy! Dummy!" She never turned her head.

"Bow legs! Bow legs!" Nothing. She just rocked on, the chin straps of her baby-boy hat swaying from side to side. I think we were wrong. I think she could hear and didn't let on. And it shames me even now to think there was somebody in there after all who heard us call her those names and couldn't tell on us.

We got along all right, Roberta and me. Changed beds every night, got F's in civics and communication skills and gym. The Bozo was disappointed in us, she said. Out of 130 of us state cases, 90 were under twelve. Almost all were real orphans with beautiful dead parents in the sky. We were the only ones dumped and the only ones with F's in three classes including gym. So we got along – what with her leaving whole pieces of things on her plate and being nice about not asking questions.

I think it was the day before Maggie fell down that we found out our mothers were coming to visit us on the same Sunday. We had been at the shelter twenty-eight days (Roberta twenty-eight and a half) and this was their first visit with us. Our mothers would come at ten o'clock in time for chapel, then lunch with us in the teachers' lounge. I thought if my dancing mother met her sick mother it might be good for her. And Roberta thought her sick mother would get a big bang out of a dancing one. We got excited about it and curled each other's hair. After breakfast we sat on the bed watching the road from the window. Roberta's socks were still wet. She washed them the night before and put them on the radiator to dry. They hadn't, but she put them on anyway be-cause their tops were so pretty – scalloped in pink. Each of us had a purple construction-paper basket that we had made in craft class. Mine had a yellow crayon rabbit on it.

Roberta's had eggs with wiggly lines of color. Inside were cellophane grass and just the jelly beans because I'd eaten the two marshmallow eggs they gave us. The Big Bozo came herself to get us. Smiling she told us we looked very nice and to come downstairs. We were so surprised by the smile we'd never seen before, neither of us moved.

"Don't you want to see your mommies?"

I stood up first and spilled the jelly beans all over the floor. Bozo's smile disappeared while we scrambled to get the candy up off the floor and put it back in the grass.

She escorted us downstairs to the first floor, where the other girls were lining up to file into the chapel. A bunch of grown-ups stood to one side. Viewers mostly. The old biddies who wanted servants and the fags who wanted company looking for children they might want to adopt. Once in a while a grandmother. Almost never anybody young or anybody whose face wouldn't scare you in the night. Because if any of the real orphans had young relatives they wouldn't be real orphans. I saw Mary right away. She had on those green slacks I hated and hated even more now because didn't she know we were going to chapel? And that fur jacket with the pocket linings so ripped she had to pull to get her hands out of them. But her face was pretty — like always, and she smiled and waved like she was the little girl looking for her mother — not me.

I walked slowly, trying not to drop the jelly beans and hoping the paper handle would hold. I had to use my last Chiclet[6] because by the time I finished cutting everything out, all the Elmer's was gone. I am left-handed and the scissors never worked for me. It didn't matter, though; I might just as well have chewed the gum. Mary dropped to her knees and grabbed me, mashing the basket, the jelly beans, and the grass into her ratty fur jacket.

"Twyla, baby. Twyla, baby!"

I could have killed her. Already I heard the big girls in the orchard the next time saying, "Twyyyyyla, baby!" But I couldn't stay mad at Mary while she was smiling and hugging me and smelling of Lady Esther dusting powder. I wanted to stay buried in her fur all day.

To tell the truth I forgot about Roberta. Mary and I got in line for the traipse into chapel and I was feeling proud because she looked so beautiful even in those ugly green slacks that made her behind stick out. A pretty mother on earth is better than a beautiful dead one in the sky even if she did leave you all alone to go dancing.

I felt a tap on my shoulder, turned, and saw Roberta smiling. I smiled back, but not too much lest somebody think this visit was the biggest thing that ever happened in my life. Then Roberta said, "Mother, I want you to meet my roommate, Twyla. And that's Twyla's mother."

I looked up it seemed for miles. She was big. Bigger than any man and on her chest was the biggest cross I'd ever seen. I swear it was six inches long each way. And in the crook of her arm was the biggest Bible ever made.

Mary, simple-minded as ever, grinned and tried to yank her hand out of the pocket with the raggedy lining — to shake hands, I guess. Roberta's mother looked down at me

---

6. **Chiclet:** A brand of chewing gum, manufactured as small pellets.

and then looked down at Mary too. She didn't say anything, just grabbed Roberta with her Bible-free hand and stepped out of line, walking quickly to the rear of it. Mary was still grinning because she's not too swift when it comes to what's really going on. Then this light bulb goes off in her head and she says "That bitch!" really loud and us almost in the chapel now. Organ music whining; the Bonny Angels singing sweetly. Everybody in the world turned around to look. And Mary would have kept it up – kept calling names if I hadn't squeezed her hand as hard as I could. That helped a little, but she still twitched and crossed and uncrossed her legs all through service. Even groaned a couple of times. Why did I think she would come there and act right? Slacks. No hat like the grandmothers and viewers, and groaning all the while. When we stood for hymns she kept her mouth shut. Wouldn't even look at the words on the page. She actually reached in her purse for a mirror to check her lipstick. All I could think of was that she really needed to be killed. The sermon lasted a year, and I knew the real orphans were looking smug again.

We were supposed to have lunch in the teachers' lounge, but Mary didn't bring anything, so we picked fur and cellophane grass off the mashed jelly beans and ate them. I could have killed her. I sneaked a look at Roberta. Her mother had brought chicken legs and ham sandwiches and oranges and a whole box of chocolate-covered grahams. Roberta drank milk from a thermos while her mother read the Bible to her.

Things are not right. The wrong food is always with the wrong people. Maybe that's why I got into waitress work later – to match up the right people with the right food. Roberta just let those chicken legs sit there, but she did bring a stack of grahams up to me later when the visit was over. I think she was sorry that her mother would not shake my mother's hand. And I liked that and I liked the fact that she didn't say a word about Mary groaning all the way through the service and not bringing any lunch.

Roberta left in May when the apple trees were heavy and white. On her last day we went to the orchard to watch the big girls smoke and dance by the radio. It didn't matter that they said, "Twyyyyyla, baby." We sat on the ground and breathed. Lady Esther. Apple blossoms. I still go soft when I smell one or the other. Roberta was going home. The big cross and the big Bible was coming to get her and she seemed sort of glad and sort of not. I thought I would die in that room of four beds without her and I knew Bozo had plans to move some other dumped kid in there with me. Roberta promised to write every day, which was really sweet of her because she couldn't read a lick so how could she write anybody. I would have drawn pictures and sent them to her but she never gave me her address. Little by little she faded. Her wet socks with the pink scalloped tops and her big serious-looking eyes – that's all I could catch when I tried to bring her to mind.

I was working behind the counter at the Howard Johnson's on the Thruway just before the Kingston exit.[7] Not a bad job. Kind of a long ride from Newburgh, but okay once I got there. Mine was the second night shift – eleven to seven. Very light until a Greyhound checked in for breakfast around six-thirty. At that hour the sun was all the

---

7. **Thruway . . . Kingston exit:** The New York State Thruway, a limited access toll road, runs near Kingston and Newburgh, cities north of New York City.

way clear of the hills behind the restaurant. The place looked better at night — more like shelter — but I loved it when the sun broke in, even if it did show all the cracks in the vinyl and the speckled floor looked dirty no matter what the mop boy did.

It was August and a bus crowd was just unloading. They would stand around a long while: going to the john, and looking at gifts and junk-for-sale machines, reluctant to sit down so soon. Even to eat. I was trying to fill the coffee pots and get them all situated on the electric burners when I saw her. She was sitting in a booth smoking a cigarette with two guys smothered in head and facial hair. Her own hair was so big and wild I could hardly see her face. But the eyes. I would know them anywhere. She had on a powder-blue halter and shorts outfit and earrings the size of bracelets. Talk about lipstick and eyebrow pencil. She made the big girls look like nuns. I couldn't get off the counter until seven o'clock, but I kept watching the booth in case they got up to leave before that. My replacement was on time for a change, so I counted and stacked my receipts as fast as I could and signed off. I walked over to the booth, smiling and wondering if she would remember me. Or even if she wanted to remember me. Maybe she didn't want to be reminded of St. Bonny's or to have anybody know she was ever there. I know I never talked about it to anybody.

I put my hands in my apron pockets and leaned against the back of the booth facing them.

"Roberta? Roberta Fisk?"

She looked up. "Yeah?"

"Twyla."

She squinted for a second and then said, "Wow."

"Remember me?"

"Sure. Hey. Wow."

"It's been a while," I said, and gave a smile to the two hairy guys.

"Yeah. Wow. You work here?"

"Yeah," I said. "I live in Newburgh."

"Newburgh? No kidding?" She laughed then a private laugh that included the guys but only the guys, and they laughed with her. What could I do but laugh too and wonder why I was standing there with my knees showing out from under that uniform. Without looking I could see the blue and white triangle on my head, my hair shapeless in a net, my ankles thick in white oxfords. Nothing could have been less sheer than my stockings. There was this silence that came down right after I laughed. A silence it was her turn to fill up. With introductions, maybe, to her boyfriends or an invitation to sit down and have a Coke. Instead she lit a cigarette off the one she'd just finished and said, "We're on our way to the Coast. He's got an appointment with Hendrix."[8] She gestured casually toward the boy next to her.

"Hendrix? Fantastic," I said. "Really fantastic. What's she doing now?"

Roberta coughed on her cigarette and the two guys rolled their eyes up at the ceiling.

---

8. **Hendrix:** Jimi Hendrix (1942–1970), the influential singer and guitarist who gained enormous popularity in Europe and the United States during the 1960s.

"Hendrix. Jimi Hendrix, asshole. He's only the biggest — Oh, wow. Forget it."

I was dismissed without anyone saying goodbye, so I thought I would do it for her.

"How's your mother?" I asked. Her grin cracked her whole face. She swallowed. "Fine," she said. "How's yours?"

"Pretty as a picture," I said and turned away. The backs of my knees were damp. Howard Johnson's really was a dump in the sunlight.

James is as comfortable as a house slipper. He liked my cooking and I liked his big loud family. They have lived in Newburgh all of their lives and talk about it the way people do who have always known a home. His grandmother has a porch swing older than his father and when they talk about streets and avenues and buildings they call them names they no longer have. They still call the A & P[9] Rico's because it stands on property once a mom and pop store owned by Mr. Rico. And they call the new community college Town Hall because it once was. My mother-in-law puts up jelly and cucumbers and buys butter wrapped in cloth from a dairy. James and his father talk about fishing and baseball and I can see them all together on the Hudson in a raggedy skiff. Half the population of Newburgh is on welfare now, but to my husband's family it was still some upstate paradise of a time long past. A time of ice houses and vegetable wagons, coal furnaces and children weeding gardens. When our son was born my mother-in-law gave me the crib blanket that had been hers.

But the town they remembered had changed. Something quick was in the air. Magnificent old houses, so ruined they had become shelter for squatters and rent risks, were bought and renovated. Smart IBM people moved out of their suburbs back into the city and put shutters up and herb gardens in their backyards. A brochure came in the mail announcing the opening of a Food Emporium. Gourmet food it said — and listed items the rich IBM crowd would want. It was located in a new mall at the edge of town and I drove out to shop there one day — just to see. It was late in June. After the tulips were gone and the Queen Elizabeth roses were open everywhere. I trailed my cart along the aisle tossing in smoked oysters and Robert's sauce and things I knew would sit in my cupboard for years. Only when I found some Klondike ice cream bars did I feel less guilty about spending James's fireman's salary so foolishly. My father-in-law ate them with the same gusto little Joseph did.

Waiting in the check-out line I heard a voice say, "Twyla!"

The classical music piped over the aisles had affected me and the woman leaning toward me was dressed to kill. Diamonds on her hand, a smart white summer dress. "I'm Mrs. Benson," I said.

"Ho. Ho. The Big Bozo," she sang.

For a split second I didn't know what she was talking about. She had a bunch of asparagus and two cartons of fancy water.

"Roberta!"

"Right."

---

9. **A & P:** The name of a supermarket chain owned by the Great Atlantic and Pacific Tea Company.

"For heaven's sake. Roberta."

"You look great," she said.

"So do you. Where are you? Here? In Newburgh?"

"Yes. Over in Annandale."[10]

I was opening my mouth to say more when the cashier called my attention to her empty counter.

"Meet you outside." Roberta pointed her finger and went into the express line.

I placed the groceries and kept myself from glancing around to check Roberta's progress. I remembered Howard Johnson's and looking for a chance to speak only to be greeted with a stingy "wow." But she was waiting for me and her huge hair was sleek now, smooth around a small, nicely shaped head. Shoes, dress, everything lovely and summery and rich. I was dying to know what happened to her, how she got from Jimi Hendrix to Annandale, a neighborhood full of doctors and IBM executives. Easy, I thought. Everything is so easy for them. They think they own the world.

"How long," I asked her. "How long have you been here?"

"A year. I got married to a man who lives here. And you, you're married too, right? Benson, you said."

"Yeah. James Benson."

"And is he nice?"

"Oh, is he nice?"

"Well, is he?" Roberta's eyes were steady as though she really meant the question and wanted an answer.

"He's wonderful, Roberta. Wonderful."

"So you're happy."

"Very."

"That's good," she said and nodded her head. "I always hoped you'd be happy. Any kids? I know you have kids."

"One. A boy. How about you?"

"Four."

"Four?"

She laughed. "Step kids. He's a widower."

"Oh."

"Got a minute? Let's have a coffee."

I thought about the Klondikes melting and the inconvenience of going all the way to my car and putting the bags in the trunk. Served me right for buying all that stuff I didn't need. Roberta was ahead of me.

"Put them in my car. It's right here."

And then I saw the dark blue limousine.

"You married a Chinaman?"

"No," she laughed. "He's the driver."

"Oh, my. If the Big Bozo could see you now."

---

10. **Annandale:** Annandale-on-Hudson, an affluent town across the Hudson River and north of Newburgh.

We both giggled. Really giggled. Suddenly, in just a pulse beat, twenty years disappeared and all of it came rushing back. The big girls (whom we called gar girls — Roberta's misheard word for the evil stone faces described in a civics class) there dancing in the orchard, the ploppy mashed potatoes, the double weenies, the Spam with pineapple. We went into the coffee shop holding on to one another and I tried to think why we were glad to see each other this time and not before. Once, twelve years ago, we passed like strangers. A black girl and a white girl meeting in a Howard Johnson's on the road and having nothing to say. One in a blue and white triangle waitress hat — the other on her way to see Hendrix. Now we were behaving like sisters separated for much too long. Those four short months were nothing in time. Maybe it was the thing itself. Just being there, together. Two little girls who knew what nobody else in the world knew — how not to ask questions. How to believe what had to be believed. There was politeness in that reluctance and generosity as well. Is your mother sick too? No, she dances all night. Oh — and an understanding nod.

We sat in a booth by the window and fell into recollection like veterans.

"Did you ever learn to read?"

"Watch." She picked up the menu. "Special of the day. Cream of corn soup. Entrées. Two dots and a wriggly line. Quiche. Chef salad, scallops . . ."

I was laughing and applauding when the waitress came up.

"Remember the Easter baskets?"

"And how we tried to *introduce* them?"

"Your mother with that cross like two telephone poles."

"And yours with those tight slacks."

We laughed so loudly heads turned and made the laughter harder to suppress.

"What happened to the Jimi Hendrix date?"

Roberta made a blow-out sound with her lips.

"When he died I thought about you."

"Oh, you heard about him finally?"

"Finally. Come on, I was a small-town country waitress."

"And I was a small-town country dropout. God, were we wild. I still don't know how I got out of there alive."

"But you did."

"I did. I really did. Now I'm Mrs. Kenneth Norton."

"Sounds like a mouthful."

"It is."

"Servants and all?"

Roberta held up two fingers.

"Ow! What does he do?"

"Computers and stuff. What do I know?"

"I don't remember a hell of a lot from those days, but Lord, St. Bonny's is as clear as daylight. Remember Maggie? The day she fell down and those gar girls laughed at her?"

Roberta looked up from her salad and stared at me. "Maggie didn't fall," she said.

"Yes, she did. You remember."

"No, Twyla. They knocked her down. Those girls pushed her down and tore her clothes. In the orchard."

"I don't — that's not what happened."

"Sure it is. In the orchard. Remember how scared we were?"

"Wait a minute. I don't remember any of that."

"And Bozo was fired."

"You're crazy. She was there when I left. You left before me."

"I went back. You weren't there when they fired Bozo."

"What?"

"Twice. Once for a year when I was about ten, another for two months when I was fourteen. That's when I ran away."

"You ran away from St. Bonny's?"

"I had to. What do you want? Me dancing in that orchard?"

"Are you sure about Maggie?"

"Of course I'm sure. You've blocked it, Twyla. It happened. Those girls had behavior problems, you know."

"Didn't they, though. But why can't I remember the Maggie thing?"

"Believe me. It happened. And we were there."

"Who did you room with when you went back?" I asked her as if I would know her. The Maggie thing was troubling me.

"Creeps. They tickled themselves in the night."

My ears were itching and I wanted to go home suddenly. This was all very well but she couldn't just comb her hair, wash her face, and pretend everything was hunky-dory. After the Howard Johnson's snub. And no apology. Nothing.

"Were you on dope or what that time at Howard Johnson's?" I tried to make my voice sound friendlier than I felt.

"Maybe, a little. I never did drugs much. Why?"

"I don't know; you acted sort of like you didn't want to know me then."

"Oh, Twyla, you know how it was in those days: black — white. You know how everything was."

But I didn't know. I thought it was just the opposite. Busloads of blacks and whites came into Howard Johnson's together. They roamed together then: students, musicians, lovers, protesters. You got to see everything at Howard Johnson's and blacks were very friendly with whites in those days. But sitting there with nothing on my plate but two hard tomato wedges wondering about the melting Klondikes it seemed childish remembering the slight. We went to her car, and with the help of the driver, got my stuff into my station wagon.

"We'll keep in touch this time," she said.

"Sure," I said. "Sure. Give me a call."

"I will," she said, and then just as I was sliding behind the wheel, she leaned into the window. "By the way. Your mother. Did she ever stop dancing?"

I shook my head. "No. Never."

Roberta nodded.

"And yours? Did she ever get well?"

She smiled a tiny sad smile. "No. She never did. Look, call me, okay?"

"Okay," I said, but I knew I wouldn't. Roberta had messed up my past somehow with that business about Maggie. I wouldn't forget a thing like that. Would I?

Strife came to us that fall. At least that's what the paper called it. Strife. Racial strife. The word made me think of a bird — a big shrieking bird out of 1,000,000,000 B.C. Flapping its wings and cawing. Its eye with no lid always bearing down on you. All day it screeched and at night it slept on the rooftops. It woke you in the morning and from the *Today* show to the eleven o'clock news it kept you an awful company. I couldn't figure it out from one day to the next. I knew I was supposed to feel something strong, but I didn't know what, and James wasn't any help. Joseph was on the list of kids to he transferred from the junior high school to another one at some far-out-of-the-way place and I thought it was a good thing until I heard it was a bad thing. I mean I didn't know. All the schools seemed dumps to me, and the fact that one was nicer looking didn't hold much weight. But the papers were full of it and then the kids began to get jumpy. In August, mind you. Schools weren't even open yet. I thought Joseph might be frightened to go over there, but he didn't seem scared so I forgot about it, until I found myself driving along Hudson Street out there by the school they were trying to integrate and saw a line of women marching. And who do you suppose was in line, big as life, holding a sign in front of her bigger than her mother's cross? MOTHERS HAVE RIGHTS TOO! it said.

I drove on, and then changed my mind. I circled the block, slowed down, and honked my horn.

Roberta looked over and when she saw me she waved. I didn't wave back, but I didn't move either. She handed her sign to another woman and came over to where I was parked.

"Hi."

"What are you doing?"

"Picketing. What's it look like?"

"What for?"

"What do you mean, 'What for?' They want to take my kids and send them out of the neighborhood. They don't want to go."

"So what if they go to another school? My boy's being bussed too, and I don't mind. Why should you?"

"It's not about us, Twyla. Me and you. It's about our kids."

"What's more *us* than that?"

"Well, it is a free country."

"Not yet, but it will be."

"What the hell does that mean? I'm not doing anything to you."

"You really think that?"

"I know it."

"I wonder what made me think you were different."

"I wonder what made me think you were different."

"Look at them," I said. "Just look. Who do they think they are? Swarming all over the place like they own it. And now they think they can decide where my child goes to school. Look at them, Roberta. They're Bozos."

Roberta turned around and looked at the women. Almost all of them were standing still now, waiting. Some were even edging toward us. Roberta looked at me out of some refrigerator behind her eyes. "No, they're not. They're just mothers."

"And what am I? Swiss cheese?"

"I used to curl your hair."

"I hated your hands in my hair."

The women were moving. Our faces looked mean to them of course and they looked as though they could not wait to throw themselves in front of a police car, or better yet, into my car and drag me away by my ankles. Now they surrounded my car and gently, gently began to rock it. I swayed back and forth like a sideways yo-yo. Automatically I reached for Roberta, like the old days in the orchard when they saw us watching them and we had to get out of there, and if one of us fell the other pulled her up and if one of us was caught the other stayed to kick and scratch, and neither would leave the other behind. My arm shot out of the car window but no receiving hand was there. Roberta was looking at me sway from side to side in the car and her face was still. My purse slid from the car seat down under the dashboard. The four policemen who had been drinking Tab in their car finally got the message and strolled over, forcing their way through the women. Quietly, firmly they spoke. "Okay, ladies. Back in line or off the streets."

Some of them went away willingly; others had to be urged away from the car doors and the hood. Roberta didn't move. She was looking steadily at me. I was fumbling to turn on the ignition, which wouldn't catch because the gearshift was still in drive. The seats of the car were a mess because the swaying had thrown my grocery coupons all over it and my purse was sprawled on the floor.

"Maybe I am different now, Twyla. But you're not. You're the same little state kid who kicked a poor old black lady when she was down on the ground. You kicked a black lady and you have the nerve to call me a bigot."

The coupons were everywhere and the guts of my purse were bunched under the dashboard. What was she saying? Black? Maggie wasn't black.

"She wasn't black," I said.

"Like hell she wasn't, and you kicked her. We both did. You kicked a black lady who couldn't even scream."

"Liar!"

"You're the liar! Why don't you just go on home and leave us alone, huh?"

She turned away and I skidded away from the curb.

The next morning I went into the garage and cut the side out of the carton our portable TV had come in. It wasn't nearly big enough, but after a while I had a decent sign: red spray-painted letters on a white background – AND SO DO CHILDREN****. I meant just to go down to the school and tack it up somewhere so those cows on the picket line across the street could see it, but when I got there, some ten or so others had already assembled – protesting the cows across the street. Police permits and every-thing. I got in line and we strutted in time on our side while Roberta's group strutted on theirs. That first day we were all dignified, pretending the other side didn't exist. The second day there was name calling and finger gestures. But that was about all. People changed signs from time to time, but Roberta never did and neither did I. Actually my sign didn't make sense without Roberta's. "And so do children what?" one of the women on my side asked me. Have rights, I said, as though it was obvious.

Roberta didn't acknowledge my presence in any way and I got to thinking maybe she didn't know I was there. I began to pace myself in the line, jostling people one minute and lagging behind the next, so Roberta and I could reach the end of our respective lines at the same time and there would be a moment in our turn when we would face each other. Still, I couldn't tell whether she saw me and knew my sign was for her. The next day I went early before we were scheduled to assemble. I waited until she got there before I exposed my new creation. As soon as she hoisted her MOTHERS HAVE RIGHTS TOO I began to wave my new one, which said, HOW WOULD YOU KNOW? I know she saw that one, but I had gotten addicted now. My signs got crazier each day, and the women on my side decided that I was a kook. They couldn't make heads or tails out of my brilliant screaming posters.

I brought a painted sign in queenly red with huge black letters that said, IS YOUR MOTHER WELL? Roberta took her lunch break and didn't come back for the rest of the day or any day after. Two days later I stopped going too and couldn't have been missed because nobody understood my signs anyway.

It was a nasty six weeks. Classes were suspended and Joseph didn't go to anybody's school until October. The children — everybody's children — soon got bored with that extended vacation they thought was going to be so great. They looked at TV until their eyes flattened. I spent a couple of mornings tutoring my son, as the other mothers said we should. Twice I opened a text from last year that he had never turned in. Twice he yawned in my face. Other mothers organized living room sessions so the kids would keep up. None of the kids could concentrate so they drifted back to *The Price Is Right* and *The Brady Bunch.* When the school finally opened there were fights once or twice and some sirens roared through the streets every once in a while. There were a lot of photographers from Albany. And just when ABC was about to send up a news crew, the kids settled down like nothing in the world had happened. Joseph hung my HOW WOULD YOU KNOW? sign in his bedroom. I don't know what became of AND SO DO CHILDREN****. I think my father-in-law cleaned some fish on it. He was always puttering around in our garage. Each of his five children lived in Newburgh and he acted as though he had five extra homes.

I couldn't help looking for Roberta when Joseph graduated from high school, but I didn't see her. It didn't trouble me much what she had said to me in the car. I mean the kicking part. I know I didn't do that, I couldn't do that. But I was puzzled by her telling me Maggie was black. When I thought about it I actually couldn't be certain. She wasn't pitch-black, I knew, or I would have remembered that. What I remember was the kiddie hat, and the semicircle legs. I tried to reassure myself about the race thing for a long time until it dawned on me that the truth was already there, and Roberta knew it. I didn't kick her; I didn't join in with the gar girls and kick that lady, but I sure did want to. We watched and never tried to help her and never called for help. Maggie was my dancing mother. Deaf, I thought, and dumb. Nobody inside. Nobody who would hear you if you cried in the night. Nobody who could tell you anything important that you could use. Rocking, dancing, swaying as she walked. And when the gar girls pushed her down, and started roughhousing, I knew she wouldn't scream, couldn't — just like me — and I was glad about that.

We decided not to have a tree, because Christmas would be at my mother-in-law's house, so why have a tree at both places? Joseph was at SUNY New Paltz and we had to economize, we said. But at the last minute, I changed my mind. Nothing could be that bad. So I rushed around town looking for a tree, something small but wide. By the time I found a place, it was snowing and very late. I dawdled like it was the most important purchase in the world and the tree man was fed up with me. Finally I chose one and had it tied onto the trunk of the car. I drove away slowly because the sand trucks were not out yet and the streets could be murder at the beginning of a snowfall. Downtown the streets were wide and rather empty except for a cluster of people coming out of the Newburgh Hotel. The one hotel in town that wasn't built out of cardboard and Plexiglas. A party, probably. The men huddled in the snow were dressed in tails and the women had on furs. Shiny things glittered from underneath their coats. It made me tired to look at them. Tired, tired, tired. On the next corner was a small diner with loops and loops of paper bells in the window. I stopped the car and went in. Just for a cup of coffee and twenty minutes of peace before I went home and tried to finish everything before Christmas Eve.

"Twyla?"

There she was. In a silvery evening gown and dark fur coat. A man and another woman were with her, the man fumbling for change to put in the cigarette machine. The woman was humming and tapping on the counter with her fingernails. They all looked a little bit drunk.

"Well. It's you."

"How are you?"

I shrugged. "Pretty good. Frazzled. Christmas and all."

"Regular?" called the woman from the counter.

"Fine," Roberta called back and then, "Wait for me in the car."

She slipped into the booth beside me. "I have to tell you something, Twyla. I made up my mind if I ever saw you again, I'd tell you."

"I'd just as soon not hear anything, Roberta. It doesn't matter now, anyway."

"No," she said. "Not about that."

"Don't be long," said the woman. She carried two regulars to go and the man peeled his cigarette pack as they left.

"It's about St. Bonny's and Maggie."

"Oh, please."

"Listen to me. I really did think she was black. I didn't make that up. I really thought so. But now I can't be sure. I just remember her as old, so old. And because she couldn't talk — well, you know, I thought she was crazy. She'd been brought up in an institution like my mother was and like I thought I would be too. And you were right. We didn't kick her. It was the gar girls. Only them. But, well, I wanted to. I really wanted them to hurt her. I said we did it, too. You and me, but that's not true. And I don't want you to carry that around. It was just that I wanted to do it so bad that day — wanting to is doing it."

Her eyes were watery from the drinks she'd had, I guess. I know it's that way with me. One glass of wine and I start bawling over the littlest thing.

"We were kids, Roberta."

"Yeah. Yeah. I know, just kids."

"Eight."

"Eight."

"And lonely."

"Scared, too."

She wiped her cheeks with the heel of her hand and smiled. "Well, that's all I wanted to say."

I nodded and couldn't think of any way to fill the silence that went from the diner past the paper bells on out into the snow. It was heavy now. I thought I'd better wait for the sand trucks before starting home.

"Thanks, Roberta."

"Sure."

"Did I tell you? My mother, she never did stop dancing."

"Yes. You told me. And mine, she never got well." Roberta lifted her hands from the tabletop and covered her face with her palms. When she took them away she really was crying. "Oh shit, Twyla. Shit, shit, shit. What the hell happened to Maggie?"

[1983]

Sylvia Plath

[1932–1963]

Sylvia Plath was born in Boston, Massachusetts, on October 27, 1932. She was the first of two children of Aurelia Schober Plath, a former high-school teacher, and Otto Emil Plath, a professor of German and biology at Boston University. Plath's father, an immigrant from the Prussian area of Germany, spent much of his time doing research on bumblebees, his scientific specialization. In 1940, he refused to seek medical treatment for what proved to be diabetes and died after the amputation of a gangrenous leg. Emotionally and economically devastated by the loss, the family was forced to move from its seaside home in Winthrop to Wellesley, Massachusetts. A brilliant student who loved art, music, and writing, Plath attended public schools in Wellesley and went to Smith College on a scholarship in the fall of 1950, shortly after the first of several of her stories appeared in *Seventeen* magazine. As an undergraduate, she edited the *Smith Review* and published poems in the *Atlantic Monthly, Harper's,* and *Mademoiselle,* for which she served as a guest editor during June 1953. Despite her remarkable successes, she was increasingly anxious about her progress. When

Sylvia Plath

This photograph of Plath was taken during the intense period of writing that preceded her death in 1963, when she was only thirty years old.

she returned home from her internship at *Mademoiselle*, Plath learned that she had not been accepted into a summer-school course in fiction writing at Harvard. She consequently became so severely depressed that she tried to commit suicide by taking an overdose of sleeping pills. Following several months of treatment at a private psychiatric hospital, she returned to Smith, from which she graduated summa cum laude in 1955. She also won numerous awards, including a Fulbright Fellowship to study at Cambridge University in England.

Plath produced a remarkable body of work before her death less than eight years later. At a party in Cambridge, she met the rising young English poet Ted Hughes, and they were married in June 1956. After she earned her master's degree in 1957, the couple moved to the United States, where Plath taught for a year at Smith before she and Hughes moved to Boston. They met a number of American poets, and Plath took a poetry-writing workshop taught by Robert Lowell. She fulfilled a lifelong dream by publishing several poems in the *New Yorker*, and Plath made further strides as a poet during the fall of 1959, which she and Hughes spent at Yaddo, an artists' colony in Saratoga Springs, New York. By then, she was pregnant, and they decided to return to England. Their daughter, Frieda Rebecca Hughes, was born there on April 1, 1960, a few months before Plath's first book, *The Colossus and Other Poems*, was published in London. The following year, she completed an autobiographical novel, and she began sustained work on a new collection of poetry after she and Hughes bought an old house in a small village in Devon. For a time, life in the country went well, and their son, Nicholas Farrar Hughes, was born there in January 1962. Six months later, however, Plath discovered that Hughes was having an affair, and they separated. Struggling with ill health, isolation, and the challenges of keeping up an old house and caring for her children, Plath nonetheless adhered to a rigorous schedule in which she wrote from four to eight o'clock each morning. "I am writing the best poems of my life," she told a friend in October. She moved with her children to London in December, a month before the publication of her novel, *The Bell Jar*. Outwardly, Plath seemed optimistic about the future, and she continued to write new poems until February 11, 1963, when she committed suicide by breathing the toxic fumes from an unlit gas oven in the kitchen of her small apartment in London.

The handling of Plath's literary estate became a source of heated controversy. Because she died without a will and was still married to Hughes, he became her literary executor. He edited a collection of poems Plath left behind at her death, *Ariel* (1965), which established her as a major poet. As Hughes later admitted, however, he altered her original arrangement and omitted some poems that he described as "personally aggressive," replacing them with other late poems by Plath. Until his death in 1998, Hughes carefully controlled access to Plath's papers and bound journals, at least one of which he destroyed, and he published several more volumes of her writings: two collections of poetry, *Crossing the Water* (1971) and *Winter Trees* (1972); a children's book, *The Bed Book* (1976); and a collection of short stories and prose pieces, *Johnny Panic and the Bible of Dreams*

We know her because the shape of her words contains the shape of our lives.

–Dave Smith

(1979). He also edited her *Collected Poems* (1981), for which Plath was posthumously awarded the Pulitzer Prize. Before his death, Hughes authorized the opening of several volumes of Plath's journals he had previously sealed, and a complete edition of the surviving manuscripts was published in 2000. Plath's daughter, Frieda Hughes, later published a facsimile of the famous manuscript her mother left behind at her death, *Ariel: The Restored Edition* (2004).

Plath's Poetry. The precocious Plath, who published her first poem in a Boston newspaper when she was eight years old and as an undergraduate published poems in several national magazines, began to recast herself as poet after her graduation from college in 1955. She experimented with a wide array of traditional forms and techniques in the tightly controlled poems in her first collection, *The Colossus* (1960), which received several positive reviews in England and was subsequently published in the United States in 1962. In some of the later poems in that volume, Plath began to employ a looser, more colloquial language that captured what she described as her "humor and oddness." The poems she wrote during the last two years of her life display an even more striking departure from her early work. Influenced in part by Robert Lowell's *Life Studies* (1959), Plath wrote a series of raw, realistic, and deeply personal poems, some of which were posthumously published in her collection *Ariel* (1965). In his introduction to the volume, Lowell observed that in her late poems "Sylvia Plath becomes herself, becomes something imaginary, newly, wildly, and subtly created — hardly a person at all, or a woman, certainly not another 'poetess,' but one of those super-real, hypnotic, classical heroines." Of those poems, two of the most famous are the pseudo-autobiographical "Daddy" and "Lady Lazarus," fierce dramatic monologues in which the speaker addresses her Prussian father, cast as a Nazi, and evokes images of the Holocaust. As the following selection illustrates, in other late poems Plath explored a range of subjects, including birth, motherhood, the painful lot of women, and the psychically charged landscapes of the natural world. The texts of the following poems, dated and arranged in the order of their composition, are taken from her *Collected Poems*, edited by Ted Hughes (1981).

bedfordstmartins.com/
americanlit *for research*
links on Plath

MORNING SONG

Love set you going like a fat gold watch.
The midwife slapped your footsoles, and your bald cry
Took its place among the elements.

Our voices echo, magnifying your arrival. New statue.
In a drafty museum, your nakedness   5
Shadows our safety. We stand round blankly as walls.

I'm no more your mother
Than the cloud that distills a mirror to reflect its own slow
Effacement at the wind's hand.

All night your moth-breath   10
Flickers among the flat pink roses. I wake to listen:
A far sea moves in my ear.

One cry, and I stumble from bed, cow-heavy and floral
In my Victorian nightgown.
Your mouth opens clean as a cat's. The window square   15

Whitens and swallows its dull stars. And now you try
Your handful of notes;
The clear vowels rise like balloons.

19 February 1961

[1965, 1981]

BLACKBERRYING

Nobody in the lane, and nothing, nothing but blackberries,
Blackberries on either side, though on the right mainly,
A blackberry alley, going down in hooks, and a sea
Somewhere at the end of it, heaving. Blackberries
Big as the ball of my thumb, and dumb as eyes   5
Ebon[1] in the hedges, fat
With blue-red juices. These they squander on my fingers.
I had not asked for such a blood sisterhood; they must love me.
They accommodate themselves to my milkbottle, flattening their sides.

Overhead go the choughs[2] in black, cacophonous flocks —   10
Bits of burnt paper wheeling in a blown sky.
Theirs is the only voice, protesting, protesting.
I do not think the sea will appear at all.
The high, green meadows are glowing, as if lit from within.
I come to one bush of berries so ripe it is a bush of flies,   15

---

1. **Ebon:** A poetic term for dark brown or black.
2. **choughs:** Black birds of the crow family.

Hanging their bluegreen bellies and their wing panes in a Chinese screen.
The honey-feast of the berries has stunned them; they believe in heaven.
One more hook, and the berries and bushes end.

The only thing to come now is the sea.
From between two hills a sudden wind funnels at me,   20
Slapping its phantom laundry in my face.
These hills are too green and sweet to have tasted salt.
I follow the sheep path between them. A last hook brings me
To the hills' northern face, and the face is orange rock
That looks out on nothing, nothing but a great space   25
Of white and pewter lights, and a din like silversmiths
Beating and beating at an intractable metal.

23 September 1961

[1962, 1981]

MIRROR

I am silver and exact. I have no preconceptions.
Whatever I see I swallow immediately
Just as it is, unmisted by love or dislike.
I am not cruel, only truthful —
The eye of a little god, four-cornered.   5
Most of the time I meditate on the opposite wall.
It is pink, with speckles. I have looked at it so long
I think it is a part of my heart. But it flickers.
Faces and darkness separate us over and over.

Now I am a lake. A woman bends over me,   10
Searching my reaches for what she really is.
Then she turns to those liars, the candles or the moon.
I see her back, and reflect it faithfully.
She rewards me with tears and an agitation of hands.
I am important to her. She comes and goes.   15
Each morning it is her face that replaces the darkness.
In me she has drowned a young girl, and in me an old woman
Rises toward her day after day, like a terrible fish.

23 October 1961

[1963, 1981]

DADDY[1]

You do not do, you do not do
Any more, black shoe
In which I have lived like a foot
For thirty years, poor and white,
Barely daring to breathe or Achoo.   5

Daddy, I have had to kill you.
You died before I had time ——
Marble-heavy, a bag full of God,
Ghastly statue with one gray toe[2]
Big as a Frisco seal[3]   10

And a head in the freakish Atlantic
Where it pours bean green over blue
In the waters off beautiful Nauset.[4]
I used to pray to recover you.
Ach, du.[5]   15

In the German tongue, in the Polish town
Scraped flat by the roller
Of wars, wars, wars.
But the name of the town is common.
My Polack[6] friend   20

Says there are a dozen or two.
So I never could tell where you
Put your foot, your root,
I never could talk to you.
The tongue stuck in my jaw.   25

It stuck in a barb wire snare.
Ich,[7] ich, ich, ich,
I could hardly speak.

---

1. **Daddy:** In a script for a planned broadcast for the British Broadcasting Company, Plath wrote: "Here is a poem spoken by a girl with an Electra complex. Her father died while she thought he was God. Her case is complicated by the fact that her father was also a Nazi and her mother very possibly part Jewish. In the daughter the two strains marry and paralyze each other — she has to act out the awful little allegory once over before she is free of it."
2. **one gray toe:** Plath's father developed gangrene in his foot, the result of diabetes, and died after amputation surgery in 1940.
3. **Frisco seal:** The large harbor seals native to San Francisco Bay.
4. **Nauset:** An area on the Atlantic Ocean side of Cape Cod, Massachusetts.
5. **Ach, du:** Oh, you (German).
6. **Polack:** Derogatory name for a person of Polish descent.
7. **Ich:** I (German).

I thought every German was you.
And the language obscene   30

An engine, an engine
Chuffing me off like a Jew.
A Jew to Dachau, Auschwitz, Belsen.[8]
I began to talk like a Jew.
I think I may well be a Jew.   35

The snows of the Tyrol,[9] the clear beer of Vienna
Are not very pure or true.
With my gipsy ancestress and my weird luck
And my Taroc pack and my Taroc pack[10]
I may be a bit of a Jew.   40

I have always been scared of *you,*
With your Luftwaffe,[11] your gobbledygoo.
And your neat mustache
And your Aryan eye, bright blue.[12]
Panzer-man,[13] panzer-man, O You ——   45

Not God but a swastika
So black no sky could squeak through.
Every woman adores a Fascist,
The boot in the face, the brute
Brute heart of a brute like you.   50

You stand at the blackboard,[14] daddy,
In the picture I have of you,
A cleft in your chin instead of your foot
But no less a devil for that, no not
Any less the black man who   55

Bit my pretty red heart in two.
I was ten when they buried you.
At twenty I tried to die
And get back, back, back to you.
I thought even the bones would do.   60

---

8. **Dachau, Auschwitz, Belsen:** Nazi death camps in which millions of Jews were killed during World War II.
9. **Tyrol:** A mountainous Alpine region in western Austria.
10. **Taroc pack:** Similar to tarot cards, used for fortune-telling.
11. **Luftwaffe:** The name of the German air force during World War II.
12. **Aryan eye, bright blue:** In Nazi ideology, Aryans were members of a superior German race characterized by blonde hair and blue eyes.
13. **Panzer-man:** Panzer was the German designation for a tank or armored forces during World War II.
14. **blackboard:** Plath's father was a biology professor at Boston University.

But they pulled me out of the sack,
And they stuck me together with glue.
And then I knew what to do.
I made a model of you,
A man in black with a Meinkampf[15] look   65

And a love of the rack and the screw.
And I said I do, I do.
So daddy, I'm finally through.
The black telephone's off at the root,
The voices just can't worm through.   70

If I've killed one man, I've killed two —
The vampire who said he was you
And drank my blood for a year,
Seven years, if you want to know.
Daddy, you can lie back now.   75

There's a stake in your fat black heart[16]
And the villagers never liked you.
They are dancing and stamping on you.
They always *knew* it was you.
Daddy, daddy, you bastard, I'm through.   80

12 October 1962

[1965, 1981]

---

15. **Meinkampf:** My struggle (German), the title of Adolf Hitler's autobiography, *Mein Kampf* (1925).
16. **There's a stake . . . heart:** An allusion to the folklore that the only way to destroy a vampire is to drive a stake into its heart.

LADY LAZARUS[1]

I have done it again.
One year in every ten
I manage it —

---

1. **Lady Lazarus:** The title alludes to the biblical story in which Lazarus, the brother of Mary, is raised from the dead by Jesus (John 11:39–55). In a script for a planned broadcast for the British Broadcasting Company, Plath wrote: "The speaker is a woman who has the great and terrible gift of being reborn. The only trouble is, she has to die first. She is the phoenix, the libertarian spirit, what you will. She is also just a good, plain, very resourceful woman."

A sort of walking miracle, my skin
Bright as a Nazi lampshade,[2]   5
My right foot

A paperweight,
My face a featureless, fine
Jew linen.

Peel off the napkin   10
O my enemy.
Do I terrify? ——

The nose, the eye pits, the full set of teeth?
The sour breath
Will vanish in a day.   15

Soon, soon the flesh
The grave cave ate will be
At home on me

And I a smiling woman.
I am only thirty.   20
And like the cat I have nine times to die.

This is Number Three.
What a trash
To annihilate each decade.

What a million filaments.   25
The peanut-crunching crowd
Shoves in to see

Them unwrap me hand and foot[3] ——
The big strip tease.
Gentlemen, ladies   30

These are my hands
My knees.
I may be skin and bone,

Nevertheless, I am the same, identical woman.
The first time it happened I was ten.   35
It was an accident.

---

2. **a Nazi lampshade:** According to some reports, the Nazis used the skin of death-camp victims to make lampshades during World War II.
3. **unwrap me hand and foot:** When the resurrected Lazarus emerges from his tomb, he is "bound hand and foot with graveclothes," which Jesus tells the people to remove. See note 1.

The second time I meant
To last it out and not come back at all.
I rocked shut

As a seashell.   40
They had to call and call
And pick the worms off me like sticky pearls.

Dying
Is an art, like everything else.
I do it exceptionally well.   45

I do it so it feels like hell.
I do it so it feels real.
I guess you could say I've a call.

It's easy enough to do it in a cell.
It's easy enough to do it and stay put.   50
It's the theatrical

Comeback in broad day
To the same place, the same face, the same brute
Amused shout:

"A miracle!"   55
That knocks me out.
There is a charge

For the eyeing of my scars, there is a charge
For the hearing of my heart ——
It really goes.   60

And there is a charge, a very large charge
For a word or a touch
Or a bit of blood

Or a piece of my hair or my clothes.
So, so, Herr Doktor.[4]   65
So, Herr Enemy.

I am your opus,
I am your valuable,
The pure gold baby

---

4. **Herr Doktor:** Mr. Doctor, a respectful title for a physician (German).

That melts to a shriek.   70
I turn and burn.
Do not think I underestimate your great concern.

Ash, ash[5] –
You poke and stir.
Flesh, bone, there is nothing there ——   75

A cake of soap,
A wedding ring,
A gold filling.[6]

Herr God, Herr Lucifer
Beware   80
Beware.

Out of the ash
I rise with my red hair
And I eat men like air.[7]

23–29 October 1962

[1965, 1981]

---

5. **Ash, ash:** A reference to the ashes of those who were gassed and cremated in the Nazi death camps.
6. **A cake of soap . . . gold filling:** The Nazis made soap from the human fat of death-camp victims, whose wedding rings and gold tooth fillings were melted down into gold bars.
7. **Out . . . air:** The phoenix is a mythical bird with red and gold plumage, the colors of the rising sun. After living for centuries, it burns itself on a funeral pyre and is reborn from the ashes.

John Updike

[b. 1932]

John Updike's genius is best excited by the lyric possibilities of tragic events that, failing to justify themselves as tragedy, turn unaccountably into comedies.

—Joyce Carol Oates

John Hoyer Updike was born on March 18, 1932, in Reading, Pennsylvania. He was the only child of Wesley Russell Updike, a high-school mathematics teacher, and Linda Grace Hoyer Updike, a homemaker and department-store clerk who dreamed of becoming a writer. The family lived with her parents in the small town of Shillington until 1945, when to Updike's deep distress they moved to an isolated farm in nearby Plowville. In his memoirs, *Consciousness* (1989), Updike recalled that his childhood was defined by his Lutheran upbringing, the source of his ongoing concern with the decline of religious faith, and his severe case of psoriasis, a skin disease that made him deeply self-conscious. At the same time, he suggested that "whenever in my timid life I have shown some courage and originality it has been because of my skin." His mother encouraged his interest in writing and art, and Updike decided that he would become a famous cartoonist for magazines such as the *New Yorker*. An outstanding student, he went to Harvard University on a full scholarship in 1950. He majored in English and contributed articles, cartoons, and sketches to the undergraduate humor magazine, the *Harvard Lampoon*. At the end of his junior year, he married Mary Pennington, a student at Radcliffe, then a women's college affiliated with Harvard. Updike graduated from Harvard summa cum laude in 1954 and won a fellowship to study at the Ruskin School of Drawing and Fine Art in Oxford, England. But he turned to writing when one of his stories was accepted by the *New Yorker*, which hired Updike as a staff writer after he and his wife returned from England in 1955.

After two years with the magazine, for which he wrote the popular column "Talk of the Town," Updike resigned to devote himself full-time to writing in 1957. Leaving New York City, he moved his family to Ipswich, a coastal town north of Boston. By 1960, he and his wife had four children. A disciplined and prolific writer, Updike initially supported the family by selling essays, poems, and especially stories to the *New Yorker*. His first book of poetry, *The Carpentered Hen and Other Tame Creatures* (1958), was swiftly followed by his first novel, *The Poorhouse Fair*, and the first of his numerous collections of stories, *The Same Door*, both of which were published in 1959. A Guggenheim Fellowship supported his work on his acclaimed novel *Rabbit, Run* (1960), in which Updike introduced his best-known character, Harry "Rabbit" Angstrom, a self-centered former high-school athlete who struggles to come to terms with the responsibilities of marriage and fatherhood. *The Centaur* (1963), a modernist novel weaving together Greek mythology and the story of a schoolteacher and his son, based on Updike's relationship with his father, won the National Book Award. Updike continued to draw upon his personal past in stories and in a novel about his relationship with his mother, *Of the Farm* (1965). He turned his attention to the social and sexual dislocations of the troubled present in *Couples* (1968), an unusually explicit novel about marital infidelity set in suburban New England. The book was on the *New York Times* bestseller list for nearly a year, and Updike was featured on the cover of *Time* magazine in April 1968.

Updike has remained one of the most prominent and successful writers in the United States. He continued his chronicle of Harry Angstrom's life and times in *Rabbit Redux* (1971) and later in two Pulitzer Prize–winning novels, *Rabbit Is Rich* (1981) and *Rabbit at Rest* (1990). In 1974, Updike and his wife separated, and he began a new life with his second wife, Martha Ruggles Bernhard, in Georgetown, Massachusetts. Further exploring the theme of adultery, Updike recast Nathaniel Hawthorne's *The Scarlet Letter* in a trilogy of novels, *A Month of Sundays* (1975), *Roger's Version* (1986), and *S.* (1988). Although he is most often thought of as the novelist of white suburban life, Updike ventured into very different terrain in *The Coup* (1978), a novel about a dictator in a mythical African nation, and later in *Brazil* (1994). Although the reception of his late work has been mixed, critics praised *In the Beauty of the Lilies* (1996), his ambitious novel about the decline of an American family through four generations, from 1910 to 1990. Still experimenting with various forms and techniques, Updike

John Updike
Gwendolyn Stewart took this photograph of the famous and best-selling author at his home in Ipswich, Massachusetts, in 1972. The normally clean-shaven Updike told the photographer, "I broke my foot so I grew a beard."

tried his hand at a postmodern novel in *Gertrude and Claudius* (1999), a prequel to Shakespeare's *Hamlet*. Updike's diverse recent work also includes his seventh collection of poetry, *Americana and Other Poems* (2001), a collection of stories about one of the recurrent characters in his fiction, *The Complete Henry Beck* (2001), and a novel told from the point of view of an American-born Islamic fundamentalist and would-be suicide bomber, *Terrorist: A Novel* (2007). The author of over fifty books, including more than twenty novels, Updike lives with his wife in Beverly Farms, Massachusetts.

Updike's "A & P." In the introduction to his collection *The Early Stories, 1953–1975* (2003), Updike fondly recalled his early career in Ipswich, Massachusetts, where he moved from New York City with his growing family in 1957. "Out there was where I belonged, immersed in the ordinary, which careful explication would reveal to be extraordinary," he affirmed. He thus described writing his numerous stories on a manual typewriter in a small room "where my only duty was to describe reality as it had come to me — to give the mundane its beautiful due." Updike's sensitivity to the particulars of time and place, as well as his ability to discover something remarkable amid seemingly commonplace characters, events, and settings, is revealed in "A & P," one of his most popular and frequently anthologized stories. Written in 1960 and published the following year in the *New Yorker*, the story is narrated by Sammy, who describes a few momentous minutes in an otherwise uneventful day back when he was nineteen and working as a cashier in a supermarket in suburban New England. At the end of this coming-of-age story, Sammy makes a crucial decision, the motivation, nature, and consequences of which may well be fully understood by him only in retrospect. The text is taken from *Pigeon Feathers and Other Stories* (1962).

bedfordstmartins.com/ americanlit for research links on Updike

A & P[1]

In walks these three girls in nothing but bathing suits. I'm in the third checkout slot, with my back to the door, so I don't see them until they're over by the bread. The one that caught my eye first was the one in the plaid green two-piece. She was a chunky kid, with a good tan and a sweet broad soft-looking can with those two crescents of white just under it, where the sun never seems to hit, at the top of the backs of her legs. I stood there with my hand on a box of HiHo crackers trying to remember if I rang it up or not. I ring it up again and the customer starts giving me hell. She's one of these cash-register-watchers, a witch about fifty with rouge on her cheekbones and no eyebrows, and I know

---

1. **A & P:** The name of a supermarket chain owned by the Great Atlantic and Pacific Tea Company.

it made her day to trip me up. She'd been watching cash registers for fifty years and probably never seen a mistake before.

By the time I got her feathers smoothed and her goodies into a bag — she gives me a little snort in passing, if she'd been born at the right time they would have burned her over in Salem[2] — by the time I get her on her way the girls had circled around the bread and were coming back, without a pushcart, back my way along the counters, in the aisle between the checkouts and the Special bins. They didn't even have shoes on. There was this chunky one, with the two-piece — it was bright green and the seams on the bra were still sharp and her belly was still pretty pale so I guessed she just got it (the suit) — there was this one, with one of those chubby berry-faces, the lips all bunched together under her nose, this one, and a tall one, with black hair that hadn't quite frizzed right, and one of these sunburns right across under the eyes, and a chin that was too long — you know, the kind of girl other girls think is very "striking" and "attractive" but never quite makes it, as they very well know, which is why they like her so much — and then the third one, that wasn't quite so tall. She was the queen. She kind of led them, the other two peeking around and making their shoulders round. She didn't look around, not this queen, she just walked straight on slowly, on these long white prima-donna legs. She came down a little hard on her heels, as if she didn't walk in her bare feet that much, putting down her heels and then letting the weight move along to her toes as if she was testing the floor with every step, putting a little deliberate extra action into it. You never know for sure how girls' minds work (do you really think it's a mind in there or just a little buzz like a bee in a glass jar?) but you got the idea she had talked the other two into coming in here with her, and now she was showing them how to do it, walk slow and hold yourself straight.

She had on a kind of dirty-pink — beige maybe, I don't know — bathing suit with a little nubble all over it and, what got me, the straps were down. They were off her shoulders looped loose around the cool tops of her arms, and I guess as a result the suit had slipped a little on her, so all around the top of the cloth there was this shining rim. If it hadn't been there you wouldn't have known there could have been anything whiter than those shoulders. With the straps pushed off, there was nothing between the top of the suit and the top of her head except just *her,* this clean bare plane of the top of her chest down from the shoulder bones like a dented sheet of metal tilted in the light. I mean, it was more than pretty.

She had sort of oaky hair that the sun and salt had bleached, done up in a bun that was unravelling, and a kind of prim face. Walking into the A & P with your straps down, I suppose it's the only kind of face you *can* have. She held her head so high her neck, coming up out of those white shoulders, looked kind of stretched, but I didn't mind. The longer her neck was, the more of her there was.

She must have felt in the corner of her eye me and over my shoulder Stokesie in the second slot watching, but she didn't tip. Not this queen. She kept her eyes moving across the racks, and stopped, and turned so slow it made my stomach rub the inside of my

---

2. **Salem:** A town in Massachusetts famous for a notorious series of witchcraft trials in 1692.

apron, and buzzed to the other two, who kind of huddled against her for relief, and then they all three of them went up the cat-and-dog-food-breakfast-cereal-macaroni-rice-raisins-seasonings-spreads-spaghetti-soft-drinks-crackers-and-cookies aisle. From the third slot I look straight up this aisle to the meat counter, and I watched them all the way. The fat one with the tan sort of fumbled with the cookies, but on second thought she put the package back. The sheep pushing their carts down the aisle — the girls were walking against the usual traffic (not that we have one-way signs or anything) — were pretty hilarious. You could see them, when Queenie's white shoulders dawned on them, kind of jerk, or hop, or hiccup, but their eyes snapped back to their own baskets and on they pushed. I bet you could set off dynamite in an A & P and the people would by and large keep reaching and checking oatmeal off their lists and muttering "Let me see, there was a third thing, began with A, asparagus, no, ah, yes, applesauce!" or whatever it is they do mutter. But there was no doubt, this jiggled them. A few houseslaves in pin curlers even looked around after pushing their carts past to make sure what they had seen was correct.

You know, it's one thing to have a girl in a bathing suit down on the beach, where what with the glare nobody can look at each other much anyway, and another thing in the cool of the A & P, under the fluorescent lights, against all those stacked packages, with her feet paddling along naked over our checkerboard green-and-cream rubber-tile floor.

"Oh Daddy," Stokesie said beside me. "I feel so faint."

"Darling," I said. "Hold me tight." Stokesie's married, with two babies chalked up on his fuselage already, but as far as I can tell that's the only difference. He's twenty-two, and I was nineteen this April.

"Is it done?" he asks, the responsible married man finding his voice. I forgot to say he thinks he's going to be manager some sunny day, maybe in 1990 when it's called the Great Alexandrov and Petrooshki Tea Company or something.

What he meant was, our town is five miles from a beach, with a big summer colony out on the Point, but we're right in the middle of town, and the women generally put on a shirt or shorts or something before they get out of the car into the street. And anyway these are usually women with six children and varicose veins mapping their legs and nobody, including them, could care less. As I say, we're right in the middle of town, and if you stand at our front doors you can see two banks and the Congregational church and the newspaper store and three real-estate offices and about twenty-seven old freeload-ers tearing up Central Street because the sewer broke again. It's not as if we're on the Cape; we're north of Boston and there's people in this town haven't seen the ocean for twenty years.

The girls had reached the meat counter and were asking McMahon something. He pointed, they pointed, and they shuffled out of sight behind a pyramid of Diet Delight peaches. All that was left for us to see was old McMahon patting his mouth and looking after them sizing up their joints. Poor kids, I began to feel sorry for them, they couldn't help it.

Now here comes the sad part of the story, at least my family says it's sad, but I don't think it's so sad myself. The store's pretty empty, it being Thursday afternoon, so there was nothing much to do except lean on the register and wait for the girls to show up again. The whole store was like a pinball machine and I didn't know which tunnel they'd come out of. After a while they come around out of the far aisle, around the light bulbs, records at discount of the Caribbean Six or Tony Martin Sings or some such gunk you wonder they waste the wax on, sixpacks of candy bars, and plastic toys done up in cellophane that fall apart when a kid looks at them anyway. Around they come, Queenie still leading the way, and holding a little gray jar in her hand. Slots Three through Seven are unmanned and I could see her wondering between Stokes and me, but Stokesie with his usual luck draws an old party in baggy gray pants who stumbles up with four giant cans of pineapple juice (what do these bums *do* with all that pineapple juice? I've often asked myself) so the girls come to me. Queenie puts down the jar and I take it into my fingers icy cold. Kingfish Fancy Herring Snacks in Pure Sour Cream: 49¢. Now her hands are empty, not a ring or a bracelet, bare as God made them, and I wonder where the money's coming from. Still with that prim look she lifts a folded dollar bill out of the hollow at the center of her nubbled pink top. The jar went heavy in my hand. Really, I thought that was so cute.

Then everybody's luck begins to run out. Lengel comes in from haggling with a truck full of cabbages on the lot and is about to scuttle into that door marked MANAGER behind which he hides all day when the girls touch his eye. Lengel's pretty dreary, teaches Sunday school and the rest, but he doesn't miss that much. He comes over and says, "Girls, this isn't the beach."

Queenie blushes, though maybe it's just a brush of sunburn I was noticing for the first time, now that she was so close. "My mother asked me to pick up a jar of herring snacks." Her voice kind of startled me, the way voices do when you see the people first, coming out so flat and dumb yet kind of tony, too, the way it ticked over "pick up" and "snacks." All of a sudden I slid right down her voice into her living room. Her father and the other men were standing around in ice-cream coats and bow ties and the women were in sandals picking up herring snacks on toothpicks off a big glass plate and they were all holding drinks the color of water with olives and sprigs of mint in them. When my parents have somebody over they get lemonade and if it's a real racy affair Schlitz in tall glasses with "They'll Do It Every Time" cartoons stencilled on.

"That's all right," Lengel said. "But this isn't the beach." His repeating this struck me as funny, as if it had just occurred to him, and he had been thinking all these years the A & P was a great big dune and he was the head lifeguard. He didn't like my smiling — as I say he doesn't miss much — but he concentrates on giving the girls that sad Sunday-school-superintendent stare.

Queenie's blush is no sunburn now, and the plump one in plaid, that I liked better from the back — a really sweet can — pipes up, "We weren't doing any shopping. We just came in for the one thing."

"That makes no difference," Lengel tells her, and I could see from the way his eyes went that he hadn't noticed she was wearing a two-piece before. "We want you decently dressed when you come in here."

"We *are* decent," Queenie says suddenly, her lower lip pushing, getting sore now that she remembers her place, a place from which the crowd that runs the A & P must look pretty crummy. Fancy Herring Snacks flashed in her very blue eyes.

"Girls, I don't want to argue with you. After this come in here with your shoulders covered. It's our policy." He turns his back. That's policy for you. Policy is what the kingpins want. What the others want is juvenile delinquency.

All this while, the customers had been showing up with their carts but, you know, sheep, seeing a scene, they had all bunched up on Stokesie, who shook open a paper bag as gently as peeling a peach, not wanting to miss a word. I could feel in the silence everybody getting nervous, most of all Lengel, who asks me, "Sammy, have you rung up their purchase?"

I thought and said "No" but it wasn't about that I was thinking. I go through the punches, 4, 9, GROC, TOT — it's more complicated than you think, and after you do it often enough, it begins to make a little song, that you hear words to, in my case "Hello (*bing*) there, you (*gung*) hap-py *pee*-pul (*splat*)!" — the *splat* being the drawer flying out. I uncrease the bill, tenderly as you may imagine, it just having come from between the two smoothest scoops of vanilla I had ever known were there, and pass a half and a penny into her narrow pink palm, and nestle the herrings in a bag and twist its neck and hand it over, all the time thinking.

The girls, and who'd blame them, are in a hurry to get out, so I say "I quit" to Lengel quick enough for them to hear, hoping they'll stop and watch me, their unsuspected hero. They keep right on going, into the electric eye; the door flies open and they flicker across the lot to their car, Queenie and Plaid and Big Tall Goony-Goony (not that as raw material she was so bad), leaving me with Lengel and a kink in his eyebrow.

"Did you say something, Sammy?"

"I said I quit."

"I thought you did."

"You didn't have to embarrass them."

"It was they who were embarrassing us."

I started to say something that came out "Fiddle-de-doo." It's a saying of my grandmother's, and I know she would have been pleased.

"I don't think you know what you're saying," Lengel said.

"I know you don't," I said. "But I do." I pull the bow at the back of my apron and start shrugging it off my shoulders. A couple customers that had been heading for my slot begin to knock against each other, like scared pigs in a chute.

Lengel sighs and begins to look very patient and old and gray. He's been a friend of my parents for years. "Sammy, you don't want to do this to your Mom and Dad," he tells me. It's true, I don't. But it seems to me that once you begin a gesture it's fatal not to go through with it. I fold the apron, "Sammy" stitched in red on the pocket, and put it on the counter, and drop the bow tie on top of it. The bow tie is theirs, if you've ever wondered. "You'll feel this for the rest of your life," Lengel says, and I know that's true, too, but remembering how he made that pretty girl blush makes me so scrunchy inside I punch the No Sale tab and the machine whirs "pee-pul" and the drawer splats out. One advantage to this scene taking place in summer, I can follow this up with a clean exit, there's no fumbling around getting your coat and galoshes, I just saunter into the electric eye in my white shirt that my mother ironed the night before, and the door heaves itself open, and outside the sunshine is skating around on the asphalt.

I look around for my girls, but they're gone, of course. There wasn't anybody but some young married screaming with her children about some candy they didn't get by the door of a powder-blue Falcon station wagon. Looking back in the big windows, over the bags of peat moss and aluminum lawn furniture stacked on the pavement, I could see Lengel in my place in the slot, checking the sheep through. His face was dark gray and his back stiff, as if he'd just had an injection of iron, and my stomach kind of fell as I felt how hard the world was going to be to me hereafter.

[1961, 1962]

Amiri Baraka
(LeRoi Jones)

[b. 1934]

Everett LeRoy Jones was born in Newark, New Jersey, on October 7, 1934, to Coyette LeRoy Jones, a postal worker, and Anna Lois Jones, a social worker. In a 1998 interview, Baraka recalled that his parents had strongly encouraged their children to excel:

> [T]hey always told me: y'all are the smartest colored kids on the planet. They gave me piano lessons, trumpet lessons, drum lessons, piano lessons, painting lessons. I used to sing *Ave Maria* with my sister. I used to recite the Gettysburg Address every Lincoln's birthday in a Boy Scout suit for about six years – this was my mama. The point is that for them two Negroes right there, they knew what they were going to do, they were going to give us all the information in the world, and they was going to equip us to go out and fight the White people.

Amiri Baraka

Leroy McLucas took this photograph of Baraka (then LeRoi Jones) in 1965, the year the prominent poet and playwright moved to Harlem to lead the emerging Black Arts Movement.

Baraka, an outstanding student who began writing stories at an early age, graduated in 1951 from a predominantly white high school and was awarded a science scholarship at the Newark campus of Rutgers University. There, he made the first change to his name, altering the spelling of his first name to "LeRoi." In 1952, he decided to attend an all-black school and transferred to Howard University in Washington, D.C., where he studied music, especially blues and jazz, and worked with the poet Sterling Brown. Baraka, however, found the conservative atmosphere of the school oppressive and was bored by his studies. In 1954, during his senior year, he flunked out and joined the air force.

While he was stationed in Puerto Rico, Baraka read constantly and began writing poetry. In his autobiography, he later said that he realized that he could never write like the white poets whose work regularly appeared in the *New Yorker*. He consequently determined to find outlets that would be receptive to his very different voice. After his term of enlistment ended in 1957, he settled in bohemian Greenwich Village, where he met and was influenced by a number of avant-garde and Beat poets, including Allen Ginsberg. In 1958, Baraka married Hettie Cohen, a Jewish intellectual with whom he founded Totem Press and the literary magazine *Yugen*. He also published poetry in other little magazines such as *Naked Ear* and *Kulchur*. With the help of Langston Hughes, who admired one of his poems, Baraka was awarded a creative-writing fellowship, and his poems appeared in the influential anthology *The New American Poetry: 1945-1960* (1960). In 1961, he published his first book of poetry, *Preface to a Twenty Volume Suicide Note*. That year, he and the Beat poet Diane di Prima established the *Floating Bear*, an underground newsletter of Greenwich Village, and formed an experimental theatrical group, the New York Poets Theatre. In addition to his classic study *Blues People: Negro Music in White America* (1963), Baraka wrote several short plays about the oppression of black people in the United States, including *Dutchman*, an explosive drama that made him famous when it was produced and published in 1964. His growing engagement in the civil rights struggle was also revealed in his second collection of poems, *The Dead Lecturer* (1964), and in an autobiographical novel in which he explored issues of racial consciousness and identity, *The System of Dante's Hell* (1965).

Baraka's later writings have been strongly shaped by his radical politics. In 1965, following the assassination of his hero Malcolm X, Baraka effectively turned his back on the white world and renounced his earlier, bohemian life in Greenwich Village. Leaving his white wife and their two daughters, he moved to Harlem, where he and other artists formed the Black Arts Repertory Theatre/School in the spring of 1965. The short-lived organization was a key institution in the development of the Black Arts Movement, and Baraka's Black Nationalist ideals also found expression in a series of experimental stories, *Tales* (1967), in *Four Black Revolutionary Plays* (1968), and in two new collections of his poetry, *Black Magic* (1969) and *It's Nation Time* (1970). Meanwhile, he married the poet Sylvia Robinson in 1966, and they moved back to Newark, New Jersey. To affirm their African heritage and Black Nationalist beliefs, they adopted Bantuized Muslim names, Amina Baraka and Iamamu Ameer Baraka, later Amiri Baraka. In 1974, however, he publicly declared that Black Nationalism was a form of racism and became a Third World Marxist. The first of his numerous socialist works was a collection of poetry, *Hard Facts* (1975), published the year he began teaching at the State University of New York in Stony Brook. He was also a frequent lecturer at the Jack Kerouac School of Disembodied Poetics, cofounded by his old friend Allen Ginsberg. Following his arrest during an alleged dispute with his wife, Baraka was sentenced to serve time in a halfway house, where he wrote *The Autobiography of LeRoi Jones/Amiri Baraka* (1984; expanded 1997). He continued to pub-

In Africa, a griot is the cultural historian. He or she must remember what the people were like so those people can learn who they are and what they can become. Amiri Baraka is, absolutely, a griot.

—*Maya Angelou*

lish essays, plays, and poetry, notably *WISE, WHY'S, Y's* (1995), part of a poem in progress on the African American experience. While serving as the Poet Laureate of New Jersey in 2002, Baraka wrote a controversial poem, "Somebody Blew Up America," in response to the September 11 attacks on the World Trade Center. Many viewed the poem as anti-Semitic, but Baraka vigorously defended himself, calling the criticism "an attempt to repress and stigmatize independent thinkers everywhere." Prompted by the governor, the state senate abolished the position of Poet Laureate in 2003. Baraka's most recent work is a critically acclaimed collection of stories dating from 1974 to the present, *Tales of the Out and the Gone* (2006).

Baraka's *Dutchman.*   This play was first performed on March 24, 1964, at the Cherry Lane Theatre, an Off-Broadway theater founded by a group of artists in the 1920s and long known for fostering the development of experimental drama in the United States. *Dutchman* was the final play of a triple bill, following one-act plays by the Irish playwright Samuel Beckett and the Spanish playwright Fernando Arrabal. Baraka's searing study of racism and repressed black rage stole the show and generated intense controversy. The reviewer for the *New York Times* wrote that everything about the play was "designed to shock — its basic idea, its language and its murderous rage." At the same time, *Dutchman* won the Off-Broadway Theater

Dutchman

The first production of Baraka's acclaimed play, which was directed by Edward Parone and produced by Edward Albee, Richard Barr, and Clinton Wilder, featured Robert Hooks as Clay and Jennifer West as Lula.

bedfordstmartins.com/ americanlit for research links on Baraka

Award (Obie) for Best American Play of 1963–64. Five years later, the theater critic for the *New York Times* called *Dutchman* "the best short play ever written in this country," adding that "black playwrighting began a new era with its production, an era that has not yet ended and has not yet seen the play's equal." Baraka, who has said that the play "is about the difficulty of becoming a man in America," dramatizes a fateful encounter in the subway between a twenty-year-old black male, Clay, and an older white woman, Lula. Despite its realistic setting, the style of the play is essentially antinaturalistic, combining poetic language, rich symbolism, and a range of mythological associations, including the temptation scene in the Garden of Eden. Baraka originally planned to call the play "The Flying Dutchman," a reference to the legend of a spectral ship doomed endlessly to sail the seas unless its captain is released from the curse by the love of a faithful woman. In a recent interview, Baraka explained: "You know the 'Dutchman' was really the train; that was the flying in it. But then there was a lot of ambiguity in it in my mind. I didn't know if I wanted the train to be the Dutchman or the dude to be the Dutchman or the woman to be the Dutchman." The text is taken from its first publication in *Dutchman and The Slave* (1964).

DUTCHMAN

CHARACTERS

CLAY, *twenty-year-old Negro*
LULA, *thirty-year-old white woman*
RIDERS OF COACH, *white and black*
YOUNG NEGRO
CONDUCTOR

In the flying underbelly of the city. Steaming hot, and summer on top, outside. Underground. The subway heaped in modern myth.

Opening scene is a man sitting in a subway seat, holding a magazine but looking vacantly just above its wilting pages. Occasionally he looks blankly toward the window on his right. Dim lights and darkness whistling by against the glass. (Or paste the lights, as admitted props, right on the subway windows. Have them move, even dim and flicker. But give the sense of speed. Also stations, whether the train is stopped or the glitter and activity of these stations merely flashes by the windows.)

The man is sitting alone. That is, only his seat is visible, though the rest of the car is outfitted as a complete subway car. But only his seat is shown. There might be, for a time, as the play begins, a loud scream of the actual train. And it can recur throughout the play, or continue on a lower key once the dialogue starts.

The train slows after a time, pulling to a brief stop at one of the stations. The man looks idly up, until he sees a woman's face staring at him through the window, when it realizes that the man has noticed the face, it begins very premeditatedly to smile. The man smiles too, for a moment, without a trace of self-consciousness. Almost an instinctive though undesirable response. Then a kind of awkwardness or embarrassment sets in, and the man makes to look away, is further embarrassed, so he brings back his eyes to where the face was, but by now the train is moving again, and the face would seem to be left behind by the way the man turns his head to look back through the other windows at the slowly fading platform. He smiles then; more comfortably confident, hoping perhaps that his memory of this brief encounter will be pleasant. And then he is idle again.

SCENE I

Train roars. Lights flash outside the windows.

LULA *enters from the rear of the car in bright, skimpy summer clothes and sandals. She carries a net bag full of paper books, fruit, and other anonymous articles. She is wearing sunglasses, which she pushes up on her forehead from time to time.* LULA *is a tall, slender, beautiful woman with long red hair hanging straight down her back, wearing only loud lipstick in somebody's good taste. She is eating an apple, very daintily. Coming down the car toward* CLAY.

She stops beside CLAY'S *seat and hangs languidly from the strap, still managing to eat the apple. It is apparent that she is going to sit in the seat next to* CLAY, *and that she is only waiting for him to notice her before she sits.*

CLAY *sits as before, looking just beyond his magazine, now and again pulling the magazine slowly back and forth in front of his face in a hopeless effort to fan himself. Then he sees the woman hanging there beside him and he looks up into her face, smiling quizzically.*

LULA: Hello.
CLAY: Uh, hi're you?
LULA: I'm going to sit down. . . . O.K.?
CLAY: Sure.
LULA: (*Swings down onto the seat, pushing her legs straight out as if she is very weary*) Oooof! Too much weight.
CLAY: Ha, doesn't look like much to me. (*Leaning back against the window, a little surprised and maybe stiff*)
LULA: It's so anyway. (*And she moves her toes in the sandals, then pulls her right leg up on the left knee, better to inspect the bottoms of the sandals and the back of her heel. She appears for a second not to notice that* CLAY *is sitting next to her or that she has spoken to him just a second before.* CLAY *looks at the magazine, then out the black*

window. As he does this, she turns very quickly toward him) Weren't you staring at me through the window?

CLAY: *(Wheeling around and very much stiffened)* What?

LULA: Weren't you staring at me through the window? At the last stop?

CLAY: Staring at you? What do you mean?

LULA: Don't you know what staring means?

CLAY: I saw you through the window . . . if that's what it means. I don't know if I was staring. Seems to me you were staring through the window at me.

LULA: I was. But only after I'd turned around and saw you staring through that window down in the vicinity of my ass and legs.

CLAY: Really?

LULA: Really. I guess you were just taking those idle potshots. Nothing else to do. Run your mind over people's flesh.

CLAY: Oh boy. Wow, now I admit I was looking in your direction. But the rest of that weight is yours.

LULA: I suppose.

CLAY: Staring through train windows is weird business. Much weirder than staring very sedately at abstract asses.

LULA: That's why I came looking through the window . . . so you'd have more than that to go on. I even smiled at you.

CLAY: That's right.

LULA: I even got into this train, going some other way than mine. Walked down the aisle . . . searching you out.

CLAY: Really? That's pretty funny.

LULA: That's pretty funny. . . . God, you're dull.

CLAY: Well, I'm sorry, lady, but I really wasn't prepared for party talk.

LULA: No, you're not. What are you prepared for? *(Wrapping the apple core in a Kleenex and dropping it on the floor)*

CLAY: *(Takes her conversation as pure sex talk. He turns to confront her squarely with this idea)* I'm prepared for anything. How about you?

LULA: *(Laughing loudly and cutting it off abruptly)* What do you think you're doing?

CLAY: What?

LULA: You think I want to pick you up, get you to take me somewhere and screw me, huh?

CLAY: Is that the way I look?

LULA: You look like you been trying to grow a beard. That's exactly what you look like. You look like you live in New Jersey with your parents and are trying to grow a beard. That's what. You look like you've been reading Chinese poetry and drinking luke-warm sugarless tea. *(Laughs, uncrossing and recrossing her legs)* You look like death eating a soda cracker.

CLAY: *(Cocking his head from one side to the other, embarrassed and trying to make some comeback, but also intrigued by what the woman is saying . . . even the sharp city coarseness of her voice, which is still a kind of gentle sidewalk throb)* Really? I look like all that?

LULA: Not all of it. (*She feints a seriousness to cover an actual somber tone*) I lie a lot. (*Smiling*) It helps me control the world.

CLAY: (*Relieved and laughing louder than the humor*) Yeah, I bet.

LULA: But it's true, most of it, right? Jersey? Your bumpy neck?

CLAY: How'd you know all that? Huh? Really, I mean about Jersey . . . and even the beard. I met you before? You know Warren Enright?

LULA: You tried to make it with your sister when you were ten. (CLAY *leans back hard against the back of the seat, his eyes opening now, still trying to look amused*) But I succeeded a few weeks ago. (*She starts to laugh again*)

CLAY: What're you talking about? Warren tell you that? You're a friend of Georgia's?

LULA: I told you I lie. I don't know your sister. I don't know Warren Enright.

CLAY: You mean you're just picking these things out of the air?

LULA: Is Warren Enright a tall skinny black black boy with a phony English accent?

CLAY: I figured you knew him.

LULA: But I don't. I just figured you would know somebody like that. (*Laughs*)

CLAY: Yeah, yeah.

LULA: You're probably on your way to his house now.

CLAY: That's right.

LULA: (*Putting her hand on Clay's closest knee, drawing it from the knee up to the thigh's hinge, then removing it, watching his face very closely, and continuing to laugh, perhaps more gently than before*) Dull, dull, dull. I bet you think I'm exciting.

CLAY: You're O.K.

LULA: Am I exciting you now?

CLAY: Right. That's not what's supposed to happen?

LULA: How do I know? (*She returns her hand, without moving it, then takes it away and plunges it in her bag to draw out an apple*) You want this?

CLAY: Sure.

LULA: (*She gets one out of the bag for herself*) Eating apples together is always the first step. Or walking up uninhabited Seventh Avenue in the twenties on weekends.[1] (*Bites and giggles, glancing at Clay and speaking in loose singsong*) Can get you involved . . . boy! Get us involved. Um-huh. (*Mock seriousness*) Would you like to get involved with me, Mister Man?

CLAY: (*Trying to be as flippant as Lula, whacking happily at the apple*) Sure. Why not? A beautiful woman like you. Huh, I'd be a fool not to.

LULA: And I bet you're sure you know what you're talking about. (*Taking him a little roughly by the wrist, so he cannot eat the apple, then shaking the wrist*) I bet you're sure of almost everything anybody ever asked you about . . . right? (*Shakes his wrist harder*) Right?

CLAY: Yeah, right. . . . Wow, you're pretty strong, you know? Whatta you, a lady wrestler or something?

---

1. **Or walking . . . weekends:** At the time, the west twenties was a primarily commercial area whose major business buildings were on Seventh Avenue.

LULA: What's wrong with lady wrestlers? And don't answer because you never knew any. Huh. (*Cynically*) That's for sure. They don't have any lady wrestlers in that part of Jersey. That's for sure.

CLAY: Hey, you still haven't told me how you know so much about me.

LULA: I told you I didn't know anything about *you* . . . you're a well-known type.

CLAY: Really?

LULA: Or at least I know the type very well. And your skinny English friend too.

CLAY: Anonymously?

LULA: (*Settles back in seat, single-mindedly finishing her apple and humming snatches of rhythm and blues song*) What?

CLAY: Without knowing us specifically?

LULA: Oh boy. (*Looking quickly at Clay*) What a face. You know, you could be a handsome man.

CLAY: I can't argue with you.

LULA: (*Vague, off-center response*) What?

CLAY: (*Raising his voice, thinking the train noise has drowned part of his sentence*) I can't argue with you.

LULA: My hair is turning gray. A gray hair for each year and type I've come through.

CLAY: Why do you want to sound so old?

LULA: But it's always gentle when it starts. (*Attention drifting*) Hugged against tenements, day or night.

CLAY: What?

LULA: (*Refocusing*) Hey, why don't you take me to that party you're going to?

CLAY: You must be a friend of Warren's to know about the party.

LULA: Wouldn't you like to take me to the party? (*Imitates clinging vine*) Oh, come on, ask me to your party.

CLAY: Of course I'll ask you to come with me to the party. And I'll bet you're a friend of Warren's.

LULA: Why not be a friend of Warren's? Why not? (*Taking his arm*) Have you asked me yet?

CLAY: How can I ask you when I don't know your name?

LULA: Are you talking to my name?

CLAY: What is it, a secret?

LULA: I'm Lena the Hyena.

CLAY: The famous woman poet?

LULA: Poetess! The same!

CLAY: Well, you know so much about me . . . what's my name?

LULA: Morris the Hyena.

CLAY: The famous woman poet?

LULA: The same. (*Laughing and going into her bag*) You want another apple?

CLAY: Can't make it, lady. I only have to keep one doctor away a day.

LULA: I bet your name is . . . something like . . . uh, Gerald or Walter. Huh?

CLAY: God, no.

LULA: Lloyd, Norman? One of those hopeless colored names creeping out of New Jersey. Leonard? Gag. . . .

CLAY: Like Warren?

LULA: Definitely. Just exactly like Warren. Or Everett.[2]

CLAY: Gag. . . .

LULA: Well, for sure, it's not Willie.

CLAY: It's Clay.

LULA: Clay? Really? Clay what?

CLAY: Take your pick. Jackson, Johnson, or Williams.

LULA: Oh, really? Good for you. But it's got to be Williams. You're too pretentious to be a Jackson or Johnson.

CLAY: Thass right.

LULA: But Clay's O.K.

CLAY: So's Lena.

LULA: It's Lula.

CLAY: Oh?

LULA: Lula the Hyena.

CLAY: Very good.

LULA: (*Starts laughing again*) Now you say to me, "Lula, Lula, why don't you go to this party with me tonight?" It's your turn, and let those be your lines.

CLAY: Lula, why don't you go to this party with me to night, Huh?

LULA: Say my name twice before you ask, and no huh's.

CLAY: Lula, Lula, why don't you go to this party with me tonight?

LULA: I'd like to go, Clay, but how can you ask me to go when you barely know me?

CLAY: That is strange, isn't it?

LULA: What kind of reaction is that? You're supposed to say, "Aw, come on, we'll get to know each other better at the party."

CLAY: That's pretty corny.

LULA: What are you into anyway? (*Looking at him half sullenly but still amused*) What thing are you playing at, Mister? Mister Clay Williams? (*Grabs his thigh, up near the crotch*) What are *you* thinking about?

CLAY: Watch it now, you're gonna excite me for real.

LULA: (*Taking her hand away and throwing her apple core through the window*) I bet. (*She slumps in the seat and is heavily silent*)

CLAY: I thought you knew everything about me? What happened? (LULA *looks at him, then looks slowly away, then over where the other aisle would be. Noise of the train. She reaches in her bag and pulls out one of the paper books. She puts it on her leg and thumbs the pages listlessly,* CLAY *cocks his head to see the title of the book. Noise of the train.* LULA *flips pages and her eyes drift. Both remain silent*) Are you going to the party with me, Lula?

---

2. **Everett:** Baraka's birth name was Everett LeRoy Jones.

LULA: (*Bored and not even looking*) I don't even know you.

CLAY: You said you know my type.

LULA: (*Strangely irritated*) Don't get smart with me, Buster. I know you like the palm of my hand.

CLAY: The one you eat the apples with?

LULA: Yeh. And the one I open doors late Saturday evening with. That's my door. Up at the top of the stairs. Five flights. Above a lot of Italians and lying Americans. And scrape carrots with. Also . . . (*Looks at him*) the same hand I unbutton my dress with, or let my skirt fall down. Same hand. Lover.

CLAY: Are you angry about anything? Did I say something wrong?

LULA: Everything you say is wrong. (*Mock smile*) That's what makes you so attractive. Ha. In that funny-book jacket with all the buttons. (*More animate, taking hold of his jacket*) What've you got that jacket and tie on in all this heat for? And why're you wearing a jacket and tie like that? Did your people ever burn witches or start revolutions over the price of tea? Boy, those narrow-shoulder clothes come from a tradition you ought to feel oppressed by. A three-button suit. What right do you have to be wearing a three-button suit and striped tie? Your grandfather was a slave, he didn't go to Harvard.

CLAY: My grandfather was a night watchman.

LULA: And you went to a colored college where everybody thought they were Averell Harriman.[3]

CLAY: All except me.

LULA: And who did you think you were? Who do you think you are now?

CLAY: (*Laughs as if to make light of the whole trend of the conversation*) Well, in college I thought I was Baudelaire.[4] But I've slowed down since.

LULA: I bet you never once thought you were a black nigger. (*Mock serious, then she howls with laughter.* CLAY *is stunned but after initial reaction, he quickly tries to appreciate the humor.* LULA *almost shrieks*) A black Baudelaire.

CLAY: That's right.

LULA: Boy, are you corny. I take back what I said before. Everything you say is not wrong. It's perfect. You should be on television.

CLAY: You act like you're on television already.

LULA: That's because I'm an actress.

CLAY: I thought so.

LULA: Well, you're wrong. I'm no actress. I told you I always lie. I'm nothing, honey, and don't you ever forget it. (*Lighter*) Although my mother was a Communist. The only person in my family ever to amount to anything.

---

3. **Averell Harriman:** The son of a wealthy railroad tycoon, Harriman (1891–1986) was a businessman and politician who twice ran for president and served as the U.S. ambassador to the Soviet Union and Great Britain.

4. **Baudelaire:** The influential French poet Charles Baudelaire (1821–1867), best known for his collection *Les Fleurs du Mal* ("Flowers of Evil"), published in 1857.

CLAY: My mother was a Republican.

LULA: And your father voted for the man rather than the party.

CLAY: Right!

LULA: Yea for him. Yea, yea for him.

CLAY: Yea!

LULA: And yea for America where he is free to vote for the mediocrity of his choice! Yea!

CLAY: Yea!

LULA: And yea for both your parents who even though they differ about so crucial a matter as the body politic still forged a union of love and sacrifice that was destined to flower at the birth of the noble Clay . . . what's your middle name?

CLAY: Clay.

LULA: A union of love and sacrifice that was destined to flower at the birth of the noble Clay Clay Williams. Yea! And most of all yea yea for you, Clay Clay. The Black Baudelaire! Yes! (*And with knifelike cynicism*) My Christ. My Christ.

CLAY: Thank you, ma'am.

LULA: May the people accept you as a ghost of the future. And love you, that you might not kill them when you can.

CLAY: What?

LULA: You're a murderer, Clay, and you know it. (*Her voice darkening with significance*) You know goddamn well what I mean.

CLAY: I do?

LULA: So we'll pretend the air is light and full of perfume.

CLAY: (*Sniffing at her blouse*) It is.

LULA: And we'll pretend the people cannot see you. That is, the citizens. And that you are free of your own history. And I am free of my history. We'll pretend that we are both anonymous beauties smashing along through the city's entrails. (*She yells as loud as she can*) GROOVE!

Black

SCENE II

Scene is the same as before, though now there are other seats visible in the car. And throughout the scene other people get on the subway. There are maybe one or two seated in the car as the scene opens, though neither CLAY *nor* LULA *notices them,* CLAY'S *tie is open.* LULA *is hugging his arm.*

CLAY: The party!

LULA: I know it'll be something good. You can come in with me, looking, casual and significant. I'll be strange, haughty, and silent, and walk with long slow strides.

CLAY: Right.

LULA: When you get drunk, pat me once, very lovingly on the flanks, and I'll look at you cryptically, licking my lips.

CLAY: It sounds like something we can do.

LULA: You'll go around talking to young men about your mind, and to old men about your plans. If you meet a very close friend who is also with someone like me, we can stand together, sipping our drinks and exchanging codes of lust. The atmosphere will be slithering in love and half-love and very open moral decision.

CLAY: Great. Great.

LULA: And everyone will pretend they don't know your name, and then . . . (*She pauses heavily*) later, when they have to, they'll claim a friendship that denies your sterling character.

CLAY: (*Kissing her neck and fingers*) And then what?

LULA: Then? Well, then we'll go down the street, late night, eating apples and winding very deliberately toward my house.

CLAY: Deliberately?

LULA: I mean, we'll look in all the shopwindows, and make fun of the queers. Maybe we'll meet a Jewish Buddhist and flatten his conceits over some very pretentious coffee.

CLAY: In honor of whose God?

LULA: Mine.

CLAY: Who is . . . ?

LULA: Me . . . and you?

CLAY: A corporate Godhead.

LULA: Exactly. Exactly. (*Notices one of the other people entering*)

CLAY: Go on with the chronicle. Then what happens to us?

LULA: (*A mild depression, but she still makes her description triumphant and increasingly direct*) To my house, of course.

CLAY: Of course.

LULA: And up the narrow steps of the tenement.

CLAY: You live in a tenement?

LULA: Wouldn't live anywhere else. Reminds me specifically of my novel form of insanity.

CLAY: Up the tenement stairs.

LULA: And with my apple-eating hand I push open the door and lead you, my tender big-eyed prey, into my . . . God, what can I call it . . . into my hovel.

CLAY: Then what happens?

LULA: After the dancing and games, after the long drinks and long walks, the real fun begins.

CLAY: Ah, the real fun. (*Embarrassed, in spite of himself*) Which is . . . ?

LULA: (*Laughs at him*) Real fun in the dark house. Hah! Real fun in the dark house, high up above the street and the ignorant cowboys. I lead you in, holding your wet hand gently in my hand . . .

CLAY: Which is not wet?

LULA: Which is dry as ashes.

CLAY: And cold?

LULA: Don't think you'll get out of your responsibility that way. It's not cold at all. You Fascist! Into my dark living room. Where we'll sit and talk endlessly, endlessly.

CLAY: About what?

LULA: About what? About your manhood, what do you think? What do you think we've been talking about all this time?

CLAY: Well, I didn't know it was that. That's for sure. Every other thing in the world but that. (*Notices another person entering, looks quickly, almost involuntarily up and down the car, seeing the other people in the car*) Hey, I didn't even notice when those people got on.

LULA: Yeah, I know.

CLAY: Man, this subway is slow.

LULA: Yeah, I know.

CLAY: Well, go on. We were talking about my manhood.

LULA: We still are. All the time.

CLAY: We were in your living room.

LULA: My dark living room. Talking endlessly.

CLAY: About my manhood.

LULA: I'll make you a map of it. Just as soon as we get to my house.

CLAY: Well, that's great.

LULA: One of the things we do while we talk. And screw.

CLAY: (*Trying to make his smile broader and less shaky*) We finally got there.

LULA: And you'll call my rooms black as a grave. You'll say, "This place is like Juliet's tomb."[5]

CLAY: (*Laughs*) I might.

LULA: I know. You've probably said it before.

CLAY: And is that all? The whole grand tour?

LULA: Not all. You'll say to me very close to my face, many, many times, you'll say, even whisper, that you love me.

CLAY: Maybe I will.

LULA: And you'll be lying.

CLAY: I wouldn't lie about something like that.

LULA: Hah. It's the only kind of thing you will lie about. Especially if you think it'll keep me alive.

CLAY: Keep you alive? I don't understand.

LULA: (*Bursting out laughing, but too shrilly*) Don't understand? Well, don't look at me. It's the path I take, that's all. Where both feet take me when I set them down. One in front of the other.

CLAY: Morbid. Morbid. You sure you're not an actress? All that self-aggrandizement.

LULA: Well, I told you I wasn't an actress . . . but I also told you I lie all the time. Draw your own conclusions.

CLAY: Morbid. Morbid. You sure you're not an actress? All scribed? There's no more?

---

5. **Juliet's tomb:** In the final scene of Shakespeare's *Romeo and Juliet*, Romeo finds Juliet asleep in her family's tomb. Believing her to be dead, he drinks poison. When she awakens and finds him dead, she stabs herself to death with his dagger.

LULA: I've told you all I know. Or almost all.

CLAY: There's no funny parts?

LULA: I thought it was all funny.

CLAY: But you mean peculiar, not ha-ha.

LULA: You don't know what I mean.

CLAY: Well, tell me the almost part then. You said almost all. What else? I want the whole story.

LULA: (*Searching aimlessly through her bag. She begins to talk breathlessly, with a light and silly tone*) All stories are whole stories. All of 'em. Our whole story . . . nothing but change. How could things go on like that forever? Huh? (*Slaps him on the shoulder, begins finding things in her bag, taking them out and throwing them over her shoulder into the aisle*) Except I do go on as I do. Apples and long walks with deathless intelligent lovers. But you mix it up. Look out the window, all the time. Turning pages. Change change change. Till, shit, I don't know you. Wouldn't, for that matter. You're too serious. I bet you're even too serious to be psychoanalyzed. Like all those Jewish poets from Yonkers,[6] who leave their mothers looking for other mothers, or others' mothers, on whose baggy tits they lay their fumbling heads. Their poems are always funny, and all about sex.

CLAY: They sound great. Like movies.

LULA: But you change. (*Blankly*) And things work on you till you hate them. (*More people come into the train. They come closer to the couple, some of them not sitting, but swinging drearily on the straps, staring at the two with uncertain interest*)

CLAY: Wow. All these people, so suddenly. They must all come from the same place.

LULA: Right. That they do.

CLAY: Oh? You know about them too?

LULA: Oh yeah. About them more than I know about you. Do they frighten you?

CLAY: Frighten me? Why should they frighten me?

LULA: 'Cause you're an escaped nigger.

CLAY: Yeah?

LULA: 'Cause you crawled through the wire and made tracks to my side.

CLAY: Wire?

LULA: Don't they have wire around plantations?

CLAY: You must be Jewish. All you can think about is wire. Plantations didn't have any wire. Plantations were big open whitewashed places like heaven, and everybody on 'em was grooved to be there. Just strummin' and hummin' all day.

LULA: Yes, yes.

CLAY: And that's how the blues was born.

LULA: Yes, yes. And that's how the blues was born. (*Begins to make up a song that becomes quickly hysterical. As she sings she rises from her seat, still throwing things out*

---

6. **Jewish poets from Yonkers:** Yonkers, a large city two miles north of New York City, once had a substantial Jewish population.

of her bag into the aisle, beginning a rhythmical shudder and twistlike wiggle, which she continues up and down the aisle, bumping into many of the standing people and tripping over the feet of those sitting. Each time she runs into a person she lets out a very vicious piece of profanity, wiggling and stepping all the time) And that's how the blues was born. Yes. Yes. Son of a bitch, get out of the way. Yes. Quack. Yes. Yes. And that's how the blues was born. Ten little niggers sitting on a limb, but none of them ever looked like him. (*Points to* CLAY, *returns toward the seat, with her hands extended for him to rise and dance with her*) And that's how blues was born. Yes. Come on, Clay. Let's do the nasty. Rub bellies. Rub bellies.

CLAY: (*Waves his hands to refuse. He is embarrassed, but determined to get a kick out of the proceedings*) Hey, what was in those apples? Mirror, mirror on the wall, who's the fairest one of all? Snow White, baby, and don't you forget it.

LULA: (*Grabbing for his hands, which he draws away*) Come on, Clay. Let's rub bellies on the train. The nasty. The nasty. Do the gritty grind, like your ol' rag-head mammy. Grind till you lose your mind. Shake it, shake it, shake it, shake it! OOOOweeee! Come on, Clay. Let's do the choo-choo train shuffle, the navel scratcher.

CLAY: Hey, you coming on like the lady who smoked up her grass skirt.

LULA: (*Becoming annoyed that he will not dance, and becoming more animated as if to embarrass him still further*) Come on, Clay . . . let's do the thing. Uhh! Uhh! Clay! Clay! You middle-class black bastard. Forget your social-working mother for a few seconds and let's knock stomachs. Clay, you liver-lipped white man. You would-be Christian. You ain't no nigger, you're just a dirty white man. Get up, Clay. Dance with me, Clay.

CLAY: Lula! Sit down, now. Be cool.

LULA: (*Mocking him, in wild dance*) Be cool. Be cool. That's all you know . . . shaking that wildroot cream-oil on your knotty head, jackets buttoning up to your chin, so full of white man's words. Christ. God. Get up and scream at these people. Like scream meaningless shit in these hopeless faces. (*She screams at people in train, still dancing*) Red trains cough Jewish underwear for keeps! Expanding smells of silence. Gravy snot whistling like sea birds. Clay. Clay, you got to break out. Don't sit there dying the way they want you to die. Get up.

CLAY: Oh, sit the fuck down. (*He moves to restrain her*) Sit down, goddamn it.

LULA: (*Twisting out of his reach*) Screw yourself, Uncle Tom.[7] Thomas Woolly-Head. (*Begins to dance a kind of jig, mocking Clay with loud forced humor*) There is Uncle Tom . . . I mean, Uncle Thomas Woolly-Head. With old white matted mane. He hobbles on his wooden cane. Old Tom. Old Tom. Let the white man hump his ol' mama, and he jes' shuffle off in the woods and hide his gentle gray head. Ol' Thomas Woolly-Head. (*Some of the other riders are laughing now. A drunk gets up and joins* LULA *in her dance, singing, as best he can, her "song."* CLAY *gets up out of his seat and visibly scans the faces of the other riders*).

---

7. **Uncle Tom:** The central character in Harriet Beecher Stowe's antislavery novel *Uncle Tom's Cabin* (1852). In the twentieth century, *Uncle Tom* became a derogatory term for black men who were considered to be fawning or servile to white people.

CLAY: Lula! Lula! (*She is dancing and turning, still shouting as loud as she can, The drunk too is shouting, and waving his hands wildly*) Lula . . . you dumb bitch. Why don't you stop it? (*He rushes half stumbling from his seat, and grabs one of her flailing arms*)

LULA: Let me go! You black son of a bitch. (*She struggles against him*) Let me go! Help! (CLAY *is dragging her towards her seat, and the drunk seeks to interfere. He grabs* CLAY *around the shoulders and begins wrestling with him.* CLAY *clubs the drunk to the floor without releasing* LULA, *who is still screaming,* CLAY *finally gets her to the seat and throws her into it*)

CLAY: Now you shut the hell up. (*Grabbing her shoulders*) Just shut up. You don't know what you're talking about. You don't know anything. So just keep your stupid mouth closed.

LULA: You're afraid of white people. And your father was. Uncle Tom Big Lip!

CLAY: (*Slaps her as hard as he can, across the mouth,* LULA'S *head bangs against the back of the seat. When she raises it again,* CLAY *slaps her again*) Now shut up and let me talk. (*He turns toward the other riders, some of whom are sitting on the edge of their seats. The drunk is on one knee, rubbing his head, and singing softly the same song. He shuts up too when he sees* CLAY *watching him. The others go back to newspapers or stare out the windows*) Shit, you don't have any sense, Lula, nor feelings either. I could murder you now. Such a tiny ugly throat. I could squeeze it flat, and watch you turn blue, on a humble. For dull kicks. And all these weak-faced ofays[8] squatting around here, staring over their papers at me. Murder them too. Even if they expected it. That man there . . . (*Points to well-dressed man*) I could rip that *Times* right out of his hand, as skinny and middle-classed as I am, I could rip that paper out of his hand and just as easily rip out his throat. It takes no great effort. For what? To kill you soft idiots? You don't understand anything but luxury.

LULA: You fool!

CLAY: (*Pushing her against the seat*) I'm not telling you again, Tallulah Bankhead![9] Luxury. In your face and your fingers. You telling me what I ought to do. (*Sudden scream frightening the whole coach*) Well, don't! Don't you tell me anything! If I'm a middle-class fake white man . . . let me be. And let me be in the way I want. (*Through his teeth*) I'll rip your lousy breasts off! Let me be who I feel like being. Uncle Tom. Thomas. Whoever. It's none of your business. You don't know anything except what's there for you to see. An act. Lies. Device. Not the pure heart, the pumping black heart. You don't ever know that. And I sit here, in this buttoned-up suit, to keep myself from cutting all your throats. I mean wantonly. You great liberated whore! You fuck some black man, and right away you're an expert on black people. What a lotta shit that is. The only thing you know is that you come if he bangs you hard enough. And that's all.

---

8. **ofays:** A derogatory term for white people.
9. **Tallulah Bankhead:** Bankhead (1903–1968), an actress who was born into a prominent Alabama family, was known for her uninhibited personality and theatrical public life.

The belly rub? You wanted to do the belly rub? Shit, you don't even know how. You don't know how. That ol' dipty-dip shit you do, rolling your ass like an elephant. That's not my kind of belly rub. Belly rub is not Queens.[10] Belly rub is dark places, with big hats and overcoats held up with one arm. Belly rub hates you. Old bald-headed four-eyed ofays popping their fingers . . . and don't know yet what they're doing. They say, "I love Bessie Smith."[11] And don't even understand that Bessie Smith is saying, "Kiss my ass, kiss my black unruly ass." Before love, suffering, desire, anything you can explain, she's saying, and very plainly, "Kiss my black ass." And if you don't know that, it's you that's doing the kissing.

Charlie Parker?[12] Charlie Parker. All the hip white boys scream for Bird. And Bird saying, "Up your ass, feeble-minded ofay! Up your ass." And they sit there talking about the tortured genius of Charlie Parker. Bird would've played not a note of music if he just walked up to East Sixty-seventh Street[13] and killed the first ten white people he saw. Not a note! And I'm the great would-be poet. Yes. That's right! Poet. Some kind of bastard literature . . . all it needs is a simple knife thrust. Just let me bleed you, you loud whore, and one poem vanished. A whole people of neurotics, struggling to keep from being sane. And the only thing that would cure the neurosis would be your murder. Simple as that. I mean if I murdered you, then other white people would begin to understand me. You understand? No. I guess not. If Bessie Smith had killed some white people she wouldn't have needed that music. She could have talked very straight and plain about the world. No metaphors. No grunts. No wiggles in the dark of her soul. Just straight two and two are four. Money. Power. Luxury. Like that. All of them. Crazy niggers turning their backs on sanity. When all it needs is that simple act. Murder. Just murder! Would make us all sane. (*Suddenly weary*) Ahhh. Shit. But who needs it? I'd rather be a fool. Insane. Safe with my words, and no deaths, and clean, hard thoughts, urging me to new conquests. My people's madness. Hah! That's a laugh. My people. They don't need me to claim them. They got legs and arms of their own. Personal insanities. Mirrors. They don't need all those words. They don't need any defense. But listen, though, one more thing. And you tell this to your father, who's probably the kind of man who needs to know at once. So he can plan ahead. Tell him not to preach so much rationalism and cold logic to these niggers. Let them alone. Let them sing curses at you in code and see your filth as simple lack of style. Don't make the mistake, through some irresponsible surge of Christian charity, of talking too much about the advantages of Western rationalism, or the

---

10. **Belly rub is not Queens:** The belly rub was a sensuous dance associated with jazz and African Americans. The population of Queens, the largest of the five boroughs of New York City, was predominantly white in the 1960s.

11. **Bessie Smith:** Smith (1894–1937), one of the most acclaimed and successful singers of the 1920s, was nicknamed "Empress of the Blues."

12. **Charlie Parker:** The saxophonist Charles "Bird" Parker Jr. (1920–1955), an influential musician who pioneered and popularized the form of jazz known as bebop or bop.

13. **East Sixty-seventh Street:** The Upper East Side is among the wealthiest sections of New York City.

great intellectual legacy of the white man, or maybe they'll begin to listen. And then, maybe one day, you'll find they actually do understand exactly what you are talking about, all these fantasy people. All these blues people. And on that day, as sure as shit, when you really believe you can "accept" them into your fold, as half-white trusties late of the subject peoples. With no more blues, except the very old ones, and not a watermelon in sight, the great missionary heart will have triumphed, and all of those ex-coons will be stand-up Western men, with eyes for clean hard useful lives, sober, pious and sane, and they'll murder you. They'll murder you, and have very rational explanations. Very much like your own. They'll cut your throats, and drag you out to the edge of your cities so the flesh can fall away from your bones, in sanitary isolation.

LULA: (*Her voice takes on a different, more businesslike quality*) I've heard enough.

CLAY: (*Reaching for his books*) I bet you have. I guess I better collect my stuff and get off this train. Looks like we won't be acting out that little pageant you outlined before.

LULA: No. We won't. You're right about that, at least. (*She turns to look quickly around the rest of the car*) All right! (*The others respond*)

CLAY: (*Bending across the girl to retrieve his belongings*) Sorry, baby, I don't think we could make it. (*As he is bending over her, the girl brings up a small knife and plunges it into* CLAY's *chest. Twice. He slumps across her knees, his mouth working stupidly*)

LULA: Sorry is right. (*Turning to the others in the car who have already gotten up from their seats*) Sorry is the rightest thing you've said. Get this man off me! Hurry, now! (*The others come and drag* CLAY's *body down the aisle*) Open the door and throw his body out. (*They throw him off*) And all of you get off at the next stop. (LULA *busies herself straightening her things. Getting everything in order. She takes out a notebook and makes a quick scribbling note. Drops it in her bag. The train apparently stops and all the others get off, leaving her alone in the coach.*

Very soon a young Negro of about twenty comes into the coach, with a couple of books under his arm. He sits a few seats in back of LULA. *When he is seated she turns and gives him a long slow look. He looks up from his book and drops the book on his lap. Then an old Negro conductor comes into the car, doing a sort of restrained soft shoe, and half mumbling the words of some song. He looks at the young man, briefly, with a quick greeting*)

CONDUCTOR: Hey, brother!

YOUNG MAN: Hey. (*The conductor continues down the aisle with his little dance and the mumbled song,* LULA *turns to stare at him and follows his movements down the aisle. The conductor tips his hat when he reaches her seat, and continues out the car*)

Curtain

[1964]

Audre Lorde

[1934–1992]

Audrey Geraldine Lorde was born in Harlem in New York City on February 18, 1934. She was the third daughter of Linda Belmar and Frederic Byron Lorde, immigrants from the Caribbean island of Grenada who struggled to earn a living in the Depression-era United States. Lorde recalled that as a child she altered her first name to "Audre" because she preferred its sound and "did not like the tail of the Y hanging down below the line in Audrey." She attended Roman Catholic grammar schools and then passed the entrance examination to Hunter High School, an elite public school for girls on the Upper East Side of Manhattan. The rebellious Lorde became part of a group who called themselves "The Branded" and who were actively involved in the school's literary magazine, the *Argus*. When the editor of the magazine rejected one of her poems, Lorde sent it to *Seventeen* magazine, where it was published shortly before her graduation in 1951. After a year at Hunter College, she dropped out and worked in a factory in Connecticut and later in a health center in New York City, where she was active in radical politics and the bohemian "gay-girl" scene in Greenwich Village. Following a pivotal visit to Mexico, where Lorde said that she confirmed her identity as a poet and a lesbian, she returned to Hunter College in 1955. She graduated in 1959 with a degree in literature and philosophy and then attended Columbia University. She earned a master's degree in library science in 1961 and took a position at the Mount Vernon Public Library in New York City.

During the following decade, Lorde actively began to pursue her true calling as a poet and a teacher. In 1962, she entered into an open marriage with a white lawyer, Edward Ashley Rollins, a bisexual man with whom she had a daughter in 1963 and a son in 1964. Meanwhile, several of her poems appeared in *Sixes and Seven* (1962), an anthology of poetry by African Americans published by the small Heritage Press in London, and Langston Hughes included two of her poems in his anthology *New Negro Poets, U.S.A.* (1964). The Poets Press, founded by one of her friends from high school, the Beat poet Diane di Prima, published Lorde's first book of poems, *The First Cities.* About the time it appeared early in 1968, she spent six weeks as the poet in residence at Tougaloo College, a historically black college in Jackson, Mississippi. There, Lorde discovered her love of teaching and became involved with a woman, Frances Clayton, a white professor of psychology on exchange from Tougaloo's sister institution, Brown University. After Lorde returned home to New York City, she separated from her husband and established a new home with her children and Clayton. Lorde also gave up library work and taught at the City College of New York and Herbert H. Lehman College before joining the English department at John Jay College of Criminal Justice in 1970. That year, her second collection of poetry, *Cables to Rage*, was published by the Heritage Press. It was distributed in the United States by the small Broadside Press, an offshoot of the Black Arts Movement, which published Lorde's next two volumes of

Audre Lorde
Dagmar Schultz took this photograph of Lorde in the early 1970s, when she was beginning to gain widespread recognition as a poet and activist.

poetry: *From a Land Where Other People Live* (1973), which was nominated for a National Book Award, and *The New York Head Shop and Museum* (1974).

As both a writer and an activist, Lorde thereafter reached an increasingly wide audience. Beginning with *Coal* (1976), which included some poems from her first two collections, all of her later collections of poetry were published by the prominent firm of W. W. Norton. She drew on African mythology in her next collection *The Black Unicorn* (1978), of which her friend Adrienne Rich wrote: "Refusing to be circumscribed by any simple identity, Audre Lorde writes as a Black woman, a mother, a daughter, a Lesbian, a feminist, a visionary; poems of elemental wildness and healing, nightmare and lucidity." In 1979, Lorde spoke to a crowd of one hundred thousand people gathered for the first March on Washington for Gay and Lesbian Rights. She returned to her alma mater, Hunter College, as a professor of English in 1980, at the beginning of a remarkably productive decade. She published two acclaimed works of nonfiction, *The Cancer Journals* (1980), an account of her treatment for breast cancer and a protest against the silence surrounding the disease, and an autobiography, or what Lorde called a "biomythography," *Zami: A New Spelling of My Name* (1982). In addition to collections of her essays and speeches, *Sister Outsider* (1984) and *A Burst of Light* (1988), Lorde also published *Chosen Poems Old and New* (1982), primarily a selection from her first five volumes of poetry, and a widely admired collection of new poems, *Our Dead Behind Us* (1986). Her long-term partnership with Clayton ended, and Lorde established a home in St. Croix in the Virgin Islands with her new partner, the social scientist Gloria Joseph. In an African ceremony on St. Croix, Lorde took the name Gambda Adisa, meaning "Warrior: She Who Makes Her Meaning Known." Lorde prepared a final edition of her poems, *Undersong: Chosen Poems Old and New*, which was published a few months before she died of liver cancer at her home on St. Croix on November 17, 1992.

Lorde's Poetry.   Lorde once observed that "poets must teach what they know, if we are all to continue being." An outspoken lesbian and black feminist, she also passionately believed in the power of words and the potential of poetry to combat racial and sexual oppression, as well as global injustice. She was consequently an exacting practitioner of her craft, a poet whose idiomatic and deceptively simple free verse is often remarkable for the density of its language, imagery, and metaphor. In fact, Lorde demanded so much of her poems that she continued to revise some of them up until the time of her death. "The process of revision is, I believe, crucial to the integrity and lasting power of a poem," she observed in the introduction to her final collection, *Undersong*. "The problem in reworking any poem is always when to let go of it, refusing to give in to the desire to have that particular poem *do it all*, say it all, become the mythical, unattainable Universal Poem." Lorde added that she always began the process of revision by asking herself two questions: "What did I want my readers to feel? And, second, What was the work of this poem (its task in

bedfordstmartins.com/ americanlit for research links on Lorde

the world)?" The texts of the following poems, all of them her final versions, are taken from *Undersong: Chosen Poems, Old and New* (1992), with the exception of "Stations," which is from the *Collected Poems of Audre Lorde* (1997).

COAL

I   is the total black
being spoken
from the earth's inside.

There are many kinds of open
how a diamond comes   5
into a knot of flame
how sound comes into a word
colored
by who pays what for speaking.

Some words are open   10
diamonds on a glass window
singing out within the crash
of passing sun
other words are stapled wagers
in a perforated book   15
buy and sign and tear apart
and come whatever wills all chances
the stub remains
an ill-pulled tooth
with a ragged edge.   20

Some words live in my throat
breeding like adders
others
know sun
seeking like gypsies   25
over my tongue
to explode through my lips
like young sparrows
bursting from shell.

Some words   30
bedevil me.

Love is a word, another kind of open.
As the diamond comes
into a knot of flame

I am Black   35
because I come from the earth's inside
take my word for jewel
in the open light.

[1962, 1992]

THE WOMAN THING

The hunters are back
from beating the winter's face
in search of a challenge or task
in search of food
making fresh tracks   5
for their children's hunger
they do not watch the sun
they cannot wear its heat
for a sign of triumph
or freedom.   10

The hunters are treading heavily
homeward through snow
marked by their own bloody footprints.
Emptyhanded   the hunters return
snow-maddened   15
sustained by their rages.

In the night after food they will seek
young girls for their amusement.
Now the hunters are coming
and the unbaked girls   20
flee from their angers.

All this day I have craved
food for my child's hunger
emptyhanded
the hunters come shouting   25
injustice drips from their mouths
like stale snow
melted in sunlight.

The woman thing
my mother taught me   30
bakes off its covering of snow
like a rising Blackening sun.

[1964, 1992]

BLACK MOTHER WOMAN

I cannot recall you gentle
yet through your heavy love
I have become
an image of your once-delicate flesh
split with deceitful longings.   5

When strangers come and compliment me
your aged spirit takes a bow
jingling with pride
but once you hid that secret
in the center of your fury   10
hanging me
with deep breasts and wiry hair
your own split flesh
and long-suffering eyes
buried in myths of little worth.   15

But I have peeled away your anger
down to its core of love
and look mother
I am   a dark temple
where your true spirit rises   20
beautiful   tough as chestnut
stanchion against nightmares of weakness
and if my eyes conceal
a squadron of conflicting rebellions
I learned from you   25
to define myself
through your denials.

[1971, 1992]

STATIONS

Some women love
to wait
for life   for a ring
in the June light   for a touch
of the sun to heal them   for another   ·5
woman's voice   to make them whole
to untie their hands
put words in their mouths
form to their passages   sound

to their screams   for some other sleeper   10
to remember   their future   their past.

Some women wait for their right
train   in the wrong station
in the alleys of morning
for the noon to holler   15
the night come down.

Some women wait for love
to rise up
the child of their promise
to gather from earth   20
what they do not plant
to claim pain for labor
to become
the tip of an arrow   to aim
at the heart of now   25
but it never stays.

Some women wait for visions
that do not return
where they were not welcome
naked   30
for invitations to places
they always wanted
to visit
to be repeated.

Some women wait for themselves   35
around the next corner
and call the empty spot peace
but the opposite of living
is only not living
and the stars do not care.   40

Some women wait for something
to change   and nothing
does change
so they change
themselves.   45
                                        [1986, 1997]

Don DeLillo

[b. 1936]

Don DeLillo was born to Italian immigrant parents on November 20, 1936, in the Bronx, a borough of New York City. Intensely private, DeLillo has offered only a few details about his early life. He says that he spent most of his time shooting pool or playing cards and street games with friends in the Italian American neighborhood where he grew up. Raised as a Roman Catholic, he graduated from Cardinal Hayes High School in 1954 and attended nearby Fordham, the Jesuit University of New York. He studied history, philosophy, and theology, but he disliked college and learned only "by rote," as DeLillo has put it. At the same time, he excitedly discovered the work of William Faulkner, Ernest Hemingway, and especially James Joyce. "I learned to see something in language that carried a radiance, something that made me feel the beauty and fervor of words, the sense that a word has a life and a history," DeLillo recalled in a 1993 interview. When he graduated in 1958 with a major in communication arts, he moved to Manhattan. Failing to get a job in publishing, as he had hoped, he found work as a copywriter for an advertising agency and spent his free time at jazz clubs, foreign films, galleries, and the Museum of Modern Art. He was also writing, and he published his first short story in the literary magazine *Epoch* in 1960.

Don DeLillo
This photograph of DeLillo was taken in 1992, by which time he was firmly established as one of the most prominent and influential postmodern writers in the United States.

After publishing several additional stories, DeLillo quit his job in 1964 to devote himself to writing fiction. He supported himself by doing freelance writing while working on his first novel, *Americana* (1971), the story of a television executive who seeks to connect with himself and his country by making a private film during a trip across the United States. Following up on the modest success of the novel, DeLillo published *End Zone* (1972), a sports novel in which he used football as a metaphor of contemporary American life, and *Great Jones Street* (1973), the story of a rock star who tries to preserve his own music in the face of the commercial pressures of popular culture. The book received solid reviews, and DeLillo's fiction appeared in prominent magazines such as *Esquire*, *Sports Illustrated*, the *New Yorker*, and the *Atlantic Monthly*. In 1975, DeLillo married Barbara Bennett, a banker who later became a landscape architect. After spending a year studying the history of mathematics, he published *Ratner's Star*

(1976), a book about a child prodigy who interprets a mathematical message from space. After that venture into science fiction, DeLillo experimented with another popular genre, the thriller, in *Players* (1977) and *Running Dog* (1978). In 1979, he was awarded a Guggenheim Fellowship, which enabled him and his wife to live in Greece for the next three years, during which time they traveled widely in the Middle East and India. "What I found was that all this traveling taught me how to see and hear all over again," he observed in a 1982 interview. "I think the most important thing is what I felt in hearing people and watching them gesture — in listening to the sound of Greek and Arabic and Hindi and Urdu." Both the limitations and potentially liberating power of language are central concerns in his novel *The Names* (1982), the story of an expatriate American businessman who becomes obsessed with a mysterious cult in Greece.

Since then, DeLillo has enjoyed widespread critical acclaim and growing commercial success. After he and his wife returned to the United States, they settled in a modest suburb of New York City. He won the National Book Award for *White Noise* (1985), a satirical novel about a professor of "Hitler Studies" at a college in a small midwestern town that is evacuated after toxic gas is released in an industrial accident. That breakthrough novel, which gained him a much wider audience, was followed by his bestseller *Libra* (1988), a nonfiction novel about the assassination of President John F. Kennedy, and *Mao II* (1991), a novel about a reclusive writer caught up in efforts to free a hostage held by terrorists. Although the reviews of both books were generally favorable, even some otherwise admiring reviewers and readers were put off by the characters and plots of his sprawling narratives. In reply to a question from a member of a reading club, DeLillo in 1995 observed that "well-behaved books with neat plots and worked-out endings seem somewhat quaint in the face of the largely incoherent reality of modern life," adding that rather than plot or character "it is language, in its beauty, its ambiguity and its shifting textures, that drives my work." Certainly, language was a driving force in his epic novel *Underworld* (1997), a sweeping saga of American life and cultural history from the 1950s to the 1990s. In a poll of writers, editors, and critics conducted by the *New York Times* in 2006, *Underworld* was named runner-up to Toni Morrison's *Beloved* as "the single best work of American fiction published in the last twenty-five years." DeLillo's recent work includes *Cosmopolis* (2003), a novel about a billionaire speculator caught up in a chaotic day in the stock market and streets of New York City, and *Falling Man* (2007), his acclaimed novel about a survivor's experience during and in the aftermath of the attacks on the World Trade Center on September 11, 2001.

bedfordstmartins.com/ americanlit *for research links on DeLillo*

DeLillo's "Videotape."   On one level, this is an apparently simple story about a family outing in a car, during which a young girl passes the time by using a video camera and inadvertently captures a violent incident on tape, recalling the famous Zapruder film of the assassination of President John F. Kennedy. Indeed, the tape rather than the event is the central subject of "Videotape," whose narrator has watched it again and again on the evening news. DeLillo's compressed narrative of postmodern life is consequently less a story in the conventional sense than an examination of our fascination with images of violence and the relationship between the technology of videotape and the actions and events it appears simply to record. Asked in a 1997 interview why film rather than books is so central in his work, DeLillo replied:

> Because this is the age of images, I suppose, and much that is different about our time can be traced to the fact that we are on film, a reality that did not shape, instruct, and haunt previous cultures. I suppose film gives us a deeply self-conscious sense, but beyond that it's simply such a prevalent fact of contemporary life that I don't think any attempt to understand the way we live and the way we think and the way we feel about ourselves can proceed without a deep consideration of the power of the image.

"Videotape," which was originally published in the final issue of the international literary quarterly *Antaeus*, was reprinted in *Harper's* magazine and later in a prestigious annual collection honoring the best work published by small presses and literary journals, *The Pushcart Prize XX* (1996). DeLillo slightly revised the story as the opening chapter of part two of his novel *Underworld* (1997). The text is taken from *Antaeus*, Autumn 1994.

Videotape

It shows a man driving a car. It is the simplest sort of family video. You see a man at the wheel of a medium Dodge.

It is just a kid aiming her camera through the rear window of the family car at the windshield of the car behind her.

You know about families and their video cameras. You know how kids get involved, how the camera shows them that every subject is potentially charged, a million things they never see with the unaided eye. They investigate the meaning of inert objects and dumb pets and they poke at family privacy. They learn to see things twice.

It is the kid's own privacy that is being protected here. She is twelve years old and her name is being withheld even though she is neither the victim nor the perpetrator of the crime but only the means of recording it.

It shows a man in a sport shirt at the wheel of his car. There is nothing else to see. The car approaches briefly, then falls back.

You know how children with cameras learn to work the exposed moments that define the family cluster. They break every trust, spy out the undefended space, catching Mom coming out of the bathroom in her cumbrous robe and turbaned towel, looking bloodless and plucked. It is not a joke. They will shoot you sitting on the pot if they can manage a suitable vantage.

The tape has the jostled sort of noneventness that marks the family product. Of course the man in this case is not a member of the family but a stranger in a car, a random figure, someone who has happened along in the slow lane.

It shows a man in his forties wearing a pale shirt open at the throat, the image washed by reflections and sunglint, with many jostled moments.

It is not just another video homicide. It is a homicide recorded by a child who thought she was doing something simple and maybe halfway clever, shooting some tape of a man in a car.

He sees the girl and waves briefly, wagging a hand without taking it off the wheel — an underplayed reaction that makes you like him.

It is unrelenting footage that rolls on and on. It has an aimless determination, a persistence that lives outside the subject matter. You are looking into the mind of home video. It is innocent, it is aimless, it is determined, it is real.

He is bald up the middle of his head, a nice guy in his forties whose whole life seems open to the hand-held camera.

But there is also an element of suspense. You keep on looking not because you know something is going to happen — of course you do know something is going to happen and you do look for that reason but you might also keep on looking if you came across this footage for the first time without knowing the outcome. There is a crude power operating here. You keep on looking because things combine to hold you fast — a sense of the random, the amateurish, the accidental, the impending. You don't think of the tape as boring or interesting. It is crude, it is blunt, it is relentless. It is the jostled part of your mind, the film that runs through your hotel brain under all the thoughts you know you're thinking.

The world is lurking in the camera, already framed, waiting for the boy or girl who will come along and take up the device, learn the instrument, shooting old Granddad at breakfast, all stroked out so his nostrils gape, the cereal spoon baby-gripped in his pale fist.

It shows a man alone in a medium Dodge. It seems to go on forever.

There's something about the nature of the tape, the grain of the image, the sputtering black-and-white tones, the starkness — you think this is more real, truer-to-life than anything around you. The things around you have a rehearsed and layered and cosmetic look. The tape is superreal, or maybe underreal is the way you want to put it. It is what lies at the scraped bottom of all the layers you have added. And this is another reason why you keep on looking. The tape has a searing realness.

It shows him giving an abbreviated wave, stiff-palmed, like a signal flag at a siding.

You know how families make up games. This is just another game in which the child invents the rules as she goes along. She likes the idea of videotaping a man in his car. She has probably never done it before and she sees no reason to vary the format or terminate early or pan to another car. This is her game and she is learning it and playing it at the same time. She feels halfway clever and inventive and maybe slightly intrusive as well, a little bit of brazenness that spices any game.

And you keep on looking. You look because this is the nature of the footage, to make a channeled path through time, to give things a shape and a destiny.

Of course if she had panned to another car, the right car at the precise time, she would have caught the gunman as he fired.

The chance quality of the encounter. The victim, the killer, and the child with a camera. Random energies that approach a common point. There's something here that speaks to you directly, saying terrible things about forces beyond your control, lines of intersection that cut through history and logic and every reasonable layer of human expectation.

She wandered into it. The girl got lost and wandered clear-eyed into horror. This is a children's story about straying too far from home. But it isn't the family car that serves as the instrument of the child's curiosity, her inclination to explore. It is the camera that puts her in the tale.

You know about holidays and family celebrations and how somebody shows up with a camcorder and the relatives stand around and barely react because they're numbingly accustomed to the process of being taped and decked and shown on the VCR with the coffee and cake.

He is hit soon after. If you've seen the tape many times you know from the handwave exactly when he will be hit. It is something, naturally, that you wait for. You say to your wife, if you're at home and she is there, Now here is where he gets it. You say, Janet, hurry up, this is where it happens.

Now here is where he gets it. You see him jolted, sort of wire-shocked – then he seizes up and falls toward the door or maybe leans or slides into the door is the proper way to put it. It is awful and unremarkable at the same time. The car stays in the slow lane. It approaches briefly, then falls back.

You don't usually call your wife over to the TV set. She has her programs, you have yours. But there's a certain urgency here. You want her to see how it looks. The tape has been running forever and now the thing is finally going to happen and you want her to be here when he's shot.

Here it comes, all right. He is shot, head-shot, and the camera reacts, the child reacts – there is a jolting movement but she keeps on taping, there is a sympathetic response, a nerve response, her heart is beating faster but she keeps the camera trained on the subject as he slides into the door and even as you see him die you're thinking of the girl. At some level the girl has to be present here, watching what you're watching, unprepared – the girl is seeing this cold and you have to marvel at the fact that she keeps the tape rolling.

It shows something awful and unaccompanied. You want your wife to see it because it is real this time, not fancy movie violence – the realness beneath the layers of cosmetic perception. Hurry up, Janet, here it comes. He dies so fast. There is no accompaniment of any kind. It is very stripped. You want to tell her it is realer than real but then she will ask what that means.

The way the camera reacts to the gunshot – a startle reaction that brings pity and terror into the frame, the girl's own shock, the girl's identification with the victim.

You don't see the blood, which is probably trickling behind his ear and down the back of his neck. The way his head is twisted away from the door, the twist of the head gives you only a partial profile and it's the wrong side, it's not the side where he was hit.

And maybe you're being a little aggressive here, practically forcing your wife to watch. Why? What are you telling her? Are you making a little statement? Like I'm going to ruin your day out of ordinary spite. Or a big statement? Like this is the risk of existing. Either way you're rubbing her face in this tape and you don't know why.

It shows the car drifting toward the guardrail and then there's a jostling sense of two other lanes and part of another car, a split-second blur, and the tape ends here, either because the girl stopped shooting or because some central authority, the police or the district attorney or the TV station, decided there was nothing else you had to see.

This is either the tenth or eleventh homicide committed by the Texas Highway Killer. The number is uncertain because the police believe that one of the shootings may have been a copycat crime.

And there is something about videotape, isn't there, and this particular kind of serial crime? This is a crime designed for random taping and immediate playing. You sit there and wonder if this kind of crime became more possible when the means of taping and playing an event — playing it immediately after the taping — became part of the culture. The principal doesn't necessarily commit the sequence of crimes in order to see them taped and played. He commits the crimes as if they were a form of taped-and-played event. The crimes are inseparable from the idea of taping and playing. You sit there thinking that this is a crime that has found its medium, or vice versa — cheap mass production, the sequence of repeated images and victims, stark and glary and more or less unremarkable.

It shows very little in the end. It is a famous murder because it is on tape and because the murderer has done it many times and because the crime was recorded by a child. So the child is involved, the Video Kid as she is sometimes called because they have to call her something. The tape is famous and so is she. She is famous in the modern manner of people whose names are strategically withheld. They are famous without names or faces, spirits living apart from their bodies, the victims and witnesses, the underage criminals, out there somewhere at the edges of perception.

Seeing someone at the moment he dies, dying unexpectedly. This is reason alone to stay fixed to the screen. It is instructional, watching a man shot dead as he drives along on a sunny day. It demonstrates an elemental truth, that every breath you take has two possible endings. And that's another thing. There's a joke locked away here, a note of cruel slapstick that you are completely willing to appreciate. Maybe the victim's a chump, a dope, classically unlucky. He had it coming, in a way, like an innocent fool in a silent movie.

You don't want Janet to give you any crap about it's on all the time, they show it a thousand times a day. They show it because it exists, because they have to show it, because this is why they're out there. The horror freezes your soul but this doesn't mean that you want them to stop.

[1994]

Michael S. Harper

[b. 1938]

Michael S. Harper was born on March 18, 1938, in Brooklyn, New York. He was the second of three children of Katherine Johnson Harper, a medical stenographer, and Walter Warren Harper, a post office supervisor. The couple owned a large collection of musical recordings, and as a child Harper took the subway into Manhattan to hear jazz musicians such as Charlie Parker. When he was thirteen, his family moved to Los Angeles, settling in a predominantly white neighborhood where "black houses were being bombed," as Harper noted in an interview in 1990. He also confronted racism at the local public high school, in which he was placed on a vocational track until his parents intervened. Following his graduation in 1955, Harper worked part-time in the post office while taking classes at Los Angeles City College, a community college from which he received an Associate of Arts degree in 1959. He then enrolled at Los Angeles State College (now California State University, Los Angeles), where he came under the tutelage of a remarkable group of writers teaching in the English department, including the British dramatist and novelist Christopher Isherwood. "He encouraged me to write one-act plays about jazz musicians," Harper recalled; "he encouraged me to capture their language, their idioms in wild scenes." With the help of his professors, Harper was admitted to the Writers' Workshop at the University of Iowa in 1961. The only black student in the program, he lived in segregated housing, haunted the library, and "contemplated my isolation when I wasn't selling pennants on Saturday afternoons," as he wryly observed. Most of all, he added, "I learned to cope and bide my time."

After a year at Iowa, from which he received his MFA in 1963, Harper pursued a career as a poet and teacher. His first teaching positions were at community colleges in California, where he married Shirley Anne Buffington in 1965. They later had five children, two of whom died in infancy from acute respiratory distress syndrome (ARDS). Meanwhile, Harper's poetry regularly appeared in literary journals such as the *Carolina Quarterly* and the *Negro Digest*. The prestigious magazine *Poetry* published six of his poems in 1968, and Harper was subsequently a poet in residence at Reed College and Lewis and Clark College in Oregon before he was hired as an associate professor of English at California State College at Hayward (now California State University, East Bay). Harper achieved his major breakthrough when the poet Gwendolyn Brooks, one of the judges of the U.S. Poetry Prize sponsored by the University of Pittsburgh, fought for the publication of his book *Dear John, Dear Coltrane* (1970). The volume, which was nominated for a National Book Award, is widely regarded as one of the most important collections of African American poetry to be published after World War II. During a year's leave from teaching, he wrote the poems in his second collection, *History Is Your Own Heartbeat* (1971), which was published about the time he went to Brown University as an

Michael Harper

LaVerne Harrell Clark took this photograph in 1973, while Harper was in Tucson to give a reading at the University of Arizona Poetry Center.

associate professor of English. Since then, he has published nine more volumes of poetry, including *Images of Kin* (1977), which was nominated for a National Book Award, *Healing Song for Inner Ear* (1985), and *Honorable Amendments* (1995), which was selected by Gwendolyn Brooks for the George Kent Poetry Award.

Harper has also played a significant role in efforts to recover the work of earlier writers and to display the richness of the African American literary tradition. "In the beginning I never found poems in the American literary pantheon about the things I knew best," he stated in 1993. "I decided that I would at least do my part and try to put some of those poems in there." Two of the earlier poets he most admired were his close friends Robert Hayden and Sterling Brown. Harper published a limited edition of Hayden's *American Journal* (1978) and later edited a special issue of *Obsidian: Black Literature in Review* featuring memorial tributes to Hayden. Harper has also edited *The Collected Poems of Sterling A. Brown* (1989) and coedited three influential anthologies: *Chant of Saints: A Gathering of Afro-American Literature, Art, and Scholarship* (1979), which was widely regarded as one of the most important collections of African American materials since Alain Locke's *The New Negro* (1925); *Every Shut Eye Ain't Asleep: An Anthology of Poetry by African Americans since 1945* (1994), which was dedicated to Sterling Brown; and *The Vintage Book of African American Poetry* (2000). Harper, who has received numerous honors and was the first Poet Laureate of Rhode Island (1988–1993), is the I. J. Kapstein Professor of English at Brown University.

Harper's Poetry.   "I've enjoyed the play of putting things together that don't belong together," Harper has observed. "I'm also a narrative poet who plays with syntax for musical overtones, and I hear everything I write. For me the poem is for the ear, but not a mechanical ear, not a metronome; I love phrasing, elegant and not so elegant associations, and drive, narrative drive." As he suggests, Harper frequently juxtaposes seemingly unrelated scenes or incidents in his poems, which reveal his deep love of music, especially the blues, gospel, and jazz. In the ironic epigraph to his first book, *Dear John, Dear Coltrane* (1970), he wrote: "A friend told me / He'd risen above jazz. / I leave him there." Harper pays tribute to jazz musicians in many of his poems, and his jazz-inflected verse is characterized by its rhythmical freedom, frequent repetitions, and refrains. He has also been inspired by poets ranging from William Carlos Williams to Gwendolyn Brooks, Sterling Brown, and Robert Hayden. Like his friend and mentor Hayden, Harper has persistently explored a theme announced in the title of the first poem in the following selection, "American History," ranging from the early history and heritage of African Americans to events such as the assassination of Martin Luther King Jr., the subject of the poem "Martin's Blues." The texts of the poems are taken from *Songlines in Michaeltree: New and Collected Poems* (2000).

bedfordstmartins.com/
americanlit *for research*
links on Harper

AMERICAN HISTORY

Those four black girls blown up
in that Alabama church[1]
remind me of five hundred
middle passage blacks,[2]
in a net, under water
in Charleston harbor
so *redcoats*[3] wouldn't find them.
Can't find what you can't see
can you?

[1970, 2000]

---

1. **Those four . . . Alabama church:** On Sunday, September 15, 1963, a bomb exploded at the Sixteenth Street
Baptist Church in Birmingham, Alabama, a regular meeting place of civil rights activists such as Martin
Luther King Jr. The bombing, which killed four young girls in a Sunday-school class and injured twenty-three
other people, was widely believed to have been the work of racist whites. Although one man was tried and
received a small fine for possession of dynamite, not until 2000 did the FBI announce that the bombing had
been planned and executed by a splinter group of the Ku Klux Klan.
2. **middle passage blacks:** The middle passage was the route across the Atlantic Ocean followed by slave
ships coming from Africa to the Americas.
3. *redcoats:* During most of the American Revolution, British soldiers or "redcoats" occupied Charleston,
South Carolina.

DEAR JOHN, DEAR COLTRANE[1]

a love supreme, a love supreme
a love supreme, a love supreme[2]

Sex fingers toes
in the marketplace
near your father's church
in Hamlet, North Carolina[3] —

---

1. **Dear John, Dear Coltrane:** The saxophonist John Coltrane (1926–1967), a leading figure in avant-garde jazz
in the 1950s and 1960s.
2. **a love supreme:** Coltrane's *A Love Supreme*, a four-part suite his quartet recorded in 1964, is widely
regarded as one of the greatest of all jazz albums. In his liner notes, Coltrane explains: "During the year
1957, I experienced by the grace of God, a spiritual awakening which was to lead me to a richer, fuller, more
productive life." In gratitude for that epiphany, which had helped him overcome his addiction to alcohol and
heroin, Coltrane made *A Love Supreme* as "a humble offering to Him."
3. **Sex . . . North Carolina:** "Dear John, Dear Coltrane" begins with a reference to Sam Hose, who was
lynched and dismembered in the Atlanta riot of 1906. . . . The black church was a haven and revolutionary
outpost for uncensored ideas, both of forgiveness and responsibility. [Harper's note] Coltrane was raised in a
deeply religious Christian home in Hamlet, North Carolina.

witness to this love   5
in this calm fallow
of these minds,
there is no substitute for pain:
genitals gone or going,
seed burned out,   10
you tuck the roots in the earth,
turn back, and move
by river through the swamps,
singing: *a love supreme, a love supreme;*
what does it all mean?   15
Loss, so great each black
woman expects your failure
in mute change, the seed gone.
You plod up into the electric city —
your song now crystal and   20
the blues. You pick up the horn
with some will and blow
into the freezing night:
a love supreme, a love supreme —

Dawn comes and you cook   25
up the thick sin 'tween
impotence and death, fuel
the tenor sax cannibal
heart, genitals, and sweat
that makes you clean —   30
a love supreme, a love supreme —

Why you so black?
cause I am
why you so funky?
cause I am   35
why you so black?
cause I am
why you so sweet?
cause I am
why you so black?   40
cause I am
a love supreme, a love supreme:

So sick
you couldn't play *Naima*,[4]
so flat we ached   45
for song you'd concealed
with your own blood,
your diseased liver gave
out its purity,
the inflated heart   50
pumps out, the tenor kiss,
tenor love:
a love supreme, a love supreme –
a love supreme, a love supreme –

[1970, 2000]

---

4. **So sick . . . *Naima*:** "Naima" is a song Coltrane wrote and named for his first wife. It is Coltrane, himself, who is singing. [Harper's note] Coltrane continued to perform until his death from liver cancer in 1967.

MARTIN'S BLUES[1]

He came apart in the open,
the slow motion cameras
falling quickly
neither alive nor kicking;
stone blind dead   5
on the balcony
that old melody
etched his black lips
in a pruned echo:
We shall overcome   10
some day[2] *–*
Yes we did!
Yes we did!

[1971, 2000]

---

1. **Martin's Blues:** "Martin's Blues" was written in the idiom of a children's ditty and found a place in the skipping rope games of preadolescents forced to grow up too soon. [Harper's note] Martin Luther King Jr. (1929-1968) was shot and killed by an assassin as he stood on a motel balcony in Memphis, Tennessee, on April 4, 1968.
2. ***We shall overcome / some day*:** Adopted from gospel songs, "We Shall Overcome" became the anthem of the civil rights movement.

"BIRD LIVES": CHARLES PARKER IN ST. LOUIS[1]

Last on legs, last on sax,
last in Indian wars, last on *smack*,
Bird is specious, *Bird* is alive,
horn, unplayable, before, after,
right now: it's heroin time: 5
smack, in the melody a trip,
smack, in the Mississippi;
smack, in the drug merchant trap;
smack, in St. Louis, Missouri.

We knew you were through —   10
trying to get out of town,
unpaid bills, connections
unmet, unwanted, unasked,
Bird's in the last arc
of his own light: *blow Bird!*   15
And you did —
screaming, screaming, baby,
for life, after it, around it,
screaming for life, *blow Bird!*

What is the meaning of music?   20
What is the meaning of war?
What is the meaning of oppression?
Blow Bird! Ripped up and down
into the interior of life, the pain,
Bird, the embraceable you,[2]   25
how many brothers gone,
smacked out: blues and racism,
the hardest, longest penis
in the Mississippi urinal:
Blow Bird!   30

Taught more musicians, then forgot,
space loose, fouling the melodies,
the marching songs, the fine white

---

1. *"Bird Lives"*: **Charles Parker in St. Louis:** "Bird Lives" was scribbled on walls during the forties as an anthem of freedom from restrictions, including racial bigotry. The scene is St. Louis in the early fifties in a Mafia-controlled nightclub where Parker is expected to enter the establishment through the kitchen, not the front door. After two consecutive incidents in which Bird overturned (by accident) a huge vat of tomato paste on the kitchen floor, he was instructed to use the front — hence a special brand of desegregation was instituted in the Gateway to the West. [Harper's note] The saxophonist Charles "Bird" Parker Jr. (1920–1955) was an influential musician who pioneered and popularized the form of jazz known as bebop or bop.
2. **embraceable you:** One of Parker's most famous recordings was his version of "Embraceable You," a popular song composed in 1928 by George and Ira Gershwin.

geese from the plantations,
syrup in this pork barrel,   35
Kansas City, the even teeth
of the mafia, the big band:
Blow Bird! Inside out Charlie's
guts, *Blow Bird!* get yourself killed.

In the first wave, the musicians,   40
out there, alone, in the first wave;
everywhere you went, Massey Hall,
Sweden, New Rochelle, *Birdland,*
nameless bird, Blue Note, Carnegie,
tuxedo junction, out of nowhere,   45
confirmation, confirmation, confirmation:[3]
Bird Lives! Bird Lives! and you do:
Dead —

[1971, 2000]

---

3. **everywhere you went . . . *confirmation*:** Harper alludes to Massey Hall in Toronto, Canada, where Parker recorded a famous concert with Dizzy Gillespie in 1951; Sweden, where Parker recorded a concert in 1950; two nightclubs in New York City, Birdland, which was named for Parker, and the Blue Note; and Carnegie Hall, where Parker made his last known live recording in 1954. "Tuxedo Junction" and "Out of Nowhere" are jazz standards, as is "Confirmation," which Parker composed in 1946.

Raymond Carver

[1938-1988]

Raymond Clevie Carver Jr. was born on May 25, 1938, in Clatskanie, Oregon. He was the first of two sons of "R. C." Carver, a sawmill worker, and Ella Casey Carver, a waitress. Struggling to support themselves and their infant son in the small logging town, the couple moved to Yakima, Washington, in 1941. Carver's happiest memories of his difficult childhood were of listening breathlessly while his alcoholic father told wonderful stories, and Carver remained an avid participant in storytelling exchanges throughout his life. After his graduation from high school in 1956, he worked as a deliveryman and took classes at Yakima Community College. In 1957, he married his sixteen-year-old high-school girlfriend, Maryann Burk. She was pregnant with their first child, born later that year, and they had a second child in 1958. They moved to Paradise, California, where Carver enrolled as a part-time student at Chico State College (now California State University, Chico). Under the tutelage of the novelist John Gardner, Carver began to write fiction and founded a literary magazine, *Selection*, where his first story appeared in 1961. By then, he had transferred to Humboldt State College (now California State University, Humboldt), from which he graduated in 1963. With the aid of a small fellowship, he studied for a year at the Writers' Workshop at the University of Iowa.

Raymond Carver

Marion Ettlinger took this photograph of Carver in 1984, when the celebrated short-story writer was one of the most famous authors in the United States.

But there simply was not enough money to support the family, so he and his wife returned with their two young children to California. "We became displaced people like so many other people in California," Carver recalled:

> We lived in various and sundry places, from Los Angeles to Eureka. We worked all the time. It was strictly blue-collar stuff, like cleaning up in fast-food places. Things would come along that we thought would improve our lot and we'd pack up our kids and the belongings. We'd move on and it would begin all over again. I wasn't doing much writing. I scarcely had time to turn around or draw a breath.

Despite the financial pressures and other obstacles, Carver somehow managed to establish himself as a writer. Several of his early stories appeared in small literary journals such as *Toyon* and *December*, and one of them was selected for inclusion in the *Best American Short Stories 1967*. Although he and his wife were forced to file for bankruptcy in the spring of 1967, their fortunes began to improve when Carver was hired as a textbook editor at Science Research Associates in Palo Alto, California. There, he became friends with Gordon Lish, who had previously edited avant-garde literary magazines and who soon became the influential fiction editor of the men's magazine *Esquire*. Carver's first book of poetry, *Winter Insomnia*, was published by a small college press in 1970, and his major break-through came the following year, when the first of his stories appeared in *Esquire*. Carver, who had worked so hard to earn a college degree and never completed his MFA, now began a career as a teacher of creative writing at the University of California, Santa Cruz, at Berkeley, and back at the Writers' Workshop. During the fall of 1974, he commuted between his jobs at Iowa and the University of California, Santa Barbara, but Carver was drinking so heavily and missing so many classes that he was forced to resign from both positions in December. He and his wife once again filed for bankruptcy, and the unemployed Carver wrote little, though in 1976 he published another collection of poetry, *At Night the Salmon Move*, and his first collection of short stories, *Will You Please Be Quiet, Please?*, which was nominated for a National Book Award.

Carver salvaged the remainder of his brief but brilliant literary career when he stopped drinking in 1977. Estranged and later divorced from his wife, he met the poet Tess Gallagher, with whom he began to live in 1979. He was the distinguished writer in residence at the University of Texas, El Paso, from 1978 to 1980, when he and Gallagher accepted positions in the creative writing program at Syracuse University. Carver published two major collections of his influential stories, *What We Talk About When We Talk About Love* (1981) and *Cathedral* (1983), which was nominated for a Pulitzer Prize. He also published *Fire: Essays, Poems, Stories* (1983). Carver resigned from Syracuse in 1984, after he received a five-year "Livings" fellowship from the American Academy and Institute of Arts and Letters. Seeking escape from the glare of his subsequent celebrity, he and Gallagher began to spend most of their time at her secluded house overlooking the Puget Sound in Port Angeles, Washington. There, he wrote

His great gift is for writing stories that create meaning through their form.

–Marilynne Robinson

mostly essays, reviews, and especially poems, which were collected in *Where the Water Comes Together* (1986), *Ultramarine* (1987), and the post-humously published *A New Path to the Waterfall* (1989). His final published story appeared in the *New Yorker* in June 1987, a few months before Carver, a heavy smoker, began treatment for lung cancer. With Gallagher's help, he put together his last collection of stories, *Where I'm Calling From* (1988). Carver and Gallagher were married in June, two months before his death on August 2, 1988. At a memorial service, Robert Gottlieb, then the editor of the *New Yorker*, stated: "America has just lost the writer it could least afford to lose."

Carver's "Are These Actual Miles?"   This story was first published as "What Is It?" in May 1972 in *Esquire*, a magazine for men noted for publishing the work of both established and emerging writers. From 1969 to 1976, its fiction editor was Gordon Lish, who strongly promoted Carver's early work, much of which appeared in *Esquire*. "What Is It?" was subsequently included under that title in the *O. Henry Prize Stories 1973* and in Carver's first collection of stories, *Will You Please Be Quiet, Please?* (1976). But he changed the title to "Are These Actual Miles?" when he revised the story for his final collection, *Where I'm Calling From* (1988). The title is a question the sales manager of a used-car dealership asks about the car that he has bought from the bankrupt central character in the story, Leo, and his wife, Toni. As several critics have suggested, the question metaphorically calls attention to the wear and tear of the many miles their marriage has accumulated, the heavy toll taken on it by financial problems, infidelities, and lack of communication. The painful story, which was inspired in part by what Carver described as the "hardscrabble" life that he and his first wife experienced during the first decade of their marriage, also displays his trademark "minimalism," the term most often used to describe the spare language and taut style of his early stories. "I always overwrite, and I have to go back and cut," Carver observed in an interview shortly before his death in 1988. "Especially in the early days, when a ten-page story might have represented a thirty-page original one — I'd go through twenty drafts." The text is taken from *Where I'm Calling From: New and Selected Stories* (1988).

bedfordstmartins.com/ *americanlit* *for research links on Carver*

ARE THESE ACTUAL MILES?

Fact is the car needs to be sold in a hurry, and Leo sends Toni out to do it. Toni is smart and has personality. She used to sell children's encyclopedias door to door. She signed him up, even though he didn't have kids. Afterward, Leo asked her for a date, and the date led to this. This deal has to be cash, and it has to be done tonight. Tomorrow somebody they owe might slap a lien on the car. Monday they'll be in court, home free — but word on them went out yesterday, when their lawyer mailed the letters of intention. The hearing on Monday is nothing to worry about, the lawyer has said. They'll be asked some questions, and they'll sign some papers, and that's it. But sell the convertible, he said — today, *tonight*. They can hold onto the little car, Leo's car, no problem. But they go into court with that big convertible, the court will take it, and that's that.

Toni dresses up. It's four o'clock in the afternoon. Leo worries the lots will close. But Toni takes her time dressing. She puts on a new white blouse, wide lacy cuffs, the new two-piece suit, new heels. She transfers the stuff from her straw purse into the new patent-leather handbag. She studies the lizard makeup pouch and puts that in too. Toni has been two hours on her hair and face. Leo stands in the bedroom doorway and taps his lips with his knuckles, watching.

"You're making me nervous," she says. "I wish you wouldn't just stand," she says. "So tell me how I look."

"You look fine," he says. "You look great. I'd buy a car from you anytime."

"But you don't have money," she says, peering into the mirror. She pats her hair, frowns. "And your credit's lousy. You're nothing," she says. "Teasing," she says and looks at him in the mirror. "Don't be serious," she says. "It has to be done, so I'll do it. You take it out, you'd be lucky to get three, four hundred and we both know it. Honey, you'd be lucky if you didn't have to pay *them*." She gives her hair a final pat, gums her lips, blots the lipstick with a tissue. She turns away from the mirror and picks up her purse: "I'll have to have dinner or something, I told you that already, that's the way they work, I know them. But don't worry, I'll get out of it," she says. "I can handle it."

"Jesus," Leo says, "did you have to say that?"

She looks at him steadily. "Wish me luck," she says.

"Luck," he says. "You have the pink slip?" he says.

She nods. He follows her through the house, a tall woman with a small high bust, broad hips and thighs. He scratches a pimple on his neck. "You're sure?" he says. "Make sure. You have to have the pink slip."

"I have the pink slip," she says.

"Make sure."

She starts to say something, instead looks at herself in the front window and then shakes her head.

"At least call," he says. "Let me know what's going on."

"I'll call," she says. "Kiss, kiss. Here," she says and points to the corner of her mouth. "Careful," she says.

He holds the door for her. "Where are you going to try first?" he says. She moves past him and onto the porch.

Ernest Williams looks from across the street. In his Bermuda shorts, stomach hanging, he looks at Leo and Toni as he directs a spray onto his begonias. Once, last winter, during the holidays, when Toni and the kids were visiting his mother's, Leo brought a woman home. Nine o'clock the next morning, a cold foggy Saturday, Leo walked the woman to the car, surprised Ernest Williams on the sidewalk with a newspaper in his hand. Fog drifted, Ernest Williams stared, then slapped the paper against his leg, hard.

Leo recalls that slap, hunches his shoulders, says, "You have someplace in mind first?"

"I'll just go down the line," she says. "The first lot, then I'll just go down the line."

"Open at nine hundred," he says. "Then come down. Nine hundred is low bluebook, even on a cash deal."

"I know where to start," she says.

Ernest Williams turns the hose in their direction. He stares at them through the spray of water. Leo has an urge to cry out a confession.

"Just making sure," he says.

"Okay, okay," she says. "I'm off."

It's her car, they call it her car, and that makes it all the worse, They bought it new that summer three years ago. She wanted something to do after the kids started school, so she went back selling. He was working six days a week in the fiber-glass plant. For a while they didn't know how to spend the money. Then they put a thousand on the convertible and doubled and tripled the payments until in a year they had it paid. Earlier, while she was dressing, he took the jack and spare from the trunk and emptied the glove compartment of pencils, matchbooks, Blue Chip stamps. Then he washed it and vacuumed inside. The red hood and fenders shine.

"Good luck," he says and touches her elbow.

She nods. He sees she is already gone, already negotiating.

"Things are going to be different!" he calls to her as she reaches the driveway. "We start over Monday. I mean it."

Ernest Williams looks at them and turns his head and spits. She gets into the car and lights a cigarette.

"This time next week!" Leo calls again. "Ancient history!"

He waves as she backs into the street. She changes gear and starts ahead. She accelerates and the tires give a little scream.

In the kitchen Leo pours Scotch and carries the drink to the backyard. The kids are at his mother's. There was a letter three days ago, his name penciled on the outside of the dirty envelope, the only letter all summer not demanding payment in full. We are having fun, the letter said. We like Grandma. We have a new dog called Mr. Six. He is nice. We love him. Good-bye.

He goes for another drink. He adds ice and sees that his hand trembles. He holds the hand over the sink. He looks at the hand for a while, sets down the glass, and holds out the other hand. Then he picks up the glass and goes back outside to sit on the steps. He recalls when he was a kid his dad pointing at a fine house, a tall white house surrounded by apple trees and a high white rail fence. "That's Finch," his dad said admiringly. "He's been in bankruptcy at least twice. Look at that house." But bankruptcy is a company collapsing utterly, executives cutting their wrists and throwing themselves from windows, thousands of men on the street.

Leo and Toni still had furniture. Leo and Toni had furniture and Toni and the kids had clothes. Those things were exempt. What else? Bicycles for the kids, but these he had sent to his mother's for safekeeping. The portable air-conditioner and the appliances, new washer and dryer, trucks came for those things weeks ago. What else did they have? This and that, nothing mainly, stuff that wore out or fell to pieces long ago. But there were some big parties back there, some fine travel. To Reno and Tahoe, at eighty with the top down and the radio playing. Food, that was one of the big items. They gorged on food. He figures thousands on luxury items alone. Toni would go to the grocery and put in everything she saw, "I had to do without when I was a kid," she says. "These kids are not going to do without," as if he'd been insisting they should. She joins all the book clubs. "We never had books around when I was a kid," she says as she tears open the heavy packages. They enroll in the record clubs for something to play on the new stereo. They sign up for it all. Even a pedigreed terrier named Ginger. He paid two hundred and found her run over in the street a week later. They buy what they want. If they can't pay, they charge. They sign up.

His undershirt is wet; he can feel the sweat rolling from his underarms. He sits on the step with the empty glass in his hand and watches the shadows fill up the yard. He stretches, wipes his face. He listens to the traffic on the highway and considers whether he should go to the basement, stand on the utility sink, and hang himself with his belt. He understands he is willing to be dead.

Inside he makes a large drink and he turns the TV on and he fixes something to eat. He sits at the table with chili and crackers and watches something about a blind detective. He clears the table. He washes the pan and the bowl, dries these things and puts them away, then allows himself a look at the clock.

It's after nine. She's been gone nearly five hours.

He pours Scotch, adds water, carries the drink to the living room. He sits on the couch but finds his shoulders so stiff they won't let him lean back. He stares at the screen and sips, and soon he goes for another drink. He sits again. A news program begins — it's ten o'clock — and he says, "God, what in God's name has gone wrong?" and goes to the kitchen to return with more Scotch. He sits, he closes his eyes, and opens them when he hears the telephone ringing.

"I wanted to call," she says.

"Where are you?" he says. He hears piano music, and his heart moves.

"I don't know," she says. "Someplace. We're having a drink, then we're going someplace else for dinner. I'm with the sales manager. He's crude, but he's all right. He bought the car. I have to go now. I was on my way to the ladies and saw the phone."

"Did somebody buy the car?" Leo says. He looks out the kitchen window to the place in the drive where she always parks.

"I told you," she says. "I have to go now."

"Wait, wait a minute, for Christ's sake," he says. "Did somebody buy the car or not?"

"He had his checkbook out when I left," she says. "I have to go now. I have to go to the bathroom."

"Wait!" he yells. The line goes dead. He listens to the dial tone. "Jesus Christ," he says as he stands with the receiver in his hand.

He circles the kitchen and goes back to the living room. He sits. He gets up. In the bathroom he brushes his teeth very carefully. Then he uses dental floss. He washes his face and goes back to the kitchen. He looks at the clock and takes a clean glass from a set that has a hand of playing cards painted on each glass. He fills the glass with ice. He stares for a while at the glass he left in the sink.

He sits against one end of the couch and puts his legs up at the other end. He looks at the screen, realizes he can't make out what the people are saying. He turns the empty glass in his hand and considers biting off the rim. He shivers for a time and thinks of going to bed, though he knows he will dream of a large woman with gray hair. In the dream he is always leaning over tying his shoelaces. When he straightens up, she looks at him, and he bends to tie again. He looks at his hand. It makes a fist as he watches. The telephone is ringing.

"Where are you, honey?" he says slowly, gently.

"We're at this restaurant," she says, her voice strong, bright.

"Honey, which restaurant?" he says. He puts the heel of his hand against his eye and pushes.

"Downtown someplace," she says. "I think it's New Jimmy's. Excuse me," she says to someone off the line, "is this place New Jimmy's? This is New Jimmy's, Leo," she says to him. "Everything is all right, we're almost finished, then he's going to bring me home."

"Honey?" he says. He holds the receiver against his ear and rocks back and forth, eyes closed. "Honey?"

"I have to go," she says. "I wanted to call. Anyway, guess how much?"

"Honey," he says.

"Six and a quarter," she says. "I have it in my purse. He said there's no market for convertibles. I guess we're born lucky," she says and laughs. "I told him everything. I think I had to."

"Honey," Leo says.

"What?" she says.

"Please, honey," Leo says.

"He said he sympathizes," she says. "But he would have said anything." She laughs again. "He said personally he'd rather be classified a robber or a rapist than a bankrupt. He's nice enough, though," she says.

"Come home," Leo says. "Take a cab and come home."

"I can't," she says. "I told you, we're halfway through dinner."

"I'll come for you," he says.

"No," she says. "I said we're just finishing. I told you, it's part of the deal. They're out for all they can get. But don't worry, we're about to leave. I'll be home in a little while." She hangs up.

In a few minutes he calls New Jimmy's. A man answers. "New Jimmy's has closed for the evening," the man says.

"I'd like to talk to my wife," Leo says.

"Does she work here?" the man asks. "Who is she?"

"She's a customer," Leo says, "She's with someone. A business person."

"Would I know her?" the man says. "What is her name?"

"I don't think you know her," Leo says.

"That's all right," Leo says. "That's all right. I see her now."

"Thank you for calling New Jimmy's," the man says.

Leo hurries to the window. A car he doesn't recognize slows in front of the house, then picks up speed. He waits. Two, three hours later, the telephone rings again. There is no one at the other end when he picks up the receiver. There is only a dial tone.

"I'm right here!" Leo screams into the receiver.

Near dawn he hears footsteps on the porch. He gets up front the couch. The set hums, the screen glows. He opens the door. She bumps the wall coming in. She grins. Her face is puffy, as if she's been sleeping under sedation, She works her lips, ducks heavily and sways as he cocks his fist.

"Go ahead," she says thickly. She stands there swaying. Then she makes a noise and lunges, catches his shirt, tears it down the front. "Bankrupt!" she screams. She twists loose, grabs and tears his undershirt at the neck. "You son of a bitch," she says clawing.

He squeezes her wrists, then lets go, steps back, looking for something heavy. She stumbles as she heads for the bedroom. "Bankrupt," she mutters. He hears her fall on the bed and groan.

He waits awhile, then splashes water on his face and goes to the bedroom. He turns the lights on, looks at her, and begins to take her clothes off. He pulls and pushes her from side to side undressing her. She says something in her sleep and moves her hand. He takes off her underpants, looks at them closely under the light, and throws them into a corner. He turns back the covers and rolls her in, naked. Then he opens her purse. He is reading the check when he hears the car come into the drive.

He looks through the front curtain and sees the convertible in the drive, its motor running smoothly, the headlamps burning, and he closes and opens his eyes. He sees a tall man come around in front of the car and up to the front porch. The man lays something on the porch and starts back to the car. He wears a white linen suit.

Leo turns on the porch light and opens the door cautiously. Her makeup pouch lies on the top step. The man looks at Leo across the front of the car, and then gets back inside and releases the handbrake.

"Wait!" Leo calls and starts down the steps. The man brakes the car as Leo walks in front of the lights. The car creaks against the brake. Leo tries to pull the two pieces of his shirt together, tries to bunch it all into his trousers.

"What is it you want?" the man says. "Look," the man says, "I have to go. No offense. I buy and sell cars, right? The lady left her makeup. She's a fine lady, very refined. What is it?"

Leo leans against the door and looks at the man. The man takes his hands off the wheel and puts them back. He drops the gear into reverse and the car moves backward a little.

"I want to tell you," Leo says and wets his lips.

The light in Ernest Williams' bedroom goes on. The shade rolls up.

Leo shakes his head, tucks in his shirt again. He steps back from the car. "Monday," he says.

"Monday," the man says and watches for sudden movement.

Leo nods slowly.

"Well, goodnight," the man says and coughs. "Take it easy, hear? Monday, that's right. Okay, then." He takes his foot off the brake, puts it on again after he has rolled back two or three feet. "Hey, one question. Between friends, are these actual miles?" The man waits, then clears his throat. "Okay, look, it doesn't matter either way," the man says. "I have to go. Take it easy." He backs into the street, pulls away quickly, and turns the corner without stopping.

Leo tucks at his shirt and goes back in the house. He locks the front door and checks it. Then he goes to the bedroom and locks that door and turns back the covers. He looks at her before he flicks the light. He takes off his clothes, folds them carefully on the floor, and gets in beside her. He lies on his back for a time and pulls the hair on his stomach, considering. He looks at the bedroom door, outlined now in the faint outside light. Presently he reaches out his hand and touches her hip. She does not move. He turns on his side and puts his hand on her hip. He runs his fingers over her hip and feels the stretch marks there. They are like roads, and he traces them in her flesh. He runs his fingers back and forth, first one, then another. They run everywhere in her flesh, dozens, perhaps hundreds of them. He remembers waking up the morning after they bought the car, seeing it, there in the drive, in the sun, gleaming.

[1972, 1988]

Gloria Anzaldúa

[1942-2004]

Gloria Evangelina Anzaldúa was born on September 26, 1942, on a ranch settlement called Jesus Maria in the Rio Grande valley of south Texas. She was the eldest of four children born to tenant farmers, Urbano and Amalia Anzaldúa. From an early age, Anzaldúa was an avid reader, and books at once exposed the injustices in her world and opened up new horizons for her. "One day when I was about seven or eight, my father dropped on my lap a 25 cent pocket western, the only type of book he could pick up at a drugstore," she recalled in an autobiographical essay, "La Prieta" (1981):

> The act of reading forever changed me. In the westerns I read, the house servants, the villains and the cantineras (prostitutes) were all Mexicans. But I knew that the first cowboys (vaqueros) were Mexicans, that in Texas we outnumbered the Anglos, that my grandmother's ranch lands had been ripped off by the greedy Anglo. Yet in the pages of these books, the Mexican and Indian were vermin. The racism I would later recognize in my schoolteachers and never be able to ignore again I found in that first western I read.

When Anzaldúa was eleven, her family moved to a farm outside Hargill, Texas, close to the border with Mexico. She and her siblings continued to work in the fields while they attended segregated schools in Hargill and later in Edinburgh, Texas. When her father died suddenly of a heart attack

Gloria Anzaldúa

Margaret Randall took this photograph of Anzaldúa, a writer, scholar, and radical activist best known for her influential book *Borderlands/La Frontera* (1987).

Her early death reminds me to remind myself and my colegas (colleagues) that our most important obligation is to finish our work, to honor our writing, to return to our desk and honor her life by doing this.

—Sandra Cisneros

in 1956, Anzaldúa was devastated, but she continued her reading and study. "Books saved my sanity, knowledge opened the locked places in me and taught me first how to survive and then how to soar," she wrote in 1987.

Anzaldúa was determined to gain an education and to educate others. After her graduation from high school, she attended Texas Women's University before transferring to a college closer to home, Pan American University (now the University of Texas-Pan American), from which she graduated with a BA in English, art, and secondary education in 1969. For the next four years, she taught at public schools in Texas while earning an MA during the summers at the University of Texas at Austin. From June 1973 to September 1974, she was the state director of migrant education in Indiana. When she returned, she became a PhD candidate in comparative literature and an instructor at the University of Texas, Austin. But her professors there discouraged her interests in feminist theory and the emerging field of Chicana/o studies, so she moved to California in 1977. She supported herself by giving lectures and teaching at several schools, including San Francisco State University. She also became involved in the Feminist Writer's Guild. Frustrated by the inability of some white feminists to recognize the additional obstacles faced by women of color, she published "Speaking in Tongues: A Letter to Third World Women Writers." Anzaldúa included the essay in a multigenre anthology she coedited with writer Cherríe Moraga, *This Bridge Called My Back: Writings by Radical Women of Color* (1981). After the small feminist press that published the book folded, a new edition was brought out in 1983 by the first press exclusively devoted to publishing works by women of color, the Kitchen Table/Women of Color Press, founded by Barbara Smith and Audre Lorde. The groundbreaking anthology exerted a profound influence on feminist theory and the direction of the women's movement, and it later received an American Book Award, designed to honor the multicultural diversity of American writing, from the Before Columbus Foundation.

Anzaldúa subsequently became widely known as an activist, cultural critic, feminist theorist, and writer. In 1987, she published her most acclaimed and influential work, *Borderlands/La Frontera: The New Mestiza*, an innovative collection of poetry and prose in which she explored the history and culture of the "third country," as she described the border between Mexico and the United States. Anzaldúa also developed a radical theory that challenged what she viewed as the binary, either/or conceptions of both race and sexuality in the Europeanized West. The book was later included in the *Hungry Mind Review*'s list of the "100 Best 20th-Century American Books of Fiction and Nonfiction," as well as in the "Alternate Canon," a list of 150 of the world's great books compiled by the *Utne Reader*. In the final years of her life, Anzaldúa published two children's books and a collection of her interviews, *Interviews/Entrevistas* (2000), as well as the anthologies *Making Face, Making Soul: Haciendo Caras* (1990) and *this bridge we call home: radical visions for transformation* (2002), which she coedited with AnaLouise Keating. Anzaldúa was completing her doctoral dissertation when she died of complications resulting from diabetes on May 15, 2004.

Anzaldúa's "El sonavabitche."   In the preface to *Borderlands*, where this poem was first published, Anzaldúa defined herself as a new *mestiza*, a "border woman" who had grown up "between two cultures, the Mexican (with a heavy Indian influence) and the Anglo (as a member of a colonized people in our own territory)." As she explained, however, the psychological, sexual, and spiritual borderlands she explored in the book are "present wherever two or more cultures edge each other, where people of different races occupy the same territory, where under, lower, middle and upper classes touch, where the space between two individuals shrinks with intimacy." Just as she challenged rigid classifications of class, culture, race, and sexuality, Anzaldúa rejected strict generic distinctions in *Borderlands*, an innovative collection of autobiographical and historical essays, lyrical prose sketches, and poetry. She also employed a hybrid language derived from different forms of English and Spanish, a rich dialect Anzaldúa called Chicano Spanish and others have called "Spanglish." In her first-person narrative poem "El sonavabitche," which was inspired by Anzaldúa's experiences working as an educator among migrant workers in Indiana during the early 1970s, she exposes the brutality, exploitation, and racism in a "borderland" far from the actual border between the United States and Mexico. The text is taken from the first edition of *Borderlands/La Frontera: The New Mestiza* (1987).

bedfordsmartins.com/ americanlit for research links on Anzaldúa

EL SONAVABITCHE

(for Aishe Berger)

    Car flowing down a lava of highway
    just happened to glance out the window
    in time to see brown faces bent backs
    like prehistoric boulders in a field
    so common a sight no one   5
    notices
    blood rushes to my face
    twelve years I'd sat on the memory
    the anger scorching me
    my throat so tight I can   10
    barely get the words out.

I got to the farm
in time to hear the shots

ricochet off barn,
spit into the sand,   15
in time to see tall men in uniforms
thumping fists on doors
metallic voices yelling Halt!
their hawk eyes constantly shifting.

    When I hear the words, *"Corran muchachos"*[1]   20
    I run back to the car, ducking,
    see the glistening faces, arms outflung,
    of the *mexicanos*[2] running headlong
    through the fields
    kicking up clouds of dirt   25

see them reach the tree line
foliage opening, swishing closed behind them.
I hear the tussling of bodies, grunts, panting
squeak of leather squawk of walkie-talkies
sun reflecting off gunbarrels   30
    the world a blinding light
    a great buzzing in my ears
    my knees like aspens in the wind.

    I see that wide cavernous look of the hunted
    the look of hares   35
    thick limp blue-black hair
    The bare heads humbly bent
    of those who do not speak
    the ember in their eyes extinguished.

I lean on the shanty wall of that migrant camp   40
north of Muncie, Indiana.
Wets, a voice says.
I turn to see a Chicano[3] pushing
the head of his *muchachita*[4]
back into the *naguas*[5] of the mother   45
a tin plate face down on the floor
tortillas scattered around them.
His other hand signals me over.

---

1. ***"Corran muchachos"***: "Run boys" (Spanish). [Anzaldúa's note]
2. **mexicanos**: Mexicans.
3. **Chicano**: A Mexican American male, probably derived from the Spanish *mejicano*, "Mexican."
4. **muchachita**: Little girl (Spanish). [Anzaldúa's note]
5. **naguas**: Skirt (Spanish). [Anzaldúa's note]

He too is from *el valle de Tejas*[6]
I had been his kid's teacher. 50
I'd come to get the grower
to fill up the sewage ditch near the huts
saying it wouldn't do for the children
to play in it.
> Smoke from a cooking fire and 55
> shirtless *niños*[7] gather around us.

> *Mojados*,[8] he says again,
> leaning on his chipped Chevy station wagon
> Been here two weeks
> about a dozen of them. 60
> The *sonavabitche* works them
> from sunup to dark – 15 hours sometimes.
> *Como mulas los trabaja*
> *no saben como hacer la perra.*[9]
> Last Sunday they asked for a day off 65
> wanted to pray and rest,
> write letters to their *familias.*
> *¿Y sabes lo que hizo el sonavabitche?*[10]
> He turns away and spits.
> Says he has to hold back half their wages 70
> that they'd eaten the other half:
> sack of beans, sack of rice, sack of flour.
> *Frijoleros sí lo son*[11] but no way
> could they have eaten that many *frijoles.*
> I nod. 75

Como le dije, son doce[12] – started out 13
five days packed in the back of a pickup
boarded up tight
fast cross-country run no stops
except to change drivers, to gas up 80
no food they pissed into their shoes –

---

6. *el valle de Tejas*: Rio Grande Valley in Texas (Spanish). [Anzaldúa's note]
7. *niños*: Children (Spanish).
8. *Mojados*: Wetbacks, undocumented workers, illegal immigrants from Mexico and parts south (Spanish). [Anzaldúa's note]
9. *Como mulas . . . la perra*: He works them like mules. They don't know how to make the work easier for themselves (Spanish). [Anzaldúa's note]
10. *¿Y sabes lo que hizo . . . ?*: And you know what he did (Spanish). [Anzaldúa's note]
11. *Frijoleros sí lo son*: Bean eaters they are (Spanish). [Anzaldúa's note]
12. *Como le dije, son doce*: Like I told you, they're 12 (Spanish). [Anzaldúa's note]

those that had *guaraches*[13]
slept slumped against each other
sabe Dios[14] where they shit.
One smothered to death on the way here.   85

    Miss, you should've seen them when they
    stumbled out.
    First thing the *sonavabitche* did was clamp
    a handkerchief over his nose
    then ordered them stripped   90
    hosed them down himself
    in front of everybody.
    They hobbled about
    learning to walk all over again.
    Flacos con caras de viejos   95
    aunque la mitá eran jóvenes.[15]

Como le estaba diciendo,[16]
today was payday.
You saw them, *la migra*[17] came busting in
waving their *pinche pistolas.*[18]   100
Said someone made a call,
what you call it? Anonymous.
Guess who? That *sonavabitche*, who else?
Done this three times since we've been coming here
Sepa Dios[19] how many times in between.   105
    Wets, free labor, *esclavos.*[20]
    Pobres jijos de la chingada.[21]
    This the last time we work for him
    no matter how *fregados*[22] we are
    he said, shaking his head,
    spitting at the ground.   110
    Vámonos, mujer, empaca el mugrero.[23]

---

13. *guarache*: Sandal (Spanish). [Anzaldúa's note]
14. *sabe Dios*: God knows (Spanish). [Anzaldúa's note]
15. *Flacos . . . jóvenes*: Skinny with old faces though half were youths (Spanish). [Anzaldúa's note]
16. *Como le estaba diciendo*: As I was telling you (Spanish). [Anzaldúa's note]
17. *la migra*: Slang for immigration officials (Spanish). [Anzaldúa's note]
18. *pinche pistolas*: Bloody guns (Spanish).
19. *Sepa Dios*: God may know (Spanish).
20. *esclavos*: Slaves (Spanish). [Anzaldúa's note]
21. *Pobres jijos de la chingada*: Poor sons of the fucked one (Spanish). [Anzaldúa's note]
22. *fregados*: Poor, beaten, downtrodden, in need (Spanish). [Anzaldúa's note]
23. *Vámonos, mujer, empaca el mugrero*: Let's go, woman, pack our junk (Spanish). [Anzaldúa's note]

He hands me a cup of coffee,
half of it sugar, half of it milk
my throat so dry I even down the dregs.
It has to be done.   115
Steeling myself
I take that walk to the big house.

Finally the big man lets me in.
How about a drink? I shake my head.
He looks me over, opens his eyes wide   120
and smiles, says how sorry he is immigration
is getting so tough
a poor Mexican can't make a living
and they sure do need the work.
My throat so thick the words stick.   125
He studies me, then says,
Well, what can I do you for?
I want two weeks wages
including two Saturdays and Sundays,
minimum wage, 15 hours a day.   130
I'm more startled than he.
Whoa there, sinorita,
wets work for whatever you give them
the season hasn't been good.
Besides most are halfway to Mexico by now.   135
Two weeks wages, I say,
the words swelling in my throat.

    Miss uh what did you say your name was?
    I fumble for my card.
    You can't do this,   140
    I haven't broken no law,
    his lidded eyes darken, I step back.
    I'm leaving in two minutes and I want cash
    the whole amount right here in my purse
    when I walk out.   145
    No hoarseness, no trembling.
    It startled both of us.

You want me telling every single one
of your neighbors what you've been doing
all these years? The mayor, too?   150
Maybe make a call to Washington?
Slitted eyes studied the card again.
They had no cards, no papers.

I'd seen it over and over.
Work them, then turn them in before paying them.   155

    Well, now, he was saying,
    I know we can work something out,
    a sweet young thang like yourself.
    Cash, I said. I didn't know anyone in D.C.
    now I didn't have to.   160
    You want to keep it for yourself?
    That it? His eyes were pin pricks.
    Sweat money, Mister, blood money,
    not my sweat, but same blood.
    Yeah, but who's to say you won't abscond with it?   165
    If I ever hear that you got illegals on your land
    even a single one, I'm going to come here
    in broad daylight and have you
    hung by your balls.
    He walks slowly to his desk.   170
    Knees shaking, I count every bill
    taking my time.

[1987]

Alice Walker

[b. 1944]

Alice Malsenior Walker was born on February 9, 1944. She was the last of six children born to Willie Lee and Minnie Grant Walker, sharecroppers in Eatonville, Georgia. Despite resistance from her husband, Walker's mother was determined to educate their youngest daughter and enrolled her in the first grade when she was only four. In 1952, Walker was blinded in her right eye when her brother accidentally shot her with his BB gun while they were playing cowboys and Indians. The injury traumatized Walker, who felt that the scar tissue was ugly and who began spending most of her time alone, reading and writing poems. In 1961, she graduated from high school as the class valedictorian and received a scholarship to Spelman College,

Alice Walker

This photograph of Walker was taken in the 1980s, following the publication of her best-selling novel *The Color Purple* (1982).

a historically black college for women in Atlanta. She became deeply involved in the civil rights movement, met Martin Luther King Jr. and heard him deliver his famous "I Have a Dream" speech at the March on Washington for Jobs and Freedom in 1963. That year, she won a scholarship and transferred to Sarah Lawrence College in Bronxville, New York. After a trip to Africa, Walker discovered she was pregnant. In despair, she contemplated suicide but instead had an abortion and wrote a story, "To Hell with Dying," which she gave to one of her teachers at Sarah Lawrence, the writer Muriel Rukeyser. Rukeyser sent the story to Langston Hughes, who later included it in *Best Short Stories by Negro Writers* (1967).

After her graduation from college in 1965, Walker devoted much of her time to politics, teaching, and writing. She married Mel Levanthal, a white civil rights lawyer, and they moved to Jackson, Mississippi. While teaching as a writer in residence at the historically black Jackson State College (now University) and Tougaloo College, Walker published her first volume of poems, *Once* (1968), and wrote her first novel, *The Third Life of Grange Copeland* (1970), the story of three generations of a black family in a small town in Georgia. About the time she finished the novel in 1969, Walker gave birth to a daughter and began work as the history consultant to a Head Start program in Mississippi. Two years later, she was awarded a fellowship at Radcliffe College in Cambridge, Massachusetts, and she subsequently taught at Wellesley College and the University of Massachusetts, Boston. In 1973, she published another collection of poetry, *Revolutionary Petunias*, and her first book of short stories, *In Love and Trouble*. In the process of doing research for one of her stories, she discovered the writer Zora Neale Hurston, whom she described as a "cultural Revolutionary," and whose works had a profound impact on Walker. She famously located Hurston's unmarked grave in Florida, where Walker arranged for a headstone to honor her literary "foremother." Walker returned briefly to Mississippi, where she completed a semiautobiographical novel about a woman who grows up in Georgia and becomes involved in the civil rights movement, *Meridian* (1976). By the time it was published, however, Walker had become frustrated with the slow progress of the movement in Mississippi and moved to New York City, where she became an editor of the feminist magazine *Ms.*

Following her divorce from Mel Levanthal, Walker moved with her daughter to northern California in 1978. During her first years there, she edited a collection of Hurston's works, *I Love Myself When I Am Laughing* (1979). Walker also published a volume of poems about the experiences of black women, *Good Night, Willie Lee, I'll See You in the Morning* (1979), and her second collection of short stories, *You Can't Keep a Good Woman Down* (1981). In what proved to be a crucial turning point in her career, she also wrote her most famous and celebrated work, *The Color Purple* (1982), an unconventional novel in which the central character, Celie, tells the painful story of her life through ninety letters addressed to God. The searing saga of a black woman's struggle for independence was awarded the

The rhythms of Alice Walker's prose are beautiful and characteristic, flexible, vigorous, easy, the gait of a hunting lion.
–Ursula K. Le Guin

Pulitzer Prize and later made into a hit movie produced by Steven Spielberg and starring Whoopi Goldberg, Oprah Winfrey, and Danny Glover. Following the publication of her ambitious novel *The Temple of My Familiar* (1989), whose narrative spans 500,000 years and ranges from Africa to the United States, Walker turned to the taboo subject of female circumcision in her next novel, *Possessing the Secret of Joy* (1992). She and a friend, Pratibha Parmar, produced a documentary about female genital mutilation in Africa, and Walker wrote an account of the making of the film, *Warrior Marks* (1993). She also wrote *The Same River Twice* (1996), about the filming of *The Color Purple.* Since then, Walker has published several collections of essays, poems, and stories, as well as a novel about a woman's spiritual pilgrimage through nature, *Now Is the Time to Open Your Heart* (2004). Her most recent book is a collection of essays on environmentalism, politics, and spirituality, *We Are the Ones We Have Been Waiting For* (2006).

*bedfordstmartins.com/
americanlit* for research
links on Walker

Walker's "Everyday Use." This story first appeared in *Harper's* magazine in April 1973, in advance of its publication in Walker's first book of stories, *In Love and Trouble*, which she dedicated, in part, to the memory of three African American writers: Zora Neale Hurston, Nella Larsen, and Jean Toomer. In "Everday Use," Walker developed one of the central themes of her work, the vital but unacknowledged tradition of black women's art, represented in the story by quilts handed down from generation to generation. In an essay in her collection *In Search of Our Mother's Gardens: Womanist Prose* (1983), Walker recalls that she once saw a magnificent quilt, "obviously the work of a person of powerful imagination and deep spiritual feeling," in the Smithsonian Institution in Washington:

> Below this quilt I saw a note that says it was made by "an anonymous Black woman in Alabama, a hundred years ago." If we could locate this "anonymous" black woman from Alabama, she would turn out to be one of our grandmothers — an artist who left her mark in the only materials she could afford, and in the only medium her position in society allowed her to use.

In "Everyday Use," Walker also drew upon her childhood memories of the visits home by her brilliant and accomplished older sister, who, as she wrote in her poem "For My Sister Molly Who in the Fifties,"

> FOUND ANOTHER WORLD
> Another life   With gentlefolk
> Far less trusting
> And moved and moved and changed
> Her name.

The text of the story is taken from *In Love and Trouble: Stories of Black Women* (1973).

EVERYDAY USE

for your grandmama[1]

I will wait for her in the yard that Maggie and I made so clean and wavy yesterday afternoon. A yard like this is more comfortable than most people know. It is not just a yard. It is like an extended living room. When the hard clay is swept clean as a floor and the fine sand around the edges lined with tiny, irregular grooves, anyone can come and sit and look up into the elm tree and wait for the breezes that never come inside the house.

Maggie will be nervous until after her sister goes: she will stand hopelessly in corners, homely and ashamed of the burn scars down her arms and legs, eying her sister with a mixture of envy and awe. She thinks her sister has held life always in the palm of one hand, that "no" is a word the world never learned to say to her.

You've no doubt seen those TV shows where the child who has "made it" is confronted, as a surprise, by her own mother and father, tottering in weakly from backstage. (A pleasant surprise, of course: What would they do if parent and child came on the show only to curse out and insult each other?) On TV mother and child embrace and smile into each other's faces. Sometimes the mother and father weep, the child wraps them in her arms and leans across the table to tell how she would not have made it without their help. I have seen these programs.

Sometimes I dream a dream in which Dee and I are suddenly brought together on a TV program of this sort. Out of a dark and soft-seated limousine I am ushered into a bright room filled with many people. There I meet a smiling, gray, sporty man like Johnny Carson[2] who shakes my hand and tells me what a fine girl I have. Then we are on the stage and Dee is embracing me with tears in her eyes. She pins on my dress a large orchid, even though she has told me once that she thinks orchids are tacky flowers.

In real life I am a large, big-boned woman with rough, man-working hands. In the winter I wear flannel nightgowns to bed and overalls during the day. I can kill and clean a hog as mercilessly as a man. My fat keeps me hot in zero weather. I can work outside all day, breaking ice to get water for washing; I can eat pork liver cooked over the open fire minutes after it comes steaming from the hog. One winter I knocked a bull calf straight in the brain between the eyes with a sledge hammer and had the meat hung up to chill before nightfall. But of course all this does not show on television. I am the way my daughter would want me to be: a hundred pounds lighter, my skin like an uncooked barley pancake. My hair glistens in the hot bright lights. Johnny Carson has much to do to keep up with my quick and witty tongue.

But that is a mistake. I know even before I wake up. Who ever knew a Johnson with a quick tongue? Who can even imagine me looking a strange white man in the eye? It seems to me I have talked to them always with one foot raised in flight, with my head

---

1. *for your grandmama:* In the first printing of the story in *Harper's* magazine, the dedication read: "A legacy for the child who will live it."
2. **Johnny Carson:** Carson (1925–2005) was the popular host of NBC's *The Tonight Show* from 1962 to 1992.

turned in whichever way is farthest from them. Dee, though. She would always look any-one in the eye. Hesitation was no part of her nature.

"How do I look, Mama?" Maggie says, showing just enough of her thin body envel-oped in pink skirt and red blouse for me to know she's there, almost hidden by the door.

"Come out into the yard," I say.

Have you ever seen a lame animal, perhaps a dog run over by some careless person rich enough to own a car, sidle up to someone who is ignorant enough to be kind to him? That is the way my Maggie walks. She has been like this, chin on chest, eyes on ground, feet in shuffle, ever since the fire that burned the other house to the ground.

Dee is lighter than Maggie, with nicer hair and a fuller figure. She's a woman now, though sometimes I forget. How long ago was it that the other house burned? Ten, twelve years? Sometimes I can still hear the flames and feel Maggie's arms sticking to me, her hair smoking and her dress falling off her in little black papery flakes. Her eyes seemed stretched open, blazed open by the flames reflected in them. And Dee. I see her standing off under the sweet gum tree she used to dig gum out of; a look of concentra-tion on her face as she watched the last dingy gray board of the house fall in toward the red-hot brick chimney. Why don't you do a dance around the ashes? I'd wanted to ask her. She had hated the house that much.

I used to think she hated Maggie, too. But that was before we raised the money, the church and me, to send her to Augusta to school. She used to read to us without pity; forcing words, lies, other folks' habits, whole lives upon us two, sitting trapped and ignorant underneath her voice. She washed us in a river of make-believe, burned us with a lot of knowledge we didn't necessarily need to know. Pressed us to her with the serious way she read, to shove us away at just the moment, like dimwits, we seemed about to understand.

Dee wanted nice things. A yellow organdy dress to wear to her graduation from high school; black pumps to match a green suit she'd made from an old suit somebody gave me. She was determined to stare down any disaster in her efforts. Her eyelids would not flicker for minutes at a time. Often I fought off the temptation to shake her. At sixteen she had a style of her own: and knew what style was.

I never had an education myself. After second grade the school was closed down. Don't ask me why: in 1927 colored asked fewer questions than they do now. Sometimes Maggie reads to me. She stumbles along good-naturedly but can't see well. She knows she is not bright. Like good looks and money, quickness passed her by. She will marry John Thomas (who has mossy teeth in an earnest face) and then I'll be free to sit here and I guess just sing church songs to myself. Although I never was a good singer. Never could carry tune. I was always better at a man's job. I used to love to milk till I was hooked in the side in '49. Cows are soothing and slow and don't bother you, unless you try to milk them the wrong way.

I have deliberately turned my back on the house. It is three rooms, just like the one that burned, except the roof is tin; they don't make shingle roofs any more. There are no real windows, just some holes cut in the sides, like the portholes in a ship, but not round and not square, with rawhide holding the shutters up on the outside. This house is in a pasture, too, like the other one. No doubt when Dee sees it she will want to tear it down. She wrote me once that no matter where we "choose" to live, she will manage to come see us. But she will never bring her friends. Maggie and I thought about this and Maggie asked me, "Mama, when did Dee ever *have* any friends?"

She had a few. Furtive boys in pink shirts hanging about on washday after school. Nervous girls who never laughed. Impressed with her they worshiped the well-turned phrase, the cute shape, the scalding humor that erupted like bubbles in lye. She read to them.

When she was courting Jimmy T she didn't have much time to pay to us, but turned all her faultfinding power on him. He *flew* to marry a cheap city girl from a family of ignorant flashy people. She hardly had time to recompose herself.

When she comes I will meet — but there they are!

Maggie attempts to make a dash for the house, in her shuffling way, but I stay her with my hand. "Come back here," I say. And she stops and tries to dig a well in the sand with her toe.

It is hard to see them clearly through the strong sun. But even the first glimpse of leg out of the car tells me it is Dee. Her feet were always neat-looking, as if God himself had shaped them with a certain style. From the other side of the car comes a short, stocky man. Hair is all over his head a foot long and hanging from his chin like a kinky mule tail. I hear Maggie suck in her breath. "Uhnnnh," is what it sounds like. Like when you see the wriggling end of a snake just in front of your foot on the road. "Uhnnnh."

Dee next. A dress down to the ground, in this hot weather. A dress so loud it hurts my eyes. There are yellows and oranges enough to throw back the light of the sun. I feel my whole face warming from the heat waves it throws out. Earrings gold, too, and hanging down to her shoulders. Bracelets dangling and making noises when she moves her arm up to shake the folds of the dress out of her armpits. The dress is loose and flows, and as she walks closer, I like it. I hear Maggie go "Uhnnnh" again. It is her sister's hair. It stands straight up like the wool on a sheep. It is black as night and around the edges are two long pigtails that rope about like small lizards disappearing behind her ears.

"Wa-su-zo-Tean-o!" she says, coming on in that gliding way the dress makes her move. The short stocky fellow with the hair to his navel is all grinning and he follows up with "Asalamalakim, my mother and sister!" He moves to hug Maggie but she falls back, right up against the back of my chair. I feel her trembling there and when I look up I see the perspiration falling off her chin.

"Don't get up," says Dee. Since I am stout it takes something of a push. You can see me trying to move a second or two before I make it. She turns, showing white heels through her sandals, and goes back to the car. Out she peeks next with a Polaroid. She stoops down quickly and lines up picture after picture of me sitting there in front of the house with Maggie cowering behind me. She never takes a shot without making sure the house is included. When a cow comes nibbling around the edge of the yard she snaps it and me and Maggie *and* the house. Then she puts the Polaroid in the back seat of the car, and comes up and kisses me on the forehead.

Meanwhile Asalamalakim is going through motions with Maggie's hand. Maggie's hand is as limp as a fish, and probably as cold, despite the sweat, and she keeps trying to pull it back. It looks like Asalamalakim wants to shake hands but wants to do it fancy. Or maybe he don't know how people shake hands. Anyhow, he soon gives up on Maggie.

"Well," I say. "Dee."

"No, Mama," she says. "Not 'Dee,' Wangero Leewanika Kemanjo!"

"What happened to 'Dee'?" I wanted to know.

"She's dead," Wangero said. "I couldn't bear it any longer, being named after the people who oppress me."

"You know as well as me you was named after your aunt Dicie," I said. Dicie is my sister. She named Dee. We called her "Big Dee" after Dee was born.

"But who was *she* named after?" asked Wangero.

"I guess after Grandma Dee," I said.

"And who was she named after?" asked Wangero.

"Her mother," I said, and saw Wangero was getting tired. "That's about as far back as I can trace it," I said. Though, in fact, I probably could have carried it back beyond the Civil War through the branches.

"Well," said Asalamalakim, "there you are."

"Uhnnnh," I heard Maggie say.

"There I was not," I said, "before 'Dicie' cropped up in our family, so why should I try to trace it that far back?"

He just stood there grinning, looking down on me like somebody inspecting a Model A car.[3] Every once in a while he and Wangero sent eye signals over my head.

"How do you pronounce this name?" I asked.

"You don't have to call me by it if you don't want to," said Wangero.

"Why shouldn't I?" I asked. "If that's what you want us to call you, we'll call you."

"I know it might sound awkward at first," said Wangero.

"I'll get used to it," I said. "Ream it out again."

Well, soon we got the name out of the way. Asalamalakim had a name twice as long and three times as hard. After I tripped over it two or three times he told me to just call him Hakim-a-barber. I wanted to ask him was he a barber, but I didn't really think he was, so I didn't ask.

"You must belong to those beef-cattle peoples down the road," I said. They said "Asalamalakim" when they met you, too, but they didn't shake hands. Always too busy: feeding the cattle, fixing the fences, putting up salt-lick shelters, throwing down hay. When the white folks poisoned some of the herd the men stayed up all night with rifles in their hands. I walked a mile and a half just to see the sight.

Hakim-a-barber said, "I accept some of their doctrines, but farming and raising cattle is not my style." (They didn't tell me, and I didn't ask, whether Wangero (Dee) had really gone and married him.)

---

3. **Model A car:** The redesigned successor to the hugely successful Model T, or "Tin Lizzie," which had been produced by the Ford Motor Company from 1908 through 1927.

We sat down to eat and right away he said he didn't eat collards and pork was unclean. Wangero, though, went on through the chitlins and corn bread, the greens and everything else. She talked a blue streak over the sweet potatoes. Everything delighted her. Even the fact that we still used the benches her daddy made for the table when we couldn't afford to buy chairs.

"Oh, Mama!" she cried. Then turned to Hakim-a-barber. "I never knew how lovely these benches are. You can feel the rump prints," she said, running her hands underneath her and along the bench. Then she gave a sigh and her hand closed over Grandma Dee's butter dish. "That's it!" she said. "I knew there was something I wanted to ask you if I could have." She jumped up from the table and went over in the corner where the churn stood, the milk in it clabber by now. She looked at the churn and looked at it.

"This churn top is what I need," she said. "Didn't Uncle Buddy whittle it out of a tree you all used to have?"

"Yes," I said.

"Uh huh," she said happily. "And I want the dasher, too."

"Uncle Buddy whittle that, too?" asked the barber.

Dee (Wangero) looked up at me.

"Aunt Dee's first husband whittled the dash," said Maggie so low you almost couldn't hear her. "His name was Henry, but they called him Stash."

"Maggie's brain is like an elephant's," Wangero said, laughing. "I can use the churn top as a centerpiece for the alcove table," she said, sliding a plate over the churn, "and I'll think of something artistic to do with the dasher."

When she finished wrapping the dasher the handle stuck out. I took it for a moment in my hands. You didn't even have to look close to see where hands pushing the dasher up and down to make butter had left a kind of sink in the wood. In fact, there were a lot of small sinks; you could see where thumbs and fingers had sunk into the wood. It was beautiful light yellow wood, from a tree that grew in the yard where Big Dee and Stash had lived.

After dinner Dee (Wangero) went to the trunk at the foot of my bed and started rifling through it. Maggie hung back in the kitchen over the dishpan. Out came Wangero with two quilts. They had been pieced by Grandma Dee and then Big Dee and me had hung them on the quilt frames on the front porch and quilted them. One was in the Lone Star pattern. The other was Walk Around the Mountain. In both of them were scraps of dresses Grandma Dee had worn fifty and more years ago. Bits and pieces of Grandpa Jarrell's Paisley shirts. And one teeny faded blue piece, about the size of a penny matchbox, that was from Great Grandpa Ezra's uniform that he wore in the Civil War.

"Mama," Wangero said sweet as a bird. "Can I have these old quilts?"

I heard something fall in the kitchen, and a minute later the kitchen door slammed.

"Why don't you take one or two of the others?" I asked. "These old things was just done by me and Big Dee from some tops your grandma pieced before she died."

"No," said Wangero. "I don't want those. They are stitched around the borders by machine."

"That'll make them last better," I said.

"That's not the point," said Wangero. "These are all pieces of dresses Grandma used to wear. She did all this stitching by hand. Imagine!" She held the quilts securely in her arms, stroking them.

"Some of the pieces, like those lavender ones, come from old clothes her mother handed down to her," I said, moving up to touch the quilts. Dee (Wangero) moved back just enough so that I couldn't reach the quilts. They already belonged to her.

"Imagine!" she breathed again, clutching them closely to her bosom.

"The truth is," I said, "I promised to give them quilts to Maggie, for when she marries John Thomas."

She gasped like a bee had stung her.

"Maggie can't appreciate these quilts!" she said. "She'd probably be backward enough to put them to everyday use."

"I reckon she would," I said. "God knows I been saving 'em for long enough with nobody using 'em. I hope she will!" I didn't want to bring up how I had offered Dee (Wangero) a quilt when she went away to college. Then she had told me they were old-fashioned, out of style.

"But they're *priceless!*" she was saying now, furiously; for she has a temper. "Maggie would put them on the bed and in five years they'd be in rags. Less than that!"

"She can always make some more," I said. "Maggie knows how to quilt."

Dee (Wangero) looked at me with hatred. "You just will not understand. The point is these quilts, *these* quilts!"

"Well," I said, stumped. "What would *you* do with them?"

"Hang them," she said. As if that was the only thing you *could* do with quilts.

Maggie by now was standing in the door. I could almost hear the sound her feet made as they scraped over each other.

"She can have them, Mama," she said, like somebody used to never winning anything, or having anything reserved for her. "I can 'member Grandma Dee without the quilts."

I looked at her hard. She had filled her bottom lip with checkerberry snuff and it gave her face a kind of dopey, hangdog look. It was Grandma Dee and Big Dee who taught her how to quilt herself. She stood there with her scarred hands hidden in the folds of her skirt. She looked at her sister with something like fear but she wasn't mad at her. This was Maggie's portion. This was the way she knew God to work.

When I looked at her like that something hit me in the top of my head and ran down to the soles of my feet. Just like when I'm in church and the spirit of God touches me and I get happy and shout. I did something I never had done before: hugged Maggie to me, then dragged her on into the room, snatched the quilts out of Miss Wangero's hands and dumped them into Maggie's lap. Maggie just sat there on my bed with her mouth open.

"Take one or two of the others," I said to Dee.

But she turned without a word and went out to Hakim-a-barber.

"You just don't understand," she said, as Maggie and I came out to the car.

"What don't I understand?" I wanted to know.

"Your heritage," she said. And then she turned to Maggie, kissed her, and said, "You ought to try to make something of yourself, too, Maggie. It's really a new day for us. But from the way you and Mama still live you'd never know it."

She put on some sunglasses that hid everything above the tip of her nose and her chin.

Maggie smiled; maybe at the sunglasses. But a real smile, not scared. After we watched the car dust settle I asked Maggie to bring me a dip of snuff. And then the two of us sat there just enjoying, until it was time to go in the house and go to bed.

[1973]

Tim O'Brien

[b. 1946]

William Timothy O'Brien Jr. was born on October 1, 1946, in Austin, Minnesota. He was the first of three children of military veterans of World War II, William Timothy O'Brien, an insurance salesman, and Ava E. Schultz O'Brien, an elementary school teacher. In 1956, the family moved to Worthington, Minnesota, known as the "Turkey Capital of the U.S." With the encouragement of his parents, O'Brien became an avid reader and began to write stories at an early age. After his graduation from high school in 1964, he enrolled at Macalester College in St. Paul, Minnesota, where he majored in political science and was deeply involved in politics and protests against the Vietnam War. In 1968, he graduated summa cum laude and was admitted to graduate school at Harvard University. A few weeks later, however, O'Brien was drafted into the army. Because of his opposition to the war, he considered going to Canada, but after agonizing over the decision he reported for duty, received basic training at Fort Lewis, Washington, and was sent to Vietnam. During his thirteen months there, he served with an infantry brigade that was engaged in constant combat in Quang Ngai Province, and O'Brien was awarded a Combat Infantry Badge, a Purple Heart, and the Bronze Star. But he was appalled by the brutality of the conflict, the devastation of the country, and the dislocation of the Vietnamese, and O'Brien was even more fiercely opposed to the war by the time he ended his tour of duty in Vietnam.

Tim O'Brien

This photograph of O'Brien was taken the year he published his novel *July, July* (2002), a chronicle of the lives of a generation still struggling with the legacy of the Vietnam War.

Following his discharge from the army, O'Brien sought to take up his civilian life where he had left off and entered the doctoral program in political science at Harvard in 1970. Although he was not planning on a literary career, he felt compelled to write about what he had witnessed in Vietnam. Drawing upon the journals he had kept during his months there, O'Brien wrote an unflinching memoir of his experiences, *If I Die in a Combat Zone, Box Me Up and Ship Me Home* (1973). The year it was published, he married Ann Weller, an editorial assistant at a publishing company. While pursuing his studies at Harvard, O'Brien spent two summers as an intern at the *Washington Post*, and he worked as a national affairs reporter for the newspaper during 1973-74. He subsequently abandoned work on his doctoral dissertation to write his first novel, *Northern Lights* (1975), which revolves around the conflicts between two brothers, one a veteran and the other a protester of the Vietnam War, living in a small town in northern Minnesota. O'Brien returned to the scenes of the war in *Going After Cacciato* (1978), a surrealistic novel about an infantry squad sent to bring back a soldier who deserts his unit in Vietnam and sets off on an 8,000-mile trek to attend the peace talks in Paris. The novel won the National Book Award, and O'Brien began to publish regularly in the *Atlantic Monthly, Esquire, Harper's,* and the *New Yorker*. Many critics were disappointed by O'Brien's ambitious chronicle of American life in the era of the cold war, *The Nuclear Age* (1985). But he followed it with his greatest triumph to date, *The Things They Carried* (1990), an internationally acclaimed sequence of stories about the Vietnam War.

That war and its aftermath have remained central themes in O'Brien's work. Shortly before he went to Vietnam in 1990, his first visit since his tour of duty ended twenty years earlier, the *New York Times* published an interview with O'Brien entitled "A Storyteller for the War That Won't End." Following the emotionally difficult visit, he wrote *In the Lake of the Woods* (1995), a novel about a politician who has sought to erase his role in one of the most brutal incidents of the Vietnam War, the My Lai Massacre of 1968. But the war played a minor role in *Tomcat in Love* (1998), a comic novel about a recently divorced professor of linguistics that was published the year before O'Brien accepted a position as an endowed chair in creative writing at Southwest Texas State University (now Texas State University-San Marcos). By then, he was divorced from his first wife, and he married Meredith Hale Baker in 2001. His most recent novel is *July, July* (2002), about the college reunion of a group of former friends from the class of 1969, the year O'Brien was sent to Vietnam.

O'Brien's "The Things They Carried." Describing the factors that made him a writer, O'Brien has stated: "I had a desire to write from the time I was a little kid and then something collided with that desire — namely Vietnam — and I had to write about it. It moved from desire to imperative. I couldn't *not* write." In the view of many critics and readers, his writing about the war is most powerful in "The Things They Carried." First published in the August 1986 issue of *Esquire*, a magazine for men long noted for featuring distinguished work of fiction and nonfiction, the story won a National Magazine Award. It was also the title story of *The Things They Carried*, a sequence of vignettes in which a semifictional narrator named "Tim O'Brien" explores the nature of both war and the war story. Although the story is deeply rooted in his experiences as an in-

bedfordstmartins.com/ americanlit for research links on O'Brien

fantryman in Vietnam and is laced with the military terminology and soldier slang of the period, O'Brien has emphasized the universal dimensions
of "The Things They Carried." "The title is meant to refer to all of us," he
told an interviewer in 2003. "[It's about] the spiritual, the emotional, and
the psychological baggage we all carry. . . . You sort of accumulate more
and more of these spiritual burdens the longer you live and they help
define who we are, what our yearnings are, what makes us happy and what
doesn't." The text is taken from *The Things They Carried* (1990).

THE THINGS THEY CARRIED

First Lieutenant Jimmy Cross carried letters from a girl named Martha, a junior at
Mount Sebastian College in New Jersey. They were not love letters, but Lieutenant Cross
was hoping, so he kept them folded in plastic at the bottom of his rucksack. In the late
afternoon, after a day's march, he would dig his foxhole, wash his hands under a can-
teen, unwrap the letters, hold them with the tips of his fingers, and spend the last hour
of light pretending. He would imagine romantic camping trips into the White Mountains in New Hampshire. He would sometimes taste the envelope flaps, knowing her
tongue had been there. More than anything, he wanted Martha to love him as he loved
her, but the letters were mostly chatty, elusive on the matter of love. She was a virgin, he
was almost sure. She was an English major at Mount Sebastian, and she wrote beautifully about her professors and roommates and midterm exams, about her respect for
Chaucer and her great affection for Virginia Woolf.[1] She often quoted lines of poetry;
she never mentioned the war, except to say, Jimmy, take care of yourself. The letters
weighed 10 ounces. They were signed Love, Martha, but Lieutenant Cross understood
that Love was only a way of signing and did not mean what he sometimes pretended it
meant. At dusk, he would carefully return the letters to his rucksack. Slowly, a bit distracted, he would get up and move among his men, checking the perimeter, then at full
dark he would return to his hole and watch the night and wonder if Martha was a virgin.

The things they carried were largely determined by necessity. Among the necessities
or near-necessities were P-38 can openers, pocket knives, heat tabs, wristwatches, dog
tags, mosquito repellent, chewing gum, candy, cigarettes, salt tablets, packets of Kool-
Aid, lighters, matches, sewing kits, Military Payment Certificates, C rations, and two or
three canteens of water. Together, these items weighed between 15 and 20 pounds,
depending upon a man's habits or rate of metabolism. Henry Dobbins, who was a big
man, carried extra rations; he was especially fond of canned peaches in heavy syrup
over pound cake. Dave Jensen, who practiced field hygiene, carried a toothbrush, dental
floss, and several hotel-sized bars of soap he'd stolen on R&R[2] in Sydney, Australia. Ted

---

1. **Chaucer . . . Woolf:** The medieval English poet Geoffrey Chaucer (c. 1343–1400), author of *The Canterbury
Tales*, and the English novelist and feminist critic Virginia Woolf (1882–1941).
2. **R &R:** Rest and recreation, the informal term for a temporary leave during a one-year tour of duty in
Vietnam.

Lavender, who was scared, carried tranquilizers until he was shot in the head outside the village of Than Khe in mid-April. By necessity, and because it was SOP,[3] they all carried steel helmets that weighed 5 pounds including the liner and camouflage cover. They carried the standard fatigue jackets and trousers. Very few carried underwear. On their feet they carried jungle boots – 2.1 pounds – and Dave Jensen carried three pairs of socks and a can of Dr. Scholl's foot powder as a precaution against trench foot. Until he was shot, Ted Lavender carried six or seven ounces of premium dope which for him was a necessity. Mitchell Sanders, the RTO,[4] carried condoms. Norman Bowker carried a diary. Rat Kiley carried comic books. Kiowa, a devout Baptist, carried an illustrated New Testament that had been presented to him by his father who taught Sunday school in Oklahoma City, Oklahoma. As a hedge against bad times, however, Kiowa also carried his grandmother's distrust of the white man, his grandfather's old hunting hatchet. Necessity dictated. Because the land was mined and booby-trapped, it was SOP for each man to carry a steel-centered, nylon-covered flak jacket, which weighed 6.7 pounds, but which on hot days seemed much heavier. Because you could die so quickly, each man carried at least one large compress bandage, usually in the helmet band for easy access. Because the nights were cold, and because the monsoons were wet, each carried a green plastic poncho that could be used as a raincoat or groundsheet or makeshift tent. With its quilted liner, the poncho weighed almost two pounds, but it was worth every ounce. In April, for instance, when Ted Lavender was shot, they used his poncho to wrap him up, then to carry him across the paddy, then to lift him into the chopper that took him away.

They were called legs or grunts.

To carry something was to hump it, as when Lieutenant Jimmy Cross humped his love for Martha up the hills and through the swamps. In its intransitive form, to hump meant to walk, or to march, but it implied burdens far beyond the intransitive.

Almost everyone humped photographs. In his wallet, Lieutenant Cross carried two photographs of Martha. The first was a Kodacolor snapshot signed Love, though he knew better. She stood against a brick wall. Her eyes were gray and neutral, her lips slightly open as she stared straight-on at the camera. At night, sometimes, Lieutenant Cross wondered who had taken the picture, because he knew she had boyfriends, because he loved her so much, and because he could see the shadow of the picture-taker spreading out against the brick wall. The second photograph had been clipped from the 1968 Mount Sebastian yearbook. It was an action shot – women's volleyball – and Martha was bent horizontal to the floor, reaching, the palms of her hands in sharp focus, the tongue taut, the expression frank and competitive. There was no visible sweat. She wore white gym shorts. Her legs, he thought, were almost certainly the legs of a virgin, dry and without hair, the left knee cocked and carrying her entire weight, which was just over one hundred pounds. Lieutenant Cross remembered touching that left knee. A dark theater, he remembered, and the movie was *Bonnie and Clyde*, and Martha wore a tweed skirt, and during the final scene, when he touched her knee, she turned and

---

3. **SOP:** Standard operating procedure.
4. **RTO:** Radiotelephone operator.

looked at him in a sad, sober way that made him pull his hand back, but he would always remember the feel of the tweed skirt and the knee beneath it and the sound of the gunfire that killed Bonnie and Clyde, how embarrassing it was, how slow and oppressive.[5] He remembered kissing her good night at the dorm door. Right then, he thought, he should've done something brave. He should've carried her up the stairs to her room and tied her to the bed and touched that left knee all night long. He should've risked it. Whenever he looked at the photographs, he thought of new things he should've done.

What they carried was partly a function of rank, partly of field specialty.

As a first lieutenant and platoon leader, Jimmy Cross carried a compass, maps, code books, binoculars, and a .45-caliber pistol that weighed 2.9 pounds fully loaded. He carried a strobe light and the responsibility for the lives of his men.

As an RTO, Mitchell Sanders carried the PRC-25 radio, a killer, 26 pounds with its battery.

As a medic, Rat Kiley carried a canvas satchel filled with morphine and plasma and malaria tablets and surgical tape and comic books and all the things a medic must carry, including M&M's[6] for especially bad wounds, for a total weight of nearly 20 pounds.

As a big man, therefore a machine gunner, Henry Dobbins carried the M-60, which weighed 23 pounds unloaded, but which was almost always loaded. In addition, Dobbins carried between 10 and 15 pounds of ammunition draped in belts across his chest and shoulders.

As PFCs or Spec 4s,[7] most of them were common grunts and carried the standard M-16 gas-operated assault rifle. The weapon weighed 7.5 pounds unloaded, 8.2 pounds with its full 20-round magazine. Depending on numerous factors, such as topography and psychology, the riflemen carried anywhere from 12 to 20 magazines, usually in cloth bandoliers, adding on another 8.4 pounds at minimum, 14 pounds at maximum. When it was available, they also carried M-16 maintenance gear — rods and steel brushes and swabs and tubes of LSA oil — all of which weighed about a pound. Among the grunts, some carried the M-79 grenade launcher, 5.9 pounds unloaded, a reasonably light weapon except for the ammunition, which was heavy. A single round weighed 10 ounces. The typical load was 25 rounds. But Ted Lavender, who was scared, carried 34 rounds when he was shot and killed outside Than Khe, and he went down under an exceptional burden, more than 20 pounds of ammunition, plus the flak jacket and helmet and rations and water and toilet paper and tranquilizers and all the rest, plus the unweighed fear. He was dead weight. There was no twitching or flopping. Kiowa, who saw it happen, said it was like watching a rock fall, or a big sandbag or something — just boom, then down — not like the movies where the dead guy rolls around and does fancy spins and goes ass over teakettle — not like that, Kiowa said, the poor bastard just flat-fuck fell. Boom. Down. Nothing else. It was a bright morning in mid-April. Lieutenant Cross felt

---

5. **A dark theater . . . slow and oppressive:** In the violent final scene of the movie *Bonnie and Clyde* (1967), the bodies of the Depression-era robbers writhe in slow motion under a hail of machine-gun bullets.
6. **M & M's:** Grimly humorous slang for medical supplies or drugs in pill form.
7. **PFCs or Spec 4s:** Private first class and the rank immediately above, specialist fourth class, the most common ranks in the Vietnam-era army.

the pain. He blamed himself. They stripped off Lavender's canteens and ammo, all the heavy things, and Rat Kiley said the obvious, the guy's dead, and Mitchell Sanders used his radio to report one U.S. KIA[8] and to request a chopper. Then they wrapped Lavender in his poncho. They carried him out to a dry paddy, established security, and sat smoking the dead man's dope until the chopper came. Lieutenant Cross kept to himself. He pictured Martha's smooth young face, thinking he loved her more than anything, more than his men, and now Ted Lavender was dead because he loved her so much and could not stop thinking about her. When the dustoff arrived, they carried Lavender aboard. Afterward they burned Than Khe. They marched until dusk, then dug their holes, and that night Kiowa kept explaining how you had to be there, how fast it was, how the poor guy just dropped like so much concrete. Boom-down, he said. Like cement.

In addition to the three standard weapons — the M-60, M-16, and M-79 — they carried whatever presented itself, or whatever seemed appropriate as a means of killing or staying alive. They carried catch-as-catch-can. At various times, in various situations, they carried M-14s and CAR-15s and Swedish Ks and grease guns and captured AK-47s and Chi-Coms and RPGs and Simonov carbines and black market Uzis and .38-caliber Smith & Wesson handguns and 66 mm LAWS and shotguns and silencers and blackjacks and bayonets and C-4 plastic explosives. Lee Strunk carried a slingshot; a weapon of last resort, he called it. Mitchell Sanders carried brass knuckles. Kiowa carried his grandfather's feathered hatchet. Every third or fourth man carried a Claymore antipersonnel mine — 3.5 pounds with its firing device. They all carried fragmentation grenades — 14 ounces each. They all carried at least one M-18 colored smoke grenade — 24 ounces. Some carried CS or tear gas grenades. Some carried white phosphorus grenades. They carried all they could bear, and then some, including a silent awe for the terrible power of the things they carried.

In the first week of April, before Lavender died, Lieutenant Jimmy Cross received a good-luck charm from Martha. It was a simple pebble, an ounce at most. Smooth to the touch, it was a milky white color with flecks of orange and violet, oval-shaped, like a miniature egg. In the accompanying letter, Martha wrote that she had found the pebble on the Jersey shoreline, precisely where the land touched water at high tide, where things came together but also separated. It was this separate-but-together quality, she wrote, that had inspired her to pick up the pebble and to carry it in her breast pocket for several days, where it seemed weightless, and then to send it through the mail, by air, as a token of her truest feelings for him. Lieutenant Cross found this romantic. But he wondered what her truest feelings were, exactly, and what she meant by separate-but-together. He wondered how the tides and waves had come into play on that afternoon along the Jersey shoreline when Martha saw the pebble and bent down to rescue it from geology. He imagined bare feet. Martha was a poet, with the poet's sensibilities, and her feet would be brown and bare, the toenails unpainted, the eyes chilly and somber like

---

8. **KIA:** Killed in action.

the ocean in March, and though it was painful, he wondered who had been with her that afternoon. He imagined a pair of shadows moving along the strip of sand where things came together but also separated. It was phantom jealousy, he knew, but he couldn't help himself. He loved her so much. On the march, through the hot days of early April, he carried the pebble in his mouth, turning it with his tongue, tasting sea salt and moisture. His mind wandered. He had difficulty keeping his attention on the war. On occasion he would yell at his men to spread out the column, to keep their eyes open, but then he would slip away into daydreams, just pretending, walking barefoot along the Jersey shore, with Martha, carrying nothing. He would feel himself rising. Sun and waves and gentle winds, all love and lightness.

What they carried varied by mission.

When a mission took them to the mountains, they carried mosquito netting, machetes, canvas tarps, and extra bug juice.

If a mission seemed especially hazardous, or if it involved a place they knew to be bad, they carried everything they could. In certain heavily mined AOs,[9] where the land was dense with Toe Poppers and Bouncing Betties,[10] they took turns humping a 28-pound mine detector. With its head-phones and big sensing plate, the equipment was a stress on the lower back and shoulders, awkward to handle, often useless because of the shrapnel in the earth, but they carried it anyway, partly for safety, partly for the illusion of safety.

On ambush, or other night missions, they carried peculiar little odds and ends. Kiowa always took along his New Testament and a pair of moccasins for silence. Dave Jensen carried night-sight vitamins high in carotene. Lee Strunk carried his slingshot; ammo, he claimed, would never be a problem. Rat Kiley carried brandy and M&M's candy. Until he was shot, Ted Lavender carried the starlight scope, which weighed 6.3 pounds with its aluminum carrying case. Henry Dobbins carried his girlfriend's pantyhose wrapped around his neck as a comforter. They all carried ghosts. When dark came, they would move out single file across the meadows and paddies to their ambush coordinates, where they would quietly set up the Claymores and lie down and spend the night waiting.

Other missions were more complicated and required special equipment. In mid-April, it was their mission to search out and destroy the elaborate tunnel complexes in the Than Khe area south of Chu Lai. To blow the tunnels, they carried one-pound blocks of pentrite high explosives, four blocks to a man, 68 pounds in all. They carried wiring, detonators, and battery-powered clackers. Dave Jensen carried earplugs. Most often, before blowing the tunnels, they were ordered by higher command to search them, which was considered bad news, but by and large they just shrugged and carried out orders. Because he was a big man, Henry Dobbins was excused from tunnel duty. The others would draw numbers. Before Lavender died there were 17 men in the platoon, and

---

9. **AOs:** Areas of operation.
10. **Toe Poppers and Bouncing Betties:** Small booby traps that explosively amputate toes or wound feet and antipersonnel mines from which a second charge is propelled upward and set to explode at about waist level.

whoever drew the number 17 would strip off his gear and crawl in headfirst with a flash-light and Lieutenant Cross's .45-caliber pistol. The rest of them would fan out as secu-rity. They would sit down or kneel, not facing the hole, listening to the ground beneath them, imagining cobwebs and ghosts, whatever was down there – the tunnel walls squeezing in – how the flashlight seemed impossibly heavy in the hand and how it was tunnel vision in the very strictest sense, compression in all ways, even time, and how you had to wiggle in – ass and elbows – a swallowed-up feeling – and how you found yourself worrying about odd things: Will your flashlight go dead? Do rats carry rabies? If you screamed, how far would the sound carry? Would your buddies hear it? Would they have the courage to drag you out? In some respects, though not many, the waiting was worse than the tunnel itself. Imagination was a killer.

On April 16, when Lee Strunk drew the number 17, he laughed and muttered some-thing and went down quickly. The morning was hot and very still. Not good, Kiowa said. He looked at the tunnel opening, then out across a dry paddy toward the village of Than Khe. Nothing moved. No clouds or birds or people. As they waited, the men smoked and drank Kool-Aid, not talking much, feeling sympathy for Lee Strunk but also feeling the luck of the draw. You win some, you lose some, said Mitchell Sanders, and sometimes you settle for a rain check. It was a tired line and no one laughed.

Henry Dobbins ate a tropical chocolate bar. Ted Lavender popped a tranquilizer and went off to pee.

After five minutes, Lieutenant Jimmy Cross moved to the tunnel, leaned down, and examined the darkness. Trouble, he thought – a cave-in maybe. And then suddenly, without willing it, he was thinking about Martha. The stresses and fractures, the quick collapse, the two of them buried alive under all that weight. Dense, crushing love. Kneel-ing, watching the hole, he tried to concentrate on Lee Strunk and the war, all the dan-gers, but his love was too much for him, he felt paralyzed, he wanted to sleep inside her lungs and breathe her blood and be smothered. He wanted her to be a virgin and not a virgin, all at once. He wanted to know her. Intimate secrets: Why poetry? Why so sad? Why that grayness in her eyes? Why so alone? Not lonely, just alone – riding her bike across campus or sitting off by herself in the cafeteria – even dancing, she danced alone – and it was the aloneness that filled him with love. He remembered telling her that one evening. How she nodded and looked away. And how, later, when he kissed her, she received the kiss without returning it, her eyes wide open, not afraid, not a virgin's eyes, just flat and uninvolved.

Lieutenant Cross gazed at the tunnel. But he was not there. He was buried with Martha under the white sand at the Jersey shore. They were pressed together, and the pebble in his mouth was her tongue. He was smiling. Vaguely, he was aware of how quiet the day was, the sullen paddies, yet he could not bring himself to worry about matters of security. He was beyond that. He was just a kid at war, in love. He was twenty-four years old. He couldn't help it.

A few moments later Lee Strunk crawled out of the tunnel. He came up grinning, filthy but alive. Lieutenant Cross nodded and closed his eyes while the others clapped Strunk on the back and made jokes about rising from the dead.

Worms, Rat Kiley said. Right out of the grave. Fuckin' zombie.

The men laughed. They all felt great relief.

Spook city, said Mitchell Sanders.

Lee Strunk made a funny ghost sound, a kind of moaning, yet very happy, and right then, when Strunk made that high happy moaning sound, when he went *Ahhooooo*, right then Ted Lavender was shot in the head on his way back from peeing. He lay with his mouth open. The teeth were broken. There was a swollen black bruise under his left eye. The cheekbone was gone. Oh shit, Rat Kiley said, the guy's dead. The guy's dead, he kept saying, which seemed profound — the guy's dead. I mean really.

The things they carried were determined to some extent by superstition. Lieutenant Cross carried his good-luck pebble. Dave Jensen carried a rabbit's foot. Norman Bowker, otherwise a very gentle person, carried a thumb that had been presented to him as a gift by Mitchell Sanders. The thumb was dark brown, rubbery to the touch, and weighed four ounces at most. It had been cut from a VC[11] corpse, a boy of fifteen or sixteen. They'd found him at the bottom of an irrigation ditch, badly burned, flies in his mouth and eyes. The boy wore black shorts and sandals. At the time of his death he had been carrying a pouch of rice, a rifle, and three magazines of ammunition.

You want my opinion, Mitchell Sanders said, there's a definite moral here.

He put his hand on the dead boy's wrist. He was quiet for a time, as if counting a pulse, then he patted the stomach, almost affectionately, and used Kiowa's hunting hatchet to remove the thumb.

Henry Dobbins asked what the moral was.

Moral?

You know. *Moral.*

Sanders wrapped the thumb in toilet paper and handed it across to Norman Bowker. There was no blood. Smiling, he kicked the boy's head, watched the flies scatter, and said, It's like with that old TV show — Paladin. Have gun, will travel.[12]

Henry Dobbins thought about it.

Yeah, well, he finally said. I don't see no moral.

There it *is*, man.

Fuck off.

They carried USO[13] stationery and pencils and pens. They carried Sterno, safety pins, trip flares, signal flares, spools of wire, razor blades, chewing tobacco, liberated joss sticks and statuettes of the smiling Buddha, candles, grease pencils, *The Stars and Stripes*, fingernail clippers, Psy Ops leaflets,[14] bush hats, bolos, and much more. Twice a week, when the resupply choppers came in, they carried hot chow in green mermite cans and large canvas bags filled with iced beer and soda pop. They carried plastic water

---

11. **VC:** Viet Cong.

12. **Have gun, will travel:** The motto of the man named "Paladin," a professional gunfighter in the popular western television series *Have Gun, Will Travel* (1957–63).

13. **USO:** United Service Organizations, a private organization that provides recreational and morale-boosting services to members of the military.

14. ***The Stars and Stripes*** . . . **Psy Ops leaflets:** A daily newspaper published for the U.S. military and leaflets dropped or distributed as part of psychological operations aimed at the enemy.

containers, each with a two-gallon capacity. Mitchell Sanders carried a set of starched tiger fatigues for special occasions. Henry Dobbins carried Black Flag insecticide. Dave Jensen carried empty sandbags that could be filled at night for added protection. Lee Strunk carried tanning lotion. Some things they carried in common. Taking turns, they carried the big PRC-77 scrambler radio, which weighed 30 pounds with its battery. They shared the weight of memory. They took up what others could no longer bear. Often, they carried each other, the wounded or weak. They carried infections. They carried chess sets, basketballs, Vietnamese-English dictionaries, insignia of rank, Bronze Stars and Purple Hearts, plastic cards imprinted with the Code of Conduct. They carried diseases, among them malaria and dysentery. They carried lice and ringworm and leeches and paddy algae and various rots and molds. They carried the land itself — Vietnam, the place, the soil — a powdery orange-red dust that covered their boots and fatigues and faces. They carried the sky. The whole atmosphere, they carried it, the humidity, the monsoons, the stink of fungus and decay, all of it, they carried gravity. They moved like mules. By daylight they took sniper fire, at night they were mortared, but it was not battle, it was just the endless march, village to village, without purpose, nothing won or lost. They marched for the sake of the march. They plodded along slowly, dumbly, leaning forward against the heat, unthinking, all blood and bone, simple grunts, soldiering with their legs, toiling up the hills and down into the paddies and across the rivers and up again and down, just humping, one step and then the next and then another, but no volition, no will, because it was automatic, it was anatomy, and the war was entirely a matter of posture and carriage, the hump was everything, a kind of inertia, a kind of emptiness, a dullness of desire and intellect and conscience and hope and human sensibility. Their principles were in their feet. Their calculations were biological. They had no sense of strategy or mission. They searched the villages without knowing what to look for, not caring, kicking over jars of rice, frisking children and old men, blowing tunnels, sometimes setting fires and sometimes not, then forming up and moving on to the next village, then other villages, where it would always be the same. They carried their own lives. The pressures were enormous. In the heat of early afternoon, they would remove their helmets and flak jackets, walking bare, which was dangerous but which helped ease the strain. They would often discard things along the route of march. Purely for comfort, they would throw away rations, blow their Claymores and grenades, no matter, because by nightfall the resupply choppers would arrive with more of the same, then a day or two later still more, fresh watermelons and crates of ammunition and sunglasses and woolen sweaters — the resources were stunning — sparklers for the Fourth of July, colored eggs for Easter — it was the great American war chest — the fruits of science, the smokestacks, the canneries, the arsenals at Hartford, the Minnesota forests, the machine shops, the vast fields of corn and wheat — they carried like freight trains; they carried it on their backs and shoulders — and for all the ambiguities of Vietnam, all the mysteries and unknowns, there was at least the single abiding certainty that they would never be at a loss for things to carry.

After the chopper took Lavender away, Lieutenant Jimmy Cross led his men into the village of Than Khe. They burned everything. They shot chickens and dogs, they trashed the village well, they called in artillery and watched the wreckage, then they marched for several hours through the hot afternoon, and then at dusk, while Kiowa explained how Lavender died, Lieutenant Cross found himself trembling.

He tried not to cry. With his entrenching tool, which weighed five pounds, he began digging a hole in the earth.

He felt shame. He hated himself. He had loved Martha more than his men, and as a consequence Lavender was now dead, and this was something he would have to carry like a stone in his stomach for the rest of the war.

All he could do was dig. He used his entrenching tool like an ax, slashing, feeling both love and hate, and then later, when it was full dark, he sat at the bottom of his foxhole and wept. It went on for a long while. In part, he was grieving for Ted Lavender, but mostly it was for Martha, and for himself, because she belonged to another world, which was not quite real, and because she was a junior at Mount Sebastian College in New Jersey, a poet and a virgin and uninvolved, and because he realized she did not love him and never would.

Like cement, Kiowa whispered in the dark. I swear to God — boom, down. Not a word.

I've heard this, said Norman Bowker.

A pisser, you know? Still zipping himself up. Zapped while zipping.

All right, fine. That's enough.

Yeah, but you had to see it, the guy just —

I *heard*, man. Cement. So why not shut the fuck *up*?

Kiowa shook his head sadly and glanced over at the hole where Lieutenant Jimmy Cross sat watching the night. The air was thick and wet. A warm dense fog had settled over the paddies and there was the stillness that precedes rain.

After a time Kiowa sighed.

One thing for sure, he said. The lieutenant's in some deep hurt. I mean that crying jag — the way he was carrying on — it wasn't fake or anything, it was real heavy-duty hurt. The man cares.

Sure, Norman Bowker said.

Say what you want, the man does care.

We all got problems.

Not Lavender.

No, I guess not, Bowker said. Do me a favor, though.

Shut up?

That's a smart Indian. Shut up.

Shrugging, Kiowa pulled off his boots. He wanted to say more, just to lighten up his sleep, but instead he opened his New Testament and arranged it beneath his head as a pillow. The fog made things seem hollow and unattached. He tried not to think about Ted Lavender, but then he was thinking how fast it was, no drama, down and dead, and how it was hard to feel anything except surprise. It seemed unchristian. He wished he could find some great sadness, or even anger, but the emotion wasn't there and he couldn't make it happen. Mostly he felt pleased to be alive. He liked the smell of the New Testament under his cheek, the leather and ink and paper and glue, whatever the chemicals were. He liked hearing the sounds of night. Even his fatigue, it felt fine, the stiff muscles and the prickly awareness of his own body, a floating feeling. He enjoyed not being dead. Lying there, Kiowa admired Lieutenant Jimmy Cross's capacity for grief. He wanted to share the man's pain, he wanted to care as Jimmy Cross cared. And yet when he closed his eyes, all he could think was Boom-down, and all he could feel was the pleasure of having his boots off and the fog curling in around him and the damp soil and the Bible smells and the plush comfort of night.

After a moment Norman Bowker sat up in the dark.

What the hell, he said. You want to talk, *talk.* Tell it to me.

Forget it.

No, man, go on. One thing I hate, it's a silent Indian.

For the most part they carried themselves with poise, a kind of dignity. Now and then, however, there were times of panic, when they squealed or wanted to squeal but couldn't, when they twitched and made moaning sounds and covered their heads and said Dear Jesus and flopped around on the earth and fired their weapons blindly and cringed and sobbed and begged for the noise to stop and went wild and made stupid promises to themselves and to God and to their mothers and fathers, hoping not to die. In different ways, it happened to all of them. Afterward, when the firing ended, they would blink and peek up. They would touch their bodies, feeling shame, then quickly hiding it. They would force themselves to stand. As if in slow motion, frame by frame, the world would take on the old logic — absolute silence, then the wind, then sunlight, then voices. It was the burden of being alive. Awkwardly, the men would reassemble them-selves, first in private, then in groups, becoming soldiers again. They would repair the leaks in their eyes. They would check for casualties, call in dustoffs, light cigarettes, try to smile, clear their throats and spit and begin cleaning their weapons. After a time someone would shake his head and say, No lie, I almost shit my pants, and someone else would laugh, which meant it was bad, yes, but the guy had obviously not shit his pants, it wasn't that bad, and in any case nobody would ever do such a thing and then go ahead and talk about it. They would squint into the dense, oppressive sunlight. For a few moments, perhaps, they would fall silent, lighting a joint and tracking its passage from man to man, inhaling, holding in the humiliation. Scary stuff, one of them might say. But then someone else would grin or flick his eyebrows and say, Roger-dodger, almost cut me a new asshole, *almost.*

There were numerous such poses. Some carried themselves with a sort of wistful res-ignation, others with pride or stiff soldierly discipline or good humor or macho zeal. They were afraid of dying but they were even more afraid to show it.

They found jokes to tell.

They used a hard vocabulary to contain the terrible softness. *Greased* they'd say. *Offed, lit up, zapped while zipping.* It wasn't cruelty, just stage presence. They were actors. When someone died, it wasn't quite dying, because in a curious way it seemed scripted, and because they had their lines mostly memorized, irony mixed with tragedy, and because they called it by other names, as if to encyst and destroy the reality of death itself. They kicked corpses. They cut off thumbs. They talked grunt lingo. They told stories about Ted Lavender's supply of tranquilizers, how the poor guy didn't feel a thing, how incredibly tranquil he was.

There's a moral here, said Mitchell Sanders.

They were waiting for Lavender's chopper, smoking the dead man's dope.

The moral's pretty obvious, Sanders said, and winked. Stay away from drugs. No joke, they'll ruin your day every time.

Cute, said Henry Dobbins.

Mind blower, get it? Talk about wiggy. Nothing left, just blood and brains.

They made themselves laugh.

There it is, they'd say. Over and over — there it is, my friend, there it is — as if the repetition itself were an act of poise, a balance between crazy and almost crazy, knowing without going, there it is, which meant be cool, let it ride, because Oh yeah, man, you can't change what can't be changed, there it is, there it absolutely and positively and fucking well *is*.

They were tough.

They carried all the emotional baggage of men who might die. Grief, terror, love, longing — these were intangibles, but the intangibles had their own mass and specific gravity, they had tangible weight. They carried shameful memories. They carried the common secret of cowardice barely restrained, the instinct to run or freeze or hide, and in many respects this was the heaviest burden of all, for it could never be put down, it required perfect balance and perfect posture. They carried their reputations. They carried the soldier's greatest fear, which was the fear of blushing. Men killed, and died, because they were embarrassed not to. It was what had brought them to the war in the first place, nothing positive, no dreams of glory or honor, just to avoid the blush of dishonor. They died so as not to die of embarrassment. They crawled into tunnels and walked point and advanced under fire. Each morning, despite the unknowns, they made their legs move. They endured. They kept humping. They did not submit to the obvious alternative, which was simply to close the eyes and fall. So easy, really. Go limp and tumble to the ground and let the muscles unwind and not speak and not budge until your buddies picked you up and lifted you into the chopper that would roar and dip its nose and carry you off to the world. A mere matter of falling, yet no one ever fell. It was not courage, exactly; the object was not valor. Rather, they were too frightened to be cowards.

By and large they carried these things inside, maintaining the masks of composure. They sneered at sick call. They spoke bitterly about guys who had found release by shooting off their own toes or fingers. Pussies, they'd say. Candy-asses. It was fierce, mocking talk, with only a trace of envy or awe, but even so the image played itself out behind their eyes.

They imagined the muzzle against flesh. So easy: squeeze the trigger and blow away a toe. They imagined it. They imagined the quick, sweet pain, then the evacuation to Japan, then a hospital with warm beds and cute geisha nurses.

And they dreamed of freedom birds.

At night, on guard, staring into the dark, they were carried away by jumbo jets. They felt the rush of takeoff. *Gone!* they yelled. And then velocity — wings and engines — a smiling stewardess — but it was more than a plane, it was a real bird, a big sleek silver bird with feathers and talons and high screeching. They were flying. The weights fell off; there was nothing to bear. They laughed and held on tight, feeling the cold slap of wind and altitude, soaring, thinking *It's over, I'm gone!* — they were naked, they were light and free — it was all lightness, bright and fast and buoyant, light as light, a helium buzz in the brain, a giddy bubbling in the lungs as they were taken up over the clouds and the war, beyond duty, beyond gravity and mortification and global entanglements — *Sin loi!* [15] they yelled. *I'm sorry, motherfuckers, but I'm out of it, I'm goofed, I'm on a space cruise, I'm gone!* — and it was a restful, unencumbered sensation, just riding the light waves, sailing that big silver freedom bird over the mountains and oceans, over America, over the farms and great sleeping cities and cemeteries and highways and the golden arches of McDonald's, it was flight, a kind of fleeing, a kind of falling, falling higher and higher, spinning off the edge of the earth and beyond the sun and through the vast, silent vacuum where there were no burdens and where everything weighed exactly nothing — *Gone!* they screamed. *I'm sorry but I'm gone!* — and so at night, not quite dreaming, they gave themselves over to lightness, they were carried, they were purely borne.

On the morning after Ted Lavender died, First Lieutenant Jimmy Cross crouched at the bottom of his foxhole and burned Martha's letters. Then he burned the two photographs. There was a steady rain falling, which made it difficult, but he used heat tabs and Sterno to build a small fire, screening it with his body, holding the photographs over the tight blue flame with the tips of his fingers.

He realized it was only a gesture. Stupid, he thought. Sentimental, too, but mostly just stupid.

Lavender was dead. You couldn't burn the blame.

Besides, the letters were in his head. And even now, without photographs, Lieutenant Cross could see Martha playing volleyball in her white gym shorts and yellow T-shirt. He could see her moving in the rain.

When the fire died out, Lieutenant Cross pulled his poncho over his shoulders and ate breakfast from a can.

There was no great mystery, he decided.

In those burned letters Martha had never mentioned the war, except to say, Jimmy, take care of yourself. She wasn't involved. She signed the letters Love, but it wasn't love, and all the fine lines and technicalities did not matter. Virginity was no longer an issue. He hated her. Yes, he did. He hated her. Love, too, but it was a hard, hating kind of love.

The morning came up wet and blurry. Everything seemed part of everything else, the fog and Martha and the deepening rain.

---

15. **Sin loi!:** I'm sorry! (Vietnamese).

He was a soldier, after all.

Half smiling, Lieutenant Jimmy Cross took out his maps. He shook his head hard, as if to clear it, then bent forward and began planning the day's march. In ten minutes, or maybe twenty, he would rouse the men and they would pack up and head west, where the maps showed the country to be green and inviting. They would do what they had always done. The rain might add some weight, but otherwise it would be one more day layered upon all the other days.

He was realistic about it. There was that new hardness in his stomach. He loved her but he hated her.

No more fantasies, he told himself.

Henceforth, when he thought about Martha, it would be only to think that she belonged elsewhere. He would shut down the daydreams. This was not Mount Sebastian, it was another world, where there were no pretty poems or midterm exams, a place where men died because of carelessness and gross stupidity. Kiowa was right. Boom-down, and you were dead, never partly dead.

Briefly, in the rain, Lieutenant Cross saw Martha's gray eyes gazing back at him.

He understood.

It was very sad, he thought. The things men carried inside. The things men did or felt they had to do.

He almost nodded at her, but didn't.

Instead he went back to his maps. He was now determined to perform his duties firmly and without negligence. It wouldn't help Lavender, he knew that, but from this point on he would comport himself as an officer. He would dispose of his good-luck pebble. Swallow it, maybe, or use Lee Strunk's slingshot, or just drop it along the trail. On the march he would impose strict field discipline. He would be careful to send out flank security, to prevent straggling or bunching up, to keep his troops moving at the proper pace and at the proper interval. He would insist on clean weapons. He would con-fiscate the remainder of Lavender's dope. Later in the day, perhaps, he would call the men together and speak to them plainly. He would accept the blame for what had hap-pened to Ted Lavender. He would be a man about it. He would look them in the eyes, keeping his chin level, and he would issue the new SOPs in a calm, impersonal tone of voice, a lieutenant's voice, leaving no room for argument or discussion. Commencing immediately, he'd tell them, they would no longer abandon equipment along the route of march. They would police up their acts. They would get their shit together, and keep it together, and maintain it neatly and in good working order.

He would not tolerate laxity. He would show strength, distancing himself.

Among the men there would be grumbling, of course, and maybe worse, because their days would seem longer and their loads heavier, but Lieutenant Jimmy Cross reminded himself that his obligation was not to be loved but to lead. He would dispense with love; it was not now a factor. And if anyone quarreled or complained, he would simply tighten his lips and arrange his shoulders in the correct command posture. He might give a curt little nod. Or he might not. He might just shrug and say, Carry on, then they would saddle up and form into a column and move out toward the villages west of Than Khe.

[1986, 1990]

Leslie Marmon Silko

[b. 1948]

Leslie Marmon Silko was born on March 5, 1948, in Albuquerque, New Mexico, to Leland Howard Marmon, a photographer, and Mary Virginia Leslie Marmon, who lived on the Laguna Pueblo Reservation about fifty miles west

Leslie Marmon Silko

LaVerne Harrell Clark took this photograph of Silko in 1992, following her presentation at a literary festival featuring Native American writers at the University of Arizona.

of Albuquerque. "We are mixed bloods — Laguna, Mexican, and white," Silko affirmed in 1975. "All those languages, all those ways of living are combined, and live somewhere on the fringes of all three. But I don't apologize for this any more — not to whites, not to full bloods — our origin is unlike any other. My poetry, my storytelling, rise out of this source." In the matriarchal and matrilineal society of the Laguna, Silko lived in an extended family that included her grandmothers and aunts, who spoke the original language of the Santa Ana Pueblo. Silko grew up listening to their stories and learning to ride a horse, to hunt, and to herd cattle. She attended an Indian boarding school and later a Roman Catholic school in Albuquerque. Partly in rebellion against the strict rules of the school, Silko created and designed her own magazine, *Nasty Asty*, in which she published an off-color joke that had been circulating throughout the school. As she recalled, she was nearly expelled for the incident, which taught her an important lesson about the weight and power of the written word. In 1964, Silko enrolled at the University of New Mexico. She was married briefly to Richard C. Chapman, with whom she had a son. Following her graduation in 1969, the year she published her first short story, she enrolled in the university's American Indian Law School Fellowship Program.

Disillusioned by the treatment of minorities under the American legal system, Silko determined to use her abilities at storytelling as a means of fighting injustice in the United States. She left law school and began graduate work in English at the University of New Mexico. In 1971, she took a job as a teacher at a community college on a Navaho reservation in Arizona. That year, she was awarded a National Endowment for the Arts Discovery Grant, which freed her for writing, and she met and married John Silko. The year after their son was born in 1972, they moved to Ketchikan, Alaska, where Silko's husband worked for Alaska Legal Services. Although she found the climate and geography difficult to endure, her years there were very productive. In 1974, she published six stories, including one of her most widely read works, "Yellow Woman," as well as her first collection of poetry, *Laguna Woman: Poems* (1974). After she returned to the Laguna Pueblo, she was awarded the prestigious Pushcart Prize for Poetry in 1977. That year, she published her novel *Ceremony* (1977), a moving account of a traumatized Native American veteran who returns to the Southwest after being held in a Japanese prisoner of war camp during World War II. In 1978, Silko accepted an invitation to teach creative writing at the University of Arizona. She began corresponding with the poet James Wright, with whom she became close professional friends until his death from cancer in 1980. His widow, Anne Wright, edited a prize-winning collection of their letters, *With the Delicacy and Strength of Lace: Letters Between Leslie Marmon Silko and James Wright* (1986).

Silko's later works reveal her growing interest in history, mythology, and the interplay among writing, oral storytelling, and images. In 1978, she was filmed in conversation with other writers, reading her works, and telling stories in a video issued by the University of Arizona, *Running on the Edge of the Rainbow: Laguna Stories and Poems.* Silko subsequently founded the Laguna Film Project, and in 1980 she and Denis Carr produced a film entitled *Estoyehmuut and the Gunnadeyah* ("Arrowboy and the Destroyers"). She wove together stories, poems, and family photographs in her acclaimed collection *Storyteller* (1981). Although her personal life was clouded by the collapse of her second marriage, Silko was awarded a prestigious MacArthur Prize Fellowship, the so-called genius grant, which provided funding for five years of creative work. Silko spent the decade researching and writing her controversial novel *Almanac of the Dead* (1991), the apocalyptic story of a revolt in which indigenous peoples seek to regain their ancestral lands from corrupt whites after centuries of brutal exploitation by the European conquerors of the Americas. Silko's recent works include *Sacred Water* (1993), a collection of photographs and essays about the ecology of southern Arizona; *Yellow Woman and a Beauty of the Spirit: Essays on Native American Life Today* (1996); and *Gardens in the Dunes* (1999), a historical novel about the far-ranging travels of two displaced Native American girls who seek to return to their home in the Southwest. A recipient of the Native Writers' Circle of the Americas award for lifetime achievement, Silko lives on her ranch near Tucson, Arizona.

Silko's "Yellow Woman." This story, which was first published in the anthology *The Man to Send Rain Clouds: Contemporary Stories by American Indians* (1974), is regarded by many readers as Silko's defining work. Inspired by stories she heard as a child growing up in the Laguna Pueblo Reservation about Yellow Woman, or Kochininako, the story is told by a woman who wanders off, meets and is seduced by a mysterious man, and accompanies him into the mountains before returning home to her husband, child, and family. The seemingly simple and straightforward narrative raises complex questions, as the narrator seeks to come to terms with her identity, her sexuality, and her place in the world. Rejecting narrowly feminist readings of the story, Silko told a reviewer in 1986:

> The kinds of things that cause white upper-middle-class women to flee the home for a while to escape or get away from domination and powerlessness and inferior status, vis-à-vis the husband, and the male, those kinds of

bedfordstmartins.com/ ***americanlit*** *for research links on Silko*

forces are not operating, they're not operating at all. What's operating in those stories of Kochininako is this attraction, this passion, this connection between the human world and the animal and spirit worlds.

In the story, Silko also explores the nature and function of storytelling, which in Laguna culture, she has observed, is "a whole way of seeing yourself, the people around you, your life, the place of your life in the bigger context, not just in terms of nature and location but in terms of what has gone on before, what's happened to other people. It's a whole way of being." The text is taken from Silko's collection *Storyteller* (1981).

Yellow Woman

What Whirlwind Man Told Kochininako, Yellow Woman[1]
    I myself belong to the wind
    and so it is we will travel swiftly
    this whole world
    with dust and with windstorms.

My thigh clung to his with dampness, and I watched the sun rising up through the tamaracks and willows.[2] The small brown water birds came to the river and hopped across the mud, leaving brown scratches in the alkali-white crust. They bathed in the river silently. I could hear the water, almost at our feet where the narrow fast channel bubbled and washed green ragged moss and fern leaves. I looked at him beside me, rolled in the red blanket on the white river sand. I cleaned the sand out of the cracks between my toes, squinting because the sun was above the willow trees. I looked at him for the last time, sleeping on the white river sand.

I felt hungry and followed the river south the way we had come the afternoon before, following our footprints that were already blurred by lizard tracks and bug trails. The horses were still lying down, and the black one whinnied when he saw me but he did not get up — maybe it was because the corral was made out of thick cedar branches and the horses had not yet felt the sun like I had. I tried to look beyond the pale red mesas to the pueblo.[3] I knew it was there, even if I could not see it, on the sandrock hill above the river, the same river that moved past me now and had reflected the moon last night.

The horse felt warm underneath me. He shook his head and pawed the sand. The bay whinnied and leaned against the gate trying to follow, and I remembered him asleep in the red blanket beside the river. I slid off the horse and tied him close to the other horse, I walked north with the river again, and the white sand broke loose in footprints over footprints.

---

1. **Kochininako, Yellow Woman:** Many stories about this powerful female figure, always told from her point of view, are part of the Laguna and Acoma Pueblo cultures of New Mexico.
2. **tamaracks and willows:** Trees that flourish in boggy areas and on river banks.
3. **pueblo:** Village (Spanish), usually used to denote a Native American settlement of adobe houses built by one of several groups of Pueblo people in the Southwest.

"Wake up."

He moved in the blanket and turned his face to me with his eyes still closed. I knelt down to touch him.

"I'm leaving."

He smiled now, eyes still closed. "You are coming with me, remember?" He sat up now with his bare dark chest and belly in the sun.

"Where?"

"To my place."

"And will I come back?"

He pulled his pants on. I walked away from him, feeling him behind me and smelling the willows.

"Yellow Woman," he said.

I turned to face him. "Who are you?" I asked.

He laughed and knelt on the low, sandy bank, washing his face in the river. "Last night you guessed my name, and you knew why I had come."

I stared past him at the shallow moving water and tried to remember the night, but I could only see the moon in the water and remember his warmth around me.

"But I only said that you were him and that I was Yellow Woman — I'm not really her — I have my own name and I come from the pueblo on the other side of the mesa. Your name is Silva and you are a stranger I met by the river yesterday afternoon."

He laughed softly. "What happened yesterday has nothing to do with what you will do today, Yellow Woman."

"I know — that's what I'm saying — the old stories about the ka'tsina spirit[4] and Yellow Woman can't mean us."

My old grandpa liked to tell those stories best. There is one about Badger and Coyote who went hunting and were gone all day, and when the sun was going down they found a house. There was a girl living there alone, and she had light hair and eyes and she told them that they could sleep with her. Coyote wanted to be with her all night so he sent Badger into a prairie-dog hole, telling him he thought he saw something in it. As soon as Badger crawled in, Coyote blocked up the entrance with rocks and hurried back to Yellow Woman.

"Come here," he said gently.

He touched my neck and I moved close to him to feel his breathing and to hear his heart. I was wondering if Yellow Woman had known who she was — if she knew that she would become part of the stories. Maybe she'd had another name that her husband and relatives called her so that only the ka'tsina from the north and the storytellers would know her as Yellow Woman. But I didn't go on; I felt him all around me, pushing me down into the white river sand.

Yellow Woman went away with the spirit from the north and lived with him and his relatives. She was gone for a long time, but then one day she came back and she brought twin boys.

---

4. **ka'tsina spirit:** According to Pueblo mythology, the ka'tsina is a good spirit, closely associated with water or rain, who selects a female figure and endows her with special powers.

"Do you know the story?"

"What story?" He smiled and pulled me close to him as he said this. I was afraid lying there on the red blanket. All I could know was the way he felt, warm, damp, his body beside me. This is the way it happens in the stories, I was thinking, with no thought beyond the moment she meets the ka'tsina spirit and they go.

"I don't have to go. What they tell in stories was real only then, back in time immemorial, like they say."

He stood up and pointed at my clothes tangled in the blanket. "Let's go," he said.

I walked beside him, breathing hard because he walked fast, his hand around my wrist. I had stopped trying to pull away from him, because his hand felt cool and the sun was high, drying the river bed into alkali. I will see someone, eventually I will see someone, and then I will be certain that he is only a man — some man from nearby — and I will be sure that I am not Yellow Woman. Because she is from out of time past and I live now and I've been to school and there are highways and pickup trucks that Yellow Woman never saw.

It was an easy ride north on horseback. I watched the change from the cottonwood trees along the river to the junipers that brushed past us in the foothills, and finally there were only piñons, and when I looked up at the rim of the mountain plateau I could see pine trees growing on the edge. Once I stopped to look down, but the pale sandstone had disappeared and the river was gone and the dark lava hills were all around. He touched my hand, not speaking, but always singing softly a mountain song and looking into my eyes.

I felt hungry and wondered what they were doing at home now — my mother, my grandmother, my husband, and the baby. Cooking breakfast, saying, "Where did she go? — maybe kidnapped." And Al going to the tribal police with the details: "She went walking along the river."

The house was made with black lava rock and red mud. It was high above the spreading miles of arroyos and long mesas. I smelled a mountain smell of pitch and buck brush. I stood there beside the black horse, looking down on the small, dim country we had passed, and I shivered.

"Yellow Woman, come inside where it's warm." He lit a fire in the stove. It was an old stove with a round belly and an enamel coffeepot on top. There was only the stove, some faded Navajo blankets, and a bedroll and cardboard box. The floor was made of smooth adobe plaster, and there was one small window facing east. He pointed at the box.

"There's some potatoes and the frying pan." He sat on the floor with his arms around his knees pulling them close to his chest and he watched me fry the potatoes. I didn't mind him watching me because he was always watching me — he had been watching me since I came upon him sitting on the river bank trimming leaves from a willow twig with his knife. We ate from the pan and he wiped the grease from his fingers on his Levi's.

"Have you brought women here before?" He smiled and kept chewing, so I said, "Do you always use the same tricks?"

"What tricks?" He looked at me like he didn't understand.

"The story about being a ka'tsina from the mountains. The story about Yellow Woman."

Silva was silent; his face was calm.

"I don't believe it. Those stories couldn't happen now," I said.

He shook his head and said softly, "But someday they will talk about us, and they will say, 'Those two lived long ago when things like that happened.'"

He stood up and went out. I ate the rest of the potatoes and thought about things — about the noise the stove was making and the sound of the mountain wind outside. I remembered yesterday and the day before, and then I went outside.

I walked past the corral to the edge where the narrow trail cut through the black rim rock, I was standing in the sky with nothing around me but the wind that came down from the blue mountain peak behind me. I could see faint mountain images in the distance miles across the vast spread of mesas and valleys and plains. I wondered who was over there to feel the mountain wind on those sheer blue edges — who walks on the pine needles in those blue mountains.

"Can you see the pueblo?" Silva was standing behind me.

I shook my head. "We're too far away."

"From here I can see the world." He stepped out on the edge. "The Navajo reservation begins over there." He pointed to the east. "The Pueblo boundaries are over here." He looked below us to the south, where the narrow trail seemed to come from. "The Texans have their ranches over there, starting with that valley, the Concho Valley. The Mexicans run some cattle over there too."

"Do you ever work for them?"

"I steal from them," Silva answered. The sun was dropping behind us and the shadows were filling the land below. I turned away from the edge that dropped forever into the valleys below.

"I'm cold," I said, "I'm going inside." I started wondering about this man who could speak the Pueblo language so well but who lived on a mountain and rustled cattle. I decided that this man Silva must be Navajo, because Pueblo men didn't do things like that.

"You must be a Navajo."

Silva shook his head gently. "Little Yellow Woman," he said, "you never give up, do you? I have told you who I am. The Navajo people know me, too." He knelt down and unrolled the bedroll and spread the extra blankets out on a piece of canvas. The sun was down, and the only light in the house came from outside — the dim orange light from sundown.

I stood there and waited for him to crawl under the blankets.

"What are you waiting for?" he said, and I lay down beside him. He undressed me slowly like the night before beside the river — kissing my face gently and running his hands up and down my belly and legs. He took off my pants and then he laughed.

"Why are you laughing?"

"You are breathing so hard."

I pulled away from him and turned my back to him.

He pulled me around and pinned me down with his arms and chest. "You don't understand, do you, little Yellow Woman? You will do what I want."

And again he was all around me with his skin slippery against mine, and I was afraid because I understood that his strength could hurt me. I lay underneath him and I knew that he could destroy me. But later, while he slept beside me, I touched his face and I had a feeling — the kind of feeling for him that overcame me that morning along the river. I kissed him on the forehead and he reached out for me.

When I woke up in the morning he was gone. It gave me a strange feeling because for a long time I sat there on the blankets and looked around the little house for some object of his — some proof that he had been there or maybe that he was coming back. Only the blankets and the cardboard box remained. The .30-30 that had been leaning in the corner was gone, and so was the knife I had used the night before. He was gone, and I had my chance to go now. But first I had to eat, because I knew it would be a long walk home.

I found some dried apricots in the cardboard box, and I sat down on a rock at the edge of the plateau rim. There was no wind and the sun warmed me. I was surrounded by silence. I drowsed with apricots in my mouth, and I didn't believe that there were highways or railroads or cattle to steal.

When I woke up, I stared down at my feet in the black mountain dirt. Little black ants were swarming over the pine needles around my foot. They must have smelled the apricots. I thought about my family far below me. They would be wondering about me, because this had never happened to me before. The tribal police would file a report. But if old Grandpa weren't dead he would tell them what happened — he would laugh and say, "Stolen by a ka'tsina, a mountain spirit. She'll come home — they usually do." There are enough of them to handle things. My mother and grandmother will raise the baby like they raised me. Al will find someone else, and they will go on like before, except that there will be a story about the day I disappeared while I was walking along the river. Silva had come for me; he said he had. I did not decide to go. I just went. Moon-flowers blossom in the sand hills before dawn, just as I followed him. That's what I was thinking as I wandered along the trail through the pine trees.

It was noon when I got back. When I saw the stone house I remembered that I had meant to go home. But that didn't seem important any more, maybe because there were little blue flowers growing in the meadow behind the stone house and the gray squirrels were playing in the pines next to the house. The horses were standing in the corral, and there was a beef carcass hanging on the shady side of a big pine in front of the house. Flies buzzed around the clotted blood that hung from the carcass. Silva was washing his hands in a bucket full of water. He must have heard me coming because he spoke to me without turning to face me.

"I've been waiting for you."

"I went walking in the big pine trees."

I looked into the bucket full of bloody water with brown-and-white animal hairs floating in it. Silva stood there letting his hand drip, examining me intently.

"Are you coming with me?"

"Where?" I asked him.

"To sell the meat in Marquez."⁵

"If you're sure it's O.K."

"I wouldn't ask you if it wasn't," he answered.

---

5. **Marquez:** A town north of the Laguna pueblo in New Mexico.

He sloshed the water around in the bucket before he dumped it out and set the bucket upside down near the door. I followed him to the corral and watched him saddle the horses. Even beside the horses he looked tall, and I asked him again if he wasn't Navajo. He didn't say anything; he just shook his head and kept cinching up the saddle.

"But Navajos are tall."

"Get on the horse," he said, "and let's go."

The last thing he did before we started down the steep trail was to grab the .30-30 from the corner. He slid the rifle into the scabbard that hung from his saddle.

"Do they ever try to catch you?" I asked.

"They don't know who I am."

"Then why did you bring the rifle?"

"Because we are going to Marquez where the Mexicans live."

The trail leveled out on a narrow ridge that was steep on both sides like an animal spine. On one side I could see where the trail went around the rocky gray hills and disappeared into the southeast where the pale sandrock mesas stood in the distance near my home. On the other side was a trail that went west, and as I looked far into the distance I thought I saw the little town. But Silva said no, that I was looking in the wrong place, that I just thought I saw houses. After that I quit looking off into the distance; it was hot and the wildflowers were closing up their deep-yellow petals. Only the waxy cactus flowers bloomed in the bright sun, and I saw every color that a cactus blossom can be; the white ones and the red ones were still buds, but the purple and the yellow were blossoms, open full and the most beautiful of all.

Silva saw him before I did. The white man was riding a big gray horse, coming up the trail towards us. He was traveling fast and the gray horse's feet sent rocks rolling off the trail into the dry tumbleweeds. Silva motioned for me to stop and we watched the white man. He didn't see us right away, but finally his horse whinnied at our horses, and he stopped. He looked at us briefly before he lapped the gray horse across the three hundred yards that separated us. He stopped his horse in front of Silva, and his young fat face was shadowed by the brim of his hat. He didn't look mad, but his small, pale eyes moved from the blood-soaked gunny sacks hanging from my saddle to Silva's face and then back to my face.

"Where did you get the fresh meat?" the white man asked.

"I've been hunting," Silva said, and when he shifted his weight in the saddle the leather creaked.

"The hell you have, Indian. You've been rustling cattle. We've been looking for the thief for a long time."

The rancher was fat, and sweat began to soak through his white cowboy shirt and the wet cloth stuck to the thick rolls of belly fat. He almost seemed to be panting from the exertion of talking, and he smelled rancid, maybe because Silva scared him.

Silva turned to me and smiled. "Go back up the mountain, Yellow Woman."

The white man got angry when he heard Silva speak in a language he couldn't understand. "Don't try anything, Indian. Just keep riding to Marquez. We'll call the state police from there."

The rancher must have been unarmed because he was very frightened and if he had a gun he would have pulled it out then. I turned my horse around and the rancher yelled, "Stop!" I looked at Silva for an instant and there was something ancient and dark — something I could feel in my stomach — in his eyes, and when I glanced at his hand I saw his finger on the trigger of the .30-30 that was still in the saddle scabbard. I slapped my horse across the flank and the sacks of raw meat swung against my knees as the horse leaped up the trail. It was hard to keep my balance, and once I thought I felt the saddle slipping backward; it was because of this that I could not look back.

I didn't stop until I reached the ridge where the trail forked. The horse was breathing deep gasps and there was a dark film of sweat on its neck. I looked down in the direction I had come from, but I couldn't see the place. I waited. The wind came up and pushed warm air past me. I looked up at the sky, pale blue and full of thin clouds and fading vapor trails left by jets.

I think four shots were fired — I remember hearing four hollow explosions that reminded me of deer hunting. There could have been more shots after that, but I couldn't have heard them because my horse was running again and the loose rocks were making too much noise as they scattered around his feet.

Horses have a hard time running downhill, but I went that way instead of uphill to the mountain because I thought it was safer. I felt better with the horse running southeast past the round gray hills that were covered with cedar trees and black lava rock. When I got to the plain in the distance I could see the dark green patches of tamaracks that grew along the river; and beyond the river I could see the beginning of the pale sandrock mesas. I stopped the horse and looked back to see if anyone was coming; then I got off the horse and turned the horse around, wondering if it would go back to its corral under the pines on the mountain. It looked back at me for a moment and then plucked a mouthful of green tumbleweeds before it trotted back up the trail with its ears pointed forward, carrying its head daintily to one side to avoid stepping on the dragging reins. When the horse disappeared over the last hill, the gunny sacks full of meat were still swinging and bouncing.

I walked toward the river on a wood-hauler's road that I knew would eventually lead to the paved road. I was thinking about waiting beside the road for someone to drive by, but by the time I got to the pavement I had decided it wasn't very far to walk if I followed the river back the way Silva and I had come.

The river water tasted good, and I sat in the shade under a cluster of silvery willows. I thought about Silva, and I felt sad at leaving him; still, there was something strange about him, and I tried to figure it out all the way back home.

I came back to the place on the river bank where he had been sitting the first time I saw him. The green willow leaves that he had trimmed from the branch were still lying there, wilted in the sand. I saw the leaves and I wanted to go back to him — to kiss him and to touch him — but the mountains were too far away now. And I told myself, because I believe it, he will come back sometime and be waiting again by the river.

I followed the path up from the river into the village. The sun was getting low, and I could smell supper cooking when I got to the screen door of my house. I could hear their voices inside — my mother was telling my grandmother how to fix the Jell-O and my husband, Al, was playing with the baby. I decided to tell them that some Navajo had kidnaped me, but I was sorry that old Grandpa wasn't alive to hear my story because it was the Yellow Woman stories he liked to tell best.

[1974, 1981]

Joy Harjo

[b. 1951]

Joy Harjo was born on May 9, 1951, in Tulsa, Oklahoma. Her mother, Wynema Baker Foster, was of mixed Cherokee and French ancestry, and her father, Allen W. Foster, was a Muscogee Creek and a descendant of powerful leaders of his tribe, including Menewa, who resisted the forced removal of the Alabama Creeks from their native lands to Indian Territory (now Oklahoma) during the 1830s. Harjo, an enrolled member of the Muscogee Creek tribe, explained in an interview in 1992: "I was not brought up traditionally Creek, was raised in the north side of Tulsa in a neighborhood where there lived many other mixed-blood Indian families. My neighbors were Seminole Indian, Pawnee, other tribes, and white." When she was sixteen, Harjo moved to New Mexico to study art at the Institute of American Indian Arts. The next year, she had her first child, a son, and her second child, a daughter, was born four years later. As a single parent, Harjo struggled to earn a living, working as a waitress and a gas-station attendant. But she enrolled at the University of New Mexico, where she concentrated in art before transferring to the English department to become a creative-writing major because, as she has explained, "I found that language, through poetry, was taking on more magical qualities than my painting. I could say more when I wrote." She published a chapbook of poetry, *The Last Song* (1975), graduated in 1976, and then continued her studies in the Writers' Workshop at the University of Iowa.

Joy Harjo
LaVerne Harrell Clark took this photograph at the Isleta Pueblo outside Albuquerque, New Mexico, in 1975, the year Harjo published her first collection of poetry, *The Last Song*.

After she received an MFA in 1978, Harjo returned to teach and write in the Southwest. She taught at the Institute of American Indian Arts before becoming an instructor of creative writing at Arizona State University in 1978, the year she published her second collection of poetry, *What Moon Drove Me to This?* Five years later, she published one of her most critically acclaimed collections, *She Had Some Horses* (1983), poems in which she explored the trials of women and the long struggle of Native Americans for survival in the United States. Harjo gained widespread recognition with the publication of her next collections of poetry, *Secrets from the Center of the World* (1989), *In Mad Love and War* (1990), for which she was awarded the Poetry Society of America's William Carlos Williams Award, and *The Woman Who Fell from the Sky* (1994). Her recent books include an anthology she coedited with Gloria Bird, *Reinventing the Enemy's Language: Contemporary Native Women's Writings of North America* (1997), which Alice Walker called "one of the most significant anthologies ever to be published in English." Harjo, whose grandmother played the saxophone in Indian Territory during the early 1900s, took up the instrument and has made two recordings combining music and poetry, *Letter from the End of the Twentieth Century* (1997) and *Native Joy for Real* (2004). She has also made a recording of her readings of the poems in *She Had Some Horses* (2006). Harjo has taught at the University of Colorado–Boulder, the University of Arizona, UCLA, and she is currently a professor at the University of New Mexico. When she is not teaching, performing with her band, Poetic Justice, or on tour giving poetry readings, Harjo lives in Hawaii. In addition to her other writings, she maintains a Web log at www.joyharjo.com/, on which she regularly reports on her travels and other events.

I turn and return to Harjo's poetry for her heartbreaking, complex witness and for her world-remaking language: precise, unsentimental, miraculous.
—Adrienne Rich

Harjo's Poetry. Harjo has explained that, because she did not study or begin to write poetry until she was in her twenties, she has been less influenced by "conventional English-language poetry" than by contemporary poets and prose writers such as Simon Ortiz, N. Scott Momaday, Leslie Marmon Silko, Audre Lorde, and Alice Walker. Harjo has also suggested that her poems derive from the Native American heritage of storytelling and her tribal memory. "It is Creek, and touches in on the larger tribal continental memory and the larger human memory, global," she has observed. "It's not something I consciously chose; I mean, I am not a full blood, but it was something that chose me, that lives in me, and I cannot deny it." The following selection of poems indicates some of the persistent themes in her work: the clash between Native American culture and contemporary American society, the function and meaning of history, and the importance and beauty of the land. Harjo's early training in art and her interest in music are evident in the sharp visual imagery and musical rhythms of the poems, which range from free-form meditations on history and place to compressed prose poems celebrating the enduring landscape of the Southwest. The texts are taken from her collection *How We Became Human: New and Selected Poems* (2002).

bedfordstmartins.com/americanlit for research links on Harjo

NEW ORLEANS

This is the south. I look for evidence
of other Creeks,[1] for remnants of voices,
or for tobacco brown bones to come wandering
down Conti Street, Royal, or Decatur.[2]
Near the French Market[3] I see a blue horse   5
caught frozen in stone in the middle of
a square. Brought in by the Spanish on
an endless ocean voyage he became mad
and crazy. They caught him in blue
rock, said   10
       don't talk.

I know it wasn't just a horse
              that went crazy.

Nearby is a shop with ivory and knives.
There are red rocks. The man behind the   15
counter has no idea that he is inside
magic stones. He should find out before
they destroy him. These things
have memory,
      you know.   20

I have a memory.
              It swims deep in blood,
a delta in the skin. It swims out of Oklahoma,
deep the Mississippi River. It carries my
feet to these places: the French Quarter,[4]   25
stale rooms, the sun behind thick and moist
clouds, and I hear boats hauling themselves up
and down the river.

My spirit comes here to drink.
My spirit comes here to drink.   30
Blood is the undercurrent.

---

1. **Creeks:** Native Americans who lived in the southeastern part of the United States until the 1830s, when the federal government forcibly removed them to the "Indian Territory," present-day Oklahoma.
2. **Conti Street, Royal, or Decatur:** Streets in the French Quarter section of New Orleans. [Harjo's note]
3. **French Market:** An open market that has been in operation since New Orleans began as a city in 1718. [Harjo's note]
4. **French Quarter:** The original city of New Orleans, which was founded by the French Mississippi Company in 1718, was centered on the land known as the French Quarter, a twelve-by-nine-block area on the Mississippi River.

There are voices buried in the Mississippi mud.
There are ancestors and future children
buried beneath the currents stirred up by
pleasure boats going up and down.   35
There are stories here made of memory.

I remember DeSoto.[5] He is buried somewhere in
this river, his bones sunk like the golden
treasure he traveled half the earth to find,
came looking for gold cities, for shining streets   40
of beaten gold to dance on with silk ladies.

He should have stayed home.

         (Creeks knew of him for miles
         before he came into town.
         Dreamed of silver blades   45
         and crosses.)

And knew he was one of the ones who yearned
for something his heart wasn't big enough
to handle.

         (And DeSoto thought it was gold.)   50

The Creeks lived in earth towns,
         not gold,
     spun children, not gold.
That's not what DeSoto thought he wanted to see.
The Creeks knew it, and drowned him in   55
    the Mississippi River
         so he wouldn't have to drown himself.

Maybe his body is what I am looking for
as evidence. To know in another way
that my memory is alive.   60
But he must have got away, somehow,
because I have seen New Orleans,
the lace and silk buildings,

---

5. **DeSoto:** Hernando deSoto [c. 1496-1542] was the first European contact with the Mvskoke Creek tribe. He landed on the western coast of Florida in 1539, bringing with him wishes and dreams for riches, an attitude of entitlement (backed up with an army in armor, mounted on horses), and numerous diseases for which the Creeks had no immunity. Usually it is just the Cherokee whose forced migration from east to west is recognized as "*The Trail of Tears*," but there were many tribes forced west, including the Mvskoke Creeks. The removal took place in stages. Some groups were taken by a southern route through New Orleans, brought up the Mississippi River on steamboats to the Arkansas River. The *Monmouth* was one of the contracted boats. On July 31, 1836, it was being piloted recklessly by a drunk crew when it collided with the *Trenton*, another steamboat. The *Monmouth* broke up and sank, killing over three hundred of the migrating Creeks. Many of those who survived were badly scalded by hot water. [Harjo's note]

trolley cars on beaten silver paths,
graves that rise up out of soft earth in the rain,   65
shops that sell black mammy dolls
holding white babies.

And I know I have seen De Soto,
        having a drink on Bourbon Street,
        mad and crazy   70
        dancing with a woman as gold
        as the river bottom.

                            [1983, 2002]

ANCHORAGE[1]

for Audre Lorde[2]

This city is made of stone, of blood, and fish.
There are Chugatch Mountains to the east
and whale and seal to the west.
It hasn't always been this way, because glaciers
who are ice ghosts create oceans, carve earth   5
and shape this city here, by the sound.
They swim backwards in time.

Once a storm of boiling earth cracked open
the streets, threw open the town.
It's quiet now, but underneath the concrete   10
is the cooking earth,
            and above that, air
which is another ocean, where spirits we can't see
are dancing   joking   getting full
on roasted caribou, and the praying   15
goes on, extends out.

Nora[3] and I go walking down 4th Avenue
and know it is all happening.
On a park bench we see someone's Athabascan[4]

---

1. **Anchorage:** On March 27, 1964, the second most powerful earthquake in recorded history devastated Anchorage [Alaska]. It registered 9.2 on the Richter scale and lasted approximately 4 to 6 minutes. More than a hundred people died, most of them from the tsunami that followed with huge waves of terrible power on the Pacific coast from Alaska all the way to Crescent City, California. The death toll could have been much worse had there been a denser population. It was the houses of the rich . . . that tumbled into the ocean during that shaking of the earth. [Harjo's note]
2. **Dedication:** Audre Lorde was a warrior-poet who inspired many in her intense well-lived life as a black, lesbian human rights artist. [Harjo's note] See Lorde, pp. 1415–20.
3. **Nora:** Nora Dauenhauer is a fine Tlinget poet and translator of Tlinget literature. [Harjo's note] The Tlingets are a people native to the southeast coast and islands of Alaska.
4. **Athabascan:** Athabascan speakers encompass an extensive group from the Chipewyan, Kutchin, Carrier,

grandmother, folded up, smelling like 200 years   20
of blood and piss, her eyes closed against some
unimagined darkness, where she is buried
in an ache in which nothing makes sense.

We keep on breathing, walking, but softer now,
the clouds whirling in the air above us.   25
What can we say that would make us understand
better than we do already?
Except to speak of her home and claim her
as our own history, and know that our dreams
don't end here, two blocks away from the ocean   30
where our hearts still batter away at the muddy shore.

And I think of the 6th Avenue jail,[5] of mostly native
and black men, where Henry told about being shot at
eight times outside a liquor store in L.A., but when
the car sped away he was surprised he was alive,   35
no bullet holes, man, and eight cartridges strewn
on the sidewalk all around him.

Everyone laughed at the impossibility of it,
but also the truth. Because who would believe
the fantastic and terrible story of all of our survival   40
those who were never meant
                                            to survive?
                                                        [1983, 2002]

---

and Sarsi peoples (in Canada), to the Tlinget (in Alaska), the chasta-Costa (in Oregon), and the Hoopa (in California), to the Navajo (in New Mexico, Arizona, and Utah) and the Apache (in New Mexico, Arizona, Utah, Oklahoma, and Texas). [Harjo's note]
5. **6th Avenue jail:** The old city jail, which has now been replaced by a new correctional facility in Anchorage. As Harjo indicates in her notes to the poem, she first visited the city as "a visiting poet in one of the many national programs for taking poetry into the prisons."

IF YOU LOOK WITH THE MIND OF THE SWIRLING EARTH

If you look with the mind of the swirling earth near Shiprock[1]
you become the land, beautiful. And understand how three
crows at the edge of the highway, laughing, become three crows
at the edge of the world, laughing.

                                                        [1989, 2002]

---

1. **Shiprock:** *Shiprock* or *Naat'aani Neez* is a large Navajo community in the northwest part of New Mexico. It is marked by a huge rock that appears to look like a ship. *Naat-aani* means boss, chief, or leader. *Neez* means tall. [Harjo's note]

THIS LAND IS A POEM

This land is a poem of ochre and burnt sand I could never write, unless paper were the sacrament of sky, and ink the broken line of wild horses staggering the horizon several miles away. Even then, does anything written ever matter to the earth, wind, and sky?

[1989, 2002]

Rita Dove

[b. 1952]

Rita Frances Dove was born in Akron, Ohio, on August 28, 1952. She was the second of four children of Elvira Hord and Ray Dove, the first African American chemist at the Goodyear Tire and Rubber Company. Their home was filled with books and music, and Dove was trained as a musician and an opera singer. She wrote poetry as a child, but she first thought of becoming a writer when one of her high-school teachers took her to a book signing where Dove met the poet John Ciardi. "Here was a living, breathing, walking, joking person, who wrote books," she recalled in a 1994 interview:

> And for me, it was that I loved to read but I always thought that the dream was too far away. The person who had written the book was a god, it wasn't a person. To have someone actually in the same room with me, talking, and you realize he gets up and walks his dog the same as everybody else, was a way of saying, "It is possible. You can really walk through that door too."

Rita Dove

Her husband Fred Viebahn took this recent photograph of Dove, who in 1993 became the first African American to be appointed Poet Laureate of the United States.

In 1970, Dove was named a Presidential Scholar, one of the top one hundred high-school seniors in the country, and enrolled at Miami University of Ohio, where she majored in English. After she graduated summa cum laude in 1973, she was awarded a Fulbright Fellowship and studied modern European literature at the University of Tübingen, Germany. When she returned, she enrolled in the Writers' Workshop at the University of Iowa and received an MFA in 1977. While at Iowa, Dove met Fred Viebahn, a German writer who was a Fulbright Fellow in the International Program. They married in 1979, the year before Dove published her first book of poems, *The Yellow House on the Corner* (1980).

The publication launched Dove's distinguished career as a writer and teacher. She joined the faculty of Arizona State University and worked on a collection of poems about her experiences in Europe, *Museum* (1983). That year, Dove gave birth to her only child, a daughter, and she was awarded a Guggenheim Fellowship. She wrote a collection of short stories, *Fifth Sunday* (1985), which was followed by a sequence of poems based on the lives and marriage of her maternal grandparents, *Thomas and Beulah* (1986). Dove consequently became the second African American woman (the first was Gwendolyn Brooks) to win the Pulitzer Prize for Poetry. In 1989, she joined the faculty of the University of Virginia and published another collection of poems, *Grace Notes.* Her next book was a novel about a young African American puppeteer, *Through the Ivory Gate* (1992). In 1993, the same year that Toni Morrison was awarded the Nobel Prize for Literature, Dove became the first African American Poet Laureate of the United States. But she continued to work in a variety of genres, publishing a play set on a southern plantation in the 1820s, *The Darker Face of the Earth* (1994); a volume of essays, *The Poet's World* (1995); a song cycle for soprano and orchestra, *Seven for Luck* (1998); and two collections of poetry, *Mother Love* (1995) and *On the Bus with Rosa Parks* (1999). Dove and her husband have become devotees of ballroom dancing, the subject of many of the poems in her recent collection *American Smooth* (2004). The recipient of numerous awards and honorary degrees, Dove lives in Charlottesville, Virginia, where she writes each night at an oak desk built for her by her father and where she is the Commonwealth Professor of English at the University of Virginia.

bedfordstmartins.com/
americanlit for research
links on Dove

Dove's Poetry.　"Poetry is language at its most distilled and most powerful," Dove has observed. Certainly, her technically accomplished poems display the rhythmical resources of language, including colloquial black speech, and the concentrated power of imagery and metaphor. In contrast to many of her contemporaries, Dove has frequently employed traditional poetic forms such as the sonnet, but she has freely adapted those forms to her own distinctive purposes and subjects. Although she has written poems on a wide range of topics, one of her central concerns is the past, especially the cultural heritage and often painful history of African Americans. The first three poems in the following selection — a remembrance of the radical black abolitionist David Walker and two monologues spoken by slaves — are from Dove's first collection, *The Yellow House on the Corner* (1980). Dove, an accomplished singer who has collaborated on a number of musical compositions based on her work, has also written numerous poems about music and musicians. "Canary," a tribute to the jazz singer Billie Holiday, is from Dove's collection *Grace Notes* (1989). The final poem in the selection is "History," a sonnet from a collection of poems in which Dove explores the relations between mothers and daughters, *Motherhood* (1995).

DAVID WALKER (1785-1830)[1]

Free to travel, he still couldn't be shown how lucky
he was: *They strip and beat and drag us about*
like rattlesnakes. Home on Brattle Street, he took in the sign
on the door of the slop shop.[2] All day at the counter —
white caps, ale-stained pea coats. Compass needles,   5
eloquent as tuning forks, shivered, pointing north.
Evenings, the ceiling fan sputtered like a second pulse
Oh Heaven! I am full!! I can hardly move my pen!!!

On the faith of an eye-wink, pamphlets were stuffed
into trouser pockets. Pamphlets transported   10
in the coat linings of itinerant seamen, jackets
ringwormed with salt traded drunkenly to pursers
in the Carolinas, pamphlets ripped out, read aloud:
Men of colour, who are also of sense.
Outrage. Incredulity. Uproar in state legislatures.   15

We are the most wretched, degraded and abject set
of beings that ever lived since the world began.
The jewelled canaries in the lecture halls tittered,
pressed his dark hand between their gloves.
Every half-step was no step at all.   20
Every morning, the man on the corner strung a fresh
bunch of boots from his shoulders. "I'm happy!" he said.
"I never want to live any better or happier than
when I can get a-plenty of boots and shoes to clean!"

A second edition. A third.   25
The abolitionist press is *perfectly appalled.*[3]
Humanity, kindness and the fear of the Lord
does not consist in protecting devils. A month —

---

1. **David Walker (1785-1830):** Walker, a free black man who was born in Wilmington, North Carolina, became a major force in the antislavery movement after settling in Boston in the 1820s. He delivered lectures, wrote articles for *Freedom's Journal*, the first African American newspaper in the United States, and published *An Appeal to the Colored Citizens of the World* (1829), a militant pamphlet in which he attacked racism and urged slaves to revolt against their masters. The italicized passages in the poem are quotations from *An Appeal*.
2. **Home . . . slop shop:** Walker operated a "slop shop," a store selling cheap, second-hand clothing, on Brattle Street. He sewed copies of *An Appeal* into the linings of trousers and jackets he sold to sailors, who smuggled the pamphlets into ports in the South. Georgia consequently put a bounty on Walker's head and made it a crime punishable by death to possess or distribute *An Appeal*.
3. *perfectly appalled:* Walker's fiery rhetoric and his endorsement of violent means to end slavery troubled white abolitionists such as the Quaker Benjamin Lundy.

his person (is that all?) found face-down
in the doorway at Brattle Street,   30
his frame slighter than friends remembered.[4]

[1980]

---

4. A month . . . remembered: Walker was found dead in the doorway of his shop a month after he published
the third edition of *An Appeal* in 1830. Many believed that he had been poisoned.

THE HOUSE SLAVE

The first horn lifts its arm over the dew-lit grass
and in the slave quarters there is a rustling —
children are bundled into aprons, cornbread

and water gourds grabbed, a salt pork breakfast taken.
I watch them driven into the vague before-dawn   5
while their mistress sleeps like an ivory toothpick

and Massa dreams of asses, rum and slave-funk.
I cannot fall asleep again. At the second horn,
the whip curls across the backs of the laggards —

sometimes my sister's voice, unmistaken, among them.   10
"Oh! pray," she cries. "Oh! pray!" Those days
I lie on my cot, shivering in the early heat,

and as the fields unfold to whiteness,
and they spill like bees among the fat flowers,
I weep. It is not yet daylight.   15

[1980]

KENTUCKY, 1833

It is Sunday, day of roughhousing. We are let out in the
woods. The young boys wrestle and butt their heads together
like sheep — a circle forms; claps and shouts fill the air.
The women, brown and glossy, gather round the banjo player,
or simply lie in the sun, legs and aprons folded. The weather's   5
an odd monkey — any other day he's on our backs, his cotton eye
everywhere; today the light sifts down like the finest cornmeal,
coating our hands and arms with a dust. God's dust, old woman
Acker says. She's the only one who could read to us from the
Bible, before Massa forbade it. On Sundays, something hangs   10
in the air, a hallelujah, a skitter of brass, but we can't
call it by name and it disappears.

Then Massa and his gentlemen friends come to bet on the boys.
They guffaw and shout, taking sides, red-faced on the edge of
the boxing ring. There is more kicking, butting, and scuffling —   15
the winner gets a dram of whiskey if he can drink it all in
one swig without choking.

Jason is bucking and prancing about — Massa said his name
reminded him of some sailor, a hero who crossed an ocean,
looking for a golden cotton field.[1] Jason thinks he's been   20
born to great things — a suit with gold threads, vest and all.
Now the winner is sprawled out under a tree and the sun, that
weary tambourine, hesitates at the rim of the sky's green light.
It's a crazy feeling that carries through the night; as if the
sky were an omen we could not understand, the book that, if we   25
could read, would change our lives.

[1980]

---

1. **a hero . . . golden cotton field:** In Greek mythology, Jason leads the Argonauts in a voyage to retrieve the Golden Fleece, the magical fur of a golden ram that is guarded by a dragon in a distant land called Colchis.

CANARY

for Michael S. Harper[1]

Billie Holiday's burned voice
had as many shadows as lights,
a mournful candelabra against a sleek piano,
the gardenia her signature under that ruined face.[2]

(Now you're cooking, drummer to bass,   5
magic spoon, magic needle.
Take all day if you have to
with your mirror and your bracelet of song.)

Fact is, the invention of women under siege
has been to sharpen love in the service of myth.   10

If you can't be free, be a mystery.

[1989]

---

1. **Dedication:** Michael S. Harper (b. 1938) is an African American poet who has written several tributes to masters of jazz (see pp. 1427-33).
2. **Billy Holiday's burned voice . . . ruined face:** Born Eleanora Fagan, Holiday (1915-1959) was a celebrated jazz singer who performed with white gardenias in her hair and was known to her fans as "Lady Day." In the years before her early death at age forty-four, her voice and her face began to show the wear and tear of alcohol and narcotics abuse.

HISTORY

Everything's a metaphor[1] some wise
guy said, and his woman nodded, wisely.
Why was this such a discovery
to him? Why did history
happen only on the outside?   5
She'd watched an embryo track an arc
across her swollen belly from the inside
and knew she'd best
think *knee*, not *tumor* or *burrowing mole*, lest
it emerge a monster. Each craving marks   10
the soul: splashed white upon a temple the dish
of ice cream, coveted, broken in a wink,
or the pickle duplicated just behind the ear. *Every wish*
will find its symbol, the woman thinks.

[1995]

---

1. **Everything's a metaphor:** An often repeated statement widely attributed to the German writer and theorist Johann Wolfgang von Goethe (1749–1832).

Sandra Cisneros

[b. 1954]

Sandra Cisneros is one of the most brilliant of today's young writers. Her work is sensitive, alert, nuanceful . . . rich with music and picture.
—Gwendolyn Brooks

Sandra Cisneros was born on December 20, 1954, in Chicago, Illinois, the only daughter of the seven children of Elvira Cordero Anguiano and Alfredo Cisneros Del Moral, an upholsterer born in Mexico. During her childhood, the family traveled frequently to visit her paternal grandparents in Mexico City. Each time they returned, Cisneros has recalled, they had to find "yet another Chicago flat, another Chicago neighborhood, another Catholic school." She felt isolated by the constant dislocations, as well as by her position as the only sister of six brothers, who "had their own conspiracies and allegiances, leaving me odd-woman-out-forever." Although her mother was a high-school dropout, she got her children library cards before they could read, and she strongly encouraged her daughter to achieve academically. Excused from household chores, Cisneros retreated to her room with her books. She wrote some poetry in high school but did not begin to write seriously until she was a student at Loyola University Chicago. When she graduated in 1976, she enrolled in the Writers' Workshop at the University of Iowa, where she was keenly aware of her differences from other students: "My classmates were from the best schools in the country. They had been bred as fine hot-house flowers. I was a yellow weed among the city's cracks." Although she was not happy at

Iowa, Cisneros credits the experience with helping her find a literary voice in her "place of difference," and she graduated with an MFA in 1978.

Despite some significant early accomplishments, Cisneros struggled for more than a decade to earn a reputation and a living as a writer. She first returned to her parents' home in Chicago and taught at the Latino Youth Alternative High School. Her poems appeared in small literary magazines such as *Quarterly West* and *Nuestro*, and she published a chapbook of poetry, *Bad Boys* (1980). She soon began work on a novel about a girl growing up in a run-down Spanish-speaking neighborhood in Chicago, *The House on Mango Street* (1984). The reviews were generally enthusiastic, and the novel won an American Book Award. Eager to live independently of her family, Cisneros moved to Texas after she received a Texas Institute of Letters Dobie Paisano Fellowship in 1986. She once again received laudatory reviews for her first collection of poems, *My Wicked, Wicked Ways* (1987). But she could not find a job in Texas, where Cisneros wanted to stay, and took a teaching position at California State University, Chico. A National Endowment for the Arts Fellowship enabled her to complete *Woman Hollering Creek*, a collection of lyrical sketches and stories set in Chicago, Texas, and Mexico. Cisneros subsequently became the first Mexican American woman to receive a contract for a book about Mexican Americans from a major publishing company, Random House. The company published the collection in 1991 and reissued *The House on Mango Street*, which became a bestseller. Speaking about her success with her characteristic humor in Chicago in 1992, Cisneros quipped: "I've been publishing for fifteen years. One press account said I was an overnight success. I thought that was the longest night I've ever spent."

Since 1992, Cisneros has been living and writing full-time in San Antonio, Texas. In 1994, she published her second collection of poetry, *Loose Woman*, as well as a book for children, *Hairs/Pelitos*. The next year, she was awarded a prestigious MacArthur Prize Fellowship, the so-called genius grant, which provides funding for five years of creative work. Her most recent book is a multigenerational novel about a Mexican American family, *Caramelo* (2002). In an autobiographical statement on her Web site (www.sandracisneros.com), the intensely private Cisneros offers some glimpses into her present life:

> I live with many creatures little and large — six dogs (Beto, Dante, Lolita, Chamaco, Valentina P-nut Butter, and Barney Fife), four cats (Gato Perón, Pánfilo, Apolonia, and Lulu), and a parrot named Agustina. I am nobody's mother, nobody's wife, am happily single and live with the love of my life.

Sandra Cisneros

The Associated Press photographer Eric Gay took this portrait of Cisneros in San Antonio, Texas, where the award-winning poet and short-story writer has lived since 1992.

Cisneros's "Mericans." In 1991, this story appeared in both a special fiction issue of *Ms.* magazine and Cisneros's *Woman Hollering Creek*. Most of the stories in the collection concern the lives of Mexican American girls and women living, both literally and figuratively, in the borderland between Mexico and the United States. Cisneros uses the setting to explore complex issues of Chicana identity, issues that she handles with a good deal of humor in "Mericans," a vignette about Mexican American children enduring a family visit to Mexico. In the story, which opens with a reference by the young female narrator to her "awful grandmother," Cisneros also pokes fun at what she has described as one of the "sacred cows" of Chicana literature. "In Chicana writing the love between a grandmother and a granddaughter is holier than the relationship between a mother and a daughter because the mother and daughter have to deal with the reality of the everyday, whereas the grandmother can be revered from afar," Cisneros observed in an interview in 2002. "Especially if she's dead, she becomes this mythic symbol in Chicana literature. But I hate when I see any kind of cliché occurring in writing, so that's why she's a wonderful cliché for me to throw rocks at." The text is taken from *Woman Hollering Creek and Other Stories* (1991).

**bedfordstmartins.com/
americanlit** *for research
links on Cisneros*

MERICANS

We're waiting for the awful grandmother who is inside dropping pesos into *la ofrenda* box before the altar to La Divina Providencia.[1] Lighting votive candles and genuflecting. Blessing herself and kissing her thumb. Running a crystal rosary between her fingers. Mumbling, mumbling, mumbling.

There are so many prayers and promises and thanks-be-to-God to be given in the name of the husband and the sons and the only daughter who never attend mass. It doesn't matter. Like La Virgen de Guadalupe,[2] the awful grandmother intercedes on their behalf. For the grandfather who hasn't believed in anything since the first PRI elections.[3] For my father, El Periquín,[4] so skinny he needs his sleep. For Auntie Light-skin, who only a few hours before was breakfasting on brain and goat tacos after dancing all night in the pink zone.[5] For Uncle Fat-face, the blackest of the black sheep — *Always remember your Uncle Fat-face in your prayers.* And Uncle Baby — *You go for me, Mamá — God listens to you.*

The awful grandmother has been gone a long time. She disappeared behind the heavy leather outer curtain and the dusty velvet inner.[6] We must stay near the church en-

---

1. *la ofrenda* **box . . . La Divina Providencia:** The offering box in the church of The Divine Providence (Spanish).

2. **La Virgen de Guadalupe:** According to Roman Catholic tradition, the Virgin Mary, the mother of Jesus Christ, appeared in 1531 to Juan Diego, a Chichimeca convert to Christianity, and told him that she wanted a church built at Tepeyac, Mexico. The miracle of Guadalupe was officially recognized by the Vatican in 1745, and the Virgin of Guadalupe is an important religious and cultural symbol to many Mexican people. Icons, or paintings of her, are often used in churches as aids to devotion.

3. **PRI elections:** *El Partido Revolucionario Institucional* (Institutional Revolutionary Party), or PRI, is a powerful political party in Mexico. Formed to serve the interests of labor unions, peasant organizations, and the poor, the party won its first elections in 1929 as the *Partido National Revolucionario* (National Revolutionary Party).

4. **El Periquín:** Derived from *perico*, a parrot (Spanish).

5. **pink zone:** The Zona Rosa (Pink Zone), a social and tourist center in Mexico City.

6. **She disappeared . . . inner:** A description of the church's confessional, an enclosed booth in which the priest sits to hear people confess their sins.

trance. We must not wander over to the balloon and punch-ball vendors. We cannot spend our allowance on fried cookies or Familia Burrón comic books or those clear cone-shaped suckers that make everything look like a rainbow when you look through them. We cannot run off and have our picture taken on the wooden ponies. We must not climb the steps up the hill behind the church and chase each other through the cemetery. We have promised to stay right where the awful grandmother left us until she returns.

There are those walking to church on their knees. Some with fat rags tied around their legs and others with pillows, one to kneel on, and one to flop ahead. There are women with black shawls crossing and uncrossing themselves. There are armies of penitents carrying banners and flowered arches while musicians play tinny trumpets and tinny drums.

La Virgen de Guadalupe is waiting inside behind a plate of thick glass. There's also a gold crucifix bent crooked as a mesquite tree when someone once threw a bomb. La Virgen de Guadalupe on the main altar because she's a big miracle, the crooked crucifix on a side altar because that's a little miracle.

But we're outside in the sun. My big brother Junior hunkered against the wall with his eyes shut. My little brother Keeks running around in circles.

Maybe and most probably my little brother is imagining he's a flying feather dancer, like the ones we saw swinging high up from a pole on the Virgin's birthday. I want to be a flying feather dancer too, but when he circles past me he shouts, "I'm a B-Fifty-two bomber, you're a German," and shoots me with an invisible machine gun. I'd rather play flying feather dancers, but if I tell my brother this, he might not play with me at all.

"*Girl.* We can't play with a *girl.*" *Girl.* It's my brothers' favorite insult now instead of "sissy." "You *girl,*" they yell at each other. "You throw that ball like a *girl.*"

I've already made up my mind to be a German when Keeks swoops past again, this time yelling, "I'm Flash Gordon. You're Ming the Merciless and the Mud People."[7] I don't mind being Ming the Merciless, but I don't like being the Mud People. Something wants to come out of the corners of my eyes, but I don't let it. Crying is what *girls* do.

I leave Keeks running around in circles – "I'm the Lone Ranger, you're Tonto."[8] I leave Junior squatting on his ankles and go look for the awful grandmother.

Why do churches smell like the inside of an ear? Like incense and the dark and candles in blue glass? And why does holy water smell of tears? The awful grandmother makes me kneel and fold my hands. The ceiling high and everyone's prayers bumping up there like balloons.

If I stare at the eyes of the saints long enough, they move and wink at me, which makes me a sort of saint too. When I get tired of winking saints, I count the awful grandmother's mustache hairs while she prays for Uncle Old, sick from the worm,[9] and Auntie Cuca, suffering from a life of troubles that left half her face crooked and the other half sad.

---

7. **Flash Gordon . . . Mud People:** Science-fiction characters in the comic strip, film serials, and 1950s television series *Flash Gordon.*

8. **Lone Ranger . . . Tonto:** *The Lone Ranger* was a 1950s television series about the adventures of a crusading Texas Ranger and his "trusty scout," the Native American Tonto.

9. **the worm:** An intestinal parasite.

There must be a long, long list of relatives who haven't gone to church. The awful grandmother knits the names of the dead and the living into one long prayer fringed with the grandchildren born in that barbaric country with its barbarian ways.

I put my weight on one knee, then the other, and when they both grow fat as a mattress of pins, I slap them each awake. *Micaela, you may wait outside with Alfredito and Enrique.* The awful grandmother says it all in Spanish, which I understand when I'm paying attention. "What?" I say, though it's neither proper nor polite. "What?" which the awful grandmother hears as "*¿Güat?*" But she only gives me a look and shoves me toward the door.

After all that dust and dark, the light from the plaza makes me squinch my eyes like if I just came out of the movies. My brother Keeks is drawing squiggly lines on the concrete with a wedge of glass and the heel of his shoe. My brother Junior squatting against the entrance, talking to a lady and man.

They're not from here. Ladies don't come to church dressed in pants. And everybody knows men aren't supposed to wear shorts.

"*¿Quieres chicle?*"[10] the lady asks in a Spanish too big for her mouth.

"*Gracias.*"[11] The lady gives him a whole handful of gum for free, little cellophane cubes of Chiclets, cinnamon and aqua and the white ones that don't taste like anything but are good for pretend buck teeth.

"*Por favor,*" says the lady. "*¿Un foto?*"[12] pointing to her camera.

"*Sí.*"

She's so busy taking Junior's picture, she doesn't notice me and Keeks.

"Hey, Michele, Keeks. You guys want gum?"

"But you speak English!"

"Yeah," my brother says, "we're Mericans."

We're Mericans, we're Mericans, and inside the awful grandmother prays.

[1991]

---

10. *¿Quieres chicle?*: Would you like some chewing gum? (Spanish).
11. *Gracias*: Thank you (Spanish).
12. *Por favor . . . ¿Un foto?*: If you please, a photo? (Spanish).

Martín Espada

[b. 1957]

Martín Espada was born on August 7, 1957, in Brooklyn, New York. He was the youngest of three children of Marilyn Levine Espada, the daughter of a working-class Jewish family, and Frank Espada, whose impoverished family had migrated from Puerto Rico when he was nine. "My father's social class was defined by the opportunities denied him because of racism, and the opportunities he created for himself in spite of racism," Espada explained in "Zapata's Disciple and Perfect Brie," an autobiographical essay dedicated to Frank Espada. "His experiences – the frustrations and rages, the stubborn resistance, the dignity of his defiance – formed the environment in which I evolved, as son and poet, contributing to my awareness of class and its punishments." Frank Espada became a radical political activist and an important bridge between the Puerto Rican and African American communities during the civil rights struggle in New York City. Working as an electrical contractor to support the family, he later became a successful photographer, and the family moved from Brooklyn to Valley Stream, Long Island. Espada, who was then thirteen, recalls that "being Puerto Rican in effect canceled out whatever middle-class trappings we had acquired for ourselves," and that he confronted racial obscenities and violence at his all-white high school. In response, he began to write poetry "to explain myself to myself," but he was "a spectacularly marginal student" who "wandered in and out of school, from job to job." Although he briefly attended the University of Maryland, Espada remained deeply alienated and dropped out after a creative-writing teacher told him that his poetry was "too hostile."

A turning point in Espada's life came when a family friend gave him a copy of the anthology *Latin American Revolutionary Poetry* (1974). Inspired by the poems, he returned to college in 1978, this time enrolling at the University of Wisconsin, Madison. As a history major, he studied American foreign policy and Latin America, and he spent the summer of 1982 working as a radio journalist in Nicaragua. When he returned to Madison, he published his first book, *The Immigrant Iceboy's Bolero* (1982). The title poem was about the brutal work his father had done after his arrival in the United States, and the volume included photographs by Frank Espada. After Espada's graduation from college, he enrolled in law school at Northeastern University. He received his law degree in 1985 and married Katherine Gilbert, a sociologist. Espada worked as a lawyer for several years, practicing in low-income, Spanish-speaking communities in Boston. He also published poetry in a variety of literary magazines and participated in poetry readings, often at Latino community centers. His second book of poetry, *Trumpets from the Islands of Their Eviction* (1987), was hailed by a reviewer in the *New York Times* as the work of "an astonishingly bold young poet." While helping to organize a conference in Boston, Espada met the influential Puerto Rican poet Clemente Soto Vélez. Their friendship and Espada's abiding interest in his Puerto Rican heritage and Latino history inspired many of the poems in his next collection, *Rebellion Is the Circle of a Lover's Hands* (1990), for which he won the first PEN/Revson Fellowship for Poetry. In their citation, the judges wrote: "The greatness of Espada's art, like all great arts, is that it gives dignity to the insulted and the injured of the earth."

In 1993, Espada joined the faculty of the University of Massachusetts, Amherst, where he teaches courses in poetry and creative writing in the Department of English. Since then, he has edited three anthologies of poetry, including *El Coro: A Chorus of Latino and Latina Poetry* (1998). He

Martín Espada
Paul Shoul took this photograph of Espada about the time he published his revolutionary collection of poetry *Rebellion Is the Circle of a Lover's Hands* (1990).

Martín Espada wields his poetry like a flint, striking sparks, cutting to the bone. To read this work is to be struck breathless, and surely, to come away changed.

–Barbara Kingsolver

has also published a collection of essays, *Zapata's Disciple* (1998), as well as five more collections of poetry: *City of Coughing and the Dead Radiators* (1993); *Imagine the Angels of Bread* (1996), which won an American Book Award; *A Mayan Astronomer in Hell's Kitchen* (2000); *Alabanza: New and Selected Poems* (2003), which received the Paterson Award for Sustained Literary Achievement; and, most recently, *The Republic of Poetry* (2006).

Espada's Poetry.   Espada has said that he views his work as part of a radical poetic tradition that goes back to Walt Whitman and encompasses Carl Sandburg, Langston Hughes, and Allen Ginsberg, as well as the Chilean poet Pablo Neruda (1904–1973). Like the North American poets he admires, Espada employs rhythmic free verse and vernacular speech, sometimes laced with Spanish words and phrases. And, like Neruda, as Espada told an interviewer in 2003, he is committed to "poetry of advocacy," to "speaking on behalf of those without an opportunity to be heard." He explained that the single most important idea in his poetry is "the struggle for justice, being able to talk about justice in philosophical terms, in aesthetic terms, in practical terms." That theme is reflected in the poems selected here, ranging from "Bully," an ironic meditation on the history of the American conquest of Puerto Rico and the subsequent "invasion" of the United States by Puerto Ricans, to "Alabanza: In Praise of Local 100," which is widely regarded as the most powerful poem inspired by the attack on the World Trade Center on September 11, 2001. In an interview on PBS on the second anniversary of the attacks, the journalist Ray Suarez asked him, "Why do we need poetry at a time like this?" Espada responded:

> Poetry humanizes. Poetry gives a human face to a time like this. Poetry gives eyes and a mouth and a voice to a time like this. Poetry records a time like this for future generations who want to know about a time like this in terms of the five senses, and in terms of the soul, I think.

The texts are taken from his collection *Alabanza: New and Selected Poems, 1982–2002* (2003).

bedfordstmartins.com/ americanlit for research links on Espada

BULLY[1]

Boston, Massachusetts, 1987

In the school auditorium,
the Theodore Roosevelt statue
is nostalgic
for the Spanish-American war,
each fist lonely for a saber   5
or the reins of anguish-eyed horses,
or a podium to clatter with speeches
glorying in the malaria of conquest.

But now the Roosevelt school
is pronounced *Hernández*.[2]   10
Puerto Rico has invaded Roosevelt
with its army of Spanish-singing children
in the hallways,
brown children devouring
the stockpiles of the cafeteria,   15
children painting Taíno[3] ancestors
who leap naked across murals.

Roosevelt is surrounded
by all the faces
he ever shoved in eugenic spite[4]   20
and cursed as mongrels, skin of one race,
hair and cheekbones of another.

Once Marines tramped
from the newsreel of his imagination;
now children plot to spray graffiti   25
in parrot-brilliant colors
across the Victorian mustache
and monocle.

[1990, 2003]

---

1. **Bully:** One of the favorite expressions of Theodore Roosevelt (1858–1919), the twenty-sixth president of the United States. Roosevelt first gained fame as one of the commanders of the First United States Volunteer Cavalry, called the "Rough Riders," during the Spanish-American War of 1898. After he returned home, Roosevelt declared: "I've had a bully time and a bully fight." In the treaty that ended the war, Spain ceded control of its overseas colonies to the United States, which subsequently annexed Puerto Rico, the Philippines, and Guam.
2. **Hernández:** Refers here to the great Puerto Rican composer, Rafael Hernández. [Espada's note] The Roosevelt Elementary School was renamed the Rafael Hernández School and reorganized in the 1970s as a result of the efforts by community activists to provide a school that would serve the needs of the increasing Latino school population in the Roxbury section of Boston.
3. **Taíno:** Original indigenous inhabitants of Puerto Rico, decimated by the Spanish. [Espada's note]
4. **eugenic spite:** Roosevelt was a firm believer in the "science" of eugenics, a theory that the human race could be improved by controlling the reproduction of "inferior" races or groups of people.

LATIN NIGHT AT THE PAWNSHOP

Chelsea, Massachusetts,
Christmas, 1987

The apparition of a salsa[1] band
gleaming in the Liberty Loan
pawnshop window:

Golden trumpet,
silver trombone,
congas, maracas,[2] tambourine,
all with price tags dangling
like the city morgue ticket
on a dead man's toe.

[1990, 2003]

---

1. **salsa:** Popular dance music that evolved in the Latino community of New York in the late 1960s. [Espada's note]
2. **congas, maracas:** A conga is a tall drum of African origin, and maracas are a pair of hollow gourd-shaped containers filled with beans or pebbles that are shaken as a percussion instrument.

FEDERICO'S GHOST

The story is
that whole families of fruitpickers
still crept between the furrows
of the field at dusk,
when for reasons of whiskey or whatever   5
the cropduster plane sprayed anyway,
floating a pesticide drizzle
over the pickers
who thrashed like dark birds
in a glistening white net,   10
except for Federico,
a skinny boy who stood apart
in his own green row,
and, knowing the pilot
would not understand in Spanish   15
that he was the son of a whore,
instead jerked his arm
and thrust an obscene finger.

The pilot understood.
He circled the plane and sprayed again,   20
watching a fine gauze of poison

drift over the brown bodies
that cowered and scurried on the ground,
and aiming for Federico,
leaving the skin beneath his shirt   25
wet and blistered,
but still pumping his finger at the sky.

[1990, 2003]

ALABANZA: IN PRAISE OF LOCAL 100

*for the 43 members of Hotel Employees and Restaurant Employees
Local 100, working at the Windows on the World restaurant,
who lost their lives in the attack on the World Trade Center*

Alabanza.[1] Praise the cook with a shaven head
and a tattoo on his shoulder that said *Oye,*[2]
a blue-eyed Puerto Rican with people from Fajardo,[3]
the harbor of pirates centuries ago.
Praise the lighthouse in Fajardo, candle   5
glimmering white to worship the dark saint of the sea.
Alabanza. Praise the cook's yellow Pirates cap
worn in the name of Roberto Clemente,[4] his plane
that flamed into the ocean loaded with cans for Nicaragua,
for all the mouths chewing the ash of earthquakes.   10
Alabanza. Praise the kitchen radio, dial clicked
even before the dial on the oven, so that music and Spanish
rose before bread. Praise the bread. *Alabanza.*

Praise Manhattan from a hundred and seven flights up,
like Atlantis glimpsed through the windows of an ancient aquarium.   15
Praise the great windows where immigrants from the kitchen
could squint and almost see their world, hear the chant of nations:
*Ecuador, México, Republica Dominicana,
Haiti, Yemen, Ghana, Bangladesh.*
Alabanza. Praise the kitchen in the morning,   20
where the gas burned blue on every stove
and exhaust fans fired their diminutive propellers,
hands cracked eggs with quick thumbs

---

1. *Alabanza*: Praise; sometimes used in a religious sense. From "alabar," to celebrate with words. [Espada's note]
2. *Oye*: Literally "listen"; the equivalent of "hey." [Espada's note]
3. Fajardo: Port city on the northeast coast of Puerto Rico. [Espada's note]
4. Roberto Clemente: Hall of Fame baseball player from Puerto Rico who died in a plane crash delivering relief supplies to earthquake victims in Nicaragua. [Espada's note]

or sliced open cartons to build an altar of cans.
Alabanza. Praise the busboy's music, the *chime-chime*   25
of his dishes and silverware in the tub.
Alabanza. Praise the dish-dog, the dishwasher
who worked that morning because another dishwasher
could not stop coughing, or because he needed overtime
to pile the sacks of rice and beans for a family   30
floating away on some Caribbean island plagued by frogs.[5]
Alabanza. Praise the waitress who heard the radio in the kitchen
and sang to herself about a man gone. *Alabanza.*

After the thunder wilder than thunder,
after the shudder deep in the glass of the great windows,   35
after the radio stopped singing like a tree full of terrified frogs,
after night burst the dam of day and flooded the kitchen,
for a time the stoves glowed in darkness like the lighthouse in Fajardo,
like a cook's soul. Soul I say, even if the dead cannot tell us
about the bristles of God's beard because God has no face,   40
soul I say, to name the smoke-beings flung in constellations
across the night sky of this city and cities to come.
Alabanza I say, even if God has no face.

Alabanza. When the war began, from Manhattan and Kabul
two constellations of smoke rose and drifted to each other,   45
mingling in icy air, and one said with an Afghan tongue:
Teach me to dance. We have no music here.
And the other said with a Spanish tongue:
I will teach you. Music is all we have.

[2003]

---

5. **plagued by frogs:** In Puerto Rico, the native coqui frog lives in densities of up to 8,000 an acre and increased to even larger numbers after Hurricane Hugo in 1989. The frog, known for its loud call, is a voracious predator of insects, consequently disrupting the food supply for birds and other wildlife

Sherman Alexie

[b. 1966]

Sherman Alexie Jr. was born on October 7, 1966, in Wellpinit, a town on the Spokane Indian Reservation in eastern Washington. His father, a Coeur d'Alene Indian, was a logger and a truck driver; his mother, of Spokane Indian descent, worked as a clerk and seamstress to help support the family. Alexie was born with hydrocephalus, fluid in the brain, and at the age of six months underwent major surgery to correct the condition. He was not expected to survive the surgery without serious mental and physical handicaps, but he suffered only an enlarged skull and some minor side effects. The size of his head caused the children in his tribal school at Wellpinit to call him "The Globe," and Alexie responded by withdrawing into the books he found at the library and by developing a quick wit. "Humor is self-defense on the rez," he said in an interview in 1999. "You make people laugh and you disarm them. You sort of sneak up on them. You can say controversial or rowdy things and they'll listen or laugh." Because he wanted to have a mainstream education, Alexie transferred to a high school in Reardon, Washington, after he completed the eighth grade. Although he once again felt isolated, this time because he was the only Indian at the school, he excelled at basketball, served as class president, and was a member of the debating team. After his graduation in 1985, he went to Gonzaga University in Spokane, Washington. He began drinking heavily and dropped out after two years. He moved to Seattle, where he worked as a busboy until he decided to give college another try at Washington State University.

Sherman Alexie
Rex Rystedt took this photograph of Alexie in 1995, the year the acclaimed young poet and fiction writer published his first novel, *Reservation Blues*.

Alexie, who enrolled as a premed major, soon discovered his protean artistic talents. In a poetry-writing workshop, he was deeply inspired by reading a volume of Native American poetry, *Songs from This Earth on Turtle's Back* (1983). "I saw my life in poems and stories for the very first time," he recalled years later. With the encouragement of his professor, Alexie began writing poems and graduated with a degree in American studies in 1991. Alexie began publishing his poems in various literary journals, and the small Hanging Loose Press published his first collection of poetry, *The Business of Fancydancing* (1992). His career was launched when the volume was enthusiastically reviewed in the *New York Times*, and he swiftly published three more collections of poetry: *I Would Steal Horses* (1992), *First Indian on the Moon* (1993), and *Old Shirts and New Skins* (1993). He also published *The Lone Ranger and Tonto Fistfight in Heaven* (1993), a collection of related stories about contemporary life on the Spokane Indian reservation that was a finalist for a PEN/Hemingway Award. Alexie then wrote two acclaimed novels: *Reservation Blues* (1995), the exuberant saga of an all-Indian blues band named Coyote Spring; and *Indian Killer* (1996), a grim account of the racial strife generated by a serial killer terrorizing Seattle. Alexie also began to branch out into other art forms. He and the Colville Indian songwriter Jim Boyd made a soundtrack to accompany *Reservation Blues*, and Alexie wrote the screenplay and was deeply involved in the production of a feature film based on his stories, *Smoke Signals*. The movie, the first made by an all-Indian crew and creative team, won a series of awards at the Sundance Film Festival in 1998.

Since then, Alexie has become one of the most prominent writers in the United States. In June 1999, he was featured in a special Summer Fiction Edition, "20 Writers for the 21st Century," of the *New Yorker.* "Forgive the immodesty, but I think it's much more important for an Indian like me to be in the *New Yorker* magazine than it is for me or an Indian to be in a museum," he replied to an interviewer who asked him about Native American culture being relegated to museums.

> I think it's more important to change the possibilities of what an Indian is and can be right now. I love museums, but for me the greatest part of all this is I'm a completely active member of the culture. We're not separate, we're not removed, we're an integral and living part of the culture.

Certainly, his work has given prominence to the contemporary lives and culture of Native Americans. Alexie wrote the screenplay and made his directorial debut in a movie about a gay Indian poet in search of his identity, *The Business of Fancydancing* (2002), which premiered at the Sundance Film Festival in 2002. He also published three more books of poetry and two more award-winning collections of stories, *The Toughest Indian in the World* (2000) and *Ten Little Indians* (2003). In 2007, Alexie published *In Flight*, a novel about a half-Irish, half–Native American boy who travels back and forth through time to witness and participate in some of the most brutal events of American history, as well as his first novel for young adults, *The Absolutely True Story of a Part-Time Indian.* When he is not on tour giving readings and performances, Alexie lives with his wife and two sons in Seattle.

*bedfordstmartins.com/
americanlit* for research
links on Alexie

Alexie's "What You Pawn I Will Redeem." First published in the *New Yorker* in April 2003, this story appeared later that year in Alexie's third collection of short stories, *Ten Little Indians.* (In a typically ironic gesture, he included only nine stories in the collection, the title of which evokes the familiar nursery song "Ten Little Indians.") "What You Pawn I Will Redeem," which displays Alexie's abiding interest in the everyday experiences of Native Americans, his keen ear for dialogue, and his sardonic humor, was singled out for inclusion in two prestigious collections, *Best American Short Stories* (2004) and the *O. Henry Prize Stories 2005.* One of the jurors for the O. Henry Prize, the novelist Ann Patchett, admiringly observed of the story:

> Like me, Sherman Alexie is in love with his homeless Spokane Indian narrator and so he simply steps aside to let his character have every inch of the stage. . . . Alexie follows this man through his world not as a character but as a human being. Every turn in his day is unexpected and true. As I read I was moved by sorrow, compassion, and joy. . . . We are lucky when we get that much from life — we should be nothing short of rapturous when we get it from short fiction.

The text is taken from *Ten Little Indians* (2003).

WHAT YOU PAWN I WILL REDEEM

Noon

One day you have a home and the next you don't, but I'm not going to tell you my particular reasons for being homeless, because it's my secret story, and Indians have to work hard to keep secrets from hungry white folks.

I'm a Spokane Indian boy, an Interior Salish,[1] and my people have lived within a one-hundred-mile radius of Spokane, Washington, for at least ten thousand years. I grew up in Spokane, moved to Seattle twenty-three years ago for college, flunked out within two semesters, worked various blue- and bluer-collar jobs for many years, married two or three times, fathered two or three kids, and then went crazy. Of course, "crazy" is not the official definition of my mental problem, but I don't think "asocial disorder" fits it, either, because that makes me sound like I'm a serial killer or something. I've never hurt another human being, or at least not physically. I've broken a few hearts in my time, but we've all done that, so I'm nothing special in that regard. I'm a boring heartbreaker, at that, because I've never abandoned one woman for another. I never dated or married more than one woman at a time. I didn't break hearts into pieces overnight. I broke them slowly and carefully. I didn't set any land-speed records running out the door. Piece by piece, I disappeared. And I've been disappearing ever since. But I'm not going to tell you any more about my brain or my soul.

I've been homeless for six years. If there's such a thing as being an effective homeless man, I suppose I'm effective. Being homeless is probably the only thing I've ever been good at. I know where to get the best free food. I've made friends with restaurant and convenience store managers who let me use their bathrooms. I don't mean the public bathrooms, either. I mean the employees' bathrooms, the clean ones hidden in the back of the kitchen or the pantry or the cooler. I know it sounds strange to be proud of, but it means a lot to me, being truthworthy enough to piss in somebody else's clean bathroom. Maybe you don't understand the value of a clean bathroom, but I do.

Probably none of this interests you. I probably don't interest you much. Homeless Indians are everywhere in Seattle. We're common and boring, and you walk right on by us, with maybe a look of anger or disgust or even sadness at the terrible fate of the noble savage. But we have dreams and families. I'm friends with a homeless Plains Indian[2] man whose son is the editor of a big-time newspaper back east. That's his story, but we Indians are great storytellers and liars and mythmakers, so maybe that Plains Indian hobo is a plain old everyday Indian. I'm kind of suspicious of him, because he describes himself only as Plains Indian, a generic term, and not by a specific tribe. When I asked him why he wouldn't tell me exactly what he is, he said, "Do any of us know exactly what we are?" Yeah, great, a philosophizing Indian. "Hey," I said, "you got to have a home to be

---

1. **Interior Salish:** The collective name for the five tribes, including the Spokane, of an Indian nation that occupied lands in the interior of British Columbia stretching south into the present-day United States.
2. **Plains Indian:** The generic term for a member of any of a large number of North American tribes that occupied the area stretching from the Rio Grande River Valley north through the Great Plains into central Canada.

that homely." He laughed and flipped me the eagle and walked away. But you probably want to know more about the story I'm really trying to tell you.

I wander the streets with a regular crew, my teammates, my defenders, and my posse. It's Rose of Sharon, Junior, and me. We matter to one another if we don't matter to anybody else. Rose of Sharon is a big woman, about seven feet tall if you're measuring overall effect, and about five feet tall if you're talking about the physical. She's a Yakama Indian of the Wishram variety.[3] Junior is a Colville,[4] but there are about 199 tribes that make up the Colville, so he could be anything. He's good-looking, though, like he just stepped out of some "Don't Litter the Earth" public-service advertisement. He's got those great big cheekbones that are like planets, you know, with little moons orbiting around them. He gets me jealous, jealous, and jealous. If you put Junior and me next to each other, he's the Before Columbus Arrived Indian, and I'm the After Columbus Arrived Indian. I am living proof of the horrible damage that colonialism has done to us Skins. But I'm not going to let you know how scared I sometimes get of history and its ways. I'm a strong man, and I know that silence is the best way of dealing with white folks.

This whole story started at lunchtime, when Rose of Sharon, Junior, and I were panning the handle down at Pike Place Market. After about two hours of negotiating, we earned five dollars, good enough for a bottle of fortified courage from the most beautiful 7-Eleven in the world. So we headed over that way, feeling like warrior drunks, and we walked past this pawnshop I'd never noticed before. And that was strange, because we Indians have built-in pawnshop radar. But the strangest thing was the old powwow-dance regalia[5] I saw hanging in the window.

"That's my grandmother's regalia," I said to Rose of Sharon and Junior.

"How do you know for sure?" Junior asked.

I didn't know for sure, because I hadn't seen that regalia in person ever. I'd seen only photographs of my grandmother dancing in it. And that was before somebody stole it from her fifty years ago. But it sure looked like my memory of it, and it had all the same colors of feathers and beads that my family always sewed into their powwow regalia.

"There's only one way to know for sure," I said.

So Rose of Sharon, Junior, and I walked into the pawnshop and greeted the old white man working behind the counter.

"How can I help you?" he asked.

"That's my grandmother's powwow regalia in your window," I said. "Somebody stole it from her fifty years ago, and my family has been looking for it ever since."

The pawnbroker looked at me like I was a liar. I understood. Pawnshops are filled with liars.

"I'm not lying," I said. "Ask my friends here. They'll tell you."

---

3. **Yakama Indian of the Wishram variety:** The Wishram is one of the tribes of the Yakama confederation, which occupied lands in present-day Oregon and Washington.
4. **Colville:** The Colville confederation includes twelve tribes that occupied lands in present-day central and eastern Washington and Canada.
5. **powwow-dance regalia:** The decorative clothing worn by dancers participating in a powwow, a traditional Native American ceremony. The regalia serves as a form of tribal identity and is often personalized to reflect the circumstances of an individual's life.

"He's the most honest Indian I know," Rose of Sharon said.

"All right, honest Indian," the pawnbroker said. "I'll give you the benefit of the doubt. Can you prove it's your grandmother's regalia?"

Because they don't want to be perfect, because only God is perfect, Indian people sew flaws into their powwow regalia. My family always sewed one yellow bead somewhere on their regalia. But we always hid it where you had to search hard to find it.

"If it really is my grandmother's," I said, "there will be one yellow bead hidden somewhere on it."

"All right, then," the pawnbroker said. "Let's take a look."

He pulled the regalia out of the window, laid it down on his glass counter, and we searched for that yellow bead and found it hidden beneath the armpit.

"There it is," the pawnbroker said. He didn't sound surprised. "You were right. This is your grandmother's regalia."

"It's been missing for fifty years," Junior said.

"Hey, Junior," I said. "It's my family's story. Let me tell it."

"All right," he said. "I apologize. You go ahead."

"It's been missing for fifty years," I said.

"That's his family's sad story," Rose of Sharon said. "Are you going to give it back to him?"

"That would be the right thing to do," the pawnbroker said. "But I can't afford to do the right thing. I paid a thousand dollars for this. I can't give away a thousand dollars."

"We could go to the cops and tell them it was stolen," Rose of Sharon said.

"Hey," I said to her, "don't go threatening people."

The pawnbroker sighed. He was thinking hard about the possibilities.

"Well, I suppose you could go to the cops," he said. "But I don't think they'd believe a word you said."

He sounded sad about that. Like he was sorry for taking advantage of our disadvantages.

"What's your name?" the pawnbroker asked me.

"Jackson," I said.

"Is that first or last?" he asked.

"Both."

"Are you serious?"

"Yes, it's true. My mother and father named me Jackson Jackson. My family nickname is Jackson Squared. My family is funny."

"All right, Jackson Jackson," the pawnbroker said. "You wouldn't happen to have a thousand dollars, would you?"

"We've got five dollars total," I said.

"That's too bad," he said and thought hard about the possibilities. "I'd sell it to you for a thousand dollars if you had it. Heck, to make it fair, I'd sell it to you for nine hundred and ninety-nine dollars. I'd lose a dollar. It would be the moral thing to do in this case. To lose a dollar would be the right thing."

"We've got five dollars total," I said again.

"That's too bad," he said again and thought harder about the possibilities. "How about this? I'll give you twenty-four hours to come up with nine hundred and ninety-nine dollars. You come back here at lunchtime tomorrow with the money, and I'll sell it back to you. How does that sound?"

"It sounds good," I said.

"All right, then," he said. "We have a deal. And I'll get you started. Here's twenty bucks to get you started."

He opened up his wallet and pulled out a crisp twenty-dollar bill and gave it to me. Rose of Sharon, Junior, and I walked out into the daylight to search for nine hundred and seventy-four more dollars.

1:00 P.M.

Rose of Sharon, Junior, and I carried our twenty-dollar bill and our five dollars in loose change over to the 7-Eleven and spent it to buy three bottles of imagination. We needed to figure out how to raise all that money in one day. Thinking hard, we huddled in an alley beneath the Alaska Way Viaduct and finished off those bottles one, two, and three.

2:00 P.M.

Rose of Sharon was gone when I woke. I heard later she had hitchhiked back to Toppenish and was living with her sister on the reservation.

Junior was passed out beside me, covered in his own vomit, or maybe somebody else's vomit, and my head hurt from thinking, so I left him alone and walked down to the water. I loved the smell of ocean water. Salt always smells like memory.

When I got to the wharf, I ran into three Aleut cousins[6] who sat on a wooden bench and stared out at the bay and cried. Most of the homeless Indians in Seattle come from Alaska. One by one, each of them hopped a big working boat in Anchorage or Barrow or Juneau, fished his way south to Seattle, jumped off the boat with a pocketful of cash to party hard at one of the highly sacred and traditional Indian bars, went broke and broker, and has been trying to find his way back to the boat and the frozen north ever since.

These Aleuts smelled like salmon, I thought, and they told me they were going to sit on that wooden bench until their boat came back.

"How long has your boat been gone?" I asked.

"Eleven years," the elder Aleut said.

I cried with them for a while.

"Hey," I said. "Do you guys have any money I can borrow?"

They didn't.

3:00 P.M.

I walked back to Junior. He was still passed out. I put my face down near his mouth to make sure he was breathing. He was alive, so I dug around in his blue-jean pockets and found half a cigarette. I smoked it all the way down and thought about my grandmother.

---

6. **Aleut cousins:** The Aleuts are natives of the Aleutian Islands and other parts of western Alaska.

Her name was Agnes, and she died of breast cancer when I was fourteen. My father thought Agnes caught her tumors from the uranium mine on the reservation. But my mother said the disease started when Agnes was walking back from the powwow one night and got run over by a motorcycle. She broke three ribs, and my mother said those ribs never healed right, and tumors always take over when you don't heal right.

Sitting beside Junior, smelling the smoke and salt and vomit, I wondered if my grandmother's cancer had started when somebody stole her powwow regalia. Maybe the cancer started in her broken heart and then leaked out into her breasts. I know it's crazy, but I wondered if could bring my grandmother back to life if I bought back her regalia.

I needed money, big money, so I left Junior and walked over to the Real Change office.

4:00 P.M.

"Real Change is a multifaceted organization that publishes a newspaper, supports cultural projects that empower the poor and homeless, and mobilizes the public around poverty issues. Real Change's mission is to organize, educate, and build alliances to create solutions to homelessness and poverty. They exist to provide a voice to poor people in our community."

I memorized Real Change's mission statement because I sometimes sell the newspaper on the streets. But you have to stay sober to sell it, and I'm not always good at staying sober. Anybody can sell the newspaper. You buy each copy for thirty cents and sell it for a dollar and keep the net profit.

"I need one thousand four hundred and thirty papers," I said to the Big Boss.

"That's a strange number," he said. "And that's a lot of papers."

"I need them."

The Big Boss pulled out the calculator and did the math. "It will cost you four hundred and twenty-nine dollars for that many," he said.

"If I had that kind of money, I wouldn't need to sell the papers."

"What's going on, Jackson-to-the-Second-Power?" he asked. He is the only one who calls me that. He is a funny and kind man.

I told him about my grandmother's powwow regalia and how much money I needed to buy it back.

"We should call the police," he said.

"I don't want to do that," I said. "It's a quest now. I need to win it back by myself."

"I understand," he said. "And to be honest, I'd give you the papers to sell if I thought it would work. But the record for most papers sold in a day by one vendor is only three hundred and two."

"That would net me about two hundred bucks," I said.

The Big Boss used his calculator. "Two hundred and eleven dollars and forty cents," he said.

"That's not enough," I said.

"The most money anybody has made in one day is five hundred and twenty-five. And that's because somebody gave Old Blue five hundred-dollar bills for some dang reason. The average daily net is about thirty dollars."

"This isn't going to work."

"No."

"Can you lend me some money?"

"I can't do that," he said. "If I lend you money, I have to lend money to everybody."

"What can you do?"

"I'll give you fifty papers for free. But don't tell anybody I did it."

"Okay," I said.

He gathered up the newspapers and handed them to me. I held them to my chest. He hugged me. I carried the newspapers back toward the water.

5:00 P.M.

Back on the wharf, I stood near the Bainbridge Island Terminal and tried to sell papers to business commuters walking onto the ferry.

I sold five in one hour, dumped the other forty-five into a garbage can, and walked into the McDonald's, ordered four cheeseburgers for a dollar each, and slowly ate them.

After eating, I walked outside and vomited on the sidewalk. I hated to lose my food so soon after eating it. As an alcoholic Indian with a busted stomach, I always hope I can keep enough food in my stomach to stay alive.

6:00 P.M.

With one dollar in my pocket, I walked back to Junior. He was still passed out, so I put my ear to his chest and listened for his heartbeat. He was alive, so I took off his shoes and socks and found one dollar in his left sock and fifty cents in his right sock. With two dollars and fifty cents in my hand, I sat beside Junior and thought about my grandmother and her stories.

When I was sixteen, my grandmother told me a story about World War II. She was a nurse at a military hospital in Sydney, Australia. Over the course of two years, she comforted and healed U.S. and Australian soldiers.

One day, she tended to a wounded Maori[7] soldier. He was very dark-skinned. His hair was black and curly, and his eyes were black and warm. His face was covered with bright tattoos.

"Are you Maori?" he asked my grandmother.

"No," she said. "I'm Spokane Indian. From the United States."

"Ah, yes," he said. "I have heard of your tribes. But you are the first American Indian I have ever met."

"There's a lot of Indian soldiers fighting for the United States," she said. "I have a brother still fighting in Germany, and I lost another brother on Okinawa."

"I am sorry," he said. "I was on Okinawa as well. It was terrible." He had lost his legs to an artillery attack.

---

7. **Maori:** The aboriginal people of New Zealand.

"I am sorry about your legs," my grandmother said.

"It's funny, isn't it?" he asked.

"What's funny?"

"How we brown people are killing other brown people so white people will remain free."

"I hadn't thought of it that way."

"Well, sometimes I think of it that way. And other times, I think of it the way they want me to think of it. I get confused."

She fed him morphine.

"Do you believe in heaven?" he asked.

"Which heaven?" she asked.

"I'm talking about the heaven where my legs are waiting for me."

They laughed.

"Of course," he said, "my legs will probably run away from me when I get to heaven. And how will I ever catch them?"

"You have to get your arms strong," my grandmother said. "So you can run on your hands."

They laughed again.

Sitting beside Junior, I laughed with the memory of my grandmother's story. I put my hand close to Junior's mouth to make sure he was still breathing. Yes, Junior was alive, so I took his two dollars and fifty cents and walked to the Korean grocery store over in Pioneer Square.

7:00 P.M.

In the Korean grocery store, I bought a fifty-cent cigar and two scratch lottery tickets for a dollar each. The maximum cash prize was five hundred dollars a ticket. If I won both, I would have enough money to buy back the regalia.

I loved Kay, the young Korean woman who worked the register. She was the daughter of the owners and sang all day.

"I love you," I said when I handed her the money.

"You always say you love me," she said.

"That's because I will always love you."

"You are a sentimental fool."

"I'm a romantic old man."

"Too old for me."

"I know I'm too old for you, but I can dream."

"Okay," she said. "I agree to be a part of your dreams, but I will only hold your hand in your dreams. No kissing and no sex. Not even in your dreams."

"Okay," I said. "No sex. Just romance."

"Good-bye, Jackson Jackson, my love, I will see you soon."

I left the store, walked over to Occidental Park, sat on a bench, and smoked my cigar all the way down.

Ten minutes after I finished the cigar, I scratched my first lottery ticket and won nothing. So I could win only five hundred dollars now, and that would be just half of what I needed.

Ten minutes later, I scratched my other lottery ticket and won a free ticket, a small consolation and one more chance to win money.

I walked back to Kay.

"Jackson Jackson," she said. "Have you come back to claim my heart?"

"I won a free ticket," I said.

"Just like a man," she said. "You love money and power more than you love me."

"It's true," I said. "And I'm sorry it's true."

She gave me another scratch ticket, and I carried it outside. I liked to scratch my tickets in private. Hopeful and sad, I scratched that third ticket and won real money. I carried it back inside to Kay.

"I won a hundred dollars," I said.

She examined the ticket and laughed. "That's a fortune," she said and counted out five twenties. Our fingertips touched as she handed me the money. I felt electric and constant.

"Thank you," I said and gave her one of the bills.

"I can't take that," she said. "It's your money."

"No, it's tribal. It's an Indian thing. When you win, you're supposed to share with your family."

"I'm not your family."

"Yes, you are."

She smiled. She kept the money. With eighty dollars in my pocket, I said good-bye to my dear Kay and walked out into the cold night air.

8:00 P.M.

I wanted to share the good news with Junior. I walked back to him, but he was gone. I later heard he had hitchhiked down to Portland, Oregon, and died of exposure in an alley behind the Hilton Hotel.

9:00 P.M.

Lonely for Indians, I carried my eighty dollars over to Big Heart's in South Downtown. Big Heart's is an all-Indian bar. Nobody knows how or why Indians migrate to one bar and turn it into an official Indian bar. But Big Heart's has been an Indian bar for twenty-three years. It used to be way up on Aurora Avenue, but a crazy Lummi Indian[8] burned that one down, and the owners moved to the new location, a few blocks south of Safeco Field.

I walked inside Big Heart's and counted fifteen Indians, eight men and seven women. I didn't know any of them, but Indians like to belong, so we all pretended to be cousins.

---

8. **Lummi Indian:** One of the more than twenty small tribes of the Salish, who occupied the area around Puget Sound in present-day Washington State.

"How much for whiskey shots?" I asked the bartender, a fat white guy.

"You want the bad stuff or the badder stuff?"

"As bad as you got."

"One dollar a shot."

I laid my eighty dollars on the bar top.

"All right." I said. "Me and all my cousins here are going to be drinking eighty shots. How many is that apiece?"

"Counting you," a woman shouted from behind me, "that's five shots for everybody."

I turned to look at her. She was a chubby and pale Indian sitting with a tall and skinny Indian man.

"All right, math genius," I said to her and then shouted for the whole bar to hear. "Five drinks for everybody!"

All of the other Indians rushed the bar, but I sat with the mathematician and her skinny friend. We took our time with our whiskey shots.

"What's your tribe?" I asked them.

"I'm Duwamish,"[9] she said. "And he's Crow."[10]

"You're a long way from Montana," I said to him.

"I'm Crow," he said. "I flew here."

"What's your name?" I asked them.

"I'm Irene Muse," she said. "And this is Honey Boy."

She shook my hand hard, but he offered his hand like I was supposed to kiss it. So I kissed it. He giggled and blushed as well as a dark-skinned Crow can blush.

"You're one of them two-spirits, aren't you?" I asked him.

"I love women," he said. "And I love men."

"Sometimes both at the same time," Irene said.

We laughed.

"Man," I said to Honey Boy. "So you must have about eight or nine spirits going on inside of you, enit?"

"Sweetie," he said, "I'll be whatever you want me to be."

"Oh, no," Irene said. "Honey Boy is falling in love."

"It has nothing to do with love," he said.

We laughed.

"Wow," I said. "I'm flattered, Honey Boy, but I don't play on your team."

"Never say never," he said.

"You better be careful," Irene said. "Honey Boy knows all sorts of magic. He always makes straight boys fall for him."

"Honey Boy," I said, "you can try to seduce me. And Irene, you can try with him. But my heart belongs to a woman named Kay."

"Is your Kay a virgin?" Honey Boy asked.

---

9. **Duwamish:** A tribe that originally occupied the area of present-day Seattle, Washington.
10. **Crow:** The *Apsaalooke*, which English-language speakers translated as "crow" or "bird people," a tribe that occupied lands in present-day Wyoming and Montana.

We laughed.

We drank our whiskey shots until they were gone. But the other Indians bought me more whiskey shots because I'd been so generous with my money. Honey Boy pulled out his credit card, and I drank and sailed on that plastic boat.

After a dozen shots, I asked Irene to dance. And she refused. But Honey Boy shuffled over to the jukebox, dropped in a quarter, and selected Willie Nelson's "Help Me Make It Through the Night." As Irene and I sat at the table and laughed and drank more whiskey, Honey Boy danced a slow circle around us and sang along with Willie.

"Are you serenading me?" I asked him.

He kept singing and dancing.

"Are you serenading me?" I asked him again.

"He's going to put a spell on you," Irene said.

I leaned over the table, spilling a few drinks, and kissed Irene hard. She kissed me back.

10:00 P.M.

Irene pushed me into the women's bathroom, into a stall, shut the door behind us, and shoved her hand down my pants. She was short, so I had to lean over to kiss her. I grabbed and squeezed her everywhere I could reach, and she was wonderfully fat, and every part of her body felt like a large, warm, and soft breast.

Midnight

Nearly blind with alcohol, I stood alone at the bar and swore I'd been standing in the bathroom with Irene only a minute ago.

"One more shot!" I yelled at the bartender.

"You've got no more money!" he yelled.

"Somebody buy me a drink!" I shouted.

"They've got no more money!"

"Where's Irene and Honey Boy?"

"Long gone!"

2:00 A.M.

"Closing time!" the bartender shouted at the three or four Indians still drinking hard after a long hard day of drinking. Indian alcoholics are either sprinters or marathon runners.

"Where's Irene and Honey Bear?" I asked.

"They've been gone for hours," the bartender said.

"Where'd they go?"

"I told you a hundred times, I don't know."

"What am I supposed to do?"

"It's closing time. I don't care where you go, but you're not staying here."

"You are an ungrateful bastard. I've been good to you."

"You don't leave right now, I'm going to kick your ass."

"Come on, I know how to fight."

He came for me. I don't remember what happened after that.

4:00 A.M.

I emerged from the blackness and discovered myself walking behind a big warehouse. I didn't know where I was. My face hurt. I touched my nose and decided it might be broken. Exhausted and cold, I pulled a plastic tarp from a truck bed, wrapped it around me like a faithful lover, and fell asleep in the dirt.

6:00 A.M.

Somebody kicked me in the ribs. I opened my eyes and looked up at a white cop.

"Jackson," said the cop. "Is that you?"

"Officer Williams," I said. He was a good cop with a sweet tooth. He'd given me hundreds of candy bars over the years. I wonder if he knew I was diabetic.

"What the hell are you doing here?" he asked.

"I was cold and sleepy," I said. "So I laid down."

"You dumb-ass, you passed out on the railroad tracks."

I sat up and looked around. I was lying on the railroad tracks. Dockworkers stared at me. I should have been a railroad-track pizza, a double Indian pepperoni with extra cheese. Sick and scared, I leaned over and puked whiskey.

"What the hell's wrong with you?" Officer Williams asked. "You've never been this stupid."

"It's my grandmother," I said. "She died."

"I'm sorry, man. When did she die?"

"1972."

"And you're killing yourself now?"

"I've been killing myself ever since she died."

He shook his head. He was sad for me. Like I said, he was a good cop.

"And somebody beat the hell out of you," he said. "You remember who?"

"Mr. Grief and I went a few rounds."

"It looks like Mr. Grief knocked you out."

"Mr. Grief always wins."

"Come on," he said, "let's get you out of here."

He helped me stand and led me over to his squad car. He put me in the back. "You throw up in there," he said, "and you're cleaning it up."

"That's fair," I said.

He walked around the car and sat in the driver's seat. "I'm taking you over to detox," he said.

"No, man, that place is awful," I said. "It's full of drunk Indians."

We laughed. He drove away from the docks.

"I don't know how you guys do it," he said.

"What guys?" I asked.

"You Indians. How the hell do you laugh so much? I just picked your ass off the railroad tracks, and you're making jokes. Why the hell do you do that?"

"The two funniest tribes I've ever been around are Indians and Jews, so I guess that says something about the inherent humor of genocide."

We laughed.

"Listen to you, Jackson. You're so smart. Why the hell are you on the streets?"

"Give me a thousand dollars, and I'll tell you."

"You bet I'd give you a thousand dollars if I knew you'd straighten up your life."

He meant it. He was the second-best cop I'd ever known.

"You're a good cop," I said.

"Come on, Jackson," he said. "Don't blow smoke up my ass."

"No, really, you remind me of my grandfather."

"Yeah, that's what you Indians always tell me."

"No, man, my grandfather was a tribal cop. He was a good cop. He never arrested people. He took care of them. Just like you."

"I've arrested hundreds of scumbags, Jackson. And I've shot a couple in the ass."

"It don't matter. You're not a killer."

"I didn't kill them. I killed their asses. I'm an ass-killer."

We drove through downtown. The missions and shelters had already released their overnighters. Sleepy homeless men and women stood on corners and stared up at the gray sky. It was the morning after the night of the living dead.

"Did you ever get scared?" I asked Officer Williams.

"What do you mean?"

"I mean, being a cop, is it scary?"

He thought about that for a while. He contemplated it. I liked that about him.

"I guess I try not to think too much about being afraid," he said. "If you think about fear, then you'll be afraid. The job is boring most of the time. Just driving and looking into dark corners, you know, and seeing nothing. But then things get heavy. You're chasing somebody or fighting them or walking around a dark house and you just know some crazy guy is hiding around a corner, and hell yes, it's scary."

"My grandfather was killed in the line of duty," I said.

"I'm sorry. How'd it happen?"

I knew he'd listen closely to my story.

"He worked on the reservation. Everybody knew everybody. It was safe. We aren't like those crazy Sioux or Apache[11] or any of those other warrior tribes. There's only been three murders on my reservation in the last hundred years."

"That is safe."

---

11. **Sioux or Apache:** Sioux is the collective name for a confederation of three tribes, the Lakota, Dakota, and Nakota, who occupied a vast area in the northern Great Plains. The Apache included several bands and tribes that lived in the American Southwest and northern Mexico. Like the Sioux, the Apache were nomadic hunters who fiercely resisted the incursions of European settlers into their traditional lands and hunting grounds.

"Yeah, we Spokane, we're passive, you know? We're mean with words. And we'll cuss out anybody. But we don't shoot people. Or stab them. Not much, anyway."

"So what happened to your grandfather?"

"This man and his girlfriend were fighting down by Little Falls."

"Domestic dispute. Those are the worst."

"Yeah, but this guy was my grandfather's brother. My great-uncle."

"Oh, no."

"Yeah, it was awful. My grandfather just strolled into the house. He'd been there a thousand times. And his brother and his girlfriend were all drunk and beating on each other. And my grandfather stepped between them just like he'd done a hundred times before. And the girlfriend tripped or something. She fell down and hit her head and started crying. And my grandfather knelt down beside her to make sure she was all right. And for some reason, my great-uncle reached down, pulled my grandfather's pistol out of the holster, and shot him in the head."

"That's terrible. I'm sorry."

"Yeah, my great-uncle could never figure out why he did it. He went to prison forever, you know, and he always wrote these long letters. Like fifty pages of tiny little handwriting. And he was always trying to figure out why he did it. He'd write and write and write and try to figure it out. He never did. It's a great big mystery."

"Do you remember your grandfather?"

"A little bit. I remember the funeral. My grandmother wouldn't let them bury him. My father had to drag her away from the grave."

"I don't know what to say."

"I don't, either."

We stopped in front of the detox center.

"We're here," Officer Williams said.

"I can't go in there," I said.

"You have to."

"Please, no. They'll keep me for twenty-four hours. And then it will be too late."

"Too late for what?"

I told him about my grandmother's regalia and the deadline for buying it back.

"If it was stolen," he said, "then you need to file reports. I'll investigate it myself. If that thing is really your grandmother's, I'll get it back for you. Legally."

"No," I said. "That's not fair. The pawnbroker didn't know it was stolen. And besides, I'm on a mission here. I want to be a hero, you know? I want to win it back like a knight."

"That's romantic crap."

"It might be. But I care about it. It's been a long time since I really cared about something."

Officer Williams turned around in his seat and stared at me. He studied me.

"I'll give you some money," he said. "I don't have much. Only thirty bucks. I'm short until payday. And it's not enough to get back the regalia. But it's something."

"I'll take it," I said.

"I'm giving it to you because I believe in what you believe. I'm hoping, and I don't know why I'm hoping it, but I hope you can turn thirty bucks into a thousand somehow."

"I believe in magic."

"I believe you'll take my money and get drunk on it."

"Then why are you giving it to me?"

"There ain't no such thing as an atheist cop."

"Sure there is."

"Yeah, well, I'm not an atheist cop."

He let me out of the car, handed me two fives and a twenty, and shook my hand. "Take care of yourself, Jackson," he said. "Stay off the railroad tracks."

"I'll try," I said.

He drove away. Carrying my money, I headed back toward the water.

8:00 A.M.

On the wharf, those three Aleut men still waited on the wooden bench.

"Have you seen your ship?" I asked.

"Seen a lot of ships," the elder Aleut said. "But not our ship."

I sat on the bench with them. We sat in silence for a long time. I wondered whether we would fossilize if we sat there long enough.

I thought about my grandmother. I'd never seen her dance in her regalia. More than anything, I wished I'd seen her dance at a powwow.

"Do you guys know any songs?" I asked the Aleuts.

"I know all of Hank Williams," the elder Aleut said.

"How about Indian songs?"

"Hank Williams is Indian."

"How about sacred songs?"

"Hank Williams is sacred."

"I'm talking about ceremonial songs, you know, religious ones. The songs you sing back home when you're wishing and hoping."

"What are you wishing and hoping for?"

"I'm wishing my grandmother was still alive."

"Every song I know is about that."

"Well, sing me as many as you can."

The Aleuts sang their strange and beautiful songs. I listened. They sang about my grandmother and their grandmothers. They were lonely for the cold and snow. I was lonely for everybody.

10:00 A.M.

After the Aleuts finished their last song, we sat in silence. Indians are good at silence.

"Was that the last song?" I asked.

"We sang all the ones we could," the elder Aleut said. "All the others are just for our people."

I understood. We Indians have to keep our secrets. And these Aleuts were so secretive that they didn't refer to themselves as Indians.

"Are you guys hungry?" I asked.

They looked at one another and communicated without talking.

"We could eat," the elder Aleut said.

11:00 A.M.

The Aleuts and I walked over to Mother's Kitchen, a greasy diner in the International District. I knew they served homeless Indians who'd lucked into money.

"Four for breakfast?" the waitress asked when we stepped inside.

"Yes, we're very hungry," the elder Aleut said.

She sat us in a booth near the kitchen. I could smell the food cooking. My stomach growled.

"You guys want separate checks?" the waitress asked.

"No, I'm paying for it," I said.

"Aren't you the generous one," she said.

"Don't do that," I said.

"Do what?" she asked.

"Don't ask me rhetorical questions. They scare me."

She looked puzzled, and then she laughed.

"Okay, Professor," she said. "I'll only ask you real questions from now on."

"Thank you."

"What do you guys want to eat?"

"That's the best question anybody can ask anybody," I said.

"How much money you got?" she asked.

"Another good question," I said. "I've got twenty-five dollars I can spend. Bring us all the breakfast you can, plus your tip."

She knew the math.

"All right, that's four specials and four coffees and fifteen percent for me."

The Aleuts and I waited in silence. Soon enough, the waitress returned and poured us four coffees, and we sipped at them until she returned again with four plates of food. Eggs, bacon, toast, hash-brown potatoes. It is amazing how much food you can buy for so little money.

Grateful, we feasted.

Noon

I said farewell to the Aleuts and walked toward the pawnshop. I later heard the Aleuts had waded into the saltwater near Dock 47 and disappeared. Some Indians said the Aleuts walked on the water and headed north. Other Indians saw the Aleuts drown. I don't know what happened to them.

I looked for the pawnshop and couldn't find it. I swear it wasn't located in the place where it had been before. I walked twenty or thirty blocks looking for the pawnshop, turned corners and bisected intersections, looked up its name in the phone books, and asked people walking past me if they'd ever heard of it. But that pawnshop seemed to have sailed away from me like a ghost ship. I wanted to cry. Right when I'd given up, when I turned one last corner and thought I might die if I didn't find that pawnshop, there it was, located in a space I swore it hadn't been filling up a few minutes before.

I walked inside and greeted the pawnbroker, who looked a little younger than he had before.

"It's you," he said.

"Yes, it's me," I said.

"Jackson Jackson."

"That is my name."

"Where are your friends?"

"They went traveling. But it's okay. Indians are everywhere."

"Do you have my money?"

"How much do you need again?" I asked and hoped the price had changed.

"Nine hundred and ninety-nine dollars."

It was still the same price. Of course it was the same price. Why would it change?

"I don't have that," I said.

"What do you have?"

"Five dollars."

I set the crumpled Lincoln on the countertop. The pawnbroker studied it.

"Is that the same five dollars from yesterday?"

"No, it's different."

He thought about the possibilities.

"Did you work hard for this money?" he asked.

"Yes," I said.

He closed his eyes and thought harder about the possibilities. Then he stepped into his back room and returned with my grandmother's regalia.

"Take it," he said and held it out to me.

"I don't have the money."

"I don't want your money."

"But I wanted to win it."

"You did win it. Now, take it before I change my mind."

Do you know how many good men live in this world? Too many to count!

I took my grandmother's regalia and walked outside. I knew that solitary yellow bead was part of me. I knew I was that yellow bead in part. Outside, I wrapped myself in my grandmother's regalia and breathed her in. I stepped off the sidewalk and into the intersection. Pedestrians stopped. Cars stopped. The city stopped. They all watched me dance with my grandmother. I was my grandmother, dancing.

[2003]

American Contexts

"Inventing the Truth": The Contemporary Memoir

"This is the age of the memoir," William Zinsser observes in his introduction to a collection of essays by some skilled practitioners of the form,
Inventing the Truth: The Art and Craft of Memoir. In fact, various kinds
of autobiographical writings have played a significant role in the development of American literature and culture since the earliest European
settlement of what became the United States. Two of the most prominent
genres in colonial New England were the captivity narrative and the
Puritan spiritual autobiography, as exemplified by Jonathan Edwards's
Personal Narrative. Benjamin Franklin, who was himself a child of Puritanism, refashioned such narratives to very different ends in his *Autobiography,* the account of his material progress and rise from obscurity to
fame in the British colonies of North America. After the Revolution, among
the most important weapons in the abolitionist crusade were slave narratives, including works by Olaudah Equiano, Frederick Douglass, and
Harriet Jacobs, which continued to shape the African American literary
tradition long after slavery ended. Many works of American fiction are
autobiographical in nature, including *Adventures of Huckleberry Finn,*
which Mark Twain first called "Huck Finn's Autobiography." Twain subsequently wrote his own autobiography, as did his contemporaries Henry
Adams and Henry James, as well as a host of twentieth-century writers

such as Gertrude Stein, Zora Neale Hurston, Richard Wright, and Arthur Miller.

The contemporary memoir is a distinct form of autobiography, a term that was not used to identify such first-person narratives until early in the nineteenth century. If Franklin had published what later editors named his *Autobiography*, he would no doubt have called the work his "Memoirs," a term then used to describe accounts of the public life and achievements of significant historical figures, usually men. In contrast, the contemporary memoir most often concerns experiences and events of personal rather than historical significance. Describing the writing of her memoir, a portion of which is included in the following section, Annie Dillard explained:

> It isn't an autobiography, and it isn't "memoirs." I wouldn't dream of writing my memoirs; I'm only forty years old. Or my autobiography; any chronology of my days would make very dull reading – I've spent about thirty years behind either a book or a desk. The book I am writing is an account of a childhood in Pittsburgh, Pennsylvania, where I grew up.

Her comment calls attention to important characteristics of the contemporary memoir, which frequently focuses on childhood experiences made meaningful and compelling through the artistry of the author. Many of those who have been drawn to the form have also written novels, and the densely detailed rendering of past experience in the memoir frequently seems as much the product of imagination as memory, which is also inevitably limited and fallible. The memoir, however, may be understood to aim at something other than simple accuracy or historical truth. As N. Scott Momaday observes in the selection from his memoir included in this section, "Memory begins to qualify the imagination, to give it another formation, one that is peculiar to the self."

Questions about truth or authenticity have not impeded the remarkable emergence of the memoir, which during the last thirty years or so has become one of the most popular of all literary forms. That popularity is perhaps not too difficult to understand, since every individual has a story, and the memoir implicitly asserts the potential value and significance of that story. Indeed, as the works in the following section reveal, the memoir opens up a wide range of experience to both writers and readers. There is a sharp contrast, for example, between Annie Dillard's *An American Childhood*, an account of her sheltered early life in an affluent area of Pittsburgh, and the memoir of another white writer who grew up at the same time, David Mamet's "The Rake," in which he recounts deeply painful scenes of domestic abuse during his childhood in suburban Chicago. The other works illuminate strikingly different backgrounds, cultures, and experiences: N. Scott Momaday's complex ancestry and early life on Indian reservations in *The Names*; Maxine Hong Kingston's struggle against the sexism of her Chinese emigrant community in *The Woman Warrior*; bell hooks's experience of growing up in an oppressive home in the racially segregated South in *Bone Black*; and Gary Soto's childhood in a poor Latino community and later courtship of a young Japanese woman in "Like Mexicans." All of these works offer artistic pleasures as well as the satisfaction of intimately sharing another's experience, which is doubtless one of the main attractions of the memoir. Taken together, these works not only enrich our sense of what constitutes an "American" experience but they also expand our sense of what it means to *be* an American in the United States.

bedfordstmartins.com/ americanlit for research links on the authors in this section

N. Scott Momaday

[b. 1934]

Navarre Scott Momaday was born in 1934 in Lawton, Oklahoma, and grew up in both non-Indian communities and on several reservations in the Southwest before attending a military academy in Virginia. After receiving a BA at the University of New Mexico, Momaday briefly attended law school at the University of Virginia before entering Stanford University, where he specialized in American poetry and received a PhD in English in 1964. Since then, he has published more than a dozen books, including literary criticism, autobiographical writings, collections of poetry, and novels, the first of which, *House Made of Dawn*, won the Pulitzer Prize in 1969. That has often been cited as a breakthrough event for Native American literature. As Momaday emphasizes, however, his own perspective is broadly multicultural. "I grew up in two worlds and straddle both those worlds even now," he has observed. The evolution of his complex sense of self — as a Native American intensely proud of his Kiowa heritage and as a Western man with a deep love of English literature — is at the center of his memoir *The Names*. "It is a search and a celebration, a book of identities and sources," Wallace Stegner observed in his review in the *New York Times*. "Out of ordinary materials — genealogy, tribal tales, memories of a boyhood in Oklahoma, at Ship Rock in the Navajo country and at Jemez pueblo, where his parents taught school — he has built a mystical, provocative book." In the first part of the book, Momaday explores those sources, tracing the ancestry of his parents: Al Momaday, christened Alfred Scott Mammedaty, a Kiowa who grew up on the reservation in the Rainy Mountain area of Oklahoma; and Natachee Scott, "a southern belle" from Kentucky whose maternal grandmother was a Cherokee and who came "to see herself as an Indian." In the second part, Momaday turns to other crucial sources of his identity, the early memories and imaginings described in the following excerpt from *The Names: A Memoir* (1976).

N. Scott Momaday

This photograph of the prominent novelist, painter, poet, and scholar was taken in 1990.

Five Generations

The Names includes numerous family photographs, including this group portrait
of Momaday's Kiowa relatives, which precedes the following selection from part 2
of the book. Momaday identifies the figures as Kau-au-ointy, "Cry of the Goose,"
his great-great-grandmother; Keahdinekeah, "Throwing It Down," his great-
grandmother; Mammedaty, "Walking Above," his grandfather; Clara, his aunt;
and her son Marland.

From THE NAMES: A MEMOIR

In my earliest years I traveled a number of times from Oklahoma to the Navajo reservation in New Mexico and Arizona and back again. The two landscapes are fixed in my
mind. They are separate realities, but they are sometimes confused in my memory. I
place my feet in the plain, but my prints are made on the mountain.

I was much alone. I had no brothers or sisters, and as it happened in my childhood,
much of it, my peers were at removes from me, across cultures and languages. I had to
create my society in my mind. And for a child this kind of creation is accomplished easily enough. I imagined much.

When I was three years old my head must have been full of Indian as well as English
words. The sounds of both Kiowa and Navajo are quite natural and familiar to me, and

even now I can make these sounds easily and accurately with my voice, so well established are they in my ear. I lived very close to these "foreign" languages, poised at a crucial time in the learning process to enter into either or both of them wholly. But my mother was concerned that I should learn English as my "native" language, and so English is first and foremost in my possession. My mother's love of books, and of English literature in particular, is intense, and naturally she wanted me to share in it. I have seen Grendel's shadow on the walls of Canyon de Chelly, and once, having led the sun around Hoskinini Mesa, I saw Copperfield at Oljeto Trading Post.[1]

In 1936 Haske Noswood, a Navajo friend, invited my parents and me to come to Gallup, New Mexico, where my mother and father hoped to find work in the Indian Service. We arrived at the time of Naa'ahoohai, the old celebration of the Navajos which had by that time become the Intertribal Indian Ceremonial. The Navajos came from far and wide to Gallup, which is called in Navajo Na'nizhoozhi, the "place of the bridge" on the Rio Puerco. We lived in the Del Mar Hotel, across from the old Harvey House on the Santa Fe Railroad, and I slept in a bureau drawer. My father found a temporary job: He painted signs for the traders in the Ceremonial exhibit hall at fifty cents a sign. And later he got on as a truck dispatcher with the Roads Department, Indian Service, at Shiprock, which is called in Navajo Naat'aaniineez (literally "tall chief"; the town takes its name from the great monolith that stands nearby in an arid reach of the San Juan Basin). The name Shiprock, like other Anglicizations in this region, seems incongruous enough, but from certain points of view — and from the air, especially — the massive rock Naat'aaniineez resembles very closely a ship at sea. Soon thereafter my mother was offered the job of switchboard operator at Shiprock Agency, which she accepted, and we were a solvent and independent entity. My parents have told me time and again what an intoxication were those days, and I think back to them on that basis; they involve me in a tide of confidence and well-being. What on earth was not possible? I must have been carried along in the waves of hope and happiness that were gathered in the hearts of my young and free and beautiful parents.

In the years between 1936 and 1943 we lived on the Navajo reservation at Shiprock, New Mexico, and at Tuba City, then Chinle, Arizona. There were in that span of time a number of sojourns away from home — to Oklahoma, to Kentucky, even to Louisiana (where my aunt Ethel lived at the time), and for several months my mother and I, while my father waited in Oklahoma to be drafted into the army (it turned out that he wasn't drafted, though the war was raging then), lived on the San Carlos Apache reservation in

---

1. **I have seen . . . Oljeto Trading Post:** Grendel is a monster killed by Beowulf in the Old English epic *Beowulf*, composed between 800 and 1000. Canyon de Chelly, which is most famous for the cliff dwellings and rock art created by the Anasazi peoples between 400 and 1300, is now part of the Navajo Reservation in northeastern Arizona and southern Utah. In the 1860s, when Colonel Kit Carson led a campaign against the Navajo in the canyon, the revered Chief Hoskinini led some of his people to safety in Monument Valley, the location of the Oljeto Trading Post. Copperfield is the autobiographical character in *David Copperfield* (1850), by the British novelist Charles Dickens (1812–1870).

the southeastern quadrant of Arizona — but "home" was particularly the Navajo country, Dine bikeyah. My earliest playmates and schoolmates were Navajo children and the children of Indian Service employees. Just at the time I was learning to talk, I heard the Navajo language spoken all around me. And just as I was coming alive to the wide world, the vast and beautiful landscape of Dine bikeyah *was* my world, all of it that I could perceive.

Memory begins to qualify the imagination, to give it another formation, one that is peculiar to the self. I remember isolated, yet fragmented and confused, images — and images, shifting, enlarging, is the word, rather than moments or events — which are mine alone and which are especially vivid to me. They involve me wholly and immediately, even though they are the disintegrated impressions of a young child. They call for a certain attitude of belief on my part now; that is, they must mean something, but their best reality does not consist in meaning. They are not stories in that sense, but they are storylike, mythic, never evolved but evolving ever. There are such things in the world: it is in their nature to be believed; it is not necessarily in them to be understood. Of all that must have happened to and about me in those my earliest days, why should these odd particulars alone be fixed in my mind? If I were to remember other things, I should be someone else.

There is a room full of light and space. The walls are bare; there are no windows or doors of which I am aware. I am inside and alone. Then gradually I become aware of another presence in the room. There is an object, something not extraordinary at first, something of the room itself — but what I cannot tell. The object does not matter at first, but at some point — after a moment? an hour? — it moves, and I am unsettled. I am not yet frightened; rather I am somewhat surprised, vaguely anxious, fascinated, perhaps. The object grows; it expands farther and farther beyond definition. It is no longer an object but a mass. It is so large now that I am dwarfed by it, reduced almost to nothing. And *now* I am afraid, nearly terrified, and yet I have no will to resist; I remain attentive, strangely curious in proportion as I am afraid. The huge, shapeless mass is displacing all of the air, all of the space in the room. It swells against me. It is soft and supple and resilient, like a great bag of water. At last I am desperate, desperately afraid of being suffocated, lost in some dimple or fold of this vague, enormous thing. I try to cry out, but I have no voice.

Restore my voice for me.

How many times has this memory been nearly recovered, the definition almost realized! Again and again I have come to that awful edge, that one word, perhaps, that I cannot bring from my mouth. I sometimes think that it is surely a name, the name of someone or something, that if only I could utter it, the terrific mass would snap away into focus, and I should see and recognize what it is at once; I should have it then, once and for all, in my possession.

. . .

It is a bright, hot day, but the arbor is cool. The smooth gray wood of the benches is cool to the touch. The worn patchwork covers are cool and soft. The red, hard-packed earth of the floor is dark and cool. It is quiet and sleepy inside. I love this place. I love the cool well water that I bring in a dipper to my mouth.

One time the creek was backed up, and my dad . . .
Was it that time he saw the animal, the . . .
Yes, that was it; that was the time.

We set out, my father and I, in the afternoon. We walk down the long grade to the ravine that runs diagonally below, up again and through the brambles. The sun burns my skin. I feel the stiff spines and furry burrs at my legs and hear the insects humming there all around. We walk down into the shadows of Rainy Mountain Creek. The banks are broad and the mud is dry and cracked, broken into innumerable large facets like shards of pottery, smooth, delicately curved, where the water has risen and then withdrawn and the sun has baked the bank. The water is brown and runs very slowly at the surface; here and there are glints of light and beams that strike through the trees and splash on the rocks and roots and underbrush. We cross the creek on a log and climb up the west bank where the woods are thicker. There is a small clearing, and inside the clearing is a single tree that was bent down to the ground and tied as a sapling; and so it remains curved, grown over in a long, graceful arc, its nimble new branches brushing whorls on the ground. It is one of my delights, for it is a wonderful, lively swing. My father lifts me up and I take hold of the slender, tapered trunk, and then he pulls me down and lets me go. I spring up, laughing, laughing, and bob up and down.

We continue on, through fields now, to "across the creek," as the house there was always called when I was a child. It is Keahdinekeah's house, built for her by my grandfather; but when you are a child you don't think of houses as possessions; it does not occur to you that anyone has ownership in them. "Across the creek" is where Justin Lee lives, a cousin not much older than I, with his sister, Lela, and his parents, Jim and Dorothy Ware, and his grandmother Keahdinekeah.

It seems reasonable to suppose that I visited my great-grandmother on other occasions, but I remember only this once, and I remember it very well. My father leads me into her room. It is dark and close inside, and I cannot see until my eyes become accustomed to the dim light. There is a certain odor in the room and not elsewhere in the house, the odor of my great-grandmother's old age. It is not unpleasant, but it is most particular and exclusive, as much hers as is her voice or her hair or the nails of her hands. Such a thing has not only the character of great age but something also of the deep self, of one's own dignity and well-being. Because of this, I believe, this old blind woman is like no one I have ever seen or shall ever see. To a child her presence is formidable. My father is talking to her in Kiowa, and I do not understand what is being said, only that the talk is of me. She is seated on the side of her bed, and my father brings me to stand directly in front of her. She reaches out for me and I place my hands in hers. *Eh neh neh neh neh.* She begins to weep very softly in a high, thin, hollow voice. Her hands are little and soft, so soft that they seem not to consist in flesh and bone, but in the softest fiber, cotton or fine wool. Her voice is so delicate, so surely expressive of her deep feelings. Long afterwards I think: That was a wonderful and beautiful thing that happened in my life. There, on that warm, distant afternoon: an old woman and a child, holding hands across the generations. There is great good in such a remembrance; I cannot imagine that it might have been lost upon me.

[1976]

Maxine Hong Kingston

[b. 1940]

Maxine Hong Kingston

Christopher Felver, who has spent his life photographing people he calls "creative revolutionaries," took this photograph of Kingston in Oakland, California, in 2001.

Maxine Hong Kingston was born in 1940 in Stockton, California, the first of six children born in the United States to immigrants from China. Although she could not speak English until she started school, Kingston was an outstanding student and won a scholarship to the University of California, Berkeley, where she received a BA in English in 1962 and later returned to earn a teaching certificate in 1965. Since then, she has had a distinguished career as a writer, publishing several books of fiction and nonfiction, including *Veterans of War, Veterans of Peace* (2006), a collection of writings by members of Kingston's healing workshops for veterans, their families, and others suffering from the trauma of war and violence. Kingston taught school while writing her first two books, *The Woman Warrior* (1976) and *China Men* (1980), both of which won a National Book Critics Circle Award. She had originally conceived of them as a single long book, but Kingston decided to divide the manuscript into two books, exploring first her female and then her male ancestors. As those linked books reveal, Kingston's childhood and identity were powerfully shaped by a number of factors: American racism and the sexism of her own family and community; the bitter silence of her father, who had been trained as a scholar of traditional Chinese classics; and the example of her formidable mother, who had been a doctor in China but who worked as a laundress and maid in the United States. She is the dominant presence in *The Woman Warrior*, which takes its title from one of her mother's fantastic "talk stories," narratives of legendary figures, female ancestors, and her earlier life in China. "She said I would grow up a wife and a slave, but she taught me the song of the woman warrior, Fa Mu Lan," Kingston recalls, suggesting the connections between such stories and both her own storytelling and the passionate revolt described in the following section from *The Woman Warrior: Memoirs of a Girlhood Among Ghosts* (1976).

From THE WOMAN WARRIOR:
MEMOIRS OF A GIRLHOOD AMONG GHOSTS

My American life has been such a disappointment.

"I got straight A's, Mama."

"Let me tell you a true story about a girl who saved her village."

I could not figure out what was my village. And it was important that I do something big and fine, or else my parents would sell me when we made our way back to China. In China there were solutions for what to do with little girls who ate up food and threw tantrums. You can't eat straight A's.

When one of my parents or the emigrant villagers said, " 'Feeding girls is feeding cowbirds,' " I would thrash on the floor and scream so hard I couldn't talk. I couldn't stop.

"What's the matter with her?"

"I don't know. Bad, I guess. You know how girls are. 'There's no profit in raising girls. Better to raise geese than girls.' "

"I would hit her if she were mine. But then there's no use wasting all that discipline on a girl. 'When you raise girls, you're raising children for strangers.' "

"Stop that crying!" my mother would yell. "I'm going to hit you if you don't stop. Bad girl! Stop!" I'm going to remember never to hit or to scold my children for crying, I thought, because then they will only cry more.

"I'm not a bad girl," I would scream. "I'm not a bad girl. I'm not a bad girl." I might as well have said, "I'm not a girl."

"When you were little, all you had to say was 'I'm not a bad girl,' and you could make yourself cry," my mother says, talking-story about my childhood.

I minded that the emigrant villagers shook their heads at my sister and me. "One girl — and another girl," they said, and made our parents ashamed to take us out together. The good part about my brothers being born was that people stopped saying, "All girls," but I learned new grievances. "Did you roll an egg on *my* face like that when *I* was born?" "Did you have a full-month party for *me*?" "Did you turn on all the lights?" "Did you send *my* picture to Grandmother?" "Why not? Because I'm a girl? Is that why not?" "Why didn't you teach me English?" "You like having me beaten up at school, don't you?"

"She is very mean, isn't she?" the emigrant villagers would say.

"Come, children. Hurry. Hurry. Who wants to go out with Great-Uncle?" On Saturday mornings my great-uncle, the ex-river pirate, did the shopping. "Get your coats, whoever's coming."

"I'm coming. I'm coming. Wait for me."

When he heard girls' voices, he turned on us and roared, "No girls!" and left my sisters and me hanging our coats back up, not looking at one another. The boys came back with candy and new toys. When they walked through Chinatown, the people must have said, "A boy — and another boy — and another boy!" At my great-uncle's funeral I secretly tested out feeling glad that he was dead — the six-foot bearish masculinity of him.

I went away to college — Berkeley in the sixties[1] — and I studied, and I marched to change the world, but I did not turn into a boy. I would have liked to bring myself back as a boy for my parents to welcome with chickens and pigs. That was for my brother, who returned alive from Vietnam.

If I went to Vietnam, I would not come back; females desert families. It was said, "There is an outward tendency in females," which meant that I was getting straight A's for the good of my future husband's family, not my own. I did not plan ever to have a husband. I would show my mother and father and the nosey emigrant villagers that girls have no outward tendency. I stopped getting straight A's.

And all the time I was having to turn myself American-feminine, or no dates.

There is a Chinese word for the female I — which is "slave." Break the women with their own tongues!

I refused to cook. When I had to wash dishes, I would crack one or two. "Bad girl," my mother yelled, and sometimes that made me gloat rather than cry. Isn't a bad girl almost a boy?

"What do you want to be when you grow up, little girl?"

"A lumberjack in Oregon."

Even now, unless I'm happy, I burn the food when I cook. I do not feed people. I let the dirty dishes rot. I eat at other people's tables but won't invite them to mine, where the dishes are rotting.

If I could not-eat, perhaps I could make myself a warrior like the swordswoman who drives me. I will — I must — rise and plow the fields as soon as the baby comes out.

Once I get outside the house, what bird might call me; on what horse could I ride away? Marriage and childbirth strengthen the swordswoman, who is not a maid like Joan of Arc. Do the women's work; then do more work, which will become ours too. No husband of mine will say, "I could have been a drummer, but I had to think about the wife and kids. You know how it is." Nobody supports me at the expense of his own adventure. Then I get bitter: no one supports me; I am not loved enough to be supported. That I am not a burden has to compensate for the sad envy when I look at women loved enough to be supported. Even now China wraps double binds around my feet.

---

1. **Berkeley in the sixties:** The University of California, Berkeley, was a center of social and political protests during the 1960s.

When urban renewal tore down my parents' laundry and paved over our slum for a parking lot, I only made up gun and knife fantasies and did nothing useful.

From the fairy tales, I've learned exactly who the enemy are. I easily recognize them — business-suited in their modern American executive guise, each boss two feet taller than I am and impossible to meet eye to eye.

I once worked at an art supply house that sold paints to artists. "Order more of that nigger yellow, willya?" the boss told me. "Bright, isn't it? Nigger yellow."

"I don't like that word," I had to say in my bad, small-person's voice that makes no impact. The boss never deigned to answer.

I also worked at a land developers' association. The building industry was planning a banquet for contractors, real estate dealers, and real estate editors. "Did you know the restaurant you chose for the banquet is being picketed by CORE and the NAACP?"[2] I squeaked.

"Of course I know." The boss laughed. "That's why I chose it."

"I refuse to type these invitations," I whispered, voice unreliable.

He leaned back in his leather chair, his bossy stomach opulent. He picked up his calendar and slowly circled a date. "You will be paid up to here," he said. "We'll mail you the check."

If I took the sword, which my hate must surely have forged out of the air, and gutted him, I would put color and wrinkles into his shirt.

It's not just the stupid racists that I have to do something about, but the tyrants who for whatever reason can deny my family food and work. My job is my own only land.

To avenge my family, I'd have to storm across China to take back our farm from the Communists; I'd have to rage across the United States to take back the laundry in New York and the one in California. Nobody in history has conquered and united both North America and Asia. A descendant of eighty pole fighters, I ought to be able to set out confidently, march straight down our street, get going right now. There's work to do, ground to cover. Surely, the eighty pole fighters, though unseen, would follow me and lead me and protect me, as is the wont of ancestors.

Or it may well be that they're resting happily in China, their spirits dispersed among the real Chinese, and not nudging me at all with their poles. I mustn't feel bad that I haven't done as well as the swordswoman did; after all, no bird called me, no wise old people tutored me. I have no magic beads, no water gourd sight, no rabbit that will jump in the fire when I'm hungry. I dislike armies.

I've looked for the bird. I've seen clouds make pointed angel wings that stream past the sunset, but they shred into clouds. Once at a beach after a long hike I saw a seagull, tiny as an insect. But when I jumped up to tell what miracle I saw, before I could get the words out I understood that the bird was insect-size because it was far away. My brain had momentarily lost its depth perception. I was that eager to find an unusual bird.

---

2. **CORE and the NAACP:** Two major civil rights organizations: the Congress of Racial Equality, established in 1942 by students at the University of Chicago, and the National Association for the Advancement of Colored People, founded by W. E. B. Du Bois, Ida Wells Barnett, and others in New York City in 1909.

The news from China has been confusing. It also had something to do with birds. I was nine years old when the letters made my parents, who are rocks, cry. My father screamed in his sleep. My mother wept and crumpled up the letters. She set fire to them page by page in the ashtray, but new letters came almost every day. The only letters they opened without fear were the ones with red borders, the holiday letters that mustn't carry bad news. The other letters said that my uncles were made to kneel on broken glass during their trials and had confessed to being land-owners. They were all executed, and the aunt whose thumbs were twisted off drowned herself. Other aunts, mothers-in-law, and cousins disappeared; some suddenly began writing to us again from communes or from Hong Kong. They kept asking for money. The ones in communes got four ounces of fat and one cup of oil a week, they said, and had to work from 4 A.M. to 9 P.M. They had to learn to do dances waving red kerchiefs; they had to sing nonsense syllables. The Communists gave axes to the old ladies and said, "Go and kill yourself. You're useless." If we overseas Chinese would just send money to the Communist bank, our relatives said, they might get a percentage of it for themselves. The aunts in Hong Kong said to send money quickly; their children were begging on the sidewalks, and mean people put dirt in their bowls.

When I dream that I am wire without flesh, there is a letter on blue airmail paper that floats above the night ocean between here and China. It must arrive safely or else my grandmother and I will lose each other.

My parents felt bad whether or not they sent money. Sometimes they got angry at their brothers and sisters for asking. And they would not simply ask but have to talk-story too. The revolutionaries had taken Fourth Aunt and Uncle's store, house, and lands. They attacked the house and killed the grandfather and oldest daughter. The grandmother escaped with the loose cash and did not return to help. Fourth Aunt picked up her sons, one under each arm, and hid in the pig house, where they slept that night in cotton clothes. The next day she found her husband, who had also miraculously escaped. The two of them collected twigs and yams to sell while their children begged. Each morning they tied the faggots on each other's back. Nobody bought from them. They ate the yams and some of the children's rice. Finally Fourth Aunt saw what was wrong. "We have to shout 'Fuel for sale' and 'Yams for sale,' " she said. "We can't just walk unobtrusively up and down the street." "You're right," said my uncle, but he was shy and walked in back of her. "Shout," my aunt ordered, but he could not. "They think we're carrying these sticks home for our own fire," she said. "Shout." They walked about miserably, silently, until sundown, neither of them able to advertise themselves. Fourth Aunt, an orphan since the age of ten, mean as my mother, threw her bundle down at his feet and scolded Fourth Uncle, "Starving to death, his wife and children starving to death, and he's too damned shy to raise his voice." She left him standing by himself and afraid to return empty-handed to her. He sat under a tree to think, when he spotted a pair of nesting doves. Dumping his bag of yams, he climbed up and caught the birds. That was where the Communists trapped him, in the tree. They criticized him for selfishly taking food for his own family and killed him, leaving his body in the tree as an example. They took the birds to a commune kitchen to be shared.

It is confusing that my family was not the poor to be championed. They were executed like the barons in the stories, when they were not barons. It is confusing that birds tricked us.

What fighting and killing I have seen have not been glorious but slum grubby. I fought the most during junior high school and always cried. Fights are confusing as to who has won. The corpses I've seen had been rolled and dumped, sad little dirty bodies covered with a police khaki blanket. My mother locked her children in the house so we couldn't look at dead slum people. But at news of a body, I would find a way to get out; I had to learn about dying if I wanted to become a swordswoman. Once there was an Asian man stabbed next door, words on cloth pinned to his corpse. When the police came around asking questions, my father said, "No read Japanese, Japanese words. Me Chinese."

I've also looked for old people who could be my gurus. A medium with red hair told me that a girl who died in a far country follows me wherever I go. This spirit can help me if I acknowledge her, she said. Between the head line and heart line in my right palm, she said, I have the mystic cross. I could become a medium myself. I don't want to be a medium. I don't want to be a crank taking "offerings" in a wicker plate from the frightened audience, who, one after another, asked the spirits how to raise rent money, how to cure their coughs and skin diseases, how to find a job. And martial arts are for unsure little boys kicking away under fluorescent lights.

I live now where there are Chinese and Japanese, but no emigrants from my own village looking at me as if I had failed them. Living among one's own emigrant villagers can give a good Chinese far from China glory and a place. "That old busboy is really a swordsman," we whisper when he goes by, "He's a swordsman who's killed fifty. He has a tong ax in his closet." But I am useless, one more girl who couldn't be sold. When I visit the family now, I wrap my American successes around me like a private shawl; I *am* worthy of eating the food. From afar I can believe my family loves me fundamentally. They only say, "When fishing for treasures in the flood, be careful not to pull in girls," because that is what one says about daughters. But I watched such words come out of my own mother's and father's mouths; I looked at their ink drawing of poor people snagging their neighbors' flotage with long flood hooks and pushing the girl babies on down the river. And I had to get out of hating range. I read in an anthropology book that Chinese say, "Girls are necessary too"; I have never heard the Chinese I know make this concession. Perhaps it was a saying in another village. I refuse to shy my way anymore through our Chinatown, which tasks me with the old sayings and the stories.

The swordswoman and I are not so dissimilar. May my people understand the resemblance soon so that I can return to them. What we have in common are the words at our backs. The idioms for *revenge* are "report a crime" and "report to five families." The reporting is the vengeance — not the beheading, not the gutting, but the words. And I have so many words — "chink" words and "gook" words too — that they do not fit on my skin.

[1976]

Annie Dillard

[b. 1945]

Annie Dillard was born in 1945 in Pittsburgh, Pennsylvania. She was the first of three daughters of affluent parents who strongly encouraged her curiosity and creativity. By the time she was sixteen, however, she began

Annie Dillard

This photograph was taken at the time Dillard published her memoir, *An American Childhood* (1987).

to rebel against the confines of her comfortable world, which was bordered by the country club, her private school, and the Presbyterian Church. She attended Hollins College in Virginia, where the landscape of the Roanoke Valley inspired her first book, *Pilgrim at Tinker's Creek* (1974). It won the Pulitzer Prize for general nonfiction and established her reputation as a major nature writer. But she has published a wide array of works, including two novels, most recently *The Maytrees* (2007); several collections of essays; and her celebrated memoir, *An American Childhood.* In his review in the *New York Times*, Noel Perrin observed: "She is one of those people who seem to be more fully alive than most of us, more nearly wide-awake than human beings generally get to be." In the following extract, Dillard recalls an early stage of her awakening to the world and its complications, when she was ten years old and her restless father embarked on a solo boat trip from Pittsburgh to New Orleans. The text is taken from the first edition of *An American Childhood* (1987).

From An American Childhood

In 1955, when I was ten, my father's reading went to his head.

My father's reading during that time, and for many years before and after, consisted for the most part of *Life on the Mississippi.*[1] He was a young executive in the old family firm, American Standard; sometimes he traveled alone on business. Traveling, he checked into a hotel, found a bookstore, and chose for the night's reading, after what I fancy to have been long deliberation, yet another copy of *Life on the Mississippi.* He brought all these books home. There were dozens of copies of *Life on the Mississippi* on the living-room shelves. From time to time, I read one.

Down the Mississippi hazarded the cub riverboat pilot, down the Mississippi from St.

---

1. *Life on the Mississippi:* Mark Twain's popular 1883 book was an expanded version of his *Old Times on the Mississippi* (1875), a series of magazine sketches about his experiences as a steamboat pilot before the Civil War (see pp. 71–93).

1534

Louis to New Orleans. His chief, the pilot Mr. Bixby, taught him how to lay the boat in her marks and dart between points; he learned to pick a way fastidiously inside a certain snag and outside a shifting shoal in the black dark; he learned to clamber down a memorized channel in his head. On tricky crossings the leadsmen sang out the soundings, so familiar I seemed to have heard them the length of my life: "Mark four! . . . Quarter-less-four! . . . Half three! . . . Mark three! . . . Quarter-less . . ."[2] It was an old story.

When all this reading went to my father's head, he took action. From Pittsburgh he went down the river. Although no one else that our family knew kept a boat on the Allegheny River, our father did, and now he was going all the way with it. He quit the firm his great-grandfather had founded a hundred years earlier down the river at his family's seat in Louisville, Kentucky; he sold his own holdings in the firm. He was taking off for New Orleans.

New Orleans was the source of the music he loved: Dixieland jazz, O Dixieland. In New Orleans men would blow it in the air and beat it underfoot, the music that hustled and snapped, the music whose zip matched his when he was a man-about-town at home in Pittsburgh, working for the family firm; the music he tapped his foot to when he was a man-about-town in New York for a few years after college working for the family firm by day and by night hanging out at Jimmy Ryan's on Fifty-second Street with Zutty Singleton, the black drummer who befriended him, and the rest of the house band. A certain kind of Dixieland suited him best. They played it at Jimmy Ryan's, and Pee Wee Russell and Eddie Condon played it too — New Orleans Dixieland chilled a bit by its journey up the river, and smoothed by its sojourns in Chicago and New York.[3]

Back in New Orleans where he was headed they would play the old stuff, the hot, rough stuff — bastardized for tourists maybe, but still the big and muddy source of it all. Back in New Orleans where he was headed the music would smell like the river itself, maybe, like a thicker, older version of the Allegheny River at Pittsburgh, where he heard the music beat in the roar of his boat's inboard motor; like a thicker, older version of the wide Ohio River at Louisville, Kentucky, where at his family's summer house he'd spent his boyhood summers mucking about in boats.

Getting ready for the trip one Saturday, he roamed around our big brick house snapping his fingers. He had put a record on: Sharkey Bonano, "Li'l Liza Jane."[4] I was reading

---

2. **"Mark four! . . . Quarter-less":** A member of the crew calls out the "soundings," or depth of the water, to the steamboat pilot in a passage from *Life on the Mississippi.*

3. **New Orleans . . . Chicago and New York:** Dixieland jazz developed in New Orleans at the beginning of the twentieth century and later spread to Chicago and New York City. After its heyday in the 1920s and 1930s, the jazz style underwent a revival in the late 1940s and 1950s. Jimmy Ryan's was a New York nightclub on Fifty-second, or "Swing Street," as the block between Fifth and Sixth avenues was known in the 1940s and 1950s. Zutty Singleton (1898-1975) was a drummer who worked with a number of jazz bands and musicians, including Louis Armstrong. White musicians who played Dixieland included the clarinetist Pee Wee Russell (1906-1969) and Eddie Condon (1905-1973), a pianist and bandleader who also owned a jazz club in New York City.

4. **"Li'l Liza Jane":** A popular tune recorded by Sharkey Bonano (1904-1972), a trumpeter, bandleader, and singer who was a major figure in early Dixieland jazz and owned a club in New York City in the early 1950s.

Robert Louis Stevenson on the sunporch: *Kidnapped*.[5] I looked up from my book and saw him outside; he had wandered out to the lawn and was standing in the wind between the buckeye trees and looking up at what must have been a small patch of wild sky. Old Low-Pockets. He was six feet four, all lanky and leggy; he had thick brown hair and shaggy brows, and a mild and dreamy expression in his blue eyes.

When our mother met Frank Doak, he was twenty-seven: witty, boyish, bookish, unsnobbish, a good dancer. He had grown up an only child in Pittsburgh, attended Shady Side Academy, and Washington and Jefferson College[6] in Pennsylvania, where he studied history. He was a lapsed Presbyterian and a believing Republican. "Books make the man," read the blue bookplate in all his books. "Frank Doak." The bookplate's wood-cut showed a square-rigged ship under way in a steep following sea. Father had hung around jazz in New York, and halfheartedly played the drums; he had smoked marijuana, written poems, begun a novel, painted in oils, imagined a career as a riverboat pilot, and acted for more than ten seasons in amateur and small-time professional theater. At American Standard, Amstan Division, he was the personnel manager.

But not for long, and never again; Mother told us he was quitting to go down the river. I was sorry he'd be leaving the Manufacturers' Building downtown. From his office on the fourteenth floor, he often saw suicides, which he reported at dinner. The suicides grieved him, but they thrilled us kids. My sister Amy was seven.

People jumped from the Sixth Street bridge into the Allegheny River. Because the bridge was low, they shinnied all the way up the steel suspension cables to the bridge towers before they jumped. Father saw them from his desk in silhouette, far away. A man vigorously climbed a slanting cable. He slowed near the top, where the cables hung almost vertically; he paused on the stone tower, seeming to sway against the sky, high over the bridge and the river below. Priests, firemen, and others — presumably family members or passersby — gathered on the bridge. In about half the cases, Father said, these people talked the suicide down. The ones who jumped kicked off from the tower so they'd miss the bridge, and fell tumbling a long way down.

Pittsburgh was a cheerful town, and had far fewer suicides than most other cities its size. Yet people jumped so often that Father and his colleagues on the fourteenth floor had a betting pool going. They guessed the date and time of day the next jumper would appear. If a man got talked down before he jumped, he still counted for the betting pool, thank God; no manager of American Standard ever wanted to hope, even in the smallest part of himself, that the fellow would go ahead and jump. Father said he and the other men used to gather at the biggest window and holler, "No! Don't do it, buddy, don't!" Now

---

5. **Kidnapped:** One of the most popular books by Robert Louis Stevenson (1850–1894), this historical novel recounts the adventures of a boy who is kidnapped and placed aboard a slave ship, from which he escapes and later leads his pursuers in a breathless flight across Scotland.
6. **Shady Side Academy, and Washington and Jefferson College:** Established in 1883, Shady Side Academy is a private school in Fox Chapel, an affluent suburb of Pittsburgh. Washington and Jefferson College is a liberal arts college thirty miles south of Pittsburgh.

he was leaving American Standard to go down the river, and he was a couple of bucks in the hole.

While I was reading *Kidnapped* on this Saturday morning, I heard him come inside and roam from the kitchen to the pantry to the bar, to the dining room, the living room, and the sunporch, snapping his fingers. He was snapping the fingers of both hands, and shaking his head, to the record — "Li'l Liza Jane" — the sound that was beating, big and jivey, all over the house. He walked lightly, long-legged, like a soft-shoe hoofer barely in touch with the floor. When he played the drums, he played lightly, coming down soft with the steel brushes that sounded like a Slinky falling,[7] not making the beat but just sizzling along with it. He wandered into the sunporch, unseeing; he was snapping his fingers lightly, too, as if he were feeling between them a fine layer of Mississippi silt. The big buckeyes outside the glass sunporch walls were waving.

A week later, he bade a cheerful farewell to us — to Mother, who had encouraged him, to us oblivious daughters, ten and seven, and to the new baby girl, six months old. He loaded his twenty-four-foot cabin cruiser with canned food, pushed off from the dock of the wretched boat club that Mother hated, and pointed his bow downstream, down the Allegheny River. From there it was only a few miles to the Ohio River at Pittsburgh's point, where the Monongahela came in. He wore on westward down the Ohio; he watched West Virginia float past his port bow and Ohio past his starboard. It was 138 river miles to New Martinsville, West Virginia, where he lingered for some races. Back on the move, he tied up nights at club docks he'd seen on the charts; he poured himself water for drinks from dockside hoses. By day he rode through locks, twenty of them in all. He conversed with the lockmasters, those lone men who paced silhouetted in overalls on the concrete lock-chamber walls and threw the big switches that flooded or drained the locks: "Hello, up there!" "So long, down there!"

He continued down the river along the Kentucky border with Ohio, bumping down the locks. He passed through Cincinnati. He moved along down the Kentucky border with Indiana. After 640 miles of river travel, he reached Louisville, Kentucky. There he visited relatives at their summer house on the river.

It was a long way to New Orleans, at this rate another couple of months. He was finding the river lonesome. It got dark too early. It was September; people had abandoned their pleasure boats for the season; their children were back in school. There were no old salts on the docks talking river talk. People weren't so friendly as they were in Pittsburgh. There was no music except the dreary yacht-club jukeboxes playing "How Much Is That Doggie in the Window?"[8] Jazz had come up the river once and for all; it wasn't still coming, he couldn't hear it across the water at night rambling and blowing and banging along high and tuneful, sneaking upstream to Chicago to get educated. He

---

7. **a Slinky falling:** The Slinky, a coil-shaped and springlike metal toy that could "walk" down stairs, was very popular in the 1950s.
8. **"How Much Is That Doggie in the Window?":** This novelty song recorded by the singer Patti Page (b. 1927) reached number one on the music sales charts in 1953.

wasn't free so much as loose. He was living alone on beans in a boat and having witless conversations with lockmasters. He mailed out sad postcards.

From phone booths all down the Ohio River he talked to Mother. She told him that she was lonesome, too, and that three children — maid and nanny or no — were a handful. She said, further, that people were starting to talk. She knew Father couldn't bear people's talking. For all his dreaminess, he prized respectability above all; it was our young mother, whose circumstances bespoke such dignity, who loved to shock the world. After only six weeks, then — on the Ohio River at Louisville — he sold the boat and flew home.

I was just waking up then, just barely. Other things were changing. The highly entertaining new baby, Molly, had taken up residence in a former guest room. The great outer world hove into view and began to fill with things that had apparently been there all along: mineralogy, detective work, lepidopterology, ponds and streams, flying, society. My younger sister Amy and I were to start at private school that year: the Ellis School, on Fifth Avenue. I would start dancing school.

Children ten years old wake up and find themselves here, discover themselves to have been here all along; is this sad? They wake like sleepwalkers, in full stride; they wake like people brought back from cardiac arrest or from drowning: *in medias res*,[9] surrounded by familiar people and objects, equipped with a hundred skills. They know the neighborhood, they can read and write English, they are old hands at the commonplace mysteries, and yet they feel themselves to have just stepped off the boat, just converged with their bodies, just flown down from a trance, to lodge in an eerily familiar life already well under way.

I woke in bits, like all children, piecemeal over the years. I discovered myself and the world, and forgot them, and discovered them again. I woke at intervals until, by that September when Father went down the river, the intervals of waking tipped the scales, and I was more often awake than not. I noticed this process of waking, and predicted with terrifying logic that one of these years not far away I would be awake continuously and never slip back, and never be free of myself again.

Consciousness converges with the child as a landing tern touches the outspread feet of its shadow on the sand: precisely, toe hits toe. The tern folds its wings to sit; its shadow dips and spreads over the sand to meet and cup its breast.

Like any child, I slid into myself perfectly fitted, as a diver meets her reflection in a pool. Her fingertips enter the fingertips on the water, her wrists slide up her arms. The diver wraps herself in her reflection wholly, sealing it at the toes, and wears it as she climbs rising from the pool, and ever after.

I never woke, at first, without recalling, chilled, all those other waking times, those similar stark views from similarly lighted precipices: dizzying precipices from which the distant, glittering world revealed itself as a brooding and separated scene — and so

---

9. *in medias res*: In the middle (Latin).

let slip a queer implication, that I myself was both observer and observable, and so a possible object of my own humming awareness. Whenever I stepped into the porcelain bathtub, the bath's hot water sent a shock traveling up my bones. The skin on my arms pricked up, and the hair rose on the back of my skull. I saw my own firm foot press the tub, and the pale shadows waver over it, as if I were looking down from the sky and remembering this scene forever. The skin on my face tightened, as it had always done whenever I stepped into the tub, and remembering it all drew a swinging line, loops connecting the dots, all the way back. You again.

[1987]

David Mamet

[b. 1947]

David Mamet was born in 1947 on the South Side of Chicago. After his parents divorced, his mother remarried and moved with Mamet and his sister to the suburb of Olympia Fields. Mamet had a difficult relationship with his stepfather and soon returned to live with his father in Chicago. He became interested in acting and drama, and he wrote a play for his senior thesis at Goddard College, where it was performed in 1968. Following his graduation, Mamet worked at a variety of jobs before he was invited back to teach at Goddard in the early 1970s. He formed a theater company and began to write plays, some of which were performed in Chicago. His major breakthrough came in 1977, when his play *American Buffalo* was produced in New York City and subsequently won a New York Drama Critics Award. In 1986, he won a Pulitzer Prize for his play *Glengarry Glen Ross*. Mamet, a prolific playwright who is internationally known for his challenging and unflinching dramas, has also written screenplays, novels, and essays on a wide range of topics. In the following brief memoir, he recalls the difficult family life he and his sister endured in the suburbs with their mother and abusive stepfather — an "emotional hurricane," as his sister once described it in an interview. Mamet's skills as a playwright are reflected in the intense scenes and dramatic structure of "The Rake," the text of which is taken from its first publication in *Harper's* magazine, June 1992.

David Mamet

Steve Liss took this photograph of Mamet in 1990, shortly before the award-winning playwright published "The Rake."

The Rake: A Few Scenes from My Childhood

There was the incident of the rake and there was the incident of the school play, and it seems to me that they both took place at the round kitchen table.

The table was not in the kitchen proper but in an area called "the nook," which held its claim to that small measure of charm by dint of a waist-high wall separating it from an adjacent area known as the living room.

All family meals were eaten in the nook. There was a dining room to the right, but, as in most rooms of that name at that time and in those surroundings, it was never used.

The round table was of wrought iron and topped with glass; it was noteworthy for that glass, for it was more than once and rather more than several times, I am inclined to think, that my stepfather would grow so angry as to bring some object down on the glass top, shattering it, thus giving us to know how we had forced him out of control.

And it seems that most times when he would shatter the table, as often as that might have been, he would cut some portion of himself on the glass, or that he or his wife, our mother, would cut their hands on picking up the glass afterward, and that we children were to understand, and did understand, that these wounds were our fault.

So the table was associated in our minds with the notion of blood.

The house was in a brand-new housing development in the southern suburbs. The new community was built upon, and now bordered, the remains of what had once been a cornfield. When our new family moved in, there were but a few homes in the development completed, and a few more under construction. Most streets were mud, and boasted a house here or there, and many empty lots marked out by white stakes.

The house we lived in was the development's Model Home. The first time we had seen it, it had signs plastered on the front and throughout the interior telling of the various conveniences it contained. And it had a lawn, and was one of the only homes in the new community that did.

My stepfather was fond of the lawn, and he detailed me and my sister to care for it, and one fall afternoon we found ourselves assigned to rake the leaves.

Why this chore should have been so hated I cannot say, except that we children, and I especially, felt ourselves less than full members of this new, cobbled-together family, and disliked being assigned to the beautification of a home that we found unbeautiful in all respects, and for which we had neither natural affection nor a sense of proprietary interest.

We went to the new high school. We walked the mile down the open two-lane road on one side of which was the just-begun suburban community and on the other side of which was the cornfield.

The school was as new as the community, and still under construction for the first three years of its occupancy. One of its innovations was the notion that honesty would be engendered by the absence of security, and so the lockers were designed and built both without locks and without the possibility of attaching locks. And there was the corresponding rash of thievery and many lectures about the same from the school administration, but it was difficult to point with pride to any scholastic or community tradition supporting the suggestion that we, the students, pull together in this new, utopian way. We were, in school, in an uncompleted building in the midst of a mud field in the midst of a cornfield. Our various sports teams were called The Spartans; and I played on those teams, which were of a wretchedness consistent with their novelty.

Meanwhile my sister interested herself in the drama society. The year after I had left the school she obtained the lead in the school play. It called for acting and singing, both of which she had talent for, and it looked to be a signal triumph for her in her otherwise unremarkable and unenjoyed school career.

On the night of the play's opening she sat down to dinner with our mother and our stepfather. It may be that they ate a trifle early to allow her to get to the school to enjoy the excitement of the opening night. But however it was, my sister had no appetite, and she nibbled a bit at her food, and then she got up from the table to carry her plate back to scrape it in the sink, when my mother suggested that she sit down, as she had not finished her food. My sister said she really had no appetite, but my mother insisted that, as the meal had been prepared, it would be good form to sit and eat it.

My sister sat down with the plate and pecked at her food and she tried to eat a bit, and told my mother that, no, really, she possessed no appetite whatever, and that was due, no doubt, not to the food, but to her nervousness and excitement at the prospect of opening night.

My mother, again, said that, as the food had been cooked, it had to be eaten, and my sister tried and said that she could not; at which my mother nodded. She then got up from the table and went to the telephone and looked the number up and called the school and got the drama teacher and identified herself and told him that her daughter wouldn't be coming to school that night, that, no, she was not ill, but that she would not be coming in. Yes, yes, she said, she knew that her daughter had the lead in the play, and, yes, she was aware that many children and teachers had worked hard for it, et cetera, and so my sister did not play the lead in her school play. But I was long gone, out of the house by that time, and well out of it. I heard that story, and others like it, at the distance of twenty-five years.

In the model house our rooms were separated from their room, the master bedroom, by a bathroom and a study. On some weekends I would go alone to visit my father in the city and my sister would stay and sometimes grow frightened or lonely in her part of the house. And once, in the period when my grandfather, then in his sixties, was living with us, she became alarmed at a noise she had heard in the night; or perhaps she just became lonely, and she went out of her room and down the hall, calling for my mother, or my stepfather, or my grandfather, but the house was dark, and no one answered.

And, as she went farther down the hall, toward the living room, she heard voices, and she turned the corner, and saw a light coming from under the closed door in the master bedroom, and heard my stepfather crying, and the sound of my mother weeping. So my sister went up to the door, and she heard my stepfather talking to my grandfather and saying, "Jack. Say the words. Just say the words . . ." And my grandfather, in his Eastern European accent, saying, with obvious pain and difficulty, "No. No. I can't. Why are you making me do this? Why?" And the sound of my mother crying convulsively.

My sister opened the door, and she saw my grandfather sitting on the bed, and my stepfather standing by the closet and gesturing. On the floor of the closet she saw my mother, curled in a fetal position, moaning and crying and hugging herself. My stepfather was saying, "Say the words. Just say the words." And my grandfather was breathing fast and repeating, "I can't. She knows how I feel about her. I can't." And my stepfather said, "Say the words, Jack. Please. Just say you love her." At which my mother would moan louder. And my grandfather said, "I can't."

My sister pushed the door open farther and said — I don't know what she said, but she asked, I'm sure, for some reassurance, or some explanation, and my stepfather turned around and saw her and picked up a hairbrush from a dresser that he passed as he walked toward her, and he hit her in the face and slammed the door on her. And she continued to hear "Jack, say the words."

She told me that on weekends when I was gone my stepfather ended every Sunday evening by hitting or beating her for some reason or other. He would come home from depositing his own kids back at their mother's house after their weekend visitation, and would settle down tired and angry, and, as a regular matter on those evenings, would find out some intolerable behavior on my sister's part and slap or hit or beat her.

Years later, at my mother's funeral, my sister spoke to our aunt, my mother's sister, who gave a footnote to this behavior. She said when they were young, my mother and my aunt, they and their parents lived in a small flat on the West Side. My grandfather was a salesman on the road from dawn on Monday until Friday night. Their family had a fiction, and that fiction, that article of faith, was that my mother was a naughty child. And each Friday, when he came home, his first question as he climbed the stairs was, "What has she done this week . . . ?" At which my grandmother would tell him the terrible things that my mother had done, after which she, my mother, was beaten.

This was general knowledge in my family. The footnote concerned my grandfather's behavior later in the night. My aunt had a room of her own, and it adjoined her parents' room. And she related that each Friday, when the house had gone to bed, she, through the thin wall, heard my grandfather pleading for sex. "Cookie, please." And my grandmother responding, "No, Jack." "Cookie, please." "No, Jack." "Cookie, please."

And once, my grandfather came home and asked, "What has she done this week?" and I do not know, but I imagine that the response was not completed, and perhaps hardly begun; in any case, he reached and grabbed my mother by the back of the neck and hurled her down the stairs.

And once, in our house in the suburbs there had been an outburst by my stepfather directed at my sister. And she had, somehow, prevailed. It was, I think, that he had the facts of the case wrong, and had accused her of the commission of something for which she had demonstrably had no opportunity, and she pointed this out to him with what I can imagine, given the circumstances, was an understandable, and, given my prejudice, a commendable degree of freedom. Thinking the incident closed she went back to her room to study, and, a few moments later, saw him throw open her door, bat the book out of her hands, and pick her up and throw her against the far wall, where she struck the back of her neck on a shelf.

She was told, the next morning, that her pain, real or pretended, held no weight, and that she would have to go to school. She protested that she could not walk, or, if at all, only with the greatest of difficulty and in great pain; but she was dressed and did walk to school, where she fainted, and was brought home. For years she suffered various headaches; an X-ray taken twenty years later for an unrelated problem revealed that when he threw her against the shelf he had cracked her vertebrae.

When we left the house we left in good spirits. When we went out to dinner, it was an adventure, which was strange to me, looking back, because many of these dinners ended with my sister or myself being banished, sullen or in tears, from the restaurant, and told to wait in the car, as we were in disgrace.

These were the excursions that had ended, due to her or my intolerable arrogance, as it was then explained to us.

The happy trips were celebrated and capped with a joke. Here is the joke: My step-father, my mother, my sister, and I would exit the restaurant, my stepfather and mother would walk to the car, telling us that they would pick us up. We children would stand by the restaurant entrance. They would drive up in the car, open the passenger door, and wait until my sister and I had started to get in. They would then drive away.

They would drive ten or fifteen feet, and open the door again, and we would walk up again, and they would drive away again. They sometimes would drive around the block. But they would always come back, and by that time the four of us would be laughing in camaraderie and appreciation of what, I believe, was our only family joke.

We were raking the lawn, my sister and I. I was raking, and she was stuffing the leaves into a bag. I loathed the job, and my muscles and my mind rebelled, and I was viciously angry, and my sister said something, and I turned and threw the rake at her and it hit her in the face.

The rake was split bamboo and metal, and a piece of metal caught her lip and cut her badly.

We were both terrified, and I was sick with guilt, and we ran into the house, my sister holding her hand to her mouth, and her mouth and her hand and the front of her dress covered in blood.

We ran into the kitchen where my mother was cooking dinner, and my mother asked what happened.

Neither of us, myself out of guilt, of course, and my sister out of a desire to avert the terrible punishment she knew I would receive, neither of us would say what occurred.

My mother pressed us, and neither of us would answer. She said that until one or the other answered, we would not go to the hospital; and so the family sat down to dinner where my sister clutched a napkin to her face and the blood soaked the napkin and ran down onto her food, which she had to eat; and I also ate my food and we cleared the table and went to the hospital.

I remember the walks home from school in the frigid winter, along the cornfield that was, for all its proximity to the city, part of the prairie. The winters were viciously cold. From the remove of years, I can see how the area might and may have been beautiful. One could have walked in the stubble of the cornfields, or hunted birds, or enjoyed any of a number of pleasures naturally occurring.

[1992]

bell hooks

[b. 1952]

bell hooks — who was born Gloria Watkins in 1952 — later adopted an unconventional form of the name of her maternal great-grandmother, a woman who was apparently as outspoken as her namesake. After growing

bell hooks

This photograph of hooks, who has described herself as a "Black woman intellectual, revolutionary activist," was taken in the 1980s.

up in a poor black area of Hopkinsville, Kentucky, hooks went to Standford University, where she received her BA in 1973. She earned an MA in 1976 from the University of Wisconsin, Madison, and a PhD in 1983 from the University of California, Santa Cruz, where she wrote her dissertation on the works of Toni Morrison. Even before she completed her graduate work, she published her first book, *Ain't I a Woman: Black Women and Feminism* (1981), and most of her more than thirty books have focused on issues of race and feminism. She is also the author of a volume of poems and two memoirs, *Bone Black* (1996) and *Wounds of Passion: A Writing Life* (1997). In her preface to the former volume, hooks describes it as "the story of girlhood rebellion, of my struggle to create identity distinct from and yet inclusive of the world around me." Certainly, what emerges from that account is both her growing separation from her world — sometimes rendered in third-person descriptions of her earlier self — and her inclusive portrait of family, home, and community, the focus of the following sections from *Bone Black: Memories of Girlhood* (1996).

From BONE BLACK: MEMORIES OF GIRLHOOD

33

It may have been the pretend Tom Thumb wedding[1] she had to participate in during first grade. It may have been that the tearing of her red crepe-paper bridesmaid dress convinced her she would fail at marriage just as she had failed at the pretend wedding. She knew that the pretend marriage had made her suspicious — nothing about it had been enjoyable. Whenever she thought of marriage she thought of it for someone else, someone who would make a beautiful bride, a good wife. From her perspective the problem

---

1. **Tom Thumb wedding:** Charles Sherwood Stratton (1838–1883), who was a dwarf, gained international fame as "General Tom Thumb," a singer, dancer, and actor employed by the famous showman P. T. Barnum. Stratton's marriage to Lavinia Warren, who was also a dwarf, made front-page news in 1863.

with marriage was not the good wife, but the lack of the good husband. She is sixteen years old. Her mother is telling her again and again about the importance of learning to cook, clean, etc., in order to be a good wife. She stomps upstairs shouting, I will never be married! I will never marry! When she comes back downstairs she must explain why, she must find words — Seems like, she says, stammering, marriage is for men, that women get nothing out of it, men get everything. She did not want the mother to feel as if she was saying unkind things about her marriage. She did not want the mother to know that it was precisely her marriage that made it seem like a trap, a door closing in a room without air.

She could not tell her mother how she became a different person as soon as the husband left the house in the morning, how she became energetic, noisy, silly, funny, fussy, strong, capable, tender, everything that she was not when he was around. When he was around she became silent. She reminded her daughter of a dog sitting, standing obediently until the master, the head of the house, gave her orders to move, to do this to do that, to cook his food just so, to make sure the house was clean just so. Her bed was upstairs over their bedroom. She never heard them making fun sounds. She heard the plaintive pleading voice of the woman — she could not hear what she was asking for, begging for, but she knew that the schoolbooks, the bit of pocket money, the new dresses, the *everything* had to be paid for with more than money, with more than sex.

Whatever joy there was in marriage was something the women kept to themselves, a secret they did not share with one another or their daughters. She never asked where the joy was, when it appeared, why it had to be hidden. She was afraid of the answer. They agreed with her when she said marriage was not a part of her dreams. They said she was too thin, lacking the hips, breasts, thighs that men were interested in. But more importantly she was too smart, men did not like smart women, men did not like a woman whose head was always in a book. And even more importantly men did not like a woman who talked back. She had been hit, whipped, punished again and again for talking back. They had said they were determined to break her — to silence her, to turn her into one of them.

She answers her mother back one day in the father's presence. He slaps her hard enough to make her fall back, telling her Don't you ever let me hear you talking to your mother like that. She sees pride in the mother's face. She thinks about the ways he speaks to her, ways that at this moment do not matter. He has taken a stand in her honor against the daughter. She has accepted it. This, the daughter thinks, must be a kind of marriage — and she hopes never to bear a daughter to sacrifice in the name of such love.

34

Wash day is a day of hard work. The machine is old and must be filled with water from buckets. Mama does most of the work. We love to stand and watch her put the clothes through the wringer after they are rinsed in huge tin buckets of water. They are the buckets we once took baths in when we were small children living on the hill. At night in the kitchen we would take turns being washed, washing. We think having our bodies washed by someone else's hands is one of the real pleasures of life. We have to grow older and bathe alone. We do — locking ourselves in to make sure no one joins us, witnesses the experience we were once more than willing to share. Everyone is irritable on wash day, especially in winter. The damp from the water and the cold enters our bones, chilling us. Clothes must be hung on the lines before we go to school. Our hands freeze as we hang piece after piece. Our feet feel the wet in the grass seeping through the thin soles of our shoes. Hanging piece after piece we move in slow motion hoping that we can go to school before the basket is empty. Mama warns us that we had better hang everything, that she does not care if we are late. In summer the clean clothes hanging in the fresh air are like rows of blossoming flowers. In winter they are like dead things frozen and cold. We bring the heavy work pants into the house frozen and stand them up in the bathtub where they will slowly thaw.

Washing means ironing. We come home from school knowing that the ironing board will stand ready, that the iron will be hot. Sometimes mama will still be ironing, her face hot, her feet hurting. We will stand and watch, telling her about our day. She will tell us who will begin ironing first. We learn to iron by pressing sheets. We do not know why sheets that are not even wrinkled must be ironed. Mama says it is practice. We especially hate ironing our father's underwear and pajamas. We especially hate being told that nothing was ironed correctly, that we must do the entire basket again.

It is my turn to iron. I can do nothing right. Before I begin I am being yelled at. I hear again and again that I am crazy, that I will end up in a mental institution. This is my punishment for wanting to finish reading before doing my work, for taking too long to walk down the stairs. Mama is already threatening to smack me if I do not stop rolling my eyes and wipe that frown off my face. It is times like these that I am sorry to be alive, that I want to die. In the kitchen with my sisters, she talks on and on about how she cannot stand me, about how I will go crazy. I am warned that if I begin to cry I will be given something to cry about. The tears do not fall. They stand in my eyes like puddles. They keep me from seeing where the ironing is going. I want them to shut up. I want them to leave me alone. I shout at them Leave Me Alone! I sit the hot iron on my arm. Already someone is laughing and yelling about what the crazy fool has done to herself. Already I have begun to feel the pain of the burning flesh. They do not stop talking. They say no one will visit me in the mental hospital. Mama says it does not matter about the pain, I must finish ironing the clothes in my basket.

35

Miss Rhobert lives around the corner in one of the storybook houses — white white with green grass, red brick steps, and matching porch furniture. Of course she never sits on the porch as that is the kind of thing the common folk do. She is not common. She comes from a long line of folks who look white. When we were small children we thought they were the color of pigs in storybooks. We know now that they are the black landowners, business people. We know now that they stand between white folks and real black folks. Like gossip, white folks spread their messages to us through them. They hate both white folks and dark black people. They hate white folks for having what they want. They hate dark black folks for reminding the world that they are colored and thus keeping them from really getting what they want. They never pass for white. They do not want to live in white communities and be treated like second-class citizens, like poor white folks are treated. They want to live in the heart of black communities where they will be looked up to, envied, where their every move will be talked about.

Miss Rhobert is one of them. She is unmarried and getting on in age. She will never marry because no one is good enough they say. She will never marry because no one has asked her they say. She was my first grade teacher. She lives alone. She has divided her house into two flats. She lives in one. Her roomers, all single men, live in the other. They live together without really seeing one another. They may not bring their women to stay. When they are gone she must look elsewhere for comfort, protection, for knowledge that she is not alone. She suggests to my mother that I should come stay nights with her, that in exchange she will give a few dollars a week and sometimes help with the buying of schoolbooks. Going to her house after dinner is a way to avoid conflict. She and I have little to say to one another. We will eat candy or ice cream, watch TV, and go to bed. I must sleep in the same bed with her. I hide myself in the corner of the bed near the wall and pretend I am not there. She sleeps soundly, snoring, her mouth open. When she pays me I will hand the money to mama who will determine what I need, how it will be spent. The money brings me no pleasure. I am never free to choose what to buy. When I assert my right to choose she never lets me forget.

Nights at Miss Rhobert's I learn the art of being present and not present at the same time. It is the art of being a good servant. It is knowing what it is to stay in one's place. I do not speak unless I am spoken to. I do not converse, I answer back in short sentences. When I laugh it sounds as though I am afraid. Sometimes I bring a book to read. This sign that I am not always a servant, not always in my place, leads her to make conversation. She wants to know what is being talked about at my house, who is doing what. I learn the art of avoiding answering her questions directly. When we are not watching television we play Scrabble. She likes to play for money. I do not as I am afraid to win. Since she has never learned to drive a car Miss Rhobert cannot go out at night unless someone comes for her. Sometimes, every now and then, she leaves me alone for a few minutes. The muscles in my body relax, I am no longer invisible in my chair. I am grateful for the silence. Mama decides for me that I am too old for this job. My younger sister takes my place.

36

When we first meet I am shy. She reminds me of the small brown bird I held in my hand days ago. We were in the backyard playing when we saw the bird on the fence. It seemed to be waiting for me. When I held it in my hand I could feel the quivering, the heartbeat. It was so alive and so delicate that I felt responsible and afraid. I put it back on the fence and waited until it flew away. To me she is that bird given human form. Miss Willie Gray is a brown-skinned woman with gray hair. She is in her nineties. She is afflicted with palsy. These are her words. Affliction makes me think of church and the Bible. She moves her arms as though they are wings continually flapping. She has learned to anticipate the trembling movement — to see it as a sign that she is still alive. The movements do not bother me. They remind me of the bird flying away. She wants to fly and cannot. We both agree that it is not a sad thing for she is able to be independent, to move around, to cook for herself, to plant a garden. She is alone, old, and happy. She tells me always, Who could ask for anything more.

They say she never married because she was too attached to her father. I believe them because she talks to me endlessly about him. She tells me how he bought the grocery store and let her work in it even though it was not considered the proper thing for a lady to do. She told me how he died and left the store to her along with money and land. She tells me that she would have given all those things away if only he could have remained alive. Her mother had died when they were still girls. She took over the running of the house. In those days she said it was a common thing for the eldest daughter to house-keep until a new wife could be found. Her father never found a new wife though he had women. She stayed to housekeep and care for him until he died. She never wanted to marry. She fascinates me because all the other independent unmarried women are schoolteachers who began work in those days when the law required them to remain single. She never tires of telling me that it is her choice to remain single and alone.

She is not always alone. I am hired to come and stay nights, to do chores in the day, to go to the store now and then. At her house I have my own bed. I can read all night long and books are in every room. We both love to lie in bed and read. She reads *True Confessions*.[2] Although I buy them at the store I do not read them. She has a copy of Milton's *Paradise Lost*[3] which I read again and again. Her books are all hardback. They are mainly popular novels. She no longer reads them. She tells me I can read them whenever I want. We are good company for each other. Now and then I must leave my bed to get water or medicine for her. She never goes anywhere. She stays in her yard and in her garden. She loves to walk up and down the rows of growing things. I tell her that I did this all the time when I was younger. Now I sit on the fence and watch.

They would like to put her in a home, a place where they would not have to worry about her. They say that they are worried that she might fall down and hurt herself. She says they want her house, her money. She intends to stay in her house alone until she dies. She tells me that to leave her house and go to an old folk's home would be the end. In a harsh voice she wants me to tell her why they cannot leave her in peace. I remain silent, listening, watching the flapping wings.

37

Her brother's room has become her room. He has become a man and gone away to do what men do — to be a soldier. A dark room with no windows, cold in winter, cool in sum-

---

2. *True Confessions*: A popular women's magazine of "true stories" and melodramatic fiction first published in 1922.
3. *Paradise Lost*: An epic about the fall of Adam and Eve and their expulsion from the Garden of Eden by the English poet John Milton (1608-1674).

mer, it is her place of refuge and recovery. The tensions of high school, family, friend-ship can all be released there. She can hide from the loneliness inside. She can pretend. She can read all night long. To them she is the problem child, the source of all their pain. Everyone else gets along well together. She is the one who is no fun, who makes trouble. Before he goes she and her five sisters share upstairs rooms — six girls in two rooms. Four in the front room and two in the back. For years her first bed is just as you come up the stairs. Beds are placed in strange ways in the room because the ceilings slope like an attic. It is near a window that reaches from low ceiling to the floor. All night she can gaze out watching the stars, watching the lights in the neighbor's windows, watching birds, watching rain. It is her only private space. All her favorite things live there with her — books, paintbrushes, diaries.

She is not very tidy. Her corner, like all the other spaces in the room, is crammed full with things. When her mother sweeps under the bed they are all outraged, embarrassed. These upstairs rooms are painted pink. She hates the color pink. Grown-ups think it should be her favorite color. Pink innocence, pink dreams, pink the color of something alive but not quite allowed to be fully living. She liked deep reds, black, dark greens. They would never let the rooms be painted another color. All girls want a pink room — she and her sisters should be content, happy to live in a world of pink. To her younger sisters, she is the one who is different. They cannot sleep at night because she is always crying. They demand that their mother make her stop crying. She learns to hold her tears, to keep them silent until everyone is sound asleep and the house is still. She cries about not being able to do anything right, about not fitting in, about being unfairly pun-ished, about being punished.

When an older sister leaves home she is first moved to the back room, sharing it. Her younger sisters are glad to see her go. She is not at home in her new space. It can never be truly hers, so completely did it bear the mark of the oldest sister. In that room her secrets are always found. Her diaries are read, her hidden money stolen, her clothes dis-appearing. Everything that is private someone will find and hang on the line like wet clothes for everyone to see. They love the pain it causes her. They resent her for needing so badly to shut them out. In this room she hardly ever cries. She stays awake nights talking to god, trying to find this stranger that will understand, that will make every-thing right. Perhaps she cries less because all the sounds made in this room can be heard by her parents lying in their bed underneath. There are no more problems with her keeping the lights on — her older sister, when she is home, does not care. Once she falls asleep nothing and no one disturbs her. Anyway, the space belonged to her oldest sister. It was her things that were everywhere; she invaded other people's things and made them her own.

Finally mama decides she should move downstairs. They give her the boy's room, not because she is the oldest of the youngest, not because she is deserving, but because she is the problem, the one no one can stand. She is to live in exile. They are glad to see her go, they feel as if something had died that they had long waited to be rid of but were not free to throw away. Like in church, they excommunicate her.

[1996]

Gary Soto

[b. 1952]

Gary Soto

Soto's wife, Carolyn, took this recent photograph of the poet, novelist, and memoirist.

Gary Soto was born in 1952 in Fresno, California, the second of three children of Mexican American parents whose own parents had immigrated to the San Joaquin Valley during the Great Depression. As a child he displayed little interest in books or school, but he began to read contemporary literature at Fresno City College, where he went to study geography in 1970. "I discovered the novelist Gabriel García Márquez, and I was hooked," Soto recalls in an interview published on his Web site. "I wanted to make writing my life." From Fresno, he went on to earn a BA in 1974 from California State University, Fresno, and an MFA in creative writing from the University of California, Berkeley, in 1976. He published *The Elements of San Joaquin*, the first of his ten collections of poetry, in 1982. He has also written novels, a memoir, and autobiographical essays, as well as numerous works for children and young adults. The popularity of the latter is not surprising, given the keen and sympathetic insight into the world of childhood and young adulthood Soto displays in the following essay, one of the "Recollections and Short Essays" gathered together in his collection *The Effects of Knut Hamsun on a Fresno Boy* (2000).

LIKE MEXICANS

My grandmother gave me bad advice and good advice when I was in my early teens. For the bad advice, she said that I should become a barber because they made good money and listened to the radio all day. "Honey, they don't work como burros,"[1] she would say every time I visited her. She made the sound of donkeys braying. "Like that, honey!" For the good advice, she said that I should marry a Mexican girl. "No Okies, hijo"[2] — she would say — "Look my son. He marry one and they fight everyday about I don't know what and I don't know what." For her, everyone who wasn't Mexican, black, or Asian were Okies. The French were Okies, the Italians in suits were Okies. When I asked about Jews, whom I had read about, she asked for a picture. I rode home on my bicycle and

---

1. **como burros:** Like donkeys (Spanish).
2. **hijo:** Son (Spanish). "Okies" was the name given to displaced farmers who fled the Dust Bowl of Oklahoma and the Great Plains and migrated to the West Coast, especially California, during the Great Depression.

returned with a calendar depicting the important races of the world. "Pues sí, son Okies también!"[3] she said, nodding her head. She waved the calendar away and we went to the living room where she lectured me on the virtues of the Mexican girl: first, she could cook and, second, she acted like a woman, not a man, in her husband's home. She said she would tell me about a third when I got a little older.

I asked my mother about it — becoming a barber and marrying Mexican. She was in the kitchen. Steam curled from a pot of boiling beans, the radio was on, looking as squat as a loaf of bread. "Well, if you want to be a barber — they say they make good money." She slapped a round steak with a knife, her glasses slipping down with each strike. She stopped and looked up. "If you find a good Mexican girl, marry her of course." She returned to slapping the meat and I went to the backyard where my brother and David King were sitting on the lawn feeling the inside of their cheeks.

"This is what girls feel like," my brother said, rubbing the inside of his cheek. David put three fingers inside of his mouth and scratched. I ignored them and climbed the back fence to see my best friend, Scott, a second-generation Okie. I called him, and his mother pointed to the side of the house where his bedroom was a small aluminum trailer, the kind you gawk at when they're flipped over on the freeway, wheels spinning in the air. I went around to find Scott pitching horseshoes.

I picked up a set of rusty ones and joined him. While we played, we talked about school and friends and record albums. The horseshoes scuffed up dirt, sometimes ringing the iron that threw out a meager shadow like a sundial. After three argued-over games, we pulled two oranges apiece from his tree and started down the alley still talking school and friends and record albums. We pulled more oranges from the alley and talked about who we would marry. "No offense, Scott," I said with an orange slice in my mouth, "but I would never marry an Okie." We walked in step, almost touching, with a sled of shadows dragging behind us. "No offense, Gary," Scott said, "but I would *never* marry a Mexican." I looked at him: a fang of orange slice showed from his munching mouth. I didn't think anything of it. He had his girl and I had mine. But our seventh-grade vision was the same: to marry, get jobs, buy cars and maybe a house if we had money left over.

We talked about our future lives until, to our surprise, we were on the downtown mall, two miles from home. We bought a bag of popcorn at Penney's and sat on a bench near the fountain watching Mexican and Okie girls pass. "That one's mine." I pointed with my chin when a girl with eyebrows arched into black rainbows ambled by. "She's cute," Scott said about a girl with yellow hair and a mouthful of gum. We dreamed aloud, our chins busy pointing out girls. We agreed that we couldn't wait to become men and lift them onto our laps.

But the woman I married was not Mexican but Japanese. It was a surprise to me. For years, I went about wide-eyed in my search for the brown girl in a white dress at a dance. I searched the playground at the baseball diamond. When the girls raced for grounders, their hair bounced like something that couldn't be caught. When they sat together in

---

3. **Pues sí, son Okies también!:** Well yes, they are Okies too! (Spanish).

the lunchroom heads pressed together, I knew they were talking about us Mexican guys. I saw them and dreamed them. I threw my face into my pillow, making up sentences that were good as in the movies.

But when I was twenty, I fell in love with this other girl who worried my mother, who had my grandmother asking once again to see the calendar of the Important Races of the World. I told her I had thrown it away years before. I took a much-glanced-at snapshot from my wallet. We looked at it together, in silence. Then grandma reclined in her chair, lit a cigarette, and said, "Es pretty." She blew and asked with all her worry pushed up to her forehead: "Chinese?"

I was in love and there was no looking back. She was the one. I told my mother who was slapping hamburger into patties. "Well, sure if you want to marry her," she said. But the more I talked, the more concerned she became. Later I began to worry. Was it all a mistake? "Marry a Mexican girl," I heard my mother say in my mind. I heard it at breakfast. I heard it over math problems, between Western Civilization and cultural geography. But then one afternoon while I was hitchhiking home from school, it struck me like a baseball in the back: my mother wanted me to marry someone of my own social class — a poor girl. I considered my fiancée, Carolyn, and she didn't look poor, though I knew she came from a family of farm workers and pull-yourself-up-by-your-boot-straps ranchers. I asked my brother, who was marrying Mexican poor that fall, if I should marry a poor girl. He screamed "Yeah" above his terrible guitar playing in his bedroom. I considered my sister who had married Mexican. Cousins were dating Mexican. Uncles were remarrying poor women. I asked Scott, who was still my best friend, and he said, "She's too good for you, so you better not."

I worried about it until Carolyn took me home to meet her parents. We drove in her Plymouth until the houses gave way to farms and ranches and finally her house fifty feet from the highway. When we pulled into the drive, I panicked and begged Carolyn to make a U-turn and go back so we could talk about it over a soda. She pinched my cheek, calling me a "silly boy." I felt better, though, when I got out of the car and saw the house: the chipped paint, a cracked window, boards for a walk to the back door. There were rusting cars near the barn. A tractor with a net of spiderwebs under a mulberry. A field. A bale of barbed wire like children's scribbling leaning against an empty chicken coop. Carolyn took my hand and pulled me to my future mother-in-law who was coming out to greet us.

We had lunch: sandwiches, potato chips, and iced tea. Carolyn and her mother talked mostly about neighbors and the congregation at the Japanese Methodist Church in West Fresno. Her father, who was in khaki work clothes, excused himself with a wave that was almost a salute and went outside. I heard a truck start, a dog bark, and then the truck rattle away.

Carolyn's mother offered another sandwich, but I declined with a shake of my head and a smile. I looked around when I could, when I was not saying over and over that I was a college student, hinting that I could take care of her daughter. I shifted my chair. I saw newspapers piled in corners, dusty cereal boxes and vinegar bottles in corners. The wallpaper was bubbled from rain that had come in from a bad roof. Dust. Dust lay on lamp shades and window sills. These people are just like Mexicans, I thought. Poor people.

Carolyn's mother asked me through Carolyn if I would like a *sushi*. A plate of black and white things were held in front of me. I took one, wide-eyed, and turned it over like a foreign coin. I was biting into one when I saw a kitten crawl up the window screen over the sink. I chewed and the kitten opened its mouth of terror as she crawled higher, wanting in to paw the leftovers from our plates. I looked at Carolyn, who said that the cat was just showing off. I looked up in time to see it fall. It crawled up, then fell again.

We talked for an hour and had apple pie and coffee, slowly. Finally, we got up with Carolyn taking my hand. Slightly embarrassed, I tried to pull away but her grip held me. I let her have her way as she led me down the hallway with her mother right behind me. When I opened the door, I was startled by a kitten clinging to the screen door, its mouth screaming "cat food, dog biscuits, *sushi* . . ." I opened the door and the kitten, still holding on, whined in the language of hungry animals. When I got into Carolyn's car, I looked back: The cat was still clinging. I asked Carolyn if it was possibly hungry, but she said the cat was being silly. She started the car, waved to her mother, and bounced us over the rain-poked drive, patting my thigh for being her lover baby. Carolyn waved again. I looked back, waving, then gawking at a window screen where there were now three kittens clawing and screaming to get in. Like Mexicans, I thought. I remembered the Molinas and how the cats clung to their screens — cats they shot down with squirt guns. On the highway, I felt happy, pleased by it all. I patted Carolyn's thigh. Her people were like Mexicans, only different.

[2000]

reserved. Originally published in *The New Yorker.* Reprinted by permission.

Raymond Carver. "Are These Actual Miles?" from *Where I'm Calling From.* Copyright © 1976, by Raymond Carver. Reprinted by permission of Grove/Atlantic, Inc.

Sandra Cisneros. "Mericans" from *Woman Hollering Creek.* Copyright © 1991 by Sandra Cisneros. Published by Vintage Books, a division of Random House, Inc., New York and originally in hardcover by Random House, Inc. Reprinted by permission of Susan Bergholz Literary Services, New York. All rights reserved.

Hart Crane. "The Broken Tower," "To the Brooklyn Bridge," and "Voyages I-VI" from *Complete Poems of Hart Crane* by Hart Crane, edited by Marc Simon. Copyright 1933, 1958, 1966 of Liveright Publishing Corporation. Copyright © 1986 by Marc Simon. "Modern Poetry" from *The Complete Poems and Selected Letters and Prose of Hart Crane* by Hart Crane, edited by Brom Weber. Copyright 1933, 1958, 1966 by Liveright Publishing Corporation. Copyright 1952 by Brom Weber. All used by permission of Liveright Publishing Corporation.

Countee Cullen. "Heritage," "For Paul Laurence Dunbar," "From the Dark Tower," and "Yet Do I Marvel" from *My Soul's High Song: The Collected Writings of Countee Cullen, Voice of the Harlem Renaissance*, edited by Gerald Early. Reprinted by permission of Thompson and Thompson and the Amistad Research Foundation, Tulane University.

E. E. Cummings. "[anyone lived in a pretty how town]," "[Buffalo Bill 's]," "[the Cambridge ladies who live in furnished souls]," "[i sing of Olaf glad and big]," "[i thank You God for most this amazing]," "[in Just-]," "[my sweet old etcetera]," "[next to of course god america i]," and "[you shall above all things be glad and young.]" from *Complete Poems: 1904-1962* by E. E. Cummings, edited by George J. Firmage. Copyright 1923, 1925, 1926, 1931, 1935, 1938, 1939, 1940, 1944, 1945, 1946, 1947, 1948, 1949, 1950, 1951, 1952, 1953, 1954, © 1955, 1956, 1957, 1958, 1959, 1960, 1961, 1962, 1963, 1966, 1967, 1968, 1972, 1973, 1974, 1975, 1976, 1977, 1978, 1979, 1980, 1981, 1982, 1983, 1984, 1985, 1986, 1987, 1988, 1989, 1990, 1991 by the Trustees for the E. E. Cummings Trust. Copyright © 1973, 1976, 1978, 1979, 1981, 1983, 1985, 1991 by George James Firmage. Used by permission of Liveright Publishing Corporation.

H.D. (Hilda Doolittle). "Helen" from *Collected Poems, 1912-1944*, copyright © 1982 by The Estate of Hilda Doolittle. Reprinted by permission of New Directions Publishing Corp.

Donald Davidson. Excerpt from "A Mirror for Artists" from *I'll Take My Stand: The South and the Agrarian Tradition.* Reprinted by permission of Louisiana State University Press.

Don DeLillo. "Videotape" reprinted with the permission of Scribner, an imprint of Simon & Schuster Adult Publishing Group, from *Underworld* by Don DeLillo. Copyright © 1997 by Don DeLillo. Originally appeared in *Antaeus*, Fall 1994. All rights reserved.

Annie Dillard. Excerpt from pp. 15-19 of *An American Childhood* by Annie Dillard, copyright © 1987 by Annie Dillard. Reprinted by permission of HarperCollins Publishers

John Dos Passos. "1919 – Two Portraits" from *New Masses*, 1931, subsequently published as "The House of Morgan, 1919." "Vag" from *The New Republic*, July 22, 1936, later published as the last chapter of *The Big Money.* Both from *USA* by John Dos Passos, copyright 1930, 1932, 1933, 1934, 1936, 1937 by John Dos Passos. Copyright 1946 by John Dos Passos and Houghton Mifflin Company. Copyright © renewed 1958, 1960 by John Dos Passos. "The Writer as Technician" from *American Writers Congress*, edited by Harry Hart et al. Copyright 1935. All reprinted by permission of Lucy Dos Passos Coggin.

Rita Dove. "David Walker (1795-1830)," "The House Slave," and "Kentucky, 1833" from *The Yellow House on the Corner*, Carnegie Mellon University Press, © 1980 by Rita Dove. Reprinted by permission of the author. "Canary" from *Grace Notes* by Rita Dove. Copyright © 1989 by Rita Dove. "History" from *Mother Love* by Rita Dove. Copyright © 1995 by Rita Dove. Both used by permission of W. W. Norton & Company, Inc.

T. S. Eliot. "Burnt Norton" from *Four Quartets* by T. S. Eliot, copyright 1936 by Harcourt, Inc., and renewed 1964 by T. S. Eliot. "Journey of the Magi" from *Collected Poems 1909-1962* by T. S. Eliot, copyright 1936 by Harcourt, Inc. and renewed 1964 by T. S. Eliot. Reprinted by permission of the publisher and Faber and Faber Ltd.

Ralph Ellison. "The Invisible Man" from "Battle Royal," copyright 1948 by Ralph Ellison from *Invisible Man* by Ralph Ellison. Reprinted by permission of Random House, Inc.

Martín Espada. "Alabanza: In Praise of Local 100," "Bully," "Federico's Ghost," and "Latin Night at the Pawnshop" from *Alabanza* by Martín Espada. Copyright © 2003 by Martín Espada. Used by permission of W. W. Norton & Company, Inc.

William Faulkner. "Barn Burning" copyright 1950 by Random House, Inc., copyright renewed 1977 by Jill Faulkner Summers. "That Evening Sun" copyright 1931 and renewed 1959 by William Faulkner. Both stories are from *Collected Stories of William Faulkner* by William Faulkner. Used by permission of Random House, Inc.

Robert Frost: "Desert Places," "The Gift Outright," "Nothing Gold Can Stay," and "Stopping by Woods on a Snowy Evening" from *The Poetry of Robert Frost,* edited by Edward Connery Lathem. Copyright © 1923, 1947, 1969 by Henry Holt and Company, Copyright 1951 by Robert Frost, © 1975 by Lesley Frost Ballantine. "The Figure a Poem Makes" from *Selected Prose of Robert Frost* edited by Hyde Cox and Edward Connery Lathem. Copyright 1939, 1967 by Henry Holt and Company. Reprinted by permission of Henry Holt and Company.

Jun Fujita. "Chicago River," "Diminuendo," "Michigan Boulevard," and "My Sister" from *Tanka: Poems in Exile* copyright 1923 by Covici-McGee Co.

Allen Ginsberg. *Howl* from *Collected Poems 1947-1980.* Copyright © 1955 by Allen Ginsberg. Reprinted by permission of HarperCollins Publishers.

Michael Gold. "Proletarian Realism" from "Notes of the Month" in *New Masses,* September 1930. Reprinted by permission of International Publishers Corporation, Inc.

Rodolfo "Corky" Gonzales. "I am Joaquin" from *I Am Joaquin/Yo Soy Joaquin.* Bantam Books, 1967.

Joy Harjo. "If You Look with the Mind of the Swirling Earth" and "This Land Is a Poem" by Joy Harjo from *Secrets from the Center of the World* by Joy Harjo and Stephen Strom. Copyright © 1989 The Arizona Board of Regents. Reprinted by permission of the University of Arizona Press. "Anchorage" and "New Orleans" from *She Had Some Horses,* Third Edition, by Joy Harjo. Copyright © 1983,

1997 Thunder's Mouth Press. Reprinted by permission of Seal / Thunder's Mouth, a member of Perseus Books Group.

Michael S. Harper. "American History," " 'Bird Lives': Charles Parker in St. Louis," "Dear John, Dear Coltrane," and "Martin's Blues" from *Songlines in Michaeltree: New and Collected Poems.* Copyright 2000 by Michael S. Harper. Used with permission of the poet and the University of Illinois Press.

Robert Hayden. "Middle Passage" copyright © 1962, 1966 by Robert Hayden from *Collected Poems of Robert Hayden* by Robert Hayden, edited by Frederick Glaysher. Used by permission of Liveright Publishing Corporation.

Ernest Hemingway. "Big Two-Hearted River," Parts I and II, reprinted with the permission of Scribner, an imprint of Simon & Schuster Adult Publishing Group, from *The Short Stories of Ernest Hemingway.* Copyright 1925 Charles Scribner's Sons. Copyright renewed 1953 by Ernest Hemingway.

bell hooks. Chapters 33-37 from *Bone Black: Memories of Girlhood* by bell hooks. Copyright 1996 by Gloria Watkins. Reprinted by permission of Henry Holt and Company.

Langston Hughes. "The Negro Artist and the Racial Mountain" first published in *The Nation,* June 23, 1926. Copyright © 1926 by Langston Hughes. Reprinted by permission of Harold Ober Associates Incorporated. "Afro-American Fragment," "Angels Wings," "Brass Spittoons," "Down and Out," "Jazzonia," and "Mulatto" edited by Arnold Rampersad with David Roessel, Assoc.; "Christ in Alabama," "Dream Boogie," and "Harlem (2)" copyright 1951 by Langston Hughes; "Cross" copyright © 1994 by The Estate of Langston Hughes; "I, Too" and "The Weary Blues" copyright © 1994 by The Estate of Langston Hughes from *The Collected Poems of Langston Hughes* by Langston Hughes, edited by Arnold Rampersad with David Roessel, Associate Editor, copyright © 1994 by The Estate of Langston Hughes. Used by permission of Alfred A. Knopf, a division of Random House, Inc.

Zora Neale Hurston. Excerpt from "Characteristics of Negro Expression" from *Negro* by Nancy Cunard. Copyright 1934. Reprinted by permission of The Continuum International Publishing Group.

Maxine Hong Kingston. Excerpt from *The Woman Warrior* by Maxine Hong Kingston, copyright

© 1975, 1976 by Maxine Hong Kingston. Used by permission of Alfred A. Knopf, a division of Random House, Inc.

Ursula K. Le Guin. "She Unnames Them" from *Buffalo Gals and Other Animal Presences.* Copyright © 1985 by Ursula K. Le Guin; first appeared in *The New Yorker*; reprinted by permission of the Author and the Author's agents, the Virginia Kidd Agency, Inc.

Audre Lorde. "Black Mother Woman" copyright © 1992, 1973 by Audre Lorde. "Coal" copyright © 1973, 1970, 1968 by Audre Lorde. "The Woman Thing" copyright © 1973, 1970, 1968 by Audre Lorde. All from *Undersong: Chosen Poems Old and New* by Audre Lorde. "Stations" copyright © 1986 by Audre Lorde from *The Collected Poems of Audre Lorde* by Audre Lorde. All used by permission of W. W. Norton & Company, Inc.

Amy Lowell. "Meeting-House Hill" from *The Complete Poetical Works of Amy Lowell.* Copyright © 1955 by Houghton Mifflin Company, renewed 1983 by Houghton Mifflin Company, Brinton P. Roberts and G. D'Andelot Belin, Esq. Reprinted by permission of Houghton Mifflin Company.

Robert Lowell. "For the Union Dead," "Memories of West Street and Lepke," "Skunk Hour," and "Waking Early Sunday Morning" from *Collected Poems* by Robert Lowell. Copyright © 2003 by Harriet Lowell and Sheridan Lowell. Reprinted by permission of Farrar, Straus and Giroux, LLC.

Mina Loy. "Love Songs I–XIII" (1923) from *The Lost Lunar Baedeker* by Mina Loy. Works of Mina Loy copyright © 1996 by the Estate of Mina Loy. Introduction and edition copyright © 1996 by Roger L. Conover. Reprinted by permission of Farrar, Straus and Giroux, LLC. From "Modern Poetry" (*Charm*, April 1925) is reprinted courtesy of Roger L. Conover for the Estate of Mina Loy.

Bernard Malamud. "The First Seven Years" from *The Magic Barrel* by Bernard Malamud. Copyright © 1950, 1958, renewed 1977, 1986 by Bernard Malamud. Reprinted by permission of Farrar, Straus and Giroux, LLC.

David Mamet. "The Rake" first published in *Harper's*, June 8, 1992, pp. 69-72. Copyright © 1992 by David Mamet. Reprinted by permission of The Wylie Agency.

Edna St. Vincent Millay. "Justice Denied in Massachusetts" and "To Inez Milholland" from *Collected Poems.* Copyright © 1928 and 1995 by Edna St. Vincent Millay and Norma Millay Ellis. Reprinted by permission of Elizabeth Barnett, Literary Executor, The Millay Society.

Arthur Miller. *Death of a Salesman* by Arthur Miller, copyright 1949, renewed © 1977 by Arthur Miller. Used by permission of Viking Penguin, a division of Penguin Group (USA) Inc.

N. Scott Momaday. Excerpt from *The Names: A Memoir*, 1976 (Harper & Row), reprinted by permission of the author.

Marianne Moore. "What Are Years?" reprinted with the permission of Scribner, an imprint of Simon & Schuster Adult Publishing Group, from *The Collected Poems of Marianne Moore* by Marianne Moore. Copyright © 1941 by Marianne Moore; copyright renewed © 1969 by Marianne Moore. "To a Snail" reprinted with the permission of Scribner, an imprint of Simon & Schuster Adult Publishing Group from *The Collected Poems of Marianne Moore* by Marianne Moore. Copyright © 1935 by Marianne Moore; copyright renewed 1963 by Marianne Moore and T. S. Eliot. All rights reserved.

Toni Morrison. "Recitatif" copyright © 1983 by Toni Morrison. Reprinted by permission of International Creative Management, Inc.

Tim O'Brien. "The Things They Carried" from *The Things They Carried* by Tim O'Brien. Copyright © 1990 by Tim O'Brien. Reprinted by permission of Houghton Mifflin Company. All rights reserved.

Flannery O'Connor. "A Good Man Is Hard to Find" from *A Good Man Is Hard to Find and Other Stories*, copyright 1953 by Flannery O'Connor and renewed 1981 by Regina O'Connor. Reprinted by permission of Harcourt, Inc.

Tillie Olsen. "I Stand Here Ironing" from *Tell Me a Riddle.* Copyright © 1956, 1957, 1960, 1961 by Tillie Olsen. Reprinted by permission of the Elaine Markson Literary Agency.

Sylvia Plath. "Daddy," "Lady Lazarus," and "Morning Song" from *Ariel: Poems* by Sylvia Plath. Copyright © 1961, 1962, 1963, 1964, 1965, 1966 by Ted Hughes. Foreword by Robert Lowell. "Blackberrying" and "Mirror" from *Crossing the Water* by Sylvia Plath. Copyright © 1971 by Ted Hughes. Reprinted by permission of HarperCollins Publishers and Faber and Faber Ltd.

Katherine Anne Porter. "Flowering Judas" from *Flowering Judas and Other Stories*, copyright

1930 and renewed 1958 by Katherine Anne Porter, reprinted by permission of Harcourt, Inc.

Charles Reznikoff. "Testimony" from *The Poems of Charles Reznikoff* by Charles Reznikoff, edited by Seamus Cooney. Reprinted by permission of David R. Godine, Publisher, Inc. Copyright © 2005 by the estate of Charles Reznikoff.

Adrienne Rich. "Diving into the Wreck" copyright © 2002 by Adrienne Rich, copyright © 1973 by W. W. Norton & Company, Inc. "Power" copyright © 2002 by Adrienne Rich, copyright © 1978 by W. W. Norton & Company, Inc. "Trying to Talk with a Man" copyright © 2002 by Adrienne Rich, copyright © 1973 by W. W. Norton & Company, Inc. "A Valediction Forbidding Mourning" copyright © 2002 by Adrienne Rich, copyright © 1971 by W. W. Norton & Company, Inc. All from *The Fact of a Doorframe: Selected Poems 1950-2001* by Adrienne Rich. Used by permission of the author and W. W. Norton & Company, Inc.

Theodore Roethke. "Cuttings" copyright 1948 by Theodore Roethke. "Cuttings (later)" copyright 1948 by Theodore Roethke. "The Far Field" copyright © 1962 by Beatrice Roethke, Administratrix of the Estate of Theodore Roethke. "I Knew a Woman" copyright © 1954 by Theodore Roethke. "My Papa's Waltz" copyright 1942 by Hearst Magazines, Inc. "Root Cellar" copyright 1943 by Modern Poetry Asssociation, Inc. "The Waking" copyright 1953 by Theodore Roethke. All from *Collected Poems of Theodore Roethke* by Theodore Roethke. Used by permission of Doubleday, a division of Random House, Inc.

Leslie Marmon Silko. "Yellow Woman" copyright © 1981 by Leslie Marmon Silko. Reprinted from *Storyteller* by Leslie Marmon Silko, published by Seaver Books, New York, New York.

Gary Snyder. "Beneath My Hand and Eye the Distant Hills, Your Body" by Gary Snyder from *The Back Country*, copyright © 1968 by Gary Snyder. "Ripples on the Surface" from *No Nature* by Gary Snyder. Copyright © 1992 by Gary Snyder. Used by permission of Pantheon Books, a division of Random House, Inc. "Wave" from *Regarding Wave*, copyright © 1970 by Gary Snyder. Reprinted by permission of New Directions Publishing Corp. "Axe Handles" and "Riprap" from *Riprap and Cold Mountain Poems* by Gary Snyder. Copyright © 2003 by Gary Snyder. Reprinted by permission of Counterpoint.

Gary Soto. "Like Mexicans" from *The Effects of Knut Hamsun on a Fresno Boy: Recollections and Short Essays* by Gary Soto. Copyright © 1983, 2001 by Gary Soto. Reprinted by permission of Persea Books, Inc. (New York).

Gertrude Stein. Excerpt from "Composition as Explanation" from *What Are Masterpieces* by Gertrude Stein. Reprinted by permission of the Estate of Gertrude Stein, through its Literary Executor, Mr. Stanford Gann, Jr. of Levin & Gann, P.A.

John Steinbeck. "Flight" from *The Long Valley* by John Steinbeck, copyright 1938, renewed © 1966 by John Steinbeck. Used by permission of Viking Penguin, a division of Penguin Group (USA) Inc.

Wallace Stevens. "The Idea of Order at Key West" and "The Plain Sense of Things" copyright 1936 by Wallace Stevens and renewed 1964 by Holly Stevens. "Of Modern Poetry" copyright 1942 by Wallace Stevens and renewed 1970 by Holly Stevens. All from *The Collected Poems of Wallace Stevens* by Wallace Stevens, copyright 1954 by Wallace Stevens and renewed 1982 by Holly Stevens. Used by permission of Alfred A. Knopf, a division of Random House, Inc.

Jean Toomer. "Blood-Burning Moon," "Portrait in Georgia," and "Seventh Street" from *Cane* by Jean Toomer. Copyright 1923 by Boni & Liveright, renewed 1951 by Jean Toomer. Used by permission of Liveright Publishing Corporation.

Mark Twain. "The War Prayer" from *Europe and Elsewhere* by Mark Twain, edited by Albert Bigelow Paine. Copyright 1923 by Mark Twain Company, renewed 1951 by Mark Twain Company.

John Updike. "A & P" from *Pigeon Feathers and Other Stories* by John Updike. Copyright © 1962 and renewed 1990 by John Updike. Used by permission of Alfred A. Knopf, a division of Random House, Inc.

Alice Walker. "Everyday Use" from *In Love & Trouble: Stories of Black Women*, copyright © 1973 by Alice Walker. Reprinted by permission of Harcourt, Inc.

Eudora Welty. "A Worn Path" from *A Curtain of Green and Other Stories*, copyright 1941 and renewed 1969 by Eudora Welty. Reprinted by permission of Harcourt, Inc.

Tennessee Williams. *Portrait of a Madonna* by Tennessee Williams, from *27 Wagons Full of*

Image Credits

AMERICAN LITERATURE 1914-1945

Pages 498-99: Gottscho-Schleisner Collection, Library of Congress Prints and Photographs Division

Pages 500 and 502 (detail): Brown Brothers

Page 509: Marcel Duchamp, *Nude Descending a Staircase, No. 2*, Philadelphia Museum of Art: The Louise and Walter Arensberg Collection, 1950 / © 2007 Artists Rights Society (ARS), New York / ADAGP, Paris / Succession Marcel Duchamp

Page 510: Billy Rose Theatre Division, The New York Public Library for the Performing Arts, Astor, Lenox and Tilden Foundations

Page 511: Michigan State University Libraries

Pages 501 (detail) and 515: Detail from Winold Reiss, *Dawn in Harlem*, courtesy of Renate Reiss

Page 516: Private Collection, Peter Newark American Pictures / The Bridgeman Art Library

Page 518: Matthew J. & Arlyn Bruccoli Collection of F. Scott Fitzgerald, University of South Carolina

Page 519: Ladies Home Journal, August 1924

Pages 505 (detail) and 522: Ben and Beatrice Goldstein Foundation Collection, Library of Congress Prints and Photographs Division

Pages 506 (detail) and 523: Library of Congress Prints and Photographs Division

Pages 507 (detail) and 524: Library of Congress Prints and Photographs Division

Page 526: Farm Security Administration–Office of War Information Photograph Collection, Library of Congress Prints and Photographs Division

Pages 508 (detail) and 527: Library of Congress Prints and Photographs Division

Page 528: Aaron Douglas: *Poetry*, Fisk University Galleries, Nashville, Tennessee

Page 531: Yale Collection of American Literature, Beinecke Rare Book and Manuscript Library

Page 532: Janet Flanner-Solita Solano Collection, Library of Congress Prints and Photographs Division

Page 534 (upper left): Yale Collection of American Literature, Beinecke Rare Book and Manuscript Library

Page 534 (lower left): Yale Collection of American Literature, Beinecke Rare Book and Manuscript Library

Page 534 (upper right): Harry Ransom Humanities Research Center, The University of Texas at Austin

Pages 503 (detail) and 534 (lower right): General Research & Reference Division, Schomburg Center for Research in Black Culture, The New York Public Library, Astor, Lenox and Tilden Foundations

Page 539: Provided by Harry Ransom Humanities Research Center, The University of Texas at Austin, from *The Literary Essays of Ezra Pound*, copyright © 1973 by The Estate of Ezra Pound

Page 570: National Association for the Advancement of Colored People Records, Library of Congress Prints and Photographs Division

Page 572: "The Creation," illustrations by Aaron Douglas, from *God's Trombones* by James Weldon Johnson, copyright 1927 The Viking Press, Inc., renewed © 1955 by Grace Nail Johnson. Used by permission of Viking Penguin, a division of Penguin Group (USA) Inc.

Page 575: Houghton Library, Harvard University

Page 581: Photograph from the Jones Library, Amherst, Massachusetts, reproduced by permission of the Estate of Robert Frost

Pages 502 (detail) and 595: Records of the Harmon Foundation, Manuscript Division of the Library of Congress

Page 599: Bettmann / Corbis

Page 605: Reproduced by permission of The Huntington Library, San Marino, California

Page 619: Reproduced courtesy of Roger Lloyd Conover

Page 621: Reproduced courtesy of Roger Lloyd Conover

Page 627: William Carlos Williams, photograph by Charles Sheeler. Copyright © 1926 Reprinted with permission of New Directions Publishing.

Page 629: The Metropolitan Museum of Art, Alfred Stieglitz Collection, 1949 (49.59.1) Image © The Metropolitan Museum of Art

Page 641: Time & Life Pictures / Getty Images

Page 643: Yale Collection of American Literature, Beinecke Rare Book and Manuscript Library

Page 651: Yale Collection of American Literature, Beinecke Rare Book and Manuscript Library

Page 658: The Rosenbach Museum & Library

Page 666: From the *Chicago Tribune* Sunday Magazine, July 24, 1955

Page 669: Hulton Archive / Getty Images

Page 677: Facsimile of first manuscript page from *The Waste Land* by T. S. Eliot. From the Henry W. and Albert A. Berg Collection of English and American Literature, The New York Public Library, Astor, Lenox and Tilden Foundations, reproduced by permission of Faber & Faber Ltd, publishers of *The Waste Land.*

Page 704: Corbis

Page 710: Corbis

Page 716: Reproduced from a copy of the photograph (bMS AM 1823.7) missing from the archive of the Houghton Library, Harvard University

Page 719: By permission of the Houghton Library, Harvard University/bMS AM 1892.14

Page 726: Mandeville Special Collections Library, University of California at San Diego

Page 735: Columbia University Libraries

Page 745: Howard University

Pages 506 (detail) and 747: Yale Collection of American Literature, Beinecke Rare Book and Manuscript Library

Page 752: Yale Collection of American Literature, Beinecke Rare Book and Manuscript Library

Pages 504 (detail) and 755: Yale Collection of American Literature, Beinecke Rare Book and Manuscript Library

Page 765: Yale Collection of American Literature, Beinecke Rare Book and Manuscript Library

Pages 501 (detail) and 772: Sheaffer-O'Neill Collection, Connecticut College, copyright Leona Rust Egan

Page 774: Music Division, The New York Public Library for the Performing Arts, Astor, Lenox and Tilden Foundations

Page 776: Henry W. and Albert A. Berg Collection of English and American Literature, The New York Public Library, Astor, Lenox and Tilden Foundations

Page 777: Columbia University Libraries

Pages 502 (detail) and 778: Sheaffer-O'Neill Collection, Connecticut College

Page 780: Henry W. and Albert A. Berg Collection of English and American Literature, The New York Public Library, Astor, Lenox and Tilden Foundations

Page 782: Billy Rose Theatre Division, The New York Public Library for the Performing Arts, Astor, Lenox and Tilden Foundations

Page 793: Henry W. and Albert A. Berg Collection of English and American Literature, The New York

Public Library, Astor, Lenox and Tilden Foundations

Page 795: Yale Collection of American Literature, Beinecke Rare Book and Manuscript Library

Page 818: © Museo Thyssen-Bornemisza, Madrid

Page 821: Stuart Davis, *New York–Paris, No. 1*, 1931. Collection of the University of Iowa Museum of Art, Iowa City, IA 1955.5

Page 823: Grambs Aronson (Blanche Mary Grambs)

Page 825: Art © T. H. Benton and R. P. Benton Testamentary Trusts / UMB Bank Trustee / Licensed by VAGA, New York, NY, from the Ben and Beatrice Goldstein Foundation Collection, Library of Congress Prints and Photographs Division

Page 834: Courtesy of Vanderbilt University Special Collections and University Archives

Page 835: Labadie Collection, University of Michigan

Pages 501 (detail) and 847: Yale Collection of American Literature, Beinecke Rare Book and Manuscript Library

Pages 506 (detail) and 849: Courtesy of The Bancroft Library, University of California, Berkeley

Page 855: © 2007 Estate of Pablo Picasso / Artists Rights Society (ARS), New York from The Metropolitan Museum of Art, Bequest of Gertrude Stein, 1946 (47.106). Image © The Metropolitan Museum of Art

Page 858: Photography Collection, Miriam and Ira D. Wallach Division of Art, Prints and Photographs, The New York Public Library, Astor, Lenox and Tilden Foundations. © 2007 Georgia O'Keeffe Museum / Artists Rights Society (ARS), New York

Page 860: Courtesy of John D. Maines

Page 869: © Estate of George Platt Lynes from Papers of Katherine Anne Porter, Special Collections, University of Maryland Libraries

Page 880: Carl Van Vechten Photograph Collection, Library of Congress Prints and Photographs Division

Page 891: Yale Collection of American Literature, Beinecke Rare Book and Manuscript Library

Page 893: Trinity College Library, Hartford, Connecticut

Page 898: The María Cristina Mena Chambers Papers, Recovering the U.S. Hispanic Library Heritage Project, University of Houston

Page 905: Bettmann / Corbis

Artist's permission, courtesy Mary Boone Gallery, New York. Gelatin silver print (composite of three photographs) 76¼ × 39½. Milwaukee Art Museum. Gift of Contemporary Art Society, M1987.13.

Page 1079: © Mary Randlett. Used by permission of the photographer, courtesy Special Collections, University of Washington Libraries.

Page 1088: Library of Congress Prints and Photographs Division

Page 1090: Jacket design by Cynthia Krupat from *The Complete Poems 1927-1979* by Elizabeth Bishop. Cover design copyright © 1982 by Cynthia Krupat. The original watercolor by Elizabeth Bishop was drawn in Mexico in 1942. Reprinted by permission of Farrar, Straus and Giroux, LLC.

Page 1098: Billy Rose Theatre Division, The New York Public Library for the Performing Arts, Astor, Lenox and Tilden Foundations

Page 1101: Photofest

Page 1111: Courtesy, National Bahá'í Archives, United States

Page 1120: Unknown photographer

Page 1128: © Terrence Spencer / Time & Life Pictures / Getty Images

Page 1134: Photographs and Prints Division, Schomburg Center for Research in Black Culture, The New York Public Library, Astor, Lenox and Tilden Foundations. By permission of the Gordon Parks Foundation.

Page 1136: Invisible Man cover copyright 1952 by Random House, Inc. from *Invisible Man* by Ralph Ellison. Used by permission of Random House, Inc. Photograph courtesy of Kazoo Books.

Pages 1044 (detail) and 1147: David Lees / Corbis

Pages 1042 (detail) and 1157: © Associated Press (AP)

Page 1175: © Associated Press (AP)

Page 1177: © Eileen Darby Images, Inc.

Page 1253: By permission of Houghton Library Harvard University

Page 1255: © North Wind Picture Archives / Alamy

Pages 1042 (detail) and 1267: © Hulton Archive / Getty Images

Page 1273: Copyright Marilyn Sanders

Page 1285: Time & Life Pictures / Getty Images

Page 1302: Courtesy Flannery O'Connor Collection, Georgia College & State University Library, Milledgeville, GA

Page 1315: © Allen Ginsberg / Corbis

Page 1317: Kim Kulish / Corbis

Page 1327: © John Jonas Gruen / Hulton Archive / Getty Images

Page 1333: New York World-Telegram and the Sun Newspaper Photograph Collection, Library of Congress Prints and Photographs Division

Page 1335: Photofest

Page 1342: Library of Congress Prints and Photographs Division

Page 1349: © Marian Wood Kolisch

Page 1354: © Allen Ginsberg / Corbis

Page 1360: © Jerry Bauer

Page 1365: © Bernard Gotfryd / Getty Images

Pages 1045 (detail) and 1380: Bettmann / Corbis

Page 1391: © Gwendolyn Stewart

Page 1397: © Associated Press (AP)

Page 1399: Photofest

Page 1415: © Dagmar Schultz / Courtesy Audre Lorde Collection, Spelman College

Page 1421: Sophie Bassouls / Corbis Sygma

Page 1427: © LaVerne Harrell Clark

Page 1433: © Marion Ettlinger

Page 1441: © Margaret Randall, Photograph Courtesy The Benson Collection, University of Texas Libraries

Pages 1047 (detail) and 1448: Hulton Archive / Getty Images

Page 1457: © Marion Ettlinger

Page 1472: © LaVerne Harrell Clark

Pages 1049 (detail) and 1481: © LaVerne Harrell Clark

Pages 1050 (detail) and 1487: © Fred Viebahn

Page 1493: AP Images / Eric Gay

Page 1497: © Paul Shoul

Pages 1050 (detail) and 1503: Hulton Archive / Getty Images

Page 1523: © Hulton Archive / Getty

Page 1524: Courtesy N. Scott Momaday. Used by permission. All rights reserved.

Page 1528: Christopher Felver / Corbis

Page 1534: © Jerry Bauer

Page 1539: Time & Life Pictures / Getty Images

Page 1544: © Pinderhughes Photography, Inc.

Pages 1051 (detail) and 1550: Courtesy of Gary Soto

Index of Authors and Titles